AWARDS, HONORS & PRIZES

AWARDS, HONORS & PRIZES

An International Directory of Awards and Their Donors Recognizing Achievement In Advertising, Architecture, Arts and Humanities, Business and Finance, Communications, Computers, Consumer Affairs, Ecology, Education, Engineering, Fashion, Films, Journalism, Law, Librarianship, Literature, Medicine, Music, Performing Arts, Photography, Public Affairs, Publishing, Radio and Television, Religion, Science, Social Science, Sports, Technology, and Transportation

VOLUME 2
INTERNATIONAL

26th EDITION

TARA ATTERBERRY
PROJECT EDITOR

THOMSON
GALE™

Detroit • New York • San Francisco • New Haven, Conn. • Waterville, Maine • London

THOMSON
GALE

Awards, Honors and Prizes, 26th Edition
Volume 2: International

Editorial
Tara Atterberry, Matthew Miskelly, Kristy Swartout, Verne Thompson

Editorial Support Services
Charles Beaumont

Composition and Electronic Prepress
Evi Seoud

Manufacturing
Rita Wimberley

For more information, contact
Thomson Gale
27500 Drake Rd.
Farmington Hills, MI 48331-3535
Or you can visit our Internet site at
http://www.gale.com

978-0-7876-7808-1 (Set) 0-7876-7808-2 (Set)
978-0-7876-7809-8 (Vol. 1) 0-7876-7809-0 (Vol. 1)
978-0-7876-7810-4 (Vol. 2) 0-7876-7810-4 (Vol. 2)
ISSN 0196-6316

Printed in the United States of America
10 9 8 7 6 5 4 3 2 1

Contents

United States and Canadian awards are covered in Volume 1

Volume 2: International

Highlights . . . vii
Introduction . . . ix
User's Guide . . . xi

Descriptive Listings by Country

Argentina . . . 1
Australia . . . 2
Austria . . . 36
Barbados . . . 41
Belarus . . . 41
Belgium . . . 41
Bolivia . . . 53
Brazil . . . 53
Bulgaria . . . 55
Burkina Faso . . . 57
Chile . . . 57
China, *See* People's Republic of China
Colombia . . . 57
Costa Rica . . . 59
Cote d'Ivoire . . . 60
Croatia . . . 60
Cuba . . . 61
Cyprus . . . 61
Czech Republic . . . 61
Denmark . . . 63
Egypt . . . 66
Estonia . . . 66
Finland . . . 67
France . . . 70
Germany . . . 96
Ghana . . . 118
Greece . . . 118
Guatemala . . . 120
Hungary . . . 120
Iceland . . . 122
India . . . 122
Indonesia . . . 135
Iran . . . 135
Ireland . . . 135
Israel . . . 139
Italy . . . 141
Jamaica . . . 152
Japan . . . 152
Kenya . . . 162
Korea, *See* Republic of Korea
Kuwait . . . 163
Lithuania . . . 163
Luxembourg . . . 164
Malaysia . . . 164
Malta . . . 165
Mexico . . . 166
Moldova . . . 168
Monaco . . . 168
Morocco . . . 169
Nepal . . . 169
Netherlands . . . 169
New Zealand . . . 180
Nigeria . . . 187
Norway . . . 188
Pakistan . . . 189
People's Republic of China . . . 190
Peru . . . 191
Philippines . . . 191
Poland . . . 194
Portugal . . . 196
Republic of Korea . . . 199
Republic of South Africa . . . 200
Romania . . . 211
Russia . . . 211

St. Lucia . . . 212
Saudi Arabia . . . 212
Senegal . . . 212
Serbia . . . 213
Singapore . . . 213
Slovakia . . . 214
Slovenia . . . 215
South Africa, *See* Republic of South Africa
Spain . . . 216
Sri Lanka . . . 221
Sweden . . . 221
Switzerland . . . 227
Taiwan . . . 242
Thailand . . . 242
Turkey . . . 243
United Kingdom . . . 244
Uruguay . . . 357
Vanuatu . . . 357
Vatican City . . . 357
Venezuela . . . 358
Zimbabwe . . . 358

Indexes

Subject Index of Awards . . . 361
Organization Index . . . 413
Award Index . . . 485

Volume 2 of *Awards, Honors & Prizes (AHP)* is the single most comprehensive source of information on awards offered by organizations in more than 80 countries outside of the United States and Canada. These awards recognize achievements in all fields of human endeavor, including:

- Advertising
- Agriculture
- Arts and Humanities
- Botany
- Business and Finance
- Communications
- Computers
- Conservation
- Ecology
- Education
- Engineering
- Environment
- Ethics
- Fashion
- Films
- Journalism
- Law
- Library Science
- Literature
- Management
- Medical Research
- Music
- Performing Arts
- Photography
- Public Affairs
- Publishing
- Radio and Television
- Religion
- Safety
- Science
- Social Science
- Sports
- Technology
- Transportation

Volume 2 provides contact information for more than 7,400 organizations and awards. (For information on awards given by organizations in the United States and Canada, consult Volume 1 of *AHP*.)

Features of This Edition

AHP continues to track trends in award giving, which in turn reflect the current values and priorities of society. This edition features listings for new awards under organizations in such fields as art, literature, education, and science, and covering such contemporary issues as the environment, religion, AIDS, national security, and international relations. *AHP* also lists e-mail and website addresses for more than 6,700 organizations.

Many Uses for *AHP*

Awards, Honors & Prizes can be used:

- by organizations, associations, and individuals to locate information on awards in a particular field of interest or that are mentioned in the media;
- by organizations and individuals to determine their eligibility for particular awards;
- by organizations to provide guidance in establishing a new award or expanding an existing program; and
- by employers in evaluating the significance of the awards listed on a job applicant's resume.

Available in Electronic Formats

Licensing. *Awards, Honors and Prizes* is available for licensing. The complete database is provided in a fielded format and is deliverable on such media as disk or CD-ROM. For more information, contact Gale's Business Development Group at 1-800-877-GALE, or visit us on our web site at www.gale.com/bizdev.

The greatest of humankind's efforts have long provided occasion for recognition and celebration. From the ancient Greek Olympics to the new Lemelson-MIT Prize for Invention and Innovation, societies worldwide continue to acknowledge extraordinary accomplishment in all fields of human endeavor.

Awards, Honors & Prizes seeks to honor individuals and groups who foster intellectual growth, set records, stimulate creativity, demonstrate courage, and inspire and encourage humanitarian efforts and international understanding. Following is a representative sampling of established awards designed to confer such recognition.

Science and Technology

- The Lemelson-MIT Prize for Invention and Innovation seeks to raise the status and visibility of American inventors and innovators. The annual award carries a $500,000 award for U.S. citizens who have shown excellence in creativity, invention, and/or innovation in the fields of medicine and health care, energy and environment, telecommunications and computing, consumer products, and durable goods and industrial products.
- Excellence in the field of aerospace engineering is rewarded by a gold medal and $100,000 by the American Institute of Aeronautics and Astronautics' Walter J. and Angeline H. Crichlow Trust Prize.
- Important work in applied or industrial physics is honored by the Institut de France, which each year presents the Prix Mesucora.

Education

- The Thomas J. Brennan Award, given by the Astronomical Society of the Pacific, recognizes high school astronomy teachers for excellence in teaching.
- Students in the ninth and tenth grades are given monetary awards for excellence in analytical thinking and writing through the Anthem Essay Contest, which is sponsored by the Ayn Rand Institute.

International Relations

- A monetary prize of 5,000,000 Japanese yen is awarded annually by the Victor Company of Japan to the person, company, or group that best demonstrates the importance of international contribution and cooperation.
- The John D. and Catherine T. MacArthur Foundation awards grants of $10,000 to $15,000 to support intellectual and scientific efforts for research and policy analysis in the countries of the former Soviet Union to scholars, journalists, policy analysts and other citizens residing in the territory of the former Soviet Union.
- The Edouard Saouma Award includes a monetary prize of $25,000 for the regional institution that has managed a particularly efficient project funded by the Food and Agriculture Organization of the United Nations.

Journalism

- The Goldsmith Prize in Investigative Reporting honors journalists whose investigative reporting best promotes more effective and ethical conduct of government, public policy making, or political practice.
- The National Lesbian and Gay Journalists Association presents the annual Crossroads Market/NLGJA Prize for excellence in print journalism on issues concerning the gay and lesbian community.

Arts and Entertainment

- The Truman Capote Awards for Literary Criticism in memory of Newton Arvis honor lifetime achievement and the best book of general literary criticism. The lifetime achievement award, administered by Stanford University, is bestowed every four years and carries a $100,000 cash prize. The best book prize of $50,000 is awarded annually by the University of Iowa, Iowa Writer's Workshop.
- The Australia Council for the Arts honors artists who have made a great contribution to the recognition of aboriginal and Torres Strait Island art and culture in the wider community at both the national and international levels with its Red Ochre Award. This award, which includes a cash prize of $50,000, was established to mark the International Year for the World's Indigenous People.

Sports

- The ESPY Awards, established by ESPN Inc., honor excellence in 34 categories of sports performance.
- The United States Olympic Committee established the Robert J. Kane Award to recognize athletes who have distinguished themselves in Olympic Festival competition by exemplifying the spirit and ideals of the Olympic movement.

News reports, by their very nature, frequently convey information that is less than welcome to world audiences. War, civil unrest, political upheaval, crime, health and environmental concerns, and other issues and events claim a majority of media attention. Perhaps that is why news of awards and their recipients, often featured prominently in print and broadcast media reporting, comes as a welcome change.

Humankind has long celebrated achievement of all kinds and in every field, from art and literature to science and technology. Individuals of all ages and from all walks of life are recognized when they transcend the boundaries of the ordinary to provide encouragement and inspiration by establishing new records, exploring new frontiers, demonstrating extraordinary courage, challenging the intellect, establishing new standards of excellence, creating beauty, or improving the quality of everyday life.

Awards, Honors & Prizes (AHP), now in its 26th edition, continues to provide perspective on the variety, scale, significance, and number of awards given throughout the world to acknowledge distinguished achievement. Volume 1 of *AHP* is the single major source of descriptive information on awards bestowed in all subject areas by organizations, foundations, corporations, universities, and government bodies in the United States and Canada. Volume 2 covers international awards.

Content and Arrangement

Volume 1 of *Awards, Honors & Prizes* comprises descriptive listings for awards and their administering organizations, and three indexes.

Descriptive Listings are arranged alphabetically by administering organization; entries for the awards administered by each organization are listed alphabetically following organization entries.

Subject Index of Awards classifies awards by their principal areas of interest.

Organization Index provides an alphabetical listing of all organizations appearing in both volumes that administer or sponsor awards, including alternate and foreign names.

Award Index provides an alphabetical listing of all award names, including alternate, former, and popular names listed in both volumes.

Preparation of This Edition

The 26th edition of *Awards, Honors & Prizes* represents the revision and updating of the previous edition. Information was obtained via survey mailings and follow-up correspondence and electronic mail as well as through the websites of administering organizations.

Volume 1 Covers U.S. and Canadian Awards

Information on awards given by organizations located in the United States and Canada is available in Volume 1 of *AHP*. It provides descriptive information on more than 17,200 awards and organizations, foundations, universities, corporations, and government bodies located in the United States and Canada.

Acknowledgments

The editors are grateful to the large number of individuals in organizations throughout the world who generously responded to our requests for updated information. Without their cooperation, this book would not be possible.

Comments and Suggestions Welcome

If you are interested in additional information about *AHP*, are interested in information about other Gale business products, if your award is listed in *AHP* and you have a question pertaining to your profile, or if you would like your award listed, please contact **Tara Atterberry, Project Editor, *Awards, Honors, and Prizes*.**

Thomson Gale
27500 Drake Rd.
Farmington Hills, MI 48331-3535
Phone: (248)699-GALE
Toll-free: 800-347-GALE
Fax: (248) 699-8075
E-mail: Tara.Atterberry@Thomson.com
URL: http://www.gale.com

Descriptive Listings

The descriptive listings are arranged alphabetically by administering organization; entries on the awards administered by each organization follow that organization's listing.

The organization and award entries shown below illustrate the kind of information that is or might be included in these entries. Each item of information is preceded by a number and is explained in the paragraph of the same number following the sample entry.

Sample Entry

1 ★4266★
2 Canadian Parks/Recreation Association
3 (Association Canadienne des Loirsirs/Parc)
4 333 River Rd.
Vanier City, ON, Canada K1L 8H9
5 Phone: (613)748-5651
6 Free: 800-748-5600
7 Fax: (613)748-5652
8 E-mail: par@rec.assn.can
9 Home Page: http://www.can.park.rec
10 Formerly: (1980) Canadian Parks Association
11 ★4267★ **12** Award of Merit **13** (Prix de Merite)
14 To give national recognition for meritorious achievements at the municipal, regional, or provincial levels that have made significant and distinct contributions to the furtherance of some aspect of local parks/recreation. Canadian individuals or organizations are eligible. The deadline for applications is February 15. **15** A wood plaque is **16** awarded annually. **17** Established in 1965. **18** Sponsored by the Canadian Park Service. **19** (Discontinued in 1985). **20** Formerly: (1982) Canadian Park Service Award.

Descriptions of Numbered Elements

1 Organization Entry Number: Entries for administering organizations are listed alphabetically, each followed by an alphabetical listing of its awards. All entries—organization and award—are numbered in a single sequence. These numbers are used as references in the indexes. Organization entry numbers are preceded by a horizontal rule across the column.

2 Organization Name: The name of the organization administering the awards that follow.

3 Organization Name in Alternate Language(s): The name of the organization is given in up to two additional languages, when provided by the organization.

4 Mailing Address: The organization's permanent mailing address for information on awards.

5 Telephone Number: The telephone number(s) for the administering organization.

6 Toll-free Number: The toll-free telephone number for the administering organization.

7 Fax Number: The facsimile number for the administering organization.

8 E-mail: When provided in source material, electronic mail numbers are listed.

9 Home Page: Whenever possible, the home page or URL (universal resource locator) for Internet access to organization sites is provided.

10 Former Name of Organization: The former name of the organization is provided if the name has changed, the organization merged, or the organization absorbed another organization. The year the name change occurred is also provided, when available.

11 Award Entry Number: Entries on awards are listed alphabetically following the entry for their administering organization. All entries—organization and award—are numbered in a single sequence. These numbers are used as references in the indexes.

12 Award Name: Name of the award, honor, or prize is listed in English whenever possible.

13 Award Name in Alternate Language(s): The award name is provided in up to two additional languages, when provided by the organization.

14 Purpose of Award and Eligibility Criteria: The description of the award indicates the purpose for which it is given, the criteria for eligibility, whether one can apply or must be nominated for the award, and the application or nomination deadline.

15 Character: Identifies the nature of the award, such as a medal, monetary award, certificate, inclusion in a hall of fame, or the presentation of a lecture.

16 Frequency: Information on the frequency of award presentation and the occasion on which it is presented.

17 Year Established: The year the award was established and in whose honor or memory it is presented.

18 Sponsor: The sponsor or co-sponsor of an award, if it is an organization other than the administering organization.

19 Status: If an award has been discontinued or is currently inactive, the year it was discontinued or last presented may be provided.

20 Former Name: The former name of an award and the year of the name change, if provided.

Indexes

Subject Index of Awards

The Subject Index of Awards classifies all awards described in this volume by their principal areas of interest. The index contains more than 400 subject headings. Identically named awards are followed by an indented alphabetical list of the organizations administering an award by that name. Each award is indexed under all relevant headings. The index also contains numerous cross-references to direct users to related topics. Awards are listed alphabetically under each subject heading, and the number following an award name identifies that award's entry in the descriptive listings portion of this volume.

Organization Index

The alphabetical Organization Index provides access to all sponsoring and administering organizations listed in both volumes, as well as to organization acronyms and alternate-language and former names. Index references include the volume in which the organization appears and book entry numbers in the descriptive listings section. In the case of sponsoring organizations, citations are to the specific awards they sponsor.

Award Index

The Award Index provides an alphabetical listing of all award names listed in both volumes, as well as alternate-language, former, and popular award names, such as the Oscars and Tonys. In the case of generic award names (e.g., Gold Medal, Achievement Award, Grand Prize), the award name is followed by an alphabetical listing of the organizations administering an award by that name.

References to the volume in which the award may be found followed by the award's entry number in the descriptive listings section follow each award citation.

Volume 2
International

Argentina

• 1 •
Academia Nacional de Agronomia y Veterinaria
Dr. Norberto Ras, Pres.
Avda. Alvear 1711, 2 piso
1014 Buenos Aires, Argentina
Phone: 54 1 48124168
Phone: 54 1 48154616
Fax: 54 1 48124168
E-mail: info@anav.org.ar
Home Page: http://www.anav.org.ar

• 2 • Dr. Antonio Pires Prize (Premio Dr. Antonio Pires)
In recognition of superior research, education, and development in agronomy and veterinary sciences. Awarded biennially in odd-numbered years. Established in honor of Dr. Antonio Pires.

• 3 • Antonio J. Prego Prize (Premio Ing. Agr. Antonio J. Prego)
For recognition of soil and water conservation and reclamation. Awarded biennially in even-numbered years. Established in 1994.

• 4 • Premio Academia Nacional de Agronomia y Veterinaria
For recognition of individuals or institutions that have contributed to progress in agriculture. Awarded biennially in odd-numbered years. Established in 1969 by the Academy as its highest award.

• 5 • Premio al Desarrollo Agropecuario
For recognition of individuals or institutions who have contributed to national agriculture. Awarded biennially in even-numbered years. Established in 1977 by Massey Ferguson Argentina s.a. Formerly: (1998) Premio Massey Ferguson.

• 6 • Premio Bayer en Ciencias Veterinarias
For recognition of contributions to veterinary science. Awarded biennially in odd-numbered years. Established in 1976 by Bayer Argentina.

• 7 • Premio Bolsa de Cereales de Buenos Aires
For recognition of contributions to the production, industrialization, and commercialization of grains. Awarded biennially in odd-numbered years. Established in 1979 by Bolsa de Cereales de Buenos Aires on the occasion of the 125th anniversary of its founding.

• 8 • Premio Fundacion Alfredo Manzullo
For recognition of persons who have contributed to the field of public health. Awarded biennially in odd-numbered years. Established by Fundacion Manzullo in 1975.

• 9 • Premio Jose Maria Bustillo
For recognition of an outstanding contribution in the field of agricultural economics. Awarded biennially in even-numbered years. Established in 1975 by Maria Luisa Devoto de Bustillo in memory of her husband, Jose Maria Bustillo.

• 10 •
Academia Nacional de la Historia de la Republica Argentina
Lic. Dora B. Pinola, Sec.
Balcarce 139
C1064AAC Buenos Aires, Argentina
Phone: 54 4343 4416
Fax: 54 4343 4416
E-mail: admite@an-historia.org.ar
Home Page: http://www.an-historia.org.ar

• 11 • Premio Enrique Pena
For recognition of the best historical work on the discovery, conquest, and settlement of the Rio de Plata. University students are eligible. Certificates are awarded annually. Established in 1944 in memory of the scholar, Dr. Enrique Pena.

• 12 • Premio Academia Nacional de la Historia
For recognition of the best works concerning the history of Argentina from its beginning until 1950. Published or unpublished works are eligible. A monetary prize and a certificate are awarded annually for first, second, and third place winners. Established in 1964 in honor of the founding of Argentina.

• 13 • Premio al Egresado con Mejor Promedio en las Carreras de Historia
Developed by the Academia Nacional de Historia and given to the best in their specialty. Awarded annually.

• 14 •
Argentine Paleontological Association (Asociacion Paleontologica Argentina)
Dr. Sergio Vizcaino, Contact
Maipu 645, piso 1
1006 Buenos Aires, Argentina
Phone: 54 11 43267463
Fax: 54 11 43267463
E-mail: secretaria@apaleontologica.org.ar
Home Page: http://www.apaleontologica.org.ar

• 15 • Premio Florentino Ameghino
To reward and encourage the publication of original research by young people in the Association's magazine *Ameghiniana*. Members who are 35 years of age or younger when they submitted their manuscripts for publication are eligible. A diploma is awarded annually. Established in 1975 in honor of Florentino Amegkino.

• 16 •
Argentine Society of Geographical Studies (Sociedad Argentina de Estudios Geograficos)
Prof. Delia M. Marinelli De Cotroneo, Pres.
Rodriguez Pena 158, 4 piso, Dep 7
1020 Buenos Aires, Argentina
Phone: 54 11 43712076
Phone: 54 11 43730588
Fax: 54 11 43712076
E-mail: gaeasaeg@ciudad.com.ar
Home Page: http://www.gaea.org.ar

• 17 • Premio Dr. Carlos A. Biedma
Annual award of recognition. Established in 1953.

• 18 • Premio Francisco P. Moreno Award
Annual award of recognition. Established in 1952.

Awards are arranged in alphabetical order below their administering organizations

• 19 • **Premio Consagracion a la Geografia**

Annual award of recognition for scholars. Established in 1984.

• 20 •
Argentinian Association of Dermatology (Asociacion Argentina de Dermatologia)
Dr. Lidia Ester Valle, Pres.
Mexico 1720
1100 Buenos Aires, Argentina
Phone: 54 11 43812737
Phone: 54 11 43831153
Fax: 54 11 43812737
E-mail: info@aad.org.ar
Home Page: http://www.aad.org.ar

• 21 • **Argentinean Association of Dermatology Awards**

To recognize dermatologists in Argentina. Awarded annually.

• 22 •
Liga Argentina Contra la Tuberculosis
Dr. Vicente Donato, Med.Dir.
Uriarte 2477
Capital Federal
C1425FNI Buenos Aires, Argentina
Phone: 54 4777 4447
Fax: 54 4774 9145
E-mail: lalat@pinos.com
Home Page: http://www.lalat.org.ar

• 23 • **Premio Profesor Dr. Ricardo Hansen**

For recognition of achievements in the antituberculosis fight. The best scientific free work on phthisio-pneumonology is eligible. A medal is awarded biennially. Established in 1966 in honor of Dr. Ricardo L. Hansen.

Australia

• 24 •
Academy of the Social Sciences in Australia
Mr. John M. Beaton BA, Exec.Dir.
28 Balmain Crescent
GPO Box 1956
Canberra, Australian Capital Territory 2601, Australia
Phone: 61 2 62491788
Fax: 61 2 62474335
E-mail: assa.secretariat@anu.edu.au
Home Page: http://www.assa.edu.au/

• 25 • **Academy Award for Scholarship**

Recognizes a young scholar. A medal is awarded annually for scholarship.

• 26 •
Accordion Society of Australia
Elizabeth Jones, Federal Pres.
60 Richard Ave.
Earlwood, New South Wales 2206, Australia
Phone: 61 2 97182609
Fax: 61 2 97182609
E-mail: fisaccord@hotmail.com
Home Page: http://www.accordions.com/asa

• 27 • **National Champion**

Annual award of recognition.

• 28 •
Accounting and Finance Association of Australia and New Zealand
Cheryl Umoh, Exec. Dir.
Level 1, 156 Bouverie St.
Carlton, Victoria 3053, Australia
Phone: 61 3 93495074
Fax: 61 3 93495076
E-mail: info@afaanz.org
Home Page: http://www.afaanz.org

• 29 • **Education Award**

• 30 • **Manuscript Award**

• 31 • **PhD Scholarships**

For PhD students within Australia.

• 32 • **Practice Award**

• 33 • **Research Award**

• 34 •
Adult Learning Australia
Ron Anderson, Exec.Dir.
GPO Box 260
Canberra, Australian Capital Territory 2601, Australia
Phone: 61 2 62749500
Fax: 61 2 62749513
E-mail: info@ala.asn.au
Home Page: http://www.ala.asn.au

• 35 • **Adult Learners Week**

This international festival of adult learning celebrates and promotes lifelong learning, whether at home, at work, or in the community. A variety of awards are presented to individuals and organizations. Held annually. Established in Australia in 1995.

• 36 •
The Age
250 Spencer St.
PO Box 257C
Melbourne, Victoria 3001, Australia
Phone: 61 3 9604 1136
Fax: 61 3 9601 2332
E-mail: inquiries@theage.com.au
Home Page: http://www.theage.com.au

• 37 • **Book of the Year Awards**

For recognition of Australian books of outstanding literary merit which best express Australia's identity and prevailing concerns. Two prizes are awarded: one to a novel or other work of imaginative writing, and the other to a non-fiction work. The prize for the work of imaginative writing is awarded to a novel, a collection of short stories, or a collection of poetry. The prize for the non-fiction work is awarded to the book considered the best biography, autobiography, the best history, or the best scholarly work of social, political or topical interest. Works must have been published during the preceding year and written by Australian citizens. Two monetary prizes (one of $3,000, and one of $4,000 for the book named *The Age* Book of the Year) are awarded annually at a literary luncheon. Established in 1974.

• 38 •
Allen & Unwin Pty. Ltd.
Paul Donovan, Mng.Dir.
PO Box 8500
St. Leonards, New South Wales 1590, Australia
Phone: 61 2 8425 0100
Fax: 61 2 9906 2218
E-mail: frontdesk@allen-unwin.com.au
Home Page: http://www.allenandunwin.com

• 39 • ***The Australian*/Vogel Literary Award**

To encourage young Australian writers of unpublished fiction, history, or biography manuscripts. Australian residents under 35 years of age are eligible. Manuscripts with a maximum of 100,000 and a minimum of 30,000 words must be submitted by May 31. A monetary prize of A$20,000 is awarded annually. Established in 1979 by Niels Stevens of Vogel's Australia.

• 40 •
ANZIAM - Australian and New Zealand Industrial and Applied Mathematics
Australian Mathematical Society
Dr. W. Summerfield, Sec.
School of Mathematical and Physical Sciences
Univ. of Newcastle
Callaghan, New South Wales 2308, Australia
Phone: 61 2 4921 5530
Fax: 61 2 4921 6898
E-mail: anziam_sec@austms.org.au
Home Page: http://www.anziam.org.au

• 41 • **ANZIAM Medal**

To recognize outstanding service to the profession of applied mathematics in Australia, through research achievements and activities enhancing applied or industrial mathematics. Members of ANZIAM are eligible. Awarded biennially. Established in 1995.

• 42 • **T. M. Cherry Student Prize**

For recognition of the best student paper presented at the annual conference of ANZIAM. Any postgraduate student whose higher degree

Awards are arranged in alphabetical order below their administering organizations

thesis has not been submitted more than three calendar months before the commencement of the annual conference is eligible. A monetary prize is awarded annually at the conference. Established in 1969 and renamed in 1976 in memory of T. M. Cherry, one of Australia's leading applied mathematicians.

• 43 • J.H. Michell Medal
For outstanding new researchers in industrial and applied mathematics who are in the first ten years of their research careers. They must be members of ANZIAM, and a significant proportion of their research must have been carried out in Australia or New Zealand. Awarded annually.

• 44 •
Appita - Technical Association for the Australian and New Zealand Pulp and Paper Industry
Ralph Coghill, Exec.Dir.
Ste. 47, Level 1
255 Drummond St.
Carlton, Victoria 3053, Australia
Phone: 61 3 93472377
Fax: 61 3 93481206
E-mail: admin@appita.com
Home Page: http://www.appita.com

• 45 • Technical Association of the Australian and New Zealand Pulp and Paper Industry Awards
To recognize individuals who work to promote the industrial application of the pulp and paper industry. The association bestows three awards annually: the L. R. Benjamin Medal (for scientific or technological excellence); the Oertel Nadebaum Distinguished Service Award (for outstanding voluntary service to Appita); and Jasper Mardon Prize (for the best paper).

• 46 •
Art Gallery of New South Wales
Edmund Capon, Dir.
Art Gallery Rd.
The Domain
Sydney, New South Wales 2000, Australia
Phone: 61 2 9225 1700
Fax: 61 2 9225 6226
E-mail: artmail@ag.nsw.gov.au
Home Page: http://www.artgallery.nsw.gov.au

• 47 • Archibald Prize
For recognition of a portrait painting of a distinguished person in art, letters, science, or politics. A monetary prize of $35,000 (AUD) is awarded annually. Applicants must have been a resident of Australia for twelve months prior to closing date. Established in 1921 by a bequest of J.F. Archibald, in trust of the Perpetual Trustee Company.

• 48 • Photographic Portrait Prize
Promotes contemporary portrait photography and excellence in all forms of still photo-based art. Entries that embrace new and innovative approaches to an established photographic genre are particularly encourage. A prize of A$15,000 is awarded annually.

• 49 • Sulman Prize
For recognition of a subject or genre painting. A monetary prize of $10,000 (AUD) is awarded annually. Applicants must have been a resident in Australia for a period of five years prior to the closing date.

• 50 • The Wynne Prize
Awarded to the best landscape painting of Australian scenery or the best figure sculpture. First awarded in 1897, it has a prize of $15,000 (AUD).

• 51 •
Association for Tertiary Education Management
Giles Pickford, Contact
PO Box 6050
O'Connor, Australian Capital Territory 2602, Australia
Phone: 61 2 62155300
Fax: 61 2 62155262
E-mail: atem1@bigpond.com
Home Page: http://www.atem.edu.au

• 52 • ATEM Fellow
To recognize the efforts of members to pursue their professional development and to improve administrative practice within the profession. Candidates must have been Associate Fellows for at least two years while engaged in the profession of tertiary education management.

• 53 •
Association for the Study of Australian Literature
Peter Kirkpatrick, Pres.
English School of Humanities and Social Sciences
Charles Sturt University
Locked Bag 588
GPO Box U1987
Wagga Wagga, New South Wales 2678, Australia
Phone: 61 2 69332465
Fax: 61 2 69332792
E-mail: dgilbey@csu.edu.au
Home Page: http://www.asc.uq.edu.au/asal

Absorbed: (1982) Australian Literature Society.

• 54 • Australian Literature Society Gold Medal
For recognition of an outstanding literary work published in Australia during the previous calendar year between January 1 and December 31. Nominations are accepted. A monetary prize and a medal are awarded annually at the annual conference of the Association. Established in 1928. Additional information is available from Monash University, English Dept., Wellington Road, Clayton, VIC 3168, Australia, phone: 3 565 4000. Formerly: (1982) Herbert Crouch Medal.

• 55 • Mary Gilmore Award
For recognition of the best first book of poetry published in Australia in the preceding calendar year. Nominations are accepted, but not required. A monetary prize and a gold medal are awarded annually at the Annual conference of the Association. Established in 1985 in honor of Mary Gilmore, an Australian poet.

• 56 • Walter McRae Russell Award
For recognition of the best book of literary scholarship on an Australian subject published in the preceding two calendar years. Nominations are accepted, but not required. A monetary prize is awarded annually at the Annual Conference of the Association. Established in honor of Walter McRae Russell, last president of the Australian Literature Society.

• 57 • A.A. Phillips Prize
To recognize a work of outstanding achievement in the field of Australian literary scholarship. A monetary award of about $500 is presented on occasion. The award has been made only once - to W.H. Wilde, Barry Andrews and Joy Hooton for the *Oxford Companion to Australian Literature* in 1986.

• 58 •
Association of Consulting Engineers of Australia
Megan Motto, Oper.Mgr.
PO Box 1002
North Sydney, New South Wales 2059, Australia
Phone: 61 2 99224711
Fax: 61 2 99572484
E-mail: acea@acea.com.au
Home Page: http://www.acea.com.au

• 59 • Awards for Excellence
To recognize engineering and technical consultants who maintain high ethical and professional standards and work to ensure the status of the engineering profession. Held annually.

• 60 •
Association of Track and Field Statisticians
Paul Jenes, Pres.
23-25 Grandview Rd.
Warrandyte
Warrandyte, Victoria 3113, Australia
Phone: 61 3 98441644
Fax: 61 3 98441863
E-mail: jenes@ausport.gov.au
Home Page: http://easyweb.easynet.co.uk/~rsparks/atfs.htm

• 61 • Association of Track and Field Statisticians Honorary Member
For recognition of service to the Association in particular or to track and field athletics in general. The Executive Committee nominates individuals who are voted upon at the convention. Winners are not subject to payment of dues. Awarded biennially in even-numbered years. Established in 1958.

• 62 •
Astronomical Society of Australia
Prof. Gary Da Costa, Pres.
PO Box 76
University of Sydney
Epping, New South Wales 1710, Australia
Phone: 61 2 93513184
Fax: 61 2 93517726
E-mail: gdc@mso.anu.edu.au
Home Page: http://asa.astronomy.org.au

• 63 • David Allen Prize
Recognizes a published article which portrays an astronomical theme in an exciting and educative way. Awarded biennially in odd-numbered years.

• 64 • The Bok Prize
To recognize the best third- or fourth-year undergraduate student essay or project. A bronze medal and cash prize of $500 is awarded annually.

• 65 • The Ellery Lectureship
Recognizes outstanding contributions in astronomy or related fields. Awarded biennially in odd-numbered years.

• 66 • Charlene Heisler Prize
To recognize the most outstanding PhD thesis in astronomy or a closely related topic. A certificate and cash prize of $500 is awarded annually. Established in 2000.

• 67 • The Page Medal
Recognizes excellence in amateur astronomy. Awarded biennially in even-numbered years.

• 68 •
Astronomical Society of New South Wales
Margaret Streamer, Pres.
GPO Box 1123
Sydney, New South Wales 2001, Australia
Phone: 61 2 45721568
Fax: 61 2 96881161
E-mail: secretary@asnsw.com
Home Page: http://www.asnsw.com

• 69 • Crago Award

• 70 • McNiven Medal

• 71 • Southern Cross Award

• 72 •
Audiological Society of Australia
Jim Brown, Pres.
Ste. 7, 476 Canterbury Rd.
Forest Hill, Victoria 3131, Australia
Phone: 61 3 94164606
Fax: 61 3 94164607
E-mail: info@audiology.asn.au
Home Page: http://www.audiology.asn.au

• 73 • Certificate of Outstanding Service
For outstanding contributions to the profession of audiology.

• 74 • Fellows of the Audiological Society of Australia

• 75 • President's Distinguished Service Award
For services to ASA and the profession, through achievements and endeavors that have led to recognition of ASA as a professional body of audiology.

• 76 •
Australasian Corrosion Association
Mal Brooks, Exec. Officer
PO Box 112
Kerrimuir, Victoria 3129, Australia
Phone: 61 3 98904833
Fax: 61 3 98907866
E-mail: aca@corrosion.com.au
Home Page: http://www.corrosion.com.au

• 77 • Australasian Corrosion Association Awards
To recognize contributions by individuals who work to decrease the cost of damage due to corrosion in Australasia. The following awards are presented: Arthur C. Kennett Memorial Award, Recipients Medal, Life Membership, Corrosion Medal, and the ACA Research Award.

• 78 •
Australasian Federation of Family History Organisations
Mrs. Lesle Berry, Pres.
PO Box 3012
Weston Creek, Australian Capital Territory 2611, Australia
Phone: 61 4 00913866
E-mail: secretary@affho.org
Home Page: http://www.affho.org

• 79 • Award for Meritorious Service to Family History
Recognizes contributions to Australasian genealogy. Awarded triennially.

• 80 •
Australasian Fleet Managers Association
PO Box 7272
Melbourne, Victoria 3004, Australia
Phone: 61 3 98666056
Fax: 61 3 98661304
E-mail: info@afma.net.au
Home Page: http://www.afma.net.au

• 81 • Fleet Environment Award
For outstanding achievement in corporate Fleet Environment practices.

• 82 • Fleet Manager of the Year
For an individual who demonstrates excellence in the field of Fleet Management.

• 83 • Fleet Safety Award
For the organization that demonstrates best practice in Fleet Safety.

• 84 •
Australasian Menopause Society
Vivien Wallace, Exec. Off.
PO Box 1228
Buderim, Queensland 4556, Australia
Phone: 61 7 46134788
Fax: 61 7 46134988
E-mail: ams@netlink.com.au
Home Page: http://www.menopause.org.au

• 85 • Australasian Menopause Society Scientific Award
For the most meritorious contribution to the field of menopause by an Australian investigator.

• 86 • Barbara Gross Award
For best overall free communication or poster by any delegate.

• 87 • Jean Hailes Memorial Prize
For best free communication by a young delegate.

• 88 • Novo Nordisk Award
To a distinguished person in the field of menopause, who has given much of their life to making a significant contribution to this field.

• 89 •
Australasian Political Studies Association
Dr. Judith Brett, Pres.
Dept. of Politics
La Trobe Univ.
Bundoora, Victoria 3086, Australia
Phone: 61 3 94792691
E-mail: j.brett@latrobe.edu.au
Home Page: http://auspsa.anu.edu.au

• 90 • Crisp Medal
For recognition of originality and intellectual contribution of a work in political science published during the preceding three years. Citizens or permanent residents of Australia or New Zealand are eligible for nomination. Individuals who have held a doctorate for ten years or more or whose first appointment to a tenurable post at atertiary institution was ten or more years ago are not eligible. The deadline for submissions is July 15. A monetary prize of $500 (Australian) and a medal are awarded annually at the Annual General Meeting of the Association. Established in 1988 by the Association and the Commonwealth Bank of Australia in memory of Leslie Finlay Crisp, Foundation Professor of Political Science at Canberra University College (later The Australian National University) and Chairman of the Board of the Commonwealth Bank of Australia from 1975 until his death in 1984.

• 91 • Women and Politics Prize
For recognition of the best unpublished work on women and politics and to promote the study of women and politics. Works between 5,000 and

Awards are arranged in alphabetical order below their administering organizations

10,000 words may be submitted by July 31. A monetary award of $1,000 (Australian) and publication in *Australian Journal of Political Science* or the *Australian Quarterly* are awarded biennially. Established in 1981. Co-sponsored by the Women's Caucus of the Australian Political Studies Association and the Institute of Public Administration (Australia).

• 92 •
Australasian Society of Clinical and Experimental Pharmacologists and Toxicologists
Andrew Somogyi, Pres.
4/184 Main St.
Lilydale, Victoria 3140, Australia
Phone: 61 3 97397697
Fax: 61 3 97397076
E-mail: ascept@meetingsfirst.com.au
Home Page: http://www.ascept.org

• 93 • **ASCEPT New Investigator Awards**
To members who are not more than 6 years postdoctoral; or not more than 6 years post fellowship of an appropriate college for medical graduates; or not more than 6 years post award of a higher or bachelor degree in dentistry or veterinary science.

• 94 • **ASCEPT Student Travel Awards**
For member student.

• 95 • **Denis Wade Johnson and Johnson New Investigators Awards**
To new investigators in clinical and experimental pharmacology and toxicology.

• 96 • **ASCEPT Michael Rand Medal**
To a member whose research has made an outstanding contribution to the disciplines of clinical and experimental pharmacology or toxicology.

• 97 •
Australia Council
PO Box 788
Performing Arts Board
Strawberry Hills, New South Wales 2012, Australia
Phone: 61 2 9509000
Fax: 61 2 9509111
Home Page: http://www.ozco.gov.au

• 98 • **Don Banks Music Award**
To recognize the finest Australian composers and to provide them with the means whereby they may devote one year fully to composition. Composers must apply by April 15. A monetary prize of $60,000 (Australian) is awarded annually. Established in 1984 in honor of Don Banks, an Australian composer and the first chairperson of the Music Board. Formerly: (1997) Don Banks Composer Fellowship.

• 99 •
Australia Council
Literature Board
Jennifer Bott, CEO
PO Box 788
Operations Section
PO Box 788
Strawberry Hills, New South Wales 2012, Australia
Phone: 61 2 92159000
Fax: 61 2 92159111
E-mail: mail@ozco.gov.au
Home Page: http://www.ozco.gov.au

• 100 • **Writers' Emeritus Award**
To acknowledge the achievements of eminent literary writers over the age of 65 who have made outstanding and lifelong contributions to Australian literature. Literary excellence, importance of previous work and financial situation of the writer are the selection criteria. Nominated writers must have produced a critically acclaimed body of work over a long creative life and be able to document that their maximum annual income is less than $40,000. A monetary prize of up to $50,000 is awarded annually.

• 101 •
Australia Council for the Arts
Visual Arts/Craft Board
Jennifer Bott, CEO
372 Elizabeth St.
Surry Hills, New South Wales 2010, Australia
Phone: 61 2 92159000
Fax: 61 2 92159111
E-mail: mail@ozco.gov.au
Home Page: http://www.ozco.gov.au

• 102 • **Ros Bower Memorial Award**
To recognize distinguished efforts in fostering and furthering the philosophies and principles by artsworkers or organizations espoused by Ros Bower, founding Director of the Community Cultural Development Board. A monetary prize of $50,000 is awarded annually.

• 103 • **Red Ochre Award**
To honor artists who have made a great contribution to the recognition of Aboriginal and Torres Strait Island art and culture in the wider community at both the national and international level. A monetary award of $50,000 per year for up to three years is presented. Established in 1993.

• 104 • **Visual Arts Emeritus Award**
To acknowledge the achievements of eminent visual artists or craftspeople over the age of 60 who have made outstanding and lifelong contributions to visual arts and craft in Australia. The award is made to a visual artist or craftsperson whose contributions to the arts merits greater public recognition, and whose life and work continues to inspire Australians. Artists over 60 years of age working in any relevant area may be nominated. A monetary prize of $40,000 is awarded annually.

• 105 • **Visual Arts Emeritus Medal**
To honor the professional achievements of writers, curators, administrators, and advocates who have made major contributions throughout their careers to Australian visual art and craft. A monetary prize of $10,000 is awarded annually. Established in 1993.

• 106 •
Australia Department of Veterans' Affairs
De-Anne Kelly, Min.
PO Box 21
Woden 2606, Australia
Phone: 61 4902646
Fax: 61 4997427
E-mail: feedback@dva.gov.au
Home Page: http://www.dva.gov.au

• 107 • **Storywriting and Art Competition**
To provide therapeutic activity for eligible members of the ex-service community. Writing awards are given in the following categories: True War Experiences, True Life Experiences, Fiction, Poetry, and a special category. Art awards are given in the following categories: Oil Painting (novice and experienced), Other Media, and All Media. Craft awards are given in the following categories: Textile/Fibre, Needlework, Ceramics/Glass, and Wood. Photography awards are given in the following categories: War/Armed Services and Open. The Sir Edward Herring Memorial Prize is given for the overall outstanding entry. Monetary prizes totaling more than $5,000, trophies, and ribbons are awarded annually. Established in 1962.

• 108 •
Australian Academy of Science
Prof. Sue Serjeantson, Exec.Sec.
GPO Box 783
Canberra, Australian Capital Territory 2601, Australia
Phone: 61 2 62475777
Fax: 61 2 62574620
E-mail: aas@science.org.au
Home Page: http://www.science.org.au

• 109 • **Burnet Lecture**
Recognizes biological research of high standing. Awarded every two years in odd numbered years. Established in 1971 in honor of Sir MacFarlane Burnet.

• 110 • **Fenner Medal**
Recognizes biology research, except biomedical sciences. Scientists under the age of 40 who are normally residents of Australia are eligible. Research must have been conducted mainly in Australia. An honorarium of $1000 and a medal is awarded annually. Established in 2000.

• 111 • **R.J.W. Le Fevre Memorial Prize**
Recognizes the achievements of young researchers in chemistry, particularly physical chemistry. Scientists not more than 40 years of age are eligible. A monetary prize of $3,000 is awarded annually. Established in 1989 in memory of the late Professor R.J.W. Le Fevre.

• 112 • Flinders Medal and Lecture
Recognizes high standing scientific research in the field of physical science. An honorarium of $200 (Australian), a medal, honorary recognition, and an invitation to present the Matthew Flinders Lecture are awarded every other year, alternating with the Burnet Lecture. Established in 1956.

• 113 • Gottschalk Medal
Recognizes outstanding research in the medical sciences. Scientists who are under 40 years of age and not Fellows of the Academy and who have completed most of the research in Australia are eligible. An honorarium of $1000 and a medal is awarded annually. Established in 1976 by Dr. A. Gottschalk.

• 114 • Hannan Medal
To recognize a scientist for distinguished research carried out mainly in Australia in statistical science. Work carried out during the entire career of the candidates will be considered, but special weight will be given to their recent research. The award is given biennially in odd-numbered years, rotating among the following three categories: statistical science, pure mathematics, and applied and computational mathematics. Established in 1994 in honor of the late E.J. Hannan, Professor and Professor Emeritus of Statistics of the Australian National University.

• 115 • Dorothy Hill Award
Supports research in Earth sciences. Female researchers under the age of 40 are eligible. Candidates are normally Australian residents who have conducted research mainly in Australia. $5000 is awarded annually. Established in 2002 in honor of Professor Dorthy Hills.

• 116 • Jaeger Medal
Recognizes outstanding investigations into the solid earth or its oceans. Investigations carried out in Australia or having some connection with Australian earth science are eligible. A medal is normally awarded biennially in odd-numbered years. Established in 1991 to honor the late John Conrad Jaeger.

• 117 • Haddon King Medal
Recognizes original and sustained contributions to earth and related sciences of particular relevance to the discovery, evaluation, and exploitation of mineral deposits, including the hydrocarbons. Scientist residents of Australia and elsewhere are eligible. Deadline for nominations is May 12. A medal is awarded biennially in odd-numbered years. Established in 1993 in honor of the late Haddon Forrester King.

• 118 • Lyle Medal
Recognizes outstanding research in mathematics or physics. The research must have been completed during the previous five years, largely in Australia. A bronze medal and honorary recognition are awarded usually biennially. Established in 1931 in honor of Sir Thomas Ranken Lyle, FRS.

• 119 • Mawson Lecture
Recognizes contributions to the field of Earth Science. Australian scientists are eligible. An honorarium of $200, a bronze medal, and an invitation to deliver the Lecture at the convention of the Geological Society of Australia are awarded biennially in even numbered years. Established in 1979 in honor of Sir Douglas Mawson, FAA FRS.

• 120 • Moran Medal for Statistical Science
To recognize a scientist for distinguished research carried out mainly in Australia, in one or more of the fields of applied probability, biometrics, mathematical genetics, psychometrics, and statistics. Candidates must be no more than 40 years of age, or have significant interruptions to a research career. A monetary award of $1,000 and a medal are awarded biennially in odd-numbered years. Established in 1990 to honor the late Professor P.A.P. Moran.

• 121 • Pawsey Medal
Recognizes contributions to research in physics. Scientists under 40 years of age and citizens of Australia are eligible. The research must be carried out mainly in Australia. $1000 (Australian) and a medal are awarded annually. Established in 1965 in honor of Dr. Pawsey and his contributions to science in Australia.

• 122 • Selby Fellowship
To recognize distinguished overseas scientists and to enable them to undertake public lectures and visit scientific centers in Australia. Travel expenses and a daily living allowance are awarded annually. Financed through the Selby Scientific Foundation.

• 123 • Ian Wark Medal and Lecture
To recognize a scientist for a contribution to the prosperity of Australia where such prosperity is attained through the advance of scientific knowledge or its application, or both. Also, to focus attention on applications of scientific discoveries that have benefited the community. A medal and lecture are awarded biennially in even numbered years. Established in 1987 in memory of Sir Ian Wark, whose work was at the interface of science and industry.

• 124 • Frederick White Prize
Recognizes scientific research achievement in the fields of mathematics, physics, astronomy, chemistry, and terrestrial and planetary sciences. Australian scientists under the age of 40 are eligible. Research must have been conducted in Australia. $3000 (Australian) is awarded biennially. Established in 1981 by Sir Frederick White.

• 125 •
Australian Academy of the Humanities
Christine Barnicoat, Admin. Officer
GPO Box 93
Canberra, Australian Capital Territory 2601, Australia
Phone: 61 2 61259860
Phone: 61 2 61258950
Fax: 61 2 62486287
E-mail: christine.barnicoat@anu.edu.au
Home Page: http://www.humanities.org.au

• 126 • Crawford Medal
To recognize the outstanding achievements of scholars in the humanities in Australia. Australian humanities scholar in the early career stages are eligible. In making the award, the Council of the Academy shall take into account the actual or potential contributions of the research to the enrichment of cultural life in Australia. The medal is awarded biennially. Established in 1992. Contact Jesse Boyd at 02 6125 8965 for additional information.

• 127 •
Australian Acoustical Society
Mr. David Watkins, Gen.Sec.
PO Box 903
Castlemaine, Victoria 3450, Australia
Phone: 61 3 54706381
Fax: 61 3 54706381
E-mail: generalsecretary@acoustics.asn.au
Home Page: http://www.acoustics.asn.au

• 128 • President's Prize
Recognizes the best paper presented at annual conference. Awarded annually.

• 129 •
Australian-American Fulbright Commission
Mark Darby, Exec. Dir.
Level 1, 6 Napier Close
PO Box 9541
Deakin, Australian Capital Territory 2600, Australia
Phone: 61 2 6260 4460
Fax: 61 2 6260 4461
E-mail: fulbright@fulbright.com.au
Home Page: http://www.fulbright.com.au

• 130 • Fulbright Awards - American Program
For American scholars (4-6 months) and American postgraduates (8-12 months) to undertake study or research in Australia. Open to any American citizen not residing in Australia. See http://www.fulbright.com.au for details.

• 131 • Fulbright Awards - Australian Program
For Australian scholars, professionals, postdoctoral fellows, and postgraduates to undertake 3 to 12 months study or research in the United States. Open to all Australian citizens. More information is available at http://www.fulbright.com.au.

• 132 •
Australian and New Zealand Association for the Advancement of Science
Robert Perrin, Sec.
University of Adelaide
Adelaide, South Australia 5005, Australia
Phone: 61 8 83034965
Phone: 61 8 83742203
Fax: 61 8 83034965
E-mail: info@anzaas.org.au
Home Page: http://www.anzaas.org.au

• 133 • ANZAAS Medal
To recognize an individual for outstanding achievements in science. Individuals who normally reside in Australia or New Zealand may be nominated. A medal is awarded annually. Established in 1965.

• 134 • Mueller Medal
For recognition of important contributions to anthropological, botanical, geological or zoological science. Preference is given to work having special reference to Australasia. There is no restriction on eligibility for the award. A medal is awarded annually. Established in 1902.

• 135 •
Australian and New Zealand Society of Respiratory Science
Kevin R. Gain PhD, Website Coor.
Royal Perth Hospital
GPO Box 2213
Perth, Western Australia 6847, Australia
Phone: 61 8 92242887
Fax: 61 8 92242385
E-mail: kevin.gain@health.wa.gov.au
Home Page: http://www.anzsrs.org.au

• 136 • Bird Young Investigator Award
For research done by young investigators and presented at the annual scientific meeting of the society.

• 137 • Compumedics Poster Prize
For the best poster presentation at the annual scientific meeting of the society.

• 138 • Life Membership
For contributions to the society.

• 139 • Research/Educational Awards
Awards of recognition.

• 140 • Society Medal
For scientific contributions to the profession.

• 141 • Technipro Best Oral Presentation
For the best oral presentation at the annual scientific meeting of the society.

• 142 •
Australian Association of the Deaf
Ann Darwin, Pres.
PO Box 1083
Stafford
Stafford, Queensland 4053, Australia
Phone: 61 7 33578266
Phone: 61 7 33578277
Fax: 61 7 33578377
E-mail: aad@aad.org.au
Home Page: http://www.aad.org.au

• 143 • Dorothy Shaw Deaf Australian of the Year Award
Recognizes a deaf person who has made an outstanding contribution to the Deaf Community. In addition, the Dorothy Shaw Deaf Youth of the Year is also honored. Awarded annually.

• 144 •
Australian Business Limited Incorporating the State Chamber of Commerce (NSW)
Mark Bethwaite, Managing Dir./CEO
Australian Business Centre
140 Arthur St.
North Sydney, New South Wales 2060, Australia
Fax: 61 1 300655277
Home Page: http://www.australianbusiness.com.au

• 145 • Business Innovation
For the successful implementation of a demonstrably Australian innovation.

• 146 • Education and Training
For an Australian company.

• 147 • Export and Trade
For an Australian company.

• 148 • President's Prize for Best Regional Business
For an outstanding company.

• 149 •
Australian Chess Federation
Paul Broekhuyse, Contact
19 Gill Ave.
Avoca Beach, New South Wales 2251, Australia
Phone: 61 2 43824525
Home Page: http://www.auschess.org

• 150 • Koshnitsky Medal
Annual award of recognition for chess administration on a national or state level.

• 151 • Purdy Medal
Annual award of recognition for outstanding contribution as a player or journalist.

• 152 • Steiner Medal
Annual award of recognition for the Australian chess player with the greatest impact or notable achievement.

• 153 •
Australian Cinematographers Society
William Bruce Hillyard, Sec.
42 Sawyer Ln.
Artarmon, New South Wales 2064, Australia
Phone: 61 2 99066262
Fax: 61 2 99063430
E-mail: info@cinematographer.org.au
Home Page: http://www.acs.asn.au

• 154 • Milli Award
For recognition of the best achievement in cinematography by an Australian cinematographer. Membership in the Society is necessary for consideration in any category. Awards maybe given in the following categories: (1) Experimental & Specialized Cinematography (2) TV Station Breaks & Promos; (3) Music Clips (4) Newsgathering; (5) News Magazine (6) TV Magazine (7) Current Affairs; (8) Wildlife & Nature Films; (9) Commercials for Cinema & TV; (10) Corporate Productions; (11) Training & Education; (12) Documentaries for Cinema & TV; (13) Dramatised Documentaries; (14) Fiction Drama Shorts for Cinema & TV; (15) Telefeatures, TV Drama & Mini-Series; and (16) Feature Productions for Cinema. A trophy is awarded annually. Established in 1968.

• 155 •
Australian College of Educators
Cheryl O'Connor, CEO
PO Box 323
Deakin West, Australian Capital Territory 2600, Australia
Phone: 61 2 62811677
Fax: 61 2 62851262
E-mail: ace@austcolled.com.au
Home Page: http://www.austcolled.com.au

• 156 • College Medal
For recognition of an outstanding contribution to education in Australia. Australian citizens or long-term residents of Australia may be nominated for the Award. Selection is made by a committee. A medal and framed citation are awarded annually at the College national conference. Established in 1981. Formerly: (2006) Australian College of Education Medal.

• 157 • Fellowship of the Australian College of Education
For recognition of a distinctive contribution to the advancement of education. College members must be nominated for selection by a committee. A parchment is awarded annually at the College national conference. Established in 1959.

• 158 •
Australian College of Rural and Remote Medicine
David Campbell, Pres.
GPO Box 2507
Brisbane, Queensland 4001, Australia
Phone: 61 7 31058200
Fax: 61 7 31058299
E-mail: acrrm@acrrm.org.au
Home Page: http://www.acrrm.org.au

• 159 • Distinguished Service Awards
For fellows, members or nonmedical persons who have provided specific and significant contributions to rural and remote medicine.

• 160 • Honorary Fellowship
For individuals who have provided significant contributions to the organization.

• 161 • Honorary Membership
For distinguished or significant service to the organization.

• 162 • John Flynn Scholarships
For aspiring rural doctors.

• 163 • Life Fellowship
For fellows who have rendered outstanding and meritorious service to the College.

• 164 • Medical Rural Bonded Scholarship Scheme
For new medical students prepared to commit to at least six years of rural practice once they completed their basic medical and postgraduate training.

• 165 • MedicarePlus Procedural Training Grants
For support to procedural rural doctors in upgrading their skills in anaesthetics, obstetrics and surgery.

• 166 • Rural Australia Medical Undergraduate Scholarship Scheme
For students with rural background who enter and complete their study of medicine.

• 167 •
Australian Council for Educational Leaders
Jenny Lewis, Exec. Officer
PO Box 4268
Winmalee, New South Wales 2777, Australia
Phone: 61 2 47517974
Fax: 61 2 47517974
E-mail: acel@pnc.com.au
Home Page: http://www.acel.org.au

• 168 • Gold Medal
Recognizes outstanding contributions to the study and practice of educational administration. Educators are eligible. Awarded annually.

• 169 • Nganakarrawa Award
Recognizes general excellence in educational administration and significant contributions to ACEA. Awarded annually.

• 170 •
Australian Council for International Development
Gaye Hart, Exec.Dir.
Private Bag 3
Deakin, Australian Capital Territory 2600, Australia
Phone: 61 2 62851816
Fax: 61 2 62851720
E-mail: main@acfid.asn.au
Home Page: http://www.acfid.asn.au

• 171 • ACFOA Human Rights Award
Recognizes substantial contribution towards sustainable human development. Individuals are eligible. A trophy is awarded annually.

• 172 •
Australian Council of Women and Policing
Narelle Beer, Sec.
PO Box 3994
Manuka, Australian Capital Territory 2603, Australia
Phone: 61 2 62842923
E-mail: acwap@ozemail.com.au
Home Page: http://www.auspol-women.asn.au

• 173 • Bravery Award
For a woman who demonstrates great commitment, courage and determination in improving the lives of people.

• 174 • Excellence in Research on Improving Policing For Women Award
For an outstanding research in women policing.

• 175 • Most Outstanding Female Administrator
To a woman For making a significant impact on the lives of many women within the police service.

• 176 • Most Outstanding Female Investigator
For a young woman who has been outstanding in her work investigating violence against women.

• 177 • Most Outstanding Female Leader
For a woman who demonstrates excellent leadership in a team.

• 178 •
Australian Direct Marketing Association
Rob Edwards, CEO
GPO Box 3895
Sydney, New South Wales 2001, Australia
Phone: 61 2 92775400
Fax: 61 2 92775410
E-mail: info@adma.com.au
Home Page: http://www.adma.com.au

• 179 • Australian Direct Marketing Awards

• 180 • Awards for Excellence

• 181 • Young Direct Marketer of the Year

• 182 •
Australian Entertainment Industry Association
Brendan Schwab, Chief Exec.
Level 1, 15-17 Queen St.
608 St. Kilda Rd.
Melbourne, Victoria 3000, Australia
Phone: 61 3 96141111
Fax: 61 3 96141166
E-mail: aeia@aeia.org.au
Home Page: http://www.aeia.org.au

• 183 • Helpmann Awards
To recognize distinguished artistic achievement and excellence in the performing arts in Australia. Productions of theatre, musical theatre, opera, ballet or dance, contemporary and classical music, visual or physical theatre, comedy, special events, new works, and children's presentations are eligible. In addition, the James Cassius Award is bestowed in recognition of outstanding contribution to the Australian Live Performance Industry. Awarded annually. Established in 2001 in honor of Sir Robert Helpmann.

• 184 •
Australian Federation of University Women
Rosemary Everett, Sec.
LPO Box 8334
Canberra, Australian Capital Territory 2601, Australia
Phone: 61 2 61250393
Fax: 61 2 61250393
E-mail: afuw@anu.edu.au
Home Page: http://www.afuw.org.au

Formerly: (1989) Australian Federation of University Women - South Australia.

• 185 • AFUW-SA Inc. Trust Fund Bursary
To assist women with study towards a Master's degree by course work at a recognized higher education institution in Australia. Applicants must have an honors degree or equivalent and not be employed full-time. There is no restriction on age or field of study. The deadline is March 1. A monetary award of up to $3,000 Australian is presented annually in June. Established in 1991.

Awards are arranged in alphabetical order below their administering organizations

• 186 • Thenie Baddams Bursary
To assist women with research towards a Master's by research or Ph.D. degree at a recognized higher education institution in Australia. Applicants must have completed one year of postgraduate research. There is no restriction on age or field of study. A monetary award of up to $6,000 Australian is presented. Established in 1986 to honor Thenie Baddams, President of AFUW from 1982 to 1985.

• 187 • Cathy Candler Bursary
To assist women or men of any nationality complete a master's or Ph.D. degree by research at a recognized higher education institution in South Australia. Applicants must have completed one year of post-graduate research. There is no restriction on age or field of study. Students in full-time employment are not eligible and evidence of enrollment must be provided at time of application. The deadline is March 1. One monetary award of $2,500 Australian is awarded annually.

• 188 • Barbara Crase Bursary
To assist women or men of any nationally complete a master's or Ph.D. degree by research at a recognized higher education institution in South Australia. Applicants must have completed one year of post-graduate research. There is no restriction on age or field of study. Students in full-time employment are not eligible and evidence of enrollment must be provided at time of application. The deadline is March 1. One monetary award of $2,500 Australian is awarded annually.

• 189 • Diamond Jubilee Bursary
To assist women or men of any nationality complete a master's or Ph.D. degree by course work at a recognized higher education institution in South Australia. There is no restriction on age or field of study. Students in full-time employment are not eligible and evidence of enrollment must be provided at time of application. Applicants must have an honors degree or equivalent. The deadline is March 1. One monetary award of $2,000 Australian is awarded annually.

• 190 • Jean Gilmore Bursary
To assist women with research towards a Master's by research or Ph.D. degree at a recognized higher education institution in Australia. Applicants must have completed one year of postgraduate research. There is no restriction on age or field of study. A monetary award of up to $6,000 Australian is presented annually in June. Established in 1969 to honor Jean Gilmore, President of the AFUW from 1965 to 1968.

• 191 • Doreen McCarthy Bursary
To assist women or men of any nationality to complete a master's degree by course work at a recognized higher education institution in South Australia. Applicants must have completed one year of post-graduate research. There is no restriction on age or field of study. Applicants must have an honors degree or equivalent and have completed one year of study. Students in full-time employment are not eligible and evidence of enrollment must be provided at time of application. The deadline is March 1. One monetary award of $2,500 is awarded annually.

• 192 • Padnendadlu Graduate Bursary
To assist indigenous Australian women to complete postgraduate study at a recognized higher education institution in South Australia. There is no restriction on age or field of study. Students in full-time employment are not eligible and evidence of enrollment must be provided at time of application. Applicants must have an honors degree or the equivalent and have completed one year of postgraduate research. The deadline is 1 March each year. A monetary award of $2,500 Australian is awarded annually. Established in 1997 as a result of the 30th Triennial Conference of the AFUW.

• 193 • Winifred E. Preedy Post-Graduate Bursary
To assist women who are or have been students in the Faculty of Dentistry in The University of Adelaide at the time of application to further their studies at postgraduate level in Dentistry or a related field. Applicants must have completed one year of their postgraduate degree. Applications must be submitted by March 1. A monetary award of A$5,000 is presented annually. Established in 1992 from the bequest of Winifred E. Preedy BDS (1901-1989), a devoted Life Member of AFUWSA Inc., who graduated in 1927, the second woman to graduate BDS in The University of Adelaide.

• 194 • Georgina Sweet Fellowship
Assists women in carrying out some advanced study or research in Australia for a period of four to twelve months. Application deadline is July 31 in the year of the offer. A fellowship of $6000 Australian is awarded biennially. Established in 1965 in honor of Dr. Georgina Sweet, a foundation member and an active member of the Victorian Branch of the Federation. Application papers are available from The Fellowship Convener, PO Box 14, Bullcreek, WA 6149 Australia.

• 195 •
Australian Film Institute
Robyn Young, Awards Coord.
236 Dorcas St.
South Melbourne, Victoria 3205, Australia
Phone: 61 3 96961884
Fax: 61 3 96967972
E-mail: info@afi.org.au
Home Page: http://www.afi.org.au

• 196 • AFI Awards - The Australian Film Institute Awards
For recognition of achievement and excellence in film and television production. Films must be either produced in Australia using a significant Australian cast (if applicable), key creative production personnel and facilities, or must be an official Australian co-production. Formerly: (2004) Emirates AFI Awards (The Australian Film Awards).

• 197 • Byron Kennedy Award
To recognize an individual working in any area of the Australian film or television industry, whose quality of work is marked by the pursuit of excellence. A monetary award of $10,000 and a trophy are presented. Established in 1984. Formerly: (2004) Byron Kennedy Memorial Prize.

• 198 • Raymond Longford Award
For recognition of an individual who has made a significant contribution to Australian filmmaking. A trophy is awarded annually. Established in 1968.

• 199 •
Australian Honours Secretariat
Secretary, Order of Australia
Government House
Canberra, Australian Capital Territory 2600, Australia
Phone: 61 2 6283 3604
Fax: 61 2 6283 3620
Home Page: http://www.gg.gov.au/textonly/honours.html
Formerly: (1995) Council for the Order of Australia.

• 200 • Ambulance Service Medal
To recognize distinguished service by members of Australian full-time and volunteer ambulance services. Recommendations are made by the responsible Minister to the Governor-General for approval. A medal in silver and bronze tones is awarded when merited. Established in 1999.

• 201 • Anniversary of National Service 1951-1972 Medal
To commemorate the service of persons who gave service under the National Service Act 1951, as the act was in force from time to time between 1951 and 1972, or who gave other service in discharge of the obligations to serve under that Act. The award is made by the Governor-General or his/her delegate. Established in 2001.

• 202 • Australian Antarctic Medal
To recognize outstanding service in scientific research or exploration, or in support of such work, in connection with Australian Antarctic expeditions. Recommendations are made by the responsible Minister to the Governor-General for approval. Awards are normally announced annually on June 21, Midwinter's Day, which is a traditional day of celebration for Antarctic expedition members. Established in 1987.

• 203 • Australian Bravery Decorations
To recognize Australian citizens and others for acts of bravery in other than warlike situations. There are five grades of award that can be made to individuals. The Cross of Valour - for acts of the most conspicuous courage in circumstances of extreme peril. The Star of Courage - for acts of conspicuous courage in circumstance of great peril. The Bravery Medal - for acts of bravery in hazardous circumstances. The Commendation for Brave Conduct - for other acts of bravery

Awards are arranged in alphabetical order below their administering organizations

which are considered worthy of recognition. The Group Citation for Bravery - for collective acts of bravery. Each decoration may be awarded posthumously. Nominations can be made by members of the public and are considered by the Australian Bravery Decorations Council. Established in 1975.

• 204 • Australian Cadet Forces Service Medal

To recognize 15 years of efficient service by officers and instructors in the Australian Cadet Force. A nickel-silver medal is awarded when merited; a clasp is awarded for each additional five years of qualifying service. Recommendations are made by the Chief of the Defence Force or his/her delegate to the Governor-General for approval. Established in 1999.

• 205 • Australian Fire Service Medal

To recognize distinguished service by members of Australian full-time and volunteer fire services. Recommendations are made by the responsible Minister to the Governor-General for approval. An annual quota exists for each fire service. Established in 1988.

• 206 • Australian Police Medal

To recognize distinguished service by members of Australian police forces. Recommendations are made by the responsible Minister to the Governor-General for approval. An annual quota exists for each police service. Established in 1986.

• 207 • Australian Service Medals

To recognize service in prescribed areas. The Australian Active Service Medal 1945-1975 and the Australian Active Service Medal are given to recognize service in a prescribed warlike operation (the latter recognizes service from 1975 onwards). The Australian Service Medal 1945-1975 and the Australian Service Medal are given to recognize service in a declared peacekeeping or non-warlike operation. Awards are made by the Governor-General on the recommendation of the Chief of the Defence Force or his/her delegate. The four medals were established between 1988 and 1997.

• 208 • Australian Sports Medal

To recognize individuals who have made a contribution to Australian sport as a current of former participant or through the provision of support service to Australian sport. Medals are made by the Governor-General's recommendation to the Prime Minister or a person authorized by the Prime Minister. Established in 1999.

• 209 • Centenary Medal

To commemorate 100 years of federation and to acknowledge the challenges of the new century by recognizing citizens and other people who made a contribution to Australian society or government. Awards are made by the Governor-General on the recommendation of the Prime Minister or a person authorized in writing by the Prime Minister to make a recommendation. Established in 2001.

• 210 • Champion Shots Medal

To honor winners in the annual target shooting contest with standard issue weapons conducted by each arm of the Defence Force. Three medals (one for each Service) are awarded annually. The award is made with a clasp to denote the year of the competition and any subsequent award to the same person is made in the form of another clasp. Awards are made by the Governor-General on the recommendation of the Chief of the Defence Force or his/her delegate. Established in 1988.

• 211 • Civilian Service Medal 1939-1945

To recognize the service of civilians who served in Australia during World War II in organizations that were subject to military-like arrangements and conditions of service, in arduous circumstances, in support of the war effort. A bronze medal portraying the Southern Cross and surrounded by Golden Wattle is awarded. Established in 1994.

• 212 • Conspicuous Service Decorations

To recognize outstanding or meritorious achievement or devotion to duty in nonwarlike situations by members of the Defence Force and certain others. The Conspicuous Service Cross is given for outstanding devotion to duty or outstanding achievement in the application of exceptional skills, judgment, or dedication in nonwarlike situations. The Conspicuous Service Medal is also given for meritorious achievement or devotion to duty in nonwarlike situations. Each decoration may be awarded posthumously. The awards are made by the Governor-General on the recommendation of the Minister for Defence. Established in 1989.

• 213 • Defence Long Service Medal

To recognize 15 years of efficient service by members of the Australian Defence Force. Recommendations are made by the Chief of the Defence Force or his/her delegate to the Governor-General for approval. Members of philanthropic organizations who are serving with the Australian Defence Force are eligible for nomination. A clasp is awarded for each additional five years of qualifying service. Established in 1982.

• 214 • Distinguished Service Decorations

To recognize members of the Defence Force and certain others for distinguished command and leadership in action or distinguished performance of duties in warlike operations. There are three levels of awards. The Distinguished Service Cross is given for distinguished command and leadership in action. The Distinguished Service Medal is given for distinguished leadership in action. The Commendation for Distinguished Service is given for distinguished performance of duties in warlike operations. Each decoration may be awarded posthumously. The awards are made by the Governor-General on the recommendation of the Minister for Defence. Established in 1991.

• 215 • Emergency Services Medal

To recognize distinguished service by members of emergency services across Australia, and people who are involved in emergency management, training, or education. Recommendations are made by the responsible Minister to the Governor-General for approval. Established in 1999.

• 216 • Gallantry Decorations

To recognize members of the Defence Force and certain others who perform acts of gallantry in action. There are four levels of awards. The Victoria Cross for Australia is given for acts of valour or self-sacrifice. The Star of Gallantry is given for acts of great heroism or conspicuous gallantry in action in circumstances of great peril. The Medal for Gallantry is given for acts of gallantry in action in hazardous circumstances. The Commendation for Gallantry is given for other acts of gallantry that are considered worthy of recognition. Each decoration may be awarded posthumously. The awards are made by the Governor-General on the recommendation of the Minister for Defence. The Governor-General may also delegate his power to make immediate awards to military commanders in the field. Established in 1991.

• 217 • Humanitarian Overseas Service Medal

To recognize emergency humanitarian service in hazardous conditions outside Australia. A medal is awarded when merited; clasps denote the area of prescribed service. Established in 1999.

• 218 • International Force East Timor Medal

To recognize service by members of the Australian Defence Force who served in East Timor during the International Force East Timor (INTERFET) campaign (Sept. 1999-April 2000). The medal may also be awarded to members of an allied country's INTERFET operation. Awards are made by the Governor-General on the recommendation of the Chief of the Defence Force or his/her delegate. Established in 2000.

• 219 • National Medal

This, AustraliaKs most awarded civilian medal, is given to recognize long service in the Australian Defence Force, including part-time and volunteer service, members of the Australian Protective Service, correctional and emergency services, and volunteer search and rescue groups. Many, but not all, eligible groups are uniformed. Fifteen yearsK service is required to qualify. A circular bronze medal is awarded when merited; a clasp is awarded for each additional ten years of qualifying service. Established in 1975.

• 220 • Nursing Service Cross

To recognize outstanding performance of nursing duties in both operational and nonoperational situations by members of the Defence Force and certain others. The decoration may be awarded posthumously. Awards are made by the Governor-General on the recommendation of the Minister for Defence. Established in 1989.

Awards are arranged in alphabetical order below their administering organizations

• 221 • **Order of Australia**

For recognition of achievement and merit in service of Australia. The Order of Australia consists of a General Division and a Military Division. Australian citizens, including members of the Defence Force, are eligible to be appointed to the Order as members in the General Division. Persons other than Australian citizens are eligible to be appointed to the Order as honorary members in the General Division or may be appointed a member if it is desirable that the person be honored by Australia. The Medal of the Order in the General Division may be awarded to Australian citizens and other persons. In the General Division, appointments are made in the following categories: Companions or honorary Companions - for eminent achievement and merit of the highest degree in service to Australia or to humanity at large; Officers or honorary Officers - for distinguished service of a high degree to Australia or to humanity at large; Members or honorary Members - for service in a particular locality or field of activity or to a particular group; and Medal of the Order - for service worthy of particular recognition. Any person or organization may submit to the Secretary of the Order for consideration by the Council a nomination of an Australian citizen for appointment to the Order as a member in the General Division or a nomination of a person for the award of the Medal of the Order in the General Division. Members of the Defence Force are eligible to be appointed to the Order as members in the Military Division. Members of the armed forces of a country other than Australia are eligible to be appointed to the Order as honorary members in the Military Division. In any calendar year, the number of appointments (other than honorary appointments) to the Military Division shall not exceed one-tenth of one percent of the average number of persons who were members of the Defence Force on each day of the immediately preceding year. The Medal of the Order in the Military Division may be awarded to members of the Defence Force. In the Military Division, appointments are made in the following categories: Companions or honorary Companions - for eminent service in duties of great responsibility; Officers or honorary Officers - for distinguished service in responsible positions; Members or honorary Members - for exceptional service or performance of duty; and Medal of the Order - for meritorious service or performance of duty. Upon the recommendation of the Minister for Defence, appointments as members or honorary members of the Order in the Military Division and awards of the Medal of the Order in the Military Division are made with the approval of the Sovereign, by Instruments signed by the Governor-General. Appointments in both Divisions are announced each year on Australia Day (January 26) and on the celebration of The Queen's Birthday in June. Established in 1975.

• 222 • **Police Overseas Service Medal**

To recognize service with international peacekeeping organizations by officers of Australian police forces. The award is made with a clasp to denote the area of prescribed service and any subsequent award to the same person is made in the form of a further clasp with the prescribed service appropriately inscribed. Awards are made by the Governor-General on the recommendation of the Chief Officer of an Australian police force. Established in 1991.

• 223 • **Public Service Medal**

To recognize outstanding service by members of Australian public services and other government employees, including those in local government. Recommendations are made by the responsible Minister to the Governor-General for approval. An annual quota exists for each government public service. Established in 1989.

• 224 • **Unit Citations**

To recognize gallantry in action or outstanding service in warlike operations by units of the Defence Force and/or units of the defence forces of other countries. The Unit Citation for Gallantry is given for extraordinary gallantry in action and the Meritorious Unit Citation is given for sustained outstanding service in warlike operations. Each citation consists of a certificate of citation to the Unit signed by the Governor-General and insignia for each recipient. Insignia may be awarded posthumously. The award is made by the Governor-General on the recommendation of the Minister for Defence. Established in 1991.

• 225 • **Vietnam Logistic and Support Medal**

To recognize service in Vietnam between May 29, 1964 and January 27, 1973. Qualifying service includes: 28 days in ships or craft on inland waters or off the coast of Vietnam; one day or more on the posted strength of a unit or formation on land; one operational sortie over Vietnam or Vietnamese waters by aircrew on the posted strength of a unit; or official visits either continuous or aggregate of 30 days. Established in 1968. Formerly: (1995) Vietnam Medal.

• 226 •

Australian Hotels Association (NSW)
John Torpe, Pres.
Level 5, 8 Quay St. Prince Ctre.
Sydney, New South Wales 2000, Australia
Phone: 61 2 92816922
Fax: 61 2 92811857
E-mail: admin@aha-nsw.asn.au
Home Page: http://www.aha-nsw.asn.au

• 227 • **Best Dance Venue**

For hotels that have an area devoted to dancing.

• 228 • **Best General Entertainment Amusement Venue**

For hotels that provide a selection of non musical entertainment and amusement For patrons.

• 229 • **Best Practices**

For hotels that demonstrate success in environmentally sympathetic operation and innovative approach to increasing health and safety awareness.

• 230 • **Outstanding Achievement in Patron Transport Safety**

For hotels that demonstrate achievement in the safe transportation of patrons.

• 231 • **Outstanding Community Service**

For hotels that play a strong role in the community

• 232 •

Australian Institute of Agricultural Science and Technology
Allan R. Jones, CEO/Ed.
AIAST
Level 2/21 Burwood Rd.
Hawthorn, Victoria 3122, Australia
Phone: 61 3 98153600
Fax: 61 3 98153633
E-mail: members@aiast.com.au
Home Page: http://www.aiast.com.au

• 233 • **Medal of Agriculture**

Annual award of recognition for service to agricultural science. Established in 1941.

• 234 •

Australian Institute of Building
Thomas John Morris, Pres.
GPO Box 1467
Canberra, Australian Capital Territory 2610, Australia
Phone: 61 2 62477433
E-mail: ausbuild@aib.org.au
Home Page: http://www.aib.org.au

• 235 • **Chapter Award**

For best graduate student in endorsed courses.

• 236 • **Professional Excellence in Building Awards**

• 237 • **Florence Taylor Medal**

To the best apprentice in each state.

• 238 •

Australian Institute of Energy
Mr. Colin Paulson, Sec.
PO Box 268
Toukley, New South Wales 2263, Australia
Phone: 61 2 43931114
Fax: 61 2 43931114
E-mail: aie@aie.org.au
Home Page: http://www.aie.org.au

• 239 • **Australian Institute of Energy Medal**

For recognition of achievement in the field of energy. Members only may be nominated. A medal is awarded when merited. Established in 1980.

• 240 •
Australian Institute of Genealogical Studies
Glen Turnbull, Pres.
41 Railway Rd.
PO Box 339
Blackburn, Victoria 3130, Australia
Phone: 61 3 98773789
Fax: 61 3 98779066
E-mail: info@aigs.org.au
Home Page: http://www.aigs.org.au

• 241 • **Alexander Henderson Award**
To recognize the best family history published in Australia, improve the quality of published family histories, and encourage people to write their family history. Any writer is eligible. The deadline is November 30. A trophy is awarded annually. Established in 1974 in honor of Alexander Henderson, an Australian pioneer genealogist.

• 242 •
Australian Institute of Landscape Architects
Petra Weisner, Office Mgr.
GPO Box 1646
Canberra, Australian Capital Territory 2601, Australia
Phone: 61 2 62489970
Fax: 61 2 62497337
E-mail: admin@aila.org.au
Home Page: http://www.aila.org.au

• 243 • **Award for Excellence in Landscape Architecture**
For outstanding projects from each of the categories of design, planning, environment, and research.

• 244 • **Commendation Award in Landscape Architecture**
For projects deemed to be worthy of commendation.

• 245 • **Merit Award in Landscape Architecture**
For projects deemed to be of a meritorious nature.

• 246 • **National Award in Landscape Architecture**
For outstanding achievement in landscape architecture.

• 247 •
Australian Institute of Nuclear Science and Engineering
Dennis Mather, Scientific Sec.
Private Mail Bag No. 1
Menai, New South Wales 2234, Australia
Phone: 61 2 97173376
Fax: 61 2 97179268
E-mail: ainse@ansto.gov.au
Home Page: http://www.ainse.edu.au

• 248 • **AINSE Awards**

• 249 • **AINSE Gold Medal**
For excellence in research.

• 250 • **AINSE Post Graduate Research Awards**
For postgraduate students whose research projects are associated with nuclear science or its applications.

• 251 •
Australian Institute of Physics
David Jamieson, Pres.
PO Box 82
Parkville, Victoria 3052, Australia
Phone: 61 3 93266669
Fax: 61 3 93267272
E-mail: aip@aip.org.au
Home Page: http://www.aip.org.au

• 252 • **Award for Outstanding Service to Physics in Australia**
To recognize outstanding service to the profession of physics. Society members are eligible for nomination. Nominations are called for in May or June of each year. Awarded annually. Established in 1996.

• 253 • **Walter Boas Medal**
For recognition of original research by an Australian in physics. A medal is awarded annually. Institute members who are also Australian citizens are eligible. Self nominations and nominations from other members are accepted. Established in 1984 in honor of Walter Boas.

• 254 • **Bragg Gold Medal for Excellence in Physics**
To recognize the student who is judged to have completed the most outstanding PhD in physics under the auspices of an Australian university and whose degree has been approved in the previous thirteen months. Awarded annually. Established in 1992 to commemorate the work of W. L. and W. H. Bragg.

• 255 • **Harrie Massie Medal and Prize**
Recognizes an Australian physicist or a non-Australian physicist working or residing in Australia for contributions to physics or its applications. Applicants must be members of the Australian Institute of Physics or the Institute of Physics (England). A medal is awarded annually. Established in 1988 in honor of Sir Harrie Massey.

• 256 • **Alan Walsh Medal for Service to Industry**
Recognizes research and/or development leading to patents, processes, or inventions that influence an industrial process. Physists who have resided in Australia for at least five years of the preceding seven years prior to application date are eligible. A trophy is awarded every two years.

• 257 •
Australian Institute of Professional Photography
PO Box 2137
Fitzroy, Victoria 3065, Australia
Fax: 61 3 94210227
E-mail: admin@aipp.com.au
Home Page: http://www.aipp.com.au

• 258 • **Australian Commercial/Industrial Photographer of the Year**
For exemplary works of a commercial/industrial photographer member.

• 259 • **Australian Landscape Photographer of the Year**
For exemplary works of a landscape photographer member.

• 260 • **Australian Professional Photographer of the Year**
To the most outstanding professional photographer member.

• 261 • **Australian Professional Photography Awards**
To the most outstanding photographers in different categories.

• 262 • **Joanne Felk Award**
Award of recognition.

• 263 • **Tertiary Institute Award**
Award of recognition.

• 264 •
Australian Institute of Quantity Surveyors
Mr. Terry Sanders, Gen.Mgr.
PO Box 301
Deakin West, Australian Capital Territory 2600, Australia
Phone: 61 2 62822222
Fax: 61 2 62852427
E-mail: contact@aiqs.com.au
Home Page: http://www.aiqs.com.au

• 265 • **National President's Award**
Annual award of recognition. Top students in Quantity Surveying degree courses are eligible.

• 266 •
Australian Institute of Radiography
Mr. Emile Badawy, Exec.Officer
PO Box 1169
Collingwood, Victoria 3066, Australia
Phone: 61 3 94193336
Fax: 61 3 94160783
E-mail: enquiries@a-i-r.com.au
Home Page: http://www.a-i-r.com.au

• 267 • **Nicholas Outterside Medallion**
For the promotion of radiography. Up to three medals are awarded annually. Established in 1982.

• 268 •
Australian Library and Information Association
Jennefer Nicholson, Exec.Dir.
PO Box 6335
Kingston, Australian Capital Territory 2604, Australia
Phone: 61 2 62158222
Fax: 61 2 62822249
E-mail: enquiry@alia.org.au
Home Page: http://www.alia.org.au

Formerly: (1988) Library Association of Australia.

• 269 • **H. C. L. Anderson Award**
To recognize an individual who has rendered outstanding service to librarianship or to the library profession in Australia, or to the theory or practice of librarianship. Professional members of the Association who hold overseas qualifications in librarianship or archives that are recognized as professional qualifications by a Library Association or Archives Association in the country concerned are eligible. Any member of the Association or the Council of a Division may nominate persons for this award. A statuette is awarded annually. Established in 1973 to honor Henry Charles Lennox Anderson.

• 270 • **Ellinor Archer Pioneer Award**
To recognize an individual who has rendered outstanding service to a library or libraries, the promotion of a library or libraries, to the theory or practice of librarianship, or an associated field such as systems, conservation, management, or bibliography. Individuals who are employed in libraries and who are not eligible for Associateship of the Association are eligible. Any member of the Association or the Council of a Division may nominate persons for this award. A statuette is awarded annually. Established in 1984 to honor Mary Ellinor Lucy Archer. Formerly: (2006) Ellinor Archer Award.

• 271 • **Australian Library and Information Association Fellow**
Recognizes distinguished contribution to the theory of practice of library and information science. Nominees must have at least eight years' standing as a professional member of the Association. Any professional member(s) of the Association; be at least 30 years of age; and be a personal member of the Association or the Council of a Division may nominate a professional member for this distinction. A certificate is awarded irregularly. Established in 1963.

• 272 • **Redmond Barry Award**
To recognize outstanding service to the promotion of a library or of libraries, to the Association, to the theory or practice of librarianship, or to an associated field such as bibliography. Individuals who are not eligible to be professional members of the Association and who are not employed in a library are eligible. Any member of the Association or the council of a Division may nominate persons for this award. A statuette is awarded annually. Established in 1973 to honor Sir Redmond Barry.

• 273 • **Maria Gemenis Award**
To recognize an outstanding contribution by a member in an information management role or special library environment. Only members of the ALIA Information Online Group section may be nominated. Awarded annually. Established in 1983 to honor Maria Gemenis.

• 274 • **Letter of Recognition**
To recognize a person or an institution or organization that has rendered a significant, specific service to a library or libraries, to the Association, or to the promotion or development of libraries or library science, or who has over a period demonstrated significant service above the call of duty in these fields. The Letter of Recognition is not available routinely to people working in or with libraries or with the Association who are retiring or to office bearers of the Association who are finishing their term of office. Any member of the Association or the Council of a Division may nominate persons for this award. A Letter of Recognition is awarded irregularly. Established in 1985.

• 275 • **Library Technician of the Year**
To recognize outstanding contributions to the advancement of library technicians and/or the Library Technicians Section of the ALIA. A trophy and a citation are awarded annually. Established in 1989.

• 276 • **Metcalfe Award**
For recognition of the most outstanding essay or other piece of work on any topic of interest to library and information services submitted by a student taking a first award course in library and information science. Entries must be pieces of work of publishable or reproducible standard and up to 5,000 words in length. Winning entries are published by the Association. Entries close on August 1 each year. A medallion is awarded annually. Established in 1984 in memory of John Wallace Metcalfe and his contribution to librarianship and library education. Formerly: (2006) Metcalfe Medallion.

• 277 • **Study Grant Awards**
To provide support for practicing librarians/information professionals wishing to undertake a study project. The Association's intention in offering study grants is to provide an opportunity for librarians to undertake projects they would otherwise be unable to do because of the time and costs involved. A practicing librarian in a supervisory or middle management position, with a minimum of three years' experience in library and information work is eligible. Applications must be submitted by August 31 each year. Monetary awards of up to $5,000 are presented annually. Established in 1984.

• 278 • **WA Special Librarian of the Year Award**
To recognize outstanding contribution to the library profession by a special librarian. Nominees must be members of the ALIA Special Libraries Section, WA Group and have demonstrated a willingness to share professional expertise and to participate in formal and informal networking activities, good management practices, and successful promotion of the library. A trophy and cash prize of $250 are awarded annually.

• 279 •
Australian Mammal Society
Lynne Selwood, Pres.
Department of Biological Sciences
Monash University
Wellington Rd.
Clayton, Victoria 3186, Australia
Phone: 61 3 99055623
Fax: 61 3 99055613
E-mail: andrea.taylor@sci.monash.edu.au
Home Page: http://www.australianmammals.org.au

• 280 • **Adolph Bolliger Award**
For best talk by student.

• 281 • **Ellis Troughton Memorial Award**
For outstanding service to Australian mammalogy.

• 282 •
Australian Mathematical Society
Dr. A. Howe, Treas.
Department of Mathematics
Australian Natl. Univ.
Canberra, Australian Capital Territory 0200, Australia
Phone: 61 2 61258922
Fax: 61 2 61258923
E-mail: treasurer@austms.org.au
Home Page: http://www.austms.org.au/

• 283 • **Australian Mathematical Society Medal**
For recognition of distinguished research in the mathematical sciences. Members who have not reached the age of forty at the beginning of the year in which the Council makes the award are eligible. A significant portion of the work should have been carried out in Australia. A medal is awarded annually. Established in 1981.

• 284 • **Bernhard H. Neumann Prize**
For recognition of the best student talk at the annual meeting. Students (part-time or full-time) who are members of the Society are eligible. A monetary prize of $250 (Australian) and a certificate are awarded each year at the annual meeting. Established in 1985 in honor of Professor Bernhard H. Neumann.

• 285 •
Australian Military Medicine Association
Russell Schedlich, Pres.
133 Harrington St.
Hobart, Tasmania 7000, Australia
Phone: 61 3 62347844
Fax: 61 3 62345958
E-mail: secretariat@amma.asn.au
Home Page: http://www.amma.asn.au

• 286 • AMMA Journal Editor's Prize
To the best paper published in the AMMA journal by an AMMA member.

• 287 • Weary Dunlop Award
For best original paper presented.

• 288 •
Australian Mushroom Growers Association
Sherilynn LeFeuvre, Exec. Asst.
Locked Bag 3
Windsor, New South Wales 2756, Australia
Phone: 61 2 45776877
Fax: 61 2 45775830
E-mail: info@amga.asn.au
Home Page: http://www.mushrooms.net.au

• 289 • Australian Mushroom Growers Award for Best Menu Using Mushrooms
For the best menu using mushrooms.

• 290 • Meat Livestock Australia Award for Best Dish Using Beef and Mushrooms
For the best dish using beef and mushrooms.

• 291 • Meat Livestock Australia Award for Best Dish Using Lamb and Mushrooms
For the best dish using lamb and mushrooms.

• 292 •
Australian Music Centre
PO Box N690
18 Hickson Rd.
PO Box N690
Grosvenor Place, New South Wales 1220, Australia
Phone: 61 2 92474677
Fax: 61 2 92412873
E-mail: info@amcoz.com.au
Home Page: http://www.amcoz.com.au

• 293 • APRA/Australian Music Centre Classical Music Awards
To recognize distinguished contributions to Australian classical music. Eleven awards are presented annually: 1. Instrumental Work of the Year; 2. Orchestral Work of the Year; 3. Vocal or Choral Work of the Year; 4. Best composition by an Australian composer; 5. Best performance of an Australian composition; 6. Outstanding contribution by an organization; 7. Outstanding contribution by an individual; 8. Outstanding contribution to Australian music in education; 9. Outstanding contribution to Australian music in a Regional Area; 10. Long-term contribution to the advancement of Australian music; and 11. Distinguished Services to Australian Music. Established in 1988.

• 294 • Australian Music Center Awards
To recognize outstanding achievements in the creation, presentation, promotion and support for Australian Music - National and State/Territory Awards. Nominations are made by members of the Australian Music Center, And Assessment of Nominations carried out by state/territory and Nationals Panels made up of composers, performers, critics and musicologists. Awarded annually.

• 295 •
Australian National Sportfishing Association
Geoff Hawkins, Chm.
PO Box 328
Rasmussen
Matraville, New South Wales 2036, Australia
Phone: 61 7 47231406
E-mail: webmaster@ansa.com.au
Home Page: http://www.ansa.com.au

• 296 • Most Meritorious Capture Award
To recognize the most meritorious capture for the fishing competition year. The award encompasses both Seniors and Juniors and can be awarded for Freshwater and Saltwater captures. Awarded annually.

• 297 •
Australian National University
Canberra, Australian Capital Territory 0200, Australia
Phone: 61 2 6125 5111
Fax: 61 2 6125 5448
E-mail: enquiries@anu.edu.au
Home Page: http://www.anu.edu.au

• 298 • J. G. Crawford Award
To recognize the author of a research paper making a substantial and original contribution to scholarship on Japan or on Australia-Japan relations. Younger and new scholars developing a specialization in the areas of study specified are encouraged to apply. To be eligible for consideration, the paper should address some aspect of the operation of the Japanese economy or economic policy, or Japan's international relations or relations with Australia, or the political environment affecting these affairs. The value of the award is determined each year by a judging panel and in recent years has been $2000. Papers published, written for publication, or unpublished, but written the year of the award are eligible for nomination. Other conditions are: (1) Papers must be in English and either typed or printed (2) Applicants must be Australian or Japanese citizens, permanent residents or scholars working in Australia (3) Persons who have had a PhD or graduate qualification in the relevant area for more than seven years will not normally be eligible for the award (4) The paper should be journal length (400-10,000 words) (5) A 100 word synopsis of the paper must also be submitted (6) Candidates must submit three copies of both the paper and the synopsis, and (7) submissions are limited to one entry per person. Where possible, the paper selected for the award will be published by the Australia-Japan Research Centre as part of its *Pacific Economic Papers* series, subject to certain conditions. Papers already published in the series in the year of the award that meet the conditions of eligibility will automatically be considered for the award. Established 1987. Additional information is available from Centre Administrator, Australia-Japan Research Centre, phone: 612 6125 3780.

• 299 •
Australian Neuroscience Society
Glenda Halliday, Pres.
2A Athelney Ave.
PO Box 2331
Kent Town, South Australia 5071, Australia
Phone: 61 8 83620038
Fax: 61 8 83620038
E-mail: ans@sallyjayconferences.com.au
Home Page: http://www.ans.org.au

• 300 • A.W. Campbell Award
For the best contribution by a member of the society over the first 5 post doctoral years.

• 301 • Distinguished Achievement Award
For outstanding contribution to neuroscience.

• 302 • Paxinos-Watson Prize
For the most significant, refereed paper in the neurosciences.

• 303 • Sir Grafton Elliot Smith Award
For the best essay on a neuroscience topic written by a student member.

• 304 • Student Poster Prize
For the best poster presentation by a student member at the annual meeting.

• 305 • Istvan Tork Prize
For the best oral presentation by a student member at the annual meeting.

• 306 •
Australian Nuclear Association
Dr. Clarence J. Hardy, Contact
PO Box 445
Sydney, New South Wales 1499, Australia
Phone: 61 2 95796193
Fax: 61 2 95706473
E-mail: cjhardy@ozemail.com.au
Home Page: http://www.nuclearaustralia.org.au

• 307 • Australian Nuclear Association Annual Award
Recognizes major contributions in the nuclear field. Awarded annually.

• 308 •
Australian Numismatic Society
Rod Sell, Contact
PO Box 366
Brookvale, New South Wales 2100, Australia
Phone: 61 2 94517896
Fax: 61 2 94023788
E-mail: rod.sell@elderwyn.com
Home Page: http://www.the-ans.com

• 309 • Australian Numismatic Society Bronze Medal
For recognition of noteworthy services to Australian Numismatic Society and numismatics research. Only members of the Society are eligible. Established in 1983.

• 310 • Gold Medal and Fellowship of the Society
For recognition of long and distinguished service to the Society and numismatics research. Only members of the Society are eligible. Established in 1968.

• 311 • Silver Medal and Associate Fellowship of the Society
For recognition of long and distinguished service to the Society and numismatics research. Only members of the Society are eligible. Established in 1968.

• 312 •
Australian Optical Society
John Holdsworth, Sec.
School of Mathematical and Physical Sciences
University of Newcastle
Callaghan, New South Wales 2308, Australia
Phone: 61 2 49215436
Fax: 61 2 49216907
E-mail: john.holdsworth@newcastle.edu.au
Home Page: http://aos.physics.mq.edu.au

• 313 • AOS Medal
For outstanding contribution to the field of optics.

• 314 • Postgraduate Student Prize
For distinguished postgraduate students.

• 315 • Technical Optics Award
For young optical worker with significant achievement in technical optics.

• 316 • Warsash/AOS Student Prize
For the best student research proposal based on scientific merit.

• 317 •
Australian Orthopaedic Association
Helen C. Beh, CEO/Sec.
Ground Fl., William Bland Ctre.
229 Macquarie St.
Sydney, New South Wales 2000, Australia
Phone: 61 2 92333018
Fax: 61 2 92218301
E-mail: admin@aoa.org.au
Home Page: http://www.aoa.org.au

• 318 • Allan Frederick Dwyer Prize
For the best paper presented at the registrars' conference.

• 319 • Evelyn Hamilton Award
For the best scientific paper.

• 320 • Gordon Kerridge Prize
For the best paper, which manifests an analytical approach to the clinical practice of orthopaedic surgery.

• 321 •
Australian Petroleum Production and Exploration Association
Belinda Robinson, Chief Exec.
GPO Box 2201
Canberra, Australian Capital Territory 2601, Australia
Phone: 61 2 62470960
Fax: 61 2 62470548
E-mail: appea@appea.com.au
Home Page: http://www.appea.com.au

• 322 • K.A. Richards Scholarship

• 323 • Reg Sprigg Medal
For outstanding service in oil and gas exploration and production industry.

• 324 • Tony Noon Scholarship
For a post graduate student.

• 325 • Lewis G. Weeks Medal
For outstanding contribution to the art, science, and practice of petroleum exploration.

• 326 •
Australian Psychological Society
PO Box 38
Flinders Ln., PO
Melbourne, Victoria 8009, Australia
Phone: 61 3 86623300
Fax: 61 3 96636177
E-mail: contactus@psychology.org.au
Home Page: http://www.psychology.org.au

• 327 • Alastair Heron Prize
To a member of the APS College of Clinical Psychologists For applied research of exceptional quality in the area of normal adult ageing or age-related dementias.

• 328 • APS College of Forensic Psychologists (NSW Section) Annual Awards
For excellence in Forensic psychology.

• 329 • APS Colleges Award of Distinction
For individuals who made outstanding contributions to their specialist field.

• 330 • APS Ethics Prize
To APS members and subscribers who have made a significant scholarly, research, pedagogical or professional contribution in the areas of professional or research ethics.

• 331 • APS Prize
For academic excellence in an APS-accredited course.

• 332 • Award For Excellent PhD Thesis in Psychology
To an outstanding research in psychology by candidates who have completed a PhD at an Australian University within the last calendar year.

• 333 • Children's Peace Literature Award
To one or more Australian authors of books For children that encourage the peaceful resolution of conflict.

• 334 • COP Excellence Awards
For an exceptional achievement in the profession of organizational psychology.

• 335 • Distinguished Scientific Contribution Award
To distinguished theoretical or empirical contributions to psychology by psychologists at mid or later career stage.

• 336 • Early Career Awards
For excellence in scientific achievement in psychology.

• 337 • Elaine Dignan Award
Proposed and endorsed by the women and psychology interest group.

• 338 •
Australian Publishers' Association
Susan Bridge, Chief Exec.
89 Jones St., Ste. 60
Ultimo, New South Wales 2007, Australia
Phone: 61 2 92819788
Fax: 61 2 92811073
E-mail: apa@publishers.asn.au
Home Page: http://www.publishers.asn.au

• 339 • Book Design Awards
For recognition of excellence in book design in Australia. Entries must be published and designed in Australia, but may be printed anywhere. Awarded annually. For full details, the Association invites you to visit www.publishers.asn.au.

• 340 •
Australian Red Cross Society
Robert Tickner, CEO
PO Box 196
Carlton, Victoria 3053, Australia
Phone: 61 3 93451800
Fax: 61 3 93482513
E-mail: inatinfo@redcross.org.au
Home Page: http://www.redcross.org.au

• 341 • Distinguished Service, Long Service

• 342 • Honorary Life Member

• 343 • Meritorious Service

Awards are arranged in alphabetical order below their administering organizations

• 344 • **Florence Nightingale Award**

• 345 •
Australian Science Teachers Association
Paul Carnemolla, Pres.
PO Box 334
Deakin West, Australian Capital Territory 2600, Australia
Phone: 61 2 62829377
Fax: 61 2 62829477
E-mail: asta@asta.edu.au
Home Page: http://www.asta.edu.au

• 346 • **Distinguished Service Award**
For ongoing distinguished service to ASTA and the profession.

• 347 • **Honorary Life Membership**
For outstanding contribution to the achievement of ASTA goals.

• 348 • **Most Valuable Paper**
For the most valuable paper published in quarterly journal of ASTA.

• 349 • **Service Award**
For service to ASTA and the profession.

• 350 •
Australian Secondary Principals Association
Peter Martin, Contact
Unit 2/13/21 Vale St.
North Melbourne, Victoria 3051, Australia
Phone: 61 3 93268077
Fax: 61 3 93268147
E-mail: aspasec@aspa.asn.au
Home Page: http://www.aspa.asn.au

• 351 • **Life Membership**
Recognizes individuals who have rendered great service to the Association. Awarded periodically.

• 352 •
Australian Severe Weather Association
Anthony Cornelius, Pres.
227/16 Cotham Rd.
Kew, Victoria 3101, Australia
E-mail: aussky@hotmail.com
Home Page: http://www.severeweather.asn.au

• 353 • **Award for Excellence in Storm Reporting**
For severe thunderstorm weather reporting and analysis of damage.

• 354 • **Award of Achievement**
For significant contribution to the Australian weather community.

• 355 • **Jester of the Year**
For members who have done something embarrassingly funny.

• 356 • **Outstanding ASWA Participation**
For outstanding participation in ASWA groups, functions, and activities.

• 357 •
Australian Singing Competition
Vivian Zeltzer, Coordinator
67 Castlereagh St., Level 4
Sydney, New South Wales 2000, Australia
Phone: 61 2 9231 4293
Fax: 61 2 9221 8201
E-mail: asc@aussing.com.au
Home Page: http://www.aussing.com.au

• 358 • **Mathy and Opera Awards**
This, the richest and most prestigious singing competition in Australia is held to encourage professional careers and to recognize exceptional classical singing talent. Submission deadline varies, see entry form for exact date. Numerous scholarships and awards are presented annually, including the Marianne Mathy Scholarship of $30,000 and travel opportunities for an Australian singer under 26 years of age. Opera Awards are open to singers who have had a professional association with one of Australia's opera companies and are nominated by a professional opera company. Established in 1982.

• 359 •
Australian Skeptics - NSW Branch
Dr. Martin Hadley, Pres.
PO Box 268
Roseville, New South Wales 2069, Australia
Phone: 61 2 94172071
Fax: 61 2 94177930
E-mail: nsw@skeptics.com.au
Home Page: http://www.skeptics.com.au

• 360 • **Bent Spoon Award**
Recognizes the perpetrator of the most preposterous piece of paranormal of pseudo-scientific work in the preceding year. Awarded annually. Established in 1982.

• 361 •
Australian Small Animal Veterinary Association
Matthew Retchford, Pres.
Unit 40, 2A Herbert St.
St. Leonards, New South Wales 2065, Australia
Phone: 61 2 94315090
Fax: 61 2 94379068
E-mail: asava@ava.com.au
Home Page: http://www.ava.com.au/main.php?c=1

• 362 • **AVP Awards**

• 363 • **Distinguished Scientific Contribution Award**

• 364 • **Distinguished Service Award**

• 365 • **Small Animal Practitioner of the Year**

• 366 •
Australian Society for Medical Research
Dr. Catherine West, Senior Exec. Officer
145 Macquarie St.
Sydney, New South Wales 2000, Australia
Phone: 61 2 92565450
Fax: 61 2 92520294
E-mail: asmr@world.net
Home Page: http://www.asmr.org.au

• 367 • **Merck Sharp and Dohme Florey Medal**
To honor an Australian for a milestone achievement in biomedical science and human health advancement arising from research carried out in Australia. A monetary prize of $25,000 is awarded annually. Established in 1998. Sponsored by Merck Sharp & Dohme.

• 368 • **Research Grant**
A monetary award is presented annually.

• 369 •
Australian Society for Parasitology
Dr. Malcolm Jones, Sec.
Queensland Institute of Medical Research Herston
PO Box E240
Brisbane, Queensland 4006, Australia
Phone: 61 7 33620405
Fax: 61 7 33620104
E-mail: malcolmj@qimr.edu.au
Home Page: http://parasite.org.au

• 370 • **Bancroft - Mackerras Medal**
For recognition of achievements in the science of parasitology. Members of the Society must be nominated by September 30 each year. A medal is awarded each year when merited at the annual general meeting of the Society. Established in 1982 in honor of the Bancroft and Mackerras families.

• 371 • **John Frederick Adrian Sprent Prize**
For recognition of an outstanding Ph.D. thesis in parasitology published during the preceding three years. Members of the Society may apply. A monetary prize and medal are awarded triennially. Established in 1987.

• 372 •
Australian Society of Archivists
Kim Eberhard, Pres.
PO Box 77
Dickson, Australian Capital Territory 2602, Australia
Phone: 61 7 38758705
Fax: 61 7 38758764
E-mail: ozarch@velocitynet.com.au
Home Page: http://www.archivists.org.au

• 373 • **Australian Society of Archivists Honorary Member**
Conferred by a two-thirds majority vote at a general meeting of the society, upon the recommendation of the council, in recognition of services to the society or to the profession. Honorary members are entitled to all rights and privileges of professional membership without payment or subscriptions. Established in 1975.

• 374 • **Distinguished Achievement Award**
Conferred on a member who has been mainly or solely responsible for an outstanding development or achievement in archives work. Awarded when merited every year. The Council accepts recommendations from the Awards Committee. Established 1993. Formerly: (2000) Laureateship of the Australian Society of Archivists.

• 375 • **Fellowship of the Australian Society of Archivists**
Conferred on a professional member of the Society who has given at least ten years of distinguished service to the profession, to the theory, teaching or practice of archives work, or to writing about archives. Established 1993.

• 376 • **Margaret Jennings Award**
Recognizes an outstanding student in each accredited diploma course in archives administration. The award consists of a certificate, one year's membership in the society, and a cheque for $100. Awarded annually to one or more recipients. Established in 1989.

• 377 • **Mander Jones Awards**
Named in honor of the late Phyllis Mander Jones, awarded in four different categories for writings about archives in Australia, or by Australians: (1) publication making the greatest contribution to Archives of a related field in Australia written by or on a corporate body; (2) publication making the greatest contribution to archives or a related field in Australia written by a person in their own right (3) best finding aid to an archival collection held by an Australian institution or about Australia produced by an organization deemed eligible for Category A Institutional Membership; (4) best article about archives or a related field written by an Australian in a journal not primarily intended for archivists or record managers; (5) best article about archives or a related field written by an Australian in an archives or records management journal (6) best article about archives or a related field written by a student (not more than 5000 words) in an entry level archives or records management course in Australia. Awarded when merited every year. Established in 1996.

• 378 • **Sharman Award**
To recognize the significant contribution over the years by Robert Charles "Bob" Sharman to the Australian Society of Archivists and the archival cause generally in Australia. The award is in the form of financial assistance for selected members of the ASA to attend the annual conference. Established in 2000.

• 379 •
Australian Teachers of Media
Amber Nelson, Education Officer
PO Box 2211
St. Kilda, Victoria 3182, Australia
Phone: 61 3 95349986
Fax: 61 3 95372325
E-mail: atom@atomvic.org
Home Page: http://www.atomvic.org/indexbody.html

• 380 • **Australian Teachers of Media Awards**
To promote the educational use of film and video; to give recognition to film and videomakers in this field; to assist teachers in selecting new, innovative and quality programs for the classroom; to encourage the pursuit of excellence in the production of educational resources; and to highlight the importance of media education. Awards are given in the following categories: Short Fiction; Animation; General Documentary; Science and Environment; Social Issues; Education Resource; Training/Instruction; Subject Specific; Secondary Student Production; Tertiary Student Production; Children's Television; Television Drama; Television Series/Serial; Television Documentary; and the Australian Multimedia Award. In addition, The Gold Atom is awarded to the best film or video from all finalists, special prizes are presented to two individual film and video makers, and awards are presented for the two best productions in the primary and secondary student categories. Films and videotapes under 60 minutes produced during the twelve months preceding the award are eligible. Awarded annually. Established in 1982.

• 381 •
Australian Veterinary Association
Margaret Conley, Contact
2A Herbert St., Unit 40
St. Leonards, New South Wales 2065, Australia
Phone: 61 2 94315000
Fax: 61 2 94379068
E-mail: members@ava.com.au
Home Page: http://www.ava.com.au

• 382 • **Gilruth Prize**
To recognize an individual for meritorious service to veterinary science in Australia. Awarded annually. Established in 1953 to honor Dr. J.A. Gilruth, Dean of the Faculty of Veterinary Science of the University of Melbourne, the first Chief of the Division of Animal Health of the CSIRO, and an outstanding veterinary authority.

• 383 • **Kendall Oration and Medal**
To recognize outstanding Australian veterinarians. A medal is awarded when merited at the annual conference of AVA. Established in 1930 by the five sons of Dr. W.T. Kendall to honor his memory. Dr. William Tyson Kendall migrated to Australia in 1880 and he made a unique contribution to veterinary science in Australia.

• 384 • **Don Kerr Veterinary Student Award**
Commemorates the work of the late Don Kerr, who died in November 1992 while serving as President of the Association. Conferred upon a final year veterinary student from one of the veterinary schools for academic achievement and exceptional commitment to cattle medicine. A one-year membership and monetary prize of $50 is awarded annually.

• 385 • **Kesteven Medal**
To recognize Australian veterinarians for distinguished contributions to international veterinary science in the fields of technical and scientific assistance to developing countries. A medal is presented each year at the annual general meeting of the Australian Veterinary Association or the Australian College of Veterinary Scientists at which the recipient may be invited to speak briefly about his or her work. The award was inaugurated by the late Dr. K.V.L. Kesteven, and first awarded in 1980. Sponsored by the Australian College of Veterinary Scientists.

• 386 • **Meritorious Service Award**
To recognize service by members to the Association, regional divisions, branches, or special interest groups. The award may also be made to persons who are not eligible for membership in the Association but who have provided meritorious service to it. Established in 1978.

• 387 •
Australian Water Association
Ian Jarman, COO
PO Box 388
Artarmon, New South Wales 1570, Australia
Phone: 61 2 94131288
Fax: 61 2 94131047
E-mail: ijarman@awa.asn.au
Home Page: http://www.awa.asn.au

• 388 • **Peter Hughes Award**
Recognizes outstanding contributions to the water industry. Awarded biennially.

• 389 • **Stockholm Junior Water Prize**
Recognizes high school seniors for a water science project. Awarded periodically.

• 390 • **Undergraduate Water Prize**
For a final-year student in an Australian university undertaking a thesis or project related to water. Awarded periodically.

• 391 • **Water Environment Merit Award**
Recognizes corporate contributions to water and the environment. Awarded biennially.

• 392 •
Australian Widescreen Association
Tony Andrews, Sec.
Box 292
Mooroolbark, Victoria 3138, Australia
Phone: 61 3 9739 6960
E-mail: scopeawa@bigpond.com
Home Page: http://www.users.bigpond.net.au/awa/awa.htm

• 393 • **Australian International Widescreen Festival**
Held annually in October to encourage the amateur use of Widescreen in Standard 8, Super-8, 16mm, movies and video, and to encourage slides taken with Widelux/Horizont panoramic cameras, and SLRs with anamorphic lenses as well as 35mm cameras with in-camera panoramic masking. Application, films must be photographed in widescreen format of not less than 2:1 ratio and videos in not less than 1.8:1. Three trophies are awarded for the Best Film at the Festival, best slide set, and best individual slide. Established in 1971. Sponsored by AGFA, Photo Express, and Crawford Productions. Additional information is available from Brian P. Beatty, 6 Menwood Street, Forest Hill, VIC 3131, Australia.

• 394 •
Australian Writers' Guild
Megan Elliott, Exec.Dir.
8/50 Reservoir St.
Surry Hills, New South Wales 2010, Australia
Phone: 61 2 92811554
Fax: 61 2 92814321
E-mail: admin@awg.com.au
Home Page: http://www.awg.com.au

• 395 • **Awgie Awards**
For recognition of excellence in scriptwriting for stage, film, radio, and television. Members of the Guild who are Australian citizens may submit scripts that have been produced during the preceding calendar year. Awgie statuettes are awarded in the following categories: (1) Best Script of the Year; (2) documentary; (3) children's drama and theatre for young people (original/adaptation); (4) comedy review/sketch material (any medium); (5) television series episode; (6) television serial episode; (7) television comedy; (8) television mini-series (adapted); (9) television mini-series (original); (10) telemovie (adapted); (11) telemovie (original); (12) original work for the stage; (13) short film and feature screenplay; (14) theater-in-education/community theater; (15) radio drama (original); (16) radio drama (adaptation); (17) Dorothy Crawford Award for a member of the industry who has furthered the cause of Australian writing for stage or screen; (18) Monte Miller Memorial Award for the best unproduced script by an Associate Member; (19) Frank Parsons Award for a special contribution to Australian comedy; (20) Richard Lane Award for long-standing service and dedication to the Guild; and (21) Hector Crawford Award for a significant contribution to the craft via a body of script editing work. The Major Awgie Award is presented when merited to an outstanding winner from the category winners. Awarded annually in a presentation ceremony which alternates between Melbourne and Sydney. Established in 1968.

• 396 •
Brisbane Writers Festival
Michael Campbell, Dir.
PO Box 3453
South Brisbane, Queensland 4101, Australia
Phone: 61 7 3255 0254
Fax: 61 7 3255 0362
E-mail: info@brisbanewritersfestival.com.au
Home Page: http://www.brisbanewritersfestival.com.au
Formerly: Brisbane Warana Festival Ltd..

• 397 • **Steele Rudd Award**
To recognize the best collection of short stories. Australian collections published in the preceding twelve months must be submitted by the end of April each year. A monetary award of $15,000 is presented annually at the opening of the Bruhane Writers Festival in Brisbane each September. Sponsored by the Queensland Government.

• 398 •
Cardiac Society of Australia and New Zealand
Mrs. Lynne Portelli, Exec. Officer
145 Macquarie St.
Sydney, New South Wales 2000, Australia
Phone: 61 2 92565452
Fax: 61 2 92477916
E-mail: csanz@racp.edu.au
Home Page: http://www.csanz.edu.au

• 399 • **R. T. Hall Prize**
To recognize an individual investigator or group of investigators for work that advances knowledge of the cardiovascular system and its diseases and is published in a scientific journal or journals during the three-year period preceding the closing date. The work must have originated in Australia or New Zealand but the investigators need not be members of The Society. The deadline for entry is September 30. A monetary prize of $3,000 (Australian) is awarded annually. Established in 1961 by the R.T. Hall Trust Fund in honor of R. T. Hall.

• 400 • **Ralph Reader Prize**
To recognize the best individual presentation by an investigator in the Clinical and Basic Science sections at the Annual Scientific Meeting of the Cardiac Society. Applicants must be domiciled in Australia or New Zealand and still be in training. Applicants must be Advanced Trainees or Research Fellows in cardiology or cardiac surgery; or an Affiliate Member of the Society, which includes undergraduate students, nurses and technicians; or Scientist, up to and including the level of post-doctoral Fellow. A monetary prize of $1,000 (Australian) is awarded annually. Established in 1981 in honor of Dr. Ralph Reader, CMG, FRACP.

• 401 •
Chartered Institute of Logistics and Transport in Australia
Mrs. Dianne Davis, Administration Mgr.
PO Box A2333
149 Castlereagh St.
Sydney, New South Wales 1235, Australia
Phone: 61 2 92677538
Fax: 61 2 92644738
E-mail: cilta@bigpond.net.au
Home Page: http://ciltia.com.au

• 402 • **Australian Transport Industry Award**
To recognize an outstanding, innovative contribution to the improvement of Australian transport. Improvements developed within Australia, related to all modes of transport that are not detrimental to the environment may be submitted by July 31 for consideration. An engraved bronze plaque is awarded annually. Established in 1977.

• 403 •
Children's Book Council of Australia
Marc Macleod, Pres.
PO Box 3203
Norwood, South Australia 5067, Australia
Phone: 61 8 83322845
Fax: 61 8 83330394
E-mail: office@cbc.org.au
Home Page: http://www.cbc.org.au

• 404 • **Book of the Year Award: Early Childhood**
Recognizes outstanding books of fiction, drama, or poetry for children who are at the pre-reading or early reading stages. They may be picture books, picture story books, or blocks in which illustrations play a substantial part in the story telling or concept development. Only books published in the English language or bilingual books where one language is English may be entered. Books in manuscript form or other nonbook materials are not eligible. Books must be published between January 1 and December 31 of the year prior to the award. The creator must be of Australian nationality or a resident in Australia.

• 405 • **Book of the Year Award: Older Readers**
To recognize outstanding books that generally require mature reading ability to appreciate the topics, themes, and the scope of emotional involvement. Only books published in the English language or bilingual books where one language is English may be entered. Books in manuscript form or other nonbook materials are not eligible. Books must have been published in Australia between January 1 and December 31 of the year prior to the awards. The creators must be of Australian nationality or a resident in Australia for at least two years prior to December 31 in the year of publication. A monetary prize and a medal are awarded annually. Established in 1946.

Awards are arranged in alphabetical order below their administering organizations

• 406 • Book of the Year Award: Younger Readers
For recognition of books for readers who have developed independent reading skills but are still developing in literary awareness. Only books published in the English language or bilingual books where one language is English may be entered. Books in manuscript form or other nonbook materials are not eligible. Books must have been published in Australia between January 1 and December 31 of the year prior to the awards. The creators must be of Australian nationality or a resident in Australia for at least two years prior to December 31 in the year of publication. A monetary prize and a medal are awarded annually. Established in 1982.

• 407 • Lady Cutler Award
For recognition of distinguished service to children's literature in New South Wales. Service should be well beyond a professional association with children's literature. The contributions should be primarily in New South Wales, and sympathetic to the aims of the Council. A trophy, citation certificate, and gift are awarded annually at the Lady Cutler Dinner. Established in 1981 in honor of the late Lady Cutler, Patron of the Children's Book Council and wife of Sir Roden Cutler, former governor of New South Wales.

• 408 • Picture Book of the Year Award
To recognize outstanding books in which the author and illustrator achieve artistic and literary unity; or in wordless books, where the story, theme, or concept is unified solely through illustrations. Only books published in the English language or bilingual books where one language is English may be entered. Books in manuscript form or other nonbook materials are not eligible. Books must have been published between January 1 and December 31 of the year prior to the award. The creator must be of Australian nationality or a resident in Australia for at least two years prior to December 31 in the year of publication. A monetary prize and a medal are awarded annually. Established in 1952. The Visual Arts Board Awards have also been given from 1974 to 1976. From 1977 they have been divided amongst the winning illustrators in the Picture Book of the Year Awards. From 1989, the award is presented to the winning illustrator and also to the author who is not the illustrator of a text.

• 409 • Eve Pownall Award for Information Books
To recognize outstanding nonfiction books that present well-authenticated data in combination with imaginative presentation and variation of style. Only books published in the English language or bilingual books where one language is in English may be entered. Books in manuscript form or other non-book materials are not eligible. Books must have been published between January 1 and December 31 of the year prior to the award. The creators must be of Australian nationality or a resident of Australia for at least two years prior to December 31 of the year of publication. A monetary prize and a medal are awarded annually. Established in 1988 in honor of Eve Pownall, the late Australian award-winning children's author.

• 410 •
City of Greater Dandenong
397 Springvale Rd.
PO Box 200
Dandenong, Victoria 3175, Australia
Phone: 61 3 9239 5100
Fax: 61 3 9239 5196
E-mail: council@cgd.vic.gov.au
Home Page: http://www.greaterdandenong.com

• 411 • Greater Dandenong Short Story Competition
For recognition of excellence in Australian writing. Entries from Australian citizens may be submitted between April 1 and June 30 annually. All entries must be accompanied by an official entry form. The following prizes are awarded: Open Award - $3,000, for stories between 1,000 and 3,000 words; Local Writers' Award - total of $1,000, for stories between 1,000 and 3,000 words; First Language Award - total of $1,000, for stories between 1,000 and 3,000 words; Young Writers' Award - $550 total, for 14-18 year olds and 8-13 year olds; and the English as a Second Language Encouragement Award - $1,000 total, for stories between 250 and 1,000 words. Established in 1981. Formerly: (1994) City of Springvale Short Story Awards.

• 412 •
Cladan Cultural Exchange Institute of Australia
Claire Dan, Mng.Dir.
PO Box 420
Double Bay 1360, Australia
Phone: 61 2 9326 2405
Fax: 61 2 9326 2604
E-mail: sipca@bigpond.com
Home Page: http://www.sipca.com.au

• 413 • Sydney International Piano Competition of Australia
Held every four years. The next Competition is in 2008 (July 2-19 inclusive). To encourage the careers of young concert pianists, to promote professional development, and to provide performance opportunities. The Competition is open to artists of any nationality, between 17 and not more than 30 years of age. The deadline for application is usually seven months prior to each Competition. The following monetary prizes in Australian dollars are awarded: (1) First prize - The Council of the City of Sydney Prize - $25,000; (2) Second prize - Yamaha Music Australia Pty. Ltd. $12,000; (3) Third prize Theme & Variations - $6,000; (4) Fourth prize Mr. Phillip Rowe Prize - $4,000; (5) Fifth prize - Hunt and Hunt - $2,500; (6) Sixth prize - J. Albert & Son Pty Ltd. - $1,500. In addition, there are special prizes totaling $75,000.

• 414 •
Confectionery Manufacturers of Australasia
David Greenwood, CEO
PO Box 1307
Camberwell, Victoria 3124, Australia
Phone: 61 3 98131600
Fax: 61 3 98825473
E-mail: cma@candy.net.au
Home Page: http://www.candy.net.au

• 415 • Craig Award
For the best student in the CMA's practical skills confectionery short course.

• 416 • Sollich Award
For best students in the practical confectionery subject.

• 417 • Alfred Stauder Award
For significant contribution to the confectionery industry.

• 418 •
Convoy for Kids
Jan Maher, Contact
PO Box 85
Park Orchards, Victoria 3114, Australia
Phone: 61 3 98762983
Fax: 61 3 98762383
E-mail: admin@convoyforkids.org
Home Page: http://www.convoyforkids.org

• 419 • Convoy For Kids Grant
For childhood asthma research.

• 420 • The Distinguished Award of Honour For Service to Children's Charities
For long term voluntary work connected with Convoy For Kids.

• 421 • Life Governor
For long term exemplary service to Convoy For Kids.

• 422 • Memorial William John Bond Safe Driver of the Year
For the truck driver who drives safely and is (not at fault accident free), courteous to workmates, customers and others on the road.

• 423 • Most Outstanding Volunteer
For outstanding service to Convoy For Kids above and beyond what is expected of a volunteer.

• 424 • President's Choice Award
For outstanding service to Convoy For Kids.

• 425 • Truck Awards
For the best truck in each nominated section.

• 426 • **Youth Ambassador**
For children with asthma or another disability or illness who are an inspiration to other children and adults.

• 427 •
Cooperative Research Centre for Polymers
Sue Beck, Executive Assistant
32 Business Park Dr.
Notting Hill, Victoria 3168, Australia
Phone: 61 9 5588111
Fax: 61 9 5588122
E-mail: polymers@crcp.com.au
Home Page: http://www.crcp.com.au

• 428 • **CRC for Polymers Prize**
To recognize a report based on project work in any field of polymer science or engineering. The competition is open to all students who have completed a research project as part of the requirement for a Bachelors or Honours degree in a relevant area of engineering, materials science, or chemistry during the year. Candidates must be members of the Royal Australian Chemical Institute or the New Zealand Institute of Chemistry. A monetary prize of $1,500 and travel expenses are awarded annually.

• 429 •
Delta Society Australia
John Cornwall, Gen.Mgr.
Ste. 706, 74 Pitt St.
Sydney, New South Wales 2000, Australia
Phone: 61 2 92313218
Fax: 61 2 92232382
E-mail: deltasoc@hotkey.net.au
Home Page: http://www.deltasocietyaustralia.com.au

• 430 • **Julie Mandile Award**
To recognize a volunteer for outstanding services to the Pet Partners Program. Awarded annually.

• 431 •
Dromkeen Collection Art Gallery
1012 Kilmore Rd.
Riddells Creek, Victoria 3431, Australia
Phone: 61 3 5428 6799
Fax: 61 3 5428 6830
E-mail: dromkeen@scholastic.com.au
Home Page: http://www.scholastic.com.au/common/dromkeen

• 432 • **Dromkeen Librarian's Award**
To recognize a teacher, teacher/librarian, or a children's librarian currently working within or outside the educational systems for the important role of introducing children to literature. The award is presented each December at the Dromkeen Literary Luncheon. Established in 1994.

• 433 • **Dromkeen Medal**
To recognize an individual for an outstanding contribution to children's literature in Australia. A bronze medal, designed by Robert Ingpen, is awarded annually in March. Established in 1982 in memory of Courtney Thomas Oldmeadow, the founder of Dromkeen.

• 434 •
Eaglehawk Dahlia and Arts Festival
David Richards, Pres.
PO Box 21
Eaglehawk, Victoria 3556, Australia
Phone: 61 5446 1515
E-mail: lauriep@housethirtysix.com
Home Page: http://dahlia.bendigo.net.au

• 435 • **Literary Competition**
To recognize outstanding literature. Australian citizens are eligible for original, unpublished works on an Australian theme. The following awards are presented: Rolf Boldrewood Award for a short story on any topic. First prize is $200 and a certificate; second prize is $50; and Allan Llewellyn Award for Bush verse with an Australian theme, written in rhyme and traditional metre. First prize is $150 and a certificate; second prize is $50. The deadline for applications is January 31. Awarded at the Eaglehawk Dahlia and Arts Festival. For additional information, contact Ms. Ruth Claridge, Literary Committee Chairperson.

• 436 •
Endocrine Society of Australia
David Phillips, Sec.
145 Macquarie St.
Sydney, New South Wales 2000, Australia
Phone: 61 2 92565405
Fax: 61 2 92518174
E-mail: esa@racp.edu.au
Home Page: http://www.endocrinesociety.org.au

• 437 • **Mayne Pharma Bryan Hudson Clinical Endocrinology Award**
For the best clinical research presentation.

• 438 • **Novartis Junior Scientist Award**
For the best abstract presentation.

• 439 • **Servier Young Investigator Award**
For the best published scientific paper.

• 440 • **Travel Grants**
To younger members of the Society.

• 441 •
English Association Sydney
Dr. Robert Jackson, Sec.
PO Box 91
Wentworth Bldg.
Sydney, New South Wales 2006, Australia
Phone: 61 02 98682897
E-mail: randmjackson@optusnet.com.au
Home Page: http://english.arts.unsw.edu.au

• 442 • **H. M. Butterley - F. Earle Hooper Award**
To encourage and promote the career of a promising Australian creative writer or literary critic who is not yet established. Previously unpublished writers who have had an article, story or poem published in the Association's literary journal, *Southerly*, during the year of the award are eligible. The writer of the best such article/story/poem is selected by a judge who is appointed by the Association and who is a distinguished writer, critic or academic. A monetary prize is awarded annually at the annual dinner. Established in 1969 in memory of the life and work of two pioneer members of the Association, H.M. Butterley, Honorary Secretary of the Association from 1930 to 1961, and Miss F. Earle Hooper, a Foundation member from 1923 and an active member of the Executive Committee from 1936 to 1945.

• 443 •
Farrer Memorial Trust
B.D. Buffier, Dir.Gen.
% New South Wales Dept. of Primary Industries, Agricultur
PO Box K220
Haymarket, New South Wales 1240, Australia
Phone: 61 2 6391 3100
Fax: 61 2 6391 3336
E-mail: nsw.agriculture@agric.nsw.gov.au
Home Page: http://www.agric.nsw.gov.au/reader/farrer-memorial-trust

• 444 • **Farrer Memorial Medal**
To provide encouragement and inspiration to those engaged in agricultural science and to recognize an individual who has rendered distinguished service in agricultural science in Australia in the fields of research, education, or administration. The recipient of the medal is invited to deliver an oration on a topical subject of his own choice. Established in 1936 in memory of William James Farrer, plant breeder.

• 445 •
Feline Control Council of Western Australia
Joyce McLeavy, Sec.
PO Box 915
Cannington, Western Australia 6109, Australia
Phone: 61 8 93565742
Fax: 61 8 93565742
E-mail: jwheeler@iinet.net.au
Home Page: http://members.tripod.com/~fccwa

• 446 • **Cat of the Year Awards**
Awards are given for best entire, kitten, desexed, and domestic felines. Awarded annually.

• 447 •
Fellowship of Australian Writers NSW
Ken Challenor, Pres.
PO Box 488
NSW Writers Centre, Rm. 36
Rozelle, New South Wales 2039, Australia
Phone: 61 2 98101307
Fax: 61 2 98101307
E-mail: faw1@bigpond.com
Home Page: http://www.fawnsw.org

• 448 • Marjorie Barnard Short Story Award
To recognize the author of an outstanding short story (under 3,000 words). A monetary prize of $500 is awarded biennially in odd-numbered years at the Annual Members' Lunch.

• 449 • Tom Collins Poetry Award
Annual award to recognise, promote and reward the literary art of poetry. Entries must be postmarked/submitted by December 31st. A total monetary award of $2,000AUD is presented. For guidelines and conditions/entry form; send a SASE to: TCPP Competition Secretary, PO Box 312, Cottesloe, WA 6911, Australia or email; fawwa@iinet.net.au or download; www.fawwa.iinet.net.au.

• 450 • Lyndall Hadow/Donald Stuart Short Story Award
Annual award to recognise, promote and reward the literary art of short story writing. Entries must be submitted/postmarked by June 30 each year. A total monetary award of $600AUD is presented. For guidelines and conditions/entry form; send a SASE to: HSSS Competition Secretary, PO Box 312 Cottesloe, WA 6911, Australia; or email; fawwa@iinet.net.au or download at; www.fawwa.iinet.net.au.

• 451 • Walter Stone Memorial Award
For recognition of a monograph, biography, or bibliography dealing with some aspect of Australian literature. A monetary prize of A$500 is awarded biennially at the Seminar in October. Established in 1984 in honor of Walter Stone, publisher, and president of City Regional FAW and NSW State Council FAW.

• 452 • Wooden Horse Award
To recognize a first professionally published work. Works are judged by a committee appointed by the State Council. A carved wooden horse is awarded annually.

• 453 •
FIBA Oceana
Steve Smith, Sec.Gen.
PO Box 174
Toormina, New South Wales 2452, Australia
Phone: 61 2 66586110
Fax: 61 2 65586114
E-mail: obcbask@tpg.com.au
Home Page: http://www.fibaoceana.com

• 454 • Competitions
To promote basketball in the Pacific region. Awards are presented.

• 455 •
Field Naturalists Club of Victoria
Karen Muscat, Pres.
1 Gardenia St.
Locked Bag 3
Blackburn, Victoria 3130, Australia
Phone: 61 3 9877 9860
Fax: 61 3 9877 9860
E-mail: fncv@vicnet.net.au
Home Page: http://home.vicnet.net.au/~fncv

• 456 • Australian Natural History Medallion
For recognition of the most meritorious contribution to the understanding of Australian natural history. A person of any age may be nominated by May 1 of any year for a contribution made in the preceding ten year period. A medal is awarded annually. Established in 1940 by Mr. J.K. Moir.

• 457 •
Film and Television Institute of Western Australia
Graeme Sward, CEO
92 Adelaide St.
PO Box 579
Fremantle, Western Australia 6959, Australia
Phone: 61 8 9431 6700
Fax: 61 8 9335 1283
E-mail: fti@fti.asn.au
Home Page: http://www.fti.asn.au

• 458 • West Australia Film Awards
For recognition of excellence, innovation, and talent in film or video making. Awards are given in the Industry Section, for commercial theatrical releases or significant television transmission and the Early Career Section for students who have not achieved commercial credits. In addition, individuals are eligible for the Outstanding Contribution to Industry Award and the Young Filmmaker of the Year. Held annually. Established in 1979. Formerly: (1998) Western Australia Film and Video Festival.

• 459 •
Foundation for Australian Literary Studies
Peter Pierce, Exec. Dir.
Rm. A4.112
McGregor Rd.
School of Humanities
James Cook University
Smithfield, Queensland 4878, Australia
Phone: 61 7 4042 1497
Fax: 61 7 4042 1290
E-mail: peter.pierce@jcu.edu.au
Home Page: http://www.faess.jcu.edu.au/soh/fals
Formerly: Townsville Foundation for Australian Literary Studies.

• 460 • Colin Roderick Award
For recognition of the best book published each year in Australia that deals with any aspect of Australian life. Publications entered may be in any field of Australian writing and may be in verse or prose. Publications considered must be published in Australia, even though they may be printed elsewhere, and deal with some aspect of Australian life. A publication or any number of publications may be entered by any author or publisher by February 28 of the year following the year of publication. A monetary prize of $10,000 Australian is awarded at the annual dinner of the Foundation. Since 1980, the winner has also received the H. T. Priestley Memorial Medal. Established in 1967. Formerly: (1995) Townsville Foundation for Australian Literary Studies Award; (2006) Colin Roderick Prize.

• 461 • Colin Roderick Lectures
To foster the study of Australian literature in the University and the wider community. To date, forty of these series of lectures have been delivered and published in the Foundation's monograph series, and they have made a significant contribution to the critical discussion of Australian literature. Awarded annually. Established in 1966.

• 462 •
Geological Society of Australia
Sue Fletcher, Business Mgr.
301 George St., Ste. 706
Sydney, New South Wales 2000, Australia
Phone: 61 2 92902194
Fax: 61 2 92902198
E-mail: info@gsa.org.au
Home Page: http://www.gsa.org.au

• 463 • GSA Young Author's Award
For the best paper

• 464 • Joe Harms Medal
For excellence in mineral exploration.

• 465 • Stillwell Award
For best paper published in Australian Journal of Earth Sciences.

• 466 • SW Carey Medal
To a person distinguished in the field of tectonics.

• 467 • W. R. Brown Medal
To a person distinguished For contributions to the geological sciences.

• 468 •
Girls' Brigade Australia
Renelle Neale, Natl. Admin.
PO Box 211
Blacktown, New South Wales 2148, Australia
Phone: 61 2 96223055
Fax: 61 2 96223088
E-mail: gbaust@bigpond.net.au
Home Page: http://girls.brigadeaustralia.org

Awards are arranged in alphabetical order below their administering organizations

• 469 • **Girl's Service Award**
For an excellent Girls Brigade member.

• 470 • **Leader's Service Award**
For an outstanding leader.

• 471 • **Pioneer Pin**
For an outstanding member who has served six months in a company in the brigade.

• 472 • **Queen's Award**
For someone who holds the pioneer pin at the time of assessment and must have earned Gold Service Award for at least three years.

• 473 •
Historical Radio Society of Australia
Warwick V. Woods, Pres.
PO Box 2283
Melbourne, Victoria 3149, Australia
Phone: 61 3 95391117
E-mail: hrsa_asn@hrsa.asn.au
Home Page: http://www.hrsa.asn.au

• 474 • **Life Membership**
Recognizes major contributions to the goals of the Society. Awarded periodically.

• 475 •
Institute of Australian Geographers
Stewart Williams, Treas./Membership Sec.
School of Geography and Environmental Studies
Univ. of Tasmania
Private Bag 78
Hobart, Tasmania 7001, Australia
Phone: 61 3 62261866
Phone: 61 3 62261866
Fax: 61 3 62262989
E-mail: stewart.williams@utas.edu.au
Home Page: http://www.iag.org.au

• 476 • **Fellowship of the Institute of Australian Geographers**
For distinguished service to the institute.

• 477 • **Griffith Taylor Medal**
For distinguished contributions to geography in Australia.

• 478 • **IAG Postgraduate Award**
For work undertaken during own research For a higher degree; the paper could be submitted during the period of enrollment but should not be submitted later than one year after the award of the degree.

• 479 • **Professional Service Award**
For a distinguished contribution to geographical education or For the advancement of geographical practice in Australia; each nominee should have a continuous record of IAG membership of not less than five years.

• 480 •
Institute of Chartered Accountants in Australia
Graham Meyer, CEO
37 York St., Level 9
Sydney, New South Wales 2000, Australia
Phone: 61 2 92905660
Phone: 61 2 92901344
Fax: 61 2 92624841
E-mail: support@icaa.org.au
Home Page: http://charteredaccountants.com.au

• 481 • **Meritorious Service Award**
For service to the profession.

• 482 • **President's Prize**
For service to the profession.

• 483 •
Institute of Materials Engineering Australasia
Ms. Maruta Rodan, CEO
PO Box 19
Parkville, Victoria 3052, Australia
Phone: 61 3 93267266
Fax: 61 3 93267272
E-mail: imea@materialsaustralia.com.au
Home Page: http://www.materialsaustralia.com.au

Formerly: Australasian Institute of Metals; Insititute of Metal and Materials Australasia.

• 484 • **Claude A. Stewart Award**
For an individual, group of individuals, company, or organization that has made a significant contribution to the industrial practice of metallurgy or materials engineering. The principal evidence may be other than published papers. Open to members and non-members of the Institute. A bronze sculpted palque and a certificate setting out the citation are awarded. May be awarded once per calendar year. Established in 1965.

• 485 •
Institution of Engineers Australia/ Engineers Australia
Dr. Peter Taylor, Chief Exec.
11 Natl. Circuit
Engineering House
Barton, Australian Capital Territory 2600, Australia
Phone: 61 2 62706555
Fax: 61 2 62731488
E-mail: memberservices@engineersaustralia.org.au
Home Page: http://www.engineersaustralia.org.au

• 486 • **Agricultural Engineering Award**
For recognition of a project, invention, design, or manufacturing process that represents a significant agricultural engineering achievement and that has been completed within the previous two years. A monetary award and a plaque are awarded biennially. Established in 1986.

• 487 • **G.N. Alexander Medal**
To honor the author of the best paper on hydrology and/or water resources published in an IE Aust publication. It is usually awarded every 18 months. The first award was given in 1988, with selection responsibility being with the National Committee on Water Engineering.

• 488 • **Australian Engineering Excellence Awards**
To reward achievement, promote better engineering, show the community how good engineering creates wealth and improves living standards, and encourage young people to join the profession. Given annually, entries comprise the winning entrants from the Divisional competitions over the previous two years. A special issue of *Engineers Australia* gives details of all the entries. An award is given in each of the following categories: building and civil design; engineering products; engineering project management; engineering reports, procedures, and systems; environmental engineering; manufacturing facilities; public works; research; resource development; and the Sir William Hudson Award for the overall winner.

• 489 • **Award for Achievement in Engineering Enterprise**
To recognize a corporate member of the Institution who, by personal endeavors, has significantly contributed to an enterprise built around the successful commercialization of innovative engineering endeavor. A memento is presented as a recognition of the award. Established in 1986.

• 490 • **C.N. Barton Medal**
To recognize James Cook University of North Queensland engineering students. The award is based on a final year project and selection is made on appraisal by faculty staff. A medal and a cash prize of $200 are awarded annually. Established in 1972.

• 491 • **O. F. Blakey Memorial Prize**
For recognition of the best prepared paper of approximately 20 minutes duration delivered on an engineering subject to a meeting of the Western Australian Division by a graduate or student member of that Division. In the event of there being more entries than can be conveniently heard in one evening, pre-selection is carried out. A significant proportion of the points are awarded for the standard of presentation of the paper. The prize consists of the O.F. Blakey Memorial Medal and a monetary award of $250. Awarded annually. Established in 1955 in memory of Professor O.F. Blakey, the first Professor of Civil Engineering at the University of Western Australia, who was a Councillor of the Institution from 1936 to 1951, Chairman of the former Perth Division in 1936 and 1942, and President of the Institution in 1945.

• 492 • **John A. Brodie Medal**
For recognition of a paper in chemical engineering considered superior by the College of Chemical Engineers. The award is not limited to members of the Institution. A bronze medal is

awarded annually. Established in 1963 in honor of J.A. Brodie, a leading industrial innovator.

• 493 • Frederick Brough Memorial Prize
For recognition of the best prepared paper of approximately 20 minutes duration delivered on any engineering subject by a graduate or student member of the Tasmania Division. A monetary prize of $250 and a medal are awarded annually. Established in 1949 in memory of Mr. Frederick Brough who was Honorary Secretary of the Tasmania Division from 1929 until his death in 1948. He was a member of the staff of the Hydro-Electric Commission from 1920 to 1947.

• 494 • W.P. Brown Medal
To recognize final-year engineering students at the Swinburne College of Technology. Awarded on the basis of academic record and involvement in extra-curricular activities and special projects. Selection is made by a Faculty/Campus Chapter Panel. A medal and a cash prize of $200 are awarded annually. Established in 1977.

• 495 • R. W. Chapman Medal
For recognition of a paper on structural engineering considered the best by the College of Civil Engineers. Members of the Institution are eligible. A bronze medal is awarded annually. Established in 1935 in memory of Sir Robert Chapman, President of the Institution in 1922.

• 496 • Chemeca Medal
This, the most prestigious award in the profession of chemical engineering in Australia, is given for achievement and distinction in the profession. This award is not limited to members of the three sponsoring associations. A medal is awarded annually at the Chemeca Conference. Sponsored by The Institution of Engineers, Australia, Chemical College, The Institution of Chemical Engineers, ANC, and The Royal Australian Chemical Institute, Industrial Chemical Division.

• 497 • College of Electrical Engineers Student Prizes
To raise the profile of the Institution and the Electrical College in electrical engineering schools of tertiary institutions, thereby encouraging students to become members. The college provides funds on the basis of $400 per electrical engineering school, to divisional electrical branches for allocation as appropriate to local circumstances. Established in 1990.

• 498 • Arthur Corbett Medal
To honor the top student graduating in engineering from the Australian Defence Force Academy of the University of New South Wales. A medal and a cash prize of $200 are awarded annually. Between 1971 and 1985, the award was made for the best final year engineering student from the Royal Military College Duntroon.

• 499 • J.M.C. Corlette Medal
To annually recognize a final year student who completes the Bachelor of Engineering degree with First Class Honors at the University of Newcastle. A medal and a cash prize of $200 are awarded annually. Established in 1961.

• 500 • J.H. Curtis Medal
To recognize Queensland University of Technology engineering students. The award is based on a final year project and selection is made on appraisal by the faculty staff. A medal and a cash prize of $200 are awarded annually. Established in 1973.

• 501 • E. H. Davis Memorial Lecture
To recognize a person selected for a distinguished recent contribution to the theory and practice of geomechanics in Australia. The selected lecturer is presented with a framed certificate. Established in 1985 in honor of E.H. Davis, who achieved eminence in the field of geomechanics.

• 502 • Russell Dumas Medal
To recognize University of Western Australia engineering students. The award is made annually to the student completing the Bachelor of Engineering degree at the University who, in the opinion of the Board of Examiners in Engineering, has given the best academic performance in the final year of the course. A medal and a cash prize of $200 are awarded annually. Established in 1970.

• 503 • L.R. East Medal
To honor final-year engineering students at the University of Melbourne. Based on academic record and involvement in extra-curricular activities and special projects. A medal and a cash prize of $200 are awarded annually. Selection is made by a Faculty/Campus Chapter Panel. Established in 1977.

• 504 • Engineering 2000 Awards
To recognize and to promote the advancement of women in engineering. A broad ranging series of initiatives are considered: an organization's internal promotional program, policies proposed or introduced to create a stimulus to women to enter the profession, and career path development in the engineering profession based on the special needs of women. Established in 1990.

• 505 • Esso Award
For recognition of significant ongoing contributions to chemical engineering through innovations or a series of related publications over a number of years. A monetary prize of $2,500 is awarded. Established in 1990.

• 506 • Faldt Guthrie Medal
To recognize University College of Central Queensland engineering students. The award is based on a final year project and selection is made on appraisal by faculty staff. A medal and a cash prize of $200 are awarded annually. Established in 1973.

• 507 • Ian Henderson Memorial Prize
For recognition of the best of a group of papers, each of approximately 20 minutes duration, on an engineering subject delivered to a single meeting of the Newcastle Division by a graduate or student member of the Division. In the event of there being more than four entries in any one year, pre-selection is carried out. Twenty-five percent of the points are awarded for the standard of presentation of the paper. A monetary prize of $250 and a medal are awarded annually. Established in 1977 in memory of Mr. I.F.G. Henderson who was employed by BHP Company Ltd. for over 45 years, and who was closely associated with the Newcastle Division for many years until his death in 1975.

• 508 • Institution of Engineers Medal
To recognize and acknowledge a notable engineering contribution to the economic or social development of Australia. The award may be given to an individual or to an organization. Exceptional performance in one or a number of the following areas is considered: development or application of engineering technology, contributing to Australia's economic performance, implementation of policies leading to industrial development or enhanced quality of life, achievement in the education of young Australians, or contributing toward the development of a technical-literate society. Up to four medals are awarded annually. Established in 1989.

• 509 • Australian Geomechanics Award - John Jaeger Memorial Award
To recognize and promote contributions of the highest order in the field of Australian geomechanics. Contributions may take the form of papers published in any publication of the Society, Institution, or Institute or presented at any meeting, conference, or symposium of one of these bodies. Papers may also be the design, construction, or supervision of any project in the field of geomechanics. The award is not restricted to members of the Australian Geomechanics Society. Nominations should be made by at least three persons (not necessarily members), to the Secretary of the National Committee of the Society six months prior to the Conference at which the award is to be presented. A bronze medallion is awarded every four years. Established in 1980 in memory of Professor John Conrad Jaeger, who was Professor of Geophysics and Geochemistry at the Australian National University from 1953 until his death in 1979. Professor Jaeger's work of the greatest importance related to the physics of heat flow and rock mechanics and he published several classic books in this field. He became a Fellow of the Australian Academy of Science in 1954 and a Fellow of the Royal Society in 1970. Sponsored by the Australian Geomechanics Society, a joint organization of The Institution of Engineers, Australia and The Australasian Institute of Mining and Metallurgy.

• 510 • K. Johinke Medal
To annually recognize a final year engineering student at the University of South Australia who is selected on the basis of personality and a high level of academic attainment. A medal and a

cash prize of $200 are awarded annually. Established in 1977.

• 511 • George Julius Medal
For recognition of a paper on mechanical engineering considered the best by the College of Mechanical Engineers. Members of the Institution are eligible. A bronze medal is awarded annually. Established in 1955 in memory of George Julius, inventor of the automatic totalizator and President of the Institution in 1925. Formerly: (1976) Mechanical Engineering Prize.

• 512 • Allen Knight Medal
To honor the engineering student at the University of Tasmania, who on the appraisal of the faculty staff, shows the highest degree of proficiency in the subject of engineering design in the final year of the course. A medal and a cash prize of $200 are awarded annually. Established in 1963.

• 513 • Ian Langlands Medal
To honor final-year engineering students at Monash University. The award is based on academic record and involvement in extra-curricular activities and special projects. A medal and a cash prize of $200 are awarded annually. Established in 1977.

• 514 • Digby Leach Medal
To recognize a final year student at Curtin University of Technology on the basis of interest in the Institution, academic record, and qualities of leadership. A medal and a cash prize of $200 are awarded annually. Established in 1968.

• 515 • Local Government Engineering Medal
To recognize the engineer responsible for the design/project judged to be the best of those completed in the last two years. The award consists of a bronze medal and a certificate. Awarded biennially.

• 516 • John Madsen Medal
For recognition of a paper on electrical engineering considered the best by the College of Electrical Engineers. Members and non-members are eligible. A bronze medal is awarded annually. Established in 1927. Renamed in 1976 to honor Sir John Madsen, one of Australia's great electrical engineers and foundation professor of Electrical Engineering at the University of Sydney. Sponsored by Engineers Australia, the Electrical Energy Society of Australia, and NHP.

• 517 • A. G. M. Michell Medal
For recognition of a significant contribution through technical innovation to the science or practice of mechanical engineering, or for notable and sustained leadership pertaining to mechanical engineering. A bronze medal is awarded annually. Established in 1978 in honor of Anthony George Maldon Michell, Australia's outstanding mechanical engineer, and inventor of the tilting-pad thrust bearing and the viscometer. Michell also developed hydraulic power transmissions and designed a series of crank less engines.

• 518 • John Monash Medal
For recognition of the best paper on multi-disciplinary engineering. Members of the Institution are eligible. A bronze medal is awarded annually. Established in 1976 in honor of Sir John Monash, Australia's greatest military commander and an outstanding engineer.

• 519 • National Excellence Awards for Engineering Journalism
To encourage and enhance the reporting of engineering issues to the public. Awards are presented in three categories: the print media, radio and television. A monetary award of $1,000 and a suitably inscribed medal are awarded in each category. Established in 1990.

• 520 • W.H.R. Nimmo Medal
To recognize University of Queensland engineering students. The award is based on a final year project and selection is made on faculty appraisal. A medal and a cash prize of $200 are awarded annually. Established in 1976.

• 521 • Sir Arvi Parbo Medal
To annually recognize a final year engineering student at the University of Adelaide who is selected on the basis of personality and high level of academic attainment. A medal and a cash prize of $200 are awarded annually. Established in 1977.

• 522 • R. W. Parsons Memorial Prize
To recognize a graduate or student member of the South Australian Division for the best prepared paper of approximately 20 minutes duration delivered on an engineering subject. In the event of there being more entries than can be conveniently heard in one evening, pre-selection of the papers is carried out. A significant proportion of the points awarded are for the standard of presentation of the paper. A monetary prize of $250 and a medal are awarded annually. Established in 1962 in memory of Mr. R.W. Parsons, a former Principal of the South Australian School of Mines (1940-1960) and a former Director of the South Australian Institute of Technology (1960-1961). Parsons was a Councillor of the Institution from 1947 to 1961, Chairman of the former Adelaide Division in 1943 and President of the Institution in 1955.

• 523 • President's Prize
To recognize corporate members of the Institution who have made a major effort in promulgating the contribution that the engineering profession makes to the general welfare of the Australian people. A medal and a certificate are awarded annually. Established in 1990.

• 524 • R.A. Priddle Medal
To honor, on the recommendation of the Dean of the Faculty of Engineering, the candidate working toward a Bachelor of Engineering degree at the University of Sydney who shows the greatest proficiency. A medal and a cash prize of $200 are awarded annually. Established in 1978.

• 525 • Professional Engineer of the Year
To recognize a corporate member of the Institution for competence and significant achievement in community affairs, a demonstrated understanding of the role and purpose of the engineering profession within society, proficiency in the use of communication and managerial skills in engineering projects, and/or effective communication with the mass media.

• 526 • Queensland Division Chemical Branch Award
To recognize a chemical engineering student at the University of Queensland. A monetary award of $100 is presented.

• 527 • Railway Engineering Award
For recognition of an outstanding contribution to railway engineering in Australia. A monetary prize of $2000 and a plaque are awarded. Established in 1984 by the Institution's National Committee on Railway Engineering.

• 528 • Peter Nicol Russell Memorial Medal
This, the most prestigious award of the Institution, is given for notable contributions to the science and practice of engineering in Australia. Fellows of the Institution who are at least 45 years of age are eligible. A bronze medal is awarded annually. Established in 1923 in memory of Peter Nicol Russell, a Sydney industrialist who made major donations to the cause of engineering education in Australia.

• 529 • W.E. Sansum Medal
To recognize aeronautical engineering students at the University of Canberra. Based on academic record and involvement in extra-curricular activities and special projects. Awarded annually. Established in 1988 after the late Air Commodore "Bill" Sansum, who was elected as a Fellow of the Institution in 1981, was Chairman of the Canberra Branch of the Royal Aeronautical Society in 1987-1988, and Chairman of the Canberra Division of the Institution in 1988.

• 530 • M. A. Sargent Medal
To recognize the outstanding Australian electrical engineer of the year. Selection of the recipient is based on: a highly significant contribution, through technical innovation to the science or practice of electrical engineering; long-standing eminence in science or practice of electrical engineering; exceptional and sustained management or leadership relating to electrical engineering; or a notable combination of the foregoing qualities. A bronze medal is awarded. Established in 1989.

• 531 • Norman Selfe Medal
To recognize the best final-year project of the Bachelor of Engineering (Maritime) at Australian Maritime College. A medal and a cash prize of $200 are awarded annually. The medal is

named in honor of Norman Selfe, who was a great promoter of technical education.

• 532 • **Shedden Uhde Medal and Prize**
To recognize the members of The Institution of Chemical Engineers or the College of Chemical Engineers, their practical services to the profession, and the practice of chemical engineering in Australia. Achievements may be in technical, marketing, or management fields and nominations may be made either by individuals themselves or by others. The award is donated by Shedden Pacific and consists of a medal and a cash prize of $1,000. Awarded annually.

• 533 • **Kevin Stark Memorial Award**
To encourage excellence in coastal and ocean engineering. Any author who has a paper published in a forthcoming Australasian Conference on Coastal and Ocean Engineering, sponsored biennially by the National Committee on Coastal and Ocean Engineering, is eligible. The award is in the form of an engraved bronze medal. Awarded to one or more recipients in odd-numbered years. Established in 1993.

• 534 • **A.E. Stohr Medal**
To recognize final-year engineering students at the Ballarat University College. Based on academic record and involvement in extra-curricular activities and special projects. Selection is made by the Faculty/Ballarat Group Panel. A medal and a cash prize of $200 are awarded annually. Established in 1977.

• 535 • **D. H. Trollope Medal**
For recognition of the best doctoral thesis in the discipline of geomechanics. It is not limited to members of the Institution. A bronze medal is awarded biennially. Established in 1987.

• 536 • **Warman International Students Design Award Competition**
To recognize outstanding third-year Mechanical Engineering Students. All recognized engineering teaching institutions may submit a team for the national award after conducting in-house competitions to ascertain their representations. A separate design problem is set each year. Awarded annually. Sponsored by Warman International.

• 537 • **W. H. Warren Medal**
For recognition of a paper on civil engineering considered the best by the College of Civil Engineers. Members of the Institution are eligible. A bronze medal is awarded annually. Established in 1929 in honor of W.H. Warren, the First President of the Institution and first professor of Engineering at the University of Sydney.

• 538 • **G.R. Wilmoth Medal**
To recognize University College of Southern Queensland engineering students. The award is based on a final year project and selection is made on appraisal by faculty staff. A medal and a cash prize of $200 are awarded annually. Established in 1974.

• 539 • **Young Engineers Speaking Competition**
To recognize outstanding young speakers. Division winners are funded to attend the National Engineering Conference. A monetary prize and a certificate are awarded annually. Established in 1989.

• 540 • **Young Professional Engineer of the Year**
Mirrors the Professional Engineer of the Year Award in its criteria but relates to graduate members of the Institution within six years of graduating. Awarded annually.

• 541 •
International Association of Volcanology and Chemistry of the Earth's Interior
(Association Internationale de Volcanologie et de Chimie de l'Interieur de la Terre)
Prof. Stephen McNutt, Sec.Gen.
PO Box 185
Campbell, Australian Capital Territory 2612, Australia
Phone: 61 2 62487407
Fax: 61 2 62487407
E-mail: members@iavcei.org
Home Page: http://www.iavcei.org

• 542 • **Thorarinsson Medal**
For recognition of excellence in volcanological research. A medal and $2,000 US for travel expenses is awarded every four years at the IAVCEI General Assembly. Established in 1987 in honor of Professor Sigurdur Thorarinsson of Reykjavik University.

• 543 • **Wager Medal**
For recognition of outstanding contributions to the study of volcanic rocks. Scientists under 40 years of age on December 31 of the year preceding the award are eligible. A monetary prize of $2,000 US to attend the IAVCEI General Assembly, where the award is presented, is awarded every four years. Established in 1975 by the Volcanology Subcommittee of the Royal Society (London) to commemorate the work of the late Professor L. R. Wager. Formerly: (1994) Wager Prize.

• 544 •
International Cost Engineering Council
Robyne Nash, Administrator
PO Box 301
Deakin West, Australian Capital Territory 2600, Australia
Phone: 61 2 62822222
Fax: 61 2 62852427
E-mail: icec@icoste.org
Home Page: http://www.icoste.org

• 545 • **Distinguished International Fellow**
Recognizes outstanding service to profession. Awarded biennially.

• 546 • **Jan Korevaar Outstanding Paper Award**
Presented to the author of the outstanding paper of each biennial congress.

• 547 •
International League of Associations for Rheumatology
Prof. Peter Brooks M.D., Pres.
Edith Cavell Bldg.
Royal Brisbane Hospital
Brisbane, Queensland 4029, Australia
Phone: 61 7 33655106
Fax: 61 7 33655533
E-mail: p.brooks@mailbox.uq.edu.au
Home Page: http://www.ilar.org

• 548 • **CIBA-GEIGY-ILAR International Rheumatism Award**
Award of recognition.

• 549 •
International Union of Microbiological Societies
(Union Internationale des Societes de Microbiologie)
Prof. John Mackenzie, Sec.Gen.
Dept. of Microbiology and Parasitology
University of Queensland
Curtin University
Brisbane, Queensland 04072, Australia
Phone: 61 8 92661640
Fax: 61 8 92661650
E-mail: j.mackenzie@curtin.edu.au
Home Page: http://www.iums.org

• 550 • **Arima Award for Applied Microbiology**
To recognize an individual for contributions to applied microbiology. A monetary award, a plaque, and travel expenses to present a lecture are awarded every three years at the International Congress. Established in 1989 to honor Professor Kli Arima, former president of IUMS.

• 551 • **Stuart Mudd Award for Studies in Basic Microbiology**
To recognize an individual for contributions to basic microbiology. A monetary award, a plaque, and travel expenses to present a lecture are awarded every three years at the International Congress. The recipient also become a Fellow in the World Academy of Art and Science. Established in 1978 to honor Professor Stuart Mudd.

• 552 • **Van Niel International Prize for Studies in Bacterial Systematics**
To recognize an individual for contributions to bacterial systematics. A monetary award of approximately $2,000 is presented every three years at the International Congress. Established in 1986 by Dr. Vic Skerman to honor Professor Van Niel. The International Committee of Systematic Bacteriology plays an advisory role in the award program.

• 553 •
Katanning Shire Council
Bruce Gilbert, Community Dvlp. Officer
16-24 Austral
PO Box 130
Katanning, Western Australia 6317, Australia
Phone: 61 8 9821 4200
Fax: 61 8 9821 1458
E-mail: cso@katanning.wa.gov.au
Home Page: http://www.katanning.wa.gov.au

• 554 • Katanning Art Prize
To recognize and acquire contemporary art works to add to the Katanning Shire Council's collection of art works. Applications may be submitted by the beginning of October. Awards are presented in various categories, and total $9,000. Awarded in October of in odd-numbered years. Established in 1979.

• 555 •
Grace Leven Prize for Poetry Trust
% Perpetual Trustee Company
39 Hunter St.
GPO Box 4171
Sydney, New South Wales 2001, Australia
Phone: 61 2 92293925
Fax: 61 2 92328936
E-mail: investments@perpetual.com.au
Home Page: http://www.perpetual.com.au

• 556 • Grace Leven Prize for Poetry
For recognition of the best volume of poetry published during the twelve months immediately preceding the year the award is made. Writers must be Australian-born and writing as Australians, or naturalized in Australia and resident in Australia for not less than ten years. A monetary prize of A$200 is awarded annually. Established in 1947 at the bequest of William Baylebridge.

• 557 •
Paul Lowin Trust
% Perpetual Trustee Company
39 Hunter St.
GPO Box 4171
Sydney, New South Wales 2001, Australia
Phone: 61 2 92293925
Fax: 61 2 92328936
E-mail: investments@perpetual.com.au
Home Page: http://www.perpetual.com.au

• 558 • Paul Lowin Orchestral Prize
To recognize an outstanding musical composition. Applicants must be at least 18 years of age and Australian citizens of at least three years at the closing date for entries. Compositions must not be completed earlier than the end of the previous competition and may have been performed in public or broadcast. Orchestral works must be for at least 30 players and 15 independent lines. The work must at least be 12 minutes in duration, and use orchestral forces (exceeding those of a classical or chamber orchestra) of a size up to the normal complement of a modern symphony orchestra using as a guide the instrumental strengths of the Melbourne Symphony Orchestra or the Sydney Symphony Orchestra. The work may be with or without instrumental soloists, but works for the string ensemble alone will not be considered. The work may include vocal soloists and/or choral, electronically produced or prerecorded elements. The winner will receive $25,000. Established under the will of Paul Lowin, an Australian businessman who loved music.

• 559 • Paul Lowin Song Cycle Prize
To recognize an outstanding music composition. Applicants must be at least 18 years of age and Australian citizens of at least three years at the closing date for entries. Compositions must not be completed earlier than the close of the previous competition. Entrants may use existing and/or specially composed lyrics. The composer and lyricist(s) may be different people. The lyrics should have some similarity or unity in thought and feeling. The work may be for a single voice, more than one, or a group of voices or choir. They may be unaccompanied, or accompanied by an instrument or ensemble. A monetary award of $15,000 is presented triennially. Established under the will of Paul Lowin, an Australian businessman who loved music.

• 560 •
Media, Entertainment and Arts Alliance
Mr. Christopher Warren, Federal Sec.
245 Chalmers St.
Redfern, New South Wales 2016, Australia
Phone: 61 2 93330999
Fax: 61 2 93330933
Home Page: http://www.alliance.org.au

• 561 • W.G. Walkley Awards for Journalism
For recognition of the best examples of Australian journalism. Best Business Report is open to entries from 33 categories of business journalism. In addition to awards in each category are several special awards: the Gold Award for the top winner among all categories; the Journalism Leadership Award for outstanding acts of courage and bravery in the practice of journalism; and the Most Outstanding Contribution to Journalism Award to recognize long-term commitment and achievement in the industry. Awarded annually. Established in 1956 by Sir William Gaston Walkley, founder of Ampol Petroleum and one of the pioneers of oil exploration in Australia. The Media, Entertainment and Arts Alliance is the trustee and administrator of the awards.

• 562 •
Melbourne International Film Festival
207 Johnston St., 1st Fl.
PO Box 2206
Fitzroy, Victoria 3065, Australia
Phone: 61 3 9417 2011
Fax: 61 3 9417 3804
E-mail: miff@melbournefilmfestival.com.au
Home Page: http://www.melbournefilmfestival.com.au

• 563 • Melbourne International Film Festival Shorts Awards
To give encouragement, recognition and reward to short film makers. Short films less than 60 minutes in length are eligible. The deadline for entry is March 31. The following prizes are awarded: (1) Erwin Rado Prize: Best Australian Short (Sponsored by Film Victoria) - $5,000 (Australian); (2) The City of Melbourne Award for Best Film (Grand Prize) - $7,000 (Australian); (3) Front Page Management Ltd. Award for Best Fiction Film $3,000 (Australian); (4) The *Herald and Weekly Times* Award for Best Documentary - $3,000 (Australian); (5) The Schwartz Publishing Award for Best Experimental Film - $3,000 (Australian); (6) The Kino Cinemas Award for the Best Student Film - $3,000 (Australian); (7) Best Animated Film - $3,000 (Australian); (8) Melbourne Airport Award for Emerging Australian Filmmaker - $5,000; and (9) Nova Cinemas Award for Creative Excellence in Australian File - $3,000. Awarded annually. Established in 1962.

• 564 •
National Association for the Visual Arts
Tamara Winikoff, Exec. Dir.
PO Box 60
Potts Point, New South Wales 1335, Australia
Phone: 61 2 93681900
Fax: 61 2 93586909
E-mail: nava@visualarts.net.au
Home Page: http://www.visualarts.net.au

• 565 • Australian Visual Artists' Benevolent Fund
To Australian visual arts practitioner.

• 566 • Pat Corrigan Artists' Grant
To Australian artists.

• 567 • Freedman Foundation Traveling Scholarship for Emerging Artists
To Australian artists.

• 568 • Marketing Grant for NSW Artists
To Australian artists.

• 569 • Windmill Trust Scholarship
To Australian artists.

• 570 •
National Health and Medical Research Council
Prof. Alan Pettigrew, CEO
GPO Box 9848
Canberra, Australian Capital Territory 2601, Australia
Phone: 61 2 62899184
Phone: 61 2 62891555
Fax: 61 2 62899517
E-mail: exec.sec@nhmrc.gov.au
Home Page: http://www.nhmrc.gov.au

Awards are arranged in alphabetical order below their administering organizations

• 571 • Neil Hamilton Fairley Fellowships
To provide training in scientific research methods, including those of the social and behavioral sciences, which can be applied to any area of clinical or community medicine. Fellowships are not restricted to medical and dental graduates. In considering applications, the Council places emphasis on the applied value of the proposed research training, with preference given to persons who already have research experience and are seeking advanced study not available in Australia. To be eligible to apply, candidates must: hold appropriate qualifications; hold a doctorate; have demonstrated their interest in, and ability to pursue, a career in research and/or teaching in the specific fields of applied health science and be currently engaged in such activities in Australia; not have more than two years' postdoctoral experience since the most recent doctoral award at the time of the application; be Australian citizens or be graduates from overseas, with permanent Australian resident status, not under bond to any foreign government; provide a specific study plan within a clearly defined area; organize affiliation with an overseas investigator/institution to carry out the study; and have reasonable prospects of a responsible position in Australia, on completion of the fellowship. The deadline for applications is July 31. The fellowships are usually awarded for a period of four years; the first two years are spent overseas and the remainder in Australia. The fellowships are named after the late Sir Neil Hamilton Fairley, an Australian scientist whose research in areas of preventive and tropical medicine received international acclaim.

• 572 • Dora Lush Biomedical Postgraduate Scholarships
To encourage science honors or equivalent graduates of outstanding ability to gain full time medical research experience. All candidates must enroll for a higher degree. Scholarships are held within Australia. Those eligible to apply are: Australian citizens who have already completed a science honors degree (or equivalent) at the time of submission of the application; and science honors graduates and unregistered medical or dental graduates from overseas who have permanent resident status and are currently residing in Australia. The deadline for applications is July 31. A stipend is awarded with allowances for consumables and conference travel.

• 573 • C. J. Martin Overseas Biomedical Fellowship
To enable fellows to work overseas on specific research projects within the biomedical sciences under nominated advisers. These fellowships are offered to a limited number of young persons of outstanding ability who wish to make medical research a full time career. To be eligible to apply, candidates must: hold a doctorate in a medical, dental, or related field of research or have submitted a thesis for such by December of the year of application. No offer of award is made unless written confirmation of submission is received; be actively engaged in such research in Australia; not have more than two years' post-doctoral experience at the time of the application; and be Australian citizens or be graduates from overseas, with permanent Australian resident status, not under bond to any foreign government. Candidates enrolled for a doctorate at the time of applying for this fellowship are expected to complete the degree successfully before the award can be taken up. The deadline for applications is July 31. The fellowships are usually awarded for a period of four years; two years are spent overseas and the remainder in Australia. The fellowships are named after the late Sir Charles Martin, a British scientist who had a profound influence on medical research and teaching in Australia early this century. Formerly: (2006) C. J. Martin Fellowships.

• 574 • Medical and Dental Postgraduate Research Scholarships
To assist medical or dental graduates to gain full time research experience. All candidates must enroll for a higher degree. The scholarships are held within Australia. Those eligible to apply are: Australian citizens who are graduates registered to practice within Australia, with the proviso that Dental Postgraduate Research Scholarships may be awarded prior to graduation provided that evidence of high quality work is shown; and overseas graduates who hold a qualification that is registered for practice in Australia and who have permanent resident status and are currently residing in Australia. The deadline for applications is June 30. A stipend is awarded for consumables and conference travel. The usual maximum period of the award is three years.

• 575 •
National Library of Australia
Jan Fullerton, Dir.Gen.
Parkes Pl.
Canberra, Australian Capital Territory 2600, Australia
Phone: 61 2 6262 1111
Fax: 61 2 6257 1703
E-mail: exec@nla.gov.au
Home Page: http://www.nla.gov.au

• 576 • Australian Audio Book of the Year
To improve the quality of audio books produced in Australia; to give recognition to quality audio books produced in Australia; and to promote the availability of audio books in Australia. Audio books produced in Australia during the preceding year may be submitted by the producers. A trophy is awarded annually. Established in 1988. Co-sponsored by the Commonwealth of Australia Department of Community Services and Health; and the Chief Librarian, Disability Services Section. Formerly: (1990) National Audio Book of the Year Award.

• 577 • Harold White Fellowship
To promote the library as a centre of scholarly activity and research; to encourage scholarly and literary use of the collections and the production of publications based on them; and to publicize the library's collections. Open to established scholars, writers and librarians of any nationality. Grant-in-aid and traveling expenses are awarded annually. Established in 1984 to honor Sir Harold White, former National Librarian.

• 578 •
National Space Society of Australia
Kirby Ikin, Chm.
GPO Box 7048
Sydney, New South Wales 2001, Australia
Phone: 61 2 91504553
E-mail: nssa@nssa.com.au
Home Page: http://nssa.com.au

• 579 • Activist of the Year
For a member's dedication and proactive service to the goal of the society.

• 580 • Chapter of the Year
For chapter activities and development.

• 581 • Outstanding Service Award
For contribution and personal service to the society.

• 582 • Space Pioneer Award
For long and outstanding service to the domestic space industry.

• 583 •
New South Wales Ministry for the Arts
Robert L. Adby, Dir.Gen.
Level 9, St. James Centre
111 Elizabeth St.
PO Box A226
Sydney, New South Wales 1235, Australia
Phone: 61 2 9228 5533
Fax: 61 2 9228 4722
E-mail: mail@arts.nsw.gov.au
Home Page: http://www.arts.nsw.gov.au

• 584 • Fellowships and Scholarships
The New South Wales Government offers each year a number of fellowships and scholarships to writers and artists living in New South Wales. No age restrictions apply to any fellowships or scholarships. The following awards are presented: New South Wales Travelling Art Scholarship $25,000; New South Wales Writer's Fellowship - $10,000; New South Wales History Fellowship - $10,000; Robert Helpmann Scholarship alternates biennially with the Rex Cramphorn Theater Scholarship, $15,000; New South Wales Women and Arts Fellowship - $15,000; David Paul Landa Music Scholarship for Pianists (biennial) - $25,000; New South Wales Government and Frederick May Foundation Scholarship $5,000; and Paul Lowin Composition Awards (triennial) - Orchestra Prize of $45,000 and Song Cycle Prize of $20,000.

• 585 • New South Wales Premier's Literary Awards
To honor distinguished achievement by Australian writers in the following categories of writing: fiction, nonfiction, poetry, children's books, and play and scriptwriting. Writers must be residents of Australia. Works may be nominated by writers or publishers. The following prizes are awarded:

Christina Stead Prize - $20,000, for fiction; Douglas Stewart Prize - $20,000, for nonfiction; Kenneth Slessor Prize - $15,000, for poetry; Ethel Turner Prize - $15,000, for children's writing; Play Award - $15,000; Script Writing Award - $15,000; Ethnic Affairs Commission Award - $10,000; Gleebrooks Award - $5,000; Special Award $5,000; and Book of the Year Award - $2,000. Awarded annually. Established in 1979 by the New South Wales Government.

• 586 •
Northern Territory Library
Jo McGill, Dir.
GPO Box 42
Darwin, Northern Territory 0801, Australia
Phone: 61 8922 0785
Fax: 61 8922 0760
E-mail: ntlinfo.dcdsca@nt.gov.au
Home Page: http://www.dcdsca.nt.gov.au/dcdsca/intranet.nsf/pages/ntl_home

• 587 • Arafura Short Story Award
To provide encouragement for writers of short stories. Open to Northern Territory residents only. Each entry must be an original story, essay or poem, not previously published. Preference will be given to stories and essays not exceeding 3000 words and to poems not exceeding 300 lines. Three copies of each entry must be submitted for each section. All entries must be typed on one side of the sheet and double spaced. The title of the work should appear on the manuscript, but not the author's name. A monetary prize of $1,000 is awarded annually. Established in 1984.

• 588 • Award for Aboriginal and Torres Strait Islander Writers
To recognize Aboriginal or Torres Strait Islander writers for short stories, poems or narratives, including testimony material. Open to Northern Territory residents only. Each entry must be an original story, essay or poem, not previously published. Preference will be given to stories and essays not exceeding 3000 words and to poems not exceeding 300 lines. Three copies of each entry must be submitted for each section. All entries must be typed on one side of the sheet and double spaced. The title of the work should appear on the manuscript, but not the author's name. A monetary award of $1,000 is awarded annually.

• 589 • Northern Territory Literary Awards
To encourage Territorians to express their creative and essay writing talents while promoting literacy and literary excellence. The following awards are presented: Chief Minister's History Book, Charles Darwin University Essay Award, Dymocks Aboriginal Torres Strait Islander Writers' Award, Dymocks Arafura Short Story Award, Dymocks Red Earth Poetry Award, and the Kath Manzie Youth Literary Award. Over $5,000 in prize money is awarded annually. The winners of each category receive a cheque and a certificate.

• 590 • Red Earth Poetry Award
To provide encouragement for writers of poetry. Open to Northern Territory residents only. Each entry must be an original story, essay or poem, not previously published. Preference will be given to stories and essays not exceeding 3000 words and to poems not exceeding 300 lines. Three copies of each entry must be submitted for each section. All entries must be typed on one side of the sheet and double spaced. The title of the work should appear on the manuscript, but not the author's name. Established in 1984.

• 591 •
Pacific Area Newspaper Publishers' Association
Alan Armsden, CEO
PO Box 6425
S Sydney Business Hub
Alexandria, New South Wales 2015, Australia
Phone: 61 2 83386300
Fax: 61 2 83386311
E-mail: panpa@panpa.org.au
Home Page: http://www.panpa.org.au

• 592 • Hegarty Prize
To recognize management potential in young newspaper executives. Awarded annually. Established in 1987

• 593 • Newspaper of the Year Award
To recognize excellent in pre-production and production of newspapers. It rewards high quality results in registration, dot gain, color density, blank density, cut off accuracy, fold, pin marks and tears, and ink set-off. Awards in six circulation categories are presented annually.

• 594 •
Packaging Council of Australia
Gavin Williams, CEO
Level 3
15-17 Park St.
South Melbourne, Victoria 3205, Australia
Phone: 61 3 96901955
Fax: 61 3 96903514
E-mail: packcoun@packcoun.com.au
Home Page: http://www.packcoun.com.au

• 595 • Australian Packaging Awards
For the industry that has made a contribution to the packaging industry.

• 596 • Packaging Achiever Awards
For substantial contribution to the packaging industry.

• 597 • Southern Cross Package Design Awards
For innovative and interesting packaging design by students.

• 598 •
Pharmacy Guild of Australia
Mr. Stephen G. Greenwood, Exec.Dir.
15 National Circuit
PO Box 7036
Canberra, Australian Capital Territory 2610, Australia
Phone: 61 2 62701888
Fax: 61 2 62701800
E-mail: guild.nat@guild.org.au
Home Page: http://www.guild.org.au

• 599 • Honorary Life Member
For recognition of distinguished service to the pharmacy profession over an extensive period or distinguished service to the community by a pharmacist over an extensive period. A certificate is awarded annually when merited. Established in 1929 by The Federated Pharmaceutical Service Guild of Australia.

• 600 •
Property Council of Australia
Peter Verwer, Chief Exec.
11 Barrack St., Level 1
Sydney, New South Wales 2000, Australia
Phone: 61 2 90331900
Fax: 61 2 90331991
E-mail: info@propertyoz.com.au
Home Page: http://www.propertyoz.com.au

• 601 • Property Council Rider Hunt Awards
To recognize outstanding property development in each Australian state and territory. Judging criteria include economic and financial factors; owner and user satisfaction; industry and community perceptions; efficiency of operation and maintenance; adaptability, quality of design and finish; quality of services; facilities for occupants; and environmental sustainability. Trophies are awarded annually. Co-sponsored by the Property Council of Australia and Rider Hunt.

• 602 •
Queensland Secondary Principals Association
Deb Ward, Sec.
PO Box 1726
Southport, Queensland 4215, Australia
Phone: 61 7 55091222
Fax: 61 7 55091200
E-mail: dward18@eq.edu.au
Home Page: http://www.pa.ash.org.au/qspa

• 603 • QSPA Achievement Award
For members with significant contribution to the work of QSPA in recent years.

• 604 • QSPA Award for Leadership in the Profession
For members who demonstrated strong and effective professional leadership.

• 605 • **QSPA Lifetime Achievement**
For members with significant contribution to Queensland public education.

• 606 •
RMIT University
GPO Box 2476V
Melbourne, Victoria 3001, Australia
Phone: 61 3 9925 2000
Fax: 61 3 9663 2764
Home Page: http://www.rmit.edu.au

• 607 • **J. N. McNichol Prize**
For recognition of achievement and to encourage professional development in the field of technology. Nominees must have exhibited outstanding academic achievement, leadership potential, initiative, and successful completion of an undergraduate course at the Royal Melbourne Institute of Technology. A monetary award, medal, and certificate are awarded annually. Established in 1976 by E. J. Reilly in memory of J. N. McNicol for his assistance and encouragement to students.

• 608 • **Francis Ormond Medal**
To recognize a member of the Institute's academic, teaching, or general staff who has served the Institute with distinction or has given meritorious service which has not been recognized by the Institute by any other honorary award. A medal is awarded annually. Established in 1983 in memory of Francis Ormond, founder of the Institute and president of the Council (1882-1889).

• 609 •
Royal Australasian College of Dental Surgeons
Dr. David H. Thomson, Pres.
64 Castlereagh St., Level 6
Sydney, New South Wales 2000, Australia
Phone: 61 2 92323800
Phone: 61 2 92323059
Fax: 61 2 92218108
E-mail: registrar@racds.org
Home Page: http://www.racds.org

• 610 • **F. G. Christensen Memorial Prize**
For recognition of a candidate who gains the highest marks in the College's Primary Examination. A dentist who is enrolled with the College, and has passed the Primary Examination is eligible. A monetary prize of $500 and a bronze medallion are awarded annually on the recommendation of the examiners. Established in 1971 by the late Dr. F.G. Christensen.

• 611 • **Kenneth J. G. Sutherland Prize**
For recognition of a candidate who gains the highest marks in General Dentistry by demonstrating eminence in the elective section of the College's General Stream Final Examination. A dentist, who is enrolled in the College and is eligible to take the Final Examination held in late January each year is eligible. A monetary prize pf $500 and the College Medal are awarded annually when merited at Scientific Meetings of the College. Established in 1987 by Emeritus Professor Kenneth J.G. Sutherland, AM.

• 612 •
Royal Australasian College of Surgeons
Mr. Russell Stitz, Pres.
College of Surgeons' Gardens
Spring St.
Melbourne, Victoria 3000, Australia
Phone: 61 3 92491200
Fax: 61 3 92491219
E-mail: college.sec@surgeons.org
Home Page: http://www.surgeons.org

• 613 • **John Mitchell Crouch Fellowship**
To recognize an individual who, in the opinion of the Council, is making an outstanding contribution to the advancement of surgery or anesthesia. The individual must be working actively in his/her field, and the award must be used to assist the continuation of this work. Fellows of the RACS and ANZCA who are graduates of Australian or New Zealand Medical Schools, resident in Australia or New Zealand, are eligible. Graduates from other countries are eligible if domiciled in Australia or New Zealand for five years or more. A fellowship of approximately $50,000 (Australian) is awarded annually. Established in 1978 by Mrs. Elisabeth Unsworth, in memory of her son, John Mitchell Crouch, a young Fellow of the College, who died early in his career.

• 614 •
Royal Australian Chemical Institute
Dr. Greg Simpson, Pres.
21 Vale St.
North Melbourne, Victoria 3051, Australia
Phone: 61 3 93282033
Fax: 61 3 93282670
E-mail: member@raci.org.au
Home Page: http://www.raci.org.au

• 615 • **Applied Research Medal**
For recognition of a significant contribution towards the development of innovation in applied research, or in industrial fields. Members of the Institute are eligible. An honorarium of $250 (Australian) and a bronze medal are awarded annually. Established in 1980. Each award of the medal is named for a distinguished chemist.

• 616 • **Biota Award for Medicinal Chemistry**
To encourage the design and development by younger chemists of small molecules as potential therapeutic agents for medicinal chemistry. The Medal will be awarded to the chemist judged to be responsible for the best drug design and development paper published, patent taken out, or commercial-in-confidence report concerning small molecules as potential therapeutic agents. Only members of the RACI under the age of 35 are eligible. A monetary prize of $5,000 Australian and a medal are awarded annually. The recipient shall deliver a lecture on the topic of the award at a RACI meeting or a division meeting.

• 617 • **Citations for Contributions to Chemistry and the Chemical Profession**
To honor individuals who make substantial contributions to chemistry and especially to the progress of the profession over a period of many years. To provide recognition of these contributions, the Institute has initiated a series of citations. The awarding of citations are based on contributions to research, development or application of chemistry; contributions to chemistry in other disciplines or technologies; contributions to chemical education; contributions to the promotion of chemistry; service to RACI. Up to three citations may be awarded in a calendar year.

• 618 • **Cornforth Medal**
To recognize an RACI member for the most outstanding Ph.D. thesis submitted in a branch of chemistry, chemical science, or chemical technology in the previous 13 months. A candidate's degree must have been approved by the governing body of an Australian University, although not necessarily conferred, in the previous 13 months. No candidate may be nominated more than once. Each Australian university may nominate one candidate through the Deputy Vice-Chancellor (Research) or person holding the equivalent office of the University. A bronze relief medal and cash prize are awarded annually.

• 619 • **Distinguished Fellowship Award**
For recognition of highly distinguished contributions to the profession in academia, government or industry and the Institute. Awarded to an individual on, or very close to, retirement from principal professional role. Restricted to Fellows of the Institute. Usually not more than three fellowships are awarded per year. Established in 1996.

• 620 • **Leighton Memorial Medal**
For recognition of eminent services to chemistry in its broadest sense. A medal is awarded annually in May. The medal is silver and has a particularly beautiful design showing a profile of Leighton on the obverse, and a design symbolizing the chemical industry on the reverse. Established in 1965 in honor of A.E. Leighton.

• 621 • **Masson Memorial Scholarship Prize**
To facilitate further study in the field of chemistry. Open to financial candidates wishing to proceed to BSc Honours or the fourth year of a BSc Honours course or the first postgraduate year following 4-year courses such as BAppScience, BSc (Industrial Chemistry), BSc (Chemical Engineering) or BE (Chemical Engineering) or their equivalent, at their own or any other approved institution. A monetary prize of $500 is awarded annually. Established as a memorial to the late Sir David Orme Masson, Founder of the Institute.

• 622 • **C. S. Piper Prize**
To recognize a RACI member for the best published original research work carried out mainly in Australia in the fields of either soil chemistry or

the mineral nutrition of plants. The successful candidate will deliver a lecture on the occasion of the presentation of the award and may be invited to lecture to other branches of the Institute. A medal, a monetary prize of $8,000, plus $2,000 travel expenses, if required, are awarded biennially in even-numbered years when merited.

• 623 • Rennie Memorial Medal
For recognition of published research. Members of the Institute who have less than 8 years of professional experience since completing their degree, have contributed towards the development of some branch of chemical science can apply. Applications due on February 28 each year. A medal is awarded annually. Established in 1931 in honor of E.H. Rennie.

• 624 • H. G. Smith Memorial Award
To recognize the individual who has contributed the most to the development of some branch of chemical science. The contribution is judged by research work published or accepted for publication during the ten years immediately preceding the award. Most of the work should have been done in Australia while the candidate was an Institute member. An honorarium and a bronze medal are awarded annually. Applications due by February 28 of each year. Established in 1929 in memory of H.G. Smith. Formerly: (2006) H. G. Smith Medal.

• 625 • Wolskel Industrial Chemistry Essay Award
To recognize an essay relating industrial chemistry to logic and/or economics. The competition is open to all Australian citizens. Essays should be between 5,000 and 15,000 words and include a synopsis of approximately 100 words. A monetary prize of $750 is awarded.

• 626 •
Royal Australian Institute of Architects
2A Mugga Way
PO Box 3373
Manuka, Australian Capital Territory 2603, Australia
Phone: 61 2 62731548
Fax: 61 2 62731953
E-mail: national@raia.com.au
Home Page: http://www.architecture.com.au/

• 627 • National Architecture Awards
To recognize achievement in architecture. The following awards are presented: Commercial Award - to recognize outstanding commercial products; Interior Architecture Award - to recognize interiors completed for commercial or other purposes, new building interiors, or interior refurbishment of existing buildings; International Award established in 1991 to recognize the overseas work of RAIA Member architects in many parts of the world; Lachlan Macquarie Award for Conservation established in 1982 to recognize conservation and restoration, both domestic and commercial, where the work has led to the restoration or conservation of the building with due consideration for its historic purpose; President's Award for Recycled Buildings established in 1985 to recognize residential and nonresidential renovation projects; Robin Boyd Award for Housing - established in 1981 to recognize residential work, including both completed new buildings and extensions (not including such major projects as hotels); Sir Zelman Cowen Award for Public Buildings - established in 1981 to recognize nonresidential work including commercial-, institutional-, and recreational-type projects, both new and extensions; and Walter Burley Griffin Award for Urban Design - established in 1989 to recognize excellence in the field of design of civic amenities. of civic amenities.

• 628 • RAIA Gold Medal
To recognize architects who have given distinguished service to the architectural profession by designing or executing buildings of high merit, or who have produced work of great distinction resulting in the advancement of architecture. Architects in countries within the Australian sphere of influence are eligible. A gold medal is awarded annually at the general meeting. Established in 1960.

• 629 •
Royal Geographical Society of Queensland
Keith Smith, Sec.
237 Milton Rd.
Milton, Queensland 4064, Australia
Phone: 61 7 33682066
Fax: 61 7 33671011
E-mail: admin@rgsq.org.au
Home Page: http://www.rgsq.org.au

• 630 • J. P. Thomson Medal
For recognition of scholarship and contribution to the study of geography as exemplified by the life of Dr. J. P. Thompson. The following criteria are considered: research that has advanced knowledge of the discipline of geography or advanced the understanding of the importance of the role of geography in daily life; teaching or writing that has contributed to geographical education, including the development or application of techniques that have promoted the progress or application of geographical studies; and activities in fields not necessarily identified as geography that are clearly influenced by a geographical outlook or knowledge. Established in 1901 to honor James Park Thompson. Formerly: J. P. Thompson Foundation Gold Medal.

• 631 •
Royal New South Wales Bowling Association
John Archer, State Pres.
PO Box A2186
Sydney, New South Wales 1235, Australia
Phone: 61 2 92834555
Fax: 61 2 92834252
E-mail: rnswba@rnswba.org.au
Home Page: http://www.rnswba.org.au

• 632 • Bowler of the Year

• 633 • Charity of the Year
For deserving charity.

• 634 • Junior Bowler of the Year

• 635 • Senior Bowler of the Year

• 636 •
Royal Society of New South Wales
Irene Kelly, Off.Man.
121 Darlington Rd.
University of Sydney
Darlington 2006, Australia
Phone: 61 2 9036 5282
Fax: 61 2 9036 5309
E-mail: info@nsw.royalsoc.org.au
Home Page: http://nsw.royalsoc.org.au

• 637 • Walter Burfitt Prize
To recognize the worker whose contributions published during the past six years are deemed of the highest scientific merit in pure or applied science. Only investigations described for the first time and carried out by the author resident in Australia or New Zealand are considered. The prize is awarded triennially when merited. Established in 1957 as a result of generous gifts by Dr. and Mrs. W. F. Burfitt.

• 638 • Clarke Medal
For recognition of distinguished work in the natural sciences done in or on the Australian Commonwealth and its territories in one of the following three categories: geology, mineralogy, and natural history. A medal is awarded annually when merited. Established in 1878 in memory of Reverend William Branwhite Clarke, Vice-President of the Society, 1866-1878.

• 639 • Clarke Memorial Lecture
To recognize an individual for advancement in geology. Awarded biennially. The lectures are published in the Society's Journal.

• 640 • James Cook Medal
For recognition of outstanding contributions to science and human welfare in and for the Southern Hemisphere. A medal is awarded annually when merited. Established in 1947.

• 641 • Edgeworth David Medal
To recognize Australian research workers under the age of 35 for work done mainly in Australia or its territories, or for contributions to the advancement of Australian science. A medal is awarded annually when merited. Established in 1948.

• 642 • Liversidge Lectureship
To recognize an individual for outstanding research in chemistry. Awarded biennially. Established under the terms of a bequest by Prof. Archibald Liversidge. The lectures are published in the Society's Journal.

• 643 • Archibald D. Olle Prize
To recognize the member of the Society who has submitted the best paper during the year. A cash award of $500 is given. Established in 1956. Established under the terms of a bequest by Mrs. A. D. Olle.

• 644 • Walter Poggendorf Lecture
To recognize an individual for outstanding achievement in agriculture. The recipient is chosen by the council to present a memorial lecture. Established in 1987 to honor Walter Hans Georg Poggendorff. The lectures are published in the Society's Journal.

• 645 • Pollock Memorial Lecture
Awarded approximately every four years n memory of Prof. J.A. Pollock, Dse, FRS, Professor of Physics, University of Sydney (1899-1922). Sponsored by the Royal Society of N.S.W. and the University of Sydney. Established 1949. The Lectures are published in the Society's Journal.

• 646 • Society's Medal
To recognize a member of the Society for meritorious contributions to the advancement of science, including administration and organization of scientific endeavour, and for recognition of services to the Society. A medal is awarded annually when merited. Established in 1882.

• 647 •
Royal Society of South Australia
Dr. John H. Love, Sec.
N Terr.
Adelaide, South Australia 5000, Australia
Phone: 61 8 82235360
E-mail: roysocsa@adam.com.au
Home Page: http://www.agwine.adelaide .edu.au/industry/rssa

Formerly: (1880) Adelaide Philosophical Society.

• 648 • HG Andrewartha Medal
Recognizes outstanding contributions to research by a scientist aged a maximum of 40 years in the year of the award. Candidates should demonstrate a clear connection with South Australia by research field or employment. Selection is based on published research within the fields covered by the activities of the Society.

• 649 • Postgraduate Student Prize
Students in the natural sciences throughout South Australia are invited to present their research at an Ordinary meeting of the Society. Six to eight students are selected to make presentations throughout the year on the basis of their submitted abstract. The student adjudged to have made the best presentation receives free membership of the Society for one year, a one year subscription to the *Transactions of the Royal Society of South Australia*, and a cash prize. Established in 2000.

• 650 • The Publication Medal
Recognizes the most outstanding paper published in the *Transactions of the Royal Society of South Australia*. Authors aged 40 or younger who are Fellows of the Society are eligible. Also encourages and rewards high quality scientific publication by younger scientists. Awarded as meritted.

• 651 • Verco Medal
For recognition of distinguished scientific work published by a member of the Society. The Council of the Society makes the award on the recommendation of the Society's awards committee, which considers members of the Society who have been nominated by fellow members. A medal is awarded annually when merited. Established in 1928 in honor of Sir Joseph Verco (1851-1933). Formerly: (2006) Sir Joseph Verco Medal.

• 652 •
The Royal Society of Victoria
Prof. Bruce Livett, Pres.
Royal Society's Hall
9 Victoria St.
Melbourne, Victoria 3000, Australia
Phone: 61 3 9663 5259
Fax: 61 3 9663 2301
E-mail: rsv@sciencevictoria.org.au
Home Page: http://www.sciencevictoria.org .au

• 653 • Research Medal
For recognition of scientific research of outstanding merit in one of the following four categories: biological sciences (non-human)- agriculture, biochemistry, botany, forestry, physiology, zoology, and related (non-human) sciences; earth sciences - geology, geochemistry, geochronology, geophysics, planetary physics, meteorology, oceanography, physical geography, and related sciences; physical sciences - astronomy, chemistry, engineering, mathematics, physics, and related sciences; and human health or medical sciences (human)- genetics, immunology, human physiology, human anatomy, pathology, necrology, epidemiology, parasitology, nuclear medicine, and related human sciences. The work must have been carried out in or on Australia with preference given to work done in Victoria or about Victoria. A silver medal is awarded annually at the Medal Lecture. Established in 1959, the centenary year of the society.

• 654 •
Royal Society of Western Australia
C. Walker, Pres.
℅ Western Australian Museum
Francis St.
Locked Bag 49
Welshpool, Western Australia 6986, Australia
Phone: 61 9 4272771
Fax: 61 9 3288686
E-mail: rswa@museum.wa.gov.au
Home Page: http://www.ecu.edu.au/pa/rswa

• 655 • Royal Society of Western Australia Medal
To provide recognition for distinguished work in natural and agricultural science connected with Western Australia. There are no restrictions on eligibility. A sterling silver medallion is awarded and a cash award of $250 at the discretion of the council of the Society every year. Established in 1924.

• 656 •
Royal Western Australian Historical Society
Prof. Reginald Appleyard, Pres.
Stirling House
49 Broadway
Nedlands, Western Australia 6009, Australia
Phone: 61 8 93863841
Fax: 61 8 93863309
E-mail: histwest@git.com.au
Home Page: http://www.histwest.git.com.au

• 657 • A. E. Williams History Prize
To recognize the best paper submitted on any aspect of Western Australian history. Open to members of Historical Societies and secondary school students of years 10 to 12 in Western Australia. A monetary award of $400 is awarded annually. Established in 1990.

• 658 •
Royal Zoological Society of New South Wales
Prof. Shelley Burgin, Pres.
PO Box 20
Mosman, New South Wales 2088, Australia
Phone: 61 2 9969 7336
E-mail: office@rzsnsw.org.au
Home Page: http://www.rzsnsw.org.au

• 659 • Whitley Awards
For recognition of outstanding publications (printed or electronic) on Australasian fauna or the history of Australasian zoology during the preceding year. Applications must be submitted by May 30. Awards may be presented in the following categories: best children's book, best field guide, best illustrated book, best reference book, best textbook, best zoological history book, best zoological periodical, and other appropriate categories. A silver medal is awarded to the author of the outstanding book; the publisher receives a certificate and citation. Certificates of commendation are awarded to category winners. Established in 1978 to honor Gilbert Whitley (1903-1975), an Australian zoologist. Additional information is available from Royal Zoological Society of NSW, PO Box 20, Mosman 2088, Australia.

• 660 •
St. Kilda Film Festival
Paul Harris, Festival Dir.
Private Bag No. 3
St. Kilda, Victoria 3182, Australia
Phone: 61 3 9209 6711
Fax: 61 3 9209 6790
E-mail: filmfest@portphillip.vic.gov.au
Home Page: http://www.stkildafilmfestival.com.au

• 661 • **St. Kilda Film Festival**
For recognition of the best Australian independent short film. A monetary prize of $10,000 is awarded annually for the City of Port Phillip Prize of Best Short Film. Other monetary prizes are awarded in various categories. Held annually. Established in 1984.

• 662 •
Sir Henry Royce Memorial Foundation
David Jones, Chair
GPO Box 4139
Sydney, New South Wales 2001, Australia
Phone: 61 2 92314688
Fax: 61 2 92215459
E-mail: email@royce.org.au
Home Page: http://www.royce.org.au

• 663 • **IIE Sir Henry Royce Award for Achievement**
To recognize a young engineering or information technology professional—who has shown excellence in the previous year in his or her work in industry or for the profession. A monetary award of £250, a medal, and a certificate are presented when merited. Established in 1990.

• 664 •
Society for Engineering in Agriculture
Mike Collins, Chm.
Engineers Australia
11 National Circuit
Barton, Australian Capital Territory 2600, Australia
Phone: 61 2 62706588
Fax: 61 2 62732358
E-mail: mcollins@agric.wa.gov.au
Home Page: http://www.ncea.org.au/seag/seag.htm

• 665 • **Agricultural Engineering Award**
Recognizes significant national contributions to the field. Only members are eligible. Awarded biennially.

• 666 •
Society of Automotive Engineers (Australasia)
Mr. Stuart Charity, Exec.Dir.
Ste. 3, 21 Vale St.
North Melbourne, Victoria 3051, Australia
Phone: 61 3 93267166
Fax: 61 3 93267244
E-mail: enquiries@sae-a.com.au
Home Page: http://www.sae-a.com.au

• 667 • **O'Shannessy Award**
For recognition of an outstanding paper delivered to the Society or published in the journal. Australian Automotive Engineers are eligible. Rodda Award and J.E. Batchelor Award winners are ineligible. Nominees must be less than 30 years of age. Awarded annually.

• 668 • **Rodda Award**
To recognize a member of the Society who submitted an outstanding written paper concerned with the original work and ideas in the fields of design, development, research or management relevant to the automotive industry. Awarded annually.

• 669 •
Society of Women Writers, Victoria Branch
Janet Howie, Pres.
% Judy Bartosy, Secretary
73 Church Rd.
Carrum, Victoria 3197, Australia
Phone: 61 3 9772 2389
E-mail: jmhowie@bigpond.com
Home Page: http://home.vicnet.net.au/~swwvic

• 670 • **Alice Award**
For recognition of a distinguished and long-term contribution to literature by an Australian woman. Selection is by nomination. A non-acquisitive statuette (The Alice) designed by Alan Ingham accompanied by a hand-lettered certificate are awarded every two years at the biennial conference. Established in 1978 by the Federal Council to commemorate fifty years of the Society (1925-1975) and the late Alice Booth, a former school teacher and member of the Society in New South Wales.

• 671 •
South Australia Arts and Industry Development
Greg Mackie, Exec.Dir.
West's Coffee Palace
110 Hindley St.
GPO Box 2308
Adelaide, South Australia 5001, Australia
Phone: 61 8 8463 5444
Fax: 61 8 8463 5420
E-mail: webmaster.art@saugov.sa.gov.au
Home Page: http://www.arts.sa.gov.au

• 672 • **Festival Awards for Literature**
To recognize distinguished Australian writing in the novel and short story form, poetry, children's literature, non-fiction, multimedia, and unpublished non-fiction. The deadline for submissions is November 1 of odd years. The following awards are presented: National Fiction Award - for a published novel or a collection of short stories, $15,000; the John Bray National Poetry Award - for a published collection of poems or for a single poem of substantial length, $15,000; National Non-fiction Award for a published work of nonfiction, $15,000; National Children's Book Award - for a published work of fiction or nonfiction, $15,000; the Jill Blewett Playwright's Award (National) - for a play script performed by a professional theatre company, or a professional production unit, in South Australia, $15,000; Faulding Multimedia Award - to recognize excellence in multimedia $10,000; Wirra Wirra Wakefield Press for best unpublished non-fiction manuscript, $10,000; Carclew Fellowship - a six-month fellowship - open to South Australian writers for young people, $15,000; and the Barbara Hanrahan Fellowship, $15,000 - a six-month fellowship - open to South Australian writers of poetry and creative prose. Awarded biennially during Writers' Week as part of the Adelaide Festival. Established in 1976. Premier's Literary Award - best of winners in all published categories - an additional $5,000 on top of category prize.

• 673 • **Premier's Literary Award**
To recognize the most outstanding published work submitted to the Festival Awards for Literature. A monetary prize of $10,000 is awarded.

• 674 •
South Australian Photographic Federation
Daniel Pangrazio, Pres.
PO Box 2204
Kent Town, South Australia 5071, Australia
Phone: 61 8 8331 9770
E-mail: info@sapf.org.au
Home Page: http://www.sapf.org.au

• 675 • **Interphot - Adelaide International Exhibition of Photography**
For recognition of outstanding photography. Awards are given in the following categories: Monochrome Prints, Contemporary Prints, Pictorial Color Slides, Contemporary Slides, Nature Prints, Wild Life Prints, Wild Life Slides, Nature Slides, and Color Prints. Entries must be submitted by mid-June. PSA medals, APS plaques, SAPF plaques, FIAP medals and ribbons, and Kodak awards are presented annually. Established in 1964.

• 676 •
Sport Australia Hall of Fame
Robert Lay, CEO
PO Box 104
Caulfield East, Victoria 3145, Australia
Phone: 61 3 9572 4600
Fax: 61 3 9572 5400
E-mail: mail@sahof.org.au
Home Page: http://www.sahof.org.au

• 677 • **Sport Australia Hall of Fame**
For recognition of outstanding achievement in Australian sport (Member), and in functions associated with Australian sporting achievement, such as sports administration, coaching, science, or media (Associate Member). Nominations may be submitted by anyone but must be endorsed by the relevant national sporting association or the Hall of Fame Selection Committee. A medal is awarded to Members; a certificate is awarded to Associate Members. Awarded annually. Established in 1985 by Garry Jeffery Daly. In 1995, the program was placed under the management of the National Sport Australia Hall of

Fame Trust. To date, 263 members and 102 Associate Members have been selected.

• 678 •
State Library of New South Wales
Macquarie St.
Sydney, New South Wales 2000, Australia
Phone: 61 2 9273 1414
Fax: 61 2 9273 1255
E-mail: library@sl.nsw.gov.au
Home Page: http://www.sl.nsw.gov.au

• 679 • C. H. Currey Memorial Fellowship
To encourage the writing of Australian history from the original sources. A monetary prize of $20,000, is awarded annually. Established in 1975 in honor of Charles Herbert Currey, an Australian historian.

• 680 • Nancy Keesing Fellowship
For research into any aspect of Australian life and culture using the resources of the state library of New South Wales, Australia. A monetary prize of $10,000 is awarded annually. Established in 1994 in honor of Nancy Keesing, author and poet.

• 681 • Nita B. Kibble Literary Award
To encourage Australian women writers, to advance Australian literature, and to benefit the community. A monetary prize is awarded annually. Established by Nita May Dobbie in memory of her aunt, the first woman appointed a librarian in the State Library of New South Wales.

• 682 •
State Library of Victoria
328 Swanston St.
Melbourne, Victoria 3000, Australia
Phone: 61 3 9669 9676
Fax: 61 3 9639 4189
E-mail: pla@slv.vic.gov.au
Home Page: http://www.slv.vic.gov.au/pla

Formerly: (1997) Australia Arts Victoria.

• 683 • Victorian Premier's Literary Awards
An annual award for recognition of achievement in Australian literature in the following categories: fiction; nonfiction; poetry; drama; young adult literature; unpublished fiction manuscript, essay, and screenwriting. The following monetary prizes are awarded; Vance Palmer Prize for Fiction $30,000; Nettie Palmer Prize for Nonfiction - $30,000; Louis Esson Prize for Drama - $15,000; C.J. Dennis Prize for Poetry - $15,000; The Prize for Young Adult Fiction $15,000; The Dinny O'Hearn/SBS Prize for Literary Translation - $15,000; Alfred Deaken Prize for an Essay Advancing Public Debate - $15,000; Prize for an Unpublished Manuscript by an Emerging Victorian Writer - $15,000; Village Roadshow Prize for Screen Writing $15,000; Prize for a First Book of History - $15,000; Prize for Indigenous Writing - $15,000; Prize for Science Writing - $15,000. Established in 1985. Guidelines Available from pla@slv.vic.gov.au or 011 61 03 9669 9734. Awards are open to Australian citizens or residents, except for the Unpublished Manuscript Prize which is only open to unpublished writers living in the state of Victoria, Australia.

• 684 •
State Library of Western Australia
Alexander Library Bldg.
Perth Cultural Centre
Perth, Western Australia 6000, Australia
Phone: 61 8 9427 3330
Fax: 61 8 9427 3336
E-mail: info@liswa.wa.gov.au
Home Page: http://www.liswa.wa.gov.au/pba.html

Formerly: (2004) Library and Information Service of Western Australia.

• 685 • Western Australian Premier's Book Awards
To honor and celebrate the literary achievements of Western Australian writers. Entrants must have been born in Western Australia, usually reside there, have lived in Western Australia for 10 years at some stage, or have Western Australia as the primary focus of their work. Awards are presented in the following categories: Poetry, Fiction, Non-Fiction, Children's Books, Young Adults Books, Scripts (for scripts written for theatre, radio, film or television) and Premier's Prize is awarded to the overall winner, selected from the winners of the six categories. Monetary awards of Aus.$7,500 for each category and Aus.$20,000 for the Premier's Prize. Presented in October. Established in 1982. Formerly: Western Australia Week Literary Awards.

• 686 •
Sydney Cultural Council
St. Martins Tower, Level 12
31 Market St.
Sydney, New South Wales 2000, Australia
Phone: 61 2 9261 8366
Fax: 61 2 9261 8161
E-mail: info@culturalcouncil.org.au
Home Page: http://www.culturalcouncil.org.au

Formerly: (1975) City of Sydney Eisteddfod.

• 687 • John Allison City of Sydney Piano Scholarship
To encourage professional piano development. Contestants must be between 16 and 22 years of age. Both amateur and professional pianists, men and women (a) born in Australia or New Zealand; or (b) naturalized citizens of Australia who have been domiciled in Australia or New Zealand for at least six years may enter. Finalists will perform their own choice of one major work with a performance time of minimum 14 and maximum 22 minutes. A scholarship totaling A$11,500 is awarded annually. Established in 1982. Formerly: City of Sydney Eisteddfod Pianoforte Scholarship; (1998) City of Sydney Piano Scholarship.

• 688 • Choral Awards
To recognize school community choirs competing in the McDonald's Performing Arts Challenge. Awarded are presented annually the first, second, and third place winners in 13 categories. Formerly: (1998) Citibank Choral Awards.

• 689 • McDonald's Ballet Scholarship
To encourage professional development in ballet. Dancers who are amateur or professional, male or female, between 15 and 19 years of age are eligible. Dancers must be citizens or permanent residents of Australia of New Zealand or have lived in these countries for more than three years. Two $12,000 scholarships are awarded annually - to a male and a female dancer. The overall winner also receives a cash prize of $3,000. The scholarships may be used to pursue studies in Australia or overseas. The winner also receives a professional portfolio of studio photographs and the opportunity of a short secondement to the Royal Danish Ballet. Six finalists' awards of $500 each are also awarded. This award is one of several given under the McDonald's City of Sydney Performing Arts Challenge Program. Established in 1974. Formerly: Rothmans Foundation Ballet Scholarship; (1998) GIO Australia Ballet Scholarship.

• 690 • McDonald's Operatic Aria
To encourage professional vocal development. Both amateur and professional singers, men and women (a) born in Australia or New Zealand; or (b) naturalized citizens of Australia who have been domiciled in Australia or New Zealand for at least six years are eligible. No previous winners are eligible. The age limit is 32 years of age on December 31. The following prizes are awarded: (1) Grand Prize - a monetary prize of $5,000, a scholarship of $30,000, return overseas economy air fare, a portfolio of professional studio photographs, and a studio recording; (2) Second Prize - $5,000; (3) six finalists - $1,000 each; and (4) eight semi-finalists $500 each. Awarded annually. Established in 1933. Formerly: Sydney *Sun* Aria Contest.

• 691 •
Sydney Film Festival
Antony Jeffrey, Gen.Mgr.
PO Box 96
Strawberry Hills, New South Wales 2012, Australia
Phone: 61 2 9280 0511
Fax: 61 2 9280 1520
E-mail: info@sydneyfilmfestival.org
Home Page: http://www.sydneyfilmfestival.org

• 692 • CRC Multicultural Award
To recognize the best film produced in Australia during the preceding year among the Dendy Award finalists that reflects the cultural diversity of Australia. Maximum running time is 59 minutes. To qualify, the film must meet one of the following criteria: treat issues arising from the Australian immigration and settlement process; address general issues in one or more cross-cultural settings; or contain material or languages that celebrate the cultural and linguistic diversity of Australia. A monetary award of

$4,000 is awarded annually in one of the following categories: documentary, fiction, and general, for films concerned with exploring the formal possibilities of film as an end in itself or made as a personal response to some area of the filmmaker's experience where articulating that response is an end in itself. Established in 1992. Sponsored by Community Relations Commission for a Multicultural New South Wales.

• 693 • Dendy Awards for Australian Short Films
To recognize the best films made in Australia during the preceding year. Maximum running time is 59 minutes at 24 frames per second. Films produced by television stations or made for a television series are not eligible. The following prizes are awarded for monetary awards of $2,500 each: Best Film in the Documentary Category; Best Film in the Fiction under 15 minutes category; Best Film in the fiction over 15 minutes category; Award for Best Film in the General category. Sponsored by Dendy Cinema, Sydney. The awards are presented during the opening night ceremony of the Sydney Film Festival. Established in 1974. Awarded annually. Formerly: (1988) Greater Union Awards; (1974) Benson and Hedges Awards.

• 694 • Rouben Mamoulian Award
Awarded for best Australian Short Film or Documentary as chosen by an international panel from finalists of the Dendy Awards at the Sydney Film Festival. A monetary prize of $3,000 is awarded annually.

• 695 •
Symphony Services Australia
Denis Daniels, Mng.Dir.
GPO Box 9994
Sydney, New South Wales 2001, Australia
Phone: 61 2 8333 1651
Fax: 61 2 8333 1678
E-mail: info@symphony.net.au
Home Page: http://www.symphony.net.au

Formerly: (1983) Australian Broadcasting Commission.

• 696 • Young Performers Awards
To encourage professional development of young solo musicians. Awards are presented in three categories: strings, keyboard, and instrumental. Individuals under 18 and 30 years of age who are citizens or permanent residents of Australia are eligible. A monetary prize of $5,000 is presented to the best performer in each category. The overall winner is designated the Young Performer of the Year and receives a monetary award of a further $ 5,000 and concert engagements with Symphony Australia orchestras. Awarded annually. Established in 1944. Formerly: (1986) ABC Young Performers' Competition; (1985) Instrumental and Vocal Competition; (1967) ABC Concerts and Vocal Competition.

• 697 •
Tasmanian Canine Association
Mr. Kerry Smith, Exec. Officer
Royal Showgrounds
PO Box 116
PO Box 116
Glenorchy, Tasmania 7010, Australia
Phone: 61 3 62729443
Fax: 61 3 62730844
E-mail: tca@iprimus.com.au
Home Page: http://www.tascanineassoc.org

• 698 • Distinguished Service Award
Annual award of recognition.

• 699 •
Trust Co.
Jonathan Sweeney, Mng.Dir.
Level 4, 35 Clarence St.
GPO Box 2000
Sydney, New South Wales 2001, Australia
Phone: 61 300 132 075
Fax: 61 2 8295 8693
E-mail: info@trust.com.au
Home Page: http://www.permanentgroup.com.au

• 700 • Miles Franklin Literary Award
To encourage and assist the advancement of Australian literature and for recognition of a novel or play that portrays an aspect of Australian life. Novels must be first published during the year preceding the award. A monetary prize of $28,000 (Australian) is awarded annually. Deadline is December 14. Established in 1957 in memory of Miles Franklin, an Australian author.

• 701 • Portia Geach Memorial Award
For recognition of the best portraits painted from life of a man or woman distinguished in art, letters, or the sciences. Any female artist, resident in Australia during the preceding twelve months, who was born in Australia or was British born or has become a naturalized Australian and whose place of domicile is Australia is eligible. A monetary prize of $18,000 is awarded annually. Established in 1965 by a bequest of Miss Florence Kate Geach, who died in 1962, in memory of her sister, Portia Geach.

• 702 •
Turner Syndrome Association of Australia
Glenn Fisher, Exec.Dir.
PO Box 112
French's Forest, New South Wales 1640, Australia
Phone: 61 9 4524196
Fax: 61 2 99754037
E-mail: turnersyn@netpro.net.au
Home Page: http://www.turnersyndrome.org.au

• 703 • Mandy Award
Awarded to an individual who supported individuals with Turner syndrome.

• 704 •
TV Week
35-51 Mitchell St.
McMahons Point, New South Wales 2060, Australia
Phone: 61 2 9464 3300
Fax: 61 2 9464 3375
Home Page: http://tvweek.ninemsn.com.au

Formerly: (1995) Southdown Press.

• 705 • *TV Week* Logie Awards
To acknowledge and honor Australia's most popular television performers and programs, along with outstanding contributions in all areas - from news and public affairs, to light entertainment and drama. The program or performance must have occurred during the calendar year for which the awards are presented. Awards are given in the following categories: Public Voted Awards - Most Popular Personality on Australian TV, Most Popular Actor and Actress on Australian TV, Most Popular Comedy Personality, Most Popular Sports Program, Most Popular Comedy Program, Most Popular Light Entertainment/Program, Most Popular Light Entertainment Personality, Most Popular Sports Event, Most Popular Series, Most Popular Children's Program, Most Popular Public Affairs Program, and Most Popular New Talent in Australia; Most Popular Lifestyle/Information Program Most Popular Series, Most Popular Sports Event, and Panel Voted Awards - Hall of Fame, Most Outstanding Actor and Actress, Most Outstanding Achievement in Public Affairs, Most Outstanding Documentary (Series or Program), Most Outstanding Achievement in News, Most Outstanding Achievement in Sports, Most Outstanding Achievement in Drama, and Most Outstanding Achievement in Comedy. Statuettes, including Silver TV Week Logie Awards for Australia's most popular actor and actresses, and a Gold TV Week Logie Award for Australian television's most popular personality are awarded annually. Established in 1958. The TV Week Logie Award is named after Scottish John Logie Baird, the inventor of television.

• 706 •
Tweed Shire Council
Civic and Cultural Centre
Turnbulgum Rd.
PO Box 816
Murwillumbah, New South Wales 2484, Australia
Phone: 61 2 6670 2400
Fax: 61 2 6670 2429
E-mail: tsc@tweed.nsw.gov.au
Home Page: http://www.tweed.nsw.gov.au

• 707 • Doug Moran National Portrait Prize
For recognition of portraits by and of Australian citizens or permanent residents. Winners receive $100,000 (Australian) and 30 finalists receive $1,000 (Australian). Finalists tour nationally in Australia. Final judging is conducted by an international judge. The winning painting becomes part of Tweed River Regional Art Gallery's Portrait Collection. Awarded biennially; annually beginning in 2000. Established in 1988.

Formerly: (1995) Douglas J. Moran Portraiture Prize.

• 708 •
University of Melbourne
Assessment Research Centre
Faculty of Education
Parkville, Victoria 3010, Australia
Phone: 61 3 83448200
Fax: 61 3 83448790
E-mail: arc@edfac.unimelb.edu.au
Home Page: http://www.edfac.unimelb.edu .au/LED/ARC/

• 709 • National Assessment Awards
For excellence in assessment practice. Awarded annually. Established in 1997.

• 710 •
University of Melbourne
Faculty of Arts
Prof. Belinda Probert, Dean
Old Arts Bldg., Rm. 104
Melbourne, Victoria 3010, Australia
Phone: 61 3 8344 5321
Phone: 61 3 8344 5321
Fax: 61 3 9347 0424
E-mail: arts-enquiries@unimelb.edu.au
Home Page: http://www.arts.unimelb.edu .au

• 711 • Wesley Michel Wright Prize for Poetry
For recognition of a composition of original English verse or poetry by an Australian citizen. Poems with a minimum of 50 lines must be submitted by July 31. A monetary prize varying between $1,000 and $1,500 Australian is awarded annually. Established in 1982 by Wesley Michel Wright.

• 712 •
University of Melbourne
Faculty of Science
Prof. Peter Rathjen, Contact
Old Geology Bldg., Ground Fl.
Melbourne, Victoria 3010, Australia
Phone: 61 3 8344 6404
Fax: 61 3 8344 5803
E-mail: science-queries@unimelb.edu.au
Home Page: http://www.science.unimelb .edu.au

• 713 • David Syme Research Prize
For recognition of the best original research in biology, chemistry, geology, or physics during the previous two years. Preference is given to work of value to the industrial and commercial interests of Australia. A monetary prize of A$11,000 and a bronze medallion are awarded annually. Established in 1904 by David Syme.

• 714 •
University of New South Wales
Student Information and Systems Office
Sydney, New South Wales 2052, Australia
Phone: 61 2 9385 1000
Fax: 61 2 9385 1252
E-mail: sisinfo@unsw.edu.au
Home Page: http://www.unsw.edu.au

• 715 • The Silver Dirac Medal
For recognition of contributions to the advancement of theoretical physics. The individual selected to deliver the Dirac Lecture receives a silver medal. Awarded at least biennially. Established in 1979 by the University of New South Wales to commemorate the only visit to Australasia of Professor P.A.M. Dirac, 1975, organized by the University. Co-sponsored by the Australian Institute of Physics (NSW Branch).

• 716 •
Victorian Artists Society
John Hunt, Pres.
430 Albert St.
East Melbourne, Victoria 3002, Australia
Phone: 61 3 96621484
Fax: 61 3 96622343
E-mail: vicarists@vicnet.net.au
Home Page: http://home.vicnet.net.au/ ~vicart

• 717 • Artist of the Month
Monthly award of recognition.

• 718 • Artist of the Year
Annual award of recognition.

• 719 •
Vietnam Veterans Association of Australia - National Council
Geoff Trevor-Hunt, Natl. Sec.
PO Box 8108
Warnbro, Western Australia 8108, Australia
Phone: 61 8 95940429
Fax: 61 8 95940429
E-mail: vvaasec@bigpond.com
Home Page: http://www.vvaa.org.au

• 720 • Air Medal
For any member of the Armed Forces of the United States for meritorious achievement while participating in aerial flight.

• 721 • Army Commendation Medal
For meritorious service by members of the Armed Forces.

• 722 • Bronze Star
For meritorious achievement.

• 723 • Silver Star
For serving with friendly forces against an opposing armed enemy force.

• 724 •
Warringah Council
Stephen Blackadder, Gen.Mgr.
Civic Centre
725 Pittwater Rd.
Dee Why, New South Wales 2099, Australia
Phone: 61 2 9942 2111
Fax: 61 2 9971 4522
E-mail: council@warringah.nsw.gov.au
Home Page: http://www.warringah.nsw.gov .au

Awards discontinued.

• 725 • Australia Day Awards
To honor individuals and organizations that epitomize the pursuit of excellence, commitment to a tolerant and diverse society, a fair go, and public service. Special awards include Citizen of the Year Award, Young Citizen of the Year Award, and Community Event of the Year. Awarded annually.

• 726 • Garden Awards
To honor the best gardens in a variety of gardens. Open to all residents, businesses, and schools who have a great garden they want to share with others in the area. Awarded annually.

• 727 • Outstanding Community Service Awards
Given to residents or non-residents of Warringah who should be rewarded for their longstanding efforts in helping the community. Up to ten residents and one non-resident will be recognized and honored for their involvement in voluntary community service. Awarded annually.

• 728 •
Weed Society of Victoria
Ros Shepherd, Sec.
PO Box 987
Frankston, Victoria 3199, Australia
Phone: 61 3 95762949
Fax: 61 3 95762949
E-mail: secwssv@surf.net.au
Home Page: http://www.wsvic.org.au

• 729 • Honorary Membership
The Society can elect people who have made a major contribution to the Society and to Weed Science as Honorary Members.

• 730 • Weed Book Prize
Recognizes excellence in some part of course work. Students studying weed science subjects at the Melbourne University Institutes of Land and Food Resources are eligible. Awarded annually. The award is usually for an outstanding weed collection.

• 731 •
Welding Technology Institute of Australia
Anne Rorke, Contact
PO Box 6165
Silverwater, New South Wales 1811, Australia
Phone: 61 2 97484443
Fax: 61 2 97482858
E-mail: info@wtia.com.au
Home Page: http://www.wtia.com.au

• 732 • **Dr. Wilfred Chapman Award**
Recognizes an individual who has made outstanding contribution to welding progress in Australia. Awarded annually.

• 733 • **Linde Gas/WTIA Young Tradesperson of the Year**
Recognizes an up-and-coming young welder. Awarded annually.

• 734 • **A. Ramsay Moon Award**
Recognizes the author of a technical welding paper. Awarded annually.

• 735 • **Florence Taylor Award**
Recognizes an individual who has a made a notable contribution to the science of welding. Awarded annually.

• 736 •
Women's Electoral Lobby - Australia
Trish Collins, Chair
PO Box 191
Civic Square, Australian Capital Territory 2608, Australia
Phone: 61 2 62476679
Fax: 61 6 2474669
E-mail: wel@wel.org.au
Home Page: http://www.wel.org.au

• 737 • **Commonwealth Office of the Status of Women Award**
Recipient must represent a broad range of women's issues. A monetary award is given annually.

• 738 •
Young Australians Best Book Award Council
Graham Davey, Pres.
PO Box 238
Kew, Victoria 3101, Australia
Phone: 61 3 9889 7749
Fax: 61 3 9889 3665
E-mail: yabbabooks@yahoo.com
Home Page: http://home.vicnet.net.au/~yabba

• 739 • **Young Australians Best Book Award**
To encourage Victorian children to read Australian children's fiction and to give them the chance to choose that which they like best. Australian books nominated may be picture story or fiction for older readers or younger readers, published in the preceding ten years, and not previously a YABBA winner. Nominations must be submitted by the end of the first school term. Young Victorian readers in grades 1 through 9 may vote. A citation, reading "From YABBA Council and the Children of Victoria," is awarded annually to the winning authors in each category. Established in 1985.

Austria

• 740 •
Alpinale Film Festival
Alexander Strolz, Chm.
Postfach 161
A-6700 Bludenz, Austria
Phone: 43 5552 30290
Fax: 43 5552 30290
E-mail: office@alpinale.net
Home Page: http://www.alpinale.net

• 741 • **Alpinale International Film Festival**
To recognize the best films of the festival, and to promote independent filmmakers. Independent movies and productions of all categories may be submitted. The Golden Unicorn, the heraldic figure of the Alpine town Bludenz, is awarded in such categories as Children*Ks* film, Shorts, Audience choice, Animation, Student film, Professional film, and Prize of the Jury. Held annually. Established in 1982.

• 742 •
Amt der Salzburger Landesregierung Kulturabteilung
Franziskanergasse 5a
Postfach 527
A-5010 Salzburg, Austria
Phone: 43 662 8042 2035
Fax: 43 662 8042 3070
E-mail: buergerbuero@salzburg.gv.at

• 743 • **Rauriser Literaturpreis**
To recognize a first book of prose by a German-speaking author. A monetary prize of 7,300 euros and a certificate are presented annually. Established in 1972.

• 744 • **Georg Trakl Prize for Poetry (Georg Trakl Preis fur Lyrik)**
To recognize an outstanding German-speaking poet. A monetary award of 7,300 euros and a certificate are presented every few years to commemorate Georg Trakl's (1887-1914) date of birth or death. Established in 1952.

• 745 •
Amt der Tiroler Landesregierung, Kulturabteilung
Dr. Christoph Mader, Contact
Sillgasse 8
A-6020 Innsbruck, Austria
Phone: 43 512 5083752
Fax: 43 512 5083755
E-mail: kultur@tirol.gv.at
Home Page: http://www.tirol.gv.at/themen/kultur

• 746 • **Alpenlandischer Volksmusikwettbewerb**
To further the development of folk music among young people. Performers who are between 7 and 25 years of age and who are from Austria, Switzerland, South Tyrol, and Bavaria may apply. A plaque and a document are awarded biennially in even-numbered years. Established in 1974.

• 747 • **Emil Berlanda Preis**
For recognition of a contribution to the promotion and interpretation of contemporary music. Selection is by nomination. A monetary prize is awarded biennially. Established in 1982 by Magdalena Berlanda and the Kulturabteilung in memory of Emil Berlanda (1905-1960), one of Tyrol's most important composers in the first half of the twentieth century.

• 748 • **Grosse Literaturstipendien des Landes Tirol**
For recognition of achievements in contemporary literature. Individuals from the Tyrol are eligible. Two monetary prizes are awarded biennially. Established in 1991.

• 749 • **Jakob Stainer Preis**
For recognition of a contribution to the promotion of early music. Individuals from Tyrol and South Tyrol who are active in the field of early music may be nominated. A monetary prize is awarded biennially. Established in 1983 in memory of Jakob Stainer (1617-1683), world-famous violin maker, who was born in Absam near Innsbruck.

• 750 • **Tiroler Landespreis fur Kunst**
For recognition of achievement in the arts. Artists from the Tyrol and South Tyrol may be nominated. A monetary prize is awarded annually. Established in 1984. Formerly: (1983) Wurdigungspreis des Landes Tirol fur Literatur, Musik etc..

• 751 • **Tiroler Landespreis fur Wissenschaft**
For recognition of achievement in the fields of humanities or science. Candidates from the Tyrol and South Tyrol may be nominated. A monetary prize is awarded annually. Established in 1984.

• 752 • **Wurdigungspreis fur Erwadisenenbieolung des Landes Tirol**
For recognition of achievement in adult education. A monetary prize is awarded when merited.

• 753 •
Association of Austrian Librarians (Vereinigung Osterreichischer Bibliothekarinnen und Bibliothekare)
Werner Schlacher, Exec. Officer
Universitaetsplatz 3
A-8010 Graz, Austria
Phone: 43 316 3801419
Fax: 43 316 384987
E-mail: werner.schlacher@kfunigraz.ac.at
Home Page: http://uibk.ac.at/

Awards are arranged in alphabetical order below their administering organizations

• 754 • **Dr. Josef Bick Ehrenmedaille**
For recognition of special service to librarianship in Austria. Members of the Society are eligible. Gold, silver, and bronze medals are awarded biennially in even-numbered years. Established in 1966 in honor of Dr. Josef Bick, former director of the Austrian national library.

• 755 •
Austria Ministry of Economic Affairs
Dr. Martin Bartenstein, Min.
Stubenring 1
A-1011 Vienna, Austria
Phone: 43 1 711000
Fax: 43 1 7137995
E-mail: service@bmwa.gv.at
Home Page: http://www.bmwa.gv.at

• 756 • **National Prize for Advertising (Staatspreise fur Werbung)**
For recognition of an ordering enterprise or advertising agency for an outstanding advertising campaign. Certificates are awarded. Established in 1972.

• 757 • **National Prize for Consulting (Staatspreis fur Consulting)**
For recognition of outstanding consulting. Applications are accepted. Trophies and certificates are awarded annually. Established in 1990.

• 758 • **National Prize for the Most Beautiful Book (Staatspreis fur das Schonste Buch)**
For recognition of the best designed books. Austrian publishing houses are eligible. Five monetary prizes and honorary recognition are awarded annually. Established in 1953. Formerly known as Most Beautiful Books of Austria (Staatspreis fur die Schonsten Bucher Osterreichs).

• 759 •
Austrian Booksellers' and Publishers' Association
(Hauptverband des Osterreichischen Buchhandels)
Dr. Inge Kralupper, Contact
Grunangergasse 4
A-1010 Vienna, Austria
Phone: 43 1 5121535
Fax: 43 1 5128482
E-mail: hvb@buecher.at
Home Page: http://www.buecher.at

• 760 • **Ehrenpreis des Osterreichischen Buchhandels**
To honor a person who, with his written word, has contributed to achieving tolerance and peace in Europe. Awarded annually. Established in 1991.

• 761 •
Austrian Broadcasting Corporation
(Landesstudio Oberosterreich)
Iris Mayr, Contact
ORF/Prix Ars Electronica
Europaplatz 3
A-4010 Linz, Austria
E-mail: iris.mayr@aec.at
Home Page: http://www.aec.at/en/prix/index.asp

• 762 • **Prix Ars Electronica - International Competition for Cyberarts**
Open to artists, scientists, researchers, and developers. Three monetary prizes are awarded in each of the following categories: Net Vision/Net Excellence, Interactive Art, and Digital Music; Six in the category of Computer Animation/Visual Effects; and as many as 12 Honorary Mentions. Sponsored by jet2web Internet, Voestapline, the City of Linz, and the Province of Upper Austria.

• 763 •
Austrian Computer Society
(Osterreichische Computer Gesellschaft)
Dr. Walter Grafendorfer, CEO
Wollzeile 1-3
A-1010 Vienna, Austria
Phone: 43 1 51202350
Fax: 43 1 51202359
E-mail: ocg@ocg.at
Home Page: http://www.ocg.at

• 764 • **Heinz Zemanek Award**
Recognizes an outstanding researcher in information and computer science. A monetary prize of 2,000 4,000 euros is awarded biennially.

• 765 •
Austrian P.E.N. Centre
Rosl Merdinger, Exec. Officer
Bankgasse 8
A-1010 Vienna, Austria
Phone: 43 1 5334459
Fax: 43 1 5328749
E-mail: info@penclub.at
Home Page: http://www.penclub.at

• 766 • **Franz Theodor Csokor Prize**
To recognize and encourage quality playwriting in Austria. Awarded when merited. Named after renowned Austrian dramatist, Franz Theodor Csokor.

• 767 •
Cultural Department of the Municipality of Spittal and the Singkreis Porcia
(Kulturamt Spittal und Singkreis Porcia)
Burgplatz 1
A-9800 Spittal an der Drau, Austria
Phone: 43 4762 5650223
Fax: 43 47 623237
E-mail: tourismusbuero@spittal-drau.at

• 768 • **International Competition for Choirs (Internationaler Chorbewerb)**
For recognition of outstanding mixed choirs. Awards are given in the categories of choral works (classical and modern) and folksong. The choir should not have more than 45 singers or less than 16, and they must be amateurs. Qualities considered by the jury are: innovation, general choral sound, dynamic flexibility, and rhythm and style. Deadline for entry is January 31. Monetary prizes are given. Established in 1964. Sponsored by the Federal Ministry of Education and Arts, the Regional Government of Carinthia, Austrian Radion-Studio Carinthia, Singkreis Porcia-Spittal an der Drau and the Cultural Department of the Municipality of Spittal an der Drau.

• 769 •
European Coordinating Committee for Artificial Intelligence
Dr. Robert Milne, Contact
% Werner Horn, Chai
Department of Medical Cybernetics and Artificial Intelligenc
Medical University, Vienna
Freyung 6
A-1010 Vienna, Austria
Phone: 43 1 4277 63114
Fax: 43 1 4277 9631
E-mail: eccai-www@eccai.org
Home Page: http://www.eccai.org

• 770 • **European Coordinating Committee for Artificial Intelligence Awards**
To recognize and encourage scientific and technological advances in the field of artificial intelligence. Awards include Travel Grants, Dissertation Awards, and Fellows Program. Awards are bestowed biennially at the European Conference on Artificial Intelligence.

• 771 •
European Federation for Medicinal Chemistry
Gerhard Ecker, Sec.-Treas.
University of Vienna
Althanstrasse 14
A-1090 Vienna, Austria
Phone: 43 1 427755110
Fax: 43 1 42779551
E-mail: info@efmc.info
Home Page: http://www.efmc.info

• 772 • **Nauta Award on Pharmacochemistry**
For outstanding achievements in the field of Medicinal Chemistry of a scientist working in Europe or European scientist abroad.

• 773 • **Prous Science Award on New Technologies in Drug Discovery**
For a scientist, without restrictions regarding nationality, who has made a discovery, evaluation or use of new technologies.

• 774 • **UCB Award for Excellence in Medicinal Chemistry**
For a scientist, without restrictions regarding nationality, who has made an outstanding research in the field of Medicinal Chemistry.

• 775 •
European Money and Finance Forum
(Societe Universitaire Europeenne de Recherches Financieres)
Mr. Edward H. Hochreiter, Sec.Gen.
Otto Wagner-Platz 3
A-1090 Vienna, Austria
Phone: 43 1 404207206
Fax: 43 1 404207298
E-mail: suerf@oenb.at
Home Page: http://www.suerf.org

• 776 • **Marjolin Prize**
Recognizes the best paper for the colloquium. Persons under the age of 40 are eligible. Awarded periodically.

• 777 •
Festival of Nations, Ebensee
(Festival der Nationen)
Erich Riess, Contact
Gaumbergstrasse 82
A-4060 Linz, Austria
Phone: 43 732 666 2666
Fax: 43 732 673 693
E-mail: eva-video@netway.at
Home Page: http://www.8ung.at/filmfestival

• 778 • **International Competition for Film and Video**
For recognition of non-commercial amateur films and videos. The following formats are eligible: super 8 and 16mm films, and all video systems (preferably VHS and S-VHS). Films must not run over 30 minutes. The following awards are presented: The Austrian Education and Art Minister's Prize; the Ebenseer Bear in Gold, Silver, and Bronze; Special Awards for Best Experimental Film; the Best Youth Film (under 21 years); Special Award for Best Film of the Competition - an invitation for free participation in the Festival of Nations the next year; and Cups and Certificates. Awarded annually. Established in 1972 by Franz David.

• 779 •
Filmfestival of Nations
Erich Reiss, Dir.
Gaumbergstrasse 82
A-4060 Linz, Austria
Phone: 43 732 673 693
Fax: 43 732 666 2666
E-mail: eva-video@netway.at
Home Page: http://www.8ung.at/filmfestival

• 780 • **Ebenseer Bear**
The rankings for the top three films are in Gold, Silver, and Bronze. All non-commercial films and videos are qualified to participate without restriction of topic, and the film must not be over two years old. The duration must be no more than 30 minutes. A jury selects the winner and the jury has the right to ask the author to participate in the deliberations.

• 781 •
International Association for Cereal Science and Technology
Dr. Roland E. Poms, Sec.Gen.
Marxergasse 2
A-1030 Vienna, Austria
Phone: 43 1 70772020
Fax: 43 1 70772040
E-mail: gen.sec@icc.or.at
Home Page: http://www.icc.or.at

• 782 • **Clyde H. Bailey Medal**
To honor an outstanding scientist in the field of cereal science. Individuals may be nominated. A medal is awarded when merited, usually at the Cereal and Bread Congresses. Established in 1970 in memory of Dr. Clyde H. Bailey, a past president of the Association and renowned cereal scientist.

• 783 • **The Harold Perten Award**
For recognition of outstanding achievements in the furtherance of cereal science. A monetary prize of $3,000 US is awarded annually at ICC meetings. Established in 1989 by Ing. Harald Perten. Sponsored by the Harald Perten Foundation. This award can be shared.

• 784 • **Friedrich Schweitzer Medal**
To honor distinguished service in furthering the aims and ideals of the ICC. The Medal is normally awarded annually at ICC meetings. Established in 1989 in memory of one of the founders of the Association, Prof. Dr. Friedrich Schweitzer, who served as President and Secretary General, and was renowned as a cereal scientist worldwide.

• 785 •
International Association for Pattern Recognition
Ms. Linda O'Gorman, Sec.
Vienna University of Technology
Institute of Computer Aided Automation
Pattern Recognition and Image Processing Group
A-1040 Vienna, Austria
Phone: 43 1 5880118350
Phone: 44 208 3989240
Fax: 43 1 5880118392
E-mail: krw@prip.tuwien.ac.at
Home Page: http://www.iapr.org

• 786 • **King-Sun Fu Prize**
To recognize an individual for outstanding technical contributions to the field of pattern recognition. A certificate and monetary prize is awarded biennially.

• 787 •
International Association for Plant Taxonomy
(Association Internationale pour la Taxonomie Vegetale)
Dr. Tod Stuessy, Sec.Gen
Rennweg 14
A-1030 Vienna, Austria
Phone: 43 1 427754098
Fax: 43 1 427754099
E-mail: office@iapt-taxon.org
Home Page: http://www.botanik.univie.ac.at/iapt/

• 788 • **Engler Gold Medal**
For recognition of an outstanding contribution to plant taxonomy. Members of the prize committee are not eligible and applications are not accepted. A gold medal is awarded every six years at the International Botanical Congresses. Established in 1987 in honor of Adolf Engler. A silver medal was established in 1990 and is awarded every year as a commendation to notable plant taxonomy books and their authors.

• 789 •
International Conference of Labour and Social History
Eva Himmelstoss, Gen. Sec.
Wipplinger Str. 8
A-1010 Vienna, Austria
Phone: 43 1 2289469
Fax: 43 1 2289469
E-mail: ith@doew.at
Home Page: http://www.ith.or.at

• 790 • **Kathe-Leichter-Preis**
For women's research.

• 791 • **Rene Kuczynski Prize**
For outstanding publications in the field of social history.

• 792 • **Herbert Steiner Prize**
For outstanding research works in German or English on resistance, persecution, exile and labour history.

• 793 •
International Federation for Information Processing
(Federation Internationale pour le Traitement de l'Information)
K. Brunnstein, Pres.
Hofstrasse 3
A-2361 Laxenburg, Austria
Phone: 43 2236 73616
Fax: 43 2236 736169
E-mail: ifip@ifip.or.at
Home Page: http://www.ifip.or.at

• 794 • **Isaac L. Auerbach Award**
To recognize individuals whose service in support of IFIP in its mission is deemed to be extraordinary by their peers. A medal and an honorarium are awarded biennially in even-numbered years.

• 795 • Outstanding Service Award
In recognition of services rendered to IFIP by Technical Committee and Working Group members not normally eligible for the Silver Core Award. Certificates are awarded to one or more recipients each year.

• 796 • Silver Core Award
For recognition of services rendered to IFIP. Silver Core pins and certificates are given. Established in 1974.

• 797 •
International Federation of Purchasing and Supply Management
(Federation Internationale de l'Approvisionnement et de l'Achat)
W. Jack Wagner, Contact
Laurenzenvorstadt 90
CH-5001 Aarau, Austria
E-mail: info@ifpmm.org
Home Page: http://www.ifpmm.org

• 798 • Garner-Themoin Medal
To recognize an individual for an outstanding contribution to international purchasing and materials management. A medal and a plaque are presented annually. Established in 1976 to commemorate two outstanding personalities, Mr. Garner from the United Kingdom, and Mr. Themoin from France.

• 799 • Maple Leaf Award
To increase the availability of written communication world wide. A technical paper is selected in the competition. A monetary prize, a plaque, and a diploma are presented annually. Established in 1977. The winning paper is normally published.

• 800 •
International Fritz Kreisler Competition
Susanne Nitsch, Sec.
Postfach 76
A-1030 Vienna, Austria
Phone: 43 2252 41003
Fax: 43 2252 21993
E-mail: office@fritz-kreisler.music.at
Home Page: http://www.fritz-kreisler.music.at

• 801 • Fritz Kreisler International Competition Prizes
To provide recognition for the best violin and viola performance. Monetary prizes and concert appearances are awarded every four years. Monetary awards are given to the six finalists. The winners of the first three prizes perform the final round in the Great Hall of the Wiener Konzerthaus with the Vienna Symphonic Orchestra. A solo performance is provided for the first prize winner. Established in 1979 in memory of Fritz Kreisler, the Austrian violinist and composer.

• 802 •
International Institute for Applied Systems Analysis
(Institut International pour l'Analyse des Systemes Appliques)
Prof. Leen Hordijk, Dir.
Schlossplatz 1
A-2361 Laxenburg, Austria
Phone: 43 2236 807477
Fax: 43 2236 807201
E-mail: inf@iiasa.ac.at
Home Page: http://www.iiasa.ac.at

• 803 • Distinguished Principal Founding Member
For recognition of exemplary dedication to the ideals of the charter and support for the objectives of the institute, as well as distinguished accomplishments in promoting the research of the institute. Established in 1987.

• 804 • Honorary Scholar
For recognition of outstanding contributions made to the development of the Institute and to the advancement of its objectives. Honorary recognition is awarded when merited. Established in 1975.

• 805 • Peccei Scholarship
To recognize outstanding contributions of participants of the Young Scientists Summer Program (YSSP). A monthly scholarship for three months and travel expenses are awarded annually. Established in 1984 to commemorate Aurelio Peccei's contributions towards understanding global problems and promoting research through multinational collaboration.

• 806 •
International Music and Media Centre
(Internationales Musikzentrum Wien)
Franz Patay, Sec. Gen.
Stiftgasse 29
A-1070 Vienna, Austria
Phone: 43 1 889 0315
Fax: 43 1 889 031577
E-mail: office@imz.at
Home Page: http://www.imz.at

• 807 • Dance Screen Award
To stimulate and disseminate the production of audiovisual dance programs. Awards are given in the following categories: Stage Recording/Studio Adaptation, Camera Re-work, Screen Choreography, and Documentary. The competition is open to dance films, dance videos, and television programs on dance and ballet completed during the previous year. The deadline for entry is February 28. A monetary prize of $15,000 is awarded annually. Established in 1990 by the IMZ.

• 808 •
International Organization of Supreme Audit Institutions
(Organisation Internationale des Institutions Superieures de Control des Finances Publiques)
Dr. Josef Moser, Sec.Gen.
Dampfschiffstrasse 2
Postfach 240
A-1033 Vienna, Austria
Phone: 43 1 711718178
Fax: 43 1 7180969
E-mail: intosai@rechnungshof.gv.at
Home Page: http://www.intosai.org

• 809 • Jorg Kandutsch Preis
To recognize important achievements and contributions in the field of auditing by supreme audit institutions. Nominations may be made for achievements or contributions in the three calendar years preceding the year of INTOSAI's triennial Congress. A wall plaque is awarded triennially. Established in memory of Dr. Jorg Kandutsch, former Secretary General of INTOSAI.

• 810 • Elmer B. Staats Award
To encourage excellence in the writing of articles for the *International Journal of Government Auditing.* Authors of articles published in the journal in the three calendar years preceding the year of the triennial Congress are eligible for nomination. A sterling silver medallion and a scroll suitable for framing are awarded triennially. Established in 1983 in memory of Dr. Elmer B. Staats, former comptroller general of the United States, and former chairman of the Journal's Board of Editors. Formerly: (2006) Elmer B. Staats International Journal Award.

• 811 •
International Press Institute
Johann P. Fritz, Dir.
Spiegelgasse 2
A-1010 Vienna, Austria
Phone: 43 1 5129011
Fax: 43 1 5129014
E-mail: ipi@freemedia.at
Home Page: http://www.freemedia.at

• 812 • Free Media Pioneer
Recognizes outstanding achievements for press freedom. Awarded annually.

• 813 •
International Union of Forest Research Organizations
(Union Internationale des Instituts de Recherches Forestieres)
Dr. P. Mayer, Exec.Sec.
Hauptstrasse 7
1140 Vienna, Austria
Phone: 43 1 87701510
Fax: 43 1 877015150
E-mail: office@iufro.org
Home Page: http://www.iufro.org

• 814 • **Certificate of Appreciation**

To express appreciation for a significant contribution to the organization or activities of IUFRO, including conducting scientific meetings, hosting excursions, and supporting a cooperative research program. A certificate is awarded when merited.

• 815 • **Scientific Achievement Award**

Selection is based on research results published in scientific journals, proceedings of scientific meetings, appropriate patents, or in books, which clearly demonstrate the importance of the advancement of forestry, forestry research, and forest products. made by a member of the parent organization, by a leader of Divisions, Subject, or Project Groups, Working Parties, and by other officers and knowledgeable persons associated with the Union (but no self-nominations). Nominations and supporting documents are sent to the Chairperson of the IUFRO Honors and Awards Committee approximately 15 months before a IUFRO World Congress. Awards consisting of a cash honorarium, a medal, and a scroll are presented every five years at the Congress. Established in 1971.

• 816 •

Ludwig Boltzmann Association - Austrian Society for the Promotion of Scientific Research
Institute for Clinical Neurobiology
(Ludwig Boltzman Gesellschaft - Osterreichische Vereinigung zur Forderung)
Dr. Christian Konrad, Pres.
Operngasse 6/5. Stock
1010 Vienna, Austria
Phone: 43 1 5132750
Fax: 43 1 5132310
E-mail: office @ludwigboltzmanngesellschaft.at
Home Page: http://www .ludwigboltzmanngesellschaft.at

• 817 • **Alzheimer Obelisk**

To promote research in Alzheimer*K*s and related diseases.

• 818 •

Rural Youth Europe
Mrs. Sabine Klocker, Sec.Gen.
Schauflergasse 6
A-1014 Vienna, Austria
Phone: 43 1 534418600
Fax: 43 1 534418609
E-mail: office@ruralyoutheurope.com
Home Page: http://www.ruralyoutheurope .com

• 819 • **Rural Youth Europe Awards**

To further the work of 4H Clubs and related rural and farming organizations by recognizing young people living in rural areas. Presented annually.

• 820 •

Stadt Villach
Rathausplatz 1
A-9500 Villach, Austria
Phone: 43 4242 205
Fax: 43 4242 205 1899
E-mail: service@villach.at
Home Page: http://www.villach.at

• 821 • **Kulturpreis der Stadt Villach**

For recognition of cultural and scientific achievements reflecting the cultural life of the city of Villach. A monetary prize is awarded annually. Established in 1986 by the Magistrat Villach. The prize was awarded for the first time in 1986.

• 822 • **Paracelsusring der Stadt Villach**

For recognition of scientific or artistic achievements in the spirit of Paracelsus. A golden ring is awarded normally every three years. Established in 1953 by the City of Villach in honor of Theophrastus Bombastus von Hohenheim, called Paracelsus; and of his father, Wilhelm Bombast von Hohenheim, who lived and worked in Villach for 32 years. Sponsored by the City of Villach.

• 823 •

UNESCO International Book Committee
% Karin Sollat, Gen.Sec.
Mayerhofgasse
A-1041 Mayerhofgasse, Austria
Phone: 43 5050359
Fax: 43 505035917
E-mail: kidllit@netway.at

• 824 • **International Book Award**

For recognition of outstanding services to the cause of books and literacy, including library services, encouragement of reading habits, imaginative bookselling, and promotion of international cooperation. Authors, publishers, translators, book designers, and printers are eligible. Honorary recognition is awarded annually. The selection of the winner is made by the International Book Committee, an interprofessional body representing publishers, authors, librarians, booksellers, and other members of the international book community.

• 825 •

University Mozarteum, Salzburg
Schrannengasse 10a
A-5020 Salzburg, Austria
Phone: 43 662 6198
Fax: 43 662 6198 3033
E-mail: presse@moz.ac.at
Home Page: http://www.moz.ac.at

• 826 • **International Mozart Competition (Internationaler Mozart Wettbewerb)**

For recognition of outstanding singers, composers, pianoforte, violinists, and pianists, at the competition. Musicians of all nationalities are eligible. Established in 1975 in memory of Wolfgang Amadeus Mozart. Details not set at time of publication. Inquire for details.

• 827 •

University of Music and Dramatic Arts in Graz
(Hochschule fur Musik und Darstellende Kunst, Graz)
Prof. Dr. Otto Kolleritsch, Rector
Leonhardstr. 15
A-8010 Graz, Austria
Phone: 43 316 3891310
Fax: 43 316 3891710
E-mail: info@kug.ac.at
Home Page: http://www.kug.ac.at

• 828 • **Franz Schubert and the Music of Modern Times International Competition (Internationaler Wettbewerb Franz Schubert und die Musik des 20 Jahrhunders)**

For recognition of an outstanding performance in three categories of voice, piano, viola, and string quartet. Held annually. Established in 1989 in memory of Franz Schubert.

• 829 •

Vienna Chamber Opera
(Wiener Kammeroper)
Isabella Gabor, Gen.Mgr.
Fleischmarkt 24
A-1010 Vienna, Austria
Phone: 43 1 512 01077
Fax: 43 1 512 010030
E-mail: gabor@wienerkammeroper.at
Home Page: http://www.wienerkammeroper .at

• 830 • **International Hans Gabor Belvedere Singing Competition (Internationaler Belvedere Wettbewerb fur Opernsanger Wien)**

To encourage the professional development of opera singers. Women under 33 and men under 35 of any nationality may apply to the Competition office in Vienna by June 20. All participants receive certificates, and diplomas are awarded to the finalists. First, second and third place winners receive monetary prizes. The following special prizes are awarded: Mozart Opera Prize - for the best Mozart interpreter, donated by the Austrian Ministry for Science and Research. This prize-winner is selected by a Jury of professors from the Austrian Music Schools of Vienna, Salzburg, and Graz; *Opernwelt* Prize - consists of an article on one of the participants in the Competition to be published in this opera magazine. The choice of the singer is the decision of the chief editor of *Opernwelt*; *Kurier* Prize - for the winner chosen by the audience after the Opera House Concert. Donated by the Austrian newspaper, *Kurier*, Japan Prize - donated by Mr. Shimkichi Nakajima, Chairman of the "World-wide Madame Butterfly Competition," Tokyo. A winner of his choice will be invited to several recitals in Japan; Prague Opera Prize National Opera House Prague offers a guest appearance to one or two finalists. The choice of the singers is the decision of Mr. Tomas Karlicek from PRAGOKONCERT; and Newport Festival Prize - donated by General Manager Mark Malkovich III, Newport Festival, Rhode Island. The winner of the first prize is invited to an appearance at the Festival. Awarded annually. Established in

1982 by Profess or Hans Gabor, General Manager of the Vienna Chamber Opera. Sponsored by OMV. Formerly: (2006) International Belvedere Competition for Opera Singers.

• 831 •
Vienna University of Music and Dramatic Arts
(Hochschule fur Musik und Darstellende Kunst, Wien)
Elga Ponzer, Sec. Gen.
Lothinger Str. 18
A-1030 Vienna, Austria
Phone: 43 71155 6050
Fax: 43 71155 6059
E-mail: ponzer@mdw.ac.at
Home Page: http://www.beethoven-comp.at

• 832 • **International Beethoven Piano Competition**
(Internationaler Beethoven Klavierwettbewerb)
To encourage the professional development of young pianists. Musicians between 17 and 32 years of age are eligible. The Competition is held quadrennally exclusively dedicated to the work of Ludwig van Beethoven. The next competition will take place in 2009. Established in 1961. Sponsored L. Boesendorfer GmbH and others.

• 833 •
World Association for the History of Veterinary Medicine
Prof. Dr. Gerhard Forstenpointner, Pres.
% Dr. G. Weissengruber, Sec.
Dept. of Anatomy
University of Veterinary Medicine, Vienna
Veterinaerplatz 1
A-1210 Vienna, Austria
Phone: 43 1 25077 2503
Fax: 43 1 25077 2590
E-mail: gerald.weissengruber@vu-wien.ac.at
Home Page: http://www.wahvm.vet.uu.nl

• 834 • **Cheiron Medal**
To recognize individuals for contributions of special merit involving the advancement of the history of veterinary medicine. A medal and a certificate are awarded at meetings of the World Association; as a rule, not more than two medals are awarded annually. Established in 1989 to commemorate the 20th anniversary of the Association.

Barbados

• 835 •
Barbados Association of Medical Practitioners
Mr. Selwyn Ferdinand, Pres.
BAMP Complex
Spring Garden
St. Michael, Barbados
Phone: 246429-7569
Fax: 246435-2328
E-mail: info@bamp.org.bb
Home Page: http://www.bamp.org.bb

• 836 • **Practitioner*K*s Award for Excellence**
Recognizes contributions to health care/medical education in Barbados. Awarded annually.

• 837 •
Barbados National Trust
William Gollop, Gen.Mgr.
Wildey Great House
Wildey
St. Michael, Barbados
Phone: 246426-2412
Phone: 246436-9033
Fax: 246429-9055
E-mail: natrust@sunbeach.net
Home Page: http://trust.funbarbados.com

• 838 • **Barbados National Trust**
Annual award of recognition. For buildings of historical and architectural interest.

• 839 •
Barbados Union of Teachers
Ms. Undene Whittaker, Pres.
PO Box 58
Welches
St. Michael, Barbados
Phone: 246436-6139
Phone: 246427-8510
Fax: 246426-9890
E-mail: but4@hotmail.com
Home Page: http://www.butbarbados.org

• 840 • **President's Award**
Recognizes outstanding service in education. Awarded annually.

• 841 •
Caribbean Association of Home Economists
Sonja Lewis, Pres.
Samuel Jackman Prescod Polytechnic
Wildey
St. Michael, Barbados
Phone: 246426-1920
Fax: 246436-8643
E-mail: cahe1972@yahoo.com
Home Page: http://www.maxpages.com/cahe

• 842 • **Hazel Hatcher International Award**
For the members of the Home Economics fraternity.

• 843 • **Gwendolyn Tonge Scholarship Award**

• 844 • **Beryl Wood Book Grant**
To a paying member for four consecutive years; currently enrolled in second year or above of undergraduate study towards a bachelor's degree related to Home Economics at an accredited institution.

Belarus

• 845 •
National Academy of Sciences of Belarus
Mikhail V. Myasnikovich, Pres.
66 Independence Ave.
Praspekt Franciska Skaryny
220072 Minsk, Belarus
Phone: 375 172 841801
Phone: 375 172 324161
Fax: 375 172 842816
E-mail: academy@mserv.bas-net.by
Home Page: http://www.ac.by

• 846 • **Best Scientific Work**
Biennial monetary prize. Inquire for additional information.

• 847 • **Best Scientific Work of a Young Scientist**
Biennial monetary prize. Inquire for additional information.

• 848 • **Best Student Scientific Work**
Biennial monetary prize. Inquire for additional information.

Belgium

• 849 •
Brussels International Festival of Fantastic Film
Georges Delmote, Chair
Rue de la Comtesse de Flandre 8
B-1020 Brussels, Belgium
Phone: 32 2 201 1713
Fax: 32 2 201 1469
E-mail: annie@bifff.org
Home Page: http://www.bifff.org

• 850 • **Brussels International Festival of Fantastic Film**
(Festival International du Film Fantastique, de Science-Fiction, et Thriller de Bruxelles)
For recognition of outstanding fantasy and science fiction films. The following prizes are awarded: LaCorbeau Grand Prix - a monetary prize of $8,000 and a sculpture of Joseph Henrion; Prix des Televisions Europeen (short); Prix du Public du Meilleur Court-Metrage Europeen (short); two Prix Special du Jury Sculptures; and Le Pegase Prize of the Audience- a sculpture of Daniel Monic. Awarded annually. Established in 1983. A Make-up Competition is also held. First, second, and third prizes are given for amateur, semi- professional, and monster categories. Formerly: (2006) Brussels International Festival of Fantasy, Thriller, and Science-Fiction Films.

• 851 •
Eureka
Heikki Kotilainen, Head of the Eureka Secretariat
rue Neerveld, 107
B-1200 Brussels, Belgium
Phone: 32 2 7770971
Fax: 32 2 7707495
E-mail: michael.vieillefosse@es.eureka.be
Home Page: http://www.eureka.be

Formerly: Eureka Secretariat.

• 852 • Lillehammer Award
To recognize an excellent environmentally-oriented project. A monetary prize of 10,000 Euro is awarded annually.

• 853 •
European Aquaculture Society
Alistair Lane, Exec.Dir.
Slijkensesteenweg 4
B-8400 Oostende, Belgium
Phone: 32 59 323859
Fax: 32 59 321005
E-mail: eas@aquaculture.cc
Home Page: http://www.easonline.org

Formerly: (1984) European Mariculture Society.

• 854 • Honorary Life Members
For recognition of achievement in aquaculture. Awarded periodically. Established in 1976.

• 855 •
European Association for the Promotion of Poetry
(Association Europeénne pour la Promotion de la Poesie)
Poezie Centrum Vrijdagmarkt 36
B-9000 Gent, Belgium
Phone: 32 9 2252225
Fax: 32 9 2259054
E-mail: info@peoziecentrum.be
Home Page: http://www.poeziecentrum.be

• 856 • European Music and Poetry Competitions
To recognize individuals involved in poetry and to promote a widespread knowledge of European languages and ideas. European music and poetry competitions are held triennially.

• 857 •
European Baseball Confederation
(Confederation Europeenne de Baseball)
Gaston Panaye, Sec.-Treas.
Thonetlaan 52
B-2050 Antwerp, Belgium
Phone: 32 3 2190440
Fax: 32 3 7727727
E-mail: info@baseballeurope.com
Home Page: http://www.baseballeurope.com

• 858 • European Baseball Championships (Campionato Europeo Baseball)
For recognition of the national team that wins the European Championship. Awarded annually. Established in 1954. In addition, a Cup of Cups, the CEB-Cup, Junior European Baseball Champion, European Cadets, and European Juvenile Championships are awarded.

• 859 • European Baseball Cup
Awarded annually to the National Club Champions. Established in 1963.

• 860 •
European Chemical Industry Council
Alain Perroy, Dir.Gen.
Avenue Van Nieuwenhuyse 4
B-1160 Brussels, Belgium
Phone: 32 2 6767211
Fax: 32 2 6767300
E-mail: mail@cefic.be
Home Page: http://www.cefic.org

• 861 • Annual Science Award
For best project on chemistry teaching.

• 862 •
European Disposables and Nonwovens Association
Mr. Pierre Wiertz, Gen.Mgr.
157 Ave. Eugene Plasky
B-1030 Brussels, Belgium
Phone: 32 2 7349310
Phone: 32 2 7401823
Fax: 32 2 7333518
E-mail: info@edana.org
Home Page: http://www.edana.org

• 863 • INDEX Awards for Advances in Nonwovens
To recognize manufacturers and converters of nonwoven fabrics used in medicine and industry. A diploma and statuette are awarded to one recipient in each of seven categories. Presented at the triennial congress. Formerly: (1995) European Disposables and Nonwovens Association Awards.

• 864 •
European Express Association
Glen Hodgson, Contact
118 Ave. de Cortenberg
B-1000 Brussels, Belgium
Phone: 32 2 7379576
Fax: 32 2 7379501
E-mail: ghodgson@hillandknowlton.com
Home Page: http://www.euroexpress.org

• 865 • Hermes Award
Recognizes outstanding contribution to the development of the express delivery industry. Awarded annually.

• 866 •
European Nuclear Society
(Europaische Kernenergie-Gesellschaft)
Dr. Peter Haug, Sec.Gen.
Rue de la Loi 57
B-1040 Brussels, Belgium
Phone: 32 2 5053050
Fax: 32 2 5023902
E-mail: ens@euronuclear.org
Home Page: http://www.euronuclear.org

• 867 • European Nuclear Society Awards
To recognize scientific and engineering progress in the peaceful use of nuclear energy. Awards include the PIME Communications Award (for communications excellence) and the Jan Runermark Award (for service by a member of the young generation). Awards are presented annually.

• 868 •
European Oncology Nursing Society
Yvonne Wengstrom, Pres.
Ave. E Mounier 83/8
B-1200 Brussels, Belgium
Phone: 32 2 7799923
Fax: 32 2 7799937
E-mail: eons@village.uunet.be
Home Page: http://www.cancerworld.org

• 869 • Distinguished Merit Award
For outstanding contribution to the advancement of cancer nursing.

• 870 • Excellence in Education Grant
For nurses in educational setting in the area of oncology nursing.

• 871 • Excellence in Patient Education Award
For individual nurses or organizations.

• 872 • Novice Research Award
For enthusiastic young researchers.

• 873 •
European Society for Engineering Education
(Societe Europeenne pour la Formation des Ingenieurs)
Francoise Come, Sec.Gen.
119, rue de Stassart
B-1050 Brussels, Belgium
Phone: 32 2 5023609
Fax: 32 2 5029611
E-mail: info@sefi.be
Home Page: http://www.ntb.ch/sefi/

• 874 • Leonardo da Vinci Medal
This is the highest award of recognition that can be bestowed by the Society. Established in 1983.

• 875 •
European Society for Therapeutic Radiology and Oncology
Michel Taillet, Exec.Dir.
Ave. E Mounierlaan 83
B-1200 Brussels, Belgium
Phone: 32 2 7759340
Fax: 32 2 7795494
E-mail: info@estro.be
Home Page: http://www.estro.be

• 876 • Awards of the ESTRO
For recognition of contributions to improve the standards of cancer treatment. Several awards are presented annually, including the Breur Award Lecture, Marie Curie Medal, Jack Fowler Award, and the Emmanuel van der Schueren Award.

• 877 •
European Society of Anaesthesiology
24 rue des Comediens
Westfalische Wilhelms-Universitat
Klinik f. Anasthesiologie u.oper. Intensivmedizin
B-1000 Brussels, Belgium
Phone: 32 2 7433290
Fax: 32 2 7433298
E-mail: secretariat.esa@euronet.be
Home Page: http://www.euroanesthesia.org

• 878 • Research Grants
To promote anaesthesiarelated research in Europe, and to encourage anaesthesiologists to extend the frontiers of their practice or understanding. Awards are made to a sponsoring institution, not to individuals or to departments. Any qualified member of a sponsoring institution in one of the European countries that is represented on the ESA Council may apply. Two types of grants are awarded: Project grants, of up to 60,000 euro each, to support work of up to two years duration; and Research support grants, for amounts up to 15,000 euro, to assist work in progress or pilot studies. Established in 1987 by ICI Germany. Formerly: (97) ZENECA Research Scholarship.

• 879 •
European Society of Comparative Physiology and Biochemistry
Andre Pequeux PhD, Gen.Sec.
Laboratory of Animal Physiology
University of Liege
22, quai Van Beneden
B-4020 Liege, Belgium
Phone: 32 43 665046
Fax: 32 43 665020
E-mail: a.pequeux@ulg.ac.be
Home Page: http://www.escpb.org

• 880 • ESCPB Grant for Young Scientists
To scientists for doctoral work.

• 881 •
European Society of Intensive Care Medicine
Suzanne Smitz-De Smet, Exec. Officer
40 Ave. Joseph Wybran
B-1070 Brussels, Belgium
Phone: 32 2 5590350
Phone: 32 2 5590355
Fax: 32 2 5270062
E-mail: public@esicm.org
Home Page: http://www.esicm.org

• 882 • Yearly Award for Young ICU Investigators
To enable young doctors to work full-time in a different intensive care unit (ICU) or laboratory. Candidates must be members of the Society, be European doctors, and be under the age of 40. A monetary prize of 20,000 euros is presented annually.

• 883 •
Federation of European Cancer Societies
Francois Isabelle, Admin. Asst.
Ave. E Mounier 83
B-1200 Brussels, Belgium
Phone: 32 2 7750201
Fax: 32 2 7750200
E-mail: kathleen@fecs.be
Home Page: http://www.fecs.be

• 884 • FECS Clinical Research Award
To individuals for outstanding international contribution to the integration of scientific research in the field of cancer.

• 885 • FECS/EJC Award
For a young scientist or doctor in the field of clinical oncology research.

• 886 • Pezcoller Foundation - FECS Recognition for Contribution to Oncology
To an individual for his/her dedication to the improvement of cancer treatment, care and research.

• 887 •
Federation of European Direct Marketing
Ara Cinar, Chm.
Tervurenlaan 439 Ave. de Tervuren
B-1150 Brussels, Belgium
Phone: 32 2 7794268
Fax: 32 2 7794269
E-mail: info@fedma.org
Home Page: http://www.fedma.org

• 888 • Best of Europe - International Direct Marketing Awards
(Concours International de campagnes de Marketing Direct)
For recognition of the best direct marketing campaigns in Europe. Awards are given in the following categories: consumer products, consumer services, business-to-business products, business-to-business services, non-profit, and multinational campaigns. Gold, silver, and bronze prizes, special awards, and letters of distinction are awarded annually. Established in 1976.

• 889 •
Flanders International Film Festival - Ghent
(Internationaal Filmfestival van Vlaanderen - Gent)
Jacques Dubrulle, Mng.Dir.
Leeuwstraat, 40b
B-9000 Gent, Belgium
Phone: 32 9 242 8060
Fax: 32 9 221 9074
E-mail: info@filmfestival.be
Home Page: http://www.filmfestival.be

Formerly: International Flanders Film Festival - Ghent.

• 890 • Impact of Music on Film Competition
(Competitie de Impact van Muziek op Film)
For recognition of achievement in incorporating music into film. Non-musical fiction films are eligible. International jury awards Best Film (24,790 euro), Best Music or application of Music (Georges Delerue Award 11,155 euro), Sabam Author Prize (11,155 euro) and Best Director (Robert Wise Prize 3,718 euro). Selection is by the festival organizing committee. the International Film Festival of Flanders - Ghent. Sponsored by the City of Ghent, the Ministry of Flemish Culture, the Ministry of Economic Affairs, and many private sponsors.

• 891 • Joseph Plateau Prize
(Joseph Plateauprijzen)
For recognition of a Belgian filmmaker's contributions to the development of national cinema. Awards are given in the following categories: Best Belgian Film; Best Belgian Director; Best Actor in a Belgian Film; Best Actress in a Belgian Film; Best Belgian Television Film; Joseph Plateau Life Achievement Award (International Award); Joseph Plateau Music Award (International Award); and Joseph Plateau Audience Award (Best Box-Office of a Belgian Film). A trophy resembling Plateau's device is awarded annually. Established in 1985 in honor of Joseph Plateau, a Belgian physicist who discovered the principle of the eye's inertia and Thus was one of the ground layers of cinema.

• 892 •
Fonds National de la Recherche Scientifique
M.J. Simoen, Sec.Gen.
Rue d'Egmont 5
B-1000 Brussels, Belgium
Phone: 32 2 504 9211
Fax: 32 2 504 9292
E-mail: mjsimoen@fnrs.be
Home Page: http://www.fnrs.be

• 893 • InBev-Baillet Latour Health Prize
To recognize individuals working in the field of scientific research and its practical applications. The prize recognizes the scientific merit of the winner and should assist him or her in the pursuit

of his or her work. A monetary prize of 150,000 euros is awarded annually.

• 894 •
Francqui Foundation
(Fondation Francqui)
Luc Eyckmans, Exec.Dir.
Rue Defacqz 1
B-1000 Brussels, Belgium
Phone: 32 2539 3394
Fax: 32 2537 2921
E-mail: francquifoundation@skynet.be
Home Page: http://www.francquifoundation.be

• 895 • Francqui Prize
(Prix Francqui)
To recognize a Belgian scholar who has contributed to the prestige of Belgium. Awards are given in alternate years in the following categories: exact sciences, human sciences, biology and medical sciences. Candidates under 50 years of age may be nominated by a former prize winner or two members of a Belgian Academy. A monetary prize of $100 (European) is awarded annually. Established in 1932.

• 896 •
International Association for the Study of Clays
(Association Internationale pour l'Etude des Argiles)
Prof. Robert A. Schoonheydt, Sec.Gen.
Department of Interphase Chemistry
Katholieke Universiteit Leuven
Kasteelpark Arenberg 23
B-3001 Leuven, Belgium
Phone: 32 16 321592
Phone: 32 16 321610
Fax: 32 16 321998
E-mail: robert.schoonheydt@agr.kuleuven.ac.be
Home Page: http://www.agr.kuleuven.ac.be/intorg/aipea/aipea.htm

• 897 • AIPEA Medals
To honor clay scientists in recognition of their contributions to clay science. A maximum of two medals are awarded quadrennially.

• 898 • Bradley Award
To enable young clay scientists to attend the International Conference for the purpose of presenting his or her paper. A travel stipend of up to $1,000 is awarded annually.

• 899 •
International Association of Professional Numismatists
(Association Internationale des Numismates Professionnels)
Mr. JL Van der Schueren, Gen.Sec.
14, Rue de La Bourse
B-1000 Brussels, Belgium
Phone: 32 2 5133400
Fax: 32 2 5122528
E-mail: iapnsecret@compuserve.com
Home Page: http://www.iapn.ch

• 900 • Medal of Honor
For recognition of distinguished service by a member of the numismatic trade profession. A medal is awarded.

• 901 •
International Association of Sedimentologists
(Association Internationale de Sedimentologistes)
Prof.Dr. Patrick Jacobs, Treas.
Department of Geology and Soil Science
Ghent University
Krijgslaan 281-S8
B-9000 Gent Cedex, Belgium
Phone: 32 9 2644651
Phone: 32 9 2644665
Fax: 32 9 2644943
E-mail: patric.jacobs@ugent.be
Home Page: http://www.blacksci.co.uk/uk/society/ias

• 902 • Honorary Membership
Awarded to members who have given outstanding service to the association. Awarded periodically when merited. Established in 1975.

• 903 • International Association of Sedimentologists Grants
To promote the study of sedimentology and the interchange of research, particularly where international cooperation is desirable.

• 904 • Sorby Medal
This, the highest honor of the IAS, is given to recognize scientists of eminent distinction in sedimentology. Awarded every four years. Established in 1978.

• 905 •
International Biennials of Poetry
(Biennales Internationales de Poesie)
Jacques Lion, Dir.Gen.
SABAM
75-77 rue d'Arlon
B-1040 Brussels, Belgium
Phone: 32 2 2868211
Fax: 32 2 22300589
E-mail: info@sabam.be
Home Page: http://www.sabam.be

• 906 • Grand Prix des Biennales Internationales de Poesie
To recognize living poets of any nationality whose works have significantly influenced world poetry. A monetary prize is awarded biennially. Established in 1951 by the International House of Poetry. Sponsored by SABAM (Societe Belge des Auteurs, Compositeurs et Editeurs).

• 907 •
International Bureau for Precast Concrete
(Bureau International du Beton Manufacture)
Mr. E. Dano, Sec.Gen.
12, rue Volta
B-1050 Brussels, Belgium
Phone: 32 2 7356069
Fax: 32 2 7347795
E-mail: mail@febe.be
Home Page: http://www.bibm.org

• 908 • BIBM Awards
To award exceptional application of precast concrete or project in view of improving quality and furthering development. Awarded triennially.

• 909 •
International Classical Guitar Competition
Rue de Jumet 108
B-6041 Charleroi, Belgium
Phone: 32 71 355320
Fax: 32 71 355320
E-mail: info@printemps-guitare.be
Home Page: http://www.printemps-guitare.be

• 910 • Concours International Printemps de la Guitare
For recognition of outstanding performances on the guitar. Solo guitarists under 32 years of age are eligible to apply by June 30. Five monetary prizes totaling 13,000 euros are awarded biennially in even-numbered years. Established in 1988.

• 911 •
International Council of Graphic Design Associations
(Conseil International des Associations Graphiques)
Thierry Van Kerm, Dir.
PO Box 5
Forest 2
B-1190 Brussels, Belgium
Phone: 32 2 3445843
Fax: 32 2 3447138
E-mail: secretariat@icograda.org
Home Page: http://www.icograda.org

• 912 • International Council of Graphic Design Associations Excellence Awards
For recognition of achievement in the field of graphic design. Professional graphic designers are eligible for nomination by the proposal of member societies. Also, individuals, institutions, and companies who have made outstanding contributions to graphic design may be recommended by the board of the association. A trophy and diploma are awarded. Established in 1983.

• 913 • International Council of Graphic Design Associations President's Trophy
For recognition of contributions to the work and aims of the association in the field of graphic design. Professional graphic designers, design administrators and others are eligible. A trophy

and diploma are awarded biennially at the general assembly. Established in 1970.

• 914 •
International Diabetes Federation
(Federation Internationale du Diabete)
Luc Hendrickx, Exec.Dir.
Ave. Emile de Mot 19
B-1000 Brussels, Belgium
Phone: 32 2 5385511
Fax: 32 2 5385114
E-mail: info@idf.org
Home Page: http://www.idf.org

• 915 • **Educational Foundation Grants**
To provide education and training of health care professionals in the field of practical care and management of diabetes mellitus. Applications must be submitted. A monetary award for travel to a training center is awarded annually. The IDF Education Foundation was formally established in 1992.

• 916 •
International Lace Biennial, Contemporary Art
Ave. du Port, 86
B-1000 Brussels, Belgium
Phone: 32 2 770 8670
Fax: 32 2 770 8670
E-mail: c.delwiche@dbk.be
Home Page: http://www.dbk.be

• 917 • **Queen Fabiola Prize**
To honor lace-makers whose work reflects both complete mastery of the craft and new forms of artistic expression. Individuals exhibiting at the International Biennial of Lace Making are eligible. Her Majesty Queen Fabiola awards the Queen Fabiola Prize at the opening of the exhibition of laces selected for display and awards. The Golden Bobbin, Silver Bobbin, and Bronze Bobbin awards are also awarded at the start of the exhibition. Established in 1983.

• 918 •
International League Against Epilepsy
Delphine Sartiaux, Proj. Mgr.
Ave. Marcel Thiry 204
B-1200 Brussels, Belgium
Phone: 32 2 7749547
Fax: 32 2 7749690
E-mail: dsartiaux@ilaey.org
Home Page: http://www.ilae-epilepsy.org

• 919 • **Ambassador Award**
For outstanding international contributions to activities advancing the cause of epilepsy.

• 920 • **Lifetime Achievement Award**
For a person with a record of achievement in the work against epilepsy.

• 921 • **Michael Prize Award**
For the best scientific and clinical research promoting the further development of epitomology.

• 922 • **Social Achievement Award**
To an individual who has carried out outstanding activities aimed at the social benefit of people with epilepsy.

• 923 •
International Navigation Association - Belgium
(Association Internationale de Navigation)
Louis van Schel, Sec.Gen.
Graaf de Ferraris Bldg., 11th Fl.
Blvd. du Roi Albert II 20, Box 3
B-1000 Brussels, Belgium
Phone: 32 2 5537160
Phone: 32 2 5537157
Fax: 32 2 5537155
E-mail: info@pianc-aipcn.org
Home Page: http://www.pianc-aipcn.org

• 924 • **Dapaepe-Willems Award**
To encourage young engineers, research workers, and others to pursue studies in the fields of interest to the Association and to submit articles on these subjects suitable for publication in the *PIANC Bulletin.* Members of PIANC or individuals sponsored by a member who are under the age of 35 may submit articles and application forms to the General Secretariat of PIANC before December 31 of the year preceding the awarding of the prize. A monetary award (amount determined each year), a five-year membership, and an invitation to present the paper at the Annual Meeting are awarded annually at the General Assembly. Established in 1984 in memory of Professor Gustave Willems, President of PIANC from 1956 until his death in 1982. Formerly: (2006) Gustave Willems Prize.

• 925 •
International Society for Military Law and Law of War
(Societe Internationale de Droit Militaire et de Droit de la Guerre)
Ludwig van der Veken, Sec.Gen.
Avenue de Renaissance 30
B-1000 Brussels, Belgium
Phone: 32 2 7376178
Phone: 32 2 7376177
Fax: 32 2 7376178
E-mail: soc-mil-law@planetinternet.be
Home Page: http://www.soc-mil-law.org

• 926 • **Scientific Prize/Prix Ciardi**
To the author of a substantative and original study in the fields.

• 927 •
International Society of Orthopaedic Surgery and Traumatology
(Societe Internationale de Chirurgie Orthopedique et de Traumatologie)
Maurice Hinsenkamp, Sec.Gen.
Rue Washington, 40-B.9
B-1050 Brussels, Belgium
Phone: 32 2 6486823
Fax: 32 2 6498601
E-mail: hq@sicot.org
Home Page: http://www.sicot.org

• 928 • **Lester ELowe Memorial Scholarship**
For trainees.

• 929 • **SICOT/SIROT Award**
For author of research in orthopaedics of traumatology.

• 930 •
International Union of Radio Science
(Union Radio Scientifique Internationale)
Prof. Paul Lagasse, Sec.Gen.
Sint-Pietersnieuwstraat 41
Universiteit Gent
B-9000 Gent, Belgium
Phone: 32 9 2643320
Fax: 32 9 2644288
E-mail: ursi@intec.rug.ac.be
Home Page: http://www.ursi.org

• 931 • **John Howard Dellinger Gold Medal**
For recognition of outstanding work in radio science, preferably in radio wave propagation. Work must have been carried out during the six-year period preceding the year of the URSI General Assembly at which the medal is presented. A medal is awarded triennially at the URSI General Assembly. Established in 1966 by the United States Member Committee of URSI in honor of Professor John Howard Dellinger, Honorary President of URSI. Administered by the U.S. Member Committee of URSI, % the National Academy of Sciences, Washington, D.C. 20418.

• 932 • **Issac Koga Gold Medal**
For recognition of outstanding work in radio science carried out by a young scientist. Candidates must be 35 years of age or younger and the work must have been carried out during the six-year period preceding the year of the URSI General Assembly at which the medal is presented. A medal is awarded triennially at the URSI General Assembly. Established in 1984 by the URSI Member Committee in Japan in honor of Professor Issac Koga, Honorary President of URSI. Administered by the URSI Member Committee in Japan, % the Science Council, Tokyo, Japan.

• 933 • **Balthasar van der Pol Gold Medal**
For recognition of outstanding work in radio science. Work must have been carried out in the six-year period preceding the year of the General Assembly at which the Medal is awarded. A medal with an effigy of Professor van der Pol is awarded every three years and presented on the occasion of the General Assembly. Established in 1963 in memory of Professor Balthasar van der Pol, Honorary President of the Union, by his widow, Mrs. P. Le Corbeiller-Posthuma.

• 934 •
King Baudouin Foundation
(Fondation Bonderjnstichting)
rue Brederodestraat 21
B-1000 Brussels, Belgium
Phone: 32 2 5111840
Fax: 32 2 5115221
E-mail: info@kbs-frb.be
Home Page: http://www.kbs-frb.be

• 935 • **King Baudouin International Development Prize**
To recognize persons or organizations, without regard to national origin, who have made a substantial contribution to the development of the Third World or towards the cooperation and good relations between industrialized and developing countries, and among their peoples. Particular importance is attached to activities having a multiplier effect and those which make it possible for the populations of the Third World to provide for themselves by their own development. Individuals or organizations may be nominated. A monetary prize is awarded biennially. Established in 1978.

• 936 •
Le Soir
S. A. Rossel & Cie
Daniel Van Wylick, Editor-in-Chief
Place de Louvain 21
B-1000 Brussels, Belgium
Phone: 32 2 225 5312
Fax: 32 2 225 5903
E-mail: internet@lesoir.be
Home Page: http://www.lesoir.be

• 937 • **Prix Victor Rossel**
For recognition of an outstanding novel or collection of short stories written in French by a Belgian citizen. Works published during the preceding twelve months are considered. A monetary prize is awarded annually in December. Established in 1938 by M. Th. Rossel, managing editor of Rossel & Cie; M. Lucien Fuss, director of *Le Soir*, and M. Charles Breisdorff, Chief editor, in memory of Victor Rossel, the son of the founder of *Le Soir*.

• 938 •
League of Families
(Ligue des Familles)
127, rue du Trone
B-1050 Brussels, Belgium
Phone: 32 2 507 7211
Fax: 32 2 507 7200
E-mail: redaction@leligueur.be
Home Page: http://www.liguedesfamilles.be

• 939 • **Prix Bernard Versele**
To encourage reading among children and to promote books of high literary, artistic, and educational value, not necessarily those best known on the market. Books are pre-selected by specialists in literature from those written in French and published during the preceding year. About 50,000 children from 3 to 14 years of age vote for the best liked children's books. Awards are given for books for children in the following age categories: from 3 years, from 5 years, from 7 years, from 9 years, and from 11 years. Five monetary prizes are awarded annually in June. Established in 1979 in memory of Bernard Versele, a young psychologist, who dedicated his professional life to children.

• 940 •
Mechelen Festival
(Festival van Mechelen)
Kortrijksesteenweg 90h
9830 Sint-Martens-Latem
B-2800 Mechelen, Belgium
Phone: 32 9 3800855
Fax: 32 15 433755
E-mail: coordinatiesv@festival.be

• 941 • **International Diaporama Festival (Festival International de Diaporamas)**
For recognition of outstanding audio-visuals (slide series with sound). Diaporamas are works that join to the beauty of the form a valid content, story, song, information, music, illustration, message, etc. The deadline for entries is January 20. A Grand Prize of the City of Mechelen is awarded for the overall winner. Awarded biennially. Established in 1966.

• 942 •
George Montefiore Foundation
A.I.M. General Secretariat
31, rue Saint Gilles
B-4000 Liege, Belgium
Phone: 32 4 222 29 46
Fax: 32 4 222 23 88
E-mail: info@aim.skynet.be
Home Page: http://www.aimontefiore.org/fondation

• 943 • **George Montefiore Foundation Prize**
(Prix de la Fondation George Montefiore)
To recognize an individual who has made significant contributions to the advancement of the technology of electricity through scientific or engineering inventions or innovations. Self-nominations will not be accepted. A monetary prize of 150,000 Euro is awarded every five years.

• 944 •
North Atlantic Treaty Organisation
(Organisation du Traite de l'Atlantique Nord - Bruxelles)
Jaap de Hoop Scheffer, Sec.Gen.
NATO Headquarters
Blvd. Leopold III
B-1110 Brussels, Belgium
Phone: 32 2 2410040
Fax: 32 2 7284579
E-mail: natodoc@hq.nato.int
Home Page: http://www.nato.int

• 945 • **Manfred Worner Essay Awards**
To honor the memory of the late Secretary General by focusing attention on leadership in the transformation of the Alliance, including efforts at extending NATO's relations with CEE countries and promoting the principals and image of the Transatlantic Partnership. Two awards are presented in this international competition: the Junior NATO Manfred Worner Essay Award and the Senior NATO Manfred Worner Essay Award. The Junior Award is open to academics, researchers, and writers from both NATO and Partner countries, aged between 20 and 35; a prize of 5,000 Euro is awarded to the individual who submits the best essay on a topic of relevance to the Alliance. The Senior Award is open to academics, researchers, and writers from both NATO and Partner countries, aged 35 years and older, who are already established in the field of international security policy; a prize of 10,000 Euro is awarded to the individual who submits the best essay on a topic of relevance to the Alliance. Awarded annually. Established in 1995. Formerly: (2005) Manfred Worner Fellowship.

• 946 •
Queen Elisabeth International Music Competition of Belgium
(Concours Musical International Reine Elisabeth de Belgique)
Michel-Etienne Van Neste, Sec.Gen.
20, rue aux Laines
B-1000 Brussels, Belgium
Phone: 32 2 213 4050
Fax: 32 2 514 3297
E-mail: info@qeimc.be
Home Page: http://www.cmireb.be

• 947 • **Queen Elisabeth International Music Competition of Belgium Prizes**
For recognition of the best performances on piano, violin, singing, and occasionally for composition. In 1999, the competition features piano and composition, in 2000, singing, and in 2001, violin and composition. Pianists and violinists must be 31 years of age or under to compete. Singers must be under 32 years to compete. The deadline for application is January 15. Monetary prizes and diplomas are awarded for piano, violin, and voice. A monetary award is presented for composition. Award winners are also given the opportunity for concerts, recitals, and recordings. Awarded every four years for each discipline. Established in 1951.

• 948 •
Royal Academy of Dutch Language and Literature
(Koninklijke Academie voor Nederlandse Taal-en Letterkunde)
Prof. Georges De Schutter, Sec.
Koningstraat 18
B-9000 Gent, Belgium
Phone: 32 9 2659340
Fax: 32 9 2659349
E-mail: info@kantl.be
Home Page: http://www.kantl.be

• 949 • **Lode Baekelmans Prize**
For recognition of the best literary work in Dutch, including novels, poetry, plays, radio-plays, and essays dealing with the sea, sailors, navigation, harbors, or a related topic. Belgian nationals are eligible. A monetary prize of 1860 Euro is

awarded every other third year. Established in 1940.

• 950 • **Dr. Karel Barbier Prize**
For recognition of the best historical novel written in Dutch based on Belgium History. Short stories and romanticized biographies are considered. Belgian nationals are eligible. A monetary prize of 1,000 Euro is awarded every other second year. Established in 1927.

• 951 • **August Beernaert Prize**
For recognition of the best literary work, irrespective of the genre, that is written in Dutch. Published or unpublished works by Belgian nationals are eligible. A monetary prize of 1240 Euro is awarded every other second year. Established in 1912.

• 952 • **Karel Boury Prize**
For recognition of the best unpublished Flemish school songs or folk songs (at least two). The author may choose the text of the songs. Belgian nationals are eligible. A monetary prize of 500 Euro is awarded every fourth year. Established in 1909.

• 953 • **Arthur H. Cornette Prize**
For recognition of the best essay written in Dutch. Descriptions, compilations, biography, academic and scientific dissertations aren't allowed. Belgian nationals are eligible. A monetary prize is awarded every fifth year. Established in 1950.

• 954 • **Nestor de Tiere Prize**
For recognition of the best play written in Dutch during the last two years. Belgian nationals are eligible. A monetary prize of 2,000 francs is awarded every other second year. Established in 1930.

• 955 • **Joris Eeckhout Prize**
For recognition of the best literary essay about an author. Works written in Dutch and a minimum 100 pages in length are considered. Belgian national are eligible. A monetary prize is awarded every other second year. Established in 1937.

• 956 • **Prof. Leon Elaut Prize**
For recognition of the best dissertation in the field of the cultural history of Flanders from 1815 till 1940 in connection with the Flemish movement. A monetary prize of 2480 Euro is awarded every other second year. Established in 1981.

• 957 • **Guido Gezelle Prize**
For recognition of the best volume of Dutch poetry that is published or in manuscript form. Belgian nationals are eligible. A monetary prize is awarded every other fifth year. Established in 1941.

• 958 • **Maurice Gilliams Prize**
For recognition of the best volume of poetry, essay about poetry, or complete poetical works, written in Dutch, without regard to the nationality of the author. Works may be published or in manuscript form. A monetary prize is awarded every fourth year. Established in 1985.

• 959 • **Noordstar - Dr. Jan Grauls Prize**
For recognition of the best essay in the field of Dutch linguistics and folklore. Writings on semantics, onomastics, dialectology, and studies on proverbs and purism are preferred. Essays written in Dutch that are published or in manuscript form are considered. Belgian nationals are eligible. A monetary prize is awarded every five years. Established in 1973.

• 960 • **Arthur Merghelynck Prize**
For recognition of the two best literary works in either prose or poetry form. Works written in Dutch that are published or in manuscript form are considered. Belgian nationals are eligible. A monetary prizes each for prose and for poetry are awarded every other third year. Established in 1946.

• 961 • **Ary Sleeks Prize**
For recognition of the best novel, volume of short stories, or essay written in Dutch. Candidates must be Belgian nationals and may not have been awarded a prize before. A monetary prize is awarded every other third year. Established in 1974.

• 962 • **Karel van de Woestijne Prize**
For recognition of an outstanding contribution to the study of the works of Karel van de Woestijne. A presentation of the complete works or a publication of exceptional importance is considered. A monetary prize of 100,000 francs is awarded every other fifth year. Established in 1980.

• 963 • **Jozef Van Ginderachter Prize**
For recognition of the best literary, historical, art-historical, linguistic publication, or a work of folklore glorifying the province of Brabant, preferably the cantons of Asse and Vilvoorde. Individuals, periodicals, or institutions that have published works in the above mentioned fields are eligible. A monetary prize is awarded every other fourth year. Established in 1935.

• 964 • **Jozef Vercoullie Prize**
For recognition of the best doctoral dissertation in the field of Dutch philology presented in a Belgian university. A literary and a linguistic study can be alternately considered for the award. Belgian nationals are eligible. A monetary prize is awarded every other fourth year. Established in 1938.

• 965 • **Leonard Willems Prize**
For recognition of an outstanding contribution to the Middle Dutch literary studies, either by the presentation of complete works, or by a publication of exceptional importance. Belgian nationals of Flemish background are eligible. A monetary prize is awarded every other second year. Established in 1961.

• 966 •
Royal Academy of Medicine
(Koninklijke Academie voor Geneeskunde van Belgie)
Palais des Academies
rue Ducale 1
B-1000 Brussels, Belgium
Phone: 32 2 5502255
Fax: 32 2 5502265
E-mail: academie.de.medecine@beon.be
Home Page: http://www.rami.ie

• 967 • **Prijs Jan-Frans Heymans**
For recognition of an original paper dealing with experimental pharmacy or chemistry. Reports must be written by a medical doctor in Dutch, English, or German. A monetary prize is awarded biennially.

• 968 • **Prijs Albert Van Dyck**
To recognize an investigator in basic or clinical science who has acquired special merit in the study of leukemia or another disease that is considered incurable or fatal. Unpublished manuscripts as well as published work written in Dutch, French, English, or German are considered. A monetary prize is awarded triennially.

• 969 • **Prijs Franz Van Goidsenhoven**
For recognition of an original paper dealing with clinical medicine, particularly, internal medicine. Manuscripts must be written in Dutch, French, English, or German. A monetary prize is awarded triennially.

• 970 • **Prijs J. B. Van Helmont**
For recognition of an original paper dealing with general pathology, biophysics, or biochemistry. Reports must be written in Dutch, French, English, or German. A monetary prize is awarded triennially.

• 971 •
Royal Academy of Science, Humanities and Fine Arts of Belgium
Division of Fine Arts
Leo Houziaux, Sec.
Palais des Academies
rue Ducale 1
B-1000 Brussels, Belgium
Phone: 32 2 550 2213
Fax: 32 2 550 2205
E-mail: arb@cfwb.be
Home Page: http://www.cfwb.be/arb

• 972 • **Prix Charles Caty**
To recognize a painter who has studied regularly and successfully at the Academy of Fine Arts at Mons. A monetary prize is awarded triennially. Established in 1956.

• 973 • **Prix Emma du Cayla-Martin**
To recognize the work of a painter not yet awarded by the Academy. A monetary prize of 2,500 euros is awarded biennially in odd-numbered years. Established in 1991.

• 974 • Prix Arthur DeGreef
For recognition of the best musical composition for piano solo conceived in the true tradition of the instrument and not aiming at virtuosity. Belgian composers are eligible. A monetary prize of 50,000 Belgian francs is awarded biennially. Established in 1989.

• 975 • Prix Baron Horta
To recognize the designer of an architectural work that has already been built or studied as a project. The finished work must have been constructed in one of the Common Market countries, or the project must have been planned for construction in Common Market countries. Architects of any nationality are eligible. A monetary prize is awarded every five years. Established in 1966.

• 976 • Prix Constant Montald
For recognition of a large fresco or a mural in oils, leaded glass, or tapestry, portraying human figures. The work must be at least one meter high. A monetary prize is awarded triennially. Established in 1946.

• 977 • Prix Ernest Acker
For recognition of an architectural project presented to the Academy on a subject chosen by the Classe des Beaux-Arts. Young Belgian architects are eligible. A monetary prize is awarded triennially. Established in 1922.

• 978 • Prix Gustave Camus
To recognize a Belgian painter who has already accomplished a notable work. A monetary prize is awarded biennially.

• 979 • Prix Irene Fuerison
For recognition of the best unpublished musical composition in the following categories: chamber music, orchestral music, vocal music, and electronic music. Young Belgian musicians or foreign musicians less than 50 years of age who have been residents of Belgium for three years are eligible. Awards are given in alternate years for chamber music, orchestral music, vocal music, and electronic music. A monetary prize of is awarded biennially. Established in 1932.

• 980 • Prix Jacques Lavalleye-Coppens
For recognition of achievements in the fields of archaeology, art history, or restoration of monuments. Awards are given in alternate years to the Belgian author or authors or the foreign author for the best published or unpublished work on archaeology or art history of ancient Southern Netherlands and the ancient ecclesiastic principalities of Liege and Stavelot; and the author of the best work on restoration of monuments or works of art erected or preserved in Belgium. A monetary prize is awarded biennially. Established in 1972.

• 981 • Prix Jos Albert
To encourage the work of a Belgian painter of the representational trend. A monetary prize is awarded annually. Established in 1982.

• 982 • Prix Joseph-Edmond Marchal
To recognize the author of the best work, published or manuscript, on national antiquities or archaeology. A monetary prize is awarded every five years. Established in 1918.

• 983 • Prix Jules Raeymaekers
To encourage an artistic activity that uses color as its form of expression. A monetary prize is awarded triennially. Established in 1981.

• 984 • Prix Louise Dehem
To recognize a painter who has been out of a fine arts school or an academy less than ten years and whose works, preferably human figures or still life, have been shown publicly and have revealed a truly artistic temperament. A monetary prize is awarded biennially. Established in 1928.

• 985 • Prix Paul Artot
To recognize the painter of a fresco or oil painting. The theme of the painting must be expressed by human figures. Belgian artists under the age of 40 are eligible. A monetary prize is awarded biennially. Established in 1959.

• 986 • Prix Paul Bonduelle
To recognize the originator(s) of a great architectural project. The subject is decided by the Classe des Beaux-Arts. Belgian architects who are not members of the Academy are eligible. A monetary prize is awarded triennially. Established in 1962.

• 987 • Prix Pierre Carsoel
For recognition of the most technically and artistically successful work conceived and executed by an architect during the preceding five year period. Belgian architects are eligible. A monetary prize of is awarded every five years. Established in 1928.

• 988 • Prix Rene Janssens
To recognize outstanding Belgian painters. Awards are given in alternate years to a painter who has excelled at portraits and a painter who has excelled at paintings of interiors. An individual's entire work is considered. A monetary prize is awarded triennially. Established in 1934.

• 989 • Prix Egide Rombaux
To recognize a sculptor for a work on a subject chosen by the Academy in decorative or monumental art. Belgian sculptors between 30 and 40 years of age are eligible. A monetary prize is awarded triennially. Established in 1952.

• 990 • Prix Emile Sacre
To recognize the painter of the most noteworthy work that was executed and publicly displayed during the preceding six year period. A monetary prize is awarded every six years. Established in 1914.

• 991 •
Royal Academy of Science, Humanities and Fine Arts of Belgium
Division of Humanities
Leo Houziaux, Sec.
Palais des Academies
rue Ducale 1
B-1000 Brussels, Belgium
Phone: 32 2 550 2213
Fax: 32 2 550 2205
E-mail: arb@cfwb.be
Home Page: http://www.cfwb.be/arb

• 992 • Fondation Edmond Fagnan
To encourage travel for Muslim and Semitic studies and to facilitate the publication of original work. Belgian and French researchers are eligible. A monetary prize of 1250 Euro is awarded annually. Established in 1926.

• 993 • Fondation Ernest Mahaim
To encourage studies on political economics and international law. Applications may be submitted by January 1. A monetary prize of 1500 Euro is awarded every five years. Established in 1936.

• 994 • Fondation Ernest Mahaim et Emile Waxweiler
For recognition in the field of social science, particularly on the subject of social organization. Monetary prizes totaling 2,500 Euro are awarded annually.

• 995 • Fondation Henri Pirenne
To assist travel for study or research in Belgium or another country, particularly studies concerning the history of Belgium. A monetary prize of 1250 Euro is awarded triennially. Established in 1923.

• 996 • Prix Joseph Houziaux
For recognition of a work in romance philology or in dialects of Belgo-Romance. All nationalities are eligible. Work with curriculum must be submitted by December 30. 1500 Euro is awarded triennially. Established in 1994.

• 997 • Prix Adelson Castiau
For recognition of the best work which has as its object or its effect the promotion of social progress. Belgian authors are eligible. A monetary prize of 1500 Euro is awarded triennially. Established in 1902.

• 998 • Prix Anton Bergmann
For recognition of a historical work or monograph on a Flemish town or community of any size in Belgium. Authors of any nationality may submit works written in Dutch and edited in Belgium or the Low Countries. A monetary prize of 1250 Euro is awarded every five years. Established in 1875.

• 999 • **Prix Auguste Teirlinck**
For recognition of a contribution to Dutch literature. A monetary prize of 1250 Euro is awarded every five years. Established in 1907.

• 1000 • **Prix baron de Saint-Genois**
To recognize the author of the best historical or literary work written in Dutch. A monetary prize of 1,250 euros is awarded every five years. Established in 1867.

• 1001 • **Prix Charles Duvivier**
For recognition of the best work on the history of Belgian or foreign law, or on the history of Belgian political, judicial, or administrative institutions. Belgian authors are eligible. A monetary prize is awarded triennially. Established in 1905.

• 1002 • **Prix de Psychologie**
For recognition of the best doctoral thesis on scientific psychology, earned in a Belgian university by a Belgian citizen during the three preceding years. A monetary prize is awarded triennially. Established in 1961.

• 1003 • **Prix de Stassart**
To recognize a noted Belgian. The award is given in alternate years to: (1) historians; (2) writers; and (3) scientists and artists. A monetary prize is awarded every six years. Established in 1851.

• 1004 • **Prix de Stassart pour Histoire Nationale**
For recognition of an outstanding contribution to national history. A monetary prize of 1,500 Euro is awarded every six years. Established in 1859.

• 1005 • **Prix Emile de Laveleye**
To recognize a scholar whose total work has brought about important progress in political economy and social science, including finance, international and public law, and general or national politics. Living Belgian or foreign scholars are eligible. A monetary prize of 1750 Euro is awarded every six years. Established in 1895.

• 1006 • **Prix Ernest Discailles**
For recognition of the best work on the history of French literature or on contemporary history. Awards are given in alternate years in the following categories: (1) history of French literature; and (2) contemporary history. Belgians are eligible for the former, and foreigners who are studying or have studied at the University of Ghent are eligible for the latter. A monetary prize of 1500 Euro is awarded every five years. Established in 1907.

• 1007 • **Prix Eugene Goblet d'Alviella**
For recognition of the best work of a strictly scientific and objective character on the history of religions. Belgian authors are eligible. A monetary prize of 1500 Euro is awarded every five years. Established in 1926.

• 1008 • **Prix Eugene Lameere**
For recognition of the best history textbook for Belgian primary and secondary schools and colleges of education, in which illustrations play an important part in making the text understandable. A monetary prize of 1250 Euro is awarded every five years. Established in 1902.

• 1009 • **Prix Franz Cumont**
For recognition of a work on the ancient history of religion or science in the Mediterranean basin before Mohammed. Belgian or foreign authors are eligible. A monetary prize of 2500 Euro is awarded triennially. Established in 1937.

• 1010 • **Prix Henri Lavachery**
For recognition of a written work or filmed commentary on ethnology. Belgian authors may submit works written in French and published in the preceding five years. A monetary prize of 1500 Euro is awarded every five years. Established in 1967.

• 1011 • **Prix Herman Schoolmeesters**
For recognition of a manuscript or printed work useful in promoting small and medium-sized firms. A monetary prize of 1500 Euro is awarded every five years. Established in 1943.

• 1012 • **Prix Joseph De Keyn**
For recognition of works by Belgian authors on secular instruction and education. Awards are given in alternate years in the following categories: (1) works useful for primary schools; and (2) works on secondary instruction or education, including industrial art. A monetary prize of 1750 Euro is awarded annually. Established in 1880.

• 1013 • **Prix Joseph Gantrelle**
For recognition of a work in classical philology. Belgian authors are eligible. A monetary prize of 1500 Euro is awarded biennially. Established in 1890.

• 1014 • **Prix Jules Duculot**
For recognition of a manuscript or printed work on the history of philosophy. Belgians or foreigners with a degree from a Belgian university may submit works written in French. A monetary prize of 3000 Euro is awarded every five years. Established in 1966.

• 1015 • **Prix Leon Leclere**
For recognition of the best manuscript or printed work on national or general history. First works by a young historian are eligible. A monetary prize of 1500 Euro is awarded every five years. Established in 1928.

• 1016 • **Prix Polydore de Paepe**
For recognition of the best account of a spiritualist philosophy founded on pure reason or experience. Preference is given to works which develop the principles stated by Paul Le Monyne in *De l'Idee de Dieu, sa transformation, ses consequences morales et sociales.* Belgian or foreign authors are eligible. A monetary prize of 1250 Euro is awarded every five years. Established in 1907.

• 1017 • **Prix Suzanne Tassier**
To recognize a woman who has obtained her doctorate at a Belgian university, and who has written an important scientific work in the fields of history, philology, law, or the social sciences. If no worthy work is found in these categories, a work on natural, medical, or mathematical sciences will be considered. A monetary prize of 1750 Euro is awarded biennially. Established in 1956.

• 1018 • **Prix Tobie Jonckheere**
For recognition of a manuscript or printed work on the science of education. A monetary prize of 1500 Euro is awarded triennially. Established in 1957.

• 1019 • **Prix Victor Tourneur**
To encourage numismatic and sigillographical studies, and to encourage the art of medal making. A monetary prize of 1500 Euro is awarded alternately every five years by the Classe des Lettres and the Classe des Beaux Arts. Established in 1954.

• 1020 •
Royal Academy of Science, Humanities and Fine Arts of Belgium
Division of Sciences
Leo Houziaux, Sec.
Palais des Academies
rue Ducale 1
B-1000 Brussels, Belgium
Phone: 32 2 550 2213
Fax: 32 2 550 2205
E-mail: arb@cfwb.be
Home Page: http://www.cfwb.be/arb

• 1021 • **Jean-Marie Delwart Foundation Prize**
For recognition of the best works in the field of chemical communication between organisms (including human beings) or in the field of human ethology and cultural anthropology. Two monetary prizes of $10,000 are awarded triennially. Established in 1993.

• 1022 • **Fondation Jean de Meyer**
To provide for research in the field of biological physical-chemistry, especially human physiology, cardiology, endocrinology and hormones. Belgian researchers or foreigners studying at Universite Libre de Bruxelles, who are less than 35 years of age are eligible. A monetary prize of 2250 Euro is awarded triennially.

• 1023 • **Fondation Jean Lebrun**
For recognition of the best works on biogeography and ecology. Scientists from French-speaking research institutions of Belgium are eligible. A monetary prize of 2000 Euro is awarded biennially. Established in 1987.

• 1024 • Fondation Max Poll
For recognition of the best work on zoology (systematic, comparative anatomy, zoo geography, or animal ecology). Reserved for researchers of Belgian French-speaking or Zairian universities. A monetary prize of 2500 Euro is awarded triennially. Established in 1991.

• 1025 • Fondation Octave Dupont
To recognize projects of fundamental scientific research in the fields of human an animal physiology and physiopathology. Reserved for Belgian French-speaking scientists. A subsidy of 8000 Euro is presented every eight years. Next prize to be awarded in 2013. Established in 1989.

• 1026 • Fondation Camille Liegeois
To provide for research or scientific travels by Belgians less than 35 years of age. The award is given alternately by the Classe des Sciences and the Classe des Lettres et des Sciences morales et politiques. A monetary prize of 1300 Euro is awarded triennially.

• 1027 • Prix Adolphe Wetrems
For recognition of the most useful discoveries or inventions made during the preceding year in: (1) the mathematical and physical sciences; and (2) the natural sciences. Belgian scientists are eligible. Two monetary prizes of 1250 Euro each are awarded annually. Established in 1926.

• 1028 • Prix Agathon De Potter
For recognition of outstanding research work in: (1) astronomy; (2) physics; (3) mathematics; (4) chemistry; (5) mineralogy; (6) animal biology; and (7) plant biology. Belgian researchers are eligible. Monetary prizes of 1000 Euro each are awarded triennially. Sponsored by Fondation Agathon De Potter. Established in 1918.

• 1029 • Prix Albert Brachet
For recognition of the best work on embryology, preferably causal embryology. Work published during the preceding three-year period in French, Flemish, German, English or Italian, is eligible. A monetary prize of 1800 Euro is awarded triennially. Established in 1930.

• 1030 • Prix Auguste Sacre
For recognition of an invention bringing about real and important progress in mechanical engineering, in any type of industry, or for any work on mechanical engineering containing new and valuable theories. Belgian researchers are eligible. A monetary prize of 1800 Euro is awarded every six years. Established in 1906.

• 1031 • Prix Baron Van Ertborn
For recognition of the best published work on geology. Belgian authors who are not members of the Academy are eligible. A monetary prize of 1250 Euro is awarded biennially. Established in 1939.

• 1032 • Prix Charles Lagrange
For recognition of the best mathematical or experimental work contributing to the progress of mathematical knowledge in the world. Belgian or foreign researchers are eligible. A monetary prize of 1250 Euro is awarded every four years. Established in 1904.

• 1033 • Prix Charles Lemaire
For recognition of the best published report on public works related preferably to experiences and practical works on engineering or theoretical research on the resistance of materials, the stability of buildings, or hydraulics. A monetary prize of 1250 Euro is awarded biennially. Established in 1894.

• 1034 • Prix de Boelpaepe
For recognition of an important discovery likely to bring about progress in photography. The work can be on the properties of emulsions, and physico-chemical techniques used in photographic processes, or can be used for a new development in photography that may add to scientific progress. Belgian researchers are eligible. A monetary prize of 2000 Euro is awarded biennially. Established in 1927.

• 1035 • Prix de la Belgica
To recognize a scholar or a group of scholars who have successfully devoted themselves to scientific research inside the Antarctic Polar Circle. Scientists of all nationalities are eligible. Surplus funds of the foundation may be given to subsidize oceanographic work by Belgians. A gold medal is awarded every five years. Established in 1959.

• 1036 • Prix de l'adjudant Hubert Lefebvre
For recognition of the best published work on botany, or to help a scientist undertake research in botany. Belgian researchers are eligible. A monetary prize of 1250 Euro is awarded triennially. Established in 1883.

• 1037 • Prix Dubois - Debauque
For recognition of the best works relating to the production of electrical currents by living organisms, and the nature of these currents. Belgian or foreign scientists are eligible. A monetary prize of 1250 Euro is awarded every four years. Established in 1936.

• 1038 • Prix Edmond de Selys Longchamps
For recognition of the best original work on present day Belgian fauna. If no entry on this subject is deemed worthy, works on Belgian fauna in the past or on the fauna of Zaire will be considered. Belgian and foreign researchers are eligible. A monetary prize of 2000 Euro is awarded every five years. Established in 1904.

• 1039 • Prix Edouard Mailly
To recognize a scientist who has contributed to progress in astronomy or has helped spread interest in and knowledge of this science. Belgian or naturalized Belgian scientists are eligible. A monetary prize of 1250 Euro is awarded every four years. Established in 1892.

• 1040 • Prix Emile Laurent
For recognition of outstanding work in the field of botany. Awards are given in alternate years for: (1) the best work on the flora or vegetation of Zaire (including works on the anatomy and physiology of plants from Zaire); and (2) the best work on botany including agriculture and horticulture. Belgian researchers are eligible. A monetary prize of 1000 Euro is awarded every four years. Established in 1910.

• 1041 • Prix Eugene Catalan
To recognize a Belgian or French scholar who has made important progress in pure mathematics. Works must be submitted in French and must have been published during the five preceding years. A monetary prize of 1500 Euro is awarded every five years. Established in 1964.

• 1042 • Prix Francois Deruyts
To recognize one or more authors who have made progress in synthetic or analytic superior geometry. Belgian researchers are eligible. A monetary prize of 1250 Euro is awarded every four years. Established in 1906.

• 1043 • Prix Frederic Swarts
To reward the best work, published or in manuscript form, in the field of pure or industrial chemistry. The work has to be written in French or in Flemish and must be the work of a Belgian citizen who holds an engineering degree from one of the Belgian universities of the Ecole des Mines de Mons, and who graduated in the preceding eight years. If the prize is not awarded for two consecutive periods, it may be awarded to a chemist with a doctorate. A monetary prize of 1250 Euro is awarded biennially. Established in 1938.

• 1044 • Prix Georges Vanderlinden
For recognition of the best discovery or the most noteworthy work in the physical sciences, in particular, radio-electricity. The prize is given alternately for national and international works. For the national competition, the work should be written in French or Dutch. For the international competition, the work should be in English, German, or Italian. A monetary prize of 1500 Euro is awarded biennially. Established in 1932.

• 1045 • Prix Henri Buttgenbach
For recognition of studies on mineralogy, petrography and paleontology that are based on materials gathered in Belgium. Belgian scientists are preferred. Dutch, French, or English scientists can be considered. A monetary prize of 1250 Euro is awarded triennially. Established in 1945.

• 1046 • Prix Jacques Deruyts
For recognition of progress in mathematical analysis. Belgian researchers are eligible. A

monetary prize of 1250 Euro is awarded every four years. Established in 1948.

• 1047 • Prix Joseph Schepkens
For recognition of work in the field of botany or agronomical research. Awards are given in alternate years for: (1) the best experimental work on the genetics of plants, particularly highly cultivated plants; (2) the best work on phytopathology and applied entomology; and (3) agronomical research. Monetary prizes of 1250 Euro each are awarded triennially. Established in 1921.

• 1048 • Prix Lamarck
For recognition of morphological works published in French or Flemish and dealing with a zoological group including humans. All the author's work must have brought to light the greatest number of facts and new explanations on animal evolution or zoological phylogeny. A monetary prize of 1300 Euro is awarded every five years. Established by Paul Pelseneer. Established in 1914.

• 1049 • Prix Leo Errera
To recognize the author or authors of the best original work on general biology. A monetary prize of 1500 Euro is awarded triennially. Established in 1909.

• 1050 • Prix Leon et Henri Fredericq
To recognize a scholar who has distinguished himself by original experimental research in physiology or any related science (biochemistry, biophysics, pharmacodynamics, molecular biology, etc.). Belgian and foreign scientists whose research is done in a Belgian laboratory are eligible. Individuals must be under 45 years of age. A monetary prize of 2500 Euro is awarded biennially. Established in 1968.

• 1051 • Prix Paul and Marie Stroobant
To recognize the Belgian or French scientist who has written the best theoretical or observational work on astronomy. A monetary prize of 1200 Euro is awarded biennially. Established in 1950.

• 1052 • Prix Paul Fourmarier
To recognize a scholar who, during the preceding ten years, has made important discoveries or has brought about considerable progress in theoretical concepts in the geological sciences. Work in geology and its applications, petrography, relations with the creation and evaluation of mineral masses, physical geography, paleontology, or understanding of the general evolution of the earth is eligible. A gold medal is awarded every ten years. Established in 1856.

• 1053 • Prix Pol and Christiane Swings
For recognition of outstanding research in the field of astrophysics. Scientists who are not older than 40 years of age are eligible. The prize is awarded in alternate years to a Belgian and to a foreigner. A monetary prize of 1750 Euro is awarded every four years. Established in 1976.

• 1054 • Prix Professeur Louis Baes
For recognition of the best discovery or the most noteworthy studies on elasticity, plasticity, resistance of materials, the stability of buildings and the calculation of machine parts, including theoretical and practical applications. Candidates must be from Common Market countries and papers must be in French. A monetary prize of 1100 Euro is awarded biennially. Established in 1962.

• 1055 • Prix Theophile de Donder
For recognition of the best original work on mathematical physics. Candidates under 40 years of age are eligible. A monetary prize of 1500 Euro is awarded triennially. Established in 1957.

• 1056 • Prix Theophile Gluge
For recognition of the best work on physiology. Belgian and foreign researchers are eligible. A monetary prize of 1250 Euro is awarded biennially. Established in 1906.

• 1057 • Pierre-Joseph and Edouard Van Beneden Prize
To recognize the author or authors of the best original manuscript or published work on embryology or cytology during the preceding three-year period. Belgian or foreign researchers are eligible. A monetary prize of 1800 Euro is awarded triennially. Established in 1915 by P. Nolf.

• 1058 •
Royal Academy of Sciences, Humanities and Fine Arts of Belgium
(Academie Royale des Sciences, des Lettres at des Beaux-Arts de Belgique)
Paleis der Academies
rue Ducale 1
B-1000 Brussels, Belgium
Phone: 32 2 5502211
Fax: 32 2 5502205
E-mail: arb@cfwb.be
Home Page: http://www.arb.cfwb.be

• 1059 • Antwoorden Prijsvragen, Klasse der Letteren
For recognition in the humanities. Established in 1941.

• 1060 • Antwoorden Prijsvragen, Klasse der Schone Kunsten
For recognition in the field of music and the fine arts. Established in 1942.

• 1061 • Antwoorden Prijsvragen, Klasse der Wetenschappen
For recognition in the field of science. Established in 1941.

• 1062 • Belgica Prize
For scientific research of the Antarctic Polar circle interior.

• 1063 • Boelpaepe Prize
Fo an original contribution to photography and other Forms of imagery.

• 1064 • Albert Brachet Prize
For the best work in embryology.

• 1065 • Henri Buttgenbach Prize
To an author of the best work in the field of mineralogy, petrography or palaeontology.

• 1066 • Octaaf Callebaut Prize
For recognition of contributions to the relief of food problems in the Third World. A monetary prize of 1,250 euros is awarded. Established in 1988.

• 1067 • Eugene Catalan Prize
To a Belgian or French scholar who made a significant progress in pure mathematical sciences.

• 1068 • Jozef Coppens Prize
For recognition in the fields of history of Leuven University, history of Bible exegesis, or Old Testament studies. A monetary prize of 1,250 euros is awarded.

• 1069 • Charles De Clercq Prize
For recognition in the field of religious history of Flanders. A monetary prize of 1,250 euros is awarded. Established in 1987.

• 1070 • Octave Dupont Prize
To recognize an outstanding contribution to human and animal physiology and physiopathology. A monetary prize of 79,325 euros is awarded every eight years. Established in 1991.

• 1071 • Paul Fourmarier Prize
For valuable work in the field of geological sciences.

• 1072 • Jan Gillis Prize
For recognition in the fields of history and/or philosophy of post-Renaissance science. A monetary prize of 1,250 euros is awarded. Established in 1969.

• 1073 • Rene Lenaerts Prize
For recognition in the field of musical science. A monetary prize of 2,500 euros is awarded. Established in 1991.

• 1074 • MacLeod Prijs
For recognition in the field of biology. A monetary prize of 750 euros is awarded. Established in 1951.

• 1075 • Henri Schoutedenprijs
For recognition in zoology, such as the study of fauna, preferably African, systematics, ecology, ethology, or animal anatomy. A monetary prize of 1,250 euros is awarded. Established in 1963.

• 1076 • Floris van der Mueren Prize
For recognition in the field of musicology. A monetary prize of 750 euros is awarded. Established in 1976.

• 1077 • Paul van Oyeprijs
For recognition in the field of biology, hydro biology, biogeography, and systematics of protista or of invertebrates. A monetary prize of 750 euros is awarded. Established in 1969.

• 1078 • Henri L. Vanderlinden Prize
For recognition in the field of astronomy. A monetary prize of 1,250 euros is awarded.

• 1079 •
Royal Carillon School Jef Denyn
(Koninklijke Beiaardschool Jef Denijn)
Frederik de Merodestraat 63
B-2800 Mechelen, Belgium
Phone: 32 15 204792
Fax: 32 15 203176
E-mail: info@beiaardschool.be
Home Page: http://www.beiaardschool.be

• 1080 • International Carillon Competition - Queen Fabiola (Internationale Beiaardwedstrijd Koningin Fabiola)
For recognition of outstanding performance of original carillon compositions. Carillonneurs from all over the world may participate. All candidates must present nine original carillon compositions, including three baroque, three romantic, and three modern works. All compositions must be of a very high virtuosity level. The following prizes are awarded: first prize - a monetary prize, a bronze bell in a frame, diploma, and a concert tour through Belgium; second prize - a monetary prize plus a medal and diploma; third prize - a monetary prize plus a medal and diploma; fourth prize - a monetary plus a diploma; fifth prize - a monetary prize plus a diploma; and sixth prize - a monetary prize plus a diploma. Application forms are due before March 31. Established in 1987 under the patronage of Her Majesty Queen Fabiola. Held every five years.

• 1081 • International Contest for Carillon Composition
For recognition of a composition for a four octave carillon (c tot c''''), three pages minimum, lasting a maximum of eight minutes. The composer has free choice of a musical form in Category I. In Category II, the carillon compositions are based on an old folksong or use a folksong as a basic element. Compositions already published, performed, or sent in on the occasion of previous competitions are not allowed, and not more than one work by the same composer may obtain a prize. The following monetary prizes, each of them with a diploma, may be awarded: Category I: first prize - Jef Denyn Prize; second prize Stad Mechelen Prize; third prize Carillon School Prize; and Category II: first prize - Staf Nees Prize; and second prize Tower and Carillon Prize. Awarded every five years. Established in 1952. Formerly: Internationale Kompositiewedstrijd voor Beiaard.

• 1082 •
Royal Film Archive of Belgium
(Cinematheque Royale)
Hotel van Cleve
Ravensteinstraat 3
B-1000 Brussels, Belgium
Phone: 32 2 551 1900
Fax: 32 2 551 1904
E-mail: filmarchief@ledoux.be
Home Page: http://www.cinematheque.be

• 1083 • Age d'Or Prize
To promote the creation and distribution of films that depart from all cinematographic conformities by the originality, the oddity of their substance, and form. Competing films must be longer than 60 minutes and completed in the preceding three years. The films must be presented in their original and uncut version. If not in English, French, or Dutch, the films must be subtitled in one of these languages. A monetary prize is awarded to the winning film chosen from one of five films awarded the Royal Film Archive of Belgium's Prizes for the Distribution of Quality Films in Belgium. This sum is given to the Belgian distributor, who may, within one year, present proof of genuine distribution in Belgium and of possession of a print of the film in its original version, subtitled in French and Dutch. Another monetary prize is divided into two parts and are awarded to the producer and director. Formerly: Prix de l'Age d'Or.

• 1084 • Prizes for the Distribution of Quality Films in Belgium (Premies voor de verspreiding van de betere film in Belgie)
To provide recognition for quality films of any country, longer than 60 minutes, whose innovative nature makes their release problematic; and to recognize the Belgian distributors who may, within one year of the award, present proof of distribution of these films in Belgium in original and uncut versions with French and Dutch subtitles. Five monetary awards are awarded annually. In Addition, one film from among these 5 award winners is singled out by the jury for the Age d'or Prize.

• 1085 •
Sarton Committee of the University of Ghent
(Sarton Comite van de Rijksuniversiteit Gent)
Blandijberg 2
B-9000 Ghent, Belgium
Phone: 32 9 264 9584
Fax: 32 9 264 4174
E-mail: sarton@webtec.be
Home Page: http://sarton.ugent.be

• 1086 • Sarton Chair (Sarton Leersoel)
For recognition of achievement in the history or philosophy of science. Individuals proposed by two scientists by January of each year are eligible. A certificate and medal are awarded annually. Established in 1986 by the University of Ghent in honor of George Sarton.

• 1087 • Sarton Medal (Sarton Medaille)
For recognition of a contribution to a field of activity in the history or philosophy of science and for encouragement in that field. Individuals proposed by two scientists by January of each year are eligible. A certificate and medal are awarded annually. Established in 1986 by the University of Ghent in honor of George Sarton.

• 1088 •
SECO: Technical Control Bureau for Construction
(Bureau de Controle Technique pour la Construction)
rue d'Arlon 53
B-1040 Brussels, Belgium
Phone: 32 2 238 22 11
Fax: 32 2 238 22 61
E-mail: mail@seco.be
Home Page: http://www.seco.be
Formerly: Bureau of Security Control of Construction.

• 1089 • Magnel Prize
For recognition of scientific work in the area of safety control of construction that has practical application for the field. The research results must be written in French, Dutch, German, or English. The author must be attached to a university or a research institute of a member country of the European Union, and must be no older than 40 years of age. A monetary award of 10,000 Euro is awarded every four years. Established in 1964.

• 1090 • Verdeyen Prize for Soil Mechanics
For recognition of scientific research on soil mechanics, with practical application for control and safety of constructions. The work must be written in French, Dutch, German, or English. Research workers not older than 40 years of age are eligible. A monetary award of 7,500 Euro is awarded every four years. Established in 1974.

• 1091 •
SIGNIS
Robert Molhant, Sec.Gen.
15, rue du Saphir
B-1030 Brussels, Belgium
Phone: 32 2 7349708
Phone: 32 2 7343526
Fax: 32 2 7343207
E-mail: sg@signis.net
Home Page: http://www.signis.net
Formerly: (2001) International Catholic Organization for Cinema and Audiovisual.

• 1092 • Ecumenical Prize
For recognition of films from any country that promotes human and spiritual values. A bronze medal is awarded at film festivals throughout the world, such as Cannes, Locarno, Montreal, Moscow, Berlin, and others. Established in 1974.

Awards are arranged in alphabetical order below their administering organizations

• 1093 • OCIC-Prize

To encourage the circulation, promotion, and production of valuable films promoting human and spiritual values. Films presented at film festivals throughout the world where the OCIC has a panel of judges are eligible. A bronze medal is awarded at the Festivals such as Ouagadougou, Troia, Amiens, Venice, Carthage, Havana, and others. Established in 1947.

• 1094 •
Societe Royale de Chimie
% Anne Choprix, Sec.
Universite Libre de Bruxelles
Ave. F.D. Roosevelt 50
CP 160/07
B-1050 Brussels, Belgium
Phone: 32 2 650 5208
Fax: 32 2 650 5184
E-mail: src@ulb.ac.be
Home Page: http://www.src.be

Formerly: (1986) Societe Chimique de Belgique.

• 1095 • Prix Paul Janssen

To honor a young French (part Belgian) researcher for his contribution in the field of therapeutical chemistry. To be eligible, a researcher must submit a Ph.D. thesis or a scientific published paper in organic chemistry, biochemistry, chemical biology. The candidate cannot be older than 35 years of age and must be a Society member. A monetary prize is awarded biennially.

• 1096 • Prix Triennal de la Societe Royale de Chimie

To honor a chemist whose work has received international recognition. Members of the Society of any nationality who are living permanently in Belgium or Belgian chemists living abroad are eligible. The candidate cannot be older than 40 years of age, and must have been a Society member for at least five years. A monetary prize is awarded triennially.

• 1097 •
Societe Royale des Sciences de Liege
Univ. of Liege, Institut de Mathematique
Campus d Sart Tilman B37
B-4000 Liege, Belgium
Phone: 32 4 3669371
Phone: 32 4 3669371
Fax: 32 4 3669547
E-mail: srsl2@ulg.ac.be
Home Page: http://www.srsl-ulg.net

• 1098 • Prizes of the 150th Anniversary of the RSSL

To recognize an individual or a group for outstanding contributions in mathematics, physics, chemistry, or biology. Individuals who are less than 35 years of age are eligible. The following awards are presented every five years: Prix Edouard Van Beneden - for contributions in biology, Prix Lucien Godeaux - for mathematics, Prix Louis d'Or - for chemistry, and Prix Pol Swings - for physics. Established in 1985.

• 1099 •
Unda International Catholic Association for Radio and Television
(Unda Association Catholique Internationale pour la Radio et la Television)
15, rue de Saphir
B-1030 Brussels, Belgium
Phone: 32 2 7349708
Fax: 32 2 7347018
E-mail: sg@signis.net
Home Page: http://www.signis.net

• 1100 • Unda Dove
(Colombe Unda)

To recognize radio and television programs of high technical quality that convey a spiritual message at the International Television Festival of Monte Carlo. Applications are accepted. Awards are presented for fiction programs and current affairs. A trophy is awarded annually in February. Established in 1962.

• 1101 •
The University Foundation
(Fondation Universitaire)
Eric de Keuleneer, Exec.Dir.
rue d'Egmont 11
B-1000 Brussels, Belgium
Phone: 32 2 545 0400
Fax: 32 2 513 6411
E-mail: fu.us@universityfoundation.be
Home Page: http://www .universitairestichting.be

• 1102 • Emile Bernheim European Prizes
(Prix Europeens Emile Bernheim)

To recognize works on European integration. A prize is awarded for a work helping those who are engaged in implementation of European integration, especially in the framework of the Common Market. The applicant must be a senior researcher from a Belgian university. A monetary prize of $10,000 (European) is awarded every two years. Established in 1954. A second prize is awarded to a student or junior researcher at a Belgian academic institution for a project related to European integration. A monetary prize of $2,500 (European) is awarded every two years. Established in 1955.

• 1103 • Fernand Collin Prijs

For recognition of an original manuscript or printed work that is an important contribution to science. A Belgian with a degree in law or economics, received from a Belgian university less than 20 years before, may submit a work that must be written in Dutch. A monetary prize and the title, Laureaat van de Fernand Colin Prijs, are awarded biennially. Established in 1962.

• 1104 •
University of Limburg
(Rijksuniversiteit Limburg)
Universitaire Campus, Gebouw D
PO Box 616
B-3590 Diepenbeek, Belgium
Phone: 32 11 268111
Fax: 32 11 268199
E-mail: info@luc.ac.be
Home Page: http://www.luc.ac.be

• 1105 • Catharina Pijlsprijs
(Catharine Pijls Prize)

To recognize scientists who have made fundamental contributions to the health sciences, and to encourage professional development of the health sciences. A monetary award is presented at the convention. Established in 1984 by the Catharina Pijls Foundation, Maastricht.

Bolivia

• 1106 •
HelpAge International - Latin America Regional Development Centre
Valerie Mealla, Rep.
Casilla 2217
La Paz, Bolivia
Phone: 591 2 2410583
Fax: 591 2 2410957
E-mail: helpage.bolivia@alamo.entelnet .com

• 1107 • Leslie Kirkley Fellowship

Recognizes outstanding service to senior citizens. Awarded annually.

• 1108 •
Kennel Club Boliviano
Luis Alberto Quiroga Arce, Natl.Pres.
Av. Oquendo, S-0149, piso 3, of. 21
Loayza esq Juan de la Riva
Casilla 11030
Cochabamba, Bolivia
Phone: 591 44543156
Fax: 591 44543156
E-mail: kcbnac@supernet.com.bo

• 1109 • Ranking Champion

To recognize the highest ranked dog of the year. Established in 1987.

Brazil

• 1110 •
Brazil Office of the President
Luis Inacio Lula da Silva, Pres.
Palacio do Planalto
Praca des Tres Poderes
70150-900 Brasilia, Federal District, Brazil
Phone: 55 61 2232714
E-mail: protocolo@planalto.gov.br
Home Page: http://www.planalto.gov.br

• 1111 • Oswaldo Cruz Prize

To recognize outstanding accomplishments in the field of medicine and biology.

Awards are arranged in alphabetical order below their administering organizations

• 1112 • National Order of the Southern Cross

To recognize individuals or groups of foreigners for outstanding accomplishments in the fields of education, science, literature, art and culture related to Brazil. The order is conferred in five classes: Grand Collar, Grand Cross, Official, and Knight. Established in 1971.

• 1113 • Order of Rio Branco

For recognition of outstanding service to the Brazilian nation by a citizen or a foreigner. The order is conferred in five classes: Grand Cross, Grand Official, Knight Commander, Official, and Knight. Established in 1963.

• 1114 • Roquette Pinto Prize

To provide recognition for the best adaptation from a book to a film scenario by a Brazilian author.

• 1115 •
Brazilian Academy of Letters
(Academia Brasileira de Letras)
Avenida Presidente Wilson 203, Castelo
20030-021 Rio de Janeiro, Rio de Janeiro, Brazil
Phone: 55 21 39742500
E-mail: academia@academia.org.br
Home Page: http://www.academia.org.br

• 1116 • Afonso Arinos Prize

For recognition of the best work of fiction published or written during the two years preceding the year of award. A monetary prize is awarded annually.

• 1117 • Arthur Azevedo Prize

For recognition of the best works of drama, history of the theatre, and theatrical criticism. A monetary prize is awarded annually.

• 1118 • Olavo Bilac Prize

For recognition of the best book of poetry. A monetary prize is awarded annually.

• 1119 • Monteiro Lobato Prize

For recognition of the best works of children's literature. A monetary prize is awarded annually.

• 1120 • Machado de Assis Prize

This, one of Brazil's highest literary awards, is given to recognize an outstanding Brazilian writer for the sum of his work. A monetary prize of 200,000 Brazilian cruzeiros is awarded annually. Established in 1943.

• 1121 •
Brazilian Agricultural Research Corporation
(Empresa Brasileira de Pesquisa Agropecuaria)
Silvio Crestana, Dir./Pres.
Parque Estacao Biologica - PqEB
SAIN - Av. W3 Norte
Cx. Postal 040315
70770-901 Brasilia, Federal District, Brazil
Phone: 55 61 34484433
Fax: 55 61 33471041
E-mail: sac@embrapa.br
Home Page: http://www.embrapa.br

• 1122 • Frederico de Menezes Veiga Prize
(Premio Frederico de Menezes Veiga)

To recognize scientists for significant contributions to the development of agricultural research. One researcher from EMBRAPA and one from other Brazilian research institutions are eligible for the prize. Nomination is by scientists or research institutions by January 1. A monetary prize of US $2,000, a gold medal, and a diploma are awarded annually. Established in 1975 in honor of Frederico de Menezes Veiga, a sugarcane breeder who made important contributions to Brazilian agriculture.

• 1123 •
Brazilian Metallurgy and Materials Association
(Associacao Brasileira de Metalurgia e Materiais)
Raquel Sturlini, Contact
Rua Antonio Comparato, 218
Campo Belo
04605-030 Sao Paulo, Sao Paulo, Brazil
Phone: 55 11 55364333
Fax: 55 11 50444273
E-mail: abm@abmbrasil.com.br
Home Page: http://www.abmbrasil.com.br

• 1124 • Gold Medal

Recognizes an individual providing outstanding service to the association. Awarded annually.

• 1125 • Silver Medal

Recognizes outstanding service to the association. Applicants must be association members. Awarded periodically.

• 1126 •
Brazilian Packaging Association
(Associacao Brasileira de Embalagem)
Fabio Mestriner, Pres.
Rua Oscar Freire 379, 15 andar, cj 152
01426-001 Sao Paulo, Sao Paulo, Brazil
Phone: 55 11 30829722
Fax: 55 11 30819201
E-mail: abre@abre.org.br
Home Page: http://www.abre.org.br

• 1127 • Brazilian Packaging and Design Awards

Annual award of recognition for packaging design in a variety of categories.

• 1128 •
International Association of Gerontology and Geriatrics
Dr. Gloria Gutman, Pres.
Rua Hilario de Gouveia 66 / 1102 - Copacabana
Simon Fraser University at Harbour Centre
2800 - 515 W Hastings St.
22040-020 Rio de Janeiro, Brazil
Phone: 55 21 22351510
E-mail: iagg@iagg.com.br
Home Page: http://www.iagg.com.br

• 1129 • Ewald W. Busse Research Awards

To promote international research in gerontology. Awards shall be selected on an international basis. Two awards are given biennially, one recognizing a researcher from the social/behavioral sciences and the other from the biomedical sciences. Awards of US$4,000 plus $3,000 for travel expenses to the conference are supported from an endowment made by Gerontology International in honor of Ewald W. Busse M.D., past president of the Association and founding director of the Duke Aging Center. Established in 1987.

• 1130 • Presidential Award

To recognize individuals who have contributed to the enhancement and dignity of the International Association of Gerontology through specific tasks, such as acting as former officers. The awards are presented to those devoted to enhancing the AssociationKs international recognition, promoting research in the aging field, and preserving the historical background of the Association. The President of the Association is responsible for the nomination. Established in 1993.

• 1131 •
International Seaweed Association
Prof. Eurico C. Oliveira, Sec.
Instituto de Biociencias
Universidade de Sao Paulo
C. postal 11461
05422-970 Sao Paulo, Sao Paulo, Brazil
Phone: 55 11 30917630
Phone: 55 11 30917540
Fax: 55 11 30917547
E-mail: euricodo@usp.br
Home Page: http://www.isaseaweed.org

• 1132 • International Seaweed Association Awards

To recognize scientific and commercial communities for contributions to the management of seaweed resources. Awards are presented triennially at the International Seaweed Symposium.

Awards are arranged in alphabetical order below their administering organizations

• 1133 •
Museum of Modern Art of Sao Paulo
(Museu de Arte Moderna de Sao Paulo)
Milu Vilella, Exec.Dir.
Parque do Ibirapuera, gate 3
04094-000 Sao Paulo, Sao Paulo, Brazil
Phone: 55 11 5549 9688
Fax: 55 11 5549 2342
E-mail: conselho.diretoria@mam.org.br
Home Page: http://www.mam.org.br

• 1134 • **Panorama Brasilian Art**
(Panorama de Arte Brasileira)
To provide for acquisition of works of art for the museum and for recognition of outstanding art in the categories of: painting, sculpture and objects, and art on paper. Monetary prizes are awarded biennially to two to four artists. Established in 1969.

• 1135 •
Sao Paulo International Film Festival
(Mostra Internacional de Cinema Em Sao Paulo)
R. Antonio Carlos, 288
01309-010 Sao Paulo, Sao Paulo, Brazil
Phone: 55 11 3141 0413
Fax: 55 11 3266 7066
E-mail: info@mostra.org
Home Page: http://www2.uol.com.br/mostra

• 1136 • **Sao Paulo International Film Festival**
For recognition of the best films of the festival. Feature films or shorts not previously shown in Brazil must be submitted by August 13. The festival has two sections: the International Perspective and the New Filmmakers Competition for films by new directors. In the first week of the Festival, the public chooses ten films, and the jury chooses the final winners in the second week. The Bandeira Paulista, a flag of Sao Paulo stylized by the designer, Tomie Ohtake, is awarded annually. The Public Award and the Critic Award are also presented. Established in 1977 by Leon Cakoff. The festival will be held from October 19 through November 1.

• 1137 •
Villa-Lobos Museum
(Museu Villa-Lobos)
Turibio Santos, Dir.
Rua Sorocaba, 200
22271-110 Botafogo, Rio de Janeiro, Brazil
Phone: 55 21 2266 1024
Fax: 55 21 2266 1024
E-mail: mvillalobos@museuvillalobos.org.br
Home Page: http://www.museuvillalobos.org.br

• 1138 • **International Villa-Lobos Guitar Competition**
(Concorso Internacional de Violao Villa-Lobos)
To recognize the best guitarist in the competition, and to encourage the development of Villa-Lobos works and Brazilian works in general. Guitarists of any age may submit entries and tapes by April 20. The following monetary prizes are awarded biennially: (1) First prize - $3,000 US; and (2) Second prize - $2,000 US. Established in 1971 by Museu Villa-Lobos in honor of Heitor Villa-Lobos.

• 1139 • **International Villa-Lobos Piano Competition**
(Concurso Internacional de Piano Villa-Lobos)
To recognize the best pianist in the competition, and to encourage the development of Villa-Lobos works and Brazilian works in general. Pianists of any age may submit entries and tapes by April 20. The following prizes are awarded: (1) first prize - 200,000,00 Brazilian cruzeiros; (2) second prize - 100,000,00 Brazilian cruzeiros; and (3) third prize - 50,000,00 Brazilian cruzeiros. Semi finalists may be awarded Distinctions. The winner also accepts the commitment to perform a pre-selected work by Villa-Lobos with orchestra. Established in 1974 by Museu Villa-Lobos in honor of Heitor Villa-Lobos.

Bulgaria

• 1140 •
Boris Christoff International Competition for Young Opera Singers Foundation
Plamen Djouroff, Chm.
41, Tzar Boris III Blvd.
BG-1612 Sofia, Bulgaria
Phone: 359 2 9515903
Fax: 359 2 9521558
E-mail: borischristoff@abv.bg
Home Page: http://www.borischristoff.dir.bg

• 1141 • **Boris Christoff International Competition for Young Opera Singers - Sofia**
(Concours International de Jeunes Chanteurs d'Opera)
For recognition of the achievements of young opera singers. Singers of all nationalities can take part in the Competition. Men may not be older than 35, and women not older than 33 years of age. The Competition takes place in three stages; the third one involves singing a principal part in a regular performance of the Sofia National Opera. The Grand Prix of Sofia consists of a monetary prize of 5,000 USD, a gold medal, a gold ring, and a diploma. The following prizes are also awarded to both men and women: (1) First prize - 2,500 USD, a gold medal, and a diploma; (2) Second prize - 1,500 USD, a silver medal, and a diploma; and (3) Third prize 1,000 levas, a bronze medal, and a diploma. The winners are offered invitations for guest performances in Bulgaria and other countries of Europe. Awarded every four years. Established in 1961.

• 1142 •
Bulgarian Academy of Sciences
(Balgarska Akademija na Naukite)
Acad. Ivan Juchnovski, Pres.
Acad. G. Bonchev Str. Bl. 25-A
BG-1113 Sofia, Bulgaria
Phone: 359 2 708494
Fax: 359 2 707273
Home Page: http://www.bas.bg

• 1143 • **Bulgarian Academy of Science Honorary Badge - Marin Drinov Medal**
To recognize Bulgarian and foreign scientists as well as outstanding cultural workers on the occasion of their jubilees for major scientific achievements and considerable contributions to Bulgarian science. Selection is made by the Bulgarian Academy of Science Presidium or the Presidium Bureau at the proposal of the Scientific Secretariat, the Research Centres or the independent scientific organizations attached to the Presidium. A medal with the relief image of Prof. Marin Drinov, first president of the Academy, a certificate of merit, and an honorary badge are awarded. The medal was established in 1975, and the honorary badge in 1981.

• 1144 • **Cyril and Methodius Prize**
For recognition of research representing a considerable original scientific contribution in the field of old Bulgarian writing, literature, and culture. A diploma and honorary recognition were awarded annually on the day of commemoration of Bulgarian education and culture, the Slav alphabet and the Bulgarian press, May 24. Established in 1971.

• 1145 •
Bulgarian National Television
(Bulgarska Natcionalna Televiziya)
International Relations Dept.
29 San Stefano Str.
BG-1504 Sofia, Bulgaria
Phone: 359 2 9461034
Fax: 359 2 9461034
E-mail: intr@bnt.bg
Home Page: http://www.bnt.bg
Formerly: (1995) Bulgarian Television and Radio.

• 1146 • **Golden Antenna International Television Festival**
(Zlatnata Antena)
To stimulate the development of entertainment musical genres for juvenile and adult audiences. It is recommended that the programs offered have their own national identity. The submitted programs should not exceed 60 minutes and should have been produced during the preceding year. Each television organization, associated television organization within a television company, or independent producer may present their programs in two categories: (1) Programs for adults with the following divisions Shows and Concerts; Operas, Musicals, and Ballets; Video Clips; Profiles and Musical Documentaries; and Sketches and other entertainment programs. (2) Programs for children with the following divisions - Shows and Concerts; Operas, Musicals,

and Ballets; Video Clips; and Educational Programs, Profiles, and Musical Documentaries. Deadline for entry forms is May 30. The programs will be nominated by an international jury of five members. The following prizes are awarded: for Category One - Grand Prize, The Golden Antenna; and Special Prix (for each division). For Category Two - Grand Prix, The Golden Antenna; and Special Prix (for each division). Established in 1988.

• 1147 • Golden Chest International Television Festival (Zlatnata Rakla)

To promote international television cooperation and a better knowledge of achievements in the field of television drama and to expand contacts between authors and producers from across the world. Productions must be on a contemporary theme and must be based on a literary work of national origin; plays written for television; TV-versions of theatre plays or television dramatizations. The programs may not offend the dignity of any country or nation, nor may they propagate violence, pornography, or religious fanaticism. The award is given in two categories: (1) Television drama for adults (running time of up to 100 minutes); and (2) Television drama for children and adolescents (70 minutes). The productions must have been released during the preceding year. Programs that have already won international awards and programs containing advertisements are not eligible. The following prizes are awarded: Category One - The Golden Chest Prize and the Special Prize of the Novotel Plovdiv. Category Two The Golden Chest Prize and the Special Prize of the Plovdiv Municipality. Other prizes may be awarded for special achievements in both categories: best actor; best actress; best child actor (awarded by the Union of Bulgarian Actors); best scriptwriter; best director; best director of photography; best set director (awarded by the Union of Bulgarian Filmmakers). The juries awarding the prizes shall be a seven-member international jury for Category One, and a five-member international jury for Category Two. Established in 1968 by Bulgarian Television.

• 1148 •

Bulgarian Orienteering Federation
Todor Kazakov, Sec.
Bul Vassil Levski 75
Box 427
BG-1000 Sofia, Bulgaria
Phone: 359 2 9300613
Fax: 359 2 9874427
Home Page: http://www.bgof.org/eng.htm

• 1149 • Top 10 Orienteers

Award of recognition for the biggest account of points gathered. Presented annually.

• 1150 •

Bulgarian Red Cross
Hristo Paunov, Chm.
76 James Boucher Blvd.
1407 Sofia, Bulgaria
Phone: 359 2 665249
Phone: 359 2 657185
Fax: 359 2 656139
E-mail: secretariat@redcross.bg
Home Page: http://www.redcross.bg/index_en.php

• 1151 • Gold Medal

Recognizes contributions to Red Cross activities. Awarded periodically.

• 1152 •

International Festival of Red Cross and Health Films
% Bulgarian Red Cross National Headquarters
Festival Directorate
76, James Boucher Blvd.
BG-1407 Sofia, Bulgaria
Phone: 359 2 8164 755
Fax: 359 2 8164 611
E-mail: v.peeva@redcross.bg
Home Page: http://www.redcross.bg

• 1153 • International Festival of Red Cross and Health Films

To recognize the best films on topical Red Cross, health, ecological and humanitarian subjects. Films produced during the preceding two years by the International Institutions and National Red Cross and Red Crescent Societies, by film production companies, television studios and other institutions, are eligible. Films can be entered in the following two categories: (1) Non-fiction Red Cross and Health Films for Cinema and Television (under 60 min.) - (a) Films promoting the ideas of the Red Cross and Red Crescent; (b) Popular-science, documentary, animation films and spots on health and ecological subjects; and (c) Scientific and instructional films; and (2) Feature Films - (a) Feature films for the cinema - 35 mm; and (b) TV dramas and parts of serials. The films judged to be the best in their category and subgroup, are awarded the following prizes: (1) Non-fiction Red Cross and Health Films for Cinema and Television - (a) Golden Ship Grand Prix of the President of the Bulgarian Red Cross for the best film in the category; (b) Grand Prix of the League of Red Cross and Red Crescent Societies for the best Red Cross film; (c) Special Prize for the best health or ecological film; and (d) Special Prize for the best scientific or instructional film. First and Second prizes of Gold and Silver medals are also awarded for each of the subgroups; and (2) Feature Films - (a) Grand Prix for the best feature film for the cinema; (b) Grand Prix for the best TV drama; (c) Prize for the best direction; (d) Prize for the best actress; (e) Prize for the best actor; and (f) Special Prize of the League of Red Cross and Red Crescent Societies for the best film with humanitarian character. A Special Prize is awarded by the World Health Organization for the best film on Communication for Health. In addition, the FIPRESCI (International Federation of Cinema Press) Prize and the CIDALC (International Committee for the Dissemination of Art and Literature through Cinema) Prize are awarded. Participation Diplomas are presented to all films shown in competition during the Festival. Awarded biennially. Established in 1965. Sponsored by The League of Red Cross and Red Crescent Societies, the International Committee of the Red Cross, and the World Health Organization.

• 1154 •

President of the Republic of Bulgaria
Georgi Parvanov, Pres.
Dondukov Boulevard 2
BG-1123 Sofia, Bulgaria
Phone: 359 2 9239 333
Fax: 359 2 8034 18
E-mail: press@president.bg
Home Page: http://www.president.bg

• 1155 • Madarski Konnik Order

To recognize foreign diplomatic representatives, public figures, private persons, and soldiers who have rendered great services to the establishment, by strengthening and maintaining friendly relations with the People's Republic of Bulgaria. Honorary recognition and the Order are awarded.

• 1156 • Stara Planina Order

To recognize foreign heads of state or government, ministers, diplomats, political, public, cultural and economic figures for their contributions to the establishment, strengthening and maintaining close and friendly relations with the People's Republic of Bulgaria, and for the strengthening of peace between peoples. Bulgarian ambassadors may also be recognized. Honorary recognition and a medal with or without a ribbon are awarded.

• 1157 •

Varna International Ballet Competition
(Concours International de Ballet, Varna)
6 Serdika St., 1st Fl.
BG-1000 Sofia, Bulgaria
Phone: 359 2 9883377
Fax: 359 2 9861901
E-mail: varna_ibc@mail.bol.bg
Home Page: http://www.varnaibc.org

• 1158 • Varna International Ballet Competition (Concours International de Ballet, Varna)

For recognition of outstanding ballet dancers. Men and women dancers from all nationalities can take part in the Competition. Awards are presented in two independent classes: (1) Class A (Seniors) - for ballet dancers not older than 26 years of age; and (2) Class B (Juniors) - for boys and girls from 14 to 19 years of age. Competitors under 19 years of age who wish to compete in Class A - Seniors should receive special permission from the international jury. If the candidates decide to dance a pas de deux in one of the three stages of the competition, the ballet couples may be formed from one and the same class or from the two different classes. The candidates have to perform five pieces. The following prizes are awarded in Class A - Seniors: (1) Laureate of the International Ballet Competition and the Grand Prix of Varna - 20,000 leva, a gold medal and a diploma; (2) First Prizes (one for men and one for women) - 15,000 leva each, a gold medal, and a diploma; (3) two Second Prizes - 10,000 leva each, a silver medal, and a diploma; (4) Third Prize - 8,000 leva, a bronze medal, and a diploma; (5) Special Prize Nina Ricci - 12,000 leva, a commemorative medal and a diploma; and (6) Special Prize Repetto - 12,000 leva, a commemorative medal and a diploma. The following prizes are awarded in Class B - Juniors: (1) Excellent Performer of the International Ballet Competition and Special Distinction of the Youth Organization of Varna 10,000 leva, a diploma, concerts, and a medal; (2) First Class Awards (one for girls and one for boys) - 6,000 leva each, a diploma and a medal; (3) two Second Class Awards - 4,000 leva each, a diploma and a medal; and (4) two Third Class Awards - 2,000 leva each, a diploma and a medal. Special awards, token awards and distinctions are also awarded. Awarded biennially. Established in 1964. Varna is one of four locations for the International Ballet Competition, the others being Moscow, USSR; Jackson, Mississippi, U.S.A.; and Helsinki, Finland.

Burkina Faso

• 1159 •
Panafrican Film and Television Festival of Ouagadougou
(Festival Panafricain du Cinema et de la Television de Ouagadougou)
Sec.Gen. of the Festival
01 BP 2505
Ouagadougou 01, Burkina Faso
Phone: 226 50 307538
Fax: 226 50 312509
E-mail: sg@fespaco.bf
Home Page: http://www.fespaco.bf

• 1160 • **Panafrican Film and Television Festival of Ouagadougou (Festival Panafrican du Cinema de Ouagadougou et de la Television de Ouagadougou)**
For recognition of the full-length African film deemed by the jury to be the best account of the African cultural identity or social realities. A monetary award and the Yennenga Stallion Trophy are awarded biennially in odd-numbered years. Established in 1972 by the government of Burkina Faso to honor Princess Yennenga, Mossi's ancestor, who fought and won battles contributing to the growth of her father's kingdom.

Chile

• 1161 •
Chile Ministerio de Educacion
Sergio Bitar, Min.
Direccion de Bibliotecas
Archivos y Museos
Ave. Libertador Bernardo O'Higgins No. 651
Santiago 1371, Chile
Phone: 56 2 3904 000
Fax: 56 2 6381975
E-mail: bndir@oris.renib.d
Home Page: http://www.mineduc.cl/biblio

• 1162 • **Premio Nacional de Ciencias**
To recognize Chilean scientists for outstanding work in the field of pure and applied sciences of humanity and the environment. A monetary award is presented biennially in odd-numbered years.

• 1163 • **Premio Nacional de Literatura**
To recognize a Chilean author of distinction in any of the literary fields of the novel, poetry, theater, essay, and literary criticism. Chilean writers must be nominated by an accredited academic institution and three or more people associated with the prize. A monetary prize and a certificate are awarded biennially in even-numbered years. Established in 1942 by Por Ley de la Republica.

• 1164 • **Premio Nacional de Periodismo**
To recognize a Chilean journalist distinguished by his or her method of communication or expression and for significant support of written or audiovisual journalism. A monetary prize is awarded biennially in odd-numbered years.

• 1165 •
Engineers' Association of Chile
Fernando Garcia, Pres.
Ave. Santa Maria 508
Providencia
Santiago, Chile
Phone: 56 2 4221140
Fax: 56 2 4221012
E-mail: soporte@ingenieros.cl
Home Page: http://www.ingenieros.cl

• 1166 • **Premio Nacional**
Recognizes contributions to the engineering field. Awarded annually.

• 1167 •
Fundacion Pablo Neruda
Juan Agustin Figueroa, Pres.
Fernando Marquez de la Plata 0192
Santiago, Chile
Phone: 56 2 777 8741
Fax: 56 2 737 8712
E-mail: comunicaciones@fundacionneruda.org
Home Page: http://www.fundacionneruda.org

• 1168 • **Premio Pablo Neruda**
To promote literary creativity among authors under 40 years of age. A monetary prize of $3,000 is awarded annually. Established in 1987 in memory of Pablo Neruda, the Chilean author.

• 1169 •
Service of Peace and Justice
(Servicio Paz y Justicia)
Fernando Aliaga, Exec. Officer
Cienfuego 85
Casilla 139-3
Santiago, Chile
Phone: 56 2 6972001
Fax: 56 2 6727608
E-mail: serpaj@cmet.net
Home Page: http://www.geocities.com/serpaj_cl/serpaj_2.html

• 1170 • **National Award for the Protection of Environment**
Recognizes outstanding community work. Awarded annually.

Colombia

• 1171 •
Academia Colombiana de Ciencias Exactas, Fisicas y Naturales
Moises Wassermann, Pres.
Av. El Dorado Cra. 50
Insituto Nacional de Salud
Bogota, Colombia
Phone: 57 1 222 1059
Fax: 57 1 224 3186
E-mail: mwasserm@colciencias.gov.co
Home Page: http://www.accefyn.org.co

• 1172 • **Colombian Academy of Exact, Physical and Natural Sciences to the Integral Work of a Scientist**
For the best scientific paper presented by a young Columbian. Awards are given in alternative years for Biology, Physics, Chemistry, and Mathematics. Unpublished, or published within the last two years, works done by Colombian scientists under 35 years of age are considered. A monetary prize of about $3,500 (U.S.) is awarded annually.

• 1173 •
Colombia Ministry of Foreign Affairs
Palacio de San Carlos
Calle 10, No. 5-51
Bogota, Colombia
Phone: 57 5 662008
Fax: 57 5 666444
E-mail: cancilleria@minrelext.gov.co
Home Page: http://www.minrelext.gov.co

• 1174 • **Cruz de Boyaca**
This is the highest national award of Colombia. To recognize officers of the Armed Forces, officials of the government, and citizens of Colombia or other friendly countries who distinguish themselves for heroism and a spirit of international brotherhood. The following awards are presented: Great Collar; Great Extraordinary Cross; Great Cross; Great Official Cross; Silver Cross; and Commander, Official and Knight Crosses. Awarded when merited. Established in 1919. These awards were originally created by the liberator, Simon Bolivar in 1828 to honor the efforts and sacrifices of those who aided him, and were re-established on the centenary of the Battle of Boyaca.

• 1175 • Order of San Carlos
To recognize citizens of Colombia and foreigners, mostly diplomats (both civilian and military) who have contributed to the improvement of relations between their countries and Colombia. A medal is awarded in seven classes: Collar; Great Cross with Golden Plaque; Great Cross; Great Official; Commander; Official; and Knight. Awarded irregularly. Established in 1954.

• 1176 •
Colombia Ministry of National Defence
Centro Administrativo Nacional
Avda Eldorado, 2
Bogota, Colombia
Phone: 57 1 2884184
E-mail: webmaster@mindefensa.gov.co
Home Page: http://www.mindefensa.gov.co

• 1177 • Medalla Militar Francisco Jose de Caldas
To recognize officials of the military forces who obtained the title of Military Professor, and alumni of the Escuela Superior de Guerra. Gold, silver, and bronze medals and a diploma are awarded annually.

• 1178 • Medalla Militar Soldado Juan Bautista Solarte Obando
To recognize the best soldier or sailor in each contingent of the Armed Forces who has distinguished himself by his excellent conduct, military qualities, ability to learn, and comradeship. A silver medal and a diploma are awarded annually.

• 1179 • Medalla Servicios Distinguidos a la Aviacion Naval
To recognize members of the Armed Forces for outstanding service.

• 1180 • Medalla Servicios Distinguidos en Orden Publico
To recognize members of the Armed Forces who have given their services to maintain public order, and who are outstanding for valor in action, above the normal call of duty. A Teutonic Cross and a diploma are awarded when merited.

• 1181 • Medalla Servicios Distinguidos la Fuerza de Superficie
To recognize members of the Armed Forces for outstanding service.

• 1182 • Medalla Tiempo de Servicio
To give public recognition to military personnel who have given distinguished service for at least 15 years. Gold, antique gold, silver, and bronze medals are awarded annually.

• 1183 • Orden del Merito Aeronautico Antonio Ricaurte
For recognition of members of the Colombian Air Force who have performed outstanding heroic and professional acts and contributed to the greatness of the nation. Awards are given in the following classes: (1) Great Cross; (2) Great Official; (3) Knight; and (4) Companion. A medal and a diploma are awarded annually. Established in 1948.

• 1184 • Orden del Merito Militar Antonio Narino
This, the highest award for military virtues, is conferred on the military and civilian personnel of the Colombian Military Forces. Awards are given in the following classes: (1) Great Cross; (2) Great Official; (3) Commander; (4) Official; (5) Knight; and (6) Companion. A medal and a diploma are awarded annually.

• 1185 • Orden del Merito Naval Almirante Padilla
For recognition of members of the Navy for outstanding services to the nation. Awards are given in the following classes: (1) Great Cross; (2) Great Official; (3) Official; and (4) Companion. A cross and a diploma are awarded annually.

• 1186 • Orden del Merito Sanitario Jose Fernandez Madrid
For recognition of personnel of the Health Section of the Armed Forces for extraordinary services in their profession. Awards are given in the following classes: (1) Grand Cross; (2) Grand Officer; (3) Office; (4) Knight; (5) Member; and (6) Commander. A medal and a diploma are awarded annually.

• 1187 • Orden Militar San Mateo
To recognize members of the Armed Forces who have performed historic acts of valor in defense of the nation. Awards are given in the following classes: (1) First Class Cross; (2) Second Class Cross; and (3) Third Class Cross. A cross and a diploma are awarded annually. Established in 1913.

• 1188 • Servicios Distinguidos a la Fuerza Submarina
To recognize members of the Armed Forces for outstanding service.

• 1189 • Medalla al Merito Logistico y Administrativo Contralmirante Rafael Tono
To recognize members of the Armed Forces for outstanding service. Awarded when merited.

• 1190 •
Colombia Ministry of Transportation
Avenida el Dorado
Bogota, Colombia
Phone: 57 1 3240800
Fax: 57 1 2215767
E-mail: mintrans@mintransporte.gov.co
Home Page: http://www.mintransporte.gov.co

• 1191 • Orden al Merito Julio Garavito
To recognize the merits of certified Colombian engineers who have rendered distinguished service to the nation. The following orders may be awarded: (1) Gran Cruz con Placa de Oro - the Great Cross with the Plaque of Gold. This may be awarded only to former Colombian presidents; (2) Gran Cruz the Great Cross is presented to those who have held the offices of the Minister of Dispatch, President of the Society of Colombian Engineers, Rector of the University, and Manager of the Department of Public Decentralization; (3) Gran Oficial - the Plaque of the Great Official is presented to those who have held the offices of Secretary General, Director of the Ministry, president of some society of engineers, of an academic group, or a national servant such as a congressional representative, or those who have merited the title of Professor Emeritus or won some of the prizes conferred by the Colombian Society of Engineers; (4) Cruz de Plata - the silver cross is presented to official organizations or jurists who have distinguished themselves in service to the country; (5) Cruz de Comendador - the Cross of Commendation is presented to those who have served as chief of a branch of the Ministry or the equivalent, a noted public servant or jurist, university professor of engineering, or persons of equivalent status; (6) Cruz Oficial - the Official Cross is presented to those who have served as chiefs of a Division of the Ministry, or its equivalent, members of professional councils of engineering and architecture, or held other public office; and (7) Cruz de Caballero - the Knight's Cross is presented to those who are judged by the Order's council to be deserving of the honor through professional service. Awarded annually. Established in 1963 by the President of the Republic.

• 1192 •
Alejandro Angel Escobar Foundation
(Fundacion Alejandro Angel Escobar)
Camila Botero, Dir.
Calle 26, No. 4A-45 Piso 10
Torre A 406
Bogota, Colombia
Phone: 57 1 281 8574
Fax: 57 1 243 3104
E-mail: faae@cable.net.co
Home Page: http://faae.org.co

• 1193 • Alejandro Angel Escobar Prizes (Premios de Beneficencia Alejandro Angel Escobar)
To recognize individuals who have performed outstanding works of public charity which will have lasting results in Colombia, such as work for hospitals, asylums, orphanages, leprosy centers, and schools and camps for poor children. A monetary prize of 35 million Colombian pesos, a silver medal, and a diploma are awarded annually. Established in 1954 by Dr. Angel Escobar in his will.

• 1194 •
National Academy of Medicine
(Academia Nacional de Medicina)
Cra. 7, No. 69-05
Bogota, Colombia
Phone: 57 1 3458890
E-mail: acadmed@cable.net.co
Home Page: http://anm.encolombia.com

• 1195 • **Concurso Nacional de Obras Medicas (National Contest of Medical Research Works)**
For recognition of achievements in Colombian medicine. Students and faculty of universities or institutions of higher learning who present original and unpublished works are eligible for awards. A monetary prize of 2,500,000 Colombian pesos, a medal and a diploma are awarded irregularly. Established in 1979. Additional information is available from Salvat Editores Colombiana, Division Medicina, Cra. 10a, No. 19-65, P-5 Bogota, Colombia, phone: 1 284 58 01.

• 1196 •
Pontificia Universidad Javeriana
Carrera 7, No. 40-62
Apartado Aereo 56710
Bogota, Colombia
Phone: 57 1 3208320
Fax: 57 1 2853348
E-mail: puj@javercol.javeriana.edu.co
Home Page: http://www.javeriana.edu.co

• 1197 • **Felix Restrepo Medal (Distincion Felix Restrepo)**
To acknowledge special bonds between the University and its graduates (Gold Class), and nongraduated benefactors (Silver Class). The Bronze Class is granted to celebrities who visit the University. Established 1990.

• 1198 •
Universidad del Valle
Calle 13 No. 100-00
Cali, Colombia
Phone: 57 2 3212100
Fax: 57 2 3398520
Home Page: http://www.univalle.edu.co

• 1199 • **Gran Cruz de la Universidad del Valle**
For recognition of outstanding services to the University by those serving on the staff, or for outstanding investigations and intellectual contributions by members of the University community. Faculty members who have been retired for over a year, who have been residents of the state of Valle for more than fifteen years, and who hold no public office are eligible. A cross is awarded annually. Established in 1954.

Costa Rica

• 1200 •
Costa Rica Ministry of Culture, Youth and Sport
Guido Saenz, Min.
Apartado 10227
San Jose 1000, Costa Rica
Phone: 506 331471
Fax: 506 337066
E-mail: mincjd@costarricense.cr
Home Page: http://www.mcjdcr.go.cr

• 1201 • **Aquileo J. Echeverria Prize**
To recognize Costa Rican citizens for excellence in the fields of literature (novel, short story, poetry, essay, scientific literature); history; theatre; music; and fine arts. Monetary prizes of 250,000 colones divided amongst the selected works, the total sum of awards not exceeding 8,000,000 Costa Rican colones, and a certificate are awarded annually. Established in 1962.

• 1202 • **Joaquin Garcia Monge Prize**
To recognize a foreign or Costa Rican journalist for promoting and disseminating literary, scientific and artistic works of Costa Ricans, or for pointing out cultural values of Costa Rica. Monetary prize of 818,800 colones and honorary recognition are awarded annually.

• 1203 • **Premio Nacional de Ciencias y Tecnologia Clodomiro Picado Twight**
For recognition of works in science and technology in the interest of Costa Rican cities. Costa Rican citizens under 36 years of age are eligible. Monetary prizes of 679,000 Costa Rican colones are awarded in alternate fields annually. Established in 1976.

• 1204 • **Premio Nacional de Periodismo Pio Viquez**
To recognize a journalist for outstanding contributions. Monetary prizes of 250,000 Costa Rican colones are awarded annually. Established in 1972.

• 1205 • **Premio Nacional de Teatro**
For recognition of achievement in the theatre. The following awards are presented: (1) Premio Olga Zuniza - best young actress; (2) Premio Eugenio Arias - best young actor; (3) best actress; (4) best actor; (5) best supporting actress; (6) best supporting actor; (7) best director; (8) best scenario; and (9) best theatrical group. Monetary prizes of 250,000 Costa Rican colones and a plaque are awarded annually. Established in 1972.

• 1206 •
Inter-American Institute for Cooperation on Agriculture
(Instituto Interamericano de Cooperacion para la Agricultura)
600 m. noreste del Cruce Ipis
Coronado, San Isidro de Coronado
Apto. 6742-1000
San Jose, Costa Rica
Phone: 506 2160222
Fax: 506 2160258
E-mail: iica.cr@iica.int
Home Page: http://www.iica.int/costarica

• 1207 • **Inter-American Agricultural Award for Young Professionals (Premio Agricola Interamericano para Profesionales Jovenes)**
To recognize young professionals in the agricultural sciences who have distinguished themselves in any of the areas covered by IICA's programs and who have demonstrated an outstanding willingness to serve, exceptional initiative and dedication in working for the well-being of the rural population, and an ability to program and carry out activities that contribute to improving methods used in agriculture and in social and enterprise systems. Candidates must be under 35 years of age at the time of nomination. A monetary award of $10,000 US and a certificate are presented biennially honoring only one candidate per IICA area. Established in 1976.

• 1208 • **Inter-American Agricultural Medal (Medalla Agricola Interamericano)**
For international recognition of those professionals who have distinguished themselves through outstanding contributions to the development of agriculture and the improvement of rural life in the Americas. Professionals who work or have worked in any of the fields covered by the programs of the Inter-American Institute for Cooperation on Agriculture are eligible, regardless of age, sex, profession, occupation, nationality, residence or other factors. A gold medal and a certificate are presented biennially. Established in 1957.

• 1209 • **Inter-American Award for the Participation of Women in Rural Development (Premio Interamericano a la Participacion de la Mujer en el Desarrollo Rural)**
For international public recognition of those women who have distinguished themselves through important contributions to the rural development process in general, and to improving the quality of life, in particular, in their own countries or in other countries in the Americas. A gold medal and a certificate are presented biennially. Established in 1979.

• 1210 •
Inter-American Institute for Cooperation on Agriculture - Costa Rica
(Instituto Interamericano de Cooperacion para la Agricultura)
Chelston W.D. Brathwaite, Dir. Gen.
PO Box 55-2200
San Isidro de Coronado
San Jose, Costa Rica
Phone: 506 2160222
Fax: 506 2160233
E-mail: iicahq@iica.ac.cr
Home Page: http://www.iica.int

• 1211 • **Inter-American Agricultural Award for Young Professionals**

• 1212 • **Inter-American Agricultural Medal**
To scientists.

• 1213 • **Inter-American Award for the Participation of Women in Rural Development**

Awards are arranged in alphabetical order below their administering organizations

Cote d'Ivoire

• 1214 •
Africa Rice Center
(Centre du riz pour l'Afrique de l'Ouest)
Dr. Kanayo F. Nwanze, Dir.Gen.
BP 2551
Bouake 01, Cote d'Ivoire
Phone: 225 31659300
Fax: 225 31659311
E-mail: warda@cgiar.org
Home Page: http://www.warda.cgiar.org/

• 1215 • **King Baudouin Award of EGIAR 2000**
Award of recognition. Inquire for additional details.

Croatia

• 1216 •
Croatian Chess Federation
(Hrvatski Sahovski Savez)
Sindik Ervin, Gen.Sec.
Trg. Sportova 11
CT-10000 Zagreb, Croatia
Phone: 385 1 3012352
Phone: 385 91 3837613
Fax: 385 1 3012352
E-mail: hss@zg.htnet.hr
Home Page: http://www.crochess.com

• 1217 • **Cups**
Awards of recognition. Presented annually in the categories of best team, best player, best senior, and best junior.

• 1218 •
Croatian Library Association
(Hrvatsko Bibliotekarsko Drustvo)
Alemka Belan-Simic, Pres.
% National and University Library
Hrvatske bratske zajednice 4
CT-10000 Zagreb, Croatia
Phone: 385 1 615 9320
Fax: 385 1 615 9320
E-mail: hkd@nsk.hr
Home Page: http://www.hkdrustvo.hr

• 1219 • **Kukuljevic's Charter (Kukuljevic Charter)**
For recognition of achievement in librarianship to prominent librarians with many years of experience (age 50 and older). Society membership is necessary for consideration. A charter is awarded at the CLA convention irregularly. Established in 1968 in honor of Croatia's meritorious bibliophile and bibliographer Ivan Kukuljevic Sakcinski (1816-1889).

• 1220 • **Nagrada Eva Verona Award**
Recognizes achievement in librarianship to young librarians (age 35 or younger). Society membership is necessary for consideration. A charter is awarded at the CLA convention every two years. The award has been named by the professor Eva Verona, PhD (1905-1996), who was Croatia's eminent librarian and scientist in the field of cataloging. Established in 1998.

• 1221 •
Croatian National Theatre Split
(Hrvatsko narodno kazaliste Split)
Trg Gaje Bulata 1
Porinova 4
CT-21000 Split, Croatia
Phone: 385 21 344 999
Fax: 385 21 344 999
E-mail: webmaster@hnk-split.hr
Home Page: http://www.hnk-split.hr

• 1222 • **MarulKs Days Festival**
To celebrate Croatian drama, the festival is a part of a wider cultural event organized and centered on the work of Marko Marulic, a writer considered to be the father of Croatian literature. The festival takes place every year in late April. Bronze sculptures created by Kazimir Hraste are awarded annually. Established in 1991.

• 1223 • **Split Summer Festival (Splitsko ljeto)**
To recognize achievement in opera, drama and ballet programs of the festival. It takes place every year from July 14 to August 14. Bronze sculptures by Vasko Lipovac are awarded annually. Established in 1984 by the journal *Danas,* in memory of Marko Marulic, the first writer on Croatian language. Sponsored by the Split newspaper, *Slobodna Dalmacija.*

• 1224 •
Croatian Pharmaceutical Society
(Hrvatsko Farmaceutsko Drustvo)
Masarykova 2/II
HR-10000 Zagreb, Croatia
Phone: 385 1 4872849
Fax: 385 1 4872853
E-mail: sluter@pharma.hr
Home Page: http://public.srce.hr/acphee/hfd.html

Formerly: (1991) Farmaceutsko drustvo Hrvatske.

• 1225 • **Julije Domac Medal (Medalja Julije Domac)**
For recognition of a contribution to the development of pharmaceutical science and the profession. Members of the Society are eligible. A medal is awarded annually when merited. Established in 1955 in memory of Julije Domac, professor of The Pharmaceutical Faculty in Zagreb, Institute for Pharmacognosy (1886 to 1924).

• 1226 •
International Animated Film Association
(Association Internationale du Film d'Animation)
Vesna Dovnikovic, Gen.Sec.
Hrvatskog proljeca 36
CT-10040 Zagreb, Croatia
Phone: 385 1 2991395
Fax: 385 1 2991395
E-mail: secretary@asifa.net
Home Page: http://asifa.net

• 1227 • **ASIFA Special Award (Prix Special ASIFA)**
To recognize a film or person or entity for the best contribution to international understanding through the art of animation. Nomination may be made to the ASIFA Board. Established in 1985.

• 1228 •
International Federation for Medical and Biological Engineering
(Federation Internationale de Genie Medical et Biologique)
Ratko Magjarevic, Sec. Gen.
Faculty of Electrical Engineering and Computing
Univ. of Zagreb
Unska 3
HR-10000 Zagreb, Croatia
Phone: 385 1 6129938
Fax: 385 1 6129652
E-mail: office@ifmbe.org
Home Page: http://www.ifmbe.org

• 1229 • **The IFMBE Otto Schmitt Award**
For exceptional contributions to the advancement of the field of medical and biological engineering.

• 1230 • **The IUPESM Awards of Merit**
For medical physicists and biomedical engineers who have established distinguished careers in medical physics and biomedical engineering.

• 1231 • **Nightingale Award**
To the best paper in the federation's journal.

• 1232 • **John E. Read Medal**
For distinguished contribution to international law and organizations.

• 1233 • **Sylvie Gravel Prize**
For the best postgraduate thesis in public or private international law.

• 1234 • **The IFMBE Vladimir K. Zworykin Award**
For outstanding research contributions in the field of medical and biological engineering.

• 1235 •
Republic of Croatia Ministry of Science, Education and Sports
(Republika Hrvatska)
Stanislava Rogic, Sec.Gen.
Trg hrvatskih velikana 6
CT-10000 Zagreb, Croatia
Phone: 385 1 4569 000
Fax: 385 1 4617 962
E-mail: office@mzos.hr
Home Page: http://www.mzos.hr

• 1236 • **Annual Award for Junior Researchers**
To recognize prominent work of young researchers, publishing a prominent article in a

journal with an international review or in a journal of corresponding excellence, or for publishing a book. Each year 7,000 Kuna is awarded.

• 1237 • **Annual Award for Popularization and Promotion of Science**
To recognize contribution in spreading scientific knowledge through popular presentation of valuable professional and scientific knowledge and other forms of presentation in the following fields: natural sciences; biomedical sciences; technical sciences; biotechnical sciences; social sciences; and the humanities. A monetary award equal to 7,000 Croatian kuna is awarded; up to three awards shall be awarded annually for all fields.

• 1238 • **Annual Science Award**
To recognize important scientific achievement, scientific innovation, and application of results obtained by scientific-research activities in the following fields: natural sciences, biomedical sciences, technical sciences, biotechnical sciences, social sciences and humanities. A Monetary award equal to 10,000 Croation kuno is awarded. Up to three awards can be awarded annually for each scientific field.

• 1239 • **Ivan Filipovic Award**
To recognize research work in the field of education and teaching, the promotion of pedagogical theory and practice, and the development of educational systems in general. A monetary prize of 5,000 dinars is awarded annually. An additional prize of 20,000 dinars is given annually for life-long contributions to teaching. Awarded annually. Established in 1964.

• 1240 •
Zagreb World Festival of Animated Films
(Svjetski Festival Animiranih Filmova, Zagreb)
Margit Antauer, Mng.Dir.
Kneza Mislava 18
CT-10000 Zagreb, Croatia
Phone: 385 1 4501 190
Fax: 385 1 4501 193
E-mail: animafest@kdz.hr
Home Page: http://www.animafest.hr

• 1241 • **World Festival of Animated Films**
(Svjetski Festival Animiranih Filmova)
To promote and advance the art and production of animated film in general, recalling the past through national, personal, or thematic retrospectives, and to assess recent worldwide film production via both competitive and non-competitive programs. Awards are given for various categories in both feature films and short films. In addition, such special awards as a Lifetime Achievement Award are presented. Held biennially in even-numbered years. Established in 1972.

Cuba

• 1242 •
International Association of Crime Writers
(Asociacion International de Escritores Policiacos)
Jose Latour, Contact
Apartado Postal No. 6067
Havana 10600, Cuba
Phone: 53 78816176
Fax: 53 78816176
E-mail: alaiep@cubarte.cult.cu
Home Page: http://jmc.ou.edu/AIEP

• 1243 • **Dashiell Hammett Award**
To recognize literary excellence in the field of crime writing, as reflected in a book published in the English language in the United States and/or Canada during the preceding year. Only U.S. or Canadian citizens or permanent residents are eligible. A statuette is awarded annually.

Cyprus

• 1244 •
International Federation of Sports Medicine
(Federation Internationale de Medecine du Sport)
PO Box 25137
Nicosia 1307, Cyprus
Phone: 357 22 663762
Fax: 357 22 664669
E-mail: sportsmedicine@cytanet.com.cy
Home Page: http://www.fims.org

• 1245 • **Gold Medal**
To recognize outstanding contributions to sports medicine over a period of years in leadership, education, research and practice. Nominations may be made by the Executive Committee to the Council of Delegates. A gold medal is presented biennially when the Council of Delegates meets. Established in 1932.

Czech Republic

• 1246 •
Academy of Sciences of the Czech Republic
(Akademie Ved Ceske Republiky)
Prof. Jiri Niederle, Contact
Narodni tr. 3
CZ-117 20 Prague 1, Czech Republic
Phone: 42 224240532
Phone: 42 221403111
Fax: 42 224240608
E-mail: info@cas.cz
Home Page: http://www.cas.cz/

• 1247 • **Academy of Sciences of the Czech Republic Awards**
Recognizes outstanding results to young scientists for popularization of science, medals are given for major contributions to science. Monetary awards are given three times per year.

• 1248 •
Czech Chemical Society
(Ceska Spolecnost Chemicka)
Marketa Blahova, Sec.
Novotneho Lavka 5
CZ-116 68 Prague 1, Czech Republic
Phone: 42 2 21082383
Phone: 42 2 22220184
Fax: 42 2 22220184
E-mail: csch@csch.cz
Home Page: http://www.csch.cz

• 1249 • **Alfred Bader Prize**
To recognize young Czech organic and bio-organic chemists for scientific achievement. Awarded to two individuals annually.

• 1250 • **Hanus Medal**
This, the highest award bestowed by the Society, recognizes high scientific achievements in chemistry. Awarded to one or more recipients annually.

• 1251 •
Czech Chopin Society
(Spolecnost Fryderyka Chopina v CSSR)
Prof. Ivan Klansky, Pres.
Chopin House
Hlavni 47
CZ-353 01 Marianske Lazne, Czech Republic
Phone: 42 354 622617
Fax: 42 354 622617
E-mail: info@chopinfestival.cz
Home Page: http://www.chopinfestival.cz

• 1252 • **Chopin Piano Competition**
(Cena Chopinovy klavirni souteze)
To encourage students of music, between the ages of 15 to 25, who are citizens of the Czech Republic and from any music school, conservatory, or academy. A monetary prize and a plaque are awarded biennially. Established in 1962 by the Chopin Society in memory of Frederik Chopin, a Polish composer who visited Marienbad in 1836. Sponsored by the cultural and social centre in Marianske Lazne/ Marienbad.

• 1253 •
Czech Radio, Radio Prague
(Cesky Rozhlas, Praga)
Vinohradska 12
CZ-120 99 Prague 2, Czech Republic
Phone: 42 2 2155 29317
Fax: 42 2 2155 2903
E-mail: cr@radio.cz
Home Page: http://www.radio.cz

• 1254 • **Concertino Prague International Radio Competition for Young Musicians**
(Mezinarodni rozhlasova soutez Mladych hudebniku Concertino Praga)
To recognize young talented musicians and enable them to compare their skills on an international scale, to acquaint the broad radio audiences with their performances, and to assist in establishing contacts among the youngest artis-

Awards are arranged in alphabetical order below their administering organizations

tic generation. The competition is open to soloists in the categories of piano, violin, and violoncello. Musicians no older than 16 years of age are eligible. Candidates take part in the competition through tape recordings sent in by radio organizations associated in the European Broadcasting Union. Each radio organization can enter one participant in each competition category. In case one of the three instruments is not represented, the second competitor may be admitted for one of the remaining categories. The selection of soloists whose performances have to be judged is made by the participating radio organization itself. The deadline for sending in the application is April 30. The deadline for submitting recordings is August 31. In each competition category, the jury awards first and second prizes. On consideration, the jury may award an honorary diploma to runners-up whose score comes close to those of the first and second prize winners. The winners, first, and second prize laureates are invited by the organizer to perform at public concerts in Prague and at the South Bohemia Concertino Praga Festival to defend their victory. The concerts are offered to members of the broadcasting unions for live or delayed broadcasts. Expenses for the winners' stay in Prague and at the South Bohemian Concertino Praga Festival, and travel to and from the Festival are paid by Czech Radio. Awarded annually. Established in 1966.

• 1255 •
Czech Television
Jiri Janecek, Dir.Gen.
Kavci hory
CZ-140 70 Prague 4, Czech Republic
Phone: 42 261 131 111
Fax: 42 261 218 599
E-mail: info@ceskatelevize.cz
Home Page: http://www.ceskatelevize.cz

Formerly: Czechoslovak Television, Prague.

• 1256 • **International Television Festival Golden Prague**
(Mezinarodni Televizni Festival Zlata Praha)
To present television music programs, promote their international exchanges, and initiate production of original programs created for the television medium. The competition is divided into two categories: Dramatic music programs, including operas, operettas, musicals, singspiels, and dance programs presented on television or produced for television; and concert works and other types of music programs, including portraits of musicians, documentary music programs, and other such programs created by television or film techniques. In both categories, programs may be shown which are parts of serials but form separate artistic wholes, and can be judged separately. Recommended footage is 10 minutes minimum and 90 minutes maximum for dramatic music programs, and 60 minutes for concert works and other types of music programs. Applicants may enter programs in both categories. Any television organization (broadcasting television programs) can take part in the festival as well as producer companies, provided that they submit applications in keeping with the rules of the competition. The Golden Prague trophy and a monetary prize of 10,000 DM are awarded. In each category, the "Czech Crystal" is awarded to the best program. In each category, three honorable mentions can be awarded. Deadline for entries is February 10.

• 1257 •
Festa Musicale
PO Box 55
CZ-771 11 Olomouc, Czech Republic
Phone: 42 585 237 373
Fax: 42 585 237 373
E-mail: festamusicale@atlas.cz
Home Page: http://www.festamusicale.cz

• 1258 • **Iuventus Mundi Cantat Competition**
For recognition of achievement in the singing competition, Iuventus Mundi Cantat. Members of choirs of all categories, including pre-school children's choir; children's choirs; selected choirs; boys' choirs; youth choirs; women choirs; men's choirs; and others are eligible. Winners are awarded by jury according to their gained points. Gold, silver, and bronze medals are awarded biennially at the Festival "Holidays of Songs." Established in 1987 by the Ministry of Culture.

• 1259 •
International Union of Speleology
(Union Internationale de Speleologie)
Pavel Bosak, Sec. Gen.
Geological Institute
Academy of Sciences
Rozvojova 135
CZ-165 02 Prague, Czech Republic
Phone: 42 2 72772795
Phone: 42 2 20922392
Fax: 42 2 20922670
E-mail: bosak@gli.cas.cz
Home Page: http://www.uis-speleo.org

• 1260 • **IUS Poster Prize**

• 1261 • **IUS Prize for the Most Significant Discovery**

• 1262 • **IUS Prize for the Most Significant Publication on a Cave or Karst Topic**

• 1263 •
Prague Spring International Music Festival
(Mezinarodni hudebni festival Prazske jaro)
Ing. Roman Belor, Dir.
Hellichova 18
CZ-118 00 Prague 1, Czech Republic
Phone: 42 257 312547
Fax: 42 257 313725
E-mail: info@festival.cz
Home Page: http://www.festival.cz

• 1264 • **Prague Spring International Music Competition**
(Mezinarodni hudebni soutez Prazske jaro)
For recognition of an outstanding performance in the field of music by young talent. Categories change annually, and there may be more than one category within any given competition. The competition in 2000 is for conducting and cello. Monetary awards are given in the amounts of 200,000 Czechoslovak crowns for first place, 70,000 Czechoslovak crowns for second. Additional prizes and engagements are awarded. Awarded annually. Established in 1948. Sponsored by the Ministry of Culture.

• 1265 •
Society for Geology Applied to Mineral Deposits
(Societe de Geologie Appliquee aux Gites Mineraux)
Jan Pasava, Exec. Sec.
Czech Geological Survey
Klarov 131/3
CZ-118 21 Prague, Czech Republic
Phone: 42 2 51085506
Fax: 42 2 51818748
E-mail: secretary@e-sga.org
Home Page: http://www.e-sga.org

• 1266 • **Best Referee Award from Mineralum Deposits**
Award of recognition.

• 1267 • **Mineralium Deposita Best Paper Award**
For mineralium deposita paper.

• 1268 • **SGA Young Scientist Award**
To a young scientist who contributed significantly to the understanding of mineral deposits.

• 1269 •
Society of Czech Architects
(Obec Architektu)
Karee Doubner, Pres.
Revolucni 23
CZ-110 15 Prague 1, Czech Republic
Phone: 42 257 535025
Phone: 42 257 535024
Fax: 42 257 535033
E-mail: obecarch@architekt.cz
Home Page: http://www.architekt.cz

Formerly: (1990) Union of Czech Architects.

• 1270 • **Grand Prix Annual Prize of the Society of Czech Architects**
(Cena Obce Architektu za Realizaci Roku)
For recognition of contemporary national architecture in the fields of new buildings, reconstructions, interior design, town planning, landscape architecture, and garden design. The competition is open to projects designed by Czech or foreign architects and created in the territory of the Czech Republic. Established in 1993.

Denmark

• 1271 •
Association of European Toxicologists and European Societies of Toxicology
Prof. Hermann Autrup MD, Pres.
Dept. of Environmental and Occupational Medicine
University of Arhus
Vennelyst Blvd. 6
8000 Arhus, Denmark
Phone: 45 89426180
Fax: 45 89426199
E-mail: ha@mil.au.dk
Home Page: http://www.eurotox.com

• 1272 • **Merit Award**
Award of recognition. Toxicologist with an outstanding careers are eligible. Awarded annually.

• 1273 • **Young Scientist's Poster Award**
Recognizes an outstanding poster on the results of experimental investigation. Scientist age 35 or under at the annual congress are eligible. Awarded annually.

• 1274 • **Gerhard Zbinden Memorial Lecture Award**
Recognizes outstanding research contribution recently made to drug and/or chemical toxicology. Awarded annually.

• 1275 •
Danish Academy of Technical Sciences (Akademiet for de tekniske Videnskaber)
Klaus H. Ostenfeld, Pres./CEO
266 Lundtoftevej
DK-2800 Lyngby, Denmark
Phone: 45 45881311
Fax: 45 45881351
E-mail: atvmail@atv.dk
Home Page: http://www.atv.dk

• 1276 • **Knud Lind Larsen Prize**
Recognizes a young Danish chemistry researcher who is outstanding in the field and shows potential for future growth. Awarded biennially.

• 1277 •
Danish Association for International Cooperation - Denmark (Mellemfolkeligt Samvirke)
Bjorn Forde, Sec.Gen.
Borgergade 14
DK-1300 Copenhagen K, Denmark
Phone: 45 77310000
Fax: 45 77310101
E-mail: ms@ms.dk
Home Page: http://www.ms.dk

• 1278 • **MS-Prize**
A monetary prize is given annually. Inquire for additional details.

• 1279 •
Danish Association of the Specialist Press (Dansk Fagpresse)
Mr. Christian Kierkegaard, Dir.
Pressens Hus
Skindergade 7
DK-1159 Copenhagen K, Denmark
Phone: 45 33974000
Fax: 45 33912670
E-mail: df@danskfagpresse.dk
Home Page: http://www.danskfagpresse.dk

• 1280 • **Anders-Bording Prisen**
To recognize a freelance journalist. Awarded annually.

• 1281 •
Danish Jazz Federation (Dansk Jazzforbund)
Nytorv 3, 3 sal.
DK-1450 Copenhagen, Denmark
Phone: 45 33 454300
Fax: 45 33 454311
E-mail: info@djazz.dk
Home Page: http://dansk.jazz.dk

Formerly: (1997) Danish Jazz Center; Danish Jazz Association.

• 1282 • **Jazzpar Prize**
To recognize an internationally known and fully active jazz artist who especially deserves further recognition. A monetary prize of 200,000 Danish kroner, a statuette, a prize concert tour, and recordings are awarded annually. Established in 1988. Sponsored by the Scandinavian Tobacco Company.

• 1283 •
Danish Library Association (Danmarks Biblioteksforening)
Vesterbrogade 20, 5 sal
DK-1620 Copenhagen V, Denmark
Phone: 45 33250935
Fax: 45 33257900
E-mail: dbf@dbf.dk
Home Page: http://www.dbf.dk/

• 1284 • **R. Lysholt Hansens Bibliotekspris**
To recognize special achievement in library or cultural work. Nominations must be submitted. A monetary award is presented annually when merited. Established in 1983 to honor R. Lysholt Hansen.

• 1285 • **Edvard Pedersens Biblioteksfonds Forfatterpris**
To recognize outstanding authors. A monetary award is presented annually. Established in 1986 to honor Edvard Pedersen.

• 1286 •
Danish Samoyed Club (Samojedhunde Klubben I Danmark)
Eva Nielsen, Pres.
Hollose Gade 42
DK-3210 Vejby, Denmark
Phone: 45 48702408
E-mail: formand@samojed.dk
Home Page: http://www.samojed.dk

• 1287 • **Samoyed of the Year: Male, Female, Veteran, Senior, and Danish Champion in Sledge Racing**
A trophy is awarded annually.

• 1288 •
Danish Women's Society (Dansk Kvindesamfund)
Karen Hallberg, Pres.
Niels Hemmingsensgade 10
DK-1153 Copenhagen K, Denmark
Phone: 45 33157837
Fax: 45 33157837
E-mail: kontor@kvindesamfund.dk
Home Page: http://www.kvindesamfund.dk

• 1289 • **Mathilde Award**
Presented to people who have made outstanding contributions to women's struggle for equality. Awarded to one or more recipients annually.

• 1290 •
Danish Writers Association (Dansk Forfatterforening)
Knud Vilby, Chm.
Strandgade 6
DK-1401 Copenhagen K, Denmark
Phone: 45 32955100
Phone: 45 32955989
Fax: 45 32540115
E-mail: danskforfatterforening @danskforfatterforening.dk
Home Page: http://www .danskforfatterforening.dk/

• 1291 • **Emil Aarestrup Prize**
To recognize a poet. A monetary prize of 5,000 Danish kroner and a medal are awarded annually. Established in 1950 in commemoration of the Danish lyric poet, Carl Ludwig Emil Aarestrup.

• 1292 • **Dansk Oversaetterforbunds Aerespris**
For recognition of an outstanding translation of foreign literature into Danish. A monetary prize of 30,000 Danish kroner and a diploma are awarded annually. Established in 1954. Sponsored by Denmark - Ministry of Cultural Affairs.

• 1293 • **Holberg Medal**
To provide recognition for outstanding contributions to Danish literature. A monetary prize of 30,000 Danish kroner and a medal are awarded annually.

• 1294 • **Martin Andersen Nex Prize**
To recognize the author of an outstanding work of literature. A monetary prize of 5,000 Danish kroner is awarded annually. Established in 1956 to commemorate the Danish socialist writer, Nex, who spent the last years of his life in Dresden.

• 1295 •
Dansk Journalistforbund
Lars Poulsen, Contact
Gammel Strand 46
DK-1202 Copenhagen K, Denmark
Phone: 45 33428000
Fax: 45 33428003
E-mail: dj@journalistforbundet.dk
Home Page: http://www.journalistforbundet.dk

• 1296 • **Cavling Prize**
For outstanding journalism. Awarded annually.

• 1297 • **Carsten Nielsen Prize**
Award of recognition. A monetary prize of 20,000 kroner is awarded annually.

• 1298 •
European Thyroid Association
(Association Europeenne Thyroide)
Prof. Albert Burger, Sec.-Treas.
Endocrine Division
Department of Medicine P2132
National University Hospital
Blegdamsvej 9
DK-2100 Copenhagen, Denmark
Phone: 45 35452337
Fax: 33 35452240
E-mail: enquiries@eurothyroid.com
Home Page: http://www.eurothyroid.com

• 1299 • **European Thyroid Association Awards**
To recognize physicians and research scientists who are involved in work on the thyroid gland and its diseases. The following awards are presented: Henning Prize, Harington-De Visscher Prize, Lissitzky Career Award, Merck KGaA Prize, and the M. Pierre Koenig/Organon/Nourpharma Poster Prize.

• 1300 •
Federation of Danish Architects
(Danske Arkitekters Landsforbund/Akademisk Arkitektforening)
Strandgade 27A
DK-1401 Copenhagen K, Denmark
Phone: 45 32 836900
Fax: 45 32 836901
E-mail: aa@dal-aa.dk
Home Page: http://dal-aa.dk/aa

• 1301 • **Kaleidoscope of Honor (Aereskalejdoskop)**
For recognition of achievement in architecture. Public authorities, institutions or private persons who have set or solved architectural tasks in an inspiring way within one or more of the fields of architecture are eligible for nomination. A trophy is awarded annually. Established in 1979.

• 1302 •
Geological Society of Denmark
(Dansk Geologisk Forening)
Geologisk Museum
Oster Voldgade 5-7
DK-1350 Copenhagen K, Denmark
Phone: 45 3532 2354
Fax: 45 3532 2325
E-mail: sekretariat@2dgf.dk
Home Page: http://www.2dgf.dk

• 1303 • **Steno Medal (Steno Medaljen)**
To recognize contributions within the field of geological sciences. The medal is awarded to foreigners and, in special cases, also to Danes. A gold medal is awarded at least every fifth year. Established in 1969 in the memory of Niels Stensen (Nicolai Stenonis) on the tercentary of the publication of his "De solido intra solidum naturaliter contento dissertationis prodromus."

• 1304 •
Gyldendaal
Nordisk Forlag A/S
Klareboderne 3
DK-1001 Copenhagen K, Denmark
Phone: 45 33 755555
Fax: 45 33 755556
E-mail: gyldendal@gyldendal.dk
Home Page: http://www.gyldendal.dk

• 1305 • **Soren Gyldendal Prisen**
To recognize authors of fiction or of scientific or educational work. A writer in the middle of his or her creative process is eligible. A monetary prize of 100,000 Danish kroner is awarded annually. Established in 1958 in memory of Soren Gyldendal, founder of Gyldendal, in connection with his birthday, April 12 (1742).

• 1306 •
International Association of Geodesy
(Association Internationale de Geodesie)
C.C. Tscherning, Gen.Sec.
Juliane Maries Vej 30
University of Copenhagen
DK-2100 Copenhagen O, Denmark
Phone: 45 35 320600
Fax: 45 35 365357
E-mail: iag@gfy.ku.dk
Home Page: http://www.iag-aig.org

• 1307 • **Guy Bomford Prize**
For recognition of outstanding individual contributions to geodetic studies. Individuals under 40 years of age are eligible. A monetary prize of $2,000 is awarded every four years at the General Assembly. Established in 1975 in honor of Brigadier Guy Bomford, formerly President of the International Association of Geodesy and Chairman of the British National Committee.

• 1308 •
International Society for Neurochemistry
(Societe Internationale de Neurochimie)
Dr. Arne Schousboe, Pres.
Dept. of Pharmacology
Danish University of Pharmaceutical Sciences
2 Universitsparken
DK-2100 Copenhagen, Denmark
Phone: 45 35306330
Fax: 45 35306021
E-mail: as@dfuni.dk
Home Page: http://www.neurochem.org

• 1309 • **Young Scientist Award**
To recognize individuals for outstanding contributions to neuroscience. Scientists who are less than 35 years of age may be nominated. A travel award is presented biennially. Established in 1989.

• 1310 •
Nicolai Malko International Competition for Young Conductors
Mikael Beier, Gen.Sec.
Rosenorns Alle 22
DK-1999 Frederiksberg C, Denmark
Phone: 45 3520 6371
Fax: 45 3520 6321
E-mail: malko@dr.dk
Home Page: http://www.dr.dk/malko

• 1311 • **Nicolai Malko International Competition for Young Conductors**
For recognition of the best performance of young conductors between 20 and 31 years of age. The following monetary awards are presented: first prize - $10,000 U.S.; second prize - 40,000 Danish kroner; third prize - 30,000 Danish kroner; fourth prize - 20,000 Danish kroner; fifth prize - 15,000 Danish kroner; and sixth prize - 10,000 Danish kroner. Awarded triennially. Established in 1965. Sponsored by Danmarks Radio and the Nicolai Malko Foundation. Application form due before January 15. Brochure available by request to Malko Secretariat.

• 1312 •
Carl Nielsen International Music Competitions
(Internationale Carl Nielsen Musik Konkurrencer)
Minna Jeppesen, Admin.
Odense Symphony Orchestra
Claus Bergs Gade 9
DK-5000 Odense C, Denmark
Phone: 45 6612 0057
Fax: 45 6591 0047
E-mail: orchestra@odensesymfoni.dk
Home Page: http://www.odensesymfoni.dk

• 1313 • **Carl Nielsen International Music Competitions (De Internationale Carl Nielsen Musik Konkurrencer)**
To recognize musicians of outstanding talent under 30 years of age and of all nationalities. Three separate competitions are held, for violin, clarinet, and flute. Monetary prizes totaling ap-

proximately DKK350,000 and concert engagements are awarded. Held every four years. Established in 1980 to honor the Danish composer Carl Nielsen.

• 1314 •
Novo Nordisk Foundation
Gert Almind, Dir.
Brogardsvej 70
Post Box 71
DK-2820 Gentofte, Denmark
Phone: 45 444 39035
Fax: 45 444 39098
E-mail: nnfond@novo.dk
Home Page: http://www.novonordiskfonden.dk

• 1315 • **H. C. Jacobaeus Lectures**
The lectures should be held in Scandinavian university cities or other European cities with association to medical research. The subject of the lectures should be within the field of physiology or endocrinology. A monetary award of 50,000 Danish kroner is presented in connection with the lecture. Awarded annually. Established in 1939.

• 1316 • **August Krogh Prize**
For recognition of outstanding research in medical sciences. Any Danish doctor is eligible. A monetary award of 100,000 Danish kroner is awarded annually. Established in 1969.

• 1317 • **Novo Nordisk Foundation Lecture**
For recognition of outstanding scientific work within the field of diabetes research and/or treatment. A monetary award of 50,000 Danish kroner is presented annually to an active outstanding Nordic scientist. The lecture is given in connection with the annual meeting of the Scandinavian Society for the Study of Diabetes (SSSD). Established in 1995.

• 1318 • **Novo Nordisk Prize**
To recognize a considerable contribution in the field of medical science. A monetary personal award of 250,000 Danish kroner and an award of 750,000 Danish kroner to be used for research is presented annually to a scientist working in a Danish university or institution.

• 1319 •
Odense Film Festival
Cecilia Lidin, Dir.
Norregade 36-38
DK-5100 Odense C, Denmark
Phone: 45 66 131372
Fax: 45 65 910144
E-mail: filmfestival@odense.dk
Home Page: http://www.filmfestival.dk

• 1320 • **Odense International Film Festival**
For recognition of outstanding films in the following categories: Fairy tale films, including live or animated films of 45 minutes maximum running time and experimental/imaginative films. The following awards are presented: Most Imaginative Film - 15,000 Danish kroner; Most Surprising Film - 15,000 Danish kroner; Personal prizes of each member of the jury 5,000 Danish kroner. Awarded annually. Established in 1975.

• 1321 •
Odense International Organ Competition and Festival
Kultursekretariatet
Norregade 36-38
DK-5100 Odense M, Denmark
Phone: 45 5194 1816
E-mail: jr@organcompetition.dk
Home Page: http://www.organcompetition.dk

• 1322 • **International Organ Competition, Odense**
For recognition of young organists of all nationalities. The deadline for application is April 1. The following prizes are awarded biennially: first prize - 40,000 Danish kroner; second prize - 15,000 Danish kroner; third prize - 10,000 Danish kroner; and fourth prize - 5,000 Danish kroner. Organ pipes with inscription are also awarded. Special prize for the best performance of the Danish piece - 5,000 Danish kroner. The organ pipes are donated by the organ-builder, Marcussen and Son, Aabenraa. Established in 1986 under the patronage of His Royal Highness, Prince Henrik of Denmark.

• 1323 •
The Royal Danish Academy of Fine Arts
Akademiraadet
Kongens Nytorv 1
Postboks 9042
DK-1022 Copenhagen, Denmark
Phone: 45 33 744910
Fax: 45 33 156841
E-mail: info@akademiraadet.dk
Home Page: http://www.akademiraadet.dk

• 1324 • **Thorvald Bindesboll Medal**
To recognize an individual for an achievement of high value within the fields of applied art and industrial graphic art. Individuals who are not members of the Council of the Academy are eligible. A bronze medal designed by the sculptor and painter, Poul Gernes, is awarded when merited. Established in 1979 in commemoration of the 75th anniversary of the printing of Thorvald Bindesboll's label for "Carlsberg Pilsner."

• 1325 • **Eckersberg Medal**
To recognize an individual for an achievement of high artistic value within the fine arts or the architectural arts. Individuals who are not members of the Council of the Academy are eligible. A bronze medal, designed by the medallist Harald Conradsen, is awarded when merited. Established in 1883 in memory of C. V. Eckersberg, a painter, on the occasion of the centenary of his birth.

• 1326 • **C. F. Hansen Medal**
This, the highest honor that the Academy awards an architect, is given for distinguished achievement in the architectural arts. Individuals who are not members of the Council of the Academy at the time are eligible. A silver medal is awarded when merited. Established in 1830.

• 1327 • **N. L. Hoyen Medal**
To recognize an individual for an achievement of high value within research, interpretation, or procurement of the fine arts. Individuals who are not members of the Council of the Academy are eligible. A medal is awarded when merited. Established in 1979 in memory of N. L. Hoyen, a professor at the Royal Academy of Fine Arts 150 years ago (in the 1830s).

• 1328 • **Thorvaldsen Medal**
This, the highest honor that the Academy can award a sculptor and a painter, is given for distinguished achievement in the fine arts. Individuals who are not members of the Council of the Academy are eligible. A silver medal, designed by the medallist Chr. Christensen and cast in 1838, is awarded when merited. Established in 1838 in honor of the sculptor, Bertel Thorvaldsen, on the occasion of the receipt of his works from Rome.

• 1329 •
Royal Danish Geographical Society
(Kongelige Danske Geografiske Selskab)
Prof. Bjarne Holm Jakobsen, Sec.Gen.
Oster Voldgade 10
DK-1350 Copenhagen K, Denmark
Phone: 45 35322558
Fax: 45 35322501
E-mail: kb@geogr.ku.dk
Home Page: http://www.geogr.ku.dk/dkgs/

• 1330 • **Vitus Bering Medal (Vitus Bering Medaillen)**
For recognition of outstanding performance in the geographical sciences. Geographers of any nation are eligible. A medal is awarded when merited. Established in 1941.

• 1331 • **Egede Medal (Egede Medaillen)**
For recognition of geographical investigations and research in the Arctic areas. Geographers and Arctic scientists are eligible. A medal is awarded when merited. Established in 1916.

• 1332 • **Galathea Medal (Galathea Medaillen)**
For recognition of geographical investigations and research outside the Arctic areas. Geographers of any nation are eligible. A medal is awarded when merited. Established in 1916.

• 1333 •
Scandinavian Packaging Association (Samarbetsorganisationen for Emballagefragor i Skandinavien)
Jens Christian Sorensen, Chm.
PO Box 141
DK-2630 Taastrup, Denmark
Phone: 45 72203150
Fax: 45 72203185
E-mail: et@teknologisk.dk
Home Page: http://www.teknologisk.dk/emballage-transport

• 1334 • **Scanstar Packaging Competition**
For recognition in the field of packaging. Awarded annually. Established in 1968.

• 1335 •
Leonie Sonnings Music Foundation (Leonie Sonnings Musikfond)
Bente Legarth, Sec.
Ved Stranden 18
Postboks 2034
DK-1012 Copenhagen 1061 K, Denmark
Phone: 45 77304050
Fax: 45 77304077
E-mail: bente.legarth@dlanordic.dk
Home Page: http://www.sonningmusik.dk

• 1336 • **Leonie Sonning Music Prize (Leonie Sonnings Musikpris)**
For recognition of outstanding achievement in music. Composers, conductors, musicians, and singers are eligible for consideration. A monetary award of 300,000 Danish kroner and a diploma are awarded annually. Established in 1959 by Mrs. Leonie Sonning.

• 1337 •
University of Copenhagen (Kobenhavns Universitet)
The Sonning Foundation
Norregade 10
PO Box 2177
DK-1017 Copenhagen K, Denmark
Phone: 45 3532 2626
Fax: 45 3532 2628
E-mail: ku@ku.dk
Home Page: http://www.ku.dk/sonning-fonden

• 1338 • **Sonning Prize**
To recognize a man or woman who has made an outstanding contribution toward the advancement of European civilization. Recommendations for candidates are invited from European universities. A monetary prize of 500,000 Danish kroner is awarded biennially on April 19, Mr. Sonning's birthday, biennially in even-numbered years. Established in 1949 in memory of C.J. Sonning, a writer and editor; first given as a special award to Winston Churchill in 1950.

• 1339 •
World Small Animal Veterinary Association
Dr. Anne Sorensen, Sec.
Strandbovej 73
Hvidovre
DK-2650 Copenhagen, Denmark
Phone: 45 36 494861
Phone: 45 36 162700
Fax: 45 36 162606
E-mail: fasanne@tiscali.dk
Home Page: http://www.wsava.org

• 1340 • **Waltham International Award for Scientific Achievement**
For recognition of outstanding contributions by a veterinarian who has had a significant impact on the advancement of knowledge concerning the cause, detection, cure and/or control of disorders of companion animals. The recipient is chosen on the basis of contributions published in scientific journals or books, and/or information presented at veterinary congresses. Veterinarians with outstanding records of achievement must be nominated by February. A monetary award of £1,000, a plaque, and travel and registration for the World Congress are awarded annually. Established in 1984. Sponsored by Waltham Worldwide.

• 1341 • **Waltham Service to the Profession Award**
For recognition of exemplary service by a veterinarian who has fostered and enhanced the exchange of scientific and cultural ideas throughout the veterinary small animal world. The recipient is chosen on the basis of service to local, state, national, and international organizations that have catalyzed scientific meetings, exchange of information, and international good will for the benefit of the profession world wide. A monetary award of £1,000, a plaque, and travel and registration for the congress are awarded annually. Established in 1984. Sponsored by Waltham Worldwide.

• 1342 • **WSAVA Hills Excellence in Veterinary Healthcare Award**
Recognizes the outstanding work of veterinarians in promoting companion animal healthcare and the family-pet veterinary bond through a special sensitivity to both clients and patients and through leading edge clinical nutrition, advanced medical and surgical techniques, aimed to help enrich and lengthen the special relationship between animals and their pets. Established in 2001. Sponsored by Hills Pet Nutrition.

• 1343 • **WSAVA Paatsama Award**
For excellence in the field of canine or feline medicine or surgery, with a preference for orthopaedics. Presented to a clinical researcher. Established in 2001. Sponsored by WSAVA.

Egypt

• 1344 •
Egyptian Ophthalmological Society
Dr. Karem A. Kolkailah, Pres.
42 Kasr El-Einy St.
Dar El Hekma
Cairo, Egypt
Phone: 20 2 7923941
Phone: 20 2 7923942
Fax: 20 2 7941538
E-mail: eos@eyegypt.com
Home Page: http://www.eyegypt.com

• 1345 • **The Opthalmological Gold Medal**
For recognition of major services and activities in the Society and ophthalmology. Members of the Society who are over 50 years of age are considered for services and activities other than scientific activities. A gold medal is awarded when merited. Established in 1943.

Estonia

• 1346 •
Estonian Academy of Sciences (Eesti Teaduste Akadeemia)
Richard Villems, Pres.
Kohtu 6
EE-10130 Tallinn, Estonia
Phone: 372 6 442129
Phone: 372 6 451925
Fax: 372 6 451805
E-mail: foreign@akadeemia.ee
Home Page: http://www.akadeemia.ee

• 1347 • **Nikolai Alumae Medal**
To recognize excellence in research in engineering and informatics. Awarded every four years.

• 1348 • **Paul Ariste Medal**
To recognize excellence in research in the humanities and social sciences. Awarded every four years.

• 1349 • **Karl Ernst von Baer Medal**
To recognize excellence in research in biology. Awarded every four years.

• 1350 • **Medal of the Estonian Academy of Sciences**
To recognize individuals for outstanding services in development of Estonian science or in helping its development, as well as for services in performance of tasks of the Academy. Awarded periodically.

• 1351 • **Karl Schlossmann Medal**
To recognize excellence in research in natural sciences. Awarded every four years.

• 1352 • **Bernhard Schmidt Prize**
To recognize young scientists and engineers for excellent results in applied sciences and innovation. Awarded biennially.

• 1353 • **Student Research Prize**
To recognize students for outstanding results in scientific work and to stimulate independent research of talented and capable students. A monetary award is given annually.

• 1354 •
Estonian Education Personnel Union
(Eesti Haridustootajate Liit)
Sven Rondik, Chm.
Gonsiori St. 21
10147 Tallinn, Estonia
Phone: 372 6419803
Phone: 372 6419967
Fax: 372 6419802
E-mail: ehl@online.ee
Home Page: http://www.online.ee/~ehl

• 1355 • **Teacher of the Year Award**
Recognizes effective work on the professional level and activeness on the social level. Awarded annually.

Finland

• 1356 •
Committee of 100 in Finland
(Suomen Sadankomitealiitto)
Jessica Suni, Gen.Sec.
Rauhanasema
Veturitori 3
FIN-00520 Helsinki, Finland
Phone: 358 9 141336
Fax: 358 9 147297
E-mail: sadankomitea@sadankomitea.org
Home Page: http://www.sadankomitea.org

• 1357 • **Peace Award of Committee of 100**
Annual award of recognition for individuals or groups who have advanced the principle of nonviolence in the world.

• 1358 •
Design Forum Finland
Mikko Kalhama, Managing Dir.
Erottajankatu 7
FIN-00130 Helsinki, Finland
Phone: 358 9 6220810
Fax: 358 9 62208181
E-mail: info@designforum.fi
Home Page: http://www.designforum.fi

• 1359 • **Estlander Prize**
For organizations promoting design in significant ways.

• 1360 • **Fennia Prize**
For companies that excel in design.

• 1361 • **Kaj Franck Design Prize**
For a distinguished designer or team.

• 1362 • **Young Designer of the Year Prize**
For a promising young designer.

• 1363 •
European Rhinologic Society
Dr. M. Rautiainen MD, Pres.
KNK-Klinikka, Tays, PL 2000
Ph. Van Leydenlan 15
FIN-33521 Tampere, Finland
Phone: 31 24 3614450
Fax: 31 24 3540251
E-mail: markus.rautiainen@tt.tays.fi
Home Page: http://www.europeanrhinologicsociety.org

• 1364 • **European Rhinologic Society Prizes**
To stimulate and recognize young scientists; prizes for clinical and basic research in rhinology are awarded biennially during the European Rhinologic Congress. They include a monetary prize and cancellation of registration fee. Established in 1986.

• 1365 •
Family Federation of Finland
Helena Hiila, Mng.Dir.
PO Box 849
FIN-00101 Helsinki, Finland
Phone: 358 9 228050
Phone: 358 9 616221
Fax: 358 9 6121211
E-mail: central.office@vaestoliitto.fi
Home Page: http://www.vaestoliitto.fi

• 1366 • **Elsa Enajarvi-Haavio Award**
Recognizes work for family welfare. Awarded every other year. Established in 2001.

• 1367 • **V.J. Sukeslained Award**
Recognizes work on family expense studies, family expense settlements. Awarded every five years. Established in 2001.

• 1368 •
Fine Arts Association of Finland
(Suomen Taideyhdistys)
Maija Tanninen-Mattila, Sec.
Nervanderinkatu 3
FIN-00100 Helsinki, Finland
Phone: 358 9 4542060
Fax: 358 9 45420610
E-mail: info@taidehalli.fi
Home Page: http://www.suomentaideyhdistys.fi

• 1369 • **Artist Awards**
To young artists.

• 1370 • **Ducat Award**
To young artists under age 35.

• 1371 • **Honouree Award**
To an artist or person in the arts field.

• 1372 • **Edward Richter Award**
For critics in fine arts.

• 1373 •
Finland Ministry of Defense
Thomas Sund, Information Off.
Etelainen Makasiinikatu 8
PO Box 31
FIN-00131 Helsinki, Finland
Phone: 358 9 16001
Fax: 358 9 1608 8244
E-mail: puolustusministerio@defmin.fi
Home Page: http://www.defmin.fi

• 1374 • **Order of the Cross of Liberty**
To recognize, during war or peace, members of the Armed Forces of Finland for military merit; to recognize civilians who work for the Armed Forces or who work in favor of the Armed Forces for services rendered to the Armed Forces; to recognize "in time of war" units of the Armed Forces as well as organizations and establishments of Finland; and to recognize foreigners for service to Finland. The Grand Cross of the Order of Freedom, the Cross of Freedom, first, second, third, and fourth class and the Medal of Freedom are awarded to military persons. The Medal of Merit is awarded to civilians. In addition, the following special decorations of the Order are awarded: Mannerheim Cross, first class, to members of the Armed Forces for extraordinary courage during military operations; Cross of Mannerheim, second class, to members of the Armed Forces for extraordinary courage during military operations. An individual may receive this cross more than once; Medal of Freedom with a rosette, to a superior commander of a unit composed of different armies for recognition of the execution of a military operation selected by the Grand Master; Medal of Merit in gold, for recognition of particularly remarkable merit chosen by the Grand Master of the Order; Cross of Mourning, to a parent of a combatant killed in action; and Medal of Mourning, to a parent of a person who dies during wartime while serving the National Defense. The Cross of the Order with a two edged sword is white enamel cross-bordered with gold, with a rose herald in the center; the medal is silver with a lion in the center. Established in 1918 by Baron Gustaf Mannerheim, former President of the Republic, and formed into a permanent military order in 1940.

• 1375 • **Order of the Lion of Finland**
For recognition of civilians and military of outstanding merit. Foreigners may also be recognized by this order. The President of the Republic confers the Order. The Order consists of the seven classes: Commander Grand Cross; Commander, First Class; Commander; Pro Finlandia Medal of the Order; Knight, First Class; Knight of the Order; and Cross of Merit of the Order. The cross is white enamel bordered with gold and has a lion in gold in the center; the medal is silver and has a gold lion in the center. Established in 1942 by Risto Ryti, President of the Republic.

• 1376 • **Order of the White Rose of Finland**
To recognize citizens of Finland and foreigners for special service to the country. The Chief of State of Finland has the right to confer the deco-

ration. The Order consists of the following classes: Commanders Grand Cross; Commanders, first class and second class; Chevaliers, first class and second class; Insigne of Merit; Medal, first class with a cross of gold; and Medals, first and second class. The cross of the order is white enamel bordered with gold and has a rose heraldry in the center; the Medal is silver with a rose in the center. Established in 1919 by the Baron Gustaf Mannerheim, former President of the Republic.

• 1377 •
Finnish Amateur Radio League
(Suomen Radioamatooriliitto ry)
Annika Wahlstrom, Sec.
PO Box 44
FIN-00441 Helsinki, Finland
Phone: 358 9 5625973
Phone: 358 9 5625973
Fax: 358 9 5623987
E-mail: hq@sral.fi
Home Page: http://www.sral.fi

• 1378 • **The Lakes of Finland Award**
For radio stations.

• 1379 • **The OH Awards**
For amateur radio operators, radio clubs and short wave listeners.

• 1380 • **The OH County Award**
For workers in OH counties.

• 1381 • **The OHA Plaques**
For amateur radio operators, radio clubs and short wave listeners in Finland.

• 1382 • **OHA-VHF Award**
For workers in VHF, UHF and SHF bands. For amateur radio station

• 1383 •
Finnish Association of Designers Ornamo
(Teollisuustaiteen Liitto Ornamo)
Paivi Bergroth, Pres.
Unioninkatu 26
FIN-00130 Helsinki, Finland
Phone: 358 9 6877740
Fax: 358 9 68777468
E-mail: office@ornamo.fi
Home Page: http://www.ornamo.fi

• 1384 • **Best Student Paper Award**
For the best paper delivered at the society's annual conference.

• 1385 • **Fashion Designer of the Year, MTO**
Award of recognition.

• 1386 • **Industrial Designer of the Year TKO**
Award of recognition.

• 1387 • **Interior Award SIO**
Award of recognition.

• 1388 • **Partisan of the Year Award, TAIKO**
Award of recognition.

• 1389 • **Textile Designer of the Year, TEXO**
Award of recognition.

• 1390 •
Finnish Cultural Foundation
(Suomen Kulttuurirahasto)
Dr. Antti Arjava, Sec.Gen.
Blvd. 5A
PO Box 203
FIN-00121 Helsinki, Finland
Phone: 358 9 612810
Fax: 358 9 640474
E-mail: info@skr.fi
Home Page: http://www.skr.fi

• 1391 • **Mirjam Helin International Singing Competition**
(Kansainvalinen Mirjam Helin laulukilpailu)
To recognize the winners of the international singing competition and to provide grants for promising young singers. The competition is open to women 31 years of age or under and to men 33 years of age or under regardless of nationality. Held every five years. Established in 1981 by Mrs. Mirjam Helin who endowed the Finnish Cultural Foundation with the special Mirjam and Hans Helin Fund.

• 1392 •
Finnish Paper Engineers' Association
(Finska Pappesingeniorsforeningen)
Markku Karlsson, Chm.
PO Box 118
00171 Helsinki, Finland
Phone: 358 9 1326696
Fax: 358 9 630365
E-mail: info@papereng.fi
Home Page: http://www.papereng.fi

• 1393 • **Andritz Oy Award**
For outstanding academic work dealing with fibre processes

• 1394 • **Association Plaquette of Merit**
For outstanding contributions done in the association's field

• 1395 • **Lampen Medal**
For outstanding technical and scientific work contributed to the Association.

• 1396 • **Stenback Plaquette**
For outstanding work done in the association's field.

• 1397 •
Finnish Society of Sciences and Letters
(Finska Vetenskaps-Societeten-Societas Scientiarum Fennica)
Prof. Carl G. Gahmberg, Sec.
Mariankatu 5A
FIN-00170 Helsinki 17, Finland
Phone: 358 9 633005
Fax: 358 9 661065
E-mail: soc.deleg@tsv.fi
Home Page: http://pro.tsv.fi/fvs/

• 1398 • **Professor Magnus Ehrnrooth Prize**
To recognize outstanding contributions to the fields of chemistry, mathematics, and physics (categories alternate each year). A monetary award of 12,000 Euro is presented annually.

• 1399 • **Professor Theodor Homen Prize**
To recognize outstanding research contributions in the fields of physics and Finnish history (category alternates each year the award is presented). Members of the Society may submit nominations. A monetary award of 15,000 Euro is presented triennially.

• 1400 • **E. J. Nystrom Prize**
(Professor E. J. Nystroms Prize)
To recognize outstanding scientific contributions. Members of the Society may submit nominations. A monetary award of 20,000 Euro is presented annually. Established in 1962 to honor Professor E. J. Nystrom, former president of the Society, who died in 1960.

• 1401 • **Upper Secondary School Teachers Prizes**
Recognizes excellent teaching in schools. Two monetary awards of 5,000 Euro are presented annually, one for teachers of science and the other for teachers of the humanities or social science. Established in 1998.

• 1402 •
Foundation for the Promotion of Finnish Music
(Luovan saveltaiteen edistamissaatio)
Kai Amberta, Sec.Gen.
Lauttasaarentie 1
FIN-00200 Helsinki, Finland
Phone: 358 9 6810 1313
Fax: 358 9 6820 770
E-mail: info@fimic.fi
Home Page: http://www.luses.fi

• 1403 • **Foundation for the Promotion of Finnish Music Grants**
(Apuraha tai Palkinto)
For recognition of teachers of music, representatives of the science of music, composers, performers of music, and persons who have in other ways meritoriously promoted music in Finland. Only Finnish citizens are eligible. Grants are available in the following categories: production of recordings; marketing of recordings; concerts; travel; publication, marketing, and export of sheet music, training events, and research in

musical culture; working; and commission. Monetary awards are presented every year on the birthday of Jean Sibelius, the famous Finnish composer. Established in 1955 by the Finnish Parliament which donated the basic capital for the establishment of the Foundation on the occasion of the 90th birthday of Professor Jean Sibelius, who died in 1957.

• 1404 •
GRAFIA - The Finnish Association of Graphic Design
(Grafia - Graafisen Suunnittelun Jarjesto)
Uudenmaankatu 11 B 9
SF-00120 Helsinki, Finland
Phone: 358 9 601941
Phone: 358 9 601942
Fax: 358 9 601140
E-mail: grafia@grafia.fi
Home Page: http://www.grafia.fi

• 1405 • The Best of Finnish Graphic Design and Advertising Competition
To recognize creative designers working in graphic design, illustration, layout and book jacket and package design. The following awards are presented: Golden Award, Silver Award, Platinum Award, and Junior Award. Held annually.

• 1406 •
Helsinki International Ballet Competition
Juhani Terasvuori, Dir.
% Nordic Dance Management
Villa Polaris
Koivukuja 14
FIN-03100 Nummela, Finland
Phone: 358 9 568 20220
Fax: 358 9 568 20220
E-mail: ballet@balcomphel.fi
Home Page: http://www.balcomphel.fi

• 1407 • Helsinki International Ballet Competition
For recognition of outstanding ballet performances. The Competition is open to dancers of all nationalities. All participants must be qualified by the selection committee. Qualifications are based on recommendations from their directors/teachers or ITI Centres. The competitors are judged individually and in two divisions: (1) Junior Division - age 15 to 18; and (2) Senior Division - age 19 to 25 at the time of the Competition. Various monetary prizes are awarded, including a grand prize of 10,000 euros. Established in 1984. Helsinki is one of the six locations for the International Ballet Competition, the others being Moscow, USSR; Jackson, Mississippi, U.S.A.; Varna, Bulgaria; New York; and Paris.

• 1408 •
International Federation of the Phonographic Industry - Finland
Arto Alaspaa, Sec.Dir.
Yrjonkatu 3 B
FIN-00120 Helsinki, Finland
Phone: 358 9 68034050
Fax: 358 9 68034055
E-mail: ifpi@ifpi.fi
Home Page: http://www.ifpi.fi

• 1409 • Emma Muuvi Awards
To recognize the best artists in the Finnish music industry. Awarded annually.

• 1410 •
International Paulo Cello Competition
(Naantalin Musiikkijuhlat)
Arto Noras, Artistic Dir.
Paulo Foundation
Mikonkatu 3B
PL 1105
FIN-00101 Helsinki, Finland
Phone: 358 40 528 4876
Fax: 358 9 2243 2879
E-mail: cello@paulo.fi
Home Page: http://www.cellocompetitionpaulo.org
Formerly: Naanteli Music Festival.

• 1411 • International Paulo Cello Competition
(Kansainvalinen Paulon Sellokilpailu)
For recognition of outstanding cello performances. The competition is open to cellists of all nationalities between ages 16 and 33. Six monetary prizes totaling 42,000 euros are awarded. Held every five years. Established in 1991. Sponsored by the Paulo Foundation.

• 1412 •
International Society for Human and Animal Mycology
(Societe Internationale de Mycologie Humaine et Animales)
Prof. Malcolm Richardson PhD, Gen.Sec.
PO Box 21
University of Leeds
00014 Helsinki, Finland
Phone: 358 9 19126894
Fax: 358 9 19126382
E-mail: malcolm.richardson@helsinki.fi
Home Page: http://www.isham.org

• 1413 • Lucille K. Georg Award
For recognition of achievement in medical and veterinary mycology. Members of the Society may be nominated by a specially appointed Awards Committee. Monetary awards and a medallion are awarded every three or four years at the Society Congress. Established in 1964 in honor of Dr. Lucille K. Georg, formerly at the Center for Disease Control, in Atlanta, Georgia, U.S.A.

• 1414 •
Sigrid Juselius Foundation
Aleksanterinkatu 48 B
FIN-00100 Helsinki, Finland
Phone: 358 9 634461
Fax: 358 9 634502
Home Page: http://www.sigridjuselius.net

• 1415 • Medical Research Grants
To enable Finnish researchers to conduct medical research. Resources are allocated only to Senior and Advanced Researchers and for work of established staff of universities. Awarded annually. Established in 1930 by Fritz Arthur Juselius.

• 1416 •
Alfred Kordelin Foundation
Mariankatu 7A3
FIN-00170 Helsinki, Finland
Phone: 358 9 6840 1200
Fax: 358 9 6840 1246
E-mail: toimisto@kordelin.fi
Home Page: http://www.kordelin.fi

• 1417 • Kordelin Prize
For recognition of outstanding contributions to Finnish culture and literature. A number of monetary prizes and an honorary prize are awarded annually.

• 1418 •
Lahti Organ Festival
Vapaudenkatu 6
FIN-15110 Lahti, Finland
Phone: 358 3 877 230
Fax: 358 3 877 2320
E-mail: office@lahtiorgan.fi
Home Page: http://www.lahtiorgan.fi

• 1419 • International Lahti Organ Competition
(Lahden Kansainvalinen Urkukilpailu)
To recognize outstanding organists. Competitors must be under 33 years of age. Held every four years. Established in 1973.

• 1420 •
Lappeenranta City Orchestra
(Lappeenrannan Kaupunki)
Valtakatu 58
FIN-53100 Lappeenranta, Finland
Phone: 358 5 6162362
Phone: 358 5 6677830
Fax: 358 5 6162236
E-mail: marja.anttila@lappeenranta.fi
Home Page: http://www.lappeenranta.fi

• 1421 • Lappeenranta National Singing Competition
(Lappeenrannan Valtakunnalliset Laulukilpailut)
To recognize the best male and female singers in Finland. Female Finnish singers under 30 years of age and male Finnish singers under 32 years of age may apply. Monetary awards are

Awards are arranged in alphabetical order below their administering organizations

presented triennially. In addition, special prizes are available. Established in 1969.

• 1422 •
Oulu International Children's Film Festival
Sauli Pesonen, Exec.Dir.
Hallituskatu 7
FIN-90100 Oulu, Finland
Phone: 358 8 8811293
Fax: 358 8 8811290
E-mail: oek@outfilmcenter.inet.fi
Home Page: http://www.ouka.fi/oek

• 1423 • **Star Boy Award**
To recognize the director of the best children's film at the festival. A monetary award and a statuette are awarded annually. Established in 1992 by *Kaleva Newspaper.*

• 1424 •
Jean Sibelius International Violin Competition
Mikko Heinio, Chm.
PO Box 31
SF-00101 Helsinki, Finland
Phone: 358 50 408 4335
Fax: 358 10 850 4760
E-mail: violin.competition@kolumbus.fi
Home Page: http://www.siba.fi/sibeliuscompetition

• 1425 • **International Jean Sibelius Violin Competition**
To recognize the best violinists of the Competition. Violinists of any nationality born in 1975 or later are eligible. Monetary prizes totaling 47,000 Euro are awarded every five years. In addition, the Finnish Broadcasting Company awards 2,000 Euro for the best performance of the Sibelius Violin Concerto; the Sibelius family awards 1,000 Euro to second-round finalists; and the city of Jarvenpaa grants a special prize of 1,500 Euro. Established in 1965 to commemorate one hundred years after the birth of Jean Sibelius by the Sibelius Society of Finland.

• 1426 •
Tampere Film Festival
(Tampereen elokuvajuhlat)
Juhani Alanen, Exec.Dir.
Tullikamarinaukio 2
PO Box 305
FIN-33101 Tampere, Finland
Phone: 358 3 223 5681
Fax: 358 3 223 0121
E-mail: office@tamperefilmfestival.fi
Home Page: http://www.tamperefilmfestival.fi

Formerly: (1980) Society for Film Art in Tampere.

• 1427 • **Tampere International Short Film Festival (Tampereen Kansainvaliset lyhytelokuvajuhlat Grand Prix)**
For recognition of short films in a national and international competition of a high standard that have a human theme and seek new forms of cinematic expression. Films produced during the two years preceding the festival are eligible in the following categories: animated films, documentary films, and fiction films. An international jury awards the following prizes for the film directors: Grand Prix - a monetary award of 5000 Euros and a "Kiss" statuette; Category Prizes three monetary prizes of 1500 Euros each and a "Kiss" Statuette; The Special Prize of the Jury - a monetary prize of 1500 Euros and a "Kiss" statuette; and Diplomas of Merit. Held annually in March. Established in 1970.

France

• 1428 •
Academie d'Agriculture de France
18, rue de Bellechasse
F-75007 Paris, France
Phone: 33 1 47051037
Fax: 33 1 45550978
Home Page: http://www.academie-agriculture.fr

• 1429 • **Academie d*K*Agriculture de France Medailles**
To recognize students graduating first in their classes from the National Agronomy Institute Paris-Grignon and the National School of Agriculture at Montpellier or Rennes. The following medals are awarded annually: Medaille Tisserand, Medaille d'Or, Medaille de Vermeil, and Medaille d'Argent.

• 1430 • **Prix de la Fondation Xavier Bernard**
To recognize the authors of the best work in applied research in the fields of vegetable and animal production. Works should contribute to the advancement of agriculture, to better quantity and quality yields, or to the struggle against pests and diseases. Studies of rural economics of agricultural production (administration of agricultural production as well as the professional sectors) and the economics of agricultural product distribution (patterns of consumption, research to open up new avenues of trade, conditions of production, etc.) are considered. One or two prizes of 3,050 euros are awarded annually. Jointly administered by the Fondation Xavier-Bernard and the Bureau d'Academie d'Agriculture de France. Established in 1955.

• 1431 • **Prix Jean Dufrenoy**
For recognition of researchers active in a sensitive, agronomic field that is emerging with practical applications in agriculture and French farm production. French researchers under 40 years of age are eligible. One or two monetary prizes of 4,575 euros and a medal are awarded annually at Seance Solennelle. Established in 1973 by Marie-Louise Dufrenoy in memory of her brother, Jean Dufrenoy, a member of the Academy.

• 1432 •
Academie des Beaux-Arts
Institut de France
23, Quai de Conti
F-75006 Paris Cedex 06, France
E-mail: contact@academie-des-beaux-arts.fr
Home Page: http://www.academie-des-beaux-arts.fr

• 1433 • **Prix Francoise Abella**
To provide financial assistance to a student of architecture. Awarded annually.

• 1434 • **Prix Antoine-Nicolas Bailly**
For recognition of an architectural work or a publication on architecture. For two consecutive times, the prize is awarded to a French architect; then on the third time, to a French author. A monetary prize is awarded periodically, when the funds permit it.

• 1435 • **Prix Jean Jacques Berger**
For recognition of the most outstanding work of art concerning the city of Paris or serving as a decoration in Paris. A monetary prize is awarded every five years by the Academie des Beaux Arts. Awarded periodically, when the funds permit it.

• 1436 • **Prix Claude Berthault**
To recognize painters, sculptors, or architects who have created a beautiful work of art or decoration in the best French spirit. Artists born in France are eligible. A monetary prize is awarded annually. Awarded by the Fondation de Madame Claude Berthault.

• 1437 • **Prix Karl Beule**
To recognize a painter for a remarkable Oriental style. Painters who exhibited at the Salon des Artistes Francais and have received no other awards are considered. A monetary prize is awarded periodically, when the funds permit it.

• 1438 • **Prix Georges Bizet**
To recognize a composer who has produced a notable work during the preceding five years. Men under 41 years of age are eligible. A monetary prize is awarded periodically, when the funds permit it.

• 1439 • **Prix Bordin**
For recognition of the best book on painting, sculpture, engraving, architecture, or music. Awards are given in alternate years in the categories of painting, sculpture, engraving, architecture, and music. A monetary prize is awarded periodically, when the funds permit it.

• 1440 • **Prix Leclerc-Maria Bouland**
To recognize a painter who has received a mark of distinction at the Salon des Artistes Francais. French painters, under 30 years of age, without fortune, are eligible. A monetary prize is awarded periodically, when the funds permit it.

• 1441 • Prix Andre Caplet
To recognize a music composer for the remarkable quality of his work. Composers of less than 40 years of age are eligible. A monetary prize is awarded biennially.

• 1442 • Prix Alphonse Cellier
To recognize a painter who is a student of l'Ecole des Beaux-Arts and is less than 30 years of age. Awarded annually.

• 1443 • Prix Paul Chabas
To recognize a painter whose work is marked by interesting, imaginative qualities. A monetary prize is awarded periodically, when the funds permit it, at the Salon de la Societe des Artistes francais.

• 1444 • Prix Chartier
For recognition of a chamber music composition. French composers are eligible. A monetary prize is awarded periodically, when the funds permit it.

• 1445 • Prix Gustave Courtois
For recognition of a painting, a nude, or a portrait accepted by the Salon des Artistes francais or the Societe Nationale. A monetary prize is awarded periodically, when the funds permit it.

• 1446 • Prix Maxime David
For recognition of the best portrait miniature shown at the Salon des Artistes Francais. A monetary prize is awarded periodically, when the funds permit it.

• 1447 • Prix Desprez
For recognition of a work by a sculptor. French artists under 35 years of age may submit work completed in France during the preceding two years. A monetary prize is awarded periodically, when the funds permit it.

• 1448 • Prix Rene Dumesnil
To recognize composers or writers of works on music. Awards are given in alternate years to the author of a work of music criticism or musicology and the author of a musical composition. A monetary prize is awarded annually.

• 1449 • Prix Auguste Durand et Edouard Ordonneau
For recognition of a copper-plate engraving exhibited at the Salon des Artistes Francais. A monetary prize is awarded periodically, when the funds permit it.

• 1450 • Prix Jacques Durand
For recognition of a symphonic work or a work of chamber music. French authors may submit published or unpublished compositions. A monetary prize is awarded periodically, when the funds permit it.

• 1451 • Prix Gabriel Ferrier
For recognition of a painting exhibited at the Salon de la Societe des Artistes francais. Paintings of figures or history are considered. An artist may be awarded the prize for several years. A monetary prize is awarded periodically, when the funds permit it.

• 1452 • Prix Achille Fould-Stirbey
For recognition of a painting of excellent design and color in the grand French humanist tradition. An artist may receive the prize only one time. Three monetary prizes are awarded annually at the Salon des Artistes francais.

• 1453 • Grand Prix d'Architecture
To recognize architects or architectural students under 35 years of age for outstanding work. The competition consists of three phases: candidates submit a draft on the subject proposed by the Academy, 20 candidates who have the most interesting drafts submit a sketch, and 10 candidates who have the best sketches submit an architectural project. The architect of the best project is the grand prize winner. Monetary prizes are awarded annually. Established in 1975.

• 1454 • Prix Haumont
For recognition of a painting of a landscape with figures. French artists under 30 years of age are eligible. A monetary prize is awarded periodically, when the funds permit it.

• 1455 • Prix Houllevigue
For recognition of a remarkable work of painting, sculpture, architecture, engraving, or musical composition; or, for a book on art or art history. A monetary prize is awarded periodically, when the funds permit it.

• 1456 • Prix Jules et Louis Jeanbernat et Barthelemy de Ferrari Doria
For recognition of a work on art by a young French author. A monetary prize is awarded every five years by the Academie des Beaux Arts. Awarded periodically, when the funds permit it. Established by Emmanuel Jeanbernat, in memory of his two sons, who died for France.

• 1457 • Prix du Baron de Joest
For recognition of a discovery or work in the field of art history that is most useful to the public good. A monetary prize is awarded periodically, when the funds permit it.

• 1458 • Prix Achille Leclere
For recognition of the best architectural project on a specific subject assigned by the Academy. Architects under 31 years of age are eligible. Collaboration in the execution of the projects is not permitted. The prize may not be awarded to the same person more than once. A monetary prize is awarded periodically, when the funds permit it.

• 1459 • Prix Hector Lefuel
For recognition of a painting, sculpture, work of architecture, or musical composition. Awards are given in alternate years in the categories of painting, sculpture, architecture, and musical composition. A monetary prize is awarded periodically, when the funds permit it.

• 1460 • Prix Henri Lehmann
To recognize a painter who has completed a work that protests the most eloquently against the degradation of art. Paintings or cartoons by artists under 25 years of age are considered. A monetary prize is awarded periodically, when the funds permit it.

• 1461 • Prix Troyon et Edouard Lemaitre
For recognition of a landscape painting. Artists under 30 years of age who are exhibited at the Salon des Artistes Francais are eligible. A monetary prize is awarded periodically, when the funds permit it.

• 1462 • Prix Paul Marmottan
For recognition of a book on art. A monetary prize is awarded annually.

• 1463 • Prix Maurice R.D.
To recognize an artist exhibiting at the Salon des Artistes francais who is noted for the seriousness and the conscience of his work. A monetary prize is awarded periodically, when the funds permit it.

• 1464 • Prix Meurand
To recognize a young landscape or historical painter whose talent has been recognized at the Salon des Artistes Francais. A monetary prize is awarded periodically, when the funds permit it.

• 1465 • Prix Monbinne
To recognize the composer of a comic opera performed for the first time during the past two years, or a symphonic work if a worthy comic opera has not been written. The symphony may be purely instrumental or with a chant, preferably a religious composition. A monetary prize is awarded periodically, when the funds permit it.

• 1466 • Prix Alphonse de Neuville et Sanford Saltus
For recognition of a military painting exhibited at the expositions of the Salon des Artistes Francais. A monetary prize is awarded periodically, when the funds permit it.

• 1467 • Prix Nicolo
For recognition of the best melodic composition. A monetary prize is awarded periodically, when the funds permit it.

• 1468 • Prix Pinet
For recognition of an original engraving exhibited at the Salon des Artistes Francais. A monetary prize is awarded periodically, when the funds permit it.

• 1469 • Prix Eugene Piot
For recognition of a sculpture or painting of a nude child. Awards are given in alternate years in the categories of sculpture and painting. A monetary prize is awarded periodically, when the funds permit it.

• 1470 • Prix Bastien-Lepage
To recognize a French painter who has an exhibition at the Salon des Artistes Francais. A monetary prize is awarded annually.

• 1471 • Prix Breaute
For recognition of a painting, a sculpture, or an engraving exhibited at the Salon de la Societe des Artistes francais. Awards are given in alternate years between painting, sculpture, and engraving. Awarded annually.

• 1472 • Prix Brizard
To recognize an exhibitor of an oil painting at the Salon des Artistes Francais who is under 28 years of age. To be eligible, a painter must be French or a naturalized citizen. Awards are given in alternate years in landscape and seascape genres. Paintings that place third and above at the Exposition are eligible. A monetary prize is awarded periodically, when the funds permit it.

• 1473 • Prix Catenacci
For recognition of outstanding contributions in the categories of interior or exterior ornamentation of a building, garden, or public square and publication of deluxe illustrated books. Two equal monetary prizes are awarded periodically, when the funds permit it.

• 1474 • Prix Chaudesaigues
To recognize a young architect. French architects who are under 32 years of age may submit sketches on the assigned subject. The 12 candidates who have the best sketches are invited to present a project based on their sketch. A monetary prize is awarded periodically, when the funds permit it.

• 1475 • Prix Colmont
To recognize a painter, sculptor or an engraver exhibiting a work at the Salon de la Societe des Artistes francais. Awards are given in alternate years to a painter, a sculptor, and an engraver. A monetary prize is awarded annually.

• 1476 • Prix Dagnan-Bouveret
For recognition of a painting, a nude, a portrait, or a simple head, shown at the Salon des Artistes Francais. Members of the Institut de France are not eligible. A monetary prize is awarded annually.

• 1477 • Prix de la Societe Francaise de Gravure
For recognition of copper-plate engravings exhibited at the Salon des Artistes Francais. A monetary prize is awarded periodically, when the funds permit it.

• 1478 • Prix des Cathedrales
For recognition of a religious sculpture. French sculptors under 30 years of age are eligible. A monetary prize is awarded periodically, when the funds permit it. Established by J.B. Dampt, a member of the Institute de France.

• 1479 • Prix Doublemard
To recognize a young sculptor who is preparing for the Rome competition. A monetary prize is awarded periodically, when the funds permit it.

• 1480 • Prix Duc
To encourage advanced study of architecture. A monetary prize is awarded periodically, when the funds permit it.

• 1481 • Prix Dumas-Millier
To recognize a painter or a sculptor. French artists over 45 years of age whose work is inspired by the traditions of the l'Ecole francaise are eligible. Awards are given in alternate years to a painter and a sculptor. A monetary prize is awarded annually.

• 1482 • Prix et Fondations Concernant l'Academie de France a Rome
To recognize painters, sculptors, architects, and engravers. Prizes awarded and Foundations awarding prizes are as follows: Fondation Pinette; Fondation Chedanne; Prix Injalbert; Fondation Jean-Paul Alaux; Fondation Daumet; Fondation Redon; Fondation de Mme. Veuve Beule; Fondation Gustave Clausse; Fondation Gustave Germain; Fondation Marmottan; and Fondation de Caen. Monetary awards are for study at the Academie de France in Rome. Aside from the prize of the Fondation de Caen, which is awarded annually, the prizes are awarded periodically, when the funds permit it. Established in 1666.

• 1483 • Prix Le Guay-Lebrun
To recognize an artist under 40 years of age for a painting, sculpture, or drawing exhibited at the Salon des Artistes Francais. Prizes are awarded in alternate years in the categories of painting, sculpture, and drawing. A monetary prize is awarded periodically, when the funds permit it.

• 1484 • Prix Susse Freres
To recognize a sculptor for a work in high relief of which the gestures and faces reflect a human sentiment. Sculptors born in France, between the ages of 27 and 35 who are exhibited at the Salon des Artistes Francais are eligible. A monetary prize is awarded periodically, when the funds permit it.

• 1485 • Prix Jean Reynaud
For recognition of the most noteworthy and original work of art produced during the preceding five years. Members of the Institute are not eligible. A monetary prize is awarded periodically, when the funds permit it.

• 1486 • Prix Richtenberger
For recognition of the best book on the history of 14th, 15th, or 16th century painting. A monetary prize is awarded periodically, when the funds permit it.

• 1487 • Prix Rossini
For recognition of a composition of lyric or religious music; and for recognition of a poetic work of less than two hundred lines of verse, destined to be set to music. A monetary prize is awarded periodically, when the funds permit it.

• 1488 • Prix de Composition Musicale Marcel Samuel-Rousseau
For recognition of a lyric work that has one or several acts. The competition is open to all French composers who are at least 35 years of age. A monetary prize of 6,000 francs is awarded triennially.

• 1489 • Prix Rouyer
For recognition of a survey of French architecture. A monetary prize is awarded periodically, when the funds permit it.

• 1490 • Prix Ruhlmann
To recognize a student architect for the best project in interior design. A monetary prize is awarded periodically, when the funds permit it.

• 1491 • Prix Ary Scheffer
For recognition of the best copperplate engraving exhibited at the Salon des Artistes Francais. A monetary prize is awarded periodically, when the funds permit it.

• 1492 • Prix Florent Schmitt
For recognition of distinguished composers. French composers who are over 45 years of age are eligible. Three monetary prizes are awarded periodically, when the funds permit it.

• 1493 • Prix Thorlet
To encourage scholarly works on the history of art, in particular on painting. A monetary prize is awarded periodically, when the funds permit it.

• 1494 • Prix Ch. M. Tornov-Loeffler
For recognition of the best musical composition of the past two or four years. Composers who are descended from at least four French generations are eligible. A monetary prize is awarded periodically, when the funds permit it.

• 1495 • Prix Frederic et Jean de Vernon
To recognize French sculptors and engravers under 40 years of age. Awards are given in alternate years to a sculptor and an engraver. A monetary prize is awarded annually.

• 1496 • Prix de Dessin Pierre David Weill
For recognition of excellence in drawing competitions. Artists must be under 30 years of age and, if foreigners, must have lived at least one

year in France. All drawing techniques are allowed with the exception of water color, gouache and pastel. Monetary prizes are awarded annually. At least the 50 best entries are publicly exhibited. Established in 1971. Sponsored by the Pierre David - Weill Foundation.

• 1497 • Prix de Portrait Paul-Louis Weiller
For recognition of a painted portrait or a sculpted bust. Awards are given in an international contest in alternate years in the categories of portrait painting and sculpture. A monetary prize is awarded to an artist of any age; two monetary prizes to artists under 35 years of age; and two monetary prizes to artists under 30 years of age. All works which pass the first selection are exhibited publicly. Awarded annually. Established by Paul Louis Weiller, a member of the l'Academie des Beaux Arts.

• 1498 • Prix Paul-Louis Weiller
To recognize painters, sculptors, engravers, and musical composers for overcoming a handicap and accomplishing outstanding work. Awards are given in alternate years to painters or sculptors and engravers or musical composers. Two monetary prizes are awarded annually.

• 1499 • Prix Georges Wildenstein
To recognize the artists, including painters, sculptors, architects, engravers, musicians and filmmakers, who were granted a fellowship by the French government and a residence in the Casa de Velasquez in Madrid. A monetary prize is awarded annually.

• 1500 •
Academie des Inscriptions et Belles-Lettres
Jean Richard, Pres.
Institut de France
23, quai de Conti
F-75006 Paris, France
Phone: 33 1 4441 4310
Fax: 33 1 4441 4311
E-mail: j.leclant.aibl@dial.oleane.com
Home Page: http://www.aibl.fr

• 1501 • Prix de la Fondation Emile Benveniste
For recognition of a work in comparative grammar of Indo-European languages and Iranian linguistics.

• 1502 • Prix Bordin
For recognition of studies in the following categories: (1) Classical antiquity; (2) Oriental; and (3) Medieval and Renaissance civilization. A monetary prize is awarded alternately in the three categories. Awarded annually.

• 1503 • Prix Brunet
For recognition of the best scholarly bibliographic works published in the preceding three years. A monetary prize is awarded triennially.

• 1504 • Prix Honore Chavee
To encourage work in linguistics and, in particular, research on Romance languages. A monetary prize is awarded biennially.

• 1505 • Prix de la Fondation Louis de Clercq
For recognition of a work in Oriental archaeology.

• 1506 • Prix Charles Clermont-Ganneau
For recognition of a work or collection of studies on the epigraphy of semitic people (from Syria, Phoenicia, Palestine, Cyprus, Carthage and other Punic colonies) or on the ancient history of these regions (studies on Syrian history may only go up to the Crusades). A monetary prize is awarded every five years. Established by the Duke of Loubat.

• 1507 • Concours des Antiquites de la France
For recognition of the best works (manuscripts or publications within the preceding two years) on French antiquities. Works on numismatics are not accepted. Three medals are awarded annually.

• 1508 • Prix Alfred Croiset
For recognition of a work or collection of printed works studying Greek language and literature (excluding modern Greek literature or works on epigraphy). A monetary prize is awarded every five years. Established by the Duke of Loubat.

• 1509 • Prix Estrade-Delcros
For recognition of a work re-examining the arrangement of studies by the Academy. The award is not to be divided. A monetary prize is awarded every five years.

• 1510 • Prix Charles and Marguerite Diehl
For recognition of a published work on Byzantine history or the history of Byzantine art. The work must be written in French. A monetary prize is awarded biennially.

• 1511 • Prix Edmond Drouin
For recognition of a manuscript or published work on Oriental numismatics. Authors without regard to nationality are eligible. A monetary prize is awarded every four years.

• 1512 • Prix Duchalais
For recognition of the best work on the numismatics of the Middle Ages appearing in the preceding two years. A monetary prize is awarded biennially.

• 1513 • Prix Raoul Duseigneur
For recognition of work on Spanish art and archaeology from the beginning of history to the end of the 16th century, or on the artistic, archaeological treasures of these epochs in the public or private Spanish collections. A monetary prize is awarded triennially. Established by the Marquise Arconati-Visconti.

• 1514 • Prix Alfred Dutens
For recognition of the most useful work on linguistics. A monetary prize is awarded every ten years.

• 1515 • Prix Louis Fould
For recognition of the best work on the history of drawing up to the end of the 16th century. A monetary prize is awarded biennially.

• 1516 • Prix Roman et Tania Ghirshman
For recognition of the best publication on pre-Islamic Iran. Works may be written on the history of civilization, the history of religion or art, numismatics, or the epigraphy or philology of Elamit, old-Persian, Armenian, Greek or Pahlavi writings. French or foreign authors are eligible. A monetary prize is awarded annually.

• 1517 • Prix Herbert Allen Giles
For recognition of a work on China, Japan or the Far East. A monetary prize is awarded biennially.

• 1518 • Prix du Baron de Joest
To recognize an individual who has made a discovery or written a book best serving the public interest during the preceding year. A monetary prize is awarded annually and is given alternately by one of the five Academies of the Institut.

• 1519 • Prix Stanislas Julien
For recognition of the best work related to China. A monetary prize is awarded annually.

• 1520 • Prix du Duc de Loubat
For recognition of the best work on the history, geography, and archaeology of the New World. A monetary prize is awarded triennially.

• 1521 • Prix Gaston Maspero
For recognition of a work or collection of works on Ancient Egypt. A monetary prize is awarded every five years. Established by the Duke of Loubat.

• 1522 • Prix Antoine Meillet
For recognition of an original work on comparative grammar or general linguistics. The author need not be French. A monetary prize is awarded every five years. Established in 1979.

• 1523 • Prix Gustave Mendel
For recognition of a detailed scientific catalogue, written in French, of part or of a whole collection of Ancient Greek monuments or objects. If no such catalogue is submitted, a scientific work on Greek archaeology is considered. A monetary prize is awarded annually. Established by Louis Gaillet-Billotteau.

• 1524 • Medaille Georges Perrot
For recognition of the best work on the history of ancient art or Greek archeology. A medal is awarded biennially.

• 1525 • Prix Allier de Hauteroche
For recognition of the best work on ancient numismatics appearing during the preceding two years. A monetary prize is awarded biennially.

• 1526 • Prix Ambatielos
For recognition of a work on the history or archaeology of Greece appearing during the preceding year. A monetary prize is awarded annually.

• 1527 • Prix de Chenier
To recognize the author of the best method for teaching Greek or for the work that seems the most useful for studying Greek language and literature. A monetary prize is awarded every five years.

• 1528 • Prix de La Fons-Melicocq
For recognition of the best work on the history and the antiquities of Picardy and Ile-de-France (except Paris). A monetary prize is awarded biennially.

• 1529 • Prix de La Grange
For recognition of the publication of a previously unpublished poem of an early poet of France. If no unpublished work is submitted, the prize may go to the best work on a published poem of the early poets. A monetary prize is awarded annually.

• 1530 • Prix Delalande-Guerineau
For recognition of work on the Orient published during the two years preceding the award. A monetary prize is awarded biennially.

• 1531 • Prix Gabriel-Auguste Prost
To recognize the author of the best historical work on Metz or neighboring areas. A monetary prize is awarded annually.

• 1532 • Prix Gustave Schlumberger
For recognition of studies in the following categories: (1) Byzantine History; (2) Byzantine Archeology; and (3) the history and archaeology of the Latin Orient. A monetary prize is awarded alternately in the three categories. Awarded annually.

• 1533 • Prix de la Fondation Emile Senart
For recognition of a study of ancient India.

• 1534 • Prix Emile Le Senne
To encourage historical, archaeological, artistic or iconographic studies on Paris and the Seine department. A monetary prize is awarded biennially.

• 1535 • Prix Toutain-Blanchet
For recognition of work either on the history of Ancient Gaul, before the advent of Clovis (485 A.D.), or on the history of Northern Africa before the end of the Byzantine domination (715 A.D.). A monetary prize is awarded triennially.

• 1536 • Prix Adolphe Noel des Vergers
For recognition of archeological studies or excavations. A monetary prize is awarded every six years.

• 1537 •
Academie des Sciences
Jean Dercourt, Sec.
Institut de France
23, quai de Conti
F-75006 Paris, France
Phone: 33 1 4441 4367
Fax: 33 1 4441 4363
E-mail: disc@academie-sciences.fr
Home Page: http://www.academie-sciences.fr

• 1538 • Prix Anatole et Suzanne Abragam
For recognition of a researcher under 40 years of age in the field of physics. A monetary prize is awarded biennially in even-numbered years. Established in 1987.

• 1539 • Prix Alcan-Pechiney
To recognize young researchers with doctorates, whose work has contributed to progress in the aluminum industry or, more broadly, the field of metallurgy. The selection is made by a commission composed of members of the Academy or members of CADAS. A monetary prize is awarded annually. Established in 1986.

• 1540 • Prix Louis Armand
For recognition of a young researcher (30 years of age or older) for an outstanding work in the field of applied mathematics, mechanical engineering, physics, chemistry, biology, or earth science. A monetary prize is awarded biennially in odd-numbered years. Established in 1987 by the Association des Amis de Louis Armand.

• 1541 • Prix Louis-Daniel Beauperthuy
For recognition of work in epidemiology that contributes to the amelioration of the human condition. A monetary prize is awarded biennially in even-numbered years. Established in 1982.

• 1542 • Prix Henri Becquerel
To encourage scientific progress. A monetary prize is awarded quadriennially. Established in 1905 by Jean Becquerel in memory of Henri Becquerel, his father and secretary of the Academie des Sciences.

• 1543 • Prix Jean-Jacques Berger
To recognize outstanding contributions concerning the city of Paris. The award is given in alternate years by the Academie des Sciences, Academie francaise, Academies des Inscriptions et Belles-Lettres, Academie des Beaux-Arts, and Academie des Sciences Morales et Politiques. The prize is not to be divided. If there is not a work that merits the prize, the value of the prize is used to encourage the best works nominated. A monetary prize is awarded. Established in 1881.

• 1544 • Prix de Madame Claude Berthault
For recognition of a scientific work that increases the influence of the French nation. French citizens are eligible. A monetary prize is awarded annually. Established in 1921.

• 1545 • Prix Berthelot
To recognize a scientist who has received a prize for chemistry during the preceding year. The Berthelot Medal is awarded annually. Established in 1902.

• 1546 • Prix Paul Bertrand
For recognition of outstanding work in paleobotany or stratigraphic geology dedicated to coal-bearing formations. Awards are given in alternate years in the two categories. If there are no candidates in these disciplines, the award goes to a work of anatomy or descriptive botany. A monetary prize is awarded triennially. Established in 1960.

• 1547 • Prix Binoux
For recognition of outstanding work in geography, navigation, or the history or philosophy of science. Awards are given in alternate years. A monetary prize is awarded biennially. Established in 1889.

• 1548 • Prix Edmond Brun
For recognition of work in the mechanics of fluids, thermics, or astronautics. A monetary prize is awarded annually. Established in 1980.

• 1549 • Prix Carriere de Mathematiques
For recognition of work in mathematics. A monetary prize is awarded every four years. Established in 1932.

• 1550 • Prix Elie Cartan
To recognize a mathematician who has introduced new ideas or solved a difficult problem. Individuals over 45 years of age of any nationality are eligible. A monetary prize is awarded triennially. Established in 1980.

• 1551 • Prix Auguste Chevalier
To recognize the author of one or more works relating to plants (systems, biology, and geography) of tropical and subtropical French-speaking countries, in particular to plants from West Africa. A monetary prize is awarded biennially. Established in 1955.

• 1552 • Prix Clavel-Lespiau
For recognition of work in organic chemistry. A monetary prize is awarded biennially. Established in 1979.

• 1553 • Prix Le Conte
For recognition of discoveries and of new applications in mathematics, physics, chemistry, natural history, and medical science. A monetary prize is awarded triennially. Established in 1876.

• 1554 • Prix Jean Dagnan-Bouveret
To encourage medical studies. A monetary prize is awarded biennially. Established in 1924.

• 1555 • Prix Dandrimont-Benicourt
For recognition of research in the field of cancer. A monetary prize is awarded annually. Established in 1990.

• 1556 • Prix Ernest Dechelle
For recognition of the work of a French scientist in the field of mathematics, physics, astronomy, and natural science. Awards are given in alternate years by the division of mathematics and physics; and the division of chemistry, natural science, biology, and medicine. A monetary prize is awarded annually. Established in 1943.

• 1557 • Prix Georges Deflandre et Marthe Deflandre-Rigaud
For recognition of a work in micro-paleontology, concerning in particular: evolution, phylogenesis, ontogenesis, ecology, paleobiology, or morphology. Scientists without regard to nationality or age are eligible. A monetary prize is awarded triennially. Established in 1970.

• 1558 • Prix Deslandres
For recognition of the best work in spectral analysis and its applications. French or foreign scientists are eligible. A monetary prize is awarded biennially. Established in 1946.

• 1559 • Prix Charles Dhere
For recognition of work in biochemistry. A monetary prize is awarded biennially in odd-numbered years. Established in 1955.

• 1560 • Prix Paul Doisteau - Emile Blutet
The purpose of the prize is decided during the year preceding its award by the Academie. A monetary prize awarded annually. Established in 1954.

• 1561 • Prix Rene Dujarric de la Riviere
For recognition of work in biology with application to rural economics and veterinary medicine. A monetary prize is awarded quadriennially. Established in 1970.

• 1562 • Prix Leon-Alexandre Etancelin
To encourage or recognize discoveries valuable to humanity, primarily in the fight against cancer and other incurable diseases. French citizens or research work done by a French institute or laboratory are eligible. A monetary award is awarded every five years. Established in 1945.

• 1563 • Fondation Andre-Romain Prevot
To recognize a French bacteriologist whose research has increased our knowledge of bacteria. The Louis Pasteur Medal is awarded annually when merited. Established in 1978.

• 1564 • Prix Foulon
For recognition of outstanding work in the fields of botany, rural economics, zoology, and neuroscience. Monetary awards are given annually. Established in 1940.

• 1565 • Prix du Gaz de France
For recognition of French researchers or researchers from the European Community in the fields of engineering, chemistry, materials, energy, or first matter that contributes to an increase in knowledge of interest to the gas industry. A monetary prize is awarded annually. Established in 1987.

• 1566 • Prix Jean-Marie Le Goff
To encourage research in biological chemistry, in particular the study of red blood cells in diabetics and the physiological and therapeutic properties of cobalt and its derivatives. A monetary prize is awarded quadrennially. Established in 1950.

• 1567 • Prix Grammaticakis-Neuman
For recognition of the best work in organic chemistry concerning photochemistry or spectrochemistry, experimental chemistry, mathematical applications in biology, or the philosophy of science. Awards are given alternately in the categories of organic chemistry, mathematical applications in biology (preferably human physiology), and the philosophy of science (preferably the pragmatic approach). A monetary prize is awarded annually. In addition, in the area of organic chemistry concerning photochemistry or spectrochemistry, a monetary prize is awarded annually. Established in 1982.

• 1568 • Prix Leon Grelaud
To recognize the author of a work most significant in the study of the upper atmosphere, either by stratospheric devices or other means. A monetary prize is awarded every eight years. Established in 1947.

• 1569 • Prix Philippe A. Guye
For recognition of work in the field of physical chemistry. A monetary prize is awarded biennially in even-numbered years. Established in 1941.

• 1570 • Prix James Hall
For recognition of the best doctoral thesis in geology written during the 10-year period preceding the award. A monetary prize is awarded biennially. Established in 1911.

• 1571 • Fondation de Madame Edmond Hamel
To recognize hydrography engineers for distinguished work in their field. The Prix Alexandre Givry is awarded every 10 years. Established in 1928.

• 1572 • Prix Fernand Holweck
For recognition of outstanding research in physics. Awards are given in alternate years in the categories of radiation physics and physics of the globe. A monetary prize is awarded triennially. Established in 1946.

• 1573 • Prix Charles Jacob
For recognition of a work, theoretical or applied, in the field of earth sciences. French or foreign scientists are eligible. A monetary prize is awarded biennially. Established in 1965.

• 1574 • Prix Max-Fernand Jayle
For recognition of original research in the biochemistry or the physiology of sexual hormones, in particular, research on the function of reproduction of mammals, primates, and humans. French citizens who are at least 45 years of age are eligible. The prize is not be divided. A monetary prize is awarded biennially in even-numbered years. Established in 1981.

• 1575 • Prix Paul Fallot-Jeremine
To aid young geologists at the beginning of their research; principally, to permit them to accomplish geological studies at a site. Candidates of any nationality or sex should present a recommendation from a professor or researcher familiar with their work. A scholarship is awarded biennially in even-numbered years. Established in 1953.

• 1576 • Prix Alexandre Joannides
For recognition of scientific, medical, or other research useful to the public good. The prize is awarded alternately by the division of chemistry and natural sciences and the division of mathematics and physics. A monetary prize is awarded annually. Established in 1958.

• 1577 • Prix Emile Jungfleisch
To recognize a Frenchman for important work or discoveries in organic chemistry. A monetary prize is awarded biennially in odd-numbered years. Established in 1923.

• 1578 • Prix L. La Caze
For recognition of outstanding work in the field of physics, chemistry, or physiology. All nationalities are eligible. A monetary prize is awarded quadriennially. Awarded alternately by the Commission for physics, chemistry, and physiology. Established in 1865.

• 1579 • Prix du Docteur et de Madame Henri Labbe
For recognition of scientific work in biochemistry and nutrition. Monetary prize is awarded for each achievement in biochemistry and for work in nutrition are awarded annually. Established in 1948.

• 1580 • Prix Lallemand

For recognition of outstanding work in the different fields of astronomy. Preference is given to works that have application in some other field. Individuals or teams are eligible. A monetary prize is awarded biennially in odd-numbered years. Established in 1990 and awarded for the first time in 1992.

• 1581 • Prix Lamb

For recognition of the best studies on the national defense of France. A monetary prize is awarded biennially in odd-numbered years. Established in 1938.

• 1582 • Prix Langevin

For recognition of outstanding work by a mathematician, chemist, physicist, or biologist. A monetary prize is awarded annually. Established through the initiative of Paul Langevin in 1945 in memory of the French scholars killed by the Germans from 1940 to 1945, and to reward works in the disciplines to which those scholars contributed.

• 1583 • La Medaille Laplace

To recognize the student graduating with the highest rank from the School of Polytechnic Sciences. A silver-gilt medal with the likeness of M. de Laplace is awarded annually by the President of the Academie des Sciences. Established in 1836.

• 1584 • Prix Alphonse Laveran

To recognize French doctors who have made the most progress in exotic pathology. A monetary prize is awarded every 10 years. Established in 1946.

• 1585 • Prix Marie Leon-Houry

To recognize the doctor, chemist, or scientist who contributes the most to the conquest of cancer and tuberculosis. A monetary prize is awarded every 10 years. Established in 1942.

• 1586 • Prix Richard Lounsbery

For recognition of research in medicine and biology. Scientists under 40 years of age are eligible. A monetary prize of $50,000 is awarded annually. The prize is awarded alternately by the National Academy of Sciences in Washington, D.C., U.S.A., and by the Academie des Sciences in Paris. Established in 1978 and first awarded in 1979 in Washington.

• 1587 • Prix Leon Lutaud

For recognition of work that makes progress in a discipline of geology. A monetary prize is awarded biennially in even-numbered years. Established in 1982 on the occasion of the election of Jean Aubouin to l'Academie des Sciences. Sponsored by Comite National Francais de Geologie.

• 1588 • Prix Adrien Constantin de Magny

To recognize a craftsman or scientist whose practical works are considered remarkable by the Academie. Individuals are not required to have a diploma to be eligible. A monetary prize is awarded biennially. Established in 1963 by the Fondation Rheims.

• 1589 • Prix Paul Marguerite de la Charlonie

For recognition of original research in chemistry, agriculture, and physics. Awards are given in alternate years in the following categories: chemistry, agriculture, and physics. A monetary prize is awarded annually. Established in 1902.

• 1590 • Prix Charles-Leopold Mayer

To encourage and support fundamental research, particularly in the fields of biology, biochemistry, and biophysics. The prize, awarded without regard to country or nationality, may not be given to the same nationality two years in a row. Research that may lead to a discovery or invention to synthesize nucleoproteins, similar to the living cell, or to reveal the fundamental workings of cellular life is considered. Candidates must be 65 years of age or younger. A monetary prize is awarded annually. Established in 1960.

• 1591 • Prix Georges Millot

To recognize the author of a work in the field of geochemistry in one of the many areas of earth science, including geology, sedimentology, oceanology, pedology, metallurgy, and ecology. The Prix de Geochimie is awarded triennially. Established in 1979.

• 1592 • Prix Michel Monpetit

To recognize a French researcher or engineer in the field of computer sciences or automation. The judges are guided by such factors as the originality of basic ideas and the serious nature of the work, the confirmation of the results obtained, and the possibility of its practical application in the French computer sciences and automation industries. A monetary prize is awarded annually. Established in 1977 by the Institut National de Recherche en Informatique et en Automatique and le Club de la Peri-Informatique.

• 1593 • Prix Montyon de Physiologie

For recognition of the most useful work on experimental physiology. A monetary prize is awarded biennially. Established in 1818.

• 1594 • Prix Victor Noury

To encourage the development of scientific culture in its most diverse forms. French citizens over the age of 45 are eligible. A monetary prize is awarded every five years. Established in 1917.

• 1595 • Prix Henri de Parville

For recognition of outstanding work in the fields of mechanics or physics. Awards are given in alternate years in the two categories. A monetary prize is awarded biennially. Established in 1891.

• 1596 • Prix Paul Pascal

For recognition of research work in physical chemistry, particularly in magnetochemistry and its eventual extensions. Young or middle-aged researchers are eligible. A monetary prize is awarded annually. Established in 1972.

• 1597 • Prix Petit d'Ormoy

For recognition of works of theory and application of science to medicine, mechanics, and industry. Awards are given in alternate years in the following categories: mathematics and physics; and chemistry and natural sciences. A monetary prize is awarded every four years. Established in 1875.

• 1598 • Prix Ivan Peyches

For recognition of work that studies the condition and usefulness of solar energy or similar applied science fields. A monetary prize is awarded annually. Established in 1978.

• 1599 • Prix Plumey

To recognize an individual who perfects steam engines or other devices that contribute to the progress of navigation. A monetary prize is awarded biennially in odd-numbered years. Established in 1859.

• 1600 • Prix Ayme Poirson

For recognition of work on the applications of science to industry. A monetary prize is awarded biennially in even-numbered years. Established in 1965.

• 1601 • Prix Andre Policard-Lacassagne

To recognize a young French or foreign scientist who has accomplished distinguished work in biochemistry, biophysics, or physical chemistry conducting research in France in these fields. Scientists under the age of 40 who do not belong to the Academie des Sciences are eligible. A monetary prize is awarded quadriennially. Established in 1958.

• 1602 • Prix Ampere d'Electricite de France

To recognize one or several French scientists for remarkable research work in the field of mathematics or physics, fundamental or applied. A monetary prize is awarded annually. Established in 1974 by Electricite de France in memory of the scientist, Ampere, whose 200th birthday was celebrated in 1975.

• 1603 • Prix Antoine d'Abbadie

For recognition of work in astronomy or geophysics. An award is given in alternate years in the categories of astronomy and geophysics. A monetary prize is awarded biennially in even-numbered years. Established in 1899 as an astronomy prize and changed in 1976, when the l'Observatoire d'Abbadie closed.

• 1604 • Prix Artur du Fay
For recognition of work on the movement of solid bodies. A monetary prize is awarded every 10 years. Established in 1912.

• 1605 • Prix Blaise Pascal du GAMNI-SMAI
To recognize one or several researchers for a remarkable work done in France using the applied numerical methods of the Science of Engineering. A monetary prize is awarded annually. Established in 1984 by le Groupement pour l'Avancement des Methodes Numerique de l'Ingenieur (GAMNI) and the Societe de Mathematiques appliques et Industrielles (SMAI).

• 1606 • Prix Charles-Louis de Saulses de Freycinet
To aid scientists whose resources are insufficient to permit them to pursue their scientific research, or to encourage research or work profitable to health or progress. A monetary prize is awarded biennially in odd-numbered years. Established in 1925.

• 1607 • Prix de l'Ecole Centrale
To recognize the first place graduate at l'Ecole Centrale des Arts et Manufactures. A monetary prize is awarded annually. Established in 1964.

• 1608 • Prix de l'Institut Francais du Petrole
To recognize a French or foreign researcher or research team for a scientific work that contributes to progress in understanding techniques directly or indirectly of interest to the hydrocarbon industry. Techniques concerning action that satisfies the needs of humanity for energy and its products and materials while respecting the environment are eligible. A monetary prize is awarded annually. Established in 1990 and awarded for the first time in 1994.

• 1609 • Prix des Sciences de la Mer
To recognize research works in physical oceanography, marine ecology, chemistry, and biology. A monetary award is given biennially. Established in 1992.

• 1610 • Prix du Commisariat a l'Energie Atomique
To recognize one or several Frenchmen for an important scientific or technical discovery in the following fields: physics, mechanics, astronomy, and their applications; and chemistry, biology, human biology, and medical sciences, as well as their applications. The Academie awards an equal number of prizes in each of the two fields. A monetary prize is awarded annually. Established in 1977 by the Commissioner of Atomic Energy.

• 1611 • Prix Fonde par l'Etat
For recognition of outstanding works in mathematics and physics and their applications; or for works in the chemical, natural, biological, and medical sciences and their applications. Each year, the prize is awarded on alternating topics: mathematics, physics, chemistry, and biology. A monetary prize is awarded annually. Established in 1975.

• 1612 • Prix France Telecom
To award one or more researchers or engineers for research work in telecommunications. A monetary award is given annually.

• 1613 • Prix Jean Cuvillier
For recognition of the best work of a young micro-paleontologist of any nationality. A monetary prize is awarded triennially. Established in 1970.

• 1614 • Prix Lazare Carnot
To recognize excellent research works. A monetary award is given biennially in odd-numbered years. Established in 1992.

• 1615 • Prix Octave Mirbeau et Valentine Allorge
To honor authors of works on cryptograms. A monetary award is given every four years. Established in 1990.

• 1616 • Prix Pierre Desnuelle
To recognize works by biological chemists. A monetary award is given every four years. Established in 1991.

• 1617 • Prix Gustave Ribaud
For recognition of work in the area of thermal exchanges or high frequency. Awards alternate between the fields of applied physics and theoretical physics. A monetary prize is awarded every four years. Established in 1965.

• 1618 • Prix L. E. Rivot
To recognize the four students who graduate from l'Ecole polytechnique in first and second place in the department of mines and the department of bridges and highways. Monetary prizes for first place and second place are awarded annually. The prize is to be used to buy science books, and for travel expenses for study. Established in 1890.

• 1619 • Prix Gaston Rousseau
To provide recognition for scientific research leading toward an improvement in human welfare, and especially toward the cure of diseases, such as cancer. A scientist or a team of scientists working in the same field (without respect to nationality) are eligible. A monetary prize is awarded biennially. Established in 1970 and first awarded in 1978.

• 1620 • Prix Gustave Roussy
For recognition and encouragement of cancer research. A monetary prize is awarded triennially. Established in 1967.

• 1621 • Prix Gabrielle Sand et Marie Guido Triossi
To recognize a scientist for an invention for the good of mankind. Awards are given in alternate years in the categories of mathematics, physics, and chemistry and natural sciences. A monetary prize is awarded every four years. Established in 1939.

• 1622 • Prix Servant
For recognition of outstanding works in mathematics and physics. A monetary prize is awarded annually, alternating between the two topics. Established in 1952.

• 1623 • Prix Victor Thebault
To recognize the author of an original study or interesting work in arithmetic or geometry. Preference is given to primary or secondary school teachers. A monetary prize is awarded every nine years. Established in 1943.

• 1624 • Prix Thorlet
For recognition of outstanding scientific work. A monetary prize is awarded annually. Established in 1912.

• 1625 • Prix Roy Vaucouloux
To encourage and assist research in the field of biology, preferably on the nature of cancer or its treatment. French scientists or a French laboratory is eligible, however, the prize is not to be divided. A monetary prize is awarded biennially in even-numbered years. Established in 1926.

• 1626 • Prix Leon Velluz
For recognition of a discovery in chemistry or organic biochemistry leading to human therapy. The prize is not to be divided, but may be awarded to a team for a discovery. A monetary prize is awarded biennially in odd-numbered years. Established in 1982.

• 1627 • Prix Alfred Verdaguer
For recognition of a remarkable work in art, literature, or science. A monetary prize is awarded annually in one of the three fields. Established in 1948 by a large bequest of Alfred Verdaguer.

• 1628 • Prix Aniuta Winter-Klein
To recognize young researchers whose work contributes to the knowledge or application of the physical chemistry of the solid noncrystalline vitreous state. Individuals of any nationality and residence are eligible. The winner gives one or two lectures in memory of Aniuta Winter Klein. A monetary prize is awarded biennially in even-numbered years. Established in 1982.

• 1629 • Prix Nicolas Zvorikine
For recognition of a scientific or practical study on ameliorating the economic condition of the small farmer. Consideration is given particularly to studies on developing market gardening and breeding, on using winter leisure time for handicrafts, or on spreading electric power. The work should be sufficiently developed to be used as a model. French or Russian citizens are eligible. A monetary prize and a book are awarded every seven years. Established in 1937.

• 1630 •
Academie des Sciences Morales et Politiques
Jean Tulard, Pres.
Institut de France
23, quai de Conti
F-75006 Paris, France
Phone: 33 1 4441 4326
Fax: 33 1 4441 4327
E-mail: secretaireperpetuel@asmp.fr
Home Page: http://www.asmp.fr

• 1631 • **Prix Dupin Aine**
For recognition of the best work on civil law, Roman law, criminal law, corporate law, customary law, history of law, the laws of nations, or statute law. The prize can be divided between two winners. A monetary prize is awarded triennially.

• 1632 • **Prix Audiffred**
For recognition of a published work that inspires love of ethics and virtue, spurns egoism and envy, and instills patriotism; and for recognition of the greatest and most beautiful self-sacrifice or devotion to any field. A monetary prize is awarded annually.

• 1633 • **Prix Odilon Barrot**
For recognition of the best work on juries, both criminal and civil and for recognition of the most practical and liberal work on decentralization of government. A monetary prize is awarded triennially.

• 1634 • **Prix Felix de Beaujour**
To recognize the author of the best treatise that contributes to the solution of the plight of the poor in different countries, particularly France. A monetary prize is awarded every five years.

• 1635 • **Prix Paul Leroy-Beaulieu**
To recognize and encourage effective publicity in favor of increasing the French birth rate and defending the rights and interests of large and average families. A monetary prize is awarded triennially.

• 1636 • **Prix de la Fondation Claude Berthault**
For recognition of an artistic or scientific work that increases the reputation of the French nation. Families of farmers or sailors of the coast of the Marche on the ocean, with preference given to veterans of World War I are eligible. A monetary prize of 3,000 francs is awarded annually.

• 1637 • **Prix Robert Blanche**
For recognition of a work of philosophy on the subject of logic or epistemology. Awarded every four years.

• 1638 • **Bourse Marcelle Blum**
To provide the opportunity for studies in female psychology. Awarded annually.

• 1639 • **Prix Bordin**
For recognition of papers on subjects touching the public interest, the good of humanity, the progress of science, and national honor. Awards are given in alternate years by the following sections of the academy: philosophy, morals, legislation, political economy, and history. A monetary prize is awarded biennially.

• 1640 • **Prix Carlier**
For recognition of the best treatise on new methods to improve moral and material conditions of the largest social class in Paris. A monetary prize is awarded annually.

• 1641 • **Prix Rene Cassin**
For recognition of a legal work of value or to recognize the author of an action or work of civic merit. A monetary prize is awarded triennially.

• 1642 • **Prix Gustave Chaix d'Est Ange**
For recognition of a work of documentary history about the Chartists movement. A monetary prize is awarded annually.

• 1643 • **Prix Jean-Baptiste Chevallier**
For recognition of the best work on the defense of private property and the laws pertaining to it in the French Civil Code. French writers are eligible. A monetary prize is awarded triennially.

• 1644 • **Prix Corbay**
For recognition of a useful contribution in the fields of science, art, law, agriculture, industry, or business.

• 1645 • **Prix Victor Cousin**
To recognize the author of a treatise on the history of ancient philosophy. A monetary prize is awarded triennially.

• 1646 • **Prix Crouzet**
For recognition of the best treatise on philosophical or religious questions exclusively from the point of view of natural religion without any diversion into the area of the supernatural. A monetary prize is awarded every five years.

• 1647 • **Prix Dagnan-Bouveret**
To encourage the study of psychology and for recognition of a work in psychology. A monetary prize is awarded biennially in odd-numbered years. Established by the parents of M. Dagnan-Bouveret, who died for France.

• 1648 • **Prix Bigot de Morogues**
For recognition of the best work on poverty in France and remedies for that poverty. A monetary prize is awarded every ten years.

• 1649 • **Prix Victor Delbos**
For recognition of publications that promote spiritual life and religious philosophy in the past and future. A monetary prize is awarded biennially.

• 1650 • **Prix de la Fondation du Chanoine Delpeuch**
For recognition of a contribution to the moral, intellectual, and religious development of France. A monetary prize of 2,000 francs is awarded annually.

• 1651 • **Prix Demolombe**
To recognize an author whose works are within the scope of the academie. Awards are given in alternate years in the following categories: philosophy, morality, law, political economy, and history and geography. Monetary awards are presented by one of the five sections of the academie. Awarded every four years.

• 1652 • **Prix Joseph du Teil**
For recognition of a work on diplomatic history. A monetary prize is awarded annually.

• 1653 • **Prix Dulac**
For recognition of acts of courage or devotion. Members of the police or military are eligible. A monetary prize is awarded annually.

• 1654 • **Prix Charles Dupin**
For recognition of the best treatise or work on statistics or political economics. A monetary prize is awarded every six years.

• 1655 • **Prix Lucien Dupont**
To recognize an individual who by some action has contributed to the elimination of legal and administrative procedures and formalities that complicate the life of a citizen. A monetary prize is awarded annually.

• 1656 • **Prix Joseph Dutens**
For recognition of the best book or treatise related to political economics, or its history and applications. A monetary prize is awarded every five years.

• 1657 • **Prix Adrien Duvand**
For recognition of the best work on civic and moral education in a democracy. A monetary prize is awarded biennially.

• 1658 • **Prix Leon Faucher**
For recognition of a treatise on a question of political economics or on the life of a famous economist. A monetary prize is awarded triennially.

• 1659 • **Prix Jean Finot**
For recognition of a work with profoundly humanitarian social tendencies. A monetary prize is awarded biennially.

• 1660 • **Prix Marcel Flach**
For recognition of a work on the history of Alsace after 1648. A monetary prize is awarded biennially. Established by Madame Jacques Flach at the bequest of her husband, a member of the academie.

• 1661 • Prix Edmond Freville
For recognition of the best original work, book, or article that discusses the organization, function, or work of the ministries of defense, Army or Navy. The work may deal with topics such as central administration, commanding, officers, troops, and different services. Works written in French and published in the preceding two years are considered. A monetary prize is awarded annually.

• 1662 • Prix Gallet
To recognize the Catholic person or group having contributed the most to the improvement of French law and organization as it relates to the Catholic point of view. French citizens are eligible. A monetary prize is awarded annually.

• 1663 • Prix Gegner
To recognize a philosopher-writer whose works contribute to the progress of positive science. A monetary prize is awarded triennially.

• 1664 • Prix Auguste Gerard
For recognition of a work on the diplomatic history of France, England, Russia, Italy, Japan, Belgium, the United States, or the Balkan States that were allied with France during World War I. Works written in French are considered. A monetary prize is awarded every five years.

• 1665 • Prix Emile Girardeau
For recognition of a work or treatise on the subject of economics or sociology. A monetary prize is awarded annually.

• 1666 • Prix Grammaticakis-Neuman
For recognition of an outstanding work of pragmatic philosophy. Awards are given in alternate years by the following sections of the academy: philosophy, morals, and political economy. A monetary prize is awarded. Established in 1985.

• 1667 • Grand Prix de l'Academie des Sciences Morales et Politiques
To recognize an individual for an outstanding career and work in the field of philosophy, law, economics, or history. A monetary prize is awarded. Established in 1984.

• 1668 • Prix Joseph Hamel
For recognition of a work on commercial financial law. A monetary prize is awarded biennially.

• 1669 • Prix Jules et Louis Jeanbernat et Barthelemy de Ferrari Doria
For recognition of a work of literature, art, or science by a young French author. Monetary awards are given in alternate years by one of the five academies: Academie francaise, Academie des Inscriptions et Belle-Lettres, Academie des Sciences, Academie des Beaux-Arts, and Academie des Sciences Morales et Politiques.

• 1670 • Prix de Joest
For recognition of a discovery or written work that is most useful for the public good. A monetary prize is awarded every five years.

• 1671 • Prix Koenigswarter
For recognition of the best book on the history of law published during the preceding five years. A monetary prize is awarded every five years.

• 1672 • Prix Charles Lambert
To recognize the author of the best published study or manuscript on the future of spiritualism. A monetary prize is awarded triennially.

• 1673 • Prix Docteur Rene-Joseph Laufer
For recognition of the best work on social prophylaxis. A monetary prize is awarded biennially.

• 1674 • Prix Jules Lefort
To recognize the author or authors of working manuscripts on private and social insurance for the common classes, and on mutuality and future planning among the common social classes. A monetary prize is awarded every ten years. Established by M. and Mme. Lefort in memory of their son, Jules Lefort.

• 1675 • Prix Ernest Lemonon
For recognition of a work concerning contemporary foreign politics or contemporary French or foreign economics and social questions. A monetary prize is awarded annually.

• 1676 • Prix Charles Leveque
For recognition of a work on methaphysics published during the preceding four years. A monetary prize is awarded every four years.

• 1677 • Prix Drouyn de Lhuys
For recognition of a published or unpublished work on history. A monetary prize is awarded annually.

• 1678 • Prix Louis Liard
For recognition of a work on education, philosophy, or the history of philosophy, using rational or experimental methods and marked by precision results. A monetary prize is awarded triennially.

• 1679 • Prix Limantour
For recognition of the best work on law, history, or political economy. Prizes are awarded in alternate years in the following categories: law by the Legislative Section, history by the History Section, and political economics by the Political Economics Section. Work published in the past three years is eligible. A monetary prize is awarded biennially.

• 1680 • Prix Charles Lyon-Caen
To recognize the author of a work on philosophy, moral sciences, law, political economics, or history. Prizes are awarded in alternate years in the following categories: philosophy, moral sciences, law, political economics, and history. A monetary prize is awarded triennially. Established by friends and associates of M. Charles-Lyon Caen on the occasion of the 40th anniversary of his election to the academy.

• 1681 • Prix Maisondieu
To recognize the author or founder of a work that contributes to the improvement of the conditions of the working classes. A monetary prize is awarded biennially.

• 1682 • Prix Malouet
To recognize a secondary school teacher in France with at least four children of whose professional merits and devotion to family deserve public recognition. A monetary prize is awarded annually.

• 1683 • Prix Zerilli Marimo
To recognize an outstanding liberal economist. A monetary prize is awarded. Established in 1984.

• 1684 • Prix Georges Mauguin
For recognition of a scholarly work on Napoleon Bonaparte or his era. A monetary prize is awarded biennially in odd-numbered years.

• 1685 • Prix Gabriel Monod
For recognition of a published work on the sources of the national history of France, or on any subjects favored by Gabriel Monod. A monetary prize is awarded triennially.

• 1686 • Prix General Muteau
To recognize individuals or institutions who have contributed to the glory of France by their heroism, actions, or writings. A monetary prize is given annually.

• 1687 • Prix Le Dissez de Penanrun
For recognition of works published during the preceding six years on a topic proposed by one of the five sections of the academie. Monetary prizes are awarded in alternate years by one of the five sections of the academie. Awarded annually.

• 1688 • Prix Paul-Michel Perret
For recognition of a book on history. Books published during the preceding three years are eligible. A monetary prize is awarded annually. Established by Madame Dupont de Latuillerie in memory of her son.

• 1689 • Prix Le Fevre-Deumier de Ports
For recognition of a remarkable work on mythology, philosophy, or comparative religion. A monetary prize is awarded every ten years.

• 1690 • Prix Paul Vigne d'Octon
To recognize the author, preferably a physician, who has demonstrated through his writings his

professional behavior and life, an authentic and tangible devotion to the cause of progress of human relationships or of relationships between groups of human beings. A monetary prize is awarded biennially.

• 1691 • **Prix Ugo Papi - Gaston Leduc**
For recognition of an outstanding work on economy. A monetary prize is awarded. Established in 1985.

• 1692 • **Prix Lucien de Reinach**
For recognition of a work on the overseas territories written in French during the preceding two years. A monetary prize is awarded biennially in odd-numbered years.

• 1693 • **Prix Rossi**
For recognition of the best treatise on a question of social and political economics. A monetary prize is awarded annually.

• 1694 • **Prix Joseph Saillet**
For recognition of the best work on a subject of rationalist moral philosophy or scientific morality, independent of any religious ideas. Published or unpublished works written in French may be submitted. All nationalities are eligible. A monetary prize is awarded annually.

• 1695 • **Prix Berriat Saint-Prix**
For recognition of the best work on divorce legislation in France by its merit to restrict the number of divorces and keep the family whole. A monetary prize is awarded every five years.

• 1696 • **Prix Saintour**
For recognition of works of philosophy, morality, law, political economy, or history and geography. Monetary awards are given in alternate years by one of the five sections of the academie. Awarded biennially.

• 1697 • **Prix Eugene Salvan**
For recognition of an act of courage or self-sacrifice. A monetary prize is awarded every five years.

• 1698 • **Prix Stassart**
For recognition of the best oration of a moralist or for recognition of a work on a question of morality. A monetary prize is awarded every six years.

• 1699 • **Prix Tanesse**
To recognize an individual who contributed the most to improving the condition of women during the preceding three years. A monetary prize is awarded triennially.

• 1700 • **Prix Henri Texier II**
For recognition of a work to preserve the beauty of France. Awarded annually.

• 1701 • **Prix Henri Texier**
To recognize the author of a treatise on individual freedom and in support of actions directed toward the defense of individual liberty. A monetary prize is awarded annually.

• 1702 • **Prix Ernest Thorel**
For recognition of the best work designed to educate the people. Pamphlets or books of current reading, other than textbooks are considered. A monetary prize is awarded biennially.

• 1703 • **Prix Thorlet**
For recognition of virtue, social work, or scholarship in the field of history or art. Preference is given to a painter. A monetary prize is awarded biennially in odd-numbered years.

• 1704 • **Prix Maurice Travers**
For recognition of works relative to international public or private law, or comparative law; or for works on diplomatic history. Prizes are awarded in alternate years in international public or private law or comparative law and diplomatic history. A monetary prize is awarded biennially.

• 1705 • **Prix Blaise des Vosges**
For recognition of the best treatise, manuscript, or book published in French having as its object the moral and material improvement of industrial and agricultural workers through instruction, unionization, or any other means. Individuals are eligible without regard to nationality. A monetary prize is awarded triennially.

• 1706 • **Prix Wolowski**
For recognition of a work of law or political economy published during the preceding eight years. Awards are given in alternate years in law and political economy. A monetary prize is awarded every four years.

• 1707 •
Amaury Sport Organisation
2, rue Rouget de Lisle
F-92130 Issy les Moulineaux, France
Phone: 33 1 4133 1400
E-mail: asopresse@aso.fr
Home Page: http://www.aso.fr

• 1708 • **Tour de France**
This, the world's most prestigious bicycle endurance race, is open to the world's top men's professional cycling teams, the Tour is a 22-day cycling race that covers approximately 4,000 kilometers during the month of July. Monetary prizes in excess of 3 million Euros are awarded. Held annually in July. Established in 1903.

• 1709 •
Amiens International Film Festival
(Festival International du Film d'Amiens)
Jean-Pierre Bergeon, Festival Dir.
% MCA
Place Leon Gontier
F-80000 Amiens, France
Phone: 33 2 2713570
Fax: 33 2 2925304
E-mail: contact@filmfestamiens.org
Home Page: http://www.filmfestamiens.org

• 1710 • **Amiens International Film Festival**
(Festival International du Film d'Amiens)
For recognition of the best quality film produced during the previous year. A Golden Unicorn trophy is awarded for the Best Fiction Feature Film, the Best Short Film, and the Best Actor and Actress. Awarded annually. Established in 1980.

• 1711 •
Association Aeronautique et Astronautique de France
6 rue Galilee
F-75782 Paris Cedex, France
Phone: 33 1 5664 1230
Fax: 33 1 5664 1231
E-mail: secr.exec@aaaf.asso.fr
Home Page: http://www.aaaf.asso.fr

• 1712 • **Grand Prix**
To recognize a person who has gained distinction through his or her works or services rendered to aeronautics or astronautics. Citizens of France or other countries are eligible. A medal and a diploma are awarded annually. Established in 1973.

• 1713 • **Prix d'Aeronautique**
To recognize an individual who has gained distinction through his or her work in the field of aeronautics. French citizens are eligible. A medal and a diploma are awarded annually. Established in 1974.

• 1714 • **Prix d'Astronautique**
To recognize an individual for outstanding work in the field of astronautics. A medal and a diploma are awarded annually. Established in 1974.

• 1715 • **Prix des Jeunes**
To recognize an individual who has distinguished himself through scientific work, originality of writings, or an enterprising spirit. Individuals under 30 years of age are eligible. A monetary prize and a diploma are awarded annually. Established in 1973.

• 1716 •
Association du Prix Albert Londres
Ange Casta, Pres.
% 5 Avenue Vepnsquez
38, rue du Faubourg Saint - Jacques
F-75008 Paris, France
Phone: 33 1 56695858
Fax: 33 1 56995859
E-mail: ange.casta@scam.fr
Home Page: http://www.scam.fr

• 1717 • **Prix Albert Londres**
To recognize outstanding French speaking reporters under 40 years of age. Two monetary prizes are awarded annually, one for journalism and one for an audiovisual film. Established in 1933 by Florise Martinet-Londres in memory of her father, the journalist who disappeared during the fire of the ship, *Georges Philippar*, in the Red Sea in 1932.

• 1718 •
Association of National Olympic Committees
(Association des Comites Nationaux Olympiques)
Gunilla Lindberg, Sec.Gen.
54, ave. Hoche
F-75008 Paris, France
Phone: 33 1 56605280
Fax: 33 1 56605555
E-mail: info@acnolympic.org
Home Page: http://www.acnolympic.org

• 1719 • **Merit Awards**
Recognizes merits in support of ANOC and it members. A plaque and laurel chains are presented to laureates. Awarded to one or more recipients annually. Established in 1983.

• 1720 •
Association of Schools of Public Health in the European Region
(Association des Ecoles de Sante Publique de la Regional Europeenne)
Thierry Louvet, Exec. Dir.
14, rue du Val d'Osne
94415 Saint-Maurice Cedex, France
Phone: 33 1 43966459
Fax: 33 1 43966463
E-mail: aspher@aspher.ensp.fr
Home Page: http://www.aspher.org

• 1721 • **Andrija Stampar Medal**
To recognize a distinguished person for excellence in the field of public health. Awarded annually.

• 1722 •
L'Atelier Imaginaire
BP 2
F-65290 Juillan, France
Phone: 33 62320370
Fax: 33 62320370
E-mail: atelier.imaginaire@wanadoo.fr
Home Page: http://perso.orange.fr/atelier .imaginaire

• 1723 • **Concours Promethee**
To recognize a French novelist who has never been published. Publication of the novel is awarded annually. Established in 1977.

• 1724 • **Concours Max-Pol Fouchet**
To recognize a French poet who is unknown or unrecognized. Publication of the first manuscript is awarded annually. Established in 1981.

• 1725 •
Automobile Club de l'Ouest
Claude Barre, Mng.Dir.
Circuit des 24 heures
F-72019 Le Mans Cedex 2, France
Phone: 33 2 4340 2424
Fax: 33 2 4340 2415
E-mail: tickets@lemans.org
Home Page: http://www.lemans.org/univers _accueil

• 1726 • **Le Mans 24-hour Grand Prix d'Endurance**
To recognize the winning team in a 24 hour endurance race on the famous Sarthe track located 3 miles south of Le Mans, France. The track, which is part raceway and part roadway, is 13.535 km (8.5 miles) long. The race is held annually in June. Established in 1923.

• 1727 •
Cafe des Deux Magots
6 Place Saint Germain des Pres
F-75006 Paris, France
Phone: 33 145485525
Fax: 33 145493139
E-mail: cafk.lesdeuxmagots@free.fr
Home Page: http://www.lesdeuxmagots .com

• 1728 • **Deux Magots Literary Prize**
(Prix des Deux-Magots)
For recognition of an avant-garde book by a young writer. The selection is made by a jury of 13 judges, as was the first prize in 1933. A monetary prize of 7700 Euro is awarded annually in January at the Cafe des Deux Magots, named after *The Two Magots of China,*, a successful play in 1813. Established in 1933 by Henri Philippon with writers, painters, and sculptors who frequented the cafe and each provide monetary contributions for the prize.

• 1729 •
Cannes International Film Festival
(Festival International du Film)
Gilles Jacob, Pres.
3 rue Amelie
F-75007 Paris, France
Phone: 33 1 5359 6100
Fax: 33 1 5359 6110
E-mail: festival@festival-cannes.fr
Home Page: http://www.festival-cannes.fr

• 1730 • **Cannes International Film Festival**
(Festival International du Film, Cannes)
To recognize feature films and shorts. The Festival aims to focus attention on works of quality in order to contribute to the progress of the motion picture arts and to encourage the development of the film industry throughout the world. Films must have been produced during the year prior to entry in the Festival. The following awards are presented for feature-length films: Palme d'Or - for the best feature; Prix du Jury - for the film that shows the most originality; Best Performance by an Actress; Best Performance by an Actor; Best Director; Best Screenplay; and the Grand Prize. The Short Film Palme d*K*Or is awarded for short subjects. Held annually in May. Established in 1946.

• 1731 •
Cinema du Reel
% Bibliotheque Publique d'Information
Centre Pompidou
25, rue Beaubourg
F-75191 Paris Cedex 04, France
Phone: 33 1 44781233
Fax: 33 1 44781215
E-mail: cinereel@bpi.fr
Home Page: http://www.bpi.fr

• 1732 • **International Film Festival of Visual Anthropology and Social Documentation**
(Festival International du Film Ethnographique et Sociologique Cinema du Reel)
For recognition of the best ethnological or sociological documentary. Films produced during the preceding year are eligible. The following monetary prizes are awarded: Prix Cinema du Reel; Prix du Court Metrage for the best short film; Prix des Bibliotheques;Prix du Patrimoine; Prix Louis Marcorelles by the Ministere des Affaires Etrangeres; Prix Joris Ivens; and Prix de la Scam. Held annually. Established in 1979.

• 1733 •
COGEDIM
Jean-Claude Borda, Pres.
153, rue de la Pompe
F-75784 Paris Cedex 16, France
E-mail: jcborda@cogedim.fr
Home Page: http://www.cogedim.fr

• 1734 • **Prix COGEDIM**
To recognize young architects who have not had a contract for a major real estate development during the preceding year. The first prize is the development of apartments in Paris. Awarded annually.

• 1735 •
Committee on Space Research
(Comite pour la Recherche Spatiale)
A. Janofsky, Assoc.Dir.
51, blvd. de Montmorency
F-75016 Paris, France
Phone: 33 1 45250679
Fax: 33 1 40509827
E-mail: cospar@cosparhq.org
Home Page: http://www.cosparhq.org

• 1736 • **COSPAR Space Science Award**
To honor a scientist who has made outstanding contributions to space science. All scientists working in fields covered by COSPAR are eligible. Awarded biennially in even-numbered years at the COSPAR Scientific Assembly. Established in 1984.

• 1737 • **Distinguished Service Medal**
To recognize extraordinary services rendered to COSPAR over many years. Awarded when merited. Established in 1992.

• 1738 • **International Cooperation Medal**
Given for significant contributions, by an individual or a group, to the promotion of international scientific cooperation. Awarded biennially in even-numbered years. Established in 1984.

• 1739 • **Massey Award**
In recognition of outstanding contributions to the development of space research, interpreted in the widest sense, in which a leadership role is of particular importance. Awarded biennially in even-numbered years. Established in 1990. Awarded jointly with the Royal Society of London.

• 1740 • **William Nordberg Medal**
To honor distinguished contributions to the application of space science in a field covered by COSPAR. Awarded biennially in even-numbered years. Established in 1988.

• 1741 • **Vikram Sarabhai Medal**
To recognize exceptional contributions to space research in developing countries. Awarded biennially in even-numbered years jointly with the Indian Space Research Organization. Established in 1990.

• 1742 • **Zeldovich Medals**
To acknowledge excellence and achievements of young scientists. One medal is awarded for each COSPAR Scientific Commission. Awarded biennially in even-numbered years. Established in 1990. Awarded jointly with the Russian Academy of Sciences.

• 1743 •
Concours Internationaux de la Ville de Paris
(Concours International de Violoncelle Rostropovitch)
Acanthes
3 rue des Couronnes
F-75020 Paris, France
Phone: 33 1 4033 4535
Fax: 33 1 4033 4538
E-mail: civp@civp.com
Home Page: http://www.civp.com

Formerly: (2004) Rostropovitch International Competitions.

• 1744 • **International Martial Solal Piano-Jazz Competition**
For recognition of outstanding jazz piano performances. The competition is open to pianists 35 years old or younger. Awarded every four years. Next competition is Autumn 2006.

• 1745 • **International Maurice Andre Trumpet Competition**
For recognition of outstanding trumpet performances. The competition is open to trumpet players 30 years old or younger. Awarded every three years.

• 1746 • **International Oliver Messiaen Competition for Interpertation of Contemporary Music**
Recognizes outstanding interpertation of contemporary music. The competition is open to musicians 33 years old or younger. Awarded every three years. Next competition Autumn 2007.

• 1747 • **International Organ Competition**
For recognition of outstanding organ performances. The competition is open to organists of any nationality who is 35 years of age or younger. The following awards are given: (1) Grand Prix de la Ville de Paris for interpretation (9,000 euros), second prize (6,000 euros), third prize (2,500 euros), Grand Prix de la Ville de Paris for improvisation (5,000 euros), Jean Guillou Prize (1,500 euros), and prize for the most promising contestant (1,500 euros). Awarded every three years as part of the Concours Internationaux de la Ville de Paris.

• 1748 • **International Violin and Bow Making Competition**
Recognizes outstanding violin and bow making. Open to professional violin and bow makers of all ages. Prizes are awarded in each of the following categories: instruments and bows, violin, viola. cello, and doublebass. Awarded every five years. Next competition in Autumn 2009.

• 1749 • **Jean-Pierre Rampal International Flute Competition**
For recognition of outstanding flute performances. The competition is open to flutists 30 years old or younger. The following awards are given (1) Grand Prix de la Ville de Paris; Second Grand Prize; (3) Third Prize; (4) Fourth Prize; (5) Special Prize for the best execution of the commissioned work; (6) Special Prize for the most promising contestant; additional awards are also given. Awarded every three years.

• 1750 • **Rostropovitch International Cello Competition**
(Concours International de Violoncelle Rostropovitch)
For recognition of outstanding cello performances. The competition is open to cellists 33 years of age or under. The following prizes are awarded: (1) Grand Prix de la Ville de Paris; (2) Second Grand Prize; (3) Third Prize; (4) Fourth Prize; (5) Fifth Prize; (6) Sixth Prize; (7) Prize for the Best Interpretation; (8) Prize for the Most Promising Contestant; and (9) the Pierre Fournier Prize for the best interpretation in the second round. Held every four years. Established in 1978.

• 1751 •
Cooperation Centre for Scientific Research Relative to Tobacco
(Centre de Cooperation pour les Recherches Scientifiques Relatives au Tabac)
Francois Jacob, Gen.Sec.
11 rue du Quatre Septembre
F-75002 Paris, France
Phone: 33 1 58625870
Fax: 33 1 58625879
E-mail: coresta.foj@wanadoo.fr
Home Page: http://www.coresta.org/

• 1752 • **CORESTA Prize**
(Prix CORESTA)
For recognition of achievement in tobacco science or technology. A monetary prize of about Euro 10,000, a diploma, and travel are presented biennially in even-numbered years at a Congress. Established in 1978. Formerly: (1978) Philip Morris International Prize.

• 1753 •
Council of Europe
(Conseil de l'Europe)
Terry Davis, Sec.Gen.
European Directive for the Quality of Medicines
F-67075 Strasbourg Cedex, France
Phone: 33 3 88412000
Fax: 33 3 88412781
E-mail: info@pheur.org
Home Page: http://www.coe.int

• 1754 • **Council of Europe Museum Prize**
To honor a museum judged to have made an original contribution to the preservation of the European heritage. The prize consists of a bronze statuette donated by the Spanish Artist Joan Miro and a monetary award of roughly 5,000 Euros. The winning museum is selected by the Parliamentary Assembly's Committee on Culture, Science and Education. Awarded annually. Established in 1977.

• 1755 • Europe Prize

Awarded to a local or regional municipality for active promotion of the European ideal through such activities as twinnings, European events, and exchange visits. The winning authority is chosen by the Parliamentary Assembly's Committee on the Environment, Regional Planning and Local Authorities, and receives a trophy (retained for one year), a bronze medal and a diploma. A cash prize of Euro 7,600 is awarded to the winning municipality, to be spent on a study visit in Europe by some of its young citizens. Awarded annually. Established in 1955.

• 1756 • European Diploma of Protected Areas

The Committee of Ministers awards this diploma on the advice of the Committee for the Activities of the Council of Europe in the field of Biological and Landscape Diversity. Awarded to natural parks, reserves, or sights of international importance which meet certain criteria for safeguarding the natural heritage, and takes their scientific, cultural, and recreational value into account. Established in 1965.

• 1757 • Prix Europa

To promote the creativity and diversity of European television, radio, and Internet products. Producers, broadcasting organizations, and associations of broadcasting organizations are eligible. Categories include Internet, Radio Drama, Radio Documentary, TV Fiction, TV Documentary, TV Multicultural Programs, and TV Current Affairs. Awarded annually.

• 1758 •

European Association for Geochemistry
Bruce Yardley, Pres.
1381 rue de la Piscine, BP 53
38041 Grenoble, France
E-mail: b.yardley@earth.leeds.ac.uk
Home Page: http://www.lmtg.obs-mip.fr/user/eag

• 1759 • Geochemistry Fellows

For outstanding scientists who have made major contributions to the field of geochemistry.

• 1760 • Houtermans Medal

To outstanding young scientists for their contributions to geochemistry.

• 1761 • Urey Medal

To outstanding senior scientists for their lifelong contributions to geochemistry.

• 1762 •

European Association of Organic Geochemists
Dr. Sylvie Derenne, Sec.
Ecole Nationale Superieure de Chimie de Paris
F-75231 Paris Cedex 05, France
Phone: 33 1 43295102
Fax: 33 1 43257975
E-mail: sderenne@ext.jussieu.fr
Home Page: http://eaog.ncl.ac.uk

• 1763 • Travel Scholarships

To foster international exchange, to provide young scientists the opportunity to undertake research in a country other than their own, through utilizing facilities in a host laboratory, and to exchange ideas, expertise, and techniques. Eligible students are those in the last stages of their Ph.D. studies in the field of Organic Geochemistry/Biogeochemistry (i.e. within one year of completion of their thesis) or newly qualified Ph.D.s who wish to work on a project related to their thesis. Several scholarships are available each year, the value of each is up to 3800 Euro.

• 1764 •

European Association of Radiology
Prof. Guy Frija, Sec.Gen.
Societe Francaise de Radiologie
20 ave. Rapp
Freiburger Str. 32
75007 Paris, France
Phone: 33 1 53595969
Fax: 33 1 53595960
E-mail: sfr@sfradiologie.org
Home Page: http://www.ear-online.org

• 1765 • Medaille Boris Rajewsky

For recognition of scientific or professional contributions to European radiology. A medal is awarded to one or more recipients annually. Established in 1972.

• 1766 •

European Environmental Mutagen Society
Dr. Robert A. Baan, Treas.
Unit of Carcinogen Identification and Evaluation
Intl. Agency for Research on Cancer
150 cours Albert Thomas
F-69008 Lyon, France
Phone: 33 4 72738659
Fax: 33 4 738319
E-mail: baan@iarc.fr
Home Page: http://193.51.164.11/eems

• 1767 • Frits Sobels Award

For recognition of an excellent scientific contribution in the field of environmental mutagenesis. The EEMS Awards Committee makes the selection. A monetary prize of 3,000 Euro is awarded and travel expenses are awarded annually. Established in 1986. Formerly: (1997) EEMS Award.

• 1768 •

European Geosciences Union
5, rue Rene Descartes
67084 Strasbourg, France
Phone: 33 3 90240058
Fax: 33 3 88603887
E-mail: egu@eost.u-strasbg.fr
Home Page: http://www.copernicus.org/EGS/EGS.html

• 1769 • Julius Bartels Medal

To recognize scientists for their outstanding achievements in solar-terrestrial sciences. Established in 1996 in honor of the scientific achievements of Julius Bartels.

• 1770 • Sir David Robert Bates Medal

To recognize scientists for their exceptional contributions to planetary and solar system sciences. Awarded annually. Established in 1992 by the Section on Planetary and Solar System Sciences in recognition of the Scientific and editorial achievements of Sir David Robert Bates.

• 1771 • Vilhelm Bjerknes Medal

To recognize distinguished research in atmospheric science. Established in 1995 by the Section on Oceans and Atmosphere (OA) in recognition of the scientific achievements of Vilhelm Bjerknes.

• 1772 • Beno Gutenberg Medal

To recognize individuals for their outstanding contributions to solid earth geophysics. Established in 1996 in honor of the scientific achievements of Beno Gutenberg.

• 1773 • Arthur Holmes Medal and Honorary Membership

This, one of the three equally-ranked most prestigious awards bestowed by the Union, is given to recognize a scientist who has achieved exceptional international standing in Solid Earth Geosciences through merit and scientific achievements. The recipients may be citizens of any country in the world. The medal may be jointly awarded to two scientists or more, whether they have worked together or not in the case of simultaneous and identical or complementary discoveries. The medal, bearing a likeness of Arthur Holmes and the recipient's name, both engraved, is awarded annually either for a specific major discovery or for the achievement of a life-time career.

• 1774 • Honorary Member

The Honorary Membership is the most prestigious award made by the Society. It is reserved for scientists who have achieved exceptional international standing in geophysics, defined in its widest sense. Established in 1973.

• 1775 • Milutin Milankovitch Medal

To recognize scientists for their outstanding achievements in climatological sciences. Awarded annually. Established in 1993 by the Section on Oceans and Atmosphere in recognition of the scientific and editorial achievements of Milutin Milankovitch.

• 1776 • Fridtjof Nansen Medal

To recognize distinguished research in oceanography. Established in 1996 in honor of the scientific achievements of Fridtjof Nansen.

• 1777 • Louis Neel Medal

To recognize scientists for outstanding achievements in the fertilization of the Earth Sciences by the transfer and application of fundamental theory and/or experimental techniques of solid state physics, as defined in its broadest sense. Awarded annually. Established in 1993 by the Section on Solid Earth Geophysics in recognition of the scientific achievements of Louis Eugene Felix Neel, who shared the 1970 Nobel Prize of Physics for his fundamental research and discoveries concerning antiferromagnetism.

• 1778 • Outstanding Young Scientist Award
To recognize scientific achievements in any field made by a scientist who is under 35 years of age. The award may be made jointly to two scientists. A certificate, cash prize of 500 euros, and an invitation to make a presentation of the scientific work at the EUG biennial meeting is awarded in odd-numbered years.

• 1779 • Runcorn-Florensky Medal
To recognize distinguished research in planetary and solar system science (solid). Awarded annually. Formerly: Keith Runcorn Travel Award.

• 1780 • Sergey Soloviev Medal
To recognize scientists for their exceptional contributions to natural hazards and their research into improving our knowledge of basic principles, as well as for the assessment and proper mitigation of hazards in view of environmental protection and the integrity of human life and socio-economic systems. Established in 1996 in honor of Sergey Soloviev.

• 1781 • Alfred Wegener Medal and Honorary Membership
This, one of the three equally-ranked most prestigious awards bestowed by the Union, is given to recognize a scientist who has achieved exceptional international standing in atmospheric, hydrological, or ocean sciences. The recipients may be citizens of any country in the world. The medal may be jointly awarded to two scientists or more, whether they have worked together or not in the case of simultaneous and identical or complementary discoveries. The medal, bearing a likeness of Alfred Wegener and the recipient's name, both engraved, is awarded annually either for a specific major discovery or for the achievement of a life-time career.

• 1782 • Young Scientists Publication Awards
To recognize young scientists in the geophysical disciplines for outstanding contributions to the EGS scientific journals. Awarded annually. Established in 1990.

• 1783 • Young Scientists Travel Awards
To enable European scientists or young scientists working in Europe to attend the scientific conferences of the Society by providing a financial contribution to the cost of travel and free registration. Established in 1977.

• 1784 •
European Physical Society
Mr. David Lee, Sec.Gen.
6 rue des Freres Lumiere
BP 2136
F-68060 Mulhouse Cedex, France
Phone: 33 3 89329440
Fax: 33 3 89329449
E-mail: d.lee@uha.fr
Home Page: http://www.eps.org

• 1785 • Accelerator Prize
To recognize an individual in the early part of his/her career having made a recent, original contribution to the accelerator field, as well as to recognize an individual for outstanding work in the accelerator field with no age limit. A cash prize and diploma are awarded to a recipient in each category biennially. Awarded by the Accelerators Division.

• 1786 • Hewlett-Packard Europhysics Prize
For recognition of outstanding achievement in solid state physics. Europeans must be nominated by August 31. Nominations are submitted to the EPS Secretariat for the Selection Committee. A monetary prize and a certificate are awarded annually at the Conference. Established in 1975.

• 1787 • High Energy and Particle Physics Prize
For recognition of important contributions to theoretical or experimental particle physics. Awarded to one or more individuals in the area of physics of condensed matter, specifically work leading to advances in the fields of electronic, electrical and materials engineering. Nominations are invited. A monetary prize is awarded at the EPS HEPP Conference. Established in 1989 by the EPS High Energy and Particle Physics (HEPP) Division. Sponsored by Cray Research France, Digital Equipment Corporation Europe (Switzerland), Interatom (Federal Republic of Germany), Le Croy Corporation (USA), Philips (The Netherlands), Siemens AG (Federal Republic of Germany), and Thomson Tubes Electroniques (France).

• 1788 • Quantum Electronics Prize
To recognize one or more individuals who have contributed to the development of quantum electronics, basic physics optics or applied research. Awarded biennially, the recipient received a medal and a diploma.

• 1789 •
Festival du Court Metrage en Plein Air
4, rue Hector Berlioz
F-38000 Grenoble, France
Phone: 33 4 7654 4351
Fax: 33 4 7651 2443
E-mail: contactfestivalgnb@yahoo.fr
Home Page: http://www.chez.com/festivalcinema

• 1790 • Festival du Court Metrage en Plein Air
For recognition of short French films. The following prizes are awarded: Grand Prix de la Ville de Grenoble; Prix du Conseil General; Prix Canal; Prix d'Aide a la Creation - grants or tools given by technical industries to aid in future productions; Prix Fuji - for quality film technique; Coupe Juliet Berto; Prix de la Presse; and Prix Public. Awarded annually. Established in 1977.

• 1791 •
Festival du Film Court de Villeurbanne
Laurent Hughues, Contact
117 Cours Emile Zola
F-69100 Villeurbanne, France
Phone: 33 4 7893 4265
Fax: 33 4 7243 0962
E-mail: lezola@wanadoo.fr
Home Page: http://www.lezola.com

• 1792 • Festival du Film Court de Villeurbanne
To recognize the best French-spoken short film made during the preceding year. The following prizes are awarded: Grand Prix de la Ville de Villeurbanne, Prix de Gnseil Regional, Prix Fuji, Prix Pyral, Prix du Public, and Prix TPS. Awarded annually. Established in 1980. Sponsored by the City of Villeurbanne, Region Rhone-Alpes Geonseil General du Rhone, France - Ministry of Culture and Communication, Centre National de la Cinematographie, and Groupement Regional d'Action Cinematographique.

• 1793 •
Festival International de Musique de Besancon et de Franche-Comte
3 bis, rue leonel de Moustier
F-25000 Besancon, France
Phone: 33 81250580
Fax: 33 81815215
E-mail: contact@festival-besancon.com
Home Page: http://www.besancon.com

• 1794 • Besancon International Competition for Young Conductors (Concours International de Jeunes Chefs d'Orchestre Besancon)
To recognize the aptitudes of young artists for conducting, rather than to check their technical knowledge. Individuals who are less than 35 years of age are eligible. A monetary prize and opportunities to conduct various orchestras are awarded annually. Established in 1951.

• 1795 • Besancon International Competition of Music Composition (Concours International de Composition Musicale)
To recognize an outstanding music composition for an orchestra. The contest is open to composers of any nationality who are under 40 years of age. Recipients are awarded Prize of the Festival of Besancon and a monetary prize. The piece that wins first place is played at the final session of the Young Conductors Contest of the

Awards are arranged in alphabetical order below their administering organizations

Music Festival of Besancon the following year. Awarded annually. Established in 1988.

• 1796 •
Festival International du Film de Vol Libre
Marie-Claude Previtali, Press Off.
Office du tourisme
F-38660 St. Hilaire du Touvet, France
Phone: 33 4 7608 3399
Fax: 33 4 7697 2056
E-mail: sthilairedutouvet@wanadoo.fr
Home Page: http://www.coupe-icare.org

• 1797 • **International Free Flight Film Festival**
For the promotion of all forms films dealing with air, wind, and flight. Film topics can include, but are not limited to: aerial sports, hot-air balloons, human-powered aircraft, sail planes, bungee jumping, base jumping, kites, boomerangs,—motorized gliders, aerial acrobatics, and birds or related species. The following prizes are awarded: Grand Prix du Festival, Prix du Public, Prix de la Critique, Mention Special du Jury, Mention Reportage, Prize for the Best Film Script, Prize for the Best Artistic Film, Prize for the Best Documentary or News Film, and Prize for the Best Advertising Film. Trophies are awarded annually in September. Established in 1983.

• 1798 •
Festival of Underwater Images
(Festival Mondial de l'Image Sous-Marine)
62, ave. des Pins du Cap
F-06160 Antibes, France
Phone: 33 4 9361 4545
Fax: 33 4 9367 3493
E-mail: spondyle@wanadoo.fr
Home Page: http://www.divernet.com/festival

Formerly: (2004) World Festival of Underwater Pictures.

• 1799 • **Festival of Underwater Images (Festival Mondial de l'Image Sous-Marine)**
For recognition of the best underwater film or video of the year. At least 40 percent of the film or video must be underwater shots. Films may be entered in Beta (three-quarter inch, 16mm, or 35mm), or VHS (8mm or Super 8). Gold, silver, and bronze Flipper trophies are awarded in each category. Monetary prizes are awarded. In addition, a slide competition, a black and white and color photography competition, and a slideshow competition are held. Gold, silver, and bronze Diver trophies are awarded in each category. The French Association of Conchology Prize is awarded to the best slide print that, while presenting strong aesthetic qualities, serves to increase knowledge of the world of mollusks. The City of Antibes Prize is awarded for the best examples of color and black and white photography. Each year the festival also awards: World Book Prize of Underwater Pictures for the best book of pictures of the year; Prix Corail du Livre (French language production); La Musique et la Mer; APNEA Sub-Aqua Documentary Prize; CD-ROM Underwater Prize - to promote the interactive works on CD-ROM dealing with the underwater world; and Underwater Television Productions - News Prize, Fiction Prize, Documentary Prize. Awarded annually. Established in 1974. Sponsored by the Spondyle Club and La Ville d'Antibes.

• 1800 •
Florilege Vocal de Tours
Christian Balandras, Dir.
Hotel de Ville
Rue des Minimes
BP 1452
F-37014 Tours Cedex 1, France
Phone: 33 2 4721 6526
Fax: 33 2 4721 6771
E-mail: florilege.vocal@free.fr
Home Page: http://www.florilegevocal.com

Formerly: Rencontres Internationales de Chant Choral de Tours.

• 1801 • **International Choral Competition of Tours (Concours International de Chant Choral de Tours)**
For recognition of outstanding choral music sung "a cappella" by four categories of singing groups: mixed choirs; equal voice ensembles; mixed voice ensembles; and free program. Monetary prizes are awarded in each category; the best choirs of each category also present a closing concert. At the close of the concert the following prizes are awarded: European Grand Prix for Choral Singing, Grand Prix de la Ville de Tours, Prix du Public, Prix Special Renaissance, Prize for a First Production Work, and Prix du Ministre de la Culture. Held annually at Pentecost. Established in 1972 by Claude Panterne.

• 1802 •
Fondation de la Maison de la Chimie
P. Potier, Pres.
Maison de la Chimie
28, rue St. Dominique
F-75007 Paris, France
Phone: 33 1 40622700
Fax: 33 1 40629521
E-mail: presidence@maisondelachimie.com
Home Page: http://www.maisondelachimie.asso.fr

• 1803 • **Grand Prix de la Fondation de la Maison de la Chimie**
For recognition of original work in the field of chemistry that benefits humanity, society, or nature. Candidates must be nominated by a learned society or a national or international scientific organization. A monetary prize of 30,000 euros is awarded annually to one or more recipients. Established in 1988.

• 1804 •
Fondation Feneon
Cabinet du Recteur de l'Academie de Paris
47, rue des Ecoles
F-75005 Paris, France
Phone: 33 1 40462015
Fax: 33 1 40462010

• 1805 • **Prix Felix Feneon**
To assist young writers, painters, or sculptors to pursue their literary or artistic education. Candidates must be younger than 35 years of age. Painters and sculptors must already have exhibited works and writers must have one published work written in French to be considered. Two monetary awards are awarded, one to a writer and the other an artist. Awarded annually in November. Established in 1949 by Rectorat de l'Academie de Paris in memory of Felix Feneon, chronicler and critic of art.

• 1806 • **Prix Henri Hertz**
For recognition of literary, historical, or artistic works that make better known or understood the civic and ethical preoccupations of Henri Hertz. Awarded annually. Established in 1986 by the Chancellerie des Universites de Paris in memory of Henri Hertz (1875-1966).

• 1807 •
Fondation Napoleon
Thierry Lentz, Dir.
148, bld Haussmann
F-75008 Paris, France
Phone: 33 1 5643 4600
Fax: 33 1 4293 2351
E-mail: lentz@napoleon.org
Home Page: http://www.napoleon.org

• 1808 • **Grands Prix de la Fondation Napoleon**
For recognition of the best work written concerning the First Empire (Napoleon I) or the Second Empire (Napoleon III). Works written during the preceding year November 1 to October 31 are eligible. A monetary prize is awarded annually. Established in 1978 in memory of Napoleon I and Napoleon III. Formerly: (1990) Grand Prix du Souvenir Napoleonien.

• 1809 •
France Ministry of Defense
14, rue Saint Dominique
F-75700 Paris, France
Phone: 33 1 42193011
Home Page: http://www.defense.gouv.fr

• 1810 • **Croix de Guerre**
To recognize fighting units for feats of arms and acts of devotion. Civilians, men or women, towns, various institutions, in combat areas, and foreigners mentioned in Army orders as having rendered distinguished services in the front line are eligible. The holders of the Croix de Guerre do not constitute an order and have no degrees of rank; the number of clasps attached to the ribbon being the only token of special distinction. The medal, Florentine bronze, 35 millimeters in diameter, consists of a cross with four branches supported on two crossed swords. On the obverse, there is an effigy of the Republic wearing a Phrygian (Liberty) cap, a wreath of laurel, and the inscription "Republicque Francaise." On the reverse, there is the date. Established in 1915; confirmed in 1921 for Theaters of Overseas Operations and again in September 1939.

• 1811 • Medaille Militaire
To reward acts of bravery and distinguished military service by noncommissioned officers and soldiers. The award is by decree of the President of the Republic. Established in 1852.

• 1812 • Prix Science et Defense
For recognition of outstanding research work or studies which advance the science and technology in fields pertaining to national defense. A monetary prize is awarded annually. Established in 1983.

• 1813 •
French Chemical Society
Jean-Claude Brunie, Gen.Sec.
250, rue Saint Jacques
F-75005 Paris, France
Phone: 33 1 4046 7160
Fax: 33 1 4046 7161
E-mail: sfc@sfc.fr
Home Page: http://www.sfc.fr

• 1814 • Grand Prix de Chimie Industrielle
To recognize an industrial researcher for an important contribution in the field of industrial chemistry. A monetary prize is awarded when merited. Established in 1988. Co-sponsored by the Societe de Chimie Industrielle. Formerly: Grand Prix de la Societe de Chimie.

• 1815 • Prix Le Bel
For recognition of research contributions in the field of stereo chemistry or on a subject of particular interest to Le Bel. A monetary prize is awarded annually. Established in 1942 in memory of Le Bel, a benefactor of the Societe.

• 1816 • Prix Pierre Sue
For recognition in the field of chemistry. A prize is awarded annually. Established in 1964 in memory of Pierre Sue, Secretary General of the Society from 1962 to 1967.

• 1817 •
French Foundation for Medical Research
(Fondation pour la Recherche Medicale)
Pierre Joly, Pres.
54, rue de Varenne
75335 Paris Cedex 07, France
Phone: 33 1 44397575
Fax: 33 1 44397599
Home Page: http://www.frm.org

• 1818 • Prix Marguerite Delahautemaison
To recognize an individual for outstanding contributions to laboratory research. French laboratory researchers are eligible. The award is presented in alternate years in the following categories: nephrology research and cancer research. A monetary award of 9,000 euros is presented biennially. Established in 1977.

• 1819 • Grand Prix
To recognize outstanding research of an individual, a team, or several researchers. A monetary award is awarded biennially in even-numbered years. Established in 1981.

• 1820 • Prix Raymond Rosen
For recognition of outstanding research in cancer. Well-known French researchers are eligible. A monetary prize of 30,000 euros is awarded annually

• 1821 •
French League for Animal Rights
(Ligue Francaise des Droits de l'Animal)
39, rue Claude Bernard
F-75005 Paris, France
Phone: 33 1 47079899
Fax: 33 1 47079998
E-mail: lfda@league-animal-rights.org
Home Page: http://league-animal-rights.org

• 1822 • Prix de Biologie Alfred Kastler
To encourage research and experimental methods that are not traumatic for animals. French-speaking researchers in the fields of biology, medicine, pharmacy, and veterinary research are eligible. A monetary prize of 25,000 francs is awarded annually. Established in 1985 in memory of Professor Alfred Kastler, French winner of the 1966 Nobel Prize of Physics and president of the League from 1979 to 1984. Formerly: Prix Alfred Kastler.

• 1823 •
French Ministry of Culture and Communication
Michele Alliott-Marie, Minister
DIC
3, rue de Valois
F-75042 Paris Cedex 01, France
Phone: 33 1 40158778
Fax: 33 1 42869736
E-mail: atelier.dic@culture.gouv.fr
Home Page: http://www.culture.gouv.fr

• 1824 • Order of the Academic Palms (Palmes Academiques)
To reward distinguished service in public education. The Order consists of the grades of Chevalier, Officer, and Commander. Nominees should have rendered at least 15 years of service in public education to be nominated for the grade of Chevalier and at least five years for the grades of Officer and Commander. Awarded semiannually. The Order was established on October 4, 1955, to replace the honorary distinctions of the Academic Palms, which had been founded in 1808.

• 1825 •
French National Center for Scientific Research
(Centre National de la Recherche Scientifique)
Herve Mathieu, Sec.Gen.
Mission de l'Information Scientifique et Technique
3, Rue Michel-Ange
F-75794 Paris Cedex 16, France
Phone: 33 1 4496 4000
Fax: 33 1 4496 5390
E-mail: webcnrs@cnrs-dir.fr
Home Page: http://www.cnrs.fr

• 1826 • Bronze Medal
To recognize young researchers for their first work, usually a thesis, which shows promise and encourages them to continue their work. Research fields cover all disciplines. A bronze medal is awarded annually to approximately 40 researchers. Established in 1954.

• 1827 • Gold Medal
To recognize an internationally renowned scientist who has made an outstanding contribution to the advancement and worldwide impact of French research. Research fields cover all disciplines. A gold medal is awarded annually. Established in 1954.

• 1828 • Silver Medal
To recognize researchers in mid-career whose works are nationally and internationally renowned for their originality, quality, and importance. Research fields cover all disciplines. A silver medal is awarded annually to approximately 15 scientists. Established in 1954.

• 1829 •
Geological Society of France
(Societe Geologique de France)
Jean-Pierre Brun, Pres.
77, rue Claude-Bernard
F-75005 Paris, France
Phone: 33 1 4331 7735
Fax: 33 1 4535 7910
E-mail: accueil@sgfr.com
Home Page: http://sgfr.free.fr

• 1830 • Prix Barbier
For recognition in the field of civil engineering, hydrogeology, metallurgy, and mineral substances. A medal is awarded biennially. Established in 1987 by a gift of R. Barbier.

• 1831 • Prix Barrabe
For recognition of methods in the fields of physics, chemistry, numerics, geophysics, and planetology. A medal is awarded biennially. Established in 1962 by Madame Barrabe.

• 1832 • Prix Leon Bertrand
To recognize a geologist for work in the field of applied geology. Members of the Society are eligible. Awarded biennially in even-numbered years. Established in 1949 by Leon Bertrand.

Awards are arranged in alphabetical order below their administering organizations

• 1833 • Prix Jacques Bourcart
For recognition in the fields of geology concerning sediment and the oceans. A medal is awarded biennially in even-numbered years. Established in 1976.

• 1834 • Prix Raymond et Madeleine Furon
For recognition in the field of endogenous geology. A medal is awarded biennially in odd-numbered years. Established in 1977 by Raymond Furon.

• 1835 • Prix de Lamothe
For recognition in the fields of geology, micropaleontology, and biostratigraphy. A medal is awarded biennially. Established in 1935 by a bequest of L.J. de Lamothe.

• 1836 • Prix Georges Millot
To recognize individuals for distinguished scientific or technical work, particularly in the earth sciences. Individuals who have developed applications of earth sciences, given service to the Academy, or demonstrated scientific research in laboratories, institutes, or French offices are eligible. A medal is awarded in even-numbered years, alternating with the Prix Prestwich. Established in 1979 by George Millot.

• 1837 • Prix Fontannes
To recognize the French author of the best stratigraphic work published during the last five years. A medal is awarded biennially. Established in 1888 by a bequest of F. Fontannes.

• 1838 • Prix Gaudry
This, the greatest distinction of the Society, is given to recognize a French or foreign geologist or paleontologist. A diploma is awarded. Established in 1910 by a bequest of A. Gaudry.

• 1839 • Prix Gosselet
For recognition of a work of applied geology. A medal is awarded every four years. Established in 1910 by Jules Gosselet.

• 1840 • Prix Prestwich
To encourage new research and to recognize one or several geologists, men or women from a country other than France, who have displayed a zeal for the progress of the science of geology. A medal is awarded biennially in odd-numbered years, alternating with the Prix Georges Millot. Established in 1902 by a bequest of Sir J. Prestwich.

• 1841 • Prix Viquesnel
To encourage geological studies and to recognize the author of a work published in the *Bulletin* or the *Memoires*. Members of the Society of any nationality are eligible. Awarded biennially in odd-numbered years. Established in 1875 by Madame Viquesnel.

• 1842 • Prix Wegmann
For recognition of a work concerning the history of geology. Awarded periodically. Established in 1984 by a bequest of E. Wegmann.

• 1843 • Prix Fondation Pierre Pruvost
For recognition in the field of structural geology. A medal is awarded biennially. Established in 1960 by Pierre Pruvost.

• 1844 • Prix van Straelen
To recognize the best paper in the field of either Earth surface or inner-Earth geology, with the topics alternating each year. A monetary prize of 2,287 euros is awarded annually. Established in 1993 in memory of Professor Victor Van Straelen.

• 1845 •
Guilde Europeenne du Raid
Patrick Edel, Dir.
11, rue de Vaugirard
F-75006 Paris, France
Phone: 33 1 4326 9752
Fax: 33 1 4634 7545
E-mail: guilde@club-internet.fr
Home Page: http://www.la-guilde.org

• 1846 • International Adventure Film Festival
(Les Ecrans De L'Aventure)
For recognition of documentary 16mm films or videos about any kind of adventure, such as mountain expeditions, arctic travels, sailing races around the world, ballooning, underwater diving, speleology, outstanding sport performances, and any dramatic events that are milestones in adventurism. Within this framework, the festival attempts to bring together the best of recently produced or non-released films from all parts of the world. Among the prizes awarded are: Toison d'Or for the best adventure documentary film; Jury*K*s Special Prize; Jean-Marc Boivin Prize for the genuineness and ethical dimension of the adventure; Adventurer of the Year; Peter Bird*K*s Trophy for perseverance and tenacity in an adventure; Alain Bombard Prize for adventure with a teaching value; Dijon Young Jury*K*s Prize; and Young Director Prize. Held annually. Established in 1977. Sponsored by Dijon - Bourgogne. Formerly: Festival Internationl du Film d'Aventure de la Plagne.

• 1847 •
Human Rights Institute of the Bar of Bordeaux
Maison de l'Avocat
18-20 Rue du Marechai-Joffre
F-33000 Bordeaux, France
Phone: 33 556 442076
Fax: 33 656 791433
E-mail: idhbb@idhbb.org
Home Page: http://www.idhbb.org

• 1848 • Ludovic-Trarieux International Human Rights Prize
Awarded to a lawyer, regardless of nationality or Bar, who has encountered personal suffering through the defense of human rights, the supremacy of law, or the struggle against racism, and intolerance of any form. A monetary prize is awarded annually. Co-sponsored by the European Bar Human Rights Institute.

• 1849 •
Institut de Biologie Physico-Chimique
13, rue Pierre et Marie Curie
F-75005 Paris, France
Phone: 33 1 5841 5000
Fax: 33 1 5841 5020
E-mail: www@ibpc.fr
Home Page: http://www.ibpc.fr

• 1850 • Prix Nine Choucroun
To recognize a young researcher for work in the field of physical-chemical biology. Researchers under 30 years of age are eligible. A monetary prize of 4,000 euros is awarded annually. Established in 1986.

• 1851 •
Institut de France
23, quai de Conti
F-75006 Paris, France
Phone: 33 1 4441 4441
Fax: 33 1 4441 4341
E-mail: fondations@institut-de-france.fr
Home Page: http://www.institut-de-france.fr

• 1852 • Prix d'Aumale
For recognition of outstanding intellectual works or for recognition of first efforts that deserve encouragement. The prize may be awarded posthumously to assist the family. Awarded by any of the five academies of the Institut.

• 1853 • Prix Georges Bizet
For recognition of a music composer. Awarded biennially by the Academie des Beaux-Arts.

• 1854 • Prix Jeanne Burdy
To recognize a painter. Awarded biennially on the recommendation of the Academie des Beaux-Arts by the Institut. Established in 1983.

• 1855 • Prix Hercule Catenacci
To encourage the publication of beautifully illustrated books of poetry, literature, history, archaeology, or music. Each of three Academies awards this prize annually.

• 1856 • Prix Jaffe
To encourage students and teachers of science to undertake experiments destined to aid humanity. A monetary prize of 1400 Euro is awarded by the Institut on the recommendation of the Academie des Sciences.

• 1857 • Prix Jules et Louis Jeanbernat et Barthelemy de Ferrari Doria
To recognize a young French author for a book of literature, science, or art. The prize is awarded alternately by each of the five Acade-

mies. Established by Emmanuel Jeanbernat in memory of her two sons who died for France.

• 1858 • Prix Germaine-Andre Lequeux
To recognize a French researcher for work in the field of science or literature that is unselfish or useful. Awarded annually. Established in 1982.

• 1859 • Prix Memain-Pelletier
To recognize a scholar or physician who, by his works or discoveries, has contributed the most to relieve humanity of the many maladies that afflict it. A prize is awarded by the Institut on the recommendation of the Academie des Sciences.

• 1860 • Prix Balleroy
For recognition of a poet and a painter. The prize is awarded alternately to a poet by the Academie Francaise and to a painter by the Academie des Beaux-Arts. Unknown or little known artists who have talent are eligible. Awarded annually.

• 1861 • Prix Osiris
For recognition of a discovery or outstanding work in the field of science, literature, art, industry, or generally any field that affects the public. Awarded every three years by a special commission whose members are from each of the five Academies.

• 1862 • Prix Volney
For recognition of a work of comparative philology. Awarded by the Institut on the recommendation of the Academie des Inscriptions et Belles Lettres.

• 1863 • Prix Alfred Verdaguer
For recognition of outstanding work in the arts, literature, or science. Recommendations are offered alternately by the Academie Francaise, the Academie des Sciences, and the Academie des Inscriptions et des Belles-Lettres.

• 1864 •
International Academy of Astronautics
(Academie Internationale d'Astronautique)
Dr. Jean-Michel Contant, Sec.Gen.
6 rue Galilee
PO Box 1268-16
F-75766 Paris Cedex 16, France
Phone: 33 1 47238215
Fax: 33 1 47238216
E-mail: sgeneral@iaanet.org
Home Page: http://www.iaanet.org

• 1865 • Book Awards
To recognize individuals who have made contributions over a lifetime to the advancement of space science and technology and the peaceful uses of outer space. Awards are presented in each of four categories: basic science, engineering science, life science, and social science. In addition, the Luigi Napolitano Book Award is presented to a non-member for excellence in any field related to science. Established in 1986.

• 1866 • International Academy of Astronautics Section Awards
To recognize individuals who have made contributions over a lifetime to the advancement of space science and technology and the peaceful uses of outer space. A certificate is awarded in each of four categories: basic science, engineering science, life science, and social science. Awarded annually at the honor luncheon of the IAA. Established in 1985.

• 1867 • Luigi Napolitano Award
To recognize excellence in a recent publication (less than three years) made by an individual or a group non-member of the Academy in any field related to space. Awarded annually. Established in 1992.

• 1868 • Von Karman Award
This, the highest award of the IAA, is given to recognize individuals who have made contributions over a lifetime to the advancement of space science and technology and the peaceful uses of outer space. Nominations are made by the Awards Committee of the International Academy of Astronautics. A certificate is awarded annually at the honor luncheon of the IAA. Established in 1982 in honor of the birth of Theodore von Karman (1881-1963).

• 1869 •
International Animated Film Festival
(Festival International du Cinema d'Animation - Annecy)
Serge Bromberg, Dir.
% Conservatoire d'art et d'histoire
18 avenue du Tresum
BP 399
F-74013 Annecy, France
Phone: 33 450100900
Fax: 33 450100970
E-mail: info@annecy.org
Home Page: http://www.annecy.org

• 1870 • Annecy International Animated Film Festival
(Festival International du Cinema d'Animation Annecy)
For recognition of outstanding animated films. Categories include short films, feature films, TV series, TV specials, educational/industrial/scientific films, advertising films, music video, graduation films, and series for the Internet. The jury may award the following official prizes: Best Poster, Audio-Visual Prize from the Ministry of Agriculture, Special ASIFA Prize. Held annually. Established in 1956.

• 1871 •
International Association of Cancer Registries
(Association Internationale des Registres du Cancer)
Dr. D.M. Parkin, President
150 cours Albert Thomas
F-69372 Lyon Cedex 08, France
Phone: 33 4 72738485
Fax: 33 4 72738650
E-mail: whelan@iarc.fr
Home Page: http://www.iacr.com.fr

• 1872 • Honorary Member
For recognition of achievement in the field of cancer registration. Nominations must be made by a member or members of the Association. A certificate is awarded annually at scientific meetings of the Association. Established in 1980.

• 1873 •
International Association of Hydrological Sciences
(Association Internationale des Sciences Hydrologiques)
Dr. Pierre Hubert, Sec.Gen.
Ecole des Mines de Paris
35 rue Saint Honore
F-77305 Fontainebleau, France
Phone: 33 1 64694740
Fax: 33 1 64694703
E-mail: iahs@ensmp.fr
Home Page: http://iahs.info

• 1874 • International Hydrology Prize
To recognize an individual who has made an outstanding contribution to hydrology such as confers on the candidate universal recognition of his international stature. The contribution should have an identifiable international dimension extending beyond both the country of normal work and the specific field of interest of the candidate. The contribution may have been made through scientific work, as evidenced by the publication in international journals of scientific literature of a high standard, and/or through practical work, as evidenced by reports of the projects concerned. Preference should be given to candidates who have contributed through both scientific and practical work. The Prize may be awarded to hydrologists of long international standing or to those who, while having gained such standing only recently, exhibit the qualities of international leadership in the science and practice of hydrology. An active involvement in the work of IAHS and other international organizations in the field of hydrology should be counted as an advantage. A silver medal is presented annually. Established in 1981. Sponsored by UNESCO and World Meteorological Organization.

• 1875 • Tison Award
To promote excellence in research by young hydrologists. Outstanding papers published by IAHS in a period of two years previous to the deadline for nominations are eligible. Candidates for the award must be under 41 years of age at the time their paper was published. A monetary prize of $750 and a citation are

awarded annually during either an IUGG/IAHS General Assembly or an IAHS Scientific Assembly.

• 1876 •
International Association of Paediatric Dentistry
Mrs. Gerald Z. Wright, Sec.Gen.
L'Avant Ctre.
13, chemin du Levant
F-01210 Ferney-Voltaire, France
Phone: 33 4 50426994
Fax: 33 4 50405555
E-mail: iapd@fdiworldental.org
Home Page: http://www.iapdworld.org

• 1877 • **Bright Smiles, Bright Futures Award**
To stimulate the development of innovative programs worldwide, and to facilitate information sharing and transfer in children's dentistry. Awarded at the biennial congress.

• 1878 • **Bengt Magnusson Memorial Prize**
Recognizes the best essay in the field of child dental health. Supporting members are eligible. Awarded periodically.

• 1879 •
International Astronautical Federation
(Federation Internationale d'Astronautique)
Mr. Yves Beguin, Exec.Dir.
8-10, rue Mario Nikis
F-75015 Paris, France
Phone: 33 1 45674260
Fax: 33 1 42732120
E-mail: yves.beguin@iafastro.org
Home Page: http://www.iafastro.com

• 1880 • **Allan D. Emil Memorial Award**
For recognition of an outstanding contribution in space science, space technology, space medicine, or space law which involved the participation of more than one nation and/or which furthered the possibility of greater international cooperation in astronautics. An IAF member society may make nominations. A monetary award of $1,000 US and a diploma are awarded annually during the IAF Congress. Established in 1977 in memory of Allan D. Emil.

• 1881 •
International Automobile Federation
(Federation Internationale de l'Automobile)
8, place de la Concorde
F-75008 Paris, France
Phone: 33 1 42659951
Fax: 33 1 49249800
Home Page: http://www.fia.com

• 1882 • **Championships, Cups, and Trophies**
Championships recognize the winners of the following races: the European Rally Championship, the African Continent Rally Challenge, the Middle East Rally Championship, the Asia Pacific Rally Championship, the Asia-Pacific Touring Car, the European Championships for Autocross and Rallycross Drivers, the European Hill Climb Championship and Challenge, the European Challenge for Historic Touring Cars, and the European Drag Racing Championship. The following cups and trophies are also awarded: the FIA World Cup for Cross Country Rallies, the FIA Marathon Trophy, the Touring Car World Cup, the European 1600 Cup for Autocross, the European Truck Racing Cup, the Electro Solar Cup, the FIA Intercontinental Formula 3 Cup, the European Trophy for Historic Sports Car, the Cup for Historic Grand Touring Cars, the Cup for Thoroughbred Grand Prix Cars, the Lurani Trophy for Formula Junior Class, the European Historic Rally Trophy, the Inter Nations Cup for Rallycross, and the European Drag Racing Championship.

• 1883 • **Formula One World Champion**
To recognize the winning driver of the Series of Formula One races. A prize is also given to the manufacturers. Established in 1950.

• 1884 • **World Rally Champion**
To recognize the winning driver of the World Rally and the manufacturer of the winning automobile.

• 1885 •
International Consultative Research Group on Rapeseed
(Groupe Consultatif International de Recherche sur le Colza)
Andre Pouzet, Sec.
12 Ave. George
V-75008 Paris, France
Phone: 33 1 56895705
Fax: 33 1 56895704
E-mail: lot@cetiom.fr
Home Page: http://www.cetiom.fr/gcirc

• 1886 • **International Rapeseed Award**
Recognizes an outstanding researcher. The Eminent Scientist Award is presented quadrennially.

• 1887 •
International Council on Monuments and Sites
(Conseil International des Monuments et des Sites)
Susan Denyer, Contact
49-51 rue de la Federation
F-75015 Paris, France
Phone: 33 1 45676770
Fax: 33 1 45660622
E-mail: secretariat@icomos.org
Home Page: http://www.international.icomos.org

• 1888 • **Gazzola Prize**
(Prix Gazzola)
To recognize a person or group of persons whose life's work has furthered the aims and objectives of ICOMOS, and the defense of conservation and restoration of historic monuments and sites. Members of ICOMOS may be nominated. A monetary prize of US $10,000, a commemorative medal, and a diploma are awarded triennially on the occasion of the General Assembly of ICOMOS. Established in 1979 in honor of Piero Gazzola, one of the founders of ICOMOS and its first President.

• 1889 •
International Festival of Maritime and Exploration Films
(Festival International du Film Maritime et d'Exploration)
14, rue Peiresc
F-83000 Toulon, France
Phone: 33 1 9492 9922
Fax: 33 1 9491 3565
E-mail: festi.film@wanadoo.fr
Home Page: http://www.fifme.com

• 1890 • **International Festival of Maritime, Exploration, and Environmental Films**
(Festival International du film Maritime et d'Exploration)
For recognition of outstanding films on the theme of the sea or exploration that were produced during the preceding three years. Films are divided in the following categories: scientific, exploration, fiction, sports, and advertising. Applications must be submitted by early September (films must be submitted by August 16). A jury selects the films. The Gold Anchor (Ancre d'Or), the Silver Anchor (Ancre d'Argent), and the Bronze Anchor (Ancre de Bronze) are awarded annually. In addition, the following prizes are awarded: (1) the Special Rolex Prize for Underwater Nature Preservation (Grand Prix Rolex pour la Protection du Monde Sous-Marin); (2) the Young Film Maker's Prize (Prix de la Federation Francaise d'Etudes et Sports Sous-Marins), offered by the French Underwater Sports and Studies Federation; (3) the Prix de la ville de Toulon for best scientific film; (4) the Prix de la Confederation Mondiale des Activites Subaquatiques (World Confederation of Underwater Activities); (5) the Prix pour le Meilleur Film d'Exploration; (6) the Prix de la Presse (Press Prize); (7) the Prix du Public (Public Prize); (8) the Prix Francois de Roubaix for the best musical accompaniment; and (9) the Prix de la Marine Nationale. Established in 1954 by Dr. Jacques-Henri Baixe, Toulon City French Navy.

• 1891 •
International Finn Association
Corinne McKenzie, Exec.Dir.
3, imp. De la bousquette
F-66370 Pezilla-la-Riviere, France
Phone: 33 46 8924895
Fax: 33 46 8380913
E-mail: 106453.577@compuserve.com
Home Page: http://www.finnclass.org

• 1892 • **World Championship**
To recognize an individual for achievement in sailing. The Finn Gold Cup is awarded annually in July. Established in 1956 by Tony Mitchell.

• 1893 •
International Hotel and Restaurant Association
David McMillan, CEO
48, Blvd. de Sebastopol
75003 Paris, France
Phone: 33 1 44889220
Fax: 33 1 44889230
E-mail: david.mcmillan@ih-ra.com
Home Page: http://www.ih-ra.com

• 1894 • **Environmental Award**
To recognize a hotel that has made outstanding efforts to protect the environment. Awarded annually. Sponsored by American Express Ltd. Established in 1990.

• 1895 •
International Institute of Refrigeration
(Institut International du Froid)
Didier Coulomb, Dir.
177, blvd. Malesherbes
F-75017 Paris, France
Phone: 33 1 42273235
Fax: 33 1 47631798
E-mail: iifiir@iifiir.org
Home Page: http://www.iifiir.org

• 1896 • **Gustav Lorentzen Medal**
Established in 1997 to honor the memory of Prof. Gustav Lorentzen, Honorary President of the IIR. Awarded to a person with outstanding and original achievements in academic or industrial research, innovation or development, in all fields of refrigeration, thus promoting creativity and renewal in the fields of competence of the IIR. Winner will receive a medal, certificate, 8000 euros (minus travel expenses, accommodation costs and registration fees for the Congress, which the winner must attend, and at which winner may make a short speech). Candidates are not limited to individuals from IIR member countries, however, active officers of the IIR are not eligible. Nomination shall be supported by a sponsor who is a member of an IIR commission.

• 1897 •
International Institute of Welding
(Institut International de la Soudure)
M. Beaufils, CEO
ZI Paris Nord 2
BP 50362
F-95942 Roissy Cedex, France
Phone: 33 1 49903608
Fax: 33 1 49903680
E-mail: iiw@wanadoo.fr
Home Page: http://www.iiw-iis.org/

• 1898 • **Yoshiaki Arata Award**
Recognizes a person who has realized outstanding achievements in fundamental researches in welding science and technology and its allied areas and which has been recognized as a great contribution to the progress of welding engineering and related fields. A monetary prize of $5,000 is awarded annually.

• 1899 • **Edstrom Medal**
Recognizes persons who have made an exceptional and distinguished contribution which furthers, in a significant manner, the aims and objectives of the IIW. The contribution may be related to any aspect of IIW business and can come from individuals either actively engaged in the IIW or those who are not usually associated with IIW affairs. A medal is awarded annually.

• 1900 • **Henry Granjon Prize**
To recognize authors of papers devoted to research into welding technology or a related subject, ultimately to stimulate interest in welding and allied processes among young people. Papers (thesis, research reports, state-of-the-art surveys) must be single authored, based on recent work carried out in a University, other appropriate Institutions, or in Industry. The work must fall within four categories of technology related to joining, surfacing, or cutting: Joining and fabrication technology; Materials behavior and weldability; Design and structural integrity; and Human related subjects. A plaque is awarded annually in each category. Established in 1991 to honor Henri Granjon of Institut de Soudure, Paris.

• 1901 • **Guerrera Medal**
Recognizes one engineer or technician especially responsible for the Fabrication of an outstanding welded construction of particular interest. Judged from the point of view of design, or materials or fabrication methods. A gold medal is awarded every three years. Established in 2000.

• 1902 • **Andre Leroy Prize**
Recognizes education in the field of welding. Awarded to large circulation multi media document, including video and computer programs, intended for use in education and training in any aspect of welding and allied processes, including brazing, hot spraying, thermal cutting, at any level, including engineers, technicians, and welders. A medal is awarded in even years. Established in 1980 in honor of Andre Leroy.

• 1903 • **Evgenij Paton Prize**
Recognizes an individual who has made a significant contribution to science and technology through their life time dedication. Work must be in the areas of applied research and development in the field of advanced technologies, materials and equipment for welding and allied processes. A medal, diploma, and a visit of E.O Pateon Electric Welding Institute in Kiev Ukraine are awarded every even year.

• 1904 • **Arthur Smith Award**
Given to an individual who has given dedicatied service to the IIW enabled the objective of the Institute to be significantly advanced. Recipients are individuals who have contributed to the activities of the Institute for a significant number of years, particularly in the work of Commissions. A silver plate is awarded annually.

• 1905 • **Thomas Medal**
Recognizes an individual who has been involved in IIW/ISO international standards activities. Requires the presentation of a lecture that illustrates the incorporation of global studies in the standardization of welding technology. A medal is awarded annually. Established in 1998.

• 1906 •
International Organisation of Vine and Wine
(Organisation Internationale de la Vigne et du Vin)
Federico Castellucci, Dir.Gen.
18, rue d'Aguesseau
F-75008 Paris, France
Phone: 33 1 44948080
Fax: 33 1 42669063
E-mail: oiv@oiv.int
Home Page: http://www.oiv.int

• 1907 • **Grand Prix**
To recognize an individual who makes a significant scholarly contribution to viticulture and enology. Awarded annually.

• 1908 •
International Radiation Protection Association
Mr. Jacques Lochard, Exec. Officer
Rte. du Panorama
BP 48
F-92263 Fontenay-aux-Roses Cedex, France
Phone: 33 1 58357467
Fax: 33 1 40849034
E-mail: irpa.exof@irpa.net
Home Page: http://www.irpa.net

• 1909 • **Sievert Award**
For recognition of contributions to radiological protection. A monetary prize and a certificate are awarded at the International IRPA Congress, which is held every three or four years. Established in 1973 in honor of Rolf Sievert. Additional information is available from Dr. C.A.M. Webb, Chairman of the Sievert Award Committee, Radiation Safety Section, Div. of Nuclear Safety, Wagramerstrasse 5, PO Box 100, Vienna, Austria A-1400.

• 1910 •
International Real Estate Federation - France
(Federation Internationale des Professions Immobilieres)
Mme. Evelyne Vivier, Sec.Gen.
23 ave. Bosquet
F-75007 Paris, France
Phone: 33 1 42606720
Fax: 33 1 42606722
E-mail: fiabci-france@noos.fr
Home Page: http://www.fiabci.com

• 1911 • **Prix d'Excellence**
Given to those outstanding real estate developments which show excellence in all aspects of their creation from initial design through con-

struction, financials, marketing, community benefit and environmental impact. Awards are made each year in a maximum of seven categories (residential, retail, office-industrial, public sector, rural, specialized, leisure), and are presented at the annual FIABCI World Congress in May annually.

• 1912 •
International Social Science Council
(Conseil International des Sciences Sociales)
Dr. Ali Kazancigil, Sec.Gen.
1, rue Miollis
F-75732 Paris Cedex 15, France
Phone: 33 1 45684860
Phone: 33 1 45682829
Fax: 33 1 45667603
E-mail: issc@unesco.org
Home Page: http://www.unesco.org/ngo/issc

• 1913 • **Stein Rokkan Prize in Comparative Social Science Research**
For recognition of a contribution in comparative social science research in either manuscript or book form; and to encourage younger scholars. Submissions cab be either an unpublished manuscript of book length or a printed book or collected works published within the past two years. Candidates must be under 40 years of age at the time of the award presentation. The laureate will receive a diploma and a cash prize of $4,000 jointly awarded by the International Social Science Council and the Conjunto Universitario Candido Mendes of Brazil. Awarded biennially in even-numbered years. Established in 1980.

• 1914 •
International Sunflower Association
Mr. Andre Pouzet, Sec.-Treas.
12 Ave George V
F-75008 Paris, France
Phone: 33 1 56895705
Fax: 33 1 56895704
E-mail: isa@cetiom.fr
Home Page: http://www.cetiom.fr/isa/

• 1915 • **Pustovoit Award**
To recognize outstanding contributions in theoretical or applied research in any field dealing with sunflowers (for example, but not limited to: genetics, breeding, physiology, chemistry, phyto-pathology, crop science, entomology, weed science, oil technology, etc.) that have stimulated the development of the sunflower crop and enriched the literature. A plaque will normally be awarded every four years, to coincide with the International Sunflower Conference. Established in 1979.

• 1916 •
International Union Against Tuberculosis and Lung Disease
(Union Internationale Contre la Tuberculose et les Maladies Respiratoires)
Asma Sony, Pres.
68 Blvd. St. Michel
F-75006 Paris, France
Phone: 33 1 44320360
Fax: 33 1 43299087
E-mail: union@iuatld.org
Home Page: http://www.iuatld.org

• 1917 • **The Princess Chichibu Memorial TB Global Award**
To a person who has shown great achievements in anti-tuberculosis activities.

• 1918 • **Public Health Prize**
To health workers.

• 1919 • **Scientific Prize**
To a young researcher.

• 1920 • **The Union Medal**
To members who have made outstanding contributions to the control of tuberculosis or nontuberculous lung disease.

• 1921 •
International Union of Architects
(Union Internationale des Architectes)
Jaime Lerner, Pres.
51 Rue Raynouard
75016 Paris, France
Phone: 33 1 45243688
Fax: 33 1 45240278
E-mail: uia@uia-architectes.org
Home Page: http://www.uia-architectes.org

• 1922 • **Sir Patrick Abercrombie Prize**
For recognition of outstanding work in the field of town planning or territorial development. Awarded triennially at the Congress of the Union. Established in 1961 in memory of Sir Patrick Abercrombie, first president of the UIA.

• 1923 • **Gold Medal for Outstanding Architectural Achievement**
This, the highest individual award of the UIA, is bestowed upon an architect or group of architects for outstanding contributions to architecture and design excellence over an extended period of time. A jury of international renown selects the Gold Medalist from nominations submitted by UIA National Sections. A gold medal is awarded triennially. Established in 1984.

• 1924 • **Sir Robert Matthew Prize**
For recognition of an outstanding improvement in the quality of human settlements. Awarded triennially at the Congress of the Union. Established in 1978 in memory of Sir Robert Matthew, a past president of the UIA.

• 1925 • **Auguste Perret Prize**
For recognition of a project which is particularly remarkable for applied technology in architecture. Awarded triennially at the Congress of the Union. Established in 1961 in memory of Auguste Perret, a past honorary president of the UIA.

• 1926 • **Jean Tschumi Prize**
For recognition of architectural criticism or architectural education. Awarded triennially at the Congress of the Union. Established in 1967 in memory of John Tschumi, a past president of the UIA.

• 1927 •
International Women's Film Festival
(Festival International de Films de Femmes de Creteil et du Val de Marne)
Jackie Buet, Dir.
Maison des Arts
Place Salvador Allende
F-94000 Creteil, France
Phone: 33 1 4980 3898
Fax: 33 1 4399 0410
E-mail: filmsfemmes@wanadoo.fr
Home Page: http://www.filmsdefemmes.com

• 1928 • **International Women's Film Festival of Creteil and Val-de-Marne (Festival International de Films de Femmes de Creteil et du Val de Marne)**
For recognition of films directed by one or several women and to encourage distribution of films in France. Films are entered in three categories: Full-length fiction films; full-length documentary films; and short length fiction and documentary films. The entry deadline is December 30. The following monetary prizes are awarded: Grand Prix du Jury for a full-length film; Prix du Jury for a full-length fiction film; Prix Canal for a short-length fiction film; Prix de l'Association des Femmes Journaliste for the full-length documentary films; and Prix du Public in all three categories with one prize for a French short-length film and another for a foreign short-length film. In addition, the Prix du Jury de l'Universite Paris may be awarded for a European short-length film. Awarded annually. Established in 1978.

• 1929 •
International Henri Langlois Encounters Poitiers International Film Schools Festival (Rencontres Internationales Henri Langlois)
Denis Garnier and Bertrand Lecerf, Dir./Gen.Coor.
Le Theatre Scene Nationale de Poitiers
1 place du Marechal Leclerc
F-86000 Poitiers, France
Phone: 33 5 49031890
Fax: 33 5 49031899
E-mail: festival.rihl@letheatre-poitiers.com
Home Page: http://www.rihl.org

• 1930 • Festival du Film d'Etudes Cinematographiques
For recognition of the best films made in a film school or workshop. The following awards are presented: Grand Prize, Special Jury Prize, Best Directing Prize, Public Prize, Best Script Writing, Directors' Prize, Students' Prize, French Critics' Prize, and SACEM Prize. Monetary prizes and trophies are awarded annually in March. Established in 1977.

• 1931 •
Marguerite Long and Jacques Thibaud International Competition
(Concours International Marguerite Long - Jacques Thibaud)
Roland Faure, Pres.
32, avenue Matignon
F-75008 Paris, France
Phone: 33 1 4266 6680
Fax: 33 1 4266 0643
E-mail: longthi@club.internet.fr
Home Page: http://www.concours-long-thibaud.org

• 1932 • Marguerite Long and Jacques Thibaud International Competition (Concours International Marguerite Long et Jacques Thibaud)
To recognize the best young piano and violin performers. The Competition is open to young pianists or violinists of all nationalities until 30 years of age. Awarded twice over a three-year period (one year for piano, and the next year for violin; during the third year, a gala concert for the young winners is presented by the older winners). Established in 1943 by Marguerite Long and Jacques Thibaud. Co-sponsored by the France Ministry of Culture, Ville de Paris, Fujisankei Communications International, and Radio-France.

• 1933 •
Maisons de la Presse
Seddif
52, rue Jacques Hillairet
F-75012 Paris, France
E-mail: francois-xavier.bricout@seddif.fr
Home Page: http://www.maisondelapresse.tm.fr

• 1934 • Prix des Maisons de la Presse
To provide recognition for a book of fiction and nonfiction of outstanding quality. Two prizes are awarded annually. Established in 1969.

• 1935 •
Observ'ER
(Observatoire des Energies Renouvelables)
146 rue de L 'Universite
F-75007 Paris, France
Phone: 33 1 44180080
Fax: 33 1 44180036
E-mail: observ.er@energies-renouvelables.org
Home Page: http://observ-er.org

• 1936 • Habitat Solaire, Habitat d'aujourd'hui
For recognition of individuals who have constructed or occupied buildings created successfully by solar architecture principles. Awards are given for individual houses, apartment housing and all types of professional buildings. Co-sponsored by Observ'ER, Ademe, the French Ministry of Environment, the Camif Group and Electricite de France. Held annually. Formerly: (1998) Maisons solaire, maisons, d'aujourd'hui.

• 1937 •
Prix Cazes
Claude Guittard, Gen.Mgr.
Brasserie Lipp
151, boulevard Saint Germain
F-75006 Paris, France
Phone: 33 1 45485391
Fax: 33 1 45443320
E-mail: ilalipp@ila-chateau.com
Home Page: http://www.ila-chateau.com/Lipp

• 1938 • Prix Cazes - Brasserie Lipp
For recognition of a novel, an essay, a biography, a historical documentary, or an anthology of short stories of excellent literary quality. The work must be written in French and must not have won a major literary prize before. A monetary prize is awarded annually in March. Established in 1935 by Marcellin Cazes, owner of the Brasserie Lipp, a restaurant frequented by writers and artists. Sponsored by the Brasserie Lipp.

• 1939 •
Prix du Jeune Ecrivain
6, ave Roger Tissandie
BP 40055
F-31602 Muret, France
Phone: 33 561 561315
Fax: 33 561 510292
E-mail: prix.du.jeune.ecrivain@wanadon.fr
Home Page: http://perso.wanadoo.fr/prix.du.jeune.ecrivain

• 1940 • Prix du Jeune Ecrivain
For recognition of outstanding writing by a young French writer between 15 and 25 years of age. Unpublished works of prose, such as short stories, drama, or fiction are eligible. Publication of the work is awarded annually in May and edited by Le Mercure de France. Established in 1985. Co-sponsored by Fondation BNP Paribas.

• 1941 • Prix du Jeune Ecrivain Francophone
For recognition of outstanding writing by a young, French-speaking writer between 15 and 27 years of age who lives outside France. Unpublished works such as short stories, drama, or fiction are eligible. Publication of the work is awarded annually in May. Established in 1985.

• 1942 •
Prix Theophraste Renaudot
Tour Eve
3610 La Defense
F-92800 Puteaux, France
E-mail: celine-albin.faivre@club-internet.fr
Home Page: http://prixrenaudot.free.fr

• 1943 • Prix Theophraste Renaudot
To provide recognition for a novelist showing talent and originality. Novels published during the preceding year are considered by a jury of 10 members. A luncheon in the winner's honor and honorary recognition are awarded annually at the Restaurant Drouan at the same time as the Prix Goncourt. Established in 1925.

• 1944 •
Rencontres Internationales de la Photographie
Francois Barre, Pres.
10 rond point des Arenes
BP 96
F-13200 Arles, France
Phone: 33 90967606
Fax: 33 90499439
E-mail: prix@rencontres-arles.com
Home Page: http://www.rencontres-arles.com

• 1945 • Prix du Livre de Photographie/ Arles Book Award (Prize of the Photo Book)
To recognize the publisher of the best photography book of the year. The prize aims to promote the quality of photography publishing and to encourage production. French publishers and photographers as well as those from abroad are eligible. It can also reward an exhibition catalog. A monetary prize of 10,000 euros, divided between the publisher and the photographer, is awarded each July. Established in 1974.

• 1946 •
Sauve Qui Peut le Court Metrage
Jean-Claude Saurel, Pres.
6 place Michel-de-L'Hospital
F-63058 Clermont-Ferrand Cedex 1, France
Phone: 33 473 916573
Fax: 33 473 921193
E-mail: info@clermont-filmfest.com
Home Page: http://www.clermont-filmfest.com

• 1947 • Clermont-Ferrand International Short Film Festival (Festival International du Court Metrage de Clermont-Ferrand)
To recognize short films in the international competition. The following prizes are awarded: Grand Prize; Audience Prize, Special Jury Prize, Best Soundtrack Creation, Best Animation Film, Canal+ Award, Youth Jury Prize, Press Prize, and Special Mentions of the Jury. Held annually. Established in 1988.

Awards are arranged in alphabetical order below their administering organizations

• 1948 • Clermont-Ferrand National Short Film Festival (Festival National du Court Metrage de Clermont-Ferrand)

To recognize short films in the national competition. The following prizes are awarded: Grand Prize; Audience Prize, Special Jury Prize, Best First Film, Best Actor and Actress, Best Soundtrack Creation, Best Animation Film, Canal+ Award, ProcirepKs Award for Best Producer, FNAC Award, Youth Jury Prize, Press Prize, and Special Mentions of the Jury. Held annually. Established in 1978.

• 1949 •
Societe Astronomique de France
3, rue Beethoven
F-75016 Paris, France
Phone: 33 1 4224 1374
Fax: 33 1 4230 7547
E-mail: saf@calva.net
Home Page: http://www.saf-lastronomie.com

• 1950 • Medaille des Soixantenaire et Fondation Manley-Bendall

To recognize individuals who have been members of the Society for sixty years. A bronze medal is awarded annually. Established in 1957.

• 1951 • Prix Georges Bidault de l'Isle

To encourage young people who show a special talent for astronomy or meteorology. Individuals are chosen from participants at courses and conferences, collaboration at the Observatory, or through communications in the bulletin during the preceding year. A bronze medal is awarded annually. Established in 1925.

• 1952 • Plaquette du Centenaire de Camille Flammarion

For recognition of long and continuous service to the Society. A silver plaque is awarded annually. Established in 1956.

• 1953 • Prix Gabrielle et Camille Flammarion

For recognition of an important discovery and marked progress in astronomy or in a sister science, to aid an independent researcher, or to assist a young researcher to begin work in astronomy. A silver medal is awarded annually. Established in 1930.

• 1954 • Prix Edmond Girard

To encourage a beginning vocation in astronomy or scientific exploration of the sky above the Observatoire de Juvisy. A medal is awarded annually. Established in 1974.

• 1955 • Prix Marius Jacquemetton

For recognition of a work or research by a member of the Society, a student, or a young astronomer. A silver medal is awarded annually.

• 1956 • Prix Jules Janssen

This, the highest award of the Society, is given for recognition of outstanding work in the field of astronomy. The award is given alternately to a professional French astronomer and a foreign one. A medal is awarded annually. Established in 1897.

• 1957 • Prix Dorothea Klumpke - Isaac Roberts

To encourage the study of the wide and diffuse nebulae of William Herschel, the obscure objects of Barnard, or the cosmic clouds of R.P. Hagen. A silver medal is awarded biennially in even-numbered years. Established in 1931.

• 1958 • Medaille des Anciens Presidents

For recognition of past presidents of the Society when they leave office. A silver medal is awarded every three years.

• 1959 • Prix Marcel Moye

To recognize a young member of the Society for his or her observations. Individuals must be 25 years of age or less. A silver medal is awarded annually. Established in 1946.

• 1960 • Prix des Dames

To recognize women for service to the Society. A silver medal is awarded annually. Established in 1897 by three women.

• 1961 • Prix Henri Rey

For recognition of an important work in astronomy. A silver medal is awarded annually. Established in 1926.

• 1962 • Prix Julien Saget

To recognize an amateur for his or her remarkable astronomic photography. A bronze medal is awarded annually. Established in 1969.

• 1963 • Prix Viennet-Damien

For recognition of a beautiful piece of optics or for some work in this branch of astronomy. A silver medal is awarded in odd-numbered years when merited, alternating with the Prix Dorothea Klumpke-Isaac Roberts.

• 1964 •
Societe de Chimie Therapeutique
Joelle Mayrargue, Sec.Gen.
Secretariat Gen.
Faculte de Pharmacie
5, rue Jean-Baptiste Clement
F-92296 Chatenay-Malabry, France
Phone: 33 1 4683 5684
Fax: 33 4 4683 5323
E-mail: sct@sct.asso.fr
Home Page: http://www.sct.asso.fr

• 1965 • Lecon Paul Ehrlich

In order to give a well known scientist the opportunity to deliver a lecture on new trends in medicinal chemistry, during Recontres internationals de Chimie Therapeutique, the annual meeting of S.C.T. A monetary prize was established in 1989. The award is given in honor of Paul Ehrlich, a great scientist in medicinal chemistry. Sponsored by the Association Paul Neumann.

• 1966 • Prix Charles Mentzer des Rencontres de Chimie Therapeutique

To recognize a researcher or a team of researchers for work in the field of therapeutic chemistry. Members of the Society may submit nominations. A monetary prize is awarded biennially in even-numbered years. Established in 1974 in honor of Charles Mentzer, a researcher in therapeutic chemistry.

• 1967 • Prix d'Encouragement a la recherche en Chimie Therapeutique

To provide encouragement for a young researcher in therapeutic chemistry to create new medicines. A monetary prize is awarded annually. Established in 1985.

• 1968 •
Societe de Pathologie Exotique
P. Saliou, Pres.
Institut Pasteur
25, rue du Docteur Roux
F-75724 Paris, France
Phone: 33 1 4566 8869
Fax: 33 1 4566 4485
E-mail: socpatex@pasteur.fr
Home Page: http://www.pathexo.fr

• 1969 • Bourse de la SPE

To encourage a young researcher in the field of pathology. A monetary prize of is awarded every two years. Established in 1997.

• 1970 • Medaille d'Or

For recognition of exceptional merit in the field of exotic pathology. A medal is awarded periodically at the convention of the Society. Established in 1908.

• 1971 •
Societe des Auteurs, Compositeurs et Editeurs de Musique
Bernard Miyet, Pres.
225, av. Charles de Gaulle
F-92528 Neuilly-sur-Seine Cedex, France
Phone: 33 1 47154715
Fax: 33 1 47154802
E-mail: drim@sacem.fr
Home Page: http://www.sacem.fr

• 1972 • Grand Prix de la Chanson Francaise

For recognition of the best French songwriter. A monetary prize and a medal are awarded annually in December. Established in 1982.

• 1973 • Grand Prix de la Musique Symphonique

For recognition in the field of symphonic music. A monetary prize and a medal are awarded annually in December. Established in 1982.

• 1974 • Grand Prix de l'Edition Musicale
To recognize a French music publisher. A medal is awarded annually in December. Established in 1984.

• 1975 • Grand Prix de l'Humour
For recognition in the field of comedy. A monetary prize and a medal are awarded annually in December. Established in 1983.

• 1976 • Grand Prix des Poetes
For recognition in the field of poetry. A monetary prize and a medal are awarded annually in December. Established in 1982. Formerly: Grand Prix de la Poesie.

• 1977 • Grand Prix du Jazz
To recognize an outstanding jazz composer. A monetary prize and a medal are awarded annually in December. Established in 1982.

• 1978 •
Societe Francaise d'Acoustique
Philippe Blanc-Benon, Pres.
23 avenue Brunetiere
F-75017 Paris, France
Phone: 33 1 4888 9059
Fax: 33 1 4888 9060
E-mail: sfa4@wanadoo.fr
Home Page: http://www.sfa.asso.fr

• 1979 • Prix Chavasse
To recognize young scientific researchers in the field of acoustics. Members of SFA who are around 40 years old are eligible for consideration. Awarded annually. Established in 1948 by Professor Chavasse, the founder of GALF. Formerly: Prix Chavasse - GALF.

• 1980 • Prix Philips
To recognize young scientific researchers in the field of acoustics. Members of SFA are eligible for consideration. Awarded periodically. Established in 1948 by Professor Chavasse, the founder of GALF. Formerly: Prix Philips.

• 1981 • Prix et Medailles de la SFA
To recognize scientific researchers of international fame in the field of acoustics. Individuals need not be members to be eligible for consideration. Two medals, one to a Frenchman and one to a citizen of another country, are awarded annually. Established in 1948 by Professor Chavasse, the founder of GALF.

• 1982 • Prix Yves Rocard
To recognize a young scientific worker in the general field of acoustics. Individuals around 30 years of age and at the doctorate level are eligible. Awarded annually. Formerly: (1995) Prix Jeune Chercheur.

• 1983 • Prix Thomson Sintra
For recognition of scientific work in the field of submarine acoustics. Individuals around 30 years of age and at the doctorate level are eligible. Awarded periodically.

• 1984 •
Society of Dramatic Authors and Composers
(Societe des Auteurs et Compositeurs Dramatiques)
Oliver Carmet, Dir.Gen.
11 bis, rue Ballu
F-75442 Paris Cedex 09, France
Phone: 33 1 40234444
Fax: 33 1 45267428
E-mail: secretariat.general@sacd.fr
Home Page: http://www.sacd.fr

• 1985 • Grand Prix
To recognize the most outstanding playwright or a composer on the basis of his entire dramatic work. A monetary prize is awarded annually.

• 1986 • Prix Nouveau Talent
To recognize new talent in theatre, music, cinema, television, radio, and dance. Monetary prizes are awarded annually in each category.

• 1987 •
Jean-Pierre Taieb
24, rue du Coteau
F-92370 Chaville, France
Phone: 33 47507763

• 1988 • Prix Julia Verlanger
To recognize a novel of science fiction or heroic fantasy selected by readers as the best of the year. French editions are eligible. A monetary prize of FF 10,000 is awarded annually. Established in 1986 by Jean Pierre Verlanger in memory of his wife, Julia Verlanger, also known under the pseudonym of Gilles Thomas, one of the first women authors of science fiction and fantastic novels in France.

• 1989 •
UNESCO
Koichiro Matsuura, Dir.Gen.
7, place de Fontenoy
F-75352 Paris, France
Phone: 33 1 4568 1000
Fax: 33 1 4567 1690
Home Page: http://www.unesco.org

• 1990 • International Simon Bolivar Prize
For recognition of activity of outstanding merit that, in accordance with the ideals of Simon Bolivar, has contributed to the freedom, independence, and dignity of peoples and to the strengthening of solidarity among nations; and has fostered their development or facilitated the establishment of a new international economic, social, and cultural order. Such activity may take the form of intellectual or artistic creation, a social achievement, or the mobilization of public opinion. A monetary prize of $25,000 is awarded triennially. Established in 1983. Sponsored by the Government of Venezuela.

• 1991 • Carlos J. Finlay Prize
To promote research and development in microbiology by rewarding a person or group of persons for an outstanding contribution in that field. Member states of UNESCO make the nominations. A monetary prize of $5,000 and a silver medal are awarded biennially in odd-numbered years coinciding with the year of UNESCO's General Conference. Established in 1977 in memory of Carlos J. Finlay, a Cuban scientist whose discoveries led to the conquest of yellow fever.

• 1992 • Nessim Habif Prize
To recognize the authors of outstanding textbooks for use in developing countries and to encourage the production in developing countries of good textbooks that are objective, balanced, and up-to-date in content and pedagogically sound in presentation. Awards are made in successive years to authors of textbooks published in member states of UNESCO in Asia, Africa, Arab States, and Latin America. The awards are open only to authors who have prepared textbooks for use in one of the countries in the regions to be selected annually. Prizes may be awarded either to a single textbook or to several textbooks that constitute a series. A monetary prize of $10,000 is awarded annually. Established in 1962 by a bequest of Nessim Habif who died at St. Maurice, Switzerland, in 1960.

• 1993 • Felix Houphouet-Boigny Peace Prize
To honor individuals, bodies, or institutions that have made a significant contribution to promoting, seeking, safeguarding, or maintaining peace through education, science, and culture. Nominations may be made by Member States and nongovernmental organizations as well as other specified groups. A monetary prize of 120,000 euros, a gold medal, and a certificate are awarded annually. Established in 1989.

• 1994 • Javed Husain Prize for Young Scientists
For recognition of outstanding pure or applied research carried out by young scientists. Eligible applicants include individuals who, in the opinion of the jury, have done the most to advance the progress of scientific research as judged by the quality of their publications and/or patents; or individuals whose age does not exceed 35 years at the time of announcement of the Prize. Research specifically aimed at the development of weapons or other military devices shall not be considered for the Prize. A monetary prize representing half the biennial interest earned from the Fund, a medal, and a certificate are awarded biennially in odd-numbered years. Established in 1987 by a donation made by Dr. Javed Husain, an Indian physicist who has held university professional posts in Saudi Arabia and the United States.

• 1995 • IPDC - UNESCO Prize for Rural Communication
For recognition of meritorious and innovative activity in improving communication in rural

communities, chiefly in the developing countries. Nationals of UNESCO Member States or institutions or organizations that have their headquarters in those States are eligible. They must have adopted one or more particularly outstanding measure to promote rural communication in the spirit of UNESCO's ideals by such means as: furthering the use of local newspapers, films, radio, television, and/or multi-media programmes; furthering the use of traditional forms of communication; and implementing new plans with a view to the full use or improvement of communication and its techniques and methods in ways adapted to the rural environment. A monetary prize of $20,000 (US) is awarded biennially in odd-numbered years. Established in 1985.

• 1996 • Kalinga Prize for the Popularization of Science

For recognition of outstanding interpretation of science to the general public. Persons actively involved in the promotion of public understanding of science and technology are eligible. National Commissions for UNESCO make the nominations. A monetary prize, a medal, and a plaque are awarded annually. Established in 1951 by Mr. B. Patnaik, an Indian industrialist. The prize is named after the ancient Indian emperor who in the second century BC renounced war and devoted his power to the development of science, culture, and education.

• 1997 • The International Jose Marti Prize

In recognition of an activity of outstanding merit in accordance with the ideals and spirit of Jose Marti (Struggle for Liberty) contributing to unity and integration of countries in Latin America/Caribbean; and the preservation of identities. A monetary prize of $5,000 is awarded biennially in odd-numbered years to coincide with the meeting of the General Conference. Established in 1995 in honor of the centenary of the death of Jose Marti.

• 1998 • Sultan Qaboos Prize for Environmental Preservation

For recognition of outstanding contributions by individuals, groups of individuals, institutes, or organizations in the management or preservation of the environment, consistent with the policies, aims, and objectives of UNESCO, and in relation to the organization's programs in this field (i.e., environmental and natural resources research, environmental education and training, creation of environmental awareness through the preparation of environmental information materials, and activities aimed at establishing and managing protected areas such as Biosphere Reserves and Natural World Heritage Sites). A monetary prize of $20,000 US is awarded biennially in odd-numbered years. Established in 1989.

• 1999 • UNESCO Award for Distinguished Services to Physical Education and Sport

For recognition of distinguished services to physical education and sport in accordance with the principles of the International Charter of Physical Education and Sport adopted by the General Conference of UNESCO at its twentieth session. The award is given in two different categories: to an institution or body that has made an outstanding contribution to the development of physical education and sport for all; and to a person who, by his or her active participation, has made a significant contribution to the development of physical education and sport for all. Candidates are selected by the Member States of UNESCO. A diploma of honor and medal are awarded biennially. Established in 1985.

• 2000 • UNESCO Crafts Prize

For recognition of the efforts of craftworkers who, by trying out different forms and techniques, have contributed to the creation of original models in their respective trades. The purpose of the Prize is to stimulate creativity among craftworkers and to encourage new initiatives in creative work in the crafts. Nominations are submitted to the Director-General of UNESCO by the appropriate bodies of Member States responsible for national participation in the regional crafts exhibition. The Prize-winner must have produced a particularly conspicuous and original work in one of the creative crafts trades. A monetary prize of $10,000 is awarded annually on the occasion of a regional crafts exhibition. Established in 1990.

• 2001 • UNESCO - International Music Council Music Prize

To recognize musicians or musical institutions whose works or activities have contributed to the enrichment and development of music, and have served peace, understanding between peoples, international cooperation, and the other purposes proclaimed by the United Nations Charter and UNESCO's Constitution. Nationals of, or institutions having their headquarters in Member States of UNESCO are eligible. The winners shall be selected from among: composers, for their work as a whole; individual performers and ensembles, for their performances as a whole; musicologists and music critics, for their research or criticism as a whole: teachers, for their teaching as a whole; and public figures and musical institutions, for their activities in the service of music as a whole. A diploma, medal, and monetary prize of 2,500 euros are awarded annually to one or two recipients. Established in 1975. Co-sponsored by the International Music Council. Formerly: (1978) International Music Council Prize.

• 2002 • UNESCO Literacy Prizes

For recognition of the services of institutions, organizations, or individuals displaying outstanding merit and achieving particularly effective results in contributing to the fight for literacy. The following prizes are awarded: International Reading Association Literacy Award; Noma Literacy Prize; King Sejong Literacy Prize; Nessim Habif Prize; and Malcolm Adiseshiah International Literacy Prize. Monetary prizes are awarded annually. The International Reading Association Literacy Award and the Noma Prize were established in 1979 and 1980 respectively.

• 2003 • UNESCO Prize for Human Rights Education

To recognize teaching institutions, organizations, or persons having made a particularly efficient, exemplary, and genuine contribution to the development of the teaching of human rights. Nominations can be presented by governments of Member States, by intergovernmental organizations, and by non-governmental international organizations with consultative and mutual information status with UNESCO, as well as national and international institutions of human rights teaching and training. A monetary prize of $10,000 is awarded biennially in even-numbered years. Established in 1978 on the occasion of the 30th anniversary of the Universal Declaration of Human Rights.

• 2004 • UNESCO Prize for Landscape Architecture

To recognize a student in landscape architecture, who is the author of a work inspired specifically by the aims of UNESCO. The winner is selected by the Director General from the winners of the international competition in landscape architecture organized by the International Federation of Landscape Architects. The prize-winner must be a national of a Member State of UNESCO. A monetary prize of $3,500 is awarded annually. Established in 1989.

• 2005 • UNESCO Prize for Peace Education

For recognition of a particularly outstanding example of activity designed to alert public opinion and mobilize the conscience of mankind in the cause of peace. The following criteria are considered: the mobilization of the consciences in the cause of peace; the implementation, at international or regional level, of programs of activity designed to strengthen peace education by enlisting the support of public opinion; the launching of important activities contributing to the strengthening of peace; education action to promote human rights and international understanding; the promotion of public awareness of the problems of peace through the media and other effective channels; and any other activity recognized as essential to the construction of the defenses of peace in the minds of men. Member states of UNESCO, intergovernmental organizations, non-governmental organizations granted consultative status with UNESCO, and persons whom the Director-General deems qualified in the field of peace may nominate an individual, a group of individuals, or an organization considered to merit the distinction of this Prize by virtue of their activities. A monetary prize is awarded biennially in even-numbered years. Established in 1980 by the Japan Shipbuilding Industry Foundation.

• 2006 • UNESCO Science Prize

To recognize a person or group of persons for an outstanding contribution, through the application of science and technology, to the development of a developing member state or region, especially in the fields of scientific and technological research and education, or in the fields of engineering and industrial development. Nomination is by governments of UNESCO member states and non-governmental organizations having consultative status with UNESCO. A monetary prize of $15,000, a medal, and a plaque are awarded biennially. Established in 1967.

• 2007 •
Union des Annonceurs
Gerard Noel, Contact
53, Ave. Victor Hugo
F-75116 Paris, France
Phone: 33 1 4500 7910
Fax: 33 1 4500 5579
E-mail: infos@uda.fr
Home Page: http://www.uda.fr

• 2008 • **Phenix UDA**
For recognition of the actions of the most highly skilled sponsors of enterprises for their undertakings, and to promote new techniques of communication and new talents among those who daily witness the increasing integration of enterprises into the life of the city. Awards are given in the following categories: culture, heritage, humanitarian causes, audiovisual programs, adventure, sport, education, and environment. A trophy is awarded annually in each category as well as honorable mention and Special Jury Prizes.

• 2009 •
Union of International Fairs
(Union des Foires Internationales)
Vincent Gerard, Mng.Dir.
35 bis, rue Jouffroy-d'Abbans
F-75017 Paris, France
Phone: 33 1 42679912
Fax: 33 1 42271929
E-mail: info@ufinet.org
Home Page: http://www.ufinet.org

• 2010 • **Union of International Fairs Awards**
To recognize international organizers of trade fairs, exhibitions, and hall-owners. Awards include the Marketing Award, which recognizes the best marketing initiatives undertaken by exhibition professionals, and the Operations Award, which recognizes the best initiatives related to operations. Awarded annually.

• 2011 •
Vieilles Maisons Francaises
Philippe Toussaint, Pres.
93, rue de l'Universite
F-75007 Paris, France
Phone: 33 1 4062 6171
Fax: 33 1 4551 1226
E-mail: revue@VMF.net
Home Page: http://www.vmf.net

• 2012 • **Concours Annuel de Sauvegarde**
For recognition of outstanding contributions to the safeguarding of old French houses. A monetary prize of 15,000 euros is awarded annually. Established in 1966.

• 2013 •
World Association of Newspapers
(Association Mondiale des Journaux)
Timothy Balding, Dir.Gen.
7 Rue Geoffroy St. Hilaire
F-75005 Paris, France
Phone: 33 1 47428500
Fax: 33 1 47424948
E-mail: contact_us@wan.asso.fr
Home Page: http://www.wan-press.org

• 2014 • **Golden Pen of Freedom Award**
Presented to individuals, groups, or institutions working for freedom of the press. Awarded annually.

• 2015 •
World Federation of Engineering Organisations
(Federation Mondiale des Organisations d'Ingenieurs)
Mr. Pierre-Edouard de Boigne, Exec.Dir.
Maison de l'UNESCO
1 rue Miollis
Cedex 15
F-75732 Paris, France
Phone: 33 1 45684846
Phone: 33 1 45684847
Fax: 33 1 43062927
E-mail: peb.fmoi@unesco.org
Home Page: http://www.wfeo.org

• 2016 • **WFEO Award for Engineering Excellence**
Biennial award of recognition.

• 2017 • **WFEO Medal of Excellence in Engineering Education**
Biennial award of recognition.

• 2018 •
World Federation of Journalists and Travel Writers
1279 Chemin Aurelien
F-83470 St. Maximin la Sainte Saume, France
Phone: 33 4 94 597070
E-mail: christine.richter@free.fr

• 2019 • **Golden Apple**
Recognition destinations and individuals promoting tourism. Awarded annually.

• 2020 •
World Veterans Federation
(Federation Mondiale des Anciens Combattants)
Marek Hagmajer, Sec.Gen.
17, rue Nicolo
F-75116 Paris, France
Phone: 33 1 40726100
Fax: 33 1 40728058
E-mail: wvf@wvf-fmac.org
Home Page: http://www.wvf-fmac.org

• 2021 • **Rehabilitation Prize**
To recognize an individual or an organization for services of international value rendered in the field of rehabilitation. Selection is by nomination. The deadline depends on the dates of the General Assembly. In recent years, certificates or scrolls bearing individual citations have been awarded to two or more persons triennially at the WVF General Assembly. Established in 1953.

Germany

• 2022 •
Association for Aerosol Research
(Gesellschaft fur Aerosolforschung)
Gunthard Metzig, Treas.
Postfach 3640
D-76021 Karlsruhe, Germany
Phone: 49 7247 824800
Fax: 49 7247 824857
E-mail: gunthard.metzig@ftu.fzk.de
Home Page: http://www.gaef.de

• 2023 • **International Aerosol Fellow Award**
For outstanding contribution to Aerosol Science and Technology through research, technical development education and service.

• 2024 • **Junge Award**
For an individual who has shaped a completely new field of aerosol science and/or technology.

• 2025 • **Smoluchowski Award**
To a young scientist for excellent aerosol research.

• 2026 •
Association of Pulp and Paper Chemists and Engineers in Germany
(Verein der Zellstoff-und Papier-Chemiker und-Ingenieure)
Wilhelm Busse, Exec.Dir.
Emilstrasse 21
D-64293 Darmstadt, Germany
Phone: 49 6151 33264
Fax: 49 6151 311076
E-mail: zellcheming@zellcheming.de
Home Page: http://www.zellcheming.com

• 2027 • **Walter Brecht Denkmunze**
For recognition of outstanding technical and scientific contributions to the paper industry. Scientists without regard to nationality are eligible. A medal with a portrait of Walter Brecht, and, on the reverse, the name of the association and the inscription "for outstanding technical and scientific achievement in the field of the paper industry" is awarded periodically. Established in 1976.

• 2028 • **Hans Clemm Denkmunze**
For recognition of achievements in the field of pulp and paper technology or for special contributions to the Association. Scientists without regard to nationality are eligible. A medal showing the bust of Hans Clemm, and on the reverse a narrow oak-leaf wreath, the name of the Association, and the inscription "in recognition of out-

standing service" is awarded periodically. Established in 1936.

• 2029 • Goldene Vereinsnadel
For recognition of long years of outstanding service to the Association. Members without regard to nationality are eligible. A gold pin with the insignia of the Association is awarded periodically. Established in 1970.

• 2030 • Goldener Ehrenring fur Papiergeschichte
For recognition of outstanding, investigative work in the area of the history of paper. Scientists without regard to nationality are eligible. A gold ring with a reproduction of the old watermark "P" is awarded periodically. Established in 1954.

• 2031 • Georg Jayme Denkmunze
For recognition of outstanding technical and scientific achievements which promote research and development of the pulp chemistry. Scientists without regard to nationality are eligible. A medal showing the bust of Georg Jayme, and on the reverse, the emblem of the association and the inscription "in recognition of outstanding service" is awarded periodically. Established in 1989.

• 2032 • Eugen Lendholt Denkmunze
For recognition of outstanding technical or scientific work which promotes the sodium pulp and sulphate pulp and paper industry. Scientists without regard to nationality are eligible. A medal is awarded periodically. Established in 1957.

• 2033 • Alexander Mitscherlich Denkmunze
For recognition of outstanding scientific or technical achievements which further the pulp and paper industry. Scientists without regard to nationality are eligible. A medal showing the bust of Alexander Mitscherlich, and on the reverse a narrow wreath of oak-leaves, the name of the organization, and the inscription "in recognition of outstanding contributions" is awarded periodically. Established in 1936 in memory of Alexander Mitscherlich, founder of the Sulfite-cellulose industry.

• 2034 • Dr. Edmund Thiele Denkmunze
For recognition of outstanding achievement in the fields of synthetic fibers, rayons or film production. The award is usually given for a significant publication of the preceding year but can be given in special cases for a scientist's entire body of research. Scientists without regard to nationality are eligible. A medal showing the bust of Edmund Thiele, and on the reverse a narrow oak-leaf wreath, the name of the Association, and the inscription "in recognition of outstanding service" is awarded periodically. Established in 1937.

• 2035 •
International Johann Sebastian Bach Competition
(Internationaler Johann-Sebastien-Bach-Wettbewerb)
Prof. Dr. Christoph Wolff, Dir.
Thomaskirchhof 15/16
D-04109 Leipzig, Germany
Phone: 49 341 9137 0
Fax: 49 341 9137 305
E-mail: info@bach-leipzig.de
Home Page: http://www.bach-leipzig.de

• 2036 • International Johann Sebastian Bach Competition
To recognize the best performers of the Competition in the following categories: flute, harpsichord, piano, organ, voice, violin, and cello. Soloists of all nations who are between the ages of 16 and 32 are eligible. Eighteen monetary prizes and special prizes and performing certificates and honorary diplomas are also awarded. The Festival is held every two years in three of the disciplines as above. Established in 1950 by the Leipzig City Council.

• 2037 •
Bavarian Academy of Fine Arts
(Bayerische Akademie der Schonen Kunste)
Prof. Dr. Dieter Borchmeyer, Pres.
Max Joseph-Platz 3
D-80539 Munich, Germany
Phone: 49 89 2900770
Fax: 49 89 29007723
E-mail: info@badsk.de
Home Page: http://www.badsk.de

• 2038 • Horst Bienek Preis fur Lyrik
To recognize outstanding poetry. A monetary award is presented annually. Established in 1991 to honor Horst Bienek. Sponsored by the Horst Bienek Stiftung.

• 2039 • Grosser Literaturpreis der Bayerischen Akademie der Schonen Kunste
To recognize an author for his or her literary work. A monetary prize is awarded annually. Established in 1950. Formerly: (1986) Literaturpreis der Bayerische Akademie der Schonen Kunste.

• 2040 • Adelbert-von-Chamisso-Preis der Robert Bosch Stiftung
To recognize outstanding contributions to German literature from foreign authors. A monetary award is presented annually. Established in 1985 to honor Adelbert von Chamisso. Sponsored by the Robert Bosch Stiftung.

• 2041 • Friedrich Ludwig von Sckell-Ehrenring
To recognize extraordinary achievements in landscape architecture. A golden ring designed by Franz Rickert is awarded biennially. Established in 1967 to honor Friedrich Ludwig von Sckell, landscape architect, who planned the "English Garden" in Munich.

• 2042 •
Bavarian Academy of Sciences and Humanities
(Bayerische Akademie der Wissenschaften)
Christian Mende, Chm.
Marstallplatz 8
D-80539 Munich 22, Germany
Phone: 49 89 230310
Fax: 49 89 23031100
E-mail: info@badw.de
Home Page: http://www.badw.de

• 2043 • Bavarian Academy of Science Prize
For recognition of an outstanding achievement in science. A monetary prize is awarded irregularly when merited. Established in 1956 by the Foundation for the Advancement of Science in Bavaria.

• 2044 • Bene merenti Medals
For recognition of outstanding work for the Academy. Gold, silver, and bronze medals are awarded irregularly; the gold is seldom awarded, while the silver is awarded most years. Established in 1759.

• 2045 • Arnold Sommerfeld Preis
For recognition of outstanding achievement in science. A monetary prize is awarded annually. Established 1993.

• 2046 • Max Weber Preis
For recognition of outstanding achievement in humanities. A monetary prize is awarded annually. Established 1993.

• 2047 •
Berlin International Film Festival
(Internationale Filmfestspiele Berlin)
Dr. Thomas Kostlin, Mng.Dir.
Potsdamer Str. 5
D-10785 Berlin, Germany
Phone: 49 30 259 20 0
Fax: 49 30 259 20 299
E-mail: info@berlinale.de
Home Page: http://www.berlinale.de

• 2048 • Berlin International Film Festival
(Internationale Filmfestspiele Berlin)
To recognize the best feature and short films which are not only of interest to selected and expert audiences, but also films of quality that reach a wide public. The competition is limited to feature films and short films (less than 15 minutes) produced during the year preceding the Festival, not having been released outside their countries of origin, and not having participated in another competition or film festival. Priority is given to films not yet released. The following prizes are awarded for feature films for the producers: (1) Golden Berlin Bear - for the best feature-length film; (2) Silver Berlin Bear - The Jury Grand Prix; (3) Silver Berlin Bear - for the

best director; (4) Silver Berlin Bear - for the best actress; (5) Silver Berlin Bear - for the best actor; (6) Silver Berlin Bear - for an outstanding individual contribution; (7) Silver Berlin Bear for the best fil music (8) the Alfred Bauer Prize; and Special Mentions. The following prizes are awarded for short films: (1) Golden Berlin Bear for the best short film; and (2) the Silver Berlin Bear for a special film. In collaboration with the European Academy for Film and Television in Brussels, the Jury awards the Blue Angel to a European film. Other prizes of various organizations also awarded at the Berlin International Film Festival include: the Prize of the Churches, including a monetary award, to one competition film and two films from the International Forum of Young Cinema (IFYC); FIPRESCI Prize to one competition film, one film from the IFYC, and one film from the International Panorama, a selection of films of the festival that showcase new directors whose films address current issues or socially relevant topics; Readers Prizes of the *Berliner Morgenpost*; Prize of the German Art Film Theatre Association; CICAE Prizes (International Confederation of Art Cinemas); Prize of UNICEF; Prize of the Berlin Children's Jury; and Gay Teddy Bear (International Gay & Lesbian Film Festival Association). Awarded annually in February. Established in 1951.

• 2049 •
Bertelsmann Stiftung
(Bertelsmann Stiftung)
Ines Koring, Proj.Dir.
Postfach 103
Carl-Bertelsmann-Strasse 256
D-33311 Gutersloh, Germany
Phone: 49 5241 8181171
Phone: 49 5241 8181372
Fax: 49 5241 81681171
E-mail: ines.koring@bertelsmann.de
Home Page: http://www.neue-stimmen.de

• 2050 • **Neue Stimmen - International Singing Contest**
(Neue Stimmen - Internationaler Gesangswettbewerb)
For recognition of young opera singers. Female singers who are 30 years of age or younger, and male singers who are 32 years of age or younger may submit applications. The following monetary awards are presented biennially: first prize - 10,000 Euro; second prize - 7500 Euro; third prize - 6000 Euro; 4th, 5th, and 6th prize - 3000 Euro each. Plus: Audience Prize, CD/DVD recording Neue Stimmen 2005, radio and television broadcast, possible participation in one of the master classes Neue Stimmen. Established in 1987. Additional information is available from Ines Koring, Program Director, Bertelsmann Stiftung.

• 2051 •
Bob und Schlittenverband fur Deutschland e.V.
Stefan Krauss, Sec.Gen.
An der Schiettstatte 6
83471 Berchtesgaden, Germany
Phone: 49 8652 95880
Fax: 49 8652 958822
E-mail: info@bsd-portal.de
Home Page: http://www.bsd-portal.de

• 2052 • **Badge of Honour in Gold, Silver and Bronze**
Recognizes sporting successes. Three medals are awarded annually.

• 2053 •
Braun GmbH
Bernard Wild, Chm.
Frankfurter Strasse 145
D-61476 Kronberg, Germany
Phone: 49 6173 300
Fax: 49 6173 302875
E-mail: info@braunprize.com
Home Page: http://www.braunprize.com

• 2054 • **Braun Prize**
To recognize the creativity of young designers and the richness of their ideas. Awarded biennially in odd-numbered years.

• 2055 •
Braunschweig City Cultural Office
(Stadt Braunschweig-Kulturamt)
Platz der Deutschen Einheit, 1
38100 Braunschweig, Germany
Phone: 49 531 470 1
Fax: 49 531 151 12
E-mail: stadt@braunscheig.de
Home Page: http://www.braunschweig.de

• 2056 • **Friedrich-Gerstaecker-Preis**
To recognize living authors of young peoples' books which convey adventures in the wide world with captivating style, as did world traveler/author Friedrich Gerstaecker, a citizen of Braunschweig. The book, written in German, must have been published within the preceding three years. A monetary prize is awarded biennially. Established in 1947.

• 2057 •
Brigitte
Andreas Lebert, Ed.
Am Baumwall 11
D-20444 Hamburg, Germany
Phone: 49 40 37030
Fax: 49 40 3703 5679
E-mail: infoline@brigitte.de
Home Page: http://www.brigitte.de

• 2058 • **Bettina Von-Arnim Prize**
To encourage young short story writers. Awarded biennially with a monetary price. Established in 1991.

• 2059 •
Bundesvereinigung Deutscher Apothekerverbande
Heinz-Gunter Wolf, Pres.
Jagerstrasse, 49/50
D-10117 Berlin, Germany
Phone: 49 30 400 040
Fax: 49 30 400 04598
E-mail: abda@abdaapponet.de
Home Page: http://www.abda.de

• 2060 • **Ehrennadel der Deutschen Apotheker**
To recognize an outstanding German pharmacist. A lapel pin and a certificate are awarded at infrequent intervals. Established in 1975.

• 2061 • **Hans Meyer Medaille**
For recognition of service to the German pharmaceutical profession and pharmaceutical medicine. A silver medal and a certificate are awarded annually. Established in 1971 by the executive councils of the Professional Association of German Pharmacists, and the Federal Chamber of Pharmacists.

• 2062 •
Centre of Films for Children and Young People in Germany
(Kinder-und Jugendfilmzentrum in Deutschland)
Horst Schafer, Ldr.
Kuppelstein 34
D-42857 Remscheid, Germany
Phone: 49 2191 794233
Fax: 49 2191 793230
E-mail: info@kjf.de
Home Page: http://www.kjf.de

• 2063 • **Deutscher Jugend-Video-Preis**
To promote qualified videos for children and young people among the commercial video programs. Awards are given in two categories: Videos for Children and Videos for Young People. Videos are suggested to a jury when they are in distribution or on sale during the current award year. Monetary prizes and an honorable mention are awarded in each category. Awarded annually. Established in 1985 and announced by Bundesministerium fer Familie, Senioren, Frauen und Jugend (Federal Minister for Family Seniors, Women, and Youth).

• 2064 •
Chopin-Gesellschaft in der Bundesrepublik Deutschland
John F.-Kennedy-Haus
Kasinostrasse 3
D-64293 Darmstadt, Germany
Phone: 49 6151 25957
Fax: 49 6151 25957
E-mail: i.hoerl@chopin-gesellschaft.de
Home Page: http://www.chopin-gesellschaft.de

Awards are arranged in alphabetical order below their administering organizations

• 2065 • **European Chopin Piano Competition (Europaischer Chopin-Klavierwettbewerb)**
To promote outstanding Chopin interpretation and to prepare artists for the Warsaw Chopin Competition. The competition is open to pianists studying or having studied in a European country for at least two semesters or one year, and who are not older than 30 years of age. Monetary prizes are awarded triennially. Established in 1983.

• 2066 •
Cologne International Pianoforte Competition - Foundation Tomassoni
Dr. Heike Sauer, Press Off.
Dagobertstrasse 38
D-50668 Cologne, Germany
Phone: 49 221 912818 105
Fax: 49 221 912818 106
E-mail: sauer@mhs-koeln.de
Home Page: http://www.mhs-koeln.de

• 2067 • **Cologne International Pianoforte Competition (Internationalen Klavierwettbewerb Koln)**
To recognize and promote young piano performers. Pianists of all nationalities between 18 and 29 years of age are eligible. Monetary prizes are awarded every four years. Established in 1980 by Caterina Tomassoni in memory of her sister.

• 2068 •
Cologne International Violin Competition (Internationaler Violinwettbewerb Koln)
Dr. Heike Sauer, Press Off.
Hochschule fur Musik Koln
Foundation Georg Kulenkampff
Dagobertstrasse 38
D-50668 Cologne, Germany
Phone: 49 221 912818 105
Fax: 49 221 912818 106
E-mail: esser@mhs-koeln.de
Home Page: http://www.mhs-koeln.de

• 2069 • **Cologne International Violin Competition (Internationaler Violinwettbewerb Koln)**
To recognize outstanding violin performance and to encourage professional development. All violinists up to 30 years of age may submit applications by June 15. Monetary prizes are awarded every four years. Established in 1982 by Prof. Dr. Caspar and Dr. Angela Kulenkampff in memory of Georg Kulenkampff.

• 2070 •
Cologne International Vocal Competition (Internationaler Violinwettbewerb Koln)
Dr. Heike Sauer, Press Off.
% Hochschule fur Musik Koln
Dagobertstrasse 38
D-50668 Cologne, Germany
Phone: 49 221 912818 103
Fax: 49 221 912818 139
E-mail: sauer@mhs-koeln.de
Home Page: http://www.mhs-koeln.de

Formerly: (2004) Cologne International Singing Competition.

• 2071 • **Cologne International Vocal Competition**
To recognize outstanding singing performance and to encourage professional development. All singers up to 30 years of age are eligible. Monetary prizes are awarded every four years. Established in 1198 by Helga and Paul Hohnen. In cooperation with the town Bergheim, near Cologne, "singing prize of the city Bergheim" will be awarded at the same time. Formerly: (2004) Cologne International Singing Competition.

• 2072 •
Dechema - Society for Chemical Engineering and Biotechnology
Dr. Christina Hirche, Public Relations
Theodor-Heuss-Allee 25
D-60486 Frankfurt am Main, Germany
Phone: 49 69 75640
Fax: 49 69 7564 201
E-mail: press@dechema.de
Home Page: http://www.dechema.de

• 2073 • **DECHEMA Award of the Max-Buchner-Forschungsstiftung**
For outstanding, published research in the fields of applied chemistry, process engineering, biotechnology and chemical apparatus. Preference is given to younger scientists whose work is fundamentally important and successfully combines theory with practical application. Awarded annually.

• 2074 • **Student Awards**
To recognize graduates in technical chemistry, chemical process engineering/chemical engineering, and biotechnology who have distinguished themselves by their outstanding academic performance achieved in a remarkably short period of study. Awarded annually.

• 2075 •
Deutsche Akademie der Naturforscher Leopoldina
Prof. Dr. Volker ter Meulen, Pres.
Archiv fur Geschichte der Naturforschung u. Medizin
Emil-Abderhalder-Str. 37
Postfach 110543
D-06019 Halle/Saale, Germany
Phone: 49 345 472390
Fax: 49 345 4723919
E-mail: leopoldina@leopoldina-halle.de
Home Page: http://www.leopoldina.uni-halle.de

• 2076 • **Leopoldina Prize for Junior Scientists**
To recognize men or women who have made a distinguished achievement in natural sciences, medical science, or the history of science and who are under the age of 30. A monetary prize is awarded biennially in odd-numbered years. Established in 1993.

• 2077 •
Deutsche Gesellschaft fur Parasitologie
Prof. Dr. Brigitte Frank, Mgr.
% Prof. Dr. Brigitte Frank
Universitat Hohenheim
FG Parasitologie
D-70599 Stuttgart, Germany
Phone: 49 711 459 2277
Fax: 49 711 459 2276
E-mail: brifrank@uni-hohenheim.de
Home Page: http://www.dgparasitologie.de

• 2078 • **Karl Asmund Rudolphi Medal (Carl-Asmund-Rudolphi-Medaille)**
For recognition of outstanding scientific achievement in the area of parasitological research and its application. Scientists not older than 38 years who are involved in the field of biology and medical science are eligible. A monetary prize of 500 euros is awarded annually. Established in 1986 in memory of Carl Asmund Rudolphi (1771-1832), a scientist in the area of parasitological research and its application.

• 2079 •
Deutsche Meteorologische Gesellschaft
Marion Schnee, Sec.
% Freie Universitat Berlin
Carl-Heinrich-Becker-Weg 6-10
D-12165 Berlin, Germany
Phone: 49 30 7970 8324
Fax: 49 30 7919 002
E-mail: sekretariat@dmg-ev.de
Home Page: http://www.dmg-ev.de

• 2080 • **Albert Defant-Medaille**
For recognition of outstanding scientific achievement in physical oceanography. Awarded triennially. Established in 1985 in honor of Albert Defant.

• 2081 • Deutsche Meteorologische Gesellschaft Ehrenmitgliedschaft
To honor members of the meteorological society for special service to meteorology or to the organization. A certificate is awarded when merited. Established in 1966.

• 2082 • Forderpreis
To recognize young meteorologists for outstanding achievement in the field. Works that are completed by individuals under 35 years of age and that have been published are considered. There may be no more than three years between publication and awarding of the prize. A monetary prize is awarded annually. Established in 1966. Formerly: Deutsche Meteorologische Gesellschaft e.V. Jugendpreis.

• 2083 • Alfred Wegener-Medaille
To recognize persons for exemplary service and contributions to meteorological science. A medal is awarded triennially. Established in 1966 in honor of Alfred Wegener.

• 2084 •
Deutsche Mineralogische Gesellschaft
Dr. Frank E. Brenker, Ed.
℅ Dr. Frank Brenker
Institut fur Geologie und Mineralogie
Universitat zu Koln
Zulpicherstr. 49 b
D-50574 Cologne, Germany
Phone: 49 221 470 6113
Fax: 49 221 470 5199
E-mail: dmg@min.uni-koeln.de
Home Page: http://www.dmg-home.de

• 2085 • Georg-Agricola-Medaille
For recognition of outstanding contributions in the field of applied (industrial) mineralogy. Individuals must be nominated. A bronze medal is awarded at the convention. Established in 1974 in honor of Georg Argricola.

• 2086 • Viktor-Moritz-Goldschmidt Preis
For recognition of important scientific contributions of younger scientists. Members of the Society, generally younger than 40 years of age, must be nominated. A monetary prize is awarded at the convention. Established in 1957 in honor of Victor Moritz Goldschmidt.

• 2087 • Paul Ramdohr Prize
Award of recognition. A monetary prize of 1,000 euros is awarded.

• 2088 • Abraham-Gottlob-Werner Medaille
For recognition of outstanding scientific contributions to mineralogy. Individuals must be nominated. Gold and silver medals are awarded at the convention. Established in 1950 in honor of Abraham Gottlob Werner.

• 2089 •
Deutsche Physikalische Gesellschaft
Rathausplatz 2-4
D-53604 Bad Honnef, Germany
Phone: 49 2224 9519518
Fax: 49 2224 951519
E-mail: presse@dpg-physik.de
Home Page: http://www.dpg-physik.de

• 2090 • Max-Born-Preis
For recognition of outstanding scientific contributions to physics. Awards are given in alternate years to German and British physicists by the combined British Institute of Physics and the Deutsche Physikalische Gesellschaft. A monetary prize, a silver medal bearing the likeness of Mr. Born (designed by his daughter, Mrs. Margaret Pryce) on one side and a formula on the other, and a certificate are awarded annually. Established in 1972.

• 2091 • Otto-Hahn-Preis fur Chemie und Physik
To recognize German individuals who have performed a unique service to the development of chemistry, physics, or applied research. A monetary prize of 50,000 Euros, a gold medal bearing the likeness of Mr. Hahn on one side, and a certificate are awarded by the Deutscher Zentralausschuss fur Chemie and the Deutsche Physikalishe Gesellschaft when merited. Established in 1955.

• 2092 • Gustav-Hertz-Preis (Physik-Preis)
To recognize a recently completed, outstanding publication by a younger physicist. A prize is awarded in both experimental and theoretical physics when merited. A monetary prize and a certificate are awarded annually. Established in 1941. Formerly: Preis der Deutschen Physikalische Gesellschaft.

• 2093 • Gentner-Kastler-Prize
To recognize alternately French and German physicists for outstanding contributions to physics. A monetary prize, a silver medal bearing the likeness of Mr. Gentner and Mr. Kastler on one side, and a certificate are awarded annually by the Societe Francaise de Physique and the Deutsche Physikalische Gesellschaft. Established in 1984.

• 2094 • Medaille fur Naturwissenschaftliche Publizistik
For recognition of journalistic achievement contributing to the expansion of natural scientific physical thought in the German-speaking realm. A silver medal and a certificate are awarded when merited. Established in 1984.

• 2095 • Max-Planck-Medaille
For recognition of outstanding theoretical work in quantum theory. A gold medal bearing the likeness of Mr. Planck on one side and a certificate are awarded annually. Established in 1928.

• 2096 • Robert-Wichard-Pohl-Preis
For recognition of outstanding achievements in physics, especially radiation and other disciplines of science and technology and the dissemination of scientific knowledge through the teaching of physics. A monetary prize and a certificate are awarded annually when merited. Established in 1979.

• 2097 • Karl-Scheel-Preis
For recognition of published works in the field of physics. Young physicists in Berlin are eligible. A monetary prize, a bronze plaque, and a certificate are awarded annually. Established in 1946 by the Physical Society of Berlin.

• 2098 • Walter-Schottky-Preis fur Festkorperforschung
For recognition of outstanding publications and research in solid state physics by a younger scientist. A monetary prize of 15,000 Euros and a certificate are awarded annually. Established in 1972. Sponsored by Siemens AG.

• 2099 •
Deutsches Forum fur Figurentheater und Puppenspielkunst e.V.
Annette Dabs, Mng.Dir.
Hattinger Str. 467
D-44795 Bochum 1, Germany
Phone: 49 234 47720
Fax: 49 23447735
E-mail: info@fidena.de
Home Page: http://www.dfp.fidena.de

• 2100 • Fritz Wortelmann Preis of the City of Bochum for Amateur Puppetry (Fritz Wortelmann-Preis der Stadt Bochum fur das Amateur-Figurentheater)
To recognize the best groups of amateur puppeteers. Monetary prizes are awarded biennially in November. Established in 1959.

• 2101 •
Electric Power Society
Association of German Electrical Engineers
VDE Headquarters
Stresemannallee 15
D-60596 Frankfurt am Main, Germany
Phone: 49 69 63080
Fax: 49 69 6312925
E-mail: service@vde.com
Home Page: http://www.vde.com/vde

• 2102 • Herbert-Kind-Preis der ETG
For recognition of outstanding academic achievement. Students of electrical power engineering may be nominated. A monetary prize and a certificate of award are presented annually. Established in 1982 in memory of Dr. Herbert Kind.

• 2103 • VDE/ETG Award
For recognition of excellence in scientific publications in the field of electric power. Members of the Society under the age of 40 are eligible. A monetary prize of 3,000 Euros and a certificate

are awarded several times a year. Established in 1975. Formerly: (2006) Literaturpreis der ETG.

• 2104 •
European Association for the Study of Diabetes
Dr. Viktor Joergens MD, Exec.Dir.
Rheindorfer Weg 3
D-40591 Dusseldorf, Germany
Phone: 49 221 7584690
Fax: 49 221 75846929
E-mail: secretariat@easd.org
Home Page: http://www.easd.org

• 2105 • **Claude Bernard Lecture**
To recognize an individual's innovative leadership and outstanding contributions to the advancement of knowledge in the field of diabetes mellitus and related diseases. Members may submit nominations by April 15. Travel expenses to the annual meeting of EASD and the Claude Bernard Medal are awarded annually. Established in 1969 by the Paul Neumann Laboratory, in Paris, France.

• 2106 • **Eli Lilly/EASD Research Fellowship in Diabetes and Metabolism**
To encourage research in the field of diabetes and metabolism and to promote excellence in medical education in Europe. Applications may be made by European members of the EASD under the age of 40 who hold an M.D. degree or European equivalent. The deadline is February 15. A fellowship of $35,000 is awarded. Established in 1991.

• 2107 • **Minkowski Prize**
For recognition of outstanding publications that increase knowledge concerning diabetes mellitus. Research must be carried out in Europe by a person normally a resident in Europe, who is under the age of 40. Nominations may be submitted by members by February 15. A monetary prize of $20,000, a certificate, and travel expenses to the annual meeting of EASD are awarded annually. Established in 1966 by Farbwerke Hoechst AG.

• 2108 • **Castelli Pedroli Prize**
For recognition of work concerned with the histopathology, pathogenesis, prevention, and treatment of the complications of diabetes mellitus. Works published in internationally recognized scientific journals during the previous five-year period are considered. Members of the Association who are residents in Europe may be nominated by members only by February 15. A monetary prize is awarded each year at the annual meeting. In addition, the winner is named the Golgi Lecturer and presents a lecture. Established in 1986 by the family of the late Maria Carla Castelli Pedroli in honor of Camillo Golgi.

• 2109 • **Albert Renold Fellowship**
To encourage young European investigators to visit another laboratory or laboratories to gain experience in new techniques and methodology, to receive postdoctoral training or to carry out collaborative research. Members under 40 years of age may apply by February 15. One Fellowship of is awarded annually. Established in memory of Professor Albert Ernst Renold (1923-1988), the founding Secretary of the European Association for the Study of Diabetes.

• 2110 •
European Athletic Association
(Association Europeenne d'Athletisme)
Till Lufft, Gen.Sec.
Alsfelder Strasse 27
D-64289 Darmstadt, Germany
Phone: 49 6151 7708023
Phone: 49 6151 7708030
Fax: 49 6151 770811
E-mail: generalsekretariat@leichtathletik.de
Home Page: http://www.european-athletics.org

• 2111 • **Waterford Crystal European Athlete of the Year Award**
Recognizes outstanding athletic performances. Awarded annually.

• 2112 •
European Behavioral Pharmacology Society
W.J. Schmidt, Pres.
Department of Neuropharmacology
University Tubingen
Auf der Mogenstelle 28 E
D-72076 Tubingen, Germany
Phone: 49 7071 2974571
Fax: 49 7071 295144
E-mail: president@ebps.org
Home Page: http://www.ebps.org

• 2113 • **Distinguished Achievement Award**
To individuals with achievements in the field of research, teaching or in in the promotion of behavioral pharmacology.

• 2114 • **Poster Prizes**
To individuals presenting a poster at the organization's biennial meeting.

• 2115 • **Young Scientist Award**
To young individuals with an achievement in the field of research.

• 2116 •
European Federation of Corrosion
(Federation Europeenne de la Corrosion)
Gerhard Kreysa, Gen.Sec.
Theodor-Heuss-Allee 25
D-60486 Frankfurt am Main, Germany
Phone: 49 69 7564209
Phone: 49 69 7564143
Fax: 49 69 7564299
E-mail: meier@dechema.de
Home Page: http://www.efcweb.org/

• 2117 • **Cavallaro Medal**
For recognition of outstanding achievement in basic research in the field of corrosion and corrosion protection. Awarded biennially. Established in 1965 by the Universite de Ferrara in memory of Professor Leo Cavallaro, founder of the Center for the Study of Corrosion.

• 2118 • **European Corrosion Medal**
For recognition of achievements by a scientist, or group of scientists in the application of corrosion science in the chemical, petroleum, and nuclear industries. The recipients must be of a nationality(ies) corresponding to one, or more, of the member Societies of the EFC and the work must be conducted within a European country. Proposals for recipients may be submitted mainly by the EFC member Societies; selection is by a Jury. A medal and diploma are awarded biennially when merited. Established in 1985 by DECHEMA.

• 2119 • **Marti I. Franques Medal**
For recognition of outstanding contributions to the advancement of science and technology of corrosion through international cooperation with the EFC, transfer of knowledge, and education. Established by the Sociedad Espanola de Quimica Industrial and awarded for the first time in 1993.

• 2120 •
European Meteorological Society
Martina Junge, Exec. Sec.
Freie Universitat Berlin
Carl-Heinrich-Becker-Weg 6-10
D-12165 Berlin, Germany
Phone: 49 30 79708328
Phone: 49 30 83871205
Fax: 49 30 7919002
E-mail: ems-sec@met.fu-berlin.de
Home Page: http://www.emetsoc.org

• 2121 • **EMS Media Award**
For outstanding broadcast meteorologist.

• 2122 • **Student/Young Scientist Travel Award**
For young participants at various conferences.

• 2123 • **Young Scientist Award**
For outstanding young scientist.

• 2124 •
European Molecular Biology Organization
Prof. Frank Gannon, Exec.Dir.
Meyerhofstr. 1
D-69117 Heidelberg, Germany
Phone: 49 6221 88910
Fax: 49 6221 8891200
E-mail: embo@embo.org
Home Page: http://www.embo.org

• 2125 • **EMBO Medal**
For recognition of contributions in Western Europe to the development of molecular biology. European citizens under the age of 40 are eligible. A monetary prize of and a medal are awarded annually. Established in 1986.

• 2126 •
European Society for Microcirculation
Dr. Axel R. Pries PhD, Gen.Sec.
Dept. of Physiology-CBF
Charite Berlin
Arnimallee 22
14195 Berlin, Germany
Phone: 49 30 84451632
Phone: 49 30 84451631
Fax: 49 30 84451634
E-mail: esmmail@charite.de
Home Page: http://www.medizin.fu-berlin.de/esm

• 2127 • **Lars-Erik Gelin Conference Travel Award**
Together with the submission of an abstract for an international conference of the ESM, young scientists may apply for a travel grant which will cover the registration fee and support their travel costs. Prices are awarded on the basis of the quality of the submitted abstracts. Awarded to one or more recipients biennially in even-numbered years.

• 2128 • **Honorary Membership of the ESM**
To award researchers who have been active in microcirculatory research for a long time (they may be retired from their professional duties). Honorary membership may be awarded upon suggestion by national societies or individual members.

• 2129 • **Malpighi Medal**
Recognizes scientific achievements of a long scientific career. A medal is awarded annually.

• 2130 • **Van Leeuwenhoek Distinctive Travel Award**
To allow researchers entering the area of microcirculatory and vascular biology research to visit research laboratories in order to learn new techniques and discuss topics, methods and perspectives with established researchers. The award entails a monetary donation. Personal applications as well as suggestions are invited.

• 2131 •
European Union of Music Competition for Youth
(Europaische Union der Musikwettbewerbe fur die Jugend)
Dr. Eckart Rohlfs, Sec.Gen.
Postf. 662205
D-81219 Munich, Germany
Phone: 49 89 871002 50
Phone: 49 89 871002 42
Fax: 49 89 87100290
E-mail: info@emcy.org
Home Page: http://www.emcy.org

• 2132 • **European Music Prize for Youth**
Annual award of recognition.

• 2133 •
European Water Pollution Control Association
Theodor-Heuss-Allee 17
D-53773 Hennef, Germany
Phone: 49 2242 872189
Fax: 49 2242 872135
E-mail: ewa@atv.de
Home Page: http://www.EWAonline.de

• 2134 • **William Dunbar Medal**
To recognize applied technology development in the field of waste water treatment and water protection. A gold medal, certificate, and monetary prize of 5,000 euros are awarded triennially. Established in 1973.

• 2135 •
Fair and Exhibition Association
(Fachverband Messe-und Ausstellungsbau)
Mrs. Eefie Adler, Contact
Berliner Str. 26
D-33378 Rheda-Wiedenbruck, Germany
Phone: 49 5242 94540
Fax: 49 5242 945410
E-mail: exhibition@famab.de
Home Page: http://www.famab.de

• 2136 • **ADAM Award**
Annual award of recognition.

• 2137 •
Filmfest Munchen
(Internationales Festival der Filmhochschulen Munchen)
Andreas Strohl, CEO
% Internationale Muenchner Filmwochen
Sonnenstrasse 21
D-80331 Munich, Germany
Phone: 49 89 3819040
Fax: 49 89 38190426
E-mail: info@filmfest-muenchen.de
Home Page: http://www.filmfest-muenchen.de

• 2138 • **Munich International Filmschool Festival**
(Internationales Festival der Filmhochschulen Munchen)
To encourage the professional development of young filmmakers. Films by film students can only be entered by the respective film schools. Film equipment and filmstock are awarded for the various prizes and special prizes. Awarded annually. Established in 1981. Prizes are sponsored by private companies, television stations, etc.

• 2139 •
Foerderkreis Deutscher Schriftsteller in Baden-Wuerttemberg
Meike Gerhardt, Mng.Dir.
Gartenstr. 58
D-76135 Karlsruhe, Germany
Fax: 49 711 6365364
E-mail: info@schriftsteller-in-bawue.de
Home Page: http://www.schriftsteller-in-bawue.de

• 2140 • **Thaddaeus-Troll-Preis**
For recognition of German writers in the field of literature. Baden-Wuerttemberg authors are eligible. An endowment of $10,000 and a certificate are awarded annually. Established in 1981 in memory of Thaddaeus-Troll who was dedicated to promoting young literary talent. Cosponsored by Ministerium Fuer Wissenschaft, Forschung und Kunst Baden-Wuerttemberg and Foerderkreis Deutscher Schriftsteller.

• 2141 •
Foundation of Lower Saxony
(Stiftung Niedersachsen)
Linda Anne Engelhardt, Exec.Dir.
Sophienstrasse 2
Kunstlerhaus
D-30159 Hannover, Germany
Phone: 49 511 990 5413
Fax: 49 511 314 499
E-mail: info@violin-competition.de
Home Page: http://www.violin-competition.de

• 2142 • **Hanover International Violin Competition**
(Internationaler Violin-Wettbewerb Hannover)
To encourage professional development of young violinists and to recognize their achievements. The competition is open to violinists of all nationalities between 16 and 30 years of age. Monetary prizes totaling 75,000 euros are awarded, as well as recording contracts and concert debuts. Awarded triennially. Established in 1991 and dedicated to Joseph Joachim.

• 2143 •
German Academy of Language and Poetry
(Deutsche Akademie fur Sprache und Dichtung)
Dr. Bernd Busch, Gen.Sec.
Gluckert-Haus
Alexandraweg 23
D-64287 Darmstadt, Germany
Phone: 49 6151 40920
Fax: 49 6151 409299
E-mail: sekretariat@deutscheakademie.de
Home Page: http://www.deutscheakademie.de

• 2144 • **Georg-Buchner-Preis**
To recognize writers and poets whose works further the cultural heritage of Germany. A monetary prize is awarded annually. Established in 1923 for the arts and literature, and changed to a literature prize in 1951.

• 2145 • **Sigmund-Freud-Preis**
For recognition of a scientific work which constitutes an effective piece of prose. A monetary is awarded annually. Established in 1964.

• 2146 • **Friedrich-Gundolf-Preis fur die Vermittlung deutscher Kultur im Ausland**
To recognize persons who have rendered outstanding service to the promulgation of German culture on foreign soil. A monetary prize of

12,500 Euros is awarded annually. Established in 1964.

• 2147 • Johann-Heinrich-Merck Preis

For recognition of works of literary criticism and essays. A monetary prize of $20,000 (DM) is awarded annually. Established in 1964.

• 2148 • Johann-Heinrich-Voss-Preis fur Uebersetzung

For recognition of excellence in translation of a life's work and also individual works of poetry, drama, or essays. A monetary prize of 15,000 Euros is awarded biennially in odd-numbered years. Established in 1958.

• 2149 •
German Adult Education Association
(Deutscher Volkshochschul-Verband)
Ulrich Aengenvoort, Dir.Gen.
Obere Wilhelm-Strasse 32
D-53225 Bonn, Germany
Phone: 49 228 975690
Fax: 49 228 9756930
E-mail: info@dvv-vhs.de
Home Page: http://vhs-dvv.server.de

• 2150 • Adolf Grimme Preis

Recognizes outstanding educational television programs. Awarded annually.

• 2151 •
German Agricultural Society
(Deutsche Landwirtschafts-Gesellschaft)
Dr. Reinhard Grandke, Dir.
Eschborner Landstrasse 122
D-60489 Frankfurt, Germany
Phone: 49 69 24788257
Fax: 49 69 24788123
E-mail: k-m.lueth@dlg-frankfurt.de
Home Page: http://www.dlg.org

• 2152 • International DLG Prize (Internationaler DLG-Preis)

For recognition of exceptional professional and honorary achievement in agriculture and its related industry and to provide further and supplementary training. Individuals who are 18 to 36 years of age may be nominated by SEPTEMBER 30. The following grants for training are awarded: (1) Junior-Prize, for individuals 18-24 years of age - $2,500; (2) Supplemental Training Prize, for individuals 24-36 years of age - $4,000. Established in 1986 by Deutsche Landwirtschafts-Gesellschaft on the occasion of its 100-year anniversary.

• 2153 •
German Association for Water, Wastewater and Waste
Dr. van Riesen, Managing Dir.
Theodor-Heuss-Allee 17
D-53773 Hennef, Germany
Phone: 49 22 428720
Fax: 49 22 42872135
E-mail: atvorg@atv.de
Home Page: http://www.atv.de/

• 2154 • Ernst-Kuntze Prize

For a practitionerKs thesis in the field of wastewater. A monetary prize of 5,000 euros is awarded annually.

• 2155 •
German Bunsen Society for Physical Chemistry
Dr. Heinz Behret, Mgr.
Varrentrappstrasse 40-42
D-60486 Frankfurt am Main 90, Germany
Phone: 49 69 7917 201
Fax: 49 69 7917 450
E-mail: h.behret@bunsen.de
Home Page: http://www.bunsen.de

Formerly: Deutsche Elektrochemische Gesellschaft.

• 2156 • Bonhoeffer-Eucen-Scheibe Memorial Lecture

To recognize and to disseminate the results of outstanding work in physical chemistry by lectures. Established in 1995.

• 2157 • Paul Bunge Prize

The Hans R. Jenemann Foundation honors work in the area of scientific historic instruments, jointly with Gesellschaft Deutscher Chemiker. Established in 1992. Awarded annually.

• 2158 • Theodor Foerster Memorial Lecture

For recognition of outstanding work in the area of photochemistry. A lecture and travel expenses are awarded. Established to honor Theodor Foerster. Awarded jointly with the Gesellschaft Deutscher Chemiker.

• 2159 • Wilhelm Jost Memorial Lecture

Established by H. Roeck, jointly with and under administration of the Akademie der Wissenschaften, Goettingen. Annual proposal of a lecturer by the Bunsen-Gesellschaft. Honors the famous physicochemist W. Jost and lectures are given in the university cities of Jost's work.

• 2160 • Nernst - Haber - Bodenstein-Preis

For recognition of achievement in physical chemistry. Younger scientists who are less than 40 years of age are eligible. A monetary award is presented annually. Established in 1953 by German industry.

• 2161 •
German Chemical Society
(Gesellschaft Deutscher Chemiker)
Prof. Dr. Henning Hopf, Pres.
Varrentrappstrasse 40-42
Postfach 90 04 40
D-60444 Frankfurt am Main, Germany
Phone: 49 69 7917 0
Fax: 49 69 7917 232
E-mail: gdch@gdch.de
Home Page: http://www.gdch.de

• 2162 • Arfvedson-Schlenk-Preis

To honor outstanding scientific and technical achievements in the field of lithium chemistry. A monetary award is given.

• 2163 • Gmelin-Beilstein-Denkmunze

For special recognition of contributions to chemical literature or the history of chemistry, hence also the goals of the German Chemical Society. German and non-German chemists are eligible. A monetary award and a silver medal are awarded every few years. Established in 1954 by Hoechst AG.

• 2164 • Carl-Duisberg-Gedachtnispreis

For recognition of research in chemistry. Younger scientists qualified as university lecturers are eligible. A monetary award is given annually.

• 2165 • Carl-Duisberg-Plakette

For recognition of special contributions to the advancement of chemistry and the goals of the society. A gold plaque is awarded. Established in 1953 by Bavarian AG.

• 2166 • Emil-Fischer-Medaille

For recognition of the best work in the field of organic chemistry. German chemists are eligible. A monetary award and a gold medal are awarded every few years.

• 2167 • Fresenius-Preis

For recognition of special contributions to the scientific development of analytical chemistry. A monetary award and a gold medal are awarded every few years. Established in 1961.

• 2168 • Horst Pracejus-Preis

For eminent contributions to the advancement of research in chirality. A monetary award is given.

• 2169 • Wilhelm-Klemm-Preis

For recognition of outstanding work in the field of inorganic chemistry. German and non-German scientists are eligible. A monetary award and a gold medal are awarded. Established in 1984 by Degussa AG.

• 2170 • Joseph-Konig-Gedenkmunze

For recognition of special contributions to the scientific development of food chemistry and for the advancement and recognition of food chemistry. German and non-German scientists are eligible. A monetary award and a bronze medal are awarded every few years.

• 2171 • Richard-Kuhn-Medaille

For recognition of special contributions in the area of biochemistry. German and non-German scientists are eligible. A monetary award and a gold medal are awarded biennially. Established in 1968 by BASF AG.

• 2172 • Liebig-Denkmunze

For recognition of outstanding achievements by German chemists. A monetary award and a silver medal are given biennially in even-numbered years.

• 2173 • Preis der Gesellschaft Deutscher Chemiker fur Journalistein und Schriftsteller (Preis der Gesellschaft Deutcher Chemiker fur Schriftsteller)
For recognition of outstanding publications that inform the public about problems of chemistry and their solutions. Journalists and authors are eligible. A monetary award is presented. Established in 1980.

• 2174 • Hermann-Staudinger-Preis
For recognition of contributions in the field of macromolecular chemistry. German and foreign scientists are eligible. A monetary award and a gold medal are awarded biennially. Established in 1970 by BASF AG.

• 2175 • Alfred-Stock-Gedachtnispreis
For recognition of an outstanding independent scientific experimental investigation in the field of inorganic chemistry. A monetary award and a gold medal are awarded biennially when merited. Established in 1950.

• 2176 • Adolf-von-Baeyer-Denkmunze
For recognition of the best published work of the preceding year in the area of organic chemistry, especially on experimental dye or pharmaceutical chemistry, or for contributions to the German chemical industry through the discovery of organic preparations, important dyes or pharmaceutical preparations, perfumes or other products. German chemists are eligible. A monetary prize (Bayer AG) and a gold medal are awarded every few years. Established in 1910 by Carl Duisberg.

• 2177 • August-Wilhelm-von-Hofmann-Denkmunze
Non-German chemists and German scientists who are not chemists but who have made special contributions to chemistry are eligible. A gold medal is awarded irregularly every two or three years.

• 2178 • Otto-Wallach-Plakette
For recognition of special achievement in the field of volatile oils, terpenes, and polyterpenes or in the area of biochemical attractants and deterrents. Younger European scientists are eligible. A monetary award and a gold medal are awarded irregularly. Established in 1964 by DRAGOCO and Gerberding & Company.

• 2179 • Wohler-Preis "Ressourcenschonende Prozesse"
For recognition of achievements in chemistry, chemical technology, and similar fields which improve the use of materials and reduce waste, solvents, energy, or hazards. A monetary award is given.

• 2180 • Karl-Ziegler-Preis
For recognition of outstanding research in the area of organo-metallic chemistry, especially catalysis. German and non-German scientists are eligible. A monetary award and a gold medal are awarded at intervals of several years.

• 2181 •
German Design Council
(Rat fur Formgebung)
Andrej Kupetz, Contact
Neue Dependance/Messengelande
Ludwig-Erhard-Anlage 1
D-60327 Frankfurt am Main, Germany
Phone: 49 69 7474860
Fax: 49 69 74748619
E-mail: info@german-design-council.de
Home Page: http://www.german-design-council.de

• 2182 • Design Prize of the Federal Republic of Germany (Designpreis der Bundesrepublik Deutschland)
To recognize the best in German product and communication design. Entries are judged on creative and technical innovation, design strategy, utility, human benefits, and sustainability. To be considered, products must be nominated by the Ministers or Senators for Economics and Culture of the German Lander and the Federal Minister of Economics and Employment. Awarded biennially. Established in 1991 by the German Ministry of Economic Affairs. Formerly: (1990) Bundespreis Gute Form.

• 2183 •
German Direct Marketing Association
(Deutscher Direktmarketing Verband)
Hasengartenstr. 14
65189 Wiesbaden, Germany
Phone: 49 611 9779314
Fax: 49 611 9779399
E-mail: info@ddv.de
Home Page: http://www.ddv.de

• 2184 • E-Talents Award
For young multimedia talents that create interactive solutions for the web and mobile applications.

• 2185 • Alfred Gerardi Memory Prize
For best dissertation about direct marketing.

• 2186 • German Direct Marketing Award
For outstanding direct marketing campaigns.

• 2187 •
German Geological Society
(Deutsche Geologische Gesellschaft)
Frau Karin Sennholz, Sec.
Stilleweg 2
Postfach 510153
D-30655 Hannover, Germany
Phone: 49 511 6432507
Fax: 49 511 6432304
E-mail: k.sennholz@bgr.de
Home Page: http://www.dgg.de

• 2188 • Herman Credner Preis
For a geologist or geoscientist. A monetary prize is awarded annually.

• 2189 • Teichmueller Stipendium
For geologist or geoscientist. A monetary prize is awarded annually.

• 2190 •
German Informatics Society
(Gesellschaft fuer Informatik)
Joerg Maas, CEO
Wissenschaftszentrum
Ahrstr. 45
D-53175 Bonn, Germany
Phone: 49 228 302145
Phone: 49 228 302146
Fax: 49 228 302167
E-mail: info@gi-ev.de
Home Page: http://www.gi-ev.de

• 2191 • Konrad-Zuse-Medaille
Recognizes an outstanding contributor to computer science. Awarded biennially.

• 2192 •
German Language Society
(Gesellschaft fur Deutsche Sprache)
Dr. Karin M. Eichoff-Cyrus, Exec.Dir.
Spiegelgasse 13
D-65183 Wiesbaden, Germany
Phone: 49 61199955
Fax: 49 6119995530
E-mail: sekr@gfds.de
Home Page: http://www.gfds.de

• 2193 • Medienpreis fur Sprachkultur
For the promotion of media communications, journalism, radio, and television, and for recognition of outstanding endeavors in promoting the German language. A certificate and a gift are awarded biennially. Established in 1985.

• 2194 • Alexander Rhomberg Preis
For the encouragement of young journalists, and for the cultivation and promotion of the German language. A monetary prize of 5,000 euros is awarded biennially in even-numbered years. Established in 1994 as an extension of the Medienpreis fur Sprachkultur.

• 2195 •
German Medical Association
(Bundesarztekammer)
Prof. Dr. Jorg-Dietrich Hoppe, Pres.
Herbert-Lewin-Platz 1
Postfach 120 864
D-10589 Berlin, Germany
Phone: 49 30 4004 560
Fax: 49 30 4004 56388
E-mail: info@baek.de
Home Page: http://www.bundesaerztekammer.de

• 2196 • **Paracelsus Medaille**
This, the highest honor of the Assembly, is given for recognition of outstanding medical achievement, contributions to the medical profession, and notable advances in the science of medicine. Doctors are eligible. A medal and a certificate are awarded annually. Established in 1952.

• 2197 • **Ernst-von-Bergmann-Plakette**
For recognition of outstanding contributions in the field of CME. Individuals of all lands are eligible. A medal and certificate are awarded annually. Established in 1962.

• 2198 •
German National Mathematical Society
(Deutsche Mathematiker Vereinigung)
Roswitha Jahnke, Sec.
Mohrenstr. 39
D-10117 Berlin, Germany
Phone: 49 30 20372306
Fax: 49 30 20372307
E-mail: dmv@wias-berlin.de
Home Page: http://www.mathematik.de/DMV

• 2199 • **George-Cantor-Medal**
For an individual characterized by outstanding scientific achievements in mathematics and has been connected to the German linguistic area.

• 2200 • **Journalists Prize**
For special activities of journalists in promoting mathematics.

• 2201 • **Media Prize**
For special activities in popularization of mathematics.

• 2202 •
German Organization of Endocrinology
(Deutsche Gesellschaft fur Endokrinologie)
Schering AG
13342 Berlin, Germany
Phone: 49 30 46815802
Fax: 49 30 46818056
Home Page: http://www.endonews.org

• 2203 • **Merck European Thyroid Von-Basedow-Research Prize**
For recognition of outstanding work on the thyroid. Scientists residing in Europe who are 40 years of age or younger are eligible. Monetary prize of $10,000 is awarded annually. Established in 1977 by the E. Merck Company in Darmstadt.

• 2204 • **Schoeller-Junkmann-Preis**
To recognize young European scientists under 40 years of age for outstanding papers in the field of endocrinology. Both clinical and experimental papers from the various fields of endocrinology are considered, with the exception of papers on diabetes mellitus and on the thyroid gland, since these particular fields are covered by other awards. A monetary prize of $10,000 is awarded. In exceptional cases, the Jury may decide to share the award. Awarded annually. Established in 1967 by Schering AG Berlin and Bergkamen.

• 2205 • **Von-Recklinghausen-Preis**
For recognition of outstanding work in the field of clinical and experimental research on osteopathy and ca-metabolism. Scientists residing in Europe who are 40 years of age are eligible. A monetary prize of $5,000 is awarded annually. Established in 1987 by Henning/Merrell Dow, Berlin.

• 2206 •
German OrnithologistsK Society
(Deutsche Ornithologen-Gesellschaft)
Prof. Dr. Franz Bairlein, Pres.
% Institut fur Vogelforschung
Vogelwarte Helgoland
An der Vogelwarte 21
D-26386 Wilhelmshaven, Germany
Phone: 49 4423 914148
Fax: 49 4421 968955
E-mail: geschaeftsstelle@do-g.de
Home Page: http://www.do-g.de

• 2207 • **Foerderpreis der Werner-Sunkel-Stiftung**
To support work on bird migration and bird banding. Members of the German Ornithological Society (DOG) may be nominated. A monetary prize of 26,000 Euro is awarded biennially. Established in 1985 by Mrs. Sunkel in honor of Werner Sunkel.

• 2208 • **Ornithologen-Preis**
For recognition of important accomplishments in ornithological research. Selection is by nomination. A monetary prize of 5,000 Euro, a medal, and a diploma are awarded annually or biennially. Established in 1985 by Klaus Schmidt-Koenig.

• 2209 • **Erwin-Stresemann-Foerderung**
For recognition of an important ornithological research or publication. The author must be a member of DOG, may be of any nationality and under 40 years of age. A monetary prize of 5,000 Euro, a medal, and a diploma are awarded biennially in odd-numbered years. Established in 1969.

• 2210 • **Preis der Horst Wiehe-Stiftung**
For recognition of a scientific contribution to bird ecology. A monetary prize of 26,000 Euro and a diploma are awarded biannually. Established in 1993.

• 2211 •
German Phytomedical Society
(Deutsche Phytomedizinische Gesellschaft)
Dr. Falko Feldmann, Mgr.
% Biologische Bundesanstalt fur Land- und Forstwirtschaft
Messeweg 11/12
D-38104 Braunschweig, Germany
Phone: 49 531 2993213
Fax: 49 531 2993019
E-mail: geschaeftsstelle@dpg.phytomedizin.org
Home Page: http://www.phytomedizin.org

• 2212 • **Inhaber de Otto-Appel-Denkmunze**
To honor extraordinary scientific and organistic work in plant pathology. A medal is awarded annually. Established in 1959 in memory of Otto Appel, past master in plant pathology in Germany.

• 2213 • **Anton-de-Bary-Medaille**
To promote international research in phytopathology. A medal is awarded annually. Established in 1989 in memory of Anton de Bary (who died in 1888), mycologist and one of the founders of plant pathology.

• 2214 • **Julius-Kuhn-Preis**
To promote research in phytopathology. Scientists who are under 40 years of age are eligible. A monetary prize is awarded biennially. Established in 1978 in memory of Julius Kuhn (1825-1910), founder of the German plant pathology.

• 2215 •
German Publishers and Booksellers Association
(Boersenverein des Deutschen Buchhandels e.V.)
Eugen Emmerling, Hd., Info. Dept.
Grosser Hirschgraben 17 - 21
D-60311 Frankfurt am Main, Germany
Phone: 49 69 13060
Fax: 49 69 1306201
E-mail: info@boev.de
Home Page: http://www.boersenverein.de
Formerly: German Booksellers Association.

• 2216 • **Peace Prize of the German Book Trade**
(Friedenpreis des Deutschen Buchhandels)
To recognize people of any nationality or religion who have made noteworthy contributions to literature, science, and art in the service of peace. A monetary prize of $15,000 is awarded annually during the Frankfurt Book Fair. Established in 1950 by a group of publishers.

• 2217 •
German Research Foundation
(Deutsche Forschungsgemeinschaft)
Reinhard Grunwald, Sec. Gen.
Kennedyallee 40
D-53175 Bonn, Germany
Phone: 49 228 8851
Fax: 49 228 8852777
E-mail: postmaster@dfg.de
Home Page: http://www.dfg.de

• 2218 • **Copernicus Award**
For young researchers.

• 2219 • **Gerhard Hess Programme**
For young scientists who have achieved outstanding scientific and academic results.

• 2220 • **Heinz Maier-Leibnitz Prize**
For young scientists who excel in research work.

• 2221 • **Albert Maucher Prize in Geoscience**
For outstanding geoscientists.

• 2222 • **Eugen and Ilse Seibold Prize**
For outstanding scientists.

• 2223 • **Gottfried Wilhelm Leibniz Prize**
For scientific excellence of a scientist.

• 2224 •
German Shoe Industry Association
(Hauptverband der Deutschen Schuhindustrie)
Philipp Urban, Contact
Waldstrasse 44
D-63065 Offenbach, Germany
Phone: 49 69 8297410
Fax: 49 69 812810
E-mail: info@hds-schuh.de
Home Page: http://www.hds-schuh.de

• 2225 • **Footwear Fashion Future Award**
Recognizes an outstanding young footwear designer. A monetary prize of 5,000 euros is awarded biennially.

• 2226 •
German Society for Biochemistry and Molecular Biology
(Gesellschaft fur Biochemie und Molekularbiologie)
Tino Apel, Contact
Morfelder Landstr. 125
D-60598 Frankfurt am Main, Germany
Phone: 49 69 660 5670
Fax: 49 69 660 56722
E-mail: info@gbm-online.de
Home Page: http://www.gbm.uni-frankfurt.de

• 2227 • **Otto-Warburg-Medaille**
For recognition in the field of biochemistry. Individuals must be nominated. A medal and document are awarded annually. Established in 1963.

• 2228 •
German Society for Fat Science
(Deutsche Gesellschaft fur Fettwissenschaft e.V.)
Dr. Frank Amoneil, Mng.Dir.
Varrentrappstr. 40-42
D-60486 Frankfurt am Main, Germany
Phone: 49 69 7917529
Fax: 49 69 7917564
E-mail: info@dgfett.de
Home Page: http://www.dgfett.de

• 2229 • **Kaufmann Memorial Lecture**
For outstanding research in the fat science field. The honoree presents a lecture at the convention. Established in 1972 in memory of H. P. Kaufmann, the society's founder.

• 2230 • **H. P. Kaufmann Prize**
For recognition of outstanding work in the field of fat and fat product chemistry and technology. Included are studies of fatty acids and their derivatives, as well as related materials and their uses. Members of related sciences are eligible, particularly chemists, biologists, medical and pharmaceutical scientists, and engineers under age 35. A maximum of two candidates may win. A monetary prize, a plaque and a certificate are awarded. Established in 1972 in memory of the society's founder and president, H. P. Kaufmann.

• 2231 • **W. Normann Medal**
To recognize superior research on fats and fat products in science and technology or to recognize an individual considered worthy by the society for his or her contributions to the advancement of the science of lipids. Scientists of any nationality are eligible. Two medals and certificates may be awarded annually. Established in 1940 in memory of Dr. Wilhelm Normann, a pioneer in the research of fat hardening.

• 2232 •
German Society for Mining, Metallurgy, Resource and Environmental Technology
Dr. Ing. Kunibert Hanusch, Pres.
Paul Ernst Strasse 10
D-38678 Clausthal-Zellerfeld, Germany
Phone: 49 5323 93790
Fax: 49 5323 937937
E-mail: gdmb@gdmb.de
Home Page: http://www.gdmb.de

Formerly: German Society of Metallurgical and Mining Engineers.

• 2233 • **Georg Agricola Denkmuenze**
To recognize outstanding achievement in the area of metallurgy and mining engineering whereby substantial advancement in the scientific, practical, or economic aspects of this field has been reached. Mature, experienced scientists or industrial workers of any nationality are eligible. A silver medal with a portrait of Georg Agricola on a chain is awarded biennially. Established in 1924.

• 2234 • **Paul Grunfeld Prize**
(Paul Grunfeld-Preis)
To recognize young engineers and scientists in the field of special metals in Europe. Individuals from Europe who are under 35 years of age may be nominated by the GDMB Committee for Special Metals. A monetary prize and a plaque are awarded biennially at the general assembly of GDMB. Established in 1986 by Ernst Grunfeld, London (Metallurgy) in memory of his father, Paul Grunfeld. The Metals Society (UK) awards the same prize.

• 2235 • **Reden Plakette**
To recognize students of metallurgy and mining at German technical universities who have passed their examinations with honors. A brass plaque is awarded. Established in 1935; and re-established in 1948.

• 2236 •
German Society for Non-Destructive Testing
(Deutsche Gesellschaft fur Zerstorungsfreie Prufung e.V.)
Jorg Volker, Pres.
Max-Planck-Strasse, 6
D-12489 Berlin, Germany
Phone: 49 30 67807 0
Fax: 49 30 67807 109
E-mail: mail@dgzfp.de
Home Page: http://www.dgzfp.de

• 2237 • **Berthold-Preis**
For recognition of achievement in non-destructive testing and of the promotion of this field. Individuals under 40 years of age may submit an application. A monetary prize is awarded annually at the convention. Established in 1973 in honor of Professor Dr. Rudolf Berthold, founder of the Society.

• 2238 • **Schiebold-Gedenkmunze**
For recognition of achievement in non-destructive testing. Students of universities and institutes of technology up to 30 years of age having finished a scholarly paper or thesis may submit an application. A commemorative medal together with a monetary prize is awarded annually at the convention. Established in 1996 in honor of Professor Dr. Ernst Schiebold, a pioneer of non-destructive testing.

• 2239 •
German Society for Social Scientific Sexuality Research
(Deutsche Gesellschaft fur Sozialwissenschaftliche Sexualforschung e.V.)
Rolf Gindorf, Contact
Gerresheimer Str 20
D-40211 Dusseldorf, Germany
Phone: 49 211 354591
Fax: 49 211 360777
E-mail: sexualforschung@sexologie.org
Home Page: http://www.sexologie.org

Awards are arranged in alphabetical order below their administering organizations

• 2240 • Magnus Hirschfeld Award
One medal given for sexuality research and one medal given for sexuality reform.

• 2241 •
German Society of Glass Technology
(Deutsche Glastechnische Gesellschaft)
Dr. Ulrich Roger Mng.Di, Contact
Siemensstrasse 45
D-63071 Offenbach, Germany
Phone: 49 69 975 8610
Fax: 49 69 975 86199
E-mail: info@hvg.dgg.de
Home Page: http://www.hvg-dgg.de

• 2242 • Adolf-Dietzel-Industriepreis der DGG
For recognition of valuable work in the committees of the Society and to provide an incentive for younger glass workers. A monetary prize and a glass box are awarded biennially. Established in 1952, renamed in 1995. Formerly: (1995) Industriepreis fur technisch-wissenschaftliche Arbeiten.

• 2243 • Goldener Gehlhoff-Ring
To recognize people who have contributed significantly to the development of the Society and those who have tried to improve deficiencies in glass manufacturing, science, and technology. A gold ring is awarded when merited. Established in 1950.

• 2244 •
German Society of Nutrition
(Deutsche Gesellschaft fur Ernahrung)
Karl-Heinz Solter, Mgr.
Godesberger Allee 18
D-53175 Bonn, Germany
Phone: 49 228 3776 600
Fax: 49 228 3776 800
E-mail: webmaster@dge.de
Home Page: http://www.dge.de

• 2245 • Journalist Prize
(Journalistenpreis of the DGE)
For recognition of journalists, reporters, and authors of press, radio, and television for contributions in the field of nutrition. The jury consists of members of the German Nutrition Society, sciences, consumer societies, nutrition industry, and the German Nutrition Foundation. Monetary prizes are awarded in four categories: daily newspapers, journals, radio, and television. A monetary prize of 2,000 Euros is awarded annually. Established in 1989.

• 2246 • Hans Adolf Krebs-Preis
To encourage young scientists in the field of nutrition and food sciences. A monetary is awarded every four years. Sponsored by the Stiftung zur Forderung der DGE (German Nutrition Foundation) since 1981.

• 2247 • Max Rubner-Preis
For recognition and promotion of research that contributes to the development of preventive and practical dietetics for physicians. A monetary prize is awarded every four years. Sponsored by the German Nutrition Foundation since 1988.

• 2248 •
German Society of Pediatrics and Adolescent Medicine
(Deutsche Gesellschaft fur Kinderheilkunde und Jugendmedizin e.V)
Dr. Gabriele Olsbrich, Mgr.
Eichendorfffstrasse, 13
D-10115 Berlin, Germany
Phone: 49 30 308 7779 0
Fax: 49 30 308 7779 99
E-mail: info@dgkj.de
Home Page: http://www.dgkj.de

• 2249 • Adalbert Czerny Preis
To stimulate research in pediatrics. Pediatricians from German speaking countries are eligible. A monetary prize of 10000 Euro and a medal are awarded annually. Established in 1961.

• 2250 • Otto Heubner Preis
For recognition of scientific achievements of the members of the German Pediatric Association. A gold medal is awarded triennially. Established before the First World War and renewed in 1953.

• 2251 •
German Society of Plastic and Reconstructive Surgery
(Deutsche Gesellschaft fur Plastische und Wiederherstellungschirurgie e.V.)
Elise-Averdieck-Str 17
D-27342 Rotenburg, Germany
Phone: 49 4261 772127
Phone: 49 4261 772126
Fax: 49 4261 772128
E-mail: info@dgpw.de
Home Page: http://www.dgpw.de

• 2252 • Hans von Seemen Preis
To encourage professional development in the field of plastic and reconstructive surgery. Work published during the preceding two years and submitted to the Society is eligible. A monetary prize and a diploma are awarded biennially. Established in 1984 in honor of Hans von Seemen, founder of the Society.

• 2253 •
Gesellschaft Deutscher Naturforscher und Arzte
Prof. Dr. Konrad Sandhoff, Pres.
Hauptstrasse 5
D-53604 Bad Honnef, Germany
Phone: 49 2224 980713
Fax: 49 2224 980789
E-mail: info@gdnae.de
Home Page: http://www.gdnae.de

• 2254 • Lorenz Oken Medaille
For recognition of the writing and/or editing of publications for the promotion of the general understanding, general knowledge, and the image of the natural sciences and medicine, and for contributions that promote the image of the organization. Selection is by nomination. A gold medal and a document are awarded biennially. Established in 1984 in memory of Lorenz Oken, who founded the Association by initiating the first meeting of German natural scientists and physicians in Leipzig in 1822.

• 2255 •
Gesellschaft fur Chemische Technik und Biotechnologie
Dr. Christina Hirche, Public Relations Off.
Theodor-Heuss-Allee 25
D-60486 Frankfurt am Main, Germany
Phone: 49 69 75640
Fax: 49 69 7564201
E-mail: internetinfo@dechema.de
Home Page: http://www.dechema.de

• 2256 • ACHEMA Plaque in Titanium
(ACHEMA-Plakette in Titan)
For recognition of outstanding service to DECHEMA, in particular to the ACHEMA Exhibition-Congresses, and to the DECHEMA's nonprofit scientific activities. The plaque is awarded triennially. The ACHEMA Plaque was founded by DECHEMA in 1970 to commemorate the 50th Jubilee of the ACHEMA Exhibition-Congress and was first awarded during the ACHEMA of 1973.

• 2257 • Jochen Block Prize
For research and development by young scientists (maximum of 35 years of age) in the field of catalysis. The prize consisting of a certificate and a monetary award is awarded in irregular intervals. Established in 1996. Sponsored by DECHEMA Subject Group Catalysis.

• 2258 • DECHEMA Honorary Membership
(DECHEMA Ehrenmitgliedschaft)
For recognition of outstanding supporters of chemical equipment manufacture, chemical engineering, and biotechnology or to the society itself. Highest award of DECHEMA.

• 2259 • DECHEMA Medal
(DECHEMA-Medaille)
For recognition of outstanding achievement in the field of chemical apparatus technology. The DECHEMA Medal is traditionally awarded triennially during ACHEMA International Meeting on Chemical Engineering and Biotechnology to one outstanding scientist each in the fields of engineering, chemistry, and biotechnology. Established in 1951.

• 2260 • DECHEMA Preis der Max Buchner Forschungsstiftung
For recognition of an outstanding and already published research and development work in the field of chemical apparatus, and its fundamentals in technical chemistry, the materials sciences, measurement and control technology, process engineering, and biotechnology on chemical apparatus or plant development. Preference is given to the works of younger scientists of demonstrated merit from whom further

development and application in chemical engineering can be expected. A monetary prize, a gold medal, and a certificate are awarded annually. Established in 1950.

• 2261 • Hellmuth Fischer-Medaille
To recognize primarily younger scientists whose works have advanced the science of electrochemistry, corrosion, or corrosion protection or works that have led to its exemplary application in industrial practice. A medal is given triennially. Established in 1988.

• 2262 • Alwin Mittasch-Medaille
For recognition of scientific works that broaden the fundamentals of catalysis, or their exemplary application in industry. The work must have been conducted in a European country. A medal is awarded triennially. Established in 1988. Cosponsored by the BASF Aktiengesellschaft.

• 2263 • Otto Roelen Medal
For essential innovations in homogeneous catalysis, like introduction of a new process to industrial application, investigations of kinetics and mechanisms or improving the knowledge base of homogeneous catalysis. The work must have been conducted in an European country by a young scientist. The prize consists of a medal and cash and is awarded biannually. Established in 1997. Cosponsored by Hoechst AG.

• 2264 •
Goethe Institute
(Goethe Institut)
Prof. Dr. Jutta Limbach, Pres.
Dachauer Str., 122
D-80637 Munich, Germany
Phone: 49 89 159210
Fax: 49 89 15921450
E-mail: info@goethe.de
Home Page: http://www.goethe.de

• 2265 • Goethe Medaille
To recognize of outstanding services in the promotion of international cultural exchange, especially in the field of promoting the German language in foreign countries. Special literary, scientific, pedalogical, or organizational achievement that promotes interaction between the cultures of Germany and the host country are considered. Individuals of any nationality are eligible, but Germans only as an exception. Every year, a maximum of five medals, and certificates are awarded at the official presentation taking place on March 22. Established in 1954.

• 2266 •
Gutenberg Society
(Gutenberg-Gesellschaft)
Jens Beutel, Pres.
Liebfrauenplatz 5
D-55116 Mainz, Germany
Phone: 49 6131 226420
Fax: 49 6131 233530
E-mail: gutenberg-gesellschaft@freenet.de
Home Page: http://www.gutenberg-gesellschaft.uni-mainz.de

• 2267 • Gutenberg Award (Gutenberg-Preis)
To recognize exceptional achievements relating to in artistic, technical, and scholarly fields. Individuals in the fields of typeface design, typography, printing, and printing technology and scholars in bibliographic studies from all over the world may be nominated. A monetary award and a diploma are presented biennially. Established in 1968 by the Gutenberg Society and the City of Mainz on the Rhine in memory of Johannes Gutenberg, master printer and inventor of moveable type in Mainz, 500 years after his death in 1468 A.D.

• 2268 •
Helmholtz Fonds
Prof. Dr. Ernst O. Gobel, Pres.
% Physikalisch-Technische Bundesanstalt
Bundesallee 100
D-38116 Braunschweig, Germany
Phone: 49 531 592 3004
Fax: 49 531 592 3003
E-mail: helmholtz-fonds@ptb.de
Home Page: http://www.helmholtz-fonds.de

• 2269 • Helmholtz Prize (Helmholtz-Preis)
For recognition of outstanding research in the fields of: precision measuring technology, metrology in medicine and environment protection, and informatics and mathematics in precision measurement techniques. Physicists and engineers, either working or cooperating with scientists in the Federal Republic of Germany are eligible. A monetary and a certificate is awarded every two years. Established in 1973, and named after the first president of the Physikalisch-Technische Reichsanstalt, Dr. Herrman von Helmholtz (1821-1894).

• 2270 •
IFRA
Reiner Mittelbach, CEO
Washingtonplatz 1
D-64287 Darmstadt, Germany
Phone: 49 6151 7336
Fax: 49 6151 733800
E-mail: info@ifra.com
Home Page: http://www.ifra.com

• 2271 • International Newspaper Color Quality Club Awards
Recognizes excellence in color print quality. Awarded biennially in even-numbered years.

• 2272 •
Information Technology Society
(Informationstechnische Gesellschaft im Verband der Elektrotechnik Elektronik Informationstechnik)
Volker Schanz, Gen.Mgr.
Stresemannallee 15
D-60596 Frankfurt am Main, Germany
Phone: 49 69 6308 360
Fax: 49 69 6312 925
E-mail: itg@vde.com
Home Page: http://www.vde.com/VDE_EN/Technical+Societies/ITG.htm

• 2273 • Forderpreis der ITG
For recognition of excellent scientific dissertations in the field of telecommunication. Members of the Society under 30 years of age are eligible. A monetary prize and a certificate of award are presented up to three times per year. Established in 1993.

• 2274 • Karl Kupfmuller Prize (Karl-Kupfmuller-Preis der ITG)
For recognition of outstanding significant technical or scientific achievements or contributions in the field of telecommunications engineering. Individuals may be nominated. A monetary prize and a certificate of award are presented every four years. Established in 1984 in memory of Karl Kuepfmueller, Professor of Engineering.

• 2275 •
International Academy of Cytology
Volker Schneider MD, Sec.Gen.
Burgenderster. 1
D-79104 Freiburg, Germany
Phone: 49 761 2923801
Fax: 49 761 2923802
E-mail: centraloffice@cytology-iac.org
Home Page: http://www.cytology-iac.org

• 2276 • Maurice Goldblatt Cytology Award
To recognize an individual(s) for outstanding contributions to the advancement of cytologic science and research in applied cellular studies. A medal is awarded annually at the International Congress of Cytology where the honoree delivers the Golodblatt Lecture of the Congress. Established in 1960 to honor Maurice Goldblatt, the Chairman of the Board of the Cancer Research Foundation of the University of Chicago, for his dedication to career research.

• 2277 • International Cytotechnology Award of the IAC
To recognize outstanding achievement and contribution by persons who have distinguished themselves as cytotechnologists. Technologists, educators, researchers and administrators are eligible. Nominations are accepted from members (MIAC, PMIC or CMIAC) or fellows (FIAC or CFIAC) of IAC. A medal, a diploma and an honorarium are awarded at the triennial International Congress of Cytology. Awardees also present a special lecture during the meeting at which they are honored. Established in 1975 through a gift from the Tutorials of Cytology, Chicago, Illinois.

• 2278 •
International Association for Sports and Leisure Facilities
(Internationale Vereinigung Sport- und Freizeiteinrichtungen)
Siegfried Hoymann, Hon.Sec.Gen.
Carl-Diem-Weg 3
D-50933 Cologne, Germany
Phone: 49 221 4912991
Fax: 49 221 4971280
E-mail: iaks@iaks.info
Home Page: http://www.iaks.info

• 2279 • **IOC/IAKS Award**
Recognizes exemplary architecture of sports and leisure facilities already in operation. Medals in gold, silver and bronze are awarded biennially in odd-numbered years. Established in 1987. Co-sponsored by the International Olympic Committee (IOC).

• 2280 •
International Association of Empirical Aesthetics
(Association Internationale d'Esthetique Experimentale
Associazione Internationale Di Estetica Empirica)
PD Dr. Holger Hoege, Sec.Gen.
University of Oldenburg
Dept. of Psychology
Post Box 2503
D-26111 Oldenburg, Germany
Phone: 49 441 7985510
Fax: 49 441 798195510
E-mail: holger.hoege@uni-oldenburg.de
Home Page: http://www.science-of-aesthetics.org

• 2281 • **Alexander Gottlieb Baumgarten Award**
Recognizes outstanding young scientists. Awarded biennially in even-numbered years. Established in 2002.

• 2282 • **Gustav Theodor Fechner Award**
Recognizes scientific contribution to the field of empirical/experimental aesthetics. Awarded biennially in even-numbered years. Established in 1996.

• 2283 • **Sir Francis Galton Award**
For scientific contribution to the field of empirical aesthetics. Awarded biennially in even-numbered years. Established in 1996.

• 2284 •
International Association of Political Consultants
Volker Riegger, Pres.
% Volker Riegger, Pres.
Romanstrasse 16
D-80639 Munich, Germany
Phone: 49 89 163 99 000
Fax: 49 89163 99 0010
Home Page: http://www.iapc.org

• 2285 • **International Democracy Award**
To recognize an individual or organization for courageously fostering, promoting, and sustaining the democratic process anywhere in the world. The Democracy medal, a bronze medal with a burnished rendering of the Acropolis etched in relief, and a certificate are awarded annually. Established in 1982.

• 2286 •
International Colour Association
(Association Internationale de la Couleur)
% LMT Lichtmesstechnik GmbH Berlin
Helmholtzstrasse 9
D-10587 Berlin, Germany
Phone: 49 303934028
Fax: 49 303918001
E-mail: alessi@image.kodak.com
Home Page: http://www.aic-colour.org

• 2287 • **Judd AIC Award**
For recognition of research in color in all aspects, and its application to science, art, and industry. A plaque is awarded biennially. Established in 1973 by Mrs. Judd in honor of Dr. Deane B. Judd, internationally acclaimed authority on color and one of the founders of the Association.

• 2288 •
International Commission of Agricultural Engineering
(Commission Internationale du Genie Rural)
Dr. Peter Schulze Lammers, Sec.Gen.
Nussallee 5
D-53115 Bonn, Germany
Phone: 49 228 732389
Phone: 49 228 732597
Fax: 49 228 739644
E-mail: cigr@uni-bonn.de
Home Page: http://www.cigr.org

• 2289 • **Armand Blanc Prize**
(Prix Armand Blanc)
To recognize the best paper presented at CIGR Congresses by a young student or agricultural engineer. Citizens of CIGR member countries who are not more than 30 years of age may submit papers on a topic dealing with the Congresses' program. A medal and expenses are awarded every five years on the occasion of each CIGR Congress. Established in 1964 to honor Armand Blanc, Honorary General Director of Agricultural Engineering and Hydraulics, founder-member and former President of CIGR.

• 2290 •
International Council of Christians and Jews
(Internationalen Rat der Christen und Juden)
Rev. Friedhelm Pieper, Gen.Sec.
Martin Buber House
Werlestrasse 2
Postfach 1129
D-64629 Heppenheim, Germany
Phone: 49 6252 93120
Phone: 49 6252 93120
Fax: 49 6252 68331
E-mail: info@iccj-buberhouse.de
Home Page: http://www.jcrelations.net

• 2291 • **International Council of Christians and Jews International Sternberg Award**
For recognition of sustained intellectual contribution to the furtherance of interreligious understanding, particularly, but not exclusively, in the field of Jewish-Christian relations. One or more individuals, institutions, or organizations may be recognized for achievements of international significance with impact beyond the recipient's own country. A monetary prize awarded annually when merited. Established in 1985 by Sir Sigmund Sternberg, K.C.S.G., J.P.

• 2292 •
International Council of Environmental Law
(Conseil International du Droit de l'Environnement)
Dr. H.E. Amado Tolentino Jr., Exec.Gov.
Godesberger Allee 108-112
D-58175 Bonn, Germany
Phone: 49 228 2692240
Phone: 49 228 2692228
Fax: 49 228 2692251
E-mail: icel@intlawpol.org

• 2293 • **Elizabeth Haub Prize for Environmental Diplomacy**
For recognition of practical accomplishments in the field of environmental diplomacy. Awarded by the ICEL and Pace University, New York.

• 2294 • **Elizabeth Haub Prize for Environmental Law**
For recognition of practical accomplishments in the field of environmental law. No restrictions exist as to membership or citizenship. A jury composed of representatives of ICEL and of the Universite Libre de Bruxelles makes the selection. A monetary prize to be used for specified purposes associated with environmental law and a gold medal are awarded annually. Established in 1974 by the ICEL and the Universite Libre de Bruxelles in honor of Elizabeth Haub.

• 2295 •
International Council of Sport Science and Physical Education
Prof.Dr. Gudrun Doll-Tepper, Pres.
Hanns Braun Strasse
Friesenhaus II
14053 Berlin, Germany
Phone: 49 30 36418850
Phone: 49 30 36418853
Fax: 49 30 8056386
E-mail: icsspe@icsspe.org
Home Page: http://www.icsspe.org
Formerly: (1983) International Council of Sport and Physical Education.

• 2296 • **Philip Noel Baker Research Award**
To recognize an individual for both scientific work and personal contribution to the Council's activities. A diploma is awarded annually. Established in 1969 to honor Lord Philip Noel Baker, first president of ICSSPE and Laureat of the Nobel Prize for Peace. Additional information is available from www.icsspe.org.

• 2297 • ICSSPE Sport Science Award of the IOC President

To recognize outstanding scientific achievements in the field of sport and physical education. A $5,000 grant is awarded in alternative years in two areas: biomedical sciences, and social/human sciences. Accomplishments in the following areas are considered which: (1) study the development of the Olympic movement and world sport and their impact upon peace and international understanding; (2) substantially contribute to the knowledge of sport and physical education in general and in their various branches; (3) study the implications of life-long participation in sport on personality development and health; or (4) contribute to the further development of sport science and its disciplines. Additional information is available from www.icsspe.org.

• 2298 •
International Cryogenic Engineering Committee
Hans Quack, Sec.
% Dr. Hans Quack, Sec.
Munchner Platz 3
Schumann-Bau, A 204
D-01062 Dresden, Germany
Phone: 49 351 463 32548
Fax: 49 351 463 37247
E-mail: quack@memkn.mw.tu-dresden.de
Home Page: http://www.tu-dresden.de/mwiem/kkt/icec.html

• 2299 • Mendelssohn Award

For recognition in the field of cryogenic engineering. A medal is awarded.

• 2300 •
International Ecology Institute
Prof. O. Kinne, Dir.
% Inter-Research
Nordbunte 23
D-21385 Oldendorf/Luhe, Germany
Phone: 49 4132 7127
Fax: 49 4132 8883
E-mail: ir@int-res.com
Home Page: http://www.int-res.com/eci

• 2301 • Ecology Institute Prize

To recognize ecologists for outstanding scientific achievements who are able and willing to provide a critical synthesis and evaluation of their field of expertise, addressing an audience beyond narrow professional borderlines. In an annually rotating pattern, awards are presented in the fields of marine, terrestrial, and limnetic ecology. All ecologists engaged in scientific research are eligible. Nominations must be submitted by September 30. A $6,000 stipend is awarded annually. In addition, the winner of the prize is requested to author a 200 to 300 printed-page book, to be published by ECI in the series *Excellence in Ecology* and to be made available world-wide at cost price. The Ecology Institute Prize is considered unique for two reasons: it was established and is financed by research ecologists, and the prize gives and takes, by both honoring the recipient and requiring him or her to serve science. Established in 1984 by Prof. Otto Kinne.

• 2302 • IRPE Prize International Recognition of Professional Excellence

To recognize a young ecologist under the age of 40 who has conducted and published uniquely independent, original, and/or challenging research efforts representing an important scientific breakthrough. Nominations must be submitted by September 30. A $3,000 stipend is awarded when merited.

• 2303 •
International Film Festival Mannheim - Heidelberg
(Internationale Filmwoche Mannheim)
Dr. Michael Koetz, Dir.
Collini-Center, Galerie
D-68161 Mannheim, Germany
Phone: 49 621 102943
Fax: 49 621 291564
E-mail: ifmh@mannheim-filmfestival.com
Home Page: http://www.mannheim-filmfestival.com

• 2304 • International Filmfestival Mannheim/Heidelberg
(Internationale Filmwoche Mannheim)

To recognize outstanding films. This small but well-known film festival is one of the oldest in the Federal Republic of Germany. Since 1994, its venues have been in the cities of Mannheim and Heidelberg. Films must be German premiers unawarded in other European Festivals such as Cannes (all sections), Berlin (all sections), Locarno (competition), and Venice (competition). New features form the backbone of the competitive festival, which prides itself on making artistic discoveries and supporting independent filmmaking. Films must be submitted by August 1. Awards are presented in the following categories: Best Feature Film, for films at least 70 minutes in length; Best Documentary, for documentary films at least 30 minutes in length; the International Short Film Prize, for the best short film in any genre no longer than 30 minutes; and the Special Prize in Memoriam of Rainer Werner Fassbinder, for the film with the most unique narrative structure at least 60 minutes in length; and Special Awards. Awarded annually. Formerly: Mannheim International Filmweek.

• 2305 •
International Institute of Public Finance
(Institut International de Finances Publiques)
Birgit Schneider, Exec.Sec.
University of Saarland
PO Box 151150
D-66041 Saarbrucken, Germany
Phone: 49 681 3023653
Fax: 49 681 3024369
E-mail: schneider@iipf.net
Home Page: http://www.iipf.net

• 2306 • Best Paper Award

Recognizes the best paper presented at annual conference. Awarded annually.

• 2307 •
International Luge Federation
(Federation Internationale de Luge de Course)
Josef Fendt, Pres.
Rathausplatz 9
D-83471 Berchtesgaden, Germany
Phone: 49 8652 66960
Fax: 49 8652 66969
E-mail: office@fil-luge.org
Home Page: http://www.fil-luge.org

• 2308 • Continental Champion

Award of recognition.

• 2309 • Fair-Play Trophy

• 2310 •
International Music Competition of the ARD
(Internationaler Musikwettbewerb ARD)
Sir Colin David, Contact
Bayerischer Rundfunk
D-80300 Munich, Germany
Phone: 49 89 5900 2471
Fax: 49 89 5900 3573
E-mail: ard.musikwettbewerb@brnet.de
Home Page: http://www.br-online.de/kultur-szene/klassik_e/pages/ard/ard.html

• 2311 • Internationaler Musikwettbewerb der ARD
(Munich International Music Competition of the Broadcasting Stations of the Federal Republic of Germany (ARD))

For recognition of the best performers of the musical competition. Awards are given in various categories. Soloists must be between 17 and 30 years of age; singers (female) between 20 and 30 years of age; singers (male) between 20 and 32 years; duos and trios between 17 and 32 years of age; windquintets between 17 and 35 years of age (two members of the ensemble can be 35 years); and the string quartet between 17 and 35 years of age, with the total of the four musicians' ages no more than 120. The competitors are judged for technique, musicality, and artistic personality. Musicians of all nationalities are eligible. Monetary prizes are awarded and invitations are extended to give concerts and make recordings and television performances. Awarded annually. Established in 1952.

• 2312 •
International Robert Schumann Competition (Internationale Robert-Schumann-Wettbewerbe)
Stadt Zwickau
Kulturbuero
muentstrasse 12
D-08056 Zwickau, Germany
Phone: 49 375 212636
Fax: 49 375 834130
E-mail: kulturbuero@zwickau.de
Home Page: http://www.zwickau.de

• 2313 • **International Robert Schumann and Piano and Song Competition**
For recognition of the best performances of Schumann's piano works and songs (lieder). The following prizes are awarded: first place - a monetary prize and a gold medal; second place - a monetary prize and a silver medal; third place - a monetary prize and a bronze medal; and a special monetary prize. Held annually.

• 2314 • **International Robert Schumann Choir Competition**
For recognition of the best music performance of Schumann's work and contemporary compositions. Amateur male, female, and mixed choirs are eligible. Held annually.

• 2315 •
International Short Film Festival, Oberhausen (Internationale Kurzfilmtage Oberhausen)
Dr. Lars Henrik Gass, Mng.Dir.
Grillostr. 34
D-46045 Oberhausen, Germany
Phone: 49 208 8252652
Fax: 49 208 8255413
E-mail: info@kurzfilmtage.de
Home Page: http://www.kurzfilmtage.de

• 2316 • **International Short Film Festival Oberhausen (Internationale Kurzfilmtage Oberhausen)**
For recognition of documentaries, short feature films, student films, animated films, and experimental films. Discussions, retrospectives, and information screenings are held as part of the Festival. A special emphasis is on young filmmakers and their first films. Films must not be longer than 35 minutes and must have been produced during the two years preceding the Festival for films from outside Germany, and during the past year for films from Germany. Videos and computer animation are accepted. The deadline for entries is February 1. The following awards are presented by the International Jury: Grand Prize of the City of Oberhausen; Best Documentary; the Owlglass Prize for the most humorous film; the Ministry of Urban Development, Culture and Sports of North Rhine-Westphalia Award for the best film in the field of educational politics; awarded by the ministry of Urban Development, Culture and Sports of North Rhine - Westphalia; and the Alexander S. Scotti Prize for the best film on the subject of old age and death awarded by Mrs. Elizabeth Scotti. Several film associations send their own juries to the festival to present the following awards: the Prize of the FIPRESCI (International Federation of the Cinematographic Press); Prize of the Catholic Film Association; Prize of INTERFILM (Jury of the Protestant Film Work); FICC Prize (Jury of the Federation Internationale des Cine Clubs); Prize for the Best German Short Film - awarded by the Association of German Film Journalists; and Prize of the Children's Cinema - by a jury of Oberhausen children. The Festival also gives a special prize to a short film not sufficiently recognized by any of the juries. Other special prizes are also given. Awarded annually in April. Foreign contributions are selected in the producing countries. Established in 1954. Formerly: (1991) International West German Short Film Festival, Oberhausen.

• 2317 •
International Society for Aerosols in Medicine (Societas Internationalis Aerosolibus in Medicina)
William D. Bennett, Gen. Sec.
Wohraer Str. 37
D-35285 Gemunden, Germany
Phone: 49 6453 648180
Fax: 49 6453 6481822
E-mail: office@isam.org
Home Page: http://www.isam.org

• 2318 • **ISAM Career Achievement Award**
For a senior investigator whose body of work demonstrates a lifetime of outstanding achievement in aerosol science.

• 2319 • **Thomas T. Mercer Award**
For achievement of excellence in the field of medical aerosols.

• 2320 • **Student Research Award**
To an investigator who is currently a full time student enrolled in an MD, PhD or Masters program who demonstrated outstanding independent research in the field of aerosols.

• 2321 • **Young Investigator Award**
For a scientist age not over 40 years for significant contributions to the field of aerosols in medicine.

• 2322 •
International Society of Psychoneuroendocrinology
Ned H. Kalin, Pres.
% Dirk Hellhammer, Pres.
Department of Psychobiology
University of Trier
D-54286 Trier, Germany
Phone: 49 651 201 2929
Fax: 49 651 201 2934
E-mail: hellman@uni-trier.de
Home Page: http://www.ispne.org

• 2323 • **Curt P. Richter Prize**
To recognize an outstanding paper on psychoneuroendocrinology. Manuscripts may be submitted by January 1 by authors under 40 years of age. An honorarium of US $1,000 and a travel grant of up to US $1,000 to attend the International Congress are awarded annually. The winning paper is considered for publication in the Journal *Psychoneuroendocrinology*. Established in 1979 to honor Curt Richter. Sponsored by Pergamon Press and the International Society of Psychoneuroendocrinology. Additional information is available from David Saphler, PhD, Department of Pharmacology, 1501 Kings Hwy., PO Box 33932, Shreveport, LA 71130-3932.

• 2324 •
International Society on Toxinology
Prof. Dietrich Mebs, Sec.
Zentrum der Rechtsmedizin
University of Frankfurt
Kennedyalle 104
D-60596 Frankfurt, Germany
Phone: 49 69 63017563
Fax: 49 69 63015882
E-mail: mebs@em.uni-frankfurt.de
Home Page: http://www.toxinology.org

• 2325 • **Redi Award**
For recognition of outstanding contributions to the knowledge of natural-occurring poisons and venoms. Individuals without regard to nationality may be nominated and voted upon by present and past officers of the Society and past awardees. A monetary award, a plaque, a leather bound illuminated manuscript noting the accomplishments of the awardee, and travel expenses are awarded every three years at the International Congress. Established in 1967 in honor of Francisco Redi, an Italian anatomist of the 17th century who showed it was venom, not spirits, that were transferred from snake to victim.

• 2326 •
International Solar Energy Society
Mr. Rian van Staden, Exec.Dir.
Villa Tannheim
Wiesentalstrasse 50
D-79115 Freiburg, Germany
Phone: 49 761 459060
Fax: 49 761 4590699
E-mail: hq@ises.org
Home Page: http://www.ises.org

• 2327 • **Achievement Through Action Award**
To recognize an individual, a group, or corporate body that has made an important contribution to the harnessing of solar energy for practical use or is proposing a new concept, development or product for the same purpose. Members and non-members may be nominated by October 31 in even-numbered years. The prize money may be divided among the recipients or used to pay for some specific research program or equipment. A monetary award and certificate are presented biennially at the International Congress. Established in 1983 in the memory of Christopher A. Weeks.

• 2328 • **Farrington Daniels Award**
For recognition of outstanding contributions to science, technology, or engineering of solar energy applications leading toward ameliorating the conditions of humanity, and for furthering this cause through the International Solar Energy Society. Members may be nominated by October 31 in even-numbered years. A certificate is presented biennially at the International Congress. The recipient of the award is invited to deliver an address on a topic of his or her choice in the field of solar energy application at the international meeting at which the award is conferred. Established in 1974 in memory of Professor Emeritus Farrington Daniels of the University of Wisconsin.

• 2329 •
International Youth Library
(Internationale Jugendbibliothek)
Dr. Barbara Scharioth, Dir.
Schloss Blutenburg
D-81247 Munich, Germany
Phone: 49 89 8912110
Fax: 49 89 8117553
E-mail: bib@ijb.de
Home Page: http://www.ijb.de

• 2330 • **White Ravens**
(Die Weissen Raben)
To promote high quality children's books of international interest. About 250 children's books, by authors and illustrators from all over the world, are given recognition. Children's books submitted by publishers during the year prior to the award are considered. White Ravens books are listed in the annual international selected bibliography and exhibited during the Children's Book Fair in Bologna, Italy, and thereafter upon request in libraries and other institutions. Awarded annually. Established in 1984.

• 2331 •
Internationales Filmwochenende Wurzburg
Friedenstr. 19
D-97072 Wurzburg, Germany
Phone: 49 931 15077
Fax: 49 931 15078
E-mail: info@filmwochenende-wuerzburg .de
Home Page: http://www.wuerzburg.de/ifw

• 2332 • **Audience Prizes**
To recognize and honor the best films as chosen by the audience. Only films by invited directors are eligible for the award. Monetary prizes are awarded for the Best Film, Best Children's Film, and Best Short Film. Presented annually at the festival. Established in 1989.

• 2333 • **Prize for Children's Film**
A monetary prize is awarded at the annual festival.

• 2334 • **Prizes for Short Films**
A monetary prize is awarded for two to three short films at the annual festival.

• 2335 •
Justus-Liebig-Universitat-Giessen
Prof. Dr. Stefan Hormuth, Pres.
Ludwigstrasse 23
D-35390 Giessen, Germany
Phone: 49 614990
Fax: 49 6419912259
E-mail: praesident@admin.uni-giessen.de
Home Page: http://www.uni-giessen.de
Formerly: Academia Ludoviciana Gissensis.

• 2336 • **Ludwig Schunk Prize for Medicine**
(Ludwig Schunk-Preis fur Medizin)
To recognize outstanding scientific achievement in medicine and to promote young medical researchers. Awarded in alternate years to nonresident Germans or foreign citizens and university scientists or resident Germans. A monetary is awarded annually. Established in 1982 by Firma Schunk & Ebe GmbH.

• 2337 •
Kiel Institute for World Economics
(Institut fur Weltwirtschaft an der Universitat Kiel)
Prof. Dennis Snower, Pres.
Duesternbrooker Weg 120
D-24105 Kiel, Germany
Phone: 49 431 881 41
Fax: 49 431 85853
E-mail: info@ifw-kiel.de
Home Page: http://www.uni-kiel.de/ifw

• 2338 • **Bernhard-Harms-Preis**
For recognition of special research achievements in the field of international economics. Professors who have distinguished themselves through extraordinary achievement in the field of international economics or individuals in the business world who have made significant contributions to the improvement of world economic relations are eligible. Individuals are nominated by a nomination committee. A monetary award of and a medal are presented biennially at Kieler Woche. Established in 1964 in memory of Bernhard Harms, professor of economics and the founder of the Kiel Institute of World Economics. Sponsored by Gesellschaft zur Forderung des Instituts fur Weltwirtschaft. In addition, the Bernhard-Harms-Medaille, established in 1980, is awarded at irregular intervals.

• 2339 •
Konrad Adenauer Foundation - Germany
(Konrad Adenauer Stiftung)
Dr. Bernhard Vogel MdL, Pres.
Rathausallee 12
D-53757 St. Augustin, Germany
Phone: 49 2241 2460
Fax: 49 2241 246591
E-mail: zentrale@kas.de
Home Page: http://www.kas.de

• 2340 • **Literaturpreis der Konrad-Adenauer-Stiftung**
For outstanding literary works. A monetary prize is given annually.

• 2341 • **Lokaljournalistenpreis des Konrad-Adenauer-Stiftung**
Annual monetary award for local journalism.

• 2342 •
Landeshauptstadt Munchen
Kulturreferat
Rindermarkt 3-4
D-80313 Munich, Germany
Phone: 49 89 233 00
Fax: 49 89 264 58
E-mail: rathaus@muenchen.de
Home Page: http://www.muenchen.info

• 2343 • **Kultureller Ehrenpreis**
To recognize a person of international prominence for their cultural or scientific achievements. A monetary prize of $10,000 is awarded annually. Established in 1958.

• 2344 • **LiteraVision Preis**
To recognize an outstanding television program or movie covering books or writers. German-speaking individuals and programs are eligible. Two monetary awards of 5,000 Euros are presented annually. Established in 1991.

• 2345 • **Promotional Prizes**
To honor outstanding contributions to German culture in various fields of the arts. Monetary prizes are awarded annually in film, art, music, and dance.

• 2346 • **Scholarships of the City of Munich**
To honor outstanding contributions to German culture in the fields of literature, fine arts, music, theater, and dance. A number of scholarships of various amounts are awarded annually. Established in 1991.

• 2347 • **Geschwister-Scholl-Preis**
To honor a book that presents intellectually important insights on civic freedom, morality, and aesthetics. A monetary prize of $10,000 is awarded annually. Established in 1980. Co-sponsored with the Bavarian Publishers and Booksellers Association.

• 2348 •
Landschaftsverband Westfalen-Lippe
Frank Tafertshofer, Contact
Freiher-vom-Stein-Platz 1
D-48145 Munster, Germany
Phone: 49 2 51 59101
Fax: 49 2 51 5913300
E-mail: lwl@lwl.org
Home Page: http://www.lwl.org
Formerly: (1953) Provinzialverband Westfalen.

• 2349 • **Annette von Droste Hulshoff Preis**
For recognition of special achievement in poetry written in either high or low German. Every third time it can be awarded for creative musical achievement. Recipients must be natives or res-

idents of the Westfalian Lippe region of Germany. A monetary prize and a certificate are awarded biennially. Established in 1946 by the Provinzialverband Westfalen in memory of the German and Westfalian poetess, Annette von Droste-Hulshoff (1797-1848). Formerly: Westfaelischer Literaturpreis.

• 2350 • **Konrad von Soest Preis**
For recognition of special achievement in the field of fine and graphic arts. Recipients must be natives or residents of the Westfalian - Lippe region of Germany. A monetary prize and a certificate are awarded biennially. Established in 1952 by the Provinzialverband Westfalen in memory of the great Westfalian medieval artist, Konrad von Soest (about 1400). Formerly: Westfaelischer Kurstpreis.

• 2351 •
Leipzig College of Graphic Arts and Book Design
Academy of Visual Arts
(Hochschule fur Grafik und Buchkunst Leipzig)
Waechterstrasse 11
D-04107 Leipzig, Germany
Phone: 49 341 21350
Fax: 49 341 2135166
E-mail: hgb@hgb-leipzig.de
Home Page: http://www.hgb-leipzig.de

• 2352 • **Walter Tiemann Award**
To recognize the design achievements of typographers and illustators. One to three different titles published within the preceding two years may be submitted. A small sculpture and monetary prizes are awarded. Established in 1992 in honor of Walter Tiemann, a teacher and the rector from 1920 to 1945 at the former Leipzig Academie for Graphic Arts and Book Production, now College of Graphic Arts and Book Design, Leipzig.

• 2353 •
Magistrat der Universitatsstadt Giessen
Heinz-Peter Haumann, Contact
Sudanlage 5
Berliner Platz 1
D-35390 Giessen, Germany
Phone: 49 641 3061000
Fax: 49 641 3062001
E-mail: internetredaktion@giessen.de
Home Page: http://www.giessen.de

• 2354 • **Hedwig-Burgheim Medaille**
To recognize an individual who has demonstrated outstanding ability to communicate and foster understanding between people for the betterment of humanity. Awarded every two years by the city of Giessen. Established in 1981 in memory of the pedagogue Hedwig Burgheim who was murdered in the concentration camp of Auschwitz.

• 2355 •
Max-Eyth-Gesselschaft Agrartechnik im VDI
(Max-Eyth Society for Agricultural Engineering of the VDI)
Dr. A. Herrmann, Contact
Postfach 10 11 39
D-40002 Dusseldorf, Germany
Phone: 49 211 6214372
Fax: 49 211 6214177
E-mail: meg@vdi.de
Home Page: http://www.vdi.de/meg

• 2356 • **Max-Eyth-Gedenkmunze**
Annual award of recognition.

• 2357 •
Medical Women's International Association
Dr. Waltraud Diekhaus, Sec.Gen.
Wilhelm-Brand-Str. 3
D-44141 Dortmund, Germany
Phone: 49 231 9432771
Phone: 49 231 9432772
Fax: 49 231 9432773
E-mail: secretariat@mwia.net
Home Page: http://www.mwia.net

• 2358 • **Honorary Member**
To recognize a member of a National Association or individual member who has rendered to the Association or the medical profession any outstanding services. A gilded MWIA brooch and a certificate of Honorary Membership in the organization are conferred at each Congress, every three years. Established in 1929.

• 2359 • **Member of Honour**
To recognize an individual who is not a member of the Association and who has rendered to the Association or the medical profession outstanding services. A gilded MWIA brooch and a certificate of Member of Honour in the organization are conferred at each congress, every three years. Established in 1987.

• 2360 •
Ministry of Science, Research and the Arts of the State of Baden-Wurttemberg
Dr. Gunter Schanz, Press Off.
Koenigstr. 46
D-70173 Stuttgart 10, Germany
Phone: 49 711 279 0
Fax: 49 711 279 3081
E-mail: presse@mwk.bwl.de
Home Page: http://www.mwk-bw.de

• 2361 • **Johann-Peter-Hebel-Preis**
For recognition of literary work. German-speaking authors from the Alemannian regions or whose works give them a special connection there, and authors who have distinguished themselves in the cultivation of Hebel's legacy or German literature in general are eligible for consideration. A monetary prize is awarded biennially on May 10 (Hebel's birthday). Established in 1936 by Land Baden in memory of the German poet Johann Peter Hebel (1760-1826).

• 2362 •
Musikschule der Stadt Ettlingen
Pforzheimer Strasse 25
D-76275 Ettlingen, Germany
Phone: 49 7243 101312
Fax: 49 7243 101436
E-mail: musikschule@ettlingen.de
Home Page: http://www.musikschule-ettlingen.de

• 2363 • **Ettlingen International Competition for Young Pianists (Internationaler Wettbewerb fur Junge Pianisten Ettlingen)**
To recognize outstanding young pianists. Pianists of all nationalities are eligible. Awards are given in two categories: those up to 15 years of age and those up to 20 years of age. A monetary award is given to the first place winner in the younger age group, and the older age group. Special prizes are also given. Awarded biennially. Established in 1988.

• 2364 •
Okomedia Institut for Environmental Media
Karina Juchelka, Dir.
Nussmannstr. 14
D-79098 Freiburg, Germany
Phone: 49 761 52024
Fax: 49 761 555724
E-mail: info@oekomedia-institut.de
Home Page: http://www.oekomedia-institut.de

• 2365 • **International Environmental Film Festival (Internationale Tage des Okologischen Films)**
For recognition of outstanding contemporary ecological films. In addition, there are film productions on specialized issues: nature films, films on conservation and environmental issues, TV Productions, and Children's Films. Seven prizes are awarded: Golden Lynx for the Best Artistic Achievement; Golden Lynx for the Best Journalistic Achievement; Golden Lynx for the Best Nature Film; Lynx for the Best Children's Film; Special Prize of the Federal Ministry of Environment, Conservation and Nuclear Reactor Safety; European Television Prize; and the Film Prize of the Archdiocese of Freiburg. Awarded annually. Established in 1984. Formerly: Freiburg Ecological Film Festival; (2000) OKOMEDIA International Ecological Film Festival.

• 2366 •
Paleontological Society
(Palaontologische Gesellschaft)
℅ Dr. Bettina Reichenbacher, Pres.
Dept. fur Geo- und Umweltwissenschaften
Ludwig-Maximilians-Universitat Munchen
Richard-Wagner-Str. 10
D-80333 Munich, Germany
Phone: 49 89 2180 6603
E-mail: b.reichenbacher@lrz.uni-muenchen.de
Home Page: http://www.palaeo.de/palges

• 2367 • Karl Alfred von Zittel Medaille
For recognition of exceptional merits in paleontology by amateurs. A certificate and a medal are awarded annually at the convention of the Society. Established in 1984 in honor of Professor Dr. Karl Alfred von Zittel (1839-1904) of Munich, a famous palaeontologist and author of an internationally known handbook.

• 2368 •
Paneuropean Union
(Internationale Paneuropa Union)
Otto Von Habsburg, Pres.
Karlstra Be 57
D-80335 Munich, Germany
Phone: 49 89 554683
Fax: 49 89 594768
E-mail: info@paneuropa.org
Home Page: http://www.paneuropa.org/intl/en/

• 2369 • Coudenhove-Kalergi Award
To recognize outstanding efforts to unite all European peoples into a nonpartisan political and economic union based on principles of liberty, self-determination, and Christian values. Awarded annually.

• 2370 •
Pressamt der Stadt Nurnberg
Funferplatz 2
D-90403 Nurnberg, Germany
E-mail: lisa.treiber-zimmer@stadt.nuernberg.de

• 2371 • Nuremberg International Human Rights Award
To recognize a film in the Festival that combines quality of form with humane thought and social commitment, independently of the scale of production and its public reception. A trophy and monetary prize of 5,000 euros is awarded annually.

• 2372 •
Prix Jeunesse Foundation
Ursula von Zallinger, Gen.Sec.
% Bayerischer Rundfunk
Rundfunkplatz 1
D-80300 Munich, Germany
Phone: 49 89 5900 2058
Fax: 49 89 5900 3053
E-mail: info@prixjeunesse.de
Home Page: http://www.prixjeunesse.de

• 2373 • Prix Jeunesse International Munchen
To stimulate production of more and better children's and youth programs, to develop internationally applicable standards for such programs, to awaken and deepen understanding among young people of all nations, and to intensify international program exchange. Television programs for children and young people, including fiction (animation, drama, story-telling, light entertainment) and nonfiction (documentary, magazines, mixed forms, natural history, etc.) are considered in the following categories: up to 7 years of age, 7 to 12 years of age, and 12 to 17 years of age. Telecasters authorized under national and international law to operate broadcasting services may enter programs and send experts to the contest. All programs must have been produced and broadcast within the two years preceding the contest. A nomination committee chooses the finalists from among the nominees. All programs not selected for the contest are passed on to the Video-Bar. The prize winning programs at the PRIX JEUNESSE INTERNATIONAL contest are not chosen by a jury; rather, all participants accredited by the Contest Management are invited to join in the vote for the prize winning programs. Six prizes are awarded biennially. A trophy, and a "kinetic object" created out of stainless steel and acrylic, are awarded in each category. UNICEF and the German UNESCO Commission award Special Prizes at the PRIX JEUNESSE INTERNATIONAL contest. The Special Prize of the International Advisory Board is awarded to an outstanding program produced by a television organization with restricted production means. Awarded biennially. Established in 1964 by the Free State of Bavaria, City of Munich, Bayerischer Rundfunk; in 1971 Zweites Deutsches Fernsehen joined the foundation; and in 1991 Bayerische Landeszentrale fur Neue Medien. The PRIX JEUNESSE Foundation is a member of the International Council of WATCH - The World Alliance of Television of Children.

• 2374 •
International Joseph A. Schumpeter Society
(Internationale Joseph A. Schumpeter Gesellschaft)
Prof. Dr. Horst Hanusch, Sec.Gen.
% Dr. H. Hanusch, Sec.-Gen.
Chair of Economics V
University of Augsburg
D-86135 Augsburg, Germany
Phone: 49 821 598 4179
Fax: 49 821 598 4229
E-mail: horst.hanusch@wiwi.uni-augsburg.de
Home Page: http://www.wiwi.uni-augsburg.de/vwl/hanusch/iss

• 2375 • Schumpeter Prize (Schumpeter-Preis)
For recognition of a recent scholarly contribution in economics on a designated topic related to Schumpeter's work. Applications are accepted. A monetary prize of 10,000 Euro is awarded biennially at the convention. Established in 1986 in honor of Joseph Alois Schumpeter. Sponsored by *Wirtschaftswoche*, a German economic weekly. Additional information is available from Horst Hanusch, Secretary General, Universitaet Augsburg, Wiso-Fakultaet, Universitaetsstr. 16, 86135 Augsburg, Germany.

• 2376 •
Society for Medicinal Plant Research
(Gesellschaft fur Arzneipflanzenforschung)
Dr. Renate Seitz, Sec.
Emmeringerstr. 11
D-82275 Emmering, Germany
Phone: 49 8141 613749
Fax: 49 8141 613749
E-mail: ga-secretary@ga-online.de
Home Page: http://www.ga-online.org
Formerly: German Society for Medicinal Plant Research.

• 2377 • Egon Stahl Award (Egon Stahl Preis)
To honor and encourage younger scientists in the field of pharmacognosy (pharmaceutical biology) and analytical phytochemistry. A monetary award and a silver medal are presented to scientists not older than 40 years of age, and a monetary prize and a bronze medal are presented to scientists not older than 30 years of age. Awarded annually. Established in 1955 to honor Egon Stahl, founder of the Prize, on his 60th birthday.

• 2378 •
Society for Spinal Research
(Gesellschaft fur Wirbelsaulenforschung)
Prof. Dr. H. Sturz, Contact
Orthopadische Klinik
Justus Liebig University
Paul Meimberg Str. 3
35392 Giessen, Germany
Phone: 49 4721 49746
Fax: 49 641 9942 909
E-mail: Dr.Peter-Edelmann@t-online.de
Home Page: http://gwsf.de

• 2379 • Georg-Schmorl-Preis
To recognize physicians for outstanding publications in the field of spinal column research. A monetary prize of at least 1000 Euro is awarded biennially. Established in 1963 to honor pathologist Georg Schmorl.

• 2380 •
Society for the Scientific Investigation of Para-Sciences
(Gesellschaft zur Wissenschaftlichen Untersuchung von Parawissenschaften)
Amardeo Sarma, Exec.Dir.
Arheilger Weg 11
D-64380 Rossdorf, Germany
Phone: 49 6154 695021
Fax: 49 6154 695022
E-mail: info@gwup.org
Home Page: http://www.gwup.org

• 2381 • GWUP Prize
Recognizes outstanding contribution to science and critical thinking, including inquiry into paranormal claims. Awarded annually.

Awards are arranged in alphabetical order below their administering organizations

• 2382 •
Society of German Cooks
(Verbandder Koche Deutschlands)
Reinhold Metz, Pres.
Steinlestrasse 32
D-60596 Frankfurt am Main, Germany
Phone: 49 69 630006 0
Fax: 49 69 630006 10
E-mail: koeche@vkd.com
Home Page: http://www.vkd.com

• 2383 • **Culinary Olympics**
To recognize outstanding culinary ability. The competition is built around research and development and the establishment of food trends for the future. Medals are awarded. The Culinary Olympics are held every four years. Winners of the other international regional competitions participate: Culinary World Cup (Luxembourg), Salon Culinaire Mondial (Basel, Switzerland), Food & Hotel Asia Competition (Singapore), Culinary Arts Salon (USA), Hotelympia (London), Chef Ireland (Ireland), and Culinary Masters (Canada). Established in 1900.

• 2384 •
Stadt Buxtehude
Helmar Putz, Contact
Postfach 1555
D-21605 Buxtehude, Germany
Phone: 49 41615010
Fax: 49 4161501318
E-mail: stadtverwaltuug@buxtehude.de
Home Page: http://www.stadt.buxtehude.de

Formerly: (1981) Buchhandlung Ziemann & Ziemann, Buxtehude.

• 2385 • **Buxtehuder Bulle**
For recognition of the best book of the year for young people. Books written in German, and published during the preceding year are considered. A monetary of $5,000 and a plaque are awarded annually. Established in 1971 by Winfried Ziemann in honor of Ferdinand, the peace-loving bull in a famous children's story.

• 2386 •
Stadt Dortmund
Friedensplatz 3
D-44122 Dortmund, Germany
Phone: 49 231 50 29731
Fax: 49 231 50 22497
E-mail: redaktion@dortmund.de
Home Page: http://www.dortmund.de

• 2387 • **Literature pveis der Stadt Dortmund - Nelly-Sachs-Preis**
For recognition of personal achievement that has promoted the cultural relationship between people by stressing the ideals of tolerance and reconciliation. A monetary prize is awarded biennially. Established in 1961.

• 2388 •
Stadt Mannheim
Rathaus E 5
D-68159 Mannheim 1, Germany
Phone: 49 621 2930
Fax: 49 621 2939532
E-mail: masta@mannheim.de
Home Page: http://www.mannheim.de

• 2389 • **Konrad Duden Preis der Stadt Mannheim**
For recognition of an outstanding contribution to the German language. The prize is non-competitive. A monetary is awarded biennially. Established in 1960 in memory of Konrad Duden (1829-1911), a linguist and authority on German orthography. Co-sponsored by the Bibliographic Institute of Mannheim.

• 2390 •
Stadt Pforzheim, Kulturamt
Marktplatz 1
D-75175 Pforzheim, Germany
Phone: 49 7231 390
Fax: 49 7231 392303
E-mail: presse@stadt-pforzheim.de
Home Page: http://www.pforzheim.de

• 2391 • **Reuchlinpreis der Stadt Pforzheim**
For recognition of a work in the humanities that represents an advancement. Works in German are nominated by the Heidelberg Academy of Sciences and the Lord Mayor of Pforzheim. A monetary award is awarded biennially when merited. Established in 1955. Sponsored by the City Council of Pforzheim.

• 2392 •
Stadt Schweinfurt
Stadtarchiv und Stadtbibliothek
Friedrich-Ruckert Bau
Martin Luther Platz 20
D-97421 Schweinfurt, Germany
Phone: 49 9721 51382
Fax: 49 9721 51728
E-mail: stadtarchiv@schweinfurt.de
Home Page: http://www.schweinfurt.de

• 2393 • **Carus Preis**
To recognize distinguished scientists of any nationality for research in the field of natural sciences and medicine. A monetary of $10,000 and a certificate are awarded biennially. Established in 1961. Given jointly with the Carus Medal of the Leopoldina Academy of Researchers in Natural Sciences.

• 2394 •
Alfred Ttoepfer Stiftung F.V.S.
Sybylle Schmietendorf, Sec.
Georgsplatz 10
D-20099 Hamburg, Germany
Phone: 49 40 334020
Fax: 49 40 335860
E-mail: schmietendorf@toepfer-fvs.de
Home Page: http://www.toepfer-fvs.de

• 2395 • **Hamburg Max Brauer Prize**
To recognize personalities and institutions in the Free Hanseatic City of Hamburg who have rendered outstanding services to the cultural, scientific, or intellectual life of the city. A monetary prize of 15,000 euros is awarded annually. First awarded in 1993.

• 2396 • **Hansischer Goethe Prize**
To provide recognition for overriding humanitarian achievements in Europe. A monetary prize of 25,000 Euros is awarded biennially in Hamburg.

• 2397 • **Herder Prizes**
To provide recognition for outstanding work by individuals from Albania, Belarus, Bosnie-kercegovine, Bulgaria, Croatia, the Czech Republic, Estonia, Greece, Hungary, Latvia, Lithuania, Poland, Romania, Slovakia, Slovenia, Ukraine, and the remains of Yugoslavia, who have contributed to the preservation and renewal of the European cultural heritage. Seven monetary prizes are awarded annually through the University of Vienna, Austria. Established in 1964.

• 2398 • **Alexander Petrowitsch Karpinskij Prize**
The Karpinskij Prize recognizes outstanding accomplishments in the field of science, ecology, and protection of the environment and the nature in the C.I.S. A monetary prize is awarded annually. Established in 1985.

• 2399 • **Montaigne Prize**
To recognize eminent Europeans from Romance-language speaking countries who further European humanitarian values in the sphere of literature, the arts, or the humanities. A monetary prize of 20,000 Euros is awarded annually through the University of Tubingen. Established in 1968.

• 2400 • **Wilhelm Leopold Pfeil Prize**
To provide recognition for exemplary forestry practice in Europe. A monetary prize of 2,000 is awarded annually. Established in 1963.

• 2401 • **Alexander Puschkin Prize**
To recognize extraordinary works in modern Russian literature. A monetary prize of 15,000 Euros is awarded annually in cooperation with the Russian PEN Club in Moscow. Established in 1989.

• 2402 • **Fritz Schumacher Prize**
To provide recognition for outstanding work in the preservation of monuments, architecture, urban areas, and the management of land areas. Established in 1949. A monetary prize is awarded annually since 1960 through the Technical University of Hanover, from 1950 until 1955 through the University of Hamburg.

• 2403 • **Shakespeare Prize**
To recognize individuals in Great Britain who have rendered distinguished services in the field

of literature, the humanities, and the visual arts. A monetary prize of $20,000 is awarded annually, along with an $11,040 scholarship to study at a German academy or university. Established in 1937 and re-established in 1967.

• 2404 • Henrik Steffens Prize
To recognize cultural achievements in the Scandinavian countries. A monetary prize of 20,000 euros is awarded annually in Kiel or Lubeck through the Christian Albrechts University, Kiel. Established in 1935-36 and re-established in 1965.

• 2405 • Heinrich Tessenow Gold Medal
To recognize achievements in the field of handicraft and industrial design. Awarded annually. Co-sponsored with the Heinrich-Tessenow-Gesellschaft in Dresden-Hellerau.

• 2406 • Justus Von Liebig Prize
To provide recognition for outstanding achievements in practical agriculture in Europe or in scientific or technical work in the field. A monetary prize of $15,000 is awarded biennally through the Agricultural Faculty of the University of Kiel. Established in 1949.

• 2407 • Freiherr Von Stein Prize
To recognize exemplary or innovative contributions to the common good achieved by individuals, groups, or institutions in the new German Lander, notably through the solution of economic, social, and cultural problems resulting from the reunification of Germany. A monetary prize is awarded annually through the Humboldt University, Berlin. Established in 1954.

• 2408 •
Stiftung Internationaler Karlspreis zu Aachen
Bernd Vincken, Mng.Dir.
Theaterstr. 67
D-52062 Aachen, Germany
Phone: 49 241 401 7770
Fax: 49 241 401 7771
E-mail: info@karlspreis.de
Home Page: http://www.karlspreis.de

• 2409 • International Charlemagne Prize of Aachen
(Internationaler Karlspreis zu Aachen)
For recognition of the most notable achievement in encouraging international understanding and cooperation in the European sphere through political, economic, and literary endeavors. Individuals without respect to nationality, religion, or race who further the idea of the creation of the United States of Europe are eligible. A monetary prize an illuminated document, and a medallion, one side of which is embossed with the ancient Aachen City seal dating from the 12th century, and the reverse side, which contains an inscription concerning the winner of the prize, are awarded annually. Established in 1949 by a number of public-minded Aachen citizens. Formerly: (1988) Internationalen Karlpreis der Stadt Aachen.

• 2410 •
Stress and Anxiety Research Society
Petra Buchwald PhD, Sec.-Treas.
Heinrich-Heine Universitat
Erziehungswissenschaftliches Institut
Universitatsstr. 1
D-40255 Dusseldorf, Germany
Phone: 49 202 4392301
Fax: 49 211 8113468
E-mail: buchwald@phil.fak.uni-duesseldorf.de
Home Page: http://www.star-society.org

• 2411 • Life Time Career Award
For outstanding research in the field of stress, emotions, and health.

• 2412 • Young Scientific Career Award
For promising young researchers.

• 2413 • Young Scientific Career Award - Light
For promising accounting students.

• 2414 •
Stuttgart City Council
(Landeshauptstadt Stuttgart)
Kulturamt
Marktplatz M1
D-70173 Stuttgart, Germany
Phone: 49 711 2160
Fax: 49 711 216 4773
E-mail: post@stuttgart.de
Home Page: http://www.stuttgart.de

• 2415 • Johann Friedrich von Cotta Literary and Translation Prize of Stuttgart City
(Literaturpreis der Landeshauptstadt Stuttgart)
For recognition of achievement in German literature or for translation into German. A monetary prize of 20,000 Euro is awarded triennially to a writer and a translator. Established in 1978. Formerly: (2004) Stuttgart Literary Prize.

• 2416 • Hegel-Preis der Landeshauptstadt Stuttgart
For recognition of an outstanding contribution to the advancement of human sciences. A monetary prize of 12,000 Euro and a certificate are awarded triennially. Established in 1967.

• 2417 • Otto Hirsch Medaille
To recognize exceptional merits in the field of Christian-Jewish cooperation and understanding. A certificate and medal are awarded annually. Established in 1985.

• 2418 • Hans-Molfenter-Preis der Landeshauptstadt Stuttgart/Galerie
For recognition of artistic achievement in fine arts in the Baden-Wurttemberg region. A monetary prize of 12,000 Euro is awarded triennially. Established in 1983 in memory of the Stuttgart artist, Hans Molfenter (1884-1979).

• 2419 • Umweltpreis der Landeshauptstadt Stuttgart
For recognition of outstanding contributions to the retention of the natural environment of Stuttgart or the improvement of environmental conditions. Candidates must be residents, employees in, or businessmen of the city. Monetary prizes and certificates are awarded biennially. Established in 1985.

• 2420 •
Stuttgart International Festival of Animated Film
(Internationales Trickfilm Festival Stuttgart)
Gabriele Roemeyer, Mng.Dir.
Breitscheidstrasse 4
D-70174 Stuttgart, Germany
Phone: 49 711 92546 100
Fax: 49 711 92546 150
E-mail: roethemeyer@festival-gmbh.de
Home Page: http://www.itfs.de

• 2421 • International Festival of Animated Film Stuttgart
(Internationales Trickfilm Festival Stuttgart)
For recognition of outstanding animated short films produced in the previous 12 months. The following prizes are awarded: the Grand Prix (15,000 euros), SWR Audience Award (6,000 euros), International Promotion Award (10,000), Award for Best Student Film (2,500 euros), Award for Best Animated ChildrenKs Film (4,000 euros), Award for Best Animated Feature Film (2,500 euros), and the Award for Best Animated TV series (2,500 euros). Held annually. Established in 1990.

• 2422 •
Taxpayers Association of Europe
(Bund der Steuerzahler Europa)
Rolf von Hohenhau, Pres.
Nymphenburger Strasse 118
D-80636 Munich, Germany
Phone: 49 89 12600820
Phone: 49 89 12600811
Fax: 49 89 12600847
E-mail: info@taxpayers-europe.org
Home Page: http://www.taxpayers-europe.org

• 2423 • Taxpayers Award
Annual award of recognition.

• 2424 •
Transparency International - Germany
(Transparency International Deutschland e.V.)
Dr. Dagmar Schroder, Mng.Dir.
Alte-Schonhauser-Str. 44
D-10119 Berlin, Germany
Phone: 49 30 5498980
Fax: 49 30 54989822
E-mail: office@transparency.de
Home Page: http://www.transparency.de

• 2425 • Integrity Awards
Recognizes courage and determination in fighting corruption around the world. Awarded annu-

Awards are arranged in alphabetical order below their administering organizations

ally to one or more recipients. Established in 2000.

• 2426 •
Underground Transportation Research Association
(Studiengesellschaft fur Unterirdische Verkehrsanlagen)
Prof.Dr. Alfred Haack, Mng.Dir.
Mathias-Bruggen-Strasse 41
D-50827 Cologne, Germany
Phone: 49 221 597950
Fax: 49 221 5979550
E-mail: info@stuva.de
Home Page: http://www.stuva.de

• 2427 • **STUVA Prize**
Recognizes innovations in the field of underground construction. Awarded biennially.

• 2428 •
Universitat Karlsruhe (Technische Hochschule)
Prof. Dr. Horst Hippler, Pres.
Kaiserstrasse 12
D-76131 Karlsruhe, Germany
Phone: 49 721 6080
Fax: 49 721 6084290
E-mail: rektor@verwaltung.uni-karlsruhe.de
Home Page: http://www.uni-karlsruhe.de

• 2429 • **Heinrich Hertz Preis**
For recognition of an outstanding scientific and technological achievement in the field of energy technology. Contributions may be of a technological or technical economic character, or relate to work in experimental or theoretical physics. They should have led to important new findings and developments or be conducive to new developments. A monetary prize of 10,000 Euros and a medal are awarded. Established in 1975 to commemorate the 150th anniversary of the University of Karlsruhe.

• 2430 •
Verband Hannoverscher Warmblutzuechter
Friedrich Jahncke Buckau, Chm.
Postfach 1743
D-27267 Verden, Germany
Phone: 49 4231 6730
Fax: 49 4231 67312
E-mail: hannoveraner@hannoveraner.com
Home Page: http://www.hannoveraner.com

• 2431 • **Hanoverian Stallion of the Year**
Annual award of recognition.

• 2432 •
Alexander von Humboldt-Stiftung Foundation
Dr. Georg Schutte, Gen.Sec.
Jean-Paul-Strasse 12
D-53173 Bonn, Germany
Phone: 49 228 8330
Fax: 49 228 833199
E-mail: info@avh.de
Home Page: http://www.avh.de

• 2433 • **Fellowship for Japan-Related Research**
To enable young German scholars, up to 32 years in age, to conduct research in Japan for a period of 12 to 24 months. Open to all disciplines. Applications are coordinated by the Alexander von Humboldt Foundation on behalf of the Japan Society for the Promotion of Science. The following assistance is provided: basic fellowship, housing allowance, health insurance, travel expenses, and special Japanese language courses in Japan. Up to 30 fellowships are awarded annually.

• 2434 • **Humboldt Research Fellowships**
To enable highly qualified foreign scholars holding doctorate degrees to carry out a research project in the Federal Republic of Germany. Individuals under the age of 40 from any discipline may submit applications at any time during the year. Scholars from all nations are eligible. Application requirements include: an examination equivalent to the doctorate degree (Ph.D., C.Sc., or equivalent); high academic qualifications; academic publications; a detailed research plan; command of the German language (humanities scholars); and at least command of the English language for science scholars (including medicine and engineering). Up to 600 fellowships for six to twelve months are awarded annually. Family allowance, travel expenses, grants for language classes and monthly monetary prizes are awarded.

• 2435 • **Feodor Lynen Research Fellowships**
To enable German scholars, not over age 38, to conduct research abroad in cooperation with a former Humboldt Fellow or Awardee. Open to all disciplines. Application requirements include a doctorate degree, high academic qualifications, a detailed research proposal approved by the host, and a good knowledge of English or the respective country's language. Fellowships are for a period of one to four years. A monthly stipend, travel expenses, and assistance upon return are awarded. Up to 150 fellowships are given annually.

• 2436 • **Max Planck Research Award**
To recognize outstanding achievements of internationally renowned foreign and German scientists of any academic discipline and to promote intensive cooperation between foreign and German scientists. German or foreign scholars (generally full/associate professors) of any age may be nominated by eminent German scholars (in special cases more than one German and/or foreign scholar may be nominated). They are granted for a period of up to five years to cover short-term research stays at the partner institute, travel expenses, expenses for conferences and workshops, and additional expenses for materials, equipment, and research assistance. Co-sponsored by the Max Planck Society.

• 2437 • **Philipp Franz von Siebold Award**
To recognize a Japanese scholar who has played an important part in promoting understanding between Japan and the Federal Republic of Germany. Awardees spend a lengthy research period in Germany and receive a monetary prize. A grant of 50,000 euros is awarded annually. Established in 1978.

• 2438 • **Alexander von Humboldt Award for Scientific Cooperation**
To encourage scientific cooperation between Germany and other countries. World-renowned researchers of any age specially engaged in bilateral scientific cooperation in any discipline are eligible. Nominations of foreign scholars are directed by German researchers to the Alexander von Humboldt Foundation, which is entrusted with the selection and administration. The selection of the German scholars is coordinated by partner organizations in other countries. Agreements with counterparts exist in Australia, Belgium, Brazil, Canada, Chile, China, Finland, France, Hungary, India, Israel, Japan, Korea, Netherlands, New Zealand, Poland, South Africa, Spain, Sweden, and Taiwan. The award consists of a prize and invitation for a period of several months to do research work in the partner's country.

• 2439 •
Wissenschaftsstadt Darmstadt (Stadt Darmstadt)
% Magistrat, Hauptamt
Postfach 11 07 80
Luisenplatz 5
W-64283 Darmstadt, Germany
Phone: 49 6151 131
Fax: 49 6151 13 3777
E-mail: info@darmstadt.de
Home Page: http://www.darmstadt.de

• 2440 • **Ricarda-Huch-Preis**
For recognition of outstanding literary works that support German culture and freedom. A monetary prize is awarded triennially. Established in 1978 in memory of the uprising June 17, 1953 and the poetess Ricarda Huch who stood up against the Nazi oppression and for cultural freedom.

• 2441 • **Kunstpreis der Stadt Darmstadt**
To recognize outstanding artists of the city. Individuals, under 50 years of age, who enter the art exhibition and who have not previously won prizes, are eligible. A monetary prize, a certificate, and travel costs are awarded annually. The prize may be divided. Established in 1955.

• 2442 • **Literarischer Marz**
For recognition of the most outstanding young lyric authors of the biennial lyric festival, "The Last Week in March." German speaking lyricists, under 35 years of age, who have won no previous prizes are eligible. Awarded biennially. Established in 1978.

• 2443 • **Johann-Heinrich-Merck Ehrung**
To recognize individuals for contributions in various fields such as science, art, economics, and architecture. Awarded several times annually.

Established in 1955. Additional information is available from phone: 6151 13 2315.

• 2444 •
World Veterinary Poultry Association (Asociacion Mundial Veterinaria de Avicola)
Dr. U. Heffels-Redmann, Sec.-Treas.
Clinic for Birds, Reptiles, Amphibians and Fish
Justus Liebig University
Frankfurter Str. 91
D-35392 Giessen, Germany
Phone: 49 641 9938452
Phone: 49 641 9938430
Fax: 49 641 201548
E-mail: ursula.heffels-redmann@vetmed.uni-giessen.de
Home Page: http://www.wvpa.net

• 2445 • **Houghton Lecture Award**
To recognize innovative contributions to any branch of research concerned with poultry diseases. Nominees must be under 45 years of age at the time of the relevant congress. The travel expenses to the WVPA Congress will be met, and a memento will be awarded. In addition, the registration fee will be waived and a contribution made to the cost of the recipient's accommodations and subsistence. Awarded in odd-numbered years at the WVPA Congress. Established in 1993.

• 2446 • **Bart Rispens Award**
For recognition of achievements in the field of avian diseases. The authors of the best papers published in *Avian Pathology* during the preceding two calendar years are eligible. A monetary award, medallion, and a certificate are awarded biennially. Established in 1975 in honor of Dr. Bart Rispens.

Ghana

• 2447 •
West African Examinations Council
Matthew P. Ndure, Registrar
PO Box GP 125
Accra, Ghana
Phone: 233 21 248967
Fax: 233 21 222905
E-mail: waechqrs@africaonline.com.gh
Home Page: http://www.waecheadquarters-gh.org/index.html

• 2448 • **Distinguished Friends of Council Award**
Award of recognition for individuals who have made outstanding contributions to the achievement of the Council's objectives in The Gambia, Ghana, Liberia, Nigeria, or Sierra Leone. Nominations are submitted from the National Committee in each member country. The award consists of a plaque and a citation, and is awarded at a ceremony during the Annual Council Meeting in March.

• 2449 • **Excellence Award**
To encourage excellence, integrity, and high performance among candidates. Awarded annually to the best five candidates in the West African Senior School Certificate Examination. A cash prize and certificate of excellence are presented to the 1st, 2nd and 3rd-place candidates. The best male and female candidates are also rewarded. Presented in March at the Annual Council Meeting.

Greece

• 2450 •
Athenaeum International Cultural Center
Louli Psychouli, Pres.
3, Adrianou St.
GR-105 55 Athens, Greece
Phone: 30 210 321 1987
Phone: 30 210 321 1155
Fax: 30 210 321 1196
E-mail: athenm@attglobal.net
Home Page: http://www.athenaeum.ids.gr

• 2451 • **Maria Callas Grand Prix for Opera, Oratorio-Lied**
To recognize outstanding singers. Male singers not older than 32 years of age and female singers not older than 30 years of age are eligible. Awards are presented in three categories: Opera Singers - female; Opera Singers male; and Oratorio-Lied. Prizes are given in each category: Opera Singers - female; Opera Singers male; Alexandra Trianti Grand Prix. In addition, concert appearances are arranged for prize winners. Awarded biennially in odd-numbered years. The Maria Callas International Music Competitions were established in 1975. Formerly: (1994) Maria Callas International Opera, Oratorio-Lied Competition.

• 2452 • **Maria Callas Grand Prix for Piano**
To recognize outstanding pianists. Pianists of all nationalities up to 30 years of age are eligible. Entries must be submitted by mid December. One Grand Prix, the Maria Callas Gold Medal (instituted by the Municipality of Athens), and a diploma are awarded. In addition, concert appearances are arranged for Grand Prix winner. Finalists receive distinctions, a silver medal, and a diploma. Awarded biennially in even-numbered years. The Maria Callas International Music Competitions were established in 1975. Formerly: (1994) Maria Callas International Piano Competition.

• 2453 •
Circle of the Greek Children's Book
Loty Petrovits, Pres.
Bouboulinas 28
GR-106 82 Athens, Greece
Phone: 30 210 8222 296
Fax: 30 210 8222 296
E-mail: kyklos@greekibby.gr
Home Page: http://www.greekibby.gr

• 2454 • **Book Prizes**
To recognize the writers and illustrators of the best Greek children's book of the previous year. Greek citizens must submit books published in the previous calendar year by December 31. Monetary prizes are awarded in four categories: authors of books for younger children, authors of books for intermediate readers, authors of books for older children and young adults, and illustrators. Presented annually on April 2, the International Children's Book Day. Established in 1988.

• 2455 • **Penelope Delta Award**
To recognize a distinguished writer of Greek children's books for the entire body of his or her work. Greek citizens must be nominated. A diploma is awarded annually. Established in 1988 in memory of Penelope Delta (1874-1941), a famous Greek writer for children.

• 2456 •
Greek Alzheimer's Association
Mr. Nina Kotras, Exec.Dir.
Charisio Old People's Home
Terma Dimitriou Charisi
A. Toumba
Thessaloniki
GR-54352 Hellas, Greece
Phone: 30 2310 925802
Phone: 30 2310 909000
Fax: 30 2310 925802
E-mail: info@alzheimer-hellas.gr
Home Page: http://www.alzheimer-hellas.gr

• 2457 • **Award of the Greek Alzheimer's Association**
Annual award of recognition. Associations and individuals helping the association are eligible.

• 2458 •
Near East/South Asia Council of Overseas Schools
David Chojnacki, Exec.Dir.
% American College of Greece
Gravias 6
Aghia Paraskevi
GR-153 42 Athens, Greece
Phone: 30 210 600 9821
Fax: 30 210 600 9928
E-mail: nesa@nesacenter.org
Home Page: http://www.nesacenter.org

• 2459 • **NESA Awards**
To promote cooperation among international English language schools in the Near East and in southern Asia. The following awards are presented: Stanley Haas/Luke Hansen Student Award and the Margaret Sanders Foundation International Schools Scholarship (for students), NESA Community Service Awards (for school projects and programs), and the Finis Engleman Award (for distinguished international educators).

• 2460 •
Alexander S. Onassis Public Benefit Foundation
Anthony S. Papadimitriou, Pres.
Athens Office
7 Eschinou St.
GR-105 58 Athens, Greece
Phone: 30 210 3713 000
Fax: 30 210 3713 013
E-mail: pubrel@onassis.gr
Home Page: http://www.onassis.gr

• 2461 • **Onassis Award for Culture (Letters, Arts and Humanities)**
A monetary award of $250,000, a gold, silver, and bronze medal, and a scroll are awarded in Athens, Greece. Established in 1979 by the Board of Directors of the Foundation according to the will of Aristotle Onassis. Formerly: Onassis Prize for Man and Culture - Olympia.

• 2462 • **Onassis Award for International Understanding and Social Achievement**
To recognize individuals for their cultural, professional, and social contributions to international understanding. Nominees must actively participate in their relevant activities and must not be in the course of retirement. Nominations are accepted from individuals as well as institutions. A monetary prize of $250,000 is awarded when merited. Established in 1979.

• 2463 • **Onassis Award for the Environment**
To recognize individuals or organizations for a notable contribution in the field of the protection of the natural environment. Nominations and applications to the International Committee for the Onassis Prizes are accepted from individuals and organizations. A monetary prize of $250,000, a silver medal, and a scroll are awarded when merited in Athens, Greece. Established in 1988. Formerly: Onassis Prize for Man and His Environment - Delphi.

• 2464 • **Onassis International Cultural Competition Prizes**
To honor outstanding work in the arts and humanities through international competitions. Each prize of all four Cultural Competition Prizes (in the fields of Theatre, Music, Choreography and Painting) includes a gold plaque (1st Prize), a silver plaque (2nd Prize) and a bronze plaque (3rd Prize), accompanied by a scroll that will be awarded to each Prize-winner during the official Ceremony. Established in 1997.

• 2465 •
Radio Amateur Association of Greece
PO Box 3564
GR-10210 Athens, Greece
Phone: 30 1 5226516
Fax: 30 1 5226505
E-mail: raag@raag.org
Home Page: http://www.raag.org

• 2466 • **Alexander the Great Award**
For listeners or radio amateurs who have confirmed contacts with countries that were crossed by Alexander the Great.

• 2467 • **The Ancient Greek Cities Award**
For radio amateur listeners who had contacts with stations near ancient Greek cities.

• 2468 • **Athenian Award**
For working and confirming twenty-five different stations located in greater Athens.

• 2469 • **Athens Summer Olympic Games Award**
For listeners or radio amateurs who had contacts with different Greek stations in a given period of time.

• 2470 • **Greek Islands Award**
For confirming and working ten contacts with at the very least three different groups of Greek islands.

• 2471 • **RAAG Award**
For those who worked and confirmed contacts with at least seven Greek stations from the nine SV call areas.

• 2472 •
Thessaloniki International Film Festival (Centre du Cinema Grec)
Despina Mouzaki, Dir.
9 Alexandras Ave.
GR-114 73 Athens, Greece
Phone: 30 210 8706 000
Fax: 30 210 6448 143
E-mail: info@filmfestival.gr
Home Page: http://www.filmfestival.gr

• 2473 • **Thessaloniki Film Festival**
To encourage the production of films and to recognize short and feature length documentary films. The Ministry of Culture awards the Golden Alexander to the outstanding film overall, and awards three monetary prizes for the best film in each category. The awards are given to the directors and producers. In addition, a prize is given for: (1) Best first feature film; (2) Best Screenplay; (3) Best Actor; (4) Best Supporting Actor; (5) Best Actress; (6) Best Supporting Actress; (7) Best Music; (8) Best Sound; (9) Best Makeup; (10) Best Costumes; (11) Best Technical Contribution; and (12) Best Editing. The Jury of the Festival presents honorary awards in the following categories: (1) Grand Prize for the best feature film; (2) Grand Prize for the best documentary; (3) Best Director; (4) Best Director for a first feature film; (5) Best Photography; (6) Best Actress; (7) Best Actor; (8) Best Screenplay; and (9) prizes for music, costumes, editing, decoration, sound, makeup, special effects and supporting roles. Held annually in October. Established in 1959 by the International Fair of Thessaloniki.

• 2474 •
World Chess Federation (Federation Internationale des Echecs)
Julius Filo, VP
9 Singrou Ave.
11743 Athens, Greece
Phone: 30 210 9212047
Fax: 30 210 9212859
E-mail: office@fide.com
Home Page: http://www.fide.com

• 2475 • **Chess World Champions**
For recognition of the winner of the Individual World Championship. Champions have been recognized since 1886.

• 2476 • **FIDE Master**
For recognition of achievement in the game of chess. The title FIDE Master is awarded for any of the following: a rating of at least 2300 based on the completion of at least 24 related games (the national federation is responsible for the payment of the fee established in the financial regulations); first place in the IBCA World Junior Championship with a rating of 2205; first place in the World Championships, Continental Championships, or the Arab Championships in specific age groups (in the event of a tie in either the Continental or Arab Championships, each of the tied players shall be awarded the title of FIDE Master - subject to a maxium of three players); a score of 50 percent or better on the Zonal Tournament of at least nine games; and runners-up of the IBCA World Championship with a rating of 2205. A title, a medal, and a diploma are awarded annually. Established in 1946.

• 2477 • **Gold Diploma of Honor**
To recognize an exceptional contribution to international chess over a period of years. A plaque is awarded annually by the FIDE Congress. Established in 1980.

• 2478 • **Grandmaster**
For recognition of achievement in the game of chess. The title Grandmaster is given for any of the following: two or more Grandmaster results in events covering at least 24 games and a rating of at least 2500 in the current FIDE Rating List, or within seven years of the first title result; qualification for the Candidates Competiton for the World Championship; one Grandmaster result in a FIDE Internzonal tournament; first place in the Women's World Championship or World Junior Championship; first place in the Continental Junior Championship or the Women's Candidates Tournament is equivalent to one nine-game Grandmaster result; a tie for first place in the World Junior Championship (equivalent to one nine-game Grandmaster result); and one 13-game Grandmaster result in the Olympiad, which leads to the award of a full title. A title, a medal, and a diploma are awarded annually. Established in 1946.

• 2479 • **International Arbiter**
To recognize individuals knowledgeable of the Laws of Chess and Federation Regulations for chess competitions. The title of International Ar-

biter is awarded for all of the following: knowledge of the laws of chess and Federation Regulations; knowledge of at least one official Federation language; objectivity; and experience as chief or deputy arbiter in at least four Federation rated events, such as the following: the final of the National Individual Adult Championship (not more than two), all official Federation tournaments and matches, international title tournaments and matches, and international chess festivals with at least 100 contestants. Awarded annually.

• 2480 • International Master
For recognition of achievement in the game of chess. The title International Master is given for any of the following: two or more International Master results in events covering at least 24 games, and a rating of at least 2400 in the current FIDE Rating List, or within seven years of the first title result; first place in one of the following events: Women's Candidates Tournament, Zonal Tournament, Continental Individual Championship, Continental Individual Junior Championship, Arab Individual and Junior Championships, Centroamerican-Caribbean Junior Championship, World Under-18 Championship, International Braille Chess Association World (IBCA) Championship (champion is given a rating of 2205), and International Committee of Silent Chess World Championship (in the event of a tie for first place in any of the above listed events, each of the tied players shall be awarded the title - subject to a maximum of three players); the top three medalist in the World Junior Championship; qualification for the Interzonal Tournament of the World Championship cycle; one International Master result in the cycle of the Individual World Championship, of at least 13 games; a score of 66 2/3 percent or better in a Zonal Tournament of at least nine games; first place in the World Under-16 Championship and the Continental Under-18 and Under-16 Championships (equivalent to one nine-game International Master result); and one 13-game International Master result in the Olympaid, which leads to the award of the full title. A title, a medal, and a diploma are awarded annually. Established in 1946.

• 2481 • Woman FIDE Master
To recognize the achievements of a female in the game of chess. The title of Woman FIDE Master is given for any of the following: a rating of at least 2100 after the completion of at least 24 games (the national federation is responsible for the payment of the fee established by the financial regulations); first place in any of the following events: World Girls' Championships in specific age groups, Continental Women's Championship, Arab Women's Championship, Continental Girls Championship in specific age groups, and IBCA Women's World Championship with a rating of at least 2005 (in the event of a tie for first place in any of the above events, each of the tied players will receive the title of WFM - subject to a maximum of three players); and a score of 50 percent or better in a Woman's Zonal tournament of at least nine games. A title, a medal, and a diploma are awarded annually.

• 2482 • Woman Grandmaster
To recognize the achievement of a female in the game of chess. The title of Woman Grandmaster is given for any of the following: two or more Woman Grandmaster results in events covering at least 24 games and a rating of at least 2300 in the FIDE Rating List, or within seven years of the first title result; qualification for the Candidates Competition for the Women's World Championship; one Woman Grandmaster result in the cycle of the Individual Women's World Championship, of at least 13 games; first place in the World Girls Championship (equivalent to one nine-game Woman Grandmaster result); first place in the Continental Girls Championship (equivalent to one nine-game WGM result); and one 13-game Woman Grandmaster result in the Olympiad, which leads to a full title. A title, a medal, and diploma are awarded annually.

• 2483 • Woman International Master
To recognize the achievement of a female in the game of chess. The title of Woman International Master is given for any of the following: two or more WIM results in events covering at least 24 games and a rating of at least 2200 in the FIDE Rating List, within seven years of the first title result; qualification for the Interzonal Tournament for the Women's World Championship; first place in any of the following events: Continental Women's Championship, Arab Women's Championship, World Girls Under-18 Championship, Continental Girls Under-20 Championship. In the event of a tie in any of the above events, each of the tied players will be awarded the title of WIM (subject to a maximum of three players); top three medalists in the World Girl Under-20 Championship; one WIM result in the cycle of the Individual Women's World Championship, of not less than 13 games; a score of 66 2/3 percent or better in a Women's World Championship Zonal Tournament of at least 9 games; first place in the World Girls Under-16 Championship and the Continential Girls Under-18 and Under-16 Championships is equivalent to one 9-game WIM result; or one 13-game WIM result in the Olympiad will result in th award of a full title. A title, medal, and diploma are awarded annually.

Guatemala

• 2484 •
American Chamber of Commerce of Guatemala
(Camara de Comercio Guatemalteco-Americana)
Carolina Castellanos, Exec.Dir.
5 Av. 5-55, zona 14. Torre 1
Nivel 5 Europlaza
01014 Guatemala City, Guatemala
Phone: 502 23333899
Fax: 502 23683536
E-mail: director@guatemalanamcham.com
Home Page: http://www.amchamguate.com

• 2485 • AmCham Annual Awards
To recognize a person who makes efforts in promoting trade and investment. Awarded annually.

Hungary

• 2486 •
Association of Hungarian Geophysicists
(Magyar Geofizikusok Egyesulete)
Fo utca 68
H-1027 Budapest, Hungary
Phone: 36 1 2019815
E-mail: geophysic@mtesz.hu
Home Page: http://www.ggki.hu/MGE/mgr.html

• 2487 • Best First Presentation
To recognize the best first presentation by a junior member at the biannual meeting of young geophysicists. Awarded at the annual General Meeting.

• 2488 • Best Papers of the Year
To recognize the two best papers of the year published by members of the association in one of the Hungarian geophysical journals (*Magyar Geofizika, Geophysical Transactions, Acta Geodaetica, Geophysica et Montanistica*). Awards are presented for the best theoretical paper and for best case history at the annual General Meeting.

• 2489 • Laszlo Egyed Medal
(Egyed Laszlo emlekerem)
For recognition of outstanding professional performance in the field of geophysics, in honor of Hungarian geophysicist Lazlo Egyed. The award may be awarded for an outstanding performance in any special area of geophysics; for achievements in the teaching of geophysics; for writing and editing special geophysics papers; and for lifetime service in the profession. Established in 1985, the award is given biennially.

• 2490 • Lorand Eotvos Medal
For recognition of achievements in research, in both theoretical and practical geophysics, during the past six years. Hungarian geophysicists who are regular members of the association are eligible. A medal with the figure of R. Eotvos on one side is awarded triennially. Established in 1957.

• 2491 • Honorary Membership
For recognition of outstanding achievements in geophysics and related sciences, or in attainment of the association's purposes. Both Hungarian and foreign citizens are eligible. Honorary memberships are awarded triennially. Established in 1954.

• 2492 • Janos Renner Medal
For recognition of outstanding performance within and on behalf of the Association. The medal may be awarded for significant social activities; for merits shown in organizing and developing Association activities; and for research in scientific history. In honor of Janos Renner, a renowned Hungarian geophysicist. Awarded annually. Established in 1985.

• 2493 •
Budapest City Council
V. Varoshaz utca 9-11
H-1840 Budapest V, Hungary
E-mail: info@budapest.hu
Home Page: http://www.budapest.hu

• 2494 • **Pro Urbe Budapest Award**
To recognize the achievement of outstanding results, lasting value, and respect. Up to six prizes of 400,000 forints and a medal are awarded annually on November 17, Budapest Day.

• 2495 •
Ferenc Liszt Society, Budapest
(Liszt Ferenc Tarsasag)
Klara Hamburger, Sec.Gen.
Voeroesmarty utca 35
H-1064 Budapest, Hungary
Phone: 36 1 342 1573
Fax: 36 1 342 1573
E-mail: hambivan@axelero.hu
Home Page: http://www.bmc.hu/lisztsociety

• 2496 • **Ferenc Liszt International Record Grand Prix**
(Nemzetkoezi Liszt Hanglemez Nagydij)
To provide recognition for outstanding artistic and technical contributions in the field of recording, compact discs and video tapes containing Liszt's works that are produced by record companies throughout the world. A bronze Liszt plaque in a case and a diploma are awarded annually on October 22, Liszt's birthday. Established in 1975 in memory of Ferenc Liszt (1811-1886).

• 2497 •
Hungarian Publishers and Booksellers Association
Istvan Bart, Pres.
Kertesz u. 41, I/4
H-1073 Budapest, Hungary
Phone: 36 1 3432540
Fax: 36 1 3432541
E-mail: mkke@mkke.hu
Home Page: http://www.mkke.hu

• 2498 • **Book of the Year**
For recognition of the best published book of the year in all categories of literature. Held annually. Co-sponsored by Artisjus, Hungarian Organization for Defence of Copyright.

• 2499 •
Hungarian Real Estate Association
(Magyar Ingatlanszovetseg)
Zoltan Szekeres, Sec.Gen.
Margit krt. 43-45
H-1024 Budapest, Hungary
Phone: 36 1 3267776
Phone: 36 1 3151039
Fax: 36 1 3151038
E-mail: hrea@euroweb.hu
Home Page: http://webcei.com/hrea.htm

• 2500 • **Best Appraiser of the Year**
Annual award of recognition.

• 2501 • **Best Broker of the Year**
Annual award of recognition.

• 2502 • **Best Developer of the Year**
Annual award of recognition.

• 2503 •
Hungarofest
(Interart Festivalkozpont)
Otto Bence, Mng.Dir.
Rakoczi u. 20
H-1072 Budapest, Hungary
Phone: 36 1 266 2669
Fax: 36 1 269 2053
E-mail: info@hungarofest.hu
Home Page: http://www.hungarofest.hu
Formerly: (1989) Interconcert Festival Bureau.

• 2504 • **Budapest International Music Competition**
To recognize the best performer of the Competition. Awards are given alternately in the following categories: the Pablo Casals Violoncello Competition; the Jozsef Szigeti Violin Competition; Liszt - Piano Competition; an Organ Competition "in memoriam Ferenc Liszt". Individuals must apply to the competition by May 1. More than one prize is awarded to recognize different instruments. Established in 1933. Sponsored by the Municipal Council of Budapest and the Ministry for Culture and Education.

• 2505 •
International Association of Hungarian Studies
(Association Internationale des Etudes Hongroises)
Jozsef Jankovics, Sec.Gen.
Pf.34
H-1250 Budapest, Hungary
Phone: 36 1 3559930
Fax: 36 1 3559930
E-mail: magyarsagtudomanyi.tars@axelero.hu
Home Page: http://www.bibl.u-szeged.hu/filo

• 2506 • **John Lotz Commemorative Medal**
(Lotz Janos Emlekerem)
To recognize scholars living outside of Hungary for an outstanding contribution to the teaching of Hungarian Studies in the fields of Hungarian language, literature, and ethnography. A special award committee makes the nomination. A medal is awarded every five years on the occasion of the general meetings of IAHS. Established in 1981 in memory of John Lotz (1913-1973), a Hungarian philologist, linguist, and educator.

• 2507 •
International Measurement Confederation
(Internationale Messtechnische Konfoderation)
Ms. Karolina Havrilla, Exec.Sec.
PO Box 457
H-1371 Budapest V, Hungary
Phone: 36 1 3531562
Phone: 36 1 4747966
Fax: 36 1 3531562
E-mail: imeko@axelero.hu
Home Page: http://www.imeko.org

• 2508 • **Gyorgy Striker Junior Paper Award**
To recognize a junior author under the age of 35 who presents a paper reflecting a deep understanding of the scope of a World Congress. A diploma and $1,000 is awarded at the Closing Session of the World Congress. Established in 1992.

• 2509 •
International Sport Press Association
(Association Internationale de la Presse Sportive)
Mr. Togay Bayatli, Pres.
Hold u. 1
H-1054 Budapest, Hungary
Phone: 36 1 3112689
Phone: 36 1 3019289
Fax: 36 1 3533807
E-mail: aips@axelero.hu
Home Page: http://www.aips-media.com

• 2510 • **AIPS Awards**
For recognition of worldwide achievement in sports. Awards are given in the following categories: Best Male Athlete, Best Female Athlete, Best Sports Team, and Best Press Facilities. Trophies are awarded annually during the AIPS Congress. Established in 1977.

• 2511 •
International Weightlifting Federation
Dr. Tamas Ajan, Pres.
Istvanmezei ut 1-3
H-1146 Budapest, Hungary
Phone: 36 1 3530530
Phone: 36 1 3318153
Fax: 36 1 3530199
E-mail: iwf@iwf.net
Home Page: http://www.iwf.net

• 2512 • **Award of Merit**
To recognize individuals for outstanding service to the development of the sport of weightlifting. Proposals to confer the award must be submitted by the national or continental federations or executive board members.

• 2513 • **The IWF Order**
A gold, silver, and bronze award given to IWF members who have served on the Executive Board or IWF Committees for a specified amount of time and a specified number of terms.

Iceland

• 2514 •
Icelandic Radio Amateurs
(Islenskir Radioamatorar)
PO Box 1058
IS-121 Reykjavik, Iceland
E-mail: ira@ira.is
Home Page: http://www.ira.is

• 2515 • **The Iceland Award**
For being able to contact or hear Icelandic amateur radio stations within one year

• 2516 • **Iceland on Six Meters Award**
For being able to contact or hear Icelandic amateur radio stations on six meters

• 2517 • **Icelandic JOTA Award**
For contacting Icelandic JOTA amateur radio stations

• 2518 • **Icelandic Radio Amateurs Award**
For radio amateurs outside Iceland.

• 2519 • **IRA Worked All Nordic Countries Award**
For licensed radio amateurs.

• 2520 • **IRA Zone 40 Award**
For being able to contact with each of the countries specified by the club.

India

• 2521 •
Aeronautical Society of India
H.C. Bhatia, Admin.Sec.
13-B, Indraprastha Estate
New Delhi 110 002, Delhi, India
Phone: 91 11 23370058
Phone: 91 11 23370516
Fax: 91 11 23370768
E-mail: aerosoc@bol.net.in
Home Page: http://csirwebistad.org/aesi

• 2522 • **Excellence in Aerospace Education**
To recognize an outstanding contribution in the field of aerospace education. Individuals actively engaged in the teaching profession in the aeronautical field are eligible. A monetary award of 10,000.00 rupees is presented annually at the annual meeting. Established in 1991.

• 2523 • **Dr. V. M. Ghatage Award**
For recognition of an outstanding contribution in the field of design, development, manufacture, operation, training, maintenance and allied areas in aviation and space. Scientific and technical institutions are invited to make recommendations to an Awards Committee, upon whose recommendation the Council makes the final decision. A monetary prize of 10,000.00 rupees is awarded annually. Established in 1984 in honor of Dr. V.M. Ghatage, on the occasion of his 75th birthday, by his students and colleagues.

• 2524 • **Indigenisation of Aeronautical Equipment Award**
Recognizes outstanding achievements in indigenisdion of aeronautical equipment, including ground handling equipment. A monetary prize of 10,000 rupees is awarded annually. Established in 1994 by S.I.A.T.L.

• 2525 • **Swarna Jayanti Award**
For outstanding contribution by a young achiever in the field of aviation, aeronautics, or aerospace. A monetary prize of 25,000 rupees is awarded annually. Established in 1999 on the golden jubilee of the society.

• 2526 • **National Aeronautical Prize**
For recognition of an outstanding fundamental and applied work in aeronautical science and technology. A monetary prize of 50,000 rupees is awarded annually. Established in 1988 by the Aeronautics Research & Development Board, Ministry of Defence of the Government of India, New Delhi.

• 2527 • **Production Technology Award**
Recognizes outstanding technicians. A monetary prize of 10,000 rupees is awarded annually. Established in 1993.

• 2528 • **Dr. Biren Roy Space Science and Design Award**
To encourage Indian space scientists and to recognize an outstanding contribution in space science. The Awards Committee selects the nominees and makes recommendations to the Council for a final decision. A monetary prize of 10,000 rupees is awarded annually. Established in 1985 by Dr. Biren Roy (Charitable) Trust, Roy Mansions, Behala, Calcutta - 34, well known for its grants for medical relief and scientific progress.

• 2529 • **Dr. Biren Roy Trust Award**
For recognition of an outstanding contribution in the field of design, development, manufacture, operation, training, maintenance and allied areas in aviation and space. Scientific and technical institutions are invited to make recommendations to an Awards Committee, upon whose recommendation the Council makes the final decision. A monetary prize of 10,000 rupees is awarded annually. Established in 1983 by Dr. Biren Roy (Charitable) Trust, Calcutta.

• 2530 •
All India Management Association
G.K. Nischol, Dir. Gen.
Mgt. House
14 Institutional Area
Lodi Rd.
New Delhi 110 003, Delhi, India
Phone: 91 11 24617354
Phone: 91 11 24618107
Fax: 91 11 24626689
E-mail: dg@aima-ind.org
Home Page: http://www.aima-ind.org

• 2531 • **ELCINA Awards**
For electronics and information technology companies.

• 2532 • **JRD TATA Corporate Leadership Award**
For corporate leaders.

• 2533 • **AIMA - Dr. J.S. Juneja Award for Creativity and Innovation**
For small enterprises.

• 2534 • **Lifetime Achievement Award for Management**
For corporate leaders.

• 2535 • **Public Service Excellence Award**
For outstanding individuals.

• 2536 •
All India Radio
(Akashvani)
Akashvani Bhavan, Rm. 204
PO Box 500
New Delhi 110 001, India
Phone: 91 11 382021
Fax: 91 11 2342 1062
E-mail: airlive@air.org.in
Home Page: http://allindiaradio.org

• 2537 • **Akashvani Annual Awards**
To encourage producers to develop first rate programs and to explore new areas in broadcasting. All stations of All India Radio and staff working at various radio stations are entitled to participate. Outstanding plays, documentaries, musical productions and innovative programs as well as topical documentaries, Yuv Vani and family welfare programs are considered. A choral singing competition is also held as part of the Akashvani Awards Scheme. The competition is open to two age groups of 5 to 12 years and 12 to 17 years. In each category, two prizes are given: (1) the first prize - 5,000 rupees for producer, and 3,000 rupees for the production team; and (2) the second prize - 3,000 rupees for the producer and 2,400 rupees for the production team. For a play, the authors/adaptors also get a first prize of 3,500 rupees and second prize receives 2,000 rupees. Similarly, for music the author and composers also win a first prize of 2,000 rupees each, and second prize of 1,000 rupees each; (3) The Special Prize for Yuv Vani is 3,000 rupees for the producer and 2,400 rupees for the production team; (4) The Special Prizes for Special Topic Documentary and Family Welfare Program are 5,000 rupees for the producer and 3,000 rupees for the production team in each category; (5) the prize-winning Choral Singing Children's groups are awarded a first prize of 5,000 rupees and second prize of 3,000 rupees for each age group; and (6) Akashvan Annual Award for the Best Commercial Broadcasting Service Centre - a running trophy, established in 1987. Under this scheme, running trophies are given every year to stations for the first prize winning entries in each cate-

Awards are arranged in alphabetical order below their administering organizations

gory of the program. Awarded annually. Established in 1974.

• 2538 • Akashvani Annual Awards for Technical Excellence

To encourage competition and recognize merit in both technology and techniques of broadcasting. The following awards are presented: (1) Best Maintained Station - one in each of the four zones; one shield and one trophy for each zone; (2) Best Installed Project - one in each of the four zones; one shield and one trophy for each zone; (3) Best Designed and Constructed Building - one shield and one trophy each to the architectural and engineering divisions; (4) Best Technical Innovation/Import Substitution - a monetary award of 3,000 rupees and two commendation awards of 1,000 rupees each; (5) Best Technical Paper - a monetary award of 3,000 rupees; (6) Best Research Work - a monetary award of 3,000 rupees; (7) Best Maintained Station amid difficult stations - one shield and trophy; and (8) Best Import Substitution - a monetary award of 3,000 rupees and two commendation awards of 1,000 rupees each. Awarded annually. Established in 1979.

• 2539 •

Anuvibha - Anuvrat Global Organization (Anuvrat Vishva Bharati (Anuvibha))
% Dr. S.L. Gandhi
PO Box 1003
Gandhinager Post Office
Jaipur 302 015, India
Phone: 91 141 2707347
Fax: 91 141 2710118
E-mail: slgandhi@hotmail.com
Home Page: http://www.anuvibha.org

• 2540 • Anuvrat Award for International Peace

To promote world peace by honoring people who work for it. An international committee, consisting of eminent people committed to nonviolence, selects an individual who has made a significant contribution to world peace by means of nonviolence through his writings, speeches, and dialogues. The people who endeavor to reduce conflict by removing the causes that promote it are also considered for this award. A medal, plaque, and citation are awarded annually. Established in 1987.

• 2541 •

Association of Gerontology India
M.K. Thakur, Pres.
Department of Zoology
Banaras Hindu Univ.
Varanasi 221005, Uttar Pradesh, India
Phone: 91 542 2307149
E-mail: mkt_bhu@yahoo.com
Home Page: http://www.iagg.com.br/webforms

• 2542 • Biology Award

For young workers below age 40.

• 2543 • Medical Award

For young workers below age 40.

• 2544 • Psycho-social Award

For young workers below age 40.

• 2545 •

Bighelp for Education
Sarojini Maturi, Managing Trustee
Sandhya Apts., Flat No. 202
Bhagyanagar Colony
Hyderabad 500072, Andhra Pradesh, India
Phone: 91 40 23061061
E-mail: info@bighelp.org
Home Page: http://www.bighelp.org

• 2546 • Kancharla Award For Excellence

• 2547 • Maturi Award for Excellence

Fo the student who scores highest marks in 10th class out of all schools in Pylon and Hilcolony.

• 2548 • Nannidar Award for Excellence

To the student who scores highest marks in 10th class out of all non-residential schools in Vijayapuri South.

• 2549 • Pothuganti Award for Excellence

To the student who scores highest marks in 7th class out of all non-residential schools in Hilcolony.

• 2550 •

Children's Film Society, India
Films Div. Complex
24 G. Deshmukh Marg
Bombay 400 026, India
Phone: 91 22 23802870
Fax: 91 22 23805610
E-mail: ncyp@bom3.vsnl.net.in
Home Page: http://www.childrensfilm.org

• 2551 • International Children's Film Festival of India

For recognition of outstanding films for children. The objects of the festival are to promote and encourage the Children's Film Movement, to foster a closer relationship among the international fraternity of children's film makers and organizations and to afford them an opportunity to exchange their films, and to exhibit the best of the children's films from different countries of the world with a view to promote international understanding and brotherhood among the children of the world. There are three sections at the festival: competitive, information Asian Panorama, and market. The following awards are presented: Golden Elephant Award for the Best Live-Action Feature Length Film - 100,000 rupees; Silver Elephant Award for the Best Short Film - 50,000 rupees; Silver Elephant Award for the Second Best Live-Action Feature-Length Film 50,000 rupees; Silver Elephant Award for the Best Animation Film - 50,000 rupees; Silver Elephant Award for the Best Puppet Film; Silver Elephant Award for the Best Director - 50,000 rupees; Silver Elephant Award for the Best Child Artist; Silver Elephant Award for the Best Cinematographer; Silver Elephant Award for the Special Jury Prize - 50,000 rupees; and Golden Plaque Award for the Most Popular Children's Film determined by a jury of 15 children. Held biennially in odd-numbered years. Established in 1979.

• 2552 •

Council of EU Chambers of Commerce in India
Dr. Kant Singh, Sec.Gen.
Y.B. Chavan Centre, 3rd Fl.
General Bhosale Marg
Bombay 400 021, Maharashtra, India
Phone: 91 22 2854563
Fax: 91 22 2854564
E-mail: ceuc@vsnl.com
Home Page: http://www.euindiachambers.com

• 2553 • Impresa Europe Awards

To recognize European ventures in India that have proven to give substantial contribution to the improvement of bilateral business by projecting India as an ideal location for investment, and to recognize the performance of Indian companies in exports to or imports from the European Union. Four awards are presented annually.

• 2554 •

Fertiliser Association of India
Shri Viren Kaushik, Dir.Gen.
10 Shaheed Jit Singh Marg
New Delhi 110 067, Delhi, India
Phone: 91 11 6567144
Phone: 91 11 6517305
Fax: 91 11 6960052
E-mail: fai@vsnl.com
Home Page: http://www.fadinap.org/india

• 2555 • Award for Production, Promotion, and Marketing of Biofertilizer

To encourage and recognize quality production, promotion, and marketing of biofertilizer. A plaque and monetary prize of 15,000 rupees are awarded annually. Co-sponsored by National Fertilisers Ltd.

• 2556 • Golden Jubilee Awards

To recognize individuals for outstanding work in the field of fertilizer use in India. Awards are presented in three categories: Excellence for the Best Work Done in the Field of Effects of Long-Term Fertilizer Use on Soil Health and Crop Productivity; Outstanding Doctoral Research in Fertilizer Usage, and Award on Transfer of Improved Farm Technologies. Awarded annually.

• 2557 • IMPHOS-FAI Award on the Role of Phosphorus on Yield and Quality of Crops

To encourage and recognize outstanding fundamental or applied research work done on phosphorus. A gold medal and monetary prize of 15,000 rupees are awarded annually. Co-sponsored by the World Phosphate Institute of Casablanca, Morocco.

• 2558 • PPIC-FAI Award
To encourage and recognize outstanding fundamental or applied research work done on management and balanced use of inputs. A gold medal and monetary award of 10,000 rupees are awarded annually. Co-sponsored by the Potash and Phosphate Institute of Canada (PPIC).

• 2559 • TSI-FAI Award on Plant Nutrient Sulphur
To recognize an individual for outstanding work done in India on plant nutrient sulphur. A gold medal and monetary award of 13,000 rupees is presented biennially. Sponsored by The Sulphur Institute (TSI) of Washington DC.

• 2560 •
Gem and Jewelry Export Promotion Council
Shri Bakul R. Mehta, Chm.
5th Fl., Diamond Plz.
391-A Dr. Dadasaheb Bhadkamkar Marg
Bombay 400 004, Maharashtra, India
Phone: 91 22 23821801
Phone: 91 22 23821801
Fax: 91 22 23808752
E-mail: gjepc@vsnl.com
Home Page: http://www.gjepc.org

• 2561 • Costume and Fashion Jewelry
Award of recognition.

• 2562 • Cut and Polished Colored Gemstones
Award of recognition.

• 2563 • Cut and Polished Diamonds
Award of recognition.

• 2564 • Cut and Polished Synthetic Stones
Award of Recognition.

• 2565 • Pearls
Award of recognition.

• 2566 • Plain Gold Jewelry
Award of recognition.

• 2567 • Plain Precious Metal Jewelry
Award of recognition.

• 2568 • Sales to Foreign Tourists
Award of recognition.

• 2569 • Silver Jewelry
Award of recognition.

• 2570 • Studded Gold Jewelry
Award of recognition.

• 2571 • Studded Precious Metal Jewelry
Award of recognition.

• 2572 •
India Ministry of Science and Technology
CSIR Bldg.
Rafi Marg
New Delhi 110 001, India
Phone: 91 11 3711744
E-mail: dgcsir@csir.res.in
Home Page: http://mst.nic.in

• 2573 • Bhatnagar Award
To recognize an Indian National for outstanding work in the following scientific disciplines: (1) physical sciences; (2) biological sciences; (3) engineering sciences; (4) medical sciences; (5) mathematical sciences; and (6) earth sciences and chemistry. Scientists under the age of 45 are eligible. A monetary prize of 200,000 rupees is awarded annually. Established in 1967.

• 2574 •
India Office of the Prime Minister
South Block
Raisina Hill
New Delhi 110 011, India
Phone: 91 11 23012312
Fax: 91 11 23019545
Home Page: http://pmindia.nic.in

• 2575 • Ashoka Chakra
For the recognition of the most conspicuous bravery or some daring or preeminent act of valor or self-sacrifice on land, at sea or in the air. Members of the military are eligible.

• 2576 • Ati Vishisht Seva Medal
To recognize personnel of all three Services for distinguished service of the most exceptional order.

• 2577 • Bharat Ratna
For recognition of exceptional service in the advancement of art, literature and science, and for recognition of public service of the highest order. Individuals without distinction of race, occupation, position or sex are eligible. A decoration made of bronze, and worn around the neck is awarded. The award may be given posthumously. The names of the persons upon whom the decoration is conferred are published in the Gazette of India, and a register of all such recipients is maintained by the Office of the President. Awarded annually by the President on the Republic Day.

• 2578 • Kirti Chakra
For recognition of conspicuous gallantry. Members of the military are eligible.

• 2579 • Maha Vir Chakra
This, the second highest decoration for valor, is given for acts of conspicuous gallantry in the presence of the enemy, whether on land, at sea, or in the air. Members of the military are eligible.

• 2580 • Padma Bhushan (Lotus Decoration)
For recognition of distinguished service of a high order in any field, including service rendered by government servants. Any person without distinction of race, occupation, position or sex shall be eligible for the award which may be awarded posthumously. The names of the persons, upon whom the decoration is conferred, is published in the Gazette of India and a register of all such recipients of the award is maintained under the direction of the President. A decoration of bronze with gold embossing is awarded annually by the President.

• 2581 • Padma Shri
For recognition of distinguished service in any field, including service rendered by government servants. Any person without distinction of race, occupation, position or sex shall be eligible for the award which may be awarded posthumously. The names of the persons, upon whom the decoration is conferred, is published in the Gazette of India and a register of all such recipients of the award is maintained under the direction of the President. A decoration made of bronze with stainless steel embossing is awarded annually by the President.

• 2582 • Padma Vibhushan
For recognition of exceptional and distinguished service in any field, including service rendered by Government servants. Any person without distinction of race, occupation, position or sex is eligible for the award which may be awarded posthumously. The names of the persons, upon whom the decoration is conferred, is published in the Gazette of India and a register of all recipients is maintained under the direction of the President. A decoration of toned bronze with embossing in white gold is awarded annually by the President.

• 2583 • Param Vir Chakra
This, the highest decoration for valor, is given for the most conspicuous bravery of some daring or pre-eminent act of valor or self-sacrifice in the presence of the enemy, whether on land, at sea or in the air. Members of the military are eligible.

• 2584 • Param Vishisht Seva Medal
To recognize personnel of all three Services for distinguished service of the most exceptional order.

• 2585 • Shaurya Chakra
For recognition of an act of gallantry. Members of the military are eligible.

• 2586 • Vir Chakra
This, the third in the order of valor awards, is given for acts of gallantry in the presence of the enemy, whether on land, at sea or in the air. Members of the military are eligible.

• 2587 • Vishisht Seva Medal
To recognize personnel of all three Services for recognition of distinguished service.

• 2588 •
Indian Adult Education Association
17-B Indraprastha Marg
New Delhi 110 002, India
Phone: 91 11 3319282
Phone: 91 11 3722206
Fax: 91 11 3366306
E-mail: iaea@vsnl.com

• 2589 • **Nehru Literacy Award**
For recognition of an outstanding contribution to the promotion of literacy and adult education in India. Individuals or institutions are eligible. A monetary award of 21,000 rupees, a plaque, a citation, and a shawl are awarded annually. Established in 1968.

• 2590 •
Indian Council for Cultural Relations
Shri Krishan Kant, Pres.
Azad Bhavan
Indraprastha Estate
New Delhi 110002, Delhi, India
Phone: 91 11 3318421
Phone: 91 11 3318303
Fax: 91 11 3370732
E-mail: iccr@vsnl.com
Home Page: http://education.vsnl.com/iccr

• 2591 • **Jawaharlal Nehru Award for International Understanding**
To recognize a person who has contributed to the promotion of international understanding, goodwill, and friendship among peoples of the world. Individuals may be nominated regardless of nationality, race, creed, or sex. Work achieved within the five years preceding nomination is considered. A monetary prize of about rupees 15 lakhs and a citation are awarded annually. Established in 1965 by the Government of India as a tribute to the memory of Jawaharlal Nehru, independent India's first Prime Minister and his life long dedication to the cause of world peace and international understanding. Sponsored by the Government of India.

• 2592 •
Indian Council of Agricultural Research
Sharad Pawar, Pres.
Krishi Bhavan, Dr. Rajendra Prasad Rd.
New Delhi 110 001, Delhi, India
Phone: 91 11 2388991
Fax: 91 11 387293
Home Page: http://www.icar.org.in

• 2593 • **Dr. Rajendra Prasad Award**
To provide recognition for the best book in the agricultural sciences. Awarded annually.

• 2594 •
Indian Council of Medical Research
Prof. N.K. Ganguly, Dir.Gen.
V. Ramalingaswami Bhawan
Ansari Nagar
New Delhi 110029, Delhi, India
Phone: 91 11 26588895
Phone: 91 11 26588980
Fax: 91 11 26588713
E-mail: icmrhqds@sansad.nic.in
Home Page: http://icmr.nic.in

• 2595 • **Professor B. K. Aikat Oration Award**
To recognize an eminent scientist for outstanding work carried out in the field of tropical diseases. The criteria for award of the prize are the significance and value of the addition to existing knowledge contributed by a worker in the field of tropical diseases in which he has been actively engaged over a number of years and has shown sustained activity in research. A monetary prize of 3,000 rupees is awarded biennially.

• 2596 • **Dr. B. R. Ambedkar Centenary Award for Excellence in Biomedical Research**
To recognize excellence in any field of biomedical research, as evidenced by scientific publications in internationally recognized journals, and contribution to advancement of knowledge and/or improvements in medical practices and health programs. Researchers of any age may be nominated. A monetary prize is awarded biennially. Established in 1991-1992 as part of the Dr. Ambedkar Birth Centenary Celebrations.

• 2597 • **Basanti Devi Amir Chand Prize**
For recognition of work of outstanding merit in any subject in the field of biomedical science, including clinical research. Senior research workers of more than 10 years are eligible. The criteria for award of the prize are the significance and value of the addition to existing knowledge contributed by a worker in a particular field in which he has been actively engaged over a number of years and has shown sustained activity in research. A monetary prize of 5,000 rupees is awarded annually.

• 2598 • **Shakuntala Amir Chand Prizes**
For recognition of the best published research on any subject in the field of biomedical sciences, including clinical research. Clinical research covers research into the mechanism and causation of diseases and its prevention and cure, and includes work on patients in hospitals, field studies in epidemiology and social medicine, and observations in general practice. Both medical and non-medical graduates are eligible. Prizes awarded to Indian nationals for work done in any institution in India. Work started in India but completed abroad will not be acceptable. Papers published both in Indian and foreign journals in the previous two years are considered for the award. Four monetary prizes of 1,500 rupees each are awarded annually.

• 2599 • **BGRC Silver Jubilee Oration Award**
To recognize an eminent scientist for outstanding work carried out in the field of haematology and immunohaematology. The criteria for award of the prize are the significance and value of the addition to existing knowledge contributed by a worker in this specialty in which he has been actively engaged over a number of years and has shown sustained activity in research. A monetary prize of 5,000 rupees is awarded biennially.

• 2600 • **Chaturvedi Ghanshyam Das Jaigopal Memorial Award**
To recognize an eminent scientist for outstanding work carried out in the field of immunology. The criteria for award of the prize are the significance and value of the addition to existing knowledge contributed by a worker on a subject in which he has been actively engaged over a number of years and has shown sustained activity in research. A monetary prize of 3,000 rupees is awarded biennially.

• 2601 • **Chaturvedi Kalawati Jagmohan Das Memorial Award**
For recognition of research in the field of cardiovascular diseases. Eminent scientists, preferably medical persons, are eligible. The criteria include the significance and value of addition to existing knowledge contributed by a worker in cardiovascular diseases in which he or she has been actively engaged over a number of years and has shown sustained activity in research. A monetary prize of 2,000 rupees and a gold medal are awarded triennially.

• 2602 • **Dr. Dharamvir Datta Memorial Oration Award**
To recognize a scientist (medical or non-medical) below 40 years of age for work carried out in the last five years in India in the field of liver diseases. The criteria include significance and value of addition to existing knowledge contributed by a worker in this specialty, with special reference to application of findings to clinical hepatology. A monetary prize of 3,000 rupees is awarded biennially.

• 2603 • **Dr. H. B. Dingley Memorial Award**
To recognize individuals for outstanding contribution to research in the field of Paediatrics by Indian scientists below the age of 40 years. The work to be assessed would be research work carried out in India and published in scientific journals during the 3 years preceding the year for which the award is to be given.

• 2604 • **Smt. Swaran Kanta Dingley Oration Award**
To recognize an eminent scientist for outstanding contribution in the field of reproductive biology. The work should highlight the underlying mechanisms and/or prevention of the various diseases related to reproductive science. A certificate of honor and monetary prize of 20,000 rupees is awarded biennially in odd-numbered years. Established in 1984.

• 2605 • ICMR Prize for Biomedical Research Conducted in Underdeveloped Areas

To recognize an eminent scientist for outstanding contributions in any field of biomedical sciences. The criteria for award of the prize are the significance and value of biomedical research carried out by a worker based in under-developed parts of the country, or for work carried out in under-developed parts of the country over a period of five years preceding the year for which the award is to be given. A monetary prize of 5,000 rupees is awarded annually.

• 2606 • ICMR Prize for Biomedical Research for Scientists Belonging to Under-Privileged Communities

To recognize an eminent scientist for outstanding contributions in any field of the biomedical sciences. The criterion for award of the prize is the significance and value of addition to existing knowledge contributed by a worker in the particular field in which he has been actively engaged over a number of years and has shown sustained activity in research. Scientists belonging to under privileged communities are eligible. A monetary prize of 5,000 rupees is awarded annually.

• 2607 • Dr. M. O. T. Iyengar Memorial Award

To recognize an eminent scientist for an outstanding contribution in the fields of malaria, filariasis, plague or medical entomology. The criteria for award of the prize are the significance and value of the addition to existing knowledge contributed by a worker in any of the fields of malaria, filariasis, plague or medical entomology in which he has been actively engaged over a number of years and has shown sustained activity in research. A monetary prize of 4,000 rupees is awarded annually.

• 2608 • Dr. C. G. S. Iyer Oration Award

To recognize a scientist under the age of 40 for an outstanding contribution in the field of leprosy. The criterion for award of the prize is the significance and value of the addition to existing knowledge contributed by a worker in this specialty in which he/she has been actively engaged over a number of years and has shown sustained activity in research. A monetary prize of 1,500 rupees is awarded biennially.

• 2609 • JALMA Trust Fund Oration Award in the Field of Leprosy

For recognition of outstanding work carried out in the field of leprosy. The criterion for award of the prize is the significance and value of addition to existing knowledge contributed by a worker on any aspect of leprosy in which he or she has been actively engaged over a number of years and has shown sustained activity in research. A monetary prize of 5,000 rupees and a medal are awarded annually.

• 2610 • Lala Ram Chand Kandhari Award

To recognize an eminent scientist for new outstanding research in the fields of dermatology and sexually transmitted diseases. The criteria for the award are the significance and value of the addition to existing knowledge contributed by the worker on a subject in which he has been actively engaged over a number of years and has shown sustained activity in research. A monetary prize of 5,000 rupees is awarded biennially.

• 2611 • Kshanika Oration Award to a Woman Scientist for Research in the Field of Biomedical Sciences

To recognize an eminent woman scientist for outstanding work carried out in any branch of biomedical science, contributing to the alleviation of human suffering. The criteria for award of this prize are the significance and value of the addition to existing knowledge contributed by her in any field of biomedical sciences in which she has been actively engaged over a number of years and has shown sustained activity in research. A monetary prize of 5,000 rupees is awarded annually.

• 2612 • Prof. Surindar Mohan Marwah Award

To recognize an Indian scientist for significant contribution to the field of geriatrics, through sustained research in India on the problems of the aged as evidenced by research papers in science publications. The subject matter could be biomedical or psychosocial research on problems of the aged, both basic and applied. A monetary prize of 20,000 rupees is awarded biennially.

• 2613 • Dr. Kamala Menon Medical Research Award

To recognize an eminent scientist, preferably a medical person, for outstanding contributions to the field of internal medicine and pediatrics. Awards are given in alternate years in the following categories: internal medicine, and pediatrics. The criterion for award of the prize is the significance and value of addition to existing knowledge contributed by a worker on a subject in which he or she has been actively engaged over a number of years and has shown sustained activity in research. A monetary prize of 5,000 rupees is awarded annually.

• 2614 • Amrut Mody-Unichem Prize for Research in Cardiology, Neurology and Gastroenterology

To recognize an eminent scientist for outstanding work carried out in the fields of cardiology and neurology, and gastroenterology. Awards are given in alternate years in the following categories: cardiology and neurology; and gastroenterology. The criteria for award of the prize are the significance and value of the addition to existing knowledge contributed by a worker on a subject in which he has been actively engaged over a number of years and has shown sustained activity in research. A monetary prize of 10,000 rupees is awarded annually.

• 2615 • Amrut Mody-Unichem Prize for Research in Maternal and Child Health and Chest Diseases

To recognize eminent scientists for outstanding work carried out in the fields of maternal and child health, and chest diseases. Awards are given in alternate years in the following categories: maternal and child health, and chest diseases. The criteria for award of the prize are the significance and value of the addition to existing knowledge contributed by a worker on a subject in which he has been actively engaged over a number of years and has shown sustained activity in research. A monetary prize of 10,000 rupees is awarded annually.

• 2616 • Dr. V. N. Patwardhan Prize in Nutritional Sciences

For recognition of outstanding work carried out in India on fundamental, clinical or field studies in nutritional sciences. Eminent scientists, not older than 40 years of age, are eligible. The criteria for the award of the prize are the contribution of a worker to nutritional sciences in which he or she has been actively engaged over a number of years and has shown sustained activity in research. A monetary prize of 7,000 rupees is awarded biennially.

• 2617 • Dr. D. N. Prasad Memorial Oration Award

To recognize an Indian scientist for significant contribution to research in the field of pharmacology, carried out in India, as evidenced by research papers and innovations. The criteria for the award will be the significance and value of addition to existing knowledge in research in pharmacology. A monetary prize of 20,000 rupees and a medal are awarded biennially.

• 2618 • Dr. P. N. Raju Oration Award

For recognition of outstanding work of national importance in the field of medicine or public health. Eminent scientists, preferably medical specialists, are eligible. A monetary prize of 5,000 rupees and an invitation to deliver a lecture are awarded biennially.

• 2619 • Dr. T. Ramachandra Rao Award

To recognize a young scientist under the age of 40 for an outstanding contribution in the field of medical entomology. The criterion for award of the prize is the significance and value of the addition to existing knowledge contributed by a worker in this specialty in which he/she has been actively engaged over a number of years and has shown sustained activity in research. A monetary prize of 3,000 rupees is awarded biennially.

• 2620 • Tilak Venkoba Rao Award

To recognize an eminent scientist for research in the field of psychological medicine and reproductive physiology. Awards are given in alternate years in the following categories: psychological medicine and reproductive physiology. The criterion for the award is the significance of contribution to existing knowledge by a worker who has been actively engaged in research on the subject over a number of years. A monetary prize of 5,000 rupees is awarded annually.

• 2621 • Dr. Y. S. Narayana Rao Oration Award in Microbiology

For recognition of outstanding work in the field of microbiology. The criteria for the award of the prize are the significance and value of the addition to existing knowledge contributed by a worker in the field of microbiology in which he has been actively engaged over a number of years and has shown sustained activity in research. Eminent scientists are eligible. A monetary prize of 4,000 rupees is awarded biennially.

• 2622 • Dr. Vidya Sagar Award

To recognize an eminent scientist for outstanding contributions made in the field of mental health. The criteria for award of the prize are the significance and value of the addition to existing knowledge contributed by a worker in the field of mental health in which he has been actively engaged over a number of years and has shown sustained activity in research. A monetary prize of 5,000 rupees is awarded biennially.

• 2623 • Sandoz Oration Award for Research in Cancer

For recognition of an outstanding contribution toward the control, prevention, and cure of cancer that is recognized nationally and internationally. Eminent scientists are eligible. A monetary prize of 2,500 rupees is awarded biennially.

• 2624 • Smt. Kamal Satbir Award

To recognize individuals for outstanding contribution to research on non-tuberculosis chest diseases, especially respiratory allergy and chronic obstructive lung diseases, pertaining to mechanism and causation of diseases, their prevention and/or management. The work to be assessed would be the research carried out in India and published in scientific journals during the three years preceding the year for which the award is to be given. A monetary prize of 5,000 rupees is awarded annually.

• 2625 • M. N. Sen Oration Award for Practice of Medicine

For recognition of outstanding work in medical practice medical practice (clinical, laboratory or therapeutic). Eminent scientists are eligible. The criterion for award of the prize is the significance and value of addition to existing knowledge contributed by a worker to the practice of medicine in which he or she has been actively engaged over a number of years and has shown sustained activity in research. A monetary prize of 5,000 rupees is awarded biennially.

• 2626 • Dr. M. K. Seshadri Prize in the Field of Practice of Community Medicine

To recognize an eminent scientist or institution whose original work has led to useful inventions in, or otherwise significantly contributed to, the practice of community medicine. A monetary prize of 10,000 rupees and a gold medal are awarded biennially.

• 2627 • Raja Ravi Sher Singh of Kalsia Memorial Cancer Research Award

For recognition of outstanding work in the experimental or clinical aspects of cancer, or in the organization of any service or research program in cancer prevention and treatment. Young physicians under 40 years of age are eligible for work done in the preceding year. A monetary prize of 2,000 rupees is awarded biennially.

• 2628 • Maj. Gen. Saheb Singh Sokhey Award

To recognize a scientist below the age of 40 years for his or her outstanding contribution to the field of communicable diseases. The facets of work to be considered could be basic or applied research that adds to the knowledge on the mechanism and causation of communicable diseases, their prevention and/or their management. The work to be assessed would be the research carried out in India and published in scientific journals, during the three years preceding the year for which the award is to be given. A certificate of honor and monetary prize of 10,000 rupees is awarded annually. Established in 1988.

• 2629 • Dr. J. B. Srivastav Award in the Field of Virology

To recognize an eminent scientist for outstanding work in virology. The criterion for award of the prize is the significance and value of addition to existing knowledge contributed by a worker in virology in which he or she has been actively engaged over a number of years and has shown sustained activity in research. A monetary prize of 10,000 rupees is awarded biennially.

• 2630 • Prof. B. C. Srivastava Foundation Award

To recognize a scientist under 40 years of age for work in the field of community medicine in medical colleges/recognized institutions. The criterion for the award is the significance of research contributions to the practice of community medicine by a worker. A monetary prize of 5,000 rupees is awarded biennially.

• 2631 • Dr. Prem Nath Wahi Award for Cytology and Preventive Oncology

To recognize an eminent scientist for outstanding contribution in the field of basic and/or clinical cytology, and/or preventive oncology. The criterion for the award is the significance and value of addition to existing knowledge contributed by a worker on the subject in which he or she has been actively engaged over a number of years and has shown sustained activity in research. A monetary prize of 30,000 rupees is awarded biennially.

• 2632 •

Indian Dairy Association
Mr. Animesh Banerjee, Pres.
Ida House
Sector IV, R.K. Puram
New Delhi 110 022, Delhi, India
Phone: 91 11 6170781
Phone: 91 11 6165237
Fax: 91 11 2617419
E-mail: ida@nde.vsnl.net.in
Home Page: http://www.indairyasso.org

• 2633 • Best Paper Award

To encourage the dissemination of scientific information. Papers published in the IDA-periodicals, such as *Indian Dairyman* and *Indian Journal of Dairy Science*, are considered. A monetary award and a certificate are presented annually during the Dairy Industry Conference. Established in 1991.

• 2634 • Dr. Kurien Award

To recognize the achievement of dedicated individuals and institutions and to provide impetus for further progress in every field associated with Indian dairying. A monetary prize of 100,000 rupees and a citation are awarded biennially at the time of the Dairy Industry Conference. The first Dr. Kurien Award was given in 1991.

• 2635 • Patrons and Fellows

For recognition of outstanding achievements in the field of dairy science and the dairy industry. Nomination is required. A plaque and citation are awarded from time to time to Patrons and Fellows at the general body meeting or any other important function. Established in 1978.

• 2636 •

Indian Institute of Architects
Balbir Verma, Pres.
Prospect Chambers Annex
Dr. D.N. Rd., Ft.
Bombay 400001, Maharashtra, India
Phone: 91 22 22046972
Phone: 91 22 22046972
Fax: 91 22 22832516
E-mail: iia@vsnl.com
Home Page: http://www.iia-india.org

• 2637 • Baburao Mhatre Gold Medal

To a distinguished architect or man of science who has produced works which promote or facilitate the knowledge of architecture or the various branches of science connected therewith.

• 2638 • Dharmasthala Manjunatheswara Award

For works that are carried out in rural or semi-urban areas For a building or project of any size which reflects outstanding qualities in architecture.

• 2639 • Madhav Achwal Gold Medal

For a teacher, professor, lecturer or administrator who has made a lasting and dedicated contribution of architectural education and community service.

• 2640 • Piloo Mody Surfa Coats Awards
To student For the best project work during its 4th year.

• 2641 • Snowcem Award
For creative excellence and/or unique contribution in the field of architecture.

• 2642 •
Indian Institute of Metals
Shri J.C. Marwah, Hon.Sec.
Plot 13/4, Block AQ, Sector V
Salt Lake City
Calcutta 700091, West Bengal, India
Phone: 91 33 23679768
Phone: 91 33 23677089
Fax: 91 33 23675335
E-mail: iiom@cal2.vsnl.net.in
Home Page: http://www.iim-india.org

• 2643 • Vidya Bharati Prize
To recognize four students who secure highest marks in order of merit in the final B. Tech. B.E./ B.Sc. Eng. in Metallurgy.

• 2644 • Bhoruka Gold Medal
For recognition of significant contributions to process control and development systems in the field of metallurgical industry. A gold medal is awarded. Established by the House of Bhoruka Steel, Bangalore, in memory of P. D. Agarwal's efforts on the industrial front.

• 2645 • Binani Gold Medal
To recognize the contributions made in the non-ferrous group through their reference work and published in the Transactions of the Institute. A gold medal is awarded. Established in 1959 by the House of Binanis.

• 2646 • G. D. Birla Memorial Gold Medal
To recognize a distinguished research worker for continuing and outstanding research work in the field of materials sciences and technology. A medal is awarded. Established in memory of the industrialist, G. D. Birla.

• 2647 • A. K. Bose Medal
To recognize the best Mechanical Engineering Thesis. Established in 1972 in honor of the late Dr. A. K. Bose.

• 2648 • Bralco Gold Medal
To recognize contributions made to the development of the non-ferrous metal industry. A medal is awarded. Established in 1972 by Bralco Metal Industries, Bombay.

• 2649 • Essar Gold Medal
To recognize outstanding contributions to metallurgical industries in general and in the field of secondary steel making, particularly electrometallurgy.

• 2650 • Sir Padamji Ginwala Gold Medal
To recognize a candidate securing the highest marks in the Associate Membership Examination (Part-I) of the Institute. A gold medal is awarded. Established in 1963 in memory of Sir Padamji Ginwala, Ex-President of IIM.

• 2651 • Hindustan Zinc Gold Medal
To recognize distinguished personalities for significant contributions to non-ferrous metallurgical industries and to advance the art and science relating to non-ferrous metallurgical industries. A medal is awarded.

• 2652 • Honorary Member
To recognize distinguished service to the metallurgical profession and to the IIM.

• 2653 • Indian Institute Metals Platinum Medal
To recognize an eminent metallurgist for his outstanding contributions to the metallurgical profession and to create an incentive by the recognition of such a contribution. A medal is awarded.

• 2654 • O. P. Jindal Gold Medal
To recognize outstanding contributions to the development of ferrous metals and alloys. Established in 1996.

• 2655 • MECON Award
To recognize outstanding contributions in the development of process engineering and equipment. Established in 1984 by Metallurgical and Engineering Consultants (India) Limited (MECON).

• 2656 • Metallurgist of the Year Award
To recognize contributions to the science and technology of metals. Five awards of 75,000 rupees each are awarded annually.

• 2657 • Quality Awards
To give recognition to the Ferrous and Non-Ferrous divisions of the IIM for the quality, highest product development, profit making, and environmental performances during the previous year. Awarded annually.

• 2658 • Rolling Trophy
To recognize chapters for overall performance and for enrolling the maximum number of new members.

• 2659 • Sail Gold Medal
To recognize the best paper published in the Transactions of the Institute during the preceding year. A medal is awarded. Established in 1933 by Steel Authority of India, Ltd., New Delhi. Formerly: Kamani Gold Medal.

• 2660 • Steel Eighties Award
For recognition of a significant contribution to the steel making technology. A monetary prize is awarded.

• 2661 • Tata Gold Medal
To recognize a distinguished personality actively connected with the metallurgical industry. A medal is awarded. Established in 1980 in honor of Mr. J. R. D. Tata.

• 2662 • Young Metallurgist of the Year Award
To recognize contributions to the science and technology of metals by a young metallurgist. Three awards of 31,000 rupees each are awarded annually.

• 2663 •
Indian Merchants' Chamber
P.N. Mogre, Sec. Gen.
IMC Bldg., IMC Marg
Churchgate
Bombay 400 020, Maharashtra, India
Phone: 91 22 2046633
Fax: 91 22 2048508
E-mail: imc@imcnet.org
Home Page: http://www.IMCnet.org

• 2664 • Community Welfare Award
For outstanding contribution by an individual, firm, association, social welfare organization, relief organization or voluntary organization.

• 2665 • Contribution by Business Community Award
For outstanding contribution by a businessman or executive.

• 2666 • Environment, Agriculture, and Rural Development Award
For outstanding contribution in the field of control of air and water pollution, rural development, and agriculture.

• 2667 • Industry and Technology Award
For any original research, discovery, invention scientific and technical.

• 2668 • Platinum Jubilee Endowment Trust Award
For outstanding contribution towards alleviation of human suffering or any other socially desirable cause.

• 2669 • Promotion of Savings, Consumer Protection, and Export PerFormance Award
For outstanding contribution towards promotion savings, consumer protection, and enhancing export perFormance.

Awards are arranged in alphabetical order below their administering organizations

• 2670 •
Indian National Science Academy
Shri S.K. Sahni, Exec.Sec.
Bahadur Shah Zafar Marg
New Delhi 110 002, Delhi, India
Phone: 91 11 23221931
Phone: 91 11 23221950
Fax: 91 11 23235648
E-mail: insa@giasdl01.vsnl.net.in
Home Page: http://www.insa.ac.in

• 2671 • **Dr. Nitya Anand Endowment Lecture**
To recognize a scientist under 50 years of age who has done outstanding work in any area of biomedical research including new drug development. The award is based on work done in India during the previous 10 years. Nominations for consideration for the award are invited from the Fellowship. The lecture is delivered in any institution involved in work in this area but not in the award winner's own institution. The lecturer is paid 25,000 rupees including funds for journeys performed to deliver the lecture. Awarded biennially. Established in 1986 out of an endowment of 130,000 rupees by the Organizing Committee to celebrate the 60th birthday of Dr. Nitya Anand, an eminent chemist and a Fellow of the Academy. The funds came from Dr. Nitya Anand's friends, students and admirers in academic institutions and the pharmaceutical industry.

• 2672 • **Aryabhata Medal**
For recognition of achievement in any branch of science. A copper medal (gold plated) is awarded biennially. Established in 1977.

• 2673 • **Prof. R. K. Asundi Memorial Lecture**
To recognize persons who have made outstanding contributions in the field of spectroscopy. The lecturer is paid an honorarium of Rs. 5,000 and travel expenses for journeys performed to deliver the lecture. Awarded every four years. Established in 1983 from an endowment of 21,000 rupees by the Asundi Endowment Fund to commemorate Professor R.K. Asundi, a Fellow of the Academy, distinguished for research in spectroscopy.

• 2674 • **INSA - Vainu Bappu Memorial Award**
To recognize an astronomer/astrophysicist of international recognition. A monetary award of 25,000 rupees and a bronze medal are awarded. Established in 1985 from an endowment by Mrs. Sunanna Bappu, mother of the late Dr. M.K.V. Bappu, an eminent astronomer and Fellow of the Academy. Awarded triennially. When awarded to a foreign scientist, the international airfare is paid by the Academy.

• 2675 • **Professor Sadhan Basu Memorial Lecture**
To recognize a scientist who has made outstanding contributions in the field of chemical science. An honorarium of 25,000 rupees and travel expenses for journeys performed to deliver the lecture are awarded. Awarded triennially. Established in 1993. First awarded in 1996.

• 2676 • **Homi J. Bhabha Medal**
For recognition of work in the field of experimental physics. A copper medal (silver plated) is awarded triennially. Established in 1978.

• 2677 • **Professor K.P. Bhargava Memorial Medal**
To recognize eminent scientist who has done outstanding work in the area of Basic Medical Sciences. Applicants must be under the age of 50. A monetary prize of 10,000 rupees and a bronze medal are awarded triennially. Established in 1992 out of an endowment of 50,000 rupees made by Mrs. Savitri Bhargava, to commemorate the memory of the late Professor K.P Bhargava, an eminent Pharmacologist and distinguished Fellow of the Academy. The first award was given in 1996.

• 2678 • **Professor Krishna Sahai Bilgrami Memorial Medal**
To recognize a sceintist who has made outstanding contributions in the field of plant sciences including agriculture and forestry. A monetary prize of 25,000 rupees and a bronze medal are awarded triennially. Established in 1998.

• 2679 • **Satyendranath Bose Medal**
For recognition of achievement in the field of theoretical physics. A copper medal (silver plated) is awarded triennially. Established in 1977.

• 2080 • **Anil Kumar Bose Memorial Award**
For recognition of the best research paper published in a reputable journal by a recipient of the INSA Medal for Young Scientists on work done in India within five years from the date of receipt of the INSA Young Scientist Medal. Two monetary prizes of 1,000 rupees and a bronze medal are awarded in physical sciences and biology.

• 2681 • **Jagdish Chandra Bose Medal**
For recognition of contributions to biochemistry, biophysics, molecular biology, and related fields. A copper medal (silver plated) is awarded triennially. Established in 1977.

• 2682 • **Dr. Guru Prajad Chatterjee Memorial Lecture**
For recognition of outstanding contributions in engineering sciences. The lecture is to be given once every five years. The lecturer is paid an honorarium of Rs. 5,000/- and travel expenses for journeys made to deliver the lecture. Established in 1979 from an endowment of 15,000 rupees by Dr. G.P. Chatterjee and Mrs. Suniti Chatterjee to commemorate Dr. Guru Prasad Chatterjee, an eminent metallurgist and Fellow of the Academy.

• 2683 • **Bashambar Nath Chopra Lecture**
For recognition of a distinctive contribution in any branch of biological sciences. The lecturer is paid an honorarium of 5,000 rupees besides expenses for the journey to deliver the award lecture. Awarded triennially. Established in 1968 from an endowment of 10,000 rupees in memory of Dr. B.N. Chopra by his family.

• 2684 • **Indira Gandhi Prize for Popularization of Science**
To encourage and recognize popularization of science in any Indian language including English. The nominee must have had a distinguished career as a writer, editor, journalist, lecturer, radio or television program director, science photographer or as an illustrator, which has enabled him/her to interpret science (including medicine), research and technology to the public. He/she should have a knowledge of the role of science, technology and research in the enrichment of cultural heritage and in the solution of problems of humanity. The prize is open to any Indian national residing in the country. A monetary prize of 10,000 rupees and a bronze medal are awarded. Established in 1986. Established in 1986.

• 2685 • **Golden Jubilee Commemoration Medal for Biology**
For recognition in the field of biological sciences. A copper medal (silver plated) is awarded triennially. Established in 1986.

• 2686 • **Golden Jubilee Commemoration Medal for Chemistry**
For recognition in the field of chemical sciences. A copper medal (silver plated) is awarded triennially. Established in 1986.

• 2687 • **Bires Chandra Guha Memorial Lecture**
To recognize a scientist who has made an outstanding contribution in the field of biochemistry, nutrition, food and allied sciences. The lecturer is paid an honorarium of 5,000 rupees and expenses for the journey to deliver the award lecture. Awarded triennially. Established in 1965 from an endowment of 10,000 rupees by Dr. (Mrs.) Phulrenu Guha in memory of her husband, Professor Bires Chandra Guha, FNA.

• 2688 • **Chandrakala Hora Memorial Medal**
To recognize an eminent scientist who has done outstanding work in the development of fisheries, aquatic biology, and related areas in India during the five years preceding the year of award. A bronze medal is awarded every five years. Established in 1945 from an endowment of Rs. 3,000/- by Dr. and Mrs. S.L. Hora in memory of their daughter.

• 2689 • **INSA Medal for Young Scientists**
For recognition of outstanding work in the field of science and technology. Any citizen of India below the age of 32 is eligible for nomination. Bronze medals and a cash prize of 25,000 rupees (maximum 15 awards per year however, in

extraordinary cases when exceptionally good scientists have been identified for recognition, this number may be increased to 20) are awarded annually. In addition, in exceptional cases, the recipient may be considered for start-up research support with seed money.

• 2690 • Daulat Singh Kothari Memorial Lecture Award

To recognize a scientist who has made an outstanding contribution to any branch of science. A lectureship and an honorarium of 5,000 rupees are awarded triennially. Established in 1993 from the General Funds of the Academy in the memory of the late Professor Daulat Singh Kothari, an esteemed Fellow and a past President of the Academy. The first award was made in 1996.

• 2691 • K. S. Krishnan Memorial Lecture

To recognize a scientist who has made an outstanding contribution to any branch of science. A lectureship and an honorarium of 5,000 rupees are awarded triennially (two awards: one in biological sciences and one in physical sciences). Established in 1965 in memory of Professor Kariamanikkam Srinivasa Krishnan, a Fellow of the Academy. Established in 1969.

• 2692 • Prof. L. S. S. Kumar Memorial Award

To recognize a recipient of INSA Medal for Young Scientists in the disciplines of Plant Sciences, Animal Sciences and Agriculture by rotation. In case of more than one person being recommended by the Sectional Committee for the award of the INSA Medal for Young Scientists, the person who is first in order of merit in the list is given the award. A monetary award of 1,000 rupees is awarded annually. Established in 1986.

• 2693 • Prasanta Chandra Mahalanobis Medal

For recognition of an outstanding contribution to the advancement of engineering and technology. A copper medal (silver plated) is awarded triennially. Established in 1978.

• 2694 • Prof. Panchanan Maheshwari Memorial Lecture

To recognize persons who have made outstanding contributions in any area of plant sciences. The lecture is to be given once every four years and is held alternately with the T.S. Sadasivan Lecture. The lecturer is paid an honorarium of Rs. 5,000/- besides travel expenses to deliver the lecture. Established in 1984 from an endowment of 26,200 rupees by the colleagues and friends of the late Professor Panchanan Maheshwari, a distinguished botanist and a Fellow of the Academy.

• 2695 • Meghnad Saha Medal

For recognition of a distinguished contribution to science. A copper medal (gold plated) is awarded biennially. Established in 1958.

• 2696 • Sisir Kumar Mitra Memorial Lecture

For recognition of a distinguished contribution to any branch of the sciences. A lectureship and an honorarium of 5,000 rupees are awarded triennially (two awards: one for biological sciences and the other for physical sciences). Established in 1963 in memory of Professor Sisir Kumar Mitra, a foundation fellow and past president of the Academy.

• 2697 • Professor K. Naha Memorial Medal

To recognize eminent scientist who has done outstanding work in the area of Earth Science. A monetary prize of 25,000 rupees and a bronze medal are awarded triennially. Established in 1996 from an endowment of 3.00 lakhs by the family members of Professor Naha to commemorate the memory of late Professor K. Naha, an eminent geologist of our country. The first award was made in 1998.

• 2698 • Professor Vishnu Vasudeva Narlikar Memorial Lecture

To recognize scientist who has made outstanding contributions in the field of Applied Mathematics, including Gravitational Theory. The lecturer is paid an honorarium of 25,000 rupees plus travel expenses for journeys performed to deliver the lecture. Awarded triennially. Established in 1992 out of an endowment of 1 lakh rupees by the family members and a close friend of late Professor V. V. Narlikar to commemorate him. Established in 1994.

• 2699 • Professor Vishwa Nath Memorial Lecture

To recognize scientist who have made outstanding contribution in the field of cell biology. Nominees must be under the age of 50. An honorarium of 25,000 rupees and travel expenses for journeys performed to deliver the lecture are awarded. Awarded triennially. Established in 1992. First awarded in 1995.

• 2700 • Jawaharlal Nehru Birth Centenary Lectures

To recognize an Indian scientist. Up to two lecturers receive an honorarium of 5,000 rupees each and travel expenses for delivering the lectures.

• 2701 • Jawaharlal Nehru Birth Centenary Medal

For recognition of international cooperation in science and technology. Scientists of all nations are eligible. A bronze medal, citation and travel expenses are awarded annually. Established in 1989.

• 2702 • Jawaharlal Nehru Birth Centenary Visiting Fellowship

To select scientists to visit scientific institutions in other countries for a period of up to 4 weeks. Travel and per diem expenses are awarded.

• 2703 • Professor Brahm Prakash Memorial Medal

To recognize eminent scientist who has done outstanding work in any area of Engineering and Technology. A monetary prize of 10,000 rupees and a bronze medal are awarded triennially. Established in 1987 from an endowment 25,000 rupees from Mrs. R. Brahm Prakash and 29,003 rupees subsequently dontated by friends of late Dr. Brahm Prakash, an eminent Fellow of the Academy. The first award was given in 1989.

• 2704 • Prof. M. R. N. Prasad Memorial Lecture

To recognize an individual who has made an outstanding contribution in the field of animal physiology in its widest sense. The lecture is to be given once in three years. An honorarium of 10,000 rupees and travel expenses are awarded triennially. Established in 1989.

• 2705 • Prize for Material Sciences

For recognition of outstanding contributions in materials science. Any citizen of India is eligible for consideration for the prize for outstanding work done in India. A monetary prize of 10,000 rupees is awarded biennially. Established in 1986 from an endowment of 50,000 rupees by the Organizing Committee of the International Conference on the Application of Mossbauer Effect, held in 1981.

• 2706 • Professor Shambu Nath De Memorial Lecture

To recognize scientist who has made outstanding contributions in the field of Microbiology in the widest sense. The lecturer is paid an honorarium of 10,000 rupees plus travel expenses for journeys performed to deliver the lecture. Awarded triennially. Established in 1992 out of an endowment of 50,000 rupees by the Organizing Committee of the VIII International Specialised Symposium on Yeasts on behalf of the Association of Microbiologists of India to commemorate Professor S.N. De Distinguished scientist for his research in Microbiology. The first award was made in 1993.

• 2707 • Prof. G. N. Ramachandran 60th Birthday Commemoration Medal

To recognize an individual who has made outstanding contributions in the field of molecular biology, biophysics and crystallography. The lecture is to be given once in three years. The lecturer is awarded a bronze medal, a monetary prize of 25,000 rupees, and travel expenses. Established in 1989.

• 2708 • Chandrasekhara Venkata Raman Medal

For recognition of contributions to the promotion of science. Scholars who have done outstanding work in any branch of science are eligible. A copper medal (silver plated) is awarded biennially. Established in 1979.

• 2709 • K. R. Ramanathan Medal

For recognition in the field of atmospheric sciences and meteorology. A cooper medal (silver plated) is awarded triennially. Established in 1987.

• 2710 • Prof. K. Rangadhama Rao Memorial Lecture

To recognize a person who has done exemplary work in the field of spectroscopy. A lectureship and an honorarium of Rs. 5,000/- are awarded every four years alternately with the Professor Rk Asundi Memorial Lecture. Established in 1979 from the endowment of 10,000 rupees in memory of Dr. K. Rangadhama Rao, an eminent physicist and a distinguished Fellow of the academy, by his students.

• 2711 • Dr. Biren Roy Memorial Lecture

To recognize a scientist who has made outstanding contributions in the filed of physics and engineering, including aeronautics. An honorarium of 25,000 rupees and travel expenses for journeys performed to deliver the lecture are awarded. Awarded triennially. Established in 1993. First awarded in 1995.

• 2712 • Prof. T. S. Sadasivan Lecture

To recognize persons who have made outstanding contributions in any field of botany. The lecturer is paid an honorarium of Rs. 5,000/- besides travel expenses to deliver the lecture. Awarded every four years alternatively with the Professor P. Maheshuari Memorial Lecture. Established in 1982 from an endowment of 25,000 rupees by the Professor T.S. Sadasivan Endowment Committee to commemorate Professor T.S. Sadasivan, a Fellow of the Academy distinguished for research in physiological plant pathology.

• 2713 • Professor Shyam Bahadur Saksena Memorial Medal

To recognize eminent scientist who had done outstanding work in any branch of Botany. A monetary prize of 10,000 rupees and a bronze medal are awarded triennially. Established in 1989 from an endowment of 50,000 rupees by Mrs. Sarla Saksena to commemorate the memory of late Professor Shyam Bahadur Saksena, a distinguished botanist and Fellow of the Academy. The first award was given in the year 1990.

• 2714 • Professor T. R. Seshadri Seventieth Birthday Commemoration Medal

For recognition of meritorious work in any branch of chemistry and chemical technology. Eminent chemists of Indian nationality are eligible. A monetary prize of 5,000 rupees and a bronze medal are awarded triennially. Established in 1971 by an endowment of 10,000 rupees by the students of Professor T. R. Seshadri, an eminent organic chemist and a Fellow of the Academy.

• 2715 • Dr. Jagdish Shankar Memorial Lecture

Recognizes a scientist who has made outstanding contributions in the field of Chemical Sciences. Established in 1992. First awarded in 1994.

• 2716 • Shanti Swarup Bhatnagar Medal

For recognition of an outstanding contribution to any branch of science. A copper medal (gold plated) is awarded biennially. Established in 1959.

• 2717 • Shri Dhanwantari Prize

To recognize an eminent scientist who has done outstanding work in the field of medical sciences in its widest sense including research in drugs and methodology of Ayurveda. This includes research in medical as well as chemical, physical and biological sciences aimed at the amelioration of human suffering. Its scope shall also include any outstanding discovery in drugs, mode of treatment, or inventions considered as a landmark in medical sciences in its widest sense. A monetary prize of 5,000 rupees and a bronze medal are awarded. Established in 1969 by an endowment of 18,500 rupees by Shri A.K. Asundi in memory of his youngest daughter, Shrimati Akkadevi.

• 2718 • Silver Jubilee Commemoration Medal

For recognition of an outstanding contribution to the agricultural sciences and applied sciences. A copper medal (silver plated) is awarded triennially. Established in 1970.

• 2719 • Srinivasa Ramanujan Medal

For recognition of outstanding work in the field of mathematics or a related subject. A copper medal (silver plated) is awarded triennially. Established in 1962.

• 2720 • Dr. Yellapragada SubbaRow Memorial Lecture

To recognize a scientist who has made outstanding contributions in the field of biomedical science. An honorarium of 25,000 rupees and travel expenses for journeys performed to deliver the lecture are awarded. Awarded triennially. Established in 1995. First awarded in 1996.

• 2721 • Sunder Lal Hora Medal

To recognize a scientist who has distinguished himself in plant and animal sciences. A copper medal (silver plated) is awarded triennially. Established in 1960.

• 2722 • Professor S. Swaminathan 60th Birthday Commemoration Lecture

To recognize scientist who has made outstanding contributions in the field of Chemical Sciences. The lecturer is paid an honorarium of 10,000 rupees plus travel expenses for journeys performed to deliver the lecture. Awarded biennially. Established in 1990 out of an endowment of 75,000 rupees by Professor S. Swaminathan 60th Birthday Commemoration Committee. The first award was made in 1992.

• 2723 • Professor Har Swarup Memorial Lecture

For recognition of outstanding contributions in the field of zoology. The lecture is to be given once in five years. The lecturer is paid an honorarium of Rs. 5,000/- besides travel expenses for journeys performed to deliver the lecture. Established in 1981 from an endowment of 10,000 rupees by Dr. (Mrs.) Savitri Swarup to commemorate Professor Har Swarup, a Fellow of the Academy distinguished for his researches on endocrinology, physiology and developmental biology.

• 2724 • Prof. B. D. Tilak Lecture

To recognize persons who have made outstanding contributions to rural economy and life through innovative and effective application of science and technology. The lecturer is paid an honorarium Rs. 10,000/- besides travel expenses for journeys performed to deliver the lecture. Awarded annually. Established in 1982 from an endowment of 100,000 rupees by Professor B.D. Tilak Scientific Research and Education Trust, % National Chemical Laboratory, Pune, to commemorate Professor B.D. Tilak, a Fellow of the Academy, distinguished for research in the field of dyestuffs chemistry and organic chemical technology.

• 2725 • Dr. T.S. Tirumurti Memorial Lecture

To recognize persons who have made outstanding contributions in the field of medical sciences. The lecturer is paid an honorarium Rs. 5,000/ besides travel expenses for journeys performed to deliver the lecture. Awarded biennially. Established in 1985 from an endowment of 25,000 rupees by Mrs. Janaki Ramachandran, daughter of the late Dr. T.S. Tirumurti, who made notable contributions to pathology and medicine and was a Foundation Fellow of the Academy.

• 2726 • Vishwakarma Medal

To recognize eminent scientists who have done outstanding work or whose discovery or invention has led to the start of a new industry in India or to a significant improvement of an existing process resulting in a cheaper or better product. A monetary prize of 7,500 rupees and a bronze medal are awarded triennially. Established in 1976 from an endowment of 30,000 rupees by Dr. P.B. Sarkar, FNA.

• 2727 • Darashaw Nosherwanji Wadia Medal

To recognize an individual who has done outstanding work in the field of earth sciences (geology, geophysics, geography). A copper medal (silver plated) is awarded triennially. Established in 1977.

• 2728 • S. H. Zaheer Medal

To recognize an individual who has made outstanding contributions in the field of engineering and technology. A copper medal (silver plated) is awarded triennially. Established in 1980.

• 2729 •
Indian Pharmaceutical Association
S.D. Joag, Hon.Gen.Sec.
Kalina
Santa Cruz
Bombay 400 098, Maharashtra, India
Phone: 91 22 26671072
Fax: 91 22 26670744
E-mail: ipacentr@mtnl.net.in
Home Page: http://www.indianpharma.org

• 2730 • **Eminent Pharmacist Award**
Tor outstanding pharmacists.

• 2731 • **IJPS Best Paper Award**
For pharmaceutical scientists.

• 2732 • **IRF Lifetime Achievement Award**
For senior pharmacists.

• 2733 • **Prof. M.L. Khorana Memorial Award**
For students.

• 2734 • **Prof. M.L. Schroff Award**
For students.

• 2735 •
Indian Physics Association
Dr. V.C. Sahni, Pres.
PRIP Shed, Rm. No. 4
Bhabha Atomic Research Centre
Trombay
Bombay 400085, Maharashtra, India
Phone: 91 22 25505138
Fax: 91 22 25505151
E-mail: ipa@hbcse.tifr.res.in
Home Page: http://www.tifr.res.in/~ipa

• 2736 • **R. D. Birla Award**
To provide recognition for achievement in the field of physics. The Sarbadhikari Gold Medal is awarded. Established in 1980.

• 2737 •
Indian Science Congress Association
Prof. B.P. Chatterjee, Gen.Sec.
14 Dr. Biresh Guha St.
Calcutta 700017, West Bengal, India
Phone: 91 33 22402551
Phone: 91 33 22474530
Fax: 91 33 22402551
E-mail: iscacal@vsnl.net
Home Page: http://www.sciencecongress.org

• 2738 • **Prof. Hira Lal Chakravarty Awards**
To recognize talented young scientists doing significant research in the field of botany within the country. Candidates must be under 40 years of age on December 31 of the preceding year for the Award and must have a Ph.D. degree in any branch of botany, either pure or applied. The awards are given for original, independent, published work carried out in India within three years prior to the award. Applications must be submitted by July 15. A monetary prize of 4,000 rupees and a certificate are awarded annually during the Inaugural Function of the Congress. Two awards are presented. Established in 1984 from a donation received from Professor Hira Lal Chakravarty and Smt. Toru Chakravarty in honor of Professor Hira Lal Chakravarty.

• 2739 • **G. P. Chatterjee Memorial Award**
To recognize a distinguished scientist for his/her outstanding original contribution related to some aspect of the Science of Man. Award is given annually. The awardee may deliver a lecture at the annual session of the Indian Science Congress Association on the subject of his/her specialization. A monetary prize of 10,000 rupees is awarded. Nominations must be received by July 31. Established in 1981.

• 2740 • **Dr. B. C. Deb Memorial Award for Popularisation of Science**
To recognize an Indian national who has sustained interest for popularizing science. The candidate must have a degree in science/technology, be under 45 years old and should have ten years experience in publishing articles/monographs/books for popularizing science. A monetary prize of 5,000 rupees and a plaque is awarded. The recipient will also deliver a lecture on the topic of his/her contributions during the Science Congress. Nominations must be submitted before July 31. Established in 1994-95.

• 2741 • **Dr. B. C. Deb Memorial Award for Soil/Physical Chemistry**
To recognize outstanding contributions in any branch of Soil/Physical Chemistry. Candidates must have published research papers either independently or as a research guide and the research work must have been carried out in India. Candidate also must have a Ph.D. in any branch of Soil/Physical Chemistry and be under 45 years old. A monetary prize of 5,000 rupees and a plaque is awarded. The recipient will also deliver a lecture on the topic of his/her contributions during the Science Congress. Nominations must be received by July 31. Established in 1994-95.

• 2742 • **Raj Kristo Dutt Memorial Award**
The awardee may deliver a lecture on the topic of his/her specialization during the Science Congress. A monetary prize of 10,000 rupees and a plaque is awarded. Nominations for the award will be invited from members of ISCA Council. The lecture is held biennially. Established in 1991.

• 2743 • **B. C. Guha Memorial Lecture**
The topic of the lecture should have some relevance to the science of nutrition and is to be delivered during the annual session of the Indian Science Congress Association. A monetary prize of 3,000 rupees and a plaque is awarded annually. Nomination for the lecture will be invited from the members of the ISCA Council. Established in 1965.

• 2744 • **Asutosh Mookerjee Memorial Award**
To honor a distinguished scientist of the country. A gold medal is awarded annually. Nominations must be received by July 31. The award is in memory of Sir Asutosh Mookerjee, the first General President of Association and a great educationist of the country. Established in 1988.

• 2745 • **Jawaharlal Nehru Birth Centenary Award**
Two awards are given annually by the Association. Each award has a monetary prize of 10,000 rupees and a plaque. Each recipient will be asked to speak, one on Science and Nation Building in the Indian Context and the other on Outstanding Contributions in Science. Nominations must be submitted by July 31. The awards commemorate the birth centenary of the late Indian Prime Minister, Pandit Jawaharlal Nehru.

• 2746 • **Platinum Jubilee Lectures**
Two lectures in each section are organized by the Association at the Science Congress Session annually. A monetary prize of 2,000 rupees is awarded. Established in 1988 to commemorate the platinum jubilee of the Association.

• 2747 • **C. V. Raman Birth Centenary Award**
To honor a distinguished scientist of the country. A gold medal is awarded annually. Each awardee may be requested to deliver a lecture at the headquarters of a Regional Chapter of ISCA or ISCA Headquarters. Nominations must be received by July 31. Established in 1989.

• 2748 • **Srinivasa Ramanujan Birth Centenary Award**
To honor a distinguished scientist of the country. A gold medal is awarded annually. Nominations must be submitted by July 31. The award was established in 1989 to commemorate the birth of the Indian mathematician Srinivasa Rmamnujan. Each awardee may be requested to deliver a lecture at the headquarters of a Regional Chapter of ISCA or ISCA headquarters.

• 2749 • **Professor R. C. Shah Memorial Lecture**
To recognize an individual who publishes outstanding research papers in any field of organic, pharmaceutical and biological chemistry either independently or under supervisors in India. Award is given annually and candidates should be under 45 years old. A monetary prize of 5,000 rupees and a plaque is awarded. The recipient will deliver a lecture on the topic of his/her contributions in the section of Chemistry during the Science Congress. Nominations must be submitted by July 31. Established in 1989.

• 2750 • **Professor Umakant Sinha Memorial Award**
To recognize an individual's original independent published work in a discipline of Plant Sciences related to Biochemistry, Biophysics Molecular biology or Molecular Genetics applied to

plant sciences. The award is given annually and candidates must be under 40 years old. The recipient has to deliver a lecture on his/her specialization during the Science Congress. A monetary prize of 4,000 rupees and a certificate is awarded. Nominations must be received by July 31. Established in 1991.

• 2751 • **Pran Vohra Award**
To recognize an individual for contributions in Agricultural Science. Candidates must be under 35 years of age on December 31 of the preceding year of the award and have a PhD degree in agricultural sciences from any university or institution in India. Only research carried out in India is considered. A monetary prize of 5,000 rupees and a certificate is awarded annually. Last date of application July 15 each year. The awardee is required to deliver a lecture on the topic of his/her specialization. Established in 1989.

• 2752 • **Young Scientists' Awards**
To encourage young scientists. Candidates must be under 30 years of age and members of the Association. The papers submitted for consideration must not be submitted for any other awards and the work must have been carried out in India. A monetary prize of 25,000 rupees and a Certificate of Merit are awarded annually to 14 recipients, one for each Section of the Association. Established in 1981.

• 2753 •
Indian Society of Agricultural Economics
Dr. V.G. Mutalik-Desai, Hon.Sec.-Treas.
46-48 Esplanade Mansions
Mahatma Gandhi Rd.
Bombay 400 001, Maharashtra, India
Phone: 91 22 22842542
Fax: 91 22 22838790
E-mail: isae@bom7.vsnl.net.in

• 2754 • **Dr. D. K. Desai Prize Award**
Recognizes the best articles published in the *Indian Journal of Agricultural Economics.* A monetary prize is awarded annually.

• 2755 • **Dr. S. R. Sen Prize**
Biennial award for a book on agricultural economics and rural development published by an Indian author below the age of 45 years on the date of publication of the book.

• 2756 •
Indian Society of Soil Science
R.K. Rattan, Sec.
Division of Soil Science and Agricultural Chemistry
Indian Agricultural Research Inst.
New Delhi 110012, Delhi, India
Phone: 91 11 25841991
Fax: 91 11 25841529
E-mail: isss@vsnl.com
Home Page: http://www.isss-india.org

• 2757 • **Best Doctoral Research Presentation Award**

• 2758 • **Fellowship Award**

• 2759 • **Honorary Membership**

• 2760 • **International Congress Commemoration**

• 2761 • **Young Scientist Award**

• 2762 • **Zonal Awards**

• 2763 •
Institution of Electronics and Telecommunication Engineers
D.P. Sehgal PVSM, Pres.
2 Institutional Area
Lodi Rd.
New Delhi 110 003, Delhi, India
Phone: 91 11 24631810
Phone: 91 11 24631810
Fax: 91 11 24649429
E-mail: ietend@bol.net.in
Home Page: http://www.iete.org

• 2764 • **IETE-Prof. S.V.C. Aiya Memorial Award**
To a person For providing guidance in electronics and telecommunication research work.

• 2765 • **IETE-Bimal Bose Award**
To a person For original outstanding contributions in the field of power electronics.

• 2766 • **IETE-Hari Ramji Toshniwal Gold Medal**
To a person For outstanding innovative ideas having practical application in industry.

• 2767 • **IETE-Ram Lal Wadhwa Gold Medal**
To a professional, For outstanding contributions in the field of electronics and telecommunications engineering during the last ten years.

• 2768 • **IETE-Prof. S.N. Mitra Memorial Award**
To a person For outstanding contributions and leadership role in radio broadcast science and technology during the last ten years.

• 2769 • **IETE-Flt. Lt. Tanmaya Singh Dandass Memorial Award**
To a person or group of persons For outstanding contributions in the field of Avionics, covering education, research, design, development and production.

• 2770 • **IETE-Prof. K. Sreenivasan Memorial Award**
For outstanding perFormance in teaching electronics and telecommunication engineering.

• 2771 • **IETE-Lal. C. Verman Award**
To a person For outstanding contributions in the areas of standardization, quality control and precision measurements, during the last ten years.

• 2772 •
International Association of Women in Radio and Television
Jai Chandiram, Pres.
D-2D Munirka
DDA Flats
New Delhi 110 067, Delhi, India
Phone: 91 11 26171259
E-mail: jaichandiram@vsnl.net
Home Page: http://www.iawrt.org

• 2773 • **IAWRT Awards**
To recognize female producers, directors, and journalists in radio and television. Awarded biennially.

• 2774 •
Jamnalal Bajaj Foundation
Bajaj Bhawan, 2nd Fl.
Jamnalal Bajaj Marg
226 Nariman Point
Bombay 400 021, India
Phone: 91 22 2202 3626
Fax: 91 22 2202 2238
Home Page: http://www.indianngos.com/ngosection/awardsjamnalalbajaj2.html

• 2775 • **International Award for Promoting Gandhian Values Outside India**
To recognize an outstanding contribution, made outside India, to any of the following: promotion of peace and harmony among people and friendliness among nations through application of the Gandhian philosophy of truth and non-violence; ending exploitation in any form and seeking solutions to social, cultural, economic, and political problems through Gandhian principles and constructive programs; and innovative work in social organizations with intention to promote Gandhian values of purity of means and ends by awakening moral conscience, fostering community self-reliance, and bringing about harmony of human life with nature. Individuals must be nominated, in writing, by persons belonging to any of the following categories: former members of the Selection Committee for the Award; persons who have received the Award in the past; members of National Parliaments; recipients of the Nobel Peace Prize; the Secretary General of the United Nations and other leaders or officials of international organizations whose aims are consistent with the objects of the Award; Presidents and Vice-Chancellors of universities and professors of political science, philosophy, religion, economics, sociology, education, rural development, natural sciences, environment, and ecology; heads of Indian embassies and missions in India and abroad and India's permanent representatives to the UNO and similar world organizations; heads of academic institutions and social work organizations; and any other person whom the Trustees may wish to invite to submit proposals for the Award. Self-nominations are not accepted. A monetary award equivalent of Rs. 2 lakhs in for-

eign currency, a trophy, and a citation are given annually. The award is presented November 4 at the Foundation. Established in 1988 to commemorate the birth centenary of Jamnalal Bajaj, a close associate of Mahatma Gandhi.

• 2776 • Jamnalal Bajaj Foundation Awards

To recognize the outstanding contribution of individuals. Three awards are given to individuals in India: Award for Outstanding Contribution in the Field of Constructive Work; Award for Application of Science & Technology for Rural Development; Award for Outstanding Contribution to Uplift the Welfare of Women and Children. A fourth award, the International Award for Promoting Gandhian Values Outside India, is presented to residents outside of India. The awards carry a citation, a trophy, and a monetary award presented at a special function held on or around the 4th of November every year.

• 2777 •
National Academy of Music, Dance and Drama
Rabindra Bhavan
Ferozeshah Rd.
New Delhi 110 001, India
Phone: 91 11 2338 7246
Fax: 91 11 2338 5715
E-mail: sangeetnatak@bol.net.in
Home Page: http://www.sangeetnatak.com

• 2778 • Sangeet Natak Akademi Fellowships

To recognize the services and achievements of eminent artists in the performing arts. Winners are selected by the General Council of the Akademi. A purse of 25,000 rupees and a woolen shawl are awarded on special occasions such as the 10th Anniversary, 20th Anniversary, Silver Jubilee, etc. A maximum of 30 fellowships may be awarded to living recipients, past and present. Established in 1960.

• 2779 •
Operational Research Society of India
Manjusri Basu PhD, Honorary Sec.
39, Mahanirvan Rd.
Calcutta 700029, West Bengal, India
Phone: 91 33 24644213
E-mail: orsihq39@dataone.in
Home Page: http://www.ifors.org/national/India.shtml

• 2780 • Prof. M.N. Gopalan Award

For best doctoral thesis presented.

• 2781 • Prof. N.K. Jaiswal Memorial Award

For best theoretical paper presented.

• 2782 • Prof. B.G. Raghavendra Memorial Award

For best student paper presented.

• 2783 •
Optical Society of India
Prof. L.N. Hazra, Gen.Sec.
Department of Applied Physics
Calcutta University
92, Acharya Prafulla Chandra Rd.
Calcutta 700 009, India
Phone: 91 33 23508386
E-mail: osi@cucc.ernet.in
Home Page: http://www.osikerala.org/osi.htm

• 2784 • Optical Society of India Award

To recognize a scientist of Indian origin having made significant contribution in the field of optics and optoelectronics. Candidates must have been members of the OSI for at least last three consecutive years and must have a membership for at least ten years in total.

• 2785 • Satgur Prasad-Prag Parmeshwari Devi Memorial Award

To recognize the best presentation of a research paper at the Symposium of the OSI. Candidates must be under 30 years of age.

• 2786 • Harvans Singh Memorial Award

Recognizes the article published in the *Journal of Optics*. Scientists under 30 years of age are eligible. Awarded periodically.

• 2787 •
Organisation of Pharmaceutical Producers of India
Mr. Ranjit Shahani, Pres.
Peninsula Chambers, Ground Fl.
Ganpatrao Kadam Marg, Lower Parel
Bombay 400 013, Maharashtra, India
Phone: 91 22 24918123
Phone: 91 22 24912486
Fax: 91 22 24915168
E-mail: indiaoppi@vsnl.com
Home Page: http://www.indiaoppi.com

• 2788 • Best Vendor Award

Annual awards of recognition. Two outstanding vendors are honored per year.

• 2789 •
Sahitya Akademi - India's National Academy of Letters
(Sahitya Akademi)
Rabindra Bhavan
35 Ferozeshah Rd.
New Delhi 110 001, India
Phone: 91 11 338 6626
Fax: 91 11 338 2428
E-mail: secy@sahitya-akademi.org
Home Page: http://www.sahitya-akademi.org

• 2790 • Bhasha Samman

To recognize writers, scholars, editors, collectors, performers, or translators who have done considerable contribution to the propagation, modernization or enrichment of the languages that are not recognized by the Sahity Akademi. Three to four monetary prizes of 50,000 rupees are given annually.

• 2791 • Sahitya Akademi Awards

To recognize outstanding writers for books of high literary merit written in each of the 22 languages of India that are recognized by the Academy. Indian nationals only are eligible. A monetary prize of 50,000 rupees and an inscribed copper plaque are awarded annually by the President of the Sahitya Akademi.

• 2792 • Sahitya Akademi Fellowship

This, the highest literary honor in India, is conferred on persons of undisputed eminence in literature. The highest standard of Fellowship is ensured by limiting the number of living Fellows to 21 at any one time. An inscribed copper plaque is presented to the Fellows, along with a shawl by the President of the Akademi.

• 2793 • Sahitya Akademi Translation Prize

To encourage translation activity in India. This award is given for the best translated creative and critical works in the 22 languages recognized by the Academy. Both the translator and the original author should be Indian nationals. A monetary prize of 15,000 rupees and an inscribed copper plaque are presented annually by the President of the Sahitya Akademi. Established in 1989.

• 2794 •
Society of Biological Chemists, India
C.M. Gupta, Dir./Pres.
Indian Institute of Science
Bangalore 560 012, Karnataka, India
Phone: 91 80 23601412
Fax: 91 80 23601412
E-mail: sbci@satyam.net.in
Home Page: http://www.iisc.ernet.in/sbci

• 2795 • A. Krishnamurthy Award

For the best paper published in an Indian journal.

• 2796 • C.R. Krishnamurthy Award

For the best work done in the field of biochemistry and allied sciences in India

• 2797 • P.B. Rama Rao Memorial Award

For the best work done in the field of biochemistry and allied sciences in India.

• 2798 • P.S. Sarma Memorial Award

For the best work done in the field of biochemistry and allied sciences in India.

• 2799 • Prof. M. Shadakshara Swamy Endowment Lecture Award

For eminent teachers in biological chemistry and allied sciences at the postgraduate level in Indian universities, deemed universities and institutions of higher learning For their contributions in teaching and research.

• 2800 • Sreenivasaya Memorial Award
For the best work done in the field of biochemistry and allied sciences in India.

• 2801 •
Sulabh International Social Service Organisation
B.B. Sahay, Hon.Chm.
Sulabh Bhawan
Mahavir Enclave
Palam Dabri Marg
New Delhi 110 045, Delhi, India
Phone: 91 11 25032617
Phone: 91 11 25031518
Fax: 91 11 25034014
E-mail: sulabh1@nde.vsnl.net.in
Home Page: http://www.sulabhinternational.org

• 2802 • Global Sanitation Award
To recognize an organization for its critical role in the promotion of hygiene, environmental sanitation, and social justice. A gold medal and monetary prize are awarded annually. Established in 2002.

• 2803 •
Tibetan Youth Congress
Kalsang Phuntsok Gordukpa, Pres.
PO Box Mcleod Ganj
Dharamsala 176 219, Himachal Pradesh, India
Phone: 91 1892 221554
Phone: 91 1892 221239
Fax: 91 1892 221849
E-mail: tyc@vsnl.com
Home Page: http://www.tibetanyouthcongress.org

• 2804 • Culture and Literature Award
Recognizes outstanding contribution to the field of Tibetan literature and culture. Applicants must be Tibetan citizens. Awarded triennially.

• 2805 • Social Service Award
Triennial award of recognition.

• 2806 •
Urological Society of India
Ajay Kumar, Honorary Sec.
Palm View Hospital
Ambedkar Park
Khajpura
Patna 800014, Bihar, India
Phone: 91 612 2598738
Phone: 91 612 2598738
Fax: 91 612 2597969
E-mail: drajaypatna@rediffmail.com

• 2807 • Member Travel Fellowship
For an individual who has been a full member For a minimum of three years.

• 2808 • Dr. G.M. Phadke Oration
For the best orator.

• 2809 • Late G.M. Phadke Travelling Award
For a senior post graduate student.

• 2810 • President's Gold Medal
For a member's outstanding contribution to the progress of urology in India.

• 2811 • Dr. R. Sitharman Memorial Essay Competition
For the best essay written by a member of the society.

• 2812 • Teacher Travel Fellowship Award
For a teacher in urology.

• 2813 •
World Association for Small and Medium Enterprises
Dr. Arun Agrawal, Sec.Gen.
Plot 4, Sector 16A
Noida 201 301, India
Phone: 91 120 2515241
Fax: 91 120 2515243
E-mail: wasme@vsnl.com
Home Page: http://www.wasmeinfo.org

• 2814 • Legion of Honor Award
For recognition of outstanding achievement in the field of small and medium enterprises. Individuals who have at least 15 years of uninterrupted service to the small and medium enterprises sector in any part of the world either at national, regional, or global level irrespective of age, religion, or citizenship are eligible. A gold medal and a citation are awarded biennially. Established in 1980.

Indonesia

• 2815 •
Gadjah Mada University
Center for Population and Policy Studies
Bulaksumur G-7
55281 Yogyakarta, Indonesia
E-mail: agusdwi@cpps.or.id
Home Page: http://www.cpps.or.id

• 2816 • Masri Singarimbun Research Awards
To enhance the opportunities of junior researchers in Indonesia and to develop networking among advanced researchers concerned with reproductive health issues.

• 2817 •
Indonesian Planned Parenthood Association
(Perkumpulan Keluarga Berencana Indonesia)
Inne Silviane, Contact
Jalan Hang Jebat III/F3
PO Box 6017
Kebayoran Baru
12120 Jakarta, Indonesia
Phone: 62 21 7394123
Phone: 62 21 7207372
Fax: 62 21 7253172
E-mail: pkbinet@link.net.id
Home Page: http://www.pkbi.or.id

• 2818 • IPPA Award
Awarded for outstanding policy. A medal is presented annually.

Iran

• 2819 •
Children's Book Council of Iran
Ms. N. Ansari, Gen.Sec.
PO Box 13145-133
PO Box 13145-133
Tehran, Iran
Phone: 98 21 6408074
Phone: 98 21 6950217
Fax: 98 21 6415878
E-mail: anmo@kanoon.net
Home Page: http://www.schoolnet.ir/~cbc

• 2820 • CBCI Award
(Jayezeye Shoraye Ketabe Koudak)
For recognition of a contribution in the field of children's literature in Iran. Iranian writers, illustrators, and translators are eligible. A plaque or diploma is awarded annually at the Founding Day Celebration. Established in 1971 by A. Yamini Sharif.

Ireland

• 2821 •
Arts Council of Ireland
Patricia Quinn, Dir.
70 Merrion Sq.
Dublin 2, Dublin, Ireland
Phone: 353 1 6180200
Fax: 353 1 6761302
E-mail: info@artscouncil.ie
Home Page: http://www.artscouncil.ie

• 2822 • Macaulay Fellowship
To further the liberal education of young creative artists. Awards are given in alternate years in the following categories: visual arts, music composition, and literature. Artists born in Ireland who are under 30 years of age on June 30 or under 35 in exceptional circumstances are eligible. A monetary award of 5,000 euros is awarded annually. Established in 1958 by W.B. Macaulay in honor of President Sean T. O'Kelly.

• 2823 • Marten Toonder Award
For recognition of works by an artist of established reputation in the fields of literature, music composition, or visual arts. Awards are given in alternate years in the three categories. A mone-

tary prize of 10,000 euros is awarded triennially. Established in 1977 by Marten Toonder, a Dutch author.

• 2824 •
AXA Dublin International Piano Competition
AXA Insurance
Dublin Rd.
Bray, Wicklow, Ireland
Phone: 353 1 272 1523
Fax: 353 1 272 1508
E-mail: pianos@iol.ie
Home Page: http://www.axadipc.ie

Formerly: (1995) GPA Dublin International Piano Competition - Guradian Dublin International Piano Competition.

• 2825 • **AXA Dublin International Piano Competition**
For recognition of outstanding piano performances. Professional pianists between 17 and 30 years of age are eligible. The following prizes are awarded: first prize - 12,000 Euro; second prize - 9500 Euro; third prize 6000 Euro; fourth prize - 5000 Euro; fifth prize 3500 Euro; sixth prize 2500 Euro; 1500 Euro to the best placed Irish competitor; six prizes of 900 Euro to the semi-finalists; and twelve prizes of 500 Euro each to those eliminated after the second round. A Kawai piano, debut recitals in London, New York, and other major cities as well as a substantial list of engagements are also awarded to the first prize winner. Held triennially. Established in 1988. Sponsored by AXA Insurance.

• 2826 •
Cork Film Festival
Eimear OKBrien, Press Off.
Emmet House
Emmet Pl.
Cork, Ireland
Phone: 353 21 427 1711
Fax: 353 21 427 5945
E-mail: info@corkfilmfest.org
Home Page: http://www.corkfilmfest.org

Formerly: (1997) Cork International Film Festival.

• 2827 • **Cork International Film Festival**
To recognize and reward excellence in the making of short films. To be eligible, films must have been completed in the two years prior to the festival and be 30 minutes or less in duration. The following awards are presented: Best International Short film; Best European Short Film; Best Irish Short Film; Claire Lynch Award for Irish shorts by first-time directors; Made in Cork Award; Youth Jury Award; Outlook Award; Gradam Gael Linn Award for the best short in the Irish language; Audience Awards; and the Best of Festival award. Held annually. Established in 1956.

• 2828 •
Cork International Choral Festival
Festival House
15 Grand Parade
Cork, Ireland
Phone: 353 21 4223 535
Fax: 353 21 4223 536
E-mail: chorfest@iol.ie
Home Page: http://www.corkchoral.ie

• 2829 • **Cork International Choral Festival**
To recognize outstanding choirs. Choirs must be organized for at least one calendar year prior to the festival. All members, except the conductor, must be amateurs. Awards are presented in the following categories: school choirs (equal and mixed voice); youth choirs; chamber choirs; female voice choirs; mixed voice choirs; light, jazz, and popular music; and church music. In addition, the following awards are presented: Trofai Chumann Naisiunta na gCor (the Association of Irish Choirs Trophy) for the best performance of a part-song in the school competitions section of the festival; Irish Federation of Musicians & Associated Professions Trophy for the best performance of a part-song in Irish in the school competitions of the festival; John Cunningham Trophy for the best school choir; Trofai Cuimhneachain Philib Ui Laoghaire (The Pilib O'Laoghaire Memorial Trophy) for the best performance of a part-song in Irish in the national adult competitions of the festival; John Mannion Memorial Trophy for the best part-song by a chamber choir; Perpetual Trophy for the Performance of Irish Contemporary Choral Music; and Victor Leeson Perpetual Trophy for the best overall choir in the festival. Held annually. Established in 1954. Formerly: Cork International Choral and Folk Dance Festival.

• 2830 • **Fleischmann International Trophy Competition**
This competition is held as part of the Cork International Choral Festival. It is open to any choir of international standing, with a minimum of 20 and a maximum of 70 voices. First prize is 2,500 euros, second prize is 1,850 euros, and third prize is $1,250 euros. In addition, the following awards are presented: Lady Dorothy Mayer Memorial Trophy, Schuman/Europe Trophy, Heinrich Schutz Perpetual Trophy, International Jury Award, and the P.E.A.C.E. Trophy. Held annually. Established in 1989.

• 2831 •
European Association for Computer Assisted Language Learning
June Thompson, Sec.
Dept. of Language and Cultural Studies
Univ. of Limerick
Limerick HU6 7RX, Limerick, Ireland
Phone: 353 61 202251
Phone: 44 1482 466373
Fax: 353 61 202556
E-mail: margaret.gammell@ul.ie
Home Page: http://www.hull.ac.uk/cti/eurocall/

• 2832 • **EUROCALL Research Award**
Recognizes an outstanding original article on computer-assisted and technology-enhanced language learning. Awarded annually.

• 2833 •
European Health Management Association
Philip C. Berman, Dir.
Vergemount Hall
Clonskeagh
Dublin 6, Ireland
Phone: 353 1 283 9299
Fax: 353 1 283 8653
E-mail: info@ehma.org
Home Page: http://www.ehma.org

Formerly: (1987) European Association of Programmes in Health Services Studies.

• 2834 • **Baxter Award for Healthcare Management in Europe**
To recognize an outstanding publication and/or practical contribution to excellence in healthcare management in Europe. Contributions can be in any of the following fields: management development initiatives, health services research, or innovations in management practice. Books, articles, or papers submitted must have been published within the last two years. The deadline is January 31st. A monetary award of $5,000 is presented at the Annual Conference of the EHMA. Established in 1986, the award is sponsored by Baxter Healthcare.

• 2835 •
Institute for Numerical Computation and Analysis
Dr. Diarmuid Herlihy, Hon.Sec.
19 Silchester Rd.
Glenageary
Dublin 2, Dublin, Ireland
Phone: 353 1 2804838
Fax: 353 1 2804838
E-mail: info@incaireland.org
Home Page: http://www.incaireland.org

• 2836 • **Victor W. Graham Perpetual Trophy**
To recognize a school teacher in Ireland for achievement in applied mathematics. Awarded annually.

• 2837 •
Institute of Chemistry of Ireland
(Institiuid Ceimice Na hEireann)
P.E. Childs MA, Pres.
PO Box 9322
Cardiff Ln.
Dublin 2, Dublin, Ireland
E-mail: info@instituteofchemistry.org
Home Page: http://www.instituteofchemistry.org

• 2838 • **Boyle-Higgins Award**
For research work carried out in chemistry.

• 2839 • **ICI Annual Award for Chemistry**
For major contribution to the area of chemistry.

• 2840 • **ICI-FOSS Golden Jubilee Award**
For best article and abstract on a chemistry-based topic.

• 2841 • **Second Level Education Award**
For students achieving the highest marks in Ireland.

• 2842 •
International Bureau for Epilepsy
(Bureau International pour l'Epilepsie)
Ms. Ann Little, Administration Mgr.
253 Crumlin Rd.
Dublin 12, Dublin, Ireland
Phone: 353 1 4560298
Fax: 353 1 4554648
E-mail: ibedublin@eircom.net
Home Page: http://www.ibe-epilepsy.org

• 2843 • **Ambassador for Epilepsy Award**
Award of recognition. For service to the epilepsy movement. Awarded biennially.

• 2844 • **Award for Social Accomplishment**
For those who have performed outstanding activities aimed at the social benefit of people with epilepsy. A scroll and monetary prize of $1,000 is awarded annually.

• 2845 •
International Songwriters' Association - Ireland
(Association Internationale des Cordeliers)
James D. Liddane, Chm.
PO Box 46
Limerick, Limerick, Ireland
Phone: 353 61 228837
Fax: 352 61 229464
E-mail: jliddane@songwriter.iol.ie
Home Page: http://www.songwriter.co.uk/

• 2846 • **International Songwriters' Association Awards**
To recognize songwriters, music publishers, and recording executives. The Association organizes competitions and bestows awards.

• 2847 •
International Union for Quaternary Research
(Union Internationale pour l'Etude du Quarternaire)
Prof. Peter Coxon, Sec.Gen.
Dept. of Geography
Museum Bldg.
Trinity Coll.
Dublin 2, Dublin, Ireland
Phone: 353 1 6081213
Fax: 47 648211
E-mail: pcoxon@tcd.ie
Home Page: http://www.inqua.tcd.ie/

• 2848 • **Honorary Member**
To recognize individuals for contributions to quaternary research. Lifetime membership is awarded when merited.

• 2849 •
Irish Amateur Rowing Union
Rachel Maher, Administrator
Block 13
Joyce Way
Parkwest Business Park
Nangor Rd.
Dublin 12, Dublin, Ireland
Phone: 353 1 6251130
Phone: 353 1 4501633
Fax: 353 1 6251131
E-mail: info@iaru.ie
Home Page: http://www.iaru.ie

• 2850 • **Rowing Awards**
Award of recognition for performance in rowing. Awarded annually.

• 2851 •
Irish Astronomical Association
Mr. D. Collins, Sec.
3 Vaddegan Ave.
Glengormley
Antrim BT36 7SP, Ireland
Phone: 353 1 2980181
E-mail: iaa2000@btinternet.com
Home Page: http://www.btinternet.com/~jimmyaquarius/

• 2852 • **Aidan P. Fitzgerald Award**
Award of recognition for outstanding service to the association. Awarded periodically.

• 2853 •
Irish Defence Forces
Lt.Gen. Jim Sreenan, Chief of Staff
Parkgate
Dublin 8, Ireland
Phone: 353 1 804 2690
Fax: 353 1 677 9018
E-mail: armypr@iol.ie
Home Page: http://military.ie

• 2854 • **Military Medal for Gallantry (An Bonn Mileata Calmachta)**
This, the highest military honor in the State, is given in recognition of the performance of any act of exceptional bravery or gallantry (other than one performed while on war service) arising out of, or associated with military service, and involving risk to life or limb above and beyond the call of duty. The medal may be awarded in three classes: with honor, with distinction, and with merit. Established in 1944.

• 2855 •
Irish Security Industry Association
Mr. Barry Brady, Exec.Dir.
21 Waterloo Rd.
Dublin 4, Dublin, Ireland
Phone: 353 1 8493426
Phone: 353 1 6070198
Fax: 353 1 8492402
E-mail: info@isia.ie
Home Page: http://www.isia.ie

• 2856 • **ISIA Awards**
Annual awards of recognition for police and community groups. The following awards are presented: Community Person of the Year, National Courage Award, Security Officer of the Year, and the Premier Award.

• 2857 •
The Irish Times
Geraldine Kennedy, Ed.
10-16 D'Olier St.
Dublin 2, Ireland
Phone: 353 1 675 8000
Fax: 353 1 677 3282
E-mail: enquiries@irish-times.com
Home Page: http://www.ireland.com

• 2858 • ***The Irish Times* Literature Prizes**
For recognition of a work of fiction, non-fiction, and poetry. To qualify, the works must be written in the English or Irish language and published in the United States, Ireland, or Britain during the preceding year. A monetary prize is awarded in each category annually. Established in 1988. Sponsored by *The Irish Times*.

• 2859 •
Irish United Nations Veterans Association
Michael Butler, Sec.
Arbour House
Mountemple Rd.
Dublin 7, Dublin, Ireland
Phone: 353 1 6791262
Fax: 353 1 6704015
Home Page: http://www.iunva.com

• 2860 • **Service Medal**
Award of recognition for two years of service to the association.

• 2861 •
Irish Youth Foundation
Liam O'Dwyer, Chief Exec.
Unit 39 Boeing Rd.
Airways Industrial Estate
Santry
Dublin 17, Dublin, Ireland
Phone: 353 1 6055580
Fax: 353 1 6055528
E-mail: info@iyf.ie
Home Page: http://www.iyf.ie

• 2862 • **Irish Youth Foundation Award**
Award of recognition for nongovernmental organizations working with disadvantaged young people. Presented three times per year.

• 2863 •
Monaghan Photographic Society
Belbroid Centre
North Rd.
Monaghan, Monaghan, Ireland
E-mail: info@monaghanphotographicsociety.com
Home Page: http://www.monaghanphotographicsociety.com/index2.html

Awards are arranged in alphabetical order below their administering organizations

• 2864 • **Life Membership**
Awarded to members for outstanding contributions.

• 2865 •
Physical Education Association of Ireland (Cumann Corpoideachais na hEireann)
Dr. Ciaran MacDonncha, Pres.
University of Limerick
The National Technology Park
Limerick, Limerick, Ireland
Phone: 353 61 330442
Phone: 353 61 202867
E-mail: info@peai.org
Home Page: http://www.peai.org

• 2866 • **Honorary Member**
To recognize an individual for outstanding contributions to the development of physical education in Ireland. Present members of the Association must be nominated by the Awards Committee and approved by the annual general meeting. A plaque is awarded when merited. Established in 1985.

• 2867 •
Pitch and Putt Union of Ireland (Aontas Teilgin Agus Amais na h'Eireann)
Michael Murphy, Hon.Sec.
Sport HQ
13 Joyce Way
Park West
Dublin 12, Dublin, Ireland
Phone: 353 1 6251110
Fax: 353 1 6251111
E-mail: ppui@iol.ie
Home Page: http://www.iol.ie/ppui/

• 2868 • **Club Development Award**
Given to clubs for improvement of facilities and/or purchase of equipment. Awarded annually.

• 2869 •
Royal Academy of Medicine in Ireland
John J. O'Connor, Gen.Sec.
6 Kildare St.
20-22 Lower Hatch St.
Dublin 2, Dublin, Ireland
Phone: 353 1 6767650
Phone: 353 1 6623706
Fax: 353 1 6611684
E-mail: secretary@rami.ie
Home Page: http://www.rami.ie

• 2870 • **Donal Burke Memorial Lecture**
An invitation lecture organized by the Section of General Practice of the Royal Academy of Medicine in Ireland. A monetary award and a silver medal are awarded annually. The first lecture was given in 1984.

• 2871 • **Conway Lecture**
To encourage research in the biological sciences. Workers in the biological sciences who are nominated by two Fellows of the Academy are eligible. A monetary award and a silver medal are awarded annually. Established in 1977 by the Biological Sciences Section of the Academy in memory of Edward J. Conway, FRS.

• 2872 • **Graves Lecture**
To encourage clinical research in Ireland. Doctors under 40 years of age who are nominated by two Fellows of the Academy and whose research has been carried out wholly or partly in Ireland are eligible. A monetary award and a silver medal are awarded annually. Established in 1960 by the Royal Academy of Medicine and the Medical Research Council of Ireland in memory of Robert Graves.

• 2873 • **Saint Luke's Lecture**
To encourage research in the field of oncology. Doctors who are nominated by two Fellows of the Academy and whose research has been carried out wholly or partly in Ireland are eligible. A monetary award and a silver medal are awarded annually. Established in 1975 by The Royal Academy of Medicine and Saint Luke's Hospital.

• 2874 • **Silver Medal**
Awarded to the recipients of the Graves Lecture (of clinical interest embodying original research) and the St. LukeKs Lecture (in the field of oncology). Awarded annually.

• 2875 •
Royal Dublin Society
Fiona Sheridan, Marketing Exec.
Ballsbridge
Dublin 4, Dublin, Ireland
Phone: 353 1 6680866
Fax: 353 1 6604014
E-mail: info@rds.ie
Home Page: http://www.rds.ie

• 2876 • **Dublin Horse Show**
For recognition of outstanding exhibits, horses, and riders entered in horse show competitions. Awards are presented in the categories of international jumping, national jumping, showing classes, Samsung Super League, and Hunt Chase. Held annually. Established in 1868.

• 2877 • **Royal Dublin Society Crafts Competition**
For recognition of original crafts of outstanding merit in the following categories: ceramics; glass; gold, silver, and other metals; blacksmithing; wood; rod, rush, and straw; leather; jewelry; weaving; musical instruments; furniture; knitting; embroidery; calligraphy and lettering; printed textiles; patchwork and quilting; and lace. The Competition is open to all craftworkers and designers in Ireland including students and apprentices. The following special awards are presented: Muriel Gahan Scholarship or Development Grant - sponsored by the Irish American Cultural Institute; California Gold Medal a gold medal awarded to the winner of a Class award whose work is considered by the judges to be of outstanding merit; Crafts Council of Ireland Purchase Award; Medal for Traditional Country Craft - sponsored by Country Markets Ltd.; and Lillias Mitchell Prize - for a weaver enlarging his or her vision by research into spinning, weaving, or dyeing (must submit both written and practical work). Royal Dublin Society certificates are given to prizewinners in all categories. The present Crafts Competition was established in 1967 as a replacement for the National Arts Competition, which was held from 1923 until 1967. Sponsored by the Educational Building Society.

• 2878 •
Royal Horticultural Society of Ireland
John Markham, Chm.
Cabinteely House
The Park
Cabinteely
Dublin 18, Dublin, Ireland
Phone: 353 1 2353912
Fax: 353 1 2353912
E-mail: info@rhsi.ie
Home Page: http://www.rhsi.ie

• 2879 • **Banksian Medal**
Annual award of recognition for contribution to horticulture in Ireland. Instituted in 1920 in commemoration of Sir Joseph Banks, one of the founders of the Society.

• 2880 •
Royal Irish Academy (Acadamh Rioga na Heireann)
Patrick Buckley, Exec.Sec.
19 Dawson St.
Dublin 2, Dublin, Ireland
Phone: 353 1 6762570
Phone: 353 1 6764222
Fax: 353 1 6762346
E-mail: info@ria.ie
Home Page: http://www.ria.ie

• 2881 • **Eoin O'Mahony Bursary**
To assist Irish scholars undertaking overseas research on historical subjects of Irish interest. Preference will be given to projects concerning family history, in particular those which are associated with the "wild geese". Special consideration will be given to those who have been active in local learned societies. One or two travel bursaries of are awarded annually. Established in 1978 by friends of the late Eoin O'Mahony, Barrister-at-Law, Knight of Malta, and genealogist who died in 1970.

• 2882 •
Scouting Ireland CSI
Eamonn Lynch, CEO
Larch Hill
Dublin 16, Ireland
Phone: 353 1 4956300
Fax: 353 1 4956301
E-mail: questions@scouts.ie
Home Page: http://www.scouts.ie i

• 2883 • **Honour Award**
Recognizes adults for service under difficult conditions. Gold, silver, and bronze honour awards are awarded when merited, as is the

Chief Scout*K*s Commendation of Honour. Awarded when merited.

• 2884 • Merit Awards
Recognizes adults for service and exceptional character. Gold, silver, and bronze merit awards are awarded when merited, as are the Chief Scout*K*s Commendation and the Thanks Badge.

• 2885 • Service Awards
To recognize adults for service in any recognized Scout or Guide association. A gold award is presented for 25 years of service; silver awards for 15 and 20 years of service; and bronze awards for 5 and 10 years of service. Awarded when merited.

• 2886 •
Shark Awards Festival
Steve Shanahan, CEO
% Institute of Advertising Practitioners in Ireland
8 Upper Fitzwilliam St.
Dublin 2, Ireland
Phone: 353 1 676 5991
Fax: 353 1 661 4589
E-mail: sharks@iapi.com
Home Page: http://www.iapi.ie

• 2887 • Shark Awards, the International Advertising Festival of Ireland
For recognition of the best commercials produced for television, cinema, and radio. Entries must advertise consumer or capital goods, consumer services, or public services and social welfare. Entries are accepted from advertising agencies, production companies, advertisers, and recording studios. Shark Awards*w* are presented in dozens of categories. In addition, the following awards are presented: Grand Prix, for best campaign overall; Palme d'Or, for best production company; Irish Radio Industry Creative Prize; and the Brian Cronin Award for best writing. Held annually in September. Established in 1962. Formerly: (1988) Irish Advertising Awards Festival.

• 2888 •
Tennis Ireland
Mr. Des Allen, CEO
Dublin City University
Glasnevin
Dublin 9, Dublin, Ireland
Phone: 353 1 8844010
Fax: 353 1 8844013
E-mail: info@tennisireland.ie
Home Page: http://www.tennisireland.ie

Formerly: (1995) Irish Lawn Tennis Association.

• 2889 • Raymond Egan Memorial Trophy
To recognize an individual for a contribution to tennis. Players, officials, and administrators at any level may be nominated by a club or a representative body before December 31. A perpetual trophy is awarded annually. Established in 1985 to honor Raymond Egan.

• 2890 •
Traditional Irish Music, Singing and Dancing Society
(Comhaltas Ceoltoiri Eireann)
Senator Labhras O'Murchu, Dir.
32 Belgrave Sq.
Monkstown, Dublin, Ireland
Phone: 353 1 2800295
Fax: 353 1 2803759
E-mail: enquiries@comhaltas.com
Home Page: http://www.comhaltas.com

Formerly: Traditional Irish Singing and Dancing Society.

• 2891 • Traditional Irish Music, Singing and Dancing Awards
To recognize Irish musicians, singers, dancers, and those who wish to promote the Irish tradition of music. The Society sponsors music competitions and bestows awards.

Israel

• 2892 •
Arthur Rubinstein International Music Society
Idith Zvi, Dir.
PO Box 6018
PO Box 6018
IL-61060 Tel Aviv, Israel
Phone: 972 3 6856684
Phone: 972 3 6856628
Fax: 972 3 6854924
E-mail: competition@arims.org.il
Home Page: http://www.arims.org.il/competition2005/pages/english/index.php

• 2893 • Arthur Rubinstein International Piano Master Competition in Conjuction with the Israel Philharmonic Orchestra
To foster young pianists with outstanding musicianship and a talent for persuasive, versatile rendering and creative interpretation of works, ranging from the pre-classical to the contemporary. The competition also aims to establish a world forum for fostering talented and aspiring young interpreters and promoting their future artistic careers. The International Jury's task is to select pianists with more than average concert standard, who have attained a mature intellectual and emotional response to music. The Competition is open to pianists of all nationalities between 18 and 32 years of age. The Screening Committee prefers candidates who have either won top prizes at other important international competitions or who have been recommended specifically by world renowned artists. Six monetary prizes and medals are awarded at the discretion of the Jury: (1) The Arthur Rubinstein Award - $25,000 and a gold medal - first prize; (2) $15,000 and a silver medal - second prize; (3) $10,000 and a bronze medal - third prize; and (4) $3,000 each fourth, fifth, and sixth prizes. The Competition's Secretariat undertakes to help promote the artistic careers of the prize winners by recommending them for engagements with leading orchestras, concert managements and recording companies. Prizes are awarded triennially by the President of the State of Israel at the Laureates Gala Concert in Tel Aviv. Established in 1973.

• 2894 •
Association for Civil Rights in Israel
(Haagudah Lezechuyot Haezrach Beyisrael)
Vered Livne, Contact
PO Box 34510
PO Box 34510
IL-91000 Jerusalem, Israel
Phone: 972 2 6521218
Fax: 972 2 6521219
E-mail: mail@acri.org.il
Home Page: http://www.acri.org.il

• 2895 • Emil Grunzweig Human Rights Award
To recognize an individual or NGO that has made a unique contribution to the advancement of human rights in Israel. Awarded annually.

• 2896 •
Mordechai Bernstein Literary Prizes Association
(Aguda l'Haanakat Prasim Sifrutiim Al Shem Mordechai Bernstein)
Book Publishers Association of Israel
29 Carlebach St.
PO Box 20123
61201 Tel Aviv, Israel
Phone: 972 3 5614121
Fax: 972 3 5611996
E-mail: info@tbpai.co.il
Home Page: http://www.tbpai.co.il

• 2897 • Award for Literary Criticism (Pras l'Bikoret Sifrutit)
To recognize an outstanding newspaper book review of an original Hebrew novel, play, poetry, or short story in the daily Hebrew press. A monetary prize of 10,000 NS is awarded biennially. Established in 1979 to honor Mordechai Bernstein, an Israeli author.

• 2898 • Award for Original Hebrew Novel (Pras l'Roman Ivri Mekori)
To encourage authors under the age of 50 who write Hebrew novels. A monetary award of 50,000 NS is presented biennially. Established in 1977 to honor Mordechai Bernstein, an Israeli author.

• 2899 • Award for Original Hebrew Poetry (Pras l'Sefer Shira Ivri Mekori)
To encourage Hebrew poets under the age of 50. A monetary award of 25,000 NS is presented biennially. Established in 1981 to honor of Mordechai Bernstein, an Israeli author.

• 2900 • First Novel Award
Recognizes the first novel written in Hebrew by an immigrant new to Israel. A monetary award of 20,000 NW is presented biennially. Established in 1999 in honor of Mordechai Bernstein, an Israeli author.

• 2901 • First Poetry Book Award
Recognizes a first poetry book in Hebrew by an immigrant new to Israel. A monetary award of

20,000 NS is presented biennially. Established in 1999 in honor of Mordechai Bernstein, an Israeli author.

• 2902 • Hebrew Play Award
Recognizes an outstanding Hebrew play. A monetary award of 10,000 NS is presented biennially. Established in 1999 in honor of Mordechai Bernstein, an Israeli author.

• 2903 •
International Harp Contest in Israel
(Concours International de Harpe en Israel)
4, Aharonowitz St.
63566 Tel Aviv, Israel
Phone: 972 3 5280233
Fax: 972 3 6299524
E-mail: harzimco@netvision.net.il
Home Page: http://harpcontest-israel.org.il

• 2904 • International Harp Contest in Israel
(Concours International de Harpe en Israel)
To encourage and recognize excellence in playing the harp. Harpists of all nationalities under 35 years of age are eligible. The following prizes are awarded: first prize - Lyon and Healy Concert Grand Harp; second prize, (the Rosalind G. Weindling Prize) - $5,000; a third prize of $3,000 (in memory of Rachel Graetz); and also the Aharon Tzvi & Mara Propes Prize of $1,500 for an Israeli work. Established in 1959 by Aharon Zvi Propes and the Israel Festival.

• 2905 •
Israel Democracy Institute
Prof. Arye Carmon, Pres.
4 Pinsker St.
PO Box 4702
91046 Jerusalem, Israel
Phone: 972 2 530 0888
Fax: 972 2 530 0837
E-mail: info@idi.org.il
Home Page: http://www.idi.org.il

• 2906 • Democracy Award
To recognize a figure of international stature in recognition of his or her significant contribution to strengthening democracy. Awarded annually.

• 2907 •
Israel Geological Society
Yossi Yechieli, Pres.
PO Box 1239
IL-91000 Jerusalem, Israel
E-mail: gsi@igs.org.il
Home Page: http://www.igs.org.il/eng/index.asp

• 2908 • Professor Raphael Freund Award
For an excellent publication in Earth Sciences.

• 2909 • Dr. Peretz Grader Award
For original work in Earth Sciences.

• 2910 • Society Awards
For outstanding research achievement.

• 2911 •
Israel Mathematical Union
Sergiu Hart, Pres.
Institute of Mathematics
The Hebrew University of Jerusalem
Givat Ram Campus
IL-91904 Jerusalem, Israel
E-mail: imu@imu.org.il
Home Page: http://imu.org.il

• 2912 • Erdos Prize
To an Israeli mathematician (pure, applied or from computer science), with preference to candidates up to the age of 40.

• 2913 • Levitzki Prize in Algebra
To a young Israeli mathematician for research in algebra or related areas.

• 2914 • Haim Nessyahu Prize in Mathematics
For excellent dissertation in mathematical sciences.

• 2915 •
Israel Museum
James S. Snyder, Dir.
Public Affairs Dept.
PO Box 71117
Hakiryah
91710 Jerusalem, Israel
Phone: 972 2 6708811
Fax: 972 2 5631833
E-mail: oritar@imj.org.il
Home Page: http://www.imj.org.il

• 2916 • Honorary Fellow
To recognize individuals for outstanding contributions to art and the Israel Museum. Awarded when merited.

• 2917 • Jesselson Prize for Contemporary Judaica Design
To recognize and encourage the design of modern Jewish ceremonial objects, using various materials. Established in 1986 by Ludwig and Erica Jesselson.

• 2918 • Gerard Levy Prize for a Young Photographer
In recognition of achievement by a young, promising Israeli photographer. A monetary award and a certificate are presented annually. Established in 1982 by Gerard Levy of France.

• 2919 • Ya'akov Meshorer Prize
Recognizes outstanding scholars in the field of numismatics. Established in 2001.

• 2920 • Percia Schimmel Award for Distinguished Contribution to Archaeology
For recognition of achievement in the field of archaeology in Eretz-Israel and the Lands of the Bible. A monetary award, a certificate, and a gold-plated engraved medal are presented annually. Established in 1979 by Norbert Schimmel (U.S.A.) in memory of his mother, Percia Schimmel.

• 2921 • The Wolgin Foundation/Israel Museum Fellowships
Provides opportunities for qualified curators, scholar, and research professional to research the rich and diverse collections of the Israel Museum. Awarded annually. Established in 2001.

• 2922 •
Israel Society for Biochemistry and Molecular Biology
Prof. Etana Padan, Pres.
PO Box 9095
IL-52190 Ramat Efal, Israel
Phone: 972 3 6355038
Fax: 972 3 5351103
E-mail: mrgzur@bezeqint.net
Home Page: http://www.weizmann.ac.il/isbmb

• 2923 • Hestrin Prize
(Pras Hestrin)
For recognition of achievement in the field of biochemistry. Israeli citizens under 42 years of age may be nominated. A monetary prize and a plaque are awarded biennially. Established in 1964 in memory of Professor Shlomo Hestrin.

• 2924 •
Jerusalem International Book Fair
PO Box 775
91007 Jerusalem, Israel
Phone: 972 2 629 7922
Fax: 972 2 624 3144
E-mail: jerfairs@jerusalem.muni.il
Home Page: http://www.jerusalembookfair.com

• 2925 • Editorial Fellowship Program
To enable selected editors with at least six to 12 years of experience from the United States and Europe to attend the fair to get to know the Israeli publishing scene and to meet colleagues from different countries. Established in 1985.

• 2926 • Jerusalem Prize for the Freedom of the Individual in Society
To recognize a world-renowned author who has contributed to the world's understanding of the freedom of the individual in society. Winner is chosen by a distinguished panel of judges. A monetary prize of $5,000, a citation from the City of Jerusalem, and travel expenses are awarded biennially by the Mayor of Jerusalem at the Jerusalem International Book Fair. The Fair, held in odd-numbered years, is open to the public for browsing and purchasing. This is not an open prize; applications are not accepted. Established in 1963 by the Jerusalem Municipality.

• 2927 •
Zalman Shazar Center for Jewish History
(Merkaz Zalman Shazar Le'Historia Yehudit/ Ha'Hevra Ha'Historit Ha 'Israelit)
Zvi Yekutiel, Exec.Dir.
22 Rashba St.
PO Box 4179
91041 Jerusalem, Israel
Phone: 972 2 565 0444
Fax: 972 2 671 2388
E-mail: shazar@shazar.org.il
Home Page: http://www.shazar.org.il

• 2928 • Zalman Shazar Award for Research in Jewish History (Pras Zalman Shazar Le'heker Toldot Am Israel)
For recognition of achievement in research on Jewish history. A research work of at least 320 pages in Hebrew, in the form of a manuscript or book that has been printed no later than two years before the application, is eligible for consideration. A monetary prize of $1,500 is awarded annually in October on the memorial date of the late Zalman Shazar in October. Established in 1983 in memory of Zalman Shazar, former president of Israel.

• 2929 •
Tel Aviv Museum of Art
Prof. Mordechai Omer, Dir.
27 Shaul Hamelech Blvd.
64329 Tel Aviv, Israel
Phone: 972 3 6077 000
Fax: 972 3 695 8099
E-mail: daria@tamuseum.com
Home Page: http://www.tamuseum.com

• 2930 • Dr. Haim Gamzu Prize
For recognition in the field of the arts. Awarded annually. Established in 1984.

• 2931 • Nathan Gottesdiener Prize
To recognize an Israeli artist. Awarded annually.

• 2932 • Eugene Kolb Prize
For recognition of a work of Israeli graphic art. Awarded annually. Established in 1983.

• 2933 • Mendel and Eva Pundik Prize
To provide for the acquisition of Israeli art. Awarded annually. Established in 1984.

• 2934 •
U.S.-Israel Binational Science Foundation
Dr. Yair Rotstein, Exec.Dir.
PO Box 45086
IL-91450 Jerusalem, Israel
Phone: 972 2 5828239
Phone: 972 2 5635440
Fax: 972 2 5828306
E-mail: bsf@bsf.org.il
Home Page: http://www.bsf.org.il

• 2935 • Prof. E. D. Bergmann Memorial Award
To encourage and assist young scientists. Any U.S. or Israeli BSF grantee under 35 years of age, who received his or her doctoral degree within the previous five years, is eligible. Awards are given to outstanding projects selected by a committee. These awards are in addition to the regular grant. Established in 1977 in memory of Ernst D. Bergmann.

• 2936 • Prof. Henry Neufeld Memorial Research Grant
To encourage young scientists in the health sciences. The BSF grantee proposing the most outstanding and original project in health science will be selected by a committee. The award is given in addition to the regular BSF grant. Established in 1987 in memory of Professor Henry Neufeld.

• 2937 •
Wolf Foundation
(Keren Wolf)
Yaron E Gruder, Dir.Gen.
39 Hama*Kapilim* Str.
Herzlia Pituach
PO Box 398
46103 Herzlia Bet, Israel
Phone: 972 9 9557120
Fax: 972 9 9541253
E-mail: wolffund@netvision.net.il
Home Page: http://www.wolffund.org.il

• 2938 • The Wolf Prizes
To recognize outstanding scientists and artists irrespective of nationality, race, color, religion, sex, or political views, for achievements in the interest of humankind and friendly relations among peoples. Individuals may be nominated by universities, academies of science, and former recipients by August 31. The recipients are selected by international prize committees. The Prize in each area consists of a diploma and $100,000 (US) equally divided among co-recipients. Awards are given in the fields of agriculture, physics, chemistry, medicine, and mathematics. There may be a sixth prize for the arts (music, painting, sculpture, architecture), or one of the five science prizes may be awarded for art rather than science. Official presentation of the prizes takes place at the Knesset (Israel's Parliament) and the winners are presented their awards by the President of the State in a special ceremony. The Wolf Foundation was established in 1978 by the Israeli chemist, Dr. Ricardo Wolf.

• 2939 •
Yad Vashem
Avner Shalev, Chm.
PO Box 3477
91034 Jerusalem, Israel
Phone: 972 2 644 3400
Fax: 972 2 644 3443
E-mail: general.information@yadvashem .org.il
Home Page: http://www.yadvashem.org

• 2940 • Bergson Award
Awarded for a term paper on the Holocaust.

• 2941 • Brandt Award
Award for children's Holocaust literature.

• 2942 • Buchman Award
Award for literature/research on the Holocaust.

• 2943 • Najmann Award
Award for excellence in the field of Holocaust education.

• 2944 • Uveeler Award
Award for outstanding papers.

Italy

• 2945 •
Abdus Salam International Centre for Theoretical Physics
Strada Costiera 11
34014 Trieste, Italy
Phone: 39 40 2240111
Fax: 39 40 224163
E-mail: sci_info@ictp.it
Home Page: http://www.ictp.it

• 2946 • Dirac Medal
For recognition of significant contributions to theoretical physics and mathematics. Selection is by nomination. The Dirac Medals are not awarded to Nobel laureates or Wolf Foundation Prize winners. Awarded annually. The winners are announced on August 8, Dirac's birthday. Established in 1985 in honor of Paul Adrien Maurice Dirac (United Kingdom), Nobel Laureate for physics.

• 2947 • ICO-ICTP Prize
To recognize a researcher under 40 years of age from a developing country who has made significant contributions to the field of optics. A certificate, $1000 and an invitation from ICTP to attend and deliver a lecture at the next conference on optics is awarded. Sponsored by the Abdus Salam International Centre for Theoretical Phusics (ICTP) and the International Commission for Optics (ICO).

• 2948 • ICTP Prize
To recognize an outstanding and original contribution made by a scientist from and working and living in a developing country in a particular field of physics and mathematics. Individuals under 45 years of age are eligible. A monetary award of US$1,000, a medal, and a certificate are awarded annually. Established in 1982.

• 2949 • Ramanujan Prize for Young Mathematicians
Awarded to a researcher less than 45 years old from a developing country, who has conducted outstanding research in mathematics in a developing country.

• 2950 • **Training and Research at Italian Libraries**
Awarded to physicists/mathematicians from developing countries with a minimum of a MSc degree and two years of working experience in relevant field.

• 2951 •
Academia Musicale Chigiana
Via di Citta 89
53100 Siena, Italy
Phone: 39 0577 22091
Fax: 39 0577 288124
E-mail: accademia.chigiana@chigiana.it
Home Page: http://www.chigiana.it

• 2952 • **Premio Internazionale Accademia Musicale Chigiana Siena**
For recognition of achievement in music. The award is presented in alternate years to violinists and pianists . Musicians under the age of 35 may be nominated. A monetary prize and a sculpture by Fritz Konig are awarded annually in the summer. Established in 1982 by a private German donor.

• 2953 •
Academy of Sciences for the Developing World
Prof. Mohamed Hag Ali Hassan, Exec.Dir.
International Centre for Theoretical Physics
Strada Costierra 11
I-34014 Trieste, Italy
Phone: 39 40 2240327
Phone: 39 40 2240686
Fax: 39 40 224559
E-mail: info@twas.org
Home Page: http://www.twas.org

• 2954 • **Celso Furtado Prize in Political Economy**
To recognize an individual whose work has made a fundamental contribution to the understanding and promotion of the socio-economic development of countries in the south. A monetary prize of $10,000 and a plaque are awarded triennially. Administered by the Third World Network of Scientific Organizations and funded by the government of Brazil. Established in honor of Celso Furtado, a leading Brazilian economist.

• 2955 • **Prize for Young Scientists**
To recognize young scientists from developing countries who have made outstanding contributions to the advancement of science. Candidates, typically under the age of 40, must be nationals of developing countries as well as working and living in those countries. A monetary prize of $2,000 is awarded annually.

• 2956 • **Prize in Agricultural Sciences**
To recognize scientists from developing countries who have made outstanding contributions to the advancement of the agricultural sciences. Candidates must be nationals of developing countries as well as working and living in those countries. A monetary prize of $10,000 and a medal are awarded annually.

• 2957 • **Prize in Chemistry**
To recognize scientists from developing countries who have made outstanding contributions to the advancement of science in chemistry. Candidates must be nationals of developing countries as well as working and living in those countries. A monetary prize of $10,000 and a medal are awarded annually.

• 2958 • **Prize in Earth Sciences**
To recognize scientists from developing countries who have made outstanding contributions to the advancement of the earth sciences. Candidates must be nationals of developing countries as well as working and living in those countries. A monetary prize of $10,000 and a medal are awarded annually.

• 2959 • **Prize in Engineering Sciences**
To recognize scientists from developing countries who have made outstanding contributions to the advancement of the engineering sciences. Candidates must be nationals of developing countries as well as working and living in those countries. A monetary prize of $10,000 and a medal are awarded annually.

• 2960 • **Trieste Science Prize**
To recognize scientists from developing countries who have made outstanding contributions to the advancement of the agricultural sciences. Two prizes are awarded annually in rotation among various fields of science: agricultural sciences; biological sciences; chemical sciences; earth, space, ocean, and atmospheric sciences; engineering sciences; mathematics; medical sciences; and physics and astronomy. Each prize carries a $50,000 monetary award.

• 2961 • **TWAS Award in Basic Medical Sciences**
To recognize scientists from developing countries who have made outstanding contributions to the advancement of basic medical sciences. Candidates for the awards must be nationals of developing countries and, as a rule, working and living in those countries. Fellows of the Third World Academy of Sciences are not eligible. Nominations must be submitted by March 31. A monetary award of $10,000 and a medal are presented annually.

• 2962 • **TWAS Award in Biology**
To recognize scientists from developing countries who have made outstanding contributions to the advancement of science in biology. Candidates for the awards must be nationals of developing countries and, as a rule, working and living in those countries. Fellows of the Third World Academy of Sciences are not eligible. Nominations must be submitted by March 31. A monetary award of $10,000 and a medal are presented annually.

• 2963 • **TWAS Award in Chemistry**
To recognize scientists from developing countries who have made outstanding contributions to the advancement of science in chemistry. Candidates for the awards must be nationals of developing countries and, as a rule, working and living in those countries. Fellows of the Third World Academy of Sciences are not eligible. Nominations must be submitted by March 31. A monetary award of $10,000 and a medal are presented annually.

• 2964 • **TWAS Award in Mathematics**
To recognize scientists from developing countries who have made outstanding contributions to the advancement of science in mathematics. Candidates for the awards must be nationals of developing countries and, as a rule, working and living in those countries. Fellows of the Third World Academy of Sciences are not eligible. Nominations must be submitted by March 31. A monetary award of $10,000 and a medal are presented annually.

• 2965 • **TWAS Award in Physics**
To recognize scientists from developing countries who have made outstanding contributions to the advancement of science in physics. Candidates for the awards must be nationals of developing countries and, as a rule, working and living in those countries. Fellows of the Third World Academy of Sciences are not eligible. Nominations must be submitted by March 31. A monetary award of $10,000 and a medal are presented annually.

• 2966 •
Accademia delle Scienze di Torino
Prof. Pietro Rossi, Pres.
Via Maria Vittoria 3
I-10123 Turin, Italy
Phone: 39 011 5620047
Fax: 39 011 532619
E-mail: info@accademia.csi.it
Home Page: http://www .accademiadellescienze.it

• 2967 • **Premio Herlitzka**
For recognition of outstanding work in physiology during the preceding ten academic years. Proposals are admitted only upon invitation by the Academy. A monetary prize is awarded every four years. Established in 1986.

• 2968 • **Premio Internazionale Ferrari-Soave**
To honor a scientist who has achieved particular distinction in research in biological sciences during the ten years preceding the prize. The prize is awarded by rotation for work in human biology, vegetal biology, animal biology, and cell biology. Nominations are admitted only upon invitation by the Academy. A monetary prize is awarded every two or four years. Established in 1994.

• 2969 • **Premio Internazionale Panetti-Ferrari (Professor Modesto Panetti International Prize with Gold Medal)**
To honor a scientist who has particularly distinguished himself or herself in work in applied mechanics during the ten years preceding the prize. Scientists who are not national or foreign mem-

bers of the Academy are eligible to be proposed by national and foreign members of the Classe di Scienze Fisiche, Matematiche e Naturali of the Accademia delle Scienze di Torino as well as presidents of scientific Italian and foreign academies. Proposals are admitted only upon invitation by the Academy. A monetary award and a gold medal are awarded biennially in odd-numbered years. Established in 1998 by the merger of two awards honoring Professors Modesto Panetti and Carlo Ferrari.

• 2970 •
Accademia Nazionale dei Lincei
Prof. Giovanni Conso, Pres.
Palazzo Corsini
Via della Lungara 10
I-00165 Rome, Italy
Phone: 39 06 680271
Fax: 39 06 6893616
E-mail: segreteria@lincei.it
Home Page: http://www.lincei.it

• 2971 • National Institute of Insurance International Prizes
(Premio Internazionali dell' Instituto Nazionale delle Assicurazioni)
To recognize a person of renown in the insurance field. A monetary prize of 25,000 euros is awarded annually on a rotating basis in four categories: law; economics, finance, and statistics; mathematics and technique; and in a different area from the other three. (If none is available, then one of the three categories is used.) The emphasis is upon private insurance. Established in 1962.

• 2972 • National Prize of the President of the Republic
(Premio Nazionale del Presidente della Repubblica)
For recognition of research and publications. The award is given in alternate years in the following fields: physics, mathematics, and natural sciences; and moral sciences, history, and philology. Italian scientists are nominated by Academy members, who themselves may not be considered for an award. A monetary prize is awarded annually. Established in 1949.

• 2973 • Premio Dotte Giuseppe Borgia
For recognition of outstanding contributions to the physical sciences, natural sciences, and mathematics or to the historical and moral sciences. Research, scientific inventions, or literary work may be submitted. Italians under the age of 35 are eligible. A monetary prize is awarded annually on a rotating basis between scientific and literary works, with every fifth year devoted to research or scientific inventions. Established in 1955.

• 2974 • Premio Maria Teresa Messori Roncaglia and Eugenio Mari
To honor, in alternate years, a scientist or a person of letters. Members of the Academy are not eligible. A monetary prize is awarded annually. Established in 1971.

• 2975 • Premio Giorgio Maria Sangiorgi
For recognition of original research on the history and ethnology of Africa. A monetary prize is awarded biennially. Established in 1972.

• 2976 •
Accademia Pontaniana
Via Mezzocannone 8
I-80134 Naples, Italy
Phone: 39 081 5527549
Fax: 39 081 5527549
E-mail: accponta@tin.it
Home Page: http://www.pontaniana.unina.it

• 2977 • Premio Tenore
For recognition in the fields of science, literature, and fine arts. A monetary prize is awarded annually.

• 2978 •
Archivio Disarmo
Prof. Fabrizio Battistelli, Sec.Gen.
Piazza Cavour 17
I-00193 Rome, Italy
Phone: 39 6 36000343
Phone: 39 6 36000344
Fax: 39 6 36000345
E-mail: archidis@pml.it
Home Page: http://www.archiviodisarmo.it

• 2979 • Colombe D'Oro per la Pace
Recognizes a journalist who wrote pro-peace. Also recognizes an outstanding international personality involved in peace processes. Awarded annually.

• 2980 •
Associazione Compagnia Jazz Ballet
Largo Francia 113
I-10138 Turin, Italy
Phone: 39 011 6500253
Fax: 39 011 6500254
E-mail: info@adrianacava.it
Home Page: http://www.adrianacava.it

• 2981 • International Festival of Modern Jazz Dance
(Festival Internazionale di Danza Modern-Jazz)
To encourage young choreographers. The competition is open to Italian and foreign choreographers 18 years of age. The deadline for entry is December 21. Monetary prizes, trophies, and plaques are awarded annually. Established in 1982 by Adriana Cava.

• 2982 •
Associazione Culturale Antonio Pedrotti
Lucio Chiricozzi, Pres.
Centro S. Chiara-via S. Croce 67
I-38100 Trento, Italy
Phone: 39 0461 231223
Fax: 39 0461 232592
E-mail: pedrotticompetition@fastwebnet.it
Home Page: http://concorsopedrotti.isite.it

• 2983 • Antonio Pedrotti International Competition for Orchestra Conductors
(Concurso Internazionale per Direttori d'Orchestra Antonio Pedrotti)
To encourage professional activity of young orchestra conductors. Applicants must be between 18 and 35 years of age. Monetary prizes totaling 16,000 euros are awarded. The first prize includes concerts with many orchestras. Held biennially in even-numbered years. Established in 1989 by Andrea Mascagni.

• 2984 •
Associazione Culturale Ennio Flaiano e *Oggi E Domani*
Via Beato Nunzio Sulprizio 16
I-65126 Pescara, Italy
Phone: 39 085 4517898
Fax: 39 085 4517909
E-mail: flaiano@webzone.it
Home Page: http://www.premioflaiano.it

• 2985 • Premio Internazionale Ennio Flaiano
To provide recognition for outstanding works in the following fields: literature, theater, film, and television. Applications must be submitted for the theater award. Nominations must be submitted for the other areas. A monetary award and a silver trophy designed by Giuseppe di Prinzio are awarded annually. Established in 1974 by Dr. Edoardo Tiboni, editor of *Oggi E Domani*.

• 2986 •
Associazione Internazionale Guido Dorso
Antonio Pisanti, Sec.Gen.
Corso Umberto I, 22
I-80138 Naples, Italy
Phone: 39 081 5527744
Fax: 39 081 5525511
E-mail: info@assodorso.it
Home Page: http://www.assodorso.it
Formerly: (1990) Centro Studi Nuovo Mezzogiorno.

• 2987 • Premio Internazionale di Meridionalistica Guido Dorso
For recognition of achievement in, or contribution to, political, economic, managerial, scientific, cultural, educational, and publishing activities, specifically focused on southern Italy's growth. Applications must be submitted for the "ordinaria" section, and for the other sections nomination is necessary. Monetary prizes and trophies are awarded annually in the autumn. Established in 1970 by Dott. Nicola Squitieri in honor of Guido Dorso.

• 2988 •
Associazione Musicale di Monza
Vile Brianza 31
I-20052 Monza, Italy
Phone: 39 02 382278
Fax: 39 02 2610492
E-mail: info@concorsosalagallo.com
Home Page: http://www.concorsosalagallo.com

• 2989 • Rina Sala Gallo International Piano Competition (Concorso Pianistico Internazionale Rina Sala Gallo)

For recognition of outstanding piano performances. The competition is open to pianists of all nationalities who are between 15 and 30 years of age, provided they have not won the first prize in any of the previous Rina Sala Gallo competitions. The deadline for entry is May 31. Monetary prizes are awarded biennially in even-numbered years. Established in 1970.

• 2990 •
Associazione per il Disegno Industriale
Alessandra Fossati, Sec.Gen.
Via Bramante 29
I-20154 Milan, Italy
Phone: 39 02331 0241
Fax: 39 023310 0878
E-mail: lettere@adi-design.org
Home Page: http://www.adi-design.org

• 2991 • Premio Compasso d'oro ADI

For recognition in the field of Italian industrial design. Awarded triennially. Established in 1954.

• 2992 •
Bagutta Restaurant
Via Bagutta 14
I-20121 Milan, Italy
Phone: 39 02 76000 902
Fax: 39 02 799613
E-mail: segreteria@bagutta.it
Home Page: http://www.bagutta.it

• 2993 • Bagutta Prize

This, one of Italy's oldest and most prestigious literary awards, is given for recognition of the best book of the year in several categories. Established and young distinguished authors of many literary forms, including the novel, poetry, and journalism are eligible. Submissions are not accepted. A monetary award and honorary recognition are awarded annually at Bagutta, a small restaurant at Via Baguttain, Milan. Established in 1927.

• 2994 •
Bergamo Film Meeting
Fiametta Girola, Gen.Sec.
Via G. Reich, 49
I-24020 Torre Bololone (BG), Italy
Phone: 39 035 363087
Fax: 39 035 341255
E-mail: info@bergamofilmmeeting.it
Home Page: http://www.alasca.it/bfm

• 2995 • Rosa Camuna

To recognize and honor films of high quality and art for sale and distribution in Italy. Participating films are included by invitation of the organizers. Films must not have been previously released in Italy nor have been shown in any other Italian film festival. The deadline is January 31. Three plaques are awarded annually in March at the end of the Bergamo Film Meeting Festival - a gold, silver, and bronze Rosa Camuna, the symbol of Regione Lombardia. Established in 1983. Sponsored by Regione Lombardia.

• 2996 •
A. Boito Conservatory of Music Parma (Conservatorio di Musica A. Boito di Parma)
Via del Conservatorio 27/A
I-43100 Parma, Italy
Phone: 39 521 282204
Fax: 39 521 200398
E-mail: direzione.con-pr@iol.it

• 2997 • Franz Liszt International Piano Competition - Mario Zanfi Prize (Concorso Internazionale Pianistico Liszt - Premio Mario Zanfi)

To recognize young pianists in a competition that is dedicated entirely to Liszt. Pianists who are 16 to 32 years of age as of the first day of the competition may apply. Award winners participate in the final concert and must be available for a 15-day period, after the end of the Mario Zanfi Prize is awarded. Held triennially. Established in 1981 by a bequest from the pianist, Mario Zanfi, to establish a competition dedicated entirely to Liszt.

• 2998 •
Busoni International Piano Competition Foundation
(Concorso Pianistico Internazionale Ferrucio Busoni)
Andrea Bonatta, Artistic Dir.
% Conservatorio Statale di Musica C. Monteverdi
Piazza Domenicani 25
PO Box 368
I-39100 Bolzano, Italy
Phone: 39 0471 976568
Fax: 39 0471 326127
E-mail: info@concorsobusoni.it
Home Page: http://www.concorsobusoni.it

• 2999 • F. Busoni Prize (Premio F. Busoni)

To recognize the best pianists of the competition. Pianists of all nationalities between 15 and 32 years of age are eligible to apply by May 31. The following prizes are awarded: Busoni Prize - a monetary prize and contracts for 60 concerts with symphony orchestras and organizations; second prize; third prize; fourth prize; fifth prize; sixth prize. Diplomas and certificates are also presented to the finalists. Awarded every two years. Established in 1949. Sponsored by Italy - the President of the Council of Ministers, Italy - Ministry of Education, and the Municipality of Bolzano.

• 3000 •
Camerata Musicale Barese
Via Sparano 141
I-70121 Bari, Italy
Phone: 39 080 5211908
Fax: 39 080 5237154
E-mail: camerata.musicale@tiscalinet.it
Home Page: http://www.itineraweb.com/italiano/certenotti/5bi5cam.htm

• 3001 • Concorso Internazionale di Chitarra Mauro Giuliani

To encourage professional development of guitarists. Applications are accepted. Monetary prizes, guitars, diplomas of merit, and concerts in Italian society are awarded annually. Established in 1980 in memory of Mauro Giuliani. Sponsored by the Ministers of Benie le Attivita Cultuzali, Provincia Bari.

• 3002 •
Campiello Foundation
(Fondazione Il Campiello)
Andrea Riello, Pres.
Vio Torino, 151 C
I-30172 Mestre-Venice, Italy
Phone: 39 041 2517511
Fax: 39 041 2517576
E-mail: campiello@confindustria.veneto.it
Home Page: http://www.premiocampiello.org

• 3003 • Campiello Prize (Premio Campiello)

To provide recognition for the best Italian prose works of the year. Books of fiction by Italian citizens published during the preceding 12 months are considered. Five monetary prizes and plaques are awarded with additional money for the super prize winner. A monetary prize is awarded annually for the super prize. Established in 1963 by Mario Valeri Manera, Associazioni Industriali del Veneto.

• 3004 •
Grinzane Cavour Prize Association
(Associazione Premio Grinzane Cavour)
Via Montebello 21
I-10124 Turin, Italy
Phone: 39 011 8100 111
Fax: 39 011 8125 456
E-mail: info@grinzane.net
Home Page: http://www.grinzane.net

• 3005 • Grinzane Cavour Prize (Premio Grinzane Cavour)

To encourage the diffusion of reading, especially of contemporary fiction. Literary critics, scholars, writers, journalists, and people in the world of Italian culture judge the books together with high school students in Italy and in Italian schools abroad. Monetary prizes are awarded annually in six categories: (1) contemporary Italian fiction; (2) contemporary foreign fiction translated into Italian; (3) best literary translation into Italian; (4) one international prize for the complete works of a foreign writer; (5) one award for the first novel of a young author, aged less than 40; (6) one award for the best essay on music.

International versions of the award are also bestowed: the Grizane Cavour Prize Moscow, Prix Grizane France, Grizane Cavour Prize La Habana, and Grizane Cavour Prize Montevideo. Established in 1982 by Prof. Giuliano Soria.

• 3006 •
Centro di Cultural Scientifica "Alessandro Volta"
Villa Olmo - Via Cantoni 1
22100 Como, Italy
Phone: 39 31 579811
Fax: 39 31 573395
E-mail: info@controvolta.it
Home Page: http://www.centrovolta.it

• 3007 • **Premio Triennale per la Fisica Francesco Somaini**

For recognition in the field of physics. Monetary prizes totaling 10 million euro are awarded triennially.

• 3008 •
Cinema Giovani- Torino Film Festival
(Festival Internazionale Cinema Giovani)
Gianni Rondolino, Pres.
Via Monte di Pieta 1
I-10121 Turin, Italy
Phone: 39 011 5623309
Fax: 39 011 5629796
E-mail: info@torinofilmfest.org
Home Page: http://www.torinofilmfest.org

• 3009 • **Turin International Film Festival (Festival Internazionale Cinema Giovani)**

For recognition of outstanding films submitted to the Festival. Prizes are awarded in two competitions: International Feature Films Competition and International Short Films Competition. Two special jury awards are also given.

• 3010 •
Club Tenco
Via Matteotti, 226
I-18038 San Remo, Italy
Phone: 39 0184 505011
Fax: 39 0184 577289
E-mail: club@clubtenco.org
Home Page: http://www.clubtenco.org

• 3011 • **Premio Tenco**

For recognition of musical artists who have always worked in the musical world with cultural, poetic and social aims. Musical performers may be nominated. A trophy is awarded annually in October. Established in 1974 in honor of Luigi Tenco. Sponsored by the San Remo Municipality.

• 3012 •
Concorso Ettore Pozzoli
Mrs. Lia Diotti, Sec.
Via Paradiso 6
20038 Seregno, Italy
Phone: 39 0362 222914
Fax: 39 0362 222914
E-mail: info@concorsopozzoli.it
Home Page: http://www.concorsopozzoli.it

• 3013 • **Ettore Pozzoli International Piano Competition (Concorso Pianistico Internazionale Ettore Pozzoli)**

For recognition of outstanding pianists. Pianists of any nationality who are 32 years of age or younger may participate in the competition. The deadline for entry is May 30. The following prizes are awarded: (1) Pozzoli Prize 14,000 euros, and the recording and printing of a Compact Disk; (2) Second Prize 6,000 euros; (3) Third Prize 3,000 euros; and Special Prizes of 1,000 euros. Held annually.

• 3014 •
Concorso Pianistico Internazionale Alessandro Casagrande
% Comune di Terni
Vico San Lorenzo 1
I-05100 Terni, Italy
Phone: 39 0744 549713
Fax: 39 0744 549723
E-mail: concasag@tin.it
Home Page: http://www .concorsocasagrande.org

• 3015 • **Alessandro Casagrande International Piano Competition (Concorso Pianistico Internazionale Alessandro Casagrande)**

To recognize and encourage young pianists. Pianists of any nationality under 30 years of age are eligible. Concert engagements and monetary awards are presented. Awarded biennially. Established in 1966 by the Municipality of Terni.

• 3016 •
Courmayeur Noir in Festival
Patricia Wachter, Public Relations
Via Panaro, 17
I-00199 Rome, Italy
Phone: 39 06 8603 111
Fax: 39 06 8621 3298
E-mail: noir@noirfest.com
Home Page: http://www.noirfest.com

Formerly: Noir International Festival.

• 3017 • **International Mystery Festival**

To recognize and promote outstanding film achievement in various mystery genres (crime story, suspense, thriller, horror, fantasy, spy story, etc.) in Italy and throughout the world. The following prizes are awarded: Black Lyon for best film; Napapijri Award for best leading actress/actor; Optical Special Citation Award at jury's discretion; Audience Award for audience favorite; and Mystery Award for best short film. The application deadline is November 15. Trophies are awarded annually. Established by Mr. Giorgio Gosetti in 1991.

• 3018 •
Cultural Association "Rodolfo Lipizer" (Associazione Culturale "Rodolfo Lipizer")
Prof. Lorenzo Qualli, Pres.
Via don Giovanni Bosco 91
I-34170 Gorizia, Italy
Phone: 39 0481 547863
Fax: 39 0481 536710
E-mail: lipizer@lipizer.it
Home Page: http://www.lipizer.it

• 3019 • **International Violin Competition Rodolfo Lipizer Prize (Concorso Internazionale di Violino Premio Rodolfo Lipizer)**

To promote Rodolfo Lipizer's work and help the debut of young concert artists. The Competition is open to violinists of all nationalities who were born after September 18, 1970. The deadline is April 30. Cash awards and concert engagements are awarded annually. Established in 1982 by Professor Lorenzo Qualli, an ex-pupil of Rodolfo Lipizer. First prize is 8000 lira (indivisible), with diploma and silver medal offered by the President of the Italian Republic. Second prize is 4500 lira and a diploma. Third prize is 2800 lira and a diploma. Fourth prize is 2000 lira and a diploma. Fifth prize is 1500 lira and a diploma. Sixth prize is 1200 lira and a diploma. 12 special prizes are also awarded.

• 3020 •
Ente David di Donatello
Gian Luigi Rondi, Pres.
Via di Villa Patrizi 8
I-00161 Rome, Italy
Phone: 39 06 4402766
Fax: 39 06 8411746
E-mail: segreteria@daviddidonatello.it
Home Page: http://www.daviddidonatello.it

• 3021 • **David Film Awards (Premi David di Donatello per la Cinematografia Internazionale)**

For recognition of outstanding Italian films; and to stimulate, with the collaboration of authors, critics, technicians, and personalities of industry, culture, and the arts, an adequate form of competition in the sphere of cinematographic production. The Premi David di Donatello are awarded for Italian films and for foreign films. A reproduction of the famous David statue by Donatello is awarded annually in a variety of categories. Established in 1954/55 under the sponsorship of the President of the Italian Republic.

• 3022 •
European Association for Animal Production
(Federation Europeenne de Zootechnie)
Valerie Vigne, Contact
Via G. Tomassetti 3
00161 Rome, Italy
Phone: 39 6 86329141
Fax: 39 6 86329263
E-mail: eaap@eaap.org
Home Page: http://www.eaap.org

• 3023 • **Distinguished Service Award**
To recognize outstanding contributions in the service of European and Mediterranean animal production and science. Individuals retired from active service may be nominated. A silver medal and diploma are awarded a maximum of three times in one year when merited. Established in 1989.

• 3024 • **A. M. Leroy Fellowship**
To recognize an individual for significant contributions to research or development in the animal sector in Europe and the Mediterranean Basin. By nomination only. A silver plaque and diploma are awarded annually when merited. Established in 1989 by E.A.A.P. to honor Prof. A. M. Leroy.

• 3025 • **Young Scientist Awards**
For recognition of the best scientific/technical paper in the field of animal production presented at the annual meeting of each one of the seven commissions of the organization. Individuals under 30 years of age are chosen by the Commission Boards. Scientific/technical papers are considered. Between 12 and 20 trophies and diplomas are awarded annually. Established in 1983. Formerly: (1995) EAAP Annual Meeting Awards.

• 3026 •
European Bridge League
(Ligue Europeenne de Bridge)
Gianarrigo Rona, Pres.
Via Ciro Menotti 11/C
I-20129 Milan, Italy
Phone: 39 2 70000333
Fax: 39 2 70001398
E-mail: ebl@federbridge.it
Home Page: http://www.eurobridge.org

• 3027 • **European Bridge Champion**
To recognize the country whose bridge team wins the European Bridge Championships. The Championships are held biennially in odd-numbered years. Medals are awarded. Established in 1940.

• 3028 •
European Commission - DG Development
Phone: 33 1 4004 9933
Fax: 33 1 3429 2477
Home Page: http://www.nataliprize.info

• 3029 • **Lorenzo Natali Prize for Journalists**
To recognize journalists writing on topics of human rights and democracy in the developing world. A total of 50,000 euros is awarded annually to outstanding works of print and online journalism in Africa, Europe, the Middle East, Asia, and Latin America/Caribbean.

• 3030 •
European Hotel Managers Association
Barbara Valzania, Sec.Gen.
Hotel Quirinale
Via Nazionale 7
I-00184 Rome, Italy
Phone: 39 6 4707
Phone: 39 6 4707
Fax: 39 6 4820099
E-mail: secretariat.ehma@ehma.com
Home Page: http://www.ehma.com

• 3031 • **European Hotel Manager of the Year**
Annual award of recognition. Awarded to EHAM General Managers.

• 3032 •
European Society for Cardiovascular Surgery
(Societe Europeenne de Chirurgie Cardiovasculaire)
Prof. Claudio Muneretto, Gen.Sec.
Spedali Civili, U.D.A. Cardiochirurgia
P.le Spedali Civili 1
I-25123 Brescia, Italy
Phone: 39 30 3996400
Phone: 39 30 3996401
Fax: 39 30 3996096
E-mail: munerett@master.cci.unibs.it
Home Page: http://www.escvs.org/

• 3033 • **Reynaldo Dos Santos Prize**
To recognize cardiac and vascular surgeons who are involved in the study of cardiovascular diseases. Researchers under the age of 36 are eligible. A monetary award of 2,500 euros is awarded biennially in even-numbered years.

• 3034 •
European Society of Biomechanics
Dr. Marco Viceconti, Sec.Gen.
Laboratorio di Tecnologia Medica
Instituti Ortopedici Rizzoli
Via di Barbiano
1/10 Bologna, Italy
Phone: 39 51 6366865
Fax: 39 51 6366863
E-mail: secretary.general@esbiomech.org
Home Page: http://www.esbiomech.org

• 3035 • **ESB Clinical Biomechanics Award**
Recognizes biomechanics research of exceptional clinical relevance. Awarded biennially.

• 3036 • **ESB Student Award**
Recognizes biomechanics research of research students. Awarded biennially.

• 3037 • **S. M. Perren Research Award**
To recognize the first author of the best scientific paper. An honorarium of 10,000 Swiss francs and invitation to present a lecture are awarded biennially in even-numbered years. Formerly: (2002) ESB Research Award.

• 3038 • **Poster Award**
To stimulate the quality of the poster presentations on biomechanics. Winning posters are selected based on clarity of presentation and scientific quality. A monetary prize of 300 Euro and a certificate are awarded at each biannual congress of the ESB.

• 3039 •
European Structural Integrity Society
Giuseppe Ferro, Sec.
Dept. of Structural Engineering and Geotechnics
Politecnico di Torino
Corso Duca degli Abruzzi, 24
10129 Turin, Italy
Fax: 39 11 5644899
E-mail: carpinteri@polito.it
Home Page: http://www.esisweb.org

• 3040 • **Award of Merit**
For outstanding technical excellence in fracture mechanics and good citizenship within ESIS.

• 3041 • **The Griffith Medal**
For outstanding research in the field of fracture mechanics.

• 3042 • **Honorary Membership Award**
For outstanding original technical contributions to fracture mechanics and good service to the international fracture mechanics community.

• 3043 • **The Wohler Award**
For outstanding research in the field of fracture mechanics.

• 3044 •
Festival dei Popoli - International Review of Social Documentary Film
(Festival dei Popoli - Rassegna Internazionale del Film di Documentazione Sociale)
Giorgio Bonsanti, Pres.
Borgo Pinti 82 rosso
I-50121 Florence, Italy
Phone: 39 055 244778
Fax: 39 055 241364
E-mail: festivaldeipopoli@festivaldeipopoli.191.it
Home Page: http://www.festivaldeipopoli.org

Awards are arranged in alphabetical order below their administering organizations

• 3045 • Festival dei Popoli

For recognition of outstanding social documentary films dealing with social anthropological, political, and historical topics, as well as art, music, and cinema. Films must be completed in the previous year. The following awards are presented: Best Documentary, Best Research, and Best Anthropological Film. Awarded annually. Established in 1959. Formerly: (1987) Marzocco d'Ora.

• 3046 •
Focolare Movement - Italy
(Movimento dei Focolari)
Via di Frascati 306
I-00040 Rocca di Papa, Italy
Phone: 39 6 947989
Fax: 39 6 949320
E-mail: sif@focolare.org
Home Page: http://www.focolare.org

• 3047 • Luminosa Award for Unity

Recognizes outstanding contributions to the cause of unity among religion, ethnic groups, and related organizations. Awarded annually. Established in 1998.

• 3048 •
Fondazione Arturo Toscanini
Palazzo Marchi
Strada della Repubblica 57
I-43100 Parma, Italy
Phone: 39 052 1391311
Fax: 39 052 1391312
E-mail: fondazione@toscanini.dsnet.it
Home Page: http://www.fondazione-toscanini.it

Formerly: Orchestra Sinfonica dell'Emilia-Romagna Arturo Toscanini.

• 3049 • Goffredo Petrassi International Competition for Composers (Concorso Internazionale di Composizione Goffredo Petrassi)

To encourage professional development and to recognize outstanding composers. Musicians of all nationalities under 30 years of age are eligible. Monetary prizes and publication of the winning compositions by Ricordi Publishers, and performances are awarded. Established in 1986 to honor Goffredo Petrassi.

• 3050 • Arturo Toscanini International Competition for Conductors (Concorso Internazionale di Direzione d'Orchestra Arturo Toscanini)

To encourage professional development and to recognize outstanding conductors of orchestras. Three monetary prizes and diplomas of merit, and engagements are awarded triennially. Established in 1985 in memory of Arturo Toscanini who was born in Parma.

• 3051 •
Fondazione Russolo-Pratella
Via Bagaini 6
I-21100 Varese, Italy
Phone: 39 0332 237245
Fax: 39 0332 280331
E-mail: up.luino@libero.it
Home Page: http://luigi.russolo.free.fr/fondation.html

• 3052 • Concorso Internazionale Luigi Russolo

To recognize outstanding young composers and programmers of electroacoustic music. Participants in the International Competition of electroacoustic, analogic, and digital music who are under 35 years of age are eligible. Each competitor can participate with one or more compositions in the following categories: analogic or digital electroacustic music; electroacoustic music with instruments or voice; electroacoustic music for the radio. Certificates and CDs (recorded from the competition) are awarded, and one individual receives a scholarship for one month to work in the G.M.E.M. of Marsiglia Research Center. Awarded annually. Established in 1979 in honor of the futuristic composer, Luigi Russolo (1885-1947).

• 3053 •
Food and Agriculture Organization of the United Nations
(Organisation des Nations Unies pour l'alimentation et l'agriculture)
Dr. Jacques Diouf, Dir.Gen.
Via delle Terme di Caracalla
I-00100 Rome, Italy
Phone: 39 06 57051
Fax: 39 06 57053152
E-mail: webmaster@fao.org
Home Page: http://www.fao.org

• 3054 • A. H. Boerma Award

To recognize journalists who have helped to focus public attention on important aspects of the world food problem and have stimulated interest in and support for measures leading to their solutions. An article, articles, and productions in television and radio may be submitted by nationals of any member country of FAO. A monetary prize of $10,000 US and a scroll describing the recipient's achievements are awarded biennially during the FAO conference year. Established in 1975 in honor of Mr. Addeke H. Boerma, Director-General of FAO from 1968 to 1975.

• 3055 • Edouard Saouma Award

To recognize a regional institution that managed a particularly efficient project funded under FAO's Technical Cooperation Programme. A monetary prize of $25,000 is awarded biennially. Established in 1993 to honor Mr. Edouard Saouma, who served as Director General of FAO from 1976 to 1993.

• 3056 • B. R. Sen Award

To recognize FAO field officers who have made outstanding contributions to the advancement of the country or countries to which he/she was assigned. Candidates must have served in the year for which the Award is granted and must have at least two years' continuous service in the field. All FAO field officers are eligible. The Award consists of a medal bearing the recipient's name, a scroll describing achievements, a cash prize of US $5,000 and round-trip airfare to FAO headquarters in Rome for the recipient and spouse. Awarded annually.

• 3057 •
Inter Press Service International Association
Mario Lubetkin, Dir.Gen.
Via Panisperna 207
I-00184 Rome, Italy
Phone: 39 6 485692
Fax: 39 6 4817877
E-mail: headquarters@ips.org
Home Page: http://www.ips.org

• 3058 • IPS Award

Honors outstanding accomplishments in international journalism and the promotion of democracy and human rights. Awarded annually. Established in 1985.

• 3059 •
International Association of Philatelic Experts
(Association Internationale des Experts en Philatelie)
Dr. Wolfgang Hellrigl, Pres.
PO Box 349
I-39100 Bozen, Italy
Phone: 39 471 972575
Fax: 39 471 972575
E-mail: hellrigl@tin.it

• 3060 • Hunziker Medal

To recognize a significant literary contribution or research work concerned with forgeries or philatelic expertising, or for expertising activities. Awarded annually.

• 3061 •
International Balzan Foundation
(Fondazione Internazionale Balzan)
Bruno Bottai, Pres.
Piazzetta Umberto Giordano 4
I-20122 Milan, Italy
Phone: 39 02 7600 2212
Fax: 39 02 7600 9457
E-mail: balzan@balzan.it
Home Page: http://www.balzan.it

• 3062 • Balzan Prize (Premio Balzan)

To promote the most deserving humanitarian and cultural works throughout the world, regardless of nationality, race, or religion. Prizes are awarded for literature, moral sciences, and the arts; physical, mathematical, and natural sciences and medicine; and a special prize for humanity, peace, and brotherhood among peoples. These are Italy's most prestigious academic awards. Up to four monetary prizes may be awarded annually. The special prize for peace is awarded at intervals of not less than three years. Established in 1961 by Eugenio Balzan.

• 3063 •
International Centre for the Study of the Preservation and Restoration of Cultural Property
Via di San Michele 13
I-00153 Rome, Italy
Phone: 39 6 585331
Fax: 39 6 585533 49
E-mail: iccrom@iccrom.org
Home Page: http://www.iccrom.org

• 3064 • ICCROM Award
For recognition of a person with exceptional talent in the field of preservation, protection, and restoration of cultural property who has contributed in an exceptional way to the development of ICCROM. The ICCROM Council makes nominations. A bronze sculpture by Peter Rockwell and a citation are awarded biennially at the General Assembly in November. Established in 1979.

• 3065 • Media Save Art Award
An international press competition for articles dealing with the preservation of cultural heritage. The competition is held every two years and is open to journalists worldwide. The award and cash prizes are presented at the ICCROM General Assembly.

• 3066 •
International Competition of Ceramic Arts: "Premio Faenza"
(Manifestazioni Internazionali della Ceramica)
Dr. Pier Antonio Rivola, Pres.
% Museo Internazionale delle Ceramiche
via Campidori 2
I-48018 Faenza, Italy
Phone: 39 0546 697315
Fax: 39 0546 27141
E-mail: concorso@micfaenza.org
Home Page: http://www.racine.ra.it/micfaenza

• 3067 • International Ceramic Art Competition
(Concorso Internazionale della Ceramica d'Arte)
To encourage the search for new creative expression, new techniques, and new materials, involving artists and ceramists worldwide in the renewal of creative forms and modes. The Competition is open to single artists or teams of artists. Countries, ministries, cultural organizations, category associations etc., may arrange the participation of national groups. Cash prizes and medals are awarded biennially. Established in 1938. Sponsored by the City of Faenza.

• 3068 •
International Ergonomics Association
Peirre Falzon, Pres.
ISTC-CNR
Via San Marcelino della Battaglia 44
00185 Rome, Italy
Phone: 39 6 44362366
Fax: 39 6 44595243
E-mail: iea.secr@istc.cnr.it
Home Page: http://www.iea.cc

• 3069 • Distinguished Service Award
For outstanding contribution to the promotion, development, and advancement of IEA.

• 3070 • Ergonomics Development Award
For contribution that advances the existing ergonomics sub-specialty or opens up a new area of ergonomics research or application.

• 3071 • K.U. Smith Student Paper Award
For deserving student responsible For an application or contribution to ergonomics.

• 3072 • Liberty Mutual Prize in Occupational Safety and Ergonomics
For outstanding original research leading to the reduction or mitigation of work related injuries and/or advancement of theory, understanding, and development of occupational safety research.

• 3073 • Outstanding Educators Award
For outstanding contribution in the area of ergonomics education.

• 3074 • President's Award
For outstanding contribution to ergonomics.

• 3075 •
International Federation of Beekeepers' Associations
(Federation Internationale des Associations d'Apiculture)
Riccardo Jannoni-Sebastianini, Sec.Gen.
Corso Vittorio Emanuele 101
I-00186 Rome, Italy
Phone: 39 6 6852286
Fax: 39 6 6852286
E-mail: apimondia@mclink.it
Home Page: http://www.apimondia.org

• 3076 • International Federation of Beekeepers' Associations Medals
To recognize national beekeepers associations, and to encourage the dissemination of information regarding new techniques, the results of scientific research, and economic developments in beekeeping. The Federation sponsors competitions, conducts symposia, and bestows awards on occasion of the biennial International Apicultural Congress in odd-numbered years.

• 3077 •
International Federation of Clinical Chemistry and Laboratory Medicine
(Federation Internationale de Chimie Clinique)
Jocelyn M.B. Hicks, Pres.
Via Carlo Farini 81
I-20159 Milan, Italy
Phone: 39 2 66809912
Fax: 39 2 60781846
E-mail: ifcc@ifcc.org
Home Page: http://www.ifcc.org

• 3078 • IFCC Distinguished Clinical Chemist Award
For an individual who has made an outstanding contribution to the science of Clinical Chemistry and Laboratory Medicine.

• 3079 • IFCC Distinguished International Services Award
For an individual who has made unique contributions to the promotion and understanding of Clinical Chemistry and Laboratory Medicine.

• 3080 • IFCC Travelling Lectureship

• 3081 •
International Institute of Humanitarian Law
(Institut International de Droit Humanitaire)
Dr. Stefania Baldini, Sec.Gen.
Villa Ormond
Corso Cavallotti 113
I-18038 Sanremo, Italy
Phone: 39 184 541848
Fax: 39 184 541600
E-mail: sanremo@iihl.org
Home Page: http://web.iihl.org

• 3082 • Prize for the Promotion, Dissemination and Teaching of International Humanitarian Law
For recognition of the promotion, dissemination, and teaching of international humanitarian law. Any person or institution whose activities have contributed to the promotion, dissemination, or teaching of international humanitarian law may be nominated. A diploma is awarded annually. Established in 1980.

• 3083 •
International Sport Film Festival of Palermo
(Rassegna di Palermo/International Sportfilmfestiva)
Via Nobici Gianarrio 32
I-90141 Palermo, Italy
Phone: 39 91 611 4968
Fax: 39 91 611 4968
E-mail: sporfile@tin.it
Home Page: http://www.sportfilmfestival-palermo.com

• 3084 • **International Prize Paladino D'Oro**
(Premio Internazionale Paladino D'Oro)
To encourage a deeper comparison between films and video works on the subject of sports. Feature films, short films (of no more than 30 minutes in length), and videos produced within the last three years are eligible. Nominations are determined by a selection committee and winners by the International Jury. Film and video submission deadline is July 31. A summary of the plot (either in Italian, French, or English) and at least five photographs must accompany submission. A Golden Paladino trophy with a monetary prize is awarded for film, and a Silver Paladino trophy with a monetary prize is awarded for short films and video. A participation diploma is given to all nominees. Established in 1981 by Dr. Vito Maggio.

• 3085 •
International TourFilm Festival
(Festival Internazionale del Film Turistico)
Antonio Conte, Gen.Mgr.
Via Fogliano, 24
I-00199 Rome, Italy
Phone: 39 06 86206635
Fax: 39 06 86200070
E-mail: tour.marketing@flashenet.it
Home Page: http://www.tourfilmfestival.it

• 3086 • **Premio Varese**
For recognition of the best tourist film. A gold medal is awarded annually. Established in 1982 by Antonio Conte. Sponsored by Azienda di Promozione Turistica di Varese. Formerly: Airone.

• 3087 •
Istituto Internazionale delle Comunicazioni
Prof. Ugo Marchese, Pres.
Via Pertinace
Villa Piaggio
I-16125 Genoa, Italy
Phone: 39 010 2722383
Fax: 39 010 2722183
E-mail: info@iicgenova.it
Home Page: http://www.iicgenova.it

• 3088 • **Columbus Prize**
To provide recognition for important research in the communications field (sea, land, air space, mail and telecommunications). Monetary prizes are awarded annually.

• 3089 •
Istituto Nazionale di Studi Romani
Prof. Mario Mazza, Pres.
Piazza dei Cavalieri di Malta 2
I-00153 Rome, Italy
Phone: 39 06 5743442
Fax: 39 06 5743447
E-mail: studiromani@studiromani.it
Home Page: http://www.studiromani.it

• 3090 • **Certamen Capitolinum**
To provide recognition for the best works on the Latin language and literature. Teachers, scholars, and students are eligible. The competition is held annually. Established in 1950.

• 3091 •
Istituto Paolo VI: International Centre for Study and Documentation
(Istituto Paolo VI: Centro Internazionale di Studi e Documentazione)
Dr. Giuseppe Camadini, Pres.
Via Gezio Calini 30
I-25121 Brescia, Italy
Phone: 39 30 3756468
Phone: 39 30 2807336
Fax: 39 30 46597
E-mail: info@istitutopaolovi-bs.org
Home Page: http://www.istitutopaolovi-bs.org

• 3092 • **International Paul VI Prize**
Presented for contributions to religious research. Awarded periodically.

• 3093 •
Italian Association for Metallurgy
(Associazione Italiana di Metallurgia)
Fabio Salina, Treas
Piazzale R. Morandi 2
I-20121 Milan, Italy
Phone: 39 02 7602 1132
Fax: 39 02 7602 0551
E-mail: aim@aimnet.it
Home Page: http://www.aimnet.it

• 3094 • **Aldo Dacco Award**
To recognize the best paper dealing with the various techniques used in ferrous and nonferrous foundries.

• 3095 • **Felice de Carli Award**
To recognize outstanding students in metallurgy. New graduates in the last year of study are eligible.

• 3096 • **Federico Giolitti Steel Medal**
(Medaglia d'Acciaio Federico Giolitti)
To recognize a major contribution to the steel plants industry. A steel medal with the portrait of the metallurgist, Federico Giolitti, is awarded triennially. Established in 1958 in memory of Federico Giolitti, a metallurgist and first professor of metallurgy at the Politechnical School of Turin.

• 3097 • **Italian Association for Metallurgy Awards**
To recognize individuals for contributions to materials science and technology that promote progress in traditional and advanced metallurgy. Awards are given biennially.

• 3098 • **Luigi Losana Gold Medal**
(Medaglia d'oro Luigi Losana)
To recognize an Italian or foreign researcher for an outstanding contribution to the knowledge of metals. During the year preceding the award, the Board designates the country whose researcher shall be chosen. The Gold Medal Luigi Losana is awarded at least every three years. Established in 1950.

• 3099 • **Eugenio Lubatti Award**
To recognize the best paper dealing with electrothermic processes.

• 3100 • **Medaglia d'Oro AIM**
To recognize outstanding contributions to the field of metallurgy.

• 3101 •
Italian Chemical Society
(Societa Chimica Italiana)
Prof. Francesco de Angelis, Contact
Viale Liegi 48c
I-00198 Rome, Italy
Phone: 39 06 8549691
Fax: 39 06 8548734
E-mail: soc.chim.it@agora.stm.it
Home Page: http://www.sci.uniba.it

• 3102 • **Medaglia Stanislao Cannizzaro**
For recognition in the field of chemistry. A medal is awarded at the National Congress of the Societa Chimica Italiana. Established in 1956.

• 3103 • **Medaglia d'oro Domenico Marotta**
Recognizes distinguished persons for their achievements in the field of chemistry and in promoting chemistry. A medal is awarded at the Society's national congress. Established in 1962.

• 3104 • **Medaglia d'oro Giulio Natta**
Recognizes distinguished researchers for their achievements in the field of chemistry. A medal is awarded at the Society's national congress. Established in 1991.

• 3105 • **Medaglia Emanuele Paterno**
For recognition of outstanding achievement in chemistry. A medal is awarded in occasion of a national congress of the Societa Chimica Italiana. Established in 1923.

• 3106 •
Italian Mathematical Union
(Unione Matematica Italiana)
Giuseppe Anichini, Sec.
Dipartimento di Matematica - Universita
Piazza Porta S. Donato 5
I-40126 Bologna, Italy
Phone: 39 51 243190
Fax: 39 51 4214169
E-mail: umi@dm.unibo.it
Home Page: http://www.dm.unibo.it/~umi/

• 3107 • **Premio Giuseppe Bartolozzi**
For recognition of achievement in the field of mathematics. Italian citizens under 33 years of age must apply or be nominated. A monetary prize of 1,500 euros is awarded biennially in odd-numbered years. Established in 1969 in honor of the Giuseppe Bartolozzi family.

• 3108 • Premio Renato Caccioppoli
For recognition of achievement in the field of mathematics. Italian citizens under 38 years of age must apply or be nominated. A monetary prize of 10,000 euros is awarded every four years. Established in 1960 in honor of Renato Caccioppoli's brother.

• 3109 • Premio Tricerri
For recognition of achievement in the field of differential geometry. Candidates must have graduated in either mathematics or physics from an Italian university in the last three years. A monetary prize is awarded biennially. Established in 1995 in honor of Franco Tricerri.

• 3110 •
Italian PEN Club
Via Mangili 2
I-20121 Milan, Italy
Phone: 39 2 654421
Fax: 39 2 654421
E-mail: penclub@tiscali.it
Home Page: http://web.tiscali.it/pen_club_it/

Formerly: PEN Club Italiano.

• 3111 • Italian PEN Prize
To recognize the poem, novel, or essay voted by Italian PEN members as most outstanding. A monetary prize is awarded in the medieval village of Campiano (Parma) in September. Established in 1991.

• 3112 •
Italian Society of Ecology
(Societa Italiana di Ecologia)
Prof. Amalia Virzo De Santo, Pres.
Area Parco delle Science 33/A
Universita di Parma
I-43100 Parma, Italy
Phone: 39 521 905609
Fax: 39 521 905402
E-mail: site@dsa.unipr.it
Home Page: http://www.dsa.unipr.it/site

• 3113 • Roberto Marchetti Award
Recognizes the provider of the best scientific contribution at the national congress. Awarded periodically.

• 3114 •
Pezcoller Foundation
(Fondazione Pezcoller)
Marco Clerici, Sci.Dir.
Via Dordi 8
I-38100 Trento, Italy
Phone: 39 0461 980250
Fax: 39 0461 980350
E-mail: pezcoller@pezcoller.it
Home Page: http://www.pezcoller.it

• 3115 • FECS-Pezcoller Recognition for Contribution to Oncology
To recognize a single individual health worker (scientist, medical doctor, biologist, nurse, etc.) for a contribution to the development of oncology and the dedication of his/her professional life to the fight against cancer. The selection of the awardee is made by an International Committee appointed by the FECS Federation of European Cancer Societies with the agreement of the Council of the Pezcoller Foundation. The winner gives his/her award lecture during the ECCO European Cancer Conference and receives an award of 30,000 Euro at a ceremony at the Foundation's headquarters. Awarded biennially in odd-numbered years. Established in 1987.

• 3116 • AACR-Pezcoller International Award for Cancer Research
Recognizes a scientist who has made a major scientific discovery in the field of cancer. Nominations must be made by a scientist of repute who is or was affiliated with a University, Academy, or Institution. Selection is made by an International Committee from the AACR American Association for Cancer Research. $75,000 is awarded annually. Nomination deadline is October. For additional information contact the American Association for Cancer Research at (215)440-9313 or e-mail at www.fortson@aacr.org.

• 3117 •
Concorso Internazionale di Chitarra Classica Michele Pittaluga Premio Citta' Di Alessandria
Piazza Garibaldi 16
I-15100 Alessandria, Italy
Phone: 39 0131 235507
Fax: 39 0131 251207
E-mail: concorso@pittaluga.org
Home Page: http://www.pittaluga.org

• 3118 • Michele Pitaluga International Composition Competition for Classical Guitar
For promote, on a biennial basis, contemporary repertoire for guitar. The theme of each award varies based on the selection of the sponsor. The first prize is 4,500 Euro. Held biennially. Established in 1997.

• 3119 • Michelle Pittaluga International Classical Guitar Competition - City of Alessandria Award
(Concorso Internazionale di Chitarra Classica "Michele Pittaluga" Premio Citta' di Alessandria)
For recognition of outstanding performance on the classical guitar. Soloists of any nationality under 30 years of age are eligible. Monetary prizes totally 23,000 euros are awarded annually in September. Established in 1968.

• 3120 •
Pordenone Silent Film Festival
(Le Giornate del Cinema Muto)
David Robinson, Dir.
% Cineteca del Friuli
Via G. Bini, Palazzo Gurisatti
I-33013 Gemona (UD), Italy
Phone: 39 0432 980458
Fax: 39 0432 970542
E-mail: info.gcm@cinetecadelfriuli.org
Home Page: http://www.cinetecadelfriuli.org/gcm

• 3121 • Jean Mitry Award
(Premio Jean Mitry)
To recognize individuals or institutions distinguished for their contribution to the reclamation and appreciation of silent cinema. Selection is by nomination. A monetary prize, a plaque, and travel are awarded annually. Established in 1986; in 1989, the award was dedicated to the memory of Jean Mitry. Sponsored by the Provincia di Pordenone.

• 3122 •
Riccione per il Teatro
% Municipio
Viale Vittorio Emanuele II, 2
47838 Riccione, Italy
Phone: 39 54 694425
Phone: 39 54 695746
Fax: 39 54 475816
E-mail: info@riccinoeteatro.it
Home Page: http://www.riccioneteatro.it

• 3123 • Premio Riccione per il Teatro
To recognize the author of a play who offers a distinctive contribution to the Italian theater and to the development of contemporary playwriting. Plays by an Italian author that have never been performed may be submitted by April 15. Previous winners as well as works that have won other awards are not eligible. A monetary prize and a monetary contribution for the production of the play are awarded biennially in odd-numbered years. If there is no work deserving a prize, the jury may award other prizes, among which is the Paolo Bignami Prize. Established in 1947. Formerly: (1995) Premio Riccione Ater.

• 3124 • Premio Piervittorio Tondelli
To recognize an author of Italian plays whose age is below 30. A contribution for the production of the play is awarded biennially. Established in honor of Piervittorio Tondelli, a young writer and playwright who died in 1992. Established in 1994.

• 3125 •
Societa del Quartetto
Alberto Cataneo, Contact
Cso. XX Settembre 44
I-21052 Busto Arsizio, Italy
Phone: 39 0331 638395
Fax: 39 0331 623069
E-mail: info@societadelquartetto.it
Home Page: http://www.societadelquartetto.it

• 3126 • Gian Battista Viotti International Music and Dance Competition (Concorso Internazionale di Musica e Danza G. B. Viotti)

To provide recognition for the best music performances in the three following categories: (1) Vocal; (2) Piano; and (3) Chamber Music or Cello (Biennial). Age limits: Opera Singing 35, Piano 30, Chamber Music 32, Cello 30. The categories vary each year. Monetary prizes, medals and concert performance opportunities are awarded annually. Established in 1950 by Joseph Robbone.

• 3127 •
Societa Geologica Italiana
Dipartimento di Scienze della Terra
Universita La Sapienza
Piazzale Aldo Moro 5, Box 11
I-00185 Rome, Italy
Phone: 39 6 4959390
Fax: 39 6 49914154
E-mail: sgi@socgeol.it
Home Page: http://www.socgeol.it

• 3128 • Premio Giorgio Dal Piaz

For recognition in the field of geology. Awarded biennially.

• 3129 •
Sondrio Festival, the International Festival of Documentary Films on Parks
(Comune di Sondrio Mostra Internazionale dei Documentari sui Parchi)
Documentation Center on Protected Areas
Via Perego 1
I-23100 Sondrio, Italy
Phone: 39 342 526260
Fax: 39 342 526260
E-mail: info@sondriofestival.it
Home Page: http://www.sondriofestival.it

• 3130 • City of Sondrio Gold Plaque (Targa D'Oro Citta Di Sondrio)

For recognition of achievement in documentary films on the subject of parks and protected areas. The City of Sondrio Gold Plaque (the Invitational Award) and the Special Award of Stelvio National Park are presented annually. Other prizes are also awarded by the Festival Jury. The winners receive a plaque, and the winner of the Invitational Award also receives a week's stay in Sondrio. Applications must be submitted by May 15. Held annually in October.

• 3131 •
Strega Alberti Benevento
Piazza Vittoria Colonna, 8
I-82100 Benevento, Italy
Phone: 39 0824 54292
Fax: 39 0824 21007
E-mail: info@strega.it
Home Page: http://www.strega.it

• 3132 • Strega Prize

To recognize an Italian novel published during the preceding year. The winner is selected by a grand jury of approximately 400 persons. A monetary prize is awarded annually at the Villa Giulia, one of the most fascinating buildings of the Rome Renaissance. Established in 1947 by the Strega liquor producer, Guido Alberti, and the Italian writers, Goffredo and Maria Bellonci.

• 3133 •
Teatro Municipale Valli
(Fondazione I Teatri)
Piazza Martiri del 7 Luglio, no. 7
I-42100 Reggio Emilia, Italy
Phone: 39 0522 458811
Fax: 39 0522 458922
E-mail: uffstampa@iteatri.re.it
Home Page: http://www.iteatri.re.it

• 3134 • "Premio Paolo Borciani" - International String Quartet Competition (Concorso Internazionale per Quartetto d'Archi)

To recognize outstanding string quartets of any nationality. Individual members must be 35 years of age or younger; the total age of the ensemble must not exceed 120 years. First place receives the Premio Paolo Borciani, 19,000 euros, and contracts for international tours; second place receives 13,800 euros; third place receives 6,600 euros; and a Special Prize is awarded for best performance. Held annually. Established in 1987.

• 3135 •
Trento International Film Festival of Mountains and Exploration
(Trento Filmfestival Internazionale Montagna Esplorazione)
Italo Zandonello Callegher, Pres.
Centro S. Chiara
Via S. Croce 67
I-38100 Trento, Italy
Phone: 39 0461 986120
Fax: 39 0461 237832
E-mail: mail@trentofestival.it
Home Page: http://www .mountainfilmfestival.trento.it

• 3136 • Trento International Film Festival of Mountain and Exploration (Trento Filmfestival Internazionale Montagna Esplorazione)

To provide recognition for the best 35 and 16mm feature or documentary films or videotapes on mountains or exploration. Films about mountains must contribute to the spread of knowledge and protection of all aspects of the mountains: environmental, social, cultural, alpinistic, excursion and sport. Films on exploration or environmental protection must document little known or completely unknown places (including the universe outside the earth) or document scientific research on anthropological, ecological, physical, archeological, naturalistic, or faunistic subjects. Adventure and sport films must illustrate the skill and daring in adventure and the peaceful message of sport activities in the natural environment. Films may be submitted by March 20; applications must be received by March 10. Accepted films compete for the following awards: (1) Gran Premio Citta di Trento - Gold Gentian and a monetary prize - for the film with high artistic qualities that best reflects the aims and values which inspire the Festival. The Gran Premio does not exclude the winner from the other awards; (2) Italian Alpine Club Prize - Gold Gentian and Lr5,000,000 for the best film on alpinism; (3) Silver Gentian - for the best fiction or documentary film; (4) Silver Gentian - for the best film on mountains; (5) Silver Gentian - for the best film on exploration and/or environmental conservation; (6) Silver Gentian - for the best film of ethnographic interest and scientific value; (7) Special Prize - for the best photography; and (8) Special Prize for the best film by an Italian director. The following awards are given by specific organizations with their own juries: (1) U.I.A.A. Prize of the International Union of Alpinistic Associations - for the best film portraying an important, modern and genuine mountaineering venture on any mountain in the world; (2) CONI Prize - the Italian National Olympic Committee Cup for the best film portraying a mountain sport discipline; (3) F.I.S.I. Prize the Italian Federation of Winter Sports - for a film capable of representing the great thrill of winter sports and the pleasure of practicing them; (4) Carlo Mauri Memorial Trophy - for the best film on adventurous exploration; (5) Vallis Agri Prize - for the film that best exalts mountain agriculture and work; (6) Antonio Pascatti Rotary Prize - for a film that exalts friendship and solidarity in the mountain world, features the internationality of alpinism, and highlights the service of spirit and humanity in the mountains; (7) RAI Prize - for the best television reporting; (8) Gold Butterfly of Trentino Prize For the best film which advocates the tourist promotion of a mountain area and exalts its environmental and cultural features; (9) Bruno Cagol Press Prize - for the film that best meets the objectives of the Festival; (10) Folklife Museum of Trentino Prize - for the film that best describes, with ethnographic and anthropological accuracy, the usage and custom of the mountain people. Awarded annually. Established in 1952.

• 3137 •
Ufficio Stampa - Casino de la Vallee E Manifestatzioni
Via Italo Mus
I-11027 Saint Vincent, Italy
Phone: 39 0166 5221
Fax: 39 0166 511616
E-mail: marketing@casinodelavallee.it
Home Page: http://www.casinodelavallee.it

• 3138 • Premio Saint-Vincent per il Cinema Italiano

Italian top award (named Grolla D'Oro) in pure gold is presented for the best film, actor, actress, music, director, screenplay, producer, director of photography, and career. Awarded annually.

• 3139 •
University of Bologna
(Universita degli Studi di Bologna)
Via Zamboni 33
I-40126 Bologna, Italy
Phone: 39 051 2099111
Fax: 39 051 2099104
E-mail: orp@aema.unibo.it
Home Page: http://www.unibo.it

• 3140 • **Giosue Carducci Prize (Premi Giosue Carducci)**
To recognize a researcher who has published a work on the life and work of the poet, Giosue Carducci. A monetary prize is awarded every five years. Established in 1957 in memory of the poet, Giosue Carducci, who won the Nobel Prize in 1906.

• 3141 •
Villa I Tatti
Harvard University Center for Italian Renaissance Studies
Joseph Connors, Dir.
Via di Vincigliata 26
I-50135 Florence, Italy
Phone: 39 055 603251
Fax: 39 055 603383
E-mail: info@itatti.it
Home Page: http://www.itatti.it

• 3142 • **Villa I Tatti Fellowships**
To provide fellowships for post-doctoral scholars doing advanced research in any aspect of the Italian Renaissance. These are normally reserved for scholars in the early stages of their career. Candidates of any nationality are eligible to apply by October 15. Each Fellow is offered a place to study, use of the Biblioteca and Fototeca Berenson, lunches on weekdays, various other privileges of membership in the I Tatti community, and an opportunity to meet scholars from various countries working in related fields. Awarded annually.

• 3143 •
World Association for Animal Production
Assefaw Medhin Tewolde, Pres.
Via G. Tomassetti 3 - 1/A
Via Nomentana 134
00161 Rome, Italy
Phone: 39 6 44202639
Fax: 39 6 86329263
E-mail: waap@waap.it
Home Page: http://www.waap.it

• 3144 • **International Animal Agriculture Award**
Award of recognition. Inquire for additional information.

Jamaica

• 3145 •
Institute of Jamaica
10-16 East St.
Kingston, Jamaica
Phone: 876922-0620
Fax: 876922-1147
E-mail: ioj.jam@mail.infochan.com
Home Page: http://www.instituteofjamaica.org.jm

• 3146 • **Musgrave Medals**
This, Jamaica's highest cultural honor, is awarded for recognition of achievement in the fields of art, science, and literature. Gold, silver, and bronze medals are awarded to one or more recipients annually. Established in 1889 in memory of Sir Anthony Musgrave, former Governor of Jamaica who founded the Institute of Jamaica in 1879.

• 3147 •
Jamaica Exporters Association
Mrs. Pauline Gray, Exec. Officer
PO Box 9
PO Box 9
Kingston, Jamaica
Phone: 876927-6238
Phone: 876927-6786
Fax: 876927-5137
E-mail: infojea@exportja.org
Home Page: http://www.exportjamaica.org

• 3148 • **Champion Exporter**
To recognize a company excelling at exporting. Awarded annually.

• 3149 •
Jamaica Hotel and Tourist Association
Horace Peterkin CD, Pres.
2 Ardenne Rd.
Kingston 10, Jamaica
Phone: 876926-3635
Phone: 876920-3482
Fax: 876929-1054
E-mail: info@jhta.org
Home Page: http://www.jhta.org

• 3150 • **Abe Issa Award for Excellence**
Annual award of recognition.

• 3151 • **Ground Transportation Company of the Year**
Annual award of recognition.

• 3152 • **Hotel Worker of the Year**
Annual award of recognition.

• 3153 • **Hotelier of the Year**
Annual award of recognition.

• 3154 •
Jamaica Teachers' Association
Adolph Cameron, Sec. Gen.
97 Church St.
Kingston, Jamaica
Phone: 876922-1385
Phone: 876922-1386
Fax: 876922-3257
E-mail: jta@cwjamaica.com
Home Page: http://www.jamaicateachers.org.jm

• 3155 • **Ben Hawthorne Award**
For members who have given 20 or more years of outstanding service to education.

• 3156 • **Edith-Dalton James Award**
For a member who has rendered more than 25 years of service to education.

• 3157 • **Roll of Honour Award**
For an outstanding service to the association.

• 3158 • **R.C. Tavares Award**
For members who are under 40 years old and have been teachers for not less than 10 years.

• 3159 •
Private Sector Organisation of Jamaica
Ms. Greta Bogues, Exec.Dir.
39 Hope Rd.
Kingston 10, Jamaica
Phone: 876927-6957
Phone: 876978-6795
Fax: 876927-5137
E-mail: psojinfo@psoj.org
Home Page: http://www.psoj.org

• 3160 • **Private Sector Hall of Fame**
Recognizes outstanding contribution to the development of private sectors as well as the nation. Awarded annually. Established in 1992.

Japan

• 3161 •
The Asahi Glass Foundation
Keiichi Uchida, Exec.Dir.
Science Plaza, 2nd Fl.
5-3, Yonbancho
Chiyoda-ku
Tokyo 102-0081, Japan
Phone: 81 3 5275 0620
Fax: 81 3 5275 0871
E-mail: post@af-info.or.jp
Home Page: http://www.af-info.or.jp

• 3162 • **Blue Planet Prize**
To recognize outstanding environmental contributions by individuals or institutions of any nationality. The award is offered to spur research and activity in global environmental issues. The deadline each year for nomination is October 15. Two monetary awards of 50 million yen each are presented annually. Established in 1992.

• 3163 •
Asia/Pacific Cultural Centre for UNESCO
Sato Kunio, Dir.Gen.
Japan Publishers Bldg.
6 Fukuromachi
Shinjuku-ku
Tokyo 162-8484, Japan
Phone: 81 3 32694435
Fax: 81 3 32694510
E-mail: general@accu.or.jp
Home Page: http://www.accu.or.jp
Formerly: Asian Cultural Centre for UNESCO.

• 3164 • **Noma Concours for Picture Book Illustrations**
To recognize illustrators of children's picture books in Africa, the Arab states, Latin America and the Caribbean, and the Asia/Pacific countries. The following prizes are awarded biennially: Grand Prix - US $3,000 and a gold medal; two second prizes - US $1,000 and a silver

medal each; ten runners-up - US $300 and a medal each; and twenty encouragement prizes - a medal each.

• 3165 •
Asian Productivity Organization
Shigeo Takenaka, Sec.Gen.
1-2-10 Hirakawacho, Chiyoda-ku
1-2-10 Hirakawa-cho Chiyoda-ku
Tokyo 102-0093, Japan
Phone: 81 3 52263920
Fax: 81 3 52263950
E-mail: apo@apo-tokyo.org
Home Page: http://www.apo-tokyo.org

• 3166 • APO National Awards
To recognize outstanding contributions to the cause of productivity promotion. A medal is awarded every five years. Established in 1985. Formerly: (1986) APO Special National Award.

• 3167 • APO Regional Award
To recognize outstanding contributions to the cause of productivity promotion. A medal is awarded every five years. Established in 1978. Formerly: (1986) APO Award.

• 3168 •
Ceramic Society of Japan
(Nippon Seramikkusu Kyokai)
Yoshinori Kokubu, Exec.Dir.
22-17 Haykunin-cho 2-chome
Shinjuku-ku
Tokyo 169-0073, Japan
Phone: 81 3 33625234
Fax: 81 3 33625714
Home Page: http://www.ceramic.or.jp

• 3169 • CerSJ Awards
Recognizes excellence in ceramic science and technology, as well as contributions to the Society. Awarded annually.

• 3170 •
Chemical Society of Japan
(Nippon Kagakukai)
Dr. Shinji Murai, Pres.
1-5, Kanda-Surugadai
Chiyoda-ku
Tokyo 101-8307, Japan
Phone: 81 3 3292 6161
Fax: 81 3 3292 6318
E-mail: info@chemistry.or.jp
Home Page: http://www.chemistry.or.jp

• 3171 • Award for Young Chemists in Technical Development
To recognize chemists under 40 years of age who have made distinguished contributions in the field of chemical industry. Society members are eligible. A plaque and a certificate are awarded to one or more recipients annually. Established in 1995.

• 3172 • Chemical Society of Japan Award
For recognition of a distinguished contribution in the field of pure and applied chemistry. Society members are eligible. A plaque and certificate is awarded annually. Established in 1948.

• 3173 • Chemical Society of Japan Award for Chemical Education
For recognition of a distinguished contribution in the field of chemical education. Society members are eligible. A plaque and a certificate is presented annually. Established in 1976.

• 3174 • Chemical Society of Japan Award for Distinguished Technical Achievements
To recognize individuals who have supported research and development works by their distinguished technical achievements. A plaque and a certificate are presented annually. Established in 1981.

• 3175 • Chemical Society of Japan Award for Technological Development
For recognition of a distinguished contribution to technological development in the chemical industry. Industries in Japan are eligible. A plaque and a certificate are awarded annually. Established in 1951.

• 3176 • Chemical Society of Japan Award for Young Chemists
To recognize chemists under 35 years of age who have made distinguished contributions in the field of pure and applied chemistry. Society members are eligible. A plaque and a certificate are awarded annually. Established in 1951.

• 3177 • Chemical Society of Japan Award of Merit for Chemical Education
To recognize teachers who have made a distinguished contribution in the practice of chemical education. Society members and members of the Division of Chemical Education are eligible. A plaque and a certificate are presented annually. Established in 1983.

• 3178 •
Denstu Inc.
(Kabushiki Kaisha Dentsu)
Tateo Mataki, Pres.
1-8-1 Higashi-shimbashi
Minato-ku
Tokyo 105-7001, Japan
Phone: 81 3 6216 5111
Home Page: http://www.dentsu.com

• 3179 • Dentsu Advertising Awards (Kokoku Dentus Sho)
To raise the standard of advertising creativity in Japan in the Japanese language only. Awards are given for excellence in ad planning and technique in the following divisions: newspaper, magazine, poster, radio, television, and sales promotion. Ads that appeared in Japan during the year from April 1 to March 31 may be submitted by advertisers. Monetary awards, including 1 million yen for the "Grand Prix", are awarded annually in July. Established in 1948.

• 3180 •
Fujihara Foundation of Science
Oji Bldg.
Ginza 3-7-12
Chuo-ku
Tokyo 104, Japan
Phone: 81 3 3561 7736
Fax: 81 3 3561 7860
Home Page: http://www.fujizai.or.jp

• 3181 • Fujihara Award
To recognize Japanese scientists who have contributed most to the advancement of science in the fields of mathematics, physics, engineering, chemistry, biology, agriculture, or medicine. Nominations may be submitted by February 28. Two monetary prizes of 10,000,000 yen each and gold medals are awarded annually. Established in 1959 in honor of Ginjro Fujihara, former President of Oji Paper Manufacturing Company.

• 3182 •
Hiroshima International Animation Festival
4-17 Kako-Machi
Naka-ku
Hiroshima 730-0812, Japan
Phone: 81 82 245 0245
Fax: 81 82 245 0246
E-mail: hiroanim@urban.ne.jp
Home Page: http://www.urban.ne.jp/home/hiroanim

• 3183 • International Animation Festival in Japan, Hiroshima
To promote the development and international exchange of animation art, and to promote world peace through animation. Entry works must be on either film or videotape (including computer animation). The running time must be within 30 minutes and works must be completed during the preceding two years. Films should be in 16mm or 35mm format with a 3m leader. Videotapes must be on standard 3/4-inch cassette (either NTSC, PAL, or SECAM) or on Betacam (only NTSC acceptable). The deadline for entry forms is March 21, and the deadline for submitting films/videos is in April 21. The following prizes are awarded biennially in August: Grand Prize 1,000,000 yen; Hiroshima Prize - 1,000,000 yen; Debut Prize - 500,000 yen; Special International Jury Prize(s); Prize(s) for Outstanding Work(s). Also, the Organizing Committee welcomes any organization wishing to present its own special awards. Established in 1985 by Hiroshima City, The Hiroshima City Foundation for Promotion of Cultural Activities, and ASIFA (Association Internationale du Film d' Animation)-Japan.

• 3184 •
Honda Foundation
Hiromori Kawashima, Pres.
2-6-20 Yaesu
Chuo-ku
Tokyo 104-0028, Japan
Phone: 81 3 3274 5125
Fax: 81 3 3274 5103
E-mail: kyt06402@niftyserve.or.jp
Home Page: http://wwwsoc.nii.ac.jp/hf

• 3185 • **Honda Prize**
To recognize a distinguished contribution in the field of "Eco-technology," a new concept of technology which does not pursue efficiency and profits alone, but is geared toward harmony with the environment surrounding human activities. The award was established to spread this concept of eco-technology. Individuals and organizations, regardless of nationality, are eligible. Nominations must be submitted by March 31. A monetary award of 10,000,000 yen, a medal, and a certificate are awarded annually on November 17. Established in 1980 to honor Soichiro Honda, the founder of Honda Motor Company.

• 3186 •
Hosei University
International Center
(Hosei Daigaku Kokusaikouryu Center)
2-17-1 Fujimi
Chiyoda-ku
Tokyo 102-8160, Japan
Phone: 81 3 3264 9662
Fax: 81 3 3238 9873
E-mail: ic@hosei.ac.jp
Home Page: http://www.hosei.ac.jp/ic

• 3187 • **Hosei International Fund Foreign Scholars Fellowship**
To assist young scholars to carry out non-degree research programs in the areas of humanities, social and natural sciences, and engineering. Positions are not available in medical or veterinary sciences, pharmacology, nursing, agriculture, marine sciences, home economics, fine arts, or crafts. To be eligible, an individual must be under 35 years of age and non-Japanese nationality, must have an advanced academic degree (Master's or Doctorate), and be proficient in Japanese or English. The application deadline is May 31. A monthly allowance of 210,000 yen and a travel allowance are awarded to three scholars annually. Established in 1982 on the occasion of the 100th year anniversary of Hosei University.

• 3188 •
The Inamori Foundation
Kazuo Inamori, Pres.
620 Suiginya-cho
Shimogyo-ku
Kyoto 600-8411, Japan
Phone: 81 75 353 7272
Fax: 81 75 353 7270
E-mail: sec@inamori-f.or.jp
Home Page: http://www.inamori-f.or.jp

• 3189 • **Kyoto Prizes**
For recognition of outstanding contributions in the following three categories: Advanced Technology, Basic Sciences, and Creative Arts and Moral Sciences. Nominations are requested by the Foundation from individuals selected from: representatives of learned societies, presidents, deans, and professors at leading universities; directors of leading research institutions and academies; members and associate members of scientific and cultural academies; former recipients of the Kyoto Prizes and other international prizes; and other individuals of equivalent stature. A monetary prize of 50,000,000 Japanese yen for each category, a gold medal, and a certificate are awarded annually in November. Established in 1985.

• 3190 •
Institute of Electronics, Information and Communication Engineers
Tatsuo Izawa, Pres.
Kikai-Shinko-Kaikan Bldg., 2nd Fl.
5-8, Shibakoen 3 chome
Minato-ku
Tokyo 105-0011, Japan
Phone: 81 3 34336691
Fax: 81 3 34336659
E-mail: office@ieice.org
Home Page: http://www.ieice.org

• 3191 • **Achievement Award**
Award of recognition.

• 3192 • **Best Paper Award**
To outstanding authors of papers published in the IEICE Transaction.

• 3193 • **Distinguished Achievement and Contributions Award**
For outstanding contribution to the study of electronic engineering.

• 3194 • **Inose Paper Award**
To author of the most outstanding paper.

• 3195 • **Young Researchers' Award**
Awarded to promising upcoming scientists and engineers.

• 3196 •
International Association of Ports and Harbors
(Kokusai Kowan Kyokai)
Dr. Satoshi Inoue, Sec.Gen.
7th Fl., S Tower, New Pier Takeshiba
1-16-1 Kaigan
Minato-ku
Tokyo 105-0022, Japan
Phone: 81 3 54032770
Fax: 81 3 54037651
E-mail: info@iaphworldports.org
Home Page: http://www.iaphworldports.org

• 3197 • **Essay Contest**
To contribute to the efficiency of ports in developing countries by conducting an essay contest for personnel from IAPH member ports in the aforementioned areas. As the Association is celebrating its 50th anniversary in 2005, the contest in this term is special in that it is open to all those employed by its members and that cash prizes are increased more than the previous ones. Applicants should be those personnel from developing ports that are IAPH members. The first prize winner receives the Akiyama Prize, consisting of US $2,000, a silver medal, a certificate, and an invitation to the Association's conference with airfare and hotel accommodation provided. A second prize of US $1,500, and third prize of US $1,000, are also awarded. Held biennially.

• 3198 •
International Association of Traffic and Safety Sciences
(Kokusai Kotsu Anzen Gakkai)
Mutsuo Kurokawa, Sec.Gen.
6-20-2-chome, Yaesu
Chuo-ku
Tokyo 104-0028, Japan
Phone: 81 3 32737884
Fax: 81 3 32727054
E-mail: iatss@db3.so-net.ne.jp
Home Page: http://www.iatss.or.jp

• 3199 • **International Association of Traffic and Safety Sciences Award**
For recognition of research on traffic and traffic safety.

• 3200 •
Irino Prize Foundation
JML Seminar, Yoshiro Irino Institute of Music
5-22-2 Matsubara
Setagaya-Ku
Tokyo 156-0043, Japan
Phone: 81 3 3323 0646
Fax: 81 3 3325 5468
E-mail: info@jml-irino.jp
Home Page: http://www.jml-irino.jp/IrinoPrize

• 3201 • **Irino Prize**
To be awarded to young composers who challenge new direction, broader and innovation for future possibilities. Individuals of any nationality who are less than 35 years of age for Chamber and 40 years of age for Orchestra by June 23 each year may submit Chamber compositions that had their first performance during the preceding year. Orchestral compositions must be 10-20 minutes in duration, unpublished, not yet performed, and must not have received any prize. The deadline is April 30. Chamber music compositions should be scored for not more than twelve players with or without tape. Instrumental music with live-computer component can be submitted. Tape music without an instrumental component cannot be submitted. Any duration is accepted. The competition rotates annually for an orchestral work and a chamber work. Monetary awards are alternated -650,000 yen is presented for the Prize for Orchestral Work, and 200,000 yen for the Prize for Chamber Orchestra. The winning orchestral composition is performed by the New Japan Philharmonic Orches-

tra. The International Composers Competition was established in 1980 to honor late Yoshiro Irino, the greatly celebrated composer.

• 3202 •
Iron and Steel Institution of Japan
Yasuo Uchinaka, Exec.Dir.
2nd Fl., Niikura Bldg.
2 Kanda-Tsukasacho 2-chome
Chiyoda-ku
Tokyo 101-0048, Japan
Phone: 81 3 52097011
Fax: 81 3 32571110
E-mail: admion@isij.or.jp
Home Page: http://www.isij.or.jp

• 3203 • Asada Medal
For recognition of an important contribution to interdisciplinary fields of iron and steel. One award is presented annually.

• 3204 • Hattori Prize
For recognition of contributions to the steel industry. Awarded annually.

• 3205 • Honorary Member
To recognize individuals who have contributed to the steel industry of Japan and have honorable fame in the industry. Honorary members are nominated by the council. Awarded annually.

• 3206 • Meritorious Prize for Scientific Achievement
To recognize excellent achievements in scientific and technological research on iron and steel. Three awards are presented each year.

• 3207 • Mishima Medal
For recognition of important inventions and research in the field of cast steel, magnets, heat treatment and metal forming as well as the commercialization of these fields. Three awards are presented annually.

• 3208 • Nishiyama Medal
For recognition of contributions to the steel industry. One award is presented annually.

• 3209 • Satomi Prize
For recognition of important research in metal surface treatment. Open only to ISIJ members and associated researchers. One award is presented annually.

• 3210 • Tawara Gold Medal
To recognize a member, regardless of nationality, who has rendered outstanding contributions to the development of science and technology, and has an internationally established fame. A certificate of merit and a gold medal are awarded.

• 3211 • G. Watanabe Medal
For recognition of contributions to the steel industry. One award is presented annually.

• 3212 •
Japan Academy
(Nippon Gakushiin)
Saburo Nagakura, Pres.
7-32 Ueno Park
Taito-ku
Tokyo 110-0007, Japan
Phone: 81 3 3822 2101
Fax: 81 3 3822 2105
E-mail: international@japan-acad.go.jp
Home Page: http://www.japan-acad.go.jp

• 3213 • Duke of Edinburgh Prize for the Japan Academy
(Nippon Gakushiin Ejinbara-ko Sho)
For recognition of outstanding scientific achievement in connection with the protection of wildlife and preservation of species. The prize is awarded on the recommendation of the members of the Academy. A monetary award of 500,000 yen and a memorial medal (the Duke of Edinburgh Prize) provided by His Royal Highness Prince Philip, Duke of Edinburgh, Honorary Member of the Academy, are awarded biennially. Established in 1987.

• 3214 • Imperial Prize
(Onshi Sho)
For recognition of outstanding papers, books, treatises, and other scientific achievements. Two Imperial Prizes, one in the field of humanities and social sciences and another in the field of pure and applied sciences are awarded to those already nominated for the Japan Academy Prize for that year. Two memorial vases are given by the Emperor in addition to the Japan Academy Prize. Awarded annually. Established in 1910.

• 3215 • Japan Academy Prize
(Nippon Gakushiin Sho)
This, the highest award of the Academy, is given to recognize outstanding papers, books, treatises, and other scientific achievements. No more than nine prizes may be awarded on the recommendation of the members of the Academy. Usually four prizes are given for distinguished works in the humanities and social sciences, and five for works in pure and applied sciences. Members of the Academy may not be nominated. Members of the Japan Academy may recommend Japanese scientists for the award. A monetary prize of 500,000 yen and a medal are awarded to each winner annually. Established in 1911.

• 3216 •
Japan Art Association
Toranomon Asahi Bldg., 6F
1-11-3 Nishi-shinbashi
Minato-ku
Tokyo 150-0001, Japan
Phone: 81 3 5251 2245
Fax: 81 3 5251 2247
E-mail: jaapi@po.iijnet.or.jp
Home Page: http://www.praemiumimperiale.org

• 3217 • Praemium Imperiale
To honor artistic values and contributions of surpassing importance in the arts beyond the boundaries of nations and races. These international awards are given to anyone in the world in the following areas: sculpture, painting, music, architecture, and theatre and film. Recipients are selected on the basis of recommendations of an appointed panel of advisors. A monetary prize of 15,000,000 yen and a medal are awarded in each category annually. Established in 1988 in memory of His Imperial Highness Prince Takamatsu. The prize reflects Japan's growing global commitment to support of the arts, and is a reminder that a nation's cultural heritage is as precious as its economic accomplishments could ever be. (First awarded in the autumn of 1989.)

• 3218 •
Japan Association for International Horse Racing
Kinya Okamoto, Pres./COO
JRA Bldg., 6th Fl.
1-1-19 Nishi-Shimbasi Minato-ku
Tokyo 105 0003, Japan
Phone: 81 3 35038221
Fax: 81 3 35038226
E-mail: jair@jair.jrao.ne.jp
Home Page: http://www.jair.jrao.ne.jp

• 3219 • Best Jockey - Races Won
For the most outstanding jockey.

• 3220 • Best Trainer - Training Technique
For the best training in horseracing.

• 3221 •
Japan Construction Mechanization Association
(Nihon Kensetsu Kikai-ka Kyokai)
Yuichi Amano, Dir.
ShibaKoen 3-5-8
Minato-ku
Tokyo 105-0011, Japan
Phone: 81 3 34331501
Phone: 81 90 23071767
Fax: 81 3 34320289
Home Page: http://www.jcmanet.or.jp

• 3222 • Chairman's Award
Annual award of recognition. Established in 1988.

• 3223 •
Japan Craft Beer Association
Mr. Ryouji R. Oda, Chm.
2F Pinemall
Matsunouchi
Ashiya City 659-0094, Japan
Phone: 81 797 316911
Fax: 81 797 236701
E-mail: mail@beertaster.org
Home Page: http://www.beertaster.org

• 3224 • Japan Beer Cup
Recognizes the best beer in each of several categories, including English light ale, German ale, wheat beer, and American lager. Gold, silver, and bronze medals are presented in each category annually. Established in 1998.

• 3225 •
Japan Design Foundation
3-1-800 Umeda, 1-chome
Kita-ku
Osaka 530-0001, Japan
Phone: 81 6 6346 2612
Phone: 81 6 6346 2613
Fax: 81 6 6346 2615
E-mail: info@jdf.or.jp
Home Page: http://www.jdf.or.jp

• 3226 • International Design Competition Osaka
To honor individuals, groups and organizations (companies, governmental bodies, research institutes, educational organizations, etc.) from around the world who have made outstanding contributions to the advancement and development of culture and human society through design activities. Winners are chosen from among candidates nominated by internationally prominent designers, journalists, design educators, and those well-informed and experienced in design and design-related fields. A diploma, an invitation to the Citation Ceremony where the award is presented, and an exhibition of the work are awarded biennially in odd-numbered years. Established in 1981.

• 3227 •
Japan Fashion Color Association
(Nihon Ryukoshoku Kyokai)
Hiroshi Kozuka, Sec. Gen.
Fukushima Bldg. 6F
1-5-3, Nihonbashi-Muromachi
Chuo-ku
Tokyo 103-0022, Japan
Phone: 81 3 32421680
Fax: 81 3 32421686
E-mail: info@jafca.org
Home Page: http://www.jafca.org

• 3228 • Auto Color Designers' Selection
For excellence in exterior/interior color, color planning, and technology design.

• 3229 • Bunka Women's University Selection Award
For the best design that will be chosen by the university's representatives.

• 3230 • Fashion Color Award
For the best design and color that represent a car's character.

• 3231 • Grand Prize
For the best overall design in auto color.

• 3232 •
Japan Foundation
(Kokusai Koryu Kikin)
Kazuo Ogoura, Pres.
Ark Mori Bldg.
1-12-32 Akasaka
Minato-ku
Tokyo 107-6021, Japan
Phone: 81 3 5562 3480
Fax: 81 3 5562 3492
Home Page: http://www.jpf.go.jp

• 3233 • Japan Foundation Awards (Kokusai Koryu Kikin Sho)
To recognize individuals and organizations at home and abroad who have made outstanding contributions to cultural exchange and mutual understanding between Japan and other countries. The awards are made in recognition of these achievements, and to encourage the recipients in future endeavors. Individuals and groups who are considered to have made especially remarkable contributions and who continue to exert a strong influence in these directions are eligible. A monetary prize of 5,000,000 yen for each winner is awarded annually. Established in 1973.

• 3234 • Japan Foundation Special Prizes (Kokusai Koryu Shorei Sho)
To recognize individuals and organizations at home and abroad who have made outstanding contributions to cultural exchange and mutual understanding between Japan and other countries. The awards are made in recognition of these achievements, and to encourage the recipients in future endeavors. Individuals and groups who are recognized to have achieved remarkable accomplishments and who are expected to make significant contributions in the same direction in the future are eligible. A monetary award of 3,000,000 yen for each winner is awarded annually. Established in 1974.

• 3235 • Prizes for the Promotion of Community-Based Cultural Exchange (Chiiki Koryu Shinko Sho)
To recognize contributions by domestic private organizations engaged in regionally-based international exchange activities in Japan. The award is designed to encourage such initiatives and thus, on a national level, to promote a greater diversification of international activities overall. A monetary prize of 1,500,000 yen for each winner is awarded annually. Established in 1985.

• 3236 •
Japan Industrial Design Promotion Organization
Yoshinobu Tanaka, Gen.Mgr., Promotion Dir.
World Trade Center Bldg., Annex 4th Fl.
2-4-1, Hamamatsu-cho
Minato-ku
Tokyo 105-6190, Japan
Phone: 81 3 34355633
Phone: 81 3 34355634
Fax: 81 3 34327346
E-mail: soumu@jidpo.or.jp
Home Page: http://www.jidpo.or.jp

• 3237 • Good Design Award
For industrial design. Awarded annually.

• 3238 •
Japan International League of Artists
(Kokusai Geijutsu Renmei)
Kazuhiko Hattori, Chm.
1-34-8 Shinjuku Gyoen-mae Bldg. 2F
Shinjuku
Shinjuku-ku
Tokyo 160-0022, Japan
Phone: 81 3 3356 4033
Fax: 81 3 3356 5780
E-mail: music@jila.co.jp
Home Page: http://www.jila.co.jp

• 3239 • Tokyo International Competition for Chamber Music Composition
To expand the field of chamber music and promote the development of quality work. Composers of all ages and nationalities are eligible to enter. A 15,000 yen application fee must be submitted along with a chamber music composition (duet to sextet) under 12 minutes. Up to 3 works per applicant are accepted. Instruments should be selected from the following: Flute, Oboe, Clarinet, Bassoon, Horn. Saxophone, Trumpt, Trombone, Tuba. Guitar, Harp, Piano, Violin, Viola, Violoncella, Contrabass, and Vocal. The following monetary prizes are awarded: first prize - 200,000 yen; second prize - 100,000 yen; and runner ups commemorative prizes. Awarded biennially. Formerly: Tokyo International Competition for Guitar Compositions.

• 3240 •
Japan Newspaper Publishers and Editors Association
(Nihon Shinbun Kyokai)
Tsuneo Watanabe, Chm.
Nihon Press Center Bldg.
2-2-1, Uchisaiwai-cho
Chiyoda-ku
Tokyo 100-8543, Japan
Phone: 81 3 35914401
Phone: 81 3 35913462
Fax: 81 3 35916149
E-mail: s_intl@pressnet.or.jp
Home Page: http://www.pressnet.or.jp

• 3241 • Nihon Shinbun Kyokai Awards (Shinbum Kyokai Sho)
For recognition of distinguished contributions towards promoting the credibility and authority

of newspapers, news agencies, and broadcasting organizations in the eyes of the general public. Members of the Association are eligible. Certificates and medals are given in the following categories: editorial field, management and business field, and technical field. Awarded annually. Established in 1957.

• 3242 •
Japan Office of the Prime Minister
Junichiro Koizumi, Prime Minister
Decoration Bureau
1-6-1 Nagata-cho
Chiyoda-ku
Tokyo 100-8968, Japan
Phone: 81 3 3581 2361
Home Page: http://www.kantei.go.jp

• 3243 • Collar of the Supreme Order of the Chrysanthemum
For recognition of great service to the country. The Collar ranks highest in the line of Japanese honors, and is followed by Grand Cordon of the Supreme Order of the Chrysanthemum; First Class Order of the Rising Sun with Paulownia Flowers; First Class Order of the Rising Sun; First Class Order of the Precious Crown; First Class Order of the Sacred Treasure; Order of Culture; and Medal of Honor with Red Ribbon. Established in 1888.

• 3244 • Grand Cordon of the Supreme Order of the Chrysanthemum
The Supreme Order of the Chrysanthemum is the highest order of Japan, and is given to recognize individuals who have rendered illustrious service to the country. Foreign heads of state and statesmen as well as Japanese statesmen are eligible. The Collar or the Grand Cordon of the Order is awarded twice a year. Established in 1876 by Emperor Meiji.

• 3245 • Medals of Honor
To recognize Japanese or foreign citizens who have saved human lives, set an example to the people by industrious diligence to their duties, or rendered valuable services in fields of culture and education. Medals with red, green, yellow, purple, blue, and dark blue ribbons are presented.

• 3246 • Order of Culture
To recognize Japanese citizens who have rendered outstanding contributions in the fields of science, literature, painting, sculpture, architecture, music, and drama. There is no class distinction, since it is believed that there should be no distinctions made for cultural services. The orange flower design of the Order symbolizes culture and in the center of the petals of a white cloisonne finish with gold edges there are crescent jades surrounded by 20 tiny gold balls, symbolizing a stamen. Approximately five orders are presented annually. Established in 1937.

• 3247 • Order of the Paulownia Flowers
To recognize men of Japanese or foreign origin for great service to Japan. Established in 1888 as an Order ranking higher than the First Class of the Order of the Rising Sun.

• 3248 • Order of the Precious Crown
To recognize non-Japanese women for distinguished service. The Order is divided into eight classes. A badge and a star are awarded when merited. Established in 1888 by Emperor Meiji.

• 3249 • Order of the Rising Sun
For recognition of meritorious service to the country. Men or women of Japanese or foreign origin are eligible. This Order is divided into eight classes. A badge and a star are awarded. The Order is awarded twice a year when merited. Established in 1875 by Emperor Meiji.

• 3250 • Order of the Sacred Treasure
To recognize men and women of Japanese or foreign origin who have rendered distinguished services to Japan. This Order is divided into eight classes. A badge and a star are awarded. The design of the Order features the sacred mirror of the Grand Shrine of Ise, surrounded by profuse shafts of light. Established in 1888 by Emperor Meiji.

• 3251 •
Japan Oil Chemists' Society
Yoshio Ohta, Managing Dir./Sec. Gen.
Nihonbashi 3-13-11
Chuo-ku
Tokyo 103-0027, Japan
Phone: 81 3 32717463
Fax: 81 3 32717464
E-mail: yukagaku@jocs-office.or.jp
Home Page: http://wwwsoc.nii.ac.jp/jocs

• 3252 • Emeritus Membership

• 3253 • JOCS Award for Industrial Technologies

• 3254 • JOCS Award for Merit

• 3255 • JOCS Award for Progress of Studies

• 3256 • JOCS Award for Prominent Studies

• 3257 • Journal of Oleoscience Editors Award

• 3258 • Oleoscience Editors Award

• 3259 • Young Fellows Award

• 3260 •
Japan Society for the Promotion of Science
(Nihon Gakujutsu Shinko-kai)
Motoyuki Ono, Pres.
Yamato Bldg.
5-3-1 Kojimachi
Chiyoda-ku
Tokyo 102-8471, Japan
Phone: 81 3 32631721
Fax: 81 3 32221986
Home Page: http://www.jsps.go.jp

• 3261 • International Prize for Biology (Kokusai Seibutsugaku-sho)
To recognize an individual for an outstanding contribution to the advancement of research in fundamental biology. The specialty within the field of biology for which the Prize is awarded is decided upon annually. There are no restrictions on the nationality of the recipient. Nominations must be submitted by relevant organizations and authoritative individuals by May 7. A monetary award of 10,000,000 yen, a medal, and an Imperial gift are awarded annually in Tokyo in the autumn. The Prize is normally made to one individual. In the event of a Prize being shared by two or more individuals, each receives a medal and an equal share of the monetary prize. Established in 1985 to celebrate the sixty-year reign of His Majesty the Emperor Showa of Japan and to commemorate the Emperor's long-time devotion to research in biology.

• 3262 •
Japan Society of Mechanical Engineers
(Nihon Kikai Gakkai)
Shinanomachi Rengakan Bldg., 5 Fl.
Shinanomachi 35, Shinjuku-ku
Tokyo 160-0016, Japan
Phone: 81 3 53603500
Fax: 81 3 53603508
E-mail: wwwadmin@jsme.or.jp
Home Page: http://www.jsme.or.jp/

• 3263 • Medal for Outstanding Paper
For recognition of outstanding technical papers and for recognition of achievement in developing new techniques in the field of mechanical engineering. Members are eligible. A medal and certificate of merit are awarded annually at the Plenary Meeting. Established in 1958.

• 3264 •
Japanese Advertising Agencies' Association
Kunihiko Ohata, Exec.Dir.
Dentsu Ginza Bldg.
7-4-17 Ginza
Chuo-Ku
Tokyo 104-0061, Japan
Phone: 81 3 55680876
Fax: 81 3 55680889
E-mail: info@jaaa.ne.jp
Home Page: http://www.jaaa.ne.jp

• 3265 • Yoshida Hideo Memorial Award
Recognizes a person who contributed to the improvement and development in the advertis-

ing industry. Awarded annually. Established in 1964.

• 3266 •
Japanese Association of University Women
Sachiko Abe, Chair
11-6-101 Samoncho
Shinjuku-ku
Tokyo 160-0017, Japan
Phone: 81 3 33582882
Fax: 81 3 33582889
E-mail: jauw@jauw.org
Home Page: http://www3.tky.3web.ne.jp/~jauw

• 3267 • **Dr. Holmes Scholarship**

• 3268 • **International Scholarship**

• 3269 • **National Scholarship**

• 3270 •
Japanese Biochemical Society
Shigekazu Nagata, Pres.
25-16 Hongo 5-chome
Bunkyo-ku
Tokyo 113-0033, Japan
Phone: 81 3 38151913
Fax: 81 3 38151934
E-mail: jbs-ho@jbsoc.or.jp
Home Page: http://www.soc.nii.ac.jp/jbiochem

• 3271 • **Shorei-Sho/Young Investigator Awards**
To encourage the professional development of young biochemists. Members who are under 40 years of age are eligible. A monetary prize of 100,000 yen and a plaque are awarded annually to one or more recipients in October. Established in 1955 by Professor Soda Tokuro.

• 3272 •
Japanese Society of Applied Entomology and Zoology
Yukio Ishikawa, Contact
1-43-11 Komagome
Toshima-ku
Tokyo 170-8484, Japan
Fax: 81 29 8388837
E-mail: aez_sg@naro.affrc.go.jp
Home Page: http://odokon.ac.affrc.go.jp

• 3273 • **Nippon Oyo Dobutsu Konchu Gakkai Sho**
For recognition of achievement in the field of applied entomology and zoology. Society members must be nominated by a member of the board. A monetary prize, a medal, and a diploma are awarded annually at the convention. Established in 1957.

• 3274 • **Nippon Oyo Dobutsu Konchu Gakkai Shoreisho**
For recognition of excellent achievements of young scientist in the field of applied Entomology and Zoology. Society members under the age of 40 are eligible. Applicants must be nominated by a member of the board. A monetary prize and a diploma are awarded annually at the convention. Established in 2001.

• 3275 •
Japanese Society of Fisheries Science
(Nippon Suisan Gakkai)
Katsumi Aida, Pres.
4-5-7 Konan, Minato
Tokyo 108-8477, Japan
Phone: 81 3 34712165
Fax: 81 3 34712054
E-mail: fishsci@d1.dion.ne.jp
Home Page: http://www.miyagi.kopas.co.jp/JSFS/e-main.shtml

• 3276 • **The JFSF Award for Achievement in Technical Research**
For exceptional achievements of practical use in any field of fisheries science.

• 3277 • **The JFSF Award for Encouragement of Young Investigators**
For members less than 37 years old, with honorable research contributions and in anticipation of future progress in their areas of excellence.

• 3278 • **The JSFS Award for Scientific Achievement**
For excellent scientific research in any particular field of fisheries science.

• 3279 • **The Tauchi Memorial Award**
For brilliant contributions in physical sciences related to fishing technology, fisheries management and seafood technology.

• 3280 •
Kinokuniya Co.
Kimiyoshi Yoshioka, Pres.
3-13-11 Higashi
Shibuya-ku
Tokyo 150-8513, Japan
Phone: 81 3 54695901
Fax: 81 3 33540405
E-mail: info@kinokuniya.co.jp
Home Page: http://www.kinokuniya.co.jp

• 3281 • **Kinokuniya Theatre Awards**
For recognition of achievement in theater. Actors, playwrights, stage designers, and directors of outstanding performances, plays, and theatrical productions may be honored. A monetary prize of 2,000,000 yen is awarded to a company, and prizes of 500,000 yen and remembrances are awarded to individuals. Awarded annually. Established in 1966.

• 3282 •
Kobe International Flute Competition
Soichi Minegishi, Chm.
% Kobe Cultural Foundation
4-2-2 Kusunoki-cho
Chuo-ku
Kobe-shi
Hyogo 650-0017, Japan
Phone: 81 78 351 3535
Fax: 81 78 351 3121
E-mail: info@kobe-bunka.jp
Home Page: http://www.kobe-bunka.jp/flute/yoko/youkou_e.html

• 3283 • **Kobe International Flute Competition**
For recognition of outstanding performance on the flute. Individuals between 16 and 32 years of age are eligible to apply by January 31. The following monetary prizes are awarded: first prize - 2,000,000 yen; second prize - 1,000,000 yen; third prize - 500,000 yen; fourth, fifth, and sixth prizes - 200,000 yen each; diplomas of merit; and special awards. Awarded every four years. Established in 1985.

• 3284 •
Kobe YMCA Cross Cultural Center
Kazuko Sumino, Prog.Dir.
Shose Plaza 4 Fl., 7-1-9 Hosoda-cyo
Nagata-ku
Kobe 653-0835, Japan
Phone: 81 78 6467100
Fax: 81 78 6467200
E-mail: kccc@gaea.ocn.ne.jp
Home Page: http://kobecrp.at.infoseek.co.jp/index.html

• 3285 • **Kobe City International Association Scholarship**
To provide academic financial assistance to undergraduate or graduate students. Awarded annually.

• 3286 •
Kodansha Ltd.
Sawako Noma, Pres.
Otowa Daini Bldg.
2-12-21 Otowa
Bunkyo-ku
Tokyo 112-8001, Japan
Phone: 81 3 3946 6201
Fax: 81 3 3944 9915
Home Page: http://www.kodanclub.com

• 3287 • **Kodansha Manga Award**
To provide recognition for the best cartoon book of the year. A monetary prize of 1,000,000 yen, a certificate, and a bronze statue are awarded annually. Formerly known as Kodansha Prize for Cartoon Book. Established in 1977. Formerly: (1995) Kodansha Prize for Cartoon Book.

• 3288 • **Noma Award for the Translation of Japanese Literature**
For recognition of outstanding translations of modern Japanese literature. A monetary prize of

$10,000 is awarded annually. Established in 1989.

• 3289 • Noma Literacy Prize

To provide recognition for the best novel published during the year. A monetary award of 3,000,000 yen and a medal are awarded annually. Established in 1941.

• 3290 • Yoshikawa Eiji Prize for Literature
(Yoshikawa Eiji Bungaku Sho)

To provide recognition for the most popular novel criticism published during the year. A monetary prize of 3,000,000 yen and a medal are awarded annually. Established in 1967.

• 3291 •
Mathematical Society of Japan
(Nihon Sugakukai)
Yoko Hannuki, Sec.
1-34-8 Taito
Taito-ku
Tokyo 110-0016, Japan
Phone: 81 3 38353483
Fax: 81 3 38353485
Home Page: http://wwwsoc.nii.ac.jp/msj6/math

• 3292 • Nihon Sugakukai Iyanaga Sho

To encourage and recognize young mathematicians who contributed significantly to the development of mathematics. Members under 40 years of age may be nominated. A monetary prize of 100,000 yen, a Certificate of Merit and an invitation to a plenary address at the annual meeting are awarded in April at the annual meeting. Established in 1973 by the Mathematical Society of Japan with a donation from Professor Shokichi Iyanaga. The award is named for Professor Shokichi Iyanaga.

• 3293 •
Mita Society for Library and Information Science
(Mita Toshokan Joho Gakkai)
Nobuyuki Midorikawa, Chm.
% School of Library and Information Science
Keio University
2-15-45 Mita
Minato-ku
Tokyo 108-8345, Japan
Phone: 81 3 34533920
Fax: 81 3 54271578
E-mail: mslis@slis.keio.ac.jp
Home Page: http://wwwsoc.nii.ac.jp/mslis

• 3294 • Mita Society for Library and Information Science Prize
(Mita Toshokan Joho Gakkai-Sho)

For recognition of achievement in the field of library and information science. Papers published in the *Library and Information Science* are eligible for consideration. A monetary prize is awarded annually at the Society convention. Established in 1977.

• 3295 •
The Naito Foundation
42-6, Hongo 3
Bunkyo-ku
Tokyo 113-0033, Japan
Phone: 81 3 3813 3005
Fax: 81 3 3811 2917
E-mail: info@naito-f.or.jp
Home Page: http://www.naito-f.or.jp

• 3296 • Research Prize
(Naito Kinen Kagaku Shinko Sho)

For recognition of outstanding contributions to the advancement of the life sciences. Directors and trustees of the Foundation, and societies in the field of life science may submit recommendations by November 10. A monetary prize of 3,000,000 yen and a gold medal are awarded annually. Established in 1969 by Toyoji Naito.

• 3297 •
NHK - Japan Broadcasting Corporation
(Nippon Hoso Kyokai)
Japan Prize Contest Secretariat
2-2-1 Jinnan
Shibuya-ku
Tokyo 150-8001, Japan
Phone: 81 3 34656199
Fax: 81 3 34811800
E-mail: japan-prize@media.nhk.or.jp
Home Page: http://www.nhk.or.jp/jp-prize/

• 3298 • NHK Japan Prize
(Prix Japon - Concours International de Programmes Educatifs)

To recognize the best educational broadcast program that is judged to have the highest educational value and demonstrates the important role and potential in broadcasting. Broadcasting organizations, or unions or associations of such organizations that provide coverage nationwide, from any country or territory with membership in the International Telecommunications Union (ITU), and authorized by the competent authority to operate a broadcasting service are eligible to participate. In addition, cable TV enterprises or equivalent organizations transmitting programs, educational institutions, or educational research bodies producing educational programs for the purpose of broadcasting, as well as independent producers operating with the same objective, are eligible to participate. There are four categories for television program entries: preschool education - programs intended for children up to six years old; primary education - programs intended for children 6-12 years old; secondary education - programs intended for those 12-17 years old; and adult education - intended for those 18 or older. Programs must have been broadcast during the period from September 1 of the preceding year to August 31 of the year that the contest is held. Each program must not exceed 60 minutes in duration. The major prizes in the Japan Prize Contest are: Japan Prize - awarded to the program of outstanding excellence that is judged to have the highest educational; Prizes for Programs of Outstanding Excellence in Each Category include: The Minister for Foreign Affairs Prize, The Minister of Education Prize, The Minister of Posts and Telecommunications Prize, and the Governor of Tokyo Prize; Prizes Awarded to Programs of Merit in Each Category include: The Hoso Bunka Foundation Prize (preschool education), The Japan Association for Education Broadcasting Prize (primary education), The Maeda Prize (secondary education), and the Abe Prize (adult education); The UNICEF Prize - for a program that best presents the life and environment of children in developing countries; The Japan Foundation's President's Prize - for a program that is judged to best contribute to international cultural exchange and cooperative spirit; and the Award of Special Commendation - for four programs, one from each category, that have made significant contributions to the educational demands of the participating countries. The Contest has been held annually since 1991. Established in 1965.

• 3299 •
NHK Symphony Orchestra, Tokyo
2-16-49 Takanawa
Minato-ku
Tokyo 108, Japan
Phone: 81 3 57938111
Fax: 81 3 34430278
E-mail: nhksym@blue.ocn.ne.jp
Home Page: http://www.nhkso.or.jp

• 3300 • Otaka Prize

To recognize a composer of classical music. Monetary prizes of 300,000 yen are awarded annually.

• 3301 •
Niwano Peace Foundation
(Niwano Heiwa Zaidan)
Kinjirou Niwano, Chm.
Shamvilla Catherina, 5th Fl.
1-16-9, Shinjuku
Shinjuku-ku
Tokyo 160-0022, Japan
Phone: 81 3 32264371
Phone: 81 3 32264372
Fax: 81 3 32261835
E-mail: info@npf.or.jp
Home Page: http://www.npf.or.jp/

• 3302 • Niwano Peace Prize

To recognize an individual or organization that is making a significant contribution to world peace through promoting inter-religious cooperation. The Foundation solicits nominations from people of recognized intellectual stature around the world. A prize of 20 million yen, a medal, and a certificate are awarded annually. Established in 1983.

• 3303 •
Oita Sports Association for the Disabled
Katsusada Hirose, Pres.
% Japan Sun Industries
1393 Kamegawa, Beppu
Oita 874-0011, Japan
Phone: 81 977 668646
Fax: 81 977 670453
E-mail: info@wheelchair-marathon.com
Home Page: http://www.wheelchair-marathon.com

• 3304 • **Oita International Wheelchair Marathon**
To encourage people with physical disabilities in Japan and other countries and territories for further social participation, and to deepen citizens' understanding toward persons with disabilities through wheelchair racing. Disabled persons over 16 years of age using a wheelchair may apply by August 31. Trophies are awarded to the top 10 runners, cups to the male and female winners of the total marathon, medals to the top runners of the four classes, and certificates are awarded to all who complete the course. Awarded annually. Established in 1981 by Hiramatsu Morihiko, Oita Prefectual Governor. Sponsored by Sony, Honda, OMRON Co., Mitsubishi Corp. et al.

• 3305 •
Pharmaceutical Society of Japan
(Nippon Yakugakkai)
Ms. Keiko Kubonoya, Public Relation Associate
12-15, Shibuya 2-chome, Shibuya-ku
Shibuya-ku
Tokyo 150-0002, Japan
Phone: 81 3 34063321
Fax: 81 3 34981835
E-mail: koho_win@pharm.or.jp
Home Page: http://www.pharm.or.jp/index_e.html

• 3306 • **Award for Divisional Scientific Contributions**
(Nihon Yakugakkai Gakujutsukokensho)
To recognize a contribution to a divisional field of the pharmaceutical sciences. Society members are eligible. A monetary prize and a medal are awarded annually. Established in 1994.

• 3307 • **PSJ Award**
(Nihon Yakugakkai sho)
For recognition of achievement in the field of pharmaceutical sciences. Society members are eligible. A monetary prize and a medal are awarded annually. Established in 1921.

• 3308 • **PSJ Award for Drug Research and Development**
(Nihon Yakugakkai Gijutsusho)
For recognition of achievement in the field of research and development of a new drug (including intermediates of a new drug, diagnostic reagent, etc.). Society members and non-members are eligible. A monetary prize and a medal are awarded annually. Established in 1987.

• 3309 • **PSJ Award for Young Scientists**
(Nihon Yakugakkai Shoreisho)
To encourage research development. Society members under 40 years of age are eligible. Society members eligible will be required to be under 38 years of age. A monetary prize and a medal are awarded annually. Established in 1955.

• 3310 •
Phytopathological Society of Japan
(Nippon Shokubutsu-Byori Gakkai)
Noriyuki Doke, Pres.
Shokubo Bldg.
1-43-11 Komagome
Toshima-ku
Tokyo 170-8484, Japan
Phone: 81 3 3943 6021
Fax: 81 3 3943 6086
E-mail: byori@juno.ocn.ne.jp
Home Page: http://ppsj.ac.affrc.go.jp/ppsj_e/index_e.html

• 3311 • **Fellow of the Phytopathological Society of Japan**
For recognition of achievement in phytopathology, or for contributions to the Society. A monetary award of 100,000 yen, a certificate, and a watch are awarded annually. Established in 1953.

• 3312 • **Young Scientist Award**
To encourage professional development in the field of phytopathology. A monetary award of 50,000 yen, a certificate, and a medal are awarded annually. Established in 1953.

• 3313 •
Recording Industry Association of Japan
Mr. Osamu Sato, Chm./CEO
11 Fl., Kita-Aoyama Yoshikawa Bldg.
2-12-16 Kita-Aoyama
Minato-ku
Tokyo 107-0061, Japan
Phone: 81 3 64060510
Fax: 81 3 64060520
E-mail: info@riaj.or.jp
Home Page: http://www.riaj.or.jp/e

• 3314 • **Japan Gold Disk Award**
Recognizes singers and musicians in various categories. Awards are given annually.

• 3315 •
Sapporo Sports Promotion Corporation
1-5 Nakajimakoen
Chuo-ku
Sapporo 064-0931, Japan
Phone: 81 11 5305550
Fax: 81 11 5305551
E-mail: kikau@mx.asahi-np.co.jp
Home Page: http://www.sspc.or.jp

• 3316 • **Sapporo International Ski Marathon**
For promotion of cross-country skiing, and to recognize the winners of 50 km and 25 km cross country marathon races. Open to both men and women over 19 years of age, (50 km); and over 16 years of age (25 km). The 10k and 5k races have no age limit. Certificates, diplomas, and some extra prizes are awarded annually. Established in 1981.

• 3317 •
The Science and Technology Foundation of Japan
Masao Ito, Pres.
Akasaka Twin Tower E., 13F
417-22 Akasaka 2-chome
Minato-ku
Tokyo 107-0052, Japan
Phone: 81 3 5545 0551
Fax: 81 3 5545 0554
E-mail: info@japanprize.jp
Home Page: http://www.japanprize.jp

Formerly: (1983) Japan Prize Preparatory Foundation.

• 3318 • **Japan Prize**
This, the most prestigious and honored scientific prize in Japan, is given to recognize scientists and technologists from all parts of the world. It is awarded to persons recognized as having served the cause of peace and prosperity for mankind through original and outstanding achievements in science and technology which have advanced the frontiers of knowledge in these fields. No distinctions are made as to nationality, occupation, race or sex, but only living persons may be named Japan Prize Laureates. Award categories change annually. Awards have been presented in the following areas: Information and Communication; Biotechnology in Medicine; Preventive Medicine; Materials Processing Technology; Energy Technology; Psychology and Psychiatry; and others. The award categories for 2000 are City Planning and Host Defense. Two laureates are selected each year. A monetary award of 50 million yen (about $420,000), a medal and a certificate are awarded in April during Japan Prize Week. Established in 1982. The first awards were presented in 1985.

• 3319 •
Society for Biotechnology, Japan
Yasuo Igarashi, Pres.
2-1 Yamadaoka, Suita
Osaka 565-0871, Japan
Phone: 81 6 68762731
Fax: 81 6 68792034
E-mail: sbbj@bio.eng.osaka-u.ac.jp
Home Page: http://wwwsoc.nii.ac.jp/sfbj

• 3320 • **Eda Award**
To members For contributing to the progress of theory or technology regarding brewing.

• 3321 • **Excellent Paper Award**
For several papers published in JBB that have prominently contributed to the progress of biotechnology

• 3322 • **Industrial Achievement Award**
To members For outstanding contributions to industrial research and development in the field of biotechnology.

Awards are arranged in alphabetical order below their administering organizations

• 3323 • **Saito Award**
To young researchers For contributing to the progress of basic studies in the field of biotechnology.

• 3324 • **Society Award**
To members For outstanding contributions in the field of biotechnology.

• 3325 • **Terui Award**
To young researchers For contributing to progress in the field of biochemical engineering.

• 3326 • **Young Asian Biotechnologist Prize**
To young scientists in Asia other than Japan, who have achieved outstanding accomplishments in the field of biotechnology.

• 3327 •
Society of Heating, Airconditioning and Sanitary Engineers of Japan
(Kuki-Chowa Eisei Kogakkai)
1-8-1 Kita-Shinjuku, Shinjuku-ku
Tokyo 169-0074, Japan
Phone: 81 3 33638261
Fax: 81 3 33638266
E-mail: jigyou03@shase.or.jp
Home Page: http://www.shasej.org

• 3328 • **Award of Specialty**

• 3329 • **Award of Technical Paper**

• 3330 • **Award of Technology**

• 3331 • **Shinohara Memorial Award**
To outstanding technical paper and accomplishment on equipment technology.

• 3332 •
Suntory Foundation
Suntory Annex 9F
2-1-5, Dojima
Kita-Ku
Osaka 530-8204, Japan
Phone: 81 6 6342 6221
Fax: 81 6 6342 6220
E-mail: sfnd@suntory-foundation.or.jp
Home Page: http://www.suntory.co.jp/sfnd

• 3333 • **Suntory Prize for Community Cultural Activities**
To recognize individuals and organizations for outstanding contributions to the cultural life of their communities. Wide-ranging activities intended for the creation or furtherance of local cultures are eligible for this prize, such as arts, literature, publication, succession of traditions, beautification of environment, and even food, shelter, and clothing, as well as international exchange and community activities. Awarded annually. Established in 1979.

• 3334 • **Suntory Prize for Social Sciences and Humanities**
To recognize pioneering achievements by rising critics and researchers in the following four fields: political science and economics, literary and art criticism, life and society, and history and civilization. The work must have been published in Japanese during the preceding year. Awarded annually. Established in 1979.

• 3335 •
Tokyo International Film Festival
Tsuguhiko Kadokawa, Chm.
Tsukiji Yasuda Bldg., 5F
2-15-14 Tsukiji
Chuo-ku
Tokyo 104-0045, Japan
Phone: 81 3 3524 1081
Fax: 81 3 3524 1087
E-mail: info@tiff-jp.net
Home Page: http://www.tiff-jp.net

• 3336 • **Tokyo International Film Festival**
To promote cultural exchange, friendship, mutual understanding and cooperation among the nations of the world through films, as well as to raise the motion picture arts and sciences and develop the international film industry. The Festival consists of the following competitive sections: (1) The International Competition; and (2) Young Cinema. Films produced in 35mm or 70mm during the 18 months preceding the Festival that have not won an award at other competitive events may be entered by June 10 in the International Competition. The following prizes are awarded: (1) Tokyo Grand Prix - a statuette sculpted by the late Sebo Kitamura; (2) Special Jury Prize; (3) Best Director; (4) Best Actress; (5) Best Actor; (6) Best Artistic Contribution; and (7) Best Screenplay. Each winner receives a trophy and a diploma. The Young Cinema Festival section is designed to encourage the development of world cinema arts by providing promising young international filmmakers, upon whose cinematic talents the film industries of tomorrow depend, with venues for interchange and competition. Film directors satisfying either one of the following categories are eligible: (a) under 35 years of age and directed no more than five commercially exploited films; or (b) made debut as a film director with this entry film. Films must be submitted by June 5. The international jury of Young Cinema will then judge the winners to receive two awards from those four film candidates: (1) Sakura Gold - for one film, with the prize money of 20,000,000 yen to the director; and (2) Sakura Silver - for one film, with the prize money of 10,000,000 yen to the director. Established in 1985. The festival is held biennially.

• 3337 •
Tokyo International Music Competition
Hiroyasu Kobayashi, Pres.
% Min-On Concert Association
8 Shinano-machi
Shinjuku-ku
Tokyo 160-8588, Japan
Phone: 81 3 5362 3400
Fax: 81 3 5362 3401
E-mail: competition@min-on.or.jp
Home Page: http://www.min-on.or.jp/competition

• 3338 • **Tokyo International Music Competition**
(Internationaler Musikwettbewerb Tokyo)
For recognition of outstanding work in the field of music. Individuals of any nationality may enter. The following awards are presented: (1) a monetary award of 2,000,000 yen, a certificate and medal - first place; (2) 1,000,000 yen, a certificate, and a medal - second place; (3) 500,000 yen, a certificate and a medal - third place. Awarded annually. Established in 1966. Mr. Hideo Saito was instrumental in the establishment of the contest. 300,000 yen and a certificate to the second place winner; and (3) 200,000 yen and a certificate to the third place winner. An airline ticket to the value of 500,000 yen will be presented to the first place winner or to the contestant judged most superior by Lufthansa German Airlines, a sponsor of the competition. A supplementary prize of 500,000 yen will be presented to the first place winner or to the contestant judged most superior by Family Mart Co., Ltd., another competition sponsor. Awarded annually. Established in 1966. Mr. Hideo Saito was instrumental in the establishment of the contest.

• 3339 •
Union of Japanese Scientists and Engineers
1-2-1, Koenji-Minami
Suginami-ku
Tokyo 166-0003, Japan
Phone: 81 3 53789812
Fax: 81 3 53781220
E-mail: juse@juse.or.jp
Home Page: http://www.juse.or.jp

• 3340 • **Deming Prize**
(Demingu Sho)
This, the most prestigious industrial award in Japan, is given to recognize companies that demonstrate their commitment to quality control. Until recently the Deming Prize was restricted to Japanese companies, as its initial purpose was to encourage the development of quality control in Japan. In recent years, however, strong interest in the Deming Application Prize has been shown by non-Japanese companies. Basic regulations have been revised to allow the acceptance of overseas companies as candidates since 1987. The following awards are presented: (1) The Deming Prize for Individual Person: (a) to a person who shows excellent achievement in the theory or application of statistical quality control; or (b) to a person who makes an outstanding contribution to the dissemination of statistical quality control; (2) The Deming Application Prizes: (a) The Deming Ap-

Awards are arranged in alphabetical order below their administering organizations

plication Prize is awarded to the enterprise (or public institution) which achieves in the designated year the most distinctive improvement of performance through the application of statistical quality control; (b) The Deming Application Prize for Small Enterprise is awarded to a small- or medium-sized enterprise which achieves in the designated year the most distinctive improvement of performance through the application of statistical quality control; (c) The Deming Application Prize for Divisions is awarded to a division of an enterprise (or a public institution) which achieves in the designated year the most distinctive improvement of performance through the application of statistical quality control; and (3) Quality Control Award for Factory. A monetary award of 500,000 yen and a medal are awarded annually for the Deming Prize for Individual Person. Established in 1951 to recognize Dr. W. Edwards Deming, an American statistician and proponent of quality control techniques who presented a series of lectures in Japan in 1950.

• 3341 • **Japan Quality Medal**
To further develop the world of quality control. Created to commemorate the first International Conference on Quality Control (ICQC), held in October 1969 in Tokyo, and to maintain an upgrade the spirit of the conference long into the future. Recipients may reapply five years after winning.

• 3342 •
Victor Company of Japan
3-2-4 Kasumigaseki, Kazan Bldg. 3F
Chiyoda-ku
Tokyo 100, Japan
Home Page: http://www.jvc-victor.co.jp/

• 3343 • **Tokyo Video Festival**
For recognition of outstanding achievement in making video compositions. Compositions produced with a video camera may be entered in: (1) Division I (No limitation) - Compositions in any style or any theme are acceptable, in two categories: (a) art-inspired type; and (b) general type; and (2) Division II (Video Letter Exchange) - Compositions that explore the possibilities of video as a means of two-way communication. The following prizes are awarded: (1) Video Grand Prix - $3,500, 10-day round-trip to Japan, a trophy and a citation; (2) JVC President Award - $3,500, 10-day round-trip to Japan, a trophy and a citation; (3) Works of Excellence - $1,500 and $2,000 equivalent in JVC video equipment, a trophy and a citation; (4) Works of Special Distinction - $800 and a citation; and (5) Special Merit Awards - $300 and a citation. Awarded annually, usually in November. Established in 1978.

• 3344 • **Yomiuri International Cooperation Prize**
(Yomiuri Kokusai Kyoryoku Sho)
To recognize the person, company, or group which best showed the importance of contribution and cooperation to the international society. A monetary prize of 5,000,000 Japanese yen is awarded annually. Established in 1994 to commemorate the 120th anniversary of the Yomiuri Shimbun.

• 3345 •
Waseda University
(Waseda Daigaku)
Office of International Exchange
1-104, Totsuka-machi
Shinjuku-ku
Tokyo 169-8050, Japan
Phone: 81 3 3203 4141
Fax: 81 3 3202 8638
E-mail: koho@list.waseda.jp
Home Page: http://www.waseda.jp

• 3346 • **Award for Distinguished Services to Art**
(Geijyutsu Korosha)
To honor alumni who have made a distinguished contribution to the promotion of art. Individuals must be over 70 to be eligible. A gold medal and honorable mention are awarded when merited. Established in 1982.

• 3347 • **Okuma Academic Commemorative Prize**
(Okuma Gakujutsu Kinensho)
To recognize faculty members whose research achievements have been recognized as distinguished, and who have greatly contributed to the progress in the field of study. A monetary award of 1,000,000 yen and honorable mention are presented annually. Established in 1958 in memory of Marquis Shigenobu Okuma, founder of the University.

• 3348 • **Okuma Academic Encouragement Prize**
(Okuma Gakujutsu Shoreisho)
To recognize faculty members who have obtained outstanding research results. A monetary award of 500,000 yen plus honorable mention are presented annually. Established in 1958 in memory of Marquis Shigenobu Okuma, founder of the University.

• 3349 • **Azusa Ono Memorial Awards**
In memory of the late Azusa Ono, who is long remembered with reverence as a co-founder of Waseda University and for the specific purpose of elevating the Waseda Spirit. Awards are presented during graduation ceremonies to individual students (or student groups) who have distinguished themselves or have made outstanding contributions in the fields of academic studies, art, and sports during the previous year. Azusa Ono Memorial Awards for Academic Studies are given to students whose dissertations, graduation theses or seminar reports have been recognized as outstanding in quality. Azusa Ono Memorial Awards for Art are given to students whose art productions have been recognized as outstanding in quality. Azusa Ono Memorial Awards for Sports are given to students who have established a world record or the equivalent in various athletic events. Established in 1959.

• 3350 •
World Association of Societies of Pathology and Laboratory Medicine
Dr. Henry Travers, Sec.-Treas.
WASPaLM Administrative Office
5F Takahashi Bldg., 1-7-1
Sarugakucho Chiyoda-ku
Tokyo 101-0064, Japan
Phone: 81 3 32950351
Fax: 81 3 32950352
E-mail: waspalm@jscp.org
Home Page: http://www.waspalm.org

• 3351 • **Gold-Headed Cane**
For recognition of a special contribution to the World Association. The former president of the World Association is ordinarily nominated for this award by the Awards Committee. A gold headed cane and a certificate are awarded when merited at the convention. Established in 1969.

• 3352 • **Gordon Signy Foreign Fellowship**
To foster cooperation between members, sponsor congresses and conventions, and improve standards in anatomic and clinical pathology by furthering the training of a pathologist from a developing country. Awarded periodically.

• 3353 •
Yomiuri Shimbun
1-7-1 Otemachi
Chiyoda-ku
Tokyo 100-8055, Japan
Phone: 81 3 3216 8744
Fax: 81 3 3216 8749
E-mail: int@yomiuri.com
Home Page: http://www.yomiuri.co.jp

• 3354 • **Yomiuri International Cartoon Contest**
(Yomiuri Kokusai Manga Taisho)
To recognize outstanding works of cartoon and to raise the standard in the field. Individuals, both professionals and amateurs, from any country in the world are eligible. The following monetary prizes are awarded: Grand Prize - 1,000,000 Japanese yen; Hidezo Kondo - 500,000 Japanese yen; Gold prize - 300,000 Japanese yen; and Special prize of the Selection Committee - 200,000 Japanese yen. Medals are also awarded. Established in 1979.

Kenya

• 3355 •
International Centre of Insect Physiology and Ecology
Dr. Christian Borgemeister, Dir.Gen./CEO
PO Box 30772-00100
Nyayo Stadium
Nairobi, Kenya
Phone: 254 20 8632000
Phone: 254 20 802501
Fax: 254 20 8632001
E-mail: dg@icipe.org
Home Page: http://www.icipe.org

• 3356 • **Outstanding Researcher**
Recognizes an outstanding researcher. Selection is based on originality, impact, and contribution to ICIPE's goals. Awarded periodically.

• 3357 •
Kenya Institute of Management
Mr. Mwangi Ngumo, Exec.Dir./CEO
Kapiti Rd.
Belle Vue, South C
PO Box 43706
Nairobi, Kenya
Phone: 254 20 607714
Phone: 254 20 604307
Fax: 254 20 607268
E-mail: info@kim.ac.ke
Home Page: http://www.kim.ac.ke

• 3358 • **Company of the Year Awards**
To identify and publicly recognize companies that demonstrate excellence and integrity in their management practices. Companies are grouped in the following sectors: Service; Manufacturing; Small and Medium Enterprises; and Parastatals. Awarded annually. Established in 2000.

• 3359 •
Kenya National Academy of Sciences
Ministry of Research, Science and Technology
Utalii House, Rm. 812
Utalii St.
PO Box 39450
Nairobi, Kenya
Phone: 254 20 311714
Fax: 254 20 311715
E-mail: sceretariat@knascience.org
Home Page: http://www.knas.g3z.com

• 3360 • **Honorary Fellow**
To recognize an individual for an outstanding contribution to science and technology.

• 3361 •
Kenyan Publishers Association
Mrs. Lynnette Kariuki, Exec.Sec.
PO Box 42767
Nairobi, Kenya
Phone: 254 20 3752344
Fax: 254 20 3754076
E-mail: info@kenyabooks.org
Home Page: http://www.kenyabooks.org

• 3362 • **Jomo Kenyatta Prize for Literature**
Recognizes the best newly published book. A monetary prize is given biennially.

• 3363 •
Kenyan Section of the International Commission of Jurists
Ms. Samuel Mbithi, Exec.Dir.
PO Box 59743
Kileleshwa
Nairobi, Kenya
Phone: 254 20 575981
Phone: 254 20 575982
Fax: 254 20 575982
E-mail: info@icj-kenya.org
Home Page: http://www.icj-kenya.org

• 3364 • **Jurist of the Year Award**
Recognizes an outstanding jurist who champions human rights. Awarded annually. Established in 1993.

• 3365 •
United Nations Environment Programme (Programme des Nations Unies pour l'Environnement)
Klaus Toepfer, Exec.Dir.
United Nations Ave., Gigiri
PO Box 30552
Nairobi, Kenya
Phone: 254 20 621234
Fax: 254 20 624489
E-mail: eisinfo@unep.org
Home Page: http://www.unep.org

• 3366 • **UNEP Sasakawa Environment Prize**
For recognition of achievement or contribution of the global level in the field of the environment. A monetary prize of $200,000 is awarded annually. Established in 1983 by a $1,000,000 endowment from the Japanese Shipbuilding Industry. The prize is today supported by the Nippon Foundation.

• 3367 • **United Nations Environment Program Awards**
To recognize individuals and organizations who have made outstanding contributions to the protection and improvement of the environment. To date, seven hundred individuals and organizations from every continent have been recognized in both the youth and adult categories.

Kuwait

• 3368 •
Organization of Arab Petroleum Exporting Countries (Organization de Paises Arabes Exportadores de Petroleo)
Abdul-Aziz A. Al-Turki, Sec.Gen.
PO Box 20501
Safat 13066, Kuwait
Phone: 965 4844500
Fax: 965 4815747
E-mail: oapec@qualitynet.net

• 3369 • **OAPEC Award for Scientific Research**
To promote and encourage scientific research by recognizing the outstanding research paper on a specified topic. Papers may be submitted by May 31 of even-numbered years. A monetary award and certificate are presented every two years at the end of even-numbered years. The certificate is presented a year later. Established in 1985.

• 3370 •
Regional Organization for the Protection of the Marine Environment
Dr. Abdul Rahman Al-Awadi, Exec.Sec.
PO Box 26388
Safat 13124, Kuwait
Phone: 965 5312140
Phone: 965 5312142
Fax: 965 5324172
E-mail: ropme@qualitynet.net
Home Page: http://www.ropme.com

• 3371 • **Environment Prize**
For outstanding contribution to environment protection in the region. A monetary prize is given annually.

Lithuania

• 3372 •
Academy of Sciences, Lithuania (Mokslu Akademija)
Prof. Zenonas Rokus Rudzikas, Pres.
Gedimino pr.3
LT-01103 Vilnius, Lithuania
Phone: 370 8 5 261 3651
Fax: 370 8 5 261 8464
E-mail: prezidiumas@ktl.mii.lt
Home Page: http://neris.mii.lt/LMA

• 3373 • **Kazimiero Barsauskas premija**
For recognition of achievements in electronics and electromechanics. Applications are accepted. A monetary prize of 2,000 litas is awarded every four years. Established in 1994 in honor of Kazimieras Barsauskas, a famous specialist of electrotechnics.

• 3374 • **Povilo Brazdziunas premija**
For recognition of achievements in experimental physics. Applications are accepted. A monetary prize of 2,000 litas is awarded every four years. Established in 1994 in honor of Povilas Brazdziunas, a well-known physicist.

• 3375 • **Kazimiero Buga premija**
For recognition of achievements in linguistics. Applications are accepted. A monetary prize of 2,000 litas is awarded every four years. Established in 1994 in honor of Kazimieras Buga, a famous Lithuanian linguist.

• 3376 • **Juozo Dalinkevicius premija**
For recognition of achievements in geosciences. Applications are accepted. A monetary prize of 2,000 litas is awarded every four years. Established in 1994 in honor of Juozas Dalinkevicius, a well-known Lithuanian geologist.

• 3377 • **Simono Daukantas premija**
For recognition of achievements in historical sciences. Applications are accepted. A monetary prize of 2,000 litas is awarded every four years.

Established in 1994 in honor of Simonas Daukantas, a famous Lithuanian historian.

• 3378 • Teodor Grotthuss premija

For recognition of achievements in electrochemistry. Applications are accepted. A monetary prize of 1,000 German marks is awarded every four years. Established in 1994 in honor of Teodor Grotus, a famous scientist.

• 3379 • Tado Ivanausko premija

For recognition of achievements in biology and environmental protection. Applications are accepted. A monetary prize of 2,000 litas is awarded every four years. Established in 1982 in honor of Tadas Ivanauskas, a well-known Lithuanian naturalist academician. Sponsored by the State Committee for Protection of Nature.

• 3380 • Adolfo Jucys premija

For recognition of achievements in theoretical physics. Applications are accepted. A monetary prize of 2,000 litas is awarded every four years. Established in 1994 in honor of Adolfas Jucys, a well-known Lithuanian physicist.

• 3381 • Vinco Kreve-Mickevicius premija

For recognition of achievements in literature. Applications are accepted. A monetary prize of 2,000 litas is awarded every four years. Established in 1994 in honor of Vincas-Kreve Mickevicius, a famous Lithuanian writer, and first president of the Lithuanian Academy of Sciences.

• 3382 • Jono Krisciunas premija

For recognition of achievements in agricultural sciences. Applications are accepted. A monetary prize of 2,000 litas is awarded every four years. Established in 1994 in honor of Jonas Krisciunas, a famous agriculturalist.

• 3383 • Vlado Lasas premija

For recognition of achievements in medicine. Applications are accepted. A monetary prize of 2,000 litas is awarded every four years. Established in 1994 in honor of Vladas Lasas, a well-known Lithuanian physician.

• 3384 • Juozo Matulis premija

For recognition of achievements in chemistry. Applications are accepted. A monetary prize of 2,000 litas is awarded every four years. Established in 1994 in honor of Juozas Matulis, a well-known Lithuanian chemist and former president of the Lithuanian Academy of Sciences.

• 3385 • Albino Rimka premija

For recognition of achievements in economics. Applications are accepted. A monetary prize of 2,000 litas is awarded every four years. Established in 1994 in honor of Albinas Rimka, a famous Lithuanian economist.

• 3386 • Kazimiero Simonaviciaus premija

For recognition of achievements in mechanical sciences. Applications are accepted. A monetary prize of 2,000 litas is awarded every four years. Established in 1995 in honor of Kazimieras Simonavicius, a famous artillery engineer, and the inventor of multi-staged rockets.

• 3387 • Pranciskaus Sivickis premija

For recognition of achievements in zoology. Applications are accepted. A monetary prize of 2,000 litas is awarded every four years. Established in 1982 in honor of P. Sivickis, a famous scientist and organizer of investigations in experimental zoology.

Luxembourg

• 3388 •

European Table Tennis Union
Mrs. Jeanny Dom, Gen.Sec.
37, Esplanade de la Moselle
L-6637 Wasserbillig, Luxembourg
Phone: 352 22 3030
Phone: 352 22 3031
Fax: 352 22 3060
E-mail: ettu@pt.lu
Home Page: http://www.ettu.org

• 3389 • European Competitions

To recognize the winners of the biennial tournament for senior citizens and the annual European Youth Championship.

• 3390 •

Federation Internationale de l'Art Photographique
Emile Wanderscheid, Pres.
32, rue du Baumbusch
L-8213 Mamer, Luxembourg
Phone: 352 310863
Fax: 352 312299
E-mail: info@fiap.net
Home Page: http://www.fiap.net

• 3391 • World Cup

For recognition of outstanding photography in the following categories: monochrome prints, color prints, and color slides. National Societies affiliated with FIAP may enter biennial international photographic contests between national photographic societies.

• 3392 •

Vatel-Club Luxembourg
Armand Steinmetz, Pres.
BP 271
L-9003 Ettelbruck, Luxembourg
Phone: 352 802453
Fax: 352 809897
E-mail: secretary@vatel.lu
Home Page: http://www.vatel-club.lu

• 3393 • Culinary World Cup

To recognize outstanding culinary ability. The competition is built around research and development and establishing food trends for the future. Medals are awarded at the EXPOGAST trade show held quadrennially in Luxembourg. Established in 1980.

Malaysia

• 3394 •

Asia-Pacific Association of Forestry Research Institutions
Dr. Sim Heok-choh, Exec.Dir.
Universiti Putra Malaysia
Kepong
52109 Selangor, Malaysia
Phone: 60 3 62722516
Phone: 60 3 62773207
Fax: 60 3 62773249
E-mail: secretariat@apafri.org
Home Page: http://www.apafri.org

• 3395 • Dr. Y.S. Rao Forestry Research Award

For outstanding work on problem solving forestry research with significant practical application value. Awarded triennially.

• 3396 •

Asia-Pacific Broadcasting Union
David Astley, Sec.Gen.
PO Box 1164
59700 Kuala Lumpur, Malaysia
Phone: 60 3 22823592
Fax: 60 3 22825292
E-mail: info@abu.org.my
Home Page: http://www.abu.org.my/

• 3397 • ABU Engineering Award

To encourage technical writing in broadcast engineering. ABU members in are eligible. A monetary prize of $400 US and a certificate for the Best Paper and two prizes of $300 each and certificates for the commended papers contributed to the bimonthly publication *ABU Technical Review* are awarded annually. Established in 1973.

• 3398 • ABU Prizes for Radio and Television Programs

For recognition of the high standard of a production in the field of radio and television programs. Prizes are awarded in the following categories for radio: Drama, Infotainment; News & Documentary; Children and Youth; and External Broadcasts; and in the following categories for television: Drama; Entertainment; Children and Youth; News & Documentary; and Sports. Awarded annually. Established in 1964.

• 3399 • Dennis Anthony Memorial Award

For the Best news coverage of the year by a member of Asiavision, the daily news exchange among member stations of the Asia-Pacific Broadcasting Union (ABU). Awarded annually. Sponsored by CNN, who selects the winner. Named after a former ABU Senior Officer, News, who died in 1996.

• 3400 •
Asian Association of Management Organisations
Dr. Jamshed J. Irani, Pres.
Management House
227 Jalan Ampang
50450 Kuala Lumpur, Malaysia
Phone: 60 3 21645255
Fax: 60 3 21643171
E-mail: aamo@mim.edu
Home Page: http://www.aamo.net

• 3401 • **MBA (International Management) Best Student Award**
Award of recognition for the top student in the masterKs level program. Presented bimonthly. Co-administered by RMIT University.

• 3402 •
Asian Football Confederation
Peter Velappan, Gen.Sec.
AFC House Jalan 1/155B
Bukit Jalil
57000 Kuala Lumpur, Malaysia
Phone: 60 3 89943388
Fax: 60 3 89942689
E-mail: media@the-afc.com
Home Page: http://www.the-afc.com

• 3403 • **Annual Awards**
To recognize outstanding performance. The following awards are presented at an annual ceremony: Goal of the Year; Referee of the Year; Assistant Referee of the Year; Women's Team of the Year; Fairplay Award; Football Writer of the Year; Young Player of the Year; Coach of the Year; Team of the Year; and Player of the Year.

• 3404 •
International Badminton Federation
3 1/2 Miles, Jalan Cheras
5600 Kuala Lumpur, Malaysia
E-mail: ibf@internationalbadminton.org
Home Page: http://www.worldbadminton.net

• 3405 • **Certificate of Commendation**
To be awarded, where appropriate, to commercial undertakings and other external organizations that have rendered significant services to the game. Nominations to be made by Member Associations. Service shall have been for a period of at least three years and will have made a significant contribution to the nominating organization. Awarded annually to multiple recipients.

• 3406 • **Distinguished Service Award**
For recognition of major support in the development of badminton. Nominations must be made by resolution of a standing committee of the Council. Awarded annually to one or more recipients.

• 3407 • **IBF Distinguished Service Award**
For recognition of a long and distinguished service to the game of badminton in an international context. Awarded annually. Established in 1985.

• 3408 • **IBF Meritorious Service Award**
For recognition of a long and meritorious service to the game of badminton in a national context, or for outstanding service as a court official. Awarded annually. Established in 1985.

• 3409 • **International Badminton Federation Distinguished Service Award**
For recognition of long and/or distinguished service to badminton throughout the world. Long service means at least fifteen years in international play and/or administration. Distinguished service, where less than fifteen years involvement is not fulfilled, means a service which is clearly distinguished in an international sense. All nominations must be presented to the Council which approves the award to each person. The decision must be unanimous in every case. A certificate and a lapel badge are awarded biannually. Established in 1985.

• 3410 • **Meritorious Service Award**
For recognition of long and meritorious service to badminton. Long service means at least fifteen years. Nominations should preferably be received from the nominee's National Organization but the Council may dispense with the requirement. A certificate and a lapel badge are awarded when merited. Established in 1985.

• 3411 • **Herbert Scheele Trophy**
For recognition of outstandingly exceptional services to badminton. A trophy and certificate are awarded when merited. Established in 1986 in memory of Herbert Scheele, past honorable secretary of the Federation (1937-1976).

• 3412 •
Malaysian Rubber Products Manufacturers Association
Mr. Kong Ping Yee, Exec.Dir.
1A, Jalan USJ 11/1J
Subang Jaya
47620 Petaling Jaya, Malaysia
Phone: 60 3 56316150
Fax: 60 3 56316152
E-mail: mrpma@po.jaring.my
Home Page: http://www.mrpma.com

• 3413 • **Honorary Life President**
For exceptional contributions to the rubber industry.

• 3414 •
Olympic Council of Malaysia
(Majlis Olimpik Malaysia)
Kok Chi Sieh, Sec. Gen.
Mezzanine Fl., Wisma OCM
Hang Jebat Rd.
MY-50150 Kuala Lumpur, Malaysia
Phone: 60 3 27152802
Phone: 60 3 27152804
Fax: 60 3 27152801
E-mail: secretariat@olympic.org.my
Home Page: http://www.olympic.org.my

• 3415 • **Hall of Fame**
For athletes with outstanding sporting achievements and sports officials with excellent contributions and services to the development of sports in Malaysia.

• 3416 • **Tan Sri Alex Lee Athletes Scholarship Awards**
For present and former national athletes to pursue further education.

• 3417 • **Olympian of the Year Award**
To a male athlete and a female athlete with the best performance in a multisports game for the year.

• 3418 •
World Association of Industrial and Technological Research Organizations (Association Mondiale des Organisations de Recherche Industrielle et Technologique)
Goey Peck Sim, Acting Sec.Gen.
SIRIM Berhad
1, Persiaran Dato' Menteri, Sec. 2
PO Box 7035
40911 Shah Alam, Malaysia
Phone: 60 3 55446635
Fax: 60 3 55446735
E-mail: info@waitro.sirim.my
Home Page: http://www.waitro.org

• 3419 • **Award of Honour**
To recognize organizations or individuals making substantial contribution to the achievement of WAITRO's aims. Awarded biennially in even-numbered years.

Malta

• 3420 •
Institute of Maltese Journalists
(Institut Tal-Gurnalisti Maltin)
Mr. Joe A. Vella, Sec.Gen.
104 Old Mint St.
Valletta CMR 01, Malta
Phone: 356 21316958
Phone: 356 373826
Fax: 356 249290
E-mail: institute.of.maltese.journalists@gmail.com
Home Page: http://www.maltapressclub.org.mt

• 3421 • Malta Journalism Awards
To recognize excellence by Maltese journalists. A gold medal is awarded in various categories. In addition, the overall Journalist of the Year is presented. Awarded annually.

• 3422 •
Malta Amateur Cine Circle
PO Box 450
Valletta CMR 01, Malta
Phone: 356 222345
Fax: 356 225047
E-mail: macc@global.net.mt
Home Page: http://www.global.net.mt/macc

• 3423 • Golden Knight International Amateur Film and Video Festival
To encourage professional development of the short film and video. Any number of films and videos which are preferably not longer than 30 minutes may be submitted. Productions entered in past Golden Knight Festivals are not accepted. Entries may be on Super 8mm, Single-8, 16mm or VHS videotape, in color or black/white, and on any subject. The deadline for submission of entry forms films/videos is September 15. The Festival is divided into three classes: Class A - Amateur productions by individuals, groups or clubs made for pleasure with no commercial purpose in mind; Class B - Productions made by film-school students during their studies; and Class C - Any production which does not qualify under Class A or Class B. The following awards are presented: Golden Knight, which is retainable, and a Certificate of Merit - for the Best Productions in Class A, B and C; Silver Knight, which is retainable, and a Certificate of Merit - for the second place entry in Class A and B; Bronze Knight which is retainable, and a Certificate of Merit in Class A and B; Malta Amateur Cine Circle Trophy, retainable for one year, and a Certificate of Merit - for the Best Entry (film or video) in Class A from a resident of Malta; Sultana Cup, retainable for one year, and a Certificate of Merit - to the entry which best extols the merits of Malta from some particular aspect, applicable to one entry from any class; and Highly Commended Certificates - to entries of outstanding merit. Awarded annually in November. Established in 1961. The President of Malta is a patron. Formerly: Golden Knight International Amateur Film Festival.

• 3424 •
The Office of the Prime Minister of Malta
Auberge De Castille
Valletta CMR 02, Malta
Phone: 356 22 001 400
Fax: 356 22 001 467
E-mail: joseph.fiott@magnet.mt
Home Page: http://www.opm.gov.mt/the.prime.minister.htm

• 3425 • Malta Self-Government Reintroduction Seventy-Fifth Anniversary Medal
To recognize persons living on the 7th of June, 1996 who at any time since the 1st of November, 1921, was, or is, a Member of the Senate, Legislative Assembly or House of Representatives.

• 3426 • Medal for Bravery (Midalja ghall-Qlubija)
To recognize a Maltese citizen for exceptional bravery. A medal is awarded by the President of the Republic of Malta, on the written advice of the Prime Minister, when merited and may be awarded posthumously. Established in 1975 by the Government of Malta.

• 3427 • Medal for Service to the Republic (Midalja ghall-Qadi tar-Repubblika)
To recognize distinguished service to Malta. Maltese citizens are eligible, and citizens of other countries are eligible on an honorary basis. A medal is awarded by the President of the Republic of Malta when merited (on the written advice of the Prime Minister). No more than 10 awards may be made in one year, and the total number of recipients may not exceed 100. Established in 1975 by the Government of Malta.

• 3428 • National Order of Merit
To recognize Maltese citizens who distinguish themselves in different fields of endeavor. Maltese citizens may be appointed members of the Order and honorary memberships may be conferred on foreign nationals who have distinguished themselves by their service in the promotion and fostering of international relations or who have earned the respect and gratitude of the people of the Maltese Islands. There are four grades of the Order: Companion of Honor, Companion, Officer, and Member. Established in 1990 by the Government of Malta as a consolidation of the Gieh ir-Repubblika Act, 1975.

• 3429 • Xirka Gieh ir-Repubblika
Induction to this honor society recognizes distinguished persons who have demonstrated merit in the service of Malta or of humanity. Maltese citizens may be appointed members of the Society and others may be appointed honorary members by the President of the Republic of Malta on the written advice of the Prime Minister. The total membership is limited to 20 persons. New appointments are made only when a vacancy occurs. Established in 1975.

Mexico

• 3430 •
Asociacion Nacional de Actores
Altamarino No. 126
01300 San Rafael, Federal District, Mexico
Phone: 52 5 7050624
E-mail: casting@anda-actores.com.mx
Home Page: http://famosos.tripod.com.mx/loscomediantes/id11.html

• 3431 • Magda Donato Prize (Premio Magda Donato)
For recognition of outstanding contributions of a primarily humanistic nature, through exacting and beautiful language, to the knowledge and proper valuation of the great cultures. A monetary prize of 2,000,000 Mexican pesos and a certificate are awarded annually. Established in 1977.

• 3432 •
Asociacion Nacional de la Publicidad
Lic. Francioli Vazquez, Pres.
UXMAL 620
Col. Vertiz Narvarte
06700 Mexico City, Federal District, Mexico
Phone: 52 5605 7001
Fax: 52 5605 0821
E-mail: gerentegeneral@anp.com.mx
Home Page: http://www.anp.com.mx

• 3433 • Premio Nacional
To recognize the most outstanding marketers of media publicity with the theme of popular consumption or representatives of industrial products or services. A gold statue is awarded annually in the categories of radio, television, the press, or audiovisual media in general. Established in 1950.

• 3434 •
Centre for Latin American Monetary Studies
(Centro de Estudios Monetarios Latinoamericanos)
Dr. Kenneth G. Coats Spry, Dir.Gen.
Durango 54
Col. Roma
06700 Mexico City, Durango, Mexico
Phone: 52 55 55330300
Phone: 52 55 55255921
Fax: 52 55 55254432
E-mail: rodriguez@cemla.org
Home Page: http://www.cemla.org

• 3435 • Rodrigo Gomez Prize
Recognizes outstanding contributions in the areas of economic, jury, finance, and monetary studies. Awarded annually.

• 3436 •
Chemical Organization of Mexico
(Sociedad Quimica de Mexico)
Av. Barranca del Muerto No. 26
Credito Constructor, Delegacion Benito Juarez
CP 03940 Mexico City, Federal District, Mexico
Phone: 52 5 3860255
Fax: 52 5 3862905
Home Page: http://www.sqm.org.mx

• 3437 • Andres Manuel del Rio National Prize in Chemistry (Premio Nacional de Quimica Andres Manuel del Rio)
To recognize chemistry professionals who have contributed extraordinarily towards raising the quality and the prestige of the chemistry profession in Mexico. Awards are made in two categories: academic and industrial. Members of the Society must make nominations by June 30. Medals and diplomas are awarded annually to one or more recipients. Established in 1964 in memory of Andres Manuel del Rio (1764-1849), the discoverer of the element Vanadium, atomic number 23, in 1801.

Awards are arranged in alphabetical order below their administering organizations

• 3438 •
Cineteca Nacional
Magdalena Acosta, Dir.Gen.
av. Mexico-Coyoacan 389
03300 Mexico City, Federal District, Mexico
Phone: 52 55 1253 9390
Fax: 52 55 5688 4211
E-mail: cineteca@cinetecanacional.net
Home Page: http://www.cinetecanacional.net

• 3439 • **Salvador Toscano Medal**
(Medalla Ing. Salvador Toscano)
For recognition of outstanding contributions to cinematography in industry. Awarded annually. Established in 1982.

• 3440 •
Consejo Nacional de Ciencia y Tecnologia
Gustavo Adolfo Chapela, Dir.Gen.
Av. Insurgentes Sur No. 1582
Col. Credito Constructor
Del. Benito Juarez
03940 Mexico City, Federal District, Mexico
Phone: 52 55 53227700
Home Page: http://www.conacyt.mx

• 3441 • **Premio Nacional de Ciencia y Tecnologia de Alimentos**
To recognize outstanding work and stimulate research in the field of nutrition. Awards are given in the following categories: (1) Premio Nacional al Merito; (2) Professional; and (3) Student. Awarded annually.

• 3442 •
Fundacion Miguel Aleman
Fernando Castro, Dir.Gen.
Ruben Dario 187
Del Miguel Hidalgo
11570 Mexico City, Federal District, Mexico
Phone: 52 5 5317065
Fax: 52 5 2501043
Home Page: http://www.miguelaleman.org.mx

• 3443 • **Premio Miguel Aleman Valdes**
To recognize and stimulate young researchers and to promote research in the knowledge, prevention, and control of the principal maladies affecting the country's health. Mexican citizens under 40 year of age who are registered researchers in the biological, biomedical, and technological sciences are eligible. A monetary prize of 25,000 Mexican pesos and the support of the project is awarded annually. Established in 1985.

• 3444 •
Gobierno del Estado de Morelos
Cuernavaca, Morelos, Mexico
E-mail: modernizacion@morelos.gob.mx
Home Page: http://www.morelos.gob.mx/

• 3445 • **Gilberto Figueroa Nogueron Prize**
(Premio Gilberto Figueroa Nogueron)
To recognize the most outstanding journalist. A monetary prize is awarded annually by the state of Morelos. Established in 1989.

• 3446 •
Instituto Cultural Domecq, A.C.
Viena 161 Esq. Mina
Col. del Carmen Covoacan
04100 Mexico City, Federal District, Mexico
Phone: 52 5 19977404
Fax: 52 5 6590695
E-mail: rentas@globaltec.com.mx
Home Page: http://www.mexico-tenoch.com

• 3447 • **Mozart Medal**
To recognize young musicians for their talent in music composition, direction, and interpretation. Mexican composers who are under 35 years of age are eligible. A monetary prize of 3,000,000 Mexican pesos is awarded. Established in 1991 to commemorate the bicentennial of the death of Mozart.

• 3448 •
Inter-American Society of Cardiology
(Sociedad Interamericana de Cardiologia)
Dr. J. Antonio Gonzalez-Hermosillo MD, Sec.-Treas.
Instituto Nacional de Cardiologia
Calle Jaun Bardiano 1
14080 Mexico City, Federal District, Mexico
Phone: 52 55 55732911
Phone: 52 55 55133740
Fax: 52 55 55135177
E-mail: soinca@mail.cpesa.com.mx
Home Page: http://www.soinca.org

• 3449 • **Professor Ignacio Chavez Young Investigator Award**
(Premio Joven Investigador Profesor Ignacio Chavez)
To recognize the best cardiological work presented at the Interamerican Congress of Cardiology. The Congress is held every two years in a city of the continent (America).

• 3450 •
Mexican Academy of Sciences
(Academia Mexicana de Ciencias)
Dr. Octavio Paredes, Pres.
Calle Cypresses s/n
Km 23.5 de la carretera federal Mexico-Cuernavaca
San Andres Totoltepec
14400 Tlalpan, Federal District, Mexico
Phone: 52 5 849 4905
Fax: 52 5 584 95112
E-mail: academia@amc.unam.mx
Home Page: http://www.unam.mx/academia

Formerly: (1997) Academy of Scientific Research; Academia de la Investigacion Cientifica.

• 3451 • **Scientific Research Prizes**
(Premios de Investigacion Cientifica)
For recognition of contributions to scientific research in the following areas: (1) natural sciences; (2) social sciences; (3) exact sciences; (4) technological innovation. Scientists and researchers working permanently in Mexico and under 40 years of age are eligible. The awards are given for a complete career rather than for a single publication or research paper. A monetary prize in Mexican pesos and a diploma are awarded annually for each field. The monetary prize changes every year. Established in 1961.

• 3452 • **Weizmann Prizes**
(Premios Weizmann de la Academia Mexicana de Ciencias)
For recognition of the best doctoral thesis in the field of: (1) natural sciences and (2) exact sciences. Originality and scientific importance are considered. Individuals under 35 years of age are eligible for thesis research done in Mexico and the degree must be conferred by a Mexican institution. A monetary prize in Mexican pesos and a diploma is awarded for each thesis annually. Established in 1986. Formerly: (1997) Weizmann Prizes of the Academy of Scientific Research (Premios Weizmann de la Academia de la Investigacion Cientifica).

• 3453 •
Mexico Ministry of Foreign Affairs
Ricardo Flores Magon, no. 1
Col. Guerrero
Tlatelolco
06995 Mexico City, Federal District, Mexico
Phone: 52 55 5063 3000
Home Page: http://www.sre.gob.mx

• 3454 • **Mexican Order of the Aztec Eagle**
(Orden Mexicana del Aguila Azteca)
For recognition of outstanding services to Mexico and humanity by persons of foreign nationality. The following awards are presented in military and civil classes: (1) a chain with an insignia of honor (el collar) - to chiefs of states; (2) a cross - to heads of governments or prime ministers; (3) a sash - to ministers, secretaries of state and ambassadors; (4) a medal - to under secretaries, special envoys and ministers plenipotenciary; (5) a plaque - to charge d'affairs; (6) a badge (la venera) - to public officials in foreign chanceries and members of diplomatic missions; and (7) an insignia - to others the Award Council wants to honor. Awarded when merited. No more than 415 may be awarded. Established in 1933.

• 3455 •
United Nations High Commission for Refugees - Regional Office Mexico
Roberto Rodriguez, Regional Rep.
Presidente Masaryk No. 29, Piso 6
Col. Palmas Polanco
11560 Polanco, Federal District, Mexico
Phone: 52 5 2639864
Phone: 52 5 2639863
Fax: 52 5 2509203
E-mail: mexme@unhcr.ch
Home Page: http://www.unhcr.ch

• 3456 • **Nansen Refugee Award**
To recognize individual or organizations that have distinguished themselves in work on behalf of refugees. A medal and monetary prize of $100,000 is awarded annually. Established in 1954. Formerly: (2006) Nansen Medal.

• 3457 •
World Boxing Council
(Consejo Mundial de Boxeo)
Jose Sulaiman, Pres.
Genova 33, Oficina 503
Colonia Juarez
Cuauhtemoc
06600 Mexico City, Federal District, Mexico
Phone: 52 55 5525 3787
Fax: 52 55 5207 7172
E-mail: info@wbcboxing.com
Home Page: http://www.wbcboxing.com

• 3458 • **World Boxing Council Awards**
To recognize the winners of world boxing title fights.

• 3459 •
World Cultural Council
(Consejo Cultural Mundial)
Dr. Lillyan Hernandez, Sec.Gen.
Apartado Postal 11-823
Monterrey NL
CP 06101 Mexico City, Federal District, Mexico
Phone: 52 55 55892907
Fax: 52 55 55898857
E-mail: wcc@axtel.net
Home Page: http://www.consejoculturalmundial.org

• 3460 • **Albert Einstein World Award of Science**
To recognize individuals for scientific and technological achievements that have brought progress to science and benefit to humankind. Candidates must be nominated. A monetary prize of US$10,000, a medal, and a diploma are awarded annually. Deadlines are April 30 and November 30.

• 3461 • **Jose Vasconcelos World Award of Education**
To recognize an educator, an authority in the field of teaching, or a legislator of education policies who has had a significant influence on the advancement of human culture. Candidates must be nominated. A monetary prize of US$10,000, a medal, and a diploma are awarded biennially.

• 3462 • **Leonardo da Vinci World Award of Arts**
To recognize artists, avant guardists, or art authorities whose works constitute a significant contribution to the artistic legacy of the world. A monetary prize of US$10,000, a medal, and a diploma are awarded biennially.

Moldova

• 3463 •
Football Association of Moldova
Pavel Cebanu, Pres.
str. Tricolorului 39
MD-2012 Chisinau, Moldova
Phone: 373 2 247878
Fax: 373 2 247890
E-mail: fmf@mfotbal.mldnet.com
Home Page: http://www.fmf.md/news_en.htm

• 3464 • **Champion Cup Holder**
Recognizes the best team clubs in all divisions. Awarded annually.

Monaco

• 3465 •
International Association of Athletics Federations
(Association Internationale des Federations di Athletisme)
Pierre Weiss, Gen.Dir.
17 rue Princesse Florestine
BP 359
MC-98007 Monaco Cedex, Monaco
Phone: 377 93 108888
Fax: 377 93 159515
E-mail: headquarters@iaaf.org
Home Page: http://www.iaaf.org

• 3466 • **World Athletics Series**
Competitions include the IAAF World Cross Country Championships, IAAF/Coca World Road Relay Championships, IAAF World Junior Championships, IAAF Grand Prix Final, IAAF World Cup in Athletics, IAAF World Half Marathon Championships, IAAF World Indoor Championships, IAAF World Marathon Cup, and IAAF World Cup of Race Walking. Gold, silver, and bronze medals are awarded for every event in every competition.

• 3467 • **World Championships**
To recognize men and women for accomplishments in track and field. Competition is held in the following events: 100 meters, 200 meters, 400 meters, 800 meters, 1,500 meters, 5,000 meters, 10,000 meters, marathon, decathlon (men), heptathlon (women), 3,000-meter steeplechase (men), 10 km walk (women), 20 and 50km walk (men), 110 and 400 hurdles, 4x100 and 4x400 relays, high jump, pole vault (men), long jump, triple jump, shot, discus, hammer (men), and javelin. Medals are awarded every four years. The World Marathon Cup is also awarded.

• 3468 •
Monte Carlo Television Festival
(Festival de Television de Monte Carlo)
Lynnette Parsons, Competition Coord.
% Monaco Mediax
4 blvd. du Jardin Exotique
MC-98000 Monte Carlo, Monaco
Phone: 377 9310 4060
Fax: 377 9350 7014
E-mail: info@tvfestival.com
Home Page: http://www.tvfestival.com

Formerly: International Television Festival of Monte Carlo.

• 3469 • **Monte Carlo Television Festival (Festival International de Television de Monte Carlo)**
For recognition of the best television programs. The competition is held in four categories: television series, news, mini-series, and television films. Nymph Awards are presented in a variety of subcategories. In addition, the following awards are presented: International TV Audience Award, URTI Prize, Red Cross International Committee Prize, Signis Prize, Prince Ranier III Special Prize, and the AMADE-UNESCO Prize, for a film that deals with an issue of human relations and whose plot and treatment neither feature violence nor excite to it. Awarded annually in February. Established in 1961. Formerly: International Television Festival of Monte Carlo.

• 3470 •
Prince Pierre Foundation of Monaco
4, boul. des Moulins
MC-98000 Monte Carlo, Monaco
Phone: 377 9315 8515
Fax: 377 9350 6694
E-mail: jlfroment@fondationprincepierre.mcmc
Home Page: http://www.fondationprincepierre.mc

• 3471 • **International Prize for Contemporary Art**
To recognize a work of contemporary art that was created in the previous two years. The winner receives a monetary prize of 15,000 euros and exhibition of the whole selected works is held in Monte Carlo. Awarded annually. Established in 1965.

• 3472 • **Prix de Composition Musicale**
To recognize a contemporary music work created during the last year. Composers of any nationality are eligible. Candidatures are not admitted. A monetary prize of 15,000 Euro and a medal bearing the effigy of H. S. H. Prince Pierre de Monaco are awarded in the spring of each year. Established in 1960.

• 3473 • **Prix Litteraire Prince Pierre-de-Monaco**
To recognize an author who writes in the French language and who is already internationally known for the whole of his or her works. A monetary prize of 15,000 Euro and a medal bearing the effigy of H. S. H. Prince Pierre de Monaco

are awarded in the spring of each year. Established in 1951.

Morocco

• 3474 •
World Phosphate Institute
(Institut Mondial du Phosphate)
Tayeb Mrabet, Sec.Gen.
3 rue Abdelkader Al Mazini
BP 15963
Casablanca 20001, Morocco
Phone: 212 2248 4122
Fax: 212 2248 4121
E-mail: imphos@casanet.net.ma
Home Page: http://www.imphos.org
Formerly: World Phosphate Rock Institute.

• 3475 • **IMPHOS-FAI Award**
To recognize achievements in phosphate fertilizer research during the past five years. Granted annually to one or more researchers in the Indian subcontinent who have contributed to the advancement of knowledge on phosphate fertilizers and their application in India. Formerly: (2004) World Phosphate Institute Awards.

Nepal

• 3476 •
Handicraft Association of Nepal
(Nepal Hastakala Udhyog Sangh)
Dilip Khalal, Exec. Sec.
PO Box 784
13, Upama Marg, Taphathali
Ward No. 11
Kathmandu, Nepal
Phone: 977 1 4245467
Phone: 977 1 4244231
Fax: 977 1 4222940
E-mail: han@wlink.com.np
Home Page: http://www.nepalhandicraft.org

• 3477 • **Best Craftsmanship**
For the best handicraft's uniqueness and export possibility.

• 3478 • **Best Entrepreneurship**
For operating the enterprise in an exemplary manner.

• 3479 • **Top Exporter**
For the highest exporter among members.

• 3480 •
Nepal Association of Tour and Travel Agents
Mr. Rabi Paudel, Pres.
Gairidhara Rd.
PO Box 362
Goma Ganesh, Naxal
Kathmandu, Nepal
Phone: 977 1 419409
Phone: 977 1 418661
Fax: 977 1 418684
E-mail: nata@mail.com.np
Home Page: http://www.nata.org.np

• 3481 • **Bhaskar Award**
To recognize a national figure who has made an outstanding contribution towards consolidating the tourism industry of the country. Awarded biennially.

• 3482 • **Sagarmatha Award**
To recognize an international figure who has made an outstanding contribution towards the tourism industry. Awarded biennially.

Netherlands

• 3483 •
Algemeen Nederlands Verbond
Jan van Nassaustraat 109
NL-2596 BS The Hague, Netherlands
Phone: 31 70 3245514
Fax: 31 70 3246186
E-mail: info@algemeennederlandsverbond.org
Home Page: http://www.algemeennederlandsverbond.org

• 3484 • **Visser-Nederlandia Prijzen**
To encourage playwriting in the Netherlands. A monetary prize of 8000 Euro is awarded biennially.

• 3485 •
Anna Bijns-Stichting
Bogortuin 187
NL-1019 PE Amsterdam, Netherlands
Phone: 31 6 5239 1770
E-mail: fleurspeet@annabijnsprijs.nl
Home Page: http://www.annabijnsprijs.nl

• 3486 • **Anna Bijnsprijs**
Recognizes a Dutch woman author for works of prose, poetry, or essay. Awarded biennially. Established in 1986.

• 3487 •
Carnegie Foundation
(Carnegie Stichting)
Carnegieplein 2
NL-2517 KJ The Hague, Netherlands
Phone: 31 70 3024242
Fax: 31 70 3024178
E-mail: peacepalace@carnegie-stichting.nl
Home Page: http://www.carnegie-stichting.nl

• 3488 • **Wateler Peace Prize**
(Wateler-Vredesprijs)
To recognize an individual or institution having rendered the most valuable service in the cause of world peace, or having contributed to finding a means of combating war. A monetary prize is awarded annually in alternate years to a Dutch and a foreign person or organization. Established in 1927 by a bequest to the Carnegie Foundation from J. G. D. Wateler, a Dutch citizen who died in 1927.

• 3489 •
Chancery of Netherlands Orders
(Kanselarij der Nederlandse Orden)
Nassaulaan 18
PO Box 30436
NL-2500 GK The Hague, Netherlands
Phone: 31 70 375 1200
Fax: 31 70 365 2923
E-mail: infor@kanselaeij.nl
Home Page: http://www.lintjes.nl

• 3490 • **Military Order of William**
(Militaire Willems-Orde)
To recognize Netherlanders or foreigners for conspicuous gallantry in the presence of the enemy. Awarded in four classes. Dutch citizens have to start as Knights 4th class, but can be promoted for further acts of bravery to Knight 3rd Class, Knight 2nd Class and Knight Commander. Such promotions are relatively rare. Established in 1815. (The ranking of the Orders of Knighthood is: (1) Military Order of William; (2) Order of the Netherlands Lion and (3) Order of Orange-Nassau).

• 3491 • **Order of Orange-Nassau**
(Orde van Oranje-Nassau)
To recognize Dutch citizens or foreigners who have made themselves particularly deserving towards the Dutch people and the State, or towards society. This Order has six classes:Grand Cross;Grand Officer;Commander; Officer;Knight;and Member. Awarded in two divisions: with swords, for military recipients; and a general division for others. Established in 1892.

• 3492 • **Order of the Golden Ark**
To recognize outstanding service to the conservation of wildlife and the natural environment. Established in 1972 by H.R.H. Prince Bernhard of the Netherlands, founder-President of the World Wildlife Fund. (The Order of the Golden Ark is a private award of H.R.H. Prince Bernhard of the Netherlands and does not belong to the Netherlands' Orders of Knighthood).

• 3493 • **Order of the Netherlands Lion**
To recognize Netherlanders who have displayed tested patriotism, unusual dedication and loyalty in the carrying out of their civil duties, or extraordinary skill and performance in the sciences and arts. This Order, in exceptional cases, is given to foreigners, and consists of three classes: Grand Cross; Commander; and Knight. Established in 1815.

• 3494 •
Collective Promotion of the Dutch Book
(Stichting Collectieve Propaganda van het Nederlandse Boek)
Postbus 10576
NL-1001 EN Amsterdam, Netherlands
Phone: 31 20 6264971
Fax: 31 20 6231696
E-mail: info@cpnb.nl
Home Page: http://www.cpnb.nl

• 3495 • Golden Kiss (Gouden Zoen)
For recognition of the most outstanding books written for children between the ages of 12 and 15. Books must have been published in the Netherlands within the preceding year and must have been written originally in Dutch. A golden kiss/medal and a monetary prize and two Silver Kisses are awarded annually. Established in 1997.

• 3496 • Prijs van de Jonge Jury
Dutch children between the ages of 12 and 15 elect the best Dutch book for children. Books must have been published during the previous year in the Netherlands. Established in 1998.

• 3497 • Prijs van de Nederlandse Kinderjury
To recognize the best children books that were published during the preceding year in two age categories (6 to 9 years and 9 to 12 years). The prize is awarded by Dutch children ages six to twelve. Two diplomas are awarded annually. Established in 1988.

• 3498 • Trouw Publieksprijs voor het Nederlandse Boek
For recognition of the best general book published in Dutch during the preceding year. The prize is based on the results of a nationwide poll. The public chooses from 6 best selling titles nominated by a committee of booksellers. The winning author receives a monetary award, a sculpture of Jeroen Henneman and the right to carry the title "Book of the Year."

• 3499 •
Conamus
(Stichting Conamus)
PO Box 929
NL-1200 AX Hilversum, Netherlands
Phone: 31 35 621 8748
Fax: 31 35 621 2750
E-mail: info@conamus.nl
Home Page: http://www.conamus.nl

• 3500 • Conamus Export Prize
To recognize Dutch performers based on the figures of records-sales abroad. These figures are obtained from records companies, music publishers, and personal or business managers of qualifying artists. A trophy is awarded annually.

• 3501 • Conamus Golden Harp
This, the highest award in light music in Holland, recognizes individuals who have contributed to national light music in exceptional ways. A trophy is awarded annually.

• 3502 • Pop Award
To recognize the Dutch artist who made the biggest contribution to Dutch pop music in the previous year. Awarded annually.

• 3503 • Silver Harp
To encourage young Dutch artists in the field of entertainment who are expected to develop into credits to their trade. A trophy is awarded annually.

• 3504 •
Dutch Cancer Society
(Nederlandse Kankerbestirijding -KWF)
P.N.M. Creijghton, Sec.
PO Box 75508
Sophialaan 8
NL-1075 BR Amsterdam, Netherlands
Phone: 31 20 5700500
Fax: 31 20 6750302
E-mail: info@kwfkankerbestrijding.nl
Home Page: http://www .kwfkankerbestrijding.nl

Formerly: (1995) Stichting Koningin Wilhelmina Fonds.

• 3505 • Dutch Cancer Society Press Award
Granted to a natural person or corporation body which by means of journalism has contributed in an exceptional way to either disseminating knowledge about cancer among the public or to improvement of the patient with cancer and his next of kin. Established in 2001 by a proposal of the 1999 winner of the of. Dr. P Muntendamprijs award. Will be awarded for five years.

• 3506 • Prof. Dr. P. Muntendamprijs
For recognition of contributions to the fight against cancer in the Netherlands, in the fields of cancer research, treatment, nursing, professional and non-professional care of cancer patients, journalism, public information, patient education, or in organizational aspects. There are no restrictions as to age. Nominations may be made by anyone or any group before March 1. A scroll and bronze plaque are awarded annually at the convention of members of the Society. The winner may allocate $30,000 to goal within the field of cancer control after board approval. Established in 1975 in memory of Professor Dr. P. Muntendam, former President of the Board of the Society. the Board of the Society.

• 3507 •
Dutch International Vocal Competition - Hertogenbosch
(Internationaal Vocalisten Concours 's-Hertogenbosch)
Marc Versteeg, Mgr.
Postbus 1225
NL-5200 BG S-Hertogenbosch, Netherlands
Phone: 31 73 6900999
Fax: 31 73 6901166
E-mail: info@ivc.nu
Home Page: http://www.ivc.nu

• 3508 • Dutch International Vocal Competition - Hertogenbosch (Internationaal Vocalisten Concours 's-Hertogenbosch)
For recognition of oratorio, opera and lied singers of any nationality under the age of 35 who enter the competition in one of the following voices: soprano, mezzosoprano/contralto, tenor, and baritone/bass. The deadline for entries for live auditions is September 1. A First Prize of 20,000 US dollars is offered to the winners in all categories. Other prizes, varying from 2,000 to 5,000 US dollars are offered for outstanding interpretations of arias and lieder as well as a Press and Public Prize. The Grand Prix award (the Prize of the City of 's-Hertogenbosch) is awarded to the singer who merits a special distinction for her/his artistic and technical qualities and is the highest distinction for the best vocalist of the competition. Since the competition began, this special distinction has been given to 23 singers. The Competition was established in 1954 and is held annually. Sponsored by the Municipality of 's-Hertogenbosch and other private sponsors.

• 3509 •
Edison Awards
(Edison Stichting)
Albertus Perkstraat 36
NL-1217 NT Hilversum, Netherlands
Phone: 31 35 625 4411
Fax: 31 35 625 4410
E-mail: info@nvpi.nl
Home Page: http://www.edisonaward.nl

• 3510 • Edison Classical Music Award
To recognize a classical (sound carrier) production for its artistic value. Awarded annually with a statue. Established in 1960.

• 3511 • Edison Popular Music Award
To recognize a pop music (sound carrier) production for its artistic value. Awarded annually with a statue. Established in 1960. Formerly: Edison Populair - Awards for Popular Music.

• 3512 •
Edmond Hustinx Foundation
Home Page: http://www.hustinxstichting.nl

• 3513 • Peter Debye Prize
For recognition of the scientist(s) who has/have made a fundamental contribution to medical research, forming a link between medicine and the basic disciplines. The particular subject is fixed once every two or three years. A monetary award of 10,000 euros and a charter are presented biennially or triennially. Established in 1977 in honor of the physicist Peter J. W. Debye (1884-1966), who was awarded the Nobel Prize for chemistry in 1936.

• 3514 • Edmond Hustinx Prize for Science
To recognize a scientific researcher working or studying at or attached to Maastricht University. The award aims to underscore the significance of science practice and to accentuate the importance for South-Limburg society of the training supplied by the faculties of the University of Maastricht. In judging the research, special consideration goes to scientific level, originality, innovative character, and applicability in practice. A monetary prize of 7,5000 euros is awarded biennially.

• 3515 • Edmond Hustinx Prize - Playwrights
This prize is meant to honour talented authors of stage plays and radio or television plays for their work. Here the board of The Edmond Hustinx foundation decided deliberately that the jury would preferably reward authors who still have a certain development ahead of them. It is during the biennial meeting of the Colloquium of Dutch-language playwrights from Belgium and the Netherlands that the Edmond Hustinx prize for playwrights is awarded in each case, presented alternately to a Belgian and a Dutch writer.

• 3516 • Edmond Hustinx Prize - Science
This prize is meant to honour talented authors of stage plays and radio or television plays for their work. Here the board of The Edmond Hustinx foundation decided deliberately that the jury would preferably reward authors who still have a certain development ahead of them: people who are at the start of the start of their careers.

• 3517 • Edmond Hustinx Prize - Visual Arts
With this prize, the board wants to stimulate artists who live in Maastricht or in the region around Maastricht or who otherwise have a relationship with Maastricht and who have not yet reached the age of 35.

• 3518 •
Erasmus Prize Foundation
(Stichting Praemium Erasmianum)
Prof. M. Sparreboom, Dir.
Jan van Goyenkade 5
NL-1075 HN Amsterdam, Netherlands
Phone: 31 20 675 2753
Fax: 31 20 675 2231
E-mail: spe@erasmusprijs.org
Home Page: http://www.erasmusprijs.org

• 3519 • Erasmus Prize (Praemium Erasmianum)
To honor persons or institutions that have made an exceptionally important contribution to European culture or the social science field. Nominations are made by the Board. A monetary prize is awarded annually when possible. Established in 1958 by H. R. H. Prince Bernhard of the Netherlands.

• 3520 •
ESOMAR: World Association of Opinion and Marketing Research Professionals
Jose Wert Ortega, Pres.
Vondelstraat 172
NL-1054 GV Amsterdam, Netherlands
Phone: 31 20 6642141
Fax: 31 20 6642922
E-mail: email@esomar.org
Home Page: http://www.esomar.org

• 3521 • ESOMAR Awards
For recognition of the best papers presented at the ESOMAR annual congress. Original, unpublished papers may be submitted. Awards are presented in four categories: The Fernanda Monti Award for the best overall paper, The ESOMAR award for the best methodological paper of technical and innovative interest, and The ESOMAR Award for the best case history showing an interesting application of research which is helpful to research users. Awarded annually. Established in 1978.

• 3522 • John and Mary Goodyear Award
To recognize the best international research paper presented at ESOMAR events. Original, unpublished papers dealing with international research or being of strong relevance to international research; presented at the ESOMAR Congress, ESOMAR Conferences and other major conferences, seminars, symposia, and other events, which ESOMAR will hold alone or in cooperation with other organizations in a given calendar year. The award carries a prize of 3500 Euro, and is awarded annually. Established in 1999.

• 3523 •
Europa Nostra Pan European Federation for Heritage
Lange Voorhout 35
NL-2514 EC The Hague, Netherlands
Phone: 31 70 3024057
E-mail: office@europanostra.org
Home Page: http://www.europanostra.org

• 3524 • European Union Prize for Cultural Heritage/Europa Nostra Awards
To promote high standards of conservation practice, to stimulate the exchange of knowledge and experience throughout Europe, and to encourage further efforts through the power of example. Monetary prizes are awarded in the following categories: Conservation of architectural heritage, cultural landscapes, collections of works of art, and archaeological sites; Outstanding study in the field of cultural heritage; and Dedicated service to heritage conservation by individuals or groups. Awarded annually. Established in 2002.

• 3525 • Medal of Honour
To recognize individuals for sustained and exemplary contribution to the protection and/or enhancement of EuropeKs cultural heritage, both built and natural. Awarded to one or more recipients annually.

• 3526 • Restoration Fund Grant
To financially support the restoration of part of a privately owned, endangered European building or site having architectural and historical value. Up to 20,000 euros is awarded annually. Established in 1984.

• 3527 •
European Association for Distance Learning
Kees Veen, Exec.Dir.
Nuwendoorn 16
NL-1613 LD Grootebroek, Netherlands
Phone: 31 22 8521546
Fax: 31 22 8522626
E-mail: kveen@eadl.org
Home Page: http://www.eadl.org

• 3528 • Roll of Honor
For extraordinary merit and achievement in the field of distance learning. A plaque is awarded annually.

• 3529 •
European Association of Geoscientists and Engineers
Gareth Williams, Pres.
PO Box 59
NL-3990 DB Houten, Netherlands
Phone: 31 30 6354055
Phone: 31 30 6354066
Fax: 31 30 6343524
E-mail: eage@eage.org
Home Page: http://www.eage.nl

• 3530 • Conrad Schlumberger Award
Recognizes outstanding contribution over a period of time to the scientific and technical advancement of geophysics or other service to the geophysical community. Awarded annually.

• 3531 • Arie van Weelden Award
Recognizes an individual under age 30 for significant contributions to one or more of the disciplines of the Association. Awarded annually.

• 3532 •
European Federation of Food Science and Technology
Prof. Brian M. McKenna BE, Pres.
PO Box 17
NL-6700 AA Wageningen, Netherlands
Phone: 31 317 476457
Fax: 31 317 475347
E-mail: info@effost.org
Home Page: http://www.effost.org

• 3533 • Young Scientist Award
Recognizes an outstanding early-career scientist, mid-career scientist, and height-of-career scientist. Awarded annually.

• 3534 •
European Hematology Association
Ans Steuten, Exec. Mgr.
Westblaak 71
NL-3012 KE Rotterdam, Netherlands
Phone: 31 10 4361760
Fax: 31 10 4361817
E-mail: info@ehaweb.org
Home Page: http://www.ehaweb.org

• 3535 • Jose Carreras-EHA Award
To an established/active investigator who has made a large contribution to hematology.

• 3536 • EHA Clinical Research Grants
For clinical research in patients with hematological diseases.

• 3537 • EHA-Jose Carreras Young Investigator Fellowship Program
To promising young investigators.

• 3538 • EHA Research Fellowships
For young basic and clinical researchers both in the field of malignant and non-malignant hematology.

• 3539 •
European Institute of Public Administration (Institut Europeen d'Administration Publique)
Prof. Gerard Druesne MD, Dir.-Gen.
O.L. Vrouweplein 22
PO Box 1229
NL-6201 BE Maastricht, Netherlands
Phone: 31 43 3296222
Fax: 31 43 3296296
E-mail: eipa@eipa-nl.com
Home Page: http://www.eipa.nl

• 3540 • Alexis de Tocqueville Prize
To recognize one or more persons, or a group of people, whose work and commitment have made a considerable contribution to improving public administration in Europe. Awarded biennially in odd-numbered years. Established in 1987.

• 3541 •
European Organization for Caries Research (Organisme Europeen de Recherche sur la Carie)
Dr. Hans de Soet, Sec.Gen.
Department Oral Microbiology, ACTA
Free University
vd Boechorststraat 7, km B-342
NL-1081 Amsterdam, Netherlands
Phone: 31 20 4448679
Fax: 31 20 4448318
E-mail: jj.desoet@vumc.nl
Home Page: http://www.orca-caries-research.org

• 3542 • ORCA Rolex Prize
For recognition of merit in any aspect of caries research. The field of scientific investigation from which a recipient is selected should be as broad as possible. A Rolex watch is awarded annually. Established in 1964.

• 3543 • ORCA-Zsolnay Prize
To recognize outstanding contributions to the field of dental caries research. Candidates need not be members. An individually made object of Zsolnay Porcelain, in Hungary, is awarded annually.

• 3544 •
Fleuroselect
Gianni Bernardotto, Pres.
Parallel Boulevard 214d
NL-2202 HT Noordwijk, Netherlands
Phone: 31 71 3649101
Fax: 31 71 3649102
E-mail: info@fleuroselect.com
Home Page: http://www.fleuroselect.com

Formerly: European Organization for Testing New Flower Seeds.

• 3545 • Fleuroselect Gold Medal
To recognize good performance and the presentation of the best new flower seeds of exceptional quality. Society members are eligible. A medal is awarded annually at the convention. Established in 1970.

• 3546 • Fleuroselect Quality Award
To recognize novelties and new varieties of flower seeds that are found to be improvements in comparison to an existing assortment. Winning varieties may carry the Fleuroselect Quality Mark logo. Awarded annually.

• 3547 •
Cesar Franck Organ Competition Committee (Projectgroup Cesar Franck Orgel Concours)
Santpoorterstroat 10
NL-2023 ND Haarlem, Netherlands
Phone: 31 23 5252766
E-mail: info@cesarfranckcompetition.org
Home Page: http://www.cesarfranckcompetition.org

• 3548 • Cesar Franck Organ Competition (Cesar Franck Orgelconcours)
For recognition of outstanding organists. Monetary prizes are given for first, second, and third place. Three finalists receive an invitation to play at St. Bavo's Cathedral, and the first prize winner is awarded a recording for Dutch radio. In addition, the best Tournemire-player of the finalists receives a monetary prize. Held triennially. Established in 1976.

• 3549 •
Frans Hals Museum
Michiel Kersten, Press Off.
Groot Heiligland 62
Postbus 3365
NL-2001 DJ Haarlem, Netherlands
Phone: 31 23 511 5775
Fax: 31 23 511 5776
E-mail: franshalsmuseum@haarlem.nl
Home Page: http://www.franshalsmuseum.nl

• 3550 • Jacobus van Looyprijs
To recognize an author/visual artist. A monetary prize and an exhibition in the Frans Hals Museum are awarded every five years. Established in 1985.

• 3551 •
French Embassy in the Netherlands
Jean-Michel Gaussot, Ambassador
Cultural Department
Smidsplein 1
NL-2514 BT The Hague, Netherlands
Phone: 31 70 312 5800
Fax: 31 70 312 5824
E-mail: info@ambafrance-nl.org
Home Page: http://www.ambafrance-nl.org

• 3552 • Descartes Huygens Award
To recognize a Dutch and a French senior scientist for their scientific achievements and contribution to the development of the cooperation between the two countries. A monetary prize is awarded annually to cover the expenses of a 6 months research stay in the partner country. Established in 1995.

• 3553 • Prix des Ambassadeurs
To recognize a Dutch author for a book, alternatively fiction and no-fiction. A monetary prize is awarded. Established in 1983.

• 3554 •
Gaudeamus Foundation (Stichting Gaudeamus)
Henk Heuvelmans, Dir.
Swammerdamstraat 38
NL-1091 RV Amsterdam, Netherlands
Phone: 31 20 6947349
Fax: 31 20 6947258
E-mail: info@gaudeamus.nl
Home Page: http://www.gaudeamus.nl

• 3555 • The Gaudeamus Prize
Serves as a commission for a new composition which will be premiered during the International Gaudeamus Music Week the following year. Awarded annually. Established in 1948.

• 3556 • International Gaudeamus Interpreters Competition
To stimulate young musicians to play contemporary music. Ensembles and soloists who are 35 years of age or less perform a program of contemporary music (after 1940) including two Dutch works. Four monetary prizes are awarded biennially in the spring. Established in 1963 in cooperation with the Rotterdam Arts Foundation.

• 3557 • International Gaudeamus Music Week
To stimulate the writing of new compositions by young composers. Individuals 30 years of age or less may submit compositions by January 31. The Gaudeamus Prize is awarded as a commission to write a new composition for an opera and musical. Awarded annually at the end of the Music Week in September. Established in 1948.

• 3558 •
Hague Academy of International Law
Peace Palace
Carnegieplein 2
NL-2517 KJ The Hague, Netherlands
Phone: 31 70 302 4242
E-mail: registration@hagueacademy.nl
Home Page: http://www.hagueacademy.nl

• 3559 • **Hague Academy of International Law Scholarships**
To provide scholarships for study at the Academy. Candidates must apply by March 1. No more than two scholarships can be granted to students from each country during the same year. Four residential scholarships are also awarded to doctoral candidates whose theses are in an advanced stage of preparation. Only candidates from developing countries who reside in their home country and who do not have access to scientific sources are eligible.

• 3560 •
Holland Animation Film Festival
Hoogt 4
NL-3512-GW Utrecht, Netherlands
Phone: 31 30 2331 733
Fax: 31 30 2331 079
E-mail: info@haff.nl
Home Page: http://haff.awn.com

• 3561 • **Holland Animation Film Festival**
To promote commissioned animated film and the individual talent of the animation filmmaker. The Joop Geesink Prize is presented for applied animation, which includes announcements, titles, education and information films, clips, use of tricks in films, and commercials affected by a technique other than live action. The prizes are presented biennially in the following categories: publicity and promotional films, music videos, educational and information films, station calls/idents and film leaders, and campaigns. One Grand Prix award is presented to the best film or video selected from the above categories. Entry forms must be submitted by September 1, and films for the competition entered by October 15. Established in 1985.

• 3562 •
Edmond Hustinx Foundation
Hondertmarkt 446
Postbus 333
NL-6200 AH Maastricht, Netherlands
Phone: 31 43 214473
E-mail: info@hustinxstichting.nl
Home Page: http://www.hustinxstichting.nl

• 3563 • **Edmond Hustinxprijs**
To recognize Dutch and Belgian authors of plays and television dramas. A jury makes the selection. Two prizes are awarded biennially, one to someone Dutch and one to someone Flemish. This award is given jointly with the Algemeen Nederlands Verbond and Stichting Dramaastricht.

• 3564 •
International Association for Engineering Geology and the Environment (Association Internationale de Geologie de l'Ingenieur)
Dr. Niek Rengers, Pres.
International Institute for Aerospace Survey and Earth Sciences ITC
Hengelosestraat 99
PO Box 6
7500 AA Enschede, Netherlands
E-mail: rengers@itc.nl
Home Page: http://www.civil.ntua.gr/IAEG.html

• 3565 • **International Association for Engineering Geology and the Environment Awards**
To recognize individuals for research and study in various engineering-geological problems. The Hans Cloos Medal recognizes an engineering geologist of outstanding merit, and the Richard Wolters*K* Prize recognizes meritorious scientific achievement by a younger member of the profession. Awarded biennially in even-numbered years.

• 3566 •
International Association for the Evaluation of Educational Achievement (Association Internationale pour l'Evaluation du Rendement Scolaire)
Barbara Malak-Minkiewicz, Mgr. of Membership Relations
Herengracht 487
NL-1017 BT Amsterdam, Netherlands
Phone: 31 20 6253625
Fax: 31 20 4207136
E-mail: department@iea.nl
Home Page: http://www.iea.nl

• 3567 • **IEA - Bruce H. Choppin Memorial Award**
For recognition of achievement in empirical research using data from studies conducted by the Association. The competition is open to persons from any nation who have completed a master's or doctoral thesis within the preceding three years that used data collected in connection with any IEA study, and that used statistical methods to analyze the data. Applications are accepted by March 31 of each year. A certificate is awarded annually. Established in 1983 in honor of Bruce H. Choppin. Additional information is available from Dr. Barbara Malak-Miukiewicz, IEA at the above address.

• 3568 •
International Bird Strike Committee
Dr. Luit Buurma, Chm.
PO Box 20703
NL-2500 ES The Hague, Netherlands
Phone: 31 70 3396346
Fax: 31 70 3396347
E-mail: sup.ops@dopklu.af.dnet.mindef.nl
Home Page: http://www.int-birdstrike.com

• 3569 • **Mike Kuhring Award**
Recognizes individuals for achievements toward improved flight safety concerning the bird problems of aviation. Awarded biennially in even-numbered years. Established in 1979.

• 3570 •
International Board on Books for Young People - Dutch Section
Mr. Toin Duijx, Contact
PO Box 17162
NL-1000JDD Amsterdam, Netherlands
Phone: 31 206363708
E-mail: ibby-nederalnd@planet.nl
Home Page: http://www.ibby.org

• 3571 • **Jenny Smelik/IBBY Prize**
To recognize alternately an author and an illustrator of children's books who contribute to a better understanding of minorities. Selection is by nomination and application. Applications must be made before February 1 of each year. A monetary prize is awarded biennially by the Dutch section of IBBY. Established in 1983 by Klasina Smelik in honor of the children's book author, Jenny Smelik-Kiggen. Sponsored by Klasina Smelik Stichting. Formerly: Jenny Smelik-Kiggenprijs.

• 3572 •
International Cartographic Association (Association Cartographique Internationale)
Ferjan Ormeling, Sec.Gen.
Utrecht University
Heidelberg laan 2
PO Box 80115
NL-3508 TC Utrecht, Netherlands
Phone: 31 30 2531373
Phone: 31 30 2540604
Fax: 31 30 2532044
E-mail: f.ormeling@geog.uu.nl
Home Page: http://www.icaci.org

• 3573 • **Honorary Fellowship**
To recognize individuals who have contributed to ICA affairs. Presented quadrennially.

• 3574 • **Carl Mannerfelt Medal**
To recognize cartographers of outstanding merit who have made significant contributions of an original nature to the field of cartography. Awarded on rare occasions.

• 3575 •
International Documentary Film Festival - Amsterdam
Ally Derks, Contact
Kleine-Gartmanplantsoen 10
NL-1017 RR Amsterdam, Netherlands
Phone: 31 20 627 3329
Fax: 31 20 638 5388
E-mail: info@idfa.nl
Home Page: http://www.idfa.nl
Formerly: (1989) Netherlands Film Institute.

• 3576 • International Documentary Film Festival Amsterdam
To encourage the making of professional documentaries. Documentaries of any length, in 35mm or 16mm with combined optical or magnetic sound-track, may be submitted. Films must have been produced during the 15 months preceding the festival. Participating films must not have been screened in the Netherlands before. Films should be submitted in their original version with English subtitles. The Joris Ivens Film Prize, a monetary award, is presented. Established in 1988.

• 3577 •
International Federation for Housing and Planning
(Federation Internationale pour l'Habitation, l'Urbanisme et l'Amenagement des Territoires)
Marc Mosheuvel, Sec.Off.
Wassenaarseweg 43
2596 CG The Hague, Netherlands
Phone: 31 70 3244557
Phone: 31 70 3281504
Fax: 31 70 3282085
E-mail: info@ifhp.org
Home Page: http://www.ifhp.org

• 3578 • International Film/Video Competition
For recognition of the best film/video made every two years in the fields of housing and/or planning. The Competition is open to anyone. The International Award Jury will select three best films and/or videos (prizes to total approximately $10,000). An additional three to eight mentions will be selected. Held in even-numbered years.

• 3579 •
International Federation of Library Associations and Institutions
Peter Johan Lor, Sec.Gen.
Postbus 95312
NL-2509 CH The Hague, Netherlands
Phone: 31 70 3140884
Phone: 31 70 3140755
Fax: 31 70 3834827
E-mail: ifla@ifla.org
Home Page: http://www.ifla.org

• 3580 • Hans-Peter Geh Grant
To sponsor a librarian from the former Soviet Union, including the Baltic States, to attend an IFLA Seminar or Conference. Awarded annually. Established in 1991.

• 3581 • International Federation of Library Associations Honorary Fellow
For recognition of outstanding contributions to librarianship. Awarded when merited.

• 3582 • International Federation of Library Associations Honorary President
For recognition of outstanding service. Awarded when merited.

• 3583 • International Federation of Library Associations Medal
For recognition of outstanding service in the field of librarianship. There are no age, society, or citizenship restrictions. A medal and scroll are awarded in odd-numbered years at the conference. IFLA's Council may also confer the title of Honorary Fellow of IFLA. Established in the 1930s.

• 3584 • Dr. Shawky Salem Conference Grant
To enable one expert in library science, who is a national of an Arabic country, to attend an IFLA Conference. A grant is awarded periodically.

• 3585 • Guust van Wesemael Literary Prize
To aid a public or school library in a developing country to perform activities in the field of literacy: collection development, promotion, training, policy development, or otherwise. A monetary prize of 3,000 Euro is awarded annually.

• 3586 • Margaret Wijnstroom Fund
To support IFLA's Regional Offices, to involve librarians from developing world in the work of IFLA's professional groups, and to support projects in the developing world. A grant is awarded periodically.

• 3587 •
International Fiscal Association
(Association Fiscale Internationale)
Prof. Maarten J. Ellis, Contact
World Trade Center
Beursplein 37
PO Box 30215
NL-3001 DE Rotterdam, Netherlands
Phone: 31 10 4052990
Fax: 31 10 4055031
E-mail: n.gensecr@ifa.nl
Home Page: http://www.ifa.nl

• 3588 • Mitchell B. Carroll Prize
For recognition of the work of young individuals under 35 years of age working or studying in the field of international fiscal law. Papers written in English, French, or German devoted to international fiscal law, comparative tax law, or national tax law having an important relationship with fiscal law in foreign countries are accepted. A monetary prize and a medal are awarded annually. Established in 1947 in memory of Dr. Mitchell B. Carroll.

• 3589 •
International Institute for Geo-Information Science and Earth Observation
Martien Molenaar, Rector
PO Box 6
NL-7500 Enschede, Netherlands
Phone: 31 53 4874444
Fax: 31 53 4874400
E-mail: pr@itc.nl
Home Page: http://www.itc.nl

• 3590 • ITC Educational Award
For a staff member who has a proven record of excellent performance in education.

• 3591 • ITC Research Award

• 3592 • Klaas Jan Beek Award
For best thesis.

• 3593 •
International Korfball Federation
Dr. Jan C. Fransoo, Pres.
PO Box 85394
PO Box 85394
NL-3508 AJ Utrecht, Netherlands
Phone: 31 30 6566354
Fax: 31 30 6570468
E-mail: office@ikf.org
Home Page: http://www.ikf.org

• 3594 • International Korfball Federation Badge of Honour
For recognition of a contribution to a field of activity over a period of time. Individuals may apply. A badge of honor is awarded at the annual general meeting. Established in 1946.

• 3595 • International Korfball Federation Honorary Member
For recognition of a contribution to a field of activity over a period of time (more than 12 years). Three Pin of Merit for recognition of a contribution to a field of activity over a period of time (more than 6 years). Awarded at the annual general meeting. Established in 1995.

• 3596 •
International Pharmaceutical Federation
(Federation Internationale Pharmaceutique)
A.J.M. Hoek, Gen.Sec.
PO Box 84200
NL-2508 AE The Hague, Netherlands
Phone: 31 70 3021970
Fax: 31 70 3021999
E-mail: fip@fip.org
Home Page: http://www.fip.org

• 3597 • Awards in Recognition of Excellence
To recognize outstanding achievements in the fields of pharmaceutical practice and pharmaceutical sciences. The following awards are presented by the Federation: Honorary President, Andre Bedat Award, Host-Madsen Medal, Honorary Member, Distinguished Practice Award, Distinguished Science Award, Lifetime Achievement in the Pharmaceutical Practice Award, Lifetime Achievement in the Pharmaceutical Science Award, and Bio-Tech Award. A commemorative gift, and travel expenses to the FIP Congress are presented annually to the winners of the awards.

• 3598 • Andre Bedat Award
To recognize a pharmacist, or a person eligible to be licensed as a pharmacist, who is an outstanding practitioner and has made significant

contributions to pharmacy at the international level. Candidates may be nominated by June 30 of the year preceding that in which the award will be presented. A winner is determined by the Board of Pharmaceutical Practice. An engraved steel plaque, and the recipient's travel expenses are awarded biennially at an FIP Congress. Established in 1986 to honor Andre Bedat, president of FIP from 1978 to 1986.

• 3599 • **FIP Fellowships**
To permit the recipient to perform research and/or be trained outside his/her own home country. The subject of research or training must be in line with the objectives of the Foundation. Anyone employed in either the practice of pharmacy or the pharmaceutical sciences may apply. Selection is based on: originality/ novelty and creativity; relevance to the Foundation's objectives and current priorities; conciseness and clarity of presentation; application's qualifications and background; demonstration that the project is innovative and needed; the international character of the project; appropriateness of the project design to the stated goals; methods of evaluation, including both the monitoring of project developments and the achievement of project goals; specificity and practicality of the project schedule; specificity and practicality of the budget; and documentation of the institutional commitments (funds, materials, facilities, and/or personnel provided).

• 3600 • **Host-Madsen Medal**
To recognize pharmacists who have particularly distinguished themselves by their work in the field of pharmaceutical sciences and to encourage pharmacists in scientific research. Scientists from any country are eligible. Nominations may be submitted by members of the Federation and the Board of Pharmaceutical Sciences makes the selection. A gold medal is awarded biennially and there may be more than one medal given. Established in 1955, and awarded for the first time to Dr. Host-Madsen to honor his services to the Federation.

• 3601 •
International Pharmaceutical Students' Federation
Katja Hakkarainen, Pres.
PO Box 84200
NL-2508 AE The Hague, Netherlands
Phone: 31 70 3021992
Fax: 31 70 3021999
E-mail: ipsf@ipsf.org
Home Page: http://www.ipsf.org

• 3602 • **Honorary Life Member**
For recognition of outstanding service to the Federation. Individuals with two years of service to the Federation are considered. A plaque is awarded at the annual Congress. Established in 1949.

• 3603 •
International Society for Contemporary Music - Netherlands
H. Heuvelmans, Sec.Gen.
Swammerdamstraat 38
NL-1091 RV Amsterdam, Netherlands
Phone: 31 20 6947349
Fax: 31 20 6947258
E-mail: info@iscm.nl
Home Page: http://www.iscm.nl

• 3604 • **International Society for Contemporary Music Honorary Member**
For recognition of outstanding accomplishment in the field of contemporary music.

• 3605 •
International Society for Sexual Medicine
Robert von Hinke Kessler, Exec. Dir.
PO Box 97
NL-3950 AB Maarn, Netherlands
Phone: 31 343 441761
Fax: 31 343 442043
E-mail: secretariat@issm.info
Home Page: http://www.issm.info

• 3606 • **Ginesty Award**
For the best basic science manuscript on the physiology, biochemistry, pharmacology, or anatomy.

• 3607 • **Tanagho Award**
For best innovative research.

• 3608 • **Zorgniotti Award**
For clinical investigation of erectile dysfunction.

• 3609 •
International Society for the Study of Hypertension in Pregnancy
Eric Steegers, Sec.-Treas.
Sophia Children's Hospital, Rm. SK-4130
Dr. Molewaterplein 60
NL-3015 GJ Rotterdam, Netherlands
Phone: 31 10 4636886
Fax: 31 10 4636815
E-mail: s.breur@atserasmusmc.nl
Home Page: http://www.isshp.com

• 3610 • **Chesley Award**
To a member's sustained contribution to research in preeclampsia.

• 3611 • **Taylor and Francis Award**
To the most outstanding abstract.

• 3612 • **Young Investigator Travel Award**
To promising young researchers.

• 3613 • **Zuspan Award**
For the most outstanding clinical work done by a young investigator.

• 3614 •
International Society of Blood Transfusion (Societe Internationale de Transfusion Sanguine)
Dr. Paul F.W. Strengers, Sec.Gen.
Jan van Goyenkade 11
NL 1075 HP Amsterdam, Netherlands
Phone: 31 20 6793411
Fax: 31 20 6737306
E-mail: isbt@eurocongres.com
Home Page: http://www.isbt-web.org

• 3615 • **Jean Julliard Prize**
For recognition of recently completed scientific work on blood transfusion and related subjects. In general, the prize is awarded to one individual; in special cases, the prize may be shared by more than one scientist. Scientists under 40 years of age may submit manuscripts. A monetary prize of 3,000 Swiss francs and a certificate are awarded biennially in even-numbered years. Established in 1964 in memory of Jean Julliard, the first secretary general of the Society.

• 3616 •
International Statistical Institute (Institut International de Statistique)
Daniel Berze, Contact
428 Prinses Beatrixlaan
PO Box 950
NL-2270 AZ Voorburg, Netherlands
Phone: 31 70 3375737
Fax: 31 70 3860025
E-mail: isi@cbs.nl
Home Page: http://www.cbs.nl/isi

• 3617 • **Jan Tinbergen Awards for Young Statisticians from Developing Countries**
To encourage the professional development of statisticians. Individuals under the age of 32 who are residents of developing countries are eligible to submit a paper on any topic within the broad field of statistics. A monetary prize and travel expenses to attend the ISI Biennial Session and to present the winning paper are awarded biennially. Established in 1981. Formerly: (1995) Competition for Young Statisticians from Developing Countries.

• 3618 •
International World Games Association
Co Koren, Sec.Gen.
Office of the IWGA Secretary General
Slot Aldeborglaan 33
NL-6432 JM Hoensbroek, Netherlands
Phone: 31 45 5631089
Fax: 31 45 5631079
E-mail: sec@worldgames-iwga.org
Home Page: http://www.worldgames-iwga.org

• 3619 • **World Games Competitions**
International Sports Federations organize annual World Games Competitions.

• 3620 •
Liszt Competition Foundation
Muziekcentrum Vredenburg
Quinten Peelen, Exec.Dir.
PO Box 550
NL-3500 AN Utrecht, Netherlands
Phone: 31 3 0286 2229
Fax: 31 3 0231 6522
E-mail: liszt.competition@vredenburg.nl
Home Page: http://www.liszt.nl

• 3621 • **International Franz Liszt Piano Competition**
(International Franz Liszt Pianoconcours)
For recognition of an extraordinary interpretation of the piano music by Franz Liszt, and as a contribution for further study. Candidates should be no younger than 16 years of age and no older than 30 years of age. First place receives 20,000 euros and concert engagements; second place receives 10,000 euros and concert engagements; third place receives 5,000 euros and concert engagements; the Press Prize of 5,000 euros is awarded for the best interpretation of the *Sonata in B Minor*, the Henk de by Incentive Prize of 2,500 euros is awarded to the best non-finalist competitor under 22 years old; and the CenE Bankiers Audience Award of 2,500 euros is awarded to the audience favorite. Awarded triennially. Established in 1986.

• 3622 •
Nederlandse Taalunie
Lange Voorhout 19
Postbus 10595
NL-2501 HN The Hague, Netherlands
Phone: 31 70 346 9548
Fax: 31 70 365 9818
E-mail: info@taalunie.org
Home Page: http://taalunieversum.org/taalunie

• 3623 • **Prijs der Nederlandse Letteren**
For recognition of contributions to poetry and prose. A monetary award of 16,000 Euro is awarded every three years. Originally established by the ministries of culture of Belgium and the Netherlands.

• 3624 •
Nederlandse Triathlon Bond
Mrs. Christie Brouwer, Contact
PO Box 30202
NL-1303 AE Almere, Netherlands
Phone: 31 36 7501520
Fax: 31 36 7501527
E-mail: info@nedtriathlonbond.org
Home Page: http://www.nedtriathlonbond.org

• 3625 • **Thea Sybesma Award**
Recognizes the best female of the international championship. Awarded annually.

• 3626 •
Nederlandse Vereniging voor Weer- en Sterrenkunde
Mat Drummen, Contact
Zonnenburg 2
NL-3512 NL Utrecht, Netherlands
Phone: 31 30 2311360
Fax: 31 30 2342852
E-mail: info@dekoepel.nl
Home Page: http://www.dekoepel.nl

• 3627 • **Dr. J. van der Bilt prijs**
Recognizes the promotion of popular astronomy. Awarded annually to one or two recipients. Established in 1945.

• 3628 •
Netherlands Design Institute
(Vormgevingsinstituut)
Patricia Ruisch, Info. Officer
Keizersgracht 609
NL-1017 DS Amsterdam, Netherlands
Phone: 31 20 5516500
Fax: 31 20 6201031
Home Page: http://www.design-inst.nl

• 3629 • **Theo Limperg Prize**
Recognizes an industrial designer utilizing originality. Awarded biennially.

• 3630 •
Netherlands Film Festival
(Stichting Nederlandse Film Festival)
Frans Afman, Chm.
PO Box 1581
NL-3500 BN Utrecht, Netherlands
Phone: 31 30 230 3800
Fax: 31 30 230 3801
E-mail: info@filmfestival.nl
Home Page: http://www.filmfestival.nl

Formerly: (1997) Dutch Film Festival Foundation.

• 3631 • **Grand Prix of the Dutch Film Golden Calf**
(Grote Prijs van de Nederlandse Film Gouden Kalf)
For recognition of achievements in or contributions to Dutch film. Awards may be given in the following categories: best Dutch feature film; best Dutch short film; best documentary short; best male acting performance; best female acting performance; best director; best documentary feature; best television-play; best acting performance television play; best film musician; and exceptional contribution to the Dutch film culture. Monetary prizes and trophies in the form of a Golden Calf are awarded annually at the Film Festival in Utrecht. Founded in 1981.

• 3632 •
Netherlands Psychiatric Association
(Nederlandse Vereniging voor Psychiatrie)
PO Box 20062
NL-3502 LB Utrecht, Netherlands
Phone: 31 30 2823 303
Fax: 31 30 2888 400
E-mail: nvvp@xs4all.nl
Home Page: http://www.nvvp.net

• 3633 • **Ramaermedaille**
To recognize a citizen of the Netherlands who has produced the most meritorious contribution to psychiatric science, in particular to clinical psychiatry. A specially appointed committee makes the selection. A medal is awarded biennially. Established in 1918 by the Nederlandse Vereniging voor Psychiatrie en Neurologie in honor of Dr. J. N. Ramaer, founder of the Netherlands Psychiatric Association.

• 3634 •
Netherlands Society for English Studies
Dr. Roger Eaton, Sec.-Treas.
Dept. of English
Univ. of Amsterdam
Spuistraat 210
NL-1012 VT Amsterdam, Netherlands
Phone: 31 20 5253819
E-mail: roger.eaton@hum.uva.nl
Home Page: http://nses.let.uu.nl

• 3635 • **Graduation Prize**
To recognize the graduate in English studies who produced the finest dissertation or final project. Awarded biennially.

• 3636 • **NSES Award**
To recognize an individual for journalistic contribution to English studies. Awarded biennially.

• 3637 •
Permanent Court of Arbitration
(Cour permanente d'arbitrage)
Gertie Burgers, Office Mgr.
Peace Palace
Carnegieplein 2
NL-2517 KJ The Hague, Netherlands
Phone: 31 70 3024165
Phone: 31 70 3024242
Fax: 31 70 3024167
E-mail: bureau@pca-cpa.org
Home Page: http://www.pca-cpa.org

• 3638 • **Financial Assistance Fund for Settlement of International Disputes**
Awarded to developing countries in need of financial assistance for resolution of disputes under PCA auspices.

• 3639 •
Poetry International Foundation
(Stichting Poetry International)
Piet Holthuis, Pres.
Eendrachtsplein 4
NL-3012 LA Rotterdam, Netherlands
Phone: 31 10 2822 777
Fax: 31 10 444 4305
E-mail: info@poetry.nl
Home Page: http://www.poetry.nl

• 3640 • **Poetry International Festival**
To recognize outstanding poets. Alongside the nightly international series of readings, the festival offers a variety of related activities: poetry and music projects, exhibitions, and a series of lectures on famous poets. The C. Buddingh Prize for New Dutch Poetry is presented. The Festival is held annually. Established in 1970.

• 3641 •
Rijksakademie van Beeldende Kunsten
Janwillem Schrofer, Pres.
Sarphatistraat 470
NL-1018 GW Amsterdam, Netherlands
Phone: 31 20 527 0300
Fax: 31 20 527 0301
E-mail: info@rijksakademie.nl
Home Page: http://www.rijksakademie.nl

• 3642 • **Prix de Rome Fine Art**
This, the largest prize for young artists and architects in the Netherlands, is presented to recognize and encourage artists under 35 years of age. Individuals of Dutch nationality or those who have lived and worked in Holland for a minimum of two years are eligible. The Prix de Rome is awarded until this year in ten areas of art and architecture. In a five-year cycle two fields are covered annually: and Art in the Open; Painting and Theatre/Visual Arts; Architecture and Urban Design & Landscape Architecture; and Photography and Film & Video; Sculpture and Art in the Open; Drawing and Printmaking. Monetary prizes are awarded annually for first, second and third place. Established in 1870 by King William III of the Netherlands and based on the French example at the Academie des Beaux Arts.

• 3643 •
Rotterdam Arts Council
(Rotterdamse Kunststichting)
Mauritsweg 35
PO Box 2800
NL-3000 CV Rotterdam, Netherlands
Phone: 31 10 4335833
Fax: 31 10 4135195
E-mail: rks@rks.nl

• 3644 • **Pierre Bayle Prijs**
For recognition of outstanding and constructive (written) criticism in the arts and literature. Monetary awards are given annually in alternating years in the following categories: (1) Architecture; (2) Film; (3) Music; (4) Theater; (5) Fine Arts; (6) Dance; and (7) Literature. Established in 1955 in memory of Pierre Bayle, a French philosopher and critic.

• 3645 •
Royal Dutch Geographical Society
(Koninklijk Nederlands Aardrijkskundig Genootschap)
Mr. E.A.G. Postma, Dir.
Postbus 80123
NL-3508 TC Utrecht, Netherlands
Phone: 31 30 2534056
Phone: 31 30 2532757
Fax: 31 30 2535523
E-mail: info@knag.nl
Home Page: http://www.knag.nl

• 3646 • **Glazen Globe**
(Glass Globe)
To recognize authors of youth literature for contributions to the understanding of the world in which children live. Books that help children understand other cultures are considered. A specially designed globe of glass is awarded biennally. Established in 1987.

• 3647 •
Royal Netherlands Academy of Arts and Sciences
(Koninklijke Nederlandse Akademie van Wetenschappen)
Drs. K. Jongbloed, Contact
Postbus 19121
NL-1000 GC Amsterdam, Netherlands
Phone: 31 20 5510700
Fax: 31 20 6204941
E-mail: knaw@bureau.knaw.nl
Home Page: http://www.knaw.nl

• 3648 • **Buys Ballot Medal**
To recognize a scientist for outstanding work in the field of meteorology. A gold medal is awarded every ten years. Established in 1888 in memory of Professor C.H.D. Buys Ballot (1817-90). (Discountined)

• 3649 • **M. W. Beijerinck Virology Medal**
For recognition of outstanding work in the field of virology. A gold medal is awarded triennially. Established in 1965.

• 3650 • **De la Court Prizes**
For conspicuous achievements by non-salaried researchers in the fields of humanities and social sciences. Awarded biennially. Established in 1985.

• 3651 • **Dr. A.H. Heineken Prize for Art**
For recognition of promising and established artists working in the Netherlands. A monetary prize is awarded biennially. Financed by the Alfred Heineken Fondsen Foundation. Established in 1988. Formerly: (1995) Amsterdam Prize for Art.

• 3652 • **Dr. H. P. Heineken Prize for Biochemistry and Biophysics**
For recognition of exceptional discoveries in the fields of biochemistry and biophysics, including microbiology and the physiology of seed germination. A monetary prize and a crystal trophy are awarded biennially at a special session of the Royal Netherlands Academy of Arts and Sciences. Established in 1963 by Heineken N.V. in memory of Dr. H.P. Heineken, past president of Heineken Brewery. Sponsored by the Dr. H.P. Heineken Foundation.

• 3653 • **Dr. A.H. Heineken Prize for Environmental Sciences**
To recognize scientists or institutions for significant contributions to a better relation between man and his natural environment in one of the following fields: the natural sciences, engineering sciences, or the social sciences. A monetary prize is awarded biennially. Financed by the Alfred Heineken Fondsen Foundation. Established in 1990. Formerly: (1995) Amsterdam Prize for the Environment.

• 3654 • **Dr. A.H. Heineken Prize for History**
For recognition of work in the field of European history from antiquity to the present day. Preference is given to work which makes a significant contribution to an understanding of Europe generally. A monetary prize is awarded biennially. Financed by the Alfred Heineken Fondsen Foundation. Established in 1990. Formerly: (1995) Amsterdam Prize for History.

• 3655 • **Dr. A.H. Heineken Prize for Medicine**
For recognition of outstanding scientific research in the field of medicine. A monetary prize is awarded biennially. Financed by the Alfred Heineken Fondsen Foundation. Established in 1989. Formerly: (1995) Amsterdam Prize for Medicine.

• 3656 • **Gilles Holst Medal**
For recognition of outstanding contributions to applied chemistry and applied physics by Dutch scientists. A gold medal is awarded every four years. Established in 1939.

• 3657 • **Lorentz Medal**
To recognize a scientist for contributions to the field of physics. A gold medal is awarded every four years. Established in 1926 in memory of Professor H.A. Lorentz (1853-1928).

• 3658 • **Netherlands Fund for Chemistry Prize**
To recognize a Dutch researcher for a project completed during the previous five years in the field of scientific and technical chemistry. Established in 1952 by Professor Dr. A.F. Holleman.

• 3659 • **Bakhuis Roozeboom Medal**
To recognize a scientist for outstanding contributions to the field of chemistry, particularly phase theory. A gold medal is awarded every four/five years. Established in 1911 in memory of Professor H.W. Bakhuis Roozeboom (1854-1907).

• 3660 • Van Leeuwenhoek Medal
To recognize a scientist for outstanding work in the field of microscopic organisms. A gold medal is awarded every ten years. Established in 1877 in memory of the Dutch microbiologist, Antonie van Leeuwenhoek (1632-1723).

• 3661 •
Scheveningen International Music Competition
(Scheveningen Internationaal Muziek Concours)
Gevers Deynootweg 970 Z
Scheveningen
NL-2586 BW The Hague, Netherlands
Phone: 31 70 3525100
Fax: 31 70 3522197

• 3662 • Scheveningen International Music Competition
To encourage professional development in the field of music. The competition features different musical instruments each year. Performers must be 28 years of age or under. Applications are accepted. Five monetary prizes and certificates are awarded annually. Established in 1987 by the Adama Zijlstra Foundation.

• 3663 •
Sikkens Foundation
(Stichting Sikkensprys)
Rijksstraatweg 31
Postbus 3
NL-2170 BA Sassenheim, Netherlands
Phone: 31 71 308 2809
Fax: 31 71 308 2725
E-mail: sikkensfoundation@planet.nl
Home Page: http://www.sikkens.com

• 3664 • Piet Mondriaan Lecture
To recognize an artist who raised and articulated, at an early stage, the problems of modern art through his or her work and writings. The focus is on the visual arts, either independently or in relation to other fields of study. Awarded biennially. Established in 1979.

• 3665 • Sikkens Prize
To stimulate social, cultural, and scientific developments in society in which color plays a specific part. Awarded biennially. Established in 1959 by A. M. Mees, director of Sikkens Sassenheim. Formerly: Stichting Sikkensprijs.

• 3666 •
Society of Netherlands Literature
(Maatschappij der Nederlandse Letterkunde)
Universiteitsbibliotheek Leiden
Witte Singel 27
PO Box 9501
NL-2300 RA Leiden, Netherlands
Phone: 31 715144962
Fax: 31 715272836
E-mail: mnl@library.leidenuniv.nl
Home Page: http://www.leidenuniv.nl/host/mnl

• 3667 • Henriette de Beaufort-prijs
To recognize the author of a biographical work. A monetary prize is awarded every three years, alternately, to a Dutch and a Flemish author. Established in 1986.

• 3668 • Dr. Wijnaendts Francken-prijs
For recognition of a literary work in the following categories: essays in literary criticism, and cultural history. A monetary prize is awarded in each of the two categories alternately. The prize is awarded triennially. The work must have been published during the preceding six years. Established in 1935.

• 3669 • Henriette Roland Holst-prijs
To recognize a literary work that appeared in Dutch prose, poetry or drama, reflecting social concerns. The work must have been published within the preceding six years. A monetary prize is awarded triennially.

• 3670 • Frans Kellendonk-prijs
To recognize an author, preferably 40 years of age or younger, of literary works (prose, essay, theater, or poetry) reflecting intellectual independency and an original view on social or existential questions. A monetary prize is awarded biennially in odd-numbered years. Established in 1993.

• 3671 • Kruyskamp-prijs
To recognize an author in the field of lexicography, lexicology, or edition and annotation of old Dutch texts. A monetary prize is awarded triennially. Established in 1992.

• 3672 • Prijs voor Meesterschap
To recognize authors in the fields of creative writing, philology, and literature and history. A gold medal is awarded every five years.

• 3673 • Lucy B. and C. W. Van der Hoogt-prijs
To encourage poets or writers of literary works written in the Dutch or South Africans languages. The work must not have been published more than two years before the award is given. A monetary prize is awarded annually. Established in 1925.

• 3674 •
Stichting Internationaal Orgelconcours
Anton Pauw, Contact
Stadhuis
Postbus 3333
NL-2001 DH Haarlem, Netherlands
Phone: 31 23 511 5733
Fax: 31 23 511 5743
E-mail: organfestival@haarlem.nl
Home Page: http://www.organfestival.nl

• 3675 • International Organ Improvisation Competition
(Stichting Internationaal Orgelconcours)
To recognize outstanding organists. The deadline for applications is December 15. A monetary prize is awarded to the winner and each finalist receives a monetary. Awarded biennially. Established in 1951. Sponsored by Ahrend Groep N.V., Amsterdam.

• 3676 •
Tilburg University
Faculty of Arts
Waeandelaan 2
PB 90153
NL-5000 LE Tilburg, Netherlands
Phone: 31 13 466 9111
Fax: 31 13 466 3110
E-mail: uvt@uvt.nl
Home Page: http://www.uvt.nl

• 3677 • E. du Perron Award
(E. Du Perron-Prijs)
For recognition of achievements in the cultural field concerned with improving the mutual understanding between ethnic groups. Selection is by nomination. A monetary prize of 850 Euro is awarded annually. Established in 1986 in honor of E. Du Perron. Sponsored by the City Council of Tilburg.

• 3678 •
Vereniging van Schouwburg en Concertgebouwdirecties
Johannes Vermeerstraat 55
NL-1071 DM Amsterdam, Netherlands
Phone: 31 20 664 7211
Fax: 31 20 675 2691
E-mail: info@vscd.nl
Home Page: http://www.vscd.nl

• 3679 • Prosceniumprijs
To recognize a person or group for distinguished contribution to directing of drama, costumes, or the music of a Dutch stage production. A bronze figurine by the sculptor, Jan Spiering, is given together with the other Dutch theatre prizes. Every year, three are set up for: (1) stage; (2) dance; (3) youth theatre; and (4) mime and cabaret. In addition, the organization also gives a gold and silver Krommert Award for theatre technique.

• 3680 •
Vereniging van Schrijvers en Vertalers
Mariette Stroeken, Sec.
De Lairessestraat 125
NL-1075 HH Amsterdam, Netherlands
Phone: 31 20 6240803
Fax: 31 20 6247755
E-mail: bureau@vsenv.nl
Home Page: http://www.schrijversenvertalers.nl

• 3681 • Charlotte Kohler Prize
(Charlotte Kohlerprijs)
To recognize the author of a Dutch novel, poetry, or drama. A monetary prize of 5,000 euros is awarded annually. Sponsored by Stichting Charlotte Kohler.

• 3682 •
WMC Foundation
(Stichting Wereld Muziek Concours Kerkrade)
Oranjestraat 2a
PO Box 133
NL-6460 AC Kerkrade, Netherlands
Phone: 31 45 545 5000
Fax: 31 45 535 3111
E-mail: info@wmc.nl
Home Page: http://www.wmc.nl

• 3683 • **International Conductors' Competition**
For recognition of outstanding conducting. Participation is open to conductors of woodwind and brassbands, Continental-style brassbands and other brassbands, who are not older than 33 years of age. Each candidate must be able to communicate in one of the following languages: Dutch, English, or German. The following prizes are awarded: First Prize - a Gold Baton; Second Prize - a Silver Baton; and Third Prize - a Bronze Baton. Awarded every four years.

• 3684 • **Kerkrade World Music Contest (Wereld Muziek Concours Kerkrade)**
For recognition of outstanding amateur bands and orchestras. Participants may enter one or more of the following competitions: concert competitions - participation in the concert competition is open to the following amateur orchestral categories: symphonic windbands, including harmony-orchestras of the French and Dutch variety as well as American style symphonic windbands; brassbands of the continental type, also known as fanfare orchestras; and brassbands of the English type; counter competition for the drumband - sector - participation is open to the drum-ensembles of various compositions, such as percussion ensembles, mallet ensembles and fife piccolo bands marching competitions participation in the marching competitions is open to all bands of the above mentioned categories and drumbands of various compositions, such as drum and bugle bands, pipebands, etc.; concert competition for the Drumband-Sector - participation is open to drum-ensembles of various compositions, such as percussion ensembles, mallet ensembles and fife and piccolo bands; show competitions - participation in the show competitions is open to bands and orchestras with or without majorettes and/or showgirls; and marching parade is open to marching bands and orchestras with a minimum of 24 musicians; the marching parade has only one division. A first prize with distinction, first prize, second prize, and third prize are awarded every four years in each competition.

• 3685 •
World Association of Research Professionals
Jose Wert Ortega, Pres.
Vondelstraat 172
NL-1054 GV Amsterdam, Netherlands
Phone: 31 20 6642141
Fax: 31 20 6642922
E-mail: customerservice@esomar.org
Home Page: http://www.esomar.org

• 3686 • **Fernanda Monti Award**
For market research. A monetary award is given annually.

• 3687 •
World Ploughing Organisation
(Organisation Mondiale de Labourage)
D E Johnson, Treas.
Grolweg 2
NL-6964 BL Hall, Netherlands
Phone: 31 313 619634
Fax: 31 313 619735
E-mail: hans.spieker@worldploughing.org
Home Page: http://www.worldploughing.org

• 3688 • **World Ploughing Championship Awards (Weltmeister im Pflugen)**
To encourage improved skills of ploughing the land, and to recognize the highest standards of soil tillage. Individuals qualify through local, regional, and national matches to enter the world championship. The following prizes are awarded for conventional plowing: Golden Plough Trophy for the champion; Silver Rose Bowl for the runner-up; Friendship Trophy for the third place winner and Golden Furrows Challenge Trophy for reversible champion. Awarded annually. Established in 1952.

• 3689 •
World Press Photo
Michiel Munneke, Mng.Dir.
Jacob Obrechtstraat 26
NL-1071 KM Amsterdam, Netherlands
Phone: 31 20 676 6096
Fax: 31 20 676 4471
E-mail: office@worldpressphoto.nl
Home Page: http://www.worldpressphoto.nl

• 3690 • **World Press Photo Contest**
For recognition of the best press photographs of the preceding year. Single pictures and picture stories (or sequences), black-and-white or color, prints or 35mm slides may be entered in the following categories: General News - planned and/or organized events; Spot News - unscheduled events for which no advance planning was possible; People in the News pictures or stories of people playing a part in the news; Sports - action or feature pictures or stories; The Arts - any performance, development, or highlight in fashion, architecture, visual and performing arts, etc.; Portraits- pictures or stories which portray public figures, celebrities, or people in general; Science and Technology - any achievement, development, or highlight in science or technology; Nature and the Environment - natural or environmental subjects, e.g., flora and fauna, landscapes, ecology, etc.; Daily Life - pictures or stories illustrating the richness and diversity of everyday life. A series is limited to 12 pictures. The World Press Photo of the Year Award will honor the photographer whose photograph can be rightfully regarded as the photographic encapsulation of the year - a photograph which represents an issue, situation, or event of great journalistic importance and that clearly demonstrates an outstanding level of visual perception and creativity. The photographer receives the Premier Award - a cash prize, a Diploma of Excellence, and an invitation to Amsterdam, including a return flight and hotel accommodation, to attend the awards ceremony at the end of April. First prize winners in each category of best single picture and best picture story receive the "Golden Eye", a cash prize, a Grand Diploma, and an invitation to Amsterdam (with the same details as above). Second and third prize winners receive the "Golden Eye" and a Diploma. An additional prize is the World Press Photo Children's Award, given for the best press photo of the year as selected by an international children's jury. The winner receives the "Golden Eye", a cash prize, and an invitation to Amsterdam (with the same details as above).

• 3691 •
World Wide Video Festival
Tom van Diet, Dir.
Keizersgracht 462
NL-1016 GE Amsterdam, Netherlands
Phone: 31 20 421 3815
Fax: 31 20 421 3828
E-mail: tomvanvliet@wwvf.nl
Home Page: http://www.wwvf.nl

Formerly: Stichting Kijkhuis.

• 3692 • **World Wide Video Festival**
For recognition of achievement in the field of video, videotapes, CD-ROMs, performances, installations, internet productions, and to encourage professional development. Independent video productions, videotapes, CD-ROMs, performances, installations, internet productions not shown in Holland publicly and not older than a year are eligible. Established in 1975. Sponsored by the Min. van OCenW, Mondriaan Stichting, and others.

• 3693 •
Worldwide Association of Self-Adhesive Labels and Related Products
J.H.M. Lejeune, Contact
PO Box 85612
NL-2508 CH The Hague, Netherlands
Phone: 31 70 3123910
Fax: 31 70 3636348
E-mail: info@finat.com
Home Page: http://www.finat.com

Formerly: (2003) International Federation of Manufacturers and Converters of Pressure-S - ensitive and Heatseals on Paper and Other Base Materials.

• 3694 • **Self-Adhesive Labelling Awards**
For recognition of research to improve the quality and utilization of pressure-sensitive and heatseal materials. The organization holds competitions and presents awards.

New Zealand

• 3695 •
Association of Consulting Engineers New Zealand
Mike Connolly, CEO
PO Box 10247
PO Box 10247
Wellington, New Zealand
Phone: 64 4 4721202
Fax: 64 4 4733814
E-mail: service@acenz.co.nz
Home Page: http://www.acenz.org.nz

• 3696 • **Awards of Excellence**
Made to projects of ACENZ members that show excellence in consulting engineering. The award is given annually at the conference in August and is for ACENZ members only. The awards are made at the Gold, Silver, and Merit levels to recognize innovation, excellence in technique, excellence in business relationships, community benefit, environmental sensitivity, and fair methods. The award is a framed certificate presented to the consultant firm and the client who commissioned the project. A magazine is published highlighting all entries.

• 3697 • **President's Award**
Made to an individual within the membership who has provided outstanding support to the association. May be, but is not required to be, awarded at the annual conference in August, and the winner is selected by the President and given a plaque.

• 3698 • **Student Award**
Recognizes excellence in report writing based on the report on a work experience project. Students attending Universities offering four-year engineering degrees are eligible. One student from each University is awarded a framed certificate and monetary prize annually.

• 3699 •
Booksellers New Zealand
Mrs. Linda Henderson, CEO
PO Box 13248
Johnsonville
Wellington, New Zealand
Phone: 64 4 4785511
Fax: 64 4 4785519
E-mail: enquiries@booksellers.co.nz
Home Page: http://www.booksellers.co.nz

• 3700 • **Montana New Zealand Book Awards**
Recognizes outstanding adult books published in New Zealand. Awarded annually. Inquire for application details.

• 3701 •
Buddle Findlay/Sargeson Trust
PricewaterhouseCoopers Tower
188 Quay St.
Auckland 1010, New Zealand
Phone: 64 9 358 2555
Fax: 64 9 358 2055

• 3702 • **Buddle Findlay Sargeson Fellowship**
To recognize and encourage a fiction writer of proven ability. New Zealand citizens are eligible. Accommodation in a furnished flat in central Auckland for nine months, plus an annual stipend of $10,000 (New Zealand). Established in 1987 by the Sargeson Trust to honor the New Zealand fiction writer, Frank Sargeson. Cosponsored by Buddle Findlay New Zealand Lawyers.

• 3703 •
Canterbury Historical Association
Judy Robertson, School Administrator
Dept. of History
Univ. of Canterbury
Private Bag 4800
Christchurch 1, New Zealand
Phone: 64 3 3642104
Fax: 64 3 3642003
E-mail: judy.robertson@canterbury.ac.nz
Home Page: http://www.hist.canterbury.ac.nz

• 3704 • **J. M. Sherrard Awards**
To encourage scholarly research and publication in the field of New Zealand regional and local history. Amateur and professional historians are eligible. All history titles included in the National Bibliography for the preceding two years are considered. A monetary award of approximately NZ$1,000 is awarded biennially as one major award, and may be divided equally among as many as four winners. Established in 1972 in honor of J. M. Sherrard.

• 3705 •
Christian Booksellers Association of New Zealand
John Jernnings, Sec.
45A Callender Tce
Paraparaumu 6010, New Zealand
Phone: 64 4 9020579
Fax: 64 4 9023659
E-mail: info@cba.net.nz
Home Page: http://www.cba.net.nz

• 3706 • **Christian Album of the Year**
To the Christian album considered to have the greatest impact on the listener during the previous 12 months,

• 3707 • **Christian Book of the Year**
To the Christian book considered to have the most impact on readers during the previous 12 months.

• 3708 • **Exhibitor of the Year**
For exhibitors.

• 3709 • **New Zealand Christian Book of the Year**
To the Christian publication published in New Zealand, or written by a resident in New Zealand at the time of publication.

• 3710 • **Salesperson of the Year**
for salespersons

• 3711 • **Young Persons Book of the Year**
To the publication targeted at young people which has had the greatest impact on the reader during the previous 12 months.

• 3712 •
Designers Institute of New Zealand
Cathy Veninga, Exec.Dir.
PO Box 5521
Wellesley St.
Auckland, New Zealand
Phone: 64 9 303 1356
Fax: 64 9 303 1357
E-mail: info@dinz.org.nz
Home Page: http://www.dinz.org.nz

Formerly: New Zealand Society of Industrial Design.

• 3713 • **BesT Design Awards**
To recognize professional designers, students, and organizations in New Zealand and to strengthen the design profession by promoting high standards in the design field, including graphic, product, and interior design. Several awards are presented annually, including Best of Discipline, Best of Category, Student Awards, Outstanding Achievement Award, and the John Britten Award. Established as the National Graphic Design Awards in 1976.

• 3714 •
Habitat for Humanity - New Zealand
Elgin Graham, Exec. Dir.
11 Marewa Rd.
Greenlane
Auckland, New Zealand
Phone: 64 9 5294111
Fax: 64 9 5295111
E-mail: admin@habitatnz.co.nz
Home Page: http://www.habitatnz.co.nz

• 3715 • **Construction Award**

• 3716 • **Distinguished Volunteer Award**

• 3717 • **Partnership Development Award**

• 3718 •
Health Research Council of New Zealand
Bruce A. Scoggins, Chief Exec.
PO Box 5541
Wellesley St.
Auckland, New Zealand
Phone: 64 9 3035200
Fax: 64 9 3779988
E-mail: info@hrc.govt.nz
Home Page: http://www.hrc.govt.nz

• 3719 • **HRC Postdoctoral Fellowship**
To PhD holders doing public health research.

Awards are arranged in alphabetical order below their administering organizations

• 3720 • **Liley Medal for Health Research**
For outstanding contribution to health and medical sciences.

• 3721 • **Macdiarmid Young Scientist of the Year**
For best communication of research, including techniques and outcomes.

• 3722 •
Historical Branch Advisory Committee
Historical Branch
Department of Internal Affairs
PO Box 805
Wellington, New Zealand
Phone: 64 4 4940630
Fax: 64 4 4957212
E-mail: kathryn.hastings@dia.govt.nz
Home Page: http://www.dia.govt.nz

• 3723 • **Awards in History**
To encourage and support research into, and the writing of, the history of New Zealand. Applications from researchers and writers of projects relating to New Zealand history are eligible. Assistance is not normally available for projects that are eligible for university research funds, nor for university theses. Grants totaling $80,000 to $90,000 are awarded annually in December. Established in 1989. Funded by the New Zealand History Research Trust Fund.

• 3724 • **Awards in Oral History**
To provide financial help for projects using oral resources relating to the history of New Zealand/Aoetearoa and New Zealand's close connections with the Pacific. Awards are made to individuals, groups, communities, and institutions. Available to those normally resident in New Zealand. Grants are awarded annually. Established in 1990 by the Australian people to commemorate New Zealand's sesquicentennial. Funded by the Australian Sesquicentennial Gift Trust for Awards in Oral History.

• 3725 •
Institute of Chartered Accountants of New Zealand
Garry Muriwai, CEO
Level 2, Cigna House
40 Mercer St.
PO Box 11342
Wellington 6034, New Zealand
Phone: 64 4 4747840
Fax: 64 4 4998033
E-mail: registry@icanz.co.nz
Home Page: http://www.icanz.co.nz

• 3726 • **Annual Report Awards**
To encourage quality, excellence, integrity, and communication in annual reports. All companies producing annual reports are eligible. Awarded annually.

• 3727 • **Chartered Accountant of the Year**
To recognize chartered accountants for their contribution to the accounting profession, community involvement, and specialist expertise. Also awarded is the Accounting Technician of the Year. Awarded annually.

• 3728 •
Institution of Professional Engineers New Zealand
PO Box 12241
Wellington, New Zealand
Phone: 64 4 4739444
Fax: 64 4 4748933
E-mail: ipenz@ipenz.org.nz
Home Page: http://www.ipenz.org.nz

• 3729 • **Angus Award**
To recognize the author of the best paper submitted during the three years preceding the date of the award on a subject possessing a substantial mechanical interest. Members are eligible. A monetary prize and a certificate are awarded annually. Established in 1959 and endowed by the late P.R. Angus, a former Chief Mechanical Engineer of the New Zealand Railways, and a Past-President of the Institution.

• 3730 • **John Cranko Memorial Award**
To recognize members of the Institution and/or the New Zealand Institute of Refrigeration Heating and Air Conditioning Engineers. Awarded when merited. Established in 1979 as a memorial by friends, clients, and family of John Eardley Cranko after his death in August, 1978. Co-sponsored by the New Zealand Institute of Refrigeration Heating and Air Conditioning Engineers.

• 3731 • **Dobson Lecture**
A public lecture on a subject of current public interest related to engineering. Established in 1974.

• 3732 • **Environmental Award**
To recognize predominantly engineering work that best exemplifies care for and consideration of environmental values. Account is taken of the indentification of environmental values in the design, the manner in which the resulting problems were resolved, and the overall contribution of the end result to environmental values and public enjoyment. Projects to qualify for the award do not have to be of national importance but must be of significance in their immediate locality. An individual or public or private body is eligible and, in the case of an individual, the person need not necessarily be an engineer or a member of the Institution. A plaque is presented to the individual or organization responsible for the work. In addition, a certificate is presented to the person or persons predominantly responsible for the design and execution of the project. Awarded biennially. Established in 1971.

• 3733 • **Freyssinet Award**
To recognize a member of the Institution for the best paper published during the three years preceding the year for which the award is made on a subject dealing with some aspects of engineering, structural design, or erection. A monetary prize and a certificate are awarded annually. Established in 1965 in memory of Eugene Freyssinet, a French engineer. Sponsored by the New Zealand Concrete Society and the Cement and Concrete Association of New Zealand.

• 3734 • **Fulton-Downer Award**
To recognize the best papers on technical subjects presented at the annual IPENZ Conference. Two awards are given: the Fulton-Downer Gold Medal and a monetary prize are awarded to the member winner and the Fulton-Downer Silver Medal and a monetary prize are awarded to the student or graduate member. Awarded annually. Established in 1929 by a bequest from the late J.E. Fulton to which was added, in 1973, a donation from A.F. Downer.

• 3735 • **Furkert Award**
For recognition of the best paper by a member submitted within the three years preceding the date of the award on a subject dealing with the action of water on the faces of nature, particularly such faces of nature as are connected with the works of man. A monetary prize and a certificate are awarded annually. Established in 1951 by the late F.W. Furkert, a former Engineer-in-Chief of the Ministry of Works and Past-President of the Institution.

• 3736 • **Hopkins Lecture**
To encourage discussion of engineering within the profession and to encourage public understanding of engineering issues. The lecture is given by an eminent speaker with a high reputation in his field and with a knowledge of engineering, although not necessarily an engineer. The lecture is held each year in Christchurch and covers broad and social engineering issues rather than being purely technical. Established in 1978 by the Institution and the University of Cambridge in honor of Professor H.J. Hopkins.

• 3737 • **IPENZ Craven Post-Graduate Research Scholarship**
To encourage research in engineering, particularly that which may have application to the future development of New Zealand. Candidates who are taking the final examination for the Degree of Bachelor of Engineering at the University of Auckland or the University of Canterbury, and also graduates in engineering of any university within the British Commonwealth are eligible. The scholarship of $2,000 is tenable for one year and shall be held by a candidate who during the tenure of his scholarship is pursuing postgraduate studies for a Masters degree in engineering at either the University of Auckland or the University of Canterbury. Awarded annually. Established in 1980.

• 3738 • **IPENZ Structural Award**
To recognize the best paper published by the Institution during the three-year period ending on July 31 preceding the conference at which the award is made on some aspect of structural engineering design or construction in which materials other than prestressed or reinforced concrete fulfill a major role. Awarded annually. Established in 1988.

• 3739 • MacLean Citation

To recognize persons who have rendered exceptional and distinguished service to the profession. A citation is awarded when merited. Established in 1954 in memory of Francis William MacLean, a former President of the Institution, who displayed exceptional devotion to the profession of engineering and to his fellow engineers.

• 3740 • New Zealand Young Engineer of the Year Award

To recognize the nation's outstanding young engineers. Applicants should be less than 35 years old. Applicants must demonstrate that they have been involved in and excelled in the areas of academia, community involvement, environmental and engineering contributions or have managed a project. Awarded annually.

• 3741 • W. L. Newnham Memorial Lecture

An annual lecture series, given on the first day of the Institution's annual conference. Established in 1970.

• 3742 • Evan Parry Award

For recognition of the best paper by a member on an electrical engineering subject submitted to the Institution during the three years preceding the date of the award. A monetary award and a certificate are awarded annually. Established in 1965 by the late R.S. Maunder, a Past-President of the Institution, in memory of Evan Parry, a former Chief Electrical Engineer of the Public Works Department. Sponsored by Electricorp Production.

• 3743 • President's Award

To recognize a member or group of members who has done something outstanding particularly in the role of the engineers public service. The award is made from time to time at the sole discretion of the President. Established in 1990.

• 3744 • Professional Commitment Award

To recognize a corporate member of the Institution for his continuing contribution to the profession of engineering, to the activities of the Institution, and to society. The recipient should be over the age of 40 years. The following attributes are sought in nominees for this award: upholding the image of the profession, publicizing engineering achievement and promoting the interests of the profession and industry, emphasis of the Institution's code of ethics and the profession's expertise and experience, encouragement to young people to enter the profession and young engineers to take an active role in Institution affairs, participation in community affairs, assistance with career counseling and recruitment to the Institution, and dissemination of technical and welfare information within the profession. A certificate is presented annually at the Institution's annual conference. Established in 1981 by R.J. McCarten.

• 3745 • Rabone Award

To recognize members submitting papers of exceptional merit which do not come within the conditions of other awards or which otherwise justify recognition. The paper must be published by the Institution during the three year period ending July 31 preceding the conference at which the award is given. A monetary award and a certificate are presented annually. Established in 1932. In 1969, the award was endowed to recognize papers of special merit by members under 40 years of age in categories other than those covered by the awards existing at the time.

• 3746 • Skellerup Award

To recognize the member presenting the best paper during the three years preceding the year of the award on a subject dealing with the development of New Zealand's natural resources or the development of New Zealand's chemical process industry. The paper must be published by the Institution during the five year period ending July 31 preceding the conference at which the award is given. A monetary prize and a certificate are awarded annually. Established in 1977 in memory of George Waldemar Skellerup, who initiated development of Lake Grassmore Solar Salt Works. Sponsored by Dominion Salt Limited.

• 3747 • Student Design Competition

To recognize and foster the steel design abilities of undergraduate engineers. In judging the award, consideration will be given to the project design, the business case, and the presentation and communication of ideas. The award consists of a trophy, cash prize, and certificate/s. There is a total prize pool of $3,000 ($2,000 for the winner and $500 for each of the two runners-up). FinalistsK reasonable travel and entry expenses will also be met to enable them to attend the IPENZ Awards Dinner during the IPENZ annual Convention. Awarded annually. Sponsored by Meridian Energy.

• 3748 • Turner Lecture

To promote and extend the knowledge of contract, particularly relating to building and engineering. Established in 1985 by C.W.O. Turner.

• 3749 •

Library and Information Association of New Zealand
Rob Arlidge, Business Development Mgr.
PO Box 12-212
Wellington, New Zealand
Phone: 64 4 4735834
Fax: 64 4 4991480
E-mail: office@lianza.org.nz
Home Page: http://www.lianza.org.nz

Formerly: (1995) New Zealand Library Association.

• 3750 • Russell Clark Award

For recognition of the most distinguished illustrations in a children's book with or without text. The illustrator must be a citizen of New Zealand, and the book must have been published during the preceding year. A monetary award and a bronze medal are presented annually. Established in 1975 in memory of Russell Clark (1905-1966), a New Zealand illustrator, artist and sculptor.

• 3751 • Esther Glen Award

To recognize the author of the most distinguished contribution to literature for children. Authors of books published during the preceding year who are citizens or residents of New Zealand are eligible. A monetary award and a bronze medal are awarded annually. Established in 1945 in memory of Esther Glen (1881-1940), a New Zealand journalist and editor active in promoting children's literature.

• 3752 • LIANZA Young People's Nonfiction Award

To recognize a distinguished contribution to nonfiction for young people. Citizens or residents of New Zealand are eligible. A monetary award and a medal are presented annually. Established in 1986.

• 3753 • Te Kura Pounamu Award

To recognize a distinguished contribution written in Te Reo Maori to the literature for children or young people. Awarded annually. Established in 1995.

• 3754 •

Logistics and Transport New Zealand
Marilyn Henderson, Administration Mgr.
PO Box 1281
Shortland St.
Auckland, New Zealand
Phone: 64 9 3684970
Fax: 64 9 3684971
E-mail: info@cilt.co.nz
Home Page: http://www.ltnz.org.nz

• 3755 • Award for Most Meritorious Paper/Presentation

For a paper presented to the meeting of CILTNZ. A trophy is awarded annually.

• 3756 • Chartered Institute of Transport Annual Innovation Award

Awarded annually for the best example of innovation in transport in New Zealand. Criteria include economic benefits and originality. The award takes the form of a trophy.

• 3757 • Ministry of Transport Award for Best Student Research

For the best undergraduate student research project/paper at the 300 level. A monetary award of $2,000 is given annually.

• 3758 • Norman Spencer Memorial Award

For personal achievements, and service to the institute, the profession, and the community in the field of transport, including expertise, experience and other criteria. A trophy is awarded annually.

Awards are arranged in alphabetical order below their administering organizations

• 3759 •
New Zealand Academy of Fine Arts
Nahleen Markham, Mgr.
1 Queens Wharf
Wellington, New Zealand
Phone: 64 4 4998807
Fax: 64 4 4992612
E-mail: nzafa@xtra.co.nz
Home Page: http://www.nzafa.com

• 3760 • **Governor General Art Award**
To recognize New Zealand artists whose works are considered to be of merit, and worthy of recognition, and to enable exceptionally promising exhibitors to work towards further development within their chosen medium. The following awards are given: Governor General Art Award - to give recognition to New Zealand artists who consistently produce work of the highest standard, and who through their work have contributed towards the development of the visual arts in New Zealand. Awarded biennially in even-numbered years. Established in 1983.

• 3761 •
New Zealand Archaeological Association
Moira White, Sec.
PO Box 6337
Dunedin, New Zealand
E-mail: moira.white@otagomuseum.govt.nz
Home Page: http://www.nzarchaeology.org

• 3762 • **Groube Fieldwork Award**
For the most remarkable contribution to field work in archaeology.

• 3763 • **Public Archaeology Award**
For outstanding efforts in public archaeology.

• 3764 •
New Zealand Association of Scientists
Dr. Hamish Campbell, Pres.
PO Box 1874
Wellington, New Zealand
Phone: 64 4 3895096
Fax: 64 4 3895096
E-mail: nzas@rsnz.org
Home Page: http://nzas.rsnz.org

• 3765 • **Foundation for Research Science and Technology Science Communicator Awards**
To provide recognition for outstanding research work in the fields of natural, physical, or social sciences. Individuals less than 40 years of age are eligible. An engraved medal is awarded annually. Established in 1951.

• 3766 • **Sir Ernest Marsden Medal for Outstanding Service to Science**
For recognition of a meritorious contribution to the cause and/or the development of science. Any person who has made an outstanding contribution to science is eligible. An engraved medal is awarded annually. Established in 1973.

• 3767 • **New Zealand Association of Scientists Research Medal**
To encourage public appreciation of scientific objectives, methods and achievements through recognition of outstanding science communication by scientists in newspapers, magazines, and broadcasting. Items produced in New Zealand for a general audience by a scientist (understood to include technologists) are eligible. Persons employed in a journalistic capacity are ineligible. A monetary award of $1,000 (New Zealand), and two merit awards of $100 (New Zealand) each are presented annually at the annual general meeting of the Association. Established in 1990.

• 3768 •
New Zealand Dental Association
Dr. David G. Crum, Exec.Dir.
PO Box 28-084
Remuera
Auckland 1136, New Zealand
Phone: 64 9 5242778
Fax: 64 9 5205256
E-mail: nzdainfo@nzda.org.nz
Home Page: http://www.nzda.org.nz

• 3769 • **New Zealand Dental Association Awards**
To recognize registered dental practitioners in New Zealand. Awards include the Research Foundation Awards of up to $10,000, as well as the Outstanding Young Dentist Award. Presented annually.

• 3770 •
New Zealand Geographical Society
Peter Holland, Pres.
City Campus
Univ. of Auckland
Private Bag 92019
Auckland, New Zealand
Phone: 64 9 3737599
Fax: 64 9 3737434
E-mail: nzgs@auckland.ac.nz
Home Page: http://www.nzgs.co.nz

• 3771 • **Distinguished Geographer Medal**
For significant contribution to geography by a New Zealander. Awarded biennially.

• 3772 •
New Zealand Ice Cream Manufacturers Association
Jenny de Lisle, Exec.Sec.
PO Box 9364
Wellington, New Zealand
Phone: 64 4 3851410
Fax: 64 4 3843980
E-mail: info@nzicecream.org.nz
Home Page: http://www.nzicecream.org.nz

• 3773 • **Ice Cream Awards**
Recognizes outstanding product competition. Awarded annually.

• 3774 •
New Zealand Law Society
Alan Ritchie, Exec.Dir.
PO Box 5041
Wellington 6145, New Zealand
Phone: 64 4 4727837
Fax: 64 4 4737909
E-mail: inquiries@lawyers.org.nz
Home Page: http://www.lawyers.org.nz

• 3775 • **The Centennial Maori Scholarship**
For Maori students.

• 3776 • **The Centennial Scholarship**
For law students.

• 3777 • **Cleary Memorial Prize**
For a newly-admitted practitioner who shows the most promise of service to and through the profession.

• 3778 •
New Zealand Microbiological Society
Ralph Jack, Sec.
PO Box 56
Dunedin 9001, New Zealand
Phone: 64 3 4793140
Fax: 64 3 4798540
E-mail: ralph.jack@stonebow.otago.ac.nz
Home Page: http://www.nzms.org.nz

• 3779 • **Life Membership Award**

• 3780 • **Student Prize**

• 3781 • **Student Travel Award**

• 3782 •
New Zealand Olympic Committee
Barry Maister, Sec.Gen.
PO Box 643
Wellington, New Zealand
Phone: 64 4 3850070
Fax: 64 4 3850090
E-mail: office@olympic.org.nz
Home Page: http://www.olympic.org.nz

• 3783 • **Sir Lance Cross Memorial Cup**
Recognizes individuals involved in the media. Awarded semiannually.

• 3784 • **Lonsdale Cup**
Recognizes the most outstanding athlete. Awarded annually.

• 3785 •
New Zealand Psychological Society
Angie Fussell, Exec.Dir.
PO Box 4092
Wellington, New Zealand
Phone: 64 4 4734884
Fax: 64 4 4734889
E-mail: office@psychology.org.nz
Home Page: http://www.psychology.org.nz

• 3786 • **C.J. Adcock Award**
To the most valuable contribution in any of the areas like philosophy of science, psychological theory, personality, cybernetics, cognition, perception, linguistics and the use of multivariate statistical techniques.

• 3787 • **Best Student Conference Paper Prizes**
For student subscribers who present the best paper at the society's annual conference.

• 3788 • **G.V. Goddard Award**
For excellence in research in the areas of biopsychology, experimental psychology, and neuro-psychology.

• 3789 • **Hunter Award**
for excellence in research in psychology

• 3790 • **Jamieson Award**
For significant contributions to industrial/organizational psychology in New Zealand.

• 3791 • **The President's (Maori) Scholarship**
To Maori, post-graduate (Masters of higher level Psychology degree) university students.

• 3792 • **Public Interest Award**
For valuable contributions to psychology.

• 3793 •
New Zealand Society of Authors
Liz Allen, Exec.Dir.
PO Box 67013
Mt. Eden
Auckland 1030, New Zealand
Phone: 64 9 3568332
Fax: 64 9 6308077
E-mail: nzsa@clear.net.nz
Home Page: http://www.authors.org.nz

Formerly: (1995) PEN New Zealand, Inc..

• 3794 • **NZSA Lilian Ida Smith Award**
To assist Society of Authors members 35 years of age or older to embark on or further a literary career. An award of $3,000 NZ is made biennially to assist a writer in the completion of a specific writing project. Projects may be nonfiction, fiction, poetry, or drama for children or adults. Recipients must be NZSA (PEN NZ Inc.) members. Application deadline is September 30. Established in 1986 from a bequest made by Lillian Ida Smith, a music teacher who had an interest in the arts.

• 3795 •
New Zealand Society of Soil Science
Trish Fraser, Contact
Crop and Food Research
PB 4704
Christchurch, New Zealand
Phone: 64 6 3256400
Fax: 64 6 3252074
E-mail: fraserp@crop.cri.nz
Home Page: http://nzsss.rsnz.org

• 3796 • **L.C. Blakemore Award**
For outstanding performance in soil science technical support.

• 3797 • **Fellow of the NZ Society of Soil Science**
To fellows for research, technology, teaching, extension and/or the advancement of soil science.

• 3798 • **Morice Fieldes Memorial Award**
For recognition of exceptional merit in a PhD thesis.

• 3799 • **M.L. Leamy Award**
To the author of the most meritorious contribution to soil science published in the last three years.

• 3800 • **Sir Theodore Rigg Memorial Award**
For recognition of exceptional merit in a masterate thesis.

• 3801 • **Summit Quinphos Award**
For contributions to New Zealand soil science arising from a doctorate study.

• 3802 • **Norman Taylor Memorial Lecture**
For outstanding contributions to soil science in New Zealand.

• 3803 • **T.W. Walker Prizes**
For best student oral paper and best student poster prizes at the main biennial conference held by the Society.

• 3804 •
New Zealand Theatre Federation
Jannat Aitchinson, Contact
Rm. 304, Second Fl., Cranmer Centre
Post Box 3037
Christchurch Mail Centre
Christchurch, New Zealand
Phone: 64 3 3772 303
Fax: 64 3 3772 305
E-mail: nztfnat@xtra.co.nz
Home Page: http://www.theatrenewzealand.co.nz

• 3805 • **Festival of Community Theatre**
To recognize an outstanding theatre. Amateur societies may enter. The festival is organized on a national basis on three levels: district, regional, and national. Awards presented are as follows: The Bryan Aitken Award for best youth production; awards for best male and female best actor, and best new director; award for best technical production; Playwrights Association of New Zealand Award for best play in the national final; and the Book of Honor for the overall winner. Awarded annually. Formerly: (1997) Annual One Act Play Festival Award.

• 3806 • **Olga E. Harding Trophy**
To recognize an original play written by a New Zealand playwright participating in the Festival of Community Theatre. Awarded annually. Established in 1986 in honor of Olga E. Harding, who contributed to amateur theatre in New Zealand. Formerly: Shell Playwriting Award.

• 3807 •
New Zealand Trade and Enterprise
Fiona Acheson, Dir. of Communications
PO Box 8680
Symonds St.
Auckland, New Zealand
Phone: 64 9 3664768
Fax: 64 9 3664767
E-mail: mediaenquiries@nzte.govt.nz
Home Page: http://www.nzte.govt.nz

• 3808 • **Agritechnology, Life Sciences and Biotechnology Exporter of the Year**
To recognize the top New Zealand exporters. Awarded annually. Established in 1965.

• 3809 • **Creative Exporter of the Year**
To recognize top New Zealand exporters.

• 3810 • **Information, Communications and Technology Exporter of the Year**
To recognize the top New Zealand exporters.

• 3811 • **Specialised Manufacturing Exporter of the Year**
To recognize the top New Zealand Exporters.

• 3812 • **Wood Building and Interiors Exporter of the Year**
To recognize the top New Zealand exporters.

• 3813 •
New Zealand Water and Wastes Association
Simon Carlaw, Chief Exec.
PO Box 1316
Wellington, New Zealand
Phone: 64 4 8025262
Fax: 64 4 8025272
E-mail: water@nzwwa.org.nz
Home Page: http://www.nzwwa.org.nz

• 3814 • **Association Medal**
For a member's extraordinary personal contribution and dedication to the water environment.

• 3815 • Best Operations Paper
For the best written and presented paper at a NZWWA Operations Workshop.

• 3816 • Brian Brown Award
For the best paper presented on a water or environmental engineering topic at an association sponsored conference.

• 3817 • Hynds-NZWWA Paper of the Year Award
For the best technical and presented paper at the NZWWA Annual Conference.

• 3818 • Michael Taylor Award
For the winning paper where significant advances have been demonstrated in potable, agricultural or industrial water supply engineering or science.

• 3819 • Operators Award
For efforts made in solving an operating difficulty or problem at a water or wastewater treatment plant.

• 3820 • Ronald Hicks Memorial Award
For a paper that presents significant solutions to sewage treatment or water pollution problems in New Zealand.

• 3821 •
Physiological Society of New Zealand
Assoc.Prof. Simon Malpas, Sec.
Department of Physiology
Medical School
University of Auckland
PO Box 92019
Auckland, New Zealand
Fax: 64 9 3737499
E-mail: s.malpas@auckland.ac.nz
Home Page: http://www.bioeng.auckland.ac.nz/psnz/www/index.php

• 3822 • Mary Bullivant Student Prize
Recognizes the best presentation at the annual conference. A certificate and monetary award of $100 is presented annually.

• 3823 • John Hubbard Memorial Prize
Recognizes excellence in studies toward a PhD degree. Awarded annually. Established in 1997.

• 3824 •
Playmarket
Andrew Caisley, Pres.
Level 2, 16 Cambridge Terr.
PO Box 9767, Te Aro
Wellington, New Zealand
Phone: 64 4 382 8462
Fax: 64 4 382 8461
E-mail: info@playmarket.org.nz
Home Page: http://www.playmarket.org.nz

• 3825 • Bruce Mason Playwrighting Award
To recognize the work on an outstanding emerging New Zealand playwright. The recipient will receive a full-length commission and an annual playreading. Awarded annually. Established in 1983 to honor Bruce Mason, one of New Zealand's finest playwrights and theater critics. Formerly: *The Dominion Sunday Times* Bruce Mason Playwrights Award.

• 3826 •
Population Association of New Zealand
Ward Friesen, Pres.
University of Auckland
Private Bag 92019
Auckland, New Zealand
Phone: 64 9 3737599
Fax: 64 9 3737434
E-mail: w.friesen@auckland.ac.nz
Home Page: http://panz.rsnc.org

• 3827 • Statistics New Zealand/Jacoby Prize
Recognizes the best essay written during a course of university study on a population topic. Awarded annually. The cash prize is $250 with a copy of the latest New Zealand official yearbook and demographic trends, plus a year's membership in PANZ and publication of the winning essay in the New Zealand population review. Formerly: (2004) Jacoby Prize.

• 3828 • Statistics New Zealand - Jacoby Student Essay Competition
For the best essay written during a course of university study on a population topic. Open to students throughout New Zealand. Essays are submitted in the form in which they were presented during the course of study.

• 3829 •
Restaurant Association of New Zealand
Alistair Rowe, CEO
PO Box 8287
Symonds St.
Auckland 1, New Zealand
Phone: 64 9 6388403
Fax: 64 9 6384209
E-mail: restaurant.assoc@xtra.co.nz
Home Page: http://www.restaurantnz.co.nz

• 3830 • Continuing Education Grant
To culinary professionals.

• 3831 • Hospitality Business Scholarships
To industry professionals who are studying For a graduate/post graduate HSI level 4 programme or equivalent

• 3832 • Merit Scholarships For Hospitality Students
to individuals pursuing level 4 hospitality units.

• 3833 • Merit Scholarships For Secondary School Students
For commitment in tertiary hospitality education and career in the hospitality/foodservice industry

• 3834 • Tutor Work Study Grant
For recipients who wish to gain knowledge and insight into today's work environment

• 3835 •
Royal New Zealand Aero Club
David Bishop, Exec.Sec
Box 1191
Blenheim, New Zealand
Phone: 64 7 8346284
Fax: 64 7 8435514
E-mail: rnzac@xtra.co.nz
Home Page: http://www.rnzac.org.nz

• 3836 • Aero Engine Services Trophy
For recognition of achievement in aerobatics by nonprofessional pilots. Entrants in the competition are eligible. A trophy is awarded annually. Established in 1969.

• 3837 • Airways Corporation Trophy
For recognition of achievement in general flying. Entrants in the competition are eligible. A cup is awarded annually. Established in 1991 by Airways Corporation of New Zealand Ltd.

• 3838 • Airwork Cup
For recognition of achievement in aircraft preflight inspection. Affiliated club members not competing for the CAA. Trophy are eligible. A cup is awarded annually. Presented in 1987 by Airwork Ltd.

• 3839 • D.M. Allen Memorial Cup
For recognition of achievement in aerobatics for New Zealand professional club pilots. Entrants in the competition are eligible. A cup is awarded annually. Established in 1949 in honor of D.M. Allan.

• 3840 • Jean Batten Memorial Trophy
For recognition of achievement in takeoff, circuit, preflight inspection, and landing. Female pilots of affiliated clubs who hold student pilot licenses are eligible. A monetary grant and trophy are awarded annually. Established in 1989 in honor of Jean Batten.

• 3841 • Bledisloe Aviation Trophy
For recognition of achievement in airmanship, landings, and navigation for pilots who have gone solo in the preceding year. A trophy is awarded annually. Established in 1934. Presented by the Governor-General of N.Z. & Lady Bledisloe.

• 3842 • Sir Francis Boys Cup
For recognition of achievement in takeoff, circuit, and landing for club-trained pilots. Entrants in the competition are eligible. A cup is awarded annually. Established in 1931. Prsented by Sir

Francis Boys K.B.E. First President of New Zealand Aero Club.

• 3843 • **CAA Trophy**
For recognition of achievement in aircraft pre-flight inspections. All RNZAC National Championship competing pilots are eligible. A trophy is awarded annually. Presented by the Civil Aviation Authority 1985.

• 3844 • **Cory - Wright Cup**
For recognition of achievement in aerobatics for club-trained pilots. Entrants in the competition are eligible. A cup is awarded annually. Established in 1931. in memory of Cyril W. Cory-Wright.

• 3845 • **Oscar Garden Trophy**
For recognition of achievement in full panel instrument flying. Entrants in the competition are eligible. A trophy is awarded annually. Established in 1975. Won by Oscar Garden in 1931-presented to RNZAC in 1975. Formerly: Air Service Training Blind Flying Trophy.

• 3846 • **Gloucester Navigation Trophy**
For recognition of achievement in direct route navigation for holders of a commercial pilot's license. Entrants in the competition are eligible. A trophy is awarded annually. Established in 1950. To commemorate the visit of the Duke of Gloucester 1934-35.

• 3847 • **Jubilee Trophy**
For recognition of achievement in aerobatic flying. Any licensed pilots of affiliated clubs are eligible. A trophy is awarded annually. Presented in 1978.

• 3848 • **W. A. Morrison Trophy**
For recognition of achievement in three aircraft flying in formation. Private or commercial pilot license holders in affiliated clubs are eligible. A trophy is awarded annually. Presented by WA Morrison 1981.

• 3849 • **New Zealand Herald Challenge Trophy**
For recognition of achievement in navigation, pilotage, and landing for nonprofessional pilots. Entrants in the competition are eligible. A trophy is awarded annually. Established in 1947. Presented by Wilson & Houghton Ltd.

• 3850 • **New Zealand Wings Trophy**
For recognition of achievement in landing, formation flying, and aerobatics. Entrants in the competition are selected by the aero club bodies of New Zealand and Australia. The competition is conducted in New Zealand and Australia on a "year about" basis. A trophy is awarded annually. Established in 1993.

• 3851 • **Newman Cup**
For recognition of achievement in takeoff, circuit, and landing for women pilots. Entrants in the competition are eligible. A cup is awarded annually. Established in 1935. Presented by Mrs. T. Newman.

• 3852 • **North Shore Trophy**
For recognition of achievement for the most points amassed by a club at the RNZAC Annual National Championships. Clubs with pilots competing at the National Championships are eligible. A trophy is awarded annually. Presented by the North Shore Aero Club-1988.

• 3853 • **Rotorua Trophy**
For recognition of achievement in a mock bombing competition. Student or private pilot license holders who are Club members are eligible. A trophy is awarded annually. Established in 1981 by the Rotorua Aero Club.

• 3854 • **G. M. Spence Trophy**
For recognition of achievement in forced landings. Entrants in the competition are eligible. A trophy is awarded annually. Established in 1935 by G.M. Spence.

• 3855 • **Waitemata Aero Club Cup**
For recognition of achievement in CIVA Sportsman aerobatics. Entrants in the competition are eligible. A trophy is awarded annually. Established in 1993.

• 3856 • **Wanganui Trophy**
For recognition of achievement in a low-flying competition. The competition is open to pilots of affiliated clubs who hold a commercial pilot's license and who are not in full-time employment as pilots. A trophy is awarded annually. Established in 1989. Presented by the Wanganui Aero Club.

• 3857 • **Ivon Warmington Trophy**
For recognition of achievement in liferaft dropping from a plane. Club pilots who hold private pilot licenses are eligible. A trophy is awarded annually. Presented in 1975 by Mr. I. Warmington D.F.C.

• 3858 • **Wigram Cup**
For recognition of achievement in landing, instrument flying, and noninstrument circuit flying for nonprofessional pilots. Entrants in the competition are eligible. A cup is awarded annually. Established in 1931. Presented by Sir Henry Wigram.

• 3859 • **Wigram Cup (Sub-Competition) - Instrument Flying**
For recognition of achievement in flying using a limited panel of flight instruments. Entrants in the competition are eligible. A cup is awarded annually. Established in 1955. originally for aerobotics changed to Instrument Flying in 1963 Presented by M.N. McLaren.

• 3860 • **Wigram Cup (Sub-Competition) - Junior Landing**
For recognition of achievement in landing. Entrants in the competition are eligible. A cup is awarded annually. Established in 1956. Presented by J.R. Franklin.

• 3861 • **Wigram Cup (Sub-Competition) - Non-instrument Circuits**
For recognition of achievement in flying two circuits without the assistance of flight instruments. Entrants in the competition are eligible. A cup is awarded annually. Established in 1956 originally for bombing-changed to Non-instrument Circuits in 1981.

• 3862 • **Wigram Cup (Sub-Competition) - Senior Landing**
For recognition of achievement in landing. Entrants in the competition are eligible. A cup is awarded annually. Established in 1956.

• 3863 •
Royal Society of New Zealand
Jez Watson, Pres.
4 Halswell St., Thorndon
PO Box 598
Wellington 6001, New Zealand
Phone: 64 4 472 7421
Fax: 64 4 473 1841
E-mail: thompson@rsnz.govt.nz
Home Page: http://www.rsnz.org

• 3864 • **Leonard Cockayne Memorial Lecture**
For encouragement of botanical research in New Zealand. An invitation to deliver a lecture is awarded triennially. Established in 1964 to commemorate the life and work of the late Leonard Cockayne.

• 3865 • **E. R. Cooper Memorial Medal and Prize**
For the encouragement of scientific research in the fields of physics or engineering. The award consists of a medal and prize - a book or books, suitably inscribed - and is made every two years to the persons who, in the opinion of the Selection Committee, published the best single account of original research in physics or engineering. Preference is given to contributions to the development of New Zealand natural resources. Established in 1958 by the Dominion Physical Laboratory in memory of E. R. Cooper.

• 3866 • **Charles Fleming Award for Environmental Achievement**
To recognize individuals, groups, or organizations who have achieved distinction in the protection, maintenance, management, improvement, or understanding of the environment. Nominations may be made by New Zealand citizens. A monetary grant, a plaque, and an expense paid lecture tour are awarded triennially.

• 3867 • **Hamilton Memorial Prize**
For the encouragement of beginners in scientific research in New Zealand or in the islands of the South Pacific. Works published within seven years preceding the last day of January prior to the annual meeting where the award is made are eligible. Such publications must include the

first investigation published by the candidate. Candidates for the prize must send an intimation of candidature to the Executive Officer before June 30, with two copies of each published work. In addition, any fellow or member may nominate one or more candidates for the prize.

• 3868 • Hector Memorial Medal and Prize

To recognize advancement and achievement, on a rotating basis, in the following scientific areas: plant sciences, chemical sciences, human sciences, solid earth sciences, mathematical sciences, physical sciences, engineering sciences, and animal sciences. Investigators working within New Zealand are considered for the award. A monetary prize of $500 and a bronze medal are awarded annually. Established in 1910 by the Hector Memorial Fund of the New Zealand Institute in memory of Sir James Hector, K.C.M.G., M.D., F.R.S., the second President of the New Zealand Institute.

• 3869 • Hutton Memorial Medal and Prize

To recognize and encourage research in zoology, botany, or geology in New Zealand. Researchers who have received the greater part of their education in New Zealand or who have resided in New Zealand for not less than ten years are eligible for the award. A bronze medal and grants are awarded triennially. Established in 1909 by the New Zealand Institute in memory of Professor Sir Frederick Wollaston Hutton, F.R.S., its first President.

• 3870 • New Zealand Science and Technology Medals

To recognize individuals who have made exceptional contributions to New Zealand society and culture through activities in the fields of science and technology. A medal is awarded for each of the following types of achievement: (1) for eminent research by a person or a group in any field of science or technology that is recognized internationally and that has contributed to public awareness of the field concerned; (2) for conspicuous, continuing contributions to science and technology over an extended period; and (3) for outstanding specific contributions to the advancement of science and technology, including an excellent piece of research, an outstanding inventions or technological innovation, or exceptional service to a society or institution. Bronze medals and up to 10 silver medals are awarded annually.

• 3871 • New Zealand Science, Mathematics and Technology Teacher Fellowship

To enable outstanding teachers to further understand the role of science, mathematics, social science, and technology in New Zealand's economy and society, and to provide them with new experiences outside the classroom that can enable them to become more effective science teachers. Primary, intermediate, or secondary school teachers of science, mathematics, and technology are eligible. Awarded annually.

• 3872 • T. K. Sidey Medal and Prize

For the promotion and encouragement of scientific research in the study of light visible and invisible, and other solar radiations in relation to human welfare, or, at the discretion of the Society, of research on radiations of any kind. A medal and monetary prize, not be less than $200, are awarded at irregular intervals as the state of the fund permits. Established in 1933 by the transfer to the New Zealand Institute of £500 collected to commemorate the passing of the Summer-Time Act (1927) through the instrumentality of Sir Thomas A. Sidey.

• 3873 • Thomson Medal

For recognition of outstanding contributions to the organization, administration, or application of science. Established in 1985 to commemorate the contributions made to science by George Malcolm Thomson (1848-1933) and his son, James Allan Thomson (1881-1928). Both are former Presidents of the Royal Society of New Zealand. Establishment of the medal was made possible by the generosity of A. P. Thomson, son of J. A. Thomson.

• 3874 •
Tourism Industry Association New Zealand
Fiona Luhrs, CEO
4th Fl., Tourism and Travel House
79 Boulcott St.
PO Box 1697
Wellington, New Zealand
Phone: 64 4 499 0104
Fax: 64 4 499 0827
E-mail: info@tianz.org.nz
Home Page: http://www.tianz.org.nz

• 3875 • New Zealand Tourism Awards

To encourage and recognize excellence in tourism and tourist products in New Zealand; to improve and enhance the quality of the New Zealand tourism experience offered; and to encourage significant initiatives taken by individuals and/or organizations to develop tourism and tourist products in New Zealand. Open to any individual, company or organization. Awards are judged in a variety of categories; in addition, several special awards are presented. Held annually. Established in 1955.

• 3876 •
University of Otago
PO Box 56
Dunedin, New Zealand
Phone: 64 3 479 1100
Fax: 64 3 474 1607
E-mail: university@otago.ac.nz
Home Page: http://www.otago.ac.nz

• 3877 • Philip Neill Memorial Prize in Music

For recognition of excellence in original composition. The test is the composition of a work in a form of structure prescribed by the examiners, such prescription to vary from year to year. The competition is open to all past and present students of a university in New Zealand, but a winner of the prize in any year is not eligible to compete again until five complete years have elapsed since the year the candidate was awarded the prize. A monetary prize is awarded annually. Established in 1943 in memory of Philip Foster Neill, a medical student of the University of Otago, by his sister.

• 3878 •
Women's Studies Association
Prue Hyman, Committee Member
PO Box 5043
Wellington, New Zealand
Phone: 64 4 4635285
E-mail: prue.hyman@vuw.ac.nz
Home Page: http://www.womenz.org.nz/wsa

• 3879 • RoseMary Seymour Award

For a research or archive project that meets aims of the organization. A monetary award is given annually.

Nigeria

• 3880 •
Action Health - Nigeria
Mrs. Nike O. Esiet, Exec.Dir.
17 Lawal St.
Off Oweh St.
Fadeyi
Lagos, Lagos, Nigeria
Phone: 234 1 7743745
Phone: 234 1 2881103
Fax: 234 1 3425496
E-mail: info@actionhealthinc.org
Home Page: http://www.actionhealthinc.org

• 3881 • Teenage Festival of Life Award

Award of recognition. For writers of outstanding poems, songs, and plays on the subject of youth health. Awarded annually.

• 3882 •
African Reinsurance Corp.
(Societe Africaine de Reassurance)
Bakary Kamara, Managing Dir.
Plot 1679 Karimu Kotun St.
Victoria Island
Private Mail Bag 12765
Lagos, Lagos, Nigeria
Phone: 234 1 2663323
Phone: 234 1 2626660
Fax: 234 1 2663282
E-mail: info@africa-re.com
Home Page: http://www.africa-re.com

• 3883 • Standard and Poor's BBB Rating

To rate companiesK ability to pay interest and repay on the principal of a given obligation. The BBB+ rating is considered goodw in those regards.

• 3884 •
Nigerian Association of Chambers of Commerce, Industry, Mines, and Agriculture
Mr. L.O. Adekunle, Dir.Gen.
15 A Ikorodu Rd.
Maryland By-Pass
Private Mail Bag 12816
Lagos, Lagos, Nigeria
Phone: 234 1 4964727
Phone: 234 1 4964737
Fax: 234 1 4964737
E-mail: naccima@pinet.com.ng
Home Page: http://www.nigeriabusinessinfo.com/naccima.htm

• 3885 • **Honorary Life Officer**
Recognizes the outstanding businessperson or entrepreneur. Awarded periodically.

• 3886 •
West African College of Surgeons
(College Ouest Africain des Chirurgiens)
Dr. Christopher Bode, Gen.Sec.
W African Health Committee Bldg.
6 Taylor Dr., Edmond Crescent
Private Mail Bag 1067
Yaba, Lagos, Nigeria
Phone: 234 1 3425016
Phone: 234 1 4710872
Fax: 234 1 2693705
E-mail: info@wacs-coac.org
Home Page: http://www.wacs-coac.org

• 3887 • **Best Paper Award**
For recognition of the best paper presented at scientific meeting. Grants and scholarships are also awarded.

Norway

• 3888 •
Association for Promotion of Skiing
(Foreningen til Ski-Idrettens Fremme)
Kongevei 5
N-0787 Oslo 3, Norway
Phone: 47 2 2292 3200
Fax: 47 2 2292 3250
E-mail: skif@skiforeningen.no
Home Page: http://www.skiforeningen.no

• 3889 • **Holmenkoll Medal (Holmenkollmedaljen)**
To recognize outstanding skiers and to promote the sport of skiing. Individuals who have been active in skiing in Holmenkollen for at least one year are eligible. Awarded to one or more recipients annually. Established in 1895.

• 3890 • **Holmenkollen Ski Festival**
To recognize outstanding skiers at the annual Ski Festival. The following events are held: Combined, Jump, Men's 50 Km, Men's 18 Km, Men's 15 Km, Women's 30, Women's 20 Km, Women's 10 Km, Women's 5 Km, Women's Relay and Men's Relay. The Trophy of Holmenkollen (Holmenkollpokal) is awarded annually. Established in 1892.

• 3891 •
Association of Consulting Engineers, Norway
(Radgivende Ingeniorers Forening)
Siri Legernes, Contact
Essendrops gate 3
Postboks 5491 Majorstuen
N-0305 Oslo 1, Norway
Phone: 47 22 853570
Fax: 47 22 853571
E-mail: rif@rif.no
Home Page: http://www.rif.no

• 3892 • **Vannprisen**
Recognizes outstanding work in the field of water engineering. Awarded annually.

• 3893 •
Bergen International Festival
(Festspillene I Bergen)
Per Boye Hansen, Festival Dir.
Vagsallmenningen 1
PO Box 183
Sentrum
N-5804 Bergen, Norway
Phone: 47 55 210630
Fax: 47 55 210640
E-mail: festsipllene@fib.no
Home Page: http://www.fib.no

• 3894 • **Robert Levins Festspillfond**
To encourage and promote a higher level of quality among younger, Norwegian pianists. Norwegian citizens are eligible. A monetary prize of 15,000 Norwegian kroner is awarded annually during the Festival in May/June. Established in 1985 in honor of Robert Levin.

• 3895 • **Operasangerinnen Fanny Elstas Fond**
To encourage, promote and improve Norwegian vocal music, both composition and singing. Stipends, scholarships, and invitations to master classes are awarded annually during the Festival in May/June. Established in 1979 in honor of Fanny Elsta.

• 3896 • **Sigbjorn Bernhoft Osas Festspillfond**
For recognition of outstanding achievements within the field of Norwegian folk-music. A monetary prize is awarded annually during the Festival in May/June. Established in 1986 in honor of Sigbjorn Bernhoft Osa.

• 3897 •
Birkebeiner-Rennet
Tone Lien, Contact
Postboks 144
N-2451 Rena, Norway
Phone: 47 62 442900
Fax: 47 62 442901
E-mail: renn@birkebeiner.no
Home Page: http://www.birkebeiner.no/renn

• 3898 • **Birkebeinerrennet Ski Race**
To recognize the best skiers in a 35-mile cross country race. Cups, trophies, and plaques are awarded annually. Established in 1932.

• 3899 •
International Council for Open and Distance Education
(Conseil International de l'Enseignement a Distance)
Reidar Roll, Sec.Gen.
Lilleakerveien 23
N-0283 Oslo 4, Norway
Phone: 47 22 062630
Fax: 47 22 062631
E-mail: icde@icde.org
Home Page: http://www.icde.org

• 3900 • **Prize of Excellence**
To recognize for excellence and dedication to distance education. Awarded annually in three categories: individual, institutional, and lifelong contributions to the field.

• 3901 •
Norway Ministry of Foreign Affairs
Anne Lene Sandsten, Press Off.
7 juni plassen
Victoria Terrasse
POB 8114 Dep.
N-0032 Oslo, Norway
Phone: 47 22 243600
Fax: 47 22 249580
E-mail: post@mfa.no
Home Page: http://odin.dep.no/ud/engelsk/index-b-n-a.html

• 3902 • **Royal Norwegian Order of Merit**
To recognize foreign nationals and Norwegian nationals living permanently abroad for outstanding service to Norway. It may also be given to foreign civil servants in Norway for diplomatic/consular service, as well as to Norway's honorary consuls. The Order has five classes: Grand Cross, Commander with Stars, Commander, Officer and Knight. The insignia of Officer of the Royal Norwegian Order of Merit ("Ridder I" in Norwegian) consists of a gold cross. The insignia of Knight ("Ridder" in Norwegian) are silver. Established in 1985.

• 3903 • **Royal Norwegian Order of St. Olav**
To recognize Norwegian citizens for outstanding service to their native country and humanity. A decoration and a diploma are awarded when merited in the following classes: Grand Cross with Collar; Grand Cross; Commander with Star; Commander; Knight First Class; and Knight. Awarded when merited. Established in 1847 by King Oscar I.

• 3904 • **St. Olav Medal**
To recognize individuals who have promoted knowledge of Norway abroad or have strengthened the cultural ties between Norwegian emigrants and their home country. The medal is

Awards are arranged in alphabetical order below their administering organizations

silver. Awarded when merited. Established in 1939 by H.M. King Haakon VII.

• 3905 •
Norwegian International Film Festival
(Norske Filmfestivalen)
Gunnar Johan Lovvik, Festival Dir.
PO Box 145
N-5501 Haugesund, Norway
Phone: 47 52 743370
Fax: 47 52 743371
E-mail: info@filmfestivalen.no
Home Page: http://www.filmfestivalen.no

• 3906 • Amanda Award for Cinematographic Merit (Amanda Film - OG Fjernsynspris)
For recognition of outstanding achievement in the preceding season's (July-July) national film and television production. Norwegian film productions may be submitted to the appointed "Amanda" jury/juries. Awards are given in the following categories: Best Norwegian Feature, Best Nordic Feature, Best Documentary, Best Artistic Short Film, Best Actor, Best Actress, Best Professional Achievement, Best Foreign Feature, Best TV-drama, Gullklapperen (Honorary Award to Filmmakers), and Amanda-Komiteens Aerespris (Special Honorary Award). A bronze statuette awarded annually. Established in 1985.

• 3907 •
Norwegian Press Association
(Norsk Presseforbund)
Radhusgatan 17
Postboks 46 Sentrum
N-0101 Oslo 1, Norway
Phone: 47 22 405040
Fax: 47 22 405055
E-mail: pfu@presse.no
Home Page: http://www.presse.no

• 3908 • Grand Journalism Prize (Den Store Journalistprisen)
For recognition of outstanding efforts in journalism by Norwegian citizens. A monetary prize of 100,000 kroner and a plaque are awarded annually when merited. Established in 1991. Sponsored by the Norwegian Union of Journalists, the Editors Association, the Norwegian Newspaper Publishers Association, and the Norwegian Broadcasting Corporation.

• 3909 •
The Norwegian Short Film Festival
(Stiftelsen Kortfilmfestivalen)
Torun Nyen, Gen.Mgr.
Filmens Hus
Dronningensgt. 16
N-0152 Oslo, Norway
Phone: 47 22 474646
Fax: 47 22 474690
E-mail: kortfilm@kortfilmfestivalen.no
Home Page: http://www.kortfilmfestivalen.no

• 3910 • Short Film Festival Prize (Stiftelsen Kortfilmfestivalen)
To recognize the best short film of the Festival. The film director must be a Norwegian citizen. A monetary award of 20,000 Norwegian kroner and a trophy of a director's chair in gold are awarded. Established in 1983.

• 3911 •
Norwegian Society of Financial Analysts
(Norske Finansanalytikeres Forening)
Gunnar Winther, Sec.Gen.
PO Box 1276 VIKA
N-0111 Oslo, Norway
Phone: 47 22 129210
Fax: 47 22 129211
E-mail: nff@finansanalytiker.no
Home Page: http://www.finansanalytiker.no

• 3912 • Stockman Award
To recognize those companies listed on the Oslo stock Exchange that provide the best investor relations efforts to the capital market. Two awards are presented annually, one in the Open Class and the other for smaller and mid-sized companies.

• 3913 •
The Queen Sonja International Music Competition
Universitetsgaten nr 14
N-0164 Oslo, Norway
Phone: 47 2299 2105
Fax: 47 2299 2101
E-mail: secretariat@queen-sonja-competition.no
Home Page: http://www.queen-sonja-competition.no
Formerly: Crown Princess Sonja International Music Competition.

• 3914 • Queen Sonja International Music Competition
To recognize promising young singers. The following prizes are awarded: First prize NOK 125,000 and concert engagements; second prize NOK 75,000; third prize NOK 50,000. In addition, the Troldhaugen Grieg Prize is awarded. Held biennially in odd-numbered years. Established in 1995.

• 3915 •
Thorolf Rafto Foundation for Human Rights
Arne Liljedahl Lynngard, Chm.
Menneskerettighetenes plass 1
N-5007 Bergen, Norway
Phone: 47 5521 0950
Fax: 47 5521 0959
E-mail: secretariat@rafto.no
Home Page: http://www.rafto.no

• 3916 • Professor Thorolf Rafto Memorial Prize
To recognize an individual or organization that is an active participant in the struggle for the ideals and principles of spiritual, political, and economic freedom. Awarded annually.

Pakistan

• 3917 •
Iqbal Academy Pakistan
Academy Block, 6th Fl.
Aiwan-i-Iqbal Complex
Egerton Rd.
Lahore, Pakistan
Phone: 92 42 6314 510
Fax: 92 42 6314 496
E-mail: iqbalacd@lhr.comsats.net.pk
Home Page: http://www.allamaiqbal.com

• 3918 • International Iqbal Award
For promotion and recognition of original research work of high caliber to a foreign national in the field of Iqbal studies. A monetary prize and a medal are awarded triennially. Established in 1977 by the President of Pakistan in honor of Dr. Sir Allama Mohammad Iqbal. Sponsored by the Pakistan Ministry of Education.

• 3919 • National Iqbal Award
Awarded to Pakistani nationals in the field of Iqbal studies. A monetary prize and a medal are awarded triennially.

• 3920 •
Pakistan Academy of Sciences
Prof. Atta-ur-Rahman, President
3-Constitution Ave., Sector G-5/2
Islamabad 44000, Pakistan
Phone: 92 51 920 4657
Fax: 92 51 9225 159
E-mail: pasisb@yahoo.com
Home Page: http://www.paspk.org

• 3921 • Pakistan Institute of Sciences Gold Medal
To recognize achievements in scientific and technological research in various disciplines of science, and in engineering and technology for those who have developed patents and processes of far-reaching national importance. Medals are given in the following categories: (1) Physical/Biological Science; (2) Physical/Biological Science (for scientists under 40 years of age); (3) Engineering and Technology; (4) Water Management; (5) Agricultural Science; (6) Energy; and (7) Earth Sciences. Pakistani scientists must be nominated by a Fellow of the Academy or rector/head of a university or scientific organization, within the time period specified. A gold medal is awarded annually at an investiture ceremony. Established in 1967 in the sciences, with the additional categories added in 1975 and 1990.

• 3922 •
Pakistan Television Corp.
Muhammad Arshad Khan, Mng.Dir.
Federal TV Complex
Constitution Ave.
PO Box 1221
Islamabad, Pakistan
Phone: 92 51 9208655
Fax: 92 51 9203406
E-mail: fakhar@ptv.com.pk
Home Page: http://ptv.com.pk

• 3923 • PTV National Awards
To recognize achievement in the field of television production, and to encourage professionals in that field. Directors, producers, cameramen, engineers, designers and other professionals including writers, actors, composers, singers, and instrumentalists are eligible. Nominations, based on outstanding performances and productions in the preceding years, are accepted. Monetary awards, trophies, and certificates are awarded annually. Established in 1980.

China, People's Republic of

• 3924 •
Chartered Institute of Management Accountants - Hong Kong Division
Ms. Juliee P.L. Tan, Mgr.
Jardine House
14th Fl., Stes. 1414-1415
139 Hennessy Rd.
Wanchai
Hong Kong, People's Republic of China
Phone: 852 25112003
Fax: 852 25074701
E-mail: juliee.tan@cimaglobal.com
Home Page: http://www.cimaglobal.com

• 3925 • Management Accounting Award
Recognizes exceptional CIMA publications and recommended readings for CIMA exams. Awarded annually.

• 3926 •
Chinese Mathematical Society
Lan Wen, Pres.
No. 55, Zhong Guan Cun East Rd.
Hai Dian District
Beijing 100080, People's Republic of China
Phone: 86 10 62551022
Phone: 86 10 62651420
Fax: 86 10 62618463
E-mail: cms@math.ac.cn
Home Page: http://www.cms.org.cn

• 3927 • Shiing S. Chern Mathematics Award
For young and middle-aged Chinese mathematicians who have made distinguished research works.

• 3928 • Hua Loo-keng Mathematics Award
To the individual deemed to have made lifetime achievements in mathematical research and mathematical education.

• 3929 • Zhong Jiaqing Mathematics Award
To the outstanding MSC and PhD graduates of mathematics.

• 3930 •
Composers and Authors Society of Hong Kong
Prof. Chan Wing Wah, Chm.
18/F Universal Trade Centre
3 Arbuthnot Rd.
Central
Hong Kong, People's Republic of China
Phone: 852 28463268
Fax: 852 28463261
E-mail: general@cash.org.hk
Home Page: http://www.cash.org.hk

• 3931 • Hall of Fame Award
Recognizes achievements and contribution to local music scenes. Awarded annually.

• 3932 •
Federation of Hong Kong Industries
Mr. Robin Chiu, Dir.Gen.
Hankow Centre, 4th Fl.
5-15 Hankow Rd.
Tsim Sha Tsui, Kowloon
Hong Kong, People's Republic of China
Phone: 852 27323188
Fax: 852 27213494
E-mail: fhki@fhki.org.hk
Home Page: http://www.fhki.org.hk

• 3933 • Young Industrialist Awards of Hong Kong
To recognize outstanding industrialists for their achievements and commitment to manufacturing industry and to encourage them to further contribute their expertise to the territory's economic development. Industrialists who have resided in Hong Kong for more than seven years and are between the ages of 21 and 45 are eligible for nomination. A trophy is awarded annually.

• 3934 •
Hong Kong Film Awards Association Ltd.
Michelle Tsang, Admin.Mgr.
Rm 304 Ashley Centre
25 Ashley Rd.
Tsimshatsui, Kowloon, People's Republic of China
Phone: 852 2367 7892
Fax: 852 2723 9597
E-mail: hkfaa@hkfaa.com
Home Page: http://www.hkfaa.com

Formerly: (1994) Hong Kong International Film Festival.

• 3935 • Hong Kong Film Awards
To promote Hong Kong films in Hong Kong and abroad, to recognize local film professionals, to encourage professional development, and to promote film culture. Awards are given in the following categories: Best Film, Best Director, Best Actor, Best Actress, Best Supporting Actor, Best Supporting Actress, Best New Performer, Best Screenplay, Best Cinematography, Best Film Editing, Best Art Direction, Best Costume and Makeup Design, Best Action Choreography, Best Original Film Score, and Best Original Film Song. All films with a general release in the preceding year are considered. Trophies are awarded annually at the award ceremony. Established in 1982. Formerly: Hong Kong International Film Festival.

• 3936 • Hong Kong Independent Short Film Competition/Urban Council Short Film Awards
To promote quality non-commercial short films and encourage creature independent production in Hong Kong. Films must be directed by Hong Kong residents with Hong Kong identity cards and must be no longer than 60 minutes in length. Films that have already received awards in a competitive film festival or that have previously been submitted to the competition are not eligible. Films must have been produced on or after April 1 of the year preceding the award. Awards are presented for fiction, animation, documentary, and experimental. The following awards are presented: Gold Award - $30,000 prize and a trophy for the best film; Silver Award - $20,000 prize and a trophy; and merit awards. Winning and selected films are shown at the Hong Kong International Film Festival. Application deadline is October 20. Awarded annually in the spring. Established in 1992.

• 3937 •
Hong Kong Management Association
Elizabeth S.C. Shing JP, Dir. Gen.
W Haking Management Development Center
Fairmont House, 14th Fl.
8 Cotton Tree Dr.
Central
Hong Kong, People's Republic of China
Phone: 852 27663303
Fax: 852 28684387
E-mail: hkma@hkma.org.hk
Home Page: http://www.hkma.org.hk/front.asp

• 3938 • Award for Excellence in Training
Award of recognition.

• 3939 • Award for Marketing Excellence
Award of recognition.

• 3940 • Best Annual Reports Awards
Award of recognition.

• 3941 • Distinguished Salesperson Award
Award of recognition.

• 3942 • HKMA Quality Award
Award of recognition.

• 3943 • Hong Kong Management Game Award
Award of recognition. 32842 HKPC HX

Awards are arranged in alphabetical order below their administering organizations

• 3944 •
Hong Kong Productivity Council
Mr. K.K. Yeung, Exec.Dir.
HKPC Bldg.
78 Tat Chee Ave.
Kowloon
Hong Kong, People's Republic of China
Phone: 852 27885678
Phone: 852 27886128
Fax: 852 27885900
E-mail: hkpcenq@hkpc.org
Home Page: http://www.hkpc.org

• 3945 • **Hong Kong Awards for Industries**
To recognize outstanding achievements of Hong Kong enterprises in their move toward higher technology and higher value-added activities. Awards are presented in seven categories: Consumer product design, Machinery and equipment design, Customer service, Environmental performance, Innovation and creativity, Productivity and Quality, and Technological Achievement. Awarded annually. Established in 2005.

• 3946 •
International Federation of the Phonographic Industry - Hong Kong
Ricky Fung, CEO
Room 3705, Hopewell Center
183 Queen's Road East
Wanchai
Hong Kong, People's Republic of China
Phone: 852 28655863
Fax: 852 28666859
E-mail: main@ifpihk.org.hk
Home Page: http://www.ifpihk.org

• 3947 • **Gold Disc Award**
Awarded when merited to a pop music recording selling 25,000 copies in Hong Kong and/or 10,000 copies internationally. Additional awards are also awarded in the classical, extended play, and multi-unit set categories.

• 3948 • **Platinum Disc Award**
Awarded when merited to a pop music recording selling 50,000 copies in Hong Kong and/or 20,000 copies internationally. Additional awards are also awarded in the classical, extended play, and multi-unit set categories.

• 3949 •
Organizing Committee of the Shanghai Television Festival
Jessica Wu, Exec.
11/F STV Mansions
298 Wei Hai Rd.
Shanghai 200041, People's Republic of China
Phone: 86 21 6253 7115
Fax: 86 21 6255 2000
E-mail: stvf@public.sta.net.cn
Home Page: http://11th.stvf.com

• 3950 • **Magnolia Prize**
To recognize outstanding television achievement at the Shanghai Television Festival. Awards are presented in the following categories: Best TV Film; Best Director; Best Actor; Best Actress; Best Screenplay; Best Social Documentary; Best History & Biography Documentary; Best Nature Documentary; and Best Asian Documentary. Magnolia and Nomination cups are awarded annually at the closing ceremony of the Festival. Established in 1986.

• 3951 •
Young Women's Christian Association - Hong Kong
Alice Yuk Tak Fun, Gen.Sec.
No. 1 MacDonnell Rd., 3rd Fl.
Hong Kong, People's Republic of China
Phone: 852 34761300
Fax: 852 25244237
E-mail: ywca@ywca.org.hk
Home Page: http://www.ywca.org.hk

• 3952 • **Outstanding Young Woman Volunteers Award**
Recognizes outstanding voluntary service for five or more years. Women volunteers are eligible. Awarded biennially.

Peru

• 3953 •
Latin American Phytopathology Association
(Asociacion Latinoamericana de Fitopatologia)
Dr. Eduardo R. French, Exec.Sec.
Apartado 1558
Av. La Molina 1895
Lima 12, Peru
Phone: 51 1 3496017
Phone: 51 1 3495783
Fax: 51 1 3175326
E-mail: e.french@cgiar.org
Home Page: http://www.fitopatologia.org

• 3954 • **Honorary Member**
Recognizes an outstanding phytopathological researcher or teacher. Awarded when merited.

• 3955 •
Peruvian Association for Conservation of Nature
(Asociacion Peruana para la Conservacion de la Naturaleza)
Silvia Sanchez, Pres.
Parque Jose de Acosta 187
Magdelena del Mar
Lima 17, Peru
Phone: 51 1 2460094
Phone: 51 1 2645804
Fax: 51 1 4420911
Home Page: http://www.apeco.org.pe

• 3956 • **Global 500**
Recognizes exemplary efforts of NGOs in the areas of conservation of natural resources. Awarded annually.

• 3957 •
Regional Centre for Seismology for South America
(Centro Regional de Sismologia para America del Sur)
Alberto A. Giesecke, Exec.Dir.
Apartado 14-0363
Lima, Peru
Phone: 51 1 2256283
Phone: 51 1 2245144
Fax: 51 1 2245144
E-mail: giescere@ceresis.org
Home Page: http://www.ceresis.org

• 3958 • **CERESIS Award (Premio Ceresis)**
For recognition of exceptional contributions to the advancement of seismology and related fields, relevant to South America. Selection is by nomination and unanimous approval of the member states. A plaque and a diploma are awarded biennially. Established in 1979.

Philippines

• 3959 •
Asia-Pacific Council of American Chambers of Commerce
George M. Drysdale, Chm./CEO
Marsman Drysdale Group
Penthouse, Philam Tower
8767 Paseo de Roxas
Makati City 1200, Philippines
Phone: 63 2 8930000
Phone: 63 2 8930111
Fax: 63 2 8930999
E-mail: apcac@amcham.org.hk
Home Page: http://www.apcac.org

• 3960 • **APCAC Award**
To recognize an individual or organization that has furthered free and fair trade in the Asia-Pacific region. Awarded annually.

• 3961 •
Asian Medical Student's Association-Philippines
Rosita Alyssa M. Baua, Contact
Faculty of Medicine and Surgery
Univ. of Santo Tomas
Espana
Manila 1008, Philippines
Phone: 63 2 4372987
Phone: 63 2 7313126
Fax: 63 2 6812514
E-mail: rbaua_amsaphil@yahoo.com
Home Page: http://www.amsa-int.org/

• 3962 • **Best Research Paper Award**
Recognizes an outstanding research paper. Winners are selected by presentation and contest. Awarded annually.

• 3963 •
Association of Development Financing Institutions in Asia and the Pacific
Orlando P. Pena, Sec.Gen.
2nd Fl., Skyland Plz.
Sen. Gil Puyat Ave.
Makati City 1200, Philippines
Phone: 63 2 8161672
Phone: 63 2 8442424
Fax: 63 2 8176498
E-mail: inquire@adfiap.org
Home Page: http://www.adfiap.org

• 3964 • **Asian Banking Awards**
Recognizes and honors Asian banks for outstanding, innovative, and world-class products, services, projects, and programs implemented during the year. Awards are presented in eight categories: SME financing, development project financing, fund sourcing, micro-finance, human resource management, marketing and public relations, customer service, and operational efficiency. Awarded annually. Established in 1998.

• 3965 • **Honorary Member**
For recognition of achievement or contribution to the advancement of the development banking profession in the Asia-Pacific region. Individuals may be nominated if they have gained recognition in the field on development banking because of any of the following services: they have created, developed, and actualized an innovative concept, system, or technology that has been responsible for the improvement of development financing in the region; they have been the leading figure in the founding, development, and the operation of a pioneering institution that provides either development, financing or support, and assistance to other development financing institutions; or they have been recognized by peers and the leaders of their country for outstanding contributions to the field of development financing. A life-time membership in the Association is awarded when merited. Established in 1983.

• 3966 •
Association of Southeast Asian Institutions of Higher Learning
Dr. Teresita U. Quirino PhD, Pres.
363 P. Casal St.
Quiapo
Manila, Philippines
Fax: 63 2 7343714
E-mail: tesyquirino@pacific.net.ph
Home Page: http://www.asaihl.org

• 3967 • **Association of Southeast Asian Institutions of Higher Learning Awards**
To recognize individuals for teaching, research, and public service. The Association sponsors competitions and gives fellowships.

• 3968 •
International Federation of Asian and Western Pacific Contractors' Associations
Rogelio M. Murga, Pres.
3rd Fl. Padilla Bldg., Emerald Ave.
Ortigas Ctr.
Emerald Ave.
Pasig, Philippines
Phone: 63 2 6312782
Phone: 63 2 6312789
Fax: 63 2 6312773
E-mail: ifawpca@mozcom.com
Home Page: http://www.ifawpca.org

• 3969 • **Builders' Awards**
To promote the development of operational and technical advancement in the field of construction, and to encourage the involvement of the construction industry in national welfare. Association members are eligible. A gold or silver medal is awarded in two classifications, Building Construction and Civil Engineering Construction, at the Association's convention. Established in 1964.

• 3970 • **IFAWPCA-Atsumi Award**
To recognize a person or a group of persons for meritorious services in the promotion of the construction industry in each IFAWPCA member nation. Established in 1993 by Mr. Takeo Atsumi (Japan), a past president of IFAWPCA.

• 3971 • **IFAWPCA-CHOI Construction Fieldman Award**
To encourage the development of construction field management systems, procedures, construction methods, and techniques; and to promote the cause of man-made power training. Candidates may be nominated. A monetary award or a citation is presented annually at the convention. Established in 1982 by Mr. Choi Chong-Whan, Past President of IFAWPCA, and President of Samwhan Corporation of Korea.

• 3972 •
National Commission for Culture and the Arts
Cecile Guidote-Alvarez, Exec.Dir.
633 NCAA Bldg.
General Luna St.
Intramuros
Manila, Philippines
Phone: 63 2527 2192
Fax: 63 2527 2194
E-mail: info@ncca.gov.ph
Home Page: http://www.ncca.gov.ph

• 3973 • **CCP Awards for the Arts (Gawad CCP Para sa Sining)**
To recognize Filipino artists or group of artists who have made outstanding contributions to their particular art form. The award is given in three categories. Category A: Artists or group of artists who have/had consistently produced outstanding works in their particular art form or have/had evolved a distinct style or technique that enriches the development of their particular art form; and artists or group of artists who are nationally recognized as outstanding in their field by virtue of winning in prestigious national or international art or literary competitions or being acknowledged as such by critic circles or by their peers. Category B: Artists or group of artists who have made outstanding contributions to the culture of the region of their birth or residence through: Outstanding works that cull and draw inspiration from the cultural heritage, tradition and experiences of the people of their region or locality; outstanding works that manifest or develop a particular style or form significant to their particular region or locality; trailblazing works contemporaneous or innovative in style or form but somehow incorporating elements of their region's heritage and tradition; pioneering or innovative works that have influenced the other artists of their region to explore and develop a particular style or form significant to their locality or have/had inspired revitalization or art-making in their region; outstanding works that draw national attention or popularize particular aesthetic forms indigenous or endemic to the region; outstanding work/works that has/have earned for the regional artists national or international prestige and honor in reputable or recognized national or international art and literary competition, thereby bringing honor not only to themselves but to the other artists and the people of their region as well. Category C: Outstanding cultural workers who, through their works either in research, curatorship or administration have helped to develop or enrich particular art forms or Philippine culture in general. Each awardee receives a medal of recognition, honor, and distinction designed by National Artist Napoleon Abueva, a citation scroll, and a gift check of 10,000.00 pesos.

• 3974 • **National Living Treasures Award (Gawad Manlilikha Ng Bayan (GAMABA))**
To recognize the vital role of the traditional Filipino artist in preserving and developing their indigenous artistic heritage, and to honor artists for their technical skills and outstanding creativity. It is the policy of the State to preserve and promote traditional, folk, and indigenous arts, whether visual, performing or literary, for their cultural and social value, and to honor and support artists for their contribution to the national heri tage by ensuring their creative and technical skills are encouraged and passed on to future generations. Awarded annually. Established in 1992.

• 3975 •
National Research Council of the Philippines (Pambansang Sanggunian sa Pananaliksik ng Pilipinas)
Dr. Paciente Cordero Jr., Exec.Dir.
Patrocinio Valenzuela Hall
General Santos Ave.
Bicutan
Taguig, Philippines
Phone: 63 2 8376141
Phone: 63 2 8376142
Fax: 63 2 8376143
E-mail: nrcpinfo@dost.gov.ph

Awards are arranged in alphabetical order below their administering organizations

• 3976 • **Achievement Awards**
Recognizes exemplary achievement in the sciences. Awards are presented in the categories of mathematics, medicine, pharmaceuticals, biology, agriculture/forestry, social sciences, engineering/industrial research, physics, chemistry, humanities, and Earth and space sciences. Awarded annually.

• 3977 •
Carlos Palanca Foundation
Ground Floor, CPJ Bldg.
105 Carlos Palanca, Jr. St.
Legaspi Village
Makati City 1229, Philippines
Phone: 63 2 818 3681
Fax: 63 2 817 4045
E-mail: cpawards@info.com.ph

• 3978 • **Carlos Palanca Memorial Awards for Literature**
For recognition of outstanding literature in English, Filipino, and Regional languages (Hiligaynon, Iluko, Cebuano). Awards are presented in nine categories: short stories, short stories for children, poetry, essays, one-act plays, full-length plays, teleplays, and screenplays. In addition, the Futuristic Fiction Award for short stories and the Kabataan Essay Award for authors under 18 years of age are presented. Cash prize, certificate, and medallion are awarded annually.

• 3979 •
Philippine Association of the Record Industry
Ronald Aniceto, Exec.Dir.
Greenhills Mansion, Ste. 207
37 Annapolis St., Greenhills
San Juan
Manila, Philippines
Phone: 63 2 7250770
Phone: 63 2 7258754
Fax: 63 2 7250786
E-mail: ronald_aniceto@pari.com.ph
Home Page: http://www.pari.com.ph

• 3980 • **AWIT Awards**
To recognize Filipino performing artists and others involved in Filipino recorded music. Awards are given in dozens of subcategories within the broader divisions of Performance, Creativity, Technical Achievement, Album Packaging, and Music Videos. Awarded annually.

• 3981 •
Philippines Department of Science and Technology
Dr. Estrella F. Alabastro, Sec.
DOST Bldg.
Gen. Santos Ave.
Bicutan, Taguig
Metro Manila 1631, Philippines
Phone: 63 2 837 2071
Fax: 63 2 837 8937
E-mail: spu@dost.gov.ph
Home Page: http://www.dost.gov.ph

• 3982 • **Gawad AGKATEK (Agham, Kapaligiran at Teknolohiya)**
To strengthen the role of science clubs in the promotion of public understanding of science and technology (STE) in the community and to encourage science club members to initiate/undertake community-based projects on STE. Awards are given separately to elementary and secondary science club projects. Screenings are conducted in the regional and national levels. Trophies, plaques and cash prizes are awarded to winning science clubs, their science club advisers and schools. Special awards of sustainability are given out every three years to winning projects which have been well-sustained throughout the years and to science clubs which have consistently performed as excellent promoters of the public understanding of STE. First implemented in 1994 with the Philippines' Department of Science and Technology-Science Education Institute as organizer and the Department of Education, Culture and Sports as cooperating agency.

• 3983 • **Outstanding Youth Science Researchers**
To recognize Philippine youth under the age of 21 who demonstrate scientific talent with constructive and innovative creativity and to encourage pursuit of research and development. Competitors are screened from a series of Science Fairs held at the school, division, regional, interregional and national levels. Only the First Place winners qualify for the next higher level of competition. The following National prizes are awarded in the elementary, secondary and tertiary categories: monetary prizes to the top three winners; medals to all the national finalists; trophies to the top three winners; plaques of recognition to the schools and advisers of the top three winners. In addition, a special award is given by APPROTECH ASIA to the best project undertaken and presented by a female researcher. Beginning SY 1995-96, the search is held biennially. Established in 1969 by the Science and Technology-Science Education Institute and co-sponsored by the Department of Education, Culture and Sports and Pilipinas Shell Foundation. Formerly: (1983) The Outstanding Young Scientists (TOYS).

• 3984 • **Philippine Mathematical Olympiad**
To recognize secondary students with mathematical talents. Certificates of achievement, monetary prizes, trophies, medals, and plaques are awarded annually. Established in 1984. Jointly sponsored by the Philippines' Department of Science and Technology-Science Education Institute, Department of Education, Culture, and Sports, the Mathematical Society of the Philippines, and the PCI Bank Group.

• 3985 • **Philippine Physics Olympiad**
To recognize Philippine secondary school students with talent in physics and to stimulate the improvement of physics education. Certificates of merit, monetary prizes, trophies, medals, and plaques are given biennially. Established in 1992. Sponsored jointly by the Philippines' Department of Science and the Science and Technology-Science Education Institute, the Department of Education, Culture, and Sports, and the Samahang Pisika ng Pilipinas.

• 3986 • **Dr. Juan S. Salcedo Jr. Science Education Award**
For recognition of outstanding contributions made by science or mathematics teachers or supervisors in advancing science/mathematics instruction in the areas of research, development of instructional materials and teaching/learning aids, use of innovative teaching strategies, and meaningful involvement in professional activities that contributed to the promotion of science and technology consciousness. Filipino citizens who teach full-time science or math in the elementary or secondary level in any public or government-recognized private school in the country, may be nominated by the school administrator. At the college level, nomination is limited to institutions offering science/math teacher education degree programs. Monetary prizes, a Presidential Gold Medallion and certificates of recognition for the nominating school are awarded biennially. Established in 1985 in honor of Dr. Juan S. Salcedo Jr., a Philippine national scientist. Sponsored by Philippines' Department of Science and Technology-Science Education Institute in cooperation with the Philippines - Department of Education, Culture, and Sports. Formerly: (1990) Search for Outstanding Contributions to Science Education.

• 3987 •
Ramon Magsayay Award Foundation
Ground Floor, Ramon Magsayay Center
1680 Roxas Blvd.
PO Box 3350
Manilla, Philippines
Phone: 632 521 3166
Fax: 632 521 8105
E-mail: webmaster@rmaf.org.ph
Home Page: http://www.rmaf.org.ph

• 3988 • **Ramon Magsaysay Award**
Awarded to individuals and organizations in Asia whose civic contributions and leadership exemplify the greatness of spirit, integrity, and devotion to freedom of Ramon Magsaysay, former president of the Philippines who died tragically in an airplane crash. Often regarded as the Nobel Prizes of Asia, these awards are presented in six categories: Government service; Public service; Community leadership; Journalism, literature, and creative communication arts; Peace and international understanding; and Emergent leadership. Awarded annually. Established in 1957.

• 3989 •
Southeast Asian Regional Center for Graduate Study and Research in Agriculture
Arsenio M. Balisacan, Dir.
College 4031
Los Banos
Laguna 4031, Philippines
Phone: 63 49 5362365
Phone: 63 49 5362363
Fax: 63 49 5367097
E-mail: post@agri.searca.org
Home Page: http://www.searca.org

• 3990 • **SEARCA Graduate Scholarship**
To enable would-be leaders in agriculture and natural resource management to pursue graduate studies.

• 3991 • **SEARCA PhD Research Scholarship**
For graduate research in Southeast Asian agricultural competitiveness and natural resource management.

• 3992 • **SEARCA Professorial Chairs**
To promote research in agriculture and rural development and natural resource management.

• 3993 • **SEARCA Seed Fund for Research and Training**
To support catalytic research and training projects in agriculture competitiveness and natural resource management.

Poland

• 3994 •
Bellona Publishing House
ul. Grzybowska 77
PL-00-844 Warsaw, Poland
Phone: 48 22 6202044
Fax: 48 22 6522695
E-mail: biuro@bellona.pl
Home Page: http://www.bellona.pl

• 3995 • **Medal for Participation in the Battle for Berlin**
(Medal Za Udzial w Walkach o Berlin)
To recognize participants in the Battle for Berlin. Established in 1966.

• 3996 •
Central Institute for Labour Protection National Research Institute
Czerniakowska 16
00-701 Warsaw, Poland
Phone: 48 22 6234601
Fax: 48 22 6233693
E-mail: oinip@ciop.pl
Home Page: http://www.ciop.pl

• 3997 • **PRO LABORE SECURO Statuette**
Recognizes extraordinary public service in aid of the protection of man in the working environment. Awarded annually.

• 3998 •
Cracow International Festival of Short Films
Janusz Nowak, Dir.
ul. Pychowicka 7
PL-30-364 Krakow, Poland
Phone: 48 12 2671355
Fax: 48 12 2674440
E-mail: festiwal@apollofilm.pl
Home Page: http://www.cracowfilmfestival.pl

• 3999 • **Cracow International Festival of Short Films**
For recognition of short films of all kinds, especially those which, in their human, social and artistic aspects, reveal the changes, trends and achievements of the 20th century. The following prizes are awarded: (1) Grand Prix - a Golden Dragon statuette and 5,000$ for the best film; (2) Special Prizes - Silver Dragon statuettes and 2,000$ each; (3) Main Prizes - Bronze dragon statuettes and monetary prizes of 2,000$ each; (4) Award of FICC; (5) Award of Prof. B. Chromy (Statuette); (6) International Federation of Cinematographic Press (FIPRESCI Diploma) - for the best short. Awarded annually in June. Established in 1961. Sponsored by the Ministry of Culture and Art and the City Council of Cracow.

• 4000 •
Frederick Chopin Society
(Towarzystwo imienia Fryderyka Chopina)
Albert Grudzinski, Dir.
Ostrogski Castle
Okolnik 1 St.
PL-00-368 Warsaw, Poland
Phone: 48 22 8275471
Phone: 48 22 8279589
Fax: 48 22 8279599
E-mail: info@chopin.pl
Home Page: http://www.chopin.pl

• 4001 • **Grand Prix du Disque Frederic Chopin**
To recognize an outstanding recording of a work by Chopin. Established in 1985.

• 4002 • **International Frederic Chopin Piano Competition**
To recognize an outstanding recording of a work by Chopin. Pianists of all nationalities between 18 and 28 years of age may apply. The award is given out every five years, with the next one being awarded in the year 2000. The deadline for the next competition is March 1, 2000. The following prizes are awarded: first prize - $25,000 American dollars and a gold medal; second prize - $20,000 American dollars and a silver medal; third prize - $15,000 American dollars and a bronze medal; fourth prize $11,000 American dollars; fifth prize - $8,000 American dollars; sixth prize $6,000 American dollars; Award for Best Performance of a Polonaise $5,000 American dollars; Polish Radio Award for the Best Performance of Mazurkas -$5,000 American dollars; and the National Philharmonic Award for the Best Performance of a Concerto - $5,000 American dollars. Additional awards sponsored by private individuals from Poland and other countries and by institutions are presented. Established in 1927 by Professor Jerzy Zurawlew in memory of Frederic Chopin.

• 4003 •
International Print Triennial Society - Krakow
(Stowarzyszenie Miedzynarodowe Triennale Grafiki)
Prof. Witold Skulicz, Pres.
Ul. Dunajewskiego 2/6
31-133 Krakow, Poland
Phone: 48 12 4221903
Fax: 48 12 4217123
E-mail: smtg@triennial.cracow.pl
Home Page: http://www.triennial.cracow.pl
Formerly: (1966) International Print Biennale.

• 4004 • **International Print Triennial (Miedzynarodowe Triennale Grafiki Krakow)**
For recognition of outstanding prints, unique-copy prints, monotypes, c omputer prints and creative photography. Monetary awards are presented for the grand prix and ex-aequo special awards. Exhibits include International Print Triennial; Integrafia - World Award Winners Gallery, Katowice; Polish Print Triennial, Katawice; Triennial Colour in Graphic Art, Torun; Mini Triennial Continents, Jelenia FGora; and International Triennial Cracow - Nuremberg. Awarded triennially. Established in 1966. Sponsored by the Ministry of Culture and Art. Formerly: (1966) International Print Biennale.

• 4005 •
Ministry of Justice, Poland
Institute of Forensic Research
ul. Westerplatte 9
31-033 Krakow, Poland
Phone: 48 12 4228755
Fax: 48 12 4223850
E-mail: ies@ies.krakow.pl
Home Page: http://www.ies.krakow.pl

• 4006 • **Robel Award**
For the best MSc thesis in forensic sciences.

• 4007 •
Office of the President of the Republic of Poland
(Kancelaria Prezydenta Rzeczypospolitej Polskiej)
Krakowski Przedmiescie 48/50
PL-00-071 Warsaw, Poland
Phone: 48 22 695 2900
Fax: 48 22 695 2238
Home Page: http://www.prezydent.pl

• 4008 • **Cross of Merit (Krzyz Zaslugi)**
For recognition of civilians or military for merit to the country or its citizens beyond their normal duty. Three grades exist: gold, silver, and bronze. The Cross of Merit for Bravery and the Cross of Merit with Swords are awarded when merited. Established in 1923.

Awards are arranged in alphabetical order below their administering organizations

• 4009 • **Cross of Merit for Bravery**
(Krzyz Zaslugi za Dzielnosc)
For recognition of accomplishments by members of the police, customs service, and frontier corps for acts of bravery at the risk of their lives in defense of law, state frontier, or human life or property. A cross is awarded when merited. Established in 1928.

• 4010 • **Cross of Merit with Swords**
(Krzyz Zaslugi z Mieczami)
For recognition of heroism and bravery during war but not on the field of battle. Gold, silver, and bronze crosses are awarded when merited. Established in 1942.

• 4011 • **Cross of Valour**
(Krzyz Walecznych)
To recognize individuals for acts of valor while serving with peacekeeping mission of the United Nations. A bronze cross is awarded when merited. Established in 1920.

• 4012 • **Medal for Long Marital Life**
(Medal Za Dlugoletnie Pozycie Malzenskie)
To recognize couples who have been happily married for 50 years. A medal is awarded when merited. Established in 1960.

• 4013 • **Medal for Sacrifice and Courage**
(Medal Za Ofiarnosc i Odwage)
To recognize individuals who have risked their lives saving human life or property at the risk of their own lives. A medal is awarded when merited. Established in 1960.

• 4014 • **Order of Merit of the Republic of Poland**
(Order Zaslugi Rzeczypospolitej Polskiej)
For recognition of outstanding political, social, economic, or cultural activities that have contributed to the development of international cooperation and friendship between Poland and other nations. Foreign citizens or Poles living abroad are eligible. A medal is awarded when merited. Established in 1974.

• 4015 • **Order of Polish Rebirth**
(Order Odrodzenia Polski)
Also known as Poland Restored, this order is presented in recognition of important contributions in the following fields: education, science, culture and arts, national economy, governmental service, and social activity. A medal is awarded in five classes when merited. Established in 1921.

• 4016 • **Order of the White Eagle**
To recognize outstanding military and civilian contribution for glory and advantage of Republic of Poland during war or peace. A red and white gold badge is awarded when merited. Established in 1705.

• 4017 • **War Order Virtuti Militari**
(Order Wojenny Virtuti Militari)
For recognition of outstanding heroism and bravery during the war and for distinguished military merit. A cross is awarded in five classes when merited. Established in 1792 by King Stanislav August Poniatowski, and first awarded to Prince Josef Poniatowski and Tadeusz Kosciuszko.

• 4018 •
PEN Club - Poland
(Polski PEN)
Wladyslav Bartoszewski, Pres.
Krakowskie Przedmiescie 87/89
PL-00-079 Warsaw, Poland
Phone: 48 22 826 5784
Fax: 48 22 828 2823
E-mail: penclub@ikp.atm.com.pl
Home Page: http://www.penclub.atomnet.pl

• 4019 • **Polish PEN Centre Prizes**
For recognition of outstanding contributions to Polish literature. The following prizes are awarded: prize for translators of Polish literature into foreign languages, established in 1948; prize for translators of foreign literature into Polish, established in 1949; Jan Parandowski Prize, established in 1988; literary prize for editors, established in 1978; Ksawery Pruszynski Prize, established in 1988; Jan Strzelecki Prize, established in 1990; Commander Kazimierz Szczesny Prize, established in 1989; and special prize, established in 1989.

• 4020 •
Phytochemical Society of Europe
Prof. Wieslaw Oleszek, Sec.Gen.
Inst. of Soil Science and Plant Cultivation
Dept. of Biochemistry
ul. Czartoryskich 8
PL-24-100 Pulawy, Poland
Phone: 48 81 8863421
Fax: 48 81 8864547
E-mail: wo@iung.pulawy.pl
Home Page: http://www
.phytochemicalsociety.org

• 4021 • **Phytochemical Society of Europe Medal**
To recognize individuals who have made an outstanding contribution to the Society or to the furtherance of plant science in general. The medal, which is struck in silver, shows an oak tree, representing plant science superimposed on a map of Europe. Awarded periodically. Established in 1986.

• 4022 •
Polish Actors Association
(Zwiazek Artystow Scen Polskich)
Olgierd Lukaszewicz, Pres.
Al. Ujazdowskie 45
PL-00-536 Warsaw, Poland
Phone: 48 22 6293271
Phone: 48 22 6293271
Fax: 48 22 6214820
E-mail: zasp@zasp.pl
Home Page: http://www.zasp.pl

• 4023 • **Arion Prize**
For lifetime achievement in opera singing.

• 4024 • **Andrew Nordelli Prize**
For the best debut.

• 4025 • **L. Schiller Award**
For excellence in acting or directing.

• 4026 • **Terpsychsna Prize**
For lifetime achievement in dancing or choreography.

• 4027 • **Janusz Warnecki Prize for a Part in Radio Drama**
Award of recognition.

• 4028 • **Jacek Woszczerowicz Prize**
For supporting actor.

• 4029 • **ZASP President's Award**
For the best graduate of Drama School.

• 4030 •
Polish Chemical Society
(Polskie Towarzystwo Chemiczne)
Pawel Kafarski, Pres.
ul. Freta 16
PL-00-227 Warsaw, Poland
Phone: 48 22 831304
Fax: 48 22 831304
E-mail: pawel.kafarski@pwr.wroc.pl
Home Page: http://www.ptchem.lodz.pl

• 4031 • **Jan Harabaszewski Medal**
For recognition of outstanding contributions to the field of chemistry education. Nominees for the awards are named by the Presidium of General Council of the Society or by Division of Educational Chemistry. A medal is awarded annually. Established in 1989 in honor of Jan Harabaszewski, a Polish scientist.

• 4032 • **Honorary Membership**
To recognize distinguished chemists, regardless of their nationality and affiliation, for outstanding scientific achievements and contributions to the development of the Society and chemistry in Poland. Nominees for the awards are named by the Presidium of General Council of the Society or by its regional councils and are determined by the General Assembly.

• 4033 • **Stanislaw Kostanecki Medal**
For recognition of contributions to the fields of physical and inorganic chemistry. Nominees for the awards are named by the Presidium of General Council of the Society or by its regional councils.

• 4034 • **Maria Sklodowska-Curie Medal**
In recognition of outstanding foreign chemists who have made significant contributions to science and/or technology and have strong ties with Polish chemical institutions, particularly ac-

ademic. Awarded annually by the General Assembly of the Society. Formerly: Polish Chemical Society Medal.

• 4035 • Jedrzej Sniadecki Medal
For recognition of superior scientific achievements. Nominees for the awards are named by the Presidium of General Council of the Society or by its regional councils.

• 4036 • Jan Zawidzki Medal
For recognition of outstanding contributions to the fields of physical and inorganic chemistry. Nominees for the awards are named by the Presidium of General Council of the Society or by its regional councils.

• 4037 •
Polish Composers Union
(Zwiazek Kompozytorow Polskich)
Jerzy Kornowicz, Pres.
Rynek Starego Miasta 27
PL-00-272 Warsaw, Poland
Phone: 48 22 831 1634
Fax: 48 22 831 1741
E-mail: zkp@zkp.org.pl
Home Page: http://www.zkp.org.pl

• 4038 • Tadeusz Baird Memorial Competition for Young Composers (Konkurs Mlodych Kompozytorow im. Tadeusza Bairda)
For recognition of outstanding young composers. Polish citizens who are 35 years of age or younger are eligible. Monetary prizes are awarded annually in November. Established in 1958 by the Board of the Polish Composers Union and renamed in 1990 in honor of Tadeusz Baird.

• 4039 • Polish Composers Union Prize (Nagroda Zwiazku Kompozytorow Polskich)
For recognition of outstanding achievements in creating and performing music, in musicology, and in organizing activities. Polish citizens are eligible. A monetary award and a diploma are presented annually in January. Established in 1949 by the Polish Composers Union to commemorate the liberation of Warsaw on January 17, 1945.

• 4040 •
Polish Medical Association
(Polski Towarzystwo Lekarskie)
Jerzy Woy-Wojciechowski, Pres.
Al. Ujazdowskie St. 24
PL-00-478 Warsaw, Poland
Phone: 48 22 6288699
Phone: 48 22 6272988
Fax: 48 22 6288699
E-mail: ptl@interia.pl

• 4041 • Gloria Medicinae Award
Recognizes eminent merits in medical sciences. A medal is awarded annually. Established in 1990.

• 4042 •
Polish Organization for Commodity Science
(Polskie Towarzystwo Towaroznawcze)
ul. H. Sienkiewicza 4
PL-30-033 Krakow, Poland
Phone: 48 12 6167519
Phone: 48 12 6167519
Fax: 48 12 335733
E-mail: adamczyw@ae.krakow.pl
Home Page: http://www.ae.krakow.pl/

• 4043 • Honorary Member
For recognition of a special activity and achievements in the development of commodity science, particularly in raising the quality of goods. A diploma is awarded every five years. Established in 1970.

• 4044 •
Polish Physical Society
(Polskie Towarzystwo Fizyczne)
Prof. Maciej Kolwas, Pres.
ul. Hoza 69
PL-00-681 Warsaw, Poland
Phone: 48 22 5532166
Fax: 48 22 6212668
E-mail: ptf@mech.pw.edu.pl
Home Page: http://ptf.fuw.edu.pl

• 4045 • Award for Promotion of Physics
For the promotion of physics and of the public understanding of physics. A monetary prize and certificate are awarded.

• 4046 • Grzegorz Bialkowski Prize
For outstanding teacher of physics. A monetary prize and certificate are awarded.

• 4047 • Honorary Membership
Given by the general ensemble of the Society when merited.

• 4048 • Arkadiiusz Piekara Prize
For outstanding masters thesis for physics. A monetary prize and certificate are awarded.

• 4049 • Polish-German Marian Smoluchowski-Emil Warburg Physics Prize
For outstanding contributions to pure or applied physics. Awarded to Polish and German physicists alternately every two years. 1000 ECU (given by the Meyer-Viol Foundation), a silver medal, and a certificate are awarded.

• 4050 • Marian Smoluchowski Medal (Medal Mariana Smoluchowskiego)
For recognition of a splendid contribution to science and to international scientific cooperation in physics. Scientists may be nominated. A medal and a special diploma in Polish and Latin are awarded annually when merited. Established in 1967 in memory of Marian Smoluchowski, a Polish physicist famous for his achievements in the kinetic theory of matter.

• 4051 • Special Award
For special services for physics and Polish Physical Society. A monetary prize and certificate are awarded.

• 4052 • Wojciech Rubinowicz Scientific Prize
For outstanding achievements in physics. A monetary prize and certificate are awarded.

• 4053 •
Warsaw Philharmonic
(Filharmonia Narodowa w Warszawie)
Antoni Wit, General and Artistic Dir.
% National Orchestra and Choir of Poland
ul. Jasna 5
PL-00-950 Warsaw, Poland
Phone: 48 22 55 17 111
Fax: 48 22 55 17 200
E-mail: sekretariat@filharmonia.pl
Home Page: http://www.filharmonia.pl

• 4054 • Witold Lutoslawski International Composers Competition (Miedzynarodowy Konkurs Kompozytorski im-Witolda Lutoslawskiego)
To recognize outstanding compositions. Compositions may be submitted in the following categories: symphony orchestra; choir and symphony orchestra; solo voice or voices and symphony orchestra; solo instrument or instruments and symphony orchestra; and choir, solo voice or voices and symphony orchestra. Composers of all ages and nationalities may submit scores by December 31. Pieces not performed in public and not rewarded at any other competition are eligible. Three monetary prizes ranging from $1,000 to $3,000 and performance of the winning pieces are awarded biennially. Established in 1988. For more information contact the Secretary of the International Witold Lutoslawski Composer's Competition.

Portugal

• 4055 •
CINANIMA - International Animated Film Festival Portugal
(CINANIMA - Festival Internacional de Cinema de Animacao)
Apartado 43
Rua 62, 251
P-4501 Espinho Codex, Portugal
Phone: 351 2 734 4611
Fax: 351 2 734 6015
E-mail: cinanima@mail.telepac.pt
Home Page: http://www.awn.com/cinanima

• 4056 • CINANIMA
To encourage the development of and to recognize outstanding animated films. Films produced for cinema or television in 35mm (optical sound), 16mm (optical or magnetic sound), and video U-matic 3/4 (PAL, SECAM, NTSC) U-matic HB/SP (PAL), and VHS multi-system made during the preceding two years are eligible. A trophy is presented in the following categories: best film up to 6 minutes; best film between 6 and 13 minutes; best film between 13 and 26 minutes; best film between 26 and 52 minutes; Long Feature; Publicity and Institutional; First Film; Didactic and

Information; Title Sequence (for cinema and television); and Series (for cinema and television). Established in 1977 by NASCENTE - Cooperative Society with Cultural Purposes.

• 4057 •
Cinema Novo Fantasporto
Rua Anibal Cunha 84, sala 1.6
P-4050-048 Porto, Portugal
Phone: 351 2220 76050
Fax: 351 2220 76059
E-mail: info@fantasporto.online.pt
Home Page: http://www.fantasporto.online.pt

• 4058 • **Oporto International Film Festival - Fantasporto (Festival Internacional de Cinema do Porto - Fantasporto)**
To promote imaginary films on an international level that seek new forms and methods of film-making, and in which the creative powers of the imagination have a treatment of quality. The Festival has four sections: Retrospective Section, Informative Section, Competitive Section, and Portuguese Cinema. Trophies are awarded annually in the following categories: Fantasporto Best Film Award, Best Director, Best Actor, Best Actress, Best Screenplay, Best Special Effects, Best Short Film, Special Award - to a film whose artistic and technical aspects present a high level of originality, New Directors Award, Critics Award, and Audience Award. Diplomas are given to all films participating in the competitive section. The Festival is held annually in February. Established in 1980 by the magazine, *Cinema Novo*.

• 4059 •
European Association for Signal, Speech and Image Processing
(Association Europeenne de Traitement de Signaux)
Sergios Theodoridis, Pres.
% Paulo L. Correia, Sec.-Treas.
Instituto de Telecomunicacoes
Instituto Superior Tecnico
P-1049-001 Lisbon 13, Portugal
E-mail: paulo.correia@lx.it.pt
Home Page: http://www.eurasip.org

Formerly: (1998) European Association for Signal Processing.

• 4060 • **European Association for Signal, Speech and Image Processing Awards**
To recognize engineers, scientists, and industrial firms for contributions to signal processing. Awards for meritorious service, group technical achievement, individual technical achievement, and best papers are presented biennially. Established in 1986.

• 4061 •
International Road Safety Organization
(La Prevention Routiere Internationale)
Jose Trigoso, Pres.
Estrada da Luz, 90-1st Fl.
1600-160 Lisbon, Portugal
Phone: 351 21 7222230
Fax: 351 21 7222232
E-mail: info@lapri.org
Home Page: http://www.lapri.org

• 4062 • **PRI Service Medal**
To recognize an outstanding commitment to international road safety. Awarded annually.

• 4063 •
International Society for Rock Mechanics
(Societe Internationale de Mecanique des Roches)
Dr. Luis Nolasco Lamas, Sec.Gen.
Avenida do Brasil 101
P-1700-066 Lisbon Codex, Portugal
Phone: 351 21 8443419
Phone: 351 21 8443385
Fax: 351 21 8443021
E-mail: isrm@lnec.pt

• 4064 • **Muller Award**
To recognize an individual for a contribution in the field of rock mechanics. Nominations or applications must be submitted 18 months in advance of the ISRM Congress. A medal and travel expenses are awarded every four years at the ISRM Congress. Established in 1991 to honor Prof. Leopold Muller.

• 4065 • **Manuel Rocha Medal**
For recognition of an outstanding doctoral thesis in the field of rock mechanics that is accepted during the two years preceding the conferment. A monetary prize, a bronze medal, and travel expenses to receive the award are presented annually. Established in 1982 in honor of Manuel Rocha, past president of the Society and Portuguese scientist.

• 4066 •
Madeira, Regional Secretary of Tourism and Culture
(Madeira, Secretaria Regional do Turismo e Cultura)
Avenido Arriaga 16
P-9004-519 Funchal, Portugal
Phone: 351 291 211 900
Fax: 351 291 232 151
E-mail: info@madeiratourism.org
Home Page: http://www.madeiratourism.org

• 4067 • **Estrelicia Dourada**
For recognition of a contribution to tourism activities and to encourage professional development in the field of tourism. Nomination is by the Tourism Authority. A trophy is awarded when merited. Established in 1982 by the Tourism Authority of the Regional Government of Madeira.

• 4068 • **Medalha de Merito Turistico**
To recognize individuals or associations for their outstanding contributions and dedication to the tourism of Madeira. Individuals or associations may be nominated by the Tourism Authority. A medal is awarded when merited. Established in 1982 by the Tourism Authority of the Regional Government of Madeira.

• 4069 •
Municipality of Lisbon
(Camara Municipal de Lisboa)
Antonio Carmona Rodrigues, Pres.
Dept. of Cultural Patrimony
Palacio dos Concelho
Praca do Municipio
P-1100-365 Lisbon, Portugal
Phone: 351 213 227000
Fax: 351 213 227008
E-mail: geral@cm-lisboa.pt
Home Page: http://www.cm-lisboa.pt

• 4070 • **Premio Municipal Francisco da Conceicao Silva de Espacos Interiores Abertos ao Publico**
To recognize the best project of construction, adaptation or recovery of an interior space. Hotels, theaters, cinemas, banks, and other buildings open to the public are eligible. A monetary award is presented annually at a special ceremony at City Hall. Established in 1989 by Francisco da Conceicao Silva, an important figure of modern Portuguese architecture.

• 4071 • **Premio Municipais Joshua Benoliel de Fotografia**
To recognize a photographer for the best color, and black and white photography. Portuguese citizens are eligible. A monetary award is awarded annually in each category, at a special ceremony at City Hall. Established in 1989 in memory of Joshua Benoliel, journalist and photographer (1873-1939), whose work marks the beginning of photographic history in Portugal.

• 4072 • **Premio Municipal Alfredo Marceneiro de Fado**
To recognize the best Portuguese folk song. Unedited folk songs with a duration of 3-6 minutes may be submitted. A monetary award is presented annually at a special ceremony at City Hall. Established in 1989 in memory of Alfredo Duarte Marceneiro (1891-1982), a distinguished Portuguese folk singer.

• 4073 • **Premio Municipal Augusto Vieira da Silva de Investigacao**
To recognize the best research work on the subject of Lisbon. Unedited works may be submitted. Portuguese citizens are eligible. A monetary award is presented annually, at a special ceremony at City Hall. Established in 1989 in memory of Augusto Vieira da Silva (1869-1951), a distinguished scholar on the history of Lisbon.

• 4074 • **Premio Municipal Carlos Botelho de Pintura**
To recognize the best painting on the subject of Lisbon. Portuguese painters may submit appli-

cations. A monetary award is presented annually, at a special ceremony at City Hall. Established in 1989 in memory of Carlos Botelho (1899-1982), a well-known Portuguese painter known as the "painter of Lisbon."

• 4075 • Premio Municipal Fernando Amado de Encenacao Teatral

To recognize the best staging exhibited in Lisbon during the preceding year. A monetary award is presented annually, at a special ceremony at City Hall. Established in 1989 in memory of Fernando Alberto da Silva Amado (1899-1968), critic, dramatist, politician, author of *O Livro e o Pensador*, *O Segredo de Polichinelo*, and teacher of theatre in school arts.

• 4076 • Premio Municipal Joao Baptista Rosa de Video

To recognize the best video on the subject of Lisbon. Unedited videos with a duration of 20-30 minutes may be submitted. A monetary award is presented annually, at a special ceremony at City Hall. Established in memory of Joao Baptista Rosa (1925- 1982), journalist, producer, television and cinema reporter and the author of *A Pintura de Vieira da Silva* and *Azulejos Portugueses*. His work marks a significant moment in Portuguese cinema.

• 4077 • Premio Municipal Jorge Colaco de Azulejaria

For recognition of the best work in decorative glazed-tiles used on the facade of a building constructed in Lisbon during the preceding year. A monetary prize is divided among the author of the work, the author of the project of the building and the makers of the glazed tiles. Awarded annually. Established in 1985. Renamed in 1989 to honor Jorge Colaco (1868-1942), a distinguished caricaturist and tile-maker, whose tiles decorate Windsor Palace, the medical school at Lisbon, and Sao Bento Station at Porto.

• 4078 • Premio Municipal Jose Simoes de Almeida de Escultura

To recognize the best piece of sculpture. Portuguese sculptors are eligible. A monetary award is presented annually, at a special ceremony at City Hall. Established in 1989 in memory of Jose Simoes de Almeida (18441926), a sculptor famous for *Duque de Terceira*, and *O Genio da Vitoria* (Restauradores), among others.

• 4079 • Premio Municipal Julio Cesar Machado de Jornalismo

For recognition of the best report on Lisbon published in newspapers or magazines during the preceding year. Portuguese journalists are eligible. A monetary prize is awarded annually. Established in 1951 in memory of Julio Cesar Machado (1835-1890), a well-known Lisbon journalist. Re-established in 1982.

• 4080 • Premio Municipal Julio de Castilho de Olisipografia

For recognition of the best research work on the history or archaeology of Lisbon published during the preceding year. Portuguese scholars are eligible. A monetary prize is awarded annually. Established in 1939 in memory of the Viscount of Castilho, Julio de Castilho, a distinguished scholar and writer, particularly on the history of Lisbon. Re-established in 1982.

• 4081 • Premio Municipal Maria Leonor Magro de Radio

To recognize the best radio broadcast on the subject of Lisbon. A monetary award is presented annually, at a special ceremony at City Hall. Established in 1989 in memory of Maria Leonor Magro (1920-1988), journalist, producer, and one of the most popular figures of Portuguese broadcasting.

• 4082 • Premio Municipal Rafael Bordalo Pinheiro de Banda Desenhada, Cartoon e Caricaturista

To recognize the best work of animated cartoon and caricature. Portuguese citizens are eligible. A monetary award is presented annually, at a special ceremony at City Hall. Established in 1989 in memory of Rafael Bordalo Pinheiro, the most popular Portuguese caricaturist (1846-1905).

• 4083 • Premio Municipal Roberto de Araujo Pereira de Design

To recognize the best design project which tends to improve the Lisbon urban context. A monetary award is awarded annually, at a special ceremony at City Hall. Established in 1989 to honor Roberto de Araujo Pereira, painter, scenographist, and a pioneer of Portuguese design.

• 4084 • Premio Valmor e Municipal de Arquitectura

To recognize the owner of and the architect responsible for a building which unites esthetic and architectonic values, constructed or restored in Lisbon during the preceding year. Portuguese architects are eligible. A monetary prize is awarded annually. Established in 1903 to honor the Viscount Valmor (1837-1897), public benefactor.

• 4085 • Premios Municipais Eca de Queiroz de Literatura

For recognition of the best work in poetry, the best novel, the best literary or biographical essay and the best theatrical play published (first edition) during the preceding year. Portuguese writers are eligible. Monetary prizes are awarded annually. Established in 1982. Renamed in 1989 to honor Eca de Queiroz (1845-1900), one of the most important Portuguese writers.

• 4086 • Premios Municipais Joly Braga Santos de Musica

To recognize the best symphony and chamber music composition. Unedited works may be submitted. A monetary prize is presented annually, at a special ceremony at City Hall. Established to honor Joly Braga Santos, a distinguished composer, teacher and orchestrator.

• 4087 • Premios Municipais Palmira Bastos e Antonio Silva de Interpretacao Teatral

To recognize the best theatrical interpretation made by an actor and an actress in Lisbon during the preceding year. Portuguese performers are eligible. A monetary award is awarded to both an actor and an actress. Awarded annually at a special ceremony at City Hall. Established in 1989 in memory of Palmira Bastos (1875-1967) and Antonio Silva (1886-1971), two important figures in Portuguese theater and cinema.

• 4088 •
Portugal State Secretariat of Culture
Palacio Nacional da Ajuda
P-1300-018 Lisbon, Portugal
Phone: 351 1 213614538
Fax: 351 1 213636668
E-mail: ministro@mc.ga.pt

• 4089 • Camoes Prize (Premio Luis de Camoes)

For recognition of the work of any writing in Portuguese, regardless of the author's nationality, published inside or outside of Portugal. Authors from all countries whose official language is Portuguese are eligible: Portugal, Brazil, Angola, Cabo-Verde, Guine-Bissau, Mozambique, and Sao Tome. A monetary prize of 100,000 euros is awarded annually. Established in 1988 by the Ministries of Culture in Portugal and Brazil.

• 4090 • Concurso Literario Dr. Joao Isabel

To recognize short stories. Monetary prizes are given.

• 4091 • Literary Premio Matilde Rosa Araujo

To recognize authors of children*K*s books. Awarded triennially. Established in 2000.

• 4092 • Premio Carlos Bonvalot

To recognize artistic creation in the categories of fiction narrative, poetry, and arts. Awarded triennially. Established in 2000.

• 4093 • Premio do Mar Rei D. Carlos

To recognize authors of oceanographical research. Awarded annually. Established in 1995.

• 4094 • Premio Literario Branquinho da Fonseca

To recognize a science fiction story. Awarded annually. Established in 1995.

Korea, Republic of

• 4095 •
Federation of Asian Chemical Societies
Junghun Suh, Pres.
Dept. of Chemistry
Seoul Natl. Univ.
Seoul 151-747, Republic of Korea
Phone: 82 2 8862184
Fax: 82 2 8743704
E-mail: jhsuh@snu.ac.kr
Home Page: http://www.facs-as.org

• 4096 • **Distinguished Contribution to Advancement in Chemical Education**
For contributions to chemical education in Asian region.

• 4097 • **Distinguished Contribution to Economic Advancement Award**
For contributions of outstanding chemists in the Asia-Pacific region.

• 4098 • **Foundation Lectureship Award**
To a lecturer who has made an outstanding contribution to the chemistry.

• 4099 • **Young Chemist Award**
To individual in the field of inorganic chemistry whose age not exceed to 40 years.

• 4100 •
International Judo Federation
(Federation Internationale de Judo)
Dr. Hedi Dhouib, Gen.Sec.
Doosan Tower 33rd Fl.
18-12, Ulchi-Ro-6-Ka, Chung-Ku
Seoul 100-730, Republic of Korea
Phone: 82 2 33981017
Phone: 82 2 33981018
Fax: 82 2 33981020
E-mail: info@ijf.org
Home Page: http://www.ijf.org

• 4101 • **International Judo Federation Awards**
To promote the spread and development of the spirit and techniques of judo by sponsoring world championships. Awards include the Gold Award, Silver Award, and Bronze Award. Awarded annually when merited.

• 4102 •
Korean Chemical Society
Si Young Oh, Exec. Dir.
The Korea Science and Technology Center, No. 703
635-4 Yeoksam-Dong
Gangnam-Gu
Seoul 135-703, Republic of Korea
Phone: 82 2 34533781
Fax: 82 2 34533785
E-mail: webmaster@kcsnet.or.kr
Home Page: http://www.kcsnet.or.kr

• 4103 • **Academic Excellency Prize**
To chemists who have performed excellent research in chemical technology.

• 4104 • **Award for Advancement of Industry**
To chemists who have made contribution in the advancement and development of the Korean chemical technology.

• 4105 • **Award for Advancement of Science**
To chemists who have published excellent research in the journals of KCS.

• 4106 • **Award for Chemical Education**
To teachers who have made distinguished achievement in the advancement of chemical education.

• 4107 • **Award for Excellent Research Paper**
To chemists who have published the paper most frequently cited in the journals of KCS.

• 4108 • **Japanese SICOT Scholarship**
For young orthopaedic surgeons.

• 4109 • **KCS Merit Award**
Awarded for distinguished achievement in the advancement and development of KCS.

• 4110 • **SEAMEO Service Award**
For government officials of member countries.

• 4111 •
Korean Culture and Arts Foundation
1-130 Dongsoong-Dong
Chongro-Ku
Seoul 110-510, Republic of Korea
Phone: 82 2 7604563
Fax: 82 2 7604684
E-mail: young@kcaf.or.kr
Home Page: http://www.kcaf.or.kr

• 4112 • **Korean Literature Translation Award**
To encourage people engaged in the translation and publication of Korean literature into other languages. There is no restriction on the number of books or literary genres. The grand prize winner will receive $50,000 and two work-of-merit prize winners will receive $10,000. If there is no work of sufficient merit for the grand prize, the finest entry will be awarded $30,000. Awarded biennially in odd-numbered years. Established in 1970.

• 4113 •
Music Association of Korea
Choi Gyu-Yong, Sec.Gen.
1-117 Tong-Sung Dong, Chong-Ro Ku
Seoul 110-510, Republic of Korea
Phone: 82 2 7448060
Fax: 82 2 7412378
Home Page: http://www.mak.or.kr/english/e-index.htm

• 4114 • **Korean Composition Awards**
To encourage and contribute to professional development in the field of Korean music. Applicants must be Korean. Works composed and performed within five years, including the year the award is given, that are more than 10 minutes duration may be submitted by late September. The following awards are presented: (1) The Most Outstanding Award 3,000,000 won for one, plus a concert; (2) The Outstanding Award - 2,000,000 won, plus a concert engagement, for six in the categories of Korean Classical Music and Western Music. Awarded annually from 1977 to 1982, and biennially since 1982.

• 4115 • **Seoul International Music Festival Awards**
To recognize top musicians performing at the Festival. Held biennially. Established in 1993.

• 4116 • **Student Competition for Overseas Music Study Award**
To recognize outstanding student musicians. Awarded annually. Established in 1982.

• 4117 •
National Academy of Sciences of the Republic of Korea
Kim Tae-kil, Pres.
San 94-4, Banpo 4-dong
Seocho-gu
Seoul 137-044, Republic of Korea
Phone: 82 2 5340737
Phone: 82 2 5940321
Fax: 82 2 5373183
E-mail: academ@nas.go.kr
Home Page: http://nas.go.kr

• 4118 • **National Academy of Sciences Award**
For scientific accomplishment. A monetary prize is given annually.

• 4119 •
World Taekwondo Federation
Mr. Dong-Hoo Moon, Sec.Gen.
5th Fl., Diplomatic Ctr. 1376-1
Seocho 2-Dong
Seocho-Gu
Seoul 137-863, Republic of Korea
Phone: 82 2 5662505
Phone: 82 2 5575446
Fax: 82 2 5334728
E-mail: wtf@unitel.co.kr
Home Page: http://www.wtf.org

• 4120 • World Taekwondo Federation Competitions
To promote taekwondo internationally. World and Continental Taekwondo Championships are held, including the Asian, European, Pan American, African, and CISM (World Military) championships.

South Africa, Republic of

• 4121 •
Actuarial Society of South Africa
Wim Els, Exec. Dir.
PO Box 4464
Cape Town 8000, Republic of South Africa
Phone: 27 21 5095242
Phone: 27 21 5097697
Fax: 27 21 5090160
E-mail: philentia@assa.org.za
Home Page: http://www.assa.org.za

• 4122 • Best First-Time Paper
For an outstanding first-time author.

• 4123 • Murray Medal
For excellent ASSA members.

• 4124 • President's Prize
For young writers of ASSA.

• 4125 • The Swiss Re Award
For a meritorious paper on risk management.

• 4126 •
Animal Feed Manufacturers Association
Hansie Bekker, Gen.Mgr.
PO Box 8144
Centurion 0046, Republic of South Africa
Phone: 27 12 6639097
Phone: 27 12 6639361
Fax: 27 12 6639612
E-mail: admin@afm.co.za
Home Page: http://www.afma.co.za

• 4127 • Koos van der Merwe Prize
For best final year student in animal nutrition. One scholarship is awarded annually.

• 4128 • Barney van Niekerk/AFMA Technical Person of the Year
Recognizes technical contributions within the industry. A trophy and monetary prize are awarded annually.

• 4129 •
Association of South African Quantity Surveyors
(Vereniging van Suid-Afrikaanse Bourekenaars)
PO Box 3527
Halfway House 1685, Republic of South Africa
Phone: 27 315 4140
Fax: 27 315 3785
E-mail: association@asaqs.co.za
Home Page: http://www.asaqs.co.za

• 4130 • Gold Medal of Honour
This, the Association's highest honor, is given for outstanding service to the building industry in general and to quantity surveying in particular. Members are eligible. A gold medal and a citation are awarded when merited. Established in 1977.

• 4131 •
Astronomical Society of Southern Africa
Mr. C.L. Rijsdijk, VP
PO Box 9
Observatory 7935, Republic of South Africa
Phone: 27 21 4470025
Fax: 27 21 4473639
E-mail: assa@saao.ac.za
Home Page: http://da.saao.ac.za/assa

• 4132 • Gill Medal
For recognition of services to astronomy. Preference is given to work done in Southern Africa. Society members and non-members are eligible. Not more than one award is made in any year. Established in 1955, the medal commemorates Sir David Gill, HM Astronomer at the Cape.

• 4133 • McIntyre Award
For recognition of significant contributions to astronomy in the form of: (1) a work to be published or which has been published in book form; or (2) a journal of recognized standing within the previous five years. Living persons of any nationality are eligible. The award derived from the interest on the bequest made to the Society by the late Donald G. McIntyre, is awarded irregularly.

• 4134 •
Botanical Society of South Africa
(Botaniese Vereniging van Suid-Afrika)
Eugene Moll, Chm.
Private Bag X 10
Claremont 7735, Republic of South Africa
Phone: 27 21 7972090
Fax: 27 21 7972376
E-mail: info@botanicalsociety.org.za
Home Page: http://www.botanicalsociety.org.za

• 4135 • Bolus Medal
To an amateur botanist who has made a significant contribution through publications.

• 4136 • Botanical Society Certificate of Merit
To a member of the Society where the Council would like to acknowledge the valuable contribution made to the promotion of the flora of Southern Africa.

• 4137 • Botanical Society Flora Conservation Medal
To any person who has contributed considerably towards the preservation and conservation of the flora of Southern Africa.

• 4138 • Dudley D'Ewes Medal
To any person who effectively promotes the flora of Southern Africa and its conservation through the media.

• 4139 • Denys Heesom Medal
To any person or organization that has made a significant contribution to the eradication of alien vegetation in Southern Africa.

• 4140 • Honorary Life Membership
To any member of the Botanical Society who has rendered exceptional services to the Society or one of its branches.

• 4141 • Cythna Letty Medal
To any person who has made a significant contribution to the promotion of South African Flora through the medium of published botanical illustrations.

• 4142 • Marloth Medal
To any amateur or professional botanist who has produced scientific literature of a popular nature to stimulate public interest.

• 4143 • Percy Sergeant Medal
To any person who effectively promotes the flora of Southern Africa and its conservation through the medium of photography.

• 4144 • Scelpe Award
For the best article in Veld and Flora in any given year covering any aspect of horticulture.

• 4145 •
Businesswomen's Association
Namane Magau, Pres.
Office 230, Killarney Mall
No. 60 Riviera Rd.
Killarney, Republic of South Africa
Phone: 27 11 4860186
Fax: 27 86 6125752
E-mail: info@bwasa.co.za
Home Page: http://www.bwasa.co.za

• 4146 • Businesswoman of the Year
For South African women business leaders, in recognition of their achievements in their respective business careers.

• 4147 • BWA Bursary
For deserving post graduate women students taking up a business related course.

• 4148 • Regional Business Achievers Award
For emerging businesswomen who have succeeded in starting small businesses in the region despite the disadvantages that they had to face.

Awards are arranged in alphabetical order below their administering organizations

• 4149 •
Cape Tercentenary Foundation
Postnet Ste. 354
Private Bag X16
Costantia 7874, Republic of South Africa
Phone: 27 21 683 3990
Fax: 27 21 671 6404
E-mail: info@cape300foundation.org.za
Home Page: http://www.cape300foundation.org.za

• 4150 • Molteno Medal Awards of Excellence and Merit
To provide recognition for outstanding services to the cultural, artistic, historic, dramatic and conservation fields. Persons who have rendered outstanding services in one of the activities in which the Foundation is interested are eligible. Monetary awards and certificates are presented annually, usually in February. Established in 1953. For additional information contact The Secretary.

• 4151 •
Concrete Society of Southern Africa
Irma Dyssel, Contact
PO Box 168
Halfway House
Gauteng 1685, Republic of South Africa
Phone: 27 12 8091824
Fax: 27 12 8091823
E-mail: concretesociety@telkomsa.net
Home Page: http://www.concretesociety.co.za/inland_awards

• 4152 • Achiever of the Year
Award of recognition. Presented at the annual banquet.

• 4153 • Chairman's Award
To recognize the greatest contribution made to the achievement of excellence in the use or application of concrete made by a hands-on operative. Awarded annually by the Inland Branch. Established 1996.

• 4154 • Concrete Achiever of the Year
For recognition of the person doing the most to promote the use of concrete and the standards of excellence in its use. Awarded annually. Established in 1982.

• 4155 • Concrete Person of the Year Awards
For recognition of the person doing the most to promote the use of concrete and the standards of excellence in its use. Awarded by three branches: Kwazula Natal, Western Cape, and Eastern Cape.

• 4156 • Fulton Award
To recognize professionals, contractors, and owners for their outstanding achievements and determination to challenge new frontiers. Awarded in various categories biennially in odd-numbered years.

• 4157 •
Direct Selling Association - South Africa
Jean McKenzie, Mgr.
Private Bag 34
Auckland Park 2006, Republic of South Africa
Phone: 27 11 7265300
Fax: 27 11 7268421
E-mail: assoc@jcci.co.za
Home Page: http://www.dsasa.co.za

• 4158 • Hall of Fame Award
For outstanding service and contribution to the association and the direct selling industry.

• 4159 • Personality of the Year
For excellence in performance, participation, and achievement.

• 4160 • Special Honorary Member Award
For an individual who has rendered outstanding service to the association and the direct selling industry for a long period of time.

• 4161 •
Dorper Sheep Breeders' Society of South Africa
(Dorpers Skaaptelersgenootskap van Suid-Afrika)
Milne Charlotte, Breed Dir.
42 Van Reenen St.
PO Box 26
Middelburg 5900, Republic of South Africa
Phone: 27 49 84222241
Phone: 27 83 9682249
Fax: 27 49 84223589
E-mail: dorperinfo@adsactive.com
Home Page: http://studbook.co.za/society/dorper/frame.html

• 4162 • Honorary Certificate
Recognizes outstanding contributions to Dorper breed. Awarded annually.

• 4163 •
Durban International Film Festival
University of Kwazulu-Natal
Center for Creative Arts, Memorial Tower Bldg.
Howard College Campus
Durban 4041, Republic of South Africa
Phone: 27 31 2602506
Fax: 27 31 2603074
E-mail: diff@ukzn.ac.za
Home Page: http://www.cca.ukzn.ac.za

• 4164 • Durban International Film Festival Awards
To honor outstanding achievement in film. Awards are presented for best film, best director, best documentary, public's choice, and a special jury award. Certificates are awarded in each category annually during the festival. Established in 1978.

• 4165 •
Economic Society of South Africa
Raymond Parsons PhD, Pres.
PO Box 73354
Lynnwood Ridge 0040, Republic of South Africa
Phone: 27 12 4203525
Fax: 27 12 3625266
E-mail: saje@up.ac.za
Home Page: http://www.essa.org.za

• 4166 • Founders' Medal for Doctors' Degree Thesis
For economic research of outstanding quality conducted at a South African university.

• 4167 • Founders' Medal for Masters' Degree Dissertation
For economic research of outstanding quality conducted at a South African university.

• 4168 • J.J.I. Middleton Award
To the author of the best paper published in the journal during the year.

• 4169 •
English Academy of Southern Africa
Liz Fick, Admin.Mgr.
PO Box 124
Wits 2050, Republic of South Africa
Phone: 27 11 7179339
Fax: 27 11 7179339
E-mail: englishacademy@societies.wits.ac.za
Home Page: http://www.englishacademy.co.za

• 4170 • English Academy Medal
To recognize an individual who has conspicuously served the cause of English over a number of years, or performed signal service in the cause of English. A medal is awarded annually. Established in 1989.

• 4171 • Percy FitzPatrick Award for Youth Literature
Recognizes achievement by Southern African writers publishing in Southern Africa in the field of children's books. Sponsored by Media Tenor South Africa and the Institute for Media Analysis. Formerly: (2006) Percy FitzPatrick Prize.

• 4172 • Thomas Pringle Award
For recognition of work written in English and published in newspapers and periodicals in Southern Africa. Material published in the following categories is considered: reviews of books, plays, films, and television in newspapers or periodicals; literary articles or substantial book reviews; articles on language, the teaching of English, and educational topics in academic, teachers', and other journals, and in newspapers; short stories and one act plays in periodicals; and poetry in periodicals (a single poem could be sufficient for an award). The first category is considered annually for an award. The other four categories are considered in alternate years over a two-year period. Monetary prizes

and an illuminated certificate are awarded. A maximum of three awards is made annually. Sponsored by the State Lottery.

• 4173 • Olive Schreiner Prize

To recognize the first major work in English by a new South African writer. Awards are given in one of three categories: poetry, drama, and prose (rotating in the order given). South Africans and Namibians are eligible for work published in South Africa. A monetary prize of 5000 rand and an illuminated certificate are awarded annually. Established in 1961 by the South African Academy for Sciences and Arts and transferred in 1972 to the English Academy of Southern Africa. Sponsored by the State Lottery.

• 4174 •
Exhibition Association of Southern Africa
Mandy O'Connor, Gen.Mgr.
PO Box 2632
Halfway House
Gallagher House, Level 3
Midrand 1685, Republic of South Africa
Phone: 27 11 8057272
Fax: 27 11 8057273
E-mail: exsa@exsa.co.za
Home Page: http://www.exsa.co.za

• 4175 • Exhibition of the Year

To recognize individuals and companies for outstanding performance in exhibiting. Awards are presented in size categories within the larger classifications of Trade, Consumer, Trade & Consumer, Confex, and New Exhibition. Awarded annually.

• 4176 •
Fertilizer Society of South Africa
(Die Misstofvereniging van Suid-Afrika)
Dr. G.J. van der Linde, Dir.
PO Box 75510
Lynnwood Ridge 0040, Republic of South Africa
Phone: 27 12 3491450
Fax: 27 12 3491463
E-mail: fssamvsa@mweb.co.za
Home Page: http://www.fssa.org.za

Awards discontinued.

• 4177 • Gold Medal Award
(MVSA Goue Medalje)

For recognition of contributions to agriculture in South Africa over a long period of time. The deadline for nomination is August. A medal is awarded annually at the general meeting of the Society. Established in 1968.

• 4178 • Silver Medal Award
(MVSA Silwer Medalje vir Navorsing)

For recognition of contributions to crop production and soil fertility research over a long period of time. The nomination deadline falls in August. A medal is awarded annually at the general meeting of the Society. Established in 1968.

• 4179 •
Free Market Foundation of Southern Africa
Leon Louw, Exec.Dir.
PO Box 785121
Sandton 2146, Republic of South Africa
Phone: 27 11 884 0270
Fax: 27 11 884 5672
E-mail: fmf@mweb.co.za
Home Page: http://www.freemarketfoundation.com

• 4180 • Free Market Award

To honor individuals who have made an outstanding contribution to the cause of economic freedom in South Africa. Selection is by nomination. A certificate and Kruger Rand are awarded annually. Established in 1980.

• 4181 •
Genealogical Society of South Africa
Marilyn Coetzee, Sec.
Ste. 143
Postnet X2600
Houghton 2041, Republic of South Africa
Phone: 27 12 3488253
Phone: 27 12 4603632
E-mail: secretary@ggsa.info
Home Page: http://www.rootsweb.com/~zafgssa

• 4182 • Genealogist of the Year

Annual award of recognition.

• 4183 •
Geological Society of South Africa
Leopold Bosch, Exec.Mgr.
PO Box 61809
Marshalltown 2107, Republic of South Africa
Phone: 27 11 4923370
Fax: 27 11 4923371
E-mail: info@gssa.org.za
Home Page: http://www.gssa.org.za/index.php

• 4184 • Corstorphine Medal

To provide recognition for the best student thesis embodying the results of original research on geological subjects. Students of any university in Southern Africa are eligible. A bronze medal is awarded annually when merited. Established in 1925 to honor Geo. S. Corstorphine, Honorary Editor of the *Transactions of the Geological Society of South Africa* (1903-1905 and 1910-1915).

• 4185 • Draper Memorial Medal

For recognition of a past record of research with particular reference to the advancement of South African geology. Members of the Society for at least five years are eligible. A bronze medal showing a bust of Dr. David Draper, the first Honorary Secretary of the Society, is awarded annually. Established in 1932.

• 4186 • Geological Society of South Africa Honorary Member

To recognize outstanding contributions to the field of geology. Awarded when merited, the recipient receives a certificate.

• 4187 • Geological Society of South Africa Honours Award

To recognize a member or group of members of the Society who has made a particularly meritorious contribution to the Geological Society of South Africa or the Geological Fraternity of South Africa. A shield on which the recipient's name is inscribed is awarded when merited. Established in 1978.

• 4188 • Geological Society of South Africa Jubilee Medal

For recognition of a paper of particular merit published by the Society in any year. Members of the Society are eligible. A gold medal weighing one ounce is awarded annually. Established in 1945 on the 50th anniversary of the founding of the Society.

• 4189 • DeBeers Alex L. du Toit Memorial Lecture

To recognize an individual who has distinguished him or herself in the fields in which Alex Du Toit was active, i.e. continental drift, geology of South Africa and particularly its relation to hydrology, and archaeology. If circumstances permit, and at the discretion of the Council, the lecturer alternates from South Africa and overseas. Awarded biennially. Established in 1949 to honor the life and work of Dr. Alexander Logi Du Toit, distinguished South African geologist.

• 4190 •
Grahamstown Foundation
1820 Settlers National Monument
PO Box 304
Grahamstown 6140, Republic of South Africa
Phone: 27 46 603 1100
Fax: 27 46 603 1173
E-mail: admin@foundation.org.za
Home Page: http://www.foundation.org.za

Formerly: (1995) Eighteen-twenty Foundation.

• 4191 • Standard Bank Young Artist Awards

For recognition of outstanding contributions to South African visual and performing arts. Individuals under 40 years of age are eligible. Awards are given in the following categories: (1) music; (2) visual; (3) drama; and (4) dance. Individuals must be nominated by the Arts Festival Committee. A monetary award, a sponsored exhibition or production at the Standard Bank National Arts Festival, and a national tour are awarded annually. Established in 1981. Sponsored by the Standard Bank Investment Corporation.

• 4192 •
Grassland Society of Southern Africa
Freyni Du Toit, Contact
PO Box 41
Hilton
Pietermaritzburg 3245, Republic of South Africa
Phone: 27 83 2567202
Fax: 27 88 333903113
E-mail: admin@gssa.co.za
Home Page: http://www.gssa.co.za

• 4193 • **Grassland Society of Southern Africa Awards**
To recognize individuals interested in grassland (or rangeland) science. Young scientists (under 35 years old) who have made outstanding contributions in the field are eligible. Top performers in the final year of study, or postgraduate students, at academic institution in southern Africa are rewarded with a medal.

• 4194 •
Hiking South Africa
(Voetslaan Suid-Afrika)
Ste. 23
Postnet X108
Centurion 0046, Republic of South Africa
Phone: 27 12 3270083
E-mail: christine.frost@pfizer.com
Home Page: http://www.linx.co.za/trails/info/hikefed.html

Formerly: (2003) Hiking Federation of Southern Africa.

• 4195 • **Honorary Membership Award**
Recognizes individuals who have rendered exceptional service to the federation and to hiking. Awarded periodically.

• 4196 •
Institute of Landscape Architects of South Africa
(Instituut van Landskapargitekte van Suid Afrika)
Debbie Bredenkamp, Contact
PO Box 78
Groenkloof 0027, Republic of South Africa
Phone: 27 12 3472325
Fax: 27 12 3472325
E-mail: ilasa@ilasa.co.za
Home Page: http://www.ilasa.co.za

• 4197 • **Merit Award**
Recognizes outstanding landscape architecture projects, studies, and research. Awarded in various categories biennially in odd-numbered years.

• 4198 •
Institution of Municipal Engineering of Southern Africa
Ta Van Der Walt, Pres.
PO Box 10011
Meerensee 3901, Republic of South Africa
Phone: 27 35 7531639
Fax: 27 35 7531639
E-mail: imesa@imesa.org.za
Home Page: http://www.imesa.org.za

• 4199 • **Best Engineering Achievements Awards**
For the most innovative project in the field of municipal engineering.

• 4200 • **Best Exhibition Stall Awards**
For the best small and large stands.

• 4201 • **Best Papers Award**
For a technical paper with the highest quality.

• 4202 • **Journal Awards**
For the best publication in the Institution's journal.

• 4203 • **Retail Store Design and Layout Award**
For retailers who used innovative layout and design.

• 4204 •
International Confederation for Thermal Analysis and Calorimetry
(Confederation Internationale d'Analyse Thermique)
Prof. Michael Brown, Sec.
Chemistry Dept.
Rhodes University
Grahamstown 6140, Republic of South Africa
E-mail: m.brown@ru.ac.za
Home Page: http://www.ictac.org

Formerly: (1993) International Confederation for Thermal Analysis.

• 4205 • **International Confederation for Thermal Analysis DuPont Award**
For recognition of an outstanding contribution to the science of thermal analysis and/or leadership in the profession of thermal analysis. Selection is by nomination. An honorarium of $1,000 US, a plaque, and expenses to attend the International Conference on Thermal Analysis are awarded every four years. Established in 1977.

• 4206 • **Young Scientist Award**
To encourage young scientists early in their careers to consider and utilize thermoanalytical methods. Scientists under 35 years of age are eligible. All necessary financial support to attend the ICTA Congress is awarded every four years. Established in 1985.

• 4207 •
International Federation of Audit Bureaux of Circulations
(Federation Internationale des Bureaux de Justification de la Diffusion)
Graham A. Langmead, CEO
Central Office
27 Kyle Cres.
The Inandas
Sandton 2196, Republic of South Africa
Phone: 27 11 8842323
Fax: 27 11 8842323
E-mail: info@ifabc.org
Home Page: http://www.ifabc.org

• 4208 • **Awards of Merit**
Recognizes notable contributions to the aims and objectives of IFABC. Members and individuals are eligible. Awarded biennially.

• 4209 •
International Federation of Interior Architects/Designers
(Federation Internationale des Architectes d'Inter)
Chris Buchanan, Sec.Gen.
PO Box 91640
Auckland Park
Johannesburg 2006, Republic of South Africa
Phone: 27 11 8888211
Fax: 27 11 8888212
E-mail: ifichris@uskonet.com
Home Page: http://www.ifiworld.org

• 4210 • **IFI Award**
To recognize a person or an institution for a contribution to the advancement of the profession of interior architecture/interior design, education, (interior) architecture, or philosophy. Citizens of, or institutions established in the country where a biennial IFI Congress is being held, are eligible. Nominations are made by the host member of IFI. Established in 1985. IFI also endorses international design competitions that comply with its guidelines. For more information, please contact the IFI Secretariat in Amsterdam.

• 4211 •
National Wool Growers' Association of South Africa
(Nasionale Wolkwekersvereniging van Suid-Afrika)
Dr. Arno Moore, Mgr.
PO Box 2242
Port Elizabeth 6056, Republic of South Africa
Phone: 27 41 541536
Phone: 27 41 541537
Fax: 27 41 545698
E-mail: nwga@nwga.co.za
Home Page: http://www.nwga.co.za/

• 4212 • **Golden Ram Award (Goueram-Toekenning)**
To recognize members of the Association who have delivered exceptional service to the wool industry. The Central Executive may nominate presidents of the Association, or persons who

have delivered exceptional service to the industry. A medal and certificate are awarded when merited at the Congress. Established about 1964.

• 4213 •
Occupational Therapy Association of South Africa
Dr. Kitty Uys, Pres.
964 Schoeman St.
PO Box 11695
Hatfield 0028, Republic of South Africa
Phone: 27 12 365 1327
Fax: 27 86 651 5438
E-mail: otasa@otasa.org.za
Home Page: http://www.otasa.org.za

• 4214 • **Marie du Toit Award**
Encourages newly qualified occupational therapists to contribute to the body of knowledge of occupational therapy profession by studying the effect and outcomes of their occupational therapy interventions.

• 4215 •
Onderstepoort Veterinary Institute
Agricultural Research Council
1134 Part St., Hatfield
PO Box 8783
Pretoria 0001, Republic of South Africa
Phone: 27 12 427 9700
Fax: 27 12 342 3948
Home Page: http://www.arc.agric.za

• 4216 • **Theiler Memorial Trust Award**
Recognizes significant contribution in veterinary research.

• 4217 •
Parasitological Society of Southern Africa
(Parasitologiese Vereniging van Suidelike Afrika)
Sonja Matthee, Contact
Department of Biology
PO Box 139
Isando 1600, Republic of South Africa
Phone: 27 12 5215795
Fax: 27 12 5214246
E-mail: pking@medunsa.ac.za
Home Page: http://www.parsa.ac.za

• 4218 • **Elsdon-Dew Medal**
Award of recognition for distinguished service in parasitology. Awarded periodically.

• 4219 • **W.O. Neitz Junior Medal/Senior Medal**
Recognizes the best postgraduate thesis MSc, PhD, or DSc respectively. Awarded periodically.

• 4220 •
Physiology Society of Southern Africa
Kathy H. Myburgh, Pres.
Department of Physiological Sciences
Stellenbosch Univ.
Private Bag X1
Matieland 7602, Republic of South Africa
Phone: 27 21 8083149
Fax: 27 21 8083145
E-mail: khm@sun.ac.za
Home Page: http://academic.sun.ac.za/med_physiology/pssa.htm

• 4221 • **Honorary Life Membership Award**
Fo senior members of the PSSA for achievements and/or service to the physiology community.

• 4222 • **Johnny van der Walt Award**
For best student poster at the annual conference.

• 4223 • **Wyndham Award**
For best student oral presentation at the annual conference.

• 4224 •
Professional Hunters' Association of South Africa
Stewart Dorrington, Pres.
PO Box 10264
Centurion 0046, Republic of South Africa
Phone: 27 12 6672048
Fax: 27 12 6672049
E-mail: phasa@pixie.co.za
Home Page: http://www.phasa.co.za

• 4225 • **Nature Conservation Officer of the Year**
For outstanding officer.

• 4226 • **Uncle Stevie Award**

• 4227 • **Coenraad Vermaak Award**
For person with outstanding service to PHASA.

• 4228 • **Wildlife Utilisation Award**
For person who made an outstanding contribution to wildlife.

• 4229 •
Public Relations Institute of Southern Africa
(Openbare Skakelinstituut van Suidelike Afrika)
Margaret Moscardi, Dir.
PO Box 2825
Pinegowrie 2123, Republic of South Africa
Phone: 27 11 3261262
Fax: 27 11 3261259
E-mail: info@prisa.co.za
Home Page: http://www.prisa.co.za

• 4230 • **Prism Awards**
To recognize public relations and communication professionals who have successfully incorporated strategy, creativity, and professionalism into public relations and communication programs and strategies that showcase a successful public relations campaign. Awards are presented in 20 categories each year.

• 4231 •
Publishers' Association of South Africa
Dudley Schroeder, Exec.Dir.
PO Box 15277
Vlaeberg 8018, Republic of South Africa
Phone: 27 21 4262728
Phone: 27 21 4261726
Fax: 27 21 4261733
E-mail: pasa@publishsa.co.za
Home Page: http://www.publishsa.co.za

• 4232 • **Sefika Award**
To recognize the best publisher of educational books. Awarded annually.

• 4233 •
Recording Industry of South Africa
Nono Suntele, Communications Off.
PO Box 367
Randburg 2125, Republic of South Africa
Phone: 27 11 8861342
Fax: 27 11 8864169
E-mail: nono@risa.org.za
Home Page: http://www.risa.org.za

• 4234 • **Best Engineer**

• 4235 • **Best Original Score/Soundtrack**
For best original score for a South African composed stage musical, motion picture or television production.

• 4236 • **Best Producer**

• 4237 • **Best Selling Release**
For the best album released in a year.

• 4238 •
Republic of South Africa Department of Sport and Recreation
Rev. Makhenkesi Stofile, Min.
Oranje Nassau Bldg., 3rd Fl.
188 Schoeman St.
Private Bag X896
Pretoria 0001, Republic of South Africa
Phone: 27 12 334 3100
Fax: 27 12 321 8493
Home Page: http://www.srsa.gov.za

• 4239 • **Presidential Sports Award (Gold)**
To recognize an individual and/or national team for achievements in sport of the highest international order. This includes an improvement of an existing world record or the winning of a world championship in an established prestige sport or other achievements equivalent to these. South

African citizens are eligible. A gold medal is awarded when merited. Formerly: (1995) State President's Sport Award.

• 4240 • **Presidential Sports Award (Silver)**

For recognition of competitive sports achievements within and outside the boundaries of the Republic of South Africa. The award recognizes coaches who brought about outstanding sports achievements by South African sportspersons at international and/or national level, and sports administrators/referees/umpires who contributed to the promotion and furtherance of the sport concerned. It also recognizes national sports teams for achievements in recognized competitive sports at international and/or national level as well as persons who have through their public actions and international esteem prompted and/or popularized sport in South Africa and/or internationally without being directly involved in sports. A silver medal is awarded when merited. Formerly: (1995) South African Sports Merit Award.

• 4241 •

Royal Society of South Africa
D.E. Rawlings, Pres.
P.D. Hahn Bldg., University of Cape Town
PO Box 594
Cape Town 8000, Republic of South Africa
Phone: 27 21 6502543
Fax: 27 21 6502710
E-mail: roysoc@science.uct.ac.za
Home Page: http://www.rssa.uct.ac.za

• 4242 • **John F. W. Herschel Medal**

To recognize persons or teams who have made outstanding contributions in a wide range of fields, especially those of a multidisciplinary scientific nature that have been completed in South Africa or that are relevant to South Africa. A medal is awarded annually when merited. Established in 1984 in honor of John F. W. Herschel, a scientist and a renowned polymath.

• 4243 • **S. Meiring Naude Medal**

To recognize persons or teams who have made outstanding contributions to science, especially those of a multidisciplinary scientific nature that have been completed in South Africa or that are relevant to South Africa. Scientists under 35 years of age who are residents or who are visiting South Africa are eligible. A medal is awarded annually when merited. Established in 1984 in honor of Stefan Meiring Naude, a renowned South African scientist, discoverer of the N15 isotope, and past president of the Society.

• 4244 •

SA Holstein Friesland Society
(Friestelersvereniging van Suid-Afrika)
52 Aliwal St.
PO Box 544
Bloemfontein 9300, Republic of South Africa
Phone: 27 51 447 9123
Fax: 27 51 430 4224
E-mail: info@saholstein.co.za
Home Page: http://www.saholstein.co.za

• 4245 • **Gold Medal**

To encourage and improve the breeding of Friesland cattle in South Africa, and maintain unimpaired the purity of the breed. Friesland cattle at the various agricultural schools and colleges throughout the Republic of South Africa are considered. Friesland shields are awarded annually.

• 4246 •

Society of Medical Laboratory Technologists of South Africa
(Vereniging van Geneeskundige Laboratorium Tegnoloe van Suid-Afrika)
Mr. Donald J. Alexander, Admin.Mgr.
PO Box 6014
Roggebaai 8012, Republic of South Africa
Phone: 27 21 4194857
Fax: 27 21 4212566
E-mail: smltsa@iafrica.com
Home Page: http://www.smltsa.org.za

• 4247 • **Abbott Award**

To recognize young virologists who have contributed to the field of virology through research and developmental projects. A monetary prize of 2000 rand is awarded annually. Sponsored by Abbott Diagnostics. Formerly: National SMLTSA Virology Prize.

• 4248 • **Abbott Award for Innovative Research and Development in Virology**

To recognize innovative research and development in virology. A monetary prize of R2000.00 is awarded biennially, in addition to a commemorative plaque. Sponsored by Abbott Laboratories S.A. (PTY) LTD, Diagnostic Division.

• 4249 • **Irene Aitken Memorial Award**

To recognize a member of the SMLTSA for papers, posters, or publications in a recognized journal on haematological subjects. The recipient must be qualified for a period of at least 5 years. Preference is given to original work. Business class return airfare from JHB to London to attend a congress or for further study, and a certificate are awarded annually. The award is presented at the National Congress of the SMLTSA. If no congress is held that year, the presentation is made at an appropriate regional or branch function.

• 4250 • **Bactlab Systems Gold Award**

To recognize the person who made significant contributions to the academic improvement of posters presented in either of the following categories: microbiology, serology, or flow-cytometry. Preference will be given to original work. The recipient should be a member in good standing of the SMLTSA and must have been qualified for a period of at least 3 years. The recipient is not restricted to the number of awards. A check for 500 rand, a floating trophy, and a miniature are awarded biannually at the SMLTSA National Congress. Sponsored by Bactlab Systems (Pty.) Ltd.

• 4251 • **Bactlab Systems Premier Award for Best Paper**

To recognize the person who has contributed most to improving the standard of academic papers in the category of microbiology. Preference will be given to authors or co-authors who have completed their papers with minimal outside help. The recipient should be a member of the SMLTSA in good standing and should have been qualified for a period of at least 5 years. The prize, which is awarded annually, includes a return airfare to the U.S. to present a paper or poster at either the American Society for Microbiology Congress or the American Society of Medical Technologists Annual Congress. The prize also included a floating trophy, miniature, and certificate. Sponsored by Bactlab Systems (Pty.) Ltd.

• 4252 • **Bayer Diagnostics Academic Achievement Award**

To recognize the author or co-author of a paper published in any recognized journal or presentation at Congress in the fields of haematology, immunology clinical chemistry, or laboratory computers. Candidates must show why the award should be made to them, how the award will be used, and what benefit will be gained from it. 5,000 rand is awarded biannually toward study or as a travel grant to further professional career. Presented at the National Congress of the SMLTSA. Sponsored by Bayer SA.

• 4253 • **Bayer/Sakura Histology Achievement Award**

To recognize achievement in the field of histology. A monetary award of 600 rand is awarded annually at the National Congress. If no congress is held that year, then presentation is made at an appropriate regional or branch meeting. Sponsored by Bayer SA and Sakura Europe. Formerly: (1995) Bayer-Mills Histology Award; (1995) Ames Histology Award.

• 4254 • **Dade Behring Award**

To recognize the best immunology student. 500 rand is awarded to the student and 250 rand is awarded to the branch at which the student is a member. Awards are presented annually at the National Congress. If a Congress is not held that year, the prize will be presented at an appropriate regional or branch meeting.

• 4255 • **Joseph Prize**

To recognize the author or authors of the highest standard paper published in *Medical Technology: SA Journal*. A monetary prize of 800 rand is presented at SMLTSA National Congress.

• 4256 • Labotec-Shandon Award for Achievement in the Field of Cytology
To recognize achievement in the field of cytology, service to the profession, original research, and publication of outstanding papers. A monetary prize of 1,000 rand is awarded biannually at the SMLTSA National Congress. Formerly: (1995) Premier Technology Shandon Award.

• 4257 • Merck Award
To recognize the most successful candidate in the categories of cytopathology or microbiology. A monetary prize of 1,000 rand is awarded biannually at the National Congress of the SMLTSA.

• 4258 • Roche Award
To recognize a member of the Society who has contributed most significantly toward the aims of medical technology. A prize of 1,000 rand is awarded biennially. Sponsored by Roche Diagnostics. Formerly: (2006) Boehringer Mannheim S.A. Award.

• 4259 • SA Scientific Award
To recognize the Technologist of the Year. 1,000 rand is awarded annually at the National Congress. If no congress is held that the year, the presentation will be made at an appropriate regional or branch function.

• 4260 • Technologist of the Year
Award to the technologist of the year. A monetary prize of R1000 and a plaque are awarded biennially at a National Congress. Administered by the SA Scientific Group.

• 4261 • Thistle Student Award
To recognize the academic achievement of students at the relevant Technikon. Recipient must be a pre-diplomat and must have been a member of the Society for a period of not less than one year. A trophy, which remains the property of the relevant Branch, a miniature, and 100 rand is awarded annually. Formerly: (1995) Wellcome Diagnostics Student Award.

• 4262 •
Society of South African Geographers
Prof. M.E. Meadows, Pres.
Dept. of Geography
University of the Free State
PO Box 399
Bloemfontein 9300, Republic of South Africa
Phone: 27 51 4012184
Fax: 27 51 4013816
E-mail: britss.sci@mail.uovs.ac.za
Home Page: http://www.ssag.co.za

Formerly: (1995) South African Geographical Society.

• 4263 • Society of South African Geographers Fellow
For recognition of sustained and outstanding intellectual contributions and productivity in any field of geography as demonstrated in a substantial number of scholarly publications. Nominations are accepted by the Fellowships Committee at least two months before the annual general meeting (customarily held in August of any year). A citation and an illuminated certificate are awarded when merited. Established in 1975.

• 4264 •
South African Academy of Science and Arts
Prof. L.R. McFarlane, Contact
Private Bag XII
Arcadia 0007, Republic of South Africa
Phone: 27 12 3285082
Fax: 27 12 3285091
E-mail: akademie@cis.co.za
Home Page: http://www.akademie.co.za

• 4265 • Alba Bouwer Prize for ChildrenKs Literature
For recognition of Afrikaans literature for children in the category 7-12 years of age. A prize is awarded triennially.

• 4266 • Gold Medal for Achievement in the Natural Sciences
To recognize meritorious work in the field of the natural sciences, technology, or medical science. It is awarded for outstanding work of practical discovery (or application) and expertise, based on scientific and/or experimental principles. A gold medal is awarded annually.

• 4267 • Havenga Prize
For recognition of original research in the natural sciences and/or the field of technology. The prize is awarded alternately in three main fields: (1) Biological sciences; (2) Human natural sciences, and (3) Mathematical, chemical, and physical sciences. A gold medal is awarded annually.

• 4268 • Hertzog Prize for Literature
For recognition of the best literary work written in Afrikaans during the three years preceding the award. The prize rotates in the following categories: poetry, drama, and prose. A monetary prize of 17,000 rand is awarded annually.

• 4269 • Tienie Holloway Medal
To recognize writers who have written the best work in Afrikaans for children, primarily under eight years of age. A gold medal is awarded every three years.

• 4270 • C. J. Langenhoven Prize
For recognition of outstanding scientific and/or creative work, including lexicography in Afrikaans. Awarded every three years.

• 4271 • D. F. Malan Medal
For recognition of outstanding contributions in the advancement of the Afrikaans language and culture. A gold medal is awarded every three years in memory of Dr. D.F. Malan for his outstanding services in the advancement of the Afrikaans language and culture.

• 4272 • Eugene Marais Prize
For recognition of an early or first work in belles lettres written in the Afrikaans language. A monetary prize of 10,000 rand is awarded annually.

• 4273 • Medal of Honor for the Performing and Visual Arts
For recognition of achievement in the following fields: music, dramatic arts, film art, painting, sculpture, architecture, weaving, ceramics, mosaics, photography, advertising, and animated films. Awarded annually.

• 4274 • Medal of Honor for the Scientific Promotion and Development of Subjects
To recognize scientific promotion and development of a specific subject in any of the education sectors, from early childhood education to higher education. Awarded annually.

• 4275 • Medal of Honor in the Natural Sciences and Technology
For recognition of achievement in any field of study in the physical sciences and technique not already covered by the named prizes. Awarded periodically.

• 4276 • Medal of Honour for Afrikaans Television (Prize for Television and Radio)
Awarded annually, alternately for dramas or documentary programs. Individuals may be nominated. A monetary award is presented annually. Established in 1961. Formerly: (2004) Prys vir Televisie en Radio.

• 4277 • Gustav Preller Prize
To provide recognition for works of literary science and criticism in Afrikaans. A monetary prize is awarded every three years.

• 4278 • Prize for Translated Work
To recognize a translation from any language into Afrikaans of a work of prose, poetry, or drama. A monetary prize is awarded triennially. Established in 1948.

• 4279 • PUK-Councilers Prize
To encourage amateur talent of school pupils from grades 10-12. The prizes are awarded alternately in the following categories: poetry, drama, and prose. Monetary prizes of 1000 rand are awarded annually. Also known as the Poort-Prize. Formerly: (2004) South African Academy of Science and Arts Literary Prize.

• 4280 • Scheepers Prize for Youth Literature
To provide recognition for the advancement of Afrikaans literature for young people. Works must be of literary and educational value to the young reader and aimed at the older child. A monetary prize is awarded every three years, since 1974. Established in 1956.

Awards are arranged in alphabetical order below their administering organizations

• 4281 • Senior Captain Scott Commemoration Medal

To recognize a biologist in southern Africa who has attained outstanding achievements in his or her field of work. Awarded annually.

• 4282 • Junior Captain Scott Commemorative Medal

To recognize the best dissertation submitted at a South African university for an M.Sc. degree. Awarded alternately in the animal and plant sciences.

• 4283 • Stals Prize for the Humanities

To recognize an outstanding publication or a series of outstanding publications preferably, but not exclusively, in Afrikaans. The prize is awarded in 14 fields that rotate every three years. Awarded annually.

• 4284 • M. T. Steyn Prize for Natural Science and Technical Achievement

For recognition of leadership at the highest level in the fields of natural sciences and technology. The prize may be awarded only once to a candidate, as it is regarded as a seal of excellence on his or her career. A gold medal is awarded annually. Established in 1964.

• 4285 • Albert Strating Prize for Preventive Medicine

To recognize outstanding contributions to a branch or branches of preventive medicine that can be regarded as significant in the promotion of the health of the community and the prevention of illness. A medal is awarded every three years. Established in 1993 in honor of Dr. Albert Strating.

• 4286 • D. F. du Toit-Malherbe Prize for Genealogical Research

To provide recognition for publications of a high standard in Afrikaans in the field of genealogy. Awarded triennially.

• 4287 • Frans du Toit Medal for Business Leadership

To recognize an individual for creative contributions to South African business, sustained contribution over a long period to the areas in which Frans du Toit was engaged, and leadership and the impetus for further development of those areas that he inspired. A gold medal is awarded annually.

• 4288 • Totius Prize for Theology and Study of the Original Languages of the Bible

For recognition of publications in Afrikaans in the field of Christian theology and the original languages of the Bible. Awarded biennially.

• 4289 • Toon Van Den Heever Prize for Jurisprudence

To provide recognition for original legal works in Afrikaans or full-length articles of outstanding quality in Afrikaans that have appeared in accredited law journals. Awarded every three years.

• 4290 • Dominee Pieter van Drimmelen Medal

To recognize the work of an individual in the following fields: translation of the Bible, theological textbooks in Afrikaans for use by university students, published books of sermons, religious teaching, and the writing, translation, composition, and improvement of Afrikaans psalms and hymns. Awarded annually.

• 4291 • N. P. van Wyk Louw Medal

To recognize an individual for a creative contribution to the development, organization, and sustained extension of a branch/branches of the human sciences. The contribution must be fundamental and important to the promotion of the human sciences and to their successful application in the national interest. A medal is awarded annually. Established in 1991 in honor of N. P. van Wyk Louw, Afrikaans poet, dramatist, essayist, and man of letters (1906-1970).

• 4292 • Markus Viljoen Medal for Journalism

To provide recognition for work of long duration and high standard in Afrikaans journalism. A gold medal is awarded every three years.

• 4293 •
South African Association for Food Science and Technology
Jean Venter, Natl. Sec.
PO Box 868
Ferndale 2160, Republic of South Africa
Phone: 27 11 7891384
Fax: 27 11 7891385
E-mail: saafost@vdw.co.za
Home Page: http://www.saafost.org.za

• 4294 • Best Paper Presented Award

• 4295 • Best Poster Award

• 4296 • Best Student Award

• 4297 • Koeppen Memorial Scholarship

For students who have registered for masters or doctorate degrees in the Department of Food Science.

• 4298 • Study Grants

• 4299 •
South African Association for Learning and Educational Difficulties
PO Box 2404
Clareinch 7740, Republic of South Africa
Phone: 27 21 762 6306
Fax: 27 21 762 6306
E-mail: info@saaled.org.za
Home Page: http://www.saaled.org.za

• 4300 • SAALED Bursary

To encourage students to engage in further study in the field of disadvantaged/learning-disabled children. Full- and part-time students applying for a course at Tertiary institutions are eligible; preference is given to Association members. A monetary prize of 3000 rand is awarded annually. Established in 1986. Formerly: .

• 4301 •
South African Association of Botanists
Mrs. Mariana Smith, Sec.
PO Box 3268
Matieland 7602, Republic of South Africa
E-mail: forsaab@mweb.co.za
Home Page: http://anubis.ru.ac.za/saab/saab.htm

• 4302 • Bronze Medal

For recognition of an outstanding thesis on a botanical subject resulting in a doctorate degree at a Southern African University. A bronze medal is awarded annually. Established in 1977.

• 4303 • Gold Medal for Botany

For recognition of outstanding botanical research. The premier award for Botany in South Africa. A gold medal is awarded annually. Established in 1972.

• 4304 • Senior Medal for Botany

For recognition of outstanding research and/or other contributions to advancement of botany in South Africa. A silver medal is awarded annually. Established in 1977.

• 4305 •
South African Association of Consulting Engineers
Graham Pirie, Exec.Dir.
PO Box 68482
Bryanston
Johannesburg 2021, Republic of South Africa
Phone: 27 11 4632022
Fax: 27 11 4637383
E-mail: general@saace.co.za
Home Page: http://www.saace.co.za

• 4306 • SAACE Excellence Awards

To recognize outstanding achievement of member firms of the SAACE and to their clients in the following categories: Technical Excellence, Business Excellence, Young Company of the Year, Visionary Client of the Year, Journalism award for the Advancement of the consulting engineering industry. The award is framed display certificate identifying the winner and category. The SAACE was established in 1952.

• 4307 •
South African Association of Women Graduates
Margaret Edwards, Pres.
PO Box 1879
Gauteng 2008, Republic of South Africa
Fax: 27 11 4532500
E-mail: elsemari@web.co.za
Home Page: http://ifuw.org/southafrica

• 4308 • **International Award**
To a foreign student enrolled in a South African university.

• 4309 • **Isie Smuts Fellowship**
For postgraduate study in any field.

• 4310 • **Hansi Pollak Fellowship**
For post graduate research.

• 4311 • **SAAUW Fellowship**
For post graduate research.

• 4312 • **Bertha Stoneman Fellowship**
For research in biology.

• 4313 •
South African Chemical Institute
(Suid-Afrikaanse Chemiese Instituut)
Sadhna Gajoo-Naidoo, Sec.
PO Box 407
Private Bag X3
Wits 2050, Republic of South Africa
Phone: 27 11 7176741
Fax: 27 11 7176779
E-mail: saci@aurum.wits.ac.za
Home Page: http://www.saci.co.za

• 4314 • **Chemical Education Medal**
To recognize a person who has made an outstanding contribution to chemical education, as judged by works published within the previous five years. Published works may be in any form and may be related to any level or education context. The deadline for applications and nominations is March 31. A medal struck in silver bearing the Institute's crest and name on the obverse is awarded.

• 4315 • **Industrial Chemistry Medal**
To recognize an individual who has conducted novel research or enhanced existing chemical research in a particular field in an industrial laboratory that is judged to be of outstanding merit, taking into account the benefits to the individual's company and the chemical community at large. The deadline for nominations and applications is March 31. A medal struck in silver bearing the Institute's crest and name on the obverse is awarded.

• 4316 • **Merck Medal**
To recognize the senior author of a research paper that has been published in the *South African Journal of Chemistry* and is considered to have made the most significant contribution to scientific knowledge in that field of chemistry. Each year, the award is considered for papers in one of the following four fields of chemistry: analytical, organic, physical, and inorganic, in the defined sequence. A gold medal is awarded annually when merited. Established in 1961. Sponsored by Merck & Co. Formerly: (2006) AECI Medal.

• 4317 • **James Moir Medal**
To recognize the best BSc Honours student in chemistry at each University, and the best BTech student in chemistry at each Technikon, or University or Institute of Technology. To be eligible for the award the student must have achieved a minimum final pass mark of 75 percent. One medal shall be available for award annually for each University, Technikon, and University or Institute of Technology in the Republic of South Africa.

• 4318 • **Raikes Medal**
To recognize an individual whose original chemical research shows outstanding promise, as adjudged by publication in reputable journals. The research must have been performed in South Africa. Individuals under the age of 35 on March 31 during the year of the award may be nominated by a member of the South African Chemical Institute, or may apply. A gold medal is awarded annually when merited. Established in 1960 in honor of Humphrey Raikes, a former professor of Chemistry at the University of the Witwatersrand.

• 4319 • **Sasol Post-Graduate Medal**
To recognize students who are engaged in research towards the M.Sc. or PhD degree in Chemistry, or the Master's Diploma of a Technikon, and who are considered to be young, innovative chemists. A maximum of five silver medals are available to be awarded annually, and the award is accompanied by a cash prize of 1000 rand. Established in 1984. Sponsored by Sasol Ltd..

• 4320 • **South African Chemical Institute Gold Medal**
To recognize an individual whose scientific contributions in the field of chemistry or chemical technology are adjudged to be of outstanding merit. A member of the South African Chemical Institute may nominate individuals. A gold medal is awarded annually when merited. Established in 1967.

• 4321 • **Hendrik Van Eck Medal**
To recognize a member of the Institute who has made exceptional contributions in the business or industrial sectors and/or to the community as a whole in South Africa. Members of the South African Chemical Institute may be nominated by a member of the SACI. A gold medal is awarded annually when merited. Established in 1983 in honor of Hendrik van Eck, a major South African industrialist.

• 4322 •
South African Dental Association
Neil Campbell, CEO
Private Bag 1
Houghton
Gauteng 2041, Republic of South Africa
Phone: 27 11 4845288
Phone: 27 11 4845289
Fax: 27 11 6425718
E-mail: neil@sada.co.za
Home Page: http://www.sadanet.co.za

• 4323 • **Business Leader Awards**
For the number one business leader.

• 4324 • **Dentistry Development Fund Scholarship for the Development of a Research Technique for Dentistry.**

• 4325 • **Distinguished Service Award of SADA**

• 4326 • **Premier Award of SADA**

• 4327 • **Research and Education in Dentistry Fund for Post Graduate Studies in Dental Education**

• 4328 • **Research Grant**
16750

• 4329 • **Travel Grant**

• 4330 •
South African Institute of Architects
Mrs. Su Linning, Exec. Officer
Private Bag X10063
Randburg 2125, Republic of South Africa
Phone: 27 11 7821315
Fax: 27 11 7828771
E-mail: admin@saia.org.za
Home Page: http://www.saia.org.za

• 4331 • **Architectural Critics and Writers Award**
For recognition of a distinguished contribution to architectural criticism and/or writing. Established in 1977.

• 4332 • **Gold Medal for Architecture**
For recognition of an outstanding contribution to architecture through practice and design. Members of the Institute are eligible. A silver gilt medal is awarded when merited. Established in 1958.

• 4333 • **Patron of Architecture Award**
For recognition of achievement in architecture and allied fields. An individual, government, department, or other organization is eligible. Awarded when merited. Established in 1981.

• 4334 • **South African Institute of Architects Award for Excellence**
For outstanding contributions to the field of architecture.

• 4335 • **South African Institute of Architects Award of Merit**
To recognize good design or a significant contribution in the field of architecture.

• 4336 • **South African Institute of Architects Best Student Award**
Awarded to the best student, based on highest academic achievement over the final two years of study for the professional degree in architecture with a minimum average over the two years of 70%. A commemorative certificate plues a cash prize is awarded, when merited.

• 4337 • **South African Institute of Architects Medal of Distinction**
For recognition of services to the profession of architecture. Members of the Institute are eligible. A medal is awarded when merited. Established in 1981.

• 4338 •
South African Institute of Electrical Engineers
Prof. Bea Lacquet, Pres.
PO Box 751253
Gardenview 2047, Republic of South Africa
Phone: 27 11 4873003
Fax: 27 11 4873002
E-mail: smitha@saiee.org.za
Home Page: http://www.saiee.org.za

• 4339 • **South African Institute of Electrical Engineers Awards**
For recognition of worthy papers, contributions, and other items of interest published in the Institute's *Transactions.* The following awards are presented: PresidentKs Award, Engineer of the Year Award, and Young Achievers Award. Monetary awards or certificates and medals are awarded annually.

• 4340 •
South African National Council for the Blind
514 Bailey's Muckleneuk
Pretoria 0181, Republic of South Africa
Phone: 27 12 352 3811
Fax: 27 12 346 4699
E-mail: admin@sancb.co.za

• 4341 • **R. W. Bowen Medal**
For recognition of lifelong meritorious service to the visually disabled people of South Africa. South Africans from all walks of life may be nominated. A medal and citation are awarded biennially. Established in 1962 in memory of R. W. Bowen, a blinded veteran of the 1914-1918 War, and first chairman of the South African National Council for the Blind.

• 4342 •
South African National Defence Force
% Department of Defense Information Centre
Private Bag X161
Pretoria 0001, Republic of South Africa
Phone: 27 12 3556321
Fax: 27 12 3556398
E-mail: info@mil.za
Home Page: http://www.dod.mil.za

• 4343 • **General Service Medal**
To recognize members of the SA Defence Force who have rendered service as part of military operations within the borders of the Republic of South Africa for the prevention or suppression of terrorism or internal disorder or who have served for the preservation of life, health or property, or maintenance of essential services, including the maintenance of law and order or the prevention of crime in co-operation with the South Africa Police. A silver medal displaying a pentagon and wreath, worn from an orange, white, and blue ribbon is bestowed. Established January 1983.

• 4344 • **Military Merit Medal**
To recognize members of the SA Defence Force who have distinguished themselves by the rendering of services of a high order. A medal worn from a blue and red striped ribbon is bestowed. A bar is presented for successive awards. Formerly: C SADF Commendation Medal; Chief of the South African Defense Force Commendation Medal.

• 4345 • **Unitas Medal**
A round bronze medal depicting a seven-pointed star with a Greek lower-case alpha in the center worn from a light blue, green, and white ribbon is bestowed. Established in 1994 to commemorate the new constitutional dispensation introduced in South Africa.

• 4346 •
South African Society for Enology and Viticulture
(Suid Afrikaanse Wingerd en Wynkundevereniging)
Ilse Trautmann, Pres.
PO Box 2092
Dennesig 7601, Republic of South Africa
Phone: 27 21 8093123
Phone: 27 21 8093123
Fax: 27 21 8896335
E-mail: sasev@arc.agric.za
Home Page: http://www.sasev.co.za

• 4347 • **Medal of Merit**
To a person who made an exceptional contribution over many years to the industry.

• 4348 • **SASEV Award**
To the most outstanding scientific contribution published in the journal or the most outstanding innovation in the industry.

• 4349 • **SASEV Journal Prize**
For the best article in the annual journal.

• 4350 • **SASEV Prize**
For individuals who made advances in research and innovation.

• 4351 • **SASEV Student Prize**
For the top students of University of Stellenboch and Elsenburg College.

• 4352 • **SASEV Table Grape Award**
To the most outstanding scientific contribution published in journal or the most outstanding innovation in table and raisin grape industry.

• 4353 • **Michael A.J. Sweeney Award**
For the best papers presented at the annual Graphics Interface Conference.

• 4354 •
South African Society of Music Teachers
(Die Suid-Afrikaanse Vereniging van Musiekonderwysers)
Jaco Van Der Merwe, Exec.Dir.
PO Box 20573
Noordbrug 2522, Republic of South Africa
Phone: 27 18 2991699
Fax: 27 18 2991699
E-mail: sasmt@samusicteacher.org.za
Home Page: http://www.samusicteacher.org.za

• 4355 • **Ellie Marx Memorial Scholarship**
To recognize an exceptionally talented young South African student, who shows promise of becoming an outstanding solo performer, and to provide for study of the performance of stringed musical instruments (particularly the violin). Individuals who have studied a stringed instrument in South Africa for three years and who are under 25 years of age are eligible. A monetary prize of 3,000 rand is awarded. Established in 1960 by Ellie Marx. Awarded biennially.

• 4356 •
South African Sugar Technologists' Association
Danile Macdonald, SASTA Administrator
% SA Sugarcane Research Institute
Private Bag X02
Mount Edgecombe 4300, Republic of South Africa
Phone: 27 31 593205
Fax: 27 31 595406
E-mail: sasta@sugar.org.za
Home Page: http://www.sasta.co.za

• 4357 • **Gold Medal**
For recognition of outstanding contributions to technology in the South African sugar industry. Members of the Association are eligible. A gold medal is awarded periodically at the annual general meeting. Established in 1968.

• 4358 •
South African Veterinary Association
Dr. Colin Cameron, CEO
PO Box 25033
Monument Park
Pretoria 0105, Republic of South Africa
Phone: 27 12 3461150
Phone: 27 12 3461151
Fax: 27 12 3462929
E-mail: savf@sava.org.za
Home Page: http://www.sava.co.za

• 4359 • **Boswell Award**
To recognize members for selfless and eminent service rendered to the profession through the SAVA. The award may be bestowed upon more than one person in a particular year.

• 4360 • **South African Veterinary Association Gold Medal**
Awarded to any person resident in South Africa, or a veterinarian who is not resident in South Africa but who is a member of the SAVA, in recognition of outstanding scientific achievement and advancement of veterinary science. The medal will only be awarded once to a particular person.

• 4361 •
Southern Africa Association for the Advancement of Science
(Suider-Afrika Genootskap vir die Bevordering van die Wetenskap)
Mrs. S.A. Korsman, Contact
PO Box 366
Irene 0062, Republic of South Africa
Phone: 27 12 6672544
Fax: 27 12 6672544
E-mail: s2a3@global.co.za
Home Page: http://s2a3.up.ac.za

• 4362 • **British Association Medal**
Recognizes exceptional scientific achievement, international participation and publications. Applicants must be under 40 years if age. Awarded annually.

• 4363 • **Bronze Medal**
To recognize the student at each South African university who has submitted the best MasterKs dissertation in one of the branches of science, either natural or human sciences. Awarded annually.

• 4364 • **South African Association for the Advancement of Science Certificate of Merit**
To recognize persons who have contributed to the advancement of science in South Africa. Awarded when merited.

• 4365 • **South African Medal**
Recognizes exceptional scientific achievement, international participation and publications. Awarded annually.

• 4366 •
Southern African Society for Plant Pathology
Prof. Z.A. Pretorius, Pres.
Dept. of Plant Sciences
Univ. of the Free State
PO Box 339
Bloemfontein 9300, Republic of South Africa
Phone: 27 51 4012466
Phone: 27 51 4012514
Fax: 27 51 4488772
E-mail: pretorza.sci@mail.uovs.ac.za
Home Page: http://www.saspp.co.za

Formerly: South African Society for Plant Pathology and Microbiology; South African Society for Plant Pathology.

• 4367 • **Fellow of the Society**
For recognition of service to the Society and to teaching and/or research in plant pathology. Individuals who have ten years of uninterrupted membership may be nominated by the members and elected by the Council. A certificate is awarded when merited. Established in 1984.

• 4368 • **Honorary Member**
For recognition of an outstanding contribution to plant pathology or the Society. Election is by ballot at the annual general meeting. A certificate is awarded when merited. Established in 1963.

• 4369 • **Christiaan Hendrik Persoon Medal**
For recognition of an outstanding achievement in the field of plant pathology. Nominations are accepted. A medal is awarded triennially when merited. Established in 1979.

• 4370 •
Sunday Times Business Times
Editor
PO Box 1742
Saxonworld 2132, Republic of South Africa
Phone: 27 11 2803000
Fax: 27 11 2805150
E-mail: sundaytimes@sundaytimes.co.za
Home Page: http://www.sundaytimes.co.za

• 4371 • **Top 100 Companies Award**
To recognize Johannesburg Stock Exchange-listed companies that have achieved high returns for shareholders over a five-year period. Companies are ranked in the top 100 companies by average annual compound rate of return to shareholders. A certificate is awarded annually. Established in 1968.

• 4372 •
Tafelberg Publishers Ltd.
Michelle Cooper, Contact
PO Box 879
Capetown 8000, Republic of South Africa
Phone: 27 21 406 3003
Fax: 27 21 406 3812
E-mail: tafelbrg@tafelberg.com
Home Page: http://www.nb.co.za/Tafelberg/tbSplash.asp

• 4373 • **W. A. Hofmeyr Prize (W. A. Hofmeyr-prys)**
To recognize the best literary work in Afrikaans published in the preceding year by one of the publishers in the Nasionale Pers group which consists of Tafelberg Publishers, Human and Rousseau, J. L. van Schaik, Via Afrika, Jonathan Ball Publishers, Queillere Publisher & Kwela Books. A monetary prize of 5,000 rand and a gold medal are awarded annually. Established in 1954 in memory of W. A. Hofmeyr, a past Chairman of the Nasionale Pers group.

• 4374 • **Recht Malan Prize (Recht Malan-prys)**
For recognition of the most deserving book of non-fiction in Afrikaans or English published in the preceding year by the publishing houses of the Nasionale Boekhandel Publishing Group. A monetary prize of 7,500 rand is awarded annually. Established in 1978 in memory of Recht Malan, a past Chairman of the Nasionale Pers group.

• 4375 •
Water Institute of Southern Africa
(Water Instituut van Suidelike Africa)
PO Box 6011
Halfway House 1685
Johannesburg 1685, Republic of South Africa
Phone: 27 11 8053537
Fax: 27 11 3151258
E-mail: wisa@wisa.or.za
Home Page: http://www.wisa.org.za

• 4376 • **Dr. G. G. Cillie Award**
To recognize the best contribution to anaerobic research in Southern Africa by a university student. A floating trophy, a book prize valued at 250 Rand, and a certificate are awarded annually. Established in 1989 to honor the research contributions on water treatment by Dr. G. G. Cillie.

• 4377 • **Umgeni Award**
To encourage excellence in the fields of water science and engineering by recognizing a paper that makes a noteworthy contribution to water science and engineering. Members are eligible for papers published through WISA. A monetary award of 1,000 rand is awarded annually. Established in 1988 to mark the inauguration of the Water Institute of Southern Africa. Sponsored by Umgeni Water.

Awards are arranged in alphabetical order below their administering organizations

• 4378 • **Wilson Award (Wilson - Toekenning)**

To recognize the combined competence and initiative of the owner and works manager of a Waste Water Treatment Works, having a total design capacity of up to 25,000 kl/day average DWF. The criteria that are considered include treatment and operating efficiency, maintenance and servicing, laboratory control, housekeeping, safety, and administration. A certificate is awarded biennially at the Conference. Established in 1976 to honor Dr. Harold Wilson (1887-1974), a founding member and first Chairman of the South African Branch of the Institute of Water Pollution Control in 1937.

• 4379 •
Zoological Society of Southern Africa (Dierkundige Vereniging van Suidelike Afrika)
Dr. Colleen Downs, Treas.
Dept. of Zoology and Entomology
University of Natal
Private bag X01
Scottsville 3209, Republic of South Africa
Phone: 27 33 2605323
Phone: 27 33 2605127
Fax: 27 33 2605105
E-mail: downs@zoology.unp.ac.za
Home Page: http://www.zssa.co.za

• 4380 • **Award to the Most Outstanding Third Year Student in Zoology**

Awarded each year to the best third-year and honors students in zoology at each of the universities in southern Africa. Each student also receives free membership for one year. Awards are based on the recommendation of department heads. Awarded annually. Formerly: Certificate of Merit.

• 4381 • **Gold Medal**

To recognize a zoologist of exceptional merit in the field of zoology in southern Africa. A medal is awarded annually if merited. Established in 1970.

• 4382 • **Stevenson - Hamilton Award**

To recognize an amateur zoologist for exceptional contributions to zoology in southern Africa. Individuals may be nominated by members of the Society before May of each year. A medal is awarded annually if merited. Established in 1988.

Romania

• 4383 •
General Association of Engineers in Romania
Mihai Mihaita, Pres.
Str. Dumitru
Ghiata Nr. 22
Turnu Severin
R-70179 Bucharest, Romania
Phone: 40 52 341063
Fax: 40 52 341063
Home Page: http://inginerie.protectia-mediului.ro

• 4384 • **AGIR's Prize**

Annual grant. Inquire for additional information.

• 4385 •
Romanian Academy (Academia Romana)
Eugen Simion, Pres.
Calea Victoriei 125
Sector 1
RO-71102 Bucharest 1, Romania
Phone: 40 1 2128640
Phone: 40 1 2129757
Fax: 40 1 2116608
E-mail: solunca@acad.ro
Home Page: http://www.acad.ro

• 4386 • **Aurel Vlaicu Prize**

For recognition of an outstanding contribution to technology. A monetary prize of 1,000,000 lei and a diploma are awarded annually. Established in 1948.

• 4387 •
Women's Association of Romania (Asociatia Femeilor din Romania)
Liliana Pagu, Pres.
Post Office No. 37
PO Box 80
R-71102 Bucharest, Romania
Phone: 40 21 3159859
Fax: 40 21 3159859
E-mail: afr@afr.ro
Home Page: http://www.afr.ro

• 4388 • **Honour Diploma**

Recognizes meritorious activity. Awarded annually.

Russia

• 4389 •
Interfest: Moscow International Film Festival
Nikita Mikhalkov, Pres.
Khokhlovsky per., 10/1
109028 Moscow, Russia
Phone: 7 95 917 2486
Fax: 7 95 916 0107
E-mail: info@miff.ru
Home Page: http://www.miff.ru

Formerly: Sovinterfest.

• 4390 • **Moscow International Film Festival**

To provide recognition for the best full-length feature films (only full-length films admitted). The following prizes are awarded: (1) Grand Prize - for the best feature film, awarded statuette of St. George; (2) Special Prize of the Jury; (3) Best actor; (4) Best actress; (5) Best director's work; and (6) special prize for the best film to the director. Awarded annually. Established in 1959.

• 4391 •
International Tchaikovsky Competition
ul. Neglinnaya 15
103051 Moscow, Russia
Phone: 7 95 9259649
Fax: 7 95 2889588
Home Page: http://www.tchaikovsky-competition.ru

• 4392 • **International Tchaikovsky Competition**

To recognize the best pianists, violinists, cellists, and vocalists of the Competition. Prizes are also awarded for meritorious performances of Tchaikovsky's music. Instrumentalists who are between 18 and 32 years of age and singers between 18 and 34 years of age are eligible. The Organizing Committee of the International Tchaikovsky Competition offers eight prizes and four certificates to pianists; eight prizes and four certificates to violinists; eight prizes and four certificates to cellists; six prizes and two certificates to female singers, and six prizes and two certificates to male singers. The following monetary awards are presented: (1) First Prize - 5,000 rubles and a Gold Medal; (2) Second Prize - 4,000 rubles and a Silver Medal; (3) Third Prize - 3,000 rubles and a Bronze Medal; (4) Fourth Prize - 2,400 rubles and an honorary badge; (5) Fifth Prize - 2,000 rubles and an honorary badge; (6) Sixth Prize 1,600 rubles and an honorary badge; (7) Seventh Prize - 1,200 rubles and an honorary badge; and (8) Eighth Prize - 800 rubles and an honorary badge. The recipients of certificates receive a prize of 250 rubles each. A prize of 250 rubles is also awarded in each group to the best performer of obligatory work by a Soviet composer. In the solo voice group, a prize is also awarded for the best performance of compositions by M. Mussorgsky. The first three laureates are engaged in concert tours in the USSR. The Competition is held every four years. Established in 1958.

• 4393 •
Russian Academy of Sciences
Leninskii ave. 14
GSP 1
119991 Moscow, Russia
Phone: 7 95 938 0309
Fax: 7 95 938 1844
E-mail: info@pran.ru
Home Page: http://www.ras.ru

• 4394 • **Lomonosov Gold Medal**

For recognition of outstanding works in the natural, physical, and social sciences. Two gold medals with the profile of the Russian scientist, M.V. Lomonosov, are awarded annually: one to a Soviet scientist; and one to a foreign scholar. Established in 1956 by the Council of Ministers of the USSR. First awarded in 1959.

• 4395 • **L. A. Spendiarov International Geological Prize**

For recognition of advanced scientific research, and to strengthen international cooperation in the field of geosciences. Citizens of the country which is the organizer of the International Geological Congress at which the prize is awarded are eligible. A monetary prize and a diploma are awarded every four years. Established in 1897 by A. Spendiarov, in memory of his son, Leonid A. Spendiarov, who perished during a geological excursion at the 7th IGC in St. Petersburg.

• 4396 •
Russian Academy of Sciences
Section of Social Science
Leninskii ave. 14
GSP 1
GSP-1
V-71
119991 Moscow, Russia
Phone: 7 95 938 0309
Fax: 7 95 938 1844
E-mail: info@pran.ru
Home Page: http://www.ras.ru

• 4397 • **Alexander Sergeovich Pushkin Prize**
To recognize Soviet scientists for outstanding work in the Russian language and literature. A monetary prize of 2,000 rubles is awarded triennially. Established in 1969 by the Council of Ministers. Administered by the Division of Literature and Language.

St. Lucia

• 4398 •
Saint Lucia Tourist Board
Mr. Kirby Allian, Contact
PO Box 221
Vide Bouteille
Castries, St. Lucia
Phone: 758452-4094
Phone: 758452-5978
Fax: 758453-1121
E-mail: kallain@stlucia.org
Home Page: http://www.stlucia.org

• 4399 • **Sent Lisi Par Excellence Awards**
Recognizes significant contribution to the development of the tourism industry. Tourism industry professionals are eligible. Awarded annually.

Saudi Arabia BANKISLAMI JEDDAH

• 4400 •
Islamic Development Bank
Dr. Abderrahim Omrana, Bank Sec./Dir.
PO Box 5925
Jeddah 21432, Saudi Arabia
Phone: 966 2 6361400
Fax: 966 2 6366871
E-mail: idbarchives@isdb.org
Home Page: http://www.isdb.org

• 4401 • **Islamic Development Bank Prizes in Islamic Economics and Islamic Banking**
To recognize, reward, and encourage creative efforts of outstanding merit in the fields of Islamic economics and Islamic banking. Such efforts may take the form of research, teaching, training, mobilization of intellectual and scientific capabilities that would contribute to the promotion of Islamic values in economics and banking, or any other related activity. Individuals, universities, academic, financial, and Islamic institutions throughout the world may nominate whoever they deem eligible. One prize is awarded annually, alternating between Islamic economics and Islamic banking. A monetary award of 30,000 Islamic dinars (equivalent to US $42,250 approximately) and a citation are awarded for each. Established in 1986.

• 4402 •
King Faisal Foundation
(Al Amanah Al Ammah Li Jaezat Al Malik Faisal Al Alamiyyah)
Prince Khalid Al-Faisal, Dir.Gen.
PO Box 352
Riyadh
Riyadh 11411, Saudi Arabia
Phone: 966 1 465 2255
Fax: 966 1 465 6524
E-mail: info@kff.com
Home Page: http://www.kff.com

• 4403 • **King Faisal International Prize for Arabic Language and Literature**
(Jaezat Al Malik Faisal Al Alamiyyah Lil Adab Al Arabi)
To provide recognition for achievement in the field of Arabic literature, and to encourage studies and creativity in this field. Individuals may be nominated by universities, academies, educational institutions, and research centers throughout the world. A monetary award of U.S. $200,000 a certificate, and a gold medal are awarded annually in a special official ceremony. Established in 1977, and first awarded in 1980 in memory of King Faisal Ibn Abdul Azia al-Saud, former King of Saudi Arabia.

• 4404 • **King Faisal International Prize for Islamic Studies**
(Jaezat Al Malik Faisal Al Alamiyyah Lil Derasat Al Islamiyyah)
To recognize individuals for scientific activities in the field of Islamic Studies. Scholars may be nominated by universities, academies, educational institutions, and research centers throughout the world. A monetary award of U.S. $200,000, a certificate, and a gold medal are awarded annually in a special official ceremony. Established in 1977, and first awarded in 1979 in memory of the late King Faisal Ibn Abdul Azia al-Saud, former King of Saudi Arabia.

• 4405 • **King Faisal International Prize for the Service of Islam**
(Jaezat Al Malik Faisal Al Alamiyyah Li Khidmt Al Islam)
To recognize individuals who have performed exceptional services for the benefit of Islam and Muslims. Individuals may be nominated by Islamic organizations, societies, and unions from all parts of the world. A monetary award of U.S. $200,000, a certificate, and a gold medal are awarded annually in a special official ceremony. Established in 1977, and first awarded in 1979 in memory of King Faisal Ibn Abdul Azia al-Saud, former King of Saudi Arabia.

• 4406 • **King Faisal International Prize in Medicine**
(Jaezat Al Malik Faisal Al Alamiyyah Lil Tib)
To recognize individuals for a published work in the field of medicine leading to the benefit of mankind and the enrichment of human thought. Individuals may be nominated by universities, academies, educational institutions, and research centers throughout the world. A monetary award of U.S. $200,000, a certificate, and a gold medal are awarded annually in a special official ceremony. Established in 1980, and first awarded in 1982 in memory of King Faisal Ibn Abdul Azia al-Saud, former King of Saudi Arabia.

• 4407 • **King Faisal International Prize in Science**
(Jaezat Al Malik Faisal Al Alamiyyah Lil Ulum)
To recognize individuals for a published work in the field of science leading to the benefit of mankind and the enrichment of human thought. Individuals may be nominated by universities, academies, educational institutions, and research centers throughout the world. The deadline for submissions is September 1. A monetary award of U.S. $200,000, a certificate, and a gold medal are awarded annually in a special official ceremony. Established in 1976, and first awarded in 1983 in memory of King King Faisal ibn Abd Al Aziz, former King of Saudi Arabia.

• 4408 •
Organization of Islamic Capitals and Cities
Omar Abdullah Kadi, Sec.Gen.
PO Box 13621
Jeddah 21414, Saudi Arabia
Phone: 966 2 69821414
Fax: 966 2 6981053
E-mail: secrtriat@oicc.org
Home Page: http://www.oicc.org

Formerly: (1984) Islamic Capitals Organization.

• 4409 • **Organization of Islamic Capitals and Cities Awards**
To recognize outstanding achievements in the domains of writing, accomplishments, translation, and projects in the fields of architecture, urban planning, environment, services, organization, and municipal legislation. They aim at encouraging municipalities and local authorities and individuals to contribute effectively to the achievement of sustainable urban development and the preservation of the heritage and the identity of Islamic cities. Prizes are awarded every three years.

Senegal

• 4410 •
Hope Unlimited
(Espoir Sans Frontieres)
Etienne Sokeng, Pres.
BP 12241
Sicap Sacre Coeur I No. 8250
Dakar, Senegal
Phone: 221 8256699
Fax: 221 8256699

Awards are arranged in alphabetical order below their administering organizations

• 4411 • **Certificate of Satisfaction**
Award if recognition for donators and active members. Presented annually.

Serbia

• 4412 •
International Jeunesses Musicales Competition
(Muzicka Omaladina Srbije)
Terazije 26/II
YU-11000 Belgrade, Serbia
Phone: 381 11 686 380
Fax: 381 11 3610 596
E-mail: ijmcbyu@music-competition.co.yu
Home Page: http://www.music-competition.co.yu

• 4413 • **International Jeunesses Musicales Competition - Belgrade (Concours International des Jeunesses Musicales - Belgrade)**
For recognition of outstanding performance in the field of music. The categories change annually, rotating between solo voice; piano and piano trio; violincello and guitar; and violin and string quartet. Performers and composers under the age of 30 are eligible; for singers and chamber ensembles, no performer should be over the age of 35. Three cash prizes are awarded in each category; several special prizes are also awarded. Held annually. Established in 1969.

Singapore

• 4414 •
Association of Accredited Advertising Agents Singapore
No. 06-04 Dapense Bldg.
158 Cecil St.
Singapore, Singapore
Phone: 65 68360600
E-mail: info@4as.org.sg
Home Page: http://www.4as.org.sg

• 4415 • **Creative Excellence in Business Advertising Awards**
These awards, known as the CEBA Awards, are given to recognize the best business-to-business advertising campaigns. Winners in each category receive Tiffany trophies, with the Best of Show receiving a cash prize of $25,000. Awarded annually. Established in 1996.

• 4416 • **William D. Littleford Award for Corporate Community Service**
To recognize companies, organizations, or individuals that are involved in active community service programs aimed at alleviating critical social problems. Awarded annually.

• 4417 • **Timothy White Award**
To recognize a business-to-business editor who serves as the consciencew of the industry he or she serves, and fearlessly supports important industry causes in writing, speeches, and personal interactions. Awarded annually. Established in honor of the late *Billboard* editor, Timothy White.

• 4418 •
Association of Small and Medium Enterprises
Gary Law, Exec. Dir.
167 Jalan Bukit Merah
Tower 4, 03-13
Singapore 150167, Singapore
Phone: 65 65130388
Fax: 65 65130399
E-mail: sme@asme.org.sg
Home Page: http://www.asme.org.sg

• 4419 • **Entrepreneur of the Year Award**
For business professionals who have exhibited outstanding performance in entrepreneurship.

• 4420 • **Singapore Promising Brand Award**
For enterprises that performed outstandingly in building and communicating their brand names.

• 4421 • **Woman Entrepreneur of the Year Award**
For successful women entrepreneurs.

• 4422 •
National Book Development Council of Singapore
Li Kok Lim, Chm.
Natl. Library Board
50 Geylang E Ave., 1
Singapore 389777, Singapore
Phone: 65 68488290
Fax: 65 67429466
E-mail: info@bookcouncil.sg
Home Page: http://www.bookcouncil.sg

• 4423 • **Book Awards of the National Book Development Council of Singapore**
To develop local literary talent in the field of creative and noncreative writing in any of the four official languages (Malay, English, Chinese, and Tamil), and to stimulate public interest in and support for local literary achievements. Works published during the two years preceding the award year are eligible. The awards are given in five categories: fiction, poetry, nonfiction, children's and young people's books, and drama. Only first editions of original books by Singapore citizens or permanent residents published locally or abroad are eligible. An author who has received a National Book Development Council of Singapore Book Award is eligible for the same award again, upon the unanimous vote of the panel of judges. Translations, edited works, treatises, or research works written for a university degree or examination are not eligible. Works by any serving members of the National Book Development Council of Singapore are not eligible. As many as 20 monetary prizes of 2,000 Singapore dollars and a souvenir are awarded biennially at a separate ceremony. Established in 1976. Since 1996, Times Publishing Group sponsors the fiction and children's and young people's books in English, Singapore Press Holding sponsors the nonfiction category in English, and Lee Foundation Singapore sponsors the fiction and children's and young people's books in Chinese.

• 4424 • **Singapore Literature Prize**
To provide incentives and public support for creative writing and the development of Singapore literature in English. To discover and encourage new writing talents as well as to support the continued commitment to writing by already published writers. Held annually for unpublished works. The prize are S$10,000, a trophy and a souvenir for the Singapore Literature prize; S$5,000 and a souvenir for the Merit prize; S$1,000 and a souvenir for the Commendation prize. Established in 1991. Sponsored by SNP Corporation.

• 4425 •
Singapore Computer Society
Lee Kwok Cheong, Pres.
53/53A Neil Rd.
Singapore 088891, Singapore
Phone: 65 6 2262567
Fax: 65 6 2262569
E-mail: scs.secretariat@scs.org.sg
Home Page: http://www.scs.org.sg

• 4426 • **Friend of IT**
For a non IT professional who has championed the innovative and broad use of IT for the benefit of the industry or a community.

• 4427 • **Person of the Year**
For an individual who has made outstanding contributions to IT industry in Singapore.

• 4428 • **Young Professional of the Year**
For an individual who has made notable contributions to IT industry.

• 4429 •
Singapore Exhibition Services Pte. Ltd.
Goldbell Towers, 11th Fl.
47 Scotts Rd.
Singapore 228233, Singapore
Phone: 65 6738 6776
Fax: 65 6732 6776
E-mail: events@sesallworld.com
Home Page: http://www.sesallworld.com

• 4430 • **FHA Culinary Challenge**
To recognize outstanding culinary ability. The following competition components are featured: (1) Battle for the Lion; (2) National Team Challenge comprised of the Best National Dessert Award, Best National Cold Display, Best National Hot Cooking Award, Kimberly Clark Award for Best Hygiene Practices, and the Best National Team Award; (3) Gourmet Team Challenge; (4) Dream Team Challenge; and (5) Individual Challenge - competitions in a series of categories, both practical and display. Held biennially in even-numbered years. Formerly known as Salon Culinaire. Formerly: (2006) FHA International Salon Culnaire.

• 4431 •
Singapore Industrial Automation Association
Elizabeth Chin, Exec.Dir.
71 Ubi Crescent, No. 06-06
Excalibur Centre
Singapore 408571, Singapore
Phone: 65 67491822
Fax: 65 68413986
E-mail: secretariat@siaa.org
Home Page: http://www.esiaa.com

• 4432 • **Industrial Automation Award**
Awarded annually to recognize innovative system integrators.

• 4433 •
Singapore National Committee of the International Water Association
Prof. S.L. Ong, Pres.
Div. of Environmental Science and Engineering
Natl. Univ. of Singapore
10 Kent Ridge Crescent
Kent Ridge
Singapore 119260, Singapore
Phone: 65 68742890
Fax: 65 67744202
E-mail: eseongsl@nus.edu.sg
Home Page: http://www.iawq.org.uk

• 4434 • **Honorary Member**
Recognizes outstanding contribution in the field of environmental engineering. Awarded periodically to one or more recipients.

• 4435 •
World Organization of Family Doctors
Dr. Alfred W.T. Loh, CEO
Coll. of Medicine Bldg.
16 Coll. Rd. 01-02
Singapore 169854, Singapore
Phone: 65 62242886
Fax: 65 63242029
E-mail: admin@wonca.com.sg
Home Page: http://www.globalfamilydoctor.com

• 4436 • **WONCA Foundation Award**
To foster and maintain high standards of care in general practice/family medicine by enabling physicians to travel to appropriate countries to instruct in general practice/family medicine, and appropriate physicians from developing countries to spend time in areas where they may develop special skills and knowledge in general practice/family medicine. Awarded triennially at the world conference. Established by a donation from the Royal College of General Practitioners.

Slovakia

• 4437 •
Bibiana, International House of Art for Children
(Bibiana, Medzinarodny dom umenia pre deti)
Panska 41
815 39 Bratislava, Slovakia
Phone: 421 2 5443 1308
Fax: 421 2 5443 4986
E-mail: bibiana@bibiana.sk
Home Page: http://www.bibiana.sk

• 4438 • **The Most Beautiful and the Best Children's Books in Slovakia**
(Najkrajsia a najlepsia detska kniha jari, leta, jesene a zimy na Slovensku)
To recognize Slovak publishing companies for the most artistically valuable books produced for children and youth. A plaque is awarded each spring, summer, autumn, and winter. Established in 1990.

• 4439 •
Ekotopfilm: International Festival of Professional Films
(Mezinarodni festival filmu a televiznich poradu o zivotnim prostredi Ekofilm)
Zadunajska cesta 12
851 01 Bratislava 1, Slovakia
Phone: 421 2 6353 0336
Fax: 421 2 6353 0333
E-mail: ekotopfilm@ekotopfilm.sk
Home Page: http://www.ekotopfilm.sk

• 4440 • **Ekotopfilm Festival**
To recognize technological and economic integration of evolution along with sustaining the ecological balance in nature of professional films, television, and video programs. Accepted titles are submitted to the contest are evaluated by the International Jury. The Grand Prize is awarded in addition to six top prizes in six categories, an International Jury Prize, the Prize of the Festival Director, and prizes for artistic creativity. Held annually. Established in 1974.

• 4441 •
Ministry of Culture of the Slovak Republic
(Slovakia Ministerstvo Kultury Slovenskej Republik)
Nora Slovakova, Contact
Nam. SNP No. 33
813 31 Bratislava, Slovakia
Phone: 421 2 59391 155
Fax: 421 2 59391 174
E-mail: mksr@culture.gov.sk
Home Page: http://www.culture.gov.sk

• 4442 • **International Biennial of Illustrations Bratislava**
For recognition of the best illustrations in children's books. Illustrations which have won national or international awards, and those which have not yet received any prizes are eligible. The following prizes are awarded: (1) Grand Prix - a trophy and 35,000 Czechoslovak crowns; (2) five Golden Apples and 15,000 Czechoslovak crowns each; (3) ten plaques and 5,000 Czechoslovak crowns each; and (4) four honorary diplomas. Awarded biennially.

• 4443 •
Music Centre Slovakia
Michalska 10
815 36 Bratislava, Slovakia
Phone: 421 2 5290 4811
Fax: 421 2 5443 0379
E-mail: hc@hc.sk
Home Page: http://www.slovkoncert.sk

Formerly: Slovkoncert, Czechoslovakia Artists Agency; NMC-Slovkoncert, Slovak Artist Management.

• 4444 • **International Rostrum of Young Performers/UNESCO**
(Medzinarodna tribuna mladych interpretov/UNESCO)
To promote outstanding young artists by helping them gain access to the concert or operatic stage at the beginning of their artistic careers. The IRP is divided into Concert Rostrum for instrumentalists and concert singers. Candidates under the age of 30 who are nominated by a radio corporation must submit sound recordings. On the basis of the audition of the sound recording, 12 young soloists and chamber ensembles are selected. A diploma, a plaque, and the distribution of recording and publicity material through the International Music Council and UNESCO, Paris, are presented biennially. Winners of the prizes are given the title, Laureate. Established in 1969 by the International Music Council. Sponsored by UNESCO. Additional information is available from International Music Council Paris, Guy Hout, Executive Secretary, 1 rue Miollis, 75 732 Paris, France, or Dr. Izabela Pazitkova, Hd. of Bratislava Music Festival Secretariat, coordinator IRP/TIJI/, Michalska 10, 815 36 Bratislava, SR.

• 4445 •
Slovak Physical Society
(Slovenska Fyzikalna Spolocnost)
Dalibor Krupa, Sec.
Slovak Academy of Sciences
Dubravska cesta 9
SK-845 27 Bratislava, Slovakia
Phone: 421 2 59410514
Phone: 421 2 59410514
Fax: 421 2 54776085
E-mail: sfs@savba.sk
Home Page: http://sfs.savba.sk

• 4446 • **Competition of Scientific Papers of Young Physicists**
For research in physics.

• 4447 • **Honorable Member**
For promotion of physics and Slovak Physical Society.

• 4448 • **Slovak Physical Society Award**
For scientific contribution to physics in fundamental and applied research.

Awards are arranged in alphabetical order below their administering organizations

• 4449 • Slovak Physical Society Medal

For general contribution to physics in Slovakia.

• 4450 • Young Physics Students Competition

For outstanding young physics students.

• 4451 •
Slovak Television
(Slovenska televizia, Bratislava)
Mlynska dolina
845 45 Bratislava, Slovakia
Phone: 421 2 6061 1111
Fax: 421 2 6061 4192
E-mail: prixdanube@stv.sk
Home Page: http://www.stv.sk

• 4452 • Prix Danube Festival, Bratislava

To encourage quality television production for children and youth. The Festival takes place under the motto: "In furtherance of a progressive relationship of children and youth to life". The competition is divided into five categories: documentary and informative programs; magazine programs; fiction programs; animated programs; and independent producers. Each participating television organization may enter the competition in the first four categories with independent entries, or individual parts of a serial, the total duration of which must not exceed 120 minutes. Independent producers may enter their own category. It is possible to submit several entries in one category. Only original television programs produced during the preceding two years and telecast in the respective country are eligible for entry. The official languages of the Festival are Slovak, English, French, and German. Entry forms must be submitted by May 15. Two tapes must be received by June 1. Personal entry forms of the participants must be received by August 15. The following awards are presented: Danube Prize - the main prize awarded in each category by the two international juries; Honorable Mention - awarded in each category for outstanding individual achievements of the creators of the program or for the program itself; Critics Prize - by the International Jury of Journalists; CIFEJ Prize - Centre International des Films pour Enfants et Jeunesse; Prize of the Mayor of the Bratislava City - by the Jury of Independent Producers; Prize of Janko Hrasko - by the Children's Jury; and the Prize of USTT and Literary Fund - by the Jury of the Union of Slovak Television Artists. The entries that have not been selected for the competition will be presented in the non-competitive informative section Videokiosk. The Festival is organized under the patronage of the President of the National Counsil of the Slovak Republic, and occurs biennially. Established in 1971.

Slovenia

• 4453 •
European Society for Noninvasive Cardiovascular Dynamics
Dr. Susara Juznic DSc, Sec.-Treas.
Institute of Physiology
Faculty of Medicine
Zaloska 4
SLO-1100 Ljubljana, Slovenia
Phone: 386 1 5437500
Phone: 386 1 4259404
Fax: 386 1 5437501
E-mail: esnicvd@mf.uni-lj.si
Home Page: http://animus.mf.uni-lj.si/~esnicvd

Formerly: (1978) European Society for Ballistocardiography and Cardiovascular Dynamics.

• 4454 • Burger Award

To recognize scientists who have contributed to important and generally accepted progress in the field of noninvasive cardiography. Selection is by nomination. A medal is awarded approximately every five years at a meeting of the Society. Established in 1975 in honor of Professor H. C. Burger, the founder of medical physics in the Netherlands.

• 4455 • Young Scientist Award in Noninvasive Cardiovascular Dynamics

To recognize young scientists who have contributed to noninvasive cardiovascular dynamics. Individuals under 35 years of age may be nominated. A certificate is awarded every five years at a meeting of the Society. Established in 1991.

• 4456 •
International Centre of Graphic Arts
(Mednarodni Graficni Likovni Center)
Lili Sturm, Contact
Pod turnom 3
SLO-1000 Ljubljana, Slovenia
Phone: 386 1 241 3800
Fax: 386 1 241 3821
E-mail: lili.sturm@mglc-lj.si
Home Page: http://www.mglc-lj.si

• 4457 • International Biennial of Graphic Art
(Biennale Internationale de Gravure)

For recognition of achievement in the field of graphic art. Both black-and-white and color reproductive printmaking techniques (monotype excluded) are taken into consideration, regardless of style and technical execution. Medals are awarded for the Grand Prix and for second and third prizes. The Grand Prix d'Honneur (Grand Prize of Honor) is given to artists who prove their constant high level during the years of participating in the biennial. Held in odd-numbered years. Established in 1955.

• 4458 •
Olympic Committee of Slovenia
(Olimpijski komite slovenije)
Tone Jagodic, Sec. Gen.
Celovska 25
SLO-1000 Ljubljana, Slovenia
Phone: 386 1 2306000
Phone: 386 1 2306027
Fax: 386 1 2306000
E-mail: info@olympic.si
Home Page: http://www.olympic.si

• 4459 • Honorary Members of NOC of Slovenia

• 4460 • Letter of Merit

• 4461 • Olympic Torch

• 4462 •
Slovene Writers' Association
(Drustvo Slovenskih Pisateljev)
Tomsiceva 12
1001 Ljubljana, Slovenia
Phone: 386 1 251 4144
Fax: 386 1 421 6430
E-mail: dsp@drustvo-dsp.si
Home Page: http://www.drustvo-dsp.si

• 4463 • Vilenica International Literary Prize

To recognize exceptional artistic achievements in poetry, fiction, drama and essay writing. Central European authors are eligible to compete for the award, which is bestowed as part of the Vilenica International Literary Festival. A monetary award is presented annually in September. Two other awards are presented at the festival: the Crystal Vilenica and the Young Vilenica awards. Established in 1986.

• 4464 •
Slovenian Pharmaceutical Society
(Pharmaceutical Society of Slovenia)
Jelka Dolinar, Sec.Gen.
Dunajska 184a
SLO-1000 Ljubljana, Slovenia
Phone: 386 1 569 2601
Fax: 386 1 569 2602
E-mail: jelk.dolinar@sfd.si
Home Page: http://www.farmacevtsko-drustvo.si

• 4465 • Minarikovo Odlicje
(Award of Minarik)

For recognition of achievement in the field of pharmacy. A plaque and trophy are awarded annually. Established in 1975 in honor of Franc Minarik, a world famous person in the history of pharmacy.

• 4466 •
Union of Associations of Slovene Librarians
(Zveza Bibliotekarskih Drustev Slovenije)
Dr. Melita Ambrozic, Pres.
Turjaska 1
SL-1000 Ljubljana, Slovenia
Phone: 386 1 2001193
Phone: 386 1 5861309
Fax: 386 1 4257293
E-mail: zveza-biblio.ds-nuk@quest.arnes.si
Home Page: http://www.zbds-zveza.si

• 4467 • **Copova Diploma**
For recognition of an outstanding contribution in the field of libraries. Members of the Association are eligible. A plaque and a diploma are awarded annually. Established in 1967 in honor of Matija Cop (1797-1835), Slovenian librarian.

• 4468 • **Pavle Kalan Fund Award**
To recognize the best written text in the field of library information systems. A biennial award and grant established in 1974 in honor of Pavle Kalan (1900-1974), Slovenian librarian.

• 4469 • **Stepinsnki Fund Award**
Award that encourages the development and professional work in the field of mobile librarianship. Awarded to main libraries for a specific professional achievement. Established in honor of the first Slovene librarian, Lovro Stepisnik (1834-1912).

Spain

• 4470 •
Asamblea de Directores-Realizadores Cinematograficos y Audiovisuales Espanoles (ADIRCAE)
San Lorenzo 11
E-28004 Madrid, Spain
Phone: 34 91 319 6844
Fax: 34 91 319 6844
Home Page: http://asambleadedirectoresyrealizadorescinematograf.visualnet.com

• 4471 • **ADIRCAE Prizes**
(Premios ADIRCAE)
For recognition of outstanding contributions to film and television. Awards are given for directing and acting. Members are eligible. Trophies are awarded annually. Established in 1985.

• 4472 •
Ayuntamiento de Benicasim
C/Medico Segarra 4
E-12560 Benicasim (Castello), Spain
Phone: 34 9643 00962
Fax: 34 9630 3432
E-mail: secretaria@benicassim.org
Home Page: http://www.benicassim.org

• 4473 • **Francisco Tarrega International Guitar Competition**
(Certamen Internacional de Guitarra Francisco Tarrega)
To promote the interpretation of works for guitar, especially those of Francisco Tarrega by concert guitar players. Guitarists who are 32 years of age or under may enter. Awarded annually. Established in 1966 in honor of the guitarist, Francisco Tarrega.

• 4474 •
Bioelectrochemical Society
Prof. Miguel A. De La Rosa, Contact
Department of Biochemistry
Faculty of Biology
Apartado 1095
E-41080 Seville, Spain
Phone: 34 95 4489506
Fax: 34 95 4460065
E-mail: marosa@cica.es
Home Page: http://www.bes-online.usf.edu

• 4475 • **Luigi Galvani Prize**
To recognize young scientists who have documented an outstanding contribution to biochemistry or bioenergetics. Eligible candidates must have achieved a PhD and must be younger than 35 years of age. A monetary prize of 1,000 euros, a citation, and an invitation to present a lecture are awarded biennially.

• 4476 •
Canarias Mediafest - International Canary Islands Video and Multimedia Festival
(Festival Internacional de Video de Canarias)
Centro Cultural Ciudad Alta.
C/ Cadiz 34
E-35012 Las Palmas de Gran Canaria, Spain
Phone: 34 928 250587
Fax: 34 928 254629
E-mail: audiovisuales@grancanaria.com
Home Page: http://www.canariasmediafest.org

• 4477 • **Mediafest, the Gran Canaria International Festival of Arts and Digital Cultures**
(Festival Internacional de Video de Canarias)
Awards are given in seven categories: Video art; Digital art for multimedia or Internet; Experimental or artistic documentary; 2D or 3D animation; Produced multimedia, multi-channel, or performance installation; New audiovisual creation formats for mobile platforms; Media art project for creators under the age of 30. Held biennially in even-numbered years. Established in 1988.

• 4478 •
Editorial Planeta SA
Diagonal, 662-664
E-08034 Barcelona, Spain
Phone: 34 93 2285800
Fax: 34 93 2177140
Home Page: http://www.editorial.planeta.es

• 4479 • **Azorin Prize**
To recognize a novel written in Spanish. Awarded annually. Established in 1994.

• 4480 • **Premi de les Lletres Catalanes Ramon Llull**
To recognize an author of any nationality for an outstanding novel of at least 200 pages, written in Catalonian Spanish, and to promote the production of novels in Catalonian Spanish. A monetary prize is awarded annually. Established in 1968, and re-established in 1980.

• 4481 • **Premi Josep Pla**
To recognize prose works in any of the genres. Awarded annually. Established in 1969.

• 4482 • **Premio Apel-les Mestres**
To recognize creative work performed in the field of illustrated books. Established in 1980.

• 4483 • **Premio Biblioteca Breve**
To recognize the creators of the new narrative and consolidated aesthetic criteria which today still influences our way of understanding reading and its personal emotions. Awarded annually. Established in 1998.

• 4484 • **Premio de Novela Fernando Lara**
Annual award of recognition. Established by the Jose Manuel Lara Foundation and Editorial Planeta in 1996. Named in honor of the youngest son of Jose Manuel Lara Hernandez.

• 4485 • **Premio Espasa Ensayo**
To recognize the Spanish authors who have written works which offer an in-depth, critical view of subjects of interest in our society. Awarded annually.

• 4486 • **Premio Espiritualidad**
To promote the creation and diffusion of those works which foster the search for inner knowledge, the concerns and the deepest values of the human being, recreating a transcendental dimension in everyday reality. Awarded annually. Established in 1999.

• 4487 • **Premio Nadal**
For novels written in Spanish. Awarded annually.

• 4488 • **Premio Planeta de Novela**
(Premio Planeta de Novela)
For recognition of the best unpublished novel. Writers of Spanish speaking countries who write in Castillian Spanish are eligible. The prize must be awarded each year. Established in 1952 by Jose Manuel Lara Hernandez, director of Editorial Planeta.

• 4489 • **Premio Primavera de Novela**
To recognize a Spanish novel. A monetary prize is awarded annually; the work is also published in the Espasa Narrativa collection.

• 4490 •
European Society for Cognitive Psychology
Maria Teresa Bajo, Pres.
Dep. de Psicologia Exp.
Universidad de Granada
Campus Univers. de Cartuja
18011 Granada, Spain
E-mail: mbajo@ugr.es
Home Page: http://www.escop.org

• 4491 • **Paul Bertelson Award**
To honor scientists at a relatively early stage of their scientific career who have made an outstanding contribution to European Cognitive Psychology. Candidates should normally have completed their doctoral thesis no more than 8 years before nomination, and be under 35 years of age. However, the committee does not wish to discriminate against researchers who have, for example, taken maternity leave or made career switches. Awarded annually.

• 4492 •
Festival de Cine de Alcala de Henares
Laura Olaizola, Contact
34 Plaza del Empecinado 1
E-28801 Alcala de Henares, Spain
Phone: 34 91 879 7380
Fax: 34 91 879 7381
E-mail: festival@alcine.org
Home Page: http://www.alcine.org

• 4493 • **Festival de Cine de Alcala de Henares**
For recognition of outstanding short films. The Comunidad de Madrid Prize, as well as a first prize, second prize, third prize, and the honorable mention, Pantalla Abierta Award, are awarded. The Certamen Nacional de Cortomrtrajes Award is also given.

• 4494 •
Film Festival of Huesca
(Certamen Internacional de Films Cortos, Ciudad de Huesca)
Jose Maria Escriche, Pres.
Avda. Parque 1, no. 2
E-22002 Huesca, Spain
Phone: 34 974 212582
Fax: 34 974 210065
E-mail: info@huesca-filmfestival.com
Home Page: http://www.huesca-filmfestival.com

• 4495 • **Huesca International Short Film Contest**
(Certamen International de Films Cortos, Ciudad de Huesca)
To promote the diffusion of short films in Spain. Any Spanish foreign short film accepted by the Selection Committee can take part in the Contest. Although there are no restrictions in the choice of theme, those that deal exclusively with tourism or publicity cannot be presented. The following prizes are awarded annually: Prix Ciudad de Huesca, Golden Danzante - to the most outstanding film; Silver Danzante; Bronze Danzante; Premio Cacho Pallero - to the best Iberoamerican short film; Premio Jinete Iberico; and Premio "Casa De America".

• 4496 •
Fundacion Principe de Asturias
Jose Ramon Alvarez, Pres.
General Yague, 2
Principado de Asturias
E-33004 Oviedo, Spain
Phone: 34 985 258755
Fax: 34 985 242104
E-mail: info@fpa.es
Home Page: http://www.fundacionprincipedeasturias.org

• 4497 • **Prince of Asturias Awards (Premios Principe de Asturias)**
For recognition of scientific, technical, cultural, social, and humanistic work performed by individuals, groups, or institutions worldwide. The following awards are given: (1) Prince of Asturias Award for Communications and Humanities; (2) Prince of Asturias Award for the Arts; (3) Prince of Asturias Award for Letters; (4) Prince of Asturias Award for Social Sciences; (5) Prince of Asturias Award for Technical and Scientific Research; (6) Prince of Asturias Award for Sports; (7) Prince of Asturias Award for International Cooperation; and (8) Prince of Asturias Award for Concord. A monetary prize and a sculpture by Joan Miro are awarded annually to each winner. All the prizes are presented by His Royal Highness The Prince of Asturias in a solemn academic act held in Ovedio. Established in 1981.

• 4498 •
Gijon International Film Festival
(Festival Internacional de Cine para la Juventud de Gijon)
Alvarez Garaya 2, 6 planta
PO Box 76
E-33201 Gijon, Spain
Phone: 34 985 182 940
Fax: 34 985 182 944
E-mail: info@gijonfilmfestival.com
Home Page: http://www.gijonfilmfestival.com
Formerly: (1986) Certamen Internacional de Cine para la Infancia y la Juventud de Gijon.

• 4499 • **Gijon International Film Festival for Young People**
(Festival Internacional de Cine para la Juventud de Gijon)
For recognition of the best full-length and short films for young people. Films may be entered by countries, organizations, and individuals that are specially adapted to young people. Long or short films in 35mm and 16mm made during the preceding year may be submitted by September 15. Exhibitors must submit their films in Spanish, French, or English, or subtitled in any one of these three languages. Worldwide producers and distributors are invited to select one or several films to participate. Awarded annually. Established in 1962.

• 4500 •
Grupo Prisa: Promotora de Informaciones SA
Gran via 32
E-28013 Madrid, Spain
Phone: 34 91 330 1000
Fax: 34 91 330 1088
E-mail: digital@elpais.es
Home Page: http://www.prisa.es

• 4501 • **Ortega y Gasset Awards for Journalism**
For recognition of outstanding articles that have appeared in a Spanish-language newspaper or magazine in any country during the previous year. Particular attention is given to investigative reporting, journalistic innovation, and the development of new professional techniques. A monetary prize if 15,000 euros and a sculpture by Eduardo Chillida are awarded annually. Established in 1983 in honor of Jose Ortega y Gasset, Spanish philosopher and journalist.

• 4502 •
Iberoamerican Film Festival - Huelva
(Festival Internacional de Cine Iberoamericano de Huelva)
Alberto Maeso, Press Off.
Casa Colon
Plaza del Punto, s/n
E-21003 Huelva, Spain
Phone: 34 959 210299
Fax: 34 959 210173
E-mail: festival@festicinehuelva.com
Home Page: http://www.festicinehuelva.com

• 4503 • **Iberoamerican Film Festival (Festival Internacional de Cine Iberoamericano)**
For recognition of outstanding films from Latin America and the Spanish peninsula. Held annually. Established in 1975.

• 4504 •
International Association of Hydraulic Engineering and Research
Dr. Christopher B. George, Exec.Dir.
Paseo Bajo Virgen del Puerto, 3
28005 Madrid, Spain
Phone: 34 91 3357908
Phone: 34 91 3357919
Fax: 34 91 3357935
E-mail: iahr@iahr.org
Home Page: http://www.iahr.org

• 4505 • **Honorary Member**
For recognition of individuals who have made outstanding contributions to hydraulic research. Awarded biennially during IAHR Biennial Congresses.

• 4506 • **IAHR-APD Award**
To encourage the presentation of research results on hydraulics and water resources at the biennial regional congresses of the Asian and Pacific Regional Division (APD) of IAHR. The awards are conferred to the authors of the two

Awards are arranged in alphabetical order below their administering organizations

papers judged as the most outstanding presented during the APD Congress. One award is given to the author of the best paper from the host country and the other to the author from outside the host country. A bronze plaque and certificate are awarded biennially. Established in 1983.

• 4507 • **IAHR Lecturer Award**

To provide an institute of research or higher learning with an IAHR lecturer. The lecturer is appointed by the Secretary-General. Individuals may apply by August 31. The award consists of a maximum of US$2,500 travel allowance, an honorarium of US$2,500, and a certificate. Awarded annually. Established in 1985.

• 4508 • **Arthur Thomas Ippen Award**

To recognize a member of IAHR who has developed an outstanding record of accomplishment as demonstrated by research, publications, and/or conception and design of significant engineering hydraulic works; and who holds great promise for a continuing level of productivity in the field of basic hydraulic research and/or applied hydraulic engineering. IAHR members may submit nominations. Preference is given to members under 40 years of age. An honorarium of $1,000 is awarded biennially at the IAHR Congress. The recipient delivers the Arthur Thomas Ippen Lecture. Established in 1977 to honor Professor Ippen, IAHR President (1959-1963), IAHR Honorary Member (1963-1974), and for many decades an inspirational leader in fluids research, hydraulic engineering, and international cooperation and understanding.

• 4509 • **John F. Kennedy Student Paper Competition**

To recognize outstanding student papers. Selection is based on written and oral presentations. A monetary award and a plaque are awarded at the Congress closing ceremony. Additional monetary awards and certificates are presented to runners-up. Awarded biennially in odd-numbered years. Established in 1992 in memory of Professor John F. Kennedy, IAHR President (1979-1983) and honorary member (1989-1991), remembered particularly for his efforts to foster younger-member membership and participation.

• 4510 • **Harold Jan Schoemaker Award**

To recognize the most outstanding paper that was published in the IAHR *Journal of Hydraulic Research* during the preceding two-year period. IAHR members may submit candidates for nomination by December 15. A bronze medal and a certificate are awarded biennially in odd-numbered years. Established in 1980 in memory of Prof. Schoemaker, Secretary (1960-1979) who guided the *Journal of Hydraulic Research* in its formative years.

• 4511 •

International Canoe Federation
(Federation Internationale de Canoe)
Ulrich Feldhoff, Pres.
C/Antracita, 7, 4th Fl.
E-28045 Madrid, Spain
Phone: 34 91 5061150
Phone: 34 91 5061151
Fax: 34 91 5061155
E-mail: message@canoeicf.com
Home Page: http://www.canoeicf.com

• 4512 • **World Championships**

To promote canoeing and its related activities including racing, slalom, marathons, canoe-polo, and sailing. World Championships are held in flatwater racing, slalom racing, wildwater racing, marathon racing, and dragonboat racing.

• 4513 •

International Commission for Optics
(Commission Internationale d'Optique)
Prof. Maria L. Calvo, Sec.
Departamento de Optica
Facultad de Fisicas
Universidad Complutense de Madrid
Ciudad Universitaria, s/n
E-28040 Madrid Cedex, Spain
Phone: 34 91 3944684
Phone: 34 91 3944555
Fax: 34 91 3944683
E-mail: mlcalvo@fis.ucm.es
Home Page: http://www.ico-optics.org

• 4514 • **Galileo Galilei Award**

For recognition of outstanding contributions to the field of optics that are achieved under comparatively unfavorable circumstances. The Galileo Galilei Medal, funding of registration and approved local expenses at the next Ico General meeting, and special attention and appropriate measures of ICO to support the future activities of the award winner have been presented annually since 1994.

• 4515 • **International Commission for Optics Prize**

To recognize an individual for outstanding achievement in the field of optics. Individuals under 40 years of age are eligible. A monetary award of $1,000 and a medal are presented annually. Established in 1982.

• 4516 •

International Festival of Documentary and Short Film - Bilbao
(Festival Internacional de Cine de Bilbao Documental y Cortometraje)
Colon de Larreategui, 37-4 drcha.
Apro. de correos 579
E-48009 Bilbao, Spain
Phone: 34 94 4248698
Fax: 34 94 4245624
E-mail: info@zinebi.com
Home Page: http://www.zinebi.com

• 4517 • **Bilbao International Festival of Documentary and Short Films**
(Festival Internacional de Cine de Bilbao Documental y Cortometraje)

For recognition of the best documentary and short fiction or animated films. Foreign films produced within the preceding two years and films from Spain produced within the preceding year must be entered by producers. The maximum duration of the films is thirty minutes. The following awards are presented: Gran Premio del Festival de Bilbao; Gran Premio de Cine Espanol; Gran Premio de Cine Vasco; Mikeldi de Oro for the categories of documentary, fiction, and animation; Premio Mikeldi Plata for the categories of documentary, fiction, and animation; and Silver Caravel of the Instituto Iberoamericano De Cooperacion (ICI). Held annually. Established in 1958.

• 4518 •

International Sociological Association
(Association Internationale de Sociologie Asociacion Internacional de Sociologia)
Izabela Barlinska, Exec.Sec.
Faculty Political Sciences and Sociology
University Complutense
E-28223 Madrid, Spain
Phone: 34 91 3527650
Fax: 34 91 3524945
E-mail: isa@cps.ucm.es
Home Page: http://www.ucm.es/info/isa

• 4519 • **Worldwide Competition for Junior Sociologists**

To recognize young scholars engaged in social research. Individuals under 35 years of age who hold a Master's degree (or an equivalent graduate diploma) in sociology or in a related discipline may submit essays focusing on socially relevant issues. Essays may be written in one of the following languages: English, French, Spanish (the three languages of the ISA) as well as Arabic, Chinese, German, Italian, Japanese, Portuguese, and Russian. A Merit Award certificate, a four-year membership in the ISA, and an invitation to attend the World Congress, of Sociology are awarded every four years. Established in 1987.

• 4520 •

Jaen International Piano Competition
(Concurso Internacional de Piano Premio Jaen)
Palacio Provincial
Plaza de San Francisco s/n
E-23071 Jaen, Spain
Phone: 34 953 248056
Fax: 34 953 248010
E-mail: cultura@promojaen.es
Home Page: http://www.dipujaen.com/premiopiano/principal.dip

• 4521 • **Jaen Prize**

To recognize excellent pianists. Open to pianists of any nationality under the age of 36. Additional prizes are the Rosa Sabater Prize for the best interpreter of Spanish music, the Contemporary Music Award for the best performer of the compulsory piece, and the XL Anniversary Prize for

Awards are arranged in alphabetical order below their administering organizations

the best interpreter of a piece by Joaquin Reyes. Deadline for applications is August 1. Held annually.

• 4522 •
Juventudes Musicales de Espana
Cristina Aparicio, Admin.Dir.
C/Marina, 164 principal 3a
E-08013 Barcelona, Spain
Phone: 34 93 2449050
Fax: 34 93 2659080
E-mail: info@jmspain.org
Home Page: http://www.jmspain.org

• 4523 • **Concurso Permanente de Jovenes Interpretes**
To recognize and encourage the artistic development of young Spanish musicians. Musicians in the following areas are eligible: accordion, harp, voice, chamber ensembles, choral ensembles, flute, guitar, organ, percussion, trombone, French horn, trumpet, violin, piano, and cello. Spanish citizens under 24 years of age may apply. Established in 1978. Sponsored by the Spanish Ministry of Culture.

• 4524 •
Mostra de Valencia, Cinema del Mediterrani
Juan Piquer, Dir.
Plaza del Arzobispo 2
E-46003 Valencia, Spain
Phone: 34 96 3921506
Fax: 34 96 3915156
E-mail: festival@mostravalencia.com
Home Page: http://www.mostravalencia.com

• 4525 • **Valencia Film Festival (Mostra de Valencia, Palmero de Oro)**
For recognition of the best Mediterranean film presented in the competition, and to encourage Mediterranean cinematography. The Festival is composed of the following sections: Official Section, Informative Section, Special Section, Retrospective, Homage, Director's Retrospective, Spanish Cinema, Actor/Actress Tribute, and Festival for Children. Feature films made in the Mediterranean area during the preceding year may enter the competition. The Palmera de Oro of 40,000 euros, Palmera de Plata of 25,000 euros; and Palmera de Bronce of 10,000 euros are awarded annually, in addition to various other monetary prizes, trophies, and plaques. Established in 1980 by Fundacion Municipal de Cine and the Town Council of Valencia.

• 4526 •
Organization for the Phyto-Taxonomic Investigation of the Mediterranean Area (Organisation pour l'Etude Phyto-Taxonomique de la Region Mediterraneenne)
Prof. Jose Maria Iriondo, Sec.
E.U.I.T. Agricola
Universidad Politecnica de Madrid
Ciudad Universitaria
Ciudad Universitaria s/n
E-28040 Madrid, Spain
Phone: 34 91 3365462
Fax: 34 91 3365656
E-mail: iriondo@ccupm.upm.es
Home Page: http://www.bgbm.fu-berlin.de/OPTIMA/

• 4527 • **OPTIMA Gold Medal**
For recognition of an outstanding contribution to the phytotaxonomy of the Mediterranean area. Individuals must not be members of the OPTIMA Prize Commission to be eligible for the award. A medal is awarded triennially, at the OPTIMA meetings. Established in 1977.

• 4528 • **OPTIMA Silver Medal**
For recognition of the authors of the best papers or books on the phytotaxonomy of the Mediterranean area, published in the three years preceding the award. Individuals must not be current members of the OPTIMA Prize Commission or the OPTIMA International Board to be eligible for the award. Medals are awarded triennially at the OPTIMA meetings. Established in 1977.

• 4529 •
Fernando Rielo Foundation
Jorge Juan 82, no. 1, 6
E-28009 Madrid, Spain
Phone: 34 915 754091
Fax: 34 915 780772
E-mail: fundacion@rielo.com
Home Page: http://www.rielo.com

• 4530 • **World Mystical Poetry Prize**
For recognition of outstanding mystical poetry (poetry expressing humanity's spiritual values in their profound religious significance). Any previously unpublished poem or group of poems with a total length of 600 to 1300 lines and written or translated into Spanish is eligible. The deadline is October 15. A monetary prize of 7,000 euros and publication of the entry are awarded annually. Established in 1981 by Fernando Rielo, Spanish philosopher and poet.

• 4531 •
Royal Academy of Pharmacy (Real Academia de Farmacia)
Monica de Villar, Sec.
Calle de la Farmacia 9-11
E-28004 Madrid, Spain
Phone: 34 9153 10307
Fax: 34 9153 10306
E-mail: fundacion@ranf.com
Home Page: http://www.ranf.com

• 4532 • **Premio Carlos del Castillo Leiva**
To recognize outstanding research in pharmacy's tools technics. A monetary prize of 600 euros is awarded annually.

• 4533 • **Premio Colegio Oficial de Farmaceuticos de Madrid**
For recognition of the best scientific and professional work by a pharmacist of Madrid. The deadline for submission is October 24. A monetary prize of 3,000 euros is awarded annually.

• 4534 • **Premio Consejo General de Colegios de Farmaceuticos**
For recognition in the field of pharmaceuticals. The deadline for submission is September 29. A monetary prize of 3,000 euros is awarded annually.

• 4535 • **Premio Real Academia Nacional de Farmacia**
For recognition of outstanding personal research in the field of pharmacology. The deadline for submission is September 29. Sponsored by Mr. Juan Abelle, a monetary prize of 6,000 euros is awarded annually.

• 4536 • **Premio Santos Ruiz**
To recognize the best doctoral thesis written by a member of the faculty of pharmacy at the Universidad Complutense de Madrid. The cost of the title of Doctor in Pharmacy is awarded annually. The deadline for submission is September 29.

• 4537 •
San Sebastian International Film Festival
Mikel Olaciregui, Dir.
PO Box 397
E-20080 San Sebastian, Spain
Phone: 34 943 481212
Fax: 34 943 481218
E-mail: ssiff@sansebastianfestival.com
Home Page: http://www.sansebastianfestival.com

• 4538 • **San Sebastian International Film Festival Awards**
To recognize superb international films in an official competitive section, an unofficial section, and a variety of retrospectives. Many awards are presented each year, including the Golden Shell, Special Jury Award, Silver Shell Awards for the best actress, actor, and director, Award for the Best Photography, and a Jury Award. A special jury award, the New Directors Prize, of approximately $160,000 is presented to the producer and director of a first or second work presented in the Official Section. Awarded annually.

• 4539 •
Paloma O'Shea Santander International Piano Competition
(Concurso Internacional de Piano de Santander Paloma O'Shea)
Secretariat General
Hernan Cortes, 3 entlo
E-39003 Santander, Spain
Phone: 34 942 311415
Fax: 34 42 314816
E-mail: concurso@aebeniz.com
Home Page: http://www.albeniz.com

Formerly: (1995) Santander International Piano Competition.

• 4540 • **Paloma O'Shea Santander International Piano Competition (Concurso Internacional de Piano de Santander Paloma O'Shea)**
To recognize pianists of the younger generation whose talent ensures an interesting artistic career. Its principal goal is to present them to the music world and assist them in developing their careers. The competition is open to pianists under age 29 of any nationality. The competition consists of three phases: First phase - recital and chamber music (quintet for piano and strings); Second phase - semifinals, six participants, concerto with chamber orchestra and recital; Third phase - three participants, concerto with symphony orchestra. First Prize consists of US $46,000, concerts and recitals throughout the world with presentations in main musical cities, recording of a compact disc and Kawai RX-3 grand piano. Second Prize is a silver medal and US $19,000, concerts in Spain and aboard. Third Prize is a bronze medal and US $7,000, with concerts in Spain. Held annually.

• 4541 •
Spanish Royal Society of Physics
(Real Sociedad Espanola de Fisica)
G. Delgado Barrio, Pres.
Facultades de Ciencias Fisicas
Universidad Complutense de Madrid
E-28040 Madrid, Spain
Phone: 34 91 3944359
Fax: 34 91 3944162
E-mail: rsef@fis.ucm.es
Home Page: http://www.ucm.es/info/rsef

• 4542 • **Medalla de la Real Sociedad Espanola de Fisica**
Recognizes research and scientific findings in the field of physics. Awarded annually to one or more recipients.

• 4543 • **Premio a Investigadores Noveles**
Recognizes scientific merit and publications. A monetary prize is given annually to one or more recipients.

• 4544 •
Torello International Festival of Mountain and Adventure Films
Joan Salarrich, Dir.
PO Box 19
Anselm Clave 5, 3er
E-08570 Torello (Barcelona), Spain
Phone: 34 93 8504321
Fax: 34 93 8504321
E-mail: info@torellomountainfilm.com
Home Page: http://www.torellomountainfilm.com

Formerly: Torello Excursionist Center.

• 4545 • **Torello International Festival of Mountain and Adventure Films (Concours International de Cinema de la Montagne Vila de Torello)**
An international film contest of mountain cinema. Films related to mountains and ecology, such as alpinism, climbing, excursions, expeditions, mountain sports, skiing, speleology, and protection of nature, flora, and fauna are considered. The following prizes are awarded: Grand Prix Vila de Torello - Gold Edelweiss and a monetary prize to the best film; Silver Edelweiss and a monetary prize to the best mountaineering film; Silver Edelweiss and a monetary prize to the best mountain environment film; Silver Edelweiss and a monetary prize to the best film of mountain sports; Silver Edelweiss and a monetary prize for the jury prize; Medal Federacion Espanola de Montanismo and a monetary prize for the best film by a Spanish director; and Silver Edelweiss and a monetary prize for best script. Awarded annually. Established in 1983. Formerly: (1997) Festival de Cinema de Montagne.

• 4546 •
Tusquets Editores S.A.
Cesare Cantu, 8
E-08023 Barcelona, Spain
Phone: 34 93 253 0400
Fax: 34 93 417 6703
E-mail: general@tusquets-editores.es
Home Page: http://www.tusquets-editores.es

• 4547 • **Premio Comillas de Biografia, Autobiografia y Memorias**
To promote unpublished biographies, memoirs, and autobiographies written in Spanish language. A monetary award and a trophy are presented annually when merited. Established in 1988.

• 4548 • **Vertical Smile La Sonrisa Vertical (Premio La Sonrisa Vertical)**
To promote the knowledge of great erotic authors and revitalize this marginal genre of Castilian literature. Works must be written in Spanish to be considered. A monetary award and an art object are awarded annually in January. Established in 1978 in honor of Lopez Barbadillo, the first to publish a collection of erotic narratives.

• 4549 •
University of Barcelona
University of Barcelona
Gran Via de les Corts Catalanes, 585
08007 Barcelona, Spain
Home Page: http://www.ub.edu

• 4550 • **Premio Sent Sovi**
For recognition of prose works of any genre in which gastronomy plays an essential role. Awarded annually. Established in 1998. Cosponsored by the Fundacion Ferrer Sala-Freixenet.

• 4551 •
Valladolid International Film Festival
(Semana Internacional de Cine de Valladolid)
Juan Carlos Frugone, Dir.
Calle Leopoldo Cano, s/n, 4th Fl.
PO Box 646
E-47003 Valladolid, Spain
Phone: 34 983 426460
Fax: 34 983 426461
E-mail: festvalladolid@seminci.com
Home Page: http://www.seminci.com

• 4552 • **Valladolid International Film Festival**
For recognition of the best films of the festival. An international jury decides the winners of the following awards from those feature-lengths and shorts selected for participation in competition in the official section: Golden Spike and Silver Spike to the two best feature-lengths. The Spanish distributor of the winner of the Golden Spike receives $40,000 US; Prize to the Best New Director, competing with a first or second feature-length receives $10,000 US; Best Actress; Best Actor; Best Director of Photography Award; Golden Spike and Silver Spike to the two best short films. The filmmaker of the top prizewinner receives $10,000 US; Jury Prize to short and feature-length films. Awarded annually. Established in 1956 by Antolin de Santiago y Juarez.

• 4553 •
Francisco Vinas International Singing Competition
(Concurs Internacional de Cant Francesc Vinas)
Manuel Garcia Gascons, Org. Sec.
Bruc 125
E-08037 Barcelona, Spain
Phone: 34 934578646
Fax: 34 934574364
E-mail: info@francisco-vinas.com
Home Page: http://www.francisco-vinas.com

• 4554 • **Francisco Vinas International Singing Contest (Concurs Internacional de Cant Francesc Vinas)**
To encourage talented young singers all over the world. Female singers between 18 and 32 years of age, and male singers between 20 and 35 years of age are eligible. A monetary prize of 11,000 Euro and a gold plated silver medal are

Awards are arranged in alphabetical order below their administering organizations

awarded to the grand prize winners in the male and female categories. Other official, special, and extraordinary prizes including scholarships are awarded. The competition is held annually, usually in January. Established in 1963 by Dr. Jacinto Vilardell in memory of Francisco Vinas, a well-known Catalan opera tenor.

Sri Lanka

• 4555 •
Institution of Engineers, Sri Lanka
120/15 Wijerama Mawatha
Colombo 7, Sri Lanka
Phone: 94 11 2698426
Fax: 94 11 2699202
E-mail: iesl@slt.lk
Home Page: http://www.iesl.lk

• 4556 • **Ceylon Development Engineering Award**
To recognize the author(s) of the best article in the quarterly journal, *Engineer*, published each year. Expertise in the relevant field is necessary for consideration. A monetary prize of 3,000 Sri Lanka rupees is awarded annually at the convention. Established in 1980. Sponsored by the Ceylon Development Engineering Company, Ltd.

• 4557 • **Junior Inventor of the Year E. C. Fernando Memorial Award**
To encourage originality and inventiveness of technical minded and talented students. Sri Lankan students between 12 and 20 years of age must be nominated. Monetary prizes, medals, and certificates are awarded annually. Established in 1988. Co-sponsored by Lanka Electricity Company (Private) Ltd.

• 4558 • **T. P. de S. Munasinghe Memorial Award**
To recognize the best student in civil engineering at the Institution Part II Examination. Students must obtain a minimum average of 65 percent marks and should have passed the Part I Examination or be exempted from it. A monetary prize of 1,000 Sri Lanka rupees is awarded annually at the convention. Established in 1984 in honor of T.P. de S. Munasinghe, a Fellow and past president of the Institution. Sponsored by Mrs. T.P. de S. Munasinghe and family.

• 4559 • **Professor E. O. E. Pereira Award**
To recognize the author(s) of the best paper in the field of engineering at the annual convention of the Institution. Members of the Institution may submit papers by June 30 every year. Books or publications valued at 1,000 Sri Lanka rupees are awarded annually at the convention. Established in 1973 in honor of Professor E.O.E. Pereira, first Dean, Faculty of Engineering and first Engineer Vice Chancellor of the Peradeniya Campus of the University of Ceylon.

• 4560 • **Aylet Lily Perera Memorial Award**
For recognition of achievement in the Institution Part II Examination in Mechanical Engineering. Individuals who pass all subjects and reach an aggregate of 65 percent are eligible. Books are awarded annually at the convention. Established in 1987 in honor of Mrs. Aylet Lilly Perera, mother of L.R.L. Perera, past president of the Institution.

• 4561 • **State Development and Construction Corporation Award**
To recognize the author(s) of the best article in the field of engineering in the quarterly journal, *Engineer.* Associate Members (under 35 years) of the Institution are eligible. A monetary prize of 1,000 Sri Lanka rupees is awarded annually at the convention. Established in 1980. Sponsored by the State Department and Construction Corporation, Sri Lanka.

• 4562 • **D. J. Wimalasurendra Memorial Award**
To recognize the best student in electrical engineering at the Institution's Part II Examination. Students must obtain a minimum average of 65 percent marks and should have passed the Part I Examination or be exempted from it. A monetary prize of 1,000 Sri Lanka rupees is awarded annually at the convention. Established in 1984 in honor of D.J. Wimalasurendra, a member of the Institution and an electrical engineer who is considered the father of hydro-electricity in Sri Lanka.

• 4563 •
Samasevaya
Samson Jayasinghe, Nat.Sec.
30/2 Pallansena South
Anuradhapura Road
Kochchikade 11540, Sri Lanka
Phone: 94 31 77951
Fax: 94 31 77951
E-mail: samasevaya@lanka.com.lk

• 4564 • **Samashuri**
Peace award granted to persons who work for peace in Sri Lanka.

• 4565 •
Sri Lanka Association for the Advancement of Science
Dr. Lochana Gunaratna, Gen.Pres.
120/10 Vidya Mawatha
Colombo 7, Sri Lanka
Phone: 94 1 691681
Phone: 94 1 688740
Fax: 94 1 691681
E-mail: slaas@itmin.com
Home Page: http://www.naresa.ac.lk/slaas/organis.htm

• 4566 • **Environmental Award**
To recognize significant contributions in sustainable management of the environment. Students, individuals, organizations, and institutions in both the public and private sector are eligible. Awarded annually.

• 4567 • **General Research Committee Award**
Recognizes the best total research contribution by a Sri Lankan scientist. Awarded annually.

• 4568 • **Manamperi (Engineering) Award**
To recognize the best undergraduate engineering research project carried out at a Faculty of Engineering in a Sri Lankan university. Awarded annually.

• 4569 • **Physical Science Award**
To recognize undergraduate students or recent graduates who have completed research projects (individual) in the field of Physics, Computer Science, Mathematics, or Statistics as a partial requirement for BSc degree in a Sri Lankan university during the previous year. Awarded annually.

• 4570 •
United Nations Association in the Democratic Socialist Republic of Sri Lanka
(Sri Lanka Eksath Jatheenge Sangamaya)
Kumaran Fernando, Sec.Gen.
National Secretariat General
39/1 Cyril Jansz Mawatha
Panadura 12500, Sri Lanka
Phone: 94 38 2232123
Phone: 94 38 2243080
Fax: 94 38 2232123
E-mail: unasl@slt.lk
Home Page: http://www.unasl.org

• 4571 • **Study Circles Challenge Trophies**
To recognize the annual work of the five best UNA Study Circles in participating high schools for the previous year by the awarding of trophies. Certificates are also awarded to the teachers-in-charge of the same five best Study Circles all taking place at the Sri Lanka National Observance of United Nations Day, which has been conducted by the association without a break since 1950. Certificates are also presented for the following inter Study Circles: General Knowledge Contest on the UN; General Knowledge Quiz on International Flags, National Emblems, Coats-of-Arms, and National Anthems of UN member States.

Sweden

• 4572 •
Blekinge County Council
(Landstinget Blekinge)
Kansliet
S-371 81 Karlskrona, Sweden
Phone: 46 455 731000
Fax: 46 455 80250
E-mail: landstinget.blekinge@ltblekinge.se
Home Page: http://www.ltblekinge.se

• 4573 • **Blekinge County Council Prize for Environmental Control (Blekinge lans landstings Miljo vardspris)**
To stimulate environmental protection in Blekinge county. A monetary prize of 50,000 Swedish kronor is awarded annually. Established in 1986.

• 4574 •
Carina Ari Foundation
(Carina Ari Stiftelsen)
Prof. Bengt Hager, Chm.
% Carina Ari Library of Dance
PO Box 27032
S-102 51 Stockholm, Sweden
Phone: 46 8 662 6570
Fax: 46 8 662 6571
E-mail: info@carina.se
Home Page: http://www.carina.se

• 4575 • **Carina Ari Medal of Merit**
(Carina Ari Medaljen)
For recognition of outstanding contributions to the art of dance in Sweden. A gold medal is awarded. Established in 1961 in memory of Carina Ari, a Swedish ballerina and choreographer of international career, especially in Paris in the 1920s and 1930s.

• 4576 •
Charta 77 Foundation
Jan Kacer, Mgr.
Melantrichova 5
CS-110 00 Prague, Sweden
Phone: 42 224 214 452
Fax: 42 224 213 647
E-mail: charta77@bariery.cz
Home Page: http://www.bariery.cz

• 4577 • **Dr. Frantisek Kriegel Prize**
(Cena Frantisek Kriegel)
For recognition of contributions to the human and civil rights movement and civil courage in the Czech Republic and the Slovak Republic. Individuals who promote human rights and civic freedom are considered. A monetary award of 100,000 czech crowns and a diploma are awarded annually. Established in 1987 in memory of Frantisek Kriegel (1908-1978), a promoter of Prague spring and the only leader who refused to sign the acceptance of Soviet rule in August 1968.

• 4578 • **Jaroslav Seifert Prize**
(Cena Jaroslava Seiferta)
For recognition of the best work in Czech and Slovak literature. A monetary award of 250,000 Czech crowns and a diploma made by one of the well known Czechoslovak artists are awarded. Established in 1986 in memory of Jaroslav Seifert, Nobel Prize Winner (1984) and Czech poet.

• 4579 •
European Society for Clinical Virology
Annika Linde, Pres.
Swedish Inst. for Infectious Disease Control
Dept. of Epidemiology
SE-17182 Solna, Sweden
Phone: 46 8 4572360
Fax: 46 8 300626
E-mail: annika.linde@smi.ki.se
Home Page: http://www.escv.org

• 4580 • **Abbott Award**
For original contributions in the area of viral diagnosis.

• 4581 • **Heine-Medin Medal**
To young promising scientist.

• 4582 •
European Sports Press Union
(Union Europeenne de la Presse Sportive)
Lingonvagen 9
S-76010 Bergshamra, Sweden
Phone: 46 176 260547
Fax: 46 176 260032
E-mail: uepsrelations@ueps-media.com
Home Page: http://www.ueps-media.com

• 4583 • **European Sportsman and Sportswoman of the Year**
(Sportive et Sportif Europeen de l'Annee)
To honor the best male and female European athlete of the year. A trophy is awarded annually. Established in 1983.

• 4584 •
Federation of International Bandy
Seppo Vaihela, VP
PO Box 78
S-641 21 Katrineholm, Sweden
Phone: 46 150 72212
Phone: 46 150 72207
Fax: 46 150 72201
E-mail: jchedenstrom@comcast.net
Home Page: http://www.internationalbandy.com

• 4585 • **Competitions and Tournaments**
To promote the game of Bandy, a sport related to ice hockey, but played on a larger ice rink, with 11 players on a team, using a plastic ball and curved sticks and no play behind goals. The Federation sponsors the Senior World Championship and a Junior Boys Championship for boys between 17 and 19 years of age. Awarded biennially. Established in 1957.

• 4586 • **IBF Gold Medal**
For recognition of contributions to the sport of bandy.

• 4587 •
International Association of Theatre for Children and Young People
(Association Internationale du Theatre pour l'Enfance et la Jeunesse)
Niclas Malmcrona, Sec.Gen.
Box 6033
S-121 06 Johanneshov, Sweden
Phone: 46 8 6598633
Fax: 46 8 6598901
E-mail: sec.gen@assitej.org
Home Page: http://www.assitej.org

• 4588 • **Honorary President's Award**
To recognize an artist or company who has achieved noteworthy excellence in theatre for children and young people. Awarded triennially.

• 4589 •
International Braille Chess Association
(Association Internationale des Echecs en Braille)
Jan Berglund
Kiorningsgatan 1
SE16931 Virebersvagen 5, Sweden
Phone: 46 723248614
Fax: 46 18128910
E-mail: prawnik@idn.org.pl
Home Page: http://cross.idn.org.pl/ibca_en.htm

• 4590 • **Chess Olympiad for the Blind**
To promote individual and team tournaments in chess for the blind. Awards are given to tournament winners.

• 4591 •
International Commission for the Eriksson Prize Fund
Prof. Berndt Gerhardson, Exec. Officer
Plant Pathology and Biocontrol Unit
Swedish University of Agicultural Sciences
PO Box 7035
SE-750 07 Uppsala, Sweden
Phone: 46 18 671600
Fax: 46 18 671690
E-mail: berndt.gerhardson@vpat.slu.se

• 4592 • **Jakob Eriksson Prize**
For recognition of research in mycology, plant pathology, or virus diseases. A gold medal and monetary prize are awarded to a researcher every five to six years at the International Congress of Plant Pathology. Established in 1923 by the Botanical Section of the International Union of Biological Sciences in honor of Prof. Jakob Eriksson.

• 4593 •
International Commission on Physics Education
Prof. Gunnar Tibell, Chm.
Department of Radiation Sciences
Uppsala University
PO Box 535
SE-75121 Uppsala, Sweden
Phone: 46 18 4713849
Fax: 46 18 4713513
E-mail: gtibell@tsl.uu.se
Home Page: http://web.phys.ksu.edu/ICPE

• 4594 • **ICPE Medal**
Recognizes outstanding contribution to physics education. A medal is awarded triennially. Established in 1979.

• 4595 •
International Research Group on Wood Preservation
(Groupe International de Recherches sur la Preservation du Bois)
Mr. Joran Jermer, Sec.Gen.
IRG Secretariat
SE-10044 Stockholm, Sweden
Phone: 46 8 101453
Fax: 46 8 108081
E-mail: irg@sp.se
Home Page: http://irg-wp.com

• 4596 • **Ron Cockcroft Award**
To promote international wood preservation research through the Research Group by assisting selected individuals to attend IRG congresses. The award is intended to be particularly available to postgraduate students and active young scientists and also non-members who otherwise cannot attend an IRG meeting. Applications must be submitted by December 15. Travel assistance is awarded annually prior to each congress. Established in 1988 in memory of Ron Cockcroft, secretary-general of the IRG.

• 4597 • **IRG Travel Award**
Contributes to the realization of the scientific objectives of the IRG. Missions shall strengthen the networks by allowing scientists to go to a laboratory in another country or in some instances within their own country, to learn a new technique or to make measurements using instruments and/or methods not available in their own laboratory. The applicant will normally be a scientist or student establishing himself/herself in the field of wood preservation, or in a field related directly to wood preservation interests. The host institution can be public or private, but most have a member of IRG on staff, or be a sponsor member of the IRG.

• 4598 •
National Association of Swedish Architects
(Svenska Arkitekters Riksforbund)
Norrlandsgatan 18, 2 tr
S-111 43 Stockholm, Sweden
Phone: 46 8 6792760
Fax: 46 8 6114930
E-mail: sat@sar.se
Home Page: http://www.sar.se

• 4599 • **Kasper Salin Prize**
(Kasper Salinpriset)
For recognition of the best Swedish architecture. Any building completed during the preceding year is eligible for consideration. A plaque is awarded annually. Established in 1961 by the Kasper Salin Foundation in memory of Kasper Salin, a city planning architect of Stockholm, Sweden (1898-1919).

• 4600 •
Nobel Foundation
Mr. Michael Sohlman, Sec.
Sturegatan 14
Box 5232
SE-102 45 Stockholm, Sweden
Phone: 46 8 6630920
Fax: 46 8 6603847
E-mail: comments@nobelprize.org
Home Page: http://nobelprize.org/

• 4601 • **Bank of Sweden Prize in Memory of Alfred Nobel**
For recognition of contributions in the field of economic sciences. A monetary prize of 7,400,000 Swedish kronor, a gold medal and a diploma are awarded annually by the Royal Swedish Academy of Sciences. Instituted in 1968 by the Central Bank of Sweden at their tercentary, which placed an annual amount of money at the disposal of the Nobel Foundation as the basis for a prize to be awarded in economic sciences.

• 4602 • **Nobel Peace Prize**
To recognize an individual who is a champion of peace, and who has done the most for the promotion of the fraternity of nations, for the abolition or reduction of standing armies, and for the holding and promotion of peace congresses. A monetary prize of 7,400,000 Swedish kronor, a gold medal, and a diploma are awarded annually by the Norwegian Nobel Committee, 19 Drammensveien, N-0255 Oslo 2, Norway. First awarded in 1901.

• 4603 • **Nobel Prize for Chemistry**
To recognize the individual who has made the most important discovery or improvement in the field of chemistry. A monetary prize of 7,400,000 Swedish kronor, a gold medal, and a diploma are awarded annually. First awarded in 1901. Presented by the Royal Swedish Academy of Sciences, PO Box 50005, S-1043 05 Stockholm.

• 4604 • **Nobel Prize for Literature**
To recognize a person who has produced the most distinguished work of an idealistic nature in the field of literature. Authors, regardless of nationality, are considered for their complete work. A monetary prize of 7,400,000 Swedish kronor, a gold medal, and a diploma are awarded annually. First awarded in 1901.

• 4605 • **Nobel Prize for Physics**
To recognize an individual who has made the most important discovery or improvement in the domain of physics. A monetary prize of 7,400,000 Swedish kronor, a gold medal, and a diploma are awarded annually. First awarded in 1901.

• 4606 • **Nobel Prize for Physiology or Medicine**
To recognize an individual who has made the most important discovery in the field of physiology and medicine. A monetary prize of 7,400,000 Swedish kronor, a gold medal and a diploma are awarded annually. Established in 1895 and first awarded in 1901. The prize is presented by the Nobel Assembly at the Karolinska Institute, Box 60250, S-104 01 Stockholm.

• 4607 •
Nordic Africa Institute
(Nordiska Afrikainstitutet)
Carin Norberg, Dir.
PO Box 1703
S-751 47 Uppsala, Sweden
Phone: 46 18 562200
Fax: 46 18 562290
E-mail: nai@nai.uu.se
Home Page: http://www.nai.uu.se

• 4608 • **African Guest Researchers' Scholarship**
For senior researchers.

• 4609 • **Nordic Guest Researchers' Scholarship**
For senior scholars.

• 4610 • **Study Scholarship**
For social science research on Africa.

• 4611 • **Travel Scholarship**
For research based at Nordic University.

• 4612 •
Nordic Council
(Nordiska Radet - Sweden)
Rannveig Gudmundsottir, Pres.
Store Strandstraede 18
DK-1253 Copenhagen, Sweden
Phone: 45 3396 0200
Fax: 45 3396 0202
E-mail: nordisk-rad@norden.org
Home Page: http://www.norden.org

• 4613 • **Nordic Council Literature Prize (Nordiska Radets Litteraturpris)**
To increase the interest in the literature of the Nordic countries. Works by living authors from Nordic countries (Denmark, Finland, Greenland, Iceland, Norway, and Sweden), which have been produced during the preceding two years are eligible. The literary work may be in one of the languages of the Nordic region, including Faeroese, Greenlandic, and Sami. A monetary prize of 350,000 Danish kroner is presented annually at the time of the Nordic Council's session. Established in 1962 by the Nordic governments.

• 4614 • **Nordic Council Music Prize (Nordisk Rads Musikpris)**
To recognize a living Nordic composer for a recent musical work and in alternate years a living Nordic performer. The selection is made by NOMUS - Nordic Music Committee, which is an expert committee consisting of two members from each Nordic country. Candidates for the prize are nominated by the delegates of the respective countries. A monetary prize of 350,000

Awards are arranged in alphabetical order below their administering organizations

Danish kroner is awarded annually. Established in 1965. Sponsored by the Nordic Council.

• 4615 •
Olof Palme Memorial Fund for International Understanding and Common Security
PO Box 836
S-101 36 Stockholm, Sweden
Phone: 46 8 677 5790
Fax: 46 8 677 5771
E-mail: palmefonden@palmecenter.se
Home Page: http://www.palmefonden.se

• 4616 • **Olof Palme Memorial Fund Scholarships**
To encourage the study of peace and disarmament and for work against racism and hostility to foreigners. Scholarships are awarded twice a year. Established in 1986.

• 4617 • **Olof Palme Prize**
For recognition of an outstanding achievement in the areas of peace, disarmament, international understanding and common security. The Board of the Fund makes the selection. A monetary prize of $50,000 and diploma are awarded annually. Established in 1987 in honor of Olof Palme, former Prime Minister of Sweden.

• 4618 •
Right Livelihood Awards Foundation
PO Box 15072
S-104 65 Stockholm, Sweden
Phone: 46 8 702 0340
Fax: 46 8 702 0338
E-mail: info@rightlivelihood.se
Home Page: http://www.rightlivelihood.se

• 4619 • **Right Livelihood Award**
To honor and support those working on exemplary and practical solutions to the real problems in the world today, thereby forming an essential contribution to making life more whole and healing our planet. The awards have become known as the Alternative Nobel Prize. Selection is by a jury that accepts nominations (no self-nomination). Three monetary prizes totaling approximately $230,000 and one honorary award are presented annually in Stockholm, Sweden. The cash prizes are for a specific project, not for personal use. Established in 1980 by Jakob von Uexkull, a Swedish-German writer, philatelic expert, Chairman of the Foundation, and former member of the European Parliament.

• 4620 •
Royal Academy of Letters, History and Antiquities
(Kungliga Vitterhets Historie och Antikvitets Akademien)
Ulf Sporrong, Sec. Gen.
Box 5622
S-114 86 Stockholm, Sweden
Phone: 46 8 4404280
Fax: 46 8 4404290
E-mail: kansli@vitterhetsakad.se
Home Page: http://www.vitterhetsakad.se

• 4621 • **The Rettig Prize**
For outstanding or promising scholarrs in clinical microbiology and/or infectious diseases.

• 4622 •
Royal Physiographic Society in Lund
(Kungliga Fysiografiska Sallskapet i Lund)
Stortorget 6
S-222 23 Lund, Sweden
Phone: 46 132528
Fax: 46 131944
E-mail: kansli@fysiografen.se
Home Page: http://www.fysiografen.org

• 4623 • **Sven Berggrens pris**
For meritorious service to Swedish science, trade, and industry. Awarded annually. Established in 1995.

• 4624 • **Rolf Dahlgrens Pris**
For meritorious work on the systematics and evolution of the flowering plants. International prize, awarded triennially. Established in 1990.

• 4625 • **Engestromska medaljen for tillampad naturvetenskap**
For recognition in the field of applied science. A medal is awarded triennially. Established in 1917.

• 4626 • **Fabian Gyllenbergs pris**
For recognition of the best thesis in the field of chemistry in the last three years at the University of Lund. Awarded triennially the award carries a cash prize of 55,000 kroner. Established in 1972.

• 4627 • **Assar Haddings pris**
For recognition in the field of geology. Awarded triennially. Established in 1959.

• 4628 • **Bengt Jonssons pris**
For recognition of meritorious work in the field of botany by young scientists at the University of Lund. Awarded every five years. Established in 1940.

• 4629 • **Minnesmedaljen i guld**
For recognition of outstanding merit in the fields of science and medicine. Established in 1915.

• 4630 • **Rosens Linnemedalj**
For recognition in the field of botany. A gold medal is awarded triennially. Established in 1939.

• 4631 • **Thunbergmedaljen**
For recognition in the field of physiology. Scandinavian scientists are eligible. A medal is awarded biennially. Established in 1954.

• 4632 • **Wilhelm Westrups beloning**
For recognition in the field of applied science, especially benefitting the economy of the Swedish province of Skane (Scania). Awarded every five years. Established in 1923.

• 4633 •
Royal Swedish Academy of Engineering Sciences
(Ingenjorsvetenskapsakademien)
Lena Treschow Torrell, Pres.
Grev Turegatan 14
Box 5073
S-102 42 Stockholm, Sweden
Phone: 46 8 791 2900
Fax: 46 8 611 5623
E-mail: info@iva.se
Home Page: http://www.iva.se

• 4634 • **Brinell Medal**
For research and publication in mining, metallurgy, and processing of iron and steel. A gold medal is awarded intermittently. Established as an international prize in 1954.

• 4635 • **Royal Swedish Academy of Engineering Sciences Great Gold Medal**
This, the highest award of the academy, is given to recognize outstanding scientific and technological achievements within the academy's sphere of activity. Another medal, the Gold Medal, is given for meritorious contributions in the academy's sphere of activity. Awarded annually. Established in 1921.

• 4636 •
Royal Swedish Academy of Sciences
(Kungl. Vetenskapsakademien)
Jan Lindsten, Pres.
PO Box 50005
S-104 05 Stockholm, Sweden
Phone: 46 8 6739500
Fax: 46 8 155670
E-mail: info@kva.se
Home Page: http://www.kva.se

• 4637 • **Crafoord Prize**
For recognition of excellence in mathematics, astronomy, biosciences (particularly ecology), geosciences, and polyarthritis. A monetary prize of approximately $500,000 and a gold medal are awarded annually. Established in 1980 by Anna-Greta and Holger Crafoord, chairman of the medical supply firm Gambro AB, to help the areas of science not covered by the Nobel prizes.

• 4638 • **Gregori Aminoffs Pris**
For recognition of an outstanding documented, individual contribution in the field of crystallography, including areas concerned with the dynamics of the formation and dissolution of crystal structures. Eatsblished in 1979.

• 4639 • **Nobel Prizes**
The Nobel Prizes in physics and chemistry have been awarded by the Academy since their inception in 1901. Since 1968 the Prize in Economic Sciences in Memory of Alfred Nobel has also been awarded by the Academy. The prize-giving ceremony takes place on December 10,

the anniversary of Nobel's death. (The prizes are described under the Nobel Foundation in Sweden.)

• 4640 • Soderbergs Pris
To recognize a Swedish citizen or resident of Sweden for outstanding work in economic science or law. Awarded every other year.

• 4641 • Sture Centerwalls Pris
To recognize conservationists who best promote the protection of animal life in Sweden.

• 4642 • Wahlbergska Minnesmedaljen I guld
For recognition of accomplishment in the natural sciences. Open to Swedish or foreign citizens. Awarded every fifth year.

• 4643 •
Scandinavian Research Council for Criminology
(Nordiska Samarbetsradet for Kriminologi)
Mia Soderbarj, Exec. Sec.
Kriminologiska Institutionen
Stockholm University
S-106 91 Stockholm, Sweden
Phone: 46 8 164674
Fax: 46 8 157881
E-mail: mia.soderbarj@crim.su.se
Home Page: http://www.nsfk.org

• 4644 • Research and Travel Grants
To promote contributions in the field of criminology. Research grants are awarded to Scandinavian researchers implementing comparative projects in criminology. Only projects with a clear Scandinavian relevance are supported, such as replications of studies between countries, cooperation between researchers from at least two countries, and literature reviews on the Scandinavian level. Studies involving only one country can be supported if their aim is to fill a gap in Scandinavian research, or if their results are likely to be relevant to researchers in other Scandinavian countries. Research projects are usually thematic and are awarded annually; travel grants are administered on an ongoing basis.

• 4645 •
Swedish Academy
(Svenska Akademien)
Horace Engdahl, Sec.
Kallargrand 4
PO Box 2118
S-103 13 Stockholm, Sweden
Phone: 46 8 555 12500
Fax: 46 8 555 12549
E-mail: sekretariat@svenskaakademien.se
Home Page: http://www.svenskaakademien.se

• 4646 • Carl Akermarks Stipendium
For recognition of outstanding achievements in Swedish theatre. Five monetary prizes of 20,000 Swedish kronor are awarded annually. Established in 1984 by Carl Akermark.

• 4647 • Ida Backmans Stipendium
For recognition of a work of Swedish literature or journalism that represents an idealistic view of the world. A monetary prize of 35,000 Swedish kronor is awarded biennially. Established in 1953 by Ida Backman in memory of the Swedish writers, Gustaf Froding (1860-1911) and Selma Lagerlof (1858-1940).

• 4648 • Bellmanpriset
To recognize a truly outstanding Swedish poet. A monetary prize of 125,000 Swedish kronor is awarded annually. Established in 1920 by the Swedish painter, Anders Zorn.

• 4649 • Beskowska resestipendiet
For recognition of a literary work by a Swedish writer. A monetary prize of 30,000 Swedish kronor for travel expenses is awarded biennially. Established in 1873 by Bernhard von Beskow.

• 4650 • Blomska stipendiet
For recognition of scientific work on the Swedish language. A monetary prize of 25,000 Swedish kronor is awarded annually. Established in 1945 by Edward and Eva Blom.

• 4651 • Gerard Bonniers Pris
To recognize promising young writers. Two monetary prizes of 30,000 Swedish kronor each are awarded annually. Established in 1992.

• 4652 • Doblougska priset
For recognition of outstanding literary works by Norwegian and Swedish writers. Two monetary prizes of 60,000 Swedish kronor each are awarded annually for each category. Established in 1951.

• 4653 • Signe Ekblad-Eldhs pris
To recognize an eminent Swedish writer. A monetary prize of 80,000 Swedish kronor is awarded annually. Established in 1960.

• 4654 • Lydia och Herman Erikssons stipendium
For recognition of poetry or prose by a Swedish author. A monetary prize of 60,000 Swedish kronor is awarded biennially. Established in 1976.

• 4655 • Finlandspriset
For recognition of important achievements in promotion of Swedish culture in Finland. Finnish citizens are eligible. A monetary prize of 50,000 Swedish kronor is awarded annually. Established in 1966.

• 4656 • Karin Gierows pris
To recognize Swedish journalists who promote knowledge by means of writing. Three monetary prizes of 25,000 Swedish kronor each are awarded annually. Established in 1976 by Karl Ragnar Gierow.

• 4657 • Gun och Olof Engqvists stipendium
For recognition of a work of Swedish literature, or to recognize a journalist who writes about Swedish culture. A monetary prize of 100,000 Swedish kronor is awarded annually. Established in 1975 by Gun and Olof Engqvist.

• 4658 • Axel Hirschs pris
For recognition of biographical or historical work by Swedish writers or scientists. Monetary prizes totaling 140,000 Swedish kronor are awarded annually. Established in 1967.

• 4659 • Kallebergerstipendiet
For recognition of a work of prose or poetry. A monetary prize of 30,000 Swedish kronor is awarded annually. Established in 1977 by Gosta Ronnstrom and Tekla Hansson.

• 4660 • Kellgrenpriset
For recognition of important achievements in any of the fields of the Academy. A monetary prize of 125,000 Swedish kronor is awarded annually. Established in 1979 by Karl Ragnar Gierow.

• 4661 • Ilona Kohrtz' stipendium
For recognition of a work of prose or poetry in Swedish. A monetary prize of 20,000 Swedish kronor is awarded annually. Established in 1962.

• 4662 • Kungliga priset
For recognition of a contribution to Swedish culture or for a literary or artistic work. A monetary prize of 40,000 Swedish kronor is awarded annually. Established in 1835 by King Karl XIV Johan of Sweden.

• 4663 • Nordiska Priset
For recognition of important achievements in any of the fields of interest of the Academy. Citizens of any of the Scandinavian countries are eligible. A monetary prize of 250,000 Swedish kronor is awarded annually. Established in 1986 by the Academy in connection with its 200th anniversary.

• 4664 • Oversattarpris
For recognition of the best translations of foreign literature into the Swedish language. Translations in other humanistic disciplines are also eligible. A monetary prize of 40,000 Swedish kronor is awarded annually. Established in 1953.

• 4665 • Margit Pahlsons pris
For recognition of works on linguistics or Swedish language cultivation. A monetary prize of 100,000 Swedish kronor is awarded annually. Established in 1981 by Ms. Margit Pahlson.

• 4666 • Birger Scholdstroms pris
For recognition of a work on the history of literature, or for a biography written by a Swedish author. A monetary prize of 30,000 Swedish

kronor is awarded every four years. Established in 1960.

• 4667 • Schuckska priset
For recognition of a work on the history of Swedish literature. A monetary prize of 60,000 Swedish kronor is awarded annually. Established in 1946.

• 4668 • Sprakvardspris
For recognition of outstanding works on linguistics or language cultivation by a Swedish author. A monetary prize of 25,000 Swedish kronor is awarded annually. Established in 1953.

• 4669 • Stiftelsen Natur och Kulturs oversattarpris
For recognition of good translations of foreign literature into Swedish or of Swedish literature into foreign languages. Two monetary prizes of 40,000 Swedish kronor are awarded annually. Established in 1985 by the Natur och Kultur Foundation.

• 4670 • Stipendium ur Lena Vendelfelts minnesfond
For recognition of a literary work, particularly poetry. A monetary prize of 30,000 Swedish kronor is awarded annually. Established in 1981 by Mr. and Mrs. Erik Vendelfelt.

• 4671 • Stora priset
For recognition of an outstanding contribution to Swedish culture. A gold medal is awarded when merited. During the 20th century, 20 persons received the medal. Established in 1786 by King Gustavus III of Sweden.

• 4672 • Svenska Akademiens pris for introduktion av svensk kultur utomlands
To recognize important contributions to the introduction of Swedish culture abroad. Two monetary prizes of 30,000 Swedish kronor each are awarded annually. Established in 1992.

• 4673 • Svenska Akademiens Svensklararpris
To recognize teachers for stimulating young people's interest in the Swedish language and literature. Three monetary prizes of 25,000 Swedish kronor each are awarded annually. Established in 1987 by the Crafoord Foundation.

• 4674 • Svenska Akademiens Teaterpris
To recognize actors, actresses, producers, and playwrights who have made outstanding achievements in the Swedish theater. A monetary prize of 50,000 Swedish kronor is awarded annually. Established in 1966.

• 4675 • Tolkningspris
For recognition of translations of Swedish literature into foreign languages. A monetary prize of 40,000 Swedish kronor is awarded annually. Established in 1965.

• 4676 • Zibetska Priset
For recognition of a work on the history or culture of the period of King Gustavus III, or for a literary work with special regard to this period. A monetary prize of 30,000 Swedish kronor is awarded every second year. Established in 1809 in memory of King Gustavus III.

• 4677 •
Swedish Academy of Pharmaceutical Sciences
(Apotekarsocieteten)
Wallingatan 26a
PO Box 1136
S-111 81 Stockholm, Sweden
Phone: 46 8 723 5000
Fax: 46 8 205511
E-mail: apotekarsocieteten@swepharm.se
Home Page: http://www.swepharm.se

• 4678 • Scheelepriset
(Scheele Award)
For recognition of outstanding scientific contributions in the field of pharmaceutical sciences. A monetary prize of 200,000 Swedish kronor and a medal are awarded and the winner presents the Scheele Memorial Lecture. Awarded annually in October/November in connection with the annual congress. Established in 1961 in memory of C. W. Scheele (1742-1786).

• 4679 •
Swedish Federation of Film and Video Amateurs
(Sveriges Film- och Videofoerbund)
Mike Rasanen, Pres.
Torsgatan 73
S-113 37 Stockholm, Sweden
Phone: 46 175 62311
E-mail: sfv@filmkrets.se
Home Page: http://www.filmkrets.se

• 4680 • UNICA Medal
(UNICA-medaljen)
To recognize an individual or an organization that has contributed to the spread of amateur film/video making. Nominations are accepted for Swedish people living anywhere and people living in Sweden. A medal is awarded annually. Established in 1980.

• 4681 •
Swedish Film Institute
(Svenska Filminstitutet)
Ase Kleveland, Dir.Gen.
Filmhuset
Borgvagen 1-5
PO Box 27126
S-102 52 Stockholm, Sweden
Phone: 46 8 665 1100
Fax: 46 8 666 3760
E-mail: info@sfi.se
Home Page: http://www.sfi.se

Awards discontinued.

• 4682 • Ingmar Bergman Plaquette
For recognition of an outstanding artistic and/or technical contribution to the cinematographic art. Swedish or foreign filmmakers are eligible. A plaquette and cash amount are awarded annually. Established in 1978.

• 4683 • Golden Bug Statuette
(Guldbaggar)
For recognition of meritorious contributions to Swedish film. Awards are given in the following categories: Best Picture, Best Director, Best Actor, Best Actress, Best Support Actor, Best Support Actress, Best Manuscript, Best Cameraman, Best Foreign Film, Best short time. Special Golden Bug Award may be given for important contributions to the Swedish cinema. Seven to eleven Golden Bug Statuettes are awarded annually. Established in 1963.

• 4684 •
Swedish Library Association
(Svensk Biblioteksforening)
Box 3127
S-103 62 Stockholm, Sweden
Phone: 46 8 54513230
Fax: 46 8 54513231
E-mail: info@biblioteksforeningen.org
Home Page: http://www.biblioteksforeningen.org

• 4685 • Aniara Prize
(Aniara Priset)
For recognition of the best book written in Swedish by a Swedish author. A trophy is awarded annually. Established in 1974 in honor of Swedish author, Harry Martinsson, and his book *Aniara*.

• 4686 • Elsa Beskow Plaque
(Elsa Beskow Plaketten)
To recognize the illustrator of the best children's book published during the preceding year. A plaque of glass is awarded annually. Established in 1958 in honor of Elsa Beskow, well known children's book designer.

• 4687 • Nils Holgersson Plaque
(Nils Holgersson Plaketten)
To recognize the author of the best book for youth published during the preceding year. A plaque of glass is awarded annually. Established in 1950 in honor of Swedish author, Selma Lagerlof.

• 4688 •
Swedish Society of Aeronautics and Astronautics
(Flygtekniska Foreningen)
Gote Marcusson, Sec.
% Swedish Space Corp.
Box 4207
S-171 04 Solna, Sweden
Phone: 46 8 7672950
Fax: 46 8 987069
E-mail: sekr@flygtekniskaforeningen.org
Home Page: http://www.flygtekniskaforeningen.org

• 4689 • Thulinmedaljen

For recognition of outstanding achievement in the field of aeronautics. The following awards are presented: a gold medal for achievement of the highest merit; a silver medal for an independent work, thesis, or design to aeronautical development; and a bronze medal for the furtherance of the goals of the Society. Awarded annually. The bronze medal may be given more often. Established in 1944 by Tord Angstrom.

• 4690 •
Swedish Society of Crafts and Design (Foreningen Svensk Form)
Ewa Kumlin, Mng.Dir.
Holmamiralens vag 2
S-111 49 Stockholm, Sweden
Phone: 46 8 463 3130
Fax: 46 8 644 2285
E-mail: info@svenskform.se
Home Page: http://www.svenskform.se

• 4691 • Excellent Swedish Design Prize (Utmarkt Svensk Form)

For recognition of outstanding Swedish design products during the preceding year. Products should be well designed and of high quality with regard to function, materials, and manufacture. The jury also takes resources and environmental factors into account. The products should be produced in quantity and available on the market. Products may be entered by application or nomination. Swedish manufacturers and designers are eligible. Plaques are awarded annually. Established in 1983. Formerly: Excellence in Swedish Design Prize.

• 4692 •
Uppsala International Short Film Festival
Niclas Gillberg, Festival Dir.
PO Box 1746
S-751 47 Uppsala, Sweden
Phone: 46 18 120025
Fax: 46 18 121350
E-mail: info@shortfilmfestival.com
Home Page: http://www.shortfilmfestival.com

• 4693 • Uppsala Short Film Festival

To recognize outstanding films and to encourage professional development. The deadline is July 25. Awards are presented in the following categories: Fiction Films A (maximum 20 minutes), Fiction Films B (20-60 minutes), Animation Films (maximum 60 minutes), Documentary Films (maximum 60 minutes), Experimental Films (maximum 60 minutes), and Children's Films (maximum 60 minutes). The Uppsala Filmkaja statuette is awarded annually. Established in 1983.

Switzerland

• 4694 •
Aga Khan Trust for Culture
℅ Aga Khan Development Network
1-3 Avenue de la Paix
PO Box 2049
CH-1211 Geneva, Switzerland
Phone: 41 22 909 7200
Fax: 41 22 909 7292
E-mail: information@aiglemont.org
Home Page: http://www.akdn.org/agency/aktc.html

• 4695 • Aga Khan Award for Architecture

For recognition of architectural excellence; to nurture a heightened awareness of Islamic culture within the architectural profession, related disciplines, and society; and to encourage buildings for tomorrow's needs. In its selection process, the independent master jury considers the context in which architecture is practiced, and the social, economic, technical, and environmental factors to which the project responds. Particular consideration is given to those projects that use available resources and initiatives appropriately and creatively, that meet both the functional and cultural needs of their users, and that have the potential to stimulate related development elsewhere. Projects that have been completed within the past twelve years and that have been in use for at least one year may be nominated. The projects must be located in the Islamic world or intended for use primarily by Muslims. Monetary prizes totaling $500,000 US, trophies, and certificates are awarded to those contributors including architects, construction professionals, craftsmen, and clients who are considered most responsible for the success of a project. Awarded triennially. Established in 1977 by His Highness the Aga Khan, chairman of the Award Steering Committee.

• 4696 •
American Citizens Abroad
Karl Jauch, Exec.Dir.
5, Rue Liotard
CH-1202 Geneva, Switzerland
Phone: 41 22 3400233
Fax: 41 22 3400233
E-mail: info.aca@gmail.com
Home Page: http://www.aca.ch

• 4697 • Eugene Abrams Award

To honor an American citizen residing abroad who, through voluntary work, has made an exceptional contribution to his or her community. The purpose of the award is to acknowledge publicly meritorious voluntary work performed by Americans abroad in fields such as education, health care, care of children or the elderly, among many others as well as original initiatives taken for the benefit of a community or group of people abroad. Awarded annually.

• 4698 • Thomas Jefferson Award

To recognize outstanding service to American citizens overseas by a US State Department employee. Awarded annually. Established in 1994 to commemorate the 250th anniversary of the birth of Thomas Jefferson, America's first Secretary of State, who himself lived outside the new republic for many years in order to promote its interests.

• 4699 •
Marcel Benoist Foundation (Marcel Benoist Stiftung)
Jean-Francois Conscience Ph.D, Exec. Sec.
Federal Office for Education and Science
Hallwylstrasse 4
CH-3003 Berne, Switzerland
Phone: 41 31 322 9675
Fax: 41 31 322 7854
E-mail: info@marcel-benoist.ch
Home Page: http://www.marcel-benoist.org

• 4700 • Marcel Benoist Prize

To recognize outstanding scientific research in Switzerland. Scholars living in Switzerland are eligible. A monetary prize is awarded annually. Established in 1920.

• 4701 •
Concours de Geneve (Concours International d'Execution Musicale - Geneve)
Francois Duchene, Pres.
8 rue Bovy Lysberg
CH-1204 Geneva, Switzerland
Phone: 41 22 328 6208
Fax: 41 22 328 4366
E-mail: music@concoursgeneve.ch
Home Page: http://www.concoursgeneve.ch

• 4702 • International Competition for Musical Performers - Geneva (Concours International d'Execution Musicale - Geneve)

For recognition of the best musical performances of the Competition. Male voices (35 years and under), female voices (32 years and under), and instruments (30 years and under), must submit registration forms by May 31. Awards are given in alternate years in the following categories: voice, harp, clarinet; and trombone, contrabass, oboe-treble, violin. The following prizes are awarded: first prize - 15,000 Swiss francs; second prize - 10,000 Swiss francs; and third prize - 8,000 Swiss francs. Also awarded are: Prix Suisse - 10,000 Swiss francs, International Music Award - 30,000 Swiss francs, Prix de l'Association des Musiciens de Geneve - 2,000 Swiss francs, and Prix Paul Streit - 3,000 Swiss francs. A Rolex watch is also presented to each first prize winner. Competitions are held annually. Established in 1939 by Dr. F. Liebstoeckl and H. Gagnebin.

• 4703 •
Conference of European Churches
Rev. Keith W. Clements, Gen.Sec.
PO Box 2100
PO Box 2100
150 route de Ferney
CH-1211 Geneva 2, Switzerland
Phone: 41 22 7916111
Fax: 41 22 7916227
E-mail: cec@cec-kek.org
Home Page: http://www.cec-kek.org

• 4704 • **John Templeton Award for European Religion Writer of the Year**
To honor journalists who write about religion in the secular press with accuracy, impartiality, and an ecumenical spirit. A monetary prize of 5,000 Swiss francs is awarded annually. Sponsored by the John Templeton Foundation.

• 4705 • **John Templeton European Film Prize**
Award of recognition for films that bring Christian values to public attention. Awarded annually.

• 4706 •
European Broadcasting Union
(Union Europeenne de Radio-Television)
David Lewis, Governance, Spokesman
Ancienne Rte. 17A
CP 45
CH-1218 Grand-Saconnex, Switzerland
Phone: 41 22 7172111
Fax: 41 22 7474000
E-mail: ebu@ebu.ch
Home Page: http://www.ebu.ch

• 4707 • **Geneva-Europe Prizes**
To assist in discovering new talents and to stimulate the growth of audiovisual culture in Europe. The following awards are presented: the Assistance Prizes for Television Writing (bursaries) and the Grand Prize for Television Writing. The following awards will be presented at a public ceremony: Assistance Prizes - a training period and a monetary award every second year; and the Grand Prize for Television Writing - a monetary award every year.

• 4708 • **Grand Prix Eurovision for Young Dancers**
To encourage the rising generation of performers of dance. This competition will include all genres of dance from classical ballet to every kind of contemporary dance including jazz and hip hop. Folkdance, however, is not included in this competition. Contestants must be aged 20 or under. Held biennially in odd-numbered years.

• 4709 • **Grand Prix Eurovision for Young Musicians**
To encourage the rising generation of performers of classical music. Contestants must be aged 19 or under. Held biennially in odd-numbered years.

• 4710 • **Grand Prix of the Eurovision Song Contest**
To encourage the creation of original songs. Awarded annually. Established in 1956. Additional information is available from Christine Marchal-Ortiz, phone: 22 7172414; fax: 22 7172810.

• 4711 • **Prix Ex Aequo - International Children's and Youth Radio Drama Festival**
To promote the creation of works in the field of children's and youth radio drama; to stimulate the international exchange of radio drama productions, text and artists; and to stimulate the exchange of theoretical and technical expertise at an international level. The festival is open to all Active and Associate EBU Members organizations. Organizations may submit programs in radio drama aimed at children and young people. Programs should have been first produced and broadcasted since the previous festival. Each organization may submit two programs for each category that do not exceed 90 minutes. The festival will be held biennially in Bratislava, Slovakia. There are two categories for the contest; radio fairy tales/radio plays for children and radio plays for youth. In each category, an award will be given to an organization for the best fairy tale or children's radio play and for the best youth radio play. In each category an award will be given to an individual creator for the exceptional artistic execution of a fairy tale or children's radio play and for the exceptional artistic execution of a youth radio play.

• 4712 •
European Society of Clinical Microbiology and Infectious Diseases - Switzerland
Peter Schoch, Managing Dir.
PO Box 6
CH-4005 Basel, Switzerland
Phone: 41 61 6867799
Fax: 41 61 6867798
E-mail: info@escmid.org
Home Page: http://www.escmid.org

• 4713 • **ESCMID Research Fellowships**
For young investigators.

• 4714 • **ESCMID Turning the Tide of Resistance Research Grant**
For research in the field of antibiotic resistance.

• 4715 • **ESCMID Young Investigator Awards for Research in Clinical Microbiology and Infectious Diseases**
To individuals for excellence in research.

• 4716 •
Federation Aeronautique Internationale
Pierre Portmann, Pres.
Ave. Mon Repos 24
CH-1005 Lausanne, Switzerland
Phone: 41 21 3451070
Fax: 41 21 3451077
E-mail: executiveboard@fai.org
Home Page: http://www.fai.org

• 4717 • **Aeromodelling Gold Medal**
To recognize aeromodellers of an FAI member for outstanding merit in organization activities. Recipients must have: fulfilled at least twice the function of Competition Director or a similar function at World or European Championships; or fulfilled at least three times the function of an FAI jury member at World or European Championships; or fulfilled at least five times the function of a judge or a similar function at World or Continental Championships; or served at least three years as a delegate to the FAI Aeromodelling Commission, or served another function therein; or shown outstanding merits in developing aeromodelling by organizational activities. Awarded annually. Established in 1987.

• 4718 • **Air Sport Medal**
To recognize individuals or groups for outstanding services in connection with air sport activities. Any number of medals may be given annually for work in FAI Commissions and Committees; organizing World and Continental championships; training and education of new pilots, parachutists, or aeromodellers; or promoting aviation in general and especially with young people. Awarded annually. Established in 1991, the 100th anniversary of Lilienthal's first flights.

• 4719 • **Antonov Aeromodelling Diploma**
To recognize technical innovations in aeromodelling. Each year an active member of the FAI may submit the name of one candidate by November 15. The Antonov Diploma can be granted more than once to the same person for different technical innovations made in different years. A diploma donated by the National Aeroclub of Russia is awarded annually. Established in 1987.

• 4720 • **Leon Biancotto Aerobatics Diploma**
To recognize individuals or organizations that have contributed significantly to the sport of aerobatics. Awarded annually if merited. Established in 1993.

• 4721 • **Louis Bleriot Medal**
To recognize the holders of the highest records for speed, altitude, and distance in a straight line attained in the previous year by light aircraft. Three medals are awarded annually (unless the records of the preceding year have not been broken). Established in 1936 in memory of Louis Bleriot, an aviation pioneer and vice president of FAI.

• 4722 • **Bronze Medal**
To recognize individuals who have rendered eminent services to the FAI in administrative work, in commissions or committees, or in organizations of international sporting competitions. The award is decided by the Council by a simple majority vote. A medal is awarded annually upon proposal by the Secretary General of FAI. Established in 1962.

Awards are arranged in alphabetical order below their administering organizations

• 4723 • Colibri Microlight Diploma
To recognize outstanding contributions to the development of microlight aircraft by action, work, achievements, initiative, or devotion. Each active member of the FAI may submit the name of a candidate. Only one Diploma may be awarded annually. Established in 1983. Formerly: The Colibri Diploma.

• 4724 • Leonardo Da Vinci Parachuting Diploma
To recognize a male or female parachutist. Eligible candidates include those who have: obtained at least three times consecutively the title of National Parachuting Champion; or obtained at least once the title of World Absolute Parachuting Champion and at least twice the title of Combined Champion at an international parachuting competition; or successfully fulfilled the function of Chief Judge at least twice at an international competition and at least once at a World Parachuting Championship; or fulfilled at least three times consecutively the function of International Judge at a World Parachuting Championship; or established at least three World Parachuting records; fulfilled at least twice the function of Competition Director at an International Parachuting Contest and at least once at a World Parachuting Championship; or been or nominated Honorary President of the FAI Parachuting Commission; or been for at least 10 consecutive years, and still are a national delegate to the FAI Parachuting Commission. A diploma may be awarded annually. Established in 1970.

• 4725 • De La Vaulx Medal
To recognize the holders of absolute world records achieved during the previous year. A medal or several medals may be awarded annually. Established in 1933 in memory of Comte de La Vaulx, a founder-member and President of FAI.

• 4726 • Diploma for Outstanding Airmanship
For recognition of a pilot or flight crew on an aircraft in sub-orbital flight for a feat of outstanding airmanship having occurred during one of the previous two years and that resulted in the saving of life, or that was carried out with that objective. Eligible nominees include pilots, flight crew, or any person being temporarily in charge of an aircraft in the air. A pilot or crew engaged in a routine search and rescue mission is not eligible. A diploma may be awarded annually. Established in 1985.

• 4727 • Yuri A. Gagarin Gold Medal
To recognize the astronaut who, in the previous year, has accomplished the highest achievement in the conquest of space. An active member may submit one candidate of the same nationality. The medal may be awarded posthumously. A gold medal may be awarded annually. Established in 1968 in memory of Astronaut Yuri A. Gagarin, who performed the first human space flight in 1961 and who lost his life in an aircraft accident while carrying out a training flight.

• 4728 • Gold Air Medal
This medal, one of FAI's two highest awards, is given for recognition of outstanding contributions to the development of aeronautics through activities, work, achievements, initiative, or devotion to the cause of aviation. Active members may submit one candidate who is of the same nationality. The medal may be awarded posthumously. A gold medal is awarded annually. Established in 1924.

• 4729 • Gold Parachuting Medal
For recognition of an outstanding accomplishment in parachuting. Contributions in the realm of sport, safety, or, at the option of the Commission, an invention are considered. Each year, an active member of the FAI may submit the name of one candidate who is not a member of the FAI Parachute Commission. A medal may be awarded annually. Established in 1968.

• 4730 • Gold Rotorcraft Medal
To reward a particularly remarkable achievement in rotorcraft, including the use of a sporting vehicle or eminent services to the development of rotorcraft over an extended period of time. A medal is awarded annually if merited. Established in 1993.

• 4731 • Gold Space Medal
This medal, one of FAI's two highest awards, is awarded to individuals who have contributed greatly to the development of astronautics by their activities, work, achievements, initiative, or devotion to the cause of space. An active member may submit one candidate of the same nationality. The medal may be awarded posthumously. A gold medal is awarded annually. Established in 1963.

• 4732 • Hang Gliding Diploma
To recognize an individual who has made an outstanding contribution to the development of hang gliding by initiative, work, or leadership in flight achievements. Nominations are accepted by the FAI Hang Gliding Commission. A diploma may be awarded annually. Established in 1979.

• 4733 • Honorary Group Diploma
To recognize a group of people who has made notable contributions to the progress of aeronautics or astronautics during the previous year or years. Each year, an active member of the FAI may submit the names of two candidates, one for aeronautics and one for astronautics. Established in 1965.

• 4734 • V. M. Komarov Diploma
To recognize astronauts and members of multiseater crews for outstanding achievements in the exploration of outer space during the previous year. Each year, an active member of the FAI may submit the name of two astronauts (multi-spaceship crews) from his country. A diploma or diplomas may be awarded annually. Established in 1970 in memory of V. M. Komarov, the cosmonaut who participated in the World Space record flight of Voskhod 1 in 1964 and who lost his life while on duty on a cosmic flight.

• 4735 • Korolev Diploma
To recognize technicians or engineers who, having worked in orbit or on a celestial body in building structures and/or equipment or in a non-planned restoration or repair of a broken device to make possible the continuation of a mission, have shown human work in space. Only one Diploma is awarded each year. Established in 1988.

• 4736 • Lilienthal Gliding Medal
For recognition of a particularly remarkable performance in gliding or for eminent services to gliding over a long period of time. A glider pilot who has broken an international record during the past year, made a pioneer flight during the past year, or has given eminent services to gliding over a long period of time and is still an active glider pilot is eligible. Each year, an active member of the FAI may submit the name of one candidate. A medal may be awarded annually. Established in 1938.

• 4737 • Charles Lindbergh General Aviation Diploma
For recognition of a significant contribution for more than 10 years to the progress and success of general aviation in either its sporting or transportation manifestations or in the work of international bodies; or to recognize technical breakthroughs in the field of General Aviation as an incentive toward general progress and for the purpose of stimulating research and development of new concepts and equipment contributing to operational efficiency and flight safety. One diploma is awarded annually. Established in 1983.

• 4738 • Pepe Lopes Hang Gliding Medal
To recognize outstanding contributions to sportsmanship or international understanding in the sport of hang gliding. Awarded annually when merited. Established in 1993 in memory of Pedro Paulo ("Pepe") Lopes, World Hang Gliding Champion in 1981.

• 4739 • Pelagia Majewska Gliding Medal
To recognize a female glider pilot for a particularly remarkable performance in gliding during the past year, or eminent services to gliding over a long period of time. Each year any FAI member may submit the name of one candidate to be considered and acted upon by the FAI Gliding Commission and the Council. A medal is awarded annually. Established in 1989 following a proposal by the Aero Club of Poland in memory of Madame Pelagia Majewska, eminent Polish glider pilot who was awarded the Lilienthal Medal in 1960, holds 17 world gliding records, and lost her life in an air accident in 1988.

• 4740 • Henry Mignet Diploma
To recognize the amateur aircraft builder who has constructed an aircraft of a new design with notable improvements. To qualify, the aircraft must have outstanding performance and low

fuel consumption at cruising speed, low noise level, and safe handling characteristics. A diploma may be awarded annually. Established in 1984.

• 4741 • Montgolfier Ballooning Diploma
To recognize each of the following: the best sporting performance in the previous Montgolfier year of a gas balloonist; the best sporting performance in the previous Montgolfier year of a hot air balloonist; and a major contribution to the development of the sport of ballooning in general. Sporting performances, including; records for distance, altitude, duration, and precision of landing: number of ascents; hours of flying; or any other performance that might be judged by the FAI Ballooning Commission to be most meritorious may be submitted for consideration. Three diplomas are awarded annually if merited. Established in 1960.

• 4742 • Nile Gold Medal
For recognition of distinguished work in the field of aerospace education, particularly during the preceding year. A person, group of persons, or organization is eligible. Each active member of the FAI may propose one candidate each year. A gold medal is presented annually by the Aero Club of Egypt. Established in 1972.

• 4743 • Odyssey Diploma
To recognize a person or a group of persons whose actions, achievements, or works on earth, in space, or on a celestial body have safeguarded or may safeguard human life in space. Each year, an FAI member may submit the name of one candidate before the end of January. Awarded annually. Established in 1988.

• 4744 • Alphonse Penaud Aeromodelling Diploma
To recognize an aeromodeller of FAI members who have: obtained at least three times consecutively the title of National Champion or at least once obtained the title of World Champion; or established at least three world records; or been at least twice Competition Director or a similar function at world and/or continental championships; or been at least three times an FAI jury member at world and/or continental championships; or been at least three times an FAI judge at world and/or continental championships; or been at least for three years Delegate of their NAC to CIAM; or shown outstanding merits in developing aeromodelling as a sport, technique, or organization. A diploma is awarded annually. Established in 1979.

• 4745 • Phoenix Diploma
For recognition of the best reconstruction or restoration of a vintage (more than 30 years old) aircraft achieved by an amateur. Each active member may submit the name of one candidate. A diploma may be awarded annually. Established in 1978.

• 4746 • Santos-Dumont Gold Airship Medal
To recognize Alberto Santos-Dumont for his contributions to the development and the sport of flying airships. A medal may be awarded on recommendation of the Ballooning Commission to reward: the best sporting performance in the previous Montgolfier year in airships; and a major contribution to the development of the sport of airship flying in general. Each year an FAI member may submit the name of one candidate. A medal is awarded annually when merited. Established in 1994.

• 4747 • Paul Tissandier Diploma
For recognition of distinguished service to the cause of aviation in general and sporting aviation in particular. Each active member of the FAI may submit the name of a candidate. A diploma is awarded annually. Established in 1952 in memory of Paul Tissandier, Secretary General of FAI from 1919 to 1945.

• 4748 • Andrei Tupolev Aeromodelling Diploma
For recognition of an outstanding record performance in aeromodelling. Each year an active member of the FAI may submit the name of one candidate. Only one Diploma is awarded annually. Established in 1989.

• 4749 • Andrei Tupolev Aeromodelling Medal
To recognize aeromodellers who, in the same year, win the World and National Aeromodelling Championships in the same class of models. One medal is awarded each year. Established in 1989.

• 4750 • Young FAI Artists Contest
To make the children of FAI-member countries more familiar with aeronautics and astronautics. Winners are chosen from three age classes: 6-9, 10-13, and 14-17. Gold, silver, and bronze FAI medals and a diploma are awarded to three winners in each age class at the Annual General Conference. Established in 1986. Sponsored by the FAI Aerospace Education Committee (CIEA) with the help of national and regional aero clubs.

• 4751 •
Federation Internationale de Football Association
Joseph S. Blatter, Pres.
FIFA House
Hitzigweg 11
PO Box 85
CH-8030 Zurich, Switzerland
Phone: 41 43 222 7777
Fax: 41 43 222 7878
E-mail: contact@fifa.org
Home Page: http://www.fifa.com

• 4752 • FIFA Futsal (Indoor Football) World Championship
To recognize the futsal (indoor football/soccer) champions. Awarded every four years. Established in 1989 in Holland. Formerly: FIFA Five-a-Side (Indoor Football) World Championship.

• 4753 • FIFA U-17 World Championship
To recognize the football (soccer) champions in the tournament. Awarded biennially. Established in 1985 in China. Formerly: FIFA U-17 World Tournament.

• 4754 • FIFA Women's World Cup
To recognize the women's football (soccer) champions. Established in China in 1991. Awarded every four years.

• 4755 • FIFA World Cup Trophy
For recognition of the world football (soccer) champions. A gold trophy is engraved with winning team's name and a replica in gold plate is awarded at the tournament held every four years. Established in 1930. Formerly: Jules Rimet Cup.

• 4756 • Olympic Football Tournaments (Men and Women)
To recognize the football (soccer) champions in the Olympic Games. Awarded every four years. The Olympics were established in 1896. Football was first included in the program in 1904. Players may be professional but under 23 years old with the exception of 3 overage players. Women's football tournament was introduced in Atlanta at the 1996 Olympics.

• 4757 • World Youth Championship for the FIFA/Coca-Cola Cup
To recognize the world youth football (soccer) champions. Awarded biennially. Established in 1977 in Tunisia.

• 4758 •
Federation Internationale de Natation Amateur
(Federation Internationale de Natation Amateur)
Ave. de l'Avant-Poste 4
CH-1005 Lausanne, Switzerland
Phone: 41 21 310 4710
Fax: 41 21 312 6610
Home Page: http://www.fina.org

• 4759 • FINA Prize
This, the highest award of the swimming world, is given to recognize individuals or organizations, within or outside FINA, who have contributed to the activities and development of the FINA disciplines through their interest, performance, and influence. The FINA Prize is awarded annually. In addition, FINA Gold Pins, FINA Silver Pins, FINA Diplomas or Certificates of Merit, and FINA Honor Plaques are awarded when deemed appropriate by the FINA Bureau. Established in 1973. Formerly: (1985) FINA Prize Eminence.

• 4760 •
Geza Anda Foundation
Ruth Bossart, Sec.
Bleicherweg 18
CH-8002 Zurich, Switzerland
Phone: 41 1 205 1423
Fax: 41 1 205 1205
E-mail: info@gezaanda.ch
Home Page: http://www.gezaanda.ch

• 4761 • **Geza Anda International Piano Competition**
(Concours Geza Anda)
To sponsor young pianists in the musical spirit of Geza Anda. Pianists who are under 32 years of age are eligible. Besides concert engagements in international music centers for the three prize winners and free management services during three years, the following monetary prizes are awarded: 30,000 Swiss francs - first prize; 20,000 Swiss francs - second prize; and 10,000 Swiss francs - third prize. The following special prizes are also awarded: such as the Geza Anda Audience Prize and the Mozart-Prize awarded by the Musikkollegium Winterthur. Awarded triennially. Established in 1978 by the Geza Anda Foundation in memory of Geza Anda, a pianist.

• 4762 •
Gottlieb Duttweiler Institut
David Bosshart, CEO
Langhaldenstrasse 21
Postfach 531
CH-8803 Rueschlikon, Switzerland
Phone: 41 44 724 6111
Fax: 41 44 724 6262
E-mail: info@gdi.ch
Home Page: http://www.gdi.ch
Formerly: (2004) Green Meadow Foundation.

• 4763 • **Gottlieb Duttweiler Prize**
For recognition of individuals who have made a commendable contribution, either academic or in practice, toward the realization of a cultural, social, or economic environment that permits self-expression and participation by all in its continual shaping. A monetary prize is awarded every two to three years. Established in 1958 on the occasion of the 70th anniversary of Gottlieb Duttweiler, the founder of Migros.

• 4764 •
Clara Haskil Association
Patrick Peikert, Dir.
31, rue du Conseil
Case postale 234
CH-1800 Vevey, Switzerland
Phone: 41 21 922 6704
Fax: 41 21 922 6734
E-mail: clara.haskil@bluewin.ch
Home Page: http://www.regart.ch/clara-haskil

• 4765 • **Clara Haskil Competition**
(Concours Clara Haskil)
To recognize and help a young pianist whose approach to piano interpretation is "of the same spirit that constantly inspired Clara Haskil and that she illustrated so perfectly." Male and female pianists from any country who are 27 years of age or younger are eligible to apply by July 1. A monetary prize of 20,000 Swiss francs, a broadcasted public concert (together with the other finalists), a concert engagement during the Festival, and concerts at other music centers in Europe are awarded biennially in August. Established in 1963 by the Clara Haskil Association and the Lucerne Festival in memory of Clara Haskil, a Romanian pianist famous for her interpretive skills. From 1973 through 1984 the Competition was organized by the Montreux-Vevey Music Festival. Since 1985, the Competition has been organized independently.

• 4766 •
Institute of International Law
(Institut de Droit International)
Mrs. Isabelle Gerardi, Asst.
132 rue de Lausanne
33, route de Suisse
CH-1211 Geneva 21, Switzerland
Phone: 41 22 9085720
Phone: 41 22 9085720
Fax: 41 22 9085710
E-mail: gerardi@hei.unige.ch
Home Page: http://www.idi-iil.org/

• 4767 • **James Brown Scott Prizes**
For recognition of contributions to international law in theory and practice. Thirteen prizes are designed to reward the authors of the best dissertations devoted to a specific topic of public international law. These prizes bear the following names: Prix Andres Bello, Prix Carlos Calvo, Prix Grotius, Prix Francis Lieber, Prix Frederic de Martens, Prix Mancini, Prix Samuel Pufendorf, Prix Louis Renault, Prix G. Rolin-Jaequemyns, Prix Emer de Vattel, Prix Vitoria, Prix John Westlake, and Prix Henri Wheaton. The prizes are offered for competition in rotation so that one prize may, where appropriate, be awarded every four years. The prize awarded in 1950 bore the name of Grotius. Thereafter, the order of rotation was in the alphabetical order of the names. The competition is open to any person, except members and former members, associates and former associates of the institute. Dissertations must be submitted by December 31 of the preceding year. The topic and the ammount suggested for the Prize are printed each year in the *Annuaire de l'Institut de Droit international.* This information can be obtained through the Secretariat of the Institute. The prizes were established in 1931 by James Brown Scott in memory of his mother and his sister, Jeannette Scott.

• 4768 •
Interactive Publishing GmbH
Bettina Tamo, Mng.Dir.
Schonbuhlstrasse 10
CH-8032 Zurich, Switzerland
Phone: 41 1256 7088
Fax: 41 1256 7080
E-mail: info@iptop.com
Home Page: http://www.interactivepublishing.net

• 4769 • **IP Top Awards**
To highlight the best interactive publishing ventures from all European countries, in all languages and formats, reflecting a need for a European voice in matters digital. Entries are judged upon content, interactivity, innovation, and community features. Awarded annually in the categories of: Financial Content, News Content, Sports Content, Corporate Communications, Entertainment, Documentary/Reports, and Content Development. Established in 1998.

• 4770 •
International 5.5 Class Association
Thomas Sprecher, Pres.
Kesslerstrasse 14
CH-8702 Zollikon, Switzerland
Phone: 41 1 3901470
Fax: 41 1 3901471
E-mail: t.sprecher@bluewin.ch
Home Page: http://www.5point5.org

• 4771 • **World Champion**
Recognizes the winner of the World Championship. A trophy is awarded annually.

• 4772 •
International Association for Bridge and Structural Engineering
(Internationale Vereinigung fur Bruckenbau und Hochbau)
Alain Golay, Exec.Dir.
ETH-Honggerberg
CH-8093 Zurich, Switzerland
Phone: 41 44 6332647
Fax: 41 44 6331241
E-mail: secretariat@iabse.org
Home Page: http://www.iabse.org

• 4773 • **IABSE Outstanding Structure Award**
Recognizes not necessarily the largest, longest, highest, but clearly the most remarkable, innovative, creative, or otherwise stimulating structures. Established in 1998.

• 4774 • **IABSE Prize**
To honor an individual early in his or her career for an outstanding achievement in the field of structural engineering. Members forty years of age or younger are eligible. A medal and a certificate are awarded annually at the conference. Established in 1983.

• 4775 • **International Award of Merit in Structural Engineering**
For recognition of outstanding contributions in the field of construction engineering, with special reference to their usefulness to society. Contributions may include the following aspects: planning, design, and construction; materials and equipment; and education, research, government, and management. Structural engineers who are members or non-members of the Association are eligible. A medal and a certificate are awarded annually at the conference. Established in 1975.

• 4776 • Outstanding Paper Award
To recognize an outstanding article published in *Structural Engineering International.* Awarded annually. Established in 1993.

• 4777 •
International Association for the Study of Insurance Economics
(Association International pour l'Etude de l'Economie de l'Assurance)
Mr. Patrick Liedtke, Sec.Gen.
53 Rte. de Malagnou
CH-1208 Geneva, Switzerland
Phone: 41 22 7076600
Fax: 41 22 7367536
E-mail: secretariat@genevaassociation.org
Home Page: http://www.genevaassociation.org

• 4778 • Ernst Meyer Prize
(Prix Ernst Meyer)
To recognize university research work that makes a significant and original contribution to the study of risk and insurance economics. Students or researchers may apply for the award mainly by the presentation of a Ph.D. thesis. A monetary prize of 5,000 Swiss francs is awarded annually. Established in 1974 by the Geneva Association. The award honors Ernst Meyer, former Managing Director of the Allianz and founding father of the Geneva Association. The Association also awards research grants and subsidies for thesis publication.

• 4779 •
International Basketball Federation
(Federation Internationale de Basketball)
Mr. Patrick Baumann, Sec.Gen.
8, Ch. De Blandonnet
Vernier
CH-1214 Geneva, Switzerland
Phone: 41 22 5450000
Fax: 41 22 5450099
E-mail: info@fiba.com
Home Page: http://www.fiba.com

• 4780 • Order of Merit
For outstanding contributions to basketball and sports in general. Awarded annually.

• 4781 • Radomir Shaper Prize
Recognizes individuals who have distinguished themselves in the field of basketball rules. Awarded periodically.

• 4782 •
International Board on Books for Young People
(Union Internationale pour les livres de jeunesse)
Leena Maissen, Exec.Dir.
Nonnenweg 12
Postfach
CH-4003 Basel, Switzerland
Phone: 41 61 2722917
Fax: 41 61 2722757
E-mail: ibby@ibby.org
Home Page: http://www.ibby.org
Formerly: (1989) International Board on Books for Young People (IBBY) - Canadian Section.

• 4783 • Claude Aubry Award
(Prix Claude Aubry)
For recognition of achievement in the field of Canadian children's literature. Canadian citizens who have made lasting and significant contributions to the development and/or promotion of Canadian children's literature are eligible for the award. A monetary award of $1,000 is presented biennially. Established in 1981 in honor of Claude Aubry, a Canadian author and librarian.

• 4784 • Elizabeth Mrazik-Cleaver Canadian Picture Book Award
(Prix Elizabeth Mrazik Cleaver pour le meilleur livre d'images canadien)
For recognition of excellence in the area of the Canadian picture books and to give some financial support to Canadian illustrators of children's books. Living Canadian citizens who are illustrators of picture books published in Canada in English or French during the previous calendar year are eligible. A monetary award of $1,000 and a certificate are awarded annually. Established in 1986 by Elizabeth Cleaver, an internationally known illustrator of Canadian picture books, who died in 1985, and left in her will the original fund of $10,000 for the establishment of the award. Administered by IBBY Canada.

• 4785 • Frances E. Russell Award
(Prix Frances E. Russell)
To encourage research in Canadian children's literature. Applicants must be Canadian citizens or landed immigrants and must submit applications by September 30. A grant of $1,000 is awarded annually. Established in 1982 by Marjorie Russell in memory of Frances E. Russell. Administered by IBBY Canada.

• 4786 •
International Catholic Union of the Press
(Union Catholique Internationale de la Presse)
Joseph C. Chittilappilly, Sec. Gen.
Case Postale 197
CH-1211 Geneva, Switzerland
Phone: 41 22 7340017
Fax: 41 22 7340053
E-mail: helo@ucip.ch
Home Page: http://www.ucip.ch

• 4787 • Titus Brandsma Award
To a catholic journalist or publisher who has suffered persecution.

• 4788 • Gold Medal Award
To individual, group or institutions who championed the freedom of opinion in the fullest sense.

• 4789 • International Award for Photojournalism
For a professional photojournalist.

• 4790 • International Media Awards

• 4791 •
International Committee of the Red Cross
(Comite International de la Croix-Rouge)
J. Kellenberger, Pres.
19, Avenue de la Paix
CH-1202 Geneva, Switzerland
Phone: 41 22 734 6001
Fax: 41 22 733 2057
E-mail: webmaster.gva@icrc.org
Home Page: http://www.icrc.org

• 4792 • Florence Nightingale Medal
(Medaille Florence Nightingale)
To recognize qualified male or female nurses and voluntary nursing aides who are active members or regular helpers of a National Red Cross or Red Crescent Society, or of an affiliated medical or nursing institution, for having distinguished themselves in time of peace or war, by exceptional courage and devotion to wounded, sick, or disabled persons or to civilian victims of a conflict or disaster and by exemplary services or creative and pioneering spirits in the areas of public health or nursing education. The medal may be awarded posthumously if the prospective recipient has fallen on active service. The award is presented by the International Committee of the Red Cross (ICRC) on proposals made to it by National Red Cross and Red Crescent Societies. The deadline is March 12 of odd numbered years. A medal and a diploma are awarded biennially. The medal is silver-gilt with a portrait of Florence Nightingale and the words "Ad memoriam Florence Nightingale 1820-1910" inscribed on the obverse, and "Pro vera misericordia et cara humanitate perennis decor universalis" on the reverse. The name of the holder and the date of the award are engraved in the center. The medal is attached by a red and white ribbon to a laurel crown surrounding a red cross. No more than 50 medals are issued at any one distribution. Established in 1912 by contributions from National Societies of the Red Cross in memory of the distinguished services of Florence Nightingale for the improvement of the care of the wounded and sick.

• 4793 • Paul Reuter Prize
To recognize a work aimed at improving knowledge or understanding of international humanitarian law. The work must either be unpublished or have been published since the closing date for submissions for the previous award. The deadline for applications is September 15. A

monetary prize of 5,000 Swiss francs is awarded triennially. Established in 1983.

• 4794 •
International Exhibition Logistics Associates
Hans R. Brauchli, Exec.Dir.
PO Box 30
CH-1218 Grand-Saconnex, Switzerland
Phone: 41 22 9200119
Fax: 41 22 9200209
E-mail: info@iela.ch
Home Page: http://www.iela.org

• 4795 • **International Exhibition Logistics Associates Awards**
To recognize outstanding contributions in the field of exhibition organization. Awarded annually at the Congress.

• 4796 •
International Federation of Consulting Engineers
(Federation Internationale des Ingenieurs Conseils)
Richard A. Kell, Pres.
World Trade Center II
PO Box 311
CH-1215 Geneva 15, Switzerland
Phone: 41 22 7994900
Fax: 41 22 7994901
E-mail: fidic@fidic.org
Home Page: http://www.fidic.org

• 4797 • **Louis Prangey Award**
Recognizes significant contribution to the consulting industry. Awarded annually.

• 4798 •
International Federation of Sound Hunters
(Federation Internationale des Chasseurs de Son)
Helmut Weber, Sec.Gen.
Riedernrain 264
CH-3027 Bern, Switzerland
Phone: 41 31 991 6240
Fax: 41 31 950 3330
E-mail: weber@soundhunters.com
Home Page: http://www.soundhunters.com

• 4799 • **Jean Thevenot Medal**
(Medaille Jean Thevenot)
To encourage sound and video recording. Entries for the international contest are considered. A monetary prize, medal, trophy, and equipment are awarded annually. The Jean Thevenot Medal is awarded when merited. The contest was established in 1951 and the medal in 1984 in honor of Jean Thevenot, founder of FICS. Additional information is available from Mr. The General Secretary, Helmut Weber, Riedernrain 264, CH-3027 Bern, Switzerland.

• 4800 •
International Federation of Standards Users
E. Patrikeev, Sec.
1 Rue de Varembe
Casa Postale 56
CH-1211 Geneva 20, Switzerland
Phone: 41 22 7490331
Phone: 41 22 7490111
Fax: 41 22 749 0155
E-mail: ifan@iso.org
Home Page: http://www.ifan.org

• 4801 • **Georges Garel Award**
Presented to individuals for their outstanding services to the international community of standards users. Awarded periodically.

• 4802 •
International Federation of University Women - Switzerland
(Federation Internationale des Femmes Diplomees des Universites)
Murielle Joye, Sec.Gen.
8, rue de l'Ancien-Port
CH-1201 Geneva, Switzerland
Phone: 41 22 7312380
Fax: 41 22 7380440
E-mail: info@ifuw.org
Home Page: http://www.ifuw.org

• 4803 • **International Federation of University Women Awards Competition**
To biennialy encourage advanced scholarship by enabling university women to undertake original research in some country other than that in which they have received their education or habitually reside. Deadline falls between mid-September and early October of the year preceding the awards. Applicants must be members of the Federation and be well started on the research program. A fellowship is not awarded for the first year of a Ph.D. program. The following fellowships and grants are awarded biennially: IFUW Ida Smedley MacLean International Fellowship - 8,000 Swiss francs; CFUW A. Vibert Douglas International Fellowship - $12,000 Canadian; British Federation Crosby Hall Fellowship - £2,500; IFUW-JAUW Peace Fellowship $10,000 US; and a number of Winifred Cullis and Dorothy Leet Grants - stipend is determined according to need, normally between 3,000 and 6,000 Swiss francs. The Winifred Cullis Grants assist women graduates to obtain specialized training essential to their research; train in new techniques in the humanities, social sciences, and natural sciences; and carry out independent research, including completion of a piece of research well advanced. The Dorothy Leet Grants assist women graduates of countries with a comparatively low per capita income. Grants are also given to other women graduates who wish to work as experts in these countries or whose research is of value to such countries. For further information for U.S. residents, contact AAUW/IFUW Liaison American Association of University Women, 1111 16th St., NW, Washington, D.C. 20036; for all others, contact IFUW headquarters. American Association of University Women, 1111 16th St., NW, Washington, D.C. 20036; for all others, contact IFUW headquarters.

• 4804 •
International Festival of Mountain and Environment Films
(Festival International du Film Alpin et de l'Environment de Montagne, Les Diablerets, Suisse)
Charles Pascal Ghiringhelli, Pres.
CP 3
CH-1865 Les Diablerets, Switzerland
Phone: 41 24 492 2040
Fax: 41 24 492 2348
E-mail: info@fifad.ch
Home Page: http://www.fifad.ch

• 4805 • **International Festival of Mountain Environment and Alpine Films, Les Diablerets, Switzerland**
(Festival International du Film Alpin et de l'Environement de Montagne, Les Diablerets, Suisse)
To encourage and develop the production of films which will stimulate, both in Switzerland and abroad, an interest in the Alps and in the people who live and work in the mountains. An "Alpine Film" is to be understood as any film or video tape with action situated in the mountains, and a "Mountain Environment Film" as any production focusing attention on, or portraying, a place or region which deserves to be preserved or which is already protected. The entries are divided into three categories: (1) Identity of the mountain life (specificities, testimonies, traditions, habits, and customs); (2) Sports activities in mountains; and (3) Safeguard of the environment of mountains. The Festival is open to all filmmakers, professional, free-lance, or amateurs. Films must be submitted in 16mm or 35mm formats, with optical magnetic or double band (sepmag) sound. Videotapes should be system VHS (Pal, Secam, NTSC) or Betcam SP (Pal). The following prizes are awarded: (1) Grand Prix du Festival des Diablerets - for the film receiving the unanimous votes of the Jury. The winning of this prize automatically excludes the film from consideration for further awards (except the Public's Prize); (2) Diables d'Or - one Diable (Devil) for each of the three categories; (3) Grain d'Or - to a film that offers something new for adventure films; (4) Special Prizes donated by various organizations outside the Festival, who stipulate the rules for the award; and (5) Public's Prize - awarded by the Festival Organizing Committee according to votes received from the public after each viewing. Established in 1975.

• 4806 •
International Handball Federation
(Federation Internationale de Handball)
Hasan Moustafa, Pres.
Peter Merian-Strasse 23
CH-4002 Basel, Switzerland
Phone: 41 61 2289040
Fax: 41 61 2289055
E-mail: ihf.office@ihf.ch
Home Page: http://www.ihf.info

• 4807 • Hans-Baumann-Trophy

To recognize the member association of the IHF that has most successfully contributed to the development and propagation of handball in their country or in the whole world. A trophy is awarded biennially at the ordinary IHF Congress. Established in memory of Hans Baumann, second president of the International Handball Federation.

• 4808 •

International Ice Hockey Federation
Jan-Ake Edvinsson, Gen.Sec.
Brandschenkestr. 50
Postfach
CH-8039 Zurich, Switzerland
Phone: 41 1 5622200
Phone: 41 1 5622229
Fax: 41 1 5622239
E-mail: office@iihf.com
Home Page: http://www.iihf.com

• 4809 • International Ice Hockey Federation Championships

To encourage the playing of ice hockey by organizing regular international competitions and championships. European Championships have been held since 1910, and World Championships since 1920.

• 4810 •

International Institute for Promotion and Prestige
(Institut International de Promotion et de Prestige)
Dr. Bernard Fourquet, Sci.Dir.
1, rue de Varembe
CH-1202 Geneva, Switzerland
Phone: 41 22 733 8614
Fax: 41 22 734 2538
E-mail: info@iipp.org
Home Page: http://www.iipp.org

• 4811 • International Institute for Promotion and Prestige Awards

To honor and encourage individuals, groups, firms, and institutions that contribute to international exchange and work to improve living conditions for all mankind in industrial, scientific, and technological areas. Awards are presented in the following categories: economics and industrial fields; scientific and technological fields; humanitarian and social fields and cultural and tourism fields. Established in 1967.

• 4812 •

International Motorcycle Federation
(Federation Internationale de Motocyclisme)
Guy Maitre, CEO
11, route de Suisse
CH-1295
CH-1295 Mies, Switzerland
Phone: 41 22 950 9500
Fax: 41 22 950 9501
E-mail: info@fim.ch
Home Page: http://www.fim.ch

• 4813 • Environmental Award

To reward a significant contribution to environmental protection, such as prevention of oil and fuel leakage, litter, and inordinate sound levels. A trophy and monetary prize of $5,000 are awarded when merited. Established in 1995.

• 4814 • FIM Fair Play Trophy (Trophee du Fairplay FIM)

For recognition of fair play in the world of motorcycling. Awarded when merited. Established in 1983.

• 4815 • Gold Medal of the FIM

For recognition of outstanding accomplishments in the sport of motorcycling. Awarded when merited. Established in 1963.

• 4816 • Prix du Merite Motocycliste

For recognition of contributions to the sport of motorcycling. Gold, silver, and bronze medals are awarded when merited. Established in 1983.

• 4817 • World Motorcycle Championships

To encourage and draw up regulations for the sport of motorcycling in all of its disciplines by controlling worldwide through its members the application of rules, standards, and, in particular, its codes. The FIM is the sole international authority empowered to control international motorcycling activities organized under its jurisdiction throughout the world. The official titles of World Championships, Intercontinental Championships, Continental Championships, and FIM Prize Events, in all disciplines of the motorcycle sport belong to the FIM. Motorcycle World Championship events held each year determine: Road Racing World Champions, World Champions Motocross and Supercross, Trial World Champions, Enduro World Champions, and World Track Racing Champions.

• 4818 •

International Olympic Committee
(Comite International Olympique)
Jacques Rogge, Pres.
Chateau de Vidy
Case Postale 356
CH-1007 Lausanne, Switzerland
Phone: 41 21 6216111
Fax: 41 21 6216216
Home Page: http://www.olympic.org/uk/organisation/ioc/index_uk.asp

• 4819 • Olympiart

To recognize an artist who has distinguished him/herself through the creation of works of outstanding aesthetic qualities in the field of the visual and plastic arts, architecture, literature, or music, and for his/her interest in youth, peace, and sport. Established in 1992.

• 4820 • Olympic Cup (Coupe Olympique)

For recognition of an institution or association with a general reputation for merit and integrity that has been active and efficient in the service of sport and has contributed substantially to the development of the Olympic Movement. The Cup remains at the Chateau de Vidy, and a reproduction is awarded annually. Established by the Baron de Coubertin in 1906.

• 4821 • Olympic Medals and Diplomas (Medailles et Diplomes Olympique)

To recognize winners of individual and team events at the summer and winter Olympics. The following awards are given: first prize - a silver-gilt medal and a diploma; second prize - a silver medal and a diploma; and third prize - a bronze medal and a diploma. The medals must bear the name of the sport concerned and be fastened to a detachable chain or ribbon to be hung around the neck of the athlete. Diplomas, not medals, are also awarded for the fourth, fifth, sixth, seventh and eighth places, if any. All participants in a tie for first, second and third places are entitled to receive a medal and a diploma. The names of all winners are inscribed upon the walls of the main stadium where the Olympic Games have taken place. Awarded every four years. Established in 1896.

• 4822 • Olympic Order (Ordre Olympique)

To recognize an individual who has illustrated the Olympic ideal through his action, has achieved remarkable merit in the sporting world, or has rendered outstanding services to the Olympic cause, either through his own personal achievement or his contribution to the development of sport. Nominations are proposed by the Olympic Order's Council and decided upon by the Executive Board. Active members of the IOC may not be admitted as such into the Olympic Order. From 1974 through 1984, the award was presented in three Orders: gold, silver and bronze. Since 1984, there has been no distinction between the silver and bronze Order. The insignia of the Olympic Order and the diploma are conferred upon the recipient by the President, by a member of the IOC nominated by him, or, failing that, by someone approved by the President. Awarded annually. Established in 1974.

• 4823 •

International Organization for Succulent Plant Study
(Internationale Organisation fur Sukkulentenforschung)
Dr. T. Bolliger, Treas.
Sukkulenten-Sammlung Zurich
Mythenquai 88
CH-8002 Zurich, Switzerland
Phone: 41 22 3486162
Fax: 41 22 3486162
E-mail: secretariat@iosweb.org
Home Page: http://www.iosweb.org/

• 4824 • Cactus d'Or (Golden Cactus)

For recognition of contributions to the scientific knowledge of succulent plants by exploration in the field. Nomination is by the Executive Board of the organization. A trophy is awarded biennially in even-numbered years. Established in

1978 by HRH Princess Grace of Monaco. Sponsored by the City Council of Monaco.

• 4825 •
International Peace Bureau
(Bureau International de la Paix)
Colin Archer, Gen.Sec.
41, rue de Zurich
CH-1201 Geneva, Switzerland
Phone: 41 22 7316429
Phone: 41 22 7414010
Fax: 41 22 7389419
E-mail: mailbox@ipb.org
Home Page: http://www.ipb.org

• 4826 • **Sean MacBride Peace Prize**
Recognizes outstanding work for peace/human rights. Awarded annually.

• 4827 •
International Quorum of Film and Video Producers
Denny Ranson, Exec.Dir.
Ruetistrasse 26
CH-8207 Zolliken, Switzerland
E-mail: simona@playground-media.com
Home Page: http://www.iqfilm.org/

• 4828 • **One World Award**
To recognize a film that demonstrates international cooperation and understanding. Awarded annually as part of the International Film and Video Festival.

• 4829 •
International Road Transport Union
(Union International des Transports Routiers)
Martin Marmy, Sec.Gen.
3 rue de Varembe
CH-1211 Geneva 20, Switzerland
Phone: 41 22 9182700
Fax: 41 22 9182741
E-mail: iru@iru.org
Home Page: http://www.iru.org

• 4830 • **Grand Prix d'Honneur**
To recognize an act of outstanding bravery by a professional road transport driver of a bus, coach, or truck accomplished in the course of professional duties. Candidates may be nominated by IRU member associations (in the United States, the America Trucking Association-ATA). A monetary prize, a diploma, and a gold button badge are awarded biennially at the IRU Congress. Established in 1967.

• 4831 •
International Service for Human Rights - Switzerland
Mr. Christopher Sidoti, Dir.
PO Box 16
PO Box 16
CH-1211 Geneva, Switzerland
Phone: 41 22 7335123
Fax: 41 22 7330826
E-mail: inf@ishr-sidh.ch
Home Page: http://www.ishr.ch

• 4832 • **Human Rights Award**
Recognizes exceptional contributions to the work of the UN Commission on Human Rights. Diplomats and UN experts are eligible. Awarded annually if merited.

• 4833 •
International Skating Union
Mr. Fredi Schmid, Gen.Sec.
Chemin de Primerose 2
CH-1007 Lausanne, Switzerland
Phone: 41 21 6126666
Fax: 41 21 6126677
E-mail: info@isu.ch
Home Page: http://www.isu.org

• 4834 • **Speed and Figure Skating Championships**
To recognize the winners of the speed skating and figure skating championships. The following Speed Skating Championships are held: (1) World Speed Skating Championship for Ladies and Men; (2) European Speed Skating Championships for Ladies and Men; (3) World Sprint Speed Skating Championships for Ladies and Men; (4) World Junior Speed Skating Championships for Ladies and Men; (5) World Single Distance Championships for Ladies and Men; (6) European Short Track Speed Skating Championships for Ladies and Men; (7) World Short Track Speed Skating Team Championships; and (8) World Junior Short Track Speed Skating Championships for Ladies and Men. The following Figure Skating Championships are held for Men, Ladies, Pairs and Dance: (1) World Figure Skating Championships; (2) European Figure Skating Championships; and (3) World Junior Figure Skating Championships. Awarded annually. Established in 1906.

• 4835 •
International Ski Federation
(Federation Internationale de Ski)
Gian Franco Kasper, Pres.
Marc Hodler House
Blochstr. 2
CH-3653 Oberhofen, Switzerland
Phone: 41 33 2446161
Fax: 41 33 2446171
E-mail: mail@fisski.ch
Home Page: http://www.fis-ski.com

• 4836 • **Alpine World Cup Champions**
To recognize the men's and women's overall champion in the ski racing competition. In addition, the following awards are presented: Alpine World Cup Medals - to recognize men and women in four categories: slalom, giant slalom, downhill, and super 6; The Nations Cup - to recognize the country whose skiers accumulate the most points in the competition; World Cup Jumping Leaders - established in 1981; Nordic World Cup Leaders - established in 1974; Nordic Combined World Cup Leaders established in 1984; and Skier of the Year - established in 1975. Awarded annually. Established in 1967.

• 4837 •
International Society for Engineering Education
(Internationale Gesellschaft fur Ingenieurpadagogik)
F. Flueckiger, Pres.
University of Applied Sciences of Southern Switzerland
Galleria 2, Via Cantonale
CH-6928 Manno, Switzerland
Phone: 41 91 6108580
Fax: 41 91 6108581
E-mail: info@igip.info
Home Page: http://www.igip.info

• 4838 • **IGIP Award**
(IGIP-Preis)
To honor outstanding scientific or practical works in the field of engineering education. A monetary award is presented biennially. Established in 1986.

• 4839 •
International Society of Electrochemistry
Dr. Roscoe S. Wolfville, Sec.Gen.
Ave. Vinet 19
CH-1004 Lausanne, Switzerland
Fax: 41 21 6483975
E-mail: info@ise-online.org
Home Page: http://www.ise-online.org

• 4840 • **Electrochimica Acta Gold Medal**
To recognize contributions in the field of electrochemistry. Work must have been completed in the past two years. A certificate and medal are awarded biennially in even-numbered years.

• 4841 • **Hans-Jurgen Engell Prize**
Recognizes work in the field of corrosion, electrodeposition, or surface treatment. Applicants must be young electrochemists. Awarded annually.

• 4842 • **Frumkin Memorial Medal**
Recognizes outstanding contributions of a living individual over his/her life in the field of fundamental electrochemistry. Awarded biennially in odd-numbered years.

• 4843 • **Oronzio and Niccolo De Nora Foundation Prize of ISE on Electrochemical Energy Conversion**
Recognizes recent application-oriented achievements in the field of electrochemical energy conversion. Applicants must be under the age of 35 on January 1 of the year of the award. Awarded annually.

• 4844 • Oronzio and Niccolo De Nora Foundation Prize of ISE on Electrochemical Technology and Engineering
Recognizes recent application-oriented achievements in the field of electrochemical technology and engineering. Applicants must be under the age of 35 on January 1 of the year of the award. Awarded annually.

• 4845 • Oronzio and Niccolo De Nora Foundation Young Author Prize
Recognizes published work in the areas of corrosion, electrodeposition or surface treatment. Applicants must be electrochemists under the age of 30. Awarded annually.

• 4846 • Prix Jacques Tacussel
Recognizes contributions to an electrochemical technique. Awarded biennially in odd-numbered years.

• 4847 • Tajima Prize
Recognizes the work of young electrochemists. Applicants must be under the age of 40. Winners are selected based on published work. Awarded annually if merited.

• 4848 • Klaus-Jurgen Vetter Prize for Electrochemical Kinetics
Recognizes excellence in the field of electrochemical kinetics. Applicants must be under the age of 40. Awarded biennially in odd-numbered years.

• 4849 •
International Society of Surgery
(Societe Internationale de Chirurgie)
Prof.Dr. Felix Harder, Sec.Gen.
Netzibodenstr. 34
PO Box 1527
CH-4133 Pratteln, Switzerland
Phone: 41 61 8159666
Phone: 41 61 8159667
Fax: 41 61 8114775
E-mail: surgery@iss-sic.ch
Home Page: http://www.iss-sic.ch

• 4850 • Robert Danis Prize
To recognize the surgeon/author of the most important and personal work in connection with surgical treatment of fractures (orthopaedic treatment excluded). Surgeon nationals of one of the countries represented at the ISS/SIC are eligible. Work can be in connection with either technics, clinics, or experimentation. Prize winners are awarded at the biennial World Congresses of Surgery. Awarded biennially. Established in 1947.

• 4851 • Rene Leriche Prize
For recognition of the most valuable work on the surgery of arteries, veins, or the heart which has appeared in the previous few years. Awarded biennially. Established in 1947. Prize winners are awarded at the biennial World Congresses of Surgery.

• 4852 • Prize of the Societe Internationale de Chirurgie
To recognize the surgeon who has a published work that has made the most notable and useful contribution to surgical science. The prize winner need not necessarily be a member of the Society. Nominations are considered and voted upon at the meeting of the Executive Committee that is always held before the General Assembly of the Congress. Prize winners are awarded biennially at the World Congress of Surgery and receive a medal. Established in 1953.

• 4853 •
International Table Tennis Federation
(Federation Internationale de Tennis de Table)
Mr. Adham Sharara, Pres.
Chemin dela Roche, 11
Renens
CH-1020 Lausanne, Switzerland
Phone: 41 21 3407090
Fax: 41 21 3407099
E-mail: ittf@ittf.com
Home Page: http://www.ittf.com

• 4854 • Merit Award
Recognizes an individual with a long period of service. Awarded periodically.

• 4855 •
International Union Against Cancer
(Union Internationale Contre le Cancer)
Mrs. Isabel Mortara, Exec.Dir.
3, rue du Conseil General
CH-1205 Geneva, Switzerland
Phone: 41 22 8091811
Fax: 41 22 8091810
E-mail: info@uicc.org
Home Page: http://www.uicc.org/

• 4856 • American Cancer Society International Cancer Research Fellowships
To enable senior investigators from any country, who have been actively engaged in cancer research for at least five years, to work in collaboration with outstanding scientists. The fellowships are not for postdoctoral or special training but for original work in the basic, clinical or behavioral areas of cancer research. The applications deadline is October 1. Between 12 to 15 Fellows are selected annually from about 50 candidates. The average award value for a 12 month fellowship is $30,000 US. Sponsored by the American Cancer Society. Formerly: American Cancer Society Eleanor Roosevelt International Cancer Fellowships.

• 4857 • Asia-Pacific Cancer Society Training Grants (APCASOT)
To assist the work of voluntary cancer societies in the Asian-Pacific region by providing their English-speaking staff and accredited volunteers with non-medical training opportunities in: prevention & early detection education programs; non-medical patient services; advocacy; fundraising; behavioral research; media relations; organization & managerial skills; and surveillance of cancer statistics at established cancer societies in Australia and others in the region. Grants cover a duration of one to two weeks, and training at two societies is encouraged. Three to five fellowships with an average value of US $1,800 are awarded each year. Applications must be submitted by September 15. Funded by the William Rudder Memorial Fund.

• 4858 • International Cancer Research Technology Transfer Project
To enable scientifically or medically qualified investigators and specialists from any country who are actively engaged in cancer research or clinical management in the field to spend time in an appropriate foreign institution to exchange information on new or improved techniques, to compile data in the basic, clinical or behavioral areas of cancer research, or to acquire knowledge and skills of appropriate, up-to-date clinical management techniques. Applications may be submitted at any time of the year. Awards are for one to three months. Contributions are awarded towards living costs. Between 120 and 150 awards are made each year. The average award value is $3,000 for travel and 1 month stipend. Funded jointly by the Office of International Affairs at the National Cancer Institute of the United States of America, and by certain Member Organizations of the UICC.

• 4859 • International Oncology Nursing Fellowships
To provide an opportunity for qualified nurses to augment their professional knowledge and experience through a short-term observership at a renowned comprehensive cancer centre in North America or the United Kingdom. English-speaking registered nurses, who are actively engaged in the management of cancer patients in their home institutes and who come from regions of the world where specialist cancer nursing training is not yet widely available, are eligible to apply, as are established oncology nurses who wish to disseminate their skills in these regions. Applications, complete with all supporting documentation, must be received by the UICC Geneva Office by November 15. About five fellowships with an average value of $2,800 US are awarded annually. Sponsored by the Oncology Nursing Society (U.S.A.).

• 4860 • Yamagiwa-Yoshida Memorial International Cancer Study Grants
To enable cancer investigators from any country who are actively engaged in cancer research to undertake joint research/study abroad or to establish bilateral research projects, including advanced training in experimental methods and special techniques. The applications deadline is January 1 or July 1. On average 15 grants with a value for 3 months of $10,000 are made annually. Selections take place twice a year, in spring and autumn. Sponsored by the Japan National Committee for UICC and the Toray Industries Inc., and Kyowa Hakko Kogyo Co. Ltd. in Tokyo.

• 4861 •
Fondation Louis Jeantet de Medecine
Prof. Bernard C. Rossier, Contact
Case postale 270
CP 270
CH-1211 Geneva 17, Switzerland
Phone: 41 22 7043636
Fax: 41 22 7043637
E-mail: info@jeantet.ch
Home Page: http://www.jeantet.ch

• 4862 • Louis-Jeantet Prize for Medicine (Prix Louis-Jeantet de medecine)
To enable researchers to continue biomedical research projects, either fundamental or clinical, of a very high level. Individuals or groups must be proposed by scientists, doctors, or institutions who are familiar with the work of the candidates. To be eligible, researchers must be working in a European country that is a member of the Council of Europe. The deadline for entry is February 15. Monetary awards amounting to a maximum of 2 million Swiss francs are awarded annually. Established in 1986.

• 4863 •
Locarno Internationale Film Festival
(Festival Internazionale del Film Locarno)
Marco Solari, Pres.
Via Ciseri 23
CH-6601 Locarno, Switzerland
Phone: 41 91 756 2121
Fax: 41 91 756 2149
E-mail: info@pardo.ch
Home Page: http://www.pardo.ch

• 4864 • Locarno International Film Festival (Festival Internazionale de Film Locarno)
For recognition of outstanding films by new directors and growing national film industries. Films may be submitted by producers, television networks as co-producers, or official national or professional organizations from each country. The following prizes are awarded: the Grand Prize of the Festival the Golden Leopard and the Grand Prize of the City of Locarno (30,000-50,000 Swiss francs) to the best film in competition; the Silver Leopard and the Prize of the City of Locarno (15,000-20,000 Swiss francs) to the first or second feature of a director; the Grand Prize of the Award Committee - the Silver Leopard and the Prize of the City of Locarno (15,000-20,000 Swiss francs) for a film of a director of new cinema; Jury Special Award Swissair/Crossair Special Prize (10,000 Swiss francs) for the film that best translates the spirit of communication among peoples and cultures; the Bronze Leopard for an actress in a competing film; the Bronze Leopard for an actor in a competing film. The Leopard sculpture, designed by the Swiss artist Remo Rossi, is awarded annually in August. Established in 1946 by the town of Locarno, the canton of Tessin, and the Swiss Government.

• 4865 •
Martin-Bodmer-Stiftung fur einen Gottfried Keller-Preis
% Thomas Bodmer
PO Box 1425
CH-8032 Zurich, Switzerland
E-mail: info@gottfried-keller-preis.ch
Home Page: http://www.gottfried-keller-preis.ch

• 4866 • Gottfried Keller Prize
To recognize authors of Switzerland and literature on Switzerland. Selection is by nomination. A monetary award of 25,000 Swiss francs is presented biennially. Established in 1921 by Martin Bodmer on the 102nd anniversary of the birth of Gottfried Keller.

• 4867 •
Max Schmidheiny Foundation
(Max Schmidheiny Stiftung)
Prof. Dr. Peter Gomez, Chm.
University of St. Gallen
PO Box 1045
CH-9001 St. Gallen, Switzerland
Phone: 41 71 227 2070
Fax: 41 71 227 2075
E-mail: msf@ms-foundation.org
Home Page: http://www.ms-foundation.org

• 4868 • Freedom Prize (Freiheitspreis)
To promote and encourage especially praiseworthy efforts to preserve and develop the free market economy and society and, in particular, endeavors to safeguard personal liberty and individual responsibility, and to guarantee social security. To ensure that support is given with complete objectivity, an independent international group of experts is appointed to examine and evaluate all achievements submitted for awards. Scientists, politicians, journalists and/or entrepreneurs, as well as any individual with a special commitment to the cause of liberty, are eligible. A monetary prize of 100,000 Swiss francs and certificate are awarded annually in May. Established in 1977 by Dr. h.c. Max Schmidheiny. Formerly: Max Schmidheiny Prize for Free Enterprise and Political Liberty.

• 4869 •
Montreux Choral Festival
(Rencontres chorales internationales de Montreux)
Case Postale 1526
CH-1820 Montreaux 1, Switzerland
Phone: 41 21 966 5550
Fax: 41 21 966 5569
E-mail: montreuxchoralfestival@bluewin.ch
Home Page: http://www.choralfestival.ch

• 4870 • Montreux Choral Festival (Rencontres chorales internationales de Montreux)
To enable choral groups from all over the world to meet in friendly competition. Each choir is free to take part in the contest and have its performance judged by the votes of the jury and the public or to perform outside the contest. The maximum time allowed is 20 minutes of actual music. The following prizes are awarded: The Jury's Prize - 8,000 Swiss francs; The Public's Prize - 2,000 Swiss francs; The OCTM Prize (Montreux Convention and Tourist Bureau) - 2,000 Swiss francs is awarded each year to one of the following: mixed voice choir, male voice choir, or ladies and children's choirs; and The Editions Barenreiter, Basle & Kassel Prize - 2,000 Swiss francs. Awarded annually. Established in 1964 by Paul-Andre Gaillard.

• 4871 •
Office for the Coordination of Humanitarian Affairs - Geneva
(Bureau de la Coordination des Affaires Humanitaires)
Siergio Vieira de Mello, Under-Sec.Gen.
Palais des Nations
CH-1211 Geneva 10, Switzerland
Phone: 41 22 9171234
Fax: 41 22 9170023
E-mail: ochagva@un.org
Home Page: http://ochaonline.un.org

• 4872 • Sasakawa - DHA Disaster Prevention Award
To promote advocacy and awareness among affected communities on disaster prevention issues worldwide. A monetary award of $5,000 is given annually. Established in 1986.

• 4873 •
Office of the Mayor of Zurich
(Prasidialabteilung der Stadt Zurich)
Postfach
Wilhelmstrasse 10
CH-8022 Zurich, Switzerland
Phone: 41 1 2799111
Fax: 41 1 2725664
E-mail: musik.literature@prd.stzh.ch

• 4874 • Kunstpreis der Stadt Zurich
For recognition of achievement in art, music, film, or literature. Citizens of Zurich are eligible. A monetary award of 50,000 Swiss francs is awarded annually. Established in 1932.

• 4875 •
Paul Guggenheim Foundation
(Fondation Paul Guggenheim)
% Graduate Institute of International Studies
11A, avenue de la Paix
CH-1202 Geneva 21, Switzerland
Phone: 41 22 9085700
Fax: 41 22 9085710
E-mail: info@hei.uniqe.ch

• 4876 • Paul Guggenheim Prize (Prix Paul Guggenheim)
To encourage young academics by awarding a prize for a first major monograph in the field of public international law (except European law). By application only. A prize of 15,000 Swiss francs is awarded biennially. Established in 1979 in honor of Paul Guggenheim, an outstanding Swiss international lawyer.

• 4877 •
Prix de Lausanne
Patricia Leroy, Sec.Gen.
Palais de Beaulieu
Av. Bergieres 6
CH-1004 Lausanne, Switzerland
Phone: 41 21 643 2405
Fax: 41 21 643 2409
E-mail: contact@prixdelausanne.org
Home Page: http://www.prixdelausanne.org

• 4878 • **Prix de Lausanne**
To help promising young dancers between 15 and 17 years of age to embark on a professional career. Up to nine scholarships for a year's study in a world renowned school of dance or ballet company are awarded. Winners choose the school or the company they wish to attend from a list furnished by the competition. Established in 1973 by Philippe Braunschweig.

• 4879 •
Rolex Awards for Enterprise
PO Box 1311
CH-1211 Geneva 26, Switzerland
Phone: 41 22 302 2200
Fax: 41 22 302 2585
E-mail: secretariat@rolexawards.com
Home Page: http://www.rolexawards.com

• 4880 • **Rolex Awards for Enterprise**
To encourage outstanding personal enterprise and to provide financial support for the implementation of projects. These should break new ground in one of the following major sectors of human endeavor: Science and Medicine, Technology and Innovation, Exploration and Discovery, the Environment, and Cultural Heritage. Projects must expand knowledge of our world, improve the quality of life on the planet, or contribute to the betterment of humankind. The only language accepted is English. Only one application may be submitted by any one person or by any one group. Five monetary awards, each consisting of $100,000 and a specially engraved gold Rolex chronometer are awarded every two years. are awarded every two years. Ten awards of $25,000 each and a steel and gold chronometer are also awarded to runners-up. Established in 1976 by Montres Rolex S.A., Geneva, on the occasion of the 50th anniversary of the invention of the Rolex Oyster, the world's first waterproof wrist watch. Contact the Rolex Awards for information on deadlines for applications.

• 4881 •
Rose d'Or Festival
(Societe Suisse de Radiodiffusion et Television et la Ville de Montreux)
Georges Luk, CEO
PO Box 5511
CH-3001 Bern 8, Switzerland
Phone: 41 31 318 3737
Fax: 41 31 318 3736
E-mail: info@rosedor.com
Home Page: http://www.rosedor.ch

Formerly: Swiss Broadcasting Corporation and the City of Montreux.

• 4882 • **Golden Rose of Montreux Award**
To promote a better knowledge of light entertainment programs on an international level, to assist program exchanges, and to encourage the creation of original works of high quality. Light entertainment programs are judged in the following categories: Music - songs, light music, jazz, pop, rock, and variety shows; Comedy - humor and situation comedy; and Miscellaneous - any entry not included in Music or Comedy such as game shows, circus, and light entertainment documentaries. Eligible recipients fall into two categories: Broadcasters - organizations which operate a television service of national importance may enter one program in each category. In the case of countries where there are several television organizations linked by a national association, this association, representing all the organizations, shall be entitled to enter one program in each category; and Independent Producers - independent producers may enter one program in the category of their choice. Competitors should select the most suitable category. The presented programs can be intended for any kind of transmission and must have been produced or televised for the first time in the 14 months. Entries composed of several parts of the same program are not eligible. The length of the program must be at least 20 minutes but not more than 60 minutes. Edited versions of longer programs are permitted. Entries are submitted to an international pre-selection committee which will then determine the programs to be presented in the official selection. Deadline for inscriptions is February 10 and deadline for material is February 24. Programs admitted to the competition are submitted to three international juries, one for each category. Each jury can award two prizes in its category: First Prize The Silver Rose; Second Prize - The Bronze Rose. In the Comedy category, the First Prize is the special prize of the City of Montreaux. At the end of this competition, the three First Prize winners then compete for the Golden Rose of Montreaux Award which goes to the best entertainment program of all categories. This award also carries a monetary prize of 10,000 Swiss francs. In addition, the program which best reflects human values can be awarded the Prixa UNDA; this prize can be awarded along with the Rose.

• 4883 • **Press Prize for Broadcasters and Producers**
For recognition of the program selected as outstanding by the journalists accredited to the Golden Rose of Montreux contest. Awards are given in two categories, Official Television Organization and Independent Producer. The Press is composed of trade press and newspaper journalists and TV critics who must sign a statement agreeing to watch all programs accepted for the contest, and must attend the first meeting of the Press jury. Not more than one-third of the total members of the Press jury may come from any one country. Journalists who have assisted in any capacity in the production of a program shown at the contest may not be members of the Press jury. The Press Prize, a golden rose, is presented at the same time as the presentation of the awards made by the International jury. Established in 1961.

• 4884 •
Swiss Academy of Medical Sciences
(Schweizerische Akademie der Medizinischen Wissenschaften)
Prof. Werner Stauffacher, Pres.
Petersplatz 13
CH-4051 Basel, Switzerland
Phone: 41 61 2699030
Fax: 41 61 2699039
E-mail: mail@samw.ch
Home Page: http://www.samw.ch

• 4885 • **Robert Bing Prize**
To encourage younger scientists, up to 45 years of age, who have done outstanding work that has helped in the recognition, treatment and cure of neurological diseases. Nominations or personal applications are accepted. A monetary prize and a certificate are awarded biennially. Established in 1956 by Professor Robert Bing. Deadline for application is July 31.

• 4886 • **Theodore Ott Prize**
(Prix Theodore Ott)
To encourage established, internationally recognized scientists and medical researchers who have performed outstanding scientific work in basic neurology research. Nominations or personal applications are accepted. A monetary prize will be awarded approximately every five years. Established in 1992.

• 4887 •
Swiss Association for Theatre Studies
(Schweizerische Gesellschaft fur Theaterkultur)
Susan Moser, Contact
Lothringerstrasse 55
Postfach 1807
CH-4056 Basel, Switzerland
Phone: 41 61 321 1060
Fax: 41 61 321 1075
E-mail: theater@theater.ch
Home Page: http://www.theater.ch

• 4888 • **Hans Reinhart Ring**
To recognize an artist for an outstanding theatrical performance. Swiss stage artists or foreign artists performing in Switzerland are eligible. A gold ring is awarded annually. Established in 1957 in memory of the ring's founder, Winterthur poet, Hans Reinhart.

• 4889 •
Swiss Chemical Society
Prof. Georg Frater, Pres.
Schwarztorstrasse 9
CH-3007 Bern, Switzerland
Phone: 41 31 310 4090
Fax: 41 31 312 1678
E-mail: info@swiss-chem-soc.ch
Home Page: http://www.nscs.ch

Formerly: Swiss Chemical Society; Swiss Association of Chemists.

• 4890 • **Grammaticakis-Neumann Prize**
Awarded annually to a young scientist (under 40 years old) who carries out an excellent research

Awards are arranged in alphabetical order below their administering organizations

program in photochemistry, photophysics or molecular photobiology.

• 4891 • **Dr. Max Luthi Award (Prix Dr. Max-Luthi)**
To recognize the author of a work of exceptional quality in the Department of Chemistry in a technical Swiss school. Applications must be filed by December. A medal and monetary prize of 1,000 Swiss francs are awarded annually.

• 4892 • **Paracelsus-Preis**
For recognition of outstanding research in the field of chemistry. A monetary prize, a medal and a diploma are awarded biennially. Established in 1938 in honor of Paracelsus. The award carries a prize of 20,000 Swiss frabcs and a medal.

• 4893 • **Sandmeyer Prize (Prix Sandmeyer)**
To recognize a researcher or a group of researchers for outstanding work in the chemical industry field or studies. The work must take place in Switzerland, or in a foreign country by a group of researchers with participation of Swiss citizens. Application deadline is October. A monetary prize of 10,000 Swiss francs for individuals (20,000 for teams) is awarded annually.

• 4894 • **Werner-Preis**
To recognize a young scientist who has obtained very good research results in the field of chemistry. A monetary prize of 10,000 Swiss francs, a medal, and a diploma are awarded annually. Established in 1915 in honor of Professor Werner. In 1966, a one-time Golden Werner-Medaille was awarded.

• 4895 •
Swiss Federal Institute of Technology Zurich
(Eidgenossische Technische Hochschule Zurich)
Raemistr. 101
CH-8092 Zurich, Switzerland
Phone: 41 1 632 1111
Fax: 41 1 632 1077
Home Page: http://www.ethz.ch

• 4896 • **Heinrich Hatt-Bucher Prize**
For recognition of outstanding student scientific work in the final diploma in the field of architecture and civil engineering. Monetary prizes of 5,000, 4,000, and 3,000. Swiss francs, respectively, are awarded annually at ETH-Day (Dies-Academicus). Established in 1986 by Heinrich Ernst Hatt-Bucher.

• 4897 • **Georg A. Fischer-Preis**
For recognition of outstanding student scientific works. In particular, diploma theses or doctoral dissertations in mechanical engineering are considered. Monetary prizes of 2,500 to 5,000 Swiss francs are awarded to one or more candidates annually on ETH-Day (Dies Academicus) and Promotion-Day. Established in 1970 by Mrs. Katja Fischer in honor of Mr. Georg A. Fischer, a mechanical engineer at ETH.

• 4898 • **Hilti-Preis**
For recognition of a scientifically outstanding diploma or Ph.D. thesis in applied research. A prize of 5,000 Swiss francs is awarded annually on the ETH-Day (Dies Academicus) or at a Promotion Ceremony. Established in 1989 by Hilti AG, Schaan, FL.

• 4899 • **Otto Jaag-Gewasserschutz-Preis**
For recognition of outstanding student scientific works, particularly for diploma theses or doctoral dissertations in protection of water. A monetary prize of 1,000 Swiss francs is awarded annually on ETH-Day (Dies Academicus). Established in 1980 in honor of Professor Dr. Otto Jaag.

• 4900 • **Fritz Kutter-Preis**
For recognition of an outstanding diploma or Ph.D. thesis in computer science, with a significant contribution in information processing or a valuable implementation of know-how, at a Swiss University or Swiss Federal Institute of Technology. A monetary prize of 10,000 francs is awarded. Established in 1975.

• 4901 • **Latsis-Preis**
For recognition of outstanding scientific work. Candidates who are 40 years of age and younger are eligible. The candidates are evaluated by the Research Committee of the ETH Zurich. A monetary prize of 25,000 Swiss francs is awarded annually. Established in 1984 by Fondation Latsis Internationale in honor of Dr. John Latsis. Sponsored by Forschungskommission ETH Zurich.

• 4902 • **Ruzicka-Prize (Ruzicka-Preis)**
For recognition of an outstanding work in the field of chemistry. Work that has already been published and completed in Switzerland or by a Swiss national abroad under 40 years of age is eligible. A monetary prize, medal, document, and colloquium are awarded annually in September. Established in 1957 by Schweizerische Chemische Industrie in memory of Dr. Leopold Ruzicka, winner of the Nobel Prize for Chemistry, 1945.

• 4903 • **Willi Studer Preis**
To recognize the best diploma in the year of every department of Swiss Federal Institute of Technology. A monetary prize of 2,500 Swiss francs is awarded annually on ETH-Day (Dies Academicus).

• 4904 •
Swiss Graphic Designers
Erika Remund Jagne, Mng.Dir.
Limmatstr. 63
CH-8005 Zurich, Switzerland
Phone: 41 1 2724555
Fax: 41 1 2725282
E-mail: info@sgd.ch
Home Page: http://www.sgd.ch

Formerly: Arbeitsgemeinschaft Schweizer Grafiker.

• 4905 • **Design Competitions**
To recognize contributions by certified graphic designers through association sponsored competitions. Prizes include the Joseph Binder Award, Swiss Poster Award, and ADC Swiss Award. Formerly: Arbeitsgemeinschaft Schweizer Grafiker Competitions.

• 4906 •
Swiss Music Edition
(Schweizer Musikedition)
Postfach 7851
CH-6000 Lucerne 7, Switzerland
Phone: 41 41 210670
Fax: 41 41 210670
E-mail: mail@musicedition.ch
Home Page: http://www.musicedition.ch

• 4907 • **Swiss Music - Edition (Schweizer Musikedition)**
To recognise the publication of compositions of contemporary music. Swiss citizens or other citizens living in Switzerland are eligible.

• 4908 •
Universal Postal Union
(Union Postale Universelle)
T.E. Leavey, Dir.Gen.
Case Postale 13
CH-3000 Bern 15, Switzerland
Phone: 41 31 3503111
Fax: 41 31 3503110
E-mail: info@upu.int
Home Page: http://www.upu.int

• 4909 • **International Letter-Writing Competition for Young People**
To develop young people's facility in composition and the subtlety of their thought and to contribute to the strengthening of international friendship which is one of the essential missions of the Universal Postal Union. Individuals who are 15 years of age and under may participate in the Competition organized at the national level by Postal Administrations belonging to the UPU. Letters may be submitted until April 30 each year. Gold-plated, silver and bronze medals, diplomas, and postage stamp albums are awarded annually. A jury of UNESCO, which chooses the winning letters, also awards three bronze medals. Ceremonies are organized by the winning Postal Administrations and prizes are presented to the winners on October 9, the anniversary of the founding of the UPU. Established in 1972.

• 4910 •
University of Basel
(Universitat Basel)
Prof. Dr. Ulrich Gabler, Dean
Petersplatz 1
CH-4003 Basel, Switzerland
Phone: 41 61 267 3111
Fax: 41 61 267 3003
E-mail: medico@ubach.umibas.ch
Home Page: http://www.unibas.ch

• 4911 • **Amerbach-Preis**
For recognition of the best essay written by a young scholar. Students or alumni of the various departments of the University are eligible. A monetary award of 5,000 Swiss francs and a medal are awarded annually on the occasion of the Dies Academicus. Established in 1962.

• 4912 •
Visions du Reel International Documentary Film Festival
Jean Schmutz, Pres.
18 rue Juste-Olivier
CP 593
CH-1260 Nyon, Switzerland
Phone: 41 22 365 4455
Fax: 41 22 365 4450
E-mail: docnyon@visionsdureel.ch
Home Page: http://www.visionsdureel.ch

• 4913 • **Visions du Reel International Documentary Film Festival**
To recognize documentary films on an international perspective. Works are classified into the International Competition, New Perceptions (beginning, self-taught, and student filmmaker), and the Showcase of Swiss Film Industry (best of recent Swiss productions). Monetary prizes accompany Visions du Reel prizes. Prizes are awarded annually.

• 4914 •
Ernst von Siemens Music Foundation
(Ernst Von Siemens-Musikstiftung)
Ute Vollmar, Mgr.
% KPMG Fides
D4 Platz 5
CH-6039 Root/Lucerne, Switzerland
Phone: 41 41 368 3838
Fax: 41 41 368 3888
E-mail: rossnagl@evs-musikstiftung.ch
Home Page: http://www.evs-musikstiftung.ch

• 4915 • **Ernst von Siemens Music Prize (Ernst von Siemens-Musikpreis)**
For recognition of an outstanding achievement in music. Famous composers or performers from anywhere in the world are eligible. A monetary prize of 150,000 Euro is awarded annually. Established 1972. In addition, each year around 1.5 million Euro is awarded for specified purposes to music institutions, ensembles and individuals, in Germany and abroad, who have made a special contribution to contemporary music.

• 4916 •
World Commission on Protected Areas
(Commission des Pares Nationaux et)
David Sheppard, Dir.
IUCN
28, Rue Mauverney
CH-1196 Gland, Switzerland
Phone: 41 22 9990160
Phone: 41 22 9990015
Fax: 41 22 9990015
E-mail: wcpa@iucn.org
Home Page: http://www.iucn.org/about/

• 4917 • **Fred M. Packard International Parks Merit Award**
For outstanding achievement in protected areas. Awarded semiannually to one or more recipients.

• 4918 •
World Conservation Union
(Union Mondiale pour la Nature)
Valli Moosa, Pres.
Rue Mauverney 28
CH-1196 Gland, Switzerland
Phone: 41 22 999 0000
Fax: 41 22 999 0002
E-mail: mail@iucn.org
Home Page: http://www.iucn.org

• 4919 • **Honorary Membership**
To recognize individuals for outstanding service in the field of conservation of nature and natural resources. Awarded when merited.

• 4920 • **Fred M. Packard International Parks Merit Award/World Commission on Protected Areas**
To recognize park wardens, rangers, and managers from anywhere in the world for contributions in the following areas: valor; advocacy for parks and their values; innovative management; communicating park ideals and objectives to the public; conscientious application to park work in the face of difficult and dangerous circumstances; teaching and training park personnel; research; and administrative service. Awards are given in the following categories: (1) Valor - to recognize personnel who have acted with physical or moral courage beyond the call of duty; (2) Service - to recognize personnel for long and distinguished service; (3) Special Achievement - to recognize personnel for outstanding performance, although their jobs did not call for acts of personal bravery or daring. Nominations are accepted. A certificate and medal are presented. In some cases, a monetary award is also presented. Established in 1979 and now given in honor of Fred M. Packard, who initiated the award. Formerly: (1982) Valor Award.

• 4921 • **John C. Phillips Memorial Medal**
For recognition of distinguished service in international conservation. A sterling silver medal is awarded triennially at ordinary sessions of the IUCN General Assembly. Established in 1963 by Friends of John C. Phillips and the American Committee for International Wild Life Protection in memory of John C. Phillips, distinguished United States naturalist, explorer, author and conservationist.

• 4922 • **Peter Scott Medal for Conservation Merit**
To recognize highly significant achievement in conservation in however small a field. Accomplishments to be recognized may involve one or more specific events, or they may reflect sustained activity over a period of time. The recipient may be one or more individuals, an organization or an institution. The achievement, though perhaps modest in absolute terms, shall be recognizable as a particularly significant and noteworthy contribution to the conservation of wild fauna and flora, especially (but not limited to) endangered and threatened taxa and those subject to exploitation by man. The award is given periodically by the Chairman of the Species Survival Commission on the recommendation of the commission Steering Committee. It consists of a medal, certificate and citation together with such other tangible recognition as may be deemed appropriate.

• 4923 • **Tree of Learning Award**
To recognize individuals who have contributed to environmental protection through education and communications. The prize is awarded every three years at the IUCN members' assembly of the World Conservation Congress. Awarded to one or more recipients.

• 4924 •
World Health Organization
(Organisation Mondiale de la Sante)
Jong-wook Lee, Dir.Gen.
20, ave. Appia
CH-1211 Geneva 27, Switzerland
Phone: 41 22 7912111
Fax: 41 22 7913111
E-mail: info@who.int
Home Page: http://www.who.int

• 4925 • **Leon Bernard Foundation Prize**
For recognition of outstanding service in the field of social medicine. No condition is made as to age, sex, profession, or nationality. Only nominations put forward by national health administrations of WHO Member States and by former recipients of the awards are acceptable. A monetary prize of 2,500 Swiss francs and a bronze medal are awarded biennially. Established in 1948.

• 4926 • **Darling Foundation Prize**
For recognition of outstanding work in the control of malaria. Only nominations put forward by national health administrations of WHO Member States and by former recipients of the award are acceptable. A monetary award of 2,500 Swiss francs and a bronze medal are awarded irregularly. Established in 1948 in memory of Dr. Samuel Taylor Darling, a noted malaria researcher.

• 4927 • **Ihsan Dogramaci Family Health Foundation Fellowship and Prize**
For recognition of outstanding services in the field of family health. Only nominations put forward by national health administrations of WHO member states and by former recipients of the award are acceptable. A monetary prize of $20,000 and a bronze medal are awarded biennially in odd-numbered years. Established in 1980. Formerly: (1996) Child Health Foundation Prize.

• 4928 • **Jacques Parisot Foundation Fellowship**
To support research in social medicine or public health. The regional offices of the WHO are invited in turn to submit candidatures. A fellowship of $5,000 and a bronze medal are awarded biennially in even-numbered years. Established in 1969.

• 4929 • **Sasakawa Health Prize**
To recognize an individual, institution, or nongovernmental organization for outstanding innovative work in health development. Only nominations put forward by national health administrations of WHO Member States and by former recipients of the award are acceptable. A monetary prize of $100,000 and a crystal statuette are awarded annually. Established in 1984 upon the initiative of Mr. Ryoichi Sasakawa of Japan, a great supporter of WHO, and President of the Sasakawa Memorial Health Foundation.

• 4930 • **Dr. A. T. Shousha Foundation Prize and Fellowship**
For recognition of outstanding contribution to health development. Only nominations put forward by national health administrations of WHO member states and by former recipients of the award are acceptable. A monetary award of 2,500 Swiss francs, a certificate, and a plaque from the founder are awarded annually; the fellowship of $15,000 is awarded approximately every six years. Established in 1993.

• 4931 •
World Health Organization
International Agency for Research on Cancer
(International Mondiale de la Sante Centre International de Recherche sur le Cancer)
Jong-wook Lee M.D., Dir.Gen.
20, ave. Appia
CH-1211 Geneva 27, Switzerland
Phone: 41 22 7912111
Fax: 41 22 7913111
E-mail: info@who.int
Home Page: http://www.who.int

• 4932 • **Research Training Fellowships**
To provide training in cancer research. Junior scientists who are actively engaged in research in medical or allied sciences, and wish to pursue a career in cancer research are eligible. Candidates may be accepted in the following fields: environmental carcinogenesis including biostatistics and epidemiology of cancer, all aspects of chemical and viral carcinogenesis cell biology, cell genetics, molecular biology, and mechanisms of carcinogenesis. The number of awards is determined by the available funds. A one-year fellowship that is tenable at the Agency in Lyon or in any country and institution abroad where suitable research facilities and material exist, a stipend, and travel costs for the fellow and, in certain circumstances, for one dependent are awarded annually. Established in 1966 by the World Health Organization.

• 4933 •
World Meteorological Organization
(Organisation Meteorologique Mondiale)
Mr. Michel Jarraud, Sec.Gen.
7 bis Ave. de la Paix
CP 2300
CH-1211 Geneva 2, Switzerland
Phone: 41 22 7308111
Fax: 41 22 7308181
E-mail: wmo@wmo.int
Home Page: http://www.wmo.ch

• 4934 • **International Meteorological Organization Prize**
For recognition of outstanding work in the field of meteorology or in any related field. A monetary prize of SFr 10,000, a gold medal, and a parchment scroll with a citation are given annually. Established in 1956 to commemorate the International Meteorological Organization which was established in 1873, and succeeded by the WMO in 1950.

• 4935 • **Norbert Gerbier-Mumm International Award**
To encourage and reward an original scientific paper on the influence of meteorology in a particular field of the physical, natural, or human sciences, or on the influence of one of these sciences on meteorology. The award aims at stimulating interest in such research in support of WMO programs. Only papers published during the 18-month period immediately preceding the year when the award is made are eligible for consideration. A medal bearing the likeness of Mr. Norbert Gerbier and 7,600 Euro are awarded annually. Established in 1987.

• 4936 • **Prof. Dr. Vilho Vaisala Award**
To encourage and stimulate interest in important research programs in the field of instruments and methods of observation in support of WMO programs. Scientists may submit papers through the Permanent Representatives of Member States with WMO by November 30. A monetary prize of $5,000, a medal, and a diploma are awarded annually. Established in 1986 in honor of Dr. Vilho Vaisala, founder of the Vaisala Oy.

• 4937 • **WMO Research Award for Young Scientists**
To encourage young scientists, preferably in developing countries, who are working in the fields of meteorology and hydrology. Individuals who are under 35 years of age may be nominated by Permanent Representatives of Member States with WMO. A monetary award of $1,000 and a citation are awarded annually. Established in 1970.

• 4938 •
World Organization of the Scout Movement
Dr. Missoni, Sec.Gen.
Honors and Awards Committee
Case Postale 91
CH-1211 Geneva 4, Switzerland
Phone: 41 22 705 1010
Fax: 41 22 705 1020
E-mail: worldbureau@world.scout.org
Home Page: http://www.scout.org

• 4939 • **Bronze Wolf (Loup de Bronze)**
To recognize an individual for outstanding services of the most exceptional character to the world scout movement. A bronze medal in the form of an wolf is awarded triennially at the World Scout Conferences. Established in 1935 by Robert Baden-Powell, founder of the Scout movement.

• 4940 •
Worlddidac Foundation
Beat Jost, Exec.Dir.
Bollwerk 21
CH-3001 Bern, Switzerland
Phone: 41 31 311 7682
Fax: 41 31 312 1744
E-mail: info@worlddidac.org
Home Page: http://www.worlddidac.org

• 4941 • **Worlddidac Award**
To promote the quality improvement and the creativity of the international educational materials industry. The products entered are divided into the following product groups: school supplies, vocational and scientific equipment, visual and audiovisual media, furniture/equipment, printed and published products, informatics and multimedia technologies. There is a further classification into entry groups based on the educational level of the respective products: preschools, elementary schools, secondary/senior schools, universities, institutes of technology, professional training and further education, and special education. Products newly released in the past two years are eligible. Gold, silver, bronze award certificates are presented biennially at the International Exhibition for Educational Materials and Professional Training WORLDDIDAC in Basel, Switzerland. For additional information Please visit our website at www.worlddidac.org/award. Established in 1984.

• 4942 •
WWF International
Dr. Claude Martin, Dir.Gen.
Av. du Mont-Blanc
CH-1196 Gland, Switzerland
Phone: 41 22 364 9111
Fax: 41 22 364 8836
E-mail: userid@wwfnet.org
Home Page: http://www.panda.org
Formerly: World Wildlife Fund.

• 4943 • Duke of Edinburgh Conservation Medal

To recognize individuals for outstanding achievements in conservation. Awarded annually.

• 4944 • Gold Panda Award

This, WWF's highest award, is given for highly meritorious and strictly personal services to the conservation of wildlife and natural resources. Nominations are made, screened, and judged through an internal consultative process. A gold medal is awarded annually. Established in 1970.

• 4945 • Roll of Honour

A posthumous honor for people having rendered outstanding services to the cause of conservation, not only to WWF. Awarded when merited. Established in 1973.

• 4946 • WWF Award for Conservation Merit

To recognize grassroots conservation work that has significantly contributed to local conservation and conservation achievement over a long period. Individuals, groups, and institutions or associations are eligible.

• 4947 •
Y's Men International
Benson Wabule, Int.Pres.
9 Ave Ste-Clotilde
CH-1205 Geneva, Switzerland
Phone: 41 22 809 1530
Fax: 41 22 809 1539
E-mail: ihq@ysmen.org
Home Page: http://www.ysmen.org

• 4948 • Harry M. Ballantyne Award

This, the highest honor of the Y's Men International, is given to recognize especially deserving friends of Y's Men International who over a long period of time have rendered service of special value and helpfulness to the Y's Men's movement. A medal, a trophy, and a framed diploma are awarded annually. Established in 1957 by Harry M. Ballantyne.

Taiwan

• 4949 •
Center for Chinese Studies
Dr. Juang Fang-rung, Dir.
20 Chungshan South Rd.
Taipei 10001, Taiwan
Phone: 886 2 2314 7321
Fax: 886 2 2371 2126
E-mail: ccswww@msg.ncl.edu.tw
Home Page: http://ccs.ncl.edu.tw

Formerly: (1987) Resource and Information Center for Chinese Studies.

• 4950 • Research Grant Program to Assist Foreign Scholars in Chinese Studies

To enhance scholarly communication in the field of Chinese studies and encourage foreign scholars of Chinese studies to carry out research work in the Republic of China. PhD candidates, assistant professors, associate professors, professors, and researchers at institutes who plan to do research in the R.O.C. are eligible to apply. Research grants for 3 to 12 months are awarded annually. The amount of each grant is determined by the candidate's rank at the time of application. Established in 1988 by the R.O.C. Center for Chinese Studies.

• 4951 •
Taipei Golden Horse Film Festival
3 F, No. 37, Sec. 1 Kaifeng St.
Taipei 100, Taiwan
Phone: 886 2 388 3880
Fax: 886 2 370 1616
E-mail: festival@goldenhorse.org.tw
Home Page: http://www.goldenhorse.org.tw

Formerly: Taipei International Film Exhibition.

• 4952 • Golden Horse Awards

To encourage film production in Taiwan and Hong Kong. The Festival is comprised of three major events each year: Golden Horse Awards - a prestigious competition designed to promote the production of Chinese-language cinema; International Film Exhibition - a non-competitive annual showcase of a wide range of the most outstanding films from around the world to enhance the public's appreciation of cinematic art and to foster understanding among diverse cultures; and Chinese Film Exhibition a showcase of Chinese films retrospectively on different topics, recent products and overseas Chinese film production. Awards are given in the following categories: Best Picture, Best Short Film, Best Documentary as well as Best Animation. Individual Awards are given for Best Director, Best Leading Actor/Actress, Best Supporting Actor/Actress, Best New Performer, Best Original Screenplay, Best Screenplay Adaptation, Best Cinematography, Best Visual Effects, Best Art Direction, Best Make Up & Costume Design, Best Action Choreography, Best Original Film Score, Best Original Film Song, Best Editing, and Best Sound Effects. Special awards include Taiwanese Film of the Year and Taiwanese Filmmaker of the Year. A non-competition award is given to the Audience Choice Award. Held annually. Established in 1980.

• 4953 •
Taiwan Ministry of Education
Cheng-seng Tu, Min.
Bureau of International Cultural and Educational Relations
No. 5, Jungshan S Rd.
Taipei 100, Taiwan
Phone: 886 2 2356 6051
Fax: 886 2 2397 6977
E-mail: mail@mail.moe.gov.tw
Home Page: http://www.edu.tw

• 4954 • Literature and Art Award

For recognition of contributions to literature and the arts. Awards are given in the following categories: literature; drama; music; art; calligraphy; dance; and photography. A monetary award of 100,000 new Taiwan dollars and a gold medal are awarded in each field annually.

• 4955 •
Taiwan Pediatric Association
Fu-Yuan Huang, Pres.
10-1F, No. 69, Hang-Chow S Rd. Sect. 1
Taipei 100, Taiwan
Phone: 886 2 23516446
Fax: 886 2 23516448
E-mail: pediatr@pediatr.org.tw
Home Page: http://www.pediatr.org.tw

• 4956 • E. Mead Johnson Award for Research in Pediatrics

To recognize clinical and laboratory research achievements in pediatrics. Two awards are presented annually, consisting of a plaque, $15,000 honorarium, and travel expenses to present review at the SocietyKs annual meeting.

Thailand

• 4957 •
Bangkok Bank Public Co. Ltd.
Kosit Panpiempras, Exec.Chm.
333 Silom Rd.
Bangkok 10500, Thailand
Phone: 66 2231 4333
Fax: 66 2231 4742
E-mail: info@bangkokbank.com
Home Page: http://www.bangkokbank.com

• 4958 • BuaLuang Art Competition Prize

To encourage students at secondary level, to display their talent and to promote Thai traditional music. A monetary award and a Bullang Trophy are rewarded annually. In cooperation with the National Youth Bureau.

• 4959 •
Southeast Asian Ministers of Education Organization
Edilberto C. de Jesus, Dir.
Mom Luang Pin Malakul Centenery Bldg., 4th Fl.
920 Sukhumvit Rd.
Bangkok 10110, Thailand
Phone: 66 2 3910144
Phone: 66 2 3910554
Fax: 66 2 3812587
E-mail: secretariat@seameo.org
Home Page: http://www.seameo.org

• 4960 • Jasper Fellowship

For research completed within the last three years and written in English, by a researcher who is a scientist and/or scholar and a national of SEAMEO member states.

• 4961 •
United Nations Economic and Social Commission for Asia and the Pacific
Mr. Kim Hak-Su, Exec.Sec.
The United Nations Bldg.
Rajadamnern Nok Ave.
Bangkok 10200, Thailand
Phone: 66 2 881234
Fax: 66 2 881000
E-mail: unescap@unescap.org
Home Page: http://www.unescap.org

• 4962 • HRD Award
Recognizes social development in Asia and Pacific. Awarded annually.

Turkey

• 4963 •
***Cumhuriyet* Newspaper**
(Cumhuriyet Matbaacilik ve Gazetecilik T.A.S.)
Yenigun A.s, Turkocagi Cad. 39/41
Cagaloglu
TR-34334 Istanbul, Turkey
Phone: 90 212 5120505
Fax: 90 212 5138595
E-mail: Hikmet.Cetinkaya@planet.com.tr
Home Page: http://www.cumhuriyet.com.tr

• 4964 • Yunus Nadi Yarismasi (Yunus Nadi Prize)
To encourage the literary and intellectual development of the new generation of Turkish people. All professional or non-professional persons interested can apply for the award. A monetary award of 10,000,000 Turkish liras is given to the winner in each of the eight categories: short stories, novel, poetry, poster, photography, cartoon, long footage film scenario, and study on social sciences. Awarded annually on June 29. Established in 1946-47 in memory of Yunus Nadi, founder of *Cumhuriyet* Newspaper. Formerly: (1990) Yunus Nadi Gift.

• 4965 •
International Centre for Heat and Mass Transfer
Mauricio Cumo, Pres.
Mechanical Engineering Department
Middle East Technical University
TR-06531 Ankara, Turkey
Phone: 90 312 210 1429
Fax: 90 312 210 1331
E-mail: ichmt@ichmt.org
Home Page: http://www.ichmt.org

• 4966 • Fellowship Awards
For recognition of a contribution to a field of heat and mass transfer science and for enhancement of the progress in scientific and technological cooperation connected to the ICHMT activities. Awarded to no more than two individuals each year. Established in 1975.

• 4967 • Luikov Medal
For recognition of an outstanding contribution to the heat and mass transfer science and art. Nominations are accepted by January. A medal is awarded biennially in even-numbered years. Established in 1975 in honor of A.V. Luikov.

• 4968 •
International Society for Photogrammetry and Remote Sensing
Orhan Altan, Sec.Gen.
% Orhan Altan, Sec.-Gen.
Dept. of Geodesy and Photogrammetry
Faculty of Civil Engineering
Istanbul Technical University
TR-34469 Ayazaga-Istanbul, Turkey
Phone: 90 212 285 3810
Fax: 90 212 285 6587
E-mail: oaltan@itu.edu.tr
Home Page: http://www.isprs.org

• 4969 • Best Papers by Young Authors
Awarded to authors who are less than 35 years old and are the sole author of a high quality paper presented to the congress.

• 4970 • Brock Gold Medal Award
For recognition of an outstanding contribution to the evolution of photogrammetric theory, instrumentation, or practice. Nomination by two member societies to which the nominee does not belong is required. A gold medal is awarded every four years at the Quadrennial Congress. Established in 1956 by the American Society for Photogrammetry and Remote Sensing in honor of Dr. G.C. Brock.

• 4971 • Gino Cassinis Award
Awarded to a person who has significantly enhanced the mathematical and statistical foundations of the photogrammetry, remote sensing or spatial information sciences in the four years preceding the congress.

• 4972 • The CATCON Prizes
Awards for software.

• 4973 • Eduard Dolezal Award
Awarded to individuals or representatives of institutions.

• 4974 • Sam G. Gamble Award
For recognition of personal contributions to the administration of the Society or to the organization of activities of the Society's Commissions. Individuals irrespective of nationality are eligible. A gold pin and a certificate are awarded every four years at the Quadrennial Congress. Established in 1985 in honor of Dr. Sam G. Gamble. Sponsored by the Canadian Institute of Surveying.

• 4975 • U.V. Helava Award
Awarded to the author(s) of the most outstanding paper published exclusively in the ISPRS international Journal of Photogrammetry.

• 4976 • President's Honorary Citation
Awarded to a chairperson, co-chairperson or member of a working group of each ISPRS Technical Commission.

• 4977 • Schermerhorn Award
To recognize a Working Group member(s) who, through commitment, has achieved successful scientific meetings of a very high level during the four year Congress period. Established in 1988. Sponsored by the Netherlands Society of Photogrammetry.

• 4978 • Schwidefsky Medal
To recognize individuals who have made significant contributions to photogrammetry and remote sensing, either through the medium of publication as author or editor, or in another form. A medal is awarded at each Congress of the International Society for Photogrammetry and Remote Sensing. Established in 1988 in memory of Prof. Dr. rer. techn. Dr.-Ing. E.h. Kurt Schwidefsky, honorary member of the Society. Sponsored by the Deutsche Gesselschaft fur Photogrammetrie und Fernerkundung.

• 4979 • Otto von Gruber Award
For recognition of a significant paper on photogrammetry or an allied subject, written in the four year period preceding the Congress. A monetary award and a gold medal are awarded evey four years at the Quadrennial Congress. Established in 1964 by the ITC-Foundation (International Institute for Aerial Survey Sciences, the Netherlands) in honor of Otto von Gruber.

• 4980 • Wang Zhizhuo Award
Awarded to a person who has made significant achievement or innovation in the spatial information sciences.

• 4981 •
Istanbul Foundation for Culture and Arts (Istanbul Kultur ve Sanat Vakfi)
Istiklat Caddesi No. 146
Beyoglu
TR-34435 Istanbul, Turkey
Phone: 90 212 334 0700
Fax: 90 212 334 0716
E-mail: press.pr@iksv.org
Home Page: http://www.iksv.org

• 4982 • Istanbul International Film Festival (Uluslararasi Istanbul Film Festivali)
For recognition of contributions to the field of cinema; to encourage cooperation between the arts and the cinema; and to promote the distribution of films of outstanding quality in Turkey. The program consists of the following sections: (1) an international competition for the Golden Tulip Award open to feature films on such subjects as literary adaptations, filmed versions of the performing arts, biographies of artists and writers, and films on creativity in the arts; (2) films on a specific theme such as music and the movies; (3) tributes to directors; and (4) recent films awarded in other festivals; and (5) Turkish cinema. Feature films in 35mm with a minimum length of 1,600 m. produced during the Preceding two years are accepted to the competition.

• 4983 •
Politzer Society - International Society for Otological Surgery
Mirko Tos M.D., Contact
ENT Department
Baskent University Hospital
Bahcelievler
TR-06490 Ankara, Turkey
Phone: 90 312 2238534
Fax: 90 312 2157597
E-mail: ozgirgin@politzersociety.org
Home Page: http://www.politzersociety.org

• 4984 • **Politzer Prize**
To recognize the best clinical and science papers by scientists aged 40 years or younger. Two awards of 1,000 euros are presented biennially.

• 4985 •
Research Centre for Islamic History, Art and Culture
(Centre de Recherches sur l'histoire, l'art et la Culture Islamiques)
Mr. Acar Tanlak, Contact
PO Box 24
Besiktas
TR-80692 Istanbul, Turkey
Phone: 90 212 2591742
Phone: 90 212 2605988
Fax: 90 212 2584365
E-mail: ircica@superonline.com
Home Page: http://www.ircica.org

Formerly: (2004) International Commission for the Preservation of Islamic Cultural Heri - tage (ICPICH).

• 4986 • **International Photography Competition**
For photography in the field of Islamic heritage. Held periodically.

• 4987 •
Scientific and Technical Research Council of Turkey
(Turkiye Bilimsel ve Teknik Arastirma Kurumu)
Prof.Dr. Namik Kemal Pak, Contact
Ataturk Bulvari No. 221
Kavaklidere
TR-06100 Ankara, Turkey
Phone: 90 312 4685300
Fax: 90 312 4277489
E-mail: aysegul@tubitak.gov.tr
Home Page: http://www.tubitak.gov.tr

• 4988 • **Bilim Odulu**
(Science Award)
For recognition of contributions to scientific research at the international level, or to the development of the country. Living Turkish scientists are eligible. A monetary prize in Turkish liras, a golden plaque, and a certificate are awarded annually. Established in 1965.

• 4989 • **Tesvik Odulu**
(Junior Science Award)
To recognize and encourage the potential for future outstanding scientific contributions. Living Turkish scientists under 40 years of age are eligible. A monetary prize in Turkish liras, a silver plaque, and a certificate are awarded annually. Established in 1968.

• 4990 •
Turkish Academy of Sciences
(Turkiye Bilimler Akademisi)
Tarik Celik, VP
Ataturk Bulvari 221
Kavaklidere
TR-06100 Ankara, Turkey
Phone: 90 312 4676789
Phone: 90 312 4260394
Fax: 90 312 4673213
E-mail: tubaulus@tuba.gov.tr
Home Page: http://www.tuba.gov.tr

• 4991 • **Encouragement Award**
For outstanding contributions in social sciences.

• 4992 • **Science Award**
For outstanding contributions in social sciences.

• 4993 • **Service Award**
For outstanding contributions in social sciences.

United Kingdom

• 4994 •
Academi - Welsh National Literature Promotion Agency and Society for Authors
3rd Fl., Mount Stuart House
Mount Stuart Sq.
Cardifff CF10 5FQ, United Kingdom
Phone: 44 29 2047 2266
Fax: 44 29 20472930
E-mail: post@academi.org
Home Page: http://www.academi.org

• 4995 • **Wales Book of the Year Awards**
To recognize works of exceptional merit by Welsh authors (by birth or residence) that have been published during the previous calendar year. Works may be written in Welsh or English. Two prizes of £10,000 are awarded to the first place winners. Awarded annually. Established in 1992. Funded by the Arts Council of Wales and supported by the Welsh Books Council. Formerly: Welsh Arts Council Prizes.

• 4996 •
Academia Europaea
Dr. David Coates, Exec.Sec.
76 Portland Pl., 4th Fl.
London W1B 1NT, United Kingdom
Phone: 44 20 73235834
Fax: 44 20 73235844
E-mail: admin@acadeuro.org
Home Page: http://www.acadeuro.org

• 4997 • **Erasmus Medal**
Recognizes eminent scholarship. Awarded annually.

• 4998 • **Gold Medal**
Recognizes contributions to the development of European science and technology. Awarded periodically.

• 4999 •
Acta Materialia
Jr.
Elsevier Science Ltd.
The Boulevard
Langford Ln.
Kidlington
Oxford OX5 1GB, United Kingdom
Phone: 44 1865 843000
Fax: 44 1865 843010
Home Page: http://actamat.web.cmu.edu

• 5000 • **Gold Medal**
To recognize ability and leadership in materials research worldwide. Nominations must be made by a sponsoring or cooperating society of ACTA Materialia, Inc., by November 30. A gold medal and a certificate are presented at a major meeting of the nominating society. Awarded annually. Established in 1974.

• 5001 • **J. Herbert Hollomon Award**
To recognize contributions to understanding the interaction between materials and societal concerns, or a contribution to materials technology that has had great impact on society. Nominations must be submitted by a sponsoring or cooperating society of Acta Materialia, Inc. or by its Board of Governors by November 30. A monetary award, a piece of Steuben sculpture, and a certificate are awarded annually. Established in 1989 to honor the memory of J. Herbert Hollomon, eminent metallurgist and administrator, and principal instigator of Acta Metallurgica.

• 5002 •
Action Medical Research
Simon Moore, CEO
Vincent House
Horsham RH12 2DP, United Kingdom
Phone: 44 1403 210406
Fax: 44 1403 210541
E-mail: info@action.org.uk
Home Page: http://www.action.org.uk

Formerly: (1991) Action Research for the Crippled Child.

• 5003 • **Duncan Guthrie Training Fellowship**
For the most outstanding Research Training Fellow in Child Health appointed each year by Action Research and first awarded in 1996. It is funded by the Duncan Guthrie Memorial Fund, which was set up to commemorate the founder of Action Research following his death in 1994. Direct applications are not accepted. Awards are given to current grant Holders or researchers who have held action research in the past.

• 5004 • **Harding Award**
For recognition of outstanding work of immediate or future benefit to the disabled. The award can be presented for developments in research

Awards are arranged in alphabetical order below their administering organizations

or in the general field of care for the disabled. A sculptured trophy is awarded annually. Awarded alternately by Action Research and the Royal Association for Disability and Rehabilitation. Established in 1971 in honor of Field Marshall Lord Harding of Petherton, Chairman of Action Research from 1960 to 1973.

• 5005 •
African Studies Association of the United Kingdom
Prof. Graham Furniss, Pres.
School of African and Oriental Studies
Thornhaugh St.
Russell Sq.
London WC1H 0XG, United Kingdom
Phone: 44 20 78984390
Fax: 44 20 78984389
E-mail: info@asauk.net
Home Page: http://www.asauk.net

• 5006 • Audrey Richards Prize
Recognizes the best Ph.D. thesis in the United Kingdom on African studies. Awarded biennially in even-numbered years.

• 5007 •
Air-Britain Historians
Howard J. Nash, Membership Sec.
Blacklands Ln.
Sudbourne
Woodbridge
Suffolk IP12 2AX, United Kingdom
Phone: 44 1394 450767
Fax: 44 1932 787768
E-mail: abms4@air-britain.co.uk
Home Page: http://www.air-britain.com

• 5008 • AAHS Trophy (American Aviation Historical Society)
To recognize the author of the best article or publication in *Air Britain* with a North American biased content during a given year. Originality of research and content and literary merit are the criteria considered for the award. A DC-3 trophy is presented each year at the Annual General Meeting in April. Established in 1973 by the chairman of AAHS in California to celebrate the 25th Anniversary of Air-Britain and to recognize the cooperation between the two aviation historical societies.

• 5009 •
Air League
E.R. Cox Esq., Dir.
Broadway House
Tothill St.
London SW1H 9NS, United Kingdom
Phone: 44 207 2228463
Fax: 44 207 2228462
E-mail: exec@airleague.co.uk
Home Page: http://www.airleague.co.uk

• 5010 • Air League Challenge Trophy
Awarded through annual competition among the Voluntary Gliding Schools of the (RAF) Air Cadets organization. A silver Challenge Cup is awarded annually. Established in 1921 by Major General Sir Sefton Brancker KCB AFC and Philip Foster Esq.

• 5011 • Air League Founders' Medal
For recognition of the most meritorious achievement in the field of British aviation during the year. British nationals and, exceptionally, foreign nationals are eligible. A medal is awarded annually when merited. Established in 1960 by a gift of the late Stephen Marples to commemorate the Founders of the Air League in 1909.

• 5012 • Air League Gold Medal
For outstanding service to the causes of The Air League. Established in 1998 by the Royal Force Historical Society.

• 5013 • Jeffrey Quill Medal
For an outstanding contribution to the development of air-mindedness in Britain's youth. Established in 1997 in memory of the late Jeffrey Quill.

• 5014 • Scott-Farnie Medal
To recognize work in the field of air education. Established in 1969 in memory of G. R. Scott-Farnie.

• 5015 •
Airey Neave Trust
Hannah Scott, Contact
40 Bernard St.
PO Box 36800
London WC1N 7WJ, United Kingdom
Phone: 44 20 7833 4440
E-mail: info@aireyneavetrust.org.uk
Home Page: http://www.aireyneavetrust.org.uk

• 5016 • Airey Neave Research Fellowship
To assist scholars to undertake research in the field of human freedom. Such research, in a department of the fellow's choice, will fall within the definition of helping to protect and/or enhance personal freedom under the rule of democratic law, either national or international, against the threat and consequences of political violence. It may, specifically, concentrate on a subject relating to terrorism, political violence and torture. Candidates for Masters' degrees or Doctorates are eligible, but not encouraged to apply. The amount and term of the fellowship varies. Awarded periodically as merited. Established in 1979 to honor Airey Neave, a Member of Parliament for Abingdon from 1953 until his assassination in 1979. The program was reactivated in 1988. Formerly: (1988) Airey Neave Scholarship.

• 5017 •
Aldeburgh Poetry Trust
Naomi Jaffa, Dir.
% The Cut
9 New Cut
Halesworth
Suffolk IP19 8BY, United Kingdom
Phone: 44 1986 835950
E-mail: info@thepoetrytrust.org
Home Page: http://www.aldeburghpoetryfestival.org

• 5018 • Jerwood Aldeburgh First Collection Prize
For recognition of promise and achievement in a first full collection (at least 40 pages) of poetry published in the United Kingdom and Eire in the twelve months preceding the November Aldeburgh Poetry Festival. A monetary prize of £3,000 with an invitation to take part in the following year's festival is awarded annually. Established in 1989.

• 5019 •
All England Lawn Tennis and Croquet Club
T.D. Phillips, Chm.
Church Rd.
Wimbledon
London SW19 5AE, United Kingdom
Phone: 44 20 89442244
Fax: 44 181 947 8752
E-mail: internet@aeltc.com
Home Page: http://www.wimbledon.org

• 5020 • The Championships, Wimbledon
To recognize the winners of the following tennis events: men's singles, men's doubles, women's singles, women's doubles, and mixed doubles. Trophies are awarded annually after the final of each event. Established in 1877.

• 5021 •
Alpine Garden Society
Christine McGregor, Dir.
AGS Centre
Avon Bank
Worcestershire
Pershore WR10 3JP, United Kingdom
Phone: 44 1386 554790
Fax: 44 1386 554801
E-mail: ags@alpinegardensociety.org
Home Page: http://www.alpinegardensociety.net

• 5022 • Award of Honour
For recognition of work within the Society. Awarded annually to the member, or members, who have given sterling service to the Society which merits recognition. Established in 1983.

• 5023 • Lionel and Joyce Bacon Award
A cash sum awarded annually for the best practical alpine gardening article published during the previous year in *Bulletin*.

• 5024 • Florence Baker Award
A cash sum awarded annually, for the best art work published in the *Bulletin*.

• 5025 • Clarence Elliott Memorial Award
This Cup, presented by the family of the late Clarence Elliott, is awarded annually to the person who submits the best article published in the *Bulletin* in each calendar year.

• 5026 • Lyttel Trophy
For recognition of Members of the Society for outstanding contributions to a profession or field of activity associated with Alpine plants. A trophy is presented annually. Established in the 1930s to honor the late Professor Lyttel, a former President of the Society.

• 5027 •
Amateur Entomologists' Society
Nick Holford FRES, Registrar
PO Box 8774
London SW7 5ZG, United Kingdom
E-mail: contact@amentsoc.org
Home Page: http://www.amentsoc.org

• 5028 • Ansorge Award
For junior exhibits.

• 5029 • BradFord Award
For best adult member exhibit.

• 5030 • Cribb Award
For conservation and related activities in AES.

• 5031 • Gardiner Award
For best article submitted by a young member to the AES bug club magazine.

• 5032 • Hammond Award
For best contribution to the AES bulletin.

• 5033 •
Amateur Swimming Association
David Sparkes, Chief Exec.
Harold Fern House
Derby Sq.
41 Granby St.
Loughborough LE11 5AL, United Kingdom
Phone: 44 1509 168700
Fax: 44 1509 618701
E-mail: customerservices@swimming.org
Home Page: http://www.britishswimming.org

• 5034 • Henry Benjamin National Memorial Trophy
For recognition of the club with the most points in the following National Championships and the National Winter Championships for Men, viz: 50, 100, 200, 400, 1,500 metres Freestyle; Long Distance; 100 and 200 metres Backstroke, Breaststroke and Butterfly; and 200 and 400 metres Individual Medley, Club Medley Team, and Club Freestyle Team. The total number of points obtained by the clubs either through their team or individual entries are added together on completion of the championships and the club obtaining the highest aggregate is declared the winner.

• 5035 • Mary Black Award
Recognizes a person who is a member of an affiliated club and who has given outstanding service to synchronized swimming during the year. Given by the Synchronized Swimming Committee.

• 5036 • G. Melville Clark National Memorial Trophy
For recognition of the club with the highest points in the Diving Championships. The competition for the G. Melville Clark National Memorial Trophy is open to all men's clubs or men's sections of clubs affiliated to the ASA. The competitions are confined to the following championships: All ASA Summer and Winter Diving Championships and the two principal District Diving Championships other than plain diving, which are declared by each District Association no later than June 1 in each year. The trophy is awarded annually.

• 5037 • Dawdon Trophy
For recognition of the winning club of the ASA Age Group Diving Competitions. The total number of points obtained by each club are added together on December 31 each year, and the club obtaining the highest total is declared the winner. The winning club is entitled to hold the trophy. Awarded annually.

• 5038 • Harold Fern Award
To recognize the most outstanding contribution to swimming on the national or international level through education or instructional achievement, for architectural design of swimming facilities, for writing or development of original material, or for competitive performance. Clubs, individuals, or associations (amateur and professional) may be nominated by District Associations by September 1. A monetary award of £50 and a framed certificate are presented each year in February at the annual council meeting. Established in 1961 in honor of Harold E. Fern C.B.E. J.P., Secretary to the ASA from 1921 to 1969.

• 5039 • Harold Fern National Trophy
For recognition of the club with the most points in the National Championships and the National Winter Championships for Women 50, 100, 200, 400, 800 metres Freestyle; Long Distance; 100 and 200 metres Backstroke, Breaststroke and Butterfly; and 200 and 400 metres Individual Medley, Club Medley Team, and Club Freestyle Team. The total number of points obtained by the clubs either through their team or individual entries, are added together on completion of the Championships, and the club obtaining the highest aggregate is declared the winner. The winning club is entitled to hold the Harold Fern National Trophy. Awarded annually.

• 5040 • Gemma Yates Trophy
Recognizes endeavor. Applicants must be members of an affiliated club who have overcome anything which has made it difficult for them, yet still gives 100% to the sport of synchronized swimming. Awarded annually.

• 5041 • George Hearn Trophy
To recognize the diver who is a member of a club affiliated with the ASA whose performance is adjudged by the ASA Diving Committee to be the best for the year. Awarded annually. Established to honor George Hearn, Present of the ASA in 1908.

• 5042 • Alan Hime Memorial Trophies
To recognize the male and the female swimmers who are members of a club affiliated to the ASA and whose performance is adjudged by the ASA Swimming Committee to be the best at the ASA National Winter Championships. A memento is awarded to each annually.

• 5043 • Holland Trophy
For the senior synchronized swimmer with the highest total of routine scores in the solo duet and team events at the National Championships. Awarded annually.

• 5044 • Shacklock Trophy
For the junior swimmer with the highest total of routine scores in the solo, duet, and team events at the National Championships. Awarded annually.

• 5045 • Norma Thomas National Memorial Trophy
To recognize a junior diver who is a member of a club affiliated to the ASA and whose performance is adjudged by the ASA Diving Committee to be the best for the year. Awarded annually.

• 5046 • Alfred H. Turner Award
For recognition of outstanding contributions to swimming on the national or international level, through educational or instructional achievement, for architectural design of swimming facilities, for writing or development of original material, or for competitive performance. This award is given to a female if the Harold Fern trophy is given to a male, and vice versa. Nominations may be made by district associations, clubs, individuals, and associations, both amateur and professional by September 1. A monetary award of £50 and a framed certificate are awarded each year at the annual council meeting held in February. Established in 1982 to honor Alfred H. Turner, O.B.E., A.I.B., the Honorary Treasurer from 1968 to 1985, and the President in 1982.

• 5047 • Belle White National Memorial Trophy
For recognition of the club with the highest points in the Diving Championships. All women's clubs or women's sections of clubs affiliated to the ASA are eligible. The competitions are confined to the following championships: All ASA summer and winter Champion-

ships and the two principal District Diving Championships other than plain diving, which are declared by each District Association not later than June 1 in each year. A trophy is awarded annually.

• 5048 • T. M. Yeadon Memorial Trophy
To recognize the swimmer whose performance is the best for the year as judged by the Amateur Swimming Association Committee. A trophy is presented annually. Established in 1970 in memory of T. M. Yeadon, an ASA officer and President in 1924.

• 5049 •
Anglo-Austrian Music Society
Walter J. Foster, Sec.Gen.
% Richard Tauber Prize Committee
158 Rosendale Rd.
London SE21 8LG, United Kingdom
Phone: 44 20 8761 0444
Fax: 44 20 8766 6151
E-mail: info@aams.org.uk
Home Page: http://www.aams.org.uk

• 5050 • Richard Tauber Prize
For recognition of an outstanding British or Austrian singer. Men and women ordinarily residing in Great Britain or Austria over 21 years of age, and preferably under 30 in the case of women and 32 in the case of men, are eligible. Applications must be submitted by January 28. The prize consists of £5,000 to enable the winner to prepare for a public recital in London under the auspices of the Anglo-Austrian Music Society. Established in 1950 in memory of the Austrian tenor Richard Tauber.

• 5051 •
Animal Transportation Association - European Office
Tim Harris, European Sec.
PO Box 251
Redhill RH1 5FU, United Kingdom
Phone: 44 1737 822249
Fax: 44 1737 822954
E-mail: aataeurope@aata-animaltransport.org
Home Page: http://www.aata-animaltransport.org

• 5052 • Animal Welfare Award
Recognizes a person working with animal transport/promoting animal welfare. Awarded annually.

• 5053 • Robert D. Campbell Memorial Award
To honor outstanding contributions to the humane transportation of animals. Awarded annually.

• 5054 • International Award
Recognizes outstanding contributions to the welfare of animals in international commerce. Government personnel are eligible. Awarded annually.

• 5055 • Public Service Award
To honor outstanding contributions to the humane transportation of animals. Awarded annually.

• 5056 •
Anti-Slavery International
Mary Cunneen, Dir.
Thomas Clarkson House
The Stableyard
Broomgrove Rd.
London SW9 9TL, United Kingdom
Phone: 44 20 75018920
Fax: 44 20 77384110
E-mail: antislavery@antislavery.org
Home Page: http://www.antislavery.org

• 5057 • Anti-Slavery Award
To recognize an individual or organization performing outstanding work in the fight against contemporary slavery. Applicants must have worked for a number of years on an issue related to slavery, be involved in direct intervention, be involved in an on-going campaign, and see a need for international pressure to enhance his or her work. Awarded annually. Established in 1991.

• 5058 •
Arboricultural Association
Nick Eden, Dir.
Ampfield House
Ampfield
Romsey SO51 9PA, United Kingdom
Phone: 44 1794 368717
Fax: 44 1794 368978
E-mail: admin@trees.org.uk
Home Page: http://www.trees.org.uk

• 5059 • Arboricultural Association Award
Recognizes services to arboriculture. Awarded annually.

• 5060 •
Architectural Association
Brett Steele, Dir.
36 Bedford Sq.
London WC1B 3ES, United Kingdom
Phone: 44 20 7887 4000
Phone: 44 20 7887 4111
Fax: 44 20 7414 0782
E-mail: reception@aaschool.ac.uk
Home Page: http://www.aaschool.ac.uk

• 5061 • Anthony Pott Memorial Award
To assist studies or the publication of studies related to the field of architecture. Architects and students of architecture and related subjects may apply. Candidates wishing to use the award for research rather than the publication of studies will, in their application, either have to demonstrate some pre-knowledge of the proposed field of study or satisfy the Award Committee that they are sufficiently competent to undertake new work. Projects are to be related to the subject of architecture and design, taken in its widest sense. A monetary award of £2,000 is presented biennially. Established in memory of Anthony Pott who was a student at the Architectural Association, a distinguished member of the staff of the Building Research Station, and Chief Architect of the Ministry of Education.

• 5062 • Michael Ventris Memorial Award
To promote the study of architecture and the study of Mycenaean civilization. It is intended that the award should support a specific project rather than a continuing program of study. Architects or students of not less than RIBA Intermediate status or other comparable level of achievement from all countries may apply. A monetary award of uo to £2,000 is awarded annually for each field of study. Established in 1957 in memory of Michael Ventris, in appreciation of his work in the fields of architecture and Mycenaean civilization.

• 5063 • Bernard Webb Studentship
For the encouragement of the study of architecture. Students of post graduate standing, 32 years of age and under, who are citizens of the British Commonwealth and have been members of the Architectural Association for not less than two years may apply. A stipend of £1,500 and travel expenses are awarded biennially for a three month architecture study visit, based on the British School at Rome.

• 5064 •
Army Families Federation
Sammie Crane, Chm.
Trenchard Lines
Upavon
Pewsey SN9 6BE, United Kingdom
Phone: 44 1980 615525
Fax: 44 1980 615526
E-mail: us@aff.org.uk
Home Page: http://www.army.mod.uk/aff

• 5065 • Anne Armstrong Award
To recognize an individual for outstanding contributions to the local community. A silver rose bowl is awarded biennially in odd-numbered years.

• 5066 • NAAFI/AFF Rose Bowl
To recognize an individual for outstanding contribution to the wellbeing of the quality of life of their local army community. A monetary prize of £500 and temporary possession of the Rose Bowl is awarded biennially in even-numbered years.

• 5067 •
Arts and Business
Colin Tweedy, CEO
Nutmeg House
60 Gainsford St.
Butlers Wharf
London SE1 2NY, United Kingdom
Phone: 44 20 7378 8143
Fax: 44 20 7407 7527
E-mail: head.office@aandb.org.uk
Home Page: http://www.aandb.org.uk

• 5068 • FT/ARTS And Business Awards
To recognize and encourage imaginative and effective support of the arts by commercial organizations. The Awards are open to all companies sponsoring arts events, projects, or organizations in the United Kingdom, and all companies sponsoring British arts events overseas. Nominations should be submitted on the nomination form and the major part of the sponsorship should have taken place in the 12 months prior to the closing date. The Awards are presented at a ceremony in November.

• 5069 •
Arts Council England
Peter Hewitt, Chief Exec.
14 Great Peter St.
London SW1P 3NQ, United Kingdom
Phone: 44 845 3006200
Phone: 44 20 79736564
Fax: 44 20 79736590
E-mail: enquiries@artscouncil.org.uk
Home Page: http://www.artscouncil.org.uk

• 5070 • Meyer-Whitworth Award
To help encourage the careers of playwrights from the United Kingdom who are not yet established. Plays must be in English and have been produced professionally in the United Kingdom for the first time between August 1 and July 31 of the preceding year. Directors of professional theater companies may nominate plays. Awarded annually.

• 5071 • John Whiting Award
For recognition of the best original play of the year. The award is intended to help further the careers and enhance the reputations of younger British playwrights, and to draw public attention to the importance of writers in contemporary theater. The following criteria are considered in judging a play: writing of special quality, relevance and importance to contemporary life, and potential value to the British theater. The judges shall not have regard to whether or not the play has received a production, or is likely to receive a production or publication. To be considered, British playwrights must, over the previous two years, have had either an offer of an award under the Arts Council Theatre Writing Schemes, a commission from one of those theater companies in receipt of annual subsidy from either the Arts Council or a Regional Arts Board, or a premiere production by a theater company in receipt of annual subsidy from either the Arts Council or a Regional Arts Board. No writer who has previously won the award may reapply, and no play that has previously been submitted for the award is eligible. The entry deadline is early January. A monetary prize of £6,000 is awarded annually. Established in 1965 in memory of John Whiting for his contribution to post-war British theater.

• 5072 • Raymond Williams Community Publishing Prize
To commend an outstanding creative and imaginative work which reflects the values of ordinary people and their lives, and is submitted by non-profit-making publishers producing books in mutual and cooperative ways. Awarded annually.

• 5073 •
Arts Council of Northern Ireland
(Airts Cooncil o Norlin Airlann)
MacNeice House
77 Malone Rd.
Belfast BT9 6AQ, United Kingdom
Phone: 44 1232 385200
Fax: 44 1232 661715
Home Page: http://www.artscouncil-ni.org

• 5074 • Arts Council of Northern Ireland Bursaries and Awards
To provide support for creative and performing artists active in the fields of drama and dance, music and jazz, literature, traditional arts, community arts, and visual arts. Artists who are residents in Northern Ireland for at least one year, contribute regularly to the artistic activity of the community, and who were previous award holders are eligible. Monetary awards of up to £12,000 each are awarded periodically to enable the recipients to concentrate on their work for a lengthy period. A bursary of £1,000 is also available in the field of jazz. In addition, the Council awards the British School at Rome Fellowship, and the New York Fellowship, to encourage professional development in the arts.

• 5075 •
Arvon Foundation
Stephanie Anderson, Natl.Dir.
42A Buckingham Palace Rd.
London SW1W 0RE, United Kingdom
Phone: 44 20 7931 7611
E-mail: s.anderson@arvonfoundation.org
Home Page: http://www.arvonfoundation.org

• 5076 • Arvon Foundation International Poetry Competition
For recognition of outstanding poetry submitted by individuals from Great Britain and abroad. Each entry must be written in English. The following prizes are awarded biennially: (1) First prize - £5,000; (2) Second prize - £2,500; (3) Third prize - £1,000 and (4) Fourth prizes of £500. Established in 1980. Sponsored by Duncan Lawrie Limited. Deadline is May 31.

• 5077 •
Association for Clinical Biochemists
Dr. Graham V. Groom, Senior Administrator
130-132 Tooley St.
London SE1 2TU, United Kingdom
Phone: 44 207 4038001
Fax: 44 207 4038006
E-mail: admin@acb.org.uk
Home Page: http://www.acb.org.uk

• 5078 • Association of Clinical Biochemists Foundation Award
To recognize a member of the Association, normally a resident in the British Isles, who is acknowledged as having made an outstanding contribution to clinical biochemistry. The subject matter of the Foundation Award Lecture should reflect the interests of the award recipient, and should be of a scientific nature, reflecting the state of the art in one area of clinical biochemistry. Nominations for the award may be made by any three members of the Association. The award, which is presented by the President or Chairman of the Association, comprises a suitable memento and an honorarium. Prior to the presentation, the recipient delivers the ACB Foundation Award Lecture. Awarded annually. Established in 1990 by the ACB Foundation. For more information contact Dr. D. J. Worthington, National Meetings Secretary.

• 5079 • Bayer Award
To recognize a junior member of the Association who has presented the best scientific paper at a national meeting. Members of the Association under 35 years of age are eligible to participate in the competition. A monetary award of £250 and a silver medal are awarded annually. Established in 1971 by Miles Laboratories Ltd., Ames Division. Now donated by Bayer Diagnostics UK Ltd.

• 5080 • Professors' Prize
To recognize general achievements within the field of clinical biochemistry. Clinical biochemists, or those in related fields such as molecular biology or clinical medicine, who are under 40 years of age are eligible. A diploma and an honorarium are awarded when merited. Established in 1994.

• 5081 • Roche Diagnostics Award
To finance the visit of an international scientist to give the Roche Diagnostics Award lecture at the national meeting of the Association. Individuals must be nominated. A monetary award of £2,000 for travel is presented annually. Established in 1985. Formerly: BCL Award Lecture.

• 5082 • Thermo Electron Clinical Chemistry and Automation Systems Award
To honor a medical scientist whose work has been of major importance to clinical biochemistry. Medical students whose work in practice, research, or education has led to improved international cooperation particularly in Europe may be nominated. A monetary award for travel to present the lecture is awarded annually. Established in 1981 by Kone Instruments.

• 5083 •
Association for Geographic Information
Mark Linehan, Dir.
Block C, 4th Fl., Morelands
5-23 Old St.
London EC1V 9HL, United Kingdom
Phone: 44 20 72535211
Phone: 44 20 72535211
Fax: 44 20 72514505
E-mail: info@agi.org.uk
Home Page: http://www.agi.org.uk

Awards are arranged in alphabetical order below their administering organizations

• 5084 • **Award For Technological Progress**
Award of recognition.

• 5085 • **Journalist of the Year**
Award of recognition.

• 5086 • **Surveyor Award For Local Government**
Award of recognition.

• 5087 •
Association for Heritage Interpretation
Michael H. Glen, Admin.
18 Rose Crescent
Tayinloan
Perth PH1 1NS, United Kingdom
Phone: 44 1738 621996
Fax: 44 1738 621996
E-mail: admin@heritage-interpretation.org.uk
Home Page: http://www.heritage-interpretation.org.uk

• 5088 • **Interpret Britain and Ireland Awards**
To recognize outstanding practice in interpretation throughout Britain and Ireland. Awarded annually.

• 5089 •
Association for Industrial Archaeology
Simon Thomas, Contact
School of Archaeological Studies
University of Leicester
Leicester LE1 7RH, United Kingdom
Phone: 44 116 2525337
Fax: 44 116 2525005
E-mail: aia@le.ac.uk
Home Page: http://www.industrial-archaeology.org.uk

• 5090 • **British Archaeological Awards**
To recognize good practice in the adaptive reuse of any building. Pays particular attention to ingenuity in the treatment of buildings which are difficult to convert. This award is one of roughly 12 British Archaeological Awards, which are presented every two years. Formerly: Ironbridge Award.

• 5091 • **Dorothea Award for Conservation**
To support and encourage voluntary conservation work on sites and artifacts of industrial, agricultural, and domestic importance. A plaque and monetary award of £500 are presented annually. Established in 1984.

• 5092 • **Fieldwork Award**
To recognize contributions to fieldwork in the preservation of historic industrial sites. A monetary award of £250 is presented annually.

• 5093 • **Publications Award**
To encourage high standards in local society publications sympathetic to the aims of industrial archaeology, but excluding those solely concerned with transport history. A local society is defined as being based on a town, county, district or region in England, Wales, Scotland, and Ireland, but excluding societies with a nationwide remit. Three categories exist: newsletters; journals produced on a regular basis; and occasional publications. All entries must have been published in the eighteen months prior to the year of the competition. A monetary award of £100 is awarded to the winner of each category annually.

• 5094 • **Recording and Fieldwork Award**
To recognize an industrial archeological project involving a substantial element of site recording in the field, together with supporting research. Open to all amateur and professional individuals and groups. Three awards are presented: the main award of £250 for the best piece of fieldwork submitted that year, a student award of £100 for the best entry by a student and the initiative award of £150 for innovative projects. Awarded annually.

• 5095 •
Association for Project Management
Martin Barnes, Pres.
150 W Wycombe Rd.
Buckinghamshire
High Wycombe HP12 3AE, United Kingdom
Phone: 44 845 4581944
Fax: 44 1494 528937
E-mail: info@apm.org.uk
Home Page: http://www.apm.org.uk

• 5096 • **Brian Willis Award**
To the student under the age of 30 who has achieved the highest mark of all candidates in the past year's APMP examination.

• 5097 • **Programme of the Year**
To the organisation that has achieved a common objective through effective management of a portfolio of projects.

• 5098 • **Project Manager of the Year**
To the project manager who provides the most effective demonstration of project management.

• 5099 • **Project of the Year**
To the company with the project delivered within the UK whose outcomes and results exceeded or aligned most closely to its objectives, completed or successfully commissioned during the last year.

• 5100 • **Sir Monty Finniston Award**
For an individual or organization who has made an outstanding contribution to the development of project management as a vehicle For effective change.

• 5101 •
Association for the Study of Obesity
Christine Hawkins, Sec.
20 Brook Meadow Close
Essex
Woodford Green IG8 9NR, United Kingdom
Phone: 44 20 85032042
Fax: 44 20 85032042
E-mail: chris@aso.ndo.co.uk
Home Page: http://www.aso.org.uk

• 5102 • **Best Practice Award**
To a member either as an individual or representative of a group working in the field of obesity.

• 5103 • **Student Researcher Award**
To individuals of any age but who are registered for a higher degree.

• 5104 • **Travel Fellowships**
For members.

• 5105 • **Young Achiever Award**
To a member who has made a significant contribution to scientific or clinical knowledge.

• 5106 •
Association in Scotland to Research Into Astronautics
Duncan A. Lunan, Treas.
Flat 65, Darliada House
Anderston
Glasgow G2 7PE, United Kingdom
Phone: 44 141 2217658
E-mail: astra@dlunan.freeserve.co.uk
Home Page: http://www.astra.org.uk

• 5107 • **Victor Hirt Prize**
To recognize the best individual flight at the International Rocketry Weekend Aquajet (water rocket) Contest. Awarded annually.

• 5108 • **Oscar Schwiglhofer Trophy**
To recognize the winning team in the International Rocketry Weekend Aquajet (water rocket) Contest. Awarded annually. Established in 1984.

• 5109 •
Association of British Philatelic Societies
PO Box 199
Thetford IP24 3WX, United Kingdom
E-mail: bpenquiry@ukphilately.org.uk
Home Page: http://www.ukphilately.org.uk/abps

• 5110 • **Congress Medal**
Awarded for outstaning service to British Philately at national level. The candidate must be a member of an organization affilated to the Association of British Philatelic Societies (ABPS) and there is only one recipient each year, with presention being made at the annual Philatelic Congress of Great Britian. The award is not for philatelic excellence, but for voluntary endeavours particularly at national level.

• 5111 • The Roll of Distinguished Philatelist

Established in 1921, the signing of the Roll has been regarded for many years as one of the world's pre-eminent philatelic honours. Candidates can be nominated by existing Signatories to the Roll, National Federations accredited to the Federation Internationale de Philatelie (FIP), regional UK Federations and a number of UK specified societies, should be philatelists who have been performed servies to philately, either by research work made available to others or in some public or other capacity.

• 5112 •
Association of British Travel Agents
Ian Reynolds, Ch.Exec.
68-71 Newman St.
London W1T 3AH, United Kingdom
Phone: 44 20 76372444
Fax: 44 20 76370713
E-mail: information@abta.co.uk
Home Page: http://www.abta.com

• 5113 • Gold Training Award

Recognizes exceptional levels of training. Only members are eligible. Awarded periodically.

• 5114 •
Association of Building Engineers
David R. Gibson, Chief Exec.
Lutyens House
Billing Brook Rd.
Weston Favell
Northamptonshire
Northampton NN3 8NW, United Kingdom
Phone: 44 845 1261058
Phone: 44 845 1773411
Fax: 44 1604 784220
E-mail: building.engineers@abe.org.uk
Home Page: http://www.abe.org.uk

• 5115 • Fire Safety Award

For significant contributions to fire safety, fire protection, or fire engineering. Awarded annually. Established in 1994.

• 5116 • Outstanding Service Award

To recognize a member's contribution to the advancement of the aims and the objectives of the Association. Awarded annually. Formerly: Lutyens Award.

• 5117 • Peter Stone Award

For personal service and valuable contribution to the advancement of building engineering. An engraved silver salver is awarded annually. Established in 1982.

• 5118 •
Association of Chartered Certified Accountants - United Kingdom
Helen Brand, Managing Dir.
89 Hydepark St., 2 Central Quay
Glasgow G3 8BW, United Kingdom
Phone: 44 141 5822000
Fax: 44 141 5822222
E-mail: info@accaglobal.com
Home Page: http://www.accaglobal.com

Formerly: (1974) Association of Certified Accountants.

• 5119 • Awards for Sustainability Reporting

To recognize innovative examples of corporate environmental, social and sustainability following from the success of the Environmental Reporting awards. Established in 1991.

• 5120 •
Association of Chief Police Officers of England, Wales and Northern Ireland
Mr. Chris Fox, Pres.
25 Victoria St.
London SW1H 0EX, United Kingdom
Phone: 44 20 72273434
Fax: 44 20 72273400
E-mail: info@acpo.police.uk
Home Page: http://www.acpo.police.uk

• 5121 • Provincial Police Award

For recognition of an act of bravery in support of law and order performed by a member of the public anywhere in England or Wales outside the area controlled by the Metropolitan Police and City of London Police. Individuals may be nominated. Gold and silver medals are awarded annually. Established in 1965.

• 5122 •
Association of Commonwealth Universities
Dr. John Rowett, Sec.Gen.
John Foster House
36 Gordon Sq.
London WC1H 0PF, United Kingdom
Phone: 44 20 73806700
Fax: 44 20 73872655
E-mail: info@acu.ac.uk
Home Page: http://www.acu.ac.uk

• 5123 • Canada Memorial Foundation Scholarships

To facilitate postgraduate study by U.K. students leading to a university degree in Canada. Candidates must be individuals of high academic promise and leadership potential who will play a full part in the life of the Canadian community which they visit and who will return to contribute fully to UK society. Additionally, they must be UK citizens aged 30 years or under, and hold, or expect to attain, a minimum of an upper second class degree. Awards are available for one year of taught study only at any university or other appropriate institution in Canada subject to the approval of the Canada Memorial Foundation. Awards are not offered for study at doctoral level. Awarded annually.

• 5124 • Commonwealth Scholarship and Fellowship Plan

Encourages students to study in a Commonwealth country other than their own. Applicants must be Commonwealth postgraduate students. Awarded annually.

• 5125 • Commonwealth Shared Scholarship Scheme

For study in the United Kingdom. Applicants must be students from developing Commonwealth countries with a fluency in English. Awarded annually.

• 5126 • Marshall Scholarships

Encourages U.S. graduate students to study in the U.K. Awarded annually.

• 5127 •
Association of Cost Engineers
Anne Fairless, Admin. Sec.
Lea House
5 Middlewich Rd.
Cheshire
Sandbach CW11 1XL, United Kingdom
Phone: 44 1270 764798
Fax: 44 1270 766180
E-mail: enquiries@acoste.org.uk
Home Page: http://www.acoste.org.uk

• 5128 • Graduate and Student Prize

To the best essay submitted to the council by a graduate or student member.

• 5129 • John Herbert Award

For an individual who has made a major contribution to the association.

• 5130 • Tony Jarvis Award

To the author of the best paper published in The Cost Engineer.

• 5131 • Pates Prize

For persons who contributed to the profile and advancement of the association.

• 5132 •
Association of Cricket Umpires and Scorers
Keith Smith, Gen.Sec.
PO Box 399
Cotes Heath
Surrey GU15 9JZ, United Kingdom
Phone: 44 1276 27962
Fax: 44 1276 62277
E-mail: admin@acus.org.uk
Home Page: http://www.acus.cricket.org

• 5133 • John Budgen Award

Recognizes outstanding scorers. Awarded annually.

• 5134 • Pat Cooke Award

Recognizes scoring excellence in the sport of cricket. Awarded annually.

• 5135 • **Arthur Sims Award**
Recognizes outstanding umpires. Awarded annually.

• 5136 •
Association of Cycle Traders
Anne Killick, Natl.Sec.
31a High St.
Tunbridge Wells TN1 1XN, United Kingdom
Phone: 44 1892 526081
Fax: 44 1892 544278
E-mail: enquiries@act-bicycles.com
Home Page: http://www.act-bicycles.com/2004/index.shtml

• 5137 • **CyTech Accreditation**
Recognizes competence in workshop skills. Awarded when merited.

• 5138 •
Association of Golf Writers
Andrew Farrell, Sec.
1 Pilgrims Bungalow
Mulberry Hill
Chilham CT4 8AH, United Kingdom
Phone: 44 1227 732496
Phone: 44 7711 702907
Fax: 44 1227 732496
E-mail: andyfarrell@compuserve.com

• 5139 • **Golfer of the Year**
To recognize achievement in European golf. European professional and amateur golfers (male and female) are considered. The Golf Writers' Trophy and a permanent memento are awarded annually in December. Established in 1951.

• 5140 •
Association of Interior Specialists
Mrs. Jean Birch, Chief Exec.
Olton Bridge
245 Warwick Rd.
Solihull B92 7AH, United Kingdom
Phone: 44 121 7070077
Fax: 44 121 7061949
E-mail: info@ais-interiors.org.uk
Home Page: http://ais-interiors.org.uk

Formerly: (1998) Partitioning and Interiors Association; Partitioning Industry Association.

• 5141 • **Contractors' Awards**
To promote and encourage high levels of craftsmanship in six categories: interior fit-outs, ceilings, partitioning, drywall construction, specialist joinery, and operable walls. Applicants must be association members. Certificates are presented to the winner in each category. Awarded annually.

• 5142 •
Association of National Park Authorities
Martin Fitton, Chief Exec.
126 Bute St.
Cardiff CF10 5LE, United Kingdom
Phone: 44 29 20499966
Fax: 44 29 20499980
E-mail: info@anpa.gov.uk
Home Page: http://www.anpa.gov.uk

• 5143 • **National Conservation Award**
For contributions to national parks purposes. A trophy is awarded biennially.

• 5144 •
Association of Paediatric Anaesthetists of Great Britain and Ireland
K.A. Wilkinson, Honorary Sec.
48-49 Rusell Sq.
London WC1B 4JY, United Kingdom
Phone: 44 20 79087376
Fax: 44 20 75806325
E-mail: apa@rcoa.ac.uk
Home Page: http://www.apagbi.org.uk

• 5145 • **Paediatric Anaesthesia Research Fund**

• 5146 • **Registrar Prize**

• 5147 • **Travel Grants**
For members.

• 5148 •
Association of Photographers
Martin Beckett, Pres.
81 Leonard St.
London EC2A 4QS, United Kingdom
Phone: 44 20 77396669
Fax: 44 20 77398707
E-mail: general@aophoto.co.uk
Home Page: http://www.the-aop.org

Formerly: Association of Fashion Advertising and Editorial Photographers.

• 5149 • **Assistants' Awards**
To recognize the potential of photographic assistants who will be the future's professional advertising, editorial, and creative photographers. Open to all Assistants Members who enter individual images or portfolios into four categories. Monetary prizes and certificates are awarded annually. The final exhibition is also reproduced in a 100-page catalogue published by Elfande Fine Art Publishing. Established in 1990. Formerly: Fuji/Association of Photographers Assistants' Awards.

• 5150 • **Idea Awards**
The International Digital Exhibition & Awards (IDEA) recognizes the skills of digital photographers, and was established in 1999. The choice is made on an international basis and is judged by a panel of leading digital creators, agency professionals, photographers, and designer workers in the digital realm.

• 5151 • **Photographers' Awards**
To recognize talent within the professional advertising, fashion, and editorial fields of photography. Awards include the Photographers' Awards, Document Awards, Bursary Awards, Zeitgeist Awards, Student Awards, Assistants' Awards, and the AOP Open. Gold and silver trophies and Merit certificates are awarded annually. Established in 1983. Formerly: (1990) AFAEP Awards.

• 5152 • **Student Awards**
To encourage the development of students training to succeed in fashion, advertising, and editorial photography and to creatively and technically satisfy briefs devised and judged by major photographers and art directors in fashion, advertising, and editorial photography. A monetary award and a certificate are awarded annually. Established in 1985. Sponsored by Epson. Formerly: (1990) AFAEP/Kodak Student Competition.

• 5153 •
Astrological Association of Great Britain
Roy Gillett, Pres.
Unit 168, Lee Valley Technopark
Tottenham Hale
London N17 9LN, United Kingdom
Phone: 44 20 88804848
Fax: 44 20 88804849
E-mail: office@astrologicalassociation.com
Home Page: http://www.astrologicalassociation.com

• 5154 • **Astrological Association Awards and Scholarships**
For recognition of contributions to the field of astrology. The following awards are presented: Charles Harvey Award for Exceptional Service to Astrology, Ada Philips Scholarships, and John Addey Scholarships.

• 5155 •
Austin Ten Drivers Club Ltd.
Mike Bevan, Contact
% Mike Bevan
98 Heague Rd.
Ripley DE5 3GH, United Kingdom
Phone: 44 1773 749891
Fax: 44 1773 749891
E-mail: austintensecretary@yahoo.co.uk
Home Page: http://www.austintendriversclub.com

• 5156 • **Driver of the Year**
For recognition of an outstanding driver of the Club who scores the most points in driving attendance events during the preceding year; and to encourage participation in vintage driving events. Members must use a Club eligible car (1931-39 Austin). A trophy is awarded annually.

• 5157 •
BackCare - The Charity for Healthier Backs
Ms. Nia Taylor, Ch.Exec.
16 Elmtree Rd.
Teddington TW11 8ST, United Kingdom
Phone: 44 20 8977 5474
Fax: 44 20 8943 5318
E-mail: info@backcare.org.uk
Home Page: http://www.backcare.org.uk

Formerly: (1987) Back Pain Association.

• 5158 • **National Back Pain Association Medal**
For recognition of the most outstanding scientific research paper on the subject of back pain published during the year in one or more scientific journals in the English language. The paper must have come to the attention of the awarding committee of the Society for Back Pain Research. A monetary prize of £200, a medal, and a certificate are awarded annually. Established in 1978. Formerly: (1990) Back Pain Association Medal.

• 5159 •
Badminton Association of England
John Havers, Pres.
Natl. Badminton Ctre.
Bradwell Rd.
Loughton Lodge
Milton Keynes MK8 9LA, United Kingdom
Phone: 44 1908 268400
Fax: 44 1908 268412
E-mail: enquiries@baofe.co.uk
Home Page: http://www.baofe.co.uk

• 5160 • **English Badminton Award**
To recognize long-standing exceptional service to badminton in England. An EBA badge and a certificate are presented to the recipient(s) annually. Established in 1993.

• 5161 • **Herbert Scheele Medal**
To recognize outstanding contributions to the development and administration of the sport of badminton. Consideration is given to a member of the Association or its other national governing bodies. A silver medal is presented as merited at All-England Championships. Established in 1981. The award commemorates Herbert Scheele, a one-time secretary of the Association and of the International Badminton Federation.

• 5162 •
Balint Society
Lenka Speight, Pres.
Attn: Dr. D. Watt
Tollgate Health Centre
220 Tollgate Rd.
London E6 4JS, United Kingdom
Phone: 44 20 7445 7700
Fax: 44 20 7445 7715
E-mail: david.watt@gp-f84093.nhs.uk
Home Page: http://www.balint.co.uk

• 5163 • **Balint Society Essay Prize**
To encourage understanding of doctor-patient relationships. Unpublished essays based on personal experience on an announced subject may be submitted by April 1. Medical or paramedical employment is required. A monetary prize of £600 and publication in the Journal of the Society are awarded annually in June. Established in honor of Dr. Michael Balint, a psychoanalyst of London and Budapest.

• 5164 •
Bibliographical Society - United Kingdom
Margaret Ford, Hon.Sec.
Institute of English Studies
Senate House, Rm. 304
Malet St.
London WC1E 7HU, United Kingdom
Phone: 44 20 78628679
Fax: 44 20 78628720
E-mail: secretary@bibsoc.org.uk
Home Page: http://www.bibsoc.org.uk

• 5165 • **Medal for Services to Bibliography**
For recognition of achievement in the field of bibliographical studies. Individuals are elected. A medal is awarded irregularly. Established in 1929. Formerly: Silver-gilt Medal for Bibliography.

• 5166 •
Biochemical Society - England
Dr. I. J. McEwan, Membership Sec.
59 Portland Pl.
London W1B 1QW, United Kingdom
Phone: 44 207 5805530
Fax: 44 207 6373626
E-mail: genadmin@biochemistry.org
Home Page: http://www.biochemistry.org

• 5167 • **AstraZeneca Award**
For outstanding work carried out in a laboratory situated in the UK or Irish Republic leading to advances in biochemistry related to the development and application of a new reagent or method. Awarded triennially, the recipient receives an honorarium of £1,000 and travel expenses. Established in 1995. Sponsored by AstraZeneca Pharmaceuticals.

• 5168 • **Biochemical Society Award**
An award related to bio-chemistry without being dedicated to it solely, the council decides every 2 years the topic they wish to recognize with the award lecture and prize of £2,000.

• 5169 • **Biochemical Society Travel Fund**
Available to those in their postdoctoral years, after one years membership to the society, wishing to attend scientific meetings or to make short visits to laboratories.

• 5170 • **Colworth Medal**
For recognition of work of an outstanding nature by a British biochemist. British citizens under the age of 35 at the beginning of the year that the award is made may be nominated. Those above this age limit, who have lost time early in their careers through family commitments, illness, late entry into higher education, or other good reasons, will be considered by the awards committee. A medal and honorarium of £2,000 is awarded annually. The recipient is expected to deliver a lecture. The lecture is published in *Biochemical Society Transactions*. Established in 1963 by Unilever Research Laboratory.

• 5171 • **Honorary Member**
To recognize individuals for outstanding contributions to the field of biochemistry. Awarded when merited. Established in 1969.

• 5172 • **Sir Frederick Gowland Hopkins Memorial Lecture**
To recognize an individual in the field of biochemistry. The lecturer is required to assess the impact of recent advances in his or her chosen field upon progress in biochemistry. Considerable discretion is given the lecturer in choosing the subject and the lecturer may include to discuss advances made in other fields of knowledge that have important implications on the biochemical field, as well as the effects the advances in biochemestry will have on other fields of inquiry. Biochemists of any nationality may be nominated by the awards committee. A bronze medal and an honorarium of £1,000 plus expenses are awarded every two or three years. Established in 1958 in memory of Sir Frederic Gowland Hopkins.

• 5173 • **Jubilee Lecture and Harden Medal**
To recognize a biochemist of distinction from any part of the world. Nominations are invited by the awards committee. An honorarium of £1,000 Plus, travel expenses for two lectures, one in London and one repeated outside London, are awarded. The lecture is published in *Biochemical Society Transactions.* Since 1978, the lecturer has also received the Harden Medal. Awarded every two to three years when the Hopkins Lecture is not presented. Established in 1961 to commemorate the 50th anniversary of the society.

• 5174 • **Keilin Memorial Lecture**
For recognition of work in the field of biochemistry and biology. Biochemists of any nationality may be nominated. An honorarium of £ 1,000, travel expenses, a medal, and an invitation to deliver the lecture are awarded biennially. The lecture is published in *Biochemical Society Transactions.* Established in 1964 in memory of David Keilin.

• 5175 • **Krebs Memorial Scholarship**
To provide for a post-graduate scholarship, tenable at any British University. Candidates who wish to proceed to a higher degree in biochemistry or in an allied biomedical science, but whose careers have been interrupted for non-academic reasons beyond their own control and/or who are unlikely to qualify for an award from public funds are eligible. It will cover a personal maintenance grant at an appropriate level and all necessary fees. Applications may be made at any time. Although the scholarship is primarily aimed at graduate students, the award of a post-doc-

toral fellowship might be considered for a candidate whose circumstances merit such consideration. Established in 1982 to commemorate the life and work of Sir Hans Krebs, F.R.S.

• 5176 • **Morton Lecture**
For recognition of outstanding contributions to lipid biochemistry. The Johnston Professor of Biochemistry in the University of Liverpool sits with the award committee when the Morton Lecturer is elected. An honorarium of £1,000, an invitation to deliver the lecture, and full travel expenses are awarded biennially. The lecture is published in *Biochemical Society Transactions.* Established in 1978 to honor R.A. Morton.

• 5177 • **Novartis Medal and Prize**
For recognition of outstanding research in any branch of biochemistry. Candidates of any nationality who carry out their work in the United Kingdom may be nominated. An honorarium of £2,000, a medal, and travel expenses are awarded annually. The recipient is expected to deliver a lecture. The lecture is published in *Biochemical Society Transactions.* Established in 1964 by CIBA Laboratories. Sponsored by Novartis Pharmaceuticals Lic Ltd.

• 5178 •
Bird Life International - United Kingdom
Dr. Michael Rands, Dir. & Chief Exec.
Wellbrook Ct.
Girton Rd.
Cambridge CB3 0NA, United Kingdom
Phone: 44 1223 277318
Fax: 44 1223 277200
E-mail: birdlife@birdlife.org.uk
Home Page: http://www.birdlife.org

Formerly: International Council for Bird Preservation.

• 5179 • **BP Conservation Programme**
To contribute to long-term environmental conservation and sustainable development in priority areas by encouraging and engaging potential leaders in biodiversity conservation, and providing opportunities for them to gain practical skills and experience. This is achieved through a comprehensive system of grants, advice and training. Six types of grants are offered by the Programme: Future Conservationist Awards, Conservation Follow-up Awards, and Conservation Leadership Awards, and the WCS Research Fellowship, as well as scholarships and apprenticeships. Awarded annually. Established in 1985. Sponsored by BP plc in collaboration with BirdLife International, Fauna & Flora International, Wildlife Conservation Society, and Conservation International. Award website: http://conservation.bp.com.

• 5180 •
Birkenhead Photographic Association
29 Fairview Rd.
Preston CH43 5SD, United Kingdom
Phone: 44 151 6524773
Phone: 44 151 6524773
Home Page: http://www.thebpa.com

• 5181 • **Birkenhead International Colour Salon**
For recognition of achievement in traditional (general), contemporary and nature photography. Four slides in each of 3 sections may be submitted by January. Gold, silver, and bronze medals and certificates are awarded annually. Established in 1970.

• 5182 •
BKSTS - The Moving Image Society
Wendy Laybourn, Dir.
Pinewood Studios
Bucks
Iver Heath SLO ONH, United Kingdom
Phone: 44 1753 656656
Fax: 44 1753 657016
E-mail: info@bksts.com
Home Page: http://www.bksts.com

• 5183 • **Frank Littlejohn Award**
For outstanding contribution to the art and craft of cinema projection.

• 5184 • **Charles Parkhouse Award**
For technicians who have made significant contributions in the laboratory or sound recording branches of the industry.

• 5185 • **Denis Wratten Journal Award**
For the author who has the best article published in the Society's Journal.

• 5186 •
Boardman Tasker Charitable Trust
Maggie Body, Sec.
Pound House
Llangennith
Swansea SA3 1JQ, United Kingdom
Phone: 44 1792 386215
Fax: 44 1792 386215
E-mail: margaretbody@lineone.net
Home Page: http://www.boardmantasker.com

• 5187 • **Boardman Tasker Award for Mountain Literature**
For recognition of an original literary work. The central theme must be concerned with the mountain environment. Fiction, nonfiction, drama, or poetry written (whether initially or in translation) in the English language may be nominated by publishers only. Books must have been published or distributed in the United Kingdom for the first time between November 1 of the preceding year and October 31 of the year the prize is awarded. Entries must be submitted by August 1. A monetary award of £2,000 is awarded annually in October/November. Established in 1983 in memory of Peter Boardman and Joe Tasker, authors of mountain literature who disappeared on Mt. Everest in 1982.

• 5188 •
Book Trust (England)
Helen Hayes, Contact
Book House
45 East Hill
London SW18 2QZ, United Kingdom
Phone: 44 20 8516 2977
Fax: 44 20 8516 2978
E-mail: info@booktrust.org.uk
Home Page: http://www.booktrust.org.uk

Formerly: (1986) National Book League (England).

• 5189 • **Booker Russian Novel Prize**
To stimulate wider knowledge of modern Russian fiction in the Western world, to encourage translations, and to increase sales of the books. The winner is chosen by an international panel of five judges. Established in 1991. For further information, contact Anne Riddoch, 40 York Rd., Woking, Surrey, England GU22 7XN

• 5190 • **Nestle Smarties Book Prize**
To encourage high standards and stimulate interest in books for children in three categories: 5 years and under, 6 to 8 years, and 9 to 11 years. Books published in Britain and written in English by citizens or residents of the United Kingdom are eligible. A monetary prize of £2,500 Gold Award, £1,500 Silver Award, and £500 Bronze Award, in each of the three age categories. Awarded annually in the autumn. Established in 1985 by Rowntree Mackintosh, now known as Nestle Rowntree. Formerly: Smarties Prize for Children's Books.

• 5191 • ***The Mail on Sunday* - John Llewellyn Rhys Prize**
For recognition of a memorable literary work of fiction, nonfiction, or poetry written in English and published in the UK during the current year. British or Commonwealth writers who are under 35 years of age at the time of publication are eligible. A monetary prize of £5,000 is awarded annually. Established in 1941 by the widow of John Llewellyn Rhys, an airman killed while on active duty. Formerly: (1989) John Llewellyn Rhys Memorial Prize.

• 5192 •
Booksellers Association of the United Kingdom and Ireland
Tim Godfray, Chief Exec.
Minster House
272 Vauxhall Bridge Rd.
London SW1V 1BA, United Kingdom
Phone: 44 207 8020802
Fax: 44 207 8020803
E-mail: mail@booksellers.org.uk
Home Page: http://www.booksellers.org.uk

• 5193 • **BBC Four Samuel Johnson Prize for Non-Fiction**
For recognition of the best nonfiction books. The winning author receives £30,000. Awarded annually. For further information, contact Hannah Blake, Colman Getty PR, Middlesex house 34-42 Cleveland St. London W1T 4JE Formerly: (1996) AT&T Nonfiction Award.

• 5194 • Whitbread Literary Awards

To celebrate the best contemporary British writing. Books are considered in the following categories: biography or autobiography, novel, first novel, and poetry. Authors who have been living in Great Britain or Ireland for three or more years are eligible. Selection is made from books first published in the United Kingdom or Ireland within the previous year. Works must be submitted by publishers only. The following monetary awards are presented: £5,000 each for the winner in each category, and an additional £25,000 to the overall winner, Whitbread Book of the Year, chosen from the four category winners. Awarded annually in January. Established in 1971. Additional information is available from Alan Staton, Booksellers Association, Minster House, 272 Vauxhall Bridge Road, London SW1V 1BA, Tel: 44 20 7802 0802.

• 5195 •
Brazilian Chamber of Commerce in Great Britain
Mr. Dionisio Cerqueira, Sec.
32 Green St.
London W1K 7AT, United Kingdom
Phone: 44 20 73999281
Fax: 44 20 74990186
E-mail: pavlova@brazilianchamber.org.uk
Home Page: http://www.brazilianchamber.org.uk

• 5196 • Personality of the Year Award

Recognizes contribution to strengthen business relations between Brazil and the UK. Awarded annually.

• 5197 •
Brick Development Association
Mr. M. Hayward, Contact
Woodside House
Winkfield
Berkshire
Windsor SL4 2DX, United Kingdom
Phone: 44 1344 885651
Fax: 44 1344 890129
E-mail: brick@brick.org.uk
Home Page: http://www.brick.org.uk

• 5198 • Brick Awards

To recognize and reward excellence in use of brick. Awards are presented in several categories covering different aspects of design and construction. Contact the BDA for full details.

• 5199 •
Bridport Arts Centre
South St.
Bridport DT6 3NR, United Kingdom
Phone: 44 1308 427183
Fax: 44 1308 459166
E-mail: frances@poorton.demon.co.uk
Home Page: http://www.bridportprize.org.uk

• 5200 • The Bridport Prize

To encourage people to write. Awards are given for poetry and short stories. Entries should be written in English, of the length specified in the current conditions of entry. A monetary first prize of £3,000, a second prize of £1,000, and a third prize of £500 are awarded in each category annually. Established in 1980. Formerly: Creative Writing Competition.

• 5201 •
British Academy
Mr. P.W.H. Brown, Sec.
10 Carlton House Terr.
London SW1Y 5AH, United Kingdom
Phone: 44 207 9695200
Fax: 44 207 6965300
E-mail: secretary@britac.ac.uk
Home Page: http://www.britac.ac.uk

• 5202 • Derek Allen Prize

To recognize outstanding contributions to musicology, numismatics, or Celtic Studies. Established in 1976 to commemorate Derek Fortrose Allen, former secretary of the Academy.

• 5203 • British Academy Fellow

To recognize scholars for outstanding distinctions in most branches of the humanities. Selected by the British Academy.

• 5204 • British Academy Research Awards

The British Academy awards annual research awards to British Scholars for advanced academic research in the humanities.

• 5205 • Burkitt Medal for Biblical Studies

To recognize outstanding contributions to Biblical studies. Awarded annually, the recipient receives a bronze medal. Established in 1925.

• 5206 • Grahame Clark Medal

To recognize outstanding contributions to the study of prehistoric archaeology. Awarded biennially in even-numbered years. Established in 1992.

• 5207 • Rose Mary Crawshay Prize for English Literature

To recognize women who have published an outstanding historical or critical work on English literature. Preference given to works on Byron, Shelley, or Keats. Monetary prizes totaling £1,000 are awarded annually. Established in 1888.

• 5208 • Cromer Greek Awards

To encourage students attending a recognized summer school in Greece by helping to meet travel expenses. Applications are obtainable from the British Academy, and should be submitted by May 31. Organized by the Joint Association of Classical Teachers.

• 5209 • Sir Israel Gollancz Prize

To recognize outstanding published work on early English literature or language. Awarded biennially in odd-numbered years. Established in 1995.

• 5210 • Kenyon Medal for Classical Studies

To recognize an individual for contributions to classical literature or archaeology. Established to honor Sir Frederic Kenyon, former President and secretary of the Academy.

• 5211 • Serena Medal for Italian Studies

To recognize an individual for an outstanding contribution to Italian studies. The award was first made in 1920.

• 5212 •
British Academy of Composers and Songwriters
Chris Green, CEO
British Music House
25-27 Berners St.
London W1T 3LR, United Kingdom
Phone: 44 20 76362929
Fax: 44 20 76362212
E-mail: info@britishacademy.com
Home Page: http://www.britishacademy.com

• 5213 • British Composer Awards

For the best composer.

• 5214 • Gold Badge

• 5215 • Ivor Novello

• 5216 •
British Academy of Film and Television Arts
Amanda Berry, Chief Exec.
195 Piccadilly
London W1J 9LN, United Kingdom
Phone: 44 20 77340022
Phone: 44 20 72925801
Fax: 44 20 77341792
E-mail: ruthg@bafta.org
Home Page: http://www.bafta.org

Formerly: (1976) Society of Film and Television Arts.

• 5217 • British Academy Television Awards

For recognition of outstanding television programs in the areas of performance, and craft and production. The voting lists are compiled from suggestions received from academy members throughout the year. The nominations for the Production, Direction, and Craft Awards are determined by vote. Juries decide the winner in each category. The Best Television Performance Awards are decided by membership vote. Awards are given in the following categories: Single Drama, Drama Series, Drama Serial, Factual Series, Light Entertainment Program or Series, Comedy Program or Series, Huw Wheldon Award for Best Arts Program or Series, News and Current Affairs Journalism, Actress, Actor, Light Entertainment Performance, Comedy Performance, Flaherty Documentary Award, Original Television Music, Make-up, Photography/Lighting - Factual and Fiction, Costume Design, Graphics Design, Film Sound - Factual and Fiction, Editor Factual and Fiction, Live Outside Broadcast Coverage, Design, Dennis Potter Award, Foreign Television Program Award, Television Award for Originality, Alan Clarke Award for Outstanding Creative Contribution to Television, and Richard Dimbleby Award for Outstanding Personal Contribution to Factual television. Trophies are awarded annually. Awards related to the Academy go back as far as 1947.

• 5218 • The Orange British Academy Film Awards
For recognition of outstanding films in the areas of performance, and craft and production. The voting lists are compiled from suggestions received from academy members throughout the year. The nominations for the Production, Direction, and Craft Awards are determined by vote. Juries decide the winner in each category. The Best Film and Performance Awards are decided by membership vote. Awards are given in the following categories: Film, David Lean Award for Best Achievement in Direction, Original Screenplay, Adapted Screenplay, Actress, Actor, Supporting Actress, Supporting Actor, Achievement in Film Music, Film Not in the English Language, Cinematography, Production Design, Costume Design, Editing, Sound, Best Achievement in Special Effects, Make-Up Artist, Short Film, Michael Balcon Award for Outstanding British Contribution to Cinema, Short Animated Film Award, and BAFTA Fellowship. Trophies are awarded annually. Awards related to the Academy go back as far as 1947.

• 5219 •
British Archaeological Awards
Dr. Alison Sherid, Sec.
% Dr. A. Sheridan, Sec.
Department of Archaeology
National Museums of Scotland
Chambers St.
Edinburgh EH1 1JF, United Kingdom
Phone: 44 131 247 4051
E-mail: a.sheridan@nms.ac.uk
Home Page: http://www.britarch.ac.uk/awards

• 5220 • Archaeological Book Award
For recognition of the most outstanding book that brings British archaeology to the widest audience. All books published in the last four years (for national distribution) are automatically considered. Sponsored by the Ancient & Medieval History Book Club.

• 5221 • Association for Industrial Archaeology Award
To encourage the retention of significant buildings from any period through appropriate and sensible adaptive re-use, with emphasis on innovative solutions to difficult problems and for evidence of economic sustainability. Museums and publicly-displayed sites are excluded. The deadline for entries is June 30. Awarded biennially. Sponsored by the Association for Industrial Archaeology.

• 5222 • The Channel Four Awards
For recognition of the best British-made film, video, and presentation on archeology. The deadline for entries is June 30. Awarded biennially in even-numbered years. Sponsored by Channel Four Television.

• 5223 • Finders Award
For recognition of the best non-archaeologist who, in the course of his/her normal, non-archaeological employment, finds archaeological artifacts/remains and causes them to be reported to the appropriate authorities. The deadline for entries is June 20. Awarded biennially. Sponsored by Tarmac Quarry Products Inc.

• 5224 • Heritage in Britain Award
For recognition of the best project that secures the long term preservation of a site or monument. The project may range from field monuments, ruined structures, roofed and used buildings, and gardens. Industrial monuments may include the machinery related to the structure. The deadline for entries is June 30. Awarded biennially. Sponsored by English Heritage, Historic Scotland, and Codus: Wales Historic Monuments.

• 5225 • IFA Award
To recognize the best archaeological project undertaken by a professional team or mixed professional/voluntary partnership demonstrating a commitment to recognized professional standards and ethics. Awarded biennially in even-numbered years. Sponsored by the Institute of Field Archaeologists. Formerly: ICI Award.

• 5226 • Mick Aston Presentation Award
For recognition of the best presentation of an archaeological project to the public, thus stimulating awareness of, and curiosity about, Britain's national heritage. The deadline for entries is June 30. Awarded biennially. Sponsored by Professor Mick Aston, well-known British archaeologist. Formerly: Virgin Group Award.

• 5227 • Pitt Rivers Award
For recognition of the best amateur project undertaken by a voluntary body or individual. Professional technical help is permitted. The deadline for entries is June 30. Awarded biennially. Sponsored by the Robert Kiln Trust.

• 5228 • Silver Trowel Award
For recognition of the greatest initiative and originality in archaeology. All entrants for other awards are considered automatically for this award, but additional direct entries are acceptable. The deadline for entries is June 30. Awarded biennially. Sponsored by Spear & Jackson. Formerly: Legal & General Silver Trowel Award.

• 5229 • Transco Press Award
To recognize the best article or reporting on British archeology. The deadline for entries is June 30. Awarded biennially in even-numbered years. Sponsored by Transco.

• 5230 • Wedgwood Sponsorship Award
For recognition of the best private sector sponsorship of archaeology based upon imagination, value for money, and the overall benefits to archaeology from the sponsorship. The deadline for entries is June 30. Awarded biennially. Sponsored by the Wedgwood Group. Formerly: Thames Television Award.

• 5231 • Young Archeologist of the Year Award
To recognize outstanding young archeologists. Awards are presented in two age categories: 8-12 and 13-16. Awarded biennially in even-numbered years. Sponsored by the Young Archeologists' Club.

• 5232 •
British Association for Applied Linguistics
Jeanie Taylor, Admin.
PO Box 6688
London SE15 3WB, United Kingdom
Phone: 44 207 6390090
Phone: 44 845 4568208
Fax: 44 207 6356014
E-mail: admin@baal.org.uk
Home Page: http://www.baal.org.uk

• 5233 • Book Prize
For recognition of an outstanding book in applied linguistics. Books published during the preceding calendar year are eligible. Books must be nominated by their publisher. Awarded annually. Established in 1984.

• 5234 • Postgraduate Scholarship
Assists in furthering education in applied linguistics. Applicants must be postgraduate students. Two scholarships are awarded annually.

• 5235 •
British Association of Aviation Consultants
Peter Mackenzie-Williams OBE, Hon.Sec.
22 Old Queen St.
285 Vauxhall Bridge Rd.
London SW1H 9HP, United Kingdom
Phone: 44 207 6305358
Fax: 44 207 8280667
E-mail: pmackenzie-williams@trl.co.uk
Home Page: http://www.baac.org.uk

• 5236 • Sir Peter Masefield Gold Medal
To recognize an individual for prolonged and outstanding service to aviation. A medal is awarded annually. Established in 1987.

• 5237 •
British Association of Barbershop Singers
Mike Lofthouse, Dir.
Clifton
Rickards
Whittlesford
Cambridge CB2 4YT, United Kingdom
Phone: 44 1223 833063
Fax: 44 1705 593558
E-mail: ask@singbarbershop.com
Home Page: http://www.singbarbershop.com

• 5238 • **Crawley Cup**
To recognize the winner of the British Barbershop Chorus contest. The plaque is bestowed annually at the convention. Established in 1975 in honor of the first recipients of the plaque, the Crawley Barbershop Club.

• 5239 •
British Association of Communicators in Business
Alan Peaford, Pres.
Auriga Bldg., 1st Fl., Ste. A
Davy Ave.
Knowlhill
Milton Keynes MK5 8ND, United Kingdom
Phone: 44 870 1217606
Fax: 44 870 1217601
E-mail: enquiries@cib.uk.com
Home Page: http://www.cib.uk.com

Formerly: (1996) British Association of Industrial Editors.

• 5240 • **Communicator of the Year**
For recognition of achievement in organizational communication. Established in 1976.

• 5241 • **Communicators in Business Awards**
For recognition of achievement in corporate communication journalism. Internal and external magazines, newspapers, newsletters, and other publications published during the preceding year are eligible. All entries must be printed in English, but house journals from across the world are welcome. Awards are given in the following categories: (1) Internal Newspapers; (2) Internal Magazines; (3) Internal Newsmagazines; (4) Internal newsletters; (5) External publications; (6) Financial Publications; (7) Special Publications; (8) Web Media; (9) Web Skills; (10) Audio Visual; (11) Skills (design); (12) Skills (writing); (13) Imagery and (14) Skills (printing). Trophies and certificates are awarded annually at the spring convention. Formerly known as BAIE Editing for Industry Awards. Established in 1954. Formerly: (1982) BACB National House Journal Competition; (1996) BACB Editing for Industry Awards.

• 5242 •
British Association of Dermatologists
Dr. M.J.D. Goodfield, Honorary Sec.
4 Fitzroy Sq.
London W1T 5HQ, United Kingdom
Phone: 44 207 3830266
Fax: 44 207 3885263
E-mail: admin@bad.org.uk
Home Page: http://www.bad.org.uk

• 5243 • **British Association of Dermatologists Fellowships**
To recognize undergraduates for outstanding contributions to dermatology. Awards include the Essay Prize, Elective Prize, Medical Student Project Grant, and the Intercalated Degree Grant. Awarded annually.

• 5244 •
British Association of Landscape Industries
David Spencer, Chief Exec.
Landscape House
Stoneleigh Park
Warwickshire
Coventry CV8 2LG, United Kingdom
Phone: 44 870 7704971
Fax: 44 870 7704972
E-mail: contact@bali.org.uk
Home Page: http://www.bali.org.uk

• 5245 • **National Landscape Awards**
To draw attention to the landscape industry's participation in creating an improved environment, and for recognition of the best contributions by BALI Members made to this aim. Landscape construction must have been undertaken by a BALI Member and completed within two years of the entry date to be eligible. Plaques are awarded annually at BALI's National Landscape Awards Luncheon. There is a Grand Award, for the overall winner. Established in 1976.

• 5246 •
British Astronomical Association
Tom Boles, Pres.
Burlington House
Piccadilly
London W1J 0DU, United Kingdom
Phone: 44 207 7344145
Fax: 44 207 4394629
E-mail: office@britastro.com
Home Page: http://www.britastro.org/main/index.html

• 5247 • **Lydia Brown Award for Meritorious Service**
For recognition of prolonged and valuable service to the BAA in an honorary capacity. Members of the BAA are eligible. A monetary prize and a silver-gilt medal are usually awarded biennially. Established in 1972.

• 5248 • **Walter Goodacre Medal and Gift**
For recognition of prolonged and outstanding contribution to the progress of astronomy. Members of the BAA are eligible. A monetary prize and a silver gilt medal are awarded biennially. Established in 1930.

• 5249 • **Merlin Medal and Gift**
For recognition of an outstanding discovery and contribution to astronomy. Members of the BAA are eligible. A monetary prize and a silver medal are awarded biennially. Established in 1961.

• 5250 • **Steavenson Memorial Award**
For recognition of diligence and excellence as an astronomical observer. Members of the BAA are eligible. A book chosen by the recipient is awarded annually. Established in 1975.

• 5251 •
British Blood Transfusion Society
Frank Boulton, Pres.
Greenheys
Manchester Science Park
Pencroft Way
Manchester M15 6JJ, United Kingdom
Phone: 44 161 2327999
Fax: 44 161 2327979
E-mail: bbts@bbts.org.uk
Home Page: http://www.bbts.org.uk

• 5252 • **BBTS Gold Medal**
To an individual's long standing services to the society and to the practice of blood transfusion in UK.

• 5253 • **James Blundell Award**
For original research that made a significant contribution in the field of blood transfusion.

• 5254 • **The Kenneth Goldsmith Award**
For original research in the field of blood transfusion.

• 5255 •
British Broadcasting Corp.
Michael Grade, Chm.
Broadcasting House
Portland Pl.
London W1A 1AA, United Kingdom
Phone: 44 20 7580 4468
Fax: 44 20 7765 1181
Home Page: http://www.bbc.co.uk

• 5256 • **Mastermind Award**
To recognize the winner of a television program quiz. A Caithness (engraved) Glass Trophy is awarded annually. Established in 1972.

• 5257 •
British Broadcasting Corporation and Welsh National Opera
% Anna Williams, Cardiff Singer of the World Competition
Broadcasting House
Portland Pl.
London W1A 1AA, United Kingdom
Phone: 44 20 7580 4468
Fax: 44 20 7765 1181
E-mail: anna.williams@ukonline.ca.uk
Home Page: http://www.bbc.co.uk/wales/cardiffsinger05/sites/content

• 5258 • **Cardiff Singer of the World Competition**
To recognize outstanding singers at the beginning of their professional careers. Individuals who are at least 18 years old and under 35. (One individual may represent each country in Cardiff). A monetary award of £10,000, a trophy, and a BBC engagement are awarded biennially. Established in 1983. Additional information is available from Anna Williams, Cardiff singer Of the World BBC Wales, Broadcasting House, Cardiff CF5 2YQ, United Kingdom.

• 5259 •
British Canoe Union
Paul Owen, Chief Exec.
John Dudderidge House
Adbolton Ln.
W Bridgford
West Bridgford
Nottingham NG2 5AS, United Kingdom
Phone: 44 115 9821100
Fax: 44 115 9821797
E-mail: info@bcu.org.uk
Home Page: http://www.bcu.org.uk

• 5260 • **Award for Valour**
For recognition of a canoeist whose gallantry or devotion in bringing assistance to others in an aquatic situation is considered to be of outstanding merit. The award may be made posthumously. Nominations may be submitted by a witness and, if possible, supported by a recognized agency. A citation is presented as merited. Established in 1981.

• 5261 • **Award of Honour**
For recognition of outstanding service to canoeing over a number of years, either nationally or internationally, in any branch of the sport. Nominations are accepted by organizations associated with the Union. An engraved plaque or medal, accompanied by a citation, are presented to the winner. Established in 1962.

• 5262 • **Award of Merit**
For recognition of those who have given distinguished service to canoeing, normally over a number of years. Nominations are accepted from organizations associated with the Union. A citation is presented to the winner. Established in 1969.

• 5263 •
British Cartographic Society
Ken Atherton, Admin.
1 Kensington Gore
London SW7 2AR, United Kingdom
Phone: 44 1823 665775
Fax: 44 1823 665775
E-mail: admin@cartography.org.uk
Home Page: http://www.cartography.org.uk

• 5264 • **John Bartholomew Award**
For recognition of originality and excellence in the field of thematic (non-topographic, 1:100,000 and smaller) cartography with emphasis on effective communication of the intended theme or themes. Submissions are accepted from any individual or organization by May 11 each year. A certificate and a plaque are awarded annually at the September symposium. Established in 1980. Sponsored by Collins Bartholomew.

• 5265 • **British Cartographic Society Design Award**
For recognition of the most outstanding map produced by a member. Members of the Society may apply by May 11 each year. A silver medal and a trophy are awarded annually at the September symposium. Established in 1978.

• 5266 • **Henry Johns Award**
For recognition of the most outstanding article published in *The Cartographic Journal.* A monetary prize and certificate are awarded annually at the September symposium. Established in 1975. Formerly: Survey and General Instrument Company Award; (1996) Ryser SGI.

• 5267 • **National Geographic Society Award**
To recognize students who have demonstrated outstanding achievement in cartography and its application and to encourage the completion of a first degree course or the pursuit of a post-graduate course. A £500 scholarship is awarded. Established in 1993. Sponsored by National Geographic Society.

• 5268 • **Ordnance Survey Award**
To recognize innovation in the design and presentation of spatial information with an emphasis on creativity, originality and impact of design. Entries must have been produced during a specified calendar year. They may be submitted by individual or organization. A monetary prize of £250 and an Ordnance Survey product are awarded annually or exceptionally at such other times as may be determined by the Council of the BCS.

• 5269 • **Readers Digest Student Award**
For recognition of meritorious work by cartography students. Given to United Kingdom students who have either the Ordinary BTEC certificate in Surveying and Cartography or the SCOTEC certificate in Topographic Studies, or the BTEC and SCOTEC Higher Certificates, Diploma, Degree and Post-Graduate courses. A certificate, £400 and an Atlas are awarded annually at the Society's Annual Technical Symposium in September. Established in 1997. Formerly: (1996) Keuffel and Esser Awards; (1997) British Cartographic Society Student Award; .

• 5270 •
British Cave Research Association
Mick Day, Chm.
The Old Methodist Chapel
Great Hucklow
Derbyshire
Buxton SK17 8RG, United Kingdom
Phone: 44 1298 873800
Fax: 44 1298 873801
E-mail: enquiries@bcra.org.uk
Home Page: http://www.bcra.org.uk

• 5271 • **Alex Pitcher Award**
For young cavers.

• 5272 • **Arthur Butcher Award**
For contributions to cave surveying.

• 5273 • **BCRA Research Fund**
For approved research in cave or karst related subject.

• 5274 • **Cave Radio and Electronics Group**
For achievements in the field of caving electronics.

• 5275 • **E.K. Tratman Award**
For the best piece of caving literature.

• 5276 •
British Chess Federation
Mrs. Cynthia Gurney, Mgr.
The Watch Oak
Chain Ln.
Battle TN33 0YD, United Kingdom
Phone: 44 1424 775222
Fax: 44 1424 775904
E-mail: office@bcf.org.uk
Home Page: http://www.englishchess.org.uk

• 5277 • **Book of the Year**
To recognize outstanding books on chess that were published during the year. Awarded annually.

• 5278 • **British Chess Federation Player of the Year**
For recognition of the best annual performance in chess-play. The winner is chosen by a poll of chess writers and direct members. A monetary award and a plaque are presented annually. Established in 1984.

• 5279 • **Club of the Year**
To encourage activity in chess clubs. Nominations are accepted for the award. A monetary award and a trophy are presented annually. Established in 1984.

Awards are arranged in alphabetical order below their administering organizations

• 5280 •
British Christmas Tree Growers Association
Roger Hay, Contact
13 Wolridge Rd.
Edinburgh EH16 6HX, United Kingdom
Phone: 44 131 6641100
Fax: 44 131 6642669
E-mail: rogermhay@btinternet.com
Home Page: http://www.christmastree.org.uk

• 5281 • **Best Christmas Tree**
Award of recognition. Selection is made by peer review. Presented annually.

• 5282 •
British Comparative Literature Association
Gillian Beer, Pres.
% Penny Brown, Sec.
Department of French Studies
University of Manchester
Oxford Rd.
Manchester M13 9PL, United Kingdom
E-mail: 101501.560@compuserve.com
Home Page: http://www.bcla.org

• 5283 • **John Dryden Translation Competition**
To encourage literary translation from any language into English. Literary translation includes poetry, fiction, or literary prose from any period. Translations (of up to 25 pages) must be previously unpublished. A monetary prize of £350 for First Prize and £200 for Second Prize, and £100 for Third Prize are awarded, as well as publication in *Comparative Criticism*. Established in 1983. Co-sponsored by the British Centre for Literary Translation.

• 5284 •
British Computer Society
David Clarke, Chief Exec.
1 Sanford St.
Swindon SN1 1HJ, United Kingdom
Phone: 44 1793 417417
Phone: 44 1793 417424
Fax: 44 1793 480270
E-mail: bcshq@hq.bcs.org.uk
Home Page: http://www.bcs.org.uk

• 5285 • **Wilkes Award**
To recognize the most outstanding paper in *The Computer Journal*. Authors under 30 years of age are eligible. Awarded annually, the recipient receives a monetary award and a medal.

• 5286 •
British Culinary Federation
PO Box 10532
Alcester B50 4ZY, United Kingdom
Phone: 44 1789 491218
Fax: 44 1789 491218
E-mail: secretary@britishculinaryfederation.co.uk
Home Page: http://www.britishculinaryfederation.co.uk

• 5287 • **Hotelympia Competition**
The competition, also known as the Skills for Chefs Competition, is held to recognize outstanding culinary ability. The competition is built around research and development and establishing food trends for the future. Medals are awarded. Winners participate in the Culinary Olympics held every four years in Frankfurt, Germany.

• 5288 •
British Deaf Association
Doug Alker, Chm.
1-3 Worship St.
London EC2A 2AB, United Kingdom
Phone: 44 207 5883520
Fax: 44 207 5883527
E-mail: helpline@bda.org.uk
Home Page: http://www.bda.org.uk

• 5289 • **Medal of Honour**
For recognition of services to the British deaf community. Individuals who are British or foreign, deaf or hearing, members or nonmembers may be nominated. A medal is awarded at the Congress or occasionally at a conference. Established in 1959.

• 5290 •
British Design and Art Direction
Dick Powell, Pres.
9 Graphite Sq.
Vauxhall Walk
London SE11 5EE, United Kingdom
Phone: 44 20 78401111
Fax: 44 20 78400840
E-mail: info@dandad.co.uk
Home Page: http://www.dandad.org

• 5291 • **British Design and Art Direction (D&AD) Awards**
Recognizes creative excellence in the categories of Broadcast, Print and Editorial, Digital and Wireless, 3D Design, Direct, Branding, Integrated, and Ambient. Awarded annually.

• 5292 •
British Ecological Society
Dr. Hazel J. Norman, Exec.Sec.
26 Blades Ct.
Putney
London SW15 2NU, United Kingdom
Phone: 44 208 8719797
Fax: 44 208 8719779
E-mail: info@britishecologicalsociety.org
Home Page: http://www.britishecologicalsociety.org

• 5293 • **Best Poster Prize**
To recognize the best poster by a research student at the Symposium and Annual General Meeting. Any full-time post-graduate student is eligible to enter as is anyone whose research training was completed within the past six months. Awarded annually.

• 5294 • **British Ecological Society Grants and Awards**
To provide funds for research and for attendance at meetings. Grants include: early career project grants, education innovation and research grants, workshop sponsorship, commemorative events fund, visiting speakers to student societies, specialist course grants, and student support grants.

• 5295 • **British Ecological Society President's Medal**
To recognize individuals in mid-career for exceptional achievement in ecology. Awarded biennially when merited. Established in 1987.

• 5296 • **Founders' Prize**
To recognize an outstanding ecologist, in his or her early career, who is making a significant contribution toward the science of ecology. The award is normally biennial, in tandem with the President's Medal. A monetary prize of £500 and a certificate are awarded. The recipient will be invited to give a forty-minute paper at the BES Winter Meeting.

• 5297 • **Anne Keymer Prize**
To recognize the best oral presentation by a postgraduate student at the—Annual Meeting. Those eligible to enter must present a paper at the BES—Annual Meeting and should normally be a current graduate student, or one who has recently graduated and is presenting work that was completed when they were still a student. An honorarium of £250 is presented to the winner, with two runners-up each receiving £100. Awarded annually. Named in the memory of Anne Keymer, one of the first winners of the previously-unnamed prize in 1981.

• 5298 • **Marsh Award for Ecology**
To recognize outstanding achievements and contributions to the science of ecology. Open to distinguished ecologists from around the world. An honorarium of £1,000 and a certificate are awarded.

• 5299 • **Small Ecological Project Grants**
To promote all aspects of ecological research and ecological survey. Applicants are automatically considered for Coalbourn Trust Grants. A maximum grant of £2,500 is awarded twice per year.

• 5300 •
British Endodontic Society
Annabel Thomas, Admin.
PO Box 707
Gerrards Cross SL9 0XS, United Kingdom
Phone: 44 1494 581542
Fax: 44 1494 581542
E-mail: enquiries@bes-administrator.org
Home Page: http://www.britishendodonticsociety.org

• 5301 • **General Dental Practitioner Prize**
To any member of BES working full or part time in General Dental Practice.

• 5302 • **Grant for Research Workers**
For a research being carried out in UK dental schools or research institutions by qualified dentists.

• 5303 • **Poster Prize**
For the best poster presentation of a research project.

• 5304 • **Prize for Vocational Dental Practitioners**
To vocational dental practitioners in the UK.

• 5305 •
British Federation of Film Societies
David Phillips, Treas.
The Ritz Bldg.
Mt. Pleasant Campus
Swansea Institute of Higher Education
Swansea SA1 6ED, United Kingdom
Phone: 44 1792 481170
Fax: 44 1792 462219
E-mail: bffs-admin@sihe.ac.uk
Home Page: http://www.bffs.org.uk

• 5306 • **Film Society of the Year Awards**
For recognition of outstanding achievement and/or development of an individual society. Awards are presented in the following categories: Film programming, program notes, marketing and publicity, website, community award, best new society, and best student society. Also awarded are the Engholm Prize for Film Society of the Year - the Society*K*s top award, as well as the Charles Roebuck Cup - for outstanding individual contribution. Awarded annually. Established in 1969 by Sir Basil Engholm in honor of the past chairman of the British Film Institute.

• 5307 •
British Film Institute
Amanda Nevill, Dir.
21 Stephen St.
London W1T 1LN, United Kingdom
Phone: 44 207 255 1444
E-mail: discover@bfi.org.uk
Home Page: http://www.bfi.org.uk

• 5308 • **British Film Institute Fellowships**
To provide recognition for outstanding contribution to film or television culture. Established in 1983.

• 5309 • **The British Film Institute Sutherland Trophy**
Awarded to the most original and imaginative film screened at the BFI London Film Festival. First presented in 1958 on behalf of the BFI by the Duke of Sutherland. Formerly: (1973) Sutherland Trophy.

• 5310 •
British Geotechnical Association
Michael Davies, Sec.
1 Great George St.
London SW1P 3AA, United Kingdom
Phone: 44 207 6652233
Fax: 44 207 7991325
E-mail: bga@britishgeotech.org.uk
Home Page: http://www.britishgeotech.org.uk

• 5311 • **Cooling Prize**
To honor the best presentation on a geotechnical topic. A glass decanter is awarded annually. Established in 1971.

• 5312 •
British Grassland Society
Dr. George Fisher, Pres.
PO Box 237
University of Reading
Reading RG6 6AR, United Kingdom
Phone: 44 118 9318189
Fax: 44 118 9666941
E-mail: office@britishgrassland.com
Home Page: http://www.britishgrassland.com

• 5313 • **British Grassland Society Award**
To acknowledge those who have made an outstanding contribution to the understanding or application of grassland and forage crop husbandry and technology. A member of the Society may be nominated by any one member supported by two others. A trophy is awarded annually at the Winter Meeting in December. Established in 1979.

• 5314 •
British Guild of Travel Writers
Melissa Shales, Chm.
51b Askew Crescent
London W12 9DN, United Kingdom
Phone: 44 20 87491128
Fax: 44 20 87491128
E-mail: info@virtualnecessities.com
Home Page: http://www.bgtw.metronet.co.uk

• 5315 • **Silver Otter Award**
For tourism projects abroad which benefit the local community and environment. A trophy is awarded annually.

• 5316 •
British Infection Society
Dr. Martin J. Wiselka, Sec.
Dept. of Infection and Tropical Medicine
Leicester Royal Infirmary
Infirmary Sq.
Leicester LE1 5WW, United Kingdom
Phone: 44 116 2586952
Fax: 44 116 2585067
E-mail: martin.wiselka@uhl-tr.nhs.uk
Home Page: http://www.britishinfectionsociety.org

• 5317 • **Barnett Christie Lectureship**
Annual award of recognition. Established in 1991.

• 5318 •
British Institute of Architectural Technologists
Francesca Berriman, Ch.Exec.
397 City Rd.
Islington
London EC1V 1NH, United Kingdom
Phone: 44 207 2782206
Fax: 44 207 8373194
E-mail: info@biat.org.uk
Home Page: http://www.biat.org.uk

Formerly: (1986) Society of Architectural and Associated Technicians.

• 5319 • **Award for Technical Excellence**
To recognize technical excellence and innovation in the construction industry. Open to all. The winner receives a certificate, and a plaque for permanent attachment to the project. The candidate, nominated by a third party, may be an individual, group or corporate body. Established in 1994.

• 5320 • **British Institute of Architectural Technologists Student Award**
For recognition of achievements of students in further and higher education studying a technology-based built environment subject. The judging takes place at regional and national levels. Groups undertaking project work in a recognized course should submit their entry forms by 5th May and their project work by the end of June. Plaques, certificates and cheques are awarded to students as well as one year's free associate membership of the institute. A trophy and certificate are awarded to the college. Awarded annually at a special awards ceremony. Additional information is available from the Education Department. Formerly: BIAT National Student Award.

• 5321 • **Open Award for Technical Excellence in Architectural Technology**
To recognize achievement of technical excellence in construction by illustrating the composition of ideas put into practice and presented in a working format. First prize of £1,200 is awarded annually. Established in 1994.

• 5322 •
British Institute of Non-Destructive Testing
Matt E. Gallagher, Sec.
1 Spencer Parade
Northampton NN1 5AA, United Kingdom
Phone: 44 1604 630124
Fax: 44 1604 231489
E-mail: info@bindt.org
Home Page: http://www.bindt.org

• 5323 • **John Grimwade Medal**
To recognize the best paper written in *Insight, the Journal of the British Institute of Non-Destructive Testing.* Works by any member of the Institute are automatically eligible for consider-

ation. A medal is presented at the Annual British Conference on NDT. Established in 1981 in memory of John G. Grimwade, an Honorary Fellow of the Institute.

• 5324 • Ron Halmshaw Award
In recognition of the best paper published in *Insight* on any aspect of industrial radiography or radiology, contributed by a member of the Institute of any grade in the preceding year. A certificate and monetary prize are awarded annually at the Institute's Conference. Established in 1994 by Dr. Ron Halmshaw, MBE.

• 5325 • Hugh MacColl Award
For recognition of practical innovation in nondestructive testing condition monitoring. Nominations must be submitted by December 31. A certificate is awarded and £300 is held in credit for the recipient to spend in improving his technical education. Awarded annually at the Institute's Conference. Established in 1988 in memory of Hugh MacColl, a founder member of the NDT Society of Great Britain and a pioneer of NDT education.

• 5326 • Nemet Award
To recognize examples of effective use of NDT, especially those that might encourage small firms to apply NDT methods for the first time. Nominations must be submitted by December 31. A certificate is awarded to the company operating the successful scheme, and a monetary prize of £500 to the person or persons nominated by the company as responsible for the innovation. Awarded annually at the Institute's Conference. Established in 1989 by Dr. A. Nemet.

• 5327 • Roy Sharpe Prize
To recognize a significant contribution through research and development in any branch of NDT to the benefit of industry or society. Nominations must be submitted by December 31. A certificate plus a monetary prize to the winner are presented by the sponsoring company. Awarded annually at the Institute's Conference. Established in 1989 in honor of Roy Sharpe.

• 5328 •
British Institute of Radiology
Mr. Gunter Dombrowe, Pres.
36 Portland Pl.
London W1B 1AT, United Kingdom
Phone: 44 207 3071400
Fax: 44 207 3071414
E-mail: admin@bir.org.uk
Home Page: http://www.bir.org.uk

• 5329 • Clinical MRI Prize
To recognize the best proffered paper on MRI by a BIR member at the Congress. There is no age limit but preference is given to members early in their career. A monetary prize of £50 is awarded annually.

• 5330 • Flude Memorial Prize
To recognize the member who has conducted research that has significantly advanced the science and practice of radiology. Awarded annually. Established in 1992 in honor of Royston Flude, a member of the Institute.

• 5331 • Leonard Levy Memorial Prize
To recognize the author of the best proffered paper at the Congress. Applicants must be under 40 years of age and BIR members. A monetary prize of £125 is awarded annually. Established in 1992 by Bennett Levy and Levy Hill Laboratories in memory of the late Dr Leonard Levy.

• 5332 • Stanley Melville Memorial Award
To enable members to visit institutions and clinics abroad. A monetary grant of £1,000 is awarded annually.

• 5333 • *RAD Magazine* Best Poster Prize
First, second, and third prizes are awarded annually.

• 5334 • Travel Bursaries
The following travel awards are presented annually: Philips Travel Fellowship, Nic McNally Prize for Cancer Research, GE Healthcare Fellowship, and Stanley Melville Memorial Award (see separate entry). Awarded to members ages 35 and under.

• 5335 •
British International Freight Association
Colin Beaumont, Dir.Gen.
Redfern House
Browells Ln.
Middlesex
Feltham TW13 7EP, United Kingdom
Phone: 44 20 88442266
Fax: 44 20 88905546
E-mail: bifa@bifa.org
Home Page: http://www.bifa.org

• 5336 • Freight Service Awards
Given to encourage and reward high standards and professionalism, these awards represent the ultimate recognition of special achievements in different sectors of the industry. Awards are given in the following categories: Air Freight, Deep Sea, European Logistics, Special Services, Project Forwarding, Supply Chain Management, and Training & Staff Development; the Lifetime Achievement Award and Young Freight Forwarder of the Year are also presented. Awarded annually.

• 5337 •
British Interplanetary Society
Suszann Parry, Exec.Sec.
27/29 S Lambeth Rd.
London SW8 1SZ, United Kingdom
Phone: 44 20 77353160
Fax: 44 20 78201504
E-mail: mail@bis-spaceflight.com
Home Page: http://bis-spaceflight.com

• 5338 • Space Achievement Medal
To recognize an individual for contributions of outstanding merit to astronautics. Gold, silver and bronze medals are awarded as merited. Established in 1954.

• 5339 •
British Lichen Society
Mrs. P.A. Wolseley, Sec.
Department of Botany
Natural History Museum
Cromwell Rd.
London SW7 5BD, United Kingdom
Phone: 44 207 9425617
Fax: 44 207 9425529
E-mail: bls@nhm.ac.uk
Home Page: http://www.theBLS.org.uk

• 5340 • British Lichen Society Awards
To recognize professional, academic, and amateur lichenologists involved in research. Awards are bestowed annually at the convention in January.

• 5341 •
British Llama and Alpaca Association
Jane Brown, Assoc. Sec.
Puckpitts Farm
Shipston-on-Stour
Warwickshire
Tredington CV36 4NH, United Kingdom
Phone: 44 1608 661893
Fax: 44 1608 661893
E-mail: info@alpaca.co.uk
Home Page: http://www.llama.co.uk

• 5342 • Champion Llama, Champion Alpaca

• 5343 • Felipe Benavides Rose Bowl

• 5344 •
British Long Distance Swimming Association
Dee Llewellyn, Pres.
16 Elmwood Rd.
Barnton
Cheshire
Northwich CW8 4NB, United Kingdom
Phone: 44 1606 75298
E-mail: bldsa@btinternet.com
Home Page: http://www.bldsa.org.uk

• 5345 • Avril and Allan Mitchell Trophy
For a veteran swimmer of the year.

• 5346 • Breaststroke Trophy
For a breaststroke endurance swim.

• 5347 • Elise Brook Trophy
For a junior swimmer during his or her last year as a junior.

• 5348 • Fred Slater Trophy
For the best swimmer of the year.

• 5349 • **Hans Belay Trophy**
For the swim of the year.

• 5350 • **Harry Moffat Memorial Trophy**
For services to the Pilot Lifesaver scheme.

• 5351 • **James Brennan Memorial Trophy**
For outstanding service rendered to the association.

• 5352 • **Tom Butcher Trophy**
For a junior swimmer of the year.

• 5353 •
British Medical Association
Tavistock Sq.
London WC1H 9JP, United Kingdom
Phone: 44 20 73874499
Fax: 44 20 73836400
E-mail: info.web@bma.org.uk
Home Page: http://www.bma.org.uk

• 5354 • **Brackenbury Award**
For recognition of research of immediate practical importance to public health, to a medico-political or medico-sociological problem, or to an educational question whether general medical or postgraduate. Candidates must be members of the Association. A monetary prize of £1,250 is awarded triennially.

• 5355 • **British Medical Association Medicine in the Media Award**
For recognition of films of outstanding educational merit in the fields of medicine and health education at the BMA Film and Video Competition. Films originally produced for broadcast television are eligible. Established in 1991. Formerly: ABI/BMA Trophy.

• 5356 • **John William Clark Award**
For recognition of research into the causes of blindness. Candidates must be members of the Association. A monetary prize of £6,500 is awarded annually.

• 5357 • **Vera Down Award**
For recognition of research into disseminated sclerosis, muscular dystrophy and neurological disorders. Candidates must be registered medical practitioners. A monetary prize of £10,500 is awarded annually.

• 5358 • **Gold Medal for Distinguished Merit**
To recognize individuals who have conspicuously raised the character of the medical profession by scientific work, by extra-ordinary professional services, or by special services rendered to the British Medical Association. A gold medal is awarded when merited. Established in 1877.

• 5359 • **T. P. Gunton Award**
For recognition of research into health education with special regard to the early diagnosis and treatment of cancer. Both medical and non-medical researchers are eligible. A monetary prize of £14,500 is awarded annually.

• 5360 • **Katherine Bishop Harman Award**
To assist research into the diminution and avoidance of risks to health and life in pregnancy and child-bearing. Candidates must be medical practitioners registered in the United Kingdom or any country at any time forming part of the British Empire. A monetary prize of £1,750 is awarded biennially.

• 5361 • **Nathaniel Bishop Harman Award**
For recognition of research in regard to the outcome of treatment in hospital practice. Candidates must be registered medical practitioners on the staff of a hospital in Great Britain or Northern Ireland and not members of the staff of a recognized undergraduate or post-graduate medical school. A monetary prize of £2,125 is awarded biennially in even-numbered years.

• 5362 • **Sir Charles Hastings Award**
For recognition of observation, research and record keeping in general practice. Candidates must be members of the Association and engaged in general practice. A monetary prize of £2,350 is awarded biennially.

• 5363 • **Charles Oliver Hawthorne Award**
For recognition of observation, research and record keeping in general practice. Candidates must be members of the Association and engaged in general practice. A monetary prize of £2,350 is awarded biennially.

• 5364 • **Doris Hillier Award**
For recognition of research into rheumatism, arthritis and/or Parkinson's Disease. Candidates must be registered medical practitioners. A monetary prize is awarded annually.

• 5365 • **Geoffrey Holt Award**
For recognition of research into cardiovascular and respiratory disease. Candidates must be members of the Association. A monetary prize of £3,500 is awarded annually.

• 5366 • **Insole Award**
For recognition of research into the causation, prevention or treatment of disease. Candidates must be members of the Association. A monetary prize of £750 is awarded biennially in even-numbered years.

• 5367 • **T. V. James Fellowship**
For recognition of and to assist research into the nature, causation, prevention or treatment of bronchial asthma. Members of the Association are eligible. A monetary prize of £40,000 is awarded annually.

• 5368 • **Albert McMaster Award**
For recognition of cancer research. Candidates must be members of the Association. A monetary prize of £11,250 is awarded annually.

• 5369 • **C. H. Milburn Award**
For recognition of research in medical jurisprudence and/or forensic medicine. Candidates must be registered medical practitioners. A monetary prize of £1,750 is awarded biennially.

• 5370 • **Doris Odlum Award**
For recognition of research in the field of mental health. Candidates must be medical practitioners registered in the British Commonwealth or the Republic of Ireland. A monetary prize £1,600 is awarded biennially.

• 5371 • **H. C. Roscoe Fellowship**
To promote research into the elimination of the common cold and/or diseases of the human respiratory system. Candidates must be members of the Association or non-medical scientists working in association with a member. A monetary prize of £75,000 is awarded annually.

• 5372 • **Helen Tomkinson Award**
For recognition of cancer research. Candidates must be members of the Association. A monetary prize of £11,250 is awarded annually.

• 5373 • **Edith Walsh Award**
For recognition of research in cardiovascular and respiratory disease. Candidates must be members of the Association. A monetary prize of £3,500 is awarded annually.

• 5374 • **Elizabeth Wherry Award**
For recognition of research into kidney disease. Candidates must be registered medical practitioners. A monetary prize of £7,000 is awarded annually.

• 5375 •
British Mexican Society
Mr. Manuel Monasterio, Chm.
Cameo House
Leicester Sq.
11 Bear St.
London WC2H 7AS, United Kingdom
Phone: 44 870 9220679
Fax: 44 20 77665260
E-mail: info@britishmexicansociety.org.uk
Home Page: http://www.britishmexicansociety.org.uk/

• 5376 • **Postgraduate Prize**
For recognition of the best PhD thesis on a topic relating to Mexico. The prize is open to students of any nationality and in any academic discipline. The thesis must be produced at a British university (or other institute of higher education). A monetary prize of £500 is awarded annually. Established in 1984.

• 5377 •
British Microcirculation Society
David O. Bates, Hon.Sec.
Microvascular Research Laboratories
Dept. of Physiology
Preclinical Veternary School
University of Bristol
Bristol BS2 8EJ, United Kingdom
Phone: 44 171 9289818
Fax: 44 171 9288151
E-mail: dave.bates@bristol.ac.uk
Home Page: http://www.microcirculation.org.uk

• 5378 • **Laboratory Visit Grant**
For outstanding student and postgraduate.

• 5379 • **Microcirculation Conference Grant**
For outstanding student and postgraduate.

• 5380 • **Student Assistance Scheme**
For outstanding student and postgraduate.

• 5381 •
British Music Society
Stephen Trowell, Hon.Treas.
7 Tudor Gardens
Upminster RM14 3DE, United Kingdom
Phone: 44 1708 224795
E-mail: sct.bms@amserve.com
Home Page: http://www.musicweb.uk.net/BMS

• 5382 • **British Music Society Awards**
To encourage the performance of neglected British music (especially by dead composers 1850-1950) through a contest for young performers. Students of a British music college may be nominated by the college. A certificate and recital are awarded biennially at the Society's annual general meeting. Established in 1988.

• 5383 •
British Mycological Society
Geoff Robson, Gen. Sec.
The Wolfson Wing
Jodrell Laboratory
Royal Botanic Gardens
Surrey
Guildford TW9 3AB, United Kingdom
E-mail: info@britmycolsoc.org.uk
Home Page: http://www.britmycolsoc.org.uk

• 5384 • **Berkeley Award**
For outstanding original scientific contribution to mycology.

• 5385 • **Howard Eggins Award**
To a young scientist who presents the most outstanding paper in the annual meeting.

• 5386 • **Microscopy Award**
For the best paper presented by a postgraduate student on an aspect of mycology at a meeting of the society.

• 5387 • **Undergraduate Student Bursaries**
For research in any branch of mycology.

• 5388 •
British Nuclear Energy Society
Ian Andrews, Sec.
1-7 Great George St.
London SW1P 3AA, United Kingdom
Phone: 44 207 6652241
Phone: 44 207 6652241
Fax: 44 207 7991325
E-mail: bnes@ice.org.uk
Home Page: http://www.bnes.com

• 5389 • **Conference Awards**
A limited number of awards are considered on the merit of the application. Applicants must be no more than 35 years old. Additional consideration will be given to those who intend to present their paper at the event. There are usually a maximum of four awards available per each major conference.

• 5390 • **International Conference Award**
Enables a young person to attend and thereby make a contribution and benefit from an international conference on a topic related to the science, engineering, safety, or economics of nuclear energy. Applicants must be no more than 30 years old and a member of the Society. Conference fees and living expenses are awarded annually. Established in 1998.

• 5391 •
British Numismatic Society
Dr. E. Screen, Hon.Sec.
Woburn Sq.
London WC1H 0AB, United Kingdom
Phone: 44 1223 332915
E-mail: secretary@britnumsoc.org
Home Page: http://www.britnumsoc.org

• 5392 • **John Sanford Saltus Medal**
To recognize individuals for scholarly contributions to British numismatics. Members and nonmembers are eligible. A gold medal is awarded triennially. Established in 1910 by John Sanford Saltus.

• 5393 •
British Occupational Hygiene Society
Pamela Blythe, Secretariat Mgr.
5/6 Melbourne Ct.
Millennium Way
Pride Park
Derby DE24 8LZ, United Kingdom
Phone: 44 1332 298101
Fax: 44 1332 298099
E-mail: admin@bohs.org
Home Page: http://www.bohs.org

• 5394 • **Bedford Award**
To individuals for outstanding contributions to the discipline of occupational hygiene, either in the general field or in work for the society.

• 5395 • **David Hickish Award**
For candidates who have achieved the diploma of professional competence in occupational hygiene.

• 5396 • **Ted King Award**
For candidates who have achieved the certificate of operational competence in occupational hygiene.

• 5397 • **Working for a Healthier Workplace - The Peter Isaac Award**
For individual members, or any other POOSH Professional Organisations in Occupational Safety and Health.

• 5398 • **Thomas Bedford Memorial Prize**
To the author or authors of the most outstanding paper published in the annals of occupational hygiene during the relevant period.

• 5399 •
British Origami Society
Mrs. Alex Bateman, Gen.Sec.
2A The Chestnuts
Countesthorpe
Leicester LE8 5TL, United Kingdom
Phone: 44 1494 675645
Phone: 44 116 2773870
Fax: 44 116 2773870
E-mail: pauline@trewimage.co.uk
Home Page: http://www.britishorigami.org.uk

• 5400 • **Sidney French Medal**
Recognizes outstanding contribution to origami and the society. Awarded annually to one or more recipients.

• 5401 •
British Ornithologists' Union
Mrs. G. Bonham, Admin.Sec.
Dept. of Zoology
Univ. of Oxford
South Parks Rd.
Oxford OX1 3PS, United Kingdom
Phone: 44 1 865281842
Phone: 44 1733 390392
Fax: 44 1 865281842
E-mail: bou@bou.org.uk
Home Page: http://www.bou.org.uk

• 5402 • **Godman-Salvin Medal**
To any person as a signal honor for distinguished ornithological work. Awarded periodically when merited. Established in 1922.

• 5403 • **Union Medal**
To recognize any member in recognition of eminent services to ornithology and to the Union.

Awards are arranged in alphabetical order below their administering organizations

Awarded periodically when merited. Established in 1912.

• 5404 •
British Orthodontic Society
Geoff Webb, Chm.
291 Gray's Inn Rd.
London WC1X 8QJ, United Kingdom
Phone: 44 207 8372193
Fax: 44 207 8377886
E-mail: email@bos.org.uk
Home Page: http://new.bos.org.uk

• 5405 • **Chapman Prize Essay**
To encourage professional development in the field of orthodontics. Any member or international member of the society is eligible. An article which must contain original material on an orthodontic or allied subject, not more than 8000 words must be submitted by April 30. £1,200 is awarded annually.

• 5406 • **Gunter Russell Prize**
Recognizes the best poster demonstrations at the British Orthodontic Conference. Three awards are given annually. Any member of the British Orthodontic Society is eligible. Sponsored by Hawley Russell & Baker Ltd. UK. Organized by Dr. Declan Millett. Prizes of £ 400 £250 and £150 and a figurine are awarded. An additional £50 is awarded to aid with the production of each poster. Application deadline is July 30.

• 5407 • **Houston Reserach Scholarship**
Allows research scholars to pursue an academic or clinically based research project which promotes the specialty of orthodontics. This should not be part of an Msc project undertaken during the 3 year orthodontic specialty training programme. Any member of the British Orthodontic Society is eligible. Sponsored by British Orthodontic Society.

• 5408 • **Maurice Berman Prize**
Awarded in memory of Maurice Berman. Candidates will present one case by means of well take photographic records, on 35mm slides or in Powerpoint for data projection. The initial severity of the case will be taken into consideration and the quality of the finish should exemplify the highest standard of clinical achievement for which Maurice Berman was so justly acclaimed. The candidate will present the case to the judges at the beginning of the annual British Orthodontic Conference and the winner will be expected to present the case during the Conference with a brief commentary. £1000 is awarded annually.

• 5409 • **Northcroft Memorial Lecture**
Application is by invitation only. For recognition of a contribution to orthodontics on an international basis. International reputation and original work are considered. A certificate is awarded annually when merited. Established in 1947 in honor of George Northcroft.

• 5410 • **Research and Audit Awards**
Encourages research or audit in a clinically related project of value to the orthodontic specialty. This should into be part of an MSC project undertaken in the three year training program. The orthodontist named in the application should be a Society member, but coauthors could be scientists or clinicians who are not members of the Society. Various grants are awarded annually.

• 5411 •
British Orthopaedic Foot and Ankle Society
Don McBride, Pres.
35-43 Lincoln's Inn Fields
London WC2A 3PN, United Kingdom
Phone: 44 20 74056507
E-mail: societiessec@boa.ac.uk
Home Page: http://www.bofss.org.uk

• 5412 • **Chen Memorial Prize**
For the best scientific paper presented by a trainee.

• 5413 • **Research Pump-Priming Grants**
For basic science and clinical research in foot and ankle problems in UK.

• 5414 • **Travelling Fellowships**
For new consultants.

• 5415 •
British Phonographic Industry
Andrew Yeates, Dir.Gen.
Riverside Bldg., County Hall
Westminster Bridge Rd.
London SE1 7JA, United Kingdom
Phone: 44 20 78031300
Fax: 44 20 78031310
E-mail: general@bpi.co.uk
Home Page: http://www.bpi.co.uk

• 5416 • **BRIT Awards**
To honor the best of British and international talent. Fifteen categories of awards are voted for by an academy of almost 600 people. The categories are as follows: Best British Male Solo Artist, Best British Female Solo Artist, Best British Group, Best British Album, Best British Dance Act, Best British Newcomer, Best British Producer, Best British Single by a British Artist, Best Video by a British Artist, Best International Male Solo Artist, Best International Female Solo Artist, Best International Group, Best International Newcomer, Best Soundtrack/Cast Recording, Outstanding Contribution to the British Music Industry.

• 5417 • **Certified Awards**
To measure the performance of music singles and records based on sales to the trade each week. Certification levels for Singles are: Silver 200,000 units; Gold 400,000 units; and Platinum 600,000 units. Certification levels for Albums are: Silver 60,000 units; Gold 100,000 units; and Platinum 300,000 units. Established in 1973.

• 5418 •
British Printing Industries Federation
Michael Johnson, Chief Exec.
Farringdon Pt.
29-35 Farringdon Rd.
London EC1M 3JF, United Kingdom
Phone: 44 870 2404085
Fax: 44 207 4057784
E-mail: info@britishprint.com
Home Page: http://www.britishprint.com

• 5419 • **British Book Design and Production Awards**
To recognize outstanding book design and production.

• 5420 • **Health and Safety Award**
To promote high safety standards in the printing industry. Presented as part of the annual Excellence Awards.

• 5421 • **National Business Calendar Awards**
To recognize outstanding printed calendars, to extend the use of printed business calendars, and to encourage high standards in their design and production. Awards are given in the following categories: Pictorial Bespoke Calendars; Typographic/Novelty Calendars; Stock Calendars; Robert Horne Student Calendar Awards; and Excellence in Colour Reproduction Award. A trophy is awarded to the publisher of the winning entry in each of the categories. Additionally, the photographic trophy(ies) is awarded to the photographer(s) of the best commissioned photography in a calendar selected by the judges from the trophy and certificate winners in any category. Special certificates and £100 of book tokens are also awarded at the discretion of the judges to the winning student. Awarded annually in January. Established in 1968 by the London College of Printing, BPIF, and the British Advertising Calendar Association.

• 5422 • **National Training and Development Awards**
To encourage, recognize and promote excellence in training and development throughout the printing, packaging and graphic communications industry in the UK. Four monetary awards are presented annually: Employer's Award, Individual Award, Apprentice of the Year, Digital Apprentice of the Year.

• 5423 • **UK Company of the Year**
To recognize all round business excellence in the printing, packaging, and graphic communications industry. A trophy is presented annually.

Awards are arranged in alphabetical order below their administering organizations

• 5424 •
British Psychological Society
Dr. Graham Powell, Pres.
St. Andrews House
48 Princess Rd. E
Leicester LE1 7DR, United Kingdom
Phone: 44 116 2549568
Fax: 44 116 2470787
E-mail: mail@bps.org.uk
Home Page: http://www.bps.org.uk

• 5425 • **Award for Outstanding Doctoral Research**
To recognize superb research in the field of psychology. Nominees must have had their work reported in one or more articles which have appeared in refereed journals, and must be directly derived from research for a doctoral degree in psychology. The Scientific Affairs Board awards £500 and a commemorative certificate to the winner, as well as an invitation to the Annual Conference of the Society. Awarded annually.

• 5426 • **Book Award**
To recognize the authors of recently published books that have made significant contributions to the advancement of psychology in one or more ways and are likely to achieve a noteworthy place in the literature of psychology. Candidates must be residents of the United Kingdom and must not have published their book prior to three years before the date of the award. The deadline for nominations is published in *The Psychologist* and changes every year. A monetary award of £500 and a certificate are presented at the annual conference each year.

• 5427 • **British Psychological Society Presidents' Award**
For recognition of achievement in the field of scientific research that contributes to psychological knowledge. This mid-career award is intended as a timely acknowledgement of the achievements of those currently engaged in research of outstanding quality. Candidates who are normally residents of the United Kingdom are eligible. Honorary Life Membership in the Society, a certificate, and the opportunity to present a paper at a plenary session at the Society's annual conference are awarded each year. Established in 1981.

• 5428 • **Honorary Fellow**
To recognize an individual for an entire career in the field of psychology.

• 5429 • **Honorary Life Member**
To recognize the major contribution individuals make to the development of the Society. The award consists of a commemorative certificate, free life membership of the Society, and free registration at a Society Conference each year. On occasions the award may be made to non-psychologists who have similarly made outstanding services to psychology through their involvement with the activities of the Society.

• 5430 • **Spearman Medal**
For recognition of published work of outstanding merit in psychology. Individuals with more than 10 years of full time employment or further study in psychology (or their part-time equivalent) and who reside in the United Kingdom may be nominated. A medal is awarded annually. Established in 1965.

• 5431 •
British Puppet and Model Theatre Guild
Judith Shutt, Sec.
Little Holme
Church Ln.
Thames Ditton KT7 0NL, United Kingdom
Phone: 44 20 89978336
Fax: 44 20 89978236
Home Page: http://www.puppetguild.org.uk

• 5432 • **Harlequin Award**
Recognizes outstanding contributions in marionette manipulation and presentation by UK puppeteers. Trophies are awarded semiannually.

• 5433 •
The British School at Rome
Gill Clark, Registrar
London Office at the British Academy
10 Carlton House Terrace
10 Carlton House Terr.
London SW1Y 5AH, United Kingdom
Phone: 44 20 79695202
Fax: 44 20 79695401
E-mail: bsr@britac.ac.uk
Home Page: http://www.bsr.ac.uk

• 5434 • **Abbey Fellowships in Painting**
To provide residencies to mid-career painters with an established record of achievement. Applicants must be citizens of the United Kingdom or the United States, or of other nationality provided resident in either country for at least five years. A £700 month research grant is awarded for three months. Awarded annually.

• 5435 • **Abbey Scholarship in Painting**
Recognizes exceptionally promising emergent painters, who are citizens of the UK or USA, or of other nationality provided resident in either country for at least five years. £500 per month is awarded. Application deadline is January 15. An application fee of £20 is required. Contact Jane Reid, Abbey Rome Awards, 43 Carson Rd., London SE21 8HT for additional information.

• 5436 • **Arts Council of England Helen Chadwick Fellowship**
For artists resident in the UK who have established their practices following graduation, with a project that could be realized at the Ruskin School in Oxford and BSR in Rome. £600 plus travel and materials expenses are awarded. Contact the British School at Rome for additional information.

• 5437 • **Australia Council Residencies Award**
For visual artists who are Australian citizens or have permanent resident status in Australia. $AUS3,300 is awarded. Contact Visual Arts/Craft Fund, Australia Council, PO Box 788 Strawberry Hills, NSSW 2012, Australia, for additional information; http://www.ozco.gov.au, mail@ozco.gov.au.

• 5438 • **Balsdon Fellowship**
Recognizes research on the archaeology, art history, history, society and culture of Italy from prehistory to the modern period. Applicants should be established scholars, normally in a post in a United Kingdom university. Award consists of a three-month residency, including accommodation and full board, and a research and travel grant of £ 650. Applicants must be British or Commonwealth citizens, or have been working professionally or studying at the graduate level for the last three years in the United Kingdom. Deadline: early to mid-January. awarded.

• 5439 • **Derek Hill Foundation Scholarship**
To recognize artists whose work demonstrates a proficiency in drawing and who have a commitment to portrait and landscape painting. Applicants must be or British or Irish nationality and aged 24 years or older. A six-month residency, including accommodation and full board, as well as a grant of £950 per month, are awarded annually

• 5440 • **Geoffrey Jellicoe Scholarship in Landscape Architecture**
To encourage a recent graduate or an individual in mid-career to propose a contemporary response to the Roman landscape and pursue a topic with direct bearing on modern design in the landscape. Applicants must have had a minimum of two years of post-grad work-place experience and must either be British or Commonwealth citizens or have been working professionally or studying at the graduate level for the last three years in the United Kingdom. A three-month residency, including accommodation and full board, as well as a research and travel grant of £500 per month, are awarded annually.

• 5441 • **Hugh Last Fellowship**
To encourage research on classical antiquity, excluding archaeological fieldwork and work on Roman Britain. Applicants must be established scholars normally in post in a UK university. Award consists of a three-month residency, including accommodation and full board, and a research and travel grant of £650. Applicants must be British or Commonwealth citizens, or have been working professionally or studying at the graduate level for the last three years in the United Kingdom. Deadline: early to mid-January. Awarded annually. Formerly: (2001) Hugh Last Fellowship and Hugh Last Prize.

• 5442 • Paul Mellon Centre Rome Fellowship
For research on grand tour subjects and within the field of Anglo Italian artistic and cultural relations. A four-month residency. The fellowship includes accommodation & full board at the school. For independent scholars it also provides a stipend of £6,000 plus travel to and from Rome. For scholars in full-time university employment, it offers an honorarium of £2,000, travel to and from Rome, and a sum of £6,000 towards replacement teaching costs at the fellow's home university. For further information contact: The Paul Mellon Centre for Studies in British Art, 16 Bedford Sq., London, WC1B 3JA, email info@paul-mellon-centre.ac.uk; http://www.paul-mellon-centre.ac.uk/supportf/PDFs/4rome.pdf

• 5443 • Tim Potter Memorial Award
To promote the study of Italian archaeological material by those of high academic potential who have had limited previous opportunity to visit Italy. Applicants must have graduated prior to receipt of the award, but need not be registered for postgraduate study. They must be British or Commonwealth citizens, or have been working professionally or studying at the graduate level for the last three years in the United Kingdom. A two- to four-month residency, including accommodation and full board, as well as a research and travel grant of £150 per month, are awarded annually.

• 5444 • Rome Awards
To aid in research of the archaeology, art history, society, and culture of Italy from prehistory to the modern period. Applicants must seek support from the AHRB and/or British Academy (or equivalent) and from their own university or college before applying to the BSR. The award consists of a £150 per month research grant with £180 allowed for travel. In addition, full board is covered for up to four months. Applicants must be British or Commonwealth citizens, or have been working professionally or studying at the graduate level for the last three years in the United Kingdom. Awarded annually.

• 5445 • Rome Fellowship
To support research on the archaeology, art history, society, and culture of Italy, from prehistory to the modern period. Applicants must be British or Commonwealth citizens, or have been working professionally or studying at the graduate level for the last three years in the United Kingdom. A nine-month residency, including accommodation and full board, as well as a research and travel grant of £475 per month, are awarded annually.

• 5446 • Rome Scholarship
To support research on the archaeology, art history, society, and culture of Italy, from prehistory to the modern period. Applicants must be British or Commonwealth citizens, or have been working professionally or studying at the graduate level for the last three years in the United Kingdom. A nine-month residency, including accommodation and full board, as well as a research and travel grant of £444 per month, are awarded annually.

• 5447 • Rome Scholarship in Architecture
For architects and students of architecture of at least post-diploma level. Provides accommodation and full board for between three and nine months, with a research grant of £500 per month. Applicants must be of British or Commonwealth nationality, or have been working professionally or studying at graduate level for the last three years in the UK. Application deadline is mid-January. A £25 application fee must be paid. For further information, contact the British School at Rome.

• 5448 • Rome Scholarship in Fine Arts
For contemporary artists who are establishing a significant position in their chosen field. Provides accommodation and full board in a residential studio. Research grant of £500 per month is awarded. Applicants must be of British or Commonwealth nationality, or have been working professionally or studying at graduate level for the last three years in the UK. Application deadline is early to mid-December. A £25 application fee must be paid. For further information, contact the British School at Rome.

• 5449 • Sainsbury Scholarship in Painting and Sculpture
For painters and sculptors under 28 who can demonstrate a commitment to drawing in their practice. Applicants must be of British citizens, or have been working professionally or studying at graduate level for the last three years in the UK, and must normally have or be in the final year of an MA or equivalent degree in Fine Art. Application deadline is Dearly to mid-December. A twelve-month residency, with the possible opportunity to be extended for a further nine months. Provides accommodation and full board, a grant of £750 per month, and a travel grant of £1,000. A £25 application fee must be paid. For further information, contact the British School at Rome.

• 5450 • Sargant Fellowship
Recognizes distinguished artists and architects. Three month residency, including accommodation and full board in a residential studio, plus a research grant of £2000. Application deadline is mid-December for visual artists and mid-January for architects. Contact the British School at Rome for more information.

• 5451 • Wingate Rome Scholarship in the Fine Arts
For contemporary artists establishing a significant position in their chosen field. Provides accommodation and full board in a residential studio. Research grant of £500 per month. Applicants must be living in the British Isles during the period of application. Applicants must be citizens of the UK or other commonwealth country, Ireland or Israel, or citizens of another EU country provided that they are and have been for the last three years, resident in the united kingdom. Deadline: early to mid-December. A £25 application fee must be paid. Contact the British School at Rome for more information.

• 5452 •
British Science Fiction Association
Estelle Roberts, Membership Sec.
97 Sharp St.
Newland Ave.
Hull HU5 2AE, United Kingdom
Phone: 44 1327 361661
E-mail: bsfa@enterprise.net
Home Page: http://www.bsfa.co.uk

• 5453 • BSFA Award
Recognizes the science fiction or fantasy novel, short fiction, and artwork considered the best of the year. Awarded annually.

• 5454 •
British Security Industry Association
David Dickinson, Chief Exec.
Security House
Barbourne Rd.
Worcester WR1 1RS, United Kingdom
Phone: 44 1905 21464
Fax: 44 1905 613625
E-mail: info@bsia.co.uk
Home Page: http://www.bsia.co.uk

• 5455 • BSIA Annual Security Officer Awards
Awarded for outstanding service in five categories. Regional and national awards are presented.

• 5456 • BSIA/IFSEC Security Industry Awards
To promote the highest standards of excellence in the field of security by recognizing not only the best new products developed in the last year, but also excellence in the fields of exporting, project innovation, and people within the industry. Trophies are awarded annually in several categories.

• 5457 •
British Show Pony Society
124 Green End Rd.
Sawtry
Huntingdon PE28 5XS, United Kingdom
Phone: 44 1487 831376
Fax: 44 1487 832779
E-mail: info@bsps.com
Home Page: http://www.britishshowponysociety.co.uk

• 5458 • British Show Pony Society Rosettes
To recognize a mare or gelding as the best pony of the year. Rosettes are awarded at all affiliated shows to the Champion and Reserve Show Pony, Working Hunter Pony, Show Hunter Pony, and Intermediate, Mini and Heritage Champions and Reserves.

• 5459 • Show Hunter Ponies Awards
To recognize the best ponies of the year in the following areas: (1) Novice Show Hunter Pony; and (2) Open Show Hunter Pony. A mare or gelding, four years of age or over, that has not won a first prize of £5.00 prior to October 1, and that is registered with the Society is eligible for novice classes. Awards are presented at shows of the Society, and are awarded by a panel of judges.

• 5460 • Show Ponies Awards
To provide recognition for the best show ponies of the year. The following general awards are given: (1) British show pony cups and trophies - to recognize members of the Society with ponies registered with the Society. A cup or trophy is presented annually, to be held for one year, and returned to the Society. Show ponies that are registered with the Society are eligible in the following categories: (1) Novice Show Pony - to a pony four years of age or older; (2) Three year old pony; and (3) Open Show Pony - to a pony four years of age or older. Ponies must not have won a first prize of £5.00 or over prior to October 1 to be eligible for novice classes. Cups and trophies are presented at shows of the Society, and are awarded by a panel of judges.

• 5461 • Working Hunter Ponies Awards
To recognize the best ponies of the year in the following areas: (1) Novice Working Hunter Pony; and (2) Open Working Hunter Pony. A mare or gelding four years of age or over, that has not won a first prize of £5.00 or over prior to October 1, and that is registered with the Society is eligible for novice classes. Awards are presented at shows of the Society, and are awarded by a panel of judges.

• 5462 •
British Slot Car Racing Association
Brian Saunders, Chm.
41 The Spinney
Buckinghamshire
Chesham HP5 3EX, United Kingdom
Phone: 44 1425 672060
E-mail: info@bscra.co.uk
Home Page: http://www.bscra.fsnet.co.uk

Formerly: (1983) Electric Car Racing Association.

• 5463 • National Model Car Racing Champion
For recognition of model car racing champions in 3 classes: Grand Prix, Sports/GT, and Saloon. Members of the Association who have competed in the races are eligible. Trophies are awarded annually. Established in 1964.

• 5464 •
British Small Animal Veterinary Association
Carmel T. Mooney, Pres.
Woodrow House
1 Telford Way
Waterwells Business Park
Quedgeley
Gloucester GL2 4AB, United Kingdom
Phone: 44 1452 726700
Fax: 44 1452 726701
E-mail: adminoff@bsava.com
Home Page: http://www.bsava.com

• 5465 • Amoroso Award
For recognition of outstanding contributions to small animal studies by a non-clinical member of University staff. A textbook and monetary award are presented annually.

• 5466 • Blaine Award
For recognition of outstanding contributions to the advancement of small animal medicine or surgery. Veterinarians and non-veterinarians are eligible for nomination. A plaque and a monetary award are presented annually.

• 5467 • Bourgelat Award
For recognition of outstanding contributions to the field of small animal practice. An engraved decanter and a scroll are awarded annually.

• 5468 • Dunkin Award
For recognition of the most valuable article published in the *Journal of Small Animal Practice* by a small animal practitioner during the 12 months ending on October 31. An engraved decanter and a scroll are awarded annually.

• 5469 • Melton Award
For recognition of meritorious contributions by veterinary surgeons to small animal practice. Veterinary surgeons in general practice are eligible. A scroll and monetary awarded are presented annually. Established in 1981.

• 5470 • Petsavers Award
For recognition of the best clinical research article published in the JSAP during the 12 months ending on October 31. Any author is eligible.

• 5471 • Simon Award
For recognition of outstanding contributions in the field of veterinary surgery. Members of the Association are eligible. A statuette is awarded annually.

• 5472 • J.A. Wight Memorial Award
For recognition of outstanding contributions to the welfare of companion animals. Veterinarians on the RCVS register are eligible.

• 5473 • Woodrow Award
For recognition of outstanding contributions to the field of small animal veterinary medicine. Members of the Association are eligible. A scroll is awarded annually.

• 5474 •
British Society for Antimicrobial Chemotherapy
Tracey Guest, Exec. Officer
11 The Wharf
16 Bridge St.
Birmingham B1 2JS, United Kingdom
Phone: 44 121 6330410
Fax: 44 121 6439497
E-mail: enquiries@bsac.org.uk
Home Page: http://www.bsac.org.uk

• 5475 • Garrod Medal
For recognition of achievement in the field of antimicrobial chemotherapy. Nominations are made by the Council of the Society. A medal and an invitation to present the Garrod Memorial Lecture are awarded annually. Established in 1982 in honor of L.P. Garrod, whose writing and influence on the field was important to the development of the discipline.

• 5476 •
British Society for Haematology
Daphne Harvey, Admin.
100 White Lion St.
London N1 9PF, United Kingdom
Phone: 44 20 77130990
Fax: 44 20 78371931
E-mail: info@b-s-h.org.uk
Home Page: http://www.b-s-h.org.uk

• 5477 • BSH Scientific Scholarships
For younger members of the Society and recently appointed consultants.

• 5478 • BSH Student Scholarships
For undergraduates undertaking electives in the field of haematology.

• 5479 • Eliminations of Leukaemia Fund (ELF) Travelling and Training Fellowships
For persons working in the field of haematological malignancies.

• 5480 • Mary Evelyn Lucking Prize in Medicine
For UK residents under the age of 40.

• 5481 •
British Society for Middle Eastern Studies
Robert Gleave, Exec. Dir.
Institute for Middle Eastern and Islamic Studies
University of Durham
Elvet Hill Rd.
Durham DH1 3TU, United Kingdom
Phone: 44 191 3345179
Fax: 44 191 3345661
E-mail: a.l.haysey@durham.ac.uk
Home Page: http://www.dur.ac.uk/brismes

• 5482 • Book Prize
For outstanding writer in Middle Eastern studies.

• 5483 • Leigh Douglas Memorial Prize
For the best writer in the field of social sciences, humanities or Middle Eastern.

• 5484 • Master's Scholarship
For a resident of EU and a member institution of the institute.

• 5485 • Research Student Awards
For research student who focused on Middle Eastern studies.

• 5486 •
British Society for Research on Ageing
Dr. David Kipling, Hon.Sec.
Univ. of the West of England
Coldharbour Ln.
Bristol BS16 1QY, United Kingdom
Phone: 44 29 20744847
Fax: 44 29 20744276
E-mail: info@bsra.org.uk
Home Page: http://www.bsra.org.uk

• 5487 • Lord Cohen Medal
To recognize an individual who has made a considerable contribution to ageing research, either through original discoveries or in the promotion of the subject of gerontology in its broadest aspects. The recipient is invited to give a lecture to the Society. Awarded periodically.

• 5488 •
British Society for Rheumatology
Ms. Samantha Peters, Chief Exec.
41 Eagle St.
London WC1R 4TL, United Kingdom
Phone: 44 207 2423313
Fax: 44 207 2423277
E-mail: bsr@rheumatology.org.uk
Home Page: http://www.rheumatology.org.uk

Formed by merger of: (1983) Heberden Society; British Association of Rheumatology and Rehabilitation.

• 5489 • Garrod Prize
To recognize young scientists (under age 35) working in the United Kingdom in a rheumatology department or performing work closely related to the discipline. A monetary prize of £500 and an invitation to give a presentation of the work during the Society's annual meeting are awarded annually.

• 5490 • Michael Mason Prize
For recognition of excellence in clinical or scientific research in the field of rheumatology. Members of the Society are eligible. A monetary prize of £1000 and a medal are awarded annually at the annual general meeting. Established in 1986.

• 5491 •
British Society for the History of Science
Mr. Philip Crane, Exec.Sec.
31 High St.
Stanford in the Vale
Oxfordshire
Faringdon SN7 8LH, United Kingdom
Phone: 44 1367 718963
Fax: 44 1367 718963
E-mail: bshs@bshs.org.uk
Home Page: http://www.bshs.org.uk

• 5492 • Dingle Prize
Awarded biennially for the best book on an aspect of the history of science, published in the two years since the last award was given, on a theme to be decided by the society's council. Established in 1997.

• 5493 • Singer Prize
Awarded for an unpublished essay based on original research into any aspect of the history of science, techonology, or medicine. The prize is intended for younger scholars or recent entrants into the profession. Candidates must be registered for a postgraduate degree course or have completed such in the last two years. Entry is not limited to British Nationals. The essay must not exceed 8,000 words including footnotes, and the essay must be fully documented. The essay must also be typewritten, with double spacing, and be submitted in English. The prize may be divided between two or more entrants, and it will be presented at a BSHS meeting. The winning essay will also be published in the *British Journal for the History of Science* at the discretion of the editor. A monetary prize of £300 is also part of this prize established in 1978.

• 5494 • Ivan Slade Prize
The prize is awarded for an essay, published or not, making the best critical contribution to the history of science. The award is not limited to British Nationals, but entries should be submitted in English and should have been written in the two years prior to the closing date. The essay should not exceed 10,000 words and should have an abstract of 500 words.

• 5495 •
British Society for the Study of Prosthetic Dentistry
Nick Jepson, Pres.
The Dental School
Dept. of Restorative Dentistry
Farmington Pl.
Newcastle upon Tyne B4 6NN, United Kingdom
Phone: 44 191 2227829
E-mail: n.j.a.jepson@ncl.ac.uk
Home Page: http://www.bsspd.org

• 5496 • Gold Medal
For meritorious work in the field of prosthetic dentistry.

• 5497 • Heraeus Kulzer Undergraduate Essay Prize
For the best essay on a topic selected by the Council.

• 5498 • New Graduate Prize
For new graduates.

• 5499 • Schottlander Prize
For the best 20-minute oral communication on a subject relevant to prosthetic dentistry.

• 5500 •
British Society of Animal Science
Mr. Mike A. Steele, Chief Exec.
PO Box 3
Midlothian
Penicuik EH26 0RZ, United Kingdom
Phone: 44 131 4454508
Fax: 44 131 5353120
E-mail: bsas@sac.ac.uk
Home Page: http://www.bsas.org.uk

Formerly: (1995) British Society of Animal Production.

• 5501 • Sir John Hammond Memorial Prize
To recognize an individual who works or has worked in the United Kingdom or Ireland in research, teaching, advising, farming, or affiliated professions, and has made a significant contribution to the development of animal production based on the application of knowledge of animal physiology. Individuals under 45 years of age may be nominated. Nominations need to be supported by three members of the Society and presented by 31 October. A monetary award and a certificate are presented at the annual meeting of the Society. Established in 1968 to honor Sir John Hammond.

• 5502 •
British Society of Cinematographers
Frances Russell, Sec.-Treas.
PO Box 2587
Gerrards Cross SL9 7WZ, United Kingdom
Phone: 44 1753 888052
Fax: 44 1753 891486
E-mail: bscine@btconnect.com
Home Page: http://www.bscine.com

• 5503 • Bert Easey Technical Award

• 5504 • BSC Best Cinematography Award

• 5505 • Charles Staffell Visual Effects Award

• 5506 •
British Society of Flavourists
Chris Goddard, Hon.Sec.
1 Wansford Close
Brentwood CM14 4PU, United Kingdom
Phone: 44 1277 224587
E-mail: bsfrefer@aol.com
Home Page: http://www.bsf.org.uk

• 5507 • BSF Student Bursary and Bill Waygood Memorial Lecture
To an original essay written by an undergraduate university student on a flavouring subject.

• 5508 • Hugh Davis Memorial Cup
To an outstanding flavour salesperson.

• 5509 • Bill Littlejohn Memorial Medal and lecture
To a member with an outstanding contribution to the technical, research, application or commercial aspect of the flavour industry.

• 5510 •
British Society of Magazine Editors
Gill Branston, Admin.
137 Hale Ln.
Edgware
Middlesex
Edgware HA8 9QP, United Kingdom
Phone: 44 20 89064664
Fax: 44 20 89592137
E-mail: admin@bsme.com
Home Page: http://www.bsme.com

• 5511 • British Society of Magazine Editors Awards
To honor those who have shown outstanding editing skills during the year. Any editor of a British magazine that is published at least four times per year is eligible. Awards are presented annually for Editor's Editor of the Year and Editors of the Year in the following weekly and non-weekly categories: business and professional magazines, contract magazines, current affairs magazines, entertainment magazines, lifestyle magazines, men's magazines, newspaper magazines, special interest magazines, women's magazines, and youth and children's magazines. Special awards include Launch of the Year, Magazine Website of the Year, Innovation of the Year, Brand Building Initiative of the Year, and Fiona MacPherson New Editor of the Year. Awarded annually.

• 5512 • Editors' Editor of the Year Award
For best magazine editor.

• 5513 • Innovation Writer of the Year
To highlight, reward, and encourage coverage by business press titles of the best of British innovation. Awards will be made to the writer or writers of articles that have successfully highlighted ideas, concepts, or discoveries whose commercial exploitation has added value to an institution or company and enhanced prospects for UK enterprise as a whole. The Writer of the Year will be awarded a check for £3,000 and the editor of the winning title will be awarded a check for £2,000.

• 5514 • Launch of the Year Award

• 5515 • The Magazines - Awards for Editorial and Publishing Excellence
To recognize outstanding achievement through editorial and publishing excellence over the last year. Awards are presented in 22 categories, such as Consumer Magazine of the Year, Editor of the Year, Publisher of the Year, Columnist of the Year, and Designer of the Year. Trophies are awarded to the winner in each category and certificates are awarded to runners-up. Held annually. Established in 1979.

• 5516 •
British Society of Periodontology
Anne S. Hallowes, Admin. Mgr.
44 Pool Rd.
Hartley Wintney
Hampshire
Hook RG27 8RD, United Kingdom
Phone: 44 1252 843598
Fax: 44 1252 844018
E-mail: bspadmin@btinternet.com
Home Page: http://www.bsperio.org

• 5517 • Frank Ashley Undergraduate Prize
For students in United Kingdom Dental Schools.

• 5518 • George Cross Fellowship Award
For members of the Society.

• 5519 • Marsh Midda Fellowship
For postgraduate students who are members of the Society.

• 5520 • Research Grant
For full or associate members of the BSP.

• 5521 • Sir Wilfred Fish Research Prize
For young researchers.

• 5522 •
British Society of Rehabilitation Medicine
Vera Neumann, Pres.
11 St. Andrews Pl.
London NW1 4LE, United Kingdom
Phone: 44 1992 638865
Fax: 44 1992 638905
E-mail: admin@bsrm.co.uk
Home Page: http://www.bsrm.co.uk

• 5523 • Essay Prize
For undergraduates in any British medical school.

• 5524 • Philip Nichols Prize
For original research on a subject pertinent to Rehabilitation Medicine from a clinical, medical, scientific or sociological point of view.

• 5525 • Travelling Scholarships
For travel contributing to post graduate study in Rehabilitation Medicine.

• 5526 •
British Society of Rheology
Prof. Timothy N. Phillips, Sec.
University of Wales
Department of Mathematics
Aberystwyth
Ceredigion SY23 6BZ, United Kingdom
Phone: 44 131 4495111
Fax: 44 131 4513161
E-mail: tnp@aber.ac.uk
Home Page: http://www.bsr.org.uk

• 5527 • Scott Blair Biorheology Scholarship
The award is similar to the BSR Scott Blair Scholarship, but the recipient must work in the field of biorheology. Awarded every four years. Established in 1989 to commemorate the work of the late Dr. G.W. Scott Blair, who was the first print editor of *Biorheology Journal.*

• 5528 • British Society of Rheology Annual Award
To recognize a significant or promising contribution and/or services to the advancement of rheology in any of its many aspects. Individuals, groups, or institutions are eligible. A certificate or monetary prize appropriate to the nature and significance of the contribution is awarded annually. Established in 1978.

• 5529 • British Society of Rheology Gold Medal
To recognize distinguished work in the theory and application of rheology. Individual scientists are eligible. A gold medal is awarded irregularly. Established in 1966.

• 5530 •
British Society of Scientific Glassblowers
Mr. Ian Pearson, Chm.
Glendale, Sinclair St.
Caithness
Thurso KW14 7AQ, United Kingdom
Phone: 44 1847 802629
Phone: 44 1847 895637
Fax: 44 1847 802971
E-mail: ian.pearson@ukaea.org.uk
Home Page: http://www.bssg.co.uk

• 5531 • Norman Collins Memorial Award
To provide an opportunity for experienced scientific glassblowers to demonstrate their outstanding skills in scientific glassware. All members of the society are eligible. Winners of the A.D. Wood Cup are automatically considered. A trophy to be held for one year is awarded annually at the symposium. Established in 1980 in memory of Norman Collins.

• 5532 • David Flack Memorial Award
To provide an opportunity for scientific glassblowers to express their artistic talent in the medium of glass. Members of the society are

Awards are arranged in alphabetical order below their administering organizations

eligible. A trophy to be held for one year and a pewter tankard for the winner to keep are awarded annually at the symposium. Established in 1972 in memory of David Flack, by his parents.

• 5533 • Lucy Oldfield Cup
For recognition of contributions to the society journal. A trophy and certificates of achievement are awarded annually. Established in 1982 by Dr. Lucy Oldfield.

• 5534 • Thames Valley Award
To recognize a member who has contributed most to the society. A trophy to be held for one year is awarded annually at the annual symposium. Established in 1970 by members of the Thames Valley Section of the society.

• 5535 • TSL Trophy
To encourage excellence in scientific vitreous silica glassworking. All members of the society are eligible. A trophy to be held for one year and a pewter tankard for the winner to keep are awarded annually at the symposium. Established in 1969 by Thermal Syndicate, Ltd. (TSL).

• 5536 • A. D. Wood Cup
To encourage excellence in scientific borosilicate glassworking. Members of the society who have less than three years experience are eligible. A cup to be held for one year, a replica, and a £50 prize are awarded annually at the symposium. Established in 1966 by Mr. A.D. Wood of A.D. Wood Ltd.

• 5537 •
British Sound Recording Association
Martyn Lycett, Hon. Secretary
11 Shernfold, Kent's Hill
Milton Keynes
Buckinghamshire MK7 6HR, United Kingdom
E-mail: mcl@soundhunters.com
Home Page: http://www.soundhunters.com/fbtrc

Formerly: (2004) Federation of British Tape Recordists.

• 5538 • British Amateur Recording Contest
To encourage the development of all aspects of sound and video recording by amateurs: speech and drama, reportage, documentary, music (live and electronic), technical experiment, and sounds from nature. Candidates must be citizens of the United Kingdom. Awards are presented in nine classes: Speech and Drama; Documentary; Live/Acoustic Music; Electronic/Multi-track Music; Reportage; Technical Experiment; Sounds from Nature; Themed Subject; and Free-Choice Video. Additional Special Awards are also presented. Held annually. Established in 1957 by Mr. D. Brown, editor and publisher of *Tape Recording Magazine*.

• 5539 •
British Thematic Association
John Hayward, Vice Chm.
18 Waverley Dr.
Camberley GU15 2DL, United Kingdom
Phone: 44 1276 29246
E-mail: ssasman@btinternet.com
Home Page: http://www.brit-thematic-assoc.com

• 5540 • BTA Trophy
For the best exhibit as judged by National Thematic rules. A trophy is awarded annually.

• 5541 •
British Transplantation Society
John L.R. Forsythe, Pres.
Broomhill Rd.
Triangle House
London SW18 4HX, United Kingdom
Phone: 44 20 88752430
Fax: 44 20 88752434
E-mail: secretariat@bts.org.uk
Home Page: http://www.bts.org.uk

• 5542 • BTS/Astellas and BTS/Novartis Research Fellowships
For individuals in training who are interested in transplantation.

• 5543 • BTS/Morris Travelling Fellowship
For trainees in the field of transplantation.

• 5544 • Roy Calne Award
To a member For the most outstanding contribution published in a peer review journal as a single paper.

• 5545 • St. John Ambulance Air Wing Travelling Fellowship
To workers in all aspects of transplantation For the benefit of transplant patients.

• 5546 • Wyeth Fellowship
To trainees in the field of transplantation.

• 5547 •
British Trust for Ornithology
Dr. Nick Carter, Dir. of Development
The Nunnery
Norfolk
Thetford IP24 2PU, United Kingdom
Phone: 44 1842 750050
Fax: 44 1842 750030
E-mail: info@bto.org
Home Page: http://www.bto.org

• 5548 • Jubilee Medal
For recognition of services to the trust that are not scientific. Members of the trust are eligible. A medal is awarded annually. Established in 1983 to commemorate 50 years of the BTO.

• 5549 • Bernard Tucker Medal
For recognition of scientific services. Members of the trust are eligible. A medal is awarded annually. Established in 1954 in honor of Bernard Tucker.

• 5550 •
British Turf and Landscape Irrigation Association
Martyn Jones, Sec.
41 Pennine Way
Great Eccleston
Lancashire
Preston PR3 0YS, United Kingdom
Phone: 44 1995 670675
E-mail: info@btlia.org.uk
Home Page: http://www.btlia.org.uk

• 5551 • Certificate of Merit
For member contracting companies who have attained the appropriate level of commendation from customers.

• 5552 • Individual Achievement/Personality of the Year Award
To the individual who has made a significant contribution to the industry.

• 5553 • John P. Shildrick Award
For libraries of colleges and other organizations which have been instrumental in promoting good irrigation practice.

• 5554 •
British Universities Film and Video Council
Murray Weston, Dir.
77 Wells St.
London W1T 3QJ, United Kingdom
Phone: 44 20 73931500
Fax: 44 20 73931555
E-mail: ask@bufvc.ac.uk
Home Page: http://www.bufvc.ac.uk

• 5555 • Channel 4 Archaeological Film Awards
To recognize cinematic achievements in the field of archaeology. Three categories exist: broadcast programmes, non-broadcast films or videos and ICT projects (CD-ROMs, websites or integrated multimedia packages). Entries may deal with any aspect of archaeology, including industrial archaeology, and may have been made for broadcast, educational, promotional or site-specific purposes. To be eligible they must be British-produced and have been made or broadcast during the previous two years. Winners in each of the three categories will be awarded a cash prize of £750. Part of the British Archaeological Awards.

• 5556 •
British Vacuum Council
Peter Main, Sec.
76 Portland Pl.
London W1N 3DH, United Kingdom
Phone: 44 20 74704838
Fax: 44 20 74704848
E-mail: peter.main@iop.org
Home Page: http://www.astec.ac.uk/vacsci/British-Vacuum-Council

• 5557 • **British Vacuum Council Junior Prize**
For young scientists and engineers for their outstanding work.

• 5558 • **C.R. Burch Prize**
To a resident of U.K. or Republic of Ireland, under 32 years of age.

• 5559 • **BVC Senior Prize**
For distinguished contributions to British scientific research.

• 5560 • **John Yarwood Memorial Medal**

• 5561 •
British Vehicle Rental and Leasing Association
John Lewis, Dir.Gen.
River Lodge
Badminton Ct.
Amersham HP7 0DD, United Kingdom
Phone: 44 1494 434747
Fax: 44 1494 434499
E-mail: info@bvrla.co.uk
Home Page: http://www.bvrla.co.uk

• 5562 • **BVRLA Awards**
Recognizes the manufacturer that has improved vehicle security by the greatest amount of the previous year. Awarded annually.

• 5563 •
British Veterinary Association
Henrietta Alderman, Head of Operations
7 Mansfield St.
London W1G 9NQ, United Kingdom
Phone: 44 207 6366541
Fax: 44 207 4362970
E-mail: bvahq@bva.co.uk
Home Page: http://www.bva.co.uk

• 5564 • **Harry Steele-Bodger Memorial Scholarship**
A traveling scholarship or contribution to a tour of study abroad is awarded at least once every four years. Eligible candidates include graduates of the Veterinary Schools in the United Kingdom and Ireland who have been qualified not more than three years and those who are in the year before their final year or their final year of school. The deadline for applications is April 8. Travel scholarships of £1,100 are awarded to assist a visit to a veterinary or agricultural school or research institute or some other course of study approved by the governing committee. Established in 1953 in memory of Henry W. Steele-Bodger, President of the Association from 1939 to 1941 and Chairman of the Survey Committee from 1939 to 1946, in recognition of his services to the veterinary profession and agriculture.

• 5565 •
British Wrestling Association
Yvonne Ball, Admin.
12 Westwood Ln.
Brimington
Chesterfield S43 1PA, United Kingdom
Phone: 44 1246 236443
Fax: 44 1246 236443
E-mail: admin@britishwrestling.org
Home Page: http://www.britishwrestling.org

• 5566 • **Honorary Membership for life**
Recognizes outstanding commitment to wrestling. Awarded annually.

• 5567 •
Britten-Pears Foundation
Richard Jarman, Dir.Gen.
Britten-Pears Library
Golf Ln.
Aldeburgh IP15 5PY, United Kingdom
Phone: 44 1728 451700
Fax: 44 1728 453076
E-mail: enquiries@brittenpears.org
Home Page: http://www.brittenpears.org

• 5568 • **Benjamin Britten International Composers' Competition**
To encourage young composers. Composers of all nationalities who are under 35 years of age may submit unpublished works for a specified instrumentation written during the previous three years. A monetary commission to write a work to be performed during the Aldeburgh Festival is awarded triennially. Established in 1983 to mark the seventieth anniversary of Benjamin Britten's birth.

• 5569 •
Business Archives Council
Fiona Maccoll, Mgr.
Archive Services
University of Glasgow
13 Thurso St.
Glasgow G11 6PE, United Kingdom
Phone: 44 141 3305515
Fax: 44 141 3302640
E-mail: enquiries@archives.gla.ac.uk
Home Page: http://www.archives.gla.ac.uk/bac/default.html

• 5570 • **Wadsworth Prize for Business History**
For recognition of an outstanding contribution to British business history in any one calendar year. Books or articles on British business history published during the year are eligible. A monetary prize is awarded annually. Established in 1978 upon the retirement from the Council of Professor J. E. Wadsworth after 50 years continuous association.

• 5571 •
Call Centre Association
Anne Marie Forsyth, Chief Exec.
20 Newton Pl.
Elmbank St.
Glasgow G3 7PY, United Kingdom
Phone: 44 141 5649010
Fax: 44 141 5649011
E-mail: cca@cca.org.uk
Home Page: http://www.cca.org.uk

• 5572 • **CCA Member Recognition**
Annual award of recognition.

• 5573 •
Calouste Gulbenkian Foundation
United Kingdom Branch
98 Portland Pl.
London W1B 4ET, United Kingdom
Phone: 44 20 7636 5313
Fax: 44 20 7908 7580
E-mail: info@gulbenkian.org.uk
Home Page: http://www.gulbenkian.org.uk

• 5574 • **Calouste Gulbenkian Foundation Grants**
To encourage and to provide support for programs in the arts, education, social welfare, and Anglo-Portuguese cultural relations. Grant applications for projects (not individuals) in the United Kingdom and the Republic of Ireland whose principal beneficiaries are people in these countries are accepted. Preference is given to original new developments, not yet a part of the regular running costs of an organization; to developments which are either strategic, such as practical initiatives directed to helping tackle the underlying causes of problems, or seminal, because they seem likely to influence policy and practice elsewhere; or to projects which are of more than local significance. The majority of grants are for less than £15,000. Awarded annually.

• 5575 •
Camanachd Association
(Cumunn na Camanachd)
Alastair MacIntyre, Exec.Off.
Queen Anne House
111 High St.
Fort William PH33 6DG, United Kingdom
Phone: 44 1397 703903
Fax: 44 1397 4999806
E-mail: alastairmac@shinty.com
Home Page: http://www.shinty.com

• 5576 • **Club of the Year**
Annual award of recognition.

• 5577 • **Player of the Year**
Annual award of recognition.

• 5578 •
Cambridge Philosophical Society
Prof. H. Ahmed, Pres.
Central Science Library
Arts School
Bene't St.
Cambridge CB2 3PY, United Kingdom
Phone: 44 1223 334743
E-mail: philosoc@hermes.cam.ac.uk
Home Page: http://www.cam.ac.uk/societies/cps

• 5579 • **William Bate Hardy Prize**
For recognition of the best memoir, investigation, or discovery by a member of the University of Cambridge in the field of biological science. Work published during the previous three years by members of Cambridge University is eligible. Three Fellows of the Society, nominated by the Council of the Society for each occasion, judge the work. A monetary prize is awarded triennially. Established in 1964 in memory of Sir William Bate Hardy (1864-1934).

• 5580 •
Campaign for the Protection of Rural Wales
(Ymgyrch Diogelu Cymru Wledig)
Mr. Merfyn Williams, Dir.
Ty Gwyn
31 High St.
Welshpool
Welshpool SY21 7YD, United Kingdom
Phone: 44 1938 552525
Phone: 44 1938 556212
Fax: 44 1938 552741
E-mail: info@cprw.org.uk
Home Page: http://www.cprw.org.uk

Formerly: Council for the Protection of Rural Wales.

• 5581 • **Rural Wales Award**
To recognize work by individuals and organizations that is consciously intended to enhance the appearance or amenities of the Welsh countryside. Local branches of the organization make the awards. Framed certificates and a wooden plaque are awarded annually. Established in 1984. Sponsored by the Post Office Ltd.

• 5582 •
Cancer Research U.K. Beatson Laboratories
Garscube Estate
Switchback Rd.
Bearsden
Glasgow G61 1BD, United Kingdom
Phone: 44 1413303953
Fax: 44 1419426521
E-mail: beatson@gla.ac.uk
Home Page: http://www.beatson.gla.ac.uk/

• 5583 • **John Paul Career Award**
Recognizes the most promising student at the Beatson Institute. Candidates prepare a progress report of their work, present a lecture to staff and other students, and are interviewed by a selection committee. Awarded annually.

• 5584 •
Catering Equipment Distributors Association of Great Britain
Ms. Amanda North, Sec.
PO Box 194
Bingley BD16 2XW, United Kingdom
Phone: 44 1274 826056
Fax: 44 1274 777260
E-mail: info@ceda.co.uk
Home Page: http://www.ceda.co.uk

• 5585 • **Grand Prix Awards**
The Grand Prix Awards recognize the best catering equipment installation projects undertaken in five industry sectors during the previous year. As part of the awards program, Supplier Awards are presented for heavy equipment, light equipment, and outstanding customer service. Trophies are awarded annually.

• 5586 •
Celtic Film and Television Festival
Frances Hendron, Contact
249 W George St.
Glasgow G12 4QE, United Kingdom
Phone: 44 141 302 1737
Fax: 44 141 302 1738
E-mail: mail@celticfilm.co.uk
Home Page: http://www.celticfilm.co.uk

Formerly: (1988) Association for Film and Television in the Celtic Countries.

• 5587 • **International Festival of Film and Television in the Celtic Countries**
For recognition of achievement by outstanding filmmakers and to encourage younger filmmakers. Individuals who reside or work in Celtic countries may apply. Eleven awards are presented at an annual peripatetic festival/conference.

• 5588 •
Central Chancery of the Orders of Knighthood
St. James' Palace
London SW1A 1BG, United Kingdom
Fax: 44 20 7839 2983
E-mail: centralchancery@royal.gov.uk
Home Page: http://www.royal.gov.uk

• 5589 • **Air Force Cross**
To recognize all ranks of the Royal Air Force for outstanding services in flying operations not against the enemy. It can also be awarded to equivalent ranks of the Royal Navy and the Army for similar services. Established in 1918. Administered by the Ministry of Defense.

• 5590 • **British Empire Medal**
To recognize men and women who do not qualify for the higher awards in the order of the British Empire. The British Empire Medal ceased being awarded in the United Kingdom in 1992, but is still awarded by some Commonwealth Countries.

• 5591 • **Distinguished Flying Medal**
To recognize non-commissioned ranks of the Royal Air Force for bravery in air operations against the enemy. It can also be awarded to equivalent ranks of the Royal Navy and the Army for similar services. Established in 1918. Administered by the Ministry of Defense.

• 5592 • **Distinguished Service Order**
To honor gallantry and leadership in action displayed by officers of the armed forces of the Crown. It can be awarded to officers of the Merchant Navy. It is now the only gallantry award which cannot be given posthumously. Established in 1886.

• 5593 • **George Cross**
To honor great heroism or conspicuous courage and equivalent to the rank of the Victoria Cross. It was intended primarily for civilians but is not limited to them; in practice more servicemen and women have received it than civilians. A tax-free annuity of £1,300 a year is payable to holders of the Cross. Established in 1940.

• 5594 • **George Medal**
For recognition of an act of bravery that has not been sufficiently outstanding to merit the Cross. It can be awarded to foreigners. Established in 1940.

• 5595 • **Military Cross**
To recognize all ranks for gallant and distinguished services in the presence of the enemy on land. Established in 1914. Administered by the Ministry of Defense.

• 5596 • **Most Ancient and Most Noble Order of the Thistle**
The Order consists of the Sovereign and 16 Knights. Royal Knights and Extra Knights are admitted by special statutes. The Order is conferred on the personal decision of the Sovereign. Created in 787 and revived in 1687 by James II.

• 5597 • **Most Distinguished Order of St. Michael and St. George**
For recognition of service overseas or in connection with foreign or Commonwealth affairs. The Grand Master is the Duke of Kent. Ranks in the Order, and their customary abbreviations, are: (1) Knight or Dame Grand Cross G.C.M.G.; (2) Knight or Dame Commander - K.C.M.G. or D.C.M.G.; and (3) Companion - C.M.G. Founded in 1818.

• 5598 • **Most Excellent Order of the British Empire**
To recognize civilians or service personnel for public services or other distinctions. The Grand Master is the Duke of Edinburgh. There are two divisions, military and civil. Ranks in the Order, which is open to both sexes, and the customary abbreviations, are: (1) Knight or Dame Grand Cross - G.B.E.; (2) Knight or Dame Commander - K.B.E. or D.B.E.; (3) Commander - C.B.E.; (4) Officer - O.B.E.; and (5) Member - M.B.E. Founded in 1917.

• 5599 • Most Honourable Order of the Bath
For recognition of conspicuous services to the Crown. This Order is open to both sexes. The Great Master and First or Principal Knight Grand Cross is the Prince of Wales. There are two divisions, military and civil. Ranks in the order, and their customary abbreviations, are: (1) Knight or Dame Grand Cross: G.C.B.; (2) Knight or Dame Commander: K.C.B. or D.C.B.; and (3) Companion: C.B. Established as a separate order in 1725 but with medieval origins.

• 5600 • Most Noble Order of the Garter
The Order consists of the Sovereign, the Duke of Edinburgh, the Prince of Wales, certain lineal descendants of King George I, if selected, and 24 other members (excluding other sons of the Sovereign and Ladies of the Garter). Foreigners, normally sovereigns, can be admitted as Extra Knights or Ladies. The Order is conferred on the personal decision of the Sovereign. Established in 1348.

• 5601 • Order of Merit
For recognition of eminent services rendered in the armed services, or towards the advancement of art, literature and science. It is open to both sexes. The Order is limited to 24 members, plus foreign honorary members. The insignia is awarded in either a military or a civil form. Founded in 1902.

• 5602 • Order of the Companions of Honour
For recognition of service of conspicuous national importance. The Order is open to both sexes and is limited to 65 persons. The only rank is that of Companion and the award carries no title. Founded in 1917.

• 5603 • Polar Medal
To recognize individuals who have made notable contributions to the exploration and/or knowledge of the Polar Regions and who, in so doing, have undergone the hazards and rigors imposed by a Polar environment to life and movement. Expeditioners to Polar Regions who have spent not less than twelve months in a Polar climate (usually including a winter) are eligible. A silver, octagonal medal is awarded by Her Majesty the Queen. Established in 1857 by Queen Victoria and authorized by King Edward VII in 1904. Administered by the Royal Navy Hydrographic Department.

• 5604 • Queen's Fire Service Medal
For recognition posthumously. There is also the Queen's Fire Service Medal for Distinguished Service. Instituted in 1954.

• 5605 • Queen's Gallantry Medal
To recognize acts of exemplary bravery. The medal is intended primarily for civilians but may be awarded to military personnel for actions for which purely military honors are not granted. Established in 1974.

• 5606 • Queen's Police Medal for Distinguished Service
For recognition posthumously. There is also The Queen's Police Medal for Distinguished Service. Established in 1954.

• 5607 • Royal Red Cross
To recognize exceptional services by nurses rendered in any of the fighting services. There is also a second class of award known as "Associate." Established in 1883.

• 5608 • Royal Victorian Order
To reward services to the Royal Family. The Grand Master is Queen Elizabeth The Queen Mother. Ranks in the Order, which is open to both sexes, and the customary abbreviations, are: (1) Knight or Dame Grand Cross - G.C.V.O.; (2) Knight or Dame Commander - K.C.V.O. or D.C.V.O.; (3) Commander - C.V.O.; (4) Lieutenant L. D. V.; and (5) Member 5th Class M.V.O. Established in 1896 by Queen Victoria.

• 5609 • Victoria Cross
This, the most esteemed of all British gallantry medals, is given to honor outstanding valor in the presence of the enemy. Normally intended for servicemen but it may be conferred on civilians serving under military command. A tax-free annuity of £1,300 a year is payable to holders of the Cross. Established in 1856.

• 5610 •
Challenger Society for Marine Science
Jennifer Jones, Exec.Sec.
National Oceanography Ctre.
Waterfront Campus, Rm. 251-20
Empress Dock
Southampton SO14 3ZH, United Kingdom
Phone: 44 23 80596097
Fax: 44 23 80596149
E-mail: jxj@soc.soton.ac.uk
Home Page: http://www.soc.soton.ac.uk/OTHERS/CSMS

Formerly: (1988) Challenger Society.

• 5611 • Cath Allen Prize
To encourage good poster presentations at the biennial UK Oceanography meeting. A monetary prize and a certificate are awarded biennially at the UK Oceanography meeting. Established in 1988 in honor of Dr. Catherine M. Allen. Formerly: (1991) Poster Prize.

• 5612 • Norman Heaps Prize
To encourage good presentations by young oceanographers. Individuals who are 35 years of age or younger are considered. A monetary prize and a certificate are awarded at the biennial UK Oceanography meeting. Established in 1988 in honor of Dr. Norman S. Heaps. Formerly: World Development Awards for Business.

• 5613 •
Chartered Institute of Arbitrators
Mr. Richard Rodger, Contact
Intl. Arbitration and Mediation Ctre.
12 Bloomsbury Sq.
London WC1A 2LP, United Kingdom
Phone: 44 20 74217444
Phone: 44 20 74217441
Fax: 44 20 74044023
E-mail: info@arbitrators.org
Home Page: http://www.arbitrators.org

• 5614 • PresidentKs Prize
Recognizes the student scoring the highest grade in the Award Writing Examination. Awarded annually.

• 5615 •
Chartered Institute of Building
MS. Chris Blythe, Chief Exec.
Englemere
Kings Ride
Berkshire
Ascot SL5 7TB, United Kingdom
Phone: 44 1344 630700
Fax: 44 1344 630777
E-mail: reception@ciob.org.uk
Home Page: http://www.ciob.org.uk

• 5616 • Building Manager of the Year Awards
To recognize outstanding performance in the management of building projects. Nominations are accepted for projects carried out in the United Kingdom. Awards and medals are bestowed annually. Established in 1979 in honor of Queen Elizabeth II's Silver Jubilee.

• 5617 •
Chartered Institute of Journalists
Dominic Cooper, Gen.Sec.
2 Dock Offices
Surrey Quays Rd.
London SE16 2XU, United Kingdom
Phone: 44 207 2521187
Fax: 44 207 2322302
E-mail: memberservices@ioj.co.uk
Home Page: http://www.ioj.co.uk

Formerly: Institute of Journalists.

• 5618 • Gold Medal
For recognition of outstanding service to journalism and the fundamental freedom of the press. Journalists and others of any nationality are eligible. A gold medal with the Institute emblem on the reverse and the name of the recipient, wreathed on the obverse, is awarded when merited. Established in 1963.

• 5619 •
Chartered Institute of Library and Information Professionals
Bob McKee, Chief Exec.
7 Ridgmount St.
London WC1E 7AE, United Kingdom
Phone: 44 20 7255 0500
Fax: 44 20 7255 0501
E-mail: info@cilip.org.uk
Home Page: http://www.cilip.org.uk
Formerly: (2004) Institute of Information Scientists; Library Association.

• 5620 • Jason Farradine Award
To recognize information scientists and information managers who promote the advancement of information science. Awarded annually. Co-sponsored by Kompass Publishers.

• 5621 •
Chartered Institute of Logistics and Transport
Logistics and Transport Centre
PO Box 5787
Corby NN17 4XQ, United Kingdom
Phone: 44 1536 740104
E-mail: membership@ciltuk.org.uk
Home Page: http://www.cilt.org.uk

• 5622 • Best Article in Logistics Focus
Award of recognition.

• 5623 • Excellence in Integrated Logistics Management
Awarded for outstanding achievement in integration.

• 5624 • Excellence in the Use of Human Resources in Logistics
Awarded for outstanding use the human resources management techniques and the improvement of logistics.

• 5625 • Excellence in the Use of Technology in Logistics
Awarded for the greatest achievement in the use of technological advances for logistics management.

• 5626 • Excellence in the Use of Transport in Logisitcs
Awarded for the best use of transport modes for the improvement of logistics.

• 5627 • Logistics Company of the Year
Awarded to the company who has made the greatest achievement in logistics management.

• 5628 • Logistics Dissertation of the Year
Award of recognition.

• 5629 • Young Manager of the Year Award
Awarded to a young person who has demonstrated potential and excellence.

• 5630 •
Chartered Institute of Purchasing and Supply
Ken James, Chief Exec.
Easton House
Easton on the Hill
Stamford PE9 3NZ, United Kingdom
Phone: 44 1780 756777
Fax: 44 1780 751610
E-mail: info@cips.org
Home Page: http://www.cips.org

• 5631 • CIPS Supply Managent Awards
For excellence in purchasing and supply management.

• 5632 • Swinbank Award
For long service and excellent contribution to the purchasing and supply management profession.

• 5633 •
Chartered Institution of Building Services Engineers - England
Julian Amey BA/MA, Chief Exec./Sec.
222 Balham High Rd.
Balham
London SW12 9BS, United Kingdom
Phone: 44 208 6755211
Fax: 44 208 6755449
E-mail: enquiries@cibse.org
Home Page: http://www.cibse.org

• 5634 • Barker Silver Medal
For recognition of papers contributing substantially to heating, ventilating, and air conditioning associated with the built environment. Papers that describe the author's experience in the application of engineering/scientific knowledge may be submitted. A silver medal is awarded annually when merited. Established in 1958 in honor of Mr. A. H. Barker.

• 5635 • Carter Bronze Medal
For recognition of the best paper presented to the Institution on the application and development of heating, ventilating, and air conditioning. A bronze medal and a certificate are awarded annually when merited. Established in 1977.

• 5636 • Dufton Silver Medal Award
For recognition of a paper that advances the science of building services through original research that leads to new development. A silver medal is awarded annually when merited. Established in 1958 in honor of Mr. A. F. Dufton.

• 5637 • Leon Gaster Bronze Medal
For recognition of the best paper presented to the Institution dealing with the research or theory of lighting and/or vision. A bronze medal and a certificate are awarded annually. Established in 1931 in honor of Mr. Leon Gaster.

• 5638 • Happold Brilliant Award
For recognition of teaching excellence. Given to a University running a CIBSE-accredited degree program. Awarded annually. Established 1996. Sponsored by the Happold Trust.

• 5639 • Napier - Shaw Bronze Medal
For recognition of the best paper presented to the institution dealing with the research or theory of heating, ventilating, and air conditioning. A bronze medal and a certificate are awarded annually when merited. Established before 1948.

• 5640 • Walsh - Weston Bronze Award
For recognition of the best paper presented to the Institution dealing with the development of light sources or lighting application. A bronze medal and a certificate are awarded annually. Established in 1963 in memory of Dr. J. W. T. Walsh and Mr. H. C. Weston.

• 5641 •
Chartered Institution of Water and Environmental Management
Nick Reeves, Exec. Dir.
15 John St.
London WC1N 2EB, United Kingdom
Phone: 44 207 8313110
Fax: 44 207 4054967
E-mail: admin@ciwem.org
Home Page: http://www.ciwem.org

• 5642 • CIWEM Certificate and Diploma in Environmental Management
For candidates who achieved overall highest marks in certain modules.

• 5643 • President's Award
Awarded to a member.

• 5644 • RSPB/CIWEM Living Wetlands Award
Awarded to multi-functional projects that demonstrated the sustainable use of wetland habitats.

• 5645 • World of Difference Award
For innovation in sustainable water technology.

• 5646 • Young Members' Award
Awarded to members under age 35.

• 5647 •
Chartered Insurance Institute
Dave Wilson, Pres.
20 Aldermanbury
London EC2 7HY, United Kingdom
Phone: 44 20 74174431
Fax: 44 20 74174431
E-mail: customer.serv@cii.co.uk
Home Page: http://www.cii.co.uk

• 5648 • Paul Golmick Scholarship
To enable an individual to spend not less than twelve months with an insurance office in a Eu-

ropean country other than his country of origin in order to perfect his or her knowledge of the language of that country and to become acquainted with the conduct of insurance business in that country. The scholarship is offered in alternate years to an applicant from the U.K. and to an applicant from one of a group of nominated European countries. Applicants must be under 28 years of age and employed in insurance. The closing date for applications is December 1. A scholarship of £4,500 is awarded annually.

• 5649 • **Morgan Owen Medal**

To recognize a notable essay or work of research by an individual in the field of insurance. The entry must be written in English, a minimum of 10,000 words, and unpublished prior to the competition. Fellows or Associates of the Chartered Insurance Institute are eligible. A monetary award of £2,000 and a medal are awarded annually . Established in 1933 by a bequest of O. Morgan Owen, FCII, president of the Institute in 1911.

• 5650 • **Rutter Gold Medal and Prize**

To recognize the individual with the highest score on completing the qualifying examination for fellowship of the Chartered Insurance Institute. Members of the Institute are eligible. A monetary award of £1,000 and a medal are presented annually . Established in 1914 by Sir Frederick Pascoe Rutter, FCII, President of the Institute from 1910-1911.

• 5651 •
Chartered Society of Designers
Brian Lymbery, Dir.
5 Bermondsey Exchange, 179-181
Bermondsey St.
London SE1 3UW, United Kingdom
Phone: 44 207 3578088
Fax: 44 207 4079878
E-mail: info@csd.org.uk
Home Page: http://www.csd.org.uk

• 5652 • **Chartered Society of Designers Honorary Fellow**

To recognize distinguished persons outside the design profession who have been of material assistance to design or to the Society.

• 5653 • **Chartered Society of Designers Medal**

For recognition of outstanding achievement in design. Awarded annually for a single design, a group of related designs, or as recognition of work of exemplary standard over a number of years. Professional designers from any country are eligible. Nominations must be made by September 30 to the Council only by fellows and members of the Society. Established in 1957. Formerly: (1987) SIAD Medal.

• 5654 • **Minerva Medal**

Recognizes a lifetime's achievement in design. A sterling silver medal is awarded annually.

• 5655 •
City and Guilds of London Institute
Chris Humphries, Dir.Gen.
1 Giltspur St.
London EC1A 9DD, United Kingdom
Phone: 44 20 7294 2800
Fax: 44 20 7294 2400
E-mail: enquiry@city-and-guilds.co.uk
Home Page: http://www.city-and-guilds.co.uk

• 5656 • **The Associateship of the City and Guilds of London Institute**

Conferred exclusively on the engineering graduates of the City and Guilds College, Imperial College of Science, Technology and Medicine, London University. It denotes the ability to demonstrate, to the level equivalent to that of a degree of Bachelor of Science (Engineering), Bachelor of Engineering, or Master of Engineering, the understanding and application of the principles of a branch of Engineering or of Computing Science approved by the Institute. This ability is to be demonstrated through the satisfactory completion of an approved course of full-time study of three or four year's duration and through success in the associated examinations at the City and Guilds College. A diploma is awarded that specifies the subject area of the award. Holders are entitled to use the letters ACGI after their names and to wear the approved gown, hood, and mortar board. Established in 1887.

• 5657 • **Fellowship of the City and Guilds of London Institute**

The Fellowship is the highest distinction that can be conferred by the Institute. It denotes the ability to manage people, information, and operations in complex professional or technical situations and to formulate and implement strategies at the highest levels of responsibility. This achievement is to be demonstrated over a number of years in demanding appointments. The Fellowship may be conferred *Honoris Causa* (HonFCGI) on individuals whose professional achievement and advancement have been of outstanding significance over a period of years and/or who have made an outstanding contribution to the Institute's affairs. It was, until 1990, exclusive to former students of the City and Guilds College. Since 1990, applicants for the Fellowship may come from any profession or industry. Fellows of the Institute may be of any nationality and either sex. There is no restriction on the number of Fellowships which may be conferred annually. Applicants are normally not less than 40, with 10 years in positions of the highest responsibility. They must have made an outstanding contribution to the promotion and practice of their profession and be personally sponsored by two referees of national/international standing. A diploma and designatory letters FGGI are conferred. Established in 1892.

• 5658 • **Graduateship of the City and Guilds of London Institute**

To recognize achievements in industry, commerce, and the public services. The Graduateship denotes the ability to understand and apply the principles of a technical subject or professional activity. This ability is to be demonstrated in an employment-based context through the design, development, improvement, or critical assessment of an artifact, process, system, or service. The level of competence required is that which could be expected of a graduate of a recognized European university, with several subsequent years of relevant experience. A diploma is awarded that specifies the subject area of the award. Holders are entitled to use the letters GCGI after their names and to wear the approved gown, hood, and mortar board. Established in 1990.

• 5659 • **Licentiateship of the City and Guilds of London Institute**

To recognize achievement in industry, commerce, and the public services. The Licentiateship denotes the ability to understand and practice the principles of a technical subject or professional activity. This ability must be demonstrated in the context of advanced education and training and/or of employment. A diploma is awarded that specifies the employment sector of the award. Holders are entitled to use the letters LCGI after their names and to wear the approved gown, hood, and mortar board. Established in 1979.

• 5660 • **Medals for Excellence**

To recognize the candidates who have demonstrated outstanding ability in their particular subjects. Three types of medals are awarded: Bronze - to candidates gaining a City and Guilds qualification at Level 1 or 2; Silver - to candidates gaining a City and Guilds qualification at Level 3 or 4; and Gold - to candidates gaining a City and Guilds qualification at National Vocational Qualification (NVQ) Level 5 or gaining Graduateship (GCGI), Associateship (ACGI), or Membership (MCGI) of the Institute. Medals are awarded to recognize excellence and a determined commitment to a high quality of work. To support an application, examples of work may be submitted which show: highly developed skills, outstanding knowledge of a subject directly related to the City and Guilds assessment undertaken, innovation and originality, enterprise, and versatility and adaptability. Also of relevance to an application would be examples that show a candidate has: made a significant contribution to his or her place of work, made a significant contribution to a special project, and overcome significant hardship or disability. Nominations will be accepted from any center in the UK and EC that is registered with City and Guilds. Medals will also be awarded to overseas candidates. Awarded annually.

• 5661 • **Membership of the City and Guilds of London Institute**

To recognize achievement in industry, commerce, and the public services. The Membership denotes the ability to exercise personal, professional responsibility for the design, development, or improvement of an artifact, process, system, or service. The emphasis is on individual competence and application of knowledge. The level of competence required is that which could be expected of a holder of a master's degree, with subsequent years of supervisory management or advanced technical experience, similar to that required for full membership of a major professional body. A diploma is awarded that specifies the subject area of the award. Holders are entitled to use the letters MCGI after their names and to wear the approved gown, hood, and mortar board. Established 1990.

• 5662 •
Civic Trust
Martin Bacon, Chief Exec.
Essex Hall, 1-6 Essex St.
London WC2R 3HU, United Kingdom
Phone: 44 20 75397900
Fax: 44 20 75397901
E-mail: info@civictrust.org.uk
Home Page: http://www.civictrust.org.uk

• 5663 • **Civic Trust Awards**
To stimulate improved standards in all forms of environmental design, including architecture, planning, urban, and landscape design by giving recognition to outstanding projects in these fields; and to raise awareness of the importance of high quality design in improving the environment. Any scheme, completed within two years of submission, which has contributed to the quality of townscape or landscape is eligible. The awards are run on a two-year cycle - alternating each year between metropolitan and non-metropolitan areas of Britain. A bronze plaque is awarded for award-winning schemes, and certificates for the owners, designers, and contractors of award-winning and commended schemes. Awarded annually. An illustrated report on all the successful schemes is published each year. Established in 1959.

• 5664 •
Clan Hunter Association
Madam Pauline Hunter, Clan Chief
Hunterston Castle
West Kilbride KA23 9QG, United Kingdom
Phone: 44 1407 860500
Fax: 44 1407 860792
E-mail: hunterclch@clanhunter.info
Home Page: http://www.clanhunter.com

• 5665 • **The Order of the Royal Huntsman**
For outstanding personal contributions to Clan Hunter. A plaque is awarded annually. Established in 1988.

• 5666 •
College of Piping
Robert Wallace, Prin.
16-24 Otago St.
Glasgow G12 8JH, United Kingdom
Phone: 44 141 334 3587
Fax: 44 141 337 6068
E-mail: college@college-of-piping.co.uk
Home Page: http://www.college-of-piping.co.uk

• 5667 • **Balvenie Medal**
For recognition of services to piping. A silver medal, struck in Edinburgh, which carries a likeness of William Grant, the founder of The Glenfiddich Distillery, on the face is awarded annually. Established in 1985.

• 5668 • **Glenfiddich Trophy**
For recognition of outstanding piping. There are two panels of three judges for each of the two sections of the championships: 1. Piobaireachd, with each piper submitting six tunes in advance from which the judges will select one; and 2. March, Strathspey, and Reel, with the judges selecting three tunes from those submitted. The following prizes are awarded: first overall prize - one year's retention of the Glenfiddich Trophy, £600, and an inscribed sgian dhu; second prize - £300; and third prize - £150. Additional prizes are also awarded annually. Established in 1974.

• 5669 •
Commonwealth Association of Architects
Tony Godwin, Exec.Dir.
PO Box 508
London HA8 9XZ, United Kingdom
Phone: 44 20 74903024
Fax: 44 20 72532592
E-mail: info@comarchitect.org
Home Page: http://comarchitect.org

• 5670 • **Robert Matthew Award**
For recognition of specific buildings which, in the opinion of member institutes (39 in the Commonwealth), show a significant response to the cultural, physical, and climatic context of the country. A scroll is awarded triannually at the CAA General Assembly. Established in 1965 in honor of Sir Robert Matthew, founder and first President of the Association. Formerly: (1983) CAA National Awards.

• 5671 •
Commonwealth Association of Science, Technology and Mathematics Educators
Ms. Lyn Haynes, Sec.
Commonwealth House
7 Lion Yard
Tremadoc Rd.
Clapham
London SW4 7NQ, United Kingdom
Phone: 44 20 78193932
Fax: 44 20 77205403
E-mail: natasha.ludlum@lect.org.uk
Home Page: http://www.castme.org

Formerly: (1982) Commonwealth Association of Science and Mathematics Educators.

• 5672 • **CASTME Awards**
To encourage teaching of the social significance of science, technology and mathematics around the world. The scope of the awards is interpreted broadly, and social aspects includes the relevance of science, technology and mathematics curricula to local needs and conditions and to the impact of technology, industry and agriculture on the local community. Teachers and officials (advisors, inspectors, etc.) working in primary, secondary and tertiary education in Commonwealth countries are eligible to enter. Individuals or syndicates may enter. Judging is based on the following criteria: evidence of originality and creativity; evidence of use practicability and cost effectiveness. (Entries based on ideas, proposals or general arguments which have not been tried out are not acceptable); evidence of evaluation of the idea or material in use; evidence of the social relevance of the project; and standards of presentation of the report. In addition to a small money prize donated by CASTME, a few traveling fellowships may be awarded at the discretion of the Judges. These fellowships, the gift of the Commonwealth Foundation and RASIT enable the prize-winners to do more innovative work. Awarded annually. Established in 1974. Sponsored by the Commonwealth Foundation. Formerly: (1982) CASME Award.

• 5673 •
Commonwealth Forestry Association
David Bills, Pres.
Crib
Dinchope
Shropshire
Oxfordshire
Craven Arms SY7 9JJ, United Kingdom
Phone: 44 1588 672868
Fax: 44 870 116645
E-mail: cfa@cfa-international.org
Home Page: http://www.cfa-international.org

• 5674 • **Tom Gill Memorial Award**
To encourage literary achievement in forestry related subjects. Essays may be submitted. A monetary award and a medal with Tom GillKs head and CFA logo are presented annually at each Commonwealth Forestry Conference. Bequeathed in 1972 Bequeathed by Tom Gill through his will.

• 5675 • **Queen's Award for Forestry**
To recognize an individual for mid-career forestry achievement with the potential to benefit and communicate to others in the land-based disciplines. Members of the Commonwealth between 30 and 55 years of age are eligible. A travel fellowship worth £3,000 approximately and a scroll signed by Her Majesty are awarded every 2 years. Established in 1987 by Her Majesty Queen Elizabeth.

• 5676 • **Schlich Memorial Trust Award**
To recognize services to forestry around the world. Any entrant considered by the trustees as suitable is eligible. A monetary award is presented annually. Established in 1928 in memory of Sir William Schlich former Inspector General of Forests in India.

• 5677 •
Commonwealth Foundation
Dr. Mark Collins, Dir.
Marlborough House
Pall Mall
London SW1Y 5HY, United Kingdom
Phone: 44 20 79303783
Fax: 44 20 78398157
E-mail: geninfo@commonwealth.int
Home Page: http://www.commonwealthfoundation.com

• 5678 • **Commonwealth Short Story Competition**
To recognize short stories suitable for radio. The original short stories must be in English, be no more than 4 - 5 minutes in duration, and must be previously unpublished. Commonwealth citizens are eligible. Winning stories will be read by high quality actors, recorded in the BBC World Service Studios London and broadcast throughout the Commonwealth on national broadcasting stations. First prize also consists of £2,000; three regional winners receive £500; and 22 runners-up receive £100. Awarded annually. Administered by Commonwealth Broadcasting Association

• 5679 • **Commonwealth Writers Prize**
To reward and encourage writing in all parts of the Commonwealth. A major prize of £10,000 for the best entry and an award of £3,000 for the best newly published book are awarded annually for works of fiction. These are selected from eight regional winners, who each receive prizes of £1,000. Administered by the Book Trust. Established in 1987.

• 5680 • **Fellowship Scheme to Promote Commonwealth Understanding**
To encourage professionals of influence to undertake a one-month program on Commonwealth affairs. Twelve fellowships are awarded annually. Fellowships are not available on personal application. Commonwealth institutions are invited to nominate suitable candidates for consideration by a selection committee made up of members of the Board of Governors.

• 5681 • **Fellowships in Arts and Crafts**
To promote excellence in arts and crafts and to foster Commonwealth cooperation. Ten fellowships are offered biennially to craftspeople and artists aged between 20 and 35.

• 5682 • **Medical Electives Bursaries**
To encourage medical students to undertake their elective period of work/study in a Commonwealth country other than their own. Approximately 45 bursaries of up to £1,000 each are offered annually. Administered by the Association of Commonwealth Universities.

• 5683 •
Commonwealth Games Federation
(Federation des Jeux du Commonwealth)
Michael Hooper, CEO
2nd Fl., 138 Piccadilly
Mayfair
London W1J 7NR, United Kingdom
Phone: 44 20 74918801
Fax: 44 20 74097803
E-mail: info@thecgf.com
Home Page: http://www.thecgf.com

• 5684 • **Commonwealth Games Federation**
To promote quadrennial Commonwealth games for amateur sport. Competitors representing constituent parts of the Commonwealth are eligible. Medals are awarded at victory ceremonies to three competitors in each sport.

• 5685 •
Commonwealth Pharmaceutical Association
Grace Allen Young, Pres.
1 Lambeth High St.
London SE1 7JN, United Kingdom
Phone: 44 207 7522364
Fax: 44 207 7522508
E-mail: admin@commonwealthpharmacy.org
Home Page: http://www.commonwealthpharmacy.org

• 5686 • **Albert Howells Award**
Recognizes outstanding contributions to pharmacy at the commonwealth level. Applicants must be pharmacists. Awarded annually to one or more recipients.

• 5687 •
Commonwealth Press Union - United Kingdom
Lindsay Ross, Exec.Dir.
17 Fleet St.
London EC4Y 1AA, United Kingdom
Phone: 44 207 5837733
Fax: 44 207 5836868
E-mail: lindsay@cpu.org.uk
Home Page: http://www.cpu.org.uk

• 5688 • **Astor Award**
Recognizes contribution to press freedom. Individuals exhibiting distinguished service to the commonwealth newspaper industry are eligible. Awarded biennially.

• 5689 • **Commonwealth Press Union Scholarships**
To promote high standards of journalistic ethics and literacy, and to uphold the principles of press freedom and free expression. Working journalists employed by newspapers and news agencies in membership in the Commonwealth Press Union are eligible. Fellowships and scholarships are awarded.

• 5690 •
Commonwealth Youth Programme
Andrews Simmons, Chief Programme Off.
Commonwealth Secretariat
Marlborough House, Pall Mall
London SW1Y 5HX, United Kingdom
Phone: 44 20 7747 6262
Fax: 44 20 7747 6549
E-mail: cyp@commonwealth.int
Home Page: http://www.thecommonwealth.org/CYP

• 5691 • **Commonwealth Youth Service Awards**
To recognize and reward the contribution made by young people in working collectively to develop their societies and to foster cooperation and exchange of ideas and experience among young people of the Commonwealth. Awards are made to projects nominated by governments that: are examples of effective teamwork by young people, preferably aged 15 to 25; are devised, set up and maintained by young people themselves; respond to and meet a local need; show potential for long-term effectiveness; and provide a model or inspiration to other localities both nationally and Commonwealth-wide. Applications must be passed through appropriate government departments and then to the relevant CYP Regional Center. A monetary award of £1,000 toward further development of the project and a certificate are awarded annually. In addition, personal mementos such as medallions for each member of the award-winning project teams are presented. Established in 1985.

• 5692 •
Concrete Society
Martin Powell, Chief Exec.
Riverside House
4 Meadows Business Park
Sta. Approach Blackwater
Surrey
Camberley GU17 9AB, United Kingdom
Phone: 44 1276 607140
Fax: 44 1276 607141
E-mail: enquiries@concrete.org.uk
Home Page: http://www.concrete.org.uk

• 5693 • **Concrete Society Awards**
To recognize excellence in the use of concrete in new structures, both in Civil Engineering and Building capacity. Entries have historically ranged from private houses, bridges, acoustic sound barring walls, waste water treatment works, theatre, museums, art centres, underground stations, and innovative sculpture. Criteria include excellence in the functional use of the material coupled with its harmony and appearance in the context of its surroundings, as well as workmanship and cost effectiveness. Plaques and certificates are awarded annually. Established in 1968.

• 5694 •
Conservation Foundation
David Shreeve, Exec.Dir.
1 Kensington Gore
London SW7 2AR, United Kingdom
Phone: 44 207 5913111
Fax: 44 207 5913110
E-mail: info@conservationfoundation.co.uk
Home Page: http://www.conservationfoundation.co.uk

• 5695 • **Young Scientists for Rainforests**
To enable young scientists to develop their ethno-medical research work. Grants of about £1,000 are available. Established in 1985.

• 5696 •
Thomas Cook Publishing
PO Box 227
Peterborough PE3 8SB, United Kingdom
Phone: 44 1733 416477
Fax: 44 1733 416688
E-mail: publishing-sales@thomascook.com
Home Page: http://www.thomascookpublishing.com

• 5697 • **Thomas Cook Travel Book Award**
To encourage the art of travel writing by recognizing the best travel narrative book. Books written in English and published during the preceding year may be submitted. A monetary prize of £10,000 is awarded for the best travel book. Awarded annually. Established in 1980.

• 5698 •
Dr. M. Aylwin Cotton Foundation
% Albany Trustee Co., Ltd.
PO Box 232
Newport House 15
The Grange, St. Peter Port
Guernsey GY1 4LA, United Kingdom
Phone: 44 1481 724136
Fax: 44 1481 710478
E-mail: info@cotton-foundation.org
Home Page: http://www.cotton-foundation.org

• 5699 • **Dr. M. Aylwin Cotton Foundation Fellowship Awards**
To provide fellowships for studies in the archaeology, architecture, history, language and arts of the Mediterranean. Persons engaged in academic research, normally of postdoctoral standard (although no formal academic qualifications are necessary) may apply by February 28. Fellowships are normally of one year's duration and may exceptionally be renewable. Up to £10,000 is awarded to cover the costs of accommodation, travel, photography, photocopying and all other expenses relating to the work for which the Fellowship is awarded. Fellows are expected to arrange for the publication of their research. Awarded annually. Established in 1971 by Dr. M. Aylwin Cotton.

• 5700 • **Dr. M. Aylwin Cotton Foundation Publication Grants**
To provide publication grants for studies in the archaeology, architecture, history, language, and art of the Mediterranean. Applicants, who should be either the author or the editor of the work, should supply a brief account of the proposed publication, the name of the publisher, and an estimate of the likely cost of publication. The grants are open to men and women of all nationalities. The deadline for application is February 28. The costs of publication of academic research already completed or imminently available for publication are awarded annually. Established in 1971 by Dr. M. Aylwin Cotton.

• 5701 •
Craft Guild of Chefs
Suzanne Barshall, Hd. Office Mgr.
1 Victoria Parade
331 Sandycombe Rd.
Surrey
Richmond TW9 3NB, United Kingdom
Phone: 44 208 9483870
Fax: 44 208 3326326
E-mail: sbarshall@craft-guild.org
Home Page: http://www.craft-guild.org

• 5702 • **Chef of the Year**
For a chef who demonstrates exceptional technical skills and produces food with flavor, texture, balance and style.

• 5703 • **Craft Guild of Chefs Awards**
For member and nonmember chefs.

• 5704 • **Graduate Awards**
For chefs, below 23 years old, who have 3 years experience in any sector of food service industry.

• 5705 •
Crime Writers' Association
Lindsey Davis, Chair
PO Box 6939
Birmingham B14 7LT, United Kingdom
Phone: 44 121 4442536
Fax: 44 121 4442536
E-mail: info@thecwa.co.uk
Home Page: http://www.thecwa.co.uk

• 5706 • **Cartier Diamond Dagger Award**
To recognize an author for lifetime achievement to the genre of crime writing. Selection is based on sustained excellence and significant contribution. Works can be translation but must be published in English. A diamond dagger is awarded annually. Sponsored by Cartier. Established in 1986.

• 5707 • **John Creasey Memorial Award**
For recognition of the best crime novel of the year by an author who has not been previously published. A monetary prize of £1,000 and a magnifying glass are awarded annually. Established in 1973 in memory of John Creasey, founder of Crime Writers' Association. Sponsored by Chivers Press.

• 5708 • **The CWA Gold Dagger for Nonfiction**
For recognition of the best nonfiction writing on crime. An independent panel of doctors, policemen, and other experts make the selection. A monetary prize of £2,000 and an gold-plated dagger are awarded annually. Established in 1978.

• 5709 • **Debut Dagger**
Recognizes unpublished works of crime fiction. Opening pages (up to 3000 words) of the novel and a 500 word outline of its progression must be submitted. A monterary prize of £250 is awarded. Submission deadline is August 10. A £10 entry fee must also be submitted. Sponsored by Orion. Established in 1998.

• 5710 • **Duncan Lawrie Dagger**
For recognition of the best crime novel published in the United Kingdom during the year. A monetary prize of £20,000 and an ornamental dagger is awarded annually. Sponsored by Duncan Lawrie Private Bank. Formerly: (2006) Macallan Gold Dagger For Fiction.

• 5711 • **The Ian Flemming Steel Dagger**
Recognizes contemporary thriller writing. Adventure novels, spy novels, and thrillers first published in the United Kingdom, in English between September 1st and August 31st of the judging year are eligible. £2000 is awarded annually. Suggested and sponsored by Ian Fleming (Glidrose) Publications Ltd. Established in 2002.

• 5712 • **Ellis Peters Historical Crime Award**
For writers of historical crime fiction. A monetary prize of £3,000 and an ornamental dagger are awarded annually. Established in honor of Ellis Peters. Sponsored by Estate of Ellis Peters, Headline Book Publishing, and Little, Brown & Co.

• 5713 • **Short Story Dagger**
To recognize the best published short story of the year submitted by publishers. Panels of judges vary from year to year. The winner receives £1500 and a Dagger lapel pin. Awarded annually. Established in 1993.

• 5714 •
Cromwell Association
Ms. Pat Barnes, Contact
Dawgates Cottage
Dawgates Ln.
Skegby
Sutton NG17 3DA, United Kingdom
Phone: 44 207 347341
Fax: 44 207 314095
E-mail: cromwellmuseum@cambridgeshire.gov.uk
Home Page: http://www.olivercromwell.org

• 5715 • **Cromwell Essay Competition**
For recognition of the best essay and/or artwork on the period of Oliver Cromwell and the history

of the Commonwealth and Protectorate. Students are eligible. £150 is awarded in the category of 15-18 years of age. £250 is awarded in the category of 19 years and older. Awarded biennially. Application deadline is December 31.

• 5716 •
Cystic Fibrosis Trust
Rosie Barnes, Chief Exec.
11 London Rd.
Bromley BR1 1BY, United Kingdom
Phone: 44 20 8464 7211
Fax: 44 20 8313 0472
E-mail: enquiries@cftrust.org.uk
Home Page: http://www.cftrust.org.uk

• 5717 • **John Panchaud Medallions**
For recognition of valuable service in the fight against cystic fibrosis and the Cystic Fibrosis Research Trust since its formation in 1964. Selection is by nomination. Medals and certificates are awarded occasionally. Established in 1983 with the agreement of the Panchaud family in honor of John Panchaud.

• 5718 •
Daiwa Anglo-Japanese Foundation
Prof. Marie Conte-Helm, Dir.Gen.
Daiwa Foundation Japan House
13/14 Cornwall Terrace
London NW1 4QP, United Kingdom
Phone: 44 20 7486 4348
Fax: 44 20 7486 2914
E-mail: office@dajf.org.uk
Home Page: http://www.daiwa-foundation.org.uk

• 5719 • **Daiwa Scholarships**
To enable outstanding young UK graduates of any discipline to acquire a lasting knowledge of Japanese life and culture and of spoken and written Japanese. Individuals must be citizens of the United Kingdom. Application deadline is December. Nineteen-month scholarships, including grants, tuition fees, and travel expenses, are awarded annually. One-year scholarships may be awarded to candidates with an excellent grasp of spoken and written Japanese. Awarded annually to numerous recipients. Established in 1991.

• 5720 •
Data Publishers Association
Christine Scott, Hd.
Queens House
28 Kingsway
London WC2B 6JR, United Kingdom
Phone: 44 20 74050836
Fax: 44 20 74044167
E-mail: christine.scott@dpassoc.org
Home Page: http://www.dpa.org.uk

• 5721 • **Advertising Sales Team of the Year**
For the teams that have made a significant impact on the business.

• 5722 • **Best Marketing**
For both subscription and marketing campaigns.

• 5723 • **Directory of the Year - Business**
For consistently high-quality directory, either in print or online.

• 5724 • **Directory of the Year - Consumer**
For consistently high-quality directory, either in print or online.

• 5725 • **New Product of the Year**
To a new directory, database or search engine

• 5726 • **Online Directory of the Year - Business**
For covering websites, cd, search engines or other online product offering.

• 5727 • **Online Directory of the Year - Consumer**
For covering websites, cd, search engines or other online product offering.

• 5728 • **Printer of the Year**
To a printer with a proven track record of excelling in their field.

• 5729 • **Publisher of the Year**
To the most successful publisher of the year.

• 5730 • **Subscription Sales Team of the Year**
For the teams that have made a significant impact on the business.

• 5731 • **Supplier of the Year**
To a supplier with a proven track record of excelling in their field.

• 5732 •
Delphinium Society
Mrs. Shirley E. Bassett, Membership Sec.
Summerfield
Church Rd.
Biddestone
Chippenham SN14 7DP, United Kingdom
E-mail: david.bassett@care4free.net
Home Page: http://www.backyardgardener.com/delp

• 5733 • **Delphinium Society Awards**
To encourage the culture of delphiniums and the production of new and improved varieties by sponsoring competitions. Cups, medals, and certificates of merit are awarded. No further information on awards is available for this edition.

• 5734 •
Design Council
David Kester, CEO
34 Bow St.
London WC2E 7DL, United Kingdom
Phone: 44 207 4205200
Fax: 44 207 4205300
E-mail: info@designcouncil.org.uk
Home Page: http://www.design-council.org.uk

• 5735 • **British Design Awards**
To promote the importance of good design by identifying and publicizing outstanding examples of British design within the areas of medical equipment, automotive, computer software, consumer and contract goods, and engineering products and components. Products that have been in production and service for some time and were designed by a British designer working in the U.K. or abroad, or by a designer resident in the U.K. are eligible. Certificates are awarded and publicity and the use of the British Design Award logo are also provided. Established in 1957. Formerly: Design Council Awards.

• 5736 • **Prince Philip Prize for the Designer of the Year**
To recognize the designer who has made the greatest contribution to design. A certificate is presented to the winner at a ceremony at Buckingham Palace by Prince Philip. Awarded annually. Established in 1958 in honor of Prince Philip. Additional information is available from the Design Council's Award Office. Formerly: Duke of Edinburgh's Designer's Prize.

• 5737 •
Direct Marketing Association
Janet Attwater, Head of Events
DMA House
70 Margaret Street
London W1W 8SS, United Kingdom
Phone: 44 20 7291 3343
Fax: 44 20 7291 4426
E-mail: janet@dma.org.uk
Home Page: http://www.dmaawards.org.uk

Formerly: (2004) British Direct Marketing Association.

• 5738 • **DMA Awards, in Association with Royal Mail**
To recognize outstanding work in direct marketing in each of the 32 categories such as digital media, direct mail, fund raising, and integrated campaign. The material needs to fulfill the criteria requirements for its particular category and is judged on results, strategy and creativity. Work must have appeared before August of the previous year. A Grand Prix award is presented to the overall winner for the most outstanding work selected from the winner of each category. A trophy is presented to the winner in each of the 32 categories. Awarded annually. Established in 1980 and sponsored by Royal Mail. Open to UK based companies. Formerly: BDMA/Post Office Direct Marketing Awards; (2004) DMA/Royal Mail Direct Marketing Awards.

• 5739 •
Dorset Natural History and Archaeological Society
Dorset County Museum
High West St.
Dorchester DT1 1XA, United Kingdom
Phone: 44 1305 262735
Fax: 44 1305 257180
E-mail: dorsetcountymuseum@dor-mus.demon.co.uk
Home Page: http://www.dor-mus.demon.co.uk

Formed by merger of: (1928) Dorset Natural History; Antiquarian Field Club.

• 5740 • **Mansel-Pleydell and Cecil Trusts**
To encourage papers on Dorset archaeology, geology, local and natural history, containing original research and material hitherto unpublished. Papers must be submitted by persons living in Dorset or having past or present connections with the county by December 31 in any year. A monetary prize of £1,000 is awarded annually on the last Tuesday in June. Established about 1905 in honor of J.C. Mansel-Pleydell Esq and Lord Eustace Cecil.

• 5741 •
Dracula Society
(Societe du Comte Dracula)
Dr. Tina Rath, Contact
PO Box 30848
London W12 0GY, United Kingdom
E-mail: thedraculasociety@yahoo.com
Home Page: http://www.thedraculasociety.org.uk

• 5742 • **Hamilton Deane Award**
For recognition of the most significant contribution to the gothic genre in the performing arts. Any performance or technical contribution to a production in a given year is eligible. The winner is voted upon by the members of the Society. A framed scroll is awarded annually. Established in 1974 in memory of Hamilton Deane, the dramatizer of "Dracula." Formerly: (1977) Actor of the Year Award.

• 5743 •
Dry Stone Walling Association of Great Britain
Jacqui Simkins, Sec.
Westmorland County Showground
Lane Farm
Crooklands
Milnthorpe
Cumbria LA7 7NH, United Kingdom
Phone: 44 1539 567953
Fax: 44 121 3780493
E-mail: information@dswa.org.uk
Home Page: http://www.dswa.org.uk

• 5744 • **Certificates in Dry Stone Walling**
Awarded for competency at various levels in dry stone walling. Certificates are awarded when merited.

• 5745 •
Duff Cooper Prize
54 St. Maur Rd.
London SW6 4DP, United Kingdom
Phone: 44 171 736 3729
Fax: 44 171 731 7638
Home Page: http://www.duffcooperprize.org.uk

Formerly: Duff Cooper Memorial Prize.

• 5746 • **Duff Cooper Prize**
To recognize work written in English or French on the subjects of history, biography, politics, or poetry published within the last year. A monetary award and a presentation copy of Duff Cooper's autobiography *Old Men Forget* are awarded annually. The Prize was founded by Duff Cooper's friends after his death in 1954. Duff Cooper was a statesman, diplomat and author who was born in 1890. Formerly: Duff Cooper Memorial Prize.

• 5747 •
Edinburgh Architectural Association
Colin Gilmour, Pres.
15 Rutland Sq.
Edinburgh EH1 2BE, United Kingdom
Phone: 44 131 2297545
Fax: 44 131 2282188
E-mail: mail@eaa.org.uk
Home Page: http://www.eaa.org.uk

• 5748 • **Bronze Medal**
For a building within the chapter area that has been sensitively restored converted or refurbished by a chartered architect, while at the same time demonstrating excellence in design and detail.

• 5749 • **Silver Medal**
To acknowledge and publicize excellence in architecture in a building within the chapter area.

• 5750 • **Small Projects Award**
To acknowledge and publicize excellence in architecture for a completed project within the chapter area with a contract sum of under 200,.

• 5751 •
Edinburgh Festival Fringe
Louise Page, Press Off.
180 High St.
Edinburgh EH1 1QS, United Kingdom
Phone: 44 131 2260026
Fax: 44 131 2204205
E-mail: admin@edfringe.com
Home Page: http://www.edfringe.com

• 5752 • **Perrier Award**
For recognition of the most outstanding revue/cabaret in the Edinburgh Festival Fringe. Judging is by a panel of experts and three members of the public. The winner leads the Perrier Pick of the Fringe Season at a leading London theater and receives a monetary award of £3,000. Established in 1981.

• 5753 • **Scotsman Fringe First Awards**
To encourage presentation of new works of drama. Eligible plays must have been performed not more than six times in the United Kingdom and must be entered in the Fringe Program. Awarded every week of the Fringe in August. Established in 1974.

• 5754 • **Stage Awards for Acting Excellence**
To recognize acting excellence at the Edinburgh Festival Fringe. Companies/performers listed in the Theatre section of the Fringe program will be considered. Awards are presented in two categories: Best Actor, and Best Actress. Established in 1995.

• 5755 •
Edinburgh International Film Festival
Ginnie Atkinson, Mng.Dir.
Filmhouse
88 Lothian Rd.
Edinburgh EH3 9BZ, United Kingdom
Phone: 44 131 228 4051
Fax: 44 131 229 5501
E-mail: info@edfilmfest.org.uk
Home Page: http://www.edfilmfest.org.uk

• 5756 • **Edinburgh International Film Festival**
For recognition of outstanding films screened at the Festival. The following prizes are awarded: Michael Powell Award - for the best new British feature; McLaren Award - for best new British animation; Standard Life Audience Award - audience vote; Guardian New Director's Award - recognizing innovation; Kodak U.K. Film Council Award - for best British short film; European Film Academy Short Film Award/Priz UIP - for the best new filmmaker; and Saltire Society Award - for best short documentary. eld annually. Established in 1947.

• 5757 •
Egypt Exploration Society
Dr. Patricia Spencer PhD, Sec.Gen.
3 Doughty Mews
London WC1N 2PG, United Kingdom
Phone: 44 207 2421880
Fax: 44 207 4046118
E-mail: eeslondon@talk21.com
Home Page: http://www.ees.ac.uk

• 5758 • **Egypt Exploration Society Centenary Studentship**
To encourage projects relating to the aims of the Society, which are to undertake Egyptological researches, whether in Egypt or abroad, and publish the results. Applications must be submitted by February of each year. A monetary award is presented annually in March. Established in 1984 to honor the Centenary of the Egypt Exploration Society in 1982.

Awards are arranged in alphabetical order below their administering organizations

• 5759 •
ENCAMS: Keep Britain Tidy
Elizabeth House
The Pier
Wigan WN3 4EX, United Kingdom
Phone: 44 1942 612621
Fax: 44 1942 824778
E-mail: cardbyneo@tidybritain.org.uk
Home Page: http://www.encams.org

• 5760 • **Britain in Bloom Awards**
To recognize cities, towns and villages for improvements in overall appearance through the planting of trees, shrubs, and flowers, increasing local pride in the environment, and attracting more business and tourism. Nominations may be submitted by the Tourist Boards of England, Scotland, Wales, Northern Ireland, Isle of Man, Jersey, and Guernsey. Awarded annually.

• 5761 •
Energy Institute
John Collins, Pres.
61 New Cavendish St.
London W1G 7AR, United Kingdom
Phone: 44 207 4677100
Fax: 44 207 2551472
E-mail: info@energyinst.org.uk
Home Page: http://www.energyinst.org.uk

• 5762 • **Energy Manager of the Year Award**
To individual energy professional in the field of energy management.

• 5763 • **Malchett Medal**
For outstanding work involving the scientific preparation or use of energy, the results of which have recently been made available to the community.

• 5764 • **Thring Award**
For outstanding project which demonstrates the likelihood of significant energy savings from recommendations.

• 5765 •
Engineers' Company
Robert Hawley CBE, Master
Wax Chandlers Hall
Gresham St.
London EC2V 7AD, United Kingdom
Phone: 44 20 77264830
Fax: 44 20 77264820
E-mail: clerk@engineerscompany.org.uk
Home Page: http://www.engineerscompany.org.uk

• 5766 • **The Baroness Platt of Writtle Award**
To individuals pursuing final year studies in the Engineering Council's Incorporated Engineer Grade.

• 5767 • **Cadzow Smith Award**
Tor excellence on an accredited undergraduate engineering course.

• 5768 • **The Mercia Prize - Postgraduate Bursary in Medical Engineering**
To a student under 30 years old.

• 5769 • **Service Awards**
To officers and NCOs.

• 5770 • **Young Consulting Engineers Award**
to professional engineers.

• 5771 •
England Basketball
Mr. Keith Mair, CEO
Coleridge Rd.
Stanningley
Sheffield S9 5DA, United Kingdom
Phone: 44 870 7744225
Fax: 44 870 7744226
E-mail: info@englandbasketball.co.uk
Home Page: http://www.englandbasketball.co.uk

• 5772 • **Coach of the Year**
To recognize outstanding basketball coaches. Awarded annually. Established in 1976.

• 5773 • **English Basket Ball Association Player of the Year (Men and Women)**
To recognize basketball achievement in the National Competitions. English players registered for National Competitions are eligible for the award. Trophies are presented annually. Established in 1971.

• 5774 • **Fair Play Award**
To recognize the player registered in National Competitions whose attitude and approach to basketball is the most sportsmanlike. Awarded annually. Established in 1973.

• 5775 • **National Championship Cup Finals**
To recognize the championship team from the men's and women's finals held among the National League Divisions. The George Williams Trophy is awarded annually. The Men's National Championship Cup Finals were established in 1936. The Women's National Championship Cup Finals were established in 1965. In the 1980-81 season the Women's Competition was reorganized, and two separate competitions were held - the National Cup, which is an open competition for all clubs, and the National Championship, which is a play off between the top teams in the National League.

• 5776 • **National League Player of the Year**
To recognize basketball achievement in National competitions. Any player registered for National Competitions is eligible. A memento is presented annually. Established in 1976/1977.

• 5777 •
English Centre of International PEN
Dr. Alastair Niven, Pres.
6-8 Amwell St.
London EC1R 1UQ, United Kingdom
Phone: 44 20 7713 0023
Fax: 44 20 7837 7838
E-mail: enquiries@englishpen.org
Home Page: http://www.englishpen.org

• 5778 • **J. R. Ackerley Prize for Autobiography**
For recognition of outstanding literary achievement. Trustees of the J.R. Ackerley Trust consider submissions are not required autobiographies published during the previous calendar year. A monetary prize is awarded annually at the PEN International Writers' Day. Established in 1982 to honor Joe Randolph Ackerley by his sister Nancy.

• 5779 •
English Folk Dance and Song Society
Hazel Miller, Chief Officer
Cecil Sharp House
2 Regents Park Rd.
London NW1 7AY, United Kingdom
Phone: 44 207 4852206
Fax: 44 207 2840534
E-mail: info@efdss.org
Home Page: http://www.efdss.org

• 5780 • **Gold Badge**
For recognition of an outstanding contribution to folk music or dance. A medal/badge is awarded annually to one or more recipients. Established in 1922 by the English Folk Dance Society.

• 5781 •
Entertainment and Leisure Software Publishers Association
Roger Bennett, Dir.Gen.
167 Wardour St.
London W1F 8WL, United Kingdom
Phone: 44 20 75340580
Fax: 44 20 75340581
E-mail: info@elspa.com
Home Page: http://www.elspa.com

• 5782 • **Volume Sales Achievement Award**
Recognizes retail sales of published software titles achieving 100,000 (Silver), 200,000 (Gold), and 300,000 (Platinum) units within 12 months of release.

• 5783 •
Environmental Transport Association
Tracy Philpot, Contact
68 High St.
Weybridge KT13 8RS, United Kingdom
Phone: 44 1932 828882
Fax: 44 1932 829015
E-mail: eta@eta.co.uk
Home Page: http://www.eta.co.uk

Awards are arranged in alphabetical order below their administering organizations

• 5784 • **Green Apple Awards**
To recognize motor manufacturers based on a rating of various environmental factors. Awarded annually.

• 5785 •
Ephemera Society
Lord Briggs, Pres.
PO Box 112
Middlesex
Northwood HA6 2WT, United Kingdom
Phone: 44 1923 829079
Fax: 44 1923 825207
E-mail: info@ephemera-society.org.uk
Home Page: http://www.ephemera-society.org.uk

• 5786 • **Samuel Pepys Medal**
For recognition of outstanding contributions to ephemera studies. Ephemera are defined by the Society as the "transient minor documents of everyday life." A medal is awarded approximately every two years at a special ceremony in November. The medal is a gold-plated replica of a seventeenth century ivory medallion preserved at Magdalene College, Cambridge. Established in 1980 in memory of Samuel Pepys, the British diarist and early collector of ephemera.

• 5787 •
Ergonomics Society - England
John Cotton, Business Mgr.
Elms Ct.
Elms Grove
Leicestershire
Loughborough LE11 1RG, United Kingdom
Phone: 44 1509 234904
Fax: 44 1509 235666
E-mail: ergsoc@ergonomics.org.uk
Home Page: http://www.ergonomics.org.uk

• 5788 • **Ulf Aberg Post Graduate Award**
To recognize the best postgraduate student project in ergonomics. The postgraduate project should be in an area of ergonomics; however, the postgraduate course need not be one recognized by the Society. Entries may be submitted by the student's supervisor or head of department by July 31. Winners receive a monetary award of £100. (If the subject is in the field of consumer ergonomics, then this may be supplemented by a further £25 from the Institute of Consumer Ergonomics.) In addition, a certificate and expenses to attend the Annual Dinner are awarded. Established in 1977. Formerly: (1985) Student Award - Postgraduate Division.

• 5789 • **Sir Frederic Bartlett Medal**
To honor an individual(s) who has made significant contributions to original research, the development of methodology, or application of knowledge within the field of ergonomics. Entries may be submitted by October 31. A medal, a certificate and expenses to attend the Annual Dinner are awarded annually when merited. Established in 1971. Submissions for all of the Society's awards should be sent to: Ergonomics Society Honours, The Ergonomics Society Office, Department of Human Sciences, University of Technology, Loughborough, Leics. LE11 3TU, United Kingdom.

• 5790 • **Otto Edholm Award**
To honor an individual or individuals who have made significant contributions to basic or applied research in ergonomics. Entries may be submitted by October 31. A certificate and expenses to attend the Annual Dinner are awarded. The award was established to honor Otto Edholm who was born in 1909 and studied Medicine at St George's Hospital, London.

• 5791 • **Ergonomics Society Lecturer**
A member of the Ergonomics Community is honored by giving a lecture to the Society. Quality of work and presentation ability are considered. The topic varies from year to year and when possible, takes account of contemporary issues. A plaque and travel expenses incurred within the United Kingdom are awarded annually.

• 5792 • **Ergonomics Society Special Award**
To recognize an individual, individuals, institutes or groups for service or accomplishments inappropriate for other categories of award or honor. Entries may be submitted by July 31. A certificate and expenses to attend the Annual Dinner are awarded when merited. Established in 1985.

• 5793 • **The Ergonomics Society Student Prize**
Awarded to the writer of an essay whose title is set each year by the society.

• 5794 • **Ergonomics Society's Meritorious Service Award**
To recognize an individual for unstinting and altruistic service to the Society over many years. Entries may be submitted by October 31. A certificate and expenses to attend the Annual Dinner are awarded annually when merited. Established in 1984.

• 5795 • **William Floyd Award**
Awarded to individuals, institutions or groups who have made innovative or outstanding contributions to ergonomics.

• 5796 • **Richard Clive Holman Memorial Award**
Awarded to a writer of an outstanding essay on information technology linked to ergonomics.

• 5797 • **Honorary Fellow**
To recognize an individual who has made a significant contribution to ergonomics over a long period of time and is recognized as a senior member of the ergonomics community. A certificate is awarded.

• 5798 • **Hywel Murrell Award**
To recognize the best undergraduate student project in ergonomics. The undergraduate project should be in an area of ergonomics; however, the undergraduate course need not be one recognized by the Society. Entries may be submitted by the student's supervisor or head of department by July 31. Winners receive a monetary award of £100. (If the subject is in the field of consumer ergonomics, then this may be supplemented by a further £25 from the Institute of Consumer Ergonomics.) In addition, a certificate and expenses to attend the Annual Dinner are awarded. Established in 1977. Formerly: (1984) Student Award - Undergraduate Division.

• 5799 • **Paul Branton Meritorious Service Award**
Awarded for altruistic service to the society over many years.

• 5800 • **President's Medal**
Awarded to institutions or organizational groups whose work has made a significant contribution to original research, development of methods or application of knowledge within the field of ergonomics.

• 5801 • **Thales Human Factors Integration Award**
Awarded for significant contribution to ergonomics through the integration of human factors in complex systems development.

• 5802 •
EuroBest Awards
33-39 Bowling Green Ln.
London EC1R 0DA, United Kingdom
Phone: 44 207 2393434
Fax: 44 207 2393444
Home Page: http://www.eurobest.com

• 5803 • **EuroBest Awards**
For recognition of advertising excellence for campaigns presented in Europe across a range of media categories: Print, TV/Cinema, Outdoor, Radio, Interactive, Direct, and Integrated. Trophies are awarded annually at the awards ceremony in December. Established in 1988.

• 5804 •
European Association for Cancer Research
Paul Saunders, Administrator
School of Pharmacy
University of Nottingham
Nottingham NG7 2RD, United Kingdom
Phone: 44 115 9515114
Phone: 44 115 9515116
Fax: 44 115 9515115
E-mail: paul.saunders@nottingham.ac.uk
Home Page: http://www.eacr.org

• 5805 • **Anthony Dipple Carcinogenesis Award**
Recognizes outstanding contributions to research in the field of carcinogenesis. Awarded biennially in even-numbered years. Sponsored by Oxford University Press.

• 5806 • Faustus Poster Awards
Recognizes the best poster as selected by the EACR Committee for Reviewing Posters.

• 5807 • Travel Fellowships
To enable cancer researchers, preferably under 35 years of age, to undertake further research in another location. Researchers must be sponsored by members of the Association. Fellowships of up to 2,000 euros are awarded annually.

• 5808 • Young Cancer Researcher Award
To recognize a young cancer researcher (under the age of 40) from European countries to give a presentation at an EACR meeting. A monetary prize of 2,000 Euro plus expenses (travel, accommodation and congress fees) is awarded annually.

• 5809 • Young Cancer Researcher Award Lecture
Assists young scientists to attend conferences in order to present papers. Young scientists showing active participation by submission of abstracts for poster or oral presentation at the meeting are eligible. A monetary prize of 2,000 Euro plus travel expenses to present the paper are awarded biennially in even-numbered years.

• 5810 •
European Association for Cranio-Maxillofacial Surgery
John Lowry, Sec. Gen.
PO Box 85
Midhurst GU29 9WS, United Kingdom
Phone: 44 1730 810951
Fax: 44 1730 812042
E-mail: secretariat@eacmfs.org
Home Page: http://www.eurofaces.com

• 5811 • Implant Innovations Grant
For any member who wishes to study oral and maxillofacial surgery.

• 5812 • Leibinger Prize
For trainee members who wish to spend a period of targeted education and training within Europe away from their host programs.

• 5813 • Mondeal Prize
For members who published a meritorious paper in the period leading to the biennial congress.

• 5814 • Hugo Obwegeser Scholarship
For trainee members who wish to travel to other countries to enhance their education and training.

• 5815 •
European Association for Lexicography
Dr. Rosamund Moon, Sec.-Treas.
Department of English
University of Birmingham
Great Clarendon St.
Birmingham B15 2TT, United Kingdom
Phone: 44 121 4143076
Fax: 44 121 4143298
E-mail: euralex@euralex.org
Home Page: http://www.euralex.org

• 5816 • Verbatim Award
To support unpaid lexicographical work of any type, including study. A monetary grant ranging from £250 to £1,500 is awarded annually. Established in 1990 by *Verbatim, The Language Quarterly*.

• 5817 •
European Calcified Tissue Society
Richard Eastell, Pres.
PO Box 337
Bristol BS32 4ZR, United Kingdom
Phone: 44 1454 610255
Fax: 44 1454 610255
E-mail: r.eastell@sheffield.ac.uk
Home Page: http://www.ectsoc.org

• 5818 • Alliance for Better Bone Health Iain T. Boyle Award
For young scientists who have made significant progress and contribution to the field of bone and calcified tissue.

• 5819 • ECTS Career Establishment Award
To assist newly appointed faculty members in launching a successful research career.

• 5820 • ECTS Young Investigator Awards
For young investigators who have outstanding achievement in the field of bone and calcified tissue.

• 5821 •
European Consortium for Political Research
Clare Dekker, Admin. Dir.
University of Essex
Colchester CO4 3SQ, United Kingdom
Phone: 44 1206 872501
Phone: 44 1206 872497
Fax: 44 1206 872500
E-mail: ecpr@essex.ac.uk
Home Page: http://www.essex.ac.uk/ecpr/index1.aspx

• 5822 • ECPR PhD Prize
For the best thesis.

• 5823 • Stein Rokkan Prize
For social science research.

• 5824 • Standing Group Grant
To standing groups.

• 5825 • Wildenmann Prize
To the presenter of best paper at the workshop.

• 5826 •
European Council of International Schools
Dixie McKay, Exec.Dir./CEO
21B Lavant St.
Hampshire
Petersfield GU32 3EL, United Kingdom
Phone: 44 1730 268244
Fax: 44 1730 267914
E-mail: ecis@ecis.org
Home Page: http://www.ecis.org

• 5827 • Award for the Promotion of International Education
To recognize an adult for exemplary contributions to the promotion of international education. Members may submit nominations. A plaque may be awarded annually by each ECIS member institution.

• 5828 • European Council of International Schools Awards
For recognition in the field of education.

• 5829 • Student Award for International Understanding
To recognize students who are good representatives of their countries, display a positive attitude towards the life and culture of others, have the ability to converse in at least two languages, are contributing forces in the life of the school, and have an ability to bring different people together in a sense of community, thus furthering the cause of international understanding. Nominees are selected by the student's school faculty. Awarded annually to a student in each participating member school.

• 5830 •
European Council of Town Planners (Conseil Europeen des Urbanistes)
Robert Upton, Sec.Gen.
41 Botolph Ln.
London EC3R 8DL, United Kingdom
Phone: 44 207 9299494
Fax: 44 207 9298199
E-mail: secretariat@ceu-ectp.org
Home Page: http://www.ceu-ectp.org

• 5831 • European Urban and Regional Planning Achievement Awards
To recognize planning strategies, schemes, or developments that make an outstanding contribution to the quality of life in urban and rural regions of Europe. Awarded biennially in even-numbered years.

Awards are arranged in alphabetical order below their administering organizations

• 5832 •
European Federation of Societies for Ultrasound in Medicine and Biology
Mrs. Gianna Stanford, Gen.Sec.
Carpenters Ct.
4a Lewes Rd.
Bromley BR1 2RN, United Kingdom
Phone: 44 20 84028973
Fax: 44 20 84029344
E-mail: efsumb@efsumb.org
Home Page: http://www.efsumb.org

• 5833 • **Young Investigators Award**
To recognize and encourage new work in the fields of clinical and/or basic research. Members under 35 years of age are eligible. A monetary prize is awarded annually for first and second place recipients at the Federation Congress. Established in 1990.

• 5834 •
European Information Association
Eric Davies, Coor.
St. Peter's Sq.
Manchester M2 5PD, United Kingdom
Phone: 44 1244 552137
E-mail: eiamanager@btinternet.com
Home Page: http://www.eia.org.uk

• 5835 • **EIA Awards for European Information Sources**
To published and electronic sources.

• 5836 • **EIA/European Sources Online Award**
To the person who has achieved the most in promoting and advancing access to, and the quality of, information about the European Union and the wider Europe.

• 5837 • **Helen Greer Memorial Prize**
To a European Documentation Centre or European Reference Centre librarian who has made a particularly outstanding contribution to EDC/ERC librarianship.

• 5838 •
European Orthodontic Society
Prof. Luc Dermaut, Sec.
49 Hallam St., Flat 20
London W1W 6JN, United Kingdom
Phone: 44 20 79352795
Fax: 44 20 73230410
E-mail: eoslondon@aol.com
Home Page: http://www.eoseurope.org

• 5839 • **Beni Solow Award**
Established in honor of Beni Solow's work for the *European Journal of Orthodontics*. All papers published in the journal are eligible. £2500 (approximatel 3000 Euro) and a certificate are awarded.

• 5840 • **EOS Poster Award**
Recognizes an outstanding poster presented at the meeting on any topic. Posters entered for the Houston Research Award are not eligible. Non-members of the Society are eligible. Society members are not eligible. Three awards of £500 Sterling are awarded.

• 5841 • **EOS Research Grant**
Provides funding for research grants. A maximum of £10,000 is awarded. Announcements are published in the *European Journal of Orthodontics*. Applications are taken after the announcement.

• 5842 • **Ernest Sheldon Friel Memorial Lecture**
For recognition of work in the field of orthodontics. The award is associated with a named lecture known specifically as the Friel Memorial Lecture, which is presented at an annual congress and published in the Society's journal. Established in 1973 by the family of the late Professor Ernest Sheldon Friel to commemorate his services to orthodontics and to the European Orthodontic Society of which he was a president and honorary member. The recipient receives an honorarium of £500.

• 5843 • **Grants to Eastern Europeans**
Provides Eastern European countries the chance to visit educational facilities in the West. Full-time university postgraduate teachers are eligible. £2000 Sterling is awarded. Visit is scheduled for a period of up to one month.

• 5844 • **W. J. B. Houston Research Awards**
To recognize outstanding presentations at the annual congress. Awards are presented for the best research paper and the best poster presenting the results of original research on a topic of orthodontic interest. Papers and posters must be presented in English by a member under the age of 35. A scroll and monetary award of £1,000 is presented in each category. Established in 1993 in memory of W. J. B. Houston, honorary editor and past president and secretary of the Society.

• 5845 • **W. J. B. Houston Scholarship Award**
To recognize the research worker who has submitted the best prospective research proposal to the Society. A monetary award of £30,000 is awarded every three years. Established in 1993 in memory of W.J.B. Houston, honorary editor and past president and secretary of the Society.

• 5846 •
European Parliament
London Information Office
Josep Borrell, Pres.
2 Queen Anne's Gate
London SW1H 9AA, United Kingdom
Phone: 44 20 7227 4300
Fax: 44 20 7227 4302
E-mail: eplondon@europarl.eu.int
Home Page: http://www.europarl.eu.int

• 5847 • **European Parliament Sakharov Prize for Freedom of Thought**
To provide for study or work on one of the following topics: (1) the development of East-West relations in the light of the Helsinki Final Act, in particular the third basket on cooperation in humanitarian and other fields; (2) safeguarding the freedom of scientific inquiry; (3) the defense of human rights and respect for international law; and (4) government practice as compared with the letter of constitutional provisions. A monetary prize of 50,000 Euros is awarded annually. Established in 1986. Additional information is available from European Parliament, Centre European, Kirchberg, Luxembourg L-2929.

• 5848 •
European Process Safety Centre
165-189 Railway Terrace
Rugby CV21 3HQ, United Kingdom
Phone: 44 1 788 534409
Fax: 44 1 788 551542
E-mail: lallford-epsc@icheme.org.uk
Home Page: http://www.epsc.org/

• 5849 • **EPSC Award**
Recognizes outstanding contribution to process safety in Europe. Awarded annually.

• 5850 •
European Prosthodontic Association
Jeff Wilson, Honorary Sec.
Division of Adult Dental Health
Univ. Dental Hospital
Heath Park
Cardiff CF14 4XY, United Kingdom
Phone: 44 2920 743552
Fax: 44 2920 743120
E-mail: wilsonj@cardiff.ac.uk
Home Page: http://www.epadental.org

• 5851 • **Sidney Barrett Travel Grant**
For young researchers wishing to present their research at the annual conference.

• 5852 • **EPA Poster Prize**
For best poster presentation of original research at annual conference.

• 5853 • **EPA Prize**
For best oral presentation (from entries) at conference.

• 5854 • **Rowland Fereday Award**
For international collaborative research projects.

• 5855 •
European Society for Biomaterials
Liz Tanner, Sec.
IRC in Biomedical Materials and Department of Materials
Queen Mary University of London
Mile End Rd.
London E1 4NS, United Kingdom
Phone: 44 20 78825316
Fax: 44 20 89831799
E-mail: k.e.tanner@qmul.ac.uk
Home Page: http://www.esb-news.org

• 5856 • **Jean Laray Award**
For research in biomaterials.

• 5857 • **Student Prizes**
For the best student poster and oral presentation.

• 5858 • **Student Travel Awards**
For students.

• 5859 • **George Winter Award**
For research contribution to the field of biomaterials.

• 5860 •
European Society for Paediatric Endocrinology
Franco Chiarelli, Sec. Gen.
BioScientifica
Euro House
22 Apex Ct.
Woodlands
Bristol BS32 4JT, United Kingdom
Phone: 44 1454 642246
Fax: 44 1454 642222
E-mail: espe@bioscientifica.com
Home Page: http://www.eurospe.org

• 5861 • **Andrea Prader Prize**
For lifetime achievement in teaching and research.

• 5862 • **ESPE-Hormone Research Prize**
For best original paper published.

• 5863 • **ESPE Young Investigator Award**
To a young European pediatrician For his/her scientific publications.

• 5864 • **Henning Andersen Prizes**
For the most highly rated clinical and experimental abstracts.

• 5865 • **Outstanding Clinician Award**
To outstanding clinical contribution.

• 5866 • **Research Award**
For outstanding research achievement in the field of endocrine science.

• 5867 •
European Society of Paediatric Radiology
Freddy E. Avni, Gen.Sec.
Dept. of Radiology
Great Ormond St.
Children's NHS Trust
London WC1N 3JH, United Kingdom
Phone: 44 207 4059200
E-mail: favni@ulb.ac.be
Home Page: http://www.espr.org

• 5868 • **Jacques Lefebvre Award**
To encourage professional development in the field of pediatric radiology. Members of the Society under 34 years of age may submit papers. A monetary prize is awarded annually at the Congress. Established in 1976 in memory of Dr. Lefebvre. Formerly: Prix Jacques Lefebvre.

• 5869 •
European Surfing Federation
Karen Walton, Sec.
Fistral Beach
Newquay TR7 1HY, United Kingdom
Phone: 44 1736 360250
Fax: 44 1736 381077
E-mail: colon@britsurf.demon.co.uk
Home Page: http://www.eurosurfing.org

• 5870 • **European Surfing Championships - Open Champion**
To recognize the winners of the annual European surfing championships. A trophy is awarded annually. Established in 1965.

• 5871 •
European Wound Management Association
Brian Gilchrist, Sec.
PO Box 864
London SE1 8TT, United Kingdom
Phone: 44 207 8483496
E-mail: ewma@kcl.ac.uk
Home Page: http://www.ewma.org

• 5872 • **Travel Award**
Annual award of recognition.

• 5873 •
Experimental Psychology Society
Prof. G. Altmann, Hon.Sec.
Dept. of Psychology
University of York
Heslington
York YO1 5DD, United Kingdom
Phone: 44 118 9875123
Fax: 44 118 9314404
E-mail: g.altmann@psych.york.ac.uk
Home Page: http://www.eps.ac.uk

• 5874 • **Bartlett Lecture**
For recognition of contributions to experimental psychology or cognate subjects. An honorarium, expenses for travel, and the opportunity to present a lecture are awarded annually. Established in 1971 in honor of Sir Frederic Bartlett, a British psychologist.

• 5875 • **Experimental Psychology Society Prize**
For recognition of distinguished work in experimental psychology or a cognate discipline by an individual in an early stage of his or her career. An honorarium and the opportunity to present a lecture are awarded annually. Established in 1993.

• 5876 •
Faculty of Astrological Studies
Clare Martin, Pres.
BM Box 7470
London WC1N 3XX, United Kingdom
Phone: 44 7000 790143
Fax: 44 7000 790143
E-mail: info@astrology.org.uk
Home Page: http://www.astrology.org.uk

• 5877 • **Academic Awards**
For academic excellence in exams. Monetary awards are given annually.

• 5878 •
Faculty of Building
David R. Winson, CEO
% David Winson Organisation
35 Hayworth Rd.
Sandiacre NG10 5LL, United Kingdom
Phone: 44 115 949 0641
Fax: 44 115 949 1664
E-mail: mail@faculty-of-building.co.uk
Home Page: http://www.faculty-of-building.co.uk

• 5879 • **Edwin Williams Memorial Award**
For recognition of significant advancement in urban design. The competition is limited to the planning authorities in the Greater London area at the discretion of the Faculty. An engraved plaque and citation are awarded annually. Established in 1979 in memory of Edwin Williams, who contributed to architecture and town planning in the Greater London area.

• 5880 •
Family Education Trust
Robert Whelan, Dir.
Jubilee House
19-21 High St.
Whitton
Twickenham TW2 7LB, United Kingdom
Phone: 44 20 88942525
Fax: 44 20 88943535
E-mail: robert@ukfamily.org.uk
Home Page: http://www.famyouth.org.uk

• 5881 • **Family Life Award**
Recognizes service to family and the community. Awarded annually.

• 5882 •
Federation of Children's Book Groups
Sinead Kromer, Contact
2 Bridge Wood View
Horsforth
Leeds LS18 5PE, United Kingdom
Phone: 44 113 2588910
Fax: 44 113 2588920
E-mail: info@fcbg.org.uk
Home Page: http://www.fcbg.org.uk

• 5883 • **Children's Book Award**
To recognize the achievement of authors and illustrators who give children so much pleasure, and to foster an interest in children's books among children and parents. Works of fiction suitable for children that were published for the first time in the United Kingdom in the previous year, are eligible for consideration. Entries must be submitted by December 31. A silver and oak prize valued at over £7,000 and a presentation book filled with letters, pictures, reviews, and comments from the children who are the judges are awarded to celebrate the winning book. Shortlisted authors and illustrators also receive presentation books. The "Pick of the Year" booklist is produced annually in the spring. Established in 1980.

• 5884 •
Federation of European Materials Societies
Robert Singer, Pres.
Institute of Materials, Minerals and Mining
Carlton House Terr. 1
London SW1Y 5DB, United Kingdom
Phone: 44 207 4517336
Fax: 44 207 8392289
E-mail: rfsinger@ww.uni-erlangen.de
Home Page: http://www.fems.org

• 5885 • **FEMS European Materials Medal**
For outstanding contributions to the field of materials science and engineering.

• 5886 • **FEMS Lecturer Award for Excellence in MSE**
To young materials scientists who have contributed significantly to a recently emerging topic of materials science and engineering to lecture throughout Europe.

• 5887 • **FEMS Materials Science and Technology Prize**
To young European materials scientists or engineers in recognition of a significant contribution to the field of materials and science engineering.

• 5888 •
Federation of European Societies of Plant Physiology
School of Biological Sciences, University of Bristol
Woodland Rd.
Bristol BS8 1UG, United Kingdom
Phone: 44 117 9289757
Fax: 44 117 3316771
E-mail: mike.jackson@bristol.ac.uk
Home Page: http://www.fespb.org/

• 5889 • **FESPP Award**
For recognition of outstanding scientific work in recent years. Plant biologists who are under 35 years of age may be nominated by each of the 30 national societies that constitute the federation. A diploma, plenary lecture, and travel and participation expenses and a cheque are awarded biennially. Established in 1986. Sponsored by Academic Press and Jouan, France. Additional information is available at the above address.

• 5890 •
Federation of Plastering and Drywall Contractors
Emma Tomlin, Dir.
The Bldg. Ctre.
26 Store St.
London WC1E 7BT, United Kingdom
Phone: 44 207 5803545
Fax: 44 207 5803288
E-mail: enquiries@fpdc.org
Home Page: http://www.fpdc.org

Formerly: (1995) National Federation of Plastering Contractors.

• 5891 • **Plaisterers Trophy**
To uphold the image of the plastering craft in all its diverse skills and to demonstrate the high level of craftsmanship that the plastering industry can still offer to the building industry; and for recognition of the best plastering contract executed during the entry period having regard to excellence of workmanship and service. Entries are accepted from any firm or company carrying out a plastering contract. Entries may comprise solid plastering only, fibrous plastering only, or a combination of both in any proportion; and may comprise either in total or in part traditional aspects of the craft, e.g. granolithic paving, external finishes, etc., or more recently introduced processes such as spray finishes, dry-lining etc. Contracts must be of a value of £25,000 and upwards. A trophy is awarded annually to the winner in each of a variety of categories. Organized in association with Royal Institute of British Architects and Worshipful Company of Plaisterers, and sponsored by British Gypsom.

• 5892 •
Fell Pony Society
Mr. TH Harrison, Pres.
Fell Pony Soc. Office
Ion House
Great Asby
Appleby
Cumbria CA16 6HD, United Kingdom
Phone: 44 01768 353100
Fax: 44 01768 353100
E-mail: christine@kerbeck-fell-ponies.co.uk
Home Page: http://www.fellponysociety.org

• 5893 • **Fell Pony Society Ridden Championship**
For recognition of the best Fell Pony shown under saddle. An animal must be fully pedigreed and four years old or over to be eligible. A monetary prize and a trophy are awarded annually. Established in 1973.

• 5894 •
FeRFA Resin Flooring Association
Association House
99 West St.
Farnham GU9 7EN, United Kingdom
Phone: 44 1252 739149
Fax: 44 1252 739140
E-mail: ferfa@associationhouse.org.uk
Home Page: http://www.ferfa.org.uk

• 5895 • **Contract of the Year**
For interesting projects.

• 5896 • **Contractor of the Year**
For all-round perFormance, quality and variety of technique.

• 5897 • **Manufacturer of the Year**
For innovation, new products and quality of service offered to customers.

• 5898 • **Training company of the year**
Award of recognition.

• 5899 •
Filtration Society
Prof. Richard Wakeman, Sec.
5 Henry Dane Way
Newbold
Coleorton LE67 8PP, United Kingdom
Phone: 44 1530 223124
Fax: 44 1530 223124
E-mail: r.j.wakeman@lboro.ac.uk
Home Page: http://www.filtsoc.com

• 5900 • **Filtration Society Gold Medal**
To recognize the most meritorious original paper on filtration and separation technology. A medal and a certificate are awarded biennially.

• 5901 • **H. K. Suttle Award**
To encourage and recognize the achievements of younger workers in the field of filtration and separation technology. Authors under 35 years of age may submit papers in English. A monetary prize of £500 and a certificate are awarded biennially. The award is named after the Founder-Chairman of the Society, Harold K. Suttle.

• 5902 •
Fingerprint Society
Mr. Vivienne Galloway FFS, Chair
Fingerprint Bur.
Leicestershire Constabulary
St. Johns, Enderby
Leicester LE5 9BX, United Kingdom
Phone: 44 116 2482580
E-mail: vivg@lloway.com
Home Page: http://www.fpsociety.org.uk

Formerly: (1976) National Society of Fingerprint Officers.

• 5903 • Lewis Minshall Award
For recognition of outstanding contributions to the science of fingerprints, identification, or research, world-wide. Members or non-members of the Society are eligible. A trophy is presented annually when merited at the general meeting. Established in 1980 by the widow of Detective Superintendent Lewis Minshall, Queen's Police Medal, in memory of her husband, the first president of the Fingerprint Society.

• 5904 •
Fireball International
Prospect House
Pickhill
Thirsk YO7 4JG, United Kingdom
Phone: 44 1845 567064
Fax: 44 1845 567064
E-mail: secretary@fireball-international.com
Home Page: http://www.fireball-international.com

• 5905 • Fireball Worlds Trophy
For recognition of achievement in the field of competitive sailing. A trophy is awarded annually to the world champion helmsman. Established in 1966 by Bill Kempner, D.S.C.

• 5906 •
Fitness Industry Association
Nigel Wallace MP, Exec.Dir.
4th Fl.
61 Southwark St.
London SE1 0HL, United Kingdom
Phone: 44 20 72024718
Fax: 44 20 72024701
E-mail: info@fia.org.uk
Home Page: http://www.fia.org.uk

• 5907 • FLAME (Fitness Leadership and Management Excellence) Awards
To recognize fitness facilities for excellence. Awards are presented in categories based on membership, as well as awards for the Corporate Club of the Year, Centre of the Year, and the Spirit of the FLAME. Awarded annually.

• 5908 • Marketing Genius Awards
Recognizes leadership and management excellence. Awards are presented in a number of categories annually.

• 5909 •
Flying Fifteen International
Commodore Roger Palmer, Contact
Leicester House
5, Montpelier Row
Twickenham TW1 2NQ, United Kingdom
Phone: 44 20 88922664
Fax: 44 20 88922664
E-mail: president@flying15.org.uk
Home Page: http://flying15.org

• 5910 • Flying Fifteen World Championship
For recognition of the winners of the Flying Fifteen World Championships. The International Flying Fifteen Class is a one design racing keelboat. Members of FFL affiliated associations are eligible. The following Perpetual World Championship Trophies are presented biennially: (1) UFFA Fox Trophy - for the World Champion; (2) Armada Dish (Biffa Trophy) a silver dish with historic hallmarks - for the Crew of the 1st placed boat in the Open-Champion crew; (3) Tom Ratcliff Trophy (crystal and silver swans) - 2nd overall; (4) WAFFA Salver - 3rd overall; (5) NZNFFA Trophy (kauriwood) - 4th overall; (6) Kellett Island Trophy (silver dragon) - leading overseas helm; (7) Dixon Trophy - (silver rose bowl) - winner 1st race; (8) Kinsale Yacht Club Trophy (waterford crystal) - winner 2nd race; (9) Napier Sailing Club Trophy (Maori War Canoe) - winner 3rd race; and (10) Hayling Island SC Trophy (silver wire Fifteen) - winner 7th race. Established in 1979. Additional information is available from International Sailing Federation, Ariane House, Town Quay, Southhampton, SO14 2AQ, England; Phone: 1703 635111.

• 5911 •
Folklore Society
Susan Vass, Administrator
Woburn Sq.
London WC1H 0AB, United Kingdom
Phone: 44 20 78628564
E-mail: folklore.society@talk21.com
Home Page: http://www.folklore-society.com

• 5912 • Katharine Briggs Folklore Award
To encourage a high standard of publication and scholarship in folklore. Books published for the first time in English in the United Kingdom and Ireland between June 1 and May 31 are eligible. Included are scholarly revised editions of previously published texts, but excluded are reprints or folktales retold for children. Entries should be submitted by May 31. A monetary prize and an engraved goblet are awarded annually. Established in 1982 in honor of Dr. Katharine Briggs, a distinguished English folktale and literary scholar, and a past president of the Society.

• 5913 • Coote-Lake Medal for Folklore Research
For recognition of research in the field of folklore studies and for service to the Folklore Society. Individuals must be nominated by a committee of the Society. A medal is awarded when merited. Established in 1941 by Mrs. H. A. Lake-Barnett, a treasurer and secretary of the Folklore Society, in memory of Harold Coote-Lake, the founder's brother and a treasurer and secretary of the Folklore Society.

• 5914 •
Foreign Press Association in London
Mr. Annalisa Piras, Pres.
11 Carlton House Terr.
London SW1Y 5AJ, United Kingdom
Phone: 44 20 79300445
Fax: 44 20 79250469
E-mail: secretariat@foreign-press.org.uk
Home Page: http://www.foreign-press.org.uk

• 5915 • The Foreign Press Association British Media Award
Recognizes the best foreign story in the British press. UK journalists are eligible. Awarded annually.

• 5916 •
Forensic Science Society
Mr. Jim Fraser, Pres.
Clarke House
18 A Mt. Parade
N Yorkshire
Harrogate HG1 1BX, United Kingdom
Phone: 44 1423 506068
Fax: 44 1423 566391
E-mail: membership@forensic-science-society.org.uk
Home Page: http://www.forensic-science-society.org.uk

• 5917 • Forensic Science Society Awards
To recognize forensic scientists, lawyers, pathologists, police officers, odontologicts, and police surgeons and to promote the study and application of forensic science. Society Diplomas are awarded on the basis of examination. The J. B. Firth Essay Prize, an award of £200, is awarded each year to a student studying either full- or part-time on a graduating course at a recognized institute of higher education based anywhere in the world.

• 5918 •
Fork Lift Truck Association
David Ellison, Contact
Manor Farm Bldgs.
Lasham
Alton GU34 5SL, United Kingdom
Phone: 44 1256 381441
Fax: 44 1256 381735
E-mail: mail@fork-truck.org.uk
Home Page: http://www.fork-truck.org.uk

• 5919 • Awards for Excellence
Presented for innovation, environment, ergonomics, health safety, lifetime achievement. Awarded annually.

• 5920 •
Franco-British Society
Mrs. Kate Brayn, Exec.Sec.
Linen Hall, Rm. 227
162-168 Regent St.
London W1R 5TB, United Kingdom
Phone: 44 207 7340815
Fax: 44 207 7340815
E-mail: execsec@francobritishsociety.org.uk
Home Page: http://www.francobritishsociety.org.uk

• 5921 • **Franco-British Landscape Gardening Award**
To draw attention to an outstanding horticultural achievement each year, either in Britain or France, thus encouraging and developing further contacts between the two countries in the areas of garden history and landscape design. Established in 1988.

• 5922 • **Enid McLeod Literary Prize**
To recognize the author of the work of literature that has contributed the most to Franco-British understanding. Any full length work of literature written in English by a citizen of the United Kingdom, British Commonwealth, Republic of Ireland, Pakistan, Bangladesh, or South Africa, and first published in the United Kingdom is eligible. A monetary prize is awarded annually. Established in 1983 in honor of Miss Enid McLeod.

• 5923 • **Vlado Perlemuter Piano Scholarship**
To select from auditions the British piano student, between 17 and 25 years old, whose career would benefit most from an international summer school course Academie Internationale de Musique Ravel in France. The annual winner of the scholarship receives fare, tuition, travel, and expenses to study at the Academie Internationale de Musique Maurice Ravel, St. Jean-de-Luz, near Biarritz. Established in 1983 in honor of the distinguished pianist, Vlado Perlemuter, pupil of Ravel.

• 5924 •
GARDENEX: Federation of Garden and Leisure Manufacturers
Amanda Sizer Barrett MBE, Dir.Gen.
The White House
High St.
Kent
Brasted TN16 1JE, United Kingdom
Phone: 44 1959 565995
Fax: 44 1959 565885
E-mail: info@gardenex.com
Home Page: http://www.gardenex.com/index.html

• 5925 • **Roy Hay Memorial Award**
Recognizes services rendered to British gardening industry. Awarded annually.

• 5926 •
Geological Society of London
Edmund Nickless, Exec.Sec.
Burlington House
Piccadilly
London W1J 0BG, United Kingdom
Phone: 44 20 74349944
Fax: 44 20 74398975
E-mail: enquiries@geolsoc.org.uk
Home Page: http://www.geolsoc.org.uk

• 5927 • **Aberconway Medal**
For recognition of distinguished contributions to the advancement of the profession and practice of geology. Individuals under 45 years of age may be nominated. A medal is awarded biennually. Established in 1980 by Lord Aberconway of Bodnant. Sponsored by English China Clays Ltd.

• 5928 • **Major John Sacheverell A'Deane Coke Medal**
To recognize scientists for their contributions to geology, and for recognition of significant service to geology, for example through administrative, organizational, or promotional activities resulting in benefits to the community. Also the field may be extended to include scientists whose training and interests are outside the main fields of geology but whose contributions are of great significance to our science. A medal is awarded annually.

• 5929 • **Bigsby Medal**
To recognize an individual under 45 years of age for imminent services in any department of geology. A medal is awarded biennially.

• 5930 • **Major Edward D'Ewes Fitzgerald Coke Medal**
To recognize scientists for their contributions to geology, and for recognition of significant service to geology through administrative, organizational, or promotional activities resulting in benefits to the community. Also the field may be extended to include scientists whose training and interests are outside the main fields of geology but whose contributions are of great significance to our science. A medal is awarded annually.

• 5931 • **Sue Tyler Friedman Medal**
To recognize an individual for distinguished contributions to the recording of the history of geology. Established in 1987 by a gift from a Northeastern Science Foundation of Troy, New York.

• 5932 • **Lyell Medal**
To recognize an individual who has made a significant contribution to the science by means of a substantial body of research. Workers in both pure and applied aspects of the geological sciences are eligible. A medal is awarded annually. The Lyell Fund is awarded to contributors to the earth sciences on the basis of noteworthy published research.

• 5933 • **Murchison Medal**
To recognize authors of memoirs or persons actually employed in any enquiries bearing upon the science of geology. A monetary prize and a medal are awarded annually. Established in 1873 through the will of Sir Roderick Impey Murchison (1792-1871). The Murchison Fund is also awarded to contributors to the earth sciences on the basis of noteworthy published research.

• 5934 • **President's Awards**
To recognize geologists who are under the age of 30 and who made a notable early contribution to the science. Awarded when merited. Established in 1980 by Professor Perce Allen.

• 5935 • **Prestwich Medal**
To recognize scientists who have undertaken special research bearing on stratigraphical or physical geology. A medal is awarded triennially. Established under the will of Sir Joseph Prestwich (1812-96).

• 5936 • **William Smith Medal**
For recognition of excellence in contributions to applied and economic aspects of the science. Candidates must have initiated significant contributions, which will normally take the form of published papers. Although in view of the confidential nature of the work in the case of some candidates, other criteria may be used as the basis of the award. A medal is awarded annually. Established in 1977. A William Smith Fund is also awarded to scientists under 40 years of age.

• 5937 • **Wollaston Medal**
This, the highest award of the Society, is normally given to geologists who have had a significant influence by means of a substantial body of excellent research in either or both pure and applied aspects of the science. A medal is awarded annually. The Wollaston Fund is awarded to contributors to the earth sciences on the basis of noteworthy published research.

• 5938 • **R. H. Worth Prize**
For recognition of meritorious geological research carried out by amateur geologists, or for the encouragement of geological research by amateurs.

• 5939 •
Girls' Brigade International Council
Miss Piang Chin Hee, Pres.
Challenge House
29 Canal St.
Glasgow G4 0AD, United Kingdom
Phone: 44 141 3329696
Fax: 44 141 3329696
E-mail: hq@gbic.org
Home Page: http://www.gbic.org

• 5940 • **International Award**
Award of recognition. Members of brigade over the age of 18 are eligible. Awarded annually. Established in 1968.

• 5941 • Queen's Award
Award of recognition. Members of the brigade in countries holding the Queen of England as head of state are eligible. Awarded annually.

• 5942 •
Goldsmiths' Company
R.D. Buchanan-Dunlop CBE, Contact
Goldsmiths' Hall
Foster Ln.
London EC2V 6BN, United Kingdom
Phone: 44 20 76067010
Fax: 44 20 76061511
E-mail: the.clerk@thegoldsmiths.co.uk
Home Page: http://www.thegoldsmiths.co.uk

• 5943 • Binney Memorial Award
For recognition of bravery in support of law and order within the Metropolitan and City police areas of London. Individuals must be nominated by the police. A medal and certificates of merit are awarded annually. Established in 1947 by friends of Captain Ralph Binney R.N., who was killed in an attempt to prevent a robbery in the City of London.

• 5944 •
Green Organisation
Marious Coulon, Managing Dir.
The Mill House
Mill Ln.
Earls Barton
Northampton NN6 0NR, United Kingdom
Phone: 44 1604 810507
Fax: 44 1604 810507
E-mail: go@themillbarn.free-online.co.uk
Home Page: http://www.thegreenorganisation.info

• 5945 • Green Apple Award
Recognizes outstanding eco-friendly practices. A trophy is awarded annually.

• 5946 •
Guild of Agricultural Journalists
Don Gomery, Sec.
Isfield Cottage, Church Rd.
Crowborough TN6 3SP, United Kingdom
Phone: 44 189 611618
Fax: 44 189 613394
E-mail: don.gomery@farmingline.com
Home Page: http://www.gaj.org.uk

• 5947 • Netherthorpe Award
To recognize a guild member who has made an outstanding and sustained contribution to the dissemination of knowledge and understanding about agriculture. A trophy and a certificate are bestowed annually. Established in 1977. The award honors the late Lord Netherthorpe. Additional information is available from Jessica Buss, Awards Secretary, Farmers Weekly, Quadrant House, Sutton, Surrey, SM2 5AS. Tel: 44 20 8652 4935.

• 5948 •
Guild of Food Writers
Mr. Jonathan Woods, Administrator
9 Colman House
High St.
London SE20 7EX, United Kingdom
Phone: 44 208 6590422
Fax: 44 207 6100299
E-mail: guild@gfw.co.uk
Home Page: http://www.gfw.co.uk

• 5949 • Guild of Food Writers Award
Recognizes excellence in food writing. Awarded annually.

• 5950 •
Guild of International Professional Toastmasters
Ivor Spencer, Pres.
% Ivor Spencer Enterprises Ltd.
12 Little Bornes
Dulwich
London SE21 8SE, United Kingdom
Phone: 44 20 8670 5585
Fax: 44 20 8670 0055
E-mail: ivor@ivorspencer.com
Home Page: http://www.ivorspencer.com

• 5951 • Ivor Spencer Best After Dinner Speaker of the Year
To recognize the best after dinner speaker of the year. Selection is by members of the Guild. A trophy is awarded annually. Established in 1967 by Ivor Spencer. Formerly: (1997) Guild of Professional Toastmasters Best After Dinner Speaker of the Year.

• 5952 •
Guild of Motoring Writers
Patricia Lodge, Gen.Sec.
39 Beswick Ave.
Bournemouth BH10 4EY, United Kingdom
Phone: 44 1202518808
Fax: 44 1202518808
E-mail: gensec@gomw.co.uk
Home Page: http://www.newspress.co.uk/guild

• 5953 • Driver of the Year Award
To recognize a driver for his skill, courage and endurance. Awarded annually.

• 5954 • Sir William Lyons Award
To encourage young writers in automotive journalism, and to foster interest in the motoring industry. British citizens resident in the United Kingdom between 17 and 23 years of age may submit essays. A monetary award of £1,500 is presented annually.

• 5955 • Pemberton Trophy
To recognize a Guild member for achievements in the field of motoring journalism.

• 5956 •
Guild of Registered Tourist Guides
Mr. Mehmet Ahmet, Office Mgr.
52D Borough High St.
London SE1 1XN, United Kingdom
Phone: 44 20 74031115
Fax: 44 20 73781705
E-mail: guild@blue-badge.org.uk
Home Page: http://www.blue-badge.org.uk

• 5957 • Life Fellowship
Recognizes outstanding service to the profession and the tourist industry. Complimentary membership is awarded when merited.

• 5958 •
Guild of Taxidermists
Duncan Ferguson, Contact
200 Woodhead Rd.
South Nitshill
Glasgow G53 7NN, United Kingdom
Phone: 44 141 2679445
Phone: 44 141 2679311
Fax: 44 141 2679305
E-mail: duncan.ferguson@cls.glasgow.gov.uk
Home Page: http://www.taxidermy.org.uk

• 5959 • Guild of Taxidermists Acredited Member
To recognize an individual for outstanding work in the field of taxidermy. Members of the Guild must submit six examples of their work for judging. Scrolls are presented at the Conference of the Guild. Established in 1976.

• 5960 •
Guild of Television Cameramen
Sheila Lewis, Admin. Officer
April Cottage
The Chalks
Chew Magna
Bristol BS40 8SN, United Kingdom
Phone: 44 1822 614405
Fax: 44 1822 614405
E-mail: administration@gtc.org.uk
Home Page: http://www.gtc.org.uk

• 5961 • Annual Awards
To recognize an outstanding contribution to the art of a cameraman. Awards are presented annually. The Guild presents The GTC Certificate of Merit to recognize outstanding camerawork and The GTC Seal of Approval to honor new euipment used in the industry.

• 5962 •
Guildhall School of Music and Drama
Dr. Andrew Parmley, Chm.
Silk St.
Barbican
London EC2Y 8DT, United Kingdom
Phone: 44 20 7628 2571
Fax: 44 20 7256 9438
E-mail: hswain@gsmd.ac.uk
Home Page: http://www.gsmd.ac.uk

• 5963 • **Gundhall School Gold Medal**
For recognition of outstanding performance in the fields of music and drama. In the field of music, awards are given alternately to: instrumentalists and singers. An award is given annually in drama. Individuals with a minimum of three years and a maximum of five years attendance as full-time students at the Guildhall School are eligible. Gold medals are awarded annually. Established in 1915 by Sir H. Dixon Kimber Bt., MA.

• 5964 •
Haemophilia Society
Margaret Unwin, Chief Exec.
1st Fl., Petersham House
57a Hatton Garden
London EC1N 8JG, United Kingdom
Phone: 44 207 8311020
Fax: 44 207 4054824
E-mail: info@haemophilia.org.uk
Home Page: http://www.haemophilia.org.uk

• 5965 • **Haemophilia Award**
For an individual who has made a significant contribution to the well being of people with haemophilia.

• 5966 • **Haemophilia Society Sports Award**
For young people with haemophilia or bleeding disorder who work hard at any sport.

• 5967 • **Philip Morris Art Award**
For people with haemophilia or related disorder who are studying music or another art form.

• 5968 •
Harrogate International Festival
William Culver-Dodds, Festival Dir.
Festival Office, Royal Baths
1 Victoria Ave.
Harrogate HG1 1EQ, United Kingdom
Phone: 44 1423 562303
Fax: 44 1423 521264
E-mail: info@harrogate-festival.org.uk
Home Page: http://www.harrogate-festival.org.uk

• 5969 • **Dorothy Parkinson Award for Young British Musicians**
To provide an opportunity for a young performer at the start of his professional career to perform a concert at a major British Festival. British musicians under 26 years of age are nominated by a selection panel. A monetary prize of £400 is awarded annually in August. Established in 1982 in honor of Lady Dorothy Parkinson. Sponsored by Dorothy Parkinson Memorial Trust.

• 5970 • **Clive Wilson Award for Young Musicians**
To encourage young performers at the start of their professional careers. Individuals under 28 years of age who are nominated by the Harrogate International Festival are eligible. A monetary prize is awarded annually. Established in 1990 in memory of Clive Wilson, founder of the Festival.

• 5971 •
Historical Association
Madeline Stiles, CEO
59a Kennington Park Rd.
London SE11 4JH, United Kingdom
Phone: 44 207 7353901
Fax: 44 207 5824989
E-mail: enquiry@history.org.uk
Home Page: http://www.history.org.uk

• 5972 • **Norton Medlicott Medal**
For recognition of an outstanding major contribution to the field of history. Nominations may be submitted. A medal is awarded annually. Established in 1984 in honor of Professor W. Norton Medlicott, past president of the Association.

• 5973 •
Historical Metallurgy Society
Mr. Peter Hutchison, Hon.Gen.Sec.
22 Easterfield Dr.
Southgate
Swansea SA3 2DB, United Kingdom
Phone: 44 1792 233223
Fax: 44 1792 233223
E-mail: hon-sec@hist-met.org
Home Page: http://hist-met.org

• 5974 • **Historical Metallurgy Society Grants**
To encourage the preservation and study of all aspects of metallurgical history, including the extraction of ores and minerals, the melting and working of metals, and the preservation of archaeological and historical sites and objects. Grants for research, excavations, and travel to conferences are awarded.

• 5975 •
Huddersfield Contemporary Music Festival
Susanna Eastburn, Artistic Dir.
University of Huddersfield
West Yorkshire
Huddersfield HD1 3DH, United Kingdom
Phone: 44 1484 425082
Fax: 44 1484 472597
E-mail: info@hcmf.co.uk
Home Page: http://www.hcmf.co.uk

• 5976 • **Yorkshire & Humberside Arts Young Composers Awards**
To give experience to composers aged 18 to 30 during the Huddersfield Contemporary Music Festival held in November each year. Works must be submitted by August. The opportunity to work with professional ensembles and composers during the Huddersfield Contemporary Music Festival is awarded annually, as well as the opportunity of being awarded a commission to be performed at the next year's festival. Established in 1984 by Yorkshire Arts. Bursaries available to attend Festival. Formerly: (1990) Yorkshire Arts Young Composers Competition.

• 5977 •
Humane Slaughter Association and Council of Justice to Animals
Dr. James K. Kirkwood, Ch.Exec.
The Old School
Brewhouse Hill
Wheathampstead AL4 8AN, United Kingdom
Phone: 44 1582 831919
Fax: 44 1582 831414
E-mail: info@hsa.org.uk
Home Page: http://www.hsa.org.uk

• 5978 • **Dorothy Sidley Memorial Award**
To encourage young people in the UK to take an interest in the Association's specialist area of food animal welfare, thereby improving welfare conditions for food animals and birds in livestock markets, during transit or in slaughterhouses. Students in agricultural, veterinary, or meat sciences, and trainees in the livestock and meat industries are eligible. Proposals for research programs may be submitted by April 1. A monetary award of £1,000 is presented annually. Established in 1986 in memory of Dorothy Sidley MBE, who was General Secretary of the Association for forty-eight years.

• 5979 •
Hunterian Society
11 Chandos St.
Lettsom House
Cavendish Sq.
London W19 9EB, United Kingdom
Phone: 44 20 7436 7363
E-mail: genadmin@hunteriansociety.org.uk
Home Page: http://www.hunteriansociety.org.uk

• 5980 • **Hunterian Medal**
To stimulate an original contribution in essay form on a medical scientific topic chosen by the Society. Registered Medical Practitioners in Great Britain are eligible. A gold medal is awarded annually. Established in 1984 in honor of John Hunter.

• 5981 •
Incorporated Society of Musicians
Neil Hoyle, Chief Exec.
10 Stratford Pl.
London W1C 1AA, United Kingdom
Phone: 44 20 76294413
Fax: 44 20 74081538
E-mail: membership@ism.org
Home Page: http://www.ism.org

• 5982 • **Distinguished Musician Award**
To recognize the outstanding contribution of a colleague to British musical life. A silver medallion bearing the ISM logo is awarded annually when merited. Established in 1976. Formerly: (1980) Musician of the Year.

• 5983 • **Honorary Member**
To recognize an individual who has given public service to the art of music or to kindred arts and sciences.

Awards are arranged in alphabetical order below their administering organizations

• 5984 •
Institute of Acoustics
Dr. Tony Jones, Chm.
77A St. Peter's St.
St. Albans AL1 3BN, United Kingdom
Phone: 44 1727 848195
Fax: 44 1727 850553
E-mail: ioa@ioa.org.uk
Home Page: http://www.ioa.org.uk

• 5985 • Rayleigh Medal
For recognition of outstanding contributions to acoustics by a United Kingdom and a foreign acoustician, alternately. A medal and a citation are awarded annually. Established in 1975 by the British Acoustical Society in memory of John William Strutt, Third Baron Rayleigh, a physicist and physician who won a Nobel Prize for physics in 1904.

• 5986 • Stephens Lecture
To honor distinguished acousticians. The lecture is held annually at the spring conference and is intended to be an important occasion at an IOA Meeting, marked by the presentation of a scroll to the lecturer. Established in 1984 in honor of Dr. Ray Stephens, a graduate of Imperial College, London where he subsequently created his Acoustics Research group, and also the first President of the Institute of Acoustics, which he was instrumental in creating. The Stephens Lecture was set up in honor of his eightieth birthday.

• 5987 • Tyndall Medal
For recognition of achievement and service in the field of acoustics. Citizens of the United Kingdom, preferably under the age of 40, are eligible. A medal and a citation are awarded biennially in even-numbered years. Established in 1975 by the British Acoustical Society in memory of John Tyndall (1820-1893), an experimental physicist and one of the world's most brilliant scientific lecturers.

• 5988 • A. B. Wood Medal and Prize
For recognition of distinguished contributions in the application of acoustics, with preference given to candidates whose work is associated with the sea. The prize is awarded alternately to a person domiciled in the United Kingdom, and in the United States or Canada. The Acoustical Society of America selects recipients from the United States or Canada. Individuals, preferably under 35 years of age in the year of the award, are considered. A silver-gilt medal, a parchment scroll, and a monetary prize are awarded annually. Established in 1968 by the Institute of Physics, London, in memory of Albert Beaumont Wood, a research scientist for the Admiralty on anti-submarine problems.

• 5989 •
Institute of Actuaries - United Kingdom
Caroline Instance, Chief Exec.
Staple Inn Hall
High Holborn
London WC1V 7QJ, United Kingdom
Phone: 44 207 6322100
Fax: 44 207 6322111
E-mail: institute@actuaries.org.uk
Home Page: http://www.actuaries.org.uk

• 5990 • Finlaison Medal
For recognition of services to the actuarial profession in furthering one or more of the various objectives set out in the Royal Charter. Awarded when merited. Established in 1966. Named after John Finlaison(1783-1860) first president of the Institute of Actuaries. Formerly: (1985) Silver Medal.

• 5991 • Gold Medal
For recognition of work of pre-eminent importance either in originality, content, or consequence in the actuarial field. Awarded when merited. Established in 1919.

• 5992 •
Institute of Administrative Management
David Woodgate, Chief Exec.
55-57 High Holborn
Caroline House
London WC1V 6DX, United Kingdom
Phone: 44 207 8411100
Fax: 44 207 8411119
E-mail: info@instam.org
Home Page: http://www.instam.org

• 5993 • Institute of Administrative Management Awards
To recognize professional managers and to promote and develop the science of administrative management. The Institute's educational programs can lead to the award of certificate, diploma, advanced diploma, and BA (Hons) degree in Administrative Management. Named awards include the IAM Medal, IAM Commendation, and the educational awards of Michael Guthrie Prize, A. J. Shawcross Prize, Sir Joseph Burn Prize, Leonard W. Green Prize, William Johnston Memorial Shield.

• 5994 •
Institute of Advanced Legal Studies
℅ Univ. of London
Charles Clore House
17 Russell Sq.
London WC1B 5DR, United Kingdom
Phone: 44 207 862 5800
Fax: 44 207 862 5850
E-mail: ials@sas.ac.uk

• 5995 • Howard Drake Memorial Award
To encourage collaboration and exchanges between legal scholars and law librarians, especially between those of different countries, and to promote the study of law librarianship and the training of law librarians. Established in 1978 in memory of Howard Drake, the first librarian of the Institute.

• 5996 • Georg Schwarzenberger Prize in International Law
To recognize a student in the Faculty of Laws in the University of London considered to be outstanding in the field of Public International Law. Nomination is by the heads of the five London University Law Schools. A monetary prize is awarded annually. Established in 1981 by friends and former students of Professor Georg Schwarzenberger.

• 5997 •
Institute of Cast Metal Engineers
National Metalforming Centre
47 Birmingham Rd.
West Bromwich B70 6PY, United Kingdom
Phone: 44 121 601 6979
Fax: 44 121 601 6981
E-mail: info@icme.org.uk
Home Page: http://www.ibf.org.uk

• 5998 • Institute of British Foundrymen Honorary Fellow
To recognize an individual for outstanding contributions to the cast metals industry.

• 5999 • Voya Kondic Medal
For recognition in the field of foundry education and training. Established in 1991.

• 6000 • Oliver Stubbs Medal
For recognition of achievement in the development of the cast metals industry and for imparting knowledge to fellow members of the Institute. Institute members are eligible. A medal is awarded annually. Established in 1922 by Oliver Stubbs, past president of the Institute.

• 6001 •
Institute of Chartered Accountants of Scotland
Mike Hathorn, Pres.
21 Haymarket Yards
Edinburgh EH12 5BH, United Kingdom
Phone: 44 131 3470100
Fax: 44 131 3470105
E-mail: enquiries@icas.org.uk
Home Page: http://www.icas.org.uk

• 6002 • David Bogie Prize
To recognize the candidate whose performance in the papers in Auditing is the most meritorious. An award of £85 is presented.

• 6003 • J. C. Burleigh Prize
To award the candidate whose performance in the papers in Information Systems is the most meritorious. £85 is awarded.

• 6004 • Canadian Institute of Chartered Accountants Prize
To reward the winner of the Institute's Gold Medal. A monetary award of £110 is presented. Established 1967.

• 6005 • Walid Chorbachi Prizes
To recognize the candidates who placed first, second, and third at the Test of Professional Competence. Awards of £275, £165, £110 are presented.

• 6006 • James M. Cowie Prize
To award the candidate in Part II who is judged to be second in merit for the Winter Diet. £165 is presented.

• 6007 • Guthrie Prize
To award the candidate in Part II who is fourth in order of merit in the Spring Diet. Award of £85.00 is presented.

• 6008 • Institute of Chartered Accountants of Scotland Gold Medal
To encourage the professional development of the Institute's students. The award is given to the candidate whose performance, over all parts of the Institute's professional examinations, is judged to be most meritorious. A gold medal is awarded annually. Established in 1961 by Mr. Albert J. Watson, CA. of Hillsborough, U.S.A.

• 6009 • John Mann Prize
To recognize the candidate whose performance in the papers in Taxation is the most meritorious. An award of £85 is presented.

• 6010 • Robert McArthur Prize
To award the candidate at Part II who is judged to be third in order of merit in the Spring Diet. £110 is presented.

• 6011 • Sir William McLintock Prize
To recognize the person who is second in order of merit in the Test of Professional Competence Part I. £110 is awarded annually.

• 6012 • Forbes Murphy Prize
To recognize the candidate whose performance in the Test of Professional Competence Part I is fourth in order of merit. £60 is awarded.

• 6013 • John Munn Ross Prize
To recognize the candidate whose performance was third in order of merit in the Test of Professional Competence Part I. £85 is awarded.

• 6014 • Primrose Scott Prize
To recognize the TOPP's candidate at Part II whose performance is judged to be first in order of merit. £80 is awarded. Formerly: Lady Members Group Prize.

• 6015 • Helen Sommerville Prize
To recognize the candidate in Part II of the Winter Diet who is fifth in order of merit. £60 is awarded.

• 6016 • Albert J. Watson Prize
To recognize meritorious performance in the Test of Professional Competence Part I. A prize of £220 is awarded annually.

• 6017 • C. J. Weir Prize
To recognize the candidate in Part II of the Winter Diet who is fourth in order of merit. A prize of £85 is presented.

• 6018 • The Ronald Williamson Prize
To provide recognition to the candidate whose performance in the papers in Financial Reporting is the most meritorious. £85 is awarded.

• 6019 •
Institute of Contemporary History and Wiener Library
Ben Barkow, Dir.Gen.
4 Devonshire St.
London W1W 5BH, United Kingdom
Phone: 44 20 7636 7247
Fax: 44 20 7636 6428
E-mail: info@wienerlibrary.co.uk
Home Page: http://www.wienerlibrary.co.uk

• 6020 • Fraenkel Prize in Contemporary History
To recognize outstanding work in the field of twentieth-century history. Eligible works must be finished but unpublished written in English, French, or German that cover one of the traditional fields of interest to the Wiener Library, such as political history of Central and Eastern Europe; Jewish history; the two world wars; anti-Semitism; and the ideologies and movements of political extremism and totalitarianism. The deadline is May 15. Two distinct awards are made: US $6,000, open to all entrants (length not less than 50,000 words and not more than 150,000 words); and US $4,000, open to entrants who have yet to publish a major work (length not less than 25,000 words and not more than 100,000 words). The Wiener Library may invite the winner of the award to give a public lecture in London. The Wiener Library will have the option to publish part of the award-winning work in the *Journal of Contemporary History*. Awarded annually in late summer. Established in 1989 by Ernst Fraenkel, chairman of the Institute.

• 6021 •
Institute of Domestic Heating and Environmental Engineers
Bill Bucknell FIDHE, Exec. Chm.
Unit 32C
New Forest Enterprise Center
Chapel Ln.
Totton
Southampton SO40 9LA, United Kingdom
Phone: 44 2380 668900
Fax: 44 2380 660888
E-mail: info@idhee.org.uk
Home Page: http://www.idhee.org.uk

• 6022 • Advanced Diploma
For an understanding of the design and installation of energy efficient central heating and domestic air conditioning systems.

• 6023 • Associate Member Diploma
For an understanding of the design and installation of energy efficient central heating systems.

• 6024 • Certificate in Energy Efficiency For Domestic Central Heating
Award of recognition.

• 6025 • Technician Diploma
For an understanding of the installation of energy efficient central heating systems.

• 6026 •
Institute of Entertainment and Arts Management
Shirley Carpenter, Administrator
17 Drake Close
Horsham RH12 5UB, United Kingdom
Phone: 44 870 2417248
Fax: 44 870 2417248
E-mail: admin@ieam.co.uk
Home Page: http://www.ieam.co.uk

• 6027 • Waterford Crystal Award
For outstanding service to the entertainment industry. Awarded annually.

• 6028 •
Institute of Export
Phillip Turon, Dir.
Minerva Business Park
Lynch Wood
Peterborough PE2 6FT, United Kingdom
Phone: 44 1733 404400
Fax: 44 1733 404444
E-mail: institute@export.org.uk
Home Page: http://www.export.org.uk

• 6029 • Institute of Export Prizes
For recognition of achievement in the Institute's professional examinations. Registered students are eligible. The following awards are given in each category: Professional Examination Part II in Export Management - National Westminster Bank Prize, Department of Trade and Industry Prizes, the DHL International (UK) Prize, George Lockhart Prize, and Barclay Bank Prize (Export Distribution); and Professional Examina-

tion Part I - Maerskline UK Prize, T & R (Insurance Services) Limited Prize, Alex Lawrie Factor Ltd. Prize, Clive and Twinkie Schmitthoff Prize (Principles of Law Relating to Overseas Trade), National Westminster Bank Prize (International Trade and Payments), SITPRO Prize (International Physical Distribution), Society of Shipping Executives Education Trust Prize, and British Aerospace Prize. The best student in either part one or part two is awarded the Company of World Traders Silver Salver. Monetary prizes and, in a few cases, a trophy are awarded annually.

• 6030 •
Institute of Financial Accountants
J. Malcolm Dean, Chief Exec.
Burford House
44 London Rd.
Sevenoaks TN13 1AS, United Kingdom
Phone: 44 1732 458080
Fax: 44 1732 455848
E-mail: mail@ifa.org.uk
Home Page: http://www.ifa.org.uk

Formerly: (1987) Institute of Administrative Accountants.

• 6031 • **Institute of Financial Accountants Awards**
To recognize individuals for: (1) excellence of achievement in the examinations for the awards of Associate and Fellow of the Institute; (2) outstanding contributions to the theory of accountancy; and (3) high levels of performance in the practice of the profession. Examination prizes are awarded twice a year in June and December. The prizes for Professional Qualification are book tokens. Formerly: Institute of Administrative Accountants Awards.

• 6032 •
Institute of Heraldic and Genealogical Studies
C.R. Humphery-Smith, Principal
79-82 Northgate
Canterbury CT1 1BA, United Kingdom
Phone: 44 1227 768664
Fax: 44 1227 765617
E-mail: ihgs@ihgs.ac.uk
Home Page: http://www.ihgs.ac.uk

• 6033 • **Julian Bickersteth Memorial Medal**
To honor individuals who have made significant contributions to family history studies. The Trustees of the Institute may nominate individuals. A gold medal is awarded annually when merited at the annual luncheon. Established in 1962 by Cecil R.J. Humphery-Smith in memory of Kenneth Julian Faithfull Bickersteth (1885-1962), an educator and canon of Canterbury Cathedral. The Institute also presents other awards: Fellowship; Frank Higenbottam Memorial Prize - for library work; and Dr. Peter Wren Prize - for best student.

• 6034 • **Certificates, Diplomas, and Licentiates in Genealogy and Heraldry**
To recognize achievement in genealogical study. Awarded when merited.

• 6035 •
Institute of Internal Auditors - UK and Ireland
Gail Easterbrook, CEO
13 Abbeville Mews
88 Clapham Park Rd.
London SW4 7BX, United Kingdom
Phone: 44 207 4980101
Fax: 44 207 9782492
E-mail: info@iia.org.uk
Home Page: http://www.iia.org.uk

• 6036 • **Charles Duly Award**
For the highest scoring student in the diploma examinations.

• 6037 • **Peter Hook Award**
For the highest scoring student in the advanced diploma examinations.

• 6038 • **JJ Morris Award**
To individuals who have given outstanding service to the internal auditing profession.

• 6039 • **Volunteer of the Year Award**
For consistent and effective volunteer activity to the association.

• 6040 •
Institute of Legal Cashiers and Administrators
Maria Maloney, Contact/Ed.
Marlowe House, 2nd Fl.
109 Station Rd.
Sidcup
Kent DA15 7ET, United Kingdom
Phone: 44 208 3022867
Fax: 44 208 3027481
E-mail: info@ilca.org.uk
Home Page: http://www.ilca.org.uk

• 6041 • **Wilfred Owen Awards**
Recognizes individuals for the highest examination marks at the Diploma, Associate, and Fellowship level. Medals are awarded annually.

• 6042 •
Institute of Management
Mary Chapman, Dir.Gen.
2 Savoy Ct., 3rd Fl.
Strand
London WC2R OEZ, United Kingdom
Phone: 44 20 74970580
Phone: 44 15 36204222
Fax: 44 20 74970463
E-mail: enquiries@managers.org.uk
Home Page: http://www.managers.org.uk

• 6043 • **Institute of Management Gold Medal**
For recognition of outstanding achievement in the art, science, or practice of management. Awarded annually. Established in 1980.

• 6044 •
Institute of Marine Engineering, Science and Technology
Mr. Keith Read, Dir.Gen.
80 Coleman St.
London EC2R 5BJ, United Kingdom
Phone: 44 207 3822600
Fax: 44 207 3822670
E-mail: info@imarest.org
Home Page: http://www.imare.org.uk

Formerly: (2004) Institute of Marine Engineers.

• 6045 • **Denny Gold Medal**
For recognition of the most worthy paper read to the Institute by a member during the year. Joint authors are eligible providing the first named is a member. A gold medal, certificate and a monetary prize of £300 are awarded annually.

• 6046 • **Stanley Gray Award**
To recognize the most worthy papers presented to the Institute by a member or nonmember. Awards are given in the following categories: marine technology, offshore technology, marine electrical technology, maritime technology development, conferences, and branches. A monetary prize of £500 and a certificate are awarded annually in each category. In addition, £500 and a certificate are awarded to the most worthy paper read by a member or nonmember at each conference organized by the Institute and branch meeting on any aspect of marine technology, offshore technology, or marine electrical technology.

• 6047 • **Stanley Gray Branch Award**
To recognize the most worthy papers read to the Institute by a member or non-member on any aspect of marine technology in five categories: Marine Technology, Offshore Technology, Marine Electrical Technology, Maritime Technology Development, and Branches. For each category, a monetary prize of £500 and a certificate are awarded annually.

• 6048 • **Stanley Gray Medal**
To enable post-graduate students to undertake research in approved maritime subjects. Applicants must have obtained an approved engineering degree or the DTp Extra First Class Certificate of Competency and be members of the Institute. The deadline for applications is July 31. A monetary award of £2,000 per year (for a maximum of three years) is presented annually.

• 6049 • **BMEC Donald Maxwell Award**
For recognition of the best paper presented to, or published by, the Institute by a member or nonmember of any nationality on the research and/or development of some aspect of marine equipment and its market potential. Joint au-

thors are also eligible. Papers are to be assessed by the IMarE Technical Papers and Conferences Committee, whose recommendations are passed to the Donald Maxwell Fund Trustees for approval. A monetary prize of £500 is awarded annually.

• 6050 •

Institute of Measurement and Control
Michael Yates B.A., Sec.
87 Gower St.
London WC1E 6AF, United Kingdom
Phone: 44 207 3874949
Fax: 44 207 3888431
E-mail: m.yates@instmc.org.uk
Home Page: http://www.instmc.org.uk

• 6051 • **Honeywell Prize**
To recognize the best article for publication in *Measurement and Control*, the institute journal. The criteria for the assessment of these articles is as follows: general interest to the institute's members, importance of the subject to the institute, and lucidity and originality. Awarded annually the recipient receives a monetary award of £100.

• 6052 • **Sir George Thomson Gold Medal**
For recognition of a contribution to measurement science which has resulted in fundamental improvements in the understanding of the physical world. There are no restrictions on eligibility. A gold medal is awarded every five years. Established in 1975 to honor Sir George Thomson, the first President of the institute.

• 6053 •

Institute of Physics
Prof. John Enderby CBE, Pres.
76 Portland Pl.
London W1B 1NT, United Kingdom
Phone: 44 207 4704800
Fax: 44 207 4704848
E-mail: physics@iop.org
Home Page: http://www.iop.org

• 6054 • **Max Born Medal and Prize**
In recognition of outstanding contributions to physics. A monetary prize of 1,000 Euros, a silver medal, and a certificate are awarded annually in even-numbered years to a German physicist and presented in England, and in odd-numbered years to a British physicist and presented in Germany. Established in 1972 by the Institute of Physics and the German Physical Society in memory of Max Born, a physicist who died in 1970.

• 6055 • **Charles Vernon Boys Medal and Prize**
In recognition of distinguished research in experimental physics. Candidates should not normally be over 35 years of age. A monetary prize of £1,000, a silver medal and a certificate are awarded annually. Established in 1944 by a bequest of Sir Charles Vernon Boys, former president of the Physical Society.

• 6056 • **Bragg Medal and Prize**
For distinguished contributions to the teaching of physics. A monetary prize of £1,000, a bronze medal and a certificate are awarded annually. Established in 1965 in honor of Sir Lawrence Brag, teacher and popularizer of physics.

• 6057 • **Charles Chree Medal and Prize**
For distinguished research in terrestrial magnetism, atmospheric electricity, and/or other aspects of geophysics comprising the earth, oceans, atmosphere, and solar-terrestrial problems. A monetary prize of £1,000, a silver medal, and a certificate are awarded in odd-numbered years. Established in 1939 in memory of Dr. Chree, past president of the Physical Society.

• 6058 • **Paul Dirac Medal and Prize**
For outstanding contributions to theoretical (including mathematical and computational) physics. A monetary prize of £1,000, a silver medal and a certificate are awarded annually. Established in 1987 in memory of P. A. M. Dirac, an Honorary Fellow of The Institute of Physics.

• 6059 • **Duddell Medal and Prize**
In recognition of outstanding contributions to the application of physics or contributions to the advancement of knowledge by the invention or design of scientific instruments or the discovery of materials used in their construction. A monetary prize of £1,000, a bronze medal and a certificate are awarded annually. Established in 1923 by the Physical Society in memory of William du Bois Duddell, inventor of the electromagnetic oscillograph.

• 6060 • **Glazebrook Medal and Prize**
In recognition of outstanding contributions in the organization, utilization, or application of science. A monetary prize of £1,000, a silver gilt medal and a certificate are awarded annually. Established in 1965 by the Institute of Physics and the Physical Society in honor of Sir Richard Glazebrook, the first director of the National Physical Laboratory.

• 6061 • **Guthrie Medal and Prize**
To a physicist of international reputation for contributions to physics. A monetary prize of £1,000, a silver gilt medal and a certificate are awarded annually. Established in 1914 in memory of Professor Frederick Guthrie, founder of the Physical Society.

• 6062 • **Holweck Medal and Prize**
For distinguished work in any aspect of physics that is ongoing or has been carried out within the 10 years preceding this award. A monetary prize of 1,000 Euros, a gold medal, and a scroll are awarded in odd-numbered years to a French physicist and presented in England, and in even-numbered years to a British physicist and presented in France. Established in 1945 and administered jointly by the French Physical Society and the Institute of Physics in memory of Fernand Holweck, director of the Curie Laboratory of the Radium Institute in Paris.

• 6063 • **Kelvin Medal and Prize**
To recognize an individual or team for outstanding contributions to the public understanding of physics. A bronze medal, a certificate, and a £1000 prize are awarded annually. Established in 1994.

• 6064 • **Maxwell Medal and Prize**
For contributions to theoretical physics made in the 10 years preceding the date of the award unless, in exceptional circumstances, the Council extends this period. This award is intended to recognize physicists early in their careers. A monetary prize of £1,000, a bronze medal and a certificate are awarded annually. Established in 1961.

• 6065 • **Paterson Medal and Prize**
For outstanding contributions to the utilization and application of physics, particularly in the development, invention or discovery of new systems, processes or devices, which show the succesful commercial exploitation of physics. This award is intended to recognize physicists early in their careers. A monetary prize of £1,000, a bronze medal and a certificate are awarded annually. Established in 1981 in honor of Sir Clifford Paterson, founder of GEC Research Laboratories and a past president of the Institute.

• 6066 • **Rutherford Medal and Prize**
To an individual or team in recognition of contributions to nuclear physics, elementary particle physics, or nuclear technology. A monetary prize of £1,000, a bronze medal and a certificate are awarded in even-numbered years. Established in 1939 in memory of Lord Rutherford of Nelson. Formerly: Rutherford Memorial Lecture.

• 6067 • **Simon Memorial Prize**
In recognition of distinguished work in experimental or theoretical low-temperature physics. A monetary prize of £300, a bronze plaque, and a certificate are awarded approximately every three years. Established in 1958 in memory of Sir Francis Simon.

• 6068 • **Thomas Young Medal and Prize**
To an individual or team in recognition of work in optics, including work related to physics outside the visible region. A monetary prize of £1,000, a bronze medal and a certificate are awarded in odd-numbered years. Established in 1907 as the Thomas Young Oration by the Optical Society, taken over by the Physical Society of London in 1932, and changed to its present state in 1961 by the amalgamated Institute of Physics and Physical Society. Formerly: Thomas Young Oration.

• 6069 •
Institute of Physics and Engineering in Medicine
Peter Jackson, Pres.
Fairmount House
230 Tadcaster Rd.
York YO24 1ES, United Kingdom
Phone: 44 1904 610821
Fax: 44 1904 612279
E-mail: office@ipem.ac.uk
Home Page: http://www.ipem.ac.uk/ipem_public

• 6070 • **Founders Prize**

• 6071 • **Manufacturers Prize**
31100

• 6072 • **Wisconsin Travel Award**
31100

• 6073 •
Institute of Practitioners in Advertising
John Oldfield, Membership Dir.
44 Belgrave Sq.
London SW1X 8QS, United Kingdom
Phone: 44 20 72357020
Fax: 44 20 72459904
E-mail: info@ipa.co.uk
Home Page: http://www.ipa.co.uk

• 6074 • **Effectiveness Awards**
to provide a data bank of case history material to demonstrate the contribution that advertising can make to successful marketing. The main objectives are to improve understanding of the crucial role advertising plays in marketing; to provide documented analyses of advertising effectiveness and to encourage use of methods of evaluation; and to generate objective case studies about how advertising works, which could then be used in connection with marketing training. In odd-numbered years, the contest is limited to agencies with an income under £20 million and a maximum word count of 3,000; in even-numbered years, it is open to agencies worldwide and has a maximum word count of 4,000. Winning cases are awarded between one and five stars. The overall winner is presented with the Grand Prize. The winning case studies and a selection from the commended papers are published in a book, *Advertising Works*. Presented annually. Established in 1980.

• 6075 •
Institute of Quarrying - England
Jack Berridge, Exec.Dir.
7 Regent St.
Nottingham NG1 5BS, United Kingdom
Phone: 44 115 9453880
Fax: 44 115 9484035
E-mail: mail@quarrying.org
Home Page: http://www.quarrying.org

• 6076 • **Institute of Quarrying Awards**
To recognize individuals employed in the quarrying and related industries and to promote education and training in all aspects of quarry operation and business management. Awards include Caernarfon Award, Citation Award, International Citation Award, Honorary Fellowship, McPherson Memorial Lecture, Nordberg Traveling Scholarship, and Technical Paper Awards. Presented annually.

• 6077 •
Institute of Trade Mark Attorneys
Philip Harris, Pres.
2-6 Sydenham Rd.
Surrey
Croydon CR0 9XE, United Kingdom
Phone: 44 20 86862052
Fax: 44 20 86805723
E-mail: tm@itma.org.uk
Home Page: http://www.itma.org.uk

• 6078 • **Elizabeth Bennett Memorial Prize**
For outstanding achievement in the Institute's examinations.

• 6079 • **Adrian Spencer Memorial Award**
For achieving the highest mark in the Institute's examinations.

• 6080 •
Institution of Agricultural Engineers
Christopher Whetnall, Chief Exec./Sec.
Barton Rd.
Silsoe
Bedford MK45 4FH, United Kingdom
Phone: 44 1525 861096
Fax: 44 1525 861660
E-mail: secretary@iagre.org
Home Page: http://www.iagre.org

• 6081 • **Award of Merit**
For a person who has rendered services to the institution.

• 6082 • **Bomford Trust Paper Award**
Award of recognition.

• 6083 • **Contribution to Land Based Industries Award**
Award of recognition.

• 6084 • **Honorary Fellowship**
For a person who has rendered services to the institution.

• 6085 • **Johnson New Holland Award**
For innovation by students of Agricultural Engineering or related subjects.

• 6086 • **Michael Dwyer Memorial Award**
For mid-career engineer who has made outstanding progress in the agricultural engineering industry.

• 6087 • **Sustainability in Design and Use Award**
Award of recognition.

• 6088 •
Institution of Chemical Engineers
Dr. Trevor J. Evans, Chief Exec.
Davis Bldg.
165-189 Railway Terr.
Rugby CV21 3HQ, United Kingdom
Phone: 44 1788 578214
Fax: 44 1788 560833
E-mail: pr@icheme.org
Home Page: http://www.icheme.org

• 6089 • **Brennan Medal**
To recognize the best book published by the Institution each year. Awarded annually. Established in 1988 to honor Basil Brennan, the Institution's first General Secretary.

• 6090 • **Council Medal**
To recognize a member or non-member who has given exceptional service on a special project. Awarded annually. Established in 1967.

• 6091 • **George E. Davis Medal**
For recognition of a contribution in the field of chemical engineering. Awarded every four or five years. Established in 1965 in honor of George E. Davis, the father of the discipline.

• 6092 • **Donald Medal**
To recognize an individual for outstanding services to biochemical engineering. Established in 1988 to honor Prof. Donald, a long-serving Honorary Secretary and former Ramsay Professor at University College London where biochemical engineering was first established in the United Kingdom.

• 6093 • **Ned Franklin Medal**
To recognize an individual for outstanding service in the fields of occupational health, safety, loss prevention, and care for the environment. Awarded annually. Established in 1988 to honor Ned Franklin, a past president of the institution and a major personality in the development of the nuclear power industry.

• 6094 • **Arnold Greene Medal**
For recognition of the most meritorious contribution to the progress of the institution. Awarded annually. Established in 1928 in honor of F. A. Greene, a founder member and honorable treasurer for 33 years. Formerly: (1964) Osborne Reynolds Medal.

• 6095 • **Hanson Medal**
For recognition of the best article contributed to the institution's monthly publication, *The Chemical Engineer*. A medal is awarded annually. Established in 1987.

• 6096 • John William Hinchley Medal
To recognize the best student in the graduating class at Imperial College London. Awarded annually. Established in 1988 to honor John William Hinchley, the driving force behind the founding of the institution in 1922.

• 6097 • Hutchison Medal
To recognize the author of the best paper that is either philosophical in nature or deals with practical matters. Awarded annually. Established in 1991 to honor Sir Kenneth Hutchison, former president (1959-1960) of the institution.

• 6098 • Junior Moulton Medal
For recognition of the best paper published by the institution during the year. Papers written by members under 30 years of age are considered. Awarded annually. Established in 1929.

• 6099 • Macnab Medal
For recognition of the best answer to the institution's Design Project in any year. Established in 1935 to honor William Macnab, former president of the Institution.

• 6100 • Senior Moulton Medal
For recognition of the best paper published by the institution during the year. Awarded annually. Established in 1929.

• 6101 •
Institution of Civil Engineers
Colin J. Clinton FICE, Pres.
One Great George St.
Westminster
London SW1P 3AA, United Kingdom
Phone: 44 20 72227722
Fax: 44 20 72227500
E-mail: secretariat@ice.org.uk
Home Page: http://www.ice.org.uk

• 6102 • Russell Allin Prize
To recognize an associate member or a student for a paper dealing with soil mechanics and foundations, either general or in any of their aspects, such as theory, research, design, construction, testing, or with a particular form of foundation. A monetary prize of £100 and a certificate are awarded annually. Established in 1958 in memory of Russell Allin (1881-1957), a pioneer in soil mechanics.

• 6103 • Robert Alfred Carr Premium
To recognize the author of the best paper on dock, railway, and gas engineering subjects published by the Institution during the past year. A monetary prize of £50 and a certificate are awarded annually. Established in 1963 by Robert Alfred Carr (1864-1942) in memory of his father Robert Carr and his brother Harold Oswald Carr, bothe members of the Institution.

• 6104 • Civil Engineering Manager of the Year Award
To recognize the chartered civil engineer who has shown, in a given year, the finest management qualities on a construction project. The award, which comprises a medal and £500, can be made to a manager of a huge scheme, someone responsible for a substantial element of such a scheme, or an engineer in charge of a modest site.

• 6105 • Civil Engineering Students Papers Competition
For recognition of a paper on engineering design, research, or practice. Undergraduates of universities and polytechnics in the United Kingdom may be nominated by the heads of the engineering colleges. A monetary prize and a medal are awarded annually. All authors presenting papers in the final and not awarded the medal receive a monetary prize and a certificate. Established in 1946. Formerly: (1987) Institution Medal and Premium (London Universities) Competition; (1997) Institution Medal and Premium (Universities) Competition.

• 6106 • Coopers Hill War Memorial Prize
For recognition of a paper by a corporate member published by the Institution. The award is made irrespective of the age of the author and of any other award made for the same paper. A monetary prize, medal, and certificate are awarded. Established in 1921 by the Coopers Hill Society in memory of its members and relatives of its members who fell in the First World War.

• 6107 • Crampton Prize
For recognition of the best paper, preferably on the construction, ventilation, and working of tunnels of considerable length, or on any other subject that may be selected. A monetary prize and a certificate are awarded every four years. Established in 1890 following a bequest by Thomas Russell Crampton (1816-1888).

• 6108 • Bill Curtin Medal
To recognize the best paper presented to the Institution on innovative design in civil engineering. A medal is awarded annually. Established by in 1992 by Curtins Consulting Engineers to commemorate W. G. Curtin's contribution to engineering.

• 6109 • James Alfred Ewing Medal
For recognition of contributions to the science of engineering in the field of research. Members or nonmembers of the Institution are eligible. Recommendations are made by the Institute of Civil Engineers, the Institute of Mechanical Engineers, the Royal Institution of Naval Architects, and the Institution of Electrical Engineers. A gold medal with a bronze replica is awarded annually jointly with the Royal Society. Established in 1936 in memory of Sir Alfred Ewing (1855-1935), Honorary Member.

• 6110 • James Forrest Medal
To recognize the writer of the best student or associate member's paper presented to the Institution. A monetary award and a medal are awarded annually. Established in 1897 in honor of James Forrest, secretary of the Institution (1860-1896).

• 6111 • Geotechnical Research Medal
To recognize the author(s) of the best contribution in the field of research in geotechnical engineering published by the Institution in the previous year. A medal is awarded annually. Established in 1989 following a bequest by the late A. W. Bishop.

• 6112 • Gold Medal
To recognize an individual for valuable contributions to civil engineering over many years. This may cover contributions in one or more areas, such as, design, research, development, investigation, construction, management (including project management), education, and training. Eligible candidates are those who are in the course of, or have just completed, their active careers. Awarded annually. Established in 1993.

• 6113 • Graduate and Students Papers Competition (Local Association) Competition
For recognition of a paper on engineering design, research, or practice that has been presented at a local association meeting. Nominations may be submitted by the committees of the local associations. Associate members, graduates, and students may be nominated. A monetary prize and a medal are awarded annually. All authors presenting papers at the final and not awarded the medal receive a monteray prize and a certificate. Established in 1952. Formerly: (1997) Institution Medal and Premium (Local Association) Competition.

• 6114 • Halcrow Premium
For recognition of the best paper published by the Institution on docks and harbors, tunnels, and hydroelectric projects. Corporate members are eligible. A monetary prize is awarded annually. Established in 1960 by a bequest of Sir William Halcrow, president of the Institution in 1946-1947.

• 6115 • T. K. Hsieh Award
To recognize the author of the best paper published by the institution in the field of structural and soil vibration caused by mechanical plant, winds, waves, or seismic effects. A monetary prize of £100 is awarded annually. Established in 1979 in memory of Dr. Tso Kung Hsieh.

• 6116 • Renee Redfern Hunt Memorial Prize
For recognition of the best essays written in the spring, autumn, and overseas sessions of the professional examination for corporate membership of the Institution. A monetary prize of £100 and a certificate are awarded. Established in 1982 in memory of Miss Renee Redfern Hunt, MBE, Professional Examination Officer at the Institution from 1945 until within a few months of her death in 1981.

• 6117 • James Prescott Joule Medal
For recognition of the best paper presented on an engineering subject, preferably one dealing with the transformation of energy. Associate members under 27 years of age or students of the Institution may submit papers. A medal is awarded triennially.

• 6118 • Kelvin Medal
For recognition of distinguished service in the application of science to engineering rather than to the development of physical science itself. A medal is awarded triennially. Established in 1914 in memory of Lord Kelvin, a British physicist.

• 6119 • Lindapter Award
To recognize the author of the best paper submitted to the Institution's Medal and Premium (Local Associations and Universities) Competitions. Students pursuing a course of study approved by the Institution are eligible. A monetary prize of £200 is awarded. The winner's name and that of the university/college is recorded on a trophy and displayed by that university/college for the following eight months. Sponsored by Lindapter International Ltd.

• 6120 • MERIT Competition
MERIT (Managing Engineering Resources Involves Teamwork) is a construction management simulation run by the Institution. It is open to teams of up to 6 members. The competition is played by post, with the top six teams after five rounds competing against each other at a two-day final. The winning team receives an engraved salver to be retained for one year, and a monetary prize of £2,000 is to be shared among the winners. Held annually. Established in 1988. Formerly: MERIT Game.

• 6121 • Miller Prizes
For recognition of the best papers or series of papers by associate members, graduates, or students. Certificates and 10 prizes of £100 each are awarded annually. Established by a bequest of Joseph Miller (1797-1860), who was associated with marine engine design.

• 6122 • Overseas Premium
For recognition of the best papers received during the year on a subject connected with works carried out outside the British Isles. Corporate members of the Institution are eligible. Two monetary prizes and certificates are awarded annually.

• 6123 • Frederick Palmer Prize
For recognition of a paper published by the Institution. Preference is given to papers of merit dealing with the economic and financial aspects of civil engineering. A monetary prize and a certificate are awarded annually. Established in 1960 by a bequest made by John Palmer to mark the centenary of the birth of his father, Sir Frederick Palmer (1862-1934), president of the Institution in 1926-1927.

• 6124 • Parkman Medal
For recognition of the best paper published by the Institution in the previous year on the practical aspects of the control or management of the design and/or construction of a specific scheme. A medal is awarded. Established in 1988 by the Parkman Group to commemorate their centenary.

• 6125 • Reed and Mallik Medal
To recognize the author of the best paper published in the previous year covering the construction aspects of a civil engineering project. A monetary prize and a medal are awarded annually. Established in 1983 following a donation by the Rush & Tompkins Group plc to commemorate the achievements of their civil engineering contracting subsidiary Reed and Mallik Ltd.

• 6126 • Safety in Construction Medal
To recognize the author of a paper published by the Institution in the previous year that discusses a project or feature within a project that best describes the measures taken to safeguard the health and safety of the construction team, the user, and the public. A medal is awarded annually. Established in 1992 by John Derrington, president of the Institution in 1984-1985, to foster actively improved health and safety in construction works.

• 6127 • George Stephenson Medal
For recognition in the field of civil engineering. Established in 1881.

• 6128 • Teambuild
To provide a competition for young professionals in the construction industry. Open to multidisciplinary teams of up to six members, all of whom must be 30 years of age or younger. The competition is held at the Institution over a two-day period. A monetary prize of £1,000 donated by the Worshipful Company of Constructors to the winners and £500 donated by the Worshipful Company of Chartered Architects is awarded to the teams that perform best in the Contracts Strategy Session. Each team receives a certificate. Held annually. Established in 1993 by the Institution and the Junior Liason Organization under the umbrella of the Construction Industry Council. Formerly: Build a Building Competition.

• 6129 • Telford Medal
This, the highest award of the Institution for a paper, is given to recognize a paper or series of papers presented to the Institution, irrespective of any previous recognition. Medals and monetary prizes are awarded annually when merited. Established in 1835 by a bequest made to the Institution by Thomas Telford (1757-1834), first president of the Institution. First awarded in 1837.

• 6130 • Trevithick Premium
For recognition of a paper presented to the Institution. A monetary prize is awarded triennially. Established in 1890 in memory of Richard Trevithick (1771-1833) and augmented in 1932 by a gift from Mrs. H. K. Trevithick.

• 6131 • Garth Watson Medal
To recognize dedicated and valuable service to the Institution related to any field of its activities or for a contribution to a specific Institution project by a member or a member of staff. Awarded annually. Established in 1993 in honor of Garth Watson, a respected past secretary of the Institution.

• 6132 • James Watt Medal
For recognition of papers on mechanical engineering subjects. A medal is awarded annually. Established in 1858 to honor James Watt, Scottish mechanical engineer and inventor.

• 6133 • Webb Prize
For recognition of papers on railway engineering and transportation in general. Two monetary prizes and certificates are awarded annually. Established in 1908 by a bequest of Francis William Webb (1838-1906), vice president.

• 6134 •
Institution of Diagnostic Engineers
Dr. J. Mullins, Sec.
7 Weir Rd.
Kibworth
Leicester LE8 0LQ, United Kingdom
Phone: 44 116 2796772
Fax: 44 116 2796884
E-mail: admin@diagnosticengineers.org
Home Page: http://www.diagnosticengineers.org

• 6135 • Collacott Prize
To encourage members to submit information of diagnostic interest and of value to increasing a member's store of knowledge and events that can or may occur, and of techniques of deduction. Entries should be brief and factual, preferably illustrated by line sketches. A monetary prize is awarded annually. Established in 1985.

• 6136 •
Institution of Diesel and Gas Turbine Engineers
John Blowes, Dir.Gen.
Bedford Heights
Manton Ln.
Bedford MK41 7PH, United Kingdom
Phone: 44 1234 214340
Fax: 44 1234 355493
E-mail: enquiries@idgte.org
Home Page: http://www.idgte.org

• 6137 • Percy Still Medal
To the paper of greatest interest to users.

• 6138 • Akroyd Stuart Certificate
To the paper with greatest technical merit.

Awards are arranged in alphabetical order below their administering organizations

• 6139 • John Walker Award
To the most meritorious operational notes and working cost return.

• 6140 •
Institution of Electrical Engineers - England
Sir John Chisholm, Pres.
Savoy Pl.
London WC2R 0BL, United Kingdom
Phone: 44 20 72401871
Fax: 44 20 72407735
E-mail: postmaster@iee.org.uk
Home Page: http://www.iee.org

• 6141 • Achievement Medals
For recognition of achievement in the following categories: informatics; control; power electrical engineering; science, education, or technology; engineering management, engineering design, or an area within the scope of Professional Group M2 (Engineering and Society). A person or group of persons without restriction as regards nationality, country of residence, or membership of the Institution may be considered. A maximum of five awards (one for each category) are made annually. A bronze medal engraved with the recipient's name and year of award is presented in October.

• 6142 • Benefactors Prize
To recognize meritorious students who have satisfied the Institute's educational requirements in the preceding year. Members of IEE are eligible. A monetary prize of £200 and a certificate are awarded annually in October.

• 6143 • Blumlein-Brown-Willans Premium
For recognition of papers on the science and art of television or pulse and wideband techniques. Papers published in IEE publications are eligible. A monetary prize of £150 and a certificate are awarded annually in October. Established in 1954.

• 6144 • Bridgeport Prize
To recognize the best project on quality management in an accredited engineering degree course. The following prizes are awarded annually: first prize - £250 and a certificate; second prize - £100 and a certificate; and third prize - £50 and a certificate.

• 6145 • Coopers Hill War Memorial Medal
For recognition of the best paper on a professional subject by a corporate member under 35 years of age. A monetary prize, a bronze medal, and a certificate are awarded annually by the Institution of Civil Engineers and triennially jointly with the IEE, the School of Military Engineering (Chatham) and the School of Forestry (Oxford). Established by the Coopers Hill Society in commemoration of members of the College who fell in the 1914-1918 War.

• 6146 • Divisional Premium
For recognition of papers published in IEE publications. Awards are given in the following divisions: Electronics and Communications Division (Mountbatten Premium), Control Division (F. C. Williams Premium), Informatics Division, Management Division, Power Division, Manufacturing Division, and Science, Education and Technology Division. Seven monetary awards of £500 each and a certificate are awarded annually. In addition to the Divisional Premiums, each Division may award the following Premiums of £150 each and a certificate annually: Electronics and Communications Division - Ambrose Fleming Premium, Oliver Lodge Premium, Marconi Premium, and J. J. Thomson Premium; Informatics Division - Mather Premium and Hartree Premium, Control Division Heaviside Premium, and Kelvin Premium; Management Division Lord Hirst Premium; Power Division - Crompton Premium, Sebastian Z. de Ferranti Premium, John Hopkinson Premium, and Swan Premium; and Science, Education and Technology Division Ayrton Premium, Duddell Premium, Maxwell Premium, and Snell Premium.

• 6147 • Faraday House Commemorative Prize
For recognition of the best lecture presentation by a younger member. Presentations made by members under 30 years of age at an IEE meeting are considered. A monetary prize of £150 and a certificate are awarded annually in October.

• 6148 • Faraday Medal
For recognition of notable scientific or industrial achievement in electrical engineering, or for conspicuous service rendered to the advancement of electrical science. There are no restrictions as regards nationality, country of residence, or membership in the institution. A bronze medal and vellum certificate are awarded annually in March.

• 6149 • Tony Goldsmith Cup
To recognize a young member (under 35 years) of the Institution active in the work of the Manufacturing Division for a meritorious contribution to the progress of the division. A cup, held for one year by the recipient, is presented annually in October.

• 6150 • Harry Henniker Premium
For recognition of a paper by a younger member of the Institution. Managed by IEE Scotland.

• 6151 • IERE Benefactors Premium
For recognition of a paper on the application of broadcast and communication technology, including papers on applications for educational purposes. A monetary prize of £150 is awarded annually in October.

• 6152 • J. A. Lodge Award for Medical Engineering
Recognizes an electronic or electrical engineer, up to the age of 35, who has shown promise through a significant innovation in the field of research and development in medical engineering. A monetary prize of £250 is awarded annually.

• 6153 • Manufacturing Project Prizes
To recognize the best project by a student in an accredited undergraduate degree course. Eight awards are presented annually: Jones & Shipman Prize, - £500; Sir Walter Puckey Prize - £100; Lord Austin Prize - £100; Sir Robert Telford Prize - £100; Sir Alan Veale Prize - £100; IBM MEng Project Prize - £100; Professor J. Cherry Prize - £100; and Bridgeport Prize - £250. Certificates are also awarded.

• 6154 • Measurement Prize
For recognition of a contribution to the science, art, and practice of electrical measurement. A monetary prize of £1,000 is awarded annually in December.

• 6155 • Eric Megaw Memorial Prize
To recognize the best lecture presentation and paper by a final year student of the Electrical and Electronic Engineering Department of the Queen's University of Belfast. A monetary prize of £100 and a certificate are awarded annually in March.

• 6156 • Sir Eric Mensforth International Gold Medal
To recognize outstanding contributions to the advancement of manufacturing engineering technology or manufacturing management. A gold medal is awarded annually in October.

• 6157 • Henry Nimmo Premium
For recognition of the best paper by a student on a subject within the field of electricity supply. A monetary award of £50 is given annually. Established in memory of Henry Nimmo, former chairman of the Southern Electricity Board, by its members.

• 6158 • Viscount Nuffield Silver Medal
To recognize a member of the Institution for meritorious contribution to the progress of the manufacturing profession. A silver medal is awarded annually in October.

• 6159 • Rayleigh Book Award
To recognize an outstanding book published by the IEE. A monetary award of £500 and a certificate are presented annually.

• 6160 • A. H. Reeves Premium
To recognize the best paper published in any Institution publication on digital coding. A monetary prize of £150 and a certificate are presented annually. Established in honor of Alec Harley Reeves for his work on PCM at the laboratories of STC (1902-1971).

• 6161 • Sir Henry Royce Award
To recognize a younger member who shows excellence in his or her work in industry or for the profession. A monetary prize of £250, a medal,

and a certificate are awarded annually in October.

• 6162 • **J. Langham Thompson Premium**
To recognize a paper published in the *Electronics & Communication Engineering Journal*. A monetary prize of £150 and a certificate are awarded annually. Established in 1962.

• 6163 • **J. J. Thomson Premium**
For recognition of outstanding work by a person or group of persons in electronics theory, practice, development, or manufacture. There are no restrictions regarding nationality, country of residence, or membership of the Institution. A bronze medal is awarded annually.

• 6164 • **Young Engineer of the Year**
To recognize competitors in the Altran Engineering Academy's Young Engineers of the Year competition. A monetary prize of £500 is awarded annually.

• 6165 • **Younger MembersK Award for Achievement**
Awarded for an outstanding achievement by a younger member in a field other than engineering. One medal and £500 are awarded annually.

• 6166 • **Dr. V. K. Zworykin Premium**
For recognition of papers published by the IEE on medical and biological electronics. A monetary prize of £150 is awarded annually in October. Established in 1960 by the Institution of Electronic and Radio Engineers in honor of Dr. V. K. Zworykin.

• 6167 •
Institution of Gas Engineers and Managers
John Williams, CEO
Charnwood Wing
Holywell Park
Ashby Rd.
Leicestershire
Loughborough LE11 3GH, United Kingdom
Phone: 44 1509 282728
Fax: 44 1509 283110
E-mail: general@igem.co.uk
Home Page: http://www.igem.org.uk

• 6168 • **Birmingham Medal**
To encourage the extension of the uses of coal gas. It is bestowed for originality in connection with the manufacture and application of gas, such qualification to be interpreted in its widest possible sense. Members may submit names of individuals who are members of the Institution or any of its affiliated organizations for the consideration of the Council. A medal is awarded biennially when merited. Established in 1881.

• 6169 • **Institution of Gas Engineers Bronze Medal**
For recognition of a paper accepted for presentation to and read at a General Meeting of a Gas Association in the calendar year preceding the year of the award. A Presidential Address is not eligible for the award and the author of a paper must be a member of the Gas Association before which the paper is read. A bronze medal is awarded annually. Established in 1905.

• 6170 • **Institution of Gas Engineers Gold Medal**
For recognition of a paper on any subject, accepted for presentation to and read at a General Meeting of the Institution in the calendar year preceding the year of the award. Individuals who are members of the Institution or any of its affiliated organizations are eligible. A gold medal is awarded annually. Established in 1912.

• 6171 • **Institution of Gas Engineers Silver Medal**
For recognition of a paper accepted for presentation to and read at a General Meeting of a District Section of the Institution or of an Affiliated District Association in the calendar year preceding the year of the award. A Chairman's or a Presidential Address is not eligible for the award and the author of a paper must be a member in any class of the Institution. A silver medal is awarded annually. Established in 1905.

• 6172 • **H. E. Jones London Medal**
For recognition of a paper accepted for presentation to and read at a General Meeting of the Institution in the calendar year preceding the year of the award. The paper must deal with the principles involved in the construction of works or plants for the manufacture or distribution of gas and/or the points of good management of a gas undertaking considered in relation to the management of labor, the facilitating and popularizing the use of gas for general purposes, or improvement in carbonizing and purifying processes, or in the development of residuals. Individuals who are members of the Institution or any of its affiliated organizations are eligible. A medal is awarded annually. Established in 1905.

• 6173 • **James Ransom Memorial Medals**
For recognition of the best paper presented by an Associate member (Technician Engineer Grade) of the Institution, who is registered with the Engineering Council as an Incorporated Engineer. The Medal will be awarded annually by the Council for a paper presented to any meeting of the Institution, its Sections, any affiliated body, or any other relevant meeting. To be presented in the calendar year preceding the award. Established in 1979 to honor James Ransom for his work in the field of education and training in the gas industry.

• 6174 • **Sugg Heritage Award**
For recognition of a paper judged to contribute most to the understanding of the history, traditions or aspirations and achievements of the gas industry (as defined by By-Law 1 of the Institution of Gas Engineers) as to a particular activity or period of either engineering, scientific or social import. Individuals who are members of the Institution or any of its affiliated organizations are eligible. The paper is to be selected by a Panel comprising the Chairman and two members or nominees of the Panel for the History of the Industry from those accepted for presentation to a General Meeting of a District Section or Gas Association of Great Britain or a paper accepted for presentation to a General Meeting of the Institution in the calendar year preceding the award. A trophy is presented at the Institution Annual General Meeting. Established in 1981.

• 6175 •
Institution of Incorporated Engineers
Peter Wason, Chief Exec./Sec.
Savoy Hill House
Savoy Hill
London WC2R 0BS, United Kingdom
Phone: 44 20 78363357
Fax: 44 20 74979006
E-mail: info@iie.org.uk
Home Page: http://www.iie.org.uk

• 6176 • **Caroline Haslett Memorial Trust**
To women undertaking a full time course in electronic, electrical, mechanical or allied engineering subjects.

• 6177 • **Editorial Award**
To the authors of best articles appearing in the IIE magazine.

• 6178 • **Gustave Canet Memorial Medal**
To an eminent scientist or engineer who presents the Gustave Canet Memorial Lecture.

• 6179 • **Lady Finniston Award**
To female UK residents For the first year of study on an engineering degree or HND course in any branch of engineering.

• 6180 • **Regional Achievement Award**
To a person who made the most significant contribution to the success of the IIE Regions.

• 6181 • **Regional Presentation Award**
To the person who have given the most inFormative presentation to the IIE Regions.

• 6182 • **Sir Henry Royce Memorial Medal**
To an eminent person who presents the Sir Henry Royce Memorial Lecture.

• 6183 • **Young Woman Engineer of the Year Award**
For the best female engineer.

• 6184 •
Institution of Mechanical Engineers
Sir Michael Moore KBE, Chief Exec.
1 Birdcage Walk
Westminster
Bury St. Edmunds
London SW1H 9JJ, United Kingdom
Phone: 44 20 72227899
Fax: 44 20 72224557
E-mail: membership@imeche.org.uk
Home Page: http://www.imeche.org.uk

• 6185 • Institution of Mechanical Engineers Awards
To support and encourage research and training for members. A number of awards are offered to corporate and non-corporate members, including: James Clayton Prize, James Watt International Medal, Thomas Hawksley Gold Medal, Whitworth Scholarship Awards for Engineering Apprentices, and George Stephenson Prize, among others. Monetary awards totaling £400,000 are presented annually.

• 6186 • James Watt International Medal
To recognize an individual for work as a mechanical engineer and the ability to apply science to the progress of mechanical engineering. Engineering institutions and societies of any nationality may nominate engineers who have attained international recognition. A gold medal is presented biennially. Established in 1937 in memory of James Watt, the inventor of the steam engine.

• 6187 •
Institution of Nuclear Engineers
Prof. P.A. Beeley PhD, Pres.
Allan House, 1 Penerley Rd.
London SE6 2LQ, United Kingdom
Phone: 44 208 6981500
Phone: 44 208 6956409
Fax: 44 208 6956409
E-mail: inucewh@aol.com
Home Page: http://www.inuce.org.uk

• 6188 • Graduate Award
Award of recognition.

• 6189 • Honorary Fellowship
Awarded for for distinguished service to the institution and/or the UK nuclear engineering profession and/or the international nuclear engineering profession.

• 6190 •
Institution of Occupational Safety and Health
Irene Plackett, Contact
The Grange
Highfield Dr.
Leicestershire
Wigston LE18 1NN, United Kingdom
Phone: 44 116 2573100
Fax: 44 116 2573101
E-mail: enquiries@iosh.co.uk
Home Page: http://www.iosh.co.uk

• 6191 • Lifetime Achievement Award
Recognizes individuals who have furthered the status of occupational health and safety practice. Awarded annually.

• 6192 • Practical Project Award
Annual award of recognition. Inquire for application details.

• 6193 • Technician Safety Practitioner Scholarship
Annual award of recognition. Inquire for application details.

• 6194 •
Institution of Structural Engineers
Dr. Keith Eaton, Chief Exec.
11 Upper Belgrave St.
London SW1X 8BH, United Kingdom
Phone: 44 20 72354535
Fax: 44 20 72354294
E-mail: mail@istructe.org.uk
Home Page: http://www.istructe.org.uk

• 6195 • Institution of Structural Engineers Gold Medal
This, the highest individual award is for recognition of outstanding personal contributions to the advancement of structural engineering. Individuals from anywhere in the world are eligible. A gold medal is awarded when merited. Established in 1922.

• 6196 • Institution of Structural Engineers Special Awards
For recognition of structural engineering excellence, as expressed in a physical form in an existing building or structure. Organizations from anywhere in the world are eligible. An appropriate award and a plaque are awarded when merited. Established in 1968.

• 6197 •
Intensive Care Society
Pauline Kemp, Admin. Mgr.
35 Red Lion Sq.
London WC1R 4SG, United Kingdom
Phone: 44 20 72804350
Fax: 44 20 75804369
E-mail: admin@ics.ac.uk
Home Page: http://www.ics.ac.uk

• 6198 • Intensive Care Society Research Gold Medal
To a young investigator who has shown excellence in science.

• 6199 • Research Grants
For research and education funding.

• 6200 • Visiting Scholarship
For members.

• 6201 •
International Advertising Festival
Romain Hatchuel, Managing Dir.
33-39 Bowling Green Ln.
London EC1R 0DA, United Kingdom
Phone: 44 20 72393400
Fax: 44 20 72393444
Home Page: http://www.canneslions.com

• 6202 • International Advertising Festival, Cannes
To recognize the best in world audio/visual advertising in 28 consumer products categories in the Festival. The Festival is open to advertising agencies and production houses throughout the world. All films submitted must have been produced during the preceding year. Entries must advertise consumer or capital goods or consumer services (with the exception of those entered in Category 26 - Public Service & Social Welfare - Political advertising). All work submitted must be designed for and exhibited in public cinemas or on television networks. The following prizes are awarded: Grand Prix du Festival - to entrant company for the best commercial in the Festival; Palme d'Or - offered by the city of Cannes to the production company obtaining the highest number of marks for its ten best commercials in the Festival, irrespective of whether these have been entered by the production company or the advertising agency; and Category prizes - the Jury will award Gold Lions, Silver Lions, and Bronze Lions. There is an Agency of the Year Award for the agency gaining the most number of Lions. Awarded annually. The festival is held in the 3rd week of June in Cannes, France. Established in 1953.

• 6203 •
International Aluminium Institute
(Institut International d'Aluminium)
Robert Chase, Sec.Gen.
New Zealand House, 8th Fl.
Haymarket
London SW1Y 4TE, United Kingdom
Phone: 44 207 9300528
Fax: 44 207 3210183
E-mail: iai@world-aluminium.org
Home Page: http://www.world-aluminium.org

• 6204 • Honorary Member
To recognize a person who has made a significant contribution to the work of the Institute, the furtherance of the objects of the Institute, or the furtherance of the interests of aluminum producers. Individuals may be recommended by the Board of Directors. Honorary membership and its rights are awarded when merited. Established in 1976.

• 6205 •
International Association for Religious Freedom
Daryl M. Balia, Gen.Sec.
2 Market St.
Oxford OX1 3ET, United Kingdom
Phone: 44 1865 202744
Fax: 44 1865 202746
E-mail: hq@iarf.net
Home Page: http://www.iarf.net

• 6206 • Albert Schweitzer Award
For recognition of distinguished service in promoting human rights and in serving the poor. Members of the Association may nominate individuals who have exhibited exemplary commitment in this regard. A plaque is awarded triennially, at each IARF World Congress.

Established in 1975 in memory of Albert Schweitzer.

• 6207 •
International Association for the Scientific Study of Intellectual Disabilities
(Association Internationale Pour l'Etude Scientifique de la Deficience Intellectuelle)
Prof. David Felce, Pres.
Univ. of Wales Coll. of Medicine
Meridian Ct.
North Rd.
Cardiff CF14 3BG, United Kingdom
Phone: 33 1 43851206
Fax: 33 1 49361154
E-mail: felce@cardiff.ac.uk
Home Page: http://www.iassid.org

Formerly: International Association for the Scientific Study of Mental Deficiency.

• 6208 • Awards
To encourage research in the field of mental retardation, including causes, prevention, diagnosis, evaluation, therapy, rehabilitation, management, education, and social habilitation. Awards are presented.

• 6209 •
International Association for the Scientific Study of Intellectual Disabilities - Ireland
David Felce, Pres.
Welsh Center for Learning Disabilities
Cardiff Univ.
2nd Fl., Neuadd Meirionydd
Heath Park
Cardiff CF14 4YS, United Kingdom
E-mail: felce@cardiff.ac.uk
Home Page: http://www.iassid.org

• 6210 • Distinguished Achievement Award - Research
For formulation and investigation which contributed significantly to the sciences.

• 6211 • Distinguished Achievement Award - Scientific Literature
For outstanding publication.

• 6212 • Distinguished Achievement Award - Service
For contributions to the improvement of services to persons with intellectual disability.

• 6213 • Distinguished Service Citation
For outstanding or exemplary service to the Association by a person who has served as an officer, counsellor or member of a committee.

• 6214 •
International Association for the Study of Obesity
Arne Astrup, Pres.
231 N Gower St.
London NW1 2NR, United Kingdom
Phone: 44 207 6911900
Fax: 44 207 3876033
E-mail: inquiries@iaso.org
Home Page: http://www.iaso.org

• 6215 • Andre Mayer Award
To individuals (under 40 years) for excellence in research.

• 6216 • Wertheimer Award
For excellence in research by a basic scientist.

• 6217 • Willendorf Award
For excellence in research by a clinician.

• 6218 •
International Association of Broadcasting Manufacturers
Mrs. Martin Salter, Chm.
PO Box 2264
Reading RG31 6WA, United Kingdom
Phone: 44 118 9418620
Fax: 44 118 9418630
E-mail: info@theiabm.org
Home Page: http://www.theiabm.org

• 6219 • Peter Wayne Award
To recognize the company that produced the best designed, most innovative product displayed at the annual exhibit of the International Broadcasting Convention. Awarded annually. Established in 1990.

• 6220 •
International Association of Music Libraries, Archives and Documentation Centres - United Kingdom and Ireland
Almut Boehme B.A.,, Membership Sec.
Music Collections
Natl. Library of Scotland
George IV Bridge
Edinburgh EH1 1EW, United Kingdom
Phone: 44 131 6233880
Fax: 44 131 6233701
E-mail: a.boehme@nls.uk
Home Page: http://www.iaml-uk-irl.org

• 6221 • C. B. Oldman Prize
For recognition of the best work of music bibliography, librarianship, or reference. Individuals living in the United Kingdom are eligible. A monetary prize of £200 is awarded annually at the IAML (UK) annual study weekend. Established in 1988.

• 6222 •
International Association of Professional Congress Organizers
Andre Vietor, Pres.
42 Canham Rd.
London W3 7SR, United Kingdom
Phone: 44 20 87496171
Fax: 44 20 87400241
E-mail: info@iapco.org
Home Page: http://www.iapco.org

• 6223 • International Client Award
For a society's contribution and excellence in the international meetings market.

• 6224 • National Client Award
For a society's desire to seek levels of excellence at meetings on a continual basis.

• 6225 • National Supplier Award
For excellent service provided over 15 years, based on professionalism, innovative planning, being proactive and creative, supportive and reliable.

• 6226 •
International Association of Schools of Social Work
(Association Internationale des Ecoles de Travail Social)
Lena Dominelli, Pres.
School of Social Sciences
Southampton Univ.
Highfield
Southampton SO17 1BJ, United Kingdom
Phone: 44 23 80593054
Fax: 44 23 80594800
E-mail: ld@socsci.soton.ac.uk
Home Page: http://www.iassw.soton.ac.uk

• 6227 • Katherine Kendall Award
To acknowledge significant contributions to the development of social work education at the international level. Awarded biennially in even-numbered years. Established in 1992.

• 6228 •
International Association of Technological University Libraries
Judith Palmer, Sec.
Radcliffe Science Library
University of Oxford
Parks Rd.
Oxford OX1 3QP, United Kingdom
Phone: 44 1865 272820
Fax: 44 1865 272832
E-mail: judith.palmer@bodley.ox.ac.uk
Home Page: http://www.iatul.org

• 6229 • International Association of Technological University Libraries Poster Prize
Encourages this presentation from at IATUL Conferences. The best poster presentation will be award 250 Euro annually. Established in 2000.

• 6230 •
International Bar Association
(Association Internationale du Barreau)
Mark Ellis, Exec.Dir.
1 Stephen St., 10th Fl.
London W1T 1AT, United Kingdom
Phone: 44 20 76916868
Fax: 44 20 76916544
E-mail: member@int-bar.org
Home Page: http://www.ibanet.org

• 6231 • **Bernard Simons Memorial Award**
To recognize a legal practitioner who had made a substantial contribution to the promotion, probation and the advancement of human rights. Awarded biennially in even-numbered years.

• 6232 •
International Broadcasting Convention
Aldwych House
81 Aldwych
London WC2B 4EL, United Kingdom
Phone: 44 20 7611 7500
Fax: 44 20 7611 7530
E-mail: show@ibc.org
Home Page: http://www.ibc.org

Formerly: IBC Award.

• 6233 • **IBC International John Tucker Award**
To recognize an individual, group, or organization for demonstrated excellence of innovation and the furtherance or application of media technology. A monetary prize of £5,000 and a specially commissioned sculpture in glass are awarded biennially at the convention. Established in 1984 to mark the 10th anniversary of IBC. Renamed for John Tucker in recognition for the past chairman's many years of service to the IBC. Formerly: (2006) IBC John Tucker Award.

• 6234 •
International Dance Teachers' Association
Liz Murphy, Contact
International House
76 Bennett Rd.
Brighton BN2 5JL, United Kingdom
Phone: 44 1273 685652
Fax: 44 1273 674388
E-mail: info@idta.co.uk
Home Page: http://www.idta.co.uk

• 6235 • **Classic Championship**
Recognizes outstanding dancers in ballroom and Latin dance. Awarded annually.

• 6236 • **Medalist of the Year**
Recognizes outstanding amateur dancers in various age categories. Dance students are eligible. Scholarships for dance school are awarded annually.

• 6237 • **Miss Dance of Great Britain**
Recognizes outstanding dancers. Dance students on the verge of becoming professional are eligible. Awarded annually.

• 6238 •
International Egg Commission
(Commission Internationale des Oeufs)
Neil Mackenzie, Sec.Gen.
89 Charterhouse St., 2nd Fl.
London EC1M 6HR, United Kingdom
Phone: 44 20 74903493
Fax: 44 20 74903495
E-mail: julian@internationalegg.com
Home Page: http://www.internationalegg.com

• 6239 • **International Egg Commission Promotion and Marketing Award**
For recognition of outstanding efforts in the fields of promotion and marketing of eggs. The IEC nominates a country which then selects an award winner. A trophy is presented annually. Established in 1970. Formerly: (1991) International Egg Marketing Award.

• 6240 •
International Federation for Theatre Research
(Federation Internationale pour la Recherche Theatrale)
David Whitton, Sec.Gen.
Department of European Languages and Cultures
University of Lancaster
Lancaster LA1 4YN, United Kingdom
Phone: 44 1524 592664
Fax: 44 1524 593942
E-mail: d.whitton@lancaster.ac.uk
Home Page: http://www.firt-iftr.org

• 6241 • **New Scholar's Prize**
To recognize the best essay by a new scholar under the age of 35. The essay must not exceed 4,000 words and may be written in English or French. Airfare, fees, and accommodation for the Conference, and one year's membership in the organization are awarded annually.

• 6242 •
International Federation of Air Line Pilots Associations
(Federation Internationale des Associations de Pilotes de Ligne)
Cathy Bill, Exec.Dir.
Interpilot House
Gogmore Ln.
Chertsey KT16 9AP, United Kingdom
Phone: 44 1932 571711
Fax: 44 1932 570920
E-mail: globalpilot@ifalpa.org
Home Page: http://www.ifalpa.org

• 6243 • **Polaris Award**
For recognition of acts of heroism and/or exceptional airmanship in civil aviation. Selection is by nomination. A medal is awarded annually at the Conference. Established in 1983.

• 6244 • **Clarence N. Sayen Award**
To honor a person whose personal contribution towards the achievement of the Federation's aims and objectives has been outstanding. Awarded annually. Established in 1965.

• 6245 • **Scroll of Merit**
For recognition of the sustained efforts of individuals who have served IFALPA with loyalty, honor, and distinction. Awarded to one or more recipients annually. Established in 1969.

• 6246 •
International Federation of Airworthiness
(Federation Internationale de Navigabilite Aerospatiale)
Mr. John W. Saul, Exec.Dir.
UK Secretariat
14 Railway Approach
East Grinstead RH19 1BP, United Kingdom
Phone: 44 1341 301788
Fax: 44 1342 317808
E-mail: sec@ifairworthy.org
Home Page: http://www.ifairworthy.org

Formerly: IFA International Aviation Scholarship.

• 6247 • **Len Gore Scholarship**
To encourage professional development, particularly in third world countries. Young persons who are employed by member organizations must be nominated by their companies by October each year. The award consists of one year of training by an aerospace manufacturer or airline in the United States or the United Kingdom, temporary employment by the host company, and a settling in grant of $2,000 from IFA. Awarded annually. Formerly: IFA International Aviation Scholarship.

• 6248 • **International Society of Aircraft Traders (ISTAT) Scholarship**
Each year, a candidate is selected from within IFA's membership to receive training in an airworthiness related discipline. This will be funded to the value of $5,000 p.a.

• 6249 • **Whittle Safety Award**
A selection board reviews entrants, from within the aerospace community, each year for this award, and it honors the work of Sir Frank Whittle. The winner receives a medal and a citation. Traditionally this award is presented at the annual IASS Global Safety Converence.

• 6250 •
International Federation of Automotive Engineering Societies
Ian Dickie, CEO
30 Percy St.
London W1T 2DB, United Kingdom
Phone: 44 20 7299 6630
Fax: 44 20 7299 6633
E-mail: info@fisita.com
Home Page: http://www.fisita.com

• 6251 • **FISITA Travelling Fellowship**
To enable young engineers (under age 35) to attend the Federation Internationale des Societes d'Ingenieurs des Techniques de

l'Automobile (FISITA) World Congress, which is held biennially in even-numbered years.

• 6252 •
International Federation of Business and Professional Women
DR. Antoinette Ruegg, Pres.
PO Box 568
Horsham RH13 9ZP, United Kingdom
Phone: 44 1403 739343
Fax: 44 1403 734432
E-mail: members@bpwintl.com
Home Page: http://www.bpwintl.com

• 6253 • Honor al Merito
To recognize women who have distinguished themselves through outstanding service to the business and professional women of Costa Rica. Candidates may be Costa Rican citizens or nationals of other lands. A certificate of merit is presented annually at the "Internacional Noche de las Velas." Established in 1982 in honor of Carmen Madrigal de Gennette y Mae, founder of the federation in 1970.

• 6254 •
International Federation of Clinical Neurophysiology
(Federation Internationale de Neurophysiologie Clinique)
Wendy Holloway, contact
42 Canham Rd.
London W3 7SR, United Kingdom
Phone: 44 208 7433106
Fax: 44 208 7431010
E-mail: ifcn@ifcn.info
Home Page: http://www.ifcn.info

Formerly: (1990) International Federation of Societies for Electroencephalography and Clinical Neurophysiology.

• 6255 • M. A. B. Brazier Young Investigator Award
For recognition of an original manuscript of a clinical neurophysiology study in which the applicant is the primary investigator and the first author. Neurophysiologists under 40 years of age from the North and South Americas, Australasia and Japan may apply. A monetary prize of $3,500 is awarded every four years at the international congress. Established in 1988 by Elsevier Science Publishers in honor of M.A.B. Brazier, for his work in electroencephalography and clinical neurophysiology.

• 6256 • W. A. Cobb Young Investigator Award
For recognition of an original manuscript of a clinical neurophysiology study in which the applicant is the primary investigator and the first author. Neurophysiologists under 40 years of age from Europe, Asia (except Japan), and Africa may apply. A monetary prize of $3,500 is awarded every four years at the international congress. Established in 1988 by Elsevier Science Publishers in honor of W.A. Cobb, for his work in electroencephalography and clinical neurophysiology.

• 6257 •
International Federation of Netball Associations
Anne Steele, Exec. Off.
Belle Vue Leisure Centre
Kirkmanshulme Ln.
Longsight
Manchester M12 4TF, United Kingdom
Phone: 44 161 9532459
Fax: 44 161 9532492
E-mail: ifna@btinternet.com
Home Page: http://www.netball.org

• 6258 • International Federation of Netball Associations Service Awards
For recognition of service to the game of netball on an international scale. (Netball is played outdoors or indoors using a netball or an Association football size 5.) Nominations must be submitted by members. A badge is awarded biennially. Established in 1979.

• 6259 •
International Federation of Shipmasters' Associations
(Federation Internationale des Associations de Patrons de Navires)
Capt. R. MacDonald, Sec.Gen.
202 Lambeth Rd.
London SE1 7JY, United Kingdom
Phone: 44 207 2610450
Fax: 44 207 9289030
E-mail: hq@ifsma.org
Home Page: http://www.ifsma.org

• 6260 • Honorary Membership
Recognizes extensive contributions to aims of IFSMA.

• 6261 •
International Federation of Societies of Cosmetic Chemists
Mrs. Lorna K. Weston, Sec.Gen.
G.T. House
24-26 Rothesay Rd.
Beds
Luton LU1 1QX, United Kingdom
Phone: 44 1582 726661
Fax: 44 1582 405217
E-mail: enquiries@ifscc.org
Home Page: http://www.ifscc.org

• 6262 • Congress Award and Honorary Mention
For recognition of the most meritorious paper presented at an IFSCC Congress. Papers that are original and that have important scientific content and relevance to the cosmetic and toiletry industry may be submitted nine months before a Congress meets. The IFSCC Award includes a monetary prize of 7,500 Swiss francs. Also awarded is an Honorable Mention prize of 1,000 Swiss francs, plus illuminated scrolls commending the achievment. Awarded biennially. Established in 1970.

• 6263 • Poster Prize
For recognition of the most meritorious poster presented at an IFSCC Congress. Posters that are original and that have important scientific content and relevance to the cosmetic and toiletry industry may be submitted nine months before a Congress meets. The IFSCC Award includes a monetary prize of 1,000 Swiss francs and a scroll. Awarded biennially.

• 6264 •
International Fertiliser Society - England
Chris Dawson, Sec.
PO Box 4
York Y032 5YS, United Kingdom
Phone: 44 1904 492700
Fax: 44 1904 492700
E-mail: secretary@fertiliser-society.org
Home Page: http://www.fertiliser-society.org

• 6265 • Francis New Medal
Recognizes distinction in the fertilizer field. A medal is awarded biennially.

• 6266 •
International Glaciological Society
Magnus Mar Magnusson, Sec.Gen.
Scott Polar Research Inst.
Lensfield Rd.
Cambridge CB2 1ER, United Kingdom
Phone: 44 1223 355974
Fax: 44 1223 354931
E-mail: igsoc@igsoc.org
Home Page: http://www.igsoc.org

• 6267 • Honorary Membership
For recognition of eminent contributions to the objects of the Society, namely to stimulate interest in and encourage research into all aspects of snow and ice in all countries, and to facilitate and increase the flow of glaciological ideas and information. Membership shall not exceed twelve in number. Established in 1962.

• 6268 • Richardson Medal
To recognize an individual for outstanding service to glaciology and to the Society. Awarded periodically. Established in 1993.

• 6269 • Seligman Crystal
For recognition of unique contributions to snow and ice studies that enrich the subject significantly. A hexagonal 5 1/2 inch column of crystal glass that is engraved with an ice crystal on a sloping top surface is awarded when merited. Established in 1963.

• 6270 •
International Map Collectors' Society
Roger Baskes, Pres.
104 Church Rd., Watford
London WD17 4QB, United Kingdom
Phone: 44 20 83492207
Phone: 44 77 68292066
Fax: 44 20 83469539
E-mail: jeh@harvey27.co.uk
Home Page: http://www.imcos.org

• 6271 • **International Map Collectors' Society Awards**
To promote map collecting and the study of cartography and its history. Various awards are presented annually.

• 6272 • **Helen Wallis Award**
To recognize the cartographic contribution of greatest merit and widest interest to map collectors worldwide. Awarded annually. Formerly: (2006) Tooley Award.

• 6273 •
International Menopause Society
Mrs. Jean Wright, Exec.Dir.
PO Box 687
Wray
Lancaster LA2 8WY, United Kingdom
Phone: 44 15242 21190
Fax: 44 15242 22596
E-mail: jwright.ims@btopenworld.com
Home Page: http://www.imsociety.org

• 6274 • **Bob Greenblatt Prize**
Award of recognition for basic research and clinical work. Awarded triennially.

• 6275 •
International Organ Festival at St. Albans
Ken Chaproniere, Gen.Mgr.
PO Box 80
St. Albans AL3 4HR, United Kingdom
Phone: 44 1727 844765
Fax: 44 1727 844765
E-mail: info@organfestival.com
Home Page: http://www.organfestival.com
Formerly: International Organ Festival Society.

• 6276 • **Improvisation Prize**
For recognition of outstanding organ improvisation during the St. Albans International Organ Festival Improvisation Competition. Individuals under the age of 35 may compete. A monetary prize of £4,000, a medal, and recital engagements at Ste Clotilde (Paris), Liverpool Metropolitan Cathedral, Salisbury Cathedral, Glouchester Cathedral, and St. Alban's Cathedral are presented biennially. Established in 1973 by Madame Tournemire in honor of Charles Tournemire.

• 6277 • **Interpretation Competition**
For recognition of the outstanding organ performance during the St. Albans International Organ Festival interpretation competition. Individuals under the age of 31 may compete. A monetary prize of £6,000 and recital engagements at various venues are awarded for first prize; £2,500 and recital engagements for second prize; and £500 and recital engagements for the winner of an audience prize. Held annually.

• 6278 • **Douglas May Award**
For recognition of the best performance of any competition piece in the quarterfinal and semifinal rounds given on the Society's Collins organ at St. Saviour's Church. A monetary prize of £750 is awarded to a competitor who is not the recipient of any other prize. The festival and competitions are held in July of odd-numbered years. Established in 1963 by Dr. Peter Hurford.

• 6279 •
International Police Association
John Waumsley, Intl.Sec.Gen.
Intl. Administration Ctre.
Arthur Troop House
1 Fox Rd.
West Bridgford
Nottingham NG2 6AJ, United Kingdom
Phone: 44 115 9455985
Fax: 44 115 9822578
E-mail: isg@ipa-iac.org
Home Page: http://www.ipa-iac.org

• 6280 • **World Police Prize**
In recognition of exceptional service rendered (by an individual or group) to the police or the IPA. Nominees may or may not be members of the police or the IPA. A monetary prize of 10,000 Swiss francs, a certificate, and a statuette are awarded annually. Established in 1994.

• 6281 •
International Psychoanalytical Association (Association Psychanalytique Internationale)
Claudio L. Eizirik, Pres.
Broomhills
Woodside Ln.
London N12 8UD, United Kingdom
Phone: 44 20 84468324
Fax: 44 20 84454729
E-mail: ipa@ipa.org.uk
Home Page: http://www.ipa.org.uk

• 6282 • **Elise M. Hayman Award**
For the most cogent, relevant and commendable work on the Holocaust and genocide, current or historical.

• 6283 • **Hayman Prize for Published Work Pertaining to Traumatized Children and Adults**
To the author or authors of the best paper about Holocaust effects published in a book or in a recognized psychoanalytic or other scientific journal.

• 6284 • **Psychoanalytic Training Today Award**
For the best submitted paper on the study and development of psychoanalytic training models.

• 6285 • **Cesare Sacerdoti Award**
For the best individual paper submitted by a relatively young author who is presenting a paper at an international congress for the first time.

• 6286 •
International Public Relations Association
Charles Can der Straten Waillet, Pres.
1 Dunley Hill Ct.
Ranmore Common
Surrey
Dorking RH5 6SX, United Kingdom
Phone: 44 1483 280 130
Fax: 44 1483 280 131
E-mail: iprasec@btconnect.com
Home Page: http://www.ipra.org

• 6287 • **International Public Relations Association Golden World Awards for Excellence**
To recognize and to acclaim excellent public relations programs carried out at least partially during the preceding two-year period. Business enterprises, associations, private institutions, and governments bodies anywhere in the world may submit entries. Public relations firms and consultancies can enter on behalf of clients and share honors with them. The public relations program can be of any kind and be local, regional, national, or international in scope. Entries must be submitted by January 31. Awards are presented in the following categories: overall institutional, international, public service, public affairs, issue management, emergency, community relations, employee relations, investor relations, marketing - new product, marketing - established product, marketing - new service, marketing - established service, special event/observance - under eight days, special event/observance - eight days or more, environmental, and other - aimed at dealers, members, educators, youth, or other special public. Sponsored by NEC Corp.

• 6288 • **International Public Relations Association President's Award**
To recognize contributions to a better world understanding. A trophy is awarded annually. Established in 1977.

• 6289 •
International Sheep Dog Society
J.W. Easton MBE, Chm.
Clifton House
4a Goldington Rd.
Bedford MK40 3NF, United Kingdom
Phone: 44 1234 352672
Fax: 44 1234 348214
E-mail: office@isds.org.uk
Home Page: http://www.isds.org.uk

• 6290 • **Supreme Champion**
For recognition of the achievements of the outstanding handler of a working border collie. Individuals must be members of the Society to be eligible. A monetary prize of £500 and numerous trophies are awarded annually. Established in 1930.

• 6291 • Young Handler Award
To recognize an outstanding young handler of sheep dogs. Presented annually.

• 6292 •
International Society for Soil Mechanics and Geotechnical Engineering
(Societe Internationale de Mecanique des Sols et de la Geotechnique)
Prof. R. N. Taylor, Sec.Gen.
City University
Northampton Sq.
London EC1V 0HB, United Kingdom
Phone: 44 20 70408154
Fax: 44 20 70408832
E-mail: secretariat@issmge.org
Home Page: http://www.issmge.org/

• 6293 • Kevin Nash Gold Medal
For recognition of outstanding contributions to practice, research, and teaching in the field of geotechnical engineering. Members of the Society are eligible. A medal is awarded every four years. Established in 1985 in honor of Kevin Nash, former secretary general of ISSMFE.

• 6294 •
International Society for Trenchless Technology
Mr. John Castle, Exec.Sec.
PO Box 54
Gloucestershire
Moreton-in-Marsh GL56 0ZT, United Kingdom
Phone: 44 1608 674900
Phone: 44 208 8509119
Fax: 44 1608 674707
E-mail: info@istt.co.uk
Home Page: http://www.istt.com

• 6295 • International No-Dig Award
Recognizes the most notable contribution to trenchless technology during the year. Awarded annually at the International No-Dig Conference and Exhibition. Prizes are awarded in four categories: Best Product, Best Project, Best Academic Project or Research, and Best Student. Best Student prize receives £500 plus travel costs; others receive trophy, certificate, and publicity within the industry. Established in 1986.

• 6296 •
International Society of Chemotherapy
(Societe Internationale de Chimiotherapie)
Dr. Faridah Moosdeen, Admin.Sec.
31 St. Olav's Ct.
City Business Centre
25 Lower Rd.
London SE16 2XB, United Kingdom
Phone: 44 20 72312944
Fax: 44 20 72312124
E-mail: moosdeen@ischemo.demon.co.uk
Home Page: http://www.ischemo.org

• 6297 • Hamao Umezawa Memorial Award
For recognition of outstanding research and life's work in chemotherapy. Nominations are accepted a half year before the award is given. A monetary prize, a medal, and a document are presented biennially in odd-numbered years at the International Congress of Chemotherapy. Established in 1979 in honor of Professor Dr. Hamao Umezawa as the highest award of the Society.

• 6298 •
International Society of Paediatric Oncology
(Societe Internationale d'Oncologie Pediatrique)
Prof. Alan W. Craft, Sec.Gen.
Department of Child Health
Royal Victoria Infirmary
Queen Victoria Rd.
Newcastle upon Tyne NE1 4LP, United Kingdom
Phone: 44 191 2023010
E-mail: a.w.craft@ncl.ac.uk
Home Page: http://www.siop.nl

• 6299 • Schweisguth Prize
For recognition of the best clinical or basic science contribution presented in the format of a full manuscript related to the field of pediatric oncology. The manuscript must describe work performed by a trainee while they were still in their training period and must be submitted within one year of completion of their training period. Criteria for awarding the prize include originality, completeness, scientific accuracy, and contribution to science. An all-expenses paid trip to the annual conference and presentation/publication of the winning article are awarded each year at the annual conference. Established in 1986 in honor of Dr. Odile Schweisguth, founding member and first president of the Society.

• 6300 • SIOP Awards
To stimulate the research and development of pediatric oncology by rewarding the quality of either an oral or poster presentation during annual SIOP meetings. The two highest scoring abstracts in the fields of—basic science and clinical science are presented orally during the congress. A jury selected by the Scientific Committee will judge which abstracts are worthy of the first prize. The main authors of the winning abstracts are awarded a certificate and 1,000 Euro. Awarded annually. Established in 1991. Formerly: (1998) Nycomed Prize.

• 6301 •
International Society of Typographic Designers
Erik Spiekermann, Pres.
PO Box 725
Somerset
Taunton TA2 8WE, United Kingdom
Phone: 44 20 74360984
Fax: 44 20 76377352
E-mail: mail@istd.org.uk
Home Page: http://www.istd.org.uk

• 6302 • ISTD Typographic Award
Biennial award of recognition. The winning entry is chosen by an international panel.

• 6303 •
International Tennis Federation
(Federation Internationale de Tennis)
Francesco Ricci Bitti, Pres.
Bank Ln.
Roehampton
London SW15 5XZ, United Kingdom
Phone: 44 20 88786464
Fax: 44 20 83924744
E-mail: itf@itftennis.com
Home Page: http://www.itftennis.com

• 6304 • Award for Services to the Game
For recognition of long service or special service to tennis, or to recognize individuals working closely with the ITF. Individuals may be nominated at any time. A plaque is awarded to one or more recipients each year. Established in 1979.

• 6305 • Davis Cup Award of Excellence
To honor a living player, doubles team, or captain who made a significant contribution to the Davis Cup from the country or the region in which the Final will be played. Awarded annually.

• 6306 • Fed Cup Award of Excellence
To honor a living player, doubles team, or captain who made a significant contribution to the Fed Cup from the country or the region in which the Final will be played. Awarded annually.

• 6307 • Grand Slam of Tennis
To recognize the male or female tennis player or doubles team that wins all the following championships in a calendar year: Wimbledon, the French Open, the Australian Open, and the United States Open. Awarded when merited. The first Grand Slam Champion was Don Budge, recognized in 1938.

• 6308 • Tennis World Champions
To recognize the outstanding male and female, singles and doubles, tennis players of the year. Named annually.

• 6309 •
International Trombone Association
Steven Greenall, Exec.Dir.
1 Broomfield Rd.
Coventry CV5 CJW, United Kingdom
Phone: 44 870 0052113
Fax: 44 870 0052114
E-mail: membership@trombone.net
Home Page: http://www.trombone.net

• 6310 • ITA Award
To an individual who has greatly influenced the field of trombone.

• 6311 • Neill Humfeld Award
For outstanding trombone teaching.

• 6312 • Orchestra Recognition Award
To an orchestra that has made a significant contribution to the artistic advancement of trombone performance and literature.

• 6313 •
International Tube Association
Phillip Knight, Exec.Sec.
46 Holly Walk
Leamington Spa CV32 4HY, United Kingdom
Phone: 44 1926 834681
Fax: 44 1926 314755
E-mail: ita@intras.co.uk
Home Page: http://www.itatube.org

• 6314 • Papers Award
For recognition of technical quality of papers that further tube technology and are presented at the Association's International Conference. The Hugh Sansome President's Trophy is awarded annually. Established in 1982.

• 6315 •
International Union for Vacuum Science, Technique and Applications
(Union Internationale pour la Science, la Technique et les Applications du Vide)
Dr. Ron J. Reid, Sec.Gen.
84 Oldfield Dr.
Vicars Cross
Chester CH3 5LW, United Kingdom
Phone: 44 1925 603268
Phone: 44 1244 342675
Fax: 44 70059 63675
E-mail: iuvsta.secretary.general@ronreid.me.uk
Home Page: http://www.iuvsta.org

• 6316 • Welch Foundation Scholarship
To promote international cooperation in research in the field of vacuum science and technology by providing an opportunity for promising scholars to work in a country where the scholar has not previously studied. Candidates should hold at least a BachelorKs degree, although a Doctoral degree is preferred. A research scholarship of $15,000 for one year is awarded annually in June. Established in 1969.

• 6317 •
International Union of Air Pollution Prevention and Environmental Protection Associations
Richard Mills, Dir.Gen.
44 Grand Parade
Brighton BN2 9QA, United Kingdom
Phone: 44 1273 878770
Fax: 44 1273 606626
E-mail: iuappa@nsca.org.uk
Home Page: http://www.iuappa.com

• 6318 • Christopher E. Barthel, Jr. Award
For recognition of outstanding service to the cause of clean air throughout the world over many years. Contributions of a civic, administrative, legislative, or judicial nature are considered. Nomination is by a member or contributing associate without further restriction. An illuminated parchment is awarded triennially at the World Clean Air Congress. Established in 1981 in honor of Christopher E. Barthel, Jr., a founding member of IUAPPA.

• 6319 • World Clean Air Congress Award
To recognize an individual (or group of individuals) who has made a contribution of outstanding significance internationally to the progress of science or technology pertaining to air pollution. An illuminated parchment is awarded triennially at the World Clean Air and Environmental Protection Congress. Established in 1990.

• 6320 •
International Union of Crystallography
(Union Internationale de Cristallographie)
Mr. Michael H. Dacombe, Exec.Sec.
2 Abbey Sq.
Chester CH1 2HU, United Kingdom
Phone: 44 1244 345431
Fax: 44 1244 344843
E-mail: execsec@iucr.org
Home Page: http://www.iucr.org

• 6321 • Ewald Prize
For recognition of outstanding contributions to the science of crystallography. Selection is by nomination. A monetary award of $30,000, a medal, and a certificate are awarded triennially at the International Congresses of Crystallography. Established in 1986 in honor of Professor Paul Peter Ewald, who made significant contributions to the foundations of crystallography and to the founding of the IUC.

• 6322 •
International Union of Soil Sciences
Stephen Nortcliff, Sec. Gen.
PO Box 233
Reading RG6 6DW, United Kingdom
Phone: 44 118 3786559
E-mail: iuss@reading.ac.uk
Home Page: http://www.iuss.org

• 6323 • Dokuchaev Award
For basic research in soil sciences.

• 6324 • Kubiena Medal
For outstanding and sustained performance in the discipline of soil micromorphology.

• 6325 • Liebig Award
For applied research in soil sciences.

• 6326 •
International Visual Communication Association
Wayne Drew, CEO
19 Pepper St.
Glengall Bridge
London E14 9RP, United Kingdom
Phone: 44 20 75120571
Fax: 44 20 75120591
E-mail: info@ivca.org
Home Page: http://www.ivca.org

Formed by merger of: International Television Association.

• 6327 • International Visual Communications Association Awards
For recognition of effective and excellent business communications in film, video, multimedia and live events. Twenty-five subcategories exist within the broader categories of: (1) Film, Video, and DVD; (2) Live Events; (3) Interactive Media and Websites; and (4) Production Arts and Crafts. Gold, Silver and Bronze Awards are awarded to the best entries in each category. The Grand Prix Award is selected by a jury from all the category Gold Award winners, and is awarded to the most outstanding work submitted. Additional special awards include Best Drama Award, Best Documentary Award, and the Industry Award for Effective Communication. Awarded annually. Established in 1968 by the British Industrial and Scientific Association.

• 6328 •
International Water Association
Paul Reiter, Exec.Dir.
Alliance House
12 Caxton St.
London SW1H 0QS, United Kingdom
Phone: 44 20 76545500
Fax: 44 20 76545555
E-mail: water@iwahq.org.uk
Home Page: http://www.iwahq.org.uk

• 6329 • Honorary Membership
Recognizes individuals who make outstanding contribution to IAWQ and water pollution research and control. A medal is awarded biennially.

• 6330 • Imhoff - Koch Award for Outstanding Contribution to Water Management and Science
Recognizes the individual making contribution of international impact relating to facilities involved in water quality control. A medal is awarded biennially at the World Congress. Named in honor of Dr. Karl Imhoff and Dr. Pierre Koch.

• 6331 • Samuel H. Jenkins Outstanding Service Award
Recognizes meritorious contribution and service to IAWQ. Awarded biennially at the World Congress.

• 6332 • Publishing Award
Recognizes the best paper by an IAWQ member at biennial conference. Awarded periodically.

• 6333 •
International Wine and Food Society
Philip Clark, Exec.Dir.
No. 4, St. James Sq.
London SW1Y 4JU, United Kingdom
Phone: 44 20 78275732
Fax: 44 20 78275733
E-mail: sec@iwfs.org
Home Page: http://www.iwfs.org

• 6334 • **Andre Simon Medal**
To recognize individuals for contributions to gastronomy. Society members are eligible. Gold and silver medals are awarded at the discretion of the Council; bronze medals are awarded by area committees. Established in 1960 to honor Andre Louis Simon, CBE, the first president and founder of the Society.

• 6335 •
International Youth Hostel Federation (Federation Internationale des Auberges de Jeunesse)
Rawdon Lau, Sec.Gen.
2nd Fl., Gate House
Fretherne Rd.
Welwyn Garden City AL8 6RD, United Kingdom
Phone: 44 1707 324170
Fax: 44 1707 323980
E-mail: iyhf@iyhf.org
Home Page: http://www.hihostels.com

• 6336 • **Certificate of Merit**
For recognition of service at the international level that contributes to the development of the system, and the promotion of international understanding and outdoor education. A parchment certificate with gift and an insignia plaque are awarded at the international conference or at national meetings. Established in 1981.

• 6337 •
ITV Network Limited
ITV1 Granada
Quay St.
Manchester M60 9EA, United Kingdom
Phone: 44 161 832 7211
Fax: 44 161 827 2180
E-mail: wtps@granadamedia.com
Home Page: http://www.granadatv.co.uk

• 6338 • ***What the Papers Say* Award**
For recognition of special achievement in the field of journalism. Awards are given in varying categories such as: Newspaper of the Year; Reporter of the Year; Columnist of the Year; Sports Writer of the Year; Scoop of the Year; and the Gerald Barry Award for lifetime achievement in journalism. A panel of program editors and producers makes the selections based on nominations from all the presenters of the *What the Papers Say* program during the preceding year. Awarded annually.

• 6339 •
Jerwood Charity
Roanne Dodds, Dir.
22 Fitzroy Sq.
London W1T 6EN, United Kingdom
Phone: 44 20 7388 6287
Fax: 44 20 7388 6289
E-mail: info@jerwood.org
Home Page: http://www.jerwood.org

• 6340 • **Jerwood Awards**
To recognize and encourage achievement in the arts. Numerous awards and competitions are held in various categories, including dance and choreography, drama, film, literature, music, and the visual arts. Among the most famous awards are the Jerwood Applied Arts Prize, Jerwood Painting Prize, Jerwood Choreography Award, and the Jerwood Awards for Non-Fiction.

• 6341 •
John Muir Trust
41 Commercial St.
Edinburgh EH6 6JD, United Kingdom
Phone: 44 845 4582910
Fax: 44 845 4582910
E-mail: info@johnmuiraward.org
Home Page: http://www.johnmuiraward.org

• 6342 • **John Muir Award**
To encourage the discovery and conservation of wild places, in a spirit of fun, adventure, and exploration. There are three levels of the award, encouraging a progressive involvement: Discover, Explore, Conserve, and Share. Awarded annually. Established in 1997.

• 6343 •
Jowett Car Club
Tim Brown, Chm.
52 Stratford St.
Coventry CV2 4NJ, United Kingdom
Phone: 44 1274 873959
E-mail: internationalsectionsec@jowett.org
Home Page: http://homepage.ntlworld.com/keith.clements/index.htm

• 6344 • **Horace Grimley Award**
For recognition of outstanding service to the marque and the Club. Members are eligible. A monetary prize is awarded annually at the general meeting. Established in 1985 to honor Horace Grimley, a relative of the founders of Jowett Cars Ltd. who worked for the company for 33 years and was responsible for engineering development.

• 6345 •
Karg-Elert Archive
Anthony Caldicott, Chm.
38 Lyndhurst Ave.
Twickenham TW2 6BX, United Kingdom
Phone: 44 20 88946859
Fax: 44 20 88946859
E-mail: anthony@caldicott247.fslife.co.uk
Home Page: http://www.karg-elert-archive.org.uk

• 6346 • **Honorary Membership Award**
Periodic award of recognition for performers, recording artists, and researchers.

• 6347 •
King's College London
Ms. Jennie Eldridge, Contact
King's College London
Strand
London WC2R 2LS, United Kingdom
E-mail: jennie.eldridge@kcl.ac.uk
Home Page: http://www.kcl.ac.uk

• 6348 • **Thouron Fellowship**
To provide for U.S.-U.K. student exchange and to promote good relations between people in the two countries. Provides support for British recipients to attend any of the graduate and professional schools of the University of Pennsylvania, while University of Pennsylvania recipients may study at any institution of higher education in the United Kingdom. Some 6-10 awards for fees and maintenance including travel are presented annually. Established in 1960 by Sir John Thouron.

• 6349 •
King's School
Canon Keith H. Wilkinson, Head
The Precincts
Canterbury CT1 2ES, United Kingdom
Phone: 44 1227 595501
Fax: 44 1227 595595
E-mail: headmaster@kings-school.co.uk
Home Page: http://www.kings-school.co.uk

• 6350 • **Calvin and Rose G. Hoffman Prize for Distinguished Publication on Christopher Marlowe**
For recognition of the unpublished essay that most informatively examines and discusses in depth the life and works of Christopher Marlowe and the authorship of the plays and poems now commonly attributed to William Shakespeare. The deadline for entry is September 1. A monetary prize of not less than £6,500 is awarded annually. Established in 1988 by a bequest of Calvin Hoffman in memory of Calvin and Rose G. Hoffman.

• 6351 •
Labologists Society
Dale Adams, Chm.
16 Bognor Dr.
Herne Bay
Kent CT6 8QP, United Kingdom
Phone: 44 121 4495681
E-mail: chairman@labology.org.uk
Home Page: http://www.labology.org.uk

• 6352 • **Label of the Year Competition**
To recognize excellence in label design for beer labels. Breweries in Britain may submit newly designed labels, which are judged by a small panel of Society members. First, second, and third place awards are given in four categories: Best Standard Label, Best Set of Labels, Best Commemorative Label, and Best Point of Sale

Material. Certificates are awarded annually. Established in 1983.

• 6353 •
Ladies' Golf Union
Andy Salmon, Sec./CEO
The Scores
St. Andrews KY16 9AT, United Kingdom
Phone: 44 1334 475811
Fax: 44 1334 472818
E-mail: info@lgu.org
Home Page: http://www.lgu.org

• 6354 • **Ladies' British Open Amateur Championship**
To recognize the winner of the annual amateur golf championship. A Challenge Cup is awarded. Established in 1893.

• 6355 • **Weetabix Women's British Open Championship**
To recognize the winners of the annual golf championship. Two trophies are awarded: (1) the Weetabix Trophy to the player returning the lowest score for the 72 holes, and held for one year. The winner is the Women's British Open Champion. If a professional golfer, she receives a check for the first prize, and if an amateur, a voucher; (2) Smyth Salver presented by Miss Moira Smyth to the amateur competitor returning the lowest score for the 72 holes, and held for one year. The winner also receives a voucher. The Trophies may not leave Great Britain or Ireland. In 1999, the prize fund totaled £575,000. Established in 1976.

• 6356 •
Landscape Research Group
Pauline Graham, Sec.
Department of Social Sciences & Law
Oxford Brookes University
Gipsy Ln.
Headington
Oxford OX3 0BP, United Kingdom
Phone: 44 1865 483950
Fax: 44 1865 483937
E-mail: pgraham@brookes.ac.uk
Home Page: http://www.landscaperesearch.org.uk

• 6357 • **Dissertation Prize**
Annual award of recognition. Undergraduates and postgraduates students are eligible.

• 6358 •
Lawn Tennis Association
John Crowther, Chief Exec.
Palliser Rd.
W Kensington
London W14 9EG, United Kingdom
Phone: 44 20 73817000
Fax: 44 20 73815965
E-mail: advantageclub@lta.org.uk
Home Page: http://www.lta.org.uk

• 6359 • **Lawn Tennis Association National Awards**
For recognition of performance, standards, and achievements in the field of lawn tennis. Awards are given in the following categories: Player of the Year; Junior Player of the Year; Disabled Player of the Year; Coach of the Year; Club of the Year; School of the Year; Local Authority of the Year; Volunteer of the Year; Official of the Year; and Marsh Team of the Year. Engraved cups or plates are presented to the winners annually at the LTA Awards Dinner. Established in 1982.

• 6360 •
League Against Cruel Sports
Sparling House
83-87 Union St.
London SE1 1SG, United Kingdom
Phone: 44 845 3308486
Fax: 44 20 7403 4532
E-mail: info@league.uk.com
Home Page: http://www.league.uk.com

• 6361 • **Lord Houghton Award**
For recognition of outstanding services to animal welfare. Nominations are accepted. An engraved glass bowl is presented annually at a general meeting of one of four groups. Established in 1979 by four animal welfare groups in honor of Lord Houghton of Sowerby, who pioneered the campaign to "put animals into politics." Co-sponsored by the British Union for the Abolition of Vivisection, the National Anti-Vivisection Society, and Advocates for Animals.

• 6362 • **Lord Soper Award**
For recognition of outstanding fundraising in conjunction with the promotion of the League's aims. Those with the highest income raised during one year through publicity and promotion of the League are eligible. A shield is awarded annually at the May general meeting. Established in 1987 in honor of Lord Soper, President of the League Against Cruel Sports.

• 6363 •
Leeds International Pianoforte Competition
Dame Fanny Waterman, Chm.
University of Leeds
Leeds LS2 9JT, United Kingdom
Phone: 44 113 244 6586
Fax: 44 113 244 6586
E-mail: admin@leedspiano.bdx.co.uk
Home Page: http://www.leedspiano.com

Formerly: Harveys Leeds International Pianoforte Competition.

• 6364 • **Leeds International Pianoforte Competition**
To recognize and encourage the professional development of talented young pianists. The competition is open to professional pianists of all nationalities who are under 30 years of age. The total prize money is in excess of £65,000. The first prize winner receives the Princess Mary Gold Medal and £14,000. Prizes include a Substantial number of engagements world-wide. The competition is held Triennially. Established in 1963 by Fanny Waterman and Marion Thorpe. Applications must be received by February 1, 2006. Formerly: Harveys Leeds International Pianoforte Competition.

• 6365 •
LEPRA
Terry Vasey, Chief Exec.
28 Middleborough
Colchester CO1 1TG, United Kingdom
Phone: 44 1206 216 700
Fax: 44 1206 762 151
E-mail: lepra@lepra.org.uk
Home Page: http://www.lepra.org.uk

• 6366 • **Essay Competition**
To bring leprosy to the attention of medical students. Any UK medical student may submit an essay on a subject proposed by the panel. A monetary prize is awarded annually in June. Established in 1982.

• 6367 •
Leprosy Relief Association
Terry Vasey Esq., Chief Exec.
28 Middleborough
Essex
Colchester CO1 1TG, United Kingdom
Phone: 44 1206 216700
Phone: 44 8451 212121
Fax: 44 1206 762151
E-mail: lepra@lepra.org.uk
Home Page: http://www.lepra.org.uk

• 6368 • **Dick Rees Memorial Fund**
For selected trainings that would enhance a significant contribution to the field of leprosy.

• 6369 • **St. Lazarus Garnham Fellowship**
For research in all aspects of leprosy.

• 6370 • **Student Electives Scheme**
For medical students.

• 6371 •
Leverhulme Trust
Gillian Dupin, Dir.
1 Pemberton Row
London EC4A 3BG, United Kingdom
Phone: 44 20 7822 5220
Fax: 44 20 7822 5084
E-mail: gdupin@leverhulme.ac.uk
Home Page: http://www.leverhulme.org.uk

• 6372 • **Leverhulme Memorial Lecture**
To invite a person of some distinction to deliver the triennial lecture at the University of Liverpool. Designed to reflect the wide range of the Founder's interests, the Lecture can be on any subject concerned with the economic and social problems of the day and the welfare of society at home and abroad, widely interpreted. The Trustees meet the cost of the Lecture and its publication. Established in 1968 in memory of the First Lord Leverhulme. Organized by the University of Liverpool.

• 6373 • Leverhulme Tercentenary Medal
To recognize outstanding contributions to in the field of pure or applied chemistry or engineering, including chemical engineering. A gold medal is awarded triennially. Established in 1960 by the Leverhulme Trust to commemorate the Tercentenary of the Royal Society. Sponsored by the Royal Society.

• 6374 •
Liberal International
(Internationale Liberale)
Federica Sabbati, Sec.Gen.
1 Whitehall Pl.
London SW1A 2HD, United Kingdom
Phone: 44 20 78395905
Fax: 44 20 79252685
E-mail: all@liberal-international.org
Home Page: http://www.liberal-international.org

• 6375 • Prize for Freedom
To recognize an individual for outstanding contributions to human rights and political freedoms. Selection is by nomination. A plaque is awarded annually. Established in 1985.

• 6376 •
Libertarian Alliance
Dr. Chris R. Tame, Dir.
Ste. 35
2 Landsdowne Row
London W1J 6HL, United Kingdom
Phone: 44 870 2421712
Fax: 44 207 8212031
E-mail: chris@libertarian.co.uk
Home Page: http://www.libertarian.co.uk

Formerly: (1979) Radical Libertarian Alliance.

• 6377 • Liberty Awards
To recognize individuals for contributions to the cause of liberty and freedom. A framed certificate is awarded when merited.

• 6378 •
Library and Information Research Group
Biddy Fisher, Chair
Academic Services & Development
Learning Centre
Sheffield Hallam University
Howard St.
Leslie Silver Bldg.
Sheffield S1 1WB, United Kingdom
Phone: 44 114 2252104
Fax: 44 114 2253859
E-mail: b.m.fisher@shu.ac.uk
Home Page: http://www.lirg.org.uk

• 6379 • Elsevier/LIRG Research Award
To encourage research and innovation in library and information science. Particular attention will be paid to proposals intended to improve the accessibility, retrievability, and usefulness of information. An award of up to £1,000 is awarded annually to fund research.

• 6380 •
Lichfield District Council
Donegal House
Bore St.
Lichfield WS13 6NE, United Kingdom
Phone: 44 1543 308209
Fax: 44 1543 417308
E-mail: vg@lichfield-tourist.co.uk
Home Page: http://www.lichfielddc.goc.uk

• 6381 • Lichfield Prize
To help publicize Lichfield District, and for recognition of an unpublished novel. Submissions are accepted. A monetary prize of £5,000 and the possibility of having the novel published are awarded biennially. Deadline is April 30. Established in 1989 to commemorate Lichfield's attachment to literary figures. Organized by Lichfield District Council and sponsored by booksellers James Redshaw Ltd. and Hodder and Stoughton Publishers.

• 6382 •
Lighting Association
Graham Samuel, Sec.
Stafford Park 7
Shropshire
Telford TF3 3BQ, United Kingdom
Phone: 44 1952 290905
Fax: 44 1952 290906
E-mail: enquiries@lightingassociation.com
Home Page: http://www.lightingassociation.com

Formerly: Decorative Lighting Association.

• 6383 • Student Lighting Design Awards
To recognize student designers at the start of their careers in the lighting industry. Students of design at educational institutions in the United Kingdom and Europe are eligible. Monetary prizes totalling £5,000 are awarded. Established in 1985.

• 6384 •
Linnean Society of London
Mr. Adrian Thomas, Exec.Sec.
Burlington House
Piccadilly
London W1J 0BF, United Kingdom
Phone: 44 20 74344479
Fax: 44 20 72879364
E-mail: adrian@linnean.org
Home Page: http://www.linnean.org

• 6385 • Bicentenary Medal
To recognize achievements of a biologist under the age of 40. Any biologist who is not at the time a member of the Council is eligible. A silver medal is awarded annually. Established in 1978 to commemorate the two-hundredth anniversary of the death of Linneaus.

• 6386 • H. H. Bloomer Award
To recognize an amateur naturalist who has made an important contribution to biological knowledge. The award may be given to any person not at the time a member of the Council. Presented alternately to a botanist and a zoologist. A silver medal is awarded annually. Established in 1963 from a legacy by the late Harry Howard Bloomer.

• 6387 • Linnean Medal
To recognize a botanist and/or a zoologist for service to science. Any biologist, who is not at the time a member of the Council, is eligible. A medal is awarded at the Anniversary Meeting. Established in 1888 in connection with the Centenary of the Society.

• 6388 • Irene Manton Prize
To recognize the best thesis in botany examined for a doctorate of philosophy during the year beginning in September and ending in August. It is open to candidates whose research has been carried out while registered at any institution in the United Kingdom. Theses on the full range of plant sciences are eligible. A piece of sculpture or other work of fine art is awarded, to which the Society has added £1000. A letter of recommendation and an abstract of the thesis must be submitted by September 30. Awarded annually. Established in 1990.

• 6389 • Jill Smythies Award
To recognize published illustrations, such as drawings or paintings, in aid of plant identification, with the emphasis on botanical accuracy and the accurate portrayal of diagnostic characteristics. Illustrations of cultivars of garden origin are not eligible. Individuals who are not at the time members of the Council are eligible. A silver medal and a purse are awarded, usually annually. Established in 1986 by Mr. B.E. Smythies, FLS, in honor of his wife, the late Florence Mary Smythies ("Jill"), whose career as a botanical artist was cut short by an accident to her right hand.

• 6390 •
Liverpool School of Tropical Medicine
Prof. Janet Hemingway, Dir.
Pembroke Pl.
Liverpool L3 5QA, United Kingdom
Phone: 44 151 708 9393
Fax: 44 151 705 3370
E-mail: imr@liverpool.ac.uk
Home Page: http://www.liv.ac.uk/lstm

• 6391 • Mary Kingsley Medal
For recognition of distinguished achievement in the field of tropical medicine. Scientists who have given distinguished service in this field are eligible. Awarded from time to time when merited. Established in 1903 to commemorate the work of the late Mary Kingsley in West Africa.

• 6392 •
Llangollen International Musical Eisteddfod
Gwyn L. Williams, CEO
Royal International Pavilion
Abbey Rd.
Llangollen LL20 8SW, United Kingdom
Phone: 44 1978 862000
Fax: 44 1978 862002
E-mail: info@international-eisteddfod.co.uk
Home Page: http://www.international-eisteddfod.co.uk

• 6393 • **Llangollen International Musical Eisteddfod**
For recognition of the best music and dance performances, which are based in the highest ideals of the Welsh Eisteddfod: peace and harmony between nations. The festival provides "an opportunity for peoples of the world to gather together to make music in a spirit of harmony and friendship...that we might learn to live in peaceful coexistence with one another." All competitors, except the choir conductors and accompanists, must be amateurs. Prizes are given for first, second, and third place winners in numerous categories within the broad classifications of choral music, solo music, folk dance and music, and Celtic music. In addition, the Pavarotti Trophy is awarded to the choir named the Choir of the World at Llangollen. Held annually in July. Established in 1947.

• 6394 •
London International Piano Competition
Sir Trevor Holdsworth, Pres
28 Wallace Rd.
London N1 2PG, United Kingdom
Phone: 44 20 73541087
Fax: 44 20 77041053
E-mail: ldn-ipc@dircon.co.uk
Home Page: http://www.ldn-ipc.dircon.co.uk
Formerly: London International Piano Competition.

• 6395 • **London International Piano Competition**
For recognition of outstanding piano performance. Pianists of all nationalities who are 29 years of age and under are eligible. Monetary prizes, concert engagements, and scholarships are awarded every three years. Established in 1991.

• 6396 •
London Mathematical Society
Mr. Peter R. Cooper, Exec.Sec.
De Morgan House
57-58 Russell Sq.
London WC1B 4HS, United Kingdom
Phone: 44 207 6373686
Fax: 44 207 3233655
E-mail: lms@lms.ac.uk
Home Page: http://www.lms.ac.uk

• 6397 • **Berwick Prize**
For recognition of a definite piece of mathematical research published by the Society in any of its publications during the preceding eight years. Members of the Society under age 40 are eligible. A monetary prize and a certificate are awarded biennially in odd-numbered years. Established in 1946 by Mrs. Berwick in memory of Professor William Edward Hodgson Berwick, ScD, member of the Society (1914-1944), Council (1925-1929), and Vice President (1929).

• 6398 • **Senior Berwick Prize**
For recognition of a definite piece of mathematical research published by the Society in any of its publications during the preceding eight years. Members of the Society are eligible. A monetary prize and a certificate are awarded biennially in even-numbered years. Established in 1946 by Mrs. Berwick in memory of Professor William Edward Hodgson Berwick, ScD, member of the Society (1914-1944), Council (1925-1929), and Vice President (1929).

• 6399 • **De Morgan Medal**
This, the Society's highest honor, is given for recognition of an individual's contributions to mathematics. Mathematicians who are normally resident in the United Kingdom are eligible. A gold medal is awarded triennially. Established in 1884 in memory of Professor A. De Morgan, first President of the Society.

• 6400 • **Forder Lectureship**
For recognition of contributions to, influence on, and general service to mathematics. Members of the Society who on January 1 of the year of the award are normally resident in the United Kingdom are eligible. A four-to-six week lecturing tour of most New Zealand universities is awarded biennially in odd-numbered years. Established in 1986 to honor Professor H.G. Forder, formerly of the University of Auckland and a benefactor of the London Mathematical Society.

• 6401 • **Hardy Fellowship**
To recognize a distinguished overseas mathematician who will make a significant contribution to the U.K. mathematical scene. The Fellow visits one or two institutions in the United Kingdom for an extended period. A lecture tour of 8-10 universities in the United Kingdom and Ireland, also incorporating the Hardy Lecture to the London Mathematical Society, is awarded biennially. Established in 1966 to honor Professor G.H. Hardy, LMS President (1926-28 and 1939-41), and De Morgan Medallist (1929). Formerly: (2006) Hardy Lectureship.

• 6402 • **Naylor Prize and Lectureship**
For recognition of contributions to applied mathematics and/or the applications of mathematics. Mathematicians who are normally resident in the United Kingdom in the year of the award are eligible. A monetary prize, a certificate, and an invitation to present a lecture are awarded biennially in even-numbered years. Established in 1976 in memory of Vernon Dalrymple Naylor, by his sons.

• 6403 • **Polya Prize**
For recognition of outstanding creativity in, imaginative exposition of, or distinguished contribution to mathematics within the United Kingdom. A monetary prize and a certificate are awarded triennially. Established in 1986 by a donation from Mrs. Polya in memory of Professor G. Polya, member of the London Mathematical Society (1925-1985), and Honorary Member (1956-1985).

• 6404 • **Senior Whitehead Prize**
For recognition of work in, influence on, and service to mathematics, as well as lecturing abilities. Mathematicians who are normally resident in the United Kingdom on January 1 of the year of the award are eligible. A monetary prize and a certificate are awarded biennially in odd-numbered years. Established in 1973 by Professor Whitehead's friends and a donation from Mrs. Whitehead in memory of Professor J.H.C. Whitehead, LMS President (1953-55).

• 6405 • **Whitehead Prize**
For recognition of work in and influence on mathematics, including applied mathematics, mathematical physics, and mathematical aspects of computer science. Candidates must be members of the Society under age 40 who are normally resident in the United Kingdom. A monetary prize and a certificate are awarded to up to four recipients annually. Established in 1973 by Professor Whitehead's friends and a donation from Mrs. Whitehead in memory of Professor J.H.C. Whitehead, LMS President (1953-55).

• 6406 •
London String Quartet Competition
Ruth Wheal, Gen.Mgr.
8 Woodlands Rd.
Romford RM1 4HD, United Kingdom
Phone: 44 1708 761423
Fax: 44 1708 761423
E-mail: info@playquartet.com
Home Page: http://www.lsqf.com

• 6407 • **London International String Quartet Competition**
For recognition of achievement in musical performance. String quartets of all nationalities, with an aggregate age of the members not to exceed 120 years, are eligible. The following monetary prizes are awarded: First Prize - £12,000 and the Menuhin Prize; Second Prize - £7,500; and Third Prize - £4,000. Additional special prizes include the Esterhazy Prize (£1,000) for the best performance of a Haydn quartet in the Preliminary Round; Sidney Griller Award (£1,000) for the best performance of the three compulsory pieces in the Preliminary Round; Amadeus Prize (£1,000) for the best performance of a Mozart quartet in the Preliminary Round; and the Audience Prize (£1,000) for the audience favorite among the Finalists. Professional engagements are also arranged for the first, second, and third place winners. Held triennially. Established in 1979 by Yehudi Menuhin.

• 6408 •
Making Music
James Davey, Administration Officer
2-4 Great Eastern St.
London EC2A 3NW, United Kingdom
Phone: 44 870 9033780
Fax: 44 870 9033785
E-mail: info@makingmusic.org.uk
Home Page: http://www.makingmusic.org.uk

Formerly: (2001) National Federation of Music Societies.

• 6409 • **Philip and Dorothy Green Award for Young Concert Artists**
To assist young solo performers in obtaining concert engagements at the beginning of their professional careers. Professional musicians under the age of 28 (30 for singers) who hold European Community passports and are normally residents of Great Britain are eligible. The award, consisting of concert engagements with music clubs and societies, is presented to a performer in several categories, such as piano, violin, tenor, harp, and saxophone; categories vary by year. Finalists are awarded engagements and are included in a publicity brochure circulated to 1,700 affiliated societies. Held annually. Established in 1961.

• 6410 • **Philip and Dorthy Green Award for Young Concert Artists**
Enables young musicians to obtain experience in the United Kingdom. Acceptance into the competition is by audition. Awarded annually. Established in 1961. Inquire for additional information.

• 6411 • **Sir Charles Grove Prizes**
Recognizes outstanding contribution to British music life. Individuals and groups are eligible. Nominations must be made by society members. Awarded annually. Established in 1990. Inquire for additional information.

• 6412 •
Malacological Society of London
Dr. G.B.J. Dussart PhD, Hon.Sec.
Canterbury Christ Church University College
Penrhyn Rd.
Kent CT1 1QU, United Kingdom
Phone: 44 20 85472000
Fax: 44 20 85477562
E-mail: g.b.dussart@canterbury.ac.uk
Home Page: http://www.sunderland.ac.uk/MalacSoc

• 6413 • **Malacological Society of London Annual Award**
To recognize exceptionally promising initial contributions to the study of molluscs. A monetary prize of £500 is awarded annually.

• 6414 • **Sir Charles Maurice Yonge Award**
To honor researchers for excellent achievements in the study of Bivalvia. Awarded annually.

• 6415 •
Maltsters' Association of Great Britain
Ivor R. Murrell, Dir.Gen.
31B Castlegate
Nottinghamshire
Newark NG24 1AZ, United Kingdom
Phone: 44 1636 700781
Fax: 44 1636 701836
E-mail: info@magb.org.uk
Home Page: http://www.ukmalt.com

• 6416 • **Malting Diploma**
To recognize individuals who demonstrate extensive understanding of and experience in all practical aspects of the malting process and related operations. Candidates are expected to possess a basic understanding of the scientific and engineering principles of the malting process and must have a minimum of three years' experience in the malting industry in work closely related to technical matters. A diploma is awarded to all successful examination candidates; occasionally, a tankard is awarded to the winner of the Walter Hyde Award for distinction. Held biennially in even-numbered years. Established in 1981.

• 6417 •
Man Group
Sugar Quay
Lower Thames St.
London EC3R 6DU, United Kingdom
Phone: 44 207 1441000
Fax: 44 207 2209984
Home Page: http://www.themanbookerprize.com

• 6418 • **Man Booker Prize for Fiction**
This, Britain's major literary prize for fiction, is given for recognition of a full-length novel. Publishers may submit up to two books which are written in English and have been published for the first time in the United Kingdom. Citizens of Britain or the British Commonwealth, the Republic of Ireland, and South Africa are eligible. A monetary prize of £50,000 is awarded annually. Established in 1968 by Booker plc. Formerly: Booker McConnell Prize.

• 6419 •
Marine Biological Association of the United Kingdom
Prof. Stephen J. Hawkins, Dir.
The Laboratory
Citadel Hill
Devon
Plymouth PL1 2PB, United Kingdom
Phone: 44 1752 633207
Fax: 44 1752 633102
E-mail: sec@mba.ac.uk
Home Page: http://www.mba.ac.uk

• 6420 • **Ray Lankester Investigatorship**
To advance knowledge on marine animals and plants, and to further the development of marine biology. An honorarium of £1500 per month for a maximum of five months is awarded, and winners may use laboratory facilities at MBA Plymouth. Awarded to one or two recipients annually. Established in 1911 by Dr. G.P. Bidder in honor of Sir Ray Lankester, president of the MBA.

• 6421 •
Medical Journalists' Association
Philippa Pigache, Sec.
Fairfield
Cross in Hand
Heathfield TN21 0SH, United Kingdom
Phone: 44 1435 868786
Fax: 44 1435 865714
E-mail: secretary@mja-uk.org
Home Page: http://www.mja-uk.org

• 6422 • **Medical Journalists' Association Open Book Awards**
For submitted work in the sections of professional and general reader, published for the first time during the previous year with one or two authors.

• 6423 • **Medical Journalists' Association Summer Awards**
For a body of work or unique contribution to health or medicine during the previous year; includes journalists, journal, editor, charity and champion in the health arena.

• 6424 • **Norwich Union Healthcare/ Medical Journalists' Association Awards**
For submitted pieces of work on health or medical science published or performed in the previous year in different sections of the media, general and professional.

• 6425 •
Mensa International
John Stevenage, Gen.Mgr.
Saint John's House
Saint John's Sq.
Wolverhampton WV2 4AH, United Kingdom
Phone: 44 1902 772771
Fax: 44 1902 392500
E-mail: john@mensa.org.uk
Home Page: http://www.mensa.org

• 6426 • **Mensa International Competitions**
To recognize individuals from 100 countries whose intelligence, as measured by standardized tests, is within the top 2 percent of the general population, and to promote social contact among intelligent people. Competitions are sponsored periodically and awards are given.

• 6427 •
Meteoritical Society
Dept. of Mineralogy
Cromwell Rd.
London SW7 5BD, United Kingdom
Phone: 44 171 9388800
Fax: 44 171 9389268
E-mail: secretary@meteoriticalsociety.org
Home Page: http://www.meteoriticalsociety.org

• 6428 • **Leonard Medal**
To recognize outstanding, original contributions to the science of meteoritics and closely allied fields of research. Any scientist, regardless of race, nationality, creed or sex, is eligible for nomination. A medal is awarded annually. Established in 1962 in memory of Professor Frederick C. Leonard, the Society's first president.

• 6429 •
MIND - National Association for Mental Health
Richard Brook, Ch.Exec.
15-19 Broadway
London E15 4BQ, United Kingdom
Phone: 44 20 85192122
Fax: 44 20 85221725
E-mail: contact@mind.org.uk
Home Page: http://www.mind.org.uk

• 6430 • **Book of the Year Award**
For recognition of the book that makes the greatest contribution to public understanding of the experience, nature, cause, treatment, or consequences of mental health problems. Books published in the United Kingdom must be submitted on or before December 31 each year. A monetary prize of £1,000 is awarded annually. Established in 1981 in honor of Allen Lane; sponsored by The Allen Lane Foundation. Also offered are the Champion of the Year Award and the Journalist of the Year Award.

• 6431 •
Minerals Engineering Society
Andrew W. Howells, Sec.-Treas.
2 Ryton Close
Blyth
Nottinghamshire
Worksop S81 8DN, United Kingdom
Phone: 44 1909 591787
Fax: 44 1909 591940
E-mail: secretary@mineralsengineering.org
Home Page: http://www.mineralsengineering.org

Formerly: Coal Preparation Society.

• 6432 • **Lessing Medal**
This, the Society's highest honor, is given for recognition of persons whose contributions to the field of mineral processing engineering have made them eminent in this sphere. Nominations are made in council, but may be initiated by a section committee or any group of ten members. Awarded from time to time in memory of Rudolph Lessing who, in the 1920's and 30's, was a determined advocate of the economic benefits to be obtained from coal cleaning and a pioneer in the introduction and establishment of coal preparation techniques.

• 6433 • **Papers and Publications Committee Prizes**
To recognize the authors of the best practical and theoretical papers given at National and Group meetings and submitted for publication in the Society's official journal, *Mine, Quarry & Recycling*. A prize is presented in each category at the annual meeting.

• 6434 • **Travel Award**
To subsidize an individual visit or attendance at a relevant conference or some other activity related to minerals engineering. Open to any person who is training or engaged in minerals engineering. A monetary award of £250 is awarded as merited.

• 6435 •
Mini-Basketball England
Martin Spencer, Contact
4 Fairmead Rise
Northampton NN2 8PP, United Kingdom
Phone: 44 1604 517732
E-mail: martin.spencer@mini-basketball.org.uk
Home Page: http://www.mini-basketball.org.uk

• 6436 • **Mini-Basketball Coach Award**
For a potential coach.

• 6437 • **Mini-Basketball Officiating Award**
For children and adults.

• 6438 • **Mini-Basketball Teacher Award**

• 6439 •
Motor Sports Association
Allan Dean-Lewis, Sec.
Motor Sports House
Riverside Park
Colnbrook
Slough SL3 0HG, United Kingdom
Phone: 44 1753 765000
Fax: 44 1753 682938
E-mail: msa_mail@compuserve.com
Home Page: http://www.msauk.org

• 6440 • **British Championship**
Recognizes the winners of championship competitions. Awarded annually.

• 6441 •
Mountaineering Council of Scotland
Kevin Howett, Natl. Officer
The Old Granary
W Mill St.
Perth PH1 5QP, United Kingdom
Phone: 44 1738 638227
Fax: 44 1738 442095
E-mail: info@mountaineering-scotland.org.uk
Home Page: http://www.mountaineering-scotland.org.uk

• 6442 • **Expedition Grant**
For climbing, cross country skiing expeditions whose objective is excellence and adventure. A monetary prize is given annually.

• 6443 •
Multiple Sclerosis International Federation
Christine Purdy, CEO
3rd Fl., Skyline House
200 Union St.
London SE1 0LX, United Kingdom
Phone: 44 20 76201911
Fax: 44 20 76201922
E-mail: info@msif.org
Home Page: http://www.msif.org

• 6444 • **Jean-Martin Charcot Award**
For recognition of lifetime achievement in pioneering research in multiple sclerosis. Nominations are accepted. A monetary grant of $10,000, travel expenses, and a plaque are presented biennially at the Multiple Sclerosis World Conference. Established in 1969 in honor of Professor Jean-Martin Charcot.

• 6445 • **Jacqueline du Pre Fellowship**
To support research in MS for young researchers by enabling them to undertake short visits to other MS research centers to either learn or jointly carry out research. The award is generally, but not exclusively, available for young and talented researchers from emerging countries. The two-year Fellowship includes an annual grant to cover travel and living costs, plus an additional contribution of £2,000 per year to the host research center. Established in 1999.

• 6446 • **Nicholson Award**
For recognition of a caregiver for a person with multiple sclerosis. Individuals must be recommended by national MS Society and reviewed by an awards committee. A silver plate is awarded annually.

• 6447 • **James D. Wolfensohn Award**
For recognition of an outstanding person with multiple sclerosis for his or her valuable contribution to fight MS. Individuals must be recommended by national MS Societies and reviewed by an awards committee. A monetary prize and a plaque are awarded annually with applicable travel and accommodation expenses. Presented biennially in odd-numbered years. Established in 1984.

• 6448 •
Music Industries Association - England
Mr. Paul McManus CIPD, Chief Exec.
Ivy Cottage Offices
Finch's Yard
Eastwick Rd.
Gt. Bookham
Surrey KT23 4BA, United Kingdom
Phone: 44 1372 750600
Fax: 44 1372 750515
E-mail: office@mia.org.uk
Home Page: http://www.mia.org.uk

• 6449 • **MIA Music Awards**
Annual awards that recognize innovation, commercial success and value for money. Awards cover the whole industry including contemporary and classical instruments, music publishing and outstanding individuals within the music industry.

• 6450 •
Musicians Benevolent Fund
Rosanna Preston, Chief Exec.
16 Ogle St.
London W1W 6JA, United Kingdom
Phone: 44 20 7636 4481
Fax: 44 20 7637 4307
E-mail: info@mbf.org.uk
Home Page: http://www.mbf.org.uk

• 6451 • **Musicians Benevolent Fund Awards**
To recognize excellence in the field of music. Awards include the Henry and Lily Davis Fund Awards, the H.A. Thew Fund Awards, the Miriam Licette Scholarship, the Guilhermina Suggia Gift for the Cello, the Songwriting Award, and the Peter Whittingham Jazz Award.

• 6452 •
National Association of Hospital Fire Officers
Ken Bullas, Gen.Sec.
Bolton Hospitals NHS Trust
Bolton General Hospital
Minerva Rd.
Farnworth
Bolton BL4 0JR, United Kingdom
Phone: 44 1204 390948
Fax: 44 1204 390838
Home Page: http://www.nahfo-healthfire.org.uk

• 6453 • **Merit Award**
Recognizes significant contribution to healthcare fire safety. Personnel outside of the association are eligible. Awarded annually.

• 6454 •
National Association of Licensed Paralegals
John C. Stacey-Hibbert, Gen.Sec.
9 Unity St.
Devon
Bristol BS1 5HH, United Kingdom
Phone: 44 177 9277077
Fax: 44 20 73285931
E-mail: info@national-paralegals.co.uk
Home Page: http://www.nationalparalegals.com

• 6455 • **Bronze Medal**
To recognize the student obtaining the third-highest marks for the examinations to obtain the Higher Certificate in Paralegal Studies. Awarded annually.

• 6456 • **Gold Medal**
To recognize the student obtaining the highest marks for the examinations to obtain the Higher Certificate in Paralegal Studies. Awarded annually.

• 6457 • **Silver Medal**
To recognize the student obtaining the second-highest marks for the examinations to obtain the Higher Certificate in Paralegal Studies. Awarded annually.

• 6458 •
National Association of Shopfitters
Robert Hudson, Dir.
NAS House
411 Limpsfield Rd.
Warlingham CR6 9HA, United Kingdom
Phone: 44 1883 624961
Fax: 44 1883 626841
E-mail: nas@clara.net
Home Page: http://www.shopfitters.org

• 6459 • **Design Partnership Award**
To encourage and recognize good design associated with the type of work undertaken by shopfitters. The competition is open to architects and designers practicing in the United Kingdom. The design project should be one for which the contract works have been completed and carried out in the United Kingdom by a member of the Association. The judges take into consideration the following: suitability of the design for the location and purpose of the project, choice of materials with particular reference to the needs of both design and cost effectiveness laid down in the design brief, creativity and originality in interpreting the design brief and to overcome problems inherent in the site or premises, and special design features of functional or decorative relevance. The entry judged the Best of Competition receives the overall Design Partnership Award. Awarded annually. Formerly: (1998) National Association of Shopfitters Design.

• 6460 •
National Association of Youth Orchestras
Susan White, Gen.Mgr.
Central Hall
W Tollcross
Edinburgh EH3 9BP, United Kingdom
Phone: 44 131 2211927
Fax: 44 131 2292921
E-mail: admin@nayo.org.uk
Home Page: http://www.nayo.org.uk

• 6461 • **Allianz Cornhill Musical Insurance Conducting Prize**
To encourage professional development of young British conductors. UK citizens under the age of 26 are eligible. A monetary prize of £400 is awarded biennially in even-numbered years. Established in 1988. Sponsored by Allianz Cornhill Musical Insurance. Formerly: (2004) British Reserve Insurance Conducting Prize.

• 6462 • **Allianz Cornhill Musical Insurance Youth Orchestra Awards**
To encourage youth orchestra development. Members of the Association are eligible. Five awards of £500 each are awarded annually. Established in 1990. Sponsored by Allianz Cornhill Musical Insurance. Formerly: (2004) .

• 6463 •
National Council for School Sport
Patrick Smith, Exec.Off.
95 Boxley Dr.
West Bridgford
Nottingham NG2 7GN, United Kingdom
Phone: 44 115 9231229
Fax: 44 115 9231229
E-mail: schoolsport@ntlworld.com
Home Page: http://www.ncss.org.uk

• 6464 • **Teacher's Award**
Recognizes a teacher devoting time to sports in schools. Awarded annually.

• 6465 •
National Council for the Training of Journalists
Kim Fletcher, Chm.
The New Granary
Station Rd.
Newport
Essex
Saffron Walden CB11 3PL, United Kingdom
Phone: 44 1799 544014
Fax: 44 1799 544015
E-mail: info@nctj.com
Home Page: http://www.nctj.com

• 6466 • **Harry Butler Award**
To the best shorthand note and transcription at 100% accuracy for speed of 100 words per minute.

Awards are arranged in alphabetical order below their administering organizations

• 6467 • The Eric Dobson Memorial Award
For the highest scoring candidate with a newspaper from Northumberland, Tyne and Wear, Durham and Cleveland.

• 6468 • The Johnston Press Award
For the best NCE Performance by a candidate trained at an accredited college/university in the southern region.

• 6469 • Pamela Meyrick Memorial Award
To the most promising trainee from the North of England and North Wales.

• 6470 •
National Eisteddfod of Wales
(Eisteddfod Genedlaethol Frenhinol Cymr)
40 Parc Ty Glas
Llanishen
Cardiff CF14 5WU, United Kingdom
Phone: 44 29 2076 3777
Fax: 44 29 2076 3737
E-mail: info@eisteddfod.org.uk
Home Page: http://www.eisteddfod.org.uk

• 6471 • Membership in the Gorsedd of Bards
(Aelod o Orsedd Beirdd Ynys Prydain)
In recognition of service to Wales, its language and culture, and also to honor Welshmen prominent in other fields of endeavor. Familiarity with the Welsh language, the oldest living language in Europe, is required. Membership in the Gorsedd of Bards - an association whose members consist of poets, writers, musicians, artists, and individuals who have made a distinguished contribution to the Welsh nation, language, and culture - entitles the holders to take part in the colorful ceremonial at the Royal National Eisteddfod. Bestowed annually during the first week of August. Established in 1772 by Iolo Morgannwg. Sponsored by the Gorsedd Board.

• 6472 • W. Towyn Roberts Vocal Scholarship
(Ysgoloriaeth W. Towyn Roberts)
To promote solo singing in Wales and to enable the most promising competitor in a special competition to follow a course of vocal instruction in a recognized school or college of music. The scholarship is open to those born in Wales or of Welsh parents, any person who has resided or worked in Wales for the three years prior to the date of the Eisteddfod, or any person able to speak or write the Welsh language. Competitors are expected to prepare a contrasting program of songs from different periods to be sung in Welsh. The program must include one song by a contemporary Welsh composer. A scholarship of £3,000 is awarded annually during the first week of August. Established in 1982 by W. Towyn Roberts in memory of Violet Jones, Nantclwyd, the founder's wife.

• 6473 •
National Federation of Women's Institutes
Jana Osborne, Gen.Sec.
104 New Kings Rd.
London SW6 4LY, United Kingdom
Phone: 44 171 3719300
Fax: 44 171 7363652
E-mail: hg@nfwi.org.uk
Home Page: http://www.womens-institute.co.uk

• 6474 • Lady Denman Cup
To recognize outstanding creative writing. Topics and genre vary each year, and may include short plays, poetry, Christmas carols, essays, etc. Open to all members of the Women's Institutes in England and Wales. First place winner receives a £75 book token; second place receives a £50 book token; and third place receives a £30 book token. Awarded annually.

• 6475 •
National Music Council of The United Kingdom
Fiona Harvey, Admin.
60/62 Clapham Rd.
London SW9 0JJ, United Kingdom
Phone: 44 20 78410266
Fax: 44 870 7062123
E-mail: nationalmusiccouncil@ukonline.co.uk
Home Page: http://www.musiced.org.uk

• 6476 • Local Education Authority Music Awards
To recognize local education authorities that have demonstrated imaginative, inclusive, and high quality music provision during the year. Awarded biennially.

• 6477 •
National Operatic and Dramatic Association
Mark Pemberton, Chief Exec.
NODA House
58-60 Lincoln Rd.
Peterborough PE1 2RZ, United Kingdom
Phone: 44 870 7702480
Fax: 44 870 7702490
E-mail: everyone@noda.org.uk
Home Page: http://www.noda.org.uk

• 6478 • Long Service Awards
To recognize 25 years of service by individuals who are involved in amateur stage performances. A medal and badge are awarded when merited.

• 6479 •
National Piers Society
Tim Mickleburgh, VP
4 Tyrrell Rd.
Benfleet
South Benflet
Essex SS7 5DH, United Kingdom
Phone: 44 126 8757291
Phone: 44 1472 350404
Fax: 44 207 4831902
E-mail: timmickleburgh2002@yahoo.co.uk
Home Page: http://www.piers.co.uk

• 6480 • Peter Mason Award
Recognizes engineering excellence in pier restoration. Awarded triennially.

• 6481 • Pier of the Year Award
Annual award of recognition. Voted on by membership ballot. Established in 1996.

• 6482 •
National Portrait Gallery
Sandy Nairne, Dir.
St. Martins Pl.
London WC2H OHE, United Kingdom
Phone: 44 171 3060055
Fax: 44 171 3060056
E-mail: snairne@npg.org.uk
Home Page: http://www.npg.org.uk

• 6483 • BP Portrait Award
To encourage young painters to specialize in portraiture, to foster new talent, and to help sustain Britain's long tradition of portraiture. British and Commonwealth citizens resident in the United Kingdom for at least five years, and older than 18 years of age but not over 40 years of age, are eligible. The first-place winner receives a monetary award of £25,000 and a commission for painting by the National Portrait Gallery. Additional awards are presented to several runners-up. Awarded annually in June. Established in 1980. Sponsored by British Petroleum, part of the BP Amoco group. Formerly: (1990) John Player Portrait Award; (1983) Imperial Tobacco Portrait Award.

• 6484 •
National Rifle Association
Glynn Alger, Sec.Gen.
Brookwood
Woking GU24 0PB, United Kingdom
Phone: 44 1483 797777
Fax: 44 1483 797285
E-mail: secgen@nra.org.uk
Home Page: http://www.nra.org.uk

• 6485 • Queen's Prize
To recognize an individual who has achieved the highest aggregate score in a course of rifle fire over distances of 300, 500, 600, 900, and 1,000 yards. A monetary prize of £250, a gold medal, and a badge are awarded annually on the fourth Saturday in July. Established in 1860 by H.M. Queen Victoria. The award was given as the King's Prize from 1901 through 1951. Formerly: (1951) King's Prize.

• 6486 •
National Small-Bore Rifle Association
Mrs. Graham Pound, Chm.
Lord Roberts Centre
Bisley Camp
Brookwood
Woking GU24 0NP, United Kingdom
Phone: 44 845 1306772
Fax: 44 1483 476392
E-mail: info@nsra.co.uk
Home Page: http://www.nsra.co.uk

• 6487 • **Distinguished Service Awards**
To recognize secretaries' long service to affiliated clubs and organizations. Awarded when merited.

• 6488 •
National Vegetable Society
David Thornton, Hon.Natl.Sec.
5 Whitelow Rd.
Heaton Moor
Stockport SK4 4BY, United Kingdom
Phone: 44 161 4227190
Fax: 44 161 4227190
E-mail: webmaster@nvsuk.org.uk
Home Page: http://www.nvsuk.org.uk

• 6489 • **Gold Medal**
To recognize a member who has devoted a minimum of 15 years of service to the Society, Branch, or District Association.

• 6490 • **Silver Medal**
To recognize a member who has devoted a minimum of 12 years of service to the Society, Branch, or District Association.

• 6491 •
The Natural History Museum
Dr. Michael Dixon, Dir.
BG Wildlife Photographer of the Year
Cromwell Rd.
London SW7 5BD, United Kingdom
Phone: 44 20 7942 5000
Fax: 44 20 7942 5084
E-mail: wildphoto@nhm.ac.uk
Home Page: http://www.nhm.ac.uk

Formerly: (1995) *BBC Wildlife Magazine.*

• 6492 • **BG Wildlife Photographer of the Year Competition**
To find the best wildlife pictures taken by photographers worldwide, and to emphasize through the work of such photographers the beauty, wonder, and importance of the natural world. Emphasis is placed on photographs taken in wild and free conditions. Open to all amateur and professional photographers. Up to three images photographs can be entered in each category. Color slide transparencies may be submitted only with official entry form by April 5th in the following categories: Animal Behavior: Mammals, Animal Behavior: Birds, Animal Behavior: All Other Animals, The World in Our Hands, British Wildlife, In Praise of Plants, The Underwater World, From Dusk to Dawn, Animal portraits, Urban and Garden Wildlife Composition and form and Wild Places. There are also two special awards: Eric Hosking Award and Gerald Durrell Award for endangered wildlife. The BG Wildlife Photographer of the Year will be the photographer whose individual image is judged to be the most striking and memorable. He or she will win the BG Award and £l2000.

• 6493 • **Young Wildlife Photographer of the Year Competition**
To recognize the best wildlife pictures taken by young photographers aged 17 years and under. Prints or slides of wild animals or plants or wild landscapes may be submitted by April 5. Awards are presented in the following categories: Photographer aged 10 years and under, Photographer aged 11-14 years, and Photographer aged 15-17 years. A first prize of £250 and a runner-up prize of £100 are presented in each category. The title "Young Wildlife Photographer of the Year" is awarded to the person (of any age) whose picture is judged to be the best in the competition. Winning pictures form part of a major exhibition in the Natural History Museum, London and on tour in the United Kingdom and overseas. For additional information regarding U.S. tours and entry forms, contact Sheelagh Coghlan, The Natural History Museum, Cromwell Rd., London SW7 5BD, England; Phone: 171 938 8714; Fax: 171 938 8788.

• 6494 •
Natural World
% The Wildlife Trusts
The Kiln, Waterside
Mather Rd.
Newark NG24 1WT, United Kingdom
Phone: 44 8700 367711
Fax: 44 8700 360101
E-mail: enquiry@wildlifetrusts.org
Home Page: http://www.wildlifetrusts.org

• 6495 • ***Natural World* Book Prize**
To recognize books published in the U.K. that most imaginatively promote the conservation of the natural environment and all its animals and plants. A monetary award of £5,000 is awarded and a possible £1,000 prize may be awarded to a runner-up. Awarded annually.

• 6496 •
New Statesman
John Kampfner, Ed.
52 Grosvenor Gardens, 3rd Fl.
London SW1W 0AU, United Kingdom
Phone: 44 207 7303444
Fax: 44 207 2590181
E-mail: info@newstatesman.co.uk
Home Page: http://www.newstatesman.co .uk

• 6497 • **The Upstarts Awards**
Recognizes social entrepreneurs who will launch ideas or projects to challenge social exclusion in their communities. Three awards totaling £ are awarded. Complete details and entry form can be obtained at the associations web site.

• 6498 •
Newport International Competition for Young Pianists
Arts Development
Newport City Council, Civic Centre
Newport NP20 4UR, United Kingdom
Phone: 44 1633 233328
Fax: 44 1633 232808
E-mail: piano.competition@newport.gov.uk
Home Page: http://www.newport.gov.uk/ piano

Formerly: Newport Pianoforte Competition.

• 6499 • **Newport International Competition for Young Pianists**
To provide a platform for young pianists at the start of their professional careers. Individuals must be under 25 years of age at the time of competition to be eligible. Contestants must select one piece from each of three categories: Bach, Sonatas, and Own Choice. The following monetary prizes are awarded: first prize - £5,000 as well as a series of concerts in Wales and a BBC engagement; second prize - £2,500; third prize - £1,000. The remaining semi-finalists each receive £500. The competition is held triennially. Established in 1979.

• 6500 •
Northern Arts
9-10 Osborne Terrace, Jesmond
Newcastle Upon Tyne NE2 1NZ, United Kingdom
Phone: 44 191 2816334
Fax: 44 191 2813276
E-mail: nab@norab.demon.co.uk

• 6501 • **Northern Arts Literary Fellowship**
To provide a fellowship for a period of two academic years at the Universities of Durham and Newcastle upon Tyne to allow the writer time to concentrate on new work and to encourage creative writing in each university. The Fellow must come to the Northern Arts Region to live and work. A Fellowship is awarded biennially. Established in 1967.

• 6502 •
Oil and Colour Chemists' Association
Chris Pacey-Day, Gen.Sec.
Priory House
967 Harrow Rd.
Wembley HA0 2SF, United Kingdom
Phone: 44 20 89081086
Fax: 44 20 89081219
E-mail: membership@occa.org.uk
Home Page: http://www.occa.org.uk

• 6503 • **Ellinger-Gardonyi Award**
To recognize the best paper presented at the Association's conferences and symposia. Both members and non-members are eligible. The silver medal is awarded annually. Established in 1989 in memory of Dr. M. Ellinger.

• 6504 • Jordan Award
To recognize the best paper published or submitted for publication in the Association's journal *Surface Coatings International.* Members under the age of 35 are eligible. A monetary award of £200 and a silver medal are awarded annually. Established in 1970.

• 6505 • Stern Award
To recognize the best paper, monograph, review, or special publication published by the Association during the year. Authors of any age are eligible, and need not be members of the Association. Awarded annually. Established in 1995 in memory of Dr. H.J. Stern, the Association's longest serving member and long-time member of the Publications Committee.

• 6506 •
Operational Research Society of the United Kingdom
Bob Miles, Sec./Gen.Mgr.
Seymour House
12 Edward St.
Birmingham B1 2RX, United Kingdom
Phone: 44 121 2339300
Fax: 44 121 2330321
E-mail: email@orsoc.org.uk
Home Page: http://www.orsoc.org.uk

• 6507 • Beale Medal
Recognizes sustained contributions to practice or theory of operational research. Awarded annually.

• 6508 • Goodeve Medal
Recognizes the most outstanding contribution to the philosophy, theory, or practice of operational research that was published in the *Journal of the OR Society,* the *European Journal of Information Systems,* or *OR Insight.* Awarded annually.

• 6509 • President's Medal
Annual award for the best account of OR practice given at the SocietyKs annual conference.

• 6510 •
Oppenheim-John Downes Memorial Trust
1 Dean Farrar St.
London SW1H 0DY, United Kingdom

• 6511 • Oppenheim John Downes Memorial Trust
To enable deserving artists of any kind to pursue their vocation. Artists unable to pursue their vocation by reason of their poverty are eligible to apply by October 15. The following qualifications are mandatory: Individuals must be over 30 years of age and natural born British subjects born within Great Britain, Northern Ireland, The Channel Islands, or The Isle of Man; their parents must be British subjects born within the British Isles and neither parent may be of colonial or overseas origin after 1900 (Section 34 of the Race Relations Acts applies). Monetary awards of £50 to £1,500 are presented annually in December. Established in 1969 by Mrs. G.E. Downes in honor of her father, E. Phillips Oppenheim and his grandson, John Downes.

• 6512 •
Oxford Preservation Trust
10 Turn Again Ln.
Oxford OX1 1QL, United Kingdom
Phone: 44 1865 242918
Fax: 44 1865 251022
Home Page: http://www.oxfordpreservation.org.uk

• 6513 • Environmental Awards
To recognize projects that make a significant contribution to the conservation and improvement of the built or natural environment of Oxford and its green setting. To be eligible, projects must be within the public domain and must have been completed within three years of entry. Nominations are welcome from owners, architects, and public and voluntary organizations. Entries are judged in four categories: landscape and environmental enhancement; building conservation; new buildings; and small projects. Plaques and certificates are awarded annually. Established in 1977.

• 6514 •
Palaeontological Association
Tim J. Palmer, Exec. Off.
Inst. of Geography and Earth Sciences
Univ. of Wales-Aberystwyth
Aberystwyth SY23 3DB, United Kingdom
Phone: 44 1970 627107
Fax: 44 1970 622659
E-mail: palass@palass.org
Home Page: http://www.palass.org

• 6515 • Hodson Fund
For palaeontologists, under the age of 35, who have made a notable early contribution to science.

• 6516 • Lapworth Medal
For palaeontologists who have made a significant contribution to science.

• 6517 • Sylvester-Bradley Award
for deserving amateur and professional palaeontologists.

• 6518 •
Paper Federation of Great Britain
Richard Sexton, Mgr.
Papermakers House
1 Rivenhall Rd.
Wiltshire
Swindon SN5 7BD, United Kingdom
Phone: 44 1793 889600
Fax: 44 1793 878700
E-mail: rsexton@paper.org.uk
Home Page: http://www.paper.org.uk
Formerly: British Paper and Board Makers' Association.

• 6519 • Paper Industry Gold Medal
To recognize an individual who has made an outstanding contribution to the affairs of the British paper and board industry. Individuals must be nominated by a special industry committee by November. A gold medal is awarded annually in the spring. Established in 1966 by Benn Brothers plc, and now sponsored by the Paper Industry Gold Medal Association. Formerly: *World's Paper Trade Review* Medal.

• 6520 •
Parenteral Society
Phil Greaves, Chm.
99 Ermin St.
Stratton St. Margaret
Wiltshire
Swindon SN3 4NL, United Kingdom
Phone: 44 1793 824254
Fax: 44 1793 832551
E-mail: secretary@parenteral.demon.co.uk
Home Page: http://www.parenteral.org.uk

• 6521 • George Sykes Memorial Award
To encourage the furtherance of knowledge in the field of parenteral science. Awarded annually.

• 6522 •
Parker Harris Partnership
15 Church St.
Esher KT10 8QS, United Kingdom
Phone: 44 1372 462190
Fax: 44 1372 460032
E-mail: info@parkerharris.co.uk
Home Page: http://www.parkerharris.co.uk

• 6523 • Singer Friedlander/Sunday Times Watercolour competition
Annual watercolor competition with prize money totaling £30,000. Open to artists born or resident in the U.K. Sponsored by Singer and Friedlander.

• 6524 • Hunting Art Prizes
Annual open exhibition open to all artists resident in the U.K. Monetary prizes totaling £21,500 are awarded annually. Established in 1980. Sponsored by Hunting Plc. Formerly: (1990) Hunting Group Art Prizes.

• 6525 • The Jerwood Painting Prize
Open to United Kingdom residents. No additional information available at this time.

• 6526 • The Jerwood Sculpture Prize
An award for sculptors to encourage and reward emerging talent in the crateve skill of outdoor sculpture. Open to United Kingdom residents. No additional information available at this time.

• 6527 •
Pensions Management Institute
Mrs. S.M. Howlett, Sec.Gen.
4-10 Artillery Ln.
London E1 7LS, United Kingdom
Phone: 44 207 2471452
Fax: 44 207 3750603
E-mail: enquiries@pensions-pmi.org.uk
Home Page: http://www.pensions-pmi.org.uk

• 6528 • **Associateship (APMI)**
Annual award of recognition. Individuals who have passed 9 exams and have relevant experience are eligible.

• 6529 • **Diploma in International Employee Benefits**
Annual award of recognition. Individuals who have passed 2 exams are eligible.

• 6530 •
Performance Textiles Association
Clive Moss, CEO
42 Heath St.
Tamworth B79 7JH, United Kingdom
Phone: 44 1827 52337
Fax: 44 1827 310827
E-mail: info@performancetextiles.org.uk
Home Page: http://www.performancetextiles.org.uk

• 6531 • **MUTA Safety Certificate**
For signed declaration and adherence to scheme. Awarded annually.

• 6532 •
Performing Right Society
Debby van den Berg, Communications Exec.
29-33 Berners St.
London W1T 3AB, United Kingdom
Phone: 44 20 75805544
Fax: 44 20 73064350
E-mail: info@prs.co.uk
Home Page: http://www.prs.co.uk

• 6533 • **Leslie Boosey Award**
To recognize an individual - not primarily a composer, conductor or solist - who has made an outstanding contribution to the furtherance of contemporary music and, in particular, British music. A bronze trophy specially commissioned from the distinguished sculptress Dame Elisabeth Frink is held for two years by the recipient, who also receives a medallion to keep. Awarded biennially in odd-numbered years. Established in 1980 to honor Leslie Boosey, President of Honour who died in 1979 at the age of 92.

• 6534 •
Philatelic Traders' Society
Mike Czuczman, Sec.
PO Box 371
Hampshire
Fleet GU52 6ZX, United Kingdom
Phone: 44 1252 628006
Fax: 44 1252 684674
E-mail: barbara.pts@btclick.com
Home Page: http://www.philatelic-traders-society.co.uk

• 6535 • **Stampex Exhibition Awards**
To recognize outstanding philatelic exhibits at the annual Stampex Exhibition. Two main classes of awards are presented: International Class: Prix d'Honneur - Harmers Diamond Jubilee Trophy and R.A.G. Lee International Award; and National Classes: Silver Mailcoach, National Philatelic Society Queen Elizabeth II Silver Jubilee Trophy, Royal Mail Trophy, National Postal Museum Medal, Phillips Trophy, P.T.S. Trophy, Stanley Gibbons Cup, Ebby Gerrish Trophy, Argyll Postal History Salver, Postal History Award, Philatelic Traders Cinderella Stamp Club Trophy, Link House Thematic Trophy, Aerophilatelic Class Award, British Aerophilatelic Federation Award, Albert H. Harris Literature Award, Francis Webb Memorial Trophy, B.P.E. Inter-Federation Award, William Ferris Bowl, British Caribbean Philatelic Study Group Award, H.L. Katcher Helvetia Trophy, Jack Grumbridge Pacific Island Trophy, the GBPS Hassan Shaida Trophy, and the Revenue Society of G.B. Award. Stampex is held twice per year, but the awards are presented only at the autumn event.

• 6536 •
Plain English Campaign
Chrissie Maher, Founder
New Mills
PO Box 3
High Peak SK22 4QP, United Kingdom
Phone: 44 1663 744409
Fax: 44 1663 747038
E-mail: info@plainenglish.co.uk
Home Page: http://www.plainenglish.co.uk

• 6537 • **Crystal Clear Day**
To recognize companies for their clear use of English in documents. Certificates are awarded annually in various categories. Established in 1995. Formerly: (2000) Crystal Clear Trophy; (1996) Capital Clear Trophy.

• 6538 • **Inside Write Awards**
To recognize internal government documents for their clear use of English. Awarded annually to one or more recipients. Established in 1980.

• 6539 • **Plain English Campaign Awards**
To promote the use of plain English and clear layout in forms, leaflets, and consumer agreements, and to recognize the worst and the best in official writing. Awards honoring the best writing are: Plain English Awards f or the best documents in any category; Inside Write Awards for internal government documents; Media Awards for radio, television, and newspapers; and the Plain English Web Award for the clearest website of the year. Awards for the worst writing are the Golden Bull Award for the worst forms of gobbledegook, and the Foot in Mouth Award for a baffling quote by a public figure. Trophies are presented to one or more recipients in each category annually. Established in 1980.

• 6540 •
Poetry Society
Paul Muldoon, Pres.
22 Betterton St.
London WC2H 9BX, United Kingdom
Phone: 44 207 4209880
Fax: 44 207 2404818
E-mail: info@poetrysociety.org.uk
Home Page: http://www.poetrysociety.org.uk

• 6541 • **National Poetry Competition**
For recognition of an outstanding unpublished poem. Individuals over 18 years of age who live anywhere are eligible. Entries must be submitted by October 31. Monetary prizes of £5,000 (for 1st place), £1,000 (2nd), £500 (3rd), and ten special commendations of £50 each are awarded annually. Established in 1978.

• 6542 • **Corneliu M. Popescu Prize for European Poetry Translation**
For recognition of a book of poems in translation of poetry from any European language into English. Eligible works are collections of poetry published within the previous 24 months that feature poetry translated from a European language into English.—A monetary prize of £1,500 is awarded biennially in odd-numbered years. Established in 1983 by Mihail Popescu of Romania in memory of his son, a young poet and translator who died in the 1977 Romanian earthquake at the age of 17.

• 6543 •
Police Federation of England and Wales
Mrs. Jan Berry, Chm.
15-17 Langley Rd.
Surrey
Surbiton KT6 6LP, United Kingdom
Phone: 44 208 3351000
Fax: 44 208 3992249
E-mail: info@jcc.polfed.org
Home Page: http://www.polfed.org

• 6544 • **Police Bravery Award**
Recognizes police officers who put themselves at risk of death or serious harm while performing their duties. Awarded annually to numerous recipients at the regional level, with one overall winner declared nationally.

• 6545 •
Political Studies Association
Prof. Wyn Grant, Pres.
Department of Politics
University of Newcastle
Newcastle upon Tyne NE1 7RU, United Kingdom
Phone: 44 191 2228021
Fax: 44 191 2225069
E-mail: psa@ncl.ac.uk
Home Page: http://www.psa.ac.uk

• 6546 • W. J. M. MacKenzie Book Prize
For recognition of publications in political science. Nominations by publishers are accepted. A monetary prize of £100 and a plaque are awarded annually. Established in 1987 in honor of W.J.M. MacKenzie.

• 6547 •
Polymer Machinery Manufacturers and Distributors Association
Sandy Weaver, Sec.
PO Box 2539
Rugby CV23 9YF, United Kingdom
Phone: 44 870 2411474
Fax: 44 870 2411475
E-mail: pmmda@pmmda.org.uk
Home Page: http://www.pmmda.org.uk

• 6548 • Apprentice of the Year
For a Coventry University student.

• 6549 • Designer of the Year
For designers.

• 6550 • Machinery Awards Interplas

• 6551 •
Pony Club of Great Britain
Judy Edwards, CEO
National Agricultural Centre
NAC Stoneleigh Park
Kenilworth CV8 2RW, United Kingdom
Phone: 44 2476 698300
Fax: 44 2476 696836
E-mail: enquiries@pcuk.org
Home Page: http://www.pcuk.org

• 6552 • Cubitt Award
To recognize individuals for long, devoted, and distinguished service in a voluntary capacity to the Club. Individuals who have served over 15 years, and preferably over 20 years, are eligible. A certificate and a badge are awarded annually at Council meetings. Established in 1988 to honor Colonel C. G. Cubitt, past chairman and president of the Club.

• 6553 •
Prehistoric Society
Prof. Miranda Aldhouse-Green, Pres.
University Coll. London
Institute of Archaeology
31-34 Gordon Sq.
London WC1H 0PY, United Kingdom
E-mail: prehistoric@ucl.ac.uk
Home Page: http://www.ucl.ac.uk/prehistoric

Formerly: (1935) Prehistoric Society of East Anglia.

• 6554 • R. M. Baguley Award
For recognition of an archaeological publication. Papers published in the proceedings of the Society are considered. A trophy, donated by R.M. Baguley, is awarded annually. Established in 1979.

• 6555 • Bob Smith Research Award
To fund research in the field of prehistory. Members must submit applications to the Society's research fund. A monetary award is presented annually in February. Established in 1987 by Dr. G.J. Wainwright in memory of Dr. Bob Smith.

• 6556 •
Professional Association of Nursery Nurses
Tricia Pritchard, Senior Professional Officer
2 St. James' Ct.
Friar Gate
Derby DE1 1BT, United Kingdom
Phone: 44 1332 372337
Fax: 44 1332 290310
E-mail: pann@pat.org.uk
Home Page: http://www.pat.org.uk

• 6557 • Meering Rose Bowl Award
Recognizes outstanding contribution to child welfare. Awarded when merited.

• 6558 •
Professional Golfers' Association - England
Mike Gray, Commercial Dir.
Centenary House
The Belfry
Sutton Coldfield
Birmingham B76 9PT, United Kingdom
Phone: 44 1675 470333
Fax: 44 1675 477888
E-mail: office.service@pga.org.uk
Home Page: http://www.pga.info

• 6559 • PGA Assistants Professional Championship
To recognize the winning PGA of America Assistant Professional from all 41 PGA of America sections, plus Australia, Canada, Great Britain,—and New Zealand. The winner receives $9,000 of the total purse of $100,000, plus an invitation to participate in the Australian PGA National Futures Championship. Awarded annually. Established in 1930.

• 6560 • PGA Club Professional Championship
To recognize the best players at the annual PGA Club Professional Championship. Features a total purse of more than $1.5 million that is awarded in Section, Regional, and National championships. Held annually. Established in 1968.

• 6561 • PGA Cup
To recognize the team winning the biennial competition between the United States versus Great Britain and Ireland. Held in odd-numbered years. Established in 1973.

• 6562 • Ryder Cup
To recognize the winner of a biennial professional golf team competition between the United States and Europe. The cup was donated by Samuel Ryder, a patron of professional golf in England. Held biennially in even-numbered years. Established in 1927.

• 6563 • Ryle Memorial Medal
Awarded to recognize the winner of the British Open Golf Championship. Candidates must be members of the PGA. Awarded when merited. Established in 1901.

• 6564 • Senior PGA Championship
To honor the best legendary golfer over the age of 50. Held annually. Established in 1957.

• 6565 • Braid Taylor Memorial Medal
To recognize the member of the PGA who finishes highest in the British Open Golf Championship. Candidates must have been born in the United Kingdom or Republic of Ireland, or at least one of their parents must have been. Awarded annually. Established in 1966.

• 6566 • Tooting Bec Cup
To recognize the member of the PGA who returns the lowest single round score in the British Open Golf Championship. Candidates must have been born in the United Kingdom or Republic of Ireland, or at least one of their parents must have been. Awarded annually. Established in 1901. From 1901 to 1922, prior to its association with the British Open Championship, the Tooting Bec Trophy was contested over 36 holes.

• 6567 • Harry Vardon Trophy
To recognize the winner of the European Tour Order of Merit. Awarded annually. Established in 1939 to honor Harry Vardon, an internationally famous British golfer.

• 6568 • Whitcombe Cox Trophy
To recognize the PGA Trainee of the Year who is considered by the examiners to be the best overall candidate in the final examinations. A trophy and a monetary award of £3,500 are awarded annually. The award was introduced in 1974 and the trophy was commissioned in 1991.

• 6569 •
Public Relations Consultants Association
Patrick Barrow, Dir.Gen.
Willow House
Willow Pl.
Victoria
London SW1P 1JH, United Kingdom
Phone: 44 207 2336026
Fax: 44 207 8284797
E-mail: pressoffice@prca.org.uk
Home Page: http://www.prca.org.uk

• 6570 • **Awards for Outstanding Consultancy Practice**
For recognition of achievement in the field of public relations. Members and associates of the Association are eligible. A certificate is awarded annually. Established in 1987.

• 6571 •
Quaternary Research Association
John Lowe, Pres.
Department of Geography
Royal Holloway
University of London
Egham RH4 3QR, United Kingdom
Phone: 44 1784 443565
E-mail: j.lowe@rhul.ac.uk
Home Page: http://www.qra.org.uk

• 6572 • **New Research Workers Awards**
For new or young researchers registered For a postgraduate degree.

• 6573 • **Postgraduate QRA Meetings Award**
For postgraduate members.

• 6574 • **QRA-Bill Bishop Award**
For full or part-time mphil/PhD students.

• 6575 • **Quaternary Conference Fund**
For members of the QRA with limited alternative sources of funding particularly postgraduate students.

• 6576 • **Quaternary Research Fund**
For members of the QRA. 297121

• 6577 •
Queen's Awards Office
151 Buckingham Palace Rd.
London SW1W 9SS, United Kingdom
Phone: 44 207 222 2277
Fax: 44 171 215 5770
E-mail: info@queensawards.org.uk
Home Page: http://www.queensawards.org.uk

• 6578 • **Queen's Award for Enterprise: Innovation**
For outstanding innovation, resulting in substantial improvement in business performance and commercial success, sustained over not less than two years, to levels which are outstanding for the goods or services concerned and for the size of the applicant's operations, and arising in the fields listed below, or for continuous innovation and development, resulting in substantial improvement in business performance and commercial success, sustained over not less than five years, to levels which are outstanding for the goods or services concerned and for the size of the applicant's operations, and arising in the fields listed below. Achievements may be assessed in any of the following fields: the innovation, design, production (in respect of goods), performance (in respect of services, including advise), marketing, distribution, and after-sale support of goods or services.

• 6579 • **Queen's Awards for Enterprise**
To recognize and reward outstanding achievement by U.K. companies. They are presented in three separate categories: (1) International Trade - for demonstrated growth in overseas earnings; (2) Innovation - for demonstrated commercial success through innovative products or services; and (3) Sustainable Development - for integration of environmental, social, economic, and management aspects of sustainable development into their business. The deadline for applications is October 31 of each year. A Grant of Appointment in scroll form and a stainless steel emblem of the award encapsulated in an acrylic block are presented at a ceremony by a Lord-Lieutenant on behalf of the Queen. Holders of the award, which is valid for five years from the date of the announcement, are entitled to fly the award flag and display the emblem. Awarded annually. Established in 1992. Formerly: (1999) Queen's Award for Environmental Achievement.

• 6580 • **Queen's Awards for Enterprise in Innovation**
To recognize business units for substantial improvement in business performance and commercial success, to levels that are outstanding for the size of the applicant's operations. Businesses may apply under the following criteria: (1) outstanding innovation, sustained over not less than two years; or (2) continuous innovation and development, sustained over not less than five years. Achievements may be assessed for any of the following: the invention, design, production (of goods), performance (of services, including advice), marketing, distribution, and after-sales support. Awarded annually to one or more recipients. Established in 1965. Formerly: (2001) Queen's Award for Technological Achievement.

• 6581 • **Queen's Awards for Enterprise in International Trade**
To recognize substantial growth in overseas earnings and commercial success, to levels that are outstanding for the goods or services concerned and for the size of the applicant's operations. Businesses may apply under the following criteria: (1) outstanding achievement in international trade, sustained over not less than three years; or (2) continuous achievement in international trade, sustained over not less than six years. Awarded annually to one or more recipients. Established in 1965. Formerly: (2001) Queen's Award for Export Achievement.

• 6582 • **Queen's Awards for Enterprise: International Trade**
For outstanding achievement in international trade resulting in substantial growth in overseas earnings and in commercial success, sustained over not less than three years, to levels which are outstanding for the goods or services concerned and for the size of the applicant's operations or for continuous achievement in international trade, resulting in substantial overseas earnings with growth and commercial success, sustained over not less than six years, to levels which are outstanding for the goods or services concerned and for the size of the applicant's operations.

• 6583 • **Queen's Awards for Enterprise: Sustainable Development**
For outstanding advance in sustainable development contributing to a substantial improvement in business performance and commercial success, sustained over not less than two years, to levels which are outstanding for the goods or services concerned and for the size of the applicant's operations, and arising in the fields listed below, or for continuous achievement in sustainable development, contributing to substantial improvement in business performance and commercial success, sustained over not less than five years, to levels which are outstanding for the goods or services concerned and for the size of the applicant's operations, and arising in the fields listed below. Achievements in either category may be assessed in any of the following fields: The invention, design, production(in respect of goods), performance (in respect of services, including advice), marketing, distribution, after-sales support of goods or services, and/or the management of resources (including natural, manufactured and human resources) and relationships (with people and organizations).

• 6584 •
Queen's English Society
Ms. C.P. Cawood, Membership Sec.
The Clergy House
Hide Pl.
W Chiltington
London SW1P 4NJ, United Kingdom
Phone: 44 20 76301819
E-mail: enquiries@queens-english-society.com
Home Page: http://www.queens-english-society.com

• 6585 • **The Goodchild Prize**
For excellence in writing. A monetary award is given annually.

• 6586 •
Racegoers Club
Winkfield Rd.
Ascot SL5 7HX, United Kingdom
Phone: 44 1344 625912
Home Page: http://www.racegoersclub.co.uk

Awards are arranged in alphabetical order below their administering organizations

• 6587 • Racehorse of the Year Award
For recognition of the outstanding racehorse of the year. The award originated as a publicity idea designed to stimulate public interest in horseracing. Any horse that has raced on a British racecourse during the year is eligible. A panel of journalists selects the winner. A twelve-inch bronze statuette sculpted by Jean Walwyn and entitled "The Winner" is awarded annually. Established in 1965 by the Racecourse Association which invited The Racegoers Club to take over the award in 1978.

• 6588 •
Ramsay Memorial Fellowships Trust
University College London
5 Gower St.
London WC1E 6BT, United Kingdom
Phone: 44 20 7679 7815
Fax: 44 20 7679 7327
E-mail: g.hawes@ucl.ac.uk
Home Page: http://www.ucl.ac.uk/ramsay-trust

• 6589 • Ramsay Memorial Fellowships for Postdoctoral Chemical Research
To enable the holder to devote himself or herself full-time to postdoctoral research in chemistry. Individuals preferably born within the British Commonwealth who graduated with honors in chemistry from a commonwealth university may apply by November 15. One or more Fellowships, tenable for two years in the United Kingdom, are awarded annually. Established in 1920 in memory of Sir William Ramsay, KCB FRS (1852-1916).

• 6590 •
Regional Studies Association
Sally Hardy, Chief Exec.
PO Box 2058
Seaford BN25 4QU, United Kingdom
Phone: 44 1323 899698
Fax: 44 1323 899798
E-mail: rsa@mailbox.ulcc.ac.uk
Home Page: http://www.regional-studies-assoc.ac.uk

• 6591 • Bill Ogden Memorial Prize
To recognize students for the best research paper. Publication and a monetary prize are awarded annually.

• 6592 •
Remote Sensing and Photogrammetry Society
Dr. J. Finch, Hon.Gen.Sec.
% School of Geography
University of Nottingham
University Park
Nottingham NG7 2RD, United Kingdom
Phone: 44 115 9515435
Fax: 44 115 9515249
E-mail: rspsoc@nottingham.ac.uk
Home Page: http://www.rspsoc.org

• 6593 • Len Curtis Award
For recognition of distinguished technical articles published in the *International Journal of Remote Sensing* during the previous year. Certificate and books valued at £200 are awarded annually. Formerly: (1991) Eurosense Award.

• 6594 • Poster Paper Prize
For recognition of the best poster papers presented at the Society's annual conference. The first place winner receives the Main Award (£100) and the runner-up receives the Merit Award (£25). Awarded annually.

• 6595 • Remote Sensing and Photogrammetry Society Award
This, the highest award of the Society, is given for recognition of an outstanding contribution in the field of remote sensing. A gold medal and honorary lifetime membership in the Society are awarded periodically. Formerly: (2004) Remote Sensing Society Medal.

• 6596 • Student Awards
For recognition of the best Doctoral and Masters theses on the subject of remote sensing and/or photogrammetry. Certificates and monetary awards of £500 (Doctoral) and £250 (Masters) are awarded annually.

• 6597 • Taylor and Francis Best Letter Award
For recognition of the best letter published in the *International Journal of Remote Sensing* during the previous year. A certificate and prizes valued at £100 are awarded annually.

• 6598 • E. H. Thompson Award
For recognition of the best paper published in the *Photogrammetric Record* during the previous two years. A certificate and monetary award of £200 is awarded when merited. Formerly: (2004) Remote Sensing Society President's Prize.

• 6599 •
Reuters Foundation
Rosemary Martin, Dir.
Reuters Bldg., S Colonnade
Canary Wharf
London E14 5EP, United Kingdom
Phone: 44 20 75427015
Fax: 44 20 75428599
E-mail: foundation@reuters.com
Home Page: http://www.foundation.reuters.com

• 6600 • Oxford University Fellowship
The fellowship offers outstanding journalists the opportunity to spend three months studying at Oxford University to study subjects of their choice. The fellowship is open to writers and broadcasters from the United States, including specialists in economic, environmental, medical and scientific subjects. Applicants must be citizens of the United States; full-time journalists or regular contributors to newspapers, news agencies, magazines, radio or television; established journalists with a minimum five years' professional experience and a clear commitment to a career in journalism. Fellowship covers travel expenses, tuition and monthly living expenses. Applications are due by October 31. Established in 1996.

• 6601 • Reuter Foundation Stanford Fellowship
To provide individuals an opportunity to research and create prototype technology solutions that will benefit the under-served communities in developing countries. As part of the Digital Vision Program, the fellowship supports social entrepreneurs who seek to leverage technology-based solutions in the interest of humanitarian, educational, and sustainable development goals. The nine-month fellowship is based at the Stanford Center for the Study of Language and Information on the campus of Stanford University. The Reuter Foundation pays the costs of the return fare between the Fellow's home and the University, tuition fees, and living expenses. Each Fellowship is tenable for one, two, or three academic terms. Certificates are awarded at the completion of the fellowship. Established in 1982.

• 6602 •
Rolls-Royce Enthusiasts' Club
The Hunt House
Paulerspury
Northamptonshire NN12 7NA, United Kingdom
Phone: 44 1327 811 788
Fax: 44 1327 811 797
E-mail: philiphall@rrec.org.uk
Home Page: http://www.rrec.co.uk

• 6603 • Rolls-Royce Enthusiasts Awards
To recognize winners of rallies and meets. Twenty separate classes are judged. Rolls-Royce motor cars from 1904 to the present day and Bentleys from 1933 to the present are eligible. Trophies are awarded annually.

• 6604 •
Romantic Novelists' Association
Jenny Haddon, Chm.
38 Stanhope Rd.
Hallaton
Leicestershire
Reading RG2 7HN, United Kingdom
Phone: 44 1858 555602
Fax: 44 208 3416275
E-mail: jennyhaddon@dial.pipex.com
Home Page: http://www.rna-uk.org

• 6605 • FosterGrant Reading Glasses Romantic Novel of the Year
For recognition of the best romantic novel, modern or historical, published in English in the United Kingdom during the year. A monetary award is presented annually. Established in 1960. Formerly: (1988) Parker Romantic Novel of the Year; (1988) Boots Romantic Novel of the Year; (1998) Romantic Novel of the Year.

• 6606 • Joan Hessayon New Writers' Award
To recognize new romance writers for an unpublished full-length novel. Probationary members of the RNA who submit full length manuscripts of romantic novels between September 1 and September 30 are eligible. A silver salver to be held for one year and a monetary award are presented annually in April. Established in 1961. Formerly: (1995) Nevva Muskett Award.

• 6607 •
Rough and Smooth Collie Training Association
Jean Tuck, Hon.Sec.
22 Riverview Way
Glynbridge Gardens
Cheltenham GL51 0AF, United Kingdom
Phone: 44 1889 568090
E-mail: jean@rscta.co.uk
Home Page: http://www.rscta.co.uk

• 6608 • Achievement Awards
Recognizes members achieving the highest number of club points with a rough or smooth collie in agility, breed league, obedience, and versatility. Awarded annually.

• 6609 •
Royal Academy of Arts
Sir Nicholas Grimshaw, Pres.
Burlington House
Picadilly
London W1J 0BD, United Kingdom
Phone: 44 20 73008000
Fax: 44 20 73005760
E-mail: library@royalacademy.org.uk
Home Page: http://www.royalacademy.org.uk

• 6610 • Jack Goldhill Award for Sculpture
For recognition of outstanding sculpture in each year's Royal Academy Summer Exhibition. A monetary award of £10,000 is presented annually. Established by the Jack and Grete Goldhill Charitable Trust.

• 6611 • Royal Academy Summer Exhibition
For recognition of different categories of work exhibited in the Royal Academy's annual Summer Exhibition: an open competition of works featuring painting, sculpture, architecture and engraving, print-making and draftsmanship. A total of £70,000 is awarded in prizes. Held annually. Established in 1769.

• 6612 • Charles Wollaston Award
For recognition of the most distinguished exhibit in the annual Royal Academy Summer Exhibition. A monetary award of £25,000 is awarded annually. Established in 1977 by Charles Wollaston, Esquire.

• 6613 •
Royal Academy of Dance
Luke Rittner, Chief Exec.
36 Battersea Sq.
London SW11 3RA, United Kingdom
Phone: 44 20 73268000
Fax: 44 20 79243129
E-mail: info@rad.org.uk
Home Page: http://www.rad.org.uk

• 6614 • Associate of the Royal Academy of Dance
To recognize full members over the age of 18 years who have passed the Advanced Examination or the Advanced Teaching Examination. Awarded annually by the Executive Committee.

• 6615 • Phyllis Bedells Bursary
Available to students worldwide who have completed their Intermediate Executant Examination with either Highly Commended or above. A monetary prize of £1,000 is given annually.

• 6616 • Fellow of the Royal Academy of Dance
To recognize members for outstanding service to the Academy over a long period of time. Awarded annually.

• 6617 • Honorary Fellow of the Royal Academy of Dance
To recognize non-Academy members for outstanding service over a long period of time. Awarded annually.

• 6618 • President's Award
To honor an individual from anywhere throughout the world who has given dedicated service to the Academy. Established in 1992.

• 6619 • Queen Elizabeth II Coronation Award
To recognize an individual who has made a significant contribution to the art of ballet. A plaque is awarded annually. Established in 1954 by Dame Adeline Genee, founding President of the Royal Academy of Dancing in honor of Her Majesty, Queen Elizabeth II, who succeeded her grandmother, Queen Mary, as Patron of the Academy.

• 6620 •
Royal Academy of Engineering
Philip Greenish, Chief Exec.
29 Great Peter St.
Westminster
London SW1P 3LW, United Kingdom
Phone: 44 20 72270500
Fax: 44 20 72330054
E-mail: philip.greenish@raeng.org.uk
Home Page: http://www.raeng.org.uk

Formerly: Fellowship of Engineering.

• 6621 • MacRobert Award
For recognition of an outstanding contribution by way of innovation in engineering or the physical technologies, or in the application of the physical sciences which is or will be for the benefit of the community. Entries should be submitted by March 31. A monetary prize of £50,000 and a gold medal are awarded annually. Established in 1968 by the MacRobert Trusts which were founded by Lady MacRobert of Douneside and Cromar, wife of Sir Alexander MacRobert, head of the British India Corporation.

• 6622 • President's Medal
Recognizes contributions to the Academy's aims and work. Organizations and individuals not eligible for membership in the academy are eligible. Awarded not more than once a year.

• 6623 • Prince Philip Medal
Recognizes contribution to engineering as a whole through practice, management, or education. Engineers of any nationality are eligible. Awarded periodically.

• 6624 • Silver Medal

• 6625 • Sir Frank Whittle Medal
Inquire for application details.

• 6626 •
Royal Academy of Music
Prof. Curtis Price, Principal
Marylebone Rd.
London NW1 5HT, United Kingdom
Phone: 44 20 7873 7373
Fax: 44 20 7873 3744
E-mail: e.mcfadden@ram.ac.uk
Home Page: http://www.ram.ac.uk

• 6627 • Honorary Membership
To recognize an individual not formerly a student of the Academy for outstanding contributions to music. Awarded when merited.

• 6628 •
Royal Aeronautical Society - United Kingdom
Keith Mans, Chief Exec.
4 Hamilton Pl.
London W1J 7BQ, United Kingdom
Phone: 44 207 6704300
Fax: 44 207 6704309
E-mail: raes@raes.org.uk
Home Page: http://aerosociety.com

• 6629 • Peter Allard Silver Medal
To recognize practical achievement leading to the use of composite materials in aerospace. Established in 1992. Sponsored by the Peter Allard Charitable Foundation and presented by Ricardo Group, plc.

• 6630 • Buchanan Barbour Award
To recognize outstanding achievement in civil or military aerospace medicine. Awarded annually when merited.

• 6631 • **British Bronze Medal**
For recognition of a practical contribution to the profession of aerospace. Established in 1989.

• 6632 • **British Gold Medal**
For recognition of outstanding practical achievement leading to advancement in aeronautics. A gold medal is awarded annually. Established in 1933. The medal commemorates Sir George Cayley and his first model aeroplane of 1804.

• 6633 • **British Silver Medal**
For recognition of practical achievement leading to advancement in aeronautics. A silver medal is awarded annually. Established in 1933. The medal commemorates the Henson machine of 1842 and the Stringfellow model of 1848.

• 6634 • **John Britten Prize**
To recognize the best paper on light aviation or lighter-than-air aviation published by the Society. Awarded annually.

• 6635 • **Bronze Medal**
For recognition of a work leading to an advance in aerospace. A bronze medal is awarded annually to individuals and teams. Established in 1908.

• 6636 • **Sir Vernon Brown Prize**
To recognize the best paper on aircraft operations, including maintenance, published by the Society. Awarded annually.

• 6637 • **Busk Prize**
For recognition of the best paper on aerodynamics (including flight testing) published by the Royal Aeronautical Society. Awarded annually.

• 6638 • **Sir Roy Fedden Award**
For recognition of a paper that has been written or innovative work carried out in the field of aerospace propulsion. Younger persons who are not yet recognized authorities in the subject are eligible, with the object of encouraging them in their career. Topical subjects of importance such as noise attenuation and fuel economy are considered suitable. An honorarium is awarded periodically.

• 6639 • **Flight Simulation Silver Medal**
To recognize an individual for significant long-term contributions, in an international context, in the field of flight simulation. A medal is awarded annually. Established in 1991.

• 6640 • **Gold Medal**
To recognize an individual for work of an outstanding nature in aerospace. A gold medal is awarded annually to individuals and teams. Established in 1909.

• 6641 • **Hafner VTOL Prize**
To recognize the best paper published by the Society on VTOL Technology by an individual under 30 years old. Awarded annually.

• 6642 • **Sir Robert Hardingham Presidential Sword**
To recognize a member for outstanding services to the Society over a period of time. Awarded at the discretion of the president of the Society.

• 6643 • **Hodgson Prize**
For recognition of the best paper on general subjects, such as policy, law, operations, management, education, and history, published by the Society. Awarded annually.

• 6644 • **Honorary Companionship**
For recognition of important service to the profession of aerospace by someone outside the industry. Awarded when merited to not more than three individuals. Established in 1950. Formerly: .

• 6645 • **Honorary Fellowship**
This, the greatest distinction of the Society, is given for long and distinguished contributions to aerospace. Awarded when merited. Established in 1920.

• 6646 • **Herbert Le Sueur Award**
To assist a student or graduate member where studies or experience will be enhanced by attending the European Rotorcraft Forum or similar event.

• 6647 • **Alan Marsh Award**
To recognize technical promise in the rotary wing field. A scroll and five hours of dual helicopter flying training are awarded when merited. Established in memory of Squadron Leader Henry Alan Marsh, AFC.

• 6648 • **Alan Marsh Medal**
For recognition of outstanding helicopter pilotage achievement in the field of helicopter research. British pilots are eligible. A medal is awarded annually. Established by the Helicopter Association of Great Britain (now the Rotorcraft Section of the Society) in 1955 to commemorate the work of Henry Alan Marsh, the outstanding test pilot who was killed in 1950 while flying the Cierva Air Horse, at that time the largest helicopter to be built in the United Kingdom.

• 6649 • **Handley Page Award**
For recognition of original work leading to advancement and progress in the art and science of aeronautics, with special reference to the practical application of a device, or the long-term implications of a new concept, directed towards the safety of those who work with aircraft or travel in aircraft. Only citizens of the British Commonwealth who are engaged in work preferably within the Commonwealth are eligible. A monetary prize of up to £5,000 that may be used to finance the proposed work through the provision of facilities, equipment, travel expenses, and any such means of furthering the proposal is awarded. Established in 1965 in memory of the late Sir Frederick Handley Page, in recognition of his contributions to aviation.

• 6650 • **Geoffrey Pardoe Space Award**
To recognize a significant contribution to space. Awarded annually.

• 6651 • **R38 Memorial Prize**
To recognize a paper or work on airships. Awarded annually.

• 6652 • **Frank Radcliffe Travelling Fellowship in Reliability and Quality Assurance**
To enable a lecturer to give a presentation at all universities and in the United Kingdom with aeronautical engineering courses. Awarded annually.

• 6653 • **N. E. Rowe Medals**
For recognition of the best lecture given before any branch of the Society by a young member of a branch, or of the young members section or its sub-sections. The award was instituted to encourage the younger members of the branches. Awards are given to individuals in two age categories: between 23 and 27 years of age and under 23 years of age. Medals are awarded annually. Established in 1956.

• 6654 • **Silver Medal**
To recognize work contributing to major advances in aerospace. A silver medal is awarded annually to individuals and teams. Established in 1909.

• 6655 • **Silver Turnbuckle Award**
To recognize long and valued service in the field of aircraft maintenance. Awarded annually when merited.

• 6656 • **Simms Prize**
For recognition of the best paper on electrical, electronic, and other systems (including the ground environment) published by the Royal Aeronautical Society. Awarded annually.

• 6657 • **Akroyd Stuart Prize**
For recognition of the best paper on propulsion published by the Society. Awarded annually.

• 6658 • **George Taylor (of Australia) Prize**
For recognition of the best paper on design, construction, production, and fabrication (including structures and materials) published by the Society. Awarded annually.

• 6659 • **B. W. O. Townshend Award**
To recognize a paper or device contributing to escape, survival from an aircraft and search, and rescue at sea. Awarded annually when merited.

• 6660 • **Wakefield Gold Medal**
For recognition of contributions towards safety in aerospace. A gold medal is awarded irregularly. Established in 1926 by Castrol Limited in memory of the company's founder, Viscount

Wakefield of Hythe. Sponsored by Kidde-Grininer.

• 6661 •
Royal Agricultural Society of England
Helen Tetlow, Sec.
Stoneleigh Park
Coventry CV8 2LZ, United Kingdom
Phone: 44 2476 696969
Fax: 44 2476 696900
E-mail: info@rase.org.uk
Home Page: http://www.rase.org.uk

• 6662 • **Bledisloe Gold Medal for Landowners**
To recognize a landowner for distinguished achievement in the successful land management and development of an agricultural estate in England. A gold medal, certificate, and honorary membership are awarded annually. Established in 1957 by the First Viscount Bledisloe.

• 6663 • **Sir Roland Burke Perpetual Challenge Machinery Trophy**
To recognize a British manufacturer of agricultural implements or machines which has made an outstanding impact on farming generally or on a particular branch of agriculture or horticulture. A trophy is awarded annually at the Royal Show. Established in 1970. Formerly: (1981) Burke Perpetual Challenge Trophy.

• 6664 • **Excellence in Practical Farming Award**
Founded in 1999 to reward farmers and farm managers setting a lead for others as practical farmers willing to impart their knowledge to others. Up to three awards may be made annually. A slate plaque and life membership in the society are awarded to the winners at the Scientific Awards Ceremony in London in February.

• 6665 • **Honorary Fellow**
To recognize individuals for outstanding contributions to the agricultural industry. Awarded when merited.

• 6666 • **Machinery Award Scheme**
To assist potential users of equipment by identifying machines that meet the judging criteria as soon as can be done safely. The secondary aim is to assist manufacturers to develop and make widely known that good new equipment has been independently assessed in field conditions. Entries must be complete machines, appliances, or important ancillary equipment which significantly contributes to performance or economy. The equipment should have a definite application to agriculture, horticulture, forestry or estate services. The equipment must be commercially available. The following criteria are considered: innovation, substantially improved working conditions, conservation or use of materials, bringing improved technical performance and significant improvement in performance. Gold medals, silver medals, and Awards of Merit are presented annually. Established in 1840.

• 6667 • **National Agricultural Award**
For recognintion of outstanding contributions to the advancement of agriculture in the United Kingdom. Sponsorship of the award and lecture was assumed by the society in 1999. A monetary prize, trophy, and medal are awarded annually at an award ceremony in London in October.

• 6668 • **Research Medal**
For recognition of outstanding research work carried out in the United Kingdom that has proved or is likely to be of benefit to agriculture. Workers actually engaged in active research are eligible. A monetary award of 300 guineas and a medal are awarded annually at the Scientific Awards. Established in 1954. Absorbed the Bledisloe Veterinary Award in 2003.

• 6669 • **Talbot-Ponsonby Prize for Agricultural Valuation**
Established in 1957, the award is given to the first placed candidate in the entrance examinations to the Central Association of Agricultural Valuers. A bronze medal is awarded, usually annually, at the Royal Show.

• 6670 • **Technology Award**
To recognize individuals who, working in a commercial environment, have applied scientific advance into technology through the development of a product or process, which are likely to lead to cost ëffective improvements for farmers in any aspect of practical agriculture. A monetary prize of 300 guineas and a medal are awarded annually. Established in 1985.

• 6671 •
Royal and Ancient Golf Club of St. Andrews
Right Hon. J Thomas Munro Gault DCNZM, Capt.
St. Andrews
Fife KY16 9JD, United Kingdom
Phone: 44 1334 460000
Fax: 44 1334 460001
Home Page: http://www.randa.org

• 6672 • **Open Championship**
To recognize the winner of the annual golf tournament. Amateur and professional golfers are eligible. The competition is held in three stages: Regional Qualifying Competitions, Final Qualifying Competitions, and Open Championship. A maximum of 156 competitors participate in the Open Championship. The winner is designated Champion Golfer of the Year, and receives the Championship Trophy to retain for one year along with the Championship Gold Medal. The first amateur in the Championship, unless he or she is the winner, receives a Silver Medal, provided that 72 holes have been completed. Other amateurs who complete 72 holes receive a Bronze Medal. Prize money is awarded only to professional golfers. The Champion Golfer of the Year receives £250,000 for first place. In addition, the Professional Golfers Association awards various trophies at the competition. Established in 1860 by the Prestwick Golf Club, Ayrshire, Scotland; the Championship has been organized by the Royal and Ancient Gold Club of St. Andrews since 1920.

• 6673 •
Royal Anthropological Institute of Great Britain and Ireland
Hilary Callan, Dir.
50 Fitzroy St.
London W1T 5BT, United Kingdom
Phone: 44 207 3870455
Fax: 44 207 3888817
E-mail: admin@therai.org.uk
Home Page: http://www.therai.org.uk

• 6674 • **Curl Essay Prize**
For recognition of the best essay not exceeding 10,000 words relating to the results or analysis of anthropological work. Anthropologists of any nationality may submit applications by October 31. A monetary prize of £1,100 is awarded annually. Established in 1951.

• 6675 • **J. B. Donne Essay Prize on the Anthropology of Art**
To recognize an essay on any aspect of the anthropology of art, including the visual and performing arts. The essay must be unpublished, 10,000 words or less, and available for publication by the institute. Essays must be submitted by October 31.A monetary prize of £700 is awarded biennially in odd-numbered years. Established in 1987.

• 6676 • **Amaury Talbot Prize for African Anthropology**
For recognition of the most valuable work of anthropological research published during the preceding calendar year. Preference is given to first works relating to Nigeria, and then to any other part of West Africa or West Africa in general, although works relating to other regions of Africa may also be considered. A monetary prize of £500 is awarded annually. Established in 1961.

• 6677 • **Wellcome Medal for Anthropology as Applied to Medical Problems**
To encourage the development of medical anthropology through recognition of an outstanding published work. Nominations or applications are accepted. Candidates in the early part of their careers are considered more favorably. A bronze medal and £600 are awarded biennially in even-numbered years. Established in 1931 by Sir Henry Wellcome. Sponsored by the Wellcome Trust.

• 6678 •
Royal Asiatic Society of Great Britain and Ireland
Dr. B.M.C. Brend MA, Sec.
73 Collier St.
London N1 9BE, United Kingdom
Phone: 44 207 8121495
Fax: 44 207 8370688
E-mail: info@royalasiaticsociety.org
Home Page: http://www.royalasiaticsociety.org

• 6679 • Sir Richard Burton Medal
To encourage Asian studies through travel. A medal is presented at intervals of at least three years. Established in 1923 in memory of Sir Richard Burton, the explorer.

• 6680 • Royal Asiatic Society Award
To recognize outstanding research that is considered to have contributed the most to the advancement of Asian studies. The research must be published either in books or articles, in English or as Asian texts with editorial matter in English. An award is presented every three years.

• 6681 •
Royal Association of British Dairy Farmers
Nick Everington, Chief Exec.
Dairy House, Unit 31
Stoneleigh Deer Park, Stareton
Warwickshire
Kenilworth CV8 2LY, United Kingdom
Phone: 44 845 4582711
Fax: 44 845 4582755
E-mail: office@rabdf.co.uk
Home Page: http://www.rabdf.co.uk

• 6682 • Dairy Student Award
For students with outstanding knowledge in practical dairy farming.

• 6683 • Prince Philip Award
For best presented technical exhibit at the Dairy Event.

• 6684 • Princess Royal Award
For individuals working in any sector of the dairy industry.

• 6685 •
Royal Astronomical Society
David Elliott, Exec.Sec.
Burlington House
Piccadilly
London W1J 0BQ, United Kingdom
Phone: 44 20 77343307
Phone: 44 20 77344582
Fax: 44 20 74940166
E-mail: info@ras.org.uk
Home Page: http://www.ras.org.uk

• 6686 • Chapman Medal
For recognition of specific investigations of outstanding merit in the fields of solar-terrestrial physics, including geomagnetism and aeronomy. A medal is awarded biennially. Established in 1973 to honor Professor Sidney Chapman.

• 6687 • Eddington Medal
To recognize specific investigations of outstanding merit in the field of theoretical astrophysics. A medal is awarded biennially. Established in 1953 in honor of Sir Arthur Stanley Eddington.

• 6688 • Herschel Medal
To recognize investigations of outstanding merit in observational astrophysics. A medal is awarded biennially. Established in 1974 to honor Sir William Herschel.

• 6689 • Jackson-Gwilt Medal
For recognition of the invention, improvement, or development of astronomical instrumentation or techniques; for achievement in observational astronomy; or for achievement in research into the history of astronomy. A monetary award and a bronze medal are presented at intervals of not less than two years. Established in 1897 to honor Mrs. Hannah Jackson-Gwilt.

• 6690 • Price Medal
To recognize specific work in the fields of solid-earth geophysics, oceanography, or planetary sciences. Awarded biennially. Established in 1993 to honor Professor Albert Thomas Price.

• 6691 •
Royal Bath and West of England Society
The Show Ground
Shepton Mallet BA4 6QN, United Kingdom
Phone: 44 1749 822200
Fax: 44 1749 823169
E-mail: info@bathandwest.co.uk
Home Page: http://www.bathandwest.co.uk

• 6692 • Art Scholarship
To recognize and encourage young professional artists in the United Kingdom. Individuals between 22 and 35 years of age are eligible. A monetary award of £2,750 is presented biennially.

• 6693 •
Royal College of General Practitioners
Roger Neighbour PRCGP, Pres.
14 Princes Gate
Hyde Park
London SW7 1PU, United Kingdom
Phone: 44 207 5813232
Fax: 44 207 2253047
E-mail: info@rcgp.org.uk
Home Page: http://www.rcgp.org.uk

• 6694 • Disability Care Award
to an individual or team in recognition of innovative/significant developments in the organization

• 6695 • GP Registrar Awards
For original and innovative projects undertaken during the course of vocational training in UK.

• 6696 • Patient Participation Award
To any member of the practice team, patient group, or patient of a practice.

• 6697 • Paul Freeling Award
To members of fellows of the RCGP in good standing.

• 6698 • RGCP/SAPC Elective Prize
For the best proposal by a medical student For an elective project.

• 6699 • Ros Prize
To all non-professional historians either as individuals or as a group, involved in primary health care.

• 6700 •
Royal College of Obstetricians and Gynaecologists - United Kingdom
Kim Dawson, Sec.
27 Sussex Pl.
Regent's Park
London NW1 4RG, United Kingdom
Phone: 44 207 7726200
Phone: 44 207 7726200
Fax: 44 207 7230575
E-mail: kdawson@rcog.org.uk
Home Page: http://www.rcog.org.uk

• 6701 • AGC/GVS Fellowship
To enable the recipient to visit, make contact with and gain knowledge from a specific centre offering new techniques or methods of clinical management within the specialty of obstetrics and gynaecology. Open to specialist registrars in the British Isles and, in the USA, to junior fellows or those in residency programs in obstetrics and gynaecology. A maximum of £1,000 will be awarded for traveling expenses. Established in 1990 by the American Gynecological Club (AGC) and the Gynaecological Visiting Society of Great Britain and Ireland (GVS). Formerly: USA/British Isles Visiting Fellowship.

• 6702 • Bernhard Baron Travelling Scholarship
To provide funds for short-term travel to expand the applicant's experience in areas where he or she already has experience. Fellows and members of the college may apply. Funds for travel up to £6000 are awarded annually. Established in 1953.

• 6703 • Malcolm Black Travel Fellowship
To enable a college member or fellow to travel, either to the British Isles or from the British Isles abroad, for a period of time to attend postgraduate training courses or to visit centers of research or particular expertise within the specialty of obstetrics and gynaecology. Travel and subsistence costs up to £1000 are awarded biennially. Established in 1987 by Mrs. Mattie Black in memory of her husband, Malcolm Duncan Black, a member of the college in 1935 who was elevated to the fellowship in 1947.

• 6704 • William Blair-Bell Memorial Lectureship in Obstetrics and Gynaecology
To honor members by inviting them to present lectures on either obstetrics or gynaecology, or closely related subjects. Preference is given to lectures based on original work, particularly in regard to the morphology, physiology, and pathology of the female reproductive organs, but this need not be considered an absolute condi-

tion of the appointment, particularly if the alternative be a problem connected with malignant neoplastic disease. Entries may be submitted by July 31. An honorarium of £500 is awarded to no more than two recipients each year.

• 6705 • Eden Travelling Fellowship in Obstetrics and Gynaecology
To enable the holder to visit, for a specified period of time, another department(s) of obstetrics and gynaecology or of closely related disciplines where the applicant may gain additional knowledge and experience in the pursuit of a specific research project in which he or she is currently engaged. Open to medical graduates of not less than two years' standing of any approved university. A maximum of £5,000 is awarded annually. Endowed by Dr. Thomas Watts Eden.

• 6706 • Edgar Gentilli Prize
For recognition of original work on the cause, nature, recognition, and treatment of any form of cancer of the female genital tract. All medical practitioners are eligible. The deadline is July 31. A monetary prize of £750 and book tokens of a valuing up to £250 are awarded annually. Established in 1960 by the late Mr. and Mrs. Gilbert Edgar.

• 6707 • Green-Armytage and Spackman Travelling Scholarship
To enable scholarship holders to visit centers where similar work to their own is being conducted on some particular aspect of obstetrical or gynaecological practice. Fellows and members of the college may apply. Funds for travel up to £4000 are awarded biennially in even-numbered years. Established in 1969 in honor of Mr. V. B. Green-Armytage and Colonel W. C. Spackman.

• 6708 • John Lawson Prize
Recognizes the best article on a topic of obstetrics or gynaecology derived from work carried out in Africa between the tropics of Capricorn and Cancer. The record of the work can be submitted by way of an original manuscript. If joint authorship is involved, the candidate must identify his or her involvement in the publication. A monetary prize of £100 is awarded annually.

• 6709 • Harold Malkin Prize
For recognition of the best original work of an individual while holding a registrar or senior registrar post in a hospital in the United Kingdom or the Republic of Ireland. Members or candidates for membership in the RCOG are eligible. A first place monetary prize of £250 and a second place prize of £150 are awarded annually. Established in 1971 by the late Harold Malkin.

• 6710 •
Royal College of Ophthalmologists
Kathy Evans, Chief Exec.
17 Cornwall Terr.
Regent's Park
London NW1 4QW, United Kingdom
Phone: 44 207 9350702
Fax: 44 207 9359838
E-mail: sara.felton@rcophth.ac.uk
Home Page: http://www.rcophth.ac.uk

• 6711 • International Glaucoma Association Fellowship
For clinical research in glaucoma.

• 6712 • Keeler Scholarship
To fellows, members, and affiliates of the Royal College of Ophthalmologists.

• 6713 • The Patrick Trevor-Roper Undergraduate Award
To all undergraduate and medical students from the UK and Eire only.

• 6714 •
Royal College of Physicians and Surgeons of Glasgow
Prof. Graham M. Teasdale, Pres.
232-242 St. Vincent St.
Glasgow G2 5RJ, United Kingdom
Phone: 44 141 2216072
Fax: 44 141 2211804
E-mail: e.nichol@rcpsg.ac.uk
Home Page: http://www.rcpsglasg.ac.uk

• 6715 • Ethicon Foundation Fund Traveling Fellowship
To promote international goodwill in surgery by means of grants to assist overseas travel of surgeons. Applications are accepted from surgeon fellows of the Royal College of Physicians and Surgeons of Glasgow who are in higher training posts. An award of up to £800 is granted to defray expenses of travel. Applicants are required to submit a report to the Council of the College within two months of return. Awarded annually.

• 6716 • Travelling Fellowships
To encourage the professional development of younger Fellows or Members of the College by enabling them to travel to centers of excellence to gain experience in their own fields, which will then be of benefit to their future careers. Awards of up to £2,000 for travel and expenses are awarded to up to 16 recipients annually.

• 6717 • T. C. White Prize Lecture
To recognize a dental graduate of not more than 10 years standing. An invitation to deliver a lecture on a subject related to the original work done by the prize winner is awarded annually. The value of the award is £330. Established in 1984.

• 6718 • T. C. White Travelling Fellowship
To encourage Fellows and Members in Dental Surgery of the College to further their education and experience by visits to centers abroad or in the United Kingdom. Travel expenses up to £1,750 are awarded annually. A T. C. White Visiting Scholarship is also awarded for travel in the United Kingdom.

• 6719 •
Royal College of Psychiatrists
Deborah Hart, Head, External Affairs
17 Belgrave Sq.
London SW1X 8PG, United Kingdom
Phone: 44 20 72352351
Fax: 44 20 72451231
E-mail: rcpsych@rcpsych.ac.uk
Home Page: http://www.rcpsych.ac.uk

• 6720 • Burden Research Prize
To recognize outstanding research work that has either been published, accepted for publication or presented as a paper to the learning society during the three year period ending December 31. Applicants must be registered medical practitioners, the greater part of whose time is spent working in the field of learning disabilities in the United Kingdom or the Republic of Ireland. The prize consists of an award of £1,000. Awarded annually.

• 6721 • Natalie Cobbing Travelling Fellowship
To further the training of specialists in the psychiatry of learning disability by enabling them to extend their experience with travel to appropriate centers overseas. All applicants must possess the MRCPsych and, must be working in the United Kingdom or Republic of Ireland. A fellowship of £3,000 is awarded biennially in even-numbered years.

• 6722 • Margaret Davenport Prize
To recognize the best oral or poster presentation made by a trainee or newly appointed consultant at the Residential Meeting of the Child and Adolescent Psychiatry Faculty. A monetary prize of £100 is awarded annually in memory of Dr. Margaret Davenport.

• 6723 • Philip Davis Prize
For recognition of an essay, between 4,000 and 6,000 words, on a broadly-based clinical topic relating to the care of the elderly mentally ill. Only members or inceptors of the college below the rank of consultant psychiatrist or the equivalent are eligible. A monetary prize of £300 is awarded annually. The deadline is April 30. Established in 1991 in honor of the late Dr. Philip R. H. Davis.

• 6724 • Gaskell Medal and Prize
To recognize individuals who have been qualified medical officers in one or more mental hospitals or clinics in psychiatry in the United Kingdom or elsewhere in the British Commonwealth for at least two years, and have passed the MRCPsych examination or equivalent examina-

tion within the last four years. A monetary prize of £500 and a medal are awarded annually. Established in 1886 in honor of Samuel Gaskell, Medical Superintendent of the County Asylum, Lancaster.

• 6725 • John Hamilton Traveling Fellowship

To encourage psychiatrists working in the field of forensic psychiatry to broaden their knowledge and experience through travel to recognized forensic centers. Proposals to visit forensic services which are developing in order to support, advise and teach will be considered. Candidates may wish to pursue a research topic or a comparative study. Entries are due to the Dean by August 31. A fellowship of £2,000 is awarded biennially.

• 6726 • Ferdinande Johanna Kanjilal Traveling Fellowship

To further the experience of senior trainees in psychiatry from countries overseas. A fellowship of £2,000 is awarded biennially to cover the expenses, either wholly or in part, of such trainees who wish to come to the United Kingdom or the Republic of Ireland, for a short period of further study, research or clinical training. Applicants must submit an account of their previous psychiatric experience and their training needs, and describe the way in which they consider that the use of the Fellowship might benefit the psychiatric services in their home countries. Applications are due to the Dean of the College by August 31. Named in memory of Ferdinande Johanna, wife of Dr. C. Kanijilal.

• 6727 • Laughlin Prize

To recognize the candidate who obtains the highest marks and the best recommendation from the examiners in the MRCPsych Examinations. A monetary prize of £250 is awarded twice a year after the spring and autumn examinations. Established in 1979.

• 6728 • Morris Markowe Public Education Prize

For recognition of an article on a psychiatric topic of approximately 1,000 words, suitable for publication in a regional newspaper, lay journal, the paramedical press, or a general practitioners' magazine, or an article published in the last year (between May and May) of approximately 1,000 words in the above types of publications, or an article commissioned for publication in a regional newspaper, lay journal, paramedical press, or general practitioner's magazine by the Public Education Committee. A monetary prize of £800 is awarded annually. Entries should be submitted by May 1 of each year. Established in 1989 in memory of Dr. Morris Markowe, Honorary Fellow and Registrar of the Royal College of Psychiatrists from 1972-78.

• 6729 • Moshen Naguib Memorial Prize

Trainees or new consultants presenting work undertaken during the training period are eligible, as are colleagues in Europe. An annual award of £100 is given. Formally established in 1998.

• 6730 • Brian Oliver Prize

Recognition for research in the psychiatry of learning disabilities. Applicants may be trainees or consultants in psychiatry within three years of their first consultant appointment. Submissions may take the form of an original piece of work or a literature review and may be presented in the form of an essay or dissertation. The application deadline is April 30. A monetary prize of £500 is awarded annually. Established in 1991 in memory of the late Dr. Brian Oliver, who was Honorary Secretary of the Mental Handicap Psychiatry Specialist Advisory Committee.

• 6731 • Gillian Page Prize

To recognize an original piece of work in the field of adolescent psychiatry. The work may take the form of a research project, a review, or a study of some clinical innovation. A monetary prize of L500 is awarded biennially, but may only be awarded to Members or Inceptors of the College below the rank of consultant psychiatrist or equivalent. Established in 1986.

• 6732 • Psychotherapy Prize

Offered for a paper which has either been published in the *British Journal of Psychiatry* in the preceding year, or submitted specifically for the prize by a specialist registered or by a consultant with less than two years in post at the time of submission. Essays may be in any area or discipline in Psychotherapy and should be between 2000 and 3000 words. A monetary prize of £500 is awarded biennially by the Faculty of Psychotherapy of the RCP.

• 6733 • Research Prize and Bronze Medal

For recognition of research. Members or inceptors of the College below the rank of consultant psychiatrist or equivalent at the time the research is submitted to the Royal College are eligible. Research involving collaboration between workers, whether psychiatrists or in other disciplines, may be submitted, but the prize may be shared by no more than two eligible psychiatrists. The research should be presented in the form of an essay or dissertation with accompanying tables or figures. Entries may be submitted to the Dean by April 30 of each year. A monetary prize of £5,000 and a bronze medal are awarded annually. Established in 1882.

• 6734 • Alec Shapiro Prize

To recognize the best verbal presentation and the best poster presentation. Applicants must submit an account of their previous experience in the area of learning disabilities and published or unpublished work that they feel would be an appropriate recipient of the prize by August 31. All applicants must possess the MRCPsych, be working in the UK or the Republic of Ireland, and be of SHO or Specialist Registrar status. Two prizes of £100 are awarded annually. Named in honor Dr. Alexander Shapiro, one of the great figures in the tradition of learning disabilities.

• 6735 • Standish-Barry Prize

To recognize the best results by an Irish Graduate in the MCRPsych Membership Examinations. A monetary prize of £200 is awarded annually. Established in 1998 as a result of a bequest made by Dr. Standish-Barry.

• 6736 • Woodford-Williams Prize

To recognize research in the prevention of dementia. Research involving collaboration may be submitted, but the award may be shared by no more than two eligible applicants. Submissions of recently published essays or dissertations should be between 10,000 and 30,000 words. The deadline is the end of March. A monetary award of £300 is presented every three years. Established in 1984 to honor Dr. Eluned Woodford-Williams, CBE, a pioneer of British geriatrics and former Director of the Health Advisory Service.

• 6737 •

Royal College of Radiologists - United Kingdom
Ms. Dan Garbutt, Communications Officer
38 Portland Pl.
London W1B 1JQ, United Kingdom
Phone: 44 207 6364432
Fax: 44 207 3233100
E-mail: enquiries@rcr.ac.uk
Home Page: http://www.rcr.ac.uk

• 6738 • Royal College of Radiologists Award

To recognize and advance the science and practice of radiological technology. Only members and fellows practicing in the United Kingdom are eligible. Available awards include the Couch Award, Ross Award, RAD Magazine Award, and the Rohan Williams Award. In addition, research grants, fellowships, sabbatical grants, bursaries, eponymous lectures, medals, prizes, scholarships, and traveling professorships are awarded annually.

• 6739 •

Royal College of Veterinary Surgeons
Mrs. Jill Nute, Chair of External Affairs
Belgravia House
62-64 Horseferry Rd.
London SW1P 2AF, United Kingdom
Phone: 44 207 2222001
Phone: 44 207 2222021
Fax: 44 207 2222004
E-mail: admin@rcvs.org.uk
Home Page: http://www.rcvs.org.uk

• 6740 • The Alison Alston Canine Award

To enable the holder to undertake studies related to the dog and is open to any Fellow or Member of the Royal College of Veterinary Surgeons who can show evidence of postgraduate experience in an appropriate field of veterinary science.

• 6741 • Robert Daubney Research Fellowship in Virology and Helminthology

To enable the holder to undertake a period of research in the fields of virology and helminthology. The Fellowship is open to any Fellow or member who shows evidence of postgraduate experience in an appropriate field of veterinary science. The fellowship is tenable for a maximum of three years.

• 6742 • G. Norman Hall Medal for Research into Animal Diseases
To recognize veterinary surgeons for outstanding work. The maximum age of entry for competitors is 45 by July 12 in the year of presentation. A gold medal is awarded triennially. Established in 1969 by a bequest of Dr. George Norman Alfred Hall (1885-1965).

• 6743 • Millennium Residencies in Production Animal Medicine
To provide effective collaboration between key academic and research institutions. Set up in response to growing public concerns about animal health and welfare, food hygiene and environmental protection. Monetary prizes totaling £36,000 are awarded annually.

• 6744 • John Lord Perry Research Scholarship
To assist qualified individuals to undertake studies in the fields of environmental science, public health and food hygiene, or epidemiology. Open to members of the Royal College of Veterinary Surgeons. Grants up to £18,000 are awarded annually.

• 6745 • Sir Frederick Smith Research Fellowship
To enable the holder to pursue original research or to prepare for such research in any branch of veterinary science at such place or places as may be approved by the Council. The "Miss Aleen Cust Research Fellowship" is awarded only to a member of the Royal College of Veterinary Surgeons who is a natural-born English, Scottish, Welsh or Irish man or woman and, in deciding between such candidates of equal merit, the Council shall give preference to women. Applicants must be nominated by a Professor, Reader or Lecturer of a University or College, or by a Director of a Research Institute, preferably the person who will supervise their work. The Fellowships are £1,000 per annum with up to £200 per annum available for equipment or other expenses arising from the research. Awarded annually. Established in 1955.

• 6746 • West Scholarship for Feline Research
To assist individuals engaged in research relating to the cat. Open to members of the Royal College of Veterinary Surgeons. Grants of up to £30,000 are awarded annually. Made available from funds bequeathed by the late Mr. G.P. West.

• 6747 • MacKellar Michael Wright Award
To enable graduates from any Veterinary School in the United Kingdom to undertake short-term projects when pursuing education, including activities requiring travel abroad. A monetary prize of £1,000 is awarded annually.

• 6748 •
Royal Commonwealth Society
Stuart Mole OBE, Dir.Gen.
25 Northumberland Ave.
London WC2N 5AP, United Kingdom
Phone: 44 207 9306733
Fax: 44 207 9309705
E-mail: info@rcsint.org
Home Page: http://www.rcsint.org/society

• 6749 • Commonwealth Essay Competition
To give young people an opportunity to exercise their intellect and imagination in English, the working language of the Commonwealth. Individuals must be 18 years or younger to be eligible. Essay topics are tailored to suit different interests and the four age groups, and cover social, economic, literary, and development issues in the Commonwealth. Educational trips, cash awards, and books are awarded annually. Special prizes are awarded in each age group for handicapped entrants. Held annually. Established in 1913.

• 6750 •
Royal Economic Society
Prof. Richard Portes, Sec-Gen.
London Business School
Sussex Pl.
Regent's Park
London NW1 4SA, United Kingdom
Phone: 44 207 7066783
Fax: 44 207 7241598
E-mail: eburke@london.edu
Home Page: http://www.res.org.uk

• 6751 • Conference Grant Scheme
Provides financial assistance. Society members are eligible. Awarded three times a year. Application deadlines are January 31, May 31, and September 30. Inquire for additional information.

• 6752 • Junior Fellowship Awards
Provides financial support. Students who have completed at least two years of work toward a doctoral thesis are eligible. A monetary award is given annually. A completed application and a written work of no more than 10,000 words must be submitted. Application deadline is May 10.

• 6753 • Royal Economic Society Prize
To recognize the best article published in *The Economic Journal*. Members of the Society may make submissions. A monetary prize of £3,000 is awarded annually. Established in 1990.

• 6754 •
Royal Entomological Society
Mr. W.H.F. Blakemore, Registrar
41 Queen's Gate
London SW7 5HR, United Kingdom
Phone: 44 207 5848361
Fax: 44 207 5818505
E-mail: reg@royensoc.co.uk
Home Page: http://www.royensoc.co.uk

• 6755 • Wigglesworth Lecture and Medal Award
For recognition of outstanding contributions to the field of entomology at the international level. Society members make the selection. A silver medal is awarded every four years. Established in 1980 in honor of Professor Sir Vincent Wigglesworth FRS, the first recipient.

• 6756 •
Royal Geographical Society with the Institute of British Geographers
Dr. Rita Gardner CBE, Dir./Sec.
1 Kensington Gore
London SW7 2AR, United Kingdom
Phone: 44 20 75913000
Phone: 44 20 75913004
Fax: 44 20 75913001
E-mail: info@rgs.org
Home Page: http://www.rgs.org

Formerly: (1997) Royal Geographic Society.

• 6757 • Back Award
To recognize individuals for applied or scientific geographical studies that make an outstanding contribution to the development of national or international public policy. Awarded annually when merited. Established in 1882 by Admiral Sir George Back.

• 6758 • Ralph Brown Expedition Award
For leaders of research expeditions associated with the study of rivers, wetlands, coral reefs or the shallow marine environment. Applicants may be of any nationality but must be over 25. The project can be located anywhere in the world, and must be of potential advantage to the host country. Close involvement of host country institutions is essential and strong preference will be given to teams involving host country nationals. The period of research should be at least 6 weeks. £15,000 is awarded annually.

• 6759 • Busk Medal
To recognize an individual for fieldwork abroad in geography or in a geographical aspect of an allied science. The Medal is granted irrespective of age or nationality. Individuals cannot apply for this medal. A silver medal is awarded annually. Established in 1967.

• 6760 • Monica Cole Research Grant
To recognize a female physical geographer undertaking original field research overseas. A monetary prize of £1,000 is awarded every three years.

• 6761 • Dax Copp Traveling Fellowship
To afford the opportunity of overseas travel in connection with biological study, teaching or research to those who would otherwise be unlikely to have it. Up to £500 is awarded annually and is open to any biologist. Applications are due by January 25. Named in recognition of Dax J.B. Copp, a former General Secretary of the Institute.

• 6762 • Distinguished Service Award
To recognize those whose work has substantially furthered the aims of IUFRO, such as the accomplishment of a special task, the improvement of IUFRO's organization, outstanding work as an office holder, etc. Two to three plaques are awarded annually.

• 6763 • Sir George Fordham Award for Cartobibliography
To recognize published work or research in progress in the field of cartobibliography. A monetary award of £250 is presented triennially.

• 6764 • Geographical Award
To recognize a company that has provided help for expeditions. Awarded annually. Established in 1990. Cosponsored by the Institute of British Geographers.

• 6765 • Gilchrist Fieldwork Award
To recognize small teams of qualified academics and researchers who affect important and valuable research within short and limited periods of time. It should be original and challenging research to be carried out overseas, preferably of potential applied benefit to the host country or region. It may be multi-disciplinary or devoted to a single scientific objective. Applicants should be British, undertaking a field session of over six weeks. A monetary prize of £15,000 is awarded biennially. Established in 1990.

• 6766 • Gill Memorial Award
For encouragement of geographical research in young researchers who have shown great potential. Awarded annually. Established in 1886 by the gift of Miss Gill.

• 6767 • Gold Medals
To encourage and promote geographical science and discovery. Individuals cannot apply for this medal. One gold Founder's Medal and gold Patron's Medal is awarded annually. Established in the 1830s by H. M. King William IV at the foundation of the Society.

• 6768 • Edward Heath Award
To recognize contributions to the geography of Europe or the developing world. Awarded annually. Established in 1984. Cosponsored by the Institute of British Geographers.

• 6769 • Honorary Membership
To acknowledge persons who have rendered particularly important services to the Union. A certificate is awarded annually.

• 6770 • Cherry Kearton Medal and Award
To recognize an explorer concerned with the study or practice of natural history, with a preference for those with an interest in nature photography, art, or cinematography. A monetary award and a bronze medal are awarded annually. Established in 1958 by a bequest of Mrs. Cherry Kearton to honor her late husband, Cherry Kearton.

• 6771 • Murchison Award
To recognize an individual for a publication that contributes the most to geographical science. Monetary awards for individuals to do fieldwork or for authors of memoirs are presented annually. Established in 1882 by a bequest of Sir Roderick Murchison.

• 6772 • Ness Award
To recognize explorers who have successfully popularized geography and the wider understanding of our world and its environments. Awarded annually. Established in 1953 by Mrs. Patrick Ness.

• 6773 • Cuthbert Peek Award
To recognize individuals who advance geographical knowledge of human impact on the environment through the application of contemporary methods, including those of earth observation and mapping. Awarded annually. The award may be given to the same explorer for more than one year. Established in 1883.

• 6774 • Neville Shulman Challenge Award
To further the understanding and exploration of the planet while promoting personal development through the intellectual or physical challenges involved in undertaking the research and/or expeditions. It is open to individuals or groups. The project can be desk or field based and be carried out in the United Kingdom or overseas. Applicants are required to demonstrate what new knowledge the project contributes to our understanding and exploration of the planet; why this is; and in what ways the project is intellectually or physically challenging. At least £10,000 is awarded annually.

• 6775 • Victoria Medal
To recognize an individual for conspicuous merit in scientific research in geography. Individuals cannot apply for this medal. Awarded annually. Established in 1901 to honor Queen Victoria.

• 6776 •
Royal Historical Society - United Kingdom
Joy McCarthy, Exec.Sec.
University College London
Gower St.
London WC1E 6BT, United Kingdom
Phone: 44 20 73877532
Fax: 44 20 73877532
E-mail: rhsinfo@rhs.ac.uk
Home Page: http://www.rhs.ac.uk

• 6777 • Alexander Prize
To recognize an individual for an essay on any historical subject. The essay must be by an author under 35 years of age, or be registered for a higher degree or have been registered for such a degree within the last three years. Subject to certain exceptions, the essay must be a work of original research not exceeding 8,000 words including footnotes. Works must be submitted by November 1. A monetary award of £250 and publication of the paper in the Society's *Transactions* are awarded annually. Established in 1897 by L.C. Alexander.

• 6778 • David Berry Prize
To recognize an individual for an essay on any subject dealing with Scottish history. The essay must be an unpublished work of original research. It should be between 6,000 and 10,000 words in length, and must be submitted by October 31. A monetary prize of £250 is awarded annually. Established in 1929 by David Anderson Berry in memory of his father, the Reverend David Berry.

• 6779 • Gladstone History Book Prize
To recognize an author who has written a book on any non-British historical subject. It must be the author's first solely written book, and be an original and scholarly work of historical research. Books published in the United Kingdom during the preceding calendar year must be submitted to the Society by December 31. A monetary prize of £1,000 is awarded annually.

• 6780 • Royal Historical Society/*History Today* Prize
Recognizes a paper based on original historical research. Third-year undergraduates enrolled in a higher education institution in the United Kingdom are eligible. A monetary prize of £250 and publication in *History Today* are awarded annually.

• 6781 • Whitfield Prize
To provide recognition for the best work within a field of British history. It must be the author's first solely written history book, and be an original and scholarly work of historical research. Books published in the United Kingdom during the preceding calendar year must be submitted to the Society by December 31. A monetary prize of £1,000 is awarded annually. Established in 1976 out of the bequest of the late Professor Archibald Stenton Whitfield.

• 6782 •
Royal Horticultural Society
Richard Crew, Pres.
80 Vincent Sq.
London SW1P 2PE, United Kingdom
Phone: 44 20 78344333
Phone: 44 20 78213000
E-mail: info@rhs.org.uk
Home Page: http://www.rhs.org.uk

• 6783 • Associateship of Honour
To recognize an individual for service to the field of horticulture over the course of a long period. Individuals of British nationality employed in the field of horticulture are eligible. Awarded annually to one or more recipients. The number of Associates of Honour may not exceed 100 at any given time. Established in 1930.

• 6784 • Peter Barr Memorial Cup
To recognize an individual for excellence in connection with daffodils. Awarded annually. Established in 1912 by the Trustees of the Peter Barr Memorial Fund.

• 6785 • Bowles Cup
For recognition of daffodils shown by amateurs. Three stems of each of fifteen cultivars of daffodils representing not fewer than four Divisions may be shown by an amateur. Awarded annually at the Daffodil Show. Established in 1949 by the late J.L. Richardson.

• 6786 • Reginald Cory Memorial Cup
To encourage the production of new hardy hybrids of garden origin. A plant which is raised and fulfills the following conditions is eligible: it must be either the result of a deliberate cross which, as far as is known, has not been made before or a new and distinct cultivar resulting from the deliberate repetition of a previously made cross; parent A must be a species or a subspecies; parent B must be either a different species, a subspecies of a different species, a different subspecies of the same species or a hybrid into the parentage of which has entered a species or subspecies different from parent A. The terms species and subspecies include varieties and cultivars of the species and subspecies concerned; it must be a herbaceous perennial, a shrub or a tree, grown for ornament (i.e., excluding fruits and vegetables), and be hardy in the climate of Kew; and it must have received an award at one of the Society's Shows during the current year. A cup is awarded annually. Established in 1962. Formerly: Cory Cup.

• 6787 • Devonshire Trophy
For recognition of the best exhibit of twelve daffodil cultivars representing at least three Divisions, one stem of each. Awarded annually at the Daffodil Competition. Established in 1958 by Mary, Duchess of Devonshire in memory of the 10th Duke of Devonshire, a keen daffodil grower.

• 6788 • E. H. Trophy
For recognition of the best exhibit of cut flowers shown to the Society during the year. Awarded annually. Established in 1961 by the late W.J.M. Hawkey in memory of his grandmother, mother and wife, Mrs. Elizabeth, Mrs. Ellen and Mrs. Emma Hawkey.

• 6789 • Engleheart Cup
For recognition of the best exhibit of one stem daffodils of each twelve cultivars raised by the exhibitor. Awarded annually at the Daffodil Show in April. Established in 1913.

• 6790 • Farrer Trophy
For recognition of the best exhibit of plants suitable for the rock garden or alpine house staged during the year at one of the Society's Shows. Awarded annually. Established in 1959 in memory of Reginald Farrer (1880-1920), the plant collector and authority on alpine plants.

• 6791 • Gold Veitch Memorial Medal
For recognition of contributions to the advancement of the science and practice of horticulture, and for special exhibits. Medals and prizes are awarded to one or more recipients annually. Established in 1870 in memory of James Veitch of Chelsea.

• 6792 • Gordon-Lennox Trophy
For recognition of the best exhibit of fruit or vegetables staged during the year at one of the Society's Shows. Awarded annually. Established in 1913 by the late Lady Algernon Gordon-Lennox.

• 6793 • Holford Medal
For recognition of the best exhibit of plants and/or flowers (fruit and vegetables excluded) shown by an amateur or group of amateurs at one of the Society's Shows. Awarded annually. Established in 1928 in memory of the late Sir George Holford.

• 6794 • Honorary Fellow
This, the highest honor of the Society, is given for recognition in the field of horticulture. Awarded when merited.

• 6795 • Jones-Bateman Cup
For recognition of original research in fruit culture that has added to our knowledge of cultivation, genetics, or other relative matters. The work should have been mainly carried out by the candidate in the United Kingdom, and mostly during the preceding five years. A cup is awarded triennially. The cup is held for three years by the successful candidate, who must give a bond for its safe return. When the cup is relinquished, the holder receives a Hogg Medal. Established in 1920 by Miss. Jones-Bateman, of Cae Glas, Abergele.

• 6796 • Lawrence Medal
For recognition of the best exhibit shown to the Society during the year. Awarded annually. No exhibitor may receive this medal more than once in three years. Established in 1906 to celebrate Sir Trevor Lawrence's twenty-one years' tenure of office as President of the Society.

• 6797 • Leonardslee Bowl
For recognition of the best exhibit of one bloom of each of twelve camellias. Awarded annually at the Camellia Show in April. Established by Sir Giles Loder Bt, in 1965.

• 6798 • Loder Rhododendron Cup
For recognition of the best exhibit of one truss of a Rhododendron hybrid. Awarded annually at the Rhododendron Show. Established by the late Gerald Loder (Lord Wakehurst) and transferred to the Society in 1946.

• 6799 • Lyttel Lily Cup
To recognize an individual who has done good work of some kind in connection with *Lilium, Nomocharis* or *Fritillaria.* Awarded annually. Established in 1939 by the Rev. Professor E.S. Lyttel.

• 6800 • George Moore Medal
To recognize the exhibitor of the new hybrid *Paphiopedilum, Selenipedium, Phragmipedium,* or an intergeneric hybrid between these genera that shows the greatest improvement on those of the same or similar parentage and that was submitted to the Society during the year. Awarded annually. Established in 1926 by the late G.F. Moore.

• 6801 • Richardson Trophy
For recognition of the best exhibit of twelve cultivars of daffodils, representing not fewer than three Divisions, to be selected from Division 1 t o 4, one stem of each, shown by an amateur at the Daffodil Show. Awarded annually. Established in 1976.

• 6802 • Mrs. F. E. Rivis Prize
To encourage excellence in cultivation and to recognize the gardener or other employee responsible for the cultivation of the exhibit for which the Williams Memorial Medal is awarded. Awarded annually. Established in 1960 by Miss A.K. Hincks in commemoration of her sister, Mrs. F.E. Rivis.

• 6803 • Rosse Cup
To recognize the winner of Class 8, Conifers shown for their foliage. Awarded annually at the November Ornamental Plant Competition. Established by Anne Countess of Rosse in 1980 in memory of the 6th Earl of Rosse.

• 6804 • Rothschild Challenge Cup
For recognition of the best exhibit in which rhododendrons predominate, shown to the Society during the year. Awarded annually. Established by the late Lionel de Rothschild and transferred to the Society in 1946.

• 6805 • Sewell Medal
For recognition of exhibits of plants suitable for the rock garden or alpine house. Awarded in alternate years for the finest trade exhibit at the Show in mid-April and the finest amateur exhibit of six pans of alpine plants specifically entered for the competition in the mid-April Show. Awarded annually. Established in 1929 by the late A.J. Sewell.

• 6806 • Victoria Medal of Honour
To recognize an individual as deserving of a special honor at the hands of the Society for contributions in the field of horticulture. Horticulturists who are residents of the United Kingdom are eligible. Awarded to one or more recipients each year. In total, 63 medals are awarded, symbolic of the 63 year reign of Her Majesty Queen Victoria. Established in 1897.

• 6807 • A. J. Waley Medal
To recognize a working gardener who has helped the cultivation of rhododendrons.

Awarded annually. Established in 1937 by the late Alfred J. Waley.

• 6808 • Westonbirt Orchid Medal

For recognition in the field of orchid cultivation in the following categories: to the exhibitor of the best cultivar of an orchid species or of a hybird grex that has been shown to the Society for the first time and received an award during the year or which, having received an award during the previous five years, has had the award raised during the year; for the most meritorious group of orchids staged in the Society's Halls during the year; for the most finely grown specimen orchid shown to the Society during the year; or for any scientific, literary, or any other outstanding personal achievement in connection with orchids. Awarded annually. Established in 1960 by Mr. H.G. Alexander, in commemoration of the collection of orchids made at Westonbirt.

• 6809 • Wigan Cup

For recognition of the best exhibit shown to the Society during the year by a local authority. Awarded annually. Established in 1911.

• 6810 • Williams Memorial Medal

For recognition of a group of plants and/or cut blooms of one genus (fruit and vegetables excepted) that show excellence in cultivation, staged at one of the Society's Shows during the year. Awarded annually. Established in 1896 by the Trustees of the Williams Memorial Fund in commemoration of B.S. Williams.

• 6811 • Guy Wilson Memorial Vase

For recognition of the best exhibit of six cultivars of white daffodils representing any or all of Divisions 1 to 3, three stems of each, at the Daffodil Show. Awarded annually. Established in 1982.

• 6812 •

Royal Humane Society

Maj.Gen. David Pennefather, Contact

Brettenham House

Lancaster Pl.

London WC2E 7EP, United Kingdom

Phone: 44 20 78368155

Fax: 44 20 78368155

E-mail: rhs@supanet.com

Home Page: http://www.royalhumane.org

• 6813 • Royal Humane Society Awards

To recognize individuals who, at personal risk, save or endeavor to save lives by rescues from the following dangers: drowning, accidents in ships or aircraft; cliffs or other heights; asphyxia in confined spaces, such as wells, sewers, blast furnaces and fallen earth works; electrocution; or other circumstances where risks are run and awards from other sources are not available. Life-saving is not in itself sufficient to merit a bravery award. The degree of risk is the paramount factor in awards for bravery and the skill exhibited by the rescuer is taken into consideration. Duplication of awards from other sources is avoided as far as possible. Awards are only made in exceptional circumstances when a close relationship exists between the rescued and the rescuer. British nationals, nationals of the Commonwealth, and foreign citizens where British lives are involved are eligible. Professional persons in the exercise of their calling, on or off duty, are not normally awarded. Silver and bronze medals are awarded depending on the degree of bravery. The Stanhope Gold Medal awarded, for the most meritorious case reported to the Society during the current year, is open to the Commonwealth societies of Australasia, Canada, New Zealand and New South Wales. Additional awards include the Testimonial on Vellum, "In Memoriam" Testimonial, Testimonial on Parchment, Certificate of Commendation, and Resuscitation Certificate. Awarded as merited throughout the year.

• 6814 •

Royal Incorporation of Architects in Scotland

Mary Wrenn, Chief Exec./Sec.

15 Rutland Sq.

Edinburgh EH1 2BE, United Kingdom

Phone: 44 131 2297545

Fax: 44 131 2282188

E-mail: info@rias.org.uk

Home Page: http://www.rias.org.uk

• 6815 • Sir Rowand Anderson Silver Medal

To recognize the best portfolio by a fifth-year student. Portfolios must be submitted to the Secretary of the RIAS by October 31. Candidates, who must be within a year of passing Part II, would normally be sponsored by a school of architecture. A silver medal, a certificate, and monetary prize of £1,000 are awarded annually. Established in 1966.

• 6816 • Award for Measured Drawing

To encourage and recognize measured drawing as essential to an architect's training. The committee judges competitors on the following points: the choice of architectural fabric, for the measured study, such buildings as under threat (buildings need not be old); the clarity of understanding and accuracy revealed by the drawing; and the elegance with which the analysis is presented. Student members and members of the RIAS may submit entries. Monetary awards of £100 to £200 certificates are presented annually. Formerly: RIAS/Acanthus Award for Measured Drawing.

• 6817 • Sir John Burnet Memorial Award

To test students' skill in architectural design and ability to communicate their proposals in response to a client's brief through drawings, prepared within a predetermined time limit. Competitors must be student members of the RIAS who have passed the Part I examination or equivalent and who have not passed the RIBA Part III examination or equivalent. Arrangements are made by each school to hold the *en loge*, normally in February. A monetary prize of £150 and a certificate are awarded annually.

• 6818 • Sir Robert Lorimer Memorial Award

For recognition of the best set of freelance sketches by students. Applications must be submitted by January 31 of each year. Competitors must be associate members or student members who are under the age of 29 years. The sketches should be analytical and illustrate in graphic form any architectural subject either existing or projected, and can be in any medium. A book voucher of £125 and a certificate are awarded annually. Established in 1933.

• 6819 • Thomas Ross Award

To provide for the production of a thesis or report resulting from research or study of: ancient Scottish buildings or monuments, or matters pertaining particularly to Scotland and to Scottish architecture and/or environment. Candidates must be members of the RIAS, be otherwise of graduate status, or submit other evidence of their qualifications as may satisfy the requirements of RIAS. An outline of the proposed subject of study must be submitted by January 31. A monetary prize of £600, with the possibility of additional help towards publication, and a certificate are awarded biennially. At the outset of the study, the nominee for the award is paid the sum of £300 which must be repaid if an acceptable study is not submitted within a two-year period. The final bound report must be presented for consideration by the first day in March two years following. If acceptable, the balance of £300 is paid. Awarded annually. Established in 1966.

• 6820 •

Royal Institute of British Architects

Richard Hastilow, Chief Exec.

66 Portland Pl.

London W1B 1AD, United Kingdom

Phone: 44 20 75805533

Fax: 44 20 72551541

E-mail: info@inst.riba.org

Home Page: http://www.architecture.com

• 6821 • Architecture Awards

For recognition of an outstanding building or group of buildings in the European Union completed up to two years and three months preceding the award. The architect responsible for the project must be a member of the RIBA, RIAS, or RSUA. For the purposes of these awards, the country is divided into 14 regions, and awards are given in each region at the discretion of the jury. Plaques are presented to the award winning buildings. Diplomas are given to the architect or firm of architects, the owner of the building, and the building contractor. Award-winning buildings receive a plaque. Awarded annually. Established in 1966.

• 6822 • Client of the Year Award

Recognizes the key role that a good client plays in the creation of fine architecture. Clients are nominated by members. A plaque is awarded annually.

• 6823 • Housing Design Awards
Awards are presented annually for incomplete projects or completed schemes that reflect the highest standards in housing design. Developments may consist of private or public sector new buildings, conversions, or renovation schemes in England, provided they are of four or more dwellings. Schemes including non-residential uses may be entered provided housing constitutes a major element. Criteria include: relationship to surroundings and neighborhood; response to site constraints and opportunities; layout, grouping, and landscaping; planning of roads and footpaths; handling of garages and car parking; attention to safety, security, and accessibility; external appearance and internal planning; sustainability in construction; and finishes, detailing, and workmanship. Awarded annually to multiple recipients in the two categories of incomplete and completed projects. Co-sponsored by the Office of the Deputy Prime Minister, the National House-Building Council, and the Royal Town Planning Institute.

• 6824 • Royal Gold Medal
This, the architectural world's most prestigious individual award, is given to recognize an architect, or group of architects, for work of high merit; or to recognize another distinguished person or group whose work has promoted either directly or indirectly the advancement of architecture. The award is conferred by Her Majesty, the Queen on the recommendation of RIBA. A gold medal is awarded annually. Established in 1848.

• 6825 •
Royal Institute of Navigation
(Association Internationale des Instituts de Navigation)
David Broughton, Dir.
1 Kensington Gore
London SW7 2AT, United Kingdom
Phone: 44 207 5913130
Fax: 44 207 5913131
E-mail: info@rin.org.uk
Home Page: http://www.rin.org.uk

Formerly: (1972) Institute of Navigation.

• 6826 • Fellowship
To recognize individuals who fall into one of the following categories: those who achieve distinction as professional navigators; those who contribute to navigation by invention, research, literature, or in other ways, or who achieve distinction in the field of training; or those who perform exceptional feats of navigation. Fellows of the institute may submit nominations by January 15. Awarded annually.

• 6827 • John Harrison Award
Recognizes contributions to navigation, achievements, technical papers. Awarded triennially.

• 6828 • Honorary Fellow
To recognize distinguished persons in the field of navigation. The Council of the Institute makes the selection.

• 6829 • Necho Award
Recognizes contributions to navigation, including achievements and technical papers. Awarded triennially.

• 6830 • Michael Richey Medal
To recognize the contributor of the most notable paper published in the Institute's journal in a given year. Nominations are made by the Technical Committee. Criteria considered are the significance of the work in relation to the subject, the importance of the subject, the presentation of the paper, and the originality of the approach to the subject, of the work, and of the publication. A bronze medal and certificate are awarded annually. Established in 1950.

• 6831 • Sadek Award
Recognizes outstanding technical papers. Awarded triennially.

• 6832 • Harold Spencer-Jones Gold Medal
This, the Institute's highest award, is given to recognize a particular contribution or a series of contributions made progressively over a number of years in the field of navigation. Nominations, accompanied by a statement of the candidate's claims, may be made by any member of the Institute. A Gold medal and certificate are awarded annually. Established in 1951.

• 6833 • J E D Williams Medal
To recognize an outstanding contribution to the affairs of the Institute. A Silver medal is awarded annually.

• 6834 •
Royal Institute of Oil Painters
Dennis Syrett, Pres.
17 Carlton House Terr.
London SW1Y 5BD, United Kingdom
Phone: 44 207 9306844
Fax: 44 207 8397830
E-mail: info@mallgalleries.com
Home Page: http://www.mallgalleries.org.uk

• 6835 • Winsor & Newton Young Artists Award
Annual award recognizing artists under 35 years of age.

• 6836 •
Royal Institution of Naval Architects
Mr. Trevor Blakeley, Chief Exec.
10 Upper Belgrave St.
London SW1X 8BQ, United Kingdom
Phone: 44 20 72354622
Fax: 44 20 72595912
E-mail: hq@rina.org.uk
Home Page: http://www.rina.org.uk

• 6837 • Samuel Baxter Prize
For recognition of the best paper published by the Institution on the subject of safety by a member under the age of 30. The Council considers nominations after October 31. A monetary prize of up to £100 is awarded annually.

• 6838 • Calder Prize
For recognition of the best paper published by the Institution on the subject of small or high-speed craft by a member under the age of 30 The essay may also be considered for publication in *The Naval Architect*. Submissions are accepted until September 1. A monetary prize of £100 is awarded annually.

• 6839 • William Froude Medal
To recognize a person of any nationality who, in the judgment of the Council of the Institution, has made some conspicuous contribution to naval architecture and/or shipbuilding and whose outstanding services and personal achievements in this direction merit special consideration. Nominations may be made by November. A gold medal is awarded when merited. Established in 1955.

• 6840 • Froude Research Scholarship in Naval Architecture
To enable Graduate Members of the Institution who have been offered a post-graduate place at a university in the United Kingdom to carry out research into hydrodynamics or other problems related to maritime technology. British subjects and citizens of EEC countries under the age of 30 who are members of the Institution may submit applications. Awarded annually as funds permit. Established in 1948.

• 6841 • Small Craft Group Medal
To recognize individuals for significant contributions to the development of small craft. Awarded annually.

• 6842 • Wakenham Prize
For recognition of the best paper written by a Junior Member of the Institution and accepted for publication. Individuals under the age of 30 are eligible. Books, instruments, and computer hardware or software to the value of £100 are awarded annually.

• 6843 • Sir William White Scholarship
To enable British and EEC graduate students of naval architecture or marine engineering under the age of 30, who have at some time been employed in shipbuilding or marine engineering, and who have passed with merit through an approved course of study in a university or college, to carry out research work into problems connected with the design and construction of ships and their machinery, or to follow a post-graduate advanced course of study relevant to ship technology. A scholarship of £700 per annum plus fees is awarded and is tenable for two years subject to a satisfactory report at the end of the first year. Presented annually. Established in 1915 in memory of Sir William H. White, K.C.B., LL.D. (1845-1913), who was a distinguished Director of Naval Construction and an Honorary Vice-President of The Institution of Naval Architects.

• 6844 •
Royal Life Saving Society
River House
High St.
Broom
Warwickshire B50 4HN, United Kingdom
Phone: 44 1789 773994
Fax: 44 1789 773995
E-mail: lifesavers@rlss.org.uk
Home Page: http://www.lifesavers.org.uk

• 6845 • **Mountbatten Medal**
To recognize the most gallant rescue attempt by a Royal Life Saving Society award holder in the British Commonwealth in each calendar year. Consideration for the award is given to holders of an RLSS Award. A medal and a citation are bestowed at a specially arranged presentation ceremony. Awarded annually. Established by the late Earl Mountbatten of Burma, Grand President of the RLSS.

• 6846 •
Royal Meteorological Society
Dr. Richard Pettifer, Exec.Dir.
104 Oxford Rd.
Reading RG1 7LL, United Kingdom
Phone: 44 118 9568500
Fax: 44 118 9568571
E-mail: execdir@rmets.org
Home Page: http://www.rmets.org

• 6847 • **Symons Memorial Medal**
For recognition of distinguished work in the field of meteorology. Meteorologists of any nationality are eligible. An inscribed silver gilt medal is awarded biennially in odd-numbered years. Established in 1902 in memory of George J. Symons, F.R.S.

• 6848 •
Royal Musical Association
Dr. Jeffrey Dean, Sec./Membership Administrator
4 Chandos Rd.
Chorlton-cum-Hardy
Manchester M21 OST, United Kingdom
Phone: 44 161 8617542
Fax: 44 161 8617543
E-mail: jeffrey.dean@stingrayoffice.com
Home Page: http://www.rma.ac.uk

• 6849 • **Dent Medal**
For recognition of an outstanding contribution and important original research in the field of musicology. Musicologists of any country are eligible. Candidates, who are normally under 40 years of age, are nominated by the Directorium of the International Musicological Society and the Council of the Royal Musical Association. A bronze medal is awarded annually. Established in 1961.

• 6850 •
Royal National Rose Society
Lt.Col. P. Beales, Pres.
Gardens of the Rose
Chiswell Green
Hertfordshire
St. Albans AL2 3NR, United Kingdom
Phone: 44 1727 850461
Fax: 44 1787 850360
E-mail: mail@rnrs.org
Home Page: http://www.rnrs.org

• 6851 • **Dean Hole Medal**
Recognizes an individual who has given services to the society and the rose. Awarded annually.

• 6852 •
Royal Over-Seas League
Mr. Robert F. Newell, Dir.Gen.
Over-Seas House
Park Pl.
St. James's St.
London SW1A 1LR, United Kingdom
Phone: 44 207 4080214
Fax: 44 207 4996738
E-mail: info@rosl.org.uk
Home Page: http://www.rosl.org.uk

• 6853 • **Royal Over-Seas League Music Competition**
Instrumentalists who are 28 years of age or younger, and singers 30 years of age or younger. Prospectus available November. Deadline January. The competition is open to Commonwealth citizens, including the United Kingdom and also citizens of former Commonwealth countries. Auditions February and March. The following awards are presented: (1) Solo Awards: Gold Medal and Harrods Bank First Prize - £1,500; Eagle Star Award for Keyboard £1,500; Eagle Star Award for Strings - £1,500; Coutts Bank Award for Singers - £1,500; Worshipful Company of Dyers Awards for Woodwind/Brass - £1,500; (2) Ensemble Prize: Rio Tinto Ensemble Prize and Miller Trophy - £4,000; (3) Parnell Award & JBR Trophy for an accompanist - 1,500 Bernard Shore Memorial Scholarship for a viola player (biennial) 3000. Manufacturers' Awards - the winner of each of the Main Solo Awards and the Ensemble Prize receive tokens for £100 from one of the following firms: Boosey & Hawkes, Chester Music, Oxford University Press, Novello, and Schott; (5) Overseas Awards: Overseas Prize and Overseas Trophy - £1,000; Philip Crawshaw Memorial Prize for a musician of promise from overseas - £500; Australian Musical Association Prize - £500; Tait Memorial Scholarship for an Australian Musician; Stella Murray Prize for a musician from New Zealand - £500; New Zealand Society Prize for a New Zealand pianist or wind player of promise - £500; New Zealand Society Prize for a New Zealand singer of promise - £500; and Irene Brown Memorial Prize for a New Zealand string player of promise - £500; and (6) Other Awards: Society of Women Musicians Prize for an outstanding woman musician - £500; Marisa Robles Harp Prize - £300; Joan Davies Memorial Prize - £200; Ivor Walsworth Memorial Prize for a string player of promise - £200; The Yorke Trust Prize for a double bass player - £300; Daphne Boden Prize for a harpist of promise - £200; Sir Ernest Cassel Prize for a brass player £200; and Lisa Fuchsova Prize for a chamber music pianist - £200. Awarded annually. Established in 1952.

• 6854 •
Royal Philatelic Society
Christopher Harman, Pres.
41 Devonshire Pl.
London W1G 6JY, United Kingdom
Phone: 44 207 4861044
Fax: 44 207 4860803
E-mail: secretary@rpsl.org.uk
Home Page: http://www.rpsl.org.uk

• 6855 • **Crawford Medal**
For recognition of the most valuable and original contribution to the study and knowledge of philately published in book form during the two years preceding the award. The award is open to worldwide competition. A silver gilt medal is awarded annually. Established in 1920 in honor of the 26th Earl of Crawford KT, president of the society (1910-1913).

• 6856 • **Tapling Medal**
For recognition of the best paper that is written by a fellow or member and published in the society's journal *The London Philatelist* during the two years preceding the date of the award. A silver medal is awarded annually. Established in 1920 in honor of Thomas Keay Tapling MP, Vice President of the society (1881-1891).

• 6857 • **Tilleard Medal**
For recognition of the best large display of any aspect of philately given by one or two Fellows or Members of the Society during the previous two years. A silver medal is awarded annually. Established in 1920 in honor of John Alexander Tilleard M.V.O., Honorary Secretary of the society, (1894-1913).

• 6858 •
Royal Philharmonic Society
Rosemary Johnson, Gen. Administrator
10 Stratford Pl.
London W1C 1BA, United Kingdom
Phone: 44 207 4918110
Fax: 44 207 4937463
E-mail: admin@royalphilharmonicsociety.org.uk
Home Page: http://www.royalphilharmonicsociety.org.uk

• 6859 • **Emily Anderson Prize for Violin**
Annual prize of £2,500 open to students of any nationality under the age of 21.

• 6860 • **Sir John Barbirolli Memorial**
Intended to offer financial assistance to purchase better instruments for worthy students. Priority is given to students entering into full-time study of music at Conservatoire level. Awarded annually.

• 6861 • Leslie Boosey Award
Awarded biennially in association with the Performing Right Society, the award honors an individual who has made an outstanding contribution to the furtherance of contemporary music in Britain. The recipient receives a bronze eagle commissioned from Elizabeth Frink.

• 6862 • Gold Medal
This, the Society's highest honor, is given to recognize outstanding musicianship over a period of years. A gold medal is awarded when merited. Established in 1870 to commemorate the centenary of Beethoven's birth.

• 6863 • Honorary Member
Honorary membership in the RPS is given in recognition of service to music.

• 6864 • Julius Isserlis Scholarship
To enable music students (between the ages of 15 and 25) in selected performing categories and of any nationality, but domiciled in the United Kingdom, to study outside the British Isles for two years. The scholarship is awarded by competition and candidate will be expected to prepare a recital program of 45' in duration as well as give an outline of their proposed course of study abroad and two references. A scholarship of £25,000 (£12,500 per year for two years) is awarded biennially.

• 6865 • Music Awards
For recognition of outstanding achievement in brass music. Awards are given in 14 categories, judged by experts and by the public to be the best of their kind in the United Kingdom in the preceding calendar year. The categories include awards for Audience Development, Chamger-Scale Composition, Concert Series including Festivals, Conductor, Creative Communication, Education, Ensemble, Instrumentalist, Large-Scale Composition, Opera and Music Theatre, Singer, and Young Artists. Winners receive a silver trophy. Awarded annually. Established in 1989. Formerly: RPS Charles Heidseick Award.

• 6866 •
Royal Philosophical Society of Glasgow
John Ramster, Pres.
PO Box NAT 8268
Glasgow G46 7BR, United Kingdom
Phone: 44 141 4334484
Fax: 44 141 3304112
E-mail: info@royalphil.org
Home Page: http://www.royalphil.org

• 6867 • Graham Medal
For distinction in research in a chemical discipline. Awarded biennially.

• 6868 • Kelvin Medal
Recognizes distinction in fields associated with Lord Kelvin, former Society President. Awarded annually.

• 6869 •
Royal Photographic Society of Great Britain
Roger Reynolds, Pres.
Fenton House
122 Wells Rd.
Bath BA2 3AH, United Kingdom
Phone: 44 1225 462841
Phone: 44 1225 325721
Fax: 44 1225 448688
E-mail: reception@rps.org
Home Page: http://www.rps.org

• 6870 • Centenary Medal
To recognize sustained and significant contributions to the art of photography. A gold medal (plus Honorary Fellowship) of the Society are awarded annually. Established in 1993.

• 6871 • Davies Medal
Award of recognition.

• 6872 • Terence Donovan Award
Award of recognition.

• 6873 • Fenton Medal
To recognize an individual for outstanding contributions to the work of the Society. Both members and non-members of the Society are eligible for nomination. Awarded annually to one or more recipients. Established in 1980 to honor Roger Fenton, a Society founder who, for several years after its foundation, filled the post of Honorary Secretary.

• 6874 • Honorary Fellowship
To recognize distinguished individuals having, from their position or attainments, an intimate connection with the science or fine art of photography. Both members and non-members of the Society are eligible for nomination. Awarded to up to eight recipients each year.

• 6875 • J. Dudley Johnston Award
Award of recognition.

• 6876 • Lumiere Award
Award of recognition.

• 6877 • Member's Award
To recognize members who have rendered distinguished service to the Society or to photography for a number of years. Honorary life membership is awarded when merited.

• 6878 • Odden Award
Award of recognition.

• 6879 • Progress Medal
This, the Society's premier award, recognizes an individual for any invention, research, publication, or other contribution that has resulted in an important advance in the scientific or technological development of photography or imaging in its widest sense. Both members and non-members of the Society are eligible for nominations. A silver medal is awarded annually. Established in 1878.

• 6880 • Saxby Award
Award of recognition.

• 6881 • Selwyn Award
To recognize individuals who have conducted research leading to the solution of one or more technical problems connected with imaging in general, or photography in particular. Scientists under the age of 35 are eligible. Established in 1994 in memory of E.W.H. Selwyn. Sponsored by The Imaging Science and Technology Group of The Society.

• 6882 •
Royal School of Church Music
John Harper, Dir.Gen.
Cleveland Lodge
Westhumble
Dorking RH5 6BW, United Kingdom
Phone: 44 1306 872800
Fax: 44 1306 887260
E-mail: enquiries@rscm.com
Home Page: http://www.rscm.com

• 6883 • Harold Smart Competition
To recognize composers for works tailored to the technical resources of choirs with limited ability. A monetary award of £100 and possible publication of the winning composition are awarded annually. Established in 1988 to honor Dr. Harold Smart.

• 6884 •
Royal Scottish Academy
Bruce Laidlaw, Admin.Sec.
The Mound
Edinburgh EH2 2EL, United Kingdom
Phone: 44 131 2256671
Fax: 44 131 2206016
E-mail: info@royalscottishsociety.org
Home Page: http://www.royalscottishacademy.org/pages/menu_page.html

• 6885 • Annual Exhibition
To recognize outstanding art at the Annual Exhibition. Exhibits may be submitted in oil, watercolour, acrylic, pastel, drawings, prints, sculpture and architecture. The following major awards are presented: RSA Medal for Architecture - for recognition of outstanding work, preferably a drawing, and to encourage younger architects. A gold medal is awarded annually and presented privately by the President of the Academy. Established in 1968 by an anonymous donor; RSA Guthrie Award - for the best work by a young artist (under 33 years of age who has passed the usual years of training in painting, sculpture or architecture). A monetary award of £500 and a medal are presented annually. Established in 1918 as a tribute to Sir James Guthrie, President of the RSA from 1902 to 1919; and RSA Benno Schotz Prize - for promising work by a young sculptor domiciled in Scotland. Open to artists who are under 33 years of age. A monetary award of £250 is pre-

sented annually. Established in 1965 by a donation from the sculptor, Benno Schotz. Additional awards are also presented. Held annually. Established in 1826.

• 6886 •
Royal Scottish Forestry Society
Andrew G. Little, Dir.
Hagg-on-Esk
Canonbie DG14 0XE, United Kingdom
Phone: 44 13873 71518
Fax: 44 13873 71418
E-mail: rsfs@ednet.co.uk
Home Page: http://www.rsfs.org

• 6887 • Hunter Blair Trophy
To encourage good woodland management in Scotland. Applications are accepted. A trophy is awarded annually. Established in 1964 in honor of Sir James Hunter Blair of Blairquhan. Sponsored by Royal Highland, Agricultural Society of Scotland and Scottish Woodlands Limited, Forestry Commission, Scottish Natural Heritage, Forestry and Timber Association, Institute of Chartered Foresters.

• 6888 •
Royal Scottish Geographical Society
Dr. David M. Munro PhD, Dir./Sec.
Graham Hills Bldg.
University of Strathclyde
40 George St.
Glasgow G1 1QE, United Kingdom
Phone: 44 141 5523330
Fax: 44 141 5523331
E-mail: rsgs@strath.ac.uk
Home Page: http://www.geo.ed.ac.uk/rsgs

• 6889 • Bartholomew Globe
For outstanding lifetime contributions to cartography in Scotland. Awarded periodically.

• 6890 • Centenary Medal
For recognition of outstanding contributions in the field of geographical enquiry and the development of geography as a discipline. Individuals of any nationality are eligible. A silver gilt medal is awarded annually. Established in 1931. Formerly: (1988) Research Medal.

• 6891 • Honorary Fellowship
To recognize an individual for distinguished contributions to the Society or to geography and public life in Scotland. Applications and nominations are not accepted. A certificate of Fellowship is awarded to one or more recipients each year. Established in 1888.

• 6892 • Livingstone Medal
For recognition of outstanding public service in which geography has played an important part, either by exploration, by administration, or in other areas where its principles have been applied to the benefit of the human race. Individuals of any nationality are eligible. No nominations or applications are accepted. A gold medal is awarded periodically. Established in 1901 by Mrs. A. Livingstone Bruce to honor David Livingstone.

• 6893 • Mungo Park Medal
In recognition of outstanding contributions to geographical knowledge through exploration and/or research, and/or work of a practical nature of benefit to humanity in potentially hazardous physical and/or social environments. Individuals of any nationality are eligible. A silver medal is awarded annually. Established in 1930.

• 6894 • Newbigin Prize
To recognize the author of the most meritorious learned article published in the *Scottish Geographical Journal* during the previous year, as judged by the Publication Committee of the Society. A monetary award of £100 is presented each year. Established in 1938 in memory of Marion Newbigin, Editor of the *Scottish Geographical Magazine.*

• 6895 • President's Award
To recognize the achievement of a research geographer at a mid-career stage. Awarded annually. Established in 1989.

• 6896 • Professional Associateship
To recognize professional geographers, as well as to enhance the professional status of geography, to create a forum for professional geographers, and to increase the influence of geography in relation to Scottish affairs. Individuals who have academic training as geographers, plus at least three years of relevant employment experience are eligible. Recipients are selected based on recommendations of the validating committee of the Society. Awarded when merited.

• 6897 • Scottish Geographical Medal
To recognize work of conspicuous merit within the science of geography. Research, whether in the field or otherwise, or any other contribution or cumulative service to the advancement of science is considered. Individuals of any nationality are eligible. A gold medal is awarded annually. Established in 1890. Formerly: (1933) Gold Medal.

• 6898 • XYZ Digital Award
Recognizes outstanding achievement by a younger worker in Scotland in the field of cartography and spatial information delivery. This award, in the form of a cartographic product, is sponsored by the XYZ Digital Map Co. Ltd. Awarded periodically.

• 6899 •
Royal Society
Mr. Stephen Cox, Exec.Sec.
6-9 Carlton House Terr.
London SW1Y 5AG, United Kingdom
Phone: 44 20 74512500
Fax: 44 20 79302170
E-mail: info@royalsoc.ac.uk
Home Page: http://www.royalsoc.ac.uk

• 6900 • Armourers and Brasier's Award
To recognize individuals for excellence in materials science and materials technology. A monetary prize of £2,000 and a silver medal are awarded biennially in odd-numbered years. Established in 1984 by agreement with the Worshipful Company of Armourers & Brasiers'.

• 6901 • Aventis Prizes for Science Books
To recognize the very best in popular science writing for adults and children. Two prizes are awarded annually: the General Prize, for a book intended for general readership, and the Junior Prize, for a book written for children under the age of 14. A monetary prize of £10,000 is awarded to the winner in each category, with an award of £1,000 for each of six finalists. Awarded annually. Established in 1988. Cosponsored by the Aventis Foundation.

• 6902 • Buchanan Medal
To recognize individuals for distinguished original research in the broad area of medical sciences. A silver gilt medal is awarded biennially in even-numbered years. Established in 1897.

• 6903 • Copley Medal
This, the premier award of the Society, is presented for outstanding achievements in research in any branch of science. Each year, the award alternates between the physical sciences and the biological sciences. A silver gilt medal is awarded annually. Established in 1731.

• 6904 • Darwin Medal
To recognize individuals for work of acknowledged distinction in the broad area of biology in which Charles Darwin worked, notably in evolution, population biology, organismal biology, and biological diversity. A silver medal is awarded biennially in even-numbered years. Established in 1890.

• 6905 • Davy Medal
To recognize an individual for an outstandingly important recent discovery in any branch of chemistry. A bronze medal is awarded annually. Established in 1877.

• 6906 • Michael Faraday Prize
To recognize individuals for excellence in communicating science to audiences in the United Kingdom. A monetary award of £2,500, a silver gilt medal, and an invitation to present a lecture at the Society's annual meeting are awarded each year. Established in 1986.

• 6907 • Rosalind Franklin Award
To recognize an individual for an outstanding contribution to any area of natural science, engineering, or technology (SET). Nominees are required to propose a project that they will undertake to raise the profile of women in SET in their organization or subject area. A monetary prize of £30,000 and a silver gilt medal are awarded annually.

• 6908 • Gabor Medal
To recognize an individual for distinction of work in the life sciences, particularly in the fields of genetic engineering and molecular biology. A silver gilt medal is awarded biennially in odd-numbered years. Established in 1989 in memory of Dennis Gabor, F.R.S., by his brother, Andre Gabor.

• 6909 • GlaxoSmithKline Prize and Lecture
In recognition of original contributions to medicine and veterinary sciences published within ten years from the date of the award. A monetary prize of £2,500, a gold medal, and an invitation to present a lecture are awarded biennially in odd-numbered years. Established in 1979. Co-sponsored by GlaxoSmithKline plc. Formerly: (2002) Wellcome Prize.

• 6910 • Hughes Medal
To recognize an original discovery in the physical sciences, particularly electricity and magnetism or their applications. A silver gilt medal is awarded annually. Established in 1902.

• 6911 • Kohn Award
To reward practicing scientists or science communicators in their engagement with society in matters of science and its societal dimension. A monetary prize of £2,500, a grant of £7,500 for science communication activities, and a silver gilt medal are awarded annually. Supported by the Kohn Foundation.

• 6912 • Leverhulme Medal
To recognize an outstandingly significant contribution in the field of pure or applied chemistry or engineering, including chemical engineering. A gold medal is awarded triennially. Established in 1960 on the tercentenary of the Society. Sponsored by the Leverhulme Trust Fund.

• 6913 • Mullard Award
To recognize a young individual for an outstanding academic record in any area of natural science, engineering, or technology, and whose work is currently making or has the potential to make a contribution to national prosperity in the United Kingdom. Eligible candidates are typically, though not exclusively, in their early- to mid-30s. A monetary award of £2,000, a travel grant of £1,500, and a silver gilt medal are awarded annually. Established in 1967.

• 6914 • Research Appointments/ Fellowships
The Royal Society administers grants and fellowships in most areas of science at the post-doctoral level. The following programs are administered by the Society: (1) Research Fellowships - currently over 50 research fellowships are offered each year - funded mostly from the Grant-in-aid and some from private sources, the majority of these are University Research Fellowships and Dorothy Hodgkin Fellowships; (2) Research Professorships - to those with not only a past record of excellence in research, but also an undoubted future potential for continuing long-term achievement in research of the highest quality; (3) U.K. Grants - including Brian Mercer Awards for Innovation, Dudley Stamp Memorial Fund, and Wolfson Laboratory Refurbishment Grants; and (4) International Grants - to enable U.K. scientists to collaborate with the world's leading researchers. Applicants, who must be ordinarily resident in the U.K. and preferably in the age range of 30 to 50 years, must be of Ph.D. or equivalent status, and be normally holding a tenured post in a university or polytechnic or employed as a scientist, mathematician or engineer in industry or in an industrial research organization. Awarded annually as merited.

• 6915 • Royal Medals
These medals, also known as the Queen's Medals, are given to recognize important contributions to natural and applied sciences. Three medals are presented annually, two for contributions to the advancement of natural knowledge and the other for distinguished contributions in the applied sciences. Silver medals are awarded annually by the Sovereign upon the recommendation of the Council of the Royal Society.

• 6916 • Rumford Medal
To recognize an outstandingly important recent discovery in the field of thermal or optical properties of matter made by a scientist working in Europe. A silver gilt medal is awarded biennially in even-numbered years. Established in 1800.

• 6917 • Sylvester Medal
To encourage mathematical research. A bronze medal is awarded triennially. Established in 1901.

• 6918 •
Royal Society for the Encouragement of Arts, Manufactures & Commerce
8 John Adam St.
London WC2N 6EZ, United Kingdom
Phone: 44 20 79305115
Fax: 44 20 7939 5805
E-mail: penny.egan@rsa.org.uk
Home Page: http://www.rsa.org.uk

• 6919 • Albert Medal
To acknowledge individuals, organizations, and groups that lead progress and create positive change within contemporary society to tackle some of the world's intractable problems. A gold medal is awarded annually. Established 1864 in memory of Prince Albert (1819-61), a former President of the Society.

• 6920 • Benjamin Franklin Medal
To recognize individuals, groups, and organizations that have made profound efforts to forward Anglo-American understanding in the arts, industry or commerce, or to recognize those that have made a significant contribution to global affairs through co-operation and collaboration between the United States and the United Kingdom. Awarded annually, alternately to citizens of the United States and the United Kingdom. Established in 1956.

• 6921 • Royal Designer for Industry Award
To encourage a high standard of industrial design and enhance the status of designers. It is awarded to individuals who have achieved sustained excellence in aesthetic and efficient design for industry. Such work can range from fashion to engineering, theatre to product design, graphics to environmental design. Only 200 designers may hold the distinction Royal Designer for Industry at any time. In addition, the Society confers on a limited number of distinguished international industrial designers the award of Honorary Royal Designer for Industry (HonRDI). Established in 1936.

• 6922 • Swiney Prize for a Work on Jurisprudence
For recognition of the best published work on medical and general jurisprudence. A monetary prize and a silver cup are awarded alternately in the two fields. Awarded every five years. Co-administered by the Royal College of Physicians.

• 6923 •
Royal Society for the Prevention of Accidents
Roger Vincent, Contact
Edgbaston Park
353 Bristol Rd.
Edgbaston
Birmingham B5 7ST, United Kingdom
Phone: 44 121 2482000
Fax: 44 121 2482001
E-mail: help@rospa.com
Home Page: http://www.rospa.org.uk

• 6924 • Achievement Awards
To recognize and celebrate the achievement of a very high standard of health and safety at work. The gold award is for four years; silver for three years; bronze for two years; and merit awards are for one year. In addition, the Gold Medal is awarded to winners of five consecutive Gold Awards, and the President's Award to winners of ten consecutive Gold Awards. Presented annually.

• 6925 • Distinguished Service Awards
To recognize an individual for an outstanding contribution to health and safety at work beyond one's own workplace. A Certificate and special tie are awarded to one or more recipients annually.

• 6926 • Sir George Earle Trophy
To recognize outstanding achievement in the field of occupational health and safety. Applications must be made by the last day of February each year. A trophy and a commemorative plaque are awarded annually at a special ceremony. Established in 1956 in honor of Sir George Earle, former President of the Portland Cement Company who donated the trophy.

• 6927 • Managing Occupational Road Risk Achievement Awards
To recognize good performance in the management of occupational road risk (i.e., work-related road safety) over stipulated periods of time. Gold, silver, bronze, and merit awards are presented annually to recognize periods of four years, three years, two years, and one year, respectively.

• 6928 • Norwich Union Trophy
To recognize health and safety achievements within small and medium-sized organizations (up to 250 employees). An engraved trophy is presented annually and retained by the winner for one year. Sponsored by Norwich Union.

• 6929 • Occupational Health Award
Donated by Lord Astor of Hever in 2000 to mark his term as President of the Society, the Astor Trophy is awarded annually for achievement in the management of health at work.

• 6930 • Sector Awards
To recognize the most outstanding performance in health and safety by a company or organization within a particular industry sector. Entrants must demonstrate four years consistently excellent or continuously improving health and safety performance with a high standard of safety policy and commitment. An engraved trophy is awarded annually. Established in 1993.

• 6931 • Training Trophy
To recognize the company or organization with the most effectively managed health and safety training program over the past year. Applications must be made by the last day of February each year. A trophy and a commemorative plaque are awarded annually at a special ceremony. Established in 1976 by William A. Nicol, then Chairman of Midland Assurance, Ltd. Formerly: (1990) Midland Assurance Trophy; (1984) William A. Nicol Trophy.

• 6932 •
Royal Society for the Promotion of Health
Prof. Richard Parish, CEO
38A St. George's Dr.
London SW1V 4BH, United Kingdom
Phone: 44 20 76300121
Fax: 44 20 79766847
E-mail: rsph@rsph.org
Home Page: http://www.rsph.org

Formerly: (2004) Royal Society of Health.

• 6933 • Lord Cohen Gold Medal
For recognition of outstanding work in the field of health. A gold medal is awarded triennially.

• 6934 • Donaldson Gold Medal
To recognize an outstanding worker in any of the professions and disciplines identified with health. Awarded triennially.

• 6935 • Honorary Fellows Award
To recognize any person actively engaged and distinguished in the promotion of health. Awarded annually.

• 6936 • Ian Macmillan Prize
To recognize the individual who attains the highest marks in the RSPH exams. Awarded annually.

• 6937 • Benjamin Ward Richardson Gold Medal
To recognize outstanding innovative work in the field of food hygiene. Awarded triennially.

• 6938 • J. W. Starkey Award
For outstanding work in the promotion of health and safety in medical, paramedical and psychiatric fields. A silver medal is awarded annually.

• 6939 • Vice Presidents Emiriti Award
To recognize Society members' meritorious service to the Society. Awarded annually.

• 6940 • John Edward Worth Silver Medal
For recognition of the best essay related to an aspect of health. A silver medal is awarded annually.

• 6941 •
Royal Society of British Artists
Romeo Di Girolamo, Pres.
17 Carlton House Terr.
London SW1Y 5BD, United Kingdom
Phone: 44 207 9306844
Fax: 44 207 8397830
E-mail: info@mallgalleries.com
Home Page: http://www.mallgalleries.org.uk

• 6942 • De Laszlo Medal
For recognition of the best painting or sculpture at the Society's Annual Exhibition. A medal is awarded annually. Established in 1910.

• 6943 • St. Cuthberts Mill Award for Works on Paper
To recognize the best work on paper at the Society's Annual Exhibition. Awarded annually.

• 6944 •
Royal Society of British Sculptors
Anne Rawcliffe-King, Dir.
108 Old Brompton Rd.
London SW7 3RA, United Kingdom
Phone: 44 207 3735554
Phone: 44 207 3738615
Fax: 44 207 3703721
E-mail: info@rbs.org.uk
Home Page: http://www.rbs.org.uk

• 6945 • Membership Bursary
Recognizes promise and dedication in the art form of sculpture. Awarded annually.

• 6946 •
Royal Society of Chemistry
Dr. Simon Campbell FRSC, Pres.
Burlington House
Piccadilly
London W1J 0BA, United Kingdom
Phone: 44 20 74378656
Fax: 44 20 74378883
E-mail: rsc@rsc.org
Home Page: http://www.rsc.org

Formerly: Chemical Society.

• 6947 • Adrien Albert Lectureship
To promote interest in the study of the relationship between heterocyclic chemistry and biological activity. A lectureship is awarded biennially in even-numbered years. Established from a bequest from the late Adrien Albert, professor of chemistry at the Australian National University, Canberrra and long-standing member of the Society.

• 6948 • Bader Award
To recognize an individual for eminence in organic chemistry. There is no restriction on age, but nominees must not hold or have held professorships in the British Isles. The major part of the nominee's work must have been carried out in an academic institution in the United Kingdom or Republic of Ireland, and the person must currently work in such an institution. The deadline is February 28. A monetary award of £2,000 is presented annually. Established in 1989 by an endowment from Dr. Alfred Bader.

• 6949 • Barrer Award
To recognize the most meritorious recent pure or applied work in the field of molecular sieve zeolites. Candidates under the age of 37 who were born in the United Kingdom or the Republic of Ireland, or persons of any nationality whose work is being carried out in an institution or company in the United Kingdom or Republic of Ireland are considered for the award. Applications must be submitted by December 31. An honorarium of £500 and a scroll are awarded triennially. Established in 1983. Jointly administered by the Society of Chemical Industry.

• 6950 • Beilby Medal and Prize
To recognize scientists or engineers for original work of exceptional significance in the fields of chemical engineering, applied materials science, energy efficiency, or a related topic. Preference is given to applicants under the age of 40. A monetary prize of £1,000 and a silver gilt medal are awarded annually. Established in 1924 in memory of Sir George Beilby, and coadministered by the Society of Chemical Industry and the Institute of Materials.

• 6951 • Ronald Belcher Memorial Lectureship
To encourage graduate students to make a positive contribution to, and to take an active interest in, the profession of analytical chemistry. Candidates may be nominated by any supervisor of postgraduate students registered with a higher educational establishment within the British

Isles. Nominations must be accompanied by a paper or manuscript co-authored by the student. A monetary award of £300 to assist the student to attend a national or international conference and a scroll are presented annually. The winner is also given the opportunity to present his or her work at the Research Topics Meeting. Established in 1983 in memory of Professor Ronald Belcher.

• 6952 • Bourke Lectureship
To enable distinguished scientists from overseas to lecture in the United Kingdom in the field of physical chemistry or chemical physics. An honorarium of £500, a silver medal, and a lectureship are awarded annually. Established in 1954 in memory of Lieutenant Colonel Bourke, a benefactor of the Society.

• 6953 • Robert Boyle Medal
To honor an analytical scientist working overseas who has made outstanding contributions to analytical science, principally through research, but also noting education, consultancy, and service to the profession. Restricted to scientists resident outside the U.K. A gold medal is awarded biennially in even-numbered years. Established in 1981.

• 6954 • S. F. Boys - A Rahman Lectureship
To recognize an individual for outstanding innovative research in the area of computational chemistry, including both quantum chemistry and molecular simulations. Open to individuals of any age and nationality. Membership in the Society is not a requirement. The deadline is January 31. A monetary award of £500 and a silver medal are presented biennially. Established through funds derived from the 1987 International Conference on the Impact of Supercomputers on Chemistry.

• 6955 • Carbohydrate Chemistry Award
For recognition of the most meritorious contribution to the knowledge of any aspect of carbohydrate chemistry. Members of the Royal Society of Chemists whose work was published during the year in question and the five preceding years and who are citizens of the United Kingdom or the Commonwealth are eligible. Applications must be submitted by December 31. A lecture is usually delivered at the spring meeting of the Carbohydrate Chemistry Group. A monetary prize of £500 and a silver medal are awarded biennially in even-numbered years. Established in 1970. Sponsored by Dextra Laboratories.

• 6956 • Centenary Lectureship
To promote the interchange of chemists between Britain and overseas countries. Any scientist normally working outside of Britain is eligible. Three Centenary Lectureships, including silver medals and £500, and the opportunity to visit a number of scientific centers in the British Isles are awarded annually. Established in 1949 by the British Chemical Industry to commemorate the centenary of the Chemical Society.

• 6957 • Joseph Chatt Lectureship
To recognize an individual who has made a contribution to interdisciplinary work in the areas which fall between inorganic chemistry and biochemistry and between organic, inorganic and catalytic chemistry. There are no age or nationality restrictions. Awarded annually. Established in 1995.

• 6958 • Corday-Morgan Medal and Prize
To recognize meritorious contributions to experimental chemistry. British chemists under 38 years of age are eligible. Applications must be submitted by January 31. Up to three awards, each consisting of a monetary prize of £500 and a silver medal, are presented annually for work in different branches of chemistry. Established in 1949.

• 6959 • Faraday Lectureship
To recognize a physical/theoretical chemist. A bronze medal and an invitation to present the Faraday Lecture are awarded every three years. Established in 1867 in memory of Michael Faraday, a Fellow of the Society from 1842 to 1867.

• 6960 • Flintoff Medal
For recognition of an outstanding contribution to the knowledge of the relationship between chemistry and botany. Members of the Society are eligible. A monetary prize of £500 and a medal are awarded triennially. Established in 1954 from a bequest to the Society by the late Robert Flintoff.

• 6961 • Sir Edward Frankland Fellowship
For the encouragement of research in organometallic chemistry or co-ordination chemistry of transition metals. In considering persons for the award, particular attention is paid to evidence of independent creativity in: experimental studies on organometallic chemistry, the latter defined by compounds containing metal-to-carbon bonds excluding those of boron, silicon, germanium, or phosphorus; and experimental studies in the complex compounds of transition metals, including biomimetic chemistry of metals or mechanistic studies and homogeneous catalysis by transition metal complexes. Candidates must be under 36 years of age, members of the Royal Society of Chemistry, British citizens, and working for the period of the award in a chemistry department in a university, college, or polytechnic in the United Kingdom. A prize of £2,000 is awarded biennially. Established in 1984.

• 6962 • Sir Edward Frankland Prize Lectureship
For recognition of meritorious contributions to pure and applied research in the field of organometallic chemistry as defined by compounds containing metal-to-carbon bonds, excluding those of boron, silicon, germanium, and phosphorus. There are no restrictions with regard to nationality or membership in the Society. Applications must be submitted by January 31. A monetary prize of £1,000 and an invitation to deliver a lecture are presented annually. Established in 1982.

• 6963 • Harrison Memorial Prize
To recognize a British theoretical or physical chemist who is under the age of 30. Applications must be submitted by December 31. A monetary prize of £500 and a bronze plaque are awarded annually. Established in 1922 in memory of Colonel Edward Frank Harrison, deputy comptroller of the Chemical Warfare Department.

• 6964 • Haworth Memorial Lectureship
To recognize an eminent chemist in the area of carbohydrate chemistry. The lecture deals with the advances in any subject of carbohydrate chemistry including contributions that further the better understanding of other branches of chemical science. A monetary prize of £500, a silver medal, and a lectureship are awarded biennially in odd-numbered years. Established in 1969 in memory of Sir Norman Haworth, a President of the Society.

• 6965 • Hickinbottom Fellowship
For recognition of research in organic chemistry. Persons holding a PhD or equivalent degree and working in a chemistry department in a university, polytechnic, or college in the United Kingdom or Republic of Ireland are eligible. Candidates must not be more than 36 years of age and must normally be domiciled in the British Isles. Awarded for a two-year period. Established in 1981.

• 6966 • Industrial Lectureship
For recognition of major contributions to and innovations in chemical and chemical-based industry. It also recognizes the commercial, technological, and managerial aspects of the development and application of chemical discovery to industry, as well as the purely scientific. There are no eligibility restrictions. The lectureship, a silver medal, and a monetary prize of £500 are awarded biennially. Established in 1981.

• 6967 • Industrially-Sponsored Awards
To recognize individuals who have made fundamental contributions to their respective fields of chemistry and whose work has been directed to its application. Men and women of British nationality, including Commonwealth citizens or those normally domiciled in the British Isles, are considered for the awards. Each award consists of a monetary prize of £500 and a silver medal. The sponsoring bodies are shown after the names of the individual awards: Analytical Separation Methods - Whatman plc; Carbohydrate Chemistry - Syngenta; Chemical Dynamics BP Chemicals Ltd.; Computational Chemistry GlaxoSmithKline plc; Geoffrey Barker Medal in Electrochemistry Roger Parsons; Food Chemistry Unilever R&D Colworth; Green Chemistry Rohm & Haas; Heterocyclic Chemistry Pfizer Global Research & Development; Homogeoeous Catalysis Johnson Matthey Catalysts; Mass Spectromoetry Thermo Electron; Natural Products Chemistry Vernalis; Nucleic Acids Chemistry Transgenomic Bioconsumables Ltd.; Organometallic Chemistry Davy Process Technology; Process Technology Scientific Update; Solid State Chemistry Materials Chemistry division of Johnson Matthey plc;

and Surface and Colloid Chemistry - Unilever R&D Colworth.

• 6968 • Christopher Ingold Lectureship
For recognition of exceptional contributions to the field of chemistry. The lecture should deal with the relationship between structure and reactivity in chemistry, or any aspect of this theme associated with Sir Christopher Ingold. A monetary prize of £500, a bronze medal, and a lectureship are awarded biennially. Established in 1973 in memory of Sir Christopher Ingold, President of the Society from 1952 to 1954. Formerly: Ingold-Albert Lectureship.

• 6969 • Interdisciplinary Awards
To draw attention to the importance of interdisciplinary studies, particularly those of public interest, involving chemistry and one or more other sciences, and to the Society's interest in the willingness to encourage such work that reaches across traditional boundaries; and to enable work that involves chemists working with scientists from different disciplines to be appropriately rewarded and publicized. There are neither age nor nationality restrictions for the awards, but nominees are expected to be domiciled in the United Kingdom or Republic of Ireland. The individual awards consist of an inscribed memento and an honorarium of £500, while the presentation of the award is associated with a lecture by the successful candidate forming the center place of a one-day scientific meeting. Up to three awards may be made each year. Established in 1986.

• 6970 • John Jeyes Lectureship
To recognize the individual who has made the most meritorious contributions to the general theme of "Chemistry in Relation to the Environment." A monetary prize of £500, a silver medal, and a lectureship are awarded biennially. Established in 1976 by the Jeyes Group in memory of John Jeyes.

• 6971 • Longstaff Medal
To recognize a member of the Society who has done the most to promote the science of chemistry by research. A silver medal and £500 are awarded triennially. Established in 1881 in memory of Dr. George Dixon Longstaff, an original member and benefactor of the Society.

• 6972 • Josef Loschimidt Prize
For recognition of excellence in physical organic chemistry, broadly construed to embrace organic structures, reactivity and reaction mechanisms. The major part of the work must have been conducted in an academic institution in the United Kingdom or the Republic of Ireland and the nominee must currently work in such an institution. Nominees must not hold or have held professorships in the British Isles. A monetary prize of £2,000 is awarded biennially in even-numbered years. Established by Dr. A. Bader.

• 6973 • Marlow Medal and Prize
For recognition of outstanding articles on physical chemistry or chemical physics subjects normally covered by the Faraday Division's *Transactions* journal. Members of the Faraday Division who are under 34 years of age are eligible. Applications must be submitted by January 1. A monetary prize of £500 and a medal are awarded annually. Established in 1957.

• 6974 • Meldola Medal and Prize
To recognize British chemists for promising original investigations in chemistry. British chemists under 30 years of age in the year of the award are eligible. Applications must be submitted by December 31. A monetary prize of £500 and a bronze medal are awarded annually. Established in 1921 by the Society of Maccabaeans in memory of Raphael Meldola, former President of the Society and the former Institute of Chemistry.

• 6975 • Ludwig Mond Lectureship
To recognize accomplishments in the general area of inorganic chemistry. The lectureship is open to chemists of any nationality working in the United Kingdom or overseas. The lectureship, a silver medal, and £500 are awarded biennially. Established in 1981 through an endowment from Imperial Chemical Industries.

• 6976 • Hugo Muller Lectureship
For recognition of valuable scientific endeavors. The subject of the lecture should deal with the relationship between chemistry and either botany or mineralogy. A monetary prize of £500, a silver medal, and the lectureship are awarded triennially. Established in 1918 in memory of Dr. Hugo Muller, a President of the Society.

• 6977 • Sir Ronald Nyholm Lectureship
To enable a scientist to present a lecture that deals with subjects of interest to either the Dalton Division or the Education Division, and has regard to the wide international interests of Sir Ronald Nyholm. A monetary prize of £500, a silver medal, and a lectureship are awarded annually in alternate divisions. Established in 1973 in memory of Sir Ronald Nyholm, a President of the Society.

• 6978 • Pedler Lectureship
To enable an outstanding chemist to present a lecture that deals with the description of new knowledge and the directions in which further research is desirable in any branch of organic chemistry. A monetary prize of £500, a silver medal, and a lectureship are awarded biennially. Established in 1927 in memory of Sir Alexander Pedler, a benefactor of the Society. Sponsored by Pfizer Ltd.

• 6979 • Theophilus Redwood Lectureship
To recognize a leading analytical scientist. A monetary prize of £500, an inscribed scroll, and a lectureship at the annual chemical conference are awarded each year. Established in 1972 to commemorate the 1874 formation of the Society of Public Analysts (now the Analytical Division of the Royal Society of Chemistry).

• 6980 • Robert Robinson Lectureship
To honor a distinguished scientist. The lecture should review progress in any branch of organic chemistry and is presented at the Society's annual congress. A monetary prize of £500, a silver medal, and a lectureship are awarded biennially in even-numbered years. Established in 1962 in honor of Sir Robert Robinson on his seventieth birthday.

• 6981 • Simonsen Lectureship
To provide the opportunity for younger workers of all nationalities in the field of the chemistry of natural products to present a lecture. A monetary prize of £500, a silver medal, and a lectureship are awarded triennially. Established in 1957 in memory of Sir John Simonsen, Vice President of the Society, by his wife, Lady Simonsen. Sponsored by AstraZeneca plc.

• 6982 • Society for Analytical Chemistry Silver Medal
To encourage young scientists working in any field covering the practices and teaching of the analytical sciences. Scientists under the age of 35 are eligible. A monetary prize of £500 and a silver medal are awarded annually when merited. Established in 1973.

• 6983 • Society of Analytical Chemistry Gold Medal
To honor an individual for outstanding contributions to analytical science, principally through research, but also noting education, consultancy, and service to the profession. A gold medal is awarded biennially in odd-numbered years. Established in 1964.

• 6984 • Spiers Memorial Lecture and Prize
To enable a respected chemist from the United Kingdom or overseas to present a lecture that serves as the introduction to a General Discussion. An honorarium of £500, a silver medal, and a lectureship are awarded annually. Established in 1928 by the Faraday Society in memory of F. S. Spiers, the first Secretary of the Society.

• 6985 • Tilden Lectureship
To encourage work in chemistry by young scientists. The lecture should deal with the progress in some branch of chemistry. A silver medal, monetary award of £500, and a lectureship are awarded to three recipients biennially. Established in 1939 in memory of Sir William Agustus Tilden, a President of the Society.

• 6986 •
Royal Society of Edinburgh
Prof. Gavin McCrone, Gen.Sec.
22-26 George St.
Edinburgh EH2 2PQ, United Kingdom
Phone: 44 131 2405000
Fax: 44 131 2405024
E-mail: rse@royalsoced.org.uk
Home Page: http://www.royalsoced.org.uk

• 6987 • David Anderson-Berry Medal
For recognition of recent work on the effects of X-rays and other forms of radiation on living tissues. Published work will be taken into consideration if submitted to the Society with the application. A medal is awarded every five years. Established in 1930.

• 6988 • BP Prize Lectureship in the Humanities
To recognize an individual under 40 years of age in a Scottish educational institution. Awards are given in alternate years in the following categories: languages, literature, and the arts; archaeological and historical studies; social studies; and philosophy, theology, and law. A monetary prize of £500 plus a lecture to be held at the society is awarded biennially. Established in 1990 and sponsored by British Petroleum (BP).

• 6989 • W. S. Bruce Medal
For recognition of some notable contribution to the natural sciences, such as zoology, botany, geology, meteorology, oceanography, and geography. The contributions must be in the nature of new knowledge and be the outcome of a personal visit to polar regions on the part of the recipient. The recipient should preferably be at the outset of his or her career as an investigator. Open to workers of all nationalities, with a preference for those of Scottish birth or origin. The Committee of Awards is appointed jointly by the Royal Society of Edinburgh, the Royal Physical Society, and the Royal Scottish Geographical Society. A medal is awarded every five years. Established in 1923 to commemorate the work of Dr. W. S. Bruce as an explorer and scientific investigator in polar regions.

• 6990 • Bruce-Preller Prize Lectureship
To recognize an outstanding scientist. The subject is to be, in sequence, in earth sciences, engineering sciences, medical sciences, or biological sciences. An honorarium is awarded biennially. Established in 1929 by the bequest of the late Dr. Charles Du Riche Preller.

• 6991 • Alexander Ninian Bruce Prize
For recognition of meritorious research in medical or veterinary physiology. Individuals under 40 years of age and working in a Scottish institution are eligible. A monetary prize of £250 is awarded quadriennially. Established in 1991.

• 6992 • Caledonian Research Foundation Prize Lectureship in Biomedical Sciences and Arts and Letters
To recognize an individual who has an international reputation in the fields of biological sciences and arts and letters subjects. A monetary prize of £1500 plus a lecture to be given by the winner at various locations throughout Scotland is awarded, alternating annually between Biomedical Sciences and Arts & Letters subjects. Established in 1990 and sponsored by Caledonian Research Foundation.

• 6993 • Henry Dryerre Prize Lectureship
To recognize a distinguished scholar in the field of medical research. A monetary prize of £500 plus a lecture to be held at the Society is awarded quadriennially. Established in 1991 in honor of Professor Henry Dryerre.

• 6994 • Henry Duncan Prize Lectureship
For recognition of a work of a scholar of any nationality for work of international reputation in Scottish studies. A monetary prize of £500 plus a lecture to be held at the Society is awarded triennially. Established in 1990 by Trustees Savings Bank (TSB) Scotland in memory of the Reverend Henry Duncan who founded the first TSB.

• 6995 • Gunning Victoria Jubilee Prize Lectureship
In recognition of original work in physics, chemistry, or pure or applied mathematics. A monetary prize of £500 for a lecture is awarded quadrennially to scientists resident in or connected with Scotland. Established in 1887 by Dr. R. H. Gunning.

• 6996 • Keith Medal
For recognition of a paper on a scientific subject presented to the Royal Society of Edinburgh. Preference is given to a paper containing a discovery. The medal is awarded alternately in quadrennial periods, provided papers worthy of recommendation have been communicated to the society for publications in: Proceedings A (Mathematics) or Transactions (Earth Sciences). Established in 1827.

• 6997 • MakDougall-Brisbane Prize
For promotion of research in science, either an individual engaged in scientific pursuit, a paper written on a scientific subject, or a discovery in science. Preference is given to a person working in Scotland. Awarded in successive biennial periods in the following subjects: physical sciences, engineering sciences, and biological sciences. Established in 1855.

• 6998 • Neill Medal
For recognition of a work or publication by some Scottish naturalist, on some branch of natural history completed or published within five years of the time of award. A medal is awarded triennially. Established in 1859 by a bequest from the late Dr. Patrick Neill.

• 6999 • James Scott Prize Lectureship
To provide for a lecture on the fundamental concepts of natural philosophy. Awarded quadriennially. Established in 1918 by the Trustees of the James Scott Bequest.

• 7000 •
Royal Society of Literature
Maggie Fergusson, Sec.
Somerset House
Strand
London WC2R 1LA, United Kingdom
Phone: 44 20 78454676
Fax: 44 20 78454679
E-mail: info@rslit.org
Home Page: http://www.rslit.org

• 7001 • Benson Medal
To recognize a lifetime of outstanding works of poetry, fiction, history, or belles-lettres. A silver medal is awarded periodically when merited. Established in 1916 by Dr. A. C. Benson.

• 7002 • Ondaatje Prize
For recognition of a distinguished work of fiction, non-fiction, or poetry that evokes the spirit of a place. Full-length works written by British or Irish citizens and published in the United Kingdom are eligible. A monetary prize of £10,000 is awarded annually. Established in 1966. Formerly: (2003) Winifred Holtby Memorial Prize.

• 7003 • V.S. Pritchett Memorial Prize
Recognizes an outstanding published short story. A monetary prize is given annually. Established in 1999.

• 7004 • Royal Society of Literature Ondaatji Prize
Recognizes outstanding literary work. Unpublished works are eligible. A monetary prize and publication of the winning work is awarded annually. Applications are accepted between September 1 and December 1.

• 7005 •
Royal Society of Medicine
Dr. Anne Grocock, Exec.Dir.
1 Wimpole St.
London W1G 0AE, United Kingdom
Phone: 44 207 2902900
Fax: 44 207 2902992
E-mail: joanna.rose@rsm.ac.uk
Home Page: http://www.rsm.ac.uk

• 7006 • John Arderne Medal
To recognize a recipient selected by the Council of the Section of Colonproctology for the quality of presentation and the content of a paper delivered at a meeting of the Section. The recipient must be a person who has not yet reached consultant status; exceptionally, the award may be made to a person who is not medically qualified. The successful candidate need not be a Fellow of the Royal Society of Medicine. The award consists of a medal struck in silver-gilt and an honorarium of £600. The medal and prize are presented annually to the recipient by the President of the Section at the annual dinner.

• 7007 • Colyer Prize
For recognition of the best original work in dental science completed during the previous five

Awards are arranged in alphabetical order below their administering organizations

years by a dental surgeon educated at any duly recognized dental school in Great Britain or Northern Ireland, and who has not been qualified to practice more than 10 years at the date of the award. Applications from candidates, together with a general account of their projects, must be submitted to the Prize Committee not later than March 31 preceding the date of the award. A monetary prize of £100 is awarded triennially. Established in 1926 to commemorate the twenty-five years' service of Sir Frank Colyer as Honorary Curator of the Odontological Museum. Administered by the Odontology Section.

• 7008 • A. C. Comfort Prize
For recognition of a paper on some aspects of clinical research in geriatric medicine, written by a practitioner of not more than five years' standing from qualification, or by a student or intern approaching the medical degree. A monetary prize of £200 and the cost of publishing the award-winning paper are presented annually. Established by Dr. Alex Comfort in 1981 as a memorial to his late father, A. C. Comfort. Administered by the Geriatrics and Geronology Section.

• 7009 • Dalby Prize
To encourage the science and art of otology. Persons of British nationality recommended to the Council of the Society by the President and Vice-Presidents of the Section of Otology as having published or done the best original work in otology during the previous five years are considered. The prize may be shared if, in the opinion of the Council of the Society, there are at any time two people whose work is considered to be of equal merit. A monetary prize is awarded every five years. Established in 1928 by Lady Hyacinthe Dalby, widow of William Dalby. Administered by the Otology Section.

• 7010 • Downs Travelling Scholarship
To support travel to centers of laryngology or rhinology overseas, and for recognition of a paper on a subject within the field of laryngology and rhinology submitted each year by an author of senior registrar status or by a consultant within two years of his appointment. All papers to be considered must be submitted on the understanding that the author may be required to read his or her paper at a meeting of the Section, that the decision of the judges shall be final, and that the winning paper will be offered for publication to the Editor of the Journal or the Royal Society of Medicine. A monetary prize of £1,200 is awarded annually. Established in 1980. Administered by the Laryngology and Rhinology Section.

• 7011 • Alan Edwards Prize
To advance the study of clinical medical science. Individuals who have not yet gained consultant status are eligible for the case presentation in each session adjudged most likely to advance the study of clinical medical science. A monetary prize of £25 is awarded annually. Established in 1979 in memory of Alan Edwards. Administered by the Clinical Section.

• 7012 • Ellison-Cliffe Medal and Lecture
To provide for a lecture by a medically qualified person of eminence in his or her field at the Society's House on a subject connected with the contribution of fundamental science to advances in medicine. Invitations to the Lecture are not restricted to members of the Society and special care is taken to invite scientists working in areas that could become related to medicine. A medal and expenses for the lecturer are awarded annually. Established by Percy Cliffe and his wife, Carice Ellison.

• 7013 • Norman Gamble Research Prize
For recognition of the best original work in otology completed during the four years prior to the month of October in the year of the award. The competition for this prize is open to any British subject, whether lay or medical. A monetary prize of £50 is awarded every four years. Established in 1930 by Mr. Norman Gamble.

• 7014 • Hughlings Jackson Lecture and Medal
To advance the science of neurology by providing a lecture. The Council of the Section of Neurology submits to the Council of the Society the names of three people to be invited to deliver the next lecture. A gold medal and an honorarium of not more than 100 guineas are awarded triennially. Established in 1897 in memory of Hughlings Jackson.

• 7015 • Jephcott Lecture
To provide for lectures in the field of medicine. An honorarium is awarded annually. Established in 1959.

• 7016 • Nuffield Lecture
To provide for a lecture to be delivered from time to time as decided upon by the Council of the Society (but not more than once in any calendar year) on October 10, or on the nearest suitable day in honor of Lord Nuffield and to advance the science and art of medicine. Lecturers are appointed by t he Council of the Society on the recommendation of a Committee consisting of the President of the Society for the time being, all living past presidents of the Society willing to serve, and, during the lifetime of Lord Nuffield, three other members nominated by him. A gold medal and an honorarium of 100 guineas are awarded every three to four years. Established in 1959 by Lord Nuffield.

• 7017 • Lloyds Roberts Lecture
To provide for a lecture in the field of medicine. Established in 1910 by a bequest of the late Dr. David Lloyd Roberts of Manchester.

• 7018 • Sherrington Memorial Lecture
To provide for a lecture to be delivered in April or May devoted to the advancement of the sciences of neurology and of physiology. A gold medal and an honorarium of 100 guineas are awarded every five years. Established in 1957 in memory of Sir Charles Scott Sherrington.

• 7019 • Joseph Toynbee Memorial Lectureship
To provide for a lecture in otology. The Lectureship is open, without restriction of nationality, to any person who is, in the opinion of the Selection Committee, qualified to contribute to the advancement of the science and practice of otology. An honorarium of £100 and an illuminated certificate are awarded biennially. Established jointly by the Royal College of Surgeons of England and the Royal Society of Medicine.

• 7020 • Hugh Wallace Essay and Publication Prize
For recognition of a review article written in English and not exceeding 3,500 words on a clinical subject or an essay of a speculative or philosophical nature on any aspect of dermatology. A monetary prize and publication in the Journal of the Society are awarded. Established by a bequest of Dr. Hugh Wallace. Administered by the Dermatology Section.

• 7021 • Hugh Wallace's Registrars' Prize
To recognize a dermatologist of registrar or senior registrar grade (or of equivalent academic status) considered to have made the most outstanding contribution at Section Meetings during the session preceding the year of award. A Selection Committee is established annually to submit a recommendation to the Council of the Society. A monetary prize of £50 is awarded annually. Established in honor of Hugh Wallace, a former president of the Section. Administered by the Dermatology Section.

• 7022 • Albert Wander Lecture
To provide for a lecture in the field of general practice of medicine. An honorarium is awarded annually. Established in 1963.

• 7023 • Edith Whetnall Lectureship
To provide for a lecture on a subject connected with the diagnosis, causation, prevention, and management of deafness in children, preference being given to a lecture dealing with the auditory approach. The lecturer is appointed by the Council of the Society upon the nomination of a committee. An honorarium of £100 and a bronze medal are awarded biennially. Established in 1971.

• 7024 •
Royal Society of Miniature Painters, Sculptors and Gravers
Pamela Henderson, Exec.Sec.
1 Knapp Cottages
Wyke
Gillingham SP8 4NQ, United Kingdom
Phone: 44 1747 825718
Fax: 44 1747 826835
E-mail: pamhendersons@dsl.pipex.com
Home Page: http://www.royal-miniature-society.org.uk

• 7025 • Gold Memorial Bowl
Recognizes the best piece of miniature work in any medium. Awarded annually.

Awards are arranged in alphabetical order below their administering organizations

• 7026 •
Royal Society of Portrait Painters
Andrew Festing, Pres.
% Federation of British Artists
17 Carlton House Terr.
London SW1Y 5BD, United Kingdom
Phone: 44 207 9306844
Fax: 44 207 8397830
E-mail: info@mallgalleries.com
Home Page: http://www.mallgalleries.org.uk

• 7027 • Federation of British Artists Prizes and Awards
To recognize outstanding artists. Six major prizes are offered each year: the HSBC Investment Management Prize - £4,000 for the best portrait by an artist aged 35 years and under; De Laszlo Prize - £3,000 and a silver medal to the best portrait by an artist aged 25 years and under; the Ondaatje Prize for Portraiture - £10,000 and gold medal for the most distinguished painting at the Society's annual exhibition; Prince of WalesKs Award for Portrait Drawing - £2,000 for a portrait in any recognized drawing medium; Changing Faces Prize - £2,000 for the portrait that communicates best with viewers; and the Arts Club Award one yearKs free membership in the Society.

• 7028 •
Royal Society of Tropical Medicine and Hygiene
Caryl R. Guest, Administrator
50 Bedford Sq.
London WC1B 3DP, United Kingdom
Phone: 44 20 75802127
Fax: 44 20 74361389
E-mail: mail@rstmh.org
Home Page: http://www.rstmh.org

• 7029 • Chalmers Memorial Medal
For recognition of research of outstanding merit contributing to knowledge of tropical medicine or tropical hygiene. Only individuals 46 years of age or under on the 1st of June of the year of the award are eligible. Candidates must be nominated by a Fellow of the Society no later than September 30. A silver-gilt medal is awarded annually. Established in 1923 in memory of Dr. Albert John Chalmers, who was known for his work in tropical medicine.

• 7030 • Sir Rickard Christophers Medal
For recognition of work in tropical medicine and hygiene in its broadest sense, with particular consideration given to practical and field applications. Fellows of the Society may nominate a candidate by September 30. A bronze medal is awarded triennially. Established in 1979 in memory of Sir Rickard Christophers, for a lifetime spent in the relentless and inspired pursuit of knowledge.

• 7031 • ICTP Diploma
Awarded to citizens of developing nations who are below 28 years of age and who have obtained a MSc in physics or mathematics.

• 7032 • George Macdonald Medal
For recognition of outstanding research leading to improvement of health in tropical countries. The London School Council and the Council of the Society propose the names of the candidates. A medal is awarded triennially. Established in 1968 in memory of Dr. George Macdonald, Professor of Tropical Hygiene at the London School of Hygiene and Tropical Medicine, and Director of the Ross Institute. Cosponsored by the London School of Hygiene and Tropical Medicine.

• 7033 • Donald Mackay Medal
For recognition of outstanding work in tropical health, especially relating to improvements in the health of rural or urban workers in the tropics. There are no restrictions as to the nationality or sex of the candidates. Preference will be given to suitable medically qualified candidates, but those in other disciplines are eligible. The Medal is awarded annually - in even-numbered years by the Royal Society of Tropical Medicine and Hygiene, and in odd-numbered years by the American Society of Tropical Medicine and Hygiene. Established in 1990 in memory of Dr. Donald Mackay, who was Deputy Director of the Ross Institute at the London School of Hygiene and Tropical Medicine, who died in 1981 after many years of outstanding work in tropical occupational health, especially on the tea plantations of South Asia.

• 7034 • Manson Medal
This, the Society's highest mark of distinction, is given for contribution to any branch of tropical medicine or tropical hygiene. Fellows of the Society may nominate a candidate by September 30. A bronze medal is awarded triennially. Established in 1922 in memory of Sir Patrick Manson, first president of the Society.

• 7035 • Medical Student Elective Prize
To recognize a medical student for an account of work carried out during an elective period in a tropical or developing country. The work, which may be the product of a student of any nationality, must contribute to the knowledge or understanding of tropical diseases. A monetary prize of £500 is awarded annually.

• 7036 • Research Grant
Awarded to physicists/mathematicians who have obtained their PhD not before four years.

• 7037 • Section Grant
Awarded to physicist or mathematician from a developing country who wishes to organize an international or regional conference in one of the areas of study of the ICTP.

• 7038 • Undergraduate Project Prize
To recognize an undergraduate student for an account of work carried out of relevance to tropical or developing countries. The work, which may be laboratory-based and not necessarily carried out in a tropical or developing country, should contribute to the knowledge of human or veterinary health or hygiene in the tropics. A monetary prize of £500 is awarded annually.

• 7039 •
Royal Society of Wildlife Trusts
The Kiln, Waterside
Mather Rd.
Newark
Nottinghamshire NG24 1WT, United Kingdom
Phone: 44 870 0361000
Fax: 44 870 0360101
E-mail: grants@rswt.org
Home Page: http://www.rswt.org

Formerly: (2004) Royal Society for Nature Conservation.

• 7040 • Christopher Cadbury Medal
For recognition of services to the advancement of nature conservation in the British Islands. A silver medal is awarded annually. Established in 1990 in honor of the late Christopher Cadbury, former president of the Royal Society for Nature Conservation, who retired in 1988.

• 7041 •
Royal Television Society
Simon Albury, CEO
Holborn Hall
100 Grays Inn Rd.
London WC1X 8AL, United Kingdom
Phone: 44 207 4301000
Fax: 44 207 4300924
E-mail: info@rts.org.uk
Home Page: http://www.rts.org.uk

• 7042 • Craft and Design Awards
To recognize excellence in regional or network broadcast television in England. Awards are given in the following categories: Graphic Design; Make-up Design; Costume Design; Production Design; Visual Effects; Lighting, Photography and Camera; Sound; Tape and Film Editing; and Music Awards. Additional awards that may be presented at the discretion of the Jury include the Design and Craft Innovation Award, Judges' Award, and Lifetime Achievement Award. Awards are presented annually.

• 7043 • Educational Television Awards
To recognize programs that constitute an outstanding contribution to the educational use of the broadcasting television medium. Awards are given in the following categories: Schools Television - with awards in Pre-School and Infants, Junior, Secondary Science, and Secondary Arts; Adult Educational Television - with awards in Education and Training, General, Personal Education, and Campaigns and Season; and Judge's Award. Awarded annually.

• 7044 • Programme Awards
For recognition of the best television programs during the previous year. Awards are given annually in numerous subcategories within the classifications of: Drama, Entertainment, Performance, Presenter, Factual, Children's, Nations and Regions, and Breakthrough. In ad-

dition, the Digital Channel Programme Award, International Award, and Judges' Award are also presented. Awarded annually.

• 7045 • Student Television Awards
To recognize undergraduate and graduate student programming that shows outstanding visual and aural creativity, a mastery of craft skills, innovation, and initiative. Awards are given in the following categories: Factual - to recognize a feature on a social issue or topic in documentary style; Animation - to recognize video or film imagery with associated sound track to show creative originality; and Non-Factual - to recognize drama, comedy, and narrative animation. Winners will be presented with an award at a national ceremony each year.

• 7046 • Technology Awards
To recognize an individual or team for outstanding development or innovation in engineering or operational systems, as applied to the television broadcasting chain in England, or in program production use in television studios/location areas of work. Entries will be considered in relation to introduction of new techniques, technological advances, and the uniqueness of the concept involved. Each year, awards are presented in the following categories: Consumer Electronics; Content Delivery; Content Management; Content Creation, Capture or Restoration; and Post-Production Process. Additional awards include the Research and Development Team Award, Young Technologist Award, JudgesK Award, and Lifetime Achievement Award.

• 7047 • Television Journalism Awards
To recognize creativity and excellence in news and current affairs television programs. Awards are given annually in numerous subcategories within the classifications of: News, Current Affairs, and Nations and Regions. In addition, awards are given to recognize innovation, specialist journalism, Young Journalist of the Year, Television Journalist of the Year, Camera Operator of the Year, and Presenter of the Year. Awarded annually. Established in 1978.

• 7048 • Television Sports Awards
To recognize sports news items covered by United Kingdom broadcasting organizations or agencies. Entries must be up to 15 minutes and networked. Awards are presented in the following categories: Sports Coverage, Regional Sports, Sports Presenter or Commentator, and Judges' Award. Awarded annually.

• 7049 •
Royal Town Planning Institute
Ron Tate, Pres.
41 Botolph Ln.
London EC3R 8DL, United Kingdom
Phone: 44 207 9299494
Fax: 44 207 9299490
E-mail: online@rtpi.org.uk
Home Page: http://www.rtpi.org.uk

• 7050 • George Pepler International Award
To enable individuals of any country to visit Britain for a short time to study an aspect of town and country planning or a related subject. Individuals under 30 years of age are eligible. A monetary prize of £1,500 is awarded biennially in even-numbered years. Established in 1963 by Lady Pepler in memory of Sir George Pepler, one of the Founders of the Town Planning Institute. Deadline is March 31.

• 7051 • Planning Consultancy of the Year Award
Recognizes contributions made to consultants in planning practices in the United Kingdom. Application is by nomination only. A monetary prize is given annually.

• 7052 • Young Planner of the Year Award
Recognizes outstanding young planners who made contributions to planning and to the profession in general. Institute members under the age of 35 are eligible. Awarded annually.

• 7053 •
Royal United Services Institute for Defence and Security Studies
Sir Paul Lever, Chm.
Whitehall
London SW1A 2ET, United Kingdom
Phone: 44 20 7930 5854
Fax: 44 20 7321 0943
E-mail: media@rusi.org
Home Page: http://www.rusi.org

• 7054 • Chesney Gold Medal
This, the highest honor bestowed by the Institute, is given to recognize the originator of distinguished or authoritative work or works that have added to knowledge or achieved advances in the defense and international security fields to the benefit of the U.K. and/or the Western Alliance. A gold medal is awarded when merited. Established in 1900 in memory of General Sir George Chesney, military author, reformer, and engineer.

• 7055 • Duke of Westminster Medal for Military Literature
To recognize the best book in the English language, regardless of nationality, gender, or age of the author, that represents a notable and original contribution to the study of international or national security, or the military professions. Awarded annually. Created with the support of His Grace—the Duke of Westminster.

• 7056 • Trench Gascoigne Prize
To encourage original writing on contemporary issues of defense and international security, ideally with an emphasis on the military sciences. Open to authors of any nationality, and entries are particularly welcome from members of the Armed Forces. One or more awards of £600 are awarded annually. Established in 1897 by Colonel F. C. Trench Gascoigne.

• 7057 •
Salters' Institute
Mrs. Audrey Strong, Institute Mgr.
Salters' Hall
4 Fore St.
London EC2Y 5DE, United Kingdom
Phone: 44 20 76285962
Fax: 44 20 76383679
E-mail: institute@salters.co.uk
Home Page: http://www.salters.co.uk/institute/index.htm

• 7058 • A-Level Chemistry Prizes
To recognize individuals who have achieved the highest grades in the Salters' A Level Chemistry exams. Monetary prizes totaling £300 are awarded to the top four or five candidates.

• 7059 • Chemistry Teaching Award
To recognize teachers in the UK who have made the greatest contribution to the teaching of chemistry. An annual prize of £10,000 is endowed for the teacher in the UK who has made the greatest contribution, at the end of the year under review, to the teaching of chemical sciences to any age group within the range of 5-18 years. The prize is divided with £5,000 going to the teacher and £5,000 to his/her chemistry department. Established in celebration of the 600th anniversary of the Salter Company.

• 7060 • City and Guilds Prizes
To recognize top students at each level of the Process Plant Operation Scheme. A monetary prize of £1,000 is awarded annually.

• 7061 • Jerwood Prize
To recognize achievement to date and to provide encouragement and incentive to Salters' Graduate Prizewinners to reach the top echelons of their professions. Past Salters' Graduate Prizewinners, chemists or chemical engineers, aged 30 to 35 and currently employed in industry in the UK are eligible as are those working for UK based companies abroad. Managing/Chief Executives will be invited to nominate their Salters' graduates on the basis of their achievement and ultimate potential to occupy a high profile leading position in the UK industry. A prize of £10,000 and 2 medals of £500 each will be awarded annually. Established in 1997.

• 7062 • Salters' Graduate Prizes
In recognition of academic merit in chemistry or chemical engineering at British universities and of potential to occupy a leading position in the United Kingdom chemical industry. Final year undergraduates, who must be nominated by the head of the department and who expect to graduate with honors in chemistry or chemical engineering and have the intention of taking a post in a United Kingdom chemical industry, may apply by late January each year. Monetary award of £1,000 and certificates are awarded to up to 10 recipients each year. Established in 1979.

• 7063 •
Saltire Society
Mrs. Kathleen Munro, Administrator
9 Fountain Close
22 High St.
Edinburgh EH1 1TF, United Kingdom
Phone: 44 131 5561836
Fax: 44 131 5571675
E-mail: saltire@saltiresociety.org.uk
Home Page: http://www.saltiresociety.org.uk

• 7064 • **Arts and Crafts in Architecture Award**
For recognition of works of art and craft that are designed to enhance and enrich buildings. Eligible works include sculpture, painting, tilework, ceramics, mosaic, tapestry, textile hangings, glass, plaster, metalwork, and enamel. Work must be located in Scotland and be an intrinsic part of a building or group of buildings. Awarded biennially in odd-numbered years. Established in 1971.

• 7065 • **Civil Engineering Award**
To encourage the highest standards in the design and construction of civil engineering projects completed in the previous two years in Scotland. Projects may be entered in five categories: (1) the project as a whole; (2) the design of the project; (3) the construction of the project; (4) the conservation elements of the project; and (5) the environmental sustainability construction of the project. A plaque is awarded annually to the winner in each category. Established in 1981. Co-sponsored by the Scottish Environmental Protection Agency and the Institute of Civil Engineers.

• 7066 • **Educational Publications Award**
Awarded granted jointly with the Times Educational Supplement Scotland. Encourages the best examples of published work that enhances the curriculum for Scottish schools. The work must be relevant to Scottish school children, ages 3-18. Established in 1993.

• 7067 • **Grierson Documentary Film Award**
Awarded to first and second-time short documentary filmmakers, either working in or from Scotland. Established in 1999.

• 7068 • **Housing Design Awards**
For recognition of housing design in Scotland. Entries may be submitted by owners, builders, public or semi-public bodies, and individuals who have commissioned works in Scotland, or by the architects employed by them. Awarded annually. Established in 1937.

• 7069 • **Scottish Book of the Year Awards**
For recognition of the Scottish Book of the Year and the Scottish First Book of the Year. The competition is open to any author of Scottish descent or living in Scotland, or for a book by anyone which deals with the work or life of a Scot or with a Scottish problem, event or situation. In 1988, the Award was extended to include the first published work by a new author. Entries are submitted to the Society by literary editors of leading newspapers, magazines, and periodicals. A monetary prize of £5,000 is awarded for the Book of the Year, and £1,500 for the First Book of the Year. Awarded annually. Established in 1982. Formerly: Saltire Society Scottish Literary Awards.

• 7070 • **Scottish Historical Book Award**
For recognition of a published work of Scottish historical research, including intellectual history and the history of science. Awarded periodically. Established in 1965 in memory of Agnes Mure MacKenzie. Formerly: (1998) Agnes Mure MacKenzie Award.

• 7071 • **Scottish Research Book Award**
To recognize books that represent a significant body of research, offer new insight or dimension to the subject, and add knowledge and understanding of Scotland and the Scots. Awarded annually. Established in 1998. Co-administered by the National Library of Scotland.

• 7072 • **Scottish Science Award**
To recognize individuals making a major contribution to science, whose merit has not been previously recognized by public honors or by election to one of the senior learned societies, and who are able to communicate their scientific results to the wider public. Presented within five branches of science in rotation annually: medicine and veterinary medicine, physical science and mathematics, biological sciences, earth sciences, and molecular biology. A medallion, a certificate, and a monetary prize are awarded annually. Established in 1989. Formerly: (1995) Saltire Society and The Royal Bank of Scotland - Scottish Science Award.

• 7073 • **Scottish Song Competition**
To recognize school and junior choirs singing Scottish songs who are the winners of first and second places at their local music competition festivals. Certificates are awarded annually. Established in 1975.

• 7074 •
School of Oriental and African Studies
Prof. Colin Bundy, Dir.
Thornhaugh St.
Russell Sq.
London WC1H 0XG, United Kingdom
Phone: 44 20 7637 2388
Fax: 44 20 7636 3844
E-mail: study@soas.ac.uk
Home Page: http://www.soas.ac.uk

• 7075 • **Sir Peter Parker Awards for Spoken Business Japanese**
For recognition of outstanding spoken business Japanese. Awarded annually to first, second, and third place recipients. Established in 1990. Co-sponsored by the Japan External Trade Organisation.

• 7076 •
Science Fiction Foundation
Andy Sawyer, Ed.
28 St. Johns Rd.
PO Box 123
Guildford GU2 7UH, United Kingdom
Phone: 44 151 7943142
Fax: 44 151 7942681
E-mail: asawyer@liverpool.ac.uk
Home Page: http://www.sf-foundation.org

• 7077 • **Arthur C. Clarke Award**
Award of recognition. Presented for the best science fiction novel first published in the United Kingdom. Awarded annually.

• 7078 •
Scottish Bowling Association
John Armstrong, Pres.
National Centre for Bowling, Northfield
Hunters Ave.
Ayr KA8 9AL, United Kingdom
Phone: 44 1292 294623
Fax: 44 1292 294623
E-mail: scottishbowling@aol.com
Home Page: http://www.scottish-bowling.co.uk

• 7079 • **National Championships**
For recognition of championship winners in bowling. Awards are given in the following competitions: Fours Championship, Triples Championship, Pairs Championship, Singles Championship, Seniors' Fours Championship, and Junior Singles Championship. Members of the Association are eligible. Monetary prizes, medals, and trophies are awarded annually. Established in 1892.

• 7080 •
Scottish International Piano Competition
Ian Mills, Admin.
The Mitchell Library
201 North St.
Glasgow G3 7DN, United Kingdom
Phone: 44 141 287 2857
Fax: 44 141 287 2858
E-mail: ian.mills@nycos.co.uk
Home Page: http://www.SIPC2004.org

• 7081 • **Scottish International Piano Competition**
For recognition of achievement in the piano competition. Applications are accepted from individuals up to 30 years of age of any nationality. The following monetary prizes are awarded: first prize - £10,000; second prize -£5,000; third prize - £2,500; fourth prize - £1,500; £750 for each semi-finalist; and a £500 prize for the best performance of the commissioned work. Held triennially. Established in 1986 in memory of Frederic Lamond (1868-1948).

• 7082 •
Scottish Photographic Federation
Jim Renny, Pres.
13a Allanfauld Rd.
Cumbernauld G67 1EX, United Kingdom
Phone: 44 1236 720082
E-mail: tom@tombell.co.uk
Home Page: http://www.scottish-photographic-federation.org

• 7083 • **Scottish Salon of Photography**
For recognition of outstanding photography from artists around the world. The Federation presents Gold Medals in four categories: Best Contemporary Slide, Best Traditional Slide, Best Monochrome Print, and Best Colour Print. It also presents four gold medals to Scottish residents in four categories: Best General Slide, Best Natural History Slide, Best Monochrome Print, and Best Colour Print. The Federation Internationale de l'art Photographique (FIAP) awards Gold Medals in four categories: Best Landscape Slide, Best Natural History Slide, Best Monochrome Landscape Print, and Best Colour Landscape Print. In addition, the Dumfries Octocentenary Trophy is awarded to the best entry from a Scottish Club. Held annually. Established in 1910.

• 7084 •
Social Research Association
Ceridwen Roberts, Chair
175-185, Gray's Inn Rd.
London WC1X 8UP, United Kingdom
Phone: 44 20 78120634
Fax: 44 20 88805684
E-mail: admin@the-sra.org.uk
Home Page: http://www.the-sra.org.uk

• 7085 • **Mark Abrams Prize**
To honor a piece of work that best links survey research, social policy, and social theory. Awarded annually. Established in 1986.

• 7086 •
Society for Applied Microbiology
Philip Wheat, CEO
The Blore Tower
Harpur Ctre.
Bedford MK40 1TQ, United Kingdom
Phone: 44 1234 326661
Fax: 44 1234 326678
E-mail: info@sfam.org.uk
Home Page: http://www.sfam.org.uk

• 7087 • **W. H. Pierce Memorial Prize**
To recognize a young microbiologist for a substantial contribution to bacteriology, such as publication in the *Journal of Applied Bacteriology* or a presentation at the Symposium held at the summer conference of the Society. Younger members of the Society are eligible for nomination by other members. A monetary award of £2,000 and a scroll are awarded annually. Deadline is May 1. Established in 1984 by Oxoid Ltd. in honor of W. H. (Bill) Pierce, former chief bacteriologist.

• 7088 • **Don Whitley Travel Scholarship**
To enable microbiologists to attend scientific meetings. Application by letter to Society office. Awarded annually.

• 7089 •
Society for Environmental Exploration
Ms. Eibleis Fanning, Managing Dir.
50-52 Rivington St.
London EC2A 3QP, United Kingdom
Phone: 44 207 6132422
Fax: 44 207 6132992
E-mail: info@frontier.ac.uk
Home Page: http://www.frontier.ac.uk

• 7090 • **BTEC Certificate in Expedition Management**
Award of recognition for gaining the knowledge and skills needed to manage and organize expeditions.

• 7091 • **BTEC Certificate in Tropical Habitat Conservation**
Award of recognition for gaining knowledge of management and issues relating to the conservation of tropical habitats.

• 7092 •
Society for Experimental Biology
(Societe de Biologie Experimentale)
Prof. Mike Lakin, Ch.Exec.
3, The Corronades
New Rd.
Southampton SO14 0AA, United Kingdom
Phone: 44 23 80224824
Fax: 44 23 80226312
E-mail: seb@sebiology.org
Home Page: http://www.sebiology.org

• 7093 • **Irene Manton Award**
Recognizes the best postgraduate cell, plant, and animal biology posters by a PhD student or a PhD in their first post doctoral year. Awarded annually.

• 7094 • **President's Medallist**
Recognizes research in new areas of science that have great success. Individuals under the age of 35 are eligible. Awarded annually.

• 7095 •
Society for General Microbiology
Prof. Ron S. Fraser, Exec.Sec.
Marlborough House
Basingstoke Rd.
Spencers Wood
Reading RG7 1AG, United Kingdom
Phone: 44 1189 881800
Fax: 44 1189 885656
E-mail: admin@sgm.ac.uk
Home Page: http://www.sgm.ac.uk

• 7096 • **Colworth Prize Lecture**
To recognize an individual for an outstanding contribution in an area of applied microbiology. Individuals must be nominated by two members of the Society, but the nominee need not be a member. A monetary award of £1,000 is awarded biennially. The winner gives the lecture at a Society meeting, and is usually published in a Society journal. Awarded biennially. Established in 1987. Sponsored by Colworth Laboratory of Unilever Research.

• 7097 • **Fleming Lecture**
For recognition of outstanding research in any branch of microbiology by a young scientist. Nominees should be within the first ten years after the completion of a doctorate. A monetary award of £1,000 is awarded annually. The winner gives the lecture at a Society meeting, and is usually published in a Society journal. Established in 1976 in memory of Sir Alexander Fleming, the discoverer of penicillin and first president of the Society.

• 7098 • **Fred Griffith Review Lecture**
Held biennially and commemorates the contributions of Fred Griffith to bacterial genetics. It recognizes long and distinguished contributions to microbiology. The winner receives £500 and gives a personal overview of an area of microbiology. The lecture is usually published in a society journal.

• 7099 • **Marjory Stephenson Prize Lecture**
To recognize an individual for an outstanding contribution of current importance in any area of microbiology. Individuals must be nominated by two members of the Society, but the nominee need not be a member of the society. A monetary award of £1,000 is awarded biennially. The winner gives the lecture at a Society meeting, and is usually published in a Society journal. Established in 1987 to honor Marjory Stephenson, one of the founders of the Society. Formerly: (1987) Marjory Stephenson Memorial Lecture.

• 7100 • **Peter Wildy Prize for Microbiology Education**
Awarded annually for an outstanding contribution to microbiology education, without restriction on the area of microbiology, and the award is not restricted to university teaching. Nominations for the prize must be made by two members of the society, but the nominee need not be a member of the society. The winner will receive £1000 and cannot win a second time. The recipient of the prize will be expected to give a presentationbased on an aspect of educational work for which the prize was given at a society meeting and the winner will be encouraged to publish the presentation in a society journal.

• 7101 •
Society for Medicines Research
Geoffrey Stemp PhD, Chm.
Triangle House
Broomhill Rd.
London SW18 4HX, United Kingdom
Phone: 44 208 8752431
Fax: 44 208 8752434
E-mail: secretariat@smr.org.uk
Home Page: http://www.socmr.org

Formerly: Society for Drug Research.

• 7102 • **Award for Drug Discovery**
To recognize researchers in academic institutions and the pharmaceutical industry as well as other concerned individuals. Awarded biennially in odd-numbered years.

• 7103 •
Society for Medieval Archaeology
Dr. Andrew Reynolds, Hon.Sec.
Department of Archaeology
School of Human and Environmental Sciences
The Univ. of Reading
Whiteknights
Reading RG6 6AA, United Kingdom
Phone: 44 118 3786381
Fax: 44 118 3786718
E-mail: r.l.gilchrist@reading.ac.uk
Home Page: http://www.socmedarch.org

• 7104 • **Eric Fletcher Research Award**
To provide financial assistance to young members who wish to undertake personal archaeological research. Several monetary awards between £50 and £250 are presented annually. Established in 1984 by the late Lord Fletcher, honorary vice-president of the Society. Formerly: (1983) Colt Fund.

• 7105 • **Medieval Archaeology Research Grant**
To encourage research in medieval archaeology. A cash award of up to £2,000 to be used for research is presented annually. Established in 1990.

• 7106 • **Sudreys Fund**
To encourage research in the field of Viking studies. Awardees will receive up to £500 for travel-related research. Awarded annually. Established in 1992.

• 7107 •
Society for Radiological Protection
Bryan Smith, Hon. Sec.
76 Portland Pl.
London W1B 1NT, United Kingdom
Phone: 44 1364 644487
Fax: 44 1364 644492
E-mail: admin@srp-uk.org
Home Page: http://www.srp-uk.org

• 7108 • **The Bursary Award Scheme**
For UK and overseas students.

• 7109 • **The Educational Support Scheme**
For individuals from UK and overseas.

• 7110 • **The Jack Martin Prize**
For excellence in MSc and PhD theses, or in the presentation of information at the Society's International Symposium.

• 7111 •
Society for Research into Higher Education
Helen Perkins, Dir.
76 Portland Pl.
London W1B 1NT, United Kingdom
Phone: 44 20 76372766
Fax: 44 20 76372781
E-mail: srheoffice@srhe.ac.uk
Home Page: http://www.srhe.ac.uk

• 7112 • **Society for Research into Higher Education Awards**
To recognize individuals involved in higher education research and to conduct educational programs. The Society bestows awards at its annual conference.

• 7113 •
Society for Research into Hydrocephalus and Spina Bifida
Dr. Hazel C. Jones PhD, Hon.Sec.
Gagle Brook House
Chesterton
Hampshire
Bicester OX26 1UF, United Kingdom
Phone: 44 1869 243614
Fax: 44 1420 549466
E-mail: hsec@srhsb.org
Home Page: http://www.srhsb.org

• 7114 • **Casey Holter Memorial Prize**
For recognition of an essay reporting original work bearing on the pathogenesis or treatment of hydrocephalus or spina bifida. Any professional worker in a field concerned with hydrocephalus and/or spina bifida may submit an essay in a form suitable for publication. Essays should include personal observations and experiences collected by the candidate in the course of his work and must not have been previously published. A monetary prize of £250 is awarded triennially. Established in 1966 by Mr. J. W. Holter in memory of his son.

• 7115 •
Society for the Advancement of Anaesthesia in Dentistry
Dr. David Craig, Pres.
21 Portland Pl.
London W1B 1PY, United Kingdom
Phone: 44 20 76318893
Phone: 44 1403 780465
Fax: 44 1246 208729
E-mail: saad@aagbi.org
Home Page: http://www.saaduk.org

• 7116 • **Drummond-Jackson Prize**
For recognition of the most meritorious essay on any subject related to conscious sedation, analgesia, anxiety control, or general anaesthesia for dentistry. All dental and medical undergraduates and graduates in the United Kingdom and throughout the world are eligible. A monetary prize of £1,000 is awarded triennially. Established in 1976 in memory of S.L. Drummond-Jackson, founder of SAAD, who died in 1975.

• 7117 • **SAAD Dental Student Prize**
Recognizes an outstanding essay. Dental students in the United Kingdom are eligible. An essay on the one of the following topics must be submitted: conscious sedation, analgesia, anxiety control, or general anaesthesia for dentistry. Application deadline is March 1.

• 7118 •
Society for the History of Alchemy and Chemistry
Dr. Noel Coley, Hon.Treas.
24 Kayemoor Rd.
Sutton SM2 5HT, United Kingdom
Phone: 44 20 86427437
E-mail: n.g.coley@surrey28.freeserve.co.uk
Home Page: http://www.ambix.org

• 7119 • **Partington Prize**
To recognize an original and unpublished essay on any aspect of the history of alchemy or chemistry by a young scholar. It is open to anyone with a scholarly interest in the history of alchemy or chemistry who has not reached 35 years of age, or if older, has completed a doctoral thesis in the history of science within the previous three years. A monetary prize of £350 and a certificate are awarded triennially. Established in 1975 in memory of Professor J. R. Partington.

• 7120 •
Society for the History of Natural History
Simon Chaplin, Sec.
Cromwell Rd.
London SW7 5BD, United Kingdom
E-mail: secretary@shnh.org
Home Page: http://www.shnh.org

• 7121 • **Founders' Medal**
For contribution to the study of the history or bibliography of natural history.

• 7122 • **Honorary Membership**
For persons who have performed signal services to the Society.

• 7123 • **John Thackray Medal**
For contribution to the history of natural history realized in the preceding 12 months.

• 7124 • **Alwyne Wheeler Bursary**
For original contribution to the study of the history of natural history by a person under the age of 30.

• 7125 •
Society for Theatre Research
Eileen Cottis, Hon.Sec.
1E Tavistock St.
London WC2E 7PR, United Kingdom
E-mail: e.cottis@btinternet.com
Home Page: http://www.str.org.uk

• 7126 • **William Poel Memorial Festival**
To encourage good stage speech, especially in sixteenth/seventeenth century drama. Entry is restricted to nominees from invited professional theatre schools in Great Britain. The festival currently takes place annually at the Royal National Theatre, normally in May. A small prize may be awarded at the Society's discretion. Established in 1952 by Dame Edith Evans in memory of William Poel (1852-1934), an innovative theatre director.

• 7127 • **Research Awards**
To provide for research on the history and practice of the British theatre. Private scholars, theatre professionals, academic staff, and students, unrestricted as to status or nationality, may apply for grants. Applications must be submitted by February 1. Monetary awards range from £100 to £2,000. The following grants are awarded: The Anthony Denning Award, Kathleen Barker Award, Stephen Joseph Award, John Ramsden Awards, as well as other, unnamed grants. Frequency of the grants vary.

• 7128 •
Society of Army Historical Research
Gen. Sir John Waters GCB, Chm.
National Army Museum
Royal Hospital Rd.
Chelsea
London SW3 4HT, United Kingdom
Phone: 44 207 7300717
E-mail: info@national-army-museum.ac.uk
Home Page: http://www.sahr.co.uk

• 7129 • **Templer Medal**
For recognition of the book making the most notable contribution to the history of the British Army or its predecessors and of the land forces of The Empire and Commonwealth. The award committee makes the selection from books published during the preceding calendar year that have been nominated. The medal and a cash prize of £5,000 are awarded at the annual general meeting. Established in 1982 in memory of Field Marshal Sir Gerald Templer KG, President of the Society.

• 7130 •
Society of Authors
Translators Association
Emma Boniwell, Membership Sec.
84 Drayton Gardens
London SW10 9SB, United Kingdom
Phone: 44 20 73736642
Fax: 44 20 73735768
E-mail: info@societyofauthors.org
Home Page: http://www.societyofauthors.org

• 7131 • **John Florio Prize**
For recognition of the best translation from Italian into English of an Italian work of literary merit and general interest written in the last 100 years. Works published in the United Kingdom by a British publisher during the award year and the preceding year are eligible. A monetary prize of £2,000 is awarded biennially in even-numbered years. Established in 1963 under the auspices of the Italian Institute of Culture for the United Kingdom, the British Italian Society, and the Society of Authors.

• 7132 • **Calouste Gulbertian Prize**
To recognize translations of full-length works from any period by a Portuguese national. The translation must have been first published in the UK in the award year and two preceding years. A monetary prize of £1,000 is awarded triennially.

• 7133 • **Scott Moncrieff Prize**
For recognition of the best translation from French to English of a French work of literary merit and general interest written in the last 100 years. Works published in the United Kingdom by a British publisher during the award year may be submitted by the publisher. A monetary prize of £2,000 is awarded annually. Established in 1964.

• 7134 • **Premio Valle Inclan**
To recognize translations of Spanish works. The original may be from any period or country, provided it is in the Spanish language. The translation must have been first published in the UK during the award year. A monetary prize of £1,000 is awarded annually.

• 7135 • **Schlegel - Tieck Prize**
For recognition of the best translation from German to English of a German work of literary merit and general interest written in the last 100 years. Works published in the United Kingdom by a British publisher during the award year may be submitted by the publisher. A monetary prize of £2,000 is awarded annually. Established in 1964.

• 7136 • **Bernard Shaw Prize**
To recognize translations of Swedish-language works from any period. The translation must have been first published in the UK during the award year and the two preceding years. A monetary prize of £1,000 is awarded triennially.

• 7137 • **Vondel Translation Prize**
To recognize translations of Dutch and Flemmish works of literature into English. The translation must have been first published in the United Kingdom or the United States in the award year or the preceding year and must be submitted by December 20. A monetary prize of £2,000 is awarded biennially in odd-numbered years. Established in 1995.

• 7138 •
Society of Authors - England
Emma Boniwell, Membership Sec.
84 Drayton Gardens
London SW10 9SB, United Kingdom
Phone: 44 20 73736642
Fax: 44 20 73735768
E-mail: info@societyofauthors.org
Home Page: http://www.societyofauthors.org

• 7139 • **K. Blundell Grants**
To assist young published authors working on their next book. British individuals under 40 years of age whose work contributes to the greater understanding of existing social and economic organization are eligible. The deadline is May 31. Grants range from £1,000 to £4,000. Awarded annually. Established in 1987 by Miss K. Blundell.

• 7140 • **Cholmondeley Award for Poets**
To recognize and encourage poets of any age, sex, or nationality. The complete work of the poet is considered, rather than a specific book of poetry. Submissions are not accepted. Monetary prizes totaling £8,000 are awarded annually. Established in 1966 by the Marchioness of Cholmondeley.

• 7141 • **Encore Award**
To reward the best second novel of the year. The winner will receive a monetary prize of £10,000. Awarded annually. Established in 1990. Sponsored by Miss Lucy Astor.

• 7142 • **Eric Gregory Awards**
To encourage young poets. Candidates who are British subjects by birth, residents of the United Kingdom, and under 30 years of age may submit a published or unpublished volume of belles-lettres, drama poems, or poetry. Monetary awards totaling over £24,000 are awarded annually. Established by the late Eric Gregory.

• 7143 • **Francis Head Bequest**
To provide grants to authors over 35 whose main source of income is their writing, and who, thorough physical mishap, illness, or other causes, are temporarily unable to continue writing.

• 7144 • **Richard Imison Memorial Award**
This £1,500 award is given for the best dramatic work broadcast by a writer new to radio.

• 7145 • **John Masefield Memorial Trust**
To provide occasional grants to professional poets (or their immediate dependants) who are faced with sudden financial problems. Applications are available from the society.

• 7146 • **Somerset Maugham Awards**
To recognize a promising British author for a published work in the field of poetry, fiction, criticism, biography, history, philosophy, belles-lettres, or travel. Authors must be under 35

years of age. The award is designed to encourage writers to travel and acquaint themselves with the customs of other countries, and to extend the basis and influence of British literature. Monetary awards of £12,000 are awarded annually. Established in 1946 by the late Somerset Maugham.

• 7147 • McKitterick Prize
To recognize the best first novel published by an author over the age of 40. Published and unpublished novels are eligible. A monetary prize of £4,000 is awarded annually. Established in 1990.

• 7148 • Medical Book Prizes
To recognize an author(s) or editor(s) of a medical textbook, an illustrated textbook, or a medical atlas which, in the opinion of the judges, made the greatest contribution to understanding in any particular field. Any medical or dental textbook written in English, or any illustrated book published in the United Kingdom during the preceding calendar year is eligible. Awards of £1,000 in each category are awarded annually. Established in 1983. Sponsored by the Royal Society of Medicine. Formerly: (1985) Abbott Prize; Glaxo Prize for Medical Writing.

• 7149 • Sagittarius Prize
This £4,000 award is for an excellent published first novel by an author over the age of 60. Awarded annually.

• 7150 • Tom-Gallon Award
To recognize authors of short stories. Published and unpublished works are eligible. A monetary prize of £1,000 is awarded biennially in odd-numbered years. Established in 1946.

• 7151 • Betty Trask Prize and Awards
To recognize authors under the age of 35 for a first novel, published or unpublished, of a romantic or traditional nature. British/Commonwealth citizens are eligible. Monetary awards totaling £25,000, which must be used for travel abroad, are presented annually. Established in 1983 by Margaret Elizabeth Trask, an author of romantic novels.

• 7152 • Travelling Scholarships
To enable British writers to travel abroad. Monetary awards of varying amounts are presented annually. Established in 1944.

• 7153 •
Society of Border Leicester Sheep Breeders
Nesta D. Todd, Sec.
Greenend
St. Boswells
Melrose Borders TD6 9ES, United Kingdom
Phone: 44 1835 824207
Fax: 44 1835 824207
E-mail: info@borderleicesters.co.uk
Home Page: http://www.borderleicesters.co.uk

• 7154 • Best in Breed Award
Recognize members whose sheep win championships.

• 7155 •
Society of Chemical Industry
Mr. Richard Denyer, Gen.Sec.
14-15 Belgrave Sq.
London SW1X 8PS, United Kingdom
Phone: 44 20 75981500
Phone: 44 20 75981572
Fax: 44 20 75981545
E-mail: secretariat@soci.org
Home Page: http://www.soci.org

• 7156 • Henry E. Armstrong Memorial Lecture
A lecture is delivered at intervals in memory of Professor H.E. Armstrong (1848-1937), regarded as one of the fathers of chemical engineering; it was his life's work to teach chemistry as part of an education in engineering. Awarded when merited. Established in 1943.

• 7157 • Baekeland Lecture
A lecture on the subject of synthetic resins and related matters is delivered at approximately four-year intervals. Established in 1943 to commemorate the work of Dr. Leo H. Baekeland (1863-1944) of the USA on synthetic resins.

• 7158 • Hans R. Bolliger Memorial Lecture
A lecture on a chemical aspect of health and safety. Established to commemorate Dr. Hans R. Bolliger. Awarded by SCI Health and Safety Group and the Manchester (UK) section. Established in 1977.

• 7159 • Canada International Award
To recognize an individual for outstanding service to the Canadian chemical industry in the international sphere. Awarded biennially. Established in 1975. Formerly: Canadian International Medal Lecture.

• 7160 • Canada Medal
For recognition of outstanding service to chemical industry in Canada. A medal is awarded biennially. Established in 1939 by the Canadian Section of the Society.

• 7161 • Castner Lecture and Medal
A lecture on applied electrochemistry is delivered by a person of authority. Awarded biennially. Established in 1946 to honor Hamilton Young Castner (1858-1899), a pioneer in the field of industrial electrochemistry.

• 7162 • Environment Medal
To recognize a member of the society for contributions to environmental science and/or its application. Awarded annually. Established in 1971.

• 7163 • Founder's Lecture
A lecture on colloid and surface chemistry. Established in 1970 to commemorate Sir Eric Rideal, President of the Society from 1944-46.

• 7164 • Carl Hanson Medal
To recognize an individual for achievements in solvent extraction science and technology. A medal is awarded triennially. Established in 1986 in memory of Carl Hanson, renowned for his work on all aspects of solvent extraction. Administered by the International Committee for Solvent Extraction.

• 7165 • Roland Harper Lecture
A lecture on consumer and/or sensory science. Established in 1994 to commemorate Dr. Roland Harper (1916-92), an international figure in the growth and application of sensory sciences.

• 7166 • Hilditch Memorial Lecture
A lecture delivered at intervals on a topic connected with oil and fats or applied chemistry. Awarded every two or three years. Established in 1967 in memory of Professor T.P. Hilditch (1886-1965), the first holder of the Campbell Brown Chair of Industrial Chemistry in the University of Liverpool, who made outstanding contributions to the knowledge of oils and fats.

• 7167 • Robert Horne Lecture
A lecture delivered at intervals in Bristol or in South Wales. Awarded triennially. Established in 1973 in memory of Viscount Horne, the first Chairman of the Imperial Smelting Corporation. Sponsored by the Bristol and the South Wales Sections of the society.

• 7168 • Hurter Memorial Lecture
A lecture delivered at intervals on applied chemistry. Awarded periodically. Established in 1898 by the Liverpool (UK) Section of the Society as a memorial to Dr. Ferdinand Hurter (1844-1898), an authority on the Leblanc system for soda production, in recognition of his services to applied chemistry and his contribution to the Society.

• 7169 • International Medal
To recognize any member or committee that furthers international cooperation in the Society's sphere of interest. A medal is awarded periodically. Established in 1948.

• 7170 • Lampitt Medal
For recognition of outstanding service to the society through the groups and sections. Awarded biennially. Established in 1958 to commemorate Dr. Leslie H. Lampitt, who played a major role in the society's affairs for 37 years.

• 7171 • LeSueur Memorial Lecture
A lecture delivered every two years at a meeting of the Canadian Section. Awarded biennially. Established in 1955 to honor Ernest A. Le Sueur who made many outstanding contributions to early industrial chemistry in Canada, including

the first successful commercial electrolytic cell for the manufacture of chlorine and caustic soda.

• 7172 • Leverhulme Lecture
To promote research and education in connection with the chemical industry. The lecture is delivered at three-yearly intervals. Established in 1943 by the Leverhulme Trust in memory of the first Viscount Leverhulme (1851-1925), the founder of Port Sunlight. Awarded every two or three years by the Liverpool (UK) Section.

• 7173 • Ivan Levinstein Memorial Lecture
A lecture delivered before the Manchester (UK) Section of the Society. Awarded annually. Endowed in 1946 in memory of Ivan Levinstein (1845-1916), a pioneer in the manufacture of synthetic dyestuffs.

• 7174 • Julius Lewkowitsch Memorial Lecture
A lecture delivered on any technical aspect of the natural oils and fats. Awarded every two years in London, UK. Endowed in 1980 to commemorate the work of Julius Lewkowitsch in the oils and fats field. Administered by the Oils and Fats Group Committee.

• 7175 • Lister Memorial Lecture
A lecture on chemistry and medical science. Endowed in 1944 to commemorate the first Baron Lister (1827-1912), the pioneer of antiseptic surgery.

• 7176 • Oils and Fats Group International Lecture
A lecture delivered periodically before the Oils and Fats Group of the Society. Awarded biennially. Established in 1964.

• 7177 • Purvis Memorial Award
To recognize dedication and service to the Canadian chemical industry. A plaque is presented at a dinner of the Canadian Section. Established in 1947 to commemorate Rt. Hon. Arthur B. Purvis (1890-1941).

• 7178 • Sir Eric Rideal Lecture
A lecture given by a person distinguished in colloid or interface science. The Rideal Memorial Trust was set up jointly in 1976 between the Society and the Royal Society of Chemistry to commemorate the life and work of the late Sir Eric Rideal FRS (1890-1974). Administered by the Colloid and Surface Chemistry Group.

• 7179 • Richard Seligman Lecture
A lecture delivered every two or three years on any aspect of engineering or processing in the food or beverage industries in order to advance the education of the public in such matters. Endowed in 1973 by APV Holdings Ltd. in memory of Dr. Richard Seligman, the founder of the company who had been a member of the society for over 50 years. Administered by the Food Engineering Group.

• 7180 • Separation Science Lecture
A lecture on a branch of separation science and technology. A scroll is also presented. Established in 1995.

• 7181 •
Society of Dyers and Colourists - England
Kenneth M. McGhee, Gen.Sec. & CEO
PO Box 244
Perkin House
82 Grattan Rd.
Bradford BD1 2JB, United Kingdom
Phone: 44 1274 725138
Fax: 44 1274 392888
E-mail: secretariat@sdc.org.uk
Home Page: http://www.sdc.org.uk

• 7182 • CCol ASDC Associateship
A diploma is awarded when merited to members who have passed prescribed Society examinations and have provided evidence of having satisfactory experience in colour science or technology.

• 7183 • CCol FSDC Fellowship
A diploma is awarded when merited to members who have demonstrated distinction in the knowledge and practice of colour science or colour technology.

• 7184 • George Douglas Lecture
To provide a lecture on some subject connected with the coloring or finishing of textiles. A monetary award is presented with an invitation to lecture; alternatively, the fund may be utilized for other educational purposes. Established in 1949.

• 7185 • Honorary Fellow
To recognize individuals who have contributed to the field of dyeing and coloring. Awarded when merited. Established in 1969.

• 7186 • Honorary Member
To recognize individuals who have contributed to the field of dyeing and coloring. Awarded when merited. Established in 1884.

• 7187 • LSDC Licentiateship
A diploma is awarded when merited to members who have passed the prescribed Society examinations (or possess an equivalent qualification) and who have provided evidence of having satisfactory experience in colour science or colour technology.

• 7188 • Medal of the Society of Dyers and Colourists
For recognition of exceptional services to the Society or in the interests of the tinctorial and allied industries. Gold, Silver, Bronze, and Centenary Medals are awarded annually. Established in 1908.

• 7189 • Perkin Medal
For recognition of exceptional services in the interests of the tinctorial and allied industries. A gold medal is awarded when merited. Established in 1908 in memory of Sir William Henry Perkin, the founder of the coal-tar dye industry, and President of the Society in 1907.

• 7190 • SDC Centenary Medal
Awarded to authors of papers of an educational, management or review nature published by the societ. Established in 1983.

• 7191 • Turner - Scholefield Award
To recognize an Associate under the age of 30 who has made notable and meritorious contributions to the science or technology of coloring matters or their application, or has demonstrated the ability to apply his or her knowledge and skills in an appropriate field of color science or technology. Awarded annually or when merited. Established in 1970 under the will of the late Mr. H. A. Turner in memory of Fred Scholefield.

• 7192 • Worshipful Company of Dyers Research Medal
To recognize the authors of papers embodying the results of scientific research or technical investigation connected with the tinctorial arts published in the *Journal* of the Society. A gold or silver medal is awarded annually. Established in 1908.

• 7193 •
Society of Floristry
Sue Stones MSF, Sec.
Clyrun Fach
Llansilin
Shropshire
Oswestry SY10 7JN, United Kingdom
Phone: 44 870 2410432
Fax: 44 120 2855520
E-mail: info@societyoffloristry.org
Home Page: http://www.societyoffloristry.org

• 7194 • Intermediate Certificate in Floristry
Recognizes success in examination result.

• 7195 • National Diploma of the Society of Floristry
Recognizes success in examination result.

• 7196 •
Society of Indexers
(Societe des Indexateurs)
Wendy Burrow, Admin.
Blades Enterprise Centre
John St.
Sheffield S2 4SW, United Kingdom
Phone: 44 114 2922350
Fax: 44 114 2922351
E-mail: admin@indexers.org.uk
Home Page: http://www.indexers.org.uk

• 7197 • **Carey Award**

For recognition of services to indexing. Individuals are nominated by the Council of the Society. A framed parchment is awarded when merited. Established in 1977 in honor of Gordon V. Carey, the first President of the Society.

• 7198 • **Wheatley Medal**

For recognition of an outstanding index first published in the United Kingdom during the preceding three years. Printed indexes to any type of publication must be submitted provided that the whole work (including the index), or the index alone, has originated in the United Kingdom. A medal and monetary prize of £500 is awarded annually. Established in 1962 in honor of Henry B. Wheatley, sometimes referred to as "the father of British indexing."

• 7199 •

Society of Legal Scholars in the United Kingdom and Ireland
Prof. Nick Wikeley, Hon.Sec.
School of Law
University of Southampton
Highfield
Southampton SO17 1BJ, United Kingdom
Phone: 44 2380 593416
Fax: 44 2380 593024
E-mail: secretary@legalscholars.ac.uk
Home Page: http://www.legalscholars.ac.uk

• 7200 • **Academic Purposes Fund Awards**

To support legal research and scholarship. Awarded annually.

• 7201 • **Peter Birks Book Prize**

Recognizes outstanding books by legal scholars in their early careers. Eligible authors are those that have been in full-time academic employment for not more than 15 years or are still under the age of 40. A monetary prize of £1,000 for first place and £300 for second place are awarded annually.

• 7202 •

Society of London Theatre
Richard Pulford, Chief Exec.
32 Rose St.
London WC2E 9ET, United Kingdom
Phone: 44 207 5576700
Fax: 44 207 5576799
E-mail: enquiries@solttma.co.uk
Home Page: http://www.officiallondontheatre.co.uk

Formerly: (1996) Society of West End Theatre.

• 7203 • **Laurence Olivier Awards**

To recognize distinguished artistic achievement in the West End Theatre. Awards are given in the following categories: Best Actor, Best Actress, Best Performance in a Supporting Role, Best New Play, Best New Comedy, Best Entertainment, Best Revival, Best New Musical, Outstanding Musical Production, Best Actor in a Musical, Best Actress in a Musical, Best Supporting Performance in a Musical, Best Director, Best Theatre Choreographer, Best Set Design, Best Lighting Design, Best Costume Design, Best Sound Design, Outstanding Achievement in an Affiliate Theatre, Best New Dance Production, Outstanding Achievement in Dance, Best New Opera Production, Outstanding Achievement in Opera, and the Society of London Theatre Special Award. Held annually. Established in 1976. Formerly: (1996) Society of West End Theatre.

• 7204 •

Society of Operations Engineers
22 Greencoat Pl.
London SW1P 1PR, United Kingdom
Phone: 44 20 7630 1111
Fax: 44 20 7630 6677
E-mail: soe@soe.org.uk
Home Page: http://www.soe.org.uk

Formerly: (2004) Institute of Road Transport Engineers.

• 7205 • **Mackenzie Junner Rose-Bowl Trophy**

To recognize a contribution in the field of road transport engineering. A monetary award and a trophy are presented annually. Established in memory of the Institute founder.

• 7206 •

Society of Ornamental Turners
Michael R. Windsor, Treas.
9 Rhodes Ave.
London N22 4UR, United Kingdom
Phone: 44 208 8883688
E-mail: webmaster@the-sot.com
Home Page: http://the-sot.com

• 7207 • **Cattell Cup**

To encourage the design and making of suitable apparatus for ornamental turning. Society members are eligible. A silver cup is awarded annually. Established in 1989 by Mr. S.N. Cattell.

• 7208 • **Haythornthwaite Cup**

For recognition of high practical and artistic skills in the art of both plain and ornamental turning. Members of the Society for fewer than five years are eligible. A cup is awarded annually.

• 7209 • **Howe Cup**

For recognition of high practical and artistic skills in the art of hand turning. Members of the Society are eligible. A cup is awarded annually.

• 7210 • **President's Cup**

To recognize the member who has consistently provided interesting displays at meetings during the year. Society members are eligible. A silver cup is awarded annually. Established in 1989.

• 7211 • **Tweddle Medal**

For recognition of high practical and artistic skills in the art of ornamental turning. Members of the Society are eligible. A medal is awarded annually.

• 7212 •

Society of Procurement Officers in Local Government
Peter Blanchard, Sec.
113-117 London Rd.
Stonehills
Pelaw
Gateshead
Leicester LE2 0RG, United Kingdom
Phone: 44 191 4311839
Fax: 44 191 4950933
E-mail: peterblanchard@gateshead.gov.uk
Home Page: http://www.sopo.org

• 7213 • **Awards for Outstanding Achievement in Procurement**

To recognize the variety of approaches to procurement made by local authorities. Trophies are awarded in four categories: County Council, Single-Tier (Unitary) Authority, Non-Unitary District/Borough Council, and Other (e.g., Police, Fire, Consortia). Awarded annually. Established in 2002.

• 7214 •

Society of Wildlife Artists
Andrew Stock, Pres.
17 Carlton House Terr.
London SW1Y 5BD, United Kingdom
Phone: 44 207 9306844
Fax: 44 207 8397830
E-mail: info@mallgalleries.com
Home Page: http://www.swla.co.uk

• 7215 • **Artists for Nature Foundation Award**

Presented at the Society's annual exhibition.

• 7216 • **RSPB Fine Art Award**

To honor artwork depicting wildlife subjects that is shown at the annual exhibition of the Society, which takes place each autumn at the Mall Galleries. Awarded annually.

• 7217 •

Society of Women Artists
Barbara Penketh Simpson, Pres.
1 Knapp Cottages
Wyke
Dorset
Gillingham SP8 4NQ, United Kingdom
Phone: 44 1747 825718
Fax: 44 1747 826835
E-mail: hendersons@dial.pipex.com
Home Page: http://www.society-women-artists.org.uk

• 7218 • **HRH Princess Michael of Kent Award**

Annual award of recognition for the artist with the best watercolor painting.

• 7219 • **President & Vice President's Choice Award**
Award of recognition for a painting.

• 7220 • **Barbara Tate Award**
Annual award of recognition for the artist with best oil painting.

• 7221 • **Winsor & Newton Choice Award**
Annual award of recognition for a painting.

• 7222 •
Soil Association
Tom de Pass, Marketing Coor.
40-56 Victoria St.
Bristol BS1 6BY, United Kingdom
Phone: 44 117 3145000
Fax: 44 117 3145001
E-mail: info@soilassociation.org
Home Page: http://www.soilassociation.org

• 7223 • **Loraine Award for Nature Conservation**
For recognition of an organically managed farm of up to 400 acres where profitable husbandry, the production of healthy foods, and the conservation of native wildlife work together. Awarded annually.

• 7224 • **Organic Food Awards**
To recognize, celebrate, and promote the best organic foods on the market. Held biennially in even-numbered years.

• 7225 •
Sony United Kingdom Ltd.
The Heights
Waybridge KT1B 0XW, United Kingdom
Phone: 44 1932 816000
Fax: 44 1932 817000
Home Page: http://www.sony.co.uk
Formerly: (1995) Sony Broadcast.

• 7226 • **Sony Radio Academy Awards**
For recognition of outstanding radio programs and performances in the United Kingdom. Awards are given in 29 categories among: Programme Awards, personality Awards, Production Awards, and Station Awards. Awarded annually. Established in 1983. Formerly: Imperial Tobacco Awards.

• 7227 •
Specialty Coffee Association of Europe
Colin Smith, Pres.
St. Lawrence, Kingsway
Hullbridge
Essex
Hockley SS5 6DR, United Kingdom
Phone: 44 1245 350866
Fax: 44 1245 350966
E-mail: secretary@scae.com
Home Page: http://www.scae.com

• 7228 • **Award For Enthusiasm**
For the most enthusiastic and persevering member

• 7229 • **Award For Innovation**
For being responsible For new concept, product or way of doing something differently which is of benefit to the industry.

• 7230 • **Coffee Statesmanship Award**
For furthering the interests of the industry or promoting the concept of quality coffee in a statesman like manner.

• 7231 • **Hidden Treasure Award**
For an unrecognized member who deserves greater recognition.

• 7232 • **Test of Time Award**
For an institution, person, concept or establishment that survived changes.

• 7233 • **Young Entrepreneur Award**
For young and achiever member.

• 7234 •
The Spectator
56 Doughty St.
London WC1N 2LL, United Kingdom
Phone: 44 20 7405 1706
Fax: 44 20 7242 0603
E-mail: spectator@solodigital.co.uk
Home Page: http://www.spectator.co.uk

• 7235 • **Shiva Naipaul Memorial Prize**
To recognize the writer best able to describe a visit to a foreign country or with a foreign group of people. The award is not for travel writing in the conventional sense, but for the most acute and profound observation of cultures and/or scenes evidently alien to the writer. Such scenes and/or cultures might be found as easily within the writer's native country as outside it. English language writers of any nationality under the age of 35 are eligible. Submissions must not be more than 3,000 words and must not have been previously published. A monetary prize of £3,000 is awarded annually. Established in 1986 by *The Spectator* in memory of Shiva Naipaul, a gifted writer who died at the age of 40 in 1985.

• 7236 • **Threadneedle/Spectator Parliamentarian of the Year Awards**
For recognition of parliamentary contributions. The following awards are presented: Politician of the Year, Parliamentarian of the Year, Newcomer of the Year, Inquisitor of the Year, Peer of the Year, Speech of the Year, and Minister to Watch. Awarded annually.

• 7237 •
SPNM - Promoting New Music
Jo Naish, Administrator
St. Margarets House, 4th Fl.
18-20 Southwark St.
London SE1 1TJ, United Kingdom
Phone: 44 20 7407 1640
Fax: 44 20 7403 7652
E-mail: spnm@spnm.org.uk
Home Page: http://www.spnm.org.uk
Formerly: (1998) Society for the Promotion of New Music.

• 7238 • **Composition Competitions**
To recognize and promote new music by bringing composers' works to the attention of publishers, concert promoters, and the public. The Society sponsors concerts, workshops, lectures and seminars throughout the UK. The George Butterworth Prize is awarded annually by the SPNM Artistic Director to a composer featured in SPNM events. Also administers the British Section of the International Society for Contemporary Music.

• 7239 •
Sports Journalists' Association of Great Britain
Steven Downes, Sec.
Unit 92, Capital Business Ctre.
22 Carlton Rd.
Surrey
South Croydon CR2 0BS, United Kingdom
Phone: 44 20 89162234
Fax: 44 20 89162235
E-mail: naylor@sportengland.org
Home Page: http://www.sportsjournalists.co.uk

• 7240 • **The J.L. Manning**
For services to sport outside competition.

• 7241 • **Bill Mcgowran Award**
For disabled sport personality.

• 7242 • **Sports Feature of the Year**
For outstanding sports journalist.

• 7243 • **Sports Journalism of the Year**
For sports journalist, staff or freelance contributor to UK national newspaper.

• 7244 • **Sports Personalities of the Year (Men, Women, Team)**
For reigning world champions.

• 7245 • **Sports Photographer of the Year**
For a professional photographer.

• 7246 •
Stand Magazine
Jon Glover, Mng.Ed.
School of English
Leeds University
Leeds LS2 9JT, United Kingdom
Phone: 44 113 233 4794
Fax: 44 113 233 2791
E-mail: stand@leeds.ac.uk
Home Page: http://saturn.vcu.edu/~dlatane/stand.html

• 7247 • *Stand* Poetry Competition
To encourage writers of poetry. Entries in the English language and not published, broadcast, or under consideration elsewhere must be submitted. A monetary prize and publication are awarded biennially. Additional monetary awards totaling $2,500 and one-year subscriptions are awarded. Established in 1995.

• 7248 •
Street Sled Sports Racers International
Mr. Ding Boston, Contact
33a Canal St.
Oxford OX2 6BQ, United Kingdom
Phone: 44 1865 750846
Phone: 44 1865 311179
Fax: 44 1865 426007
E-mail: dingboston@oxfordstuntfactory.com
Home Page: http://www.streetluge.co.uk

• 7249 • Street Luge Championship
Annual award of recognition for the top street luger in the United Kingdom National Championship series. Held annually. Established in 1995.

• 7250 •
Tartans of Scotland
Keith G.A. Lumsden, Registrar/Dir.
Scottish Tartans World Register
The Glack
Dunkeld PH8 0ER, United Kingdom
Phone: 44 1350 728849
Fax: 44 1350 728849
E-mail: info@tartans.scotland.net
Home Page: http://www.tartans.scotland.net

Formerly: (2001) Scottish Tartans Society.

• 7251 • Fellowship
For recognition of outstanding scholarly work in the field of Tartans and Highland Dress. Original research which makes a significant contribution is considered. The title of Fellow of the Society is awarded when merited.

• 7252 •
Tea Council
William Gorman, Exec.Dir.
9, The Courtyard
Gowan Ave.
Fulham
London SW6 6RH, United Kingdom
Phone: 44 207 3717787
Fax: 44 207 3717958
E-mail: tea@teacouncil.co.uk
Home Page: http://www.teacouncil.co.uk

• 7253 • Top Tea Place of the Year
Recognizes excellence in the service of tea. Awarded annually.

• 7254 •
Television and Radio Industries Club
George Stone, Dir.
Drake House
2 Duckling Ln.
Sawbridgeworth CM21 9QA, United Kingdom
Phone: 44 1279 721100
Fax: 44 1279 725625
E-mail: info@tric.org.uk
Home Page: http://www.tric.org.uk

Formerly: (1981) Radio Industries Club.

• 7255 • TRIC Awards
For recognition of the best in contributions in radio and television in the previous twelve months. Awards are given in 16 categories: Satellite/Digital TV Personality, Radio/Digital Radio Personality, TV Personality, Sports Presenter, Newscaster/Reporter, TV Weather Presenter, New TV Talent, TV Arts/Documentary Program, Satellite/Digital Program, Radio/Digital Program, TV Comedy Program, TV Drama Program, TV Daytime Program, TV Entertainment Program, TV Soap of the Year, and the TRIC Special Award. Monetary prizes, trophies and certificates are awarded annually. Established in 1969.

• 7256 •
TENOVUS - SCOTLAND
Edward Read, Gen.Sec.
234 St. Vincent St.
Glasgow G2 5RJ, United Kingdom
Phone: 44 1292 311276
Fax: 44 1292 311433
E-mail: gen.sec@talk21.com
Home Page: http://www.tenovus-scotland.org.uk

• 7257 • Lady Illingworth Award
Rewards a major contribution made towards improving the quality of life for the elderly. Individuals or teams that have been actively engaged in research and/or in the development of a piece of medical/dental equipment, which has resulted in the improved welfare of the elderly, the quality of life for the elderly; elderly, for the purpose of this Award is 65 years of age and over, are eligible. Work must have been carried out within the British Isles. A monetary awarded is given every five years.

• 7258 •
Lionel Tertis International Viola Competition and Workshop
Raymond Leppard, Pres.
Lionel Tertis Secretariat
Erin Arts Centre
Victoria Sq.
Port Erin IM9 6LD, United Kingdom
Phone: 44 1624 835858
Fax: 44 1624 836658
E-mail: information@erinartscentre.com
Home Page: http://www.erinartscentre.com

Formerly: Mananan Festival Trust.

• 7259 • Lionel Tertis International Viola Competition and Workshop (Internationaler Wettbewerb und Seminar fur Bratsche)
To recognize outstanding viola players. Individuals of any nationality not over 30 years of age may submit applications by March 1. The following prizes are awarded at the triennial competition: Ruth Fernoy Memorial Prize, L3000, for first place; The Artur Rubinstein Memorial Prize, L2000, for second place; and The Lillian Tertis Award, L1500, for third place.

• 7260 •
Textile Institute
Rebecca Unsworth, Information Mgr.
St. James's Bldg., 1st Fl.
Oxford St.
Manchester M1 6FQ, United Kingdom
Phone: 44 161 2371188
Fax: 44 161 2361991
E-mail: tiihq@textileinst.org.uk
Home Page: http://www.texi.org

• 7261 • Carothers Medal
To recognize creativity in the production or use of fibres. Awarded annually. Established in 1992 in memory of Wallace H. Carothers, who discovered nylon (polyamide).

• 7262 • Companion Membership
Awarded to institute members (over 40 years of age) who are considered to have substantially advanced the general interests of the textile industry. Established in 1956 and limited to 50 living members worldwide.

• 7263 • Development Award
To recognize individuals, groups, or organizations for outstanding achievements in enhancing international textile interests through commerce or marketing or economic development. Established in 1990.

• 7264 • Holden Medal
In recognition of an outstanding contribution to education for, or to the technology of, the apparel sector. Established in 1981.

• 7265 • Honorary Fellow
This, the highest honor within the Institute, is given for recognition of creativity and the advancement of knowledge achieved by an indi-

Awards are arranged in alphabetical order below their administering organizations

vidual as a result of ingenuity and application over many years. It covers all occupational areas of the Institute's work, including science, technology, marketing and management. Established in 1928.

• 7266 • Honorary Life Member
This, the highest award granted for service to the Institute, is given to recognize exceptional and sustained service to the Institute in the furtherance of its Charter objectives and to the textile industry in general. Established in 1979.

• 7267 • Institute Medal
For recognition of distinguished services to the textile industry in general, and to the Institute. Established in 1921.

• 7268 • Institute Medal for Design
To recognize professional designers or groups of designers who have devoted themselves to, and made significant contributions in the field of textile design or design management or both. Aesthetic appeal and commercial success are both taken into account. Established in 1971.

• 7269 • Jubilee Award
For recognition of successful research and invention by teams or groups of researchers working within any appropriate organization. Established in 1960 to commemorate the Institute's Golden Jubilee Year.

• 7270 • Lemkin Medal
For recognition of exceptional service to the Institute in the areas of clothing and footwear. Established in 1960.

• 7271 • Service Medal
In recognition of valuable services rendered to the Institute. Established in 1940.

• 7272 • S. G. Smith Memorial Medal
To recognize individuals for contributions to the furtherance of scientific knowledge concerned with the physical and structural properties of fibers, whether such work has been published or not. Established in 1964.

• 7273 • Warner Memorial Medal
To recognize outstanding work in textile science and technology, the results of which have been published, and particularly for work published in the *Journal of the Textile Institute.* Established in 1930.

• 7274 • Weaver's Company Medal and Prize
To recognize outstanding contributions to the weaving sector of the United Kingdom textile industry. Awarded annually. Established in 1979 by Worshipful Company Of Weavers', the oldest of the Livery Companies of the City of London.

• 7275 •
***Time Out* Communications Ltd.**
David Pepper, Mng.Dir.
Universal House
251 Tottenham Court Rd.
London W1T 7AB, United Kingdom
Phone: 44 20 7813 3000
Fax: 44 20 7813 6001
E-mail: davidpepper@timeout.com
Home Page: http://www.timeout.com

• 7276 • Live Awards
For recognition of achievement in the London theatre, dance, and comedy scene. Awards are given in the categories of nightlife, music, theatre, classical music, comedy, and dance. Plaques are awarded annually. Established in 1986. Formerly: *Time Out*/01 - for London Awards.

• 7277 • *Time Out* Eating and Drinking Awards
For recognition of outstanding area restaurants. Winners and runners-up are named annually in two categories: Best Bars and Best Cheap Eats.

• 7278 •
Tunbridge Wells International Young Concert Artists Competition
John Lill, Pres.
PO Box 10
Turnbridge Wells North TN2 5ZQ, United Kingdom
Phone: 44 1892 616844
Fax: 44 1892 616844
E-mail: info@twiyca.org
Home Page: http://www.twiyca.org

• 7279 • Tunbridge Wells International Young Concert Artists Competition
To assist young professional instrumental soloists at the outset of their careers. Candidates must be 28 years of age or younger who are professional musicians or students undertaking advanced studies in preparation for a solo career. In each category - piano, strings, and wind - a first prize (£2,000), second prize (£800), third prize (£400), and fourth prizes (£150 each) are presented. Additional prizes include the Crystal Goblet Award for the best performer overall; the Hans Romney Prize of £100 for the best performer who won no major prize; and the John Bray Accompanist Prize of £400. Held biennially in June of even-numbered years. Established in 1980.

• 7280 •
Tylers' and Bricklayers' Company
Larry Dzledzic, Pres.
Hawthorns
Claygate Ln.
Thames Ditton KT7 0DT, United Kingdom
Phone: 44 20 83390360
E-mail: dama@dama.org
Home Page: http://www.tylersandbricklayers.co.uk

• 7281 • Achievement Award

• 7282 • Better Brickwork Alliance
For an apprentice.

• 7283 • Mark Boxer Award
For services to the industry.

• 7284 •
UK Fashion Exports
Paul Alger, Exec.Dir.
5 Portland Pl.
London W1B 1PW, United Kingdom
Phone: 44 20 76365577
Fax: 44 20 76367848
E-mail: paul.alger@ukfashionexports.com
Home Page: http://www.ukfashionexports.com

• 7285 • UK Fashion Export Awards
Recognizes performance in exporting. Awarded annually. Inquire for application details.

• 7286 •
Ulster Teachers' Union
Avril Hall-Callaghan, Gen.Sec.
94 Malone Rd.
Belfast BT9 5HP, United Kingdom
Phone: 44 28 90662216
Fax: 44 28 90683296
E-mail: office@utu.edu
Home Page: http://www.utu.edu

• 7287 • Honorary Member
Recognizes special services to Northern Ireland education. An honorary membership is awarded periodically.

• 7288 • Honorary Vice President
Recognizes special services to Northern Ireland education. Awarded periodically.

• 7289 •
Union for the International Language Ido (Uniono por la Linguo Internaciona Ido)
David Weston, Sec.
24 Nunn St.
Leek ST13 8EA, United Kingdom
Phone: 44 1538 381491
Home Page: http://www.idolinguo.com

• 7290 • Award of Merit
Recognizes individuals rendering meritorious service to the Ido movement. Awarded periodically.

• 7291 •
United Kingdom Department of Trade and Industry
Sir Brian Bender, Permanent Sec.
1 Victoria St.
London SW1H 0ET, United Kingdom
Phone: 44 20 7215 5000
E-mail: dti.enquiries@dti.gsi.gov.uk
Home Page: http://www.dti.gov.uk

• 7292 • SMART Awards
To provide small firms with the necessary funding to develop innovative ideas that could lead to new products or processes. Individuals or businesses with fewer than 50 employees, located in the United Kingdom are eligible. The competition is divided into two stages. In Stage 1, winners receive 75 percent of the first £60,000 of project costs (maximum award £45,000). The selection criteria include the quality and novelty of the project; the qualifications and experience of the people involved, the significance of the project and its potential commercial benefit to the UK, the means proposed for turning the idea into a commercially successful product or process, and the financial need of the applicant in relation to the project ("Additionality"). Stage 2 is a separate competition open to winners who make satisfactory progress in Stage 1. The Stage 2 competition opens about seven months into Stage 1 and is designed to run on from a 9-15 month project. A Stage 2 Award provides 50 percent of the first £120,000 of project costs (maximum award £60,000). Awarded annually at several presentation ceremonies. Established in 1986. Formerly: (1995) Small Firms Merit Awards for Research and Technology.

• 7293 • SPUR: Support for Products Under Research
To provide help with the development of new products and processes which involve a significant technological advance. Established businesses in Great Britain with up to 250 employees and either an annual turnover not exceeding ECU 20 million or a balance sheet total not exceeding ECU 10 million are eligible. Projects must cost a minimum of £50,000 and be 6 to 36 months duration. The grant is normally 30 percent of the project costs up to a maximum grant of ECU 200,000, but SMART winners may receive a higher percentage grant rate. In addition, for a small number of exceptional projects which have a strategic significance for an industry sector and high R&D costs, there is the possibility of receiving a grant of up to £450,000 under a separate element of the scheme SPUR Plus.

• 7294 •
United Kingdom eInformation Group
Christine Baker, Honorary Sec.
The Old Chapel, Walden
West Burton
Leyburn DL8 4LE, United Kingdom
Phone: 44 1969 663749
Fax: 44 1969 663749
E-mail: cabaker@ukeig.org.uk
Home Page: http://www.ukeig.org.uk

• 7295 • Jason Farradane Award
To an individual or a group of people for outstanding work in the information field.

• 7296 • Tony Kent Strix Award
To individuals or groups for an outstanding contribution to the field of information retrieval.

• 7297 • Lever Pond's Research Fellowship

• 7298 • Student Bursary
To a student studying information management in the UK.

• 7299 • UKeiG Research Award
For small research project in the broad area of electronic information.

• 7300 •
United Kingdom Literacy Association
Lyn Overall, Gen. Sec.
4th Fl., Attenborough Bldg.
Univ. of Leicester
Leicester LE1 7RH, United Kingdom
Phone: 44 0116 2297450
Fax: 44 0116 2997451
E-mail: admin@ukla.org
Home Page: http://www.ukla.org

• 7301 • Children's Book Award

• 7302 • John Downing Award

• 7303 • Literacy Author Award

• 7304 •
Universities Federation for Animal Welfare
The Old School
Brewhouse Hill
Wheathampstead AL4 8AN, United Kingdom
Phone: 44 1582 831818
Fax: 44 1582 831414
E-mail: ufaw@ufaw.org.uk
Home Page: http://www.ufaw.org.uk

• 7305 • Small Project and Travel Awards
To support the benefit of animal welfare, particularly the welfare of farm, companion, laboratory, and captive wild animals as well as free-living wild animals whose welfare is compromised by humans. Applications may be made for the purchase of equipment, for the organisation of (and, sometimes, to support attendance at) educational meetings, lectures and courses, and for publication, translation, or transmission of information on animal welfare and for other small projects in support of UFAW's objectives. Monetary grants of up to £3,500 are awarded annually.

• 7306 • Wild Animal Welfare Award
To recognize innovations that are relevant to improving the welfare of captive wild animals, or that alleviates or prevents anthropogenic (human-induced) harm to animals in the wild. Two awards of £1,000 are presented annually. Established in 1986. Formerly: (2006) Zoo Animal Welfare Award.

• 7307 •
University of Edinburgh
Department of English Literature
David Hume Tower
George Sq.
Edinburgh EH8 9JX, United Kingdom
Phone: 44 131 650 3620
Fax: 44 131 650 6898
E-mail: english.literature@ed.ac.uk
Home Page: http://www.englit.ed.ac.uk/jtbinf.htm

• 7308 • James Tait Black Memorial Prizes
For recognition of the best biography or work of that nature, and the best work of fiction, published during the calendar year. Works of fiction and biographies written in English, originating with a British publisher, and first published in Britain in the 12-month period prior to the submission date are eligible. Two monetary prizes of £10,000 each are awarded annually. Established in 1918 in memory of James Tait Black, a partner in the publishing house of A.C. Black Ltd.

• 7309 •
University of Liverpool
John Charles Latham, COO
12 Abercromby Sq.
PO Box 147
Liverpool L69 3BX, United Kingdom
Phone: 44 151 794 2000
Fax: 44 151 708 6502
Home Page: http://www.liv.ac.uk

• 7310 • John Buchanan Prize in Esperanto
To encourage knowledge and use of Esperanto. Students or graduates of the University of Liverpool or any approved university and teachers in United Kingdom schools may submit an original composition in Esperanto and a translation from English into Esperanto on an announced subject by May 1 each year. A monetary prize of £150 is awarded annually. Established in honor of John Buchanan.

• 7311 • Felicia Hemans Prize for Lyrical Poetry
For recognition of outstanding lyrical poetry. Past and present members and students of the University of Liverpool may submit not more than one published or unpublished poem by May 1. A monetary award of £30 and a commemorative certificate are awarded annually. Established in 1899 in memory of Felicia Hemans, a poet from Liverpool.

• 7312 • Thomas Eric Peet Travelling Prize
To encourage study of Egyptology and prehistory of the Mediterranean lands and the Near East. Graduates of any British university are eligible. A travel prize of approximately £300 is awarded every five years. Established in memory of Thomas Eric Peet, Brunner Professor of Egyptology, 1919-1939.

• 7313 •
University of Oxford
Faculty of Music
Faculty Board Secretary
St. AldateKs
Oxford OX1 1DB, United Kingdom
Phone: 44 1865 276125
Fax: 44 1865 276128
E-mail: judith.philpott@music.ox.ac.uk
Home Page: http://www.music.ox.ac.uk

• 7314 • Donald Tovey Memorial Prize
To provide assistance for research in the philosophy, history, or understanding of music. Men or women without regard to nationality, age, or membership of a university are eligible. A monetary prize is awarded as funds allow.

• 7315 •
University of Sussex Library
Deborah Shorley, Librarian
Brighton BN1 9QL, United Kingdom
Phone: 44 1273 678440
Fax: 44 1273 678441
E-mail: library@sussex.ac.uk
Home Page: http://www.sussex.ac.uk/library

• 7316 • Ralph Lewis Award
To support an approved three-year program of publishing new writing. A monetary prize is awarded periodically. Established in 1984 by a bequest of Ralph Henry Lewis, author and art dealer of Brighton, East Sussex, England.

• 7317 •
Viking Society for Northern Research
Prof. David Ashurst, Asst.Sec.
Univ. Coll. London
Gower St.
University Coll. London
London WC1E 6BT, United Kingdom
Phone: 44 20 76797176
Fax: 44 20 76797755
E-mail: vsnr@ucl.ac.uk
Home Page: http://www.shef.ac.uk/viking-society

• 7318 • Viking Society for Northern Research Awards
For recognition of contributions that promote interest in the literature and antiquities of the Scandinavian North. The Research Support Fund aims to assist in the development of the study of the literature, history, language, and archaeology of early and medieval Scandanavia, including its relationship with other areas and cultures. In addition, the Margaret Orme Prize is awarded to an undergraduate or new graduate student of universities and colleges in the U.K. and Eire (other than Oxford and the University College London) for distinguished contributions to the fields of study appropriate to the SocietyKs interests; recipient receives a five-year membership in the Society and a monetary prize of £50. Awarded annually.

• 7319 •
Voice of the Listener and Viewer
Jocelyn Hay, Hon.Chm.
101 King's Dr.
Kent
Gravesend DA12 5BQ, United Kingdom
Phone: 44 1474 352835
Fax: 44 1474 351112
E-mail: info@vlv.org.uk
Home Page: http://www.vlv.org.uk

• 7320 • Awards for Excellence in Broadcasting
Recognizes the best radio and television program and personalities of the year. Awarded in various categories annually. Formerly: (2004) National Awards.

• 7321 •
Wales Craft Council
Philomena Hearn, Chair
Henfaes Ln.
Powys
Welshpool SY21 7BE, United Kingdom
Phone: 44 1938 555313
Fax: 44 1938 556237
E-mail: info@walescraftcouncil.co.uk
Home Page: http://www.walescraftcouncil.co.uk

• 7322 • Best New Products
A monetary prize is given quarterly for best at show. Inquire for additional information.

• 7323 • Best Stand
A monetary prize is given quarterly for best at show. Inquire for additional information.

• 7324 •
Welsh Books Council
(Cyngor Llyfrau Cymru)
Gwerfyl Pierce Jones, Pres.
Castell Brychan, Ceredigion
Aberystwyth SY23 2JB, United Kingdom
Phone: 44 1970 624151
Fax: 44 1970 625385
E-mail: castellbrychan@wbc.org.uk
Home Page: http://www.wbc.org.uk

Formerly: (1990) Welsh National Centre for Children's Literature.

• 7325 • Gwobrau Tir na n-Og (Tir na n-Og Awards)
To raise the standard of children's and young people's books and to encourage the buying and reading of good books. Three awards of £1,000 each are presented annually: (1) Best English-language book, fiction or non-fiction, with an authentic Welsh background; (2) Best original Welsh-language book aimed at the primary sector; and (3) Best original Welsh-language book aimed at the secondary sector. Established in 1976 by the Welsh Arts Council, the Welsh Joint Education Committee, and the Welsh Youth Libraries Group.

• 7326 • Mary Vaughan Jones Award
For recognition of outstanding services to the field of children's literature in Wales over a period of time. A silver trophy is awarded triennially in November. Established in 1985 in memory of Mary Vaughan Jones, one of the main benefactors of children's literature in Wales for a period of over 30 years.

• 7327 •
Welsh Centre for International Affairs
Stephen Thomas, Dir.
Temple of Peace
Cathays Park
Cardiff CF10 3AP, United Kingdom
Phone: 44 29 20228549
Fax: 44 29 20640333
E-mail: centre@wcia.org.uk
Home Page: http://www.wcia.org.uk

• 7328 • Development Education Grants
For UK-based school work. A monetary prize is given annually.

• 7329 •
Welsh Music Guild
(Urdd Cerddoriaeth Cymru)
John H. Lewis, Hon.Sec.
17 Penyrheol Dr.
Llanelli SA15 3NX, United Kingdom
Phone: 44 1443 730383
E-mail: guild.info@ntlworld.com
Home Page: http://www.welshmusic.org.uk

• 7330 • Tlws y Cerddor (Composers Medal)
A medal is awarded annually to the winner of the national competition.

• 7331 •
Wiener Library
Ben Barkow, Dir.
4 Devonshire St.
London W1W 5BH, United Kingdom
Phone: 44 20 7636 7247
Fax: 44 20 7636 6428
E-mail: info@wienerlibrary.co.uk
Home Page: http://www.wienerlibrary.co.uk

• 7332 • Fraenkel Prize
To recognize the author of an outstanding, unpublished work in contemporary history written in English, French, or German. Possible topics include central European and Jewish history in the 20th century, the Second World War, fascism and totalitarianism, political violence, and racism. Two awards will be granted: a prize of $6,000 is awarded for entries between 50,000 and 150,000 words, and a prize of $4,000 is awarded for entries between 25,000 and 100,000 words. The second prize is open only to entrants who have yet to publish a major work. Awarded annually.

• 7333 •
Wildlife Explorer
% Royal Society for the Protection of Birds
The Lodge
Sandy
Luton SG19 2DL, United Kingdom
Phone: 44 1767 680551
Fax: 44 1767 692365
Home Page: http://www.rspb.org.uk/youth

Formerly: (1995) Young Ornithologists' Club.

• 7334 • **Wildlife Action Awards**
For recognition of action for conservation of birds and other wildlife. Individuals under 19 years of age are eligible. Awards are granted for accomplishing up to 28 tasks in four sections: exploration, helping wildlife, environment, and communication. Gold awards are presented for accomplishing 18 tasks; silver awards for 12 tasks; and bronze awards for 6 tasks. Awarded annually. Established in 1993. Formerly: (1993) Action for Birds Award.

• 7335 •
William Hill plc
Graham Sharpe, Media Relations
Greenside House
50 Station Rd.
Wood Green
London N22 7TP, United Kingdom
Phone: 44 208 918 3600
Fax: 44 113 291 2007
E-mail: gsharpe@williamhill.co.uk
Home Page: http://www.williamhillplc.co.uk

• 7336 • **William Hill Sports Book of the Year**
To honor the best sports book of the year in the United Kingdom. Books published in the United Kingdom during the previous calendar year are eligible. A monetary prize of £16,000, a free £2,000 bet, and a leather bound book are awarded annually. Established in 1989.

• 7337 •
William Morris Society
Helen Elletson, Curator
Kelmscott House
26 Upper Mall
Hammersmith
London W6 9TA, United Kingdom
Phone: 44 20 87413735
Fax: 44 20 87485207
E-mail: uk@morrissociety.org
Home Page: http://www.morrissociety.org

• 7338 • **Peter Floud Award**
Recognizes a work in progress on a Morris subject. A monetary award is given biennially.

• 7339 •
Wolfson Foundation
8 Queen Anne St.
London W1G 9LD, United Kingdom
Phone: 44 20 7323 5730
Fax: 44 20 7323 3241
Home Page: http://www.wolfson.org.uk

• 7340 • **Wolfson History Awards**
To promote and encourage standards of excellence in the writing of history for the general public. Books published in the United Kingdom during the year are eligible. Two prizes are awarded annually, with an occasional ouevre prize given for an individualKs distinguished contribution to the writing of history. Established in 1972.

• 7341 •
Women in Publishing
Bridget Clark, Membership Sec.
PO Box 46816
London SW11 3XL, United Kingdom
Phone: 44 7956 402408
E-mail: info@wipub.org.uk
Home Page: http://www.wipub.org.uk

• 7342 • **New Venture Award**
Recognizes a pioneering woman or group of women who have embarked on a venture whose aim is to highlight the work and lives of underrepresented groups of society. An engraved silver letter opener or pen is awarded annually. Established in 1987

• 7343 • **Pandora Award**
Recognizes the promotion of positive images of women in publishing, bookselling and related trades. Individuals or organizations are eligible. A writing box which is passed on from winner to winner is awarded annually. Established in 1981.

• 7344 •
Women's Engineering Society
Cathy MacGillivray, Sec.
22 Old Queen St.
London SW1H 9HP, United Kingdom
Phone: 44 20 72331974
Fax: 44 20 72331973
E-mail: info@wes.org.uk
Home Page: http://www.wes.org.uk

• 7345 • **Bursaries**
For students, unwaged or low-waged women to attend the society's conferences. Monetary awards are given annually.

• 7346 • **Karen Burt Award**
For newly chartered outstanding woman engineers. Awarded periodically.

• 7347 • **Lady Finniston Award**
For women students facing extreme hardship due to lack of funds. Monetary awards are given periodically.

• 7348 •
Workers' Music Association
Aubrey Bowman, Pres.
12 St. Andrews Sq.
London W11 1RH, United Kingdom
Phone: 44 20 72430920
Home Page: http://www.workersmusic.co.uk

• 7349 • **John Horrocks Scholarship**
Awarded to summer school students through political and musical activity. Awarded annually.

• 7350 •
World Association of Christian Radio Amateurs and Listeners
(Association Mondiale des Radio-Amateurs et des Radioclubs Chretiens)
Shirley Jackson, Gen.Sec.
10 Grosvenor Ave.
West Yorkshire
Pontefract WF8 4QU, United Kingdom
Phone: 44 1977 705395
E-mail: cswl1199@wacral.org
Home Page: http://www.wacral.org

• 7351 • **World Association of Christian Radio Amateurs and Listeners Awards**
For recognition of individuals achieving contacts over the air with WACRAL members. Proof of contact is required. The following awards are presented: basic award - for contact with 10 members; bronze award - for contact with 25 members; silver award - for contact with 35 members; gold award - for contact with 70 members; and Heavenly Pilots - for contact with five Ministers. Plaques are presented. Established in 1968 in memory of the founder, Rev. Arthur W. Shepherd, C3NGF.

• 7352 •
World Association of Detectives
Richard D. Jacques-Turner, Exec.Dir.
PO Box 333
Brough HU15 1XL, United Kingdom
Phone: 44 1482 665577
Fax: 44 870 8310957
E-mail: wad@wad.net
Home Page: http://www.wad.net

• 7353 • **Investigator of the Year**
To recognize an individual who has demonstrated outstanding professional service in the calendar year. Awarded annually.

• 7354 • **Hal Lipset "Truth in Action" Award**
To recognize a non-member for distinguished service and contribution to the profession of private investigation, private security, or law enforcement. Awarded annually.

• 7355 • **Security Professional of the Year**
To recognize individuals who have demonstrated outstanding professional service in the calendar year. Awarded annually.

• 7356 • **Norman J. Sloan Memorial Award**
This, the AssociationKs highest honor, is awarded to a member who has contributed an exceptional amount of his or her time, energy, and effort to the betterment of the investigative or security professions. Awarded annually.

• 7357 •
World Association of Girl Guides and Girl Scouts
(Asociacion Mundial de las Guias Scouts)
Leslie Bulman, Chief Exec.
Olave Centre World Bureau
12c Lyndhurst Rd.
London NW3 5PQ, United Kingdom
Phone: 44 20 77941181
Fax: 44 20 74313764
E-mail: waggs@wagggsworld.org
Home Page: http://www.wagggsworld.org

• 7358 • **FAO-WAGGGS Nutrition Award**
Periodic award of recognition for groups organizing successful projects which enhance nutritional understanding.

• 7359 • **Olave Award**
Periodic award of recognition for groups.

• 7360 • **Wagggs Medal**
Award of recognition.

• 7361 • **Women of Outstanding Achievement**
Periodic award of recognition. Awarded to one woman from each region every three years.

• 7362 • **Young Woman of the Region**
Award of recognition for five young women once every three years.

• 7363 •
World Confederation for Physical Therapy
(Confederation Mondiale pour la Therapie Physique)
Ms. B.J. Myers, Sec.Gen.
Kensington Charity Centre
4th Fl.
Charles House
London W14 8QH, United Kingdom
E-mail: info@wcpt.org
Home Page: http://www.wcpt.org

• 7364 • **Mildred Elson Award**
To honor an individual for significant contributions to the development of physical therapy on an international basis through his or her efforts, dedication, and leadership. A plaque is awarded every four years at the International Congress. Established in 1987 by the American Physical Therapy Association in honor of Mildred Elson, first president of the Confederation.

• 7365 •
World Curling Federation
Mike Thomson, Sec.Gen.
74 Tay St.
Perth PH2 8NN, United Kingdom
Phone: 44 1738 451630
Fax: 44 1738 451641
E-mail: wcf@dial.pipex.net
Home Page: http://www.worldcurling.org

• 7366 • **World Curling Freytag Award**
Recognizes outstanding services to world curling. Awarded annually.

• 7367 •
World Dance and Dance Sport Council
(Conseil Mondiale pour la Danse de Salon et la Danse Sportive)
Mrs. P. Hines, Contact
7-8 Albert Rd.
Silvertown
South Wimbledon
London E16 2DW, United Kingdom
Phone: 44 208 5450223
Fax: 44 208 5449825
E-mail: wddscoffice@btclick.com
Home Page: http://www.wddsc.com

Formerly: International Council of Ballroom Dancing.

• 7368 • **World Championships in Ballroom and Latin Dancing**
For recognition of outstanding ballroom and Latin dancing.

• 7369 •
World Federation for Culture Collections
Dr. David Smith, Pres.
CABI Bioscience UK Ctre.
Bakeham Ln.
Egham
Surrey TW20 9TY, United Kingdom
Phone: 44 1491 829046
Phone: 44 2 2383713
Fax: 44 1491 829100
E-mail: d.smith@cabi.org
Home Page: http://www.wfcc.info

• 7370 • **Skerman Award for Microbial Taxonomy**
For recognition of a contribution by a young microbial taxonomist. Individuals under 40 years of age are eligible. A monetary prize and travel expenses are awarded every four years at the Congress of the Federation. Established in 1988 in honor of Prof. V.B.D. Skerman.

• 7371 •
World Federation of Neurology
Dr. Jun Kimura MD, Pres.
12 Chandos St.
London W1G 9DR, United Kingdom
Phone: 44 207 3234011
Fax: 44 207 3234012
E-mail: wfnlondon@aol.com
Home Page: http://www.wfneurology.org

• 7372 • **Junior Travelling Fellowship**
Recognizes a junior neurologists from developing countries. A monetary award is given annually.

• 7373 •
World Jersey Cattle Bureau
Suzanne Le Feuvre, Sec.
Royal Jersey Showground
La Rte. de la Trinite
Jersey JE3 5JP, United Kingdom
Phone: 44 1534 862327
Phone: 44 1534 860968
Fax: 44 1534 865619
E-mail: avonteur@localdial.com
Home Page: http://www.worldjerseycattle.com

• 7374 • **Distinguished Service Award**
Recognizes an individual who has made major contribution to the Jersey breed. Awarded periodically.

• 7375 •
World Petroleum Council - The Global Forum for Oil and Gas Science, Technology, Economics and Management
(Congres Mondiaux du Petrole)
Dr. Pierce Riemer, Dir.Gen.
1 Duchess St., 4th Fl., Ste. 1
London W1N 3DE, United Kingdom
Phone: 44 20 76374958
Fax: 44 20 76374965
E-mail: pierce@world-petroleum.org
Home Page: http://www.world-petroleum.org

• 7376 • **Dewhurst Lecture and Award**
Recognizes distinction in the industry. Awarded triennially.

• 7377 • **Excellence Awards**
To distinguish companies, institutions, or any public or private organization engaged in the oil and gas industry for promoting or operating with high excellence standards in two categories: Technological Development and Social Responsibility. Presented triennially.

• 7378 •
World Ship Trust - United Kingdom
Hon. Lord Greenway, Chm.
202 Lambeth Rd.
London SE1 7JW, United Kingdom
Phone: 44 207 3854267
Fax: 44 207 3854267
E-mail: worldship@lynnmallet.demon.co.uk
Home Page: http://www.worldshiptrust.org

• 7379 • **International Maritime Heritage Award**
To recognize and encourage especially meritorious ship preservation achievements on a worldwide basis. A medal is awarded at the discretion of the Trustees when merited. Established in 1980.

• 7380 •
World's Poultry Science Association
Dr. Paul M. Hocking, Pres.
Bradfield St. Clare
Bury St. Edmunds
Suffolk IP30 0EQ, United Kingdom
Phone: 44 01284 386520
Fax: 44 01284 386520
E-mail: parsonbury@hotmail.com
Home Page: http://www.wpsa-uk.com

• 7381 • **Macdougall Medal**
To recognize individuals for outstanding services to the Association. Any member of the WPSA is eligible. A gold medal is awarded intermittently by a decision of the Council of WPSA. Established in 1962 in memory of Major I. Macdougall.

• 7382 •
Worshipful Company of Glaziers' and Painters of Glass
David Eking, Clerk
The Glazier's Co.
9 Montague Close
London Bridge
London SE1 9DD, United Kingdom
Phone: 44 20 74033300
Phone: 44 20 74036652
Fax: 44 20 74036652
E-mail: info@worshipfulglaziers.com
Home Page: http://www.worshipfulglaziers.com

• 7383 • **Award For Excellence**
For student or craftsperson involved in stained glass.

• 7384 • **Ashton Hill Awards**
For student or craftsperson involved in conservation of stained glass.

• 7385 • **Stevens Competition**
For student or craftsperson involved in stained glass, age 30 or under.

• 7386 •
Worshipful Company of Scientific Instrument Makers
Neville Watson, Clerk
9 Montague Close
London SE1 9DD, United Kingdom
Phone: 44 20 74074832
Fax: 44 20 74071565
E-mail: theclerk@wcsim.co.uk
Home Page: http://www.wcsim.co.uk

• 7387 • **Sim Awards**
Annual awards of recognition. Awards are given in the forms of scholarships, bursaries, achievement.

• 7388 •
Worshipful Society of Apothecaries of London
Maj.Gen. Alan Hawley, Pres.
Apothecaries Hall
Black Friars Ln.
London EC4V 6EJ, United Kingdom
Phone: 44 20 8236 1180
Fax: 44 20 8329 3177
E-mail: clerk@apothecaries.org
Home Page: http://www.apothecaries.org

• 7389 • **Galen Medal**
This, the Society's highest honor, is given for recognition of outstanding contributions in the field of therapeutics. Individuals may be nominated by members of the Society's governing body. A medal is awarded annually. Established in 1925.

• 7390 •
Yachting Journalists' Association
Mr. Tom Willis, Membership Sec.-Treas.
22 St. Johns Rd.
Church Ln.
Arundel
Woking GU21 7SA, United Kingdom
Phone: 44 1483 751506
Fax: 44 1243 751021
E-mail: tom@yja.co.uk
Home Page: http://www.yja.co.uk

Formerly: Guild of Yachting Writers.

• 7391 • **Yachtsman of the Year Award**
For recognition of achievement in the field of boating by a British citizen during the previous year. Nominations may be made by anyone, but are shortlisted by members belonging to the Association. The entire Association votes for the final winner. The trophy, a silver navigation buoy on a sea of crystal, is awarded annually, as well as a keepsake replica for the winner. Established in 1955 by Sir Max Aitken.

• 7392 • **Young Sailor of the Year Award**
To recognize endeavor and achievement by young sailors. Open to young sailors who are under 18 years of age before December 31 of the award year and who have a British passport or are immediately eligible to receive a British passport. Nominations may be submitted by members of each of the Royal Yachting Association's 13 regions which submit one candidate each, the regional winner. The entire association votes for the final winner. A trophy, held for one year by the recipient, and cash prizes are awarded for the final three competitors. Cash prizes are held in trust by the RYA for the winners to use for approved sailing-related expenses. Awarded annually. Established in 1993.

• 7393 •
Young Concert Artists Trust
Rosemary Pickering, Chief Exec.
23 Garrick St.
London WC2E 9BN, United Kingdom
Phone: 44 20 7379 8477
Fax: 44 20 7379 8467
E-mail: info@ycat.co.uk
Home Page: http://www.ycat.co.uk

• 7394 • **Young Concert Artists Trust Award**
To recognize outstanding young musicians (instrumentalists and singers), and to promote their careers until they are established with a recognized commercial agent. Auditions are open to all instruments, but the categories vary each year. The applicants must be under 29 years for instrumentalists; under 31 for singers; and be British citizens or resident in the United Kingdom. The deadline for applications is in early February. Management services and promotion of career are awarded annually. Established in 1983 by W. H. Smith and Son, the founding sponsor. Supported by numerous trusts and foundations.

• 7395 •
Zoological Society of London
Prof. Patrick Bateson FRS, Pres.
Regent's Park
London NW1 4RY, United Kingdom
Phone: 44 20 77223333
Fax: 44 20 75865743
E-mail: enquiries@ioz.ac.uk
Home Page: http://www.zsl.org

• 7396 • **Frink Medal for British Zoologists**
To recognize professional zoologists who have made substantial and original contributions to the advancement of zoology. British citizens who are residents of the United Kingdom and whose work is based there may be nominated. A bronze medal designed by Elisabeth Frink is awarded annually when merited. Established in 1973.

• 7397 • **Thomas Henry Huxley Award**
To recognize postgraduate research students for original work in zoology. Postgraduate students attending a university in Great Britain or Northern Ireland who were awarded the Doctor of Philosophy degree during the preceding year may be nominated. A bronze medal and a sum of money are awarded annually when merited; a certificate may be awarded as an honorable mention. Established in 1961.

• 7398 • **Marsh Award for Conservation Biology**
To recognize contributions of fundamental science and its application to the conservation of animal species and habitats. A certificate and a sum of money are awarded annually when merited. Established in 1992.

Awards are arranged in alphabetical order below their administering organizations

• 7399 • Prince Philip Prize
To recognize students for an account of practical work involving some aspect of animal biology. Pupils of schools in Great Britain, Northern Ireland, the Channel Isles, and the Isle of Man who are under 19 years of age are eligible. A bronze medal and a certificate are awarded annually when merited. The winner's school will also receive an award of money to be used in promoting the teaching of animal biology. Prizes of books or a certificate may also be awarded as honorable mentions. Awarded annually. Established in 1961.

• 7400 • Stamford Raffles Award
To recognize amateur zoologists who have made distinguished contributions to zoology or to recognize professional zoologists who have made contributions outside the scope of their professional activities and principal specialization. Nominations are accepted. A bronze sculpture by Anita Mandl is awarded annually when merited. Established in 1961.

• 7401 • Scientific Medal
For recognition of distinguished work in zoology. Men and women under 40 years of age may be nominated. Up to three silver medals may be awarded each year. Established in 1938.

• 7402 • Silver Medal
To recognize persons who have contributed to the understanding and appreciation of zoology. Selection is based on such activities as public education in natural history and wildlife conservation. A silver medal is awarded periodically when merited. Nominations are requested annually. Established in 1837 and first awarded in 1847.

Uruguay

• 7403 •
International Council for Adult Education (Conseil International d'Education des Adultes)
Paul Belanger, Pres.
2069 Colonia
11200 Montevideo, Uruguay
Phone: 598 2 4010006
Fax: 598 2 4010006
E-mail: secretariat@icae.org.uy
Home Page: http://www.icae.org.uy

• 7404 • Dame Nita Barrow Award
To recognize and support regional or national adult education organizations who have made a significant contribution towards the empowerment of women in the adult education movement. All ICAE member organizations are eligible to apply. The organization must demonstrate that women's active participation has increased in leadership and decision-making roles and planning and policy advisory positions. The organization must also show that it has promoted the discussion of gender issues and their participating social movements, and included gender issues in all aspects of the organization and on agenda and programs. A monetary award of $2,000 Canadian is granted annually. Established in 1990 to honor Nita Barrow for her long-time service as President of the ICAE, her commitment to the international adult education movement, and her firm support of women's full and equal participation in organizational and global issues.

• 7405 • Nabila Breir Award
For recognition of women's organizations engaged in innovative educational programming or projects for Palestinian women. The objectives of the award are: to support women's educational programs aimed at enhancing the socioeconomic development of Palestinian communities, and the quality of life and self-sufficiency of women in particular; to provide opportunities for Palestinian women grassroots educators to exchange educational experiences with women educators from other regions; and to provide opportunities for participation in ICAE's regional and international workshops, seminars, and conferences for Palestinian women educators. A monetary prize of $2,000 Canadian is awarded annually. Established in 1987 in memory of Nabila Breir, an active member of ICAE women's program who was murdered in Beirut at the age of 42.

• 7406 • J. Roby Kidd Award
To recognize an individual or individuals who have made a particularly significant contribution to adult education at the local or national level. In particular, the aim of the award is to recognize and encourage innovative contributions of women and men, practitioners of whatever age, who could be considered as recent practitioners in adult education and thus carry out Roby Kidd's interest in attracting new people with new ideas. Individuals of any nationality, religion, race, sex, or age are eligible. A monetary award of $2,000 Canadian is granted annually. Established in memory or Roby Kidd, a pioneer in the field of adult education and founding Secretary-General of the ICAE.

Vanuatu

• 7407 •
National Spiritual Assembly of the Baha'is of Vanuatu
Charles Pierce, Sec.
PO Box 1017
Port Vila, Vanuatu
Phone: 678 22419
Fax: 678 25419
E-mail: nsavanuatu@vanuatu.com.vu
Home Page: http://www.bahai.org

• 7408 • Bertha Dobbins Award for Community Service
Annual award of recognition. Persons, groups, or organizations that have rendered significant service to the local community during the previous year are eligible. Awarded annually.

Vatican City

• 7409 •
Pontifical Academy of Sciences (Pontifica Academia delle Scienze)
Marcelo Sanchez Sorondo, Chancellor
Casina Pio IV
V-00120 Vatican City, Vatican City
Phone: 39 6 69883195
Phone: 39 6 69885416
Fax: 39 6 69885218
E-mail: academy.sciences@acdscience.va

• 7410 • Pius XI Medal
To recognize a young scientist who has distinguished himself or herself at an international level through scientific achievements. Awarded biennially. Established in 1961 by John XXIII.

• 7411 •
The Vatican
Papal Secretariat of State
I-00120 Vatican City, Vatican City
Home Page: http://www.vatican.va

• 7412 • Benemerenti Medal
To recognize a well deserving person for exceptional accomplishment and service. Men and women are eligible. Medals of gold, silver or bronze, bearing the likeness of the reigning Pope on one side and a laurel crown and the letter B on the other, are conferred by the Pope.

• 7413 • Order of Pius
For recognition of outstanding service to the Church and society. Four classes of knighthood may be awarded: (1) the Class of the Grand Collar; (2) Knights of the Grand Cross; (3) Knights of the Second Class; and (4) Commander and Knights of the Third Class. Christian or non-Christian heads of state are eligible. Membership is determined by the Pope. Pontifical Orders of Knighthood are awarded. Founded in 1847, and restricted to heads of state in 1966 by Paul VI.

• 7414 • Order of St. Gregory the Great
To recognize people who are distinguished for personal character and reputation, and for notable accomplishment. This secular honor of merit has civic and military divisions. Membership is determined by the Pope. Pontifical Orders of Knighthood are awarded. Established in 1831.

• 7415 • Order of St. Sylvester
For recognition of outstanding service to the Church. A secular honor of merit, formerly a part of the Order of the Golden Spur, is now awarded separately with three possible degrees: (1) Knights of the Grand Cross; (2) Knight Commanders, with or without emblem; and (3) Knights. Membership is determined by the Pope. Pontifical Orders of Knighthood are awarded. Established in 1841 by Gregory XVI and redefined in 1905 by Pius X.

• 7416 • Order of the Golden Spur (Golden Militia)
To recognize Christian heads of state. This secular honor of merit is one of the oldest knighthoods. The award was restricted in 1966 by Paul VI to Christian heads of state. Membership is determined by the Pope. Pontifical Orders of Knighthood are awarded. Established in 1841 by Gregory XVI as the Order of St. Sylvester. In 1905, Pius X restored the Order of the Golden Spur, separating it from the Order of Sylvester.

• 7417 • Pro Ecclesia et Pontifice Medal
For recognition of outstanding service to the Church and the papacy. Men and women are eligible. A gold medal with the likeness of Leo XIII is awarded. Established in 1888.

• 7418 • Supreme Order of Christ (Militia of Our Lord Jesus Christ)
For recognition of a Christian head of state. A secular honor of merit, originally meant to continue the suppressed Order of Templars in Portugal during the 14th and 15th centuries, this Order is now restricted to Christian heads of state. Membership in this highest and most exclusive Pontifical Order of Knighthood is determined by the Pope. Founded in 1319, and restricted to heads of state in 1966 by Paul VI.

• 7419 •
World Federation of Catholic Medical Associations
(Federation Internationale des Associations Medicales Catholiques)
Mrs. Isabelle Biondi, Exec.Dir.
Palazzo San Calisto
V-00120 Vatican City, Vatican City
Phone: 39 6 69887372
Fax: 39 6 69887372
E-mail: fiamc.va@virgilio.it
Home Page: http://www.fiamc.org

• 7420 • Pope John XXI Prize
To encourage original work in Catholic medical ethics. Medical practitioners of any nationality are eligible. A monetary prize and a medal are awarded every four years. Established in 1950 by the Portuguese Catholic doctors organization in memory of Pope John XXI, a Portuguese physician who wrote medical treatises and books.

Venezuela

• 7421 •
Academy of Physical, Mathematical and Natural Sciences
(Academia de Ciencias Fisicas, Matematicas y Naturales)
Claudio Bifano, Pres./Chm.
Palacio de las Academias
Bolsa a San Francisco
Apartado Postal No. 1421
Caracas 1010-A, Venezuela
Phone: 58 212 4822954
Phone: 58 212 4827513
Fax: 58 212 4846611
E-mail: info@acfiman.org.ve
Home Page: http://www.acfiman.org.ve

• 7422 • Juan Alberto Olivares' Foundation Award
To Venezuelan or foreign scientists.

• 7423 • Arnoldo Gabaldon Award
For Venezuelan scientists not older than 40 years of age.

• 7424 • Yearly Research Award
For scientists or technicians who represent a real and significant contribution to universal knowledge.

• 7425 •
National Council for Scientific and Technological Research
(Consejo Nacional de Investigaciones Cientificas y Tecnologicas - CONICIT)
Apartado 70617
Los Ruices
Caracas, Venezuela
Fax: 58 2 398677
E-mail: conicit@conicit.gov.ve

• 7426 • Annual Prize for Scientific Works
(Premios Anuales a los Mejores Trabajos Cientificos)
For recognition of outstanding work in scientific research in biology, medicine, physics, chemistry, mathematics, engineering, and social sciences. An indivisible monetary prize and a certificate are awarded annually in each of three categories: technological investigation, natural sciences, and social sciences.

• 7427 • National Prize of Science and Technology
(Premio Nacional de Ciencia)
For recognition of outstanding scientific research, both national and international in scope. Awarded annually. Established in 1978 by the Council.

• 7428 • Luis Zambrano National Prize for Inventive Technology
(Premio Luis Zambrano a la Inventiva Tecnologica Nacional)
To recognize scientists who promote the development of technology through invention rather than research. A monetary prize is awarded annually. Established in 1984.

Zimbabwe

• 7429 •
Computer Society of Zimbabwe
G.R. Fairall, Exec.Dir.
PO Box CY164
6 Baines Ave.
Causeway
Harare, Zimbabwe
Phone: 263 4 250489
Phone: 263 4 250490
Fax: 263 4 708861
E-mail: info@csz.org.zw
Home Page: http://www.csz.org.zw

• 7430 • J. F. Carlisle Award
Recognizes the best industry-related paper. Applicants must be association members. Awarded annually.

• 7431 • The G. R. Fairall Award
For the most outstanding contribution in the promotion of information technology to young people in Zimbabwe, not necessarily by a CSZ member.

• 7432 • PC World Award
For the best delivered paper at the annual CSZ Bulawayo Chapter seminar, not necessarily by a CSZ member. A trophy is awarded annually.

• 7433 • Jean van Vught Award
For the best delivered paper at the annual CSZ Summer school, not necessarily by a CSZ member. Awarded annually. Established in 1990.

• 7434 •
Geological Society of Zimbabwe
David Love, Sec.
PO Box CY1719
Causeway
Harare, Zimbabwe
Phone: 263 4 303211
Fax: 263 4 303557
E-mail: kevin@geology.uz.zw
Home Page: http://www.mining.co.zw/GSZ.htm

• 7435 • Phaup Award
Recognizes the author(s) of the best paper on Zimbabwean geology. Awarded annually.

• 7436 •
National Arts Council of Zimbabwe
Titus Chipangura, Dir.
Education Service Centre, 2nd Fl., East Wing
Box UA463
Union Ave.
Harare, Zimbabwe
Phone: 263 4 304 510
Fax: 263 4 304 510
E-mail: natarts@zol.co.zw
Home Page: http://www.natartszim.co.zw

• 7437 • National Arts Merit Awards
To recognize and reward talent and excellence in the fields of art and culture in Zimbabwe, and to those individuals, groups, or institutions who have spearheaded the growth of the arts and cultural sector before and after Zimbabwe's national independence. The Awards, also known as the Special Jubilee Awards, are presented in various arts disciplines that include film and television, theatre, dance, music, visual, and literary arts. Awarded annually. Established in 2002.

• 7438 •
Wildlife and Environment Zimbabwe
Jerry Gotora, Pres.
PO Box HG 966
Highlands
Harare, Zimbabwe
Phone: 263 4 747500
Phone: 263 4 747684
Fax: 263 4 747174
E-mail: zimwild@mweb.co.zw
Home Page: http://www.zimwild.co.zw

• 7439 • **Wildlife and Environment Zimbabwe Competitions**
To recognize groups and individuals united to preserve wildlife in Zimbabwe, and to encourage all Zimbabweans to take an active interest in conservation through increased public awareness and use of available conservation educational facilities, the Society sponsors an annual wildlife photography competition and an annual environmental quiz for school-age children. The Society presents four prestigious conservation awards annually to individuals and institutions.

• 7440 •
Zimbabwe Institution of Engineers
J.C. Johnston, CEO
Conquenar House
256 Samora Machel Ave. E
Harare, Zimbabwe
Phone: 263 4 746821
Fax: 263 4 746652
E-mail: zie@zarnet.ac.zw
Home Page: http://www.zie.org.zw

• 7441 • **Engineering Achievement Award**
To provide public recognition of noteworthy engineering achievements in Zimbabwe with the two-fold aim of challenging and encouraging engineers to strive for professional excellence, and drawing public attention to the contribution the engineering profession makes to the quality of life. Nominees do not have to be members of this Institution but the submission must be by a member of the Zimbabwe Institution of Engineers. Nominations for achievements in every branch of engineering and in such fields as research, invention, construction or design, amongst others may be submitted by March 31. A certificate and an inscribed plaque are awarded.

• 7442 • **P. H. Haviland Award**
To recognize an individual who has made an outstanding contribution in the field of water engineering, irrigation, or the prevention of water pollution and allied fields. Such contribution may be either in engineering or in administration and may arise from outstanding work in a person's field of employment. The award consists of a plaque, framed in wood, and a check in the value of $100.

• 7443 • **President's Commendation**
For original paper and/or article in specialized field whose criteria is not covered by other awards. Awarded annually.

• 7444 • **SKF Award**
For recognition of a service to engineering, noteworthy achievements, or unpaid social or public service. Members of any grade of the Institution are eligible for nomination by March 31. A monetary prize of $500 is awarded annually. Established in 1982 in honor of Wingquist. Formerly: (1996) Wingquist Award.

• 7445 • **K. G. Stevens Award**
To encourage the presentation of papers of outstanding merit. Corporate members of the Institution and Editorial Committee may make nominations by April 30. A monetary prize of $200 and a bookplate are awarded annually. Established in 1981 in honor of K.G. Stevens. Sponsored by K.G. Stevens Trust.

• 7446 •
Zimbabwe Scientific Association
Dr. L. Mhlanga, Pres.
PO Box CY124, Causeway
Harare, Zimbabwe
Phone: 263 4 335143
E-mail: husseiny@ecoweb.co.zw
Home Page: http://www.zarnet.ac.zw/zsa

• 7447 • **Honorary Fellow**
To recognize individuals who have actively contributed to the advancement of science in Zimbabwe. Persons of high standing who may or may not be members of the Association are eligible for nomination. A certificate and lifetime membership are awarded annually when merited. Established in 1968.

Subject Index of Awards

The Subject Index of Awards classifies all awards described in this volume by their principal areas of interest. The index contains some 400 subject headings, and each award is indexed under all relevant headings. The index also contains *see* and *see also* references. Awards are arranged alphabetically under each subject heading. Identically named awards are followed by an indented alphabetical list of the organizations administering an award by that name. The numbers following award and organization names are book entry numbers, not page numbers.

Academic achievement (*See also* Professional and personal achievement)
AGC/GVS Fellowship 6701
Benefactors Prize 6142
Eden Travelling Fellowship in Obstetrics and Gynaecology 6705
Fulbright Awards - American Program 130
Fulbright Awards - Australian Program 131
Gran Cruz de la Universidad del Valle 1199
Herbert-Kind-Preis der ETG 2102
La Medaille Laplace 1583
Masson Memorial Scholarship Prize 621
Azusa Ono Memorial Awards 3349
Postgraduate Prize 5376
Prix de l'Ecole Centrale 1607
Prix L. E. Rivot 1618
Willi Studer Preis 4903

Accounting
Annual Report Awards 3726
David Bogie Prize 6002
J. C. Burleigh Prize 6003
Business Leader Awards 4323
Canadian Institute of Chartered Accountants Prize 6004
Chartered Accountant of the Year 3727
Walid Chorbachi Prizes 6005
James M. Cowie Prize 6006
Charles Duly Award 6036
Education Award 29
Graduate and Student Prize 5128
Guthrie Prize 6007
John Herbert Award 5129
Peter Hook Award 6037
Institute of Chartered Accountants of Scotland Gold Medal 6008
Institute of Financial Accountants Awards 6031
Tony Jarvis Award 5130
Jorg Kandutsch Preis 809
Management Accounting Award 3925
John Mann Prize 6009
Manuscript Award 30
Robert McArthur Prize 6010
Sir William McLintock Prize 6011
Meritorious Service Award 481
JJ Morris Award 6038
Forbes Murphy Prize 6012
Pates Prize 5131
PhD Scholarships 31
Practice Award 32
President's Prize 482
Research Award 33
John Munn Ross Prize 6013
Primrose Scott Prize 6014
Helen Sommerville Prize 6015
Elmer B. Staats Award 810
Volunteer of the Year Award 6039
Albert J. Watson Prize 6016
C. J. Weir Prize 6017
The Ronald Williamson Prize 6018

Acoustics
Prix Chavasse 1979
Prix Philips 1980
President's Prize 128
Prix et Medailles de la SFA 1981
Rayleigh Medal 5985
Prix Yves Rocard 1982
Prix Thomson Sintra 1983
Stephens Lecture 5986
Tyndall Medal 5987
A. B. Wood Medal and Prize 5988

Actuary *See* Insurance

Administration *See* Management

Adoption *See* Family relations

Adult and continuing education
Dame Nita Barrow Award 7404
Nabila Breir Award 7405
Adolf Grimme Preis 2150
J. Roby Kidd Award 7406
Nehru Literacy Award 2589
Wurdigungspreis fur Erwadisenenbieolung des Landes Tirol 752

Advertising (*See also* Marketing; Public relations; Publicity)
Creative Excellence in Business Advertising Awards 4415
Dentsu Advertising Awards 3179
Effectiveness Awards 6074
EuroBest Awards 5803
Yoshida Hideo Memorial Award 3265
International Advertising Festival, Cannes 6202
National Business Calendar Awards 5421
National Prize for Advertising 756
Premio Nacional 3433
Shark Awards, the International Advertising Festival of Ireland 2887

Aeronautical engineering
International Society of Aircraft Traders (ISTAT) Scholarship 6248
Henry Mignet Diploma 4740
National Aeronautical Prize 2526
Frank Radcliffe Travelling Fellowship in Reliability and Quality Assurance 6652
W.E. Sansum Medal 529
Silver Turnbuckle Award 6655
George Taylor (of Australia) Prize 6658
Whittle Safety Award 6249

Aeronautics and aviation (*See also* Aeronautical engineering; Aviation safety; Flying; Helicopters)
AAHS Trophy (American Aviation Historical Society) 5008
Air League Challenge Trophy 5010
Air League Founders' Medal 5011
Air League Gold Medal 5012
Airwork Cup 3838
Leon Biancotto Aerobatics Diploma 4720
Louis Bleriot Medal 4721
British Gold Medal 6632
British Silver Medal 6633
John Britten Prize 6634
Bronze Medal
Federation Aeronautique Internationale 4722
Royal Aeronautical Society - United Kingdom 6635
Sir Vernon Brown Prize 6636
Busk Prize 6637
CAA Trophy 3843
Colibri Microlight Diploma 4723
Cory - Wright Cup 3844
De La Vaulx Medal 4725
Diploma for Outstanding Airmanship 4726
Excellence in Aerospace Education 2522
Flight Simulation Silver Medal 6639
Dr. V. M. Ghatage Award 2523
Gloucester Navigation Trophy 3846
Gold Air Medal 4728
Len Gore Scholarship 6247
Grand Prix 1712
Hafner VTOL Prize 6641
Sir Robert Hardingham Presidential Sword 6642
Hodgson Prize 6643
Honorary Group Diploma 4733
Indigenisation of Aeronautical Equipment Award 2524
Swarna Jayanti Award 2525
Herbert Le Sueur Award 6646
Charles Lindbergh General Aviation Diploma 4737
Sir Peter Masefield Gold Medal 5236
National Aeronautical Prize 2526
New Zealand Herald Challenge Trophy 3849
North Shore Trophy 3852

Aeronautics (continued)

Alphonse Penaud Aeromodelling Diploma 4744
Phoenix Diploma 4745
Polaris Award 6243
Prix d'Aeronautique 1713
Prix des Jeunes 1715
Production Technology Award 2527
Jeffrey Quill Medal 5013
R38 Memorial Prize 6651
N. E. Rowe Medals 6653
Dr. Biren Roy Memorial Lecture 2711
Dr. Biren Roy Trust Award 2529
Clarence N. Sayen Award 6244
Scott-Farnie Medal 5014
Scroll of Merit 6245
Silver Turnbuckle Award 6655
Simms Prize 6656
Akroyd Stuart Prize 6657
Thulinmedaljen 4689
Paul Tissandier Diploma 4747
B. W. O. Townshend Award 6659
Young FAI Artists Contest 4750

Aerospace (*See also* Aerospace medicine)
Activist of the Year 579
Aeromodelling Gold Medal 4717
Air Sport Medal 4718
Peter Allard Silver Medal 6629
Antonov Aeromodelling Diploma 4719
Book Awards 1865
British Bronze Medal 6631
Prix Edmond Brun 1548
Chapter of the Year 580
COSPAR Space Science Award 1736
Distinguished Service Medal 1737
Allan D. Emil Memorial Award 1880
Sir Roy Fedden Award 6638
Yuri A. Gagarin Gold Medal 4727
Dr. V. M. Ghatage Award 2523
Gold Medal 6640
Gold Space Medal 4731
Grand Prix 1712
Honorary Companionship 6644
Honorary Fellowship 6645
Honorary Group Diploma 4733
Indigenisation of Aeronautical Equipment Award 2524
International Academy of Astronautics Section Awards 1866
International Cooperation Medal 1738
Swarna Jayanti Award 2525
V. M. Komarov Diploma 4734
Korolev Diploma 4735
Mike Kuhring Award 3569
Massey Award 1739
Luigi Napolitano Award 1867
Nile Gold Medal 4742
William Nordberg Medal 1740
Odyssey Diploma 4743
Outstanding Service Award 581
Geoffrey Pardoe Space Award 6650
Prix d'Astronautique 1714
Production Technology Award 2527
Dr. Biren Roy Space Science and Design Award 2528
Dr. Biren Roy Trust Award 2529
Vikram Sarabhai Medal 1741
Silver Medal 6654
Space Achievement Medal 5338
Space Pioneer Award 582
Andrei Tupolev Aeromodelling Diploma 4748
Andrei Tupolev Aeromodelling Medal 4749
Von Karman Award 1868
Wakefield Gold Medal 6660
Young FAI Artists Contest 4750
Zeldovich Medals 1742

Aerospace medicine
Buchanan Barbour Award 6630

African art (*See also* African studies)
Molteno Medal Awards of Excellence and Merit 4150
National Arts Merit Awards 7437

African studies (*See also* African art)
African Guest Researchers' Scholarship 4608
D. F. Malan Medal 4271
Molteno Medal Awards of Excellence and Merit 4150
Nordic Guest Researchers' Scholarship 4609
Audrey Richards Prize 5006
Premio Giorgio Maria Sangiorgi 2975
Study Scholarship 4610
Amaury Talbot Prize for African Anthropology 6676
Travel Scholarship 4611

Aging (*See also* Geriatrics; Gerontology)
Leslie Kirkley Fellowship 1107
McKitterick Prize 7147

Agricultural economics
Prix de la Fondation Xavier Bernard 1430
Octaaf Callebaut Prize 1066
Prix Rene Dujarric de la Riviere 1561
Excellence in Practical Farming Award 6664
Prix Foulon 1564
Premio Jose Maria Bustillo 9
Talbot-Ponsonby Prize for Agricultural Valuation 6669
Prix Nicolas Zvorikine 1629

Agricultural education
Excellence in Practical Farming Award 6664
SEARCA Graduate Scholarship 3990
SEARCA PhD Research Scholarship 3991
SEARCA Professorial Chairs 3992
SEARCA Seed Fund for Research and Training 3993

Agricultural engineering
Agricultural Engineering Award
  Institution of Engineers Australia/Engineers Australia 486
  Society for Engineering in Agriculture 665
Armand Blanc Prize 2289
Sir Roland Burke Perpetual Challenge Machinery Trophy 6663
Machinery Award Scheme 6666
Technology Award 6670
D. H. Trollope Medal 535

Agriculture (*See also* Agricultural economics; Agricultural education; Agricultural engineering; Agronomy; Animal husbandry; Dairy industry; Forestry; Poultry science; Rural economics)
Academie dFAgriculture de France Medailles 1429
Australian Mushroom Growers Award for Best Menu Using Mushrooms 289
Prix de la Fondation Xavier Bernard 1430
Bledisloe Gold Medal for Landowners 6662
British Grassland Society Award 5313
Prix Corbay 1644
Frederico de Menezes Veiga Prize 1122
Dr. D. K. Desai Prize Award 2754
Prix Jean Dufrenoy 1431
Excellence in Practical Farming Award 6664
Farrer Memorial Medal 444
Francis New Medal 6265
Fujihara Award 3181
Gold Medal Award 4177
Golden Jubilee Awards 2556
Honorary Fellow 6665
Honorary Life Members 854
Inter-American Agricultural Award for Young Professionals
  Inter-American Institute for Cooperation on Agriculture 1207
  Inter-American Institute for Cooperation on Agriculture - Costa Rica 1211
Inter-American Agricultural Medal
  Inter-American Institute for Cooperation on Agriculture 1208
  Inter-American Institute for Cooperation on Agriculture - Costa Rica 1212
Inter-American Award for the Participation of Women in Rural Development
  Inter-American Institute for Cooperation on Agriculture 1209
  Inter-American Institute for Cooperation on Agriculture - Costa Rica 1213
International DLG Prize 2152
International Rapeseed Award 1886
Jono Krisciunas premija 3382
Prof. L. S. S. Kumar Memorial Award 2692
Loraine Award for Nature Conservation 7223
Prix Paul Marguerite de la Charlonie 1589
Meat Livestock Australia Award for Best Dish Using Beef and Mushrooms 290
Meat Livestock Australia Award for Best Dish Using Lamb and Mushrooms 291
Medal of Agriculture 233
National Agricultural Award 6667
Netherthorpe Award 5947
Organic Food Awards 7224
Pakistan Institute of Sciences Gold Medal 3921
Walter Poggendorf Lecture 644
Dr. Rajendra Prasad Award 2593
Premio Academia Nacional de Agronomia y Veterinaria 4
Premio al Desarrollo Agropecuario 5
Premio Bolsa de Cereales de Buenos Aires 7
Prize in Agricultural Sciences 2956
Research Medal
  Royal Agricultural Society of England 6668
  The Royal Society of Victoria 653
Rural Youth Europe Awards 819
Edouard Saouma Award 3055

Agriculture (continued)

B. R. Sen Award 3056
Dr. S. R. Sen Prize 2755
Silver Jubilee Commemoration Medal 2718
Silver Medal Award 4178
Technology Award 6670
TSI-FAI Award on Plant Nutrient Sulphur 2559
Justus Von Liebig Prize 2406
Prix Blaise des Vosges 1705
The Wolf Prizes 2938
World Ploughing Championship Awards 3688

Agronomy
Academie dFAgriculture de France Medailles 1429
Dr. Antonio Pires Prize 2
Antonio J. Prego Prize 3

Air pollution *See* Environmental conservation

Animated films
AFI Awards - The Australian Film Institute Awards 196
Annecy International Animated Film Festival 1870
ASIFA Special Award 1227
Bilbao International Festival of Documentary and Short Films 4517
CINANIMA 4056
Edinburgh International Film Festival 5756
Holland Animation Film Festival 3561
International Animation Festival in Japan, Hiroshima 3183
International Festival of Animated Film Stuttgart 2421
International Visual Communications Association Awards 6327
Mediafest, the Gran Canaria International Festival of Arts and Digital Cultures 4477
Odense International Film Festival 1320
The Orange British Academy Film Awards 5218
Tampere International Short Film Festival 1427
World Festival of Animated Films 1241

Anesthesiology
Drummond-Jackson Prize 7116
Research Grants 878
SAAD Dental Student Prize 7117

Animal care and training (*See also* Animal husbandry; Animal rights; Horsemanship; Poultry science; Veterinary medicine)
Achievement Awards 6608
Animal Welfare Award 5052
Adolph Bolliger Award 280
Robert D. Campbell Memorial Award 5053
Cat of the Year Awards 446
Champion Llama, Champion Alpaca 5342
Distinguished Service Award
Tasmanian Canine Association 698
World Jersey Cattle Bureau 7374
Felipe Benavides Rose Bowl 5343
Honorary Certificate 4162
International Award 5054
Prix de Biologie Alfred Kastler 1822
Julie Mandile Award 430
Public Service Award 5055
Ranking Champion 1109
Dorothy Sidley Memorial Award 5978
Small Project and Travel Awards 7305
Supreme Champion 6290
Ellis Troughton Memorial Award 281
Wild Animal Welfare Award 7306
Young Handler Award 6291

Animal husbandry
Best in Breed Award 7154
Bledisloe Gold Medal for Landowners 6662
Frederico de Menezes Veiga Prize 1122
Distinguished Service Award 3023
Gold Medal 4245
Golden Ram Award 4212
Sir John Hammond Memorial Prize 5501
Hanoverian Stallion of the Year 2431
International Animal Agriculture Award 3144
Prof. L. S. S. Kumar Memorial Award 2692
A. M. Leroy Fellowship 3024
Koos van der Merwe Prize 4127
Barney van Niekerk/AFMA Technical Person of the Year 4128
Dorothy Sidley Memorial Award 5978
Young Scientist Awards 3025

Animal rights
Lord Houghton Award 6361
Dorothy Sidley Memorial Award 5978
Lord Soper Award 6362

Anthropology
Curl Essay Prize 6674
J. B. Donne Essay Prize on the Anthropology of Art 6675
Festival dei Popoli 3045
Mueller Medal 134
Research Medal 653
Amaury Talbot Prize for African Anthropology 6676
Wellcome Medal for Anthropology as Applied to Medical Problems 6677

Antiquity
Best Referee Award from Mineralum Deposits 1266
Prix Bordin 1502
Concours des Antiquites de la France 1507
Prix Roman et Tania Ghirshman 1516
Prix Gustave Mendel 1523
Prix de La Fons-Melicocq 1528
Viking Society for Northern Research Awards 7318

Apparel *See* Fashion

Arabic culture
Fondation Edmond Fagnan 992

Archaeology
Archaeological Book Award 5220
Association for Industrial Archaeology Award 5221
R. M. Baguley Award 6554
Balsdon Fellowship 5438
Best Student Paper Award 1384
BP Prize Lectureship in the Humanities 6988
British Archaeological Awards 5090
Prix Hercule Catenacci 1855
Channel 4 Archaeological Film Awards 5555
The Channel Four Awards 5222
Grahame Clark Medal 5206
Prix de la Fondation Louis de Clercq 1505
Dr. M. Aylwin Cotton Foundation Fellowship Awards 5699
Dr. M. Aylwin Cotton Foundation Publication Grants 5700
Prix Raoul Duseigneur 1513
Egypt Exploration Society Centenary Studentship 5758
Finders Award 5223
Eric Fletcher Research Award 7104
Groube Fieldwork Award 3762
Heritage in Britain Award 5224
IFA Award 5225
Hugh Last Fellowship 5441
Prix du Duc de Loubat 1520
Mansel-Pleydell and Cecil Trusts 5740
Medieval Archaeology Research Grant 7105
Prix Gustave Mendel 1523
Mick Aston Presentation Award 5226
Medaille Georges Perrot 1524
Pitt Rivers Award 5227
Tim Potter Memorial Award 5443
Premio Municipal Julio de Castilho de Olisipografia 4080
Prix Ambatielos 1526
Prix Jacques Lavalleye-Coppens 980
Prix Joseph-Edmond Marchal 982
Public Archaeology Award 3763
Recording and Fieldwork Award 5094
Research Medal 653
Percia Schimmel Award for Distinguished Contribution to Archaeology 2920
Prix Gustave Schlumberger 1532
Prix de la Fondation Emile Senart 1533
Prix Emile Le Senne 1534
Silver Trowel Award 5228
Bob Smith Research Award 6555
Sudreys Fund 7106
DeBeers Alex L. du Toit Memorial Lecture 4189
Transco Press Award 5229
Michael Ventris Memorial Award 5062
Prix Adolphe Noel des Vergers 1536
Bernard Webb Studentship 5063
Wedgwood Sponsorship Award 5230
Young Archeologist of the Year Award 5231

Architectural criticism
Architectural Critics and Writers Award 4331
Pierre Bayle Prijs 3644
Jean Tschumi Prize 1926

Architecture (*See also* Architectural criticism; Construction; Historic preservation; Housing; Landscape architecture; Monument restoration)
Prix Francoise Abella 1433
Aga Khan Award for Architecture 4695
Sir Rowand Anderson Silver Medal 6815
Annual Exhibition 6885
Architecture Awards 6821
Arts and Crafts in Architecture Award 7064
Award for Measured Drawing 6816
Baburao Mhatre Gold Medal 2637
Prix Antoine-Nicolas Bailly 1434
Prix Claude Berthault 1436
Prix Bordin 1439
Brick Awards 5198
British Institute of Architectural Technologists Student Award 5320

Architecture (continued)

Bronze Medal 5748
Heinrich Hatt-Bucher Prize 4896
Sir John Burnet Memorial Award 6817
Civic Trust Awards 5663
Client of the Year Award 6822
Premio Municipal Francisco da Conceicao Silva de Espacos Interiores Abertos ao Publico 4070
Dr. M. Aylwin Cotton Foundation Fellowship Awards 5699
Dr. M. Aylwin Cotton Foundation Publication Grants 5700
Design Partnership Award 6459
Dharmasthala Manjunatheswara Award 2638
Eckersberg Medal 1325
Environmental Awards 6513
James Alfred Ewing Medal 6109
Harold Fern Award 5038
Fulton Award 4156
Gold Medal for Architecture 4332
Gold Medal for Outstanding Architectural Achievement 1923
Grand Prix Annual Prize of the Society of Czech Architects 1270
Grand Prix d'Architecture 1453
C. F. Hansen Medal 1326
Prix Baron Horta 975
Prix Houllevigue 1455
Housing Design Awards
Royal Institute of British Architects 6823
Saltire Society 7068
IABSE Outstanding Structure Award 4773
IFI Award 4210
Jerwood Awards 6340
Kaleidoscope of Honor 1301
Prix Achille Leclere 1458
Prix Hector Lefuel 1459
Sir Robert Lorimer Memorial Award 6818
Madhav Achwal Gold Medal 2639
Robert Matthew Award 5670
Sir Robert Matthew Prize 1924
Medal of Honor for the Performing and Visual Arts 4273
Johann-Heinrich-Merck Ehrung 2443
National Architecture Awards 627
Olympiart 4819
Order of Culture 3246
Organization of Islamic Capitals and Cities Awards 4409
Patron of Architecture Award 4333
Auguste Perret Prize 1925
Piloo Mody Surfa Coats Awards 2640
Anthony Pott Memorial Award 5061
Praemium Imperiale 3217
Premio Valmor e Municipal de Arquitectura 4084
Prix Catenacci 1473
Prix Chaudesaigues 1474
Prix COGEDIM 1734
Prix de Rome Fine Art 3642
Prix Duc 1480
Prix Ernest Acker 977
Prix et Fondations Concernant l'Academie de France a Rome 1482
Prix Paul Bonduelle 986
Prix Pierre Carsoel 987
RAIA Gold Medal 628
Thomas Ross Award 6819
Prix Rouyer 1489
Royal Academy Summer Exhibition 6611
Royal Gold Medal 6824
Prix Ruhlmann 1490
Kasper Salin Prize 4599
Fritz Schumacher Prize 2402
Sikkens Prize 3665
Silver Medal 5749
Small Projects Award 5750
Snowcem Award 2641
South African Institute of Architects Award for Excellence 4334
South African Institute of Architects Award of Merit 4335
South African Institute of Architects Best Student Award 4336
South African Institute of Architects Medal of Distinction 4337
Alfred H. Turner Award 5046
Michael Ventris Memorial Award 5062
Bernard Webb Studentship 5063
Prix Georges Wildenstein 1499
The Wolf Prizes 2938
Charles Wollaston Award 6612

Archival science *See* Library and information services

Art (*See also* African art; Art education; Art history; Design; Exhibiting; Photography; specific disciplines, e.g. Ceramics)

Annual Exhibition 6885
Antwoorden Prijsvragen, Klasse der Schone Kunsten 1060
Art Scholarship 6692
Artist of the Month 717
Artist of the Year 718
Artists for Nature Foundation Award 7215
Arts Council of Northern Ireland Bursaries and Awards 5074
Award for Distinguished Services to Art 3346
Pierre Bayle Prijs 3644
Prix Jean Jacques Berger 1435
Prix de la Fondation Claude Berthault 1636
Best Craftsmanship 3477
Best Entrepreneurship 3478
Bharat Ratna 2577
Ros Bower Memorial Award 102
British Design and Art Direction (D&AD) Awards 5291
CCP Awards for the Arts 3973
Prix Corbay 1644
Dr. M. Aylwin Cotton Foundation Fellowship Awards 5699
Dr. M. Aylwin Cotton Foundation Publication Grants 5700
Leonardo da Vinci Medal 874
J. B. Donne Essay Prize on the Anthropology of Art 6675
Oppenheim John Downes Memorial Trust 6511
Prix Raoul Duseigneur 1513
Aquileo J. Echeverria Prize 1201
Eckersberg Medal 1325
Federation of British Artists Prizes and Awards 7027
Fellowships and Scholarships 584
Fellowships in Arts and Crafts 5681
Festival dei Popoli 3045
Dr. Haim Gamzu Prize 2930
Joaquin Garcia Monge Prize 1202
Gold Memorial Bowl 7025
Nathan Gottesdiener Prize 2931
Calouste Gulbenkian Foundation Grants 5574
Dr. A.H. Heineken Prize for Art 3651
Prix Henri Hertz 1806
Honorary Fellow 2916
Prix Houllevigue 1455
N. L. Hoyen Medal 1327
HRH Princess Michael of Kent Award 7218
Edmond Hustinx Prize - Visual Arts 3517
International Ceramic Art Competition 3067
International Print Triennial 4004
International Prize for Contemporary Art 3471
Prix Jules et Louis Jeanbernat et Barthelemy de Ferrari Doria
Academie des Sciences Morales et Politiques 1669
Institut de France 1857
Kungliga priset 4662
Kunstpreis der Stadt Darmstadt 2441
Kunstpreis der Stadt Zurich 4874
Kyoto Prizes 3189
Literature and Art Award 4954
Macaulay Fellowship 2822
Prix Paul Marmottan 1462
Medal of Honor for the Performing and Visual Arts 4273
Membership Bursary 6945
Johann-Heinrich-Merck Ehrung 2443
Ya'akov Meshorer Prize 2919
Hans-Molfenter-Preis der Landeshauptstadt Stuttgart/Galerie 2418
Piet Mondriaan Lecture 3664
Doug Moran National Portrait Prize 707
Musgrave Medals 3146
National Arts Merit Awards 7437
National Living Treasures Award 3974
Olympiart 4819
Azusa Ono Memorial Awards 3349
Order of Merit 5601
Order of Polish Rebirth 4015
Order of the Netherlands Lion 3493
Panorama Brasilian Art 1134
Paracelsusring der Stadt Villach 822
Peace Prize of the German Book Trade 2216
Premio Carlos Bonvalot 4092
Premio Tenore 2977
President & Vice President's Choice Award 7219
Prince of Asturias Awards 4497
Prix de Rome Fine Art 3642
Prix de Stassart 1003
Prix Jacques Lavalleye-Coppens 980
Prix Jules Raeymaekers 983
Prix Osiris 1861
Promotional Prizes 2345
Mendel and Eva Pundik Prize 2933
Red Ochre Award 103
Prix Jean Reynaud 1485
Royal Academy Summer Exhibition 6611
RSPB Fine Art Award 7216
Scholarships of the City of Munich 2346
Prix Emile Le Senne 1534
Sikkens Prize 3665
Jill Smythies Award 6389
Konrad von Soest Preis 2350
Standard Bank Young Artist Awards 4191
Storywriting and Art Competition 107
Suntory Prize for Social Sciences and Humanities 3334
Barbara Tate Award 7220
Prix Thorlet 1703
Thorvaldsen Medal 1328
Tiroler Landespreis fur Kunst 750
Marten Toonder Award 2823

Art (continued)
Top Exporter 3479
Jacobus van Looyprijs 3550
Prix Alfred Verdaguer
Academie des Sciences 1627
Institut de France 1863
Leonardo da Vinci World Award of Arts 3462
Visual Arts Emeritus Award 104
Visual Arts Emeritus Medal 105
Winsor & Newton Choice Award 7221
Winsor & Newton Young Artists Award 6835
The Wolf Prizes 2938
The Wolgin Foundation/Israel Museum Fellowships 2921
Charles Wollaston Award 6612

Art education
Jozef Van Ginderachter Prize 963

Art history
Prix Charles and Marguerite Diehl 1510
Prix Louis Fould 1515
Prix Roman et Tania Ghirshman 1516
Prix Houllevigue 1455
Prix Jules et Louis Jeanbernat et Barthelemy de Ferrari Doria 1456
Prix du Baron de Joest 1457
Medaille Georges Perrot 1524
Prix Richtenberger 1486
Prix Thorlet 1493

Arts and humanities (*See also* Antiquity; Archaeology; Ethics; Humanities research; Museums; Philosophy; Philosophy of science; Religion)
Albert Medal 6919
Antwoorden Prijsvragen, Klasse der Letteren 1059
Artist Awards 1369
Balzan Prize 3062
Alexander Gottlieb Baumgarten Award 2281
Belgica Prize 1062
Boelpaepe Prize 1063
BP Prize Lectureship in the Humanities 6988
Albert Brachet Prize 1064
British Academy Research Awards 5204
Hedwig-Burgheim Medaille 2354
Henri Buttgenbach Prize 1065
Eugene Catalan Prize 1067
Crawford Medal 126
De la Court Prizes 3650
Ducat Award 1370
Gustav Theodor Fechner Award 2282
Paul Fourmarier Prize 1071
Benjamin Franklin Medal 6920
FT/ARTS And Business Awards 5068
Sir Francis Galton Award 2283
Honouree Award 1371
Imperial Prize 3214
International Federation of University Women Awards Competition 4803
Japan Academy Prize 3215
Molteno Medal Awards of Excellence and Merit 4150
Montaigne Prize 2399
Onassis International Cultural Competition Prizes 2464
Premio Maria Teresa Messori Roncaglia and Eugenio Mari 2974
Prince of Asturias Awards 4497
Edward Richter Award 1372
Shakespeare Prize 2403
Stals Prize for the Humanities 4283
Tiroler Landespreis fur Wissenschaft 751
Max Weber Preis 2046

Asian studies (*See also* Japanese culture)
Dennis Anthony Memorial Award 3399
APO National Awards 3166
APO Regional Award 3167
Association of Southeast Asian Institutions of Higher Learning Awards 3967
Prix Bordin 1502
Sir Richard Burton Medal 6679
Prix Herbert Allen Giles 1517
International Iqbal Award 3918
Prix Stanislas Julien 1519
National Iqbal Award 3919
Prix Delalande-Guerineau 1530
Research Grant Program to Assist Foreign Scholars in Chinese Studies 4950
Royal Asiatic Society Award 6680
Student Competition for Overseas Music Study Award 4116

Astronautics *See* Aerospace

Astrology
Academic Awards 5877

Astronomy
David Allen Prize 63
Astrological Association Awards and Scholarships 5154
INSA - Vainu Bappu Memorial Award 2674
Sir David Robert Bates Medal 1770
Medaille des Soixantenaire et Fondation Manley-Bendall 1950
Prix Georges Bidault de l'Isle 1951
Dr. J. van der Bilt prijs 3627
The Bok Prize 64
Lydia Brown Award for Meritorious Service 5247
Crafoord Prize 4637
Crago Award 69
Prix Ernest Dechelle 1556
Eddington Medal 6687
The Ellery Lectureship 65
Aidan P. Fitzgerald Award 2852
Plaquette du Centenaire de Camille Flammarion 1952
Prix Gabrielle et Camille Flammarion 1953
Gill Medal 4132
Prix Edmond Girard 1954
Walter Goodacre Medal and Gift 5248
Charlene Heisler Prize 66
Herschel Medal 6688
Jackson-Gwilt Medal 6689
Prix Marius Jacquemetton 1955
Prix Jules Janssen 1956
Prix Dorothea Klumpke - Isaac Roberts 1957
Prix Lallemand 1580
McIntyre Award 4133
McNiven Medal 70
Medaille des Anciens Presidents 1958
Merlin Medal and Gift 5249
Prix Marcel Moye 1959
The Page Medal 67
Prix Agathon De Potter 1028
Prix Antoine d'Abbadie 1603
Prix des Dames 1960
Prix du Commisariat a l'Energie Atomique 1610
Prix Edouard Mailly 1039
Prix Paul and Marie Stroobant 1051
Prix Pol and Christiane Swings 1053
Research Medal 653
Prix Henri Rey 1961
Prix Julien Saget 1962
Southern Cross Award 71
Steavenson Memorial Award 5250
Henri L. Vanderlinden Prize 1078
Prix Viennet-Damien 1963
Frederick White Prize 124

Athletics *See* Physical education; Sports; Track and field

Atmospheric science *See* Meteorology

Atomic energy (*See also* Nuclear engineering)
European Nuclear Society Awards 867

Audiology *See* Speech and hearing

Audiovisuals
Dance Screen Award 807
International Advertising Festival, Cannes 6202
International Diaporama Festival 941
Prix Albert Londres 1717
Phenix UDA 2008
Worlddidac Award 4941

Auto racing
Championships, Cups, and Trophies 1882
Driver of the Year Award 5953
Formula One World Champion 1883
Le Mans 24-hour Grand Prix d'Endurance 1726
World Rally Champion 1884

Automobile industry
Awards for Excellence 5919
BVRLA Awards 5562
Fleet Environment Award 81
Fleet Manager of the Year 82
Fleet Safety Award 83

Automobiles
British Championship 6440
Driver of the Year 5156
Horace Grimley Award 6344
Sir William Lyons Award 5954
Pemberton Trophy 5955
Rolls-Royce Enthusiasts Awards 6603
IIE Sir Henry Royce Award for Achievement 663

Automotive engineering
FISITA Travelling Fellowship 6251
O'Shannessy Award 667
Rodda Award 668

Automotive safety
PRI Service Medal 4062

Aviation *See* Aeronautics and aviation

Aviation safety
International Society of Aircraft Traders (ISTAT) Scholarship 6248
Handley Page Award 6649
Whittle Safety Award 6249

Aviation (continued)

Aviculture *See* Ornithology

Bacteriology *See* Microbiology

Badminton
Certificate of Commendation 3405
Distinguished Service Award 3406
English Badminton Award 5160
IBF Distinguished Service Award 3407
IBF Meritorious Service Award 3408
International Badminton Federation Distinguished Service Award 3409
Meritorious Service Award 3410
Herbert Scheele Medal 5161
Herbert Scheele Trophy 3411

Ballet
Associate of the Royal Academy of Dance 6614
Phyllis Bedells Bursary 6615
Fellow of the Royal Academy of Dance 6616
Grand Prix Eurovision for Young Dancers 4708
Helsinki International Ballet Competition 1407
Honorary Fellow of the Royal Academy of Dance 6617
McDonald's Ballet Scholarship 689
President's Award 6618
Queen Elizabeth II Coronation Award 6619
Varna International Ballet Competition 1158

Banking
Asian Banking Awards 3964
Honorary Member 3965
Islamic Development Bank Prizes in Islamic Economics and Islamic Banking 4401

Baseball
European Baseball Championships 858
European Baseball Cup 859

Basketball
Coach of the Year 5772
Competitions 454
English Basket Ball Association Player of the Year (Men and Women) 5773
Fair Play Award 5774
Mini-Basketball Coach Award 6436
Mini-Basketball Officiating Award 6437
Mini-Basketball Teacher Award 6438
National Championship Cup Finals 5775
National League Player of the Year 5776
Order of Merit 4780
Radomir Shaper Prize 4781

Bibliography
Redmond Barry Award 272
Prix Brunet 1503
Howard Drake Memorial Award 5995
Medal for Services to Bibliography 5165
C. B. Oldman Prize 6221
Walter Stone Memorial Award 451

Bicycling
Tour de France 1708

Biochemistry
Henry E. Armstrong Memorial Lecture 7156
Association of Clinical Biochemists Foundation Award 5078
AstraZeneca Award 5167
Bayer Award 5079
Biochemical Society Travel Fund 5169
Caledonian Research Foundation Prize Lectureship in Biomedical Sciences and Arts and Letters 6992
Jagdish Chandra Bose Medal 2681
Colworth Medal 5170
Dr. B. C. Deb Memorial Award for Soil/ Physical Chemistry 2741
Prix Charles Dhere 1559
Luigi Galvani Prize 4475
Prix Jean-Marie Le Goff 1566
Bires Chandra Guha Memorial Lecture 2687
Dr. H. P. Heineken Prize for Biochemistry and Biophysics 3652
Hestrin Prize 2923
Honorary Member 5171
Sir Frederick Gowland Hopkins Memorial Lecture 5172
Prix Max-Fernand Jayle 1574
Jubilee Lecture and Harden Medal 5173
Keilin Memorial Lecture 5174
Krebs Memorial Scholarship 5175
Richard-Kuhn-Medaille 2171
Prix du Docteur et de Madame Henri Labbe 1579
Prix Charles-Leopold Mayer 1590
Morton Lecture 5176
Novartis Medal and Prize 5177
Prix Andre Policard-Lacassagne 1601
Prix Leon et Henri Fredericq 1050
Prix Nine Choucroun 1850
Professors' Prize 5080
Research Medal 653
Roche Diagnostics Award 5081
Professor R. C. Shah Memorial Lecture 2749
Shorei-Sho/Young Investigator Awards 3271
Professor Umakant Sinha Memorial Award 2750
Thermo Electron Clinical Chemistry and Automation Systems Award 5082
Prijs J. B. Van Helmont 970
Prix Leon Velluz 1626
Otto-Wallach-Plakette 2178
Otto-Warburg-Medaille 2227
Frederick White Prize 124

Biography
J. R. Ackerley Prize for Autobiography 5778
Benson Medal 7001
James Tait Black Memorial Prizes 7308
Book of the Year Awards 37
Giosue Carducci Prize 3140
Duff Cooper Prize 5746
Dr. Wijnaendts Francken-prijs 3668
Axel Hirschs pris 4658
Somerset Maugham Awards 7146
Premio Comillas de Biografia, Autobiografia y Memorias 4547
Premios Municipais Eca de Queiroz de Literatura 4085
Prix Cazes - Brasserie Lipp 1938
Birger Scholdstroms pris 4666
Walter Stone Memorial Award 451
Strega Prize 3132
Wales Book of the Year Awards 4995
Whitbread Literary Awards 5194

Biology (*See also* Biochemistry; Biophysics; Biomedical engineering; Biotechnology; Botany; Genetics; Marine biology; Microbiology; Mycology; Nature; Ornithology; Physiology; Zoology)
Prix Louis Armand 1540
Karl Ernst von Baer Medal 1349
Bancroft - Mackerras Medal 370
Bhatnagar Award 2573
Bicentenary Medal 6385
Anil Kumar Bose Memorial Award 2680
Bruce-Preller Prize Lectureship 6990
Caledonian Research Foundation Prize Lectureship in Biomedical Sciences and Arts and Letters 6992
Jagdish Chandra Bose Medal 2681
Bashambar Nath Chopra Lecture 2683
Colombian Academy of Exact, Physical and Natural Sciences to the Integral Work of a Scientist 1172
Conway Lecture 2871
Dax Copp Traveling Fellowship 6761
Crafoord Prize 4637
Oswaldo Cruz Prize 1111
Darwin Medal 6904
Prix Georges Deflandre et Marthe Deflandre-Rigaud 1557
EMBO Medal 2125
ESCPB Grant for Young Scientists 880
Fenner Medal 110
Frits Sobels Award 1767
Fujihara Award 3181
Gabor Medal 6908
Golden Jubilee Commemoration Medal for Biology 2685
Gottschalk Medal 113
Prix Grammaticakis-Neuman 1567
William Bate Hardy Prize 5579
Hector Memorial Medal and Prize 3868
International Prize for Biology 3261
Tado Ivanausko premija 3379
Louis-Jeantet Prize for Medicine 4862
Prix de Biologie Alfred Kastler 1822
Keilin Memorial Lecture 5174
Keith Medal 6996
Kshanika Oration Award to a Woman Scientist for Research in the Field of Biomedical Sciences 2611
Prix Langevin 1582
Jean Laray Award 5856
Prix Richard Lounsbery 1586
MacLeod Prijs 1074
MakDougall-Brisbane Prize 6997
Irene Manton Award 7093
Prix Charles-Leopold Mayer 1590
Professor Vishwa Nath Memorial Lecture 2699
Pakistan Institute of Sciences Gold Medal 3921
Premio Internazionale Ferrari-Soave 2968
President's Medallist 7094
Prix Albert Brachet 1029
Prix des Sciences de la Mer 1609
Prix du Commisariat a l'Energie Atomique 1610
Prix Dubois - Debauque 1037
Prix Fonde par l'Etat 1611
Prix Lamarck 1048
Prix Leo Errera 1049
Prizes of the 150th Anniversary of the RSSL 1098
Prof. G. N. Ramachandran 60th Birthday Commemoration Medal 2707

Biology (continued)

Research Prize 3296
Karl Asmund Rudolphi Medal 2078
Henri Schoutedenprijs 1075
Scientific Research Prizes 3451
Senior Captain Scott Commemoration Medal 4281
Scottish Science Award 7072
John Frederick Adrian Sprent Prize 371
Egon Stahl Award 2377
Student Prizes 5857
Student Travel Awards 5858
David Syme Research Prize 713
TWAS Award in Biology 2962
Pierre-Joseph and Edouard Van Beneden Prize 1057
Paul van Oyeprijs 1077
Prix Roy Vaucouloux 1625
Don Whitley Travel Scholarship 7088
George Winter Award 5859
Young Investigators Award 5833

Biomedical engineering
The IFMBE Otto Schmitt Award 1229
The IUPESM Awards of Merit 1230
C. J. Martin Overseas Biomedical Fellowship 573
Nightingale Award 1231
The IFMBE Vladimir K. Zworykin Award 1234
Dr. V. K. Zworykin Premium 6166

Biophysics
Jagdish Chandra Bose Medal 2681
Dr. H. P. Heineken Prize for Biochemistry and Biophysics 3652
Prix Charles-Leopold Mayer 1590
Prix Andre Policard-Lacassagne 1601
Prix Leon et Henri Fredericq 1050
Prof. G. N. Ramachandran 60th Birthday Commemoration Medal 2707
Professor Umakant Sinha Memorial Award 2750
Prijs J. B. Van Helmont 970

Biotechnology
Henry E. Armstrong Memorial Lecture 7156
Creative Exporter of the Year 3809
DECHEMA Honorary Membership 2258
DECHEMA Medal 2259
DECHEMA Preis der Max Buchner Forschungsstiftung 2260
Eda Award 3320
Excellent Paper Award 3321
Industrial Achievement Award 3322
Poster Award 3038
Saito Award 3323
Skerman Award for Microbial Taxonomy 7370
Society Award 3324
Terui Award 3325
Young Asian Biotechnologist Prize 3326

Blindness
Australian Audio Book of the Year 576
R. W. Bowen Medal 4341
Chess Olympiad for the Blind 4590
John William Clark Award 5356

Boating (*See also* Rowing)
Award for Valour 5260
Award of Honour 5261
Award of Merit 5262
Fireball Worlds Trophy 5905
Flying Fifteen World Championship 5910
Honorary Membership 6260
Peter Mason Award 6480
Pier of the Year Award 6481
World Champion 4771
World Championship 1892
World Championships 4512
Yachtsman of the Year Award 7391
Young Sailor of the Year Award 7392

Book and newspaper design
Book Design Awards 339
British Book Design and Production Awards 5419
Walter Tiemann Award 2352

Book collecting
Christian Album of the Year 3706
Christian Book of the Year 3707
Exhibitor of the Year 3708
New Zealand Christian Book of the Year 3709
Salesperson of the Year 3710
Young Persons Book of the Year 3711

Book illustration *See* Illustration

Books *See* Publishing

Botany
Inhaber de Otto-Appel-Denkmunze 2212
Prix Paul Bertrand 1546
H. H. Bloomer Award 6386
Bolus Medal 4135
Botanical Society Certificate of Merit 4136
Botanical Society Flora Conservation Medal 4137
British Lichen Society Awards 5340
Bronze Medal 4302
W. S. Bruce Medal 6989
Cactus d'Or 4824
Prof. Hira Lal Chakravarty Awards 2738
Prix Auguste Chevalier 1551
Clarke Medal 638
Leonard Cockayne Memorial Lecture 3864
Anton-de-Bary-Medaille 2213
Dudley D'Ewes Medal 4138
Engler Gold Medal 788
Jakob Eriksson Prize 4592
Fellow of the Phytopathological Society of Japan 3311
Fellow of the Society 4367
FESPP Award 5889
Flintoff Medal 6960
Prix Foulon 1564
Gold Medal for Botany 4303
Hector Memorial Medal and Prize 3868
Denys Heesom Medal 4139
Dr. H. P. Heineken Prize for Biochemistry and Biophysics 3652
Dean Hole Medal 6851
Honorary Life Membership 4140
Honorary Member 4368
Hutton Memorial Medal and Prize 3869
Bengt Jonssons pris 4628
Julius-Kuhn-Preis 2214
Prof. L. S. S. Kumar Memorial Award 2692
Cythna Letty Medal 4141
Linnean Medal 6387
Prof. Panchanan Maheshwari Memorial Lecture 2694
Irene Manton Prize 6388
Martloth Medal 4142
Mueller Medal 134
Hugo Muller Lectureship 6976
OPTIMA Gold Medal 4527
OPTIMA Silver Medal 4528
Percy Sergeant Medal 4143
Christiaan Hendrik Persoon Medal 4369
Prix Agathon De Potter 1028
Prix de l'adjudant Hubert Lefebvre 1036
Prix Edmond de Selys Longchamps 1038
Prix Emile Laurent 1040
Prix Joseph Schepkens 1047
Research Medal 653
Rosens Linnemedalj 4630
Prof. T. S. Sadasivan Lecture 2712
Professor Shyam Bahadur Saksena Memorial Medal 2713
Scelpe Award 4144
Junior Captain Scott Commemorative Medal 4282
Senior Medal for Botany 4304
Professor Umakant Sinha Memorial Award 2750
Jill Smythies Award 6389
Egon Stahl Award 2377
Sunder Lal Hora Medal 2721
TSI-FAI Award on Plant Nutrient Sulphur 2559
Whitley Awards 659
Young Scientist Award 3312

Bowling
Bowler of the Year 632
Charity of the Year 633
Junior Bowler of the Year 634
National Championships 7079
Senior Bowler of the Year 635

Boxing
World Boxing Council Awards 3458

Bravery *See* Heroism

Bridge
European Bridge Champion 3027

Broadcast journalism
Reuter Foundation Stanford Fellowship 6601
Television Journalism Awards 7047

Broadcasting (*See also* Broadcast journalism; Cable television; Media; Radio; Sports broadcasting; Television; Video)
ABU Engineering Award 3397
Akashvani Annual Awards for Technical Excellence 2538
Awards for Excellence in Broadcasting 7320
IAWRT Awards 2773
IERE Benefactors Premium 6151
Nihon Shinbun Kyokai Awards 3241
IBC International John Tucker Award 6233
Peter Wayne Award 6219

Brotherhood
Balzan Prize 3062
Cruz de Boyaca 1174
Jawaharlal Nehru Award for International Understanding 2591

Burglar and fire alarms *See* Security

Business (*See also* Accounting; Advertising; Business history; Business journalism; Consumer affairs; Conventions; Economics; Management; Manufacturing; Marketing)
Abe Issa Award for Excellence 3150
Albert Medal 6919
Best First-Time Paper 4122
Best New Products 7322
Best Stand 7323
Business Innovation 145
Businesswoman of the Year 4146
BWA Bursary 4147
Champion Exporter 3148
CIPS Supply Managent Awards 5631
Community Welfare Award 2664
Contribution by Business Community Award 2665
Prix Corbay 1644
Education and Training 146
Entrepreneur of the Year Award 4419
Environment, Agriculture, and Rural Development Award 2666
Exhibition of the Year 4175
Export and Trade 147
Financial Assistance Fund for Settlement of International Disputes 3638
Benjamin Franklin Medal 6920
Graduateship of the City and Guilds of London Institute 5658
Ground Transportation Company of the Year 3151
Honorary Life Officer 3885
HRD Award 4962
Impresa Europe Awards 2553
Industry and Technology Award 2667
Integrity Awards 2425
Intermediate Certificate in Floristry 7194
Licentiateship of the City and Guilds of London Institute 5659
Max-Eyth-Gedenkmunze 2356
Medals for Excellence 5660
Membership of the City and Guilds of London Institute 5661
Murray Medal 4123
National Diploma of the Society of Floristry 7195
Sir Peter Parker Awards for Spoken Business Japanese 7075
Personality of the Year Award 5196
Platinum Jubilee Endowment Trust Award 2668
President's Prize 4124
President's Prize for Best Regional Business 148
Prix Herman Schoolmeesters 1011
Promotion of Savings, Consumer Protection, and Export PerFormance Award 2669
Queen's Award for Enterprise: Innovation 6578
Queen's Awards for Enterprise: International Trade 6582
Queen's Awards for Enterprise: Sustainable Development 6583
Regional Business Achievers Award 4148
Singapore Promising Brand Award 4420
Swinbank Award 5632
The Swiss Re Award 4125
Frans du Toit Medal for Business Leadership 4287
Top 100 Companies Award 4371
Woman Entrepreneur of the Year Award 4421
Young Industrialist Awards of Hong Kong 3933

Business administration *See* Management

Business history
Wadsworth Prize for Business History 5570

Business journalism
Communicators in Business Awards 5241
Sir William Lyons Award 5954
The Magazines - Awards for Editorial and Publishing Excellence 5515
Timothy White Award 4417

Cable television (*See also* Television)
NHK Japan Prize 3298

Calligraphy *See* Graphic arts

Camping *See* Recreation

Canadian literature
Claude Aubry Award 4783
Elizabeth Mrazik-Cleaver Canadian Picture Book Award 4784
Frances E. Russell Award 4785

Cancer (*See also* Radiology)
American Cancer Society International Cancer Research Fellowships 4856
Awards of the ESTRO 876
Prix Dandrimont-Benicourt 1555
Prix Marguerite Delahautemaison 1818
Anthony Dipple Carcinogenesis Award 5805
Dutch Cancer Society Press Award 3505
Prix Leon-Alexandre Etancelin 1562
Faustus Poster Awards 5806
FECS Clinical Research Award 884
FECS/EJC Award 885
FECS-Pezcoller Recognition for Contribution to Oncology 3115
Garrod Medal 5475
Edgar Gentilli Prize 6706
T. P. Gunton Award 5359
Honorary Member 1872
International Cancer Research Technology Transfer Project 4858
International Oncology Nursing Fellowships 4859
Prix Marie Leon-Houry 1585
Albert McMaster Award 5368
Prof. Dr. P. Muntendamprijs 3506
John Paul Career Award 5583
Pezcoller Foundation - FECS Recognition for Contribution to Oncology 886
Research Training Fellowships 4932
Prix Raymond Rosen 1820
Prix Gustave Roussy 1620
Saint Luke's Lecture 2873
Sandoz Oration Award for Research in Cancer 2623
Schweisguth Prize 6299
Raja Ravi Sher Singh of Kalsia Memorial Cancer Research Award 2627
SIOP Awards 6300
Helen Tomkinson Award 5372
Travel Fellowships 5807
Hamao Umezawa Memorial Award 6297
Prix Roy Vaucouloux 1625
Yamagiwa-Yoshida Memorial International Cancer Study Grants 4860
Young Cancer Researcher Award Lecture 5809

Canoeing *See* Boating

Cardiology
Burger Award 4454
Professor Ignacio Chavez Young Investigator Award 3449
R. T. Hall Prize 399
Geoffrey Holt Award 5365
Amrut Mody-Unichem Prize for Research in Cardiology, Neurology and Gastroenterology 2614
Reynaldo Dos Santos Prize 3033
Edith Walsh Award 5373
Young Scientist Award in Noninvasive Cardiovascular Dynamics 4455

Career achievement *See* Academic achievement; Professional and personal achievement

Cars *See* Automobiles

Cartography (*See also* Geography)
John Bartholomew Award 5264
Bartholomew Globe 6889
British Cartographic Society Design Award 5265
Sir George Fordham Award for Cartobibliography 6763
Fondation de Madame Edmond Hamel 1571
Henry Johns Award 5266
Honorary Fellowship 3573
International Map Collectors' Society Awards 6271
Carl Mannerfelt Medal 3574
National Geographic Society Award 5267
Ordnance Survey Award 5268
Readers Digest Student Award 5269
Helen Wallis Award 6272
XYZ Digital Award 6898

Cartoons (*See also* Animated films; Drawing; Humor)
Kodansha Manga Award 3287
Prix Henri Lehmann 1460
Yunus Nadi Yarismasi 4964
Premio Municipal Rafael Bordalo Pinheiro de Banda Desenhada, Cartoon e Caricaturista 4082
W.G. Walkley Awards for Journalism 561
Yomiuri International Cartoon Contest 3354

Catholic literature
Prix Gallet 1662

Cats *See* Animal care and training

Ceramic engineering
Adolf-Dietzel-Industriepreis der DGG 2242
Goldener Gehlhoff-Ring 2243

Ceramics (*See also* Glass)
CerSJ Awards 3169
Governor General Art Award 3760
International Ceramic Art Competition 3067
Royal Dublin Society Crafts Competition 2877

Charity activities *See* Philanthropy

Chemical engineering
Henry E. Armstrong Memorial Lecture 7156
Jochen Block Prize 2257
Brennan Medal 6089
John A. Brodie Medal 492
Chemeca Medal 496
Council Medal 6090
George E. Davis Medal 6091
DECHEMA Honorary Membership 2258
DECHEMA Medal 2259
DECHEMA Preis der Max Buchner Forschungsstiftung 2260
Donald Medal 6092
Esso Award 505
Filtration Society Gold Medal 5900
Ned Franklin Medal 6093
Arnold Greene Medal 6094
Hanson Medal 6095
John William Hinchley Medal 6096
Hutchison Medal 6097
Junior Moulton Medal 6098
Leverhulme Medal 6912
Macnab Medal 6099
Queensland Division Chemical Branch Award 526
Otto Roelen Medal 2263
Salters' Graduate Prizes 7062
Senior Moulton Medal 6100
Shedden Uhde Medal and Prize 532
Skellerup Award 3746
H. K. Suttle Award 5901

Chemical industry
Award for Young Chemists in Technical Development 3171
Baekeland Lecture 7157
Hans R. Bolliger Memorial Lecture 7158
Canada Medal 7160
Cavallaro Medal 2117
Chemical Society of Japan Award for Technological Development 3175
DECHEMA Award of the Max-Buchner-Forschungsstiftung 2073
European Corrosion Medal 2118
Hellmuth Fischer-Medaille 2261
Founder's Lecture 7163
Marti I. Franques Medal 2119
Roland Harper Lecture 7165
International Medal 7169
Leverhulme Lecture 7172
Ivan Levinstein Memorial Lecture 7173
Alwin Mittasch-Medaille 2262
James Moir Medal 4317
Purvis Memorial Award 7177
Andres Manuel del Rio National Prize in Chemistry 3437
Separation Science Lecture 7180
Hendrik Van Eck Medal 4321
Wohler-Preis "Ressourcenschonende Prozesse" 2179

Chemistry (*See also* Biochemistry; Chemical engineering; Chemical industry; Color technology; Fiber science; Geochemistry; Industrial chemistry)
A-Level Chemistry Prizes 7058
Academic Excellency Prize 4103
ACHEMA Plaque in Titanium 2256
Adrien Albert Lectureship 6947
Annual Science Award 861
Applied Research Medal 615
Arfvedson-Schlenk-Preis 2162
Prix Louis Armand 1540
Henry E. Armstrong Memorial Lecture 7156
Award for Advancement of Industry 4104
Award for Advancement of Science 4105
Award for Chemical Education 4106
Award for Excellent Research Paper 4107
Bader Award 6948
Alfred Bader Prize 1249
Prix Barrabe 1831
Barrer Award 6949
Beilby Medal and Prize 6950
Gmelin-Beilstein-Denkmunze 2163
Ronald Belcher Memorial Lectureship 6951
Prix Berthelot 1545
Biochemical Society Award 5168
Biota Award for Medicinal Chemistry 616
Bonhoeffer-Eucen-Scheibe Memorial Lecture 2156
Bourke Lectureship 6952
Boyle-Higgins Award 2838
Robert Boyle Medal 6953
S. F. Boys - A Rahman Lectureship 6954
Paul Bunge Prize 2157
Canada International Award 7159
Medaglia Stanislao Cannizzaro 3102
Carbohydrate Chemistry Award 6955
Castner Lecture and Medal 7161
Centenary Lectureship 6956
Joseph Chatt Lectureship 6957
Chemical Education Medal 4314
Chemical Society of Japan Award 3172
Chemical Society of Japan Award for Chemical Education 3173
Chemical Society of Japan Award for Distinguished Technical Achievements 3174
Chemical Society of Japan Award for Young Chemists 3176
Chemical Society of Japan Award of Merit for Chemical Education 3177
Chemistry Teaching Award 7059
Citations for Contributions to Chemistry and the Chemical Profession 617
City and Guilds Prizes 7060
Prix Clavel-Lespiau 1552
Colombian Academy of Exact, Physical and Natural Sciences to the Integral Work of a Scientist 1172
Congress Award and Honorary Mention 6262
Prix Le Conte 1553
Corday-Morgan Medal and Prize 6958
Cornforth Medal 618
Davy Medal 6905
DECHEMA Honorary Membership 2258
DECHEMA Medal 2259
Distinguished Contribution to Advancement in Chemical Education 4096
Distinguished Contribution to Economic Advancement Award 4097
Distinguished Fellowship Award 619
Carl-Duisberg-Gedachtnispreis 2164
Carl-Duisberg-Plakette 2165
Lecon Paul Ehrlich 1965
Electrochimica Acta Gold Medal 4840
Ellinger-Gardonyi Award 6503
Emeritus Membership 3252
Hans-Jurgen Engell Prize 4841
Ewald Prize 6321
Faraday Lectureship 6959
Emil-Fischer-Medaille 2166
Hellmuth Fischer-Medaille 2261
Flintoff Medal 6960
Theodor Foerster Memorial Lecture 2158
Foundation Lectureship Award 4098
Founder's Lecture 7163
Francqui Prize 895
Sir Edward Frankland Fellowship 6961
Sir Edward Frankland Prize Lectureship 6962
Fresenius-Preis 2167
Frumkin Memorial Medal 4842
Fujihara Award 3181
Prix du Gaz de France 1565
Golden Jubilee Commemoration Medal for Chemistry 2686
Prix Grammaticakis-Neuman 1567
Grammaticakis-Neumann Prize 4890
Grand Prix de la Fondation de la Maison de la Chimie 1803
Gregori Aminoffs Pris 4638
Teodor Grotthuss premija 3378
Gunning Victoria Jubilee Prize Lectureship 6995
Prix Philippe A. Guye 1569
Fabian Gyllenbergs pris 4626
Otto-Hahn-Preis fur Chemie und Physik 2091
Carl Hanson Medal 7164
Hanus Medal 1250
Jan Harabaszewski Medal 4031
Harrison Memorial Prize 6963
Haworth Memorial Lectureship 6964
Hector Memorial Medal and Prize 3868
Helmholtz Prize 2269
Prijs Jan-Frans Heymans 967
Hickinbottom Fellowship 6965
Hilditch Memorial Lecture 7166
Gilles Holst Medal 3656
Honorary Membership
International Glaciological Society 6267
Polish Chemical Society 4032
Robert Horne Lecture 7167
Horst Pracejus-Preis 2168
Hurter Memorial Lecture 7168
ICI Annual Award for Chemistry 2839
ICI-FOSS Golden Jubilee Award 2840
IFCC Distinguished Clinical Chemist Award 3078
IFCC Distinguished International Services Award 3079
IFCC Travelling Lectureship 3080
Industrial Chemistry Medal 4315
Industrial Lectureship 6966
Industrially-Sponsored Awards 6967
Christopher Ingold Lectureship 6968
Interdisciplinary Awards 6969
Prix Paul Janssen 1095
Jerwood Awards 6340
Jerwood Prize 7061
John Jeyes Lectureship 6970
JOCS Award for Industrial Technologies 3253
JOCS Award for Merit 3254
JOCS Award for Progress of Studies 3255
JOCS Award for Prominent Studies 3256
Jordan Award 6504
Wilhelm Jost Memorial Lecture 2159
Journal of Oleoscience Editors Award 3257
Prix Emile Jungfleisch 1577
Kaufmann Memorial Lecture 2229
H. P. Kaufmann Prize 2230
KCS Merit Award 4109
Wilhelm-Klemm-Preis 2169
Joseph-Konig-Gedenkmunze 2170
Stanislaw Kostanecki Medal 4033
A. Krishnamurthy Award 2795

Chemistry (continued)

C.R. Krishnamurthy Award 2796
Prix L. La Caze 1578
Prix Langevin 1582
Leighton Memorial Medal 620
LeSueur Memorial Lecture 7171
Leverhulme Medal 6912
Julius Lewkowitsch Memorial Lecture 7174
Liebig-Denkmunze 2172
Liversidge Lectureship 642
Longstaff Medal 6971
Josef Loschimidt Prize 6972
Dr. Max Luthi Award 4891
Prix Paul Marguerite de la Charlonie 1589
Maria Sklodowska-Curie Medal 4034
Marlow Medal and Prize 6973
Medaglia d'oro Domenico Marotta 3103
Juozo Matulis premija 3384
Meldola Medal and Prize 6974
Merck Medal 4316
Prix Georges Millot 1836
Ludwig Mond Lectureship 6975
Hugo Muller Lectureship 6976
Medaglia d'oro Giulio Natta 3104
Nauta Award on Pharmacochemistry 772
Nernst - Haber - Bodenstein-Preis 2160
Netherlands Fund for Chemistry Prize 3658
Nobel Prize for Chemistry 4603
Nobel Prizes 4639
W. Normann Medal 2231
Sir Ronald Nyholm Lectureship 6977
Oils and Fats Group International Lecture 7176
Oleoscience Editors Award 3258
Oronzio and Niccolo De Nora Foundation Prize of ISE on Electrochemical Energy Conversion 4843
Oronzio and Niccolo De Nora Foundation Prize of ISE on Electrochemical Technology and Engineering 4844
Oronzio and Niccolo De Nora Foundation Young Author Prize 4845
Paracelsus-Preis 4892
Partington Prize 7119
Prix Paul Pascal 1596
Medaglia Emanuele Paterno 3105
Pedler Lectureship 6978
Phytochemical Society of Europe Medal 4021
C. S. Piper Prize 622
Prix Andre Policard-Lacassagne 1601
Poster Prize 6263
Preis der Gesellschaft Deutscher Chemiker fur Journalistein und Schriftsteller 2173
Prix Agathon De Potter 1028
Prix de Boelpaepe 1034
Prix de l'Institut Francais du Petrole 1608
Prix des Sciences de la Mer 1609
Prix du Commisariat a l'Energie Atomique 1610
Prix Fonde par l'Etat 1611
Prix Frederic Swarts 1043
Prix Le Bel 1815
Prix Pierre Desnuelle 1616
Prix Pierre Sue 1816
Prix Triennal de la Societe Royale de Chimie 1096
Prize in Chemistry 2957
Prizes of the 150th Anniversary of the RSSL 1098
Prous Science Award on New Technologies in Drug Discovery 773
Raikes Medal 4318
P.B. Rama Rao Memorial Award 2797
Ramsay Memorial Fellowships for Postdoctoral Chemical Research 6589
Theophilus Redwood Lectureship 6979
Rennie Memorial Medal 623
Research Medal 653
Richardson Medal 6268
Sir Eric Rideal Lecture 7178
Robert Robinson Lectureship 6980
Bakhuis Roozeboom Medal 3659
Ruzicka-Prize 4902
Salters' Graduate Prizes 7062
Prix Gabrielle Sand et Marie Guido Triossi 1621
Sandmeyer Prize 4893
P.S. Sarma Memorial Award 2798
Sasol Post-Graduate Medal 4319
Scientific Research Prizes 3451
Second Level Education Award 2841
Seligman Crystal 6269
Professor T. R. Seshadri Seventieth Birthday Commemoration Medal 2714
Prof. M. Shadakshara Swamy Endowment Lecture Award 2799
Professor R. C. Shah Memorial Lecture 2749
Simonsen Lectureship 6981
H. G. Smith Memorial Award 624
Jedrzej Sniadecki Medal 4035
Society for Analytical Chemistry Silver Medal 6982
Society of Analytical Chemistry Gold Medal 6983
South African Chemical Institute Gold Medal 4320
Spiers Memorial Lecture and Prize 6984
Sreenivasaya Memorial Award 2800
Hermann-Staudinger-Preis 2174
Stern Award 6505
Alfred-Stock-Gedachtnispreis 2175
Student Awards 2074
David Syme Research Prize 713
Prix Jacques Tacussel 4846
Tajima Prize 4847
Dr. Edmund Thiele Denkmunze 2034
Tilden Lectureship 6985
Travel Scholarships 1763
TWAS Award in Chemistry 2963
UCB Award for Excellence in Medicinal Chemistry 774
Prix Leon Velluz 1626
Klaus-Jurgen Vetter Prize for Electrochemical Kinetics 4848
Adolf-von-Baeyer-Denkmunze 2176
August-Wilhelm-von-Hofmann-Denkmunze 2177
Otto-Wallach-Plakette 2178
Werner-Preis 4894
Prix Aniuta Winter-Klein 1628
The Wolf Prizes 2938
Young Chemist Award 4099
Young Fellows Award 3259
Young Scientist Award
International Confederation for Thermal Analysis and Calorimetry 4206
International Society for Neurochemistry 1309
Jan Zawidzki Medal 4036
Karl-Ziegler-Preis 2180

Chess
Book of the Year 5277
British Chess Federation Player of the Year 5278
Chess Olympiad for the Blind 4590
Chess World Champions 2475
Club of the Year 5279
Cups 1217
FIDE Master 2476
Gold Diploma of Honor 2477
Grandmaster 2478
International Arbiter 2479
International Master 2480
Koshnitsky Medal 150
Purdy Medal 151
Steiner Medal 152
Woman FIDE Master 2481
Woman Grandmaster 2482
Woman International Master 2483

Child welfare (*See also* Youth work)
Certificate of Satisfaction 4411
Jamnalal Bajaj Foundation Awards 2776
John Muir Award 6342

Children and youth
Ihsan Dogramaci Family Health Foundation Fellowship and Prize 4927
FAO-WAGGGS Nutrition Award 7358
Honour Award 2883
International Award 5940
Merit Awards 2884
Olave Award 7359
Prix Danube Festival, Bratislava 4452
Prix Ex Aequo - International Children's and Youth Radio Drama Festival 4711
Prix Jeunesse International Munchen 2373
Queen's Award 5941
Service Awards 2885
Women of Outstanding Achievement 7361

Children's literature
Claude Aubry Award 4783
Elsa Beskow Plaque 4686
Book Awards of the National Book Development Council of Singapore 4423
Book of the Year Award: Early Childhood 404
Book of the Year Award: Older Readers 405
Book of the Year Award: Younger Readers 406
Book Prizes 2454
Alba Bouwer Prize for ChildrenFs Literature 4265
Buxtehuder Bulle 2385
CBCI Award 2820
Children's Book Award 5883
Russell Clark Award 3750
Lady Cutler Award 407
Penelope Delta Award 2455
Dromkeen Librarian's Award 432
Dromkeen Medal 433
Festival Awards for Literature 672
Percy FitzPatrick Award for Youth Literature 4171
Friedrich-Gerstaecker-Preis 2056
Glazen Globe 3646
Esther Glen Award 3751
Golden Kiss 3495
Gwobrau Tir na n-Og 7325
Nils Holgersson Plaque 4687
Tienie Holloway Medal 4269
International Biennial of Illustrations Bratislava 4442
Mary Vaughan Jones Award 7326
LIANZA Young People's Non-fiction Award 3752

Children's (continued)
Literary Competition 435
Literary Premio Matilde Rosa Araujo 4091
Monteiro Lobato Prize 1119
The Most Beautiful and the Best Children's Books in Slovakia 4438
Elizabeth Mrazik-Cleaver Canadian Picture Book Award 4784
Nestle Smarties Book Prize 5190
New South Wales Premier's Literary Awards 585
Noma Concours for Picture Book Illustrations 3164
Carlos Palanca Memorial Awards for Literature 3978
Picture Book of the Year Award 408
Eve Pownall Award for Information Books 409
Premier's Literary Award 673
Prijs van de Jonge Jury 3496
Prijs van de Nederlandse Kinderjury 3497
Frances E. Russell Award 4785
Scheepers Prize for Youth Literature 4280
Jenny Smelik/IBBY Prize 3571
Prix Bernard Versele 939
Western Australian Premier's Book Awards 685
Whitbread Literary Awards 5194
White Ravens 2330
Young Australians Best Book Award 739

Choral music
Akashvani Annual Awards 2537
Choral Awards 688
Cork International Choral Festival 2829
Crawley Cup 5238
Fleischmann International Trophy Competition 2830
International Choral Competition of Tours 1801
International Competition for Choirs 768
Iuventus Mundi Cantat Competition 1258
Llangollen International Musical Eisteddfod 6393
Montreux Choral Festival 4870
Scottish Song Competition 7073
Harold Smart Competition 6883

Choreography
Dance Screen Award 807
Helsinki International Ballet Competition 1407
International Festival of Modern Jazz Dance 2981
Jerwood Awards 6340
Live Awards 7276
Laurence Olivier Awards 7203

Christianity (*See also* Catholic literature)
Otto Hirsch Medaille 2417
Order of Pius 7413
Order of St. Sylvester 7415
Order of the Golden Spur (Golden Militia) 7416
Pro Ecclesia et Pontifice Medal 7417
Supreme Order of Christ (Militia of Our Lord Jesus Christ) 7418
John Templeton Award for European Religion Writer of the Year 4704
John Templeton European Film Prize 4705
Totius Prize for Theology and Study of the Original Languages of the Bible 4288
Unda Dove 1100
Dominee Pieter van Drimmelen Medal 4290

Church history
International Photography Competition 4986

Cinema *See* Films

Citizenship and patriotism
Prix Audiffred 1632
Australia Day Awards 725
Prix General Muteau 1686
Order of Orange-Nassau 3491
Order of Rio Branco 1113
Order of the Netherlands Lion 3493
Royal Norwegian Order of St. Olav 3903
St. Olav Medal 3904

City management
Britain in Bloom Awards 5760
Planning Consultancy of the Year Award 7051
Young Planner of the Year Award 7052

City planning
Sir Patrick Abercrombie Prize 1922
Civic Trust Awards 5663
European Urban and Regional Planning Achievement Awards 5831
International Film/Video Competition 3578
International No-Dig Award 6295
Organization of Islamic Capitals and Cities Awards 4409
George Pepler International Award 7050
Prix de Rome Fine Art 3642
Edwin Williams Memorial Award 5879

Civil engineering (*See also* Construction)
Russell Allin Prize 6102
Australian Engineering Excellence Awards 488
Prix Barbier 1830
Heinrich Hatt-Bucher Prize 4896
Robert Alfred Carr Premium 6103
R. W. Chapman Medal 495
Civil Engineering Award 7065
Civil Engineering Manager of the Year Award 6104
Concrete Society Awards 5693
Coopers Hill War Memorial Prize 6106
Crampton Prize 6107
Bill Curtin Medal 6108
James Alfred Ewing Medal 6109
James Forrest Medal 6110
Freyssinet Award 3733
Furkert Award 3735
Geotechnical Research Medal 6111
Gold Medal 6112
Halcrow Premium 6114
T. K. Hsieh Award 6115
Renee Redfern Hunt Memorial Prize 6116
IABSE Prize 4774
Institution of Structural Engineers Gold Medal 6195
Institution of Structural Engineers Special Awards 6196
International Award of Merit in Structural Engineering 4775
Kelvin Medal 6118
Lindapter Award 6119
MERIT Competition 6120
Miller Prizes 6121
T. P. de S. Munasinghe Memorial Award 4558
New Zealand Young Engineer of the Year Award 3740
Outstanding Paper Award 4776
Overseas Premium 6122
Frederick Palmer Prize 6123
Parkman Medal 6124
Reed and Mallik Medal 6125
Prix L. E. Rivot 1618
SAACE Excellence Awards 4306
Safety in Construction Medal 6126
George Stephenson Medal 6127
Teambuild 6128
Telford Medal 6129
Trevithick Premium 6130
W. H. Warren Medal 537
Garth Watson Medal 6131
Webb Prize 6133

Civil rights and liberties (*See also* Brotherhood; Child welfare; Citizenship and patriotism; Freedom; Heroism; Human relations; Human rights; Humanitarianism; Intellectual freedom; Women's rights)
Eugene Abrams Award 4697
Fraenkel Prize in Contemporary History 6020
Thomas Jefferson Award 4698
Liberty Awards 6377

Coaching
Coach of the Year 5772

Coin collecting *See* Numismatics

Collectibles *See* Hobbies and clubs

Color technology
CCol ASDC Associateship 7182
CCol FSDC Fellowship 7183
George Douglas Lecture 7184
Ellinger-Gardonyi Award 6503
Honorary Fellow 7185
Honorary Member 7186
Jordan Award 6504
Judd AIC Award 2287
LSDC Licentiateship 7187
Medal of the Society of Dyers and Colourists 7188
Perkin Medal 7189
Sikkens Prize 3665
Turner - Scholefield Award 7191
Worshipful Company of Dyers Research Medal 7192

Comedy *See* Entertainment; Humor

Commerce *See* Business; Finance

Communications (*See also* Audiovisuals; Broadcasting; Communications technology; Human relations; Linguistics; Public relations; Public speaking)
CCA Member Recognition 5572
Columbus Prize 3088
Communicator of the Year 5240
Forderpreis der ITG 2273
International Advertising Festival, Cannes 6202
International Visual Communications Association Awards 6327

Communications (continued)
IPDC - UNESCO Prize for Rural Communication 1995
Ramon Magsaysay Award 3988
Medienpreis fur Sprachkultur 2193
Plain English Campaign Awards 6539
Prince of Asturias Awards 4497
Prix France Telecom 1612
Prix Octave Mirbeau et Valentine Allorge 1615
Alexander Rhomberg Preis 2194

Communications technology
John Howard Dellinger Gold Medal 931
IERE Benefactors Premium 6151
Issac Koga Gold Medal 932
Karl Kupfmuller Prize 2274
Balthasar van der Pol Gold Medal 933
Technology Awards 7046

Community affairs (*See also* Citizenship and patriotism; Community service; Heroism; Humanitarianism; Organizational service; Public affairs)
Fellowship Scheme to Promote Commonwealth Understanding 5680

Community service (*See also* Public service; Social service)
Ros Bower Memorial Award 102
Commonwealth Youth Service Awards 5691
William D. Littleford Award for Corporate Community Service 4416
Ramon Magsaysay Award 3988
Medals of Honor 3245
Order of Orange-Nassau 3491
Order of the Netherlands Lion 3493
Outstanding Community Service Awards 727

Composing *See* Music composition

Computer programming
Prix Ars Electronica - International Competition for Cyberarts 762

Computer science (*See also* Communications; Computer programming; Computers; Information management; Library and information services)
J. F. Carlisle Award 7430
European Coordinating Committee for Artificial Intelligence Awards 770
Victor W. Graham Perpetual Trophy 2836
Konrad-Zuse-Medaille 2191
Prix Michel Monpetit 1592
Heinz Zemanek Award 764

Computers
Friend of IT 4426
Fritz Kutter-Preis 4900
Outstanding Service Award 795
Person of the Year 4427
Silver Core Award 796
Michael A.J. Sweeney Award 4353
Volume Sales Achievement Award 5782
Wilkes Award 5285
Young Professional of the Year 4428

Concrete
BIBM Awards 908
Chairman's Award 4153
Concrete Person of the Year Awards 4155
Concrete Society Awards 5693

Conducting
Allianz Cornhill Musical Insurance Conducting Prize 6461
Besancon International Competition for Young Conductors 1794
International Competition for Musical Performers - Geneva 4702
International Conductors' Competition 3683
Nicolai Malko International Competition for Young Conductors 1311
Music Awards 6865
Antonio Pedrotti International Competition for Orchestra Conductors 2983
Prague Spring International Music Competition 1264
Leonie Sonning Music Prize 1336
Tokyo International Music Competition 3338
Arturo Toscanini International Competition for Conductors 3050

Conservation (*See also* Ecology; Energy; Environmental conservation; Environmental health; Forestry; Nature; Water conservation; Water resources; Wildlife conservation)
Christopher Cadbury Medal 7040
Council of Europe Museum Prize 1754
Duke of Edinburgh Conservation Medal 4943
Environment Prize 3371
European Diploma of Protected Areas 1756
Green Apple Awards 5784
Honorary Membership 4919
Jerwood Awards 6340
National Conservation Award 5143
Fred M. Packard International Parks Merit Award/World Commission on Protected Areas 4920
John C. Phillips Memorial Medal 4921
Peter Scott Medal for Conservation Merit 4922
Tree of Learning Award 4923
WWF Award for Conservation Merit 4946

Construction (*See also* Architecture; Civil engineering; Concrete)
Achievement Award 7281
Achiever of the Year 4152
Australian Engineering Excellence Awards 488
Award for Technical Excellence 5319
Better Brickwork Alliance 7282
Mark Boxer Award 7283
British Institute of Architectural Technologists Student Award 5320
Builders' Awards 3969
Building Manager of the Year Awards 5616
Certificates in Dry Stone Walling 5744
Chairman's Award 3222
Dr. Wilfred Chapman Award 732
Chapter Award 235
Concrete Achiever of the Year 4154
Contract of the Year 5895
Contractor of the Year 5896
Contractors' Awards 5141
Crampton Prize 6107
Fulton Award 4156
Gold Medal 6112
Gold Medal of Honour 4130
Housing Design Awards 6823
IFAWPCA-Atsumi Award 3970
IFAWPCA-CHOI Construction Fieldman Award 3971
Linde Gas/WTIA Young Tradesperson of the Year 733
Magnel Prize 1089
Manufacturer of the Year 5897
A. Ramsay Moon Award 734
Open Award for Technical Excellence in Architectural Technology 5321
Plaisterers Trophy 5891
Professional Excellence in Building Awards 236
Safety in Construction Medal 6126
Florence Taylor Award 735
Florence Taylor Medal 237
Teambuild 6128
Training company of the year 5898
Verdeyen Prize for Soil Mechanics 1090

Consulting
Awards for Excellence 59
National Prize for Consulting 757

Consumer affairs
International Advertising Festival, Cannes 6202

Conventions
International Client Award 6223
National Client Award 6224
National Supplier Award 6225

Cooking *See* Food

Copyright
E-Talents Award 2184
Alfred Gerardi Memory Prize 2185

Costume design
Laurence Olivier Awards 7203

Crafts
Best New Products 7322
Best Stand 7323
Cattell Cup 7207
Fellowships in Arts and Crafts 5681
Haythornthwaite Cup 7208
Howe Cup 7209
President's Cup 7210
Storywriting and Art Competition 107
Tweddle Medal 7211
UNESCO Crafts Prize 2000
Visual Arts Emeritus Award 104

Craftsmanship
Contractors' Awards 5141
Queen Fabiola Prize 917
Royal Dublin Society Crafts Competition 2877

Creative writing
Book of the Year Awards 37
The Bridport Prize 5200
Franz Theodor Csokor Prize 766
Lady Denman Cup 6474
Deux Magots Literary Prize 1728
Ehrenpreis des Osterreichischen Buchhandels 760
Geneva-Europe Prizes 4707
Frans Kellendonk-prijs 3670
Lichfield Prize 6381

Creative (continued)
McKitterick Prize 7147
Shiva Naipaul Memorial Prize 7235
Prijs voor Meesterschap 3672
Singapore Literature Prize 4424
Writers' Emeritus Award 100

Crime writing *See* Mystery writing

Criminology (*See also* Law enforcement)
Investigator of the Year 7353
Hal Lipset "Truth in Action" Award 7354
Lewis Minshall Award 5903
Research and Travel Grants 4644
Robel Award 4006
Security Professional of the Year 7355
Norman J. Sloan Memorial Award 7356

Culinary arts *See* Food

Culture (*See also* African studies; Asian studies; Ethnic affairs; Folklore; Islamic culture; Mythology; specific cultural groups, e.g. Arabic culture)
Book Prize 5482
Bulgarian Academy of Science Honorary Badge - Marin Drinov Medal 1143
Cyril and Methodius Prize 1144
Leigh Douglas Memorial Prize 5483
Joaquin Garcia Monge Prize 1202
Friedrich-Gundolf-Preis fur die Vermittlung deutscher Kultur im Ausland 2146
R. Lysholt Hansens Bibliotekspris 1284
International Institute for Promotion and Prestige Awards 4811
Kultureller Ehrenpreis 2343
Kulturpreis der Stadt Villach 821
Literature pveis der Stadt Dortmund - Nelly-Sachs-Preis 2387
Master's Scholarship 5484
Medals of Honor 3245
National Iqbal Award 3919
National Living Treasures Award 3974
National Order of the Southern Cross 1112
Onassis Award for Culture (Letters, Arts and Humanities) 2461
Organization of Islamic Capitals and Cities Awards 4409
E. du Perron Award 3677
Research Student Awards 5485
Scholarships of the City of Munich 2346
Geschwister-Scholl-Preis 2347
Svenska Akademiens pris for introduktion av svensk kultur utomlands 4672
The Upstarts Awards 6497
Jose Vasconcelos World Award of Education 3461

Cycling *See* Bicycling

Dairy industry
Dairy Student Award 6682
Ice Cream Awards 3773
Dr. Kurien Award 2634
Patrons and Fellows 2635
Prince Philip Award 6683
Princess Royal Award 6684

Dance (*See also* Ballet; Choreography)
Carina Ari Medal of Merit 4575
Arts Council of Northern Ireland Bursaries and Awards 5074
Pierre Bayle Prijs 3644
Classic Championship 6235
Dance Screen Award 807
Gold Badge 5780
Grand Prix 1985
Jerwood Awards 6340
Literature and Art Award 4954
Live Awards 7276
Llangollen International Musical Eisteddfod 6393
Medal of Honor for the Performing and Visual Arts 4273
Medalist of the Year 6236
Miss Dance of Great Britain 6237
Laurence Olivier Awards 7203
Prix de Lausanne 4878
Prix Nouveau Talent 1986
Promotional Prizes 2345
Scholarships of the City of Munich 2346
Split Summer Festival 1223
Traditional Irish Music, Singing and Dancing Awards 2891
Gian Battista Viotti International Music and Dance Competition 3126
World Championships in Ballroom and Latin Dancing 7368

Data base management *See* Information management

Data processing *See* Computer science

Deafness (*See also* Speech and hearing)
Certificate of Outstanding Service 73
Fellows of the Audiological Society of Australia 74
Medal of Honour 5289
President's Distinguished Service Award 75
Dorothy Shaw Deaf Australian of the Year Award 143
Edith Whetnall Lectureship 7023

Democracy *See* Freedom

Demography
Prix Paul Leroy-Beaulieu 1635
Statistics New Zealand/Jacoby Prize 3827

Dental research
Colyer Prize 7007
Medical and Dental Postgraduate Research Scholarships 574
ORCA Rolex Prize 3542
ORCA-Zsolnay Prize 3543

Dentistry (*See also* Dental research; Orthodontistry)
Bright Smiles, Bright Futures Award 1877
F. G. Christensen Memorial Prize 610
Dentistry Development Fund Scholarship for the Development of a Research Technique for Dentistry. 4324
Distinguished Service Award of SADA 4325
Drummond-Jackson Prize 7116
Frank Ashley Undergraduate Prize 5517
General Dental Practitioner Prize 5301
George Cross Fellowship Award 5518
Gold Medal 5496
Grant for Research Workers 5302
Heraeus Kulzer Undergraduate Essay Prize 5497
Lever Pond's Research Fellowship 7297
Bengt Magnusson Memorial Prize 1878
Marsh Midda Fellowship 5519
New Graduate Prize 5498
New Zealand Dental Association Awards 3769
Poster Prize 5303
Winifred E. Preedy Post-Graduate Bursary 193
Premier Award of SADA 4326
Prize for Vocational Dental Practitioners 5304
Research and Education in Dentistry Fund for Post Graduate Studies in Dental Education 4327
Research Grant
British Society of Periodontology 5520
South African Dental Association 4328
SAAD Dental Student Prize 7117
Schottlander Prize 5499
Sir Wilfred Fish Research Prize 5521
Kenneth J. G. Sutherland Prize 611
Travel Grant 4329
Travelling Fellowships 6716
T. C. White Prize Lecture 6717
T. C. White Travelling Fellowship 6718

Dermatology
Argentinean Association of Dermatology Awards 21
British Association of Dermatologists Fellowships 5243
Hugh Wallace Essay and Publication Prize 7020
Hugh Wallace's Registrars' Prize 7021

Design (*See also* Art; Architecture; Book and newspaper design; Costume design; Fiber science; Fashion; Graphic arts; Industrial design; Interior design; Jewelry design; Lighting design; Set design; Textile design)
BesT Design Awards 3713
Braun Prize 2054
Brick Awards 5198
British Academy Television Awards 5217
British Design Awards 5735
Chartered Society of Designers Honorary Fellow 5652
Chartered Society of Designers Medal 5653
Design Partnership Award 6459
Design Prize of the Federal Republic of Germany 2182
Edison Classical Music Award 3510
Edison Popular Music Award 3511
Estlander Prize 1359
Excellent Swedish Design Prize 4691
Fashion Designer of the Year, MTO 1385
Fennia Prize 1360
Kaj Franck Design Prize 1361
Dr. V. M. Ghatage Award 2523
Industrial Designer of the Year TKO 1386
Interior Award SIO 1387
International Design Competition Osaka 3226
Jerwood Awards 6340
Jesselson Prize for Contemporary Judaica Design 2917
Label of the Year Competition 6352
Theo Limperg Prize 3629
Minerva Medal 5654
National Prize for the Most Beautiful Book 758
Newspaper of the Year Award 593

Design (continued)

The Orange British Academy Film Awards 5218
Partisan of the Year Award, TAIKO 1388
Premio Municipal Jorge Colaco de Azulejaria 4077
Premio Municipal Roberto de Araujo Pereira de Design 4083
Prince Philip Prize for the Designer of the Year 5736
Dr. Biren Roy Trust Award 2529
Royal Designer for Industry Award 6921
Sikkens Prize 3665
Textile Designer of the Year, TEXO 1389
Young Designer of the Year Prize 1362

Dietetics *See* Nutrition

Diplomacy *See* International relations

Divorce *See* Family relations

Documentary films
AFI Awards - The Australian Film Institute Awards 196
Amanda Award for Cinematographic Merit 3906
Bilbao International Festival of Documentary and Short Films 4517
British Academy Television Awards 5217
City of Sondrio Gold Plaque 3130
Dance Screen Award 807
Festival dei Popoli 3045
Grand Prix of the Dutch Film Golden Calf 3631
International Adventure Film Festival 1846
International Documentary Film Festival Amsterdam 3576
International Film Festival of Visual Anthropology and Social Documentation 1732
International Filmfestival Mannheim/Heidelberg 2304
International Short Film Festival Oberhausen 2316
International Visual Communications Association Awards 6327
International Women's Film Festival of Creteil and Val-de-Marne 1928
Magnolia Prize 3950
Rouben Mamoulian Award 694
Prix Danube Festival, Bratislava 4452
Tampere International Short Film Festival 1427
Thessaloniki Film Festival 2473
Trento International Film Festival of Mountain and Exploration 3136
Uppsala Short Film Festival 4693
Visions du Reel International Documentary Film Festival 4913

Dogs *See* Animal care and training

Drama (*See also* Drama criticism; Theater)
Arts Council of Northern Ireland Bursaries and Awards 5074
Awgie Awards 395
Arthur Azevedo Prize 1117
Boardman Tasker Award for Mountain Literature 5187
Book Awards of the National Book Development Council of Singapore 4423
Nestor de Tiere Prize 954
Festival of Community Theatre 3805
Miles Franklin Literary Award 700
Golden Antenna International Television Festival 1146
Golden Chest International Television Festival 1147
Grand Prix 1985
Eric Gregory Awards 7142
Gundhall School Gold Medal 5963
Olga E. Harding Trophy 3806
Hertzog Prize for Literature 4268
Edmond Hustinxprijs 3563
Literature and Art Award 4954
Live Awards 7276
Long Service Awards 6478
MarulFs Days Festival 1222
Bruce Mason Playwrighting Award 3825
New South Wales Premier's Literary Awards 585
Order of Culture 3246
Carlos Palanca Memorial Awards for Literature 3978
Premio Nacional de Literatura 1163
Premio Riccione per il Teatro 3123
Premios Municipais Eca de Queiroz de Literatura 4085
Thomas Pringle Award 4172
Prix Ex Aequo - International Children's and Youth Radio Drama Festival 4711
Prix Nouveau Talent 1986
Prize for Translated Work 4278
Prosceniumprijs 3679
PUK-Councilers Prize 4279
Olive Schreiner Prize 4173
Scotsman Fringe First Awards 5753
Split Summer Festival 1223
Standard Bank Young Artist Awards 4191
Svenska Akademiens Teaterpris 4674
Teenage Festival of Life Award 3881
Premio Piervittorio Tondelli 3124
Victorian Premier's Literary Awards 683
Visser-Nederlandia Prijzen 3484
John Whiting Award 5071

Drama criticism
Arthur Azevedo Prize 1117
Pierre Bayle Prijs 3644
Thomas Pringle Award 4172

Drawing (*See also* Cartoons; Graphic arts; Illustration)
Governor General Art Award 3760
Derek Hill Foundation Scholarship 5439
Katanning Art Prize 554
Premio Municipal Rafael Bordalo Pinheiro de Banda Desenhada, Cartoon e Caricaturista 4082
Prix de Rome Fine Art 3642
Prix Le Guay-Lebrun 1483
St. Cuthberts Mill Award for Works on Paper 6943
Prix de Dessin Pierre David Weill 1496

Dutch literature
Lode Baekelmans Prize 949
Dr. Karel Barbier Prize 950
August Beernaert Prize 951
Anna Bijnsprijs 3486
Henriette de Beaufort-prijs 3667
Golden Kiss 3495
Henriette Roland Holst-prijs 3669
Charlotte Kohler Prize 3681
Kruyskamp-prijs 3671
Arthur Merghelynck Prize 960
Order of the Netherlands Lion 3493
Prijs der Nederlandse Letteren 3623
Prijs van de Nederlandse Kinderjury 3497
Prijs voor Meesterschap 3672
Prix des Ambassadeurs 3553
Lucy B. and C. W. Van der Hoogt-prijs 3673
Jozef Van Ginderachter Prize 963

Earth science *See* Geology and paleontology; Seismology

East European culture
Booker Russian Novel Prize 5189

Ecology (*See also* Nature)
Best Poster Prize 5293
British Ecological Society Grants and Awards 5294
British Ecological Society President's Medal 5295
Crafoord Prize 4637
Prix Georges Deflandre et Marthe Deflandre-Rigaud 1557
Ecology Institute Prize 2301
Environment Medal 7162
Fondation Jean Lebrun 1023
Founders' Prize 5296
International Environmental Film Festival 2365
International Institute for Promotion and Prestige Awards 4811
IRPE Prize International Recognition of Professional Excellence 2302
Anne Keymer Prize 5297
Roberto Marchetti Award 3113
Marsh Award for Ecology 5298
Prix Georges Millot 1591
Prix des Sciences de la Mer 1609
Small Ecological Project Grants 5299
Torello International Festival of Mountain and Adventure Films 4545
Trento International Film Festival of Mountain and Exploration 3136
Preis der Horst Wiehe-Stiftung 2210

Economic development
APO National Awards 3166
APO Regional Award 3167
Asian Banking Awards 3964
Nessim Habif Prize 1992
Honorary Member 3965
King Baudouin International Development Prize 935
Legion of Honor Award 2814
TWAS Award in Basic Medical Sciences 2961
TWAS Award in Biology 2962
TWAS Award in Chemistry 2963
TWAS Award in Mathematics 2964
TWAS Award in Physics 2965
UNESCO Science Prize 2006
Freiherr Von Stein Prize 2407

Economics (*See also* Agricultural economics; Economic development; Finance; International trade; Rural economics; Social science research)
ATEM Fellow 52
Best Paper Award 2306
Conference Grant Scheme 6751
J. G. Crawford Award 298
Prix Estrade-Delcros 1509

Economics (continued)
Prix Demolombe 1651
Distinguished Service Award 346
Prix Charles Dupin 1654
Prix Joseph Dutens 1656
Prix Leon Faucher 1658
Fondation Ernest Mahaim 993
Founders' Medal for Doctors' Degree Thesis 4166
Founders' Medal for Masters' Degree Dissertation 4167
Free Market Award 4180
Freedom Prize 4868
Celso Furtado Prize in Political Economy 2954
Prix Emile Girardeau 1665
Prix Grammaticakis-Neuman 1666
Grand Prix de l'Academie des Sciences Morales et Politiques 1667
Bernhard-Harms-Preis 2338
Honorary Life Membership 347
International Institute for Promotion and Prestige Awards 4811
Islamic Development Bank Prizes in Islamic Economics and Islamic Banking 4401
Junior Fellowship Awards 6752
Leverhulme Memorial Lecture 6372
Prix Limantour 1679
Prix Charles Lyon-Caen 1680
Prix Zerilli Marimo 1683
Johann-Heinrich-Merck Ehrung 2443
Ernst Meyer Prize 4778
J.J.I. Middleton Award 4168
Most Valuable Paper 348
National Institute of Insurance International Prizes 2971
Bank of Sweden Prize in Memory of Alfred Nobel 4601
Nobel Prizes 4639
Order of Merit of the Republic of Poland 4014
Order of Polish Rebirth 4015
Prix Le Dissez de Penanrun 1687
Premio Internazionale di Meridionalistica Guido Dorso 2987
Prix Ugo Papi - Gaston Leduc 1691
Research Medal 653
Albino Rimka premija 3385
Roll of Honour Award 3157
Prix Rossi 1693
Royal Economic Society Prize 6753
Prix Saintour 1696
Schumpeter Prize 2375
Service Award 349
Soderbergs Pris 4640
Suntory Prize for Social Sciences and Humanities 3334
Prix Wolowski 1706

Editing
British Society of Magazine Editors Awards 5511
Communicators in Business Awards 5241
International Visual Communications Association Awards 6327
Nihon Shinbun Kyokai Awards 3241
Lorenz Oken Medaille 2254
Polish PEN Centre Prizes 4019

Editorial writing
Anders-Bording Prisen 1280
Golden Apple 2019
Lokaljournalistenpreis des Konrad-Adenauer-Stiftung 2341

Education (*See also* Academic achievement; Educational research; Intellectual freedom; Learning disabled; Literacy; Scholarly works; Teaching; Training and development)
Adult Learners Week 35
Award for the Promotion of International Education 5827
BTA Trophy 5540
Canada Memorial Foundation Scholarships 5123
Chemical Education Medal 4314
Chemistry Teaching Award 7059
Commonwealth Scholarship and Fellowship Plan 5124
Commonwealth Shared Scholarship Scheme 5125
Cromer Greek Awards 5208
Development Education Grants 7328
Distinguished Friends of Council Award 2448
Prix Adrien Duvand 1657
Erasmus Medal 4997
European Council of International Schools Awards 5828
Excellence Award 2449
Family Life Award 5881
Ivan Filipovic Award 1239
Gold Medal
Academia Europaea 4998
Australian Council for Educational Leaders 168
Calouste Gulbenkian Foundation Grants 5574
Soren Gyldendal Prisen 1305
Nessim Habif Prize 1992
Ben Hawthorne Award 3155
Hodgson Prize 6643
Honorary Member 7287
Honorary Vice President 7288
International Visual Communications Association Awards 6327
Edith-Dalton James Award 3156
Jasper Fellowship 4960
Kancharla Award For Excellence 2546
Leverhulme Lecture 7172
Prix Louis Liard 1678
Life Membership 351
Ian Macmillan Prize 6936
Maturi Award for Excellence 2547
Medals of Honor 3245
Najmann Award 2943
Nannidar Award for Excellence 2548
National Order of the Southern Cross 1112
NESA Awards 2459
Nganakarrawa Award 169
NHK Japan Prize 3298
Nile Gold Medal 4742
Bill Ogden Memorial Prize 6591
Order of Polish Rebirth 4015
Order of the Academic Palms 1824
Phenix UDA 2008
Pothuganti Award for Excellence 2549
Premio Internazionale di Meridionalistica Guido Dorso 2987
President's Award 840
Prix Eugene Lameere 1008
Prix Tobie Jonckheere 1018
Prize of Excellence 3900
QSPA Achievement Award 603
QSPA Award for Leadership in the Profession 604
QSPA Lifetime Achievement 605
Andres Manuel del Rio National Prize in Chemistry 3437
Roll of Honor 3528
SEAMEO Service Award 4110
Richard Seligman Lecture 7179
R.C. Tavares Award 3158
Teacher of the Year Award 1355
J. P. Thomson Medal 630
Prix Ernest Thorel 1702
Jose Vasconcelos World Award of Education 3461
Peter Wildy Prize for Microbiology Education 7100
Worlddidac Award 4941

Education, adult and continuing *See* Adult and continuing education

Education, agricultural *See* Agricultural education

Education, art *See* Art education

Education, elementary *See* Elementary education

Education, engineering *See* Engineering education

Education, health *See* Health education

Education, higher *See* Higher education

Education, journalism *See* Journalism education

Education, legal *See* Legal education

Education, medical *See* Medical education

Education, music *See* Music education

Education, physical *See* Physical education

Education, science *See* Science education

Education, secondary *See* Secondary education

Education, special *See* Special education

Educational films
Australian Teachers of Media Awards 380
Andre Leroy Prize 1902
NHK Japan Prize 3298

Educational research
IEA - Bruce H. Choppin Memorial Award 3567
National Assessment Awards 709
Prix Victor Thebault 1623
UNESCO Prize for Human Rights Education 2003
Peter Wildy Prize for Microbiology Education 7100

Subject Index

Electrical engineering (*See also* Electronics)
Achievement Medals 6141
Benefactors Prize 6142
Blumlein-Brown-Willans Premium 6143
Bridgeport Prize 6144
College of Electrical Engineers Student Prizes 497
Coopers Hill War Memorial Medal 6145
Divisional Premium 6146
James Alfred Ewing Medal 6109
Faraday House Commemorative Prize 6147
Faraday Medal 6148
Harry Henniker Premium 6150
Herbert-Kind-Preis der ETG 2102
J. A. Lodge Award for Medical Engineering 6152
John Madsen Medal 516
Manufacturing Project Prizes 6153
Measurement Prize 6154
Eric Megaw Memorial Prize 6155
George Montefiore Foundation Prize 943
Henry Nimmo Premium 6157
Evan Parry Award 3742
Rayleigh Book Award 6159
A. H. Reeves Premium 6160
IIE Sir Henry Royce Award for Achievement 663
Sir Henry Royce Award 6161
SAACE Excellence Awards 4306
M. A. Sargent Medal 530
Simms Prize 6656
South African Institute of Electrical Engineers Awards 4339
J. Langham Thompson Premium 6162
VDE/ETG Award 2103
D. J. Wimalasurendra Memorial Award 4562
Young Engineer of the Year 6164

Electrical industry
Student Lighting Design Awards 6383

Electronics
IETE-Prof. S.V.C. Aiya Memorial Award 2764
Kazimiero Barsauskas premija 3373
Caroline Haslett Memorial Trust 6176
Cave Radio and Electronics Group 5274
Editorial Award 6177
European Association for Signal, Speech and Image Processing Awards 4060
Gustave Canet Memorial Medal 6178
IETE-Bimal Bose Award 2765
IETE-Hari Ramji Toshniwal Gold Medal 2766
Lady Finniston Award 6179
IETE-Ram Lal Wadhwa Gold Medal 2767
IETE-Prof. S.N. Mitra Memorial Award 2768
Quantum Electronics Prize 1788
Regional Achievement Award 6180
Regional Presentation Award 6181
IETE-Flt. Lt. Tanmaya Singh Dandass Memorial Award 2769
Sir Henry Royce Memorial Medal 6182
IETE-Prof. K. Sreenivasan Memorial Award 2770
J. Langham Thompson Premium 6162
J. J. Thomson Premium 6163
IETE-Lal. C. Verman Award 2771
Young Woman Engineer of the Year Award 6183
Dr. V. K. Zworykin Premium 6166

Elementary education
Prix Joseph De Keyn 1012

Emergency medicine
Ambulance Service Medal 200

Emergency services
Emergency Services Medal 215

Endocrinology
Mayne Pharma Bryan Hudson Clinical Endocrinology Award 437
Merck European Thyroid Von-Basedow-Research Prize 2203
Novartis Junior Scientist Award 438
Schoeller-Junkmann-Preis 2204
Servier Young Investigator Award 439
Travel Grants 440
Von-Recklinghausen-Preis 2205

Energy
Achievement Through Action Award 2327
Australian Institute of Energy Medal 239
Farrington Daniels Award 2328
Energy Manager of the Year Award 5762
Prix du Gaz de France 1565
Habitat Solaire, Habitat d'aujourd'hui 1936
Heinrich Hertz Preis 2429
James Prescott Joule Medal 6117
Malchett Medal 5763
Pakistan Institute of Sciences Gold Medal 3921
Prix Ivan Peyches 1598
Thring Award 5764

Energy, atomic *See* Atomic energy

Engineering (*See also* Communications technology; Electronics; Energy; Engineering education; Materials science; Mining and metallurgy; Photogrammetry; Standards; Surveying; Testing; Water resources)
ABU Engineering Award 3397
Achievement Award 3191
AGIR's Prize 4384
Nikolai Alumae Medal 1347
Andritz Oy Award 1393
The Associateship of the City and Guilds of London Institute 5656
Association Plaquette of Merit 1394
Australian Engineering Excellence Awards 488
Award for Achievement in Engineering Enterprise 489
Award of Merit 6081
Award of Specialty 3328
Award of Technical Paper 3329
Award of Technology 3330
Awards for Excellence 59
Awards of Excellence 3696
Barker Silver Medal 5634
The Baroness Platt of Writtle Award 5766
C.N. Barton Medal 490
Beilby Medal and Prize 6950
Best Engineering Achievements Awards 4199
Best Exhibition Stall Awards 4200
Best Paper Award 3192
Best Papers Award 4201
Bhatnagar Award 2573
Birmingham Medal 6168
Scott Blair Biorheology Scholarship 5527
O. F. Blakey Memorial Prize 491
Bomford Trust Paper Award 6082
A. K. Bose Medal 2647
British Society of Rheology Annual Award 5528
British Society of Rheology Gold Medal 5529
Frederick Brough Memorial Prize 493
W.P. Brown Medal 494
Bruce-Preller Prize Lectureship 6990
Bursaries 7345
Karen Burt Award 7346
Cadzow Smith Award 5767
Carter Bronze Medal 5635
Ceylon Development Engineering Award 4556
Civil Engineering Students Papers Competition 6105
Collacott Prize 6135
Conference Awards 5389
Contribution to Land Based Industries Award 6083
Cooling Prize 5311
E. R. Cooper Memorial Medal and Prize 3865
J.M.C. Corlette Medal 499
John Cranko Memorial Award 3730
J.H. Curtis Medal 500
Dapaepe-Willems Award 924
E. H. Davis Memorial Lecture 501
Distinguished Achievement and Contributions Award 3193
Distinguished International Fellow 545
Distinguished Service Award 3069
Dobson Lecture 3731
Dufton Silver Medal Award 5636
Russell Dumas Medal 502
L.R. East Medal 503
Engineering 2000 Awards 504
Engineering Achievement Award 7441
Environmental Award 3732
Ergonomics Development Award 3070
Rosalind Franklin Award 6907
Fujihara Award 3181
Fulton-Downer Award 3734
Leon Gaster Bronze Medal 5637
Prix du Gaz de France 1565
Graduate and Students Papers Competition (Local Association) Competition 6113
Faldt Guthrie Medal 506
P. H. Haviland Award 7442
Hector Memorial Medal and Prize 3868
Dr. A.H. Heineken Prize for Environmental Sciences 3653
Helmholtz Prize 2269
Ian Henderson Memorial Prize 507
Honda Prize 3185
Honorary Fellowship 6084
Hopkins Lecture 3736
Hosei International Fund Foreign Scholars Fellowship 3187
IAHR-APD Award 4506
Industrial Automation Award 4432
Inose Paper Award 3194
Institution of Engineers Medal 508
Institution of Gas Engineers Bronze Medal 6169
Institution of Gas Engineers Gold Medal 6170
Institution of Gas Engineers Silver Medal 6171

Engineering (continued)

International Association for Engineering Geology and the Environment Awards 3565
IPENZ Craven Post-Graduate Research Scholarship 3737
IPENZ Structural Award 3738
Arthur Thomas Ippen Award 4508
K. Johinke Medal 510
Johnson New Holland Award 6085
James Prescott Joule Medal 6117
Journal Awards 4202
Junior Inventor of the Year E. C. Fernando Memorial Award 4557
Allen Knight Medal 512
Jan Korevaar Outstanding Paper Award 546
K.U. Smith Student Paper Award 3071
Lady Finniston Award 7347
Lampen Medal 1395
Ian Langlands Medal 513
Digby Leach Medal 514
Liberty Mutual Prize in Occupational Safety and Ergonomics 3072
Local Government Engineering Medal 515
MacLean Citation 3739
MacRobert Award 6621
Prasanta Chandra Mahalanobis Medal 2693
MakDougall-Brisbane Prize 6997
Mendelssohn Award 2299
Sir Eric Mensforth International Gold Medal 6156
The Mercia Prize - Postgraduate Bursary in Medical Engineering 5768
Michael Dwyer Memorial Award 6086
John Monash Medal 518
Mullard Award 6913
Napier - Shaw Bronze Medal 5639
Kevin Nash Gold Medal 6293
National Excellence Awards for Engineering Journalism 519
W. L. Newnham Memorial Lecture 3741
W.H.R. Nimmo Medal 520
Orden al Merito Julio Garavito 1191
Outstanding Educators Award 3073
Pakistan Institute of Sciences Gold Medal 3921
Sir Arvi Parbo Medal 521
R. W. Parsons Memorial Prize 522
Professor E. O. E. Pereira Award 4559
Louis Prangey Award 4797
Premio Nacional 1166
President's Award
Association of Consulting Engineers New Zealand 3697
Institution of Professional Engineers New Zealand 3743
International Ergonomics Association 3074
President's Commendation 7443
President's Medal 6622
President's Prize 523
R.A. Priddle Medal 524
Prince Philip Medal 6623
Prix Blaise Pascal du GAMNI-SMAI 1605
Prix Charles Lemaire 1033
Prize in Engineering Sciences 2959
Professional Commitment Award 3744
Professional Engineer of the Year 525
Rabone Award 3745
Railway Engineering Award 527
James Ransom Memorial Medals 6173
Research Medal 653
Dr. Biren Roy Memorial Lecture 2711
Peter Nicol Russell Memorial Medal 528
SAACE Excellence Awards 4306
Bernhard Schmidt Prize 1352
Service Awards 5769
Shanti Swarup Bhatnagar Medal 2716
Shinohara Memorial Award 3331
Silver Medal 6624
SKF Award 7444
State Development and Construction Corporation Award 4561
Stenback Plaquette 1396
K. G. Stevens Award 7445
Claude A. Stewart Award 484
Percy Still Medal 6137
A.E. Stohr Medal 534
Peter Stone Award 5117
Akroyd Stuart Certificate 6138
Student Award 3698
Sugg Heritage Award 6174
Sustainability in Design and Use Award 6087
Turner Lecture 3748
UNESCO Science Prize 2006
Vannprisen 3892
John Walker Award 6139
Walsh - Weston Bronze Award 5640
WFEO Award for Engineering Excellence 2016
WFEO Medal of Excellence in Engineering Education 2017
Sir Frank Whittle Medal 6625
G.R. Wilmoth Medal 538
Young Consulting Engineers Award 5770
Young Engineers Speaking Competition 539
Young Professional Engineer of the Year 540
Young Researchers' Award 3195
S. H. Zaheer Medal 2728

Engineering, aeronautical *See* Aeronautical engineering

Engineering, agricultural *See* Agricultural engineering

Engineering, automotive *See* Automotive engineering

Engineering, biomedical *See* Biomedical engineering

Engineering, ceramic *See* Ceramic engineering

Engineering, chemical *See* Chemical engineering

Engineering, civil *See* Civil engineering

Engineering education
IGIP Award 4838
Gustav Lorentzen Medal 1896
Norman Selfe Medal 531
Student Award 3698

Engineering, electrical *See* Electrical engineering

Engineering, human *See* Human engineering

Engineering, industrial *See* Industrial engineering

Engineering, marine *See* Naval engineering

Engineering, mechanical *See* Mechanical engineering

Engineering, military *See* Military engineering

Engineering, naval *See* Naval engineering

Engineering, nuclear *See* Nuclear engineering

English history
David Berry Prize 6778
Cromwell Essay Competition 5715
Templer Medal 7129
Whitfield Prize 6781

English literature
Benson Medal 7001
Rose Mary Crawshay Prize for English Literature 5207
Gladstone History Book Prize 6779
Sir Israel Gollancz Prize 5209
Graduation Prize 3635
Enid McLeod Literary Prize 5922
NSES Award 3636

Engraving
Prix Bordin 1439
Prix Auguste Durand et Edouard Ordonneau 1449
Prix Houllevigue 1455
Prix Pinet 1468
Prix Breaute 1471
Prix Colmont 1475
Prix de la Societe Francaise de Gravure 1477
Prix et Fondations Concernant l'Academie de France a Rome 1482
Prix Ary Scheffer 1491
Prix Frederic et Jean de Vernon 1495
Prix Paul-Louis Weiller 1498
Prix Georges Wildenstein 1499

Entertainment (*See also* Animated films; Humor)
Arion Prize 4023
Bert Easey Technical Award 5503
Best Dance Venue 227
Best General Entertainment Amusement Venue 228
BSC Best Cinematography Award 5504
Golden Rose of Montreaux Award 4882
Helpmann Awards 183
Frank Littlejohn Award 5183
Andrew Nordelli Prize 4024
Outstanding Achievement in Patron Transport Safety 230
Charles Parkhouse Award 5184
L. Schiller Award 4025
Charles Staffell Visual Effects Award 5505
Terpsychsna Prize 4026
Janusz Warnecki Prize for a Part in Radio Drama 4027
Waterford Crystal Award 6027
Jacek Woszczerowicz Prize 4028
Denis Wratten Journal Award 5185

Entertainment (continued)
ZASP President's Award 4029

Entomology *See* Zoology

Entrepreneurship *See* Business

Environmental conservation
Advanced Diploma 6022
Associate Member Diploma 6023
Awards for Sustainability Reporting 5119
Christopher E. Barthel, Jr. Award 6318
Blekinge County Council Prize for Environmental Control 4573
Blue Planet Prize 3162
Britain in Bloom Awards 5760
Certificate in Energy Efficiency For Domestic Central Heating 6024
Environment Prize 3371
Environmental Award
Institution of Professional Engineers New Zealand 3732
International Hotel and Restaurant Association 1894
International Motorcycle Federation 4813
Charles Fleming Award for Environmental Achievement 3866
Ned Franklin Medal 6093
Global 500 3956
Grassland Society of Southern Africa Awards 4193
Green Apple Award 5945
Elizabeth Haub Prize for Environmental Diplomacy 2293
Elizabeth Haub Prize for Environmental Law 2294
Honda Prize 3185
Honorary Member 4434
Honorary Membership 6329
Imhoff - Koch Award for Outstanding Contribution to Water Management and Science 6330
International Festival of Mountain Environment and Alpine Films, Les Diablerets, Switzerland 4805
Tado Ivanausko premija 3379
Samuel H. Jenkins Outstanding Service Award 6331
Lillehammer Award 852
Onassis Award for the Environment 2463
Organization of Islamic Capitals and Cities Awards 4409
Fred M. Packard International Parks Merit Award 4917
Prix de l'Institut Francais du Petrole 1608
Publishing Award 6332
Sultan Qaboos Prize for Environmental Preservation 1998
Queen's Awards for Enterprise 6579
Rolex Awards for Enterprise 4880
Fritz Schumacher Prize 2402
Sorby Medal 904
Sture Centerwalls Pris 4641
Technician Diploma 6025
Umweltpreis der Landeshauptstadt Stuttgart 2419
UNEP Sasakawa Environment Prize 3366
United Nations Environment Program Awards 3367
World Clean Air Congress Award 6319
World Press Photo Contest 3690

Environmental health
Gawad AGKATEK (Agham, Kapaligiran at Teknolohiya) 3982
Sergey Soloviev Medal 1780

Epilepsy
Ambassador for Epilepsy Award 2843
Award for Social Accomplishment 2844

Equestrian *See* Horsemanship

Essays
Alexander Prize 6777
Russell Allin Prize 6102
Amerbach-Preis 4911
Barker Silver Medal 5634
David Berry Prize 6778
Blumlein-Brown-Willans Premium 6143
Robert Alfred Carr Premium 6103
Carter Bronze Medal 5635
Civil Engineering Students Papers Competition 6105
Commonwealth Essay Competition 6749
Coopers Hill War Memorial Medal 6145
Coopers Hill War Memorial Prize 6106
Arthur H. Cornette Prize 953
Crampton Prize 6107
Curl Essay Prize 6674
Bill Curtin Medal 6108
Divisional Premium 6146
J. B. Donne Essay Prize on the Anthropology of Art 6675
Dufton Silver Medal Award 5636
Aquileo J. Echeverria Prize 1201
Joris Eeckhout Prize 955
Essay Contest 3197
James Forrest Medal 6110
Dr. Wijnaendts Francken-prijs 3668
Trench Gascoigne Prize 7056
Leon Gaster Bronze Medal 5637
Graduate and Students Papers Competition (Local Association) Competition 6113
Halcrow Premium 6114
Harry Henniker Premium 6150
T. K. Hsieh Award 6115
Renee Redfern Hunt Memorial Prize 6116
IERE Benefactors Premium 6151
James Prescott Joule Medal 6117
John F. Kennedy Student Paper Competition 4509
Lindapter Award 6119
Eric Megaw Memorial Prize 6155
Johann-Heinrich-Merck Preis 2147
Miller Prizes 6121
Napier - Shaw Bronze Medal 5639
New Scholar's Prize 6241
Henry Nimmo Premium 6157
Overseas Premium 6122
Carlos Palanca Memorial Awards for Literature 3978
Frederick Palmer Prize 6123
Parkman Medal 6124
Premio Nacional de Literatura 1163
Premios Municipais Eca de Queiroz de Literatura 4085
Prix Cazes - Brasserie Lipp 1938
Reed and Mallik Medal 6125
A. H. Reeves Premium 6160
Royal Historical Society/*History Today* Prize 6780
Safety in Construction Medal 6126
Ary Sleeks Prize 961
Gyorgy Striker Junior Paper Award 2508
Telford Medal 6129
J. Langham Thompson Premium 6162
Trevithick Premium 6130
Walsh - Weston Bronze Award 5640
James Watt Medal 6132
Webb Prize 6133
Wolskel Industrial Chemistry Essay Award 625
Wooden Horse Award 452
Dr. V. K. Zworykin Premium 6166

Ethics
Premio Dotte Giuseppe Borgia 2973

Ethnic affairs (*See also* Culture)
CRC Multicultural Award 692
The G. R. Fairall Award 7431
International Film Festival of Visual Anthropology and Social Documentation 1732
Nancy Keesing Fellowship 680
Media Save Art Award 3065
PC World Award 7432
Phenix UDA 2008
Prix Henri Lavachery 1010
Jean van Vught Award 7433

European culture (*See also* East European culture)
Hamburg Max Brauer Prize 2395
Henry Duncan Prize Lectureship 6994
Erasmus Prize 3519
European Music and Poetry Competitions 856
Dr. Wijnaendts Francken-prijs 3668
Goethe Medaille 2265
Herder Prizes 2397
John Lotz Commemorative Medal 2506
Somerset Maugham Awards 7146
Membership in the Gorsedd of Bards 6471
Scottish Research Book Award 7071
Sonning Prize 1338
Henrik Steffens Prize 2404

European history
Fraenkel Prize 7332
Fraenkel Prize in Contemporary History 6020
Dr. Wijnaendts Francken-prijs 3668
Dr. A.H. Heineken Prize for History 3654
Eoin O'Mahony Bursary 2881
Premio Municipal Augusto Vieira da Silva de Investigacao 4073
Prix Anton Bergmann 998

European integration
Emile Bernheim European Prizes 1102
Coudenhove-Kalergi Award 2369
Europe Prize 1755
Herder Prizes 2397
International Charlemagne Prize of Aachen 2409

European literature (*See also* Dutch literature; English literature; French literature; Italian literature; Spanish literature)
Aniara Prize 4685
Booker Russian Novel Prize 5189
Ehrenpreis des Osterreichischen Buchhandels 760
John Lotz Commemorative Medal 2506
Nordic Council Literature Prize 4613
Rauriser Literaturpreis 743
Schlegel - Tieck Prize 7135

European (continued)
Shakespeare Prize 2403
Adelbert-von-Chamisso-Preis der Robert Bosch Stiftung 2040

Exhibiting
ADAM Award 2136
International Exhibition Logistics Associates Awards 4795
Union of International Fairs Awards 2010

Exploration (*See also* Geography)
Australian Antarctic Medal 202
Livingstone Medal 6892
Mungo Park Medal 6893
Polar Medal 5603
Rolex Awards for Enterprise 4880
Trento International Film Festival of Mountain and Exploration 3136

Export *See* International trade

Family planning
IPPA Award 2818

Family relations (*See also* Child welfare)
Prix Malouet 1682
Medal for Long Marital Life 4012

Fashion (*See also* Design; Modeling)
Auto Color Designers' Selection 3228
Bunka Women's University Selection Award 3229
Fashion Color Award 3230
Footwear Fashion Future Award 2225
Grand Prize 3231
UK Fashion Export Awards 7285

Fashion modeling *See* Modeling

Feminism *See* Women

Fencing
National Order of the Southern Cross 1112

Fiber science (*See also* Textile design; Textile industry)
George Douglas Lecture 7184
Jubilee Award 7269
S. G. Smith Memorial Medal 7272

Fiction (*See also* Science fiction; Short stories)
Afonso Arinos Prize 1116
The Australian/Vogel Literary Award 39
Award for Original Hebrew Novel 2898
Azorin Prize 4479
Bagutta Prize 2993
Benson Medal 7001
James Tait Black Memorial Prizes 7308
Boardman Tasker Award for Mountain Literature 5187
Book Awards of the National Book Development Council of Singapore 4423
Book of the Year Awards 37
Buddle Findlay Sargeson Fellowship 3702
Commonwealth Writers Prize 5679
Aquileo J. Echeverria Prize 1201
Festival Awards for Literature 672
FosterGrant Reading Glasses Romantic Novel of the Year 6605
Soren Gyldendal Prisen 1305
Joan Hessayon New Writers' Award 6606
Man Booker Prize for Fiction 6418
Somerset Maugham Awards 7146
New South Wales Premier's Literary Awards 585
Noma Literacy Prize 3289
Ondaatje Prize 7002
Carlos Palanca Memorial Awards for Literature 3978
Ellis Peters Historical Crime Award 5712
Premi de les Lletres Catalanes Ramon Llull 4480
Premi Josep Pla 4481
Premier's Literary Award 673
Premio Apel-les Mestres 4482
Premio Biblioteca Breve 4483
Premio Carlos Bonvalot 4092
Premio de Novela Fernando Lara 4484
Premio Espasa Ensayo 4485
Premio Espiritualidad 4486
Premio Nacional de Literatura 1163
Premio Nadal 4487
Premio Planeta de Novela 4488
Premio Primavera de Novela 4489
Premio Sent Sovi 4550
Premios Municipais Eca de Queiroz de Literatura 4085
Prix Cazes - Brasserie Lipp 1938
Prix des Maisons de la Presse 1934
Prix Theophraste Renaudot 1943
Prix Victor Rossel 937
Ary Sleeks Prize 961
NZSA Lilian Ida Smith Award 3794
Strega Prize 3132
Betty Trask Prize and Awards 7151
Victorian Premier's Literary Awards 683
Wales Book of the Year Awards 4995
Western Australian Premier's Book Awards 685
Whitbread Literary Awards 5194
Yoshikawa Eiji Prize for Literature 3290

Field hockey *See* Hockey

Film competitions *See* Film festivals

Film criticism
Pierre Bayle Prijs 3644

Film festivals
Alpinale International Film Festival 741
Amiens International Film Festival 1710
Audience Prizes 2332
Australian International Widescreen Festival 393
Berlin International Film Festival 2048
Bilbao International Festival of Documentary and Short Films 4517
Brussels International Festival of Fantastic Film 850
Cannes International Film Festival 1730
CINANIMA 4056
Clermont-Ferrand International Short Film Festival 1947
Clermont-Ferrand National Short Film Festival 1948
Cork International Film Festival 2827
Cracow International Festival of Short Films 3999
CRC Multicultural Award 692
Dendy Awards for Australian Short Films 693
Durban International Film Festival Awards 4164
Ebenseer Bear 780
Edinburgh International Film Festival 5756
Ekotopfilm Festival 4440
Festival de Cine de Alcala de Henares 4493
Festival du Film Court de Villeurbanne 1792
Festival du Film d'Etudes Cinematographiques 1930
Festival of Underwater Images 1799
Gijon International Film Festival for Young People 4499
Golden Horse Awards 4952
Golden Knight International Amateur Film and Video Festival 3423
Holland Animation Film Festival 3561
Hong Kong Independent Short Film Competition/Urban Council Short Film Awards 3936
Iberoamerican Film Festival 4503
Impact of Music on Film Competition 890
International Adventure Film Festival 1846
International Advertising Festival, Cannes 6202
International Animation Festival in Japan, Hiroshima 3183
International Children's Film Festival of India 2551
International Competition for Film and Video 778
International Documentary Film Festival Amsterdam 3576
International Environmental Film Festival 2365
International Festival of Animated Film Stuttgart 2421
International Festival of Film and Television in the Celtic Countries 5587
International Festival of Maritime, Exploration, and Environmental Films 1890
International Festival of Mountain Environment and Alpine Films, Les Diablerets, Switzerland 4805
International Festival of Red Cross and Health Films 1153
International Film Festival of Visual Anthropology and Social Documentation 1732
International Filmfestival Mannheim/Heidelberg 2304
International Free Flight Film Festival 1797
International Mystery Festival 3017
International Prize Paladino D'Oro 3084
International Short Film Festival Oberhausen 2316
International Women's Film Festival of Creteil and Val-de-Marne 1928
Istanbul International Film Festival 4982
Locarno International Film Festival 4864
Mediafest, the Gran Canaria International Festival of Arts and Digital Cultures 4477
Melbourne International Film Festival Shorts Awards 563
Moscow International Film Festival 4390
Munich International Filmschool Festival 2138
Odense International Film Festival 1320
Oporto International Film Festival - Fantasporto 4058
Panafrican Film and Television Festival of Ouagadougou 1160
Joseph Plateau Prize 891
Premio Varese 3086
Prize for Children's Film 2333

Film (continued)

Prizes for Short Films 2334
St. Kilda Film Festival 661
San Sebastian International Film Festival Awards 4538
Sao Paulo International Film Festival 1136
Short Film Festival Prize 3910
Star Boy Award 1423
Tampere International Short Film Festival 1427
Thessaloniki Film Festival 2473
Tokyo International Film Festival 3336
Torello International Festival of Mountain and Adventure Films 4545
Trento International Film Festival of Mountain and Exploration 3136
Turin International Film Festival 3009
Uppsala Short Film Festival 4693
Valencia Film Festival 4525
Valladolid International Film Festival 4552
Visions du Reel International Documentary Film Festival 4913
West Australia Film Awards 458
World Festival of Animated Films 1241

Films (*See also* Animated films; Audiovisuals; Cable television; Documentary films; Educational films; Entertainment; Film criticism; Film festivals; Television; Video)
ADIRCAE Prizes 4471
AFI Awards - The Australian Film Institute Awards 196
Age d'Or Prize 1083
Amanda Award for Cinematographic Merit 3906
Awgie Awards 395
Ingmar Bergman Plaquette 4682
British Film Institute Fellowships 5308
The British Film Institute Sutherland Trophy 5309
British Medical Association Medicine in the Media Award 5355
Channel 4 Archaeological Film Awards 5555
The Channel Four Awards 5222
Dance Screen Award 807
David Film Awards 3021
Ecumenical Prize 1092
Festival du Court Metrage en Plein Air 1790
Film Society of the Year Awards 5306
Golden Bug Statuette 4683
Grand Prix 1985
Grand Prix of the Dutch Film Golden Calf 3631
Hong Kong Film Awards 3935
Huesca International Short Film Contest 4495
International Film/Video Competition 3578
International Visual Communications Association Awards 6327
Cherry Kearton Medal and Award 6770
Byron Kennedy Award 197
LiteraVision Preis 2344
Raymond Longford Award 198
Medal of Honor for the Performing and Visual Arts 4273
Milli Award 154
Jean Mitry Award 3121
Yunus Nadi Yarismasi 4964
OCIC-Prize 1093
One World Award 4828
The Orange British Academy Film Awards 5218
Roquette Pinto Prize 1114
Praemium Imperiale 3217
Premio Internazionale Ennio Flaiano 2985
Premio Saint-Vincent per il Cinema Italiano 3138
Prix Nouveau Talent 1986
Prizes for the Distribution of Quality Films in Belgium 1084
Promotional Prizes 2345
Rosa Camuna 2995
Shark Awards, the International Advertising Festival of Ireland 2887
Salvador Toscano Medal 3439
UNICA Medal 4680
Prix Georges Wildenstein 1499

Finance (*See also* Accounting; Banking; Business; Economics; Financial planning; Insurance)
Bernhard-Harms-Preis 2338
Marjolin Prize 776
National Institute of Insurance International Prizes 2971
Property Council Rider Hunt Awards 601
Stockman Award 3912
Top 100 Companies Award 4371

Financial journalism *See* Business journalism

Financial law *See* Law

Financial planning
Taxpayers Award 2423

Fine arts *See* Art; Arts and humanities; Music

Fire fighting
Australian Fire Service Medal 205
Merit Award 6453
Queen's Fire Service Medal 5604

Fire prevention
EPSC Award 5849
Fire Safety Award 5115
Outstanding Service Award 5116

Firearms
Queen's Prize 6485

Fishing
Most Meritorious Capture Award 296

Fishing industry
Chandrakala Hora Memorial Medal 2688
The JFSF Award for Achievement in Technical Research 3276
The JFSF Award for Encouragement of Young Investigators 3277
The JSFS Award for Scientific Achievement 3278
The Tauchi Memorial Award 3279

Fitness *See* Health and fitness

Flying
Aero Engine Services Trophy 3836
Airways Corporation Trophy 3837
D.M. Allen Memorial Cup 3839
Jean Batten Memorial Trophy 3840
Bledisloe Aviation Trophy 3841
Sir Francis Boys Cup 3842
Leonardo Da Vinci Parachuting Diploma 4724
Oscar Garden Trophy 3845
Gold Parachuting Medal 4729
Gold Rotorcraft Medal 4730
Hang Gliding Diploma 4732
International Free Flight Film Festival 1797
Jubilee Trophy 3847
Lilienthal Gliding Medal 4736
Pepe Lopes Hang Gliding Medal 4738
Pelagia Majewska Gliding Medal 4739
Montgolfier Ballooning Diploma 4741
W. A. Morrison Trophy 3848
New Zealand Wings Trophy 3850
Newman Cup 3851
Rotorua Trophy 3853
Santos-Dumont Gold Airship Medal 4746
G. M. Spence Trophy 3854
Paul Tissandier Diploma 4747
Waitemata Aero Club Cup 3855
Wanganui Trophy 3856
Ivon Warmington Trophy 3857
Wigram Cup 3858
Wigram Cup (Sub-Competition) - Instrument Flying 3859
Wigram Cup (Sub-Competition) - Junior Landing 3860
Wigram Cup (Sub-Competition) - Non-instrument Circuits 3861
Wigram Cup (Sub-Competition) - Senior Landing 3862

Folklore
Katharine Briggs Folklore Award 5912
Coote-Lake Medal for Folklore Research 5913
Noordstar - Dr. Jan Grauls Prize 959
Trento International Film Festival of Mountain and Exploration 3136
Jozef Van Ginderachter Prize 963

Food (*See also* Dairy industry; Food processing; Nutrition; Restaurants; Wine)
Agritechnology, Life Sciences and Biotechnology Exporter of the Year 3808
Award For Enthusiasm 7228
Award For Innovation 7229
Best Paper Presented Award 4294
Best Poster Award 4295
Best Student Award 4296
A. H. Boerma Award 3054
BSF Student Bursary and Bill Waygood Memorial Lecture 5507
Chef of the Year 5702
Coffee Statesmanship Award 7230
Craft Guild of Chefs Awards 5703
Culinary Olympics 2383
Culinary World Cup 3393
Hugh Davis Memorial Cup 5508
FHA Culinary Challenge 4430
Gold Medal 6489
Graduate Awards 5704
Grand Prix Awards 5585
Bires Chandra Guha Memorial Lecture 2687
Guild of Food Writers Award 5949
Hidden Treasure Award 7231
Hotelympia Competition 5287
Japan Beer Cup 3224
Koeppen Memorial Scholarship 4297
Joseph-Konig-Gedenkmunze 2170

Food (continued)
Bill Littlejohn Memorial Medal and lecture 5509
Dr. V. N. Patwardhan Prize in Nutritional Sciences 2616
Edouard Saouma Award 3055
B. R. Sen Award 3056
Silver Medal 6490
Andre Simon Medal 6334
Study Grants 4298
Test of Time Award 7232
Young Entrepreneur Award 7233
Young Scientist Award 3533

Food processing
Clyde H. Bailey Medal 782
Oils and Fats Group International Lecture 7176
The Harold Perten Award 783
Benjamin Ward Richardson Gold Medal 6937
Friedrich Schweitzer Medal 784
Richard Seligman Lecture 7179

Food service (*See also* Restaurants)
Top Tea Place of the Year 7253

Food technology *See* Food processing

Foreign policy
Prix Lucien de Reinach 1692

Forestry (*See also* Paper industry; Wood and wood products)
Hunter Blair Trophy 6887
Certificate of Appreciation 814
Distinguished Service Award 6762
Tom Gill Memorial Award 5674
Honorary Membership 6769
Wilhelm Leopold Pfeil Prize 2400
Queen's Award for Forestry 5675
Dr. Y.S. Rao Forestry Research Award 3395
Research Medal 653
Schlich Memorial Trust Award 5676
Scientific Achievement Award 815

Freedom
Anti-Slavery Award 5057
International Simon Bolivar Prize 1990
Commonwealth Press Union Scholarships 5689
Democracy Award 2906
Free Market Award 4180
Freedom Prize 4868
Gold Medal 5618
Golden Pen of Freedom Award 2014
International Democracy Award 2285
Jerusalem Prize for the Freedom of the Individual in Society 2926
Airey Neave Research Fellowship 5016
Prize for Freedom 6375
European Parliament Sakharov Prize for Freedom of Thought 5847
Albert Schweitzer Award 6206
Prix Henri Texier 1701

French culture
Prix de la Fondation du Chanoine Delpeuch 1650
Phenix UDA 2008
Pustovoit Award 1915

French history
Prix Henri Hertz 1806
Prix Gabriel Monod 1685
Grands Prix de la Fondation Napoleon 1808
Prix de La Fons-Melicocq 1528
Prix Emile Le Senne 1534
Prix Toutain-Blanchet 1535

French literature
Concours Promethee 1723
Prix Estrade-Delcros 1509
Prix Felix Feneon 1805
Concours Max-Pol Fouchet 1724
Prix Henri Hertz 1806
Scott Moncrieff Prize 7133
Prix du Jeune Ecrivain 1940
Prix du Jeune Ecrivain Francophone 1941
Prix Ernest Discailles 1006
Prix Litteraire Prince Pierre-de-Monaco 3473
Prix Alfred Verdaguer 1863

Friendship *See* Brotherhood

Gardening *See* Horticulture

Gastronomy *See* Food; Restaurants

Genealogy
Award for Meritorious Service to Family History 79
Julian Bickersteth Memorial Medal 6033
Certificates, Diplomas, and Licentiates in Genealogy and Heraldry 6034
Genealogist of the Year 4182
Alexander Henderson Award 241
Eoin O'Mahony Bursary 2881
D. F. du Toit-Malherbe Prize for Genealogical Research 4286

Genetics
Gabor Medal 6908
Prix Joseph Schepkens 1047

Geochemistry
Environment Medal 7162
Geochemistry Fellows 1759
Houtermans Medal 1760
Urey Medal 1761
Verdeyen Prize for Soil Mechanics 1090

Geography (*See also* Cartography; Exploration)
Award For Technological Progress 5084
Back Award 6757
Vitus Bering Medal 1330
Premio Dr. Carlos A. Biedma 17
Prix Binoux 1547
W. S. Bruce Medal 6989
Busk Medal 6759
Centenary Medal 6890
Monica Cole Research Grant 6760
Distinguished Geographer Medal 3771
Egede Medal 1331
Fellowship of the Institute of Australian Geographers 476
Fondation Jean Lebrun 1023
Sir George Fordham Award for Cartobibliography 6763
Galathea Medal 1332
Geographical Award 6764
Gill Memorial Award 6766
Gold Medals 6767
Griffith Taylor Medal 477
Edward Heath Award 6768
Honorary Fellowship 6891
IAG Postgraduate Award 478
Journalist of the Year 5085
Livingstone Medal 6892
Prix du Duc de Loubat 1520
Premio Francisco P. Moreno Award 18
Mungo Park Medal 6893
Murchison Award 6771
Ness Award 6772
Newbigin Prize 6894
Cuthbert Peek Award 6773
Premio Consagracion a la Geografia 19
President's Award 6895
Professional Associateship 6896
Professional Service Award 479
Research Medal 653
Prix Saintour 1696
Scottish Geographical Medal 6897
Society of South African Geographers Fellow 4263
Surveyor Award For Local Government 5086
J. P. Thomson Medal 630
Victoria Medal 6775
Darashaw Nosherwanji Wadia Medal 2727

Geology and paleontology (*See also* Geochemistry; Geophysics; Photogrammetry; Seismology)
Aberconway Medal 5927
Major John Sacheverell A'Deane Coke Medal 5928
Premio Florentino Ameghino 15
Prix Louis Armand 1540
Prix Barbier 1830
Prix Barrabe 1831
Prix Leon Bertrand 1832
Prix Paul Bertrand 1546
Bhatnagar Award 2573
Bigsby Medal 5929
Prix Jacques Bourcart 1833
W. S. Bruce Medal 6989
Bruce-Preller Prize Lectureship 6990
CERESIS Award 3958
Clarke Medal 638
Clarke Memorial Lecture 639
Corstorphine Medal 4184
Crafoord Prize 4637
Herman Credner Preis 2188
Juozo Dalinkevicius premija 3376
Prix Georges Deflandre et Marthe Deflandre-Rigaud 1557
Dokuchaev Award 6323
Draper Memorial Medal 4185
Major Edward D'Ewes Fitzgerald Coke Medal 5930
Professor Raphael Freund Award 2908
Sue Tyler Friedman Medal 5931
Prix Raymond et Madeleine Furon 1834
Geological Society of South Africa Honorary Member 4186
Geological Society of South Africa Honours Award 4187
Geological Society of South Africa Jubilee Medal 4188
Dr. Peretz Grader Award 2909
GSA Young Author's Award 463
Assar Haddings pris 4627
Prix James Hall 1570
Hector Memorial Medal and Prize 3868
Hodson Fund 6515

Geology (continued)
Arthur Holmes Medal and Honorary Membership 1773
Honorary Member 2848
Hutton Memorial Medal and Prize 3869
International Association for Engineering Geology and the Environment Awards 3565
International Association of Sedimentologists Grants 903
International Confederation for Thermal Analysis DuPont Award 4205
Prix Charles Jacob 1573
Prix Paul Fallot-Jeremine 1575
Joe Harms Medal 464
Keith Medal 6996
Kubiena Medal 6324
Prix de Lamothe 1835
Lapworth Medal 6516
Liebig Award 6325
Prix Leon Lutaud 1587
Lyell Medal 5932
Mansel-Pleydell and Cecil Trusts 5740
Mawson Lecture 119
Prix Georges Millot
Academie des Sciences 1591
Geological Society of France 1836
Mineralium Deposita Best Paper Award 1267
Mueller Medal 134
Murchison Medal 5933
Kevin Nash Gold Medal 6293
New Research Workers Awards 6572
Pakistan Institute of Sciences Gold Medal 3921
Phaup Award 7435
Premio Giorgio Dal Piaz 3128
Postgraduate QRA Meetings Award 6573
President's Awards 5934
Prestwich Medal 5935
Prix Baron Van Ertborn 1031
Prix Fontannes 1837
Prix Gaudry 1838
Prix Gosselet 1839
Prix Henri Buttgenbach 1045
Prix Jean Cuvillier 1613
Prix Paul Fourmarier 1052
Prix Prestwich 1840
Prix Viquesnel 1841
Prix Wegmann 1842
Prix Fondation Pierre Pruvost 1843
QRA-Bill Bishop Award 6574
Quaternary Conference Fund 6575
Quaternary Research Fund 6576
Research Medal 653
Scottish Science Award 7072
SGA Young Scientist Award 1268
William Smith Medal 5936
Society Awards 2910
L. A. Spendiarov International Geological Prize 4395
Steno Medal 1303
Stillwell Award 465
Prix van Straelen 1844
SW Carey Medal 466
Sylvester-Bradley Award 6517
David Syme Research Prize 713
Teichmueller Stipendium 2189
Thorarinsson Medal 542
DeBeers Alex L. du Toit Memorial Lecture 4189
Trento International Film Festival of Mountain and Exploration 3136
W. R. Brown Medal 467
Darashaw Nosherwanji Wadia Medal 2727
Wager Medal 543
Alfred Wegener Medal and Honorary Membership 1781
Frederick White Prize 124
Wollaston Medal 5937
R. H. Worth Prize 5938
Karl Alfred von Zittel Medaille 2367

Geophysics (*See also* Physics; Geology and paleontology)
Prix Barrabe 1831
Julius Bartels Medal 1769
Sir David Robert Bates Medal 1770
Prix Leon Bertrand 1832
Best First Presentation 2487
Best Papers of the Year 2488
Vilhelm Bjerknes Medal 1771
Guy Bomford Prize 1307
Prix Jacques Bourcart 1833
Chapman Medal 6686
Charles Chree Medal and Prize 6057
Laszlo Egyed Medal 2489
Lorand Eotvos Medal 2490
Beno Gutenberg Medal 1772
Honorary Member 1774
Honorary Membership 2491
Milutin Milankovitch Medal 1775
Prix Georges Millot 1836
Louis Neel Medal 1777
Price Medal 6690
Prix Antoine d'Abbadie 1603
Prix Gosselet 1839
Prix Fondation Pierre Pruvost 1843
Janos Renner Medal 2492
Research Medal 653
Runcorn-Florensky Medal 1779
Conrad Schlumberger Award 3530
Darashaw Nosherwanji Wadia Medal 2727
Arie van Weelden Award 3531
Young Scientists Publication Awards 1782
Young Scientists Travel Awards 1783

Geriatrics (*See also* Gerontology)
Lord Cohen Medal 5487
A. C. Comfort Prize 7008
Philip Davis Prize 6723
Lady Illingworth Award 7257
Prof. Surindar Mohan Marwah Award 2612

Gerontology (*See also* Geriatrics)
Biology Award 2542
Ewald W. Busse Research Awards 1129
Bob Greenblatt Prize 6274
Ivor Novello 5215
Medical Award 2543
Presidential Award 1130
Psycho-social Award 2544

Glass (*See also* Ceramics)
Award For Excellence 7383
Norman Collins Memorial Award 5531
David Flack Memorial Award 5532
Ashton Hill Awards 7384
Lucy Oldfield Cup 5533
Royal Dublin Society Crafts Competition 2877
Stevens Competition 7385
Thames Valley Award 5534
TSL Trophy 5535
A. D. Wood Cup 5536

Golf
Club Development Award 2868
Golfer of the Year 5139
Ladies' British Open Amateur Championship 6354
Open Championship 6672
PGA Assistants Professional Championship 6559
PGA Club Professional Championship 6560
PGA Cup 6561
Ryder Cup 6562
Ryle Memorial Medal 6563
Senior PGA Championship 6564
Braid Taylor Memorial Medal 6565
Tooting Bec Cup 6566
Harry Vardon Trophy 6567
Weetabix Women's British Open Championship 6355
Whitcombe Cox Trophy 6568

Government service (*See also* Public service)
Awards for Outstanding Achievement in Procurement 7213
Ramon Magsaysay Award 3988
Malta Self-Government Re-introduction Seventy-Fifth Anniversary Medal 3425
Order of Merit of the Republic of Poland 4014
Order of Polish Rebirth 4015
Padma Bhushan 2580
Padma Shri 2581
Padma Vibhushan 2582

Graphic arts
The Best of Finnish Graphic Design and Advertising Competition 1405
Thorvald Bindesboll Medal 1324
Design Competitions 4905
International Biennial of Graphic Art 4457
International Council of Graphic Design Associations Excellence Awards 912
International Council of Graphic Design Associations President's Trophy 913
International Festival of Animated Film Stuttgart 2421
International Visual Communications Association Awards 6327
ISTD Typographic Award 6302
Eugene Kolb Prize 2932
National Training and Development Awards 5422
Prix Ars Electronica - International Competition for Cyberarts 762
Prix de Rome Fine Art 3642
Royal Dublin Society Crafts Competition 2877
Konrad von Soest Preis 2350
UK Company of the Year 5423

Greek culture
Prix Alfred Croiset 1508
Prix Gustave Mendel 1523
Prix Ambatielos 1526
Prix de Chenier 1527

Handball
Hans-Baumann-Trophy 4807

Handicapped (*See also* Blindness; Deafness; Mentally disabled; Rehabilitation and therapy; Speech and hearing)
Duncan Guthrie Training Fellowship 5003
Harding Award 5004
Nicholson Award 6446
Oita International Wheelchair Marathon 3304
James D. Wolfensohn Award 6447

Health and fitness
FLAME (Fitness Leadership and Management Excellence) Awards 5907
InBev-Baillet Latour Health Prize 893
Marketing Genius Awards 5908
Prof. Henry Neufeld Memorial Research Grant 2936
Occupational Health Award 6929
Catharina Pijlsprijs 1105

Health care (*See also* Health and fitness; Health education; Health care administration; Medicine; Preventive medicine)
Award of the Greek Alzheimer's Association 2457
Lord Cohen Gold Medal 6933
Donaldson Gold Medal 6934
Elsa Enajarvi-Haavio Award 1366
Duncan Guthrie Training Fellowship 5003
Honorary Fellows Award 6935
HRC Postdoctoral Fellowship 3719
InBev-Baillet Latour Health Prize 893
International Festival of Red Cross and Health Films 1153
Liley Medal for Health Research 3720
Macdiarmid Young Scientist of the Year 3721
Ian Macmillan Prize 6936
Sasakawa Health Prize 4929
George Sykes Memorial Award 6521
Vice Presidents Emiriti Award 6939
John Edward Worth Silver Medal 6940

Health care administration
Baxter Award for Healthcare Management in Europe 2834
Barnett Christie Lectureship 5317
Honorary Fellows Award 6935
Vice Presidents Emiriti Award 6939

Health education
T. P. Gunton Award 5359
InBev-Baillet Latour Health Prize 893
International Festival of Red Cross and Health Films 1153
Occupational Health Award 6929
Vice Presidents Emiriti Award 6939

Hearing *See* Speech and hearing

Helicopters
Alan Marsh Award 6647
Alan Marsh Medal 6648

Heroism
Ashoka Chakra 2575
Award for Valour 5260
Binney Memorial Award 5943
Cross of Merit for Bravery 4009
Cross of Merit with Swords 4010
Cross of Valour 4011
Cruz de Boyaca 1174
Diploma for Outstanding Airmanship 4726
Distinguished Service Order 5592
Prix Dulac 1653
Gallantry Decorations 216
George Cross 5593
George Medal 5594
Grand Prix d'Honneur 4830
Kirti Chakra 2578
Maha Vir Chakra 2579
Medal for Bravery 3426
Medal for Sacrifice and Courage 4013
Medals of Honor 3245
Military Medal for Gallantry 2854
Military Order of William 3490
Mountbatten Medal 6845
Florence Nightingale Medal 4792
Fred M. Packard International Parks Merit Award/World Commission on Protected Areas 4920
Param Vir Chakra 2583
Polaris Award 6243
Provincial Police Award 5121
Queen's Gallantry Medal 5605
Royal Humane Society Awards 6813
Prix Eugene Salvan 1697
Shaurya Chakra 2585
Victoria Cross 5609
Vir Chakra 2586
War Order Virtuti Militari 4017

Higher education
AFUW-SA Inc. Trust Fund Bursary 185
Association of Southeast Asian Institutions of Higher Learning Awards 3967
Thenie Baddams Bursary 186
Cathy Candler Bursary 187
College Medal 156
Barbara Crase Bursary 188
Diamond Jubilee Bursary 189
Fellowship of the Australian College of Education 157
Jean Gilmore Bursary 190
IAHR Lecturer Award 4507
Doreen McCarthy Bursary 191
Padnendadlu Graduate Bursary 192
Felix Restrepo Medal 1197
Society for Research into Higher Education Awards 7112
Georgina Sweet Fellowship 194
Thouron Fellowship 6348

Highway safety
International Association of Traffic and Safety Sciences Award 3199
PRI Service Medal 4062

Hiking *See* Recreation

Historic preservation (*See also* Monument restoration)
Association for Industrial Archaeology Award 5221
Barbados National Trust 838
Concours Annuel de Sauvegarde 2012
Dorothea Award for Conservation 5091
European Union Prize for Cultural Heritage/ Europa Nostra Awards 3524
Fieldwork Award 5092
Gazzola Prize 1888
Heritage in Britain Award 5224
ICCROM Award 3064
International Maritime Heritage Award 7379
Interpret Britain and Ireland Awards 5088
Medal of Honour 3525
Molteno Medal Awards of Excellence and Merit 4150
Onassis Award for Culture (Letters, Arts and Humanities) 2461
Publications Award 5093
Restoration Fund Grant 3526
Rural Wales Award 5581
Prix Henri Texier II 1700
Jozef Van Ginderachter Prize 963

History (*See also* Antiquity; Biography; Culture; Genealogy; Historic preservation; History of science; Medieval studies; Monument restoration; Social science research)
Prix Dupin Aine 1631
Alexander Prize 6777
Australian Society of Archivists Honorary Member 373
The Australian/Vogel Literary Award 39
Awards in History 3723
Awards in Oral History 3724
Arthur Azevedo Prize 1117
Bergson Award 2940
Book of the Year Awards 37
BP Prize Lectureship in the Humanities 6988
Brandt Award 2941
Buchman Award 2942
Prix Hercule Catenacci 1855
Prix Gustave Chaix d'Est Ange 1642
Prix Charles Clermont-Ganneau 1506
Duff Cooper Prize 5746
Jozef Coppens Prize 1068
Dr. M. Aylwin Cotton Foundation Fellowship Awards 5699
Dr. M. Aylwin Cotton Foundation Publication Grants 5700
Prix Victor Cousin 1645
C. H. Currey Memorial Fellowship 679
Charles De Clercq Prize 1069
Prix Estrade-Delcros 1509
Prix Demolombe 1651
Prix Charles and Marguerite Diehl 1510
Distinguished Achievement Award 374
Prix Joseph du Teil 1652
Aquileo J. Echeverria Prize 1201
Prof. Leon Elaut Prize 956
Fellowship 7251
Fellowship of the Australian Society of Archivists 375
Fellowships and Scholarships 584
Festival dei Popoli 3045
Prix Marcel Flach 1660
Fondation Henri Pirenne 995
Founders' Medal 7121
Fraenkel Prize in Contemporary History 6020
Prix Auguste Gerard 1664
Prix Roman et Tania Ghirshman 1516
Gladstone History Book Prize 6779
Grand Prix de l'Academie des Sciences Morales et Politiques 1667
Axel Hirschs pris 4658
Hodgson Prize 6643
Professor Theodor Homen Prize 1399
Honorary Membership 7122
Honorary Membership Award 6346
Mander Jones Awards 377
Kellgrenpriset 4660
Prix Koenigswarter 1671
Prix Drouyn de Lhuys 1677
Prix Limantour 1679
Prix du Duc de Loubat 1520

History (continued)

Prix Charles Lyon-Caen 1680
Mansel-Pleydell and Cecil Trusts 5740
Manufacturers Prize 6071
Prix Gaston Maspero 1521
Somerset Maugham Awards 7146
Prix Georges Mauguin 1684
Norton Medlicott Medal 5972
Prix Gabriel Monod 1685
Najmann Award 2943
National Prize of the President of the Republic 2972
Nordiska Priset 4663
Thomas Eric Peet Travelling Prize 7312
Premio Enrique Pena 11
Prix Le Dissez de Penanrun 1687
Samuel Pepys Medal 5786
Prix Paul-Michel Perret 1688
Premio Academia Nacional de la Historia 12
Premio al Egresado con Mejor Promedio en las Carreras de Historia 13
Premio Dotte Giuseppe Borgia 2973
Premio Municipal Julio de Castilho de Olisipografia 4080
Prijs voor Meesterschap 3672
Prix Ambatielos 1526
Prix baron de Saint-Genois 1000
Prix Cazes - Brasserie Lipp 1938
Prix Charles Duvivier 1001
Prix de Stassart 1003
Prix de Stassart pour Histoire Nationale 1004
Prix Ernest Discailles 1006
Prix Eugene Lameere 1008
Prix Jacques Lavalleye-Coppens 980
Prix Jules Duculot 1014
Prix Leon Leclere 1015
Prix Suzanne Tassier 1017
Prix Gabriel-Auguste Prost 1531
The Rettig Prize 4621
Royal Historical Society/*History Today* Prize 6780
Prix Saintour 1696
Prix Gustave Schlumberger 1532
Birger Scholdstroms pris 4666
Schuckska priset 4667
Scottish Historical Book Award 7070
J. M. Sherrard Awards 3704
Suntory Prize for Social Sciences and Humanities 3334
John Thackray Medal 7123
Prix Thorlet 1703
Prix Maurice Travers 1704
Uveeler Award 2944
Alwyne Wheeler Bursary 7124
A. E. Williams History Prize 657
Wolfson History Awards 7340
Zibetska Priset 4676

History, art *See* Art history

History, business *See* Business history

History, church *See* Church history

History, English *See* English history

History, European *See* European history

History, French *See* French history

History, Italian *See* Italian history

History, Jewish *See* Jewish history

History, military *See* Military history

History of art *See* Art history

History of science
Prix Binoux 1547
Simono Daukantas premija 3377
Dingle Prize 5492
Jan Gillis Prize 1072
Partington Prize 7119
Prix Franz Cumont 1009
Singer Prize 5493
Ivan Slade Prize 5494

Hobbies and clubs (*See also* Animal care and training; Automobiles; Book collecting; Crafts; Genealogy; Horticulture; Numismatics; Philately; Photography; Recreation)
Sidney French Medal 5400
National Model Car Racing Champion 5463

Hockey
International Ice Hockey Federation Championships 4809

Home economics (*See also* Consumer affairs)
Hazel Hatcher International Award 842
Gwendolyn Tonge Scholarship Award 843
Beryl Wood Book Grant 844

Horse racing
Best Jockey - Races Won 3219
Best Trainer - Training Technique 3220
Racehorse of the Year Award 6587

Horsemanship
British Show Pony Society Rosettes 5458
Cubitt Award 6552
Dublin Horse Show 2876
Fell Pony Society Ridden Championship 5893
Show Hunter Ponies Awards 5459
Show Ponies Awards 5460
Working Hunter Ponies Awards 5461

Horticulture
Arboricultural Association Award 5059
Associateship of Honour 6783
Award for Production, Promotion, and Marketing of Biofertilizer 2555
Award of Honour 5022
Lionel and Joyce Bacon Award 5023
Florence Baker Award 5024
Banksian Medal 2879
Peter Barr Memorial Cup 6784
Best Christmas Tree 5281
Bowles Cup 6785
Reginald Cory Memorial Cup 6786
Rolf Dahlgrens Pris 4624
Delphinium Society Awards 5733
Devonshire Trophy 6787
Dublin Horse Show 2876
E. H. Trophy 6788
Clarence Elliott Memorial Award 5025
Engleheart Cup 6789
Farrer Trophy 6790
Fleuroselect Gold Medal 3545
Fleuroselect Quality Award 3546
Franco-British Landscape Gardening Award 5921
Garden Awards 726
Gold Veitch Memorial Medal 6791
Gordon-Lennox Trophy 6792
Roy Hay Memorial Award 5925
Holford Medal 6793
Honorary Fellow 6794
Honorary Membership 729
IMPHOS-FAI Award on the Role of Phosphorus on Yield and Quality of Crops 2557
Jones-Bateman Cup 6795
King Baudouin Award of EGIAR 2000 1215
Lawrence Medal 6796
Leonardslee Bowl 6797
Loder Rhododendron Cup 6798
Lyttel Lily Cup 6799
Lyttel Trophy 5026
George Moore Medal 6800
PPIC-FAI Award 2558
Richardson Trophy 6801
Mrs. F. E. Rivis Prize 6802
Rosse Cup 6803
Rothschild Challenge Cup 6804
Sewell Medal 6805
Victoria Medal of Honour 6806
A. J. Waley Medal 6807
Weed Book Prize 730
Westonbirt Orchid Medal 6808
Wigan Cup 6809
Williams Memorial Medal 6810
Guy Wilson Memorial Vase 6811

Hotels *See* Travel

Housing (*See also* Real estate)
Construction Award 3715
Distinguished Volunteer Award 3716
Housing Design Awards 6823
International Film/Video Competition 3578
Partnership Development Award 3717

Human engineering
Ulf Aberg Post Graduate Award 5788
Sir Frederic Bartlett Medal 5789
Otto Edholm Award 5790
Ergonomics Society Lecturer 5791
Ergonomics Society Special Award 5792
Ergonomics Society's Meritorious Service Award 5794
William Floyd Award 5795
Richard Clive Holman Memorial Award 5796
Honorary Fellow 5797
Hywel Murrell Award 5798
Paul Branton Meritorious Service Award 5799
President's Medal 5800
PRO LABORE SECURO Statuette 3997
Thales Human Factors Integration Award 5801

Human relations
International Simon Bolivar Prize 1990
Hedwig-Burgheim Medaille 2354
Gottlieb Duttweiler Prize 4763
Literature pveis der Stadt Dortmund - Nelly-Sachs-Preis 2387
Olof Palme Memorial Fund Scholarships 4616
Olof Palme Prize 4617
E. du Perron Award 3677
Prix Paul Vigne d'Octon 1690

Human rights (*See also* Civil rights and liberties)
Emil Grunzweig Human Rights Award 2895
Human Rights Award 4832
Jurist of the Year Award 3364
Dr. Frantisek Kriegel Prize 4577
Ludovic-Trarieux International Human Rights Prize 1848
Sean MacBride Peace Prize 4826
The International Jose Marti Prize 1997
Lorenzo Natali Prize for Journalists 3029
Airey Neave Research Fellowship 5016
Nuremberg International Human Rights Award 2371
Prince of Asturias Awards 4497
Professor Thorolf Rafto Memorial Prize 3916
Right Livelihood Award 4619
European Parliament Sakharov Prize for Freedom of Thought 5847
UNESCO Prize for Human Rights Education 2003

Humanitarianism
Australian Bravery Decorations 203
Prix Felix de Beaujour 1634
Civilian Service Medal 1939-1945 211
Colombe D'Oro per la Pace 2979
Distinguished Service, Long Service 341
Prix Jean Finot 1659
Hansischer Goethe Prize 2396
Gold Medal 1151
Honorary Life Member 342
Humanitarian Overseas Service Medal 217
International Institute for Promotion and Prestige Awards 4811
Meritorious Service 343
Montaigne Prize 2399
Florence Nightingale Award 344
Peace Award of Committee of 100 1357
Phenix UDA 2008
Prize for the Promotion, Dissemination and Teaching of International Humanitarian Law 3082
Paul Reuter Prize 4793
Royal Norwegian Order of St. Olav 3903
Henrik Steffens Prize 2404
World Mystical Poetry Prize 4530

Humanities *See* Arts and humanities

Humanities research
British Academy Fellow 5203
Hosei International Fund Foreign Scholars Fellowship 3187
Reuchlinpreis der Stadt Pforzheim 2391

Humor (*See also* Cartoons; Entertainment)
Grand Prix de l'Humour 1975
International Short Film Festival Oberhausen 2316
Live Awards 7276

Hunting
Nature Conservation Officer of the Year 4225
Uncle Stevie Award 4226
Coenraad Vermaak Award 4227
Wildlife Utilisation Award 4228

Ice hockey *See* Hockey

Ice skating
Speed and Figure Skating Championships 4834

Illustration
Elsa Beskow Plaque 4686
The Best of Finnish Graphic Design and Advertising Competition 1405
Book of the Year Award: Early Childhood 404
Book Prizes 2454
Prix Hercule Catenacci 1855
CBCI Award 2820
Children's Book Award 5883
Russell Clark Award 3750
International Biennial of Illustrations Bratislava 4442
Elizabeth Mrazik-Cleaver Canadian Picture Book Award 4784
National Business Calendar Awards 5421
Noma Concours for Picture Book Illustrations 3164
Picture Book of the Year Award 408
Prix Catenacci 1473
Jenny Smelik/IBBY Prize 3571
White Ravens 2330
Young Australians Best Book Award 739

Individual rights *See* Civil rights and liberties

Industrial arts
Prix Joseph De Keyn 1012

Industrial chemistry
Canada International Award 7159
Castner Lecture and Medal 7161
Grand Prix de Chimie Industrielle 1814
Industrial Lectureship 6966
Industrially-Sponsored Awards 6967
LeSueur Memorial Lecture 7171
Leverhulme Lecture 7172
Ivan Levinstein Memorial Lecture 7173
Prix Frederic Swarts 1043
Wolskel Industrial Chemistry Essay Award 625

Industrial design
Thorvald Bindesboll Medal 1324
British Design Awards 5735
Good Design Award 3237
Premio Compasso d'oro ADI 2991
Prince Philip Prize for the Designer of the Year 5736
Royal Designer for Industry Award 6921
Student Lighting Design Awards 6383
Heinrich Tessenow Gold Medal 2405

Industrial engineering
Student Design Competition 3747

Industries and trades (*See also* Business; Craftsmanship; specific industries and trades, e.g. Dairy industry)
Australasian Corrosion Association Awards 77
Sven Berggrens pris 4623
Carothers Medal 7261
Prix Corbay 1644
ESB Clinical Biomechanics Award 3035
ESB Student Award 3036
Benjamin Franklin Medal 6920
Golden Ram Award 4212
Graduateship of the City and Guilds of London Institute 5658
Guild of Taxidermists Acredited Member 5959
Honorary Member 6204
INDEX Awards for Advances in Nonwovens 863
Institute of Quarrying Awards 6076
International Institute for Promotion and Prestige Awards 4811
International Medal 7169
LeSueur Memorial Lecture 7171
Licentiateship of the City and Guilds of London Institute 5659
Malting Diploma 6416
Medals for Excellence 5660
Membership of the City and Guilds of London Institute 5661
Papers Award 6314
S. M. Perren Research Award 3037
Prix Petit d'Ormoy 1597
Prix Ayme Poirson 1600
PresidentFs Prize 5614
Prix Osiris 1861
Purvis Memorial Award 7177
Queen's Awards for Enterprise 6579
Top 100 Companies Award 4371
Vishwakarma Medal 2726
Ian Wark Medal and Lecture 123

Information management
Isaac L. Auerbach Award 794
EIA Awards for European Information Sources 5835
EIA/European Sources Online Award 5836
Jason Farradane Award 7295
Jason Farradine Award 5620
Helen Greer Memorial Prize 5837
Tony Kent Strix Award 7296
Fritz Kutter-Preis 4900
Student Bursary 7298
UKeiG Research Award 7299

Innovation *See* Inventions

Instructional films *See* Audiovisuals; Educational films

Insurance
Finlaison Medal 5990
Gold Medal 5991
Paul Golmick Scholarship 5648
Prix Jules Lefort 1674
Ernst Meyer Prize 4778
National Institute of Insurance International Prizes 2971
Morgan Owen Medal 5649
Rutter Gold Medal and Prize 5650
Standard and Poor's BBB Rating 3883

Intellectual freedom
Liberty Awards 6377

Intellectual property *See* Copyright; Inventions

Intelligence *See* National security

Interior design
IFI Award 4210

International law
Mitchell B. Carroll Prize 3588
Fondation Ernest Mahaim 993

International (continued)
Hague Academy of International Law Scholarships 3559
Prize for the Promotion, Dissemination and Teaching of International Humanitarian Law 3082
Georg Schwarzenberger Prize in International Law 5996
James Brown Scott Prizes 4767

International relations (*See also* European integration; World peace)
ACFOA Human Rights Award 171
Canada Medal 7160
J. G. Crawford Award 298
Calouste Gulbenkian Foundation Grants 5574
International Award for Promoting Gandhian Values Outside India 2775
International Medal 7169
International Public Relations Association President's Award 6288
Japan Foundation Awards 3233
Japan Foundation Special Prizes 3234
King Baudouin International Development Prize 935
Jawaharlal Nehru Award for International Understanding 2591
Order of Merit of the Republic of Poland 4014
Order of San Carlos 1175
Prizes for the Promotion of Community-Based Cultural Exchange 3235
St. Olav Medal 3904
Thouron Fellowship 6348
Manfred Worner Essay Awards 945
Yomiuri International Cooperation Prize 3344

International trade
AmCham Annual Awards 2485
APCAC Award 3960
Bernhard-Harms-Preis 2338
Institute of Export Prizes 6029
Private Sector Hall of Fame 3160
Queen's Awards for Enterprise in International Trade 6581

International understanding (*See also* Brotherhood; Human relations; Humanitarianism)
International Simon Bolivar Prize 1990
Rodrigo Gomez Prize 3435
International Television Festival Golden Prague 1256
Arthur Thomas Ippen Award 4508
John F. Kennedy Student Paper Competition 4509
Ramon Magsaysay Award 3988
Onassis Award for International Understanding and Social Achievement 2462
Philipp Franz von Siebold Award 2437
Student Award for International Understanding 5829
Yomiuri International Cooperation Prize 3344

Inventions (*See also* Technology)
Junior Inventor of the Year E. C. Fernando Memorial Award 4557
MacRobert Award 6621
Paterson Medal and Prize 6065
President's Medal 6622
Prince Philip Medal 6623
Rolex Awards for Enterprise 4880
Silver Medal 6624
SMART Awards 7292
SPUR: Support for Products Under Research 7293
Vishwakarma Medal 2726
Luis Zambrano National Prize for Inventive Technology 7428

Investment *See* Finance

Irish culture
Traditional Irish Music, Singing and Dancing Awards 2891

Iron and steel industry
Asada Medal 3203
Hattori Prize 3204
Honorary Member 3205
Meritorious Prize for Scientific Achievement 3206
Mishima Medal 3207
Nishiyama Medal 3208
Satomi Prize 3209
Dr. Jagdish Shankar Memorial Lecture 2715
Tawara Gold Medal 3210
G. Watanabe Medal 3211

Islamic culture
Aga Khan Award for Architecture 4695
King Faisal International Prize for Arabic Language and Literature 4403
King Faisal International Prize for Islamic Studies 4404
King Faisal International Prize for the Service of Islam 4405

Israeli culture
Nathan Gottesdiener Prize 2931
Emil Grunzweig Human Rights Award 2895
Honorary Fellow 2916
Percia Schimmel Award for Distinguished Contribution to Archaeology 2920

Italian culture
Premio Internazionale di Meridionalistica Guido Dorso 2987
Premio Tenore 2977
Rome Awards 5444
Rome Fellowship 5445
Rome Scholarship 5446
Serena Medal for Italian Studies 5211

Italian history
Australia Council Residencies Award 5437
Balsdon Fellowship 5438
Paul Mellon Centre Rome Fellowship 5442
Tim Potter Memorial Award 5443
Rome Awards 5444
Rome Fellowship 5445
Rome Scholarship 5446
Rome Scholarship in Architecture 5447
Rome Scholarship in Fine Arts 5448
Sainsbury Scholarship in Painting and Sculpture 5449
Sargant Fellowship 5450
Villa I Tatti Fellowships 3142
Wingate Rome Scholarship in the Fine Arts 5451

Italian literature
Bagutta Prize 2993
Balsdon Fellowship 5438
Campiello Prize 3003
Grinzane Cavour Prize 3005
Certamen Capitolinum 3090
John Florio Prize 7131
Italian PEN Prize 3111
Rome Awards 5444

Japanese culture (*See also* Asian studies)
Daiwa Scholarships 5719
Japan Foundation Awards 3233
Japan Foundation Special Prizes 3234
Sir Peter Parker Awards for Spoken Business Japanese 7075
Prizes for the Promotion of Community-Based Cultural Exchange 3235
Philipp Franz von Siebold Award 2437
Suntory Prize for Community Cultural Activities 3333
Suntory Prize for Social Sciences and Humanities 3334

Jewelry design
Jerwood Awards 6340
Royal Dublin Society Crafts Competition 2877

Jewelry industry
Costume and Fashion Jewelry 2561
Cut and Polished Colored Gemstones 2562
Cut and Polished Diamonds 2563
Cut and Polished Synthetic Stones 2564
Pearls 2565
Plain Gold Jewelry 2566
Plain Precious Metal Jewelry 2567
Sales to Foreign Tourists 2568
Silver Jewelry 2569
Studded Gold Jewelry 2570
Studded Precious Metal Jewelry 2571

Jewish culture
Award for Literary Criticism 2897
Award for Original Hebrew Novel 2898
Award for Original Hebrew Poetry 2899
First Novel Award 2900
First Poetry Book Award 2901
Fondation Edmond Fagnan 992
Hebrew Play Award 2902
Otto Hirsch Medaille 2417
Jesselson Prize for Contemporary Judaica Design 2917

Jewish history
Fraenkel Prize in Contemporary History 6020
Zalman Shazar Award for Research in Jewish History 2928

Journalism (*See also* Literature; Cartoons; Editing; Editorial writing; Journalism education; Media; Publications; Radio; Television; Travel literature; specific types of journalism, e.g. Broadcast journalism)
AAHS Trophy (American Aviation Historical Society) 5008
Ida Backmans Stipendium 4647
Bagutta Prize 2993
A. H. Boerma Award 3054
Titus Brandsma Award 4787

Journalism (continued)
British Society of Magazine Editors Awards 5511
Cavling Prize 1296
Commonwealth Press Union Scholarships 5689
Gilberto Figueroa Nogueron Prize 3445
Joaquin Garcia Monge Prize 1202
Karin Gierows pris 4656
Gold Medal 5618
Gold Medal Award 4788
Grand Journalism Prize 3908
Gun och Olof Engqvists stipendium 4657
Innovation Writer of the Year 5513
International Award for Photojournalism 4789
International Media Awards 4790
The J.L. Manning 7240
Journalist Prize 2245
Kellgrenpriset 4660
Prix Albert Londres 1717
The Magazines - Awards for Editorial and Publishing Excellence 5515
Ramon Magsaysay Award 3988
Bill Mcgowran Award 7241
Medienpreis fur Sprachkultur 2193
Lorenzo Natali Prize for Journalists 3029
Netherthorpe Award 5947
Carsten Nielsen Prize 1297
Nordiska Priset 4663
Ortega y Gasset Awards for Journalism 4501
Premio Municipal Julio Cesar Machado de Jornalismo 4079
Premio Nacional de Periodismo 1164
Premio Nacional de Periodismo Pio Viquez 1204
Press Prize for Broadcasters and Producers 4883
Thomas Pringle Award 4172
Reuter Foundation Stanford Fellowship 6601
Sports Feature of the Year 7242
Sports Journalism of the Year 7243
Sports Personalities of the Year (Men, Women, Team) 7244
Television Journalism Awards 7047
Transco Press Award 5229
Markus Viljoen Medal for Journalism 4292
W.G. Walkley Awards for Journalism 561
What the Papers Say Award 6338

Journalism education
Harry Butler Award 6466
The Eric Dobson Memorial Award 6467
The Johnston Press Award 6468
Pamela Meyrick Memorial Award 6469
Oxford University Fellowship 6600

Judo *See* Martial arts

Justice *See* Civil rights and liberties

Juvenile literature *See* Children's literature

Karate *See* Martial arts

Kayak *See* Boating

Labor (*See also* Occupational health; Occupational safety)
Kathe-Leichter-Preis 790
Rene Kuczynski Prize 791
Herbert Steiner Prize 792
Prix Blaise des Vosges 1705

Landscape architecture (*See also* Horticulture)
Award for Excellence in Landscape Architecture 243
Britain in Bloom Awards 5760
Certificate of Merit 5551
Civic Trust Awards 5663
Commendation Award in Landscape Architecture 244
Dissertation Prize 6357
Environmental Awards 6513
Individual Achievement/Personality of the Year Award 5552
Geoffrey Jellicoe Scholarship in Landscape Architecture 5440
Merit Award 4197
Merit Award in Landscape Architecture 245
National Award in Landscape Architecture 246
National Landscape Awards 5245
Prix de Rome Fine Art 3642
Rural Wales Award 5581
John P. Shildrick Award 5553
UNESCO Prize for Landscape Architecture 2004
Friedrich Ludwig von Sckell-Ehrenring 2041

Language *See* Linguistics; Translations

Law (*See also* Civil rights and liberties; Consumer affairs; Copyright; Criminology; Firearms; International law; Inventions; Law enforcement; Legal education; Legal literature; Legislative improvement)
Prix Dupin Aine 1631
Elizabeth Bennett Memorial Prize 6078
BP Prize Lectureship in the Humanities 6988
Bronze Medal 6455
Prix Rene Cassin 1641
The Centennial Maori Scholarship 3775
The Centennial Scholarship 3776
Cleary Memorial Prize 3777
Prix Corbay 1644
Prix Estrade-Delcros 1509
Prix Demolombe 1651
Howard Drake Memorial Award 5995
Forensic Science Society Awards 5917
Gold Medal 6456
Grand Prix de l'Academie des Sciences Morales et Politiques 1667
Paul Guggenheim Prize 4876
Hodgson Prize 6643
Ludovic-Trarieux International Human Rights Prize 1848
C. H. Milburn Award 5369
National Institute of Insurance International Prizes 2971
Prix Le Dissez de Penanrun 1687
Prix Charles Duvivier 1001
Prix Suzanne Tassier 1017
John E. Read Medal 1232
Paul Reuter Prize 4793
Prix Saintour 1696
Scientific Prize/Prix Ciardi 926
Silver Medal 6457
Bernard Simons Memorial Award 6231
Soderbergs Pris 4640
Adrian Spencer Memorial Award 6079
Swiney Prize for a Work on Jurisprudence 6922
Sylvie Gravel Prize 1233
Prix Maurice Travers 1704
Toon Van Den Heever Prize for Jurisprudence 4289
Prix Wolowski 1706

Law enforcement
Australian Police Medal 206
Police Bravery Award 6544
Police Overseas Service Medal 222
Queen's Police Medal for Distinguished Service 5606
World Police Prize 6280

Leadership (*See also* Academic achievement; Professional and personal achievement)
Distinguished Service Decorations 214

Learning disabled
Natalie Cobbing Travelling Fellowship 6721
SAALED Bursary 4300
Alec Shapiro Prize 6734

Legal education
Academic Purposes Fund Awards 7200
Peter Birks Book Prize 7201

Legal literature
Prix Dupin Aine 1631
Prix Odilon Barrot 1633
Prix Rene Cassin 1641
Prix Jean-Baptiste Chevallier 1643
Prix Gallet 1662
Prix Joseph Hamel 1668
Prix Koenigswarter 1671
Prix Limantour 1679
Prix Charles Lyon-Caen 1680
Prix Berriat Saint-Prix 1695
Prix Maurice Travers 1704
Prix Wolowski 1706

Legislative improvement
Prix Lucien Dupont 1655

Library and information services (*See also* Bibliography; Information management; Literacy)
H. C. L. Anderson Award 269
Ellinor Archer Pioneer Award 270
Australian Library and Information Association Fellow 271
Redmond Barry Award 272
Dr. Josef Bick Ehrenmedaille 754
Carey Award 7197
Copova Diploma 4467
Howard Drake Memorial Award 5995
Elsevier/LIRG Research Award 6379
Hans-Peter Geh Grant 3580
Maria Gemenis Award 273
R. Lysholt Hansens Bibliotekspris 1284
International Book Award 824
International Federation of Library Associations Honorary Fellow 3581
International Federation of Library Associations Honorary President 3582
International Federation of Library Associations Medal 3583
Margaret Jennings Award 376
Pavle Kalan Fund Award 4468
Kukuljevic's Charter 1219
Letter of Recognition 274

Library (continued)

Library Technician of the Year 275
Metcalfe Award 276
Mita Society for Library and Information Science Prize 3294
C. B. Oldman Prize 6221
Edvard Pedersens Biblioteksfonds Forfatterpris 1285
Dr. Shawky Salem Conference Grant 3584
Sharman Award 378
Stepinsnki Fund Award 4469
Study Grant Awards 277
Nagrada Eva Verona Award 1220
WA Special Librarian of the Year Award 278
Wheatley Medal 7198
Harold White Fellowship 577
Margaret Wijnstroom Fund 3586

Library services *See* Library and information services

Lighting design
Leon Gaster Bronze Medal 5637
Laurence Olivier Awards 7203
Student Lighting Design Awards 6383
Walsh - Weston Bronze Award 5640

Linguistics
Award of Merit 7290
Prix de la Fondation Emile Benveniste 1501
Bhasha Samman 2790
Blomska stipendiet 4650
Book Prize 5233
Kazimiero Buga premija 3375
Certamen Capitolinum 3090
Prix Honore Chavee 1504
Dr. M. Aylwin Cotton Foundation Fellowship Awards 5699
Dr. M. Aylwin Cotton Foundation Publication Grants 5700
Prix Alfred Croiset 1508
Konrad Duden Preis der Stadt Mannheim 2389
Prix Alfred Dutens 1514
English Academy Medal 4170
Prix Roman et Tania Ghirshman 1516
Noordstar - Dr. Jan Grauls Prize 959
Prix Joseph Houziaux 996
Kellgrenpriset 4660
C. J. Langenhoven Prize 4270
John Lotz Commemorative Medal 2506
D. F. Malan Medal 4271
Prix Antoine Meillet 1522
National Prize of the President of the Republic 2972
Nordiska Priset 4663
Margit Pahlsons pris 4665
Postgraduate Scholarship 5234
Prijs voor Meesterschap 3672
Thomas Pringle Award 4172
Prix Joseph Gantrelle 1013
Prix Suzanne Tassier 1017
Prix Volney 1862
Alexander Sergeovich Pushkin Prize 4397
Sprakvardspris 4668
Jozef Van Ginderachter Prize 963
Verbatim Award 5816
Jozef Vercoullie Prize 964
Leonard Willems Prize 965

Literacy
International Book Award 824
Nehru Literacy Award 2589
UNESCO Literacy Prizes 2002

Literary criticism
Award for Literary Criticism 2897
Pierre Bayle Prijs 3644
Rose Mary Crawshay Prize for English Literature 5207
Prix Alfred Croiset 1508
Dr. Wijnaendts Francken-prijs 3668
Somerset Maugham Awards 7146
Walter McRae Russell Award 56
Johann-Heinrich-Merck Preis 2147
Gustav Preller Prize 4277
Premio Nacional de Literatura 1163
Thomas Pringle Award 4172
Suntory Prize for Social Sciences and Humanities 3334
Wales Book of the Year Awards 4995

Literature (*See also* Creative writing; Drama criticism; Editing; Essays; Editorial writing; Humor; Illustration; Linguistics; Literacy; Literary criticism; Mystery writing; Scholarly works; Translations; specific literary genres, e.g. Biography)
Alice Award 670
Arts Council of Northern Ireland Bursaries and Awards 5074
Australian Literature Society Gold Medal 54
Award for Aboriginal and Torres Strait Islander Writers 588
Ida Backmans Stipendium 4647
Balzan Prize 3062
Beskowska resestipendiet 4649
Bharat Ratna 2577
K. Blundell Grants 7139
Gerard Bonniers Pris 4651
Book of the Year 2498
BP Prize Lectureship in the Humanities 6988
John Buchanan Prize in Esperanto 7310
Buchman Award 2942
Georg-Buchner-Preis 2144
H. M. Butterley - F. Earle Hooper Award 442
Prix Hercule Catenacci 1855
Grinzane Cavour Prize 3005
Children's Book Award 7301
Johann Friedrich von Cotta Literary and Translation Prize of Stuttgart City 2415
Franz Theodor Csokor Prize 766
Denny Gold Medal 6045
Doblougska priset 4652
Duke of Westminster Medal for Military Literature 7055
Aquileo J. Echeverria Prize 1201
Educational Publications Award 7066
E.K. Tratman Award 5275
Signe Ekblad-Eldhs pris 4653
Encore Award 7141
Lydia och Herman Erikssons stipendium 4654
Fellowships and Scholarships 584
Miles Franklin Literary Award 700
Joaquin Garcia Monge Prize 1202
Eric Gregory Awards 7142
Grierson Documentary Film Award 7067
Grosse Literaturstipendien des Landes Tirol 748
Grosser Literaturpreis der Bayerischen Akademie der Schonen Kunste 2039
Gun och Olof Engqvists stipendium 4657
Francis Head Bequest 7143
Johann-Peter-Hebel-Preis 2361
Hertzog Prize for Literature 4268
W. A. Hofmeyr Prize 4373
Holberg Medal 1293
Ricarda-Huch-Preis 2440
The Irish Times Literature Prizes 2858
Prix Jules et Louis Jeanbernat et Barthelemy de Ferrari Doria
Academie des Sciences Morales et Politiques 1669
Institut de France 1857
Jerusalem Prize for the Freedom of the Individual in Society 2926
John Downing Award 7302
Kallebergerstipendiet 4659
Gottfried Keller Prize 4866
Kellgrenpriset 4660
Nita B. Kibble Literary Award 681
King Faisal International Prize for Arabic Language and Literature 4403
Ilona Kohrtz' stipendium 4661
Kordelin Prize 1417
Vinco Kreve-Mickevicius premija 3381
Kungliga priset 4662
Kunstpreis der Stadt Zurich 4874
Prix Germaine-Andre Lequeux 1858
Lichfield Prize 6381
Literacy Author Award 7303
Literature and Art Award 4954
Literaturpreis der Konrad-Adenauer-Stiftung 2340
Lokaljournalistenpreis des Konrad-Adenauer-Stiftung 2341
Macaulay Fellowship 2822
Machado de Assis Prize 1120
Ramon Magsaysay Award 3988
Eugene Marais Prize 4272
Somerset Maugham Awards 7146
BMEC Donald Maxwell Award 6049
McKitterick Prize 7147
Montaigne Prize 2399
Musgrave Medals 3146
Yunus Nadi Yarismasi 4964
National Order of the Southern Cross 1112
Premio Pablo Neruda 1168
New South Wales Premier's Literary Awards 585
Martin Andersen Nex Prize 1294
Nobel Prize for Literature 4604
Nordiska Priset 4663
Northern Arts Literary Fellowship 6501
Olympiart 4819
Order of Culture 3246
Order of Merit 5601
Peace Prize of the German Book Trade 2216
Edvard Pedersens Biblioteksfonds Forfatterpris 1285
A.A. Phillips Prize 57
Polish PEN Centre Prizes 4019
Gustav Preller Prize 4277
Premio do Mar Rei D. Carlos 4093
Premio Internazionale Ennio Flaiano 2985
Prince of Asturias Awards 4497
V.S. Pritchett Memorial Prize 7003
Prix Auguste Teirlinck 999
Prix baron de Saint-Genois 1000
Prix de Stassart 1003
Prix Fontannes 1837
Prix Osiris 1861

Literature (continued)

Prize for Translated Work 4278
PUK-Councilers Prize 4279
Alexander Puschkin Prize 2401
The Mail on Sunday - John Llewellyn Rhys Prize 5191
Colin Roderick Award 460
Colin Roderick Lectures 461
Royal Society of Literature Ondaatji Prize 7004
Sagittarius Prize 7149
Sahitya Akademi Awards 2791
Sahitya Akademi Fellowship 2792
Harold Jan Schoemaker Award 4510
Scholarships of the City of Munich 2346
Birger Scholdstroms pris 4666
Geschwister-Scholl-Preis 2347
Olive Schreiner Prize 4173
Schuckska priset 4667
Scottish Book of the Year Awards 7069
Jaroslav Seifert Prize 4578
Singapore Literature Prize 4424
Stipendium ur Lena Vendelfelts minnesfond 4670
Svenska Akademiens Svensklararpris 4673
Tiroler Landespreis fur Kunst 750
Marten Toonder Award 2823
Travelling Scholarships 7152
Thaddaeus-Troll-Preis 2140
Trouw Publieksprijs voor het Nederlandse Boek 3498
Guust van Wesemael Literary Prize 3585
Prix Alfred Verdaguer 1627
Vertical Smile { La Sonrisa Vertical 4548
Viking Society for Northern Research Awards 7318
Vilenica International Literary Prize 4463
Bettina Von-Arnim Prize 2058
Wales Book of the Year Awards 4995
Zibetska Priset 4676

Literature, Canadian *See* Canadian literature

Literature, Catholic *See* Catholic literature

Literature, Children's *See* Children's literature

Literature, Dutch *See* Dutch literature

Literature, English *See* English literature

Literature, European *See* European literature

Literature, French *See* French literature

Literature, Italian *See* Italian literature

Literature, legal *See* Legal literature

Literature, Mexican *See* Mexican literature

Literature, Spanish *See* Spanish literature

Literature, travel *See* Travel literature

Magazines *See* Journalism; Publications

Management (*See also* Health care administration; Human relations; Information management; Leadership; Operations research; Public administration)

APO National Awards 3166
APO Regional Award 3167
Associateship (APMI) 6528
Award for Excellence in Training 3938
Award for Marketing Excellence 3939
Baxter Award for Healthcare Management in Europe 2834
Best Annual Reports Awards 3940
Brian Willis Award 5096
Bridgeport Prize 6144
Building Manager of the Year Awards 5616
Company of the Year Awards 3358
Creative Exporter of the Year 3809
Diploma in International Employee Benefits 6529
Distinguished Salesperson Award 3941
ELCINA Awards 2531
Fellowship of the City and Guilds of London Institute 5657
Garner-Themoin Medal 798
Elizabeth Haub Prize for Environmental Law 2294
Hegarty Prize 592
HKMA Quality Award 3942
Hodgson Prize 6643
Hong Kong Awards for Industries 3945
Hong Kong Management Game Award 3943
IFAWPCA-CHOI Construction Fieldman Award 3971
Institute of Administrative Management Awards 5993
Institute of Management Gold Medal 6043
Jerwood Awards 6340
JRD TATA Corporate Leadership Award 2532
AIMA - Dr. J.S. Juneja Award for Creativity and Innovation 2533
Lifetime Achievement Award for Management 2534
Maple Leaf Award 799
Marketing Genius Awards 5908
MBA (International Management) Best Student Award 3401
Sir Eric Mensforth International Gold Medal 6156
MERIT Competition 6120
Organization of Islamic Capitals and Cities Awards 4409
Wilfred Owen Awards 6041
Parkman Medal 6124
Premio Internazionale di Meridionalistica Guido Dorso 2987
Programme of the Year 5097
Project Manager of the Year 5098
Project of the Year 5099
Public Service Excellence Award 2535
Sir Monty Finniston Award 5100

Manufacturing (*See also* Industries and trades)

Albert Medal 6919
Apprentice of the Year 6548
Craig Award 415
Designer of the Year 6549
Dr. V. M. Ghatage Award 2523
Tony Goldsmith Cup 6149
Machinery Awards Interplas 6550
Sir Eric Mensforth International Gold Medal 6156
Viscount Nuffield Silver Medal 6158
Dr. Biren Roy Trust Award 2529
Sollich Award 416
Specialised Manufacturing Exporter of the Year 3811
Alfred Stauder Award 417

Marine biology

International Seaweed Association Awards 1132
Ray Lankester Investigatorship 6420
Premio do Mar Rei D. Carlos 4093

Marine engineering *See* Naval engineering

Marketing (*See also* Advertising; Public relations; Merchandising)

Australian Direct Marketing Awards 179
Awards for Excellence 180
Best of Europe - International Direct Marketing Awards 888
DMA Awards, in Association with Royal Mail 5738
ESOMAR Awards 3521
German Direct Marketing Award 2186
Hall of Fame Award 4158
Honorary Member 4043
International Egg Commission Promotion and Marketing Award 6239
Newspaper of the Year Award 593
Personality of the Year 4159
Special Honorary Member Award 4160
Young Direct Marketer of the Year 181

Martial arts

World Taekwondo Federation Competitions 4120

Materials science (*See also* Ceramic engineering; Mining and metallurgy; Plastics and rubber)

Peter Allard Silver Medal 6629
Armourers and Brasier's Award 6900
Beilby Medal and Prize 6950
G. D. Birla Memorial Gold Medal 2646
FEMS European Materials Medal 5885
FEMS Lecturer Award for Excellence in MSE 5886
FEMS Materials Science and Technology Prize 5887
Prix du Gaz de France 1565
Gold Medal 5000
J. Herbert Hollomon Award 5001
Italian Association for Metallurgy Awards 3097
Prix Charles Lemaire 1033
Prix Professeur Louis Baes 1054
Prize for Material Sciences 2705

Mathematics (*See also* Statistics; Surveying)

ANZIAM Medal 41
Prix Louis Armand 1540
Australian Mathematical Society Medal 283
Balzan Prize 3062
Prix Barrabe 1831
Premio Giuseppe Bartolozzi 3107
Berwick Prize 6397
Senior Berwick Prize 6398
Bhatnagar Award 2573
Guy Bomford Prize 1307

Mathematics (continued)

Premio Renato Caccioppoli 3108
Prix Carriere de Mathematiques 1549
Prix Elie Cartan 1550
CASTME Awards 5672
Shiing S. Chern Mathematics Award 3927
T. M. Cherry Student Prize 42
Colombian Academy of Exact, Physical and Natural Sciences to the Integral Work of a Scientist 1172
Prix Le Conte 1553
Crafoord Prize 4637
De Morgan Medal 6399
Prix Ernest Dechelle 1556
Dirac Medal 2946
Professor Magnus Ehrnrooth Prize 1398
Erdos Prize 2912
Forder Lectureship 6400
Francqui Prize 895
Fujihara Award 3181
George-Cantor-Medal 2199
Prix Grammaticakis-Neuman 1567
Gunning Victoria Jubilee Prize Lectureship 6995
Hardy Fellowship 6401
Hector Memorial Medal and Prize 3868
Hua Loo-keng Mathematics Award 3928
ICTP Diploma 7031
ICTP Prize 2948
Zhong Jiaqing Mathematics Award 3929
Journalists Prize 2200
Keith Medal 6996
Prix Langevin 1582
Levitzki Prize in Algebra 2913
Lyle Medal 118
Media Prize 2201
J.H. Michell Medal 43
Moran Medal for Statistical Science 120
National Institute of Insurance International Prizes 2971
National Prize of the President of the Republic 2972
Naylor Prize and Lectureship 6402
Haim Nessyahu Prize in Mathematics 2914
Bernhard H. Neumann Prize 284
Nihon Sugakukai Iyanaga Sho 3292
Philippine Mathematical Olympiad 3984
Pollock Memorial Lecture 645
Polya Prize 6403
Premio Dotte Giuseppe Borgia 2973
Prix Adolphe Wetrems 1027
Prix Agathon De Potter 1028
Prix Ampere d'Electricite de France 1602
Prix Blaise Pascal du GAMNI-SMAI 1605
Prix Charles Lagrange 1032
Prix Eugene Catalan 1041
Prix Fonde par l'Etat 1611
Prix Francois Deruyts 1042
Prix Jacques Deruyts 1046
Prix Theophile de Donder 1055
Prizes of the 150th Anniversary of the RSSL 1098
Ramanujan Prize for Young Mathematicians 2949
Research Grant 7036
Research Medal 653
Dr. Juan S. Salcedo Jr. Science Education Award 3986
Prix Gabrielle Sand et Marie Guido Triossi 1621
Scientific Research Prizes 3451
Section Grant 7037
Senior Whitehead Prize 6404
Prix Servant 1622
Srinivasa Ramanujan Medal 2719
Sylvester Medal 6917
Prix Victor Thebault 1623
Training and Research at Italian Libraries 2950
Premio Tricerri 3109
TWAS Award in Mathematics 2964
Upper Secondary School Teachers Prizes 1401
Whitehead Prize 6405
The Wolf Prizes 2938

Mechanical engineering

Angus Award 3729
Prix Louis Armand 1540
Award of Merit 3040
James Alfred Ewing Medal 6109
Georg A. Fischer-Preis 4897
The Griffith Medal 3041
Honorary Membership Award 3042
Institution of Mechanical Engineers Awards 6185
Australian Geomechanics Award - John Jaeger Memorial Award 509
George Julius Medal 511
Medal for Outstanding Paper 3263
A. G. M. Michell Medal 517
Prix Henri de Parville 1595
Aylet Lily Perera Memorial Award 4560
Prix Petit d'Ormoy 1597
Premio Internazionale Panetti-Ferrari 2969
Prix Auguste Sacre 1030
Prix du Commisariat a l'Energie Atomique 1610
SAACE Excellence Awards 4306
Warman International Students Design Award Competition 536
James Watt International Medal 6186
James Watt Medal 6132
The Wohler Award 3043

Media (*See also* Cable television; Communications; Journalism; Radio; Television)

Premio Nacional 3433

Medical education

AGC/GVS Fellowship 6701
British Medical Association Medicine in the Media Award 5355
Prix Jean Dagnan-Bouveret 1554
Eden Travelling Fellowship in Obstetrics and Gynaecology 6705
Medical Electives Bursaries 5682
Medical Student Elective Prize 7035
Undergraduate Project Prize 7038

Medical journalism (*See also* Science journalism)

Dutch Cancer Society Press Award 3505
Garrod Prize 5489
Ron Halmshaw Award 5324
Michael Mason Prize 5490
Medical Book Prizes 7148
Medical Journalists' Association Open Book Awards 6422
Medical Journalists' Association Summer Awards 6423
Minkowski Prize 2107
Prof. Dr. P. Muntendamprijs 3506
Norwich Union Healthcare/Medical Journalists' Association Awards 6424

Medical research (*See also* Scientific research)

Professor B. K. Aikat Oration Award 2595
Ambassador Award 919
Basanti Devi Amir Chand Prize 2597
Shakuntala Amir Chand Prizes 2598
Dr. Nitya Anand Endowment Lecture 2671
John Arderne Medal 7006
Australasian Menopause Society Scientific Award 85
Bernhard Baron Travelling Scholarship 6702
Best Practice Award 5102
BGRC Silver Jubilee Oration Award 2599
Robert Bing Prize 4885
Alliance for Better Bone Health Iain T. Boyle Award 5818
Brackenbury Award 5354
M. A. B. Brazier Young Investigator Award 6255
Bruce-Preller Prize Lectureship 6990
Alexander Ninian Bruce Prize 6991
Donal Burke Memorial Lecture 2870
Jose Carreras-EHA Award 3535
Chalmers Memorial Medal 7029
Jean-Martin Charcot Award 6444
Chesley Award 3610
CIBA-GEIGY-ILAR International Rheumatism Award 548
W. A. Cobb Young Investigator Award 6256
Prix Le Conte 1553
Dalby Prize 7009
Chaturvedi Kalawati Jagmohan Das Memorial Award 2601
Dr. Dharamvir Datta Memorial Oration Award 2602
Peter Debye Prize 3513
Prix Marguerite Delahautemaison 1818
Smt. Swaran Kanta Dingley Oration Award 2604
Vera Down Award 5357
Downs Travelling Scholarship 7010
Henry Dryerre Prize Lectureship 6993
Jacqueline du Pre Fellowship 6445
ECTS Career Establishment Award 5819
ECTS Young Investigator Awards 5820
EHA Clinical Research Grants 3536
EHA-Jose Carreras Young Investigator Fellowship Program 3537
EHA Research Fellowships 3538
Prix Leon-Alexandre Etancelin 1562
European Thyroid Association Awards 1299
Norman Gamble Research Prize 7013
Edgar Gentilli Prize 6706
Prix Jean-Marie Le Goff 1566
Maurice Goldblatt Cytology Award 2276
Grand Prix 1819
Graves Lecture 2872
Green-Armytage and Spackman Travelling Scholarship 6707
Barbara Gross Award 86
Haemophilia Award 5965
Haemophilia Society Sports Award 5966
Jean Hailes Memorial Prize 87
R. T. Hall Prize 399
Katherine Bishop Harman Award 5360
Nathaniel Bishop Harman Award 5361
Sir Charles Hastings Award 5362
Charles Oliver Hawthorne Award 5363
Doris Hillier Award 5364
Geoffrey Holt Award 5365
Casey Holter Memorial Prize 7114

Medical (continued)

Honorary Membership of the ESM 2128
ICMR Prize for Biomedical Research Conducted in Underdeveloped Areas 2605
ICMR Prize for Biomedical Research for Scientists Belonging to Under-Privileged Communities 2606
Insole Award 5366
Intensive Care Society Research Gold Medal 6198
ISAM Career Achievement Award 2318
Dr. M. O. T. Iyengar Memorial Award 2607
Dr. C. G. S. Iyer Oration Award 2608
H. C. Jacobaeus Lectures 1315
T. V. James Fellowship 5367
Louis-Jeantet Prize for Medicine 4862
Prix Alexandre Joannides 1576
Lala Ram Chand Kandhari Award 2610
Prix de Biologie Alfred Kastler 1822
August Krogh Prize 1316
John Lawson Prize 6708
Prix Marie Leon-Houry 1585
Life Time Career Award 2411
Lifetime Achievement Award 920
Eli Lilly/EASD Research Fellowship in Diabetes and Metabolism 2106
Dora Lush Biomedical Postgraduate Scholarships 572
George Macdonald Medal 7032
Donald Mackay Medal 7033
C. J. Martin Overseas Biomedical Fellowship 573
Prof. Surindar Mohan Marwah Award 2612
Andre Mayer Award 6215
Medical and Dental Postgraduate Research Scholarships 574
Medical Research Grants 1415
Thomas T. Mercer Award 2319
Merck Sharp and Dohme Florey Medal 367
National Back Pain Association Medal 5158
Novo Nordisk Award 88
Novo Nordisk Foundation Lecture 1317
Theodore Ott Prize 4886
Paediatric Anaesthesia Research Fund 5145
Philip Morris Art Award 5967
Catharina Pijlsprijs 1105
Dr. D. N. Prasad Memorial Oration Award 2617
Prix Fonde par l'Etat 1611
Michael Prize Award 921
Dr. T. Ramachandra Rao Award 2619
Ralph Reader Prize 400
Dick Rees Memorial Fund 6368
Registrar Prize 5146
Albert Renold Fellowship 2109
Research Grant 368
Research Grants 6199
H. C. Roscoe Fellowship 5371
Prix Raymond Rosen 1820
Prix Gustave Roussy 1620
St. Lazarus Garnham Fellowship 6369
Reynaldo Dos Santos Prize 3033
Smt. Kamal Satbir Award 2624
Georg-Schmorl-Preis 2379
Ludwig Schunk Prize for Medicine 2336
Shri Dhanwantari Prize 2717
Social Achievement Award 922
Maj. Gen. Saheb Singh Sokhey Award 2628
Student Electives Scheme 6370
Student Research Award 2320
Student Researcher Award 5103
Taylor and Francis Award 3611
Dr. T.S. Tirumurti Memorial Lecture 2725
Joseph Toynbee Memorial Lectureship 7019
Travel Fellowships 5104
Travel Grants 5147
Prijs Albert Van Dyck 968
Van Leeuwenhoek Distinctive Travel Award 2130
Prix Roy Vaucouloux 1625
Visiting Scholarship 6200
Dr. Prem Nath Wahi Award for Cytology and Preventive Oncology 2631
Edith Walsh Award 5373
Wertheimer Award 6216
Elizabeth Wherry Award 5374
Willendorf Award 6217
Young Achiever Award 5105
Young Cancer Researcher Award 5808
Young Investigator Award 2321
Young Investigator Travel Award 3612
Young Scientific Career Award 2412
Young Scientific Career Award - Light 2413
Young Scientist Award 1309
Young Scientists for Rainforests 5695
Zuspan Award 3613

Medical technology (*See also* Biomedical engineering; Biotechnology)
Abbott Award 4247
Abbott Award for Innovative Research and Development in Virology 4248
Irene Aitken Memorial Award 4249
Bactlab Systems Gold Award 4250
Bactlab Systems Premier Award for Best Paper 4251
Bayer Diagnostics Academic Achievement Award 4252
Bayer/Sakura Histology Achievement Award 4253
Dade Behring Award 4254
International Cytotechnology Award of the IAC 2277
Joseph Prize 4255
Labotec-Shandon Award for Achievement in the Field of Cytology 4256
Merck Award 4257
Roche Award 4258
SA Scientific Award 4259
Technologist of the Year 4260
Thistle Student Award 4261
Dr. V. K. Zworykin Premium 6166

Medicine (*See also* Biomedical engineering; Biotechnology; Health care; Occupational health; Rehabilitation and therapy; Toxicology; specific fields of medicine, e.g. Anesthesiology)
Abbott Award 4580
Dr. B. R. Ambedkar Centenary Award for Excellence in Biomedical Research 2596
AMMA Journal Editor's Prize 286
Balint Society Essay Prize 5163
Balzan Prize 3062
Sidney Barrett Travel Grant 5851
BBTS Gold Medal 5252
Prix Louis-Daniel Beauperthuy 1541
Leon Bernard Foundation Prize 4925
Claude Bernard Lecture 2105
Best Research Paper Award 3962
Bhatnagar Award 2573
Bird Young Investigator Award 136
Malcolm Black Travel Fellowship 6703
William Blair-Bell Memorial Lectureship in Obstetrics and Gynaecology 6704
James Blundell Award 5253
BSH Scientific Scholarships 5477
BSH Student Scholarships 5478
Buchanan Medal 6902
Caledonian Research Foundation Prize Lectureship in Biomedical Sciences and Arts and Letters 6992
Carus Preis 2393
Sir Rickard Christophers Medal 7030
Compumedics Poster Prize 137
Concurso Nacional de Obras Medicas 1195
Oswaldo Cruz Prize 1111
Darling Foundation Prize 4926
Chaturvedi Ghanshyam Das Jaigopal Memorial Award 2600
Disability Care Award 6694
Distinguished Service Awards 159
Ihsan Dogramaci Family Health Foundation Fellowship and Prize 4927
E. Mead Johnson Award for Research in Pediatrics 4956
Educational Foundation Grants 915
Alan Edwards Prize 7011
Eliminations of Leukaemia Fund (ELF) Travelling and Training Fellowships 5479
Ellison-Cliffe Medal and Lecture 7012
Elsdon-Dew Medal 4218
EPA Poster Prize 5852
EPA Prize 5853
Essay Competition 6366
Ethicon Foundation Fund Traveling Fellowship 6715
European Rhinologic Society Prizes 1364
Neil Hamilton Fairley Fellowships 571
Rowland Fereday Award 5854
Francqui Prize 895
Fujihara Award 3181
Lars-Erik Gelin Conference Travel Award 2127
Lucille K. Georg Award 1413
Ginesty Award 3606
GlaxoSmithKline Prize and Lecture 6909
Gloria Medicinae Award 4041
Gold Medal for Distinguished Merit 5358
The Kenneth Goldsmith Award 5254
Gottschalk Medal 113
GP Registrar Awards 6695
Premio Profesor Dr. Ricardo Hansen 23
Heine-Medin Medal 4581
Dr. A.H. Heineken Prize for Medicine 3655
Honorary Fellowship 160
Honorary Member
Latin American Phytopathology Association 3954
Medical Women's International Association 2358
Honorary Membership 161
Hunterian Medal 5980
InBev-Baillet Latour Health Prize 893
JALMA Trust Fund Oration Award in the Field of Leprosy 2609
Jephcott Lecture 7015
John Flynn Scholarships 162
Jean Julliard Prize 3615
Junior Travelling Fellowship 7372
King Faisal International Prize in Medicine 4406
Mary Kingsley Medal 6391

Subject Index

Medicine (continued)

Kshanika Oration Award to a Woman Scientist for Research in the Field of Biomedical Sciences 2611
Vlado Lasas premija 3383
Life Fellowship 163
Life Membership 138
Lister Memorial Lecture 7175
Prix Richard Lounsbery 1586
Mary Evelyn Lucking Prize in Medicine 5480
Harold Malkin Prize 6709
Mandy Award 703
Manson Medal 7034
Marshall Scholarships 5126
Medical Rural Bonded Scholarship Scheme 164
MedicarePlus Procedural Training Grants 165
Member of Honour 2359
Member Travel Fellowship 2807
Dr. Kamala Menon Medical Research Award 2613
C. H. Milburn Award 5369
Minnesmedaljen i guld 4629
Amrut Mody-Unichem Prize for Research in Cardiology, Neurology and Gastroenterology 2614
Amrut Mody-Unichem Prize for Research in Maternal and Child Health and Chest Diseases 2615
W.O. Neitz Junior Medal/Senior Medal 4219
Nobel Prize for Physiology or Medicine 4606
Novo Nordisk Prize 1318
Nuffield Lecture 7016
Lorenz Oken Medaille 2254
John Panchaud Medallions 5717
Paracelsus Medaille 2196
Jacques Parisot Foundation Fellowship 4928
Patient Participation Award 6696
Dr. V. N. Patwardhan Prize in Nutritional Sciences 2616
Paul Freeling Award 6697
Castelli Pedroli Prize 2108
Prix Memain-Pelletier 1859
Prix Petit d'Ormoy 1597
AACR-Pezcoller International Award for Cancer Research 3116
Dr. G.M. Phadke Oration 2808
Late G.M. Phadke Travelling Award 2809
Politzer Prize 4984
Pope John XXI Prize 7420
PractitionerFs Award for Excellence 836
President's Gold Medal 2810
The Princess Chichibu Memorial TB Global Award 1917
Prix du Commisariat a l'Energie Atomique 1610
Public Health Prize 1918
Dr. P. N. Raju Oration Award 2618
Tilak Venkoba Rao Award 2620
Research/Educational Awards 139
RGCP/SAPC Elective Prize 6698
Lloyds Roberts Lecture 7017
Ros Prize 6699
Prix Gaston Rousseau 1619
Karl Asmund Rudolphi Medal 2078
Rural Australia Medical Undergraduate Scholarship Scheme 166
Ludwig Schunk Prize for Medicine 2336
Scientific Prize 1919
Scottish Science Award 7072
M. N. Sen Oration Award for Practice of Medicine 2625
Dr. A. T. Shousha Foundation Prize and Fellowship 4930
Silver Medal 2874
Dr. R. Sitharman Memorial Essay Competition 2811
Society Medal 140
Dr. J. B. Srivastav Award in the Field of Virology 2629
Andrija Stampar Medal 1721
Swiney Prize for a Work on Jurisprudence 6922
Tanagho Award 3607
Teacher Travel Fellowship Award 2812
Technipro Best Oral Presentation 141
Travel Award 5872
Travelling Fellowships 6716
TWAS Award in Basic Medical Sciences 2961
The Union Medal 1920
Premio Miguel Aleman Valdes 3443
Prijs Franz Van Goidsenhoven 969
Ernst-von-Bergmann-Plakette 2197
Albert Wander Lecture 7022
Weary Dunlop Award 287
Wellcome Medal for Anthropology as Applied to Medical Problems 6677
The Wolf Prizes 2938
WONCA Foundation Award 4436
Yearly Award for Young ICU Investigators 882
Young Investigators Award 5833
Zorgniotti Award 3608

Medicine, aerospace *See* Aerospace medicine

Medicine, emergency *See* Emergency medicine

Medicine, preventive *See* Preventive medicine

Medicine, sports *See* Sports medicine

Medicine, veterinary *See* Veterinary medicine

Medieval studies
Prix Bordin 1502

Meetings *See* Conventions

Mental health (*See also* Psychiatry)
Book of the Year Award 6430
John Hamilton Traveling Fellowship 6725
Ferdinande Johanna Kanjilal Traveling Fellowship 6726
Doris Odlum Award 5370
Dr. Vidya Sagar Award 2622
Alec Shapiro Prize 6734
J. W. Starkey Award 6938

Mentally disabled
Awards 6208
Philip Davis Prize 6723
Distinguished Achievement Award - Research 6210
Distinguished Achievement Award - Scientific Literature 6211
Distinguished Achievement Award - Service 6212
Distinguished Service Citation 6213
Brian Oliver Prize 6730

Merchandising
Fernanda Monti Award 3686
Montana New Zealand Book Awards 3700

Metallurgy *See* Mining and metallurgy

Meteorology
Award for Excellence in Storm Reporting 353
Award of Achievement 354
Buys Ballot Medal 3648
Vilhelm Bjerknes Medal 1771
W. S. Bruce Medal 6989
Deutsche Meteorologische Gesellschaft Ehrenmitgliedschaft 2081
EMS Media Award 2121
Forderpreis 2082
Prix Leon Grelaud 1568
Helmholtz Prize 2269
International Meteorological Organization Prize 4934
Jester of the Year 355
Leonard Medal 6428
Norbert Gerbier-Mumm International Award 4935
Outstanding ASWA Participation 356
K. R. Ramanathan Medal 2709
Research Medal 653
Student/Young Scientist Travel Award 2122
Symons Memorial Medal 6847
Prof. Dr. Vilho Vaisala Award 4936
Alfred Wegener-Medaille 2083
WMO Research Award for Young Scientists 4937
Young Scientist Award 2123

Mexican literature
Magda Donato Prize 3431

Microbiology
Abbott Award for Innovative Research and Development in Virology 4248
Arima Award for Applied Microbiology 550
Bactlab Systems Premier Award for Best Paper 4251
M. W. Beijerinck Virology Medal 3649
Colworth Prize Lecture 7096
ESCMID Research Fellowships 4713
ESCMID Turning the Tide of Resistance Research Grant 4714
ESCMID Young Investigator Awards for Research in Clinical Microbiology and Infectious Diseases 4715
Carlos J. Finlay Prize 1991
Fleming Lecture 7097
Fondation Andre-Romain Prevot 1563
Garrod Medal 5475
Fred Griffith Review Lecture 7098
Dr. H. P. Heineken Prize for Biochemistry and Biophysics 3652
Life Membership Award 3779
Merck Award 4257
Stuart Mudd Award for Studies in Basic Microbiology 551
W. H. Pierce Memorial Prize 7087
Professor Shambu Nath De Memorial Lecture 2706

Microbiology (continued)
Dr. Y. S. Narayana Rao Oration Award in Microbiology 2621
Marjory Stephenson Prize Lecture 7099
Student Prize 3780
Student Travel Award 3781
Technologist of the Year 4260
Van Leeuwenhoek Medal 3660
Van Niel International Prize for Studies in Bacterial Systematics 552
Don Whitley Travel Scholarship 7088
Peter Wildy Prize for Microbiology Education 7100

Microfilms *See* Information management

Military engineering
Arthur Corbett Medal 498

Military history
Duke of Westminster Medal for Military Literature 7055
Order of the White Eagle 4016
Templer Medal 7129

Military service
Air Force Cross 5589
Air Medal 720
Anniversary of National Service 1951-1972 Medal 201
Anne Armstrong Award 5065
Army Commendation Medal 721
Ashoka Chakra 2575
Ati Vishisht Seva Medal 2576
Australian Cadet Forces Service Medal 204
Australian Service Medals 207
Bronze Star 722
Champion Shots Medal 210
Chesney Gold Medal 7054
Conspicuous Service Decorations 212
Croix de Guerre 1810
Cross of Merit for Bravery 4009
Cross of Valour 4011
Defence Long Service Medal 213
Distinguished Flying Medal 5591
Distinguished Service Decorations 214
Prix Edmond Freville 1661
Gallantry Decorations 216
Trench Gascoigne Prize 7056
General Service Medal 4343
International Force East Timor Medal 218
Kirti Chakra 2578
Maha Vir Chakra 2579
Medaille Militaire 1811
Medal for Participation in the Battle for Berlin 3995
Medalla Militar Francisco Jose de Caldas 1177
Medalla Militar Soldado Juan Bautista Solarte Obando 1178
Medalla Servicios Distinguidos a la Aviacion Naval 1179
Medalla Servicios Distinguidos en Orden Publico 1180
Medalla Servicios Distinguidos la Fuerza de Superficie 1181
Medalla Tiempo de Servicio 1182
Military Cross 5595
Military Merit Medal 4344
Most Excellent Order of the British Empire 5598
NAAFI/AFF Rose Bowl 5066
Nursing Service Cross 220
Orden del Merito Aeronautico Antonio Ricaurte 1183
Orden del Merito Militar Antonio Narino 1184
Orden del Merito Naval Almirante Padilla 1185
Orden del Merito Sanitario Jose Fernandez Madrid 1186
Orden Militar San Mateo 1187
Order of Australia 221
Order of Merit 5601
Order of the Cross of Liberty 1374
Order of the Lion of Finland 1375
Param Vir Chakra 2583
Param Vishisht Seva Medal 2584
Prix Lazare Carnot 1614
Service Medal 2860
Servicios Distinguidos a la Fuerza Submarina 1188
Shaurya Chakra 2585
Silver Star 723
Medalla al Merito Logistico y Administrativo Contralmirante Rafael Tono 1189
Unit Citations 224
Unitas Medal 4345
Vietnam Logistic and Support Medal 225
Vir Chakra 2586
Vishisht Seva Medal 2587
War Order Virtuti Militari 4017

Mineralogy
Georg-Agricola-Medaille 2085
AIPEA Medals 897
Bradley Award 898
Essar Gold Medal 2649
Viktor-Moritz-Goldschmidt Preis 2086
Muller Award 4064
Hugo Muller Lectureship 6976
Prix Agathon De Potter 1028
Prix Henri Buttgenbach 1045
Paul Ramdohr Prize 2087
Manuel Rocha Medal 4065
Abraham-Gottlob-Werner Medaille 2088

Mining and metallurgy (*See also* Materials science)
Georg Agricola Denkmuenze 2233
Prix Alcan-Pechiney 1539
Prix Barbier 1830
Vidya Bharati Prize 2643
Bhoruka Gold Medal 2644
Binani Gold Medal 2645
G. D. Birla Memorial Gold Medal 2646
A. K. Bose Medal 2647
Bralco Gold Medal 2648
Brinell Medal 4634
Aldo Dacco Award 3094
Felice de Carli Award 3095
Essar Gold Medal 2649
Sir Padamji Ginwala Gold Medal 2650
Federico Giolitti Steel Medal 3096
Gold Medal 1124
Paul Grunfeld Prize 2234
Hindustan Zinc Gold Medal 2651
Historical Metallurgy Society Grants 5974
Honorary Member 2652
Robert Horne Lecture 7167
IMPHOS-FAI Award 3475
Indian Institute Metals Platinum Medal 2653
Institute of British Foundrymen Honorary Fellow 5998
Italian Association for Metallurgy Awards 3097
Australian Geomechanics Award - John Jaeger Memorial Award 509
O. P. Jindal Gold Medal 2654
Voya Kondic Medal 5999
Lessing Medal 6432
Luigi Losana Gold Medal 3098
Eugenio Lubatti Award 3099
MECON Award 2655
Medaglia d'Oro AIM 3100
Metallurgist of the Year Award 2656
Prix Georges Millot 1591
Papers and Publications Committee Prizes 6433
Quality Awards 2657
Reden Plakette 2235
Rolling Trophy 2658
Sail Gold Medal 2659
Silver Medal 1125
Steel Eighties Award 2660
Claude A. Stewart Award 484
Oliver Stubbs Medal 6000
Tata Gold Medal 2661
Travel Award 6434
Young Metallurgist of the Year Award 2662

Minority groups *See* Ethnic affairs

Modeling
Mathilde Award 1289

Monument restoration
Gazzola Prize 1888
Fritz Schumacher Prize 2402

Motion pictures *See* Films

Motorcycle racing
CyTech Accreditation 5137
FIM Fair Play Trophy 4814
Gold Medal of the FIM 4815
Prix du Merite Motocycliste 4816
World Motorcycle Championships 4817

Museums
Council of Europe Museum Prize 1754

Music (*See also* Conducting; Music competitions; Music composition; Music education; Musical instruments; Musicology; Opera; Performing arts; Recording industry; specific types of music, e.g. Choral music)
Allianz Cornhill Musical Insurance Youth Orchestra Awards 6462
Alpenlandischer Volksmusikwettbewerb 746
Emily Anderson Prize for Violin 6859
Antwoorden Prijsvragen, Klasse der Schone Kunsten 1060
APRA/Australian Music Centre Classical Music Awards 293
Arts Council of Northern Ireland Bursaries and Awards 5074
Australian Music Center Awards 294
Balvenie Medal 5667
Sir John Barbirolli Memorial 6860
Emil Berlanda Preis 747
Leslie Boosey Award 6861
Prix Bordin 1439
BRIT Awards 5416
British Composer Awards 5213
Prix Hercule Catenacci 1855

Music (continued)

Grand Prix du Disque Frederic Chopin 4001
Chopin Piano Competition 1252
Conamus Golden Harp 3501
Distinguished Musician Award 5982
Aquileo J. Echeverria Prize 1201
Emma Muuvi Awards 1409
European Music and Poetry Competitions 856
European Music Prize for Youth 2132
Fellowships and Scholarships 584
Festival dei Popoli 3045
Festival of Underwater Images 1799
Foundation for the Promotion of Finnish Music Grants 1403
Glenfiddich Trophy 5668
Gold Badge
British Academy of Composers and Songwriters 5214
English Folk Dance and Song Society 5780
Gold Medal 6862
Grand Prix 1985
Grand Prix de la Musique Symphonique 1973
Grand Prix de l'Edition Musicale 1974
Grand Prix Eurovision for Young Musicians 4709
Philip and Dorthy Green Award for Young Concert Artists 6410
Sir Charles Grove Prizes 6411
Gundhall School Gold Medal 5963
Hall of Fame Award 3931
Honorary Member
Incorporated Society of Musicians 5983
Royal Philharmonic Society 6863
Honorary Membership 6627
Impact of Music on Film Competition 890
International Society for Contemporary Music Honorary Member 3604
Julius Isserlis Scholarship 6864
Japan Gold Disk Award 3314
Jazzpar Prize 1282
Jerwood Awards 6340
John Horrocks Scholarship 7349
Kunstpreis der Stadt Zurich 4874
Kyoto Prizes 3189
Rene Lenaerts Prize 1073
Ferenc Liszt International Record Grand Prix 2496
Literarischer Marz 2442
Literature and Art Award 4954
Local Education Authority Music Awards 6476
Ellie Marx Memorial Scholarship 4355
Medal of Honor for the Performing and Visual Arts 4273
MIA Music Awards 6449
Mozart Medal 3447
Music Awards 6865
Musicians Benevolent Fund Awards 6451
National Champion 27
C. B. Oldman Prize 6221
Olympiart 4819
Order of Culture 3246
Dorothy Parkinson Award for Young British Musicians 5969
Joseph Plateau Prize 891
Pop Award 3502
Praemium Imperiale 3217
Premio Tenco 3011
Prix Nouveau Talent 1986
Promotional Prizes 2345
Prosceniumprijs 3679
Scholarships of the City of Munich 2346
Leonie Sonning Music Prize 1336
Jakob Stainer Preis 749
Standard Bank Young Artist Awards 4191
International Tchaikovsky Competition 4392
Lionel Tertis International Viola Competition and Workshop 7259
Tiroler Landespreis fur Kunst 750
Tlws y Cerddor (Composers Medal) 7330
Donald Tovey Memorial Prize 7314
Traditional Irish Music, Singing and Dancing Awards 2891
TRIC Awards 7255
Ernst von Siemens Music Prize 4915
Prix Georges Wildenstein 1499
Clive Wilson Award for Young Musicians 5970
The Wolf Prizes 2938

Music competitions (*See also* Opera; Piano competitions; Violin competitions; Vocal music)
Emily Anderson Prize for Violin 6859
International Johann Sebastian Bach Competition 2036
British Music Society Awards 5382
Budapest International Music Competition 2504
Maria Callas Grand Prix for Opera, Oratorio-Lied 2451
Concertino Prague International Radio Competition for Young Musicians 1254
Concorso Internazionale di Chitarra Mauro Giuliani 3001
Concours International Printemps de la Guitare 910
Concurso Permanente de Jovenes Interpretes 4523
European Chopin Piano Competition 2065
Cesar Franck Organ Competition 3548
Philip and Dorothy Green Award for Young Concert Artists 6409
Improvisation Prize 6276
International Carillon Competition - Queen Fabiola 1080
International Competition for Musical Performers - Geneva 4702
International Gaudeamus Interpreters Competition 3556
International Harp Contest in Israel 2904
International Jeunesses Musicales Competition - Belgrade 4413
International Lahti Organ Competition 1419
International Martial Solal Piano-Jazz Competition 1744
International Maurice Andre Trumpet Competition 1745
International Oliver Messiaen Competition for Interpertation of Contemporary Music 1746
International Organ Competition 1747
International Organ Competition, Odense 1322
International Organ Improvisation Competition 3675
International Paulo Cello Competition 1411
International Rostrum of Young Performers/ UNESCO 4444
International Villa-Lobos Guitar Competition 1138
International Violin and Bow Making Competition 1748
Internationaler Musikwettbewerb der ARD 2311
Interpretation Competition 6277
Irino Prize 3201
Kerkrade World Music Contest 3684
Kobe International Flute Competition 3283
Leeds International Pianoforte Competition 6364
Robert Levins Festspillfond 3894
Llangollen International Musical Eisteddfod 6393
London International String Quartet Competition 6407
Mathy and Opera Awards 358
Douglas May Award 6278
Carl Nielsen International Music Competitions 1313
Sigbjorn Bernhoft Osas Festspillfond 3896
Paloma O'Shea Santander International Piano Competition 4540
Michelle Pittaluga International Classical Guitar Competition - City of Alessandria Award 3119
Prague Spring International Music Competition 1264
"Premio Paolo Borciani" - International String Quartet Competition 3134
Queen Elisabeth International Music Competition of Belgium Prizes 947
Jean-Pierre Rampal International Flute Competition 1749
Rostropovitch International Cello Competition 1750
Royal Over-Seas League Music Competition 6853
Scheveningen International Music Competition 3662
Franz Schubert and the Music of Modern Times International Competition 828
International Robert Schumann Choir Competition 2314
Seoul International Music Festival Awards 4115
Student Competition for Overseas Music Study Award 4116
Francisco Tarrega International Guitar Competition 4473
International Tchaikovsky Competition 4392
Lionel Tertis International Viola Competition and Workshop 7259
Tokyo International Competition for Chamber Music Composition 3239
Tokyo International Music Competition 3338
Tunbridge Wells International Young Concert Artists Competition 7279
Young Concert Artists Trust Award 7394
Young Performers Awards 696

Music composition
Tadeusz Baird Memorial Competition for Young Composers 4038
Don Banks Music Award 98
Sir John Barbirolli Memorial 6860
Besancon International Competition of Music Composition 1795
Prix Georges Bizet
Academie des Beaux-Arts 1438
Institut de France 1853
Leslie Boosey Award 6533
Karel Boury Prize 952
British Academy Television Awards 5217
Benjamin Britten International Composers' Competition 5568

Music (continued)

Prix Andre Caplet 1441
Prix Chartier 1444
Composition Competitions 7238
Concorso Internazionale Luigi Russolo 3052
Prix Arthur DeGreef 974
Prix Rene Dumesnil 1448
Prix Jacques Durand 1450
Foundation for the Promotion of Finnish Music Grants 1403
Grand Prix de la Chanson Francaise 1972
Grand Prix du Jazz 1977
Grand Prix of the Eurovision Song Contest 4710
Prix Houllevigue 1455
International Contest for Carillon Composition 1081
International Gaudeamus Music Week 3557
International Mozart Competition 826
International Songwriters' Association Awards 2846
Irino Prize 3201
Korean Composition Awards 4114
Prix Hector Lefuel 1459
Paul Lowin Orchestral Prize 558
Paul Lowin Song Cycle Prize 559
Witold Lutoslawski International Composers Competition 4054
Macaulay Fellowship 2822
Prix Monbinne 1465
Mozart Medal 3447
Music Awards 6865
Philip Neill Memorial Prize in Music 3877
Prix Nicolo 1467
Nordic Council Music Prize 4614
Operasangerinnen Fanny Elstas Fond 3895
The Orange British Academy Film Awards 5218
Otaka Prize 3300
Goffredo Petrassi International Competition for Composers 3049
Michele Pitaluga International Composition Competition for Classical Guitar 3118
Polish Composers Union Prize 4039
Premio Municipal Alfredo Marceneiro de Fado 4072
Premios Municipais Joly Braga Santos de Musica 4086
Prix Ars Electronica - International Competition for Cyberarts 762
Prix de Composition Musicale 3472
Prix Irene Fuerison 979
Queen Elisabeth International Music Competition of Belgium Prizes 947
Prix Rossini 1487
Prix de Composition Musicale Marcel Samuel-Rousseau 1488
Prix Florent Schmitt 1492
Harold Smart Competition 6883
Leonie Sonning Music Prize 1336
Swiss Music - Edition 4907
Teenage Festival of Life Award 3881
Marten Toonder Award 2823
Prix Ch. M. Tornov-Loeffler 1494
Prix Paul-Louis Weiller 1498
Yorkshire & Humberside Arts Young Composers Awards 5976

Music education
ITA Award 6310
Neill Humfeld Award 6311
Orchestra Recognition Award 6312
UNESCO - International Music Council Music Prize 2001

Musical instruments
Sir John Barbirolli Memorial 6860
Royal Dublin Society Crafts Competition 2877

Musicology
Derek Allen Prize 5202
Dent Medal 6849
Prix Rene Dumesnil 1448
Foundation for the Promotion of Finnish Music Grants 1403
Polish Composers Union Prize 4039
UNESCO - International Music Council Music Prize 2001
Floris van der Mueren Prize 1076

Mycology
Lucille K. Georg Award 1413

Mystery writing
Cartier Diamond Dagger Award 5706
John Creasey Memorial Award 5707
Debut Dagger 5709
Duncan Lawrie Dagger 5710
The Ian Flemming Steel Dagger 5711
Dashiell Hammett Award 1243
Short Story Dagger 5713

Mythology
Prix Le Fevre-Deumier de Ports 1689

National security
Prix Lamb 1581
Prix Science et Defense 1812

Natural history *See* Science

Natural science *See* Science

Nature
Duke of Edinburgh Conservation Medal 4943
Marsh Award for Conservation Biology 7398
Natural World Book Prize 6495
WWF Award for Conservation Merit 4946

Nature photography
Birkenhead International Colour Salon 5181

Naval architecture *See* Naval engineering

Naval engineering
Samuel Baxter Prize 6837
Calder Prize 6838
Denny Gold Medal 6045
William Froude Medal 6839
Froude Research Scholarship in Naval Architecture 6840
Stanley Gray Award 6046
Stanley Gray Branch Award 6047
Stanley Gray Medal 6048
BMEC Donald Maxwell Award 6049
Prix Plumey 1599
Small Craft Group Medal 6841
Kevin Stark Memorial Award 533
Wakenham Prize 6842
Sir William White Scholarship 6843

Navigation
Lode Baekelmans Prize 949
Prix Binoux 1547
Dapaepe-Willems Award 924
Fellowship 6826
Fondation de Madame Edmond Hamel 1571
John Harrison Award 6827
Honorary Fellow 6828
Necho Award 6829
Michael Richey Medal 6830
Sadek Award 6831
Harold Spencer-Jones Gold Medal 6832
J E D Williams Medal 6833

Neurology
A.W. Campbell Award 300
Distinguished Achievement Award 301
Hughlings Jackson Lecture and Medal 7014
Amrut Mody-Unichem Prize for Research in Cardiology, Neurology and Gastroenterology 2614
Paxinos-Watson Prize 302
Sherrington Memorial Lecture 7018
Sir Grafton Elliot Smith Award 303
Student Poster Prize 304
Istvan Tork Prize 305
Young Scientist Award 1309

Newspapers *See* Journalism

Non-destructive testing *See* Testing

Nonfiction
Aventis Prizes for Science Books 6901
BBC Four Samuel Johnson Prize for Non-Fiction 5193
Boardman Tasker Award for Mountain Literature 5187
Book Awards of the National Book Development Council of Singapore 4423
Crystal Clear Day 6537
The CWA Gold Dagger for Nonfiction 5708
Festival Awards for Literature 672
Calvin and Rose G. Hoffman Prize for Distinguished Publication on Christopher Marlowe 6350
Inside Write Awards 6538
Recht Malan Prize 4374
New South Wales Premier's Literary Awards 585
Eve Pownall Award for Information Books 409
Prix des Maisons de la Presse 1934
NZSA Lilian Ida Smith Award 3794
Strega Prize 3132
Victorian Premier's Literary Awards 683
Wales Book of the Year Awards 4995
Western Australian Premier's Book Awards 685
Whitfield Prize 6781

Nuclear disarmament *See* World peace

Nuclear engineering (*See also* Atomic energy)
AINSE Awards 248
AINSE Gold Medal 249
AINSE Post Graduate Research Awards 250

Nuclear (continued)
Australian Nuclear Association Annual Award 307
Graduate Award 6188
Honorary Fellowship 6189
International Conference Award 5390
Rutherford Medal and Prize 6066

Numismatics
Australian Numismatic Society Bronze Medal 309
Prix Edmond Drouin 1511
Prix Duchalais 1512
Prix Roman et Tania Ghirshman 1516
Gold Medal and Fellowship of the Society 310
Medal of Honor 900
Prix Allier de Hauteroche 1525
Prix Victor Tourneur 1019
John Sanford Saltus Medal 5392
Silver Medal and Associate Fellowship of the Society 311

Nursing
Distinguished Merit Award 869
Excellence in Education Grant 870
Excellence in Patient Education Award 871
International Oncology Nursing Fellowships 4859
Meering Rose Bowl Award 6557
Florence Nightingale Medal 4792
Novice Research Award 872
Nursing Service Cross 220
Royal Red Cross 5607

Nutrition
B. C. Guha Memorial Lecture 2743
Journalist Prize 2245
Hans Adolf Krebs-Preis 2246
Prix du Docteur et de Madame Henri Labbe 1579
Julius Lewkowitsch Memorial Lecture 7174
Premio Nacional de Ciencia y Tecnologia de Alimentos 3441
Max Rubner-Preis 2247

Occupational health
Achievement Awards 6924
Bedford Award 5394
Distinguished Service Awards 6925
Sir George Earle Trophy 6926
Ned Franklin Medal 6093
David Hickish Award 5395
Ted King Award 5396
Working for a Healthier Workplace - The Peter Isaac Award 5397
Sector Awards 6930
Thomas Bedford Memorial Prize 5398
Training Trophy 6931

Occupational safety
Achievement Awards 6924
Distinguished Service Awards 6925
Sir George Earle Trophy 6926
Ned Franklin Medal 6093
Health and Safety Award 5420
Lifetime Achievement Award 6191
Occupational Health Award 6929
Sector Awards 6930
Training Trophy 6931

Occupational therapy *See* Rehabilitation and therapy

Oceanography
Cath Allen Prize 5611
W. S. Bruce Medal 6989
Albert Defant-Medaille 2080
Norman Heaps Prize 5612
International Festival of Maritime, Exploration, and Environmental Films 1890
Prix Georges Millot 1591
Fridtjof Nansen Medal 1776
Premio do Mar Rei D. Carlos 4093
Prix de la Belgica 1035
Prix des Sciences de la Mer 1609
Research Medal 653

Oil painting *See* Painting

Oncology *See* Cancer

Opera (*See also* Vocal music)
International Hans Gabor Belvedere Singing Competition 830
Maria Callas Grand Prix for Opera, Oratorio-Lied 2451
Boris Christoff International Competition for Young Opera Singers - Sofia 1141
Dutch International Vocal Competition - Hertogenbosch 3508
Bernhard-Harms-Preis 2338
International Gaudeamus Music Week 3557
International Rostrum of Young Performers/ UNESCO 4444
Long Service Awards 6478
Mathy and Opera Awards 358
Prix Monbinne 1465
Music Awards 6865
Neue Stimmen - International Singing Contest 2050
Laurence Olivier Awards 7203
Prix de Composition Musicale Marcel Samuel-Rousseau 1488
Split Summer Festival 1223

Operations research
Distinguished Principal Founding Member 803
Hodgson Prize 6643
Honorary Scholar 804
Peccei Scholarship 805

Ophthalmology
AOS Medal 313
International Glaucoma Association Fellowship 6711
Keeler Scholarship 6712
The Opthalmological Gold Medal 1345
The Patrick Trevor-Roper Undergraduate Award 6713
Peter Floud Award 7338
Postgraduate Student Prize 314
Technical Optics Award 315
Warsash/AOS Student Prize 316

Optics
Galileo Galilei Award 4514
ICO-ICTP Prize 2947
International Commission for Optics Prize 4515
Optical Society of India Award 2784
Satgur Prasad-Prag Parmeshwari Devi Memorial Award 2785
Harvans Singh Memorial Award 2786
Thomas Young Medal and Prize 6068

Orchestral conducting *See* Conducting

Organizational service
Harry M. Ballantyne Award 4948

Oriental culture *See* Asian studies; Japanese culture

Ornithology
BP Conservation Programme 5179
Foerderpreis der Werner-Sunkel-Stiftung 2207
Godman-Salvin Medal 5402
Jubilee Medal 5548
Ornithologen-Preis 2208
Erwin-Stresemann-Foerderung 2209
Bernard Tucker Medal 5549
Union Medal 5403
Preis der Horst Wiehe-Stiftung 2210
Wildlife Action Awards 7334

Orthodontistry
Beni Solow Award 5839
Chapman Prize Essay 5405
EOS Poster Award 5840
EOS Research Grant 5841
Ernest Sheldon Friel Memorial Lecture 5842
Grants to Eastern Europeans 5843
Gunter Russell Prize 5406
W. J. B. Houston Research Awards 5844
Houston Reserach Scholarship 5407
Maurice Berman Prize 5408
Northcroft Memorial Lecture 5409
Research and Audit Awards 5410

Orthopedics
Chen Memorial Prize 5412
Allan Frederick Dwyer Prize 318
Evelyn Hamilton Award 319
Gordon Kerridge Prize 320
Research Pump-Priming Grants 5413
Travelling Fellowships 5414

Packaging
Australian Packaging Awards 595
Brazilian Packaging and Design Awards 1127
National Training and Development Awards 5422
Packaging Achiever Awards 596
Scanstar Packaging Competition 1334
Southern Cross Package Design Awards 597
UK Company of the Year 5423

Painting (*See also* Watercolor painting)
Abbey Fellowships in Painting 5434
Abbey Scholarship in Painting 5435
Archibald Prize 47
Arts Council of England Helen Chadwick Fellowship 5436
Prix Claude Berthault 1436
Prix Karl Beule 1437
Prix Bordin 1439
Prix Leclerc-Maria Bouland 1440
BP Portrait Award 6483
BuaLuang Art Competition Prize 4958
Prix Jeanne Burdy 1854
Prix Charles Caty 972
Prix Emma du Cayla-Martin 973
Prix Alphonse Cellier 1442
Prix Paul Chabas 1443
Prix Gustave Courtois 1445

Painting (continued)

Prix Maxime David 1446
De Laszlo Medal 6942
Federation of British Artists Prizes and Awards 7027
Prix Felix Feneon 1805
Prix Gabriel Ferrier 1451
Prix Achille Fould-Stirbey 1452
Portia Geach Memorial Award 701
Governor General Art Award 3760
Prix Haumont 1454
Derek Hill Foundation Scholarship 5439
Prix Houllevigue 1455
Hunting Art Prizes 6524
Jerwood Awards 6340
The Jerwood Painting Prize 6525
The Jerwood Sculpture Prize 6526
Katanning Art Prize 554
Prix Hector Lefuel 1459
Prix Henri Lehmann 1460
Prix Troyon et Edouard Lemaitre 1461
Prix Maurice R.D. 1463
Prix Meurand 1464
Prix Constant Montald 976
Prix Alphonse de Neuville et Sanford Saltus 1466
Order of Culture 3246
Panorama Brasilian Art 1134
Photographic Portrait Prize 48
Prix Eugene Piot 1469
Praemium Imperiale 3217
Premio Municipal Carlos Botelho de Pintura 4074
Prix Balleroy 1860
Prix Bastien-Lepage 1470
Prix Breaute 1471
Prix Brizard 1472
Prix Colmont 1475
Prix Dagnan-Bouveret 1476
Prix de Rome Fine Art 3642
Prix Dumas-Millier 1481
Prix et Fondations Concernant l'Academie de France a Rome 1482
Prix Gustave Camus 978
Prix Jos Albert 981
Prix Le Guay-Lebrun 1483
Prix Louise Dehem 984
Prix Paul Artot 985
Prix Rene Janssens 988
Royal Academy Summer Exhibition 6611
Prix Emile Sacre 990
St. Cuthberts Mill Award for Works on Paper 6943
Storywriting and Art Competition 107
Sulman Prize 49
Prix de Portrait Paul-Louis Weiller 1497
Prix Paul-Louis Weiller 1498
Prix Georges Wildenstein 1499
The Wolf Prizes 2938
Charles Wollaston Award 6612
The Wynne Prize 50

Paleontology *See* Geology and paleontology

Paper industry (*See also* Forestry; Wood and wood products)

Walter Brecht Denkmunze 2027
Hans Clemm Denkmunze 2028
Goldene Vereinsnadel 2029
Goldener Ehrenring fur Papiergeschichte 2030
Georg Jayme Denkmunze 2031
Eugen Lendholt Denkmunze 2032
Alexander Mitscherlich Denkmunze 2033
Paper Industry Gold Medal 6519
Technical Association of the Australian and New Zealand Pulp and Paper Industry Awards 45
Dr. Edmund Thiele Denkmunze 2034

Parachuting *See* Flying

Parenting *See* Family relations

Parks *See* Recreation

Patents *See* Inventions

Pathology

Inhaber de Otto-Appel-Denkmunze 2212
Bourse de la SPE 1969
Gold-Headed Cane 3351
Prix Alphonse Laveran 1584
Medaille d'Or 1970
Gordon Signy Foreign Fellowship 3352
Prijs J. B. Van Helmont 970

Patriotism *See* Citizenship and patriotism

Peace *See* World peace

Pediatrics

Andrea Prader Prize 5861
Adalbert Czerny Preis 2249
Dr. H. B. Dingley Memorial Award 2603
ESPE-Hormone Research Prize 5862
ESPE Young Investigator Award 5863
Henning Andersen Prizes 5864
Otto Heubner Preis 2250
Jacques Lefebvre Award 5868
Dr. Kamala Menon Medical Research Award 2613
Outstanding Clinician Award 5865
Research Award 5866
Schweisguth Prize 6299
SIOP Awards 6300
Edith Whetnall Lectureship 7023

Performing arts (*See also* Ballet; Choreography; Costume design; Dance; Drama; Entertainment; Music; Puppetry; Theater)

Arts Council of Northern Ireland Bursaries and Awards 5074
British Academy Television Awards 5217
Conamus Export Prize 3500
Hamilton Deane Award 5742
Fellowships and Scholarships 584
Live Awards 7276
Nordic Council Music Prize 4614
The Orange British Academy Film Awards 5218
Polish Composers Union Prize 4039
Premios Municipais Palmira Bastos e Antonio Silva de Interpretacao Teatral 4087
Sangeet Natak Akademi Fellowships 2778
International Robert Schumann and Piano and Song Competition 2313
Silver Harp 3503

Personal achievement *See* Professional and personal achievement

Personal finance *See* Financial planning

Pest control *See* Public health

Petroleum industry

BTEC Certificate in Expedition Management 7090
BTEC Certificate in Tropical Habitat Conservation 7091
Dewhurst Lecture and Award 7376
Eminent Pharmacist Award 2730
Excellence Awards 7377
IJPS Best Paper Award 2731
IRF Lifetime Achievement Award 2732
H. E. Jones London Medal 6172
Prof. M.L. Khorana Memorial Award 2733
Prof. M.L. Schroff Award 2734
K.A. Richards Scholarship 322
Reg Sprigg Medal 323
Sugg Heritage Award 6174
Tony Noon Scholarship 324
Lewis G. Weeks Medal 325

Pets *See* Animal care and training

Pharmacology

Dr. Nitya Anand Endowment Lecture 2671
ASCEPT New Investigator Awards 93
ASCEPT Student Travel Awards 94
Award for Divisional Scientific Contributions 3306
Award for Drug Discovery 7102
Awards in Recognition of Excellence 3597
Andre Bedat Award 3598
Best Vendor Award 2788
Professor K.P. Bhargava Memorial Medal 2677
Distinguished Achievement Award 2113
Julije Domac Medal 1225
Ehrennadel der Deutschen Apotheker 2060
FIP Fellowships 3599
Galen Medal 7389
Prijs Jan-Frans Heymans 967
Honorary Life Member
International Pharmaceutical Students' Federation 3602
Pharmacy Guild of Australia 599
Host-Madsen Medal 3600
Albert Howells Award 5686
Denis Wade Johnson and Johnson New Investigators Awards 95
Prix de Biologie Alfred Kastler 1822
Premio Carlos del Castillo Leiva 4532
Lister Memorial Lecture 7175
Hans Meyer Medaille 2061
Minarikovo Odlicje 4465
Poster Prizes 2114
Dr. D. N. Prasad Memorial Oration Award 2617
Premio Colegio Oficial de Farmaceuticos de Madrid 4533
Premio Consejo General de Colegios de Farmaceuticos 4534
Premio Real Academia Nacional de Farmacia 4535
Prix Charles Mentzer des Rencontres de Chimie Therapeutique 1966
Prix d'Encouragement a la recherche en Chimie Therapeutique 1967
Prix Leon et Henri Fredericq 1050
PSJ Award 3307
PSJ Award for Drug Research and Development 3308
PSJ Award for Young Scientists 3309
ASCEPT Michael Rand Medal 96
Redi Award 2325

Pharmacology (continued)

Premio Santos Ruiz 4536
Scheelepriset 4678
Egon Stahl Award 2377
Young Scientist Award 2115

Philanthropy
Alejandro Angel Escobar Prizes 1193
Young Scientists for Rainforests 5695

Philatelic journalism
Hunziker Medal 3060

Philately
Congress Medal 5110
Crawford Medal 6855
The Roll of Distinguished Philatelist 5111
Stampex Exhibition Awards 6535
Tapling Medal 6856
Tilleard Medal 6857

Philology *See* Linguistics

Philosophy
Balzan Prize 3062
Prix Robert Blanche 1637
BP Prize Lectureship in the Humanities 6988
Prix Victor Cousin 1645
Prix Crouzet 1646
Prix Victor Delbos 1649
Prix Estrade-Delcros 1509
Prix Demolombe 1651
Prix Gegner 1663
Graham Medal 6867
Prix Grammaticakis-Neuman 1666
Grand Prix de l'Academie des Sciences Morales et Politiques 1667
Kelvin Medal 6868
Kyoto Prizes 3189
Prix Charles Lambert 1672
Prix Charles Leveque 1676
Prix Louis Liard 1678
Prix Charles Lyon-Caen 1680
Somerset Maugham Awards 7146
Prix Le Dissez de Penanrun 1687
Prix Jules Duculot 1014
Prix Le Fevre-Deumier de Ports 1689
Prix Polydore de Paepe 1016
Prix Joseph Saillet 1694
Prix Saintour 1696
Sarton Chair 1086
Sarton Medal 1087
Prix Stassart 1698

Philosophy of science
Prix Binoux 1547
Jan Gillis Prize 1072
Prix Grammaticakis-Neuman 1567
James Scott Prize Lectureship 6999

Photogrammetry
Best Papers by Young Authors 4969
Brock Gold Medal Award 4970
Gino Cassinis Award 4971
The CATCON Prizes 4972
Len Curtis Award 6593
Eduard Dolezal Award 4973
Sam G. Gamble Award 4974
U.V. Helava Award 4975
Poster Paper Prize 6594
President's Honorary Citation 4976
Remote Sensing and Photogrammetry Society Award 6595
Schermerhorn Award 4977
Schwidefsky Medal 4978
Student Awards 6596
Taylor and Francis Best Letter Award 6597
E. H. Thompson Award 6598
Otto von Gruber Award 4979
Wang Zhizhuo Award 4980

Photography (*See also* Nature photography; Photogrammetry; Photojournalism; Slide photography)
AIPS Awards 2510
Assistants' Awards 5149
Australian Commercial/Industrial Photographer of the Year 258
Australian Landscape Photographer of the Year 259
Australian Professional Photographer of the Year 260
Australian Professional Photography Awards 261
BG Wildlife Photographer of the Year Competition 6492
British Academy Television Awards 5217
Centenary Medal 6870
Communicators in Business Awards 5241
Davies Medal 6871
Terence Donovan Award 6872
Fenton Medal 6873
Festival of Underwater Images 1799
Governor General Art Award 3760
Honorary Fellowship 6874
Idea Awards 5150
International Visual Communications Association Awards 6327
Interphot - Adelaide International Exhibition of Photography 675
Joanne Felk Award 262
J. Dudley Johnston Award 6875
Cherry Kearton Medal and Award 6770
Gerard Levy Prize for a Young Photographer 2918
Life Membership 2864
Literature and Art Award 4954
Lumiere Award 6876
Magnolia Prize 3950
Member's Award 6877
Yunus Nadi Yarismasi 4964
National Business Calendar Awards 5421
Odden Award 6878
The Orange British Academy Film Awards 5218
Photographers' Awards 5151
Premio Municipais Joshua Benoliel de Fotografia 4071
Prix de Boelpaepe 1034
Prix de Rome Fine Art 3642
Prix du Livre de Photographie/Arles Book Award 1945
Progress Medal 6879
Saxby Award 6880
Scottish Salon of Photography 7083
Selwyn Award 6881
Sports Photographer of the Year 7245
Student Awards 5152
Tertiary Institute Award 263
World Cup 3391
Young Wildlife Photographer of the Year Competition 6493

Photojournalism
W.G. Walkley Awards for Journalism 561
World Press Photo Contest 3690

Physical education
Philip Noel Baker Research Award 2296
Honorary Member 2866
ICSSPE Sport Science Award of the IOC President 2297
UNESCO Award for Distinguished Services to Physical Education and Sport 1999

Physical fitness *See* Health and fitness

Physical medicine *See* Rehabilitation and therapy

Physical science
Bhatnagar Award 2573
Anil Kumar Bose Memorial Award 2680
Bruce-Preller Prize Lectureship 6990
Caledonian Research Foundation Prize Lectureship in Biomedical Sciences and Arts and Letters 6992
R.J.W. Le Fevre Memorial Prize 111
Foundation for Research Science and Technology Science Communicator Awards 3765
Honorary Membership 902
Lomonosov Gold Medal 4394
MakDougall-Brisbane Prize 6997
Premio Dotte Giuseppe Borgia 2973
Scottish Science Award 7072
Sorby Medal 904

Physical therapy *See* Rehabilitation and therapy

Physics
Prix Anatole et Suzanne Abragam 1538
Accelerator Prize 1785
Prix Louis Armand 1540
Prof. R. K. Asundi Memorial Lecture 2673
Award for Outstanding Service to Physics in Australia 252
Award for Promotion of Physics 4045
Prix Barrabe 1831
Homi J. Bhabha Medal 2676
Grzegorz Bialkowski Prize 4046
R. D. Birla Award 2736
Walter Boas Medal 253
Max Born Medal and Prize 6054
Max-Born-Preis 2090
Satyendranath Bose Medal 2679
Charles Vernon Boys Medal and Prize 6055
Bragg Gold Medal for Excellence in Physics 254
Bragg Medal and Prize 6056
Povilo Brazdziunas premija 3374
Prix Edmond Brun 1548
Colombian Academy of Exact, Physical and Natural Sciences to the Integral Work of a Scientist 1172
Competition of Scientific Papers of Young Physicists 4446
Prix Le Conte 1553
E. R. Cooper Memorial Medal and Prize 3865
Prix Ernest Dechelle 1556
Prix Deslandres 1558
Dirac Medal 2946
Paul Dirac Medal and Prize 6058
Duddell Medal and Prize 6059
Fellowship Awards 4966
Founders Prize 6070

Physics (continued)
Francqui Prize 895
Fujihara Award 3181
Prix du Gaz de France 1565
Glazebrook Medal and Prize 6060
Gregori Aminoffs Pris 4638
Gunning Victoria Jubilee Prize Lectureship 6995
Guthrie Medal and Prize 6061
Otto-Hahn-Preis fur Chemie und Physik 2091
Helmholtz Prize 2269
Gustav-Hertz-Preis (Physik-Preis) 2092
Hewlett-Packard Europhysics Prize 1786
High Energy and Particle Physics Prize 1787
Gilles Holst Medal 3656
Holweck Medal and Prize 6062
Prix Fernand Holweck 1572
Honorable Member 4447
Honorary Membership 4047
Hughes Medal 6910
ICTP Prize 2948
Adolfo Jucys premija 3380
Gentner-Kastler-Prize 2093
Kelvin Medal and Prize 6063
Prix L. La Caze 1578
Prix Langevin 1582
Lorentz Medal 3657
Luikov Medal 4967
Lyle Medal 118
Prix Paul Marguerite de la Charlonie 1589
Marlow Medal and Prize 6973
Harrie Massie Medal and Prize 255
Maxwell Medal and Prize 6064
Medaille fur Naturwissenschaftliche Publizistik 2094
Medalla de la Real Sociedad Espanola de Fisica 4542
Prix Georges Millot 1836
National Prize of the President of the Republic 2972
Nobel Prize for Physics 4605
Nobel Prizes 4639
Prix Henri de Parville 1595
Paterson Medal and Prize 6065
Pawsey Medal 121
Philippine Physics Olympiad 3985
Arkadiiusz Piekara Prize 4048
Max-Planck-Medaille 2095
Robert-Wichard-Pohl-Preis 2096
Polish-German Marian Smoluchowski-Emil Warburg Physics Prize 4049
Pollock Memorial Lecture 645
Premio a Investigadores Noveles 4543
Prix Agathon De Potter 1028
Prix Ampere d'Electricite de France 1602
Prix Artur du Fay 1604
Prix du Commisariat a l'Energie Atomique 1610
Prix Fonde par l'Etat 1611
Prix Georges Vanderlinden 1044
Prix Pol and Christiane Swings 1053
Prix Theophile de Donder 1055
Prizes of the 150th Anniversary of the RSSL 1098
Prof. G. N. Ramachandran 60th Birthday Commemoration Medal 2707
Prof. K. Rangadhama Rao Memorial Lecture 2710
Research Medal 653
Prix Gustave Ribaud 1617
Dr. Biren Roy Memorial Lecture 2711
Rumford Medal 6916
Rutherford Medal and Prize 6066
Prix Gabrielle Sand et Marie Guido Triossi 1621
Karl-Scheel-Preis 2097
Walter-Schottky-Preis fur Festkorperforschung 2098
Scientific Research Prizes 3451
Prix Servant 1622
The Silver Dirac Medal 715
Simon Memorial Prize 6067
Slovak Physical Society Award 4448
Slovak Physical Society Medal 4449
Marian Smoluchowski Medal 4050
Premio Triennale per la Fisica Francesco Somaini 3007
Special Award 4051
David Syme Research Prize 713
Premio Tricerri 3109
TWAS Award in Physics 2965
Alan Walsh Medal for Service to Industry 256
Frederick White Prize 124
Wisconsin Travel Award 6072
Wojciech Rubinowicz Scientific Prize 4052
The Wolf Prizes 2938
Young Physics Students Competition 4450

Physiology
Alexander Ninian Bruce Prize 6991
Mary Bullivant Student Prize 3822
Octave Dupont Prize 1070
Fondation Jean de Meyer 1022
Fondation Octave Dupont 1025
Luigi Galvani Prize 4475
Premio Herlitzka 2967
Honorary Life Membership Award 4221
John Hubbard Memorial Prize 3823
Prix Max-Fernand Jayle 1574
Prix L. La Caze 1578
Prix Montyon de Physiologie 1593
Nobel Prize for Physiology or Medicine 4606
Prix Leon et Henri Fredericq 1050
Prix Theophile Gluge 1056
Research Medal 653
Sherrington Memorial Lecture 7018
Thunbergmedaljen 4631
Johnny van der Walt Award 4222
Wyndham Award 4223

Piano competitions
John Allison City of Sydney Piano Scholarship 687
Geza Anda International Piano Competition 4761
AXA Dublin International Piano Competition 2825
International Johann Sebastian Bach Competition 2036
International Beethoven Piano Competition 832
Budapest International Music Competition 2504
F. Busoni Prize 2999
Maria Callas Grand Prix for Piano 2452
Alessandro Casagrande International Piano Competition 3015
Cologne International Pianoforte Competition 2067
Concertino Prague International Radio Competition for Young Musicians 1254
Prix Arthur DeGreef 974
Ettlingen International Competition for Young Pianists 2363
Franz Liszt International Piano Competition - Mario Zanfi Prize 2997
Rina Sala Gallo International Piano Competition 2989
Philip and Dorothy Green Award for Young Concert Artists 6409
Clara Haskil Competition 4765
International Competition for Musical Performers - Geneva 4702
International Franz Liszt Piano Competition 3621
International Frederic Chopin Piano Competition 4002
International Mozart Competition 826
International Villa-Lobos Piano Competition 1139
Internationaler Musikwettbewerb der ARD 2311
Jaen Prize 4521
Leeds International Pianoforte Competition 6364
London International Piano Competition 6395
Marguerite Long and Jacques Thibaud International Competition 1932
Newport International Competition for Young Pianists 6499
Vlado Perlemuter Piano Scholarship 5923
Ettore Pozzoli International Piano Competition 3013
Premio Internazionale Accademia Musicale Chigiana Siena 2952
Queen Elisabeth International Music Competition of Belgium Prizes 947
Royal Over-Seas League Music Competition 6853
Arthur Rubinstein International Piano Master Competition in Conjuction with the Israel Philharmonic Orchestra 2893
International Robert Schumann and Piano and Song Competition 2313
Scottish International Piano Competition 7081
Sydney International Piano Competition of Australia 413
Tunbridge Wells International Young Concert Artists Competition 7279
Gian Battista Viotti International Music and Dance Competition 3126
Young Concert Artists Trust Award 7394

Ping pong *See* Table tennis

Plastics and rubber
Baekeland Lecture 7157
Honorary Life President 3413

Plays *See* Drama; Theater

Playwriting *See* Drama

Poetry
Emil Aarestrup Prize 1291
Arvon Foundation International Poetry Competition 5076
Award for Aboriginal and Torres Strait Islander Writers 588
Award for Original Hebrew Poetry 2899
Bagutta Prize 2993
Bellmanpriset 4648
Benson Medal 7001
Horst Bienek Preis fur Lyrik 2038

Poetry (continued)
Olavo Bilac Prize 1118
Boardman Tasker Award for Mountain Literature 5187
Book Awards of the National Book Development Council of Singapore 4423
Book of the Year Awards 37
The Bridport Prize 5200
Georg-Buchner-Preis 2144
Giosue Carducci Prize 3140
Prix Hercule Catenacci 1855
Cholmondeley Award for Poets 7140
Tom Collins Poetry Award 449
Annette von Droste Hulshoff Preis 2349
Aquileo J. Echeverria Prize 1201
Lydia och Herman Erikssons stipendium 4654
European Music and Poetry Competitions 856
Festival Awards for Literature 672
Concours Max-Pol Fouchet 1724
Guido Gezelle Prize 957
Maurice Gilliams Prize 958
Mary Gilmore Award 55
Grand Prix des Biennales Internationales de Poesie 906
Grand Prix des Poetes 1976
Eric Gregory Awards 7142
Felicia Hemans Prize for Lyrical Poetry 7311
Hertzog Prize for Literature 4268
Jerwood Aldeburgh First Collection Prize 5018
Kallebergerstipendiet 4659
Frans Kellendonk-prijs 3670
Kellgrenpriset 4660
Ilona Kohrtz' stipendium 4661
Grace Leven Prize for Poetry 556
Literary Competition 435
John Masefield Memorial Trust 7145
Somerset Maugham Awards 7146
Arthur Merghelynck Prize 960
Yunus Nadi Yarismasi 4964
National Poetry Competition 6541
New South Wales Premier's Literary Awards 585
Nordiska Priset 4663
Northern Territory Literary Awards 589
Carlos Palanca Memorial Awards for Literature 3978
Poetry International Festival 3640
Corneliu M. Popescu Prize for European Poetry Translation 6542
Premier's Literary Award 673
Premio Carlos Bonvalot 4092
Premio Nacional de Literatura 1163
Premios Municipais Eca de Queiroz de Literatura 4085
Thomas Pringle Award 4172
Prix Balleroy 1860
Prix de La Grange 1529
Prize for Translated Work 4278
PUK-Councilers Prize 4279
Red Earth Poetry Award 590
Prix Rossini 1487
Olive Schreiner Prize 4173
NZSA Lilian Ida Smith Award 3794
Stand Poetry Competition 7247
Stipendium ur Lena Vendelfelts minnesfond 4670
Storywriting and Art Competition 107
Teenage Festival of Life Award 3881
Georg Trakl Prize for Poetry 744
Karel van de Woestijne Prize 962
Lucy B. and C. W. Van der Hoogt-prijs 3673
Victorian Premier's Literary Awards 683
Wales Book of the Year Awards 4995
Western Australian Premier's Book Awards 685
Whitbread Literary Awards 5194
World Mystical Poetry Prize 4530
Wesley Michel Wright Prize for Poetry 711

Police *See* Law enforcement

Polish culture
Order of Merit of the Republic of Poland 4014
Order of Polish Rebirth 4015

Political science (*See also* European integration; Foreign policy; Human relations; International relations; Legislative improvement; National security; Social science research; World peace)
Crisp Medal 90
Prix Charles Dupin 1654
Prix Joseph Dutens 1656
ECPR PhD Prize 5822
Prix Leon Faucher 1658
Prix Grammaticakis-Neuman 1666
Prix Ernest Lemonon 1675
Prix Limantour 1679
Prix Charles Lyon-Caen 1680
W. J. M. MacKenzie Book Prize 6546
Premio Internazionale di Meridionalistica Guido Dorso 2987
Prix Emile de Laveleye 1005
Stein Rokkan Prize 5823
Prix Rossi 1693
Prix Saintour 1696
Masri Singarimbun Research Awards 2816
Standing Group Grant 5824
Suntory Prize for Social Sciences and Humanities 3334
Wildenmann Prize 5825
Women and Politics Prize 91

Pollution control *See* Environmental conservation; Water conservation

Population *See* Demography; Family planning

Portuguese culture
Camoes Prize 4089

Poultry science
Houghton Lecture Award 2445
Macdougall Medal 7381
Bart Rispens Award 2446

Poverty *See* Humanitarianism

Preventive medicine
InBev-Baillet Latour Health Prize 893
Insole Award 5366
Albert Strating Prize for Preventive Medicine 4285
Younger MembersF Award for Achievement 6165

Printed materials *See* Publications

Printing industry
Gutenberg Award 2267
Health and Safety Award 5420
National Business Calendar Awards 5421
National Training and Development Awards 5422
UK Company of the Year 5423

Prints *See* Graphic arts

Professional and personal achievement (*See also* Academic achievement; Leadership)
Achievement Medals 6141
Conspicuous Service Decorations 212
Cross of Merit 4008
Essar Gold Medal 2649
Faraday Medal 6148
Hindustan Zinc Gold Medal 2651
O. P. Jindal Gold Medal 2654
Kultureller Ehrenpreis 2343
Mensa International Competitions 6426
Metallurgist of the Year Award 2656
Onassis Award for International Understanding and Social Achievement 2462
Francis Ormond Medal 608
Pro Urbe Budapest Award 2494
Sir Henry Royce Award 6161
Xirka Gieh ir-Repubblika 3429
Young Metallurgist of the Year Award 2662

Psychiatry (*See also* Mental health)
Burden Research Prize 6720
Natalie Cobbing Travelling Fellowship 6721
Margaret Davenport Prize 6722
Philip Davis Prize 6723
Gaskell Medal and Prize 6724
Laughlin Prize 6727
Morris Markowe Public Education Prize 6728
Moshen Naguib Memorial Prize 6729
Brian Oliver Prize 6730
Gillian Page Prize 6731
Psychotherapy Prize 6732
Ramaermedaille 3633
Research Prize and Bronze Medal 6733
Standish-Barry Prize 6735
Woodford-Williams Prize 6736

Psychology
C.J. Adcock Award 3786
Alastair Heron Prize 327
APS College of Forensic Psychologists (NSW Section) Annual Awards 328
APS Colleges Award of Distinction 329
APS Ethics Prize 330
APS Prize 331
Award For Excellent PhD Thesis in Psychology 332
Award for Outstanding Doctoral Research 5425
Bartlett Lecture 5874
Paul Bertelson Award 4491
Best Student Conference Paper Prizes 3787
Bourse Marcelle Blum 1638
Book Award 5426
British Psychological Society Presidents' Award 5427
Children's Peace Literature Award 333
COP Excellence Awards 334
Prix Dagnan-Bouveret 1647

Psychology (continued)
Distinguished Scientific Contribution Award 335
Early Career Awards 336
Elaine Dignan Award 337
Experimental Psychology Society Prize 5875
G.V. Goddard Award 3788
Elise M. Hayman Award 6282
Hayman Prize for Published Work Pertaining to Traumatized Children and Adults 6283
Honorary Fellow 5428
Honorary Life Member 5429
Hunter Award 3789
Jamieson Award 3790
The President's (Maori) Scholarship 3791
Prix de Psychologie 1002
Psychoanalytic Training Today Award 6284
Public Interest Award 3792
Research Medal 653
Cesare Sacerdoti Award 6285
Spearman Medal 5430

Public administration (*See also* City management; Government service; Historic preservation; Public works)
Prix Odilon Barrot 1633
Alexis de Tocqueville Prize 3540
Prix Edmond Freville 1661
Prix Charles Duvivier 1001

Public affairs (*See also* Community affairs; Consumer affairs; Housing; Leadership; Legislative improvement; Military service)
Astor Award 5688
Hans R. Bolliger Memorial Lecture 7158
Richard Seligman Lecture 7179

Public health
Brackenbury Award 5354
Buchanan Medal 6902
Ihsan Dogramaci Family Health Foundation Fellowship and Prize 4927
Dutch Cancer Society Press Award 3505
Donald Mackay Medal 7033
Prof. Dr. P. Muntendamprijs 3506
Occupational Health Award 6929
Jacques Parisot Foundation Fellowship 4928
Premio Fundacion Alfredo Manzullo 8
Dr. P. N. Raju Oration Award 2618
Dr. M. K. Seshadri Prize in the Field of Practice of Community Medicine 2626
Dr. A. T. Shousha Foundation Prize and Fellowship 4930
Prof. B. C. Srivastava Foundation Award 2630
Premio Miguel Aleman Valdes 3443

Public relations (*See also* Advertising; Publicity)
Awards for Outstanding Consultancy Practice 6570
FT/ARTS And Business Awards 5068
International Public Relations Association Golden World Awards for Excellence 6287
International Visual Communications Association Awards 6327
Prism Awards 4230
Prix Herman Schoolmeesters 1011

Public service (*See also* Community service; Government service)
Benemerenti Medal 7412
Prix Jean-Jacques Berger 1543
Bharat Ratna 2577
Prix Bordin 1639
British Empire Medal 5590
Prix Rene Cassin 1641
Collar of the Supreme Order of the Chrysanthemum 3243
Croix de Guerre 1810
Graduateship of the City and Guilds of London Institute 5658
Grand Cordon of the Supreme Order of the Chrysanthemum 3244
Prix de Joest 1670
Prix du Baron de Joest 1518
Madarski Konnik Order 1155
Licentiateship of the City and Guilds of London Institute 5659
Medal for Service to the Republic 3427
Medals for Excellence 5660
Membership of the City and Guilds of London Institute 5661
Mexican Order of the Aztec Eagle 3454
Most Ancient and Most Noble Order of the Thistle 5596
Most Distinguished Order of St. Michael and St. George 5597
Most Excellent Order of the British Empire 5598
Most Honourable Order of the Bath 5599
Most Noble Order of the Garter 5600
National Order of Merit 3428
Onassis Award for the Environment 2463
Orden al Merito Julio Garavito 1191
Order of Australia 221
Order of Pius 7413
Order of St. Gregory the Great 7414
Order of the Companions of Honour 5602
Order of the Cross of Liberty 1374
Order of the Lion of Finland 1375
Order of the Paulownia Flowers 3247
Order of the Precious Crown 3248
Order of the Rising Sun 3249
Order of the Sacred Treasure 3250
Order of the White Rose of Finland 1376
Padma Bhushan 2580
Padma Shri 2581
Padma Vibhushan 2582
President's Award 3743
Public Service Medal 223
Right Livelihood Award 4619
Royal Norwegian Order of Merit 3902
Royal Norwegian Order of St. Olav 3903
Royal Victorian Order 5608
Prix Gabrielle Sand et Marie Guido Triossi 1621
Stara Planina Order 1156
Threadneedle/Spectator Parliamentarian of the Year Awards 7236
Hendrik Van Eck Medal 4321

Public speaking
Faraday House Commemorative Prize 6147
IAHR Lecturer Award 4507
Eric Megaw Memorial Prize 6155
Ivor Spencer Best After Dinner Speaker of the Year 5951
T. C. White Prize Lecture 6717

Public works
Australian Engineering Excellence Awards 488

Publications (*See also* Travel literature)
Book Award 5426
British Society of Magazine Editors Awards 5511
The Foreign Press Association British Media Award 5915
Free Media Pioneer 812
IPS Award 3058
Anne Keymer Prize 5297
The Magazines - Awards for Editorial and Publishing Excellence 5515
Malta Journalism Awards 3421
National Prize of the President of the Republic 2972
Prix Danube Festival, Bratislava 4452
Rayleigh Book Award 6159

Publicity (*See also* Advertising; Public relations)
Lord Soper Award 6362

Publishing (*See also* Bibliography; Book and newspaper design; Book collecting; Editing; Illustration; Printing industry; Publications; Typography)
Advertising Sales Team of the Year 5721
Awards of Merit 4208
Best Marketing 5722
Book Design Awards 339
Prix Bordin 1439
British Book Design and Production Awards 5419
Directory of the Year - Business 5723
Directory of the Year - Consumer 5724
Editorial Fellowship Program 2925
Editors' Editor of the Year Award 5512
Guild of Food Writers Award 5949
Hegarty Prize 592
Innovation Writer of the Year 5513
International Book Award 824
International Newspaper Color Quality Club Awards 2271
IP Top Awards 4769
Jomo Kenyatta Prize for Literature 3362
Launch of the Year Award 5514
Ralph Lewis Award 7316
The Magazines - Awards for Editorial and Publishing Excellence 5515
Montana New Zealand Book Awards 3700
The Most Beautiful and the Best Children's Books in Slovakia 4438
National Prize for the Most Beautiful Book 758
New Product of the Year 5725
New Venture Award 7342
Nihon Shinbun Kyokai Awards 3241
Online Directory of the Year - Business 5726
Online Directory of the Year - Consumer 5727
Pandora Award 7343
Premio Internazionale di Meridionalistica Guido Dorso 2987
Printer of the Year 5728
Prix du Livre de Photographie/Arles Book Award 1945
Publisher of the Year 5729
SDC Centenary Medal 7190
Sefika Award 4232
Subscription Sales Team of the Year 5730

Publishing (continued)
Supplier of the Year 5731
Walter Tiemann Award 2352
Raymond Williams Community Publishing Prize 5072

Puppetry
Fritz Wortelmann Preis of the City of Bochum for Amateur Puppetry 2100

Quality control *See* Standards

Race relations *See* Ethnic affairs

Radio (*See also* Broadcasting; Cable television; Media; Television)
ABU Prizes for Radio and Television Programs 3398
Akashvani Annual Awards 2537
Akashvani Annual Awards for Technical Excellence 2538
Alexander the Great Award 2466
The Ancient Greek Cities Award 2467
Athenian Award 2468
Athens Summer Olympic Games Award 2469
Awgie Awards 395
Dentsu Advertising Awards 3179
Grand Prix 1985
Greek Islands Award 2470
The Iceland Award 2515
Iceland on Six Meters Award 2516
Icelandic JOTA Award 2517
Icelandic Radio Amateurs Award 2518
Richard Imison Memorial Award 7144
IRA Worked All Nordic Countries Award 2519
IRA Zone 40 Award 2520
Journalist Prize 2245
The Lakes of Finland Award 1378
Life Membership 474
Medal of Honour for Afrikaans Television 4276
Medienpreis fur Sprachkultur 2193
NHK Japan Prize 3298
The OH Awards 1379
The OH County Award 1380
The OHA Plaques 1381
OHA-VHF Award 1382
Premio Municipal Maria Leonor Magro de Radio 4081
Prix Ex Aequo - International Children's and Youth Radio Drama Festival 4711
Prix Nouveau Talent 1986
RAAG Award 2471
Shark Awards, the International Advertising Festival of Ireland 2887
Sony Radio Academy Awards 7226
TRIC Awards 7255
Unda Dove 1100
W.G. Walkley Awards for Journalism 561
World Association of Christian Radio Amateurs and Listeners Awards 7351

Radiology
David Anderson-Berry Medal 6987
The Bursary Award Scheme 7108
Clinical MRI Prize 5329
The Educational Support Scheme 7109
Flude Memorial Prize 5330
Jacques Lefebvre Award 5868
Leonard Levy Memorial Prize 5331
The Jack Martin Prize 7110
Stanley Melville Memorial Award 5332
Nicholas Outterside Medallion 267
RAD Magazine Best Poster Prize 5333
Medaille Boris Rajewsky 1765
Royal College of Radiologists Award 6738
Sievert Award 1909
Travel Bursaries 5334

Radiotherapy *See* Cancer

Railway transportation
Railway Engineering Award 527
Webb Prize 6133

Real estate (*See also* Construction; Housing)
Best Appraiser of the Year 2500
Best Broker of the Year 2501
Best Developer of the Year 2502
Prix d'Excellence 1911

Recording industry
AWIT Awards 3980
Best Engineer 4234
Best Original Score/Soundtrack 4235
Best Producer 4236
Best Selling Release 4237
BRIT Awards 5416
British Amateur Recording Contest 5538
Burkitt Medal for Biblical Studies 5205
Certified Awards 5417
Grand Prix du Disque Frederic Chopin 4001
Conamus Export Prize 3500
Gold Disc Award 3947
International Songwriters' Association Awards 2846
Ferenc Liszt International Record Grand Prix 2496
Platinum Disc Award 3948
Jean Thevenot Medal 4799

Recreation (*See also* Hobbies and clubs)
City of Sondrio Gold Plaque 3130
Honorary Membership Award 4195
Honorary Membership for life 5566
Waterford Crystal European Athlete of the Year Award 2111

Refugees *See* Humanitarianism

Rehabilitation and therapy
Mildred Elson Award 7364
Essay Prize 5523
Marie du Toit Award 4214
Philip Nichols Prize 5524
Rehabilitation Prize 2021
Travelling Scholarships 5525

Religion (*See also* Catholic literature; Christianity; Church history; Theology)
Prix Crouzet 1646
Charles De Clercq Prize 1069
Prix Victor Delbos 1649
Bertha Dobbins Award for Community Service 7408
Ecumenical Prize 1092
Prix Roman et Tania Ghirshman 1516
International Council of Christians and Jews International Sternberg Award 2291
International Paul VI Prize 3092
Malacological Society of London Annual Award 6413
OCIC-Prize 1093
Prix des Cathedrales 1478
Prix Emile de Laveleye 1005
Prix Eugene Goblet d'Alviella 1007
Prix Franz Cumont 1009
Prix Le Fevre-Deumier de Ports 1689
Albert Schweitzer Award 6206
Sir Charles Maurice Yonge Award 6414

Research (*See also* Dental research; Educational research; Humanities research; Medical research; Scientific research; Social science research)
Yoshiaki Arata Award 1898
Australian Engineering Excellence Awards 488
BCRA Research Fund 5273
Beale Medal 6507
Copernicus Award 2218
CRC for Polymers Prize 428
Dufton Silver Medal Award 5636
James Alfred Ewing Medal 6109
Leon Gaster Bronze Medal 5637
Geotechnical Research Medal 6111
Goodeve Medal 6508
John and Mary Goodyear Award 3522
Prof. M.N. Gopalan Award 2780
Stanley Gray Medal 6048
Hannan Medal 114
Gerhard Hess Programme 2219
Magnus Hirschfeld Award 2240
Prof. N.K. Jaiswal Memorial Award 2781
Heinz Maier-Leibnitz Prize 2220
Albert Maucher Prize in Geoscience 2221
Moran Medal for Statistical Science 120
Napier - Shaw Bronze Medal 5639
National Prize of the President of the Republic 2972
Okuma Academic Commemorative Prize 3347
Okuma Academic Encouragement Prize 3348
President's Medal 6509
Prix Prestwich 1840
Prof. B.G. Raghavendra Memorial Award 2782
Retail Store Design and Layout Award 4203
Scottish Research Book Award 7071
Eugen and Ilse Seibold Prize 2222
Gottfried Wilhelm Leibniz Prize 2223

Restaurants
Continuing Education Grant 3830
Hospitality Business Scholarships 3831
Merit Scholarships For Hospitality Students 3832
Merit Scholarships For Secondary School Students 3833
Time Out Eating and Drinking Awards 7277
Tutor Work Study Grant 3834

Retailing *See* Merchandising

Rhetoric *See* Public speaking

Riflery *See* Firearms; Hunting; Shooting

Rowing
Rowing Awards 2850

Rubber *See* Plastics and rubber

Rural economics
Global Sanitation Award 2802
Inter-American Agricultural Award for Young Professionals 1207
Inter-American Agricultural Medal 1208
Inter-American Award for the Participation of Women in Rural Development 1209
IPDC - UNESCO Prize for Rural Communication 1995
Prof. B. D. Tilak Lecture 2724

Safety (*See also* Environmental health; Fire fighting; Fire prevention; Security; specific types of safety, e.g. Automotive safety)
Hans R. Bolliger Memorial Lecture 7158
International Visual Communications Association Awards 6327
Magnel Prize 1089
Managing Occupational Road Risk Achievement Awards 6927
Norwich Union Trophy 6928
Practical Project Award 6192
Safety in Construction Medal 6126
Technician Safety Practitioner Scholarship 6193
Verdeyen Prize for Soil Mechanics 1090

Salesmanship *See* Marketing; Merchandising

Scholarly works
Prix d'Aumale 1852
Best Poster Prize 5293
Book of the Year Awards 37
A. K. Bose Medal 2647
Cornforth Medal 618
Prix James Hall 1570
Kenyon Medal for Classical Studies 5210
Anne Keymer Prize 5297
A.A. Phillips Prize 57
C. S. Piper Prize 622
Premio Municipal Augusto Vieira da Silva de Investigacao 4073

Science (*See also* History of science; Science education; Scientific research; Technology; specific fields of science, e.g. Astronomy)
Academy of Sciences of the Czech Republic Awards 1247
Achievement Awards 3976
Juan Alberto Olivares' Foundation Award 7422
Alzheimer Obelisk 817
Annual Award for Junior Researchers 1236
Ansorge Award 5028
Antwoorden Prijsvragen, Klasse der Wetenschappen 1061
ANZAAS Medal 133
Henry E. Armstrong Memorial Lecture 7156
Aryabhata Medal 2672
Australian Natural History Medallion 456
Baekeland Lecture 7157
Balzan Prize 3062
Professor Sadhan Basu Memorial Lecture 2675
Bavarian Academy of Science Prize 2043
Prix Henri Becquerel 1542
Bene merenti Medals 2044
Prof. E. D. Bergmann Memorial Award 2935
Berkeley Award 5384
Prix de la Fondation Claude Berthault 1636
Prix de Madame Claude Berthault 1544
Best Doctoral Research Presentation Award 2757
Best Scientific Work 846
Best Scientific Work of a Young Scientist 847
Best Student Scientific Work 848
Bharat Ratna 2577
Professor Krishna Sahai Bilgrami Memorial Medal 2678
Scott Blair Biorheology Scholarship 5527
L.C. Blakemore Award 3796
BradFord Award 5029
British Association Medal 4362
British Society of Rheology Annual Award 5528
British Society of Rheology Gold Medal 5529
British Vacuum Council Junior Prize 5557
Bronze Medal 4363
Bulgarian Academy of Science Honorary Badge - Marin Drinov Medal 1143
C.R. Burch Prize 5558
Burnet Lecture 109
BVC Senior Prize 5559
Carus Preis 2393
Castner Lecture and Medal 7161
G. P. Chatterjee Memorial Award 2739
Dr. Guru Prajad Chatterjee Memorial Lecture 2682
Fernand Collin Prijs 1103
Prix Le Conte 1553
James Cook Medal 640
Prix Corbay 1644
Cribb Award 5030
Dr. B. C. Deb Memorial Award for Popularisation of Science 2740
Prix Ernest Dechelle 1556
John Howard Dellinger Gold Medal 931
Prix Paul Doisteau - Emile Blutet 1560
Raj Kristo Dutt Memorial Award 2742
Howard Eggins Award 5385
Professor Magnus Ehrnrooth Prize 1398
Albert Einstein World Award of Science 3460
Encouragement Award 4991
Engestromska medaljen for tillampad naturvetenskap 4625
Environment Medal 7162
Environmental Award 4566
The Ergonomics Society Student Prize 5793
Michael Faraday Prize 6906
Fellow of the NZ Society of Soil Science 3797
Fellowship Award 2758
Fellowship of the City and Guilds of London Institute 5657
Morice Fieldes Memorial Award 3798
Flinders Medal and Lecture 112
Foundation for Research Science and Technology Science Communicator Awards 3765
Founder's Lecture 7163
Francqui Prize 895
Fujihara Award 3181
Arnoldo Gabaldon Award 7423
Joaquin Garcia Monge Prize 1202
Gardiner Award 5031
Gawad AGKATEK (Agham, Kapaligiran at Teknolohiya) 3982
Prix Gegner 1663
General Research Committee Award 4567
Gold Medal for Achievement in the Natural Sciences 4266
GWUP Prize 2381
Soren Gyldendal Prisen 1305
Hamilton Memorial Prize 3867
Hammond Award 5032
Hannan Medal 114
Carl Hanson Medal 7164
Roland Harper Lecture 7165
Havenga Prize 4267
Hegel-Preis der Landeshauptstadt Stuttgart 2416
Dr. A.H. Heineken Prize for Environmental Sciences 3653
John F. W. Herschel Medal 4242
HG Andrewartha Medal 648
Hilditch Memorial Lecture 7166
Dorothy Hill Award 115
Professor Theodor Homen Prize 1399
Honorary Fellow
 Kenya National Academy of Sciences - Ministry of Research, Science and Technology 3360
 Zimbabwe Scientific Association 7447
Honorary Membership 2759
Robert Horne Lecture 7167
Hurter Memorial Lecture 7168
Javed Husain Prize for Young Scientists 1994
Edmond Hustinx Prize for Science 3514
Edmond Hustinx Prize - Science 3516
Descartes Huygens Award 3552
ICPE Medal 4594
Imperial Prize 3214
INSA Medal for Young Scientists 2689
International Aerosol Fellow Award 2023
International Congress Commemoration 2760
International Federation of University Women Awards Competition 4803
International Institute for Promotion and Prestige Awards 4811
ITC Educational Award 3590
ITC Research Award 3591
IUS Poster Prize 1260
IUS Prize for the Most Significant Discovery 1261
IUS Prize for the Most Significant Publication on a Cave or Karst Topic 1262
Otto Jaag-Gewasserschutz-Preis 4899
Jaeger Medal 116
Prix Jaffe 1856
Jamnalal Bajaj Foundation Awards 2776
Klaas Jan Beek Award 3592
Japan Academy Prize 3215
Japan Prize 3318
Prix Jules et Louis Jeanbernat et Barthelemy de Ferrari Doria
 Academie des Sciences Morales et Politiques 1669
 Institut de France 1857
Junge Award 2024
Kalinga Prize for the Popularization of Science 1996
Alexander Petrowitsch Karpinskij Prize 2398
Cherry Kearton Medal and Award 6770
King Faisal International Prize in Science 4407
Haddon King Medal 117
Knud Lind Larsen Prize 1276
Issac Koga Gold Medal 932
Kohn Award 6911

Science (continued)

Daulat Singh Kothari Memorial Lecture Award 2690
K. S. Krishnan Memorial Lecture 2691
Kultureller Ehrenpreis 2343
Kulturpreis der Stadt Villach 821
Kyoto Prizes 3189
Laboratory Visit Grant 5378
La Medaille Laplace 1583
Latsis-Preis 4901
M.L. Leamy Award 3799
Leopoldina Prize for Junior Scientists 2076
Prix Germaine-Andre Lequeux 1858
LeSueur Memorial Lecture 7171
Leverhulme Tercentenary Medal 6373
Lister Memorial Lecture 7175
Lomonosov Gold Medal 4394
Prix Adrien Constantin de Magny 1588
Malpighi Medal 2129
Manamperi (Engineering) Award 4568
Mansel-Pleydell and Cecil Trusts 5740
Sir Ernest Marsden Medal for Outstanding Service to Science 3766
Medal of Honor for the Scientific Promotion and Development of Subjects 4274
Medal of Honor in the Natural Sciences and Technology 4275
Medal of Merit 4347
Medal of the Estonian Academy of Sciences 1350
Meghnad Saha Medal 2695
Johann-Heinrich-Merck Ehrung 2443
Microcirculation Conference Grant 5379
Microscopy Award 5386
Minnesmedaljen i guld 4629
Sisir Kumar Mitra Memorial Lecture 2696
Asutosh Mookerjee Memorial Award 2744
Moran Medal for Statistical Science 120
Mullard Award 6913
Musgrave Medals 3146
Professor K. Naha Memorial Medal 2697
Professor Vishnu Vasudeva Narlikar Memorial Lecture 2698
National Academy of Sciences Award 4118
National Order of the Southern Cross 1112
National Prize of the President of the Republic 2972
S. Meiring Naude Medal 4243
Jawaharlal Nehru Birth Centenary Award 2745
Jawaharlal Nehru Birth Centenary Lectures 2700
Jawaharlal Nehru Birth Centenary Medal 2701
Jawaharlal Nehru Birth Centenary Visiting Fellowship 2702
Neill Medal 6998
New Zealand Science and Technology Medals 3870
New Zealand Science, Mathematics and Technology Teacher Fellowship 3871
Prix Victor Noury 1594
E. J. Nystrom Prize 1400
Lorenz Oken Medaille 2254
Order of Culture 3246
Order of Merit 5601
Order of Polish Rebirth 4015
Order of the Netherlands Lion 3493
Outstanding Youth Science Researchers 3983
Pakistan Institute of Sciences Gold Medal 3921
Paracelsusring der Stadt Villach 822
Peace Prize of the German Book Trade 2216
Peccei Scholarship 805
Prix Petit d'Ormoy 1597
Physical Science Award 4569
Pius XI Medal 7410
Platinum Jubilee Lectures 2746
Prix Ayme Poirson 1600
Balthasar van der Pol Gold Medal 933
Postgraduate Student Prize 649
Professor Brahm Prakash Memorial Medal 2703
Premio Dotte Giuseppe Borgia 2973
Premio Internazionale di Meridionalistica Guido Dorso 2987
Premio Maria Teresa Messori Roncaglia and Eugenio Mari 2974
Premio Nacional de Ciencias 1162
Premio Nacional de Ciencias y Tecnologia Clodomiro Picado Twight 1203
Premio Tenore 2977
Prix Adolphe Wetrems 1027
Prix de Stassart 1003
Prix Osiris 1861
Prix Science et Defense 1812
Prize for Young Scientists 2955
Prize in Earth Sciences 2958
The Publication Medal 650
Alexander Sergeovich Pushkin Prize 4397
C. V. Raman Birth Centenary Award 2747
Chandrasekhara Venkata Raman Medal 2708
Srinivasa Ramanujan Birth Centenary Award 2748
Curt P. Richter Prize 2323
Sir Theodore Rigg Memorial Award 3800
Rolex Awards for Enterprise 4880
Royal Society of Western Australia Medal 655
Prix Gabrielle Sand et Marie Guido Triossi 1621
Sarton Chair 1086
Sarton Medal 1087
SASEV Award 4348
SASEV Journal Prize 4349
SASEV Prize 4350
SASEV Student Prize 4351
SASEV Table Grape Award 4352
Karl Schlossmann Medal 1351
Bernhard Schmidt Prize 1352
Science Award 4992
Selby Fellowship 122
Richard Seligman Lecture 7179
Separation Science Lecture 7180
Service Award 4993
Sim Awards 7387
Kazimiero Simonaviciaus premija 3386
Smoluchowski Award 2025
Society's Medal 646
Arnold Sommerfeld Preis 2045
South African Association for the Advancement of Science Certificate of Merit 4364
South African Medal 4365
M. T. Steyn Prize for Natural Science and Technical Achievement 4284
Student Assistance Scheme 5380
Student Research Prize 1353
Dr. Yellapragada SubbaRow Memorial Lecture 2720
Summit Quinphos Award 3801
Professor S. Swaminathan 60th Birthday Commemoration Lecture 2722
Norman Taylor Memorial Lecture 3802
Thomson Medal 3873
Prix Thorlet 1624
Prof. B. D. Tilak Lecture 2724
Tiroler Landespreis fur Wissenschaft 751
Trieste Science Prize 2960
Undergraduate Student Bursaries 5387
UNESCO Science Prize 2006
Upper Secondary School Teachers Prizes 1401
Verco Medal 651
Prix Alfred Verdaguer
Academie des Sciences 1627
Institut de France 1863
Pran Vohra Award 2751
Wahlbergska Minnesmedaljen I guld 4642
T.W. Walker Prizes 3803
Ian Wark Medal and Lecture 123
Weizmann Prizes 3452
Wilhelm Westrups beloning 4632
John Yarwood Memorial Medal 5560
Yearly Research Award 7424
Young Scientist Award 2761
Young Scientists' Awards 2752
Zonal Awards 2762

Science education

Aventis Prizes for Science Books 6901
Bragg Medal and Prize 6056
CASTME Awards 5672
Chemical Society of Japan Award for Chemical Education 3173
Chemical Society of Japan Award of Merit for Chemical Education 3177
Excellence in Aerospace Education 2522
Jan Harabaszewski Medal 4031
Medal of Honor for the Scientific Promotion and Development of Subjects 4274
New Zealand Science, Mathematics and Technology Teacher Fellowship 3871
Dr. Juan S. Salcedo Jr. Science Education Award 3986
Worlddidac Award 4941

Science fiction

Brussels International Festival of Fantastic Film 850
BSFA Award 5453
Arthur C. Clarke Award 7077
Prix Julia Verlanger 1988

Science journalism (*See also* Medical journalism)

Annual Award for Popularization and Promotion of Science 1237
Best Paper Award 2633
Forderpreis der ITG 2273
Sigmund-Freud-Preis 2145
Indira Gandhi Prize for Popularization of Science 2684
Medaille fur Naturwissenschaftliche Publizistik 2094
National Excellence Awards for Engineering Journalism 519
New Zealand Association of Scientists Research Medal 3767
Newbigin Prize 6894
Preis der Gesellschaft Deutscher Chemiker fur Journalistein und Schriftsteller 2173
Spearman Medal 5430
VDE/ETG Award 2103
Warner Memorial Medal 7273

Scientific research

Prix Anatole et Suzanne Abragam 1538

Scientific (continued)

Prix Alcan-Pechiney 1539
Annual Prize for Scientific Works 7426
Annual Science Award 1238
Award of Honour 3419
Marcel Benoist Prize 4700
Bent Spoon Award 360
Bilim Odulu 4988
Charles Vernon Boys Medal and Prize 6055
British Psychological Society Presidents' Award 5427
Bronze Medal 1826
Walter Burfitt Prize 637
Castner Lecture and Medal 7161
Charles Chree Medal and Prize 6057
Colombian Academy of Exact, Physical and Natural Sciences to the Integral Work of a Scientist 1172
Copley Medal 6903
CORESTA Prize 1752
Prix Dandrimont-Benicourt 1555
Edgeworth David Medal 641
Peter Debye Prize 3513
Jean-Marie Delwart Foundation Prize 1021
Anthony Dipple Carcinogenesis Award 5805
Neil Hamilton Fairley Fellowships 571
Faustus Poster Awards 5806
Fellowship for Japan-Related Research 2433
Carlos J. Finlay Prize 1991
Fondation Andre-Romain Prevot 1563
Gilchrist Fieldwork Award 6765
Gold Medal 1827
Henry Granjon Prize 1900
Otto-Hahn-Preis fur Chemie und Physik 2091
Hilti-Preis 4898
Prix Fernand Holweck 1572
Honorary Member 4505
Robert Horne Lecture 7167
Hosei International Fund Foreign Scholars Fellowship 3187
W. J. B. Houston Research Awards 5844
W. J. B. Houston Scholarship Award 5845
Humboldt Research Fellowships 2434
Hurter Memorial Lecture 7168
Javed Husain Prize for Young Scientists 1994
International Hydrology Prize 1874
Arthur Thomas Ippen Award 4508
Prix Paul Fallot-Jeremine 1575
Prix Alexandre Joannides 1576
Jubilee Award 7269
Prix de Biologie Alfred Kastler 1822
John F. Kennedy Student Paper Competition 4509
Fondation Camille Liegeois 1026
Feodor Lynen Research Fellowships 2435
C. J. Martin Overseas Biomedical Fellowship 573
Michael Mason Prize 5490
National Prize of Science and Technology 7427
OAPEC Award for Scientific Research 3369
Archibald D. Olle Prize 643
Outstanding Young Scientist Award 1778
Prix Paul Pascal 1596
Max Planck Research Award 2436
Prix Andre Policard-Lacassagne 1601
Prix Ampere d'Electricite de France 1602
Prix Blaise Pascal du GAMNI-SMAI 1605
Prix Charles-Louis de Saulses de Freycinet 1606
Prix de l'Institut Francais du Petrole 1608
Prix des Jeunes 1715
Research Appointments/Fellowships 6914
Andres Manuel del Rio National Prize in Chemistry 3437
Prix Gaston Rousseau 1619
Royal Medals 6915
Royal Swedish Academy of Engineering Sciences Great Gold Medal 4635
T. K. Sidey Medal and Prize 3872
Philipp Franz von Siebold Award 2437
Silver Medal 1828
Tesvik Odulu 4989
Thorarinsson Medal 542
Tison Award 1875
Travel Fellowships 5807
Van Leeuwenhoek Distinctive Travel Award 2130
Alexander von Humboldt Award for Scientific Cooperation 2438
Wager Medal 543
Wahlbergska Minnesmedaljen I guld 4642
Don Whitley Travel Scholarship 7088
Young Cancer Researcher Award Lecture 5809

Sculpture
Annual Exhibition 6885
Prix Claude Berthault 1436
Prix Bordin 1439
De Laszlo Medal 6942
Prix Desprez 1447
Prix Felix Feneon 1805
Jack Goldhill Award for Sculpture 6610
Governor General Art Award 3760
Prix Houllevigue 1455
Prix Hector Lefuel 1459
Medal of Honor for the Performing and Visual Arts 4273
Order of Culture 3246
Panorama Brasilian Art 1134
Prix Eugene Piot 1469
Praemium Imperiale 3217
Premio Municipal Jose Simoes de Almeida de Escultura 4078
Prix Breaute 1471
Prix Colmont 1475
Prix de Rome Fine Art 3642
Prix des Cathedrales 1478
Prix Doublemard 1479
Prix Dumas-Millier 1481
Prix et Fondations Concernant l'Academie de France a Rome 1482
Prix Le Guay-Lebrun 1483
Prix Susse Freres 1484
Prix Egide Rombaux 989
Royal Academy Summer Exhibition 6611
Thorvaldsen Medal 1328
Prix Frederic et Jean de Vernon 1495
Prix de Portrait Paul-Louis Weiller 1497
Prix Paul-Louis Weiller 1498
Prix Georges Wildenstein 1499
The Wolf Prizes 2938
Charles Wollaston Award 6612

Secondary education
Prix Joseph De Keyn 1012

Security (*See also* National security)
BSIA Annual Security Officer Awards 5455
BSIA/IFSEC Security Industry Awards 5456
ISIA Awards 2856

Seismology
Keith Medal 6996

Service
Centenary Medal 209
Girl's Service Award 469
Leader's Service Award 470
National Medal 219
Pioneer Pin 471
Queen's Award 472
Waggs Medal 7360
Young Woman of the Region 7362

Set design
Laurence Olivier Awards 7203

Shooting
Champion Shots Medal 210
Distinguished Service Awards 6487

Short stories
Arafura Short Story Award 587
Award for Aboriginal and Torres Strait Islander Writers 588
Dr. Karel Barbier Prize 950
Marjorie Barnard Short Story Award 448
Book of the Year Awards 37
The Bridport Prize 5200
Commonwealth Short Story Competition 5678
Commonwealth Writers Prize 5679
Concurso Literario Dr. Joao Isabel 4090
Aquileo J. Echeverria Prize 1201
Festival Awards for Literature 672
Greater Dandenong Short Story Competition 411
Lyndall Hadow/Donald Stuart Short Story Award 450
Literary Competition 435
Northern Territory Literary Awards 589
Carlos Palanca Memorial Awards for Literature 3978
Premier's Literary Award 673
Premio Literario Branquinho da Fonseca 4094
Thomas Pringle Award 4172
Prix Cazes - Brasserie Lipp 1938
Prix Victor Rossel 937
Steele Rudd Award 397
Ary Sleeks Prize 961
NZSA Lilian Ida Smith Award 3794
Storywriting and Art Competition 107
Tom-Gallon Award 7150
Bettina Von-Arnim Prize 2058
Whitbread Literary Awards 5194

Skiing
Alpine World Cup Champions 4836
Birkebeinerrennet Ski Race 3898
Holmenkoll Medal 3889
Holmenkollen Ski Festival 3890
Sapporo International Ski Marathon 3316

Slide photography
Australian International Widescreen Festival 393
Festival of Underwater Images 1799
World Cup 3391

Soccer
Annual Awards 3403
Champion Cup Holder 3464
FIFA Futsal (Indoor Football) World Championship 4752
FIFA U-17 World Championship 4753
FIFA Women's World Cup 4754
FIFA World Cup Trophy 4755
Olympic Football Tournaments (Men and Women) 4756
World Youth Championship for the FIFA/Coca-Cola Cup 4757

Social science (*See also* Anthropology; Archaeology; Criminology; Demography; Economics; Genealogy; Geography; History; Political science; Psychology; Social science research; Sociology)
Mark Abrams Prize 7085
Academy Award for Scholarship 25
Paul Ariste Medal 1348
De la Court Prizes 3650
Erasmus Prize 3519
Fondation Ernest Mahaim et Emile Waxweiler 994
Foundation for Research Science and Technology Science Communicator Awards 3765
Francqui Prize 895
Dr. A.H. Heineken Prize for Environmental Sciences 3653
Hosei International Fund Foreign Scholars Fellowship 3187
Imperial Prize 3214
International Federation of University Women Awards Competition 4803
Japan Academy Prize 3215
Alexander Petrowitsch Karpinskij Prize 2398
Lomonosov Gold Medal 4394
Prince of Asturias Awards 4497
Prix Adelson Castiau 997
Prix Emile de Laveleye 1005
Prix Suzanne Tassier 1017
Scientific Research Prizes 3451
N. P. van Wyk Louw Medal 4291

Social science research
Yunus Nadi Yarismasi 4964
Stein Rokkan Prize in Comparative Social Science Research 1913

Social service (*See also* Community affairs; Public affairs; Child welfare; Family relations; Handicapped; Social work; Youth work)
Prix Felix de Beaujour 1634
Cross of Merit 4008
Jamnalal Bajaj Foundation Awards 2776
Kobe City International Association Scholarship 3285
Lampitt Medal 7170
Max-Eyth-Gedenkmunze 2356
John Muir Award 6342
Nansen Refugee Award 3456
The Order of the Royal Huntsman 5665
Samashuri 4564
Sasakawa - DHA Disaster Prevention Award 4872
Freiherr Von Stein Prize 2407

Social work
Calouste Gulbenkian Foundation Grants 5574
International Award for Promoting Gandhian Values Outside India 2775
Jamnalal Bajaj Foundation Awards 2776
Katherine Kendall Award 6227
Medal of Honor for the Performing and Visual Arts 4273
V.J. Sukeslained Award 1367

Sociology
Prix Carlier 1640
Prix Bigot de Morogues 1648
Festival dei Popoli 3045
Prix Emile Girardeau 1665
International Film Festival of Visual Anthropology and Social Documentation 1732
Prix Docteur Rene-Joseph Laufer 1673
Leverhulme Memorial Lecture 6372
Prix Maisondieu 1681
Research Medal 653
Prix Rossi 1693
Worldwide Competition for Junior Sociologists 4519

Spanish culture
Huesca International Short Film Contest 4495
Premio Municipal Julio de Castilho de Olisipografia 4080

Spanish literature
Azorin Prize 4479
Premi Josep Pla 4481
Premio Apel-les Mestres 4482
Premio Biblioteca Breve 4483
Premio de Novela Fernando Lara 4484
Premio Espasa Ensayo 4485
Premio Espiritualidad 4486
Premio Nadal 4487
Premio Primavera de Novela 4489
Premio Sent Sovi 4550
World Mystical Poetry Prize 4530

Special education
SAALED Bursary 4300

Spectroscopy *See* Optics

Speech and hearing (*See also* Deafness)
EUROCALL Research Award 2832

Speleology *See* Geology and paleontology

Sports (*See also* Coaching; Physical education; Sports broadcasting; Sports medicine; Sportsmanship; specific sports, e.g. Auto racing)
AIPS Awards 2510
Australian Sports Medal 208
Badge of Honour in Gold, Silver and Bronze 2052
Philip Noel Baker Research Award 2296
British Championship 6440
John Budgen Award 5133
Club of the Year 5576
Commonwealth Games Federation 5684
Competitions and Tournaments 4585
Continental Champion 2308
Pat Cooke Award 5134
Sir Lance Cross Memorial Cup 3783
European Sportsman and Sportswoman of the Year 4583
Expedition Grant 6442
Fair-Play Trophy 2309
Hall of Fame 3415
William Hill Sports Book of the Year 7336
Victor Hirt Prize 5107
Honorary Members of NOC of Slovenia 4459
IBF Gold Medal 4586
ICSSPE Sport Science Award of the IOC President 2297
International Federation of Netball Associations Service Awards 6258
International Judo Federation Awards 4101
International Korfball Federation Badge of Honour 3594
International Korfball Federation Honorary Member 3595
International Prize Paladino D'Oro 3084
IOC/IAKS Award 2279
Tan Sri Alex Lee Athletes Scholarship Awards 3416
Letter of Merit 4460
Lonsdale Cup 3784
Merit Awards 1719
Oita International Wheelchair Marathon 3304
Olympian of the Year Award 3417
Olympiart 4819
Olympic Cup 4820
Olympic Medals and Diplomas 4821
Olympic Order 4822
Olympic Torch 4461
Azusa Ono Memorial Awards 3349
Phenix UDA 2008
Player of the Year 5577
Presidential Sports Award (Gold) 4239
Presidential Sports Award (Silver) 4240
Prince of Asturias Awards 4497
Samoyed of the Year: Male, Female, Veteran, Senior, and Danish Champion in Sledge Racing 1287
Oscar Schwiglhofer Trophy 5108
Arthur Sims Award 5135
Sport Australia Hall of Fame 677
Street Luge Championship 7249
Thea Sybesma Award 3625
Teacher's Award 6464
Trento International Film Festival of Mountain and Exploration 3136
UNESCO Award for Distinguished Services to Physical Education and Sport 1999
World Athletics Series 3466
World Curling Freytag Award 7366
World Games Competitions 3619

Sports broadcasting
Television Sports Awards 7048

Sports medicine
Gold Medal 1245

Sportsmanship
Fair Play Award 5774

Stamp collecting *See* Philately

Standards
Deming Prize 3340
Georges Garel Award 4801
Honeywell Prize 6051
Japan Quality Medal 3341
Sir George Thomson Gold Medal 6052

Statistics
Association of Track and Field Statisticians Honorary Member 61
Prix Charles Dupin 1654
Moran Medal for Statistical Science 120
National Institute of Insurance International Prizes 2971
Jan Tinbergen Awards for Young Statisticians from Developing Countries 3617

Steel industry *See* Iron and steel industry

Surfing
European Surfing Championships - Open Champion 5870

Surgery
Best Paper Award 3887
John Mitchell Crouch Fellowship 613
Robert Danis Prize 4850
Implant Innovations Grant 5811
Japanese SICOT Scholarship 4108
Leibinger Prize 5812
Rene Leriche Prize 4851
Lester ELowe Memorial Scholarship 928
Mondeal Prize 5813
Hugo Obwegeser Scholarship 5814
Prize of the Societe Internationale de Chirurgie 4852
Hans von Seemen Preis 2252
SICOT/SIROT Award 929
Joseph Toynbee Memorial Lectureship 7019
Travelling Fellowships 6716

Surveying
Alex Pitcher Award 5271
Arthur Butcher Award 5272
Gold Medal of Honour 4130
National President's Award 265

Swedish culture
Sven Berggrens pris 4623
Finlandspriset 4655
Gun och Olof Engqvists stipendium 4657
Kellgrenpriset 4660
Kungliga priset 4662
Nordiska Priset 4663
Stora priset 4671

Swimming (*See also* Surfing)
Avril and Allan Mitchell Trophy 5345
Henry Benjamin National Memorial Trophy 5034
Mary Black Award 5035
Breaststroke Trophy 5346
G. Melville Clark National Memorial Trophy 5036
Dawdon Trophy 5037
Elise Brook Trophy 5347
Harold Fern Award 5038
Harold Fern National Trophy 5039
FINA Prize 4759
Fred Slater Trophy 5348
Gemma Yates Trophy 5040
Hans Belay Trophy 5349
Harry Moffat Memorial Trophy 5350
George Hearn Trophy 5041
Alan Hime Memorial Trophies 5042
Holland Trophy 5043
James Brennan Memorial Trophy 5351
Shacklock Trophy 5044
Norma Thomas National Memorial Trophy 5045
Tom Butcher Trophy 5352
Alfred H. Turner Award 5046
Belle White National Memorial Trophy 5047
T. M. Yeadon Memorial Trophy 5048

Systems management *See* Information management; Operations research

Table tennis
European Competitions 3389
Merit Award 4854

Tapestry *See* Textile design

Teaching (*See also* Education)
Bragg Medal and Prize 6056
Excellence in Aerospace Education 2522
Ivan Filipovic Award 1239
Foundation for the Promotion of Finnish Music Grants 1403
Happold Brilliant Award 5638
Jerwood Awards 6340
Prix Malouet 1682
Robert-Wichard-Pohl-Preis 2096
Thomas Pringle Award 4172
Prix de Chenier 1527
SAALED Bursary 4300
Dr. Juan S. Salcedo Jr. Science Education Award 3986
Svenska Akademiens Svensklararpris 4673

Technology (*See also* Biotechnology; Computer science; Engineering; Industrial arts; Inventions; Science; Standards; Testing)
CASTME Awards 5672
CORESTA Prize 1752
Albert Einstein World Award of Science 3460
Fellowship of the City and Guilds of London Institute 5657
Rosalind Franklin Award 6907
The Gaudeamus Prize 3555
Gawad AGKATEK (Agham, Kapaligiran at Teknolohiya) 3982
Gold Medal 4357
Gold Medal for Achievement in the Natural Sciences 4266
Havenga Prize 4267
Heinrich Hertz Preis 2429
Honda Prize 3185
Honorary Fellow 3360
Information, Communications and Technology Exporter of the Year 3810
INSA Medal for Young Scientists 2689
International Association of Technological University Libraries Poster Prize 6229
Jamnalal Bajaj Foundation Awards 2776
Japan Prize 3318
Kalinga Prize for the Popularization of Science 1996
King-Sun Fu Prize 786
Kyoto Prizes 3189
MacRobert Award 6621
Prasanta Chandra Mahalanobis Medal 2693
J. N. McNichol Prize 607
Mullard Award 6913
Jawaharlal Nehru Birth Centenary Medal 2701
Francis Ormond Medal 608
Pakistan Institute of Sciences Gold Medal 3921
Robert-Wichard-Pohl-Preis 2096
Premio Nacional de Ciencias y Tecnologia Clodomiro Picado Twight 1203
President's Medal 6622
Prince Philip Medal 6623
Queen's Awards for Enterprise 6579
Queen's Awards for Enterprise in Innovation 6580
Royal Swedish Academy of Engineering Sciences Great Gold Medal 4635
Scientific Research Prizes 3451
Self-Adhesive Labelling Awards 3694
Shanti Swarup Bhatnagar Medal 2716
Silver Medal 6624
SMART Awards 7292
SPUR: Support for Products Under Research 7293
M. T. Steyn Prize for Natural Science and Technical Achievement 4284
Willi Studer Preis 4903
Prof. B. D. Tilak Lecture 2724
IBC International John Tucker Award 6233
UNESCO Science Prize 2006
Aurel Vlaicu Prize 4386
S. H. Zaheer Medal 2728
Luis Zambrano National Prize for Inventive Technology 7428

Technology, color *See* Color technology

Technology, medical *See* Medical technology

Technology, vacuum *See* Vacuum technology

Telecommunications *See* Communications

Television (*See also* Broadcasting; Cable television; Media; Radio; Video)
ABU Prizes for Radio and Television Programs 3398
ADIRCAE Prizes 4471
AFI Awards - The Australian Film Institute Awards 196
Amanda Award for Cinematographic Merit 3906
Annual Awards 5961
Awgie Awards 395
British Academy Television Awards 5217
British Film Institute Fellowships 5308
The British Film Institute Sutherland Trophy 5309
CINANIMA 4056
Craft and Design Awards 7042
Dentsu Advertising Awards 3179
Educational Television Awards 7043
EuroBest Awards 5803
Geneva-Europe Prizes 4707
Golden Antenna International Television Festival 1146
Golden Chest International Television Festival 1147
International Festival of Film and Television in the Celtic Countries 5587
International Television Festival Golden Prague 1256
International Visual Communications Association Awards 6327
Journalist Prize 2245
Byron Kennedy Award 197

Television (continued)

LiteraVision Preis 2344
Magnolia Prize 3950
Mastermind Award 5256
Medal of Honour for Afrikaans Television 4276
Medienpreis fur Sprachkultur 2193
Monte Carlo Television Festival 3469
NHK Japan Prize 3298
Panafrican Film and Television Festival of Ouagadougou 1160
Joseph Plateau Prize 891
Premio Internazionale Ennio Flaiano 2985
Press Prize for Broadcasters and Producers 4883
Prix Danube Festival, Bratislava 4452
Prix Jeunesse International Munchen 2373
Programme Awards 7044
PTV National Awards 3923
Shark Awards, the International Advertising Festival of Ireland 2887
Student Television Awards 7045
Television Journalism Awards 7047
TRIC Awards 7255
TV Week Logie Awards 705
Unda Dove 1100
W.G. Walkley Awards for Journalism 561

Tennis (*See also* Table tennis)
Award for Services to the Game 6304
The Championships, Wimbledon 5020
Davis Cup Award of Excellence 6305
Raymond Egan Memorial Trophy 2889
Fed Cup Award of Excellence 6306
Grand Slam of Tennis 6307
Lawn Tennis Association National Awards 6359
Tennis World Champions 6308

Testing
Berthold-Preis 2237
John Grimwade Medal 5323
Ron Halmshaw Award 5324
Hugh MacColl Award 5325
Nemet Award 5326
Schiebold-Gedenkmunze 2238
Roy Sharpe Prize 5327

Textile design
Institute Medal for Design 7268
Royal Dublin Society Crafts Competition 2877

Textile industry (*See also* Fiber science)
Companion Membership 7262
Development Award 7263
Holden Medal 7264
Honorary Fellow 7265
Honorary Life Member 7266
Institute Medal 7267
Jubilee Award 7269
Lemkin Medal 7270
MUTA Safety Certificate 6531
Service Medal 7271
S. G. Smith Memorial Medal 7272
Warner Memorial Medal 7273
Weaver's Company Medal and Prize 7274

Theater
Carl Akermarks Stipendium 4646
Magda Donato Prize 3431
Aquileo J. Echeverria Prize 1201
Harlequin Award 5432
Honorary President's Award 4588
Edmond Hustinx Prize - Playwrights 3515
Frans Kellendonk-prijs 3670
Kinokuniya Theatre Awards 3281
Medal of Honor for the Performing and Visual Arts 4273
Meyer-Whitworth Award 5070
New Scholar's Prize 6241
Laurence Olivier Awards 7203
Onassis International Cultural Competition Prizes 2464
Perrier Award 5752
William Poel Memorial Festival 7126
Praemium Imperiale 3217
Premio Internazionale Ennio Flaiano 2985
Premio Municipal Fernando Amado de Encenacao Teatral 4075
Premio Nacional de Teatro 1205
Prix de Rome Fine Art 3642
Hans Reinhart Ring 4888
Research Awards 7127
Scholarships of the City of Munich 2346
Stage Awards for Acting Excellence 5754
Svenska Akademiens Teaterpris 4674
Premio Piervittorio Tondelli 3124

Theology
BP Prize Lectureship in the Humanities 6988
Dominee Pieter van Drimmelen Medal 4290

Therapy *See* Rehabilitation and therapy

Third world *See* Economic development

Tourism *See* Travel

Town planning *See* City planning

Toxicology
Merit Award 1272
Redi Award 2325
Young Scientist's Poster Award 1273
Gerhard Zbinden Memorial Lecture Award 1274

Track and field
Association of Track and Field Statisticians Honorary Member 61
Top 10 Orienteers 1149
World Championships 3467

Trade *See* Business; Finance; International trade

Trade shows *See* Conventions

Trade unions *See* Labor

Trades *See* Industries and trades

Training and development
Asia-Pacific Cancer Society Training Grants (APCASOT) 4857
International Visual Communications Association Awards 6327

Translations
BTS/Astellas and BTS/Novartis Research Fellowships 5542
BTS/Morris Travelling Fellowship 5543
John Buchanan Prize in Esperanto 7310
CBCI Award 2820
Johann Friedrich von Cotta Literary and Translation Prize of Stuttgart City 2415
Dansk Oversaetterforbunds Aerespris 1292
John Dryden Translation Competition 5283
John Florio Prize 7131
Calouste Gulbertian Prize 7132
Korean Literature Translation Award 4112
Scott Moncrieff Prize 7133
Noma Award for the Translation of Japanese Literature 3288
Oversattarpris 4664
Polish PEN Centre Prizes 4019
Corneliu M. Popescu Prize for European Poetry Translation 6542
Premio Valle Inclan 7134
Prize for Translated Work 4278
Roy Calne Award 5544
Sahitya Akademi Translation Prize 2793
St. John Ambulance Air Wing Travelling Fellowship 5545
Schlegel - Tieck Prize 7135
Bernard Shaw Prize 7136
Stiftelsen Natur och Kulturs oversattarpris 4669
Tolkningspris 4675
Vondel Translation Prize 7137
Johann-Heinrich-Voss-Preis fur Uebersetzung 2148
Wyeth Fellowship 5546

Transportation (*See also* Aeronautics and aviation; Automobiles; Automotive engineering; Automotive safety; Aviation safety; Helicopters; Highway safety; Navigation; Railway transportation)
Australian Transport Industry Award 402
Award for Most Meritorious Paper/ Presentation 3755
Best Article in Logistics Focus 5622
Chartered Institute of Transport Annual Innovation Award 3756
Excellence in Integrated Logistics Management 5623
Excellence in the Use of Human Resources in Logistics 5624
Excellence in the Use of Technology in Logistics 5625
Excellence in the Use of Transport in Logisitcs 5626
Freight Service Awards 5336
Grand Prix d'Honneur 4830
Ground Transportation Company of the Year 3151
Hermes Award 865
Mackenzie Junner Rose-Bowl Trophy 7205
Logistics Company of the Year 5627
Logistics Dissertation of the Year 5628
Ministry of Transport Award for Best Student Research 3757
Norman Spencer Memorial Award 3758
STUVA Prize 2427
Young Manager of the Year Award 5629

Travel
Abe Issa Award for Excellence 3150
Best Practices 229
Bhaskar Award 3481
Sir Richard Burton Medal 6679
Certificate of Merit 6336
Environmental Award 1894
Estrelicia Dourada 4067
European Hotel Manager of the Year 3031
Gold Training Award 5113
Golden Apple 2019

Travel (continued)

Hotel Worker of the Year 3152
Hotelier of the Year 3153
Life Fellowship 5957
Medalha de Merito Turistico 4068
New Zealand Tourism Awards 3875
Outstanding Community Service 231
Sagarmatha Award 3482
Sent Lisi Par Excellence Awards 4399
Trento International Film Festival of Mountain and Exploration 3136

Travel literature
Thomas Cook Travel Book Award 5697
Somerset Maugham Awards 7146
Silver Otter Award 5315

Typography
Gutenberg Award 2267

Uniforms *See* Fashion

Unions *See* Labor

Urban development *See* City planning

Vacuum technology
Welch Foundation Scholarship 6316

Veterans *See* Military service

Veterinary medicine
The Alison Alston Canine Award 6740
Amoroso Award 5465
AVP Awards 362
Blaine Award 5466
Boswell Award 4359
Bourgelat Award 5467
Alexander Ninian Bruce Prize 6991
Cheiron Medal 834
Robert Daubney Research Fellowship in Virology and Helminthology 6741
Distinguished Scientific Contribution Award 363
Distinguished Service Award 364
Prix Rene Dujarric de la Riviere 1561
Dunkin Award 5468
Lucille K. Georg Award 1413
Gilruth Prize 382
GlaxoSmithKline Prize and Lecture 6909
G. Norman Hall Medal for Research into Animal Diseases 6742
Prix de Biologie Alfred Kastler 1822
Kendall Oration and Medal 383
Don Kerr Veterinary Student Award 384
Kesteven Medal 385
Melton Award 5469
Meritorious Service Award 386
Millennium Residencies in Production Animal Medicine 6743
John Lord Perry Research Scholarship 6744
Petsavers Award 5470
Dr. Antonio Pires Prize 2
Prof. M. R. N. Prasad Memorial Lecture 2704
Premio Bayer en Ciencias Veterinarias 6
Bart Rispens Award 2446
Scottish Science Award 7072
Dorothy Sidley Memorial Award 5978
Simon Award 5471
Small Animal Practitioner of the Year 365
Sir Frederick Smith Research Fellowship 6745
South African Veterinary Association Gold Medal 4360
Harry Steele-Bodger Memorial Scholarship 5564
Theiler Memorial Trust Award 4216
Waltham International Award for Scientific Achievement 1340
Waltham Service to the Profession Award 1341
West Scholarship for Feline Research 6746
J.A. Wight Memorial Award 5472
Woodrow Award 5473
MacKellar Michael Wright Award 6747
WSAVA Hills Excellence in Veterinary Healthcare Award 1342
WSAVA Paatsama Award 1343

Video
Australian Teachers of Media Awards 380
BRIT Awards 5416
British Academy Television Awards 5217
British Amateur Recording Contest 5538
Channel 4 Archaeological Film Awards 5555
Communicators in Business Awards 5241
Dance Screen Award 807
Deutscher Jugend-Video-Preis 2063
Ecumenical Prize 1092
Festival of Underwater Images 1799
Golden Knight International Amateur Film and Video Festival 3423
International Animation Festival in Japan, Hiroshima 3183
International Competition for Film and Video 778
International Festival of Mountain Environment and Alpine Films, Les Diablerets, Switzerland 4805
International Film/Video Competition 3578
International Prize Paladino D'Oro 3084
International Short Film Festival Oberhausen 2316
International Visual Communications Association Awards 6327
OCIC-Prize 1093
Premio Municipal Joao Baptista Rosa de Video 4076
Student Television Awards 7045
Jean Thevenot Medal 4799
Tokyo Video Festival 3343
Torello International Festival of Mountain and Adventure Films 4545
Trento International Film Festival of Mountain and Exploration 3136
UNICA Medal 4680
W.G. Walkley Awards for Journalism 561
West Australia Film Awards 458
World Wide Video Festival 3692

Visually impaired *See* Blindness

Violin competitions
Emily Anderson Prize for Violin 6859
International Johann Sebastian Bach Competition 2036
Cologne International Violin Competition 2069
Cologne International Vocal Competition 2071
Concertino Prague International Radio Competition for Young Musicians 1254
Hanover International Violin Competition 2142
International Competition for Musical Performers - Geneva 4702
International Jeunesses Musicales Competition - Belgrade 4413
International Mozart Competition 826
Internationaler Musikwettbewerb der ARD 2311
Fritz Kreisler International Competition Prizes 801
International Violin Competition Rodolfo Lipizer Prize 3019
Marguerite Long and Jacques Thibaud International Competition 1932
Carl Nielsen International Music Competitions 1313
Prague Spring International Music Competition 1264
Premio Internazionale Accademia Musicale Chigiana Siena 2952
Queen Elisabeth International Music Competition of Belgium Prizes 947
International Jean Sibelius Violin Competition 1425
Tunbridge Wells International Young Concert Artists Competition 7279
Gian Battista Viotti International Music and Dance Competition 3126

Visual arts
Australian Visual Artists' Benevolent Fund 565
Pat Corrigan Artists' Grant 566
Freedman Foundation Traveling Scholarship for Emerging Artists 567
Marketing Grant for NSW Artists 568
Windmill Trust Scholarship 569

Vocal music (*See also* Choral music; Opera)
International Johann Sebastian Bach Competition 2036
Budapest International Music Competition 2504
Maria Callas Grand Prix for Opera, Oratorio-Lied 2451
Cardiff Singer of the World Competition 5258
Dutch International Vocal Competition - Hertogenbosch 3508
Grand Prix of the Eurovision Song Contest 4710
Philip and Dorothy Green Award for Young Concert Artists 6409
Gundhall School Gold Medal 5963
Bernhard-Harms-Preis 2338
Mirjam Helin International Singing Competition 1391
International Mozart Competition 826
Internationaler Musikwettbewerb der ARD 2311
Lappeenranta National Singing Competition 1421
Llangollen International Musical Eisteddfod 6393
Mathy and Opera Awards 358
McDonald's Operatic Aria 690
Music Awards 6865
Operasangerinnen Fanny Elstas Fond 3895
Queen Elisabeth International Music Competition of Belgium Prizes 947

Vocal (continued)
Queen Sonja International Music Competition 3914
W. Towyn Roberts Vocal Scholarship 6472
Royal Over-Seas League Music Competition 6853
International Robert Schumann Choir Competition 2314
Leonie Sonning Music Prize 1336
Richard Tauber Prize 5050
International Tchaikovsky Competition 4392
Tokyo International Music Competition 3338
Tunbridge Wells International Young Concert Artists Competition 7279
Francisco Vinas International Singing Contest 4554
Gian Battista Viotti International Music and Dance Competition 3126
Young Concert Artists Trust Award 7394
Young Performers Awards 696

Walking *See* Track and field

Water conservation
Association Medal 3814
Best Operations Paper 3815
Brian Brown Award 3816
CIWEM Certificate and Diploma in Environmental Management 5642
William Dunbar Medal 2134
P. H. Haviland Award 7442
Hynds-NZWWA Paper of the Year Award 3817
Michael Taylor Award 3818
Operators Award 3819
President's Award 5643
Ronald Hicks Memorial Award 3820
RSPB/CIWEM Living Wetlands Award 5644
World of Difference Award 5645
Young Members' Award 5646

Water pollution control
Ernst-Kuntze Prize 2154

Water resources
G.N. Alexander Medal 487
Dr. G. G. Cillie Award 4376
P. H. Haviland Award 7442
Peter Hughes Award 388
IAHR-APD Award 4506
Arthur Thomas Ippen Award 4508
Pakistan Institute of Sciences Gold Medal 3921
Stockholm Junior Water Prize 389
Umgeni Award 4377
Undergraduate Water Prize 390
Water Environment Merit Award 391
Wilson Award 4378

Watercolor painting (*See also* Painting)
Singer Friedlander/Sunday Times Watercolour competition 6523
Hunting Art Prizes 6524
Katanning Art Prize 554

Waterfowl management *See* Wildlife conservation

Weather *See* Meteorology

Weightlifting
Award of Merit 2512
The IWF Order 2513

Welding
Yoshiaki Arata Award 1898
Edstrom Medal 1899
Henry Granjon Prize 1900
Guerrera Medal 1901
Andre Leroy Prize 1902
Evgenij Paton Prize 1903
Arthur Smith Award 1904
Thomas Medal 1905

Welfare *See* Child welfare; Social service

Wildlife conservation (*See also* Environmental conservation)
BG Wildlife Photographer of the Year Competition 6492
BP Conservation Programme 5179
Ralph Brown Expedition Award 6758
Duke of Edinburgh Prize for the Japan Academy 3213
Gold Panda Award 4944
Marsh Award for Conservation Biology 7398
Order of the Golden Ark 3492
Roll of Honour 4945
Neville Shulman Challenge Award 6774
Sture Centerwalls Pris 4641
Wildlife Action Awards 7334
Wildlife and Environment Zimbabwe Competitions 7439
Young Wildlife Photographer of the Year Competition 6493

Wine
Grand Prix 1907
Andre Simon Medal 6334

Women
AFUW-SA Inc. Trust Fund Bursary 185
Alice Award 670
Thenie Baddams Bursary 186
Dame Nita Barrow Award 7404
Anna Bijnsprijs 3486
Bourse Marcelle Blum 1638
Bravery Award 173
Nabila Breir Award 7405
Karen Burt Award 7346
Rose Mary Crawshay Prize for English Literature 5207
Lady Denman Cup 6474
Engineering 2000 Awards 504
European Sportsman and Sportswoman of the Year 4583
Excellence in Research on Improving Policing For Women Award 174
Fellowships and Scholarships 584
Harold Fern National Trophy 5039
FIFA Women's World Cup 4754
Rosalind Franklin Award 6907
Jean Gilmore Bursary 190
Dr. Holmes Scholarship 3267
Honor al Merito 6253
Honorary Member 2358
HRH Princess Michael of Kent Award 7218
Inter-American Award for the Participation of Women in Rural Development 1209
International Award 4308
International Federation of University Women Awards Competition 4803
International Scholarship 3268
International Women's Film Festival of Creteil and Val-de-Marne 1928
Isie Smuts Fellowship 4309
Jamnalal Bajaj Foundation Awards 2776
Nita B. Kibble Literary Award 681
Kshanika Oration Award to a Woman Scientist for Research in the Field of Biomedical Sciences 2611
Ladies' British Open Amateur Championship 6354
Lady Finniston Award 7347
Pelagia Majewska Gliding Medal 4739
Member of Honour 2359
Most Outstanding Female Administrator 175
Most Outstanding Female Investigator 176
Most Outstanding Female Leader 177
National Scholarship 3269
Newman Cup 3851
Order of the Precious Crown 3248
Padnendadlu Graduate Bursary 192
Pandora Award 7343
Hansi Pollak Fellowship 4310
Winifred E. Preedy Post-Graduate Bursary 193
President & Vice President's Choice Award 7219
Prix des Dames 1960
Prix Suzanne Tassier 1017
RoseMary Seymour Award 3879
SAAUW Fellowship 4311
Bertha Stoneman Fellowship 4312
Georgina Sweet Fellowship 194
Prix Tanesse 1699
Barbara Tate Award 7220
Weetabix Women's British Open Championship 6355
Winsor & Newton Choice Award 7221
Women and Politics Prize 91

Women's rights
Bursaries 7345
Commonwealth Office of the Status of Women Award 737
Honour Diploma 4388
New Venture Award 7342

Wood and wood products (*See also* Forestry; Paper industry)
Ron Cockcroft Award 4596
IRG Travel Award 4597
Wood Building and Interiors Exporter of the Year 3812

Work safety *See* Occupational safety

World peace
Anuvrat Award for International Peace 2540
Ehrenpreis des Osterreichischen Buchhandels 760
Felix Houphouet-Boigny Peace Prize 1993
International Award for Promoting Gandhian Values Outside India 2775
International Public Relations Association President's Award 6288
Luminosa Award for Unity 3047
Sean MacBride Peace Prize 4826
The International Jose Marti Prize 1997
Merit Awards 1719
MS-Prize 1278
National Award for the Protection of Environment 1170
Niwano Peace Prize 3302

World (continued)

Nobel Peace Prize 4602
Order of San Carlos 1175
Olof Palme Memorial Fund Scholarships 4616
Olof Palme Prize 4617
Peace Prize of the German Book Trade 2216
Study Circles Challenge Trophies 4571
UNESCO Prize for Peace Education 2005
Wateler Peace Prize 3488

Writing
The Goodchild Prize 6585
Prix Europa 1757
Statistics New Zealand - Jacoby Student Essay Competition 3828

Yachting *See* Boating

Youth achievement
Commonwealth Youth Service Awards 5691
International Letter-Writing Competition for Young People 4909
Outstanding Young Woman Volunteers Award 3952
Outstanding Youth Science Researchers 3983
Rural Youth Europe Awards 819
Te Kura Pounamu Award 3753
Teenage Festival of Life Award 3881

Youth work
Bronze Wolf 4939
Certificate of Merit 6336
Convoy For Kids Grant 419
Culture and Literature Award 2804
The Distinguished Award of Honour For Service to Children's Charities 420
Irish Youth Foundation Award 2862
Life Governor 421
Memorial William John Bond Safe Driver of the Year 422
Most Outstanding Volunteer 423
President's Choice Award 424
Social Service Award 2805
Truck Awards 425
Youth Ambassador 426

Zoology (*See also* Ornithology)
Award to the Most Outstanding Third Year Student in Zoology 4380
H. H. Bloomer Award 6386
W. S. Bruce Medal 6989
Clarke Medal 638
Fondation Max Poll 1024
Prix Foulon 1564
Frink Medal for British Zoologists 7396
Gold Medal 4381
Hector Memorial Medal and Prize 3868
Hutton Memorial Medal and Prize 3869
Thomas Henry Huxley Award 7397
International Federation of Beekeepers' Associations Medals 3076
Linnean Medal 6387
Mueller Medal 134
Nippon Oyo Dobutsu Konchu Gakkai Sho 3273
Nippon Oyo Dobutsu Konchu Gakkai Shoreisho 3274
Outstanding Researcher 3356
Prince Philip Prize 7399
Prix Agathon De Potter 1028
Prix Lamarck 1048
Stamford Raffles Award 7400
Research Medal 653
Scientific Medal 7401
Junior Captain Scott Commemorative Medal 4282
Silver Medal 7402
Pranciskaus Sivickis premija 3387
Stevenson - Hamilton Award 4382
Sunder Lal Hora Medal 2721
Professor Har Swarup Memorial Lecture 2723
Whitley Awards 659
Wigglesworth Lecture and Medal Award 6755

Organization Index

The alphabetical Organization Index provides access to all sponsoring and administering organizations listed in both volumes, as well as to organization acronyms and alternate-language and former names. In the case of a sponsoring organization, the citation is to the specific award it sponsors. Each organization name is followed by the volume in which it appears. The numbers following the volume references are book entry numbers, not page numbers.

3M Canada Vol 1: 6688
3M Company Vol 1: 156
11th Armored Cavalry's Veterans of Vietnam and Cambodia Vol 1: 1
60 Plus Association Vol 1: 3
70th Infantry Division Association Vol 1: 5
84th Infantry Division, Railsplitter Society Vol 1: 7
The 92nd Street Y Vol 1: 10
303rd Bomb Group (H) Association Vol 1: 12
A. Philip Randolph Institute Vol 1: 14
AACC International Vol 1: 16
AACE International Vol 1: 19
AAFRC Trust for Philanthropy Vol 1: 27
AAR Cadillac Manufacturing, Inc. Vol 1: 11527
AARL Foundation Vol 1: 29
AARL, The National Association for Amateur Radio Vol 1: 31
ABA Marketing Network Vol 1: 38
Abbott Diagnostics Vol 2: 4247
Abbott Laboratories Vol 1: 3762
ABC Canada Vol 1: 6704
ABC-CLIO Vol 1: 1272
Abdus Salam International Centre for Theoretical Physics Vol 2: 2945
ABET Vol 1: 40
Abraham Lincoln Association Vol 1: 43
Abrasive Engineering Society Vol 1: 46
ACA International Vol 1: 50
Acacia Fraternity Vol 1: 62
Acadamh Rioga na Heireann Vol 2: 2880
Academi - Welsh National Literature Promotion Agency and Society for Authors Vol 2: 4994
Academia Brasileira de Letras Vol 2: 1115
Academia Colombiana de Ciencias Exactas, Fisicas y Naturales Vol 2: 1171
Academia de Ciencias Fisicas, Matematicas y Naturales Vol 2: 7421
Academia de la Investigacion Cientifica Vol 2: 3450
Academia Europaea Vol 2: 4996
Academia Ludoviciana Gissensis Vol 2: 2335
Academia Mexicana de Ciencias Vol 2: 3450
Academia Musicale Chigiana Vol 2: 2951
Academia Nacional de Agronomia y Veterinaria Vol 2: 1
Academia Nacional de la Historia de la Republica Argentina Vol 2: 10
Academia Nacional de Medicina Vol 2: 1194
Academia Romana Vol 2: 4385
Academic Press Vol 2: 5889
Academie Canadienne du Cinema et de la Television Vol 1: 66
Academie d'Agriculture de France Vol 2: 1428
Academie des Beaux-Arts Vol 2: 1432
Academie des Inscriptions et Belles-Lettres Vol 2: 1500
Academie des Sciences Vol 2: 1537
Academie des Sciences Morales et Politiques Vol 2: 1630
Academie Internationale d'Astronautique Vol 2: 1864
Academie Internationale de Medecine Aeronautique et Spatiale Vol 1: 10016
Academie Royale des Sciences, des Lettres at des Beaux-Arts de Belgique Vol 2: 1058
Academy of American Poets Vol 1: 64
Academy of Applied Osteopathy Vol 1: 671
Academy of Canadian Cinema and Television Vol 1: 66
Academy of Certified Hazardous Materials Managers Vol 1: 72
Academy of Country Music Vol 1: 84
Academy of Country Music Entertainment Vol 1: 6444
Academy of Criminal Justice Sciences Vol 1: 86
Academy of Dentistry International Vol 1: 93
Academy of International Business Vol 1: 100
Academy of Marketing Science Vol 1: 103
Academy of Motion Picture Arts and Sciences Vol 1: 107
Academy of Operative Dentistry Vol 1: 112
Academy of Parish Clergy Vol 1: 116
Academy of Parish Clergy Vol 1: 116
Academy of Pharmacy Practice and Management Vol 1: 3041, 3042, 3043, 3044, 3045, 3046
Academy of Pharmacy Practice and Management; American Pharmacists Association - Vol 1: 3037
Academy of Physical, Mathematical and Natural Sciences Vol 2: 7421
Academy of Science Fiction, Fantasy, and Horror Films Vol 1: 120
Academy of Sciences for the Developing World Vol 2: 2953
Academy of Sciences, Lithuania Vol 2: 3372
Academy of Sciences of the Czech Republic Vol 2: 1246
Academy of Scientific Research Vol 2: 3450
Academy of Security Educators and Trainers Vol 1: 122
Academy of Television Arts and Sciences Vol 1: 12178
Academy of the Social Sciences in Australia Vol 2: 24
Academy of Wind and Percussion Arts Vol 1: 12736
Accademia delle Scienze di Torino Vol 2: 2966
Accademia Nazionale dei Lincei Vol 2: 2970
Accademia Pontaniana Vol 2: 2976
Accelrys Inc. Vol 1: 1501
Accordion Society of Australia Vol 2: 26
Accounting and Finance Association of Australia and New Zealand Vol 2: 28
ACM SIGCOMM Vol 1: 4825
Acoustical Society of America Vol 1: 124
Acoustical Society of America Vol 2: 5988
Acta Materialia Vol 2: 4999
Action for Nuclear Disarmament Vol 1: 18843
Action Health - Nigeria Vol 2: 3880
Action Medical Research Vol 2: 5002
Action Research for the Crippled Child Vol 2: 5002
Acton Institute for the Study of Religion and Liberty Vol 1: 135
Actors' Equity Association Vol 1: 138
Actors' Equity Foundation Vol 1: 141
Actors' Fund of America Vol 1: 146
Actors Theatre of Louisville Vol 1: 148
Actuarial Education and Research Fund Vol 1: 16478
Actuarial Society of South Africa Vol 2: 4121
Adapted Physical Activity Council Vol 1: 925
ADARA: Professionals Networking for Excellence in Service Delivery with Individuals who are Deaf or Hard of Hearing Vol 1: 150
Adelaide Philosophical Society Vol 2: 647
Ademe Vol 2: 1936
Adhesion Society Vol 1: 155
Adidas Vol 1: 13709
The Adirondack Council Vol 1: 157
ADISQ (Association Quebecoise de l'Industrie du Disque, du Spectacle et de la Video) Vol 1: 159
Admiral of the Ocean Sea Vol 1: 17713
Adoption Council of Canada Vol 1: 162
Adoptive Families Today Vol 1: 167
Adult Education of the U.S.A. Vol 1: 834
Adult Learning Australia Vol 2: 34
Advancing Canadian Entrepreneurship Vol 1: 169
Adventist World Headquarters Vol 1: 15014
Advertising Age - Crain Communications Inc. Vol 1: 175
Advertising and Design Club of Canada Vol 1: 177
Advertising Club of New York Vol 1: 179
Advertising Council Vol 1: 181

Advertising Media Credit Executives Association Vol 1: 183
Advertising Production Club of New York Vol 1: 185
Advertising Women of New York Vol 1: 187
Advocates for Animals Vol 2: 6361
AeA Vol 1: 194
Aero Club of America Vol 1: 12186
Aero Club of Egypt Vol 2: 4742
Aero Club of Poland Vol 2: 4739
Aeronautical Society of India Vol 2: 2521
Aerospace Education Foundation Vol 1: 197
Aerospace Medical Association Vol 1: 199
Aestheticians International Association Headquarters Vol 1: 214
Aesthetics International Association Vol 1: 214
Affaire de Coeur Magazine Vol 1: 216
Africa Rice Center Vol 2: 1214
Africa Travel Association Vol 1: 218
African Reinsurance Corp. Vol 2: 3882
African Studies Association Vol 1: 222
African Studies Association of the United Kingdom Vol 2: 5005
Africare Vol 1: 229
AFS Intercultural Programs Vol 1: 231
Aga Khan Trust for Culture Vol 2: 4694
AGC Education and Research Foundation Vol 1: 233
The Age Vol 2: 36
AGFA Vol 2: 393
Agfa-Gavaert Vol 1: 16253
AGFA Medical Systems Vol 1: 6266
Agilent Technologies Vol 1: 3670
Agri-Energy Roundtable Vol 1: 237
Agricultural History Society Vol 1: 239
Agricultural Institute of Canada Vol 1: 243
Aguda l'Haanakat Prasim Sifrutiim Al Shem Mordechai Bernstein Vol 2: 2896
Ahrend Groep N.V. Vol 2: 3675
AIA Pennsylvania Vol 1: 250
AICHE Vol 1: 418
AIIM - The Enterprise Content Management Association Vol 1: 252
AIM Magazine - AIM Publication Association Vol 1: 261
Air and Waste Management Association Vol 1: 263
Air-Britain Historians Vol 2: 5007
Air Force Association Vol 1: 273
Air Force Association - Aerospace Education Foundation Vol 1: 197
Air Force Association of Canada Vol 1: 312
Air Force Historical Foundation Vol 1: 314
Air League Vol 2: 5009
Air Products and Chemicals, Inc. Vol 1: 1502, 2494
Air Traffic Control Association Vol 1: 325
Air Transport World Vol 1: 340
Aircraft Owners and Pilots Association Vol 1: 342
Aircraft Technical Publishers Vol 1: 12228, 15272
Airey Neave Trust Vol 2: 5015
Airport Consultants Council Vol 1: 2407
Airports Council International - North America Vol 1: 346
Airts Cooncil o Norlin Airlann Vol 2: 5073
Airways Corporation Vol 2: 3837
Akademie Ved Ceske Republiky Vol 2: 1246
Akademiet for de tekniske Videnskaber Vol 2: 1275
Akashvani Vol 2: 2536
Akzo Nobel Inc. Vol 1: 2969
Alabama Library Association Vol 1: 350
Alabama State Poetry Society Vol 1: 13140
Alabama Writers' Forum Vol 1: 352
Alamogordo Music Theatre Vol 1: 354
Alarm and Security Association; Canadian Vol 1: 6868
Albany Institute of History and Art Vol 1: 15901
Albany Trustee Co., Ltd. Vol 2: 5698
Albany; University of Vol 1: 15901
Alberta Amateur Boxing Association Vol 1: 356
Alberta Construction Safety Association Vol 1: 362
Alberta Irrigation Projects Association Vol 1: 369
Alberta Motion Picture Industries Association Vol 1: 371
Alberta Occupational Health Nurses Association Vol 1: 373
Alberta Publishers Association Vol 1: 5835
Alberta Theatre Projects Vol 1: 378
Alcan Canada Limited Vol 1: 6898
Alco Control Company Vol 1: 4045
Alcoa Company Vol 1: 4129
Alcoa Inc. Vol 1: 380
Alcuin Society Vol 1: 384
Aldeburgh Poetry Trust Vol 2: 5017
Aldrich Chemical Company, Inc. Vol 1: 1505
Aldrich Chemical Co., Inc. Vol 1: 1517
Alexander Graham Bell Association for the Deaf and Hard of Hearing Vol 1: 386
Alfred Heineken Fondsen Foundation Vol 2: 3651, 3653, 3654, 3655
Algemeen Nederlands Verbond Vol 2: 3483, 3563
All-America Rose Selections Vol 1: 391
All-America Selections Vol 1: 395
All England Lawn Tennis and Croquet Club Vol 2: 5019
All India Management Association Vol 2: 2530
All India Radio Vol 2: 2536
Allard Charitable Foundation; Peter Vol 2: 6629
Allen & Unwin Pty. Ltd. Vol 2: 38
Alliance for Aging Research Vol 1: 9469
Alliance for Children and Families Vol 1: 397
Alliance for Children and Television Vol 1: 401
Alliance for Community Media Vol 1: 404
Alliance of Area Business Publications Vol 1: 406
Alliance of Motion Picture and Television Producers Vol 1: 408
Alliance of the American Dental Association Vol 1: 410
L'Alliance pour l'Enfant et la Television Vol 1: 401
Allianz Cornhill Musical Insurance Vol 2: 6461, 6462
Allied Artists of America Vol 1: 413
Allyn & Bacon Publishers Vol 1: 15398
Alpert Foundation; Herb Vol 1: 10803
Alpha Chi Sigma Vol 1: 415
Alpha Chi Sigma Fraternity Vol 1: 1520
Alpha Epsilon Rho; National Broadcasting Society - Vol 1: 12786
Alpha Kappa Delta Vol 1: 420
Alpha Omega Alpha Honor Medical Society Vol 1: 422
Alpha Omega Dental Fraternity Vol 1: 426
Alpha Omega International Dental Fraternity Vol 1: 426
Alpha Sigma Nu Vol 1: 5202
Alpha Tau Delta Vol 1: 429
Alpha Zeta Omega Vol 1: 434
Alpinale Film Festival Vol 2: 740
Alpine Club of Canada Vol 1: 439
Alpine Garden Society Vol 2: 5021
ALS Association, West Michigan Chapter Vol 1: 444
Altran Engineering Academy Vol 2: 6164
Aluminum Association Inc. - Extruded Products Division Vol 1: 446
Alumni Association Vol 1: 1653
Alumni Association of Princeton University Vol 1: 448
Alumni Association of the City College of New York Vol 1: 451
Alumni Federation of New York University Vol 1: 14195
Alzheimer Society of Canada Vol 1: 456
Amanah Al Ammah Li Jaezat Al Malik Faisal Al Alamiyyah; Al Vol 2: 4402
Amateur Astronomers Association Vol 1: 460
Amateur Athletic Foundation of Los Angeles Vol 1: 462
Amateur Athletic Union Vol 1: 465
Amateur Boxing Federation; United States of America Vol 1: 17716
Amateur Cinema League Vol 1: 2809
Amateur Entomologists' Society Vol 2: 5027
Amateur Hockey Association of the United States Vol 1: 18397
Amateur Softball Association of America Vol 1: 519
Amateur Swimming Association Vol 2: 5033
Amaury Sport Organisation Vol 2: 1707
Ambulatory Pediatric Association Vol 1: 525
Amelia Reynolds Long Memorial Fund Vol 1: 13158
America-Israel Cultural Foundation Vol 1: 533
America the Beautiful Fund Vol 1: 535
American Academy for Cerebral Palsy Vol 1: 537
American Academy for Cerebral Palsy and Developmental Medicine Vol 1: 537
American Academy in Rome Vol 1: 539, 18483
American Academy of Addiction Psychiatry Vol 1: 541
American Academy of Advertising Vol 1: 544
American Academy of Arts and Sciences Vol 1: 549
American Academy of Child and Adolescent Psychiatry Vol 1: 556
American Academy of Child Psychiatry Vol 1: 556
American Academy of Clinical Psychiatrists Vol 1: 559
American Academy of Clinical Toxicology Vol 1: 561
American Academy of Crown and Bridge Prosthodontics Vol 1: 621
American Academy of Dermatology Vol 1: 564
American Academy of Dramatic Arts Vol 1: 570
American Academy of Environmental Engineers Vol 1: 572
American Academy of Environmental Medicine Vol 1: 577
American Academy of Equine Art Vol 1: 581
American Academy of Facial Plastic and Reconstructive Surgery Vol 1: 591

American Academy of Family Physicians Vol 1: 597
American Academy of Fixed Prosthodontics Vol 1: 621
American Academy of Kinesiology and Physical Education Vol 1: 623
American Academy of Medical Administrators Vol 1: 625
American Academy of Neurological and Orthopaedic Surgeons Vol 1: 631
American Academy of Neurology Vol 1: 633
American Academy of Neurology Vol 1: 13463
American Academy of Nursing Vol 1: 643
American Academy of Occupational Medicine Vol 1: 1689
American Academy of Ophthalmology Vol 1: 645
American Academy of Ophthalmology and Otolaryngology Vol 1: 645
American Academy of Optometry Vol 1: 650
American Academy of Oral and Maxillofacial Radiology Vol 1: 660
American Academy of Oral Medicine Vol 1: 665
American Academy of Osteopathic Surgeons Vol 1: 1238
American Academy of Osteopathy Vol 1: 671
American Academy of Otolaryngology - Head and Neck Surgery Vol 1: 673
American Academy of Pediatrics Vol 1: 677
American Academy of Periodontology Vol 1: 721
American Academy of Physician Assistants Vol 1: 732
American Academy of Professional Coders Vol 1: 736
American Academy of Psychiatrists in Alcoholism and Addiction Vol 1: 541
American Academy of Psychiatry and the Law Vol 1: 739
American Academy of Religion Vol 1: 741
American Academy of Sanitarians Vol 1: 746
American Academy of Sleep Medicine Vol 1: 748
American Academy of Somnology Vol 1: 751
American Academy of the History of Dentistry Vol 1: 753
American Accordion Musicological Society Vol 1: 756
American Accordionists' Association Vol 1: 758
American Accounting Association Vol 1: 2461
American Adoption Congress Vol 1: 760
American Advertising Federation Vol 1: 762
American Agri-Women Vol 1: 770
American Agricultural Economics Association Vol 1: 773
American Agricultural Editors Association Vol 1: 17369
American Alliance for Health, Physical Education, Recreation and Dance Vol 1: 781
American Alliance for Theatre and Education Vol 1: 788
American Amateur Press Association Vol 1: 805
American Animal Hospital Association Vol 1: 807
American Anthropological Association Vol 1: 811
American Antiquarian Society Vol 1: 816
American Arbitration Association Vol 1: 820
American Armsport Association Vol 1: 822
American Armwrestling Association Vol 1: 822
American Art Therapy Association Vol 1: 825
American Artists Professional League Vol 1: 828
American Assembly Vol 1: 830
American Assembly for Men in Nursing Vol 1: 832
American Association for Adult and Continuing Education Vol 1: 834
American Association for Aerosol Research Vol 1: 840
American Association for Agricultural Education Vol 1: 845
American Association for Artificial Intelligence Vol 1: 849
American Association for Artificial Intelligence Vol 1: 4813
American Association for Automotive Medicine Vol 1: 4969
American Association for Cancer Research Vol 1: 857
American Association for Cancer Research Vol 2: 3116
American Association for Clinical Chemistry Vol 1: 864
American Association for Conservation Information Vol 1: 4837
American Association for Counseling and Development Vol 1: 1837
American Association for Employment in Education Vol 1: 902
American Association for Geodetic Surveying Vol 1: 904
American Association for Health Education Vol 1: 907
American Association for Laboratory Animal Science Vol 1: 913
American Association for Leisure and Recreation Vol 1: 920
American Association for Marriage and Family Therapy Vol 1: 926
American Association for Public Opinion Research Vol 1: 937
American Association for State and Local History Vol 1: 940
American Association for the Advancement of Science Vol 1: 945
American Association for the Advancement of Sciences Vol 1: 3161
American Association for the Advancement of Slavic Studies Vol 1: 955
American Association for the History of Medicine Vol 1: 962
American Association for the History of Nursing Vol 1: 970
American Association for Theatre in Secondary Education Vol 1: 788
American Association for Women in Community Colleges Vol 1: 975
American Association for Women Radiologists Vol 1: 978
American Association of Advertising Agencies Vol 1: 982
American Association of Agricultural College Editors Vol 1: 4798
American Association of Airport Executives Vol 1: 2407
American Association of Airport Executives, Great Lakes Chapter Vol 1: 986
American Association of Anatomists Vol 1: 988
American Association of Avian Pathologists Vol 1: 991
American Association of Bioanalysts Vol 1: 997
American Association of Blacks in Energy Vol 1: 999
American Association of Blood Banks Vol 1: 1002
American Association of Botanical Gardens and Arboreta Vol 1: 1019
American Association of Bovine Practitioners Vol 1: 1022
American Association of Cat Enthusiasts Vol 1: 1029
American Association of Cereal Chemists Vol 1: 16
American Association of Certified Orthoptists Vol 1: 1031
American Association of Children's Residential Centers Vol 1: 1034
American Association of Christian Schools Vol 1: 1036
American Association of College Baseball Coaches Vol 1: 1379
American Association of Colleges for Teacher Education Vol 1: 1038
American Association of Collegiate Registrars and Admissions Officers Vol 1: 1053
American Association of Community Colleges Vol 1: 12958, 12959
American Association of Community Theatre Vol 1: 1057
American Association of Cost Engineers Vol 1: 19
American Association of Critical-Care Nurses Vol 1: 1065
American Association of Dental Examiners Vol 1: 1075
American Association of Diabetes Educators Vol 1: 1077
American Association of Electromyography and Electrodiagnosis Vol 1: 1168
American Association of Endodontists Vol 1: 1084
American Association of Engineering Societies Vol 1: 1089
American Association of Family and Consumer Sciences Vol 1: 1094
American Association of Feline Practitioners Vol 1: 1101
American Association of Genito-Urinary Surgeons Vol 1: 1103
American Association of Gynecologic Laparoscopists Vol 1: 1106
American Association of Handwriting Analysts Vol 1: 1110
American Association of Healthcare Administrative Management Vol 1: 1112
American Association of Homes and Services for the Aging Vol 1: 1118
American Association of Hospital Dental Chiefs Vol 1: 1130
American Association of Hospital Dentists Vol 1: 1130
American Association of Housing Educators Vol 1: 1132
American Association of Immunologists Vol 1: 1134
American Association of Industrial Physicians and Surgeons Vol 1: 1689
American Association of Law Libraries Vol 1: 1136
American Association of Meat Processors Vol 1: 1149

American Association of Motor Vehicle Administrators Vol 1: 1160
American Association of Museums Vol 1: 1164
American Association of Neuromuscular and Electrodiagnostic Medicine Vol 1: 1168
American Association of Neuropathologists Vol 1: 1173
American Association of Nurse Anesthetists Vol 1: 1177
American Association of Nurse Attorneys Vol 1: 1185
American Association of Occupational Health Nurses Vol 1: 1188
American Association of Oral and Maxillofacial Surgeons Vol 1: 1191
American Association of Orthodontists Vol 1: 1196
American Association of Osteopathic Specialists Vol 1: 1238
American Association of Owners and Breeders of Peruvian Paso Horses Vol 1: 1202
American Association of Pathologists and Bacteriologists Vol 1: 3751
American Association of Petroleum Geologists Vol 1: 1204
American Association of Physical Anthropologists Vol 1: 1231
American Association of Physician Specialists Vol 1: 1238
American Association of Physicists in Medicine Vol 1: 1241
American Association of Physics Teachers Vol 1: 1246
American Association of Plastic Surgeons Vol 1: 1255
American Association of Poison Control Centers Vol 1: 1257
American Association of Political Consultants Vol 1: 1259
American Association of Psychiatric Administrators Vol 1: 3266
American Association of Public Health Dentistry Vol 1: 1261
American Association of Public Health Physicians Vol 1: 1263
American Association of School Administrators Vol 1: 1265
American Association of School Librarians Vol 1: 1271
American Association of School Personnel Administrators Vol 1: 1283
American Association of State Colleges and Universities Vol 1: 1285
American Association of State Highway and Transportation Officials Vol 1: 1287
American Association of Suicidology Vol 1: 1293
American Association of Surgeon Physician Assistants Vol 1: 1296
American Association of Teacher Educators in Agriculture Vol 1: 845
American Association of Teachers of German Vol 1: 1298
American Association of Teachers of Italian Vol 1: 1303
American Association of Teachers of Spanish and Portuguese Vol 1: 1305
American Association of Textile Chemists and Colorists Vol 1: 1307
American Association of the Deaf-Blind Vol 1: 1311
American Association of University Administrators Vol 1: 1313
American Association of University Professors Vol 1: 1317
American Association of University Women - Legal Advocacy Fund Vol 1: 1322
American Association of University Women Educational Foundation Vol 1: 1324
American Association of Veterinary Laboratory Diagnosticians Vol 1: 1330
American Association of Wardens and Superintendents Vol 1: 14266
American Association of Women Dentists Vol 1: 1332
American Association of Zoo Keepers Vol 1: 1334
American Association of Zoological Parks and Aquariums Vol 1: 4493
American Association on Mental Deficiency Vol 1: 1340
American Association on Mental Retardation Vol 1: 1340
American Astronautical Society Vol 1: 1343
American Astronomical Society Vol 1: 1354
American Astronomical Society Vol 1: 2541, 2542
American Auto Racing Writers and Broadcasters Association Vol 1: 1368
American Automatic Control Council Vol 1: 2471, 2495
American Award Manufacturers Association Vol 1: 5605
American Badminton Association Vol 1: 18373
American Bandmasters Association Vol 1: 1371
American Bar Association Vol 1: 1373
American Bar Association Vol 1: 13415
American Baseball Coaches Association Vol 1: 1379
American Bashkir Curly Registry Vol 1: 1389
American Basketball Association Vol 1: 12753
American Begonia Society Vol 1: 1392
American Bible Society Vol 1: 1396
American Billiard Association Vol 1: 17763
American Birding Association Vol 1: 1399
American Blade Collectors Association and *The Blade Magazine* Vol 1: 5805
American Blind Bowling Association Vol 1: 1401
American Board for Occupational Health Nurses, Inc. Vol 1: 1403
American Board of Orthodontics Vol 1: 1409
American Board of Psychological Hypnosis Vol 1: 1411
American Booksellers Association Vol 1: 1413
American Bottled Water Association Vol 1: 10273
American Bowling Congress Vol 1: 1415
American Bowling Congress Vol 1: 10276
American Breeders Service Global Vol 1: 1882
American Bridge Teachers' Association Vol 1: 1417
American Brittany Club, Heart of Illinois Vol 1: 1420
American Bureau of Shipping Vol 1: 16765
American Burn Association Vol 1: 1422
American Business Media Vol 1: 1426
American Business Women's Association Vol 1: 1429
American Camellia Society Vol 1: 1431
American Camping Association Vol 1: 1433
American Cancer Society Vol 1: 1439
American Cancer Society Vol 2: 4856
American Carbon Committee Vol 1: 1446
American Carbon Society Vol 1: 1446
American Cat Fanciers Association Vol 1: 1450
American Catholic Historical Association Vol 1: 1452
American Catholic Historical Society Vol 1: 1457
American Catholic Historical Society Vol 1: 2241
American Catholic Philosophical Association Vol 1: 1459
American Center for Children's Television - % Central Educational Network Vol 1: 1462
American Ceramic Society Vol 1: 1465
American Chamber of Commerce Executives Vol 1: 1498
American Chamber of Commerce of Guatemala Vol 2: 2484
American Chemical Society Vol 1: 1500
American Chemical Society Vol 1: 3121
American Chemical Society, Philadelphia Section Vol 1: 1586
American Chesterton Society Vol 1: 1589
American Children's Television Festival Vol 1: 1462
American Chinese Medical Society Vol 1: 7364
American Chiropractic Association Vol 1: 1591
American Cinema Editors Vol 1: 1593
American Citizens Abroad Vol 2: 4696
The American Civil Defense Association Vol 1: 1595
American Civil Liberties Union Vol 1: 1597
American Civil Liberties Union of the National Capital Area Vol 1: 1599
American Cleft Palate Education Foundation Vol 1: 7468
American College Health Association Vol 1: 1602
American College of Allergy, Asthma and Immunology Vol 1: 1609
American College of Apothecaries Vol 1: 1611
American College of Cardiology Vol 1: 1614
American College of Chest Physicians Vol 1: 1621
American College of Chest Physicians - The CHEST Foundation Vol 1: 1623
American College of Clinical Pharmacology Vol 1: 1627
American College of Dentists Vol 1: 1639
American College of Emergency Physicians Vol 1: 1645
American College of Healthcare Executives Vol 1: 1650
American College of Hospital Administrators Vol 1: 1650
American College of Legal Medicine Vol 1: 1660
American College of Legal Medicine Vol 1: 7208
American College of Managed Care Administrators Vol 1: 1664
American College of Medical Practice Executives Vol 1: 1674
American College of Musicians Vol 1: 1678
American College of Neuropsychopharmacology Vol 1: 1680

American College of Nurse-Midwives Vol 1: 1687
American College of Occupational and Environmental Medicine Vol 1: 1689
American College of Occupational Medicine Vol 1: 1689
American College of Oncology Administrators Vol 1: 1694
American College of Oral and Maxillofacial Surgeons Vol 1: 1704
American College of Physicians Vol 1: 1707
American College of Preventive Medicine Vol 1: 1721
The American College of Psychiatrists Vol 1: 1726
American College of Radiology Vol 1: 1731
American College of Surgeons Vol 1: 1734
American Community Theatre Association Vol 1: 1057
American Comparative Literature Association Vol 1: 1741
American Composers Alliance Vol 1: 1744
American Concrete Institute Vol 1: 1746
American Concrete Institute - New Jersey Chapter Vol 1: 1766
American Congress of Rehabilitation Medicine Vol 1: 1768
American Congress on Surveying and Mapping Vol 1: 1776
American Congress on Surveying and Mapping Vol 1: 13754, 13756
American Consular Association Vol 1: 2054
American Contact Dermatitis Society Vol 1: 1782
American Contract Bridge League Vol 1: 1786
American Coon Hunters Association Vol 1: 1789
American Correctional Association Vol 1: 1791
American Council for Better Broadcasts Vol 1: 13841
American Council for Polish Culture Vol 1: 1799
American Council of Christian Churches Vol 1: 1807
American Council of Engineering Companies Vol 1: 1809
American Council of Learned Societies Vol 1: 1812
American Council of the Blind Vol 1: 1814
American Council on Consumer Interests Vol 1: 1820
American Council on Education Vol 1: 1827
American Council on Industrial Arts Teacher Education Vol 1: 7926
American Council on the Teaching of Foreign Languages Vol 1: 1829
American Counseling Association Vol 1: 1837
American Craft Council Vol 1: 1849
American Crossword Puzzle Tournament Vol 1: 1853
American Crystallographic Association Vol 1: 1855
American Dairy Science Association Vol 1: 1867
American Dance Festival Vol 1: 1892
American Dance Guild Vol 1: 1895
American Darts Organization Vol 1: 1899
American Deafness and Rehabilitation Association Vol 1: 150
American Dental Association Vol 1: 1902
American Dental Hygienists' Association Vol 1: 1905
American Diabetes Association Vol 1: 1907
American Die Casting Institute Vol 1: 14292
American Dietetic Association Foundation Vol 1: 1918
American Disaster Reserve Vol 1: 1922
American Documentation Institute Vol 1: 3733
American Donkey and Mule Society Vol 1: 1931
American Economic Association Vol 1: 1934
American Educational Research Association Vol 1: 1939
American Electroplaters and Surface Finishers Society Vol 1: 1947
American Electroplaters' Society Vol 1: 1947
American Endurance Ride Conference Vol 1: 1951
American Enterprise Institute for Public Policy Research Vol 1: 1972
American Epilepsy Society Vol 1: 1974
American Equilibration Society Vol 1: 1976
American Ethical Union Vol 1: 1978
American Evaluation Association Vol 1: 1980
American Ex-Prisoners of War Vol 1: 1986
American Express Company Vol 1: 11122
American Family Therapy Academy Vol 1: 1988
American Family Therapy Association Vol 1: 1988
American Fancy Rat and Mouse Association Vol 1: 1991
American Farm Bureau Federation Vol 1: 1993
American Farm Economics Association Vol 1: 773
American Federation for Aging Research Vol 1: 1995
American Federation of Aviculture Vol 1: 1998
American Federation of Labor - Congress of Industrial Organizations Vol 1: 2000
American Federation of Mineralogical Societies Vol 1: 2002
American Federation of Police Vol 1: 3216
American Federation of Teachers, AFL-CIO Vol 1: 2004
American Feed Industry Association Vol 1: 2006
American Fence Association Vol 1: 2008
American Fighter Aces Association Vol 1: 2016
American Film Institute Vol 1: 2018
American Film Institute Alumni Association Writers Workshop Vol 1: 13949
American Finance Association Vol 1: 2020
American First Day Cover Society Vol 1: 2023
American Fisheries Society Vol 1: 2025
American Folklore Society Vol 1: 2039
American Football Coaches Association Vol 1: 2042
American Forage and Grassland Council Vol 1: 2047
American Foreign Service Association Vol 1: 2054
American Forensic Association Vol 1: 2061
American Forest and Paper Association Vol 1: 2063
American Foundation for the Blind Vol 1: 2065
American Friends of The Hebrew University Vol 1: 2071
American Fuchsia Society Vol 1: 2073
American Galvanizers Association Vol 1: 2076
American Gastroenterological Association Vol 1: 2078
American Gastroenterological Association Foundation Vol 1: 8830
American Gem Society Vol 1: 2087
American Gem Trade Association Vol 1: 2089
American Geographical Society Vol 1: 2093
American Geological Institute Vol 1: 2104
American Geophysical Union Vol 1: 2108
American Geriatrics Society Vol 1: 2125
American Group Psychotherapy Association Vol 1: 2132
American Guernsey Association Vol 1: 2134
American Guild of Organists Vol 1: 2143
American Guild of Organists, Region II Vol 1: 2151
American Gynecological and Obstetrical Society Vol 1: 2153
American Gynecological Club Vol 2: 6701
American Gynecological Society Vol 1: 2153
American Handwriting Analysis Foundation Vol 1: 2156
American Hanoverian Society Vol 1: 2159
American Headache Society Vol 1: 2161
American Health Care Association Vol 1: 2164
American Health Information Management - Wisconsin Chapter Vol 1: 2168
American Healthcare Radiology Administrators Vol 1: 2170
American Heart Association Vol 1: 2172
American Heart Association, Talbot County Branch Vol 1: 2189
American Helicopter Society Vol 1: 2191
American Hemerocallis Society Vol 1: 2207
American Hibiscus Society Vol 1: 2213
American Hiking Society Vol 1: 2215
American Historical Association Vol 1: 2224
American Historical Association Vol 1: 6557, 11346
American Historical Association, Pacific Coast Branch Vol 1: 2245
American Historical Print Collectors Society Vol 1: 2247
American Hockey Coaches Association Vol 1: 2249
American Hockey League Vol 1: 2259
American Holsteiner Horse Association Vol 1: 2281
American Home Economics Association Foundation Vol 1: 1094
American Homebrewers Association Vol 1: 2283
American Horticultural Society Vol 1: 2285
American Hospital Association Vol 1: 2301
American Hospital Radiology Administrators Vol 1: 2170
American Hosta Society Vol 1: 2310
American Hot Rod Association Vol 1: 2317
American Hotel and Lodging Association Vol 1: 2319
American Hotel & Motel Association Vol 1: 2319
American Humanist Association Vol 1: 2321
American Hungarian Foundation Vol 1: 2326
American Indian Ethnohistoric Conference Vol 1: 3702
American Indian Heritage Foundation Vol 1: 2328
American Indian Horse Registry Vol 1: 2331

American Indian Lore Association Vol 1: 13970
American Industrial Arts Student Association Vol 1: 17424
American Industrial Hygiene Association Vol 1: 2336
American Institute for Contemporary German Studies Vol 1: 2349
American Institute for Decision Sciences Vol 1: 8082
American Institute for Public Service Vol 1: 2351
American Institute of Aeronautics and Astronautics Vol 1: 2353
American Institute of Aeronautics and Astronautics Vol 1: 16581, 16589
American Institute of Aeronautics and Astronautics - Stanford University Branch Vol 1: 2421
American Institute of Architects Vol 1: 2423
American Institute of Architects Vol 1: 11334, 17332
American Institute of Architects - New York Chapter Vol 1: 2440
American Institute of Architects, Southern Arizona Vol 1: 2445
American Institute of Architects - *Sunset Magazine* Vol 1: 17329
American Institute of Architects, Tampa Bay Vol 1: 2447
American Institute of Biological Sciences Vol 1: 2450
American Institute of Building Design Vol 1: 2453
American Institute of Certified Planners Vol 1: 3198, 3199
American Institute of Certified Public Accountants Vol 1: 2455
American Institute of Chemical Engineers Vol 1: 2466
American Institute of Chemical Engineers Vol 1: 3938, 3948, 4144
American Institute of Chemists Vol 1: 2506
American Institute of Civil Engineers Vol 1: 4141
American Institute of Fishery Research Biologists Vol 1: 2510
American Institute of Graphic Arts Vol 1: 2514
American Institute of Industrial Engineers Vol 1: 9857
American Institute of Iranian Studies Vol 1: 2518
American Institute of Mechanical Engineers Vol 1: 4155
American Institute of Mining, Metallurgical, and Petroleum Engineers Vol 1: 2522
American Institute of Mining, Metallurgical and Petroleum Engineers Vol 1: 3938
American Institute of Mining, Metallurgical, and Petroleum Engineers Vol 1: 3948
American Institute of Mining, Metallurgical and Petroleum Engineers Vol 1: 4141
American Institute of Mining, Metallurgical and Petroleum Engineers; Iron and Steel Society of the Vol 1: 4895
American Institute of Mining, Metallurgical and Petroleum Engineers; Society of Petroleum Engineers of the Vol 1: 16791
American Institute of Musical Studies Vol 1: 13490
American Institute of Park Executives Vol 1: 4100
American Institute of Physics Vol 1: 2538
American Institute of Planners Vol 1: 3197
American Institute of Professional Geologists Vol 1: 2550
American Institute of Real Estate Appraisers Vol 1: 4565
American Institute of Steel Construction Vol 1: 2555
American Institute of Stress Vol 1: 2559
American Institute of Timber Construction Vol 1: 2561
American Institute of Ultrasound in Medicine Vol 1: 2563
American Intellectual Property Law Association Vol 1: 2568
American Interior Designers Vol 1: 4083
American Intraocular Implant Society Vol 1: 3900
American Iris Society Vol 1: 2572
American Irish Historical Society Vol 1: 2574
American Iron and Steel Institute Vol 1: 2576
American-Israel Numismatic Association Vol 1: 2579
American Italian Historical Association Vol 1: 2581
American Jewish Committee Vol 1: 2583
American Jewish Congress Vol 1: 2589
American Jewish Historical Society Vol 1: 2592
American Jewish Press Association Vol 1: 2598
American Judicature Society Vol 1: 2601
American Junior Golf Association Vol 1: 18943
American Junior Shorthorn Association Vol 1: 2607
American Kenpo Karate International Vol 1: 2609
American Kidney Fund Vol 1: 2611
American Kitefliers Association Vol 1: 2614
American Laryngological Association Vol 1: 2616
American Lawyers Auxiliary Vol 1: 2623
American League of Professional Baseball Clubs Vol 1: 2627
American Leather Chemists Association Vol 1: 2629
American Legion Vol 1: 2633
American Legion Auxiliary Vol 1: 2636
American Legion Baseball Vol 1: 15567
American Legion Virginia Vol 1: 2638
American Legislative Exchange Council Vol 1: 2640
American Library Association Vol 1: 2682
American Library Association - Children's Services Division Vol 1: 4917
American Library Association - Ethnic and Multicultural Information Exchange Round Table Vol 1: 2643
American Library Association - Exhibits Round Table Vol 1: 2645
American Library Association - Governance Office Vol 1: 2648
American Library Association - Intellectual Freedom Round Table Vol 1: 2667
American Library Association - International Relations Committee Vol 1: 2671
American Library Association - Library History Round Table Vol 1: 2674
American Library Association - Office for Research and Statistics Vol 1: 2679
American Library Association - Public Information Office Vol 1: 2681
American Library Association - Reference and Adult Services Division Vol 1: 2683
American Library Association - Reference and User Services Vol 1: 2683
American Library Association - Resources and Technical Services Division Vol 1: 4909
American Library Association - Social Responsibilities Round Table Vol 1: 2698
American Library Association - Young Adult Services Division Vol 1: 19079
American Library Association/Library Administration & Management Association Vol 1: 2425
American Liszt Society Vol 1: 2701
American Literary Translators Association Vol 1: 2703
American Lung Association Vol 1: 2706
American Lung Association of Eastern Missouri Vol 1: 2710
American Lung Association of Rhode Island Vol 1: 2712
American Marketing Association Vol 1: 2714
American Mathematical Association of Two-Year Colleges Vol 1: 2722
American Mathematical Society Vol 1: 2724
American Mathematical Society Vol 1: 11614, 12152, 16266
American Mathematical Society Vol 1: 16273
American Mathematical Society Vol 1: 16285
American Meat Institute Vol 1: 2729
American Meat Science Association Vol 1: 2733
American Medical Association Vol 1: 698
American Medical Association Foundation Vol 1: 2744
American Medical Technologists Vol 1: 2748
American Medical Women's Association Vol 1: 2762
American Medical Writers Association Vol 1: 2766
American Mental Health Clergy Vol 1: 3283
American Mental Health Counselors Association Vol 1: 2772
American Meteorological Society Vol 1: 2776
American MGC Register Vol 1: 2783
American Military Institute Vol 1: 16334
American Military Retirees Association Vol 1: 2785
American Mining Congress Vol 1: 13453
American Morgan Horse Association Vol 1: 2787
American Mosquito Control Association Vol 1: 2799
American Mothers Committee Vol 1: 2805
American Mothers, Inc. Vol 1: 2805
American Motion Picture Society Vol 1: 2808
American Motorcyclist Association Vol 1: 2810
American Moving and Storage Association Vol 1: 2813
American Mule Racing Association Vol 1: 2815
American Museum of Natural History Vol 1: 2828
American Music Awards Vol 1: 2833
American Music Center Vol 1: 2835
American Music Scholarship Association Vol 1: 18964
American Musical Instrument Society Vol 1: 2837
American Musicological Society Vol 1: 2841
American National Standards Institute Vol 1: 2848
American Nature Study Society Vol 1: 2858
American Neuropsychiatric Association Vol 1: 2860

American Newspaper Publishers Association Foundation Vol 1: 14220
American North Country Cheviot Sheep Association Vol 1: 2863
American Nuclear Society Vol 1: 14440
American Numismatic Association Vol 1: 2865
American Numismatic Society Vol 1: 2931
American Nursery and Landscape Association Vol 1: 8483
American Nurses Association Vol 1: 2936
American Nurses Foundation Vol 1: 2947
American Occupational Medical Association Vol 1: 1689
American Occupational Therapy Association Vol 1: 2949
American Occupational Therapy Foundation Vol 1: 2961
American Oil Chemists' Society Vol 1: 2963
American Ophthalmological Society Vol 1: 2971
American Optical Company Vol 1: 14617
American Optical Corporation Vol 1: 14604
American Optometric Association Vol 1: 2973
American Optometric Foundation Vol 1: 655
American Orchid Society Vol 1: 2978
American Ornithologists' Union Vol 1: 3003
American ORT Vol 1: 3006
American Orthopaedic Society for Sports Medicine Vol 1: 3011
American Osteopathic Academy of Orthopedics Vol 1: 3015
American Osteopathic College of Pathologists Vol 1: 3017
American Otological Society Vol 1: 3020
American Park and Recreation Society Vol 1: 3024
American Parkinson Disease Association Vol 1: 3027
American Patent Law Association Vol 1: 2568
American Peanut Council Vol 1: 3029
American Pediatric Society Vol 1: 3031
American Pet Products Manufacturer Association Vol 1: 3033
American Petanque Association U.S.A. Vol 1: 8674
American Petroleum Institute Vol 1: 3035
American Pharmacists Association - Academy of Pharmacy Practice and Management Vol 1: 3037
American Philatelic Association Vol 1: 3074
American Philatelic Congress Vol 1: 3065
American Philatelic Society Vol 1: 3074
American Philatelic Society Writers Unit Junior Division Vol 1: 11068
American Philological Association Vol 1: 3078
American Philosophical Association Vol 1: 3081
American Philosophical Society Vol 1: 3093
American Photographic Historical Society Vol 1: 3103
American Physical Society Vol 1: 3105
American Physical Therapy Association Vol 1: 3141
American Physicians Art Association Vol 1: 3158
American Physiological Society Vol 1: 3160
American Phytopathological Society Vol 1: 3185
American Phytopathological Society Vol 1: 6812, 17367
American Pianists Association Vol 1: 3195
American Planning Association Vol 1: 3197
American Plant Life Society Vol 1: 10283
American Podiatric Medical Association Vol 1: 3214
American Podiatry Association Vol 1: 3214
American Police Hall of Fame and Museum Vol 1: 3216
American Political Science Association Vol 1: 3228
American Pomological Society Vol 1: 3241
American Power Boat Association Vol 1: 3245
American Primrose Society Vol 1: 3251
American Printing History Association Vol 1: 3253
American Probation and Parole Association Vol 1: 3256
American Protestant Health Association; College of Chaplains of the Vol 1: 5307
American Psychiatric Association Vol 1: 3265
American Psychiatric Institute for Research and Education Vol 1: 3276, 3277
American Psychological Association Vol 1: 15400, 15402
American Psychological Association - Adult Development and Aging Division (Division 20) Vol 1: 3296
American Psychological Association - American Psychology-Law Society (Division 41) Vol 1: 3299
American Psychological Association - Applied Experimental and Engineering Psychology Division (Division 21) Vol 1: 3302
American Psychological Association - Behavior Analysis Division (Division 25) Vol 1: 3306
American Psychological Association - Behavioral Neuroscience and Comparative Psychology Division (Division 6) Vol 1: 3311
American Psychological Association - Committee on Ethnic Minority Affairs Vol 1: 3313
American Psychological Association - Committee on International Relations Vol 1: 3315
American Psychological Association - Committee on Women in Psychology Vol 1: 3317
American Psychological Association - Counseling Psychology Division (Division 17) Vol 1: 3320
American Psychological Association - Developmental Psychology Division (Division 7) Vol 1: 3327
American Psychological Association - Division of Family Psychology (Division 43) Vol 1: 3329
American Psychological Association - Division of State, Provincial, and Territorial Psychological Affairs (Division 31) Vol 1: 3333
American Psychological Association - Educational Psychology Division (Division 15) Vol 1: 3336
American Psychological Association - Exercise and Sport Psychology Division (Division 47) Vol 1: 3340
American Psychological Association - General Psychology Division (Division 1) Vol 1: 3342
American Psychological Association - Health Psychology Division (Division 38) Vol 1: 3347
American Psychological Association - Mental Retardation and Developmental Disabilities Division (Division 33) Vol 1: 3349
American Psychological Association - Psychologists in Public Service Division (Division 18) Vol 1: 3351
American Psychological Association - Psychology of Religion (Division 36) Vol 1: 3353
American Psychological Association - Psychotherapy Division (Division 29) Vol 1: 3356
American Psychological Association - Rehabilitation Psychology Division (Division 22) Vol 1: 3359
American Psychological Association - School Psychology Division (Division 16) Vol 1: 3361
American Psychological Association - Science Directorate Vol 1: 3363
American Psychological Association - Society for Community Research and Action (Division 27) Vol 1: 3368
American Psychological Association - Society for Military Psychology (Division 19) Vol 1: 3375
American Psychological Association - Society for the History of Psychology (Division 26) Vol 1: 3378
American Psychological Association - Society for the Psychology of Women (Division 35) Vol 1: 3380
American Psychological Association - Society for the Study of Lesbian, Gay and Bisexual Concerns (Division 44) Vol 1: 3386
American Psychological Association - Society for the Teaching of Psychology (Division 2) Vol 1: 3399
American Psychological Association - Society of Clinical Psychology (Division 12) Vol 1: 3401
American Psychological Association - Society of Consulting Psychology (Division 13) Vol 1: 3405
American Psychological Association - Society of Pediatric Psychology (Division 54) Vol 1: 3408
American Psychological Association - Society of Psychological Hypnosis (Division 30) Vol 1: 3412
American Psychological Association (Division 28) Vol 1: 3417
American Psychological Association Division of Independent Practice - Division of Independent Practice Vol 1: 3421
American Psychopathological Association Vol 1: 3425
American Public Gas Association Vol 1: 3427
American Public Health Association Vol 1: 3430
American Public Human Services Association Vol 1: 3434
American Public Power Association Vol 1: 3436
American Public Works Association Vol 1: 3450
American Rabbit Breeders Association Vol 1: 3458
American Radium Society Vol 1: 3460
American Recorder Society Vol 1: 3464

American Red Cross National Headquarters Vol 1: 3466
American Red Magen David for Israel - American Friends of Magen David Vol 1: 3476
American Rental Association Vol 1: 3478
American Revolution Round Table Vol 1: 3486
American Rhinologic Society Vol 1: 3488
American Rhododendron Society Vol 1: 3491
American Risk and Insurance Association Vol 1: 3494
American Road and Transportation Builders Association Vol 1: 3499
American Road Builders Association Vol 1: 3499
American Romanian Academy of Arts and Sciences Vol 1: 3506
American Rose Society Vol 1: 3509
American Rottweiler Club Vol 1: 3511
American Rural Health Association Vol 1: 13649
American-Scandinavian Foundation Vol 1: 3515
American Schleswig-Holstein Heritage Society Vol 1: 3517
American School and Community Safety Association Vol 1: 15902
American School and University Vol 1: 3519
American School Health Association Vol 1: 3523
American Scientific Glassblowers Society Vol 1: 3528
American Screenwriters Association Vol 1: 3531
American Sheep Industry Association Vol 1: 3539
American-Slovenian Polka Foundation Vol 1: 3547
American Society for Adolescent Psychiatry Vol 1: 3551
American Society for Advancement of Anesthesia and Sedation in Dentistry Vol 1: 3553
American Society for Aesthetic Plastic Surgery Vol 1: 3555
American Society for Aesthetics Vol 1: 3557
American Society for Aesthetics Vol 1: 11045
American Society for Bariatric Surgery Vol 1: 3559
American Society for Biochemistry and Molecular Biology Vol 1: 3561
American Society for Bioethics and Humanities Vol 1: 3569
American Society for Bone and Mineral Research Vol 1: 3573
American Society for Cell Biology Vol 1: 3584
American Society for Clinical Laboratory Science Vol 1: 3596
American Society for Clinical Pathology Vol 1: 3600
American Society for Clinical Pharmacology and Therapeutics Vol 1: 3606
American Society for Colposcopy and Cervical Pathology Vol 1: 3613
American Society for Competitiveness Vol 1: 3616
American Society for Cybernetics Vol 1: 3618
American Society for Dermatologic Surgery Vol 1: 3622
American Society for Eighteenth-Century Studies Vol 1: 3624
American Society for Engineering Education Vol 1: 3627
American Society for Engineering Management Vol 1: 3683
American Society for Enology and Viticulture Vol 1: 3694
American Society for Environmental History Vol 1: 3697
American Society for Ethnohistory Vol 1: 3702
American Society for Experimental Pathology Vol 1: 3751
American Society for Gastrointestinal Endoscopy Vol 1: 3704
American Society for Gravitational and Space Biology Vol 1: 3710
American Society for Horticultural Science Vol 1: 3717
American Society for Information Science and Technology Vol 1: 3733
American Society for Investigative Pathology Vol 1: 3751
American Society for Legal History Vol 1: 3758
American Society for Metals Vol 1: 4693
American Society for Microbiology Vol 1: 3761
American Society for Microbiology Vol 1: 17898
American Society for Nondestructive Testing Vol 1: 3773
American Society for Nutrition Vol 1: 3785
American Society for Nutritional Sciences Vol 1: 3785
American Society for Parenteral and Enteral Nutrition Vol 1: 3799
American Society for Personnel Administration Vol 1: 16230
American Society for Pharmacology and Experimental Therapeutics Vol 1: 3803
American Society for Photogrammetry and Remote Sensing Vol 2: 4970
American Society for Public Administration Vol 1: 3811
American Society for Public Administration Vol 1: 12648
American Society for Public Administration (ASPA) Vol 1: 12137
American Society for Quality Control Vol 1: 5631
American Society for Stereotactic and Functional Neurosurgery Vol 1: 3821
American Society for Testing and Materials Vol 1: 5399
American Society for the Prevention of Cruelty to Animals Vol 1: 3823
American Society for Theatre Research Vol 1: 3826
American Society for Training and Development Vol 1: 3832
American Society of Abdominal Surgeons Vol 1: 3837
American Society of Agricultural and Biological Engineers Vol 1: 3840
American Society of Agricultural Engineers Vol 1: 10215
American Society of Agronomy Vol 1: 3866
American Society of Agronomy Vol 1: 16943, 17368
American Society of Animal Science Vol 1: 3878
American Society of Association Executives Vol 1: 3894
American Society of Biological Chemists Vol 1: 3561
American Society of Business Press Editors Vol 1: 3897
American Society of Business Publication Editors Vol 1: 3897
American Society of Cataract and Refractive Surgery Vol 1: 3900
American Society of Certified Engineering Technicians Vol 1: 3903
American Society of Church History Vol 1: 3909
American Society of Civil Engineering Vol 1: 3915
American Society of Civil Engineers Vol 1: 3915, 16589
American Society of Clinical Pathologists Vol 1: 3600
American Society of Colon and Rectal Surgeons Vol 1: 3996
American Society of Composers, Authors and Publishers Vol 1: 3998
American Society of Composers, Authors and Publishers Vol 1: 7377
American Society of Criminology Vol 1: 4006
American Society of Cytopathology Vol 1: 4011
American Society of Echocardiography Vol 1: 4022
American Society of Electroencephalographic Technologists Vol 1: 4031
American Society of Electroneurodiagnostic Technologists Vol 1: 4031
American Society of Enologists Vol 1: 3694
American Society of Farm Managers and Rural Appraisers Vol 1: 4033
American Society of Furniture Designers Vol 1: 4038
American Society of Genealogists Vol 1: 4040
American Society of Golf Course Architects Vol 1: 18943
American Society of Heating, Refrigerating and Air-Conditioning Engineers Vol 1: 4042
American Society of Hematology Vol 1: 4067
American Society of Human Genetics Vol 1: 4073
American Society of Ichthyologists and Herpetologists Vol 1: 4075
American Society of Indexers Vol 1: 4081
American Society of Interior Designers Vol 1: 4083
American Society of International Law Vol 1: 4086
American Society of Journalism School Administrators Vol 1: 5332
American Society of Journalists and Authors Vol 1: 4091
American Society of Landscape Architects Vol 1: 4094
American Society of Law, Medicine and Ethics Vol 1: 4108
American Society of Limnology and Oceanography Vol 1: 4110
American Society of Magazine Editors Vol 1: 4113
American Society of Magazine Editors Vol 1: 11458
American Society of Mammalogists Vol 1: 4115
American Society of Mechanical Engineers Vol 1: 3938, 3948

American Society of Mechanical Engineers Vol 1: 4122
American Society of Mechanical Engineers Vol 1: 16589
American Society of Mining & Reclamation Vol 1: 4176
American Society of Music Arrangers and Composers Vol 1: 4180
American Society of Naturalists Vol 1: 4182
American Society of Naval Engineers Vol 1: 4186
American Society of Nephrology Vol 1: 4193
American Society of Neuroimaging Vol 1: 4201
American Society of Newspaper Editors Vol 1: 4204
American Society of Oral Surgeons Vol 1: 1191
American Society of Orthopedic Professionals Vol 1: 4210
American Society of Pharmacognosy Vol 1: 3055
American Society of Pharmacognosy Vol 1: 4212
American Society of Photogrammetry Vol 1: 4732
American Society of Physician Analysts Vol 1: 4226
American Society of Planning Officials Vol 1: 3197
American Society of Plant Biologists Vol 1: 4214
American Society of Plant Taxonomists Vol 1: 4221
American Society of Plant Taxonomists Vol 1: 5872
American Society of Psychoanalytic Physicians Vol 1: 4226
American Society of Psychopathology of Expression Vol 1: 4228
American Society of Safety Engineers Vol 1: 4230
American Society of Safety Engineers, Arkansas/Louisiana/Texas Chapter Vol 1: 4235
American Society of Sanitary Engineering Vol 1: 4237
American Society of Swedish Engineers Vol 1: 4241
American Society of Traffic and Transportation Vol 1: 4251
American Society of Transplantation Vol 1: 4243
American Society of Transportation and Logistics Vol 1: 4251
American Society of Travel Agents Vol 1: 4253
American Society of Tropical Medicine and Hygiene Vol 1: 4258
American Society of Tropical Medicine and Hygiene Vol 2: 7033
American Society of Ultrasound Technical Specialists Vol 1: 16646
American Society of Zoologists Vol 1: 16312
American Society on Aging Vol 1: 4262
American Society on Aging Vol 1: 4265
American Sociological Association Vol 1: 4274
American Solar Energy Society Vol 1: 4284
American Spaniel Club Vol 1: 4286
The American Spectator Vol 1: 4288
American Speech and Hearing Association Vol 1: 4290
American Speech Language Hearing Association Vol 1: 4290
American Spelean Historical Association Vol 1: 13791
American Spinal Injury Association Vol 1: 4295
American Sportfishing Association Vol 1: 4297
American Sports Medicine Institute Vol 1: 4299
American Sportscasters Association Vol 1: 4301
American Staffing Association Vol 1: 4308
American Statistical Association Vol 1: 4312, 7622
American Steamship and Tourist Agents Association Vol 1: 4253
American String Teachers Association Vol 1: 4319
American String Teachers Association/ National School Orchestra Association Vol 1: 4322
American Studies Association Vol 1: 4324
American Swimming Coaches Association Vol 1: 4334
American Symphony Orchestra League Vol 1: 4339
American Telephone and Telegraph Company Vol 1: 12155
American Theatre Organ Society Vol 1: 4349
American Theatre Wing Vol 1: 4353, 11261
American Therapeutic Recreation Association Vol 1: 4355
American Thyroid Association Vol 1: 4357
American Topical Association Vol 1: 4360
American Translators Association Vol 1: 4363
American Truck Historical Society Vol 1: 4368
American Trucking Associations - Safety Management Council Vol 1: 4371
American TV Commercials Festival Vol 1: 7480
American Underground Association Vol 1: 4378
American Underground Construction Association Vol 1: 4378
American Underground-Space Association Vol 1: 4378
American University - School of Public Affairs Vol 1: 4383
American Urological Association Vol 1: 4385
American Urological Association Foundation Vol 1: 4398
American Vaulting Association Vol 1: 4400
American Veterinary Medical Association Vol 1: 4402
American Water Resources Association Vol 1: 4415
American Water Works Association Vol 1: 4425
American Watercolor Society Vol 1: 4427
American Welding Society Vol 1: 4447
American Whig-Cliosophic Society Vol 1: 4474
American White American Creme Horse Registry Vol 1: 4476
American Wine Society Vol 1: 4480
American Woman's Society of Certified Public Accountants Vol 1: 4487
American Zoo and Aquarium Association Vol 1: 4493
Americanism Educational League Vol 1: 4501
America's Cup Global Information Service Vol 1: 4503
America's Foundation Vol 1: 4505
America's Junior Miss Scholarship Foundation Vol 1: 4507
Americas Society Vol 1: 4509
America's Young Woman of the Year Vol 1: 4507
Amiens International Film Festival Vol 2: 1709
Amnesty International - Canadian Section Vol 1: 4511
Amt der Salzburger Landesregierung - Kulturabteilung Vol 2: 742
Amt der Tiroler Landesregierung, Kulturabteilung Vol 2: 745
Amusement and Music Operators Association Vol 1: 4513
AMVETS - American Veterans Vol 1: 4516
Amy Foundation Vol 1: 4520
Anchor Bay Chamber of Commerce Vol 1: 4522
Ancient & Medieval History Book Club Vol 2: 5220
Ancient Mediterranean Research Association Vol 1: 4524
Anda Foundation; Geza Vol 2: 4761
Anderson Poetry Club Vol 1: 13152
Anglo-Austrian Music Society Vol 2: 5049
Anhinga Press Vol 1: 4526
Animal Behavior Society Vol 1: 4528
Animal Feed Manufacturers Association Vol 2: 4126
Animal Transportation Association - European Office Vol 2: 5051
Animal Welfare Institute Vol 1: 4532
Ann Arbor Film Festival Vol 1: 4534
Anna Bijns-Stichting Vol 2: 3485
Annenberg School for Communication Vol 1: 4539
Annual Reviews Inc. Vol 1: 12148
Anti-Defamation League Vol 1: 4541
Anti-Slavery International Vol 2: 5056
Antiquarian Field Club Vol 2: 5739
Anuvibha - Anuvrat Global Organization Vol 2: 2539
Anuvrat Vishva Bharati (Anuvibha) Vol 2: 2539
Anvil Press Vol 1: 4547
ANZIAM - Australian and New Zealand Industrial and Applied Mathematics - Australian Mathematical Society Vol 2: 40
AOAC International Vol 1: 4549
Aontas Teilgin Agus Amais na h'Eireann Vol 2: 2867
APA Committee on Ethnic Minority Affairs Vol 1: 3314
APA Committee on International Relations Vol 1: 3316
APA Committee on Women in Psychology Vol 1: 3319
Apex Awards Vol 1: 4551
APMI International Vol 1: 11704
Apotekarsocieteten Vol 2: 4677
Apotex Inc. Vol 1: 6805
Appalachian Center Vol 1: 4553
Appalachian Peace and Justice Network Vol 1: 4555
Appalachian Studies Association Vol 1: 4557
Appeal of Conscience Foundation Vol 1: 4563
Appita - Technical Association for the Australian and New Zealand Pulp and Paper Industry Vol 2: 44

Appraisal Institute Vol 1: 4565
APPROTECH ASIA Vol 2: 3983
Arab American Institute Vol 1: 4567
Arabian Sport Horse Association, Inc. Vol 1: 4569
Arango Design Foundation Vol 1: 4571
Arbeitsgemeinschaft Schweizer Grafiker Vol 2: 4904
Arboricultural Association Vol 2: 5058
Archaeological Geology Division Vol 1: 9026
Archaeological Institute of America Vol 1: 4573
Architectural Association Vol 2: 5060
Architectural League of New York Vol 1: 4586
Architectural Record Vol 1: 4588
Archival Issues Vol 1: 11757
Archivio Disarmo Vol 2: 2978
Arcos Corporation Vol 1: 4470
Arctowski Fund; Henryk Vol 1: 12144
Argentine Paleontological Association Vol 2: 14
Argentine Society of Geographical Studies Vol 2: 16
Argentinian Association of Dermatology Vol 2: 20
Argosy Foundation Contemporary Music Fund Vol 1: 7276
Aril Society International Vol 1: 4591
Arizona Authors' Association Vol 1: 4594
Arizona Geriatrics Society Vol 1: 4596
Arizona Library Association Vol 1: 4598
Arizona State Poetry Society Vol 1: 13142
Arkansas Arts Center Vol 1: 4612
Arkansas Elementary School Council - Arkansas Department of Education Vol 1: 4614
Arkansas Historical Association Vol 1: 4616
Arkansas Nurserymen's Association Vol 1: 4620
Arkansas Women's History Institute Vol 1: 4622
ARMA International - The Association of Information Management Professionals Vol 1: 4624
Armenian Behavioral Science Association Vol 1: 4631
Armstrong Memorial Research Foundation Vol 1: 4633
Army Families Federation Vol 2: 5064
Arnold Air Society Vol 1: 4635
Art Directors Club Vol 1: 4647
Art Directors Club of Toronto Vol 1: 177
Art Gallery of New South Wales Vol 2: 46
Art Niche New York Vol 1: 4652
Arthouse at the Jones Center Vol 1: 4654
Arthritis Foundation Vol 1: 4656
Arthroscopy Association of North America Vol 1: 4660
Arthur Rubinstein International Music Society Vol 2: 2892
Artisjus, Hungarian Organization for Defence of Copyright Vol 2: 2498
Artist-Blacksmith's Association of North America Vol 1: 4664
Artists and Educators Serving Young People Vol 1: 788
Artists' Fellowship Vol 1: 4667
Artists Guild of the Santa Ynez Valley Vol 1: 4670
The Artist's Magazine Vol 1: 4672
Arts and Business Vol 2: 5067
Arts and Science Center for Southeast Arkansas Vol 1: 4674
Arts Council England Vol 2: 5069
Arts Council of Ireland Vol 2: 2821
Arts Council of Northern Ireland Vol 2: 5073
Arts Council of Wales Vol 2: 4995
The Arts Guild of Old Forge Vol 1: 4676
Arts Midwest Vol 1: 4678
The ARTS of the Southern Finger Lakes Vol 1: 4680
Arvon Foundation Vol 2: 5075
The Asahi Glass Foundation Vol 2: 3161
Asamblea de Directores-Realizadores Cinematograficos y Audiovisuales Espanoles (ADIRCAE) Vol 2: 4470
Asbury Graphite Mills Vol 1: 1447
ASCAP Foundation Vol 1: 4005
Ascutney Mountain Audubon Society Vol 1: 4682
ASHBEAMS Vol 1: 5021
Asia-Pacific Association of Forestry Research Institutions Vol 2: 3394
Asia-Pacific Broadcasting Union Vol 2: 3396
Asia-Pacific Council of American Chambers of Commerce Vol 2: 3959
Asia/Pacific Cultural Centre for UNESCO Vol 2: 3163
Asian American Journalists Association Vol 1: 4684
Asian American Writers' Workshop Vol 1: 4688
Asian Association of Management Organisations Vol 2: 3400
Asian Cultural Centre for UNESCO Vol 2: 3163
Asian Football Confederation Vol 2: 3402
Asian Medical Student's Association-Philippines Vol 2: 3961
Asian/Pacific American Librarians Association Vol 1: 4690
Asian PGA Vol 1: 18943
Asian Productivity Organization Vol 2: 3165
ASM International Vol 1: 4693
ASM International Vol 1: 11820
Asociacion Argentina de Dermatologia Vol 2: 20
Asociacion Interamericana de Contabilidad Vol 1: 9990
Asociacion International de Escritores Policiacos Vol 2: 1242
Asociacion Latinoamericana de Fitopatologia Vol 2: 3953
Asociacion Mundial de las Guias Scouts Vol 2: 7357
Asociacion Mundial Veterinaria de Avicola Vol 2: 2444
Asociacion Nacional de Actores Vol 2: 3430
Asociacion Nacional de la Publicidad Vol 2: 3432
Asociacion Paleontologica Argentina Vol 2: 14
Asociacion Peruana para la Conservacion de la Naturaleza Vol 2: 3955
Asociatia Femeilor din Romania Vol 2: 4387
Aspen Filmfest Vol 1: 4712
Aspen Institute Vol 1: 4723
Aspen Technology, Inc. Vol 1: 2475
Asphalt Emulsion Manufacturer Association Vol 1: 4726
Asphalt Recycling and Reclaiming Association Vol 1: 4729
ASPRS - The Imaging and Geospatial Information Society Vol 1: 4732
Assisted Living Federation of America Vol 1: 4751
Associacao Brasileira de Embalagem Vol 2: 1126
Associacao Brasileira de Metalurgia e Materiais Vol 2: 1123
Associated Builders and Contractors Vol 1: 4753
Associated Builders and Contractors, Southeast Pennsylvania Chapter Vol 1: 4756
Associated Church Press Vol 1: 4758
Associated Colleges of the Midwest Vol 1: 4761
Associated General Contractors of Vermont Vol 1: 4763
Associated Landscape Contractors of Colorado Vol 1: 4765
Associated Medical Services Inc. Vol 1: 15760
Associated Press Managing Editors - Managing Editors Association Vol 1: 4767
Associated Taxpayers of Idaho Vol 1: 4770
Associated Writing Programs Vol 1: 4772
Associates of Brand Library and Art Center Vol 1: 4774
Association Aeronautique et Astronautique de France Vol 2: 1711
Association canadienne d'archeologie Vol 1: 6184
Association Canadienne de Cartographie Vol 1: 6382
Association canadienne de dermatologie Vol 1: 6452
Association canadienne de gerontologie Vol 1: 6253
Association Canadienne de la Construction Vol 1: 6420
L'Association Canadienne de la Maladie Coeliaque Vol 1: 6387
L'Association Canadienne de la Securite Vol 1: 6868
Association canadienne de la technologie de l'information Vol 1: 9709
Association canadienne de l'informatique Vol 1: 6576
Association Canadienne de Production de Film et de Television Vol 1: 6498
Association Canadienne de Radioprotection Vol 1: 6850
Association Canadienne De Sante Publique Vol 1: 6838
Association canadienne de science politique Vol 1: 6817
Association canadienne de soins palliatifs Vol 1: 6564
Association Canadienne de Traitement d'Images et de Reconnaissance des Formes Vol 1: 6572
Association Canadienne de Transport Industriel Vol 1: 6574
Association Canadienne d'Economique Vol 1: 6465
Association Canadienne d'Education Vol 1: 6467
Association Canadienne Des Annonceurs Vol 1: 5054
Association Canadienne des Artistes de la Scene Vol 1: 6148
Association Canadienne Des Barrages Vol 1: 6449
Association Canadienne des Educateurs en Radioffusion Vol 1: 5952
Association Canadienne des Fabricants de Produits de Quincaillerie et d'Articles Menagers Vol 1: 6547

Association Canadienne des Femmes Cadres et Entrepreneurs Vol 1: 6309
Association Canadienne des Harmonies Vol 1: 6325
Association Canadienne des Inspecteurs de Biens Immobiliers Vol 1: 6259
Association Canadienne des Journaux Vol 1: 6758
Association Canadienne des laboratories d'analyses environmentale Vol 1: 6196
Association Canadienne des Medecins Veterinaires Vol 1: 7056
Association Canadienne des Parcs et Loisirs Vol 1: 6795
Association Canadienne des Pathologistes Vol 1: 6272
Association canadienne des physiciens et physiciennes Vol 1: 6280
Association canadienne des professeures et professeurs d'universite Vol 1: 6305
L'association Canadienne des Professionnels de la Vente Vol 1: 6823
Association Canadienne des Radiodiffuseurs Vol 1: 6230
Association canadienne des radiologistes Vol 1: 6292
Association canadienne des redacteurs scientifiques Vol 1: 6864
Association canadienne des reviseurs Vol 1: 8391
Association Canadienne des Surintendants de Golf Vol 1: 6532
Association Canadienne des Technologues en Electroneurophysiologie Vol 1: 6243
Association Canadienne des Technologues en Radiation Medicale Vol 1: 6262
Association Canadienne des Therapeutes du Sport Vol 1: 6313
Association Canadienne des Veterans de la Coree Vol 1: 11163
Association Canadienne D'Histoire Ferroviaire Vol 1: 6854
Association Canadienne du Camionnage d'Entreprise Vol 1: 15241
Association Canadienne du Controle du Trafic Aerien - Section Locale 5454 des TCA Vol 1: 6175
Association Canadienne du Sport Collegial Vol 1: 6405
Association Canadienne pour la Sante Mentale Vol 1: 6711
Association Canadienne pour l'Avancement des Femmes du Sport et de l'Activite Physique Vol 1: 6215
Association Canadienne pour l'Etude du Quarternaire Vol 1: 6848
Association Cartographique Internationale Vol 2: 3572
Association catholique canadienne de la sante Vol 1: 7149
Association de la Recherche Theatrale au Canada Vol 1: 4792
Association de Musicotherapie du Canada Vol 1: 6213
L'Association des architects paysagistes du Canada Vol 1: 7007
Association des Bibliotheques de la Sante du Canada Vol 1: 6549
Association des Camps du Canada Vol 1: 6369
Association des Comites Nationaux Olympiques Vol 2: 1718
L'Association des counseillers en orientation de l'Ontario Vol 1: 14587
Association des Ecoles de Sante Publique de la Regional Europeenne Vol 2: 1720
L'Association des Forces aeriennes du Canada Vol 1: 312
Association des Infirmieres et Infirmiers du Canada Vol 1: 6768
Association des Ingenieurs-Conseils du Canada Vol 1: 5107
Association des Journalistes Automobile du Canada Vol 1: 5557
L'Association des Malentendants Canadiens Vol 1: 6541
Association des Musees Canadiens Vol 1: 6740
Association des Pharmaciens du Canada Vol 1: 6804
Association des Traducteurs et Traductrices Litteraires du Canada Vol 1: 11380
Association des universites et colleges du Canada Vol 1: 5373
L'Association du Barreau Canadien Vol 1: 6327
Association du Prix Albert Londres Vol 2: 1716
Association Europeenne d'Athletisme Vol 2: 2110
Association Europeenne de Traitement de Signaux Vol 2: 4059
Association Europeenne pour la Promotion de la Poesie Vol 2: 855
Association Europeenne Thyroide Vol 2: 1298
Association Fiscale Internationale Vol 2: 3587
Association for Aerosol Research Vol 2: 2022
Association for Asian Studies Vol 1: 4776
Association for Behavioral and Cognitive Therapies Vol 1: 4782
Association for Canadian Studies in the United States Vol 1: 4788
Association for Canadian Theatre Research Vol 1: 4792
Association for Civil Rights in Israel Vol 2: 2894
Association for Clinical Biochemists Vol 2: 5077
Association for Communication Excellence in Agriculture, Natural Resources, and Life and Human Sciences Vol 1: 4798
Association for Computer Educators Vol 1: 10051
Association for Computing Machinery Vol 1: 4804
Association for Computing Machinery Vol 1: 9806
Association for Computing Machinery - Special Interest Group on Algorithm and Computation Theory Vol 1: 4817
Association for Computing Machinery - Special Interest Group on Computer Science Education Vol 1: 4821
Association for Computing Machinery - Special Interest Group on Data Communications Vol 1: 4824
Association for Computing Machinery - Special Interest Group on Design of Communications Vol 1: 4826
Association for Computing Machinery - Special Interest Group on Hypertext, Hypermedia and the Web Vol 1: 4829
Association for Computing Machinery - Special Interest Group on Knowledge Discovery and Data Mining Vol 1: 4831
Association for Computing Machinery - Special Interest Group on Management of Data Vol 1: 4834
Association for Conservation Information Vol 1: 4837
Association for Consumer Research Vol 1: 11047
Association for Corporate Growth Vol 1: 4839
Association for Counselor Education and Supervision Vol 1: 4842
Association for Education and Rehabilitation of the Blind and Visually Impaired Vol 1: 4855
Association for Education in Journalism Vol 1: 4862
Association for Education in Journalism and Mass Communication Vol 1: 4862
Association for Educational Communications and Technology and the ECT Foundation Vol 1: 4865
Association for Evolutionary Economics Vol 1: 4880
Association for Film and Television in the Celtic Countries Vol 2: 5586
Association for Gay, Lesbian, and Bisexual Issues in Counseling Vol 1: 4882
Association for General and Liberal Studies Vol 1: 4885
Association for Geographic Information Vol 2: 5083
Association for Gerontology in Higher Education Vol 1: 4887
Association for Gravestone Studies Vol 1: 4890
Association for Healthcare Philanthropy Vol 1: 4893
Association for Heritage Interpretation Vol 2: 5087
Association for Industrial Archaeology Vol 2: 5089, 5221
Association for Investment Management and Research Vol 1: 7261
Association for Iron and Steel Technology Vol 1: 4895
Association for Library and Information Science Education Vol 1: 4905
Association for Library Collections and Technical Services Vol 1: 4909
Association for Library Service to Children Vol 1: 4917
Association for Library Trustees and Advocates Vol 1: 4933
Association for Moral Education Vol 1: 4938
Association for Preservation Technology International Vol 1: 4940
Association for Professionals in Infection Control and Epidemiology Vol 1: 4943
Association for Project Management Vol 2: 5095
Association for Promotion of Skiing Vol 2: 3888
Association for Recorded Sound Collections Vol 1: 4946
Association for Research in Ophthalmology Vol 1: 4950
Association for Research in Otolaryngology, Inc. Vol 1: 4948
Association for Research in Vision and Ophthalmology Vol 1: 4950
Association for Science Teacher Education Vol 1: 4957
Association for Social Anthropology in Oceania Vol 1: 4963

Association for Social Economics Vol 1: 4965
Association for Tertiary Education Management Vol 2: 51
Association for the Advancement of Automotive Medicine Vol 1: 4969
Association for the Advancement of Baltic Studies Vol 1: 4971
Association for the Advancement of Behavior Therapy Vol 1: 4782
Association for the Advancement of Health Education Vol 1: 907
Association for the Advancement of International Education Vol 1: 4973
Association for the Advancement of Medical Instrumentation Vol 1: 4976
Association for the Advancement of Medical Instrumentation (AAMI) Foundation Vol 1: 4983
Association for the Education of Teachers in Science Vol 1: 4957
Association for the History of Chiropractic Vol 1: 4985
Association for the Preservation of Virginia Antiquities Vol 1: 4987
Association for the Study of African American Life and History Vol 1: 2244
Association for the Study of Australian Literature Vol 2: 53
Association for the Study of Connecticut History Vol 1: 4989
Association for the Study of Obesity Vol 2: 5101
Association for Theatre in Higher Education Vol 1: 4992
Association for Women Geoscientists Vol 1: 4997
Association for Women in Communications Vol 1: 4999
Association for Women in Computing Vol 1: 5002
Association for Women in Mathematics Vol 1: 5004
Association for Women in Science Vol 1: 5007
Association for Women Veterinarians Vol 1: 5010
Association Forestiere Canadienne Vol 1: 6519
Association Francois-Xavier Bagnoud Vol 1: 9097
Association Francophone pour le Savoir Vol 1: 5013
Association in Scotland to Research Into Astronautics Vol 2: 5106
Association International du Tube Vol 2: 6313
Association International pour l'Etude de l'Economie de l'Assurance Vol 2: 4777
Association Internationale de Geodesie Vol 2: 1306
Association Internationale de Geologie de l'Ingenieur Vol 2: 3564
Association Internationale de la Couleur Vol 2: 2286
Association Internationale de la Presse Sportive Vol 2: 2509
Association Internationale de Navigation Vol 2: 923
Association Internationale de Sedimentologistes Vol 2: 901
Association Internationale de Sociologie Asociacion Internacional de Sociologia Vol 2: 4518
Association Internationale de Volcanologie et de Chimie de l'Interieur de la Terre Vol 2: 541
Association Internationale des Cordeliers Vol 2: 2845
Association Internationale des Echecs en Braille Vol 2: 4589
Association Internationale des Ecoles de Travail Social Vol 2: 6226
Association Internationale des Educateurs pour la paix Vol 1: 10198
Association Internationale des Etudes Hongroises Vol 2: 2505
Association Internationale des Experts en Philatelie Vol 2: 3059
Association Internationale des Federations di Athletisme Vol 2: 3465
Association Internationale des Instituts de Navigation Vol 2: 6825
Association Internationale des Numismates Professionnels Vol 2: 899
Association Internationale des Registres du Cancer Vol 2: 1871
Association Internationale des Sciences Hydrologiques Vol 2: 1873
Association Internationale des Technologistes de Laboratoire Medical Vol 1: 10404
Association Internationale d'Esthetique Experimentale - Associazione Internationale Di Estetica Empirica Vol 2: 2280
Association Internationale du Barreau Vol 2: 6230
Association Internationale du Film d'Animation Vol 2: 1226
Association Internationale du Film d'Animation Vol 1: 10037
Association Internationale du Theatre pour l'Enfance et la Jeunesse Vol 2: 4587
Association Internationale pour la Taxonomie Vegetale Vol 2: 787
Association Internationale pour l'Etude des Argiles Vol 2: 896
Association Internationale Pour l'Etude Scientifique de la Deficience Intellectuelle Vol 2: 6207
Association Internationale pour l'Evaluation du Rendement Scolaire Vol 2: 3566
Association mineralogique du Canada Vol 1: 11785
Association Mondial de Radios Communautarias Vol 1: 18903
Association Mondiale des Journaux Vol 2: 2013
Association Mondiale des Organisations de Recherche Industrielle et Technologique Vol 2: 3418
Association Mondiale des Radio-Amateurs et des Radioclubs Chretiens Vol 2: 7350
L'Association Motocycliste Canadienne Vol 1: 6736
Association Nationale de la Femme et du Droit Vol 1: 12712
Association of Accredited Advertising Agents Singapore Vol 2: 4414
Association of Administrative Law Judges Vol 1: 5019
Association of Air Medical Services Vol 1: 5021
Association of American Colleges and Universities Vol 1: 5027
Association of American Editorial Cartoonists Vol 1: 5029
Association of American Geographers Vol 1: 5031, 12965
Association of American Library Schools Vol 1: 4905
Association of American Medical Colleges Vol 1: 423, 5034
Association of American Publishers Vol 1: 5039
Association of American University Presses Vol 1: 5041
Association of Asphalt Paving Technologists Vol 1: 5043
Association of Austrian Librarians Vol 2: 753
Association of Behavioral Healthcare Management Vol 1: 5046
Association of Bone and Joint Surgeons Vol 1: 5048
Association of British Columbia Drama Educators Vol 1: 5050
Association of British Philatelic Societies Vol 2: 5109
Association of British Travel Agents Vol 2: 5112
Association of Building Engineers Vol 2: 5114
Association of Business Publishers Vol 1: 1426
Association of Canadian Advertisers Vol 1: 5054
Association of Canadian Archivists Vol 1: 5056
Association of Catholic Colleges and Universities Vol 1: 5060
Association of Certified Accountants Vol 2: 5118
Association of Certified Fraud Examiners Vol 1: 5063
Association of Chartered Certified Accountants - United Kingdom Vol 2: 5118
Association of Chief Police Officers of England, Wales and Northern Ireland Vol 2: 5120
Association of Children's Museums Vol 1: 5066
Association of College and Research Libraries Vol 1: 5068
Association of College and University Housing Officers International Vol 1: 5089
Association of College English Teachers of Alabama Vol 1: 5094
Association of College Unions International Vol 1: 5096
Association of Collegiate Schools of Architecture Vol 1: 2424
Association of Collegiate Schools of Architecture Vol 1: 5099
Association of Commonwealth Universities Vol 2: 5122, 5682
Association of Conservation Engineers Vol 1: 5105
Association of Consulting Engineers New Zealand Vol 2: 3695
Association of Consulting Engineers, Norway Vol 2: 3891
Association of Consulting Engineers of Australia Vol 2: 58
Association of Consulting Engineers of Canada Vol 1: 5107
Association of Consulting Foresters of America Vol 1: 5111
Association of Contingency Planners- Capital of Texas Chapter Vol 1: 5114
Association of Cooperative Educators Vol 1: 5116
Association of Cost Engineers Vol 2: 5127

Association of Cricket Umpires and Scorers Vol 2: 5132
Association of Cycle Traders Vol 2: 5136
Association of Departments of English Vol 1: 5123
Association of Development Financing Institutions in Asia and the Pacific Vol 2: 3963
Association of Directory Publishers Vol 1: 5125
Association of Earth Science Editors Vol 1: 5127
Association of Educational Publishers Vol 1: 5130
Association of Energy Engineers Vol 1: 5133
Association of Engineering Geologists Vol 1: 5135
Association of Equipment Manufacturers Vol 1: 12472
Association of European Operational Research Societies Vol 1: 10411
Association of European Toxicologists and European Societies of Toxicology Vol 2: 1271
Association of Faculties of Pharmacy of Canada Vol 1: 5940
Association of Fashion Advertising and Editorial Photographers Vol 2: 5148
Association of Field Ornithologists Vol 1: 5144
Association of Film Commissioners International Vol 1: 5146
Association of Food Journalists Vol 1: 5149
Association of Fraternity Advisors Vol 1: 5151
Association of Free Community Papers Vol 1: 5156
Association of Fundraising Professionals Vol 1: 5159
Association of Fundraising Professionals Manitoba Chapter Vol 1: 5168
Association of General Contractors of America Vol 1: 10046
Association of Gerontology India Vol 2: 2541
Association of Golf Writers Vol 2: 5138
Association of Government Accountants Vol 1: 5173
Association of Hungarian Geophysicists Vol 2: 2486
Association of Indiana Media Educators Vol 1: 5189
Association of Indians in America Vol 1: 5194
Association of Industrial Metallizers, Coaters and Laminators Vol 1: 5196
Association of Information Technology Professionals Vol 1: 5198
Association of Interior Specialists Vol 2: 5140
Association of Interpretive Naturalists Vol 1: 12345
Association of Jesuit Colleges and Universities Vol 1: 5201
Association of Jewish Center Professionals Vol 1: 5203
Association of Jewish Libraries Vol 1: 5205
Association of Late-Deafened Adults Vol 1: 5212
Association of Lunar and Planetary Observers Vol 1: 5214
Association of Management/International Association of Management Vol 1: 5216
Association of Medical Microbiology and Infectious Disease Canada Vol 1: 5218
Association of Metropolitan Planning Organizations Vol 1: 5226
Association of Microbiologists of India Vol 2: 2706
Association of Military Colleges and Schools of the United States Vol 1: 5234
Association of Military Surgeons of the United States Vol 1: 5236
Association of Municipal Recycling Coordinators Vol 1: 5263
Association of National Olympic Committees Vol 2: 1718
Association of National Park Authorities Vol 2: 5142
Association of New Jersey Environmental Commissions Vol 1: 5265
Association of North American Radio Clubs Vol 1: 5267
Association of Official Analytical Chemists Vol 1: 4549
Association of Official Seed Analysts Vol 1: 5270
Association of Oncology Social Work Vol 1: 5272
Association of Orthodox Jewish Teachers Vol 1: 5275
Association of Paediatric Anaesthetists of Great Britain and Ireland Vol 2: 5144
Association of Pediatric Oncology Nurses Vol 1: 5278
Association of Performing Arts Presenters Vol 1: 5287
Association of PeriOperative Registered Nurses Vol 1: 5290
Association of Personal Computer User Groups Vol 1: 5299
Association of Photographers Vol 2: 5148
Association of Physician Assistants in Cardiac Surgery Vol 1: 1297
The Association of Pool and Spa Professionals Vol 1: 5301
Association of Private Enterprise Education Vol 1: 5303
Association of Professional Chaplains Vol 1: 5307
Association of Professional Communication Consultants Vol 1: 5312
Association of Professional Engineers of Ontario Vol 1: 15306
Association of Professors of Higher Education Vol 1: 12313
Association of Public-Safety Communications Officials - International Vol 1: 5315
Association of Public Treasurers of the United States and Canada Vol 1: 5324
Association of Pulp and Paper Chemists and Engineers in Germany Vol 2: 2026
Association of Records Managers and Administrators Vol 1: 4624
Association of Schools of Allied Health Professions Vol 1: 5327
Association of Schools of Journalism and Mass Communication Vol 1: 5332
Association of Schools of Public Health in the European Region Vol 2: 1720
Association of Sleep Disorders Centers Vol 1: 748
Association of Small and Medium Enterprises Vol 2: 4418
Association of South African Quantity Surveyors Vol 2: 4129
Association of Southeast Asian Institutions of Higher Learning Vol 2: 3966
Association of Southern Baptist Campus Ministries Vol 1: 5334
Association of Specialized and Cooperative Library Agencies Vol 1: 5337
Association of Sports Museums and Halls of Fame Vol 1: 10243
Association of State and Provincial Psychology Boards Vol 1: 5344
Association of State and Territorial Health Officials Vol 1: 5348
Association of State and Territorial Local Liaison Officials Vol 1: 12498
Association of State Territorial and Health Officials Vol 1: 12498
Association of Steel Distributors Vol 1: 5351
Association of Surfing Professionals Vol 1: 5354
Association of Surgical Technologists Vol 1: 5356
Association of Teacher Educators Vol 1: 5358
Association of the United States Army Vol 1: 5363
Association of the Wall and Ceiling Industries - International Vol 1: 5365
Association of Third World Studies Vol 1: 5367
Association of Track and Field Statisticians Vol 2: 60
Association of Travel Marketing Executives Vol 1: 5371
Association of Universities and Colleges of Canada Vol 1: 5373
Association of University Architects Vol 1: 5376
Association of University Programs in Health Administration Vol 1: 5379
Association of Visual Language Interpreters of Canada Vol 1: 5381
Association of Women Surgeons Vol 1: 5386
Association on Handicapped Student Service Programs in Postsecondary Education Vol 1: 5390
Association on Higher Education and Disability Vol 1: 5390
Association Paul Neumann Vol 2: 1965
Association pour la microbiologie medicale et l'infectiology Canada Vol 1: 5218
Association pour l'Avancement des Sciences et des Techniques de la Documentation Vol 1: 5393
Association Psychanalytique Internationale Vol 2: 6281
Association Quebecoise des Critiques de Cinema Vol 1: 5395
Association Trends Newsweekly Vol 1: 5397
Associations des proprietaires de cinemas du Canada Vol 1: 11962
Associazione Compagnia Jazz Ballet Vol 2: 2980
Associazione Culturale Antonio Pedrotti Vol 2: 2982
Associazione Culturale Ennio Flaiano e *Oggi E Domani* Vol 2: 2984
Associazione Culturale "Rodolfo Lipizer" Vol 2: 3018
Associazione Internazionale Guido Dorso Vol 2: 2986
Associazione Italiana di Metallurgia Vol 2: 3093
Associazione Musicale di Monza Vol 2: 2988
Associazione per il Disegno Industriale Vol 2: 2990

Associazione Premio Grinzane Cavour Vol 2: 3004
ASTM International Vol 1: 5399, 17248
AstraZeneca Ltd. Vol 1: 16868
AstraZeneca Pharmaceuticals Vol 2: 5167
AstraZeneca plc Vol 2: 6981
Astrological Association of Great Britain Vol 2: 5153
Astronomical League Vol 1: 5474
Astronomical Society of Australia Vol 2: 62
Astronomical Society of New South Wales Vol 2: 68
Astronomical Society of Southern Africa Vol 2: 4131
Astronomical Society of the Pacific Vol 1: 1356, 5479
Asundi Endowment Fund Vol 2: 2673
AT&T Bell Laboratories Vol 1: 3114, 3115
L'Atelier Imaginaire Vol 2: 1722
Athenaeum International Cultural Center Vol 2: 2450
Athenaeum of Philadelphia Vol 1: 5487
Athletes in Action Vol 1: 5492
The Athletics Congress of the USA Vol 1: 18429
Atlanta Advertising Club Vol 1: 5494
Atlanta Film Festival - IMAGE Film and Video Center Vol 1: 5496
Atlanta Independent Film and Video Festival Vol 1: 5496
Atlanta Tipoff Club Vol 1: 5498
Atlantic Film Festival Association Vol 1: 5504
Atlantic Journalism Awards Vol 1: 5506
Atlantic Salmon Federation Vol 1: 5511
Atlantic Seed Association Vol 1: 5513
Atlantis Films Vol 1: 6499
Atlas Economic Research Foundation Vol 1: 5515
Atlas World Press Review Vol 1: 18994
Atomic Industrial Forum Vol 1: 14439
Attorneys Bar Association of Florida Vol 1: 5517
Audio Engineering Society Vol 1: 5519
Audiological Society of Australia Vol 2: 72
AudioVideo International Vol 1: 5525
Audubon Artists Vol 1: 5527
Audubon Naturalist Society of the Central Atlantic States Vol 1: 5529
Audubon Society of New Hampshire Vol 1: 5531
Augusta National Golf Club Vol 1: 5535
Augusta National Golf Club Vol 1: 18943
Augustan Society Vol 1: 5537
Augustinians of the Assumption Vol 1: 5539
The Austin Chronicle Vol 1: 5541
Austin Ten Drivers Club Ltd. Vol 2: 5155
Australasian Corrosion Association Vol 2: 76
Australasian Federation of Family History Organisations Vol 2: 78
Australasian Fleet Managers Association Vol 2: 80
Australasian Institute of Metals Vol 2: 483
Australasian Institute of Mining and Metallurgy Vol 2: 509
Australasian Menopause Society Vol 2: 84
Australasian Political Studies Association Vol 2: 89
Australasian Society of Clinical and Experimental Pharmacologists and Toxicologists Vol 2: 92
Australia Arts Victoria Vol 2: 682
Australia Council Vol 2: 97
Australia Council - Literature Board Vol 2: 99
Australia Council for the Arts - Visual Arts/ Craft Board Vol 2: 101
Australia Department of Veterans' Affairs Vol 2: 106
Australia-Japan Research Centre Vol 2: 298
Australian Academy of Science Vol 2: 108
Australian Academy of the Humanities Vol 2: 125
Australian Acoustical Society Vol 2: 127
Australian-American Fulbright Commission Vol 2: 129
Australian and New Zealand Association for the Advancement of Science Vol 2: 132
Australian and New Zealand Industrial and Applied Mathematics; ANZIAM - - Australian Mathematical Society Vol 2: 40
Australian and New Zealand Society of Respiratory Science Vol 2: 135
Australian Association of the Deaf Vol 2: 142
Australian Broadcasting Commission Vol 2: 695
Australian Business Limited Incorporating the State Chamber of Commerce (NSW) Vol 2: 144
Australian Chess Federation Vol 2: 149
Australian Cinematographers Society Vol 2: 153
Australian College of Educators Vol 2: 155
Australian College of Rural and Remote Medicine Vol 2: 158
Australian College of Veterinary Scientists Vol 2: 385
Australian Council for Educational Leaders Vol 2: 167
Australian Council for International Development Vol 2: 170
Australian Council of Women and Policing Vol 2: 172
Australian Direct Marketing Association Vol 2: 178
Australian Entertainment Industry Association Vol 2: 182
Australian Federation of University Women Vol 2: 184
Australian Federation of University Women - South Australia Vol 2: 184
Australian Film Institute Vol 2: 195
Australian Honours Secretariat Vol 2: 199
Australian Hotels Association (NSW) Vol 2: 226
Australian Institute of Agricultural Science and Technology Vol 2: 232
Australian Institute of Building Vol 2: 234
Australian Institute of Energy Vol 2: 238
Australian Institute of Genealogical Studies Vol 2: 240
Australian Institute of Landscape Architects Vol 2: 242
Australian Institute of Nuclear Science and Engineering Vol 2: 247
Australian Institute of Physics Vol 2: 251
Australian Institute of Physics (NSW Branch) Vol 2: 715
Australian Institute of Professional Photography Vol 2: 257
Australian Institute of Quantity Surveyors Vol 2: 264
Australian Institute of Radiography Vol 2: 266
Australian Library and Information Association Vol 2: 268
Australian Literature Society Vol 2: 53
Australian Mammal Society Vol 2: 279
Australian Maritime College Vol 2: 531
Australian Mathematical Society Vol 2: 282
Australian Military Medicine Association Vol 2: 285
Australian Mushroom Growers Association Vol 2: 288
Australian Music Centre Vol 2: 292
Australian National Sportfishing Association Vol 2: 295
Australian National University Vol 2: 297
Australian Neuroscience Society Vol 2: 299
Australian Nuclear Association Vol 2: 306
Australian Numismatic Society Vol 2: 308
Australian Optical Society Vol 2: 312
Australian Orthopaedic Association Vol 2: 317
Australian Petroleum Production and Exploration Association Vol 2: 321
Australian Psychological Society Vol 2: 326
Australian Publishers' Association Vol 2: 338
Australian Red Cross Society Vol 2: 340
Australian Science Teachers Association Vol 2: 345
Australian Secondary Principals Association Vol 2: 350
Australian Sesquicentennial Gift Trust for Awards in Oral History Vol 2: 3724
Australian Severe Weather Association Vol 2: 352
Australian Singing Competition Vol 2: 357
Australian Skeptics - NSW Branch Vol 2: 359
Australian Small Animal Veterinary Association Vol 2: 361
Australian Society for Medical Research Vol 2: 366
Australian Society for Parasitology Vol 2: 369
Australian Society of Archivists Vol 2: 372
Australian Teachers of Media Vol 2: 379
Australian Veterinary Association Vol 2: 381
Australian Water Association Vol 2: 387
Australian Widescreen Association Vol 2: 392
Australian Writers' Guild Vol 2: 394
Austria Ministry of Economic Affairs Vol 2: 755
Austrian Booksellers' and Publishers' Association Vol 2: 759
Austrian Broadcasting Corporation Vol 2: 761
Austrian Computer Society Vol 2: 763
Austrian P.E.N. Centre Vol 2: 765
Austrian Radion-Studio Carinthia Vol 2: 768
Autism Society of America Vol 1: 5546
Autodesk Canada Vol 1: 6191
Automated Imaging Association Vol 1: 5555
Automated Vision Association Vol 1: 5555
Automobile Club de l'Ouest Vol 2: 1725
Automobile Journalists Association of Canada Vol 1: 5557
Automotive Hall of Fame Vol 1: 5564
Automotive Occupant Restraints Council Vol 1: 5570
Automotive Organization Team Vol 1: 5564
Automotive Training Managers Council Vol 1: 5572
Automotive Warehouse Distributors Association Vol 1: 5574
Avanti Polar Lipids Inc. Vol 1: 3564
Aventis Foundation Vol 2: 6901
Aviation Distributors and Manufacturer Association Vol 1: 5576
Aviation Hall of Fame Vol 1: 12730

Aviation Hall of Fame and Museum of New Jersey Vol 1: 5578
Aviation Technician Education Council Vol 1: 5580
Aviation Week & Space Technology Vol 1: 5582, 8721
Avon Products, Inc. Vol 1: 5584
AVS Vol 1: 5586
Awana Clubs International Vol 1: 5601
Awards and Recognition Association Vol 1: 5605
AXA Dublin International Piano Competition Vol 2: 2824
AXA Insurance Vol 2: 2825
Aylesworth Foundation for the Advancement of Marine Science Vol 1: 8755
Ayn Rand Institute Vol 1: 5611
Ayuntamiento de Benicasim Vol 2: 4472
Azienda di Promozione Turistica di Varese Vol 2: 3086
Babson College Vol 1: 5614
Babson College - Center for Information Management Studies Vol 1: 5622
Bach Competition; International Johann Sebastian Vol 2: 2035
Bachauer International Piano Foundation; Gina Vol 1: 5625
Back Pain Association Vol 2: 5157
BackCare - The Charity for Healthier Backs Vol 2: 5157
Bactlab Systems (Pty.) Ltd. Vol 2: 4250, 4251
Badminton Association of England Vol 2: 5159
BAE Systems Vol 1: 16672
Bagnoud; Association Francois-Xavier Vol 1: 9097
Bagutta Restaurant Vol 2: 2992
Baird Corporation Vol 1: 14606
Baker and Taylor Vol 1: 1275, 15423
Baker and Taylor Company Vol 1: 8901
Baker & Taylor Co. Vol 1: 15424
Baker and Taylor Company Vol 1: 19081
Baker & Taylor Entertainment Co. Vol 1: 15419
Baker Street Irregulars Vol 1: 5627
Baldridge National Quality Program - National Institute of Standards and Technology Vol 1: 5630
Baldwin Piano and Organ Company Vol 1: 12033
Baldwin Piano Co. Vol 1: 12034
Balgarska Akademija na Naukite Vol 2: 1142
Balint Society Vol 2: 5162
Ball State University - Department of Journalism Vol 1: 5632
Ballarat University College Vol 2: 534
Ballet Makers Dance Foundation Vol 1: 7093
Balloon Federation of America Vol 1: 5643
The Banff Centre Vol 1: 5648
Banff Centre for the Arts Vol 1: 5648
Banff School of Fine Arts Vol 1: 5648
Banff World Television Festival Vol 1: 5653
Bangkok Bank Public Co. Ltd. Vol 2: 4957
Bank Marketing Association Vol 1: 38
Bank Street College Vol 1: 7339
Bank Street College of Education Vol 1: 5655
Banta Company, Inc.; George Vol 1: 18789
Baptist Communicators Association Vol 1: 5657
Baptist History and Heritage Society Vol 1: 5665
Barbados Association of Medical Practitioners Vol 2: 835
Barbados National Trust Vol 2: 837
Barbados Union of Teachers Vol 2: 839
Barbizon Vol 1: 17948
Bard; C.R. Vol 1: 4393
Barnard-Seyfert Astronomical Society Vol 1: 5669
Barnes & Noble Inc. Vol 1: 5672
Baromedical Nurses Association Vol 1: 5674
Baseball Canada Vol 1: 5676
Baseball Writers Association of America Vol 1: 5680
Baseball Writers Association of America Vol 1: 12751, 12752
BASF Aktiengesellschaft Vol 2: 2262
BASF Catalysts LLC Vol 1: 10553
Bataan Relief Organization Vol 1: 1986
Battelle Memorial Institute Vol 1: 1512
Bavarian Academy of Fine Arts Vol 2: 2037
Bavarian Academy of Sciences and Humanities Vol 2: 2042
Baxter Healthcare Vol 2: 2834
Baxter Healthcare Corp. Vol 1: 1003, 1004
Baxter International Foundation Vol 1: 16048
Bay Area Independent Publishers Association Vol 1: 5684
Bay Area Video Coalition Vol 1: 5686
Bay Chamber Concerts Vol 1: 5688
Bay Improvement Group Vol 1: 5690
Bayer Corporation Vol 1: 1083
Bayer Corporation Diagnostics Group Vol 1: 865
Bayer SA Vol 2: 4252, 4253
Bayerische Akademie der Schonen Kunste Vol 2: 2037
Bayerische Akademie der Wissenschaften Vol 2: 2042
Baytown Chamber of Commerce Vol 1: 5693
Baywood Publishing Company Vol 1: 9060
BBC Wildlife Magazine Vol 2: 6491
BC Decker Inc. Vol 1: 6550
BC Innovation Council Vol 1: 5696
BD Biosciences Vol 1: 1135
BD Diagnostic Systems Vol 1: 3764
BDA Vol 1: 5702
Bechtel Fund Vol 1: 4920
Beckton Dickinson Co. Vol 1: 4979
Becton Dickinson Consumer Products Vol 1: 1080, 1082
Before Columbus Foundation Vol 1: 5704
Belgian American Educational Foundation Vol 1: 5706
Bell Canada Vol 1: 15758
Bell Helicopter Textron Vol 1: 11512
Bell Laboratories; AT&T Vol 1: 3114, 3115
Bellarmine University Vol 1: 5708
Belleek Collectors' International Society Vol 1: 5710
Bellona Publishing House Vol 2: 3994
Benevolent and Loyal Order of Pessimists Vol 1: 5712
Benn Brothers plc Vol 2: 6519
Bennett Neuropsychiatric Research Foundation; A. E. Vol 1: 16603
Benoist Foundation; Marcel Vol 2: 4699
Benoist Stiftung; Marcel Vol 2: 4699
Bentley College - Center for Business Ethics Vol 1: 5715
Bergamo Film Meeting Vol 2: 2994
Bergen International Festival Vol 2: 3893
Berlin International Film Festival Vol 2: 2047
Bernstein; Aguda l'Haanakat Prasim Sifrutiim Al Shem Mordechai Vol 2: 2896
Bernstein Literary Prizes Association; Mordechai Vol 2: 2896
Berntsen International Inc. Vol 1: 1778
Bertelsmann Stiftung Vol 2: 2049
Best Motion Picture of the Year Vol 1: 188
Beta Alpha Psi Vol 1: 5717
Beta Beta Beta National Biological Honor Society Vol 1: 5721
Beta Gamma Sigma Vol 1: 5728
Beta Phi Mu International Library Science Honorary Society Vol 1: 2650
Bethesda Lutheran Homes and Services Vol 1: 5730
Better Business Bureau Vol 1: 5734
Better Business Bureau of Western Michigan Vol 1: 5736
Better Business Bureau Serving Upstate South Carolina Vol 1: 5738
Better Government Association Vol 1: 5740
Beverly Hills Theatre Guild Vol 1: 5743
Bibiana, International House of Art for Children Vol 2: 4437
Bibiana, Medzinarodny dom umenia pre deti Vol 2: 4437
Bibliographic Institute of Mannheim Vol 2: 2389
Bibliographical Society of Canada Vol 1: 5746
Bibliographical Society - United Kingdom Vol 2: 5164
Bienek Stiftung; Horst Vol 2: 2038
Biennales Internationales de Poesie Vol 2: 905
Big Brothers Big Sisters of America Vol 1: 5749
Big Brothers of America Vol 1: 5749
Big East Conference Vol 1: 5752
Big Muddy Film Festival Vol 1: 5755
Big Sisters International Vol 1: 5749
Bighelp for Education Vol 2: 2545
Bilingual Foundation of the Arts Vol 1: 5757
Billboard - VNU Business Publications USA Vol 1: 5759
Billiard and Bowling Institute of America Vol 1: 5762
Billiard Congress of America Vol 1: 5764
Billiard Federation of the United States of America Vol 1: 17763
Billings Preservation Society Vol 1: 5766
Bingham Memorial Fund; Worth Vol 1: 5768
Bio-Serv Inc. Vol 1: 3786
Biochemical Society - England Vol 2: 5166
Bioelectrochemical Society Vol 2: 4474
Biomedical Engineering Society Vol 1: 5770
bioMerieux Inc. Vol 1: 3765
Biometric Society Vol 1: 7622
Biophysical Society Vol 1: 5774
Biotechnology Industry Organization Vol 1: 5782
Bird Life International - United Kingdom Vol 2: 5178
Birkebeiner-Rennet Vol 2: 3897
Birkenhead Photographic Association Vol 2: 5180
Birmingham Historical Society Vol 1: 5786
Birmingham-Southern College Vol 1: 5788
BKSTS - The Moving Image Society Vol 2: 5182
Black Business and Professional Association Vol 1: 5790
Black Caucus of the American Library Association Vol 1: 5793
Black Entertainment and Sports Lawyers Association Vol 1: 5801

Black Theatre Network Vol 1: 5803
Blackwell Vol 1: 4911
Blackwell North America Inc. Vol 1: 11656
Blackwell's Book Services Vol 1: 5079
Blade Magazine Vol 1: 5805
Blekinge County Council Vol 2: 4572
Blinded Veterans Association Vol 1: 5807
Blue Ridge English as a Second Language Council Vol 1: 5812
Blue Ridge Literacy Council Vol 1: 5814
The Blues Foundation Vol 1: 5818
B'nai Brith Canada Vol 1: 5824
B'nai B'rith Hillel Foundations Vol 1: 9396
B'nai B'rith Women Vol 1: 11013
Board of Directors of City Trusts acting for the City of Philadelphia Vol 1: 5827
Boardman Tasker Charitable Trust Vol 2: 5186
Boating Industry Vol 1: 13431
Boating Writers International Vol 1: 5829
Bob und Schlittenverband fur Deutschland e.V. Vol 2: 2051
Boca Raton Historical Society Vol 1: 5831
Boehringer-Mannheim Canada Vol 1: 6988
Boeing Co. Vol 1: 16669
Boeing Defense & Space Group Vol 1: 11509
Boersenverein des Deutschen Buchhandels e.V. Vol 2: 2215
Boesendorfer GmbH; L. Vol 2: 832
Bogle Memorial Fund Vol 1: 2672
Boise Peace Quilt Project Vol 1: 5833
Boito Conservatory of Music Parma; A. Vol 2: 2996
Book of the Month Club Vol 1: 14894
Book Publishers Association of Alberta Vol 1: 5835
Book Publishers Association of Israel Vol 2: 2896
Book Trust Vol 2: 5679
Book Trust (England) Vol 2: 5188
Book Wholesalers Inc. Vol 1: 4923
Bookbuilders of Boston Vol 1: 5843
Bookbuilders West Vol 1: 5846
Booker plc Vol 2: 6418
Booklist Vol 1: 19080
Books Abroad Vol 1: 18953
Booksellers Association of the United Kingdom and Ireland Vol 2: 5192
Booksellers New Zealand Vol 2: 3699
Boone and Crockett Club Vol 1: 10211
Borden Ladner Gervais LLP Vol 1: 6645
Boris Christoff International Competition for Young Opera Singers Foundation Vol 2: 1140
Boston Association for the Education of Young Children Vol 1: 5849
Boston Athletic Association Vol 1: 5851
Boston Book Review Vol 1: 5853
Boston College - Center for Corporate Citizenship Vol 1: 5855
The Boston Globe Vol 1: 5857
Boston Municipal Research Bureau Vol 1: 5859
Boston University - Department of Athletics Vol 1: 5861
Boston University - Pike Institute on Law and Disability Vol 1: 5863
Boston University - School of Music Vol 1: 5865
Botanical Society of America Vol 1: 5867
Botanical Society of South Africa Vol 2: 4134
Botaniese Vereniging van Suid-Afrika Vol 2: 4134
Bound to Stay Bound Books, Inc. Vol 1: 4922
Bound to Stay Bound Books Inc. Vol 1: 4931
Bowling Proprietors' Association of America Vol 1: 5887
Bowling Proprietors' Association of America Vol 1: 10276
Bowling Writers Association of America Vol 1: 5891
Box Office Management International Vol 1: 10794
Boxoffice Magazine Vol 1: 5901
Boy Scouts of America Vol 1: 5904
Boys and Girls Clubs of America Vol 1: 5919
Boys Clubs of America Vol 1: 5919
BP America, Inc. Vol 1: 2472
BP Chemicals Ltd. Vol 2: 6967
BP plc Vol 2: 5179
Brain Injury Association of America Vol 1: 5925
Bralco Metal Industries Vol 2: 2648
Brandeis University Vol 1: 15721
Brandon University Vol 1: 8362
BrandWeek Magazine Vol 1: 5927
Brasserie Lipp Vol 2: 1938
The Brattle Group, Inc. Vol 1: 2021
Braun GmbH Vol 2: 2053
Braunschweig City Cultural Office Vol 2: 2055
Brazil Office of the President Vol 2: 1110
Brazilian Academy of Letters Vol 2: 1115
Brazilian Agricultural Research Corporation Vol 2: 1121
Brazilian-American Chamber of Commerce Vol 1: 5931
Brazilian Chamber of Commerce in Great Britain Vol 2: 5195
Brazilian Metallurgy and Materials Association Vol 2: 1123
Brazilian Packaging Association Vol 2: 1126
Brechner Center for Freedom of Information; Joseph L. Vol 1: 5933
Brick Development Association Vol 2: 5197
Bridge Publications Inc. Vol 1: 5935
Bridge School Foundation Vol 1: 10637
Bridport Arts Centre Vol 2: 5199
Brigham College of Fine Arts and Communications - Barlow Endowment for Music Composition Vol 1: 5937
Brigitte Vol 2: 2057
Brisbane Warana Festival Ltd. Vol 2: 396
Brisbane Writers Festival Vol 2: 396
Bristol-Myers Squibb Vol 1: 3166
Bristol-Myers Squibb Canada Co. Vol 1: 5939
Bristol Myers Squibb Canada Co. Vol 1: 6903
Bristol-Myers Squibb Oncology Vol 1: 14535
British Academy Vol 2: 5201
British Academy of Composers and Songwriters Vol 2: 5212
British Academy of Film and Television Arts Vol 2: 5216
British Archaeological Awards Vol 2: 5219
British Association for Applied Linguistics Vol 2: 5232
British Association of Aviation Consultants Vol 2: 5235
British Association of Barbershop Singers Vol 2: 5237
British Association of Communicators in Business Vol 2: 5239
British Association of Dermatologists Vol 2: 5242
British Association of Industrial Editors Vol 2: 5239
British Association of Landscape Industries Vol 2: 5244
British Association of Rheumatology and Rehabilitation Vol 2: 5488
British Astronomical Association Vol 2: 5246
British Blood Transfusion Society Vol 2: 5251
British Broadcasting Corp. Vol 2: 5255
British Broadcasting Corporation and Welsh National Opera Vol 2: 5257
British Canoe Union Vol 2: 5259
British Cartographic Society Vol 2: 5263
British Cave Research Association Vol 2: 5270
British Centre for Literary Translation Vol 2: 5283
British Chess Federation Vol 2: 5276
British Christmas Tree Growers Association Vol 2: 5280
British Columbia Historical Federation Vol 1: 5943
British Columbia Psychological Association Vol 1: 5945
British Comparative Literature Association Vol 2: 5282
British Computer Society Vol 2: 5284
British Culinary Federation Vol 2: 5286
British Deaf Association Vol 2: 5288
British Design and Art Direction Vol 2: 5290
British Direct Marketing Association Vol 2: 5737
British Ecological Society Vol 2: 5292
British Endodontic Society Vol 2: 5300
British Federation of Film Societies Vol 2: 5305
British Film Institute Vol 2: 5306, 5307
British Geotechnical Association Vol 2: 5310
British Grassland Society Vol 2: 5312
British Guild of Travel Writers Vol 2: 5314
British Gypsom Vol 2: 5891
British Industrial and Scientific Association Vol 2: 6327
British Infection Society Vol 2: 5316
British Institute of Architectural Technicians Vol 2: 5318
British Institute of Architectural Technologists Vol 2: 5318
British Institute of Non-Destructive Testing Vol 2: 5322
British Institute of Radiology Vol 2: 5328
British International Freight Association Vol 2: 5335
British Interplanetary Society Vol 2: 5337
British Italian Society Vol 2: 7131
British Lichen Society Vol 2: 5339
British Llama and Alpaca Association Vol 2: 5341
British Long Distance Swimming Association Vol 2: 5344
British Medical Association Vol 2: 5353
British Mexican Society Vol 2: 5375
British Microcirculation Society Vol 2: 5377
British Music Society Vol 2: 5381
British Mycological Society Vol 2: 5383
British Nuclear Energy Society Vol 2: 5388
British Numismatic Society Vol 2: 5391
British Occupational Hygiene Society Vol 2: 5393
British Origami Society Vol 2: 5399
British Ornithologists' Union Vol 2: 5401
British Orthodontic Society Vol 2: 5404, 5407

British Orthopaedic Foot and Ankle Society Vol 2: 5411
British Paper and Board Industry Federation Vol 2: 6518
British Paper and Board Makers' Association Vol 2: 6518
British Petroleum Vol 2: 6483, 6988
British Phonographic Industry Vol 2: 5415
British Players Vol 1: 5948
British Printing Industries Federation Vol 2: 5418
British Psychological Society Vol 2: 5424
British Puppet and Model Theatre Guild Vol 2: 5431
The British School at Rome Vol 2: 5433
British Science Fiction Association Vol 2: 5452
British Security Industry Association Vol 2: 5454
British Show Pony Society Vol 2: 5457
British Slot Car Racing Association Vol 2: 5462
British Small Animal Veterinary Association Vol 2: 5464
British Society for Antimicrobial Chemotherapy Vol 2: 5474
British Society for Cell Biology Vol 1: 3595
British Society for Haematology Vol 2: 5476
British Society for Middle Eastern Studies Vol 2: 5481
British Society for Research on Ageing Vol 2: 5486
British Society for Rheumatology Vol 2: 5488
British Society for the History of Science Vol 2: 5491
British Society for the Study of Prosthetic Dentistry Vol 2: 5495
British Society of Animal Production Vol 2: 5500
British Society of Animal Science Vol 2: 5500
British Society of Cinematographers Vol 2: 5502
British Society of Flavourists Vol 2: 5506
British Society of Magazine Editors Vol 2: 5510
British Society of Periodontology Vol 2: 5516
British Society of Rehabilitation Medicine Vol 2: 5522
British Society of Rheology Vol 2: 5526
British Society of Scientific Glassblowers Vol 2: 5530
British Sound Recording Association Vol 2: 5537
British Thematic Association Vol 2: 5539
British Transplantation Society Vol 2: 5541
British Trust for Ornithology Vol 2: 5547
British Turf and Landscape Irrigation Association Vol 2: 5550
British Union for the Abolition of Vivisection Vol 2: 6361
British Universities Film and Video Council Vol 2: 5554
British Vacuum Council Vol 2: 5556
British Vehicle Rental and Leasing Association Vol 2: 5561
British Veterinary Association Vol 2: 5563
British Wrestling Association Vol 2: 5565
Britten-Pears Foundation Vol 2: 5567
Broadcast Cable Financial Management Association Vol 1: 5950
Broadcast Education Association Vol 1: 12427
Broadcast Educators Association of Canada Vol 1: 5952
Broadcast Financial Management Association Vol 1: 5950
Broadcast Music, Inc. Vol 1: 5956
Broadcast Promotion and Marketing Executives Vol 1: 15380
Broadcasters Promotion Association Vol 1: 15380
Brodart Vol 1: 6702
Bronfman Family Foundation; Samuel and Saidye Vol 1: 5958
Brookdale Center on Aging Vol 1: 4266
Brookhaven Women in Science Vol 1: 5960
Broome County Farm Bureau Vol 1: 5962
Bross Foundation Vol 1: 5964
Brotherhood of the Knights of the Vine Vol 1: 5966
Brotherhood of Working Farriers Association Vol 1: 5968
Brown Alumni Association Vol 1: 5970
Brown Foundation; James Barrett Vol 1: 1256
Brown; James Vol 1: 13231
Brown University - Division of Biology and Medicine Vol 1: 5974
Bruner Foundation Vol 1: 5976
Brussels International Festival of Fantastic Film Vol 2: 849
Buchhandlung Ziemann & Ziemann, Buxtehude Vol 2: 2384
Buckeye Children's Book Award Council Vol 1: 5978
Bucks County Historical Society Vol 1: 5980
Budapest City Council Vol 2: 2493
Buddle Findlay New Zealand Lawyers Vol 2: 3702
Buddle Findlay/Sargeson Trust Vol 2: 3701
Budget Rent a Car Vol 1: 11193
Buffalo Audubon Society Vol 1: 5982
Builder Vol 1: 5984
Building Officials and Code Administrators International Vol 1: 5986
Building Owners and Managers Association International Vol 1: 5988
Building Stone Institute Vol 1: 6004
Bulgarian Academy of Sciences Vol 2: 1142
Bulgarian National Front Vol 1: 6006
Bulgarian National Television Vol 2: 1145
Bulgarian Orienteering Federation Vol 2: 1148
Bulgarian Red Cross Vol 2: 1150
Bulgarian Television and Radio Vol 2: 1145
Bulgarska Natcionalna Televiziya Vol 2: 1145
Bund der Steuerzahler Europa Vol 2: 2422
Bundesarztekammer Vol 2: 2195
Bundesvereinigung Deutscher Apothekerverbande Vol 2: 2059
Bureau de Controle Technique pour la Construction Vol 2: 1088
Bureau de la Coordination des Affaires Humanitaires Vol 2: 4871
Bureau International de la Paix Vol 2: 4825
Bureau International du Beton Manufacture Vol 2: 907
Bureau International pour l'Epilepsie Vol 2: 2842
Bureau of Security Control of Construction Vol 2: 1088
Burnett Fund; Carol Vol 1: 18286
Burns and Roe, Inc. Vol 1: 3671
Burroughs Bibliophiles Vol 1: 6008
Bush Artist Fellows Program - Bush Foundation Vol 1: 6011
Business Archives Council Vol 2: 5569
Business Committee for the Arts Vol 1: 6013
Business Forms Management Association Vol 1: 6017
Business Forum on Aging Vol 1: 4267
Business History Conference Vol 1: 6021
Business Marketing Association Vol 1: 6023
Business News Publishing Co. Vol 1: 13756
Business Press Editors; American Society of Vol 1: 3897
Business/Professional Advertising Association Vol 1: 6023
Business Roundtable Vol 1: 8554
Business Volunteers for the Arts/ Washington Vol 1: 6026
Business Week Vol 1: 9689
Businesswomen's Association Vol 2: 4145
Busoni International Piano Competition Foundation Vol 2: 2998
C. F. Peters Corp. Vol 1: 16026
Cabletelevision Advertising Bureau Vol 1: 6028
Cafe des Deux Magots Vol 2: 1727
Caisse de depot et placement du Quebec Vol 1: 5017
Cajal Club Vol 1: 6032
Caledonian Research Foundation Vol 2: 6992
Calendar Marketing Association Vol 1: 6035
Calgary Apartment Association Vol 1: 6037
California Academy of Sciences Vol 1: 6044
California Association of Teachers of English Vol 1: 6053
California Avocado Society Vol 1: 6046
California Federation of Mineralogical Societies Vol 1: 6048
California Healthcare Institute Vol 1: 6050
California Library Association Vol 1: 6053
California National Watercolor Society Vol 1: 13891
California Notary Association Vol 1: 13478
California Reading Association Vol 1: 6052
California School Library Association Vol 1: 6053
California School Library Association Vol 1: 6054
California Science Teachers Association Vol 1: 6056
California Sea Grant Vol 1: 6059
California Society of Anesthesiologists Vol 1: 6062
California State Beekeepers Association Vol 1: 6064
California Walnut Commission Vol 1: 6068
Call Centre Association Vol 2: 5571
Callerlab - International Association of Square Dance Callers Vol 1: 6070
Calouste Gulbenkian Foundation Vol 2: 5573
Camanachd Association Vol 2: 5575
Camara de Comercio Guatemalteco-Americana Vol 2: 2484
Camara Municipal de Lisboa Vol 2: 4069
Cambridge Center for Behavioral Studies Vol 1: 6072
Cambridge Philosophical Society Vol 2: 5578
Camerata Musicale Barese Vol 2: 3000
Camif Group Vol 2: 1936
Camp Fire Vol 1: 6074
Camp Fire USA Vol 1: 6074
Camp Fire USA, Minnesota Council Vol 1: 6077

Campaign for the Protection of Rural Wales Vol 2: 5580
Campiello Foundation Vol 2: 3002
Canada Chancellery of Honors Vol 1: 6079
Canada Council for the Arts Vol 1: 5959, 6098
Canada Safety Council Vol 1: 6125
Canada's Aviation Hall of Fame Vol 1: 6127
Canada's National Ballet School - National Ballet School Foundation Vol 1: 6129
Canada's National History Society Vol 1: 6133
Canada's Research-Based Pharmaceutical Companies Vol 1: 6136
Canada's Sports Hall of Fame Vol 1: 6138
Canadian Academy of Recording Arts and Sciences Vol 1: 6140
Canadian Acoustical Association Vol 1: 6142
Canadian Actors' Equity Association Vol 1: 6148
Canadian Adult Recreational Hockey Association Vol 1: 6151
Canadian Advanced Technology Alliance Vol 1: 6158
Canadian Aeronautics and Space Institute Vol 1: 6167
Canadian Air Traffic Control Association-CAW Local 5454 Vol 1: 6175
Canadian Alarm and Security Association Vol 1: 6868
Canadian Anesthesiologists' Society Vol 1: 6178
Canadian Animal Health Institute Vol 1: 6182
Canadian Archaeological Association Vol 1: 6184
Canadian Architect Vol 1: 6189
Canadian Association for Enterostomal Therapy Vol 1: 6192
Canadian Association for Environmental Analytical Laboratories Vol 1: 6196
Canadian Association for Health, Physical Education, Recreation and Dance Vol 1: 6198
Canadian Association for Laboratory Animal Science Vol 1: 6202
Canadian Association for Music Therapy Vol 1: 6213
Canadian Association for the Advancement of Women and Sport and Physical Activity Vol 1: 6215
Canadian Association of Aquarium Clubs Vol 1: 6219
Canadian Association of Black Journalists Vol 1: 6226
Canadian Association of Broadcasters Vol 1: 6230
Canadian Association of Career Educators and Employers Vol 1: 6237
Canadian Association of Electroneurophysiology Technologists Vol 1: 6243
Canadian Association of Geographers Vol 1: 6247
Canadian Association of Gerontology Vol 1: 6253
Canadian Association of Home and Property Inspectors Vol 1: 6259
Canadian Association of Home Inspectors Vol 1: 6259
Canadian Association of Medical Radiation Technologists Vol 1: 6262
Canadian Association of Oilwell Drilling Contractors Vol 1: 6270
Canadian Association of Pathologists Vol 1: 6272
Canadian Association of Physical Medicine and Rehabilitation Vol 1: 6274
Canadian Association of Physicists Vol 1: 6280
Canadian Association of Principals Vol 1: 6287
Canadian Association of Radiologists Vol 1: 6292
Canadian Association of Special Libraries and Information Services Vol 1: 6299
Canadian Association of University Business Officers Vol 1: 6301
Canadian Association of University Teachers Vol 1: 6305
Canadian Association of Women Executives and Entrepreneurs Vol 1: 6309
Canadian Astronomical Society Vol 1: 15739
Canadian Athletic Therapists Association Vol 1: 6313
Canadian Authors Association Vol 1: 6319
Canadian Band Association Vol 1: 6325
Canadian Bar Association Vol 1: 6327
Canadian Booksellers Association Vol 1: 6343
Canadian Broadcasting Corp. Vol 1: 6360
Canadian Brown Swiss and Braunvieh Association Vol 1: 6364
Canadian Business Press Vol 1: 6367
Canadian Camping Association Vol 1: 6369
Canadian Cardiovascular Society Vol 1: 6374
Canadian Cartographic Association Vol 1: 6382
Canadian Celiac Association Vol 1: 6387
Canadian Centre for Ecumenism Vol 1: 6390
Canadian Children's Book Centre Vol 1: 6392
Canadian Co-Operative Wool Growers Vol 1: 6396
Canadian College of Teachers Vol 1: 6399
Canadian Colleges Athletic Association Vol 1: 6405
Canadian Committee on Women's History Vol 1: 6561
Canadian Community Newspapers Association Vol 1: 6415
Canadian Conference of the Arts Vol 1: 6417
Canadian Construction Association Vol 1: 6420
Canadian Council of Christians and Jews Vol 1: 6427
Canadian Council of Land Surveyors Vol 1: 6429
Canadian Council of Professional Engineers Vol 1: 6431
Canadian Council of Technicians and Technologists Vol 1: 6440
Canadian Council on International Law Vol 1: 6442
Canadian Country Music Association Vol 1: 6444
Canadian Culinary Federation Vol 1: 6446
Canadian Daily Newspaper Publishers Association Vol 1: 6758
Canadian Dam Association Vol 1: 6449
Canadian Dermatology Association Vol 1: 6452
Canadian Down Syndrome Society Vol 1: 6459
Canadian Economics Association Vol 1: 6465
Canadian Education Association Vol 1: 6467
Canadian Environmental Network Vol 1: 6469
Canadian Federation for the Humanities and Social Sciences Vol 1: 6471
Canadian Federation of Amateur Baseball Vol 1: 6473
Canadian Federation of Biological Societies Vol 1: 6476
Canadian Federation of Chefs and Cooks Vol 1: 6446
Canadian Federation of Humane Societies Vol 1: 6480
Canadian Federation of University Women Vol 1: 6483
Canadian Fertility and Andrology Society Vol 1: 6492
Canadian Film and Television Association Vol 1: 6498
Canadian Film and Television Production Association Vol 1: 6498
Canadian Football Council Vol 1: 6501
Canadian Football League Vol 1: 6501
Canadian Forestry Association Vol 1: 6519
Canadian Foundation for Ileitis and Colitis Vol 1: 7968
Canadian Geotechnical Society Vol 1: 6521
Canadian Golf Superintendents Association Vol 1: 6532
Canadian Gospel Music Association Vol 1: 6539
Canadian Hard of Hearing Association Vol 1: 6541
Canadian Hardware and Housewares Manufacturers Association Vol 1: 6547
Canadian Health Libraries Association Vol 1: 6549
Canadian Historical Association Vol 1: 2230, 6555
Canadian HIV/AIDS Legal Network Vol 1: 6562
Canadian Hospice Palliative Care Association Vol 1: 6564
Canadian Human-Computer Communications Society Vol 1: 6568
Canadian Image Processing and Pattern Recognition Society Vol 1: 6572
Canadian Industrial Transportation Association Vol 1: 6574
Canadian Information Processing Society Vol 1: 6576
Canadian Institute for the Administration of Justice Vol 1: 6583
Canadian Institute of Energy Vol 1: 6585
Canadian Institute of Food Science and Technology Vol 1: 6588
Canadian Institute of Forestry Vol 1: 6596
Canadian Institute of Mining, Metallurgy, and Petroleum Vol 1: 6607
Canadian Institute of Public Health Inspectors Vol 1: 13118
Canadian Institute of Surveying Vol 2: 4974
Canadian Institute of Traffic and Transportation Vol 1: 6633
Canadian International Amateur Film Festival Vol 1: 6640
Canadian International Annual Film/Video Festival Vol 1: 6640
Canadian Interuniversity Sport Vol 1: 6642
Canadian Intravenous Nurses Association Vol 1: 6679
Canadian Journalists for Free Expression Vol 1: 6684
Canadian Legal Conference Vol 1: 6336

Canadian Library Association Vol 1: 6687
Canadian Library Association - Canadian Association for School Libraries Vol 1: 6695
Canadian Library Association - Canadian Association of Children's Librarians Vol 1: 6698
Canadian Library Association - Canadian Association of Public Libraries Vol 1: 6701
Canadian Library Trustees' Association Vol 1: 6703
Canadian Liver Foundation Vol 1: 6706
Canadian Mental Health Association Vol 1: 6711
Canadian Mental Health Association - Alberta Division Vol 1: 6718
Canadian Meteorological and Oceanographic Society Vol 1: 6725
Canadian Mineral Analysts Vol 1: 6734
Canadian Motorcycle Association Vol 1: 6736
Canadian Museum of Civilization Vol 1: 5959
Canadian Museums Association Vol 1: 6740
Canadian Music Competition Vol 1: 6742
Canadian National Institute for the Blind Vol 1: 6744
Canadian Nautical Research Society Vol 1: 6753
Canadian Newspaper Association Vol 1: 6758
Canadian Nuclear Society Vol 1: 6760
Canadian Nurses Association Vol 1: 6768
Canadian Nurses Foundation Vol 1: 6771
Canadian Occupational Therapy Foundation Vol 1: 6773
Canadian Organization of Medical Physicists Vol 1: 6282
Canadian Ornamental Plant Foundation Vol 1: 6779
Canadian Orthopaedic Foundation Vol 1: 6781
Canadian Paediatric Society Vol 1: 6786
Canadian Pain Society Vol 1: 6789
Canadian Parks and Recreation Association Vol 1: 6795
Canadian Parks and Wilderness Society Vol 1: 6802
Canadian Pharmacists Association Vol 1: 6804
Canadian Physiotherapy Cardio-respiratory Society Vol 1: 6806
Canadian Phytopathological Society Vol 1: 6811
Canadian Political Science Association Vol 1: 6817
Canadian Professional Sales Association Vol 1: 6823
Canadian Psychoanalytic Society Vol 1: 6825
Canadian Psychological Association Vol 1: 6829
Canadian Public Health Association Vol 1: 6838
Canadian Public Relations Society Vol 1: 6843
Canadian Quaternary Association Vol 1: 6848
Canadian Radiation Protection Association Vol 1: 6850
Canadian Railroad Historical Association Vol 1: 6854
Canadian Research Institute for the Advancement of Women Vol 1: 6859
Canadian Science Writers' Association Vol 1: 6864
Canadian Security Association Vol 1: 6868
Canadian Ski Council Vol 1: 6870
Canadian Society for Analytical Sciences and Spectroscopy Vol 1: 6873
Canadian Society for Bioengineering Vol 1: 6878
Canadian Society for Brain, Behaviour and Cognitive Science Vol 1: 6886
Canadian Society for Chemical Engineering Vol 1: 6891, 6955
Canadian Society for Chemistry Vol 1: 6897
Canadian Society for Civil Engineering Vol 1: 6911
Canadian Society for Clinical Investigation Vol 1: 6923
Canadian Society for Clinical Pharmacology Vol 1: 6928
Canadian Society for Immunology Vol 1: 6938
Canadian Society for Industrial Security Vol 1: 6942
Canadian Society for International Health Vol 1: 6946
Canadian Society for Mechanical Engineering Vol 1: 6948
Canadian Society for Medical Laboratory Science Vol 1: 6956
Canadian Society for Nutritional Sciences Vol 1: 6959
Canadian Society for the Study of Education Vol 1: 6961
Canadian Society for the Study of Higher Education Vol 1: 6966
Canadian Society of Animal Science - Agricultural Institute of Canada Vol 1: 6971
Canadian Society of Association Executives Vol 1: 6978
Canadian Society of Biblical Studies Vol 1: 6982
Canadian Society of Biochemistry, Molecular and Cellular Biology Vol 1: 6987
Canadian Society of Diagnostic Medical Sonographers Vol 1: 6989
Canadian Society of Hospital Pharmacists Vol 1: 6992
Canadian Society of Internal Medicine Vol 1: 7000
Canadian Society of Landscape Architects Vol 1: 7007
Canadian Society of Microbiologists Vol 1: 7009
Canadian Society of Petroleum Geologists Vol 1: 7012
Canadian Society of Sugar Artistry Vol 1: 7025
Canadian Society of Zoologists Vol 1: 7027
Canadian Sociology and Anthropology Association Vol 1: 7037
Canadian Sport Council Vol 1: 17146
Canadian Sport Parachuting Association Vol 1: 7041
Canadian Standards Association Vol 1: 17249
Canadian Toy Testing Council Vol 1: 7043
Canadian Trakehner Horse Society Vol 1: 7047
Canadian University Music Society Vol 1: 7054
Canadian Veterinary Medical Association Vol 1: 7056
Canadian Weekly Newspapers Association Vol 1: 6415
Canadian Wildlife Federation Vol 1: 7063
Canadian Wood Council Vol 1: 7070
Canarias Mediafest - International Canary Islands Video and Multimedia Festival Vol 2: 4476
CANARIE Vol 1: 7072
Cancer Care Ontario Vol 1: 7074
Cancer Hope Network Vol 1: 7076
Cancer Research & Prevention Foundation Vol 1: 7078
Cancer Research Foundation Vol 1: 7080
Cancer Research Institute, Inc. Vol 1: 7083
Cancer Research U.K. Beatson Laboratories Vol 2: 5582
Cannes International Film Festival Vol 2: 1729
Canola Council of Canada Vol 1: 7087
Canon Law Society of America Vol 1: 7089
Canon USA Inc. Vol 1: 15249
Canterbury Historical Association Vol 2: 3703
Cape Cod Art Association Vol 1: 7091
Cape Tercentenary Foundation Vol 2: 4149
Capezio/Ballet Makers Dance Foundation Vol 1: 7093
Capezio Foundation Vol 1: 7094
Capote Literary Trust; Truman Vol 1: 10871
Car and Driver Vol 1: 7095
Cardiac Society of Australia and New Zealand Vol 2: 398
Cardinal Health Vol 1: 888, 13716
Career College Association Vol 1: 7097
Career Communications Group Vol 1: 7099
Cargill Animal Nutrition Vol 1: 1873
Cargill Inc. Vol 1: 2966, 10082
Caribbean Association of Home Economists Vol 2: 841
Caribbean Conservation Corporation and Sea Turtle Survival League Vol 1: 7102
Caribbean Culinary Federation Vol 1: 7105
Caribbean Hotel Association Vol 1: 7104
Caribbean Hotel Council of the Caribbean Travel Association Vol 1: 7104
Caribbean Studies Association Vol 1: 7106
Carina Ari Foundation Vol 2: 4574
Carina Ari Stiftelsen Vol 2: 4574
The Caring Institute Vol 1: 7108
Caritas of Austin Vol 1: 7110
Carmel Music Society Vol 1: 7112
Carnegie Corporation of New York Vol 1: 4925
Carnegie Foundation Vol 2: 3487
Carnegie Hero Fund Commission Vol 1: 7114
Carnegie Mellon University - Software Engineering Institute Vol 1: 7116
Carnegie Museum of Art Vol 1: 7118
Carnegie Stichting Vol 2: 3487
Carolina Biological Supply Company Vol 1: 4960, 4962
Carolinas Roofing and Sheet Metal Contractors Association Vol 1: 7120
Carroll Center for the Blind Vol 1: 7122
Cartier Vol 2: 5706
Cartoonists Northwest Vol 1: 7124
CASA Association; National Vol 1: 13057
Case Western Reserve University - Physics Dept. Vol 1: 7126
Casualty Actuarial Society Vol 1: 7128
Catalyst Vol 1: 7134
Catboat Association Vol 1: 7136
Catering Equipment Distributors Association of Great Britain Vol 2: 5584
Catholic Academy for Communication Arts Professionals Vol 1: 7140
Catholic Book Club Vol 1: 7142

Catholic Broadcasting Association Vol 1: 7140
Catholic Campus Ministry Association Vol 1: 7144
Catholic Church Extension Society of the U.S.A. Vol 1: 7147
Catholic Health Association of Canada Vol 1: 7149
Catholic Hospital Association of Canada Vol 1: 7149
Catholic Kolping Society of America Vol 1: 7151
Catholic League for Religious and Civil Rights Vol 1: 7153
Catholic Library Association Vol 1: 7155
Catholic Press Association Vol 1: 7163
Catholic Theological Society of America Vol 1: 7166
Catholic University of America - Office of Alumni Relations Vol 1: 7168
Catholic War Veterans of the United States of America Vol 1: 7175
Catskill Center for Photography Vol 1: 7233
Caucus for Television Producers, Writers and Directors Vol 1: 7177
Cavour Prize Association; Grinzane Vol 2: 3004
CBS Vol 1: 14960
CDS International Vol 1: 7181
Ceilings and Interior Systems Construction Association Vol 1: 7183
Ceilings and Interior Systems Contractors Association Vol 1: 7183
Celtic Film and Television Festival Vol 2: 5586
Cement and Concrete Association of New Zealand Vol 2: 3733
Centennial Education Foundation Vol 1: 7185
Center for Advanced Study in the Behavioral Sciences Vol 1: 7187
Center for Afroamerican and African Studies Vol 1: 7189
The Center for American and International Law Vol 1: 7191
Center for Architecture Foundation Vol 1: 2441, 2443
Center for Book Arts Vol 1: 7194
Center for Chinese Studies Vol 2: 4949
Center for Christian/Jewish Understanding of Sacred Heart University Vol 1: 7196
Center for Communication Vol 1: 7198
Center for Contemporary Opera Vol 1: 7200
Center for Creative Leadership Vol 1: 7202
Center for Democratic Policy Vol 1: 7227
Center for Design of Analog-Digital Integrated Circuits Vol 1: 7205
Center for Health Law and Policy - Southern Illinois University School of Law Vol 1: 7207
Center for Human-Computer Communication - OGI School of Science and Engineering Vol 1: 7209
Center for Immigration Studies Vol 1: 7211
Center for International Studies Vol 1: 7213
Center for Latin America and Caribbean Studies Vol 1: 7215
Center for Lesbian and Gay Studies Vol 1: 7217
Center for Meteorite Studies Vol 1: 7225
Center for National Policy Vol 1: 7227
Center for Nonprofit Management Vol 1: 7229
Center for Philosophy, Law, Citizenship Vol 1: 7231
Center for Photography at Woodstock Vol 1: 7233
Center for Population Options (California) Vol 1: 11638
Center for Public Resources - CPR Legal Program Vol 1: 7937
Center for Public Safety Vol 1: 10168
Center for the Study of Canada Vol 1: 7235
Center for the Study of Science Fiction Vol 1: 7237
Center for the Study of Sport in Society Vol 1: 7240
Center for the Study of the Presidency Vol 1: 7243
Centers for Disease Control and Prevention Vol 1: 12498
Centracare Health Foundation Vol 1: 7245
Central Association of Obstetricians and Gynecologists Vol 1: 7247
Central Chancery of the Orders of Knighthood Vol 2: 5588
Central Institute for Labour Protection - National Research Institute Vol 2: 3996
Central Missouri State University Vol 1: 18248
Central New York Regional Planning and Development Board Vol 1: 7250
Central Pennsylvania Festival of the Arts Vol 1: 7252
Central Pennsylvania Paralegal Association Vol 1: 7257
Centre Canadien d'Oecumenisme Vol 1: 6390
Centre de Cooperation pour les Recherches Scientifiques Relatives au Tabac Vol 2: 1751
Centre de Recherches Mathematiques Vol 1: 6286
Centre de recherches mathematiques, Universite de Montreal Vol 1: 11616
Centre de Recherches sur l'histoire, l'art et la Culture Islamiques Vol 2: 4985
Centre du Cinema Grec Vol 2: 2472
Centre du riz pour l'Afrique de l'Ouest Vol 2: 1214
Centre for Latin American Monetary Studies Vol 2: 3434
Centre International de Criminologie Comparee Vol 1: 10297
Centre International de Recherche sur le Cancer - International Mondiale de la Sante Vol 2: 4931
Centre National de la Cinematographie Vol 2: 1792
Centre National de la Recherche Scientifique Vol 2: 1825
Centre of Films for Children and Young People in Germany Vol 2: 2062
Centro de Estudios Monetarios Latinoamericanos Vol 2: 3434
Centro di Cultural Scientifica "Alessandro Volta" Vol 2: 3006
Centro Gerontologico Latino Vol 1: 11243
Centro Regional de Sismologia para America del Sur Vol 2: 3957
Centro Studi Nuovo Mezzogiorno Vol 2: 2986
Centrum Vol 1: 6960
Century Productions Vol 1: 8710
Ceramic Society of Japan Vol 2: 3168
Certamen Internacional de Cine para la Infancia y la Juventud de Gijon Vol 2: 4498
Certamen Internacional de Films Cortos, Ciudad de Huesca Vol 2: 4494
Ceska Spolecnost Chemicka Vol 2: 1248
Cesky Rozhlas, Praga Vol 2: 1253
Cetacean Society International Vol 1: 7259
Ceylon Development Engineering Company, Ltd. Vol 2: 4556
CFA Institute Vol 1: 7261
Chain Link Fence Manufacturer Institute Vol 1: 7271
Chaine d'approvisionement et logistique Canada Vol 1: 17333
Challenger Society Vol 2: 5610
Challenger Society for Marine Science Vol 2: 5610
Chamber Music America Vol 1: 3999
Chamber Music America Vol 1: 7273
Chamber Music Society of Lincoln Center Vol 1: 7277
Chamber Music Yellow Springs Vol 1: 7279
Chamber of Commerce of Harrison County Vol 1: 7281
Champagne d'Argent Federation Vol 1: 3458
Champlin Refining and Chemicals, Inc. Vol 1: 9761
Chancery of Netherlands Orders Vol 2: 3489
Channel Four Television Vol 2: 5222
Chapin Foundation; Harry Vol 1: 18946
Charcot-Marie-Tooth Association Vol 1: 7283
Charles A. and Anne Morrow Lindbergh Foundation Vol 1: 7285
Charles S. Peirce Society Vol 1: 7287
Charlotte Touchdown Club Vol 1: 8798
Charta 77 Foundation Vol 2: 4576
Chartered Institute of Arbitrators Vol 2: 5613
Chartered Institute of Building Vol 2: 5615
Chartered Institute of Environmental Health Vol 1: 13118
Chartered Institute of Journalists Vol 2: 5617
Chartered Institute of Library and Information Professionals Vol 2: 5619
Chartered Institute of Logistics and Transport Vol 2: 5621
Chartered Institute of Logistics and Transport in Australia Vol 2: 401
Chartered Institute of Management Accountants - Hong Kong Division Vol 2: 3924
Chartered Institute of Purchasing and Supply Vol 2: 5630
Chartered Institution of Building Services Engineers - England Vol 2: 5633
Chartered Institution of Water and Environmental Management Vol 2: 5641
Chartered Insurance Institute Vol 2: 5647
Chartered Society of Designers Vol 2: 5651
Chattahoochee Valley Art Museum Vol 1: 7289
Chautauqua Center for the Visual Arts - Chautauqua Institution Vol 1: 7292
Chelsea Vol 1: 7294
Chemical Engineering - Access Intelligence Vol 1: 7296
Chemical Industry Institute of Toxicology Vol 1: 7409
The Chemical Institute of Canada Vol 1: 7299
Chemical Institute of Canada - Canadian Society for Chemical Technology Vol 1: 7307
Chemical Marketing Research Association Vol 1: 7615
Chemical Organization of Mexico Vol 2: 3436
Chemical Society Vol 2: 6946
Chemical Society of Japan Vol 2: 3170

Chemical Specialties Manufacturers Association Vol 1: 7781
Chesapeake Bay Foundation Vol 1: 7309
Chess Journalists of America Vol 1: 7312
Chevron Conservation Awards Program - Chevron Corp. Vol 1: 7314
Chevron USA Vol 1: 7314
Chian Federation of America Vol 1: 7316
The Chicago Athenaeum: Museum of Architecture and Design Vol 1: 7318
Chicago Book Clinic Vol 1: 7321
The Chicago Community Trust Vol 1: 7325
Chicago Film Critics Association Vol 1: 7328
Chicago International Children's Film Festival Vol 1: 7330
Chicago International Festival of Children's Films Vol 1: 7330
Chicago Tribune Vol 1: 7332
Chihuahuan Desert Research Institute Vol 1: 7335
Children as Teachers of Peace Vol 1: 7337
Children as the Peacemakers Vol 1: 7337
Children's Book Committee Vol 1: 7339
Children's Book Council of Australia Vol 2: 403
Children's Book Council of Iran Vol 2: 2819
Children's Book Guild of Washington, D.C. Vol 1: 7342
Children's Film Society, India Vol 2: 2550
Children's Librarians of New Hampshire Vol 1: 7344
Children's Literature Association Vol 1: 7346
Children's Literature Council of Southern California Vol 1: 7351
Children's Rights Council Vol 1: 7353
Childs Memorial Fund for Medical Research; Jane Coffin Vol 1: 7356
Chile Ministerio de Educacion Vol 2: 1161
China Stamp Society Vol 1: 7358
Chinard Prize Committee; Gilbert Vol 1: 7360
Chinese American Librarians Association Vol 1: 7362
Chinese American Medical Society Vol 1: 7364
Chinese Economists Society Vol 1: 7366
Chinese Mathematical Society Vol 2: 3926
Chivers Press Vol 2: 5707
Choate, Hall & Stewart LLP Vol 1: 7368
Choice - American Library Association Vol 1: 7370
Chopin Foundation of the United States Vol 1: 7372
Chopin-Gesellschaft in der Bundesrepublik Deutschland Vol 2: 2064
Chopin Society; Czech Vol 2: 1251
Choral Arts New England Vol 1: 7374
Chorus America Vol 1: 7376
The Chris Awards Vol 1: 7380
Christian Booksellers Association of New Zealand Vol 2: 3705
Christian Holiness Partnership Vol 1: 7388
Christian Management Association Vol 1: 7390
Christian Ministries Management Association Vol 1: 7390
The Christophers Vol 1: 7392
Chroniqueurs de la Vie au Grand Air du Canada Vol 1: 14753
Chrysler Canada Vol 1: 2263
Chugai Pharma USA LLC Vol 1: 3753
Church & Dwight Company Vol 1: 10063
Church and Synagogue Library Association Vol 1: 7394
Churches' Center for Theology and Public Policy Vol 1: 7400
Churchill Center Vol 1: 7402
Churchill Downs Inc. Vol 1: 7406
Churchill Study Unit Vol 1: 7402
CIBA Plant Protection Vol 1: 17364
CIBA Specialty Chemicals Education Foundation Vol 1: 13679, 13680
CIIT Centers for Health Research Vol 1: 7409
CINANIMA - Festival Internacional de Cinema de Animacao Vol 2: 4055
CINANIMA - International Animated Film Festival Portugal Vol 2: 4055
Cincinnati Opera Association Vol 1: 7411
Cincinnati Scholarship Association Vol 1: 18964
Cinema/Chicago Vol 1: 7413
Cinema du Reel Vol 2: 1731
Cinema Giovani- Torino Film Festival Vol 2: 3008
Cinema Novo Fantasporto Vol 2: 4057
Cinematheque Royale Vol 2: 1082
Cineteca Nacional Vol 2: 3438
Cintas Foundation, Inc. Vol 1: 9888
Circle of the Greek Children's Book Vol 2: 2453
Circumnavigators Club Vol 1: 7417
Citizens Committee for New York City Vol 1: 7419
Citizens Research Council of Michigan Vol 1: 7421
Citizens Union of the City of New York Vol 1: 7423
City and Guilds of London Institute Vol 2: 5655
City and Regional Magazine Association Vol 1: 7425
City College of New York Vol 1: 7427
City Council of Pforzheim Vol 2: 2391
City of Beverly Hills Vol 1: 7429
City of Greater Dandenong Vol 2: 410
City of Independence, Missouri Vol 1: 7431
City of Linz Vol 2: 762
City of New York Department of Cultural Affairs Vol 1: 7433
City of Ottawa Vol 1: 7435
City of Philadelphia - Greater Philadelphia First Corporation Vol 1: 9191
City of Sydney Eisteddfod Vol 2: 686
City of Toronto Vol 1: 7437, 17562
City of Yorkton Vol 1: 19078
City University of New York Graduate Center - Doctoral Theater Students Association Vol 1: 7444
Civic Trust Vol 2: 5662
Civil Aviation Medical Association Vol 1: 211
Civitan International Vol 1: 7446
Cladan Cultural Exchange Institute of Australia Vol 2: 412
Clan Hunter Association Vol 2: 5664
Clarinet International Vol 1: 10319
Clarinetwork International Vol 1: 10319
Clarke College Vol 1: 7458
Classic Car Club of America Vol 1: 7460
Classified Federation Vol 1: 14218
Clay Minerals Society Vol 1: 7463
Clear-Com Vol 1: 17950
Cleft Palate Foundation Vol 1: 7468
Clemson Architectural Foundation Vol 1: 15773
Clemson University Vol 1: 16183
The Cleveland Foundation Vol 1: 7471
Cleveland Institute of Music Vol 1: 7473
Cleveland State University Poetry Center Vol 1: 7475
Cliburn Foundation; Van Vol 1: 7478
Clio Awards Inc. Vol 1: 7480
Clowes Fund Vol 1: 1737
Club Managers Association of America Vol 1: 18943
Club Tenco Vol 2: 3010
Coal Preparation Society Vol 2: 6431
Coalition for Alternatives in Jewish Education Vol 1: 7482
Coalition for the Advancement of Jewish Education Vol 1: 7482
Coalition to Protect Maryland Burial Sites Vol 1: 7484
Coblentz Society Vol 1: 14610
Codus: Wales Historic Monuments Vol 2: 5224
COGEDIM Vol 2: 1733
Colby College - Goldfarb Center Vol 1: 7486
Coldwater Community Theater Vol 1: 7488
Coleman Chamber Music Association Vol 1: 7490
Coleopterists' Society Vol 1: 7492
Colgate-Palmolive Vol 1: 10059
Colgate-Palmolive Company Vol 1: 10056, 16870, 16871
Collective Promotion of the Dutch Book Vol 2: 3494
Collectors Club Vol 1: 7494
College and Association of Registered Nurses of Alberta Vol 1: 7496
College Art Association Vol 1: 7500
College English Association Vol 1: 7510
College Gymnastics Association Vol 1: 7515
College Language Association Vol 1: 7520
College Media Advisers Vol 1: 7524
College of American Pathologists Vol 1: 3602
College of Chaplains of the American Protestant Health Association Vol 1: 5307
College of Chemical Engineers Vol 2: 532
College of Healthcare Information Management Executives Vol 1: 9326
College of Mount Saint Joseph - Office of Alumni Relations Vol 1: 7531
College of Mount Saint Joseph on the Ohio Vol 1: 7531
College of Optometrists in Vision Development Vol 1: 7536
College of Piping Vol 2: 5666
College of Psychologists of British Columbia Vol 1: 5945
College Ouest Africain des Chirurgiens Vol 2: 3886
College Sports Information Directors of America Vol 1: 7539
College Swimming Coaches Association Vol 1: 13388
College Swimming Coaches Association of America Vol 1: 7543
Collegium Internationale Neuro-Psychopharmacologicum Vol 1: 7547
Collier Building Industry Association Vol 1: 7551
Cologne International Pianoforte Competition - Foundation Tomassoni Vol 2: 2066
Cologne International Singing Competition Vol 2: 2070
Cologne International Violin Competition Vol 2: 2068
Cologne International Vocal Competition Vol 2: 2070

Colombia Ministry of Foreign Affairs Vol 2: 1173
Colombia Ministry of National Defence Vol 2: 1176
Colombia Ministry of Transportation Vol 2: 1190
Colonial Players, Inc. Vol 1: 7553
Colonial Society of Massachusetts Vol 1: 7555
Colorado Business Committee for the Arts Vol 1: 7557
Colorado Congress of Foreign Language Teachers Vol 1: 7559
Colorado Language Arts Society Vol 1: 7562
Colorado Ranger Horse Association Vol 1: 7564
Colorado River Watch Network Vol 1: 7566
Colorado Society of Association Executives Vol 1: 7568
Columbia: A Journal of Literature and Art Vol 1: 7570
Columbia: A Magazine of Poetry and Art Vol 1: 7570
Columbia College Chicago - Theater/Music Center Vol 1: 7572
Columbia Engineering School Alumni Association Vol 1: 7574
Columbia Scholastic Press Association Vol 1: 7577
Columbia University Vol 1: 7582
Columbia University - Department of Music Vol 1: 7590
Columbia University - Graduate School of Journalism Vol 1: 4114
Columbia University - Graduate School of Journalism Vol 1: 7592
Columbia University - Lamont-Doherty Earth Observatory Vol 1: 7596
Columbia University - School of Law Vol 1: 7598
Columbia University - School of the Arts Vol 1: 7600
Columbian Squires Vol 1: 7602
Columbine Poets of Colorado Vol 1: 13143
Columbus Blues Alliance Vol 1: 7604
Columbus Foundation Vol 1: 10805
Colworth Laboratory Vol 2: 7096
Combined Organizations of Numismatic Error Collectors of America Vol 1: 7606
Combustion Institute Vol 1: 7608
Comhaltas Ceoltoiri Eireann Vol 2: 2890
Comite International de la Croix-Rouge Vol 2: 4791
Comite International des Sports des Sourds Vol 1: 10328
Comite International Olympique Vol 2: 4818
Comite pour la Recherche Spatiale Vol 2: 1735
Commemorative Air Force Vol 1: 7613
Commercial Development and Marketing Association Vol 1: 7615
Commercial Finance Association Vol 1: 7618
Commission des Pares Nationaux et Vol 2: 4916
Commission Internationale de Juristes - Section Canadienne Vol 1: 10324
Commission Internationale des Oeufs Vol 2: 6238
Commission Internationale d'Optique Vol 2: 4513
Commission Internationale du Genie Rural Vol 2: 2288
Commitment Recognition Award Vol 1: 9555
Committee for Accreditation of Canadian Medical School in Canada Vol 1: 1738
Committee of 100 in Finland Vol 2: 1356
Committee of Presidents of Statistical Societies Vol 1: 7620
Committee of Presidents of Statistical Societies Vol 1: 9910
Committee on Space Research Vol 2: 1735
Committee to Protect Journalists Vol 1: 7625
Common Cause Vol 1: 7628
Commonwealth Association for Public Administration and Management Vol 1: 7630
Commonwealth Association of Architects Vol 2: 5669
Commonwealth Association of Science and Mathematics Educators Vol 2: 5671
Commonwealth Association of Science, Technology and Mathematics Educators Vol 2: 5671
Commonwealth Bank of Australia Vol 2: 90
Commonwealth Broadcasting Association Vol 2: 5678
Commonwealth Club of California Vol 1: 7632
Commonwealth Forestry Association Vol 2: 5673
Commonwealth Foundation Vol 2: 5672, 5677
Commonwealth Games Federation Vol 2: 5683
Commonwealth Pharmaceutical Association Vol 2: 5685
Commonwealth Press Union - United Kingdom Vol 2: 5687
Commonwealth Youth Programme Vol 2: 5690
Communication Arts Vol 1: 7634
Community College Humanities Association Vol 1: 7639
Community Colleges for International Development Vol 1: 7641
Community Counselling Service Vol 1: 5161
Community Funds, Inc. Vol 1: 18292
Community Relations Commission for a Multicultural New South Wales Vol 2: 692
Compass Publications Inc. Vol 1: 11543, 13482
Composers and Authors Society of Hong Kong Vol 2: 3930
Composites Manufacturing Association of the Society of Manufacturing Engineers Vol 1: 7643
Computer and Automated Systems Association of Society of Manufacturing Engineers Vol 1: 7645
Computer Measurement Group Vol 1: 7647
Computer Professionals for Social Responsibility Vol 1: 7650
Computer Society of Zimbabwe Vol 2: 7429
Computing Research Association Vol 1: 7652
Comune di Sondrio Mostra Internazionale dei Documentari sui Parchi Vol 2: 3129
Conamus Vol 2: 3499
Conamus; Stichting Vol 2: 3499
Concord Coalition Vol 1: 7655
Concordia Historical Institute Vol 1: 7657
Concorso Ettore Pozzoli Vol 2: 3012
Concorso Pianistico Internazionale Alessandro Casagrande Vol 2: 3014
Concorso Pianistico Internazionale Ferruccio Busoni Vol 2: 2998
Concours de Geneve Vol 2: 4701
Concours de musique du Canada Vol 1: 6742
Concours International de Ballet, Varna Vol 2: 1157
Concours International de Harpe en Israel Vol 2: 2903
Concours International de Violoncelle Rostropovitch Vol 2: 1743
Concours International d'Execution Musicale - Geneve Vol 2: 4701
Concours International J. S. Bach Vol 2: 2035
Concours International Robert Schumann Vol 2: 2312
Concours Internationaux de la Ville de Paris Vol 2: 1743
Concours Musical International Reine Elisabeth de Belgique Vol 2: 946
Concrete Foundations Association Vol 1: 7659
Concrete Reinforcing Steel Institute Vol 1: 7662
Concrete Society Vol 2: 5692
Concrete Society of Southern Africa Vol 2: 4151
Concurs Internacional de Cant Francesc Vinas Vol 2: 4553
Concurso Internacional de Piano de Santander Paloma O'Shea Vol 2: 4539
Concurso Internacional de Piano Premio Jaen Vol 2: 4520
Conductors Guild Vol 1: 7664
Confectionery Manufacturers of Australasia Vol 2: 414
Confederate Air Force Vol 1: 7613
Confederate Memorial Literary Society Vol 1: 7667
Confederate Stamp Alliance Vol 1: 7670
Confederation Europeenne de Baseball Vol 2: 857
Confederation Internationale d'Analyse Thermique Vol 2: 4204
Confederation Mondiale pour la Therapie Physique Vol 2: 7363
Conference Canadienne des arts Vol 1: 6417
Conference of California Historical Societies Vol 1: 7679
Conference of European Churches Vol 2: 4703
Conference on British Studies Vol 1: 14282
Conference on Christianity and Literature Vol 1: 7688
Conference on College Composition and Communication Vol 1: 7690
Conference on College Composition and Communication Vol 1: 13019
Conference on English Education Vol 1: 13020, 13024
Conference on Lasers and Electro-Optics Vol 1: 14603
Conference on Latin American History Vol 1: 7695
Conferences and Professional Programs Community of Practice Vol 1: 18224
Congregational Christian Historical Society Vol 1: 7702
Congres Mondiaux du Petrole Vol 2: 7375
Congress of Neurological Surgeons Vol 1: 7704
Congress of Racial Equality Vol 1: 7709
The Congressional Award Foundation Vol 1: 7711

Congressional Hispanic Caucus Institute Vol 1: 7713
Congressional Medal of Honor Society Vol 1: 7716
Conjunto Universitario Candido Mendes of Brazil Vol 2: 1913
Connected International Meeting Professionals Association Vol 1: 7718
Connecticut Alliance for Music Vol 1: 7720
Connecticut Association of Assessing Officers Vol 1: 7722
Connecticut Audubon Center at Glastonbury Vol 1: 7724
Connecticut Forest and Park Association Vol 1: 7726
Connecticut League for Nursing Vol 1: 7728
Connecticut Poetry Society Vol 1: 13144
Connecticut River Watershed Council Vol 1: 7730
Conseil canadien de la securite Vol 1: 6125
Conseil Canadien des Ingenieurs Vol 1: 6431
Conseil Canadien des Techniciens et Technologues Vol 1: 6440
Conseil canadien du ski Vol 1: 6870
Conseil d'adoption du Canada Vol 1: 162
Conseil de Canola du Canada Vol 1: 7087
Conseil de la Vie Francaise en Amerique Vol 1: 7732
Conseil de l'Europe Vol 2: 1753
Conseil de recherches en sciences naturelles et en genie du Canada Vol 1: 13974
Conseil des arts de l'Ontario Vol 1: 14554
Conseil Europeen des Urbanistes Vol 2: 5830
Conseil International d Etudes Canadiennes Vol 1: 10344
Conseil International de l'Enseignement a Distance Vol 2: 3899
Conseil International d'Education des Adultes Vol 2: 7403
Conseil International des Associations Graphiques Vol 2: 911
Conseil International des Monuments et des Sites Vol 2: 1887
Conseil International des Sciences Sociales Vol 2: 1912
Conseil International du Droit de l'Environnement Vol 2: 2292
Conseil Mondiale pour la Danse de Salon et la Danse Sportive Vol 2: 7367
Consejo Cultural Mundial Vol 2: 3459
Consejo Mundial de Boxeo Vol 2: 3457
Consejo Nacional de Ciencia y Tecnologia Vol 2: 3440
Consejo Nacional de Investigaciones Cientificas y Tecnologicas - CONICIT Vol 2: 7425
Conservation and Research Foundation Vol 1: 5882
Conservation Foundation Vol 2: 5694
Conservation International Vol 2: 5179
Conservatorio di Musica A. Boito di Parma Vol 2: 2996
Conservatory of Music at Baldwin-Wallace College Vol 1: 7735
Construction Innovation Forum Vol 1: 7737
Construction Specifications Canada Vol 1: 7739
Construction Specifications Institute Vol 1: 7743
Construction Writers Association Vol 1: 7756
Consultant Dietitians in Health Care Facilities Vol 1: 7763
Consulting Engineers Council of Metropolitan Washington Vol 1: 7771
Consulting Psychologists Press Vol 1: 3321, 3323
Consumer Credit Insurance Association Vol 1: 7773
Consumer Electronics Association Vol 1: 7775
Consumer Federation of America Vol 1: 7777
Consumer Specialty Products Association Vol 1: 7781
Consumers for World Trade Vol 1: 7783
Contact Lens Manufacturer Association Vol 1: 7785
Containerization and Intermodal Institute Vol 1: 7787
Contemporary A Cappella Society of America Vol 1: 7789
Contemporary Record Society Vol 1: 7791
Continental Basketball Association Vol 1: 7794
Convoy for Kids Vol 2: 418
Cook Publishing; Thomas Vol 2: 5696
Cooper Memorial Prize; Duff Vol 2: 5745
Cooper Ohioana Library Association; Martha Kinney Vol 1: 14485
Cooper Ornithological Society Vol 1: 7802
Cooper Union for the Advancement of Science and Art Vol 1: 7809
Cooperation Centre for Scientific Research Relative to Tobacco Vol 2: 1751
Cooperative Council for Oklahoma School Administration Vol 1: 7811
Cooperative Education and Internship Association Vol 1: 7813
The Cooperative Foundation Vol 1: 5116
Cooperative Research Centre for Polymers Vol 2: 427
Coopers Hill Society Vol 2: 6106
Coopers Hill Society Vol 2: 6145
Cooperstown Art Association Vol 1: 7817
Copper Union Alumni Association Vol 1: 7819
Cork Film Festival Vol 2: 2826
Cork International Choral Festival Vol 2: 2828
Cork International Film Festival Vol 2: 2826
Cornell Laboratory of Ornithology Vol 1: 7822
Corning Inc. Vol 1: 14619
Corona Norco United Way Vol 1: 7824
Corporation Associates Vol 1: 1511
Corporation for National and Community Service Vol 1: 15142
Corporation for Public Broadcasting Vol 1: 7827
Corporation Professionnelle des Psychologues du Quebec Vol 1: 14664
Correctional Education Association - Region III Vol 1: 7830
Costa Rica Ministry of Culture, Youth and Sport Vol 2: 1200
Costume Society of America Vol 1: 7832
Cotton Foundation; Dr. M. Aylwin Vol 2: 5698
Council for Advancement and Support of Education Vol 1: 28
Council for Agricultural Science and Technology Vol 1: 7840
Council for Art Education Vol 1: 7842
Council for Art Education, Inc. Vol 1: 12280
Council for Business and Arts in Canada Vol 1: 7844
Council for Business and the Arts in Canada Vol 1: 7848
Council for Exceptional Children Vol 1: 7851
Council for Exceptional Children - Division of Learning Disabilities Vol 1: 7862
Council for Health and Human Services Ministries, United Church of Christ Vol 1: 7866
Council for Learning Disabilities Vol 1: 7868
Council for the Advancement of Science Writing Vol 1: 7872
Council for the Order of Australia Vol 2: 199
Council for the Protection of Rural Wales Vol 2: 5580
Council for Wisconsin Writers Vol 1: 7874
Council of Administrators of Special Education Vol 1: 7876
Council of Authors and Journalists Vol 1: 9033
Council of Chief State School Officers Vol 1: 7878
Council of Education Vol 1: 16359
Council of Educational Facility Planners, International Vol 1: 7881
Council of Engineering Deans of the Historically Black Colleges and Universities Vol 1: 7100
Council of EU Chambers of Commerce in India Vol 2: 2552
Council of Europe Vol 2: 1753
Council of Fashion Designers of America Vol 1: 7884
Council of Graduate Schools Vol 1: 7887
Council of Graduate Schools in the United States Vol 1: 7887
Council of Logistics Management Vol 1: 7899
Council of Natural Waters Vol 1: 10273
Council of Residential Specialists Vol 1: 7891
Council of Scientific Society Presidents Vol 1: 7894
Council of Supply Chain Management Professionals Vol 1: 7899
Council on Accreditation of Nurse Anesthesia Educational Programs Vol 1: 7902
Council on Approved Student Education Vol 1: 13061
Council on Arteriosclerosis, Thrombosis and Vascular Biology Vol 1: 2174, 2186
Council on Basic Cardiovascular Sciences Vol 1: 2182, 2185
Council on Cardiopulmonary, Perioperative and Critical Care Vol 1: 2175
Council on Cardiovascular Nursing Vol 1: 2180, 2183
Council on Cardiovascular Radiology and Intervention Vol 1: 2181
Council on Clinical Cardiology Vol 1: 2184
Council on Environmental Quality Vol 1: 8554
Council on Foreign Relations Vol 1: 7911
Council on Foundations Vol 1: 7913
Council on Governmental Ethics Laws Vol 1: 7919
Council on International Nontheatrical Events Vol 1: 7922
Council on Peace Research in History Vol 1: 14878
Council on Technology Teacher Education Vol 1: 7926
Counseil Canadien de droit International Vol 1: 6442
Count Dracula Society Vol 1: 7928

Country Markets Ltd. Vol 2: 2877
Country Music Association Vol 1: 7931
Country Music Showcase International Vol 1: 7934
Cour permanente d'arbitrage Vol 2: 3637
Courmayeur Noir in Festival Vol 2: 3016
Coutts Nijhoff International Vol 1: 5073
Cox Newspapers Vol 1: 17463
CPR Institute for Dispute Resolution Vol 1: 7937
CQ Press Vol 1: 5081
CQ, The Radio Amateur's Journal Vol 1: 7939
Cracow International Festival of Short Films Vol 2: 3998
Craft Guild of Chefs Vol 2: 5701
Crain Communications, Inc. Vol 1: 6024
Cram Co.; George F. Vol 1: 12966, 12985
Crane Duplicating Service, Inc. Vol 1: 18698
Cranial Academy Vol 1: 7949
Craniofacial Biology Group Vol 1: 10066
Crawford Productions Vol 2: 393
Cray Research France Vol 2: 1787
Creative Glass Center of America Vol 1: 7951
Creative Standards International Vol 1: 10024
Creative Studies Alumni Foundation Vol 1: 7953
Creative Writing Program Vol 1: 7955
Credit Union Executives Society Vol 1: 7957
Crime Writers' Association Vol 2: 5705
Crime Writers of Canada Vol 1: 7966
Croatian Chess Federation Vol 2: 1216
Croatian Library Association Vol 2: 1218
Croatian National Theatre Split Vol 2: 1221
Croatian Pharmaceutical Society Vol 2: 1224
Crohn's and Colitis Foundation of Canada Vol 1: 7968
Cromwell Association Vol 2: 5714
Cronkite School of Journalism and Mass Communication; Walter Vol 1: 7971
Crop Science Society of America Vol 1: 7973
Crouch Foundation; George E. Vol 1: 3129
Crown Princess Sonja International Music Competition Vol 2: 3913
The Crustacean Society Vol 1: 7985
Cryogenic Engineering Conference Vol 1: 7987
Cryogenic Society of America Vol 1: 7989
CSA/Ulrich Vol 1: 4912
CTAM - Cable and Telecommunications Association for Marketing Vol 1: 7992
Cultural Arts Council of Estes Park Vol 1: 7999
Cultural Association "Rodolfo Lipizer" Vol 2: 3018
Cultural Department of the Municipality of Spittal and the Singkreis Porcia Vol 2: 767
Cumann Corpoideachais na hEireann Vol 2: 2865
Cumhuriyet Matbaacilik ve Gazetecilik T.A.S. Vol 2: 4963
Cumhuriyet Newspaper Vol 2: 4963
Cumunn na Camanachd Vol 2: 5575
CURE Childhood Cancer Association Vol 1: 8001
Curtin University of Technology Vol 2: 514
Curtins Consulting Engineers Vol 2: 6108
Cushman Foundation for Foraminiferal Research Vol 1: 8003
Cymbidium Society of America Vol 1: 8005
Cyngor Llyfrau Cymru Vol 2: 7324
Cypress Creek Foundation for the Arts and Community Enrichment Vol 1: 8007
Cystic Fibrosis Foundation Vol 1: 8009
Cystic Fibrosis Trust Vol 2: 5716
Czech Chemical Society Vol 2: 1248
Czech Chopin Society Vol 2: 1251
Czech Radio, Radio Prague Vol 2: 1253
Czech Television Vol 2: 1255
Czechoslovak Society of Arts and Sciences Vol 1: 8013
Czechoslovak Television, Prague Vol 2: 1255
D. H. Lawrence Society of North America Vol 1: 8015
Dade Behring Inc. Vol 1: 899, 3767
Daily Racing For Vol 1: 17533
Daily Racing Form Vol 1: 17532
Dairy and Food Industries Supply Association Vol 1: 10214
The Dairy Barn: Southeastern Ohio Arts Center Vol 1: 8018
Dairy Shrine Vol 1: 13072
Daiwa Anglo-Japanese Foundation Vol 2: 5718
Dale Medical Products Vol 1: 1067
Dallas Area Paralegal Association Vol 1: 8020
Dallas Metropolitan Young Men's Christian Association Vol 1: 8022
Dallas Museum of Art Vol 1: 8024
Dallas Songwriters Association Vol 1: 8028
Dalmatian Club of America Vol 1: 8030
Dames of America; Colonial Vol 1: 16489
Damien-Dutton Society for Leprosy Aid Vol 1: 8032
Damon Runyon Cancer Research Foundation Vol 1: 8034
Dana Foundation; Charles A. Vol 1: 8036
Dance Division Vol 1: 13076
Dance Films Association Vol 1: 8038
Dance Magazine Vol 1: 8040
Dance Masters of America Vol 1: 8042
Dance Notation Bureau Vol 1: 8045
Dance Theater Workshop Vol 1: 8048
Dance/U.S.A. Vol 1: 8050
Danish Academy of Technical Sciences Vol 2: 1275
Danish Association for International Cooperation - Denmark Vol 2: 1277
Danish Association of the Specialist Press Vol 2: 1279
Danish Jazz Association Vol 2: 1281
Danish Jazz Center Vol 2: 1281
Danish Jazz Federation Vol 2: 1281
Danish Library Association Vol 2: 1283
Danish Samoyed Club Vol 2: 1286
Danish Women's Society Vol 2: 1288
Danish Writers Association Vol 2: 1290
Danmarks Biblioteksforening Vol 2: 1283
Danmarks Radio Vol 2: 1311
Dannon Institute Vol 1: 3797
Dansk Fagpresse Vol 2: 1279
Dansk Forfatterforening Vol 2: 1290
Dansk Geologisk Forening Vol 2: 1302
Dansk Jazzforbund Vol 2: 1281
Dansk Journalistforbund Vol 2: 1295
Dansk Kvindesamfund Vol 2: 1288
Danske Arkitekters Landsforbund/Akademisk Arkitektforening Vol 2: 1300
Dante Society of America Vol 1: 8052
Danube Prize Vol 2: 4452
Darien Chamber of Commerce Vol 1: 8055
Data Processing Management Association Vol 1: 5198
Data Publishers Association Vol 2: 5720
DateAble, Inc. Vol 1: 8057
Daughters of the American Revolution Vol 1: 13769
David; Pierre - Weill Foundation Vol 2: 1496
Davis Publications Vol 1: 18979
Davison Chemical Division Vol 1: 14272
Davy Devotees - The Official Fan Club for Davy Jones Vol 1: 8059
Davy Process Technology Vol 2: 6967
The Dayton Playhouse Vol 1: 8061
Dayton Repertory Theatre Vol 1: 8061
Daytona International Speedway Vol 1: 8063
D.C. Commission on the Arts and Humanities Vol 1: 8070
Deadline Club Vol 1: 8072
Deafness Research Foundation Vol 1: 8074
Death Penalty Information Center Vol 1: 8077
Decalogue Society of Lawyers Vol 1: 8079
DECHEMA Vol 2: 2118
Dechema - Society for Chemical Engineering and Biotechnology Vol 2: 2072
DECHEMA Subject Group Catalysis Vol 2: 2257
Decision Sciences Institute Vol 1: 8082
Decorative Lighting Association Vol 2: 6382
Deep Foundations Institute Vol 1: 8084
Defense Logistics Agency - United States Air Force Vol 1: 8087
Defense Research Institute Vol 1: 8129
Del Mar Fair Vol 1: 15823
Delacorte Press Vol 1: 8138
DeLaval Inc. Vol 1: 1875
Delaware Association of School Administrators Vol 1: 8140
Delaware County Historical Society Vol 1: 8142
Delaware Restaurant Association Vol 1: 8144
Deloitte Touche Tohmatsu Vol 1: 8146
Delphinium Society Vol 2: 5732
Delta Air Lines Vol 1: 12215
Delta Education Vol 1: 4958
Delta Nu Alpha Transportation Fraternity Vol 1: 8149
Delta Omicron Vol 1: 8151
Delta Pi Epsilon Vol 1: 8155
Delta Society Vol 1: 4407
Delta Society Australia Vol 2: 429
Demco Inc. Vol 1: 15420
Denmark - Ministry of Cultural Affairs Vol 2: 1292
Denstu Inc. Vol 2: 3178
Dentsply International Vol 1: 10061
Denver Film Society Vol 1: 8158
Denver Public Library - Western History/ Genealogy Department Vol 1: 8164
Denver Rocky Mountain News Vol 1: 18267
Department of the Interior Vol 1: 14883
Dermatology Foundation Vol 1: 8166
Des Moines Education Association Vol 1: 8169
Desert Fishes Council Vol 1: 8172
Design Council Vol 2: 5734
Design Forum Finland Vol 2: 1358
Designers Institute of New Zealand Vol 2: 3712
Deutsche Akademie der Naturforscher Leopoldina Vol 2: 2075
Deutsche Akademie fur Sprache und Dichtung Vol 2: 2143
Deutsche Elektrochemische Gesellschaft Vol 2: 2155

Deutsche Forschungsgemeinschaft Vol 2: 2217
Deutsche Geologische Gesellschaft Vol 2: 2187
Deutsche Gesellschaft fur Endokrinologie Vol 2: 2202
Deutsche Gesellschaft fur Ernahrung Vol 2: 2244
Deutsche Gesellschaft fur Fettwissenschaft e.V. Vol 2: 2228
Deutsche Gesellschaft fur Kinderheilkunde und Jugendmedizin e.V Vol 2: 2248
Deutsche Gesellschaft fur Parasitologie Vol 2: 2077
Deutsche Gesellschaft fur Plastische und Wiederherstellungschirurgie e.V. Vol 2: 2251
Deutsche Gesellschaft fur Sozialwissenschaftliche Sexualforschung e.V. Vol 2: 2239
Deutsche Gesellschaft fur Zerstorungsfreie Prufung e.V. Vol 2: 2236
Deutsche Glastechnische Gesellschaft Vol 2: 2241
Deutsche Landwirtschafts-Gesellschaft Vol 2: 2151
Deutsche Mathematiker Vereinigung Vol 2: 2198
Deutsche Meteorologische Gesellschaft Vol 2: 2079
Deutsche Mineralogische Gesellschaft Vol 2: 2084
Deutsche Ornithologen-Gesellschaft Vol 2: 2206
Deutsche Physikalische Gesellschaft Vol 2: 2089
Deutsche Phytomedizinische Gesellschaft Vol 2: 2211
Deutscher Direktmarketing Verband Vol 2: 2183
Deutscher Volkshochschul-Verband Vol 2: 2149
Deutscher Zentralausschuss fur Chemie Vol 2: 2091
Deutsches Forum fur Figurentheater und Puppenspielkunst e.V. Vol 2: 2099
Developing Countries Farm Radio Network Vol 1: 8175
DeVilliers Foundation Vol 1: 11298
Dextra Laboratories Vol 2: 6955
Dialogue: A Journal of Mormon Thought Vol 1: 8177
Diamond Council of America Vol 1: 8179
Dibner Fund Vol 1: 16436
Dickinson College Vol 1: 8182
Die Misstofvereniging van Suid-Afrika Vol 2: 4176
Die Suid-Afrikaanse Vereniging van Musiekonderwysers Vol 2: 4354
Dierkundige Vereniging van Suidelike Afrika Vol 2: 4379
Dietitians of Canada Vol 1: 8186
Dighton Historical Society Vol 1: 8190
Digital Equipment Corporation Europe Vol 2: 1787
Dillmans Creative Arts Foundation Vol 1: 8196
Direct Mail/Marketing Educational Foundation Vol 1: 8205
Direct Marketing Association Vol 2: 5737
Direct Marketing Association Vol 1: 8198
Direct Marketing Association of Detroit Vol 1: 8201
Direct Marketing Club of New York Vol 1: 8203
Direct Marketing Educational Foundation Vol 1: 8205
Direct Selling Association Vol 1: 8208
Direct Selling Association - South Africa Vol 2: 4157
Directors Guild of America Vol 1: 8213
Dirksen Congressional Center Vol 1: 8224
Disabled American Veterans Vol 1: 8226
Disciples Peace Fellowship Vol 1: 8229
District of Columbia Library Association Vol 1: 8231
Diving Equipment and Marketing Association Vol 1: 8233
Dixie Council of Authors and Journalists Vol 1: 9033
Doberman Pinscher Club of America Vol 1: 8235
Dr. Declan Millett Vol 2: 5406
Dr. H.P. Heineken Foundation Vol 2: 3652
Dr. James Naismith Basketball Foundation Vol 1: 8237
Doctors of the World Vol 1: 9097
Document Management Industries Association Vol 1: 8239
Documentary Film Festival - Amsterdam Vol 2: 3575
Dog Writers Association of America Vol 1: 8243
Doll Artisan Guild Vol 1: 8245
Dominican University Vol 1: 8250
Dominion Council of Canada Vol 1: 6431
Dominion Salt Limited Vol 2: 3746
Donors Forum of Wisconsin Vol 1: 8253
Donovan Memorial Foundation; William J. Vol 1: 14451
Door and Hardware Institute Vol 1: 8255
Door County Environmental Council Vol 1: 8261
Dorper Sheep Breeders' Society of South Africa Vol 2: 4161
Dorpers Skaaptelersgenootskap van Suid-Afrika Vol 2: 4161
Dorset Natural History Vol 2: 5739
Dorset Natural History and Archaeological Society Vol 2: 5739
Dow Chemical Company; The Vol 1: 1531
Dow Chemical Company Vol 1: 2474, 2501
Dow Chemical Company Foundation Vol 1: 1518, 1526, 2479
Dow Corning Corporation Vol 1: 1560
Dow Jones Newspaper Fund Vol 1: 8263
Downeast Association of Physician Assistants Vol 1: 8265
Dozenal Society of America Vol 1: 8271
Dracula Society Vol 2: 5741
Drama Desk Vol 1: 8273
The Drama League Vol 1: 8275
Dramatists Guild of America Vol 1: 8279
Dreyfus Foundation Inc.; Camille and Henry Vol 1: 1507, 1508
Dromkeen Collection Art Gallery Vol 2: 431
Drug Enforcement Administration Vol 1: 8564
Drug Strategies Vol 1: 8281
Drustvo Slovenskih Pisateljev Vol 2: 4462
Dry Stone Walling Association of Great Britain Vol 2: 5743
du Pont de Nemours and Company; E. I. Vol 1: 2473, 2497, 12146
Du Pont KEVLAR Vol 1: 10176
Dubuque Fine Arts Players Vol 1: 8283
Dubuque Fine Arts Society Vol 1: 8284
Ductile Iron Society Vol 1: 8285
Dudley Observatory Vol 1: 8287
Duff Cooper Prize Vol 2: 5745
Duke University - Center for Documentary Studies Vol 1: 8290
Duke University - Department of Physics Vol 1: 8293
Duluth Art Institute Vol 1: 8295
Dumbarton Oaks Vol 1: 8297
Duncan Guthrie Memorial Fund Vol 2: 5003
Duncan Lawrie Limited Vol 2: 5076
Duncan Lawrie Private Bank Vol 2: 5710
Dungannon Foundation - Rea Award for the Short Story Vol 1: 8300
Duodecimal Society of America Vol 1: 8271
duPont; Alfred I. Vol 1: 7585
duPont de Nemours and Co.; E. I. Vol 1: 1522
duPont de Nemours and Co.; E.I. Vol 1: 1541
Durban International Film Festival Vol 2: 4163
Dutch Cancer Society Vol 2: 3504
Dutch Film Festival Foundation Vol 2: 3630
Dutch International Vocal Competition - Hertogenbosch Vol 2: 3507
Dystrophic Epidermolysis Bullosa Research Association of America Vol 1: 8302
Dystrophie Musculaire Canada Vol 1: 12015
Eagle Forum Vol 1: 8304
Eaglehawk Dahlia and Arts Festival Vol 2: 434
Early Music America Vol 1: 8307
Earthwatch Institute Vol 1: 8311
East & West Artists Vol 1: 8314
East Carolina University - Office of Research and Scholarship Vol 1: 8316
East Coast Music Association Vol 1: 8318
East Polk County Committee of 100 Vol 1: 8327
East Tennessee Environmental Business Association Vol 1: 8329
East Texas Historical Association Vol 1: 8331
East-West News Bureau Vol 1: 14351
Easter Seals Vol 1: 8333
Eastern Apicultural Society of North America Vol 1: 8337
Eastern Association of Mosquito Control Workers Vol 1: 2799
Eastern Bird Banding Association Vol 1: 8340
Eastern Coast Breweriana Association Vol 1: 8342
Eastern College Athletic Conference Vol 1: 8345
Eastern College Athletic Conference Sports Information Directors Association Vol 1: 8347
Eastern Kentucky University Vol 1: 8350
Eastern Music Festival Vol 1: 8352
Eastern Surfing Association Vol 1: 8356
Eastman Chemical Co. Vol 1: 1513
Eastman Kodak Company Vol 1: 1538
Eastman Kodak Co. Vol 1: 10380
Eastman Kodak Company Vol 1: 18012
Eastman Kodak Company - Consumer Imaging Vol 1: 8358
Eastman Kodak Company Aerial Systems Division Vol 1: 4742
Eaton Literary Associates Vol 1: 8360
EBSCO Information Services Vol 1: 15421
EBSCO Subscription Services Vol 1: 2655

Eckhardt Gramatte National Music Competition Vol 1: 8362
Ecolab Inc. Vol 1: 10084
Ecological Society of America Vol 1: 8364
Econometric Society Vol 1: 8374
Economic History Association Vol 1: 8376
Economic Society of South Africa Vol 2: 4165
Ecumenical Council of San Diego County Vol 1: 8383
Edgar County Genealogical Society Vol 1: 8385
Edinburgh Architectural Association Vol 2: 5747
Edinburgh Festival Fringe Vol 2: 5751
Edinburgh International Film Festival Vol 2: 5755
Edison Awards Vol 2: 3509
Edison Electric Institute Vol 1: 8387
Edison Fund; Charles Vol 1: 16436
Edison Media Arts Consortium Vol 1: 8389
Edison Stichting Vol 2: 3509
Editorial Planeta Vol 2: 4484
Editorial Planeta SA Vol 2: 4478
Editors; American Society of Business Press Vol 1: 3897
Editors Association Vol 2: 3908
Editors' Association of Canada Vol 1: 8391
Edmond Hustinx Foundation Vol 2: 3512
Education Commission of the States Vol 1: 8393
Education; U.S. Department of Vol 1: 12515
Education Writers Association Vol 1: 8395
Educational Building Society Vol 2: 2877
Educational Communications Inc. Vol 1: 13008
Educational Paperback Association Vol 1: 8397
Educational Testing Service Vol 1: 8399
Educational Theatre Association Vol 1: 8402
Educators for Social Responsibility, Grand Rapids Chapter Vol 1: 8407
Edwards Trust; Margaret A. Vol 1: 19080
Eesti Haridustootajate Liit Vol 2: 1354
Eesti Teaduste Akadeemia Vol 2: 1346
Effie Awards Vol 1: 8409
Egypt Exploration Society Vol 2: 5757
Egyptian Ophthalmological Society Vol 2: 1344
E.I. du Pont de Nemours and Company Vol 1: 2480
Eidgenossische Technische Hochschule Zurich Vol 2: 4895
EIFS Industry Members Association Vol 1: 8411
Eighteen-twenty Foundation Vol 2: 4190
Eire Philatelic Association Vol 1: 8413
Eisenhower Fellowships Vol 1: 8415
Eisteddfod Genedlaethol Frenhinol Cymr Vol 2: 6470
Ekotopfilm: International Festival of Professional Films Vol 2: 4439
El Toro International Yacht Racing Association Vol 1: 8417
Elanco Vol 1: 6973
Elanco Animal Health Vol 1: 1879, 3890
Electric Car Racing Association Vol 2: 5462
Electric Power Society - Association of German Electrical Engineers Vol 2: 2101
Electrical Apparatus Service Association Vol 1: 8419
Electrical Generating Systems Association Vol 1: 8421
Electricite de France Vol 2: 1936
Electricorp Production Vol 2: 3742
Electronic Associates, Inc. Vol 1: 3646
Electronic Document Systems Foundation Vol 1: 8423
Electronic Industries Alliance Vol 1: 8426
Electronic Retailing Association Vol 1: 8428
Electronics Technicians Association, International; ETA International - Vol 1: 8535
Eli Lilly Vol 1: 6902
Eli Lilly & Co. Vol 1: 557
Eli Lilly and Company Vol 1: 4259, 8616
Elsevier Vol 1: 5077
Elsevier Ltd. Vol 1: 1581
Elsevier Science Vol 1: 16606
Elsevier Science Publishers Vol 2: 6255, 6256
Elsevier Scientific Publishing Company Vol 1: 8831
Embassy Players Vol 1: 5948
Emergency Department Nurses Association Vol 1: 8439
Emergency Medicine Residents' Association Vol 1: 8430
Emergency Nurses Association Vol 1: 8439
Employment Management Association Vol 1: 8447
Empresa Brasileira de Pesquisa Agropecuaria Vol 2: 1121
Emprise Bank of Wichita Vol 1: 11088
ENCAMS: Keep Britain Tidy Vol 2: 5759
Encylcopedia Britannica Vol 1: 2700
Endocrine Society Vol 1: 8450
Endocrine Society of Australia Vol 2: 436
Energy Institute Vol 2: 5761
Engineering College Magazines Associated Vol 1: 8459
Engineering Geology Division Vol 1: 9016
Engineering Institute of Canada Vol 1: 6915, 6917, 8461
Engineering News-Record Vol 1: 8471
Engineering Research Council Vol 1: 3658
Engineers' Association of Chile Vol 2: 1165
Engineers' Company Vol 2: 5765
Engineers' Council for Professional Development Vol 1: 40
England Basketball Vol 2: 5771
English Academy of Southern Africa Vol 2: 4169
English Association Sydney Vol 2: 441
English Centre of International PEN Vol 2: 5777
English China Clays Vol 2: 5927
English Folk Dance and Song Society Vol 2: 5779
English Heritage Vol 2: 5224
English-Speaking Union of the United States Vol 1: 8469
ENR: Engineering News-Record - The McGraw-Hill Cos., Inc. Vol 1: 8471
Ente David di Donatello Vol 2: 3020
Entertainment and Leisure Software Publishers Association Vol 2: 5781
Entertainment Merchants Association Vol 1: 8473
Entomological Foundation Vol 1: 8475
Entomological Society of America Vol 1: 8481
Entomological Society of America Vol 1: 17366
Entomological Society of Canada Vol 1: 8491
Environmental and Conservation Organization Vol 1: 8494
Environmental Business Council of New England Vol 1: 8496
Environmental Design Research Association Vol 1: 8498
Environmental Mutagen Society Vol 1: 8502
Environmental Systems Research Institute Vol 1: 4737
Environmental Tectonics Corporation Vol 1: 210
Environmental Transport Association Vol 2: 5783
Ephemera Society Vol 2: 5785
Epilepsy Foundation Vol 1: 8506
Episcopal Communicators Vol 1: 8508
Epsilon Pi Tau Vol 1: 8511
Epsilon Sigma Phi Vol 1: 8514
Epson Vol 2: 5152
Equine Guelph Vol 1: 8521
Equine Research Centre Vol 1: 8521
Erasmus Prize Foundation Vol 2: 3518
Ergonomics Society - England Vol 2: 5787
Erie Art Museum Vol 1: 8523
Erie County Historical Society Vol 1: 8525
Ernest C. Manning Awards Foundation Vol 1: 8527
Ernst & Young LLP Vol 1: 8529
Ernst Von Siemens-Musikstiftung Vol 2: 4914
Errors, Freaks and Oddities Collector's Club Vol 1: 8531
Errors, Freaks, Oddities Collectors Association Vol 1: 8531
Escobar Foundation; Alejandro Angel Vol 2: 1192
ESOMAR: World Association of Opinion and Marketing Research Professionals Vol 2: 3520
ESPN Inc. Vol 1: 8533
Espoir Sans Frontieres Vol 2: 4410
Estate of Ellis Peters Vol 2: 5712
Estee Corporation Vol 1: 1081
Estonian Academy of Sciences Vol 2: 1346
Estonian Education Personnel Union Vol 2: 1354
ETA International - Electronics Technicians Association, International Vol 1: 8535
Eta Kappa Nu Vol 1: 8537
Eugene V. Debs Foundation Vol 1: 8543
Eureka Vol 2: 851
Eureka Secretariat Vol 2: 851
EuroBest Awards Vol 2: 5802
Europa Nostra Pan European Federation for Heritage Vol 2: 3523
Europaische Kernenergie-Gesellschaft Vol 2: 866
Europaische Union der Musikwettbewerbe fur die Jugend Vol 2: 2131
European Aquaculture Society Vol 2: 853
European Association for Animal Production Vol 2: 3022
European Association for Cancer Research Vol 2: 5804
European Association for Computer Assisted Language Learning Vol 2: 2831
European Association for Cranio-Maxillofacial Surgery Vol 2: 5810
European Association for Distance Learning Vol 2: 3527
European Association for Geochemistry Vol 2: 1758
European Association for Lexicography Vol 2: 5815
European Association for Signal Processing Vol 2: 4059

European Association for Signal, Speech and Image Processing Vol 2: 4059
European Association for the Promotion of Poetry Vol 2: 855
European Association for the Study of Diabetes Vol 2: 2104
European Association for Theoretical Computer Science Vol 1: 4818
European Association of Geoscientists and Engineers Vol 2: 3529
European Association of Organic Geochemists Vol 2: 1762
European Association of Programmes in Health Services Studies Vol 2: 2833
European Association of Radiology Vol 2: 1764
European Athletic Association Vol 2: 2110
European Bar Human Rights Institute Vol 2: 1848
European Baseball Confederation Vol 2: 857
European Behavioral Pharmacology Society Vol 2: 2112
European Bridge League Vol 2: 3026
European Broadcasting Union Vol 2: 4706
European Calcified Tissue Society Vol 2: 5817
European Cancer Conference Vol 2: 3115
European Chemical Industry Council Vol 2: 860
European Commission - DG Development Vol 2: 3028
European Consortium for Political Research Vol 2: 5821
European Coordinating Committee for Artificial Intelligence Vol 2: 769
European Council of International Schools Vol 2: 5826
European Council of Town Planners Vol 2: 5830
European Disposables and Nonwovens Association Vol 2: 862
European Environmental Mutagen Society Vol 2: 1766
European Express Association Vol 2: 864
European Federation for Medicinal Chemistry Vol 2: 771
European Federation of Corrosion Vol 2: 2116
European Federation of Food Science and Technology Vol 2: 3532
European Federation of Societies for Ultrasound in Medicine and Biology Vol 2: 5832
European Geosciences Union Vol 2: 1768
European Health Management Association Vol 2: 2833
European Hematology Association Vol 2: 3534
European Hotel Managers Association Vol 2: 3030
European Information Association Vol 2: 5834
European Institute of Public Administration Vol 2: 3539
European Mariculture Society Vol 2: 853
European Meteorological Society Vol 2: 2120
European Molecular Biology Organization Vol 2: 2124
European Money and Finance Forum Vol 2: 775
European Nuclear Society Vol 2: 866
European Oncology Nursing Society Vol 2: 868
European Organization for Caries Research Vol 2: 3541
European Organization for Testing New Flower Seeds Vol 2: 3544
European Orthodontic Society Vol 2: 5838
European Parliament - London Information Office Vol 2: 5846
European Physical Society Vol 2: 1784
European Process Safety Centre Vol 2: 5848
European Prosthodontic Association Vol 2: 5850
European Rhinologic Society Vol 2: 1363
European Society for Ballistocardiography and Cardiovascular Dynamics Vol 2: 4453
European Society for Biomaterials Vol 2: 5855
European Society for Cardiovascular Surgery Vol 2: 3032
European Society for Clinical Virology Vol 2: 4579
European Society for Cognitive Psychology Vol 2: 4490
European Society for Engineering Education Vol 2: 873
European Society for Microcirculation Vol 2: 2126
European Society for Noninvasive Cardiovascular Dynamics Vol 2: 4453
European Society for Paediatric Endocrinology Vol 2: 5860
European Society for Therapeutic Radiology and Oncology Vol 2: 875
European Society of Anaesthesiology Vol 2: 877
European Society of Biomechanics Vol 2: 3034
European Society of Clinical Microbiology and Infectious Diseases - Switzerland Vol 2: 4712
European Society of Comparative Physiology and Biochemistry Vol 2: 879
European Society of Intensive Care Medicine Vol 2: 881
European Society of Paediatric Radiology Vol 2: 5867
European Sports Press Union Vol 2: 4582
European Structural Integrity Society Vol 2: 3039
European Surfing Federation Vol 2: 5869
European Table Tennis Union Vol 2: 3388
European Thyroid Association Vol 2: 1298
European Union of Music Competition for Youth Vol 2: 2131
European Water Pollution Control Association Vol 2: 2133
European Wound Management Association Vol 2: 5871
Eutectic Castolin Corporation Vol 1: 4472
Evaluation Network Vol 1: 1980
Evaluation Research Society Vol 1: 1980
Evangelical Christian Publishers Association Vol 1: 8545
Evergreen Area Chamber of Commerce Vol 1: 8547
Evidence Photographers International Council Vol 1: 8549
Executive Office of the President Vol 1: 8551
Executive Search Roundtable Vol 1: 8556
Exhibit Designers and Producers Association Vol 1: 8558
Exhibition Association of Southern Africa Vol 2: 4174
Experimental Psychology Society Vol 2: 5873
The Explorers Club Vol 1: 8560
Exploring Program of Learning for Life Vol 1: 8563
Exxon Mobil Corp. - Downstream Operations Vol 1: 8568
ExxonMobil Chemical Co. Vol 1: 1519
ExxonMobil Chemical Company Vol 1: 2475
ExxonMobil Foundation Vol 1: 1545
ExxonMobil Research and Engineering Co. Vol 1: 1555, 1567
ExxonMobil Research and Engineering Company Vol 1: 2490
ExxonMobil Research & Engineering Company Vol 1: 2504
Eye Bank Association of America Vol 1: 8570
Eye-Bank for Sight Restoration Vol 1: 8574
Fachverband Messe-und Ausstellungsbau Vol 2: 2135
Faculty of Astrological Studies Vol 2: 5876
Faculty of Building Vol 2: 5878
Fair and Exhibition Association Vol 2: 2135
Fairfield County Medical Association Vol 1: 8576
Fairleigh Dickinson University Press Vol 1: 14388
Families with Children from China - New England Vol 1: 8578
Family, Career and Community Leaders of America Vol 1: 8580
Family Education Trust Vol 2: 5880
Family Federation of Finland Vol 2: 1365
Family Firm Institute Vol 1: 8582
Family Mart Co., Ltd. Vol 2: 3338
Family Service Association of America Vol 1: 397
FARM (Farm Animal Reform Movement) Vol 1: 8589
Farmaceutsko drustvo Hrvatske Vol 2: 1224
Farrer Memorial Trust Vol 2: 443
Father's Day/Mother's Day Council - National Father's Day Committee Vol 1: 8594
Fauna & Flora International Vol 2: 5179
Federal Aviation Administration Vol 1: 15264, 15266
Federal Bar Association Vol 1: 8596
Federal Bar Council Vol 1: 8602
Federal Executive Institute Alumni Association Vol 1: 8606
Federal Ministry of Education and Arts Vol 2: 768
Federally Employed Women Vol 1: 8608
Federation Aeronautique Internationale Vol 2: 4716
Federation Canadienne de la Faune Vol 1: 7063
Federation Canadienne de la Nature Vol 1: 13978
Federation Canadienne des Archers Vol 1: 8620
Federation Canadienne des Femmes Diplomees des Universites Vol 1: 6483
Federation canadienne des societes de biologie Vol 1: 6476
Federation Culinaire Canadienne Vol 1: 6446
Federation des Jeux du Commonwealth Vol 2: 5683
Federation des Societes d'Histoire du Quebec Vol 1: 15482
Federation Europeenne de la Corrosion Vol 2: 2116

Federation Europeenne de Zootechnie Vol 2: 3022
Federation International des Societes de Recherche Operationnelle Vol 1: 10410
Federation Internationale d'Astronautique Vol 2: 1879
Federation internationale de associations vexillologiques Vol 1: 10420
Federation Internationale de Basketball Vol 2: 4779
Federation Internationale de Canoe Vol 2: 4511
Federation Internationale de Chimie Clinique Vol 2: 3077
Federation Internationale de Football Association Vol 2: 4751
Federation Internationale de Genie Medical et Biologique Vol 2: 1228
Federation Internationale de Handball Vol 2: 4806
Federation Internationale de Judo Vol 2: 4100
Federation Internationale de l'Approvisionnement et de l'Achat Vol 2: 797
Federation Internationale de l'Art Photographique Vol 2: 3390
Federation Internationale de l'art Photographique Vol 2: 7083
Federation Internationale de l'Automobile Vol 2: 1881
Federation Internationale de Luge de Course Vol 2: 2307
Federation Internationale de Medecine du Sport Vol 2: 1244
Federation Internationale de Motocyclisme Vol 2: 4812
Federation Internationale de Natation Amateur Vol 2: 4758
Federation Internationale de Navigabilite Aerospatiale Vol 2: 6246
Federation Internationale de Neurophysiologie Clinique Vol 2: 6254
Federation Internationale de Ski Vol 2: 4835
Federation Internationale de Tennis Vol 2: 6303
Federation Internationale de Tennis de Table Vol 2: 4853
Federation Internationale des Architectes d'Inter Vol 2: 4209
Federation Internationale des Associations d'Apiculture Vol 2: 3075
Federation Internationale des Associations de Controleurs du Trafic Aerien Vol 1: 10402
Federation Internationale des Associations de Patrons de Navires Vol 2: 6259
Federation Internationale des Associations de Pilotes de Ligne Vol 2: 6242
Federation Internationale des Associations Medicales Catholiques Vol 2: 7419
Federation Internationale des Auberges de Jeunesse Vol 2: 6335
Federation Internationale des Bureaux de Justification de la Diffusion Vol 2: 4207
Federation Internationale des Chasseurs de Son Vol 2: 4798
Federation Internationale des Echecs Vol 2: 2474
Federation Internationale des Femmes Diplomees des Universites Vol 2: 4802
Federation Internationale des Ingenieurs Conseils Vol 2: 4796
Federation Internationale des Professions Immobilieres Vol 2: 1910
Federation Internationale des Traducteurs Vol 1: 10416
Federation Internationale du Diabete Vol 2: 914
Federation Internationale Pharmaceutique Vol 2: 3596
Federation Internationale pour la Recherche Theatrale Vol 2: 6240
Federation Internationale pour le Traitement de l'Information Vol 2: 793
Federation Internationale pour l'Habitation, l'Urbanisme et l'Amenagement des Territoires Vol 2: 3577
Federation Mondiale de l'Hemophilie Vol 1: 18928
Federation Mondiale des Anciens Combattants Vol 2: 2020
Federation Mondiale des Organisations d'Ingenieurs Vol 2: 2015
Federation of Alberta Naturalists Vol 1: 8610
Federation of American Hospitals Vol 1: 8612
Federation of American Hospitals Vol 1: 8612
Federation of American Societies for Experimental Biology Vol 1: 8615
Federation of Analytical Chemistry and Spectroscopy Societies Vol 1: 8617
Federation of Asian Chemical Societies Vol 2: 4095
Federation of British Tape Recordists Vol 2: 5537
Federation of Canadian Archers Vol 1: 8620
Federation of Canadian Music Festivals Vol 1: 8628, 13472
Federation of Children's Book Groups Vol 2: 5882
Federation of Danish Architects Vol 2: 1300
Federation of European Cancer Societies Vol 2: 883
Federation of European Cancer Societies Vol 2: 3115
Federation of European Direct Marketing Vol 2: 887
Federation of European Materials Societies Vol 2: 5884
Federation of European Societies of Plant Physiology Vol 2: 5888
Federation of Fly Fishers Vol 1: 8630
Federation of Gay Games Vol 1: 8651
Federation of Genealogical Societies Vol 1: 8653
Federation of Historical Bottle Clubs Vol 1: 8663
Federation of Historical Bottle Collectors Vol 1: 8663
Federation of Hong Kong Industries Vol 2: 3932
Federation of International Bandy Vol 2: 4584
Federation of Jewish Men's Clubs Vol 1: 8668
Federation of Materials Societies Vol 1: 8670
Federation of Ontario Naturalists Vol 1: 14576
Federation of Plastering and Drywall Contractors Vol 2: 5890
Federation of Women Contractors Vol 1: 8672
Federation Petanque U.S.A. Vol 1: 8674
Federation pour le planning des naissances du Canada Vol 1: 15089
Feline Control Council of Western Australia Vol 2: 445
Fell Pony Society Vol 2: 5892
Fellows of the American Bar Foundation Vol 1: 8676
Fellowship of Australian Writers NSW Vol 2: 447
Fellowship of Engineering Vol 2: 6620
Fellowship of Reconciliation - USA Vol 1: 8679
Ferenc Liszt Society, Budapest Vol 2: 2495
FeRFA Resin Flooring Association Vol 2: 5894
Ferst Foundation of Atlanta Vol 1: 16056
Fertiliser Association of India Vol 2: 2554
Fertilizer Society of South Africa Vol 2: 4176
Festa Musicale Vol 2: 1257
Festival de Cine de Alcala de Henares Vol 2: 4492
Festival de Television de Monte Carlo Vol 2: 3468
Festival dei Popoli - International Review of Social Documentary Film Vol 2: 3044
Festival dei Popoli - Rassegna Internazionale del Film di Documentazione Sociale Vol 2: 3044
Festival der Nationen Vol 2: 777
Festival des Films du Monde - Montreal Vol 1: 11943
Festival du Court Metrage en Plein Air Vol 2: 1789
Festival du Film Court de Villeurbanne Vol 2: 1791
Festival Internacional de Cine de Bilbao Documental y Cortometraje Vol 2: 4516
Festival Internacional de Cine Iberoamericano de Huelva Vol 2: 4502
Festival Internacional de Cine para la Juventud de Gijon Vol 2: 4498
Festival Internacional de Video de Canarias Vol 2: 4476
Festival International de Films de Femmes de Creteil et du Val de Marne Vol 2: 1927
Festival International de Jazz de Montreal Vol 1: 8682
Festival International de Musique de Besancon et de Franche-Comte Vol 2: 1793
Festival International du Cinema d'Animation - Annecy Vol 2: 1869
Festival International du Film Vol 2: 1729
Festival International du Film Alpin et de l'Environment de Montagne, Les Diablerets, Suisse Vol 2: 4804
Festival International du Film d'Amiens Vol 2: 1709
Festival International du Film de Berlin Vol 2: 2047
Festival International du Film de Vol Libre Vol 2: 1796
Festival International du Film Maritime et d'Exploration Vol 2: 1889
Festival International du Film sur l'Art Montreal Vol 1: 10423
Festival International du Nouveau Cinema et de la Video Montreal Vol 1: 11934
Festival Internazionale Cinema Giovani Vol 2: 3008
Festival Internazionale del Film Locarno Vol 2: 4863
Festival Internazionale del Film Turistico Vol 2: 3085
Festival Mondial de l'Image Sous-Marine Vol 2: 1798
Festival of Nations, Ebensee Vol 2: 777
Festival of Underwater Images Vol 2: 1798

Festival Panafricain du Cinema et de la Television de Ouagadougou Vol 2: 1159
Festival van Mechelen Vol 2: 940
Festspillene I Bergen Vol 2: 3893
Ffederasiwn Cerddoriaeth Amatur Cymru Vol 1: 10241
FIBA Oceana Vol 2: 453
Fiber Society Vol 1: 8684
FIDIA Research Foundation Vol 1: 12154
Field Naturalists Club of Victoria Vol 2: 455
Filharmonia Narodowa w Warszawie Vol 2: 4053
Film Advisory Board Vol 1: 8686
Film and Television Institute of Western Australia Vol 2: 457
Film Festival of Huesca Vol 2: 4494
Film Music Society Vol 1: 8688
Film Safety Awards Committee Vol 1: 13655
Film Victoria Vol 2: 563
Filmfest Munchen Vol 2: 2137
Filmfestival of Nations Vol 2: 779
FilmLinc: Film Society of Lincoln Center Vol 1: 8690
Filson Historical Society Vol 1: 8692
Filtration Society Vol 2: 5899
Financial Analysts Federation Vol 1: 7261
Financial Management Association International Vol 1: 8694
Financial Planning Association Vol 1: 8696
Fine Arts Association of Finland Vol 2: 1368
Fine Arts Club of Arkansas Vol 1: 4612
Fine Arts Work Center in Provincetown Vol 1: 8698
Fingerprint Society Vol 2: 5902
Finland Ministry of Defense Vol 2: 1373
Finnish Amateur Radio League Vol 2: 1377
Finnish Association of Designers Ornamo Vol 2: 1383
Finnish Cultural Foundation Vol 2: 1390
Finnish Paper Engineers' Association Vol 2: 1392
Finnish Ski Club Vol 1: 18094
Finnish Society of Sciences and Letters Vol 2: 1397
Finska Pappesingeniorsforeningen Vol 2: 1392
Finska Vetenskaps-Societeten-Societas Scientiarum Fennica Vol 2: 1397
Fire & Aviation Management - United States Forest Service Vol 1: 8700
Fireball International Vol 2: 5904
First Data Corp. Vol 1: 9190
First Marine Aviation Force Veterans' Association Vol 1: 11504
First Special Service Force Association Vol 1: 8706
Fischetti Endowment Scholarship Fund Vol 1: 8708
Fischoff National Chamber Music Association Vol 1: 8710
Fisher Diagnostics/Fisher Healthcare Vol 1: 13716
Fisheries and Oceans Canada Vol 1: 8712
Fiterman Foundation; Miles and Shirley Vol 1: 8832, 8833
Fitness Industry Association Vol 2: 5906
Flanders International Film Festival - Ghent Vol 2: 889
Fleischner Society Vol 1: 8714
Fleuroselect Vol 2: 3544
Flexible Packaging Association Vol 1: 8716
Flight Safety Foundation Vol 1: 8719
Flight Safety Foundation Vol 1: 15269
Flint Symphony Orchestra Vol 1: 15789
Florida Alliance of Information and Referral Services Vol 1: 8728
Florida Arts Council Vol 1: 8730
Florida Association of Colleges and Universities Vol 1: 8733
Florida Association of Nonprofit Organizations Vol 1: 8735
Florida Education Fund Vol 1: 8737
Florida Federation of Music Clubs Vol 1: 8739
Florida Film Festival Vol 1: 8741
Florida Freedom of Information Clearinghouse Vol 1: 5933
Florida Institute of Oceanography Vol 1: 8744
Florida Irrigation Society Vol 1: 8746
Florida Nursery, Growers and Landscape Association Vol 1: 8748
Florida Propane Gas Association Vol 1: 8752
Florida Sea Grant Vol 1: 8754
Florida Space Coast Writers Conference Vol 1: 17063
Florida Space Grant Consortium Vol 1: 8756
Florida Sports Foundation Vol 1: 8758
Florida State Archives Vol 1: 8760
Florida State Golf Association Vol 1: 8762
Florida State Grange Vol 1: 8765
Florida State Poets Association Vol 1: 13145
Florida TaxWatch Vol 1: 8767
Florida Trail Association Vol 1: 8769
Florilege Vocal de Tours Vol 2: 1800
Flowers Canada Vol 1: 8772
Fluor Daniel, Inc. Vol 1: 2468
Flygtekniska Foreningen Vol 2: 4688
Flying Fifteen International Vol 2: 5909
Flying Physicians Association Vol 1: 8774
Focolare Movement - Italy Vol 2: 3046
Foerderkreis Deutscher Schriftsteller in Baden-Wuerttemberg Vol 2: 2139
Folger Shakespeare Library Vol 1: 8777
Folklore Society Vol 2: 5911
Follett Library Resources Vol 1: 1281
Follett Software Company Vol 1: 1279
Fondation Agathon De Potter Vol 2: 1028
Fondation BNP Paribas Vol 2: 1940
Fondation Bonderjnstichting Vol 2: 934
Fondation Canadiene du Foie Vol 1: 6706
Fondation Canadienne d'Ergotherapie Vol 1: 6773
Fondation de la Maison de la Chimie Vol 2: 1802
Fondation des Infirmieres et Infirmiers du Canada Vol 1: 6771
Fondation des Prix Michener Vol 1: 11717
Fondation du Basket-Ball Dr. James Naismith Vol 1: 8237
Fondation Emile-Nelligan Vol 1: 17672, 17673
Fondation E.W.R. Steacie Vol 1: 17287
Fondation Feneon Vol 2: 1804
Fondation Francqui Vol 2: 894
Fondation Napoleon Vol 2: 1807
Fondation Paul Guggenheim Vol 2: 4875
Fondation pour la Recherche Medicale Vol 2: 1817
Fondation Universitaire Vol 2: 1101
Fondazione Arturo Toscanini Vol 2: 3048
Fondazione I Teatri Vol 2: 3133
Fondazione Il Campiello Vol 2: 3002
Fondazione Internazionale Balzan Vol 2: 3061
Fondazione Pezcoller Vol 2: 3114
Fondazione Russolo-Pratella Vol 2: 3051
Fonds National de la Recherche Scientifique Vol 2: 892
Food and Agriculture Organization of the United Nations Vol 2: 3053
Food and Commercial Workers AFL-CIO, LU 513 T Vol 1: 8779
Food and Drug Law Institute Vol 1: 8781
Food and Process Engineering Institute Vol 1: 3850
Food Distribution Research Society Vol 1: 8783
Food Marketing Institute Vol 1: 8785
Food Processing Suppliers Association Vol 1: 3850
Foodservice and Packaging Institute Vol 1: 8790
Foodservice Consultants Society International Vol 1: 8792
Football Association of Moldova Vol 2: 3463
Football Writers Association of America Vol 1: 8796
Foothills Art Center Vol 1: 8802
Forbes Vol 1: 6015, 6016
Ford Foundation and Harvard University - Innovations Program Vol 1: 9151
Ford Library; Gerald R. Vol 1: 8805
Ford Motor Company Vol 1: 3130, 7101
Ford Motor Co. Vol 1: 13000
Fordham University - School of Law Vol 1: 8808
Foreign Affairs and International Trade Canada Vol 1: 8810
Foreign Language Association of North Dakota Vol 1: 8814
Foreign Language Learning Today Vol 1: 1830
Foreign Press Association in London Vol 2: 5914
Foreningen Svensk Form Vol 2: 4690
Foreningen til Ski-Idrettens Fremme Vol 2: 3888
Forensic Science Society Vol 2: 5916
Forest History Society Vol 1: 8817
Forest Laboratories Vol 1: 16606
Forest Landowners Association Vol 1: 8822
Forest Press, Inc.; OCLC/ Vol 1: 2653
Forge Memorial Poetry Foundation; Ellen La Vol 1: 9208
Fork Lift Truck Association Vol 2: 5918
Forsyth County Defense League Vol 1: 13961
Fort Collins Symphony Association Vol 1: 8824
Fort Scott Community College Vol 1: 8826
Foster Care Association of Oklahoma Vol 1: 8828
Foundation for Australian Literary Studies Vol 2: 459
Foundation for Digestive Health and Nutrition Vol 1: 8830
Foundation for Microbiology Vol 1: 12169
Foundation for North American Wild Sheep Vol 1: 8837
Foundation for the Promotion of Finnish Music Vol 2: 1402
Foundation of American Women in Radio and Television Vol 1: 8848
Foundation of Lower Saxony Vol 2: 2141
Four Freedoms Foundation Vol 1: 8863
Fragrance Foundation Vol 1: 8852
Fragrance Foundation and Fragrance Research Fund Vol 1: 8852
France Ministry of Culture Vol 2: 1932
France Ministry of Defense Vol 2: 1809

Franciscan Retreats Vol 1: 8857
Franciscan University of Steubenville Vol 1: 8859
Franck Organ Competition Committee; Cesar Vol 2: 3547
Franco-British Society Vol 2: 5920
Francqui Foundation Vol 2: 894
Frank Huntington Beebe Fund Vol 1: 8861
Franklin and Eleanor Roosevelt Institute Vol 1: 8863
Franklin Institute Vol 1: 8865
Franklin National Memorial; Benjamin Vol 1: 8866
Frans Hals Museum Vol 2: 3549
Fraternal Order of Police Lodge 86 Vol 1: 8869
Frederick Chopin Society Vol 2: 4000
Fredericksburg Sister City Association Vol 1: 8871
Free Market Foundation of Southern Africa Vol 2: 4179
Freedom Forum Vol 1: 8873
Freedom to Read Foundation Vol 1: 8875
Freedoms Foundation at Valley Forge Vol 1: 8877
French-American Chamber of Commerce Vol 1: 8881
French-Canadian Genealogical Society Vol 1: 8883
French Chemical Society Vol 2: 1813
French Embassy in the Netherlands Vol 2: 3551
French Foundation for Medical Research Vol 2: 1817
French, Inc.; Samuel Vol 1: 11118
French League for Animal Rights Vol 2: 1821
French Ministry of Culture and Communication Vol 2: 1823
French Ministry of Environment Vol 2: 1936
French National Center for Scientific Research Vol 2: 1825
Fresno-Madera Medical Society Vol 1: 8886
Friday Morning Music Club Vol 1: 8888
Friday Morning Music Club Foundation Vol 1: 8889
Friends of Alexandria Archaeology Vol 1: 8890
Friends of Algonquin Park Vol 1: 8892
Friends of American Writers Vol 1: 8894
Friends of Casco Bay Vol 1: 8896
Friends of Freedom Society Vol 1: 8898
Friends of Libraries U.S.A. Vol 1: 8900
Friends of Old-Time Radio Vol 1: 8904
Friends of the Chicago Public Library Vol 1: 8906
Friends of the Morrill Memorial Library Vol 1: 8908
Friends of the Pendleton District Vol 1: 8910
Friends of the Princeton University Library Vol 1: 8912
Friends of the River Vol 1: 8915
Friends of the Waterfront Vol 1: 8917
Friends Research Institute Vol 1: 3419
Friestelersvereniging van Suid-Afrika Vol 2: 4244
Fuji Photo Film Vol 1: 16745
Fujihara Foundation of Science Vol 2: 3180
Fujisankei Communications International Vol 2: 1932
Fulton Chapter, Ohio Genealogical Society Vol 1: 8919
The Fund for American Studies Vol 1: 8921
Fund for Modern Courts Vol 1: 8925
Fund for the City of New York Vol 1: 8928
Fund for UFO Research Vol 1: 8930
Fundacion Alejandro Angel Escobar Vol 2: 1192
Fundacion Ferrer Sala-Freixenet Vol 2: 4550
Fundacion Miguel Aleman Vol 2: 3442
Fundacion Pablo Neruda Vol 2: 1167
Fundacion Principe de Asturias Vol 2: 4496
Fusion Power Associates Vol 1: 8932
Gadjah Mada University - Center for Population and Policy Studies Vol 2: 2815
Gairdner Foundation Vol 1: 8936
Galaxy Pageants Inc. Vol 1: 8938
Gale Group Vol 1: 2644, 2659
The Gale Group Vol 1: 4934
Galesburg Civic Art Center Vol 1: 8940
Gallaudet University Alumni Association Vol 1: 8942
Galva Arts Council Vol 1: 8945
Galveston Historical Foundation Vol 1: 8947
Gamma Sigma Delta Vol 1: 8949
Garden Club of America Vol 1: 8951
Garden Writers Association Vol 1: 8958
The Gardeners of America/Men's Garden Clubs of America Vol 1: 8962
GARDENEX: Federation of Garden and Leisure Manufacturers Vol 2: 5924
Gas Processors Association Vol 1: 8968
Gateway Greening Vol 1: 8973
Gathering of Nations Vol 1: 8975
Gaudeamus Foundation Vol 2: 3554
Gay and Lesbian Association of Choruses Vol 1: 8977
Gazette International Networking Institute Vol 1: 15161
GE Global Research Vol 1: 1562
GE Healthcare Vol 1: 4978, 4981
Gem and Jewelry Export Promotion Council Vol 2: 2560
Gem State Award Recognition Vol 1: 9555
Gemini Industries, Inc. Vol 1: 10554
Genealogical Association of Nova Scotia Vol 1: 8979
Genealogical Society of South Africa Vol 2: 4181
General Association of Engineers in Romania Vol 2: 4383
General Aviation Manufacturer Association Vol 1: 8981
General Commission on Archives and History of the United Methodist Church Vol 1: 8983
General Electric Company Vol 1: 3650
General Electric Foundation Vol 1: 3121
General Federation of Women's Clubs Vol 1: 8986
General Mills, Inc. Vol 1: 8993
General Monitors Vol 1: 16066
General Motors Cancer Research Foundation Vol 1: 8995
General Services Administration - Financial Systems Integration Office Vol 1: 8997
Genetic Alliance Vol 1: 8999
Genetics Society of America Vol 1: 9002
Genetics Society of Canada Vol 1: 9005
Geneva Association Vol 2: 4778
Geochemical Society Vol 1: 9008
Geographical Society of Philadelphia Vol 1: 9010
Geological Society of America Vol 1: 5137
Geological Society of America Vol 1: 9014
Geological Society of Australia Vol 2: 462
Geological Society of Denmark Vol 2: 1302
Geological Society of France Vol 2: 1829
Geological Society of London Vol 2: 5926
Geological Society of South Africa Vol 2: 4183
Geological Society of Zimbabwe Vol 2: 7434
George F. Cram Co. Vol 1: 12966
Georgetown University - Institute for the Study of Diplomacy Vol 1: 9029
Georgia Public Policy Foundation Vol 1: 9031
Georgia Writers Association and Young Georgia Writers Vol 1: 9033
Germain; La Foundation Yves-Saint- Vol 1: 9729
German Academic Exchange Service Vol 1: 9035
German Academy of Language and Poetry Vol 2: 2143
German Adult Education Association Vol 2: 2149
German Agricultural Society Vol 2: 2151
German Association for Water, Wastewater and Waste Vol 2: 2153
German Booksellers Association Vol 2: 2215
German Bunsen Society for Physical Chemistry Vol 2: 2155
German Chemical Society Vol 2: 2161
German Design Council Vol 2: 2181
German Direct Marketing Association Vol 2: 2183
German Geological Society Vol 2: 2187
German Informatics Society Vol 2: 2190
German Language Society Vol 2: 2192
German Marshall Fund of the United States Vol 1: 9048
German Medical Association Vol 2: 2195
German Ministry of Economic Affairs Vol 2: 2182
German National Mathematical Society Vol 2: 2198
German Nutrition Foundation Vol 2: 2247
German Organization of Endocrinology Vol 2: 2202
German OrnithologistsF Society Vol 2: 2206
German Physical Society Vol 2: 6054
German Phytomedical Society Vol 2: 2211
German Publishers and Booksellers Association Vol 2: 2215
German Research Foundation Vol 2: 2217
German Shoe Industry Association Vol 2: 2224
German Society for Biochemistry and Molecular Biology Vol 2: 2226
German Society for Fat Science Vol 2: 2228
German Society for Medicinal Plant Research Vol 2: 2376
German Society for Mining, Metallurgy, Resource and Environmental Technology Vol 2: 2232
German Society for Non-Destructive Testing Vol 2: 2236
German Society for Social Scientific Sexuality Research Vol 2: 2239
German Society of Glass Technology Vol 2: 2241
German Society of Metallurgical and Mining Engineers Vol 2: 2232
German Society of Nutrition Vol 2: 2244
German Society of Pediatrics and Adolescent Medicine Vol 2: 2248
German Society of Plastic and Reconstructive Surgery Vol 2: 2251
Germany Philatelic Society Vol 1: 9050
Gerontological Society of America Vol 1: 9052

Gesellschaft Deutscher Chemiker Vol 2: 2157, 2158, 2161
Gesellschaft Deutscher Naturforscher und Arzte Vol 2: 2253
Gesellschaft fuer Informatik Vol 2: 2190
Gesellschaft fur Aerosolforschung Vol 2: 2022
Gesellschaft fur Arzneipflanzenforschung Vol 2: 2376
Gesellschaft fur Biochemie und Molekularbiologie Vol 2: 2226
Gesellschaft fur Chemische Technik und Biotechnologie Vol 2: 2255
Gesellschaft fur Deutsche Sprache Vol 2: 2192
Gesellschaft fur Wirbelsaulenforschung Vol 2: 2378
Gesellschaft zur Forderung des Instituts fur Weltwirtschaft Vol 2: 2338
Gesellschaft zur Wissenschaftlichen Untersuchung von Parawissenschaften Vol 2: 2380
Gesneriad Society Vol 1: 9066
Getty Grant Program Vol 1: 9068
Geyer - McAllister Publications Vol 1: 9076
Geza Anda Foundation Vol 2: 4760
Giant Schnauzer Club of America Vol 1: 9078
Gijon; Festival Internacional de Cine para la Juventud de Vol 2: 4498
Gijon International Film Festival Vol 2: 4498
Gilbert and Sullivan Society of Austin Vol 1: 9080
Gilpin County Arts Association Vol 1: 9082
Girl Scouts of the Pioneer Council Vol 1: 9084
Girls' Brigade Australia Vol 2: 468
Girls' Brigade International Council Vol 2: 5939
Givaudan Vol 1: 1553
Glass Art Society Vol 1: 9086
The Glaucoma Foundation Vol 1: 9089
GlaxoSmithKline Vol 1: 1535
GlaxoSmithKline plc Vol 2: 6909, 6967
Gleeson Library Associates Vol 1: 9091
Gleitsman Foundation Vol 1: 9093
Glencoe Vol 1: 1098
Glencoe/McGraw-Hill Company Vol 1: 3657
Global Health Council Vol 1: 9096
Global Rights Vol 1: 9098
Global Solutions Education Fund - Pittsburgh Vol 1: 9100
Global Warming International Center Vol 1: 9102
Globe and Horn Book, Inc. Vol 1: 5858
Go Kart Club of America Vol 1: 10477
Gobierno del Estado de Morelos Vol 2: 3444
Godzilla Society of North America Vol 1: 9104
Goethe-Institut Vol 1: 1299
Goethe Institut Vol 2: 2264
Goethe Institute Vol 2: 2264
Golden Gate Audubon Society Vol 1: 9106
Golden Key International Honour Society Vol 1: 9108
Golden Key National Honor Society Vol 1: 9108
Goldman Environmental Foundation Vol 1: 9111
Goldsmith-Greenfield Foundation Vol 1: 15990, 15991
Goldsmiths' Company Vol 2: 5942
Golf Course Builders Association of America Vol 1: 18943
Golf Course Superintendents Association of America Vol 1: 9113
Golf Course Superintendents Association of America Vol 1: 18943
Golf Digest Vol 1: 9118
Golf Writers Association of America Vol 1: 9122, 18943
Good Housekeeping Vol 1: 8786
Goodwill Industries International Vol 1: 9126
Google Inc. Vol 1: 4808
Gorsedd Board Vol 2: 6471
Goshen College Vol 1: 9136
Gospel Music Association Vol 1: 9138
Gottlieb Duttweiler Institut Vol 2: 4762
Government Computer News Vol 1: 9141
Government Executive - National Journal Group Inc. Vol 1: 9143
Government Finance Officers Association of United States and Canada Vol 1: 9145
Government Innovators Network Vol 1: 9151
Government Management Information Sciences Vol 1: 9153
Government of India Vol 2: 2591
Governmental Research Association Vol 1: 9158
GPA Dublin International Piano Competition - Guradian Dublin International Piano Competition Vol 2: 2824
Grace and Company; W. R. Vol 1: 14272, 14273
Grafia - Graafisen Suunnittelun Jarjesto Vol 2: 1404
GRAFIA - The Finnish Association of Graphic Design Vol 2: 1404
Graham Foundation Vol 1: 9160
Grahamstown Foundation Vol 2: 4190
Grand Aerie, Fraternal Order of Eagles Vol 1: 9162
Grand American Road Racing Association Vol 1: 8068
Graphic Arts Technical Foundation Vol 1: 9170
Graphic Design USA Vol 1: 9177
Grassland Society of Southern Africa Vol 2: 4192
Graviner, Ltd. Vol 1: 8727
Great Lakes Carbon Corporation Vol 1: 1449
Great Lakes Colleges Association Vol 1: 9179
Great Lakes Commission Vol 1: 9181
Great Lakes Fishery Commission Vol 1: 10087
Greater Haverhill Arts Association Vol 1: 9183
Greater Lynn Photographic Association Vol 1: 9185
Greater Muskegon Music Teachers Association Vol 1: 9187
Greater Omaha Sports Committee Vol 1: 9189
Greater Philadelphia Chamber of Commerce Vol 1: 9191
Greater Seattle Business Association Vol 1: 9193
Greater Vancouver Professional Theatre Alliance Vol 1: 9195
Greater Waterbury Chamber of Commerce Vol 1: 9197
Greek Alzheimer's Association Vol 2: 2456
Green Meadow Foundation Vol 2: 4762
Green Organisation Vol 2: 5944
The Greensboro Review Vol 1: 9199
Greenwich Village Society for Historic Preservation Vol 1: 9201
Greenwood Publishing Group Vol 1: 1276
Greeting Card Association Vol 1: 9203
Gregg Fund; John Robert Vol 1: 18292
Griffin Trust for Excellence in Poetry Vol 1: 9205
Grolier Educational Corp. Vol 1: 2661
The Grolier Poetry Book Shop Vol 1: 9207
Groundwater Foundation Vol 1: 9209
Group for the Use of Psychology in History Vol 1: 9213
Groupe Consultatif International de Recherche sur le Colza Vol 2: 1885
Groupe International de Recherches sur la Preservation du Bois Vol 2: 4595
Groupement Regional d'Action Cinematographique Vol 2: 1792
Grune & Statton Vol 1: 4071
Grupo Prisa: Promotora de Informaciones SA Vol 2: 4500
Gruppo Esponenti Italiani Vol 1: 9215
Guadalupe Cultural Arts Center Vol 1: 9217
Guelph Spring Festival Vol 1: 9219
Guggenheim; Fondation Paul Vol 2: 4875
Guggenheim Memorial Foundation; John Simon Vol 1: 9221
Guide Dogs of America Vol 1: 9223
Guild of Agricultural Journalists Vol 2: 5946
Guild of Catholic Lawyers Vol 1: 9225
Guild of Food Writers Vol 2: 5948
Guild of International Professional Toastmasters Vol 2: 5950
Guild of Motoring Writers Vol 2: 5952
Guild of Registered Tourist Guides Vol 2: 5956
Guild of Taxidermists Vol 2: 5958
Guild of Television Cameramen Vol 2: 5960
Guild of Yachting Writers Vol 2: 7390
Guilde Europeenne du Raid Vol 2: 1845
Guildhall School of Music and Drama Vol 2: 5962
Guitar Foundation of America Vol 1: 9227
Gulf Coast Association of Geological Societies Vol 1: 1208
Gutenberg-Gesellschaft Vol 2: 2266
Gutenberg Society Vol 2: 2266, 2267
Gyldendaal Vol 2: 1304
Gynaecological Visiting Society of Great Britain and Ireland Vol 2: 6701
Haagudah Lezechuyot Haezrach Beyisrael Vol 2: 2894
Habitat for Humanity - New Zealand Vol 2: 3714
Hacker Instruments, Inc. Vol 1: 13717
Hadassah Magazine Vol 1: 9229
Hadassah, The Women's Zionist Organization of America Vol 1: 9231
Haemophilia Society Vol 2: 5964
Hague Academy of International Law Vol 2: 3558
Haiku Literature; Museum of Vol 1: 9238
Haiku Society of America Vol 1: 9233
Hall and Company; G. K. Vol 1: 2662
Handicraft Association of Nepal Vol 2: 3476
Handweavers Guild of America Vol 1: 9240
Hannibal Arts Council Vol 1: 9243
Hanover Chamber of Commerce Vol 1: 9245
Happold Trust Vol 2: 5638
Harcourt Brace Jovanovich Vol 1: 1831
Hardwood Research Council Vol 1: 13319
Harkness Fellowships of the Commonwealth Fund Vol 1: 9247
Harlow Foundation; Bryce Vol 1: 9249
Harmony Inc. Vol 1: 9251

Harness Racing Museum and Hall of Fame Vol 1: 17933
Harness Tracks of America Vol 1: 9263
Harrassowitz Co. Vol 1: 4914
Harrogate International Festival Vol 2: 5968
Harry S. Truman Library Institute for National and International Affairs Vol 1: 9267
Harry Stephen Keeler Society Vol 1: 9269
Hartley Fund; Marcellus Vol 1: 12163
Harvard Alumni Association Vol 1: 9271
Harvard Business Review Vol 1: 9274
Harvard Business School Vol 1: 14208
Harvard University - Graduate School of Design Vol 1: 9276
Harvard University Center for Italian Renaissance Studies Vol 2: 3141
Harvard University Press Vol 1: 9278
Harvey W. Watt & Co. Vol 1: 201
Harveys Leeds International Pianoforte Competition Vol 2: 6363
Haskil Association; Clara Vol 2: 4764
The Hastings Center Vol 1: 9280
Hatebusters Incorporated Vol 1: 9282
Hauptverband der Deutschen Schuhindustrie Vol 2: 2224
Hauptverband des Osterreichischen Buchhandels Vol 2: 759
Hawaii Association of School Librarians Vol 1: 9284
Hawaii State Foundation on Culture and the Arts Vol 1: 9286
Hawk Migration Association of North America Vol 1: 9289
Hawk Mountain Sanctuary Vol 1: 9291
Hawk Mountain Sanctuary Association Vol 1: 9293
Hawley Russell & Baker Ltd. UK Vol 2: 5406
Headline Book Publishing Vol 2: 5712
Headliners Club Vol 1: 9295
Headliners Foundation Vol 1: 9295
Healing the Children, Northeast Chapter Vol 1: 9297
Health Care Exhibitors Association Vol 1: 9319
Health Education Division Vol 1: 907
Health Industry Distributors Association Vol 1: 9299
Health Information Resource Center Vol 1: 9301
Health Physics Society Vol 1: 9303
Health Research Council of New Zealand Vol 2: 3718
Health Science Communications Association Vol 1: 9308
Healthcare Convention and Exhibitors Association Vol 1: 9319
Healthcare Financial Management Association Vol 1: 9321
Healthcare Information and Management Systems Society Vol 1: 9324
HEAR Center Vol 1: 9328
HEAR Foundation Vol 1: 9328
Hearst Corporation Vol 1: 8554
Hearst Foundation; William Randolph Vol 1: 9330, 13584
Heart of Denver Romance Writers Vol 1: 9332
Heart of New England Chihuahua Club Vol 1: 9335
Heart Rhythm Association Vol 1: 9337
Heat Transfer Research, Inc. Vol 1: 2489
Heavy Specialized Carriers Conference Vol 1: 17092
Heberden Society Vol 2: 5488
Hebrew Immigrant Aid Society Vol 1: 9343
Hebrew Union College - Jewish Institute of Religion Vol 1: 9345
Heinrich-Tessenow-Gesellschaft Vol 2: 2405
The Heinz Family Foundation Vol 1: 9348
Heiser Program for Research in Leprosy and Tuberculosis Vol 1: 9354
Heisman Trophy Trust Vol 1: 9356
Helen Keller International Vol 1: 9358
Helen Keller Worldwide Vol 1: 9358
Helfer Foundation for Children and Families; Ray E. Vol 1: 528
Helicopter Association International Vol 1: 9360
Helicopter Association of America Vol 1: 9360
Helmholtz Fonds Vol 2: 2268
HelpAge International - Latin America Regional Development Centre Vol 2: 1106
Helsinki International Ballet Competition Vol 2: 1406
Hemophilia Foundation of Michigan Vol 1: 9372
Herb Society of America Vol 1: 9374
Herbert Hoover Presidential Library Association Vol 1: 9380
Herff Jones, Inc. Vol 1: 12659
Heritage Association of San Marcos Vol 1: 9382
Heritage Canada Foundation Vol 1: 9384
Heritage Center Vol 1: 9388
Heritage Toronto Vol 1: 9390
Herpetologists' League Vol 1: 9392
High Point Convention and Visitors Bureau Vol 1: 9394
Highsmith Inc. Vol 1: 1277, 6055
Highsmith, Inc. Vol 1: 15422
Hiking Federation of Southern Africa Vol 2: 4194
Hiking South Africa Vol 2: 4194
Hillel, the Foundation for Jewish Campus Life Vol 1: 9396
Hillerich and Bradsby Co. Vol 1: 17192
Hillman Foundation Inc.; The Sidney Vol 1: 9399
Hills Pet Nutrition Vol 2: 1342
Hill's Pet Nutrition, Inc. Vol 1: 4407
Hillsdale College - Center for Constructive Alternatives/The Shavano Institute Vol 1: 9401
The Hip Society Vol 1: 9403
Hiroshima International Animation Festival Vol 2: 3182
Hispanic Engineer Vol 1: 7101
Histochemical Society Vol 1: 9406
Historic Albany Foundation Vol 1: 9408
Historic American Buildings Survey Vol 1: 16559
Historic Chattahoochee Commission Vol 1: 9410
Historic Harmony Vol 1: 9412
Historic Landmarks Foundation of Indiana Vol 1: 9414
Historic Mobile Preservation Society Vol 1: 9416
Historic New Orleans Collection - Williams Prize Committee Vol 1: 9418
Historic Scotland Vol 2: 5224
Historical Association Vol 2: 5971
Historical Branch Advisory Committee Vol 2: 3722
Historical Metallurgy Society Vol 2: 5973
Historical Radio Society of Australia Vol 2: 473
Historical Society of Frederick County Vol 1: 9420
Historical Society of Michigan Vol 1: 9422
Historical Society of Palm Beach County Vol 1: 9426
Historical Society of Princeton Vol 1: 9428
History of Dermatology Society Vol 1: 9430
History of Economics Society Vol 1: 9433
History of Education Society Vol 1: 9435
History of Science Society Vol 1: 9439
History Today Vol 2: 6780
Hitachi, Ltd. Vol 1: 7912
Hobey Baker Memorial Award Vol 1: 9447
Hochschule fur Grafik und Buchkunst Leipzig Vol 2: 2351
Hochschule fur Musik und Darstellende Kunst, Graz Vol 2: 827
Hochschule fur Musik und Darstellende Kunst, Wien Vol 2: 831
Hockey Hall of Fame Vol 1: 9449
Hodder and Stoughton Publishers Vol 2: 6381
Hodson Corporation Vol 1: 16882
Hoechst AG Vol 2: 2263
Holland Animation Film Festival Vol 2: 3560
Holly Society of America Vol 1: 9453
Hollywood Foreign Press Association Vol 1: 9457
Hollywood Radio and Television Society Vol 1: 9460
Home Baking Association Vol 1: 9462
Home Builders Association of Western Massachusetts Vol 1: 9464
Home Diagnostics, Inc. Vol 1: 1078
Home Inspectors; Canadian Association of Vol 1: 6259
Honda Foundation Vol 2: 3184
Honda Motor Company. Vol 1: 4139
Honens Calgary International Piano Competition; Esther Vol 1: 9466
Honeywell Vol 1: 1504
Honeywell International Foundation Vol 1: 9468
Hong Kong Film Awards Association Ltd. Vol 2: 3934
Hong Kong International Film Festival Vol 2: 3934
Hong Kong Management Association Vol 2: 3937
Hong Kong Productivity Council Vol 2: 3944
Honolulu Board of Realtors Vol 1: 9470
Honolulu Publishing Co. Ltd. Vol 1: 9472
Honor Society of Phi Kappa Phi Vol 1: 9474
Hope Unlimited Vol 2: 4410
Horatio Alger Association of Distinguished Americans Vol 1: 9479
Horatio Alger Society Vol 1: 9481
Horizons Theatre Vol 1: 9487
Horror Writers Association Vol 1: 9489
Hosei Daigaku Kokusaikouryu Center Vol 2: 3186
Hosei University - International Center Vol 2: 3186
Hospital Financial Management Association Vol 1: 9321
Hospital Management Systems Society Vol 1: 9324
Hospitality Sales and Marketing Association International Vol 1: 9491
Hotel Sales and Marketing Association International Vol 1: 9491
Hotel Sales Management Association Vol 1: 9491

Houston International Film Festival Vol 1: 18992
Houston Symphony Vol 1: 9498
Howard Foundation; George A. and Eliza Vol 1: 9501
Hoyt Institute of Fine Arts Vol 1: 9503
Hrvatski Sahovski Savez Vol 2: 1216
Hrvatsko Bibliotekarsko Drustvo Vol 2: 1218
Hrvatsko Farmaceutsko Drustvo Vol 2: 1224
Hrvatsko narodno kazaliste Split Vol 2: 1221
Huddersfield Contemporary Music Festival Vol 2: 5975
Hudson Valley Arabian Horse Association Vol 1: 9505
Human and Ergonomics Factors Society Vol 1: 9507
Human Factors and Ergonomics Society Vol 1: 9507
Human Growth Foundation Vol 1: 9515
Human Rights and Race Relations Centre Vol 1: 9517
Human Rights Institute of the Bar of Bordeaux Vol 2: 1847
Human Rights Watch Vol 1: 9521
Humane Slaughter Association and Council of Justice to Animals Vol 2: 5977
Humane Society of the United States Vol 1: 9523
Humane Society of the United States, New England Regional Office Vol 1: 9527
Humanist Association of Salem Vol 1: 9529
The Humanitas Prize Vol 1: 9531
Humboldt Film Festival Vol 1: 9533
Hungarian Publishers and Booksellers Association Vol 2: 2497
Hungarian Real Estate Association Vol 2: 2499
Hungarofest Vol 2: 2503
The Hunger Project Vol 1: 9535
Hunt Institute for Botanical Documentation Vol 1: 9537
Hunter Charitable Foundation; K. M. Vol 1: 14561
Hunterdon Museum of Art Vol 1: 9539
Hunterian Society Vol 2: 5979
Hunting Vol 2: 6524
Hunting Retriever Club Vol 1: 17699
Huntington County Visitor and Convention Bureau Vol 1: 9541
Huntington Library Vol 1: 14286
Huntington Society of Canada Vol 1: 9543
Hustinx Foundation; Edmond Vol 2: 3562
Hyatt Foundation Vol 1: 15240
Hydrolab/Hach Corp. Vol 1: 10090
Hymn Society in the United States and Canada Vol 1: 9545
Hymn Society of America Vol 1: 9545
IADR Dental Materials Group Vol 1: 10068
Ian Fleming (Glidrose) Publications Ltd. Vol 2: 5711
IBC Award Vol 2: 6232
Iberoamerican Film Festival - Huelva Vol 2: 4502
IBM Vol 1: 9931
IBM Corporation Vol 1: 1523
Ibsen Society of America Vol 1: 9548
ICD - International Center for the Disabled Vol 1: 9550
Icelandic Radio Amateurs Vol 2: 2514
I.D., The International Design Magazine - F+ Publications Inc. Vol 1: 9552
Idaho Quality Award - Idaho Department of Commerce and Labor Vol 1: 9554
Idaho Quality Award Recognition Vol 1: 9555
IDEA Health and Fitness Association Vol 1: 9556
Iditarod Trail Committee Vol 1: 9561
IEE Scotland Vol 2: 6150
IEEE Aerospace and Electronic Systems Society Vol 1: 9794
IEEE Computer Society Vol 1: 4812
IEEE Computer Society Vol 1: 9563
IEEE Control Systems Society Vol 1: 9794
IEEE Dielectrics and Electrical Insulation Society Vol 1: 9565
IEEE Education Society Vol 1: 9568
IEEE Electromagnetic Compatibility Society Vol 1: 9570
IEEE Engineering in Medicine and Biology Society Vol 1: 9794
IEEE Industrial Electronics Society Vol 1: 9579
IEEE Industry Applications Society Vol 1: 9784
IEEE Lasers and Electro-Optics Society Vol 1: 9581
IEEE Professional Communication Society Vol 1: 9591
IES, Institute for the International Education of Students Vol 1: 9593
IFA International Aviation Scholarship Vol 2: 6246
IFRA Vol 2: 2270
Illinois Association of Meat Processors Vol 1: 9596
Illinois Association of Teachers of English Vol 1: 15573
Illinois Ethnic Consultation Vol 1: 1832
Illinois Foreign Language Teachers Association Vol 1: 1832
Illinois Library Association Vol 1: 9598
Illinois Reading Council Vol 1: 15573
Illinois School Library Media Association Vol 1: 15573
Illinois Society for Microbiology Vol 1: 9613
Illuminating Engineering Society of North America Vol 1: 9615
ILSI North America Vol 1: 3795
Ima Hogg National Young Artist Audition Vol 1: 9498
Imagine Canada Vol 1: 9621
Imaging Geospatial Information Society Vol 1: 4732
Imaging Science and Technology Group Vol 2: 6881
Immigration and Ethnic History Society Vol 1: 9624
Imperial Chemical Industries Vol 2: 6975
In-Plant Graphics Vol 1: 10566
In-Plant Management Association Vol 1: 10563
In-Plant Printing Management Association Vol 1: 10563
The Inamori Foundation Vol 2: 3188
Incorporated Society of Musicians Vol 2: 5981
Independent Accountants Association of Illinois Vol 1: 9629
Independent Colleges and Universities of Florida Vol 1: 9631
Independent Feature Project Vol 1: 9633
Independent Free Papers of America Vol 1: 9636
Independent Insurance Agents and Brokers of America Vol 1: 9638
Independent Mystery Booksellers Association Vol 1: 9646
Independent Organic Inspectors Association Vol 1: 9648
Independent Sector Vol 1: 9650
India Ministry of Science and Technology Vol 2: 2572
India Office of the Prime Minister Vol 2: 2574
India Study Circle for Philately Vol 1: 9652
Indian Adult Education Association Vol 2: 2588
Indian and Northern Affairs Canada Vol 1: 9655
Indian Arts and Crafts Association Vol 1: 9657
Indian Council for Cultural Relations Vol 2: 2590
Indian Council of Agricultural Research Vol 2: 2592
Indian Council of Medical Research Vol 2: 2594
Indian Dairy Association Vol 2: 2632
Indian Institute of Architects Vol 2: 2636
Indian Institute of Metals Vol 2: 2642
Indian Merchants' Chamber Vol 2: 2663
Indian National Science Academy Vol 2: 2670
Indian Pharmaceutical Association Vol 2: 2729
Indian Physics Association Vol 2: 2735
Indian Science Congress Association Vol 2: 2737
Indian Society of Agricultural Economics Vol 2: 2753
Indian Society of Soil Science Vol 2: 2756
Indian Space Research Organization Vol 2: 1741
Indiana Arts Commission Vol 1: 9659
Indiana Black Expo Vol 1: 9661
Indiana Holstein Association Vol 1: 9665
Indiana Library Federation Vol 1: 9667
Indiana Opera Theatre Vol 1: 9681
Indiana Repertory Theatre Vol 1: 9683
Indiana State Federation of Poetry Clubs Vol 1: 13152
Indianapolis Motor Speedway Vol 1: 9685
Indonesian Planned Parenthood Association Vol 2: 2817
Industrial Designers Society of America Vol 1: 9688
Industrial Fabrics Association International Vol 1: 9690
Industrial Research and Development Vol 1: 15502
Industrial Research Institute Vol 1: 9692
Infectious Diseases Society of America Vol 1: 9696
Information Systems Security Association Vol 1: 9701
Information Technology Association of Canada Vol 1: 9709
Information Technology Society Vol 2: 2272
Information Today Inc. Vol 1: 2649, 6689
Informationstechnische Gesellschaft im Verband der Elektrotechnik Elektronik Informationstechnik Vol 2: 2272
Inforum, A Professional Women's Alliance Vol 1: 9711
Infusion Nurses Society Vol 1: 9713
ING Foundation Vol 1: 7880
Ingenjorsvetenskapsakademien Vol 2: 4633
Ingram Book Company Vol 1: 16997
Inland Bird Banding Association Vol 1: 9715
Inland Press Association Vol 1: 9718
Innovations at U of T Vol 1: 9725

Insititute of Metal and Materials Australasia Vol 2: 483
Institiuid Ceimice Na hEireann Vol 2: 2837
Institut Aeronautique et Spatial du Canada Vol 1: 6167
Institut Canadien d Administration de la Justice Vol 1: 6583
Institut Canadien de l'immeuble Vol 1: 15570
Institut Canadien de l'Energie Vol 1: 6585
L'Institut Canadien de Science et Technologie Alimentaires Vol 1: 6588
Institut Canadien des Ingenieurs Vol 1: 8461
Institut canadien des mines, Metallurgie et Petrole Vol 1: 6607
Institut Canadien du Trafic et du Transport Vol 1: 6633
L'Institut d'administration publique du Canada Vol 1: 9930
Institut de Biologie Physico-Chimique Vol 2: 1849
Institut de Chimie du Canada Vol 1: 7299
Institut de Droit International Vol 2: 4766
Institut de France Vol 2: 1851
Institut d'Histoire de l'Amerique Francaise Vol 1: 9727
Institut et Hospital Neurologiques de Montreal Vol 1: 11938
Institut Europeen d'Administration Publique Vol 2: 3539
Institut Forestier du Canada Vol 1: 6596
The Institut Francais de Washington Vol 1: 7361
Institut fur Weltwirtschaft an der Universitat Kiel Vol 2: 2337
Institut International d'Aluminium Vol 2: 6203
Institut International de Droit Humanitaire Vol 2: 3081
Institut International de Finances Publiques Vol 2: 2305
Institut International de la Soudure Vol 2: 1897
Institut International de Promotion et de Prestige Vol 2: 4810
Institut International de Statistique Vol 2: 3616
Institut International des Sciences Humaines Integrales Vol 1: 10470
Institut International du Froid Vol 2: 1895
Institut International pour l'Analyse des Systemes Appliques Vol 2: 802
Institut Mondial du Phosphate Vol 2: 3474
L'Institut National Canadien pour les Aveugles Vol 1: 6744
Institut national de la qualite Vol 1: 13585
Institut National du Cancer du Canada Vol 1: 12844
Institut Royal d'Architecture du Canada Vol 1: 15727
Institut Tal-Gurnalisti Maltin Vol 2: 3420
Institute for Communications Law Studies Vol 1: 9732
Institute for Energy Law Vol 1: 7192
Institute for Financial Crime Prevention Vol 1: 5063
Institute for Media Analysis Vol 2: 4171
Institute for Mesoamerican Studies Vol 1: 9734
Institute for Numerical Computation and Analysis Vol 2: 2835
Institute for Operations Research and the Management Sciences Vol 1: 9737
Institute for Policy Studies Vol 1: 9752
Institute for Public Relations Vol 1: 9754
Institute for Scientific Information Vol 1: 3744, 12148, 16422
Institute for Supply Management Vol 1: 9757
Institute for the Study of Earth and Man Vol 1: 9759
Institute of Acoustics Vol 2: 5984
Institute of Actuaries - United Kingdom Vol 2: 5989
Institute of Administrative Accountants Vol 2: 6030
Institute of Administrative Management Vol 2: 5992
Institute of Advanced Legal Studies Vol 2: 5994
Institute of Advanced Philosophic Research Vol 1: 9764
Institute of Australian Geographers Vol 2: 475
Institute of British Geographers Vol 2: 6764, 6768
Institute of Cast Metal Engineers Vol 2: 5997
Institute of Certified Records Managers Vol 1: 9766
Institute of Chartered Accountants in Australia Vol 2: 480
Institute of Chartered Accountants of New Zealand Vol 2: 3725
Institute of Chartered Accountants of Scotland Vol 2: 6001
Institute of Chartered Financial Analysts Vol 1: 7261
Institute of Chemistry of Ireland Vol 2: 2837
Institute of Civil Engineers Vol 2: 7065
The Institute of Classical Architecture and Classical America Vol 1: 9768
Institute of Contemporary History and Wiener Library Vol 2: 6019
Institute of Domestic Heating and Environmental Engineers Vol 2: 6021
Institute of Early American History and Culture Vol 1: 14527
Institute of Electrical and Electronics Engineers Vol 1: 3938, 3948, 4141
Institute of Electrical and Electronics Engineers Vol 1: 9770
Institute of Electrical and Electronics Engineers Vol 1: 16439, 16589
Institute of Electrical and Electronics Engineers - Computer Society Vol 1: 9799
Institute of Electrical and Electronics Engineers - Power Engineering Society Vol 1: 9817
Institute of Electrical and Electronics Engineers Lasers and Electro-optics Society Vol 1: 14619
Institute of Electronics, Information and Communication Engineers Vol 2: 3190
Institute of Entertainment and Arts Management Vol 2: 6026
Institute of Environmental Sciences Vol 1: 9829
Institute of Environmental Sciences and Technology Vol 1: 9829
Institute of Export Vol 2: 6028
Institute of Field Archaeologists Vol 2: 5225
Institute of Financial Accountants Vol 2: 6030
Institute of Food Technologists Vol 1: 9844
Institute of Heraldic and Genealogical Studies Vol 2: 6032
Institute of Industrial Engineers Vol 1: 9857
Institute of Information Scientists Vol 2: 5619
Institute of Internal Auditors Vol 1: 9876
Institute of Internal Auditors - UK and Ireland Vol 2: 6035
Institute of International Container Lessors Vol 1: 9884
Institute of International Education Vol 1: 9887
Institute of International Law Vol 2: 4766
Institute of Jamaica Vol 2: 3145
Institute of Journalists Vol 2: 5617
Institute of Landscape Architects of South Africa Vol 2: 4196
Institute of Legal Cashiers and Administrators Vol 2: 6040
Institute of Maltese Journalists Vol 2: 3420
Institute of Management Vol 2: 6042
Institute of Management Accountants Vol 1: 9889
Institute of Management Accountants, Rochester Vol 1: 9907
Institute of Management Sciences Vol 1: 9737
Institute of Marine Engineering, Science and Technology Vol 2: 6044
Institute of Marine Engineers Vol 2: 6044
Institute of Materials Vol 2: 6950
Institute of Materials Engineering Australasia Vol 2: 483
Institute of Mathematical Statistics Vol 1: 7622
Institute of Mathematical Statistics Vol 1: 9909
Institute of Measurement and Control Vol 2: 6050
Institute of Mechanical Engineers Vol 2: 6109
Institute of Navigation Vol 2: 6825
Institute of Navigation Vol 1: 9914
Institute of Nuclear Materials Management Vol 1: 9921
Institute of Packaging Professionals Vol 1: 9925
Institute of Physics Vol 2: 6053
Institute of Physics and Engineering in Medicine Vol 2: 6069
Institute of Physics (England) Vol 2: 255
Institute of Practitioners in Advertising Vol 2: 6073
Institute of Public Administration of Canada Vol 1: 9930
Institute of Quarrying - England Vol 2: 6075
Institute of Real Estate Management Vol 1: 9933
Institute of Road Transport Engineers Vol 2: 7204
Institute of Store Planners Vol 1: 9940
Institute of Trade Mark Attorneys Vol 2: 6077
Institute of Transportation Engineers Vol 1: 9943
Institute of Turkish Studies Vol 1: 9956
Institute on Political Journalism Vol 1: 8923
Institute on Religion and Democracy Vol 1: 9958
Institutes for Journalism in Natural Resources Vol 1: 8820
Institution of Agricultural Engineers Vol 2: 6080
Institution of Chemical Engineers Vol 2: 496, 532, 6088
Institution of Civil Engineers Vol 2: 6101, 6145
Institution of Diagnostic Engineers Vol 2: 6134
Institution of Diesel and Gas Turbine Engineers Vol 2: 6136

Institution of Electrical Engineers Vol 2: 6109
Institution of Electrical Engineers - England Vol 2: 6140
Institution of Electronics and Telecommunication Engineers Vol 2: 2763
Institution of Engineers Australia/Engineers Australia Vol 2: 485
Institution of Engineers, Sri Lanka Vol 2: 4555
Institution of Gas Engineers and Managers Vol 2: 6167
Institution of Incorporated Engineers Vol 2: 6175
Institution of Mechanical Engineers Vol 2: 6184
Institution of Municipal Engineering of Southern Africa Vol 2: 4198
Institution of Nuclear Engineers Vol 2: 6187
Institution of Occupational Safety and Health Vol 2: 6190
Institution of Professional Engineers New Zealand Vol 2: 3728
Institution of Structural Engineers Vol 2: 6194
Institutional and Municipal Parking Congress Vol 1: 10538
Instituto Cultural Domecq, A.C. Vol 2: 3446
Instituto Interamericano de Cooperacion para la Agricultura Vol 2: 1206, 1210
Instituut van Landskapargitekte van Suid Afrika Vol 2: 4196
Instructional Technology Council Vol 1: 9960
Instructional Telecommunications Council Vol 1: 9960
Instrument and Measurement Science Topical Group Vol 1: 3120
Instrumentation Laboratories Vol 1: 881
Insurance and Financial Communicators Association Vol 1: 9962
Insurance Institute of America Vol 1: 13736
Insurance Marketing Communications Association Vol 1: 9964
Intel Corp. Vol 1: 15927, 15928
Intellectual Property Law Association Vol 1: 14089
Intellectual Property Owners Vol 1: 9966
Intellectual Property Owners Association Vol 1: 9966
Intelligent Community Forum Vol 1: 9968
Intensive Care Society Vol 2: 6197
Inter-American Institute for Cooperation on Agriculture Vol 2: 1206
Inter-American Institute for Cooperation on Agriculture - Costa Rica Vol 2: 1210
Inter-American Organization for Higher Education Vol 1: 9972
Inter American Press Association Vol 1: 9974
Inter-American Society of Cardiology Vol 2: 3448
Inter-Collegiate Sailing Association of North America Vol 1: 9984
Inter-Collegiate Yacht Racing Association of North America Vol 1: 9984
Inter Press Service International Association Vol 2: 3057
Inter-Society Color Council Vol 1: 9986
Interactive Publishing GmbH Vol 2: 4768
Interamerican Accounting Association Vol 1: 9990
Interart Festivalkozpont Vol 2: 2503
Interatom Vol 2: 1787
Intercollegiate Men's Chorus, An International Association of Male Choruses Vol 1: 9992
Intercollegiate Musical Council Vol 1: 9992
Intercollegiate Rowing Association Vol 1: 9994
Intercollegiate Tennis Association Vol 1: 9996
Interconcert Festival Bureau Vol 2: 2503
Interfest: Moscow International Film Festival Vol 2: 4389
InterFuture Vol 1: 10010
Internationaal Filmfestival van Vlaanderen - Gent Vol 2: 889
Internationaal Vocalisten Concours 's-Hertogenbosch Vol 2: 3507
International 5.5 Class Association Vol 2: 4770
International 210 Association Vol 1: 10012
International Academy for Child Brain Development Vol 1: 10014
International Academy of Astronautics Vol 2: 1864
International Academy of Aviation and Space Medicine Vol 1: 10016
International Academy of Cytology Vol 2: 2275
International Academy of Olympic Chiropractic Officers Vol 1: 10018
International Academy of Television Arts and Sciences Vol 1: 12178
International Academy of Trial Lawyers Vol 1: 10021
International Advertising Association Vol 1: 10023
International Advertising Festival Vol 2: 6201
International Al Jolson Society Vol 1: 10026
The International Alliance, An Association of Executive and Profession - al Women Vol 1: 10028
The International Alliance for Women Vol 1: 10028
International Alliance for Women in Music Vol 1: 10030
International Aluminium Institute Vol 2: 6203
International Amateur-Professional Photoelectric Photometry Vol 1: 10033
International American Albino Association and White Horse Ranch National Foundation Vol 1: 4476
International ANDY Awards Vol 1: 10035
International Animated Film Association Vol 2: 1226
International Animated Film Festival Vol 2: 1869
International Animated Film Society, ASIFA - Hollywood Vol 1: 10037
International Association Auto Theft Investigators Vol 1: 10045
International Association for Bridge and Structural Engineering Vol 2: 4772
International Association for Cereal Science and Technology Vol 2: 781
International Association for Computer Information Systems Vol 1: 10051
International Association for Dental Research Vol 1: 10053
International Association for Dental Research Craniofacial Biology Group Vol 1: 10070
International Association for Energy Economics Vol 1: 10072
International Association for Engineering Geology and the Environment Vol 2: 3564
International Association for Food Protection Vol 1: 10077
International Association for Great Lakes Research Vol 1: 10085
International Association for Housing Science Vol 1: 10093
International Association for Human Resource Information Management Vol 1: 10095
International Association for Impact Assessment Vol 1: 10097
International Association for Jazz Education Vol 1: 10099
International Association for Mathematical Geology Vol 1: 10101
International Association for Pattern Recognition Vol 2: 785
International Association for Plant Taxonomy Vol 2: 787
International Association for Professional Art Advisors Vol 1: 10107
International Association for Religious Freedom Vol 2: 6205
International Association for Research in Income and Wealth Vol 1: 10109
International Association for Sports and Leisure Facilities Vol 2: 2278
International Association for Structural Mechanics in Reactor Technology Vol 1: 10111
International Association for the Evaluation of Educational Achievement Vol 2: 3566
International Association for the Fantastic in the Arts Vol 1: 10113
International Association for the Scientific Study of Intellectual Disabilities Vol 2: 6207
International Association for the Scientific Study of Intellectual Disabilities - Ireland Vol 2: 6209
International Association for the Scientific Study of Mental Deficiency Vol 2: 6207
International Association for the Study of Clays Vol 2: 896
International Association for the Study of Insurance Economics Vol 2: 4777
International Association for the Study of Obesity Vol 2: 6214
International Association for the Study of Pain Vol 1: 10116
International Association for Women of Color Day Vol 1: 10122
International Association of Assessing Officers Vol 1: 10124
International Association of Astacology Vol 1: 10140
International Association of Athletics Federations Vol 2: 3465
International Association of Audio Visual Communicators Vol 1: 10142
International Association of Broadcasting Manufacturers Vol 2: 6218
International Association of Bryologists Vol 1: 10144
International Association of Business Communicators Vol 1: 10149
International Association of Business Communicators - BC Chapter Vol 1: 10153
International Association of Business Communicators Manitoba Vol 1: 10157
International Association of Cancer Registries Vol 2: 1871
International Association of Cancer Victims and Friends Vol 1: 10161
International Association of Cancer Victors and Friends Vol 1: 10161
International Association of Chiefs of Police Vol 1: 10167
International Association of Clothing Designers and Executives Vol 1: 10178

International Association of Cooking Professionals Vol 1: 10185
International Association of Correctional Officers Vol 1: 10181
International Association of Crime Writers Vol 2: 1242
International Association of Crime Writers - North American Branch Vol 1: 10183
International Association of Culinary Professionals Vol 1: 10185
International Association of Defense Counsel Vol 1: 10190
International Association of Diecutting and Diemaking Vol 1: 10192
International Association of Educators for World Peace - USA Vol 1: 10198
International Association of Emergency Managers Vol 1: 10202
International Association of Empirical Aesthetics Vol 2: 2280
International Association of Energy Economists Vol 1: 10072
International Association of Fire Chiefs Vol 1: 10206
International Association of Fire Fighters Vol 1: 10208
International Association of Fish and Wildlife Agencies Vol 1: 10210
International Association of Food Industry Suppliers Vol 1: 10214
International Association of Geodesy Vol 2: 1306
International Association of Gerontology and Geriatrics Vol 2: 1128
International Association of Golf Administrators Vol 1: 18943
International Association of Human-Animal Interaction Organizations Vol 1: 10216
International Association of Hungarian Studies Vol 2: 2505
International Association of Hydraulic Engineering and Research Vol 2: 4504
International Association of Hydrological Sciences Vol 2: 1873
International Association of Insurance Counsel Vol 1: 10190
International Association of Jazz Educators Vol 1: 10099
International Association of Lighting Designers Vol 1: 10219
International Association of Music Libraries, Archives and Documentation Centres - United Kingdom and Ireland Vol 2: 6220
International Association of Orthodontics Vol 1: 10221
International Association of Paediatric Dentistry Vol 2: 1876
International Association of Philatelic Experts Vol 2: 3059
International Association of Physicians in AIDS Care Vol 1: 10223
International Association of Pipe Smokers Clubs Vol 1: 10227
International Association of Political Consultants Vol 2: 2284
International Association of Ports and Harbors Vol 2: 3196
International Association of Professional Bureaucrats Vol 1: 10229
International Association of Professional Congress Organizers Vol 2: 6222
International Association of Professional Numismatists Vol 2: 899
International Association of Radiopharmacology Vol 1: 10232
International Association of Registered Financial Consultants Vol 1: 10234
International Association of School Librarianship Vol 1: 10237
International Association of Schools of Social Work Vol 2: 6226
International Association of Sedimentologists Vol 2: 901
International Association of Special Investigation Units Vol 1: 10241
International Association of Sports Museums and Halls of Fame Vol 1: 10243
International Association of Structural Movers Vol 1: 10245
International Association of Technological University Libraries Vol 2: 6228
International Association of Theatre for Children and Young People Vol 2: 4587
International Association of Theoretical and Applied Limnology Vol 1: 10257
International Association of Traffic and Safety Sciences Vol 2: 3198
International Association of Volcanology and Chemistry of the Earth's Interior Vol 2: 541
International Association of Wall and Ceiling Contractors Vol 1: 5365
International Association of Wildland Fire Vol 1: 10259
International Association of Women in Radio and Television Vol 2: 2772
International Association of Women Police Vol 1: 10261
International Astronautical Federation Vol 2: 1879
International Atlantic Salmon Federation Vol 1: 5511
International Automobile Federation Vol 2: 1881
International Badminton Federation Vol 2: 3404
International Balzan Foundation Vol 2: 3061
International Banana Club Vol 1: 10264
International Bar Association Vol 2: 6230
International Basketball Federation Vol 2: 4779
International Biennials of Poetry Vol 2: 905
International Bird Strike Committee Vol 2: 3568
International Black Writers and Artists Vol 1: 10267
International Bluegrass Music Association Vol 1: 10269
International Board on Books for Young People Vol 2: 4782
International Board on Books for Young People - Dutch Section Vol 2: 3570
International Board on Books for Young People (IBBY) - Canadian Section Vol 2: 4782
International Book Project Vol 1: 10271
International Bottled Water Association Vol 1: 10273
International Bowling Museum and Hall of Fame Vol 1: 10275
International Braille Chess Association Vol 2: 4589
International Bridge, Tunnel and Turnpike Association Vol 1: 10277
International Broadcasting Convention Vol 2: 6232
International Buckskin Horse Association Vol 1: 10279
International Builders Exchange Executives Vol 1: 10281
International Bulb Society Vol 1: 10283
International Bureau for Epilepsy Vol 2: 2842
International Bureau for Precast Concrete Vol 2: 907
International Burn Foundation Vol 1: 10285
International Business Council MidAmerica Vol 1: 1832
International Business Machines Vol 1: 4815
International Business Machines Corporation Vol 1: 12149
International Business Machines (IBM) Vol 1: 3123
International Camaro Club Vol 1: 10287
International Canoe Federation Vol 2: 4511
International Card Manufacturers Association Vol 1: 10289
International Cartographic Association Vol 2: 3572
The International Cat Association Vol 1: 10292
International Catholic Organization for Cinema and Audiovisual Vol 2: 1091
International Catholic Stewardship Council Vol 1: 10294
International Catholic Union of the Press Vol 2: 4786
International Center for Comparative Criminology Vol 1: 10297
International Center of Photography Vol 1: 10299
International Centre for Heat and Mass Transfer Vol 2: 4965
International Centre for Human Rights and Democratic Development Vol 1: 10301
International Centre for the Study of the Preservation and Restoration of Cultural Property Vol 2: 3063
International Centre of Graphic Arts Vol 2: 4456
International Centre of Insect Physiology and Ecology Vol 2: 3355
International Chiropractors Association Vol 1: 10303
International Christian Studies Association Vol 1: 10305
International City/County Management Association Vol 1: 10308
International Civil Aviation Organization Vol 1: 10317
International Clarinet Association Vol 1: 10319
International Clarinet Society Vol 1: 10319
International Classical Guitar Competition Vol 2: 909
International College of Angiology Vol 1: 10322
International Colour Association Vol 2: 2286
International Commission for Optics Vol 2: 2947, 4513
International Commission for the Eriksson Prize Fund Vol 2: 4591
International Commission for the Preservation of Islamic Cultural Heri - tage (ICPICH) Vol 2: 4985
International Commission of Agricultural Engineering Vol 2: 2288
International Commission of Jurists - Canadian Section Vol 1: 10324
International Commission on Physics Education Vol 2: 4593
International Commission on Radiation Units and Measurements Vol 1: 10326

International Committee of Sports for the Deaf/DEAFLYMPICS Vol 1: 10328
International Committee of Systematic Bacteriology Vol 2: 552
International Committee of the Red Cross Vol 2: 1153, 4791
International Communications Industries Association Vol 1: 10330
International Community Corrections Association Vol 1: 10332
International Competition of Ceramic Arts: "Premio Faenza" Vol 2: 3066
International Confederation for Thermal Analysis Vol 2: 4204
International Confederation for Thermal Analysis and Calorimetry Vol 2: 4204
International Conference of Building Officials Vol 1: 10334
International Conference of Labour and Social History Vol 2: 789
International Consortium of Investigative Journalists Vol 1: 10337
International Consultative Research Group on Rapeseed Vol 2: 1885
International Corrections and Prisons Association Vol 1: 10339
International Cost Engineering Council Vol 2: 544
International Council for Adult Education Vol 2: 7403
International Council for Bird Preservation Vol 2: 5178
International Council for Canadian Studies Vol 1: 10344
International Council for Health, Physical Education, Recreation, Sport, and Dance Vol 1: 10347
International Council for Open and Distance Education Vol 2: 3899
International Council for Small Business Vol 1: 10356
International Council for the Improvement of Reading Vol 1: 10571
International Council of Ballroom Dancing Vol 2: 7367
International Council of Christians and Jews Vol 2: 2290
International Council of Environmental Law Vol 2: 2292
International Council of Graphic Design Associations Vol 2: 911
International Council of Shopping Centers Vol 1: 10358
International Council of Sport and Physical Education Vol 2: 2295
International Council of Sport Science and Physical Education Vol 2: 2295
International Council of the National Academy of Television Arts and Sciences Vol 1: 10362
International Council on Hotel, Restaurant and Institutional Education Vol 1: 10364
International Council on Monuments and Sites Vol 2: 1887
International Cryogenic Engineering Committee Vol 2: 2298
International Cryogenic Materials Conference Vol 1: 10373
International Customer Service Association Vol 1: 10375
International Dairy Foods Association Vol 1: 1878
International Dairy Foods Association Vol 1: 10377
International Dance Teachers' Association Vol 2: 6234
International Diabetes Federation Vol 2: 914
International Documentary Association Vol 1: 10379
International Documentary Film Festival - Amsterdam Vol 2: 3575
International Double Reed Society Vol 1: 10382
International Downtown Association Vol 1: 10384
International Downtown Executive Association Vol 1: 10384
International Dyslexia Association Vol 1: 10386
International Ecology Institute Vol 2: 2300
International Egg Commission Vol 2: 6238
International Electrical Testing Association Vol 1: 10388
International Embryo Transfer Society Vol 1: 10390
International Ergonomics Association Vol 2: 3068
International Executive Service Corps Vol 1: 10392
International Exhibition Logistics Associates Vol 2: 4794
International Exhibitors Association Vol 1: 17569
International Facility Management Association Vol 1: 10394
International Fan Club Organization Vol 1: 10400
International Federation for Housing and Planning Vol 2: 3577
International Federation for Information Processing Vol 2: 793
International Federation for Medical and Biological Engineering Vol 2: 1228
International Federation for Theatre Research Vol 2: 6240
International Federation of Air Line Pilots Associations Vol 2: 6242
International Federation of Air Traffic Controllers' Associations Vol 1: 10402
International Federation of Airworthiness Vol 2: 6246
International Federation of Asian and Western Pacific Contractors' Associations Vol 2: 3968
International Federation of Audit Bureaux of Circulations Vol 2: 4207
International Federation of Automotive Engineering Societies Vol 2: 6250
International Federation of Beekeepers' Associations Vol 2: 3075
International Federation of Biomedical Laboratory Science Vol 1: 10404
International Federation of Business and Professional Women Vol 2: 6252
International Federation of Clinical Chemistry and Laboratory Medicine Vol 2: 3077
International Federation of Clinical Neurophysiology Vol 2: 6254
International Federation of Consulting Engineers Vol 2: 4796
International Federation of Interior Architects/Designers Vol 2: 4209
International Federation of Landscape Architects Vol 2: 2004
International Federation of Leather Guilds Vol 1: 10408
International Federation of Library Associations and Institutions Vol 2: 3579
International Federation of Manufacturers and Converters of Pressure-S - ensitive and Heatseals on Paper and Other Base Materials Vol 2: 3693
International Federation of Netball Associations Vol 2: 6257
International Federation of Operational Research Societies Vol 1: 10410
International Federation of Ophthalmological Societies Vol 1: 10412
International Federation of Purchasing and Supply Management Vol 2: 797
International Federation of Shipmasters' Associations Vol 2: 6259
International Federation of Societies for Electroencephalography and Clinical Neurophysiology Vol 2: 6254
International Federation of Societies of Cosmetic Chemists Vol 2: 6261
International Federation of Sound Hunters Vol 2: 4798
International Federation of Sports Medicine Vol 2: 1244
International Federation of Standards Users Vol 2: 4800
International Federation of the Phonographic Industry - Finland Vol 2: 1408
International Federation of the Phonographic Industry - Hong Kong Vol 2: 3946
International Federation of Translators Vol 1: 10416
International Federation of University Women - Switzerland Vol 2: 4802
International Federation of Vexillological Associations Vol 1: 10420
International Fertiliser Society - England Vol 2: 6264
International Festival of Documentary and Short Film - Bilbao Vol 2: 4516
International Festival of Films for TV Vol 1: 5653
International Festival of Films on Art Vol 1: 10423
International Festival of Maritime and Exploration Films Vol 2: 1889
International Festival of Mountain and Environment Films Vol 2: 4804
International Festival of Red Cross and Health Films Vol 2: 1152
International Film Festival Mannheim - Heidelberg Vol 2: 2303
International Finn Association Vol 2: 1891
International Fire Photographers Association Vol 1: 10426
International Fire Service Training Association Vol 1: 10428
International Fiscal Association Vol 2: 3587
International Flanders Film Festival - Ghent Vol 2: 889
International Flat Earth Research Society Vol 1: 10430
International Flat Earth Research Society Vol 1: 10430
International Fluid Power Society Vol 1: 10432
International Foodservice Manufacturer Association Vol 1: 10435
International Formalwear Association Vol 1: 10437
International Franchise Association Vol 1: 10439
International Fritz Kreisler Competition Vol 2: 800

Organization Index

International Furnishings and Design Association Vol 1: 10443
International Game Fish Association Vol 1: 10447
International Gas Turbine Institute Vol 1: 4166
International Gay and Lesbian Human Rights Commission Vol 1: 10449
International Geographical Union Vol 1: 10451
International Glaciological Society Vol 2: 6266
International Golf Federation Vol 1: 10453
International Graphoanalysis Society Vol 1: 10456
International Guild of Candle Artisans Vol 1: 10458
International Handball Federation Vol 2: 4806
International Harp Contest in Israel Vol 2: 2903
International Horn Society Vol 1: 10463
International Hot Rod Association Vol 1: 10465
International Hotel and Restaurant Association Vol 2: 1893
International House of Poetry Vol 2: 906
International House - World Trade Center Vol 1: 18982
International Ice Hockey Federation Vol 2: 4808
International Institute for Applied Systems Analysis Vol 2: 802
International Institute for Geo-Information Science and Earth Observation Vol 2: 3589
International Institute for Promotion and Prestige Vol 2: 4810
International Institute of Fisheries Economics and Trade Vol 1: 10467
International Institute of Humanitarian Law Vol 2: 3081
International Institute of Integral Human Sciences Vol 1: 10470
International Institute of Public Finance Vol 2: 2305
International Institute of Refrigeration Vol 2: 1895
International Institute of Welding Vol 2: 1897
International Institute of Wisconsin Vol 1: 10472
International Isotope Society Vol 1: 10474
International Jeunesses Musicales Competition Vol 2: 4412
International Judges Association Vol 1: 18101
International Judo Federation Vol 2: 4100
International Kart Federation Vol 1: 10477
International Korfball Federation Vol 2: 3593
International Labor Communications Association, AFL-CIO/CLC Vol 1: 10479
International Labor Press Association Vol 1: 10479
International Lace Biennial, Contemporary Art Vol 2: 916
International Lacrosse Federation Vol 1: 10482
International Landslide Research Group Vol 1: 10484
International Laser Display Association Vol 1: 10486
International Law Students Association Vol 1: 4089, 10488
International League Against Epilepsy Vol 2: 918
International League of Antiquarian Booksellers Vol 1: 10490
International League of Associations for Rheumatology Vol 2: 547
International League of Women Composers Vol 1: 10030
International Life Sciences Institute - North America Vol 1: 9846
International Life Sciences Institute - North America Vol 1: 10492
International Lightning Class Association Vol 1: 10494
International Linear Algebra Society Vol 1: 10497
International Luge Federation Vol 2: 2307
International Magnesium Association Vol 1: 10499
International Map Collectors' Society Vol 2: 6270
International Masonry Institute Vol 1: 10503
International Mathematical Union Vol 1: 10505
International Measurement Confederation Vol 2: 2507
International Medical Consultants Vol 1: 8435
International Menopause Society Vol 2: 6273
International Metallographic Society Vol 1: 4705
International Microelectronics and Packaging Society Vol 1: 10508
International Mondiale de la Sante - Centre International de Recherche sur le Cancer Vol 2: 4931
International Morab Registry Vol 1: 10512
International Motor Press Association Vol 1: 10521
International Motor Sports Association Vol 1: 10523
International Motorcycle Federation Vol 2: 4812
International Motorsports Hall of Fame and Museum Vol 1: 10525
International Music and Media Centre Vol 2: 806
International Music Competition of the ARD Vol 2: 2310
International Music Council Vol 2: 2001, 4444
International Narcotic Enforcement Officers Association Vol 1: 10527
International Navigation Association - Belgium Vol 2: 923
International Newspaper Marketing Association Vol 1: 10531
International Newspaper Promotion Association Vol 1: 10531
International Nickel Company of Canada Vol 1: 7301
International Old Lacers, Inc. Vol 1: 10534
International Olympic Committee Vol 2: 2279
International Olympic Committee Vol 2: 4818
International Optometric and Optic League Vol 1: 18921
International Organ Festival at St. Albans Vol 2: 6275
International Organ Festival Society Vol 2: 6275
International Organisation of Vine and Wine Vol 2: 1906
International Organization for Succulent Plant Study Vol 2: 4823
International Organization of Plant Biosystematists Vol 1: 10536
International Organization of Supreme Audit Institutions Vol 2: 808
International Parking Institute Vol 1: 10538
International Partnership for Service-Learning and Leadership Vol 1: 10540
International Paulo Cello Competition Vol 2: 1410
International Peace Bureau Vol 2: 4825
International Pharmaceutical Federation Vol 2: 3596
International Pharmaceutical Students' Federation Vol 2: 3601
International Planned Parenthood Federation, Western Hemisphere Region Vol 1: 10545
International Platform Association Vol 1: 10547
International Police Association Vol 2: 6279
International Polka Association Vol 1: 10549
International Precious Metals Institute Vol 1: 10552
International Press Institute Vol 2: 811
International Print Biennale Vol 2: 4003
International Print Triennial Society - Krakow Vol 2: 4003
International Professional Surfers Vol 1: 5354
International Psychoanalytical Association Vol 2: 6281
International Psychohistorical Association Vol 1: 10556
International Public Management Association for Human Resources Vol 1: 10559
International Public Relations Association Vol 2: 6286
International Publishing Management Association Vol 1: 10563
International Quorum of Film and Video Producers Vol 2: 4827
International Radiation Protection Association Vol 2: 1908
International Radio and Television Society Vol 1: 10568
International Radio and Television Society Foundation Vol 1: 10568
International Reading Association Vol 1: 10571
International Readings at Harbourfront Centre Vol 1: 10603
International Real Estate Federation - France Vol 2: 1910
International Recording Media Association Vol 1: 10605
International Recreation Association Vol 1: 18951
International Religious Liberty Association Vol 1: 10608
International Rescue Committee - USA Vol 1: 10610
International Research Group on Wood Preservation Vol 2: 4595
International Road Federation Vol 1: 10612
International Road Safety Organization Vol 2: 4061
International Road Transport Union Vol 2: 4829
International Robert Schumann Competition Vol 2: 2312
International Save the Pun Foundation Vol 1: 10614
International Sculpture Center Vol 1: 10616
International Seaweed Association Vol 2: 1131
International Section of the National Council on Family Relations Vol 1: 10621

International Service for Human Rights - Switzerland Vol 2: 4831
International Sheep Dog Society Vol 2: 6289
International Short Film Festival, Oberhausen Vol 2: 2315
International Shuffleboard Association Vol 1: 10623
International Side-Saddle Organization Vol 1: 10625
International Sign Association Vol 1: 10627
International Silo Association Vol 1: 10629
International Skating Union Vol 2: 4833
International Ski Federation Vol 2: 4835
International Slurry Surfacing Association Vol 1: 10632
International Soap Box Derby Vol 1: 10634
International Social Science Council Vol 2: 1912
International Society for Aerosols in Medicine Vol 2: 2317
International Society for Augmentative and Alternative Communication Vol 1: 10636
International Society for Burn Injuries Vol 1: 10640
International Society for Contemporary Music - Netherlands Vol 2: 3603
International Society for Developmental Psychobiology Vol 1: 10642
International Society for Education through Art Vol 1: 10645
International Society for Engineering Education Vol 2: 4837
International Society for Heart and Lung Transplantation Vol 1: 10647
International Society for Heart Transplantation Vol 1: 10647
International Society for Human and Animal Mycology Vol 2: 1412
International Society for Individual Liberty Vol 1: 10649
International Society for Iranian Studies Vol 1: 10651
International Society for Military Law and Law of War Vol 2: 925
International Society for Neurochemistry Vol 2: 1308
International Society for Performance Improvement Vol 1: 10653
International Society for Pharmaceutical Engineering Vol 1: 10661
International Society for Philosophical Enquiry Vol 1: 10666
International Society for Photogrammetry and Remote Sensing Vol 2: 4968
International Society for Quality-of-Life Studies Vol 1: 10668
International Society for Rock Mechanics Vol 2: 4063
International Society for Sexual Medicine Vol 2: 3605
International Society for Soil Mechanics and Geotechnical Engineering Vol 2: 6292
International Society for the Arts, Sciences and Technology Vol 1: 10678
International Society for the Prevention of Child Abuse and Child Neglect Vol 1: 10683
International Society for the Study of Hypertension in Pregnancy Vol 2: 3609
International Society for Traumatic Stress Studies Vol 1: 10690
International Society for Trenchless Technology Vol 2: 6294
International Society for Vehicle Preservation Vol 1: 10695
International Society of Aerosols in Medicine Vol 1: 842
International Society of Air Safety Investigators Vol 1: 10697
International Society of Appraisers Vol 1: 10699
International Society of Blood Transfusion Vol 2: 3614
International Society of Certified Electronics Technicians Vol 1: 10701
International Society of Chemical Ecology Vol 1: 10703
International Society of Chemotherapy Vol 2: 6296
International Society of Contemporary Music - League of Composers Vol 1: 10707
International Society of Crime Prevention Practitioners Vol 1: 8565
International Society of Crime Prevention Practitioners Vol 1: 10709
International Society of Dermatology Vol 1: 10717
International Society of Electrochemistry Vol 2: 4839
International Society of Explosives Engineers Vol 1: 10719
International Society of Logistics; SOLE, the Vol 1: 16945
International Society of Offshore and Polar Engineers Vol 1: 10722
International Society of Orthopaedic Surgery and Traumatology Vol 2: 927
International Society of Paediatric Oncology Vol 2: 6298
International Society of Parametric Analysts Vol 1: 10731
International Society of Phonetic Sciences Vol 1: 10734
International Society of Political Psychology Vol 1: 10738
International Society of Psychoneuroendocrinology Vol 2: 2322, 2323
International Society of Reliabilty Engineers Vol 1: 16844
International Society of Surgery Vol 2: 4849
International Society of Travel and Tourism Educators Vol 1: 10743
International Society of Tropical Dermatology Vol 1: 10717
International Society of Typographic Designers Vol 2: 6301
International Society of Weekly Newspaper Editors Vol 1: 10745
International Society of Weighing and Measurement Vol 1: 10748
International Society on Toxinology Vol 2: 2324
International Sociological Association Vol 2: 4518
International Softball Congress Vol 1: 10754
International Softball League Vol 1: 10754
International Solar Energy Society Vol 2: 2326
International Songwriters' Association - Ireland Vol 2: 2845
International Sport Film Festival of Palermo Vol 2: 3083
International Sport Press Association Vol 2: 2509
International Statistical Institute Vol 2: 3616
International Steel Guitar Convention Vol 1: 10758
International Studies Association Vol 1: 10760
International Sunfish Class Association Vol 1: 10765
International Sunflower Association Vol 2: 1914
International Surfing Association Vol 1: 10767
International Swimming Hall of Fame Vol 1: 10769
International Table Tennis Federation Vol 2: 4853
International Tape/Disc Association Vol 1: 10605
International Tchaikovsky Competition Vol 2: 4391
International Technology Education Association Vol 1: 10778
International Telephone and Telegraph Corporation Vol 1: 9771
International Television Association Vol 2: 6326
International Television Festival of Monte Carlo Vol 2: 1100, 3468
International Tennis Federation Vol 2: 6303
International Tennis Hall of Fame Vol 1: 10788
International Ticketing Association Vol 1: 10794
International TourFilm Festival Vol 2: 3085
International Trade Mart Vol 1: 18982
International Transactional Analysis Association Vol 1: 10799
International Trombone Association Vol 2: 6309
International Trumpet Guild Vol 1: 10801
International Tube Association Vol 2: 6313
International Unicycling Federation Vol 1: 10807
International Union Against Cancer Vol 2: 4855
International Union Against Tuberculosis and Lung Disease Vol 2: 1916
International Union for Quaternary Research Vol 2: 2847
International Union for Vacuum Science, Technique and Applications Vol 2: 6315
International Union of Air Pollution Prevention and Environmental Protection Associations Vol 2: 6317
International Union of Architects Vol 2: 1921
International Union of Crystallography Vol 2: 6320
International Union of Forest Research Organizations Vol 2: 813
International Union of Microbiological Societies Vol 2: 549
International Union of Pure and Applied Physics - USA Vol 1: 10809
International Union of Radio Science Vol 2: 930
International Union of Soil Sciences Vol 2: 6322
International Union of Speleology Vol 2: 1259
International Veteran Boxers Association Vol 1: 10818
International Visitors Council - Columbus Vol 1: 10825
International Visual Communication Association Vol 2: 6326
International Water Association Vol 2: 6328

International Water Resources Association Vol 1: 10827
International Weightlifting Federation Vol 2: 2511
International Wild Waterfowl Association Vol 1: 10832
International Wildlife Media Center and Film Festival Vol 1: 10838
International Wine and Food Society Vol 2: 6333
International Wizard of Oz Club Vol 1: 10840
International Women's Film Festival Vol 2: 1927
International Women's Media Foundation Vol 1: 10842
International World Games Association Vol 2: 3618
International Yacht Racing Union Vol 1: 18079
International Youth Hostel Federation Vol 2: 6335
International Youth Library Vol 2: 2329
Internationale Carl Nielsen Musik Konkurrencer Vol 2: 1312
Internationale Filmfestspiele Berlin Vol 2: 2047
Internationale Filmwoche Mannheim Vol 2: 2303
Internationale Gesellschaft fur Felsmechanik Vol 2: 4063
Internationale Gesellschaft fur Ingenieurpadagogik Vol 2: 4837
Internationale Joseph A. Schumpeter Gesellschaft Vol 2: 2374
Internationale Jugendbibliothek Vol 2: 2329
Internationale Kurzfilmtage Oberhausen Vol 2: 2315
Internationale Liberale Vol 2: 6374
Internationale Messtechnische Konfoderation Vol 2: 2507
Internationale Organisation fur Sukkulentenforschung Vol 2: 4823
Internationale Paneuropa Union Vol 2: 2368
Internationale Robert-Schumann-Wettbewerbe Vol 2: 2312
Internationale Vereinigung fur Bruckenbau und Hochbau Vol 2: 4772
Internationale Vereinigung Sport- und Freizeiteinrichtungen Vol 2: 2278
Internationalen Rat der Christen und Juden Vol 2: 2290
Internationaler Johann-Sebastien-Bach-Wettbewerb Vol 2: 2035
Internationaler Musikwettbeweb - Genf Vol 2: 4701
Internationaler Musikwettbewerb ARD Vol 2: 2310
Internationaler Pianistenwettbewerb Busoni Vol 2: 2998
Internationaler Verband Forstlicher Forschungsanstalten Vol 2: 813
Internationaler Violinwettbewerb Koln Vol 2: 2068, 2070
Internationales Festival der Filmhochschulen Munchen Vol 2: 2137
Internationales Filmwochenende Wurzburg Vol 2: 2331
Internationales Musikzentrum Wien Vol 2: 806
Internationales Trickfilm Festival Stuttgart Vol 2: 2420
Interstate Mining Compact Commission Vol 1: 10844
Inventors Clubs of America Vol 1: 10847
Inventors Workshop International Education Foundation/Entrepreneurs Workshop Vol 1: 10849
Investigative Reporters and Editors Vol 1: 10851
Investment Education Institute Vol 1: 10854
IODE - Municipal Chapter of Toronto Vol 1: 10856
IONS - Institute of Noetic Sciences Vol 1: 10858
Iota Sigma Pi Vol 1: 10860
Iowa Bankers Association Vol 1: 10868
Iowa Center for the Book Vol 1: 10870
Iowa Horse Industry Council Vol 1: 10872
Iowa Hospice Organization Vol 1: 10874
Iowa League of Cities Vol 1: 10876
Iowa Poetry Association Vol 1: 13153
Iowa School of Letters Vol 1: 10878
Iqbal Academy Pakistan Vol 2: 3917
IREM Foundation Vol 1: 9937
Irino Prize Foundation Vol 2: 3200
Irish Amateur Rowing Union Vol 2: 2849
Irish American Cultural Institute Vol 2: 2877
Irish American Cultural Institute Vol 1: 10881
Irish Astronomical Association Vol 2: 2851
Irish Defence Forces Vol 2: 2853
Irish Lawn Tennis Association Vol 2: 2888
Irish Security Industry Association Vol 2: 2855
Irish Terrier Club of America Vol 1: 10889
The Irish Times Vol 2: 2857
Irish United Nations Veterans Association Vol 2: 2859
Irish Youth Foundation Vol 2: 2861
Iron and Steel Institution of Japan Vol 2: 3202
Iron and Steel Society of the American Institute of Mining, Metallurgical and Petroleum Engineers Vol 1: 4895
Iron Mountain Inc. Vol 1: 9767
Irrigation Association Vol 1: 10898
Irwin Co.; Richard D. Vol 1: 2715
ISA - Instrumentation, Systems, and Automation Society Vol 1: 10904
Islamic Capitals Organization Vol 2: 4408
Islamic Development Bank Vol 2: 4400
Islamic Propagation Centre Vol 1: 10918
Islamic Research Foundation International Vol 1: 10920
Island Resources Foundation Vol 1: 10922
Islenskir Radioamatorar Vol 2: 2514
Israel Democracy Institute Vol 2: 2905
Israel Geological Society Vol 2: 2907
Israel Mathematical Union Vol 2: 2911
Israel Museum Vol 2: 2915
Israel Society for Biochemistry and Molecular Biology Vol 2: 2922
The Issue Exchange Vol 1: 10924
Issue Management Council Vol 1: 10924
Istanbul Foundation for Culture and Arts Vol 2: 4981
Istanbul Kultur ve Sanat Vakfi Vol 2: 4981
Istituto Internazionale delle Comunicazioni Vol 2: 3087
Istituto Nazionale di Studi Romani Vol 2: 3089
Istituto Paolo VI: Centro Internazionale di Studi e Documentazione Vol 2: 3091
Istituto Paolo VI: International Centre for Study and Documentation Vol 2: 3091
Italian Association for Metallurgy Vol 2: 3093
Italian Chemical Society Vol 2: 3101
Italian Folk Art Federation of America Vol 1: 10926
Italian Historical Society of America Vol 1: 10928
Italian Institute of Culture for the United Kingdom Vol 2: 7131
Italian Mathematical Union Vol 2: 3106
Italian PEN Club Vol 2: 3110
Italian Society of Ecology Vol 2: 3112
Italian Wine and Food Institute Vol 1: 10930
Italic Institute of America Vol 1: 10932
Italic Studies Institute Vol 1: 10932
Italy - Ministry of Education Vol 2: 2999
Italy - the President of the Council of Ministers Vol 2: 2999
Italy-America Chamber of Commerce Vol 1: 10934
ITC-Foundation Vol 2: 4979
Ittleson Foundation Vol 1: 3274
ITV Network Limited Vol 2: 6337
IUPAP Commission C2: Sun Amco Vol 1: 10816
Izaak Walton League of America Vol 1: 10936
J-Lab: The Institute for Interactive Journalism Vol 1: 10942
Jackie Robinson Foundation Vol 1: 10944
Jackson County Literacy Council Vol 1: 10947
Jaen International Piano Competition Vol 2: 4520
Jaguar Clubs of North America Vol 1: 10949
Jamaica Exporters Association Vol 2: 3147
Jamaica Hotel and Tourist Association Vol 2: 3149
Jamaica Teachers' Association Vol 2: 3154
James Beard Foundation Vol 1: 10952
James Cook University of North Queensland Vol 2: 490
Jamnalal Bajaj Foundation Vol 2: 2774
Jane Addams Peace Association Vol 1: 10959
Janssen-Ortho Inc. Vol 1: 6842, 15090
Janssen Research Council Vol 1: 7549
Japan Academy Vol 2: 3212
Japan Art Association Vol 2: 3216
Japan Association for International Horse Racing Vol 2: 3218
Japan Construction Mechanization Association Vol 2: 3221
Japan Craft Beer Association Vol 2: 3223
Japan Design Foundation Vol 2: 3225
Japan External Trade Organisation Vol 2: 7075
Japan Fashion Color Association Vol 2: 3227
Japan Foundation Vol 2: 3232
Japan Golf Tour Vol 1: 18943
Japan Industrial Design Promotion Organization Vol 2: 3236
Japan International League of Artists Vol 2: 3238
Japan National Committee for UICC Vol 2: 4860
Japan Newspaper Publishers and Editors Association Vol 2: 3240
Japan Office of the Prime Minister Vol 2: 3242
Japan Oil Chemists' Society Vol 2: 3251
Japan Prize Preparatory Foundation Vol 2: 3317
Japan Society Vol 1: 10961
Japan Society for the Promotion of Science Vol 2: 2433, 3260
Japan Society of Mechanical Engineers Vol 2: 3262

Japanese Advertising Agencies' Association Vol 2: 3264
Japanese American Citizens League Vol 1: 10963
Japanese Association of University Women Vol 2: 3266
Japanese Biochemical Society Vol 2: 3270
Japanese Shipbuilding Industry Vol 2: 3366
Japanese Society of Applied Entomology and Zoology Vol 2: 3272
Japanese Society of Fisheries Science Vol 2: 3275
Jeantet de Medecine; Fondation Louis Vol 2: 4861
Jef Denyn; Royal Carillon School Vol 2: 1079
Jefferson County Historical Commission Vol 1: 10965
Jefferson Foundation; Monticello/Thomas Vol 1: 11931
Jellinek Memorial Fund Vol 1: 10967
JEMS Communications Vol 1: 12525
Jenemann Foundation; Hans R. Vol 2: 2157
Jeppesen Sanderson, Inc. Vol 1: 12227
Jerome Foundation Vol 1: 15105
Jerusalem International Book Fair Vol 2: 2924
Jerusalem Municipality Vol 2: 2926
Jerwood Charity Vol 2: 6339
jet2web Internet Vol 2: 762
Jewelers Security Alliance Vol 1: 10969
Jewish Book Council Vol 1: 10971
Jewish Book Council/JWB (Jewish Welfare Board) Vol 1: 10971
Jewish Community Center Theatre - Eugene S. and Blanche R. Halle Theatre Vol 1: 10984
Jewish Community Centers Association Vol 1: 10986
Jewish Educators Assembly Vol 1: 10989
Jewish Federation of Metropolitan Detroit Vol 1: 10991
Jewish Foundation for Christian Resevers/ADL Vol 1: 4543
Jewish Foundation for the Righteous Vol 1: 10993
Jewish Genealogical Society of Greater Philadelphia Vol 1: 10995
Jewish Institute for National Security Affairs Vol 1: 10997
Jewish Labor Committee Vol 1: 10999
Jewish National Fund Vol 1: 11001
Jewish Peace Fellowship Vol 1: 11004
Jewish Theological Seminary Vol 1: 11006
Jewish Welfare Federation of Metropolitan Detroit Vol 1: 10991
Jewish Women International Vol 1: 11013
Job Corps Advanced Career Training Program Vol 1: 17843
Jobs for America's Graduates Vol 1: 11015
Jockey Club of Canada Vol 1: 11017
John Deere and Company Vol 1: 17982
John F. Kennedy Library Foundation Vol 1: 11019
John Muir Trust Vol 2: 6341
John Templeton Foundation Vol 1: 11021
John Wiley and Sons Inc. Vol 1: 3737
Johns Hopkins University Vol 1: 11028
Johnson & Johnson Medical Vol 1: 4945
Johnson & Johnson Oral Health Products Vol 1: 1903
Johnson Foundation; Robert Wood Vol 1: 5038, 12174, 12175
Johnson Library and Museum; Lyndon Baines Vol 1: 11030
Johnson Matthey Catalysts Vol 2: 6967
Johnson Matthey plc Vol 2: 6967
Johnson Publishing Co. Vol 1: 2700
Join Hands Day Vol 1: 11033
Joint Baltic American National Committee Vol 1: 11035
Jose Manuel Lara Foundation Vol 2: 4484
Joseph Foundation Vol 1: 9347
Joshua Slocum Society International Vol 1: 11037
Journal of Aesthetics and Art Criticism Vol 1: 11044
Journal of Consumer Research - University of Wisconsin, Madison Vol 1: 11046
Journalism Education Association Vol 1: 11048
Jowett Car Club Vol 2: 6343
Joy in Singing Vol 1: 11056
Judah L. Magnes Museum Vol 1: 11460
Jump Memorial Foundation; William A. Vol 1: 11058
Junior Achievement Vol 1: 11060
Junior Achievement of Canada Vol 1: 11062
Junior Engineering Technical Society Vol 1: 11064
Junior Golf Association of Mobile Vol 1: 11066
Junior Philatelic Society of America Vol 1: 11068
Junior Philatelists of America Vol 1: 11068
Junior Wireless Club Vol 1: 15514
Juselius Foundation; Sigrid Vol 2: 1414
Justus-Liebig-Universitat-Giessen Vol 2: 2335
Juvenile Welfare Board of Pinellas County Vol 1: 11070
Juventudes Musicales de Espana Vol 2: 4522
JWB Vol 1: 10986
K. G. Saur Publishing Vol 1: 5087
Kabushiki Kaisha Dentsu Vol 2: 3178
Kancelaria Prezydenta Rzeczypospolitej Polskiej Vol 2: 4007
Kankakee River Valley Chamber of Commerce Vol 1: 11072
Kansas Arts Commission Vol 1: 11088
Kansas City Barbeque Society Vol 1: 11075
Kansas Crop Improvement Association Vol 1: 11078
Kansas Dietetic Association Vol 1: 11080
Kansas Native Plant Society Vol 1: 11083
Kansas State University - Center for Basic Cancer Research Vol 1: 11085
Kansas Watercolor Society Vol 1: 11087
Kanselarij der Nederlandse Orden Vol 2: 3489
Kappa Alpha Theta Foundation Vol 1: 13059
Kappa Delta Pi Vol 1: 11089
Kappa Delta Rho Vol 1: 11094
Kappa Mu Epsilon Vol 1: 11096
Kappa Publishing Group Inc. Vol 1: 1854
Kappa Tau Alpha Vol 1: 11098
Karg-Elert Archive Vol 2: 6345
Katanning Shire Council Vol 2: 553
Keats-Shelley Association of America Vol 1: 11100
Keene Center of Japanese Culture; Donald Vol 1: 11103
Keep America Beautiful Vol 1: 11105
Keithley Instruments Vol 1: 9785
Keithley Instruments Inc. Vol 1: 3120
Keller Worldwide; Helen Vol 1: 9358
Kennedy Center Alliance for Arts Education Network Vol 1: 11109
Kennedy Center American College Theater Festival Vol 1: 11112
Kennedy Center for the Performing Arts; John F. Vol 1: 11121
Kennedy Center for the Performing Arts; John F. - Partners in Education Program Vol 1: 11124
Kennedy School of Government at Harvard University; John F. Vol 1: 9152
Kennel Club Boliviano Vol 2: 1108
Kent State University - Gerontology Center Vol 1: 11126
Kent State University Alumni Association Vol 1: 11128
Kentucky Arts Council Vol 1: 11130
Kentucky Psychiatric Association Vol 1: 11132
Kentucky Reading Association Vol 1: 8351
Kentucky Watercolor Society Vol 1: 11134
Kenya Institute of Management Vol 2: 3357
Kenya National Academy of Sciences - Ministry of Research, Science and Technology Vol 2: 3359
Kenyan Publishers Association Vol 2: 3361
Kenyan Section of the International Commission of Jurists Vol 2: 3363
Keramos Vol 1: 11136
Keren Wolf Vol 2: 2937
Kettering - Moraine - Oakwood Chamber of Commerce Vol 1: 11138
Keuka College Alumni Association Vol 1: 11140
Keweenaw County Historical Society Vol 1: 11146
Kidde-Graviner, Ltd. Vol 1: 8727
Kidde-Grininer Vol 2: 6660
Kiel Institute for World Economics Vol 2: 2337
Kilby International Awards Foundation Vol 1: 11148
Kiln Trust; Robert Vol 2: 5227
Kinder-und Jugendfilmzentrum in Deutschland Vol 2: 2062
King Baudouin Foundation Vol 2: 934
King County Bar Association Vol 1: 11150
King Faisal Foundation Vol 2: 4402
King's College London Vol 2: 6347
Kings County Farm Bureau Vol 1: 11155
King's School Vol 2: 6349
Kinokuniya Co. Vol 2: 3280
Kinsmen and Kinette Clubs of Canada Vol 1: 11157
Kiwanis International Vol 1: 11159
Klasina Smelik Stichting Vol 2: 3571
KM Fabrics, Inc. Vol 1: 17952
Knight Fellowships; John S. Vol 1: 11161
Knight Foundation Vol 1: 10943
Kobe International Flute Competition Vol 2: 3282
Kobe YMCA Cross Cultural Center Vol 2: 3284
Kobenhavns Universitet Vol 2: 1337
Kodak Canada Vol 1: 6500
Kodansha Ltd. Vol 2: 3286
Kohler; Stichting Charlotte Vol 2: 3681
Kohn Foundation Vol 2: 6911
Kokusai Geijutsu Renmei Vol 2: 3238
Kokusai Koryu Kikin Vol 2: 3232
Kokusai Kotsu Anzen Gakkai Vol 2: 3198
Kokusai Kowan Kyokai Vol 2: 3196
Kompass Publishers Vol 2: 5620
Kone Instruments Vol 2: 5082

Kongelige Danske Geografiske Selskab Vol 2: 1329
Koning Boudewijnstichting Vol 2: 934
Koninklijk Belgisch Filmarchief Vol 2: 1082
Koninklijk Nederlands Aardrijkskundig Genootschap Vol 2: 3645
Koninklijke Academie voor Geneeskunde van Belgie Vol 2: 966
Koninklijke Academie voor Nederlandse Taal- en Letterkunde Vol 2: 948
Koninklijke Beiaardschool Jef Denijn Vol 2: 1079
Koninklijke Nederlandse Akademie van Wetenschappen Vol 2: 3647
Konrad Adenauer Foundation - Germany Vol 2: 2339
Konrad Adenauer Stiftung Vol 2: 2339
Kordelin Foundation; Alfred Vol 2: 1416
Korea Veterans Association of Canada Vol 1: 11163
Korean Aerospace Medical Association Vol 1: 203
Korean Chemical Society Vol 2: 4102
Korean Culture and Arts Foundation Vol 2: 4111
Kosciuszko Foundation Vol 1: 11165
The Koussevitzky Music Foundations Vol 1: 11169
Kraft Foods Vol 1: 1884, 3788
Kryolan Vol 1: 17954
Kuki-Chowa Eisei Kogakkai Vol 2: 3327
Kulturamt Spittal und Singkreis Porcia Vol 2: 767
Kungl. Vetenskapsakademien Vol 2: 4636
Kungliga Fysiografiska Sallskapet i Lund Vol 2: 4622
Kungliga Vitterhets Historie och Antikvitets Akademien Vol 2: 4620
Kurt J. Lesker Co. Vol 1: 5590
La Crosse Area Development Corporation Vol 1: 11171
La Federation des Societes Canadiennes d'Assistance aux Animaux Vol 1: 6480
La Foundation Yves-Saint-Germain Vol 1: 9729
La Leche League International Vol 1: 11174
La Prevention Routiere Internationale Vol 2: 4061
La Salle College Vol 1: 11180
La Salle University Vol 1: 11180
La Societe Canadienne De La Douleur Vol 1: 6789
Labologists Society Vol 2: 6351
Labor Education and Research Project Vol 1: 11182
Labor Research Association Vol 1: 11184
Ladies Association of British Barbershop Singers Vol 1: 9257
Ladies Auxiliary Veterans of Foreign Wars Vol 1: 11187
Ladies' Golf Union Vol 2: 6353
Ladies Professional Golf Association Vol 1: 11191, 18943
Laerdal Medical Corp. Vol 1: 12523
Lafarge Canada Inc. Vol 1: 6421
Lahti Organ Festival Vol 2: 1418
Lake Placid Education Foundation Vol 1: 14133
Lakeshore Humane Society Vol 1: 11206
Lakeshore Publishing Vol 1: 13141
Lamaze International Vol 1: 11208
Lambda Kappa Sigma Vol 1: 11215
Lambda Literary Foundation Vol 1: 11218
Lamoille County Planning Commission Vol 1: 11220
Lancaster Historical Society Vol 1: 11222
Land Improvement Contractors of America Vol 1: 11224
Land OFLakes Vol 1: 15178
Land O'Lakes, Inc. Vol 1: 1880
Landeshauptstadt Munchen Vol 2: 2342
Landeshauptstadt Stuttgart Vol 2: 2414
Landesstudio Oberosterreich Vol 2: 761
Landscape Research Group Vol 2: 6356
Landschaftsverband Westfalen-Lippe Vol 2: 2348
Landstinget Blekinge Vol 2: 4572
Lane Foundation; Allen Vol 2: 6430
Langlois Encounters; International Henri - Poitiers International Film Schools Festival Vol 2: 1929
Lanka Electricity Company Vol 2: 4557
Lannan Foundation Vol 1: 11226
Lanxess Inc. Vol 1: 7304
Lappeenrannan Kaupunki Vol 2: 1420
Lappeenranta City Orchestra Vol 2: 1420
LaPrensa Vol 1: 9976
Laser Institute of America Vol 1: 11228
Lasers and Electro-optics Society; Institute of Electrical and Electronics Engineers Vol 1: 14619
Lasker Foundation; Albert and Mary Vol 1: 11230
Latin American Phytopathology Association Vol 2: 3953
Latin American Studies Association Vol 1: 11234
Latin Liturgy Association Vol 1: 11239
Latin Recording Academy Vol 1: 11241
Latino Gerontological Center Vol 1: 11243
Latrobe Area Chamber of Commerce Vol 1: 11245
Law and Society Association Vol 1: 11247
Law of Polk County Vol 1: 11252
Lawn Tennis Association Vol 2: 6358
Lawrence Foundation Vol 1: 15191
LDA Publishers Vol 1: 11254
Le College canadien des enseignantes et des enseignants Vol 1: 6399
Le Conseil des Arts du Canada Vol 1: 6098
Le Croy Corporation Vol 2: 1787
Le Giornate del Cinema Muto Vol 2: 3120
le parc jean-Drapeau Vol 1: 11937
Le Soir - Rossel & Cie; S. A. Vol 2: 936
Leadership Conference on Civil Rights Vol 1: 11256
Leadership Fort Wayne Vol 1: 11258
League Against Cruel Sports Vol 2: 6360
League of American Theatres and Producers Vol 1: 11260
League of Canadian Poets Vol 1: 11262
League of Families Vol 2: 938
League of Minnesota Cities Vol 1: 11265
League of Minnesota Poets Vol 1: 13155
League of New York Theatres and Producers, Inc. Vol 1: 11260
League of Off-Broadway Theatres and Producers Vol 1: 11406
League of Women Voters of Arkansas Vol 1: 11268
League of Women Voters of Oklahoma Vol 1: 11270
The Leakey Foundation Vol 1: 11272
Learning Disabilities Association of Arkansas Vol 1: 11274
Learning Disabilities Association of California Vol 1: 11276
Leatherneck Magazine Vol 1: 11532
Leavenworth Area Development Vol 1: 11278
Lee Foundation Singapore Vol 2: 4423
Leeds International Pianoforte Competition Vol 2: 6363
Lefthanders International Vol 1: 11280
Legal Aid Society of the Orange County Bar Association Vol 1: 11282
Legal Momentum: Advancing Women's Rights Vol 1: 11284
Legion of Valor of the United States of America Vol 1: 11288
Leica Geosystems Inc. Vol 1: 4743
Leipzig College of Graphic Arts and Book Design - Academy of Visual Arts Vol 2: 2351
Lemelson-MIT Program - Massachusetts Institute of Technology Vol 1: 11291
Lentz Peace Research Association Vol 1: 11295
Leopoldina Academy of Researchers in Natural Sciences Vol 2: 2393
LEPRA Vol 2: 6365
Leprosy Relief Association Vol 2: 6367
Les Clubs Kin du Canada Vol 1: 11157
Les Dietetistes du Canada Vol 1: 8186
Leukemia & Lymphoma Society Vol 1: 5274
Leukemia and Lymphoma Society Vol 1: 11298
Leukemia Society of America Vol 1: 11298
Leven Prize for Poetry Trust; Grace Vol 2: 555
Leverhulme Trust Vol 2: 6371
Leverhulme Trust Fund Vol 2: 6912
Lewis and Clark Trail Heritage Foundation Vol 1: 11314
LexisNexis Vol 1: 5080, 17078
Liaison Committee on Medical Education in the United States Vol 1: 1738
Liberal International Vol 2: 6374
Libertarian Alliance Vol 2: 6376
Libertarian Futurist Society Vol 1: 11318
Libertarian International Vol 1: 10649
Libertarian Party of California Vol 1: 11321
Liberty Bell Wanderers Vol 1: 11323
Liberty Seated Collectors Club Vol 1: 11325
Library Administration and Management Association Vol 1: 11327
Library and Information Association of New Zealand Vol 2: 3749
Library and Information Research Group Vol 2: 6378
Library and Information Service of Western Australia Vol 2: 684
Library and Information Technology Association Vol 1: 11337
Library Association Vol 2: 5619
Library Association of Australia Vol 2: 268
Library Directory Associates Publishers Vol 1: 11254
Library of Congress Vol 1: 11344
Library Public Relations Council Vol 1: 11348
Library Systems and Services Inc. Vol 1: 11342
Lichfield District Council Vol 2: 6380
Liederkranz Foundation Vol 1: 11351
Life Insurance Advertisers Association Vol 1: 9962
Life Office Management Association Vol 1: 11353
Lifespan, Inc. Vol 1: 1079

Lifespan/Tufts/Brown Center for AIDS Research Vol 1: 11357
Liga Argentina Contra la Tuberculosis Vol 2: 22
Lighter-Than-Air Society Vol 1: 11359
Lighting Association Vol 2: 6382
Ligue des Familles Vol 2: 938
Ligue Europeenne de Bridge Vol 2: 3026
Ligue Francaise des Droits de l'Animal Vol 2: 1821
Lilly and Company; Eli Vol 1: 1563
Lilly and Co.; Eli Vol 1: 16606
Limnological Society of America Vol 1: 4110
Lincoln Center for the Performing Arts Vol 1: 11361
Lincoln Electric Company Vol 1: 4473
Lincoln Group of New York Vol 1: 11366
Lincoln Lancaster Women's Commission Vol 1: 11368
Lincoln University of Missouri Vol 1: 11372
Lindapter International Ltd. Vol 2: 6119
Lindbergh Fund; Charles A. Vol 1: 7285
Linguistic Association of Canada and the United States Vol 1: 11374
Link Foundation Vol 1: 11376
Linnean Society of London Vol 2: 6384
Lions Club International Foundation Vol 1: 1912
Lipizzan Association of North America Vol 1: 11378
Liszt Competition Foundation - Muziekcentrum Vredenburg Vol 2: 3620
Liszt Ferenc Tarsasag Vol 2: 2495
Literary Translators Association of Canada Vol 1: 11380
Literature; Museum of Haiku Vol 1: 9238
Lithuanian American Roman Catholic Women's Alliance Vol 1: 11382
Little Big Horn Associates Vol 1: 11384
Little, Brown & Co. Vol 2: 5712
Little, Inc.; A. D. Vol 1: 2491
Little Theatre of Alexandria Vol 1: 11387
Liverpool School of Tropical Medicine Vol 2: 6390
Livestock Publications Council Vol 1: 11389
Livingston County Council on Alcohol and Substance Abuse Vol 1: 11393
Llangollen International Musical Eisteddfod Vol 2: 6392
Lo-Jack Corp. Vol 1: 10049
Locarno Internationale Film Festival Vol 2: 4863
Lockheed Martin Corp. Vol 1: 11546
Lockheed Martin Science and Engineering Service Vol 1: 208
Locus Publications Vol 1: 11395
The Loft, A Place for Writing and Literature Vol 1: 11397
The Loft Literary Center Vol 1: 11397
Logistics and Transport New Zealand Vol 2: 3754
Lomond Poets; Ben Vol 1: 13157
London International Piano Competition Vol 2: 6394
London International Piano Competition Vol 2: 6394
London Mathematical Society Vol 2: 6396
London School of Hygiene and Tropical Medicine Vol 2: 7032
London String Quartet Competition Vol 2: 6406
Long and Jacques Thibaud International Competition; Marguerite Vol 2: 1931
Long Island University, Brooklyn Campus Vol 1: 11400
Long - Jacques Thibaud; Concours International Marguerite Vol 2: 1931
LoonWatch Vol 1: 11403
Lortel Theatre; Lucille Vol 1: 11405
Los Angeles Advertising Agencies Association Vol 1: 11407
Los Angeles Athletic Club Vol 1: 11409
Los Angeles Conservancy Vol 1: 11411
Los Angeles Public Library Vol 1: 11413
Los Angeles Times Book Prizes Vol 1: 11415
Louisiana Association of School Librarians Vol 1: 11422, 11427
Louisiana Historical Association Vol 1: 9419
Louisiana Library Association Vol 1: 11417
Louisiana State Poetry Society Vol 1: 13159
Louisiana State University - U.S. Civil War Center Vol 1: 11428
Lowin Trust; Paul Vol 2: 557
Loyola University Chicago Vol 1: 11430
Ludwig Boltzman Gesellschaft Osterreichische Vereinigung zur Forderung Vol 2: 816
Ludwig Boltzmann Association - Austrian Society for the Promotion of Scientific Research - Institute for Clinical Neurobiology Vol 2: 816
Lufthansa German Airlines Vol 2: 3338
Luovan saveltaiteen edistamissaatio Vol 2: 1402
Lupus Foundation of America Vol 1: 11436
Lupus Foundation of America, Arizona Area Coordinator Vol 1: 11438
Lupus Foundation of America, Arkansas Chapter Vol 1: 11440
Lupus Foundation of Minnesota Vol 1: 11442
Lutheran Education Association Vol 1: 11444
Lutheran Historical Conference Vol 1: 11446
Lutherans Concerned/North America Vol 1: 11448
Lyme Academy College of Fine Arts Vol 1: 13693
Lynchburg Historical Foundation Vol 1: 11450
Maatschappij der Nederlandse Letterkunde Vol 2: 3666
MacArthur Foundation; John D. and Catherine T. Vol 1: 11452
The MacDowell Colony Vol 1: 11454
Macmillan Vol 1: 1098
Macworld Vol 1: 14874
Madeira, Regional Secretary of Tourism and Culture Vol 2: 4066
Madeira, Secretaria Regional do Turismo e Cultura Vol 2: 4066
Madison Square Garden Television Productions Vol 1: 11854
Magazine Publishers Association Vol 1: 11456
Magazine Publishers of America Vol 1: 11456
Magistrat der Universitatsstadt Giessen Vol 2: 2353
Magnes Museum; Judah L. Vol 1: 11459
The Magnolia Society Vol 1: 11461
Magyar Geofizikusok Egyesulete Vol 2: 2486
Magyar Ingatlanszovetseg Vol 2: 2499
Mail Systems Management Association Vol 1: 11463
Mailing and Fulfillment Service Association Vol 1: 11467
Maine Hospice Council Vol 1: 11475
Maine Journeymen Vol 1: 11477
Maine Space Grant Consortium Vol 1: 11479
Maisons de la Presse Vol 2: 1933
Majlis Olimpik Malaysia Vol 2: 3414
Majors; J. A. Vol 1: 11661
Making Music Vol 2: 6408
Malacological Society of London Vol 2: 6412
Malahat Review Vol 1: 11481
Malaysian Rubber Products Manufacturers Association Vol 2: 3412
Malice Domestic Ltd. Vol 1: 11484
Malko International Competition for Young Conductors; Nicolai Vol 2: 1310
Mallinckrodt Baker Inc. Vol 1: 1569
Malta Amateur Cine Circle Vol 2: 3422
Maltese-American Benevolent Society Vol 1: 11486
Maltsters' Association of Great Britain Vol 2: 6415
Man Group Vol 2: 6417
Mananan Festival Trust Vol 2: 7258
Manhattan College Vol 1: 11490
Manifestazioni Internazionali della Ceramica Vol 2: 3066
Manomet Bird Observatory Vol 1: 11492
Manomet Center for Conservation Sciences Vol 1: 11492
Manufacturers' Agents for the Foodservice Industry Vol 1: 11494
Manufacturers Association; Chemical Specialties Vol 1: 7781
Marconi Society Vol 1: 11502
Marian Library Vol 1: 18271
Marin Self Publishers Association Vol 1: 5684
Marin Small Publishers Association Vol 1: 5684
Marine Biological Association of the United Kingdom Vol 2: 6419
Marine Corps Aviation Association Vol 1: 11504
Marine Corps Heritage Foundation Vol 1: 11531
Marine Corps Mustang Association Vol 1: 11538
Marine Corps Reserve Association Vol 1: 11540
Marine Technology Society Vol 1: 11542
Mariological Society of America Vol 1: 11548
Marketing Science Institute Vol 1: 2721
Marketing Science Institute Vol 1: 11550
Marquette University - Department of Journalism Vol 1: 11552
Marshall Cavendish Corp. Vol 1: 2652
Martin-Bodmer-Stiftung fur einen Gottfried Keller-Preis Vol 2: 4865
Maryknoll Fathers and Brothers Vol 1: 11554
Maryknoll Lay Missioners Vol 1: 11556
Maryland Association of Private Colleges and Career Schools Vol 1: 11558
Maryland Jockey Club Vol 1: 11560
Maryland Technology Enterprise Institute Vol 1: 11564
Mason Contractors Association of America Vol 1: 11567
The Masquers Vol 1: 11569
Massachusetts Association of School Business Officials Vol 1: 11571
Massachusetts Audubon Society Vol 1: 11573
Massachusetts Conveyancers Association Vol 1: 11575
Massachusetts Council for the Social Studies Vol 1: 11577

Massachusetts Forestry Association Vol 1: 11582
Massachusetts Lodging Association Vol 1: 11584
Massachusetts Science Educators Hall of Fame Vol 1: 11586
Massachusetts Society of Professional Engineers Vol 1: 11588
Massachusetts State Poetry Society Vol 1: 13160
Massey Foundation Vol 1: 15743
Master of Professional Writing Program Vol 1: 11590
Master's Men Ministry - National Associaton of Free Will Baptists Vol 1: 11592
Materials Research Society Vol 1: 11594
Mathematical Association of America Vol 1: 11600
Mathematical Association of America Vol 1: 16273
Mathematical Programming Society Vol 1: 11612, 16269
Mathematical Society of Japan Vol 2: 3291
Mathematical Society of the Philippines Vol 2: 3984
Mathematics Research Center Vol 1: 11616
Mattel Sports Vol 1: 18941
Mature Market Resource Center Vol 1: 11620
Max-Eyth-Gesselschaft Agrartechnik im VDI Vol 2: 2355
Max-Eyth Society for Agricultural Engineering of the VDI Vol 2: 2355
Max Schmidheiny Foundation Vol 2: 4867
MC Sailing Association Vol 1: 11622
McClelland & Stewart Ltd. Vol 1: 11624
McCord Museum of Canadian History Vol 1: 11626
McGannon Communication Research Center; Donald Vol 1: 11628
McGill University - Gault Nature Reserve Vol 1: 11630
McGovern Fund for the Behavioral Sciences Vol 1: 950
McGraw-Hill Vol 1: 1098
The McGraw-Hill Companies, Inc. Vol 1: 11632
McGraw-Hill Companies Inc. Vol 1: 12411
McHose Scholarship Fund; Allen I. Vol 1: 12032
McKay Welding Products Vol 1: 4455
McKinsey Foundation for Management Research Vol 1: 9275
McKnight Foundation Vol 1: 15106
McKnight Programs in Higher Education Vol 1: 8737
McLaughlin Foundation; R. Samuel Vol 1: 15762
Mead Johnson Nutritionals Vol 1: 3794, 16149
Meade Instrument Corporation Vol 1: 5476
Meadows Foundation Inc. Vol 1: 17044
Mechelen Festival Vol 2: 940
MED Associates Vol 1: 3418
Media and Methods Magazine Vol 1: 11634
Media, Entertainment and Arts Alliance Vol 2: 560
Media Human Resources Association Vol 1: 11636
The Media Project Vol 1: 11638
Media Tenor South Africa Vol 2: 4171
Median Iris Society Vol 1: 11640
Medical-Dental-Hospital Business Associates Vol 1: 11642
Medical Education for South African Blacks Vol 1: 11647
Medical Fitness Association Vol 1: 11649
Medical Group Management Association Vol 1: 1675, 1676, 1677
Medical Journalists' Association Vol 2: 6421
Medical Library Association Vol 1: 11651
Medical Mycological Society of the Americas Vol 1: 11669
Medical Society of the State of New York Vol 1: 11672
Medical Women's International Association Vol 2: 2357
Medieval Academy of America Vol 1: 11674
Mednarodni Graficni Likovni Center Vol 2: 4456
Meeting Professionals International Vol 1: 11678
Meetings and Conventions Vol 1: 11684
Melbourne International Film Festival Vol 2: 562
Mellemfolkeligt Samvirke Vol 2: 1277
Memorial Foundation for Jewish Culture Vol 1: 11686
Memphis State Review Vol 1: 15675
Menlo Park Chamber of Commerce Vol 1: 11689
Mensa International Vol 2: 6425
Merchandise Mart Properties, Inc. Vol 1: 11692
Merck and Co. Vol 1: 3768
Merck & Co. Vol 2: 4316
Merck & Co., Inc. Vol 1: 15179
Merck Company Foundation Vol 1: 12151
Merck Frosst Canada Ltd. Vol 1: 6909
Merck Research Laboratories Vol 1: 1556, 3563
Merck Sharp & Dohme Vol 2: 367
Meridian Energy Vol 2: 3747
Merkaz Zalman Shazar Le'Historia Yehudit/ Ha'Hevra Ha'Historit Ha 'Israelit Vol 2: 2927
Merrimack Valley Chamber of Commerce Vol 1: 11694
Merriman Smith Memorial Fund Vol 1: 18729
Mesa Arts Center Vol 1: 11696
Metal Construction Association Vol 1: 11698
Metal Powder Industries Federation Vol 1: 11700
Metallurgical and Engineering Consultants (India) Limited Vol 2: 2655
Metallurgical Society Vol 1: 11800
Meteoritical Society Vol 2: 6427
MetLife Foundation Vol 1: 4264
MetLife Foundation Vol 1: 5922
MetLife Foundation Vol 1: 17510
Metropolitan Area Planning Council Vol 1: 11707
Metropolitan Opera Vol 1: 11709
Mexican Academy of Sciences Vol 2: 3450
Mexican-American Engineering Society Vol 1: 16738
Mexico Ministry of Foreign Affairs Vol 2: 3453
Meyer-Viol Foundation Vol 2: 4049
Mezinarodni festival filmu a televiznich poradu o zivotnim prostredi Ekofilm Vol 2: 4439
Mezinarodni hudebni festival Prazske jaro Vol 2: 1263
MG Drivers Club of North America Vol 1: 11711
Miami Beach Film Society Vol 1: 11713
Michael E. DeBakey International Surgical Society Vol 1: 11715
Michener Awards Foundation Vol 1: 11717
Michigan Association for Infant Mental Health Vol 1: 11720
Michigan Association for the Education of Young Children Vol 1: 11723
Michigan Competing Band Association Vol 1: 11725
Michigan Concrete Paving Association Vol 1: 11727
Michigan Department of State Police Vol 1: 11729
Michigan Mosquito Control Association Vol 1: 11734
Michigan Sea Grant Vol 1: 11736
Michigan Space Grant Consortium Vol 1: 11738
Microelectronic Devices, Circuits, and Systems Vol 1: 11740
Micronet R & D Vol 1: 11740
Mid-America Regional Council Vol 1: 11742
Mid-Atlantic States Association of Avian Veterinarians Vol 1: 11744
Middle East Report - Middle East Research and Information Project Vol 1: 11746
Middle East Studies Association of North America Vol 1: 11748
Midland-Odessa Symphony & Chorale, Inc. Vol 1: 11753
Midwest Archives Conference Vol 1: 11755
Midwest Center for Nonprofit Leadership - University of Missouri—Kansas City L.P. Cookingham Institute of Public Affairs Vol 1: 11759
Midwest Roofing Contractors Association Vol 1: 11761
Military Audiology Association Vol 1: 11763
Military Chaplains Association of the U.S.A. Vol 1: 11766
Military Operations Research Society Vol 1: 11768
Military Order of the World Wars Vol 1: 11774
Milk Industry Foundation Vol 1: 1884
Milkweed Chronicle Vol 1: 11776
Milkweed Editions Vol 1: 11776
Millbrook Society Vol 1: 11779
Miller Fellowship Fund; John William Vol 1: 11781
Miller Lite Vol 1: 13226
Milton Bradley Co. Vol 1: 13688
MIND - National Association for Mental Health Vol 2: 6429
Mind Science Foundation Vol 1: 11783
Mine Safety and Health Administration Vol 1: 13455
Mineralogical Association of Canada Vol 1: 11785
Mineralogical Society of America Vol 1: 11793
Minerals Engineering Society Vol 2: 6431
Minerals, Metals and Materials Society Vol 1: 4710
Minerals, Metals, and Materials Society Vol 1: 11800
Mini-Basketball England Vol 2: 6435
Mining and Metallurgical Society of America Vol 1: 11821
Ministarstvo Znanosti Vol 2: 1235
Ministerium Fuer Wissenschaft, Forschung und Kunst Baden-Wuerttemberg Vol 2: 2140
Ministry of Culture of the Slovak Republic Vol 2: 4441
Ministry of Justice, Poland - Institute of Forensic Research Vol 2: 4005

Ministry of Science, Research and the Arts of the State of Baden-Wurttemberg Vol 2: 2360
Minneapolis Foundation Vol 1: 11823
Minnesota Advocates for Human Rights Vol 1: 11827
Minnesota Association of Townships Vol 1: 11829
Minnesota Concrete Masonry Association Vol 1: 11831
Minnesota Conservation Federation Vol 1: 11833
Minnesota Funeral Directors Association Vol 1: 11835
Minnesota Historical Society Vol 1: 11837
Minnesota Holstein Association Vol 1: 11839
Minnesota Psychological Association Vol 1: 11843
Minnesota Stroke Association, NSA Chapters Vol 1: 11846
Minnesota; University of Vol 1: 9719
Minot State University - Northwest Art Center Vol 1: 11848
Miss America Foundation Vol 1: 11853
Miss America Organization Vol 1: 11851
Miss America Pageant Vol 1: 11851
The Miss Universe Organization Vol 1: 11854
Mississippi-Alabama Sea Grant Consortium Vol 1: 11858
Mississippi Association of Public Accountants Vol 1: 11860
Mississippi Ballet International, Inc. Vol 1: 18406
Mississippi Historical Society Vol 1: 11862
Mississippi Poetry Society Vol 1: 13162
Mississippi State Medical Association Vol 1: 11869
Mississippi State University - Cobb Institute of Archaeology Vol 1: 11871
Mississippi; University of Southern - School of Library and Information Science Vol 1: 11873
Mississippi Urban Forest Council Vol 1: 11875
Mississippi Valley Historical Association Vol 1: 14685
Missouri Archaeological Society Vol 1: 11877
Missouri Association of Meat Processors Vol 1: 11879
Missouri Association of School Librarians Vol 1: 11881
Missouri Bass Federation Vol 1: 11884
Missouri Botanical Garden Vol 1: 5878
Missouri Dental Association Vol 1: 11886
Missouri Department of Elementary and Secondary Education Vol 1: 11889
Missouri Sheriffs Association Vol 1: 11891
Missouri Southern International Piano Competition Vol 1: 11893
Mita Society for Library and Information Science Vol 2: 3293
Mita Toshokan Joho Gakkai Vol 2: 3293
Mitsubishi Chemical Company Vol 1: 2474
Mobil Oil Corporation Vol 1: 7100, 8568
Mobile Opera Guild Vol 1: 11895
The Mobius Awards Vol 1: 11897
Model A Restorers Club Vol 1: 11899
Model Missiles Association Vol 1: 12641
Model "T" Ford Club of America Vol 1: 11901
Modern Language Association of America Vol 1: 11903
The Modern Language Journal Vol 1: 11830, 11834
Mokslu Akademija Vol 2: 3372
Molson Family Foundation Vol 1: 6116
Monaghan Photographic Society Vol 2: 2863
Monash University Vol 2: 513
Monett Chamber of Commerce Vol 1: 11923
Money for Women/Barbara Deming Memorial Fund Vol 1: 11925
Monk Institute of Jazz; Thelonious Vol 1: 11927
Monsanto Agricultural Products Company Vol 1: 4218
Monsanto Co. Vol 1: 3883
Monsanto Company Vol 1: 4234
Montana Society of Certified Public Accountants Vol 1: 11929
Monte Carlo Television Festival Vol 2: 3468
Montefiore Foundation; George Vol 2: 942
Monthly Labor Review Vol 1: 17841
Monticello/Thomas Jefferson Foundation Vol 1: 11931
Montreal International Festival of New Cinema Vol 1: 11934
Montreal International Fireworks Competition Vol 1: 11936
Montreal Neurological Institute and Hospital Vol 1: 11938
Montreal Symphony Orchestra Vol 1: 11941
Montreal World Film Festival Vol 1: 11943
Montres Rolex Vol 2: 4880
Montreux Choral Festival Vol 2: 4869
Moore Fund for Writers; Jenny McKean Vol 1: 11945
Moore Medical Corp. Vol 1: 12522
Morgan Guaranty Trust Company Vol 1: 8049
Mormon History Association Vol 1: 11947
Mortar Board Vol 1: 11956
MOSAID Technologies Inc. Vol 1: 6323
Mostra de Valencia, Cinema del Mediterrani Vol 2: 4524
Mostra Internacional de Cinema Em Sao Paulo Vol 2: 1135
Mothers Against Munchausen Syndrome by Proxy Allegations Vol 1: 11958
Motion Picture Theatre Associations of Canada Vol 1: 11962
Motor and Equipment Manufacturer Association Vol 1: 11964
Motor Sports Association Vol 2: 6439
Motor Trend Vol 1: 11966
Motorcycle Safety Foundation Vol 1: 11970
Motorola Vol 1: 10175
Mounds View High School Alumni Association Vol 1: 11972
Mount Desert Island Biological Laboratory Vol 1: 11974
Mount Rogers Planning District Commission Vol 1: 11976
Mount Vernon Genealogical Society Vol 1: 11979
Mountain West Center for Regional Studies Vol 1: 11981
Mountaineering Council of Scotland Vol 2: 6441
Mountaineers Books Vol 1: 11985
Mountainfilm Vol 1: 11987
Mountainview Women's Nine Hole Golf Association Vol 1: 11989
Movies on a Shoestring Vol 1: 15693
Movimento dei Focolari Vol 2: 3046
Mr. Blackwell Vol 1: 11994
Mu Phi Epsilon Foundation Vol 1: 11997
Mu Phi Epsilon International Vol 1: 11999
Multi-Level Marketing International Association Vol 1: 12001
Multi-Unit Foodservice Operators Vol 1: 13965, 13969
Multiple Sclerosis International Federation Vol 2: 6443
Multiple Sclerosis Society of Canada Vol 1: 12005
Municipal Art Society of New York Vol 1: 12007
Municipal Council of Budapest Vol 2: 2504
Municipal Finance Officers and Association of the United States and Canada Vol 1: 9145
Municipal Treasurers Association of the United States and Canada Vol 1: 5324
Municipality of Bolzano Vol 2: 2999
Municipality of Lisbon Vol 2: 4069
Municipality of Terni Vol 2: 3015
Munson Foundation; Curtis and Edith Vol 1: 4498
Muscular Dystrophy Association Vol 1: 12013
Muscular Dystrophy Canada Vol 1: 12015
Museu de Arte Moderna de Sao Paulo Vol 2: 1133
Museu Villa-Lobos Vol 2: 1137
Museum of Comparative Zoology Vol 1: 12022
Museum of Fine Arts Vol 1: 4612
Museum of Haiku Literature Vol 1: 9238
Museum of Modern Art of Sao Paulo Vol 2: 1133
Museum of New Mexico Vol 1: 12024
Museum of Science, Boston Vol 1: 12026
Music Association of Korea Vol 2: 4113
Music Center of Los Angeles County Vol 1: 12029
Music Centre Slovakia Vol 2: 4443
Music Industries Association - England Vol 2: 6448
Music Operators Association Vol 1: 4513
Music Teachers National Association Vol 1: 12031
Musical Arts Society of New Orleans Vol 1: 12038
Musical Club of Hartford Vol 1: 12040
Musicians AFM Local 7 Vol 1: 12042
Musicians Benevolent Fund Vol 2: 6450
Musikkollegium Winterthur Vol 2: 4761
Musikschule der Stadt Ettlingen Vol 2: 2362
Muzicka Omaladina Srbije Vol 2: 4412
Mycological Society of America Vol 1: 12044
Mystery Readers International Vol 1: 12050
Mystery Writers of America Vol 1: 12052
Mystic Valley Railway Society Vol 1: 12056
Mythopoeic Society Vol 1: 12058
Naantalin Musiikkijuhlat Vol 2: 1410
Naanteli Music Festival Vol 2: 1410
NACE International: The Corrosion Society Vol 1: 12061
NAHB Research Center Vol 1: 15282
Naismith Memorial Basketball Hall of Fame Vol 1: 12069
The Naito Foundation Vol 2: 3295
NAMI Kansas-The Alliance on Mental Illness Vol 1: 12073
Napa Sonoma Wine Country Film Festival Vol 1: 12075
NASCENTE - Cooperative Society with Cultural Purposes Vol 2: 4056
Nasco International Inc. Vol 1: 10078
NASDAQ Educational Foundation Vol 1: 13037

Organization Index

Nashville Film Festival Vol 1: 12079
Nashville Songwriters Association International Vol 1: 12081
Nasionale Wolkwekersvereniging van Suid-Afrika Vol 2: 4211
NASSTRAC Vol 1: 12083
Nathan Trust; George Jean Vol 1: 12085
Nation Institute Vol 1: 12087
National Academic Advising Association Vol 1: 12089
The National Academy Vol 1: 12095
National Academy Vol 1: 12095
The National Academy of Design Vol 1: 12095
National Academy of Education Vol 1: 12123
National Academy of Engineering Vol 1: 12125
National Academy of Medicine Vol 2: 1194
National Academy of Music, Dance and Drama Vol 2: 2777
National Academy of Neuropsychology Vol 1: 12131
National Academy of Popular Music Vol 1: 12133
National Academy of Public Administration Vol 1: 12135
National Academy of Recording Arts and Sciences Vol 1: 12139
National Academy of Sciences Vol 2: 1586
National Academy of Sciences Vol 1: 12142
National Academy of Sciences - Institute of Medicine Vol 1: 12173
National Academy of Sciences of Belarus Vol 2: 845
National Academy of Sciences of the Republic of Korea Vol 2: 4117
National Academy of Television Arts and Sciences Vol 1: 12176
National Action Council for Minorities in Engineering Vol 1: 12184
National Aeroclub of Russia Vol 2: 4719
National Aeronautic Association Vol 1: 12186
National Aeronautics and Space Administration Vol 1: 12193, 14883, 18129
National Agricultural Aviation Association Vol 1: 12212
National Agricultural Center and Hall of Fame Vol 1: 12222
National Air Transportation Association Vol 1: 12224
National Alliance for Research on Schizophrenia and Depression Vol 1: 12230
National Alliance of Children's Trust Funds Vol 1: 696
National American Legion Press Association Vol 1: 12234
National Amputee Golf Association Vol 1: 12237
National and Provincial Parks Association of Canada Vol 1: 6802
National Animal Control Association Vol 1: 12240
National Anti-Vivisection Society Vol 2: 6361
National Apostolate for Inclusion Ministry Vol 1: 12247
National Arbor Day Foundation Vol 1: 12252
National Archery Association of the United States Vol 1: 12255
National Art Education Association Vol 1: 12259
National Art Materials Trade Association Vol 1: 12281
National Arts Centre Orchestra Vol 1: 12283
National Arts Club Vol 1: 12285
National Arts Council of Zimbabwe Vol 2: 7436
National Asphalt Pavement Association Vol 1: 12294
National Association for College Admission Counseling Vol 1: 12299
National Association for Environmental Education Vol 1: 14248
National Association for Equal Opportunity in Higher Education Vol 1: 12307
National Association for Ethnic Studies Vol 1: 12310
National Association for Gifted Children Vol 1: 12313
National Association for Girls and Women in Sport Vol 1: 12322
National Association for Healthcare Quality Vol 1: 12328
National Association for Hospital Development Vol 1: 4893
National Association for Humane and Environmental Education Vol 1: 12336
National Association for Industry-Education Cooperation Vol 1: 12342
National Association for Interpretation Vol 1: 12345
National Association for Public Continuing and Adult Education Vol 1: 834
National Association for Pupil Transportation Vol 1: 12349
National Association for Remedial Teaching Vol 1: 10571
National Association for Research in Science Teaching Vol 1: 12351
National Association for Search and Rescue Vol 1: 12355
National Association for Sport and Physical Education Vol 1: 12361
National Association for Stock Car Auto Racing Vol 1: 12363
National Association for the Advancement of Colored People Vol 1: 12365
National Association for the Advancement of Psychoanalysis Vol 1: 12369
National Association for the Visual Arts Vol 2: 564
National Association of Academic Advisors for Athletics Vol 1: 12371
National Association of Academies of Science Vol 1: 12374
National Association of Accountants Vol 1: 9889
National Association of Advertising Publishers Vol 1: 5156
National Association of Amateur Oarsmen Vol 1: 18044
National Association of American Composers and Conductors Vol 1: 12466
National Association of Animal Breeders Vol 1: 12376
National Association of Anorexia Nervosa and Associated Disorders Vol 1: 12380
National Association of Assessing Officers Vol 1: 10124
National Association of Athletic Development Directors Vol 1: 12382
National Association of Attorneys General Vol 1: 12390
National Association of Bar Executives Vol 1: 12392
National Association of Basketball Coaches Vol 1: 12394
National Association of Biology Teachers Vol 1: 12403
National Association of Black Journalists Vol 1: 12412
National Association of Black Social Workers Vol 1: 12415
National Association of Boards of Pharmacy Vol 1: 12424
National Association of Broadcasters Vol 1: 12426
National Association of Catholic Chaplains Vol 1: 12438
National Association of College and University Food Services Vol 1: 12440
National Association of College Auxiliary Services Vol 1: 12446
National Association of College Gymnastics Coaches Vol 1: 7515
National Association of Colleges and Teachers of Agriculture Vol 1: 14275
National Association of Collegiate Marketing Administrators Vol 1: 12449
National Association of Colored Graduate Nurses Vol 1: 2942
National Association of Community Health Centers Vol 1: 12458
National Association of Competitive Mounted Orienteering Vol 1: 12460
National Association of Composers, U.S.A. Vol 1: 12466
National Association of Conservation Districts Vol 1: 12468
National Association of Consumer Agency Administrators Vol 1: 12476
National Association of Corrosion Engineers Vol 1: 12061
National Association of Corrosion Engineers Vol 1: 12479
National Association of Counties Vol 1: 12491
National Association of Counties Vol 1: 12501
National Association of County Agricultural Agents Vol 1: 12495
National Association of County and City Health Officials Vol 1: 12497
National Association of County Engineers Vol 1: 12499
National Association of County Information Officers Vol 1: 12501
National Association of Credit Management Vol 1: 12503
National Association of Criminal Defense Lawyers Vol 1: 12505
National Association of Diaconate Directors Vol 1: 12507
National Association of Diocesan Ecumenical Officers Vol 1: 12511
National Association of Elementary School Principals Vol 1: 12513
National Association of Elementary School Principals Vol 1: 17819
National Association of Emergency Medical Technicians Vol 1: 12516
National Association of Farm Broadcasters Vol 1: 17365
National Association of Federal Credit Unions Vol 1: 12529
National Association of Federal Veterinarians Vol 1: 12533
National Association of Fleet Administrators Vol 1: 12535
National Association of Geoscience Teachers Vol 1: 12537
National Association of Government Communicators Vol 1: 12541

National Association of Greeting Card Publishers Vol 1: 9203
National Association of Health and Welfare Ministries of the United Methodist Church Vol 1: 17700
National Association of Health Underwriters Vol 1: 12545
National Association of Hispanic Journalists Vol 1: 12548
National Association of Hispanic Nurses Vol 1: 12550
National Association of Home and Workshop Writers Vol 1: 12553
National Association of Home Builders Vol 1: 12555, 15280
National Association of Hospital Fire Officers Vol 2: 6452
National Association of Housing and Redevelopment Officials Vol 1: 12561
National Association of Independent Fee Appraisers Vol 1: 12567
National Association of Independent Resurfacers Vol 1: 12569
National Association of Industrial and Office Properties Vol 1: 12571
National Association of Intercollegiate Athletics Vol 1: 12573
National Association of Intercollegiate Athletics Vol 1: 13211
National Association of Jazz Educators Vol 1: 10099
National Association of Journalism Directors Vol 1: 11048
National Association of Legal Investigators Vol 1: 12584
National Association of Licensed Paralegals Vol 2: 6454
National Association of Metal Finishers Vol 1: 12586
National Association of Mutual Insurance Companies Vol 1: 3859
National Association of Negro Business and Professional Women's Clubs Vol 1: 12593
National Association of Neonatal Nurses Vol 1: 12598
National Association of Pastoral Musicians Vol 1: 12601
National Association of Pediatric Nurse Practitioners Vol 1: 12603
National Association of Personal Financial Advisors Vol 1: 12606
National Association of Photo Equipment Technicians Vol 1: 12608
National Association of Pipe Coating Applicators Vol 1: 12610
National Association of Printing Ink Manufacturer Vol 1: 12612
National Association of Produce Market Managers Vol 1: 12615
National Association of Professional Baseball Leagues Vol 1: 12617
National Association of Professional Gardeners Vol 1: 15326
National Association of Professional Insurance Agents Vol 1: 12621
National Association of Professional Organizers Vol 1: 12625
National Association of Purchasing Management Vol 1: 9757
National Association of Quick Printers Vol 1: 15232
National Association of Railroad Passengers Vol 1: 12627
National Association of Real Estate Editors Vol 1: 12630
National Association of Realtors Vol 1: 12632
National Association of Recording Merchandisers Vol 1: 12635
National Association of Rocketry Vol 1: 12641
National Association of Sanitarians Vol 1: 13114
National Association of Scholars Vol 1: 12643
National Association of Schools and Public Affairs and Administration Vol 1: 3817
National Association of Schools of Public Affairs and Administration Vol 1: 12647
National Association of Science Writers Vol 1: 12653
National Association of Scientific Materials Managers Vol 1: 12655
National Association of Secondary School Principals Vol 1: 12657
National Association of Secondary School Principals Vol 1: 17819
National Association of Shopfitters Vol 2: 6458
National Association of Social Workers Vol 1: 12660
National Association of Social Workers, Kansas Chapter Vol 1: 12664
National Association of State Chief Information Officers Vol 1: 12666
National Association of State Information Resource Executives Vol 1: 12666
National Association of State Procurement Officials Vol 1: 12668
National Association of State Purchasing Officials Vol 1: 12668
National Association of State Units on Aging Vol 1: 12670
National Association of State Workforce Agencies Vol 1: 12672
National Association of Store Fixture Manufacturer Vol 1: 12681
National Association of Student Personnel Administrators Vol 1: 12683
National Association of Summer Sessions Vol 1: 14264
National Association of Swedish Architects Vol 2: 4598
National Association of Teachers of Singing Vol 1: 12691
National Association of Television Program Executives Vol 1: 12693
National Association of Temporary Staffing Services Vol 1: 4308
National Association of the Bureau of Animal Industry Veterinarians Vol 1: 12533
National Association of the Remodeling Industry Vol 1: 12695
National Association of Theatre Owners Vol 1: 12707
National Association of Trade and Technical Schools Vol 1: 7097
National Association of Underwater Instructors Vol 1: 12709
National Association of Women and the Law Vol 1: 12712
National Association of Women Artists Vol 1: 12714
National Association of Women Judges Vol 1: 12716
National Association of Youth Orchestras Vol 2: 6460
National Assoiation of Temporary Services Vol 1: 4308
National Athletic Trainers' Association Vol 1: 12718
National Auctioneers Association Vol 1: 12721
National Audio-Visual Association Vol 1: 10330
National Audubon Society Vol 1: 1092
National Audubon Society Vol 1: 12725
National Auto Auction Association Vol 1: 12728
National Automobile Dealers Association Vol 1: 17542
National Aviation Hall of Fame Vol 1: 12730
National Back Pain Association Vol 2: 5157
National Ballet of Canada Vol 1: 12733
National Band Association Vol 1: 12735
National Bar Association Vol 1: 12745
National Baseball Hall of Fame and Museum Vol 1: 12749
National Basketball Association Vol 1: 12753
National Beep Baseball Association Vol 1: 12766
National Biplane Association Vol 1: 12768
National Bison Association Vol 1: 12773
National Black Police Association Vol 1: 12775
National Black Programming Consortium Vol 1: 12780
National Book Critics Circle Vol 1: 12782
National Book Development Council of Singapore Vol 2: 4422
National Book Foundation Vol 1: 12784
National Book League (England) Vol 2: 5188
National Book Service Vol 1: 6690
National Book Service Vol 1: 6696
National Broadcasting Society - Alpha Epsilon Rho Vol 1: 12786
National Broiler Council Vol 1: 15180
National Buffalo Association Vol 1: 12773
National Building Museum Vol 1: 12801
National Bureau of Standards Vol 1: 5630, 17796
National Burglar and Fire Alarm Association Vol 1: 12803
National Burglar and Fire Alarm Association - National Training School (NTS) Vol 1: 12809
National Business Aircraft Association Vol 1: 12821
National Business and Disability Council Vol 1: 12812
National Business Aviation Association Vol 1: 12821
National Business Education Association Vol 1: 12830
National Cable and Telecommunications Association Vol 1: 12836
National Cancer Institute of Canada Vol 1: 12844
National Cartoonists Society Vol 1: 12848
National CASA Association Vol 1: 13057
National Catholic Band Association Vol 1: 12853
National Catholic Bandmasters' Association Vol 1: 12853
National Catholic Development Conference Vol 1: 12856
National Catholic Educational Association Vol 1: 12859
National Center for Public Productivity Vol 1: 12870

National Center for State Courts Vol 1: 12872
National Centre for Audiology Vol 1: 12877
National Cervical Cancer Coalition Vol 1: 12879
National Child Labor Committee Vol 1: 12881
National Christian College Athletic Association Vol 1: 12883
National Citizens' Coalition Vol 1: 12895
National Civic League Vol 1: 12897
National Classification Management Society Vol 1: 12899
National Collegiate Athletic Association Vol 1: 12901
National Collegiate Athletic Association Vol 1: 13208, 13213, 13218
National Collegiate Athletic Association - Division 1 Track Coaches Association Vol 1: 12907
National Commercial Finance Association Vol 1: 7618
National Commission for Culture and the Arts Vol 2: 3972
National Commission on Correctional Health Care Vol 1: 12914
National Committee for Adoption Vol 1: 12953
National Committee for Recording for the Blind Vol 1: 15574
National Committee for the Observance of Mother's Day Vol 1: 13459
National Committee on American Foreign Policy Vol 1: 12916
National Committee on Coastal and Ocean Engineering Vol 2: 533
National Committee on Water Engineering Vol 2: 487
National Communication Association Vol 1: 12920
National Community Education Association Vol 1: 12933
National Confectionery Sales Association Vol 1: 12943
National Conference of Editorial Writers Vol 1: 12414
National Consumers League Vol 1: 12945
National Coordinating Council on Emergency Management Vol 1: 10202
National Corn Growers Association Vol 1: 12948
National Corvette Restorers Society Vol 1: 12950
National Council for Adoption Vol 1: 12953
National Council for Children's Rights Vol 1: 7353
National Council for Community Behavioral Healthcare Vol 1: 12955
National Council for Community Relations Vol 1: 12975
National Council for Continuing Education and Training Vol 1: 12957
National Council for Eurasian and East European Research Vol 1: 957
National Council for Eurasian and East European Research Vol 1: 12960
National Council for GeoCosmic Research Vol 1: 12962
National Council for Geographic Education Vol 1: 12964
National Council for Interior Design Qualification Vol 1: 12973
National Council for Marketing and Public Relations Vol 1: 12975
National Council for School Sport Vol 2: 6463
National Council for Scientific and Technological Research Vol 2: 7425
National Council for Small Business Management Development Vol 1: 10356
National Council for the Social Studies Vol 1: 12980
National Council for the Training of Journalists Vol 2: 6465
National Council of College Publications Advisers Vol 1: 7524
National Council of Commercial Plant Breeders Vol 1: 7982
National Council of Commercial Plant Breeders Vol 1: 12993
National Council of Engineering Examiners Vol 1: 12997
National Council of Examiners for Engineering and Surveying Vol 1: 12997
National Council of La Raza Vol 1: 12999
National Council of Less Commonly Taught Languages Vol 1: 13005
National Council of Patent Law Associations Vol 1: 18028
National Council of Physical Distribution Management Vol 1: 7899
National Council of Secondary School Athletic Directors Vol 1: 13007
National Council of Social Security Management Associations Vol 1: 13009
National Council of Supervisors of Mathematics Vol 1: 13013
National Council of Teachers of English Vol 1: 7692
National Council of Teachers of English Vol 1: 13015
National Council on Alcoholism Vol 1: 13034
National Council on Alcoholism and Drug Dependence Vol 1: 13034
National Council on Community Services and Continuing Education Vol 1: 12957
National Council on Community Services for Community and Junior Colleges Vol 1: 12957
National Council on Economic Education Vol 1: 13036
National Council on Family Relations Vol 1: 13038
National Council on Public History Vol 1: 13045
National Council on Schoolhouse Construction Vol 1: 7881
National Council on the Aging Vol 1: 4265
National Council on the Aging Vol 1: 13051
National Council on U.S.-Arab Relations Vol 1: 13054
National Court Appointed Special Advocate Association Vol 1: 13056
National Court Reporters Association Vol 1: 13060
National Court Reporters Foundation Vol 1: 13064
National Cowboy and Western Heritage Museum Vol 1: 13067, 15705, 15706
National Cowboy Hall of Fame and Western Heritage Center Vol 1: 13067
National Cutting Horse Association Vol 1: 13070
National Dairy Shrine Vol 1: 13072
National Dance Association Vol 1: 13076
National Defense Transportation Association Vol 1: 13082
National Democratic Institute for International Affairs Vol 1: 13087
National Derby Rallies Vol 1: 13089
National Duckpin Bowling Congress Vol 1: 13091
National Economic Association Vol 1: 13093
National Eisteddfod of Wales Vol 2: 6470
National Electric Sign Association Vol 1: 10627
National Electrical Manufacturer Representatives Association Vol 1: 13095
National Electrical Testing Association Vol 1: 10388
National Electronics Sales and Service Dealers Association Vol 1: 13097
National Electronics Service Dealers Association Vol 1: 13097
National Endowment for Democracy Vol 1: 13099
National Endowment for the Arts Vol 1: 13101
National Endowment for the Arts Vol 1: 17507, 17508, 18698, 18774
National Endowment for the Humanities Vol 1: 13110
National Environmental Health Association Vol 1: 13114
National Environmental Health Association Vol 1: 14433
National Environmental, Safety and Health Training Association Vol 1: 13119
National Ethnic Coalition of Organizations Vol 1: 13124
National Farm-City Council Vol 1: 13126
National Federation of Abstracting and Information Services Vol 1: 13128
National Federation of Jewish Men's Clubs Vol 1: 8668
National Federation of Local Cable Programmers Vol 1: 404
National Federation of Music Clubs Vol 1: 7665
National Federation of Music Clubs Vol 1: 13130
National Federation of Music Societies Vol 2: 6408
National Federation of Plastering Contractors Vol 2: 5890
National Federation of Press Women Vol 1: 13132
National Federation of State High School Associations Vol 1: 13136
National Federation of State High School Athletic Associations Vol 1: 13136
National Federation of State Poetry Societies Vol 1: 13139
National Federation of the Blind Vol 1: 13190
National Federation of Women's Institutes Vol 2: 6473
National Fertilisers Ltd. Vol 2: 2555
National Field Archery Association Vol 1: 13194
National Film Board of Canada Vol 1: 17561
National Fisheries Institute Vol 1: 15951
National Fishing Lure Collectors Club Vol 1: 13196
National Flexible Packaging Association Vol 1: 8716
National Flute Association Vol 1: 13198
National Football Foundation and College Hall of Fame Vol 1: 13207

National Football Foundation and College Hall of Fame, Valley of the Sun Chapter Vol 1: 13219
National Football Foundation and Hall of Fame Vol 1: 13207
National Football League Vol 1: 13223
National Football League Players Association Vol 1: 13230
National Forensic Association Vol 1: 13234
National Forensic League Vol 1: 13236
National Forum for Black Public Administrators Vol 1: 13246
National Forum of Greek Orthodox Church Musicians Vol 1: 13249
National Foundation for Advancement in the Arts Vol 1: 13253
National Foundation for Infectious Diseases Vol 1: 13255
National Foundation for Peroneal Muscular Atrophy Vol 1: 7283
National Friends of Public Broadcasting Vol 1: 13259
National Frozen and Refrigerated Foods Association Vol 1: 13264
National Frozen Food Association Vol 1: 13264
National Funeral Directors Association Vol 1: 13266
National Genealogical Society Vol 1: 13268
National Geographic Society Vol 1: 1777
National Geographic Society Vol 2: 5267
National Glass Association Vol 1: 13282
National Golf Course Owners Association Vol 1: 18943
National Golf Foundation Vol 1: 13285, 18943
National Ground Water Association Vol 1: 13287
National Guard Association of the United States Vol 1: 13300
National Guild of Community Schools of the Arts Vol 1: 13303
National Guild of Hypnotists Vol 1: 13306
National Gymnastics Judges Association Vol 1: 13317
National Hacky Sack Footbag Players Association Vol 1: 18940, 18941
National Hardwood Lumber Association Vol 1: 13319
National Head Injury Foundation Vol 1: 5925
National Headache Foundation Vol 1: 13321
National Headliner Awards Vol 1: 13324
National Headliner Club Vol 1: 13324
National Health and Medical Research Council Vol 2: 570
National Hearing Conservation Association Vol 1: 13326
National Hemophilia Foundation Vol 1: 13331
National High School Athletic Coaches Association Vol 1: 13342
National High School Band and Choral Directors Hall of Fame Vol 1: 13344
National High School Band Directors Hall of Fame Vol 1: 13344
National High School Rodeo Association Vol 1: 13346
National Highway Traffic Safety Administration Vol 1: 10168
National Hockey League Players' Association Vol 1: 13348
National Home Fashions League Vol 1: 10443
National Home Furnishings Association Vol 1: 13350
National Home Improvement Council Vol 1: 12695
National Horseshoe Pitchers Association of America Vol 1: 13352
National House-Building Council Vol 2: 6823
National Housing Conference Vol 1: 13359
National Humanities Center Vol 1: 13362
National Independent Automobile Dealers Association Vol 1: 13364
National Indian Health Board Vol 1: 13366
National Institute for Women of Color Vol 1: 10122
National Institute of American Doll Artists Vol 1: 13368
National Institute of Ceramic Engineers Vol 1: 1477, 1481, 1495
National Institute of Governmental Purchasing Vol 1: 13370
National Institute of Mental Health Vol 1: 1685, 3293
National Institute of Nursing Research Vol 1: 13376
National Institute of Real Estate Brokers Vol 1: 7891
National Institute of Standards and Technology Vol 1: 5631
National Institutes of Health Vol 1: 8010
National Intercollegiate Soccer Officials Association Vol 1: 13379
National Interscholastic Swimming Coaches Association of America Vol 1: 13386
National Intravenous Therapy Association Vol 1: 9713
National Jewish Committee on Scouting Vol 1: 13390
National Jewish Girl Scout Committee Vol 1: 13396
National Junior College Athletic Association Vol 1: 13398
National Kidney Foundation Vol 1: 13408
National Kidney Foundation of Ohio Vol 1: 13411
National Lawyers Wives Vol 1: 2623
National Legal Aid and Defender Association Vol 1: 13413
National Library of Australia Vol 2: 575
National Library of Medicine Vol 1: 11660
National Library of Scotland Vol 2: 7071
National LP-Gas Association Vol 1: 13574
National Magazine Awards Foundation Vol 1: 13419
National Male Nurses Association Vol 1: 832
National Marine Educators Association Vol 1: 13421
National Marine Manufacturers Association Vol 1: 13427
National Marine Manufacturers Association Vol 1: 18064
National Marine Representatives Association Vol 1: 13430
National Marrow Donor Program Vol 1: 13432
National Medical Fellowships Vol 1: 13442
National Mental Health Association Vol 1: 13445
National Micrographics Association Vol 1: 252
National Migraine Foundation Vol 1: 13321
National Military Intelligence Association Vol 1: 13451
National Milk Producers Federation Vol 1: 1877
National Mining Association Vol 1: 13453
National Minority Supplier Development Council Vol 1: 13456
National Mother's Day Committee Vol 1: 13459
National Multiple Sclerosis Society Vol 1: 13461
National Municipal League Vol 1: 12897
National Museum of Racing and Hall of Fame Vol 1: 13468
National Music Council Vol 1: 13470
National Music Council of The United Kingdom Vol 2: 6475
The National Music Festival Vol 1: 13472
National Newspaper Association Vol 1: 13474
National Notary Association Vol 1: 13478
National Ocean Industries Association Vol 1: 13481
National Office Paper Recycling Project Vol 1: 13483
National Opera Association Vol 1: 13485
National Operatic and Dramatic Association Vol 2: 6477
National Organization for Human Service Education Vol 1: 13491
National Organization for Victim Assistance Vol 1: 13497
National Organization of Black Law Enforcement Executives, Central Virginia Chapter Vol 1: 13506
National Organization of Human Service Educators Vol 1: 13491
National Organization on Disability Vol 1: 13508
National Orientation Directors Association Vol 1: 13510
National Outdoor Book Awards Vol 1: 13513
National Paint and Coatings Association Vol 1: 13515
National Paperbox and Packaging Association Vol 1: 13520
National Paperbox Association Vol 1: 13520
National Park Academy of the Arts Vol 1: 13522
National Park Service Vol 1: 13534
National Parks Association Vol 1: 13530
National Parks Conservation Association Vol 1: 13530
National Peach Council Vol 1: 13535
National Peanut Council Vol 1: 3029
National Piers Society Vol 2: 6479
National Pigeon Association Vol 1: 13538
National Portrait Gallery Vol 2: 6482
National Post Vol 1: 7847
National Press Club Vol 1: 13542
National Press Foundation Vol 1: 13545, 13554
National Press Photographers Association Vol 1: 13559
National Propane Gas Association Vol 1: 13574
National Property Management Association Vol 1: 13579
National PTA - National Congress of Parents and Teachers Vol 1: 13583
National Quality Institute Vol 1: 13585
National Railroad Construction and Maintenance Association Vol 1: 13587
National Ramah Commission Vol 1: 13589
National Recreation and Park Association Vol 1: 13591
National Recreation and Parks Association Vol 1: 4100

National Recycling Coalition Vol 1: 13603
National Rehabilitation Association Vol 1: 13605
National Rehabilitation Association - Vocational Evaluation and Work Adjustment Association Vol 1: 13612
National Rehabilitation Counseling Association Vol 1: 13615
National Rehabilitation Hospital Vol 1: 13621
National Religious Broadcasters Vol 1: 13623
National Religious Vocation Conference Vol 1: 13625
National Remodeling Association Vol 1: 12695
National Research Council Vol 1: 13627
National Research Council of Canada Vol 1: 13974
National Research Council of the Philippines Vol 2: 3975
National Restaurant Association Vol 1: 13630
National Restaurant Association Educational Foundation Vol 1: 13634
National Restaurant Association Foundation Vol 1: 13634
National Retail Federation Vol 1: 13637
National Retail Merchants Association Vol 1: 13637
National Rifle Association Vol 2: 6484
National Rifle Association of America Vol 1: 13645
National Rural Health Association Vol 1: 13649
National Rural Health Care Association Vol 1: 13649
National Safety Council Vol 1: 13655
National Scale Men's Association Vol 1: 10748
National Scholastic Press Association Vol 1: 13660
National Scholastic Press Association/ Associated Collegiate Press Vol 1: 17308
National School Boards Association Vol 1: 11125
National School Plant Managers Association Vol 1: 3522
National School Public Relations Association Vol 1: 13663
National School Transportation Association Vol 1: 13667
National Science Foundation Vol 1: 13671
National Science Foundation Vol 1: 18026
National Science Foundation - National Science Board Vol 1: 13674
National Science Teachers Association Vol 1: 13677
National Scrabble Association Vol 1: 13687
National Sculpture Society Vol 1: 13689
National Sea Grant College Program Vol 1: 9182
National Security Council Vol 1: 13694
National Shellfisheries Association Vol 1: 13696
National Sheriffs' Association Vol 1: 13698
National Shorthand Reporters Association Vol 1: 13060
National Silo Association Vol 1: 10629
National Skeet Shooting Association Vol 1: 13797
National Small-Bore Rifle Association Vol 2: 6486
National Small Shipments Traffic Conference Vol 1: 12083
National Soccer Coaches Association of America Vol 1: 13707
National Society, Daughters of the American Revolution Vol 1: 13712
National Society for Histotechnology Vol 1: 13715
National Society for Park Resources Vol 1: 13724
National Society for Performance and Instruction Vol 1: 10653
National Society of Artists Vol 1: 13726
National Society of Arts and Letters Vol 1: 13728
National Society of Fingerprint Officers Vol 2: 5902
National Society of Insurance Premium Auditors Vol 1: 13735
National Society of Interior Design Vol 1: 4083
National Society of Newspaper Columnists Vol 1: 13738
National Society of Painters in Casein and Acrylic Vol 1: 13740
National Society of Professional Engineers Vol 1: 13742
National Society of Professional Surveyors Vol 1: 13753
National Society of Tole and Decorative Painters Vol 1: 16642
National Society, Sons of the American Revolution Vol 1: 13757
National Softball Congress Vol 1: 10754
National Sojourners Vol 1: 13779
National Space Club Vol 1: 13781
National Space Society of Australia Vol 2: 578
National Speakers Association Vol 1: 13783
National Speleological Society Vol 1: 13786
National Spiritual Assembly of the Baha'is of Vanuatu Vol 2: 7407
National Sporting Clays Association Vol 1: 13797
National Sports Law Institute Vol 1: 13799
National Sportscasters and Sportswriters Association Vol 1: 13802
National Spotted Saddle Horse Association Vol 1: 13805
National Starch & Chemical Company Vol 1: 1557
National Steeplechase Association Vol 1: 13808
National Stroke Association Vol 1: 13810
National Student Campaign Against Hunger and Homelessness Vol 1: 13813
National Swimming Pool Institute Vol 1: 5301
National Symphony Orchestra Association Vol 1: 13817
National Tattoo Association Vol 1: 13819
National Tattoo Club of the World Vol 1: 13819
National Taxpayers Union Vol 1: 13837
National Telecommunications Cooperative Association Vol 1: 13839
National Telemedia Council Vol 1: 13841
National Telephone Cooperative Association Vol 1: 13839
National Therapeutic Recreation Society Vol 1: 13843
National Thespian Society Vol 1: 8402
National Threshers Association Vol 1: 13851
National Tractor Pullers Association Vol 1: 13853
National Traditional Country Music Association Vol 1: 13865
National Trust for Historic Preservation Vol 1: 13868
National Turf Writers Association Vol 1: 13872
National Turf Writers Association Vol 1: 17532, 17533
National Union of Public and General Employees Vol 1: 13876
National University Extension Association Vol 1: 18208
National Urban League Vol 1: 13881
National Vegetable Society Vol 2: 6488
National Water Resources Association Vol 1: 13884
National Water Safety Congress Vol 1: 13886
National Watercolor Society Vol 1: 13891
National Weather Association Vol 1: 13893
National Wheelchair Athletic Association Vol 1: 18721
National Wheelchair Basketball Association Vol 1: 13902
National Wild Turkey Federation Vol 1: 13906
National Wildlife Federation Vol 1: 13909
National Wildlife Rehabilitators Association Vol 1: 13911
National Woman's Party Vol 1: 13915
National Women's Hall of Fame Vol 1: 13917
National Women's Political Caucus Vol 1: 13919
National Women's Studies Association Vol 1: 13922
National Wood Flooring Association Vol 1: 13927
National Wool Growers' Association of South Africa Vol 2: 4211
National Wrestling Coaches Association Vol 1: 13933
National Wrestling Hall of Fame & Museum Vol 1: 13936
National Writers Association Vol 1: 13942
National Writers Union Vol 1: 13947
National WritersF United Service Organization Vol 1: 13948
National Writers Workshop Vol 1: 13949
National Young Farmer Educational Association Vol 1: 13951
National Young Farmer Educational Association Vol 1: 13951
National Youth Bureau. Vol 2: 4958
The Nationalist Movement Vol 1: 13961
Nation's Restaurant News - Lebhar-Friedman Inc. Vol 1: 13963
NationsBank of Texas, N.A. Vol 1: 205, 207
Native American Institute Vol 1: 13970
The Natural History Museum Vol 2: 6491
Natural Resources Defense Council Vol 1: 13972
Natural Sciences and Engineering Research Council of Canada Vol 1: 13974
Natural World Vol 2: 6494
Nature Canada Vol 1: 13978
Nature Conservancy Vol 1: 13982
Nature Conservancy of Minnesota Vol 1: 13985
Nature Saskatchewan Vol 1: 13987
Nature's Window Art Gallery Vol 1: 7066
Naumburg Foundation; Walter W. Vol 1: 13993
Nautical Research Guild Vol 1: 13996

Naval Submarine League Vol 1: 13998
NCTE Research Foundation Vol 1: 13032
NEA Foundation for the Improvement of Education Vol 1: 14004
Near East/South Asia Council of Overseas Schools Vol 2: 2458
Nebraska Dressage Association Vol 1: 14009
Nebraska Hospice and Palliative Care Partnership Vol 1: 14011
Nebraska Humanities Council Vol 1: 14013
Nebraska Library Association Vol 1: 14015
Nebraska State Genealogical Society Vol 1: 14020
Nebraska State Poetry Society Vol 1: 13167
Nebraska Sustainable Agriculture Society Vol 1: 14022
NEC Corp Vol 2: 6287
NEC Corporation Vol 1: 9786
Nederlandse Kankerbestirijding -KWF Vol 2: 3504
Nederlandse Taalunie Vol 2: 3622
Nederlandse Triathlon Bond Vol 2: 3624
Nederlandse Vereniging voor Psychiatrie Vol 2: 3632
Nederlandse Vereniging voor Weer- en Sterrenkunde Vol 2: 3626
Nelligan; Fondation Emile- Vol 1: 17672, 17673
Nepal Association of Tour and Travel Agents Vol 2: 3480
Nepal Hastakala Udhyog Sangh Vol 2: 3476
Nerken School of Engineering; Albert Vol 1: 7810
Nestle Nutrition Institute Vol 1: 3798
Nestle Rowntree Vol 2: 5190
Netherlands Design Institute Vol 2: 3628
Netherlands Film Festival Vol 2: 3630
Netherlands Film Institute Vol 2: 3575
Netherlands Psychiatric Association Vol 2: 3632
Netherlands Society for English Studies Vol 2: 3634
Netherlands Society of Photogrammetry Vol 2: 4977
Networking Institute; Gazette International Vol 1: 15161
New Brunswick Institute of Agrologists Vol 1: 14025
New Delta Review Vol 1: 14028
New England Council Vol 1: 14030
New England Historic Genealogical Society Vol 1: 14032
New England Mountain Bike Association Vol 1: 14034
New England Pest Management Association Vol 1: 14036
New England Poetry Club Vol 1: 14039
New England Press Association Vol 1: 14050
New England Regional Genetics Group Vol 1: 14052
New England Theatre Conference Vol 1: 14054
New England Water Works Association Vol 1: 14059
New England Wild Flower Society Vol 1: 14068
New England Wildflower Preservation Society Vol 1: 14068
New Hampshire Association of Broadcasters Vol 1: 14075
New Hampshire Golf Association Vol 1: 14077
New Hampshire Pharmacists Association Vol 1: 14079
New Jersey Forest Stewardship Committee Vol 1: 14081
New Jersey Historical Commission Vol 1: 14083
New Jersey Hospice and Palliative Care Organization Vol 1: 14086
New Jersey Intellectual Property Law Association Vol 1: 14089
New Jersey Library Association Vol 1: 14091
New Jersey Patent Law Association Vol 1: 14089
New Jersey Poetry Society Vol 1: 13169
New Jersey Symphony Orchestra Vol 1: 14096
New Letters Vol 1: 14098
New Mexico Library Association Vol 1: 14100
New Mexico Museum of Space History Vol 1: 14102
New Mexico State Poetry Society Vol 1: 13172
New Orleans Time-Picayune Vol 1: 18728
New Peace History Society Vol 1: 14878
New Rivers Press - Minnesota State University, Moorhead Vol 1: 14104
The New School Vol 1: 14106
New School University Vol 1: 14106
New South Wales Ministry for the Arts Vol 2: 583
New Statesman Vol 2: 6496
New York Academy of Sciences Vol 1: 14108
New York Biology Teachers Association Vol 1: 14110
New York Botanical Garden Vol 1: 5877
New York Botanical Garden - Institute of Systematic Botany Vol 1: 14112
New York Civil Liberties Union Vol 1: 14115
New York Community Trust Vol 1: 9355
New York Festivals Vol 1: 14118
New York Financial Writers' Association Vol 1: 14122
New York Flute Club Vol 1: 14124
New York Foundation for the Arts Vol 1: 14126
New York Genealogical and Biographical Society Vol 1: 14128
New York International Ballet Competition Vol 1: 14130
New York Library Association Vol 1: 14132
New York Press Club Vol 1: 14134
New York Public Library Vol 1: 14145
New York Racing Association Vol 1: 14149
New York Road Runners Vol 1: 14151
New York Section of the Illuminating Engineering Society Vol 1: 9619
New York Shipping Association Vol 1: 14154
New York Society for Ethical Culture Vol 1: 14156
New York Society of Architects Vol 1: 14158
New York State Association of Criminal Defense Lawyers Vol 1: 14170
New York State Association of Foreign Language Teachers Vol 1: 1833
New York State Association of Library Boards Vol 1: 14172
New York State Council on the Arts Vol 1: 14174
New York State Court Reporters Association Vol 1: 14176
New York State Department of Health Wadsworth Center Vol 1: 14178
New York State Historical Association Vol 1: 14180
New York State Society of CPAs Vol 1: 14184
New York State Writers Institute Vol 1: 14186
The New York Times Vol 1: 14189
New York Times Digital Vol 1: 1854
New York University - Office for University Development and Alumni Relations Vol 1: 14191
New York University - Office of Advertising and Publications Vol 1: 14193
New York University Alumni Association Vol 1: 14195
New York Urban League Vol 1: 14198
New York Women in Communications, Inc. Vol 1: 14201
New York Women in Film and Television Vol 1: 18815
New Zealand Academy of Fine Arts Vol 2: 3759
New Zealand Archaeological Association Vol 2: 3761
New Zealand Association of Scientists Vol 2: 3764
New Zealand Concrete Society Vol 2: 3733
New Zealand Dental Association Vol 2: 3768
New Zealand Geographical Society Vol 2: 3770
New Zealand History Research Trust Fund Vol 2: 3723
New Zealand Ice Cream Manufacturers Association Vol 2: 3772
New Zealand Institute of Refrigeration Heating and Air Conditioning Engineers Vol 2: 3730
New Zealand Law Society Vol 2: 3774
New Zealand Library Association Vol 2: 3749
New Zealand Microbiological Society Vol 2: 3778
New Zealand Olympic Committee Vol 2: 3782
New Zealand Psychological Society Vol 2: 3785
New Zealand Society of Authors Vol 2: 3793
New Zealand Society of Designers Vol 2: 3712
New Zealand Society of Industrial Design Vol 2: 3712
New Zealand Society of Soil Science Vol 2: 3795
New Zealand Theatre Federation Vol 2: 3804
New Zealand Trade and Enterprise Vol 2: 3807
New Zealand Water and Wastes Association Vol 2: 3813
Newark Black Film Festival Vol 1: 14203
Newberry Library Vol 1: 14205
Newbury House Vol 1: 17421, 17422
Newcomen Society in North America Vol 1: 14207
Newcomen Society of the United States Vol 1: 14207
Newcomer Supply Vol 1: 13723
Newhouse Newspapers Vol 1: 18728
Newport International Competition for Young Pianists Vol 2: 6498
Newport International Competition for Young Pianists Committee Vol 2: 6498
Newport Pianoforte Competition Vol 2: 6498
Newsday Vol 1: 14209

Organization Index

Newsletter and Electronic Publishers Association Vol 1: 14211
Newsletter and Electronic Publishers Foundation Vol 1: 17103
Newspaper Association of America Vol 1: 14213
Newspaper Association of America Foundation Vol 1: 14220
Newspaper Fund Vol 1: 8263
The Newspaper Guild-CWA Vol 1: 14224
Newspaper Research Council Vol 1: 14219
NHK - Japan Broadcasting Corporation Vol 2: 3297
NHK Symphony Orchestra, Tokyo Vol 2: 3299
NHL Broadcasters' Association Vol 1: 9451
Niagara University Vol 1: 14226
Nickelodeon Vol 1: 14232
Nicolai Malko Foundation Vol 2: 1311
Nielsen International Music Competitions; Carl Vol 2: 1312
Nieman Foundation Vol 1: 14234
Nieman Foundation for Journalism at Harvard University Vol 1: 14236
Nigerian Association of Chambers of Commerce, Industry, Mines, and Agriculture Vol 2: 3884
Nihon Gakujutsu Shinko-kai Vol 2: 3260
Nihon Kensetsu Kikai-ka Kyokai Vol 2: 3221
Nihon Kikai Gakkai Vol 2: 3262
Nihon Ryukoshoku Kyokai Vol 2: 3227
Nihon Shinbun Kyokai Vol 2: 3240
Nihon Sugakukai Vol 2: 3291
Nimrod: International Journal of Prose and Poetry Vol 1: 14239
The Ninety-Nines, Inc. Vol 1: 12192
Ninety-Nines, International Organization of Women Pilots Vol 1: 14242
Nippon Gakushiin Vol 2: 3212
Nippon Hoso Kyokai Vol 2: 3297
Nippon Kagakukai Vol 2: 3170
Nippon Seramikkusu Kyokai Vol 2: 3168
Nippon Shokubutsu-Byori Gakkai Vol 2: 3310
Nippon Suisan Gakkai Vol 2: 3275
Nippon Yakugakkai Vol 2: 3305
Niwano Heiwa Zaidan Vol 2: 3301
Niwano Peace Foundation Vol 2: 3301
NMC-Slovkoncert, Slovak Artist Management Vol 2: 4443
Nobel Foundation Vol 2: 4600
Noir International Festival Vol 2: 3016
Nordic Africa Institute Vol 2: 4607
Nordic Council Vol 2: 4612, 4614
Nordiska Afrikainstitutet Vol 2: 4607
Nordiska Radet - Sweden Vol 2: 4612
Nordiska Samarbetsradet for Kriminologi Vol 2: 4643
Norfolk Southern Vol 1: 9874
Norsk Presseforbund Vol 2: 3907
Norske Filmfestivalen Vol 2: 3905
Norske Finansanalytikeres Forening Vol 2: 3911
North Alabama Tourist Association Vol 1: 14244
North American Academy of Liturgy Vol 1: 14246
North American Association for Environmental Education Vol 1: 14248
North American Association of Christians in Social Work Vol 1: 14257
North American Association of Food Equipment Manufacturers Vol 1: 14260
North American Association of Summer Sessions Vol 1: 14264
North American Association of Wardens and Superintendents Vol 1: 14266
North American Bluebird Society Vol 1: 14268
North American Catalysis Society Vol 1: 14270
North American Colleges and Teachers of Agriculture Vol 1: 14275
North American Conference on British Studies Vol 1: 14282
North American Council on Adoptable Children Vol 1: 14288
North American Die Casting Association Vol 1: 14292
North American Gladiolus Council Vol 1: 14299
North-American Interfraternity Conference Vol 1: 14301
North American Lily Society Vol 1: 14303
North American Manx Association Vol 1: 14306
North American Model Boat Association Vol 1: 14308
North American Mustang Association and Registry Vol 1: 14310
North American Mycological Association Vol 1: 14312
North American Patristics Society Vol 1: 14314
North American Peruvian Horse Association Vol 1: 14316
North American Snowsports Journalists Association Vol 1: 14322
North American Society for Oceanic History Vol 1: 14329
North American Society for Sport History Vol 1: 14331
North American Society for Sport Management Vol 1: 14333
North American Society for the Psychology of Sport and Physical Activity Vol 1: 14335
North American Trail Ride Conference Vol 1: 14339
North American Travel Journalist Association Vol 1: 14351
North American Vexillological Association Vol 1: 14353
North Atlantic Treaty Organisation Vol 2: 944
North Carolina Arts Council Vol 1: 14356
North Carolina Association of County Commissioners Vol 1: 14358
North Carolina Herpetological Society Vol 1: 14361
North Carolina Library Association Vol 1: 14363
North Carolina Literary and Historical Association Vol 1: 14367
North Carolina Utility Contractors Association Vol 1: 14374
North Dakota Long Term Care Association Vol 1: 14379
North San Antonio Chamber of Commerce Vol 1: 14381
Northcote Parkinson Fund Vol 1: 14383
Northeast Asia Council Vol 1: 4780
Northeast Louisiana Arts Council Vol 1: 14385
Northeast Modern Language Association Vol 1: 14387
Northeast Nebraska Economic Development District Vol 1: 14389
Northeastern Bird-Banding Association Vol 1: 5144
Northeastern Loggers Association Vol 1: 14391
Northern Arts Vol 2: 6500
Northern Kentucky University - Department of Theatre and Dance Vol 1: 14393
Northern Territory Library Vol 2: 586
Northport/B.J. Spoke Gallery Vol 1: 17144
Northrop Grumman Corp. Vol 1: 16916
Northrop Grumman Electronic Systems and Integration Division Vol 1: 11520
Northwest Business for Culture and the Arts Vol 1: 14395
Northwest Film Center Vol 1: 14397
Northwest Film Study Center Vol 1: 14397
Northwest Regional Spinners Association Vol 1: 14401
Northwestern University - Center for International and Comparative Studies Vol 1: 14403
Northwestern University - Office of the Provost Vol 1: 14406
Northwood University, Florida Campus Vol 1: 14409
Northwood University, Michigan Campus Vol 1: 14412
Norway Ministry of Foreign Affairs Vol 2: 3901
Norwegian Broadcasting Corporation Vol 2: 3908
Norwegian International Film Festival Vol 2: 3905
Norwegian Newspaper Publishers Association Vol 2: 3908
Norwegian Nobel Committee Vol 2: 4602
Norwegian Press Association Vol 2: 3907
The Norwegian Short Film Festival Vol 2: 3909
Norwegian Society of Financial Analysts Vol 2: 3911
Norwegian Union of Journalists Vol 2: 3908
Norwich and Norfolk Terrier Club Vol 1: 14419
NOVA Chemicals Corp. Vol 1: 7305
Novartis Pharmaceuticals Lic Ltd Vol 2: 5177
Novo Nordisk Foundation Vol 2: 1314
NSF International Vol 1: 14432
Nuclear Age Peace Foundation Vol 1: 14434
Nuclear Energy Institute Vol 1: 14439
Nutrition Professionals, Inc. Vol 1: 1886
Oak Ridge Associated Universities Vol 1: 14441
Oak Ridge National Laboratory Vol 1: 14444
Obec Architektu Vol 2: 1269
Observatoire des Energies Renouvelables Vol 2: 1935
Observ'ER Vol 2: 1935
OC Incorporated Vol 1: 11508
Occidental Petroleum Corporation Vol 1: 1525
Occupational Therapy Association of South Africa Vol 2: 4213
Ocean Conservancy Vol 1: 14446
Oceania Philatelic Society Vol 1: 16562
Ochsner Clinic Foundation Vol 1: 14448
OCLC/Forest Press, Inc. Vol 1: 2653
OCLC Online Computer Center, Inc. Vol 1: 11339
Odense Film Festival Vol 2: 1319
Odense International Organ Competition and Festival Vol 2: 1321
Office for the Coordination of Humanitarian Affairs - Geneva Vol 2: 4871

Office of Naval Research Vol 1: 3118
Office of Strategic Services Society Vol 1: 14450
Office of the Americas Vol 1: 14452
Office of the Mayor of Zurich Vol 2: 4873
Office of the President of the Republic of Poland Vol 2: 4007
The Office of the Prime Minister of Malta Vol 2: 3424
Oglebay Institute Vol 1: 14454
Ohio Academy of History Vol 1: 14456
Ohio Arts Council Vol 1: 14462
Ohio Construction Suppliers Association Vol 1: 14464
Ohio Department of Jobs and Family Services - Ohio Women's Programs Vol 1: 14466
Ohio Genealogical Society, Franklin County Vol 1: 14468
Ohio Genealogical Society, Seneca County Vol 1: 14470
Ohio Hospice and Palliative Care Organization Vol 1: 14473
Ohio Middle School Association Vol 1: 14475
Ohio Recorders Association Vol 1: 14477
Ohio State University Vol 1: 7385
Ohio State University Mershon Center Vol 1: 14479
Ohio State University Press Vol 1: 14481
Ohio University Press Vol 1: 14388
Ohio University Press and Swallow Press Vol 1: 14483
Ohioana Library Association Vol 1: 14485
Oil and Colour Chemists' Association Vol 2: 6502
Oita Sports Association for the Disabled Vol 2: 3303
Oklahoma Association of School Library Media Specialists Vol 1: 14495
Oklahoma Library Association Vol 1: 14499
Okomedia Institut for Environmental Media Vol 2: 2364
Old Dominion Kennel Club of Northern Virginia Vol 1: 14502
Old Timers Soccer Association of Maryland Vol 1: 14504
Oley Valley Combined Training Association Vol 1: 14507
Olimpijski komite slovenije Vol 2: 4458
Olin Fine Arts Center Gallery Vol 1: 14510
Oliver Trucking Vol 1: 17758
Olympic Committee of Slovenia Vol 2: 4458
Olympic Council of Malaysia Vol 2: 3414
Omaha Symphony Vol 1: 14512
Omicron Chi Epsilon Vol 1: 14514
Omicron Delta Epsilon Vol 1: 14514
Omicron Delta Gamma Vol 1: 14514
Omicron Delta Kappa Vol 1: 14517
Omicron Kappa Upsilon Vol 1: 14524
Omohundro Institute of Early American History and Culture Vol 1: 14527
OMV Vol 2: 830
Onassis Public Benefit Foundation; Alexander S. Vol 2: 2460
Oncology Nursing Foundation Vol 1: 14544
Oncology Nursing Society Vol 2: 4859
Oncology Nursing Society Vol 1: 14529
Onderstepoort Veterinary Institute - Agricultural Research Council Vol 2: 4215
One Club for Art & Copy Vol 1: 14550
One Reel Vol 1: 14552
Ontario Arts Council Vol 1: 14554
Ontario College of Art and Design Vol 1: 14567
Ontario Ministry of Citizenship and Immigration Vol 1: 14569
Ontario Ministry of Citizenship and Immigration - Ontario Honours and Awards Secretariat Vol 1: 14571
Ontario Nature Vol 1: 14576
Ontario Psychological Association Vol 1: 14585
Ontario School Counsellor's Association Vol 1: 14587
Openbare Skakelinstituut van Suidelike Afrika Vol 2: 4229
Operation Clean Government Vol 1: 14594
Operation Oswego County Vol 1: 14596
Operational Research Society of India Vol 2: 2779
Operational Research Society of the United Kingdom Vol 2: 6506
Operations Research Society of America Vol 1: 9737
Oppenheim-John Downes Memorial Trust Vol 2: 6510
Opperman Foundation; Dwight D. Vol 1: 2602
Optical Research Associates Vol 1: 17131
Optical Society of America Vol 1: 14600
Optical Society of India Vol 2: 2783
Optimist International Vol 1: 14621
Oral and Maxillofacial Surgery Foundation Vol 1: 14623
Oral-B Laboratories Vol 1: 10058
Orange Alumni Association Vol 1: 14629
Oratorio Society of New York Vol 1: 14631
Orbis Books Ltd. Vol 1: 959
Orchard Lake Schools Vol 1: 14634
Orchestra Sinfonica dell'Emilia-Romagna Arturo Toscanini Vol 2: 3048
Orchestras Canada Vol 1: 14636
Orchestre Symphonique de Montreal Vol 1: 11941
Orchestres Canada Vol 1: 14636
Order of Daedalians Vol 1: 14638
Order of St. Lazarus Vol 1: 14656
Order of the Coif Vol 1: 14658
Order of the Founders and Patriots of America Vol 1: 14660
Order Sons of Italy in America Vol 1: 14662
Ordre de Saint-Lazare au Canada Vol 1: 14656
Ordre des Psychologues du Quebec Vol 1: 14664
Oregon Blueberry Growers Association Vol 1: 14668
Oregon-California Trails Association Vol 1: 14670
Oregon Newspaper Publishers Association Vol 1: 14672
Oregon Society of Physician Assistants Vol 1: 14674
Oregon State Poetry Association Vol 1: 13181
Oregon Thoroughbred Owners and Breeders Vol 1: 14677
Organ Historical Society Vol 1: 14679
Organic Reactions, Inc. Vol 1: 1524
Organic Syntheses, Inc. Vol 1: 1524
Organisation de l'Aviation Civile Internationale Vol 1: 10317
L'Organisation des Musees Militaires du Canada Vol 1: 14703
Organisation des Nations Unies pour l'alimentation et l'agriculture Vol 2: 3053
Organisation du Traite de l'Atlantique Nord - Bruxelles Vol 2: 944
Organisation Internationale de la Vigne et du Vin Vol 2: 1906
Organisation Internationale des Institutions Superieures de Control des Finances Publiques Vol 2: 808
Organisation Meteorologique Mondiale Vol 2: 4933
Organisation Mondiale de la Sante Vol 2: 4924
Organisation Mondiale de Labourage Vol 2: 3687
Organisation of Pharmaceutical Producers of India Vol 2: 2787
Organisation pour l'Etude Phyto-Taxonomique de la Region Mediterraneenne Vol 2: 4526
Organisation Universitaire Interamericaine Vol 1: 9972
Organisme Europeen de Recherche sur la Carie Vol 2: 3541
Organization de Paises Arabes Exportadores de Petroleo Vol 2: 3368
Organization Development Institute Vol 1: 14681
Organization for the Phyto-Taxonomic Investigation of the Mediterranean Area Vol 2: 4526
Organization of American Historians Vol 1: 14685
Organization of American Historians Vol 1: 16217
Organization of Arab Petroleum Exporting Countries Vol 2: 3368
Organization of Islamic Capitals and Cities Vol 2: 4408
Organization of Military Museums of Canada Vol 1: 14703
Organization of Professional Employees of the United States Department of Agriculture Vol 1: 14705
Organizing Committee of the Shanghai Television Festival Vol 2: 3949
Orion Vol 2: 5709
Orphan Train Heritage Society of America Vol 1: 14708
Ortho Biotech Vol 1: 6996
Ortho Biotech Products LP Vol 1: 14543
Ortho Diagnostic Systems, Inc. Vol 1: 3603
Orthopaedic Research Society Vol 1: 14711
Oscars Vol 1: 188
Osteopathic Physicians and Surgeons of California Vol 1: 14717
Osterreichische Computer Gesellschaft Vol 2: 763
Oswego Heritage Council Vol 1: 14719
Ottawa Field-Naturalists' Club Vol 1: 14721
Ottawa International Animation Festival Vol 1: 14728
Ottawa Little Theatre Vol 1: 14741
Ouachita Council on Aging Vol 1: 14743
Oulu International Children's Film Festival Vol 2: 1422
Outdoor Advertising Association of America Vol 1: 14745
Outdoor Writers Association of America Vol 1: 14748
Outdoor Writers of Canada Vol 1: 14753
Outer Critics Circle Vol 1: 14756
Outfest Vol 1: 14758
Overseas Press Club of America Vol 1: 14760
Owen M. Kupferschmid Holocaust and Human Rights Project Vol 1: 14762
OX5 Aviation Pioneers Vol 1: 14764
Oxford Preservation Trust Vol 2: 6512

Oxford University Press Vol 2: 5805
Oxoid Ltd. Vol 2: 7087
Ozark Society Vol 1: 14767
Pace University Vol 2: 2293
Pacific Area Newspaper Publishers' Association Vol 2: 591
Pacific Area Travel Association Vol 1: 14771
Pacific Arts Association Vol 1: 14769
Pacific Asia Travel Association Vol 1: 14771
Pacific Coast Archaeological Society Vol 1: 14773
Pacific Northwest Association of Masters Swimmers Vol 1: 14775
Pacific Northwest Booksellers Association Vol 1: 14777
Pacific Northwest Library Association Vol 1: 14779
Pacific Northwest Writers Association Vol 1: 14781
Pacific Science Association Vol 1: 14783
Pacific Sociological Association Vol 1: 14786
Pacific Telecommunications Council Vol 1: 14791
Packaging Council of Australia Vol 2: 594
Packaging Machinery Manufacturers Institute Vol 1: 14793
The Packard Club Vol 1: 14795
Painting and Decorating Contractors of America Vol 1: 14806
Pakistan Academy of Sciences Vol 2: 3920
Pakistan Ministry of Education Vol 2: 3918
Pakistan Television Corp. Vol 2: 3922
Palaeontological Association Vol 2: 6514
Palanca Foundation; Carlos Vol 2: 3977
Palaontologische Gesellschaft Vol 2: 2366
Paleontological Research Institution Vol 1: 14808
Paleontological Society Vol 2: 2366
Paleontological Society Vol 1: 14812
Palm Springs International Film Society Vol 1: 14816
Palme Memorial Fund for International Understanding and Common Security; Olof Vol 2: 4615
Palomino Horse Breeders of America Vol 1: 14818
Pambansang Sanggunian sa Pananaliksik ng Pilipinas Vol 2: 3975
Pan-American Association of Ophthalmology Vol 1: 14824
Pan American Development Foundation Vol 1: 14826
Pan American Health and Education Foundation Vol 1: 14828
Pan American Society of the United States Vol 1: 4509
Panafrican Film and Television Festival of Ouagadougou Vol 2: 1159
Paneuropean Union Vol 2: 2368
Paper Federation of Great Britain Vol 2: 6518
Paper Industry Management Association Vol 1: 14833
Paperboard Packaging Council Vol 1: 14840
PARADE Vol 1: 10174
Paralyzed Veterans of America Vol 1: 14842
Parasitological Society of Southern Africa Vol 2: 4217
Parasitologiese Vereniging van Suidelike Afrika Vol 2: 4217
Parent Cooperative Preschools International Vol 1: 14848
Parenteral Society Vol 2: 6520
Parents' Choice Foundation Vol 1: 14853
Parents Without Partners Vol 1: 14855
The Paris Review Vol 1: 14857
Parker Harris Partnership Vol 2: 6522
Parkinson Memorial Trust; Dorothy Vol 2: 5969
Parkinson Society of Canada Vol 1: 14861
Partitioning and Interiors Association Vol 2: 5140
Partitioning Industry Association Vol 2: 5140
The Passano Foundation Vol 1: 14866
Pastel Society of America Vol 1: 14868
Patinage de Vitesse Canada Vol 1: 17121
Paul Guggenheim Foundation Vol 2: 4875
Paulo Foundation Vol 2: 1411
PC World Communications Inc. Vol 1: 14873
PCI Bank Group Vol 2: 3984
PCL Constructors Canada Inc. Vol 1: 6425
Peabody Conservatory of Music Vol 1: 14877
Peabody Institute of Johns Hopkins University Vol 1: 14876
The Peabody Institute of the City of Baltimore Vol 1: 14876
Peace History Society Vol 1: 14878
Peace Research Laboratory Vol 1: 11295
Pearl S. Buck International Vol 1: 14880
Pecora Award Committee; William T. - U.S. Department of the Interior Vol 1: 14882
Peerless Rockville Historic Preservation Vol 1: 14884
Pemiscot County Historical Society Vol 1: 14886
PEN American Center Vol 1: 14888
PEN Center U.S.A. Vol 1: 14906
PEN Club Italiano Vol 2: 3110
PEN Club - Poland Vol 2: 4018
PEN/Faulkner Foundation Vol 1: 14908
PEN New England Vol 1: 14911
PEN New Zealand, Inc. Vol 2: 3793
Pendleton District Historical, Recreational, and Tourism Commission Vol 1: 14914
Penguin Young Readers Group Vol 1: 4929
Penney Company; JC Vol 1: 18325
Pennsylvania Academy of Fine Arts Vol 1: 13693
Pennsylvania Association of Community Bankers Vol 1: 14916
Pennsylvania Association of Environmental Professionals Vol 1: 14918
Pennsylvania Association of Private School Administrators Vol 1: 14920
Pennsylvania Council on the Arts Vol 1: 14922
Pennsylvania Elks State Association Vol 1: 14924
Pennsylvania Library Association Vol 1: 14926
Pennsylvania Manufacturing Confectioners' Association Vol 1: 14928
Pennsylvania Music Educators Association Vol 1: 14930
Pennsylvania Newspaper Association Vol 1: 14932
Pennsylvania Poetry Society Vol 1: 13149
Pennsylvania School Counselors Association Vol 1: 14937
Pennsylvania School Librarians Association Vol 1: 14939
Pennsylvania Society of Anesthesiologists Vol 1: 14941
Pennsylvania Society of Newspaper Editors Vol 1: 14935, 14943
Pennsylvania Society of Physician Assistants Vol 1: 14945
Pennsylvania State Education Association Vol 1: 14947
Pennsylvania State University - College of Communications Vol 1: 14949
Pennsylvania State University - Smeal College of Business Administration - Institute for the Study of Business Markets Vol 1: 14951
Pensions Management Institute Vol 2: 6527
Penton Media Vol 1: 12084
People for Animal Rights Vol 1: 14953
People for the Ethical Treatment of Animals Vol 1: 14955
People to People International Vol 1: 14957
People's Choice Awards Vol 1: 14959
Percussive Arts Society Vol 1: 14961
Performance by an Actor in a Leading Role Vol 1: 188
Performance by an Actress in a Leading Role Vol 1: 188
Performance Textiles Association Vol 2: 6530
Performers of Connecticut Vol 1: 7720
Performing Right Society Vol 2: 6532, 6861
Pergamon Press Vol 2: 2323
Periodical Writers' Association of Canada Vol 1: 14963
Perkumpulan Keluarga Berencana Indonesia Vol 2: 2817
Permanent Court of Arbitration Vol 2: 3637
Perpetual Trustee Company Vol 2: 47
Perten Foundation; Harald Vol 2: 783
Peruvian Association for Conservation of Nature Vol 2: 3955
Peters Corp.; C. F. Vol 1: 16026
Petroleos de Venezuela, SA Vol 1: 9761
Petroleos de Venezuela, S.A. Vol 1: 9762
Pettinos Foundation; Charles E. and Joy C. Vol 1: 1448
Pezcoller Foundation Vol 2: 3114
Pfizer Vol 1: 4271, 6975, 6977
Pfizer Animal Health Vol 1: 1887
Pfizer Consumer Healthcare Vol 1: 10060
Pfizer Global Research & Development Vol 2: 6967
Pfizer Inc Vol 1: 734
Pfizer Inc. Vol 1: 1684, 9442, 10062, 12153
Pfizer Ltd. Vol 2: 6978
PGA European Tour Vol 1: 18943
PGA Tour Vol 1: 18943
PGA Tour of Australasia Vol 1: 18943
Pharmaceutical Manufacturers Association Vol 1: 14965
Pharmaceutical Research and Manufacturers of America Vol 1: 14965
Pharmaceutical Society of Japan Vol 2: 3305
Pharmaceutical Society of Slovenia Vol 2: 4464
Pharmacological Society of Canada Vol 1: 14967
Pharmacy Guild of Australia Vol 2: 598
Pharmasave Vol 1: 6805
Phi Alpha Theta Vol 1: 14974
Phi Beta Kappa Vol 1: 14986
Phi Chi Pharmacy Fraternity Vol 1: 14993
Phi Delta Chi Vol 1: 14993
Phi Delta Phi International Legal Fraternity Vol 1: 14995
Phi Lambda Upsilon Vol 1: 15000
Phi Tau Sigma Vol 1: 9849
Phi Theta Kappa, International Honor Society Vol 1: 15003
Phi Upsilon Omicron Vol 1: 15005
Philalethes Society Vol 1: 15011

Philanthropic Service for Institutions Vol 1: 15014
Philatelic Traders' Society Vol 2: 6534
Philippine Association of the Record Industry Vol 2: 3979
Philippines - Department of Education, Culture, and Sports Vol 2: 3986
Philippines Department of Science and Technology Vol 2: 3981
Philippines' Department of Science and Technology-Science Education Institute Vol 2: 3986
Philips Vol 2: 1787
Philips Electronics N.V. Vol 1: 9790
Phillips 66 National Swimming Championships Vol 1: 18417
Phillips Petroleum Company Vol 1: 18421
Phoenix Community Works Foundation Vol 1: 15016
Phoenix House Vol 1: 15018
Phoenix House Foundation Vol 1: 15018
Photo Express Vol 2: 393
Photographes Professionnels du Canada Vol 1: 15341
Photographic Art and Science Foundation Vol 1: 15020
Photographic Historical Society of Canada Vol 1: 15022
Photographic Historical Society of New York Vol 1: 3103
Photographic Society of America Vol 1: 15026
Phycological Society of America Vol 1: 15033
Physical Education Association of Ireland Vol 2: 2865
Physical Society Vol 2: 6060
Physiological Society of New Zealand Vol 2: 3821
Physiology Society of Southern Africa Vol 2: 4220
Phytochemical Society of Europe Vol 2: 4020
Phytopathological Society of Japan Vol 2: 3310
Pi Gamma Mu Vol 1: 15037
Pi Kappa Alpha Vol 1: 15039
Pi Kappa Alpha Memorial Foundation Vol 1: 15039
Pi Kappa Phi Vol 1: 15045
Pi Lambda Theta Vol 1: 15051
Pi Tau Sigma Vol 1: 4147, 4159, 4163
Piano Technicians Guild Vol 1: 15060
Pickerington Area Chamber of Commerce Vol 1: 15064
Pierce-Arrow Society Vol 1: 15066
Pierre Fauchard Academy Vol 1: 15070
Pierre Foundation of Monaco; Prince Vol 2: 3470
Pijls Foundation; Catharina Vol 2: 1105
Pilipinas Shell Foundation Vol 2: 3983
Pioneer Hi-Bred International Inc. Vol 1: 1889
Pitch and Putt Union of Ireland Vol 2: 2867
Pitcher Insurance Agency Inc. Vol 1: 15205
Pittaluga Premio Citta' Di Alessandria; Concorso Internazionale di Chitarra Classica Michele Vol 2: 3117
Pittsburgh History and Landmarks Foundation Vol 1: 15078
Pittsburgh New Music Ensemble Vol 1: 15080
Plain English Campaign Vol 2: 6536
Planck Society; Max Vol 2: 2436
Planet Drum Foundation Vol 1: 15082
Planetary Geology Division Vol 1: 9021
The Planetary Society Vol 1: 15084
Planned Parenthood Federation of America Vol 1: 15086
Planned Parenthood Federation of Canada Vol 1: 15089
Plant Growth Regulation Society of America Vol 1: 15091
Plastic Surgery Educational Foundation Vol 1: 15094
Plastics Academy Vol 1: 15098
Playboy Vol 1: 15100
Playboy Foundation Vol 1: 15102
Players Inc. Vol 1: 13231
Playmarket Vol 2: 3824
Playwrights' Center Vol 1: 15104
Please Touch Museum Vol 1: 15108
Plumsock Fund Vol 1: 18535
PMNETwork Vol 1: 15373
Podiatry Management Vol 1: 15110
Poet Lore Vol 1: 15112
Poetry Vol 1: 15114
The Poetry Center Vol 1: 15122
The Poetry Center & American Poetry Archives Vol 1: 15122
Poetry Foundation Vol 1: 15118, 15119
Poetry International Foundation Vol 2: 3639
Poetry Society Vol 2: 6540
Poetry Society of America Vol 1: 15124
Poetry Society of Michigan Vol 1: 13174
Poetry Society of Oklahoma Vol 1: 13175
Poetry Society of Tennessee Vol 1: 13176
Poetry Society of Texas Vol 1: 13177
Poetry Society of Texas Vol 1: 13183
Poets' Roundtable of Arkansas Vol 1: 13178
Poets' Study Club of Terre Haute Vol 1: 13152
Point-of-Purchase Advertising International Vol 1: 15137
Points of Light Foundation Vol 1: 15139
Points of Light Volunteer Organization Vol 1: 15139
Polaroid Foundation Vol 1: 14609
Police Federation of England and Wales Vol 2: 6543
Polish Actors Association Vol 2: 4022
Polish American Historical Association Vol 1: 15145
Polish Chemical Society Vol 2: 4030
Polish Composers Union Vol 2: 4037
Polish Genealogical Society of America Vol 1: 15149
Polish Medical Association Vol 2: 4040
Polish Organization for Commodity Science Vol 2: 4042
Polish Physical Society Vol 2: 4044
Political Studies Association Vol 2: 6545
Politzer Society - International Society for Otological Surgery Vol 2: 4983
Pollock-Krasner Foundation Vol 1: 15151
Polski PEN Vol 2: 4018
Polski Towarzystwo Lekarskie Vol 2: 4040
Polskie Towarzystwo Chemiczne Vol 2: 4030
Polskie Towarzystwo Fizyczne Vol 2: 4044
Polskie Towarzystwo Towaroznawcze Vol 2: 4042
Polymer Alliance Zone of West Virginia Vol 1: 15153
Polymer Machinery Manufacturers and Distributors Association Vol 2: 6547
Polytechnic Institute of New York Vol 1: 1859
Pontifica Academia delle Scienze Vol 2: 7409
Pontifical Academy of Sciences Vol 2: 7409
Pontificia Universidad Javeriana Vol 2: 1196
Pony Club of Great Britain Vol 2: 6551
Population Association of New Zealand Vol 2: 3826
Population Institute Vol 1: 15155
Pordenone Silent Film Festival Vol 2: 3120
Portland Opera Vol 1: 15157
Portugal State Secretariat of Culture Vol 2: 4088
Portuguese American Police Association Vol 1: 15159
Post-Polio Health International Vol 1: 15161
Postal History Society Vol 1: 15163
Postal History Society of Canada Vol 1: 15167
Postpartum Support, International Vol 1: 15170
Potamkin Foundation Vol 1: 641
Potash and Phosphate Institute of Canada Vol 2: 2558
Poteet Strawberry Festival Association Vol 1: 15173
Poultry Science Association Vol 1: 15175
Pound-American Trial Lawyers Foundation; Roscoe Vol 1: 15715
Pound Foundation; Roscoe Vol 1: 15715
Poynter Institute for Media Studies Vol 1: 15186
Practical Builder Vol 1: 15279
Prague Spring International Music Festival Vol 2: 1263
Prairie Schooner Vol 1: 15189
Prasidialabteilung der Stadt Zurich Vol 2: 4873
Pratt Institute Vol 1: 3745
Pratt Institute School of Information and Library Science Vol 1: 2672
Praxair, Inc. Vol 1: 2487
Precast/Prestressed Concrete Institute Vol 1: 15198
Precision Metalforming Association Vol 1: 15204
Prehistoric Society Vol 2: 6553
Prehistoric Society of East Anglia Vol 2: 6553
Prentice Hall Vol 1: 3652
Prentice-Hall Publishing Company Vol 1: 4810
Preservation Maryland Vol 1: 15207
Preservation Pennsylvania Vol 1: 15209
President of the Republic of Bulgaria Vol 2: 1154
President's Commission on White House Fellowships Vol 1: 15212
President's Committee on the Arts and the Humanities Vol 1: 11122
President's Council on Physical Fitness and Sports Vol 1: 15214
President's Council on Youth Fitness Vol 1: 15214
Pressamt der Stadt Nurnberg Vol 2: 2370
Primedia Magazines Inc. Vol 1: 11966
Prince Edward Island Council of the Arts Vol 1: 15216
Prince Pierre Foundation of Monaco Vol 2: 3470
Princess Grace Foundation - USA Vol 1: 15224
Princeton University - MicroFluidic Research and Engineering Laboratory Vol 1: 15228
The Print Center Vol 1: 15230

PrintImage International Vol 1: 15232
Printing Industries of America Vol 1: 15236
Pritsker Corp. Vol 1: 9872
Pritzker Architecture Prize Vol 1: 15239
Private Motor Truck Council of Canada Vol 1: 15241
Private Practice Section/American Physical Therapy Association Vol 1: 15246
Private Sector Organisation of Jamaica Vol 2: 3159
Prix Cazes Vol 2: 1937
Prix de Lausanne Vol 2: 4877
Prix du Jeune Ecrivain Vol 2: 1939
Prix Jeunesse Foundation Vol 2: 2372
Prix Theophraste Renaudot Vol 2: 1942
Pro Femina Theatre Vol 1: 9487
Pro Football Hall of Fame Vol 1: 15248
Pro Musicis Foundation Vol 1: 15251
Procter and Gamble Vol 1: 14960
Procter & Gamble Company Vol 1: 1515, 10069
Procter & Gamble Health Care Vol 1: 3062
Proctor and Gamble Denture Care Vol 1: 10064
Producers Guild of America Vol 1: 15253
Professional Aerial Photographers Association Vol 1: 15255
Professional Association of Nursery Nurses Vol 2: 6556
Professional Aviation Maintenance Association Vol 1: 15263
Professional Basketball Writers Association Vol 1: 12759
Professional Bowlers Association Vol 1: 10276
Professional Bowlers Association of America Vol 1: 15273
Professional Builder - Reed Business Information Vol 1: 15279
Professional Construction Estimators Association of America Vol 1: 15283
Professional Convention Management Association Vol 1: 15285
Professional Disc Golf Association Vol 1: 15302
Professional Engineers in Government Vol 1: 13744
Professional Engineers in Industry Vol 1: 13745
Professional Engineers Ontario Vol 1: 15306
Professional Fraternity Association Vol 1: 15311
Professional Golf Tournaments Association Vol 1: 18943
Professional Golfers' Association - England Vol 2: 6558
Professional Golfers' Association of America Vol 1: 15314, 18943
Professional Grounds Management Society Vol 1: 15326
Professional Hockey Writers' Association Vol 1: 9450
Professional Hunters' Association of South Africa Vol 2: 4224
Professional Independent Insurance Agents of Illinois Vol 1: 9641
Professional Institute of the Public Service of Canada Vol 1: 15331
Professional Insurance Marketing Association Vol 1: 15334
Professional Insurance Mass-Marketing Association Vol 1: 15334
Professional Interfraternity Conference Vol 1: 15311
Professional Landcare Network Vol 1: 15336
Professional Panhellenic Association Vol 1: 15311
Professional Photographers of America Vol 1: 15339
Professional Photographers of Canada Vol 1: 15341
Professional Photographers of Iowa Vol 1: 15344
Professional Picture Framers Association Vol 1: 15346
Professional Putters Association Vol 1: 15348
Professional Recreation Council Vol 1: 921, 923
Professional Rehabilitation Workers With the Adult Deaf Vol 1: 150
Professional Rodeo Cowboys Association Vol 1: 15350
Professional Services Management Association Vol 1: 15357
Professional Skaters Association Vol 1: 15359
Professional Women's Bowling Association Vol 1: 10276
Program to Assist Foreign Sinologists to Carry Out Research in the R.O.C. Vol 2: 4949
Programme des Nations Unies pour l'Environnement Vol 2: 3365
Progressive Education of Children in the Arts Network Vol 1: 15365
Project Censored Vol 1: 15368
Project Management Institute Vol 1: 15370
Projectgroup Cesar Franck Orgel Concours Vol 2: 3547
ProLiteracy Worldwide Vol 1: 15376
ProLiteracy Worldwide - Rochester New York Affiliate Vol 1: 15378
PROMAX Vol 1: 15380
Promega Corp. Vol 1: 3772
Promoting Enduring Peace Vol 1: 15382
Promotion Marketing Association Vol 1: 15384
Promotional Products Association International Vol 1: 15386
Property Council of Australia Vol 2: 600
ProQuest Vol 1: 1274, 1280, 14365
ProQuest Information & Learning Co. Vol 1: 4866
ProQuest/SIRS Vol 1: 2670, 4599
ProRodeo Sports News Vol 1: 15352
Prospectors and Developers Association of Canada Vol 1: 15392
Province of Upper Austria Vol 2: 762
Provinzialverband Westfalen Vol 2: 2348
Prudential Financial Vol 1: 8768
Psi Chi Vol 1: 3367
Psi Chi, National Honor Society in Psychology Vol 1: 15397
Psychological Assessment Resources, Inc. Vol 1: 3322
Psychological Dimensions of Peacework Fund Vol 1: 15413
Psychologists' Association of Alberta Vol 1: 15403
Psychologists for Social Responsibility Vol 1: 15410
Public Choice Society Vol 1: 15415
Public Library Association Vol 1: 15417
Public Relations Consultants Association Vol 2: 6569
Public Relations Institute of Southern Africa Vol 2: 4229
Public Relations Society of America Vol 1: 15425
Public Relations Society of America - Health Academy Vol 1: 15432
Public Risk Insurance Management Association Vol 1: 15434
Public Risk Management Association Vol 1: 15434
Public Utilities Communicators Association Vol 1: 18478
Publicity Club of New England Vol 1: 15437
Publishers' Association of South Africa Vol 2: 4231
Publishers Association of the South Vol 1: 15440
Publishers Association of the West Vol 1: 15442
Publishers Association; Yellow Pages Vol 1: 19044
Publishers Marketing Association Vol 1: 15444
Pudding House Publications Vol 1: 15446
Puerto Rico Manufacturers Association Vol 1: 15449
The Pulitzer Prizes - Columbia University Vol 1: 15452
Pulliam Family Vol 1: 5641
Pulmonary Hypertension Association Vol 1: 15455
Pulp and Paper Safety Association Vol 1: 15459
Puppeteers of America Vol 1: 15463
Purchasing Management Association of Boston Vol 1: 15467
Purdue University - African American Studies and Research Center Vol 1: 15469
Purina Mills Inc. Vol 1: 15178
Pushcart Press Vol 1: 15473
Pyrotechnics Guild International Vol 1: 15475
Qualcomm Inc. Vol 1: 9782
Quality Paperback Book Club Vol 1: 15477
Quarterly West Vol 1: 15480
Quaternary Geology and Geomorphology Division Vol 1: 9015
Quaternary Research Association Vol 2: 6571
Quebec Federation of Historical Societies Vol 1: 15482
Quebec Film Critics Association Vol 1: 11935
Quebec Ministere de la Culture et des Communications Vol 1: 15486
Quebec Writers' Federation Vol 1: 15492
Queen Elisabeth International Music Competition of Belgium Vol 2: 946
The Queen Sonja International Music Competition Vol 2: 3913
Queen's Awards Office Vol 2: 6577
Queen's English Society Vol 2: 6584
Queen's University Vol 1: 15494
Queensland Secondary Principals Association Vol 2: 602
Queensland University of Technology Vol 2: 500
Quilters Hall of Fame Vol 1: 15500
R & D Magazine - Reed Business Information Vol 1: 15502
Racegoers Club Vol 2: 6586
Radgivende Ingeniorers Forening Vol 2: 3891
The Radiance Technique International Association Vol 1: 15507
Radiation Research Society Vol 1: 15509
Radical Libertarian Alliance Vol 2: 6376

Radio Advertising Bureau Vol 1: 15512
Radio Amateur Association of Greece Vol 2: 2465
Radio Club of America Vol 1: 15514
Radio Creative Fund Vol 1: 15513
Radio Industries Club Vol 2: 7254
Radio Technical Commission for Aeronautics Vol 1: 15770
Radio-Television Correspondents Association Vol 1: 15531
Radio-Television News Directors Association Vol 1: 15533
Radiological Society of North America Vol 1: 15537
Rafto Foundation for Human Rights; Thorolf Vol 2: 3915
Railway Tie Association Vol 1: 15542
Rain Bird International Vol 1: 3862
Rainforest Action Network Vol 1: 15544
Rainforest Alliance Vol 1: 15546
Ramon Magsaysay Award Foundation Vol 2: 3987
Ramsay Memorial Fellowships Trust Vol 2: 6588
R&D Magazine Vol 1: 15930
Random House - Anchor Books Vol 1: 15549
Raoul Wallenberg Committee of the United States Vol 1: 15551
Raptor Research Foundation Vol 1: 15555
Rassegna di Palermo/International Sportfilmfestiva Vol 2: 3083
Rassegna Internazionale del Film di Documentazione Sociale; Festival dei Popoli - Vol 2: 3044
Rat fur Formgebung Vol 2: 2181
Ravenswood Community Council Vol 1: 15564
Rawlings Sporting Goods Inc. Vol 1: 15566
Real Academia de Farmacia Vol 2: 4531
Real Estate Institute of Canada Vol 1: 15570
Real Sociedad Espanola de Fisica Vol 2: 4541
Rebecca Caudill Young Readers' Book Award Committee Vol 1: 15572
Recording for the Blind Vol 1: 15574
Recording for the Blind and Dyslexic Vol 1: 15574
Recording Industry Association of America Vol 1: 15577
Recording Industry Association of Japan Vol 2: 3313
Recording Industry of South Africa Vol 2: 4233
Recreation Vehicle Industry Association Vol 1: 15580
Recycling Council of Alberta Vol 1: 15588
Recycling Council of Ontario Vol 1: 15590
Red Cross; International Committee of the Vol 2: 1153
Redd Center for Western Studies; Charles Vol 1: 15592
Redshaw Ltd.; James Vol 2: 6381
Reebok Human Rights Foundation Vol 1: 15600
Reference Sources Committee Vol 1: 2692
Reflectone, Inc. Vol 1: 11507
REFORMA Vol 1: 4921
REFORMA: National Association to Promote Library Services to the Spanish-Speaking Vol 1: 15602
Regional Centre for Seismology for South America Vol 2: 3957
Regional Government of Carinthia Vol 2: 768
Regional Organization for the Protection of the Marine Environment Vol 2: 3370
Regional Studies Association Vol 2: 6590
Regione Lombardia Vol 2: 2995
Rehabilitation International Vol 1: 15606
Religion Communicators Council Vol 1: 15610
Religion Newswriters Association Vol 1: 15612
Religious and Military Order of Knights of the Holy Sepulchre of Jerusalem Vol 1: 15618
Religious Communication Association Vol 1: 15620
Remodeling Vol 1: 12560
Remote Sensing and Photogrammetry Society Vol 2: 6592
Renaissance Society of America Vol 1: 15622
Rencontres chorales internationales de Montreux Vol 2: 4869
Rencontres Internationales de Chant Choral de Tours Vol 2: 1800
Rencontres Internationales de la Photographie Vol 2: 1944
Rencontres Internationales Henri Langlois Vol 2: 1929
Renewable Natural Resources Foundation Vol 1: 15625
Republic of Croatia Ministry of Science, Education and Sports Vol 2: 1235
Republic of South Africa Department of Sport and Recreation Vol 2: 4238
Republika Hrvatska Vol 2: 1235
Research and Development Associates for Military Food and Packaging Systems Vol 1: 15628
Research Centre for Islamic History, Art and Culture Vol 2: 4985
Research Corp. Vol 1: 1510
Research Corporation Vol 1: 3131
Research Society for Victorian Periodicals Vol 1: 15631
Reseau canadien de l'environment Vol 1: 6469
Reseau de radios rurales des pays en developpement Vol 1: 8175
Reseau juridique canadien VIH/SIDA Vol 1: 6562
Reserve Officer Training Corps Vol 1: 13780
Residential Meeting of the Child and Adolescent Psychiatry Faculty Vol 2: 6722
Resistance Welder Manufacturers' Association Vol 1: 4471
Resistol Hats Vol 1: 15354
Resort and Commercial Recreation Association Vol 1: 15633
Resource and Information Center for Chinese Studies Vol 2: 4949
Restaurant Association of New Zealand Vol 2: 3829
Restaurant Hospitality - Penton Media, Inc. Vol 1: 15641
Results Vol 1: 15644
Retail Advertising and Marketing Association Vol 1: 15646
Retail Advertising Conference Vol 1: 15646
Retail Council of Canada Vol 1: 15649
Reticuloendothelial Society Vol 1: 16323
Reuters Foundation Vol 2: 6599
Review of Social Economy Vol 1: 4968
Rheims; Fondation Vol 2: 1588
Rhode Island Health Center Association Vol 1: 15655
Rhode Island Turfgrass Foundation Vol 1: 15657
Rhodes 19 Class Association Vol 1: 15659
Rhododendron Species Foundation Vol 1: 15661
Ricardo Group, plc. Vol 2: 6629
Riccione per il Teatro Vol 2: 3122
Richard-Allan Scientific Vol 1: 13716
Richard III Society Vol 1: 15664
Richard III Society, American Branch Vol 1: 15663
Richard the III Foundation Vol 1: 15665
Richards Free Library Vol 1: 15667
Rider Hunt Vol 2: 601
Rider University Student Government Association Vol 1: 15669
Rielo Foundation; Fernando Vol 2: 4529
Right Livelihood Awards Foundation Vol 2: 4618
Rijksakademie van Beeldende Kunsten Vol 2: 3641
Rijksuniversiteit Limburg Vol 2: 1104
Risk and Insurance Management Society Vol 1: 15671
Rittenhouse Book Distributors, Inc. Vol 1: 11667
River City Vol 1: 15675
RMIT University Vol 2: 606, 3401
Road Racing Drivers Club Vol 1: 17202
Road Runners Club of America Vol 1: 15677
Robert A. Welch Foundation Vol 1: 18654
Robert Bosch Stiftung Vol 2: 2040
Robert F. Kennedy Memorial Vol 1: 15680
Robert Foster Cherry Awards Committee Vol 1: 15684
Roberts Theatre; Forest Vol 1: 15686
Robot Institute of America Vol 1: 15688
Robotic Industries Association Vol 1: 15688
Roche Diagnostics Vol 2: 4258
Rochester Institute of Technology Vol 1: 15690
Rochester International Amateur Film Festival Vol 1: 15692
Rochester International Film Festival Vol 1: 15692
Rock and Roll Hall of Fame and Museum Vol 1: 15694
Rockefeller Foundation Vol 1: 2233, 3088
Rockford College Vol 1: 15696
Rockwell Collins Vol 1: 2365
Rockwell International Vol 1: 3628
Rockwell International Vol 1: 12642
Rocky Mountain Coal Mining Institute Vol 1: 15698
Rocky Mountain Elk Foundation Vol 1: 15700
Rocky Mountain Masonry Institute Vol 1: 15702
Rodeo Cowboys Association Vol 1: 15350
Rodeo Historical Society Vol 1: 15704
Roger Parsons Vol 2: 6967
Rogers Endowment Fund; Hal Vol 1: 11158
Rohm & Haas Vol 2: 6967
Rohm & Haas Co. Vol 1: 1548, 1565
Rohm and Haas Co. Vol 1: 1575, 1585
Rohrer, Hibler and Replogle Vol 1: 3407
Rolex Awards for Enterprise Vol 2: 4879
Rolex Watch U.S.A. Inc. Vol 1: 11201, 11203
Rolling Stone Vol 1: 15707
Rolls-Royce Enthusiasts' Club Vol 2: 6602
Romance Writers of America Vol 1: 15709
Romanian Academy Vol 2: 4385
Romantic Novelists' Association Vol 2: 6604

Ronald McDonald House Charities Vol 1: 15712
Roosevelt Memorial Association Vol 1: 17520
Rosary College Vol 1: 8250
Roscoe Pound Institute Vol 1: 15715
Rose Brand Vol 1: 17947
Rose Brand Theatrical Fabrics, Fabrications & Supplies Vol 1: 17949
Rose d'Or Festival Vol 2: 4881
Rosenstiel Basic Medical Sciences Research Center Vol 1: 15719
Rosenthal Foundation; Richard and Hinda Vol 1: 1719
Ross Products Division, Abbott Laboratories Vol 1: 3791
Rostropovitch International Competitions Vol 2: 1743
Rotary International Vol 1: 15722
Rothko Chapel Vol 1: 15725
Rotterdam Arts Council Vol 2: 3643
Rotterdam Arts Foundation Vol 2: 3556
Rotterdamse Kunststichting Vol 2: 3643
Rough and Smooth Collie Training Association Vol 2: 6607
Royal Academy of Arts Vol 2: 6609
Royal Academy of Dance Vol 2: 6613
Royal Academy of Dutch Language and Literature Vol 2: 948
Royal Academy of Engineering Vol 2: 6620
Royal Academy of Letters, History and Antiquities Vol 2: 4620
Royal Academy of Medicine Vol 2: 966
Royal Academy of Medicine in Ireland Vol 2: 2869
Royal Academy of Music Vol 2: 6626
Royal Academy of Pharmacy Vol 2: 4531
Royal Academy of Science, Humanities and Fine Arts of Belgium - Division of Fine Arts Vol 2: 971
Royal Academy of Science, Humanities and Fine Arts of Belgium - Division of Humanities Vol 2: 991
Royal Academy of Science, Humanities and Fine Arts of Belgium - Division of Sciences Vol 2: 1020
Royal Academy of Sciences, Humanities and Fine Arts of Belgium Vol 2: 1058
Royal Aeronautical Society - United Kingdom Vol 2: 6628
Royal Agricultural Society of England Vol 2: 6661
Royal Air Force Historical Society Vol 1: 323
Royal and Ancient Golf Club of St. Andrews Vol 2: 6671
Royal Anthropological Institute of Great Britain and Ireland Vol 2: 6673
Royal Architectural Institute of Canada Vol 1: 15727
Royal Asiatic Society of Great Britain and Ireland Vol 2: 6678
Royal Association for Disability and Rehabilitation Vol 2: 5004
Royal Association of British Dairy Farmers Vol 2: 6681
Royal Astronomical Society Vol 2: 6685
Royal Astronomical Society of Canada Vol 1: 15734
Royal Australasian College of Dental Surgeons Vol 2: 609
Royal Australasian College of Surgeons Vol 2: 612
Royal Australian Chemical Institute Vol 2: 496, 614
Royal Australian Institute of Architects Vol 2: 626
Royal Bath and West of England Society Vol 2: 6691
Royal Canadian Geographical Society Vol 1: 15741
Royal Canadian Golf Association Vol 1: 18943
Royal Carillon School Jef Denyn Vol 2: 1079
Royal College of General Practitioners Vol 2: 4436
Royal College of General Practitioners Vol 2: 6693
Royal College of Obstetricians and Gynaecologists - United Kingdom Vol 2: 6700
Royal College of Ophthalmologists Vol 2: 6710
Royal College of Physicians Vol 2: 6922
Royal College of Physicians and Surgeons of Canada Vol 1: 6477, 15744
Royal College of Physicians and Surgeons of Glasgow Vol 2: 6714
Royal College of Psychiatrists Vol 2: 6719
Royal College of Radiologists - United Kingdom Vol 2: 6737
Royal College of Veterinary Surgeons Vol 2: 6739
Royal Commonwealth Society Vol 2: 6748
Royal Conservatory of Music Vol 1: 15749
The Royal Danish Academy of Fine Arts Vol 2: 1323
Royal Danish Geographical Society Vol 2: 1329
Royal Dublin Society Vol 2: 2875
Royal Dutch Geographical Society Vol 2: 3645
Royal Economic Society Vol 2: 6750
Royal Entomological Society Vol 2: 6754
Royal Film Archive of Belgium Vol 2: 1082
Royal Force Historical Society Vol 2: 5012
Royal Geographic Society Vol 2: 6756
Royal Geographical Society of Queensland Vol 2: 629
Royal Geographical Society with the Institute of British Geographers Vol 2: 6756
Royal Historical Society - United Kingdom Vol 2: 6776
Royal Horticultural Society Vol 2: 6782
Royal Horticultural Society of Ireland Vol 2: 2878
Royal Humane Society Vol 2: 6812
Royal Incorporation of Architects in Scotland Vol 2: 6814
Royal Institute of British Architects Vol 2: 5891, 6820
Royal Institute of Navigation Vol 2: 6825
Royal Institute of Oil Painters Vol 2: 6834
Royal Institution of Naval Architects Vol 2: 6109, 6836
Royal Irish Academy Vol 2: 2880
Royal Life Saving Society Vol 2: 6844
Royal Mail Vol 2: 5738
Royal Meteorological Society Vol 2: 6846
Royal Musical Association Vol 2: 6848
Royal National Rose Society Vol 2: 6850
Royal Navy Hydrographic Department Vol 2: 5603
Royal Neighbors of America Vol 1: 15751
Royal Netherlands Academy of Arts and Sciences Vol 2: 3647
Royal New South Wales Bowling Association Vol 2: 631
Royal New Zealand Aero Club Vol 2: 3835
Royal N.S. Historical Society - Genealogical Committee Vol 1: 8979
Royal Over-Seas League Vol 2: 6852
Royal Philatelic Society Vol 2: 6854
Royal Philharmonic Society Vol 2: 6858
Royal Philosophical Society of Glasgow Vol 2: 6866
Royal Photographic Society of Great Britain Vol 2: 6869
Royal Physiographic Society in Lund Vol 2: 4622
Royal School of Church Music Vol 2: 6882
Royal Scottish Academy Vol 2: 6884
Royal Scottish Forestry Society Vol 2: 6886
Royal Scottish Geographical Society Vol 2: 6888
Royal Society Vol 2: 6109, 6373, 6899
Royal Society for Nature Conservation Vol 2: 7039
Royal Society for the Encouragement of Arts, Manufactures & Commerce Vol 2: 6918
Royal Society for the Prevention of Accidents Vol 2: 6923
Royal Society for the Promotion of Health Vol 2: 6932
Royal Society for the Protection of Birds Vol 2: 7333
Royal Society of British Artists Vol 2: 6941
Royal Society of British Sculptors Vol 2: 6944
Royal Society of Canada Vol 1: 15753
Royal Society of Chemistry Vol 2: 6946
Royal Society of Edinburgh Vol 2: 6986
Royal Society of Health Vol 2: 6932
Royal Society of Literature Vol 2: 7000
Royal Society of London Vol 2: 1739
Royal Society of Medicine Vol 2: 7005, 7148
Royal Society of Miniature Painters, Sculptors and Gravers Vol 2: 7024
Royal Society of New South Wales Vol 2: 636
Royal Society of New Zealand Vol 2: 3863
Royal Society of Portrait Painters Vol 2: 7026
Royal Society of South Africa Vol 2: 4241
Royal Society of South Australia Vol 2: 647
Royal Society of Tropical Medicine and Hygiene Vol 2: 7028
The Royal Society of Victoria Vol 2: 652
Royal Society of Western Australia Vol 2: 654
Royal Society of Wildlife Trusts Vol 2: 7039
Royal Swedish Academy of Engineering Sciences Vol 2: 4633
Royal Swedish Academy of Sciences Vol 2: 4603, 4636
Royal Television Society Vol 2: 7041
Royal Town Planning Institute Vol 2: 6823, 7049
Royal United Services Institute for Defence and Security Studies Vol 2: 7053
Royal Western Australian Historical Society Vol 2: 656
Royal Zoological Society of New South Wales Vol 2: 658
RTCA Vol 1: 15770
Rudder Memorial Fund; William Vol 2: 4857
Rudolph E. Lee Gallery - College of Architecture, Arts, and Humanities Vol 1: 15772
Runyon - Walter Winchell Cancer Fund; Damon Vol 1: 8034
Rural Nurse Organization Vol 1: 15774
Rural Sociological Society Vol 1: 15776

Rural Youth Europe Vol 2: 818
Russian Academy of Sciences Vol 2: 1742, 4393
Russian Academy of Sciences - Section of Social Science Vol 2: 4396
Russian PEN Club Vol 2: 2401
Ryan Foundation; Irene Vol 1: 11119
SA Holstein Friesland Society Vol 2: 4244
SABAM Vol 2: 906
Sagebrush Book Co. Vol 1: 19085
Sagebrush Education Resources Vol 1: 4930
Sahitya Akademi Vol 2: 2789
Sahitya Akademi - India's National Academy of Letters Vol 2: 2789
Sail America Vol 1: 4503
St. Bonaventure University - Russell J. Jandoli School of Journalism and Mass Communication Vol 1: 15782
St. Cecilia Society Vol 1: 15788
St. George's Society of New York Vol 1: 15790
St. Kilda Film Festival Vol 2: 660
Saint Louis University Vol 1: 15792
Saint Lucia Tourist Board Vol 2: 4398
St. Martin's Press Vol 1: 1854
St. Nicholas Society of the City of New York Vol 1: 15797
Sakura Europe Vol 2: 4253
Sakura Finetek, USA, Inc. Vol 1: 13716
Sakura Finetek U.S.A. Inc. Vol 1: 13723
Sales and Marketing Executives International Vol 1: 15800
Sales Professionals USA Vol 1: 15802
Salina Arts and Humanities Commission Vol 1: 15804
Salmon Preservation Association for the Waters of Newfoundland Vol 1: 15806
Salon du Livre de l'Estrie Vol 1: 15810
Salon du Livre de Montreal Vol 1: 15812
Salter Company Vol 2: 7059
Salters' Institute Vol 2: 7057
Saltire Society Vol 2: 7063
Samahang Pisika ng Pilipinas Vol 2: 3985
Samarbetsorganisationen for Emballagefragor i Skandinavien Vol 2: 1333
Samasevaya Vol 2: 4563
Samojedhunde Klubben I Danmark Vol 2: 1286
San Angelo Symphony Vol 1: 15815
San Antonio Building Owners and Managers Association Vol 1: 15817
San Antonio International Piano Competition Vol 1: 15819
San Diego County Fair - Exhibits Department Vol 1: 15823
San Francisco Film Festival Vol 1: 15825
The San Francisco Foundation Vol 1: 15827
San Francisco Planning and Urban Research Association Vol 1: 15832
San Jose Astronomical Association Vol 1: 15834
San Jose State University Vol 1: 15836
San Juan 21 Class Association Vol 1: 15838
San Remo Municipality Vol 2: 3011
San Sebastian International Film Festival Vol 2: 4537
Sanford-Sprindale Rotary Vol 1: 15840
Sanofi-Synthelabo Inc. Vol 1: 14544
Santa Fe Partners in Education Vol 1: 15842
Santander International Piano Competition Vol 2: 4539
Santander International Piano Competition; Paloma O'Shea Vol 2: 4539
Sao Paulo International Film Festival Vol 2: 1135
Sapporo Sports Promotion Corporation Vol 2: 3315
Sarnoff Corporation Vol 1: 9795
Sarton Comite van de Rijksuniversiteit Gent Vol 2: 1085
Sarton Committee of the University of Ghent Vol 2: 1085
SAS Institute Inc. Vol 1: 15844
Saskatchewan Library Association Vol 1: 15846
Saskatchewan Lotteries Vol 1: 19078
Saskatchewan Motion Picture Association Vol 1: 19078
Saskatchewan Music Festival Association Vol 1: 15849
Saskatchewan Natural History Society Vol 1: 13987
Sasol Ltd. Vol 2: 4319
Sauve Qui Peut le Court Metrage Vol 2: 1946
Scandinavian Collectors Club Vol 1: 15891
Scandinavian Packaging Association Vol 2: 1333
Scandinavian Research Council for Criminology Vol 2: 4643
Scandinavian Society for the Study of Diabetes Vol 2: 1317
Scandinavian Tobacco Company Vol 2: 1282
Scarab Club Vol 1: 15896
Scarecrow Press, Inc. Vol 1: 2656
Schenectady Museum Association Vol 1: 15900
Schering-Plough Animal Health Vol 1: 7058, 7060
Schering-Plough Research Institute Vol 1: 1554, 3567
Scheveningen Internationaal Muziek Concours Vol 2: 3661
Scheveningen International Music Competition Vol 2: 3661
Schmidheiny Stiftung; Max Vol 2: 4867
Scholastic, Inc. Vol 1: 12989
Scholastic Library Publishing Vol 1: 2682
Schonstedt Instrument Co. Vol 1: 1781
School and Community Safety Society of America Vol 1: 15902
School Library Journal Vol 1: 19083
School Library Media Specialists of Southeastern New York Vol 1: 15904
School Nurses Organization of Arizona Vol 1: 15906
School Nutrition Association Vol 1: 15908
School of American Ballet Vol 1: 15916
School of American Research Vol 1: 15918
School of Natural Resources and Environment Vol 1: 18313
School of Oriental and African Studies Vol 2: 7074
Schumpeter Gesellschaft; Internationale Joseph A. Vol 2: 2374
Schumpeter Society; International Joseph A. Vol 2: 2374
Schwartz Foundation; Ruth Vol 1: 14564
Schweizer Musikedition Vol 2: 4906
Schweizerische Akademie der Medizinischen Wissenschaften Vol 2: 4884
Schweizerische Gesellschaft fur Theaterkultur Vol 2: 4887
The Science and Technology Foundation of Japan Vol 2: 3317
Science and Technology-Science Education Institute Vol 2: 3985
Science Council of Japan Vol 1: 14785
Science Fiction and Fantasy Writers of America Vol 1: 15920
Science Fiction Foundation Vol 2: 7076
Science Fiction Writers of America Vol 1: 15920
Science Fiction Writers of Earth Vol 1: 15924
Science Service Vol 1: 15926
Scientific and Technical Research Council of Turkey Vol 2: 4987
Scientific Equipment and Furniture Association Vol 1: 15929
Scientific Program Committee Vol 1: 3282
Scientific Research Society of America Vol 1: 16055
Scientific Update Vol 2: 6967
Scleroderma Foundation Vol 1: 15931
Scott Arboretum of Swarthmore College Vol 1: 15933
Scott Horticultural Foundation Vol 1: 15933
Scott Joplin International Ragtime Foundation Vol 1: 15935
Scottish Bowling Association Vol 2: 7078
Scottish Environmental Protection Agency Vol 2: 7065
Scottish International Piano Competition Vol 2: 7080
Scottish Photographic Federation Vol 2: 7082
Scottish Studies Program/Scottish Studies Foundation Vol 1: 15937
Scottish Tartans Society Vol 2: 7250
Scouting Ireland CSI Vol 2: 2882
Scrabble Players Vol 1: 13687
Screen Actors Guild Vol 1: 15939
Scribes Vol 1: 15943
Scripps School of Journalism; E. W. Vol 1: 15947
Sea Grant Association Vol 1: 15949
Search for Common Ground Vol 1: 15952
Seattle Art Museum Vol 1: 15954
Seattle International Film Festival Vol 1: 15956
Seattle Writers Association Vol 1: 15960
SECO: Technical Control Bureau for Construction Vol 2: 1088
Secondary School Admission Test Board Vol 1: 15962
Section for Women in Public Administration - Section for Women in Public Administration Vol 1: 15964
Security Equipment Industry Association Vol 1: 15968
Security Industry Association Vol 1: 15968
Selby Scientific Foundation Vol 2: 122
Semana Internacional de Cine de Valladolid Vol 2: 4551
SEMI International Vol 1: 15970
Semiconductor Equipment and Materials Institute Vol 1: 15970
Semiconductor Equipment and Materials International Vol 1: 15970
Seminar on the Acquisition of Latin American Library Materials Vol 1: 15973
Service of Peace and Justice Vol 2: 1169
Servicio Paz y Justicia Vol 2: 1169
Seventh Day Baptist Historical Society Vol 1: 15975
Severn River Association Vol 1: 15979
The Sewanee Review Vol 1: 15981
Seybold Publications Vol 1: 15983
The Shakespeare Theatre Vol 1: 15985

Organization Index

Shakespeare Theatre at the Folger Vol 1: 15985
Shark Awards Festival Vol 2: 2886
Sharp Corporation Vol 1: 16309
Shazar Center for Jewish History; Zalman Vol 2: 2927
Shell Foundation Vol 1: 1206
Shell Global Solutions Inc. Vol 1: 2470
Shell Oil Co. Vol 1: 13684
Shenango Valley Chamber of Commerce Vol 1: 15987
Shin-Norinsha Company Limited of Japan Vol 1: 3854
Shiras Institute Vol 1: 15687
Shorenstein Center on the Press, Politics and Public Policy; Joan Vol 1: 15989
Shreveport Civic Opera Vol 1: 15992
Shreveport Opera Company Vol 1: 15992
Shurgain Ltd. Vol 1: 6972
S.I.A.T.L Vol 2: 2524
Sibelius International Violin Competition; Jean Vol 2: 1424
Sibelius Society of Finland Vol 2: 1425
SID Award (Store Interior Design Award) Vol 1: 12681
Sidewise Awards for Alternate History Vol 1: 15994
Sidney-Shelby County Young Men's Christian Association Vol 1: 15996
Siemens AG Vol 2: 1787, 2098
Siena College - Department of Creative Arts Vol 1: 15998
Sierra Club Vol 1: 16000
Sigma Alpha Iota Foundation Vol 1: 16025
Sigma Alpha Iota Philanthropies, Inc. Vol 1: 16025
Sigma Delta Epsilon - Graduate Women in Science Vol 1: 16028
Sigma Diagnostics Inc. Vol 1: 13723
Sigma Gamma Tau Vol 1: 16032
Sigma Iota Epsilon Vol 1: 16034
Sigma Phi Alpha Vol 1: 16036
Sigma Phi Epsilon Fraternity Vol 1: 16038
Sigma Pi Sigma Trust Fund Vol 1: 2549
Sigma Tau Delta, the International English Honor Society Vol 1: 16040
Sigma Theta Tau International Vol 1: 16042
Sigma Xi Vol 1: 16055
Sigma Xi, The Scientific Research Society Vol 1: 16055
Sigma Zeta Vol 1: 16059
SIGNIS Vol 2: 1091
Sikkens Foundation Vol 2: 3663
Sikorsky Aircraft Vol 1: 9370
Silverfish Review Press Vol 1: 16061
Silvermine Guild Arts Center Vol 1: 16063
Simon Fraser University - Office of Vice President and Research Services Vol 1: 16065
Simon Wiesenthal Center Vol 1: 16067
Singapore Computer Society Vol 2: 4425
Singapore Exhibition Services Pte. Ltd. Vol 2: 4429
Singapore Industrial Automation Association Vol 2: 4431
Singapore National Committee of the International Water Association Vol 2: 4433
Singapore Press Holding Vol 2: 4423
Singkreis Porcia-Spittal an der Drau Vol 2: 768
Single Service Institute Vol 1: 8790
SIPA Footbags and Adidas Footbags Vol 1: 18941
Sir Henry Royce Memorial Foundation Vol 2: 662
Sister Cities International Vol 1: 16070
Sister Kenny Rehabilitation Institute Vol 1: 16072
Sixteenth Century Society and Conference Vol 1: 16074
Ski Racing Vol 1: 16082
Skills USA - VICA Vol 1: 16084
SLE Foundation Vol 1: 16087
Slipstream Vol 1: 16089
Sloan Foundation; Alfred P. Vol 1: 8929
Slobodna Dalmacija Vol 2: 1223
Slovak Physical Society Vol 2: 4445
Slovak Television Vol 2: 4451
Slovakia Ministerstvo Kultury Slovenskej Republik Vol 2: 4441
Slovene Writers' Association Vol 2: 4462
Slovenian Pharmaceutical Society Vol 2: 4464
Slovenska Fyzikalna Spolocnost Vol 2: 4445
Slovenska televizia, Bratislava Vol 2: 4451
Slovkoncert, Czechoslovakia Artists Agency Vol 2: 4443
Small Business Council of America Vol 1: 16091
Smith and Son; W. H. Vol 2: 7394
Smith Breeden Associates Inc. Vol 1: 2022
Smith Kline Corporation Vol 1: 3808
Smith Performing Arts Center; Clarice Vol 1: 16093
SmithKline Beecham Pharmaceuticals Vol 1: 206
Smithson Society; James Vol 1: 16095
Smithsonian Institution Vol 1: 16097
Smithsonian Women's Committee Vol 1: 16099
Snipe Class International Racing Association Vol 1: 16101
Snow Inc.; John Vol 1: 9097
SNP Corporation Vol 2: 4424
Soaring Society of America Vol 1: 16103
The SOCAN Foundation Vol 1: 16118
Soccer Association for Youth Vol 1: 16120
Soccer Industry Council of America Vol 1: 16123
Social Issues Resources Series Vol 1: 10238, 11418, 17437
Social Research Association Vol 2: 7084
Social Science Research Council Vol 1: 16125
Sociedad Argentina de Estudios Geograficos Vol 2: 16
Sociedad Espanola de Quimica Industrial Vol 2: 2119
Sociedad Interamericana de Cardiologia Vol 2: 3448
Sociedad Interamericana de Prensa Vol 1: 9974
Sociedad Quimica de Mexico Vol 2: 3436
Societa Chimica Italiana Vol 2: 3101
Societa del Quartetto Vol 2: 3125
Societa Geologica Italiana Vol 2: 3127
Societa Italiana di Ecologia Vol 2: 3112
Societas Internationalis Aerosolibus in Medicina Vol 2: 2317
Societas Internationalis Limnologiae Vol 1: 10257
Societe Africaine de Reassurance Vol 2: 3882
Societe Alzheimer du Canada Vol 1: 456
Societe Astronomique de France Vol 2: 1949
Societe Bibliographique du Canada Vol 1: 5746
Societe Canadienne de Fertilite et d'Andrologie Vol 1: 6492
Societe canadienne de genie chimique Vol 1: 6891
Societe Canadienne de Genie Civil Vol 1: 6911
Societe Canadienne de Genie Mecanique Vol 1: 6948
Societe Canadienne de Geotechnique Vol 1: 6521
Societe Canadienne de la Sclerose en Plaques Vol 1: 12005
Societe Canadienne de la Surete Industrielle Vol 1: 6942
Societe canadienne de medecine interne Vol 1: 7000
Societe Canadienne de Meteorologie et d'Oceanographique Vol 1: 6725
Societe Canadienne de Pediatrie Vol 1: 6786
Societe Canadienne de Pharmacologie Clinique Vol 1: 6928
Societe Canadienne de physitherapie cardio-respiatoire Vol 1: 6806
Societe Canadienne de Phytopathologie Vol 1: 6811
Societe Canadienne de Psychanalyse Vol 1: 6825
Societe Canadienne de Psychologie Vol 1: 6829
Societe canadienne de recherches cliniques Vol 1: 6923
Societe Canadienne de Sante Internationale Vol 1: 6946
Societe Canadienne de Science de Laboratoire Medical Vol 1: 6956
Societe Canadienne de Sociologie et d'Anthropologie Vol 1: 7037
Societe Canadienne de Zootechnie Vol 1: 6971
Societe Canadienne des Anesthesiologistes Vol 1: 6178
Societe canadienne des auteurs, compositeurs, et editeurs de musique Vol 1: 16118
Societe Canadienne des Directeurs d'Association Vol 1: 6978
Societe Canadienne des Etudes Bibliques Vol 1: 6982
Societe Canadienne des Microbiologistes Vol 1: 7009
Societe Canadienne des pharmaciens d'Hopitaux Vol 1: 6992
Societe Canadienne des Relations Publiques Vol 1: 6843
Societe Canadienne des Sciences de la Nutrition Vol 1: 6959
Societe Canadienne des Sciences du Cerveau, du Comportement et de la Cognition Vol 1: 6886
Societe Canadienne d'Immunologie Vol 1: 6938
Societe Canadienne du Dialogue Humaine Machine Vol 1: 6568
Societe Canadienne pour la Recherche Nautique Vol 1: 6753
Societe canadienne pour l'etude de l'education Vol 1: 6961
Societe canadienne pour l'etude de l'enseignement superieur Vol 1: 6966
Societe Chimique de Belgique Vol 2: 1094
Societe de Biologie Experimentale Vol 2: 7092
Societe de Chimie Industrielle Vol 2: 1814

Societe de Chimie Therapeutique Vol 2: 1964
Societe de Geologie Appliquee aux Gites Mineraux Vol 2: 1265
Societe de Musique des Universites Canadiennes Vol 1: 7054
Societe de Pathologie Exotique Vol 2: 1968
Societe de Pharmacologie du Canada Vol 1: 14967
Societe des Auteurs, Compositeurs et Editeurs de Musique Vol 2: 1971
Societe des Auteurs et Compositeurs Dramatiques Vol 2: 1984
Societe des Canadiennes dans la Science et la Technologies Vol 1: 16186
Societe des Indexateurs Vol 2: 7196
Societe des Ornithologistes du Canada Vol 1: 16617
Societe du Comte Dracula Vol 2: 5741
Societe Europeenne de Chirurgie Cardiovasculaire Vol 2: 3032
Societe Europeenne pour la Formation des Ingenieurs Vol 2: 873
Societe Francaise d'Acoustique Vol 2: 1978
Societe Francaise de Physique Vol 2: 2093
Societe Genealogique Canadienne-Francaise Vol 1: 8883
Societe Geologique de France Vol 2: 1829
Societe historique du Canada Vol 1: 6555
Societe Internationale de Chimiotherapie Vol 2: 6296
Societe Internationale de Chirurgie Vol 2: 4849
Societe Internationale de Chirurgie Orthopedique et de Traumatologie Vol 2: 927
Societe Internationale de Droit Militaire et de Droit de la Guerre Vol 2: 925
Societe Internationale de Mecanique des Roches Vol 2: 4063
Societe Internationale de Mecanique des Sols et de la Geotechnique Vol 2: 6292
Societe Internationale de Mycologie Humaine et Animales Vol 2: 1412
Societe Internationale de Neurochimie Vol 2: 1308
Societe Internationale de Transfusion Sanguine Vol 2: 3614
Societe Internationale d'Oncologie Pediatrique Vol 2: 6298
Societe Internationale pour l'Education Artistique Vol 1: 10645
Societe Nucleaire Canadienne Vol 1: 6760
Societe Parkinson Canada Vol 1: 14861
Societe quebecoise pour la promotion de la litterature de langue anglaise Vol 1: 15492
Societe Royale de Chimie Vol 2: 1094
Societe Royale des Sciences de Liege Vol 2: 1097
Societe Royale Du Canada Vol 1: 15753
Societe Saint-Jean-Baptiste de Montreal Vol 1: 16134
Societe statistique du Canada Vol 1: 17278
Societe Suisse de Radiodiffusion et Television et la Ville de Montreux Vol 2: 4881
Societe Universitaire Europeenne de Recherches Financieres Vol 2: 775
Society for Adolescent Medicine Vol 1: 16147
Society for Advancement of Management Vol 1: 16153
Society for American Archaeology Vol 1: 16157
Society for American Baseball Research Vol 1: 16166
Society for Applied Anthropology Vol 1: 815
Society for Applied Microbiology Vol 2: 7086
Society for Applied Spectroscopy Vol 1: 14610
Society for Applied Spectroscopy Vol 1: 16176
Society for Behavioral Pediatrics Vol 1: 16201
Society For Biomaterials Vol 1: 16182
Society for Biotechnology, Japan Vol 2: 3319
Society for Canadian Women in Science and Technology Vol 1: 16186
Society for Cinema and Media Studies Vol 1: 16190
Society for Clinical and Experimental Hypnosis Vol 1: 16193
Society for Developmental and Behavioral Pediatrics Vol 1: 16201
Society for Drug Research Vol 2: 7101
Society for Economic Botany Vol 1: 16203
Society for Engineering in Agriculture Vol 2: 664
Society for Environmental Exploration Vol 2: 7089
Society for Environmental Graphic Design Vol 1: 16206
Society for Epidemiologic Research Vol 1: 16208
Society for Ethnomusicology Vol 1: 16210
Society for Experimental Biology Vol 2: 7092
Society for Film Art in Tampere Vol 2: 1426
Society for French Historical Studies Vol 1: 7361
Society for General Microbiology Vol 2: 7095
Society for Geology Applied to Mineral Deposits Vol 2: 1265
Society for Historians of American Foreign Relations Vol 1: 16214
Society for Historical Archaeology Vol 1: 16219
Society for History in the Federal Government Vol 1: 16224
Society for Human Resource Management Vol 1: 16230
Society for Imaging Science and Technology Vol 1: 14609
Society for Imaging Science and Technology Vol 1: 16244
Society for In Vitro Biology Vol 1: 16257
Society for Industrial and Applied Mathematics Vol 1: 2726
Society for Industrial and Applied Mathematics Vol 1: 16265
Society for Industrial and Organizational Psychology Vol 1: 16287
Society for Industrial Microbiology Vol 1: 16298
Society for Information Display Vol 1: 16303
Society for Integrative and Comparative Biology Vol 1: 16312
Society for International Hockey Research Vol 1: 16314
Society for Investigative Dermatology Vol 1: 16316
Society for Italian Historical Studies Vol 1: 2241
Society for Italian Historical Studies Vol 1: 16318
Society for Judgement and Decision Making Vol 1: 16321
Society for Leukocyte Biology Vol 1: 16323
Society for Marketing Professional Services Vol 1: 16326
Society for Medical Decision Making Vol 1: 16329
Society for Medicinal Plant Research Vol 2: 2376
Society for Medicines Research Vol 2: 7101
Society for Medieval Archaeology Vol 2: 7103
Society for Military History Vol 1: 16334
Society for Mining, Metallurgy, and Exploration Vol 1: 16340
Society for Nondestructive Testing Vol 1: 3773
Society for Pediatric Dermatology Vol 1: 16365
Society for Pediatric Research Vol 1: 16368
Society for Personality and Social Psychology (Division 8) Vol 1: 16376
Society for Prevention Research Vol 1: 16379
Society for Public Health Education Vol 1: 16392
Society for Radiological Protection Vol 2: 7107
Society for Range Management Vol 1: 16400
Society for Research into Higher Education Vol 2: 7111
Society for Research into Hydrocephalus and Spina Bifida Vol 2: 7113
Society for Sedimentary Geology Vol 1: 16406
Society for Sedimentary Geology Vol 1: 16406
Society for Sedimentary Geology, Great Lakes Section Vol 1: 16417
Society for Sex Therapy and Research Vol 1: 16419
Society for Social Studies of Science Vol 1: 16421
Society for Spinal Research Vol 2: 2378
Society for Technical Communication Vol 1: 16426
Society for the Advancement of Anaesthesia in Dentistry Vol 2: 7115
Society for the Advancement of the Arts and Film Vol 1: 12076
Society for the Historians of the Early American Republic Vol 1: 16430
Society for the History of Alchemy and Chemistry Vol 2: 7118
Society for the History of Natural History Vol 2: 7120
Society for the History of Technology Vol 1: 16434
Society for the Preservation of American Business History Vol 1: 18574
Society for the Preservation of Bluegrass Music of America Vol 1: 16442
Society for the Promotion of New Music Vol 2: 7237
Society for the Psychological Study of Lesbian, Gay and Bisexual Issues Vol 1: 3388, 3395
Society for the Psychological Study of Social Issues Vol 1: 16444
Society for the Scientific Investigation of Para-Sciences Vol 2: 2380
Society for the Scientific Study of Sexuality Vol 1: 16451
Society for the Study of Amphibians and Reptiles Vol 1: 16453

Organization Index

Society for the Study of Architecture in Canada Vol 1: 16455
Society for the Study of Evolution Vol 1: 16457
Society for the Study of Midwestern Literature Vol 1: 16459
Society for the Study of Social Problems Vol 1: 16461
Society for the Study of Southern Literature Vol 1: 16466
Society for the Study of Symbolic Interaction Vol 1: 16468
Society for Theatre Research Vol 2: 7125
Society for Utopian Studies Vol 1: 16472
Society for Women in Philosophy Vol 1: 16475
Society of Actuaries Vol 1: 16477
Society of Allied Weight Engineers Vol 1: 16482
Society of American Archivists Vol 1: 16487
Society of American Business Editors and Writers Vol 1: 16500
Society of American Florists Vol 1: 16502
Society of American Foresters Vol 1: 16505
Society of American Graphic Artists Vol 1: 16516
Society of American Military Engineers Vol 1: 16518
Society of American Registered Architects Vol 1: 16537
Society of American Travel Writers Vol 1: 16539
Society of Animal Artists Vol 1: 16542
Society of Architectural and Associated Technicians Vol 2: 5318
Society of Architectural Historians Vol 1: 16550
Society of Army Historical Research Vol 2: 7128
Society of Arts and Crafts Vol 1: 16560
Society of Australasian Specialists Vol 1: 16562
Society of Australasian Specialists/ Oceania Vol 1: 16562
Society of Authors Vol 2: 7131
Society of Authors - Translators Association Vol 2: 7130
Society of Authors - England Vol 2: 7138
Society of Automotive Engineers Vol 1: 2386, 16564
Society of Automotive Engineers (Australasia) Vol 2: 666
Society of Automotive Historians Vol 1: 16595
Society of Biological Chemists, India Vol 2: 2794
Society of Biological Psychiatry Vol 1: 16602
Society of Border Leicester Sheep Breeders Vol 2: 7153
Society of Broadcast Engineers Vol 1: 16608
Society of Cable Telecommunications Engineers Vol 1: 16614
Society of Cable Television Engineers Vol 1: 16614
Society of Canadian Ornithologists Vol 1: 16617
Society of Cardiovascular Anesthesiologists Vol 1: 16619
Society of Chemical Industry Vol 2: 6949, 7155
Society of Chemical Industry - American Section Vol 1: 16621
Society of Children's Book Writers Vol 1: 16623
Society of Children's Book Writers and Illustrators Vol 1: 16623
Society of Clinical Ecology Vol 1: 577
Society of Cosmetic Chemists Vol 1: 16627
Society of Critical Care Medicine Vol 1: 16633
Society of Czech Architects Vol 2: 1269
Society of Decorative Painters Vol 1: 16642
Society of Diagnostic Medical Sonography Vol 1: 16646
Society of Die Casting Engineers Vol 1: 14292
Society of Dramatic Authors and Composers Vol 2: 1984
Society of Dyers and Colourists - England Vol 2: 7181
Society of Economic Geologists Vol 1: 16649
Society of Economic Paleontologists and Mineralogists Vol 1: 16406
Society of Environmental Graphic Designers Vol 1: 16206
Society of Environmental Toxicology and Chemistry Vol 1: 16655
Society of Experimental Test Pilots Vol 1: 16668
Society of Exploration Geo-physicists Vol 1: 16673
Society of Film and Television Arts Vol 2: 5216
Society of Fire Protection Engineers Vol 1: 16682
Society of Flight Test Engineers Vol 1: 16686
Society of Floristry Vol 2: 7193
Society of Forensic Toxicologists Vol 1: 16689
Society of General Internal Medicine Vol 1: 16691
Society of German Cooks Vol 2: 2382
Society of Heating, Airconditioning and Sanitary Engineers of Japan Vol 2: 3327
Society of Illinois Bacteriologists Vol 1: 9613
Society of Illustrators Vol 1: 16701
Society of Indexers Vol 2: 7196
Society of Legal Scholars in the United Kingdom and Ireland Vol 2: 7199
Society of London Theatre Vol 2: 7202
Society of Magazine Writers Vol 1: 4091
Society of Manufacturing Engineers - Composites Manufacturing Association Vol 1: 16703
Society of Medical Friends of Wine Vol 1: 16736
Society of Medical Laboratory Technologists of South Africa Vol 2: 4246
Society of Mexican American Engineers and Scientists Vol 1: 16738
Society of Midland Authors Vol 1: 16740
Society of Motion Picture and Television Engineers Vol 1: 16742
Society of Municipal Arborists Vol 1: 16754
Society of National Association Publications Vol 1: 16756
Society of Naval Architects and Marine Engineers Vol 1: 16589
Society of Naval Architects and Marine Engineers Vol 1: 16758
Society of Nematologists Vol 1: 16770
Society of Netherlands Literature Vol 2: 3666
Society of Nuclear Medicine Vol 1: 16776
Society of Operations Engineers Vol 2: 7204
Society of Ornamental Turners Vol 2: 7206
Society of Packaging and Handling Engineers Vol 1: 9925
Society of Pediatric Nurses Vol 1: 16782
Society of Petroleum Engineers Vol 1: 16791
Society of Petroleum Engineers of the American Institute of Mining, Metallurgical and Petroleum Engineers Vol 1: 16791
Society of Petrophysicists and Well Log Analysts Vol 1: 16809
Society of Physics Students Vol 1: 2544, 2547, 2549
Society of Physics Students Vol 1: 16814
Society of Plastics Engineers Vol 1: 16823
Society of Procurement Officers in Local Government Vol 2: 7212
Society of Professional Journalists Vol 1: 16835
Society of Publication Designers Vol 1: 16841
Society of Real Estate Appraisers Vol 1: 4565
Society of Reliability Engineers Vol 1: 16844
Society of Research Administrators Vol 1: 16846
Society of Rheology Vol 1: 16851
Society of South African Geographers Vol 2: 4262
Society of Southwest Archivists Vol 1: 16494
Society of Surgical Oncology Vol 1: 16853
Society of Systematic Biologists Vol 1: 16856
Society of Systematic Zoology Vol 1: 16856
Society of Technical Writers and Publishers Vol 1: 16426
Society of the Plastics Industry - Moldmakers Division Vol 1: 16858
Society of the Plastics Industry - Thermoforming Institute Vol 1: 16862
Society of the Silurians Vol 1: 16864
Society of Toxicology Vol 1: 16866
Society of Tribologists and Lubrication Engineers Vol 1: 16879
Society of United States Air Force Flight Surgeons Vol 1: 16887
Society of USAF Flight Surgeons of the Aerospace Medical Association Vol 1: 213
Society of Vertebrate Paleontology Vol 1: 16890
Society of West End Theatre Vol 2: 7202
Society of Wetland Scientists Vol 1: 16896
Society of Wildlife Artists Vol 2: 7214
Society of Woman Geographers Vol 1: 16906
Society of Women Artists Vol 2: 7217
Society of Women Engineers Vol 1: 16909
Society of Women Writers, Victoria Branch Vol 2: 669
Society of Wood Science and Technology Vol 1: 16917
Sociologists for Women in Society Vol 1: 16920
Software and Information Industry Association Vol 1: 16926
Soil and Water Conservation Society Vol 1: 16928
Soil Association Vol 2: 7222
Soil Conservation Society of America Vol 1: 16928
Soil Science Society of America Vol 1: 16935
SOLE, the International Society of Logistics Vol 1: 16945
Sondrio Festival, the International Festival of Documentary Films on Parks Vol 2: 3129

Sonia Shankman Orthogenic School Vol 1: 16954
Sonnings Music Foundation; Leonie Vol 2: 1335
Sonnings Musikfond; Leonie Vol 2: 1335
Sonoma County Culinary Guild Vol 1: 16956
Sons of the Republic of Texas Vol 1: 16958
Sons of the Revolution in the State of New York Vol 1: 16961
Sony Broadcast Vol 2: 7225
Sony Corporation Vol 1: 9783
Sony United Kingdom Ltd. Vol 2: 7225
Soroptimist International of the Americas Vol 1: 16963
Soul Train Music Awards Vol 1: 16966
Source Theatre Company Vol 1: 16968
Sousa Foundation; John Philip Vol 1: 16970
South African Academy of Science and Arts Vol 2: 4264
South African Association for Food Science and Technology Vol 2: 4293
South African Association for Learning and Educational Difficulties Vol 2: 4299
South African Association of Botanists Vol 2: 4301
South African Association of Consulting Engineers Vol 2: 4305
South African Association of Women Graduates Vol 2: 4307
South African Chemical Institute Vol 2: 4313
South African Dental Association Vol 2: 4322
South African Geographical Society Vol 2: 4262
South African Institute of Architects Vol 2: 4330
South African Institute of Electrical Engineers Vol 2: 4338
South African National Council for the Blind Vol 2: 4340
South African National Defence Force Vol 2: 4342
South African Society for Enology and Viticulture Vol 2: 4346
South African Society for Plant Pathology Vol 2: 4366
South African Society for Plant Pathology and Microbiology Vol 2: 4366
South African Society of Music Teachers Vol 2: 4354
South African Sugar Technologists' Association Vol 2: 4356
South African Veterinary Association Vol 2: 4358
South Asia Council Vol 1: 4779
South Atlantic Modern Language Association Vol 1: 16978
South Australia Arts and Industry Development Vol 2: 671
South Australian Photographic Federation Vol 2: 674
South Carolina Arts Commission Vol 1: 16981
South Carolina Association of School Librarians Vol 1: 16983
South Dakota Broadcasters Association Vol 1: 16985
South Dakota Library Association Vol 1: 16988
South Dakota Poetry Society Vol 1: 13182
South Dakota State Historical Society Vol 1: 16990
South Metropolitan Planning Council Vol 1: 16992
South Monmouth Board of Realtors Vol 1: 16994
Southam Vol 1: 6191
Southdown Press Vol 2: 704
Southeast Asian Ministers of Education Organization Vol 2: 4959
Southeast Asian Regional Center for Graduate Study and Research in Agriculture Vol 2: 3989
Southeast Booksellers Association Vol 1: 16996
The Southeast Review - Florida State University Vol 1: 16998
Southeastern American Society for Eighteenth-Century Studies Vol 1: 17001
Southeastern Conference Vol 1: 17003
Southeastern Library Association Vol 1: 17005
Southeastern Theatre Conference Vol 1: 17012
Southern Africa Association for the Advancement of Science Vol 2: 4361
Southern African Society for Plant Pathology Vol 2: 4366
Southern Appalachian Botanical Society Vol 1: 17020
Southern Baptist Historical Society Vol 1: 5665
Southern Conference Vol 1: 17022
Southern Economic Association Vol 1: 17031
Southern Electricity Board Vol 2: 6157
Southern Historical Association Vol 1: 17033
Southern Home Furnishings Association Vol 1: 13351
Southern Humanities Review Vol 1: 17039
Southern Methodist University - Caruth Institute for Entrepreneurship Vol 1: 17041
Southern Methodist University - Caruth Institute of Owner-Managed Business Vol 1: 17041
Southern Methodist University - Meadows School of the Arts Vol 1: 17043
Southern Poetry Review Vol 1: 17045
Southern Psychiatric Association Vol 1: 17047
Southern Regional Council Vol 1: 17049
Southern Regional Council Vol 1: 17050
The Southern Review Vol 1: 17051
Southern States Communication Association Vol 1: 17053
Southwest Review Vol 1: 17055
Southwestern Association of Naturalists Vol 1: 17058
Sovinterfest Vol 2: 4389
Space Coast Writers' Guild Vol 1: 17063
Spain-United States Chamber of Commerce Vol 1: 17065
Spanish Institute Vol 1: 17067
Spanish Ministry of Culture Vol 2: 4523
Spanish Mustang Registry Vol 1: 17069
Spanish Royal Society of Physics Vol 2: 4541
Spear & Jackson Vol 2: 5228
Special Libraries Association Vol 1: 17072
Special Libraries Association - News Division Vol 1: 17082
Special Libraries Association - Transportation Division Vol 1: 17087
Special Olympics Canada Vol 1: 17089
Specialized Carriers and Rigging Association Vol 1: 17092
Specialized Information Publishers Association Vol 1: 17103
Specialty Coffee Association of Europe Vol 2: 7227
Specialty Equipment Market Association Vol 1: 17105
Specialty Graphic Imaging Association Vol 1: 17107
Species Survival Commission Vol 2: 4922
The Spectator Vol 2: 7234
Spectroscopy Society of Pittsburgh Vol 1: 17119
Speech Association of America Vol 1: 12920
Speech Communication Association Vol 1: 12920
Speed Equipment Market Association Vol 1: 17105
Speed Skating Canada Vol 1: 17121
Spencer Foundation Vol 1: 12124
SPIE: International Society for Optical Engineering Vol 1: 17130
Spill Control Association of America Vol 1: 17138
Spina Bifida Association of Greater St. Louis Vol 1: 17140
Spitball, the Literary Baseball Magazine Vol 1: 17142
SPNM - Promoting New Music Vol 2: 7237
Spoke Gallery; B. J. Vol 1: 17144
Spolecnost Fryderyka Chopina v CSSR Vol 2: 1251
Sport Australia Hall of Fame Vol 2: 676
Sport Canada Vol 1: 17146
Sport Interuniversitaire Canadien Vol 1: 6642
Sporting Goods Agents Association Vol 1: 17157
Sporting News Vol 1: 17161
Sports Car Club of America Vol 1: 17195
Sports Federation of Canada Vol 1: 17146
Sports Illustrated Vol 1: 17225
Sports Information Directors Association Vol 1: 12582
Sports Journalists' Association of Great Britain Vol 2: 7239
The Sports Network Vol 1: 6652
Sports Philatelists International Vol 1: 17228
Sportscar Vintage Racing Association Vol 1: 17230
Springer Vol 1: 17080
Springer-Verlag Vol 1: 4807
Springfield Art Museum Vol 1: 17238
Springfield Association for Retarded Citizens Vol 1: 17240
Sprinkler Irrigation Association Vol 1: 10898
Sri Lanka Association for the Advancement of Science Vol 2: 4565
Sri Lanka Eksath Jatheenge Sangamaya Vol 2: 4570
Stadt Braunschweig-Kulturamt Vol 2: 2055
Stadt Buxtehude Vol 2: 2384
Stadt Darmstadt Vol 2: 2439
Stadt Dortmund Vol 2: 2386
Stadt Mannheim Vol 2: 2388
Stadt Pforzheim, Kulturamt Vol 2: 2390
Stadt Schweinfurt Vol 2: 2392
Stadt Villach Vol 2: 820
Stand Magazine Vol 2: 7246
Standard Bank Investment Corporation Vol 2: 4191
Standards Council of Canada Vol 1: 17242
Standards Engineering Society Vol 1: 5449
Standards Engineering Society Vol 1: 17244
Stanford University Vol 2: 6601
Stanford University - Center for Integrated Facility Engineering Vol 1: 17251

Stanford University - Stanford Center on International Conflict and Negotiation Vol 1: 17253
State Bar of California Vol 1: 17255
State Bar of Michigan Vol 1: 17258
State Debt Management Network Vol 1: 17260
State Department and Construction Corporation Vol 2: 4561
State Farm Insurance Vol 1: 18857
State Farm Insurance Co. Vol 1: 10050
State Farm Mutual Automobile Insurance Co. Vol 1: 17263
State Historical Society of Missouri Vol 1: 17265
State Library of New South Wales Vol 2: 678
State Library of Victoria Vol 2: 682
State Library of Western Australia Vol 2: 684
States Organization for Boating Access Vol 1: 17268
Statistical Society of Canada Vol 1: 17278
Statistics Society of Canada Vol 1: 7622
Status of Women Canada Vol 1: 17285
Steacie Memorial Fund; E. W. R. Vol 1: 17287
Steel Authority of India, Ltd. Vol 2: 2659
Steel Founders' Society of America Vol 1: 17289
Stein Collectors International Vol 1: 17293
Stephen Leacock Association Vol 1: 17296
Stgorz; Karl Vol 1: 4397
Stichting Collectieve Propaganda van het Nederlandse Boek Vol 2: 3494
Stichting Conamus Vol 2: 3499
Stichting Dramaastricht Vol 2: 3563
Stichting Gaudeamus Vol 2: 3554
Stichting Internationaal Orgelconcours Vol 2: 3674
Stichting Kijkhuis Vol 2: 3691
Stichting Koningin Wilhelmina Fonds Vol 2: 3504
Stichting Nederlandse Film Festival Vol 2: 3630
Stichting Poetry International Vol 2: 3639
Stichting Praemium Erasmianum Vol 2: 3518
Stichting Sikkensprys Vol 2: 3663
Stichting Wereld Muziek Concours Kerkrade Vol 2: 3682
Stiftelsen Kortfilmfestivalen Vol 2: 3909
Stiftung F.V.S.; Alfred Ttoepfer Vol 2: 2394
Stiftung Internationaler Karlspreis zu Aachen Vol 2: 2408
Stiftung Niedersachsen Vol 2: 2141
Stiftung zur Forderung der DGE Vol 2: 2246
Stowarzyszenie Miedzynarodowe Triennale Grafiki Vol 2: 4003
Stratton Mountain and Valley Community Benefit Foundation Vol 1: 17299
Street Sled Sports Racers International Vol 2: 7248
Strega Alberti Benevento Vol 2: 3131
Strem Chemicals Inc. Vol 1: 1506
Stress and Anxiety Research Society Vol 2: 2410
Structural Board Association Vol 1: 17301
Structural Engineering Institute Vol 1: 17303
Student American Veterinary Medical Association Vol 1: 17305
Student Council for Exceptional Children Vol 1: 7853
Student Press Law Center Vol 1: 17307
Studiengesellschaft fur Unterirdische Verkehrsanlagen Vol 2: 2426
Studio Museum in Harlem Vol 1: 17309
Stulberg International String Competition Vol 1: 17311
Stuttgart City Council Vol 2: 2414
Stuttgart International Festival of Animated Film Vol 2: 2420
Suburban Newspapers of America Vol 1: 17313
Successful Meetings Magazine - VNU Business Publications USA Inc. Vol 1: 17316
Sud-Chemie Inc. Vol 1: 14274
Sudler Foundation of Chicago; Louis Vol 1: 16977
Sugar Industry Technologists Vol 1: 17320
Suid-Afrikaanse Chemiese Instituut Vol 2: 4313
Suid Afrikaanse Wingerd en Wynkundevereniging Vol 2: 4346
Suider-Afrika Genootskap vir die Bevordering van die Wetenskap Vol 2: 4361
Sulabh International Social Service Organisation Vol 2: 2801
Sulphur Institute Vol 2: 2559
Sumi-e Society of America Vol 1: 17323
Summit Art Center Vol 1: 18570
Suncoast Waldorf Association Vol 1: 17325
Sundance Institute - Sundance Film Festival Vol 1: 17327
Sunday Times Business Times Vol 2: 4370
SunGard Higher Education Vol 1: 1054
Sunset Magazine Vol 1: 17329
Sunshine Tour Vol 1: 18943
Suntory Foundation Vol 2: 3332
Suomen Kulttuurirahasto Vol 2: 1390
Suomen Radioamatooriliitto ry Vol 2: 1377
Suomen Sadankomitealiitto Vol 2: 1356
Suomen Taideyhdistys Vol 2: 1368
SUPELCO, Inc. Vol 1: 1514
Supelco Inc. Vol 1: 2970
SuperGen Inc. Vol 1: 14542
Supply Chain and Logistics Canada Vol 1: 17333
Surfrider Foundation Vol 1: 17338
Surgipath Medical Industries Inc. Vol 1: 13719
Susan G. Komen Breast Cancer Foundation Vol 1: 14538, 17340
Susan Smith Blackburn Prize Vol 1: 17346
Svensk Biblioteksforening Vol 2: 4684
Svenska Akademien Vol 2: 4645
Svenska Arkitekters Riksforbund Vol 2: 4598
Svenska Filminstitutet Vol 2: 4681
Sveriges Film- och Videofoerbund Vol 2: 4679
Svjetski Festival Animiranih Filmova, Zagreb Vol 2: 1240
Swedish Academy Vol 2: 4645
Swedish Academy of Pharmaceutical Sciences Vol 2: 4677
Swedish-American Chambers of Commerce, USA Vol 1: 17348
Swedish Council of America Vol 1: 17350
Swedish Federation of Film and Video Amateurs Vol 2: 4679
Swedish Film Institute Vol 2: 4681
Swedish Library Association Vol 2: 4684
Swedish Society of Aeronautics and Astronautics Vol 2: 4688
Swedish Society of Crafts and Design Vol 2: 4690
Swinburne College of Technology Vol 2: 494
Swiss Academy of Medical Sciences Vol 2: 4884
Swiss Association for Theatre Studies Vol 2: 4887
Swiss Association of Chemists Vol 2: 4889
Swiss Broadcasting Corporation and the City of Montreux Vol 2: 4881
Swiss Chemical Society Vol 2: 4889
Swiss Federal Institute of Technology Zurich Vol 2: 4895
Swiss Graphic Designers Vol 2: 4904
Swiss Music Edition Vol 2: 4906
Swope Art Museum; Sheldon Vol 1: 17353
Sydney Cultural Council Vol 2: 686
Sydney Film Festival Vol 2: 691
Sylva Gelber Foundation Vol 1: 6108
Symphony of the Mountains Vol 1: 17355
Symphony Services Australia Vol 2: 695
Synchro Swimming U.S.A. Vol 1: 17357
Syndicat National des Employees et Employes Generaux et du Secteur Public Vol 1: 13876
Syngenta Vol 2: 6967
Syngenta Corp. Vol 1: 17364
Syngenta Crop Protection Vol 1: 3194
Syngenta Crop Protection Inc. Vol 1: 17365, 17366, 17367, 17368, 17369
SynQuest Laboratories Inc. Vol 1: 1504
System Safety Society Vol 1: 17370
Tacoma-Pierce County Sports Commission Vol 1: 17379
Tafelberg Publishers Ltd. Vol 2: 4372
Taieb; Jean-Pierre Vol 2: 1987
Taipei Golden Horse Film Festival Vol 2: 4951
Taipei International Film Exhibition Vol 2: 4951
Taiwan Ministry of Education Vol 2: 4953
Taiwan Pediatric Association Vol 2: 4955
Talbot County Arts Council Vol 1: 17381
Tall Clubs International Vol 1: 17384
Tampa Bay Business Committee for the Arts Vol 1: 17388
Tampere Film Festival Vol 2: 1426
Tampereen elokuvajuhlat Vol 2: 1426
TAPPI - Technical Association of the Pulp and Paper Industry Vol 1: 17390
Tarmac Quarry Products Inc. Vol 2: 5223
Tartans of Scotland Vol 2: 7250
TASH Vol 1: 17397
Tasmanian Canine Association Vol 2: 697
Tau Beta Pi Association Vol 1: 17400
Tau Beta Sigma Vol 1: 17405
Tau Sigma Delta Vol 1: 17408
Tax Foundation Vol 1: 17412
Taxpayers Association of Europe Vol 2: 2422
TD Financial Group Vol 1: 17297, 17298
Tea Council Vol 2: 7252
Teachers Association of Baltimore County Vol 1: 17414
Teachers of English to Speakers of Other Languages Vol 1: 17416
Teatro Municipale Valli Vol 2: 3133
Technology-Science Education Institute Vol 2: 3984
Technology Student Association Vol 1: 17424
Tel Aviv Museum of Art Vol 2: 2929
Telefilm Canada Vol 1: 19078
Television and Radio Industries Club Vol 2: 7254
Telly Awards Vol 1: 17428
Temple de la Renommee des Sports du Canada Vol 1: 6138
Temple University Vol 1: 101

Templeton Foundation; John Vol 2: 4704
Templeton Foundation; John M. Vol 1: 15617
TENN-SHARE Vol 1: 17436
Tennessee Council of Teachers of English Vol 1: 17430
Tennessee Library Association Vol 1: 17432
Tennis Ireland Vol 2: 2888
Tennis Magazine - Miller Sports Group LLC Vol 1: 17441
TENOVUS - SCOTLAND Vol 2: 7256
Teollisuustaiteen Liitto Ornamo Vol 2: 1383
Teratology Society Vol 1: 17443
Tertis International Viola Competition and Workshop; Lionel Vol 2: 7258
Test of English as a Foreign Language Vol 1: 8401
Texas Association of Bank Counsel Vol 1: 17453
Texas Association of Sports Officials - Baseball, Houston Chapter Vol 1: 17455
Texas Cable and Telecommunications Association Vol 1: 17457
Texas Council for the Social Studies Vol 1: 17459
Texas Daily Newspaper Association Vol 1: 17461
Texas Fine Arts Association, The Jones Center for Contemporary Art Vol 1: 17468
Texas Heart Institute Vol 1: 17470
Texas Independent Producers and Royalty Owners Association Vol 1: 17472
Texas Institute of Letters Vol 1: 17474
Texas Library Association Vol 1: 17487
Texas Medical Association Vol 1: 17489
Texas Oral History Association Vol 1: 17492
Texas Sign Association Vol 1: 17496
Texas Society of Architects/ AIA Vol 1: 17498
Texas Tech University - College of Mass Communications Vol 1: 17501
Textile Institute Vol 2: 7260
Textile Study Group of New York Vol 1: 17504
Theatre Communications Group Vol 1: 17506
Theatre Historical Society of America Vol 1: 17511
Theatre Library Association Vol 1: 17513
Theatre World Vol 1: 17516
Theodore Roethke Memorial Foundation Vol 1: 17518
Theodore Roosevelt Association Vol 1: 17520
Thermal Syndicate, Ltd. Vol 2: 5535
Thermo Electron Vol 2: 6967
Thermo Electron Corp. Vol 1: 1537, 13718, 13723, 17120
Thessaloniki International Film Festival Vol 2: 2472
Theta Sigma Phi Vol 1: 4999
Thibaud; Concours International Marguerite Long - Jacques Vol 2: 1931
Third World Network of Scientific Organizations Vol 2: 2954
Thistle Class Association Vol 1: 17522
Thomas Paine National Historical Association Vol 1: 17525
Thomas Wolfe Society Vol 1: 17527
Thomson Financial Vol 1: 2685
Thomson Gale Vol 1: 2696
Thomson Scientific Vol 1: 5076, 5082, 11668, 16422
Thomson Tubes Electroniques Vol 2: 1787
Thoroughbred Racing Associations Vol 1: 17531
Thurber House Vol 1: 17534
Tibetan Youth Congress Vol 2: 2803
Tilburg University Vol 2: 3676
Tile Contractors' Association of America Vol 1: 17536
Tile Heritage Foundation Vol 1: 17538
Time Inc. Vol 1: 17540
Time Out Communications Ltd. Vol 2: 7275
Times Publishing Group Vol 2: 4423
Tissue Culture Association, Inc. Vol 1: 16257
Toastmasters International Vol 1: 17544
Tokyo International Film Festival Vol 2: 3335
Tokyo International Music Competition Vol 2: 3337
Tolkien Society of America Vol 1: 12058
Toni Morrison Society Vol 1: 17546
Topps Chewing Gum Vol 1: 17548
Topps Company, Inc. Vol 1: 17548
Toray Industries Inc., and Kyowa Hakko Kogyo Co. Ltd. Vol 2: 4860
Torello Excursionist Center Vol 2: 4544
Torello International Festival of Mountain and Adventure Films Vol 2: 4544
Toronto Arts Council Foundation Vol 1: 17554
Toronto International Film Festival Group Vol 1: 17557
Toronto International Salon of Photography Vol 1: 17563
Touchdown Club Charities of Washington, D.C. Vol 1: 17565
Tourism Industry Association New Zealand Vol 2: 3874
Towarzystwo imienia Fryderyka Chopina Vol 2: 4000
Townsville Foundation for Australian Literary Studies Vol 2: 459
Towson University - College of Liberal Arts Vol 1: 17567
Trade Show Exhibitors Association Vol 1: 17569
Traditional Irish Music, Singing and Dancing Society Vol 2: 2890
Traditional Irish Singing and Dancing Society Vol 2: 2890
Transco Vol 2: 5229
Transcultural Nursing Society Vol 1: 17571
Transgenomic Bioconsumables Ltd. Vol 2: 6967
Transparency International Deutschland e.V. Vol 2: 2424
Transparency International - Germany Vol 2: 2424
Transplant Recipients International Organization Vol 1: 17574
Transport Insurance Company Vol 1: 4376
Transportation Research Board Vol 1: 17576
Travel and Tourism Research Association Vol 1: 17585
Travel Industry Association of America Vol 1: 17587
Travel Research Association Vol 1: 17585
Treasury Board of Canada Secretariat Vol 1: 17590
Tree Care Industry Association Vol 1: 17594
Trento Filmfestival Internazionale Montagna Esplorazione Vol 2: 3135
Trento International Film Festival of Mountains and Exploration Vol 2: 3135
Tri-County Arts Council Gallery Vol 1: 17596
Tri-County Specialty Contractors Association Vol 1: 17598
TRI-M Music Honor Society Vol 1: 17600
Trial Lawyers for Public Justice Vol 1: 17606
Triathlon Federation Vol 1: 18459
Tribune Entertainment Vol 1: 16966
Trident Insurance Services LLC Vol 1: 15436
Triple Crown Productions, Inc. Vol 1: 17608
Trophy Dealers of America Vol 1: 5605
True Value Hardware Stores Vol 1: 17757
Truman Good Neighbor Award Foundation; Harry S. Vol 1: 17611
Trust Co. Vol 2: 699
Trustees Savings Bank Vol 2: 6994
Tucker Music Foundation; Richard Vol 1: 17615
Tucson Arts Brigade Vol 1: 17619
Tulane University - Center for Bioenvironmental Research Vol 1: 17621
Tulsa Library Trust Vol 1: 17624, 17625
Tunbridge Wells International Young Concert Artists Competition Vol 2: 7278
Turkish Academy of Sciences Vol 2: 4990
Turkish Studies Association Vol 1: 17628
Turkiye Bilimler Akademisi Vol 2: 4990
Turkiye Bilimsel ve Teknik Arastirma Kurumu Vol 2: 4987
Turner Syndrome Association of Australia Vol 2: 702
Tusquets Editores S.A. Vol 2: 4546
TV Week Vol 2: 704
Tweed Shire Council Vol 2: 706
Twin Cities Musicians Union, Local 30-73 Vol 1: 17634
Two/Ten Foundation Vol 1: 17636
Two/Ten International Footwear Foundation Vol 1: 17636
Tylers' and Bricklayers' Company Vol 2: 7280
UCLA Alumni Association Vol 1: 17639
Ucross Foundation Vol 1: 17647
Ufficio Stampa - Casino de la Vallee E Manifestatzioni Vol 2: 3137
UK Fashion Exports Vol 2: 7284
Ukrainian Congress Committee of America Vol 1: 17649
Ukrainian Institute of America Vol 1: 17651
Ulster Teachers' Union Vol 2: 7286
Ultimate Players Association Vol 1: 17653
Unda Association Catholique Internationale pour la Radio et la Television Vol 2: 1099
Unda International Catholic Association for Radio and Television Vol 2: 1099
Unda-USA, the National Catholic Association of Broadcasters and Commun - icators Vol 1: 7140
Underfashion Club Vol 1: 17656
Underground Transportation Research Association Vol 2: 2426
Undersea and Hyperbaric Medical Society Vol 1: 17659
Undersea Medical Society, Inc. Vol 1: 17659
Underwater Society of America Vol 1: 17664
UNESCO Vol 2: 1874, 1989, 4444
UNESCO International Book Committee Vol 2: 823
Unilever Oral Care Vol 1: 10055
Unilever R&D Colworth Vol 2: 6967
Unilever Research Vol 2: 7096
Unilever Research Laboratory Vol 2: 5170
UNIMA-U.S.A., American Center of the Union Internationale de la Marionnette Vol 1: 17668
Union Catholique Internationale de la Presse Vol 2: 4786
Union des Annonceurs Vol 2: 2007

Union des Ecrivaines et Ecrivains Quebecois Vol 1: 17671
Union des Foires Internationales Vol 2: 2009
Union Europeenne de la Presse Sportive Vol 2: 4582
Union Europeenne de Radio-Television Vol 2: 4706
Union for the International Language Ido Vol 2: 7289
Union Geographique Internationale Vol 1: 10451
Union International des Transports Routiers Vol 2: 4829
Union Internationale Contre la Tuberculose et les Maladies Respiratoires Vol 2: 1916
Union Internationale Contre le Cancer Vol 2: 4855
Union Internationale de Cristallographie Vol 2: 6320
Union Internationale de Physique Pure et Appliquee Vol 1: 10809
Union Internationale de Speleologie Vol 2: 1259
Union Internationale des Architectes Vol 2: 1921
Union Internationale des Instituts de Recherches Forestieres Vol 2: 813
Union Internationale des Societes de Microbiologie Vol 2: 549
Union Internationale pour la Science, la Technique et les Applications du Vide Vol 2: 6315
Union Internationale pour les livres de jeunesse Vol 2: 4782
Union Internationale pour l'Etude du Quarternaire Vol 2: 2847
Union Mathematique Internationale Vol 1: 10505
Union Mondiale pour la Nature Vol 2: 4918
Union Mundial para la Naturaleza Vol 2: 4918
Union of Associations of Slovene Librarians Vol 2: 4466
Union of Bulgarian Actors Vol 2: 1147
Union of Bulgarian Filmmakers Vol 2: 1147
Union of Councils for Jews in the Former Soviet Union Vol 1: 17674
Union of Councils for Soviet Jews Vol 1: 17674
Union of Czech Architects Vol 2: 1269
Union of International Fairs Vol 2: 2009
Union of Japanese Scientists and Engineers Vol 2: 3339
Union Postale Universelle Vol 2: 4908
Union Radio Scientifique Internationale Vol 2: 930
Unione Matematica Italiana Vol 2: 3106
Uniono por la Linguo Internaciona Ido Vol 2: 7289
Unitarian Universalist Association of Congregations Vol 1: 17676
Unitarian Universalist Service Committee Vol 1: 17683
United Airlines Vol 1: 18207
United Church of Christ - Coordinating Center for Women in Church and Society Vol 1: 17688
United Commercial Travelers of America, Butler Council 465 Vol 1: 17690
United Daughters of the Confederacy Vol 1: 17692
United Engineering Foundation Vol 1: 17694
United HIAS Service Vol 1: 9343
United in Group Harmony Association Vol 1: 17696
United Kennel Club Vol 1: 17698
United Kingdom Department of Trade and Industry Vol 2: 7291
United Kingdom eInformation Group Vol 2: 7294
United Kingdom Literacy Association Vol 2: 7300
United Methodist Association of Health and Welfare Ministries Vol 1: 17700
United Nations Vol 1: 17703
United Nations Association in the Democratic Socialist Republic of Sri Lanka Vol 2: 4570
United Nations Association of the United States of America Vol 1: 17705
United Nations Association of the U.S.A. Vol 1: 17707
United Nations Economic and Social Commission for Asia and the Pacific Vol 2: 4961
United Nations Environment Programme Vol 2: 3365
United Nations High Commission for Refugees - Regional Office Mexico Vol 2: 3455
United Nations Population Fund Vol 1: 17709
United Parcel Service (UPS) Vol 1: 9875
United Seamen's Service Vol 1: 17711
United States Air Force Vol 1: 13632
United States Air Force Academy Vol 1: 17714
United States Amateur Boxing, Inc. Vol 1: 17716
United States Amateur Confederation of Roller Skating Vol 1: 17718
United States and Canadian Academy of Pathology Vol 1: 17720
U.S. Aquatic Sports Vol 1: 17728
United States Arms Control and Disarmament Agency Vol 1: 17735
United States Army Corps of Engineers Vol 1: 17738
U.S. Association for Blind Athletes Vol 1: 17740
United States Association of Former Members of Congress Vol 1: 17743
United States Auto Club Vol 1: 17745
United States Badminton Association Vol 1: 18373
U.S. Bicycling Hall of Fame Vol 1: 17761
United States Billiard Association Vol 1: 17763
U.S. Bureau of Mines and Explosives Engineers Vol 1: 13455
U.S. Cancellation Club Vol 1: 17765
U.S. Catholic - Claretians Publications Vol 1: 17767
U.S. Census Bureau Vol 1: 17769
United States Chess Federation Vol 1: 17771
United States Civil Defense Council Vol 1: 10202
United States Civil Service Commission Vol 1: 18013
U.S. Coast Guard Vol 1: 17773
United States Committee of the International Council on Monuments and Sites Vol 1: 17779
United States Conference of Mayors Vol 1: 17781
United States Congress - Committee on Banking, Finance, and Urban Affairs Vol 1: 17784
U.S. Council for Energy Awareness Vol 1: 14439
United States Council for International Business Vol 1: 17786
United States Council for IYDP Vol 1: 13508
United States Council of the International Chamber of Commerce Vol 1: 17786
United States Curling Association Vol 1: 17788
United States Department of Army - Civilian Marksmanship Program Vol 1: 17791
United States Department of Commerce - International Trade Administration Vol 1: 17793
United States Department of Commerce - National Institute of Standards and Technology Vol 1: 17796
United States Department of Commerce - Office of Human Resources Management Vol 1: 17806
U.S. Department of Commerce - Technology Adminisration Vol 1: 17810
United States Department of Defense - Defense Logistics Agency Vol 1: 17812
United States Department of Defense - Office of the Secretary of Defense Vol 1: 17814
U.S. Department of Education Vol 1: 12515
U.S. Department of Education - National Institute on Disability and Rehabilitation Research Vol 1: 17816
United States Department of Education - Office of Intergovernmental and Interagency Affairs Vol 1: 17818
United States Department of Education - White House Commission on Presidential Scholars Vol 1: 17820
United States Department of Energy Vol 1: 17822, 18026
United States Department of Health and Human Services Vol 1: 17824
United States Department of Health and Human Services - National Institutes of Health Vol 1: 17826
United States Department of Health and Human Services, Public Health Service - Centers for Disease Control and Prevention (CDC) Vol 1: 17828
U.S. Department of Housing and Urban Development Vol 1: 3210
United States Department of Interior Vol 1: 14882
United States Department of Justice - Federal Bureau of Investigation Vol 1: 17831
United States Department of Justice - Office of Justice Programs Vol 1: 17833
United States Department of Labor Vol 1: 17836
United States Department of Labor - Bureau of Labor Statistics Vol 1: 17840
U.S. Department of Labor - Office of Job Corps Vol 1: 17842
United States Department of Navy - U.S. Naval Observatory Vol 1: 17847
United States Department of State Vol 1: 17850
United States Department of Transportation Vol 1: 17877
United States Department of Transportation - Federal Highway Administration Vol 1: 17879

United States Department of Veterans Affairs - Regional Office Vol 1: 17881
United States Dressage Federation Vol 1: 17883
U.S. Energy Association Vol 1: 17891
United States Environmental Protection Agency Vol 1: 17893
U.S. Environmental Protection Agency - Office of Research and Development Vol 1: 17895
United States Executive Office of the President Vol 1: 12195, 17785, 17815, 17834, 17835, 17894, 18015
United States Federation for Culture Collections Vol 1: 3770
U.S. Federation for Culture Collections Vol 1: 17897
United States Fencing Coaches Association Vol 1: 17899
United States Figure Skating Association Vol 1: 17902
United States Fish and Wildlife Service - Federal Duck Stamp Program Vol 1: 17905
U.S. Forest Service - Northeastern Research Station Vol 1: 17907
U.S. Fund for UNICEF - U.S. Committee Vol 1: 17909
United States Golf Association Vol 1: 17914, 18943
United States Handball Association Vol 1: 17921
U.S. Hang Gliding Association Vol 1: 17923
United States Harness Writers' Association Vol 1: 17929
United States Hockey Hall of Fame Vol 1: 17941
U.S. Holocaust Memorial Council Vol 1: 17943
United States Institute for Theatre Technology Vol 1: 17945
U.S. Institute of Peace Vol 1: 17958
United States Intercollegiate Lacrosse Association Vol 1: 17962
U.S. International Film and Video Festival Vol 1: 17977
U.S.-Israel Binational Science Foundation Vol 2: 2934
United States Jaycees Vol 1: 17981
U.S. Junior Chamber of Commerce Vol 1: 17981
U.S. Lacrosse and The Lacrosse Museum and National Hall of Fame Vol 1: 17984
United States Lawn Tennis Association Vol 1: 18137
U.S. Marine Corps Combat Correspondents Association Vol 1: 17986
United States Masters Swimming Vol 1: 17992
U.S. Metric Association Vol 1: 17996
U.S.-Mexico Border Health Association Vol 1: 17998
United States-Mexico Chamber of Commerce Vol 1: 18000
United States Military Academy Association of Graduates Vol 1: 18002
United States Naval Institute Vol 1: 14002
United States Naval Institute Vol 1: 18004
United States Navy Vol 1: 2112
United States of America Amateur Boxing Federation Vol 1: 17716
United States of America Rugby Football Union Ltd. Vol 1: 18052
United States Office of Personnel Management Vol 1: 18013
United States Olympic Committee Vol 1: 18016
United States Orienteering Federation Vol 1: 18021
U.S. Pan Asian American Chamber of Commerce Vol 1: 18023
U.S. Particle Accelerator School Vol 1: 18025
United States Patent and Trademark Office Vol 1: 18027
United States Police Canine Association Vol 1: 18029
United States Professional Tennis Association Vol 1: 18032
United States Racquetball Association Vol 1: 18037
United States Rowing Association Vol 1: 18044
United States Rugby Football Union Vol 1: 18052
United States Sailing Association Vol 1: 18061
United States Ski and Snowboard Association Vol 1: 18080
United States Ski Association Vol 1: 18080
United States Ski Writers Association Vol 1: 14322
U.S. Small Business Administration Vol 1: 18115
United States Soccer Federation Vol 1: 18123
United States Space Foundation Vol 1: 18125
U.S. Speedskating Vol 1: 18130
U.S. Sports Acrobatics Vol 1: 18132
United States Stamp Society Vol 1: 18134
United States Synchronized Swimming Vol 1: 17357
U.S. Table Tennis Association Vol 1: 18427
United States Tennis Association Vol 1: 18137
United States Trotting Association Vol 1: 18159
United States Water Polo Vol 1: 18164
United States Women's Curling Association Vol 1: 18168
U.S. Wrestling Foundation Vol 1: 510
U.S. Yacht Racing Union Vol 1: 18061
United States Youth Soccer Association Vol 1: 18170
United Synagogue of Conservative Judaism Vol 1: 18181
United Technologies Research Center Vol 1: 14602
United Way of America Vol 1: 18183
United Way of Chester County Vol 1: 18186
United Way of the Berwick Area Vol 1: 18189
United Way of the Valley Area Vol 1: 18191
Unity-and-Diversity World Council Vol 1: 18193
Universal Oil Products Vol 1: 2484
Universal Pantheist Society Vol 1: 18195
Universal Postal Union Vol 2: 4908
Universal Ship Cancellation Society Vol 1: 18197
Universidad del Valle Vol 2: 1198
Universita degli Studi di Bologna Vol 2: 3139
Universitat Basel Vol 2: 4910
Universitat Karlsruhe (Technische Hochschule) Vol 2: 2428
Universite de Montreal; Centre de recherches mathematiques, Vol 1: 11616
Universite Libre de Bruxelles Vol 2: 2294
Universities Federation for Animal Welfare Vol 2: 7304
Universities Research Association Vol 1: 3126
University Aviation Association Vol 1: 18204
University College of Central Queensland Vol 2: 506
University College of Southern Queensland Vol 2: 538
University Continuing Education Association Vol 1: 18208
University Council for Educational Administration Vol 1: 18228
The University Foundation Vol 2: 1101
University Mozarteum, Salzburg Vol 2: 825
The University Museum Vol 1: 18334
University Musical Society Vol 1: 18232
University of Adelaide Vol 2: 521
University of Alabama at Birmingham - Department of Theatre Vol 1: 18234
University of Albany Vol 1: 15901
University of Alberta - Perinatal Research Centre Vol 1: 18236
University of Arizona - Department of Journalism Vol 1: 18238
University of Arizona - Udall Center for Studies in Public Policy Vol 1: 18240
University of Barcelona Vol 2: 4549
University of Basel Vol 2: 4910
University of Bologna Vol 2: 3139
University of British Columbia - Wine Research Centre Vol 1: 18242
University of California, Davis - Davis Arboretum Vol 1: 18244
University of California, Los Angeles - Anderson School of Management Vol 1: 18246
University of Canberra Vol 2: 529
University of Central Missouri - Art Center Gallery Vol 1: 18248
University of Chicago Vol 2: 2276
University of Chicago - Cancer Research Center Vol 1: 18250
University of Chicago - Department of Music Vol 1: 18252
University of Chicago - Medical and Biological Sciences Alumni Association Vol 1: 18254
University of Chicago Alumni Association Vol 1: 18257
University of Chicago Medical Alumni Association Vol 1: 18254
University of Chicago Press Vol 1: 18264
University of Colorado - School of Journalism and Mass Communication Vol 1: 18266
University of Colorado at Boulder - Center of the American West Vol 1: 18268
University of Copenhagen Vol 2: 1337
University of Dayton - Office of Provost Vol 1: 18270
University of Denver - Daniels College of Business Vol 1: 18272
University of Edinburgh - Department of English Literature Vol 2: 7307
University of Georgia - Artificial Intelligence Center Vol 1: 18274
University of Georgia - Department of Language and Literary Education Vol 1: 18276
University of Georgia - Grady College of Journalism and Mass Communication Vol 1: 18279
University of Georgia Press Vol 1: 18282
University of Hawaii Vol 1: 4863

University of Hawaii at Manoa - School of Communications Vol 1: 18285
University of Houston Vol 1: 7101
University of Illinois at Chicago - Center for Urban Economic Development Vol 1: 18287
University of Illinois at Urbana-Champaign - Agricultural Bioprocess Laboratory Vol 1: 18289
University of Illinois at Urbana-Champaign - College of Fine & Applied Arts Vol 1: 18291
University of Illinois at Urbana-Champaign - Graduate School of Library and Information Science Vol 1: 18293
University of Kentucky - Lucille Parker Markey Cancer Center Vol 1: 18295
University of Limburg Vol 2: 1104
University of Liverpool Vol 2: 6372, 7309
University of Louisville - College of Education and Human Development Vol 1: 18297
University of Louisville - Labor-Management Center Vol 1: 18300
University of Louisville - Louisville Presbyterian Theological Seminary Vol 1: 18302
University of Louisville - School of Music Vol 1: 18304
University of Manitoba Vol 1: 15729
University of Maryland - College of Information Studies Vol 1: 18306
University of Maryland International Music Competitions, Rossborough Festival Vol 1: 16093
University of Massachusetts Press Vol 1: 18308
University of Melbourne Vol 2: 503
University of Melbourne - Assessment Research Centre Vol 2: 708
University of Melbourne - Faculty of Arts Vol 2: 710
University of Melbourne - Faculty of Science Vol 2: 712
University of Michigan Vol 1: 18310
University of Michigan - Matthaei Botanical Gardens and Nichols Arboretum Vol 1: 18312
University of Michigan - Stephen M. Ross School of Business Vol 1: 18314
University of Michigan Press Vol 1: 18316
University of Minnesota Vol 1: 9719
University of Minnesota - Children's Literature Research Collections Vol 1: 18318
University of Minnesota - Office of the Senior Vice President for Academic Affairs and Provost Vol 1: 18321
University of Missouri-Columbia - School of Journalism Vol 1: 18323
University of Missouri—St. Louis - Center for International Studies Vol 1: 18327
University of Missouri—St. Louis - Center for Trauma Recovery Vol 1: 18329
University of Montreal Vol 1: 15730
University of Music and Dramatic Arts in Graz Vol 2: 827
University of New South Wales Vol 2: 498, 714
University of Newcastle Vol 2: 499
University of Notre Dame - News and Information Vol 1: 18331
University of Otago Vol 2: 3876
University of Oxford - Faculty of Music Vol 2: 7313
University of Pennsylvania Vol 2: 6348
University of Pennsylvania Museum of Archaeology and Anthropology Vol 1: 18334
University of Pittsburgh Press Vol 1: 18337
University of Queensland Vol 2: 520
University of Rochester Vol 1: 18340
University of San Diego - School of Law - Children's Advocacy Institute Vol 1: 18342
University of South Australia Vol 2: 510
University of Southern California - College of Letters, Arts and Sciences Vol 1: 18344
University of Sussex Library Vol 2: 7315
University of Sydney Vol 2: 524
University of Tasmania Vol 2: 512
University of Toronto - Faculty of Law Vol 1: 18346
University of Toronto - Faculty of Music Vol 1: 18348
University of Toronto - Pulp and Paper Centre Vol 1: 18350
University of Toronto - University College Vol 1: 18354
University of Toronto Law Alumni Association Vol 1: 18347
University of Virginia - Center for Russian and East European Studies Vol 1: 18356
University of Virginia - Center for South Asian Studies Vol 1: 18358
University of Western Australia Vol 2: 502
University of Wisconsin—Madison - Center for South Asia Vol 1: 18360
University of Wisconsin—Madison - Institute on Aging Vol 1: 18362
University of Wisconsin Press Vol 1: 18364
Uppsala International Short Film Festival Vol 2: 4692
Upsilon Pi Epsilon Association Vol 1: 18366
Urban Affairs Association Vol 1: 18368
Urban Land Institute Vol 1: 18371
Urdd Cerddoriaeth Cymru Vol 2: 7329
Urological Society of India Vol 2: 2806
US Black Engineer Vol 1: 7100
USA Badminton Vol 1: 18373
U.S.A. Baseball Vol 1: 18377
USA Cycling Vol 1: 18381
USA Deaf Sports Federation Vol 1: 18383
USA Diving Vol 1: 17730, 17731, 17732, 18386
USA Dry Pea and Lentil Council Vol 1: 18389
USA Hockey Vol 1: 18397
USA International Ballet Competition Vol 1: 18405
USA International Harp Competition Vol 1: 18407
USA Swimming Vol 1: 18409
U.S.A. Table Tennis Vol 1: 18427
USA Today Sports Weekly Vol 1: 16172
U.S.A. Track and Field Vol 1: 18429
USA Triathlon Vol 1: 18459
U.S.A. Wrestling Vol 1: 18462
USO of Metropolitan New York Vol 1: 18474
USSA Eastern Alpine Official's Committee Vol 1: 18088
Utah Professional Videographers Association Vol 1: 18476
Utility Communicators International Vol 1: 18478
UWO - Faculty of Applied Health Science Vol 1: 12877
Val de Marne; Festival International de Films de Femmes de Creteil et du Vol 2: 1927
Valladolid International Film Festival Vol 2: 4551
Valley Players Vol 1: 18480
Van Alen Institute Vol 1: 18482
Vancouver International Film Festival Vol 1: 18484
Varian Associates Vol 1: 5597
Varian Medical Systems Vol 1: 14541
Varna International Ballet Competition Vol 2: 1157
Vatel-Club Luxembourg Vol 2: 3392
The Vatican Vol 2: 7411
Vaughan & Bushnell Manufacturing Co. Vol 1: 12554
Veeco Instruments, Inc Vol 1: 5595
Vegetarian Resource Group Vol 1: 18486
Velo-Cardio-Facial Syndrome Vol 1: 18488
Venture Clubs Vol 1: 18491
Verband Hannoverscher Warmblutzuechter Vol 2: 2430
Verbandder Koche Deutschlands Vol 2: 2382
Verbatim, The Language Quarterly Vol 2: 5816
Verein der Zellstoff-und Papier-Chemiker und-Ingenieure Vol 2: 2026
Vereinigung Osterreichischer Bibliothekarinnen und Bibliothekare Vol 2: 753
Vereniging van Geneeskundige Laboratorium Tegnoloe van Suid-Afrika Vol 2: 4246
Vereniging van Schouwburg en Concertgebouwdirecties Vol 2: 3678
Vereniging van Schrijvers en Vertalers Vol 2: 3680
Vereniging van Suid-Afrikaanse Bourekenaars Vol 2: 4129
Vermont Business Round Table Vol 1: 18493
Vermont Chamber of Commerce Vol 1: 18495
Vermont Parent Teacher Association Vol 1: 18497
Vermont Society of Land Surveyors Vol 1: 18499
Vermont Superintendents Association Vol 1: 18501
Vernacular Architecture Forum Vol 1: 18503
Vernalis Vol 2: 6967
Vesterheim Norwegian-American Museum Vol 1: 18506
Veteran Wireless Operators Association Vol 1: 18510
Veterans for Peace Vol 1: 18514
Veterans of Foreign Wars of the United States Vol 1: 18516
Veterans of Foreign Wars of the U.S., Department of Alabama Vol 1: 18528
Veterans of Safety Vol 1: 4233
Veterans of the Office of Strategic Services in World War II Vol 1: 14450
Victor Company of Japan Vol 2: 3342
Victorian Artists Society Vol 2: 716
Vieilles Maisons Francaises Vol 2: 2011
Vienna Chamber Opera Vol 2: 829
Vienna University of Music and Dramatic Arts Vol 2: 831
Vietnam Veterans Association of Australia - National Council Vol 2: 719
Vietnamese Culture and Science Association Vol 1: 18530
Vietnamese Medical Association in the U.S.A. Vol 1: 18532
Viking Society for Northern Research Vol 2: 7317
Villa I Tatti - Harvard University Center for Italian Renaissance Studies Vol 2: 3141
Villa-Lobos Museum Vol 2: 1137

The Village Voice Vol 1: 18534
Vinas International Singing Competition; Francisco Vol 2: 4553
Vinegar Connoisseurs International Vol 1: 18536
Vinifera Wine Growers Association Vol 1: 18538
Vintage Sailplane Association Vol 1: 18542
Vintage Thunderbird Club International Vol 1: 18546
Vintage Thunderbird Club of America Vol 1: 18546
Violin Society of America Vol 1: 18548
Virginia Association of Chiefs of Police Vol 1: 18550
Virginia Association of Independent Specialized Education Facilities Vol 1: 18552
Virginia Film Office Vol 1: 18554, 18555
Virginia Interscholastic Athletic Administrators Association Vol 1: 18556
Virginia Library Association Vol 1: 18558
Virginia Peninsula Chamber of Commerce Vol 1: 18560
Virginia Quarterly Review Vol 1: 18562
Virginia Recreation and Park Society Vol 1: 18564
Virginia Volkssport Association Vol 1: 18566
Virginia Waring International Piano Competition Vol 1: 18568
Visions du Reel International Documentary Film Festival Vol 2: 4912
Visual Arts Center of New Jersey Center Vol 1: 18570
VMI Cadet Investment Group Vol 1: 18573
VMI Research Laboratories Vol 1: 18575
VM+SD Vol 1: 9941
Voestapline Vol 2: 762
Voetslaan Suid-Afrika Vol 2: 4194
Voice of the Listener and Viewer Vol 2: 7319
Voice of Youth Advocates Vol 1: 19084
von Humboldt Foundation; Alexander Vol 1: 15754
von Humboldt Foundation of New York; Alexander Vol 1: 11029
von Humboldt-Stiftung Foundation; Alexander Vol 2: 2432
von Siemens Music Foundation; Ernst Vol 2: 4914
Vormgevingsinstituut Vol 2: 3628
VSA Arts Vol 1: 18577
Wagner Society of New York Vol 1: 18580
Wales Craft Council Vol 2: 7321
Wall Colmonoy Corp. Vol 1: 4464
Wallace Reader's Digest Fund; Lila Vol 1: 18582
Walter Cronkite Endowment for Journalism and Telecommunication Vol 1: 7971
Waltham Worldwide Vol 2: 1340, 1341
WAMSO, Minnesota Orchestra Volunteer Association Vol 1: 18584
Warman International Vol 2: 536
Warner-Lambert/Parke-Davis Vol 1: 3807
Warringah Council Vol 2: 724
Warsaw Philharmonic Vol 2: 4053
Waseda Daigaku Vol 2: 3345
Waseda University Vol 2: 3345
Washington Academy of Sciences Vol 1: 18589
Washington-Baltimore Newspaper Guild Vol 1: 18591
Washington College - College Relations and Marketing Office Vol 1: 18593
Washington Craft Show Vol 1: 16099
Washington Crossing Foundation Vol 1: 18595
Washington Independent Writers Vol 1: 18597
Washington International Trade Association Vol 1: 18599
The Washington Monthly Vol 1: 18602
The Washington Post Company Educational Foundation Vol 1: 18605
Washington State Bar Association Vol 1: 18607
Washington Theatre Awards Society Vol 1: 18609
Washington University in St. Louis - Diabetes Research and Training Center Vol 1: 18611
Washington Writers' Publishing House Vol 1: 18613
Washingtonian Magazine Vol 1: 18615
Washtenaw Contractors Association Vol 1: 18617
Water Environment Federation Vol 1: 18620
Water Environment Research Foundation Vol 1: 18648
Water Institute of Southern Africa Vol 2: 4375
Water Instituut van Suidelike Africa Vol 2: 4375
Waters Corp. Vol 1: 1521, 1547
Wayne State University - Merrill-Palmer Institute Vol 1: 18650
Weatherby Health Care Vol 1: 8434
Wedding and Portrait Photographers International Vol 1: 18652
Wedding Photographers International Vol 1: 18652
Wedding Photographers of America Vol 1: 18652
Wedgwood Group Vol 2: 5230
Weed Society of Victoria Vol 2: 728
Weekly Reader Corp. Vol 1: 10585
The Welch Foundation Vol 1: 18654
Welding Technology Institute of Australia Vol 2: 731
Wellcome Trust Vol 2: 6677
Welsh Arts Council Vol 2: 7325
Welsh Books Council Vol 2: 4995, 7324
Welsh Centre for International Affairs Vol 2: 7327
Welsh Joint Education Committee Vol 2: 7325
Welsh Music Guild Vol 2: 7329
Welsh National Centre for Children's Literature Vol 2: 7324
Welsh Society of Philadelphia Vol 1: 18656
Welsh Youth Libraries Group Vol 2: 7325
West African College of Surgeons Vol 2: 3886
West African Examinations Council Vol 2: 2447
West Agro Inc. Vol 1: 1891
West Coast Book Prize Society Vol 1: 18658
West Texas Press Association Vol 1: 18667
West Virginia Children's Book Award Vol 1: 18669
West Virginia Poetry Society Vol 1: 13187
West Virginia University Reading Center Vol 1: 18669
Westchester Library Association Vol 1: 18671
Western Building Material Association Vol 1: 18673
Western Canada Wilderness Committee Vol 1: 18675
Western Economic Association International Vol 1: 18677
Western Electronic Manufacturers Association - American Electronics Association Vol 1: 194
Western History Association Vol 1: 18679
Western Interpretation Association Vol 1: 12345
Western North Carolina Historical Association Vol 1: 18692
Western Political Science Association Vol 1: 18695
Western States Advertising Agencies Association Vol 1: 11407
Western States Arts Federation Vol 1: 18697
Western Women Professional Bowlers Vol 1: 18699
Western Writers of America Vol 1: 18702
Westerners International Vol 1: 18705
Westerners International Association Vol 1: 14983
Westerville Area Chamber of Commerce Vol 1: 18710
Westminster Kennel Club Vol 1: 18712
Wexner Center for the Arts Vol 1: 18717
Wexner Foundation Vol 1: 18719
Whatman plc Vol 2: 6967
Wheelchair Sports, USA Vol 1: 18721
Whirly-Girls - International Women Helicopter Pilots Vol 1: 18723
White House Commission on Presidential Scholars Vol 1: 17820
White House Correspondents' Association Vol 1: 18726
White House News Photographers Association Vol 1: 18730
White Library; William Allen Vol 1: 18732
White School of Journalism; William Allen Vol 1: 9721
Whiting Foundation; Mrs. Giles Vol 1: 18734
Wichita Art Museum Vol 1: 11088
Wichita State University Center for Entrepreneurship Vol 1: 18736
Wiener Kammeroper Vol 2: 829
Wiener Library Vol 2: 7331
Wiesel Foundation for Humanity; Elie Vol 1: 18738
Wilcher Fund; Denny and Ida Vol 1: 16024
Wilderness Medical Society Vol 1: 18741
The Wilderness Society Vol 1: 18743
Wildlife and Environment Zimbabwe Vol 2: 7438
Wildlife Conservation Society Vol 2: 5179
Wildlife Explorer Vol 2: 7333
The Wildlife Society Vol 1: 18747
Wiley & Sons Inc.; John Vol 1: 4913, 5074
Wiley & Sons; John Vol 1: 10370, 10371
Wiley & Sons Publishing Company; John Vol 1: 3681
William Hill plc Vol 2: 7335
William Morris Society Vol 2: 7337
William T. Grant Foundation Vol 1: 18750
Williams College Vol 1: 11782
Williamson-White Medal Vol 1: 11641
Wilson Company; H. W. Vol 1: 4082, 17081
Wilson Co.; H.W. Vol 1: 2665
Wilson Ornithological Society Vol 1: 18752
Wilson Sporting Goods Company Vol 1: 1383, 10009
Winchell Cancer Fund; Damon Runyon - Walter Vol 1: 8034
Windsor Chamber of Commerce Vol 1: 18757

Wine Country Film Festival; Napa Sonoma Vol 1: 12075
Wine Spectator Vol 1: 18759
Wingfoot Lighter than Air Society Vol 1: 11359
Wings Club Vol 1: 18762
Winston Churchill Foundation Vol 1: 18764
Wire Association International Vol 1: 18766
Wireless Communications Association International Vol 1: 18769
Wisconsin Agri-Service Association Vol 1: 18771
Wisconsin Arts Board Vol 1: 18773
Wisconsin Cheese Makers' Association Vol 1: 18775
Wisconsin Educational Media Association Vol 1: 18777
Wisconsin Farm Bureau Federation Vol 1: 18779
Wisconsin Historical Society Vol 1: 18781
Wisconsin Labor History Society Vol 1: 18785
Wisconsin Library Association Vol 1: 18788
Wisconsin Park and Recreation Association Vol 1: 18792
Wisconsin Parkinson Association Vol 1: 18794
Wisconsin State Genealogical Society Vol 1: 18796
Wisconsin State Legislature Vol 1: 18774
Wissenschaftsstadt Darmstadt Vol 2: 2439
W.K. Kellogg Foundation Vol 1: 18799
WMC Foundation Vol 2: 3682
WMX Technologies, Inc. (Waste Management, Inc.) Vol 1: 17783
Wolf Foundation Vol 2: 2937
Wolfe Pack Vol 1: 18801
Wolfson Foundation Vol 2: 7339
Woman's Building - Slide Archive Vol 1: 18803
Women for Faith and Family Vol 1: 18805
Women in Agribusiness Vol 1: 18807
Women in Cable and Telecommunications Vol 1: 18809
Women in Direct Marketing International Vol 1: 18811
Women in Film Vol 1: 18813
Women in Film and Video Vol 1: 18816
Women in Film and Video/New England Vol 1: 18818
Women in Food Industry Management Vol 1: 18820
Women in Insurance and Financial Services Vol 1: 18823
Women in Literacy and Life Assembly Vol 1: 18827, 18828
Women in Livestock Development Vol 1: 18829
Women in Management Vol 1: 18831
Women in Production Vol 1: 18833
Women in Publishing Vol 2: 7341
Women in Technology International Vol 1: 18836
Women in the Wind Vol 1: 18839
Women Marines Association Vol 1: 18841
Women's Action for New Directions Vol 1: 18843
Women's All-Star Association Vol 1: 18845
Women's Art Association of Canada Vol 1: 18852
Women's Association of Romania Vol 2: 4387
Women's Bar Association of the District of Columbia Vol 1: 18854
Women's Basketball Coaches Association Vol 1: 18856
Women's Business Enterprise National Council Vol 1: 18858
Women's Caucus for Art Vol 1: 18860
Women's Caucus of the Australian Political Studies Association Vol 2: 91
Women's Electoral Lobby - Australia Vol 2: 736
Women's Engineering Society Vol 2: 7344
Women's International Bowling Congress Vol 1: 10276
Women's International League for Peace and Freedom, U.S. Section Vol 1: 18862
Women's International Network of Utility Professionals Vol 1: 18864
Women's National Book Association Vol 1: 18866
Women's Sports Foundation Vol 1: 18869
Women's Studies Association Vol 2: 3878
Women's Transportation Seminar Vol 1: 18877
Women's Veterinary Medical Association Vol 1: 5010
Wood County Historical Society Vol 1: 18881
Wood Design and Building Magazine - Dovetail Communications Vol 1: 18883
Woodrow Wilson National Fellowship Foundation Vol 1: 18885
Woodson Art Museum; Leigh Yawkey Vol 1: 18888
The Word Works Vol 1: 18890
Words+ Inc. Vol 1: 10639
Workers' Music Association Vol 2: 7348
Workforce Management - Crain Communications Inc. Vol 1: 18892
The Works Festival Vol 1: 6191
World Academy of Art and Science Vol 2: 551
World Airlines Clubs Association Vol 1: 18894
World Amateur Golf Council Vol 1: 10453
World Association for Animal Production Vol 2: 3143
World Association for Public Opinion Research Vol 1: 18896
World Association for Small and Medium Enterprises Vol 2: 2813
World Association for the Advancement of Veterinary Parasitology Vol 1: 18899
World Association for the History of Veterinary Medicine Vol 2: 833
World Association of Christian Radio Amateurs and Listeners Vol 2: 7350
World Association of Community Radio Broadcasters Vol 1: 18903
World Association of Detectives Vol 2: 7352
World Association of Girl Guides and Girl Scouts Vol 2: 7357
World Association of Industrial and Technological Research Organizations Vol 2: 3418
World Association of Newspapers Vol 2: 2013
World Association of Research Professionals Vol 2: 3685
World Association of Societies of Pathology and Laboratory Medicine Vol 2: 3350
World Atlatl Association Vol 1: 18905
World Bank Group Vol 1: 18910
World Book, Inc. Vol 1: 2666
World Book Inc. Vol 1: 2700, 7162
World Bowling Writers Vol 1: 10276, 18912
World Boxing Council Vol 2: 3457
World Chess Federation Vol 2: 2474
World Commission on Protected Areas Vol 2: 4916
World Confederation for Physical Therapy Vol 2: 7363
World Confederation of Productivity Science Vol 1: 18917
World Conservation Union Vol 2: 4918
World Council of Credit Unions Vol 1: 18919
World Council of Optometry Vol 1: 18921
World Cultural Council Vol 2: 3459
World Curling Federation Vol 2: 7365
World Dance and Dance Sport Council Vol 2: 7367
World Environment Center Vol 1: 18924
World Federation for Culture Collections Vol 2: 7369
World Federation of Catholic Medical Associations Vol 2: 7419
World Federation of Engineering Organisations Vol 2: 2015
World Federation of Estonian Women's Clubs Vol 1: 18926
World Federation of Hemophilia Vol 1: 18928
World Federation of Journalists and Travel Writers Vol 2: 2018
World Federation of Neurology Vol 2: 7371
World Federation of Neurosurgical Societies Vol 1: 18930
World Federation of Personnel Management Associations Vol 1: 18934
World Festival of Underwater Pictures Vol 2: 1798
World Folk Music Association Vol 1: 18936
The World Food Prize Foundation Vol 1: 18938
World Footbag Association Vol 1: 18940
World Golf Championships Vol 1: 18943
World Golf Hall of Fame Vol 1: 18942
World Golf Village Vol 1: 18943
World Health Organization Vol 2: 1153, 4924
World Health Organization - International Agency for Research on Cancer Vol 2: 4931
World Hunger Year Vol 1: 18944
World International Nail and Beauty Association Vol 1: 18947
World Jersey Cattle Bureau Vol 2: 7373
World Learning Vol 1: 18949
World Leisure and Recreation Association Vol 1: 18951
World Literature Today Vol 1: 18953
World Meteorological Organization Vol 2: 1874, 4933
World Methodist Council Vol 1: 18955
World Ocean and Cruise Liner Society Vol 1: 18957
World Organization for Human Potential Vol 1: 18959
World Organization of Building Officials Vol 1: 18961
World Organization of Family Doctors Vol 2: 4435
World Organization of the Scout Movement Vol 2: 4938
World Petroleum Council - The Global Forum for Oil and Gas Science, Technology, Economics and Management Vol 2: 7375
World Phosphate Institute Vol 2: 2557, 3474
World Phosphate Rock Institute Vol 2: 3474
World Piano Competition Vol 1: 18964
World Ploughing Organisation Vol 2: 3687
World Press Photo Vol 2: 3689

World Safety Organization Vol 1: 18966
World Science Fiction Society Vol 1: 18978
World Ship Trust - United Kingdom Vol 2: 7378
World Small Animal Veterinary Association Vol 2: 1339
World Taekwondo Federation Vol 2: 4119
World Teleport Association Vol 1: 18980
World Trade Center of New Orleans Vol 1: 18982
World Trade Centre Vancouver Vol 1: 18985
World Veterans Federation Vol 2: 2020
World Veterinary Poultry Association Vol 2: 2444
World Wide Video Festival Vol 2: 3691
World Wildlife Fund Vol 2: 4942
Worlddidac Foundation Vol 2: 4940
WorldFest - Houston International Film and Video Festival Vol 1: 18992
Worldpress.org - All Media Inc. Vol 1: 18994
WorldRadio Vol 1: 18996
World's Poultry Science Association Vol 2: 7380
Worldwide Association of Self-Adhesive Labels and Related Products Vol 2: 3693
Worshipful Company of Armourers & Brasiers' Vol 2: 6900
Worshipful Company of Chartered Architects Vol 2: 6128
Worshipful Company of Constructors Vol 2: 6128
Worshipful Company of Glaziers' and Painters of Glass Vol 2: 7382
Worshipful Company of Plaisterers Vol 2: 5891
Worshipful Company of Scientific Instrument Makers Vol 2: 7386
Worshipful Company Of Weavers' Vol 2: 7274
Worshipful Society of Apothecaries of London Vol 2: 7388
Worthington Pump, Inc. Vol 1: 4175
Wright State University Vol 1: 15413
Wrigley, Jr. Company; William Vol 1: 10065
Writers' Development Trust Vol 1: 19003, 19024
Writer's Digest Vol 1: 18998
Writers' Federation of Nova Scotia Vol 1: 19002
Writers Guild of Alberta Vol 1: 19005
Writers Guild of America, West Vol 1: 19009
Writers' Journal Vol 1: 19016
Writers' Trust of Canada Vol 1: 19024
Writers' Union of Canada Vol 1: 19026
Writers Workshop Vol 1: 13949
WWF International Vol 2: 4942
Wyeth Ayerst Research Vol 1: 3810
Wyeth Consumer Healthcare Vol 1: 3787
Wyeth Nutrition Vol 1: 3792
Wyeth Research Vol 1: 3420
Wyeth Vaccines Research Vol 1: 9700
WYOpoets of Wyoming Vol 1: 13189
Xavier University Vol 1: 19031
Xerox Corporation Vol 1: 3127, 3634, 14620
Xerox Corp. Vol 1: 16246
Xplor International Vol 1: 19033
XYZ Digital Map Co. Ltd. Vol 2: 6898
Yachting Journalists' Association Vol 2: 7390
Yad Vashem Vol 2: 2939
Yale Series of Younger Poets Vol 1: 19036
Yale University - Beinecke Rare Book and Manuscript Library Vol 1: 19038
Yale University - Yale Center for International and Area Studies Vol 1: 19040
Yamaha Corporation of America Vol 1: 12034, 12035
Yasme Foundation Vol 1: 19042
YBP, Inc. Vol 1: 4916
YBP Inc. Vol 1: 11336
Yellow Pages Association Vol 1: 19044
Yellow Pages Publishers Association Vol 1: 19044
Yes I Can! Foundation for Exceptional Children Vol 1: 19046
Yeshiva University Vol 1: 19055
YIVO Institute for Jewish Research Vol 1: 19057
YMCA of Greater New York Vol 1: 19070
YMCA of the United States of America Vol 1: 19073
Ymgyrch Diogelu Cymru Wledig Vol 2: 5580
Yomiuri Shimbun Vol 2: 3353
Yorkshire Terrier Club of America Vol 1: 19075
Yorkton International Short Film & Video Festival 1981 Vol 1: 19077
Yorkton Short Film & Video Festival Vol 1: 19077
Young Adult Library Services Association Vol 1: 19079
Young Adult Services Interest Group Vol 1: 6694
Young Archeologists' Club Vol 2: 5231
Young Audiences of Greater Cleveland Vol 1: 19086
Young Australians Best Book Award Council Vol 2: 738
Young Concert Artists Vol 1: 19088
Young Concert Artists Trust Vol 2: 7393
Young Menswear Association Vol 1: 19090
Young Menswear Association of the Men's Apparel Industry Vol 1: 19090
Young Ornithologists' Club Vol 2: 7333
Young Playwrights Inc. Vol 1: 19092
Young Republican National Federation Vol 1: 19094
Young Women's Christian Association - Hong Kong Vol 2: 3951
Young Women's Christian Association of Elmira and the Twin Tiers Vol 1: 19099
Young Women's Christian Association of Lubbock Vol 1: 19101
Young Women's Christian Association of San Diego County Vol 1: 19103
Young Women's Christian Association of the United States of America YWCA of the U.S.A. Vol 1: 19105
Y's Men International Vol 2: 4947
Yuki Teikei Haiku Society Vol 1: 19107
YWCA El Paso del Norte Region Vol 1: 19109
YWCA of Houston Vol 1: 19111
YWCA of the City of New York Vol 1: 19113
YWCA of Vermont Vol 1: 19116
Zagreb World Festival of Animated Films Vol 2: 1240
Zelienople-Harmony Area Chamber of Commerce Vol 1: 19118
Zen-do Kai Martial Arts Vol 1: 19120
ZENECA Pharmaceuticals Group Vol 1: 212
Zeta Phi Eta Vol 1: 800
Zijlstra Foundation; Adama Vol 2: 3662
Zimbabwe Institution of Engineers Vol 2: 7440
Zimbabwe Scientific Association Vol 2: 7446
Zisking-Somerfeld Research Foundation Vol 1: 16607
Zoll Medical Corp. Vol 1: 12517
Zoological Society of London Vol 2: 7395
Zoological Society of Southern Africa Vol 2: 4379
Zveza Bibliotekarskih Drustev Slovenije Vol 2: 4466
Zwiazek Artystow Scen Polskich Vol 2: 4022
Zwiazek Kompozytorow Polskich Vol 2: 4037

Award Index

The Award Index provides an alphabetical listing of all awards appearing in both volumes, as well as alternate-language, former, and popular award names. Identically named awards are followed by an indented alphabetical list of the organizations administering an award by that name. Each award name is followed by the volume in which it appears. The numbers following the volume references refer to award book entry numbers, not page numbers.

3M Integrity Award Vol. 1: 9926
5 Band WAZ Award Vol. 1: 7940
10 Best Cars Competition Vol. 1: 7096
50 Books/50 Covers Competition Vol. 1: 2515
50 Greatest U.S. Tennis Resorts Vol. 1: 17442
"54" Founders Award Vol. 1: 10937
125th Anniversary Medals Vol. 1: 7428
408/437 Wing Award Vol. 1: 313
500 Mile Limited Distance Horse Program Award Vol. 1: 1952
1000 Mile Horse Program Award Vol. 1: 1953
$30,000 Lemelson-MIT Student Prize Vol. 1: 11292
$100,000 Lemelson-MIT Lifetime Achievement Award Vol. 1: 11293
$500,000 Lemelson-MIT Prize Vol. 1: 11294
A. J. Shawcross Prize Vol. 2: 5993
A-Level Chemistry Prizes Vol. 2: 7058
AAAI Classic Paper Award Vol. 1: 850
AAAI Distinguished Service Award Vol. 1: 851
AAAI Effective Expository Writing Award Vol. 1: 852
AAAI Fellows Program Vol. 1: 853
AAAI Intel Science and Engineering Awards Vol. 1: 13894
AAAI Outstanding Paper Award Vol. 1: 854
AAAS Mass Media Science and Engineering Fellowship Vol. 1: 3161
AAAS Thousand Dollar Prize Vol. 1: 952
AAAS Westinghouse Award for Public Understanding of Science and Technology Vol. 1: 948
AAAS Westinghouse Science Journalism Awards - Whitaker Science Journalism Awards Vol. 1: 953
AABB-Baxter SBB Scholarship Awards Vol. 1: 1003
AABB-Baxter Transfusion Medicine Scholarship Awards Vol. 1: 1004
AACC International Scholarship Endowment Fund Vol. 1: 17
AACC Lectureship Award Vol. 1: 865
AACD Distinguished Professional Service Award Vol. 1: 1842
AACP Clinical Research Award Vol. 1: 560
AACT Fellow Vol. 1: 1058
AADA Alumni Achievement Award Vol. 1: 571
AAFP Award for Excellence in Graduate Medical Education Vol. 1: 5902
AAFP Award for National Leadership in Government Service Vol. 1: 598
AAFP Distinguished Service Award Vol. 1: 599
AAGO Prize Vol. 1: 2146
AAHS Trophy (American Aviation Historical Society) Vol. 2: 5008
AAHSA/National Organization on Disability Award Vol. 1: 1119
AALAS Animal Technician Award Vol. 1: 915
AALAS Technical Notes Award Vol. 1: 919
AALL LexisNexis Call for Papers Awards Program Vol. 1: 1137
AALL Spectrum Article of the Year Award Vol. 1: 1138
AALL/West Excellence in Marketing Award Vol. 1: 1139
AAMI Foundation Laufman-Greatbatch Prize Vol. 1: 4977
AAMI/GE Healthcare BMET of the Year Award Vol. 1: 4978
AAMR Awards Vol. 1: 1341
AANOS Scholarship Fund Vol. 1: 632
AAPA Humanitarian Physician Assistant of the Year Vol. 1: 733
AAPL Outstanding Service Award Vol. 1: 740
AAPOR Award Vol. 1: 938
Aarestrup Prize; Emil Vol. 2: 1291
AARL Foundation Grant Vol. 1: 30
AAS Individual Awards Vol. 1: 4636
AASL/EB School Library Media Program of the Year Award - AASL National School Library Media Program of the Year Award Vol. 1: 1281
AASL President's Award Vol. 1: 1275
AASL/SIRS Intellectual Freedom Award Vol. 1: 1280
AAU Media Award Vol. 1: 466
AAU Promotions Award Vol. 1: 467
AAUP Design Show Vol. 1: 5042
AAZPA Bean Award Vol. 1: 1339
Abafazi-Africana Women's Studies Essay Award Vol. 1: 13923
ABBA Awards Vol. 1: 1402
Abbey Fellowships in Painting Vol. 2: 5434
Abbey Scholarship in Painting Vol. 2: 5435
Abbott Award
  European Society for Clinical Virology Vol. 2: 4580
  Society of Medical Laboratory Technologists of South Africa Vol 2: 4247
Abbott Award; Charles Greeley Vol. 1: 4285
Abbott Award for Innovative Research and Development in Virology Vol. 2: 4248
Abbott Distinguished Research Award Vol. 1: 3162
Abbott Laboratories Award in Clinical and Diagnostic Immunology Vol. 1: 3762
Abbott Prize Vol. 2: 7148
ABBY Award Vol. 1: 1414
ABC Champion Performance Horse Vol. 1: 1390
ABC-CLIO *America: History and Life* Award Vol. 1: 14686
ABC/CLIO Leadership Grant Vol. 1: 1272
ABC Concerts and Vocal Competition Vol. 2: 696
ABC Young Performers' Competition Vol. 2: 696
ABCNews VideoSource Award Vol. 1: 10380
Abe Fellowships Vol. 1: 16126
Abe Issa Award for Excellence Vol. 2: 3150
Abe Prize Vol. 2: 3298
Abel Award; Paul Vol. 1: 15583
Abel Cultural Arts, Literature, and Music Awards; Alice Vol. 1: 2806
Abella; Prix Francoise Vol. 2: 1433
Abelson Prize; Philip Hauge Vol. 1: 946
Aberconway Medal Vol. 2: 5927
Abercrombie Prize; Sir Patrick Vol. 2: 1922
Aberdeen Memorial Trophy; Stuart W. Vol. 1: 6643
Aberg Post Graduate Award; Ulf Vol. 2: 5788
ABET Honor Roll Vol. 1: 41
ABI/BMA Trophy Vol. 2: 5355
ABOA Foundation - National Scholastic Press Association Pacemaker Awards Vol. 1: 14222
ABOHN Research Award Vol. 1: 1404
Aboriginal Canadians Scholarship Vol. 1: 13877
Aboriginal Torres Strait Islander Writers' Award; Dymocks Vol. 2: 589
Abragam; Prix Anatole et Suzanne Vol. 2: 1538
Abrams Award; Eugene Vol. 2: 4697
Abrams Award in Geriatric Clinical Pharmacology; William B. Vol. 1: 3607
Abrams Award; Talbert Vol. 1: 4733
Abrams Medal; General Creighton W. Vol. 1: 5364
Abrams Prize; Mark Vol. 2: 7085
Abromowicz Emerging Scholar Fellowship; Dina Vol. 1: 19058
ABU Engineering Award Vol. 2: 3397
ABU Prizes for Radio and Television Programs Vol. 2: 3398
Abzug Memorial Award; Martin Vol. 1: 13920
ACA Academy Scholar and Fellow Degrees Vol. 1: 51
ACA Honorary Membership Vol. 1: 5057

Academic Achievement Award Vol. 1: 4426
Academic All-American By Sport Award Vol. 1: 13401
Academic All-Canadian Awards Vol. 1: 6406
Academic Athletes of the Year (All Academic Team) Vol. 1: 12908
Academic Awards Vol. 2: 5877
Academic Excellence Award Vol. 1: 8431
Academic Excellency Prize Vol. 2: 4103
Academic Librarians' Distinguished Service Award Vol. 1: 6306
Academic Purposes Fund Awards Vol. 2: 7200
Academic/Research Librarian of the Year Award Vol. 1: 5069
Academic Scholarships Vol. 1: 9373
Academic Team-of-the-Year Vol. 1: 13399
Academic Year Grant Program Vol. 1: 9957
Academie dFAgriculture de France Medailles Vol. 2: 1429
Academy Achievement Award Vol. 1: 69
Academy and Achievement Awards Vol. 1: 67
Academy Award for Scholarship Vol. 2: 25
Academy Awards Vol. 1: 188
Academy Fellow Vol. 1: 123
Academy Fellow Award Vol. 1: 87
Academy of Authors Vol. 1: 9934
Academy of Country Music Awards Vol. 1: 85
Academy of Distinguished Entrepreneurs Vol. 1: 5615
Academy of Fellows Vol. 1: 10779
Academy of Pharmaceutical Research and Science Fellow Vol. 1: 3038
Academy of Pharmacy Practice and Management Fellow Vol. 1: 3039
Academy of Sciences of the Czech Republic Awards Vol. 2: 1247
Academy Research Grants Vol. 1: 947
Accelerator Prize Vol. 2: 1785
Access Award for Disability Issues Vol. 1: 7438
Access Awards Vol. 1: 2066
Accolades Award Vol. 1: 18810
Accomplishment Award Vol. 1: 1150
Accountant of the Year Award Vol. 1: 5718
Accountants, Bankers and Factors Division Award Vol. 1: 2590
Accounting Technician of the Year Vol. 2: 3727
ACE Award Vol. 1: 12849
ACE Eddie Awards Vol. 1: 1594
ACE Education Program Award Vol. 1: 5117
ACE Fellows Program Vol. 1: 1828
Ace of the Year Vol. 1: 11990
ACES Research Grants Vol. 1: 4843
ACFOA Human Rights Award Vol. 2: 171
ACHA Article Award Vol. 1: 1651
Acha Award for Veterinary Public Health; Pedro N. Vol. 1: 14829
ACHA World Championship Vol. 1: 1790
ACHEMA-Plakette in Titan Vol. 2: 2256
ACHEMA Plaque in Titanium Vol. 2: 2256
Achievement Award
  Alpha Omega International Dental Fraternity Vol. 1: 427
  American Academy of Ophthalmology Vol 1: 646
  American Association of Meat Processors Vol 1: 1151
  American Association of University Women Educational Foundation Vol 1: 1325
  American Fuchsia Society Vol 1: 2074
  American Meat Science Association Vol 1: 2734
  American Scientific Glassblowers Society Vol 1: 3530
  Canadian Cardiovascular Society Vol 1: 6375
  Creative Studies Alumni Foundation Vol 1: 7954
  Foundation of American Women in Radio and Television Vol 1: 8849
  Historic Chattahoochee Commission Vol 1: 9411
  Industrial Research Institute Vol 1: 9693
  Institute of Electronics, Information and Communication Engineers Vol 2: 3191
  Liberty Bell Wanderers Vol 1: 11324
  Lighter-Than-Air Society Vol 1: 11360
  National Association of County Agricultural Agents Vol 1: 12496
  National Black Police Association Vol 1: 12776
  National Junior College Athletic Association Vol 1: 13400
  National Peach Council Vol 1: 13536
  Ontario Nature Vol 1: 14577
  Professional Convention Management Association Vol 1: 15286
  Resort and Commercial Recreation Association Vol 1: 15634
  Society of Toxicology Vol 1: 16867
  Society of Women Engineers Vol 1: 16910
  Tylers' and Bricklayers' Company Vol 2: 7281
  U.S.A. Baseball Vol 1: 18378
  Virginia Volkssport Association Vol 1: 18567
Achievement Award for a Disabled Person Vol. 1: 11977
Achievement Awards
  Health Science Communications Association Vol. 1: 9309
  Heritage Canada Foundation Vol 1: 9385
  National Association of Counties Vol 1: 12492
  National Horseshoe Pitchers Association of America Vol 1: 13353
  National Research Council of the Philippines Vol 2: 3976
  Public Risk Management Association Vol 1: 15435
  Rough and Smooth Collie Training Association Vol 2: 6608
  Royal Society for the Prevention of Accidents Vol 2: 6924
Achievement Awards in Writing Vol. 1: 13016
Achievement in Communication Vol. 1: 10151
Achievement in Consumer Education Awards Vol. 1: 12477
Achievement in the Arts Award Vol. 1: 14413
Achievement Medal Vol. 1: 435
Achievement Medal: Air Force Vol. 1: 8088
Achievement Medal: Coast Guard Vol. 1: 8089
Achievement Medal: Navy - Marine Corps Vol. 1: 8090
Achievement Medals Vol. 2: 6141
Achievement of Excellence Vol. 1: 6370
Achievement of Social Studies Education General Grant Vol. 1: 12983
Achievement of the Year Award Vol. 1: 5174
Achievement Through Action Award Vol. 2: 2327
Achiever of the Year Vol. 2: 4152
Achievers of the Year Vol. 1: 9127
Achieving Chapter Excellence (ACE) Vol. 1: 11090
Achieving Excellence Awards Vol. 1: 10378
Achieving Professional Excellence in Education Administration Award Vol. 1: 1054
ACI Annual Awards Vol. 1: 4838
ACI Fellow Vol. 1: 1747
Ackerley Prize for Autobiography; J. R. Vol. 2: 5778
Ackermann Medal for Excellence in Water Management; William C. Vol. 1: 4416
ACLS/SSRC/NEH International and Area Studies Fellowships Vol. 1: 16127
ACM Fellow Vol. 1: 4805
ACMS Scientific Achievement Award Vol. 1: 7365
Acorn Poetry Award; Milton Vol. 1: 15217
ACP-CRM/CAP-CRM Prize in Theoretical and Mathematical Physics Vol. 1: 11617
ACRL Best Practices in Marketing Academic and Research Libraries Award Vol. 1: 5070
ACS Award for Computers in Chemical and Pharmaceutical Research Vol. 1: 1501
ACS Award for Creative Advances in Environmental Science and Technology Vol. 1: 1502
ACS Award for Creative Invention Vol. 1: 1503
ACS Award for Creative Work in Fluorine Chemistry Vol. 1: 1504
ACS Award for Creative Work in Synthetic Organic Chemistry Vol. 1: 1505
ACS Award for Distinguished Service in the Advancement of Inorganic Chemistry Vol. 1: 1506
ACS Award for Encouraging Disadvantaged Students into Careers in the Chemical Sciences Vol. 1: 1507
ACS Award for Encouraging Women into Careers in the Chemical Sciences Vol. 1: 1508
ACS Award for Nuclear Applications in Chemistry Vol. 1: 1578
ACS Award for Nuclear Chemistry Vol. 1: 1578
ACS Award for Outstanding Performance by Local Sections Vol. 1: 1509
ACS Award for Research at an Undergraduate Institution Vol. 1: 1510
ACS Award for Team Innovation Vol. 1: 1511
ACS Award in Analytical Chemistry Vol. 1: 1512
ACS Award in Applied Polymer Science Vol. 1: 1513
ACS Award in Chemical Education Vol. 1: 1575
ACS Award in Chromatography Vol. 1: 1514
ACS Award in Colloid and Surface Chemistry Vol. 1: 1515
ACS Award in Industrial Chemistry Vol. 1: 1516
ACS Award in Inorganic Chemistry Vol. 1: 1517
ACS Award in Organometallic Chemistry Vol. 1: 1518
ACS Award in Petroleum Chemistry Vol. 1: 1571
ACS Award in Polymer Chemistry Vol. 1: 1519
ACS Award in Pure Chemistry Vol. 1: 1520

ACS Award in Separations Science and Technology Vol. 1: 1521
ACS Award in the Chemistry of Materials Vol. 1: 1522
ACS Award in Theoretical Chemistry Vol. 1: 1523
ACSA Awards Program Vol. 1: 5100
ACSA Collaborative Practice Award Vol. 1: 5101
ACSA Creative Achievement Award Vol. 1: 5102
ACSA Faculty Design Award Vol. 1: 5103
ACSA Topaz Medallion for Excellence in Architectural Education; AIA/ Vol. 1: 2424
ACSM-CaGIS Map Design Competition Awards Vol. 1: 1777
ACT-NUCEA Innovations in Continuing Education Awards Vol. 1: 18220
ACTA Special Medallion Award Vol. 1: 326
Action for Birds Award Vol. 2: 7334
Active Duty Literary Prize Vol. 1: 13999
Activist of the Year Vol. 2: 579
Actor of the Year Award Vol. 2: 5742
Actors' Fund Medal Vol. 1: 147
ACUHO-I Award Vol. 1: 5090
ADA/EASD Trans-Atlantic Fellowship Vol. 1: 1908
ADA Foundation Award for Excellence in the Practice of Clinical Nutrition Vol. 1: 1919
ADA Foundation Awards for Excellence Vol. 1: 1919
ADA Foundation Scholarships Vol. 1: 1920
ADAM Award Vol. 2: 2136
Adams Article Prize; Percy G. Vol. 1: 17002
Adams Award; Dorothy Garrigus Vol. 1: 16049
Adams Award for Conservation Photography; Ansel Vol. 1: 16001
Adams Award in Organic Chemistry; Roger Vol. 1: 1524
Adams Award; James Luther Vol. 1: 17684
Adams Chapter Heritage Award; Mildred Vol. 1: 16043
Adams Conservation Award; Ansel Vol. 1: 18744
Adams Cup; Mrs. Charles Francis Vol. 1: 18078
Adams Lecture Award; Comfort A. Vol. 1: 4448
Adams Memorial Membership Award Vol. 1: 4449
Adams Prize; Henry Vol. 1: 16225
Adams Prize; Herbert Baxter Vol. 1: 2225
Adams Prize; Willi Paul Vol. 1: 14687
Adams Short Story Contest; Nick Vol. 1: 4762
Adams Trophy; U.S. Women's Sailing Championship - Mrs. Charles Francis Vol. 1: 18077
Adamson Award for Distinguished Service in the Advancement of Surface Chemistry; Arthur W. Vol. 1: 1525
Adapted Committee Award Vol. 1: 18410
ADARN of the Year Vol. 1: 153
Adaskin Memorial Award; Canadian Music Centre John Vol. 1: 14555
ADC Swiss Award Vol. 2: 4905
Adcock Award; C.J. Vol. 2: 3786
Addams Award; Homer Vol. 1: 4043
Addams Children's Book Award; Jane Vol. 1: 10960
Addams Medal; Jane Vol. 1: 15697
Addey Scholarships; John Vol. 2: 5154
Addis Award; Margaret Vol. 1: 12300
Additional Honours Vol. 1: 6080
A'Deane Coke Medal; Major John Sacheverell Vol. 2: 5928
Adelaide Festival Vol. 2: 672
Adelaide International Exhibition of Photography; Interphot - Vol. 2: 675
Adenauer Research Award; Konrad Vol. 1: 15754
Adhesives Award Vol. 1: 5400
Adidas Coach of the Year Vol. 1: 18171
ADIRCAE Prizes Vol. 2: 4471
Adirondack Council Annual Awards Vol. 1: 158
Adirondack Wilderness Award Vol. 1: 4677
Adirondacks National Exhibition of American Watercolors Vol. 1: 4677
Adiseshiah International Literacy Prize; Malcolm Vol. 2: 2002
Adkins Award; James C. Vol. 1: 5518
Adkins Memorial Instructor Membership Award; Howard E. Vol. 1: 4450
Adler Friend of Education Award; Lewis F. Vol. 1: 14948
Adler Lectureship Award in the Field of Materials Physics; David Vol. 1: 3106
Adler Undergraduate Book Collecting Prize; Elmer Vol. 1: 8913
Administrative Committee Prize Vol. 1: 2593
Administrative Psychiatry Award Vol. 1: 3266
Administrator Award Vol. 1: 12314
Administrator of the Year Vol. 1: 7812
AdministratorFs Award Vol. 1: 8403
Admiral of the Ocean Sea Vol. 1: 17712
Adolescent Health Award Vol. 1: 697
Adolf-Dietzel-Industriepreis der DGG Vol. 2: 2242
Adopt-Action Service Award Vol. 1: 14289
Adoption Activist Awards Vol. 1: 14289
Adoption Hall of Fame Award Vol. 1: 12954
Adrian Awards Vol. 1: 9492
Adsit Excellence in Veterinary Medical Media Award; Milton E. Vol. 1: 9314
Adult Advisor of the Year Award Vol. 1: 2866
Adult Amateur Award Vol. 1: 17884
Adult Learners Week Vol. 2: 35
Adult Volunteer of the Year Vol. 1: 2165
Advanced Ceramic Award Vol. 1: 5401
Advanced Diploma Vol. 2: 6022
Advanced Oncology Certified Nurse of the Year Award Vol. 1: 14530
Advancement of Literacy Award Vol. 1: 15418
Adventurer of the Year Vol. 2: 1846
Adventurous Programming Chamber Music Awards Vol. 1: 3999
Advertiser of the Year Vol. 1: 12813
Advertiser of the Year Award Vol. 1: 14215
Advertising Age Awards Vol. 1: 176
Advertising and Marketing Awards
National Association of Recording Merchandisers Vol. 1: 12636
Society of National Association Publications Vol 1: 16757
Advertising and Promotions Contest Awards Vol. 1: 17314
Advertising Annual Vol. 1: 7635
Advertising Awards Vol. 1: 39
Advertising Design Club of Canada Awards Vol. 1: 178
Advertising Hall of Achievement Vol. 1: 763
Advertising Hall of Fame Vol. 1: 764
Advertising Leader of the Year Award Vol. 1: 11408
Advertising Merit Awards Vol. 1: 8786
Advertising Sales Team of the Year Vol. 2: 5721
Advertising Woman of the Year Vol. 1: 189
Advisor of the Year Vol. 1: 12787
Advocacy Award Vol. 1: 10572
Advocates for Justice Award Vol. 1: 1039
AE50 Award Vol. 1: 3841
Aebersold Award; Paul C. Vol. 1: 16777
AECI Medal Vol. 2: 4316
AECT/SIRS Intellectual Freedom Award Vol. 1: 4866
AEIP Graduating Student Award Vol. 1: 5382
Aelod o Orsedd Beirdd Ynys Prydain Vol. 2: 6471
AERA - American College Testing Program Award Vol. 1: 1943
AERA - PDK Award for Distinguished Contributions Relating Research to Practice Vol. 1: 1940
AERC National Championship Vol. 1: 1960
Aereskaljedoskop Vol. 2: 1301
AERF Practitioners Award Vol. 1: 16478
Aerial Achievement Medal Vol. 1: 8091
Aero Club of America Trophy Vol. 1: 12188
Aero Engine Services Trophy Vol. 2: 3836
Aeroacoustics Award Vol. 1: 2354
Aerobics Athlete of the Year Vol. 1: 468
Aerobics Contributor of the Year Vol. 1: 469
Aerobics Man and Woman of the Year Vol. 1: 470
Aerobics Official of the Year Vol. 1: 471
Aerodynamic Measurement Technology Award Vol. 1: 2355
Aerodynamics Award Vol. 1: 2356
Aeromodelling Gold Medal Vol. 2: 4717
Aerophilatelic Class Award Vol. 2: 6535
Aerospace Communications Award Vol. 1: 2357
Aerospace Design Engineering Award Vol. 1: 2358
Aerospace Division/AIAA Educational Achievement Award Vol. 1: 3628
Aerospace Engineering Leadership Award Vol. 1: 16565
Aerospace Power Systems Award Vol. 1: 2359
Aerospace Software Engineering Award Vol. 1: 2360
AES Award Vol. 1: 5521
AES Awards of Excellence Vol. 1: 47
AES Man of the Year Award Vol. 1: 48
Aetate Award; Nostra Vol. 1: 7197
AFA Air Force Reserve Troop Carrier Wing Trophy Vol. 1: 298
AFA Newsletter Award Vol. 1: 5154
AFAEP Awards Vol. 2: 5151
AFAEP/Kodak Student Competition Vol. 2: 5152
AFAR Award of Distinction Vol. 1: 1997
Affair on the Square Art Festival Vol. 1: 7290
Affaire in the Gardens Art Show Vol. 1: 7430
Affiliate Award Vol. 1: 13979
Affiliate of the Year Award
International Society for Pharmaceutical Engineering Vol. 1: 10662
National Council of La Raza Vol 1: 13000
Affirmative Action Award; CMA Vol. 1: 2937
AFI Awards - The Australian Film Institute Awards Vol. 2: 196
AFJ Awards Competition Vol. 1: 5150
AFMA Technical Person of the Year; Barney van Niekerk/ Vol. 2: 4128

AFMC Executive Management Award Vol. 1: 274
AFMC Junior Management Award Vol. 1: 275
AFMC Middle Management Award Vol. 1: 276
AFP Award for Excellence in Fund Raising Vol. 1: 5160
AFPC/Bristol-Myers Squibb Award for Excellence in Education Vol. 1: 5940
AFRES Outstanding Unit Award Vol. 1: 277
Africa Prize for Leadership for the Sustainable End of Hunger Vol. 1: 9536
African-American Culture and Philosophy Award Vol. 1: 15470
African Guest Researchers' Scholarship Vol. 2: 4608
AFT Scholarship Vol. 1: 168
AFUD Research Scholars Vol. 1: 4399
AFUW-SA Inc. Trust Fund Bursary Vol. 2: 185
Aga Khan Award for Architecture Vol. 2: 4695
AGA Student Summer Research Fellowships Vol. 1: 8836
Agan Award; Tessie Vol. 1: 1133
Agassiz Medal; Alexander Vol. 1: 12143
Agatha Awards Vol. 1: 11485
AGC/GVS Fellowship Vol. 2: 6701
AGC/IAATI Award Vol. 1: 10046
AGCO National Student Design Competition Vol. 1: 3842
Age d'Or Prize Vol. 2: 1083
Agell Award for Excellence in Research; Gladys Vol. 1: 826
Agency Award for Excellence Vol. 1: 10560
Agency Awards Vol. 1: 9142
Agency of the Year Award Vol. 1: 12478
Aggiornamento Award Vol. 1: 7156
AGHE Award Vol. 1: 4889
Agility Award Vol. 1: 14420
AGIR's Prize Vol. 2: 4384
AGO/ECS Publishing Award in Choral Composition Vol. 1: 2144
AGO Scholarships Vol. 1: 2145
Agopoff Award; Agop Vol. 1: 12096
Agopoff Memorial Prize; Agop Vol. 1: 13690
AGPA Fellowship Vol. 1: 2133
Agribrands/Purina Technician of the Year Award Vol. 1: 6203
Agricola Denkmuenze; Georg Vol. 2: 2233
Agricola-Medaille; Georg- Vol. 2: 2085
Agricultural Bioprocess Laboratory Awards Vol. 1: 18290
Agricultural Engineering Award
  Institution of Engineers Australia/Engineers Australia Vol. 2: 486
  Society for Engineering in Agriculture Vol 2: 665
Agricultural Expressions Contest Consumer Award Vol. 1: 13952
Agricultural Expressions Contest Member Award Vol. 1: 13953
Agricultural Expressions Contest Youth Award Vol. 1: 13954
Agricultural Hall of Fame Vol. 1: 12223
Agricultural Initiative Award Vol. 1: 14026
Agricultural Institute of Canada Fellowship Vol. 1: 244
Agricultural Leadership Award Vol. 1: 14027
Agricultural Stewardship Award Vol. 1: 14023
Agrinaut Award Vol. 1: 12213
Agritechnology, Life Sciences and Biotechnology Exporter of the Year Vol. 2: 3808
Agronomic Extension Education Award Vol. 1: 3867
Agronomic Industry Award Vol. 1: 3868
Agronomic Resident Education Award Vol. 1: 3869
Agronomic Service Award Vol. 1: 3870
AGS Award for Outstanding Contributions to Gravestone Studies Vol. 1: 4891
Agusta Community Service Award Vol. 1: 9361
Agway Inc. Young Scientist Award
  American Dairy Science Association Vol. 1: 1868
  American Dairy Science Association Vol 1: 1873
AHS/Merck US Human Health Migraine and Women's Health Research Award Vol. 1: 2162
Ahwash Literary Award; K.M. Vol. 1: 11326
AIA/ACSA Award for Architectural Education Vol. 1: 2424
AIA/ACSA Topaz Medallion Vol. 1: 5100
AIA/ACSA Topaz Medallion for Excellence in Architectural Education Vol. 1: 2424
AIA/ALA Library Buildings Award Vol. 1: 2425
AIAA Foundation International Student Conference Awards Vol. 1: 2361
AIANYS Educator Award Vol. 1: 14159
AIANYS Student Award Vol. 1: 14160
AIAS/ACSA New Faculty Teaching Award
  Association of Collegiate Schools of Architecture Vol. 1: 5100
  Association of Collegiate Schools of Architecture Vol 1: 5104
AIASA Recognition Awards Vol. 1: 17427
AIB Best Paper Award Vol. 1: 101
AIBS Distinguished Scientist Award Vol. 1: 2451
AICP National Historic Planning Landmarks and Pioneers Awards Vol. 1: 3198
AICP Student Project and Outstanding Student Awards Vol. 1: 3199
AICPA Business Valuation Volunteer of the Year Award Vol. 1: 2456
Aid to Advertising Education Award
  American Advertising Federation Vol. 1: 767
  American Advertising Federation Vol 1: 767
Aide a la diffusion de films de qualite en Belgique Vol. 2: 1084
AIGA Design Leadership Award Vol. 1: 2517
AIGA Medal Vol. 1: 2516
AIIE Award for Excellence in Productivity Improvement Vol. 1: 9858
AIIM Company of Fellows Vol. 1: 253
Aikat Oration Award; Professor B. K. Vol. 2: 2595
Aikenhead Memorial Choral Scholarship; Roy Vol. 1: 15850
Aim Quarterly Magazine Short Story Award Vol. 1: 262
Aine; Prix Dupin Vol. 2: 1631
AINSE Awards Vol. 2: 248
AINSE Gold Medal Vol. 2: 249
AINSE Post Graduate Research Awards Vol. 2: 250
Ainsworth/Troester Founder's Award Vol. 1: 10348
AIPEA Medals Vol. 2: 897
AIPS Awards Vol. 2: 2510
Air Breathing Propulsion Award Vol. 1: 2362
Air Force Academy Award Vol. 1: 315
Air Force Association AFLC Logistics Executive Management Award Vol. 1: 274
Air Force Association AFLC Logistics Junior Management Awards Vol. 1: 275
Air Force Association AFLC Logistics Middle Management Award Vol. 1: 276
Air Force Association AFSC Distinguished Award for Management Vol. 1: 274
Air Force Association AFSC Junior Management Award Vol. 1: 275
Air Force Association AFSC Management Awards Vol. 1: 276
Air Force Cross Vol. 2: 5589
Air Force Institute of Technology Award Vol. 1: 316
Air Force ROTC Scholarship Vol. 1: 317
Air Force Test and Evaluation Team of the Year Award Vol. 1: 278
Air League Challenge Trophy Vol. 2: 5010
Air League Founders' Medal Vol. 2: 5011
Air League Gold Medal Vol. 2: 5012
Air Medal Vol. 2: 720
Air National Guard Unit Award Vol. 1: 279
Air Reserve Forces Meritorious Service Medal - Air Force Vol. 1: 8092
Air Service Training Blind Flying Trophy Vol. 2: 3845
Air Sport Medal Vol. 2: 4718
Air Traffic Control Specialist of the Year Award Vol. 1: 327
Air Transport World Awards Vol. 1: 341
Air War College Research and Writing Award Vol. 1: 318
Aircraft Design Award Vol. 1: 2363
Airline of the Year Vol. 1: 341
Airline Technology Achievement Award Vol. 1: 341
Airman of the Year Award Vol. 1: 8775
Airmanship Award Vol. 1: 2017
Airone Vol. 2: 3086
Airport Safety Award Vol. 1: 8720
Airway Facilities Technician of the Year Vol. 1: 328
Airway Transportation Systems Specialist of the Year Vol. 1: 328
Airways Corporation Trophy Vol. 2: 3837
Airwork Cup Vol. 2: 3838
Aisenstadt Prize; Andre Vol. 1: 11618
Aitken Award; Bryan Vol. 2: 3805
Aitken Memorial Award; Irene Vol. 2: 4249
Aiya Memorial Award; IETE-Prof. S.V.C. Vol. 2: 2764
Aizstrauts Team Sportsmanship Award; Arnie Vol. 1: 472
AJL Scholarship for Library School Students Vol. 1: 5206
Akashvani Annual Awards Vol. 2: 2537
Akashvani Annual Awards for Technical Excellence Vol. 2: 2538
Akermarks Stipendium; Carl Vol. 2: 4646
Akiyama Prize Vol. 2: 3197
AL and NL Baseball Player Comeback of the Year Vol. 1: 17162
AL and NL Comeback Players of the Year Vol. 1: 17162
AL and NL Manager of the Year Vol. 1: 17163
AL and NL Pitchers of the Year Vol. 1: 17164
AL and NL Rookie Pitchers of the Year Vol. 1: 17165

ALA/Information Today Library of the Future Award Vol. 1: 2649
ALA Library Buildings Award; AIA/ Vol. 1: 2425
ALA/Mecklermedia Library of the Future Award Vol. 1: 2649
Alabama Authors Award Vol. 1: 351
Alabama Sportswriters Hall of Fame Vol. 1: 10526
Alabama State Poetry Society Award Vol. 1: 13140
Alaska Cup Award Vol. 1: 18081
Alastair Heron Prize Vol. 2: 327
Alaux; Fondation Jean-Paul Vol. 2: 1482
Albano Memorial Award; John Vol. 1: 18592
Albers Industry Relations Award; William H. Vol. 1: 8787
Albert Award; Henry J. Vol. 1: 10553
Albert Hourani Book Award Competition Vol. 1: 11749
Albert Lectureship; Adrien Vol. 2: 6947
Albert Medal Vol. 2: 6919
Alberta Book Awards
Book Publishers Association of Alberta Vol. 1: 5836
Book Publishers Association of Alberta Vol 1: 5837
Book Publishers Association of Alberta Vol 1: 5838
Book Publishers Association of Alberta Vol 1: 5839
Book Publishers Association of Alberta Vol 1: 5840
Book Publishers Association of Alberta Vol 1: 5841
Book Publishers Association of Alberta Vol 1: 5842
Writers Guild of Alberta Vol 1: 19006
Alberta Book Design Awards Vol. 1: 5836
Alberta Emerging Publisher of the Year Vol. 1: 5837
Alberta Film and Television Awards Vol. 1: 372
Alberta Publisher of the Year Award Vol. 1: 5838
Alberto Olivares' Foundation Award; Juan Vol. 2: 7422
Alberts Award for Excellence in Science Education; Bruce Vol. 1: 3585
Albion Book Prize Vol. 1: 14283
Albrand Award for First Nonfiction; Martha Vol. 1: 14889
Albrand Award for the Art of the Memoir; Martha Vol. 1: 14890
Albright Award; Fuller Vol. 1: 3574
Albritton, Jr. Award; Claude C. Vol. 1: 9760
Album of the Year Vol. 1: 10270
Alcan Jazz Prize Vol. 1: 8683
Alcan Lecture Award Vol. 1: 6898
Alcan-Pechiney; Prix Vol. 2: 1539
Aldeburgh Poetry Festival Vol. 2: 5018
Aldrich Award; C. Anderson Vol. 1: 678
Aldrich Service Award; Robert B. Vol. 1: 8214
ALEA III International Composition Prize Vol. 1: 5866
Aleph Emblem Vol. 1: 13391
Alex Awards Vol. 1: 19080
Alex Pitcher Award Vol. 2: 5271
Alexander Award; J. Allen Vol. 1: 3529
Alexander Medal; G.N. Vol. 2: 487
Alexander Prize Vol. 2: 6777
Alexander, Sr., NAACP State Conference President's Award; Kelly M. Vol. 1: 12366
Alexander Service Award; Mary Vol. 1: 7322
Alexander the Great Award Vol. 2: 2466
Alexopoulos Prize; C. J. Vol. 1: 12045
Alfa Laval Agri Dairy Extension Award
American Dairy Science Association Vol. 1: 1869
American Dairy Science Association Vol 1: 1875
Alfano in Colorectal Surgery; Dr. Blaise F. Vol. 1: 3838
Alfond Scholar-Athlete Award; Harold Vol. 1: 13215
Alfred N. Goldsmith Award Vol. 1: 9592
Alger Awards; Horatio Vol. 1: 9480
Algood Scholarship; Emma and Meloid Vol. 1: 12416
Algren Awards for Short Fiction; Nelson Vol. 1: 7333
Alice Award
National Woman's Party Vol. 1: 13916
Society of Women Writers, Victoria Branch Vol 2: 670
Alice H. Hayden Fellowship Vol. 1: 17398
Alice Hamilton Prize Vol. 1: 3698
Alice Paul Award Vol. 1: 13916
ALISE Award for Professional Contribution to Library and Information Science Education Vol. 1: 4906
Alison Award; John R. Vol. 1: 280
All-America Awards
National Association of Intercollegiate Athletics Vol. 1: 12574
National Soccer Coaches Association of America Vol 1: 13708
All-America Basketball Team Vol. 1: 17166
All-America City Awards Vol. 1: 12898
All-America Football Team Vol. 1: 17167
All-America Honors (Men) Vol. 1: 17900
All-America Honors (Women) Vol. 1: 17901
All-America Racing Team Vol. 1: 1369
All-America Rose Selections Annual Winners Vol. 1: 392
All-America Rose Selections Certificate of Merit Vol. 1: 393
All-America Scholar-Athlete Awards Vol. 1: 12575
All-America Team
Football Writers Association of America Vol. 1: 8797
Intercollegiate Tennis Association Vol 1: 9997
All-America Teams Vol. 1: 2043
All-American Association Award Vol. 1: 473
All-American Award Vol. 1: 520
All American Awards Vol. 1: 12909
All-American Awards Vol. 1: 13401
All American Dive Team Vol. 1: 17665
All American Hall of Fame Vol. 1: 13661
All-American Soap Box Derby Vol. 1: 10635
All-Around Amateur Golden Horse Vol. 1: 14819
All-Around Cowboy Vol. 1: 15356
All-Around Golden Horse Award Vol. 1: 14820
All Around NAMAR Mustang Vol. 1: 14311
All Breed Master Judge Vol. 1: 13541
All-Breeds Awards Vol. 1: 17885
All-Canadian Awards Vol. 1: 6407
All-Defensive Team Vol. 1: 12754
All-Industry Awards Vol. 1: 11495
All-NBA Team Vol. 1: 12755
All Poets Award Vol. 1: 13141
All Sonatina, All Sonata, All Bach Programs Vol. 1: 1679
All Sport Insurance Marketing Ltd. Volunteer of the Year Award Vol. 1: 17156
All-Star Community Awards Vol. 1: 10877
All-Star Game Most Valuable Player Vol. 1: 7795
All-Tournament Teams/Outstanding Athlete Award Vol. 1: 12576
All-World Awards Vol. 1: 10755
Allain Intellectual Freedom Award; Alex P. Vol. 1: 11418
Allan Award; William Vol. 1: 4074
Allard Silver Medal; Peter Vol. 2: 6629
Allderdice Jr. Memorial Award; Charles E. Vol. 1: 7782
Allee Award; Warder Clyde Vol. 1: 4529
Allegro Award Vol. 1: 15366
Allen Award; Alfred Vol. 1: 4856
Allen Award; Alfred W. Vol. 1: 1466
Allen Award; Arthur A. Vol. 1: 7823
Allen Award for Scholarhip and Service; TESOL Virginia French Vol. 1: 17417
Allen Award; Helen Vol. 1: 163
Allen Award; Lee Vol. 1: 16167
Allen Award; Ruth Vol. 1: 3186
Allen Awards; Gracie Vol. 1: 8850
Allen Bott Creative Excellence Award; Patricia Vol. 1: 16543
Allen Leadership and Achievement Award; George Vol. 1: 17566
Allen Memorial Cup; D.M. Vol. 2: 3839
Allen Most Valuable Member Award; Clifford B. Vol. 1: 10125
Allen Prize; Cath Vol. 2: 5611
Allen Prize; David Vol. 2: 63
Allen Prize; Derek Vol. 2: 5202
Allen Scholarship; Dr. J. Frances Vol. 1: 2026
Allen Service Award; Mel Vol. 1: 4302
Allendoerfer Awards; Carl B. Vol. 1: 11601
Allentown Leadership Award Vol. 1: 6204
Allentown Talking Poster Award Vol. 1: 6205
Allhands Student Essay Competition; James L. Vol. 1: 234
Alliance Award
American Alliance for Theatre and Education Vol. 1: 801
American Alliance for Theatre and Education Vol 1: 801
Alliance of Plastics Processors Annual Recognition Vol. 1: 16859
Alliance of Plastics Processors Awards Vol. 1: 16860
Allianz Cornhill Musical Insurance Conducting Prize Vol. 2: 6461
Allianz Cornhill Musical Insurance Youth Orchestra Awards Vol. 2: 6462
Allied Arts Medal Vol. 1: 15728
Allied Industry Individual Award Vol. 1: 12214
Allied Member Award Vol. 1: 4254
Allied Signal Award for Research on Aging Vol. 1: 9469
Allied-Signal Awards Vol. 1: 2547
AlliedSignal Outstanding Student Branch Award Vol. 1: 16585
Allin Prize; Russell Vol. 2: 6102
Allis Prize for Study of Ionized Gases; Will Vol. 1: 3107
Allison Award; American Center for Children's Television - Fran Vol. 1: 1463
Allison City of Sydney Piano Scholarship; John Vol. 2: 687
Allport Intergroup Relations Prize; Gordon Vol. 1: 16445

Alluisi Award; Earl A. Vol. 1: 3303
Allwork Scholarship Grants; Eleanor Vol. 1: 2441
Ally Award Vol. 1: 14597
Allyn & Bacon Psychology Awards Vol. 1: 15398
Aloha Aina Awards Vol. 1: 9471
Alouette Award Vol. 1: 6168
Alpenlandischer Volksmusikwettbewerb Vol. 2: 746
Alpha Awards Vol. 1: 1464
Alpha Chi Sigma Award in Pure Chemistry Vol. 1: 416
Alpha Chi Sigma Scholarship Vol. 1: 417
Alpha Kappa Psi Award Vol. 1: 2721
Alpha Omega Alpha Distinguished Teacher Awards Vol. 1: 423
Alpha Omega Alpha Student Essay Award Vol. 1: 424
Alpha Sigma Nu National Jesuit Book Award Vol. 1: 5202
Alpharma Award of Excellence Vol. 1: 1023
Alpinale International Film Festival Vol. 2: 741
Alpine Club of Canada Award for Best Film on Climbing Vol. 1: 5651
Alpine World Cup Champions Vol. 2: 4836
ALS Medal for Excellence Vol. 1: 2702
ALS Service of the Year Award Vol. 1: 12517
ALSA/Econo-Clad Award for Outstanding Young Adult Reading or Literature Program Vol. 1: 19085
ALSC/Econo-Clad Literature Program Award Vol. 1: 4930
Alsobrook Industrial Minerals Distinguished Service Award; A. Frank Vol. 1: 16341
Alsop Award Vol. 1: 2630
Alston Award; Ralph E. Vol. 1: 5868
Alston Canine Award; The Alison Vol. 2: 6740
ALTA/Gale Outstanding Trustee Conference Grant Vol. 1: 4934
ALTA Outstanding Translations of the Year Vol. 1: 2704
Alter Cup; National Multihull Championship - Vol. 1: 18066
Alternative Nobel Prize Vol. 2: 4619
Altieri Outstanding Coach Award Vol. 1: 13220
Altman (Figure) Prize; Benjamin Vol. 1: 12097
Altman (Landscape) Prize; Benjamin Vol. 1: 12098
Alumae Medal; Nikolai Vol. 2: 1347
Alumni Achievement Award Vol. 1: 571
Alumni Achievement Awards Vol. 1: 7169
Alumni Career Achievement Award Vol. 1: 7532
Alumni Medal Vol. 1: 18258
Alumni PRN Grant Vol. 1: 430
Alumni/Professional Coordinator of the Year Vol. 1: 12788
Alumni Scholarship Vol. 1: 14630
Alumni Service Award Vol. 1: 452
Alumni Service Citations Vol. 1: 18259
Alumni Service Medal Vol. 1: 18260
Alumni Volunteer Leadership Award Vol. 1: 7533
Alumnus-of-the-Decade Vol. 1: 7820
Alumnus of the Year Vol. 1: 7820
Alumnus of the Year Award Vol. 1: 15783
Alumnus or Alumna of the Year Award Vol. 1: 170
Alvarez Memorial Award; Walter C. Vol. 1: 2767
Alzheimer Obelisk Vol. 2: 817
AMA/Irwin/McGraw-Hill Distinguished Marketing Educator Award Vol. 1: 2715
AMADE-UNESCO Prize Vol. 2: 3469
Amadeus Prize Vol. 2: 6407
Amado Foundation Award; Maurice Vol. 1: 10983
Amadon Grant; Dean Vol. 1: 15556
Amanda Award for Cinematographic Merit Vol. 2: 3906
Amanda Film - OG Fjernsynspris Vol. 2: 3906
AMAS Scholarship Vol. 1: 4683
Amateur Achievement Award Vol. 1: 5480
Amateur Astronomers Medal Vol. 1: 461
Amateur Athletic Fund Vol. 1: 17380
Amateur Bowler of the Year Vol. 1: 5892
Amateur Cartoonist Extraordinaire Award Vol. 1: 12849
Amateur Division Golden Horse Vol. 1: 14819
Amateur Photo Challenge Vol. 1: 15249
Amateur Wine Competition Awards Vol. 1: 4481
Ambassador Vol. 1: 2009
Ambassador Award
American Council of the Blind Vol. 1: 1819
Federation of Fly Fishers Vol 1: 8631
International League Against Epilepsy Vol 2: 919
Ambassador Award of Hospitality Vol. 1: 13635
Ambassador Book Awards Vol. 1: 8470
Ambassador for Epilepsy Award Vol. 2: 2843
Ambassador of Honor Book Awards Vol. 1: 8470
Ambassador of Hospitality Award Vol. 1: 13635
Ambassador of the Year Vol. 1: 9154
Ambedkar Centenary Award for Excellence in Biomedical Research; Dr. B. R. Vol. 2: 2596
Ambulance Service Medal Vol. 2: 200
AmCham Annual Awards Vol. 2: 2485
Ameghino; Premio Florentino Vol. 2: 15
Amelia Frances Howard-Gibbon Illustrator's Award Vol. 1: 6699
Amerbach-Preis Vol. 2: 4911
America: History and Life Award; ABC-CLIO Vol. 1: 14686
American Academy of Periodontology Student Award Vol. 1: 722
American Academy of Psychiatry and the Law Vol. 1: 3272
American Accounting Association Vol. 1: 8148
American and National League Managers of the Year Vol. 1: 17168
American and National League Relief Pitcher of the Year Vol. 1: 17169
American Architecture Awards Vol. 1: 7319
American Association of Cat Enthusiasts Annual Awards Vol. 1: 1030
American Association of Community Theatre Festival Award Vol. 1: 1059
American Association of University Women Award in Juvenile Literature Vol. 1: 14368
American Bible Society Award Vol. 1: 1397
American Book Awards Vol. 1: 5705
American Cancer Society Eleanor Roosevelt International Cancer Fellowships Vol. 2: 4856
American Cancer Society International Cancer Research Fellowships Vol. 2: 4856
American Center for Children's Television - Fran Allison Award Vol. 1: 1463
American Children's Television Festival - Fran Allison Award Vol. 1: 1463
American College of Critical Care Medicine Distinguished Investigator Award Vol. 1: 16634
American College of Legal Medicine Foundation Vol. 1: 7208
American College of Physicians Award Vol. 1: 1708
American College of Surgeons Faculty Fellowship Vol. 1: 1735
American College Theatre Festival Vol. 1: 11113
American Council of Learned Societies Fellowships Vol. 1: 1813
American Craft Council Fellows Vol. 1: 1850
American Craft Council Honorary Fellow Vol. 1: 1850
American Crossword Puzzle Champion Vol. 1: 1854
American Culinary Classic Vol. 1: 13631
American Cured Meat Championship Awards Vol. 1: 1152
American Eagle Award Vol. 1: 13471
American Education Award Vol. 1: 1266
American Egg Board Research Award Vol. 1: 15176
American Eurocopter Golden Hour Award Vol. 1: 9362
American Exemplar Medal Vol. 1: 8878
American Express Tribute Vol. 1: 18610
American Family Therapy Academy Awards Vol. 1: 1989
American Family Therapy Association Awards Vol. 1: 1989
American Feed Industry Association Award
American Dairy Science Association Vol. 1: 1870
American Feed Industry Association Vol 1: 2007
American Feed Industry Association Award in Ruminant Nutrition Research Vol. 1: 3879
American Feed Manufacturers Association Award Vol. 1: 1870
American Fellowships Vol. 1: 1327
American Friendship Medal Vol. 1: 8878
American Graphic Design Awards Vol. 1: 9178
American Head and Neck Society Vol. 1: 1738
American Hiking Society Award Vol. 1: 2216
American Historical Print Collectors Society Fellowship Vol. 1: 819
American Independent Award Vol. 1: 15958
American Indian Education Fund Vol. 1: 2329
American Indian Festival of Words Author Award Vol. 1: 17625
American International Film/Video Festival Vol. 1: 2809
American Iron and Steel Institute Medal Vol. 1: 2577
American Jazz Masters Fellowship Awards Vol. 1: 13103
American Kennel Club Career Achievement Award in Canine Research Vol. 1: 4403
American Kennel Club Excellence in Research Awards Vol. 1: 4404
American Laryngological Association Award Vol. 1: 2617

American League All-Star Team Vol. 1: 17170
American League Most Valuable Player Vol. 1: 5681
American League Rookie of the Year Vol. 1: 17171
American Legion Mercury Award Vol. 1: 2635
American Liberties Medallion Vol. 1: 2584
American Library Association Literary Awards; Black Caucus of the Vol. 1: 5795
American Mineralogist Undergraduate Award Vol. 1: 11794
American Music Awards Vol. 1: 2834
American Occupational Therapy Foundation Awards Vol. 1: 2962
American Patriots Medal Vol. 1: 8878
American Pharmacists Association Fellow Vol. 1: 3040
American Poultry Historical Society Award Vol. 1: 15177
American Preparedness Award Vol. 1: 1596
American Romanian Academy Awards Vol. 1: 3507
American Society for Eighteenth-Century Studies Fellowship Vol. 1: 819
American Society of Cytology Award for Meritorious Achievement in Cytology Vol. 1: 4018
American Society of Mammalogists Fellowship Vol. 1: 4116
American Society of Pharmacognosy Awards and Grants Vol. 1: 4213
American Society of Safety Engineers Fellow Vol. 1: 4231
American Spirit Award Vol. 1: 13638
American Stars Awards Vol. 1: 536
American Statesman Medal Vol. 1: 8878
American Therapeutic Recreation Association Awards Vol. 1: 4356
American Veterinary Medical Association Explorer Award Vol. 1: 5905
Americanism Award Vol. 1: 2639
Americanism Awards Vol. 1: 4518
Americas 2000: All Media Competition Vol. 1: 11849
Americas 2000: Paper Works Competition Vol. 1: 11850
Americas Book Award for Children's and Young Adult Literature Vol. 1: 7216
America's Cup Vol. 1: 4504
America's Democratic Legacy Award Vol. 1: 4542
AmericaFs Favorite Recipe Award Vol. 1: 8994
America's Junior Miss Vol. 1: 4508
America's Old-Time Country Music Hall of Fame Vol. 1: 13866
America's Old-Time Fiddler's Hall of Fame Vol. 1: 13867
America's Ten Outstanding Young Men Vol. 1: 17983
America's Young Woman of the Year Vol. 1: 4508
AmeriStar Package Awards Vol. 1: 9926
Ames Histology Award Vol. 2: 4253
Amgen Award Vol. 1: 3562
Amgen Outstanding Investigator Award Vol. 1: 3752
Amiens International Film Festival Vol. 2: 1710
Amir Chand Prize; Basanti Devi Vol. 2: 2597
Amir Chand Prizes; Shakuntala Vol. 2: 2598
Amirikian Memorial Maritime Welding Award; Arsham Vol. 1: 4451
Amirikian Welding Scholarship; Arsham Vol. 1: 4451
AMMA Journal Editor's Prize Vol. 2: 286
Ammann Research Fellowship in Structural Engineering; O. H. Vol. 1: 17304
Amoroso Award Vol. 2: 5465
Amory Prize; Francis Vol. 1: 550
Amos Award Vol. 1: 13475
AMS 50 Fellowships Vol. 1: 2845
AMSA International Piano Competition Vol. 1: 18965
Amsterdam Prize for Art Vol. 2: 3651
Amsterdam Prize for History Vol. 2: 3654
Amsterdam Prize for Medicine Vol. 2: 3655
Amsterdam Prize for the Environment Vol. 2: 3653
Amstutz-Williams Award Vol. 1: 1024
Amtmann Fellowship; Bernard Vol. 1: 5747
AMT's Outstanding Medical Assistant Students Vol. 1: 2755
Amundson Student Presentation Award; Terry Vol. 1: 18749
AMY Awards Vol. 1: 19091
Amy Writing Awards Vol. 1: 4521
ANAD Award Vol. 1: 12381
Anand Endowment Lecture; Dr. Nitya Vol. 2: 2671
The Ancient Greek Cities Award Vol. 2: 2467
Anda Audience Prize; Geza Vol. 2: 4761
Anda International Piano Competition; Geza Vol. 2: 4761
Anders-Bording Prisen Vol. 2: 1280
Andersen Memorial Award; William C.
American Urological Association Vol. 1: 4386
Raptor Research Foundation Vol 1: 15557
Anderson Award; Arthur R. Vol. 1: 1748
Anderson Award; Elda E. Vol. 1: 9304
Anderson Award; F. Paul Vol. 1: 4044
Anderson Award; H. C. L. Vol. 2: 269
Anderson Award; Harlan J. Vol. 1: 5402
Anderson Award; Kathleen S. Vol. 1: 11493
Anderson Award; Mayer Vol. 1: 15816
Anderson Award of Merit; Inge Vol. 1: 6450
Anderson Award; William G. Vol. 1: 782
Anderson-Berry Medal; David Vol. 2: 6987
Anderson Emerson Scholarship; Gladys Vol. 1: 10861
Anderson-Everett Award Vol. 1: 10086
Anderson Lectureship on World Food Security; Glenn Vol. 1: 6812
Anderson Lifetime Achievement Award; Eric Vol. 1: 14215
Anderson Memorial Intermediate Woodwind Scholarship; Mary Vol. 1: 15851
Anderson Memorial Senior Woodwind Scholarship; Mary Vol. 1: 15852
Anderson Prize for Violin; Emily Vol. 2: 6859
Anderson Publishing Outstanding Paper Award; William L. Simon/ Vol. 1: 90
Anderson Publishing Outstanding Student Paper Award; William L. Simon/ Vol. 1: 91
Anderson Sr. Micrographics Awards; Thomas P. Vol. 1: 254
Anderson Silver Medal; Sir Rowand Vol. 2: 6815
Anderson Trophy; Samuel E. Vol. 1: 4646
Anderson Vocal Arts Competition; Marian Vol. 1: 16094
Andes National Award; Ammon S. Vol. 1: 16033
Andrea Prader Prize Vol. 2: 5861
Andrew Mentor Award; Maureen Vol. 1: 16369
Andrews Award for Excellence in Baseball Sports Medicine; James R. Vol. 1: 4300
Andrews Bibliographical Award; Joseph L. Vol. 1: 1140
Andrews/Committee D-2 Scroll of Achievement; Syndey D. Vol. 1: 5403
Andritz Oy Award Vol. 2: 1393
Andry Award; Nicolas Vol. 1: 5049
ANDY Awards Vol. 1: 180
ANDY Awards; International Vol. 1: 10036
Angel Escobar Prizes; Alejandro Vol. 2: 1193
Angeli Contest; Marguerite de Vol. 1: 8139
Angell Comedy Fellowship Vol. 1: 9532
Angell Humanitarian Award; The David Vol. 1: 3532
Angus Award Vol. 2: 3729
Angus Medal; Robert W. Vol. 1: 6949
Anhinga Prize for Poetry Vol. 1: 4527
Aniara Priset Vol. 2: 4685
Aniara Prize Vol. 2: 4685
Animal Behavior Society Best Student Paper Award Vol. 1: 4529
Animal Control Employee of the Year Vol. 1: 12241
Animal Growth and Development Award Vol. 1: 3880
Animal Industry Service Award Vol. 1: 3881
Animal Management Award Vol. 1: 3882
Animal Physiology and Endocrinology Award Vol. 1: 3883
Animal Rights Hall of Fame Vol. 1: 8590
Animal Welfare Award
American Veterinary Medical Association Vol. 1: 4405
Animal Transportation Association - European Office Vol 2: 5052
Animated Eye Award Vol. 1: 4713
Anisfield-Wolf Book Award in Race Relations Vol. 1: 7472
Anisfield-Wolf Book Awards Vol. 1: 7472
Annecy Festival Prizes Vol. 2: 1870
Annecy International Animated Film Festival Vol. 2: 1870
Annett Award for Children's Literature; R. Ross Vol. 1: 19006
Annie Award for Best Animated Feature Vol. 1: 10038
Annie Award for Best Animated Television Commercial Vol. 1: 10039
Annie Award for Best Animated Television Production Vol. 1: 10040
Annie Award for Outstanding Individual Achievement Vol. 1: 10041
Annie Awards Vol. 1: 10044
Annin Award; Douglas H. Vol. 1: 10905
Anniversary of National Service 1951-1972 Medal Vol. 2: 201
Annual Achievement Award Vol. 1: 4867
Annual Achievement Awards Vol. 1: 3548
Annual Art Competition
The Artist's Magazine Vol. 1: 4673
Associates of Brand Library and Art Center Vol 1: 4775
Annual Art Competition and Exhibition Vol. 1: 17324
Annual Art Exhibition Vol. 1: 9184
Annual Award Vol. 1: 1896
Annual Award for Junior Researchers Vol. 2: 1236
Annual Award for Popularization and Promotion of Science Vol. 2: 1237

Award Index

Annual Awards
Asian Football Confederation Vol. 2: 3403
Guild of Television Cameramen Vol 2: 5961
Annual Awards Competition Vol. 1: 7875
Annual Awards Exhibitions Vol. 1: 4648
Annual Boat Writing Contest Vol. 1: 5830
Annual Central Prize Award and Certificate of Merit Award Vol. 1: 7248
Annual Championship Prizes Vol. 1: 8675
Annual Design Review Vol. 1: 9553
Annual Dissertation Award Vol. 1: 6887
Annual Distinction Award Vol. 1: 10094
Annual Essay Contest Vol. 1: 8262
Annual Exhibition
Allied Artists of America Vol. 1: 414
National Watercolor Society Vol 1: 13892
Royal Scottish Academy Vol 2: 6885
Annual Exhibition Awards
Audubon Artists Vol. 1: 5528
National Association of Women Artists Vol 1: 12715
National Sculpture Society Vol 1: 13690
Society of Illustrators Vol 1: 16702
Annual Gold Leaf Awards Vol. 1: 6141
Annual International Competition Vol. 1: 15231
Annual JOHS Paper Award Vol. 1: 10669
Annual Manuscript Award Vol. 1: 5719
Annual Medal Design Award Vol. 1: 2580
Annual Meeting Best Paper Award Vol. 1: 18369
Annual Meeting Competitive Paper Awards Vol. 1: 8695
Annual National Art Exhibition Vol. 1: 3159
Annual News Award Vol. 1: 10593
Annual One Act Play Festival Award Vol. 2: 3805
Annual Open Exhibition Vol. 1: 4653
Annual Open Juried Exhibition
Pastel Society of America Vol. 1: 14869
Pastel Society of America Vol 1: 14871
Annual Political Book Award Vol. 1: 18603
Annual Prize Vol. 1: 16479
Annual Prize for Scientific Works Vol. 2: 7426
Annual Report Awards Vol. 2: 3726
Annual Report Contest Award of Excellence Vol. 1: 3437
Annual School and College Publications Contest Vol. 1: 13666
Annual Science Award
European Chemical Industry Council Vol. 2: 861
Republic of Croatia Ministry of Science, Education and Sports Vol 2: 1238
Annual Tour Scholarship Vol. 1: 16558
Annual Writing Competition Vol. 1: 8244
Anonymous Prize Vol. 1: 12099
ANPA Foundation - Associated Collegiate Press Pacemakers Awards Vol. 1: 14221
ANPA Foundation - Newspaper in Education Program Excellence Award Vol. 1: 14223
Ansell Distinguished Service Award; John Vol. 1: 5953
Anson Award; Jack L. Vol. 1: 5152
Ansorge Award Vol. 2: 5028
Antarctica Service Medal Vol. 1: 8093
Anthem Essay Contest Vol. 1: 5612
Anthony Award; Susan B. Vol. 1: 19117
Anthony Memorial Award; Dennis Vol. 2: 3399
Anthropology in Media Award Vol. 1: 812
Anti-Slavery Award Vol. 2: 5057
Antonov Aeromodelling Diploma Vol. 2: 4719
Antwoorden Prijsvragen, Klasse der Letteren Vol. 2: 1059
Antwoorden Prijsvragen, Klasse der Schone Kunsten Vol. 2: 1060
Antwoorden Prijsvragen, Klasse der Wetenschappen Vol. 2: 1061
Anuvrat Award for International Peace Vol. 2: 2540
ANZAAS Medal Vol. 2: 133
ANZIAM Medal Vol. 2: 41
AOJT Awards Vol. 1: 5276
AOP Open Vol. 2: 5151
AOS Medal Vol. 2: 313
AOTA COTA/OTR Partnership Award Vol. 1: 2952
AOTOS Mariner's Plaque Vol. 1: 17713
APA/PDC Prize for Excellence and Innovation in Philosophy Programs Vol. 1: 3082
APALA Scholarship Award Vol. 1: 4691
APCAC Award Vol. 2: 3960
APEX Award Achieving Professional Excellence in Education Administration Award Vol. 1: 1054
APEX - Awards for Publication Excellence Vol. 1: 4552
Apgar Award; Virginia Vol. 1: 679
APHA/APPM Merit Awards Vol. 1: 3041
Apker Award; Leroy Vol. 1: 3108
Aplan Award Vol. 1: 9389
Aplan Award; Frank F. Vol. 1: 2523
APO Award Vol. 2: 3167
APO National Awards Vol. 2: 3166
APO Regional Award Vol. 2: 3167
APO Special National Award Vol. 2: 3166
Apollo Award
American Optometric Association Vol. 1: 2974
Arnold Air Society Vol 1: 4646
APON Distinguished Researcher Award Vol. 1: 5279
APON Excellence in Pediatric Oncology Nursing Practice Award Vol. 1: 5280
APON Local Chapter Community Service Award Vol. 1: 5281
APON Local Chapter Excellence Award Vol. 1: 5282
Apotex Award Vol. 1: 6993
Appalachian Ohio Peace Prize Vol. 1: 4556
Appeal of Conscience Award Vol. 1: 4564
Appel-Denkmunze; Inhaber de Otto- Vol. 2: 2212
Appert Award; Nicholas Vol. 1: 9845
Applause Award Vol. 1: 18859
Applebaum Composers Award; Louis Vol. 1: 14556
Applebaum Memorial Scholarship; William Vol. 1: 8784
Appleseed Award; Johnny Vol. 1: 8963
Application Award Vol. 1: 10500
Application to Practice Award Vol. 1: 11801
Applied Consumer Economics Award Vol. 1: 1821
Applied Energy Innovation Award Vol. 1: 6586
Applied Research Award Vol. 1: 17797
Applied Research Medal Vol. 2: 615
Applied Social Issues Internship Vol. 1: 16446
Appraiser of the Year Award Vol. 1: 12568
Appreciation Award Vol. 1: 11315
Apprentice of the Year
British Printing Industries Federation Vol. 2: 5422
Polymer Machinery Manufacturers and Distributors Association Vol 2: 6548
Apprenticeship Awards Vol. 1: 17599
APRA/Australian Music Centre Classical Music Awards Vol. 2: 293
APS College of Forensic Psychologists (NSW Section) Annual Awards Vol. 2: 328
APS Colleges Award of Distinction Vol. 2: 329
APS Ethics Prize Vol. 2: 330
APS Fellow Vol. 1: 3187
APS Prize Vol. 2: 331
Apsey Playwriting Award; Ruby Lloyd Vol. 1: 18235
Apt Lectureship; Leonard Vol. 1: 680
Apuraha tai Palkinto Vol. 2: 1403
Aqua Awards Vol. 1: 10274
Aqueous Show Vol. 1: 11135
Aqueous USA Competition Vol. 1: 11135
Aquinas Medal Vol. 1: 1460
ARA Annual Award Vol. 1: 3508
ARA Hall of Fame Award Vol. 1: 5606
ARA Pacis Award (Altar of Peace) Vol. 1: 10933
Arafura Short Story Award Vol. 2: 587
Arafura Short Story Award; Dymocks Vol. 2: 589
Arango Design Award Vol. 1: 4572
Arata Award; Yoshiaki Vol. 2: 1898
Arbeitsgemeinschaft Schweizer Grafiker Competitions Vol. 2: 4905
Arbor Day Awards Vol. 1: 12253
Arboricultural Association Award Vol. 2: 5059
Arbuse Gold Medal; Gussie and Samuel Vol. 1: 14131
Arbuthnot Award Vol. 1: 10573
Arbuthnot Honor Lecture Award; May Hill Vol. 1: 4918
ARCA Championship Hall of Fame Vol. 1: 10526
Archaeological Book Award Vol. 2: 5220
Archaeological Geology Division Award Vol. 1: 9026
Archaeology of Portugal Fund Vol. 1: 4574
Archambault Prize in Physical Sciences and Mathematics; Urgel Vol. 1: 5014
Archer Award; Ellinor Vol. 2: 270
Archer Award; W. Harry Vol. 1: 1705
Archer Pioneer Award; Ellinor Vol. 2: 270
Archibald Prize Vol. 2: 47
Architectural Awards Vol. 1: 9417
Architectural Critics and Writers Award Vol. 2: 4331
Architectural Portfolio Vol. 1: 3520
Architecture Awards
Royal Institute of British Architects Vol. 2: 6821
United States Institute for Theatre Technology Vol 1: 17946
Architecture Firm Award
American Institute of Architects Vol. 1: 2426
Texas Society of Architects/ AIA Vol 1: 17499
Arctowski Medal Vol. 1: 12144
Arderne Medal; John Vol. 2: 7006
Area/Regional Impact Award Vol. 1: 13367
Arena Memorial Scholarship; John Vol. 1: 11277
Arenth Excellence in Cancer Nursing Management Award; Linda Vol. 1: 14531
Arete Best of Show Award Vol. 1: 7256
Arfvedson-Schlenk-Preis Vol. 2: 2162

Argentinean Association of Dermatology Awards Vol. 2: 21
Argyll Postal History Salver Vol. 2: 6535
Ari Medal of Merit; Carina Vol. 2: 4575
Ari Medaljen; Carina Vol. 2: 4575
Arid Lands Hydraulic Engineering Award Vol. 1: 3916
Arima Award for Applied Microbiology Vol. 2: 550
Arinos Prize; Afonso Vol. 2: 1116
Arion Prize Vol. 2: 4023
Ariste Medal; Paul Vol. 2: 1348
Arizona State Poetry Society Award Vol. 1: 13142
Arizona Young Reader's Award Vol. 1: 4602
Arlt Award in the Humanities; Gustave O. Vol. 1: 7888
Armada Dish (Biffa Trophy) Vol. 2: 5910
Armand; Prix Louis Vol. 2: 1540
Armed Forces Expeditionary Medal Vol. 1: 8094
Armed Forces Joint Warfighting Essay Contest Vol. 1: 18005
Armed Forces Reserve Medal Vol. 1: 8095
Armourers and Brasier's Award Vol. 2: 6900
Armstrong Award; Anne Vol. 2: 5065
Armstrong/Kahn Award Vol. 1: 4566
Armstrong Medal Vol. 1: 15515
Armstrong Memorial Award for Outstanding Regional Coordinator; Terry Vol. 1: 2867
Armstrong Memorial Lecture; Henry E. Vol. 2: 7156
Armstrong Memorial Research Foundation Awards Vol. 1: 4634
Armstrong Playwrights Rent Award; Gordon Vol. 1: 9196
Armwrestler of the Year Vol. 1: 823
Army Commendation Medal Vol. 2: 721
Army of Occupation Medal - Army-Air Force Vol. 1: 8096
Army Reserve Components Achievement Medal Vol. 1: 8097
Arnold Air Letter Trophy Vol. 1: 4636
Arnold Award for Excellence in Aeronautical Program Management; Hap Vol. 1: 2364
Arnold Award; H. H. Vol. 1: 281
Arnold Sabre; H. H. Vol. 1: 4636
Arnow Award; Philip Vol. 1: 17837
Arpino Award Vol. 1: 14131
Arrington Award; Leonard J. Vol. 1: 11948
Arrington-Prucha Award Vol. 1: 18680
Arrowhead Biennial Exhibition Vol. 1: 8296
Arsenault Senior Arts Award; Father Adrien Vol. 1: 15218
Art Award Vol. 1: 14135
Art Competition Vol. 1: 6460
Art Directors Awards Vol. 1: 4649
Art Directors Club of Toronto Awards and Show Presentation Vol. 1: 178
Art in the Park Awards Vol. 1: 8941
Art of Listening Award Vol. 1: 9000
Art of Reporting Award Vol. 1: 9001
Art of the Automobile Competition Vol. 1: 5558
Art of the Northeast Competition Vol. 1: 16064
Art Scholarship
  Artists Guild of the Santa Ynez Valley Vol. 1: 4671
  Royal Bath and West of England Society Vol 2: 6692
Art Show and Auction Vol. 1: 9264
Art Song Festival Vol. 1: 7736
ARTBA Awards Vol. 1: 3500
Arthroscopy Research Grants Vol. 1: 4661
Arthur A. Hitchcock Award for Distinguished Service Vol. 1: 1842
Arthur Butcher Award Vol. 2: 5272
Arthur, M.D. Award; Capt. Ransom J. Vol. 1: 17993
The Arthur Quern Quality Award Vol. 1: 15672
Article Award
  Canadian Railroad Historical Association Vol. 1: 6855
  Children's Literature Association Vol 1: 7347
  Religious Communication Association Vol 1: 15621
Article of the Year Vol. 1: 6533
Article Prize
  American Philosophical Association Vol. 1: 3083
  Law and Society Association Vol 1: 11248
Artist Achievement Award Vol. 1: 5760
Artist Award for a Distinguished Body of Work Vol. 1: 7501
Artist Awards
  Fine Arts Association of Finland Vol. 2: 1369
  National Association of Teachers of Singing Vol 1: 12692
  Society of Arts and Crafts Vol 1: 16561
Artist of the Month Vol. 2: 717
Artist of the Year
  Billboard - VNU Business Publications USA Vol. 1: 5760
  Indian Arts and Crafts Association Vol 1: 9658
  Victorian Artists Society Vol 2: 718
Artist-Teacher Award Vol. 1: 4320
Artists' Fellowships Vol. 1: 14127
Artists for Nature Foundation Award Vol. 2: 7215
Artists-in-Residence Program Vol. 1: 17310
The *Artist's Magazine Annual Painting Competition* Vol. 1: 4673
The Artist's Magazine Still Life Painting Competition Vol. 1: 4673
The Artist's Magazine/Watercolor Magic Magazine Award Vol. 1: 4428
Arts and Crafts in Architecture Award Vol. 2: 7064
Arts and Tourism Grants Program Vol. 1: 9395
Arts Breakfast of Champions Vol. 1: 14396
Arts Council of England Helen Chadwick Fellowship Vol. 2: 5436
Arts Council of Northern Ireland Bursaries and Awards Vol. 2: 5074
Arts for the Parks Competition Vol. 1: 13523
ARTS Graduate Research Award Vol. 1: 6962
Arts Recognition and Talent Search (ARTS) Vol. 1: 13254
Arvin; Truman Capote Award for Literary Criticism in Memory of Newton Vol. 1: 10871
Arvon Foundation International Poetry Competition Vol. 2: 5076
Aryabhata Medal Vol. 2: 2672
ASA African American Screenwriters Scholarship Vol. 1: 3533
The ASA Award Vol. 1: 4263
ASA Hispanic Screenwriters Scholarship Vol. 1: 3534
ASA-Metlife Foundation MindAlert Awards Vol. 1: 4264
ASA National Championships Vol. 1: 521
ASA Undergraduate Student Award Vol. 1: 4265
ASABE Fellows Vol. 1: 3843
ASABE Paper Awards Vol. 1: 3844
Asada Medal Vol. 2: 3203
ASAE Fellow Vol. 1: 3895
Asali Memorial Scholarship; Joseph W. Vol. 1: 11478
ASBC - Merck Award Vol. 1: 3563
ASBMB-Merck Award Vol. 1: 3563
ASCA Awards of Excellence Vol. 1: 4335
ASCA Coaches Hall of Fame Vol. 1: 4336
ASCAP Foundation College Musical Theatre Award Vol. 1: 11117
ASCEPT New Investigator Awards Vol. 2: 93
ASCEPT Student Travel Awards Vol. 2: 94
ASCP - CAP Joint Annual Award Vol. 1: 3602
ASEM Fellows Vol. 1: 3684
ASHA Scholarship Vol. 1: 3524
Ashe Award for Courage; Arthur Vol. 1: 8534
Ashe Award for Leadership and Sportsmanship; Arthur Vol. 1: 9998
Ashford Medal; Bailey K. Vol. 1: 4259
Ashley Award; Larry Vol. 1: 6314
Ashoka Chakra Vol. 2: 2575
ASHRAE - Alco Medal for Distinguished Public Service Vol. 1: 4045
ASHRAE ASHAE - Homer Addams Award Vol. 1: 4043
ASHRAE Energy Awards Vol. 1: 4066
ASHRAE Fellow Vol. 1: 4046
ASHRAE Journal Paper Award Vol. 1: 4047
Asia-Pacific Cancer Society Training Grants (APCASOT) Vol. 2: 4857
Asian American Literary Awards Vol. 1: 4689
Asian/Asian-American Award Vol. 1: 3289
Asian Banking Awards Vol. 2: 3964
ASID Human Environment Award Vol. 1: 4084
ASIFA Special Award Vol. 2: 1227
ASJA Outstanding Author Award Vol. 1: 4093
ASJSA Citation of Merit Award Vol. 1: 5333
ASLA Medal Vol. 1: 4095
ASM Award in Applied and Environmental and Microbiology Vol. 1: 3771
ASM Fellow Vol. 1: 4694
ASM Founders Distinguished Service Award Vol. 1: 3763
ASM International and The Metallurgical Society Distinguished Lectureship in Materials and Society Vol. 1: 4710
ASME Medal Vol. 1: 4123
ASN Career Enhancement Grant Vol. 1: 4194
ASN/NKF Fellowships Vol. 1: 4195
ASN Research Scholar Award Vol. 1: 4196
ASNE Distinguished Writing Awards Vol. 1: 15187
ASNT Fellows Vol. 1: 3774
ASNT Fellowship Award Vol. 1: 3775
ASNT Gold Medal Vol. 1: 3779
ASP World Title Vol. 1: 5355
ASPA/NASPAA Distinguished Research Award Vol. 1: 12648
Aspen Filmfest Vol. 1: 4714
Aspen Gold Awards Vol. 1: 9333
ASPEN Research Scholar Award Vol. 1: 3800
Aspen Shortsfest Vol. 1: 4715
Asselin; Prix Olivar- Vol. 1: 16135
Assistant Coach of the Year Vol. 1: 13709

Assistant Coach of the Year Award Vol. 1: 9999
Assistant Referee of the Year Vol. 2: 3403
Assistants' Awards Vol. 2: 5149
Associate Member Diploma Vol. 2: 6023
Associate Member of the Year
Document Management Industries Association Vol. 1: 8240
North Carolina Utility Contractors Association Vol 1: 14375
Associate of the Royal Academy of Dance Vol. 2: 6614
Associate Remodeler of the Year Award Vol. 1: 12556
Associated American Artists Purchase Award Vol. 1: 16517
Associated Collegiate Press Pacemaker Awards Vol. 1: 14221
Associates Award Vol. 1: 12838
Associateship (APMI) Vol. 2: 6528
Associateship of Honour Vol. 2: 6783
The Associateship of the City and Guilds of London Institute Vol. 2: 5656
Association Executive of the Year Vol. 1: 5398
Association for Industrial Archaeology Award Vol. 2: 5221
Association Medal Vol. 2: 3814
Association of Clinical Biochemists Foundation Award Vol. 2: 5078
Association of Irish Choirs Trophy Vol. 2: 2829
Association of Southeast Asian Institutions of Higher Learning Awards Vol. 2: 3967
Association of Subspecialty Professors Young Investigator Award in Geriatrics Vol. 1: 13258
Association of the United States Army Awards Vol. 1: 5364
Association of the Year Vol. 1: 18430
Association of Track and Field Statisticians Honorary Member Vol. 2: 61
Association Plaquette of Merit Vol. 2: 1394
Association Silver Pin Awards Vol. 1: 474
Association Wrestling Award Vol. 1: 475
Association Youth Sport Membership Award Vol. 1: 476
Association Youth Sport Programming Award Vol. 1: 477
AST Fujisawa Fellowship in Transplantation Vol. 1: 4244
AST President's Award Vol. 1: 4245
AST Sandoz Fellowship in Transplantation Vol. 1: 4246
AST Scholarship Vol. 1: 5357
Astar Award Vol. 1: 15648
Astin Measurement Science Award; Allen V. Vol. 1: 17798
Astin - Polk International Standards Medal Vol. 1: 2849
ASTM Robert J. Painter Memorial Award; SES/ Vol. 1: 17248
Astor Award Vol. 2: 5688
Astor Award; Brooke Russell Vol. 1: 14146
Astor Award for Philanthropy; Brooke Russell Vol. 1: 7420
Astor Memorial Leadership Essay Contest; Vincent Vol. 1: 18006
Astor Trophy Vol. 2: 6929
AstraZeneca Award Vol. 2: 5167
AstraZeneca Fellowship/Faculty Transition Vol. 1: 2079
AstraZeneca Trainee Presentation Award Vol. 1: 6929
AstraZeneca Traveling Lectureship Award Vol. 1: 16868
Astrological Association Awards and Scholarships Vol. 2: 5154
Astronautics Literature Award Vol. 1: 1346
Astronomical League Award Vol. 1: 5475
Astwood Lecture Award; Edwin B. Vol. 1: 8451
ASU Commander's Cup Vol. 1: 4636
Asundi Memorial Lecture; Prof. R. K. Vol. 2: 2673
ATA National Truck Driving Championships Vol. 1: 4372
ATA National Truck Rodeo Vol. 1: 4372
AT&T Foundation Awards Vol. 1: 3674
AT&T Nonfiction Award Vol. 2: 5193
ATCA Industrial Award Vol. 1: 329
ATCA Life Cycle Management Award Vol. 1: 330
ATCA Small Business Award Vol. 1: 338
ATEM Fellow Vol. 2: 52
ATHENA Award Vol. 1: 14216
Athena Award
Kankakee River Valley Chamber of Commerce Vol. 1: 11073
North San Antonio Chamber of Commerce Vol 1: 14382
Athena Cup Vol. 1: 18179
Athenaeum Literary Award Vol. 1: 5488
Athenian Award Vol. 2: 2468
Athens Summer Olympic Games Award Vol. 2: 2469
Athlete of the Month Vol. 1: 6408
Athlete of the Year
Federation of Canadian Archers Vol. 1: 8621
Special Olympics Canada Vol 1: 17090
USA Deaf Sports Federation Vol 1: 18384
Athletes Appreciation Award Vol. 1: 18411
Athletic Director of the Year
Canadian Colleges Athletic Association Vol. 1: 6409
National High School Athletic Coaches Association Vol 1: 13343
Athletic Director of the Year Award Vol. 1: 13008
Athletic Hall of Fame Award Vol. 1: 7170
Ati Vishisht Seva Medal Vol. 2: 2576
Atkins Communications Award; George Vol. 1: 8176
Atkinson Award for Excellence in Arkansas Teaching; J.H. Vol. 1: 4617
Atkinson Memorial Award; Hugh C. Vol. 1: 5071
Atlanta Film Festival Vol. 1: 5497
Atlantic Chrysler Cup Vol. 1: 2263
Atlantic Film Festival Vol. 1: 5505
Atlantic Journalism Awards Vol. 1: 5507
Atlantic Lottery Corporation Achievement Award
Atlantic Journalism Awards Vol. 1: 5507
Atlantic Journalism Awards Vol 1: 5508
Atlas Award; Allison Vol. 1: 13433
Atlas Awards Vol. 1: 5372
Atlas Travel Marketing Executive Award Vol. 1: 5372
Atrium Award Vol. 1: 18280
Atwood Award; J. Leland Vol. 1: 2365
Atwood Award; John Leland Vol. 1: 3628
AUA Honor Awards Vol. 1: 5377
Aubry Award; Claude Vol. 2: 4783
Aubuchon Freedom of the Press Award; John R. Vol. 1: 13543
Audience and Juried Awards Vol. 1: 14759
Audience Awards Vol. 1: 8742
Audience Prize Vol. 2: 6407
Audience Prizes Vol. 2: 2332
Audiffred; Prix Vol. 2: 1632
Audubon Medal Vol. 1: 12726
Auerbach Award; Isaac L. Vol. 2: 794
Auerbach Trophy; Red Vol. 1: 12756
Aufranc Award; Otto Vol. 1: 9404
August Memorial Award; Helen Vol. 1: 3066
Augusta International Helicopter Fellowship Award; Gruppo Vol. 1: 2192
Ault Award Vol. 1: 12613
Aumale; Prix d' Vol. 2: 1852
Aurbach Lecture Award; Gerald D. Vol. 1: 8452
Aurelio Award for Altruism; Santo J. Vol. 1: 13065
Austern Memorial Writing Competition; H. Thomas Vol. 1: 8782
The Austin Chronicle Best of Austin Vol. 1: 5542
The Austin Chronicle Hot Sauce Contest Vol. 1: 5543
The Austin Chronicle Readers' Poll Music Awards Vol. 1: 5544
The Austin Chronicle Readers' Restaurant Poll Vol. 1: 5545
Austin Music Awards Vol. 1: 5544
Austin Prize; Lord Vol. 2: 6153
Australasian Corrosion Association Awards Vol. 2: 77
Australasian Menopause Society Scientific Award Vol. 2: 85
Australia Council Residencies Award Vol. 2: 5437
Australia Day Awards Vol. 2: 725
Australia/New Zealand Chapter Traveling Fellowship Vol. 1: 1736
Australian Active Service Medal Vol. 2: 207
Australian Active Service Medal 1945-1975 Vol. 2: 207
Australian Antarctic Medal Vol. 2: 202
Australian Audio Book of the Year Vol. 2: 576
Australian Bravery Decorations Vol. 2: 203
Australian Cadet Forces Service Medal Vol. 2: 204
Australian College of Education Medal Vol. 2: 156
Australian Commercial/Industrial Photographer of the Year Vol. 2: 258
Australian Direct Marketing Awards Vol. 2: 179
Australian Engineering Excellence Awards Vol. 2: 488
Australian Fire Service Medal Vol. 2: 205
Australian Geography Competition Vol. 1: 10108
Australian Institute of Energy Medal Vol. 2: 239
Australian International Widescreen Festival Vol. 2: 393
Australian Landscape Photographer of the Year Vol. 2: 259
Australian Library and Information Association Fellow Vol. 2: 271
Australian Literature Society Gold Medal Vol. 2: 54
Australian Mathematical Society Medal Vol. 2: 283
Australian Mushroom Growers Award for Best Menu Using Mushrooms Vol. 2: 289
Australian Music Center Awards Vol. 2: 294

Australian Musical Association Prize Vol. 2: 6853
Australian Natural History Medallion Vol. 2: 456
Australian Nuclear Association Annual Award Vol. 2: 307
Australian Numismatic Society Bronze Medal Vol. 2: 309
Australian Packaging Awards Vol. 2: 595
Australian Police Medal Vol. 2: 206
Australian Professional Photographer of the Year Vol. 2: 260
Australian Professional Photography Awards Vol. 2: 261
Australian Service Medals Vol. 2: 207
Australian Society of Archivists Honorary Member Vol. 2: 373
Australian Sports Medal Vol. 2: 208
Australian Teachers of Media Awards Vol. 2: 380
Australian Transport Industry Award Vol. 2: 402
Australian Visual Artists' Benevolent Fund Vol. 2: 565
The Australian/Vogel Literary Award Vol. 2: 39
Author Emeritus Award Vol. 1: 15921
Author of the Year Award
  American Society of Journalists and Authors Vol. 1: 4093
  Canadian Booksellers Association Vol 1: 6344
  Professional Convention Management Association Vol 1: 15287
Author's Awards Vol. 1: 5175
Authorship Award Vol. 1: 4488
Autism Professional of the Year Vol. 1: 5547
Auto Color Designers' Selection Vol. 2: 3228
Automated Imaging Achievement Award Vol. 1: 5556
Automotive Achievement Award Vol. 1: 11701
Automotive Aftermarket Education Award Vol. 1: 14414
Automotive Dealer Education Award Vol. 1: 14415
Automotive Hall of Fame; Induction into the Vol. 1: 5565
Automotive Industry Leader of the Year Vol. 1: 5566
Automotive Innovation Award Vol. 1: 11702
Automotive Leader of the Year Vol. 1: 5575
Automotive Man of the Year Vol. 1: 5575
Automotive Replacement Management Award Vol. 1: 14414
Automotive Training Awards Vol. 1: 5573
Autopsy Award for Pathologists-in-Training Vol. 1: 17721
Auxiliary Excellence Award Vol. 1: 2624
Avanti Award in Lipids Vol. 1: 3564
Avatar Award Vol. 1: 5951
Aventis Prizes for Science Books Vol. 2: 6901
Avery Award; Oswald Vol. 1: 9697
Aviation Ground Marine of the Year Vol. 1: 11508
Aviation Hall of Fame and Museum of New Jersey Vol. 1: 5579
Aviation Hall of Fame Award Vol. 1: 12732
Aviation Journalism Award Vol. 1: 12225
Aviation Maintenance Department Safety Award Vol. 1: 12822
Aviation Maintenance Technician of the Year Award Vol. 1: 15264
Aviation Supply Marine of the Year Vol. 1: 11527
Aviation Support Services Safety Award Vol. 1: 12823
Aviation Week & Space Technology Distinguished Service Award Vol. 1: 8721
Avioli Founders Award; Louis V. Vol. 1: 3575
Avionics Technician Award Vol. 1: 15266
AVMA Award Vol. 1: 4406
AVMA Student Chapter Certificates Vol. 1: 17306
AVP Awards Vol. 2: 362
Avril and Allan Mitchell Trophy Vol. 2: 5345
AVY Awards Vol. 1: 1999
AWAPA (Academy of Wind and Percussion Arts) Award Vol. 1: 12736
Award for Aboriginal and Torres Strait Islander Writers Vol. 2: 588
Award for Achievement in Business Growth Vol. 1: 7619
Award for Achievement in Engineering Enterprise Vol. 2: 489
Award for Achievement in Technical Services Vol. 1: 6688
Award for Advancement of Industry Vol. 2: 4104
Award for Advancement of Science Vol. 2: 4105
Award for Application of Science & Technology for Rural Development Vol. 2: 2776
Award for Association Excellence Vol. 1: 12329
Award for Behavioral Research Relevant to the Prevention of Nuclear War Vol. 1: 12145
Award for Best Practices in Human Resources and Aging Vol. 1: 4266
Award for Career Development in Honor of L.P. Cookingham Vol. 1: 10309
Award for Chemical Education Vol. 2: 4106
Award for Chemical Education Vol. 1: 7300
Award for Chemistry in Service to Society Vol. 1: 12146
Award for Community Service Vol. 1: 13283
Award for Contributions to Amateur Mycology Vol. 1: 14313
Award for Creativity in Psychiatric Education Vol. 1: 1727
Award for Distinguished Achievement in Fiber Science Vol. 1: 8685
Award for Distinguished Career Contributions to Education and Training Vol. 1: 3387
Award for Distinguished Contribution to Ethnic Minority Issues Vol. 1: 3388
Award for Distinguished Contributions to Asian Studies Vol. 1: 4777
Award for Distinguished Contributions to Education and Training Vol. 1: 3389
Award for Distinguished Contributions to Education and Training in Psychology Vol. 1: 6830
Award for Distinguished Contributions to Psychology as a Profession Vol. 1: 6831
Award for Distinguished Contributions to Psychology in the Public Interest Vol. 1: 3390
Award for Distinguished Contributions to Public or Community Service Vol. 1: 6832
Award for Distinguished Contributions to Research in Education Vol. 1: 1940
Award for Distinguished Contributions to Research in Public Policy Vol. 1: 3391
Award for Distinguished Contributions to the International Advancement of Psychology Vol. 1: 6833
Award for Distinguished Public Service
  American Mathematical Society Vol. 1: 2725
  Medical Library Association Vol 1: 11652
  United States Conference of Mayors Vol 1: 17782
Award for Distinguished Research in the Biomedical Sciences Vol. 1: 5035
Award for Distinguished Service
  American Society for Dermatologic Surgery Vol. 1: 3623
  Mathematical Association of America Vol 1: 11606
Award for Distinguished Service to Children Vol. 1: 12514
Award for Distinguished Service to Historical Recordings Vol. 1: 4947
Award for Distinguished Service to Museums Vol. 1: 1165
Award for Distinguished Service to N4A Vol. 1: 12372
Award for Distinguished Services to Art Vol. 2: 3346
Award for Divisional Scientific Contributions Vol. 2: 3306
Award for Drug Discovery Vol. 2: 7102
Award For Enthusiasm Vol. 2: 7228
Award for Environmental Achievement Vol. 1: 8717
Award For Excellence Vol. 2: 7383
Award for Excellence Vol. 1: 3431
Award for Excellence: Genealogical Methods and Sources Vol. 1: 13269
Award for Excellence: Genealogy and Family History Vol. 1: 13270
Award for Excellence in Adhesion Science Vol. 1: 156
Award for Excellence in Book Publication Vol. 1: 742
Award for Excellence in Clinical Pharmacy Practice Vol. 1: 5237
Award for Excellence in Clinical Teaching Vol. 1: 3145
Award for Excellence in Community Crime Prevention Vol. 1: 3257
Award for Excellence in Corporate Community Service Vol. 1: 15140
Award for Excellence in Encouraging Equity Vol. 1: 12404
Award for Excellence in Integrated Pest Management Vol. 1: 8476
Award for Excellence in Labor Diplomacy Vol. 1: 17851
Award for Excellence in Landscape Architecture Vol. 2: 243
Award for Excellence in Nutrition and Meat Sciences Vol. 1: 6972
Award for Excellence in Perioperative Nursing Vol. 1: 5291
Award for Excellence in Plasma Physics Research Vol. 1: 3109
Award for Excellence in Poetry for Children Vol. 1: 13017
Award for Excellence in Power Distribution Engineering Vol. 1: 9818
Award for Excellence in Productivity Improvement Vol. 1: 9858
Award for Excellence in Professional Writing Vol. 1: 1051
Award for Excellence in Storm Reporting Vol. 2: 353

Award Index

Award for Excellence in Teaching
American Academy of Religion Vol. 1: 742
Emergency Medicine Residents' Association Vol 1: 8432
Award for Excellence in Teaching Geography Vol. 1: 6248
Award for Excellence in Training Vol. 2: 3938
Award for Excellence in Workplace Volunteer Programs Vol. 1: 15140
Award For Excellent PhD Thesis in Psychology Vol. 2: 332
Award for Excellent Research Paper Vol. 2: 4107
Award for Executive Excellence Vol. 1: 7616
Award for Geography in the Service of Government or Business Vol. 1: 6249
Award for Heroism Vol. 1: 17852
Award for Humanistic Studies Vol. 1: 551
Award for Initiatives in Research Vol. 1: 12147
Award For Innovation
Canadian Colleges Athletic Association Vol. 1: 6410
Specialty Coffee Association of Europe Vol 2: 7229
Award for Innovative Management Vol. 1: 9931
Award for Lifetime Service Vol. 1: 4822
Award for Literary Criticism Vol. 2: 2897
Award for Local Sales Achievement Vol. 1: 6029
Award for Marketing Excellence Vol. 2: 3939
Award for Measured Drawing Vol. 2: 6816
Award for Meritorious Service to Family History Vol. 2: 79
Award for Most Meritorious Paper/ Presentation Vol. 2: 3755
Award for Original Hebrew Novel Vol. 2: 2898
Award for Original Hebrew Poetry Vol. 2: 2899
Award for Outstanding Achievement in International Business Vol. 1: 18983
Award for Outstanding Contribution in the Field of Constructive Work Vol. 2: 2776
Award for Outstanding Contribution to Public Understanding of the Geosciences Vol. 1: 2105
Award for Outstanding Contribution to the Adoption Community Vol. 1: 8579
Award for Outstanding Contribution to Uplift the Welfare of Women and Children Vol. 2: 2776
Award for Outstanding Contributions in Research Vol. 1: 1646
Award for Outstanding Contributions to Animal Clinical Chemistry Vol. 1: 866
Award for Outstanding Contributions to Pediatric and Maternal-Fetal Clinical Chemistry Vol. 1: 867
Award for Outstanding Doctoral Research Vol. 2: 5425
Award for Outstanding Editorial or Publishing Contributions Vol. 1: 5128
Award for Outstanding International Investigative Reporting Vol. 1: 10338
Award for Outstanding Leadership and Service to NHCA Vol. 1: 13330
Award for Outstanding Paper in *The Energy Journal* Vol. 1: 10073
Award for Outstanding Publication Vol. 1: 5129
Award for Outstanding Research Vol. 1: 6813
Award for Outstanding Research in the Pathophysiology of Osteoporosis Vol. 1: 3576
Award for Outstanding Scholastic Achievement Vol. 1: 2467
Award for Outstanding Service to Maltreated Children Vol. 1: 681
Award for Outstanding Service to Physics in Australia Vol. 2: 252
Award for Outstanding Service to the Society Vol. 1: 14069
Award for Poetry in Translation Vol. 1: 14891
Award for Private Mint Issues Vol. 1: 2868
Award for Production, Promotion, and Marketing of Biofertilizer Vol. 2: 2555
Award for Professional Excellence
CFA Institute Vol. 1: 7262
Iota Sigma Pi Vol 1: 10862
Society for Human Resource Management Vol 1: 16231
Award for Promotion of Physics Vol. 2: 4045
Award for Public Understanding of Science and Technology Vol. 1: 948
Award for Pure or Applied Inorganic Chemistry Vol. 1: 6899
Award for Research in Information Science Vol. 1: 3734
Award for Research in Psychiatry Vol. 1: 3267
Award for Research on Automotive Lubricants Vol. 1: 16566
Award for Residents Vol. 1: 17048
Award for Scene Design Vol. 1: 17947
Award for Scholarly Distinction in Geography Vol. 1: 6250
Award for Scientific Reviewing Vol. 1: 12148
Award for Service Vol. 1: 11648
Award for Service to People Vol. 1: 3917
Award for Service to Society Vol. 1: 2468
Award for Service to the Profession of Geography Vol. 1: 6251
Award for Services to the Game Vol. 2: 6304
Award for Social Accomplishment Vol. 2: 2844
Award for Special Librarianship in Canada Vol. 1: 6300
Award for Teaching Excellence in the Field of Library and Information Science Education Vol. 1: 4907
Award for Technical Excellence
American Chemical Society Vol. 1: 1566
British Institute of Architectural Technologists Vol 2: 5319
Award for Technical Innovation in Enhancing Production of Safe Affordable Food Vol. 1: 6973
Award for Technical Innovation in Industrial Engineering Vol. 1: 9859
Award For Technological Progress Vol. 2: 5084
Award for the Advancement of Surface Irrigation Vol. 1: 3845
Award for the Best Photography Vol. 2: 4538
Award for the Betterment of Humanity Vol. 1: 10670
Award for the Betterment of the Human Condition Vol. 1: 10671
Award for the Industrial Application of Science Vol. 1: 12149
Award for the Promotion of International Education Vol. 2: 5827
Award for the Public Understanding of Sociology Vol. 1: 4275
Award for the Support of Women in the Engineering Profession Vol. 1: 6432
Award for Valour Vol. 2: 5260
Award for Young Chemists in Technical Development Vol. 2: 3171
Award for Young Investigators in Dermatology Vol. 1: 565
Award for Young Leadership and Excellence Vol. 1: 5567
Award in Aeronautical Engineering Vol. 1: 12150
Award in Chemical Engineering Vol. 1: 418
Award in Chemical Engineering Practice Vol. 1: 2469
Award in Chemical Instrumentation Vol. 1: 1526
Award in Chemical Sciences Vol. 1: 12151
Award in Electrochemistry Vol. 1: 1527
Award in Forest Science Vol. 1: 16506
Award in Geriatric Oral Research Vol. 1: 10054
Award in Industrial Practice
Canadian Society for Chemical Engineering Vol. 1: 6892
Canadian Society for Chemistry Vol 1: 6900
Award in International Communication Vol. 1: 9771
Award in Magnetism Vol. 1: 10810
Award in Mathematics Vol. 1: 12152
Award in Molecular Biology Vol. 1: 12153
Award in Science Vol. 1: 14987
Award in Spectrochemical Analysis Vol. 1: 1528
Award in the Chemistry of Plastics and Coatings Vol. 1: 1513
Award in the Neurosciences Vol. 1: 12154
Award of Achievement
Australian Severe Weather Association Vol. 2: 354
La Leche League International Vol 1: 11175
Lincoln Group of New York Vol 1: 11367
Award of Appreciation
La Leche League International Vol. 1: 11176
NAMI Kansas-The Alliance on Mental Illness Vol 1: 12074
Award of Artistry Vol. 1: 1897
Award of Attainment Vol. 1: 6845
Award of Commendation Vol. 1: 7658
Award of Distinction
American Association for State and Local History Vol. 1: 941
American Orchid Society Vol 1: 2979
American Phytopathological Society Vol 1: 3188
International Technology Education Association Vol 1: 10780
The Award of Distinction Vol. 1: 94
Award of Excellence
Academy of Operative Dentistry Vol. 1: 113
Alliance for Children and Television Vol 1: 402
American Fisheries Society Vol 1: 2027
Business Forms Management Association Vol 1: 6018
Canadian Toy Testing Council Vol 1: 7044
Colorado Society of Association Executives Vol 1: 7569
ENR: Engineering News-Record - The McGraw-Hill Cos., Inc. Vol 1: 8472

Equine Guelph Vol 1: 8522
Film Advisory Board Vol 1: 8687
International Customer Service Association Vol 1: 10376
International Reading Association Vol 1: 10574
La Leche League International Vol 1: 11177
Oregon Society of Physician Assistants Vol 1: 14675
Professional Aviation Maintenance Association Vol 1: 15265
Society of Animal Artists Vol 1: 16544
Award of Excellence for Distinguished Educators Vol. 1: 13061
Award of Excellence for Innovation Vol. 1: 6796
Award of Excellence of the Pipeline Division Vol. 1: 3918
Award of Honor
American Association of Homes and Services for the Aging Vol. 1: 1120
American Dairy Science Association Vol 1: 1871
American Hospital Association Vol 1: 2302
American Hospital Association Vol 1: 2309
California Avocado Society Vol 1: 6047
National Business and Disability Council Vol 1: 12814
Award of Honour
Alpine Garden Society Vol. 2: 5022
British Canoe Union Vol 2: 5261
Canadian Air Traffic Control Association-CAW Local 5454 Vol 1: 6176
Canadian Camping Association Vol 1: 6371
Canadian Dermatology Association Vol 1: 6453
World Association of Industrial and Technological Research Organizations Vol 2: 3419
Award of Hope and Courage Vol. 1: 13811
Award of Merit
AACE International Vol. 1: 20
AIIM - The Enterprise Content Management Association Vol 1: 255
American Academy of Family Physicians Vol 1: 600
American Association for State and Local History Vol 1: 942
American Association of Botanical Gardens and Arboreta Vol 1: 1020
American College of Dentists Vol 1: 1640
American Occupational Therapy Association Vol 1: 2950
American Oil Chemists' Society Vol 1: 2964
American Orchid Society Vol 1: 2980
American Otological Society Vol 1: 3021
American Philological Association Vol 1: 3080
American Society for Information Science and Technology Vol 1: 3735
American Spaniel Club Vol 1: 4287
American Wine Society Vol 1: 4482
Association for Research in Otolaryngology, Inc. Vol 1: 4949
ASTM International Vol 1: 5404
B'nai Brith Canada Vol 1: 5825
British Canoe Union Vol 2: 5262
Canadian Air Traffic Control Association-CAW Local 5454 Vol 1: 6177
Canadian Association of Career Educators and Employers Vol 1: 6238
Canadian Dermatology Association Vol 1: 6454
Canadian Parks and Recreation Association Vol 1: 6797
Conference of California Historical Societies Vol 1: 7686
Conference of California Historical Societies Vol 1: 7687
Construction Specifications Canada Vol 1: 7740
Door and Hardware Institute Vol 1: 8256
European Structural Integrity Society Vol 2: 3040
Federation of Genealogical Societies Vol 1: 8654
Institution of Agricultural Engineers Vol 2: 6081
International Association Auto Theft Investigators Vol 1: 10047
International Federation of Air Traffic Controllers' Associations Vol 1: 10403
International Weightlifting Federation Vol 2: 2512
Lambda Kappa Sigma Vol 1: 11216
National Association of Metal Finishers Vol 1: 12587
National Commission on Correctional Health Care Vol 1: 12915
National Genealogical Society Vol 1: 13271
National Water Safety Congress Vol 1: 13887
New England Water Works Association Vol 1: 14060
North American Association of Food Equipment Manufacturers Vol 1: 14263
Ontario Psychological Association Vol 1: 14586
Pittsburgh History and Landmarks Foundation Vol 1: 15079
Polymer Alliance Zone of West Virginia Vol 1: 15154
Professional Aviation Maintenance Association Vol 1: 15266
Society for Historical Archaeology Vol 1: 16220
Society of Manufacturing Engineers - Composites Manufacturing Association Vol 1: 16704
Swedish Council of America Vol 1: 17351
Tree Care Industry Association Vol 1: 17595
Union for the International Language Ido Vol 2: 7290
Western History Association Vol 1: 18681
Award of Merit - Commercial Vol. 1: 7680
Award of Merit - Governmental Vol. 1: 7681
Award of Merit in Broadcasting Vol. 1: 15611
Award of Merit in Journalism Vol. 1: 15611
Award of Merit - Individual Vol. 1: 7682
Award of Merit - Preservation Vol. 1: 7683
Award of Merit - Scholastic/Authorship Vol. 1: 7684
Award of Meritorious Achievement Vol. 1: 11316
Award of Minarik Vol. 2: 4465
Award of Quality Vol. 1: 2981
Award of Recognition
AACE International Vol. 1: 26
La Leche League International Vol 1: 11178
Award of Recognition: AACRAO Internships Vol. 1: 1054
Award of Safety Excellence Vol. 1: 15460
Award of Special Merit Vol. 1: 15267
Award of Special Recognition Vol. 1: 12588
Award of Specialty Vol. 2: 3328
Award of Technical Paper Vol. 2: 3329
Award of Technology Vol. 2: 3330
Award of the Greek Alzheimer's Association Vol. 2: 2457
Award of Valor
American Association of Airport Executives, Great Lakes Chapter Vol. 1: 987
National Collegiate Athletic Association Vol 1: 12902
Award to Honor Excellence in Newspaper Advertising Vol. 1: 14216
Award to the Most Outstanding Third Year Student in Zoology Vol. 2: 4380
Awards Vol. 2: 6208
Awards Competition Vol. 1: 12530
Awards for Action on HIV/AIDS and Human Rights Vol. 1: 6563
Awards for Educational Excellence Vol. 1: 16232
Awards for Excellence
Association of Consulting Engineers of Australia Vol. 2: 59
Australian Direct Marketing Association Vol 2: 180
Fork Lift Truck Association Vol 2: 5919
Government Finance Officers Association of United States and Canada Vol 1: 9146
Rural Sociological Society Vol 1: 15777
Awards for Excellence in Broadcasting Vol. 2: 7320
Awards for Excellence in Cancer Research Vol. 1: 12845
Awards for Excellence in Chess Journalism Vol. 1: 7313
Awards for Excellence in Community Service, Philanthropy, and Media Vol. 1: 17341
Awards for Excellence in Conflict Resolution Vol. 1: 7938
Awards for Excellence in Distance Learning Vol. 1: 9961
Awards for Excellence in Teaching of the Classics Vol. 1: 3079
Awards for Innovation in Teaching Science Teachers Vol. 1: 4958
Awards for Outstanding Achievement Vol. 1: 6741
Awards for Outstanding Achievement in Procurement Vol. 2: 7213
Awards for Outstanding Consultancy Practice Vol. 2: 6570
Awards for Professional Publications in Agricultural Economics Vol. 1: 774
Awards for Program Excellence Vol. 1: 10312
Awards for Scientific Achievement Vol. 1: 18590
Awards for Sustainability Reporting Vol. 2: 5119
Awards in History Vol. 2: 3723
Awards in Oral History Vol. 2: 3724
Awards in Recognition of Excellence Vol. 2: 3597
Awards of Distinction
Canadian Cartographic Association Vol. 1: 6383
Society of the Plastics Industry - Moldmakers Division Vol 1: 16861
Awards of Distinction in Programs Vol. 1: 13332

Award Index

Awards of Excellence
Association for Communication Excellence in Agriculture, Natural Resources, and Life and Human Sciences Vol. 1: 4799
Association of Consulting Engineers New Zealand Vol 2: 3696
Association of Consulting Engineers of Canada Vol 1: 5108
Canadian Architect Vol 1: 6190
Canadian Public Relations Society Vol 1: 6844
Canadian Society of Landscape Architects Vol 1: 7008
International Magnesium Association Vol 1: 10502
National Association of Community Health Centers Vol 1: 12459
National Association of County Information Officers Vol 1: 12502
National Council for Community Behavioral Healthcare Vol 1: 12956
Ronald McDonald House Charities Vol 1: 15713
Treasury Board of Canada Secretariat Vol 1: 17591
Wedding and Portrait Photographers International Vol 1: 18653
Awards of Excellence in Housing and Community Development Vol. 1: 12562
Awards of Merit
American Association of Blood Banks Vol. 1: 1005
Historical Society of Michigan Vol 1: 9423
International Federation of Audit Bureaux of Circulations Vol 2: 4208
International Trumpet Guild Vol 1: 10802
Awards of Merit in Housing and Community Development Vol. 1: 12563
Awards of Recognition Vol. 1: 11541
Awards of the ESTRO Vol. 2: 876
Awards Portfolio Competition Vol. 1: 11635
Awards Program
American Hanoverian Society Vol. 1: 2160
American Holsteiner Horse Association Vol 1: 2282
Awgie Awards Vol. 2: 395
AWIT Awards Vol. 2: 3980
AWP Award Series Vol. 1: 4773
AXA Dublin International Piano Competition Vol. 2: 2825
Axelrod Award; Julius Vol. 1: 3804
Ayers Award; A. Jean Vol. 1: 2962
Aylesworth Scholarship Vol. 1: 8755
Ayrton Premium Vol. 2: 6146
Azbee Awards of Excellence Vol. 1: 3898
Azevedo Prize; Arthur Vol. 2: 1117
AzLA/SIRS Intellectual Freedom Award Vol. 1: 4599
Azorin Prize Vol. 2: 4479
Babbidge, Jr. Award; Homer D. Vol. 1: 4990
Babcock-Hart Award Vol. 1: 9846
Baber Member Booster Award; Al Vol. 1: 2869
Baber Research Grant; Carrol Preston Vol. 1: 2680
Baburao Mhatre Gold Medal Vol. 2: 2637
BACB Editing for Industry Awards Vol. 2: 5241
BACB National House Journal Competition Vol. 2: 5241
Bach Award Vol. 1: 17312
Bach Competition; International Johann Sebastian Vol. 2: 2036
Bachauer Gold Medal; Gina Vol. 1: 5626
Bachauer International Piano Competition; Gina Vol. 1: 5626
Bachus Gold Medal; Walter O. Vol. 1: 16519
Bacigalupi Program of Distinction Award; Tadini Vol. 1: 13498
Back Award Vol. 2: 6757
Back Pain Association Medal Vol. 2: 5158
Backmans Stipendium; Ida Vol. 2: 4647
Backus Award Vol. 1: 12047
Bacon Award; Lionel and Joyce Vol. 2: 5023
Bacon Award; Paul Vol. 1: 18082
Bactlab Systems Gold Award Vol. 2: 4250
Bactlab Systems Premier Award for Best Paper Vol. 2: 4251
Baddams Bursary; Thenie Vol. 2: 186
Bader Award Vol. 2: 6948
Bader Award in Bioinorganic or Bioorganic Chemistry; Alfred Vol. 1: 1529
Bader Award in Organic Chemistry; Alfred Vol. 1: 6901
Bader Prize; Alfred Vol. 2: 1249
Badge of Honour in Gold, Silver and Bronze Vol. 2: 2052
Badminton Hall of Fame Vol. 1: 18374
Baekeland Lecture Vol. 2: 7157
Baekelmans Prize; Lode Vol. 2: 949
Baer Heart Fund; Max Vol. 1: 9163
Baer Medal; Karl Ernst von Vol. 2: 1349
Baethke - Eleanor J. Carlin Award for Excellence in Academic Teaching; Dorothy E. Vol. 1: 3142
Baethke - Eleanor J. Carlin Award for Teaching Excellence; Dorothy E. Vol. 1: 3142
Bagnoud Award; Francois Xavier Vol. 1: 2193
Baguley Award; R. M. Vol. 2: 6554
Bagutta Prize Vol. 2: 2993
Baier Technical Achievement Award; Edward J. Vol. 1: 2337
Bailey Award; Alton E. Vol. 1: 2965
Bailey Award; E.G. Vol. 1: 10906
Bailey Distinguished Member Award; Marilyn and Sturges W. Vol. 1: 7464
Bailey Medal; Clyde H. Vol. 2: 782
Bailey Medal; Liberty Hyde Vol. 1: 2286
Baillie Award; Andrew D. Vol. 1: 7013
Bailly; Prix Antoine-Nicolas Vol. 2: 1434
Bainton Book Prize; Roland H. Vol. 1: 16075
Bair Endowment Award; Clifford E. Vol. 1: 13490
Baird Audience Development Gold Ribbon Awards; Audrey Vol. 1: 4340
Baird Memorial Competition for Young Composers; Tadeusz Vol. 2: 4038
Baird Oncology Excellence in Writing Award in Clinical Practice; Susan Vol. 1: 14532
Baker & Taylor Award Vol. 1: 8901
Baker and Taylor Conference Grants Vol. 1: 19081
Baker and Taylor Entertainment Audio Music/ Video Product Award Vol. 1: 15419
Baker Award; "Cannonball" Vol. 1: 8064
Baker Award; Florence Vol. 2: 5024
Baker Award for Highway Safety; J. Stannard Vol. 1: 10168
Baker Award; Ron Vol. 1: 17302
Baker Best Conference Paper Award; Merl Vol. 1: 3685
Baker Conservation Engineering Award; Eugene Vol. 1: 5106
Baker Distinguished Research Award; Dr. David F. Vol. 1: 9860
Baker Foundation for the Prevention of Blindness Fellowships; E. A. Vol. 1: 6745
Baker Memorial Award; Hobey Vol. 1: 9448
Baker Prize Award; W. R. G. Vol. 1: 9772
Baker Research Award; Philip Noel Vol. 2: 2296
Baker Scholarship; Philip E. Vol. 1: 2145
Baker Scholarship; Robert S. Vol. 1: 2145
Baker-Wilkins Award for Outstanding Deputy Chief of Mission Vol. 1: 17853
Bakjian Award; Andy Vol. 1: 18431
Balakian Citation for Excellence in Reviewing Award; Nona Vol. 1: 12783
Balasaraswati/Joy Ann Dewey Beinecke Chair for Distinguished Teaching Vol. 1: 1893
Balch Prize; Emily Clark Vol. 1: 18563
Balcon Award; Michael Vol. 2: 5218
Baldock Memorial Award; Len Vol. 1: 313
Baldrige Community Award; Malcolm Vol. 1: 9198
Baldrige National Quality Award; Malcolm Vol. 1: 5631
Baldwin Award; F. W. (Casey) Vol. 1: 6169
Baldwin Distinguished Service Award; A. Richard Vol. 1: 2966
Baldwin Fishery Science Scholarship; Norman S. Vol. 1: 10087
Baldwin Medal of Liberty Award; Roger N. Vol. 1: 1598
Balfour Scholarship Vol. 1: 14996
Balfour Silver and Golden Anniversary Award Vol. 1: 12400
Balint Memorial Award; Michael J. Vol. 1: 15822
Balint Society Essay Prize Vol. 2: 5163
Ball Memorial Award; Clifford Vol. 1: 14766
Ballantyne Award; Harry M. Vol. 2: 4948
Ballew Directing Award; Leighton M. Vol. 1: 17013
Ballot Medal; Buys Vol. 2: 3648
Balsdon Fellowship Vol. 2: 5438
Baltic Freedom Award Vol. 1: 11036
Balvenie Medal Vol. 2: 5667
Balzan Prize Vol. 2: 3062
Banbury Award; Fernley H. Vol. 1: 1530
Bancroft Award Vol. 1: 15755
Bancroft History Prize; Caroline Vol. 1: 8165
Bancroft - Mackerras Medal Vol. 2: 370
Bancroft Memorial Scholarship; Mary A. Vol. 1: 11084
Bancroft Prizes Vol. 1: 7583
Band Booster Award Vol. 1: 12737
Bandeira Paulista Vol. 2: 1136
Banff Concours International de Quatuor A Cordes Vol. 1: 5649
Banff International String Quartet Competition Vol. 1: 5649
Banff Mountain Book Festival Vol. 1: 5650
Banff Mountain Film Festival Vol. 1: 5651
Banff Mountain Photography Competition Vol. 1: 5652
Banff Rockie Award Vol. 1: 5654
Banff World Television Festival Vol. 1: 5654
Bank of America Awards for Excellence in Orchestra Education Vol. 1: 4341
Bank of Montreal Scholarship Vol. 1: 5792
Banks Music Award; Don Vol. 2: 98
Banksian Medal Vol. 2: 2879
Banner Exhibition and Competition Vol. 1: 7253
Banner Society Awards Vol. 1: 17685
Banta Awards Vol. 1: 18789
Bappu Memorial Award; INSA - Vainu Vol. 2: 2674

Barany Award for Young Investigators; Michael and Kate Vol. 1: 5775
Barbados National Trust Vol. 2: 838
Barbara Hanrahan Fellowship Vol. 2: 672
Barbara Hollander Award Vol. 1: 8583
Barbara Jordan Youth Debates on Health Vol. 1: 13244
Barbato Award; Lewis Vol. 1: 1603
Barbed Wire Award Vol. 1: 1987
Barber Award for Best Research Associate Publication; Linda D. Vol. 1: 3711
Barbier; Prix Vol. 2: 1830
Barbier Prize; Dr. Karel Vol. 2: 950
Barbirolli Memorial; Sir John Vol. 2: 6860
Barbizon Award for Lighting Design Vol. 1: 17948
Barbizon Awards for Theatrical Design Excellence Vol. 1: 11113
Barbosa Earth Fund Award; Joseph Vol. 1: 16002
Barbour Air Safety Award; Laura Taber Vol. 1: 8722
Barbour Award; Buchanan Vol. 2: 6630
Barchi Prize; Richard H. Vol. 1: 11769
Barclay Bank Prize Vol. 2: 6029
Bard Allied Professional Award; Morton Vol. 1: 13499
Bard Award; Al Vol. 1: 9493
Bardeen Award; John Vol. 1: 11802
Bareback Horse of the Year Vol. 1: 15355
Barkan Article Prize; Omer Lutfi Vol. 1: 17629
Barkan Memorial Award; Manuel Vol. 1: 12260
Barker Award; Kathleen Vol. 2: 7127
Barker Distinguished Research Contribution Award; Roger Vol. 1: 3360
Barker Medal; Geoffrey Vol. 2: 6967
Barker Silver Medal Vol. 2: 5634
Barlow Award of Honor; Thomas E. Vol. 1: 17290
Barlow International Competition Vol. 1: 5938
Barlow Memorial Award Vol. 1: 6608
Barlow Prize Vol. 1: 5938
Barnard Award; Bernard L. Vol. 1: 10126
Barnard Prize; Henry Vol. 1: 9436
Barnard Short Story Award; Marjorie Vol. 2: 448
Barnato Trophy; Woolf Vol. 1: 17196
Barneby Award; Rupert Vol. 1: 14113
Barner Teacher of the Year Award; John C. Vol. 1: 789
Barnes Award; Charles H. Vol. 1: 6824
Barnes Award; CMSAF Thomas N. Vol. 1: 282
Barnes Award for Excellence for Community History Projects; Mary Faye Vol. 1: 17493
Barnes Award for Leadership in Chemical Research Management; Earle B. Vol. 1: 1531
Barnes Award; Rudolph John Vol. 1: 15284
Barnes Life Membership Award; Charles Reid Vol. 1: 4215
Barnes Research Grant; Corinne J. Vol. 1: 16783
Barnes Student Paper Award; K.K. Vol. 1: 3864
Barnett Award; Henry L. Vol. 1: 682
Barnett Prize; Helen Foster Vol. 1: 12100
Barnhill Memorial Award; Colin Vol. 1: 5505
Barnouw Award; Erik Vol. 1: 14688
Barnum Industry Award; Harold Vol. 1: 10078
Barometer Star Poll Vol. 1: 5903
Baron Award in Fluid-Particle Systems; Thomas Vol. 1: 2470
Baron Travelling Scholarship; Bernhard Vol. 2: 6702
Barone Award; Joan Shorenstein Vol. 1: 15532
The Baroness Platt of Writtle Award Vol. 2: 5766
Barr Award
American Philatelic Congress Vol. 1: 3067
Diamond Council of America Vol 1: 8180
Barr Award; Andy Vol. 1: 5176
Barr Award; Mel Vol. 1: 13431
Barr, Jr. Award; Alfred H. Vol. 1: 7502
Barr Memorial Cup; Peter Vol. 2: 6784
Barrabe; Prix Vol. 2: 1831
Barraza Leadership Award; Maclovio Vol. 1: 13001
Barrer Award Vol. 2: 6949
Barrett-Colea Foundry Prize Vol. 1: 13690
Barrett Travel Grant; Sidney Vol. 2: 5851
Barringer Medal Vol. 1: 1104
Barringer Memorial Trophy; Lewin B. Vol. 1: 16104
Barrot; Prix Odilon Vol. 2: 1633
Barrow Award; Dame Nita Vol. 2: 7404
Barry Award Vol. 1: 1458
Barry Award; Gerald Vol. 2: 6338
Barry Award in Human Relations; Lillian and Henry Vol. 1: 15052
Barry Award; Redmond Vol. 2: 272
Barry Ohioana Award for Editorial Excellence; James P. Vol. 1: 14486
Barry Prize; Robertine Vol. 1: 6860
Barsauskas premija; Kazimiero Vol. 2: 3373
Bart Feminist Activist Award; Pauline Vol. 1: 16921
Bartels Medal; Julius Vol. 2: 1769
Bartelsmeyer Award; Ralph R. Vol. 1: 3501
Barth Volunteer Service Award; Alan and Adrienne Vol. 1: 1600
Barthel, Jr. Award; Christopher E. Vol. 2: 6318
Bartholome Award for Ethical Excellence; William G. Vol. 1: 683
Bartholomew Award; Harland Vol. 1: 3919
Bartholomew Award; John Vol. 2: 5264
Bartholomew Award; Marshall Vol. 1: 9993
Bartholomew Globe Vol. 2: 6889
Bartlett Award; Charlie Vol. 1: 9123
Bartlett Award; Ford Vol. 1: 4734
Bartlett Award; George S. Vol. 1: 1288
Bartlett Lecture Vol. 2: 5874
Bartlett Medal; Sir Frederic Vol. 2: 5789
Bartley Award; Mel W. Vol. 1: 6609
Bartok Award for Outstanding Ethnomusicological Book; Bela Vol. 1: 4004
Bartolozzi; Premio Giuseppe Vol. 2: 3107
Barton Medal; C.N. Vol. 2: 490
Barton Top Debate Speaker Award; Phyllis Flory Vol. 1: 13237
Bartow Memorial Award; Buzz Vol. 1: 11681
Bartram Memorial Education Award; Walt Vol. 1: 16705
Bartsch Award; Paul Vol. 1: 5530
Bartter Award; Frederic C. Vol. 1: 3577
Baruch Essay Contest; Bernard M. Vol. 1: 1769
Baruch University Award; Mrs. Simon Vol. 1: 17693
Baseball Outstanding Volunteer Award Vol. 1: 478
Baseball Players Scholarships Vol. 1: 17456
Baseball Research Awards Vol. 1: 16168
Basic Medical Research Award Vol. 1: 11231
Basic Research in Biological Mineralization Award Vol. 1: 10055
Basic Research in Periodontal Disease Award Vol. 1: 10056
Basic Research Prize Vol. 1: 2173
Basic Science Lecture Award Vol. 1: 4012
Bass Gold Medal; Nancy Lee and Perry R. Vol. 1: 7479
Bassett Memorial Award; Johnny F. Vol. 1: 17147
Bassford Student Award; Forrest Vol. 1: 11390
Bassow Award; Whitman Vol. 1: 14761
Bastien Memorial Cello Award; Vincent R. Vol. 1: 18585
Bastien Memorial Trophy; Aldege Baz Vol. 1: 2260
Basu Memorial Lecture; Professor Sadhan Vol. 2: 2675
Batchelder Award; Mildred L. Vol. 1: 4919
Batcher Memorial Award; Ralph Vol. 1: 15516
Bates Medal; Sir David Robert Vol. 2: 1770
Bates Memorial Award; P. H. Vol. 1: 5405
Baton Twirling Achievement Award Vol. 1: 479
Batten Awards for Excellence in Civic Journalism Vol. 1: 10943
Batten Memorial Trophy; Jean Vol. 2: 3840
Battisti Award; Eugenio Vol. 1: 16473
Battle Award; Helen I. Vol. 1: 7028
Bauer Founders Award; Louis H. Vol. 1: 200
Bauer Memorial Exhibit Award; George Vol. 1: 2870
Bauer Prize; Alfred Vol. 2: 2048
Baum Memorial Award; L. Frank Vol. 1: 10841
Bauman Award; Mary K. Vol. 1: 4857
Baumann-Trophy; Hans- Vol. 2: 4807
Baumgardner Award; Merrill Vol. 1: 12673
Baumgardt Memorial Fellowship; David Vol. 1: 3084
Baumgarten Award; Alexander Gottlieb Vol. 2: 2281
Bavarian Academy of Science Prize Vol. 2: 2043
Baxter Allegiance Prize for Health Services Research Vol. 1: 5380
Baxter American Foundation Prize Vol. 1: 5380
Baxter Award Vol. 1: 6994
Baxter Award for Healthcare Management in Europe Vol. 2: 2834
Baxter Awards; Annette K. Vol. 1: 4325
Baxter Diagnostics MicroScan Young Investigator Award Vol. 1: 3767
Baxter Prize; Samuel Vol. 2: 6837
Baxter Specialist in Blood Banking Scholarship Vol. 1: 1016
Baxter Transfusion Medicine Scholarship Vol. 1: 1016
Bayer Award Vol. 2: 5079
Bayer Awards for Outstanding Contributions to Research and Teaching Vol. 1: 18900
Bayer Crop Science Award Vol. 1: 15092
Bayer Diagnostics Academic Achievement Award Vol. 2: 4252
Bayer Inc. Awards for High School Chemistry Teachers Vol. 1: 7304
Bayer-Mills Histology Award Vol. 2: 4253

Bayer/Sakura Histology Achievement Award Vol. 2: 4253
Bayer-Snoeyenbos New Investigator Award Vol. 1: 992
Bayfield Award; St. Clair Vol. 1: 142
Bayle Prijs; Pierre Vol. 2: 3644
Baytown Chamber of Commerce Scholarship Vol. 1: 5694
BBC Four Samuel Johnson Prize for Non-Fiction Vol. 2: 5193
BBTS Gold Medal Vol. 2: 5252
BC Decker Research Paper Prize Vol. 1: 6550
BC Prize for Poetry Vol. 1: 18664
BC Science and Technology Champion of the Year Vol. 1: 5698
BCA Hall of Fame Vol. 1: 6014
The BCA Ten: Best Companies Supporting the Arts in America Vol. 1: 6015
BCL Award Lecture Vol. 2: 5081
BCRA Research Fund Vol. 2: 5273
BD Award for Research in Clinical Microbiology Vol. 1: 3764
BD Biosciences Investigator Award Vol. 1: 1135
BDA International Design Award Vol. 1: 5703
BDMA/Post Office Direct Marketing Awards Vol. 2: 5738
BEAC Broadcaster of the Year Vol. 1: 5383
Beale Medal Vol. 2: 6507
Beale Memorial Award; John A. Vol. 1: 16507
Bealer Award Vol. 1: 4665
Bealer Award of Merit; Edward C. Vol. 1: 5384
Beamish Award; Fred Vol. 1: 6902
Beamish Award; Jim Vol. 1: 6879
Bean Award; Dan Vol. 1: 18083
Bean Award; Edward H. Vol. 1: 4494
Bean Memorial Trophy; Gladys Vol. 1: 6644
Beard Award; Ralph Vol. 1: 8272
Beare Award Vol. 1: 6983
Bearns Prize in Music; Joseph H. Vol. 1: 7591
Beasley Award; Theodore P. Vol. 1: 8023
Beaubien Award Vol. 1: 5109
Beaudet Award in Orchestra Conducting; Jean-Marie Vol. 1: 6099
Beaujour; Prix Felix de Vol. 2: 1634
Beaulieu; Prix Paul Leroy- Vol. 2: 1635
Beauperthuy; Prix Louis-Daniel Vol. 2: 1541
Beautification Award Vol. 1: 8964
Bechtel Fellowship; Louise Seaman Vol. 1: 4920
Bechtel, Jr. Energy Award; Stephen D. Vol. 1: 3920
Bechtel Pipeline Engineering Award; Stephen D. Vol. 1: 3921
Beck Graduate Student Paper Award; Carl Vol. 1: 10761
Beck International Award Vol. 1: 18084
Beckenbach Book Prize Vol. 1: 11602
Becker Award; Joseph Vol. 1: 4896
Becker Distinguished Service Award; Samuel L. Vol. 1: 12921
Beckman Award; Aldo Vol. 1: 18727
Beckman Founder Award; Arnold O. Vol. 1: 10907
The Becky Award Vol. 1: 2749
Becquerel; Prix Henri Vol. 2: 1542
Becton Dickinson Career Achievement Award Vol. 1: 4979
Bedat Award; Andre
  International Pharmaceutical Federation Vol. 2: 3597
  International Pharmaceutical Federation Vol 2: 3598
Bedell Award; Arthur Sidney Vol. 1: 18621
Bedells Bursary; Phyllis Vol. 2: 6615
Bedford Award Vol. 2: 5394
Bedi-Makky Foundry Prize Vol. 1: 13690
Bee Award for Excellence in Illustrating and/or Editorial Cartooning; Noah Vol. 1: 2599
Beebe Fellowship; Frank Huntington Vol. 1: 8862
Beekeeper of the Year Vol. 1: 6065
Beekler Award; Martin V. Vol. 1: 9184
Beer and E. Russell Johnston Jr. Outstanding New Mechanics Educator Award; Ferdinand P. Vol. 1: 3629
Beer Prize; George Louis Vol. 1: 2226
Beernaert Prize; August Vol. 2: 951
Beers Award; Clifford W. Vol. 1: 13446
Beeson Career Development Awards in Aging Research; Paul B. Vol. 1: 1996
Beeson Physician Faculty Scholar in Aging Research Award; Paul Vol. 1: 1996
Beethoven Piano Competition; International Vol. 2: 832
Beethoven Scholarship; Gordon C. Wallis Memorial Intermediate Vol. 1: 15888
Beethoven Scholarship; Gordon C. Wallis Memorial Senior Vol. 1: 15889
Begay Award; Tony Vol. 1: 9389
Behavioral Science and Health Services Research Award Vol. 1: 10057
Behnke, Award; Albert R. Vol. 1: 17660
Behrens Award Vol. 1: 8745
Beigel Research Award; Hugo G. Vol. 1: 16452
Beijerinck Virology Medal; M. W. Vol. 2: 3649
Beilby Medal and Prize Vol. 2: 6950
Beilstein-Denkmunze; Gmelin- Vol. 2: 2163
Beinecke Chair for Distinguished Teaching; Balasaraswati/Joy Ann Dewey Vol. 1: 1893
Beisswenger Memorial Award; Robert H. Vol. 1: 12838
Belair Sr. Memorial-Volunteer of the Year; Denis Vol. 1: 357
Belanger; Prix Leonidas- Vol. 1: 15483
Belcher Memorial Lectureship; Ronald Vol. 2: 6951
Belford Award; Elizabeth Russell Vol. 1: 16049
Belgian American Educational Foundation Fellowships Vol. 1: 5707
Belgica Prize Vol. 2: 1062
Belin Advocacy Award; David W. Vol. 1: 12315
Belkin Memorial Award; John N. Vol. 1: 2800
Bell Award; Alexander Graham Vol. 1: 387
Bell Award; Elliott V. Vol. 1: 14123
Bell Award; Grover E. Vol. 1: 2194
Bell Canada Award in Video Art Vol. 1: 6100
Bell DHHS Youth Achievement Award (Deaf and Hard of Hearing Section); Alexander Graham Vol. 1: 388
Bell Honors; Alexander Graham Vol. 1: 389
Bell Jr. Civilian of the Year Award; Floyd R. Vol. 1: 11730
Bell, Jr. Travel Grants; Alfred D. Vol. 1: 8818
Bell Lifetime Achievement Award; Campton Vol. 1: 790
Bell Memorial Award; Lawrence D. Vol. 1: 9363
Bell Prize for Choral Conducting; Leslie Vol. 1: 14557
Bell Prize; Gordon Vol. 1: 9800
Bell Ringer Awards Vol. 1: 15438
Bell Student Prize in Speech Communication and Behavioral Acoustics; Alexander Graham Vol. 1: 12878
Bell Volta Award; Alexander Graham Vol. 1: 390
Bellarmine Medal Vol. 1: 5709
Belleau Award; Bernard Vol. 1: 6903
Belleek Hall of Fame Award Vol. 1: 5711
Beller Medal; Esther Hoffman Vol. 1: 14601
Bellflasher Award Vol. 1: 151
Bellman Control Heritage Award; Richard E. Vol. 1: 2471
Bellmanpriset Vol. 2: 4648
Bello; Prix Andres Vol. 2: 4767
Bellwether Prize for Fiction in Support of a Social Change Vol. 1: 13948
Belmont Memorial Cup; August Vol. 1: 14150
Belmont Stakes
  New York Racing Association Vol. 1: 14150
  Triple Crown Productions, Inc. Vol 1: 17609
Belpre Award; Pura Vol. 1: 4921
Belt of Orion Award for Excellence Vol. 1: 6128
Belvedere Singing Competition; International Hans Gabor Vol. 2: 830
Bemis President's Trophy; F. Gregg Vol. 1: 10013
Bemis Trophy; F. Gregg Vol. 1: 18074
Ben David Award; Mordecai Vol. 1: 19056
Benda Prize; Harry J. Vol. 1: 4778
Bendall; Medaille des Soixantenaire et Fondation Manley- Vol. 2: 1950
Bendix Automotive Electronics Engineering Award; Vincent Vol. 1: 16567
Bendix Award; Vincent
  American Society for Engineering Education Vol. 1: 3645
  American Society for Engineering Education Vol 1: 3650
Bendix Minorities in Education Award; Vincent Vol. 1: 3645
Bene Merenti de Patria; Prix Vol. 1: 16145
Bene merenti Medals Vol. 2: 2044
Benefactors Prize Vol. 2: 6142
Benemerenti Medal Vol. 2: 7412
Benet Culinary Scholarship; Jane G. Vol. 1: 16957
Benham Award; Rhoda Vol. 1: 11670
Beni Solow Award Vol. 2: 5839
Benjamin Award for Creative Publishing; Curtis G. Vol. 1: 5040
Benjamin Award; Robert Spiers Vol. 1: 14761
Benjamin Franklin Medal for Distinguished Achievement in Science Vol. 1: 3094
Benjamin Medal; L. R. Vol. 2: 45
Benjamin Memorial Award; Burton Vol. 1: 7626
Benjamin National Memorial Trophy; Henry Vol. 2: 5034
Benjamin Photo History Award; Rudolf and Hertha Vol. 1: 3104
Bennett Award; Harry Vol. 1: 1203
Bennett Award; Hugh Hammond Vol. 1: 16929
Bennett Award; John Vol. 1: 18432
Bennett Fellowship; Viscount Vol. 1: 6328

Bennett Memorial Prize; Elizabeth Vol. 2: 6078
Bennett Prize; Mrs. Louis Vol. 1: 13690
Bennett Public Service Award; Walter J. Vol. 1: 13895
Bennett Research Awards; A. E. Vol. 1: 16603
Benny Vol. 1: 15238
Benoist Prize; Marcel Vol. 2: 4700
Benoit Mid-Career Award; Anthony H. Vol. 1: 11419
Benson and Hedges Awards Vol. 2: 693
Benson Award; Clara Vol. 1: 6904
Benson Medal Vol. 2: 7001
Benson Scholarship Fund; Charles E. and Marian Vol. 1: 14465
Bent Spoon Award Vol. 2: 360
Benveniste; Prix de la Fondation Emile Vol. 2: 1501
Benz Award; Carl Vol. 1: 16596
Berakah Award Vol. 1: 14247
Berber Memorial Award; Naomi Vol. 1: 9171
Berdie Memorial Research Award; Ralph F. Vol. 1: 1838
Berens Award; Betty Vol. 1: 15360
Bereuter Accomplished Community Award; Doug Vol. 1: 14390
Berg Award; Patty Vol. 1: 11192
Berger Award; Frederick J. Vol. 1: 3630
Berger Award; Mike Vol. 1: 7593
Berger Memorial Prize; Fred Vol. 1: 3085
Berger; Prix Jean Jacques Vol. 2: 1435
Berger; Prix Jean-Jacques Vol. 2: 1543
Berggrens pris; Sven Vol. 2: 4623
Bergh Medal of Honor; Henry Vol. 1: 3824
Bergman Plaquette; Ingmar Vol. 2: 4682
Bergmann Memorial Award; Prof. E. D. Vol. 2: 2935
Bergson Award Vol. 2: 2940
Bergstrom Research Awards Vol. 1: 5145
Bering Medaillen; Vitus Vol. 2: 1330
Bering Medal; Vitus Vol. 2: 1330
Berkeley Award Vol. 2: 5384
Berkeley Memorial Award; Maureen Vol. 1: 4032
Berkman Chapter Awards; Frank W. Vol. 1: 9494
Berkner Award; Lloyd V. Vol. 1: 1344
Berlanda Preis; Emil Vol. 2: 747
Berlin Children's Jury; Prize of the Vol. 2: 2048
Berlin International Film Festival Vol. 2: 2048
Berlin Memorial Outstanding Dissertation Award; James Vol. 1: 7691
Berliner Award; Benjamin C. Vol. 1: 2982
Berliner Award; Emile Vol. 1: 5524
Berliner Morgenpost; Readers Prizes of the Vol. 2: 2048
Berling Program for Advanced German and European Studies Vol. 1: 16128
Bernabei Honor Award; Dr. Raymond Vol. 1: 13380
Bernabi Memorial Award; Emilio Vol. 1: 10557
Bernal Prize; John Desmond Vol. 1: 16422
Bernard Award; Jessie Vol. 1: 4276
Bernard Foundation Prize; Leon Vol. 2: 4925
Bernard Lecture; Claude Vol. 2: 2105
Bernard; Prix de la Fondation Xavier Vol. 2: 1430
Bernath Book Prize; Stuart L. Vol. 1: 16215
Bernath Lecture Prize; Stuart L. Vol. 1: 16216
Bernath Scholarly Article Prize; Stuart L. Vol. 1: 16217
Berne Memorial Award; Eric Vol. 1: 10800
Bernfield Memorial Award; Merton Vol. 1: 3586
Bernhard Award; Dianne B. Vol. 1: 829
Bernhard Gold Medal Award; Dianne B. Vol. 1: 14869
Bernhard-Harms-Medaille Vol. 2: 2338
Bernhardt Distinguished Service Award; Homer I. Vol. 1: 3631
Bernheim European Prizes; Emile Vol. 2: 1102
Bernheimer, Jr. Award; Leo G. fBillv Vol. 1: 11468
Bernick New Leadership Award; Paul Vol. 1: 3007
Bernstein Book Award for Excellence in Journalism; Helen B. Vol. 1: 14147
Bernstein-Crosman Scholarship Vol. 1: 12000
Bernstein Grant Vol. 1: 592
Bernstein, M.D. Award; Albion O. Vol. 1: 11673
Berntsen International Scholarship in Surveying Vol. 1: 1778
Berry Fellowship; Rosann S. Vol. 1: 16551
Berry Medal Vol. 1: 11786
Berry Medal; Albert E. Vol. 1: 6912
Berry Prize; David Vol. 2: 6778
Berry Scholar Award for Excellence in Writing; Chester A. Vol. 1: 5097
Berry Scholarship; Howard A. Vol. 1: 10541
Berryman Award for Editorial Cartoons; Clifford K. and James T. Vol. 1: 13555
Berryman Student Research Award; Doris L. Vol. 1: 13850
Berson-Yalow Award Vol. 1: 16778
Bert Easey Technical Award Vol. 2: 5503
Bertelsen Prize; Paul and Margaret Vol. 1: 12101
Bertelson Award; Paul Vol. 2: 4491
Berthault; Prix Claude Vol. 2: 1436
Berthault; Prix de la Fondation Claude Vol. 2: 1636
Berthault; Prix de Madame Claude Vol. 2: 1544
Berthelot; Prix Vol. 2: 1545
Berthold-Preis Vol. 2: 2237
Bertholf Award for Chapter Efficiency; Lloyd M. Vol. 1: 5722
Bertholf Award for Chapter Excellence; Lloyd M. Vol. 1: 5722
Berton Award; Pierre Vol. 1: 6134
Bertrand; Prix Leon Vol. 2: 1832
Bertrand; Prix Paul Vol. 2: 1546
Berwick Prize Vol. 2: 6397
Berwick Prize; Senior Vol. 2: 6398
Besancon International Competition for Young Conductors Vol. 2: 1794
Besancon International Competition of Music Composition Vol. 2: 1795
Beskow Plaketten; Elsa Vol. 2: 4686
Beskow Plaque; Elsa Vol. 2: 4686
Beskowska resestipendiet Vol. 2: 4649
BESLA Award Vol. 1: 5802
Bessaraboff Prize; Nicolas Vol. 1: 2838
Bessey Award; Charles Edwin Vol. 1: 5869
Bessie Awards Vol. 1: 8049
Best Animation Short Made for the Internet Vol. 1: 14729
Best Annual Reports Awards Vol. 2: 3940
Best Annual SIR Paper Award Vol. 1: 10672
Best Appraiser of the Year Vol. 2: 2500
Best Article Award Vol. 1: 9437
Best Article in Logistics Focus Vol. 2: 5622
Best Article of the Year Award Vol. 1: 13018
Best Bet Awards Vol. 1: 7045
Best Black/Gray Tattoo Vol. 1: 13820
Best Black/White Design Sheet Vol. 1: 13821
Best Book of the Year on the American Revolution Vol. 1: 3487
Best Book on East Texas History Vol. 1: 8332
Best Booth Award Vol. 1: 1153
Best Broker of the Year Vol. 2: 2501
Best Builder Award Vol. 1: 4764
Best Cars Vol. 1: 2784
Best Christmas Tree Vol. 2: 5281
Best Cinematography Vol. 1: 4716
Best Colored Back Piece Vol. 1: 13822
Best Colored Design Sheet Vol. 1: 13823
Best Comedy Vol. 1: 4717
Best Cover-Up Tattoo Vol. 1: 13824
Best Craftsmanship Vol. 2: 3477
Best Dance Venue Vol. 2: 227
BesT Design Awards Vol. 2: 3713
Best Developer of the Year Vol. 2: 2502
Best Dissertation Award Vol. 1: 10673
Best Doctoral Dissertation Vol. 1: 8584
Best Doctoral Dissertation Award Vol. 1: 104
Best Doctoral Research Presentation Award Vol. 2: 2757
Best Documentary
Aspen Filmfest Vol. 1: 4718
International Short Film Festival, Oberhausen Vol 2: 2316
Best Documentary Award Vol. 2: 6327
Best Drama Vol. 1: 4719
Best Drama Award Vol. 2: 6327
Best-Dressed Women Vol. 1: 11995
Best Elected Recycling Leader Vol. 1: 13604
Best Engineer Vol. 2: 4234
Best Engineering Achievements Awards Vol. 2: 4199
Best Entrepreneurship Vol. 2: 3478
Best Exhibit Booth Display Vol. 1: 5607
Best Exhibition Stall Awards Vol. 2: 4200
Best Feature-Length Mountain Film Award Vol. 1: 5651
Best Film Made for Children Vol. 1: 14730
Best Film on Mountain Culture Award Vol. 1: 5651
Best Film on Mountain Environment Award Vol. 1: 5651
Best Film on Mountain Sports Award Vol. 1: 5651
Best First Article Award Vol. 1: 14315
Best First Book Award Vol. 1: 14975
Best First Book in the History of Religions Vol. 1: 743
Best First Feature Award Vol. 1: 12076
Best First Presentation Vol. 2: 2487
Best First-Time Paper Vol. 2: 4122
Best General Entertainment Amusement Venue Vol. 2: 228
Best Gesneriad in Show Vol. 1: 9067
Best Graduate Film Vol. 1: 14731
Best Graduate Student Paper Award Vol. 1: 7511
Best Hosta in a Tour Garden Award Vol. 1: 2311
Best Hosta Seedling or Sport in a Tour Garden Award Vol. 1: 2312
Best Illustrated Children's Books of the Year Vol. 1: 14190

Award Index

Best in American Living Awards
National Association of Home Builders Vol. 1: 12557
Professional Builder - Reed Business Information Vol 1: 15280
Best in Breed Award Vol. 2: 7154
Best in Business Award Vol. 1: 5737
Best in Business Contest Vol. 1: 16501
Best in Media Award Vol. 1: 7354
Best in Show
American Physicians Art Association Vol. 1: 3159
Westminster Kennel Club Vol 1: 18713
Best in Topical Awards Vol. 1: 4361
Best Information Science Book Award Vol. 1: 3736
Best *JASIST* Paper Award Vol. 1: 3737
Best Jockey - Races Won Vol. 2: 3219
Best KidsF Menu in America Competition Vol. 1: 15642
Best Marketing Vol. 2: 5722
Best MBA Paper in Corporate Citizenship Competition Vol. 1: 5856
Best Memorial Award; Elmer S. Vol. 1: 15071
Best Memorial Breeder Trophy; John Vol. 1: 10890
Best Music Video Vol. 1: 14732
Best New Design Vol. 1: 5559
Best New Divisional Road Rally Vol. 1: 17212
Best New Products Vol. 2: 7322
Best New Regional Road Rally Program Vol. 1: 17212
Best New Technology Vol. 1: 5560
Best of Breed Vol. 1: 8031
Best of Breed or Best of Variety of Breed Vol. 1: 18714
Best of Category Awards; Intel Vol. 1: 15927
Best of Europe - International Direct Marketing Awards Vol. 2: 888
Best of Festival Awards (Grand Prix) Vol. 1: 17978
The Best of Finnish Graphic Design and Advertising Competition Vol. 2: 1405
Best of *LRTS* Award Vol. 1: 4910
Best of Saskatchewan Award Vol. 1: 19078
Best of Show Artistic Vol. 1: 15256
Best of Show Award
Minot State University - Northwest Art Center Vol. 1: 11849
Smithsonian Women's Committee Vol. 1: 16100
Best of Show Awards Vol. 1: 11328
Best of Show Commercial Vol. 1: 15257
Best of the Online Journal Award Vol. 1: 16044
Best of the Rest Award Vol. 1: 18198
Best One-Year Safety Record Award Vol. 1: 15461
Best Operations Paper Vol. 2: 3815
Best Original Score/Soundtrack Vol. 2: 4235
Best Paper Award
Canadian Fertility and Andrology Society Vol. 1: 6493
Geological Society of America Vol 1: 9018
Indian Dairy Association Vol 2: 2633
Institute of Electronics, Information and Communication Engineers Vol 2: 3192
International Cryogenic Materials Conference Vol 1: 10374
International Institute of Public Finance Vol 2: 2306
International Society of Offshore and Polar Engineers Vol 1: 10723
West African College of Surgeons Vol 2: 3887
The Best Paper Award Vol. 1: 10828
Best Paper Awards Vol. 1: 10102
Best Paper in *Geophysics* Award Vol. 1: 16674
Best Paper of the Year Award Vol. 1: 7617
Best Paper Presented at the Annual Meeting Award Vol. 1: 16675
Best Paper Presented Award Vol. 2: 4294
Best Paper Published in History of Psychology Vol. 1: 3379
Best Paper Student Presentation Vol. 1: 16418
Best Papers Award Vol. 2: 4201
Best Papers by Young Authors Vol. 2: 4969
Best Papers of the Year Vol. 2: 2488
Best Performance of a Classical Work Vol. 1: 15820
Best Performance of a Romantic Work Vol. 1: 15821
Best Portrait Tattoo Vol. 1: 13825
Best Poster Award Vol. 2: 4295
Best Poster Prize Vol. 2: 5293
Best Practice Award
Association for the Study of Obesity Vol. 2: 5102
Consultant Dietitians in Health Care Facilities Vol 1: 7764
Best Practice Award for Comprehensive Services in Education Vol. 1: 1040
Best Practice Award for Gender Equality Vol. 1: 1041
Best Practice Award for Global and International Teacher Education Vol. 1: 1042
Best Practice Award for the Innovative Use of Technology Vol. 1: 1043
Best Practice Award in Support of Diversity Vol. 1: 1044
Best Practice Award in Support of Teacher Education Accreditation Vol. 1: 1045
Best Practices Vol. 2: 229
Best Producer Vol. 2: 4236
Best Referee Award from Mineralum Deposits Vol. 2: 1266
Best Research Paper Vol. 1: 3413
Best Research Paper Award Vol. 2: 3962
Best Scientific Work Vol. 2: 846
Best Scientific Work of a Young Scientist Vol. 2: 847
Best Selling Release Vol. 2: 4237
Best Short Mountain Film Award Vol. 1: 5651
Best Sleeve Vol. 1: 13826
Best Space Operations Crew Award Vol. 1: 283
Best Stand Vol. 2: 7323
Best Stock Z28 Award Vol. 1: 10288
Best Student Vol. 1: 4720
Best Student Award Vol. 2: 4296
Best Student Conference Paper Prizes Vol. 2: 3787
Best Student Paper and Poster Awards Vol. 1: 16897
Best Student Paper Award
Academy of Marketing Science Vol. 1: 105
American Association of Petroleum Geologists Vol 1: 1205
American Society for Information Science and Technology Vol 1: 3745
Canadian Cartographic Association Vol 1: 6384
Finnish Association of Designers Ornamo Vol 2: 1384
IEEE Electromagnetic Compatibility Society Vol 1: 9571
International Institute of Fisheries Economics and Trade Vol 1: 10468
Micronet R & D Vol 1: 11741
Society of Nematologists Vol 1: 16771
Best Student Paper Awards Vol. 1: 16313
Best Student Poster Award Vol. 1: 1206
Best Student Scientific Work Vol. 2: 848
Best Subsequent Book Award Vol. 1: 14976
Best Tattooed Female Vol. 1: 13827
Best Tattooed Male Vol. 1: 13828
Best Tattooist Vol. 1: 13829
Best Television Series for Adults Vol. 1: 14733
Best Theoretical Paper Award Vol. 1: 3414
Best Theoretical Paper on Hypnosis Award Vol. 1: 16197
Best Time Saving Device Vol. 1: 10246
Best Traditional Tattoo Vol. 1: 13830
Best Trainer - Training Technique Vol. 2: 3220
Best Transaction Paper Vol. 1: 9569
Best Unique Tattoo Vol. 1: 13831
Best Unpublished Research Paper Vol. 1: 8585
Best Unrestored Award Vol. 1: 14796
Best Variegated Hosta in a Tour Garden Award Vol. 1: 2313
Best Vendor Award Vol. 2: 2788
Best Wine Lists in America Awards Vol. 1: 15643
Best Young Filmmaker Award Vol. 1: 12080
Beta Phi Mu Award Vol. 1: 2650
The Bette Moulton Award Vol. 1: 6542
Better Brickwork Alliance Vol. 2: 7282
Better Communications Contest Vol. 1: 18479
Better Newspaper Advertising Contest Vol. 1: 13476
Better Newspaper Contest Vol. 1: 13476
Better Newspapers Competition Vol. 1: 6416
Bettineski Child Advocate of the Year Award; G. F. Vol. 1: 13057
Betton Youth Exhibit Award; James L. Vol. 1: 2871
Between the Lines Award for Best Gay/ Lesbian Film Vol. 1: 4535
Beule; Fondation de Mme. Veuve Vol. 2: 1482
Beule; Prix Karl Vol. 2: 1437
Beveridge Award; Albert J. Vol. 1: 2227
Beverly Hills Theatre Guild Playwright Award Vol. 1: 5744
Beville, Jr. Award; Hugh Malcolm Vol. 1: 12427
Beydoun Memorial Award for Best International Poster; Ziad Vol. 1: 1207
Beyond Margins Award Vol. 1: 14892
BG Wildlife Photographer of the Year Competition Vol. 2: 6492
BGA Tribute Award Vol. 1: 5741
BGRC Silver Jubilee Oration Award Vol. 2: 2599
Bhabha Medal; Homi J. Vol. 2: 2676
Bharat Ratna Vol. 2: 2577
Bharati Prize; Vidya Vol. 2: 2643
Bhargava Memorial Medal; Professor K.P. Vol. 2: 2677
Bhasha Samman Vol. 2: 2790

Bhaskar Award Vol. 2: 3481
Bhatnagar Award Vol. 2: 2573
Bhatt Young Investigator Award; Pravin N. Vol. 1: 914
Bhoruka Gold Medal Vol. 2: 2644
Bialkowski Prize; Grzegorz Vol. 2: 4046
Bianchi Cup Vol. 1: 13647
Biancotto Aerobatics Diploma; Leon Vol. 2: 4720
BIBM Awards Vol. 2: 908
Bicentenary Medal Vol. 2: 6385
Bick Ehrenmedaille; Dr. Josef Vol. 2: 754
Bickel Award; John O. Vol. 1: 3922
Bickersteth Memorial Medal; Julian Vol. 2: 6033
Bicking Award; Lew Vol. 1: 13787
Bidault de l'Isle; Prix Georges Vol. 2: 1951
Biedenbach Distinguished Service Award; Joseph M. Vol. 1: 3632
Biedma; Premio Dr. Carlos A. Vol. 2: 17
Bienek Preis fur Lyrik; Horst Vol. 2: 2038
Biennale Internationale de Gravure Vol. 2: 4457
Biennial Award Vol. 1: 129
Biennial Exhibition Awards Vol. 1: 12025
Bier Award; William C. Vol. 1: 3354
Biesbroeck Prize; George Van Vol. 1: 1355
Bietila Award; Paul Vol. 1: 18085
Big Brother of the Year Vol. 1: 5750
Big East Conference Academic Awards Vol. 1: 5753
Big Muddy Film Festival Awards Vol. 1: 5756
BIG Oscars Vol. 1: 5691
Big Shoulders Award Vol. 1: 7329
Big Sister of the Year Vol. 1: 5751
Bigelow Trophy Vol. 1: 7461
Biggs Fellowship; E. Power Vol. 1: 14680
Bignami Prize; Paolo Vol. 2: 3123
Bigsby Medal Vol. 2: 5929
Bijnsprijs; Anna Vol. 2: 3486
Bikila Award; Abebe Vol. 1: 14152
Bilac Prize; Olavo Vol. 2: 1118
Bilbao International Festival of Documentary and Short Films Vol. 2: 4517
Bilgrami Memorial Medal; Professor Krishna Sahai Vol. 2: 2678
Bilim Odulu Vol. 2: 4988
Bill Mahon Trainee Presentation Award Vol. 1: 6930
Billard Award; Admiral Frederick C. Vol. 1: 13452
Billboard Music Awards Vol. 1: 5760
Billboard Radio Awards Vol. 1: 5761
Billings Good Sportsmanship Award; Bruce Vol. 1: 3512
Billingsley Memorial Scholarship; Dewayne Vol. 1: 17497
Billington Book Award; Ray A. Vol. 1: 18706
Billington Prize; Ray Allen Vol. 1: 14689
Bilson Award; Geoffrey Vol. 1: 6393
Bilt prijs; Dr. J. van der Vol. 2: 3627
Binani Gold Medal Vol. 2: 2645
Binder Award; Joseph Vol. 2: 4905
Bindesboll Medal; Thorvald Vol. 2: 1324
Bing Award; Elisabeth Vol. 1: 11209
Bing Prize; Robert Vol. 2: 4885
Bingham Fellowships for Writers; Robert Vol. 1: 14893
Bingham Medal Vol. 1: 16852
Bingham Poetry Prize Vol. 1: 5854
Bingham Prize; Worth Vol. 1: 5769
Bingham Scholarship; Seth Vol. 1: 2145
Bingham Sr. Media Award; Barry Vol. 1: 11133
Binkhorst Medal and Lecture Vol. 1: 3901
Binkley Award; Thomas Vol. 1: 8308
Binkley-Stephenson Award Vol. 1: 14690
Binney Memorial Award Vol. 2: 5943
Binoux; Prix Vol. 2: 1547
Bio-Mega/Boehringer Ingelheim Award for Organic or Bioorganic Chemistry Vol. 1: 6905
Bio-Serv Award Vol. 1: 3786
Bio-Tech Award Vol. 2: 3597
Biochemical Society Award Vol. 2: 5168
Biochemical Society Travel Fund Vol. 2: 5169
Biological Physics Prize Vol. 1: 3110
Biology Award Vol. 2: 2542
Biomedical Engineering Outstanding Educator Award Vol. 1: 3668
Biomedical Instrumentation & Technology Outstanding Paper Awards Vol. 1: 4980
bioMerieux Sonnenwirth Award for Leadership in Clinical Microbiology Vol. 1: 3765
Biota Award for Medicinal Chemistry Vol. 2: 616
Biotechnology Teaching Award Vol. 1: 12405
Birch Award; Carroll L. Vol. 1: 2763
Bird Young Investigator Award Vol. 2: 136
Birds in Art Vol. 1: 18889
Bird*F*s Trophy; Peter Vol. 2: 1846
Birdsall Prize in European Military and Strategic History; Paul Vol. 1: 2228
Birkebeinerrennet Ski Race Vol. 2: 3898
Birkenhead International Colour Salon Vol. 2: 5181
Birkhoff Prize; George David Vol. 1: 16266
Birkhoff Prize in Applied Mathematics; George David Vol. 1: 2726
Birkmaier Award for Doctoral Dissertation Research in Foreign Language Education; Emma Marie Vol. 1: 1830
Birks Book Prize; Peter Vol. 2: 7201
Birla Award; R. D. Vol. 2: 2736
Birla Memorial Gold Medal; G. D. Vol. 2: 2646
Birmingham Medal Vol. 2: 6168
BIS Bibilographic Instruction Publication of the Year Award Vol. 1: 5086
Bischoff Award; Ernst Vol. 1: 886
Bishop Award; Joan Fiss Vol. 1: 15965
Bishop, III Memorial Trophy; Louis F. Vol. 1: 18715
Bisson Award; Edmond E. Vol. 1: 16880
Bittner Extension Award in Horticulture; Carl S. Vol. 1: 3723
Bittner Service Citation for Outstanding Service in UCEA; Walton S. Vol. 1: 18209
Bizet; Prix Georges
Academie des Beaux-Arts Vol. 2: 1438
Institut de France Vol 2: 1853
Bjerknes Medal; Vilhelm Vol. 2: 1771
Black Award; Charles A. Vol. 1: 7841
Black Award for Excellence in Children's Literature; Irma S. and James H. Vol. 1: 5656
Black Award for Excellence in Children's Literature; Irma Simonton Vol. 1: 5656
Black Award for Outstanding Achievement in the Practice of Counseling Psychology; John D. Vol. 1: 3321
Black Award; Mary Vol. 2: 5035
Black Award; SETAC/EA Engineering Jeff Vol. 1: 16656
Black Caucus Certificate of Appreciation Vol. 1: 5794
Black Caucus of the American Library Association Literary Awards Vol. 1: 5795
Black Caucus of the American Library Association Trailblazer's Award Vol. 1: 5796
Black Caucus Special Recognition Plaques Vol. 1: 5797
Black Engineer of the Year Awards Vol. 1: 7100
Black Lyon Vol. 2: 3017
Black Maria Film and Video Festival; Thomas A. Edison Media Arts Consortium - Vol. 1: 8390
Black Memorial Prizes; James Tait Vol. 2: 7308
Black Prize; Duncan Vol. 1: 15416
Black Tie Award Vol. 1: 10438
Black Travel Fellowship; Malcolm Vol. 2: 6703
Blackall Machine Tool and Gage Award Vol. 1: 4124
Blackburn Prize; Susan Smith Vol. 1: 17347
Blackhorse Scholarship Vol. 1: 2
Blackwell Medal; Elizabeth Vol. 1: 2765
Blackwell's Scholarship Award Vol. 1: 4911
Blaine Award Vol. 2: 5466
Blair-Bell Memorial Lectureship in Obstetrics and Gynaecology; William Vol. 2: 6704
Blair Biorheology Scholarship; Scott Vol. 2: 5527
Blair Eminent Naturalist Award; W. Frank Vol. 1: 17059
Blair Memorial Award; W. Frank Vol. 1: 7336
Blair Service Award; Lucy Vol. 1: 3143
Blair Trophy; Hunter Vol. 2: 6887
Blake Award for Distinguished Graduate Teaching; M. A. Vol. 1: 3725
Blakemore Award; L.C. Vol. 2: 3796
Blakeslee Graduate Student Fellowships; Rennie Taylor/Alton Vol. 1: 7873
Blakey Memorial Prize; O. F. Vol. 2: 491
Blanc; Prix Armand Vol. 2: 2289
Blanc Prize; Armand Vol. 2: 2289
Blanche; Prix Robert Vol. 2: 1637
Blasters Leadership Award Vol. 1: 10720
BIAT National Student Award Vol. 2: 5320
Blaylock Medal; Selwyn G. Vol. 1: 6610
Bledisloe Aviation Trophy Vol. 2: 3841
Bledisloe Gold Medal for Landowners Vol. 2: 6662
Bledisloe Veterinary Award Vol. 2: 6668
Bledsoe Award; C. Warren Vol. 1: 4858
Blegen Award; Julius Vol. 1: 18086
Blegen Award; Theodore C. Vol. 1: 8819
Bleininger Memorial Award; Albert Victor Vol. 1: 1467
Blekinge County Council Prize for Environmental Control Vol. 2: 4573
Blekinge lans landstings Miljo vardspris Vol. 2: 4573
Blenheim Award Vol. 1: 7403
Bleriot Medal; Louis Vol. 2: 4721
Blewett Playwright's Award; Jill Vol. 2: 672
BLG Awards Vol. 1: 6645
Blick Art Materials Award; Dick Vol. 1: 14869
Blick Merchandise Award; Dick Vol. 1: 16517
Bliss Editors' Award; A. Harry Vol. 1: 13115
Bliss Medal Vol. 1: 16520
Bliss Memorial Award; Gordon M. Vol. 1: 3833
Bliss Prize Fellowship in Byzantine Studies Vol. 1: 8298
Bloch Award; Herbert Vol. 1: 4007
Block Community Lecture; I. E. Vol. 1: 16267

Block Prize; Jochen Vol. 2: 2257
Blodger Diversity Award; John D. Vol. 1: 11637
Bloem Distinguished Service Award; Delmar L. Vol. 1: 1749
Blomska stipendiet Vol. 2: 4650
Bloom Memorial Award; A. A. Vol. 1: 17637
Bloom Memorial Scholarship; Amy L. Vol. 1: 17635
Bloomer Award; H. H. Vol. 2: 6386
Bloomfield Award; John J. Vol. 1: 2338
BLS Service of the Year Award Vol. 1: 12527
Blue Angel Vol. 2: 2048
Blue Heron Award Vol. 1: 15980
Blue Pencil Awards Vol. 1: 12542
Blue Planet Prize Vol. 2: 3162
Blue Wave Awards Vol. 1: 10154
Bluebird Research Grants Vol. 1: 14269
Bluegrass Event of the Year Vol. 1: 10270
Bluegrass Music Awards Vol. 1: 16443
Blues Hall of Fame Vol. 1: 5819
Blues Music Awards Vol. 1: 5820
Blum; Bourse Marcelle Vol. 2: 1638
Blum Research Grant; Stella Vol. 1: 7833
Blumer Award; Herbert Vol. 1: 16469
Blumlein-Brown-Willans Premium Vol. 2: 6143
Blundell Award; James Vol. 2: 5253
Blundell Grants; K. Vol. 2: 7139
Blunk Memorial Award; Jim Vol. 1: 17746
Bly Cub Reporter Award; Nellie Vol. 1: 14136
BMA Hall of Fame Vol. 1: 6024
BMET of the Year Award Vol. 1: 4981
Board Citation Vol. 1: 11299
Board LeaderFs Award Vol. 1: 9128
Board of Directors Distinguished Service Award for Senior ACS Administrators Vol. 1: 1532
Board of Directors Student Paper Awards Vol. 1: 7803
Board of Governors Award Vol. 1: 5520
Board of Publications Award for the Best Paper in *Toxicological Sciences* Vol. 1: 16869
Board of Trustees Award
  American Hospital Association Vol. 1: 2303
  American Hospital Association Vol 1: 2309
Boardman Tasker Award for Mountain Literature Vol. 2: 5187
Boas Medal; Walter Vol. 2: 253
Boase Award; Arthur J. Vol. 1: 1750
Bob Sawyer Award Vol. 1: 7660
Bob Shaw Golden Age Award Vol. 1: 13832
Bobbitt National Prize for Poetry; Rebekah Johnson Vol. 1: 11345
Bobby Chapter of the Year Award; Lloyd Vol. 1: 7741
Bocher Memorial Prize Vol. 1: 2727
Bock Prize; Frederick Vol. 1: 15115
Bocking Award; Douglas Vol. 1: 5941
Bocking Memorial Award; James H. Vol. 1: 6329
Bode { Norman Holmes Pearson Prize; Carl Vol. 1: 4326
Boedecker Jr. Distinguished Service Award; Kenneth J. Vol. 1: 5406
The Boehringer Ingelheim Post-Doctoral Award Vol. 1: 14968
Boehringer Mannheim Award Vol. 1: 6988
Boehringer Mannheim S.A. Award Vol. 2: 4258
Boehringer Mannheim Student Poster Awards Vol. 1: 6988
Boeing Award for Best Paper in Image Analysis and Interpretation Vol. 1: 4735
Boelpaepe Prize Vol. 2: 1063
Boerma Award; A. H. Vol. 2: 3054
Boger Award; Robert F. Vol. 1: 7757
Bogg Memorial Award; Wm. G. Vol. 1: 7673
Boggs Award; Larry Vol. 1: 12837
Boggs Award; Lindy Vol. 1: 2951
Boggs Award; Phil Vol. 1: 18387
Boggs Service Award; Andrew T. Vol. 1: 4048
Bogie Prize; David Vol. 2: 6002
Bogin Memorial Award; George Vol. 1: 15125
Bogle/Pratt International Library Travel Fund Vol. 1: 2672
Bogomolny National Service Award; Richard J. Vol. 1: 7274
Bohlen Award; Avis Vol. 1: 2055
Boisen Professional Service Award; Anton Vol. 1: 5308
Boivin Prize; Jean-Marc Vol. 2: 1846
Bok Award; Priscilla and Bart Vol. 1: 1356
The Bok Prize Vol. 2: 64
Bold Award; Harold C. Vol. 1: 15034
Boldenweck Voice Scholarship; Elizabeth Vol. 1: 12000
Boldrewood Award; Rolf Vol. 2: 435
Boldy Memorial Award; Julian Vol. 1: 6611
Bolivar Lecture Award; Simon Vol. 1: 3268
Bolivar Prize; International Simon Vol. 2: 1990
Bolliger Award; Adolph Vol. 2: 280
Bolliger Memorial Lecture; Hans R. Vol. 2: 7158
Bolling Cross Vol. 1: 8
Bollingen Prize in Poetry Vol. 1: 19039
Bollinger Humanitarian Award; Glen H. Vol. 1: 9329
Bolt Award; CAA Carol Vol. 1: 6320
Bolton Award for Professional Excellence Vol. 1: 12393
Bolton-Johnson Prize Vol. 1: 7696
Bolton-Kinnaird Award Vol. 1: 18682
Boltzmann Medal Vol. 1: 10811
Bolus Medal Vol. 2: 4135
Bombard Prize; Alain Vol. 2: 1846
Bombardier Prize in Technological Innovation; J. Armand Vol. 1: 5015
Bomford Prize; Guy Vol. 2: 1307
Bomford Trust Paper Award Vol. 2: 6082
Bonazinga Award; Marie T. Vol. 1: 16324
Bond Award; Polly Vol. 1: 8509
Bond Memorial Consumer Award; Ethel Vol. 1: 12459
Bonder Scholarship for Applied Operations Research in Health Services; Seth Vol. 1: 9738
Bonder Scholarship for Applied Operations Research in Military Applications; Seth Vol. 1: 9739
Bonderman National Youth Theatre Playwriting Competition and Workshop; Waldo M. and Grace C. Vol. 1: 9684
Bonhoeffer-Eucen-Scheibe Memorial Lecture Vol. 2: 2156
Bonica Trainee Fellowship; John J. Vol. 1: 10117
Bonin Award; Wilbrod Vol. 1: 5941
Bonn Mileata Calmachta; An Vol. 2: 2854
Bonner Prize in Nuclear Physics; Tom W. Vol. 1: 3111
Bonniers Pris; Gerard Vol. 2: 4651
Bono Engineering Communications Award; Jack Vol. 1: 16683
Book Award
  British Psychological Society Vol. 2: 5426
  Canadian Railroad Historical Association Vol 1: 6856
  Children's Literature Association Vol 1: 7348
  New York Genealogical and Biographical Society Vol 1: 14129
  North American Society for Sport History Vol 1: 14332
  Please Touch Museum Vol 1: 15109
  The Poetry Center & American Poetry Archives Vol 1: 15123
  Religious Communication Association Vol 1: 15621
  Scribes Vol 1: 15944
  Society for American Archaeology Vol 1: 16158
  Society for Human Resource Management Vol 1: 16233
  Toni Morrison Society Vol 1: 17547
  Wisconsin State Genealogical Society Vol 1: 18797
Book Awards
  Catholic Press Association Vol. 1: 7164
  Children's Literature Council of Southern California Vol 1: 7352
  Commonwealth Club of California Vol 1: 7633
  International Academy of Astronautics Vol 2: 1865
  James Beard Foundation Vol 1: 10953
  Pacific Northwest Booksellers Association Vol 1: 14778
  South Carolina Association of School Librarians Vol 1: 16984
Book Awards of the National Book Development Council of Singapore Vol. 2: 4423
Book Cover Design of the Year Vol. 1: 5836
Book Design Awards
  Alcuin Society Vol 1: 385
  Australian Publishers' Association Vol 2: 339
Book Design of the Year Vol. 1: 5836
Book Design of the Year Award Vol. 1: 6345
Book Illustration of the Year Vol. 1: 5836
Book, Jacket and Journal Show Vol. 1: 5042
Book of Honor Vol. 2: 3805
Book-of-the-Month Club Translation Prize Vol. 1: 14894
Book of the Year
  British Chess Federation Vol. 2: 5277
  Hungarian Publishers and Booksellers Association Vol 2: 2498
Book of the Year Award
  Academy of Parish Clergy Vol. 1: 117
  Conference on Christianity and Literature Vol 1: 7689
  Healthcare Information and Management Systems Society Vol 1: 9325
  MIND - National Association for Mental Health Vol 2: 6430
Book of the Year Award: Early Childhood Vol. 2: 404
Book of the Year Award: Older Readers Vol. 2: 405
Book of the Year Award: Younger Readers Vol. 2: 406
Book of the Year Awards Vol. 2: 37

Book of the Year for Children Award Vol. 1: 6700
Book of the Year for Children Medal Vol. 1: 6700
Book Prize
American Philosophical Association Vol. 1: 3086
British Association for Applied Linguistics Vol 2: 5233
British Society for Middle Eastern Studies Vol 2: 5482
Law and Society Association Vol 1: 11250
Society for the Historians of the Early American Republic Vol 1: 16431
Book Prizes Vol. 2: 2454
Book Publishers of Texas Children's/Young People's Award Vol. 1: 17475
Book Sense Book of the Year Award Vol. 1: 1414
Bookbuilders West Book Show Vol. 1: 5847
Booker McConnell Prize Vol. 2: 6418
Booker Russian Novel Prize Vol. 2: 5189
Books Abroad/Neustadt International Prize Vol. 1: 18954
Bookseller of the Year Award Vol. 1: 6346
Boom Award; Roger W. Vol. 1: 7990
Boone and Crockett Award Vol. 1: 10211
Boone Award; Joel T. Vol. 1: 5238
Boosey Award; Leslie
Performing Right Society Vol. 2: 6533
Royal Philharmonic Society Vol 2: 6861
Booth Award; Edwin Vol. 1: 7445
Booth Awards Vol. 1: 17108
Booth Education Award; Taylor Vol. 1: 9801
Booth Scholarship Award; E.V. Vol. 1: 6957
Boothby Award; Walter M. Vol. 1: 201
Boothby - Edwards Award Vol. 1: 201
Boothman Bursary; Harry Vol. 1: 6798
Boots Romantic Novel of the Year Vol. 2: 6605
Borden Award
American Dairy Science Association Vol. 1: 1872
American Dairy Science Association Vol 1: 1880
Association of American Medical Colleges Vol 1: 5035
Borden Award in Nutrition Vol. 1: 6960
Bordin; Prix
Academie des Beaux-Arts Vol. 2: 1439
Academie des Inscriptions et Belles-Lettres Vol 2: 1502
Academie des Sciences Morales et Politiques Vol 2: 1639
Borgia; Premio Dotte Giuseppe Vol. 2: 2973
Borgman Award for Surface Design; Lynn Goodwin Vol. 1: 8019
Borman Award; Alvah K. Vol. 1: 3633
Born Award; Max Vol. 1: 14602
Born Medal and Prize; Max Vol. 2: 6054
Born-Preis; Max- Vol. 2: 2090
Borovik Award; Artyom Vol. 1: 14761
Bos Innovative Projects Grants; Candace C. Vol. 1: 7863
Bosch Foundation Fellowship Program; Robert Vol. 1: 7182
Bose Medal; A. K. Vol. 2: 2647
Bose Medal; Satyendranath Vol. 2: 2679
Bose Memorial Award; Anil Kumar Vol. 2: 2680
Boston Globe - Horn Book Awards Vol. 1: 5858
Boston Marathon Vol. 1: 5852
Boswell Award Vol. 2: 4359
Botanical Society Certificate of Merit Vol. 2: 4136
Botanical Society Flora Conservation Medal Vol. 2: 4137
Botein Fellowship; Stephen Vol. 1: 819
Bottorf Award; Jim Vol. 1: 49
Boucher-OCLC Distinguished Interlibrary Loan Library Award; Virginia Vol. 1: 2684
Bouchet Award; Edward A. Vol. 1: 3112
Bouffault International Animal Agriculture Award Vol. 1: 3884
Bouillon Award; Lincoln Vol. 1: 4049
Bouland; Prix Leclerc-Maria Vol. 2: 1440
Bound to Stay Bound Books Scholarship Vol. 1: 4922
Bourcart; Prix Jacques Vol. 2: 1833
Bourgelat Award Vol. 2: 5467
Bourke Lectureship Vol. 2: 6952
Bourne Student Poetry Award; Louise Louis/Emily F. Vol. 1: 15131
Bourse Bancroft Vol. 1: 15755
Bourse de la SPE Vol. 2: 1969
Bourse Harry Boothman Vol. 1: 6798
Bourses Commemoratives E. W. R. Steacie Vol. 1: 13977
Bourses de quatre mois Vol. 1: 11719
Boury Prize; Karel Vol. 2: 952
Boutin Division Service; Delano L. Vol. 1: 14834
Bouwer Prize for ChildrenFs Literature; Alba Vol. 2: 4265
Bouwhuis Memorial Scholarship; Rev. Andrew L. Vol. 1: 7157
Bovey Award for Leadership Support of the Arts; Edmund C. Vol. 1: 7849
Bowditch Award Lecture Vol. 1: 3163
Bowen Award; N.L. Vol. 1: 2109
Bowen Medal; R. W. Vol. 2: 4341
Bowen Memorial Award Competition; Betty Vol. 1: 15955
Bower Award and Prize for Achievement in Science Vol. 1: 8866
Bower Award for Business Leadership Vol. 1: 8867
Bower Memorial Award; Ros Vol. 2: 102
Bowie Medal; William Vol. 1: 2110
Bowie Young Investigator; Lemuel J. Vol. 1: 871
Bowis Award Vol. 1: 1728
Bowis Award; E.B. Vol. 1: 1730
Bowker Award; Isadore Gilbert Mudge - R. R. Vol. 1: 2691
Bowker/Ulrich's Serials Librianship Award Vol. 1: 4912
Bowler of the Year
Bowling Writers Association of America Vol. 1: 5893
Royal New South Wales Bowling Association Vol 2: 632
Western Women Professional Bowlers Vol 1: 18700
Bowlers of the Year Vol. 1: 18913
Bowles Cup Vol. 2: 6785
Bowling Hall of Fame and Museum Vol. 1: 10276
Bowling Magazine Writing Competition Vol. 1: 1416
Bowling Reclamation Awards; Kenes C. Vol. 1: 10845
Bowman Award; Raymond C. Vol. 1: 16245
Bowman Best of East Texas Award; Bob and Doris Vol. 1: 8332
Bowman Memorial Award for Painting; Jean Vol. 1: 582
Boxer Award; Mark Vol. 2: 7283
Boxing Hall of Fame Vol. 1: 10819
Boxing Referee Award Vol. 1: 10820
Boxing Trainer of the Year Award Vol. 1: 10821
Boxing Writer of the Year Vol. 1: 10822
Boyd Award for Housing; Robin Vol. 2: 627
Boyd Hall of Fame Award; John A. Vol. 1: 7525
Boyd Humanitarian Award; Benjamin F. Vol. 1: 14825
Boyd Literary Award; W.Y. Vol. 1: 2651
Boyer Award; Francis Vol. 1: 1973
Boyer Lecture on Public Policy; Frances Vol. 1: 1973
Boyer Medal; Marian Angell Godfrey Vol. 1: 18335
Boyle Award; Alliance for Better Bone Health Iain T. Vol. 2: 5818
Boyle Award for Distinguished Public Service; Joseph F. Vol. 1: 1709
Boyle Award; Hal Vol. 1: 14761
Boyle Gold Award and Trophy; Sister Vol. 1: 15853
Boyle-Higgins Award Vol. 2: 2838
Boyle Medal; Robert Vol. 2: 6953
Boyle Memorial Senior French Music Scholarship; Sister Geraldine Vol. 1: 15854
Boyle Memorial Senior Hayden and Mozart Scholarship; Sister Geraldine Vol. 1: 15855
Boyle/Norma Farber Award; Rosalie Vol. 1: 14040
Boynton Award; Melbourne W. Vol. 1: 1345
Boynton Award; Ruth E. Vol. 1: 1604
Boys - A Rahman Lectureship; S. F. Vol. 2: 6954
Boys & Girls Club Medallion Vol. 1: 5920
Boys' Basketball Past Chair Recognition Vol. 1: 480
Boys' Basketball Vision Award Vol. 1: 481
Boys Cup; Sir Francis Vol. 2: 3842
Boys Medal and Prize; Charles Vernon Vol. 2: 6055
Bozett Award; Dr. Fred Vol. 1: 13040
BP Conservation Programme Vol. 2: 5179
bp Nichol Chapbook Award Vol. 1: 15017
BP Portrait Award Vol. 2: 6483
BP Prize Lectureship in the Humanities Vol. 2: 6988
BPAA Special Award Vol. 1: 5890
B.P.E. Inter-Federation Award Vol. 2: 6535
Brachet Prize; Albert Vol. 2: 1064
Brackenbury Award Vol. 2: 5354
Brackett Memorial Award; Dexter Vol. 1: 14061
Braddock Award; CCCC Richard Vol. 1: 13019
Braddock Award; Richard Vol. 1: 7692
Braddom FRFDS Scholarship; Diana V. Vol. 1: 11329
BradFord Award Vol. 2: 5029
Bradford Memorial Student Poster Award; James C. Vol. 1: 17444
Bradlee Editor of the Year Award; Benjamin Vol. 1: 13556
Bradley Award Vol. 2: 898
Bradley Award; Barbara Vol. 1: 14041
Bradley Distinguished Service Award; James J. Vol. 1: 16597
Bradways Rogers Information Advancement Award; Frank Vol. 1: 11668
Brady Award; Ken Vol. 1: 11900
Brady Memorial Awards; Gerald Vol. 1: 9234
Brady/Schuster Award Vol. 1: 3418

Bragg Gold Medal for Excellence in Physics Vol. 2: 254
Bragg Medal and Prize Vol. 2: 6056
Brahce Gerontology Service Award; Carl I. Vol. 1: 11127
Brahney Scholarship; James M. Vol. 1: 10564
Brakhage Award for Best Short Subject; Stan Vol. 1: 8159
Bralco Gold Medal Vol. 2: 2648
Brand and Arik Weintraub Award; Sandra Vol. 1: 10972
Brand Award for Scenic Lighting; Rose Vol. 1: 17949
Brand Building Initiative of the Year Vol. 2: 5511
Branding Hammer Award Vol. 1: 15543
Brandsma Award; Titus Vol. 2: 4787
Brandt Award Vol. 2: 2941
Brandt Volunteer Service Award; Sandy Vol. 1: 13447
Brannon Award; R. A. Vol. 1: 12062
Brannon Award; R.A. Vol. 1: 12480
Brasile Clinician of the Year; Frank N. Vol. 1: 4356
BRASS Primark Student Travel Award Vol. 1: 2685
BRASS Thomson Financial Student Travel Award Vol. 1: 2685
Brasted Memorial Lecture Vol. 1: 1533
Brattle Prizes in Corporate Finance Vol. 1: 2021
Brauer Prize; Hamburg Max Vol. 2: 2395
Braun Award; E. Lucy Vol. 1: 8365
Braun Award; Fred Vol. 1: 18087
Braun Prize Vol. 2: 2054
Braun Prize; Karl Ferdinand Vol. 1: 16304
Braunstein Memorial Award; Jules Vol. 1: 1208
Brautigam Award; Frank C. Vol. 1: 5407
Bravery Award Vol. 2: 173
Bravo Award
Dominican University Vol. 1: 8251
Horizons Theatre Vol 1: 9488
Bray Accompanist Prize; John Vol. 2: 7279
Bray Award; Robert S. Vol. 1: 1815
Bray Graduate Fellowship in Music Education; Kenneth & Helen Vol. 1: 18349
Bray National Poetry Award; John Vol. 2: 672
Brazdziunas premija; Povilo Vol. 2: 3374
Brazier Young Investigator Award; M. A. B. Vol. 2: 6255
Brazilian Packaging and Design Awards Vol. 2: 1127
Breakthrough Awards Vol. 1: 6216
Breakthrough Director Award Vol. 1: 9634
Breasted Prize; James Henry Vol. 1: 2229
Breaststroke Trophy Vol. 2: 5346
Brechner Freedom of Information Award; Joseph L. Vol. 1: 5934
Brecht Denkmunze; Walter Vol. 2: 2027
Breed Awards Vol. 1: 14340
Breeder Awards Vol. 1: 14678
Breeder of the Year Vol. 1: 10513
Breeders' Award Vol. 1: 6220
Breeders Crop Vol. 1: 10514
Bregger Essay Award Vol. 1: 3242
Breir Award; Nabila Vol. 2: 7405
Breithaupt Award; Chef Herman Vol. 1: 10365
Breitkreutz Award; Emil Vol. 1: 482
Bremner Awards; M. D. K. Vol. 1: 754
Brennan Award for Outstanding Jurist; Hon. William J. Vol. 1: 14171
Brennan Award; Robert F. Vol. 1: 12631
Brennan Award; Thomas J. Vol. 1: 5481
Brennan Medal Vol. 2: 6089
Bretnall Award; William B. Vol. 1: 15963
Brett Award; Philip Vol. 1: 2842
Breur Award Lecture Vol. 2: 876
Brewer Prize; Frank S. and Elizabeth D. Vol. 1: 3910
Brewer Trophy; Frank G. Vol. 1: 12187
Brewster Memorial Award; William Vol. 1: 3004
Brey Award; Karl Vol. 1: 11322
Brian Brown Award Vol. 2: 3816
Brian Willis Award Vol. 2: 5096
Brice Undergraduate Leadership Award; Leonard R. Vol. 1: 16234
Brick Awards Vol. 2: 5198
Bridge Book of the Year Vol. 1: 1418
Bridge School International Scholarship Vol. 1: 10637
Bridge Software Award Vol. 1: 1418
Bridgeport Prize
Institution of Electrical Engineers - England Vol. 2: 6144
Institution of Electrical Engineers - England Vol 2: 6153
Bridges Memorial Award; Polly Vol. 1: 14341
Bridgman Memorial Award; Laura Vol. 1: 1312
The Bridport Prize Vol. 2: 5200
Brief-Writing Award Vol. 1: 15945
Brier Instructor of the Year Award; Herb S. Vol. 1: 32
Briggs Award; Charles W.
Association for Iron and Steel Technology Vol. 1: 4897
ASTM International Vol 1: 5408
Briggs Dissertation Award; George E. Vol. 1: 3304
Briggs Folklore Award; Katharine Vol. 2: 5912
Briggs Memorial Scientific Inquiry Award; Dorothy Vol. 1: 3144
Briggs Memorial Technical and Operating Medal; Charles W. Vol. 1: 17291
Brigham Award; Reuben Vol. 1: 4800
Brigham Award; Richard and Grace Vol. 1: 16598
Bright Idea Awards Vol. 1: 17462
Bright Memorial Award; Norman and Marion Vol. 1: 7308
Bright Smiles, Bright Futures Award Vol. 2: 1877
Brindley Lecture; George W. Vol. 1: 7465
Brine Awards; W. H. Vol. 1: 17963
Brinell Medal Vol. 2: 4634
Briner Nuclear Pharmacy Practice Award; William H. Vol. 1: 3042
Brink Award for Distinguished Service; Victor Z. Vol. 1: 9877
Brinker Award; Maureen Connolly Vol. 1: 18138
Brinker International Award for Breast Cancer Research Vol. 1: 17342
Brinker Outstanding Junior Girl Award; Maureen Connolly Vol. 1: 18138
Brinkhous Physician of the Year Award; Dr. Kenneth Vol. 1: 13333
Brinkhous Young Investigator Prize in Thrombosis; Kenneth M. Vol. 1: 2174
Brinkley Award; Rawn Vol. 1: 9890
Bristol Award
Canadian Society of Hospital Pharmacists Vol. 1: 6995
Infectious Diseases Society of America Vol 1: 9698
Bristol-Myers Squibb Award Vol. 1: 6995
Bristol-Myers Squibb Awards for Excellence in Medical Teaching Vol. 1: 5941
Bristol-Myers Squibb Smissman Award Vol. 1: 1534
BRIT Awards Vol. 2: 5416
Britain in Bloom Awards Vol. 2: 5760
British Academy Fellow Vol. 2: 5203
British Academy Research Awards Vol. 2: 5204
British Academy Television Awards Vol. 2: 5217
British Aerophilatelic Federation Award Vol. 2: 6535
British Aerospace Prize Vol. 2: 6029
British Amateur Recording Contest Vol. 2: 5538
British Archaeological Awards
Association for Industrial Archaeology Vol. 2: 5090
British Universities Film and Video Council Vol 2: 5555
British Association Medal Vol. 2: 4362
British Association of Dermatologists Fellowships Vol. 2: 5243
British Book Design and Production Awards Vol. 2: 5419
British Bronze Medal Vol. 2: 6631
British Caribbean Philatelic Study Group Award Vol. 2: 6535
British Cartographic Society Design Award Vol. 2: 5265
British Cartographic Society Student Award Vol. 2: 5269
British Championship Vol. 2: 6440
British Chess Federation Player of the Year Vol. 2: 5278
British Composer Awards Vol. 2: 5213
British Council Book Prize Vol. 1: 14283
British Design and Art Direction (D&AD) Awards Vol. 2: 5291
British Design Awards Vol. 2: 5735
British Ecological Society Grants and Awards Vol. 2: 5294
British Ecological Society President's Medal Vol. 2: 5295
British Empire Medal Vol. 2: 5590
British Federation Crosby Hall Fellowship Vol. 2: 4803
British Film Institute Fellowships Vol. 2: 5308
The British Film Institute Sutherland Trophy Vol. 2: 5309
British Gold Medal Vol. 2: 6632
British Grassland Society Award Vol. 2: 5313
British Institute of Architectural Technologists Student Award Vol. 2: 5320
British Lichen Society Awards Vol. 2: 5340
British Medical Association Medicine in the Media Award Vol. 2: 5355
British Music Society Awards Vol. 2: 5382
British Open Golf Championship
Professional Golfers' Association - England Vol. 2: 6563
Professional Golfers' Association - England Vol 2: 6565
Professional Golfers' Association - England Vol 2: 6566
British Psychological Society Presidents' Award Vol. 2: 5427

British Reserve Insurance Conducting Prize Vol. 2: 6461
British School at Rome Fellowship Vol. 2: 5074
British Show Pony Society Rosettes Vol. 2: 5458
British Silver Medal Vol. 2: 6633
British Society of Magazine Editors Awards Vol. 2: 5511
British Society of Rheology Annual Award Vol. 2: 5528
British Society of Rheology Gold Medal Vol. 2: 5529
British Vacuum Council Junior Prize Vol. 2: 5557
Britt Literary Award Vol. 1: 4625
Brittell OTA/OT Partnership Award; Terry Vol. 1: 2952
Britten Award; John Vol. 2: 3713
Britten International Composers' Competition; Benjamin Vol. 2: 5568
Britten Prize; John Vol. 2: 6634
Brittingham Prize in Poetry and Felix Pollak Prize in Poetry; The Vol. 1: 18365
The Brittingham Prize in Poetry and Felix Pollak Prize in Poetry Vol. 1: 18365
Britton Award for Inquiry within the English Language Arts; CEE James N. Vol. 1: 13020
Broad Axe Award Vol. 1: 7137
Broadcast Engineer of the Year Vol. 1: 16609
Broadcast Journalism Awards Vol. 1: 12014
Broadcast Media Awards for Radio and Television Vol. 1: 10575
Broadcast Media Awards for Television Vol. 1: 10575
Broadcast of the Year Vol. 1: 8319
Broadcaster of the Year
  International Bluegrass Music Association Vol. 1: 10270
  National Weather Association Vol 1: 13896
  New Hampshire Association of Broadcasters Vol 1: 14076
  South Dakota Broadcasters Association Vol 1: 16986
Broadcasting Hall of Fame Vol. 1: 12428
Brochure Award Vol. 1: 12295
Brock Gold Medal Award Vol. 2: 4970
Brodie Award in Drug Metabolism; Bernard B. Vol. 1: 3805
Brodie Medal; John A. Vol. 2: 492
Brodman Award for the Academic Medical Librarian of the Year; Estelle Vol. 1: 11653
Brody Young Investigator Award; Michael J. Vol. 1: 3164
Broida Prize; Herbert P. Vol. 1: 3113
Brokaw Award; Tom Vol. 1: 16987
Brokaw Memorial Trophy; Irving Vol. 1: 17903
Bronfenbrenner Award; Urie Vol. 1: 3328
Bronfman Award; Saidye
  Samuel and Saidye Bronfman Family Foundation Vol. 1: 5959
  Canada Council for the Arts Vol 1: 6101
Bronze Anchor Vol. 2: 1890
Bronze Anvil Awards Vol. 1: 15426
The Bronze Baby Vol. 1: 6646
Bronze Cross for Achievement Vol. 1: 11289
Bronze Good Citizenship Medal Vol. 1: 13758
Bronze Irrigation Award Vol. 1: 370
Bronze Medal
  Edinburgh Architectural Association Vol. 2: 5748
  Federation Aeronautique Internationale Vol 2: 4722
  French National Center for Scientific Research Vol 2: 1826
  National Association of Licensed Paralegals Vol 2: 6455
  Royal Aeronautical Society - United Kingdom Vol 2: 6635
  South African Association of Botanists Vol 2: 4302
  Southern Africa Association for the Advancement of Science Vol 2: 4363
  Tau Sigma Delta Vol 1: 17409
Bronze Medal Award
  Audio Engineering Society Vol. 1: 5521
  National Student Campaign Against Hunger and Homelessness Vol 1: 13814
Bronze Medal of Honor Vol. 1: 4429
Bronze Plaque Awards Vol. 1: 7382
Bronze Service Citation Vol. 1: 15072
Bronze Star Vol. 2: 722
Bronze Wolf Vol. 2: 4939
Brooker Collegiate Scholarship for Minorities; George M. Vol. 1: 9935
Brookes Award for Excellence in Journalism; Warren Vol. 1: 2641
Brooks Award for Best Graduate Paper; Juanita Vol. 1: 11949
Brooks Award for Best Undergraduate Paper; Juanita Vol. 1: 11950
Brooks Award for Excellence in Student Research; Frank G. Vol. 1: 5723
Brooks Award for Excellence in the Teaching of Culture; Nelson Vol. 1: 1831
Brooks Memorial Life Award; Charles E. Vol. 1: 8632
Brooks Moore Scholarship; Bradley Vol. 1: 11885
Brooks Undergraduate Essay Competition; F. G. Vol. 1: 5723
Brookshire Moore Superintendent of the Year Vol. 1: 14835
Broome County Farm Bureau Scholarship Vol. 1: 5963
Brophy AAO Distinguished Service Award; James E. Vol. 1: 1197
Bross Prize Vol. 1: 5965
Brosseau Memorial Award; Robert P. Vol. 1: 7744
Brough Memorial Prize; Frederick Vol. 2: 493
Broun Award; Heywood Vol. 1: 14225
Broussard Best First Book Prize; James Vol. 1: 16432
Brouwer Award; Dirk Vol. 1: 1357
Brower Environmental Journalism Award; David R. Vol. 1: 16003
Brown & Associates Award of Merit Vol. 1: 7256
Brown Award; Antoinette Vol. 1: 17689
Brown Award for Meritorious Service; Lydia Vol. 2: 5247
Brown Award; Gwilym Vol. 1: 18433
Brown Award; Howard Mayer Vol. 1: 8309
Brown Award in Biomedical Research; Malcolm Vol. 1: 6477
Brown Award; James Barrett Vol. 1: 1256
Brown Award; Ray E. Vol. 1: 5239
Brown Award; Roger J. E. Vol. 1: 6522
Brown Bear Award Vol. 1: 5971
Brown Boettner Award for Outstanding Public Education; Beth Vol. 1: 13604
Brown Book; Selena Vol. 1: 12417
Brown Expedition Award; Ralph Vol. 2: 6758
Brown Freedom Medal; Colin M. Vol. 1: 12896
Brown Grant; Amber Vol. 1: 16626
Brown IV Award of Excellence for Outstanding Community Service; James Vol. 1: 7326
Brown Medal; W.P. Vol. 2: 494
Brown Memorial Award; Dr. Charlie Vol. 1: 12710
Brown Memorial Award; J. Hammond
  Outdoor Writers Association of America Vol. 1: 14749
  Outdoor Writers Association of America Vol 1: 14749
Brown Memorial Grant; Leslie Vol. 1: 15558
Brown Memorial Public Service Award; Aaron L. Vol. 1: 12459
Brown Memorial Sportsmanship Award; Cecil J. Vol. 1: 2788
Brown Prize; John Nicholas Vol. 1: 11675
Brown Prize; Sir Vernon Vol. 2: 6636
Brown Public Service Award; James Wright Vol. 1: 8073
Brown Publication Award; James W. Vol. 1: 4868
Brown Research Recognition Award; Mary Louise Vol. 1: 1189
Brown Shield; Goodfellow Memorial Award in Voice/Chief Justice J.T. Vol. 1: 15856
Brown Trade Leadership Award; Doreen T. Vol. 1: 7784
Brown Trophy; Jack Vol. 1: 18062
Brown Volunteer/Community Service Award; H. Barksdale Vol. 1: 398
Browne Memorial Bowl; George H. Vol. 1: 17903
Brownell Media Award; Emery A. Vol. 1: 13414
Brownell Press Award; Emery A. Vol. 1: 13414
Browning Award for Excellence in Writing; Alice Vol. 1: 10268
Brownlee Fund Grants; Richard S. Vol. 1: 17266
Brownlee Memorial Scholarship; Scott Vol. 1: 11930
Brownlow Award; Louis Vol. 1: 3812
Brownlow Book Award; Louis Vol. 1: 12136
Brownlow Publication Award; Cecil A. Vol. 1: 8723
Brubaker Memorial Award; John Vol. 1: 7158
Bruce Award for Humour; Gordon Vol. 1: 14734
Bruce Medal; Catherine Wolfe Vol. 1: 5482
Bruce Medal; W. S. Vol. 2: 6989
Bruce Memorial Award; James D. Vol. 1: 1710
Bruce-Preller Prize Lectureship Vol. 2: 6990
Bruce Prize; Alexander Ninian Vol. 2: 6991
Bruel Gold Medal for Noise Control and Acoustics; Per Vol. 1: 4125
Bruemmer Award; Mary A. Vol. 1: 15793
Bruhn Prize; Erik Vol. 1: 12734
Brun; Prix Edmond Vol. 2: 1548
Brunauer Award; S. Vol. 1: 1468
Brunauer Best Paper Award Vol. 1: 1468
Bruner Award for Urban Excellence; Rudy Vol. 1: 5977
Brunet Memorial Trophy; Jean-Pierre Vol. 1: 17903
Brunet; Prix Vol. 2: 1503

Award Index

Brunetti Award; Cledo Vol. 1: 9773
Brunner Grant; Arnold W. Vol. 1: 2442
Brunnstrom Award for Excellence in Clinical Teaching; Signe Vol. 1: 3145
Bruno Cagol Press Prize Vol. 2: 3136
Bruno E. Jacob Trophy Vol. 1: 13240
Brussels International Festival of Fantastic Film Vol. 2: 850
Brussels International Festival of Fantasy, Thriller, and Science-Fiction Films Vol. 2: 850
Brya Award; Brig Gen Edward N. Vol. 1: 4644
Bryan Award; Alden Vol. 1: 829
Bryan Award for Research Excellence; Kirk Vol. 1: 9015
Bryan, Jr. Scholarships; Joseph M. Vol. 1: 8353
Bryant Award; Rachel Vol. 1: 12323
Bryant Gold Medal; Henry Grier Vol. 1: 9011
Bryant Outstanding Service Award; David C. Vol. 1: 1060
Bryson Memorial Senior Speech Arts Scholarship; L.I. Vol. 1: 15857
BSC Best Cinematography Award Vol. 2: 5504
BSF Student Bursary and Bill Waygood Memorial Lecture Vol. 2: 5507
BSFA Award Vol. 2: 5453
BSH Scientific Scholarships Vol. 2: 5477
BSH Student Scholarships Vol. 2: 5478
BSIA Annual Security Officer Awards Vol. 2: 5455
BSIA/IFSEC Security Industry Awards Vol. 2: 5456
BSS Student Research Award Vol. 1: 9053
BTA Trophy Vol. 2: 5540
BTEC Certificate in Expedition Management Vol. 2: 7090
BTEC Certificate in Tropical Habitat Conservation Vol. 2: 7091
BTS/Astellas and BTS/Novartis Research Fellowships Vol. 2: 5542
BTS/Morris Travelling Fellowship Vol. 2: 5543
BuaLuang Art Competition Prize Vol. 2: 4958
BUBBA Award Vol. 1: 17231
Buchanan Award; Paul E. Vol. 1: 18504
Buchanan Cup Vol. 1: 16039
Buchanan Medal Vol. 2: 6902
Buchanan Outstanding Chapter Award Vol. 1: 16039
Buchanan Prize in Esperanto; John Vol. 2: 7310
Buchannon Scholarship; Donald A. Vol. 1: 17843
Bucher Medal; Walter H. Vol. 1: 2111
Bucher Prize; Heinrich Hatt- Vol. 2: 4896
Buchman Award Vol. 2: 2942
Buchner-Preis; Georg- Vol. 2: 2144
Buck Award; Solon J. Vol. 1: 11838
Buckendale Lecture; L. Ray Vol. 1: 16568
Buckeye Children's Book Awards Vol. 1: 5979
Buckley Condensed Matter Prize; Oliver E. Vol. 1: 3114
Buckner Medal; Emory Vol. 1: 8603
Buckwell Memorial Scholarship; Arthur Vol. 1: 15729
Budapest International Music Competition Vol. 2: 2504
Buddingh Prize for New Dutch Poetry; C. Vol. 2: 3640
Buddle Findlay Sargeson Fellowship Vol. 2: 3702
BUDDY Award (Bringing Up Daughters Differently) Vol. 1: 11285
Budgen Award; John Vol. 2: 5133
Budget Service Award Vol. 1: 11193
Bueche Award; Arthur M. Vol. 1: 12126
Buell Award; Murray F. Vol. 1: 8366
Buerger Award; Martin J. Vol. 1: 1856
Buffalo Hall of Fame Award Vol. 1: 12774
Buga premija; Kazimiero Vol. 2: 3375
Bugnet Award for Novel; Georges Vol. 1: 19006
Build a Building Competition Vol. 2: 6128
Build America Beautiful Award Vol. 1: 11108
Builder of the Year Vol. 1: 15281
Builders' Awards Vol. 2: 3969
Builder's Choice Awards for Excellence in Design and Planning Vol. 1: 5985
Builder's Choice Design and Planning Awards Vol. 1: 5985
Building Manager of the Year Awards Vol. 2: 5616
Building of the Year Award Vol. 1: 6038
Building with Trees Awards of Excellence Vol. 1: 12254
Bulgarian Academy of Science Honorary Badge - Marin Drinov Medal Vol. 2: 1143
Bull Freedom of Information Award; John V.R. Vol. 1: 14935
Bull of the Year Vol. 1: 15355
Bullard Scholarship; Helen Vol. 1: 13369
Bullen Prize; John Vol. 1: 6556
Bullivant Student Prize; Mary Vol. 2: 3822
Bulpitt Woman of the Year Award; Mildred Vol. 1: 976
Bulwer-Lytton Fiction Contest Vol. 1: 15837
Bumbershoot, SeattleFs Music and Arts Festival Vol. 1: 14553
Bunche Award; Ralph Vol. 1: 18608
Bunche Award; Ralph J. Vol. 1: 3229
Bundespreis Gute Form Vol. 2: 2182
Bunge Prize; Paul Vol. 2: 2157
Bunka Women's University Selection Award Vol. 2: 3229
Bunn Lifetime Achievement Award Vol. 1: 12070
Bunyan Award; Paul Vol. 1: 59
Buonocore Memorial Lecturer Vol. 1: 114
Burbank Award; Luther Vol. 1: 2287
Burch Memorial Safety Award; Dr. Gary Vol. 1: 12628
Burch Prize; C.R. Vol. 2: 5558
Burchfield Award; Laverne Vol. 1: 3813
Burden Research Prize Vol. 2: 6720
Burdett, Jr. Army Aviation Flight Safety Award; Lt. Gen. Allen M. Vol. 1: 14639
Burdgick Award; Gary Vol. 1: 13090
Burdick Award for Distinguished Service to Clinical Pathology; Ward Vol. 1: 3601
Burdick-Thorne Gold Medal Vol. 1: 17312
Burdin Scholarship; Edythe G. Vol. 1: 12000
Burdy; Prix Jeanne Vol. 2: 1854
Burfitt Prize; Walter Vol. 2: 637
Burgdorf Student Science Research Competition; Otto P. Vol. 1: 14111
Burger Award Vol. 2: 4454
Burger Award in Medicinal Chemistry; Alfred Vol. 1: 1535
Burger Award; Warren E. Vol. 1: 12873
Burger Healer Award; Chief Justice Warren E. Vol. 1: 7355
Burgess Award; Ernest W. Vol. 1: 13039
Burggraf Award; Fred Vol. 1: 17577
Burgheim Medaille; Hedwig- Vol. 2: 2354
Burka Award Vol. 1: 9915
Burkan Memorial Competition; Nathan Vol. 1: 4000
Burke Essay Contest; Arleigh Vol. 1: 18007
Burke, Jr. Award; George W. Vol. 1: 18622
Burke Memorial Award; John "Sonny" Vol. 1: 18030
Burke Memorial Award; Tom Vol. 1: 17197
Burke Memorial Lecture; Donal Vol. 2: 2870
Burke Perpetual Challenge Machinery Trophy; Sir Roland Vol. 2: 6663
Burke Perpetual Challenge Trophy Vol. 2: 6663
Burket Award; Lester Vol. 1: 666
Burkett-Dodge Award Vol. 1: 18088
Burkhalter Award; Frank Vol. 1: 5658
Burkhardt Fellowship; Frederick Vol. 1: 819
Burkhardt Residential Fellowships for Recently Tenured Scholars; Frederick Vol. 1: 1813
Burkitt Medal for Biblical Studies Vol. 2: 5205
Burleigh Prize; J. C. Vol. 2: 6003
Burley Prize; Joseph Fraunhofer Award/Robert M. Vol. 1: 14606
Burn Prevention Award Vol. 1: 1423
Burn Prize; Sir Joseph Vol. 2: 5993
Burnet Lecture Vol. 2: 109
Burnet Memorial Award; Sir John Vol. 2: 6817
Burnett Prizes in Journalism Ethics; UH Journalism Carol Vol. 1: 18286
Burnett/University of Hawaii/AEJMC Prize for Excellence in Ethics; Carol Vol. 1: 4863
Burnham Award; Daniel Vol. 1: 3200
Burnham Manufacturing Management Award; Donald C. Vol. 1: 16706
Burns Award; Bernard J. Vol. 1: 9639
Burns Best of the Festival Award; Ken Vol. 1: 4536
Burr/Worzalla Award; Elizabeth Vol. 1: 18790
Burrin Award; Esther V. Vol. 1: 9668
Burroughs Life Achievement Award; Edgar Rice Vol. 1: 6009
Bursaries Vol. 2: 7345
The Bursary Award Scheme Vol. 2: 7108
Bursary Competition Vol. 1: 12284
Burt Award; Karen Vol. 2: 7346
Burton Award; Gale Cotton Vol. 1: 18089
Burton Medal; Sir Richard Vol. 2: 6679
Burwell, Jr., Award; E. B. Vol. 1: 9016
Burwell Lectureship in Catalysis; Robert Vol. 1: 14271
Busch Award; Paul L. Vol. 1: 18649
Busch Series Vol. 1: 12364
Bush Artist Fellows Program Vol. 1: 6012
Bush Award; Vannevar Vol. 1: 13675
Bush Foundation Fellowships for Artists Vol. 1: 6012
Bushkin Friend of the Foundation Award; Ellyn Vol. 1: 14533
Bushnell Trophy; Asa S. Vol. 1: 13208
Busignies Memorial Award; Henri Vol. 1: 15517
Business Achievement Awards Vol. 1: 9109
Business and Aging Awards Vol. 1: 4267
Business and Culture Award Vol. 1: 10935
Business and Industry Hall of Fame Vol. 1: 2457
Business and the Arts Awards Vol. 1: 18986
Business Aviation Meritorious Service Award Vol. 1: 8724

Business Award
Council for Exceptional Children Vol. 1: 7852
New York Press Club Vol 1: 14137
Business Awards Vol. 1: 19047
Business Excellence Award Vol. 1: 14598
Business Hall of Fame Vol. 1: 18987
Business in the Arts Award Vol. 1: 17389
Business in the Arts Awards
Business Committee for the Arts Vol. 1: 6015
Colorado Business Committee for the Arts Vol 1: 7558
Business Innovation Vol. 2: 145
Business Leader Awards Vol. 2: 4323
Business Leader of the Year Award Vol. 1: 17066
Business Leadership Award Vol. 1: 18315
Business Management Award Vol. 1: 16824
Business Marketing Doctoral Award Support Competition Vol. 1: 14952
Business of the Year Vol. 1: 8548
Business of the Year Award Vol. 1: 10710
Business Partner Award Vol. 1: 2216
Business Recognition Award Vol. 1: 1190
Business Valuation Hall of Fame Award Vol. 1: 2458
Business Volunteers for the Arts Awards Vol. 1: 6027
Businesswoman of the Year Vol. 2: 4146
Busk Medal Vol. 2: 6759
Busk Prize Vol. 2: 6637
Busoni Prize; F. Vol. 2: 2999
Busse Research Awards; Ewald W. Vol. 2: 1129
Bustad Companion Animal Veterinarian of the Year Award Vol. 1: 4407
Buszek Memorial Award; Buz Vol. 1: 8633
Butcher Medal; Goler T. Vol. 1: 4087
Butler Award; Harry Vol. 2: 6466
Butler Award; Wendell E. Vol. 1: 8750
Butler Faculty Fellowships; John Tropham and Susan Redd Vol. 1: 15599
Butler Independent Research and Creative Work Awards; John Topham and Susan Redd Vol. 1: 15598
Butler Literary Award Vol. 1: 10882
Butler Literary Awards Vol. 1: 10883
Butler Medal; Nicholas Murray Vol. 1: 7584
Butt Award in Hepatology or Nutrition; H.R. Vol. 1: 8832
Butterfield Trophy; Jack A. Vol. 1: 2261
Butterley - F. Earle Hooper Award; H. M. Vol. 2: 442
Butterworth Prize Vol. 1: 2983
Buttgenbach Prize; Henri Vol. 2: 1065
Butts-Whiting Award Vol. 1: 5098
Butzel Award; Fred M. Vol. 1: 10992
Buxtehuder Bulle Vol. 2: 2385
Buyer of the Year Award Vol. 1: 13371
BVA Achievement Award Vol. 1: 5811
BVC Senior Prize Vol. 2: 5559
BVRLA Awards Vol. 2: 5562
BWA Bursary Vol. 2: 4147
BWI Reading Program Grant Vol. 1: 4923
BWI/YALSA Collection Development Grant Vol. 1: 19082
By-Line Award Vol. 1: 11553
Byrd Young Artist Competition; William C. Vol. 1: 15789
Byrne Memorial Literary Award; Ray Vol. 1: 2872
C SADF Commendation Medal Vol. 2: 4344
CAA Awards for Adult Literature Vol. 1: 6321
CAA/Heritage Preservation Award for Distinction in Scholarship and Conservation Vol. 1: 7503
CAA National Awards Vol. 2: 5670
CAA Trophy Vol. 2: 3843
CAAO Scholarship Vol. 1: 7723
Caballo de Trabajo Award; El Vol. 1: 17071
Cabaud Memorial Award Vol. 1: 3012
Cable Book Award; Gerald Vol. 1: 16062
Cabot Prizes; Maria Moors Vol. 1: 7594
Caccioppoli; Premio Renato Vol. 2: 3108
Cactus d'Or Vol. 2: 4824
Cadbury Medal; Christopher Vol. 2: 7040
Cade Award; Tom Vol. 1: 15559
Cadmus Memorial Award; Bradford Vol. 1: 9878
Cady Award; Gilbert H. Vol. 1: 9017
Cadzow Smith Award Vol. 2: 5767
Caen Memorial Award; Herb Vol. 1: 13739
Caernarfon Award Vol. 2: 6076
CAFE Award for Scholarly Articles Vol. 1: 6963
Caffey Award for Excellence for Pre-Collegiate Teaching; W. Stewart Vol. 1: 17494
CAG Award For Contribution to Gerontology Vol. 1: 6254
CAG Distinguished Member Award Vol. 1: 6255
CAG Donald Menzies Bursary Vol. 1: 6256
CAG Honorary Member Vol. 1: 6257
Cahn Lifetime Achievement Award; Sammy Vol. 1: 12134
Caille Memorial Medal; Pierre Francois Vol. 1: 10417
Cain Memorial Award; Bruce F. Vol. 1: 858
Caitlin Peace Pipe Award Vol. 1: 13971
Cajal Medal Vol. 1: 6033
Cake Show Competition Vol. 1: 7026
The CALAS/ACSAL Travel Fellowship Award Vol. 1: 6206
Caldecott Medal; Randolph Vol. 1: 4924
Calder Cup Vol. 1: 2262
Calder Prize Vol. 2: 6838
Caldicott Leadership Award; Helen Vol. 1: 18844
Caledonian Research Foundation Prize Lectureship in Biomedical Sciences and Arts and Letters Vol. 2: 6992
California Gold Medal Vol. 2: 2877
California History Day Award Vol. 1: 7685
California Sea Grant Fellowship Vol. 1: 6060
California Young Reader Medal Vol. 1: 6053
Calihan Academic Fellowship Vol. 1: 136
Calihan Fellowships Vol. 1: 136
Calihan Lecture Vol. 1: 137
Calihan Research Fellowship Vol. 1: 136
Calihan Travel Grants Vol. 1: 136
Callan Medal; Elizabeth Vol. 1: 4430
Callas Gold Medal; Maria Vol. 2: 2452
Callas Grand Prix for Opera, Oratorio-Lied; Maria Vol. 2: 2451
Callas Grand Prix for Piano; Maria Vol. 2: 2452
Callas International Music Competitions; Maria
Athenaeum International Cultural Center Vol. 2: 2451
Athenaeum International Cultural Center Vol 2: 2452
Callas International Opera, Oratorio-Lied Competition; Maria Vol. 2: 2451
Callas International Piano Competition; Maria Vol. 2: 2452
Callaway Award; Joe A. Vol. 1: 143
Callaway Prize for the Defense of the Right to Privacy; Joe Vol. 1: 14116
Callebaut Prize; Octaaf Vol. 2: 1066
Callimaci Memorial Supporters Award; Fulvio Vol. 1: 6737
Callison Award; Charles H. Vol. 1: 12727
Calne Lectureship; The Donald Vol. 1: 14862
Calvin Award; Melvin Vol. 1: 10475
Calvo; Prix Carlos Vol. 2: 4767
Camden Freeholders Award Vol. 1: 9995
CAMEO Award Vol. 1: 14215
Camera Operator of the Year Vol. 2: 7047
Cameron Award; Jane Vol. 1: 6461
Cameron Outstanding PhD Thesis Award; T. W. N. Vol. 1: 7029
Cameron Young Investigator Award; John R. Vol. 1: 1242
Camoes Prize Vol. 2: 4089
Camp Medal; Thomas R. Vol. 1: 18623
Camp Memorial Trophy; Mary C. Vol. 1: 13648
Campbell & Company Award for Excellence in Fundraising Vol. 1: 5160
Campbell Award; A. B. Vol. 1: 12063
Campbell Award; A.B. Vol. 1: 12481
Campbell Award; A.W. Vol. 2: 300
Campbell Award; Estelle Vol. 1: 13729
Campbell Award for Distinguished Research in Social Psychology; Donald T. Vol. 1: 16377
Campbell Award; Francis Joseph Vol. 1: 5338
Campbell Award; Frank W. Vol. 1: 15168
Campbell Award of Merit; E. K. Vol. 1: 4050
Campbell Award; Roald Vol. 1: 18229
Campbell Fund; The Mona Vol. 1: 6130
Campbell; Medal in Memory of Ian Vol. 1: 2106
Campbell Memorial Award; John W.
Center for the Study of Science Fiction Vol. 1: 7238
World Science Fiction Society Vol 1: 18979
Campbell Memorial Award; Robert D. Vol. 2: 5053
Campbell Memorial Lecture; Edward DeMille Vol. 1: 4695
Campbell Outstanding Public Broadcasting Award; Elizabeth Vol. 1: 13260
Campbell Research Award; J.A. Vol. 1: 6388
Campbell Scholar-Athlete Award; William V. Vol. 1: 13215
Campbell Space Simulation Award; John D. Vol. 1: 9830
Campbell Young Investigators Award; J.A. Vol. 1: 6389
Campiello Prize Vol. 2: 3003
Campion Award; Saint Edmund Vol. 1: 7143
Campionato Europeo Baseball Vol. 2: 858
Campos Memorial Award for Best International Student Paper; Carlos Walter M. Vol. 1: 1209
Camptender Award Vol. 1: 3540
Campus Bookseller of the Year Award Vol. 1: 6347
Can-AM Civil Engineering Amity Award Vol. 1: 3923
Canada Award Vol. 1: 69
Canada Awards for Business Excellence Vol. 1: 13586
Canada Awards for Excellence Vol. 1: 13586
Canada Export Award Vol. 1: 8811
Canada International Award Vol. 2: 7159

Canada - Japan Literary Awards Vol. 1: 6102
Canada Medal Vol. 2: 7160
Canada Memorial Foundation Scholarships Vol. 2: 5123
Canada Packers' Medal Vol. 1: 6972
Canada Post Corporation Journalism Prize Vol. 1: 5507
Canada's Outstanding CEO of the Year Award Vol. 1: 7845
Canada's Sports Hall of Fame Vol. 1: 6139
Canadian Agricultural Engineering of the Year Award. Vol. 1: 6885
Canadian Architect Magazine Art of CAD Competition Vol. 1: 6191
Canadian Architect Yearbook Vol. 1: 6190
Canadian Association of Black Journalist Scholarship Vol. 1: 6227
Canadian Authors Association Award for Fiction Vol. 1: 6323
Canadian Award for Financial Reporting
Government Finance Officers Association of United States and Canada Vol. 1: 9147
Government Finance Officers Association of United States and Canada Vol 1: 9150
Canadian Basketball Hall of Fame Vol. 1: 8238
Canadian Braille Literacy Foundation Vol. 1: 6746
Canadian Business Hall of Fame Vol. 1: 11063
Canadian Car of the Year Vol. 1: 5561
Canadian Cardiovascular Society Research Achievement Award Vol. 1: 6376
Canadian Chrysler Cup Vol. 1: 2263
Canadian Coast Guard Exemplary Service Medal Vol. 1: 6081
Canadian Composers Award Vol. 1: 6326
Canadian Conservation Achievement Awards Vol. 1: 7064
Canadian Country Music Association's Awards Vol. 1: 6445
Canadian Engineers' Awards
Canadian Council of Professional Engineers Vol. 1: 6432
Canadian Council of Professional Engineers Vol 1: 6433
Canadian Council of Professional Engineers Vol 1: 6434
Canadian Council of Professional Engineers Vol 1: 6435
Canadian Council of Professional Engineers Vol 1: 6436
Canadian Council of Professional Engineers Vol 1: 6437
Canadian Council of Professional Engineers Vol 1: 6438
Canadian Council of Professional Engineers Vol 1: 6439
Canadian Football Hall of Fame and Museum Vol. 1: 6502
Canadian Forces Decoration Vol. 1: 6082
Canadian Forestry Achievement Award Vol. 1: 6597
Canadian Forestry Group Achievement Award Vol. 1: 6598
Canadian Forestry Scientific Achievement Award Vol. 1: 6599
Canadian Geotechnical Colloquium Vol. 1: 6523
Canadian Hospital Librarian of the Year Award Vol. 1: 6551
Canadian Information Productivity Awards Vol. 1: 9710
Canadian Information Technology Innovation Award Vol. 1: 6577
Canadian Institute of Chartered Accountants Prize Vol. 2: 6004
Canadian International Amateur Film Festival Vol. 1: 6641
Canadian International Annual Film/Video Festival Vol. 1: 6641
Canadian International Medal Lecture Vol. 2: 7159
Canadian Journal of Statistics Award Vol. 1: 17279
Canadian Medical Student Essay Award Vol. 1: 6275
Canadian Mineral Analysts Scholarships Vol. 1: 6735
Canadian Music Competition Vol. 1: 6743
Canadian One-Act Playwriting Competition Vol. 1: 14742
Canadian Outdoorsman of the Year Award Vol. 1: 7066
Canadian Pacific Railway Medal Vol. 1: 8462
Canadian Pediatric Society Research Award Vol. 1: 6787
Canadian Rockies Award Vol. 1: 5650
Canadian Scholarships and Fellowships Vol. 1: 18349
Canadian School Library Association Merit Award Vol. 1: 6697
Canadian Software Systems Award Vol. 1: 6578
Canadian Student Film Festival Vol. 1: 11944
Canadian Truck of the Year Vol. 1: 5562
Canal+ Award
Sauve Qui Peut le Court Metrage Vol. 2: 1947
Sauve Qui Peut le Court Metrage Vol 2: 1948
Cancer Research Awards Vol. 1: 11086
Candle Artisan of the Year Vol. 1: 10459
Candler Bursary; Cathy Vol. 2: 187
Candy Hall of Fame Vol. 1: 12944
Cane Pace Vol. 1: 18162
Canham Graduate Studies Scholarship Vol. 1: 18624
Caniff Spirit of Flight Award; Milton Vol. 1: 12731
CANMET Technology Transfer Award Vol. 1: 6612
Cann Plaque; R. C. Vol. 1: 12235
Cannes International Film Festival Vol. 2: 1730
Canning Trophy; Richard F. Vol. 1: 2264
Cannizzaro; Medaglia Stanislao Vol. 2: 3102
Cannon Award in Astronomy; Annie J. Vol. 1: 1358
Cannon Award Lecture; Physiology in Perspective: Walter B. Vol. 1: 3165
Cannon Prize Vol. 1: 12102
CAOG Awards Vol. 1: 7248
CAP Primary/Elementary Award Vol. 1: 6288
CAP Student Leadership Vol. 1: 6289
Capa Award; Corsell Vol. 1: 10300
Capa Gold Medal; Robert Vol. 1: 14761
Caparne-Welch Medal Vol. 1: 11641
Cape Cod Art Association Awards Vol. 1: 7092
Capezio Dance Award Vol. 1: 7094
Capital Clear Trophy Vol. 2: 6537
Caplet; Prix Andre Vol. 2: 1441
Capote Award for Literary Criticism in Memory of Newton Arvin; Truman Vol. 1: 10871
A Cappella Recording Awards ("CARAs"); Contemporary Vol. 1: 7790
Cappon Prize for Essay; Dorothy Churchill Vol. 1: 14099
Cappon Prize for Fiction; Alexander Patterson Vol. 1: 14099
Capra Achievement Award; Frank Vol. 1: 8215
Capron Outstanding Elementary Social Studies Teacher of the Year; Barbara J. Vol. 1: 11578
Captain Joseph H. Linnard Prize Vol. 1: 16765
CAR Coach of the Year Award Vol. 1: 18870
Car of the Year Vol. 1: 11967
Caraccio Purchase Award; Kathleen Vol. 1: 16517
Carbohydrate Chemistry Award Vol. 2: 6955
Carclew Fellowship Vol. 2: 672
Card Award; George Vol. 1: 1816
Cardiff Singer of the World Competition Vol. 2: 5258
Cardiovascular Section Young Investigator Award Vol. 1: 3166
Carducci Prize; Giosue Vol. 2: 3140
Career Achievement Award
Film Music Society Vol. 1: 8689
Professional Fraternity Association Vol 1: 15312
Career Achievement Award - Professional Theatre Vol. 1: 4993
Career Achievement Award - Teacher in Higher Education Vol. 1: 4994
Career Award Vol. 1: 8499
Career Awareness Award Vol. 1: 5731
Career Contribution Award Vol. 1: 9018
Career Development Award
American Neuropsychiatric Association Vol. 1: 2861
Transcultural Nursing Society Vol 1: 17572
Career Development Award in Skin Research Vol. 1: 8167
Career Development Awards
American Association for Cancer Research Vol. 1: 859
American Diabetes Association Vol 1: 1909
Career Development Grants Vol. 1: 1326
Career Education Citation Vol. 1: 14588
Career Enhancement Award Vol. 1: 2366
Career Grants Vol. 1: 17616
Career/Life Skills Resources Award For Excellence in Career Education Vol. 1: 14589
Career/Lifetime Achievement Award Vol. 1: 4783
Career Scientist Awards Vol. 1: 6179
Caregiver Appreciation Certificate Vol. 1: 445
Carey Award Vol. 2: 7197
Carey, Jr. Distinguished Service Award; W. N. Vol. 1: 17578
Cargill Animal Nutrition Young Scientist Award Vol. 1: 1873
Cargo Airline of the Year Vol. 1: 341
Carhartt National Team Award Vol. 1: 13347
Caribbean Hotel Association Awards Vol. 1: 7105
Caribbean Hotelier of the Year Vol. 1: 7105
Carillon School Prize Vol. 2: 1081
Caring Award Vol. 1: 7109
Caritas Medal Vol. 1: 14227
Carleton Award; Robert H. Vol. 1: 13678
Carlier; Prix Vol. 2: 1640

Carlin Award for Excellence in Academic Teaching; Dorothy E. Baethke - Eleanor J. Vol. 1: 3142
Carlin Service Award; John Vol. 1: 18045
Carlisle Award; J. F. Vol. 2: 7430
Carll Award; John Franklin Vol. 1: 16792
Carlo Mauri Memorial Trophy Vol. 2: 3136
Carlsburg Light People's Choice Award Vol. 1: 17560
Carlsen Award; Emil and Dines Vol. 1: 12103
Carlson Award; Chester F. Vol. 1: 16246
Carlson Award for Innovation in Engineering Education; Chester F. Vol. 1: 3634
Carmody-Lebo Memorial Award for Outstanding District Delegate; Helen Vol. 1: 2873
Carne Service Award; Herbert O. Vol. 1: 868
Carnegie International Exhibition Vol. 1: 7119
Carnegie Medal Vol. 1: 7115
Carnegie Medal for Excellence in ChildrenFs Video; Andrew Vol. 1: 4925
Carnegie Prize Vol. 1: 7119
Carnegie Prize; Andrew Vol. 1: 12104
Carnegie Scholarship; Herb Vol. 1: 5792
Caroline Haslett Memorial Trust Vol. 2: 6176
Carothers Medal Vol. 2: 7261
Carpenter Award; Leroy H. Vol. 1: 8422
Carpenter Award; William W. Vol. 1: 14261
Carper Award; James D. Vol. 1: 12631
Carr Flower Arranging Award; Celia Vol. 1: 8191
Carr Lifetime Achievement Award; Archie Vol. 1: 7103
Carr Music Award; Celia Vol. 1: 8192
Carr Premium; Robert Alfred Vol. 2: 6103
Carr Scholarship; Alice Vol. 1: 2625
Carreras-EHA Award; Jose Vol. 2: 3535
Carrier Award; Willis H. Vol. 1: 4051
Carriere Award; Jean P. Vol. 1: 17243
Carriere de Mathematiques; Prix Vol. 2: 1549
Carringer Mental Health Journalism Award; Helen Vol. 1: 13449
Carroll Award; Charles Vol. 1: 9226
Carroll Literary Award; John M. Vol. 1: 11385
Carroll Prize; Mitchell B. Vol. 2: 3588
The Carroll Society Vol. 1: 7123
Carron Award; I. Louis Vol. 1: 17523
Carron Keeper Vol. 1: 17523
Carrozza Scholarship Solo; Carmen Vol. 1: 759
Carski Foundation Distinguished Undergraduate Teaching Award Vol. 1: 3766
Carson Award; Rachel Vol. 1: 16423
Carson Award; SETAC Rachel Vol. 1: 16657
Carstensen Memorial Award; Vernon Vol. 1: 240
Cartan; Prix Elie Vol. 2: 1550
Carter Award; Leona Lyons Vol. 1: 2750
Carter Bronze Medal Vol. 2: 5635
Carter Logistics Readiness Award; Maj. Gen. Warren R. Vol. 1: 14640
Carter Memorial Golf Tournament; WPLGA - John Vol. 1: 18390
Carter Trophy Vol. 1: 9891
Cartier Diamond Dagger Award Vol. 2: 5706
Cartier MA Prize; Jacques Vol. 1: 6754
Cartoon Award Vol. 1: 9975
Cartwright Award; L. J. Vol. 1: 6263
Carty Award for the Advancement of Science; John J. Vol. 1: 12155
Carus Lectures Vol. 1: 3087
Carus Medal Vol. 2: 2393
Carus Preis Vol. 2: 2393
Caruso International Jazz Trumpet Solo Competition; Carmine Vol. 1: 10803
Caruthers Memorial Award; Jimmy Vol. 1: 17747
Caruthers Memorial Championship Rookie Driver of the Year Award; Jimmy Vol. 1: 17747
Carver Distinguished Service Award; W. O. Vol. 1: 5666
CASA/SME University LEAD Awards Vol. 1: 7646
Casadesus International Piano Competition; Robert Vol. 1: 7474
Casagrande International Piano Competition; Alessandro Vol. 2: 3015
Casagrande Professional Development Award; Arthur Vol. 1: 3924
Casals Violoncello Competition; Pablo Vol. 2: 2504
CASE Award of Excellence Vol. 1: 13061
CASEY Award Vol. 1: 17143
Casey/Minnesota Award; Ralph D. Vol. 1: 9719
Cash Awards Vol. 1: 17854
Cash-In-A-Flash Award Program Vol. 1: 17807
Casida Award; L. E. Vol. 1: 3885
CASME Award Vol. 2: 5672
Cass Correctional Achievement Award; E. R. Vol. 1: 1792
Cassavetes Award; John Vol. 1: 8160
Casselberry Award Vol. 1: 2618
Casselberry Fund Vol. 1: 2618
Cassels Reporter of the Year Award for Small Newspapers Vol. 1: 15613
Cassin; Prix Rene Vol. 2: 1641
Cassinis Award; Gino Vol. 2: 4971
Cassius Award; James Vol. 2: 183
Castellani - Reiss Medal and Award Vol. 1: 10718
Castle Trophy Vol. 1: 13647
Castleman Award; Benjamin Vol. 1: 17722
CASTME Awards Vol. 2: 5672
Castner Lecture and Medal Vol. 2: 7161
Caswell Screenwriting Award; Mick Vol. 1: 3535
Cat of the Year Awards Vol. 2: 446
Catalan Prize; Eugene Vol. 2: 1067
The Catalyst Award Vol. 1: 7135
Catalyst Grants Vol. 1: 15547
The CATCON Prizes Vol. 2: 4972
Category Awards Vol. 1: 12850
Catenacci; Prix Hercule Vol. 2: 1855
Caterpillar Scholars Award Vol. 1: 16707
Cattell Cup Vol. 2: 7207
Cattell Early Career Award for Programmatic Research; Raymond B. Vol. 1: 1941
Cattell Memorial Award; McKeen Vol. 1: 1628
Caty; Prix Charles Vol. 2: 972
Cauble Short Play Award; John Vol. 1: 11114
Caudill Young Readers' Book Award; Rebecca Vol. 1: 15573
Caughey Western History Association Award Vol. 1: 18683
Caulfield, Jr. Medal for Exemplary Contributions to National Water Policy; Henry P. Vol. 1: 4417
Cavallaro Medal Vol. 2: 2117
Cavanaugh Award; Catherine A. M. Vol. 1: 13730
Cavanaugh Award for Excellence in Training and Education in Aging; The Gloria Vol. 1: 4268
Cavanaugh Memorial Award; W. T. Vol. 1: 5409
Cavanaugh Memorial Prize; John Vol. 1: 13690
Cavanaugh Student Grant; William M. Vol. 1: 15439
Cave Radio and Electronics Group Vol. 2: 5274
Cavender Award of Service; Maggie Vol. 1: 12082
Cavendish Area Tourist Association Creative Writing Award for Children Vol. 1: 15219
Cavendish Excellence in Library Programming Award; Marshall Vol. 1: 2652
Caveness, M.D. Memorial Award; William Fields Vol. 1: 5926
Caves Award; Philip K. Vol. 1: 10648
Cavett Award Vol. 1: 13784
Cavin Award; Sheri Lynette Vol. 1: 4644
Cavling Prize Vol. 2: 1296
Cavour Prize; Grinzane Vol. 2: 3005
Cavour Prize La Habana; Grizane Vol. 2: 3005
Cavour Prize Montevideo; Grizane Vol. 2: 3005
Cavour Prize Moscow; Grizane Vol. 2: 3005
Cayla-Martin; Prix Emma du Vol. 2: 973
C.B. Macpherson Prize Vol. 1: 6818
CBA University Law School Essay Contest; Department of Justice - Vol. 1: 6330
CBC Literary Awards Vol. 1: 6103
CBC Radio National Competition for Amateur Choirs Vol. 1: 6361
CBC Radio National Competition for Young Composers Vol. 1: 6362
CBC Radio National Competition for Young Performers Vol. 1: 6363
CBC Radio Talent Competition Vol. 1: 6363
CBC Young Composers Competition Vol. 1: 6104
CBCI Award Vol. 2: 2820
CCA Member Recognition Vol. 2: 5572
CCAA Scholar Athlete Vol. 1: 6411
CCCC Outstanding Dissertation Award Vol. 1: 7691
CCol ASDC Associateship Vol. 2: 7182
CCol FSDC Fellowship Vol. 2: 7183
CCP Awards for the Arts Vol. 2: 3973
CCPE Faculty Teaching Award Vol. 1: 6435
CCSE Mentorship Award Vol. 1: 6964
CD-ROM Underwater Prize Vol. 2: 1799
CDADIC Awards Vol. 1: 7206
CDC Medal of Excellence Vol. 1: 17830
CDHCF Circle Award Vol. 1: 7765
CDHCF Distinguished Member Award Vol. 1: 7766
CDHCF Horizon Award Vol. 1: 7767
CDHCF Scholarship Award Vol. 1: 7768
The CDS/Honickmand First Book Prize in Photography Vol. 1: 8291
CEB-Cup Vol. 2: 858
CEBA Awards Vol. 2: 4415
CEC Outstanding Contributor Award Vol. 1: 7857
Cecil Arthritis Awards; Russell L. Vol. 1: 4657
Cecil Award in Environmental Chemical Engineering; Lawrence K. Vol. 1: 2472

Cecil Writing Awards; Russell L. Vol. 1: 4657
Celebration Awards Vol. 1: 12253
Celebrity Animal Rights Advocate of the Year Vol. 1: 8591
Cellier; Prix Alphonse Vol. 2: 1442
Cellular Toxicology Award Vol. 1: 16258
Cements Award Vol. 1: 1470
Cena Chopinovy klavirni souteze Vol. 2: 1252
Cena Frantisek Kriegel Vol. 2: 4577
Cena Jaroslava Seiferta Vol. 2: 4578
Cena Obce Architektu za Realizaci Roku Vol. 2: 1270
CenE Bankiers Audience Award Vol. 2: 3621
Cenie J. Williams Tuition Vol. 1: 12418
Census Award of Excellence Vol. 1: 17770
Centenarian Award Vol. 1: 15518
Centenary Lectureship Vol. 2: 6956
Centenary Medal
  Australian Honours Secretariat Vol. 2: 209
  Indian and Northern Affairs Canada Vol 1: 9656
  Royal Photographic Society of Great Britain Vol 2: 6870
  Royal Scottish Geographical Society Vol 2: 6890
Centennial Award Vol. 1: 6805
Centennial Award for Excellence in Teaching Vol. 1: 10863
The Centennial Maori Scholarship Vol. 2: 3775
Centennial Medal Vol. 1: 453
The Centennial Scholarship Vol. 2: 3776
Centorino Award; James Vol. 1: 13422
Central Poster Award Vol. 1: 7248
Central Prize Award Vol. 1: 7248
Centre of the Year Vol. 2: 5907
Centrum Center for Nutrition Science Award Vol. 1: 3787
Centurion Award Vol. 1: 483
Century Award
  American Numismatic Association Vol. 1: 2874
  American Public Power Association Vol 1: 3438
  Billboard - VNU Business Publications USA Vol 1: 5760
Century Awards Vol. 1: 16112
Century Club Award Vol. 1: 1380
Century Scholarship Vol. 1: 5339
CEO Recognition Award Vol. 1: 18837
CERA/Statistics Canada Research Prize and Award for Excellence Vol. 1: 6965
CERES Award Vol. 1: 18808
CERESIS Award Vol. 2: 3958
CerSJ Awards Vol. 2: 3169
Certamen Capitolinum Vol. 2: 3090
Certamen Internacional de Guitarra Francisco Tarrega Vol. 2: 4473
Certamen International de Films Cortos, Ciudad de Huesca Vol. 2: 4495
Certamen Nacional de Cortomrtrajes Award Vol. 2: 4493
Certificate in Energy Efficiency For Domestic Central Heating Vol. 2: 6024
Certificate of Achievement
  American Urological Association Vol. 1: 4387
  Herb Society of America Vol 1: 9375
Certificate of Achievement for Excellence in Financial Reporting
  Government Finance Officers Association of United States and Canada Vol. 1: 9148
  Government Finance Officers Association of United States and Canada Vol 1: 9150
Certificate of Achievement of Focused Studies Vol. 1: 118
Certificate of Appreciation
  American Occupational Therapy Association Vol. 1: 2953
  American Psychological Association - Division of Family Psychology (Division 43) Vol 1: 3330
  Blinded Veterans Association Vol 1: 5808
  Canadian Camping Association Vol 1: 6372
  Construction Specifications Institute Vol 1: 7746
  Federation of Genealogical Societies Vol 1: 8655
  Herb Society of America Vol 1: 9376
  IEEE Electromagnetic Compatibility Society Vol 1: 9572
  International Union of Forest Research Organizations Vol 2: 814
  Lakeshore Humane Society Vol 1: 11207
  Library Administration and Management Association Vol 1: 11330
  National Aeronautics and Space Administration Vol 1: 12194
  National Genealogical Society Vol 1: 13272
  National Society, Sons of the American Revolution Vol 1: 13759
  Rural Sociological Society Vol 1: 15778
  Soaring Society of America Vol 1: 16105
Certificate of Appreciation and Recognition Vol. 1: 17083
Certificate of Appreciation Award Vol. 1: 17109
Certificate of Botanical Recognition Vol. 1: 2984
Certificate of Commendation
  American Association for State and Local History Vol. 1: 943
  International Badminton Federation Vol 2: 3405
Certificate of Cultural Excellence Vol. 1: 2985
Certificate of Cultural Merit Vol. 1: 2986
Certificate of Distinguished Service Vol. 1: 13760
Certificate of Excellence in Exhibit Renovation Vol. 1: 1335
Certificate of Honor Vol. 1: 869
Certificate of Honor - HSA Vol. 1: 9456
Certificate of Horticultural Merit Vol. 1: 2987
Certificate of Merit
  American Association of Petroleum Geologists Vol. 1: 1210
  American Association of Teachers of German Vol 1: 1299
  American Institute of Aeronautics and Astronautics Vol 1: 2367
  American Red Cross National Headquarters Vol 1: 3467
  American Society for Engineering Education Vol 1: 3635
  American Society of International Law Vol 1: 4088
  British Turf and Landscape Irrigation Association Vol 2: 5551
  Canadian Public Health Association Vol 1: 6839
  Canadian Society of Diagnostic Medical Sonographers Vol 1: 6990
  Huntington Society of Canada Vol 1: 9544
  International Animated Film Society, ASIFA - Hollywood Vol 1: 10042
  International Council for Canadian Studies Vol 1: 10345
  International Youth Hostel Federation Vol 2: 6336
  Mathematical Association of America Vol 1: 11603
  Mount Vernon Genealogical Society Vol 1: 11980
  Municipal Art Society of New York Vol 1: 12008
  National Environmental Health Association Vol 1: 13116
  National Speleological Society Vol 1: 13788
  Pierre Fauchard Academy Vol 1: 15073
  Specialty Graphic Imaging Association Vol 1: 17110
  Zoological Society of Southern Africa Vol 2: 4380
Certificate of Merit for Commercial Wool Production in Canada Vol. 1: 6397
Certificate of Merit for Marching Excellence Vol. 1: 12738
Certificate of Merit for Zoo Keeper Education Vol. 1: 1336
Certificate of Outstanding Service Vol. 2: 73
Certificate of Recognition Vol. 1: 16586
Certificate of Satisfaction Vol. 2: 4411
Certificate of Service Vol. 1: 6950
Certificate of Victory Vol. 1: 13301
Certificates, Diplomas, and Licentiates in Genealogy and Heraldry Vol. 2: 6034
Certificates in Dry Stone Walling Vol. 2: 5744
Certificates of Appreciation Vol. 1: 4844
Certificates of Excellence Vol. 1: 9241
Certificates of Merit Vol. 1: 12105
Certification Award Vol. 1: 6680
Certifications of Appreciation Vol. 1: 18895
Certified Awards Vol. 2: 5417
Certified Instructor of the Year Vol. 1: 13307
Certified Residential Specialist Designation Vol. 1: 7892
Cervenka Scholarship; Arthur and Gladys Vol. 1: 16708
Cervi Award; Eugene Vol. 1: 10746
Cesery Memorial Award; Carl V. Vol. 1: 17537
Cetacean Citation Vol. 1: 7260
Cetus Corporation Biotechnology Research Award Vol. 1: 3772
Ceylon Development Engineering Award Vol. 2: 4556
CFA Distinguished Service Award Vol. 1: 7780
CFAS Award of Excellence in Reproductive Medicine Vol. 1: 6494
CFDA Fashion Awards Vol. 1: 7885
CFF/NIH Unfunded Grants Vol. 1: 8010
CFIC Book Prize Vol. 1: 7970
CFMS Scholarship Vol. 1: 6049
CFUW A. Vibert Douglas International Fellowship Vol. 2: 4803
CFUW Memorial Fellowship Award Vol. 1: 6484
CGS/Peterson's Award for Promoting an Inclusive Graduate Community Vol. 1: 7889
CGS Prize Vol. 1: 6529
CGS/UMI Distinguished Dissertation Award Vol. 1: 7890
CGSA/Toro Future Superintendent Award Vol. 1: 6534

Chabas; Prix Paul Vol. 2: 1443
Chabon Award; Irwin Vol. 1: 11210
Chaim and Simcha Tova Mizel Memorial Exhibit Award; Menachem Vol. 1: 2875
Chairman of the Board Awards Vol. 1: 5644
Chairman's Advocacy Award Vol. 1: 11300
ChairmanFs Award Vol. 1: 2850
Chairman's Award
Alcoa Inc. Vol. 1: 381
American Academy of Medical Administrators Vol 1: 626
American College of Managed Care Administrators Vol 1: 1665
American College of Oncology Administrators Vol 1: 1695
Concrete Society of Southern Africa Vol 2: 4153
CTAM - Cable and Telecommunications Association for Marketing Vol 1: 7993
Friends of the Pendleton District Vol 1: 8911
International Association of Business Communicators Vol 1: 10150
Japan Construction Mechanization Association Vol 2: 3222
National Association for the Advancement of Colored People Vol 1: 12367
National Biplane Association Vol 1: 12769
Outdoor Advertising Association of America Vol 1: 14746
Pendleton District Historical, Recreational, and Tourism Commission Vol 1: 14915
Society of Cable Telecommunications Engineers Vol 1: 16615
World Trade Centre Vancouver Vol 1: 18988
ChairmanFs Award for Career Achievement Vol. 1: 5698
Chairman's Award for Career Achievement Vol. 1: 5697
ChairmanFs Awards Vol. 1: 5302
Chairman's Citation Vol. 1: 11301
Chairman's Citation of Merit Awards Vol. 1: 331
The Chairman's Cup Vol. 1: 1000
Chairman's Professional Leadership Award Vol. 1: 1499
Chairman's Special Award Vol. 1: 17980
Chair's Award Vol. 1: 1090
Chair's Citation
American Association of Homes and Services for the Aging Vol. 1: 1121
Council of Scientific Society Presidents Vol 1: 7896
Chaix d'Est Ange; Prix Gustave Vol. 2: 1642
Chakravarty Awards; Prof. Hira Lal Vol. 2: 2738
Challenge Trophies Vol. 1: 1992
Challenger Award Vol. 1: 12843
Chalmers Award; Jean A. Vol. 1: 6363
Chalmers Memorial Medal Vol. 2: 7029
Chamber Music Performance Competition Vol. 1: 12032
Chamber Music Yellow Springs Competition Vol. 1: 7280
Chamber of Commerce Scholarship Vol. 1: 7282
Chamber Opera Competition Vol. 1: 13486
Chamber Person of the Year Vol. 1: 15988
Chamber Scholarships Vol. 1: 9246
Chamberlain Award; C. K. Vol. 1: 8332
Chambers Excellence in Air Pollution Control Award; Frank A. Vol. 1: 264
Chamorro Inter-American Relations Award; Pedro Joaquin Vol. 1: 9976
Champion Award Vol. 1: 6565
Champion Cup Holder Vol. 2: 3464
Champion Exporter Vol. 2: 3148
Champion Llama, Champion Alpaca Vol. 2: 5342
Champion of Champions Vol. 1: 3075
Champion of the Florida Trail Award Vol. 1: 8770
Champion of the Year Award Vol. 2: 6430
Champion Shots Medal Vol. 2: 210
Champions for Children Vol. 1: 8829
Champions of Excellence Vol. 1: 73
Championship Awards
National Derby Rallies Vol. 1: 13090
Spanish Mustang Registry Vol 1: 17070
Championship of Champions Vol. 1: 18062
Championship Title Vol. 1: 18948
Championships, Cups, and Trophies Vol. 2: 1882
The Championships, Wimbledon Vol. 2: 5020
Champlain Award Vol. 1: 6430
Champlin Research Award Vol. 1: 9761
Chan Scholarship; Dr. Allan P. Vol. 1: 8773
Chandler-Misener Award Vol. 1: 10088
Chandra Bose Medal; Jagdish Vol. 2: 2681
Chaney Award Vol. 1: 870
Chang Award for Lipid or Flavor Science; Stephen S. Vol. 1: 9847
Chang Award; Stephen S. Vol. 1: 2967
Chang Student Travel Grants; Incubic/Milton Vol. 1: 14603
Changing Faces Prize Vol. 2: 7027
Channel 4 Archaeological Film Awards Vol. 2: 5555
The Channel Four Awards Vol. 2: 5222
Chant Medal; C. A. Vol. 1: 15735
Chapanis Best Student Paper Award; Alphonse Vol. 1: 9508
Chapbook Competition Vol. 1: 15447
Chapelle Award for Nautical Research; Howard I. Vol. 1: 13997
Chapin Award for Volunteers in the Arts; Elizabeth Vol. 1: 7420
Chapin Award; Harold C. Vol. 1: 1308
Chapin Media Awards; Harry Vol. 1: 18945
Chapin Memorial Humanitarian Award; Harry Vol. 1: 12637
Chapin Self-Reliance Award; Harry Vol. 1: 18946
Chaplain of the Year Vol. 1: 17701
Chapline Land Stewardship Award; W. R. Vol. 1: 16401
Chapline Research Award; W. R. Vol. 1: 16402
Chapman Award; Dr. Wilfred Vol. 2: 732
Chapman Medal Vol. 2: 6686
Chapman Medal; R. W. Vol. 2: 495
Chapman Memorial Award; Charles F. Vol. 1: 13428
Chapman Memorial Award for Outstanding Contributions in Technical Services Law Librarianship; Renee D. Vol. 1: 1141
Chapman Memorial Grant; Frank M. Vol. 1: 2829
Chapman Prize Essay Vol. 2: 5405
Chapter Achievement Award Vol. 1: 18824
Chapter Activities Award Vol. 1: 1751
Chapter Activity Award Contest Vol. 1: 8597
Chapter Award Vol. 2: 235
Chapter Award for Excellence in Membership Marketing Vol. 1: 10395
Chapter Award for Excellence in Newsletter Publishing Vol. 1: 10396
Chapter Awards
Society of Cosmetic Chemists Vol. 1: 16628
Tau Beta Pi Association Vol 1: 17401
Chapter Best Speaker Award Vol. 1: 16628
Chapter Community Service Award Vol. 1: 13955
Chapter Competition Vol. 1: 9892
Chapter Education Grants Vol. 1: 5169
Chapter Event of the Year Award Vol. 1: 3738
Chapter Excellence Award
American Association of Healthcare Administrative Management Vol. 1: 1113
Oncology Nursing Society Vol 1: 14534
Chapter Excellence Awards Vol. 1: 10663
Chapter History Award Vol. 1: 5724
Chapter Hope Chest Award Vol. 1: 13462
Chapter Innovation Vol. 1: 16393
Chapter Key Awards Vol. 1: 16045
Chapter Leader of the Year Vol. 1: 11682
Chapter Member of the Year Award Vol. 1: 3739
Chapter Membership Awards Vol. 1: 601
Chapter Merit Award Vol. 1: 16628
Chapter Merit Awards Vol. 1: 4309
Chapter Merit Awards for Professional Chapters Vol. 1: 16235
Chapter Merit Awards for Students Vol. 1: 16236
Chapter MVP of the Year Vol. 1: 5115
Chapter Newsletter Awards Vol. 1: 16046
Chapter Newsletter of the Year Award Vol. 1: 4626
Chapter of Excellence Award Vol. 1: 10654
Chapter of the Year
Academy of Certified Hazardous Materials Managers Vol. 1: 74
Autism Society of America Vol 1: 5548
Information Systems Security Association Vol 1: 9702
National Space Society of Australia Vol 2: 580
Chapter of the Year
American Fence Association Vol. 1: 2010
American ORT Vol 1: 3008
ARMA International - The Association of Information Management Professionals Vol 1: 4627
National Broadcasting Society - Alpha Epsilon Rho Vol 1: 12789
National Property Management Association Vol 1: 13580
Professional Aviation Maintenance Association Vol 1: 15268
System Safety Society Vol 1: 17371
U.S. Hang Gliding Association Vol 1: 17924
Chapter of the Year Award
American Society for Information Science and Technology Vol. 1: 3740
American Society of Certified Engineering Technicians Vol 1: 3904
International Facility Management Association Vol 1: 10397
Mail Systems Management Association Vol 1: 11464
National Institute of Governmental Purchasing Vol 1: 13372
TRI-M Music Honor Society Vol 1: 17601
Chapter-of-the-Year Award Vol. 1: 9573

The Chapter of the Year Award Vol. 1: 12016
Chapter of the Year Awards Vol. 1: 4944
Chapter President Award Vol. 1: 16327
Chapter Publication of the Year Award Vol. 1: 3741
Chapter Research Advancement Award Vol. 1: 16047
Chapter Service Award Vol. 1: 5177
Chapter Website Award Vol. 1: 75
Chapters of the Year Vol. 1: 11679
Charcot Award; J. B. Vol. 1: 11038
Charcot Award; Jean-Martin Vol. 2: 6444
Chardonnay of the Century - Million Dollar Challenge Vol. 1: 18243
Charity of the Year
Canadian Association of Women Executives and Entrepreneurs Vol. 1: 6310
Royal New South Wales Bowling Association Vol 2: 633
Charles C. Curtis Religion and Hypnosis Award Vol. 1: 13308
Charles D. EdsForth Memorial Award Vol. 1: 6634
Charles Darwin University Essay Award Vol. 2: 589
Charles Laferle Memorial Award Vol. 1: 6635
The Charles Laszlo Award of Technical Excellence Vol. 1: 6543
Charles Loring Brace Award Vol. 1: 14709
Charles Tebbetts Award Vol. 1: 13309
Charles U. Letourneau Student Research Paper of the Year Vol. 1: 1666
Charlotte Kohlerprijs Vol. 2: 3681
Charlson Award; Jim Vol. 1: 5022
Charlton Lifetime Achievement Award; Thomas L. Vol. 1: 17495
Charnley Award; John Vol. 1: 9405
Chartered Accountant of the Year Vol. 2: 3727
Chartered Institute of Transport Annual Innovation Award Vol. 2: 3756
Chartered Society of Designers Honorary Fellow Vol. 2: 5652
Chartered Society of Designers Medal Vol. 2: 5653
Chartered State Association Executive Director of the Year Vol. 1: 12804
Chartered State Association of the Year Vol. 1: 12805
Chartered State Association President of the Year Vol. 1: 12806
Chartier; Prix Vol. 2: 1444
Chase Award for Excellence in Issue Management; W. Howard Vol. 1: 10925
Chase Award for Physician Executive Excellence; John D. Vol. 1: 5240
Chase Award; Joe Vol. 1: 15269
Chase Award; Joe M. Vol. 1: 8725
Chasko Award; Lawrence J. Vol. 1: 1131
Chasman Scholarship for Women; Renate W. Vol. 1: 5961
Chassis Inspectors Award Vol. 1: 9885
Chatt Lectureship; Joseph Vol. 2: 6957
Chattanooga Research Award Vol. 1: 3146
Chatterjee Memorial Award; G. P. Vol. 2: 2739
Chatterjee Memorial Lecture; Dr. Guru Prajad Vol. 2: 2682
Chauncey Award for Distonguished Service to Assessment and Education Science; Henry Vol. 1: 8400
Chautauqua International Exhibition of American Art Vol. 1: 7293
Chautauqua National Exhibition of American Art Vol. 1: 7293
Chauveau Medal; Pierre Vol. 1: 15756
Chauvenet Prize Vol. 1: 11604
Chavasse; Prix Vol. 2: 1979
Chavee; Prix Honore Vol. 2: 1504
Chavez Young Investigator Award; Professor Ignacio Vol. 2: 3449
Chavrid Award Vol. 1: 12674
Chayefsky Laurel Award for Television; Paddy Vol. 1: 19010
Chayes Award Vol. 1: 10103
CHCCS/SCDHM Achievement Award Vol. 1: 6569
CHCCS/SCDHM Service Award Vol. 1: 6570
Chedanne; Fondation Vol. 2: 1482
Cheek Exemplary Service Award; Willard D. Vol. 1: 3636
Chef Ireland
National Restaurant Association Vol. 1: 13631
Society of German Cooks Vol 2: 2383
Chef of the Year
Caribbean Hotel Association Vol. 1: 7105
Craft Guild of Chefs Vol 2: 5702
Cheiron Medal Vol. 2: 834
Chelsea Award Vol. 1: 7295
Chemeca Medal Vol. 2: 496
Chemical Education Medal Vol. 2: 4314
Chemical Industry Medal Vol. 1: 16622
Chemical Institute of Canada Awards for High School Chemistry Teachers Vol. 1: 7304
Chemical Institute of Canada Medal Vol. 1: 7301
Chemical Pioneer Awards Vol. 1: 2507
Chemical Society of Japan Award Vol. 2: 3172
Chemical Society of Japan Award for Chemical Education Vol. 2: 3173
Chemical Society of Japan Award for Distinguished Technical Achievements Vol. 2: 3174
Chemical Society of Japan Award for Technological Development Vol. 2: 3175
Chemical Society of Japan Award for Young Chemists Vol. 2: 3176
Chemical Society of Japan Award of Merit for Chemical Education Vol. 2: 3177
Chemistry Teaching Award Vol. 2: 7059
Chen Memorial Prize Vol. 2: 5412
Cheney Award; Frances Neel Vol. 1: 17433
Chennault Award; Lt. General Claire Lee Vol. 1: 284
Chennault Trophy Vol. 1: 4646
Chern Mathematics Award; Shiing S. Vol. 2: 3927
Cherry Award for Great Teachers; Robert Foster Vol. 1: 15685
Cherry Prize; Professor J. Vol. 2: 6153
Cherry Student Prize; T. M. Vol. 2: 42
Cherry Tree Marathon Vol. 1: 14153
Chesley Award Vol. 2: 3610
Chesney Gold Medal Vol. 2: 7054
Chess Championship; U.S. Vol. 1: 17772
Chess Journalist of the Year Vol. 1: 7313
Chess Olympiad for the Blind Vol. 2: 4590
Chess World Champions Vol. 2: 2475
CHEST Foundation Young Investigator Awards Vol. 1: 1622
Chester County Community Hero Vol. 1: 18187
Chester County Youth Community Hero Vol. 1: 18188
Chetwynd Award for Entrepreneurial Excellence Vol. 1: 6499
Chevalier; Prix Auguste Vol. 2: 1551
Chevallier; Prix Jean-Baptiste Vol. 2: 1643
Chevron Conservation Awards Vol. 1: 7315
Chevron - Times Mirror Magazines Conservation Awards Program Vol. 1: 7315
Chicago Award Vol. 1: 7414
Chicago Book and Media Show Vol. 1: 7323
Chicago Film Critics Awards Vol. 1: 7329
Chicago Flame Vol. 1: 7329
Chicago Folklore Prize Vol. 1: 18253
Chicago International Children's Film Festival Vol. 1: 7331
Chicago International Festival of Children's Films Vol. 1: 7331
Chicago International Film Festival Vol. 1: 7414
Chick Trophy; John Vol. 1: 2265
Chief Financial Officers Award for Distinction in Public Finance Vol. 1: 17855
Chief Justice J.T. Brown Shield; Goodfellow Memorial Award in Voice/ Vol. 1: 15856
Chief Minister's History Book Vol. 2: 589
Chief of Engineers Award of Excellence Vol. 1: 17739
Chief of Engineers Design and Environmental Awards Program Vol. 1: 17739
Chief of the South African Defense Force Commendation Medal Vol. 2: 4344
Chief ScoutFs Commendation Vol. 2: 2884
Chief ScoutFs Commendation of Honour Vol. 2: 2883
Chiiki Koryu Shinko Sho Vol. 2: 3235
Chilcote Young Investigator Award; Max E. Vol. 1: 871
Child Advocate of the Year Vol. 1: 14290
Child Award; Julia Vol. 1: 10189
Child Cookbook Award; Julia Vol. 1: 10189
Child Health Foundation Prize Vol. 2: 4927
Childers Award for Distinguished Graduate Teaching; Norman F. Vol. 1: 3725
Children Author/Illustrator Award Vol. 1: 4601
Children's ABBY Award Vol. 1: 1414
Children's Africana Book Awards Vol. 1: 223
Children's Book Award
Association of Jewish Libraries Vol. 1: 5210
Children's Book Committee Vol 1: 7340
Federation of Children's Book Groups Vol 2: 5883
South Carolina Association of School Librarians Vol 1: 16984
United Kingdom Literacy Association Vol 2: 7301
Children's Book Awards Vol. 1: 10576
Children's Book of the Year Vol. 1: 5839
Children's Book Prize Vol. 1: 18660
Children's Choice Award Vol. 1: 7046
Children's Illustrator of the Year Award Vol. 1: 6348
Children's Peace Literature Award Vol. 2: 333
Children's Sequoyah Book Award Vol. 1: 14500
Childs Award; Gayle B. Vol. 1: 18210
Chilton Prize; Ken Vol. 1: 15736
China Service Medal - Navy, Marine Corps, Coast Guard Vol. 1: 8098
China Stamp Society Award Vol. 1: 7359
Chinard Prize; The Gilbert Vol. 1: 7361
Chinese Martial Arts Leadership Award Vol. 1: 484

Chinese Martial Arts Outstanding Service Award Vol. 1: 485
Chipp Memorial Award; Rodney D. Vol. 1: 16911
Chiron Therapeutics Award for Excellence of Scholarship and Consistency of Contribution to the Oncology Nursing Literature Vol. 1: 14542
Chiron Therapeutics Chapter Excellence Award Vol. 1: 14534
Chiron Therapeutics Susan Baird Excellence in Writing Awards in Clinical Practice and Nursing Research Vol. 1: 14532
Chiropractor of the Year Vol. 1: 10304
Chisholm Award for Lifetime Achievement; Jack Vol. 1: 6500
ChM Prize Vol. 1: 2146
Choice Outstanding Academic Books and Nonprint Materials Vol. 1: 7371
Choice's Outstanding Academic Books Vol. 1: 7371
Choir of the World at Llangollen Vol. 2: 6393
Cholmondeley Award for Poets Vol. 2: 7140
Chopin Competition; Warsaw Vol. 2: 2065
Chopin; Grand Prix du Disque Frederic Vol. 2: 4001
Chopin-Klavierwettbewerb; Europaischer Vol. 2: 2065
Chopin Piano Competition
Czech Chopin Society Vol. 2: 1252
Kosciuszko Foundation Vol 1: 11166
Chopinovy klavirni souteze; Cena Vol. 2: 1252
Choppin Memorial Award; IEA - Bruce H. Vol. 2: 3567
Chopra Lecture; Bashambar Nath Vol. 2: 2683
Choral Awards Vol. 2: 688
Chorbachi Prizes; Walid Vol. 2: 6005
Chorpenning Playwright Award; Charlotte B. Vol. 1: 791
Chorus America/ASCAP Awards for Adventurous Programming Vol. 1: 7377
Choseed Research Fellowship; Prof. Bernard Vol. 1: 19059
Chow Award; Ven Te Vol. 1: 3925
Chow Memorial Endowed Lecturer Vol. 1: 10829
CHPCA Award of Excellence Vol. 1: 6566
Chree Medal and Prize; Charles Vol. 2: 6057
Chris Statuette Vol. 1: 7382
Christensen Award for Best Documentary/ Bibliography; Steven F. Vol. 1: 11951
Christensen Memorial Exhibit Award; Henry Vol. 1: 2876
Christensen Memorial Prize; F. G. Vol. 2: 610
Christian Album of the Year Vol. 2: 3706
Christian Book of the Year Vol. 2: 3707
Christian Management Award Vol. 1: 7391
Christian Stewardship Award Vol. 1: 10295
Christian Unity Award Vol. 1: 8384
Christie Lectureship; Barnett Vol. 2: 5317
Christman Award; Luther Vol. 1: 833
Christman Scholarship; Irene R. Vol. 1: 14931
Christoff International Competition for Young Opera Singers - Sofia; Boris Vol. 2: 1141
Christopher Awards Vol. 1: 7393
Christopher J. Georges Fellowship Vol. 1: 14235
Christopher Life Achievement Award Vol. 1: 7393
Christopher Spirit Award Vol. 1: 7393
Christophers Medal; Sir Rickard Vol. 2: 7030
Christopherson Lectureship Award; E. H. Vol. 1: 684
Christus Magister Award Vol. 1: 11445
Christy Award; Teresa E. Vol. 1: 971
Chrysler Triple Crown Challenge Vol. 1: 17610
Chugai Mentoring Award Vol. 1: 3753
Church Medal; Edwin F. Vol. 1: 4126
Churchill Award; H. V. Vol. 1: 5410
Churchill Award; Winston Vol. 1: 18765
Churchill Bowl Vol. 1: 6674
Ciapetta Lectureship in Catalysis; F. G. Vol. 1: 14272
CIBA Crop Protection and Sandoz Agro Vol. 1: 17369
CIBA-GEIGY Corporation Vol. 1: 17369
CIBA-GEIGY Exemplary Middle Level and High School Science Teaching Award Vol. 1: 13679
CIBA-GEIGY-ILAR International Rheumatism Award Vol. 2: 548
CIBA Specialty Chemicals Exemplary Middle Level and High School Principal Awards Vol. 1: 13679
CIBA Specialty Chemicals Exemplary Middle Level and High School Science Teaching Awards Vol. 1: 13680
CIBC National Music Festival Vol. 1: 13473
CIC Fellowship Vol. 1: 7302
CICAE Prizes (International Confederation of Art Cinemas) Vol. 2: 2048
Ciccoli Joint Operations Award Vol. 1: 4645
Cichan Award; Michael Vol. 1: 5870
Cider Maker of the Year Vol. 1: 2284
Cihon Exhibit Award; Fred Vol. 1: 2877
Cillie Award; Dr. G. G. Vol. 2: 4376
CIM Distinguished Lecturers Vol. 1: 6613
CIM Fellowship Vol. 1: 6614
CIM/NRCan Journalism Awards Vol. 1: 6615
CIM Student Essay Competition Vol. 1: 6616
CINA Incentive Maisie Townsend Scholarship Vol. 1: 6681
Cinader Award; Harvey Vol. 1: 6939
CINANIMA Vol. 2: 4056
Cincinnati Opera Education Program Vol. 1: 7412
Cinderella Stamp Club Trophy Vol. 2: 6535
CineFestival in San Antonio Vol. 1: 9218
Cinema in Industry (CINDY) Awards Vol. 1: 10143
Cinema Under the Stars Vol. 1: 11944
Cintas Foundation Fellowships Vol. 1: 9888
CIPS Supply Managent Awards Vol. 2: 5631
Circulation Council Awards Vol. 1: 14214
Circulation Federation Awards Vol. 1: 14214
Cisneros Award; Rosa Vol. 1: 10546
Citation Award
Awana Clubs International Vol. 1: 5602
Institute of Quarrying - England Vol 2: 6076
Citation for Career Achievement Vol. 1: 16319
Citation for Excellence in Community Architecture Vol. 1: 2433
Citation for Outstanding Service to the Society Vol. 1: 16743
Citation for Service Vol. 1: 8969
Citation of Excellence Vol. 1: 12739
Citation of Excellence in Advertising Vol. 1: 18625
Citation of Honor
Air Force Association Vol. 1: 285
Associated Church Press Vol 1: 4759
Citation of Merit Vol. 1: 6826
Citation of Outstanding Achievement Vol. 1: 6799
Citations for Contributions to Chemistry and the Chemical Profession Vol. 2: 617
Citations pour Service Eminent Vol. 1: 6799
Citibank Choral Awards Vol. 2: 688
Citizen Activist Award Vol. 1: 9094
Citizen Diplomat Award Vol. 1: 10826
Citizen Leadership Award Vol. 1: 12934
Citizen of the Year
American Association of Dental Examiners Vol. 1: 1076
Center for Philosophy, Law, Citizenship Vol 1: 7232
Darien Chamber of Commerce Vol 1: 8056
Kankakee River Valley Chamber of Commerce Vol 1: 11074
Vermont Chamber of Commerce Vol 1: 18496
Citizen of the Year Award Vol. 2: 725
Citizen's Award Vol. 1: 9669
City and Guilds Prizes Vol. 2: 7060
City Livability Awards Program Vol. 1: 17783
City of Antibes Prize Vol. 2: 1799
City of Excellence Awards Vol. 1: 11266
City of Sondrio Gold Plaque Vol. 2: 3130
City of Springvale Short Story Awards Vol. 2: 411
City of Sydney Eisteddfod Pianoforte Scholarship Vol. 2: 687
City of Sydney Piano Scholarship Vol. 2: 687
City of Toronto Book Awards Vol. 1: 7439
CITY-TV Award for Best Canadian First Feature Film Vol. 1: 17558
Civic Achievement Award Vol. 1: 5742
Civic Courage Award Vol. 1: 15552
Civic Leadership Award Vol. 1: 7424
Civic Trust Awards Vol. 2: 5663
Civil Air Patrol Aerospace Education Cadet of the Year Vol. 1: 286
Civil Air Patrol Cadet of the Year Vol. 1: 286
Civil Courage Prize Vol. 1: 14384
Civil Engineering Award Vol. 2: 7065
Civil Engineering Best Paper Award Vol. 1: 3637
Civil Engineering History and Heritage Award Vol. 1: 3926
Civil Engineering Manager of the Year Award Vol. 2: 6104
Civil Engineering Students Papers Competition Vol. 2: 6105
Civil Government Award Vol. 1: 3927
Civil Service Secretary of the Year; Foreign Service Office Management Specialist of the Year/ Vol. 1: 17864
Civilian Employee Awards Vol. 1: 287
Civilian Executive of the Year Vol. 1: 9142
Civilian Medal of Appreciation Vol. 1: 3217
Civilian Service Medal 1939-1945 Vol. 2: 211
CIWEM Certificate and Diploma in Environmental Management Vol. 2: 5642
CLA Book Award Vol. 1: 7521
CLA/Information Today Award for Innovative Technology Vol. 1: 6689
CLA/Meckler Award for Innovative Technology Vol. 1: 6689
CLA Service Award Vol. 1: 7522
Clagett Trophy; U.S. Sailing/Rolex Junior Women's Championship - Nancy Leiter Vol. 1: 18063
CLAGS Fellowship Vol. 1: 7218
CLAGS Student Paper Awards Vol. 1: 7219

Award Index

CLAGS Student Travel Award Vol. 1: 7220
Claiming Mule Vol. 1: 2816
Clair Jr. Award; John J. Vol. 1: 18090
Clare Glover Award Vol. 1: 12330
Clarion Awards Vol. 1: 5000
Clark Award Vol. 1: 8414
Clark Award; John Vol. 1: 6880
Clark Award; John William Vol. 2: 5356
Clark Award; Justice Tom C. Vol. 1: 8598
Clark Award; Mary Higgins Vol. 1: 12055
Clark Award; Russell Vol. 2: 3750
Clark Citizenship Award; Rhea Eckel Vol. 1: 7251
Clark, Jr. Trophy; W. Van Alan Vol. 1: 18068
Clark McCoy Service Award; Lois Vol. 1: 12356
Clark Medal; Grahame Vol. 2: 5206
Clark Medal; John Bates Vol. 1: 1935
Clark Memorial Award; F. Ambrose Vol. 1: 13809
Clark Memorial Educational Scholarship; Robert A. Vol. 1: 13716
Clark National Memorial Trophy; G. Melville Vol. 2: 5036
Clark Prize; Matt Vol. 1: 14029
Clark Professional Award; David E. Vol. 1: 3025
Clark Research Award; Kenneth E. Vol. 1: 7203
Clarke Award; Alan Vol. 2: 5217
Clarke Award; Arthur C. Vol. 2: 7077
Clarke Award; Ethel Palmer Vol. 1: 16049
Clarke Award; Polly Vol. 1: 14496
Clarke Fraser New Investigator Award; F. Vol. 1: 17445
Clarke Medal Vol. 2: 638
Clarke Memorial Award; Doug Vol. 1: 7065
Clarke Memorial Lecture Vol. 2: 639
Clarke Outstanding Educator Award; Robert B. Vol. 1: 8206
Clarke Prize; Thomas B. Vol. 1: 12106
Clarke Trophy; Robert W. Vol. 1: 2266
Classic Championship Vol. 2: 6235
Classical Fellowship Awards Vol. 1: 3196
Classified Advertising Managers Executive Order Award Vol. 1: 14215
Classified Council Awards Vol. 1: 14215
Classified Federation Awards Vol. 1: 14215
Clausse; Fondation Gustave Vol. 2: 1482
Clavel-Lespiau; Prix Vol. 2: 1552
Clay Award; Garland W. Vol. 1: 651
Claypoole, Sr. Memorial Award; Ralph O. Vol. 1: 1711
Clayton Doctoral Dissertation Proposal Award; Alden G. Vol. 1: 11551
Clayton Prize; James Vol. 2: 6185
Cleanrun Award Vol. 1: 14421
Clear-Com Intercom Systems Sound Achievement Award Vol. 1: 17950
Cleary Award; Edward J. Vol. 1: 573
Cleary Memorial Prize Vol. 2: 3777
Cleaver Club Award Vol. 1: 1155
Clements Award; Ken Vol. 1: 6302
Clemm Denkmunze; Hans Vol. 2: 2028
Clemson Awards Vol. 1: 16183
Clemson National Print and Drawing Exhibition Vol. 1: 15773
Clercq; Prix de la Fondation Louis de Vol. 2: 1505
Clermont-Ferrand International Short Film Festival Vol. 2: 1947
Clermont-Ferrand National Short Film Festival Vol. 2: 1948
Clermont-Ganneau; Prix Charles Vol. 2: 1506
Cleveland International Piano Competition Vol. 1: 7474
Cliburn International Piano Competition; Van Vol. 1: 7479
Client of the Year Award Vol. 2: 6822
Clifford Prize; James L. Vol. 1: 3625
Climatics Award Vol. 1: 9831
Cline Memorial Prize; Howard Francis Vol. 1: 7697
Clinedinst Memorial Medal; Benjamin West Vol. 1: 4668
Clinical/Biomedical Engineering Achievement Award Vol. 1: 4982
Clinical Center of Excellence Vol. 1: 18795
Clinical Excellence Award Vol. 1: 8433
Clinical Instructor of the Year Vol. 1: 7903
Clinical Instructor of the Year Award Vol. 1: 1178
Clinical Investigator Lecture Award Vol. 1: 8453
Clinical Medicine Person-in-Training Award Vol. 1: 9054
Clinical Medicine Research Award Vol. 1: 9055
Clinical MRI Prize Vol. 2: 5329
Clinical Nursing Excellence Award Vol. 1: 5241
Clinical Research Award Vol. 1: 1910
Clinical Research Award in Periodontology Vol. 1: 723
Clinical Scientist in Nephrology Fellowship Vol. 1: 2612
Clinical Surgery Fellowship Vol. 1: 14624
Clinician of the Year Award Vol. 1: 2126
Clinician Scientist Awards Vol. 1: 7075
Clinician-Scientist Scholarship Vol. 1: 3022
Clinician's Professional Enrichment Vol. 1: 6293
Clio Awards Vol. 1: 7481
Cloos Medal; Hans Vol. 2: 3565
Clore International Award; Gerald R. Vol. 1: 9129
Clowes, Jr., M.D., F.A.C.S. Memorial Research Career Development Award; George H. A. Vol. 1: 1737
Clowes Memorial Award; G. H. A. Vol. 1: 860
Clown of the Year Vol. 1: 15351
Club Achievement Awards Vol. 1: 765
Club Champion Vol. 1: 11991
Club Development Award Vol. 2: 2868
Club Member Scholarship Vol. 1: 8763
Club of the Year
British Chess Federation Vol. 2: 5279
Camanachd Association Vol 2: 5576
Club Professional Player of the Year Vol. 1: 15315
Clubok Award; Miriam Vol. 1: 13492
ClubRally Division of the Year Award Vol. 1: 17198
ClubRally Region of the Year Award Vol. 1: 17199
CMA Affirmative Action Award Vol. 1: 2937
CMA/ASCAP Awards for Adventurous Programming Vol. 1: 7275
CNRS Merit Award Vol. 1: 6755
Co-Founders Book Award Vol. 1: 18706
Co-op Feeds Young Scientist's Award Vol. 1: 6977
Co-Pilot of the Year Vol. 1: 8776
Coach of the Year
Asian Football Confederation Vol. 2: 3403
Baseball Canada Vol 1: 5677
Canadian Colleges Athletic Association Vol 1: 6412
Canadian Federation of Amateur Baseball Vol 1: 6474
Continental Basketball Association Vol 1: 7796
England Basketball Vol 2: 5772
Federation of Canadian Archers Vol 1: 8622
Ladies Professional Golf Association Vol 1: 11194
National Association of Basketball Coaches Vol 1: 12395
National Basketball Association Vol 1: 12756
National Christian College Athletic Association Vol 1: 12884
National High School Athletic Coaches Association Vol 1: 13343
Special Olympics Canada Vol 1: 17091
Speed Skating Canada Vol 1: 17122
Coach of the Year Award
American Baseball Coaches Association Vol. 1: 1381
American Hockey Coaches Association Vol 1: 2250
American Swimming Coaches Association Vol 1: 4337
Football Writers Association of America Vol 1: 8801
National Association of Intercollegiate Athletics Vol 1: 12577
National Soccer Coaches Association of America Vol 1: 13709
U.S. Aquatic Sports Vol 1: 17729
Coach of the Year Awards
American Football Coaches Association Vol. 1: 2044
National Wrestling Coaches Association Vol 1: 13934
Coal and Energy Division Distinguished Service Award Vol. 1: 16342
Coal Award Vol. 1: 6617
Coalbourn Trust Grants Vol. 2: 5299
Coan, Sr. Public Service Award; Carl A.S. Vol. 1: 13360
Coast Guard Arctic Service Medal Vol. 1: 8099
Coast Guard Essay Contest Vol. 1: 18008
Coast Guard Reserve Good Conduct Medal Vol. 1: 8100
Cobb, Jr. Award for Initiative and Success in Trade Development; Charles E. Vol. 1: 17856
Cobb Young Investigator Award; W. A. Vol. 2: 6256
Cobbing Travelling Fellowship; Natalie Vol. 2: 6721
Coble Award for Young Scholars; Robert L. Vol. 1: 1469
Coca-Cola Cup Vol. 2: 4757
Cochrane Award; Vice Admiral E. L. Vol. 1: 16759
Cochrane Sr. Scholarship Award; Thomas Vol. 1: 186
Cockayne Memorial Lecture; Leonard Vol. 2: 3864
Cockcroft Award; Ron Vol. 2: 4596
Codd Innovations Award; Edgar F. Vol. 1: 4835
Coddington Award of Merit Vol. 1: 14033
Codes and Standards Medal Vol. 1: 4134
Codie Awards Vol. 1: 16927

Coffee Statesmanship Award Vol. 2: 7230
Cogan Award Vol. 1: 4951
COGEL Award Vol. 1: 7920
Cohen Award for a Distinguished Edition of Letters; Morton N. Vol. 1: 11904
Cohen Award; Harry and Martha Vol. 1: 379
Cohen Award; Herb Vol. 1: 14633
Cohen Award; Seymour R. Vol. 1: 2619
Cohen Gold Medal; Lord Vol. 2: 6933
Cohen Medal; Lord Vol. 2: 5487
Cohen Purchase Award; Joan Vol. 1: 16517
Cohn Hope Award; Norman Vol. 1: 13462
Coif Book Award Vol. 1: 14659
Coker Award; C. F. W. Vol. 1: 16488
Colaianni Award for Excellence and Achievement in Hospital Librarianship; Lois Ann Vol. 1: 11654
Colburn Award for Excellence in Publications by a Young Member of the Institute; Allan P. Vol. 1: 2473
Colby Award Vol. 1: 3068
Colby Award; William E. Vol. 1: 16004
Cole Award; Art Vol. 1: 1061
Cole Award for Automotive Engineering Innovation; Edward N. Vol. 1: 16569
Cole Distinguished Younger Member Award; Edward N. Vol. 1: 16570
Cole Grants-in-Aid; Arthur H. Vol. 1: 8377
Cole Human Rights Award; Kitty Vol. 1: 1839
Cole Prize; Arthur H. Vol. 1: 8378
Cole Prizes in Algebra and Number Theory; Frank Nelson Vol. 1: 2728
Cole Research Grant; Monica Vol. 2: 6760
Cole Sportsmanship Award; Mark Vol. 1: 13090
Coleman-Barstow Award for Strings Vol. 1: 7491
Coleman Chamber Ensemble Competition Vol. 1: 7491
Coleman Prize; Alice Vol. 1: 7491
Coleman-Saunderson Prize for Woodwinds and Brass Vol. 1: 7491
Colen Memorial Grant; Kimberly Vol. 1: 16626
Coler - Maxwell Medal Vol. 1: 10679
Coley Award; William B. Vol. 1: 7084
Colgate-Palmolive Post-Doctoral Fellowship Award in In-Vitro Toxicology Vol. 1: 16870
Colgate-Palmolive Research Scholarship Award Vol. 1: 1333
Colgate-Palmolive/SOT Awards for Student Research Training in Alternative Methods Vol. 1: 16871
The Colibri Diploma Vol. 2: 4723
Colibri Microlight Diploma Vol. 2: 4723
Collaborative Practice Award Vol. 1: 5100
Collaborative Research Grant Vol. 1: 10118
Collaborative Research Grants Vol. 1: 9069
Collaborative School Library Media Award Vol. 1: 1273
Collacott Prize Vol. 2: 6135
Collar of the Supreme Order of the Chrysanthemum Vol. 2: 3243
Collection System Award Vol. 1: 18626
College and University Health and Safety Award Vol. 1: 1536
College Art Association/National Institute for Conservation Award Vol. 1: 7503
College Athletics Top Ten Vol. 1: 12906
College Basketball Coach of the Year Vol. 1: 17172
College Basketball Player of the Year Vol. 1: 17173
College Fiction Contest Vol. 1: 15101
College Football Coach of the Year Vol. 1: 17174
College Football Defensive Player of the Year Trophy Vol. 1: 8798
College Football Hall of Fame Vol. 1: 13209
College Football Player of the Year Vol. 1: 17175
College Journalism Competition Vol. 1: 15708
College Medal Vol. 2: 156
College of Diplomates Award Vol. 1: 13636
College of Electrical Engineers Student Prizes Vol. 2: 497
College Player of the Year Vol. 1: 18398
College Press Freedom Award Vol. 1: 17308
College Sailing Hall of Fame Vol. 1: 9985
College Scholar All-America Award Vol. 1: 13708
College Scholarship Vol. 1: 5568
College/University Distinguished Teaching Achievement Award Vol. 1: 12969
College/University Excellence of Scholarship Award Vol. 1: 12965
Collegiate Advisor Award Vol. 1: 15006
Collegiate Athlete of the Year Vol. 1: 17358
Collegiate Bowlers of the Year Vol. 1: 5894
Collegiate or University Teacher of the Year Vol. 1: 12831
Collier Award for Forest History Journalism; John M. Vol. 1: 8820
Collier Award; Margaret Vol. 1: 69
Collier Trophy; Robert J. Vol. 1: 12188
Collin Prijs; Fernand Vol. 2: 1103
Collingwood Prize Vol. 1: 3928
Collins Award Vol. 1: 5549
Collins Award; Carr P. Vol. 1: 17476
Collins Award; George R. Vol. 1: 915
Collins Award; Joseph P. Vol. 1: 13010
Collins Award; Samuel C. Vol. 1: 7988
Collins Award; W. Leighton Vol. 1: 3638
Collins Diversity Award; Marva Vol. 1: 7864
Collins, Jr. Research Promotion Award; William J. Vol. 1: 4052
Collins Memorial Award; Norman Vol. 2: 5531
Collins Poetry Award; Tom Vol. 2: 449
Cologne International Pianoforte Competition Vol. 2: 2067
Cologne International Singing Competition Vol. 2: 2071
Cologne International Violin Competition Vol. 2: 2069
Cologne International Vocal Competition Vol. 2: 2071
Colombe D'Oro per la Pace Vol. 2: 2979
Colombe Unda Vol. 2: 1100
Colombian Academy of Exact, Physical and Natural Sciences to the Integral Work of a Scientist Vol. 2: 1172
Color Slide Division Awards Vol. 1: 15027
Colposcopy Recognition Award Vol. 1: 3614
Colt Fund Vol. 2: 7104
Columbia Journalism Award Vol. 1: 7585
Columbine Poets of Colorado Award Vol. 1: 13143
Columbus Award; Christopher Vol. 1: 7381
Columbus International Film and Video Festival Vol. 1: 7385
Columbus International Film and Video Festival Vol. 1: 7382
Columbus Prize Vol. 2: 3088
Column Writing Contest Vol. 1: 13739
Colvin Award for Excellence in Individual Achievement; Ruth J. Vol. 1: 15377
Colwell Cooperative Engineering Medal; Arch T. Vol. 1: 16571
Colwell Merit Award; Arch T. Vol. 1: 16572
Colworth Medal Vol. 2: 5170
Colworth Prize Lecture Vol. 2: 7096
Colyer Prize Vol. 2: 7007
Comas Prize; Juan Vol. 1: 1232
Combat Readiness Medal Vol. 1: 8101
Comfort Prize; A. C. Vol. 2: 7008
Command, Control, Communication & Intelligence Award Vol. 1: 2368
Commandant's Aviation Trophy Vol. 1: 11505
Commandant's Distringuished Career Service Medal Vol. 1: 17774
Commandant's Superior Achievement Award (Bronze Medal) Vol. 1: 17775
Commander-in-Chief's Annual Award for Installation Excellence Vol. 1: 17815
Commander's Award for Civilian Service Vol. 1: 17776
Commander's Award for Sustained Excellence in the Federal Service Vol. 1: 17777
Commemorative Arts Awards Vol. 1: 17555
Commemorative Lecture Award Vol. 1: 1095
Commemorative Lecture Series Vol. 1: 1752
Commendation Vol. 1: 1923
Commendation Award
International Narcotic Enforcement Officers Association Vol. 1: 10528
Soil and Water Conservation Society Vol 1: 16930
Commendation Award in Landscape Architecture Vol. 2: 244
Commendation for Distinguished Service Vol. 2: 214
Commendation for Gallantry Vol. 2: 216
Commendation Medal: Navy Vol. 1: 8102
Commentary/Column Writing Vol. 1: 4205
Commercial Award Vol. 1: 2288
Commercial Horticulture Distinguished Achievement Award Vol. 1: 3718
Commercial Wine Competition Awards Vol. 1: 4483
Commission Matching Grants Vol. 1: 8978
Commissioner's Award Vol. 1: 11195
Commissioner's Congressional Leadership Award Vol. 1: 347
Commissioner's Cup Vol. 1: 17023
Commissioner's Trophy Awards Vol. 1: 5754
Commissioning Program
Chamber Music America Vol. 1: 7276
The Koussevitzky Music Foundations Vol 1: 11170
Commitment to Chicago Award Vol. 1: 7329
Committee D-12 Award Vol. 1: 5411
Committee D-20 Award of Excellence Vol. 1: 5412
Committee E-8 Fracture Mechanics Medal Vol. 1: 5413
Committee E08 Best Student Paper Award Vol. 1: 5414
Committeeman of the Year Vol. 1: 1192
Common Award for Canadian History; Lela Vol. 1: 6322
Common Ground Award for Journalism in the Middle East Vol. 1: 15953
Commonwealth Essay Competition Vol. 2: 6749
Commonwealth Fund Fellowships Vol. 1: 9248

Commonwealth Games Federation Vol. 2: 5684
Commonwealth Office of the Status of Women Award Vol. 2: 737
Commonwealth Press Union Scholarships Vol. 2: 5689
Commonwealth Scholarship and Fellowship Plan Vol. 2: 5124
Commonwealth Shared Scholarship Scheme Vol. 2: 5125
Commonwealth Short Story Competition Vol. 2: 5678
Commonwealth Writers Prize Vol. 2: 5679
Commonwealth Youth Service Awards Vol. 2: 5691
Communication Award Vol. 1: 7199
Communications Award
American Institute of Aeronautics and Astronautics Vol. 1: 2369
American Staffing Association Vol 1: 4311
Canadian Mental Health Association - Alberta Division Vol 1: 6719
Communications Center Director of the Year Vol. 1: 5316
Communications Contest Vol. 1: 13135
Communicator of Achievement Award Vol. 1: 13133
Communicator of the Year
British Association of Communicators in Business Vol. 2: 5240
National Association of Government Communicators Vol 1: 12543
Communicator of the Year Award
International Association of Business Communicators Vol. 1: 10151
National Council for Marketing and Public Relations Vol 1: 12976
Utility Communicators International Vol 1: 18479
Communicators in Business Awards Vol. 2: 5241
Community Based Program Award Vol. 1: 10711
Community College Learning Resources and Library Achievement Awards Vol. 1: 5072
Community Counselling Service Award for Outstanding Fundraising Professional Vol. 1: 5161
Community, Culture, and Prevention Science Award Vol. 1: 16380
Community Dentistry Award Vol. 1: 1903
Community Development Award Vol. 1: 14161
Community Event of the Year Vol. 2: 725
Community Health and Safety Awards Vol. 1: 10312
Community Hospital Award Vol. 1: 7249
Community Improvement Contest Vol. 1: 8987
Community Leadership Award Vol. 1: 9720
Community Leadership Awards Vol. 1: 15828
Community Partnership Awards Vol. 1: 10312
Community Partnership Program Accessible America Award Vol. 1: 13509
Community Person of the Year Vol. 2: 2856
Community Preventive Dentistry Award Vol. 1: 1903
Community Psychology Dissertation Award Vol. 1: 3369
Community Service Award Vol. 1: 6413
Community Service Award
American Academy of Facial Plastic and Reconstructive Surgery Vol. 1: 593
American Association of Critical-Care Nurses Vol 1: 1066
American Association of Homes and Services for the Aging Vol 1: 1122
American Correctional Association Vol 1: 1793
American Public Power Association Vol 1: 3439
American Society of Landscape Architects Vol 1: 4096
Florida State Grange Vol 1: 8766
Inland Press Association Vol 1: 9720
Keuka College Alumni Association Vol 1: 11141
Latrobe Area Chamber of Commerce Vol 1: 11246
Livingston County Council on Alcohol and Substance Abuse Vol 1: 11394
Mississippi State Medical Association Vol 1: 11870
National Association for Gifted Children Vol 1: 12316
National Association of Black Journalists Vol 1: 12413
National Council of Social Security Management Associations Vol 1: 13011
Sierra Club Vol 1: 16005
UCLA Alumni Association Vol 1: 17640
Community Service Awards Vol. 1: 14917
Community Sustainability Awards Vol. 1: 10312
Community Welfare Award Vol. 2: 2664
Compadre Award Vol. 1: 17071
Companion Membership Vol. 2: 7262
Company Appreciation Award Vol. 1: 15270
Company Award of Excellence Vol. 1: 12622
Company of Fellows Vol. 1: 4628
Company of the Year Award Vol. 1: 10664
Company of the Year Awards Vol. 2: 3358
Company of World Traders Silver Salver Vol. 2: 6029
Company Safety Awards Vol. 1: 14293
Comparative Physiology Section Scholander Award Vol. 1: 3167
Compass Distinguished Achievement Award Vol. 1: 11543
Compass Industrial Award Vol. 1: 11544
Compass International Award Vol. 1: 11545
Competitie de Impact van Muziek op Film Vol. 2: 890
Competition and Festival for Accordionists Vol. 1: 759
Competition Awards Vol. 1: 6221
Competition for Composers Recording Vol. 1: 7792
Competition for Performing Artists Vol. 1: 7793
Competition for Young Statisticians from Developing Countries Vol. 2: 3617
Competition of Scientific Papers of Young Physicists Vol. 2: 4446
Competitions Vol. 2: 454
Competitions and Tournaments Vol. 2: 4585
Competitive Awards Vol. 1: 13131
Competitive Student Research Award Vol. 1: 972
Competitive Workforce Award Vol. 1: 16238
Composition Competitions Vol. 2: 7238
Compton Award; Karl Taylor Vol. 1: 2539
Compton Award; Neil Vol. 1: 14768
Compumedics Poster Prize Vol. 2: 137
Computer Educator of the Year Vol. 1: 10052
Computer Entrepreneur Award Vol. 1: 9802
Computer Pioneer Award Vol. 1: 9803
Computer Science and Engineering Undergraduate Teaching Award Vol. 1: 9804
Computer Sciences Man of the Year Vol. 1: 5199
Computing in Chemical Engineering Award Vol. 1: 2474
Computing Practice Award Vol. 1: 2475
Comstock Prize in Physics Vol. 1: 12156
Comunidad de Madrid Prize Vol. 2: 4493
Conamus Export Prize Vol. 2: 3500
Conamus Golden Harp Vol. 2: 3501
Conant Award in High School Chemistry Teaching; James Bryant Vol. 1: 1537
Conant Award; James Bryant Vol. 1: 8394
Conceicao Silva de Espacos Interiores Abertos ao Publico; Premio Municipal Francisco da Vol. 2: 4070
Concerned Broadcaster of the Year Vol. 1: 12794
Concertino Prague International Radio Competition for Young Musicians Vol. 2: 1254
Concorso Internacional de Violao Villa-Lobos Vol. 2: 1138
Concorso Internazionale della Ceramica d'Arte Vol. 2: 3067
Concorso Internazionale di Chitarra Classica "Michele Pittaluga" Premio Citta' di Alessandria Vol. 2: 3119
Concorso Internazionale di Chitarra Mauro Giuliani Vol. 2: 3001
Concorso Internazionale di Composizione Goffredo Petrassi Vol. 2: 3049
Concorso Internazionale di Direzione d'Orchestra Arturo Toscanini Vol. 2: 3050
Concorso Internazionale di Musica e Danza G. B. Viotti Vol. 2: 3126
Concorso Internazionale di Violino Premio Rodolfo Lipizer Vol. 2: 3019
Concorso Internazionale Luigi Russolo Vol. 2: 3052
Concorso Internazionale per Quartetto d'Archi Vol. 2: 3134
Concorso Internazionale Pianistico Liszt - Premio Mario Zanfi Vol. 2: 2997
Concorso Pianistico Internazionale Alessandro Casagrande Vol. 2: 3015
Concorso Pianistico Internazionale Ettore Pozzoli Vol. 2: 3013
Concorso Pianistico Internazionale Rina Sala Gallo Vol. 2: 2989
Concours Annuel de Sauvegarde Vol. 2: 2012
Concours Awards Vol. 1: 18547
Concours Canadien de Journalisme Vol. 1: 6759
Concours Clara Haskil Vol. 2: 4765
Concours de musique du Canada Vol. 1: 6743
Concours des Antiquites de la France Vol. 2: 1507
Concours et Seminaire International d'alto Vol. 2: 7259
Concours Geza Anda Vol. 2: 4761
Concours International de Ballet, Varna Vol. 2: 1158
Concours International de campagnes de Marketing Direct Vol. 2: 888

Concours International de Chant Choral de Tours Vol. 2: 1801
Concours International de Chant Francisco Vinas Vol. 2: 4554
Concours International de Cinema de la Montagne Vila de Torello Vol. 2: 4545
Concours International de Composition Musicale Vol. 2: 1795
Concours International de Harpe en Israel Vol. 2: 2904
Concours International de Jeunes Chanteurs d'Opera Vol. 2: 1141
Concours International de Jeunes Chefs d'Orchestre Besancon Vol. 2: 1794
Concours International de l'Orgue a Lahti Vol. 2: 1419
Concours international de Violoncelle Paulo Vol. 2: 1411
Concours International de Violoncelle Rostropovitch Vol. 2: 1750
Concours International des Jeunesses Musicales - Belgrade Vol. 2: 4413
Concours International d'Execution Musicale - Geneve Vol. 2: 4702
Concours International Printemps de la Guitare Vol. 2: 910
Concours OSM Vol. 1: 11942
Concours Promethee Vol. 2: 1723
Concrete Achiever of the Year Vol. 2: 4154
Concrete Paving Awards Vol. 1: 11728
Concrete Person of the Year Awards Vol. 2: 4155
Concrete Society Awards Vol. 2: 5693
Concurs Internacional de Cant Francesc Vinas Vol. 2: 4554
Concurso Internacional de Piano de Santander Paloma O'Shea Vol. 2: 4540
Concurso Internacional de Piano Villa-Lobos Vol. 2: 1139
Concurso Internazionale per Direttori d'Orchestra Antonio Pedrotti Vol. 2: 2983
Concurso Literario Dr. Joao Isabel Vol. 2: 4090
Concurso Nacional de Obras Medicas Vol. 2: 1195
Concurso Permanente de Jovenes Interpretes Vol. 2: 4523
Condon Award; Edward Uhler Vol. 1: 17799
Conductor of the Year Vol. 1: 8899
Conductor's Award Vol. 1: 14097
Confederate Philatelist Writers Award Vol. 1: 7671
Conference Awards
  British Nuclear Energy Society Vol. 2: 5389
  Space Coast Writers' Guild Vol 1: 17064
Conference Contribution Award Vol. 1: 9805
Conference Grant Scheme Vol. 2: 6751
Conference on Latin American History Prize Vol. 1: 7698
Conformation Award Vol. 1: 14422
Congress Award and Honorary Mention Vol. 2: 6262
Congress Medal Vol. 2: 5110
The Congressional Award Vol. 1: 7712
Congressional Gold Medal Vol. 1: 17785
Congressional Research Awards Vol. 1: 8225
Congressional Service Award Vol. 1: 3705
Congressional Space Medal of Honor Vol. 1: 12195
CONI Prize Vol. 2: 3136
Conkling Memorial Award; Robert J. Vol. 1: 4452
Conley Award; Dean Vol. 1: 1651
Conley Award; Fred O. Vol. 1: 16825
Connare Award for Distinguished Service; Bishop William G. Vol. 1: 10296
Connecticut Poetry Society Award Vol. 1: 13144
Connell Award; W. F. Vol. 1: 5941
Connelly Award; Robert P. Vol. 1: 11160
Conners Prize for Poetry; Bernard F. Vol. 1: 14858
Connie Award Vol. 1: 7788
Connor Award; Robert D. W. Vol. 1: 14369
ConocoPhillips Performance Award Vol. 1: 18412
Conover-Porter Award Vol. 1: 224
Conrad Award/Lecturer; Miles Vol. 1: 13129
Conrady Award; A. E. Vol. 1: 17131
Conservation and Heritage Management Award Vol. 1: 4575
Conservation Award
  Federation of Fly Fishers Vol. 1: 8634
  International Wild Waterfowl Association Vol. 1: 10833
  Nature Saskatchewan Vol 1: 13988
  New England Wild Flower Society Vol 1: 14070
  Ottawa Field-Naturalists' Club Vol 1: 14722
Conservation District Awards Vol. 1: 12469
Conservation Education and Research Project Vol. 1: 7731
Conservation Guest Scholars Vol. 1: 9070
Conservation Medal Vol. 1: 14070
Conservation Teacher Awards Vol. 1: 12470
Conservation Teacher of the Year Vol. 1: 11574
Conservationist of the Year
  Chesapeake Bay Foundation Vol. 1: 7310
  Minnesota Conservation Federation Vol 1: 11834
Conservationist of the Year Award Vol. 1: 158
Considine Award; Bob
  Overseas Press Club of America Vol. 1: 14761
  St. Bonaventure University - Russell J. Jandoli School of Journalism and Mass Communication Vol 1: 15784
Conspicuous Service Cross Vol. 2: 212
Conspicuous Service Decorations Vol. 2: 212
Conspicuous Service Medal Vol. 2: 212
Construction Award Vol. 2: 3715
Construction Award Vol. 1: 1753
Construction Management Award Vol. 1: 3929
Constuction's Man of the Year Vol. 1: 8472
Consular Service Award Vol. 1: 17876
Consumer Conference Awards Vol. 1: 13367
Consumer Horticulture Distinguished Achievement Award Vol. 1: 3719
Consumer Involvement Award Vol. 1: 6712
Consumer Journalism Award Vol. 1: 13544
Consumer Participation Award Vol. 1: 6712
Consumer Plastics Product Design Award Vol. 1: 16826
Consumer Research Award Vol. 1: 11047
Container Inspectors Award Vol. 1: 9886
Conte; Prix Le Vol. 2: 1553
Contemplative Practice Fellowship Vol. 1: 1813
Contemporary A Cappella Recording Awards ("CARAs") Vol. 1: 7790
Contemporary Music Award Vol. 2: 4521
Contemporary Poetry Series Vol. 1: 18283
Contender's Award Vol. 1: 1808
Continental Casualty Award Vol. 1: 17755
Continental Champion Vol. 2: 2308
Continental Grain Company Poultry Products Research Award Vol. 1: 15183
Continuare Protessus Articulatus Excellare Vol. 1: 13785
Continuing Education Grant Vol. 2: 3830
Continuing Publication Commendation Vol. 1: 7745
Continuing Service Award Vol. 1: 12711
Contract of the Year Vol. 2: 5895
Contractor of the Year Vol. 2: 5896
Contractor of the Year Vol. 1: 11225
Contractor of the Year Award Vol. 1: 7661
Contractor of the Year Awards (CotY Awards) Vol. 1: 12696
Contractors' Awards Vol. 2: 5141
Contribution by Business Community Award Vol. 2: 2665
Contribution to Land Based Industries Award Vol. 2: 6083
Contributions to Public Awareness of the Importance of Animals in Toxicology Research Award Vol. 1: 16872
Control Systems Award Vol. 1: 9774
Convention Performers Competition Vol. 1: 13199
Convention Services Manager of the Year Vol. 1: 17317
Convoy For Kids Grant Vol. 2: 419
Conway Lecture Vol. 2: 2871
Coogler Award for Worst Book of the Year; J. Gordon Vol. 1: 4289
Cook Award; Col. Donald G. Vol. 1: 13452
Cook-Douglas Medal Vol. 1: 11641
Cook Founders Award; Pete Vol. 1: 76
Cook Medal; James Vol. 2: 640
Cook Memorial Trophy; Jim Vol. 1: 17224
Cook Prize; Gladys Emerson Vol. 1: 12107
Cook Travel Book Award; Thomas Vol. 2: 5697
Cookbook Hall of Fame Vol. 1: 10953
Cookbook of the Year Vol. 1: 10953
Cooke Award; Pat Vol. 2: 5134
Cooke Memorial Award; Sybil Vol. 1: 14742
Cooking Teacher of the Year Award
  International Association of Culinary Professionals Vol. 1: 10186
  International Association of Culinary Professionals Vol 1: 10186
Cookingham; Award for Career Development in Memory of L.P. Vol. 1: 10309
Cookson Award; Isabel Vol. 1: 5871
Cooley Award; Charles Horton Vol. 1: 16470
Cooley Award; George R.
  American Society of Plant Taxonomists Vol. 1: 4222
  Botanical Society of America Vol 1: 5872
Cooley Leadership Award; Denton A. Vol. 1: 17471
Cooley Memorial Award and Lectureship; Emily Vol. 1: 1006
Cooley Memorial Lectureship; Emily Vol. 1: 1006
Coolidge Award; Edgar D. Vol. 1: 1085
Coolidge Award; William D. Vol. 1: 1243
Cooling Prize Vol. 2: 5311
Coomaraswamy Book Prize; Ananda Kentish Vol. 1: 4779
Cooney Award; Joe Vol. 1: 12493
Coonley Medal; Howard Vol. 1: 2851
Cooper and Dale Meyers Medal; Mario Vol. 1: 4431

Cooper Architecture Award; Shirley Vol. 1: 1267
Cooper Award Vol. 1: 872
Cooper Award; Billy H. Vol. 1: 11671
Cooper Award; W. S. Vol. 1: 8367
Cooper Lecture Award; Lenna Frances Vol. 1: 1921
Cooper Memorial Medal and Prize; E. R. Vol. 2: 3865
Cooper Memorial Prize; Duff Vol. 2: 5746
Cooper Prize; Duff Vol. 2: 5746
Cooperative Research Award in Polymer Science and Engineering Vol. 1: 1538
Cooperman-Boque Awards Vol. 1: 11071
Coopers Hill War Memorial Medal Vol. 2: 6145
Coopers Hill War Memorial Prize Vol. 2: 6106
Coordinator Award Vol. 1: 7825
Coors "Man in the Can" Vol. 1: 15351
Coote-Lake Medal for Folklore Research Vol. 2: 5913
COP Excellence Awards Vol. 2: 334
Cope Award; Arthur C. Vol. 1: 1539
Cope Fund; Arthur C. Vol. 1: 1539
Cope Scholar Award; Arthur C. Vol. 1: 1540
Cope Travel Grant; Arthur C. Vol. 1: 1540
Copeland Award; Edith Moore Vol. 1: 16049
Copeland Award; L. E. Vol. 1: 1470
Copeland Scholarship; Arthur E. Vol. 1: 17741
Copeland Scholarship; Helen Vol. 1: 17742
Copernicus Award Vol. 2: 2218
Copley Medal Vol. 2: 6903
Copova Diploma Vol. 2: 4467
Copp Award; Nan Vol. 1: 6647
Copp Traveling Fellowship; Dax Vol. 2: 6761
Coppens Prize; Jozef Vol. 2: 1068
Copper Club Award/Committee B-5 Award Vol. 1: 5415
Copying Assistance Program Vol. 1: 2836
Corbay; Prix Vol. 2: 1644
Corbett Medal; Arthur Vol. 2: 498
Corbetta Concrete Constructor Award; Roger H. Vol. 1: 1754
Corbin Companion Animal Biology Award Vol. 1: 3886
Corbitt Ultra Male Runner-of-the-Year Award; Ted Vol. 1: 18434
Corcoran Award; William H. Vol. 1: 3639
Corcoran Craft Awards; William and Mary Vol. 1: 14558
Corday-Morgan Medal and Prize Vol. 2: 6958
Core Medical Residents Research Award Vol. 1: 6924
Core Student Award; Earl Vol. 1: 17021
CORESTA Prize Vol. 2: 1752
Corey Award; Albert B. Vol. 1: 944
Corey Prize in Canadian-American Relations; Albert B.
  American Historical Association Vol. 1: 2230
  Canadian Historical Association Vol 1: 6557
Cork International Choral and Folk Dance Festival Vol. 2: 2829
Cork International Choral Festival Vol. 2: 2829
Cork International Film Festival Vol. 2: 2827
Corlette Medal; J.M.C. Vol. 2: 499
Cornell Reporter of the Year Award for Mid-Sized Papers Vol. 1: 15614
Cornette Prize; Arthur H. Vol. 2: 953
Cornforth Medal Vol. 2: 618
Corporate Award
  American Association of Community Theatre Vol. 1: 1062
  Ecological Society of America Vol 1: 8368
  Ontario Nature Vol 1: 14578
  Sport Canada Vol 1: 17148
Corporate Citizenship Award Vol. 1: 9622
Corporate Club of the Year Vol. 2: 5907
Corporate/Commercial Business Flying Safety Awards Vol. 1: 12824
Corporate Environmental Achievement Award Vol. 1: 1471
Corporate Excellence Award Vol. 1: 17148
Corporate Facility Award Vol. 1: 5989
Corporate Health Achievement Award
  American College of Occupational and Environmental Medicine Vol. 1: 1690
  American College of Occupational and Environmental Medicine Vol 1: 1690
Corporate Innovation Recognition Award Vol. 1: 9775
Corporate Leadership Award
  American Institute of Graphic Arts Vol. 1: 2517
  Aspen Institute Vol 1: 4724
Corporate Recognition Award
  Autism Society of America Vol. 1: 5550
  International Microelectronics and Packaging Society Vol 1: 10509
  International Microelectronics and Packaging Society Vol 1: 10509
Corporate Sponsor of the Year Vol. 1: 12450
Corporate Technical Achievement Award Vol. 1: 1472
Corporation of the Year Vol. 1: 13458
Corps d'Elite Award Vol. 1: 7603
Correctional Officer of the Year Vol. 1: 10182
Correll Award; Erasmus Vol. 1: 11369
Corresponding Members Vol. 1: 5873
Corrigan Artists' Grant; Pat Vol. 2: 566
Corstorphine Medal Vol. 2: 4184
Cory Cup Vol. 2: 6786
Cory Memorial Cup; Reginald Vol. 2: 6786
Cory - Wright Cup Vol. 2: 3844
Cosio, RN Research Award; Mary Jo Vol. 1: 13412
COSPAR Space Science Award Vol. 2: 1736
Costa Award; Joseph Vol. 1: 13560
Costa Courtroom Photography Award; Joseph Vol. 1: 5633
Costello Fellowships; Jeanne Timmins Vol. 1: 11939
Costume and Fashion Jewelry Vol. 2: 2561
COTF Graduate Scholarships Vol. 1: 6774
COTF Research Grant Vol. 1: 6775
Cotta Literary and Translation Prize of Stuttgart City; Johann Friedrich von Vol. 2: 2415
Cotter Award; John L. Vol. 1: 16221
Cottle Honor Award; Dr. Maurice H. Vol. 1: 3489
Cotton Foundation Fellowship Awards; Dr. M. Aylwin Vol. 2: 5699
Cotton Foundation Publication Grants; Dr. M. Aylwin Vol. 2: 5700
CotY Awards Vol. 1: 12696
Couch Award Vol. 2: 6738
Coudenhove-Kalergi Award Vol. 2: 2369
Coues Award; Elliott Vol. 1: 3005
Coulee Region Entrepreneurial Awards Vol. 1: 11172
Coulter Memorial Lecturer; John Stanley Vol. 1: 1770
Council Award of Excellence Vol. 1: 8635
Council for Wisconsin Writers Major Achievement Award Vol. 1: 7875
Council Medal Vol. 2: 6090
Council Meritorious Service Award Vol. 1: 1647
Council of Europe Museum Prize Vol. 2: 1754
Council of Peers Award for Excellence/ Speaker Hall of Fame Vol. 1: 13785
Council of the Year Vol. 1: 13458
Council of the Year Award of Excellence Vol. 1: 10398
Counseling Vision and Innovation Award Vol. 1: 4845
Counselor Educator of the Year Vol. 1: 2773
Counselor of the Year Vol. 1: 2774
Counselor of the Year Award Vol. 1: 13616
Counsilman Coach of the Year Award Vol. 1: 18413
Counting Coup Award Vol. 1: 2332
Country Award Vol. 1: 15156
Country Music Association Awards Vol. 1: 7932
Country Music Hall of Fame Vol. 1: 7933
County Engineer of the Year Awards Vol. 1: 12500
Coupe Olympique Vol. 2: 4820
Courage Award Vol. 1: 1440
Courage in Journalism Awards Vol. 1: 10843
Courage to Care Award Vol. 1: 4543
Cournand and Comroe Young Investigator Award Vol. 1: 2175
Course Rally Rookie of the Year Vol. 1: 17200
Courtois; Prix Gustave Vol. 2: 1445
Cousin; Prix Victor Vol. 2: 1645
Cousins Award; Norman Vol. 1: 9101
Cousins National Chapter Award; Ruth Hubbard Vol. 1: 15399
Coutts Bank Award for Singers Vol. 2: 6853
Coutts Nijhoff International West European Specialist Study Grant Vol. 1: 5073
Couture Award for Outstanding Volunteer Service to Eastern Surfing; Dr. Colin J. Vol. 1: 8357
Covenant Awards Vol. 1: 6540
Covey Girls' Voice Scholarship Vol. 1: 15858
Cowart Plaque Vol. 1: 16521
Cowen Award for Public Buildings; Sir Zelman Vol. 2: 627
Cowie Prize; James M. Vol. 2: 6006
Cox Award; Morgan Vol. 1: 19011
Cox Award; Norman W. Vol. 1: 5667
Cox Family Rookie of the Year Award Vol. 1: 13090
CPCRS Fellowship Vol. 1: 6807
CPRS Lamp of Service Vol. 1: 6845
CPRS Lectern Vol. 1: 6845
The Crabtree Award Vol. 1: 16159
Crabtree Foundation Award; Harold Vol. 1: 12284
Cracow International Festival of Short Films Vol. 2: 3999
Crafoord Prize Vol. 2: 4637
Craft and Design Awards Vol. 2: 7042
Craft Guild of Chefs Awards Vol. 2: 5703
Crafts Council of Ireland Purchase Award Vol. 2: 2877
Crafts National Exhibition Vol. 1: 7254
Craftsman Degree Vol. 1: 13928

Craftsman of Photographic Arts Vol. 1: 15342
Craftsman Truck Series Vol. 1: 12364
Crago Award Vol. 2: 69
Craig Award Vol. 2: 415
Craig Memorial Scholarship; Bob Vol. 1: 18668
Craigie Award; Andrew Vol. 1: 5242
Crain Award; G. D. Vol. 1: 1427
Crain Jr. Award; G. D. Vol. 1: 6024
Craine Award; Zur Vol. 1: 10630
Cram Scholarships Vol. 1: 12966
Cramer Award; W. E. Vol. 1: 1473
Cramphorn Theater Scholarship; Rex Vol. 2: 584
Crampton Prize Vol. 2: 6107
Crane and Rigging Group Job of the Year Award Vol. 1: 17093
Crane and Rigging Group Safety/Safety Improvement Awards Vol. 1: 17094
Crane Distinguished Service Award; Fred C. Vol. 1: 9861
Craniofacial Biology Group Distinguished Scientist Award Vol. 1: 10058
Craniofacial Biology Research Award Vol. 1: 10058
Cranko Memorial Award; John Vol. 2: 3730
Crase Bursary; Barbara Vol. 2: 188
Crasilneck Award; Sherry K. and Harold B. Vol. 1: 16194
Crater Software Award for Best Graduate Film Vol. 1: 14731
Crave the Dave Award Vol. 1: 8060
Craven Award; Avery O. Vol. 1: 14691
Crawford Art Award; Charlotte Vol. 1: 8193
Crawford Award; Dorothy Vol. 2: 395
Crawford Award; Hector Vol. 2: 395
Crawford Award; J. G. Vol. 2: 298
Crawford Fantasy Award; William L. Vol. 1: 10114
Crawford Medal
Australian Academy of the Humanities Vol. 2: 126
Royal Philatelic Society Vol 2: 6855
Crawford Young Professional Award; Robert W. Vol. 1: 13592
Crawley Cup Vol. 2: 5238
Crawshaw Memorial Prize; Philip Vol. 2: 6853
Crawshay Prize for English Literature; Rose Mary Vol. 2: 5207
Cray Computer Engineering Award; Seymour Vol. 1: 9564
CRC for Polymers Prize Vol. 2: 428
CRC Multicultural Award Vol. 2: 692
Creasey Memorial Award; John Vol. 2: 5707
Creative Achievement Award
Association of Collegiate Schools of Architecture Vol. 1: 5100
National Association of Television Program Executives Vol 1: 12694
Creative Achievement in Reproductive Endocrinology (CARE) Award Vol. 1: 6495
Creative and Innovative Awards Vol. 1: 14265
Creative Arts Emmy Awards Vol. 1: 12178
Creative Commercial Production Awards Vol. 1: 6030
Creative Drama Award Vol. 1: 792
Creative Excellence Awards
Employment Management Association Vol. 1: 8448
Utah Professional Videographers Association Vol 1: 18477
Creative Excellence in Business Advertising Awards Vol. 2: 4415
Creative Exporter of the Year Vol. 2: 3809
Creative Ticket National Schools of Distinction Award Vol. 1: 11110
Creative Writing Competition Vol. 2: 5200
Credner Preis; Herman Vol. 2: 2188
Crescendo Award Vol. 1: 15367
Cressey Memorial Award; Donald R. Vol. 1: 5064
Cressman ACE Award Recognizing Commitment to Staff Development; Reginald J. Vol. 1: 5118
Cresta International Advertising Awards Vol. 1: 10024
Cretsos Leadership Award; James M. Vol. 1: 3742
Crew Chief of the Year Award Vol. 1: 282
Cribb Award Vol. 2: 5030
Crichlow Trust Prize; Walter J. and Angeline H. Vol. 1: 2370
Crighton Trophy; Hec Vol. 1: 6648
Criminal Investigation Award Vol. 1: 3218
Crimson Glory Award; Colonel A. T. Reid Vol. 1: 4644
Crisp Medal Vol. 2: 90
Crisp Television News Photographer of the Year; Ernie Vol. 1: 13561
The Cristy Award Vol. 1: 15673
CriticFs Choice Innovation Award Vol. 1: 9196
Crittenden Award; Eugene Casson Vol. 1: 17800
Crittenden Memorial Award; Christopher Vol. 1: 14370
Crittenden Memorial Award; John and Jessie Vol. 1: 5608
CRM-Fields-PIMS Prize Vol. 1: 11619
CRM-SSC Prize Vol. 1: 17280
Crocker Award; Allen Vol. 1: 14053
Croes Medal; J. James R. Vol. 1: 3930
Croiset; Prix Alfred Vol. 2: 1508
Croix de Guerre Vol. 2: 1810
Croke Traditional Music Award; Bernard Vol. 1: 10883
Croly/GFWC Print Journalism Award for Excellence; Jane Cunningham Vol. 1: 8988
Cromer Greek Awards Vol. 2: 5208
Crompton Premium Vol. 2: 6146
Cromwell Essay Competition Vol. 2: 5715
Cronin Award; Brian Vol. 2: 2887
Cronin Award; Joe Vol. 1: 2628
Cronin Club Award Vol. 1: 12669
Crop Science Awards Vol. 1: 7974
Crop Science Teaching Award Vol. 1: 7975
Crosby Medallion; Philip Vol. 1: 3617
Crosman Memorial Award Vol. 1: 9599
Cross Community Service; Ray H. Vol. 1: 14836
Cross Country Coach of the Year Vol. 1: 18091
Cross Memorial Cup; Sir Lance Vol. 2: 3783
Cross of Merit
Finland Ministry of Defense Vol. 2: 1375
Office of the President of the Republic of Poland Vol 2: 4008
Cross of Merit for Bravery Vol. 2: 4009
Cross of Merit with Swords Vol. 2: 4010
Cross of Mourning Vol. 2: 1374
Cross of Valour
Canada Chancellery of Honors Vol. 1: 6083
Office of the President of the Republic of Poland Vol 2: 4011
Crouch Fellowship; John Mitchell Vol. 2: 613
Crouch Medal; Herbert Vol. 2: 54
Crouzet; Prix Vol. 2: 1646
Crow Award; Horace Vol. 1: 18435
Crow Award; Jake White Vol. 1: 13367
Crowe Memorial Exhibit Award; Dr. Charles W. Vol. 1: 2878
Crowley Scholarship; Francis X.
New England Water Works Association Vol. 1: 14062
New England Water Works Association Vol 1: 14066
Crown Awards Vol. 1: 7578
Crowninshield Award; Louise du Pont Vol. 1: 13869
Cruce Trophy; Marion C. Vol. 1: 16106
Cruess Award; William V. Vol. 1: 9848
Cruickshank Alumni Leadership Award Vol. 1: 5616
Crum Distinguished Service Award; Roy W. Vol. 1: 17579
Crumbine Consumer Protection Award; Samuel J.
Foodservice and Packaging Institute Vol. 1: 8791
International Association for Food Protection Vol 1: 10079
Cruz de Boyaca Vol. 2: 1174
Cruz Prize; Oswaldo Vol. 2: 1111
Crymes TESOL Fellowship for Graduate Study; Ryan Vol. 1: 17418
Crystal Apple Award Vol. 1: 15976
Crystal Award
American Staffing Association Vol. 1: 4311
Sugar Industry Technologists Vol 1: 17321
Crystal Awards Vol. 1: 18814
Crystal Clear Day Vol. 2: 6537
Crystal Clear Trophy Vol. 2: 6537
Crystal Drop Award Vol. 1: 10830
Crystal Goblet Award Vol. 2: 7279
Crystal Prism Award Vol. 1: 190
Crystal Radio Awards Vol. 1: 12429
Crystal Vilenica Vol. 2: 4463
Crystal Vision Award Vol. 1: 5147
Crystallographic Research Grant Vol. 1: 11795
CSA Travel Research Grants Vol. 1: 7834
CSA Trophy Vol. 1: 7672
CSA/Ulrich's Serials Librarianship Award Vol. 1: 4912
CSAE/CSSBI Award Vol. 1: 6884
CSAE Fellow Vol. 1: 6881
Csallany Institutional Award for Exemplary Contributions to Water Resources Management; Sandor C. Vol. 1: 4418
CSCI Distinguished Scientist Award Vol. 1: 6925
CSI Investigator Award Vol. 1: 6940
CSI New Investigator Vol. 1: 6941
The CSIM Osler Awards Vol. 1: 7001
CSM/Roche Diagnostics Award Vol. 1: 7010
Csokor Prize; Franz Theodor Vol. 2: 766
CSPG Undergraduate Scholarship; Norcen/ Vol. 1: 7020
CSRT Essay Award Vol. 1: 6263
CSSHE Masters Thesis or Project Award Vol. 1: 6967
CSZ Popular Article Award Vol. 1: 7030
CSZ Public Education Award Vol. 1: 7031
CTAM Hall of Fame Vol. 1: 7994
CTHS Annual Awards Vol. 1: 7048
Cubitt Award Vol. 2: 6552
Cudecki International Business Award; Edwin Vol. 1: 1832

CUES Executive of the Year Vol. 1: 7958
CUES Financial Suppliers Forum Supplier of the Year Vol. 1: 7959
CUES Future Leader Award Vol. 1: 7960
CUES Golden Mirror Award Vol. 1: 7961
CUES Hall of Fame Vol. 1: 7962
CUES Marketer of the Year Vol. 1: 7963
CUES Technology Executive of the Year Vol. 1: 7964
Cugnot Award Vol. 1: 16596
Cugnot Award; Nicholas-Joseph Vol. 1: 16599
Culbertson Award; Jack A. Vol. 1: 18230
Culbertson Outstanding Volunteer Service Award; Charles V. Vol. 1: 4232
Culinary Arts Salon
National Restaurant Association Vol. 1: 13631
Society of German Cooks Vol 2: 2383
Culinary Masters
National Restaurant Association Vol. 1: 13631
Society of German Cooks Vol 2: 2383
Culinary Olympics
British Culinary Federation Vol. 2: 5287
Society of German Cooks Vol 2: 2383
Culinary World Cup
National Restaurant Association Vol. 1: 13631
Society of German Cooks Vol 2: 2383
Vatel-Club Luxembourg Vol 2: 3393
Cullis Grants; Winifred Vol. 2: 4803
Cullum Geographical Medal Vol. 1: 2094
Cultural Achievement Award Vol. 1: 1800
Cultural and Economic Diversity Award Vol. 1: 1990
Cultural Awards Vol. 1: 10883
Cultural Diversity Grant Vol. 1: 11331
Cultural Pluralism Award Vol. 1: 5328
Culture and Literature Award Vol. 2: 2804
Culver Distinguished Service Award; Essae M. Vol. 1: 11420
Cumiskey Hall of Fame; Frank J. Vol. 1: 13318
Cumming Award for Outstanding Service; Laurence G. Vol. 1: 9574
Cummings Award; Abbott Lowell Vol. 1: 18505
Cummings Memorial Award; Donald E. Vol. 1: 2339
Cumulative Contribution to Family Therapy Research Award Vol. 1: 927
Cumulative Mileage Awards Vol. 1: 14342
Cunningham Aviator of the Year Award; Alfred A. Vol. 1: 11506
Cunningham Award; Glenn Vol. 1: 18436
Cunningham Award; Les Vol. 1: 2267
Cunningham Award; Robinson- Vol. 1: 558
Cunningham Award; Thomas F. Vol. 1: 18984
Cunningham Distinguished Citizen Award Vol. 1: 15656
Cunningham Inter-American Award; Thomas F. Vol. 1: 18984
Cunningham Memorial Award; Ed Vol. 1: 14761
Cunningham Memorial International Fellowship Vol. 1: 11655
Cunningham Trophy; John Vol. 2: 2829
CUNY Student Papers Awards Vol. 1: 7221
Cup for Historic Grand Touring Cars Vol. 2: 1882
Cup for Thoroughbred Grand Prix Cars Vol. 2: 1882
Cup of Cups Vol. 2: 858
Cups Vol. 2: 1217
Curatorial Research Fellowships Vol. 1: 9071
Cured Meat Awards Vol. 1: 9597
Cured Meats Hall of Fame Vol. 1: 1154
Curie Medal; Marie Vol. 2: 876
Curl Award; Earl Vol. 1: 10749
Curl Essay Prize Vol. 2: 6674
Current Topic Award Vol. 1: 3201
Currey Book-Length Publications Award; Cecil B. Vol. 1: 5368
Currey Memorial Fellowship; C. H. Vol. 2: 679
Curti Award; Merle Vol. 1: 14692
Curtin Medal; Bill Vol. 2: 6108
Curtin Plaque Vol. 1: 16522
Curtis Award; Air Marshal W.A. Vol. 1: 313
Curtis Award; Len Vol. 2: 6593
Curtis Cup Vol. 1: 17915
Curtis Lecture Award; John A. Vol. 1: 3640
Curtis Medal; J.H. Vol. 2: 500
Cushman Award for Excellence in Foraminiferal Research; Joseph A. Vol. 1: 8004
Customer Service Award Vol. 1: 6039
Customer Service Award Vol. 1: 6579
Customer Service Excellence Award Vol. 1: 1161
Cut and Polished Colored Gemstones Vol. 2: 2562
Cut and Polished Diamonds Vol. 2: 2563
Cut and Polished Synthetic Stones Vol. 2: 2564
Cutler Award for Residential Lighting; Aileen Page Vol. 1: 9618
Cutler Award; Lady Vol. 2: 407
Cutlery Hall of Fame Vol. 1: 5806
Cutting Edge Gemstone Competition Vol. 1: 2090
Cutts Scholarships; Donna Vol. 1: 16489
CVMA Award Vol. 1: 7057
C.W. Bill Young Congressional Award Vol. 1: 13434
The CWA Gold Dagger for Nonfiction Vol. 2: 5708
CWI of the Year Award Vol. 1: 4454
Cyril and Methodius Prize Vol. 2: 1144
CyTech Accreditation Vol. 2: 5137
Cytotechnologist Award of the American Society of Cytology Vol. 1: 4013
Cytotechnologist of the Year Award Vol. 1: 4014
Cytotechnologist Scientific Presentation Award Vol. 1: 4013
CytotechnologistsF Award for Outstanding Achievement Vol. 1: 4014
Czerny Preis; Adalbert Vol. 2: 2249
Da Vinci Medal; Leonardo Vol. 1: 16435
da Vinci Medal; Leonardo Vol. 2: 874
Da Vinci Parachuting Diploma; Leonardo Vol. 2: 4724
DAAD Conference Funding Vol. 1: 9036
DAAD EMGIP-Bundestag Internship Vol. 1: 9037
DAAD German Studies Research Grant Vol. 1: 9038
DAAD Group Study Visit Vol. 1: 9039
DAAD Hochschulsommerkurse Vol. 1: 9040
DAAD Intensive Language Grant Vol. 1: 9041
DAAD Learn German in Germany Vol. 1: 9042
DAAD Prize for Distinguished Scholarship in German Studies Vol. 1: 2350
DAAD Research Grant Vol. 1: 9043
DAAD Research Internships in Science and Engineering (RISE) Vol. 1: 9044
DAAD Research Visit Grant (for Faculty) Vol. 1: 9045
DAAD Short Term Lectureship Vol. 1: 9046
DAAD Visiting Professorship Vol. 1: 9047
DAC Trophy Vol. 1: 9357
Dacco Award; Aldo Vol. 2: 3094
Dach Award for InVEST Agent of the Year Vol. 1: 9640
Dade Behring Award Vol. 2: 4254
Dade Behring MicroScan Young Investigator Award Vol. 1: 3767
Daedalian Award Vol. 1: 14643
Daedalian Civilian Air Safety Award Vol. 1: 14647
Daedalian Distinguished Achievement Award Vol. 1: 14641
Daedalian Scholarships Vol. 1: 14642
Daedalian Supply Effectiveness Award Vol. 1: 14640
Daedalian Trophy
Order of Daedalians Vol. 1: 14639
Order of Daedalians Vol 1: 14640
Order of Daedalians Vol 1: 14644
Order of Daedalians Vol 1: 14645
Order of Daedalians Vol 1: 14646
Order of Daedalians Vol 1: 14647
Order of Daedalians Vol 1: 14648
Order of Daedalians Vol 1: 14649
Order of Daedalians Vol 1: 14650
Order of Daedalians Vol 1: 14651
Order of Daedalians Vol 1: 14652
Order of Daedalians Vol 1: 14653
Order of Daedalians Vol 1: 14654
Daedalian Weapon Systems Award Vol. 1: 14643
Dagenais Award; Camille A. Vol. 1: 6913
Daggs Award; Ray G. Vol. 1: 3168
Dagnan-Bouveret; Prix Vol. 2: 1647
Dagnan-Bouveret; Prix Jean Vol. 2: 1554
Dahl Award of Merit; The Marilyn Vol. 1: 6544
Dahlgrens Pris; Rolf Vol. 2: 4624
Dahlquist Prize; Germund Vol. 1: 16268
Dain Library History Dissertation Award; Phyllis Vol. 1: 2675
Dairy Student Award Vol. 2: 6682
Daiwa Scholarships Vol. 2: 5719
Dakin Award; Thomas W. Vol. 1: 9566
Daland Prize; Judson Vol. 1: 3095
Dalby Prize Vol. 2: 7009
Dale Award; Edgar Vol. 1: 7383
Dale Medical Products Excellent Clinical Nurse Specialist Award Vol. 1: 1067
Dale Philip Award; Margaret Vol. 1: 6485
Dalinkevicius premija; Juozo Vol. 2: 3376
Dallas 100 Award Vol. 1: 17042
Dallos Award; Dr. Joseph Vol. 1: 7786
Daly Award; Sgt. Maj. Dan Vol. 1: 11532
Daly Medal; Charles P. Vol. 1: 2095
Dalziel Outstanding Guide Award; G.C.F Vol. 1: 8838
d'Alzon Medal; Emmanuel Vol. 1: 5540
Damen Award Vol. 1: 11431
Dames of America Scholarship; Colonial Vol. 1: 16489
Dameshek Award; Dr. William Vol. 1: 11302
Dameshek Prize; William Vol. 1: 4068
Damien - Dutton Award Vol. 1: 8033
D'Amour Award; O'Neil Vol. 1: 12860
Dana Award; John Cotton Vol. 1: 17073
Dana Award; Margaret Vol. 1: 5416

Dana Awards for Pioneering Achievements in Higher Education; Charles A. Vol. 1: 8037
Dana Library Public Relations Awards; John Cotton Vol. 1: 11332
Dana Publicity Award; John Cotton Vol. 1: 11332
Dance Grants Vol. 1: 15225
Dance Magazine Annual Awards Vol. 1: 8041
Dance Screen Award Vol. 2: 807
Dance/USA National Honors Vol. 1: 8051
Dandrimont-Benicourt; Prix Vol. 2: 1555
Dandurand Trophy; Leo Vol. 1: 6503
DANDY Awards Vol. 1: 14216
Danieli Young Professional Award; Chaim Vol. 1: 10691
Daniels Award; Farrington
American Association of Physicists in Medicine Vol. 1: 1244
International Solar Energy Society Vol 2: 2328
Danielson Award; Philip A. Vol. 1: 18707
Danis Prize; Robert Vol. 2: 4850
Danisco International Dairy Science Award Vol. 1: 1874
Dansk Oversaetterforbunds Aerespris Vol. 2: 1292
Danstrom Award; Charlotte Vol. 1: 18832
Dante Prize Vol. 1: 8053
Dantzig Dissertation Award; George B. Vol. 1: 9740
Dantzig Prize Vol. 1: 11613
Dantzig Prize; George B. Vol. 1: 16269
Danzig Award; Sarah Palfrey Vol. 1: 18139
Dapaepe-Willems Award Vol. 2: 924
Darbaker Prize Vol. 1: 5874
Darby Award for Inspirational Leadership and Excellence of Command; Jack N. Vol. 1: 14000
Darling Foundation Prize Vol. 2: 4926
Darling Medal for Distinguished Achievement in Collection Development in the Health Sciences; Louise Vol. 1: 11656
Darrow Student Design Competition; Carl E. Vol. 1: 2562
Dartmouth Medal Vol. 1: 2686
Darwin Lifetime Achievement Award; Charles R. Vol. 1: 1233
Darwin Medal Vol. 2: 6904
Daryl L. Cook Peer Helping Award Vol. 1: 14590
Das Jaigopal Memorial Award; Chaturvedi Ghanshyam Vol. 2: 2600
Das Memorial Award; Chaturvedi Kalawati Jagmohan Vol. 2: 2601
DASA Scholarship Vol. 1: 8141
Dasher Best Paper Award; Benjamin J. Vol. 1: 3641
Datascope Excellence in Collaboration Award - Multidisciplinary Teams Vol. 1: 1068
Datascope Excellence in Collaboration Award - Nurse to Family Vol. 1: 1069
DateAble Image Award Vol. 1: 8058
Datta Memorial Oration Award; Dr. Dharamvir Vol. 2: 2602
Daubney Research Fellowship in Virology and Helminthology; Robert Vol. 2: 6741
Daughters of Liberty Medal Vol. 1: 13761
Daukantas premija; Simono Vol. 2: 3377
Daula (Frigate Bird) Award; Manu Vol. 1: 14770
Daumet; Fondation Vol. 2: 1482
Dauphinee Volunteer of the Year; Judy Vol. 1: 15379
Davenport Award; Arthur S. Vol. 1: 5659
Davenport Memorial Exhibit Award; John S. Vol. 1: 2879
Davenport Prize; Margaret Vol. 2: 6722
Davenport Publication Award; Millia Vol. 1: 7835
David Film Awards Vol. 2: 3021
The David Green Award Vol. 1: 12017
David Medal; Edgeworth Vol. 2: 641
David; Prix Maxime Vol. 2: 1446
Davidoff National Award for Social Advocacy; Paul Vol. 1: 3202
Davids Award; Bob Vol. 1: 16169
Davidson Award; Murray Vol. 1: 685
Davidson Medal Vol. 1: 16760
Davidson Medal; George Vol. 1: 2096
Davidson Memorial Trophy; Sam Vol. 1: 6649
Davidson Practice of the Profession Award; Park O. Vol. 1: 5946
Davidson President's Award for Practical Papers; John I. Vol. 1: 4736
Davies Award; Valentine Vol. 1: 19012
Davies Medal Vol. 2: 6871
Davies Memorial Scholar Award for Scholarly Activities in Humanities and History of Medicine; Nicholas E. Vol. 1: 1712
Davila ALDA Angel Award; Robert Vol. 1: 5213
Davis and Helen Miles Davis Prize; Watson Vol. 1: 9440
Davis Article Award; Donald G. Vol. 1: 2676
Davis Award; Arthur Vining Vol. 1: 382
Davis Award; Donald E. Vol. 1: 11507
Davis Award; Henry B. Vol. 1: 4238
Davis Award; Jefferson Vol. 1: 7668
Davis Award; John P. Vol. 1: 4127
Davis Award; W. Allison and Elizabeth Stubbs Vol. 1: 12009
Davis Award; Watson Vol. 1: 3743
Davis Cup Vol. 1: 18140
Davis Cup Award Vol. 1: 9600
Davis Cup Award of Excellence Vol. 2: 6305
Davis Fund Awards; Henry and Lily Vol. 2: 6451
Davis Graduate Scholarship; Dr. Keith Vol. 1: 16035
Davis International Award in Medicine; Dr. Nathan Vol. 1: 2745
Davis, Jr. Award; Sammy Vol. 1: 16967
Davis Lecture Series; Raymond E. Vol. 1: 1752
Davis Medal; George E. Vol. 2: 6091
Davis Memorial Award; Suzanne M. Vol. 1: 17014
Davis Memorial Award; William J. Vol. 1: 18231
Davis Memorial Cup; Hugh Vol. 2: 5508
Davis Memorial Lecture; E. H. Vol. 2: 501
Davis Prize; Philip Vol. 2: 6723
Davis Prize; Watson Davis and Helen Miles Vol. 1: 9440
Davis Productivity Awards Vol. 1: 8768
Davis Silver Medal Award; A. F. Vol. 1: 4453
Davisson-Germer Prize in Atomic or Surface Physics Vol. 1: 3115
Davy Medal Vol. 2: 6905
Dawdon Trophy Vol. 2: 5037
Dawson Award for Programmatic Excellence; William Vol. 1: 5288
Dawson Medal; Sir John William Vol. 1: 15757
Day Cup; Colonel George E. Vol. 1: 4636
Day Medal; Arthur L. Vol. 1: 9019
Day Prize and Lectureship; Arthur L. Vol. 1: 12157
Daytime Emmy Awards Vol. 1: 12177
Dayton Playhouse FutureFest Vol. 1: 8062
Dayton Playhouse National Playwriting Competition Vol. 1: 8062
Daytona 200 Vol. 1: 2811
Daytona 500 NASCAR Winston Cup Series Stock Car Race Vol. 1: 8066
Daytona Gatorade Victory Lane Award Vol. 1: 8065
D.C. Awards Program Vol. 1: 19048
DC Fellowship Vol. 1: 8187
de-Bary-Medaille; Anton- Vol. 2: 2213
de Beaufort-prijs; Henriette Vol. 2: 3667
de Caen; Fondation Vol. 2: 1482
de Carli Award; Felice Vol. 2: 3095
De Clercq Prize; Charles Vol. 2: 1069
de Conway Little Medal of Honor; Helen Vol. 1: 9377
de Ferranti Premium; Sebastian Z. Vol. 2: 6146
De Florez Award for Flight Simulation Vol. 1: 2371
De Florez Award for Modeling and Simulation Vol. 1: 2371
de Florez Flight Safety Award; Admiral Luis Vol. 1: 8726
De Internationale Carl Nielsen Musik Konkurrencer Vol. 2: 1313
De la Court Prizes Vol. 2: 3650
De La Salle Medal Vol. 1: 11491
De La Vaulx Medal Vol. 2: 4725
De Laszlo Medal Vol. 2: 6942
De Laszlo Prize Vol. 2: 7027
de Martens; Prix Frederic Vol. 2: 4767
de Menezes Veiga; Premio Frederico Vol. 2: 1122
de Menezes Veiga Prize; Frederico Vol. 2: 1122
De Mille Award; Cecil B. Vol. 1: 9458
De Morgan Medal Vol. 2: 6399
de Morogues; Prix Bigot Vol. 2: 1648
de Tiere Prize; Nestor Vol. 2: 954
de Tocqueville Prize; Alexis Vol. 2: 3540
de Varona Award; Donna Vol. 1: 18874
de Vattel; Prix Emer Vol. 2: 4767
DEA Explorer Drug Abuse Prevention Service Award Vol. 1: 8564
Deadline Club Awards Vol. 1: 8073
Deaf Youth of the Year; Dorothy Shaw Vol. 2: 143
Deak Award; Francis Vol. 1: 10489
Deak Prize; Francis O. Vol. 1: 4089
Dealer and Exhibit Awards Vol. 1: 7673
Dealer and Supplier Volunteer of the Year Award Vol. 1: 5610
Dealer Awards Vol. 1: 5609
Dealer Booster Award Vol. 1: 2880
Dealer Education Award Vol. 1: 14415
Dean Award for Creative Excellence; John Vol. 1: 18993
Dean Memorial Award; H. Trendley Vol. 1: 10059
Dean Research Award; Stanley Vol. 1: 1729
Deane Award; Hamilton Vol. 2: 5742
Deaver Award; Sally Vol. 1: 18092
Deb Memorial Award for Popularisation of Science; Dr. B. C. Vol. 2: 2740
Deb Memorial Award for Soil/Physical Chemistry; Dr. B. C. Vol. 2: 2741
DeBakey Award; Michael E. Vol. 1: 11716
Deballion Medal; Mary Swords Vol. 1: 11641
DeBellis Award; Anthony Vol. 1: 5417

DeBenedetti Prize in Peace History; Charles Vol. 1: 14879
Debra Hills Fellowship Vol. 1: 15254
DebRA Research Grants Vol. 1: 8303
Debs Award; Eugene V. Vol. 1: 8544
Debut Dagger Vol. 2: 5709
Debye Award in Physical Chemistry; Peter Vol. 1: 1541
Debye Prize; Peter Vol. 2: 3513
DeCelle, Jr., Award; Robert E. Vol. 1: 18437
Dechelle; Prix Ernest Vol. 2: 1556
DECHEMA Award of the Max-Buchner-Forschungsstiftung Vol. 2: 2073
DECHEMA Ehrenmitgliedschaft Vol. 2: 2258
DECHEMA Honorary Membership Vol. 2: 2258
DECHEMA-Medaille Vol. 2: 2259
DECHEMA Medal Vol. 2: 2259
DECHEMA Preis der Max Buchner Forschungsstiftung Vol. 2: 2260
Decorative Arts Collection Awards Vol. 1: 16643
Dedicated Service Award
American Society of Mechanical Engineers Vol. 1: 4128
Society of Decorative Painters Vol 1: 16644
Dedication Award Vol. 1: 8434
Dedrick, Jr. Award; Dewey R. Vol. 1: 4239
Deen Distinguished Lectureship; Thomas B. Vol. 1: 17580
Deere Gold Medal Award; John Vol. 1: 3846
DEF Director of the Year Vol. 1: 7965
Defant-Medaille; Albert Vol. 2: 2080
Defence Long Service Medal Vol. 2: 213
Defense Distinguished Service Medal Vol. 1: 8103
Defense Meritorious Service Medal Vol. 1: 8104
Defense of Academic Freedom Award Vol. 1: 12981
Defense Superior Service Medal Vol. 1: 8105
Defensive Player of the Year
Continental Basketball Association Vol. 1: 7797
National Association of Basketball Coaches Vol 1: 12396
National Basketball Association Vol 1: 12757
DeFiore Parental Choice Advocate Award; Leonard F. Vol. 1: 12861
Deflandre et Marthe Deflandre-Rigaud; Prix Georges Vol. 2: 1557
DeForest Audion Award Vol. 1: 18511
DeForest Audion Gold Medal Award Vol. 1: 18511
DeForest Award; Lee Vol. 1: 15519
Defries Award; R. D. Vol. 1: 6840
DeGelleke Award Vol. 1: 7184
DeGolyer Distinguished Service Medal Vol. 1: 16793
DeGolyer Memorial Fund Award; Clare Hart Vol. 1: 8025
DeGreef; Prix Arthur Vol. 2: 974
deKieffer International Fellowship Award; Robert Vol. 1: 4869
Del Gaudio Award; Matthew W. Vol. 1: 14162
Delacorte Dell Yearling Contest for a First Middle-Grade Novel Vol. 1: 8139
Delahautemaison; Prix Marguerite Vol. 2: 1818
DeLaval Dairy Extension Award Vol. 1: 1875
DeLaval Inc. Dairy Extension Award Vol. 1: 1875
Delavan Award for Foreign Service Secretaries Vol. 1: 2056
Delbos; Prix Victor Vol. 2: 1649
Delcros; Prix Estrade- Vol. 2: 1509
Delegate Award Vol. 1: 8656
Dellinger Gold Medal; John Howard Vol. 2: 931
Delpeuch; Prix de la Fondation du Chanoine Vol. 2: 1650
Delphinium Society Awards Vol. 2: 5733
Delta Air Lines Puffer Award Vol. 1: 12215
Delta Art Exhibition Vol. 1: 4613
Delta Award; Penelope Vol. 2: 2455
Delta Pi Epsilon Research Awards Vol. 1: 8156
Delta Sigma Rho - Tau Kappa Alpha Trophy Vol. 1: 13240
Delwart Foundation Prize; Jean-Marie Vol. 2: 1021
DeMaio Award for Trade Union Activism; Ernest Vol. 1: 11185
DeMarco-Becket Memorial Trophy Vol. 1: 6504
DEMCO/ALA Black Caucus Award for Excellence in Librarianship Vol. 1: 5798
Demco New Leaders Travel Grant Vol. 1: 15420
Dement Academic Achievement Award; William C. Vol. 1: 749
Deming Application Prize Vol. 2: 3340
Deming Memorial Fund Grants; Money for Women/Barbara Vol. 1: 11926
Deming Prize Vol. 2: 3340
Deming Prize for Individual Person Vol. 2: 3340
Demingu Sho Vol. 2: 3340
Demmond Award; Jack W. Vol. 1: 11508
Democracy Award
Israel Democracy Institute Vol. 2: 2906
National Endowment for Democracy Vol 1: 13100
Demolombe; Prix Vol. 2: 1651
Den Store Journalistprisen Vol. 2: 3908
Dendy Award Vol. 2: 692
Dendy Awards Vol. 2: 694
Dendy Awards for Australian Short Films Vol. 2: 693
Dengo Memorial Award for Best International Paper; Gabriel Vol. 1: 1211
Denig Distinguished Service Award; Brig. Gen. Robert L. Vol. 1: 17987
Denk Scholarship for Violin, Viola, Cello; Alberta Vol. 1: 12000
Denman Cup; Lady Vol. 2: 6474
Denmark National Faculty Advisor Award; Florence L. Vol. 1: 15400
Denning Award; Anthony Vol. 2: 7127
Dennis Prospector of the Year Award; Bill Vol. 1: 15393
Dennis Scholarship; John Vol. 1: 11892
Denny Gold Medal Vol. 2: 6045
Densmore Prize; Frances Vol. 1: 2839
Dent Medal Vol. 2: 6849
Dental Trade and Industry Award of Recognition Vol. 1: 15074
Dentist of the Year Vol. 1: 11887
Dentistry Development Fund Scholarship for the Development of a Research Technique for Dentistry. Vol. 2: 4324
Dentsu Advertising Awards Vol. 2: 3179
Denver International Film Festival; Starz
Denver Film Society Vol. 1: 8159
Denver Film Society Vol 1: 8160
Denver Film Society Vol 1: 8161
Denver Film Society Vol 1: 8162
Denver Film Society Vol 1: 8163
Denyn Prize; Jef Vol. 2: 1081
Department of Defense Distinguished Service Award Vol. 1: 13083
Department of Defense Executive of the Year Vol. 1: 9142
Department of Justice - CBA University Law School Essay Contest Vol. 1: 6330
Department of Secondary School Awards Vol. 1: 12862
Department of Trade and Industry Prizes Vol. 2: 6029
Department of Transportation Award for Heroism Vol. 1: 17878
Department of Veteran's Affairs Employee of the Year Award Vol. 1: 288
Deputy Sheriff of the Year Award Vol. 1: 13699
Derleth Nonfiction Book Award; Kenneth Kingery/August Vol. 1: 7875
deRoaldes Award Vol. 1: 2620
Derwent Award; Clarence Vol. 1: 144
Desai Prize Award; Dr. D. K. Vol. 2: 2754
Desert Palm Achievement Award
Palm Springs International Film Society Vol. 1: 14817
Palm Springs International Film Society Vol 1: 14817
DESI Awards Vol. 1: 9178
Design and Application Award
International Magnesium Association Vol. 1: 10500
International Magnesium Association Vol 1: 10501
Design and Construction Excellence Awards Vol. 1: 7663
Design and Craft Innovation Award Vol. 2: 7042
Design Annual Vol. 1: 7636
Design Award
AIA Pennsylvania Vol. 1: 251
American Concrete Institute Vol 1: 1755
Chain Link Fence Manufacturer Institute Vol 1: 7272
International Magnesium Association Vol 1: 10501
Texas Society of Architects/ AIA Vol 1: 17500
Design Award Competition Vol. 1: 11699
Design Awards Vol. 1: 2446
Design Awards Competition Vol. 1: 16207
Design Competition Vol. 1: 2454
Design Competition Awards Vol. 1: 16538
Design Competitions Vol. 2: 4905
Design Council Awards Vol. 2: 5735
Design for Humanity Award Vol. 1: 4084
Design Medal Vol. 1: 4097
Design Partnership Award Vol. 2: 6459
Design Prize of the Federal Republic of Germany Vol. 2: 2182
Design Standards Award Vol. 1: 12261
Designer of Distinction Award Vol. 1: 4085
Designer of the Year Vol. 2: 6549
Designpreis der Bundesrepublik Deutschland Vol. 2: 2182
Desjardins President of the Year Award; Carolyn Vol. 1: 977
Deslandres; Prix Vol. 2: 1558
Desprez; Prix Vol. 2: 1447
Detroit Founding Chapter (Chapter 1) Scholarship Vol. 1: 16709

Deutsch Award; Karl Vol. 1: 10762
Deutsch Memorial Award; Wilbur Vol. 1: 16881
Deutsche Meteorologische Gesellschaft Ehrenmitgliedschaft Vol. 2: 2081
Deutsche Meteorologische Gesellschaft e.V. Jugendpreis Vol. 2: 2082
Deutscher Jugend-Video-Preis Vol. 2: 2063
Deutz-Allis National Student Design Competition Vol. 1: 3842
Deux Magots Literary Prize Vol. 2: 1728
Developer of the Year Vol. 1: 12572
Developing Country Literacy Project Support Grant Vol. 1: 10577
Development Award Vol. 2: 7263
Development Education Grants Vol. 2: 7328
Developmental Awards Vol. 1: 11358
Developmental Coach of the Year
USA Swimming Vol. 1: 18414
U.S.A. Wrestling Vol 1: 18463
Developmental Disabilities Awareness Award Vol. 1: 5732
Developmental Disabilities Scholastic Achievement Scholarship Vol. 1: 5733
Developmental Psychology Awards Vol. 1: 3328
DeVilliers Award Vol. 1: 11303
Devitt Distinguished Service to Justice Award; Edward J. Vol. 1: 2602
Devonshire Trophy Vol. 2: 6787
Dew Award; G. Richard Vol. 1: 14933
D'Ewes Medal; Dudley Vol. 2: 4138
Dewey Medal; Melvil Vol. 1: 2653
Dewey Scholarship Vol. 1: 14133
Dewhurst Lecture and Award Vol. 2: 7376
Dews Award for Research in Behavioral Pharmacology; P.B. Vol. 1: 3806
Dexter Prize Vol. 1: 16437
Dey Award; Joseph Vol. 1: 17916
Dharmasthala Manjunatheswara Award Vol. 2: 2638
Dhere; Prix Charles Vol. 2: 1559
DHL International (UK) Prize Vol. 2: 6029
Di Castagnola Award; Alice Fay Vol. 1: 15126
Di Valerio Technician of the Year Award; Lou Vol. 1: 3776
Diabetes Camp Educator Award Vol. 1: 1078
Diabetes Educator of the Year Award Vol. 1: 1079
Diables d'Or Vol. 2: 4805
Dialogue-Silver Foundation Awards Vol. 1: 8178
Dialogue Writing Awards Vol. 1: 8178
Diamond Anniversary Book Award Vol. 1: 12924
Diamond Clinical Fellowship in Headache Education; Seymour Vol. 1: 13322
Diamond Coach Vol. 1: 13238
Diamond ECHO Award Vol. 1: 8200
Diamond Jubilee Bursary Vol. 2: 189
Diamond Key Award Vol. 1: 13238
Diana Award Vol. 1: 4827
DiBello Memorial Exhibit Award; Gaston Vol. 1: 2881
Dibner Award for Excellence in Museum Exhibits Vol. 1: 16436
Dick Medal of Merit; Charles Vol. 1: 13301
The Dick PettiFor Memorial Award Vol. 1: 15404
Dickerman Award Lecture; Herbert W. Vol. 1: 14179
Dickerson Award; Ben F. Vol. 1: 16343
Dickinson Award; *The Writer* Magazine/ Emily Vol. 1: 15127
Dickinson College Arts Award Vol. 1: 8183
Dickinson Scholarship; Clarence Vol. 1: 2145
Dickinson Teacher of the Year Award; John Vol. 1: 594
Dickson Alumnus of the Year; Edward A. Vol. 1: 17641
Dickson Memorial Award; Donald L. Vol. 1: 17988
Dickson Memorial Award; Dorothy Stredicke Vol. 1: 3252
Dickson Scholarship; Alec and Mora Vol. 1: 10542
Dicus Award; Robert G. Vol. 1: 15247
Didactic Instructor of the Year Award
American Association of Nurse Anesthetists Vol. 1: 1179
Council on Accreditation of Nurse Anesthesia Educational Programs Vol 1: 7904
Didusch Art and History Award; William P. Vol. 1: 4388
Die Weissen Raben Vol. 2: 2330
Diederich Award Vol. 1: 9389
Diederich Landscape Award Vol. 1: 9389
Diehl; Prix Charles and Marguerite Vol. 2: 1510
Diener Award; Irving Vol. 1: 5809
Diesel and Gas Engine Power Award Vol. 1: 4142
Dietsch Sculpture Prize; C. Percival Vol. 1: 13690
Dietz Award; August Vol. 1: 7674
Dietz Service Award; Albert A. Vol. 1: 873
Digital Apprentice of the Year Vol. 2: 5422
Digital Avionics Award Vol. 1: 2372
Digital Channel Programme Award Vol. 2: 7044
Digital Innovation Fellowship Vol. 1: 1813
Dijon Young JuryFs Prize Vol. 2: 1846
Dillard Award; Harrison Vol. 1: 18438
Dillman's Scholarship Vol. 1: 8197
Dillon Medal for Research in Polymer Physics; John H. Vol. 1: 3116
The Dilys Award Vol. 1: 9647
Dimbleby Award; Richard Vol. 2: 5217
Dimock Award; Hedley S. Vol. 1: 1434
Dimock Award; Marshall E. Vol. 1: 3814
Dine Award; Joe and Laurie Vol. 1: 14761
Dinerman Award; Helen Vol. 1: 18897
Dinerman Memorial Prize; Helen S. Vol. 1: 939
Dingle Prize Vol. 2: 5492
Dingley Memorial Award; Dr. H. B. Vol. 2: 2603
Dingley Oration Award; Smt. Swaran Kanta Vol. 2: 2604
Dining Idea Exchange Contest Vol. 1: 12442
Dinkeloo Fellowship Vol. 1: 18483
Diploma for Outstanding Airmanship Vol. 2: 4726
Diploma in International Employee Benefits Vol. 2: 6529
Diploma of Honor Vol. 1: 10199
Diplomate of the American Board of Psychological Hypnosis Vol. 1: 1412
Diplomatic Security Employee of the Year Award Vol. 1: 17857
Diplome d'honneur Vol. 1: 6418
Dipple Carcinogenesis Award; Anthony Vol. 2: 5805
DiPrima Prize; Richard C. Vol. 1: 16270
Dirac Medal Vol. 2: 2946
Dirac Medal and Prize; Paul Vol. 2: 6058
Direct Marketing Woman of the Year Award Vol. 1: 18812
Director General's Award for Excellence in Human Resource Management Vol. 1: 17858
Director of the Year Vol. 1: 12790
Directorate Award Vol. 1: 10363
Director's Award
American Alliance for Theatre and Education Vol. 1: 802
American Helicopter Society Vol 1: 2193
Federation of Genealogical Societies Vol 1: 8657
National Marine Manufacturers Association Vol 1: 13429
Directors Award
Friends of Algonquin Park Vol. 1: 8893
Society of Flight Test Engineers Vol 1: 16687
Directors' Awards Vol. 1: 6143
Director's Choice Award Vol. 1: 13815
Directors Emeriti Award Vol. 1: 11362
Director's Franklin Award Vol. 1: 8701
Directors Scholarship Vol. 1: 16710
Directors Special Achievement Award Vol. 1: 8320
Directory of the Year - Business Vol. 2: 5723
Directory of the Year - Consumer Vol. 2: 5724
Disability Awareness Award Vol. 1: 14844
Disability Care Award Vol. 2: 6694
Disaster Relief Fund Grants Vol. 1: 17469
Discover America National Travel Marketing Awards Vol. 1: 17589
Discover Award Vol. 1: 5673
Discover Screenwriter Award Vol. 1: 3536
DiscovererFs Award Vol. 1: 14966
"Discovery" Award Vol. 1: 11
Discovery Prize Vol. 1: 14860
"Discovery"/*The Nation* Contest Vol. 1: 11
Dissertation Award
American Psychological Association - American Psychology-Law Society (Division 41) Vol. 1: 3300
American Society for Training and Development Vol 1: 3834
American Sociological Association Vol 1: 4277
International Society for Developmental Psychobiology Vol 1: 10643
National Association of Schools of Public Affairs and Administration Vol 1: 12649
Ohio Academy of History Vol 1: 14457
Religious Communication Association Vol 1: 15621
Society for Cinema and Media Studies Vol 1: 16191
Dissertation Award in Geographic Education Vol. 1: 12967
Dissertation Award in Nuclear Physics Vol. 1: 3117
Dissertation Competition Vol. 1: 13487
Dissertation Fellowships in American Art Vol. 1: 1813
Dissertation Prize Vol. 2: 6357
Dissertation Research Awards Vol. 1: 3364
Dissertation Research Fellowship Vol. 1: 3827
Dissertation Year Fellowship Vol. 1: 14284
Distance Learning Course Awards Vol. 1: 18211
Distinguised Service Award Vol. 1: 18920

Distinguish Service to Social Work Vol. 1: 14258
Distinguished Academic All-American Award Vol. 1: 13401
Distinguished Achievement and Contributions Award Vol. 2: 3193
Distinguished Achievement Award
Alberta Motion Picture Industries Association Vol. 1: 372
American Recorder Society Vol 1: 3465
Australian Neuroscience Society Vol 2: 301
Australian Society of Archivists Vol 2: 374
Canadian Radiation Protection Association Vol 1: 6851
Eastern College Athletic Conference Vol 1: 8346
European Behavioral Pharmacology Society Vol 2: 2113
International Bluegrass Music Association Vol 1: 10270
International Communications Industries Association Vol 1: 10331
Scarab Club Vol 1: 15897
Society of Exploration Geo-physicists Vol 1: 16676
USA Hockey Vol 1: 18399
Wings Club Vol 1: 18763
Distinguished Achievement Award for Community Service Vol. 1: 9720
Distinguished Achievement Award for Nursery Crops Vol. 1: 3720
Distinguished Achievement Award for Petroleum Engineering Faculty Vol. 1: 16794
Distinguished Achievement Award in Clinical/Pharmacotherapeutic Practice Vol. 1: 3043
Distinguished Achievement Award in Community and Ambulatory Practice Vol. 1: 3044
Distinguished Achievement Award in Extension Vol. 1: 8482
Distinguished Achievement Award in Horticultural Entomology Vol. 1: 8483
Distinguished Achievement Award in Hospital and Institutional Practice Vol. 1: 3045
Distinguished Achievement Award in Regulatory Entomology Vol. 1: 8483
Distinguished Achievement Award in Specialized Pharmaceutical Services Vol. 1: 3046
Distinguished Achievement Award in Teaching Vol. 1: 8484
Distinguished Achievement Award - Research Vol. 2: 6210
Distinguished Achievement Award - Scientific Literature Vol. 2: 6211
Distinguished Achievement Award - Service Vol. 2: 6212
Distinguished Achievement Awards Vol. 1: 2751
Distinguished Achievement Awards for Excellence in Educational Publishing Vol. 1: 5131
Distinguished Achievement Awards for Local Public Affairs Vol. 1: 9723
Distinguished Achievement in Accounting Education Award Vol. 1: 2459
Distinguished Achievement in Agriculture Award Vol. 1: 8950
Distinguished Achievement in Musical Theatre Award Vol. 1: 8276
Distinguished Achievement in RV Journalism Award Vol. 1: 15581
Distinguished Achievement in RV Standards Award Vol. 1: 15582
Distinguished Advertising Educator Award Vol. 1: 766
Distinguished Adviser Award Vol. 1: 7526
Distinguished Africanist Award Vol. 1: 225
Distinguished Alumni Award Vol. 1: 11973
Distinguished Alumni Citation Vol. 1: 12308
Distinguished Alumnus Award
American Association of State Colleges and Universities Vol. 1: 1286
Tau Beta Pi Association Vol 1: 17402
University of Maryland - College of Information Studies Vol 1: 18307
Distinguished American Award Vol. 1: 13210
Distinguished Arizonan Award Vol. 1: 13221
Distinguished Artist Award Vol. 1: 18233
Distinguished Artist Award for Lifetime Achievement Vol. 1: 7504
Distinguished Assessment Jurisdiction Award Vol. 1: 10127
Distinguished Athletic Therapy Educator Award Vol. 1: 6315
The Distinguished Award of Honour For Service to Children's Charities Vol. 2: 420
Distinguished Award of Merit Vol. 1: 1810
Distinguished Awards Vol. 1: 8878
Distinguished Awards for the Contributions to the Science and Professional of Clinical Psychology Vol. 1: 3402
Distinguished Board Member Vol. 1: 1162
Distinguished Book Award
American Alliance for Theatre and Education Vol. 1: 793
Society for Military History Vol 1: 16335
Distinguished Budget Presentation Award Vol. 1: 9149
Distinguished Canadian Retailer of the Year Award Vol. 1: 15650
Distinguished Career Award
Ambulatory Pediatric Association Vol. 1: 526
American Academy of Pediatrics Vol 1: 686
Canadian Pain Society Vol 1: 6790
Fusion Power Associates Vol 1: 8933
International Society for the Prevention of Child Abuse and Child Neglect Vol 1: 10684
Southeastern Theatre Conference Vol 1: 17015
Distinguished Career Award for the Practice of Sociology Vol. 1: 4278
Distinguished Career Contribution to Gerontology Award Vol. 1: 9056
Distinguished Career Service Awards Vol. 1: 17838
Distinguished Citizen Vol. 1: 18561
Distinguished Citizen Award Vol. 1: 12947
Distinguished Communicator Award Vol. 1: 15787
Distinguished Community Member Vol. 1: 1162
Distinguished Contribution Award
American Planning Association Vol. 1: 3203
American Urological Association Vol 1: 4389
Project Management Institute Vol 1: 15371
Psychologists for Social Responsibility Vol 1: 15411
Distinguished Contribution to Advancement in Chemical Education Vol. 2: 4096
Distinguished Contribution to Building Cultures of Peace Vol. 1: 15412
Distinguished Contribution to Child Advocacy Award Vol. 1: 3370
Distinguished Contribution to Economic Advancement Award Vol. 2: 4097
Distinguished Contribution to Family Therapy Research Award Vol. 1: 1989
Distinguished Contribution to Family Therapy Theory and Practice Award Vol. 1: 1989
Distinguished Contribution to Nursing Science Award Vol. 1: 2948
Distinguished Contribution to Practice in Community Psychology Award Vol. 1: 3371
Distinguished Contribution to Psychology and Law Vol. 1: 3301
Distinguished Contribution to Research Administration Award Vol. 1: 16847
Distinguished Contribution to Scholarship Award Vol. 1: 4280
Distinguished Contribution to Science Education Through Research Award Vol. 1: 12352
Distinguished Contribution to Social Justice Award
American Family Therapy Academy Vol. 1: 1989
American Family Therapy Academy Vol 1: 1990
Distinguished Contribution to Theory and Research in Community Psychology Award Vol. 1: 3372
Distinguished Contribution to Workplace Learning and Performance Award Vol. 1: 3835
Distinguished Contributions to Slavic Studies Award Vol. 1: 956
Distinguished Contributions to Teaching Award
American Sociological Association Vol. 1: 4279
Pacific Sociological Association Vol 1: 14787
Distinguished Contributions to the International Advancement of Psychology Vol. 1: 3316
Distinguished Convention Service Manager Award Vol. 1: 15288
Distinguished Dairy Cattle Breeder Award Vol. 1: 13073
Distinguished Dealer of the Year Vol. 1: 18674
Distinguished Dietitian of the Year Vol. 1: 11081
Distinguished Dissertation Award
Association for Canadian Studies in the United States Vol. 1: 4789
Kappa Delta Pi Vol 1: 11091
Distinguished Dissertation in Teacher Education Award Vol. 1: 5359
Distinguished Eagle Scout Award Vol. 1: 5906
Distinguished Early Career Contributions Award Vol. 1: 16288
Distinguished Economic Botanist Award Vol. 1: 16204
Distinguished Education and Behavioral Sciences Librarian Award Vol. 1: 5074
Distinguished Educator and Service Award Vol. 1: 3642
Distinguished Educator Award
American Association of Petroleum Geologists Vol. 1: 1220
American Society for Gastrointestinal Endoscopy Vol 1: 3706

National Rural Health Association Vol 1: 13650
North American Colleges and Teachers of Agriculture Vol 1: 14276
Distinguished Engineering Educator Award Vol. 1: 16912
Distinguished Extension-Industry Service Award Vol. 1: 2735
Distinguished Extension/Outreach Program Award Vol. 1: 775
Distinguished Fellow
American Economic Association Vol. 1: 1936
American Park and Recreation Society Vol 1: 3025
Society for Public Health Education Vol 1: 16394
Distinguished Fellow Award
American Council on Consumer Interests Vol. 1: 1822
History of Economics Society Vol 1: 9434
Distinguished Fellowship Vol. 1: 95
Distinguished Fellowship Award
American College of Cardiology Vol. 1: 1615
Royal Australian Chemical Institute Vol 2: 619
Distinguished Fifty-Year Member Award Vol. 1: 4053
Distinguished Flying Medal Vol. 2: 5591
Distinguished Flying Unit Plaques Vol. 1: 13301
Distinguished Forester Vol. 1: 5112
Distinguished Friend to Behavior Therapy Vol. 1: 4784
Distinguished Friends of Council Award Vol. 2: 2448
Distinguished Geographer Medal Vol. 2: 3771
Distinguished Graduate Award in Premium Auditing Vol. 1: 13736
Distinguished Grant Maker Award Vol. 1: 7914
Distinguished Grasslander Award Vol. 1: 2048
Distinguished Honor Award Vol. 1: 17859
Distinguished Humanities Education Awards Vol. 1: 7640
Distinguished Individual Service Award Vol. 1: 12419
Distinguished Informal Science Education Award Vol. 1: 13681
Distinguished Information Sciences Award Vol. 1: 5199
Distinguished International Colleague Award Vol. 1: 9509
Distinguished International Fellow Vol. 2: 545
Distinguished International Service Award Vol. 1: 8515
Distinguished Investigator Award
American College of Clinical Pharmacology Vol. 1: 1629
National Alliance for Research on Schizophrenia and Depression Vol 1: 12231
Distinguished Jurisdictional Member Vol. 1: 1162
Distinguished Leadership Award
American Association for Marriage and Family Therapy Vol. 1: 928
International Landslide Research Group Vol 1: 10485
Distinguished Leadership Award for a Citizen Planner Vol. 1: 3204
Distinguished Leadership Award for a Professional Planner Vol. 1: 3205
Distinguished Leadership Award for a Student Planner Vol. 1: 3206
Distinguished Leadership Award for an Elected Official Vol. 1: 3207
Distinguished Lecture Award Vol. 1: 813
Distinguished Lecturer Vol. 1: 10831
Distinguished Lecturer Award Vol. 1: 5771
Distinguished Lectureship Vol. 1: 17580
Distinguished Lectureships Vol. 1: 16650
Distinguished Life Member
American Ceramic Society Vol. 1: 1474
ASM International Vol 1: 4696
Distinguished Local Government Leadership Award Vol. 1: 5178
Distinguished Member
National Wrestling Hall of Fame & Museum Vol. 1: 13937
Society of Petroleum Engineers Vol 1: 16795
Distinguished Member and Fellow Award Vol. 1: 4898
Distinguished Member Award
American Congress of Rehabilitation Medicine Vol. 1: 1771
Association of Women Surgeons Vol 1: 5387
National Association for Healthcare Quality Vol 1: 12331
Professional Convention Management Association Vol 1: 15289
Society for Mining, Metallurgy, and Exploration Vol 1: 16344
Distinguished Membership Award Vol. 1: 2938
Distinguished Mentor Award
Association for Counselor Education and Supervision Vol. 1: 4846
National Council for Geographic Education Vol 1: 12968
Distinguished Mentorship in Gerontology Award Vol. 1: 9057
Distinguished Merit Award
American Association of Community Theatre Vol. 1: 1063
European Oncology Nursing Society Vol 2: 869
Distinguished Mission Support Plaques Vol. 1: 13301
Distinguished Musician Award Vol. 2: 5982
Distinguished Musician Certificate Vol. 1: 6326
Distinguished Mycologist Award Vol. 1: 12046
Distinguished Neuropsychologist Award Vol. 1: 12132
Distinguished New Engineer Award Vol. 1: 16913
Distinguished Organization Award Vol. 1: 12482
Distinguished Pathologist Award Vol. 1: 17723
Distinguished Patriot Award Vol. 1: 13762
Distinguished Peace Leadership Award Vol. 1: 14435
Distinguished Performance Award
The Drama League Vol. 1: 8277
U.S. Marine Corps Combat Correspondents Association Vol 1: 17989
Distinguished Physician Award Vol. 1: 1169
Distinguished Pi Lambda Thetan Award Vol. 1: 15053
Distinguished Play Awards Vol. 1: 794
Distinguished Police Service Award Vol. 1: 3219
Distinguished Policy Contribution Award Vol. 1: 776
Distinguished Practice Award
International Pharmaceutical Federation Vol. 2: 3597
Pacific Sociological Association Vol 1: 14788
Distinguished Principal Founding Member Vol. 2: 803
Distinguished Pro Bono Service Award Vol. 1: 17257
Distinguished Professional Contribution to Family Therapy Award Vol. 1: 929
Distinguished Professional Contributions Award Vol. 1: 16289
Distinguished Professional Contributions to Applied Research Vol. 1: 3392
Distinguished Professional Contributions to Knowledge Vol. 1: 3392
Distinguished Professional Contributions to Practice in the Public Sector Vol. 1: 3393
Distinguished Professional Contributions to Public Service Vol. 1: 3393
Distinguished Professional Service Award Vol. 1: 4847
Distinguished Professor Award Vol. 1: 5100
Distinguished Programs in Teacher Education Award Vol. 1: 5360
Distinguished Psychologist Award Vol. 1: 3357
Distinguished Psychologist of the Year Vol. 1: 3422
Distinguished Public Involvement Award Vol. 1: 14063
Distinguished Public Service Award
American Psychological Association Division of Independent Practice - Division of Independent Practice Vol. 1: 3423
Center for National Policy Vol 1: 7228
Distinguished Public Service Medal
Mineralogical Society of America Vol. 1: 11796
National Aeronautics and Space Administration Vol 1: 12196
Distinguished Quality of Life Researcher Award Vol. 1: 10674
Distinguished Recent Alumnus Award Vol. 1: 5617
Distinguished Research and Development Award Vol. 1: 10128
Distinguished Research Award
American Meat Science Association Vol. 1: 2736
National Council of Teachers of English Vol 1: 13030
Section for Women in Public Administration - Section for Women in Public Administration Vol 1: 15966
Distinguished Research in Teacher Education Award Vol. 1: 5361
Distinguished Researcher Award
American Association of Neuromuscular and Electrodiagnostic Medicine Vol. 1: 1170
Oncology Nursing Society Vol 1: 14535
Distinguished Rural Sociologist Award Vol. 1: 15779
Distinguished Salesperson Award Vol. 2: 3941
Distinguished Scholar Award
International Association of Human-Animal Interaction Organizations Vol. 1: 10217

Award Index

Keats-Shelley Association of America Vol 1: 11101
National Association for Gifted Children Vol 1: 12317
North American Society for the Psychology of Sport and Physical Activity Vol 1: 14336
Distinguished Scholarly Publication Award Vol. 1: 4280
Distinguished Scholarship Award Vol. 1: 14789
Distinguished School Administrators Award Vol. 1: 1274
Distinguished Science Award Vol. 2: 3597
Distinguished Scientific Achievement Award Vol. 1: 9305
Distinguished Scientific Award for an Early Career Contribution to Psychology Vol. 1: 3394
Distinguished Scientific Award for the Applications of Psychology Vol. 1: 3365
Distinguished Scientific Contribution Award
Australian Psychological Society Vol. 2: 335
Australian Small Animal Veterinary Association Vol 2: 363
Distinguished Scientific Contribution Award Vol. 1: 3366
Distinguished Scientific Contributions Award Vol. 1: 16290
Distinguished Scientist Award
American College of Cardiology Vol. 1: 1616
Heart Rhythm Association Vol 1: 9338
Distinguished Service
American Disaster Reserve Vol. 1: 1924
American Fence Association Vol 1: 2011
American Guernsey Association Vol 1: 2135
Association of British Columbia Drama Educators Vol 1: 5051
Foundation for North American Wild Sheep Vol 1: 8839
Distinguished Service Vol. 1: 11650
Distinguished Service/Achievement Awards Vol. 1: 16006
Distinguished Service Award
American College of Managed Care Administrators Vol. 1: 1667
American Council for Polish Culture Vol 1: 1801
American Rental Association Vol 1: 3479
Association of Medical Microbiology and Infectious Disease Canada Vol 1: 5219
Australian Science Teachers Association Vol 2: 346
Australian Small Animal Veterinary Association Vol 2: 364
Biophysical Society Vol 1: 5776
Canadian Association of University Business Officers Vol 1: 6303
International Ergonomics Association Vol 2: 3069
International Society for Quality-of-Life Studies Vol 1: 10675
National Community Education Association Vol 1: 12935
Professional Convention Management Association Vol 1: 15290
State Debt Management Network Vol 1: 17261
Distinguished Service Award
303rd Bomb Group (H) Association Vol. 1: 13
Alpine Club of Canada Vol 1: 440
American Academy of Advertising Vol 1: 545
American Academy of Medical Administrators Vol 1: 627
American Academy of Pediatrics Vol 1: 687
American Association for Agricultural Education Vol 1: 846
American Association for Clinical Chemistry Vol 1: 874
American Association of Collegiate Registrars and Admissions Officers Vol 1: 1055
American Association of Diabetes Educators Vol 1: 1080
American Association of Homes and Services for the Aging Vol 1: 1123
American Association of Motor Vehicle Administrators Vol 1: 1162
American Association of Oral and Maxillofacial Surgeons Vol 1: 1193
American Association of Petroleum Geologists Vol 1: 1212
American Association of Public Health Physicians Vol 1: 1264
American Association of School Administrators Vol 1: 1268
American Association of School Librarians Vol 1: 1275
American Association of Teachers of Italian Vol 1: 1304
American Association of University Administrators Vol 1: 1314
American Camping Association Vol 1: 1435
American Cancer Society Vol 1: 1441
American Chemical Society Vol 1: 1542
American College of Cardiology Vol 1: 1617
American College of Dentists Vol 1: 1643
American College of Dentists Vol 1: 1643
American College of Oncology Administrators Vol 1: 1696
American College of Preventive Medicine Vol 1: 1722
The American College of Psychiatrists Vol 1: 1730
American Dairy Science Association Vol 1: 1876
American Farm Bureau Federation Vol 1: 1994
American Fisheries Society Vol 1: 2028
American Forensic Association Vol 1: 2062
American Hospital Association Vol 1: 2304
American Hospital Association Vol 1: 2309
American Industrial Hygiene Association Vol 1: 2340
American Institute of Aeronautics and Astronautics Vol 1: 2373
American Institute of Biological Sciences Vol 1: 2451
American Institute of Chemical Engineers Vol 1: 2476
American Institute of Mining, Metallurgical, and Petroleum Engineers Vol 1: 2524
American Moving and Storage Association Vol 1: 2814
American Optometric Association Vol 1: 2975
American Osteopathic College of Pathologists Vol 1: 3018
American Phytopathological Society Vol 1: 3189
American Public Gas Association Vol 1: 3428
American Public Power Association Vol 1: 3446
American Public Works Association Vol 1: 3451
American School Health Association Vol 1: 3525
American Society for Bioethics and Humanities Vol 1: 3570
American Society for Engineering Education Vol 1: 3643
American Society for Gastrointestinal Endoscopy Vol 1: 3707
American Society of Abdominal Surgeons Vol 1: 3839
American Society of Heating, Refrigerating and Air-Conditioning Engineers Vol 1: 4054
American Speech Language Hearing Association Vol 1: 4291
American Urological Association Vol 1: 4390
Association for Asian Studies Vol 1: 4777
Association for Computing Machinery Vol 1: 4806
Association for Educational Communications and Technology and the ECT Foundation Vol 1: 4870
Association for Library Service to Children Vol 1: 4926
Association for Women Veterinarians Vol 1: 5011
Association of Fraternity Advisors Vol 1: 5153
Association of Free Community Papers Vol 1: 5157
Association of Professional Chaplains Vol 1: 5309
Association of Schools of Allied Health Professions Vol 1: 5329
Association of University Architects Vol 1: 5378
Black Caucus of the American Library Association Vol 1: 5799
Bookbuilders West Vol 1: 5848
California Walnut Commission Vol 1: 6069
Canadian Society of Hospital Pharmacists Vol 1: 6996
Caucus for Television Producers, Writers and Directors Vol 1: 7178
Chicago Book Clinic Vol 1: 7324
Chinese American Librarians Association Vol 1: 7363
Citizens Union of the City of New York Vol 1: 7424
Computing Research Association Vol 1: 7653
Conference on Latin American History Vol 1: 7699
Congress of Neurological Surgeons Vol 1: 7705
Congressional Hispanic Caucus Institute Vol 1: 7714
Construction Specifications Institute Vol 1: 7746
Council of Chief State School Officers Vol 1: 7879
Council of Supply Chain Management Professionals Vol 1: 7900
Dance Notation Bureau Vol 1: 8046
Deep Foundations Institute Vol 1: 8085
Easter Seals Vol 1: 8334

European Association for Animal Production Vol 2: 3023
Family, Career and Community Leaders of America Vol 1: 8581
Federally Employed Women Vol 1: 8609
Federation of Genealogical Societies Vol 1: 8658
Financial Planning Association Vol 1: 8697
Florida Association of Colleges and Universities Vol 1: 8734
Geological Society of America Vol 1: 9020
Golf Course Superintendents Association of America Vol 1: 9114
Health Science Communications Association Vol 1: 9310
Healthcare Convention and Exhibitors Association Vol 1: 9320
Heart Rhythm Association Vol 1: 9339
Illuminating Engineering Society of North America Vol 1: 9616
Independent Free Papers of America Vol 1: 9637
Institute of Nuclear Materials Management Vol 1: 9922
International Association of Cancer Victors and Friends Vol 1: 10162
International Badminton Federation Vol 2: 3406
International Institute of Fisheries Economics and Trade Vol 1: 10469
International Society for the Prevention of Child Abuse and Child Neglect Vol 1: 10685
Lamaze International Vol 1: 11209
Lewis and Clark Trail Heritage Foundation Vol 1: 11317
Lutheran Historical Conference Vol 1: 11447
Mail Systems Management Association Vol 1: 11465
Military Chaplains Association of the U.S.A. Vol 1: 11767
Military Order of the World Wars Vol 1: 11775
Minerals, Metals, and Materials Society Vol 1: 11803
Missouri Dental Association Vol 1: 11888
NACE International: The Corrosion Society Vol 1: 12064
National Air Transportation Association Vol 1: 12226
National Association for Gifted Children Vol 1: 12318
National Association for Pupil Transportation Vol 1: 12350
National Association of Academies of Science Vol 1: 12375
National Association of Animal Breeders Vol 1: 12377
National Association of Biology Teachers Vol 1: 12406
National Association of Broadcasters Vol 1: 12430
National Association of Conservation Districts Vol 1: 12471
National Association of Corrosion Engineers Vol 1: 12483
National Association of Fleet Administrators Vol 1: 12536
National Association of Realtors Vol 1: 12633
National Business Education Association Vol 1: 12832
National Council of Teachers of English Vol 1: 13021
National Court Reporters Association Vol 1: 13062
National Defense Transportation Association Vol 1: 13084
National Genealogical Society Vol 1: 13273
National Mining Association Vol 1: 13454
National Propane Gas Association Vol 1: 13575
National Retail Federation Vol 1: 13639
National School Transportation Association Vol 1: 13668
National Society of Professional Engineers Vol 1: 13743
National Therapeutic Recreation Society Vol 1: 13844
National Water Resources Association Vol 1: 13885
Ohio Academy of History Vol 1: 14458
Oncology Nursing Society Vol 1: 14536
Optical Society of America Vol 1: 14604
Pennsylvania Society of Anesthesiologists Vol 1: 14942
Professional Golfers' Association of America Vol 1: 15316
Prospectors and Developers Association of Canada Vol 1: 15394
Royal Geographical Society with the Institute of British Geographers Vol 2: 6762
School and Community Safety Society of America Vol 1: 15903
Society for Applied Spectroscopy Vol 1: 16177
Society for Medical Decision Making Vol 1: 16330
Society for Range Management Vol 1: 16403
Society for Sedimentary Geology Vol 1: 16407
Society of American Archivists Vol 1: 16490
Society of Naval Architects and Marine Engineers Vol 1: 16761
Society of Petroleum Engineers Vol 1: 16796
Society of Petrophysicists and Well Log Analysts Vol 1: 16810
Society of Research Administrators Vol 1: 16849
Society of Wood Science and Technology Vol 1: 16918
SOLE, the International Society of Logistics Vol 1: 16946
Specialty Graphic Imaging Association Vol 1: 17111
Tasmanian Canine Association Vol 2: 698
Tax Foundation Vol 1: 17413
United States Association of Former Members of Congress Vol 1: 17744
Washington International Trade Association Vol 1: 18600
The Wildlife Society Vol 1: 18748
Wine Spectator Vol 1: 18760
World Bowling Writers Vol 1: 18914
World Jersey Cattle Bureau Vol 2: 7374
Zelienople-Harmony Area Chamber of Commerce Vol 1: 19119
Distinguished Service Award for an Administrator or Supervisor Vol. 1: 12833
Distinguished Service Award for Elected County Official Vol. 1: 12494
Distinguished Service Award in Investment Education Vol. 1: 10855
Distinguished Service Award of SADA Vol. 2: 4325
Distinguished Service Award (Outside the Profession) Vol. 1: 12262
Distinguished Service Award (Within the Profession) Vol. 1: 12263
Distinguished Service Awards
Australian College of Rural and Remote Medicine Vol. 2: 159
Canadian Society for Analytical Sciences and Spectroscopy Vol 1: 6874
Distinguished Service Awards
American Catholic Historical Society Vol. 1: 1458
American Psychiatric Association Vol 1: 3269
Canadian Image Processing and Pattern Recognition Society Vol 1: 6573
National Association of Elementary School Principals Vol 1: 12514
National Center for State Courts Vol 1: 12874
National Institute of Governmental Purchasing Vol 1: 13373
National Small-Bore Rifle Association Vol 2: 6487
Royal Society for the Prevention of Accidents Vol 2: 6925
University of Chicago - Medical and Biological Sciences Alumni Association Vol 1: 18255
Distinguished Service Citation Vol. 2: 6213
Distinguished Service Citation
Acoustical Society of America Vol. 1: 125
AIIM - The Enterprise Content Management Association Vol 1: 256
American Association of Physics Teachers Vol 1: 1247
American Society for Engineering Education Vol 1: 3644
Automotive Hall of Fame Vol 1: 5569
Ecological Society of America Vol 1: 8369
Lambda Kappa Sigma Vol 1: 11217
Pierre Fauchard Academy Vol 1: 15075
Distinguished Service Contributions Award Vol. 1: 16291
Distinguished Service Cross Vol. 2: 214
Distinguished Service Decorations Vol. 2: 214
Distinguished Service in Social Welfare Award Vol. 1: 14259
Distinguished Service Key Vol. 1: 14518
Distinguished Service Key and Certificate for Retiring Continuing Educators Vol. 1: 18212
Distinguished Service, Long Service Vol. 2: 341
Distinguished Service Medal
American Legion Vol. 1: 2634
Australian Honours Secretariat Vol 2: 214
Canadian Institute of Mining, Metallurgy, and Petroleum Vol 1: 6618
Committee on Space Research Vol 2: 1737
National Aeronautics and Space Administration Vol 1: 12197
Distinguished Service Order Vol. 2: 5592
Distinguished Service Star Vol. 1: 11164
Distinguished Service to Agriculture Award Vol. 1: 4034
Distinguished Service to Children Award
National Association of Elementary School Principals Vol. 1: 12514
Parents Without Partners Vol 1: 14856

Award Index

Distinguished Service to College Award Vol. 1: 5618
Distinguished Service to Education Award Vol. 1: 12514
Distinguished Service to Families Award Vol. 1: 13040
Distinguished Service to Health Education Award Vol. 1: 908
Distinguished Service to Powder Metallurgy Award Vol. 1: 11703
Distinguished Service to Rural Life Award Vol. 1: 15780
Distinguished Service to Safety Education Vol. 1: 15903
Distinguished Service to Science Education Award Vol. 1: 13682
Distinguished Service to the Cause of Liberal Religion Vol. 1: 17677
Distinguished Service to the Cause of Unitarian Universalism Vol. 1: 17677
Distinguished Service to the RV Industry Award Vol. 1: 15583
Distinguished Society Service Award Vol. 1: 10908
Distinguished Sonographer Teacher Award Vol. 1: 4023
Distinguished Student Contribution to the Society for the Psychological Study of Lesbian, Gay and Bisexual Issues Vol. 1: 3395
Distinguished Student Paper Awards Vol. 1: 14790
Distinguished Student Scholar Award Vol. 1: 15054
Distinguished Teacher Award
- American College of Physicians Vol. 1: 1713
- American Society of Animal Science Vol 1: 3887
- Canadian Cardiovascular Society Vol 1: 6377
- Heart Rhythm Association Vol 1: 9340

Distinguished Teaching Achievement Awards Vol. 1: 12969
Distinguished Teaching Award
- American Meat Science Association Vol. 1: 2737
- National Science Teachers Association Vol 1: 13683
- Ohio Academy of History Vol 1: 14459
- UCLA Alumni Association Vol 1: 17642

Distinguished Teaching Awards
- American Agricultural Economics Association Vol. 1: 777
- Kent State University Alumni Association Vol 1: 11129

Distinguished Teaching Contributions Award Vol. 1: 16292
Distinguished Teaching in Journalism Award Vol. 1: 16836
Distinguished Teaching of Art Award Vol. 1: 7505
Distinguished Teaching of Art History Award Vol. 1: 7506
Distinguished Technical Achievement Award Vol. 1: 16811
Distinguished Technology Educator Award Vol. 1: 10781
Distinguished Topical Philatelist Award Vol. 1: 4362
Distinguished Vanguard Awards for Leadership Vol. 1: 12837
Distinguished Visual Award Vol. 1: 14935
Distinguished Volunteer Award Vol. 2: 3716
Distinguished Woman Philosopher Award Vol. 1: 16476
Distinguished Women's Awards Vol. 1: 14410
Distinguished Writing Award Vol. 1: 14935
Distinguished Writing Award in Commentary/Column Writing Vol. 1: 4205
Distinguished Writing Award in Editorial Writing Vol. 1: 4206
Distinguished Writing Award in Local Watchdog Reporting Vol. 1: 4207
Distinguished Writing Award in Non-Deadline Writing Vol. 1: 4208
Distinguished Writing Awards Vol. 1: 14934
Distinguished Young Breeder Award Vol. 1: 11840
Distribution Executive of the Year Vol. 1: 6575
Distributor of the Year Award
- Canadian Booksellers Association Vol. 1: 6349
- Multi-Level Marketing International Association Vol 1: 12002
- National Association of the Remodeling Industry Vol 1: 12697

Distributor Web Award Vol. 1: 15387
District Award Vol. 1: 14849
District Award of Merit Vol. 1: 5907
District Bulletin Award Vol. 1: 7447
District Coach of the Year Vol. 1: 12910
District Distinguished Service Awards Vol. 1: 6619
District Proficiency Medals Vol. 1: 6620
District/Section Newsletter Award Vol. 1: 9944
Distringuished Lecturer Award Vol. 1: 9582
Ditson Conductor's Award; Alice M. Vol. 1: 7586
Dittus Award; Ray Vol. 1: 14300
Divine Award; Thomas F. Vol. 1: 4966
Division I Player of the Year Vol. 1: 12397
Division II Player of the Year Vol. 1: 12398
Division III Player of the Year Vol. 1: 12399
Division Leadership and Service Award Vol. 1: 17391
Division of Medicinal Chemistry Award Vol. 1: 1543
Division of the Year Vol. 1: 18033
Division Technical Awards Vol. 1: 17392
Divisional Achievement Award Vol. 1: 17201
Divisional Contribution Award Vol. 1: 930
Divisional Premium Vol. 2: 6146
Divisional PRO Rally of the Year Vol. 1: 17212
Divisional PRO Rally Program of the Year Vol. 1: 17212
Divisions Council Awards Vol. 1: 3208
Divisions Safety Professional of the Year Vol. 1: 4234
Dix Leadership Award; Marion Quin Vol. 1: 12264
Dixon Award; Russell A. Vol. 1: 1823
Dixon Medal; John W. Vol. 1: 5364
Dixon Trophy Vol. 2: 5910
DLS Haworth Press Distance Learning Librarian Conference Sponsorship Vol. 1: 5075
DMA Annual Award Vol. 1: 8043
DMA Awards, in Association with Royal Mail Vol. 2: 5738
DMA/Royal Mail Direct Marketing Awards Vol. 2: 5738
Doane Award; D. Howard Vol. 1: 4035
Dobbelsteyn Memorial Trophy; Ernest Vol. 1: 6426
Dobbins Award for Community Service; Bertha Vol. 2: 7408
Dobbs Award; Ella Victoria Vol. 1: 15055
Dobie-Paisano Writing Fellowships Vol. 1: 17477
Doblougska priset Vol. 2: 4652
Dobson Lecture Vol. 2: 3731
Dobson Memorial Award; The Eric Vol. 2: 6467
Dobzhansky Prize; Theodosius Vol. 1: 16458
Dock Award; Lavinia L. Vol. 1: 973
Dr. David Sackett Senior Investigator Award Vol. 1: 7002
Dr. Helen Creighton Lifetime Achievement Award Vol. 1: 8321
Dr. May K. Simon Memorial Scholarship Vol. 1: 5206
Doctoral Awards Vol. 1: 457
Doctoral Awards Program Vol. 1: 1315
Doctoral Dissertation Award
- Association for Computing Machinery Vol. 1: 4807
- Council of Supply Chain Management Professionals Vol 1: 7901

Doctoral Dissertation Competition Vol. 1: 546
Doctoral Dissertation Fellowship Vol. 1: 5076
Doctoral Dissertation Grants in Women's Studies Vol. 1: 18886
Doctoral Fellowship Vol. 1: 8147
Doctoral Scholarship Awards Vol. 1: 14977
Doctorate of Bananistry Medal Vol. 1: 10265
Doctorate of Food Service Medallion Vol. 1: 14262
Documentaries of the World Vol. 1: 11944
Dodd Award; M.E. Vol. 1: 5660
Dodge Award Vol. 1: 19071
Dodge Award; Harold F. Vol. 1: 5418
Doe Lectureship; Janet Vol. 1: 11657
Doehler Award; Herman H. Vol. 1: 14294
Doerfer Engineering Concept of the Year Award
- American Society of Agricultural and Biological Engineers Vol. 1: 3844
- American Society of Agricultural and Biological Engineers Vol 1: 3862

Dog of the Year Vol. 1: 1421
Dogramaci Family Health Foundation Fellowship and Prize; Ihsan Vol. 2: 4927
Dohrenwend Lecture in Social and Community Epidemiology; Barbara Vol. 1: 3373
Doisteau - Emile Blutet; Prix Paul Vol. 2: 1560
Dokuchaev Award Vol. 2: 6323
Dole Award; Gertrude Vol. 1: 9184
Dolezal Award; Eduard Vol. 2: 4973
Doll Award; Edgar A. Vol. 1: 3350
Dolphin Award Vol. 1: 7138
Dolphin Fellowship Vol. 1: 4432
Dolphin Medal Vol. 1: 4432
Domac Medal; Julije Vol. 2: 1225
Domac; Medalja Julije Vol. 2: 1225
Domestic Alpine Coach of the Year Vol. 1: 18093
Domtar Awards of the Chemical Institute of Canada for High School Chemistry Teachers Vol. 1: 7304
Domus Dei Vol. 1: 11240
Don Banks Composer Fellowship Vol. 2: 98
Donald Medal Vol. 2: 6092
Donald National Award for Issues of Importance to Women and Families; Diana Vol. 1: 3209

Donald Smiley Prize Vol. 1: 6819
Donaldson Award of Merit; Mary Vol. 1: 15847
Donaldson Gold Medal Vol. 2: 6934
Donath Medal Vol. 1: 9028
Donato; Premio Magda Vol. 2: 3431
Donato Prize; Magda Vol. 2: 3431
Donehoo Essay Award Vol. 1: 10129
Donne Essay Prize on the Anthropology of Art; J. B. Vol. 2: 6675
Donner Medal in Canadian Studies Vol. 1: 4790
Donohue Award; Mark Vol. 1: 17202
Donor of the Year - College Division Vol. 1: 12383
Donor of the Year - University Division Vol. 1: 12384
Donovan Award; Terence Vol. 2: 6872
Donovan Award; William J. Vol. 1: 14451
Donovan Individual Achievement Award; James D. Vol. 1: 3440
Donovan Memorial Exhibit Award; William Vol. 1: 2882
Doolitte Award; Arthur K. Vol. 1: 1544
Doolittle Award; James H. Vol. 1: 16669
d'Or; Prix Louis Vol. 2: 1098
Dorcus Award; Roy M. Vol. 1: 16195
Dornstein Memorial Creative Writing Contest for Young Adult Writers; David Vol. 1: 7483
Dorothea Award for Conservation Vol. 2: 5091
D'Orta Award; Augustine Vol. 1: 8435
Dorweiler Prize Vol. 1: 7129
Doswell Award; John P. "Jack" Vol. 1: 12825
Dott, Sr., Memorial Award; Robert H. Vol. 1: 1213
Doty Research Grant Vol. 1: 17539
Doublespeak Award Vol. 1: 13022
Dougherty Award; John L. Vol. 1: 4768
Douglas Award; Marjory Stoneman Vol. 1: 13531
Douglas Award; William O. Vol. 1: 16007
Douglas Gold Medal; James Vol. 1: 2525
Douglas International Fellowship; CFUW A. Vibert Vol. 2: 4803
Douglas Lecture; George Vol. 2: 7184
Douglas Memorial Medal; R. J. W. Vol. 1: 7014
Douglas Memorial Prize; Leigh Vol. 2: 5483
Douglas Memorial Scholarship; Tommy Vol. 1: 13878
Douglass Award; Frederick Vol. 1: 14199
Douglass Foundation Graduate Business Plan Competition Vol. 1: 5619
Douglass Prize; Jane Dempsey Vol. 1: 3911
Doupe Young Investigator's Award; Joe Vol. 1: 6926
Douthit Public Service Award; Richard Vol. 1: 2217
Dove Awards Vol. 1: 9139
Dove Medal Award; Allan B. Vol. 1: 18768
Dow Creativity Center Summer Residency Fellowships; Alden B. Vol. 1: 14416
Down Award; Vera Vol. 2: 5357
Downes Jr. Memorial Award; William E. Vol. 1: 348
Downes Memorial Trust; Oppenheim John Vol. 2: 6511
Downes Resident Research Award; John J. Vol. 1: 688
Downing Award; Antoinette Forrester Vol. 1: 16552
Downing Award; C. N. Vol. 1: 6951
Downing Award; Glenn Vol. 1: 6882
Downs Intellectual Freedom Award; Robert B. Vol. 1: 18294
Downs Travelling Scholarship Vol. 2: 7010
Downtown Achievement Awards Vol. 1: 10385
Doyle Award; William H. Vol. 1: 2477
Dozier Travel Grant; Otis and Velma Davis Vol. 1: 8026
Dracup Scholarship Award; Joseph F. Vol. 1: 905
Draddy Trophy Vol. 1: 13215
Drake Memorial Award; Howard Vol. 2: 5995
Drama Desk Awards Vol. 1: 8274
Drama in Education Vol. 1: 5052
Drama League's Delia Austrian Medal for Distinguished Performance Vol. 1: 8277
Draper Medal; Henry Vol. 1: 12158
Draper Memorial Medal Vol. 2: 4185
Draper Prize; Charles Stark Vol. 1: 12127
The fDrawn to Artv Fellowship Vol. 1: 819
Dream Garden Awards Vol. 1: 17330
Dreammaker Award; Regal Cinemas Vol. 1: 12080
Drechsel Award; Helmet E. Vol. 1: 3530
Dreher Memorial Award; Raymond H. Vol. 1: 10048
Drench Fellowship; Rose and Isidore Vol. 1: 19060
Drenckhahn Scholarship Award; Vivian Vol. 1: 16395
Dresel Student Award; Peter Vol. 1: 14969
Dressage Achievement Awards Vol. 1: 14508
Drewes Scholarship; Tom and Roberta Vol. 1: 2654
Drexel Award; St. Katharine Vol. 1: 7159
Drexel Medal; Lucy Wharton Vol. 1: 18336
Dreyer Award in Applied Economic Geology; Robert M. Vol. 1: 16345
DRI Community Service Award Vol. 1: 8130
DRI Law Firm Diversity Award Vol. 1: 8131
Drilling and Completions Award Vol. 1: 16797
Drilling Engineering Award Vol. 1: 16797
Drinov Medal; Marin Vol. 2: 1143
Driscoll Fellowship; Governor Alfred E. Vol. 1: 14084
Driscoll Prize; Alfred E. Vol. 1: 14084
Driver Award; Captain William Vol. 1: 14354
Driver of the Year
Austin Ten Drivers Club Ltd. Vol. 2: 5156
Private Motor Truck Council of Canada Vol 1: 15242
Sportscar Vintage Racing Association Vol 1: 17232
Driver of the Year Award
American Trucking Associations - Safety Management Council Vol. 1: 4373
Guild of Motoring Writers Vol 2: 5953
Drivers World Champions Vol. 1: 2318
Dromkeen Librarian's Award Vol. 2: 432
Dromkeen Medal Vol. 2: 433
Drossos Award Vol. 1: 3069
Droste Hulshoff Preis; Annette von Vol. 2: 2349
Drotman Memorial Award; Jay S. Vol. 1: 3432
Drouin; Prix Edmond Vol. 2: 1511
Drum Memorial Scholarship Award; Douglas R. Vol. 1: 2786
Drummond-Jackson Prize Vol. 2: 7116
Dryburgh Memorial Trophy; Dave Vol. 1: 6505
Dryden Lectureship in Research Vol. 1: 2374
Dryden Translation Competition; John Vol. 2: 5283
Dryerre Prize Lectureship; Henry Vol. 2: 6993
Du Bois-Mandela-Rodney Fellowship Vol. 1: 7190
Du Perron-Prijs; E. Vol. 2: 3677
du Pont Trophy; Richard C. Vol. 1: 16107
du Pre Fellowship; Jacqueline Vol. 2: 6445
du Teil; Prix Joseph Vol. 2: 1652
Dublin Award; Louis I. Vol. 1: 1294
Dublin Horse Show Vol. 2: 2876
Dubner Research Prize; Ronald Vol. 1: 10119
Duboff Award; Samuel J. Vol. 1: 8926
Dubois Award; Mark Vol. 1: 8916
DuBois Career of Distinguished Scholarship Award; W.E.B. Vol. 1: 4281
Dubois-Johnson-Frazier Award Vol. 1: 4282
Ducat Award Vol. 2: 1370
Duchalais; Prix Vol. 2: 1512
Ducks Unlimited Canada WetlandFs Appreciation Writing Award Vol. 1: 14755
Duckworth Award; Muriel Vol. 1: 6861
Ductile Iron Society Annual Award Vol. 1: 8286
Duddell Medal and Prize Vol. 2: 6059
Duddell Premium Vol. 2: 6146
Duden Preis der Stadt Mannheim; Konrad Vol. 2: 2389
Dudley Instruction Librarian Award; Miriam Vol. 1: 5077
Dudley Medal; Charles B. Vol. 1: 5419
Dudrick Research Scholar Award; Stanley J. Vol. 1: 3800
Duer Scholarship Award; A. O. Vol. 1: 12578
Duffy Award Vol. 1: 10478
Dufrenoy; Prix Jean Vol. 2: 1431
Dufresne Award; A.O. Vol. 1: 6621
Dufton Silver Medal Award Vol. 2: 5636
Duggan Medal; G. H. Vol. 1: 6952
Dugger Award; Robert B. Vol. 1: 2988
Duisberg-Gedachtnispreis; Carl- Vol. 2: 2164
Duisberg-Plakette; Carl- Vol. 2: 2165
Dujarric de la Riviere; Prix Rene Vol. 2: 1561
Duke and Duchess of York Prize in Photography Vol. 1: 6105
Duke Lifeline Earthquake Engineering Award; Charles Martin Vol. 1: 3931
Duke of Edinburgh Conservation Medal Vol. 2: 4943
Duke of Edinburgh Prize Vol. 2: 3213
Duke of Edinburgh Prize for the Japan Academy Vol. 2: 3213
Duke of Edinburgh's Designer's Prize Vol. 2: 5736
Duke of Westminster Medal for Military Literature Vol. 2: 7055
Dulac; Prix Vol. 2: 1653
Duly Award; Charles Vol. 2: 6036
Dumas Medal; Russell Vol. 2: 502
Dumbarton Oaks Fellowships Vol. 1: 8299
Dumesnil; Prix Rene Vol. 2: 1448
Dumfries Octocentenary Trophy Vol. 2: 7083
DuMont Citation; Allen B. Vol. 1: 15520
Dun and Bradstreet Award for Outstanding Service to Minority Business Communities Vol. 1: 2687
Dun & Bradstreet Public Librarian Support Award Vol. 1: 2688
Dunbar Award; Dr. Bonnie J. Vol. 1: 4645
Dunbar Medal; William Vol. 2: 2134

Award Index

Dunbar Memorial Award; Walter Vol. 1: 3258
Duncan Lawrie Dagger Vol. 2: 5710
Duncan Legacy Award; Todd Vol. 1: 13490
Duncan Media Award; Cameron Vol. 1: 15645
Duncan Prize Lectureship; Henry Vol. 2: 6994
Dunham Award for Excellence in Teaching; Meneve Vol. 1: 7459
Dunkin Award Vol. 2: 5468
Dunlap Kidney Fund; D.D. Vol. 1: 9164
Dunlap Lecture Award Vol. 1: 7305
Dunleavy Award Vol. 1: 14228
Dunlop Memorial Award; Jerry Vol. 1: 9252
Dunn Award for Excellence; James Clement Vol. 1: 17860
Dunn Award; Gano Vol. 1: 7810
Dunning Award; H. A. B. Vol. 1: 3047
Dunning Prize in United States History; John H. Vol. 1: 2231
Dunsford Memorial Award; Ivor Vol. 1: 1007
Dunton Memorial Award; Loren Vol. 1: 10235
Duntov Mark of Excellence Award Vol. 1: 12951
Dupin; Prix Charles Vol. 2: 1654
DuPont Award; International Confederation for Thermal Analysis Vol. 2: 4205
DuPont Minorities in Engineering Award Vol. 1: 3645
Dupont; Prix Lucien Vol. 2: 1655
Dupont Prize; Octave Vol. 2: 1070
Dupree Prize for Research on Central Asia; Louis Vol. 1: 16129
Durand et Edouard Ordonneau; Prix Auguste Vol. 2: 1449
Durand Lectureship for Public Service Vol. 1: 2375
Durand; Prix Jacques Vol. 2: 1450
Durante Children's Fund; Jimmy Vol. 1: 9165
Durban International Film Festival Awards Vol. 2: 4164
Duseigneur; Prix Raoul Vol. 2: 1513
Dusmet World Championship Cup; Edith Oliver Vol. 1: 10495
Dussich Founder's Award; John J. P. Vol. 1: 13500
Dutch Cancer Society Press Award Vol. 2: 3505
Dutch International Vocal Competition - Hertogenbosch Vol. 2: 3508
Dutens; Prix Alfred Vol. 2: 1514
Dutens; Prix Joseph Vol. 2: 1656
Duthie Booksellers' Choice; Bill Vol. 1: 18659
Dutt Memorial Award; Raj Kristo Vol. 2: 2742
Dutton Award; Damien - Vol. 1: 8033
Duttweiler Prize; Gottlieb Vol. 2: 4763
Duvand; Prix Adrien Vol. 2: 1657
Duvernay; Prix Ludger- Vol. 1: 16136
D.W. Griffith Award Vol. 1: 8217
Dwiggins Award; William A. Vol. 1: 5844
Dwyer Scholarships; Peter Vol. 1: 6106
DX Award Vol. 1: 7941
DX Hall of Fame Vol. 1: 7942
DX Honor Roll Vol. 1: 7943
DYBWAD Humanitarian Award Vol. 1: 1341
Dyckman Award; Herbert P. Vol. 1: 1393
Dyer Aviation Education Award; Janice Marie Vol. 1: 5577
Dyer Award; Edward C. Vol. 1: 11509
Dykes Memorial Medal
American Iris Society Vol. 1: 2573
Median Iris Society Vol 1: 11641
Dymocks Aboriginal Torres Strait Islander Writers' Award Vol. 2: 589
Dymocks Arafura Short Story Award Vol. 2: 589
Dymocks Red Earth Poetry Award Vol. 2: 589
Dymond Public Service Award; J. R. Vol. 1: 14579
Dyrbye Mental Health Award; Marita Vol. 1: 6776
Dystel Prize for Multiple Sclerosis Research; John Vol. 1: 634
Dystel Prize; John Vol. 1: 13463
e-Appalachia Award for Outstanding Website Vol. 1: 4558
E. Benjamin Nelson Government Service Award Vol. 1: 9210
E-gre Vol. 1: 8363
E. H. Trophy Vol. 2: 6788
E. Mead Johnson Award for Research in Pediatrics Vol. 2: 4956
E-Talents Award Vol. 2: 2184
E3 Environmental Excellence in Exploration Award Vol. 1: 15395
EAAP Annual Meeting Awards Vol. 2: 3025
Eadie Medal; Thomas W. Vol. 1: 15758
Eagle Award
Council on International Nontheatrical Events Vol. 1: 7923
Eagle Forum Vol 1: 8305
National Association of State Workforce Agencies Vol 1: 12675
Eagle Hall of Fame Award Vol. 1: 9166
Eagle Scout Vol. 1: 5908
Eagle Scout Scholarship; Arthur M. and Berdena King Vol. 1: 13775
Eagle Star Award for Keyboard Vol. 2: 6853
Eagle Star Award for Strings Vol. 2: 6853
Eagle Trophy Vol. 1: 4646
Eagles Golden Eagle Fund Vol. 1: 9167
EAI Award Vol. 1: 3646
Earhart Medal; Amelia Vol. 1: 14243
Earl Daytona 500 Trophy; Harley J. Vol. 1: 8066
Earle Award; Wilton R. Vol. 1: 16259
Earle Trophy; Sir George Vol. 2: 6926
Early Achievement Award Vol. 1: 6791
Early Advocate of the Year Award; Joseph D. Vol. 1: 13334
Early Career Award Vol. 1: 16381
Early Career Awards Vol. 2: 336
Early Career Distinguished Scholar Award Vol. 1: 14337
Early Career Fellowship Vol. 1: 1813
Early Career Life Scientist Award Vol. 1: 3587
Early Career Teacher Grant Vol. 1: 7563
Early Leader Award Vol. 1: 12319
Early Music Brings History Alive Award Vol. 1: 8310
Early Scholar Award Vol. 1: 12320
Earn and Learn Scholarship Vol. 1: 8330
Earth Award Vol. 1: 5990
Earth Shelter and Architecture Merit Award Vol. 1: 4379
Earthcare Award Vol. 1: 16008
Earthwatch Film Award Vol. 1: 8312
EASA Exceptional Achievement and Service Award Vol. 1: 8420
East European Language Travel Grants Vol. 1: 16130
East Medal; L.R. Vol. 2: 503
Eastman Award Vol. 1: 12397
Eastman Kodak Gold Medal Award Vol. 1: 16744
Eaton Literary Awards Program Vol. 1: 8361
Eaton Memorial Trophy; Warren E. Vol. 1: 16108
Eavenson Award; Howard N. Vol. 1: 16346
EBEE Awards Vol. 1: 8497
Ebeling Fellowship; Christoph Daniel Vol. 1: 819
Ebenseer Bear Vol. 2: 780
Eberhardt Memorial Awards; Constance Vol. 1: 13490
Ebert Prize Vol. 1: 3048
Ebright Award for Outstanding Service; Harry E. Vol. 1: 1475
EBSCO ALA Conference Sponsorship Vol. 1: 2655
EBSCO Excellence in Small and/or Rural Public Library Service Award Vol. 1: 15421
EBSS Distinguished Education and Behavioral Science Librarian Award Vol. 1: 5078
Eby Memorial Award for the Art of Teaching; Harvey L. Vol. 1: 17642
ECAC-SIDA Media Award Vol. 1: 8347
Eccles Medal Vol. 1: 16947
Echeverria Prize; Aquileo J. Vol. 2: 1201
ECHO Awards; International Vol. 1: 8200
Ecke Jr. Commercial Award; Paul Vol. 1: 2288
Eckel Student Prize in Noise Control Vol. 1: 6144
Eckersberg Medal Vol. 2: 1325
Eckert - Mauchly Award Vol. 1: 9806
Eckhardt-Gramatte National Competition for the Performance of Canadian Music Vol. 1: 8363
Eckleberry Scholarship Award; Don Vol. 1: 16545
Eckler National Student Logistics Paper Award; H. James Vol. 1: 17334
Eckman Education Award; Donald P. Vol. 1: 10909
Eclipse Awards Vol. 1: 17532
Eclipse Awards for Media Vol. 1: 17533
ECMA Awards Vol. 1: 8460
Ecological Award Vol. 1: 12296
Ecological Section Best Student Presentation and Poster Awards Vol. 1: 5875
Ecology Institute Prize Vol. 2: 2301
Economic Inquiry Article Award Vol. 1: 18678
Economics and Evaluation Award Vol. 1: 16802
ECPA Christian Book Awards Vol. 1: 8546
ECPR PhD Prize Vol. 2: 5822
Ecroyd Award for Outstanding Teaching in Higher Education; Donald H. Vol. 1: 12922
ECTS Career Establishment Award Vol. 2: 5819
ECTS Young Investigator Awards Vol. 2: 5820
Ecumenical Leadership Award Vol. 1: 6391
Ecumenical Prize Vol. 2: 1092
Eda Award Vol. 2: 3320
Eddington Medal Vol. 2: 6687
Edeiken Memorial Kiteflier of the Year Award; Steven Vol. 1: 2615
Edeiken Trophy Vol. 1: 2615
Edelman Award for Achievement in Operations Research and Management Sciences; Franz Vol. 1: 9741
Edelstein Prize; Sidney Vol. 1: 16437
Eden Service Charles H. Hoens, Jr., Scholar Program Vol. 1: 5551

Eden Travelling Fellowship in Obstetrics and Gynaecology Vol. 2: 6705
Edenburn Trophy; Eddie Vol. 1: 17748
Edgars Vol. 1: 12055
Edgerton Award; Harold E. Vol. 1: 17132
Edgerton Civil Liberties Award; Henry W. Vol. 1: 1601
Edgerton-Lenker Memorial Youth Exhibit Award Vol. 1: 2883
Edholm Award; Otto Vol. 2: 5790
Edi Awards Vol. 1: 15361
Edib Adivar Scholarship; Halide Vol. 1: 17630
Edilia de Montequin Fellowship in Iberian and Latin American Architecture Vol. 1: 16557
Edinburgh International Film Festival Vol. 2: 5756
Edison Award Vol. 1: 8388
Edison Classical Music Award Vol. 2: 3510
Edison Medal Vol. 1: 9776
Edison Media Arts Consortium - Black Maria Film and Video Festival; Thomas A. Vol. 1: 8390
Edison Populair - Awards for Popular Music Vol. 2: 3511
Edison Popular Music Award Vol. 2: 3511
Edith Stevens Groundwater Hero Award Vol. 1: 9211
Editions Barenreiter, Basle & Kassel Prize Vol. 2: 4870
Editor of the Year Award Vol. 1: 6350
Editor-Publisher Award Vol. 1: 12585
Editorial and Design Award Vol. 1: 407
Editorial and Graphics Awards Vol. 1: 16757
Editorial Award
Canadian Intravenous Nurses Association Vol. 1: 6682
Institution of Incorporated Engineers Vol 2: 6177
Editorial Contest Awards Vol. 1: 17315
Editorial Excellence Award Vol. 1: 9721
Editorial Fellowship Program Vol. 2: 2925
Editor's Award Vol. 1: 10089
Editor's Editor of the Year Vol. 2: 5511
Editors' Editor of the Year Award Vol. 2: 5512
Editors of the Year Vol. 2: 5511
Edmonds Young Scholars Competition; S. Randolph Vol. 1: 5804
Edmonton Book Prize Vol. 1: 19007
EDRA Student Design Competition Vol. 1: 8500
Edstrom Medal Vol. 2: 1899
Education Achievement Award Vol. 1: 18126
Education and Training Vol. 2: 146
Education Award
Accounting and Finance Association of Australia and New Zealand Vol. 2: 29
Canadian Society for Clinical Pharmacology Vol 1: 6931
Education Award
American Association for Clinical Chemistry Vol. 1: 875
American College of Clinical Pharmacology Vol 1: 1630
American Institute of Chemical Engineers Vol 1: 2495
American Zoo and Aquarium Association Vol 1: 4495
Life Office Management Association Vol 1: 11354
New England Wild Flower Society Vol 1: 14071
Society of Forensic Toxicologists Vol 1: 16690
Society of Manufacturing Engineers - Composites Manufacturing Association Vol 1: 16711
Society of Toxicology Vol 1: 16873
Education Awards Vol. 1: 15593
Education Awards of Excellence Vol. 1: 9172
Education Council/GATF Individual Award Vol. 1: 9172
Education Excellence Award Vol. 1: 6294
Education Excellence Award Vol. 1: 13650
Education Fellowships Vol. 1: 8313
Educational Aids Blue Ribbon Awards Vol. 1: 3847
Educational Book of the Year Vol. 1: 5840
Educational Foundation Grants Vol. 2: 915
Educational Foundation Predoctoral Award Vol. 1: 5008
Educational Foundation Undergraduate Award Vol. 1: 5009
Educational Interiors Showcase Vol. 1: 3521
Educational Publications Award Vol. 2: 7066
Educational Research Award
Council of Scientific Society Presidents Vol. 1: 7895
Society of Forensic Toxicologists Vol 1: 16690
Educational Scholarship Award Vol. 1: 16784
Educational Scholarships Vol. 1: 13716
Educational Sponsorship Award Vol. 1: 12343
The Educational Support Scheme Vol. 2: 7109
Educational Television Awards Vol. 2: 7043
Educational Training Scholarship Vol. 1: 17141
Educator Award
Association of Government Accountants Vol. 1: 5179
Home Baking Association Vol 1: 9463
Minerals, Metals, and Materials Society Vol 1: 11804
Educator-Industry Award
International Association for Food Protection Vol. 1: 10078
International Association for Food Protection Vol 1: 10083
Educator of the Year
Ohio Middle School Association Vol. 1: 14476
Society of Broadcast Engineers Vol 1: 16610
Educator of the Year Award
American Woman's Society of Certified Public Accountants Vol. 1: 4489
East Texas Historical Association Vol 1: 8332
Professional Convention Management Association Vol 1: 15291
System Safety Society Vol 1: 17372
Edwards Award; Boothby - Vol. 1: 201
Edwards Award; Douglas Vol. 1: 15785
Edwards Award; Howard K. Vol. 1: 201
Edwards Award; Margaret A. Vol. 1: 19083
Edwards Industry Advancement Award; Harry H. Vol. 1: 15199
Edwards Memorial Award; Everett Eugene Vol. 1: 241
Edwards Prize; Alan Vol. 2: 7011
EEA - SHIP Award for Distinguished Service Vol. 1: 10782
Eeckhout Prize; Joris Vol. 2: 955
Eells Award for Program Excellence; Eleanor P. Vol. 1: 1436
EEMS Award Vol. 2: 1767
Effective Use of Retirement Award Vol. 1: 11142
Effectiveness Awards Vol. 2: 6074
Effie Awards Vol. 1: 8410
Efron Research Award; Daniel H. Vol. 1: 1681
Egan Memorial Trophy; Raymond Vol. 2: 2889
Egan Scholarhip Vol. 1: 14642
Egede Medaillen Vol. 2: 1331
Egede Medal Vol. 2: 1331
Egerton Gold Medal; Alfred C. Vol. 1: 7609
Eggins Award; Howard Vol. 2: 5385
Eggleston Award for Non-fiction; Wilfrid Vol. 1: 19006
Egleston Medal Vol. 1: 7575
Egoff Children's Prize; Sheila A. Vol. 1: 18660
Egyed Laszlo emlekerem Vol. 2: 2489
Egyed Medal; Laszlo Vol. 2: 2489
Egypt Exploration Society Centenary Studentship Vol. 2: 5758
EHA Clinical Research Grants Vol. 2: 3536
EHA-Jose Carreras Young Investigator Fellowship Program Vol. 2: 3537
EHA Research Fellowships Vol. 2: 3538
Ehninger Distinguished Rhetorical Scholar Award; Douglas W. Vol. 1: 12923
Ehrennadel der Deutschen Apotheker Vol. 2: 2060
Ehrenpreis des Osterreichischen Buchhandels Vol. 2: 760
Ehrlich; Lecon Paul Vol. 2: 1965
Ehrmann Cancer Fund; Eagles Art Vol. 1: 9168
Ehrnrooth Prize; Professor Magnus Vol. 2: 1398
EIA Awards for European Information Sources Vol. 2: 5835
EIA/European Sources Online Award Vol. 2: 5836
Eifler Award; Col. Carl Vol. 1: 13452
Eikenberry Voice Scholarships; Sara Vol. 1: 12000
Einbond Renku Competition; Bernard Lionel Vol. 1: 9235
Einhorn New Investigator Award Vol. 1: 16322
Einstein Award; Alfred Vol. 1: 2843
Einstein Award; Hans Albert Vol. 1: 3932
Einstein World Award of Science; Albert Vol. 2: 3460
Eisenberg National Award for Career Achievement in Medicine; John M. Vol. 1: 16692
Eisenhower Medal; Dwight D. Vol. 1: 8416
Eisenhower Medallion Vol. 1: 14958
Eisenhower Trophy Vol. 1: 10454
Eisenhower Trophy; Dwight D. Vol. 1: 13211
Eisenman Award; William Hunt Vol. 1: 4697
E.K. Tratman Award Vol. 2: 5275
Ekblad-Eldhs pris; Signe Vol. 2: 4653
Ekotopfilm Festival Vol. 2: 4440
El Angel Award Vol. 1: 5758
El Caballo de Trabajo Award Vol. 1: 17071
Elaine Dignan Award Vol. 2: 337
Elan Awards Vol. 1: 10290
Elaut Prize; Prof. Leon Vol. 2: 956
ELCINA Awards Vol. 2: 2531
Elder Grant Award; Dr. Marion Vol. 1: 6486

Award Index

Elder Medal; International Duke Vol. 1: 10413
Elder Statesman of Aviation Award Vol. 1: 12189
Eldredge Award; Bart Vol. 1: 14037
Eldredge Award; Marie H. Vol. 1: 3270
Eleazar and Rose Tartakow Levinson Prize; Samuel Vol. 1: 16438
Electro Solar Cup Vol. 2: 1882
Electrochimica Acta Gold Medal Vol. 2: 4840
Electronic Communication Award Vol. 1: 16009
Electronic Imaging Management Award Vol. 1: 257
Electronic Innovation Commendation Vol. 1: 7747
Electronic Warfare Squadron of the Year Vol. 1: 11520
Electronics Division Award Vol. 1: 1482
Elementary, Middle, and Secondary School Physical Education Teacher of the Year Vol. 1: 12362
Eli Lilly Fellowship in Infectious Diseases Vol. 1: 13257
Eli Lilly Women and Minority Travel Award Vol. 1: 17446
Eliav-Sartawi Awards for Middle East Journalism Vol. 1: 15953
Eliminations of Leukaemia Fund (ELF) Travelling and Training Fellowships Vol. 2: 5479
Elion Cancer Research Award; Gertrude Vol. 1: 861
Eliot II Scholarship; Charles Vol. 1: 11708
Eliot Leadership Award; Abigail Vol. 1: 5850
Elise Brook Trophy Vol. 2: 5347
Elizabeth N. Watrous Gold Medal Vol. 1: 12122
Elkes Research Award; Joel Vol. 1: 1682
The Ellen Vol. 1: 4721
The Ellery Lectureship Vol. 2: 65
Ellery Memorial Award; James H. Vol. 1: 2268
Ellinger-Gardonyi Award Vol. 2: 6503
Elliot-Drake Intermediate Chopin Scholarship; Janice Vol. 1: 15859
Elliot Medal; Daniel Giraud Vol. 1: 12159
Elliott-Black Award Vol. 1: 1979
Elliott Community Leadership Award; Osborn Vol. 1: 7420
Elliott Distinguished Service Award; Henry W. Vol. 1: 3608
Elliott Memorial Award; Clarence Vol. 2: 5025
Elliott Memorial Award; John Vol. 1: 1008
Elliott Prize; Van Courtlandt Vol. 1: 11676
Ellis Award; Arthur Vol. 1: 7967
Ellis Award; Perry Vol. 1: 7885
Ellis Award; Wayne P. Vol. 1: 5420
Ellis Dissertation Award; John Tracy Vol. 1: 1453
Ellis/Henderson Outdoor Writing Award Vol. 1: 7875
Ellis Island Medals of Honor Vol. 1: 13125
Ellison-Cliffe Medal and Lecture Vol. 2: 7012
Ellison Memorial Prize; Ralph W. Vol. 1: 13443
Ellison Postdoctoral Fellowship in International Infectious Diseases Vol. 1: 13257
Elmer Award Vol. 1: 11643
Elmer Award; S. Lewis Vol. 1: 2146
Elmer Huff Award For Media Resources Vol. 1: 14591
ELong Distinguished Service Award; David Vol. 1: 17335
Elsdon-Dew Medal Vol. 2: 4218
Elsevier/LIRG Research Award Vol. 2: 6379
Elsevier Research Initiative Award Vol. 1: 2080
Elsevier Research Initiative Award Vol. 1: 8831
Elsey Award; George M. Vol. 1: 3468
Elson Award; Mildred Vol. 2: 7364
Elvehjem Award for Public Service in Nutrition; Conrad A. Vol. 1: 3788
Elver Mineral Economics Award; Robert Vol. 1: 6622
Ely *Human Factors* Article Award; Jerome H. Vol. 1: 9510
Ely Lecturer; Richard T. Vol. 1: 1937
EMA Foundation School/Business Partnership Award Vol. 1: 8449
Emberson Award; Richard M. Vol. 1: 9777
EMBO Medal Vol. 2: 2125
Emens Award for Support of a Free Student Press; John R. Vol. 1: 5634
Emera Priza for Jouranlism Excellence Vol. 1: 5509
Emera Prize for Journalism Excellence Vol. 1: 5507
Emergency Medical Services Exemplary Service Medal Vol. 1: 6084
Emergency Medical Technician Gold Medal Award Vol. 1: 18517
Emergency Services Medal Vol. 2: 215
Emerging Artist of the Year Vol. 1: 10270
Emerging Company Award Vol. 1: 4840
Emerging Jockey Vol. 1: 2817
Emerging Journalist Award Vol. 1: 12413
Emerging Scholars Award Vol. 1: 18370
Emeritus Award Vol. 1: 4959
Emeritus Awards Vol. 1: 6589
Emeritus Membership Vol. 2: 3252
Emeritus Membership Vol. 1: 11756
Emerson Award; Ralph Waldo Vol. 1: 14988
Emerson Medal; Charles Alvin Vol. 1: 18627
Emerson - Thoreau Medal Vol. 1: 552
Emil Memorial Award; Allan D. Vol. 2: 1880
Eminent Ecologist Vol. 1: 8370
Eminent Pharmacist Award Vol. 2: 2730
Eminent Scientist Award Vol. 2: 1886
Eminent Service Award Vol. 1: 652
Emirates AFI Awards (The Australian Film Awards) Vol. 2: 196
Emma Muuvi Awards Vol. 2: 1409
Emme Astronautical Literature Award; Eugene M. Vol. 1: 1346
Emmett Award in Fundamental Catalysis; Paul H. Vol. 1: 14273
Emmons Award Vol. 1: 5044
Emmy Awards Vol. 1: 12178
Emmy Awards; Daytime Vol. 1: 12177
Emmy Awards; News and Documentary Vol. 1: 12180
Emmy Awards; Public and Community Service Vol. 1: 12181
Emmy Awards; Sports Vol. 1: 12182
Emperess Elizabeth National Champion Vol. 1: 10626
Employee of the Year
Council for Health and Human Services Ministries, United Church of Christ Vol. 1: 7867
National Business and Disability Council Vol 1: 12815
Employer of the Month Award Vol. 1: 3905
Employer of the Year Vol. 1: 12816
Employer of the Year Award
American Society of Certified Engineering Technicians Vol. 1: 3906
AMVETS - American Veterans Vol 1: 4517
Blinded Veterans Association Vol 1: 5810
Employer Recognition Award
American Board for Occupational Health Nurses, Inc. Vol. 1: 1405
Canadian Nurses Association Vol 1: 6769
Employer's Award Vol. 2: 5422
EMS Award Vol. 1: 8503
EMS Media Award Vol. 2: 2121
EMT-Paramedic Emergency Medical Service of the Year Award (ALS Service of the Year Award) Vol. 1: 12517
EMT-Paramedic of the Year Award Vol. 1: 12523
Enajarvi-Haavio Award; Elsa Vol. 2: 1366
Encore Award Vol. 2: 7141
Encouragement Award Vol. 2: 4991
Endeavor Student Writing Award Vol. 1: 11338
Endowment Fund Vol. 1: 3518
Endurance Champion Rider Vol. 1: 2818
Energy and Environmental Design Award Vol. 1: 9618
Energy Fellowship Program Vol. 1: 11377
Energy Innovator Award Vol. 1: 3441
Energy Manager of the Year Award Vol. 2: 5762
Energy Research and Development Award Vol. 1: 6462
Energy Scholarship Award Vol. 1: 6587
Energy Systems Award Vol. 1: 2376
Enersen Award; Lawrence Vol. 1: 12253
Engel Award; Marian Vol. 1: 19025
Engelbart Best Paper Award; Douglas Vol. 1: 4830
Engelberger Awards; Joseph F. Vol. 1: 15689
Engelberger Robotics Awards; Joseph F. Vol. 1: 15689
Engelbrecht International Activities Service Award; Richard S. Vol. 1: 18628
Engell Prize; Hans-Jurgen Vol. 2: 4841
Engen Scholarship; Allan B. Vol. 1: 14380
Engestromska medaljen for tillampad naturvetenskap Vol. 2: 4625
Engholm Prize for Film Society of the Year Vol. 2: 5306
Engineer of the Year Vol. 1: 17373
Engineer of the Year Award
American Institute of Aeronautics and Astronautics Vol. 1: 2377
South African Institute of Electrical Engineers Vol 2: 4339
Engineering 2000 Awards Vol. 2: 504
Engineering Achievement Award
American Institute of Mining, Metallurgical, and Petroleum Engineers Vol. 1: 2530
Zimbabwe Institution of Engineers Vol 2: 7441
Engineering Achievement Awards
American Society of Agricultural and Biological Engineers Vol. 1: 3848
National Association of Broadcasters Vol 1: 12431
Engineering Achievement in Radio Vol. 1: 12431
Engineering Achievement in Television Vol. 1: 12431
Engineering and Construction Contracting Division Award Vol. 1: 2478
Engineering Award Vol. 1: 12431

Engineering Excellence Award Vol. 1: 7772
Engineering Excellence Awards
American Council of Engineering Companies Vol. 1: 1811
Optical Society of America Vol 1: 14605
Engineering Manager of the Year Award Vol. 1: 3686
Engineering Materials Achievement Award Vol. 1: 4698
Engineering Medal Vol. 1: 15307
Engineering Meetings Board Outstanding Oral Presentation Award Vol. 1: 16573
England Intermediate Hayden and Mozart Scholarship; Frances Vol. 1: 15860
Engleheart Cup Vol. 2: 6789
Engleman Award; Finis Vol. 2: 2459
Engler Gold Medal Vol. 2: 788
English Academy Medal Vol. 2: 4170
English Badminton Award Vol. 2: 5160
English Basket Ball Association Player of the Year (Men and Women) Vol. 2: 5773
English Foundation Grants Vol. 1: 17695
Engstrom Award; Victor Vol. 1: 15894
Enhancement of Animal Welfare Award Vol. 1: 16874
Enlisted Essay Contest Vol. 1: 18009
Enners Award; Lt. Raymond J. Vol. 1: 17964
Ennes Scholarship Vol. 1: 16611
Ennis Award; Peter Vol. 1: 6650
Ennor Manufacturing Technology Award; William T. Vol. 1: 4129
Ensemble Company of Cincinnati Opera (ECCO) Vol. 1: 7412
Enterprise Spirit Award Vol. 1: 11139
Enterprises Award of Merit Vol. 1: 52
Entertainer of the Year Vol. 1: 10270
Enthusiast of the Year Vol. 1: 13833
Entrepreneur Award Vol. 1: 10187
Entrepreneur of the Year Vol. 1: 18821
Entrepreneur of the Year
Ernst & Young LLP Vol. 1: 8530
International Franchise Association Vol 1: 10440
Entrepreneur of the Year Award Vol. 2: 4419
Entrepreneurial Success Award Vol. 1: 18116
Entry Films Competition Vol. 1: 5756
Environment, Agriculture, and Rural Development Award Vol. 2: 2666
Environment and Energy Achievement Awards Vol. 1: 2064
Environment, Health and Safety Award Vol. 1: 16800
Environment Medal Vol. 2: 7162
Environment Prize Vol. 2: 3371
Environmental Achievement Award
Association of New Jersey Environmental Commissions Vol. 1: 5266
Canadian Construction Association Vol 1: 6421
Canadian Golf Superintendents Association Vol 1: 6535
Environmental and Exercise Physiology Section Gatorade Young Investigator Award Vol. 1: 3169
Environmental and Safety Distinguished Achievement Award Vol. 1: 16800
Environmental Award
Institution of Professional Engineers New Zealand Vol. 2: 3732
International Hotel and Restaurant Association Vol 2: 1894
International Motorcycle Federation Vol 2: 4813
Sri Lanka Association for the Advancement of Science Vol 2: 4566
Environmental Awards Vol. 2: 6513
Environmental Conservation Distinguished Service Award Vol. 1: 2526
Environmental Education Award Vol. 1: 13120
Environmental Educator of the Year Vol. 1: 7311
Environmental Excellence Award Vol. 1: 7725
Environmental Improvement Awards Program Vol. 1: 15337
Environmental Merit Award for Leadership by a Non-Profit Organization Vol. 1: 8497
Environmental Quality Research Award Vol. 1: 3871
Environmental Science Award Vol. 1: 205
Environmental Stewardship Award Vol. 1: 3541
EOS Poster Award Vol. 2: 5840
EOS Research Grant Vol. 2: 5841
Eotvos Medal; Lorand Vol. 2: 2490
EPA Poster Prize Vol. 2: 5852
EPA Prize Vol. 2: 5853
Epilepsy Foundation of America Awards Vol. 1: 8507
Epilepsy Research Award for Outstanding Contributions to the Pharmacology of Antiepileptic Drugs Vol. 1: 3807
Epilepsy Research Awards Program Vol. 1: 1975
Episteme Award Vol. 1: 16048
EPSC Award Vol. 2: 5849
The Epstein Award Vol. 1: 3537
Epstein Foundation Awards; Norma Vol. 1: 18355
Equal Employment Opportunity Award
United States Department of Commerce - National Institute of Standards and Technology Vol. 1: 17801
United States Department of State Vol 1: 17861
Equal Employment Opportunity Awards Vol. 1: 17839
Equal Employment Opportunity Medal Vol. 1: 12198
Equal Justice Award Vol. 1: 12746
Equal Opportunity/Affirmative Action Exemplary Practices Award Vol. 1: 3815
Equal Opportunity Award Vol. 1: 11286
Equal Opportunity Day Award Vol. 1: 13882
Equality Award Vol. 1: 2656
Equipment Design Award Vol. 1: 13288
ERA Awards Vol. 1: 8429
Erasmus Medal Vol. 2: 4997
Erasmus Prijs Vol. 2: 3519
Erasmus Prize Vol. 2: 3519
Erdos Prize Vol. 2: 2912
Ergonomics Development Award Vol. 2: 3070
Ergonomics Society Lecturer Vol. 2: 5791
Ergonomics Society Special Award Vol. 2: 5792
The Ergonomics Society Student Prize Vol. 2: 5793
Ergonomics Society's Meritorious Service Award Vol. 2: 5794
Ericksen Award; Anna Mae Vol. 1: 15775
Erickson Award; Bonnie Vol. 1: 9389
Erickson Continuous Service Award; James K. Vol. 1: 53
Ericson's Award for Outstanding Doll Sculpture; Rolf Vol. 1: 8246
Ericsson Gold Medal; John Vol. 1: 4242
Erikson Early Career Award; Erik H. Vol. 1: 10739
Eriksson Prize; Jakob Vol. 2: 4592
Erikssons stipendium; Lydia och Herman Vol. 2: 4654
Ernest Hemingway Foundation Award Vol. 1: 14912
Ernst-Kuntze Prize Vol. 2: 2154
ERT Scholarship; Christopher J. Hoy/ Vol. 1: 2646
Erwin Memorial Trophy; Franklin Vol. 1: 18199
ESA Honorary Membership Vol. 1: 8485
ESA Recognition Award in Entomology Vol. 1: 8486
ESA Recognition Award in Insect Physiology, Biochemistry and Toxicology Vol. 1: 8487
ESA Student Activity Award Vol. 1: 8488
Esau Award; Katherine Vol. 1: 5876
ESB Clinical Biomechanics Award Vol. 2: 3035
ESB Research Award Vol. 2: 3037
ESB Student Award Vol. 2: 3036
Eschenbach Best EMJ Journal Paper Award; Ted Vol. 1: 3687
ESCMID Research Fellowships Vol. 2: 4713
ESCMID Turning the Tide of Resistance Research Grant Vol. 2: 4714
ESCMID Young Investigator Awards for Research in Clinical Microbiology and Infectious Diseases Vol. 2: 4715
ESCPB Grant for Young Scientists Vol. 2: 880
Eskow Scholarship; Seymour Vol. 1: 10543
ESOMAR Awards Vol. 2: 3521
ESPE-Hormone Research Prize Vol. 2: 5862
ESPE Young Investigator Award Vol. 2: 5863
Espenschade Award; Park W. Vol. 1: 9832
Espirito Santo Trophy Vol. 1: 10455
Espoir Person of the Year Vol. 1: 18464
Esposito Backbone Award; Bill Vol. 1: 7540
ESPY Awards Vol. 1: 8534
ESRA Award Vol. 1: 8557
ESRI Award for Best Scientific Paper in Geographic Information Systems Vol. 1: 4737
Essar Gold Medal Vol. 2: 2649
Essay Awards Vol. 1: 9735
Essay Competition
Islamic Research Foundation International Vol. 1: 10921
LEPRA Vol 2: 6366
Essay Contest Vol. 2: 3197
Essay Contest for College Students Vol. 1: 4502
Essay Contest for Professionals in Rehabilitation Vol. 1: 1772
Essay Prize Vol. 2: 5523
Essay Prizes and Research Fellowships Vol. 1: 11782
Essey Award; Shelia Vol. 1: 635
Essig Award; Otto Vol. 1: 18439
Esso Award Vol. 2: 505
Established Investigator Award
American Heart Association Vol. 1: 2176
National Alliance for Research on Schizophrenia and Depression Vol 1: 12231
Esterhazy Prize Vol. 2: 6407
Estes Memorial Pioneer Jujitsu Award; Bud Vol. 1: 486
Estes Prize; J. Worth Vol. 1: 963

Estlander Prize Vol. 2: 1359
Estrelicia Dourada Vol. 2: 4067
Estridge, Jr. Award; Capt. W. W. Vol. 1: 18205
Etancelin; Prix Leon-Alexandre Vol. 2: 1562
ET&C Best Student Paper Award Vol. 1: 16658
Eternal Light Medal Vol. 1: 11007
Ethical Humanist Award Vol. 1: 14157
Ethicon Foundation Fund Traveling Fellowship Vol. 2: 6715
Ethnic Minority Fellowships Awards Vol. 1: 931
Ethnic Minority Honorable Mention Awards Vol. 1: 932
ETR&D Young Scholar Award Vol. 1: 4871
ETS Award for Distinguished Service to Measurement Vol. 1: 8400
Etter Early Career Award; Margaret C. Vol. 1: 1857
Etter Student Travel Award Fund; Peggy Vol. 1: 1858
Ettl Grant; Alex J. Vol. 1: 13691
Ettlingen International Competition for Young Pianists Vol. 2: 2363
Etz Chaim (Tree of Life) Award Vol. 1: 13392
Eubank Services Award; Maj. Gen. Eugene L. Vol. 1: 14644
Eubanks Award; Jackie Vol. 1: 2699
Eugene Rogers Award Vol. 1: 18676
EURO Golden Medal Vol. 1: 10411
EuroBest Awards Vol. 2: 5803
EUROCALL Research Award Vol. 2: 2832
Europa Nostra Awards; European Union Prize for Cultural Heritage/ Vol. 2: 3524
Europaischer Chopin-Klavierwettbewerb Vol. 2: 2065
Europe Prize Vol. 2: 1755
European 1600 Cup for Autocross Vol. 2: 1882
European Association for Signal, Speech and Image Processing Awards Vol. 2: 4060
European Awards Vol. 1: 10359
European Baseball Championships Vol. 2: 858
European Baseball Cup Vol. 2: 859
European Bridge Champion Vol. 2: 3027
European Chopin Piano Competition Vol. 2: 2065
European Competitions Vol. 2: 3389
European Coordinating Committee for Artificial Intelligence Awards Vol. 2: 770
European Corrosion Medal Vol. 2: 2118
European Council of International Schools Awards Vol. 2: 5828
European Diploma of Protected Areas Vol. 2: 1756
European Disposables and Nonwovens Association Awards Vol. 2: 863
European Drag Racing Championship Vol. 2: 1882
European Figure Skating Championships Vol. 2: 4834
European Film Academy Short Film Award Vol. 2: 5756
European Grand Prix for Choral Singing Vol. 2: 1801
European Historic Rally Trophy Vol. 2: 1882
European Hotel Manager of the Year Vol. 2: 3031
European Juvenile Championships Vol. 2: 858
European Music and Poetry Competitions Vol. 2: 856
European Music Prize for Youth Vol. 2: 2132
European Nuclear Society Awards Vol. 2: 867
European Rhinologic Society Prizes Vol. 2: 1364
European Speed Skating Championships for Ladies and Men Vol. 2: 4834
European Sportsman and Sportswoman of the Year Vol. 2: 4583
European Surfing Championships - Open Champion Vol. 2: 5870
European Thyroid Association Awards Vol. 2: 1299
European Tour Order of Merit Vol. 2: 6567
European Trophy for Historic Sports Car Vol. 2: 1882
European Truck Racing Cup Vol. 2: 1882
European Union Contest for Young Scientists Vol. 1: 15927
European Union Prize for Cultural Heritage/ Europa Nostra Awards Vol. 2: 3524
European Urban and Regional Planning Achievement Awards Vol. 2: 5831
Eurosense Award Vol. 2: 6593
Euverard Innovation Award Vol. 1: 5421
Evans Award; John K. Vol. 1: 10074
Evans Biography Award Vol. 1: 11982
Evans Handcart Award Vol. 1: 11983
Evans Nonfiction Prize; Hubert Vol. 1: 18661
Evans Trophy; Edward S. Vol. 1: 16107
Evanshen Trophy; Terry Vol. 1: 6506
Eva's Choice Award Vol. 1: 8247
Events of the Year Vol. 1: 18460
Everett Award; Woody Vol. 1: 3647
Ewald Prize Vol. 2: 6321
Ewing Layman Award; James Vol. 1: 16854
Ewing Lecturer; James Vol. 1: 16855
Ewing Medal; James Alfred Vol. 2: 6109
Ewing Medal; Maurice
American Geophysical Union Vol. 1: 2112
Society of Exploration Geo-physicists Vol 1: 16677
Examination Prizes Vol. 1: 2146
EXCEL Awards Vol. 1: 16757
Excellence 200 Awards Vol. 1: 18024
Excellence Award
Society of Research Administrators Vol. 1: 16848
West African Examinations Council Vol 2: 2449
Excellence Awards
British Printing Industries Federation Vol. 2: 5420
Join Hands Day Vol 1: 11034
World Petroleum Council - The Global Forum for Oil and Gas Science, Technology, Economics and Management Vol 2: 7377
Excellence in Academic Libraries Award Vol. 1: 5079
Excellence in Advanced Practice Award Vol. 1: 16785
Excellence in Aerospace Education Vol. 2: 2522
Excellence in Aviation Education Award Vol. 1: 8982
Excellence in Biotherapy Nursing Award Vol. 1: 14537
Excellence in Breast Cancer Education Award Vol. 1: 14538
Excellence in Caring Practices Award Vol. 1: 1070
Excellence in Clinical Practice Award Vol. 1: 16786
Excellence in Communication Leadership (EXCEL) Award Vol. 1: 10151
Excellence in Communications Award Vol. 1: 9364
Excellence in Communications Awards Vol. 1: 12472
Excellence in Construction Awards Vol. 1: 4754
Excellence in Craft Awards Vol. 1: 14750
Excellence in Craft Competition Vol. 1: 14752
Excellence in Economic Reporting Vol. 1: 8922
Excellence in Education Award
National Association for College Admission Counseling Vol. 1: 12301
Society of Pediatric Nurses Vol 1: 16787
Excellence in Education Award
American Association of Critical-Care Nurses Vol. 1: 1071
American Society of Cytopathology Vol 1: 4015
Life Office Management Association Vol 1: 11355
Pi Lambda Theta Vol 1: 15056
Excellence in Education Awards Vol. 1: 8424
Excellence in Education Grant Vol. 2: 870
Excellence in EIFS Construction Vol. 1: 8412
Excellence in Emerging Technology Vol. 1: 6159
Excellence in Environmental Engineering Vol. 1: 574
Excellence in Extension Award
American Association of Family and Consumer Sciences Vol. 1: 1096
American Phytopathological Society Vol 1: 3190
Excellence in Financial Journalism Award Vol. 1: 14185
Excellence in Fisheries Education Award Vol. 1: 2029
Excellence in Fusion Engineering Awards Vol. 1: 8934
Excellence in Geophysical Education Award Vol. 1: 2113
Excellence in Government Leadership Award Vol. 1: 5180
Excellence in Highway Design Awards Vol. 1: 17880
Excellence in Hot-Dip Galvanizing Awards Vol. 1: 2077
Excellence in In-Plant Promotion Award Vol. 1: 10565
Excellence in Innovation Award Vol. 1: 6422
Excellence in Integrated Logistics Management Vol. 2: 5623
Excellence in Journalism Awards Vol. 1: 16865
Excellence in Landscape Awards Vol. 1: 4766
Excellence in Local Media Award Vol. 1: 13435
Excellence in Media Award Vol. 1: 1124
Excellence in Mentorship Awards Vol. 1: 3582
Excellence in Oncology Nursing Private Practice Award Vol. 1: 14539
Excellence in Patient Education Award Vol. 2: 871
Excellence in Patient/Public Education Award Vol. 1: 14540

Excellence in Pilot Training Award Vol. 1: 12227
Excellence in Practical Farming Award Vol. 2: 6664
Excellence in Practice Award Vol. 1: 1125
Excellence in Pre-College Physics Teaching Award Vol. 1: 1248
Excellence in Professional Journalism Award Vol. 1: 13754
Excellence in Programming Award
Resort and Commercial Recreation Association Vol. 1: 15635
Resort and Commercial Recreation Association Vol 1: 15640
Excellence in Public Service Award Vol. 1: 689
Excellence in Race Relations Trophy Vol. 1: 9518
Excellence in Radiation Therapy Nursing Award Vol. 1: 14541
Excellence in Research Award Vol. 1: 16788
Excellence in Research Award
The Crustacean Society Vol. 1: 7986
Resort and Commercial Recreation Association Vol 1: 15640
Excellence in Research Awards Vol. 1: 3013
Excellence in Research on Improving Policing For Women Award Vol. 2: 174
Excellence in Science and Technology Reporting Vol. 1: 6160
Excellence in Science Award Vol. 1: 8616
Excellence in Science Teaching Awards Vol. 1: 17490
Excellence in Software Awards Vol. 1: 16927
Excellence in Sports Journalism Award Vol. 1: 7241
Excellence in Supervision Award Vol. 1: 15405
Excellence in Swedish Design Prize Vol. 2: 4691
Excellence in Teaching Award
AACC International Vol. 1: 18
American Phytopathological Society Vol 1: 3191
Excellence in Teaching in Pediatrics Vol. 1: 4024
Excellence in Teaching Veterinary Parasitology Vol. 1: 18901
Excellence in the Use of Human Resources in Logistics Vol. 2: 5624
Excellence in the Use of Technology in Logistics Vol. 2: 5625
Excellence in the Use of Transport in Logisitcs Vol. 2: 5626
Excellence in Training Vol. 1: 5313
Excellence in Ultrasound Award Vol. 1: 6991
Excellence in Undergraduate Physics Teaching Award Vol. 1: 1249
Excellence in Undergraduate Teaching Award Vol. 1: 4576
Excellence of Poster Presentation Award Vol. 1: 16408
Excellence of Scholarship and Consistency of Contributions to the Oncology Nursing Literature Award Vol. 1: 14542
Excellent Nurse Manager Award Vol. 1: 1072
Excellent Paper Award Vol. 2: 3321
Excellent Swedish Design Prize Vol. 2: 4691
Exceptional Achievement Award
Baptist Communicators Association Vol. 1: 5661
Soaring Society of America Vol 1: 16109
Exceptional Achievement Medal Vol. 1: 12199
Exceptional Administrative Achievement Medal (EAAM) Vol. 1: 12200
Exceptional Bravery Medal Vol. 1: 12201
Exceptional Engineering Achievement Medal Vol. 1: 12202
Exceptional Media Merit Award Vol. 1: 13921
Exceptional Merit Awards Vol. 1: 2752
Exceptional Scientific Achievement Medal Vol. 1: 12203
Exceptional Service Vol. 1: 1925
Exceptional Service Vol. 1: 17925
Exceptional Service Award
Association of Specialized and Cooperative Library Agencies Vol. 1: 5340
Soaring Society of America Vol 1: 16110
Exceptional Service Medal Vol. 1: 12204
Exceptional Technology Achievement Medal (ETAM) Vol. 1: 12205
Executive Board Award Vol. 1: 12302
Executive Committee Award Vol. 1: 13031
Executive of the Year
Caucus for Television Producers, Writers and Directors Vol. 1: 7179
Federal Executive Institute Alumni Association Vol 1: 8607
National Basketball Association Vol 1: 12758
Paper Industry Management Association Vol 1: 14837
Private Motor Truck Council of Canada Vol 1: 15243
Executive Service Award Vol. 1: 602
Exemplar Award Vol. 1: 7693
Exemplary Offender Program Award Vol. 1: 1794
Exemplary Program Award Vol. 1: 18213
Exemplary Research in Social Studies Award Vol. 1: 12982
Exemplary Service Award Vol. 1: 374
Exemplary Service Award Vol. 1: 2884
Exemplary State and Local Awards Program Vol. 1: 12871
Exemplary Teaching Awards Vol. 1: 603
Exhibit Award Vol. 1: 4496
Exhibition of Photography Vol. 1: 15824
Exhibition of the Year Vol. 2: 4175
Exhibitor of the Year Vol. 2: 3708
Exhibitors' Choice Awards Vol. 1: 16100
Expedition Grant Vol. 2: 6442
Experiment Citation Vol. 1: 18950
Experimental Analysis of Behavior Dissertation Award Vol. 1: 3307
Experimental Pathologist-in-Training Award Vol. 1: 3754
Experimental Psychology Society Prize Vol. 2: 5875
Explorer of the Year Vol. 1: 8566
Explorers Medal Vol. 1: 8561
EXPO Juried Competition Vol. 1: 17145
Export and Trade Vol. 2: 147
Expository Writing Award Vol. 1: 9742
Express Ranches the Great American Cowboy Award Vol. 1: 13068
Extended Neuroscience Award Vol. 1: 639
Extended Research Award Vol. 1: 1840
Extension 2000 Award Vol. 1: 1096
Extension Award Vol. 1: 3888
Extension Division Educational Materials Award Vol. 1: 3721
Extension Forester of the Year Vol. 1: 8823
EXTRA! Awards Vol. 1: 16757
Extra Mile Award Vol. 1: 5815
Extraction and Processing Distinguished Lecturer Award Vol. 1: 11805
Extraction and Processing Science Award Vol. 1: 11806
Extraction and Processing Technology Award Vol. 1: 11807
Extractive Metallurgy Division Best Paper Award
Minerals, Metals, and Materials Society Vol. 1: 11806
Minerals, Metals, and Materials Society Vol 1: 11807
ExtraOrdinary Woman of the Year Award Vol. 1: 6311
ExxonMobil Solid State Chemistry Faculty Fellowship Vol. 1: 1545
Eyck Memorial Trophy; Jim Ten Vol. 1: 9995
Faber Award; John Vol. 1: 14761
Fabri Prize; Ralph Vol. 1: 12108
Fabulous Fashion Independents Vol. 1: 11995
Face in the Crowd Vol. 1: 17226
Faculty Career Development Award for Oncology of the Head and Neck Vol. 1: 1738
Faculty Design Award Vol. 1: 5100
Faculty Development Vol. 1: 4247
Faculty Excellence Award Vol. 1: 15313
Faculty Fellowship Award Vol. 1: 7642
Faculty Publication of the Year
American College of Managed Care Administrators Vol. 1: 1668
American College of Oncology Administrators Vol 1: 1697
Faculty Research Grants Vol. 1: 7349
Faculty Service Award Vol. 1: 18214
Fagley Award; Frederick L. Vol. 1: 7703
FAGO Prize Vol. 1: 2146
Failor Award; Clarence W. Vol. 1: 1846
Fain, Jr. Award; P. Kemp Vol. 1: 8697
Fair Award; Gordon Maskew Vol. 1: 575
Fair Play Award Vol. 2: 5774
Fair-Play Trophy Vol. 2: 2309
Fairall Award; The G. R. Vol. 2: 7431
Fairbank Prize; John K. Vol. 1: 2232
Fairchild Education Achievement Award; Gen. Muir S. Vol. 1: 14645
Fairless Award; Benjamin F. Vol. 1: 2527
Fairley Award for Editorial Excellence; Tom Vol. 1: 8392
Fairley Fellowships; Neil Hamilton Vol. 2: 571
Fairplay Award Vol. 2: 3403
Faith and Family Award Vol. 1: 18806
Falcon Golden Spike Award; George Vol. 1: 12629
Faligatter Distinguished Service Award; Florence Vol. 1: 15007
Fambro Student Paper Award; Daniel B. Vol. 1: 9945
Family History Writing Contest Award of Excellence Vol. 1: 13274
Family Life Award Vol. 2: 5881
Family Physician of the Year Vol. 1: 604
Family Practice Research Presentations Vol. 1: 605
Family Psychologist of the Year Vol. 1: 3331
Fankuchen Award; Isidor Vol. 1: 1859
Fann Memorial Challenge Trophy; J. W. Vol. 1: 13806
Fantus, M.D., Medal; Bernard Vol. 1: 1009
FAO-WAGGGS Nutrition Award Vol. 2: 7358

Faraday House Commemorative Prize Vol. 2: 6147
Faraday Lectureship Vol. 2: 6959
Faraday Medal Vol. 2: 6148
Faraday Prize; Michael Vol. 2: 6906
Farber Award; Rosalie Boyle/Norma Vol. 1: 14040
Farber First Book Award; Norma Vol. 1: 15128
Farkas Performance Scholarships Vol. 1: 10464
Farm and Ranch Management Award Vol. 1: 13956
Farm Broadcaster of the Year Vol. 1: 17365
Farm-City Award Vol. 1: 13127
Farmer *English Journal* Writing Award; Paul and Kate Vol. 1: 13023
Farmer International Business Dissertation Award; Richard N. Vol. 1: 102
Farnsworth Senior Player of the Year Award; Ted Vol. 1: 10000
Farnsworth Senior Player of the Year; Ted A. Vol. 1: 10001
Faro Trophy; R. Vale Vol. 1: 15067
Farquhar Award; Francis P. Vol. 1: 16010
Farquhar Mountaineering Award; Francis P. Vol. 1: 16010
Farr Silver Medal; Bertrand Vol. 1: 2208
Farradane Award; Jason Vol. 2: 7295
Farradine Award; Jason Vol. 2: 5620
Farrall Young Educator Award; A.W. Vol. 1: 3848
Farrel Memorial Scholarship; Kenley Vol. 1: 11735
Farrell Brownfields Project of the Year; James D.P. Vol. 1: 8497
Farrell Distinguished Teacher Award; Sister Miriam Joseph Vol. 1: 12863
Farrell Young Educator Award; A. W. Vol. 1: 3849
Farrer Memorial Medal Vol. 2: 444
Farrer Trophy Vol. 2: 6790
Farrington Award of Excellence; J. D. Vol. 1: 12518
Farrow Award Vol. 1: 7404
Fashion Color Award Vol. 2: 3230
Fashion Designer of the Year, MTO Vol. 2: 1385
Fashion Fiasco of the Year Vol. 1: 11996
Fashion Forward Awards Vol. 1: 2091
Father of the Year Vol. 1: 8595
Fatigue Achievement Award Vol. 1: 5422
Fauchard Gold Medal Vol. 1: 15076
Faucher; Prix Leon Vol. 2: 1658
Faulding Multimedia Award Vol. 2: 672
Faulkes Award; W. F. Vol. 1: 13606
Faulkner Award for Excellence in Writing; Virginia Vol. 1: 15190
Faulkner Award for Fiction; PEN/ Vol. 1: 14909
Faulkner Travel Award; D. John Vol. 1: 4213
Faulstich Grand Award; Edith M. Vol. 1: 15164
Faustus Poster Awards Vol. 2: 5806
Favorite Sports Athlete Vol. 1: 14233
Favorite TV Actor Vol. 1: 14233
Favorite TV Actress Vol. 1: 14233
Fawcett Chemical Health and Safety Award; Howard Vol. 1: 1546
FBI Honorary Medals Vol. 1: 17832
FBI Medal for Meritorious Achievement Vol. 1: 17832
FBI Medal of Valor Vol. 1: 17832
FBI Memorial Star Vol. 1: 17832
FBI Shield of Bravery Vol. 1: 17832
FBI Star Vol. 1: 17832
Feasibility Grants Vol. 1: 1917
Feature Article Award Vol. 1: 15220
Feature Photo Award Vol. 1: 14138
Feature Photography Award Vol. 1: 14761
Feature Stories Awards Vol. 1: 14139
Feature Video Award Vol. 1: 14140
Features Award Vol. 1: 9977
Fechner Award; Gustav Theodor Vol. 2: 2282
FECS Clinical Research Award Vol. 2: 884
FECS/EJC Award Vol. 2: 885
FECS-Pezcoller Recognition for Contribution to Oncology Vol. 2: 3115
Fed Cup Award of Excellence Vol. 2: 6306
Fedden Award; Sir Roy Vol. 2: 6638
Federal Achievement Award Vol. 1: 16382
Federal Credit Union of the Year Vol. 1: 12530
Federal Duck Stamp Contest Vol. 1: 17906
Federal Engineer of the Year Award Vol. 1: 13744
Federal Health Care Executive Special Achievement Award Vol. 1: 2305
Federal Legislative Service Award Vol. 1: 1841
Federal Migratory Bird Hunting and Conservation Stamp Contest Vol. 1: 17906
Federal Nursing Services Award Vol. 1: 5243
Federal Political Director of the Year Award Vol. 1: 7905
Federal Property Manager of the Year Vol. 1: 13581
Federal Statesman Vol. 1: 8840
Federation Leadership Award Vol. 1: 9670
Federation of British Artists Prizes and Awards Vol. 2: 7027
Fee Outstanding Young Engineer Award; Walter Vol. 1: 9819
Fein Prize; Ruth B. Vol. 1: 2594
Feinberg Award; Frederick L. Vol. 1: 2195
Feinbloom Award; William Vol. 1: 653
Feis Award for Nonacademically-Affiliated Historians; Herbert Vol. 1: 2233
Feis Award; Herbert Vol. 1: 2233
Feitelson Research Award; Dina Vol. 1: 10578
Feldbrill National Graduate Fellowship in Orchestral Conducting; Victor Vol. 1: 18349
Feldman Award; Dr. Harold Vol. 1: 13040
Feldman Award; Fellowship Award - Hillel Vol. 1: 3554
Feldman Memorial Exhibit Award; Aaron Vol. 1: 2885
Felipe Benavides Rose Bowl Vol. 2: 5343
Felix Awards, Artistic Vol. 1: 160
Felix Awards, Industrial Vol. 1: 161
Fell Pony Society Ridden Championship Vol. 2: 5893
Fell Student Award; Honor B. Vol. 1: 16260
Fellers Award; Carl R. Vol. 1: 9849
Fellow
AACE International Vol. 1: 21
American Ceramic Society Vol 1: 1476
American Meteorological Society Vol 1: 2777
American Society for Nutrition Vol 1: 3789
ASPRS - The Imaging and Geospatial Information Society Vol 1: 4738
Canadian Phytopathological Society Vol 1: 6814
Canadian Society for Civil Engineering Vol 1: 6914
Center for Advanced Study in the Behavioral Sciences Vol 1: 7188
Engineering Institute of Canada Vol 1: 8463
Institute of Environmental Sciences and Technology Vol 1: 9833
Philalethes Society Vol 1: 15012
Society for Advancement of Management Vol 1: 16154
Society for Information Display Vol 1: 16305
Society of Broadcast Engineers Vol 1: 16612
Soil Science Society of America Vol 1: 16936
SOLE, the International Society of Logistics Vol 1: 16948
Fellow Achievement Award Vol. 1: 690
Fellow Award
American Camellia Society Vol. 1: 1432
American Society of Animal Science Vol 1: 3889
American Society of Sanitary Engineering Vol 1: 4240
American Sportfishing Association Vol 1: 4298
Institute of Industrial Engineers Vol 1: 9862
Minerals, Metals, and Materials Society Vol 1: 11808
National Association for Interpretation Vol 1: 12346
Precast/Prestressed Concrete Institute Vol 1: 15200
Project Management Institute Vol 1: 15372
Resort and Commercial Recreation Association Vol 1: 15636
Society of Allied Weight Engineers Vol 1: 16483
Society of Wetland Scientists Vol 1: 16898
Soil and Water Conservation Society Vol 1: 16931
Standards Engineering Society Vol 1: 17245
Fellow Awards Vol. 1: 9306
Fellow Designation
American Association for Agricultural Education Vol. 1: 847
Illuminating Engineering Society of North America Vol 1: 9617
Fellow Grade Membership Vol. 1: 3648
Fellow Grade of Membership
Air and Waste Management Association Vol. 1: 265
Society of Automotive Engineers Vol 1: 16574
Society of Women Engineers Vol 1: 16914
Fellow Honor Vol. 1: 12484
Fellow if the AOAO Vol. 1: 3016
Fellow Member Vol. 1: 9927
Fellow Member Award Vol. 1: 4419
Fellow Membership Vol. 1: 7367
Fellow of ESA Vol. 1: 8489
Fellow of the Academy of Professional Reporters Vol. 1: 13063
Fellow of the American Academy of Somnology Vol. 1: 752
Fellow of the American Society of Agronomy Vol. 1: 3872
Fellow of The Athenaeum Vol. 1: 5489
Fellow of the Cranial Academy Award Vol. 1: 7950

Fellow of the Crop Science Society of America Vol. 1: 7976
Fellow of the CSME Vol. 1: 6953
Fellow of the Federation Vol. 1: 10421
Fellow of the Hymn Society Vol. 1: 9546
Fellow of the Institute Vol. 1: 6590
Fellow of the Metallurgical Society Vol. 1: 11808
Fellow of the National Genealogical Society Vol. 1: 13275
Fellow of the NZ Society of Soil Science Vol. 2: 3797
Fellow of the Phytopathological Society of Japan Vol. 2: 3311
Fellow of the Royal Academy of Dance Vol. 2: 6616
Fellow of the SID Vol. 1: 16306
Fellow of the Society
 Society of Plastics Engineers Vol. 1: 16827
 Southern African Society for Plant Pathology Vol 2: 4367
Fellow of the Society
 AVS Vol. 1: 5587
 National Speleological Society Vol 1: 13789
 Society of Nematologists Vol 1: 16772
Fellow of the Society Award Vol. 1: 10510
Fellow of the Special Libraries Association Vol. 1: 17074
Fellow or Foreign Honorary Member Vol. 1: 553
Fellow Quality of Life Researcher Award Vol. 1: 10676
Fellow Recognition Award Vol. 1: 10444
Fellow Scholar Award Vol. 1: 4070
Fellows and Honorary Members Vol. 1: 11658
Fellows Award
 Nature Saskatchewan Vol. 1: 13989
 Virginia Recreation and Park Society Vol 1: 18565
Fellow's Basic Research Award Vol. 1: 16370
Fellow's Clinical Research Award Vol. 1: 16371
Fellows Medal Vol. 1: 4098
Fellows' Medal Vol. 1: 6045
Fellows of the American Statistical Association Vol. 1: 4313
Fellows of the Association Vol. 1: 4292
Fellows of the Audiological Society of Australia Vol. 2: 74
Fellows of the Biophysical Society Vol. 1: 5777
Fellows of the Canadian Nuclear Society Vol. 1: 6761
Fellows of the Metallurgical Society of AIME Vol. 1: 11808
Fellows Program Award Vol. 1: 5330
Fellowship
 American Institute of Architects Vol. 1: 2427
 Augustan Society Vol 1: 5538
 Construction Specifications Institute Vol 1: 7748
 Creative Glass Center of America Vol 1: 7952
 Royal Institute of Navigation Vol 2: 6826
 Society for Imaging Science and Technology Vol 1: 16247
 Society for Industrial Microbiology Vol 1: 16299
 Tartans of Scotland Vol 2: 7251
Fellowship and Grant Award Program Vol. 1: 8168
Fellowship Award
 Canadian College of Teachers Vol. 1: 6400
 Indian Society of Soil Science Vol 2: 2758
Fellowship Award
 American Academy of Periodontology Vol. 1: 724
 Canadian Society of Animal Science - Agricultural Institute of Canada Vol 1: 6974
 Damon Runyon Cancer Research Foundation Vol 1: 8035
 World Atlatl Association Vol 1: 18906
Fellowship Awards Vol. 1: 6180
Fellowship Awards Vol. 2: 4966
Fellowship Awards of the Jane Coffin Childs Memorial Fund for Medical Research Vol. 1: 7357
Fellowship for Community Leaders Vol. 1: 7327
Fellowship for Japan-Related Research Vol. 2: 2433
Fellowship in Aviation History Vol. 1: 319
Fellowship in Clinical Pharmacology Vol. 1: 6932
Fellowship of the Australian College of Education Vol. 2: 157
Fellowship of the Australian Society of Archivists Vol. 2: 375
Fellowship of the City and Guilds of London Institute Vol. 2: 5657
Fellowship of the Institute of Australian Geographers Vol. 2: 476
Fellowship Program Vol. 1: 1327
Fellowship Scheme to Promote Commonwealth Understanding Vol. 2: 5680
Fellowships
 American Association of Oral and Maxillofacial Surgeons Vol. 1: 1194
 National Humanities Center Vol 1: 13363
Fellowships and Scholarships Vol. 2: 584
Fellowships for Creative and Performing Artists and Writers Vol. 1: 817
Fellowships in Arts and Crafts Vol. 2: 5681
Female Athlete of the Year
 Federation of Canadian Archers Vol. 1: 8623
 Sport Canada Vol 1: 17149
Female Vocalist of the Year Vol. 1: 10270
Feminist Activist Award Vol. 1: 16921
Feminist Lecturer Award Vol. 1: 16922
Feminist Theory and Gender Studies Graduate Student Paper Award Vol. 1: 10763
Femmy Vol. 1: 17657
Femoyer Trophy; Robert E. Vol. 1: 4646
FEMS European Materials Medal Vol. 2: 5885
FEMS Lecturer Award for Excellence in MSE Vol. 2: 5886
FEMS Materials Science and Technology Prize Vol. 2: 5887
Fence Project of the Year Vol. 1: 2012
Fenderbosch Leadership Award; Henry Vol. 1: 12698
Feneon; Prix Felix Vol. 2: 1805
Fenner Medal Vol. 2: 110
Fennia Prize Vol. 2: 1360
Fenno, Jr. Book Prize; Richard F. Vol. 1: 3230
Fenton Medal Vol. 2: 6873
Fentress Memorial Award for Editorial Excellence; H. M. Vol. 1: 17463
Ferber Award for Consumer Research; Robert Vol. 1: 11047
Fereday Award; Rowland Vol. 2: 5854
Ferguson Award; Virginia Vol. 1: 16011
Ferguson Medal; Cedric K. Vol. 1: 16798
Ferguson Memorial Award; Elmer Vol. 1: 9450
Ferguson Memorial Scholarship; Jennica Vol. 1: 13191
Ferguson; Premio Massey Vol. 2: 5
Ferguson Prize; Wallace K. Vol. 1: 6558
Fergusson Excellence in Pediatric Oncology Nursing Education Award; Jean Vol. 1: 5283
Fermi Award; Enrico Vol. 1: 17823
Fern Award; Harold Vol. 2: 5038
Fern National Trophy; Harold Vol. 2: 5039
Fernanda Monti Award Vol. 2: 3686
Fernandez Award; USCU Vol. 1: 18200
Fernandez Trophy; Anthony Vol. 1: 18200
Fernbach Memorial Award; Sidney Vol. 1: 9807
Fernoy Memorial Prize; Ruth Vol. 2: 7259
Ferreira Award; Lil Vol. 1: 14797
Ferrier; Prix Gabriel Vol. 2: 1451
Ferris Bowl; William Vol. 2: 6535
Ferst Award; Monie A. Vol. 1: 16056
Feser Award; Leo Vol. 1: 9115
FESPP Award Vol. 2: 5889
Fessenden Award; Reginald Vol. 1: 16678
Fessenden Student Prize in Underwater Acoustics Vol. 1: 6145
Festival Awards for Literature Vol. 2: 672
Festival de Cine de Alcala de Henares Vol. 2: 4493
Festival de Cinema de Montagne Vol. 2: 4545
Festival dei Popoli Vol. 2: 3045
Festival du Court Metrage en Plein Air Vol. 2: 1790
Festival du Film Court de Villeurbanne Vol. 2: 1792
Festival du Film de l'Atlantique Vol. 1: 5505
Festival du Film d'Etudes Cinematographiques Vol. 2: 1930
Festival du Nouveau Cinema de Montreal Vol. 1: 11935
Festival Internacional de Cine de Bilbao Documental y Cortometraje Vol. 2: 4517
Festival Internacional de Cine Iberoamericano Vol. 2: 4503
Festival Internacional de Cine para la Juventud de Gijon Vol. 2: 4499
Festival Internacional de Cinema de Muntanya, Vila de Torello Vol. 2: 4545
Festival Internacional de Cinema do Porto - Fantasporto Vol. 2: 4058
Festival Internacional de Video de Canarias Vol. 2: 4477
Festival International de Diaporamas Vol. 2: 941
Festival International de Films de Femmes de Creteil et du Val de Marne Vol. 2: 1928
Festival International de Television de Monte Carlo Vol. 2: 3469
Festival International de Television Prague d'Or Vol. 2: 1256
Festival International du Cinema d'Animation Annecy Vol. 2: 1870
Festival International du Court Metrage de Clermont-Ferrand Vol. 2: 1947
Festival International du Film Alpin et de l'Environement de Montagne, Les Diablerets, Suisse Vol. 2: 4805

Festival International du Film, Cannes Vol. 2: 1730
Festival International du Film d'Amiens Vol. 2: 1710
Festival International du Film de Berlin Vol. 2: 2048
Festival International du Film Ethnographique et Sociologique Cinema du Reel Vol. 2: 1732
Festival International du Film Fantastique, de Science-Fiction, et Thriller de Bruxelles Vol. 2: 850
Festival International du film Maritime et d'Exploration Vol. 2: 1890
Festival International du Film sur l'Art Montreal Vol. 1: 10424
Festival Internationl du Film d'Aventure de la Plagne Vol. 2: 1846
Festival Internazionale Cinema Giovani Vol. 2: 3009
Festival Internazionale de Film Locarno Vol. 2: 4864
Festival Internazionale di Danza Modern-Jazz Vol. 2: 2981
Festival Mondial de l'Image Sous-Marine Vol. 2: 1799
Festival National du Court Metrage de Clermont-Ferrand Vol. 2: 1948
Festival of American Community Theatre Vol. 1: 1059
Festival of Community Theatre Vol. 2: 3805
Festival of the Americas Vol. 1: 18993
Festival of Underwater Images Vol. 2: 1799
Festival Panafrican du Cinema de Ouagadougou et de la Television de Ouagadougou Vol. 2: 1160
Fetch Award; Tom Vol. 1: 14798
Feuth Award; The Mimi Vol. 1: 14863
Fevre Memorial Prize; R.J.W. Le Vol. 2: 111
FHA Culinary Challenge Vol. 2: 4430
FHA International Salon Culnaire Vol. 2: 4430
FIA Intercontinental Formula 3 Cup Vol. 2: 1882
FIA Marathon Trophy Vol. 2: 1882
FIA World Cup for Cross Country Rallies Vol. 2: 1882
FIAP Medals Vol. 1: 9186
FICC Prize Vol. 2: 2316
Fiction Award
Black Caucus of the American Library Association Vol. 1: 5795
River City Vol 1: 15676
Fiction Book of the Year Award Vol. 1: 6351
Fiction Contest Vol. 1: 19017
FIDE Master Vol. 2: 2476
Fidelitas Medal Vol. 1: 14635
Field and Joe L. Franklin Award for Outstanding Achievement in Mass Spectrometry; Frank H. Vol. 1: 1547
Field Award; Carolyn W. Vol. 1: 14927
Field Award; Crosby Vol. 1: 4055
Field Awards Vol. 1: 16949
Field Maintenance Award Vol. 1: 1382
Fieldes Memorial Award; Morice Vol. 2: 3798
Fieldgate Trophy; Norm Vol. 1: 6507
Fields Medal Vol. 1: 10506
Fieldwork Award Vol. 2: 5092
Fies Award; John Vol. 1: 10335
FIFA Five-a-Side (Indoor Football) World Championship Vol. 2: 4752
FIFA Futsal (Indoor Football) World Championship Vol. 2: 4752
FIFA U-17 World Championship Vol. 2: 4753
FIFA U-17 World Tournament Vol. 2: 4753
FIFA Women's World Cup Vol. 2: 4754
FIFA World Cup Trophy Vol. 2: 4755
Fife Memorial Award; Mary Perry Vol. 1: 13731
FiFi Awards Vol. 1: 8854
Fifth Sense Commendation Vol. 1: 8853
Fifty Books of the Year Vol. 1: 2515
Fifty-Year Award Vol. 1: 8677
Fifty Year Club Vol. 1: 6623
Fifty Year Club Member Certificate Vol. 1: 2886
Fifty Year Membership Medal and Pin Vol. 1: 2887
Fight for Liberation of Bulgaria Medal Vol. 1: 6007
Fighter of the Year Award Vol. 1: 10823
Figueroa Nogueron Prize; Gilberto Vol. 2: 3445
Filene Travel Award; Adele Vol. 1: 7836
Filipovic Award; Ivan Vol. 2: 1239
Filley Memorial Awards for Excellence in Respiratory Physiology and Medicine; Giles F. Vol. 1: 3170
Film Award for the Best Commercial Film Vol. 1: 4530
Film Festival Awards Vol. 1: 4530
Film Grants Vol. 1: 15226
Film Society of the Year Awards Vol. 2: 5306
Filmmakers Showcase Award Vol. 1: 121
Filtration Society Gold Medal Vol. 2: 5900
FIM Fair Play Trophy Vol. 2: 4814
FINA Prize Vol. 2: 4759
FINA Prize Eminence Vol. 2: 4759
Financial Assistance Fund for Settlement of International Disputes Vol. 2: 3638
Financial Executive of the Year Vol. 1: 9908
Financial Management Improvement Award Vol. 1: 8998
Financial Planner of the Year Vol. 1: 12607
Financial Post Awards for Business in the Arts Vol. 1: 7847
Finch Law Day Speech Award; Judge Edward R. Vol. 1: 1374
Finch Speech Award; Judge Vol. 1: 1375
Finders Award Vol. 2: 5223
Findlay Plaque Vol. 1: 9253
Fine Art Award Vol. 1: 13834
Fine Arts Award Vol. 1: 7256
Fine Arts Work Center Fellowships Vol. 1: 8699
Fine Dining Hall of Fame Vol. 1: 13964
Fine Memorial Student Loans; Ruth Vol. 1: 8232
Fine Printing Awards Vol. 1: 10566
Finegan Standards Medal Vol. 1: 2852
Fink Prize Award; Donald G. Vol. 1: 9778
Finkelstein Award Vol. 1: 7969
Finlaison Medal Vol. 2: 5990
Finlandia Award Vol. 1: 18094
Finlandspriset Vol. 2: 4655
Finlay Prize; Carlos J. Vol. 2: 1991
Finley Award; John H. Vol. 1: 454
Finn Gold Cup Vol. 2: 1892
Finneburgh Sr. Award of Excellence; M. L. Vol. 1: 13098
Finocchiaro Award for Excellence in the Development of Pedagogical Materials; Mary Vol. 1: 17419
Finot; Prix Jean Vol. 2: 1659
FIP Fellowships Vol. 2: 3599
FIPRESCI Diploma Vol. 2: 3999
FIPRESCI Prize Vol. 2: 2048
Fipresci Prize of the International Critics Vol. 1: 17559
The Fire Department of the Year Award Vol. 1: 12018
FIRE Excellence Award Vol. 1: 14543
The Fire Fighter of the Year Award Vol. 1: 12019
Fire Safety Award Vol. 2: 5115
Fireball Worlds Trophy Vol. 2: 5905
Fireman of the Year (Relief Pitcher) Vol. 1: 17169
Fireman Prize; Bert M. Vol. 1: 18684
First Amendment Defender Award Vol. 1: 9733
First Breeding Award Vol. 1: 10834
First Class Certificate Vol. 1: 2989
First Encounter Scholarship Vol. 1: 9736
First Families Award Vol. 1: 8920
First Families of Seneca County Gold Award Vol. 1: 14471
First Families of Seneca County Silver Award Vol. 1: 14472
First Films World Competition Vol. 1: 11944
First Novel Award
Mordechai Bernstein Literary Prizes Association Vol. 2: 2900
Black Caucus of the American Library Association Vol 1: 5795
First Place Award Vol. 1: 13732
First Poetry Book Award Vol. 2: 2901
First Professional Work Award Vol. 1: 14735
First Step Award Vol. 1: 4913
First Step Award - Wiley Professional Development Grant Vol. 1: 4913
First-Time Author of the Year Award Vol. 1: 6352
First-Time Exhibitor Award Vol. 1: 16100
First-Time Student Attendee Award Vol. 1: 606
Firth Essay Prize; J. B. Vol. 2: 5917
Fischer Environmental Award; Kermit Vol. 1: 10910
Fischer Gold Medal; Helen Field Vol. 1: 2209
Fischer-Medaille; Emil- Vol. 2: 2166
Fischer-Medaille; Hellmuth Vol. 2: 2261
Fischer Memorial Award; Donn Vol. 1: 2212
Fischer-Preis; Georg A. Vol. 2: 4897
Fischer Scholarship Vol. 1: 8170
Fischetti Editorial Cartoon Competition; John Vol. 1: 8709
Fischoff National Chamber Music Competition Vol. 1: 8711
Fish Aid to Advertising Education Award; James S. Vol. 1: 767
Fish Memorial Award; Robert L. Vol. 1: 12053
Fisher Article Award; Irving Vol. 1: 14515
Fisher Award; Elaine R. "Boots" Vol. 1: 8599
Fisher Award; Eunice Vol. 1: 2314
Fisher Award for Media Support of the Arts; John P. Vol. 1: 7850
Fisher Award; Henry Johnson Vol. 1: 11458
Fisher Award; Ming Vol. 1: 5345
Fisher Awards; Bill Vol. 1: 15445
Fisher Career Grants; Avery Vol. 1: 11363
Fisher Children's Book Award; Dorothy Canfield Vol. 1: 18498
Fisher Diagnostics/Fisher Healthcare Educational Scholarship Vol. 1: 13716
Fisher Distinguished Writing Award; M. K. Vol. 1: 10954
Fisher Graduate Student Paper Prize; Sydney N. Vol. 1: 17631

Fisher Lectureship; R. A. Vol. 1: 7621
Fisher Memorial Lectureship; Jeanne Mannery Vol. 1: 6988
Fisher Memorial Lectureship; R. A. Vol. 1: 9910
Fisher Memorial Prize; John
American Society for Aesthetics Vol. 1: 3558
Journal of Aesthetics and Art Criticism Vol 1: 11045
Fisher Prize; Avery Vol. 1: 11364
Fisher Prize in Environmental Law and Public Policy; Lillian S. Vol. 1: 18241
Fisher Resident Award; Alexander A. Vol. 1: 1783
Fisher Scientific Company Award for Applied and Environmental Microbiology Vol. 1: 3771
Fisher Scientific Lecture Award Vol. 1: 6902
F.I.S.I. Prize Vol. 2: 3136
FISITA Travelling Fellowship Vol. 2: 6251
Fisk Fiction Prize Vol. 1: 5854
FIT C. B. Nathhorst Translation Prize Vol. 1: 10418
FIT - Translation Prize Vol. 1: 10418
Fiterman Clinical Research Award Vol. 1: 2081
Fiterman Foundation Award for Excellence in Clinical Research; Miles and Shirley Vol. 1: 8832
Fiterman Foundation Basic Research Awards; Miles and Shirley Vol. 1: 8833
Fitness Inspiration Award Vol. 1: 9557
Fitness Instructor of the Year Vol. 1: 9558
Fitts Education Award; Paul M. Vol. 1: 9511
Fitz Award; Mr. Vol. 1: 13873
Fitzgerald Award; Aidan P. Vol. 2: 2852
Fitzgerald Award for Ecumenism; James Vol. 1: 12512
Fitzgerald Award; James Vol. 1: 12512
Fitzgerald Coke Medal; Major Edward D'Ewes Vol. 2: 5930
Fitzgerald Rookie of the Year; Jim Vol. 1: 17203
FitzPatrick Award for Youth Literature; Percy Vol. 2: 4171
FitzPatrick Prize; Percy Vol. 2: 4171
Five Million Dollar Hall of Fame Vol. 1: 13882
Five State Exhibition Vol. 1: 11088
Five-Year Research Support Program Vol. 1: 11437
Fixed Wing Award of Excellence Vol. 1: 5023
F.L. "Gus" Cooper Award for Meritorious Service Vol. 1: 9963
FLA Annual Awards Vol. 1: 8823
Flach; Prix Marcel Vol. 2: 1660
Flack Memorial Award; David Vol. 2: 5532
Flagg Multicultural Award; Ann Vol. 1: 795
Flaherty Documentary Award Vol. 2: 5217
Flaherty Memorial Lectureship; Mara Mogensen Vol. 1: 14544
FLAME (Fitness Leadership and Management Excellence) Awards Vol. 2: 5907
Flame of Courage Award Vol. 1: 7077
Flammarion; Plaquette du Centenaire de Camille Vol. 2: 1952
Flammarion; Prix Gabrielle et Camille Vol. 2: 1953
Flanagan Award; John C. Vol. 1: 16293
Flandrin/Michon Life Achievement Award Vol. 1: 2157
Flavelle Medal Vol. 1: 15759
Fleck Award; Norma Vol. 1: 6394
Fleck Prize; Ludwik Vol. 1: 16424
Fleet Environment Award Vol. 2: 81
Fleet Manager of the Year Vol. 2: 82
Fleet Perfect Record Award Vol. 1: 13656
Fleet Safety Award
American Trucking Associations - Safety Management Council Vol. 1: 4377
Australasian Fleet Managers Association Vol 2: 83
Specialized Carriers and Rigging Association Vol 1: 17101
Fleet Safety Contests Vol. 1: 13656
Fleet Safety Improvement Award Vol. 1: 17101
Fleet Safety/Safety Improvement Awards Vol. 1: 17095
Fleet Significant Improvement Award Vol. 1: 13656
Fleischmann International Trophy Competition Vol. 2: 2830
Fleischner Awards for Outstanding Contributions to the Field of LD; Jeannette E. Vol. 1: 6888
Fleming Award; Alexander Vol. 1: 9698
Fleming Award for Environmental Achievement; Charles Vol. 2: 3866
Fleming Award; John Adam Vol. 1: 2114
Fleming Award; Myrtle Butts Vol. 1: 5832
Fleming Lecture Vol. 2: 7097
Fleming Premium; Ambrose Vol. 2: 6146
Fleming Prize; Robert Vol. 1: 6107
Flemming Steel Dagger; The Ian Vol. 2: 5711
Fletcher Achievement Award; Stevenson W. Vol. 1: 10366
Fletcher Award; George Vol. 1: 6441
Fletcher Research Award; Eric Vol. 2: 7104
Fletcher Scholar Awards Vol. 1: 7081
Fleuroselect Gold Medal Vol. 2: 3545
Fleuroselect Quality Award Vol. 2: 3546
Fleury-Mesplet Literary Prize Vol. 1: 15813
Flexner Award for Distinguished Service to Medical Education; Abraham Vol. 1: 5036
Flight Achievement Award Vol. 1: 1347
Flight Nurse of the Year Award Vol. 1: 204
Flight Simulation Silver Medal Vol. 2: 6639
Flinders Medal and Lecture Vol. 2: 112
Flinn III Award; Edward A. Vol. 1: 2115
Flintoff Medal Vol. 2: 6960
Flipper trophies Vol. 2: 1799
Flock Guardian Award Vol. 1: 3542
Floor of the Year Award Vol. 1: 13929
Florey Medal; Merck Sharp and Dohme Vol. 2: 367
Floriculture Award Vol. 1: 8751
Floriculture Hall of Fame Vol. 1: 16503
Florida Artists Hall of Fame Vol. 1: 8731
Florida Arts Recognition Awards Vol. 1: 8732
Florida Citrus Sports Scholar-Athlete Award Vol. 1: 13215
Florida Folk Heritage Awards Vol. 1: 8761
Florida Space Coast Writers Conference Awards Vol. 1: 17064
Florida State Poets Association, Inc. Award Vol. 1: 13145
Florio Prize; John Vol. 2: 7131
Flory Polymer Education Award; Paul J. Vol. 1: 1548
Floyd Award; William Vol. 2: 5795
Flude Memorial Prize Vol. 2: 5330
Fluid and Plasmadynamics Award Vol. 1: 2378
Fluid Dynamics Award Vol. 1: 2378
Fluid Dynamics Prize Vol. 1: 3118
Fluidized Processes Recognition Award Vol. 1: 2479
Fluids Engineering Award Vol. 1: 4130
Fluke Corporation Award for Excellence in Laboratory Instruction Vol. 1: 3670
Fly Neighborly Award Vol. 1: 9361
Flying Fifteen World Championship Vol. 2: 5910
Flynn Humanitarian Award; Charles H. Vol. 1: 18192
Flynn Initiative for Peace Award; William J. Vol. 1: 12917
FNAC Award Vol. 2: 1948
FNGLA Hall of Fame Vol. 1: 8749
FOCAL Award Vol. 1: 11414
Focus Award Vol. 1: 12880
Focus Awards Vol. 1: 17570
Focus on Affordability Awards Vol. 1: 5985
Focus on Education Vol. 1: 8008
Focus on World Cinema Vol. 1: 11944
Foerderpreis der Werner-Sunkel-Stiftung Vol. 2: 2207
Foerster Memorial Lecture; Theodor Vol. 2: 2158
FOI Award Vol. 1: 10852
Foliage Hall of Fame Vol. 1: 8749
Folk Heritage Award Vol. 1: 14357
Folklife Museum of Trentino Prize Vol. 2: 3136
Follett School Librarian of the Year Award Vol. 1: 4600
Follo Upper Pennisula History Award; Charles Vol. 1: 9424
Foltz Award; Clara Shortridge Vol. 1: 13415
Folz Memorial Award Vol. 1: 12952
FON Achievement Certificates Vol. 1: 14583
FON Çonservation Award Vol. 1: 14581
FON Conservation Trophy Vol. 1: 14580
FON Distinguished Service Award Vol. 1: 14579
Fondation Andre-Romain Prevot Vol. 2: 1563
Fondation Chedanne Vol. 2: 1482
Fondation Daumet Vol. 2: 1482
Fondation de Caen Vol. 2: 1482
Fondation de Mme. Veuve Beule Vol. 2: 1482
Fondation Edmond Fagnan Vol. 2: 992
Fondation Ernest Mahaim Vol. 2: 993
Fondation Ernest Mahaim et Emile Waxweiler Vol. 2: 994
Fondation Gustave Clausse Vol. 2: 1482
Fondation Gustave Germain Vol. 2: 1482
Fondation Henri Pirenne Vol. 2: 995
Fondation Jean de Meyer Vol. 2: 1022
Fondation Jean Lebrun Vol. 2: 1023
Fondation Jean-Paul Alaux Vol. 2: 1482
Fondation Marmottan Vol. 2: 1482
Fondation Max Poll Vol. 2: 1024
Fondation Octave Dupont Vol. 2: 1025
Fondation Pinette Vol. 2: 1482
Fondation Redon Vol. 2: 1482
Fones Award; Alfred C. Vol. 1: 1906
Fontaine Trophy; Frank Vol. 1: 2276
Food & Hotel Asia Competition
National Restaurant Association Vol. 1: 13631
Society of German Cooks Vol 2: 2383
Food Engineering Award Vol. 1: 10215
The Food Industry CEO of the Year Award Vol. 1: 6591
Food, Pharmaceutical and Bioengineering Division Award in Chemical Engineering Vol. 1: 2480

Food Technology Industrial Achievement Award Vol. 1: 9850
Foodservice Operator of the Year Vol. 1: 10436
Foot in Mouth Award Vol. 2: 6539
Football Writer of the Year Vol. 2: 3403
Foote Award; Lucy B. Vol. 1: 11421
Footwear Fashion Future Award Vol. 2: 2225
FOP86 Scholarship Vol. 1: 8870
Foray Award; June Vol. 1: 10043
Forbes Award; Harriette Merrifield Vol. 1: 4891
Forbes Award; Malcolm Vol. 1: 14761
Forces for Nature Award Vol. 1: 13973
Ford Award; Lester R. Vol. 1: 11605
Ford Distinguished Fellow Award; Loretta C. Vol. 1: 12604
Ford Foundation Diversity Dissertation Fellowship Vol. 1: 13628
Ford Foundation Postdoctoral Diversity Fellowships Vol. 1: 13628
Ford Foundation Predoctoral Diversity Fellowship Vol. 1: 13628
Ford II Distinguished Award for Excellence in Automotive Engineering; Henry Vol. 1: 16575
Ford Prize for Distinguished Reporting on National Defense; Gerald R. Vol. 1: 8806
Ford Prize for Distinguished Reporting on the Presidency; Gerald R. Vol. 1: 8807
Forder Lectureship Vol. 2: 6400
Forderpreis Vol. 2: 2082
Forderpreis der ITG Vol. 2: 2273
Fordham Award for Cartobibliography; Sir George Vol. 2: 6763
Fordham-Stein Prize Vol. 1: 8809
Foreign Honorary Member Vol. 1: 1938
Foreign Language and Area Studies Fellowships Vol. 1: 18361
The Foreign Press Association British Media Award Vol. 2: 5915
Foreign Service Award Vol. 1: 17862
Foreign Service National of the Year Award Vol. 1: 17863
Foreign Service Office Management Specialist of the Year/Civil Service Secretary of the Year Vol. 1: 17864
Forensic Science Society Awards Vol. 2: 5917
Forensic Sciences Award Vol. 1: 5423
Forest Capital of Canada Award Vol. 1: 6520
Forest Landowner of the Year Vol. 1: 8823
Forest Products Division Award in Chemical Engineering Vol. 1: 2481
Forest Runes Award Vol. 1: 4677
Forest Stewardhip Award Vol. 1: 13320
Foresters' Ring Vol. 1: 6605
Forestry Program Accreditation Vol. 1: 16755
Forkosch Prize; Morris D. Vol. 1: 2234
Forman Award; Jonathan Vol. 1: 578
Formation Evaluation Award Vol. 1: 16799
Formula One World Champion Vol. 2: 1883
Forrest Medal; James Vol. 2: 6110
Forrestal III, Leadership Award for Professional Ethics and Standards of Investment Practice; Daniel J. Vol. 1: 7263
Forster Award; Eric Vol. 1: 9567
Forsyth Award; Rev. Charles Vol. 1: 7145
Fort Dodge Animal Health - Bovine Practitioner of the Year Award Vol. 1: 1025
Fortescue Fellowship; Charles LeGeyt Vol. 1: 9779
Forty Year Membership Pin Vol. 1: 2888
Foss Award; Hal Vol. 1: 12357
Foss Award; Joseph J. Vol. 1: 2049
Foster Award; Eugene S. Vol. 1: 2212
Foster Fellows Visiting Scholars Program; William C. Vol. 1: 17736
FosterGrant Reading Glasses Romantic Novel of the Year Vol. 2: 6605
Fouchet; Concours Max-Pol Vol. 2: 1724
Fould; Prix Louis Vol. 2: 1515
Fould-Stirbey; Prix Achille Vol. 2: 1452
Foulois Memorial Award; Maj. Gen. Benjamin D. Vol. 1: 14646
Foulon; Prix Vol. 2: 1564
Foundation Award Vol. 1: 10569
Foundation Award for Outstanding Achievement Vol. 1: 13420
Foundation for Research Science and Technology Science Communicator Awards Vol. 2: 3765
Foundation for the Promotion of Finnish Music Grants Vol. 2: 1403
Foundation Lectureship Award Vol. 2: 4098
Foundation Prize Awards Vol. 1: 2154
Founder Award Vol. 1: 4369
FounderFs Award Vol. 1: 11179
Founder's Award
Academy of Criminal Justice Sciences Vol. 1: 88
American Academy of Neurology Vol 1: 636
American Academy of Optometry Vol 1: 654
American Alliance for Theatre and Education Vol 1: 802
American Society for Gravitational and Space Biology Vol 1: 3712
Canadian Radiation Protection Association Vol 1: 6852
Civitan International Vol 1: 7448
Military Audiology Association Vol 1: 11764
Society of Architectural Historians Vol 1: 16553
Founders Award
American Academy of Pediatrics Vol. 1: 691
American Hockey Coaches Association Vol 1: 2255
American Statistical Association Vol 1: 4314
Business Committee for the Arts Vol 1: 6014
Canadian Association of Electroneurophysiology Technologists Vol 1: 6244
Canadian Society of Biblical Studies Vol 1: 6984
CIIT Centers for Health Research Vol 1: 7410
Confederate Memorial Literary Society Vol 1: 7669
Door and Hardware Institute Vol 1: 8257
Environmental and Conservation Organization Vol 1: 8495
Health Physics Society Vol 1: 9307
Indiana Black Expo Vol 1: 9662
International Council of the National Academy of Television Arts and Sciences Vol 1: 10363
National Academy of Engineering Vol 1: 12128
National Federation of State Poetry Societies Vol 1: 13146
Niagara University Vol 1: 14229
Society For Biomaterials Vol 1: 16184
Society of Environmental Toxicology and Chemistry Vol 1: 16659
Founders' Award Vol. 1: 8404
The Founders Award
Awards and Recognition Association Vol. 1: 5608
The Packard Club Vol 1: 14799
Founders Award for Academic Excellence for Leadership of Engineering and Technical Management for Undergraduate Programs Vol. 1: 3688
Founders Award for Best Student Chapter Vol. 1: 3689
Founder's Award for Humane Excellence Vol. 1: 3825
Founders Award for Outstanding Contributions to the Field of Chemical Engineering Vol. 1: 2482
Founders Award for Painting Vol. 1: 583
Founders' Award for Public Service Vol. 1: 5162
Founders Award for Sculpture Vol. 1: 584
Founders Awards
Biophysical Society Vol. 1: 5778
Sigma Theta Tau International Vol 1: 16049
Founder's Favorite Winner Award Vol. 1: 13524
Founders Funds Vol. 1: 6958
Founder's Lecture Vol. 2: 7163
FounderFs Medal Vol. 1: 16096
Founder's Medal
Association of Military Surgeons of the United States Vol. 1: 5244
Royal Geographical Society with the Institute of British Geographers Vol 2: 6767
Founders Medal
Institute of Electrical and Electronics Engineers Vol. 1: 9780
National Academy of Engineering Vol 1: 12128
SOLE, the International Society of Logistics Vol 1: 16950
Founders' Medal Vol. 2: 7121
Founders' Medal for Doctors' Degree Thesis Vol. 2: 4166
Founders' Medal for Masters' Degree Dissertation Vol. 2: 4167
FoundersF Memorial Award Vol. 1: 8490
Founders Memorial Lecture Vol. 1: 3019
Founders of Adolescent Health Award Vol. 1: 692
Founders of SIGNA Medal Vol. 1: 11641
Founders Prize Vol. 2: 6070
Founders' Prize Vol. 2: 5296
Fountain of Universal Peace Award Vol. 1: 10200
The Fountainhead Essay Contest Vol. 1: 5613
Four Seasons Critics Awards Vol. 1: 17559
Four Wheel Drive Puller of the Year Vol. 1: 13854
Four-Year College Biology Research/Teaching Award Vol. 1: 12407
Four-Year University and College Achievement Award Vol. 1: 10744
Fourmarier Prize; Paul Vol. 2: 1071
Fournier; Prix Rodolphe- Vol. 1: 15484
Fournier Prize; Pierre Vol. 2: 1750
Fourth Estate Award Vol. 1: 2635
Fowler Award; Jack Vol. 2: 876
Fowler Award; Raymond D. Vol. 1: 3318
Fox Award; Ruth Berrien Vol. 1: 14042

Fox Communications Award; Muriel Vol. 1: 11287
Fox Founder's Award; A. Roger Vol. 1: 12519
Fox Manuscript Prize; Dixon Ryan Vol. 1: 14181
Fox, M.D. Memorial Lectureship; Everett C. Vol. 1: 566
Fox Memorial Scholarship; Don Vol. 1: 355
Fox Memorial Scholarship; Terry Vol. 1: 13879
Fox Scholarship; Virgil Vol. 1: 2145
Fox Trophy; UFFA Vol. 2: 5910
Fox Young Investigator Award; Terry Vol. 1: 12845
The Foxy Vol. 1: 11287
Foy; Prix Percy W. Vol. 1: 8884
FPGA Scholarship Program Vol. 1: 8753
FPSA-FPEI Food Engineering Award Vol. 1: 3850
Fraenkel Prize Vol. 2: 7332
Fraenkel Prize in Contemporary History Vol. 2: 6020
Fragrance Foundation Recognition Awards (FiFi Awards) Vol. 1: 8854
Fraiberg Award; Selma Vol. 1: 11721
Francis New Medal Vol. 2: 6265
Franciscan International Award Vol. 1: 8858
Franck Design Prize; Kaj Vol. 2: 1361
Franck Organ Competition; Cesar Vol. 2: 3548
Franck Orgelconcours; Cesar Vol. 2: 3548
Francke Leadership Mentor Award; Gloria Niemeyer Vol. 1: 3049
Francken-prijs; Dr. Wijnaendts Vol. 2: 3668
Franco-British Landscape Gardening Award Vol. 2: 5921
Francois Golden Medal; Jules Vol. 1: 10414
Francou Legacy; Andre Vol. 1: 15730
Francqui Prize Vol. 2: 895
Frank Ashley Undergraduate Prize Vol. 2: 5517
Frank Award for Excellence in Personality Profiles; David Vol. 1: 2599
Frank Award; Josette Vol. 1: 7340
Frank Award; Morton Vol. 1: 14761
Frank Memorial Award and Lectureship; Sally Vol. 1: 1010
Frankel Prize; Charles Vol. 1: 13113
Frankland Fellowship; Sir Edward Vol. 2: 6961
Frankland Prize Lectureship; Sir Edward Vol. 2: 6962
Franklin Award; Ben Vol. 1: 7384
Franklin Award for Federal Excess Personal Property Vol. 1: 8702
Franklin Award for Outstanding Achievement in Mass Spectrometry; Frank H. Field and Joe L. Vol. 1: 1547
Franklin Award for State Fire Assistance Vol. 1: 8703
Franklin Award for Volunteer Fire Assistance Vol. 1: 8704
Franklin Award; John A. Vol. 1: 6524
Franklin Award; Rosalind Vol. 2: 6907
Franklin Awards; Benjamin Vol. 1: 15445
Franklin Fire Service Award for Valor; International Benjamin Vol. 1: 10207
Franklin Literary Award; Miles Vol. 2: 700
Franklin Medal; Benjamin Vol. 2: 6920
Franklin Medal for Distinguished Public Service; Benjamin Vol. 1: 3096
Franklin Medal; Ned Vol. 2: 6093
Franklin Medals; Benjamin Vol. 1: 8868
Franklin Mint Exhibit Award Vol. 1: 2868
Franklin Publication Prize; John Hope Vol. 1: 4327
Franklin Service Award; Jack Vol. 1: 18046
Franques Medal; Marti I. Vol. 2: 2119
Franz Liszt International Piano Competition - Mario Zanfi Prize Vol. 2: 2997
Franzmeier Memorial Award and Lectureship; Chapman- Vol. 1: 1011
Frary Award; Francis C. Vol. 1: 383
Fraser Award for Best Book of Translation; Soeurette Diehl Vol. 1: 17478
Fraser Award; Soeurette Diehl Vol. 1: 17478
Fraser Sculpture Award; James Earle Vol. 1: 13068
Fraternalist of the Year Award Vol. 1: 15752
Fraunces Tavern Museum Book Award Vol. 1: 16962
Fraunhofer Award/Robert M. Burley Prize; Joseph Vol. 1: 14606
The Fred H. Bossons Award Vol. 1: 15674
Fred Slater Trophy Vol. 2: 5348
Frederic Ives Medal Vol. 1: 14608
Frederick Award for Outstanding Soldier Vol. 1: 8707
Frederick Dwyer Prize; Allan Vol. 2: 318
Frederick Quality of Life Lectureship; Purdue Vol. 1: 14545
Free Market Award Vol. 2: 4180
Free Media Pioneer Vol. 2: 812
Free Spirit Award Vol. 1: 8874
Freedley Memorial Award; George Vol. 1: 17514
Freedman Foundation Traveling Scholarship for Emerging Artists Vol. 2: 567
Freedom Award
Indiana Black Expo Vol. 1: 9663
International Rescue Committee - USA Vol 1: 10611
Freedom Forum Playwriting Award Vol. 1: 11115
Freedom Leadership Medal Vol. 1: 8878
Freedom Medal Vol. 1: 8864
Freedom of the Human Spirit Award Vol. 1: 9551
Freedom Prize Vol. 2: 4868
Freedom Torch Award Vol. 1: 10650
Freeman Award; Joseph T. Vol. 1: 9058
Freeman Fellowship Vol. 1: 3933
Freeman Lectureship in Geriatrics Vol. 1: 9058
Freeman Memorial Grant-in-Aid; Don Vol. 1: 16626
Freeman Scholar Award Vol. 1: 4131
Freeman Writing Award; Ned E. Vol. 1: 1817
Freese Environmental Engineering Award and Lecture; Simon W. Vol. 1: 3934
Freestyle Coach of the Year Vol. 1: 18465
Freestyle Wrestler of the Year Vol. 1: 18466
Fregault; Prix Guy et Lilianne Vol. 1: 9728
Freiburg Ecological Film Festival Vol. 2: 2365
Freight Service Awards Vol. 2: 5336
Freiheitspreis Vol. 2: 4868
Freiman Award; Frank Vol. 1: 10732
French Association of Conchology Prize Vol. 2: 1799
French Medal; Sidney Vol. 2: 5400
French Tastemaker Awards; R. T. Vol. 1: 10953
Fresenius-Preis Vol. 2: 2167
Fresno-Madera Medical Society Scholarship Vol. 1: 8887
Freud Award; Sigmund Vol. 1: 4227
Freud-Preis; Sigmund- Vol. 2: 2145
Freudenthal Medal; Alfred M. Vol. 1: 3935
Freund Award; Clement J. Vol. 1: 3649
Freund Award; Professor Raphael Vol. 2: 2908
Freville; Prix Edmond Vol. 2: 1661
Frew National Leadership Award; Stephen A. Vol. 1: 12520
Freyssinet Award Vol. 2: 3733
Frick Award; Ford C. Vol. 1: 12750
Friedberg Memorial Lecture; Arthur L. Vol. 1: 1477
Friedenpreis des Deutschen Buchhandels Vol. 2: 2216
Friedenwald Award Vol. 1: 4954
Friedenwald Memorial Award Vol. 1: 4952
Friedenwald Memorial Award; Jonas S. Vol. 1: 4952
Friedlander Award; Sheldon K. Vol. 1: 841
Friedlander/Sunday Times Watercolour competition; Singer Vol. 2: 6523
Friedman Award Medal; Lee Max Vol. 1: 2595
Friedman Essay Contest; Milton Vol. 1: 4502
Friedman Medal; Sue Tyler Vol. 2: 5931
Friedman Professional Recognition Award; Edmund Vol. 1: 3936
Friedman Young Engineer Award for Professional Achievement; Edmund Vol. 1: 3937
Friel Memorial Lecture; Ernest Sheldon Vol. 2: 5842
Friend of Automotive History Award Vol. 1: 16600
Friend of Children Award Vol. 1: 14291
Friend of Conservation Award Vol. 1: 12473
Friend of ECPN Award Vol. 1: 16383
Friend of IT Vol. 2: 4426
Friend of Libraries U.S.A. Award (Friend of the Year) Vol. 1: 8902
Friend of Recreation Vol. 1: 921
Friend of the Academy Award Vol. 1: 77
Friend of the Florida Trail Award Vol. 1: 8771
Friend of the Industry Award Vol. 1: 372
Friend of the Legal Profession Award Vol. 1: 11151
Friend of the Maine Hospice Council Award Vol. 1: 11476
Friend of the Rottweiler Award Vol. 1: 3513
Friend of the Trail Award Vol. 1: 14671
Friend of the Year Vol. 1: 8902
Friends of Casco Bay Award Vol. 1: 8897
Friends of Libraries U.S.A. Award Vol. 1: 8901
Friends of Old-Time Radio Award Vol. 1: 8905
Friends of Scholastic Journalism Vol. 1: 11049
Friends of the Dallas Public Library Award Vol. 1: 17479
Friendship Trophy Vol. 2: 3688
Friesen Award; Henry Vol. 1: 6927
Friman Best of Show Award; Elmer Vol. 1: 9314
Frink Medal for British Zoologists Vol. 2: 7396
Fris Marine Air Command and Control Unit of the Year Award; Edward S. Vol. 1: 11510
Frisch Medal Award Vol. 1: 8375
Frishmuth Memorial Award; Harriet W. Vol. 1: 4653
Frits Sobels Award Vol. 2: 1767
Fritz Medal; John Vol. 1: 3938

Front Page Award Vol. 1: 9722
Front Page Awards Vol. 1: 18592
Front Prize; Theodore Vol. 1: 10031
Frontiers in Research Award Vol. 1: 5698
Frontiers of Science and Society - Rustum Roy Lecture Vol. 1: 1478
Frosst Prize; Merck Vol. 1: 6988
Frost & Conn Inc. Booth of Distinction Vol. 1: 7256
Frost Literary Award; Dr. Lawrence A. Vol. 1: 11386
The Frost Medal Vol. 1: 15129
Froude Medal; William Vol. 2: 6839
Froude Research Scholarship in Naval Architecture Vol. 2: 6840
Frumkin Memorial Medal Vol. 2: 4842
Fry Award; F. E. J. Vol. 1: 7032
Fry Award; F.E.J. Vol. 1: 7033
Fry Lecture Award; Glenn A. Vol. 1: 655
Fry Memorial Lecture; William J. Vol. 1: 2564
Fry Victim Service Practitioner Award; Margery Vol. 1: 13501
Fryxell Award for Interdisciplinary Research Vol. 1: 16160
FT/ARTS And Business Awards Vol. 2: 5068
Fuels and Petrochemicals Division Award Vol. 1: 2483
Fuentes Fiction Award; Carlos Vol. 1: 7571
Fuertes Award; Louis Agassiz Vol. 1: 18753
Fuji/Association of Photographers Assistants' Awards Vol. 2: 5149
Fuji Gold Medal Award Vol. 1: 16745
Fujihara Award Vol. 2: 3181
Fujita Research Achievement Award; T. Theodore Vol. 1: 13897
Fukumura Award; Roy T. Vol. 1: 2990
Fulbright Awards - American Program Vol. 2: 130
Fulbright Awards - Australian Program Vol. 2: 131
Fulkerson Prize Vol. 1: 11614
Full Community Inclusion Award Vol. 1: 1341
Fuller Award; Oliver Torry Vol. 1: 4941
Fuller Award; Solomon Carter Vol. 1: 3271
Fullerton Award; Jim Vol. 1: 2251
Fulling Award; Edmund H. Vol. 1: 16205
Fulltime Homemaker Award Vol. 1: 8306
Fullum Award; Ernest F. Vol. 1: 8288
Fulrath Award; Richard M. Vol. 1: 1479
Fulton Award Vol. 2: 4156
Fulton-Downer Award Vol. 2: 3734
Fund for Educational Research and Development Vol. 1: 10990
Fund for New American Plays Vol. 1: 11122
Fund for the Advancement of Social Studies Education (FASSE) Grant Vol. 1: 12983
Fund Raiser of the Year - College Division Vol. 1: 12385
Fund Raiser of the Year - University Division Vol. 1: 12386
Funderberg Scholar Award Vol. 1: 2082
Furkert Award Vol. 2: 3735
Furlong Grant; Miriam Fay Vol. 1: 431
Furness Consumer Media Service Award; Betty Vol. 1: 7778
Furniss Book Award; Edgar S. Vol. 1: 14480
Furon; Prix Raymond et Madeleine Vol. 2: 1834
Furtado Prize in Political Economy; Celso Vol. 2: 2954
Furuseth Award; Andrew Vol. 1: 17713
Futas Catalyst for Change Award; Elizabeth Vol. 1: 2657
Future Leader Awards Vol. 1: 10493
Future Science Teacher Awards Vol. 1: 6057
Futuristic Award Vol. 1: 13147
Futuristic Fiction Award Vol. 2: 3978
Fyan Public Library Research Grant; Loleta D. Vol. 1: 2658
Gabaldon Award; Arnoldo Vol. 2: 7423
Gabbay Award in Biotechnology and Medicine; Jacob Heskel Vol. 1: 15720
Gabor Award; Dennis Vol. 1: 17133
Gabor Medal Vol. 2: 6908
Gabriel Award Vol. 1: 7141
Gabriel Award for Personal Achievement Vol. 1: 7141
Gabriel Dissertation Prize; Ralph Henry Vol. 1: 4328
Gaede-Langmuir Award Vol. 1: 5588
Gagarin Gold Medal; Yuri A. Vol. 2: 4727
Gagne Award for Graduate Student Research in Instructional Design; Robert M. Vol. 1: 4872
Gagne Family Award Vol. 1: 17123
Gahan Scholarship or Development Grant; Muriel Vol. 2: 2877
Gaige Fund Award Vol. 1: 4076
Gakreski Award; Francis S. Vol. 1: 2050
GALA (Got a Lot Accomplished) Award Vol. 1: 6580
Galantiere Award; Lewis Vol. 1: 4364
Galathea Medaillen Vol. 2: 1332
Galathea Medal Vol. 2: 1332
Galatti Award for Outstanding Volunteer Service Vol. 1: 232
Galbraith Award Vol. 1: 7706
Gale Award for Excellence in Business Librarianship; Thomson Vol. 1: 2696
Gale Award for Excellence in Reference and Adult Library Services; Thomson Vol. 1: 2697
Gale/EMIERT Multicultural Award Vol. 1: 2644
Gale Group Financial Development Award Vol. 1: 2659
Gale Outstanding Trustee Conference Grant; ALTA/ Vol. 1: 4934
Galen Medal Vol. 2: 7389
Galey, Sr. Memorial Public Service Award; John T. Vol. 1: 2551
Galileo Galilei Award Vol. 2: 4514
Galkin Award; Harry Vol. 1: 10130
Gall Jr./CIO of the Year Award; John E. Vol. 1: 9326
Gallagher Award; Mike Vol. 1: 18095
Gallagher Award; William F. and Catherine T. Vol. 1: 2067
Gallagher Distinguished Service Award; Marian Gould Vol. 1: 1142
Gallant Prize for Non-Fiction; Mavis Vol. 1: 15493
Gallantry Decorations Vol. 2: 216
Gallatin Medal; Albert Vol. 1: 14192
Gallet; Prix Vol. 2: 1662
Gallo; Concorso Pianistico Internazionale Rina Sala Vol. 2: 2989
Gallo International Piano Competition; Rina Sala Vol. 2: 2989
Galloway Spacemodeling Service Award; H. Vol. 1: 12642
Galton Award; Sir Francis Vol. 2: 2283
Galva Arts Council Scholarship Vol. 1: 8946
Galvani Prize; Luigi Vol. 2: 4475
Galvin Scholarship Vol. 1: 8171
GAMA Learn to Fly Award for Excellence in Aviation Education Vol. 1: 8982
Gamble Award; Sam G. Vol. 2: 4974
Gamble Research Prize; Norman Vol. 2: 7013
Gamzu Prize; Dr. Haim Vol. 2: 2930
Gandhi Prize for Popularization of Science; Indira Vol. 2: 2684
Gans Distinguished Overseas Lectureship; Stephen L. Vol. 1: 693
Gantt Medal; Henry Laurence Vol. 1: 4132
Garant Awards; Serge Vol. 1: 16119
Garcia Health Service Award; Louis S. Vol. 1: 12459
Garcia Monge Prize; Joaquin Vol. 2: 1202
Garcia-Tunon Memorial Award in Human Dignity; Miguel Vol. 1: 1605
Gard Superior Citizen Volunteer Award; Robert E. Vol. 1: 1064
Gard Superior Volunteer Award; Robert E. Vol. 1: 1064
Garde Nationale Trophy Vol. 1: 13301
Garden Awards Vol. 2: 726
Garden State Children's Book Awards Vol. 1: 14092
Garden State Teen Book Awards Vol. 1: 14093
Garden Trophy; Oscar Vol. 2: 3845
Gardeners of America/Men's Garden Clubs of America Scholarship Vol. 1: 8965
Gardening From the Heart Award Vol. 1: 8966
Gardiner Award Vol. 2: 5031
Gardner Foundation Scholarship Vol. 1: 9714
Gardner Leadership Award; John W. Vol. 1: 9651
Gardner Scholarship Award; Harry L. Vol. 1: 2713
Gardner Subcommittee Chairman of the Year Award; Henry A. Vol. 1: 5424
Gardner Trophy Vol. 1: 18078
Garel Award; Georges Vol. 2: 4801
Garland Commemorative Refrigeration Award for Project Excellence; Milton W. Vol. 1: 4056
Garland Educator Award; Robin F. Vol. 1: 13562
Garlick Lifetime Achievement Award; Betty Vol. 1: 11724
Garneau Medal; Francois-Xavier Vol. 1: 6559
Garner-Themoin Medal Vol. 2: 798
Garnsey Trainers Award; Glen Vol. 1: 17930
Garrett Memorial Award; Dudley (Red) Vol. 1: 2269
Garrett Turbomachinery Engineering Award; Cliff Vol. 1: 16576
Garrod Medal Vol. 2: 5475
Garrod Prize Vol. 2: 5489
Garulat Award; Bernard J. Vol. 1: 876
Garvan-John M. Olin Medal; Francis P. Vol. 1: 1549
Garvey Award; Joseph J. Vol. 1: 916
Gary Memorial Medal Vol. 1: 2578
Gas Balloon Championships Vol. 1: 5645
Gas Turbine Award Vol. 1: 4133
Gascoigne Medal; George Bradley Vol. 1: 18629
Gascoigne Prize; Trench Vol. 2: 7056
Gaskell Medal and Prize Vol. 2: 6724
Gassner Award; John Vol. 1: 14757
Gassner Memorial Playwriting Award; John Vol. 1: 14055
Gaster Bronze Medal; Leon Vol. 2: 5637

Gately Memorial Trophy; Micheal Vol. 1: 10891
Gatorade Rookie of the Year Vol. 1: 11203
Gatorade Victory Lane Award; Daytona Vol. 1: 8065
Gatorade Young Investigator Award; Environmental and Exercise Physiology Section Vol. 1: 3169
Gatzke Outstanding Dissertation Award; Dr. Donald A. Vol. 1: 1315
Gaudeamus Prize Vol. 2: 3557
The Gaudeamus Prize Vol. 2: 3555
Gaudens Award; Augustus St. Vol. 1: 7821
Gaudin Award; Antoine M. Vol. 1: 16347
Gaul Competition; Harvey Vol. 1: 15081
Gaus Award; John Vol. 1: 3231
Gauss Award; Christian Vol. 1: 14989
Gavel Award Vol. 1: 821
Gaver Scholarship; Mary V. Vol. 1: 2660
Gawad AGKATEK (Agham, Kapaligiran at Teknolohiya) Vol. 2: 3982
Gawad CCP Para sa Sining Vol. 2: 3973
Gawad Manlilikha Ng Bayan (GAMABA) Vol. 2: 3974
Gay Teddy Bear Vol. 2: 2048
Gaz de France; Prix du Vol. 2: 1565
Gazzola Prize Vol. 2: 1888
GBPS Hassan Shaida Trophy Vol. 2: 6535
GCA Award in Coastal Wetland Studies Vol. 1: 8952
GCA Awards for Summer Environmental Studies Vol. 1: 8953
GCA Awards in Tropical Biology Vol. 1: 8954
GCA Fellowship in Ecological Restoration Vol. 1: 8955
GCA Summer Scholarship in Field Botany Vol. 1: 8956
GE Healthcare Fellowship Vol. 2: 5334
GE Imagination At Work Award Vol. 1: 8994
Geach Memorial Award; Portia Vol. 2: 701
Geesink Prize; Joop Vol. 2: 3561
Gegner; Prix Vol. 2: 1663
Geh Grant; Hans-Peter Vol. 2: 3580
GEI Award Vol. 1: 9216
Geiger Award; General Roy S. Vol. 1: 11533
Geijsbeek Award; Samuel Vol. 1: 1480
Geijyutsu Korosha Vol. 2: 3346
Geilfuss Fellowship; John C. Vol. 1: 18782
Geils Memorial Award; G. Ruth Vol. 1: 9254
Geis Dissertation Award; George L. Vol. 1: 6968
Geis Memorial Award Vol. 1: 3381
Geisness Outstanding Lawyer or Non-Lawyer Award; Helen M. Vol. 1: 11152
Gelber Foundation Award; Sylva Vol. 1: 6108
Gelin Conference Travel Award; Lars-Erik Vol. 2: 2127
GEM Awards Vol. 1: 16348
Gemant Award; Andrew Vol. 1: 2540
Gemeaux Awards Vol. 1: 68
Gemenis Award; Maria Vol. 2: 273
Gemimi Humanitarian Award Vol. 1: 69
The Gemini Awards Vol. 1: 69
Gemma Yates Trophy Vol. 2: 5040
Gender Equity Architects Award Vol. 1: 1046
Gender Equity Award Vol. 1: 15156
Genealogical Publishing Company Award Vol. 1: 2689
Genealogist of the Year Vol. 2: 4182
General Aviation Award Vol. 1: 2397
General Aviation Maintenance Technician Award Vol. 1: 15266
General Aviation Service Technician Award Vol. 1: 12228
General Bryce Pow II Award Vol. 1: 316
General Contractor Award of Excellence Vol. 1: 6423
General Dental Practitioner Prize Vol. 2: 5301
General Diagnostics Lectureship in Clinical Chemistry Vol. 1: 865
General Electric Senior Research Award Vol. 1: 3650
General Knowledge Contest on the UN Vol. 2: 4571
General Knowledge Quiz on International Flags, National Emblems, Coats-of-Arms, and National Anthems of UN member States Vol. 2: 4571
General Motors Cancer Research Prize Vol. 1: 8996
General Motors Grand Jazz Award
Festival International de Jazz de Montreal Vol. 1: 8683
Festival International de Jazz de Montreal Vol 1: 8683
General Research Committee Award Vol. 2: 4567
General Service Medal Vol. 2: 4343
Genetics Society of America Medal Vol. 1: 9003
Geneva-Europe Prizes Vol. 2: 4707
The Genies Vol. 1: 70
Gentilli Prize; Edgar Vol. 2: 6706
Gentleman of the Year Award Vol. 1: 11487
Geochemistry Fellows Vol. 2: 1759
Geochimie; Prix de Vol. 2: 1591
GeoEye Award Vol. 1: 4739
Geoffroy Prize Vol. 1: 8711
Geographical Award Vol. 2: 6764
Geological Society of South Africa Honorary Member Vol. 2: 4186
Geological Society of South Africa Honours Award Vol. 2: 4187
Geological Society of South Africa Jubilee Medal Vol. 2: 4188
Georg Award; Lucille K. Vol. 2: 1413
George A. Hall/Harold F. Mayfield Award Vol. 1: 18754
George-Cantor-Medal Vol. 2: 2199
George Civilian Airmanship Award; Lt. Gen. Harold L. Vol. 1: 14647
George Croskery Memorial Award Vol. 1: 6401
George Cross Vol. 2: 5593
George Cross Fellowship Award Vol. 2: 5518
George Medal Vol. 2: 5594
George Perkins Marsh Prize Vol. 1: 3699
George Polya Lectureship Vol. 1: 11610
George R. Mach Distinguished Service Award Vol. 1: 11097
Georges Petitpas Memorial Award Vol. 1: 18935
Georgescu-Roegen Prize in Economics Vol. 1: 17032
Georgette LeMoyne; Bourse Vol. 1: 6487
Georgia Author of the Year Awards Vol. 1: 9034
Georgia Children's Book Award Vol. 1: 18277
Georgia Children's Picture Storybook Award Vol. 1: 18278
Georgia tNo Excusesv Awards Vol. 1: 9032
Georgia Poetry Society Award Vol. 1: 13148
Geosciences in the Media Award Vol. 1: 1214
Geotechnical Research Medal Vol. 2: 6111
Gerard; Prix Auguste Vol. 2: 1664
Gerardi Memory Prize; Alfred Vol. 2: 2185
Gerdes Distinguished Service Award; Betty Vol. 1: 13737
Gerharz Scholarship; Anthony Vol. 1: 11930
Gerhold Award; Clarence (Larry) G. Vol. 1: 2484
Geriatric Oral Health Care Award Vol. 1: 1904
Geriatrician/Gerontologist of the Year Vol. 1: 4597
Gerke Collegiate Artist Scholarships Vol. 1: 12000
Gerke Scholarship; Madge Cathcart Vol. 1: 12000
Germain; Fondation Gustave Vol. 2: 1482
German Direct Marketing Award Vol. 2: 2186
German Marshall Fund of the United States Fellowships and Awards Vol. 1: 9049
German Summer-Study Award Vol. 1: 1300
Germann Cup Vol. 1: 17024
Geron Corporation - Samuel Goldstein Distinguished Publication Award Vol. 1: 9059
Gerrard Award; Louise B. Vol. 1: 12671
Gerrish Trophy; Ebby Vol. 2: 6535
Gerrity Award; Thomas P. Vol. 1: 289
Gerry Fellowships; Eloise Vol. 1: 16029
Gerry Lesback Award Vol. 1: 6040
Gerschenkron Prize; Alexander Vol. 1: 8379
Gershoy Award; Leo Vol. 1: 2235
Gersoni Military Psychology Award; Charles S. Vol. 1: 3376
Gerstacker Trooper of the Year Award; Dr. Carl A. Vol. 1: 11731
Gerstaecker-Preis; Friedrich- Vol. 2: 2056
Gervais Award; Arthur J. Vol. 1: 17204
Getchell Award; Charles M. Vol. 1: 17016
Getman Award; G. N. Vol. 1: 7537
Getty Scholar Grants Vol. 1: 9072
Getty Wildlife Conservation Prize; J. Paul Vol. 1: 18991
Gezelle Prize; Guido Vol. 2: 957
GFWC Print Journalism Award for Excellence; Jane Cunningham Croly/ Vol. 1: 8988
Ghandi Peace Award Vol. 1: 15383
Ghatage Award; Dr. V. M. Vol. 2: 2523
Ghirshman; Prix Roman et Tania Vol. 2: 1516
Ghost Contest; Horror/ Vol. 1: 19018
Giant Schnauzer of the Year Vol. 1: 9079
Gibb Award; Jack Vol. 1: 14682
Gibbons Cup; Stanley Vol. 2: 6535
Gibbons Medal; James Cardinal Vol. 1: 7171
Gibbs Brothers Medal Vol. 1: 12160
Gibbs, Jr. Memorial Award; Robert H. Vol. 1: 4077
Gibson Aviation Command and Control Officer of the Year Award; Robert F. Vol. 1: 11511
Gibson Award; Arrell M. Vol. 1: 18685
Gibson Award; Charlie Vol. 1: 17233
Gibson Trophy; Frank M. Vol. 1: 6508
Giddings Award for Excellence in Education; J. Calvin Vol. 1: 1550
Gideon Prize; Miriam Vol. 1: 10031
Giegengack Award; Robert Vol. 1: 18440
Gierows pris; Karin Vol. 2: 4656
Gies Award; William John Vol. 1: 1641
Gies Foundation Award; William J. Vol. 1: 725

Award Index

Giese Structures and Environment Award; Henry Vol. 1: 3851
Giffuni Memorial Award; Andrew Vol. 1: 14869
Gift of Sight Award
Eye Bank Association of America Vol. 1: 8571
Guide Dogs of America Vol 1: 9224
Gifted Teacher Award Vol. 1: 1618
Giguere Award; John P. Vol. 1: 11512
Gijon International Film Festival for Young People Vol. 2: 4499
Gilbert Aviation Ordnance Marine of the Year Award; Gaines G. Vol. 1: 11513
Gilbert Award; G. K. Vol. 1: 9021
Gilbert Award; John Vol. 1: 12459
Gilbert Fellowship Vol. 1: 7563
Gilbert Memorial Award; Glen A. Vol. 1: 332
Gilbert Memorial Trustee Award; Gloria F. "Mike" Vol. 1: 3597
Gilbert National Leadership Award; Glenn Vol. 1: 13014
Gilbert Prize; Geoffery Vol. 1: 13201
Gilbreth Industrial Engineering Award; Frank and Lillian Vol. 1: 9863
Gilbreth Medal Vol. 1: 16155
Gilchrist Fieldwork Award Vol. 2: 6765
Giles Award; Annie T. Vol. 1: 2212
Giles; Prix Herbert Allen Vol. 2: 1517
Gill Medal Vol. 2: 4132
Gill Memorial Award Vol. 2: 6766
Gill Memorial Award; Tom Vol. 2: 5674
Gill Prize; Brendan Vol. 1: 12010
Gillet / Hugo Fox International Competition; Fernand Vol. 1: 10383
Gillet Young Artist Performance Competition; Fernand Vol. 1: 10383
Gilliams Prize; Maurice Vol. 2: 958
Gillihan Award Vol. 1: 9389
Gillingham Award; Kent K. Vol. 1: 202
Gillis Prize; Jan Vol. 2: 1072
Gilliss Award for Outstanding Service; Captain James M. Vol. 1: 17848
Gilman Award in Drug Receptor Pharmacology; Goodman and Vol. 1: 3808
Gilmore Award; Mary Vol. 2: 55
Gilmore Bursary; Jean Vol. 2: 190
Gilmore - Woman Behind the Scenes Award; Diana Fell Vol. 1: 17749
Gilpin County Arts Association Annual Members Exhibition and Sale Vol. 1: 9083
Gilruth Prize Vol. 2: 382
Giltner Memorial Trophy; Joe Vol. 1: 16111
Gilula Award; Norton B. Vol. 1: 3588
Ginesty Award Vol. 2: 3606
Gingles Award; Violet B. Vol. 1: 4618
Gingrich Memorial Life Award; Arnold Vol. 1: 8636
Ginwala Gold Medal; Sir Padamji Vol. 2: 2650
GIO Australia Ballet Scholarship Vol. 2: 689
Giolitti Steel Medal; Federico Vol. 2: 3096
Girard; Prix Edmond Vol. 2: 1954
Girardeau; Prix Emile Vol. 2: 1665
Girls' 18 National Championships Sportsmanship Award Vol. 1: 18141
Girls' Basketball National Volunteer of the Year Vol. 1: 487
Girl's Service Award Vol. 2: 469
Gitelson Essay Awards; Moses Leo Vol. 1: 7244
Gitlin Literary Prize; Zelda Vol. 1: 17528
Gitlin Literary Prize; Zelda & Paul Vol. 1: 17528
Givry; Prix Alexandre Vol. 2: 1571
Gladstone History Book Prize Vol. 2: 6779
Glaser Award; Jerome Vol. 1: 694
Glaser Award; John Vol. 1: 8891
Glaser Award; Robert J. Vol. 1: 16693
Glaser Distinguished Teacher Awards; Robert J. Vol. 1: 423
Glaser Student Essay Award; Helen H. Vol. 1: 424
Glasgow-Rubin Student Achievement Award Vol. 1: 2764
Glasgow-Rubin Student Achievement Certificate Vol. 1: 2765
Glass Dealer of the Year Vol. 1: 13284
Glass Globe Vol. 2: 3646
Glass Professional of the Year Vol. 1: 13284
Glassco Translation Prize; John Vol. 1: 11381
Glaxo Prize for Medical Writing Vol. 2: 7148
GlaxoSmithKline Prize and Lecture Vol. 2: 6909
Glazebrook Medal and Prize Vol. 2: 6060
Glazen Globe Vol. 2: 3646
Gleason Award; Henry Allan
Botanical Society of America Vol. 1: 5877
New York Botanical Garden - Institute of Systematic Botany Vol 1: 14114
Gleason Book Award; Eliza Atkins Vol. 1: 2677
Gleason Music Book Awards; Ralph J. Vol. 1: 14194
Gleed Literary Award; Danuta Vol. 1: 19027
Glen Award; Esther Vol. 2: 3751
Glen Special Award for Public Service; Peter Vol. 1: 15648
Glenfiddich Trophy Vol. 2: 5668
Glenn Award; R. A. Vol. 1: 5425
Global 500 Vol. 2: 3956
Global Citizen Award Vol. 1: 7214
Global Citizenship Award Vol. 1: 18328
Global Leaders Award Vol. 1: 15156
Global Leadership Award Vol. 1: 4725
Global Media Awards Vol. 1: 15156
Global Paragon Awards Vol. 1: 11680
Global Sanitation Award Vol. 2: 2802
Gloria Medal Vol. 1: 13693
Gloria Medicinae Award Vol. 2: 4041
Gloucester Navigation Trophy Vol. 2: 3846
Glushien Award; Anne Williams Vol. 1: 4433
Goal of the Year Vol. 2: 3403
Godbout; Prix Archange- Vol. 1: 8885
Goddard Astronautics Award Vol. 1: 2379
Goddard Award Vol. 1: 2379
Goddard Award; George W. Vol. 1: 17134
Goddard Award; G.V. Vol. 2: 3788
Goddard/Libraries Ltd. Author Awards; Judy Vol. 1: 4601
Goddard Medal Vol. 1: 16523
Goddard Memorial Scholarship; Dr. Robert H. Vol. 1: 13782
Gode Medal; Alexander Vol. 1: 4365
Godeaux; Prix Lucien Vol. 2: 1098
Godel Prize Vol. 1: 4818
Godfrey Award; Kneeland Vol. 1: 7758
Godin Award; Jean-Cleo Vol. 1: 4793
Godlove Award Vol. 1: 9987
Godman-Salvin Medal Vol. 2: 5402
Goedken Outstanding Leadership Service Award; Loras Vol. 1: 13338
Goethals Medal; George W. Vol. 1: 16524
Goethe Medaille Vol. 2: 2265
Goethe Prize; Hansischer Vol. 2: 2396
Goetze 21st Century Award; Mandy Vol. 1: 10029
Goff; Prix Jean-Marie Le Vol. 2: 1566
Golata Award; Frank Vol. 1: 8841
Gold Air Medal Vol. 2: 4728
Gold Anchor Vol. 2: 1890
Gold and Silver Medals Vol. 1: 14302
Gold Anvil Award Vol. 1: 15427
Gold Award
American Healthcare Radiology Administrators Vol. 1: 2171
Media, Entertainment and Arts Alliance Vol 2: 561
Recording Industry Association of America Vol 1: 15578
Gold Awards
Meetings and Conventions Vol. 1: 11685
Pacific Asia Travel Association Vol 1: 14772
Gold Badge
British Academy of Composers and Songwriters Vol. 2: 5214
English Folk Dance and Song Society Vol 2: 5780
Gold Ball Award Vol. 1: 16121
Gold Baton Award Vol. 1: 4342
Gold Book Awards Vol. 1: 5126
Gold Butterfly of Trentino Prize Vol. 2: 3136
Gold Camera Award Vol. 1: 17980
Gold Cane Award Vol. 1: 4391
Gold Circle Awards Vol. 1: 7579
Gold Crown Awards Vol. 1: 7578
Gold Cup Vol. 1: 3246
Gold Cup of Industry Award Vol. 1: 8328
Gold Cystoscope Award Vol. 1: 4392
Gold Diploma of Honor Vol. 2: 2477
Gold Disc Award Vol. 2: 3947
Gold Edelweiss Vol. 2: 4545
Gold Good Citizenship Medal Vol. 1: 13763
Gold-Headed Cane
Seventh Day Baptist Historical Society Vol. 1: 15977
World Association of Societies of Pathology and Laboratory Medicine Vol 2: 3351
Gold-Headed Cane Award Vol. 1: 3755
Gold Heart Award Vol. 1: 2177
Gold Insigne Vol. 1: 4510
Gold Key Award
American Congress of Rehabilitation Medicine Vol. 1: 1773
Columbia Scholastic Press Association Vol 1: 7580
Gold Key Awards
Society of Professional Journalists Vol. 1: 16838
University of Chicago - Medical and Biological Sciences Alumni Association Vol 1: 18256
Gold Keyboard Award Vol. 1: 14141
Gold Level Achievement Awards Vol. 1: 17425
Gold Lifesaving Medal Vol. 1: 8106
Gold Mailbox Award Vol. 1: 8200
Gold Medal
Academia Europaea Vol. 2: 4998
Acoustical Society of America Vol 1: 126
Acta Materialia Vol 2: 5000
American College of Radiology Vol 1: 1732
American Craft Council Vol 1: 1851
American Institute of Architects Vol 1: 2428
American Institute of Chemists Vol 1: 2508
American Irish Historical Society Vol 1: 2575
American Rhododendron Society Vol 1: 3492

Anchor Bay Chamber of Commerce Vol 1: 4523
ASM International Vol 1: 4699
Australian Council for Educational Leaders Vol 2: 168
Brazilian Metallurgy and Materials Association Vol 2: 1124
British Society for the Study of Prosthetic Dentistry Vol 2: 5496
Bulgarian Red Cross Vol 2: 1151
Canadian Association of Radiologists Vol 1: 6295
Canadian Institute of Forestry Vol 1: 6600
Chartered Institute of Journalists Vol 2: 5618
French National Center for Scientific Research Vol 2: 1827
Institute of Actuaries - United Kingdom Vol 2: 5991
Institute of Chartered Accountants of Scotland Vol 2: 6004
Institution of Civil Engineers Vol 2: 6112
International Federation of Sports Medicine Vol 2: 1245
National Association of Licensed Paralegals Vol 2: 6456
National Football Foundation and College Hall of Fame Vol 1: 13212
National Vegetable Society Vol 2: 6489
Professional Grounds Management Society Vol 1: 15327
Professional Institute of the Public Service of Canada Vol 1: 15332
Radiological Society of North America Vol 1: 15538
Royal Aeronautical Society - United Kingdom Vol 2: 6640
Royal Architectural Institute of Canada Vol 1: 15731
Royal Canadian Geographical Society Vol 1: 15742
Royal Philharmonic Society Vol 2: 6862
Royal Scottish Geographical Society Vol 2: 6897
SA Holstein Friesland Society Vol 2: 4245
Scarab Club Vol 1: 15898
Society of Manufacturing Engineers - Composites Manufacturing Association Vol 1: 16712
Society of Woman Geographers Vol 1: 16907
South African Sugar Technologists' Association Vol 2: 4357
SPIE: International Society for Optical Engineering Vol 1: 17135
Tau Sigma Delta Vol 1: 17410
Zoological Society of Southern Africa Vol 2: 4381
Gold Medal and Fellowship of the Society Vol. 2: 310
Gold Medal Award
American Academy of Periodontology Vol. 1: 726
American College of Healthcare Executives Vol 1: 1652
American Society of Naval Engineers Vol 1: 4187
Association of Canadian Advertisers Vol 1: 5055
Audio Engineering Society Vol 1: 5522
Canadian Council of Professional Engineers Vol 1: 6433
Entomological Society of Canada Vol 1: 8492
Fertilizer Society of South Africa Vol 2: 4177
International Catholic Union of the Press Vol 2: 4788
International Radio and Television Society Foundation Vol 1: 10570
Mining and Metallurgical Society of America Vol 1: 11822
National Retail Federation Vol 1: 13640
National Student Campaign Against Hunger and Homelessness Vol 1: 13815
Society of Biological Psychiatry Vol 1: 16604
Spanish Institute Vol 1: 17068
Gold Medal Award for Distinguished Archaeological Achievement Vol. 1: 4577
Gold Medal Award for Distinguished Lifetime Contributions to Canadian Psychology Vol. 1: 6834
Gold Medal Award for Technical Achievement Vol. 1: 16812
Gold Medal Awards Vol. 1: 5698
Gold Medal for Achievement in the Natural Sciences Vol. 2: 4266
Gold Medal for Architecture Vol. 2: 4332
Gold Medal for Botany Vol. 2: 4303
Gold Medal for Distinguished Achievement Vol. 1: 3036
Gold Medal for Distinguished Merit Vol. 2: 5358
Gold Medal for Distinguished Service
American Institute of Certified Public Accountants Vol. 1: 2460
Society of American Military Engineers Vol 1: 16519
Gold Medal for Excellence in Human Rights Vol. 1: 9519
Gold Medal for Excellence in Public Life Vol. 1: 9520
Gold Medal for Outstanding Architectural Achievement Vol. 2: 1923
Gold Medal of Excellence for Photography Vol. 1: 12286
Gold Medal of Honor
American Watercolor Society Vol. 1: 4434
World Federation of Neurosurgical Societies Vol 1: 18931
Gold Medal of Honor for Education Vol. 1: 12287
Gold Medal of Honor for Film/Video Vol. 1: 12288
Gold Medal of Honor for Theater/Drama Vol. 1: 12289
Gold Medal of Honor for Visual Arts Vol. 1: 12290
Gold Medal of Honour Vol. 2: 4130
Gold Medal of the FIM Vol. 2: 4815
Gold Medal Student Award Vol. 1: 6434
Gold Medallion Vol. 1: 5921
Gold Medallion Award
International Swimming Hall of Fame Vol. 1: 10770
National School Public Relations Association Vol 1: 13664
Gold Medallion Book Awards Vol. 1: 8546
Gold Medals Vol. 2: 6767
Gold Member Vol. 1: 10019
Gold Memorial Bowl Vol. 2: 7025
Gold Nibs Award Vol. 1: 2158
Gold Panda Award Vol. 2: 4944
Gold Parachuting Medal Vol. 2: 4729
Gold Plate Award Vol. 1: 10436
Gold Quill Award Vol. 1: 4036
Gold Quill Awards Vol. 1: 10158
Gold Ribbon Award for Broadcast Excellence Vol. 1: 6231
Gold Ribbon for Community Service (Radio) Vol. 1: 6232
Gold Ribbon for Community Service (Specialty/Pay/PPV) Vol. 1: 6233
Gold Ribbon for Community Service (Television) Vol. 1: 6234
Gold Ribbon for Distinguished Service Vol. 1: 6231
Gold Ribbon for Outstanding Community Service by an Individual Broadcaster Vol. 1: 6235
Gold Ribbon for Promotion of Canadian Talent (Radio) Vol. 1: 6236
Gold Rotorcraft Medal Vol. 2: 4730
Gold Screen Awards Vol. 1: 12544
Gold, Silver, and Bronze Medals Vol. 1: 8006
Gold Space Medal Vol. 2: 4731
Gold T-Square Vol. 1: 12852
Gold Training Award Vol. 2: 5113
Gold Veitch Memorial Medal Vol. 2: 6791
Gold Video Sales Award Vol. 1: 10606
Gold Wing Award Vol. 1: 12826
Goldberg Young Investigator Award; Leon I. Vol. 1: 3609
Goldblatt Cytology Award; Maurice Vol. 2: 2276
Golde Award Vol. 1: 10935
Golden Achievement Award
ISA - Instrumentation, Systems, and Automation Society Vol. 1: 10911
National School Public Relations Association Vol 1: 13665
Specialized Carriers and Rigging Association Vol 1: 17096
Golden Acorn Award Vol. 1: 11690
Golden Age Award Vol. 1: 11244
Golden Alexander Vol. 2: 2473
Golden Anniversary Award Vol. 1: 12400
Golden Anniversary Monograph Awards Vol. 1: 12924
Golden Antenna International Television Festival Vol. 2: 1146
Golden Apple
Ministry of Culture of the Slovak Republic Vol. 2: 4442
World Federation of Journalists and Travel Writers Vol 2: 2019
Golden Archer Award Vol. 1: 18778
Golden Award Vol. 1: 12447
Golden Berlin Bear Vol. 2: 2048
Golden Bobbin Vol. 2: 917
Golden Broom Award Vol. 1: 14595
Golden Bug Statuette Vol. 2: 4683
Golden Bull Award Vol. 2: 6539
Golden Cactus Vol. 2: 4824
Golden Chain Award
Nation's Restaurant News - Lebhar-Friedman Inc. Vol. 1: 13965
Nation's Restaurant News - Lebhar-Friedman Inc. Vol 1: 13968
Golden Chest International Television Festival Vol. 2: 1147
Golden Circle Award Vol. 1: 11039
Golden Cleaver Trophy Vol. 1: 1155
Golden Danzante Vol. 2: 4495
Golden Dozen Vol. 1: 10747
Golden Dragon Vol. 2: 3999
Golden Eagle Award
Council on International Nontheatrical Events Vol. 1: 7924

Society of American Military Engineers Vol 1: 16525
Wireless Communications Association International Vol 1: 18770
Golden Elephant Award Vol. 2: 2551
"Golden Eye" Vol. 2: 3690
Golden Field Award Vol. 1: 18379
Golden Furrows Challenge Trophy Vol. 2: 3688
Golden Gate Awards Vol. 1: 15826
Golden Gavel Award Vol. 1: 17545
Golden Globe Vol. 1: 9458
Golden Globe Awards Vol. 1: 9459
Golden Hammer Award Vol. 1: 15061
Golden Hammer Award for Scenic Technology Vol. 1: 17951
Golden Hammer Awards Vol. 1: 12554
Golden Heart Award Vol. 1: 15710
Golden Horse Award Vol. 1: 14820
Golden Horse Awards Vol. 2: 4952
Golden Hysteroscope Award Vol. 1: 1107
Golden Image Award
Professional Convention Management Association Vol. 1: 15292
Specialty Graphic Imaging Association Vol 1: 17112
Golden Jubilee Awards Vol. 2: 2556
Golden Jubilee Commemoration Medal for Biology Vol. 2: 2685
Golden Jubilee Commemoration Medal for Chemistry Vol. 2: 2686
Golden Key Scholar Awards Vol. 1: 9110
Golden Kiss Vol. 2: 3495
Golden Kite Awards Vol. 1: 16624
Golden Knight International Amateur Film and Video Festival Vol. 2: 3423
Golden Knight International Amateur Film Festival Vol. 2: 3423
Golden Lamp Award Vol. 1: 5132
Golden Laparoscope Award Vol. 1: 1108
Golden Lion Award Vol. 1: 6010
Golden Merit Award Vol. 1: 13669
Golden Mike Awards Vol. 1: 14076
Golden Peanut Research and Education Award Vol. 1: 3030
Golden Pen Vol. 1: 8343
Golden Pen Award Vol. 1: 3154
Golden Pen of Freedom Award Vol. 2: 2014
Golden Penguin Awards Vol. 1: 13265
Golden Plough Trophy Vol. 2: 3688
Golden Pyramid Competition Vol. 1: 15388
Golden Quill Award Vol. 1: 10747
Golden Ram Award Vol. 2: 4212
Golden Raster Award Vol. 1: 9311
Golden Reel Award Vol. 1: 70
Golden Reins Award Vol. 1: 2789
Golden Rookie of the Year; Harry Vol. 1: 15274
Golden Rose Award Vol. 1: 14043
Golden Rose of Montreaux Award Vol. 2: 4882
Golden Saddleman Award Vol. 1: 18704
Golden Score Award Vol. 1: 4181
Golden Sheaf Awards Vol. 1: 19078
Golden Sheaf Craft Awards Vol. 1: 19078
Golden Shell Vol. 2: 4538
Golden Ship Grand Prix of the President of the Bulgarian Red Cross Vol. 2: 1153
Golden Sower Awards Vol. 1: 14016
Golden Space Needle Audience Awards Vol. 1: 15957
Golden Spike Vol. 2: 4552
Golden Spikes Award Vol. 1: 18380
Golden Spur Awards Vol. 1: 18703
Golden Toonie Award Vol. 1: 7125
Golden Torch Award
Better Business Bureau Serving Upstate South Carolina Vol. 1: 5739
Insurance Marketing Communications Association Vol 1: 9965
Golden Trowel Award Vol. 1: 10504
Golden Tulip Award Vol. 2: 4982
Golden Unicorn
Alpinale Film Festival Vol. 2: 741
Amiens International Film Festival Vol 2: 1710
Golden Werner-Medaille Vol. 2: 4894
Goldene Vereinsnadel Vol. 2: 2029
Goldener Ehrenring fur Papiergeschichte Vol. 2: 2030
Goldener Gehlhoff-Ring Vol. 2: 2243
Goldhill Award for Sculpture; Jack Vol. 2: 6610
Goldman Environmental Prize Vol. 1: 9112
Goldschmidt Medal; V. M. Vol. 1: 9009
Goldschmidt Preis; Viktor-Moritz- Vol. 2: 2086
Goldsmith Award; The Kenneth Vol. 2: 5254
Goldsmith Award; Richard S. Vol. 1: 17254
Goldsmith Book Prize Vol. 1: 15990
Goldsmith Cup; Tony Vol. 2: 6149
Goldsmith Prize for Investigative Reporting Vol. 1: 15991
Goldstein Award for Washington Regional Reporting; Robin Vol. 1: 13545
Goldstein Distinguished Publication Award; Geron Corporation - Samuel Vol. 1: 9059
Goldstein Foundation Purchase Award; Ben and Beatrice Vol. 1: 16517
Goldwater Amateur Radio Award; Barry M. Vol. 1: 15521
Golf Digest - LPGA Founders Cup Vol. 1: 11196
Golf Professional of the Year Vol. 1: 15317
Golfer of the Year Vol. 2: 5139
Golgi Lecture Vol. 2: 2108
Gollancz Prize; Sir Israel Vol. 2: 5209
Golmick Scholarship; Paul Vol. 2: 5648
Golseth Young Investigator Award Vol. 1: 1171
Gomez Award; Lefty Vol. 1: 1383
Gomez Prize; Rodrigo Vol. 2: 3435
Gomulinski Community Service Award; Robert Vol. 1: 4518
Gondos Memorial Service Award; Victor Vol. 1: 16336
Gonin Medal Vol. 1: 10415
Good Conduct Medal Vol. 1: 8107
Good Design Award Vol. 2: 3237
GOOD DESIGN Competition and Exhibition Vol. 1: 7320
Good Government Pharmacist of the Year Award Vol. 1: 3050
Good Grant Award Vol. 1: 8254
Good Neighbor Award
American Red Cross National Headquarters Vol. 1: 3469
United States-Mexico Chamber of Commerce Vol 1: 18001
Good Neighbor Teacher Award Vol. 1: 17264
Good Poster Award Vol. 1: 10405
Good Samaritan Award Vol. 1: 12857
Good Servant Medal Vol. 1: 6428
Good Steward Award Vol. 1: 12253
Goodacre Medal and Gift; Walter Vol. 2: 5248
The Goodchild Prize Vol. 2: 6585
Goode Memorial Award; Harry M. Vol. 1: 9808
Goodeve Medal Vol. 2: 6508
Goodfellow Memorial Award for Senior Vocal Concert Groups Vol. 1: 15861
Goodfellow Memorial Canadian Vocal Music Scholarship Vol. 1: 15862
Goodfellow Memorial Grade A Female Voce Scholarship Vol. 1: 15863
Goodfellow Memorial Grade A Male Voice Scholarship Vol. 1: 15864
Goodfellow Memorial Lieder Voice Scholarship/Whelan Lieder Piano Scholarship Vol. 1: 15865
Goodfellow Memorial Operatic Scholarship Vol. 1: 15866
Goodfellow Memorial Oratorio Scholarship/ Helen Davis Sherry Memorial Trophy Vol. 1: 15867
Goodfellowship Award Vol. 1: 2889
Goodhue-Elkins Award Vol. 1: 5532
Goodman Award; Arnold Vol. 1: 17708
Goodman-Malamuth Outstanding Dissertation Award; Dr. Leo and Margaret Vol. 1: 1315
Goodnight Award for Outstanding Performance as a Dean; Scott Vol. 1: 12684
Goodnow Award; Frank J. Vol. 1: 3232
Goodwill Ambassadors for UNICEF Vol. 1: 17910
Goodwill Industries Volunteer Services (GIVS) Volunteer Group of the Year Vol. 1: 9130
Goodwill Industries Volunteer Services (GIVS) Volunteer of the Year Vol. 1: 9131
Goodwin Award of Merit; Charles J. Vol. 1: 3080
Goodwin Memorial Scholarship; James L. Vol. 1: 7727
Goodyear Award; John and Mary Vol. 2: 3522
Goodyear Medal; Charles Vol. 1: 1551
Gooley Humanitarian of the Year Award; Mary M. Vol. 1: 13335
Gopalan Award; Prof. M.N. Vol. 2: 2780
Gordan Book Prize; Phyllis Goodhart Vol. 1: 15623
Gordon Award; Eva L. Vol. 1: 2859
Gordon Award for Children's Science Literature; Eva L. Vol. 1: 2859
Gordon Award; Marjorie Vol. 1: 13490
Gordon Award; Seth Vol. 1: 10212
Gordon Award; Winston Vol. 1: 6747
Gordon Editor of the Year Award; Jim Vol. 1: 13563
Gordon-Lennox Trophy Vol. 2: 6792
Gordon Memorial Award; Harold R. Vol. 1: 12546
Gordon Prize; Bernard M. Vol. 1: 12129
Gordon Royal Maybee Award Vol. 1: 6592
Gore "Remember the Children" Award; Tipper Vol. 1: 13448
Gore Scholarship; Len Vol. 2: 6247
Gorgas Medal Vol. 1: 5245
Gorin Award for Outstanding Achievement in Rural Health Care; Louis Vol. 1: 13651
Gorin Award; Susan Phillips Vol. 1: 7853
Goring Award; D.A.I. Vol. 1: 18351
Gorman Trophy; Peter Vol. 1: 6651
Gospel Music Hall of Fame Vol. 1: 9140
Gospel Recorded Performance of the Year Vol. 1: 10270
Gosset Award; George R. Vol. 1: 2309
Gotham Awards
Independent Feature Project Vol. 1: 9634

Independent Feature Project Vol 1: 9635
Gotlieb Contribution Award; C. C. Vol. 1: 6581
Gottesdiener Prize; Nathan Vol. 2: 2931
Gottesfeld Award; Kenneth R. Vol. 1: 16647
Gottlieb Immerman and Abraham Nathan and Bertha Daskal Weinstein Memorial Fellowship; Abram and Fannie Vol. 1: 19061
Gottlieb Prize; Murray Vol. 1: 11659
Gottlieb Trophy; Eddie Vol. 1: 12765
Gottschalk Medal Vol. 2: 113
Gottschalk Prize; Louis Vol. 1: 3626
Gouden Zoen Vol. 2: 3495
Goueram-Toekenning Vol. 2: 4212
Gould Memorial Literary Award Vol. 1: 2890
Gould Young Composer Awards; Morton Vol. 1: 4005
Goulden Memorial Award; Loran L. Vol. 1: 8611
Governing Board's Award for the Best Paper Vol. 1: 18369
Government Affairs Award Vol. 1: 12699
Government Affairs Award of Recognition Vol. 1: 5991
Government Building Award Vol. 1: 5992
Government Civil Engineer of the Year Award Vol. 1: 3939
Government Computer News Awards Program Vol. 1: 9142
Government Executive Leadership Award Vol. 1: 9144
Government Management Information Sciences Award Vol. 1: 9155
Government Technology Leadership Award Vol. 1: 9144
Governor General Art Award
New Zealand Academy of Fine Arts Vol. 2: 3760
New Zealand Academy of Fine Arts Vol 2: 3760
Governor General's Award Vol. 1: 6135
Governor General's Awards in Commemoration of the Persons Case Vol. 1: 17286
Governor General's Awards in Visual and Media Arts Vol. 1: 6109
Governor General's International Award for Canadian Studies Vol. 1: 10346
Governor General's Literary Awards Vol. 1: 6110
Governor General's Literary Awards for Children's Literature Vol. 1: 6110
Governor General's Literary Awards for Translation Vol. 1: 6110
Governor of the Year Vol. 1: 13464
Governor of the Year Award Vol. 1: 5783
Governor's Arts Awards Vol. 1: 14175
Governor's Award for Distinguished Achievement in Culture the Arts and Humanities Vol. 1: 9287
Governor's Award for Distinguished Achievement in the Culture, Arts, and Humanities Vol. 1: 9287
Governor's Awards for History Vol. 1: 16991
Governor's Awards for the Arts Vol. 1: 8732
Governor's National Leadership Award Vol. 1: 12520
Governor's Screenwriting Competition Vol. 1: 18555
Gowdy Media Award; Curt Vol. 1: 12071
GP Registrar Awards Vol. 2: 6695
GRA Annual Awards Vol. 1: 9159
Graber Award of Special Merit; Thomas M. Vol. 1: 1198
Graber Female Student-Athlete of the Year; Betty Jo Vol. 1: 13402
Grace Award; Oliver R. Vol. 1: 7085
Grace Memorial Award; Dorman John Vol. 1: 13149
Gracies Vol. 1: 9144
Grader Award; Dr. Peretz Vol. 2: 2909
Gradiva Awards Vol. 1: 12370
Graduate and Student Prize Vol. 2: 5128
Graduate and Students Papers Competition (Local Association) Competition Vol. 2: 6113
Graduate and Undergraduate Scholarships Vol. 1: 11092
Graduate Assistantships Vol. 1: 18275
Graduate Award Vol. 2: 6188
Graduate Awards Vol. 2: 5704
Graduate Fellowship Vol. 1: 7648
Graduate Fellowship Award Vol. 1: 906
Graduate Fellowship for Confectionery Research at Penn State University Vol. 1: 14929
Graduate Fellowships Vol. 1: 9475
Graduate Fellowships in Mycology Vol. 1: 12047
Graduate of the Year Vol. 1: 9132
Graduate Research Award Vol. 1: 9864
Graduate Research Awards
AVS Vol. 1: 5589
Northwestern University - Center for International and Comparative Studies Vol 1: 14404
Graduate Research Prizes Vol. 1: 12048
Graduate Scholarship Award Vol. 1: 13924
Graduate Student Award
Canadian Society of Microbiologists Vol. 1: 7011
Dietitians of Canada Vol 1: 8188
International Precious Metals Institute Vol 1: 10554
Materials Research Society Vol 1: 11595
Society for Applied Spectroscopy Vol 1: 16178
Graduate Student Awards
Biomedical Engineering Society Vol. 1: 5772
International Association for the Fantastic in the Arts Vol 1: 10115
Graduate Student Conference Scholarship Vol. 1: 18686
Graduate Student Fellowship Vol. 1: 9583
Graduate Student Fellowship/Novartis Award Vol. 1: 16875
Graduate Student Paper Award
Canadian Geotechnical Society Vol. 1: 6525
Rural Sociological Society Vol 1: 15781
Graduate Student Paper Competition Awards Vol. 1: 6975
Graduate Student Paper Contest Vol. 1: 4700
Graduate Student Plant Breeding Award Vol. 1: 12994
Graduate Student Research Award Vol. 1: 4269
Graduate Student Research Grant Award Vol. 1: 933
Graduate Student Research Grants Vol. 1: 4223
Graduate Student Scholar Award Vol. 1: 15057
Graduate Student Scholarhip Award Vol. 1: 14978
Graduate Student Scholarship Vol. 1: 14938
Graduate Student Teaching Award Vol. 1: 14277
Graduate Studentships Vol. 1: 6707
Graduate Thesis Award Vol. 1: 7015
Graduateship of the City and Guilds of London Institute Vol. 2: 5658
Graduation Awards Vol. 1: 7854
Graduation Prize Vol. 2: 3635
Grady Award for Interpreting Chemistry for the Public; James T. Vol. 1: 1552
Grady - James H. Stack Award for Interpreting Chemistry for the Public; James T. Vol. 1: 1552
Graff Excellence Award; Margarite Ahern Vol. 1: 1406
Graffin Lectureship Award; George D. Vol. 1: 1447
Graffis Award; The Vol. 1: 13286
Graffis Award; Herb Vol. 1: 13286
Graffis Award; Joe Vol. 1: 13286
Graham and Dodd Award Vol. 1: 7264
Graham Award; Duncan Vol. 1: 15745
Graham Award for Innovation in Improving Community Health; Fred Vol. 1: 1675
Graham Award; Harry J. Vol. 1: 15468
Graham Award of Merit; James H. Vol. 1: 15746
Graham Family Physician Executive Award; Robert Vol. 1: 607
Graham Foundation Grants Vol. 1: 9161
Graham Medal Vol. 2: 6867
Graham Perpetual Trophy; Victor W. Vol. 2: 2836
Graham Prize for Health Services Research; William B. Vol. 1: 5380
Grain d'Or Vol. 2: 4805
Gramatky Memorial Award; Hardie Vol. 1: 4435
Grambs Distinguished Career Research in Social Studies Award; Jean Dresden Vol. 1: 12984
Grammaticakis-Neuman; Prix
Academie des Sciences Vol. 2: 1567
Academie des Sciences Morales et Politiques Vol 2: 1666
Grammaticakis-Neumann Prize Vol. 2: 4890
Grammy Awards Vol. 1: 12140
Gran Cruz de la Universidad del Valle Vol. 2: 1199
Gran Premio Citta di Trento Vol. 2: 3136
Gran Premio de Cine Espanol Vol. 2: 4517
Gran Premio de Cine Vasco Vol. 2: 4517
Gran Premio del Festival de Bilbao Vol. 2: 4517
Grand Award
American First Day Cover Society Vol. 1: 2024
Wine Spectator Vol 1: 18761
Grand Canyon Young Readers Award Vol. 1: 4602
Grand Champion Vol. 1: 12770
Grand Champion Primitive and Modern Equipment - U.S. and Europe Vol. 1: 18907
Grand Conceptor Award Vol. 1: 1811
Grand Concours Litteraire Vol. 1: 15811
Grand Cordon of the Supreme Order of the Chrysanthemum Vol. 2: 3244
Grand Effie Vol. 1: 8410
Grand Journalism Prize Vol. 2: 3908
Grand Jury Awards Vol. 1: 8743

Grand Master Award
Mystery Writers of America Vol. 1: 12054
Science Fiction and Fantasy Writers of America Vol 1: 15922
Grand National Exhibition Awards Vol. 1: 829
Grand National Pulling Circuit Rookie of the Year Vol. 1: 13855
Grand Prix
Association Aeronautique et Astronautique de France Vol. 2: 1712
French Foundation for Medical Research Vol 2: 1819
International Organisation of Vine and Wine Vol 2: 1907
Society of Dramatic Authors and Composers Vol 2: 1985
Grand Prix Annual Prize of the Society of Czech Architects Vol. 2: 1270
Grand Prix Award Vol. 2: 6327
Grand Prix Awards Vol. 2: 5585
Grand Prix d'Architecture Vol. 2: 1453
Grand Prix de Chimie Industrielle Vol. 2: 1814
Grand Prix de Jazz General Motors Vol. 1: 8683
Grand Prix de la Chanson Francaise Vol. 2: 1972
Grand Prix de la Fondation de la Maison de la Chimie Vol. 2: 1803
Grand Prix de la Musique Symphonique Vol. 2: 1973
Grand Prix de la Poesie Vol. 2: 1976
Grand Prix de la Societe de Chimie Vol. 2: 1814
Grand Prix de la Ville de Tours Vol. 2: 1801
Grand Prix de la Ville de Villeurbanne Vol. 2: 1792
Grand Prix de l'Academie des Sciences Morales et Politiques Vol. 2: 1667
Grand Prix de l'Edition Musicale Vol. 2: 1974
Grand Prix de l'Humour Vol. 2: 1975
Grand Prix des Biennales Internationales de Poesie Vol. 2: 906
Grand Prix des Poetes Vol. 2: 1976
Grand Prix d'Honneur Vol. 2: 4830
Grand Prix du Jazz Vol. 2: 1977
Grand Prix du Livre de Montreal Vol. 1: 15814
Grand Prix du Souvenir Napoleonien Vol. 2: 1808
Grand Prix Eurovision for Young Dancers Vol. 2: 4708
Grand Prix Eurovision for Young Musicians Vol. 2: 4709
Grand Prix of Sofia Vol. 2: 1141
Grand Prix of the Americas Vol. 1: 11944
Grand Prix of the Dutch Film Golden Calf Vol. 2: 3631
Grand Prix of the Eurovision Song Contest Vol. 2: 4710
Grand Prix of the League of Red Cross and Red Crescent Societies Vol. 2: 1153
Grand Prix Rolex pour la Protection du Monde Sous-Marin Vol. 2: 1890
Grand Prize
Carmel Music Society Vol. 1: 7113
Japan Fashion Color Association Vol 2: 3231
Grand Prize for Commissioned Animation Vol. 1: 14736
Grand Prize Winner Award Vol. 1: 13525
Grand Prizes Vol. 1: 14737
Grand Slam of Tennis Vol. 2: 6307
Grand TAM Award Vol. 1: 7995
Grandgent Award; Charles Hall Vol. 1: 8054
Grandmaster Vol. 2: 2478
GRANDY Award
Advertising Club of New York Vol. 1: 180
International ANDY Awards Vol 1: 10036
Granjon Prize; Henry Vol. 2: 1900
Grant and Peter B. Moens Award of Excellence; William F. Vol. 1: 9006
Grant Award; Eugene L. Vol. 1: 3651
Grant Faculty Scholars; William T. Vol. 1: 18751
Grant for Research Workers Vol. 2: 5302
Grant for Student Research in Mineralogy and Petrology Vol. 1: 11797
Grant for the Enhancement of Geographic Literacy Vol. 1: 12985
Grant Memorial Musical Theatre Scholarship; Regan Vol. 1: 15868
Grant Program Vol. 1: 17959
Grant to Support Costume in Small Museums Vol. 1: 7837
Grants for Arts Projects Vol. 1: 13102
Grants for Otologic and Related Science Research Projects Vol. 1: 8075
Grants-in-Aid of Research Vol. 1: 16057
Grants-in-Aid Program
Lyndon Baines Johnson Library and Museum Vol. 1: 11031
Society for the Psychological Study of Social Issues Vol 1: 16447
Grants in Herpetology
North Carolina Herpetological Society Vol. 1: 14362
Society for the Study of Amphibians and Reptiles Vol 1: 16454
Grants to Eastern Europeans Vol. 2: 5843
Graphic Designer of the Year Vol. 1: 8322
Graphoanalyst of the Year Vol. 1: 10457
Grass Roots Vol. 1: 8842
Grasselli Medal Vol. 1: 16622
Grassland Society of Southern Africa Awards Vol. 2: 4193
Grau Turfgrass Science Award; Fred V. Vol. 1: 7977
Grauls Prize; Noordstar - Dr. Jan Vol. 2: 959
Graves Lecture
Royal Academy of Medicine in Ireland Vol. 2: 2872
Royal Academy of Medicine in Ireland Vol 2: 2874
Gray Article Prize; Ralph D. Vol. 1: 16433
Gray Award; Asa Vol. 1: 4224
Gray Award; Emily M. Vol. 1: 5779
Gray Award; Eva Kenworthy Vol. 1: 1394
Gray Award; Stanley Vol. 2: 6046
Gray Branch Award; Stanley Vol. 2: 6047
Gray Citation of Merit; William S. Vol. 1: 10579
Gray/Elsevier Distinguished Educator Award; Henry Vol. 1: 989
Gray Medal Vol. 1: 10327
Gray Medal; Stanley Vol. 2: 6048
Great 8 Exhibition Vol. 1: 11088
Great American Main Street Award Vol. 1: 13870
Great Friend to Kids Award Vol. 1: 5067
Great Idea Contest Vol. 1: 10850
Great Lakes Sea Grant Network Vol. 1: 9182
Great Lakes Skakel Award Vol. 1: 1449
Great Stone Face Book Award Vol. 1: 7345
Great Swedish Heritage Award Vol. 1: 17352
Great Teachers Award Vol. 1: 14196
Greater Dandenong Short Story Competition Vol. 2: 411
Greater Lynn International Color Slide Salon Vol. 1: 9186
Greater Midwest International Art Exhibition Vol. 1: 18249
Greater Union Awards Vol. 2: 693
Greathouse Distinguished Leadership Award; Frank Vol. 1: 5181
Greathouse Medal; Walser S. Vol. 1: 4436
Greaves-Walker Award; Arthur Frederick Vol. 1: 1481
Greaves-Walker Roll of Honor Award Vol. 1: 11137
Grebe Award; Alfred H. Vol. 1: 15522
Greco-Roman Coach of the Year Vol. 1: 18467
Greco-Roman Wrestler of the Year Vol. 1: 18468
Greek Islands Award Vol. 2: 2470
Greeley Award; Horace Vol. 1: 14051
Greeley Award; Samuel Arnold Vol. 1: 3940
Green and Charles W. Ramsdell Award; Fletcher M. Vol. 1: 17034
Green Apple Award Vol. 2: 5945
Green Apple Awards Vol. 2: 5784
Green-Armytage and Spackman Travelling Scholarship Vol. 2: 6707
Green Award Vol. 1: 8793
Green Award; Brian and Maria Vol. 1: 7673
Green Award; Daniel H. Vol. 1: 5426
Green Award; Fletcher M. Vol. 1: 17034
Green Award for Technology Entrepreneurship; Cecil
BC Innovation Council Vol. 1: 5698
BC Innovation Council Vol 1: 5699
Green Award for Young Concert Artists; Philip and Dorothy Vol. 2: 6409
Green Award for Young Concert Artists; Philip and Dorthy Vol. 2: 6410
Green City Hands-On Activist Award Vol. 1: 15083
Green Codes and Standards Medal; Melvin R. Vol. 1: 4134
Green Globe Award for Environmental Achievement Vol. 1: 8717
Green Heron Award Vol. 1: 15980
Green Hotel of the Year Vol. 1: 7105
Green Journalism Awards; Charles E. Vol. 1: 9296
Green Outstanding Young Scientist Award; Gordon J. Vol. 1: 6815
Green Prize; Leonard W. Vol. 2: 5993
Green Round Hill Trophy; Colonel Vol. 1: 3247
Green School Educator Award; Elizabeth A.H. Vol. 1: 4321
Green Section Award Vol. 1: 17917
Green Star Awards Vol. 1: 15328
Greenberg Award; Noah Vol. 1: 2844
Greenberg Rabbinic Achievement Award; Rabbi Simon Vol. 1: 11008
Greenblatt Prize; Bob Vol. 2: 6274
Greene Award in Bryology; Stanley Vol. 1: 10145
Greene Awards for Food Journalism; Bert Vol. 1: 10188
Greene, Jr., Award; General Wallace M. Vol. 1: 11534
Greene Leadership Award; Dr. Patricia Vol. 1: 5284
Greene Medal; Arnold Vol. 2: 6094
Greene Memorial Award; Jerry Vol. 1: 12843

Greene Memorial United States Numismatics - YN Exhibit Award; Gordon Z. Vol. 1: 2883
Greene Telecommunications Research Fund Award; Paul F. Vol. 1: 5623
Greenfield Award; Sylvia Sorkin Vol. 1: 1245
Greenford Award; Stephen Vol. 1: 6260
Greenman Award; Jesse M. Vol. 1: 5878
The Greensboro Review Literary Awards Vol. 1: 9200
Greenwood Publishing Group Award; Louis Shores - Vol. 1: 2695
Greer Cup; Don Vol. 1: 18172
Greer Memorial Prize; Helen Vol. 2: 5837
Gregg Award; Dr. Randy Vol. 1: 6652
Gregori Aminoffs Pris Vol. 2: 4638
Gregory Award; Dr. A. B. Vol. 1: 15835
Gregory Award; Joseph T. Vol. 1: 16891
Gregory Awards; Eric Vol. 2: 7142
Gregory Medal; Herbert E. Vol. 1: 14784
Greim Distinguished Service Award; Willard N. Vol. 1: 488
Grelaud; Prix Leon Vol. 2: 1568
Grenvik Memorial Award; Christer Vol. 1: 16635
Grenzebach Awards for Outstanding Research in Philanthropy for Education; John Vol. 1: 28
Gresham Award; D. Todd Vol. 1: 11462
Gretzky Scholarship Foundation; Wayne and Walter Vol. 1: 6748
Greve Memorial Award; Belle Vol. 1: 13607
Grey Award; Earle Vol. 1: 69
Grey Cup Vol. 1: 6509
Grice Award; Winthrop W. Vol. 1: 9495
Grieg Prize; Troldhaugen Vol. 2: 3914
Grierson Documentary Film Award Vol. 2: 7067
Grierson International Gold Medal Award; John Vol. 1: 16746
Griffin Award; Charles A. Vol. 1: 917
Griffin Award for Urban Design; Walter Burley Vol. 2: 627
Griffin Poetry Prize Vol. 1: 9206
Griffin Rolex Award; Ellen Vol. 1: 11197
Griffith Award; H. Winter Vol. 1: 608
Griffith Award; Ruby Vol. 1: 5949
Griffith Medal; The Vol. 2: 3041
Griffith Review Lecture; Fred Vol. 2: 7098
Griffith Taylor Medal Vol. 2: 477
Griffiths Award Vol. 1: 10104
Griffiths Obedience Trophy; Suzanne Vol. 1: 10892
Griffiths Property Person of the Year; Jack Vol. 1: 13582
Grigsby, Jr. Award; J. Eugene Vol. 1: 12265
Grimes Award for Excellence in Chemical Engineering; William W. Vol. 1: 2485
Grimley Award; Horace Vol. 2: 6344
Grimm Leadership and Service Award; James C. Vol. 1: 5091
Grimm Prize; Harold J. Vol. 1: 16076
Grimme Preis; Adolf Vol. 2: 2150
Grimwade Medal; John Vol. 2: 5323
Grindley Medal Vol. 1: 245
Griner Award; John Vol. 1: 6979
Grinter Distinguished Service Award; Linton E. Vol. 1: 42
Griscom Award; Ludlow Vol. 1: 1400
Griswold Outstanding Air Pollution Control Official Award; S. Smith Vol. 1: 266
Gritz Award for Excellence in Public Finance; Tanya Vol. 1: 17262
Grizane France; Prix Vol. 2: 3005
Groennings Scholarship; Sven Vol. 1: 10544
Grohmann Award; H. Victor Vol. 1: 9492
Grolier Foundation Award Vol. 1: 2661
Grolier National Library Week Grant Vol. 1: 2682
Grolier Poetry Prize Vol. 1: 9208
Grolla D'Oro Vol. 2: 3138
Gross Award; Barbara Vol. 2: 86
Gross Memorial Award; Barry R. Vol. 1: 12644
Gross Restoration Award; Frank Vol. 1: 18543
Grosse Literaturstipendien des Landes Tirol Vol. 2: 748
Grosser Literaturpreis der Bayerischen Akademie der Schonen Kunste Vol. 2: 2039
Grossman Award; Louis I. Vol. 1: 1086
Grossmann Young Author Award; Marcus A. Vol. 1: 4701
Grote Prijs van de Nederlandse Film Gouden Kalf Vol. 2: 3631
Grotius; Prix Vol. 2: 4767
Grotthuss premija; Teodor Vol. 2: 3378
Groube Fieldwork Award Vol. 2: 3762
Ground Testing Award Vol. 1: 2380
Ground Transportation Company of the Year Vol. 2: 3151
Grounds Management Awards Vol. 1: 15328
Group Achievement Award
Library Administration and Management Association Vol. 1: 11333
National Aeronautics and Space Administration Vol 1: 12206
Group and Grotto Conservation Award Vol. 1: 13790
Group Trophies Vol. 1: 18715
Group Volunteer of the Year Award Vol. 1: 2166
Grove Adoption Activist Award; Judith Vol. 1: 164
Grove Prizes; Sir Charles Vol. 2: 6411
Grove-Rasmussen Memorial Award; Morten Vol. 1: 1012
Groves Fund Awards; Donald Vol. 1: 2932
Grow Award; Malcolm C. Vol. 1: 16888
Grower of the Year Award Vol. 1: 8751
Growth and Promotion Award Vol. 1: 17524
Gruber Fund Award of the AAD; Lila Vol. 1: 569
Gruber Memorial Cancer Research Award and Lectureship; Lila Vol. 1: 567
Grulee Award; Clifford G. Vol. 1: 695
Grumbacher Gold Medal Vol. 1: 14511
Grumbacher Gold Medallion Award Vol. 1: 9184
Grumbridge Pacific Island Trophy; Jack Vol. 2: 6535
Grunfeld-Preis; Paul Vol. 2: 2234
Grunfeld Prize; Paul Vol. 2: 2234
Grunzweig Human Rights Award; Emil Vol. 2: 2895
GSA Young Author's Award Vol. 2: 463
GSBA Scholarships Vol. 1: 9194
Guardia Memorial Trophy; Ed Vol. 1: 17927
Guardian New Director's Award Vol. 2: 5756
Guardian of Seniors' Rights Vol. 1: 4
Gude, Jr. Award; Adolph E. Vol. 1: 4216
Guelph Spring Festival Music Competition Vol. 1: 9220
Guenther Award in the Chemistry of Essential Oils and Related Products; Ernest Vol. 1: 1553
Guenther Award in the Chemistry of Natural Products; Ernest Vol. 1: 1553
Guerin; Prix Andre- Vol. 1: 16137
Guerrera Medal Vol. 2: 1901
Guest of Honor Vol. 1: 647
Guest of Honor Award Vol. 1: 13074
Guetzkow Prize; Harold Vol. 1: 14405
Guggenheim Memorial Foundation Fellowships; John Simon Vol. 1: 9222
Guggenheim; Prix Paul Vol. 2: 4876
Guggenheim Prize; Paul Vol. 2: 4876
Guha Memorial Lecture; B. C. Vol. 2: 2743
Guha Memorial Lecture; Bires Chandra Vol. 2: 2687
Guiding Women in Sport Vol. 1: 12324
Guild Award; Elizabeth Vol. 1: 11765
Guild of Food Writers Award Vol. 2: 5949
Guild of Professional Toastmasters Best After Dinner Speaker of the Year Vol. 2: 5951
Guild of Taxidermists Acredited Member Vol. 2: 5959
Guilday Prize; Peter Vol. 1: 1454
Guilford Undergraduate Research Awards; J. P. Vol. 1: 15401
Guilhermina Suggia Gift for the Cello Vol. 2: 6451
Guillou Prize; Jean Vol. 2: 1747
Guise Medal; Arthur B. Vol. 1: 16684
Guiteras Award; Ramon Vol. 1: 4393
Gulbenkian Foundation Grants; Calouste Vol. 2: 5574
Gulbertian Prize; Calouste Vol. 2: 7132
Guldbaggar Vol. 2: 4683
Gulf Coast 4-Star National Best Condition Award Vol. 1: 1954
Gulick Medal; Luther Halsey Vol. 1: 783
Gullo and Treiber Award Vol. 1: 14295
Gun och Olof Engqvists stipendium Vol. 2: 4657
Gundhall School Gold Medal Vol. 2: 5963
Gundolf-Preis fur die Vermittlung deutscher Kultur im Ausland; Friedrich- Vol. 2: 2146
Gung and Dr. Charles Y. Hu Award for Distinguished Service to Mathematics; Yueh-Gin Vol. 1: 11606
Gunlogson Countryside Engineering Award; G. B. Vol. 1: 3852
Gunlogson Medal; G. B. Vol. 1: 2289
Gunn Award; Ira P. Vol. 1: 7906
Gunn Conservation Award; W. W. H. Vol. 1: 14580
Gunnarson Award; Arthur B. Vol. 1: 9893
Gunnells Intellectual Freedom Award; Danny Vol. 1: 9671
Gunning Victoria Jubilee Prize Lectureship Vol. 2: 6995
Gunter Russell Prize Vol. 2: 5406
Gunter Scholarship; Connie and Robert T. Vol. 1: 16713
Gunther Award; Frank A. Vol. 1: 15523
Gunton Award; T. P. Vol. 2: 5359
Gustave Canet Memorial Medal Vol. 2: 6178
Gustin Memorial Intermediate Chopin Scholarship; The Lyell Vol. 1: 15859
Gustin Memorial Senior Chopin Scholarship; The Lyell Vol. 1: 15885
Gutenberg Award Vol. 2: 2267
Gutenberg Medal; Beno Vol. 2: 1772
Gutenberg-Preis Vol. 2: 2267
Gutenberg Prize; Johann Vol. 1: 16307
Guth Memorial Award for Interior Lighting Design; Edwin F. Vol. 1: 9618
Guthrie Award; RSA Vol. 2: 6885
Guthrie Medal and Prize Vol. 2: 6061
Guthrie Medal; Faldt Vol. 2: 506
Guthrie Prize Vol. 2: 6007
Guthrie Prize; Michael Vol. 2: 5993

Guthrie Training Fellowship; Duncan Vol. 2: 5003
Guttentag Award; Marcia Vol. 1: 1981
Guttentag Fellowship; Marcia Vol. 1: 1981
Guttmacher Award; Manfred S. Vol. 1: 3272
Guye; Prix Philippe A. Vol. 2: 1569
Guynn Family Book Scholarship Vol. 1: 12420
Guyton Awards for Excellence in Integrative Physiology; Arthur C. Vol. 1: 3171
Guze Award; Henry Vol. 1: 16196
GVPTA Career Achievement Award Vol. 1: 9196
GWA Fellow Vol. 1: 8959
GWFC Publicity Book Contest Vol. 1: 8989
GWIC Award Vol. 1: 9103
Gwobrau Tir na n-Og Vol. 2: 7325
GWUP Prize Vol. 2: 2381
Gyldendal Prisen; Soren Vol. 2: 1305
Gyllenbergs pris; Fabian Vol. 2: 4626
Gymnastics National Volunteer of the Year Vol. 1: 489
Gzowski Medal Vol. 1: 6915
Haas Award; F. Otto Vol. 1: 15210
Haas Award; Walter H. Vol. 1: 5215
Haas/Luke Hansen Student Award; Stanley Vol. 2: 2459
Haber Award; William
- American ORT Vol. 1: 3009
- Hillel, the Foundation for Jewish Campus Life Vol 1: 9397

Habermann Award; A. Nico Vol. 1: 7654
Habif Prize; Nessim Vol. 2: 1992
Habitat Solaire, Habitat d'aujourd'hui Vol. 2: 1936
Hachemeister Prize; Charles A. Vol. 1: 7130
Hacke Scholar-Teacher Award; Robert Vol. 1: 7512
Hacker Memorial Award; William J. Vol. 1: 13717
Hackney Award; L. R. Mike Vol. 1: 16484
Hackney Literary Awards Vol. 1: 5789
Hadassah Award for Excellence in Writing About Women Vol. 1: 2599
Haddings pris; Assar Vol. 2: 4627
Hadford Professional Achievement Award; Gary Vol. 1: 6582
Hadley Memorial Achievement Award; Ross Vol. 1: 17750
Hadow/Donald Stuart Short Story Award; Lyndall Vol. 2: 450
Haemophilia Award Vol. 2: 5965
Haemophilia Society Sports Award Vol. 2: 5966
Hafner VTOL Prize Vol. 2: 6641
Hagan Trophy Vol. 1: 4646
Hager Award; Herbert Vol. 1: 2991
Hague Academy of International Law Scholarships Vol. 2: 3559
Hague Award; John L. Vol. 1: 5427
Hahn-Preis fur Chemie und Physik; Otto- Vol. 2: 2091
Hahn Scholarship; Philip Vol. 1: 2145
Hahner Award; USPLTA - Carol Vol. 1: 18391
Haig-Brown Award; Roderick Vol. 1: 8637
Haight Award; Walter Vol. 1: 13874
Hailes Memorial Prize; Jean Vol. 2: 87
Haiman Award Vol. 1: 12925
Haiman Award for Distinguished Scholarship in Freedom of Expression; Franklyn S. Vol. 1: 12925
Haiman Award; Mieczyslaw Vol. 1: 15146
Haimo Award for Distinguished College or University Teaching of Mathematics; Deborah and Franklin Tepper Vol. 1: 11607
Hair Prize; Paul Vol. 1: 226
Hakanson Award; R. C. Vol. 1: 8550
Hake Basic/Applied Research Award; Don F. Vol. 1: 3308
Hakluyt Award Vol. 1: 11040
Halas Trophy; George S. Vol. 1: 13224
Halbouty Outstanding Leadership Award; Michel T. Vol. 1: 1215
Halcrow Premium Vol. 2: 6114
Hale Award; Sarah Josepha Vol. 1: 15668
Hale Prize; George Ellery Vol. 1: 1359
Halecki Award; Oscar Vol. 1: 15147
Hales Prize; Stephen Vol. 1: 4217
Haley Memorial Award for Clinical Excellence; Sarah Vol. 1: 10692
Hall Award for Library Literature; G. K. Vol. 1: 2662
Hall Award; G. Stanley Vol. 1: 3328
Hall Award; Marilyn Vol. 1: 5745
Hall Book Prize; John Whitney Vol. 1: 4780
Hall Composites Manufacturing Award; J. H. "Jud" Vol. 1: 16714
Hall Freedom Cup; George Robert Vol. 1: 4646
Hall/Harold F. Mayfield Award; George A. Vol. 1: 18754
Hall Manufacturing Award; J.H. tJudv Vol. 1: 7644
Hall Medal for Research into Animal Diseases; G. Norman Vol. 2: 6742
Hall Memorial Award; Albert H. Vol. 1: 13374
Hall Memorial Trophy; Martha Vol. 1: 10893
Hall of Champions Vol. 1: 3248
Hall of Distinguished Americans Vol. 1: 13938
Hall of Fame
- American Baseball Coaches Association Vol. 1: 1384
- American Endurance Ride Conference Vol 1: 1955
- American Fence Association Vol 1: 2013
- American Morgan Horse Association Vol 1: 2790
- American Society of Heating, Refrigerating and Air-Conditioning Engineers Vol 1: 4057
- American Theatre Organ Society Vol 1: 4350
- Art Directors Club Vol 1: 4650
- Association for the Advancement of International Education Vol 1: 4974
- Billiard Congress of America Vol 1: 5765
- Brotherhood of Working Farriers Association Vol 1: 5969
- Canadian Hardware and Housewares Manufacturers Association Vol 1: 6548
- Country Music Showcase International Vol 1: 7935
- Direct Marketing Association Vol 1: 8199
- Garden Writers Association Vol 1: 8960
- *Government Computer News* Vol 1: 9142
- Hospitality Sales and Marketing Association International Vol 1: 9496
- Information Systems Security Association Vol 1: 9703
- International Association for Jazz Education Vol 1: 10100
- International Softball Congress Vol 1: 10756
- Libertarian Futurist Society Vol 1: 11319
- Multi-Level Marketing International Association Vol 1: 12003
- National Academy of Television Arts and Sciences Vol 1: 12179
- National Auto Auction Association Vol 1: 12729
- National Baseball Hall of Fame and Museum Vol 1: 12751
- National Christian College Athletic Association Vol 1: 12885
- National Forensic League Vol 1: 13239
- National Museum of Racing and Hall of Fame Vol 1: 13469
- National Pigeon Association Vol 1: 13539
- National Sportscasters and Sportswriters Association Vol 1: 13803
- National Wheelchair Basketball Association Vol 1: 13903
- Olympic Council of Malaysia Vol 2: 3415
- OX5 Aviation Pioneers Vol 1: 14765
- Palomino Horse Breeders of America Vol 1: 14821
- Pastel Society of America Vol 1: 14870
- Percussive Arts Society Vol 1: 14962
- Pi Kappa Phi Vol 1: 15046
- Piano Technicians Guild Vol 1: 15062
- Professional Bowlers Association of America Vol 1: 15275
- Retail Advertising and Marketing Association Vol 1: 15647
- Special Libraries Association Vol 1: 17075
- Specialty Equipment Market Association Vol 1: 17106
- Speed Skating Canada Vol 1: 17124
- United States Curling Association Vol 1: 17789
- United States Racquetball Association Vol 1: 18038
- U.S. Speedskating Vol 1: 18131
- United States Water Polo Vol 1: 18165
- USA Deaf Sports Federation Vol 1: 18385
- Wheelchair Sports, USA Vol 1: 18722
- Women's All-Star Association Vol 1: 18846
- Zen-do Kai Martial Arts Vol 1: 19121

Hall of Fame Award
- American Society for Horticultural Science Vol. 1: 3722
- American Society on Aging Vol 1: 4270
- American Sportscasters Association Vol 1: 4303
- Asphalt Emulsion Manufacturer Association Vol 1: 4727
- Composers and Authors Society of Hong Kong Vol 2: 3931
- Direct Selling Association Vol 1: 8209
- Direct Selling Association - South Africa Vol 2: 4158
- International Federation of Leather Guilds Vol 1: 10409
- International Franchise Association Vol 1: 10441
- Livestock Publications Council Vol 1: 11391
- National Art Materials Trade Association Vol 1: 12282
- National Association of Pipe Coating Applicators Vol 1: 12611
- National Auctioneers Association Vol 1: 12722
- National Aviation Hall of Fame Vol 1: 12732
- National Forum for Black Public Administrators Vol 1: 13247

National High School Band Directors Hall of Fame Vol 1: 13345
National Intercollegiate Soccer Officials Association Vol 1: 13381
National Interscholastic Swimming Coaches Association of America Vol 1: 13387
National School Transportation Association Vol 1: 13670
Salmon Preservation Association for the Waters of Newfoundland Vol 1: 15807
Hall of Fame Awards
Consumer Electronics Association Vol. 1: 7776
National Academy of Recording Arts and Sciences Vol 1: 12141
United in Group Harmony Association Vol 1: 17697
Hall of Fame - Contributor Vol. 1: 17359
Hall of Fame in Philanthropy Vol. 1: 17702
Hall of Fame Museum Vol. 1: 9687
Hall of Fame of Distinguished Band Conductors Vol. 1: 12740
Hall of Fame Program Vol. 1: 12579
Hall of Flame Vol. 1: 11076
Hall of Foam Vol. 1: 8344
Hall of Honor Vol. 1: 10270
Hall of Outstanding Americans Vol. 1: 13938
Hall; Prix James Vol. 2: 1570
Hall Prize in Poetry; Donald Vol. 1: 4773
Hall Prize; R. T. Vol. 2: 399
Halle Research Award; Herman L. Vol. 1: 9051
Haller Interpretive Sculpture Award; Evelyn Vol. 1: 16546
Hallinan Award; Archbishop Paul Vol. 1: 7146
Hallmark Award Vol. 1: 15004
Halmshaw Award; Ron Vol. 2: 5324
Halmstad Prize Vol. 1: 16480
Halperin Electric Transmission and Distribution Award; Herman Vol. 1: 9781
Halpern Award for Distinguished Professional Contributions; Florence Vol. 1: 3403
Halsell Prize; Willie D. Vol. 1: 11863
Halstead Young Investigator's Award; Thora W. Vol. 1: 3713
Halverson Fair Play Award; John Vol. 1: 18039
Ham-Wasserman Lecture Vol. 1: 4069
Hamel; Fondation de Madame Edmond Vol. 2: 1571
Hamel; Prix Joseph Vol. 2: 1668
Hamer and Elizabeth Hamer Kegan Award; Philip M. Vol. 1: 16491
Hamerstrom Award; Fran and Frederick Vol. 1: 15560
Hamilton Award; Alice Vol. 1: 2341
Hamilton Award; Constance E. Vol. 1: 7440
Hamilton Award; Evelyn Vol. 2: 319
Hamilton Award; James A. Vol. 1: 1653
Hamilton Award; Jimmie Vol. 1: 4188
Hamilton Award; Mary Ellen Vol. 1: 13416
Hamilton Hospital Administrators' Book Award; James A. Vol. 1: 1653
Hamilton Memorial Award; Scott Vol. 1: 18441
Hamilton Memorial CWI of the Year Award; Dalton E. Vol. 1: 4454
Hamilton Memorial Prize Vol. 2: 3867
Hamilton Memorial Prize; Max Vol. 1: 7548
Hamilton Scholarship; Al Vol. 1: 5792
Hamilton Traveling Fellowship; John Vol. 2: 6725
Hammarksjold Award; Dag Vol. 1: 10224
Hammerman Spirit of Education Award; Harold Vol. 1: 12700
Hammett Award; Dashiell Vol. 2: 1243
Hammett Prize Vol. 1: 10184
Hamming Medal; Richard W. Vol. 1: 9782
Hammond Award Vol. 2: 5032
Hammond Memorial Prize; Sir John Vol. 2: 5501
Hammond Prize; Dr. George P. Vol. 1: 14981
Hampton Award for Excellence in Film and Digital Media; Henry Vol. 1: 7915
Hancock Brick and Tile Soil and Water Engineering Award Vol. 1: 3853
Hancock Memorial Award in Piano Vol. 1: 15869
Hancor Soil and Water Engineering Award Vol. 1: 3853
Hand Award; Judge Learned Vol. 1: 2585
Hand Award; Learned Vol. 1: 8604
Handler Memorial Award; Christina Vol. 1: 313
"Hands Across South Madison" Community Services Initiative Vol. 1: 16993
Handy Award; W. C. Vol. 1: 5820
Hanes Natural History Award; Anne Vol. 1: 14723
Hanford Sr. Distinguished Faculty Award; Lloyd D. Vol. 1: 9936
Hang Gliding Diploma Vol. 2: 4732
Hank IBA Defensive Player of the Year Vol. 1: 12396
Hanks, Jr., Scholarship in Meteorology; Howard H. Vol. 1: 2778
Hanks Memorial Award for Professional Excellence; Nancy Vol. 1: 1166
Hanlon Award Vol. 1: 8970
Hann Award; Elmer L. Vol. 1: 16762
Hannah Medal; Jason A. Vol. 1: 15760
Hannan Medal Vol. 2: 114
Hanover International Violin Competition Vol. 2: 2142
Hanover Shoe Farms Caretaker of the Year Award Vol. 1: 9265
Hanoverian Stallion of the Year Vol. 2: 2431
Hans Belay Trophy Vol. 2: 5349
Hansberger Leadership in Global Investment Profession Award; Thomas L. Vol. 1: 7265
Hansberry Playwriting Award; Lorraine Vol. 1: 11116
Hansell Publication Award; Dorothy E. Vol. 1: 1021
Hansen Award; Ann Vol. 1: 18096
Hansen Diabetes Fund; Robert W. Vol. 1: 9169
Hansen Medal; C. F. Vol. 2: 1326
Hansen; Premio Profesor Dr. Ricardo Vol. 2: 23
Hansen Student Award; Stanley Haas/ Luke Vol. 2: 2459
Hansens Bibliotekspris; R. Lysholt Vol. 2: 1284
Hanson Award; Abel Vol. 1: 5163
Hanson Fighter/Attack Squadron of the Year Award; Robert M. Vol. 1: 11514
Hanson Medal Vol. 2: 6095
Hanson Medal; Carl Vol. 2: 7164
Hanus Medal Vol. 2: 1250
Hanyo Award; George T. Vol. 1: 5590
Happold Brilliant Award Vol. 2: 5638
Harabaszewski Medal; Jan Vol. 2: 4031
Harbourfront Festival Prize Vol. 1: 10604
Hardee Dissertation of the Year Award; Melvene D. Vol. 1: 12685
Hardeman Prize; D. B. Vol. 1: 11032
Harden Medal Vol. 2: 5173
Hardesty Award; Shortridge Vol. 1: 3941
Harding Award Vol. 2: 5004
Harding Trophy; Olga E. Vol. 2: 3806
Hardinge Award; Hal Williams
American Institute of Mining, Metallurgical, and Petroleum Engineers Vol. 1: 2528
Society for Mining, Metallurgy, and Exploration Vol 1: 16349
Hardingham Presidential Sword; Sir Robert Vol. 2: 6642
Hardison Award; J. Brown Vol. 1: 15581
Hardison Jr. Poetry Prize; O. B. Vol. 1: 8778
Hardy Award; Samuel Vol. 1: 10789
Hardy Fellowship Vol. 2: 6401
Hardy Keynote Address; R. M. Vol. 1: 6526
Hardy Lectureship Vol. 2: 6401
Hardy Medal Award; Robert Lansing Vol. 1: 11809
Hardy Prize; William Bate Vol. 2: 5579
Hardy Scholarship for Professional Advancement; Patricia Vol. 1: 5170
Harger Memorial Life Award; Don Vol. 1: 8638
Hargrove Award; Bill Vol. 1: 18442
Haring Prize; Clarence H. Vol. 1: 2236
Harington-De Visscher Prize Vol. 2: 1299
Harkin Conservation Award; J. B. Vol. 1: 6803
Harkin Medal; J. B. Vol. 1: 6803
Harkness Fellowships Vol. 1: 9248
The Harlan/Teklad Speakers Award Vol. 1: 6207
Harlequin Award Vol. 2: 5432
Harley Award; Herbert Vol. 1: 2603
Harlow Business-Government Relations Award; Bryce Vol. 1: 9250
Harman Award; Katherine Bishop Vol. 2: 5360
Harman Award; Nathaniel Bishop Vol. 2: 5361
Harmers Diamond Jubilee Trophy Vol. 2: 6535
Harmon Award; Lt. Gens. Millard F. and Hubert R. Vol. 1: 14648
Harmony Queens Vol. 1: 9255
Harms-Preis; Bernhard- Vol. 2: 2338
Harness Horse of the Year Vol. 1: 18160
Harper Lecture; Roland Vol. 2: 7165
Harpers Ferry Memorial Scholarship Vol. 1: 17844
Harriman Award for Distinguished Volunteer Service Vol. 1: 3470
Harriman Award; W. Averell Vol. 1: 2057
Harriman Democracy Award; W. Averell Vol. 1: 13088
Harriman Memorial Harness Horse of the Year Trophy; E. Roland Vol. 1: 17931
Harrington Award Vol. 1: 16222
Harrington-Lux Creative Design Award; Holly Vol. 1: 9314
Harris Award Vol. 1: 12676
Harris Award; Albert J. Vol. 1: 10580
Harris Award; Charles Vol. 1: 8194
Harris Award; Gilbert Vol. 1: 14809
Harris Award; Hayden - Vol. 1: 755
Harris Literature Award; Albert H. Vol. 2: 6535
Harris Medal; Townsend Vol. 1: 455
Harris Playwright Award Competition; Julie Vol. 1: 5744
Harris Prize for Illustratied Children's Book; Christie Vol. 1: 18662

Award Index

Harris State Leadership Award; Jeffrey S. Vol. 1: 12521
Harrison Award; George T. Vol. 1: 15208
Harrison Award; John Vol. 2: 6827
Harrison Award of Merit; Bernard P. Vol. 1: 12915
Harrison Memorial Award; Bernie Vol. 1: 18592
Harrison Memorial Prize Vol. 2: 6963
Harrison Scholarship; Dalton S. Vol. 1: 8747
Harry Moffat Memorial Trophy Vol. 2: 5350
Hart Award of Merit for Lifetime Achievement; Kitty Carlisle Vol. 1: 9090
Hart Cup Award Vol. 1: 18097
Hart Graduate Scholarship; Dave Vol. 1: 17025
Hart Memorial Award; Moss Vol. 1: 14056
Hart Public Service Award; Philip Vol. 1: 7779
Hart Service Award; Ray L. Vol. 1: 744
Hart Trophy; Nelson C. Vol. 1: 6653
Hartford-Nicholsen Award Vol. 1: 16849
Hartley Diversity Award; Grant Vol. 1: 13436
Hartman Excellence in Sportswriting Award; Fred Vol. 1: 17464
Hartranft Award; Joseph B. Vol. 1: 343
Hartree Premium Vol. 2: 6146
Hartshorne Trophies Vol. 1: 17903
Hartwig Prize; Dr. Vol. 1: 2160
Harvard Alumni Association Award Vol. 1: 9272
Harvard Medal Vol. 1: 9273
Harvard-Newcomen Postdoctoral Fellowship Vol. 1: 14208
Harvest Award Vol. 1: 13626
Harvest Festival Scholarship Award Vol. 1: 18758
Harvey Award for Exceptional Service to Astrology; Charles Vol. 2: 5154
Harveys Leeds International Pianoforte Competition Vol. 2: 6364
Harwick Lifetime Achievement Award; Harry J. Vol. 1: 1676
Haseltine Memorial Fellowship in Science Writing; Nate Vol. 1: 7873
Haskell Award for Student Journalism; Douglas Vol. 1: 2443
Haskil Competition; Clara Vol. 2: 4765
Haskins Medal Vol. 1: 11677
Haslam Award for Excellence in Bookselling; Charles S. Vol. 1: 16997
Hasler Award; Maurice F. Vol. 1: 17120
Hasse Prize; Merten M. Vol. 1: 11608
Hastings Award; Sir Charles Vol. 2: 5362
Hatai Medal; Shinkishi Vol. 1: 14785
Hatch Award; James E. Vol. 1: 11515
Hatcher International Award; Hazel Vol. 2: 842
HateBuster Hero Award Vol. 1: 9283
Hatfield Award; W. Wilbur Vol. 1: 13021
Hatfield Award; William D. Vol. 1: 18630
Hat's Off! Award Vol. 1: 17473
Hattaway Marine Aviation Ground Officer of the Year Award; Earle Vol. 1: 11516
Hatton Awards Competition for Junior Investigators; Edward H. Vol. 1: 10060
Hatton Awards Competition; Pfizer Vol. 1: 10060
Hatton Memorial Grade B Male Voice Scholarship; Thomas and Don Vol. 1: 15870
Hattori Prize Vol. 2: 3204
Hattori Prize; S. Vol. 1: 10146
Haub Prize for Environmental Diplomacy; Elizabeth Vol. 2: 2293
Haub Prize for Environmental Law; Elizabeth Vol. 2: 2294
Hauer Spelean History Award; Peter M. Vol. 1: 13791
Haueter Award; Paul E. Vol. 1: 2196
Haughton Good Guy Award; Bill Vol. 1: 17932
Hauling Job of the Year Award Vol. 1: 17097
Haumont; Prix Vol. 2: 1454
Haupt Alumni Chapter Project Grants; Helen Vol. 1: 12000
Haupt Piano Scholarship; Helen Vol. 1: 12000
Havenga Prize Vol. 2: 4267
Haverhill Library Award Vol. 1: 9184
Haverland Citation Award; Harry Vol. 1: 10080
Haviland Award; P. H. Vol. 2: 7442
Hawes NEA National Heritage Award; Bess Lomax Vol. 1: 13106
Hawk Migration Association of North America Research Award Vol. 1: 9290
Hawk Mountain - Student Research Award Vol. 1: 9292
Hawkins Award; Ann T. Vol. 1: 4644
Hawksley Gold Medal; Thomas Vol. 2: 6185
Hawley Prize; Ellis W. Vol. 1: 14693
Haworth Memorial Lectureship Vol. 2: 6964
Hawryliuk Memorial Fund; Donald Vol. 1: 6552
Hawryliuk Rural and Remote Opportunities Grant; Donald Vol. 1: 6552
Hawthorne Award; Ben Vol. 2: 3155
Hawthorne Award; Charles Oliver Vol. 2: 5363
Hay Award; Louise Vol. 1: 5005
Hay Medal; Logan Vol. 1: 44
Hay Memorial Award; Roy Vol. 2: 5925
Hayden Award; Alice H. Vol. 1: 17398
Hayden - Harris Award Vol. 1: 755
Hayes Award; Sheldon G. Vol. 1: 12298
Hayes Awards; Helen Vol. 1: 18610
Hayes Student Prize Paper Award; T. Burke Vol. 1: 9820
Hayhow Award; Edgar C. Vol. 1: 1654
Hayling Island SC Trophy Vol. 2: 5910
Hayman Award; Elise M. Vol. 2: 6282
Hayman Distinguished Service Award; Harry Vol. 1: 9809
Hayman Prize for Published Work Pertaining to Traumatized Children and Adults Vol. 2: 6283
Hayman Trophy; Lew Vol. 1: 6510
Haynes Prize for Best Paper Vol. 1: 101
HaynesYoung Scientist Award; Robert H. Vol. 1: 9007
Hays Award Vol. 1: 9916
Hays Award; Hazel Vol. 1: 8559
Haythornthwaite Cup Vol. 2: 7208
Hayward Trophy Vol. 1: 16102
Hazardous Materials Manager of the Year Vol. 1: 78
Hazardous Waste Management Award Vol. 1: 18631
Hazen Education Prize; Joseph H. Vol. 1: 9441
Hazzard Voice Scholarship; Brena Vol. 1: 12000
Head Arthur Ashe Sportsmanship Award Vol. 1: 9998
Head Bequest; Francis Vol. 2: 7143
Head Book Award; Florence Roberts Vol. 1: 14487
Head of Public Service Award Vol. 1: 17592
Headliner Award
Association for Women in Communications Vol. 1: 5001
Livestock Publications Council Vol 1: 11392
Headliner Awards Vol. 1: 11373
Heads Up Award Vol. 1: 18708
Healey Health Law Teachers Award; Jay Vol. 1: 4109
Health Achievement in Occupational Medicine Award Vol. 1: 1690
Health Advocate Award Vol. 1: 2954
Health and Safety Award Vol. 2: 5420
Health Care Delivery Award Vol. 1: 527
Health Education Mentor Award Vol. 1: 16396
Health Education Professional of the Year Awards Vol. 1: 909
Health Management Research Award Vol. 1: 1655
Health Professions Education and Training Award Vol. 1: 12459
Health Research Foundation Awards Vol. 1: 6137
Health, Safety, and Environment Award Vol. 1: 16800
Health Science Award Vol. 1: 4394
Healthcare and Aging Awards Vol. 1: 4271
Healthcare Executive of the Year
American College of Managed Care Administrators Vol. 1: 1669
American College of Oncology Administrators Vol 1: 1698
Healthy Workplace Initiative Award Vol. 1: 15406
Heaps Prize; Norman Vol. 2: 5612
Hearn Trophy; George Vol. 2: 5041
Hearst Memorial Performance Award Vol. 1: 10515
Hearst/National PTA Excellence in Education Partnership Award; Phoebe Aperson Vol. 1: 13584
Heart of America Awards Vol. 1: 2637
Heart of Humanity Award Vol. 1: 18194
Heart of Molly Award Vol. 1: 9334
Heart of the Program Award Vol. 1: 15909
Heart of the Year Award Vol. 1: 2178
Heartland Arts Fund Vol. 1: 4679
Heartland Prizes Vol. 1: 7334
Heartwell Award Vol. 1: 12677
Heat Transfer & Energy Conversion Division Award Vol. 1: 2500
Heat Transfer Memorial Award Vol. 1: 4135
Heath Achievement in Literacy Award; Stan Vol. 1: 6704
Heath Award; Edward Vol. 2: 6768
Heaviest Structure Moved Not On Rubber Tired Dollies Vol. 1: 10247
Heaviest Structure Moved On Dollies Under $30000 Vol. 1: 10248
Heaviest Structure Moved On Rubber Tired Dollies Vol. 1: 10249
Heaviest Structure Moved Under $30000 Vol. 1: 10250
Heaviside Premium Vol. 2: 6146
Hebb Award for Distinguished Contributions to Psychology as a Science; Donald O. Vol. 1: 6835
Hebb Distinguished Contribution Award; Donald O. Vol. 1: 6889

Hebb Distinguished Scientific Contribution Award; D. O. Vol. 1: 3312
Hebel-Preis; Johann-Peter- Vol. 2: 2361
Hebert; Prix Louis-Phillipe- Vol. 1: 16138
Hebrew Play Award Vol. 2: 2902
Hecht Award; Max Vol. 1: 5428
Heck Prize; Mathilda Vol. 1: 18588
Heckel Award; George Baugh Vol. 1: 13516
Hector Memorial Medal and Prize Vol. 2: 3868
Hedberg Award in Energy; Hollis D. Vol. 1: 9762
Hedrick Awards; U. P. Vol. 1: 3242
Hedrick Lectureship Vol. 1: 11609
Hedwig Medal Vol. 1: 10147
Heeney Memorial Award; Robert C. Vol. 1: 12506
Heesom Medal; Denys Vol. 2: 4139
Hefley Educator of the Year Award; Sue Vol. 1: 11422
Hefner First Amendment Award; Hugh M. Vol. 1: 15103
Hegarty Prize Vol. 2: 592
Hegel-Preis der Landeshauptstadt Stuttgart Vol. 2: 2416
Heidbreder Eastman Grant; Ann Vol. 1: 11824
Heideman Award Vol. 1: 149
Heidseick Award; RPS Charles Vol. 2: 6865
Heifetz Memorial Fellowship; Vladimir and Pearl Vol. 1: 19062
Heilprin Literary Medal; Angelo Vol. 1: 9012
Heiman Impact Award for Excellence in Educational Support; John C. Vol. 1: 2486
Heimann Service Award; Jack Vol. 1: 17294
Heine-Medin Medal Vol. 2: 4581
Heineken Prize for Art; Dr. A.H. Vol. 2: 3651
Heineken Prize for Biochemistry and Biophysics; Dr. H. P. Vol. 2: 3652
Heineken Prize for Environmental Sciences; Dr. A.H. Vol. 2: 3653
Heineken Prize for History; Dr. A.H. Vol. 2: 3654
Heineken Prize for Medicine; Dr. A.H. Vol. 2: 3655
Heineman Prize for Astrophysics; Dannie N. Vol. 1: 2541
Heineman Prize for Mathematical Physics; Dannie N. Vol. 1: 2542
Heineman Trophy Vol. 1: 15648
Heinl, Jr., Award; Colonel Robert D. Vol. 1: 11535
Heinz Award in Public Policy Vol. 1: 9349
Heinz Award in Technology, the Economy and Employment Vol. 1: 9350
Heinz Award in the Arts and Humanities Vol. 1: 9351
Heinz Award in the Environment Vol. 1: 9352
Heinz Award in the Human Condition Vol. 1: 9353
Heinz III Federal Public Service Award; H. John Vol. 1: 13502
Heinz Literature Prize; Drue Vol. 1: 18338
Heinzerling Trophy; Commodore Charles E. Vol. 1: 16102
Heise Award Vol. 1: 8572
Heiskell Community Service Awards; Andrew Vol. 1: 17541
Heisler Prize; Charlene Vol. 2: 66
Heisman Memorial Trophy Vol. 1: 9357
Heizer Prize; Robert F. Vol. 1: 3703
Helava Award; U.V. Vol. 2: 4975
Helfer Award; Ray E.
  Ambulatory Pediatric Association Vol. 1: 528
  American Academy of Pediatrics Vol 1: 696
Helicopter Maintenance Award Vol. 1: 9365
Helin International Singing Competition; Mirjam Vol. 2: 1391
Hellebrandt Professional Opportunity Awards; Caroline tum Suden/Frances Vol. 1: 3181
Heller Award; Florence G. Vol. 1: 10987
Heller Prize; Dr. Bernard Vol. 1: 9346
Hellinger Award; Mark Vol. 1: 15786
Hellings Award; Susan R. Vol. 1: 12886
Hellman-Hammett Grants Vol. 1: 9522
Hellman Research Essay Award; Milo Vol. 1: 1199
Hellrung Award; Robert T. Vol. 1: 11644
Helm Award; McKay - Vol. 1: 4455
Helmerich Distinguished Author Award; Peggy V. Vol. 1: 17626
Helmholtz-Preis Vol. 2: 2269
Helmholtz Prize Vol. 2: 2269
Helmholtz-Rayleigh Interdisciplinary Silver Medal Vol. 1: 127
Helms Award for Staff and Graduate Staff; Edgar J. Vol. 1: 9133
Helpmann Awards Vol. 2: 183
Helpmann Scholarship; Robert Vol. 2: 584
Helsinki International Ballet Competition Vol. 2: 1407
Helton Manufacturing Scholarship; Clinton J. Vol. 1: 16715
Helvetia Trophy; H.L. Katcher Vol. 2: 6535
Hemans Prize for Lyrical Poetry; Felicia Vol. 2: 7311
Hemingway Foundation/PEN Award Vol. 1: 14912
Hemley Memorial Award; Cecil Vol. 1: 15130
Hemphill-Jordan Leadership Award Vol. 1: 1013
Hemphill Memorial Award; Bernice
  American Association of Blood Banks Vol. 1: 1013
  American Association of Blood Banks Vol 1: 1013
Hemschemeyer Award; Hattie Vol. 1: 1688
Hench Post-Dissertation Fellowship Vol. 1: 819
Hendershott Award; Robert Vol. 1: 2891
Henderson Award; Alexander Vol. 2: 241
Henderson Award; R.A. Vol. 1: 6869
Henderson Memorial Award; Harold G. Vol. 1: 9236
Henderson Memorial Exhibit Award; William C. Vol. 1: 2892
Henderson Memorial Grant for Foreign Experience; Mabel Vol. 1: 12000
Henderson Memorial Prize; Ian Vol. 2: 507
Henderson Scholarship; Charles Vol. 1: 2145
Henderson Service to the Section Award; Julia Vol. 1: 15967
Henderson Student Award; Edward Vol. 1: 2127
Hendrick Memorial Award for Technical Excellence; Mic Vol. 1: 10750
Hendy Award; James C. Vol. 1: 2270
Henebry Roll of Honor Award; Agnes Vol. 1: 17084
Henie Award; Sonja Vol. 1: 15362
Henk de by Incentive Prize Vol. 2: 3621
Henley Award; Butch Vol. 1: 2218
Henley Media Award; Vernon Vol. 1: 1818
Henne Award; Frances Vol. 1: 1276
Henne Research Grant; Frances Vol. 1: 19084
Henne/YALSA/VOYA Research Grant; Frances Vol. 1: 19084
Hennessy Awards Vol. 1: 13632
Hennessy Travelers Association Award of Excellence Vol. 1: 13632
Hennessy Trophy; John L. Vol. 1: 13632
Henniker Premium; Harry Vol. 2: 6150
Henning Andersen Prizes Vol. 2: 5864
Henning Prize Vol. 2: 1299
Henrich Award; Emo Vol. 1: 17300
Henry Award; Charles D. Vol. 1: 784
Henry Award; Edward C. Vol. 1: 1482
Henry Award; O. Vol. 1: 17480
Henry Award; Patrick Vol. 1: 13301
Henry Fonda Young Playwrights Project Vol. 1: 18578
Henry J. Kaiser Policy Debate Vol. 1: 13244
Henry Johns Award Vol. 2: 5266
Henry Knowles Beecher Award Vol. 1: 9281
Henry Prize Stories; O. Vol. 1: 15550
Henry Student Research Award; Ted Vol. 1: 16237
Henry Volunteer of the Year Award; Robert Lee Vol. 1: 13336
Henshall Award; Dr. James A. Vol. 1: 8639
Henshel Award; Colonel Harry D. Vol. 1: 490
Hensler Award; Bill and Sue Vol. 1: 9389
Hepburn Award for Contributions to the Health and Welfare of Children; Audrey Vol. 1: 16050
Heptathlon Award Vol. 1: 18443
Herb S. Brier Instructor of the Year Award Vol. 1: 32
Herb Society of America Grant Vol. 1: 9378
Herbert Award; John Vol. 2: 5129
Herbert Medal Vol. 1: 10284
Herbert Memorial Scholarships; Richard A. Vol. 1: 4420
Herbert Youth Exhibit Award; Alan Vol. 1: 2893
Herder Prizes Vol. 2: 2397
Hereford Airport Communication Excellence Award; Peggy Vol. 1: 349
Hereford Award for Excellence in Communications; Peggy G. Vol. 1: 349
Hering Medal; Henry Vol. 1: 13692
Hering Medal; Rudolph Vol. 1: 3942
Heritage APA Service Award Vol. 1: 3382
Heritage Award
  American Psychological Association - Society for the Psychology of Women (Division 35) Vol. 1: 3382
  Historic Harmony Vol 1: 9413
  Irish American Cultural Institute Vol 1: 10883
  Irish American Cultural Institute Vol 1: 10884
  National Dance Association Vol 1: 13077
  North American Manx Association Vol 1: 14307
Heritage Award; Doris Brown Vol. 1: 18444
Heritage Award for Outstanding Career Achievement Vol. 1: 16967
Heritage in Britain Award Vol. 2: 5224
Heritage Practice Award Vol. 1: 3382
Heritage Public Policy Award Vol. 1: 3382
Heritage Publications Award Vol. 1: 3382
Heritage Research Award Vol. 1: 3382
Heritage Toronto Awards of Merit Vol. 1: 9391
Herlitzka; Premio Vol. 2: 2967

Herman Memorial Award; M. Justin Vol. 1: 12564
Herman Memorial Award; Robert H. Vol. 1: 3790
Hermann Memorial Award; Fred Vol. 1: 9834
Hermanns International Competition; Heida Vol. 1: 7721
Hermes Award Vol. 2: 865
Herndon National Legislative Award; Maurice G. Vol. 1: 9641
Hero Awards Vol. 1: 4752
A Hero for Our Time Award Vol. 1: 15552
Hero in Medicine Award Vol. 1: 10225
Hero of Baseball Award Vol. 1: 16170
Heroes Award Vol. 1: 13437
Heroism Award Vol. 1: 8727
Heroism Medal Vol. 1: 13764
Heroy, Jr. Award for Distinguished Service to AGI; William B. Vol. 1: 2107
Herpetologists' League Award for Graduate Research Vol. 1: 9393
Herpetologists' League Student Prize Vol. 1: 9393
Herreshoff Trophy; Nathaniel G. Vol. 1: 18064
Herrick Award; Charles Judson Vol. 1: 990
Herrick Award; James B. Vol. 1: 2179
Herring Memorial Prize; Sir Edward Vol. 2: 107
Herriot Award; James Vol. 1: 9524
Herschel Medal Vol. 2: 6688
Herschel Medal; John F. W. Vol. 2: 4242
Herschfus Memorial Award Vol. 1: 667
Hersey Award; Mayo D. Vol. 1: 4136
Hershberg Award for Important Discoveries in Medicinally Active Substances; E. B. Vol. 1: 1554
Hersholt Humanitarian Award; Jean Vol. 1: 108
Herskovits Award Vol. 1: 227
Herter Award; Christian A. Vol. 1: 2058
Hertert Memorial Award; Lucien Dean Vol. 1: 998
Herty, Jr., Award; Charles W. Vol. 1: 4899
Hertz Memorial Fellowship; Aleksander and Alicja Vol. 1: 19063
Hertz Preis; Heinrich Vol. 2: 2429
Hertz-Preis (Physik-Preis); Gustav- Vol. 2: 2092
Hertz; Prix Henri Vol. 2: 1806
Hertzog Prize for Literature Vol. 2: 4268
Hervey Journalism Award; John Vol. 1: 18161
Hervey-Smallsreed Award Vol. 1: 18161
Herzberg Award Vol. 1: 6875
Herzberg Canada Gold Medal for Science and Engineering; Gerhard Vol. 1: 13975
Herzberg Medal Vol. 1: 6281
Hesburgh, CSC, Award; Theodore M. Vol. 1: 5061
HeSCA/JBC Literary Award Vol. 1: 9312
HeSCA/Marion Laboratories Print Media Festival Vol. 1: 9315
HeSCA/NCME Award Vol. 1: 9318
Hesch Memorial Scholarship; Wayne E. Vol. 1: 4514
Heschel Peace Award; Abraham Joshua Vol. 1: 11005
Hess Award; Barbara A. Vol. 1: 5024
Hess Award; Henry Vol. 1: 4137
Hess Medal; Harry H. Vol. 1: 2116
Hess Programme; Gerhard Vol. 2: 2219
Hessayon New Writers' Award; Joan Vol. 2: 6606
Heston Award for Outstanding Scholarship in Interpretation and Performance Studies; Lilla A. Vol. 1: 12926
Hestrin Prize Vol. 2: 2923
Hetherington Award Vol. 1: 624
Heubner Preis; Otto Vol. 2: 2250
Heuer Timing Road Rally Rookie Vol. 1: 17200
Hevesy Nuclear Pioneer Award; Georg Charles de Vol. 1: 16779
Hewes Design Awards; Henry Vol. 1: 4354
Hewes Memorial Award For Distinguished Volunteer Service; Bettie Vol. 1: 6720
Hewett Book Prize; Ed A. Vol. 1: 957
Hewitt and Maybelle Ellen Ball Hewitt Award; William Boright Vol. 1: 3192
Hewitt Award; Barnard Vol. 1: 3828
Hewitt Award; C. Gordon Vol. 1: 8493
Hewitt Memorial Award; Foster Vol. 1: 9451
Hewlett-Packard Europhysics Prize Vol. 2: 1786
Hexter Prize; Margaret Vol. 1: 13690
Hexter Prize; Maurice B. Vol. 1: 13690
Heymans; Prijs Jan-Frans Vol. 2: 967
HG Andrewartha Medal Vol. 2: 648
HGA Award Vol. 1: 9242
HHS Distinguished Public Service Award Vol. 1: 17825
Hi-Fi Grand Prix Awards Vol. 1: 5526
Hibiscus of the Year Award Vol. 1: 2214
Hickey Memorial Award; Joseph V. Vol. 1: 13150
Hickinbottom Fellowship Vol. 2: 6965
Hickish Award; David Vol. 2: 5395
Hickman Memorial Research Award; Susan Vol. 1: 15171
Hicks Award for Outstanding Contributions to Academic Law Librarianship; Frederick Charles Vol. 1: 1143
Hicks Graduate Scholarship; Dorothy Vol. 1: 17026
Hidden Treasure Award Vol. 2: 7231
Hideo Memorial Award; Yoshida Vol. 2: 3265
Higdon Distinguished Educator Award; Archie Vol. 1: 3652
Higenbottam Memorial Prize; Frank Vol. 2: 6033
Higgins Lectureship Award; T. R. Vol. 1: 2556
Higgins Redesign Award Vol. 1: 15206
Higginson Cinematography Award; Ed Vol. 1: 5505
High Energy and Particle Physics Prize Vol. 2: 1787
High Point Awards
North American Peruvian Horse Association Vol. 1: 14317
Oley Valley Combined Training Association Vol 1: 14509
High Point Horsemanship Award Vol. 1: 14343
High Point Performance Horse Awards Vol. 1: 14318
High Points Champion Stallion/Mare Vol. 1: 4477
High Rising Trophy - Norwich Bitch Vol. 1: 14423
High School All-American Awards Vol. 1: 18375
High School and Proprietary School Achievement Award Vol. 1: 10744
High School Athlete Award Vol. 1: 14505
High School Awards Program Vol. 1: 463
High School Essay Contest
Biotechnology Industry Organization Vol. 1: 5784
Wisconsin Labor History Society Vol 1: 18786
High School Flute Choir Competition Vol. 1: 13200
High School Literary Arts Awards and Scholarships Competition Vol. 1: 353
High School Scholar All-America Award Vol. 1: 13708
High School Science Fair National Award Vol. 1: 18632
High School Solo Competition Vol. 1: 10320
High School Soloist Competition Vol. 1: 13201
High School Student Fellowship Vol. 1: 5983
High Winds Medal Vol. 1: 4437
Higher Education Student Achievement Award Vol. 1: 12266
Higher Education Writers Award Vol. 1: 1320
Highly Commended Certificate Vol. 1: 2992
Highman Travel Grant Award Vol. 1: 9625
Highsmith Library Innovation Award Vol. 1: 15422
Highsmith Library Innovative Award Vol. 1: 9601
Highsmith Library Literature Award Vol. 1: 2662
Highsmith Research Grant Vol. 1: 1277
Highway Research Board Distinguished Service Award Vol. 1: 17579
Higuchi Research Prize; Takeru Vol. 1: 3051
Hildebrand Award in the Theoretical and Experimental Chemistry of Liquids; Joel Henry Vol. 1: 1555
Hilditch Memorial Lecture Vol. 2: 7166
Hildreth Award; Harold M. Vol. 1: 3352
Hilgard Award; Ernest and Josephine Vol. 1: 16197
Hilgard Award for Distinguished Contributions to General Psychology; Ernest R. Vol. 1: 3343
Hilgard Best Graduate Level Academic Thesis Award; E. R. Vol. 1: 3415
Hilgard Hydraulic Prize; Karl Emil Vol. 1: 3943
Hill Award; Bill Vol. 1: 13576
Hill Award; Dorothy Vol. 2: 115
Hill Award; Errol Vol. 1: 3829
Hill Award; Jimmie D. Vol. 1: 13452
Hill Award; Reuben Vol. 1: 13041
Hill Awards; Ashton Vol. 2: 7384
Hill Community Development Awards; Charlotte Vol. 1: 13262
Hill Foundation Scholarship; Derek Vol. 2: 5439
Hill New Investigator Award; Martha N. Vol. 1: 2180
Hill Sports Book of the Year; William Vol. 2: 7336
Hill Volunteer in Fund-Raising Award; Charlotte Vol. 1: 13261
The Hillenbrand Award Vol. 1: 96
Hillerman Award; Fred Vol. 1: 2993
Hillier Award; Doris Vol. 2: 5364
Hillis Achievement Award for Choral Excellence; Margaret Vol. 1: 7378
Hillman Foundation Prize Awards; Sidney Vol. 1: 9400
Hill's Animal Welfare and Humane Ethics Award Vol. 1: 808
Hilti-Preis Vol. 2: 4898
Hime Memorial Trophies; Alan Vol. 2: 5042

Hinchley Medal; John William Vol. 2: 6096
Hincks Award; C. M. Vol. 1: 6713
Hinderstein Award; Jeanette Robinson Vol. 1: 11468
Hinds Award; Julian Vol. 1: 3944
Hindustan Zinc Gold Medal Vol. 2: 2651
Hine Awards; Lewis Vol. 1: 12882
Hippocratic Oath Award Vol. 1: 10163
Hirsch Award for Excellence in Broadcasting; Harold S. Vol. 1: 14323
Hirsch Award for Excellence in Ski Photography; Harold S. Vol. 1: 14324
Hirsch Award; Harold S. Vol. 1: 14325
Hirsch Director's Award; John Vol. 1: 14559
Hirsch Medaille; Otto Vol. 2: 2417
Hirsch Prize; John Vol. 1: 6111
Hirschfeld Award; Magnus Vol. 2: 2240
Hirschfeld Award; Tomas A. Vol. 1: 8618
Hirschmann Award in Peptide Chemistry; Ralph F. Vol. 1: 1556
Hirschs pris; Axel Vol. 2: 4658
Hirsh Award Vol. 1: 1661
Hirst Premium; Lord Vol. 2: 6146
Hirt Prize; Victor Vol. 2: 5107
Hiser Exemplary Publication Award; Paul T. Vol. 1: 8512
Hislop Award for Outstanding Contributions to Professional Literature; Helen J. Vol. 1: 3147
Hispanic Engineer National Achievement Awards Vol. 1: 7101
Historic Preservation Award
Billings Preservation Society Vol. 1: 5767
Peerless Rockville Historic Preservation Vol 1: 14885
Historical Achievement Award
Ohio Academy of History Vol. 1: 14458
Ohio Academy of History Vol 1: 14460
Historical Building Award Vol. 1: 5993
Historical Category Award of Merit Vol. 1: 13526
Historical Landmarks Designation Vol. 1: 4702
Historical Metallurgy Society Grants Vol. 2: 5974
Historical Plaque Vol. 1: 14720
History Manuscript Award Vol. 1: 2381
History of Geology Award Vol. 1: 9022
History of Military Medicine Essay Award Vol. 1: 5246
Histotechnologist of the Year Award Vol. 1: 13718
Hitchcock Award; Alice Davis Vol. 1: 16554
Hitchcock Award; Edward Vol. 1: 1606
Hitchcock Distinguished Professional Service Award; Arthur A. Vol. 1: 1842
Hitchcock Landscape in Sunlight Prize; George Vol. 1: 12109
HKMA Quality Award Vol. 2: 3942
Hlushko Award to Young Co-operative Educators; William Vol. 1: 5119
Hnatyshyn Award for Law; Ramon John Vol. 1: 6331
Hoag Scholarship; Jim Vol. 1: 16995
Hoagland Award; Dennis Robert Vol. 1: 4218
Hoar Award Vol. 1: 7034
Hobart Memorial Award; W. H. Vol. 1: 4456
Hobart Seven Hats Award; Larry Vol. 1: 3442
Hobbs Award; Nicholas Vol. 1: 3374
Hobbyist of the Year Vol. 1: 6222
Hoch Distinguished Service Award; Paul Vol. 1: 1683
Hochhausen Fund for Research in Adaptive Technologyfor Blind and Visually Impaired Persons; E. (Ben) and Mary Vol. 1: 6749
Hockey Hall of Fame Award Vol. 1: 9452
Hockey Hall of Fame - Builder Category Vol. 1: 6152
Hockey Hall of Fame - International Friends Category Vol. 1: 6153
Hockey Hall of Fame - John Sergnese (Friends of CARHA) Category Vol. 1: 6154
Hockey Hall of Fame - Media Category Vol. 1: 6155
Hockey Hall of Fame - Player Category Vol. 1: 6156
Hockey Hall of Fame - Team Category Vol. 1: 6157
Hodder Cup Vol. 1: 18077
Hodges International Piano Competition/ Virginia Waring International Piano Competition; Joanna Vol. 1: 18569
Hodgins Award; Agatha Vol. 1: 7907
Hodgins Award for Outstanding Accomplishment; Agatha Vol. 1: 1180
Hodgkin Fellowships; Dorothy Vol. 2: 6914
Hodgkiss Canadian Outdoorsperson of the Year Award; Stan Vol. 1: 7066
Hodgson Distinguished Service Award; Kenneth O. Vol. 1: 14064
Hodgson Prize Vol. 2: 6643
Hodson Award; Walter D. Vol. 1: 16882
Hodson Fund Vol. 2: 6515
Hoepfner Awards; Theodore Christian Vol. 1: 17040
Hoffman Award; Anna Louise Vol. 1: 10864
Hoffman Award; Dorothy M. and Earl S. Vol. 1: 5591
Hoffman Award for the Best Postgraduate Paper; Jerome J. Vol. 1: 1109
Hoffman Award; Paul R. Vol. 1: 13613
Hoffman Award; Phillip R. Vol. 1: 3945
Hoffman-La Roche Award for Specialties in Pharmacy Practice Vol. 1: 6997
Hoffman LaRoche Award of Excellence Vol. 1: 1023
Hoffman-LaRoche Ltd. Award Vol. 1: 6903
Hoffman Memorial Award; Cecile Pollack Vol. 1: 10164
Hoffman Memorial Award; Craig Vol. 1: 17661
Hoffman Prize; Artists Fund Malvina Vol. 1: 12110
Hoffman Prize; Edward Fenno Vol. 1: 13693
Hoffman Prize for Distinguished Publication on Christopher Marlowe; Calvin and Rose G. Vol. 2: 6350
Hoffman Scholarship; Dorothy M. and Earl S. Vol. 1: 5592
Hofheimer Prize Vol. 1: 3267
Hofheimer Prize Award Vol. 1: 3267
Hofman Award; Jozef Vol. 1: 1802
Hofmann Award; Adele Dellenbaugh Vol. 1: 697
Hofmann Visiting Professor in Adolescent Medicine and Health Award; Adele D. Vol. 1: 16148
Hofmeyr Prize; W. A. Vol. 2: 4373
Hofmeyr-prys; W. A. Vol. 2: 4373
Hogan Award; Ben Vol. 1: 9124
Hogan Distinguished Service Award; John F. Vol. 1: 15534
Hogan Environmental Law Essay Contest; Roscoe Vol. 1: 15716
Hogentogler Award; C. A. Vol. 1: 5429
Hogg Medal Vol. 2: 6795
Hogg Young Artist Competition; Ima Vol. 1: 9499
Hoggard Performance Medallion; Lara Vol. 1: 11754
Hohl Service Award; Shirley Vol. 1: 3578
Hoke, Sr. Award; Henry Vol. 1: 11469
Hokin Prize; Bess Vol. 1: 15116
Holberg Medal Vol. 2: 1293
Holbrook Alumni Award; Frances Morton Vol. 1: 15008
Holden Medal Vol. 2: 7264
Holdredge Award; Claire P. Vol. 1: 5136
Hole Medal; Dean Vol. 2: 6851
Holford Medal Vol. 2: 6793
Holgersson Plaketten; Nils Vol. 2: 4687
Holgersson Plaque; Nils Vol. 2: 4687
Holiness Exponent Vol. 1: 7389
Holladay Distinguished Fellow Award; Louise and Bill Vol. 1: 4058
Hollaender Award; Alexander Vol. 1: 8504
Holland Animation Film Festival Vol. 2: 3561
Holland Award for Outstanding Achievement in Career or Personality Research; John Vol. 1: 3322
Holland Award; Maurice Vol. 1: 9694
Holland Trophy Vol. 2: 5043
Hollenback Memorial Prize Vol. 1: 115
Holley Medal Vol. 1: 4138
Holley Memorial Music Scholarship; Rick Vol. 1: 4515
Holliday Award; Polly Vol. 1: 17017
Hollister Award; Jean Vol. 1: 8436
Hollomon Award; J. Herbert Vol. 2: 5001
Holloway Distinguished Service Award; George T. Vol. 1: 12858
Holloway Medal; Tienie Vol. 2: 4269
Holly Memorial Award for Humanitarian Achievement; T. Kenyon Vol. 1: 17638
Holman Award; C. Hugh Vol. 1: 16467
Holman Memorial Award; Richard Clive Vol. 2: 5796
Holmenkoll Medal Vol. 2: 3889
Holmenkollen Ski Festival Vol. 2: 3890
Holmenkollmedaljen Vol. 2: 3889
Holmes Award; John Vol. 1: 14044
Holmes Bill of Rights Award; Oliver Wendell Vol. 1: 1601
Holmes Medal and Honorary Membership; Arthur Vol. 2: 1773
Holmes Memorial Award; Harry (Hap) Vol. 1: 2271
Holmes Pioneer Award; Joseph H. Vol. 1: 2565
Holmes Scholarship; Dr. Vol. 2: 3267
Holmes Scholarship; Sylvia Vol. 1: 9085
Holmes Travel Award; Oliver Wendell Vol. 1: 16492
Holmes - Weatherly Award Vol. 1: 17678
Holonyak Jr. Award; Nick Vol. 1: 14607
Holst Medal; Gilles Vol. 2: 3656
Holst-prijs; Henriette Roland Vol. 2: 3669
Holt Award; Geoffrey Vol. 2: 5365
Holtby Memorial Prize; Winifred Vol. 2: 7002
Holter Memorial Prize; Casey Vol. 2: 7114
Holtkamp-AGO Award in Organ Composition Vol. 1: 2147
Holweck Medal and Prize Vol. 2: 6062
Holweck; Prix Fernand Vol. 2: 1572
Holzman Distinguished Educator Award; Albert G. Vol. 1: 9865
Homebrew Club of the Year Vol. 1: 2284
Homebrewer of the Year Vol. 1: 2284
Homen Prize; Professor Theodor Vol. 2: 1399

Award Index

Homer D. Babbidge, Jr. Award Vol. 1: 4990
Homeric Award Vol. 1: 7317
Hometown Video Festival Vol. 1: 405
Homewood Chiropractic Heritage Award; Lee- Vol. 1: 4986
Honda Medal; Soichiro Vol. 1: 4139
Honda Prize Vol. 2: 3185
Honens International Piano Competition; Esther Vol. 1: 9467
Honeywell Prize Vol. 2: 6051
Hong Kong Awards for Industries Vol. 2: 3945
Hong Kong Film Awards Vol. 2: 3935
Hong Kong Independent Short Film Competition/Urban Council Short Film Awards Vol. 2: 3936
Hong Kong International Film Festival Vol. 2: 3935
Hong Kong Management Game Award Vol. 2: 3943
Honikman Volunteer Award; Jane Vol. 1: 15172
HONOLULU Magazine Fiction Contest Vol. 1: 9473
Honor al Merito Vol. 2: 6253
Honor Award
- American Academy of Otolaryngology - Head and Neck Surgery Vol. 1: 674
- American Alliance for Health, Physical Education, Recreation and Dance Vol 1: 785
- American Association for Leisure and Recreation Vol 1: 922
- ASPRS - The Imaging and Geospatial Information Society Vol 1: 4740
- Association of Indians in America Vol 1: 5195
- Black Caucus of the American Library Association Vol 1: 5795
- National Association for Girls and Women in Sport Vol 1: 12325
- National Building Museum Vol 1: 12802
- National Soccer Coaches Association of America Vol 1: 13710
- Sigma Zeta Vol 1: 16060
- Soil and Water Conservation Society Vol 1: 16932
- Tennessee Library Association Vol 1: 17434

Honor Awards Vol. 1: 1385
Honor Awards for Program Excellence Vol. 1: 5922
Honor Awards Program Vol. 1: 17808
Honor Club Awards Vol. 1: 7449
Honor Coach Award Vol. 1: 7516
Honor Coach Certificate Vol. 1: 7517
Honor Council Program Vol. 1: 10581
Honor et Veritas Award Vol. 1: 7176
Honor Medal with Crossed Palms Vol. 1: 5913
Honor Roll
- Information Systems Security Association Vol. 1: 9704
- International Buckskin Horse Association Vol 1: 10280
- Society of Motion Picture and Television Engineers Vol 1: 16747

Honor Roll Adviser Award Vol. 1: 7527
Honor Roll Award Vol. 1: 3443
Honor Roll of Champions Vol. 1: 79
Honor Roll of Excellence in Communication Vol. 1: 5314
Honor Roll of Housing Vol. 1: 13361
Honor Squadron Vol. 1: 3249
Honorable Member Vol. 2: 4447
Honorable Mention National Award for Outstanding Achievement in Metropolitan Transportation Planning - MPOs Over 200000 Vol. 1: 5227
Honorable Mentions Vol. 1: 4537
Honorary and Life Fellowships Vol. 1: 656
Honorary Award Vol. 1: 4986
Honorary Awards Vol. 1: 109
Honorary Awards to Private Citizens and Organizations Vol. 1: 17813
Honorary Certificate Vol. 2: 4162
Honorary Citations Vol. 1: 10203
Honorary Companionship Vol. 2: 6644
Honorary Distinguished Logistics Professional Vol. 1: 4252
Honorary Emeritus Membership Vol. 1: 4959
Honorary Fellow
- Acoustical Society of America Vol. 1: 128
- American Academy of Oral Medicine Vol 1: 668
- American College of Physicians Vol 1: 1714
- American College of Radiology Vol 1: 1733
- American Society of Civil Engineers Vol 1: 3946
- Association for Social Anthropology in Oceania Vol 1: 4964
- British Psychological Society Vol 2: 5428
- The Chemical Institute of Canada Vol 1: 7303
- Ergonomics Society - England Vol 2: 5797
- Geological Society of America Vol 1: 9023
- Institute of Environmental Sciences and Technology Vol 1: 9835
- Israel Museum Vol 2: 2916
- Kenya National Academy of Sciences - Ministry of Research, Science and Technology Vol 2: 3360
- Royal Agricultural Society of England Vol 2: 6665
- Royal Horticultural Society Vol 2: 6794
- Royal Institute of Navigation Vol 2: 6828
- Society for Public Health Education Vol 1: 16397
- Society of Dyers and Colourists - England Vol 2: 7185
- Society of Experimental Test Pilots Vol 1: 16670
- Textile Institute Vol 2: 7265
- Zimbabwe Scientific Association Vol 2: 7447

Honorary Fellow Award
- American Institute of Ultrasound in Medicine Vol. 1: 2566
- Society of Allied Weight Engineers Vol 1: 16485

Honorary Fellow of the College of Human Sciences Vol. 1: 10471
Honorary Fellow of the Royal Academy of Dance Vol. 2: 6617
Honorary Fellowhip Vol. 1: 1699
Honorary Fellows Vol. 1: 2197
Honorary Fellows Award Vol. 2: 6935
Honorary Fellowship
- American College of Managed Care Administrators Vol. 1: 1670
- Australian College of Rural and Remote Medicine Vol 2: 160
- Institution of Agricultural Engineers Vol 2: 6084
- Institution of Nuclear Engineers Vol 2: 6189

Honorary Fellowship
- Academy of Dentistry International Vol. 1: 97
- American Academy of Medical Administrators Vol 1: 628
- American College of Dentists Vol 1: 1642
- American College of Healthcare Executives Vol 1: 1656
- American College of Preventive Medicine Vol 1: 1725
- American Institute of Architects Vol 1: 2429
- Institute of Quarrying - England Vol 2: 6076
- International Cartographic Association Vol 2: 3573
- Royal Aeronautical Society - United Kingdom Vol 2: 6645
- Royal Photographic Society of Great Britain Vol 2: 6874
- Royal Scottish Geographical Society Vol 2: 6891

Honorary Fellowship Award
- American College of Cardiology Vol. 1: 1619
- American College of Clinical Pharmacology Vol 1: 1631

Honorary Group Diploma Vol. 2: 4733
Honorary Human Rights Award Vol. 1: 2939
Honorary Knights of the Golden Fleece Vol. 1: 6398
Honorary Life Member
- AACE International Vol. 1: 22
- American Art Therapy Association Vol 1: 827
- Association of British Columbia Drama Educators Vol 1: 5053
- Australian Red Cross Society Vol 2: 342
- British Psychological Society Vol 2: 5429
- Canadian Parks and Recreation Association Vol 1: 6800
- Canadian Public Health Association Vol 1: 6841
- Confederate Stamp Alliance Vol 1: 7675
- Directors Guild of America Vol 1: 8216
- Institute of Packaging Professionals Vol 1: 9928
- International Pharmaceutical Students' Federation Vol 2: 3602
- Pharmacy Guild of Australia Vol 2: 599
- Standards Engineering Society Vol 1: 17246
- Textile Institute Vol 2: 7266

Honorary Life Members
- American Wine Society Vol. 1: 4484
- European Aquaculture Society Vol 2: 854
- Sierra Club Vol 1: 16012

Honorary Life Membership
- Australian Science Teachers Association Vol. 2: 347
- Botanical Society of South Africa Vol 2: 4140
- Western History Association Vol 1: 18687

Honorary Life Membership
- American Hospital Association Vol. 1: 2306
- American Hospital Association Vol 1: 2309
- Canadian Health Libraries Association Vol 1: 6553
- Canadian Society of Animal Science - Agricultural Institute of Canada Vol 1: 6976
- Genealogical Association of Nova Scotia Vol 1: 8980
- International Association of Astacology Vol 1: 10141

International Public Management Association for Human Resources Vol 1: 10561
Parent Cooperative Preschools International Vol 1: 14850
Honorary Life Membership Award Vol. 2: 4221
Honorary Life Membership Award Vol. 1: 10081
Honorary Life Officer Vol. 2: 3885
Honorary Life President Vol. 2: 3413
Honorary Lifetime Member Vol. 1: 15233
Honorary Lifetime Membership Vol. 1: 17326
Honorary Lifetime Membership Award Vol. 1: 9087
Honorary Member
Air and Waste Management Association Vol. 1: 267
American Academy of Family Physicians Vol 1: 609
American Association of Neuromuscular and Electrodiagnostic Medicine Vol 1: 1172
American Bridge Teachers' Association Vol 1: 1419
American Ceramic Society Vol 1: 1483
American Concrete Institute Vol 1: 1756
American Congress on Surveying and Mapping Vol 1: 1779
American Institute of Architects Vol 1: 2430
American Institute of Professional Geologists Vol 1: 2552
American Pharmacists Association - Academy of Pharmacy Practice and Management Vol 1: 3052
American Physical Therapy Association Vol 1: 3148
American Society for Engineering Education Vol 1: 3653
American Society of Agronomy Vol 1: 3873
American Society of Civil Engineers Vol 1: 3947
American Society of Heating, Refrigerating and Air-Conditioning Engineers Vol 1: 4059
American Society of Landscape Architects Vol 1: 4099
American Society of Mechanical Engineers Vol 1: 4140
American Theatre Organ Society Vol 1: 4351
Arnold Air Society Vol 1: 4637
ASM International Vol 1: 4703
ASPRS - The Imaging and Geospatial Information Society Vol 1: 4741
Association of Asphalt Paving Technologists Vol 1: 5045
Association of Development Financing Institutions in Asia and the Pacific Vol 2: 3965
AVS Vol 1: 5593
Biochemical Society - England Vol 2: 5171
Canadian Actors' Equity Association Vol 1: 6149
Canadian Phytopathological Society Vol 1: 6816
Canadian Research Institute for the Advancement of Women Vol 1: 6862
Canadian Society of Petroleum Geologists Vol 1: 7016
Engineering Institute of Canada Vol 1: 8464
European Geosciences Union Vol 2: 1774
Garden Writers Association Vol 1: 8961
Ibsen Society of America Vol 1: 9549
Incorporated Society of Musicians Vol 2: 5983
Indian Institute of Metals Vol 2: 2652
International Aluminium Institute Vol 2: 6204
International Association of Cancer Registries Vol 2: 1872
International Association of Hydraulic Engineering and Research Vol 2: 4505
International Pharmaceutical Federation Vol 2: 3597
International Union for Quaternary Research Vol 2: 2848
Iron and Steel Institution of Japan Vol 2: 3205
ISA - Instrumentation, Systems, and Automation Society Vol 1: 10912
Latin American Phytopathology Association Vol 2: 3954
Medical Women's International Association Vol 2: 2358
National Association of Metal Finishers Vol 1: 12589
National Marine Educators Association Vol 1: 13423
National Speleological Society Vol 1: 13792
Ottawa Field-Naturalists' Club Vol 1: 14724
Phi Lambda Upsilon Vol 1: 15001
Physical Education Association of Ireland Vol 2: 2866
Polish Organization for Commodity Science Vol 2: 4043
Royal Philharmonic Society Vol 2: 6863
Sigma Delta Epsilon - Graduate Women in Science Vol 1: 16030
Sigma Phi Alpha Vol 1: 16037
Singapore National Committee of the International Water Association Vol 2: 4434
Society of American Foresters Vol 1: 16508
Society of Dyers and Colourists - England Vol 2: 7186
Society of Motion Picture and Television Engineers Vol 1: 16747
Society of Nematologists Vol 1: 16773
Soil Science Society of America Vol 1: 16937
Southern African Society for Plant Pathology Vol 2: 4368
Special Libraries Association Vol 1: 17076
Ulster Teachers' Union Vol 2: 7287
World Federation of Estonian Women's Clubs Vol 1: 18927
Honorary Member Award
American Water Resources Association Vol. 1: 4421
Association of Women Surgeons Vol 1: 5388
Ecological Society of America Vol 1: 8371
Institute of Industrial Engineers Vol 1: 9866
International Silo Association Vol 1: 10631
Honorary Member (Individual) Vol. 1: 13276
Honorary Member (Institutional) Vol. 1: 13277
Honorary Member of AIA New York State Award Vol. 1: 14163
Honorary Members of NOC of Slovenia Vol. 2: 4459
Honorary Membership
Australian College of Rural and Remote Medicine Vol. 2: 161
Indian Society of Soil Science Vol 2: 2759
Society for the History of Natural History Vol 2: 7122
Honorary Membership
ACA International Vol. 1: 54
Agricultural Institute of Canada Vol 1: 246
Alpine Club of Canada Vol 1: 441
American Association of Handwriting Analysts Vol 1: 1111
American Association of Petroleum Geologists Vol 1: 1216
American Fisheries Society Vol 1: 2030
Association of Hungarian Geophysicists Vol 2: 2491
Construction Specifications Institute Vol 1: 7749
International Association of Sedimentologists Vol 2: 902
International Federation of Shipmasters' Associations Vol 2: 6260
International Glaciological Society Vol 2: 6267
International Water Association Vol 2: 6329
National Association of Biology Teachers Vol 1: 12408
Oncology Nursing Society Vol 1: 14546
Organization of Military Museums of Canada Vol 1: 14704
Polish Chemical Society Vol 2: 4032
Polish Physical Society Vol 2: 4047
Royal Academy of Music Vol 2: 6627
Royal Geographical Society with the Institute of British Geographers Vol 2: 6769
Society for Imaging Science and Technology Vol 1: 16248
Society for Sedimentary Geology Vol 1: 16409
Society of Exploration Geo-physicists Vol 1: 16679
Society of Manufacturing Engineers - Composites Manufacturing Association Vol 1: 16716
Society of Petroleum Engineers Vol 1: 16801
Water Environment Federation Vol 1: 18633
Weed Society of Victoria Vol 2: 729
World Conservation Union Vol 2: 4919
Honorary Membership Award Vol. 2: 3042
Honorary Membership Award
American Nurses Association Vol. 1: 2938
American Welding Society Vol 1: 4457
Hiking South Africa Vol 2: 4195
International Society for the Prevention of Child Abuse and Child Neglect Vol 1: 10686
Karg-Elert Archive Vol 2: 6346
National Athletic Trainers' Association Vol 1: 12719
National Fishing Lure Collectors Club Vol 1: 13197
Society for Applied Spectroscopy Vol 1: 16179
Southeastern Library Association Vol 1: 17006
Honorary Membership Award for Meritorious Service Vol. 1: 3452
Honorary Membership for Distinguished Service Vol. 1: 6304
Honorary Membership for life Vol. 2: 5566
Honorary Membership of the ESM Vol. 2: 2128
Honorary Membership (Outstanding Contributors) Vol. 1: 12911
Honorary National Commander Vol. 1: 4638

Honorary Nurse Practitioner Award Vol. 1: 2940
Honorary Nursing Practice Award Vol. 1: 2940
Honorary President
American Pharmacists Association - Academy of Pharmacy Practice and Management Vol. 1: 3053
International Pharmaceutical Federation Vol 2: 3597
Honorary President's Award Vol. 2: 4588
Honorary Recognition Award
American Nurses Association Vol. 1: 2941
International Furnishings and Design Association Vol 1: 10445
Honorary Research Lecture Vol. 1: 3695
Honorary Scholar Vol. 2: 804
Honorary Service Awards Vol. 1: 4525
Honorary Vanguard Degree Vol. 1: 13930
Honorary Vice President Vol. 2: 7288
Honored Service Member Award Vol. 1: 16828
Honored Student Award Vol. 1: 2968
Honoree of the Year Award Vol. 1: 12717
Honors of the Association
American Speech Language Hearing Association Vol. 1: 4293
International Society of Phonetic Sciences Vol 1: 10735
Honour Award Vol. 2: 2883
Honour Diploma Vol. 2: 4388
Honourary Member Vol. 1: 15737
Honouree Award Vol. 2: 1371
Hood Award; E. I. Vol. 1: 6264
Hood Award for Diplomatic Correspondence; Edwin M. Vol. 1: 13546
Hook Award; Peter Vol. 2: 6037
Hook Industry Award; Daryl Van Vol. 1: 12441
Hook Memorial Award; Sidney
National Association of Scholars Vol. 1: 12645
Phi Beta Kappa Vol 1: 14990
Hooke Distinguished Service Award; Casey Vol. 1: 5285
Hooker of the Year Vol. 1: 13856
Hoosier Intellectual Freedom Award Vol. 1: 9672
Hooten Plaque; George W. Vol. 1: 12236
Hooters Championship Series Vol. 1: 521
Hoover Award; VFW J. Edgar Vol. 1: 18518
Hoover Book Award; Herbert Vol. 1: 9381
Hoover Humanitarian Award; Herbert Vol. 1: 5923
Hoover Medal
American Society of Civil Engineers Vol. 1: 3948
American Society of Mechanical Engineers Vol 1: 4141
Hoover Memorial Award; Herbert Vol. 1: 5923
Hoover Memorial Award; John Edgar Vol. 1: 3220
Hope Award; John Vol. 1: 5972
Hopkins Lecture Vol. 2: 3736
Hopkins Memorial Lecture; Sir Frederick Gowland Vol. 2: 5172
Hopkins Promising Poet Award; Lee Bennett Vol. 1: 10582
Hopkinson Premium; John Vol. 2: 6146
Hopkinson Trophy; Walter W. Vol. 1: 18135
Hopper Award; Grace Murray Vol. 1: 4808
Hopps Award; Hope E. Vol. 1: 16261
Hora Memorial Medal; Chandrakala Vol. 2: 2688
Horizon Award
American Association for Health Education Vol. 1: 910
League of Women Voters of Arkansas Vol 1: 11269
Horizon Scholarship Vol. 1: 14177
Horizons Grants Program Vol. 1: 15805
Hornaday Bronze and Silver Medals; William T. Vol. 1: 5909
Hornaday Gold Certificate; William T. Vol. 1: 5910
Hornaday Gold Medal; William T. Vol. 1: 5911
Hornaday Unit Award; William T. Vol. 1: 5912
Horne Lecture; Robert Vol. 2: 7167
Horne Memorial Award; John Robert Vol. 1: 12216
Horner Award; Wesley W. Vol. 1: 3949
Horner Sportsmanship Award; Frederic S. Vol. 1: 10950
Hornickel Award Vol. 1: 9389
Horning Memorial Award; Harry L. Vol. 1: 16577
Hornstein Medal in Operational Meteorology; Rube Vol. 1: 6726
Horonjeff Award of the Air Transport Division; Robert Vol. 1: 3950
Horror/Ghost Contest Vol. 1: 19018
Hors Concours Vol. 1: 11944
Horse and Rider Awards Vol. 1: 14010
Horse Awards Vol. 1: 12461
Horse Hall of Fame Vol. 1: 13071
Horse of the Year Vol. 1: 11018
Horse of the Year Awards
National Spotted Saddle Horse Association Vol. 1: 13806
United States Dressage Federation Vol 1: 17886
Horseback Hours Award Vol. 1: 2333
Horseback Miles Award Vol. 1: 2334
Horsemastership Awards Vol. 1: 2791
Horseshoe Hall of Fame Vol. 1: 13354
Horst Pracejus-Preis Vol. 2: 2168
Horta; Prix Baron Vol. 2: 975
Horticultural Communication Award Vol. 1: 2290
Horticultural Therapy Award Vol. 1: 2291
Horticulturist Award Vol. 1: 6223
Hortie Memorial - Coach of the Year; Paul Vol. 1: 358
Horton Award; Dutch Vol. 1: 5148
Horton Award; Robert E. Vol. 1: 2118
Horton Dining Awards; Loyal E. Vol. 1: 12442
Horton Medal; Robert E. Vol. 1: 2117
Horvath Memorial; Alex Vol. 1: 359
Horwitz Award for Leadership in Inter-American Health; Abraham Vol. 1: 14830
Horwitz Prize; Louisa Gross Vol. 1: 7587
Hosei International Fund Foreign Scholars Fellowship Vol. 2: 3187
Hoso Bunka Foundation Prize Vol. 2: 3298
Hospice Team Awards Vol. 1: 14087
Hospital Awards for Volunteer Excellence Vol. 1: 2307
Hospitality Business Scholarships Vol. 2: 3831
Host-Madsen Medal
International Pharmaceutical Federation Vol. 2: 3597
International Pharmaceutical Federation Vol 2: 3600
Hosto Distinguished Service Award; Lester E. Vol. 1: 12425
Hot Concepts! Awards Vol. 1: 13966
Hot Mix Asphalt Hall of Fame Vol. 1: 12297
Hotel Worker of the Year Vol. 2: 3152
Hotelier of the Year Vol. 2: 3153
Hotelympia
National Restaurant Association Vol. 1: 13631
Society of German Cooks Vol 2: 2383
Hotelympia Competition Vol. 2: 5287
Houdry Award in Applied Catalysis; Eugene J. Vol. 1: 14274
Houghton Award; Firman Vol. 1: 14045
Houghton Award; Lord Vol. 2: 6361
Houghton Lecture Award Vol. 2: 2445
Houle Award for Outstanding Literature in Adult Education; Cyril O. Vol. 1: 835
Houllevigue; Prix Vol. 2: 1455
Houphouet-Boigny Peace Prize; Felix Vol. 2: 1993
House of the Year Vol. 1: 12557
Housing Design Awards
Royal Institute of British Architects Vol. 2: 6823
Saltire Society Vol 2: 7068
Housing Person of the Year Award Vol. 1: 13361
Houston Research Award Vol. 2: 5840
Houston Research Award; Charles S. Vol. 1: 18742
Houston Research Awards; W. J. B. Vol. 2: 5844
Houston Reserach Scholarship Vol. 2: 5407
Houston Scholarship Award; W. J. B. Vol. 2: 5845
Houston State University Award; Sam Vol. 1: 3259
Houston Symphony League Concerto Competition Vol. 1: 9500
Houston Symphony Student Auditions Vol. 1: 9500
Houtermans Medal Vol. 2: 1760
Houziaux; Prix Joseph Vol. 2: 996
Hovey Trophy; Chandler Vol. 1: 18065
Howard Award; Ernest E. Vol. 1: 3951
Howard Award for Courage; Paul Vol. 1: 2663
Howard Award for Excellence in Horticulture; Nancy Putnam Vol. 1: 9379
Howard Citation of Musical Excellence for Military Concert Bands; Colonel George S. Vol. 1: 16971
Howard Fellowships Vol. 1: 9502
Howard-Gibbon Illustrator's Award; Amelia Frances Vol. 1: 6690
Howard Plaque; Mary B. Vol. 1: 12236
Howe Award Vol. 1: 9389
Howe Award; C. D. Vol. 1: 6170
Howe Award; William A. Vol. 1: 3526
Howe Cup Vol. 2: 7209
Howe Medal; Henry Marion Vol. 1: 4704
Howe Medal; Lucien Vol. 1: 2972
Howe Memorial Foundation Engineering Awards; C.D. Vol. 1: 5374
Howe Memorial Lecture Vol. 1: 4900
Howe Memorial Trophy; Henry Wainwright Vol. 1: 17903
Howell Award; A. Brazier
American Society of Mammalogists Vol. 1: 4117
Cooper Ornithological Society Vol 1: 7804

Howells Award; Albert Vol. 2: 5686
Howland Award; John Vol. 1: 3032
Howley, Sr. Prize for Research in Arthritis; Lee C. Vol. 1: 4658
Howlin' Wolf Award Vol. 1: 5821
Hoy/ERT Scholarship; Christopher J. Vol. 1: 2646
Hoyen Medal; N. L. Vol. 2: 1327
Hoyt Award; Richard M. Vol. 1: 1877
Hoyt Mid Atlantic Art Show Vol. 1: 9504
Hoyt National Drawing and Painting Show Vol. 1: 9504
HQF Career Development Grant Vol. 1: 12332
HQF New Quality Professional Grant Vol. 1: 12333
HRC Postdoctoral Fellowship Vol. 2: 3719
HRD Award Vol. 2: 4962
Hrdlicka Prize; Ales Vol. 1: 1234
HRH Princess Michael of Kent Award Vol. 2: 7218
HRLSD Exceptional Service Award Vol. 1: 5340
Hromadka Excellence in Zoo Keeping Award; Jean M. Vol. 1: 1337
Hrycak Award; John and Judy Vol. 1: 15871
HSBC Investment Management Prize Vol. 2: 7027
Hsieh Award; T. K. Vol. 2: 6115
HSMA Advertising Awards Vol. 1: 9492
Hu Award for Distinguished Service to Mathematics; Yueh-Gin Gung and Dr. Charles Y. Vol. 1: 11606
Hu Award; Shiu-ying Vol. 1: 9454
Hua Loo-keng Mathematics Award Vol. 2: 3928
Hubbard Award for Race Relations; William P. Vol. 1: 7441
Hubbard Award; Prevost Vol. 1: 5430
Hubbard Gold Award; L. Ron Vol. 1: 5936
Hubbard Memorial Prize; John Vol. 2: 3823
Hubbard Scholarship; William Peyton Vol. 1: 5792
Hubbard's Writers and Illustrators of the Future Contests; L. Ron Vol. 1: 5936
Hubbert Award; M. King Vol. 1: 13289
Hubbs Award; Carl L. Vol. 1: 8173
Hubele National Graduate Student Award; Glen E. Vol. 1: 1843
Huber Civil Engineering Research Prizes; Walter L. Vol. 1: 3952
Huber Learning Through Listening Awards; Marion Vol. 1: 15575
Huch-Preis; Ricarda- Vol. 2: 2440
HUD Secretary's Opportunity and Empowerment Award Vol. 1: 3210
Hudgens Memorial Award for Young Healthcare Executive of the Year; Robert S. Vol. 1: 1657
Hudgens Memorial Award - Young Hospital Administrator of the Year; Robert S. Vol. 1: 1657
Hudiburg Award; Everett E. Vol. 1: 10429
Hudson Award in Carbohydrate Chemistry; Claude S. Vol. 1: 1557
Hudson Award; Sir William Vol. 2: 488
Hudson Medal; Manley O. Vol. 1: 4090
Hudson Service Award; Floyd G. Vol. 1: 7869
Hueck and Norman Walford Career Achievement Awards in the Performing Arts and in Visual Arts; Paul de Vol. 1: 14560
Huesca International Short Film Contest Vol. 2: 4495
Hug Teacher of the Year Award; Clarissa Vol. 1: 7855
Huggins-Quarles Award Vol. 1: 14694
Hugh Last Fellowship and Hugh Last Prize Vol. 2: 5441
Hughes Award; Howard Vol. 1: 2198
Hughes Award; John T. Vol. 1: 13452
Hughes Award; Peter Vol. 2: 388
Hughes, Jr., Memorial Award; Daniel C. Vol. 1: 10511
Hughes Medal Vol. 2: 6910
Hughes Memorial Graduate Student Prize; Tertia M.C. Vol. 1: 6727
Hughes Memorial Scholarship; John Vol. 1: 10869
Hugo Awards Vol. 1: 18979
The Hugos: The Chicago International Television Awards Vol. 1: 7415
Hull Award; T. J. Vol. 1: 12065
Hull Award; T.J. Vol. 1: 12485
Hull-Warriner Award Vol. 1: 8280
Hulse Memorial Award; William F. Vol. 1: 5431
Human Capital Business Leader of the Year Award Vol. 1: 16238
Human Capital Leadership Awards Vol. 1: 16238
Human Kinetics Writing Awards Vol. 1: 6316
Human Needs Award Vol. 1: 1215
Human Relations Award Vol. 1: 12303
Human Rights Award
American Psychiatric Association Vol. 1: 3273
Global Rights Vol 1: 9099
International Service for Human Rights - Switzerland Vol 2: 4832
Jewish Labor Committee Vol 1: 11000
Minnesota Advocates for Human Rights Vol 1: 11828
Human Rights Prize Vol. 1: 17704
Human Spirit Award; Nashville Public Television Vol. 1: 12080
Humana Festival of New American Plays Vol. 1: 149
Humane Award
American Veterinary Medical Association Vol. 1: 4408
Canadian Veterinary Medical Association Vol 1: 7058
People for Animal Rights Vol 1: 14954
Humane Teen of the Year Award Vol. 1: 12337
Humanist Distinguished Service Award Vol. 1: 2322
Humanist Fellow Award Vol. 1: 2322
Humanist Heroine Award Vol. 1: 2323
Humanist of the Year Vol. 1: 9530
Humanist of the Year Award Vol. 1: 2324
Humanist Pioneer Award Vol. 1: 2325
Humanitarian Award
American Academy of Family Physicians Vol. 1: 610
American Cancer Society Vol 1: 1442
American Sportscasters Association Vol 1: 4304
B'nai Brith Canada Vol 1: 5826
Canadian Psychological Association Vol 1: 6836
International Association of Cancer Victors and Friends Vol 1: 10165
National Association of Recording Merchandisers Vol 1: 12637
National Press Photographers Association Vol 1: 13564
People for the Ethical Treatment of Animals Vol 1: 14956
Elie Wiesel Foundation for Humanity Vol 1: 18739
The Humanitarian Award Vol. 1: 98
Humanitarian Efforts Award Vol. 1: 675
Humanitarian Overseas Service Medal Vol. 2: 217
Humanitarian Physician Assistant of the Year Vol. 1: 733
Humanitarian Project Development Grants Vol. 1: 1624
Humanitarian Recognition Awards Vol. 1: 1625
Humanitarian Service Medal Vol. 1: 8108
Humanitas Prize Vol. 1: 9532
Humber Environmental Award for Outstanding Collaboration; Nicholas Vol. 1: 8497
Humble Award; Joe Vol. 1: 4666
Humboldt International Short Film Festival Vol. 1: 9534
Humboldt Research Fellowships Vol. 2: 2434
Hume Memorial Award; David M. Vol. 1: 13409
Hume Memorial Award for Excellence in Political Journalism; Sandy Vol. 1: 13547
Hume-Rothery Award; William Vol. 1: 11810
Hummer Award; Glen S. Vol. 1: 18415
Humorous Poetry Award Vol. 1: 13151
Humphrey Award; Hubert H. Vol. 1: 3054
Humphrey Civil Rights Award; Hubert H. Vol. 1: 11257
Humphrey Doctoral Fellowships in Arms Control and Disarmament; Hubert H. Vol. 1: 17737
Humphrey First Amendment Freedoms Prize; Hubert H. Vol. 1: 4544
Humphrey Freedom Award; John Vol. 1: 10302
Humphrey/OCLC/Forest Press Award for International Librarianship; John Ames Vol. 1: 2673
Humphrey Research Grant; Hubert Vol. 1: 15910
Humphrey Student Fellowships Vol. 1: 6443
Humphreys Scholarship; Pat Vol. 1: 6792
Humphry/Forest Press Award; John Ames Vol. 1: 2673
Hunger Cleanup Rookie of the Year Vol. 1: 13816
Hunkins Award; Ruth E. Vol. 1: 9184
Hunt Award for Administrative Excellence; Leamon R. Vol. 1: 17865
Hunt-Kelly Outstanding Paper Award Vol. 1: 4901
Hunt Memorial Award; Captain Alfred E. Vol. 1: 16883
Hunt Memorial Award; Fred T. Vol. 1: 2272
Hunt Memorial Prize; Renee Redfern Vol. 2: 6116
Hunt Trophy; Lamar Vol. 1: 13225
Hunt Young Historian Award; Rockwell D. Vol. 1: 7686
Hunter Artists Awards; K. M. Vol. 1: 14561
Hunter Award Vol. 2: 3789
Hunter Fellowship; Amy Louise Vol. 1: 18783
Hunter, Jr. Prize (Thesis Award); Charles A. Vol. 1: 2154
Hunter Memorial Award in Therapeutics; Oscar B. Vol. 1: 3610
Hunter Memorial Award; J. Norman Vol. 1: 7750

Hunter Screenwriting Scholarship; Lew and Pamela Vol. 1: 3538
Hunterdon Museum of Art Purchase Awards Vol. 1: 9540
Hunterian Medal Vol. 2: 5980
Hunting Art Prizes Vol. 2: 6524
Hunting Group Art Prizes Vol. 2: 6524
Hunting Retriever Champion Vol. 1: 17699
Huntington Award; Merritt W. Vol. 1: 2994
Huntington Medal Award; Archer M. Vol. 1: 2933
Huntington-WHA Martin Ridge Vol. 1: 18688
Hunziker Medal Vol. 2: 3060
Hurd Award; James A. Vol. 1: 5092
Hurdler of the Year Vol. 1: 18457
Hurst Prize; J. Willard Vol. 1: 11249
Hurter Memorial Lecture Vol. 2: 7168
Husain Prize for Young Scientists; Javed Vol. 2: 1994
Hustinx Prize for Science; Edmond Vol. 2: 3514
Hustinx Prize - Playwrights; Edmond Vol. 2: 3515
Hustinx Prize - Science; Edmond Vol. 2: 3516
Hustinx Prize - Visual Arts; Edmond Vol. 2: 3517
Hustinxprijs; Edmond Vol. 2: 3563
Hutchins Award; Lee M. Vol. 1: 3193
Hutchinson Award; G. Evelyn Vol. 1: 4111
Hutchison Medal Vol. 2: 6097
Hutton Memorial Award; Brig. Gen. Carl I. Vol. 1: 14649
Hutton Memorial Medal and Prize Vol. 2: 3869
Huxley Award; Thomas Henry Vol. 2: 7397
Huygens Award; Descartes Vol. 2: 3552
Hyatt Benefit to Society Award; John W. Vol. 1: 16829
Hydar Memorial Award; Eleonora Vol. 1: 7049
Hyde Award; Donald F. Vol. 1: 8914
Hyde Award; Walter Vol. 2: 6416
Hyde Graduate Student Research Award Vol. 1: 3383
Hyde Graduate Student Research Grant Vol. 1: 3384
Hyden Award; W. Vander Vol. 1: 18618
Hydraulic Structures Medal Vol. 1: 3953
Hydrology Section Award Vol. 1: 2118
Hyman Award; Women's Sports Foundation Flo Vol. 1: 18871
Hyman Ethics Award; Joseph Vol. 1: 2509
Hyman Memorial Award; Flo Vol. 1: 18871
Hynds-NZWWA Paper of the Year Award Vol. 2: 3817
Hypnosis Humanities Award Vol. 1: 13310
Hypnosis Research Award Vol. 1: 13311
IAAF/Coca World Road Relay Championships Vol. 2: 3466
IAAF Grand Prix Final Vol. 2: 3466
IAAF World Cross Country Championships Vol. 2: 3466
IAAF World Cup in Athletics Vol. 2: 3466
IAAF World Cup of Race Walking Vol. 2: 3466
IAAF World Half Marathon Championships Vol. 2: 3466
IAAF World Indoor Championships Vol. 2: 3466
IAAF World Junior Championships Vol. 2: 3466
IAAF World Marathon Cup Vol. 2: 3466
IABC Fellow Vol. 1: 10152
IABSE Outstanding Structure Award Vol. 2: 4773
IABSE Prize Vol. 2: 4774
IACP Cookbook Awards
International Association of Culinary Professionals Vol. 1: 10189
International Association of Culinary Professionals Vol 1: 10189
IACP, Division of State and Provincial Police Trooper of the Year Award Vol. 1: 10169
IACP University and College Police Section Scholarship Fund Vol. 1: 10170
IAFF International Media Awards Vol. 1: 10209
IAFIS-FPEI Food Engineering Award Vol. 1: 3850
IAG Postgraduate Award Vol. 2: 478
IAGLR/Hydrolab Best Student Paper and Poster Competition Vol. 1: 10090
IAGLR Scholarship Vol. 1: 10091
IAHR-APD Award Vol. 2: 4506
IAHR Lecturer Award Vol. 2: 4507
Iakovos' Years of Service Award; Archbishop Vol. 1: 13250
IAM Commendation Vol. 2: 5993
IAM Medal Vol. 2: 5993
Ian McRae Award Vol. 1: 6762
IASL/ProQuest SIRS International Commendation Award Vol. 1: 10238
IAWRT Awards Vol. 2: 2773
Iben Award; Icko Vol. 1: 4422
Iberoamerican Film Festival Vol. 2: 4503
IBF Distinguished Service Award Vol. 2: 3407
IBF Gold Medal Vol. 2: 4586
IBF Meritorious Service Award Vol. 2: 3408
IBM MEng Project Prize Vol. 2: 6153
Ibuka Consumer Electronics Award; Masaru Vol. 1: 9783
ICAAC Young Investigator Awards Vol. 1: 3768
ICCROM Award Vol. 2: 3064
Ice Carving Classic Vol. 1: 13633
Ice Cream Awards Vol. 2: 3773
The Iceland Award Vol. 2: 2515
Iceland on Six Meters Award Vol. 2: 2516
Icelandic JOTA Award Vol. 2: 2517
Icelandic Radio Amateurs Award Vol. 2: 2518
ICHPER-SD Biennial Distinguished Scholar Award in Health Education Vol. 1: 10349
ICHPER-SD Biennial Distinguished Scholar Award in Leisure and Recreation Vol. 1: 10350
ICHPER-SD Biennial Distinguished Scholar Award in Physical Education Vol. 1: 10351
ICHPER-SD Biennial Distinguished Scholar Award in Research Vol. 1: 10352
ICHPER-SD Biennial Distinguished Scholar in Sport and Olympic Movement Vol. 1: 10353
ICHPER-SD Biennial Outstanding Administration Award Vol. 1: 10354
ICHPER-SD Biennial Outstanding Contribution and Service Award Vol. 1: 10355
ICI Annual Award for Chemistry Vol. 2: 2839
ICI Award Vol. 2: 5225
ICI-FOSS Golden Jubilee Award Vol. 2: 2840
ICI Student Award in Applied Polymer Science Vol. 1: 1558
ICIA Excellence in the Communications Industry Achievement Awards Vol. 1: 10331
ICMR Prize for Biomedical Research Conducted in Underdeveloped Areas Vol. 2: 2605
ICMR Prize for Biomedical Research for Scientists Belonging to Under-Privileged Communities Vol. 2: 2606
ICO-ICTP Prize Vol. 2: 2947
ICO Prize Vol. 1: 10812
ICON Awards; Technology Marketing Vol. 1: 5930
ICPE Medal Vol. 2: 4594
ICPE Medal for Physics Teaching Vol. 1: 10813
ICSC Annual Awards Vol. 1: 10360
ICSSPE Sport Science Award of the IOC President Vol. 2: 2297
ICTP Diploma Vol. 2: 7031
ICTP Prize Vol. 2: 2948
ICU Design Citation Vol. 1: 16636
Ida and Henry Schuman Prize Vol. 1: 9444
IDA Awards for Design Excellence Vol. 1: 10179
IDA Distinguished Documentary Achievement Awards Vol. 1: 10380
Idaho Quality Award Vol. 1: 9555
Idea Awards Vol. 2: 5150
Iditarod Trail International Sled Dog Race Vol. 1: 9562
IEEE Education Medal Vol. 1: 9788
IEEE Life Members' Prize in Electrical History Vol. 1: 16439
IEEE Photonic Field Award Vol. 1: 9584
IERE Benefactors Premium Vol. 2: 6151
IETE-Bimal Bose Award Vol. 2: 2765
IETE-Hari Ramji Toshniwal Gold Medal Vol. 2: 2766
IFA Award Vol. 2: 5225
IFA International Aviation Scholarship Vol. 2: 6247
IFAFA Award Vol. 1: 10927
IFAWPCA-Atsumi Award Vol. 2: 3970
IFAWPCA-CHOI Construction Fieldman Award Vol. 2: 3971
IFCC Distinguished Clinical Chemist Award Vol. 2: 3078
IFCC Distinguished International Services Award Vol. 2: 3079
IFCC Travelling Lectureship Vol. 2: 3080
IFI Award Vol. 2: 4210
The IFMBE Otto Schmitt Award Vol. 2: 1229
IFUW Ida Smedley MacLean International Fellowship Vol. 2: 4803
IGIP Award Vol. 2: 4838
IGIP-Preis Vol. 2: 4838
IHIC Scholarship Vol. 1: 10873
IIE Distinguished Educator Award Vol. 1: 9865
IIE Doctoral Dissertation Award Vol. 1: 9872
IIE/Joint Publishers Book of the Year Award Vol. 1: 9867
IIE Transactions Award Vol. 1: 9868
IIE Transactions Development and Applications Paper Award Vol. 1: 9870
IIS Award Vol. 1: 10476
IJPS Best Paper Award Vol. 2: 2731
ILDA Awards Vol. 1: 10487
Illingworth Award; Lady Vol. 2: 7257
Illinois Academic Librarian of the Year Award Vol. 1: 9602
Illustration Annual Vol. 1: 7637
Image Awards
National Association for the Advancement of Colored People Vol. 1: 12367

Women in Film and Video/New England Vol 1: 18819
Image Awards Hall of Fame Vol. 1: 12367
Images Competition Vol. 1: 7255
Imagineer Awards Vol. 1: 11784
Imhoff - Koch Award for Outstanding Contribution to Water Management and Science Vol. 2: 6330
Imig Award for Distinguished Achievement in Teacher Education; David G. Vol. 1: 1047
Imison Memorial Award; Richard Vol. 2: 7144
Imitate Keeler Contest Vol. 1: 9270
Immroth Memorial Award; John Phillip Vol. 1: 2668
Impact of Music on Film Competition Vol. 2: 890
Impact of Workload on Diagnostic Accuracy Research Award Vol. 1: 4016
IMPC Award for Excellence in Parking Design Vol. 1: 10539
IMPC Award for Excellence in Parking Design and Program Innovation Vol. 1: 10539
Imperial Order Daughters of the Empire Scholarship Vol. 1: 18349
Imperial Prize Vol. 2: 3214
Imperial Tobacco Awards Vol. 2: 7226
Imperial Tobacco Portrait Award Vol. 2: 6483
IMPHOS-FAI Award Vol. 2: 3475
IMPHOS-FAI Award on the Role of Phosphorus on Yield and Quality of Crops Vol. 2: 2557
Implant Innovations Grant Vol. 2: 5811
Implications for Research and Innovations in Teaching Vol. 1: 4960
Import Car of the Year Vol. 1: 11968
Impresa Europe Awards Vol. 2: 2553
Improvisation Prize Vol. 2: 6276
In-Depth Reporting Award Vol. 1: 9978
In-House Promotional Excellence Award Vol. 1: 10565
In-Print Award Vol. 1: 10566
In-Training Award Vol. 1: 16637
InBev-Baillet Latour Health Prize Vol. 2: 893
INCO Medal Vol. 1: 6624
Independent Accountants Scholarship Award Vol. 1: 9630
Independent Investigator Award Vol. 1: 12232
Independent Research Award Vol. 1: 8157
INDEX Awards for Advances in Nonwovens Vol. 2: 863
Indian Country Officer of the Year Award Vol. 1: 10171
Indian Horse Hall of Fame Award Vol. 1: 2335
Indian Institute Metals Platinum Medal Vol. 2: 2653
Indian Student Conference Scholarship Vol. 1: 18689
Indiana Governor's Arts Awards Vol. 1: 9660
Indiana Journalism Award Vol. 1: 5635
Indiana Scholastic Journalism Award Vol. 1: 5636
Indiana State Federation of Poetry Clubs Award Vol. 1: 13152
Indianapolis 500 Vol. 1: 9686
Indianapolis Motor Speedway Hall of Fame Vol. 1: 9687
Indigenisation of Aeronautical Equipment Award Vol. 2: 2524
Individual Achievement/Personality of the Year Award Vol. 2: 5552
Individual Artist Fellowship Vol. 1: 14463
Individual Artists Fellowship and Merit Awards Vol. 1: 9288
Individual Artists Fellowships
Hawaii State Foundation on Culture and the Arts Vol. 1: 9288
Pennsylvania Council on the Arts Vol 1: 14923
Individual Award
American Printing History Association Vol. 1: 3254
British Printing Industries Federation Vol 2: 5422
Individual Citation Vol. 1: 13845
Individual of the Year Award Vol. 1: 8613
Individual Safety Advocate Award Vol. 1: 13290
Industrial Achievement Award Vol. 2: 3322
Industrial Appreciation Award Vol. 1: 23
Industrial Arts Teacher Educator of the Year Vol. 1: 7927
Industrial Automation Award Vol. 2: 4432
Industrial Chapter Scholarship Vol. 1: 10180
Industrial Chemistry Medal Vol. 2: 4315
Industrial Design Excellence Awards (IDEA) Vol. 1: 9689
Industrial Designer of the Year TKO Vol. 2: 1386
Industrial Leadership Award Vol. 1: 1348
Industrial Lectureship Vol. 2: 6966
Industrial Minerals Young Scientist Award Vol. 1: 16350
Industrial Office Park Award Vol. 1: 5994
Industrial Plastics Product Design Award Vol. 1: 16830
Industrial Research Institute Medal Vol. 1: 9695
Industrial Safety Contest Vol. 1: 4374
Industrial Scientist Award Vol. 1: 9851
Industrial Water Quality Achievement Award Vol. 1: 18634
Industrially-Sponsored Awards Vol. 2: 6967
Industriepreis fur technisch-wissenschaftliche Arbeiten Vol. 2: 2242
Industry Achievement Award
Irrigation Association Vol. 1: 10899
National Paint and Coatings Association Vol 1: 13517
Industry Advancement Award Vol. 1: 2730
Industry and Technology Award Vol. 2: 2667
Industry Appreciation Award Vol. 1: 12441
Industry Award for Effective Communication Vol. 2: 6327
Industry Award of Distinction
Health Industry Distributors Association Vol. 1: 9300
PrintImage International Vol 1: 15234
Industry Awards Vol. 1: 8750
Industry Builder Award Vol. 1: 8323
Industry Excellence Awards Vol. 1: 19045
Industry Executive of the Year Vol. 1: 9142
Industry/Government Graduate Fellowships Vol. 1: 2779
Industry Hall of Fame Vol. 1: 15389
Industry Innovation Award Vol. 1: 8210
Industry Leadership Award Vol. 1: 6183
Industry Professional of the Year Vol. 1: 8324
Industry Recognition Award Vol. 1: 10367
Industry Research Scholar Awards Vol. 1: 8834
Industry Service Award Vol. 1: 5763
Industry Specific Group of the Year Award Vol. 1: 4629
Industry Statesman Awards Vol. 1: 13518
Industry Undergraduate Scholarships Vol. 1: 2780
Infinity Awards Vol. 1: 10300
Infographics Award Vol. 1: 9979
Information, Communications and Technology Exporter of the Year Vol. 2: 3810
Information Plus Continuing Education Scholarship Vol. 1: 1278
Information Processing Public Service Award Vol. 1: 5200
Information Systems Award Vol. 1: 2382
Information Technology Pathfinder Award Vol. 1: 1279
Information Technology Scholarship Vol. 1: 17845
INFORMS Fellow Award Vol. 1: 9743
INFORMS Prize Vol. 1: 9744
ING New York City Marathon Vol. 1: 14153
Ingbar Distinguished Lectureship Award; Sidney H. Vol. 1: 4358
Ingbar Distinguished Service Award; Sidney H. Vol. 1: 8454
Ingberg Award; S. H. Vol. 1: 5432
Ingelheim Award for Organic or Bioorganic Chemistry; Boehringer Vol. 1: 6905
Ingersoll Award; E. P. Vol. 1: 16601
Ingle Award; Robert Vol. 1: 1982
Inglehart First Amendment Award; Louis E. Vol. 1: 7528
Inglis Award; Rewey Belle Vol. 1: 18828
Ingold-Albert Lectureship Vol. 2: 6968
Ingold Lectureship; Christopher Vol. 2: 6968
Initiative Awards Vol. 1: 15211
Initiative for Peace Award Vol. 1: 12917
Injalbert; Prix Vol. 2: 1482
Inklings Vol. 1: 12059
Inland Bird Banding Association Avian Research Fund Vol. 1: 9716
INMA Newspaper Marketing Awards Vol. 1: 10532
Inn of the Year Vol. 1: 14997
Inner City Physician Assistant of the Year Vol. 1: 735
Innis Aviation Command and Control Marine of the Year Award; Kenneth A. Vol. 1: 11517
Innis-Gerin Medal Vol. 1: 15761
Innovation Award Vol. 1: 17336
Innovation Award
Association for Computing Machinery - Special Interest Group on Knowledge Discovery and Data Mining Vol. 1: 4832
California School Library Association Vol 1: 6055
Direct Selling Association Vol 1: 8210
Innovation in Civil Engineering Award Vol. 1: 3954
Innovation in Higher Education Award Vol. 1: 8425
Innovation of the Year Vol. 2: 5511
Innovation of the Year Awards Vol. 1: 1126
Innovation Showcase Award Vol. 1: 12531
Innovation Writer of the Year Vol. 2: 5513
Innovations Challenge Vol. 1: 9726
Innovations in American Government Awards Vol. 1: 9152
Innovative Achievement Award Vol. 1: 6763
Innovative Applications of Artificial Intelligence Awards Vol. 1: 855
Innovative Business Solution Award Vol. 1: 16238
Innovative Contribution to Family Therapy Award Vol. 1: 1989

Award Index

Innovative Intermodal Solutions for Urban Transportation Paper Award Vol. 1: 9946
Innovative Practice Award Vol. 1: 16239
Innovative Research in Primary Care Award Vol. 1: 12459
Innovative Technology Awards Vol. 1: 18635
Innovator Award
American Society of Cataract and Refractive Surgery Vol. 1: 3902
Nation's Restaurant News - Lebhar-Friedman Inc. Vol 1: 13967
Innovator of the Year
Canadian Advanced Technology Alliance Vol. 1: 6161
R & D Magazine - Reed Business Information Vol 1: 15503
Innovator of the Year Award Vol. 1: 19034
Inose Paper Award Vol. 2: 3194
INSA Medal for Young Scientists Vol. 2: 2689
Inside Write Awards
Plain English Campaign Vol. 2: 6538
Plain English Campaign Vol 2: 6539
Insole Award Vol. 2: 5366
Institute Award Vol. 1: 6593
Institute Award for Excellence in Industrial Gases Technology Vol. 1: 2487
Institute Honor Award for Architecture Vol. 1: 2431
Institute Honor Award for Interior Architecture Vol. 1: 2432
Institute Honor Award for Regional and Urban Design Vol. 1: 2433
Institute Honors for Collaborative Achievement Vol. 1: 2434
Institute Manuscript Award Vol. 1: 14528
Institute Medal Vol. 2: 7267
Institute Medal for Design Vol. 2: 7268
Institute of Administrative Accountants Awards Vol. 2: 6031
Institute of Administrative Management Awards Vol. 2: 5993
Institute of British Foundrymen Honorary Fellow Vol. 2: 5998
Institute of Chartered Accountants of Scotland Gold Medal Vol. 2: 6008
Institute of Export Prizes Vol. 2: 6029
Institute of Financial Accountants Awards Vol. 2: 6031
Institute of Management Gold Medal Vol. 2: 6043
Institute of Metals Division Award Vol. 1: 11817
Institute of Metals Lecturer and Robert Franklin Mehl Award Vol. 1: 11811
Institute of Quarrying Awards Vol. 2: 6076
Institute Recognition Award Vol. 1: 247
Institute Service Awards Vol. 1: 15333
Institution Medal and Premium (Local Association) Competition Vol. 2: 6113
Institution Medal and Premium (London Universities) Competition Vol. 2: 6105
Institution Medal and Premium (Universities) Competition Vol. 2: 6105
Institution of Engineers Medal Vol. 2: 508
Institution of Gas Engineers Bronze Medal Vol. 2: 6169
Institution of Gas Engineers Gold Medal Vol. 2: 6170
Institution of Gas Engineers Silver Medal Vol. 2: 6171
Institution of Mechanical Engineers Awards Vol. 2: 6185
Institution of Structural Engineers Gold Medal Vol. 2: 6195
Institution of Structural Engineers Special Awards Vol. 2: 6196
Institutional Achievement Award Vol. 1: 10744
Institutional Award Vol. 1: 3255
Instruction Section Innovation Award Vol. 1: 5080
Instructional Innovation Award Vol. 1: 8083
Instructor of the Year Vol. 1: 12810
Instrumental Album of the Year Vol. 1: 10270
Instrumental and Vocal Competition Vol. 2: 696
Instrumental Group of the Year Vol. 1: 10270
Instrumental Performers of the Year Vol. 1: 10270
Integrated Young Playwrights Project Vol. 1: 18578
Integrity Award Vol. 1: 5735
Integrity Awards Vol. 2: 2425
Intel Achievement Awards Vol. 1: 15927
Intel Best of Category Awards Vol. 1: 15927
Intel Foundation Young Scientist Award Vol. 1: 15927
Intel International Science and Engineering Fair Vol. 1: 15927
Intel Science Talent Search Vol. 1: 15928
Intellectual Freedom Award
American Association of School Librarians Vol. 1: 1280
Colorado Language Arts Society Vol 1: 7563
Illinois Library Association Vol 1: 9603
Louisiana Library Association Vol 1: 11418
Intellectual Freedom Round Table State Program Award Vol. 1: 2670
Intelligent Community Awards Vol. 1: 9969
Intelligent Community of the Year Vol. 1: 9969
Intensive Care Society Research Gold Medal Vol. 2: 6198
Inter-American Agricultural Award for Young Professionals
Inter-American Institute for Cooperation on Agriculture Vol. 2: 1207
Inter-American Institute for Cooperation on Agriculture - Costa Rica Vol 2: 1211
Inter-American Agricultural Medal
Inter-American Institute for Cooperation on Agriculture Vol. 2: 1208
Inter-American Institute for Cooperation on Agriculture - Costa Rica Vol 2: 1212
Inter-American Award for the Participation of Women in Rural Development
Inter-American Institute for Cooperation on Agriculture Vol. 2: 1209
Inter-American Institute for Cooperation on Agriculture - Costa Rica Vol 2: 1213
Inter-American Awards Vol. 1: 1451
Inter-American Leadership Award Vol. 1: 14827
Inter-American Music Awards Vol. 1: 16026
Inter Nations Cup Vol. 2: 1882
Interactive Materials Festival Vol. 1: 9313
InterAd Vol. 1: 10025
Interamerica Prize Vol. 1: 9973
Intercollegiate Meat Judging Meritorious Service Award Vol. 1: 2738
Intercollegiate Pistol Championships Vol. 1: 13646
INTERCOM: International Communication Video and Interactive Media Competition Vol. 1: 7416
Interdisciplinary Award Vol. 1: 8586
Interdisciplinary Awards Vol. 2: 6969
Interior Architecture Awards of Excellence Vol. 1: 2432
Interior Award SIO Vol. 2: 1387
Interior Design Awards Vol. 1: 17331
Intermediate Certificate in Floristry Vol. 2: 7194
Internal Combustion Engine Award Vol. 1: 4142
Internationaal Vocalisten Concours 's-Hertogenbosch Vol. 2: 3508
International Academy of Astronautics Section Awards Vol. 2: 1866
International Achievement Award Vol. 1: 5182
International Achievement Awards Competition Vol. 1: 9691
International Activist Award Vol. 1: 9095
International Activities Award Vol. 1: 4060
International Adventure Film Festival Vol. 2: 1846
International Advertising Awards Vol. 1: 14119
International Advertising Festival, Cannes Vol. 2: 6202
International Advertising Festival of New York Vol. 1: 14119
International Aerosol Fellow Award Vol. 2: 2023
International Affairs Fellowship Program Vol. 1: 7912
International Aluminum Extrusion Design Competition Vol. 1: 447
International ANDY Awards Vol. 1: 10036
International Animal Agriculture Award Vol. 2: 3144
International Animation Festival in Japan, Hiroshima Vol. 2: 3183
International Arbiter Vol. 2: 2479
International Art Show by Artists with Disabilities
Minnesota Stroke Association, NSA Chapters Vol. 1: 11847
Sister Kenny Rehabilitation Institute Vol 1: 16073
International Association for Engineering Geology and the Environment Awards Vol. 2: 3565
International Association of Sedimentologists Grants Vol. 2: 903
International Association of Technological University Libraries Poster Prize Vol. 2: 6229
International Association of Traffic and Safety Sciences Award Vol. 2: 3199
International Auctioneers Championship Vol. 1: 12723
International Auditions Vol. 1: 8315
International Automotive Media Awards Vol. 1: 10696
International Award
Royal Television Society Vol. 2: 7044
South African Association of Women Graduates Vol 2: 4308
International Award
American Meat Science Association Vol. 1: 2739
Animal Transportation Association - European Office Vol 2: 5054
Family Firm Institute Vol 1: 8587

Girls' Brigade International Council Vol 2: 5940
International Association of Assessing Officers Vol 1: 10131
Parent Cooperative Preschools International Vol 1: 14851
Pro Musicis Foundation Vol 1: 15252
Society of Plastics Engineers Vol 1: 16831
Society of Tribologists and Lubrication Engineers Vol 1: 16884
System Safety Society Vol 1: 17374
International Award for Photojournalism Vol. 2: 4789
International Award for Promoting Gandhian Values Outside India
Jamnalal Bajaj Foundation Vol. 2: 2775
Jamnalal Bajaj Foundation Vol 2: 2776
International Award of Merit in Structural Engineering Vol. 2: 4775
International Awards Vol. 1: 5134
International Awards of Excellence Vol. 1: 5302
International Badminton Federation Distinguished Service Award Vol. 2: 3409
International Band Award Vol. 1: 6326
International Belvedere Competition for Opera Singers Vol. 2: 830
International Biennial of Graphic Art Vol. 2: 4457
International Biennial of Illustrations Bratislava Vol. 2: 4442
International Blindness Prevention Award Vol. 1: 648
International Bluegrass Music Awards Vol. 1: 10270
International Book Award Vol. 2: 824
International Bowling Hall of Fame Vol. 1: 18915
International Broadcasting Award Vol. 1: 9461
International Broadcasting Excellence Award Vol. 1: 12432
International Business Dissertation Award Vol. 1: 102
International Cancer Research Technology Transfer Project Vol. 2: 4858
International Carillon Competition - Queen Fabiola Vol. 2: 1080
International Ceramic Art Competition Vol. 2: 3067
International Championship Trophy Vol. 1: 9256
International Charlemagne Prize of Aachen Vol. 2: 2409
International Children's Film Festival of India Vol. 2: 2551
International Children's Peace Prize Vol. 1: 7338
International Chopin Piano Competition Vol. 1: 7373
International Choral Competition of Tours Vol. 2: 1801
International Cinema Achievement Award Vol. 1: 7929
International Citation Award Vol. 2: 6076
International Citation of Merit Vol. 1: 10583
International Client Award Vol. 2: 6223
International Coastal Engineering Award Vol. 1: 3955
International Collaborative Prevention Research Award Vol. 1: 16384
International Commission for Optics Prize Vol. 2: 4515
International Competition for Choirs Vol. 2: 768
International Competition for Film and Video Vol. 2: 778
International Competition for Musical Performers - Geneva Vol. 2: 4702
International Competition for New Instruments and Bows Vol. 1: 18549
International Composers Competition Vol. 2: 3201
International Conductors' Competition Vol. 2: 3683
International Confederation for Thermal Analysis DuPont Award Vol. 2: 4205
International Conference Award Vol. 2: 5390
International Congress Commemoration Vol. 2: 2760
International Conservation Award Vol. 1: 4497
International Contest for Carillon Composition Vol. 2: 1081
International Cooperation Award Vol. 1: 2383
International Cooperation Medal Vol. 2: 1738
International Council of Christians and Jews International Sternberg Award Vol. 2: 2291
International Council of Graphic Design Associations Excellence Awards Vol. 2: 912
International Council of Graphic Design Associations President's Trophy Vol. 2: 913
International Critics Award Vol. 1: 17559
International Cytotechnology Award of the IAC Vol. 2: 2277
International Dairy Foods Association Research Award in Dairy Foods Processing Vol. 1: 1878
International Dairy Production Award Vol. 1: 1879
International Democracy Award Vol. 2: 2285
International Dentist of the Year Vol. 1: 99
International Design and Development Awards Vol. 1: 10360
International Design Competition Osaka Vol. 2: 3226
International Diaporama Festival Vol. 2: 941
International Director's Award Vol. 1: 8406
International Dissertation Research Fellowhips Vol. 1: 16131
International DLG Prize Vol. 2: 2152
International Doctoral Scholarship for Studies Specializing in Jewish Fields Vol. 1: 11687
International Documentary Film Festival Amsterdam Vol. 2: 3576
International DXer of the Year Vol. 1: 5268
International ECHO Awards Vol. 1: 8200
International Editor of the Year Vol. 1: 18995
International Egg Commission Promotion and Marketing Award Vol. 2: 6239
International Egg Marketing Award Vol. 2: 6239
International Emmy Awards Vol. 1: 10363
International Entertainment Competition; Vivian Vivio Stolaruk Vol. 1: 759
International Environmental Film Festival Vol. 2: 2365
International Excellence in Masonry Award Vol. 1: 11568
International Exhibition Logistics Associates Awards Vol. 2: 4795
International Exhibition of Professional Photography Vol. 1: 15340
International Federation of Beekeepers' Associations Medals Vol. 2: 3076
International Federation of Library Associations Honorary Fellow Vol. 2: 3581
International Federation of Library Associations Honorary President Vol. 2: 3582
International Federation of Library Associations Medal Vol. 2: 3583
International Federation of Netball Associations Service Awards Vol. 2: 6258
International Federation of University Women Awards Competition Vol. 2: 4803
International Fellow Award Vol. 1: 16899
International Fellowship of Certified Collection Executives Vol. 1: 55
International Fellowships in Jewish Studies and Jewish Culture Vol. 1: 11688
International Festival of Animated Film Stuttgart Vol. 2: 2421
International Festival of Film and Television in the Celtic Countries Vol. 2: 5587
International Festival of Films on Art Vol. 1: 10425
International Festival of Films on Art Vol. 1: 10424
International Festival of Maritime, Exploration, and Environmental Films Vol. 2: 1890
International Festival of Modern Jazz Dance Vol. 2: 2981
International Festival of Mountain Environment and Alpine Films, Les Diablerets, Switzerland Vol. 2: 4805
International Festival of Red Cross and Health Films Vol. 2: 1153
International Film and Television Festival of New York Vol. 1: 14121
International Film and Video Festival Vol. 2: 4828
International Film Festival of Visual Anthropology and Social Documentation Vol. 2: 1732
International Film/Video Competition Vol. 2: 3578
International Filmfestival Mannheim/ Heidelberg Vol. 2: 2304
International Force East Timor Medal Vol. 2: 218
International Forestry Achievement Award Vol. 1: 6601
International Foundation Fellow Award Vol. 1: 56
International Franz Liszt Piano Competition Vol. 2: 3621
International Franz Liszt Pianoconcours Vol. 2: 3621
International Frederic Chopin Piano Competition Vol. 2: 4002
International Free Flight Film Festival Vol. 2: 1797
International Futures Award for Exceptional and Innovative Leadership in Continuing Higher Education Vol. 1: 18215
International Game Fish Association Awards Vol. 1: 10448
International Gas Turbine Institute Scholar Award Vol. 1: 4143
International Gaudeamus Interpreters Competition Vol. 2: 3556
International Gaudeamus Music Week Vol. 2: 3557
International Glaucoma Association Fellowship Vol. 2: 6711
International Gold Quill Awards Vol. 1: 10155
International Good Neighbor Award Vol. 1: 17614
International Grand Champoin Vol. 1: 4478

Award Index

International Guest Scholarships Vol. 1: 1739
International Hall of Fame Awards Vol. 1: 10848
International Harp Contest in Israel Vol. 2: 2904
International Hemophilia Training Centres Fellowships Vol. 1: 18929
International Honor Key Vol. 1: 7450
International Humanitarian Award
AARL, The National Association for Amateur Radio Vol. 1: 33
American Red Magen David for Israel - American Friends of Magen David Vol 1: 3477
International Hydrology Prize Vol. 2: 1874
International Ice Hockey Federation Championships Vol. 2: 4809
International Illumination Design Awards Program Vol. 1: 9618
International Innovation Awards Vol. 1: 7631
International Institute for Promotion and Prestige Awards Vol. 2: 4811
International Iqbal Award Vol. 2: 3918
International Jeunesses Musicales Competition - Belgrade Vol. 2: 4413
International Judo Federation Awards Vol. 2: 4101
International Juried Show Vol. 1: 18571
International Jury Award Vol. 2: 2830
International Korfball Federation Badge of Honour Vol. 2: 3594
International Korfball Federation Honorary Member Vol. 2: 3595
International Lahti Organ Competition Vol. 2: 1419
International Leadership Award
International Association for Food Protection Vol. 1: 10082
Simon Wiesenthal Center Vol 1: 16068
United States Council for International Business Vol 1: 17787
International Leadership Citation Vol. 1: 16578
International Letter-Writing Competition for Young People Vol. 2: 4909
International Map Collectors' Society Awards Vol. 2: 6271
International Marathon Swimming Hall of Fame Vol. 1: 10771
International Maritime Heritage Award Vol. 2: 7379
International Martial Solal Piano-Jazz Competition Vol. 2: 1744
International Master Vol. 2: 2480
International Maurice Andre Trumpet Competition Vol. 2: 1745
International Medal
National Society, Sons of the American Revolution Vol. 1: 13765
Society of Chemical Industry Vol 2: 7169
International Media Awards Vol. 2: 4790
International Meteorological Organization Prize Vol. 2: 4934
International Migration Summer Institute and Fellowships Vol. 1: 16132
International Motorsports Hall of Fame Vol. 1: 10526
International Mozart Competition Vol. 2: 826
International Music Award Vol. 2: 4702
International Music Council Prize Vol. 2: 2001
International Mystery Festival Vol. 2: 3017
International Navies Photo Contest Vol. 1: 18010
International New Music Competition Vol. 1: 14513
International Newspaper Color Quality Club Awards Vol. 2: 2271
International No-Dig Award Vol. 2: 6295
International Old Lacers Contest Vol. 1: 10535
International Oliver Messiaen Competition for Interpertation of Contemporary Music Vol. 2: 1746
International Oncology Nursing Fellowships Vol. 2: 4859
International Online Communication Competition Vol. 1: 16427
International Opera Singers Competition Vol. 1: 7201
International Organ Competition Vol. 2: 1747
International Organ Competition, Odense Vol. 2: 1322
International Organ Festival Vol. 2: 6277
International Organ Improvisation Competition Vol. 2: 3675
International Parking Awards for Excellence Vol. 1: 10539
International Paul VI Prize Vol. 2: 3092
International Paulo Cello Competition Vol. 2: 1411
International Photography Competition Vol. 2: 4986
International Photography Hall of Fame and Museum Vol. 1: 15021
International Planner and Supplier Award Vol. 1: 11681
International Playwrights' Competition Vol. 1: 15999
International Polka Festival Vol. 1: 10550
International Polka Music Hall of Fame Vol. 1: 10550
International Poster Award Vol. 1: 1207
International Press Freedom Award Vol. 1: 6685
International Press Freedom Awards Vol. 1: 7627
International Print Biennale Vol. 2: 4004
International Print Framing Competition Vol. 1: 15347
International Print Triennial Vol. 2: 4004
International Prize for Biology Vol. 2: 3261
International Prize for Contemporary Art Vol. 2: 3471
International Prize Paladino D'Oro Vol. 2: 3084
International Program (IP) Award Vol. 1: 6470
International Property Tax Achievement Award Vol. 1: 10132
International Public Relations Association Golden World Awards for Excellence Vol. 2: 6287
International Public Relations Association President's Award Vol. 2: 6288
International Radio Festival of New York Vol. 1: 14120
International Rapeseed Award Vol. 2: 1886
International Reading Association Literacy Award Vol. 2: 2002
International Recognition and Scholarship Award Vol. 1: 10262
International Recognition Award Vol. 1: 248
International Retailer of the Year Vol. 1: 13641
International Rostrum of Young Performers/ UNESCO Vol. 2: 4444
International Sales Executive of the Year Vol. 1: 15801
International Scholarship Vol. 2: 3268
International Scholarship Award Vol. 1: 637
International Scholarship Program Vol. 1: 8354
International Science and Engineering Fair Vol. 1: 2569
International Seaweed Association Awards Vol. 2: 1132
International Service Vol. 1: 8843
International Service in Agronomy Award Vol. 1: 3874
International Service in Crop Science Award Vol. 1: 7978
International Short Film Festival Oberhausen Vol. 2: 2316
International Short Film Prize Vol. 2: 2304
International Show and Sale Vol. 1: 2864
International Society for Contemporary Music Honorary Member Vol. 2: 3604
International Society of Aircraft Traders (ISTAT) Scholarship Vol. 2: 6248
International Soil Science Award Vol. 1: 16938
International Solo Guitar Competition Vol. 1: 9228
International Songwriters' Association Awards Vol. 2: 2846
International Space Hall of Fame Vol. 1: 14103
International Special Librarians Day Vol. 1: 17077
International Sportscasters of the Year Vol. 1: 4305
International Standard Accuracy Contests Vol. 1: 18908
International Stepping-Stone Scholarships Vol. 1: 6743
International Store Interior Design Competition Vol. 1: 9941
International Swimming Hall of Fame Vol. 1: 10772
International Technical Art Competition Vol. 1: 16428
International Technical Publications Competition Vol. 1: 16429
International Television Festival Golden Prague Vol. 2: 1256
International Television Festival of Monte Carlo Vol. 2: 3469
International Tennis Hall of Fame Vol. 1: 10790
International Travel Awards Vol. 1: 16900
International Travel Fellowship Vol. 1: 877
International Trumpet Guild Composition Contest Vol. 1: 10804
International TV Audience Award Vol. 2: 3469
International Veterinary Congress Prize Vol. 1: 4409
International Villa-Lobos Guitar Competition Vol. 2: 1138
International Villa-Lobos Piano Competition Vol. 2: 1139
International Violin and Bow Making Competition Vol. 2: 1748
International Visitor Award Vol. 1: 228
International Visual Communications Association Awards Vol. 2: 6327
International West German Short Film Festival, Oberhausen Vol. 2: 2316

International Wildlife Film Festival Vol. 1: 10839
International Women's Film Festival of Creteil and Val-de-Marne Vol. 2: 1928
International Women's Sports Hall of Fame Vol. 1: 18872
Internationale Beiaardwedstrijd Koningin Fabiola Vol. 2: 1080
Internationale Filmfestspiele Berlin Vol. 2: 2048
Internationale Filmwoche Mannheim Vol. 2: 2304
Internationale Kompositiewedstrijd voor Beiaard Vol. 2: 1081
Internationale Kurzfilmtage Oberhausen Vol. 2: 2316
Internationale Tage des Okologischen Films Vol. 2: 2365
Internationalen Karlpreis der Stadt Aachen Vol. 2: 2409
Internationalen Klavierwettbewerb Koln Vol. 2: 2067
Internationaler Beethoven Klavierwettbewerb Vol. 2: 832
Internationaler Belvedere Wettbewerb fur Opernsanger Wien Vol. 2: 830
Internationaler Chorbewerb Vol. 2: 768
Internationaler Direct Marketing Wettbewerb Vol. 2: 888
Internationaler DLG-Preis Vol. 2: 2152
Internationaler Karlspreis zu Aachen Vol. 2: 2409
Internationaler Mozart Wettbewerb Vol. 2: 826
Internationaler Musikwettbewerb der ARD Vol. 2: 2311
Internationaler Musikwettbewerb Tokyo Vol. 2: 3338
Internationaler Violin-Wettbewerb Hannover Vol. 2: 2142
Internationaler Violinwettbewerb Koln Vol. 2: 2069
Internationaler Wettbewerb Franz Schubert und die Musik des 20 Jahrhunders Vol. 2: 828
Internationaler Wettbewerb fur Junge Pianisten Ettlingen Vol. 2: 2363
Internationaler Wettbewerb und Seminar fur Bratsche Vol. 2: 7259
Internationales Festival der Filmhochschulen Munchen Vol. 2: 2138
Internationales Trickfilm Festival Stuttgart Vol. 2: 2421
Internship Vol. 1: 18882
Internship Program
Center for Human-Computer Communication - OGI School of Science and Engineering Vol. 1: 7210
Ocean Conservancy Vol 1: 14447
Sonia Shankman Orthogenic School Vol 1: 16955
Interphot - Adelaide International Exhibition of Photography Vol. 2: 675
Interpret Britain and Ireland Awards Vol. 2: 5088
Interpretation Competition Vol. 2: 6277
Interscholastic Member Recognition Award Vol. 1: 13382
InterTech Technology Awards Vol. 1: 9173
Intra-Society Merit Award Vol. 1: 8080
Inukshuk Award Vol. 1: 6339
Investigator Awards Vol. 1: 7086
Investigator of the Year Vol. 2: 7353
IOC/IAKS Award Vol. 2: 2279
IOOL Emeritus Vol. 1: 18923
Iowa Country Music Hall of Fame Vol. 1: 13866
Iowa Poetry Association Award Vol. 1: 13153
Iowa School of Letters Award for Short Fiction Vol. 1: 10879
Iowa Short Fiction Award Vol. 1: 10879
IP Top Awards Vol. 2: 4769
Ipatieff Prize Vol. 1: 1559
IPDC - UNESCO Prize for Rural Communication Vol. 2: 1995
IPENZ Craven Post-Graduate Research Scholarship Vol. 2: 3737
IPENZ Structural Award Vol. 2: 3738
IPMA Educational Award Vol. 1: 10564
IPPA Award Vol. 2: 2818
Ippen Award; Arthur Thomas Vol. 2: 4508
IPS Award Vol. 2: 3058
IR-100 Competition Vol. 1: 15505
IRA Worked All Nordic Countries Award Vol. 2: 2519
IRA Zone 40 Award Vol. 2: 2520
Irby Distinguished Service Award; Charles C. Vol. 1: 12311
IRE Awards Vol. 1: 10852
IREAD (Illinois Reading Enrichment and Development) Awards Vol. 1: 9604
IRF Lifetime Achievement Award Vol. 2: 2732
IRG Travel Award Vol. 2: 4597
Irino Prize Vol. 2: 3201
Irish Advertising Awards Festival Vol. 2: 2887
Irish Federation of Musicians & Associated Professions Trophy Vol. 2: 2829
Irish Radio Industry Creative Prize Vol. 2: 2887
Irish Research Funds Vol. 1: 10885
The Irish Times Literature Prizes Vol. 2: 2858
Irish Way Scholarships Vol. 1: 10886
Irish Youth Foundation Award Vol. 2: 2862
IRLA Award Vol. 1: 10609
Iron Eyes Cody Award Vol. 1: 11106
Ironbridge Award Vol. 2: 5090
Ironman Jockey Vol. 1: 2819
IRPE Prize International Recognition of Professional Excellence Vol. 2: 2302
Irregular Shilling Vol. 1: 5628
Irrgang Memorial Award; William Vol. 1: 4458
Irvine Memorial Award; Charles H. Vol. 1: 5433
Irving Children's Book Choice Award; Washington Vol. 1: 18672
Irving Medal of Literary Excellence; Washington Vol. 1: 15798
Irwin Award; George R. Vol. 1: 5434
Irwin/McGraw-Hill Distinguished Marketing Educator Award; AMA/ Vol. 1: 2715
Irwin Memorial Ontario Cup; Bert Vol. 1: 6738
ISA Fellow Vol. 1: 10913
Isaac Composition Contest; Merle J. Vol. 1: 4323
Isaacs Awards for Outstanding Newsletter; Marx Vol. 1: 2488
Isaacs Marine Undergraduate Research Assistant Program; John D. Vol. 1: 6061
Isakson Prize for Optical Effects in Solids; Frank Vol. 1: 3119
ISAM Career Achievement Award Vol. 2: 2318
Isbrandt Automotive Safety Engineering Award; Ralph H. Vol. 1: 16579
ISC All-World Awards Vol. 1: 10755
ISC Award Vol. 1: 9653
ISCC Service Award Vol. 1: 9989
ISCE Silver Medal Vol. 1: 10704
ISCPP National Law Enforcement Explorer Community Crime Prevention Award Vol. 1: 8565
ISEM Seed Grants Vol. 1: 9763
ISIA Awards Vol. 2: 2856
Isidor Memorial Medal; Joseph S. Vol. 1: 12111
Isie Smuts Fellowship Vol. 2: 4309
Isker Award; Colonel Rohland A. Vol. 1: 15629
Islamic Development Bank Prizes in Islamic Economics and Islamic Banking Vol. 2: 4401
ISOPE Award Vol. 1: 10724
ISOPE EUROMS Aard Vol. 1: 10725
ISOPE OMS Award Vol. 1: 10726
ISOPE PACOMS Award Vol. 1: 10727
ISP/*VM+SD* International Store Design Awards Vol. 1: 9941
ISPE Engineer of The Year Vol. 1: 10665
Israel Museum Fellowships; The Wolgin Foundation/ Vol. 2: 2921
Issaccs Trophy Vol. 1: 16102
Isserlis Scholarship; Julius Vol. 2: 6864
Istanbul International Film Festival Vol. 2: 4982
ISTD Typographic Award Vol. 2: 6302
ISTTE Awards Vol. 1: 10744
ITA Award Vol. 2: 6310
Italian Alpine Club Prize Vol. 2: 3136
Italian Association for Metallurgy Awards Vol. 2: 3097
Italian PEN Prize Vol. 2: 3111
ITC Educational Award Vol. 2: 3590
ITC Research Award Vol. 2: 3591
Itek Award Vol. 1: 16249
Ithiel de Sola Pool Award Vol. 1: 3233
Itschner Plaque Vol. 1: 16526
Ittleson Award for Research in Child and Adolescent Psychiatry; Blanche F. Vol. 1: 3274
The IUPESM Awards of Merit Vol. 2: 1230
IUPUI National Children's Theatre Playwriting Competition Vol. 1: 9684
IUS Poster Prize Vol. 2: 1260
IUS Prize for the Most Significant Discovery Vol. 2: 1261
IUS Prize for the Most Significant Publication on a Cave or Karst Topic Vol. 2: 1262
Iuventus Mundi Cantat Competition Vol. 2: 1258
Ivanausko premija; Tado Vol. 2: 3379
Ivens Film Prize; Joris Vol. 2: 3576
Ivens; Prix Joris Vol. 2: 1732
Ivers Award; William H. Vol. 1: 17269
Ives Journal Award (Engineering); Charles E. Vol. 1: 16250
Ives Medal/Jarus W. Quinn Endowment; Frederic Vol. 1: 14608
Ivor Novello Vol. 2: 5215
IWAY (Information HighWAY) Awards Vol. 1: 7073
The IWF Order Vol. 2: 2513
IWLA Conservation Award Vol. 1: 10938
IWLA Hall of Fame Award Vol. 1: 10939
Iyengar Memorial Award; Dr. M. O. T. Vol. 2: 2607
Iyer Oration Award; Dr. C. G. S. Vol. 2: 2608

Award Index

J. B. Firth Essay Prize Vol. 2: 5917
J. I. Hambleton Award Vol. 1: 8338
J. Stuart Robertson Memorial Award Vol. 1: 6636
Jaag-Gewasserschutz-Preis; Otto Vol. 2: 4899
Jackling Award; Daniel C. Vol. 1: 16351
Jackson Award; Anna M. Vol. 1: 4118
Jackson Award; Hartley H. T. Vol. 1: 4119
Jackson Award; Lawrence Vol. 1: 14964
Jackson Award; Nell Vol. 1: 12326
Jackson Award; Sara E. Vol. 1: 12807
Jackson Award; William E. Vol. 1: 15771
Jackson Awards; C. C. Vol. 1: 18445
Jackson Distinguished Service Award; Henry M. tScoopv Vol. 1: 10998
Jackson Fellowship; Beverley Vol. 1: 6488
Jackson-Gwilt Medal Vol. 2: 6689
Jackson Lecture and Medal; Hughlings Vol. 2: 7014
Jackson Literary Award; Joseph Henry Vol. 1: 15829
Jackson Memorial Intermediate Piano Scholarship Vol. 1: 15872
Jackson Memorial Music Therapy Scholarship; La Verne Vol. 1: 12000
Jackson Mid-Career Clay Scientist Award; Marion L. and Chrystie M. Vol. 1: 7466
Jackson Prize; John Brinckerhoff Vol. 1: 5032
Jackson Prize; W. Turrentine Vol. 1: 2246
Jackson Research Fellowship; Dr. Noel Vol. 1: 15658
Jackson Scholarships; Stanley Vol. 1: 19049
Jackson Social Responsibility Award; Hobart Vol. 1: 1127
Jacob Book Prize; Herbert Vol. 1: 11250
Jacob; Prix Charles Vol. 2: 1573
Jacob Scholarship; Jerry Vol. 1: 11691
Jacob Trophy; Bruno E. Vol. 1: 13240
Jacobaeus Lectures; H. C. Vol. 2: 1315
Jacobi Memorial Award; Abraham Vol. 1: 698
Jacobs Award; Alvin H. Vol. 1: 699
Jacobsen Award; Earl Grant Vol. 1: 15892
Jacobsen Scholarship; Sally S. Vol. 1: 13191
Jacobson Award for Excellence in Teaching Trial Advocacy; Richard S. Vol. 1: 15717
Jacobson Award for Women Working in Health Care Law; Elaine Osborne Vol. 1: 15718
Jacobus Award; Donald Lines Vol. 1: 4041
Jacoby Prize Vol. 2: 3827
Jacoby Prize; Statistics New Zealand/ Vol. 2: 3827
Jacoby Student Essay Competition; Statistics New Zealand - Vol. 2: 3828
Jacquemetton; Prix Marius Vol. 2: 1955
Jacquet Gold Medal and the Francis F. Lucas Award for Excellence in Metallography; Pierre Vol. 1: 4705
Jade of Chiefs Award Vol. 1: 14751
JAE Best Article Award Vol. 1: 5100
JAE Best Design Article Award Vol. 1: 5100
Jaeger Medal Vol. 2: 116
Jaeger Memorial Award; Australian Geomechanics Award - John Vol. 2: 509
Jaeger Prize; Thomas A. Vol. 1: 10112
Jaeger Student Award for Graduate Research; Robert J. Vol. 1: 9393
Jaen Prize Vol. 2: 4521
Jaezat Al Malik Faisal Al Alamiyyah Li Khidmt Al Islam Vol. 2: 4405
Jaezat Al Malik Faisal Al Alamiyyah Lil Adab Al Arabi Vol. 2: 4403
Jaezat Al Malik Faisal Al Alamiyyah Lil Derasat Al Islamiyyah Vol. 2: 4404
Jaezat Al Malik Faisal Al Alamiyyah Lil Tib Vol. 2: 4406
Jaezat Al Malik Faisal Al Alamiyyah Lil Ulum Vol. 2: 4407
Jaffe; Prix Vol. 2: 1856
Jahnigen Memorial Award; Dennis W. Vol. 1: 2128
Jahns Distinguished Lecturer in Engineering Geology Award; Richard H. Vol. 1: 5137
Jaiswal Memorial Award; Prof. N.K. Vol. 2: 2781
Jakob Memorial Award; Max Vol. 1: 4144
JALMA Trust Fund Oration Award in the Field of Leprosy Vol. 2: 2609
James Award; Edith-Dalton Vol. 2: 3156
James Award; William Vol. 1: 3355
James B. White JSA Award Vol. 1: 10970
James Beard/Perrier Jouet Restaurant Awards Vol. 1: 10955
James Beard/Seagram Restaurant Awards Vol. 1: 10955
James Beard Who's Who of Food and Beverage in America Vol. 1: 10958
James Book Award; William Vol. 1: 3344
James Brennan Memorial Trophy Vol. 2: 5351
James Fellowship; T. V. Vol. 2: 5367
James International Award; John F. Vol. 1: 4060
James Lynah Memorial Award Vol. 1: 8346
James Memorial Trophy; Eddie Vol. 1: 6511
James T. MacKenzie Memorial Award Vol. 1: 6637
James Traveling Fellowship; Olivia Vol. 1: 4578
Jameson Archival Advocacy Award; J. Franklin Vol. 1: 16493
Jameson Fellowship in American History; J. Franklin Vol. 1: 11346
Jameson Prize; J. Franklin Vol. 1: 2237
Jamestown Foundation Award Vol. 1: 14528
Jamestown Prize Vol. 1: 14528
Jamestown Scholars: Dissertation Fellowships from the National Park Service and OAH Vol. 1: 14695
Jamieson Award Vol. 2: 3790
Jamieson Fellowship; Donald Vol. 1: 6916
Jamieson Prize; Laura Vol. 1: 6863
Jamison Scholarship; Ines Pratt Vol. 1: 12000
Jamnalal Bajaj Foundation Awards Vol. 2: 2776
Jan Beek Award; Klaas Vol. 2: 3592
Janata Award; Rudolf A. Vol. 1: 8132
Jandoli Award for Outstanding Achivement in the Print Curriculum Vol. 1: 15787
Jane Addams Children's Book Award Vol. 1: 18863
Jane Memorial Award; R.S. Vol. 1: 6893
Janeway Medal Vol. 1: 3461
Janice Hines Memorial Award Vol. 1: 6777
Janssen-Ortho Award Vol. 1: 6842
Janssen; Prix Jules Vol. 2: 1956
Janssen; Prix Paul Vol. 2: 1095
Janssen Research Award Vol. 1: 542
Janssen Schizophrenia Research Award; Dr. Paul Vol. 1: 7549
Japan Academy Prize Vol. 2: 3215
Japan Association for Education Broadcasting Prize Vol. 2: 3298
Japan Beer Cup Vol. 2: 3224
Japan Foundation Awards Vol. 2: 3233
Japan Foundation Special Prizes Vol. 2: 3234
Japan Gold Disk Award Vol. 2: 3314
Japan Prize Vol. 2: 3318
Japan Quality Medal Vol. 2: 3341
Japan Society Award Vol. 1: 10962
Japan-U.S. Friendship Commission Prize for the Translation of Japanese Literature Vol. 1: 11104
Japanese SICOT Scholarship Vol. 2: 4108
Jarabak Award; Louise Ada Vol. 1: 1200
Jarvis Award; Tony Vol. 2: 5130
Jasper Fellowship Vol. 2: 4960
Javits Public Service Award; Jacob K. Vol. 1: 3275
Jay Award for Distinguished Professional Achievement; John Vol. 1: 7588
Jayanti Award; Swarna Vol. 2: 2525
Jayezeye Shoraye Ketabe Koudak Vol. 2: 2820
Jayle; Prix Max-Fernand Vol. 2: 1574
Jayme Denkmunze; Georg Vol. 2: 2031
Jazz Flute Masterclass Vol. 1: 13202
Jazz Masters Fellowships Vol. 1: 13103
Jazz Prize Vol. 1: 8683
Jazz Scholarship Vol. 1: 12000
Jazzpar Prize Vol. 2: 1282
JB Awards Vol. 1: 13231
JCPenney - University of Missouri Awards in Lifestyle Journalism Vol. 1: 18325
Jeanbernat et Barthelemy de Ferrari Doria; Prix Jules et Louis
Academie des Beaux-Arts Vol. 2: 1456
Academie des Sciences Morales et Politiques Vol 2: 1669
Institut de France Vol 2: 1857
Jeanie Voice Scholarship Vol. 1: 8740
Jeanne S. Chall Research Fellowship Vol. 1: 10584
Jeanne Scholarship; Sister Rita Vol. 1: 11052
Jeantet Prize for Medicine; Louis- Vol. 2: 4862
Jefferson Award; Thomas
American Citizens Abroad Vol. 2: 4698
Association of Private Enterprise Education Vol 1: 5304
Jefferson Awards Vol. 1: 2352
Jefferson Awards for Public Architecture; Thomas Vol. 1: 2435
Jefferson Cup Award Vol. 1: 18559
Jefferson Foundation Medal in Architecture; Thomas Vol. 1: 11932
Jefferson Foundation Medal in Law; Thomas Vol. 1: 11933
Jefferson Freedom Award; Thomas Vol. 1: 2642
Jefferson Grape-wine Loving Cup Trophy Vol. 1: 18540
Jefferson Lecture in the Humanities Award Vol. 1: 13111
Jefferson Medal Vol. 1: 14090
Jefferson Medal for Distinguished Achievement in the Arts, Humanities, or Social Sciences; Thomas Vol. 1: 3097
Jefferson Prize; Thomas Vol. 1: 16226
Jeffords, Jr. Trophy; Walter M. Vol. 1: 18715
Jeffries Aerospace Medicine and Life Sciences Research Award Vol. 1: 2384
Jeffries Award; John Vol. 1: 2384
Jelavich Book Prize; Barbara Vol. 1: 958

Jellicoe Scholarship in Landscape Architecture; Geoffrey Vol. 2: 5440
Jellinek Memorial Fund Award; E. M. Vol. 1: 10968
Jenkins Outstanding Service Award; Samuel H. Vol. 2: 6331
Jenkins Teacher of Excellence; Don Vol. 1: 17431
Jennings Award; Margaret Vol. 2: 376
Jennings Memorial Award; Charles H. Vol. 1: 4459
Jensen Award; Harry T. Vol. 1: 2199
Jensen Award; Paul Vol. 1: 15894
Jensen Memorial Trophy; Rudolf Vol. 1: 10894
Jenson Educational Stipend; Gaynold Vol. 1: 7769
Jephcott Lecture Vol. 2: 7015
Jeppson Medal; John Vol. 1: 1484
Jerard Fund Award Vol. 1: 14895
Jeremiah Award; Edward Vol. 1: 2250
Jeremiah Award/MenFs Division III Ice Hockey Coach of the Year; Edward Vol. 1: 2252
Jeremine; Prix Paul Fallot- Vol. 2: 1575
Jermias Award Vol. 1: 6985
Jernigan Scholarship; Kenneth Vol. 1: 13191
Jerome Award Vol. 1: 7160
Jerome Awards; Harry Vol. 1: 5791
Jerome Fellowships Vol. 1: 15105
Jerome Scholarships; Harry Vol. 1: 5792
Jerry Awards Vol. 1: 5300
Jerusalem Prize for the Freedom of the Individual in Society Vol. 2: 2926
Jerwood Aldeburgh First Collection Prize Vol. 2: 5018
Jerwood Awards Vol. 2: 6340
The Jerwood Painting Prize Vol. 2: 6525
Jerwood Prize Vol. 2: 7061
The Jerwood Sculpture Prize Vol. 2: 6526
Jeske Award; Walter E. Vol. 1: 14249
Jesselson Prize for Contemporary Judaica Design Vol. 2: 2917
Jessies Vol. 1: 9196
Jester of the Year Vol. 2: 355
Jesup Botanical Trophy; Ann and Phil Vol. 1: 2995
Jeter Award; Frank Vol. 1: 4801
Jewett Memorial Life Award; Lew Vol. 1: 8640
Jewish Caucus Scholarship Vol. 1: 13925
Jewish Heritage Essay Contest Vol. 1: 5277
Jeyes Lectureship; John Vol. 2: 6970
The JFSF Award for Achievement in Technical Research Vol. 2: 3276
The JFSF Award for Encouragement of Young Investigators Vol. 2: 3277
JHQ Golden Pen Award Vol. 1: 12334
Jiaqing Mathematics Award; Zhong Vol. 2: 3929
Jill Vickers Prize Vol. 1: 6820
Jindal Gold Medal; O. P. Vol. 2: 2654
The J.L. Manning Vol. 2: 7240
JNMA Awards for Medical Journalism Vol. 1: 13444
Joachim Distinguished Service Award; TAPPI Herman L. Vol. 1: 17393
Joanne Felk Award Vol. 2: 262
Joannides; Prix Alexandre Vol. 2: 1576
Job Corps Hall of Fame Vol. 1: 17846
Jobs Award Vol. 1: 14599
Jobst Foundation Prize; Conrad Vol. 1: 1774
JOCS Award for Industrial Technologies Vol. 2: 3253
JOCS Award for Merit Vol. 2: 3254
JOCS Award for Progress of Studies Vol. 2: 3255
JOCS Award for Prominent Studies Vol. 2: 3256
Joe Harms Medal Vol. 2: 464
Joe Sobek Award Vol. 1: 18040
Joest; Prix de Vol. 2: 1670
Joest; Prix du Baron de
Academie des Beaux-Arts Vol. 2: 1457
Academie des Inscriptions et Belles-Lettres Vol 2: 1518
JOFA All-American Ice Hockey Teams (College Division) Vol. 1: 2253
JOFA All-American Ice Hockey Teams (University Division) Vol. 1: 2254
Jofa-Titan/USA Hockey Distinguished Achievement Award Vol. 1: 18399
Johinke Medal; K. Vol. 2: 510
John Alexander Media Award Vol. 1: 12006
John B. Steele Distinguished Service Award Vol. 1: 6536
John Britten Award Vol. 2: 3713
John Deere Awards Vol. 1: 14278
John Downing Award Vol. 2: 7302
John Flynn Scholarships Vol. 2: 162
John G. Paterson Media Award Vol. 1: 15407
John Guice Award Vol. 1: 11959
John Horrocks Scholarship Vol. 2: 7349
John Hurdis Award Vol. 1: 17125
John McMenemy Prize Vol. 1: 6821
John Paul II Award Vol. 1: 13626
John Paul Jones - Norwich Dog Vol. 1: 14424
John S. Hewitt Team Achievement Award Vol. 1: 6764
John Tyndall Award Vol. 1: 9585
John W. Kaufmann Award Vol. 1: 7673
Johns Award; Harold E.
National Cancer Institute of Canada Vol. 1: 12845
National Cancer Institute of Canada Vol 1: 12846
Johnson Achievement Award; Alfred E. Vol. 1: 1289
Johnson AMS 50 Dissertation Fellowships; Alvin H. Vol. 1: 2845
Johnson and Johnson Medical Products Editorial Award Vol. 1: 6683
Johnson and Johnson New Investigators Awards; Denis Wade Vol. 2: 95
Johnson Annual Scholarship Winners; Edward Vol. 1: 9220
Johnson Award; Bob Vol. 1: 18400
Johnson Award; Charles A. Vol. 1: 5435
Johnson Award; Eleanor M. Vol. 1: 10585
Johnson Award for Career Contributions to Family Medicine Education; Thomas W. Vol. 1: 611
Johnson Award; G. Wesley Vol. 1: 13046
Johnson Award; John C. Vol. 1: 5725
Johnson Award; Kelly Vol. 1: 16688
Johnson Award; Lady Bird Vol. 1: 12253
Johnson Award; Larry R. Vol. 1: 13898
Johnson Award; Mrs. Lyndon B. Vol. 1: 11107
Johnson Award; Pyke Vol. 1: 17581
Johnson Award; Richard B. Vol. 1: 11576
Johnson-Cox-Frazier Award Vol. 1: 4282
Johnson Exhibition Catalogue Award; Philip Vol. 1: 16555
Johnson Health Policy Fellowships; Robert Wood Vol. 1: 12174
Johnson Honorary Member Award; Philip D. Vol. 1: 3777
Johnson Image Award; Peter H. Vol. 1: 12701
Johnson, Jr., Award; J. E. Vol. 1: 4902
Johnson Memorial Award; Palmer O. Vol. 1: 1942
Johnson Memorial Trophy; Joe Vol. 1: 6654
Johnson New Holland Award Vol. 2: 6085
Johnson Nutritionals New Investigator Award; Mead Vol. 1: 16149
Johnson Outstanding Achievement Award; A. Ivan Vol. 1: 5436
Johnson Pioneer Citation; Edgar F. Vol. 1: 15524
Johnson President's Trophy; John H. Vol. 1: 12618
Johnson Prize; Harry G. Vol. 1: 6466
Johnson Writing Award; Orinne Vol. 1: 15009
Johnston Award; J. Dudley Vol. 2: 6875
Johnston Award; William M. Vol. 1: 18142
Johnston Distinguished Lecture Award Vol. 1: 10639
Johnston Jr. Outstanding New Mechanics Educator Award; Ferdinand P. Beer and E. Russell Vol. 1: 3629
Johnston Medal; W. A. Vol. 1: 6849
Johnston Memorial Shield; William Vol. 2: 5993
Johnston Press Award; The Vol. 2: 6468
Johnston Service Award; Floyd T. Vol. 1: 5138
Johnstone III Trophy (Singlehanded); Robert L. Vol. 1: 18079
Joint AICPA/AAA Notable Contributions to Accounting Literature Award Vol. 1: 2461
Joint ASCP - CAP Award for Distinguished Service to American Pathology Vol. 1: 3602
Joint Service Achievement Medal Vol. 1: 8109
Joint Service Commendation Medal Vol. 1: 8110
Jomo Kenyatta Prize for Literature Vol. 2: 3362
Jones and Bailey K. Howard World Book Encylopedia - ALA Goal Awards; J. Morris Vol. 1: 2666
Jones & Shipman Prize Vol. 2: 6153
Jones Award; Bob Vol. 1: 17918
Jones Award; Col. James L. Vol. 1: 13452
Jones Award; Dexter Vol. 1: 13693
Jones Award for Best Work of Fiction; Jesse Vol. 1: 17481
Jones Award for Executive Leadership; Roger W. Vol. 1: 4384
Jones Award; Jesse H. Vol. 1: 17481
Jones Award; Mary Vaughan Vol. 2: 7326
Jones Awards; Mander Vol. 2: 377
Jones-Bateman Cup Vol. 2: 6795
Jones Community Service Award; Edward C. Vol. 1: 2731
Jones Distinguished Service Award; Reginald H. Vol. 1: 12185
Jones Fleet Engineer Award; Claud A. Vol. 1: 4189
Jones London Medal; H. E. Vol. 2: 6172
Jones, M.D., Award; Anson Vol. 1: 17491
Jones Memorial Scholarship; Billy Mayo/Rubin Vol. 1: 8780
Jones Prize; Alice Hanson Vol. 1: 8380
Jones Stallion Award; Jim Vol. 1: 1956
Jonssons pris; Bengt Vol. 2: 4628
Jordan Award Vol. 2: 6504

Award Index

Jordan Developing Artist Grant; Lana Vol. 1: 15805
Jordan Memorial Challenge Trophy; Lynn Vol. 1: 13806
Jorgenson Award; Wally Vol. 1: 12433
Joseph Award; Stephen Vol. 2: 7127
Joseph Award; Thomas L. Vol. 1: 4903
Joseph Prize Vol. 2: 4255
Joseph Prize for Human Rights Vol. 1: 4545
Joseph Prize; Roger E. Vol. 1: 9347
Joseph W. Rosenbluth Memorial Award Vol. 1: 4255
Joseph W. Rosenbluth Memorial Travel Agent of the Year Award Vol. 1: 4255
Joseph/Wilson Study Grant Vol. 1: 9188
Josey Scholarship Award; E. J. Vol. 1: 5800
Josie Tomforde Competition Vol. 1: 9500
Jost Memorial Lecture; Wilhelm Vol. 2: 2159
Jostens Most Improved National Midget Championship Series Driver Award Vol. 1: 17751
Joukowsky Distinguished Service Award; Martha and Artemis Vol. 1: 4579
Joule Medal; James Prescott Vol. 2: 6117
Journal Award
  National Council on Public History Vol. 1: 13046
  Society of Motion Picture and Television Engineers Vol 1: 16748
The Journal Award in Poetry Vol. 1: 14482
Journal Award (Science) Vol. 1: 16251
Journal Awards Vol. 2: 4202
Journal Certificate of Merit Vol. 1: 16748
Journal Contributor Awards Vol. 1: 4485
Journal of Advertising Best Article Award Vol. 1: 547
Journal of Allied Health Award Vol. 1: 5331
Journal of Geography Awards Vol. 1: 12970
Journal of Oleoscience Editors Award Vol. 2: 3257
Journal of Research in Science Teaching Award Vol. 1: 12353
Journal of Sedimentary Research Best Paper Award Vol. 1: 16410
Journalism Achievement Awards Vol. 1: 3556
Journalism Alumni Award Vol. 1: 5637
Journalism Award
  American Association of Petroleum Geologists Vol. 1: 1214
  American Podiatric Medical Association Vol 1: 3215
  International Association for Energy Economics Vol 1: 10074
  International Association of Assessing Officers Vol 1: 10133
Journalism Awards
  American Planning Association Vol. 1: 3211
  James Beard Foundation Vol 1: 10954
  Leukemia and Lymphoma Society Vol 1: 11304
  New York Press Club Vol 1: 14137
  Specialized Information Publishers Association Vol 1: 17104
Journalism Awards Program Vol. 1: 9331
Journalism Hall of Fame Vol. 1: 5638
Journalism Leadership Award Vol. 2: 561
Journalist of the Year
  Association for Geographic Information Vol. 2: 5085
  Automobile Journalists Association of Canada Vol 1: 5563
  Institute of Maltese Journalists Vol 2: 3421
Journalist of the Year Award
  MIND - National Association for Mental Health Vol. 2: 6430
  National Association of Black Journalists Vol 1: 12413
Journalist Prize Vol. 2: 2245
Journalistenpreis of the DGE Vol. 2: 2245
Journalists in Distress Fund Vol. 1: 6686
Journalists Prize Vol. 2: 2200
Journey Prize Vol. 1: 11625
Joy Awards; Linda Vol. 1: 5505
Joy In Singing Award Competition Vol. 1: 11057
Joynt Mentorship Award; Phyllis Vol. 1: 5385
JPA Exhibiting Award Vol. 1: 11069
JRD TATA Corporate Leadership Award Vol. 2: 2532
The JSFS Award for Scientific Achievement Vol. 2: 3278
JSID Outstanding Student Paper of the Year Award Vol. 1: 16308
Juan Embil Award Vol. 1: 5220
The Juanita Chambers Excellence in Community Service Award Vol. 1: 15408
Jubilee Award Vol. 2: 7269
Jubilee Lecture and Harden Medal Vol. 2: 5173
Jubilee Medal Vol. 2: 5548
Jubilee Trophy Vol. 2: 3847
Jucys premija; Adolfo Vol. 2: 3380
Judaica Reference Award Vol. 1: 5207
Judd AIC Award Vol. 2: 2287
Judeen Award; Erik Vol. 1: 18098
Judge Heart of New York Awards; Rev. Mychal Vol. 1: 14142
Judge of the Year
  Federation of Canadian Archers Vol. 1: 8624
  The International Cat Association Vol 1: 10293
Judge of the Year Award
  National Association of Women Judges Vol. 1: 12717
  National Court Appointed Special Advocate Association Vol 1: 13058
Judges Appreciation Award Vol. 1: 2894
JudgesF Award Vol. 2: 7046
Judges' Award
  Royal Television Society Vol. 2: 7042
  Royal Television Society Vol 2: 7044
JudgeFs Award of Merit Vol. 1: 13527
Judges' Choice Vol. 1: 15258
Judges Choice Award Vol. 1: 10460
Judges' Commendation Vol. 1: 2996
Judkins Young Clinical Investigator Award; Melvin Vol. 1: 2181
Jujitsu Outstanding Competitor Vol. 1: 491
Julien; Prix Stanislas Vol. 2: 1519
Julin Trophy; Bengt Vol. 1: 18069
Julius Medal; George Vol. 2: 511
Julius Stulberg Auditions Vol. 1: 17312
Julliard Prize; Jean Vol. 2: 3615
Jump Memorial Foundation Award; William A. Vol. 1: 11059
Jumper of the Year Vol. 1: 18457
Juneja Award for Creativity and Innovation; AIMA - Dr. J.S. Vol. 2: 2533
Junge Award Vol. 2: 2024
Jungfleisch; Prix Emile Vol. 2: 1577
Junior Athlete of the Year
  Federation of Canadian Archers Vol. 1: 8625
  United States Racquetball Association Vol 1: 18041
Junior Award Vol. 1: 4137
Junior Book Award Vol. 1: 16984
Junior Bowler of the Year Vol. 2: 634
Junior Division Award Vol. 1: 1957
Junior European Baseball Champion Vol. 2: 858
Junior Faculty Award Vol. 1: 1911
Junior Faculty Scholar Award Vol. 1: 4070
Junior Fellowship Awards Vol. 2: 6752
Junior Female Athlete of the Year Vol. 1: 17150
Junior Golf Association of Mobile Scholarship Vol. 1: 11067
Junior Golf Leader Vol. 1: 15318
Junior Grand Champion Vol. 1: 14344
Junior High Average Horsemanship Vol. 1: 14345
Junior Hobbyist Vol. 1: 6224
Junior, Intermediate, and Senior Championship Awards Vol. 1: 8418
Junior Inventor of the Year E. C. Fernando Memorial Award Vol. 2: 4557
Junior Male Athlete of the Year Vol. 1: 17151
Junior Moulton Medal Vol. 2: 6098
Junior National Championship Vol. 1: 14346
Junior National Championships Vol. 1: 18382
Junior Paper Award Vol. 1: 16767
Junior Performance Competition Vol. 1: 12033
Junior Performance Competitions Vol. 1: 12034
Junior Player Clarence Camp Scholarship Vol. 1: 8764
Junior Player of the Year Vol. 1: 18401
Junior Science Award Vol. 2: 4989
Junior Travelling Fellowship Vol. 2: 7372
Junior Triathletes of the Year Vol. 1: 18461
Junior/Young Rider Awards Vol. 1: 17887
Juniper Prize Vol. 1: 18309
Junner Rose-Bowl Trophy; Mackenzie Vol. 2: 7205
Juno Awards Vol. 1: 6141
Jupiter Award Vol. 1: 11937
Jurdant Prize in Environmental Science; Michel Vol. 1: 5016
Juried Crafts Exhibition Vol. 1: 7254
Jurist of the Year Award Vol. 2: 3364
Jury Award Vol. 2: 4538
Jury Prize for the Dance on Camera Festival Vol. 1: 8039
Just Lecture Award; E.E. Vol. 1: 3589
Justice Award
  American Judicature Society Vol. 1: 2604
  Canadian Institute for the Administration of Justice Vol 1: 6584
Justicia Award Vol. 1: 6332
Jutra Award; Claude Vol. 1: 70
Juvenile Stake Challenge Trophy Vol. 1: 13806
JVC President Award Vol. 2: 3343
K-9 Service Award Vol. 1: 3221
K-12 Dance Educator of the Year Vol. 1: 13078
K-12 Distinguished Teaching Achievement Award Vol. 1: 12969
KAB System Awards Vol. 1: 11108
Kabataan Essay Award Vol. 2: 3978
Kable Electrification Award; George W. Vol. 1: 3860
Kagin Family Paper Money Youth Exhibit Award Vol. 1: 2895
Kagy Education Award of Excellence; Frederick D. Vol. 1: 9174

Kahan Scholars Prize; Gerald Vol. 1: 3830
Kahlil Gibran Spirit of Humanity Award Vol. 1: 4568
Kahn Award; Noah A. Vol. 1: 5437
Kahuna Award Vol. 1: 10768
Kaigler; Fay B. Vol. 1: 11874
Kain Scholarhip Fund; Karen Vol. 1: 6131
Kaiser Educational Award; L. U. "Luke" Vol. 1: 11470
Kaitz Award; Idell Vol. 1: 12837
Kal Kan Award Vol. 1: 810
Kalan Fund Award; Pavle Vol. 2: 4468
Kalbache and Zara Ben Hamou Memorial Award; Azar Vol. 1: 10558
Kaleidoscope - A Fair of the Arts Vol. 1: 7290
Kaleidoscope of Honor Vol. 2: 1301
Kaletta Award; Father Paul Vol. 1: 10295
Kalinga Prize for the Popularization of Science Vol. 2: 1996
Kalish Innovative Publication Award; Richard Vol. 1: 9060
Kallebergerstipendiet Vol. 2: 4659
Kallman Executive Fellow Program; Ernest A. Vol. 1: 5716
Kalmus Gold Medal Award; Technicolor/ Herbert T. Vol. 1: 16752
Kalven, Jr., Prize; Harry J. Vol. 1: 11251
Kamani Gold Medal Vol. 2: 2659
Kammer Merit in Authorship Award; Adolph G. Vol. 1: 1691
Kammerer Award; Gladys M. Vol. 1: 3234
Kanai Award; Tsutomu Vol. 1: 9810
Kancharla Award For Excellence Vol. 2: 2546
Kandhari Award; Lala Ram Chand Vol. 2: 2610
Kandutsch Preis; Jorg Vol. 2: 809
Kane Medal; Elisha Kent Vol. 1: 9013
Kane Rising Star Award; William Vol. 1: 1723
Kanellakis Theory and Practice Award; Paris Vol. 1: 4809
Kanin Playwriting Award Program; Michael
Kennedy Center American College Theater Festival Vol. 1: 11116
Kennedy Center American College Theater Festival Vol 1: 11117
Kennedy Center American College Theater Festival Vol 1: 11120
Kanin Playwriting Awards Program; Michael Vol. 1: 11118
Kanjilal Traveling Fellowship; Ferdinande Johanna Vol. 2: 6726
Kansainvalinen Mirjam Helin laulukilpailu Vol. 2: 1391
Kansainvalinen Paulon Sellokilpailu Vol. 2: 1411
Kansas Premier Seed Grower Vol. 1: 11079
Kapell Piano Competition; University of Maryland International Piano Festival and William Vol. 1: 16094
Kapitan Award; Josef S. Vol. 1: 4904
Kaplan Award; David Vol. 1: 14761
Kaplan Award; Gordin Vol. 1: 6478
Kaplan Sportsmanship Award; Bobby Vol. 1: 18143
Kaplun Foundation Award; Morris J. and Betty
Jewish Book Council Vol. 1: 10976
Jewish Book Council Vol 1: 10979
Kapp Foundation Engineering Award; Martin S. Vol. 1: 3956
Kappa Alpha Theta Program Director of the Year Award Vol. 1: 13059
Kappa Delta Pi National Student Teacher/ Intern of the Year Award Vol. 1: 5362
Kappa Tau Alpha Research Award; Frank Luther Mott- Vol. 1: 18326
Kappe Award; Stanley E. Vol. 1: 576
Karant Award for Excellence in Aviation Journalism; Max Vol. 1: 344
Karlin Grant; Barbara Vol. 1: 16626
Karling Graduate Student Research Award; J. S. Vol. 1: 5879
Karlson Lifetime Achievement Award; Adele Vol. 1: 17241
Karlsson Award for Leadership and Achievement through Collaboration; Hans Vol. 1: 9811
Karlstrom Outstanding Educator Award; Karl V. Vol. 1: 4810
Karmel Award; Marjorie Vol. 1: 11211
Karpinskij Prize; Alexander Petrowitsch Vol. 2: 2398
Kasdan Award for Best Narrative Film; Lawrence Vol. 1: 4538
Kastler; Prix de Biologie Alfred Vol. 2: 1822
Kastler-Prize; Gentner- Vol. 2: 2093
Katanning Art Prize Vol. 2: 554
Kathe-Leichter-Preis Vol. 2: 790
Katz Award; Donald L. Vol. 1: 8971
Katz Award for Excellence in the Coverage of Immigration; Eugene Vol. 1: 7212
Katz Award; Joseph Vol. 1: 4886
Katz Basic Science Research Prize; Louis N. and Arnold M. Vol. 1: 2182
Kauffman Gold Medal; Virgil Vol. 1: 16680
Kaufman Women's Scholarship; Lucille B. Vol. 1: 16717
Kaufmann Award; Richard Harold Vol. 1: 9784
Kaufmann Memorial Lecture Vol. 2: 2229
Kaufmann Prize; H. P. Vol. 2: 2230
Kautz Merit Award; Sena Vol. 1: 9673
Kavanagh Memorial Youth Baseball Research Award; Jack
Society for American Baseball Research Vol. 1: 16168
Society for American Baseball Research Vol 1: 16171
Kay Award; Won Chuel Vol. 1: 203
Kay Cattarulla Short Story Award Vol. 1: 17482
Kay Co-Op Scholarship; E. Wayne Vol. 1: 16718
Kay Community College Scholarship; E. Wayne Vol. 1: 16719
Kay Elemetrics Award for Research in Phonetics Vol. 1: 10736
Kay Graduate Fellowship; Wayne Vol. 1: 16720
Kay High School Scholarship; E. Wayne Vol. 1: 16721
Kay Scholarship; E. Wayne Vol. 1: 16722
KCFB Scholarship Vol. 1: 11156
KCS Merit Award Vol. 2: 4109
Kean Medal; Ben Vol. 1: 4260
Keane; Award for Career Excellence in Honor of Mark E. Vol. 1: 10310
Keane Award for Excellence; Mark E. Vol. 1: 10310
Keane Distinguished Service Award; Charles V. Vol. 1: 24
Kearns Credit Executive of the Year; Alfred W. Vol. 1: 184
Kearton Medal and Award; Cherry Vol. 2: 6770
Keats/Kerlan Collection Fellowship; Ezra Jack Vol. 1: 18319
Keats Memorial Fellowship; Ezra Jack Vol. 1: 18319
Keats-Shelley Prize Vol. 1: 11102
Keefer Medal Vol. 1: 6917
Keeler Scholarship Vol. 2: 6712
Keeling Dissertation Award; William B. Vol. 1: 17586
Keep America Beautiful National Awards Vol. 1: 11108
Keepers Preservation Education Fund Fellowship Vol. 1: 16556
Keeping the Blues Alive Awards Vol. 1: 5822
Keesiing Fellowship; Nancy Vol. 2: 680
Kegan Award; Philip M. Hamer and Elizabeth Hamer Vol. 1: 16491
Kegans Award for Victims Services in Probation and Parole; Joe Vol. 1: 3260
Kegel Bowler of the Month Vol. 1: 5895
Kehoe Award of Merit; Robert A. Vol. 1: 1692
Kehoe Memorial Award; Fr. George Vol. 1: 6655
Kehrlein Award; Oliver Vol. 1: 16013
Keilin Memorial Lecture Vol. 2: 5174
Keith Medal Vol. 2: 6996
Keithley Award for Advances in Measurement Science; Joseph F. Vol. 1: 3120
Keithley Award in Instrumentation and Measurement; Joseph F. Vol. 1: 9785
Kelleher Award; Judith C. Vol. 1: 8440
Kellendonk-prijs; Frans Vol. 2: 3670
Keller Achievement Awards; Helen Vol. 1: 2068
Keller Award; Spirit of Helen Vol. 1: 9359
Keller Behavioral Education Award; Fred S. Vol. 1: 3309
Keller High Average Award; Jean-Fish-Pearl Vol. 1: 18847
Keller Prize; Gottfried Vol. 2: 4866
Keller Trophy Vol. 1: 9894
Kellett Island Trophy Vol. 2: 5910
Kelley Consumer Leadership Award; Florence Vol. 1: 12946
Kelley - Wyman Award Vol. 1: 12391
Kellgrenpriset Vol. 2: 4660
Kellogg National Leadership Program Vol. 1: 18800
Kelly Award for Cultural Leadership; Keith Vol. 1: 6419
Kelly Award; Jack Vol. 1: 18047
Kelly Award; Joe W. Vol. 1: 1757
Kelly Award; Stephen E. Vol. 1: 11457
Kelly Awards Vol. 1: 11457
Kelly Fair Play Award; Jack Vol. 1: 18017
Kelly Founders Award; John tSnooksv Vol. 1: 2255
Kelly Memorial Award; Robert Vol. 1: 13047
Kelly Memorial Prize; Joan Vol. 1: 2238
Kelly Peace Poetry Awards; Barbara Mandigo Vol. 1: 14436
Kelly Trophy; C. Markland Vol. 1: 17965
Kelman Innovator's Lecture; Charles D. Vol. 1: 3902
Kelsey Award; Guy Vol. 1: 3502
Kelvin Medal
Institution of Civil Engineers Vol. 2: 6118
Royal Philosophical Society of Glasgow Vol 2: 6868
Kelvin Medal and Prize Vol. 2: 6063
Kelvin Premium Vol. 2: 6146
Kempe Award; C. Henry Vol. 1: 10687
Kempe Lectureship Vol. 1: 10688

Award Index

Kemper Award; Edward C. Vol. 1: 2436
Kempf Fund Award for Research Development in Psychobiological Psychiatry; APIRE/ Vol. 1: 3276
Kenaga SETAC Membership Award; Eugene Vol. 1: 16660
Kendall Award; Katherine Vol. 2: 6227
Kendall Oration and Medal Vol. 2: 383
Kendall Practice Award; Henry O. and Florence P. Vol. 1: 3149
Kenna Scholar-Athlete Award; E. Douglas Vol. 1: 13215
Kennan Award for Distinguished Public Service; George F. Vol. 1: 12918
Kennedy Astronautics Award; John F. Vol. 1: 1349
Kennedy Award; Byron Vol. 2: 197
Kennedy Award; Henry L. Vol. 1: 1758
Kennedy Award; William M. Vol. 1: 16763
Kennedy Book Awards; Robert F. Vol. 1: 15681
Kennedy Center Alliance for Arts Education Network and National School Board Association Award Vol. 1: 11111
Kennedy Center Alliance for Arts Education Network/National School Boards Association Award Vol. 1: 11125
Kennedy Center Honors Vol. 1: 11123
Kennedy Center/National School Boards Association Award Vol. 1: 11125
Kennedy Citizenship Award; J. Walter Vol. 1: 12759
Kennedy Human Rights Award; Robert F. Vol. 1: 15682
Kennedy Journalism Awards; Robert F. Vol. 1: 15683
Kennedy Medal; Sir John Vol. 1: 8465
Kennedy Memorial Prize; Byron Vol. 2: 197
Kennedy Profile in Courage Award; John F. Vol. 1: 11020
Kennedy Student Paper Competition; John F. Vol. 2: 4509
Kennedy Trophy; John F. Vol. 1: 13213
Kennett Memorial Award; Arthur C. Vol. 2: 77
Kenny Award; Dr. John J. Vol. 1: 11305
Kent Award; Donald P. Vol. 1: 9061
Kent Strix Award; Tony Vol. 2: 7296
Kentucky Artists Fellowship Awards Vol. 1: 11131
Kentucky Bluegrass Awards Vol. 1: 8351
Kentucky Derby
Churchill Downs Inc. Vol. 1: 7407
Triple Crown Productions, Inc. Vol 1: 17609
Kentucky Oaks Vol. 1: 7408
Kentucky State Poetry Society Award Vol. 1: 13154
Kenyon Medal for Classical Studies Vol. 2: 5210
Keogh Award for Distinguished Public Service; Eugene J. Vol. 1: 14197
Keough Environmental Award for Government Service; Paul G. Vol. 1: 8497
Kerkrade World Music Contest Vol. 2: 3684
Kerlan Award Vol. 1: 18320
Kern Award; Donald Q. Vol. 1: 2489
Kern Award; Jim Vol. 1: 2219
Kern Lecture Award; Richard A. Vol. 1: 5247
Kerr Dissertation Award competition; Malcolm H. Vol. 1: 11750
Kerr History Prize Vol. 1: 14182
Kerr Prize; Sophie Vol. 1: 18594
Kerr Veterinary Student Award; Don Vol. 2: 384
Kerridge Prize; Gordon Vol. 2: 320
Kershner Memorial Chapter Leader Award; Marion N. Vol. 1: 11682
Kerwin Jr. Readiness Award; Walter T. Vol. 1: 13301
Kesler Memorial Achievement Award; John C. Vol. 1: 10744
Kesselring Fund Award; Joseph Vol. 1: 12291
Kesselring Prize Vol. 1: 12291
Kessler Awards; Henry H. Vol. 1: 15607
Kessler Awards in International Rehabilitation; Henry and Estelle Vol. 1: 15607
Kesteven Medal Vol. 2: 385
Ketcham Memorial Award; Albert H. Vol. 1: 1410
Ketchum Award for Outstanding Volunteer Fundraiser Vol. 1: 5164
Ketner Employee Productivity Awards Vol. 1: 14359
Kettering Award; Charles F.
American Society of Plant Biologists Vol. 1: 4219
Cooperative Education and Internship Association Vol 1: 7814
Keuffel and Esser Awards Vol. 2: 5269
Key Award Vol. 1: 15293
Key Awards Vol. 1: 3896
Keyes Award; Marjorie Hiscott Vol. 1: 6714
Keyes Medal Vol. 1: 1105
Keyhoe Journalism Award; Donald E. Vol. 1: 8931
Keymer Prize; Anne Vol. 2: 5297
Keys Roundtable Award; Ted Vol. 1: 9879
Keysa Scholarship; Louise Vol. 1: 11223
Keystone Press Awards
Pennsylvania Newspaper Association Vol. 1: 14934
Pennsylvania Newspaper Association Vol 1: 14935
Pennsylvania Society of Newspaper Editors Vol 1: 14944
Khan Prize for Fiction; Aga Vol. 1: 14859
Khona Award for Communication of Engineering Excellence; Ramesh M. Vol. 1: 1811
Kibble Literary Award; Nita B. Vol. 2: 681
Kibler Memorial Award; Robert J. Vol. 1: 12927
Kidd Award; Bruce Vol. 1: 17152
Kidd Award; J. Roby Vol. 2: 7406
Kidder Award for Eminence in the Field of American Archaeology; Alfred Vincent Vol. 1: 814
Kidder Early Career Award; Louise Vol. 1: 16448
Kideney Gold Medal Award; James William Vol. 1: 14164
Kids and Kindness Achievement Award Vol. 1: 12338
Kids/Cadet Person of the Year Vol. 1: 18469
Kiefer Safety Commendation Award; Adolph Vol. 1: 18416
Kiene Fellowship in Electrical Energy; Julia Vol. 1: 18865
Kieslowski Award for Best Foreign Feature; Krzysztof Vol. 1: 8161
Kilbourne Award; Judith Vol. 1: 6871
Kilby Awards of Excellence; Jack St. Clair Vol. 1: 11149
Kilby International Awards Vol. 1: 11149
Kilby Young Innovator Vol. 1: 11149
Kilgour Award for Research in Library and Information Technology; Frederick G. Vol. 1: 11339
Killam Memorial Prizes; Izaak Walton Vol. 1: 6112
Killam Memorial Scholarship; Elson T.
New England Water Works Association Vol. 1: 14065
New England Water Works Association Vol 1: 14066
Killam Research Fellowships; Izaak Walton Vol. 1: 6112
Kilmer Prize
American Pharmacists Association - Academy of Pharmacy Practice and Management Vol. 1: 3055
American Society of Pharmacognosy Vol 1: 4213
Kilpatrick Trophy; Macgregor Vol. 1: 2273
Kilrea Trophy; Wally Vol. 1: 2280
Kimball Innovators Award; Justin Ford
American Hospital Association Vol. 1: 2308
American Hospital Association Vol 1: 2309
Kimball Medal; George E. Vol. 1: 9745
Kimball Medallion; Miles Vol. 1: 11471
Kimber Enthusiasts Award; Cecil Vol. 1: 11712
Kimberly Cup Vol. 1: 17205
Kimbrough Fund Award; Anne Giles Vol. 1: 8027
Kimbrough Fund Award; Arch and Anne Giles Vol. 1: 8027
Kincheloe Award; Iven C. Vol. 1: 16671
Kind Children's Book Award Vol. 1: 12339
Kind-Preis der ETG; Herbert- Vol. 2: 2102
King Award; Coretta Scott Vol. 1: 2700
King Award; Dr. Lyndon Vol. 1: 7607
King Award/Jose Marti Awards; Martin Luther Vol. 1: 11401
King Award; Ted Vol. 2: 5396
King Baudouin Award of EGIAR 2000 Vol. 2: 1215
King Baudouin International Development Prize Vol. 2: 935
King Contribution Award; Billie Jean Vol. 1: 18873
King Eagle Scout Scholarship; Arthur M. and Berdena Vol. 1: 13775
King Faisal International Prize for Arabic Language and Literature Vol. 2: 4403
King Faisal International Prize for Islamic Studies Vol. 2: 4404
King Faisal International Prize for the Service of Islam Vol. 2: 4405
King Faisal International Prize in Medicine Vol. 2: 4406
King Faisal International Prize in Science Vol. 2: 4407
King, Jr. Achievement Award; Martin Luther Vol. 1: 7710
King, Jr. Award; Martin Luther Vol. 1: 8680
King, Jr. Scholarship Award; Martin Luther Vol. 1: 1795
King Management Award; Kenneth K. Vol. 1: 9134
King Medal; Haddon Vol. 2: 117
King Memorial Award; Donald Vol. 1: 17156
King Memorial Award; Robert W. Vol. 1: 5183
King Memorial Certificate; Milton W. Vol. 1: 13818
King or Queen of Bridge Award Vol. 1: 1787
King Sejong Literacy Prize Vol. 2: 2002
King-Sun Fu Prize Vol. 2: 786

Kingery/August Derleth Nonfiction Book Award; Kenneth Vol. 1: 7875
Kingery Award; W. David Vol. 1: 1485
King's Prize Vol. 2: 6485
Kingslake Medal and Prize; Rudolf Vol. 1: 17136
Kingsley Medal; Mary Vol. 2: 6391
Kinias Service Award; George A. Vol. 1: 13121
Kinkeldey Award; Otto Vol. 1: 2846
Kinley Memorial Fellowship; Kate Neal Vol. 1: 18292
Kinokuniya Theatre Awards Vol. 2: 3281
Kinsale Yacht Club Trophy Vol. 2: 5910
Kinsley Memorial Trophy; Charles A.
Photographic Society of America Vol. 1: 15027
Photographic Society of America Vol 1: 15028
Photographic Society of America Vol 1: 15029
Photographic Society of America Vol 1: 15030
Photographic Society of America Vol 1: 15032
Kintner Award for Distinguished Service; Earl Vol. 1: 8600
Kiphuth Award Vol. 1: 18417
Kiplinger Distinguished Contributions to Journalism Award Vol. 1: 13557
Kipping Award in Silicon Chemistry; Frederic Stanley Vol. 1: 1560
Kirby Award Vol. 1: 7563
Kirby Memorial Medal for Outstanding Service to Canadian Physics; Peter Vol. 1: 6282
Kirby Scholar-Athlete Award; F. M. Vol. 1: 13215
Kirby Scholar-Athlete Award; Jefferson Walker Vol. 1: 13215
Kirk Award for Outstanding Graduate Student Research; Barbara A. Vol. 1: 3323
Kirk Award; H. David Vol. 1: 165
Kirk Award; Samuel A. Vol. 1: 7865
Kirkley Fellowship; Leslie Vol. 2: 1107
Kirkley Young Investigator Award; Alexandra Vol. 1: 6782
Kirklin M.D. Award for Professional Excellence; John W. Vol. 1: 1297
Kirkpatrick Chemical Engineering Achievement Award Vol. 1: 7297
Kirsch Award; Robert Vol. 1: 11416
Kirschner Instructor Achievement Award; Fred Vol. 1: 57
Kirsner Award in Gastroenterology; J.B. Vol. 1: 8832
Kirti Chakra Vol. 2: 2578
Kishida International Award Vol. 1: 3854
Kitz Award; James M. Vol. 1: 6602
Kiwanis of Wascana Senior Cello/Viola/Double Bass Scholarship Vol. 1: 15873
Kiyoshi Tokutomi Memorial Haiku Contest Vol. 1: 19108
KKI Black Belt Certification Vol. 1: 2610
Klausmeyer Distinguished Service Award; Otto Vol. 1: 15068
Kleemeier Award; Robert W. Vol. 1: 9062
Klein Award Vol. 1: 3070
Klein Award; Lawrence R. Vol. 1: 17841
Klein Prize for Poetry; A. M. Vol. 1: 15493
Kleiner Memorial Award; Joseph J. Vol. 1: 3598
Kleinhans Fellowships Vol. 1: 15548
Kleinpeter Award; Hugh Vol. 1: 17234
Kleitman Distinguished Service Award; Nathaniel Vol. 1: 750
Klemin Award; Dr. Alexander Vol. 1: 2200
Klemm-Preis; Wilhelm- Vol. 2: 2169
Klineberg Intercultural and International Relations Award; Otto Vol. 1: 16449
Klingensmith EMS Administrator of the Year Award; William Vol. 1: 12522
Klinger Research Award; William A. Vol. 1: 235
Klinker Award; Mary T. Vol. 1: 204
Klopsteg Memorial Lecture Vol. 1: 1250
Klumpke - Isaac Roberts; Prix Dorothea Vol. 2: 1957
Klumpke-Roberts Award Vol. 1: 5483
The KM Fabrics Technical Production Award Vol. 1: 17952
K.M. Piafsky Trainee Presentation Award Vol. 1: 6933
K.M. Piasky Junior Investigator Award Vol. 1: 6934
Knacke Aerodynamic Decelerator Systems Award; Theodor W. Vol. 1: 2385
Knauss Marine Policy Fellowships; John A. Vol. 1: 11737
Knebel Best of Show Memorial Award; Clarence Vol. 1: 1156
Knee/Whitman Lifetime Achievement Award Vol. 1: 12661
Knight-Bagehot Fellowships Vol. 1: 7595
Knight-Batten Awards for Innovations in Journalism Vol. 1: 10943
Knight Essay Contest; George S. and Stella M. Vol. 1: 13775
Knight Fellowships; John S. Vol. 1: 11162
Knight Graduate Scholarship; David Vol. 1: 17027
Knight Medal; Allen Vol. 2: 512
Knight Memorial Grand Master Award; Damon
Science Fiction and Fantasy Writers of America Vol. 1: 15922
Science Fiction and Fantasy Writers of America Vol 1: 15923
Knight *NACTA Journal* Award; E. B. Vol. 1: 14279
Knight Research Grant; Elva Vol. 1: 10586
Knights of Justice Award Vol. 1: 3222
Knott Historical Contribution Award; Judge James R. Vol. 1: 9427
Knouff Line Officer of the Year Award; Scotia Vol. 1: 3261
Knowledge Industry Publications, Inc. Award for Library Literature Vol. 1: 2662
Knowles Award for Outstanding Adult Education Program Leadership; Malcolm Vol. 1: 836
Knowlton Medal Vol. 1: 11641
Knud Lind Larsen Prize Vol. 2: 1276
Knudsen Award; William S. Vol. 1: 1693
Knuth Prize; Donald E. Vol. 1: 4819
Knutson Award; Jeanne N. Vol. 1: 10740
Kobayashi Computers and Communications Award; Koji Vol. 1: 9786
Kobe City International Association Scholarship Vol. 2: 3285
Kobe International Flute Competition Vol. 2: 3283
Koch Award for Outstanding Contribution to Water Management and Science; Imhoff - Vol. 2: 6330
Koch Award; Fred Conrad Vol. 1: 8455
Koch Memorial Medal Award; Carel C. Vol. 1: 657
Kochanska Sembrich Award; Marcella Vol. 1: 1803
Kodak Coach of the Year Vol. 1: 12395
Kodak Film Raw Stock Award Vol. 1: 18993
KODAK International Educational Literature Award Vol. 1: 4742
Kodak International Newspaper Snapshot Awards Vol. 1: 8359
Kodak U.K. Film Council Award Vol. 2: 5756
Kodama Award; Benjamin Vol. 1: 2997
Kodansha Manga Award Vol. 2: 3287
Kodansha Prize for Cartoon Book Vol. 2: 3287
Koehl Award; Albert E. Vol. 1: 9497
Koenig/Organon/Nourpharma Poster Prize; M. Pierre Vol. 2: 1299
Koenigsberg Award; Nancy and Harry Vol. 1: 17505
Koenigswarter; Prix Vol. 2: 1671
Koeppen Memorial Scholarship Vol. 2: 4297
Koerner Outstanding Electrical and Computer Engineering Student Award; Alton B. Zerby and Carl T. Vol. 1: 8542
Koga Gold Medal; Issac Vol. 2: 932
Kohl Memorial Exhibit Award; Melvin and Leona Vol. 1: 2896
Kohler Prize; Charlotte Vol. 2: 3681
Kohlstedt Exhibit Award Vol. 1: 2647
Kohn Award Vol. 2: 6911
Kohrtz' stipendium; Ilona Vol. 2: 4661
Kokoku Dentus Sho Vol. 2: 3179
Kokusai Koryu Kikin Sho Vol. 2: 3233
Kokusai Koryu Shorei Sho Vol. 2: 3234
Kokusai Seibutsugaku-sho Vol. 2: 3261
Kolb Prize; Eugene Vol. 2: 2932
Kolk Air Transportation Progress Award; Franklin W. Vol. 1: 16580
Kolovakos Award; Gregory Vol. 1: 14896
Kolping Award Vol. 1: 7152
Kolstad Junior Soaring Awards Vol. 1: 16112
Kolstad Youth Scholarship Vol. 1: 16112
Komarov Diploma; V. M. Vol. 2: 4734
Komen Foundation Brinker Award for Scientific Distinction Vol. 1: 17343
Kondic Medal; Voya Vol. 2: 5999
Konheim Award; Beatrice G. Vol. 1: 1318
Konig-Gedenkmunze; Joseph- Vol. 2: 2170
Konkurs Mlodych Kompozytorow im. Tadeusza Bairda Vol. 2: 4038
Konnik Order; Madarski Vol. 2: 1155
Konrad-Zuse-Medaille Vol. 2: 2191
Koob Award; C. Albert Vol. 1: 12864
Kook Endowment Fund; Edward F. Vol. 1: 17953
Koplin Travel Award; James R. Vol. 1: 15561
Koprulu Book Prize; M. Fuat Vol. 1: 17632
Kordelin Prize Vol. 2: 1417
Korean Composition Awards Vol. 2: 4114
Korean Literature Translation Award Vol. 2: 4112
Korean Service Medal Vol. 1: 8111
Korevaar Outstanding Paper Award; Jan Vol. 2: 546
Korey Award; Saul R. Vol. 1: 639
Korn Award; Martin P. Vol. 1: 15201
Korn Founder's Award for Development of the Professional Choral Art; Michael Vol. 1: 7379
Korolev Diploma Vol. 2: 4735
Kosar Award; William F. Vol. 1: 9455
Kosar Memorial Award Vol. 1: 16252
Kosciuszko Foundation Exchange Program with Poland Vol. 1: 11167

Koshnitsky Medal Vol. 2: 150
Kosoff Memorial Literary Award; Abe Vol. 1: 2897
Kossler, USCG Award; Captain William J. Vol. 1: 2201
Kostanecki Medal; Stanislaw Vol. 2: 4033
Kothari Memorial Lecture Award; Daulat Singh Vol. 2: 2690
Kovacs Prize; Katherine Singer Vol. 1: 11905
Kovalenko Medal; Jessie Stevenson Vol. 1: 12161
Kozik Award for Environmental Reporting; Robert L. Vol. 1: 13548
KPMG Vol. 1: 9931
KPMG Peat Marwick Award Vol. 1: 18610
Kraft Community Service Award; Eve Vol. 1: 18144
Kraft Innovator Award; Jack A. Vol. 1: 9512
Kralik Distinguished Service Award; Gary M. Vol. 1: 5438
Kramer Award of Excellence; William S. Vol. 1: 14525
Kramer - John Preston Personal Service Award; Harold Vol. 1: 3444
Kramer Memorial Award; Murray Vol. 1: 5862
Kramer Scarlet Quill Award; Murray Vol. 1: 5862
Krasner Memorial Award; Jack D. Vol. 1: 3358
Kraus Award; Francis L. (Babe) Vol. 1: 17966
Krebs Memorial Scholarship Vol. 2: 5175
Krebs-Preis; Hans Adolf Vol. 2: 2246
Kreisel Award for Best First Book; Henry Vol. 1: 19006
Kreisher Award; Peter Vol. 1: 16563
Kreisler International Competition Prizes; Fritz Vol. 2: 801
Krenek Solo Competition; Ernst Vol. 1: 18569
Kressel Award; Aron Vol. 1: 9586
Kretchmer Memorial Award in Nutrition and Development; Norman Vol. 1: 3791
Kreve-Mickevicius premija; Vinco Vol. 2: 3381
Krieg Cortical Kudos Vol. 1: 6034
Kriegel Prize; Dr. Frantisek Vol. 2: 4577
Krieger Award; Richard Vol. 1: 7673
Krieghbaum Under 40 Award Vol. 1: 4864
Kris Award; Ernst Vol. 1: 4229
Krisciunas premija; Jono Vol. 2: 3382
Krishnamurthy Award; A. Vol. 2: 2795
Krishnamurthy Award; C.R. Vol. 2: 2796
Krishnan Memorial Lecture; K. S. Vol. 2: 2691
Kriske Memorial Award; George W. Vol. 1: 333
Kristol Award and Lecture; Irving Vol. 1: 1973
Krochock Award; Rich Vol. 1: 8133
Krogh Prize; August Vol. 2: 1316
Krommert Award Vol. 2: 3679
Krooss Prize for Best Dissertation in Business History; Herman E. Vol. 1: 6022
Krout Memorial Poetry Award; Helen and Laura Vol. 1: 14488
Krout Ohioana Poetry Award; Helen and Laura Vol. 1: 14488
Krueger Paper Money - YN Exhibit Award; Kurt Vol. 1: 2895
Krumbein Medal; William Christian Vol. 1: 10105
Kruszynski Achievement Award; Edward A. Vol. 1: 14296
Krutch Medal; Joseph Wood Vol. 1: 9525
Kruyskamp-prijs Vol. 2: 3671
Kryolon Makeup Design Award Vol. 1: 17954
Kryski Canadian Heritage Award; Antoinette (Nettie) Vol. 1: 19078
Krzyz Walecznych Vol. 2: 4011
Krzyz Zaslugi Vol. 2: 4008
Krzyz Zaslugi z Mieczami Vol. 2: 4010
Krzyz Zaslugi za Dzielnosc Vol. 2: 4009
Kshanika Oration Award to a Woman Scientist for Research in the Field of Biomedical Sciences Vol. 2: 2611
KSO Young People's Concerto Competition Award Vol. 1: 17356
Ku Meritorious Award; P. M. Vol. 1: 16885
K.U. Smith Student Paper Award Vol. 2: 3071
Kubasik Award; Norman Vol. 1: 878
Kubiena Medal Vol. 2: 6324
Kucharski Young Investigator Award for Research in Developmental Psychobiology; David Vol. 1: 10644
Kucyna International Composition Prize Vol. 1: 5866
Kuczynski Prize; Rene Vol. 2: 791
Kuder Early Career Scientist/Practitioner Award; Fritz and Linn Vol. 1: 3324
Kuebler Award; John R. Vol. 1: 419
Kuehl Prize for Documentary Editing; Arthur S. Link/Warren F. Vol. 1: 16218
Kuhlmann Award; Frank W. Reinhart and Henry Vol. 1: 5453
Kuhmerker Award Vol. 1: 4939
Kuhn Advocate of the Year Award; Dr. L. Michael Vol. 1: 13337
Kuhn-Medaille; Richard- Vol. 2: 2171
Kuhn-Preis; Julius- Vol. 2: 2214
Kuhring Award; Mike Vol. 2: 3569
Kuiper Prize; Gerard P. Vol. 1: 1360
Kukuljevic Charter Vol. 2: 1219
Kukuljevic's Charter Vol. 2: 1219
Kulp Memorial Award; Clarence Arthur Vol. 1: 3495
Kulp-Wright Book Award Vol. 1: 3495
Kultureller Ehrenpreis Vol. 2: 2343
Kulturpreis der Stadt Villach Vol. 2: 821
Kulzer Undergraduate Essay Prize; Heraeus Vol. 2: 5497
Kumar Memorial Award; Prof. L. S. S. Vol. 2: 2692
Kungliga priset Vol. 2: 4662
Kunitz Poetry Award; Stanley Vol. 1: 7571
Kunst Prize; Jaap Vol. 1: 16211
Kunstpreis der Stadt Darmstadt Vol. 2: 2441
Kunstpreis der Stadt Zurich Vol. 2: 4874
Kuntz '07 Award; Frank A. Vol. 1: 7172
Kupfer Award Vol. 1: 4953
Kupferschmid Memorial Lecture; Owen M. Vol. 1: 14763
Kupfmuller-Preis der ITG; Karl- Vol. 2: 2274
Kupfmuller Prize; Karl Vol. 2: 2274
Kurien Award; Dr. Vol. 2: 2634
Kusnetz Award Vol. 1: 2342
Kutter-Preis; Fritz Vol. 2: 4900
Kwapil Memorial Award; Joseph F. Vol. 1: 17085
Kwit Memorial Distinguished Service Award; Nathaniel T. Vol. 1: 1632
Kyoto Prizes Vol. 2: 3189
"L. PeRCy" Awards Vol. 1: 11349
LA/BAFTA Award for Excellence Vol. 1: 4722
La Caze; Prix L. Vol. 2: 1578
La Croix Award Vol. 1: 12609
La Guardia Award; Fiorello H. Vol. 1: 14107
La Parada Award Vol. 1: 17071
Labatt Classic Film Award; John Vol. 1: 17560
Labatt's Award for the Most Popular Film Vol. 1: 17560
Labbe Award for Contributions to Laboratory Assessment of Nutritional Status; Garry Vol. 1: 879
Labbe; Prix du Docteur et de Madame Henri Vol. 2: 1579
LABBS Trophy Vol. 1: 9257
Label of the Year Competition Vol. 2: 6352
Labor Award Vol. 1: 11186
Labor-Management Award Vol. 1: 18301
Labor Press Journalistic Awards Contest Vol. 1: 10480
Laboratory Analyst Excellence Award Vol. 1: 18636
Laboratory Innovation in Fertility and Embryology (LIFE) Award Vol. 1: 6496
Laboratory of the Year Vol. 1: 15504
Laboratory of the Year Award Vol. 1: 15930
Laboratory Visit Grant Vol. 2: 5378
Labotec-Shandon Award for Achievement in the Field of Cytology Vol. 2: 4256
Lackman Jr. Award; William F. Vol. 1: 13452
LaCorbeau Grand Prix Vol. 2: 850
Lacross Memorial Award; Nanette R. Vol. 1: 18313
Lacy Award; Alfred and Norma Vol. 1: 15993
Ladd Medal; William E. Vol. 1: 700
Ladies' British Open Amateur Championship Vol. 2: 6354
Lady Finniston Award
  Institution of Incorporated Engineers Vol. 2: 6179
  Women's Engineering Society Vol 2: 7347
Lady Members Group Prize Vol. 2: 6014
Lady of the Year Award Vol. 1: 10751
Lady Riders Challenge Trophy Vol. 1: 13806
Laerdal Award for Excellence (EMT-Paramedic of the Year Award); Asmund S. Vol. 1: 12523
Laetare Medal Vol. 1: 18332
LaFage Graduate Student Research Award; Jeffery P. Vol. 1: 8477
LaGasse Medal; Alfred B. Vol. 1: 4100
LaGrange National Vol. 1: 7291
Lahden Kansainvalinen Urkukilpailu Vol. 2: 1419
Lahm Memorial Award for Flight Safety; Brig. Gen. Frank P. Vol. 1: 14650
Lai Research Grant Award; APALA Sheila S. Vol. 1: 4692
Laidler Award; Keith Vol. 1: 6906
Laing Prize; Gordon J. Vol. 1: 18265
The Lakes of Finland Award Vol. 2: 1378
Lal Wadhwa Gold Medal; IETE-Ram Vol. 2: 2767
Lallemand; Prix Vol. 2: 1580
Lally Distinguished Alumni Merit Award; Jack and Julie Vol. 1: 15794
Lamaze Childbirth Educator Program Scholarship Vol. 1: 11212
Lamb Memorial Trophy; Charles Vol. 1: 13806
Lamb Outstanding Educator Award; Helen
  American Association of Nurse Anesthetists Vol. 1: 1181

Council on Accreditation of Nurse Anesthesia Educational Programs Vol 1: 7908
Lamb; Prix Vol. 2: 1581
Lamb Prize; W. Kaye Vol. 1: 5058
Lambacher Trophy Vol. 1: 11360
Lambda Literary Awards Vol. 1: 11219
Lambert; Prix Charles Vol. 2: 1672
Lambert/Webster Award Vol. 1: 2212
Lamberton Award for Teaching High School Science; Bernice G. Vol. 1: 18590
LaMer Award; Victor K. Vol. 1: 1561
Lamme Award; Benjamin Garver Vol. 1: 3654
Lamont Award; Dorothy J. Vol. 1: 12847
Lamont Scientist Award; Dorothy J. Vol. 1: 12845
Lamothe; Prix de Vol. 2: 1835
Lampe-Kunkle Memorial Award Vol. 1: 562
Lampen Medal Vol. 2: 1395
Lampert Memorial Award; Gerald Vol. 1: 11263
Lampert Student Writing Award; Herb Vol. 1: 6865
Lampitt Medal Vol. 2: 7170
Lancaster Award Vol. 1: 1032
Lanchester Prize; Frederick W. Vol. 1: 9746
Land Medal; Edwin H. Vol. 1: 14609
Land Medal; Vice Admiral "Jerry" Vol. 1: 16764
Land of Enchantment Book Awards Vol. 1: 14101
Land O'Lakes, Inc. Award Vol. 1: 1880
Land OFLakes/Purina Mills Teaching Award Vol. 1: 15178
Land O'Lakes/Purina Teaching Award in Dairy Production Vol. 1: 1881
Landa Music Scholarship for Pianists; David Paul Vol. 2: 584
Landis Award (Most Valuable Player); Kenesaw M. Vol. 1: 5681
Landis Medal; James N. Vol. 1: 4145
Landmark Award Vol. 1: 4101
Landmark Distinction Vol. 1: 9383
Landscape Architecture Firm Award Vol. 1: 4102
Landscape Architecture Medal of Excellence Vol. 1: 4103
Landscape Awards Vol. 1: 8751
Landscape Design Award Vol. 1: 2292
Landsteiner Memorial Award and Lectureship; Karl Vol. 1: 1014
Lane Award; Margaret T. Vol. 1: 11423
Lane Award; Richard Vol. 2: 395
Lane History Award; Helen H. Vol. 1: 8195
Lane Industrial Achievement Award; Frank E. Vol. 1: 1948
Lane Industrial Award; Frank E. Vol. 1: 1948
Lane Memorial Award; Diane Vol. 1: 12242
Lane Memorial Award; Sister M. Claude Vol. 1: 16494
Lane Prize; Ken Vol. 1: 4380
Lang Prize Paper Award; Warren R.
American Society of Cytopathology Vol. 1: 4017
American Society of Cytopathology Vol 1: 4017
Lang Resident Physician Award; Warren R. Vol. 1: 4017
Lange/CQ Press Award; Marta Vol. 1: 5081
Lange International Award; John D. Vol. 1: 12565
Lange - Paul Taylor Prize; Dorothea Vol. 1: 8292
Langelier Award for Young Professionals; Claude Vol. 1: 6801
Langenhoven Prize; C. J. Vol. 2: 4270
Langer Award; William L. Vol. 1: 9214
Langer Nuclear Codes and Standards Award; Bernard F. Vol. 1: 4146
Langevin; Prix Vol. 2: 1582
Langlands Medal; Ian Vol. 2: 513
Langmuir Award; Gaede- Vol. 1: 5588
Langmuir Award in Chemical Physics; Irving Vol. 1: 1562
Langmuir Prize in Chemical Physics; Irving Vol. 1: 3121
Lankester Investigatorship; Ray Vol. 2: 6420
Lanxess Inc. Award Vol. 1: 7304
Lapham Outstanding Service Award; Robert J. Vol. 1: 8266
Laplace; La Medaille Vol. 2: 1583
Lappeenrannan Valtakunnalliset Laulukilpailut Vol. 2: 1421
Lappeenranta National Singing Competition Vol. 2: 1421
Lapworth Medal Vol. 2: 6516
LaQue Memorial Award; Francis L. Vol. 1: 5439
Laray Award; Jean Vol. 2: 5856
Larew Memorial Scholarship in Library and Information Technology; Christian Vol. 1: 11340
Larsen-Miller Community Service Award Vol. 1: 12217
Larsen Prize; Libby Vol. 1: 10031
Larsen Turner-Ella Ruth Turner Bergera Award for Best Biography; Ella Vol. 1: 11952
Larson Award; Gustus L. Vol. 1: 4147
Larson Humanitarian Award; Barbara A. Vol. 1: 16789
Laryngological Association Award; American Vol. 1: 2617
Las Cumbres Amateur Outreach Award Vol. 1: 5484
Lasas premija; Vlado Vol. 2: 3383
Lascoff Memorial Award; J. Leon Vol. 1: 1612
Laser Institute of America Honored Speaker Award Vol. 1: 11229
Lasher-Bottorff Award Vol. 1: 993
Lashley Award; Karl Spencer Vol. 1: 3098
Lasker Award; Albert D. Vol. 1: 2187
Lasker Award for Public Service; Mary Woodard Vol. 1: 11232
Lasker Civil Liberties Award; Florina Vol. 1: 14117
Lasker Public Service Award; Albert Vol. 1: 11232
Lasker Special Achievement in Medical Science Award; Albert Vol. 1: 11233
LASL Educator's Award Vol. 1: 11422
Lasswell Award; Harold D. Vol. 1: 10741
Last Fellowship; Hugh Vol. 2: 5441
Last Fellowship; Jay and Deborah Vol. 1: 819
Latham Sportsman Service Award; Roger M. Vol. 1: 13907
Latin Grammy Awards Vol. 1: 11242
Latsis-Preis Vol. 2: 4901
Lauch Memorial Grant; Robert Vol. 1: 18581
Lauer Safety Award; A. R. Vol. 1: 9513
Laufer Award for Outstanding Scientific Achievement; Robert S. Vol. 1: 10693
Laufer; Prix Docteur Rene-Joseph Vol. 2: 1673
Laufman-Greatbatch Prize; AAMI Foundation Vol. 1: 4977
Laughlin Prize Vol. 2: 6727
Launch of the Year Vol. 2: 5511
Launch of the Year Award Vol. 2: 5514
Laureat d'Honneur Vol. 1: 10452
Laureate Awards Vol. 1: 806
Laureateship of the Australian Society of Archivists Vol. 2: 374
Laurel Award for Screen Vol. 1: 19013
Laurel Crowned Circle Award Vol. 1: 14519
Laurel Leaf Award Vol. 1: 1745
Laurels/Laureates Awards Vol. 1: 5583
Laurie Prize; James Vol. 1: 3957
Laurin Special Award; Carroll A. Vol. 1: 6783
Laursen Award; Capt. V. L. Vol. 1: 18206
Lavallee; Prix Calixa- Vol. 1: 16139
Laventhol Prize for Deadline News Reporting; Jesse Vol. 1: 15188
Laventhol Prizes for Deadline News Reporting; Jesse Vol. 1: 4209
Laver Award; Keith Vol. 1: 6780
Laveran; Prix Alphonse Vol. 2: 1584
Law Alumni Association's Distinguished Alumnus Award Vol. 1: 18347
Law Award; Frank G. Vol. 1: 4190
Law Day Vol. 1: 1375
Law Enforcement and Fire Safety Commendation Medal Vol. 1: 13766
Law Enforcement Award Vol. 1: 12777
Law Enforcement Commendation Medal Vol. 1: 13767
Law Enforcement Explorer Post Advisor Award Vol. 1: 13700
Law Enforcement Exploring Proficiency Awards Vol. 1: 8566
Law Enforcement Officer of the Year Vol. 1: 3223
Law Firm Award of Excellence Vol. 1: 11283
Law Library Journal Article of the Year Award Vol. 1: 1144
Law Library Publications Award Vol. 1: 1145
Law-Related Education Teacher of the Year Award Vol. 1: 2625
Law-Review Award Vol. 1: 15946
Lawler Award for Humanitarian Contributions within Computer Science and Informatics; Eugene L. Vol. 1: 4811
Lawn Tennis Association National Awards Vol. 2: 6359
Lawrence Foundation Award Vol. 1: 15191
Lawrence Medal Vol. 2: 6796
Lawrence Memorial Award Vol. 1: 9538
Lawrence Prize; Robert G. Vol. 1: 4794
Lawrie Factor Ltd. Prize; Alex Vol. 2: 6029
Laws of Life Essay Contest - Christian Education Movement/BT Campus World Vol. 1: 11022
Laws of Life Essay Contest - Franklin County, Tennessee Vol. 1: 11023
Laws of Life Essay Contest - Nassau, Bahamas Vol. 1: 11024
Laws of Life Essay Contest - Peale Center for Christian Living Vol. 1: 11025
Lawson Prize; John Vol. 2: 6708
Lawton Distinguished Contribution Award for Applied Gerontology; M. Powell Vol. 1: 3297
LawtonFs Heart Humanitarian Award Vol. 1: 8736
Laxdal Memorial Grade B Female Voice Scholarship; Heather Vol. 1: 15874
Laxdal Memorial Vocal Award/Golan E. Hoole Memorial Shield; Heather Vol. 1: 15875

Lay Education Project Award Vol. 1: 701
Lay Memorial Award; Herman W. Vol. 1: 5305
Layman Junior Award; Paul Nash Vol. 1: 18099
Layman of the Year Vol. 1: 11593
Layn Award; Kristine M. Vol. 1: 15229
Lazarsfeld Award for Research Vol. 1: 1983
Lazarsfeld Award; Paul F. Vol. 1: 1983
Lazarus Memorial Award Vol. 1: 2210
Lazerow Fellowship for Research in Collections and Technical Services in Academic and Research Libraries; Samuel Vol. 1: 5082
LBJ Cup Vol. 1: 4646
LDA Award for Excellence in Library Achievement Vol. 1: 11255
Le Caine Awards; Hugh Vol. 1: 16119
Le Mans 24-hour Grand Prix d'Endurance Vol. 2: 1726
Le Pegase Prize of the Audience Vol. 2: 850
Le Prix D' Excellence Aliant Vol. 1: 5510
Le Prix de IFACFAS Vol. 1: 5017
Le Sueur Award; Herbert Vol. 2: 6646
Leab and Daniel J. Leab *American Book Prices Current* Exhibition Catalogue Awards; Katharine Kyes Vol. 1: 5083
Leach Award; Victoria Vol. 1: 166
Leach Medal; Digby Vol. 2: 514
Leacock Medal for Humour; Stephen Vol. 1: 17297
Leader of the Year Award Vol. 1: 14520
Leaderle Award in Human Nutrition Vol. 1: 3787
Leaders Award Vol. 1: 1097
Leaders Recognition Society Award Vol. 1: 18825
Leader's Service Award Vol. 2: 470
Leadership Achievement Award Vol. 1: 5341
Leadership and Service Awards Vol. 1: 5091
Leadership Award
American Psychological Association - Committee on Women in Psychology Vol. 1: 3319
American Society on Aging Vol 1: 4272
Business Committee for the Arts Vol 1: 6016
Canadian Hospice Palliative Care Association Vol 1: 6567
Corona Norco United Way Vol 1: 7826
Emergency Medicine Residents' Association Vol 1: 8437
International Association of Cancer Victors and Friends Vol 1: 10166
Minerals, Metals, and Materials Society Vol 1: 11812
National Apostolate for Inclusion Ministry Vol 1: 12248
National Association for Equal Opportunity in Higher Education Vol 1: 12309
University of Toronto - Pulp and Paper Centre Vol 1: 18352
Leadership Awards
American Hospital Association Vol. 1: 2309
Fusion Power Associates Vol 1: 8935
Leadership Citation Vol. 1: 7896
Leadership Development Grants Vol. 1: 4873
Leadership for Learning Award Vol. 1: 1269
Leadership Hall of Fame Award Vol. 1: 4310
Leadership in Advancing Communications Policy Vol. 1: 5317
Leadership in Advocacy Award Vol. 1: 5318
Leadership in Human Services Vol. 1: 3435
Leadership in Legislative Service Vol. 1: 5319
Leadership in Library Acquisitions Award Vol. 1: 4914
Leadership in Oncology Social Work Award Vol. 1: 5273
Leadership in Public Service Award Vol. 1: 13642
Leadership in Regulatory Service Vol. 1: 5320
Leadership in Sport Award Vol. 1: 17153
Leading Chapter Award Vol. 1: 13241
Leading Claim Owner Vol. 1: 2820
Leading Jockey Vol. 1: 2821
Leading Producer Round Table Awards Vol. 1: 12547
Leading Trainer Vol. 1: 2822
League Executive of the Year Awards Vol. 1: 12619
League of Minnesota Poets Award Vol. 1: 13155
League Volunteer Award Vol. 1: 14097
Leahy Award; Emmett Vol. 1: 9767
Leakey Foundation Prize; L. S. B. Vol. 1: 11273
Leamy Award; M.L. Vol. 2: 3799
Lean Award; David Vol. 2: 5218
Learning and Leadership Grants Vol. 1: 14005
Learning in the Arts for Children and Youth Vol. 1: 13104
Leary Sportsmanship Award; Cissie Vol. 1: 10002
Leaurate of the Federation Vol. 1: 10422
LEAVEN Award Vol. 1: 771
Leavey Awards for Excellence in Private Enterprise Education Vol. 1: 8879
LeBonne Scholarship; Hank Vol. 1: 13191
Leclere; Prix Achille Vol. 2: 1458
Lectureship Award Vol. 1: 13323
Lectureship in Developmental and Behavioral Pediatrics Vol. 1: 16202
Lederer Award; Jerome F. Vol. 1: 10698
Lee and Perry R. Bass Gold Medal; Nancy Vol. 1: 7479
Lee Athletes Scholarship Awards; Tan Sri Alex Vol. 2: 3416
Lee Award; Carlton Vol. 1: 579
Lee Award for Metals Research; SETAC/ICA Chris Vol. 1: 16661
Lee Award; Mabel Vol. 1: 786
Lee B. Lusted Student Prizes Vol. 1: 16331
Lee Consumer Education Award; Stewart M. Vol. 1: 1824
Lee Founders Award Vol. 1: 16462
Lee Grand Prize; Norman H. Vol. 1: 2024
Lee-Homewood Chiropractic Heritage Award Vol. 1: 4986
Lee International Award; R.A.G. Vol. 2: 6535
Lee Memorial Trophy; Penny West Vol. 1: 13806
Lee Prize; Jesse Vol. 1: 8984
Leeds Award; Morris E. Vol. 1: 9785
Leeds International Pianoforte Competition Vol. 2: 6364
Leet Grants; Dorothy Vol. 2: 4803
Lefcowitz Prize; Rose Vol. 1: 15113
Lefebvre Award; Jacques Vol. 2: 5868
Lefkowitz Award Vol. 1: 14131
Lefort; Prix Jules Vol. 2: 1674
Lefsky Hort Fellowship; Vivian Vol. 1: 19064
Lefthander of the Year Award Vol. 1: 11281
Lefuel; Prix Hector Vol. 2: 1459
Legacy Fellowship Vol. 1: 819
Legal & General Silver Trowel Award Vol. 2: 5228
Legal Writing Contest Vol. 1: 10191
Legendary Station of the Year Vol. 1: 12434
Legends in Racing Hall of Honor Award Vol. 1: 1370
Leger Medal; Gabrielle Vol. 1: 9386
Leger Prize for New Chamber Music; Jules Vol. 1: 6113
Legget Medal; R. F. Vol. 1: 6527
Legion of Honor Award Vol. 2: 2814
Legion of Merit Vol. 1: 8112
Legislative Service Award Vol. 1: 13610
Legislator Award Vol. 1: 9674
Legislator of the Year Award
Biotechnology Industry Organization Vol. 1: 5785
New York Society of Architects Vol 1: 14165
Legislator of the Year Awards Vol. 1: 195
Lehman Award; Arnold J. Vol. 1: 16876
Lehman Human Relations Award; Herbert I. Vol. 1: 2586
Lehman Memorial Award; Bill Vol. 1: 12243
Lehmann Medal; Inge Vol. 1: 2119
Lehmann; Prix Henri Vol. 2: 1460
Leibinger Prize Vol. 2: 5812
Leica Geosystems Award for Best Scientific Paper in Remote Sensing Vol. 1: 4743
Leica Geosystems Internship Vol. 1: 4744
Leicht-Bowers Bowler of the Year; Barbara Vol. 1: 18848
Leighton Memorial Medal Vol. 2: 620
Leininger Leadership Award Vol. 1: 17573
Leipholz Medal Vol. 1: 6918
Leiter Clagett Trophy; U.S. Junior Women's Sailing Championship - Nancy Vol. 1: 18063
Leiter Lectureship; Joseph Vol. 1: 11660
Leiva; Premio Carlos del Castillo Vol. 2: 4532
Lejins Research Award; Peter P. Vol. 1: 1796
Leland Award; Waldo Gifford Vol. 1: 16495
Leland Memorial Prize; Waldo Gifford Vol. 1: 16495
Leland Prize; Waldo G. Vol. 1: 2239
Lemaitre; Prix Troyon et Edouard Vol. 2: 1461
LeMay Bomber Aircrew Award; General Curtis E. Vol. 1: 290
Lemay-Ohio Award Vol. 1: 4646
LeMay Services Award; Gen. Curtis E. Vol. 1: 14651
LeMay Strategic Aircrew Award; General Curtis E. Vol. 1: 290
Lembright Award; Katharine A. Vol. 1: 2183
Lemburg Award for Distinguished Service; Wayne A. Vol. 1: 2716
Lemelson-MIT Lifetime Achievement Award; $100,000 Vol. 1: 11293
Lemelson-MIT Prize; $500,000 Vol. 1: 11294
Lemelson-MIT Student Prize; $30,000 Vol. 1: 11292
Lemen Award; J. Winton Vol. 1: 13565
Lemieux Award for Organic Chemistry; R. U. Vol. 1: 6907
Lemieux Prize; Jacqueline Vol. 1: 6114
Lemkin Medal Vol. 2: 7270
Lemonon; Prix Ernest Vol. 2: 1675
Lenaerts Prize; Rene Vol. 2: 1073
Lendholt Denkmunze; Eugen Vol. 2: 2032
Lenington All-American Award Vol. 1: 2212
LeNoire Award; Rosetta Vol. 1: 139

Lentz Fellowship in Peace and Conflict Resolution Research Vol. 1: 11296
Lentz International Peace Research Award Vol. 1: 11297
Leon-Houry; Prix Marie Vol. 2: 1585
Leonard Award; Donald S. Vol. 1: 11732
Leonard Award; Richard M. Vol. 1: 16014
Leonard Holloway Award Vol. 1: 5662
Leonard Medal Vol. 2: 6428
Leonard W. Green Prize Vol. 2: 5993
Leonardo Award for Excellence Vol. 1: 10679
Leonardslee Bowl Vol. 2: 6797
Leopold-Hidy Prize Vol. 1: 3700
Leopold Memorial Award; Aldo Vol. 1: 18748
Leopold Prize; Richard W. Vol. 1: 14696
Leopoldina Prize for Junior Scientists Vol. 2: 2076
LEOS Distinguished Service Award Vol. 1: 9587
LEOS Engineering Achievement Award Vol. 1: 9588
LEOS William Streifer Award Vol. 1: 9589
Lequeux; Prix Germaine-Andre Vol. 2: 1858
Leriche Prize; Rene Vol. 2: 4851
Lerner-Gray Grant for Marine Research Vol. 1: 2830
Lerner Memorial Medal; Victor Vol. 1: 5888
Lerner-Scott Dissertation Prize Vol. 1: 14697
Lerner Student Scholarship; Irwin S. Vol. 1: 13723
Leroy Fellowship; A. M. Vol. 2: 3024
Leroy Prize; Andre Vol. 2: 1902
Les Ecrans De L'Aventure Vol. 2: 1846
Les Prix Gemeaux Vol. 1: 71
Lesbian Caucus Prize Vol. 1: 13926
Leskinen Memorial Award; Lauri W. Vol. 1: 11147
Lessing Medal Vol. 2: 6432
Lester Award; Elmer Vol. 1: 8664
Lester ELowe Memorial Scholarship Vol. 2: 928
Lester Honor Lecture Vol. 1: 3778
LeSueur Memorial Lecture Vol. 2: 7171
Leszkiewicz AADAA Award; Ted Vol. 1: 4518
Letelier - Moffitt Human Rights Awards Vol. 1: 9753
Letheren International Sport Leadership Award; Carol Anne Vol. 1: 6217
Letourneau Award Vol. 1: 1662
Letourneau Student Research Paper of the Year; Charles U. Vol. 1: 1700
Letter of Commendation Vol. 1: 13711
Letter of Distinction Vol. 1: 2836
Letter of Merit Vol. 2: 4460
Letter of Recognition
Australian Library and Information Association Vol. 2: 274
City of Toronto Vol 1: 7442
Letty Medal; Cythna Vol. 2: 4141
Leuver Exhibit Award; Robert J. Vol. 1: 2898
Leven Prize for Poetry; Grace Vol. 2: 556
Levenson Prizes for Books in Chinese Studies; Joseph Vol. 1: 4781
Leveque; Prix Charles Vol. 2: 1676
Lever Pond's Research Fellowship Vol. 2: 7297
Leverett Graduate Student Merit Award for Outstanding Achievement in Dental Public Health Vol. 1: 1262
Leverett, Jr. Environmental Science Award; Sidney D. Vol. 1: 205
Leverhulme Lecture Vol. 2: 7172
Leverhulme Medal Vol. 2: 6912
Leverhulme Memorial Lecture Vol. 2: 6372
Leverhulme Tercentenary Medal Vol. 2: 6373
Levin Award for Short Nonfiction; Kay Vol. 1: 7875
Levin Prize; Douglas Vol. 1: 6827
Levin Prize; Harry Vol. 1: 1742
LeVine Award; Bonny Vol. 1: 10442
Levine Award for Outstanding Research; Philip Vol. 1: 3603
Levine Award; P.P. Vol. 1: 994
Levine Young Clinical Investigator Award; Samuel A. Vol. 1: 2184
Levins Festspillfond; Robert Vol. 2: 3894
Levinson Award; Harry and Miriam Vol. 1: 3406
Levinson Prize Vol. 1: 15117
Levinson Prize; Samuel Eleazar and Rose Tartakow Vol. 1: 16438
Levinstein Memorial Lecture; Ivan Vol. 2: 7173
Levis Prize for Poetry; Larry Vol. 1: 15192
Levitzki Prize in Algebra Vol. 2: 2913
Levorsen Memorial Award; A. I. Vol. 1: 1217
Levy Memorial Prize; Leonard Vol. 2: 5331
Levy Memorial Scholarship; Herbert Vol. 1: 16815
Levy Prize for a Young Photographer; Gerard Vol. 2: 2918
Lewis Award; Arthur O. Vol. 1: 16474
Lewis Award for Chemical Engineering Education; Warren K. Vol. 1: 2490
Lewis Award; H.D. Vol. 1: 16969
Lewis Award; Henry Vol. 1: 14097
Lewis Award; John F. Vol. 1: 3099
Lewis Award; Ralph Vol. 2: 7316
Lewis Book Award; Gordon K. Vol. 1: 7107
Lewis Community Service Award; Helen M. Vol. 1: 4559
Lewis Environmental Merit Award for Service to the Environmental Industry; Stephen G. Vol. 1: 8497
Lewis Gold Medal; Bernard Vol. 1: 7610
Lewis Memorial Award; Richard B. Vol. 1: 4874
Lewis Memorial Executive of the Year Award Vol. 1: 15237
Lewis Memorial Lifetime Achievement Award Vol. 1: 15237
Lewis Study Grant; Lee Vol. 1: 14402
Lewkowitsch Memorial Lecture; Julius Vol. 2: 7174
LexisNexis Call for Papers Awards Program; AALL Vol. 1: 1137
LexisNexis Innovations in Technology Award Vol. 1: 17078
Lhuys; Prix Drouyn de Vol. 2: 1677
Liaison with Industry Committee Novel Disease Model Award Vol. 1: 3172
Liang Memorial Award; Ta Vol. 1: 4745
LIANZA Young People's Non-fiction Award Vol. 2: 3752
Liard; Prix Louis Vol. 2: 1678
Liberty Award Vol. 1: 9344
Liberty Awards Vol. 2: 6377
Liberty Bell Award Vol. 1: 9632
Liberty Legacy Foundation Award Vol. 1: 14698
Liberty Medal Vol. 1: 13768
Liberty Mutual Prize in Occupational Safety and Ergonomics Vol. 2: 3072
Liberty St. Video Award Vol. 1: 4535
Librarian of the Year Vol. 1: 9605
Library Buildings Awards Vol. 1: 11334
Library Hi Tech Award for Outstanding Communication for Continuing Education in Library and Information Science Vol. 1: 11341
Library Leadership Award Vol. 1: 4603
Library Public Relations Council Award Vol. 1: 11349
Library Research and Development Grants Vol. 1: 6691
Library Research Grants Vol. 1: 9073
Library Service Awards Vol. 1: 14094
Library Support Staff Scholarship Award Vol. 1: 4604
Library Technician of the Year Vol. 2: 275
Licentiateship of the City and Guilds of London Institute Vol. 2: 5659
Licette Scholarship; Miriam Vol. 2: 6451
Lichfield Prize Vol. 2: 6381
Lichten Award; Robert L. Vol. 1: 2202
Lichtenfelt Award; Richard Vol. 1: 12443
Lichtenstein Memorial Award for Distinguished Service to Philately; Alfred F. Vol. 1: 7495
Lieber Awards; Eleanor Vol. 1: 15158
Lieber Awards for Young Singers; Eleanor Vol. 1: 15158
Lieber; Prix Francis Vol. 2: 4767
Lieber Purchase Award; Judith Vol. 1: 16517
Lieberman Student Poetry Award; Elias Vol. 1: 15131
Liebig Award Vol. 2: 6325
Liebig-Denkmunze Vol. 2: 2172
Liebmann Book Award; Fred L. Vol. 1: 14166
Liechty Pro Bono Child Custody Award; Ann Vol. 1: 1376
Liegeois; Fondation Camille Vol. 2: 1026
Lienhard Award; Gustav O. Vol. 1: 12175
Lieutenant Governor's Award for Literary Excellence Vol. 1: 18663
Lieutenant Governor's Medal Vol. 1: 9387
Lieutenant-Governor's Medal for Historical Writing Vol. 1: 5944
Lieutenant GovernorFs Technology Innovation Award Vol. 1: 5698
Lieven Gevaert Medal Vol. 1: 16253
Life Achievement Award Vol. 1: 15940
Life Fellowship Vol. 2: 163
Life Fellowship Vol. 2: 5957
Life Governor Vol. 2: 421
Life Member
Canadian Actors' Equity Association Vol. 1: 6150
National Association of Metal Finishers Vol 1: 12590
Life Member Award Vol. 1: 13291
Life Membership Vol. 2: 138
Life Membership
Australian Secondary Principals Association Vol. 2: 351
Historical Radio Society of Australia Vol 2: 474
International Organization of Plant Biosystematists Vol 1: 10537
Monaghan Photographic Society Vol 2: 2864
Society of Exploration Geo-physicists Vol 1: 16681
Life Membership Award Vol. 2: 3779
Life Membership Award
American Association of Petroleum Geologists Vol. 1: 1218
Canadian Association of Career Educators and Employers Vol 1: 6239
Life Saving Vol. 1: 1926

Life Time Career Award Vol. 2: 2411
Life-Time Membership Award Vol. 1: 7936
Lifesaving and Meritorious Action Awards Vol. 1: 5913
Lifetime Achievement
Canadian Railroad Historical Association Vol. 1: 6857
Doberman Pinscher Club of America Vol 1: 8236
Lifetime Achievement Award
American Association of Colleges for Teacher Education Vol. 1: 1048
American Association of Motor Vehicle Administrators Vol 1: 1162
American Association of Zoo Keepers Vol 1: 1338
American Chesterton Society Vol 1: 1590
American College of Dentists Vol 1: 1643
American Family Therapy Academy Vol 1: 1989
American Numismatic Association Vol 1: 2899
American-Slovenian Polka Foundation Vol 1: 3549
American Society for Bioethics and Humanities Vol 1: 3571
American Society for Clinical Pathology Vol 1: 3604
American Spinal Injury Association Vol 1: 4296
Asian American Journalists Association Vol 1: 4685
Association of Medical Microbiology and Infectious Disease Canada Vol 1: 5221
Association of Southern Baptist Campus Ministries Vol 1: 5335
Association of Travel Marketing Executives Vol 1: 5372
Bay Improvement Group Vol 1: 5692
Before Columbus Foundation Vol 1: 5705
The Blues Foundation Vol 1: 5823
British International Freight Association Vol 2: 5336
Calgary Apartment Association Vol 1: 6041
Canadian Advanced Technology Alliance Vol 1: 6162
Canadian Booksellers Association Vol 1: 6353
Canadian Society for International Health Vol 1: 6947
Council of Fashion Designers of America Vol 1: 7886
Directors Guild of America Vol 1: 8217
Georgia Writers Association and Young Georgia Writers Vol 1: 9034
Glass Art Society Vol 1: 9088
Home Builders Association of Western Massachusetts Vol 1: 9465
IES, Institute for the International Education of Students Vol 1: 9594
Institution of Occupational Safety and Health Vol 2: 6191
International Association of Diecutting and Diemaking Vol 1: 10193
International Center of Photography Vol 1: 10300
International League Against Epilepsy Vol 2: 920
International Society for Traumatic Stress Studies Vol 1: 10694
Journalism Education Association Vol 1: 11050
Leukemia and Lymphoma Society Vol 1: 11306
Lupus Foundation of America, Arizona Area Coordinator Vol 1: 11439
Medical-Dental-Hospital Business Associates Vol 1: 11645
National Association of Black Journalists Vol 1: 12413
National Association of Collegiate Marketing Administrators Vol 1: 12451
National Association of Television Program Executives Vol 1: 12694
National Telecommunications Cooperative Association Vol 1: 13840
National Wildlife Rehabilitators Association Vol 1: 13912
New York Society of Architects Vol 1: 14167
Newspaper Association of America Vol 1: 14214
Newspaper Association of America Vol 1: 14217
North American Snowsports Journalists Association Vol 1: 14326
Podiatry Management Vol 1: 15111
Retail Council of Canada Vol 1: 15651
Royal Television Society Vol 2: 7042
Royal Television Society Vol 2: 7046
Scott Joplin International Ragtime Foundation Vol 1: 15936
Society for American Archaeology Vol 1: 16161
Society for Prevention Research Vol 1: 16385
Society of Wetland Scientists Vol 1: 16901
U.S. International Film and Video Festival Vol 1: 17979
Washington International Trade Association Vol 1: 18601
Zagreb World Festival of Animated Films Vol 2: 1241
Lifetime Achievement Award for Management Vol. 2: 2534
Lifetime Achievement Award in News Direction Vol. 1: 8218
Lifetime Achievement Award in Sports Direction Vol. 1: 8219
Lifetime Achievement Award in the History of Medicine Vol. 1: 964
Lifetime Achievement Award Program Vol. 1: 10516
Lifetime Achievement Awards
Columbus Blues Alliance Vol. 1: 7605
Magazine Publishers of America Vol 1: 11458
Lifetime Achievement Honor Award Vol. 1: 646
Lifetime Achievement in Contemporary Sculpture Award Vol. 1: 10617
Lifetime Achievement in the Pharmaceutical Practice Award Vol. 2: 3597
Lifetime Achievement in the Pharmaceutical Science Award Vol. 2: 3597
Lifetime Honorary Beekeeper Award Vol. 1: 6066
Lifetime Membership Award
Canadian Society for Industrial Security Vol. 1: 6943
Manufacturers' Agents for the Foodservice Industry Vol 1: 11496
Lifetime Membership Award
College English Association Vol. 1: 7513
Mothers Against Munchausen Syndrome by Proxy Allegations Vol 1: 11960
Lifetime Mentor Award Vol. 1: 949
Lifetime Sales Achievement Award Vol. 1: 17158
Light Metals Award Vol. 1: 11813
Light Metals Distinguished Service Award Vol. 1: 11814
Light Metals Division *JOM* Best Paper Award Vol. 1: 11815
Light Metals Technology Award Vol. 1: 11816
Lighten Your Life Award Vol. 1: 13156
Lighting Design Awards Vol. 1: 10220
Liley Medal for Health Research Vol. 2: 3720
Lilienfeld Student Prize Paper; Abraham Vol. 1: 16209
Lilienthal Gliding Medal Vol. 2: 4736
Liljencrantz Award; Eric Vol. 1: 206
Lillegren Award; Austin T. Vol. 1: 14297
Lillehammer Award Vol. 2: 852
Lillie Award; Ralph D. Vol. 1: 9407
Lillie Memorial Award; Howard Vol. 1: 1486
Lillo Award; John Moffat and Larry Vol. 1: 9196
Lilly and Company Research Award; Eli Vol. 1: 3769
Lilly Award in Biological Chemistry; Eli Vol. 1: 1563
Lilly/EASD Research Fellowship in Diabetes and Metabolism; Eli Vol. 2: 2106
Lilly Poetry Fellowship; Ruth Vol. 1: 15118
Lilly Poetry Prize; Ruth Vol. 1: 15119
Lilly Prize; Blake Vol. 1: 16816
Lilly Psychiatric Research Fellowship; APIRE/ Vol. 1: 3277
Lima Award for Excellence in Disaster Psychiatry; Bruno Vol. 1: 3278
Limantour; Prix Vol. 2: 1679
Limited Distance Program Award Vol. 1: 1958
Limmer Award for Best Restored Steam Engine; John F. Vol. 1: 13852
Limperg Prize; Theo Vol. 2: 3629
Lin Award; T. Y. Vol. 1: 3958
Lincoln Award; Abraham Vol. 1: 2327
Lincoln Financial Group Lincoln Douglas Debates Vol. 1: 13244
Lincoln Foodservice Award for Innovations in School Foodservice Vol. 1: 15911
Lincoln Gold Medal Award; James F. Vol. 1: 4460
Lincoln the Lawyer Award Vol. 1: 45
Lind Award; Erv Vol. 1: 522
Lind Award; Wilbur H. Vol. 1: 5987
Lindapter Award Vol. 2: 6119
Lindau Award; Alfred E. Vol. 1: 1759
Lindbergh General Aviation Diploma; Charles Vol. 2: 4737
Lindbergh Grants Vol. 1: 7286
Linde Gas/WTIA Young Tradesperson of the Year Vol. 2: 733
Lindeman Award; Raymond L. Vol. 1: 4112
Lindemann Certified Instructor of the Year; Charles F. Vol. 1: 58
Linderman Award Vol. 1: 15352
Lindgren Award; Waldemar S. Vol. 1: 16651
Lindgren Translation Prize; FIT Astrid Vol. 1: 10419
Lindquist Award; E. F. Vol. 1: 1943
Lindsay Award; R. Bruce Vol. 1: 129
Lindsay Book Prize; The Cas Vol. 1: 7035
Lindsey Award for Distinguished Research in Teacher Education; Margaret B. Vol. 1: 1049
Lindzey Dissertation Award; Gardner Vol. 1: 3345

Line Supervisor of the Year Vol. 1: 5321
Linear Algebra Prize Vol. 1: 16271
Lines Award in Astronomy; Richard D. Vol. 1: 10034
Lingeman Award; Marie Hippenstell Vol. 1: 16049
Link Award Vol. 1: 7017
Link Award; Fred M. Vol. 1: 15525
Link House Thematic Trophy Vol. 2: 6535
Link/Warren F. Kuehl Prize for Documentary Editing; Arthur S. Vol. 1: 16218
Linkiewich Memorial Scholarship; Ken Vol. 1: 6793
Linn Award; Gradam Gael Vol. 2: 2827
Linn Awards; Lawrence S. Vol. 1: 16694
Linnard Prize; American Bureau of Shipping - Captain Joseph H. Vol. 1: 16765
Linnean Medal Vol. 2: 6387
Linsley Award; Betty M. Vol. 1: 4991
Linville's R. H. Wright Award in Olfactory Research; Frank Allison Vol. 1: 16066
Lions Club International Clinical Research Program in Diabetic Eye Disease Vol. 1: 1912
Lions SightFirst Diabetic Retinopathy Research Program Vol. 1: 1912
Lipizer Prize; International Violin Competition Rodolfo Vol. 2: 3019
Lipmann Lectureship; Fritz Vol. 1: 3565
Lippert Memorial Award; George R. Vol. 1: 15969
Lipphard Award for Distinguished Service to Religious Journalism; William B. Vol. 1: 4760
Lippincott Award; Benjamin E. Vol. 1: 3235
Lippincott Award; Ellis R. Vol. 1: 14610
Lippincott Award; Joseph W. Vol. 1: 2664
Lippman Jr. USA Swimming Combined Team Traveling Trophy; William A. Vol. 1: 18418
Lipset "Truth in Action" Award; Hal Vol. 2: 7354
Lipson Memorial Fund Award; Tony Vol. 1: 18489
Liquid Tide Trans-Am Tour Vol. 1: 17208
Liscombe Trophy; Carl Vol. 1: 2280
Liskin Foundation Award; Joyce and Elliot Vol. 1: 13690
Lissitzky Career Award Vol. 2: 1299
Lissner Award; H. R. Vol. 1: 4148
List Purchase Award; Vera Vol. 1: 16517
Lister Memorial Lecture Vol. 2: 7175
Liston Award; Emil S. Vol. 1: 12580
Liszt - Piano Competition Vol. 2: 2504
Liszt International Record Grand Prix; Ferenc Vol. 2: 2496
LITA/LSSI Minority Scholarship in Library and Information Technology Vol. 1: 11342
LITA/OCLC Minority Scholarship in Library and Information Technology Vol. 1: 11343
Litehiser Award; Robert R. Vol. 1: 5440
Literacy Author Award Vol. 2: 7303
Literacy Award Vol. 1: 4935
Literacy Grant Competition Vol. 1: 9476
Literarischer Marz Vol. 2: 2442
Literary Awards
Boston Book Review Vol. 1: 5854
Friends of American Writers Vol 1: 8895
Lannan Foundation Vol 1: 11227
PEN Center U.S.A. Vol 1: 14907
Literary Competition Vol. 2: 435
Literary Contest Vol. 1: 14782
Literary Premio Matilde Rosa Araujo Vol. 2: 4091
Literature and Art Award Vol. 2: 4954
Literature Award Vol. 1: 16629
Literature Fellowships Vol. 1: 13105
Literature Paper Prize Vol. 1: 16077
Literature pveis der Stadt Dortmund - Nelly-Sachs-Preis Vol. 2: 2387
Literaturpreis der Bayerische Akademie der Schonen Kunste Vol. 2: 2039
Literaturpreis der ETG Vol. 2: 2103
Literaturpreis der Konrad-Adenauer-Stiftung Vol. 2: 2340
Literaturpreis der Landeshauptstadt Stuttgart Vol. 2: 2415
LiteraVision Preis Vol. 2: 2344
Litman Memorial Youth Exhibit Award; Charles "Cheech" Vol. 1: 2900
Little Award; Bud and Mary Vol. 1: 18100
Little Award for Chemical Engineering Innovation; Arthur Dehon Vol. 1: 2491
Little Brown Jug Vol. 1: 18162
Little Memorial Journalism Award; Jerry Vol. 1: 15678
Littleford Award for Corporate Community Service; William D. Vol. 2: 4416
Littlejohn Award; Frank Vol. 2: 5183
Littlejohn Memorial Medal and lecture; Bill Vol. 2: 5509
Littleton-Griswold Prize in American Law and Society Vol. 1: 2240
Littlewood Memorial Lecture; William
American Institute of Aeronautics and Astronautics Vol. 1: 2386
Society of Automotive Engineers Vol 1: 16581
Live Awards Vol. 2: 7276
Liversidge Lectureship Vol. 2: 642
Livesay Poetry Prize; Dorothy Vol. 1: 18664
Livi Maintenance Educator of the Year Award; Ivan D. Vol. 1: 5581
Living Hall of Fame Vol. 1: 17933
Living Lifetime Production Award Vol. 1: 2136
Livingood Lectureship; Clarence S. Vol. 1: 568
Livingston Award for Poetry; Myra Cohn Vol. 1: 7352
Livingston Awards for Young Journalists Vol. 1: 18311
Livingstone Centenary Medal; David Vol. 1: 2097
Livingstone Medal Vol. 2: 6892
Llangollen International Musical Eisteddfod Vol. 2: 6393
Llewellyn Award; Allan Vol. 2: 435
Lloyd Conservation Award; Stanley Vol. 1: 8641
Lloyd Prize; David D. Vol. 1: 9268
Lo-Jack Awards Vol. 1: 10049
Lo Medal; K.Y. Vol. 1: 8466
Lobato Prize; Monteiro Vol. 2: 1119
Local, Branch, and Regional Award Vol. 1: 1844
Local Chapter Community Project Award Vol. 1: 12702
Local Chapter Excellence Award Vol. 1: 12703
Local Chapter of the Year Vol. 1: 737
Local Chapter President Award Vol. 1: 12704
Local Committee Appreciation Vol. 1: 2901
Local Council Community Service Award Vol. 1: 10587
Local Education Authority Music Awards Vol. 2: 6476
Local Government Engineering Medal Vol. 2: 515
Local History Award Vol. 1: 8526
Local Horticulture Award Vol. 1: 2293
Local Impact Award Vol. 1: 13367
Local News Writing Awards Vol. 1: 9723
Locarno International Film Festival Vol. 2: 4864
Locher Memorial Award; John Vol. 1: 5030
Lock Endowment Awards; Ottis Vol. 1: 8332
Lockette Humanitarian Award; Rutherford B. Vol. 1: 10783
Lockette/Monroe Humanitarian Award Vol. 1: 10783
Lockhart Prize; George Vol. 2: 6029
Lockheed Award for Ocean Science and Engineering Vol. 1: 11546
Lockheed Martin Award for Ocean Science and Engineering Vol. 1: 11546
Locus Awards Vol. 1: 11396
Lode-Van-Bercken Award Vol. 1: 8181
Loder Rhododendron Cup Vol. 2: 6798
Lodge Award for Medical Engineering; J. A. Vol. 2: 6152
Lodge Premium; Oliver Vol. 2: 6146
Loeb Awards; Gerald Vol. 1: 18247
Loeb Fellowship Vol. 1: 9277
Loebner Prize for Artificial Intelligence Vol. 1: 6073
Loft-McKinght Award Vol. 1: 11398
Logistician of the Year Vol. 1: 17337
Logistics Company of the Year Vol. 2: 5627
Logistics Dissertation of the Year Vol. 2: 5628
Logistics Lessons Learned Award Vol. 1: 320
Lohse Information Technology Medal; Edward Vol. 1: 2853
Lokaljournalistenpreis des Konrad-Adenauer-Stiftung Vol. 2: 2341
Lomb Medal; Adolph Vol. 1: 14611
Lombardi Trophy; Vince Vol. 1: 13228
Lomond Poets Award; Ben Vol. 1: 13157
Lomonosov Gold Medal Vol. 2: 4394
Loncin Research Prize; Marcel Vol. 1: 9852
London Award Vol. 1: 10814
London International Piano Competition Vol. 2: 6395
London International String Quartet Competition Vol. 2: 6407
London Memorial Award; Fritz Vol. 1: 8294
Londres; Prix Albert Vol. 2: 1717
Loney Trophy; Don Vol. 1: 6656
Long and Jacques Thibaud International Competition; Marguerite Vol. 2: 1932
Long Employment Award; Wilburn H. Vol. 1: 5810
Long et Jacques Thibaud; Concours International Marguerite Vol. 2: 1932
Long-Form Award Vol. 1: 15995
Long Memorial Award; Amelia Reynolds Vol. 1: 13158
Long Poem Prize
Malahat Review Vol. 1: 11482
Malahat Review Vol 1: 11483
Long Service Awards Vol. 2: 6478
Longacre Award; Raymond F. Vol. 1: 207
Longest Structure Moved Vol. 1: 10251
Longest Structure Moved Under $30000 Vol. 1: 10252
Longevity Award Vol. 1: 2075
Longevity Awards Vol. 1: 17098
Longford Award; Raymond Vol. 2: 198
Longstaff Medal Vol. 2: 6971

Award Index

Longtime Meritorious Service Award Vol. 1: 11841
Lonsdale Cup Vol. 2: 3784
Lopes Hang Gliding Medal; Pepe Vol. 2: 4738
Loraine Award for Nature Conservation Vol. 2: 7223
Lorentz Award; Pare Vol. 1: 10380
Lorentz Medal Vol. 2: 3657
Lorentzen Medal; Gustav Vol. 2: 1896
Lorenz Memorial Medal; Frederick A. Vol. 1: 17292
Lorimer Memorial Award; Sir Robert Vol. 2: 6818
Lortel Awards; Lucille Vol. 1: 11406
Lortie; Prix Leon- Vol. 1: 16140
Los Angeles Area Emmy Awards Vol. 1: 12178
Los Angeles Times Book Prizes Vol. 1: 11416
Losana Gold Medal; Luigi Vol. 2: 3098
Loschimidt Prize; Josef Vol. 2: 6972
Losey Atmospheric Science Award Vol. 1: 2387
Losey Award; Robert M. Vol. 1: 2387
Losey Human Resource Research Award; Michael R. Vol. 1: 16240
Lotus Decoration Vol. 2: 2580
Lotz Commemorative Medal; John Vol. 2: 2506
Lotz Janos Emlekerem Vol. 2: 2506
Loubat; Prix du Duc de Vol. 2: 1520
Lougheed Memorial Award; Robert Vol. 1: 13068
Loughlin Conservation Award; Ches Vol. 1: 15808
LOUIE Awards Vol. 1: 9204
Louis/Emily F. Bourne Student Poetry Award; Louise Vol. 1: 15131
Louisiana Literary Award Vol. 1: 11424
Louisiana State Poetry Society Award Vol. 1: 13159
Louisville Award for Innovation in Financial Management Vol. 1: 9146
Louisville Grawemeyer Award in Religion Vol. 1: 18303
Lounsbery Award; Richard Vol. 1: 12162
Lounsbery; Prix Richard Vol. 2: 1586
Loup de Bronze Vol. 2: 4939
Louvain Award; The Michel Vol. 1: 12020
Love Prize in History; Walter D. Vol. 1: 14285
Love Token Society Exhibit Award Vol. 1: 2902
Lovejoy Award; Elijah Parish Vol. 1: 7487
Lovelace Award; Augusta Ada Vol. 1: 5003
Lovelace II Award; W. Randolph Vol. 1: 1350
Lovelace Scholarship Fund; Austin Vol. 1: 9547
Loveland Memorial Award; Edward R. Vol. 1: 1715
Loveless Chapter of the Year Award; Bill H. Vol. 1: 11497
Lovett Award; E. Dean Vol. 1: 1607
Low Award; George M. Vol. 1: 12207
Low-Rise Suburban Office Park Award Vol. 1: 5995
Low Space Transportation Award; George M. Vol. 1: 2388
Lowe Benston Memorial Scholarship; Dr. Margaret Vol. 1: 16187
Lowell Award; Ralph Vol. 1: 7828
Lowell Mallett Award Vol. 1: 14950
Lowell Poetry Traveling Scholarship; Amy Vol. 1: 7369
Lowell President's Award; Richard E. Vol. 1: 4730
Lowell Prize; James Russell Vol. 1: 11906
Lowenfeld Award Vol. 1: 12267
Lowenheim Memorial Award; Frederick A. Vol. 1: 5441
Lowery Memorial Award; Louis R. Vol. 1: 17990
Lowin Composition Awards; Paul Vol. 2: 584
Lowin Orchestral Prize; Paul Vol. 2: 558
Lowin Song Cycle Prize; Paul Vol. 2: 559
Lowman Award; Edward W. Vol. 1: 1775
Lowrie Leadership Development Grant; Jean Vol. 1: 10239
Lowry Award; SCN Elizabeth Vol. 1: 19078
Lowther Memorial Award; Pat Vol. 1: 11264
Loyalty Award
National Junior College Athletic Association Vol. 1: 13403
Pi Kappa Alpha Vol 1: 15040
Pi Kappa Alpha Vol 1: 15042
LPGA Hall of Fame Vol. 1: 11198
LSDC Licentiateship Vol. 2: 7187
Lubalin Award; Herb Vol. 1: 16842
Lubatti Award; Eugenio Vol. 2: 3099
Luby Sr. Hall of Fame Award; Mort Vol. 1: 5896
Lucas Award; Ferris E. Vol. 1: 13701
Lucas Award for Excellence in Metallography; Jacquet Vol. 1: 4705
Lucas Gold Medal; Anthony F. Vol. 1: 2529
Lucas Landscape Award; Homer Vol. 1: 14072
Lucas Memorial Award; Tad Vol. 1: 15705
Lucia Trade Award Vol. 1: 17349
Luck and Pluck Award Vol. 1: 9482
Luck Award; James Murray Vol. 1: 12148
Lucking Prize in Medicine; Mary Evelyn Vol. 2: 5480
Ludington Memorial Award; Jeremiah Vol. 1: 8398
Ludovic-Trarieux International Human Rights Prize Vol. 2: 1848
Ludwig Award; C.C. Vol. 1: 11267
Ludwig-Seidel Award Vol. 1: 529
Luer Award; Carlyle A. Vol. 1: 2998
Luff Award Vol. 1: 3076
Luikov Medal Vol. 2: 4967
Luke Award; Hugh J. Vol. 1: 15193
Lum Award; Louise L. and Y. T. Vol. 1: 9937
Lumen Awards Vol. 1: 9619
Lumen Christi Award Vol. 1: 7148
Lumiere Award Vol. 2: 6876
Luminaire Vol. 1: 18834
Luminosa Award for Unity Vol. 2: 3047
Luna Foreign Travel Scholarship; Lee G. Vol. 1: 13719
Lund Award; A.J. Vol. 1: 10336
Lund Public Service Award; Paul M. Vol. 1: 15428
Lundell-Bright Memorial Award Vol. 1: 5442
Lunsford Scholarship; Alfred E. Vol. 1: 2145
Lurani Trophy for Formula Junior Class Vol. 2: 1882
Lush Award in Animal Breeding; J. L. Vol. 1: 1882
Lush Biomedical Postgraduate Scholarships; Dora Vol. 2: 572
Lussi Award; Gustave Vol. 1: 15363
Lutaud; Prix Leon Vol. 2: 1587
Lutheran Educator of the Year Vol. 1: 11445
Luthi Award; Dr. Max Vol. 2: 4891
Lutoslawski International Composers Competition; Witold Vol. 2: 4054
Lutyens Award Vol. 2: 5116
Lybrand Medals Vol. 1: 9895
Lyell Medal Vol. 2: 5932
Lyle Medal Vol. 2: 118
Lyman Award; Robert J. Vol. 1: 15202
Lyman Book Awards; John Vol. 1: 14330
Lynch Award; Claire Vol. 2: 2827
Lynch Memorial Fund Award; Caitlin Vol. 1: 18490
Lynch-Staunton Awards; Victor Martyn Vol. 1: 6115
Lyndon Woodwide Solo Competition Vol. 1: 14632
Lyne Award; A.G. Vol. 1: 6276
Lynen Research Fellowships; Feodor Vol. 2: 2435
Lyon Award for Best Article of the Year; T. Edgar Vol. 1: 11953
Lyon Book Award; Thomas J. Vol. 1: 11984
Lyon-Caen; Prix Charles Vol. 2: 1680
Lyon Memorial Award; James P. Vol. 1: 8349
Lyons Award for Conscience and Integrity in Journalism; Louis M. Vol. 1: 14237
Lyons Award; Sir William Vol. 2: 5954
Lyons Memorial Award; Ronald D. Vol. 1: 17991
Lyric Poetry Award Vol. 1: 15132
Lyster Award; Theodore C. Vol. 1: 208
Lyttel Lily Cup Vol. 2: 6799
Lyttel Trophy Vol. 2: 5026
M & E Outstanding Young Professional Award Vol. 1: 16352
Maas Achievement Award; Major General Melvin J. Vol. 1: 5811
MAC Foundation Scholarship Vol. 1: 11787
MAC Poster Award Vol. 1: 3590
Macallan Gold Dagger For Fiction Vol. 2: 5710
MacAllister Awards for Opera Singers Vol. 1: 9682
MacArthur Award; Robert H. Vol. 1: 8372
MacArthur Fellows Vol. 1: 11453
MacArthur Prize Fellows Vol. 1: 11453
MacArthur Trophy Vol. 1: 13214
Macaulay Fellowship Vol. 2: 2822
Macauley Award; Alvan Vol. 1: 14800
Macavity Awards Vol. 1: 12051
Macbeth Award Vol. 1: 9988
MacBride Peace Prize; Sean Vol. 2: 4826
Maccabee Emblem Vol. 1: 13393
MacCaffree Award; Charles Vol. 1: 7544
Maccoby Book Award; Eleanor Vol. 1: 3328
MacColl Award; Hugh Vol. 2: 5325
MacConnell Award; James D. Vol. 1: 7882
Macdiarmid Young Scientist of the Year Vol. 2: 3721
Macdonald; Le Prix Sir John Vol. 1: 6560
Macdonald Medal; George Vol. 2: 7032
MacDonald Memorial Award; Thomas H. Vol. 1: 1290
MacDonald Outstanding Teacher Award; C. Holmes Vol. 1: 8538
Macdonald Prize; Sir John A. Vol. 1: 6560
Macdougall Medal Vol. 2: 7381
MacDowell Medal; Edward Vol. 1: 11455
MacEachern Award Vol. 1: 15433
Macelwane Annual Awards in Meteorology; Father James B. Vol. 1: 2781
Macelwane Medal; James B. Vol. 1: 2120
MacFarland Award; Douglas Vol. 1: 4859
MacFarlane Award; Brian Vol. 1: 16315

Machado de Assis Prize Vol. 2: 1120
Machine Design Award Vol. 1: 4149
Machinery Award Scheme Vol. 2: 6666
Machinery Awards Interplas Vol. 2: 6550
MacInnes Award; John Vol. 1: 2256
MacIntosh Award Vol. 1: 9258
Mackay Award; Roland P. Vol. 1: 639
Mackay Medal; Donald Vol. 2: 7033
Mackay Trophy Vol. 1: 12190
MacKeller Distinguished Service Award; Lillian Vol. 1: 17360
MacKenzie Award; Agnes Mure Vol. 2: 7070
MacKenzie Book Prize; W. J. M. Vol. 2: 6546
Mackey Assistance Fund Grants; Agnes K. Vol. 1: 8002
Mackie Awards; Howard Vol. 1: 6645
MacLean Award; Angus H. Vol. 1: 17679
MacLean Citation Vol. 2: 3739
MacLean International Fellowship; IFUW Ida Smedley Vol. 2: 4803
MacLenan Prize for Fiction; Hugh Vol. 1: 15493
MacLeod Prijs Vol. 2: 1074
MacMillan Awards; Sir Ernest Vol. 1: 16119
MacMillan Developer's Award; Viola R. Vol. 1: 15396
Macmillan Prize; Ian Vol. 2: 6936
Macnab Medal Vol. 2: 6099
MacNeill New Journalist Award; Jim Vol. 1: 5507
MacPhail Promotional Trophy; Larry Vol. 1: 12620
MacPherson New Editor of the Year; Fiona Vol. 2: 5511
Macquarie Award for Conservation; Lachlan Vol. 2: 627
MacRae Award in Creative Leadership; A. E. Vol. 1: 15495
MacRobert Award Vol. 2: 6621
Macromolecular Science and Engineering Award Vol. 1: 7305
Macworld Editors' Choice Awards Vol. 1: 14874
Madhav Achwal Gold Medal Vol. 2: 2639
Madison Award for Distinguished Public Service; James Vol. 1: 4475
Madison Award; James Vol. 1: 3236
Madison Medal; James Vol. 1: 449
Madison Prize; James Vol. 1: 16227
Madrina/Padrino Scholarship Vol. 1: 16739
Madsen Medal; John Vol. 2: 516
Maeda Prize Vol. 2: 3298
Maerskline UK Prize Vol. 2: 6029
Magaw Outstanding Clinical Practitioner Award; Alice Vol. 1: 1182
Magaw Outstanding Clinician Practitioner Award; Alice Vol. 1: 7909
Magazine Merit Awards Vol. 1: 16625
Magazine of the Year
National Magazine Awards Foundation Vol. 1: 13420
Society of Publication Designers Vol 1: 16843
Magazine of the Year Award Vol. 1: 3899
Magazine Website of the Year Vol. 2: 5511
The Magazines - Awards for Editorial and Publishing Excellence Vol. 2: 5515
Magellanic Premium Vol. 1: 3100
Magge Award Vol. 1: 8248
Maggie Awards Vol. 1: 15087
Maggio Award; Charles Vol. 1: 15993
Magic Lantern Vol. 1: 14352
Magid Award; Nora Vol. 1: 14897
Magida Award; Dr. Melville G. Vol. 1: 8577
Magill Distinguished Service Award; Arthur Napier Vol. 1: 6750
Magnel Prize Vol. 2: 1089
Magnolia Prize Vol. 2: 3950
Magnus Award Vol. 1: 15294
Magnussen Award; Ann Vol. 1: 3471
Magnusson Memorial Prize; Bengt Vol. 2: 1878
Magny; Prix Adrien Constantin de Vol. 2: 1588
Magruder Award; Colonel John H. Vol. 1: 11536
Magruder Scholarship; Neil Vol. 1: 11861
Magsaysay Award; Ramon Vol. 2: 3988
MaGuire Exceptional Achievement Award; James Vol. 1: 11518
Maha Vir Chakra Vol. 2: 2579
Mahalanobis Medal; Prasanta Chandra Vol. 2: 2693
Mahan Prize; Archie Vol. 1: 14612
Maharam Theatrical Design Awards Vol. 1: 4354
Maheshwari Memorial Lecture; Prof. Panchanan Vol. 2: 2694
Mahnke Multimedia Award; Carl F. and Viola V. Vol. 1: 4875
Mahoney Award; Mary Vol. 1: 2942
Mai Service Award; Ludwig Vol. 1: 4967
Maibach Travel Award; Howard Vol. 1: 1784
Maier-Leibnitz Prize; Heinz Vol. 2: 2220
Mail System Management Hall of Fame Vol. 1: 11465
Mailing Industry Ingenuity Award Vol. 1: 11472
Mailloux Award; Noel Vol. 1: 14665
Main Excellence in Clinical Practice Award; Robyn Vol. 1: 12599
Main Student Section Award; Charles T. Vol. 1: 4150
Maine Space Grant Consortium Internships Vol. 1: 11480
Maintenance/Avionics Technician Safety Award Vol. 1: 12827
Maisondieu; Prix Vol. 2: 1681
Maisonneuve; Prix Chomedey-de- Vol. 1: 16141
Maisons solaire, maisons, d'aujourd'hui Vol. 2: 1936
Majeri Award for Innovation and Leadership in Graphic Journalism; Anthony Vol. 1: 5639
Majewska Gliding Medal; Pelagia Vol. 2: 4739
Major and Regional Sports Grants Vol. 1: 8759
Major Awards Vol. 1: 6845
Major Awgie Award Vol. 2: 395
Major Benefactors Honor Award Vol. 1: 4936
Major League All-Star Team Vol. 1: 17170
Major League Baseball Player of the Year Vol. 1: 17176
Majors/MLA Chapter Project of the Year Award Vol. 1: 11661
MakDougall-Brisbane Prize Vol. 2: 6997
Make a Difference Day Awards Vol. 1: 15141
Make-Up Competition Vol. 1: 215
Makeup and Design Award Vol. 1: 9722
Making Democracy Work Award Vol. 1: 11271
Malacological Society of London Annual Award Vol. 2: 6413
Malamud Award for Short Fiction; PEN/ Vol. 1: 14910
Malan Medal; D. F. Vol. 2: 4271
Malan Prize; Recht Vol. 2: 4374
Malan-prys; Recht Vol. 2: 4374
Malchett Medal Vol. 2: 5763
Male Athlete of the Year Vol. 1: 17154
Male Team of the Year Vol. 1: 17155
Male Thrower of the Year Vol. 1: 18446
Male Vocalist of the Year Vol. 1: 10270
Malina - Leonardo Award for Lifetime Achievement; Frank J. Vol. 1: 10680
Malkin Prize; Harold Vol. 2: 6709
Malko International Competition for Young Conductors; Nicolai Vol. 2: 1311
Mallett Student Award; Dr. Marshall Vol. 1: 6265
Malloy Leadership Award; B. Charles Vol. 1: 5443
Malo Medal Award; Urbain J.H. Vol. 1: 18768
Malone Fellowship in Arab and Islamic Studies; Joseph J. Vol. 1: 13055
Malone Memorial Diving Award; Mike Vol. 1: 18388
Malone Post-Doctoral Fellows Program; Joseph J. Vol. 1: 13055
Malouet; Prix Vol. 2: 1682
Malpighi Medal Vol. 2: 2129
Malta Journalism Awards Vol. 2: 3421
Malta Self-Government Re-introduction Seventy-Fifth Anniversary Medal Vol. 2: 3425
Maltese American Scholarship Fund Vol. 1: 11488
Malting Diploma Vol. 2: 6416
Mamoulian Award; Rouben Vol. 2: 694
MAMP Scholarship Vol. 1: 11880
Man Booker Prize for Fiction Vol. 2: 6418
Man of the Year
Federation of Fly Fishers Vol. 1: 8642
International Road Federation Vol 1: 10613
Tall Clubs International Vol 1: 17385
U.S.A. Wrestling Vol 1: 18470
Man of the Year in Travel Vol. 1: 17588
Man or Woman of the Year Vol. 1: 10427
Man/Woman of the Year Awards Vol. 1: 2792
Man/Woman of Vision Vol. 1: 8575
Management Accounting Award Vol. 2: 3925
Management Achievement Awards Vol. 1: 15358
Management and Information Award Vol. 1: 16802
Management and Staff Training Vol. 1: 10340
Management Award Vol. 1: 10567
Management Division Award Vol. 1: 2492
Management Information Systems Annual Professional of the Year Award Vol. 1: 9156
Management Innovation Award Vol. 1: 10312
Manager of the Year
National Business and Disability Council Vol. 1: 12817
System Safety Society Vol 1: 17375
Manager of the Year Award
Baseball Writers Association of America Vol. 1: 5682
Mail Systems Management Association Vol 1: 11466
National Institute of Governmental Purchasing Vol 1: 13375
Managing Occupational Road Risk Achievement Awards Vol. 2: 6927
Manamperi (Engineering) Award Vol. 2: 4568

Award Index

Mance Award; Jeanne Vol. 1: 6770
Mancini; Prix Vol. 2: 4767
Mandel Young Investigator Award; Lazaro J. Vol. 1: 3173
Mandile Award; Julie Vol. 2: 430
Mandy Award Vol. 2: 703
Mangled Skyscraper Award Vol. 1: 9105
Mangold Award; Walter S. Vol. 1: 13117
Manheim Medal for Translation; Ralph Vol. 1: 14898
Mankin Award; John E. Vol. 1: 17458
Manly Memorial Medal; Charles M. Vol. 1: 16582
Mann Award for Global Health and Human Rights; Jonathan Vol. 1: 9097
Mann Citation; Margaret Vol. 1: 4915
Mann Health Human Rights Award; Jonathan Vol. 1: 10226
Mann Plaque; Emerson O. Vol. 1: 12236
Mann Plaque; R. C. Vol. 1: 12236
Mann Prize; John Vol. 2: 6009
Mannerfelt Medal; Carl Vol. 2: 3574
Mannerheim Cross Vol. 2: 1374
Mannheim International Filmweek Vol. 2: 2304
Manning Award Vol. 1: 8532
Manning Awards Vol. 1: 8528
Mannino Award for Superintendent of the Year; Ernesto Vol. 1: 4975
Mannion Memorial Trophy; John Vol. 2: 2829
Mansel-Pleydell and Cecil Trusts Vol. 2: 5740
Manson Medal Vol. 2: 7034
Manton Award; Irene Vol. 2: 7093
Manton Prize; Irene Vol. 2: 6388
Manufacturer Award Vol. 1: 13292
Manufacturer Member of the Year Vol. 1: 8240
Manufacturer of the Year Vol. 2: 5897
Manufacturers Appreciation Award Vol. 1: 17159
Manufacturers Prize Vol. 2: 6071
Manufacturing Manager of the Year/Service Sector Manager of the Year Vol. 1: 15450
Manufacturing Project Prizes Vol. 2: 6153
Manuscript Award
  Accounting and Finance Association of Australia and New Zealand Vol. 2: 30
  Canadian Association for Enterostomal Therapy Vol 1: 6193
  Phi Alpha Theta Vol 1: 14979
Many Voices Project Vol. 1: 14105
Manzie Youth Literary Award; Kath Vol. 2: 589
Maori) Scholarship; The President's (Vol. 2: 3791
MAPCCS Scholarship Program Vol. 1: 11559
Maple Leaf Award
  Canadian Society for Bioengineering Vol. 1: 6883
  International Federation of Purchasing and Supply Management Vol 2: 799
Maple/Longman Memorial Travel Grant; Robert Vol. 1: 17423
Maplehurst Trophy - Norfolk Bitch Vol. 1: 14425
Marais Prize; Eugene Vol. 2: 4272
Maravich Memorial Award; Pete Vol. 1: 12887
March Award; Francis Andrew Vol. 1: 5124
March Fong Eu Achievement Award Vol. 1: 13479
Marchetti Award; Roberto Vol. 2: 3113
Marckwardt Travel Grants; Albert H. Vol. 1: 17420
Marconi Award; Guglielmo Vol. 1: 14663
Marconi International Fellowship Vol. 1: 11503
Marconi Memorial Gold Medal of Service Vol. 1: 18512
Marconi Memorial Scroll of Honor Vol. 1: 18513
Marconi Premium Vol. 2: 6146
Marconi Prize Vol. 1: 11503
Marconi Radio Awards Vol. 1: 12434
Marcorelles; Prix Louis Vol. 2: 1732
Marcus Young Investigator Award in Basic Cardiovascular Sciences; Melvin L. Vol. 1: 2185
Mardon Prize; Jasper Vol. 2: 45
Margaret A. Johnston Memorial Teaching Excellence Award Vol. 1: 6402
Margery Boyce Vol. 1: 6258
Margolin Prize for Distinguished Business Reporting; Morton Vol. 1: 18273
Marguerite de la Charlonie; Prix Paul Vol. 2: 1589
Maria Sklodowska-Curie Medal Vol. 2: 4034
Marian Award for Priests Vol. 1: 11549
Marian Library Medal Vol. 1: 18271
Marie du Toit Award Vol. 2: 4214
Marimo; Prix Zerilli Vol. 2: 1683
Marine Aviation Logistics Squadron of the Year Vol. 1: 11507
Marine Corps Essay Contest Vol. 1: 18011
Marine Corps Expeditionary Medal Vol. 1: 8113
Marine Education Award Vol. 1: 13424
Marine Light/Attack Helicopter Squadron of the Year Vol. 1: 11512
Marine Medium Helicopter Squadron of the Year Vol. 1: 11509
Marine Wing Support Squadron of the Year Vol. 1: 11515
Mariological Award Vol. 1: 11549
Marion AxFord Award For Elementary Guidance Vol. 1: 14592
Marion; Prix Seraphin- Vol. 1: 16142
Mariucci Award; John Vol. 1: 2257
Marjolin Prize Vol. 2: 776
Mark Award Vol. 1: 7996
Mark Division of Polymer Chemistry Award; Herman F. Vol. 1: 1564
Mark Memorial Award; Peter Vol. 1: 5594
Market Development and Promotion Council Awards Vol. 1: 14217
Market Development and Promotion Federation Awards Vol. 1: 14217
Market Leadership Award Vol. 1: 341
Market Manager of the Year Vol. 1: 12616
Market Mover Award Vol. 1: 11498
Marketing Achievement Award Vol. 1: 16328
Marketing Achievement of the Year Award Vol. 1: 6354
Marketing and Publications Awards Vol. 1: 18216
Marketing Award Vol. 1: 12840
Marketing Communications Award Vol. 1: 7759
Marketing Competition Vol. 1: 12724
Marketing Computers ICON Awards Vol. 1: 5930
Marketing Genius Awards Vol. 2: 5908
Marketing Grant for NSW Artists Vol. 2: 568
Marketing Master Award Vol. 1: 14217
Marketing Methods Competition Vol. 1: 15335
Marketing Practitioner Award Vol. 1: 106
Markowe Public Education Prize; Morris Vol. 2: 6728
Marks Award; Louis B. Vol. 1: 9620
Marks of Excellence Award Vol. 1: 13248
Markwardt Award; L. J. Vol. 1: 5444
Marlow Medal and Prize Vol. 2: 6973
Marlowe Award; Donald E. Vol. 1: 3655
Marmottan; Fondation Vol. 2: 1482
Marmottan; Prix Paul Vol. 2: 1462
Marotta; Medaglia d'oro Domenico Vol. 2: 3103
The Marquette Excellence Award Vol. 1: 13814
Marquis Memorial Award; John E. Vol. 1: 1487
Marra Award; George Vol. 1: 16919
Marraro Prize; Helen and Howard R. Vol. 1: 16320
Marraro Prize; Howard R.
  American Catholic Historical Association Vol. 1: 1455
  Modern Language Association of America Vol 1: 11907
Marraro Prize in Italian History; Howard R. Vol. 1: 2241
Marriott-Carlson Award Vol. 1: 5025
Marrs Plaques; Lieutenant Theodore C. Vol. 1: 4639
Marsalis Scholarship; Wynton Vol. 1: 8355
Marschall Rhodia Award Vol. 1: 1874
Marschall - Rhone - Poulenc International Dairy Science Award Vol. 1: 1874
Marsden Award Vol. 1: 16652
Marsden Medal for Outstanding Service to Science; Sir Ernest Vol. 2: 3766
Marsh Award; Alan Vol. 2: 6647
Marsh Award for Conservation Biology Vol. 2: 7398
Marsh Award for Ecology Vol. 2: 5298
Marsh Distinguished Service Award; Burton W. Vol. 1: 9947
Marsh Fellowship for Graduate Study in Traffic and Transportation Engineering; Burton W. Vol. 1: 9948
Marsh Medal; Alan Vol. 2: 6648
Marsh Medal for Exemplary Contributions to the Protection and Wise Use of the Nation's Water Resources; Mary H. Vol. 1: 4423
Marsh Memorial Prize; James R. and Anne Steele Vol. 1: 9540
Marsh Midda Fellowship Vol. 2: 5519
Marsh Safety Award; William O. Vol. 1: 12218
Marshall Award; Louis B. Vol. 1: 11009
Marshall Award; Robert Vol. 1: 18745
Marshall Education Award; Richard Vol. 1: 880
Marshall Journalism Award; Thurgood Vol. 1: 8078
Marshall Medal; George Catlett Vol. 1: 5364
Marshall Scholarships Vol. 2: 5126
Marshall Travel Grant; Thomas F. Vol. 1: 3831
Marshall Urist Award Vol. 1: 14712
Marth Educator Award; Elmer Vol. 1: 10083
Marti Prize; The International Jose Vol. 2: 1997
Martin Award; Allie Beth Vol. 1: 15423
Martin Award; E. O. Vol. 1: 1239
Martin Award; Eric W. Vol. 1: 2768

Martin Award for Excellence in the Exhibition of Costume; Richard Vol. 1: 7838
Martin Award; G. Harold Vol. 1: 10773
Martin Award; Joseph J. Vol. 1: 3656
Martin Duberman Award Vol. 1: 7222
Martin Fellowships; C.J. Vol. 2: 573
Martin Outstanding Younger Member Award; John Vol. 1: 9836
Martin Overseas Biomedical Fellowship; C. J. Vol. 2: 573
Martin Prize; The Jack Vol. 2: 7110
Martin Trophy; Dr. Beattie Vol. 1: 6512
Martinez-Marquez Award; Guillermo Vol. 1: 12549
Martino Outstanding Contributions to Bowling Award; John O. Vol. 1: 5897
Martloth Medal Vol. 2: 4142
Marty Public Understanding of Religion Award; Martin E. Vol. 1: 745
Marucci Scholarship; Michael and Marie Vol. 1: 13191
MarulFs Days Festival Vol. 2: 1222
Marvel Creative Polymer Chemistry Award; Carl S. Vol. 1: 1565
Marvin Award; Jim Vol. 1: 11221
Marvin Grant; Walter Rumsey Vol. 1: 14489
Marvin Hall of Fame for Design Excellence; William S. Vol. 1: 5985
Marwah Award; Prof. Surindar Mohan Vol. 2: 2612
Marx Memorial Scholarship; Ellie Vol. 2: 4355
Mary Louise Brown Research Award Vol. 1: 1189
Maryknoll Mission Award Vol. 1: 11555
Maryknoll Student Essay Contest Vol. 1: 11557
Maryland Cup Vol. 1: 4646
Maryland Performance Excellence Award Vol. 1: 11565
Maryland Quality Awards Vol. 1: 11565
Marzocco d'Ora Vol. 2: 3045
Masatoshi Miyamoto Award Vol. 1: 2999
Mascoll Scholarship; Beverly Vol. 1: 5792
Masefield Gold Medal; Sir Peter Vol. 2: 5236
Masefield Memorial Trust; John Vol. 2: 7145
Mashman Safety Award; Joe Vol. 1: 9366
Maskew Fair Medal; Gordon Vol. 1: 18637
Mason Anderson Williams Award; Mary Vol. 1: 4988
Mason Award for Excellence in Jewelry Design; John C. Vol. 1: 7256
Mason Award; Jack Vol. 1: 5685
Mason Award; Karl Vol. 1: 14919
Mason Award; Peter Vol. 2: 6480
Mason Playwrighting Award; Bruce Vol. 2: 3825
Mason Prize; Michael Vol. 2: 5490
Mason Reference Award; Harold Vol. 1: 5207
Masotto Cup; Patricia L. Vol. 1: 18173
Maspero; Prix Gaston Vol. 2: 1521
Mass Communications Hall of Fame Vol. 1: 17502
Mass Communications Outstanding Alumni Awards Vol. 1: 17503
Massachusetts Bay Trophy Vol. 1: 18074
Massachusetts Hall of Fame for Science Educators Vol. 1: 11587
Massachusetts State Poetry Society Award Vol. 1: 13160
Massachusetts Tree Farmer of the Year Vol. 1: 11583
Massey Award Vol. 2: 1739
Massey-Ferguson Educational Medal Vol. 1: 3855
Massey Medal Vol. 1: 15743
Massie Medal and Prize; Harrie Vol. 2: 255
Masson Memorial Scholarship Prize Vol. 2: 621
Master Breeder Vol. 1: 2137
Master Breeder Award Vol. 1: 13540
Master Clinician Award Vol. 1: 727
Master Craftsman Degree Vol. 1: 13931
Master Endoscopist Award Vol. 1: 3708
Master Judge Award Vol. 1: 13541
Master Musician Award Vol. 1: 17602
Master of Bananistry Medal Vol. 1: 10266
Master of Photographic Arts Vol. 1: 15343
Master of the Game Award Vol. 1: 13800
Master Pastelist Vol. 1: 14871
Master Steinologist Vol. 1: 17295
Master Triathletes of the Year Vol. 1: 18461
Master Wildlife Artist Vol. 1: 18889
Masterclass Performers Competition Vol. 1: 13203
Mastermind Award Vol. 2: 5256
Masters Administrator of the Year Vol. 1: 18447
Masters Age Division Runners of the Year Vol. 1: 18448
Masters and Johnson Award Vol. 1: 16420
Masters Athlete of the Year Vol. 1: 17361
Masters Award Vol. 1: 17361
Masters Golf Tournament Vol. 1: 5536
Masters Race Walker of the Year Award Vol. 1: 18449
Master's Scholarship Vol. 2: 5484
Master's Series Award Vol. 1: 7925
Master's Thesis Award Vol. 1: 9755
Masters Thesis Research Award Vol. 1: 15409
Masters Transportation Engineering Award; Frank M. Vol. 1: 3959
Masterships Vol. 1: 1716
Masterson Award & Outstanding Women's Awards; Carroll Sterling Vol. 1: 19112
Masterworks in Masonry Awards Vol. 1: 15703
Masubuchi Award; Professor Koichi Vol. 1: 4461
Masursky Award for Meritorious Service to Planetary Science; Harold Vol. 1: 1361
Mathematical Contest in Modeling Vol. 1: 16272
Mathematics Excellence Award Vol. 1: 2723
Mather Award; Frank Jewett Vol. 1: 7507
Mather Award; Katharine and Bryant Vol. 1: 5445
Mather Award; Stephen Tyng Vol. 1: 13532
Mather Premium Vol. 2: 6146
Mathers Trophy; Frank Vol. 1: 2274
Mathews Distinguished Service Award; James K. Vol. 1: 7401
Mathewson Award; Champion H. Vol. 1: 11817
Mathiasen Award; Geneva Vol. 1: 13052
Mathilde Award Vol. 2: 1289
Mathy and Opera Awards Vol. 2: 358
Mathy Scholarship; Marianne Vol. 2: 358
Matrix Award Vol. 1: 14202
Matson Memorial Award; George C. Vol. 1: 1219
Matson Memorial Award; Theodore M. Vol. 1: 9949
Matthew Award; Robert Vol. 2: 5670
Matthew Prize; Sir Robert Vol. 2: 1924
Matthews Award; Austin- Vol. 1: 6657
Matthews Awards for Publications; Keith Vol. 1: 6756
Matthews Outstanding Chapter Award; R. C. Vol. 1: 17401
Matulis premija; Juozo Vol. 2: 3384
Maturi Award for Excellence Vol. 2: 2547
Maucher Prize in Geoscience; Albert Vol. 2: 2221
Mauchly Award; Eckert - Vol. 1: 4812
Maud Montgomery Children's Literature Award; Lucy Vol. 1: 15221
Maugham Awards; Somerset Vol. 2: 7146
Mauguin; Prix Georges Vol. 2: 1684
Maurice Berman Prize Vol. 2: 5408
Maurice R.D.; Prix Vol. 2: 1463
Maurice Rookie of the Year; Lisa Vol. 1: 18849
Maury and Hinman Research Awards Vol. 1: 18576
Mawson Lecture Vol. 2: 119
Max-Buchner-Forschungsstiftung; DECHEMA Award of the Vol. 2: 2073
Max Dawdy Scholarship Vol. 1: 2138
Max-Eyth-Gedenkmunze Vol. 2: 2356
MAXI Awards Vol. 1: 10361
Maxim Gold Medal; Hiram Percy Vol. 1: 34
Maxim Memorial Award; Hiram Percy Vol. 1: 34
Maxwell Award; BMEC Donald Vol. 2: 6049
Maxwell Medal and Prize Vol. 2: 6064
Maxwell Premium Vol. 2: 6146
Maxwell Prize for Plasma Physics; James Clerk Vol. 1: 3122
May Award; Douglas Vol. 2: 6278
May Foundation Scholarship; New South Wales Government and Frederick Vol. 2: 584
Mayborn Award for Community Leadership; Frank Vol. 1: 17465
Mayer Award; Andre Vol. 2: 6215
Mayer Award for Educational Leadership; Edward N. Vol. 1: 8207
Mayer Memorial Trophy; Lady Dorothy Vol. 2: 2830
Mayer; Prix Charles-Leopold Vol. 2: 1590
Mayfield Award Vol. 1: 7707
Mayfield Award; George A. Hall/Harold F. Vol. 1: 18754
Mayfield Cotton Engineering Award Vol. 1: 3856
Maynard Award; Harold H. Vol. 1: 2717
Maynard Book of the Year Award; H. B. Vol. 1: 9867
Maynard Prize; Isaac N. Vol. 1: 12112
Mayne Pharma Bryan Hudson Clinical Endocrinology Award Vol. 2: 437
Mayo/Rubin Jones Memorial Scholarship; Billy Vol. 1: 8780
Mayor's Arts Awards Vol. 1: 8071
Mayor's Awards for Excellence in Science and Technology Vol. 1: 7434
Mayor's Lifetime Achievement Award Vol. 1: 8162
Mayr Award in Systematic Biology; Ernst Vol. 1: 16857
Mayr Grants; Ernst Vol. 1: 12023
Mays Award; Captain "Willie" Vol. 1: 4646
Mays Award; Robin Vol. 1: 15441
Mazzetti Scholarship; Guilliano Vol. 1: 16723
MBA (International Management) Best Student Award Vol. 2: 3401
MBA Scholarship Vol. 1: 6312
MBC Paper of the Year Award Vol. 1: 3591
MBE Coordinator of the Year Vol. 1: 13458

MC National Championship Regatta Vol. 1: 11623
MCA Annual Merit Awards Program Vol. 1: 11699
McAlister Award; D.S. Vol. 1: 17028
McAllister Editorial Fellowship Vol. 1: 9077
McAnch Award Vol. 1: 7088
McArthur Prize; Robert Vol. 2: 6010
McAulay Award; John H. Vol. 1: 4860
McAuliffe Memorial Award; Christa Vol. 1: 198
McAuliffe Reach for the Stars Award; Christa Vol. 1: 12986
McAuslan First Book Prize Vol. 1: 15493
MCBA Scholarship Vol. 1: 11726
McBryde Medal; W. A. E. Vol. 1: 6908
McCaffrey Trophy; James P. Vol. 1: 6513
McCall Life Pattern Fund (Training Award) Vol. 1: 16965
McCallam Award; James A. Vol. 1: 5248
McCallum Scholarship; Heather Vol. 1: 4795
McCampbell Award; David Vol. 1: 2051
McCandless Award; Boyd R. Vol. 1: 3328
McCanse Award; Jessie Vol. 1: 13842
McCarren Award Vol. 1: 10134
McCarthy Bursary; Doreen Vol. 2: 191
McCarthy Good Guy Award; Clem Vol. 1: 17932
McCarthy Memorial Award; Domini Vol. 1: 8019
McCay Award; Windsor Vol. 1: 10044
McClarren Legislative Development Award; Robert R. Vol. 1: 9606
McClellan Award; Albert Vol. 1: 5663
McClelland and Stewart Journey Prize; The Writer's Trust of Canada/ Vol. 1: 11625
McCloskey Award; Michael Vol. 1: 16015
McCloy Memorial Award; John J. Vol. 1: 8927
McClung Award Vol. 1: 5726
McClure Award for Outstanding Environmental and Community Leadership; Tim Vol. 1: 13604
McClure Silver Ram Award Vol. 1: 3543
McCluskey Award of Excellence; Roger Vol. 1: 17752
McClusky Research Award; Dean and Sybil Vol. 1: 4876
McColl Family Fellowship Vol. 1: 2098
McCollum Award; E. V. Vol. 1: 3792
McCollum International Lectureship in Nutrition; E. V. Vol. 1: 3793
McConnell Award; Robert Earll Vol. 1: 2530
McConnell Distinguished Service Award; Douglas Rand Vol. 1: 2523
McConnell, MD Award for Excellence in Volunteerism; Jack B. Vol. 1: 2746
McConnell Scholar-Athlete Award; John M. Vol. 1: 13215
McCord National Education Award; L. P. Vol. 1: 9642
McCormack Award Vol. 1: 5349
McCormick Award for Distinguished Early Career Contributions; Earnest J. Vol. 1: 16288
McCormick - Jerome Increase Case Medal; Cyrus Hall Vol. 1: 3857
McCormick, M.D. Award; J. B. Vol. 1: 13720
McCormick Medal; Cyrus Hall Vol. 1: 3857
McCormick Memorial Diving Award; Glenn Vol. 1: 17730
McCormick Prize; Richard P. Vol. 1: 14085
McCoy Award Vol. 1: 3071
McCrae Cup Vol. 1: 6658
McCredie Award; Dr. Kenneth B. Vol. 1: 11307
McCree, Jr. Awards for the Advancement of Justice; Wade H. Vol. 1: 17259
McCulloch Award; Warren Vol. 1: 3619
McCulloch Prizes for Public Speaking; Andrina Vol. 1: 15496
McCullough Award; Constance M. Vol. 1: 10588
McCurdy Award Vol. 1: 6171
McCutcheon Marine Heavy Helicopter Squadron of the Year Award; Keith B. Vol. 1: 11519
McDaniel Ambassador Award; Durward K. Vol. 1: 1819
McDonald House Charities Grants Program; Ronald Vol. 1: 15714
McDonald's Ballet Scholarship Vol. 2: 689
McDonald's City of Sydney Performing Arts Challenge Vol. 2: 689
McDonald's Operatic Aria Vol. 2: 690
McDonald's Performing Arts Challenge Vol. 2: 688
McDonnell Award; James A. Vol. 1: 4645
McDowell Award; W. Wallace Vol. 1: 9812
McEwan Memorial Award (Masters Athlete of the Year); May Vol. 1: 17361
McFarland Award; Forest R. Vol. 1: 16583
McFarland-SABR Baseball Research Award Vol. 1: 16168
McFarlane Environmental Leadership Award; Euan P. Vol. 1: 10923
McGan Memorial Silver Antenna Award; Philip J. Vol. 1: 35
McGannon Award for Social and Ethical Relevance in Communications Policy Research; Donald Vol. 1: 11629
McGavin Award; Agnes Purcell Vol. 1: 3279
McGee Service Award; George Vol. 1: 14725
McGee Trophy; Francis J. Vol. 1: 13648
McGee Trophy; W. P. Vol. 1: 6659
McGibbon Award; Pauline Vol. 1: 14562
McGill Award; John Vol. 1: 17206
McGill Award; Ormond Vol. 1: 13312
McGillen Award; Pete Vol. 1: 14754
McGinnis Memorial Award; John H. Vol. 1: 17056
McGinnis-Ritchie Award Vol. 1: 17056
McGivern Challenge Bowl Vol. 1: 18715
McGlennon Environmental Award for Corporate Leadership; John A.S. Vol. 1: 8497
McGovern Award; James M.
Newspaper Association of America Vol. 1: 14215
Newspaper Association of America Vol 1: 14218
McGovern Award; John P. Vol. 1: 2769
McGovern Award Lectureship; John P. Vol. 1: 11662
McGovern Lecture in the Behavioral Sciences; John P. Vol. 1: 950
McGovern Umpires' Award; John T. Vol. 1: 18145
McGowan Memorial - Official of the Year; Joe Vol. 1: 360
Mcgowran Award; Bill Vol. 2: 7241
McGrand Award; Frederic A. Vol. 1: 6481
McGraw Award; James H. Vol. 1: 3657
McGraw, Jr. Prize in Education; Harold W. Vol. 1: 11633
McGraw Research Award; Curtis W. Vol. 1: 3658
McGroddy Prize for New Materials; James C. Vol. 1: 3123
McGuire Cup; James P. Vol. 1: 18174
McGuire Memorial Intermediate Piano Scholarship; Maude Vol. 1: 15876
McHenry Award; Lawrence C. Vol. 1: 638
McHugh Award; Walter P. Vol. 1: 5249
McIntyre Award Vol. 2: 4133
McIver Public Health Nurse Award; Pearl Vol. 1: 2943
McKee Award; Harley J. Vol. 1: 4942
McKee Medal; Jack Edward Vol. 1: 18638
McKee Trophy Vol. 1: 6172
McKenzie Award; Dorothy C. Vol. 1: 7352
McKenzie Award; Ken Vol. 1: 2275
McKenzie Award of Honour; R. Tait Vol. 1: 6199
McKenzie Award; R. Tait Vol. 1: 787
McKenzie Cup Vol. 1: 8643
McKenzie Plaque Vol. 1: 8643
McKinney Award; George Vol. 1: 8729
McKinney Award; William M. Vol. 1: 4202
McKinney Memorial Award; Emma C. Vol. 1: 13477
McKinsey Awards Vol. 1: 9275
McKitterick Prize Vol. 2: 7147
McKnight Advancement Grants Vol. 1: 15106
McKnight Artist Fellowships for Writers Vol. 1: 11398
McKnight Black Doctoral Fellowship Program Vol. 1: 8738
McKnight Doctoral Fellowship Program Vol. 1: 8738
McLaren Award Vol. 2: 5756
McLaren Heritage Award; Norman Vol. 1: 14738
McLaren Scholarship; GCA Interchange Fellowhip and Martin Vol. 1: 8957
McLaughlin Award of Merit; Kenneth P. Vol. 1: 13566
McLaughlin, Jr. Memorial Award; Lt. Donald Vol. 1: 17967
McLaughlin Medal Vol. 1: 15762
McLaughry Award; Tuss Vol. 1: 2045
McLemore Prize Vol. 1: 11864
McLeod Literary Prize; Enid Vol. 2: 5922
McLeod Society Trophy; Stuart Cameron Vol. 1: 9896
McLintock Prize; Sir William Vol. 2: 6011
McMaster Award; Albert Vol. 2: 5368
McMaster Gold Medal; Robert C. Vol. 1: 3779
McMillan Lecture Award; Mary Vol. 1: 3150
McMillan Undergraduate Writing Award; Mary Evelyn Vol. 1: 5095
McMullen Weapon System Maintenance Award; Maj. Gen. Clements Vol. 1: 14652
McNabnet National Award; Elaine Vol. 1: 14671
McNally Prize for Cancer Research; Nic Vol. 2: 5334
McNamara Fellowships Program; Robert S. Vol. 1: 18911
McNamee Award; Graham Vol. 1: 4306
McNamee CSJ Award; Catherine T. Vol. 1: 12865
McNaughton Exemplary Communication Award; Shirley Vol. 1: 10638
McNeer Award; Lenore Vol. 1: 13493
McNeil Medal for the Public Awareness of Science Vol. 1: 15763
McNichol Prize; J. N. Vol. 2: 607
McNiven Medal Vol. 2: 70
McParland Memorial Award Vol. 1: 6625

McPherson Memorial Lecture Vol. 2: 6076
McQuade Memorial Award; Gerard Vol. 1: 10835
McRae Russell Award; Walter Vol. 2: 56
McRitchie Writing Award; Brock Vol. 1: 14755
McWhorter Scholar-Athlete Award; H. Boyd Vol. 1: 17004
McWilliams Award; Carey Vol. 1: 3237
McWilliams Pre-Doctoral Fellowship; Margaret Vol. 1: 6489
MDS SCIEX Student Bursaries Vol. 1: 6876
Meacham Award; Monte Vol. 1: 796
Mead Award; George Herbert Vol. 1: 16471
Mead Award; Margaret
American Anthropological Association Vol. 1: 815
International Community Corrections Association Vol 1: 10333
Mead Johnson Award Vol. 1: 3794
Mead Johnson Nutritionals New Investigator Award Vol. 1: 16149
Mead Johnson Research Award in Endocrinology and Metabolism Vol. 1: 3174
Mead Prize; Sidney E. Vol. 1: 3912
Mead Prizes; Daniel W. Vol. 1: 3960
Meade Award; CEE Richard A. Vol. 1: 13024
Meade Award; George and Eleanore Vol. 1: 17322
Meadmaker of the Year Vol. 1: 2284
Meadows Award for Excellence in the Arts; Algur H. Vol. 1: 17044
Measurement Prize Vol. 2: 6154
Meat Livestock Australia Award for Best Dish Using Beef and Mushrooms Vol. 2: 290
Meat Livestock Australia Award for Best Dish Using Lamb and Mushrooms Vol. 2: 291
Meat Processing Award Vol. 1: 2740
Meats Research Award Vol. 1: 3890
Mechanic of the Year Award
Professional Aviation Maintenance Association Vol. 1: 15264
United States Auto Club Vol 1: 17753
Mechanical Engineering Prize Vol. 2: 511
Mechanics and Control of Flight Award Vol. 1: 2389
Mechelen Prize; Stad Vol. 2: 1081
MECON Award Vol. 2: 2655
Medaglia d'Acciaio Federico Giolitti Vol. 2: 3096
Medaglia d'Oro AIM Vol. 2: 3100
Medaglia d'oro Luigi Losana Vol. 2: 3098
Medaille de l'ACP pour Contribution Exceptionnelle a la Physique Vol. 1: 6284
Medaille des Anciens Presidents Vol. 2: 1958
Medaille d'Or Vol. 2: 1970
Medaille du Lieutenant-Gouverneur Vol. 1: 9387
Medaille Flavelle Vol. 1: 15759
Medaille fur Naturwissenschaftliche Publizistik Vol. 2: 2094
Medaille Gabrielle Leger Vol. 1: 9386
Medaille Henry Marshall Tory Vol. 1: 15768
Medaille Innis - Gerin Vol. 1: 15761
Medaille Jason A. Hannah Vol. 1: 15760
Medaille Jean Thevenot Vol. 2: 4799
Medaille Lorne Pierce Vol. 1: 15765
Medaille McLaughlin Vol. 1: 15762
Medaille Militaire Vol. 2: 1811
Medaille Pierre Chauveau Vol. 1: 15756
Medaille Pierre Francois Caille Vol. 1: 10417
Medaille Thomas W. Eadie Vol. 1: 15758
Medaille Tisserand Vol. 2: 1429
Medaille Willet G. Miller Vol. 1: 15764
Medailles et Diplomes Olympique Vol. 2: 4821
Medal Award Vol. 1: 16678
Medal Class Awards Vol. 1: 2793
Medal Federacion Espanola de Montanismo Vol. 2: 4545
Medal for Bravery
Canadian Institute of Mining, Metallurgy, and Petroleum Vol. 1: 6626
The Office of the Prime Minister of Malta Vol 2: 3426
Medal for Distinction in Engineering Education Vol. 1: 6435
Medal for Distinguished Philanthropy Vol. 1: 1167
Medal for Excellence in Teaching Vol. 1: 6283
Medal for Gallantry Vol. 2: 216
Medal for Lifetime Achievement in Physics Vol. 1: 6284
Medal for Long Marital Life Vol. 2: 4012
Medal for Outstanding Achievement in Industrial and Applied Physics Vol. 1: 6285
Medal for Outstanding Paper Vol. 2: 3263
Medal for Participation in the Battle for Berlin Vol. 2: 3995
Medal for Sacrifice and Courage Vol. 2: 4013
Medal for Service to the Republic Vol. 2: 3427
Medal for Services to Bibliography Vol. 2: 5165
Medal for the Advancement of Research Vol. 1: 4706
Medal in Medicine Vol. 1: 15747
Medal in Surgery Vol. 1: 15748
Medal Mariana Smoluchowskiego Vol. 2: 4050
Medal of Achievement Vol. 1: 196
Medal of Agriculture Vol. 2: 233
Medal of Appreciation Vol. 1: 13769
Medal of Bravery Vol. 1: 6085
Medal of Courage Vol. 1: 13939
Medal of Freedom Vol. 1: 8553
Medal of Honor
American Cancer Society Vol. 1: 1443
American Institute of Architects, Tampa Bay Vol 1: 2448
American Institute of Certified Public Accountants Vol 1: 2462
Electronic Industries Alliance Vol 1: 8427
Fragrance Foundation Vol 1: 8855
Herb Society of America Vol 1: 9377
Institute of Electrical and Electronics Engineers Vol 1: 9787
International Association of Professional Numismatists Vol 2: 900
Niagara University Vol 1: 14230
St. George's Society of New York Vol 1: 15791
Society of Automotive Engineers Vol 1: 16584
Medal of Honor Award Vol. 1: 2801
Medal of Honor for Career Service Vol. 1: 16813
Medal of Honor for Literature Vol. 1: 12292
Medal of Honor for Music Vol. 1: 12293
Medal of Honor for the Performing and Visual Arts Vol. 2: 4273
Medal of Honor for the Scientific Promotion and Development of Subjects Vol. 2: 4274
Medal of Honor in the Natural Sciences and Technology Vol. 2: 4275
Medal of Honour
British Deaf Association Vol. 2: 5289
Europa Nostra Pan European Federation for Heritage Vol 2: 3525
Medal of Honour for Afrikaans Television Vol. 2: 4276
Medal of Liberty Vol. 1: 1598
Medal of Merit
American Numismatic Association Vol. 1: 2903
Canadian Society of Petroleum Geologists Vol 1: 7018
Journalism Education Association Vol 1: 11051
National Sheriffs' Association Vol 1: 13702
St. Nicholas Society of the City of New York Vol 1: 15799
South African Society for Enology and Viticulture Vol 2: 4347
Medal of Military Valour Vol. 1: 6086
Medal of the Endocrine Society Vol. 1: 8455
Medal of the Estonian Academy of Sciences Vol. 2: 1350
Medal of the Society of Dyers and Colourists Vol. 2: 7188
Medal of Valor
International Narcotic Enforcement Officers Association Vol. 1: 10529
National Sheriffs' Association Vol 1: 13703
Medal of Valor Award Vol. 1: 1797
Medal Za Dlugoletnie Pozycie Malzenskie Vol. 2: 4012
Medal Za Ofiarnosc i Odwage Vol. 2: 4013
Medal Za Udzial w Walkach o Berlin Vol. 2: 3995
Medalha de Merito Turistico Vol. 2: 4068
Medalist of the Year Vol. 2: 6236
Medalja Julije Domac Vol. 2: 1225
Medalla Agricola Interamericano Vol. 2: 1208
Medalla de la Real Sociedad Espanola de Fisica Vol. 2: 4542
Medalla de Oro Vol. 1: 16739
Medalla de Plata Vol. 1: 16739
Medalla Ing. Salvador Toscano Vol. 2: 3439
Medalla Militar Francisco Jose de Caldas Vol. 2: 1177
Medalla Militar Soldado Juan Bautista Solarte Obando Vol. 2: 1178
Medalla Servicios Distinguidos a la Aviacion Naval Vol. 2: 1179
Medalla Servicios Distinguidos en Orden Publico Vol. 2: 1180
Medalla Servicios Distinguidos la Fuerza de Superficie Vol. 2: 1181
Medalla Tiempo de Servicio Vol. 2: 1182
Medallion Award
American Forage and Grassland Council Vol. 1: 2052
Council of Residential Specialists Vol 1: 7893
Medallion de Oro Vol. 1: 14319
Medallion de Plata Vol. 1: 14320
Medallion for Entrepreneurship Vol. 1: 5729
Medallion of Excellence / Community Service Vol. 1: 7714
Medallion of Excellence - Leadership Vol. 1: 7715
Medallion of Honor Vol. 1: 396
Medallion of Merit Vol. 1: 2753
Medallion School Award Vol. 1: 18494
Medals for Excellence Vol. 2: 5660
Medals of Honor Vol. 2: 3245

Award Index

Medbery Nature Landscape/Seascape Award; Lorena Vol. 1: 15028
Media All-Stars Vol. 1: 5928
Media and Methods Maxi Awards Vol. 1: 11635
Media Award
American Association of Critical-Care Nurses Vol. 1: 1073
Canadian Down Syndrome Society Vol 1: 6463
Canadian Mental Health Association Vol 1: 6715
Emergency Nurses Association Vol 1: 8441
International Society of Appraisers Vol 1: 10700
National Hearing Conservation Association Vol 1: 13327
Special Libraries Association Vol 1: 17079
Media Awards
American Academy of Nursing Vol. 1: 644
American Institute of Biological Sciences Vol 1: 2452
American Society on Aging Vol 1: 4273
Catholic Press Association Vol 1: 7165
International Association of Emergency Managers Vol 1: 10204
Plain English Campaign Vol 2: 6539
Sigma Theta Tau International Vol 1: 16051
Media Awards Competition Vol. 1: 13042
Media Awards Contest
International Association of Fire Fighters Vol. 1: 10209
International Labor Communications Association, AFL-CIO/CLC Vol 1: 10480
Media Awards for Excellence Vol. 1: 4512
Media Awards for Journalists Vol. 1: 4294
Media Citation Vol. 1: 11049
Media Commendation Awards Vol. 1: 6482
Media Contest Awards Vol. 1: 10481
Media Diversity Award Vol. 1: 6228
Media Festival Awards Vol. 1: 9314
Media-Field Award Vol. 1: 4799
Media Medal Vol. 1: 11235
Media of the Year Award Vol. 1: 10712
Media Plan of the Year Vol. 1: 5929
Media Prize Vol. 2: 2201
Media Psychology Student/Dissertation Research Award Vol. 1: 3396
Media Save Art Award Vol. 2: 3065
Mediafest, the Gran Canaria International Festival of Arts and Digital Cultures Vol. 2: 4477
Mediamaker Award Vol. 1: 5687
Median Iris Awards Vol. 1: 11641
Medical and Dental Postgraduate Research Scholarships Vol. 2: 574
Medical Award Vol. 2: 2543
Medical Book Awards Vol. 1: 2770
Medical Book Prizes Vol. 2: 7148
Medical Crew/Crew Member of the Year Award Vol. 1: 5026
Medical Education Awards Vol. 1: 702
Medical Electives Bursaries Vol. 2: 5682
Medical Executive Award Vol. 1: 1677
Medical Journalists' Association Open Book Awards Vol. 2: 6422
Medical Journalists' Association Summer Awards Vol. 2: 6423
Medical Office Building Award Vol. 1: 5996
Medical Professional Education Award Vol. 1: 13438
Medical Research Grants
Sigrid Juselius Foundation Vol. 2: 1415
SLE Foundation Vol 1: 16088
Medical Rural Bonded Scholarship Scheme Vol. 2: 164
Medical Scholars Award Vol. 1: 1913
Medical Student and Resident Travel Stipend Vol. 1: 543
Medical Student Elective Prize Vol. 2: 7035
Medical Student Essay Awards Vol. 1: 639
Medical Technologist of the Year Vol. 1: 3604
MedicarePlus Procedural Training Grants Vol. 2: 165
Medicine Pipe Bearer's Award Vol. 1: 18703
Medienpreis fur Sprachkultur Vol. 2: 2193
Medieval Archaeology Research Grant Vol. 2: 7105
Medina Award; Jose Toribio Vol. 1: 15974
Medlar Award Vol. 1: 15345
Medlicott Medal; Norton Vol. 2: 5972
Medwick Memorial Award; Lucille Vol. 1: 15133
Medzinarodna tribuna mladych interpretov/ UNESCO Vol. 2: 4444
Meek Award; Howard B. Vol. 1: 10368
Meeker Award Vol. 1: 18101
Meering Rose Bowl Award Vol. 2: 6557
Mees Medal; C. E. .K. Vol. 1: 14613
Megaw Memorial Prize; Eric Vol. 2: 6155
Meggers Award; William F. Vol. 1: 14614
Meggers Project Award; William F. and Edith R. Vol. 1: 2543
Meghnad Saha Medal Vol. 2: 2695
Mehl Award; Institute of Metals Lecturer and Robert Franklin Vol. 1: 11811
Mehl Award; Robert Franklin Vol. 1: 11811
Mehl Honor Lecture Vol. 1: 3780
Mehr Award; Robert I. Vol. 1: 3496
Meiklejohn Award for Academic Freedom; Alexander Vol. 1: 1319
Meillet; Prix Antoine Vol. 2: 1522
Meinzer Award; O. E. Vol. 1: 9024
Meiselman Memorial Award for Painting; Leonard J. Vol. 1: 585
Meiselman Memorial Award for Sculpture; Leonard J. Vol. 1: 586
Meiselman Prize; Leonard J. Vol. 1: 13690
Meiselman Representational Painting Award; Leonard Vol. 1: 16547
Meiselman Representational Sculpture Award; Leonard Vol. 1: 16548
Meisner Foundry Award; Joel Vol. 1: 13690
Meissner Prize; Leo Vol. 1: 12113
Melbourne International Film Festival Shorts Awards Vol. 2: 563
Melcher Book Award; Frederic G. Vol. 1: 17680
Melcher Scholarship; Frederic G. Vol. 1: 4927
Melchers Memorial Medal; Gari Vol. 1: 4669
Meldola Medal and Prize Vol. 2: 6974
Melezin Fellowship; Abraham and Rachela Vol. 1: 19065
Mellon Centre Rome Fellowship; Paul Vol. 2: 5442
Mellon Environmental Stewardship Award; Richard Beatty Vol. 1: 268
Mellon Post-Dissertation Fellowship Vol. 1: 818
Mellon Predoctoral Research Grant Vol. 1: 16133
Mellor Award; Sam Vol. 1: 13567
Melton Award Vol. 2: 5469
Melville Medal Vol. 1: 4151
Melville Memorial Award; Stanley Vol. 2: 5332
Member Association Award of Excellence Vol. 1: 6424
Member Association Director Award Vol. 1: 12378
Member Association Safety Awards Vol. 1: 18639
Member of Honour Vol. 2: 2359
Member of Note Vol. 1: 15063
Member of the Year
Caucus for Television Producers, Writers and Directors Vol. 1: 7180
Document Management Industries Association Vol 1: 8241
Institute of Packaging Professionals Vol 1: 9929
National Guild of Hypnotists Vol 1: 13313
National Therapeutic Recreation Society Vol 1: 13846
Ottawa Field-Naturalists' Club Vol 1: 14726
Society of Cable Telecommunications Engineers Vol 1: 16616
Member of the Year Award
ACA International Vol. 1: 59
American Probation and Parole Association Vol 1: 3262
American Society of Certified Engineering Technicians Vol 1: 3907
Dance Masters of America Vol 1: 8044
International Association of Assessing Officers Vol 1: 10135
National Weather Association Vol 1: 13899
Member of the Year - Regional Vol. 1: 6019
Member Organization of the Year Vol. 1: 18146
Member Service Award Vol. 1: 15271
Member Travel Fellowship Vol. 2: 2807
Member's Award Vol. 2: 6877
Members Award Vol. 1: 6627
Members Choice Award Vol. 1: 10461
Membership Achievement Award Vol. 1: 6845
Membership Award Vol. 1: 2390
Membership Bursary Vol. 2: 6945
Membership in Omicron Kappa Upsilon Vol. 1: 14526
Membership in the Gorsedd of Bards Vol. 2: 6471
Membership of the City and Guilds of London Institute Vol. 2: 5661
Membership Recognition Vol. 1: 5059
Membres Honoraires a Vie Vol. 1: 6800
Memorial Awards Vol. 1: 18217
Memorial Fellowship Award Vol. 1: 8715
Memorial Fellowships Vol. 1: 2582
Memorial Grants Vol. 1: 8341
Memorial Hall of Fame Award Vol. 1: 2567
Memorial Lecturer Award and Honoree Vol. 1: 2802
Memorial Life Membership Awards Vol. 1: 8644
Memorial NAMA Fellowship Vol. 1: 12047
Memorial Scholarship Vol. 1: 18725
Memorial Scholarship Awards Vol. 1: 4877
Memorial William John Bond Safe Driver of the Year Vol. 2: 422
Mendal Memorial Award in Strings and Trophy; Fred S. Vol. 1: 15877
Mendal Memorial Senior Violin Scholarship and Trophy; Mrs. Clare K. Vol. 1: 15878
Mendel Award; Osborne and Vol. 1: 3795
Mendel; Prix Gustave Vol. 2: 1523

Mendelson Memorial Awards; Robin H. Vol. 1: 3599
Mendelssohn Award Vol. 2: 2299
Mendes Award; Chico Vol. 1: 16016
Menefee Honorary Life Membership Award; Jim Vol. 1: 14347
Menninger Memorial Award; William C. Vol. 1: 1717
Menon Medical Research Award; Dr. Kamala Vol. 2: 2613
Men's Garden Clubs of America Scholarship; Gardeners of America/ Vol. 1: 8965
Men's National Championship Cup Finals Vol. 2: 5775
Mensa International Competitions Vol. 2: 6426
Mensforth International Gold Medal; Sir Eric Vol. 2: 6156
Mental Health in the Workplace Award Vol. 1: 6716
Mental Health Media Awards Vol. 1: 13449
Mention in Dispatches Vol. 1: 6087
Mentor Award
 American Association for the Advancement of Science Vol. 1: 951
 Professional Convention Management Association Vol 1: 15295
 Specialty Graphic Imaging Association Vol 1: 17113
Mentor Award in Developmental Psychology Vol. 1: 3328
Mentor-Based Minority Postdoctoral Fellowship Vol. 1: 1914
Mentor-Based Postdoctoral Fellowships Vol. 1: 1915
Mentor Series in Poetry and Creative Prose Award Vol. 1: 11399
Mentoring Award
 American Association of Critical-Care Nurses Vol. 1: 1074
 American Contact Dermatitis Society Vol 1: 1785
 Middle East Studies Association of North America Vol 1: 11751
Mentorship Award Vol. 1: 16923
Menuhin Prize Vol. 2: 6407
Menzel Award; Margaret Vol. 1: 5880
Mercer Award; George Vol. 1: 8373
Mercer Award; Henry Chapman Vol. 1: 5981
Mercer Award; Johnny Vol. 1: 12134
Mercer Award; Thomas T. Vol. 2: 2319
Mercer Awards for Innovation; Brian Vol. 2: 6914
Mercer Joint Prize; Thomas T. Vol. 1: 842
Merchandise Mart Hall of Fame Vol. 1: 11693
Merchandiser of the Year Award
 National Association of Recording Merchandisers Vol. 1: 12639
 Newspaper Association of America Vol 1: 14214
Merchandisers of the Year Vol. 1: 15319
Merchant Manufacturing Medal; M. Eugene Vol. 1: 4152
The Mercia Prize - Postgraduate Bursary in Medical Engineering Vol. 2: 5768
Merck Agvet Dairy Management Research Award Vol. 1: 1883
Merck Award Vol. 2: 4257
Merck Award for Achievement in Poultry Science Vol. 1: 15179
Merck Ehrung; Johann-Heinrich- Vol. 2: 2443
Merck European Thyroid Von-Basedow-Research Prize Vol. 2: 2203
Merck Frosst Award Vol. 1: 6998
Merck Frosst Award (Junior Scientist) Vol. 1: 14970
Merck Frosst Centre for Therapeutic Research Lecture Award Vol. 1: 6909
Merck Frosst-CSBMCB Travel Awards Vol. 1: 6988
Merck Frosst Pharmacology Fellowship Award Vol. 1: 14971
Merck KGaA Prize Vol. 2: 1299
Merck Medal Vol. 2: 4316
Merck Preis; Johann-Heinrich- Vol. 2: 2147
Merck Sharp and Dohme Florey Medal Vol. 2: 367
Merck Sharp & Dohme Lecture Award Vol. 1: 6909
Merck US Human Health Migraine and Women's Health Research Award; AHS/ Vol. 1: 2162
Mercure Awards; Pierre Vol. 1: 16119
Mercury Gold Award Vol. 1: 15513
Mercury Silver Award Vol. 1: 15513
Merenti de Patria; Prix Bene Vol. 1: 16145
Merghelynck Prize; Arthur Vol. 2: 960
Merial Preventive Medicine in Beef Award Vol. 1: 1026
Merial Preventive Medicine in Dairy Award Vol. 1: 1027
Merit Award
 American Concrete Institute - New Jersey Chapter Vol. 1: 1767
 American Forage and Grassland Council Vol 1: 2053
 American Society for Enology and Viticulture Vol 1: 3696
 Association of European Toxicologists and European Societies of Toxicology Vol 2: 1272
 Association of Official Seed Analysts Vol 1: 5271
 Canadian Athletic Therapists Association Vol 1: 6317
 City of Toronto Vol 1: 7443
 Decalogue Society of Lawyers Vol 1: 8081
 Indiana Library Federation Vol 1: 9673
 Institute of Landscape Architects of South Africa Vol 2: 4197
 International Table Tennis Federation Vol 2: 4854
 Lynchburg Historical Foundation Vol 1: 11451
 National Association of Hospital Fire Officers Vol 2: 6453
 National Junior College Athletic Association Vol 1: 13404
 Society of Cosmetic Chemists Vol 1: 16630
 Society of Toxicology Vol 1: 16877
 Society of Wetland Scientists Vol 1: 16902
 Soil and Water Conservation Society Vol 1: 16933
Merit Award for Breeders and Yorkshire Terrier Vol. 1: 19076
Merit Award for Distinguished Service as a Public Library Trustee Vol. 1: 6705
Merit Award for Excellent Arrest Vol. 1: 3224
Merit Award in Landscape Architecture Vol. 2: 245
Merit Awards
 Association of National Olympic Committees Vol. 2: 1719
 Botanical Society of America Vol 1: 5881
 Scouting Ireland CSI Vol 2: 2884
Merit Book Awards Vol. 1: 9237
Merit Citation Vol. 1: 15047
MERIT Competition Vol. 2: 6120
MERIT Game Vol. 2: 6120
Merit Medal Vol. 1: 8348
Merit of Breeding Award Vol. 1: 1932
Merit of Exhibits Vol. 1: 2904
Merit Scholarships For Hospitality Students Vol. 2: 3832
Merit Scholarships For Secondary School Students Vol. 2: 3833
Merit Shop Excellence in Construction Awards Vol. 1: 4757
Meritorious Accountant of the Americas Vol. 1: 9991
Meritorious Achievement Award
 American Association of Zoo Keepers Vol. 1: 1339
 American Industrial Hygiene Association Vol 1: 2343
Meritorious Achievement in Pessimism Vol. 1: 5713
Meritorious Award Vol. 1: 436
Meritorious Awards Vol. 1: 14657
Meritorious Honor Award Vol. 1: 17866
Meritorious Prize for Scientific Achievement Vol. 2: 3206
Meritorious Service Vol. 2: 343
Meritorious Service Award
 American Rental Association Vol. 1: 3480
 American Society of Echocardiography Vol 1: 4025
 Canadian Radiation Protection Association Vol 1: 6853
 Institute of Chartered Accountants in Australia Vol 2: 481
 International Morab Registry Vol 1: 10517
 National Guild of Hypnotists Vol 1: 13314
 States Organization for Boating Access Vol 1: 17270
Meritorious Service Award
 Alpha Omega International Dental Fraternity Vol. 1: 428
 American Association for Leisure and Recreation Vol 1: 923
 American Association of Homes and Services for the Aging Vol 1: 1128
 American Baseball Coaches Association Vol 1: 1386
 American Fisheries Society Vol 1: 2031
 American Horticultural Society Vol 1: 2294
 American Mosquito Control Association Vol 1: 2803
 American National Standards Institute Vol 1: 2854
 American Park and Recreation Society Vol 1: 3026
 American Philatelic Congress Vol 1: 3072
 Australian Veterinary Association Vol 2: 386
 Institute of Nuclear Materials Management Vol 1: 9923
 International Badminton Federation Vol 2: 3410
 National Association for Interpretation Vol 1: 12347
 National Christian College Athletic Association Vol 1: 12888
 National Council of Examiners for Engineering and Surveying Vol 1: 12998
 National Therapeutic Recreation Society Vol 1: 13847
 Nebraska Library Association Vol 1: 14017
 Society of Nematologists Vol 1: 16774
Meritorious Service Award for Community Service Vol. 1: 6436

Meritorious Service Award for Professional Service Vol. 1: 6437
Meritorious Service Awards Vol. 1: 13338
Meritorious Service Cross - Civil Division Vol. 1: 6088
Meritorious Service Cross - Military Division Vol. 1: 6089
Meritorious Service in Communications Award Vol. 1: 4037
Meritorious Service Medal
Defense Logistics Agency - United States Air Force Vol. 1: 8114
National Society, Sons of the American Revolution Vol 1: 13770
Meritorious Service Medal - Civil Division Vol. 1: 6090
Meritorious Service Medal - Military Division Vol. 1: 6091
Meritorious Service to Aviation Award Vol. 1: 12828
Meritorious Trophy Vol. 1: 5603
Meritorious Unit Citation Vol. 2: 224
Meritorius Service Vol. 1: 1927
Merlin Medal and Gift Vol. 2: 5249
Merriam Award; C. Hart Vol. 1: 4120
Merriam Award; Charles Vol. 1: 3238
Merrill Nordic Award; Al Vol. 1: 18102
Merrill-Palmer Citation Award Vol. 1: 18651
Merriman Award; Wayne Vol. 1: 14801
Merryfield Design Award; Fred Vol. 1: 3659
Mertz Trophy; Allegra Knapp Vol. 1: 18078
Merwe Award; Marina Van Der Vol. 1: 6660
Merwe Prize; Koos van der Vol. 2: 4127
Merwin Distinguished Service Award; Richard E. Vol. 1: 9813
Mesa Contemporary Arts Exhibitions Vol. 1: 11697
Meshorer Prize; Ya'akov Vol. 2: 2919
Messenger Stake Vol. 1: 18162
Metal Mining Division Award Vol. 1: 6628
The Metallurgical Society Vol. 1: 11820
Metallurgist of the Year Award Vol. 2: 2656
Metcalf Exemplary Dissertation Award; Larry Vol. 1: 12987
Metcalfe Award Vol. 2: 276
Metcalfe Medallion Vol. 2: 276
MetLife Awards for Excellence in Community Engagement Vol. 1: 4343
MetLife Foundation Extended Collaboration Grants for Artists; TCG/ Vol. 1: 17510
Metlife Foundation MindAlert Awards; ASA- Vol. 1: 4264
Metras Trophy; J. P. Vol. 1: 6661
Metro Awards Vol. 1: 18737
Metropolitan Award Vol. 1: 12401
Meurand; Prix Vol. 2: 1464
Mewaldt-King Student Research Award Vol. 1: 7805
Mexican Order of the Aztec Eagle Vol. 2: 3454
Meyer Lectureship; Adolf Vol. 1: 3280
Meyer Medaille; Hans Vol. 2: 2061
Meyer Medal for Plant Genetic Resources; Frank N. Vol. 1: 7979
Meyer Outstanding Teacher Awards; Agnes Vol. 1: 18606
Meyer Prize; Carl S. Vol. 1: 16078
Meyer Prize; Ernst Vol. 2: 4778
Meyer-Whitworth Award Vol. 2: 5070
Meyerhof Award; Geoffrey G. Vol. 1: 6528
Meyers Award; John F. Vol. 1: 12866
Meyers Medal; Mario Cooper and Dale Vol. 1: 4431
Meyerson Award; Stanley C. Vol. 1: 14633
Meyrick Memorial Award; Pamela Vol. 2: 6469
Mezinarodni hudebni soutez Prazske jaro Vol. 2: 1264
Mezinarodni rozhlasova soutez Mladych hudebniku Concertino Praga Vol. 2: 1254
Mezinarodni Televizni Festival Zlata Praha Vol. 2: 1256
MHA Best Book Award Vol. 1: 11954
MIA Music Awards Vol. 2: 6449
Miami Beach International Film Festival Vol. 1: 11714
Michael Dwyer Memorial Award Vol. 2: 6086
Michael Guthrie Prize Vol. 2: 5993
Michael Taylor Award Vol. 2: 3818
Michaels Memorial Film Award; John Vol. 1: 5756
Michal Award for Body of Work by an Emerging Director; Ray Vol. 1: 9196
Michel T. Halbouty Memorial Human Needs Award Vol. 1: 1215
Michelbacher Prize Vol. 1: 7131
Michell Medal; A. G. M. Vol. 2: 517
Michell Medal; J.H. Vol. 2: 43
Michels New Investigator Award; Eugene Vol. 1: 3151
Michelson Award; A.A. Vol. 1: 7649
Michelson Award; Albert A. Vol. 1: 7127
Michelson-Morley Award Vol. 1: 7127
Michener Award
Michener Awards Foundation Vol. 1: 11718
Michener Awards Foundation Vol 1: 11718
Michener Conservation Award; Roland Vol. 1: 7067
Michener de Journalism; Prix Vol. 1: 11718
Michener-Deacon Fellowship Vol. 1: 11719
Michigan Industrial Hygiene Society Award of Authorship Vol. 1: 2344
Mick Aston Presentation Award Vol. 2: 5226
Mickle Award; D. Grant Vol. 1: 17582
Microcirculation Conference Grant Vol. 2: 5379
Microcomputer in the Media Center Award Vol. 1: 1279
Microscopy Award Vol. 2: 5386
Mid-Career Award Vol. 1: 1825
Mid-Career Research Mentorship Award Vol. 1: 16695
Mid-Rise Suburban Office Park Award Vol. 1: 5997
Midalja ghall-Qadi tar-Repubblika Vol. 2: 3427
Midalja ghall-Qlubija Vol. 2: 3426
Middle Atlantic Section Distinguished Teaching Award Vol. 1: 3660
Middlebrooks Award; Thomas A. Vol. 1: 3961
Middleton Award; J.J.I. Vol. 2: 4168
Middleton Award; William S. Vol. 1: 17882
Midland Assurance Trophy Vol. 2: 6931
Miedzynarodowe Triennale Grafiki Krakow Vol. 2: 4004
Miedzynarodowy Konkurs Kompozytorski im-Witolda Lutoslawskiego Vol. 2: 4054
Migel Medal Vol. 1: 2069
Mignet Diploma; Henry Vol. 2: 4740
Mikeldi de Oro Vol. 2: 4517
Milankovitch Medal; Milutin Vol. 2: 1775
Milburn Award; C. H. Vol. 2: 5369
Mildenberger Outstanding NESDA Officer Award; Richard Vol. 1: 13098
Mildenberger Prize; Kenneth W. Vol. 1: 11908
Mildon Award; James R. Vol. 1: 9837
Miles Distinguished Service Award; Margaret Vol. 1: 16790
Miles - Marschall International Award Vol. 1: 1874
Milestone Award Vol. 1: 6071
Milestone Awards Vol. 1: 9425
Militaire Willems-Orde Vol. 2: 3490
Military Astronautics Award Vol. 1: 1351
Military Cross Vol. 2: 5595
Military Medal for Gallantry Vol. 2: 2854
Military Merit Medal Vol. 2: 4344
Military Order of William Vol. 2: 3490
Military Photographer of the Year Vol. 1: 13568
Milk Industry Foundation and Kraft Foods Teaching Award in Dairy Manufacturing Vol. 1: 1884
Milkweed National Fiction Prize Vol. 1: 11777
Milkweed Prize for Children's Literature Vol. 1: 11778
Mill Manager of the Year Vol. 1: 14838
Millar Award for Innovative Approaches to Adolescent Health Care; Hilary E. C. Vol. 1: 16150
Millennium Residencies in Production Animal Medicine Vol. 2: 6743
Miller Award; Carroll R. Vol. 1: 13537
Miller Award; Douglas Vol. 1: 6333
Miller Award; Elizabeth McWilliams Vol. 1: 16049
Miller Award; Frances Hubbs Vol. 1: 8174
Miller Award; George A. Vol. 1: 3346
Miller Award; Merl K. Vol. 1: 3661
Miller Award; Russell R. Vol. 1: 1633
Miller Award; Samuel Charles Vol. 1: 669
Miller Awards; Saul Vol. 1: 10481
Miller Chapter Service Awards; Susan E. Vol. 1: 16017
Miller Distinguished Service Award; George J. Vol. 1: 12971
Miller International Award; S. Ray Vol. 1: 10194
Miller Interpretive Sculpture Award; Donald Vol. 1: 16549
Miller Legal Services Award; Loren Vol. 1: 17256
Miller Lite Women's Sports Journalism Awards Vol. 1: 18876
Miller Medal; Osborn Maitland Vol. 1: 2099
Miller Medal; Willet G. Vol. 1: 15764
Miller Memorial Award; Barse Vol. 1: 4438
Miller Memorial Award; Monte Vol. 2: 395
Miller Memorial Medal Award; Samuel Wylie Vol. 1: 4462
Miller Outstanding Doctoral Dissertation Award; Gerald R. Vol. 1: 12928
Miller Prizes Vol. 2: 6121
Miller Research Award; Loye and Alden Vol. 1: 7806
Miller Scholarship; Cheryl Allyn Vol. 1: 16924
Miller Storyteller Award; Ron Vol. 1: 14755
Milli Award Vol. 2: 154
Millie Award Vol. 1: 8249
Millikan Medal; Robert A. Vol. 1: 1251
Milliken Scholarship; Ruth Vol. 1: 2145
Million Dollar Hall of Fame Vol. 1: 13882
Million Mile Club Award Vol. 1: 13657
Million Miler Award for Safety Excellence
Specialized Carriers and Rigging Association Vol. 1: 17099
Specialized Carriers and Rigging Association Vol 1: 17101

Millot; Prix Georges
Academie des Sciences Vol. 2: 1591
Geological Society of France Vol 2: 1836
Mills Award; C. Wright Vol. 1: 16463
Mills Award for Meritorious Service Vol. 1: 1648
Mills Award; Harlan D. Vol. 1: 9814
Mills Outstanding Contribution to Emergency Medicine Award; James D. Vol. 1: 1648
Millson Award for Invention; Henry E. Vol. 1: 1309
Milne Memorial Award; Jack Vol. 1: 492
Minah Distinguished Service Award; Theodore W. Vol. 1: 12444
Minarikovo Odlicje Vol. 2: 4465
Minasian Award; George T. Vol. 1: 269
Miner Award; Neil A. Vol. 1: 12538
Mineral Economics Award Vol. 1: 2531
Mineral Education Awards Vol. 1: 10846
Mineral Industry Education Award Vol. 1: 2532
Mineralium Deposita Best Paper Award Vol. 2: 1267
Mineralogical Society of America Award Vol. 1: 11798
Minerva Awards Vol. 1: 14148
Minerva Medal Vol. 2: 5654
Mini-Basketball Coach Award Vol. 2: 6436
Mini-Basketball Officiating Award Vol. 2: 6437
Mini-Basketball Teacher Award Vol. 2: 6438
Mini-Grants Vol. 1: 19050
Mining and Exploration Division Distinguished Service Award Vol. 1: 16353
Ministere des Affaires etrangeres et du Commerce international Vol. 1: 8811
Minister's Award for Consular Excellence Vol. 1: 8812
Minister's Award for Foreign Policy Excellence Vol. 1: 8813
Ministry of Transport Award for Best Student Research Vol. 2: 3757
Ministry of Urban Development, Culture and Sports of North Rhine-Westphalia Award Vol. 2: 2316
Mink Award; Walter D. Vol. 1: 11844
Minkowski Prize Vol. 2: 2107
Minks Award; Nancy Vol. 1: 2311
Minneapolis Foundation Grants Vol. 1: 11825
Minnesmedaljen i guld Vol. 2: 4629
Minnesota International Human Rights Award Vol. 1: 11828
Minnesota Masonry Project Awards Vol. 1: 11832
Minority Business Leadership Awards Vol. 1: 13457
Minority Fellowship Vol. 1: 4283
Minority Initiatives Award Vol. 1: 3152
Minority Scholarships Program for Residents and Students Vol. 1: 612
Minority Travel Fellowship Awards Vol. 1: 3175
Minshall Award; Lewis Vol. 2: 5903
Minter Award; Jerry B. Vol. 1: 15526
Mintz Award; Morton Vol. 1: 18592
Minute Award Vol. 1: 13161
Minuteman Medal Vol. 1: 13771
Minville; Prix Esdras- Vol. 1: 16143
Miriam Dudley Award for Bibliographic Instruction Vol. 1: 5077
Mishima Medal Vol. 2: 3207
Miss America Vol. 1: 11852
Miss America Woman of Achievement Award Vol. 1: 11853
Miss Dance of Great Britain Vol. 2: 6237
Miss Galaxy Vol. 1: 8939
Miss Indian World Vol. 1: 8976
Miss Tall International Vol. 1: 17386
Miss Teen USA Vol. 1: 11855
Miss Teen USA Pageant Vol. 1: 11855
Miss Universe Vol. 1: 11856
Miss Universe Pageant Vol. 1: 11856
Miss USA Vol. 1: 11857
Miss USA Pageant Vol. 1: 11857
Missile Systems Awards Vol. 1: 2391
Mission Accomplished Creative Commercial Production Awards Vol. 1: 6030
Mission Support Trophy Vol. 1: 13301
Mississippi-Alabama Sea Grant Consortium Grants Vol. 1: 11859
Mississippi Poetry Society Award Vol. 1: 13162
Missouri History Book Award Vol. 1: 17267
Missouri Honor Medal Vol. 1: 18324
Missouri Lifestyle Journalism Award Vol. 1: 18325
Missouri Southern International Piano Competition Vol. 1: 11894
Missouri State Poetry Society Award Vol. 1: 13163
Missouri Teacher of the Year Program Vol. 1: 11890
Mita Society for Library and Information Science Prize Vol. 2: 3294
Mita Toshokan Joho Gakkai-Sho Vol. 2: 3294
Mitchell Award; Gen. Billy Vol. 1: 291
Mitchell Award; General Billy Vol. 1: 291
Mitchell Award; H. L. Vol. 1: 17035
Mitchell Award; James G. Vol. 1: 13793
Mitchell Award; S. Weir Vol. 1: 640
Mitchell Bowl
Canadian Interuniversity Sport Vol. 1: 6656
Canadian Interuniversity Sport Vol 1: 6668
Mitchell City of Calgary Book Prize; W.O. Vol. 1: 19008
Mitchell Community Development Award; Jan Vol. 1: 13262
Mitchell Convention Travel Grant; Ronald W. Vol. 1: 10589
Mitchell Medal; Sydney B. Vol. 1: 11641
Mitchell Memorial Intermediate Cello/Viola/Double Bass Scholarship; Johanna Vol. 1: 15879
Mitchell Memorial Intermediate Violin Scholarship and Trophy; Robert C. Vol. 1: 15880
Mitchell National Debate Trophy; Harland B. Vol. 1: 13242
Mitchell Prize; Lillias Vol. 2: 2877
Mitchell Young Extension Worker Award; Nolan
American Society of Agricultural and Biological Engineers Vol. 1: 3848
American Society of Agricultural and Biological Engineers Vol 1: 3858
Mitra Memorial Award; IETE-Prof. S.N. Vol. 2: 2768
Mitra Memorial Lecture; Sisir Kumar Vol. 2: 2696
Mitry Award; Jean Vol. 2: 3121
Mitsakos Outstanding Social Studies Supervisor of the Year; Charles Vol. 1: 11579
Mitscherlich Denkmunze; Alexander Vol. 2: 2033
Mittasch-Medaille; Alwin Vol. 2: 2262
Mittelstadt Ski Jumping Officials Award Vol. 1: 18103
Mittlemann Achievement Award; Eugene Vol. 1: 9580
Mixon First Prize Vol. 1: 7474
Mizel Memorial Exhibit Award; Menachem Chaim and Simcha Tova Vol. 1: 2875
MLA Scholarships and Grants Vol. 1: 11663
MLM Company of the Year Vol. 1: 12004
Mobil Five-Star Award Vol. 1: 8569
Mobius Advertising Awards Vol. 1: 11898
Moch Lifetime Achievement Award; Frank J. Vol. 1: 13098
Modisette Award; James O. Vol. 1: 11425
Mody-Unichem Prize for Research in Cardiology, Neurology and Gastroenterology; Amrut Vol. 2: 2614
Mody-Unichem Prize for Research in Maternal and Child Health and Chest Diseases; Amrut Vol. 2: 2615
Moe Prize for Catalogs of Distinction in the Arts; Henry Allen Vol. 1: 14183
Moe Prize in the Humanities; Henry Allen Vol. 1: 3101
Moffat and Larry Lillo Award; John Vol. 1: 9196
Moffat - Frank E. Nichol Harbor and Coastal Engineering Award; John G. Vol. 1: 3962
Moffitt Human Rights Awards; Letelier - Vol. 1: 9753
Mohawk-Hudson Region Art Exhibition Award Vol. 1: 15901
Mohr Medal; William
Aril Society International Vol. 1: 4592
Median Iris Society Vol 1: 11641
Moir Medal; James Vol. 2: 4317
Moisseiff Award Vol. 1: 3963
Molesworth Award; Jack Vol. 1: 7673
Molfenter-Preis der Landeshauptstadt Stuttgart/Galerie; Hans- Vol. 2: 2418
Moll Memorial Quality Management Award; Dale C. Vol. 1: 7751
Mollenhoff Award for Excellence in Investigative Reporting; Clark Vol. 1: 8923
Moller/AGO Award in Choral Competition Vol. 1: 2144
Molly Awards Vol. 1: 9334
Molodovsky Award; Nicholas Vol. 1: 7266
Molotsky Award for Excellence in Coverage of Higher Education; Iris Vol. 1: 1320
Mols Award; Herbert Joseph Vol. 1: 493
Molson Prizes Vol. 1: 6116
Molteno Medal Awards of Excellence and Merit Vol. 2: 4150
Monash Medal; John Vol. 2: 518
Monbinne; Prix Vol. 2: 1465
Moncado Prizes for Best Article Vol. 1: 16337
Moncrieff Prize; Scott Vol. 2: 7133
Mond Lectureship; Ludwig Vol. 2: 6975
Mondeal Prize Vol. 2: 5813
Mondriaan Lecture; Piet Vol. 2: 3664
Monette-Roger Horwitz Dissertation Prize; Paul Vol. 1: 7223
Money for Women/Barbara Deming Memorial Fund Grants Vol. 1: 11926
Monica Browning Award Vol. 1: 4644
Monk International Jazz Competition; Thelonious Vol. 1: 11928
Monk International Jazz Instrumental Competition; Thelonious Vol. 1: 11928
Monk International Jazz Piano Competition; Thelonious Vol. 1: 11928

Award Index

Monod; Prix Gabriel Vol. 2: 1685
Monpetit; Prix Michel Vol. 2: 1592
Monroe Library Adult Services Award; Margaret E. Vol. 1: 2690
Monsanto Crop Science Distinguished Career Award Vol. 1: 7980
Montague Distinguished Resident Award in Radiation Oncology; Eleanor Vol. 1: 979
Montaigne Prize Vol. 2: 2399
Montald; Prix Constant Vol. 2: 976
Montana CPA Scholarships Vol. 1: 11930
Montana Memorial Prize; Pietro and Alfrieda Vol. 1: 13690
Montana New Zealand Book Awards Vol. 2: 3700
Monte Carlo Television Festival Vol. 2: 3469
Montefiore Foundation Prize; George Vol. 2: 943
Montefiore; Prix de la Fondation George Vol. 2: 943
Montequin Fellowship; Edilia and Francois-Auguste de Vol. 1: 16557
Montgolfier Ballooning Diploma Vol. 2: 4741
Montgolfier Trophy Vol. 1: 11360
Montgomery Child-Produced Prize; Kenneth and Harle Vol. 1: 7331
Montgomery Distinguished Service Award; Reid H. Vol. 1: 7529
Montgomery Doctoral Grant; Merle Vol. 1: 12000
Montgomery Emerging Director Prize; Kenneth and Harle Vol. 1: 7331
Montgomery Medal Vol. 1: 13301
Montgomery Memorial Trophy; Hugh R. Vol. 1: 6422
Montreal International Festival of New Cinema and Video Vol. 1: 11935
Montreal International Fireworks Competition Vol. 1: 11937
Montreal Medal Vol. 1: 7306
Montreal World Film Festival Vol. 1: 11944
Montreux Choral Festival Vol. 2: 4870
Monty Distinguished Service Award; Michael Vol. 1: 5954
Montyon de Physiologie; Prix Vol. 2: 1593
Mookerjee Memorial Award; Asutosh Vol. 2: 2744
Moon Award; A. Ramsay Vol. 2: 734
Mooney Distinguished Technology Award; Melvin Vol. 1: 1566
Moore Alumni Award; Mary Vol. 1: 4645
Moore Award Vol. 1: 1174
Moore Award for Outstanding New Academic Faculty Member; Margaret L. Vol. 1: 3153
Moore Award for Voluntary Service; Clarence H. Vol. 1: 14831
Moore Award; Harry T. Vol. 1: 8016
Moore Award; Ray Vol. 1: 14364
Moore Award; Royal N. Vol. 1: 11520
Moore Award; Velma Vol. 1: 14173
Moore Award; Virginia P. Vol. 1: 6117
Moore Medal for Paleontology; Raymond C. Vol. 1: 16411
Moore Medal; George Vol. 2: 6800
Moore Medal; Leo B. Vol. 1: 17247
Moore Memorial Award; Barrington Vol. 1: 16509
Moore Memorial Award; Robert P. Vol. 1: 12771
Moore Prize; Glover Vol. 1: 11865
Moore Writer-in-Washington; Jenny McKean Vol. 1: 11946
Moose Moss Age Group Diving Coach of the Year Award Vol. 1: 17731
Mora Award; Estela and Raul Vol. 1: 15603
Morab Horse of the Year Vol. 1: 10518
Moran Medal for Statistical Science Vol. 2: 120
Moran National Portrait Prize; Doug Vol. 2: 707
Moran Portraiture Prize; Douglas J. Vol. 2: 707
Morando Lifetime Achievement Award; Rocco V. Vol. 1: 12524
Mordica Memorial Award Vol. 1: 18767
More Medal for Book Collecting; Sir Thomas Vol. 1: 9092
Moreno Award; Premio Francisco P. Vol. 2: 18
Morey Award; George W. Vol. 1: 1488
Morey Book Award; Charles Rufus Vol. 1: 7508
Morgan Award; Frederick C. Vol. 1: 9322
Morgan Award; Joseph F. Vol. 1: 16262
Morgan Individual Achievement Award; Frederick C. Vol. 1: 9322
Morgan Medal; Philip F. Vol. 1: 18640
Morgan Medal; Thomas Hunt Vol. 1: 9004
Morgan Prize for Outstanding Research in Mathematics by an Undergraduate Student; Frank and Brennie Vol. 1: 16273
Morgan Research Award; Agnes Fay Vol. 1: 10865
Morgan Scholarship; Hazel B. Vol. 1: 12000
Morgan-Wood Medal Vol. 1: 11641
Morgenthau Award; Hans J. Vol. 1: 12919
Morgenthau Memorial Award; Hans J. Vol. 1: 12919
Morgotch Memorial Award; Larry Vol. 1: 13990
Morguard Literary Award Vol. 1: 15571
Moricoli; Research Award in Honor of John C. Vol. 1: 16832
Morin; Prix Victor- Vol. 1: 16144
Morison Prize; Samuel Eliot Vol. 1: 16338
Morlan Faculty Secretary Award; Robert L. Vol. 1: 14521
Morley Award; Colonel Bill Vol. 1: 4645
Morley Award; Elise Vol. 1: 4644
Morley CFA Award for Distinguished Service; Alfred C. fPetev Vol. 1: 7267
Morley/Montgomery Award Vol. 1: 5629
Morneau Distinguished Service Award; Robert F. Vol. 1: 12858
Morrell Memorial Award; David Vol. 1: 17207
Morrill Volunteer Award; Lisa Vol. 1: 5816
Morris Award; Arthur J. Vol. 1: 7774
Morris Award; JJ Vol. 2: 6038
Morris Award; Old Tom Vol. 1: 9116
Morris Award; Robert Vol. 1: 18657
Morris Humanitarian Award; AAMI Foundation/ ACCE Robert L. Vol. 1: 4984
Morris Memorial Prize; Lindsay Vol. 1: 13690
Morris Memorial Trophy; Ted Vol. 1: 6662
Morris Scholarship; Ruth Dean Vol. 1: 12000
Morris Student Research Award; Charles R. Vol. 1: 661
Morris Sustaining Member Award; J. W. Vol. 1: 16527
Morrison Award Vol. 1: 3891
Morrison Award; Francis Vol. 1: 15848
Morrison Communicator Award; Thomas Vol. 1: 17867
Morrison Information Management Award; Thomas Vol. 1: 17867
Morrison Jr. Award; Major Gen. John E. Vol. 1: 13452
Morrison Trophy; W. A. Vol. 2: 3848
Morrow Award; Elizabeth Cutter Vol. 1: 19114
Morrow Public Outreach Award; Douglas S. Vol. 1: 18127
MORS Prize Vol. 1: 11770
Morse Lectureship Award; Philip McCord Vol. 1: 9747
Morse Medal; Samuel Finley Breese Vol. 1: 2100
Morse Writer's Award; Robert T. Vol. 1: 3281
Morsey Award; David Vol. 1: 10306
Mortimer Memorial Silver Plated Trophy; James Vol. 1: 18716
Morton Award; Caroline French Vol. 1: 12253
Morton Award; J. Sterling Vol. 1: 12253
Morton Lecture Vol. 2: 5176
Mosaic Foundation Best of the Festival Award Vol. 1: 4536
MOSAID Technologies Award for Fiction Vol. 1: 6323
Mosby Above and Beyond Award; Senator Carolyn Vol. 1: 9664
Mosby Award; Henry S. Vol. 1: 13908
Moscow International Film Festival Vol. 2: 4390
Moseley Award; Harry G. Vol. 1: 209
Moser Memorial Trophy; Mike Vol. 1: 6663
Mosher and Frederick C. Mosher Award; William E. Vol. 1: 3816
Mosher Award; William E. Mosher and Frederick C. Vol. 1: 3816
Most Active Woman Award Vol. 1: 12219
Most Ancient and Most Noble Order of the Thistle Vol. 2: 5596
The Most Beautiful and the Best Children's Books in Slovakia Vol. 2: 4438
Most Distinguished Order of St. Michael and St. George Vol. 2: 5597
Most Distinguished Project Award Vol. 1: 2077
Most Excellent Order of the British Empire Vol. 2: 5598
Most Honourable Order of the Bath Vol. 2: 5599
Most Improved Award
Advancing Canadian Entrepreneurship Vol. 1: 171
Mountainview Women's Nine Hole Golf Association Vol 1: 11992
Pulp and Paper Safety Association Vol 1: 15462
Most Improved Chapter Award Vol. 1: 9575
Most Improved Chapter of the Year Vol. 1: 12791
Most Improved Driver Vol. 1: 17235
Most Improved Driver Award Vol. 1: 17754
Most Improved Golfer Award Vol. 1: 12238
Most Improved Player Award Vol. 1: 12760
Most Influential Women in Sport and Physical Activity Vol. 1: 6218
Most Innovative Move Vol. 1: 10253
Most Meritorious Capture Award Vol. 2: 296
Most Noble Order of the Garter Vol. 2: 5600
Most Outstanding Abstract Award Vol. 1: 3579
Most Outstanding Contribution to Journalism Award Vol. 2: 561
Most Outstanding Female Administrator Vol. 2: 175
Most Outstanding Female Investigator Vol. 2: 176
Most Outstanding Female Leader Vol. 2: 177

Most Outstanding Player Award Vol. 1: 6514
Most Outstanding Volunteer Vol. 2: 423
Most Outstanding Wrestler Vol. 1: 13935
Most Realistic Tattoo Vol. 1: 13835
Most Sportsman-like Angler Vol. 1: 15809
Most Supportive Business Advisory Board Member of the Year Award Vol. 1: 172
Most Supportive Dean or Department Chair of the Year Award Vol. 1: 173
Most Unusual Move Vol. 1: 10254
Most Valuable Paper Vol. 2: 348
Most Valuable Player Vol. 1: 7798
Most Valuable Player Award
  National Basketball Association Vol. 1: 12761
  National Wheelchair Basketball Association Vol 1: 13904
Most Valuable Player in the Rose Bowl Vol. 1: 464
Most Versatile Horse Award Vol. 1: 7565
Mostofi Distinguished Service Award; F. K. Vol. 1: 17724
Mostra de Valencia, Palmero de Oro Vol. 2: 4525
Moten Award; Ollie B. Vol. 1: 1608
Mother/Father of the Year Award Vol. 1: 13465
Mother of All Vinegar Contest Vol. 1: 18537
Mother of the Year Vol. 1: 2807
Mothers and Daughters Award Vol. 1: 13164
Motley EMT of the Year Award; Robert E. Vol. 1: 12525
Motor Carrier Officer of the Year Vol. 1: 11733
Motorcycle Safety Foundation Awards Vol. 1: 11971
Motorock Trans-Am Tour Vol. 1: 17208
Mott Jr. Park Leadership Award; William Penn Vol. 1: 13533
Mott-Kappa Tau Alpha Research Award; Frank Luther Vol. 1: 18326
Mott-KTA Research Book Award; Frank Luther Vol. 1: 11099
Mott Scholarship; Gerald O. Vol. 1: 7981
Mountainfilm in Telluride Vol. 1: 11988
Mountbatten Medal Vol. 2: 6845
Mountbatten Premium Vol. 2: 6146
Movies of the Year Vol. 1: 2019
Moye; Prix Marcel Vol. 2: 1959
Moynihan Award; Senator Daniel Patrick Vol. 1: 5228
Moynihan Cup; Laura Vol. 1: 18175
Moynihan Medal for Lifetime Public Service; Daniel Patrick Vol. 1: 7420
Mozart Medal Vol. 2: 3447
Mozart Opera Prize Vol. 2: 830
Mozart-Prize Vol. 2: 4761
Mozart Scholarship; Frances England Intermediate Hayden and Vol. 1: 15860
Mozart Scholarship; Sister Geraldine Boyle Memorial Senior Hayden and Vol. 1: 15855
MPD Outstanding Young Engineer Award Vol. 1: 16354
MPT Benchmark Award Vol. 1: 2160
Mr. Blackwell's Hall of Fame Vol. 1: 11996
Mr. OX5 Vol. 1: 14766
Mr. Pi Kappa Phi Vol. 1: 15048
Mrazik-Cleaver Canadian Picture Book Award; Elizabeth Vol. 2: 4784
MRCA Foundation Scholarships Vol. 1: 11762
MRS Medal Vol. 1: 11596
MS-Prize Vol. 2: 1278
MSD AGVET AABP Award for Excellence in Preventive Veterinary Medicine Beef Cattle Vol. 1: 1026
MSD AGVET AABP Award for Excellence in Preventive Veterinary Medicine Dairy Cattle Vol. 1: 1027
MSI Annual Doctoral Dissertation Proposal Award Vol. 1: 11551
MTNA National Student Composition Contest Vol. 1: 12037
Mu Phi Epsilon Annual Grants and Scholarships Vol. 1: 12000
Mu Phi Epsilon International Competition Vol. 1: 11998
Mudd Award for Studies in Basic Microbiology; Stuart Vol. 2: 551
Mudge Citation; Isadore Gilbert Vol. 1: 2691
Mudge - R. R. Bowker Award; Isadore Gilbert Vol. 1: 2691
Muellen Whirly-Girls Scholarship; Doris Vol. 1: 18724
Mueller Human Services Award; Sister Mary Lea Vol. 1: 7534
Mueller Lecture Award; James I. Vol. 1: 1489
Mueller Medal Vol. 2: 134
Muhlmann Prize; Maria and Eric Vol. 1: 5485
Muir Award; John
  John Muir Trust Vol. 2: 6342
  Sierra Club Vol 1: 16018
Muir Editor's Award; John B. Vol. 1: 12304
Mullard Award Vol. 2: 6913
Mullen National Arts and Humanities Award; Dorothy Vol. 1: 13593
Muller Award Vol. 2: 4064
Muller Jr. Undergraduate Business Plan Competition; John H. Vol. 1: 5620
Muller Lectureship; Hugo Vol. 2: 6976
Mulligan Education Medal; James H. Vol. 1: 9788
Mullins Award; Nicholas C. Vol. 1: 16425
Mullins Memorial Trophy; Thomas H. Vol. 1: 10895
Multi-Event Outstanding Women Award Vol. 1: 18443
Multicultural Leadership and Involvement Vol. 1: 12936
Multidisciplinary Design Optimization Award Vol. 1: 2392
Multidisclipinary Team Award Vol. 1: 10689
Multinational Force and Observers Medal Vol. 1: 8115
Mumford Prize; Erika Vol. 1: 14046
Mumm International Award; Norbert Gerbier- Vol. 2: 4935
Munasinghe Memorial Award; T. P. de S. Vol. 2: 4558
Mundt Congress Trophy; Senator Karl E. Vol. 1: 13243
Mungo Park Medal Vol. 2: 6893
Munich International Filmschool Festival Vol. 2: 2138
Munich International Music Competition of the Broadcasting Stations of the Federal Republic of Germany (ARD) Vol. 2: 2311
Municipal Chapter of Toronto IODE Children's Book Award Vol. 1: 10857
Munson Aquatic Conservation Exhibitory Award Vol. 1: 4498
Munson Award; Ida Vol. 1: 2212
Munson Jr. Award; R.W. Vol. 1: 2212
Muntendamprijs; Prof. Dr. P. Vol. 2: 3506
Murchison Award Vol. 2: 6771
Murchison Medal Vol. 2: 5933
Murdoch Award; Connie Vol. 1: 16092
Murie Award; Olaus and Margaret Vol. 1: 18746
Murofushi Research Award; Takeshi Vol. 1: 10240
Murphree Award in Industrial and Engineering Chemistry; E. V. Vol. 1: 1567
Murphy Award for Excellence in Copy Editing; John Vol. 1: 17466
Murphy Award; Glenn Vol. 1: 3662
Murphy Award; John Killam Vol. 1: 7139
Murphy Excellence in Teaching Award; Mother Evelyn Vol. 1: 8252
Murphy Memorial Award; Jack Vol. 1: 13165
Murphy Prize; Forbes Vol. 2: 6012
Murphy Scholarship; Joseph Vol. 1: 14066
Murray Award for Outstanding Philanthropist; Paschal Vol. 1: 5165
Murray Award; Henry A. Vol. 1: 16378
Murray Award; John Courtney Vol. 1: 7167
Murray Award; Robert J. Vol. 1: 15993
Murray Distinguished Educator Award; Grover E. Vol. 1: 1220
Murray - Green Award Vol. 1: 2001
Murray-Green-Meany-Kirkland Award for Community Service Vol. 1: 2001
Murray Medal Vol. 2: 4123
Murrell Award; Hywel Vol. 2: 5798
Murrow Award; Edward R.
  Corporation for Public Broadcasting Vol. 1: 7829
  Overseas Press Club of America Vol 1: 14761
Murrow Awards; Edward R. Vol. 1: 15535
Murtagh Memorial Prize; Lillian Vol. 1: 2149
Museum Acquisition Award Vol. 1: 16100
Museum Directors Award Vol. 1: 587
Museum of Haiku Literature Awards Vol. 1: 9238
Museums and Schools Partnership Award Vol. 1: 6403
Musgrave Medals Vol. 2: 3146
Music Award Vol. 1: 13166
Music Awards Vol. 2: 6865
Music Camper Citation Vol. 1: 12741
Musical Freestyle Awards Vol. 1: 17888
Musical Theater Award Vol. 1: 11117
Musician of the Year Vol. 2: 5982
Musicians Achievement Award Vol. 1: 8325
Musicians Benevolent Fund Awards Vol. 2: 6451
Muskett Award; Nevva Vol. 2: 6606
Muskie Distinguished Public Service Award; Edmund S. Vol. 1: 7228
Musselman Inspirational Swimmer Award; Dawn Vol. 1: 14776
Mustang Spirit Award Vol. 1: 11539
Mustard Seed Awards Vol. 1: 12867
MUTA Safety Certificate Vol. 2: 6531
Muteau; Prix General Vol. 2: 1686
MVSA Goue Medalje Vol. 2: 4177
MVSA Silwer Medalje vir Navorsing Vol. 2: 4178
Myer Award; Haydn Vol. 1: 7676
Myers Award for Applied Research in the Workplace; M. Scott Vol. 1: 16294
Myers Award; Paul W. Vol. 1: 292
Myers Man of the Year Award; Howdy Vol. 1: 17968
Myers Writers Award; Cordelia Vol. 1: 2955
Myhre Awards; Paul Vol. 1: 18325
Myrdal Award for Science Vol. 1: 1983
Myrdal Government Award; Alva and Gunnar Vol. 1: 1984

Award Index

Myrdal Human Service Delivery Award; Gunnar Vol. 1: 1985
Myrdal Practice Award; Alva and Gunnar Vol. 1: 1985
Mythopoeic Fantasy Awards Vol. 1: 12059
Mythopoeic Scholarship Awards Vol. 1: 12060
NAADD Postgraduate Scholarships Vol. 1: 12387
NAAFI/AFF Rose Bowl Vol. 2: 5066
Nabokov Award Vol. 1: 14899
NABS Research Grants Vol. 1: 14269
NAC Orchestra Association Award Vol. 1: 12284
NACBS-Huntington Library Fellowship Vol. 1: 14286
NACD - Allis Chalmers Conservation Teacher Awards Vol. 1: 12470
NACD Deutz/Allis Chalmers Conservation District Awards Vol. 1: 12469
Nachison Award; Judith Vol. 1: 14097
Nachtsheim Award; John Vol. 1: 5446
NACMA "Best of" Awards Vol. 1: 12452
NACMA Hall of Fame Vol. 1: 12453
NACMA/Host Communications Marketer of the Year Vol. 1: 12454
NACMA Postgraduate Scholarship Vol. 1: 12455
Nadai Medal Vol. 1: 4153
Nadebaum Distinguished Service Award; Oertel Vol. 2: 45
NADEO Annual Award for Ecumenism Vol. 1: 12512
Nadi Prize; Yunus Vol. 2: 4964
Nadi Yarismasi; Yunus Vol. 2: 4964
Nadine Williams Scholarship Vol. 1: 12000
NAE/Spencer Postdoctoral Fellowship Program Vol. 1: 12124
NAEA Art Educator of the Year Vol. 1: 12268
NAEA State/Province Newsletter Editor Award Vol. 1: 12278
Naegelin Dramatic Interpretation Contest; Lanny D. Vol. 1: 13244
Nagel Most Improved Chapter Award; R. H. Vol. 1: 17401
Nagroda Zwiazku Kompozytorow Polskich Vol. 2: 4039
Naguib Memorial Prize; Moshen Vol. 2: 6729
Nagurski Award; Bronko Vol. 1: 8798
Naha Memorial Medal; Professor K. Vol. 2: 2697
NAHWW/Stanley Awards (Stanleys) Vol. 1: 12554
NAIA Academic All-America Awards Vol. 1: 12575
NAIA - SIDA All-Sports Championship Awards Vol. 1: 12581
NAIOP Man of the Year Award Vol. 1: 12572
Naipaul Memorial Prize; Shiva Vol. 2: 7235
Naismith Award; Frances Pomeroy Vol. 1: 12072
Naismith College Coach of the Year Vol. 1: 5499
Naismith College Officials of the Year Vol. 1: 5500
Naismith College Players of the Year Vol. 1: 5501
Naismith High School Prep Player of the Year Awards Vol. 1: 5502
Naismith Outstanding Contribution to Basketball Award Vol. 1: 5503
Naismith Trophy Vol. 1: 5501
Naito Kinen Kagaku Shinko Sho Vol. 2: 3296
Najkrajsia a najlepsia detska kniha jari, leta, jesene a zimy na Slovensku Vol. 2: 4438
Najmann Award Vol. 2: 2943
Nakanishi Prize Vol. 1: 1568
Nakkula Award for Police Reporting; Al Vol. 1: 18267
NAMBA Hall of Fame Vol. 1: 14309
NAMIC Engineering Safety Award Vol. 1: 3859
Nance Award; James J. Vol. 1: 14802
Nannidar Award for Excellence Vol. 2: 2548
Nansen Award for Young Scientists; Peter Vol. 1: 18902
Nansen Medal Vol. 2: 3456
Nansen Medal; Fridtjof Vol. 2: 1776
Nansen Refugee Award Vol. 2: 3456
Napapijri Award Vol. 2: 3017
Napier Sailing Club Trophy Vol. 2: 5910
Napier - Shaw Bronze Medal Vol. 2: 5639
Napoleon; Grands Prix de la Fondation Vol. 2: 1808
Napolitano Award; Luigi Vol. 2: 1867
Napolitano Book Award; Luigi Vol. 2: 1865
Narlikar Memorial Lecture; Professor Vishnu Vasudeva Vol. 2: 2698
Narrative Screenwriting Award Vol. 1: 7387
NASAR Service Award Vol. 1: 12356
NASCAR Championships Vol. 1: 12364
NASCAR Grand National Championship Vol. 1: 8069
NASCAR Mechanics Hall of Fame; Western Auto Vol. 1: 10526
NASCAR Winston Cup Series Stock Car Race; Daytona 500 Vol. 1: 8066
NASDAQ National Teaching Awards Vol. 1: 13037
Nash Award; Ruth Lopin
Oratorio Society of New York Vol. 1: 14632
Oratorio Society of New York Vol 1: 14633
Nash Gold Medal; Kevin Vol. 2: 6293
Nash History Journal Prize Vol. 1: 14980
Nashville Film Festival Vol. 1: 12080
Nashville Public Television Human Spirit Award Vol. 1: 12080
Nashville Songwriters Association International Awards Vol. 1: 12082
NASPAA/ASPA Distinguished Research Award Vol. 1: 3817
NASPAA Public Courage Award Vol. 1: 12652
NASSTRAC Awards Program Vol. 1: 12084
Nast Award; Thomas Vol. 1: 14761
Natali Prize for Journalists; Lorenzo Vol. 2: 3029
Natelson Senior Investigation Award; Samuel Vol. 1: 881
Nath Memorial Lecture; Professor Vishwa Vol. 2: 2699
Nathan Award for Dramatic Criticism; George Jean Vol. 1: 12086
Nathan Award in Hematology/Oncology; David G. Vol. 1: 16372
National 100 Mile Award Vol. 1: 1959
National Academy of Sciences Award Vol. 2: 4118
National Academy of Sciences Award in Microbiology Vol. 1: 12169
National Academy of Western Art Exhibition Vol. 1: 13068
National Achievement Award Vol. 1: 12594
National Advisor of the Year Award Vol. 1: 432
National Aeronautical Prize Vol. 2: 2526
National Agricultural Award Vol. 2: 6667
National Amputee Golf Champion Vol. 1: 12239
National Appreciation Award Vol. 1: 12595
National Architecture Awards Vol. 2: 627
National Art Educator Award Vol. 1: 12268
National Art Honor Society Sponsor Award Vol. 1: 12269
National Arts Merit Awards Vol. 2: 7437
National Assessment Awards Vol. 2: 709
National Association of Shopfitters Design Vol. 2: 6459
National Athletic Director of the Year Vol. 1: 13008
National Audio Book of the Year Award Vol. 2: 576
National Award
American Cancer Society Vol. 1: 1443
Kennedy Center American College Theater Festival Vol 1: 11118
National Water Safety Congress Vol 1: 13888
National Award for Career Achievements in Medical Education Vol. 1: 16696
National Award for Demonstrated Leadership Vol. 1: 14852
National Award for Engineering Achievement Vol. 1: 6438
National Award for Media Excellence Vol. 1: 13594
National Award for Outstanding Achievement in Metropolitan Transportation Planning - MPOs Over 200000 Vol. 1: 5229
National Award for Outstanding Technical Merit in Metropolitan Transportation Planning - MPOs Over 200000 Vol. 1: 5230
National Award for Outstanding Technical Merit in Metropolitan Transportation Planning - MPOs Under 200000 Vol. 1: 5231
National Award for the Protection of Environment Vol. 2: 1170
National Award in Landscape Architecture Vol. 2: 246
National Awards Vol. 2: 7320
National Awards Vol. 1: 13244
National Awards Contest Vol. 1: 5000
National Awards for Education Reporting Vol. 1: 8396
National Awards for Scholarship in Medical Education Vol. 1: 16697
National Awards for Teaching Economics Vol. 1: 13037
National Awards Program
AMVETS - American Veterans Vol. 1: 4518
Canadian Band Association Vol 1: 6326
Freedoms Foundation at Valley Forge Vol 1: 8880
OX5 Aviation Pioneers Vol 1: 14766
National Back Pain Association Medal Vol. 2: 5158
National Ballet School Foundation Scholarship Vol. 1: 18853
National Band Award Vol. 1: 6326
National Book Awards Vol. 1: 12785
National Book Critics Circle Awards Vol. 1: 12783
National Book Service Teacher-Librarian of the Year Award Vol. 1: 6696
National Bowling Hall of Fame and Museum Vol. 1: 10276
National Breeders Award Vol. 1: 17934
National Business Calendar Awards Vol. 2: 5421

National Career Award Competition
National Society of Arts and Letters Vol. 1: 13729
National Society of Arts and Letters Vol 1: 13730
National Society of Arts and Letters Vol 1: 13731
National Society of Arts and Letters Vol 1: 13732
National Society of Arts and Letters Vol 1: 13733
National Society of Arts and Letters Vol 1: 13734
National Champion
Accordion Society of Australia Vol. 2: 27
U.S. Sports Acrobatics Vol 1: 18133
National Champion Bronze Statue Vol. 1: 10626
National Champions
American Darts Organization Vol. 1: 1900
San Juan 21 Class Association Vol 1: 15839
National Championship
American Baseball Coaches Association Vol. 1: 1387
American Motorcyclist Association Vol 1: 2811
Rhodes 19 Class Association Vol 1: 15660
National Championship Awards Vol. 1: 824
National Championship Cup Finals Vol. 2: 5775
National Championship Regatta Vol. 1: 9995
National Championships
American Endurance Ride Conference Vol. 1: 1960
Canadian Sport Parachuting Association Vol 1: 7042
National Collegiate Athletic Association Vol 1: 12903
National Rifle Association of America Vol 1: 13647
Scottish Bowling Association Vol 2: 7079
United States Curling Association Vol 1: 17790
USA Badminton Vol 1: 18376
USA Cycling Vol 1: 18382
National Chapter of the Year Vol. 1: 17603
National Chef of the Year Vol. 1: 6447
National Chicken Council Broiler Research Award Vol. 1: 15180
National Chopin Piano Competition Vol. 1: 7373
National Citation Vol. 1: 11957
National Citation Awards Vol. 1: 13617
National City and Regional Magazine Awards Vol. 1: 7426
National Client Award Vol. 2: 6224
National Club Championship Award (Men) Vol. 1: 18053
National Club Championship Award (Women) Vol. 1: 18054
National Club Sevens Championship Award (Men) Vol. 1: 18055
National Coach of the Year Vol. 1: 12912
National Coin Week Vol. 1: 2905
National College Championship Award Vol. 1: 18056
National College Championship Award (Women) Vol. 1: 18057
National College Football Champions Vol. 1: 12904
National Collegiate and Scholastic Swimming Trophy Vol. 1: 13388
National Collegiate Trophy Vol. 1: 7545
National CommanderFs Award Vol. 1: 4640
National Community Service Award
Jewish Theological Seminary Vol. 1: 11010
National Association of Negro Business and Professional Women's Clubs Vol 1: 12596
National Company Representative of the Year Vol. 1: 12623
National Competition Vol. 1: 1037
National Competition in Organ Improvisation Vol. 1: 2148
National Composers' Competition Vol. 1: 10708
National Congressional Award Vol. 1: 13595
National Conservation Award Vol. 2: 5143
National Contest of Medical Research Works Vol. 2: 1195
National Convention Awards Program Vol. 1: 3459
National Convention Internship Program Vol. 1: 4878
National Corn Yield Contest Vol. 1: 12949
National Corporate Humanitarian Award Vol. 1: 13596
National Council Auditions Vol. 1: 11710
National Courage Award Vol. 2: 2856
National Course Rally Manufacturer Champion Vol. 1: 17212
National Credit Executive of the Year Vol. 1: 12504
National Cup Boys Under 18 (Boys National Championship) Vol. 1: 18176
National Cup Girls Under 17 Cup Vol. 1: 18175
National Cup Girls Under 18 (Girls National Championship) Vol. 1: 18177
National Defense Service Medal Vol. 1: 8116
National Diploma of the Society of Floristry Vol. 2: 7195
National Distinguished Friends of Extension Award Vol. 1: 8516
National Distinguished Principal Award Vol. 1: 12515
National Distinguished Professional Award Vol. 1: 13597
National Distinguished Service Award
Canadian Mental Health Association Vol. 1: 6717
National Rehabilitation Counseling Association Vol 1: 13618
National Distinguished Service Ruby Award Vol. 1: 8517
National Division Art Educator Award Vol. 1: 12270
National Division Art Educator of the Year Vol. 1: 12270
National Editor's Award Vol. 1: 1114
National Endowment for the Arts Programs Vol. 1: 13102
National Endowment for the Humanities Grant Programs Vol. 1: 13112
National Endowment for the Humanities Long-Term Fellowships Vol. 1: 819
National Engineering Award Vol. 1: 1091
National Equal Employment/Affirmative Action Exemplary Practices Award Vol. 1: 3815
National Excellence Awards for Engineering Journalism Vol. 2: 519
National Exhibition of Rosemaling in the Norwegian Tradition Vol. 1: 18507
National Exhibition of Weaving in the Norwegian Tradition Vol. 1: 18508
National Exhibition of Woodworking in the Norwegian Tradition Vol. 1: 18509
National Faculty Advisor Award Vol. 1: 2393
National Family and Consumer Sciences Home Economics Teacher of the Year Award Vol. 1: 1098
National Federation of Music Clubs Awards and Scholarships Vol. 1: 13131
National Federation of the Blind Scholarship Program Vol. 1: 13191
National Field Archery Championship Vol. 1: 13195
National Film Board Award for Best Short Film Vol. 1: 17561
National Film Board Kathleen Shannon Award Vol. 1: 19078
National Film Board of Canada Prize for Creativity Vol. 1: 10424
National Film Board of Canada Public Prize Vol. 1: 14739
National Fishing Week Writing Award Vol. 1: 14755
National Food and Energy Council Electric Technology Award Vol. 1: 3860
National Footbag Championships Vol. 1: 18941
National Football League Scholar-Athlete Award Vol. 1: 13215
National Forensic Association Awards Vol. 1: 13235
National Fresenius Award Vol. 1: 15002
National Genealogical Society Quarterly Award for Excellence Vol. 1: 13278
National Genealogy Hall of Fame Vol. 1: 13279
National Geographic Society Award Vol. 2: 5267
National Gold Honor Medal Vol. 1: 3510
National Gold Pin Awards Vol. 1: 494
National Goodwill Worker of the Year Vol. 1: 9127
National Graphic Design Awards Vol. 2: 3713
National Guard Association of the United States Awards Program Vol. 1: 13301
National Headliner Awards Vol. 1: 13325
National Health Information Awards Vol. 1: 9302
National Health Law Moot Court Competition Vol. 1: 7208
National Health Leadership Award Vol. 1: 7910
National Heritage Fellowships Vol. 1: 13106
National High Point Awards Vol. 1: 12462
National High School Championships Award Vol. 1: 18058
National High School Finals Rodeo Vol. 1: 13347
National High School Flute Choir Vol. 1: 13200
National High School Journalism Teacher of the Year Vol. 1: 8264
National High School Journalist of the Year Vol. 1: 11052
National High School Sports Hall of Fame Awards Vol. 1: 13137
National High School Yearbook Adviser of the Year Vol. 1: 11053
National Homebrew Competition Awards Vol. 1: 2284
National Honor Award Vol. 1: 1437
National Honor Society Scholarship Program Vol. 1: 12658
National Honorary Member Award Vol. 1: 10866
National Honours and Awards Vol. 1: 313
National Housing Hall of Fame Vol. 1: 12558

National Housing Quality Award Vol. 1: 15282
National Human Relations Award Vol. 1: 2587
National Humane Education Achievement Award Vol. 1: 12340
National Humanitarian Award Vol. 1: 13598
National Humanities Medal Vol. 1: 13113
National Impact Award Vol. 1: 13367
National Institute of Insurance International Prizes Vol. 2: 2971
National Inventor of the Year Vol. 1: 9967
National Inventor's Hall of Fame Vol. 1: 18028
National Iqbal Award Vol. 2: 3919
National Jewish Book Award - Autobiography/ Memoir Vol. 1: 10972
National Jewish Book Award - Children's Literature Vol. 1: 10973
National Jewish Book Award - Children's Picture Book Vol. 1: 10974
National Jewish Book Award - Fiction Vol. 1: 10975
National Jewish Book Award - Holocaust Vol. 1: 10976
National Jewish Book Award in Contemporary Jewish Life and Practice Vol. 1: 10977
National Jewish Book Award in the Visual Arts Vol. 1: 10978
National Jewish Book Award - Israel Vol. 1: 10979
National Jewish Book Award - Jewish History Vol. 1: 10980
National Jewish Book Award - Jewish Thought Vol. 1: 10981
National Jewish Book Award - Scholarship Vol. 1: 10982
National Jewish Book Award - Sephardic Studies Vol. 1: 10983
National Journal Award Vol. 1: 1115
National Journalism Award Vol. 1: 5641
National Journalism Awards Vol. 1: 4686
National Junior Art Honor Society Sponsor Award Vol. 1: 12271
National Junior Team MVP Vol. 1: 5678
National Junior Tennis League Chapter of the Year Award Vol. 1: 18156
National Juried Print Exhibition Awards Vol. 1: 9540
National Kind Teacher Award Vol. 1: 12341
National Lacrosse Hall of Fame Vol. 1: 17985
National Landscape Awards Vol. 2: 5245
National Law Enforcement Saved by the Belt/ Air Bag Awards Program Vol. 1: 10172
National Leadership
Jobs for America's Graduates Vol. 1: 11016
Simon Wiesenthal Center Vol 1: 16068
National Leadership Award
Leukemia and Lymphoma Society Vol. 1: 11308
National Council for Continuing Education and Training Vol 1: 12958
National League All-Star Team Vol. 1: 17177
National League Most Valuable Player Vol. 1: 5681
National League Player of the Year
England Basketball Vol. 2: 5776
Sporting News Vol 1: 17178
National League Rookie of the Year Vol. 1: 17179
National Legislative Award Vol. 1: 15584
National Level Medal Vol. 1: 4641
National Limited Distance Mileage Champion Vol. 1: 1961
National Limited Distance Mileage Championship Vol. 1: 1960
National Literary Award Vol. 1: 13599
National Literary Contest Vol. 1: 4595
National Living Treasures Award Vol. 2: 3974
National Looking Glass Poetry Competition for a Single Poem Vol. 1: 15447
National Magazine Awards
American Society of Magazine Editors Vol. 1: 4114
National Magazine Awards Foundation Vol 1: 13420
National Mass Media Award Vol. 1: 2588
National Materials Advancement Award Vol. 1: 8671
National Mature Media Awards Program Vol. 1: 11621
National Medal Vol. 2: 219
National Medal of Arts Vol. 1: 13107
National Medal of Technology Vol. 1: 17811
National Media Awards
American College of Allergy, Asthma and Immunology Vol. 1: 1610
American Society of Colon and Rectal Surgeons Vol 1: 3997
National Member of the Year Award Vol. 1: 433
National Merit Award Vol. 1: 13383
National Meritorious Award Vol. 1: 4463
National Mileage Championship Vol. 1: 1960
National Mileage Championship Vol. 1: 1962
National Military Intelligence Association Annual Awards Vol. 1: 13452
National Milk Producers Federation Graduate Student Paper Presentation Contest in Dairy Production Vol. 1: 1885
National Minority Supplier Development Council Awards Vol. 1: 13458
National Minority Supplier Development Council Conference Vol. 1: 13458
National Model Car Racing Champion Vol. 2: 5463
National Multihull Championship - Alter Cup Vol. 1: 18066
National Music Festival Vol. 1: 8629
The National Music Festival Vol. 1: 13473
National Newspaper Awards Vol. 1: 6759
National Officials Outstanding Service Award Vol. 1: 18431
National Offshore Championship - Lloyd Phoenix Trophy Vol. 1: 18067
National One-Act Play Contest Vol. 1: 149
National One-Act Playwriting Contest Vol. 1: 8284
National Order of Merit Vol. 2: 3428
National Order of the Southern Cross Vol. 2: 1112
National Organization on Disability Award; AAHSA/ Vol. 1: 1119
National Outdoor Book Awards Vol. 1: 13514
National Outstanding Advisor Award Vol. 1: 17403
National Outstanding Young Farmer Vol. 1: 2139
National Paperboard Packaging Competition Vol. 1: 14841
National Peace Essay Contest Vol. 1: 17960
National Person of the Year Award Vol. 1: 12958
National Philatelic Society Queen Elizabeth II Silver Jubilee Trophy Vol. 2: 6535
National Philharmonic Award Vol. 2: 4002
National Poetry Competition Vol. 2: 6541
National Police Award for Traffic Safety Vol. 1: 6126
National Police Shooting Championships Vol. 1: 13648
National Post Annual Report Awards Vol. 1: 7846
National Post Awards for Business in the Arts Vol. 1: 7847
National Postal Museum Medal Vol. 2: 6535
National Preservation Honor Awards Vol. 1: 13871
National President's Award
American Association of Healthcare Administrative Management Vol. 1: 1116
Australian Institute of Quantity Surveyors Vol 2: 265
National President's Awards Vol. 1: 5184
National Print and Drawing Exhibition Vol. 1: 11850
National Print Exhibition Vol. 1: 16517
National Private Fleet Safety Awards Vol. 1: 15244
National Prize for Advertising Vol. 2: 756
National Prize for Consulting Vol. 2: 757
National Prize for the Most Beautiful Book Vol. 2: 758
National Prize of Science and Technology Vol. 2: 7427
National Prize of the President of the Republic Vol. 2: 2972
National PRO Rally of the Year Vol. 1: 17212
National Public Citizen of the Year Vol. 1: 12662
National Public Relations Achievement Award Vol. 1: 5640
National Public Service Awards Vol. 1: 12137
National Putting Championship Vol. 1: 15349
National Quality Dealer Award Vol. 1: 13365
National Radio Award Vol. 1: 12435
National Ranking Award Vol. 1: 13092
National Recognition Award Vol. 1: 1117
National Recognition Medal Vol. 1: 8878
National Recreational Fisheries Awards Vol. 1: 8713
National Recycling Coalition Annual Awards Vol. 1: 13604
National Research Competition Vol. 1: 12961
National Research Service Awards Vol. 1: 13377
National Rifle and Pistol Championship Trophy Match Vol. 1: 17792
National Scholar-Athlete Awards Vol. 1: 13215
National Scholarship Vol. 2: 3269
National Scholarships Vol. 1: 4490
National Scholastic Award Vol. 1: 15585
National Scholastic Press Association Pacemaker Awards Vol. 1: 14222
National School Library Media Program of the Year Award Vol. 1: 1281
National School Plant Manager of the Year Award Vol. 1: 3522
National Scrabble Championship Vol. 1: 13688
National Sculpture Competition Vol. 1: 13693
National Security Medal Vol. 1: 13695
National Service Award
Chamber Music America Vol. 1: 7274
Recreation Vehicle Industry Association Vol 1: 15586

Women Marines Association Vol 1: 18842
National Service Medal Vol. 1: 8878
National Ski Hall of Fame Vol. 1: 18104
National Ski Safety Award Vol. 1: 6872
National Skillbuild Competition Vol. 1: 15652
National Small Business Person of the Year Vol. 1: 18117
National Small Works Exhibition Vol. 1: 17597
National SMLTSA Virology Prize Vol. 2: 4247
National Smokey Bear Awards Vol. 1: 8705
National Soccer Hall of Fame Award Vol. 1: 18124
National Social Worker of the Year Vol. 1: 12663
National Society of Artists Awards Vol. 1: 13727
National Softball Hall of Fame Vol. 1: 523
National Sportscaster and Sportswriter of Year Vol. 1: 13804
National Sportsmanship Award Vol. 1: 18068
National Student Advertising Competition (NSAC) Vol. 1: 768
National Student Award for Excellence Vol. 1: 13725
National Student Awards Vol. 1: 5955
National Student Design Competition Vol. 1: 4104
National Student Playwriting Award Vol. 1: 11118
National Student Production Awards Competition Vol. 1: 12792
National Student Teacher/Intern of the Year Vol. 1: 11093
National Superintendent of the Year Award Vol. 1: 1270
National Supplier Award Vol. 2: 6225
National Sweepstakes Champion Vol. 1: 14348
National Take Pride in America Award Vol. 1: 536
National Target Championships Vol. 1: 12256
National Teacher of the Year Vol. 1: 7880
National TEAMS (Tests of Engineering Aptitude, Mathematics, and Science) Competition Vol. 1: 11065
National Ten-Minute Play Contest Vol. 1: 149
National Territorial Union Championship Award Vol. 1: 18059
National Torchbearer Award Vol. 1: 2613
National Touring Rally Manufacturer Champion Vol. 1: 17212
National Touring Rally of the Year Vol. 1: 17212
National Touring Rally of the Year Award Vol. 1: 17209
National Track and Field Hall of Fame Vol. 1: 18450
National Training and Development Awards Vol. 2: 5422
National Translation Award Vol. 1: 2704
National Translation Prize Vol. 1: 2705
National Transportation Award Vol. 1: 13085
National Travel Marketing Awards Vol. 1: 17589
National Treasure Award Vol. 1: 19074
National Trophy Vol. 1: 13092
National Turkey Federation Research Award Vol. 1: 15181
National Vaulting Championship Awards Vol. 1: 4401
National Vehicle Graphics Design Awards Vol. 1: 15245
National Voluntary Service Award Vol. 1: 13600
National Water and Energy Conservation Award Vol. 1: 10900
National Westminster Bank Prize Vol. 2: 6029
National Wildlife Photo Contest Vol. 1: 13910
National Wildlife Week Awards Vol. 1: 7068
National Wohelo Order Award Vol. 1: 6076
National Women's Hall of Fame Vol. 1: 13918
National Works on Paper Exhibition Vol. 1: 11850
National Young Artist Competition Vol. 1: 11754
National Young Artists Competition in Organ Performance Vol. 1: 2149
National Young Astronomer Award Vol. 1: 5476
National Youth Achievement Awards Vol. 1: 2330
National Youth Award Vol. 1: 12597
National Youth Cup Boys Vol. 1: 18178
The Nations Cup Vol. 2: 4836
NATJA Awards Competition Vol. 1: 14352
NATO Awards Vol. 1: 12708
Natta; Medaglia d'oro Giulio Vol. 2: 3104
NATTS Hall of Fame Vol. 1: 7098
Natural World Book Prize Vol. 2: 6495
Nature Conservation Officer of the Year Vol. 2: 4225
Nature Division Awards Vol. 1: 15028
Naude Medal; S. Meiring Vol. 2: 4243
Naumann - August Thienemann Medal; Einar Vol. 1: 10258
Naumburg Chamber Music Award Vol. 1: 13994
Naumburg International Competition Vol. 1: 13995
Nauta Award on Pharmacochemistry Vol. 2: 772
Nautica/U.S. SAILING Youth Championship Vol. 1: 18079
Naval and Maritime Photo Contest Vol. 1: 18012
Naval Reserve Award Vol. 1: 13452
Naval Reserve Medal Vol. 1: 8117
Navarre Medal Award; Maison G. de Vol. 1: 16631
Navigation Award (California Maritime Academy) Vol. 1: 9917
Navy Expeditionary Medal Vol. 1: 8118
Navy Occupation Service Medal - Navy-Marine Corps-Coast Guard Vol. 1: 8119
NAWL Charitable Trust Essay Competition Vol. 1: 12713
Nax Trophy Vol. 1: 2995
Naylor Prize and Lectureship Vol. 2: 6402
Naylor Working Writer Fellowship; Phyllis Vol. 1: 14900
NBA All-Rookie Team Vol. 1: 12764
NBA All-Star Team Vol. 1: 17180
NBA Coach of the Year Vol. 1: 17181
NBA Player of the Year Vol. 1: 17182
NBA Rookie of the Year Vol. 1: 17183
NCCPB Genetics and Plant Breeding Award for Industry Vol. 1: 7982
NCEA Merit Award Vol. 1: 12864
NCLA/SIRS Intellectual Freedom Award Vol. 1: 14365
NCTE/Prentice-Hall Leadership Development Award Vol. 1: 7563
NCUCA Scholarhip Vol. 1: 14376
NEA Books Across America Library Books Awards Vol. 1: 14006
NEA Challenge America Fast-Track Review Grants Vol. 1: 13108
NEA Fine Arts Grants Vol. 1: 14007
NEA Grants for Arts Projects/Access to Artistic Excellence Vol. 1: 13109
NEA/TCG Career Development Program for Designers Vol. 1: 17507
NEA/TCG Career Development Program for Directors Vol. 1: 17508
Neal National Business Journalism Awards; Jesse H. Vol. 1: 1428
Neatby en Histoire des Femmes; Le Prix Hilda Vol. 1: 6561
Neatby Prize; Hilda Vol. 1: 6561
Neave Research Fellowship; Airey Vol. 2: 5016
Neave Scholarship; Airey Vol. 2: 5016
Nebraska Hospice Volunteer of the Year Vol. 1: 14012
Nebraska State Poetry Society Award Vol. 1: 13167
Nebula Awards Vol. 1: 15923
NECCC Medal Vol. 1: 9186
Necho Award Vol. 2: 6829
Neel Medal; Louis Vol. 2: 1777
Nefesh B'Nefesh Award for the Story of Aliyah Vol. 1: 2599
Neff Distinguished Service Award; Thelma J. Vol. 1: 411
Nehru Award for International Understanding; Jawaharlal Vol. 2: 2591
Nehru Birth Centenary Award; Jawaharlal Vol. 2: 2745
Nehru Birth Centenary Lectures; Jawaharlal Vol. 2: 2700
Nehru Birth Centenary Medal; Jawaharlal Vol. 2: 2701
Nehru Birth Centenary Visiting Fellowship; Jawaharlal Vol. 2: 2702
Nehru Literacy Award Vol. 2: 2589
Neighborhood Greening Projects Vol. 1: 8974
Neil Prize for Innovation in Drug Development; Gary Vol. 1: 3611
Neill Humfeld Award Vol. 2: 6311
Neill Medal Vol. 2: 6998
Neill Memorial Prize in Music; Philip Vol. 2: 3877
Neitz Junior Medal/Senior Medal; W.O. Vol. 2: 4219
Nelson Award; Byron Vol. 1: 9119
Nelson Award for Diagnosis of Yield-Limiting Factors; Werner L. Vol. 1: 3875
Nelson Engineering Award; Carl E. Vol. 1: 258
Nelson Fellowship; Morley Vol. 1: 15562
Nelson Fly Tying Teaching Award; Dick Vol. 1: 8645
Nelson Prize; William Vol. 1: 15624
Nelson Service Award; Harold E. Vol. 1: 16685
Nelvana Grand Prize for Independent Short Animation Vol. 1: 14740
Nemet Award Vol. 2: 5326
NEMLA Book Prize Vol. 1: 14388
Nemmers Prize in Economics; Erwin Plein Vol. 1: 14407
Nemmers Prize in Mathematics; Frederic Esser Vol. 1: 14408

Award Index

NEMRA Manufacturer of the Year Vol. 1: 13096
Nemzetkoezi Liszt Hanglemez Nagydij Vol. 2: 2496
Nene Award Vol. 1: 9285
Neonatal Education Award Vol. 1: 703
Neptune Award Vol. 1: 10728
Ner Tamid (Eternal Light) Emblem Vol. 1: 13394
Nerken Award; Albert Vol. 1: 5595
Nernst - Haber - Bodenstein-Preis Vol. 2: 2160
Nero Award Vol. 1: 18802
Neruda; Premio Pablo Vol. 2: 1168
Neruda Prize for Poetry; Pablo Vol. 1: 14240
NESA Awards Vol. 2: 2459
NESA Community Service Awards Vol. 2: 2459
Nesburn Playwright Award; Dr. Henry and Lilian Vol. 1: 5744
NESDA Awards Vol. 1: 13098
Ness Award Vol. 2: 6772
Ness Book Award; Frederic W. Vol. 1: 5028
Ness Memorial Award; John Harrison Vol. 1: 8985
Nessim Habif Prize Vol. 2: 2002
Nessyahu Prize in Mathematics; Haim Vol. 2: 2914
Nester Award; William R. Vol. 1: 15042
Nestle Smarties Book Prize Vol. 2: 5190
NETA Special Service Award Vol. 1: 13121
Netherlands Fund for Chemistry Prize Vol. 2: 3658
Netherthorpe Award Vol. 2: 5947
Network Affiliate Sales Achievement Award Vol. 1: 6031
Network/Syndicated Personality of the Year Vol. 1: 12434
Networker of the Year Award Vol. 1: 738
Neue Stimmen - International Singing Contest Vol. 2: 2050
Neue Stimmen - Internationaler Gesangswettbewerb Vol. 2: 2050
Neufeld Memorial Research Grant; Prof. Henry Vol. 2: 2936
Neuharth Free Spirit of the Year Award; Al Vol. 1: 8874
Neuman Award; William F. Vol. 1: 3580
Neumann Memorial Award; Selma Vol. 1: 9499
Neumann Prize; Bernhard H. Vol. 2: 284
Neumueller Award in Optics; Julius F. Vol. 1: 658
Neustadt International Prize for Literature Vol. 1: 18954
Neuville et Sanford Saltus; Prix Alphonse de Vol. 2: 1466
Nevada Poetry Society Award Vol. 1: 13168
Nevanlinna Prize; Rolf Vol. 1: 10507
Neversink Trophy Vol. 1: 14426
Neves Memorial Scholarship; Sgt. Edward Vol. 1: 15160
Nevins Physiology and Human Environment Award; Ralph G. Vol. 1: 4061
Nevins Prize; Allan Vol. 1: 8381
New Achievers Awards Vol. 1: 1099
New American Cinema Award Vol. 1: 15958
New American Talent Show Vol. 1: 4655
New Book Award Vol. 1: 13048
New Directors Prize Vol. 2: 4538
New Directors Showcase Vol. 1: 15959
New England Book Show Vol. 1: 5845
New Englander of the Year Awards Vol. 1: 14031
New Focus Student Travel Grants Vol. 1: 14603
New Generations Award Vol. 1: 2855
New Genre Prize Vol. 1: 10031
New Graduate Prize Vol. 2: 5498
New Holland Young Researcher Award
American Society of Agricultural and Biological Engineers Vol. 1: 3848
American Society of Agricultural and Biological Engineers Vol 1: 3861
New Horizons Award for Innovation Vol. 1: 10681
New Investigator Award Vol. 1: 7003
New Investigator Awards
American Geriatrics Society Vol. 1: 2129
Mount Desert Island Biological Laboratory Vol 1: 11975
University of Wisconsin—Madison - Institute on Aging Vol 1: 18363
New Investigator Recognition Awards Vol. 1: 14713
New Investigator Research Award Vol. 1: 4945
New Jersey Poetry Society Award Vol. 1: 13169
New Leaders Travel Grant Vol. 1: 15420
New Letters Writing Awards Vol. 1: 14099
New Orleans International Piano Competition Vol. 1: 12039
New Play Project Vol. 1: 17016
New Product Award
American Association of Law Libraries Vol. 1: 1146
National Society of Professional Engineers Vol 1: 13745
New Product of the Year Vol. 2: 5725
New Product Showcase Award Vol. 1: 3034
New Professional Reporter Grant Vol. 1: 13066
New Research Workers Awards Vol. 2: 6572
New Scholar Award Vol. 1: 8017
New Scholar's Prize Vol. 2: 6241
New South Wales Premier's Literary Awards Vol. 2: 585
New Spirit of Community Partnership Awards Program Vol. 1: 9623
New Venture Award Vol. 2: 7342
New Visions Award Vol. 1: 15478
New Voices Award Vol. 1: 15479
New Writers Awards Vol. 1: 9180
New York Dance and Performance Awards (Bessie Awards) Vol. 1: 8049
New York Fellowship Vol. 2: 5074
New York International Ballet Competition Vol. 1: 14131
New York Poetry Forum Award Vol. 1: 13170
New York Press Club/AT&T Award Vol. 1: 14137
New York Women in Film and Television Post Production Completion Grants Vol. 1: 18815
New Yorker for New York Awards Vol. 1: 7420
New Zealand Association of Scientists Research Medal Vol. 2: 3767
New Zealand Chapter Traveling Fellowship; Australia/ Vol. 1: 1736
New Zealand Christian Book of the Year Vol. 2: 3709
New Zealand Dental Association Awards Vol. 2: 3769
New Zealand Herald Challenge Trophy Vol. 2: 3849
New Zealand Science and Technology Medals Vol. 2: 3870
New Zealand Science, Mathematics and Technology Teacher Fellowship Vol. 2: 3871
New Zealand Tourism Awards Vol. 2: 3875
New Zealand Wings Trophy Vol. 2: 3850
New Zealand Young Engineer of the Year Award Vol. 2: 3740
Newbery Medal; John Vol. 1: 4928
Newbigin Prize Vol. 2: 6894
Newbold V/STOL Award; F. E. Vol. 1: 2394
Newcomb Award for Research Achievement; Simon Vol. 1: 17849
Newcomb Award; James E. Vol. 1: 2621
Newcomb Award; Simon Vol. 1: 15738
Newcomb Cleveland Prize Vol. 1: 952
Newcombe Doctoral Dissertation Fellowship; Charlotte W. Vol. 1: 18887
Newcomer Award
Resort and Commercial Recreation Association Vol. 1: 15637
Resort and Commercial Recreation Association Vol 1: 15640
Newcomer Healthcare Executive of the Year Award; William Vol. 1: 629
Newcomer of the Year Vol. 1: 7799
Newcomer Supply Student Scholarship Vol. 1: 13723
Newell Award; ACM/AAAI Allen Vol. 1: 856
Newell Award; Allen Vol. 1: 4813
Newell Most Improved Chapter Award; Harvey T. Vol. 1: 15042
Newell Prize; W. W. Vol. 1: 2040
Newington Award Vol. 1: 829
Newkirk Award; Burt L. Vol. 1: 4154
Newman Award; Ewell L. Vol. 1: 2248
Newman Cup Vol. 2: 3851
Newman Graduate Research Award; Edwin B. Vol. 1: 15402
Newman Graduate Research Award; Psi Chi/ APA Edwin B. Vol. 1: 3367
Newman Speller Award; Frank Vol. 1: 12486
Newmark Medal; Nathan M. Vol. 1: 3964
Newnham Memorial Lecture; W. L. Vol. 2: 3741
Newport International Competition for Young Pianists Vol. 2: 6499
News and Documentary Emmy Awards Vol. 1: 12180
News Correspondent Award Vol. 1: 3965
News Coverage Award Vol. 1: 9980
News Picture Contest Vol. 1: 9724
Newsboy Award Vol. 1: 9483
Newsfilm Cameramen of the Year Vol. 1: 13561
Newsletter Association Journalism Awards Vol. 1: 17104
Newsletter Awards Vol. 1: 5185
Newsletter Competition
Institute of Management Accountants Vol. 1: 9897
National Genealogical Society Vol 1: 13280
Newsletter Journalism Award Vol. 1: 13549
Newsletter Journalism Awards Vol. 1: 14212
Newsletter of the Year
U.S. Hang Gliding Association Vol. 1: 17926
United States Professional Tennis Association Vol 1: 18034
Newsletter of the Year Award Vol. 1: 13721
Newsletter of the Year Merit Award Vol. 1: 13721
Newspaper Award Vol. 1: 437

Newspaper Carrier of the Year Award Vol. 1: 14214
Newspaper in Education Award Vol. 1: 9981
Newspaper in Education Program Excellence Award Vol. 1: 14223
Newspaper of the Year Award Vol. 2: 593
Newspaper of the Year Contest Vol. 1: 14936
NEWWA Scholarships Vol. 1: 14066
Nex Prize; Martin Andersen Vol. 2: 1294
Next Generation Achievement Award Vol. 1: 5292
Nextel Cup Vol. 1: 12364
Neyman Lecture Vol. 1: 9911
NFHS Citations Vol. 1: 13138
NFID - Burroughs Welcome Fund Young Investigator Awards Vol. 1: 13258
NFL All-Star Team Vol. 1: 17184
NFL Coach of the Year Vol. 1: 17185
NFL Player of the Year Vol. 1: 17186
NFL Rookie of the Year Vol. 1: 17187
Nganakarrawa Award Vol. 2: 169
NHK Japan Prize Vol. 2: 3298
NHL All-Star Team Vol. 1: 17188
NHL Coach of the Year Vol. 1: 17189
NHL Player of the Year Vol. 1: 17190
NHL Rookie of the Year Vol. 1: 17191
NHPA Scholarships Vol. 1: 14080
Nia Award Vol. 1: 12421
Nicest Studio Award Vol. 1: 13836
Nichol Chapbook Award; bp Vol. 1: 15017
Nichol Harbor and Coastal Engineering Award; John G. Moffat - Frank E. Vol. 1: 3962
Nicholas Outterside Medallion Vol. 2: 267
Nicholls Award; Percy Vol. 1: 4155
Nicholls Award; Percy W. Vol. 1: 16355
Nichols Award; Christopher D. Vol. 1: 4636
Nichols Award for Environmental Excellence; Charles Walter Vol. 1: 3453
Nichols Innovation Award; Albert L. Vol. 1: 882
Nichols Prize; Philip Vol. 2: 5524
Nicholson Award Vol. 2: 6446
Nicholson Award; J. Lee Vol. 1: 9898
Nicholson Award; Lt. Col. Arthur D. Vol. 1: 13452
Nicholson Award; Mollie Davis Vol. 1: 13733
Nicholson Distinguished Service Award; Margaret Vol. 1: 6058
Nicholson Gold Medal Award; Gunnar Vol. 1: 17394
Nicholson Memorial Scholarship in Cartography; Norman L. Vol. 1: 6385
Nicholson Non-Commissioned Officer Leadership Award; James E. Vol. 1: 11521
Nicholson Student Paper Competition; George Vol. 1: 9748
Nickelodeon Kid's Choice Awards Vol. 1: 14233
Nickens Award; Herbert W. Vol. 1: 16698
Nickerson Service Award Vol. 1: 9989
Nicklin Memorial Trophy; Jeff Vol. 1: 6515
Nicol Trophy; William A. Vol. 2: 6931
Nicolo; Prix Vol. 2: 1467
NIDRR Scholars Program Vol. 1: 17817
Niedecker Poetry Award; Lorine Vol. 1: 7875
Niederman Award; Allan and Joyce Vol. 1: 9389
Niekerk/AFMA Technical Person of the Year; Barney van Vol. 2: 4128
Nielsen International Music Competitions; Carl Vol. 2: 1313
Nielsen Prize; Carsten Vol. 2: 1297
Nieman Fellowships for Journalists Vol. 1: 14238
Nies Medal; Eric Vol. 1: 11641
Nightingale Award
Canadian Nurses Foundation Vol. 1: 6772
International Federation for Medical and Biological Engineering Vol 2: 1231
Nightingale Award; Florence Vol. 2: 344
Nightingale; Medaille Florence Vol. 2: 4792
Nightingale Medal; Florence Vol. 2: 4792
NIGP Fellow Award Vol. 1: 13374
Nihon Shinbun Kyokai Awards Vol. 2: 3241
Nihon Sugakukai Iyanaga Sho Vol. 2: 3292
Nihon Yakugakkai Gakujutsukokensho Vol. 2: 3306
Nihon Yakugakkai Gijutsusho Vol. 2: 3308
Nihon Yakugakkai sho Vol. 2: 3307
Nihon Yakugakkai Shoreisho Vol. 2: 3309
Nikolsky Honorary Lectureship; Alexander A. Vol. 1: 2203
Nile Gold Medal Vol. 2: 4742
Nimmo Medal; W.H.R. Vol. 2: 520
Nimmo Premium; Henry Vol. 2: 6157
NINDS Javits Neuroscience Investigator Award Vol. 1: 17827
Ninety-Nines NIFA Awards Vol. 1: 14243
Nininger Meteorite Award Vol. 1: 7226
Ninkasi Award Vol. 1: 2284
Niotis Cup; D. J. Vol. 1: 18178
Nippon Gakushiin Ejinbara-ko Sho Vol. 2: 3213
Nippon Gakushiin Sho Vol. 2: 3215
Nippon Oyo Dobutsu Konchu Gakkai Sho Vol. 2: 3273
Nippon Oyo Dobutsu Konchu Gakkai Shoreisho Vol. 2: 3274
Nishiyama Medal Vol. 2: 3208
Nissan - Fitzgerald Vol. 1: 17203
Nissen Award Vol. 1: 7518
Nissen-Emery Award Vol. 1: 7518
Nissim Prize; Rudolf Vol. 1: 4001
Nivaud Scholarship; Francois L. Vol. 1: 11585
Niwano Peace Prize Vol. 2: 3302
NMRT Mid-Career Award Vol. 1: 11419
Nobel; Bank of Sweden Prize in Memory of Alfred Vol. 2: 4601
Nobel Laureate Signature Award for a Graduate Student in Chemistry Vol. 1: 1569
Nobel Laureate Signature Award for Graduate Education in Chemistry Vol. 1: 1569
Nobel Peace Prize Vol. 2: 4602
Nobel Prize for Chemistry Vol. 2: 4603
Nobel Prize for Literature Vol. 2: 4604
Nobel Prize for Physics Vol. 2: 4605
Nobel Prize for Physiology or Medicine Vol. 2: 4606
Nobel Prizes Vol. 2: 4639
NOBLE Central Virginia Chapter Awards Vol. 1: 13507
Noble Educational Scholarship; Leonard Vol. 1: 13716
Noble Prize; Alfred Vol. 1: 3966
Noble Prize; Robert L. Vol. 1: 12845
NODA Scholarship Vol. 1: 13512
NOGI Awards Vol. 1: 17666
Nolin Collection Study Award; Marie-Paule Vol. 1: 11627
Nolte Award for Extraordinary Leadership; Julius M. Vol. 1: 18218
Nolting; International Award in Memory of Orin F. Vol. 1: 10311
Noma Award for the Translation of Japanese Literature Vol. 2: 3288
Noma Concours for Picture Book Illustrations Vol. 2: 3164
Noma Literacy Prize
Kodansha Ltd. Vol. 2: 3289
UNESCO Vol 2: 2002
Non-Deadline Writing Vol. 1: 4208
Non-Fiction Book of the Year Award Vol. 1: 6355
Nonfiction Award Vol. 1: 5795
Nonfiction Contest Vol. 1: 13943
Nonnenmacher Industry Service Award; Tom Vol. 1: 12570
Noranda Lecture Award Vol. 1: 6906
Norcen/CSPG Undergraduate Scholarship Vol. 1: 7020
Nordberg Medal; William Vol. 2: 1740
Nordberg Traveling Scholarship Vol. 2: 6076
Nordelli Prize; Andrew Vol. 2: 4024
Nordic Award Vol. 1: 10406
Nordic Combined World Cup Leaders Vol. 2: 4836
Nordic Council Literature Prize Vol. 2: 4613
Nordic Council Music Prize Vol. 2: 4614
Nordic Guest Researchers' Scholarship Vol. 2: 4609
Nordic World Cup Leaders Vol. 2: 4836
Nordisk Award; Novo Vol. 2: 88
Nordisk Rads Musikpris Vol. 2: 4614
Nordiska Priset Vol. 2: 4663
Nordiska Radets Litteraturpris Vol. 2: 4613
Nordlinger Child Welfare Leadership Award; Samuel Gerson Vol. 1: 399
Norkool Award; Diane Vol. 1: 5675
Norman Medal Vol. 1: 3967
Norman Scholarship; Ralph G. Vol. 1: 11275
Normann Medal; W. Vol. 2: 2231
Norris Award in Physical Organic Chemistry; James Flack Vol. 1: 1570
North American Championship Trophy Vol. 1: 10496
North American Conservation Award Vol. 1: 4499
North American Mixing Forum Award Vol. 1: 2493
North American Sculpture Exhibition Awards Vol. 1: 8803
North American Shortwave DXer of the Year Vol. 1: 5269
North Memorial Trophy; Rexford L. Vol. 1: 13315
North Shore Trophy Vol. 2: 3852
Northcroft Memorial Lecture Vol. 2: 5409
Northeast Modern Language Association Fellowship Vol. 1: 819
Northeastern Loggers' Association Awards Vol. 1: 14392
Northern Arts Literary Fellowship Vol. 2: 6501
Northern Light Award Vol. 1: 11041
Northern New England Playwrights Award Vol. 1: 18481
Northern Science Award Vol. 1: 9656
Northern Territory Literary Awards Vol. 2: 589
Northrop Distinguished Service Award; Cynthia Vol. 1: 1186
Northwest Film and Video Festival Vol. 1: 14398
Northwest Flower & Garden Show Garden Award Vol. 1: 15662
Norton Award; Andre Vol. 1: 15923
Norton Award; Joseph Vol. 1: 4883
Norton Award; Margaret Cross Vol. 1: 11757

Award Index

Norton Distinguished Ceramist Award; F. H. Vol. 1: 1490
Norton Memorial Scholarship Award for Women; Mary R. Vol. 1: 5447
Norwich Union Healthcare/Medical Journalists' Association Awards Vol. 2: 6424
Norwich Union Trophy Vol. 2: 6928
Norwood Cultural Council Grants Vol. 1: 8909
Notable Wisconsin Authors Vol. 1: 18791
Notary of the Year Award Vol. 1: 13480
Notre Dame Award Vol. 1: 18333
Noury; Prix Victor Vol. 2: 1594
NOVA Award Vol. 1: 7738
Nova Awards Vol. 1: 9266
NOVA Program of Distinction Awards Vol. 1: 13498
Novak Award Vol. 1: 137
Novartis Award; Graduate Student Fellowship/ Vol. 1: 16875
Novartis Crop Protection Agricultural Writing Awards Vol. 1: 17366
Novartis Crop Protection NAFB Farm Broadcasting Award Vol. 1: 17365
Novartis Fellowship in Transplantation Vol. 1: 4248
Novartis Junior Scientist Award Vol. 2: 438
Novartis Medal and Prize Vol. 2: 5177
Novartis Nematology Award Vol. 1: 16775
Novel Manuscript Award Vol. 1: 13944
Novella Contest Vol. 1: 15481
Novella Prize Vol. 1: 11483
Novice Award Vol. 1: 18201
Novice Research Award Vol. 2: 872
Novikoff Memorial Award; Philip A.
Canadian Public Relations Society Vol. 1: 6845
Canadian Public Relations Society Vol 1: 6846
Novo Nordisk Foundation Lecture Vol. 2: 1317
Novo Nordisk Prize Vol. 2: 1318
NovoPharm Award Vol. 1: 6999
Nowotny Excellence in Cancer Nursing Education Award; Mary Vol. 1: 14547
Noyes Award; Marcia C. Vol. 1: 11664
NPM Scholarships Vol. 1: 12602
NRCA Fellow Vol. 1: 13619
NSES Award Vol. 2: 3636
NSPCA Annual Exhibition Vol. 1: 13741
NSPE Award Vol. 1: 13746
NSPS Scholarships Vol. 1: 13755
NSTA ExploraVision Awards; Toshiba/ Vol. 1: 13685
Nuffield Lecture Vol. 2: 7016
Nuffield Silver Medal; Viscount Vol. 2: 6158
Numismatic Art Award for Excellence in Medallic Sculpture Vol. 1: 2906
Numismatic Error Collectors Exhibit Award Vol. 1: 2907
Nunn Media and Conservation Award; Carl Vol. 1: 14581
Nuremberg International Human Rights Award Vol. 2: 2371
Nurse Manager Award Vol. 1: 8442
Nurse of the Year Award Vol. 1: 13339
Nursery Extension Award for Distinguished Service to the Nursery Industry Vol. 1: 3723
Nursing Education Award Vol. 1: 8443
Nursing Excellence Awards Vol. 1: 7497
Nursing Practice Award Vol. 1: 8444
Nursing Professionalism Award Vol. 1: 8445
Nursing Research Award Vol. 1: 6794
Nursing Scholarships Vol. 1: 7729
Nursing Service Cross Vol. 2: 220
Nutrition Award Vol. 1: 704
Nutrition Education Award Vol. 1: 1081
Nutrition Professionals, Inc. Applied Dairy Nutrition Award Vol. 1: 1886
NWAA Hall of Fame Vol. 1: 18722
NWC Nonfiction Contest Vol. 1: 13943
NWC Novel Manuscript Award Vol. 1: 13944
NWC Poetry Award Vol. 1: 13945
NWC Short Story Award Vol. 1: 13946
NWRA Grants Vol. 1: 13913
Nycomed Prize Vol. 2: 6300
Nyholm Lectureship; Sir Ronald Vol. 2: 6977
Nymph Awards Vol. 2: 3469
Nyselius Award Vol. 1: 14298
Nystrom Award; J. Warren Vol. 1: 5033
Nystrom Prize; E. J. Vol. 2: 1400
Nystroms Prize; Professor E. J. Vol. 2: 1400
NZNFFA Trophy Vol. 2: 5910
O. Henry Awards Vol. 1: 15550
O. Henry Prize Stories Vol. 1: 15550
Oak Leaf Award Vol. 1: 13983
Oakley Certificate of Merit Vol. 1: 4892
Oakley Dayhoff Award; Margaret Vol. 1: 5780
OAPEC Award for Scientific Research Vol. 2: 3369
Obedience Award Vol. 1: 14427
Oberle Award for Outstanding Teaching in Grades K-12; Marcella E. Vol. 1: 12929
Oberly Award for Bibliography in the Agricultural or Natural Sciences Vol. 1: 5084
Oberly Memorial Award; Eunice Rockwell Vol. 1: 5084
Oberman and Rich Award Vol. 1: 9607
Oberst Award; Byron B. Vol. 1: 705
OBIE Awards; The Village Voice Vol. 1: 18535
Oboler Memorial Award; Eli M. Vol. 1: 2669
O'Brien Award; Jane Vol. 1: 9608
O'Brien Award; Robert F. Vol. 1: 12854
O'Brien Championship Trophy; Larry Vol. 1: 12762
Obrig Prize for Painting in Oil; Adolph and Clara Vol. 1: 12114
Observing Awards Vol. 1: 5670
Obwegeser Scholarship; Hugo Vol. 2: 5814
O'Byrne Award; Father Patrick Vol. 1: 18442
O'Callaghan Trophy; Jeremiah Vol. 1: 10896
Occupational Excellence Achievement Award Vol. 1: 13658
Occupational Health Award Vol. 2: 6929
Occupational Safety/Health Contests Vol. 1: 13658
Ocean Sciences Award Vol. 1: 2121
Oceaneering International Award Vol. 1: 17662
Ochal Award for Distinguished Service to the Profession; Bethany J. Vol. 1: 1147
Ochsner Award Relating Smoking and Health; Alton Vol. 1: 14449
OCIC-Prize Vol. 2: 1093
Ockerman State and Regional Professional Activity Award; Elbert W. Vol. 1: 1056
O'Connor Award for Short Fiction; Flannery Vol. 1: 18284
O'Connor Essay Award; Richard Vol. 1: 4662
OCTA Awards Vol. 1: 14671
OCTM Prize Vol. 2: 4870
ODAS Youth Achievement Award Vol. 1: 388
Odden Award Vol. 2: 6878
O'Dell Award; William Vol. 1: 2718
Odense International Film Festival Vol. 2: 1320
Odlum Award; Doris Vol. 2: 5370
O'Donoghue Sports Injury Research Award Vol. 1: 3014
Odyssey Diploma Vol. 2: 4743
Oelke Memorial Award for Painting; Kimbel E. Vol. 1: 588
Oenslager Scholastic Achievement Awards; Mary P. Vol. 1: 15576
Oersted Medal Vol. 1: 1252
Offender Management Reintegration Vol. 1: 10341
Offensive and Defensive Linemen of the Year Vol. 1: 13226
Office Building of the Year Vol. 1: 15818
Office of Civilian Radioactive Waste Management Graduate Fellowship Program Vol. 1: 14442
Office of Civilian Radioactive Waste Management Historically Black Colleges and Universities Undergraduate Scholarship Program Vol. 1: 14443
Office of the Americas Peace & Justice Award Vol. 1: 14453
Officer of the Year Award Vol. 1: 10263
Official of the Year
Speed Skating Canada Vol. 1: 17126
U.S.A. Wrestling Vol 1: 18471
Offshore Mechanics Scholarship Vol. 1: 10729
O'Flaherty Service Award; Fred Vol. 1: 2631
Ofsthun Award; Stan Vol. 1: 16845
Ogden Award; H. R. "Russ" Vol. 1: 5448
Ogden Memorial Prize; Bill Vol. 2: 6591
The OH Awards Vol. 2: 1379
The OH County Award Vol. 2: 1380
The OHA Plaques Vol. 2: 1381
OHA-VHF Award Vol. 2: 1382
O'Hagan Award for Short Fiction; Howard Vol. 1: 19006
Ohio Award Vol. 1: 13171
Ohioana Award for Editorial Excellence Vol. 1: 14486
Ohioana Book Awards Vol. 1: 14490
Ohioana Career Award Vol. 1: 14491
Ohioana Citations Vol. 1: 14492
Ohioana Pegasus Award Vol. 1: 14493
Oils and Fats Group International Lecture Vol. 2: 7176
Oita International Wheelchair Marathon Vol. 2: 3304
Oke Trophy; F. G. (Teddy) Vol. 1: 2276
O'Keefe Memorial Trophy; Edward Vol. 1: 10897
Oken Medaille; Lorenz Vol. 2: 2254
Okes Award; Imogene Vol. 1: 837
Oklahoma School Administrator Award Vol. 1: 14497
OKOMEDIA International Ecological Film Festival Vol. 2: 2365
Okuma Academic Commemorative Prize Vol. 2: 3347
Okuma Academic Encouragement Prize Vol. 2: 3348
Okuma Gakujutsu Kinensho Vol. 2: 3347
Okuma Gakujutsu Shoreisho Vol. 2: 3348
Olah Award in Hydrocarbon or Petroleum Chemistry; George A. Vol. 1: 1571
O'Laoghaire Memorial Trophy; Pilib Vol. 2: 2829
Olave Award Vol. 2: 7359
Old Forge Hardware Prize Vol. 1: 4677

Old Guard Prizes Vol. 1: 4156
Old Hilltop Award Vol. 1: 11561
Old Tackle Makers Vol. 1: 13197
Oldenburger Medal; Rufus Vol. 1: 4157
Oldendorf Award; William H. Vol. 1: 4203
Oldfield Cup; Lucy Vol. 2: 5533
Oldman Prize; C. B. Vol. 2: 6221
O'Leary Award; Bart Vol. 1: 12508
Oleoscience Editors Award Vol. 2: 3258
Olfactory Research Fund Sense of Smell Award Vol. 1: 8856
Olin Fellowships Vol. 1: 5512
Olin Medal; Francis P. Garvan-John M. Vol. 1: 1549
Olivarez La Raza Award; Graciela Vol. 1: 13002
Oliver Award for Sustained Excellence; Edith Vol. 1: 11406
Oliver Award; Ross L. Vol. 1: 13293
Oliver Prize; Brian Vol. 2: 6730
Oliveros Prize; Pauline Vol. 1: 10031
Olivier Awards; Laurence Vol. 2: 7203
Olle Prize; Archibald D. Vol. 2: 643
Ollie Awards Vol. 1: 1464
Olman Publishers Award; Abe Vol. 1: 12134
Olmsted Award; Frederick Law Vol. 1: 12253
Olmsted Liberal Education Award for Innovation; Sterling Vol. 1: 3663
Olmsted Medal; Frederick Law Vol. 1: 4105
Olney Medal Vol. 1: 1310
Olson Loon Research Award; Sigurd T. Vol. 1: 11404
Olson Spider Award; Harris Vol. 1: 2212
Olympian of the Year Award Vol. 2: 3417
Olympiart Vol. 2: 4819
Olympic Cup Vol. 2: 4820
Olympic Football Tournaments (Men and Women) Vol. 2: 4756
Olympic Medals and Diplomas Vol. 2: 4821
Olympic Order Vol. 2: 4822
Olympic Spirit Award Vol. 1: 18018
Olympic Torch Vol. 2: 4461
Olympique; Ordre Vol. 2: 4822
O'Mahony Bursary; Eoin Vol. 2: 2881
O'Malley Art Award Vol. 1: 10883
O'Malley Art Award Vol. 1: 10887
O'Malley Award; Diane Vol. 1: 4644
O'Malley Award; General Jerome F. Vol. 1: 293
Omega Protein Innovative Research Award Vol. 1: 3892
Omicron Delta Kappa Scholarships Vol. 1: 14522
On Behalf of Youth Award Vol. 1: 6075
On-the-Spot Awards Vol. 1: 17809
Onassis Award for Culture (Letters, Arts and Humanities) Vol. 2: 2461
Onassis Award for International Understanding and Social Achievement Vol. 2: 2462
Onassis Award for the Environment Vol. 2: 2463
Onassis Awards; Jacqueline Kennedy Vol. 1: 2352
Onassis International Cultural Competition Prizes Vol. 2: 2464
Onassis Medal; Jacqueline Kennedy Vol. 1: 12011
Onassis Prize for Man and Culture - Olympia Vol. 2: 2461
Onassis Prize for Man and His Environment - Delphi Vol. 2: 2463
Oncology Social Worker of the Year Vol. 1: 5274
Ondaatje Ballet Fund; Christopher Vol. 1: 6132
Ondaatje Prize Vol. 2: 7002
Ondaatje Prize for Portraiture Vol. 2: 7027
One-Act Playwriting Competition Vol. 1: 11388
One Club Award Vol. 1: 16019
One of a Kind Award Vol. 1: 7997
One Show Awards Vol. 1: 14551
One World Award Vol. 2: 4828
O'Neal Safety Award; Jack Vol. 1: 17755
O'Neill Award; Joseph E. Vol. 1: 13801
Ong Memorial Award; William A. "Bill" Vol. 1: 12229
Online Directory of the Year - Business Vol. 2: 5726
Online Directory of the Year - Consumer Vol. 2: 5727
Online Journalism Award Vol. 1: 13550
Ono Memorial Awards; Azusa Vol. 2: 3349
Ono Memorial Awards for Art; Azusa Vol. 2: 3349
Ono Memorial Awards for Sports; Azusa Vol. 2: 3349
Onsager Prize; Lars Vol. 1: 3124
Onshi Sho Vol. 2: 3214
Ontario College of Art & Design Scholarships Vol. 1: 14568
Ontario Medal for Firefighter Bravery Vol. 1: 14572
Ontario Medal for Good Citizenship Vol. 1: 14573
Ontario Medal for Police Bravery Vol. 1: 14574
Ontario Waste Minimization Awards Vol. 1: 15591
OPC Awards Vol. 1: 14761
Open Award for Technical Excellence in Architectural Technology Vol. 2: 5321
Open Championship Vol. 2: 6672
Open Competition Awards Vol. 1: 2794
Open Palm Award Vol. 1: 9634
Open Water Swimmer of the Year Vol. 1: 18419
Opera Production Competition Vol. 1: 13488
Operasangerinnen Fanny Elstas Fond Vol. 2: 3895
Operating Grants Vol. 1: 6708
Operational Achievement Award (Individual and Group) Vol. 1: 13900
Operator of the Year Vol. 1: 13968
Operators Award Vol. 2: 3819
Opernwelt Prize Vol. 2: 830
Opie Prize; Peter and Iona Vol. 1: 2041
Opinion Award Vol. 1: 9982
Oporto International Film Festival - Fantasporto Vol. 2: 4058
Oppenheimer Award Vol. 1: 3664
Oppenheimer Award; Ernst Vol. 1: 8456
Oppenheimer/*Newsday* Playwriting Award; George Vol. 1: 14210
Opperman Award for Judicial Excellence; Dwight D. Vol. 1: 2605
Oppermann Memorial Award for Lifetime Achievement; Martin Vol. 1: 10744
Oppy Award Vol. 1: 14210
The Opthalmological Gold Medal Vol. 2: 1345
Optical Society of India Award Vol. 2: 2784
Optical Special Citation Award Vol. 2: 3017
OPTIMA Gold Medal Vol. 2: 4527
OPTIMA Silver Medal Vol. 2: 4528
Optimas Awards Vol. 1: 18893
Optometrist of the Year Vol. 1: 18922
Optometrist of the Year Award Vol. 1: 2976
Optometry Outstanding Service and Recognition Award Vol. 1: 5258
Ora Award Vol. 1: 13397
Oral Science Research Award Vol. 1: 10069
The Orange British Academy Film Awards Vol. 2: 5218
Orban Memorial Prize; Balint Vol. 1: 728
Orbis Books Prize for Polish Studies Vol. 1: 959
Orbis Pictus Nonfiction Award Vol. 1: 13025
ORCA Rolex Prize Vol. 2: 3542
ORCA-Zsolnay Prize Vol. 2: 3543
Orchard-Hays Prize Vol. 1: 11615
Orchard Medal; William J. Vol. 1: 18641
Orchestra Recognition Award Vol. 2: 6312
Orchestral Audition and Masterclass Competition Vol. 1: 13204
Orde van Oranje-Nassau Vol. 2: 3491
Orden al Merito Julio Garavito Vol. 2: 1191
Orden del Merito Aeronautico Antonio Ricaurte Vol. 2: 1183
Orden del Merito Militar Antonio Narino Vol. 2: 1184
Orden del Merito Naval Almirante Padilla Vol. 2: 1185
Orden del Merito Sanitario Jose Fernandez Madrid Vol. 2: 1186
Orden Mexicana del Aguila Azteca Vol. 2: 3454
Orden Militar San Mateo Vol. 2: 1187
Order Odrodzenia Polski Vol. 2: 4015
Order of Australia Vol. 2: 221
Order of Canada Vol. 1: 6092
Order of Culture Vol. 2: 3246
Order of Honour Service Awards Vol. 1: 15308
Order of Magellan Vol. 1: 7418
Order of Mariposa Vol. 1: 17298
Order of Merit
  Central Chancery of the Orders of Knighthood Vol. 2: 5601
  International Basketball Federation Vol 2: 4780
  National Wrestling Hall of Fame & Museum Vol 1: 13940
  Religious and Military Order of Knights of the Holy Sepulchre of Jerusalem Vol 1: 15619
Order of Merit of the Police Forces Vol. 1: 6080
Order of Merit of the Republic of Poland Vol. 2: 4014
Order of Ontario Vol. 1: 14575
Order of Orange-Nassau Vol. 2: 3491
Order of Pius Vol. 2: 7413
Order of Polish Rebirth Vol. 2: 4015
Order of Red Triangle Vol. 1: 19072
Order of Rio Branco Vol. 2: 1113
Order of St. Gregory the Great Vol. 2: 7414
Order of St. John of Jerusalem Vol. 1: 6080
Order of St. Sylvester Vol. 2: 7415
Order of San Carlos Vol. 2: 1175
Order of Sancta Barbara Vol. 1: 6629
Order of the Academic Palms Vol. 2: 1824
Order of the Bird Vol. 1: 10230
Order of the Companions of Honour Vol. 2: 5602
Order of the Cross of Liberty Vol. 2: 1374
Order of the Eagle Vol. 1: 9
Order of the Egg Vol. 1: 10231
Order of the Golden Ark Vol. 2: 3492
Order of the Golden Microscope Vol. 1: 2754

Order of the Golden Spur (Golden Militia) Vol. 2: 7416
Order of the Lapis Lazuli Vol. 1: 8646
Order of the Lion of Finland Vol. 2: 1375
Order of the Netherlands Lion Vol. 2: 3493
Order of the Paulownia Flowers Vol. 2: 3247
Order of the Precious Crown Vol. 2: 3248
Order of the Rising Sun Vol. 2: 3249
The Order of the Royal Huntsman Vol. 2: 5665
Order of the Sacred Treasure Vol. 2: 3250
Order of the West Range Vol. 1: 15042
Order of the White Eagle Vol. 2: 4016
Order of the White Rose of Finland Vol. 2: 1376
Order of West Range Vol. 1: 15041
Order Wojenny Virtuti Militari Vol. 2: 4017
Order Zaslugi Rzeczypospolitej Polskiej Vol. 2: 4014
Ordnance Survey Award Vol. 2: 5268
Ordo Honorium Award Vol. 1: 11095
Ordre du Conseil de la Vie Francaise en Amerique Vol. 1: 7733
Ordre Olympique Vol. 2: 4822
Ordway Stewardship Award; Katherine Vol. 1: 13986
O'Reilly Award; Richard T. Vol. 1: 10036
Orenstein Memorial Convention Travel Fund; Doris Vol. 1: 5208
Orford String Quartet Scholarship Vol. 1: 14563
Organic Food Awards Vol. 2: 7224
Organist of the Year Vol. 1: 4352
Organization and Institution Citations Vol. 1: 13848
Organization of Islamic Capitals and Cities Awards Vol. 2: 4409
Organizational Award Vol. 1: 13608
Organizational Certificate of Appreciation Vol. 1: 7752
Organizational Contribution Award Vol. 1: 934
Organizing Excellence Award Vol. 1: 12626
Orlando Award; Babe Vol. 1: 10824
Orme Prize; Margaret Vol. 2: 7318
Ormond Medal; Francis Vol. 2: 608
Ornish Award; Natalie Vol. 1: 17483
Ornithologen-Preis Vol. 2: 2208
Oronzio and Niccolo De Nora Foundation Prize of ISE on Electrochemical Energy Conversion Vol. 2: 4843
Oronzio and Niccolo De Nora Foundation Prize of ISE on Electrochemical Technology and Engineering Vol. 2: 4844
Oronzio and Niccolo De Nora Foundation Young Author Prize Vol. 2: 4845
Orr Award; Joan Vol. 1: 294
Orr Award; Verne Vol. 1: 295
ORSA Prize Vol. 1: 9744
Ortega y Gasset Awards for Journalism Vol. 2: 4501
Orthopedic Allied Professional of the Year Vol. 1: 4211
Orton Award; Samuel T. Vol. 1: 10387
Orton, Jr., Memorial Lecture; Edward Vol. 1: 1491
Orville Scholarship in Meteorology; Howard T. Vol. 1: 2782
Orwell Award for Distinguished Contribution to Honesty and Clarity in Public Language; George Vol. 1: 13026
OSA Leadership Award - New Focus/ Bookham Prize Vol. 1: 14615
OSA Leadership Award/New Focus Prize Vol. 1: 14615
Osas Festspillfond; Sigbjorn Bernhoft Vol. 2: 3896
Osborne and Mendel Award Vol. 1: 3795
Osborne Award; Ernest Vol. 1: 13043
Osetek Educator Award; Edward M. Vol. 1: 1087
O'Shannessy Award Vol. 2: 667
Osler Award Vol. 1: 5941
Osler Medal; William Vol. 1: 965
OSM Standards Life Competition Vol. 1: 11942
Ostermeier Memorial Award; Rosemary and Donald Vol. 1: 13722
Osterweil Award for Poetry; Joyce Vol. 1: 14901
Ostwald Original Band Composition Award Vol. 1: 1372
OSU Photography and Cinema Alumni Society Award Vol. 1: 7385
Osuna Sportsmanship Award Vol. 1: 10003
Osuna Sportsmanship Award; Rafael Vol. 1: 10003
OTA Award of Excellence Vol. 1: 2956
Otaka Prize Vol. 2: 3300
Othmer Sophomore Academic Excellence Award; Donald F. Vol. 1: 2498
Otological Research Fellowship for Medical Students Vol. 1: 8076
O'Toole Agency Award Vol. 1: 983
O'Toole Multicultural Advertising Award Vol. 1: 984
O'Toole Public Service Award Vol. 1: 985
Otremba Memorial Award; Elke Vol. 1: 7050
Ott Award for Outstanding Contribution to Children's Literature; Helen Keating Vol. 1: 7395
Ott Prize; Theodore Vol. 2: 4886
Ottawa Architectural Conservation Awards Vol. 1: 7436
Our American Indian Heritage Award Vol. 1: 13172
Our Native American Heritage Award Vol. 1: 13172
ournier PhD Thesis Award; Alain F Vol. 1: 6571
Oustanding Service Award Vol. 1: 8677
Outdoor Classic Award Vol. 1: 13514
Outdoor Communications Awards Vol. 1: 14755
Outdoor Writing Awards Vol. 1: 14755
Outer Critics Circle Awards Vol. 1: 14757
Outgoing President Award Vol. 1: 17271
Outland Trophy
Football Writers Association of America Vol. 1: 8799
Greater Omaha Sports Committee Vol 1: 9190
Outler Prize in Ecumenical Church History; Albert C. Vol. 1: 3913
Outlook Award Vol. 2: 2827
Outreach Services Award Vol. 1: 4605
Outstanding Academic Librarian Award Vol. 1: 11426
Outstanding Achievement Vol. 1: 8844
Outstanding Achievement Award
Alliance for Children and Television Vol. 1: 403
American Association of Blood Banks Vol 1: 1015
American Psychological Association - Society for the Study of Lesbian, Gay and Bisexual Concerns (Division 44) Vol 1: 3397
Armenian Behavioral Science Association Vol 1: 4632
Canadian Association of Career Educators and Employers Vol 1: 6240
Canadian Public Relations Society Vol 1: 6845
National Association of Metal Finishers Vol 1: 12591
Renewable Natural Resources Foundation Vol 1: 15626
Society of Woman Geographers Vol 1: 16908
Treasury Board of Canada Secretariat Vol 1: 17593
Western North Carolina Historical Association Vol 1: 18693
Outstanding Achievement Award - Group Vol. 1: 2511
Outstanding Achievement Award - Individual Vol. 1: 2512
Outstanding Achievement in Adolescent Medicine Award Vol. 1: 16151
Outstanding Achievement in Law Enforcement Volunteer Programs Award Vol. 1: 10173
Outstanding Achievement in Management Award Vol. 1: 9869
Outstanding Achievement in Mentorship Vol. 1: 5293
Outstanding Achievement in Metropolitan Transportation Planning as an Elected Official Vol. 1: 5232
Outstanding Achievement in Patron Transport Safety Vol. 2: 230
Outstanding Achievement in Perioperative Clinical Nursing Education Award Vol. 1: 5294
Outstanding Achievement in Perioperative Clinical Nursing Practice Vol. 1: 5295
Outstanding Achievement in Perioperative Nursing Management Award Vol. 1: 5296
Outstanding Achievement in Perioperative Nursing Research Award Vol. 1: 5297
Outstanding Achievement in Perioperative Patient Education Vol. 1: 5298
Outstanding Achievement in the Industry Vol. 1: 10389
Outstanding Achievement in Water Quality Improvement Award Vol. 1: 18642
Outstanding Activity Awards Vol. 1: 1375
Outstanding Administrator Vol. 1: 17127
Outstanding Advertising Campaign Vol. 1: 12818
Outstanding Advising Awards Vol. 1: 12090
Outstanding Advising Program Awards Vol. 1: 12091
Outstanding Advocate Award
American Association of Nurse Attorneys Vol. 1: 1187
Easter Seals Vol 1: 8335
Outstanding Affiliate Organization Award Vol. 1: 14250
Outstanding After-School Program Award Vol. 1: 12937
Outstanding Alumni Achievement Award Vol. 1: 14417
Outstanding Americal Films of the Year Awards Vol. 1: 2019
Outstanding Animal Control Agency Award Vol. 1: 12244
Outstanding Area Advisor Vol. 1: 4642

Outstanding Article Award Vol. 1: 4092
Outstanding Article in *American Journal of Agricultural Economics* Award Vol. 1: 778
Outstanding Arts Educator Award Vol. 1: 17382
Outstanding ASWA Participation Vol. 2: 356
Outstanding Band Musician Award Vol. 1: 12742
Outstanding Biology Teacher Award Vol. 1: 12409
Outstanding Book Award
Academy of Criminal Justice Sciences Vol. 1: 89
American Educational Research Association Vol 1: 1944
Conference on College Composition and Communication Vol 1: 7694
History of Education Society Vol 1: 9438
Outstanding Book Award: General Nonfiction Vol. 1: 4093
Outstanding Box Office Award Vol. 1: 10795
Outstanding Business Leader Awards Vol. 1: 14411
Outstanding Business Person of the Year Vol. 1: 18711
Outstanding Certified Flight Instructor Award Vol. 1: 9367
Outstanding Chapter Advisor Award Vol. 1: 16817
Outstanding Chapter Advisor Award Vol. 1: 3056
Outstanding Chapter/Affiliate Award Vol. 1: 10136
Outstanding Chapter Award
Arnold Air Society Vol. 1: 4645
Eta Kappa Nu Vol 1: 8539
Outstanding Chapter Awards
American Academy of Pediatrics Vol. 1: 706
Institute of Electrical and Electronics Engineers - Power Engineering Society Vol 1: 9821
Outstanding Chapter of the Year Award Vol. 1: 1082
Outstanding Citizenship Award Vol. 1: 13772
Outstanding Civil Engineering Achievement Vol. 1: 3968
Outstanding Civitan Awareness Project Vol. 1: 7451
Outstanding Clinician Award Vol. 2: 5865
Outstanding Club Bulletin Vol. 1: 7452
Outstanding Club Publication Award Vol. 1: 2908
Outstanding Club Representative Award Vol. 1: 2909
Outstanding Clubs Vol. 1: 19095
Outstanding Collegiate Branch Award Vol. 1: 16585
Outstanding Committee Achievement Vol. 1: 2014
Outstanding Committee Chair Award Vol. 1: 8134
Outstanding Community Service Vol. 2: 231
Outstanding Community Service Award Vol. 1: 5037
Outstanding Community Service Awards Vol. 2: 727
Outstanding Community Service Project Vol. 1: 7453
Outstanding Competitor Award Vol. 1: 14327
Outstanding Component School Award Vol. 1: 14476
Outstanding Congregational Librarian Vol. 1: 7396
Outstanding Congregational Library Vol. 1: 7397
Outstanding Conservationist Vol. 1: 8845
Outstanding Continuing Education Student Awards Vol. 1: 18219
Outstanding Contribution Award
Canadian Nuclear Society Vol. 1: 6765
Canadian Sociology and Anthropology Association Vol 1: 7038
Outstanding Contribution by an Individual for Educational/Training Activities Vol. 1: 4785
Outstanding Contribution by an Organization Vol. 1: 13494
Outstanding Contribution of the Year Vol. 1: 8626
Outstanding Contribution to ACE by an Organization Vol. 1: 5120
Outstanding Contribution to ACM Award Vol. 1: 4814
Outstanding Contribution to Amateur Football Award Vol. 1: 13216
Outstanding Contribution to Campus Ministry Vol. 1: 5336
Outstanding Contribution to Co-operative Education and Training Vol. 1: 5121
Outstanding Contribution to Congregational Libraries Vol. 1: 7398
Outstanding Contribution to Forest Industry Education Vol. 1: 14392
Outstanding Contribution to Higher Education Award Vol. 1: 12686
Outstanding Contribution to Industry Award Vol. 2: 458
Outstanding Contribution to Literature or Research Award Vol. 1: 12687
Outstanding Contribution to Publishing Award Vol. 1: 5795
Outstanding Contribution to Research Award Vol. 1: 548
Outstanding Contribution to Rural Life Award Vol. 1: 15780
Outstanding Contribution to Safety Vol. 1: 14392
Outstanding Contributions in Education Vol. 1: 883
Outstanding Contributions Through Science to the Profession of Clinical Chemistry Vol. 1: 884
Outstanding Contributions to Chemistry in a Selected Area of Research Vol. 1: 885
Outstanding Contributions to Clinical Chemistry Vol. 1: 886
Outstanding Contributions to Community Education Legislation Award Vol. 1: 12938
Outstanding Contributions to Health Psychology Vol. 1: 3348
Outstanding Contributions to the IAEE Award Vol. 1: 10075
Outstanding Contributions to the Orientation Profession Award Vol. 1: 13511
Outstanding Contributions to the Profession Award Vol. 1: 10076
Outstanding Contributor Award Vol. 1: 9880
Outstanding Corporate Achievement Vol. 1: 12456
Outstanding Corporate Growth Award Vol. 1: 4841
Outstanding Corporation Award Vol. 1: 5166
Outstanding Council Award Vol. 1: 924
Outstanding County Program Awards Vol. 1: 14360
Outstanding CPA in Government Award Vol. 1: 2463
Outstanding Decision Maker Award Vol. 1: 4606
Outstanding Director of the Year Award Vol. 1: 15912
Outstanding Directorial Achievement Award for Feature Films Vol. 1: 8220
Outstanding Directorial Achievement Award for Television Vol. 1: 8221
Outstanding Directorial Achievement in Commercials Vol. 1: 8222
Outstanding Disabled Veteran of the Year Vol. 1: 8227
Outstanding Dissertation Award
American Association of Colleges for Teacher Education Vol. 1: 1050
American Psychological Association - Exercise and Sport Psychology Division (Division 47) Vol 1: 3341
American Psychological Association (Division 28) Vol 1: 3419
Association for Counselor Education and Supervision Vol 1: 4848
Outstanding Dissertation of the Year Award Vol. 1: 10590
Outstanding Doctoral Dissertation Award Vol. 1: 779
Outstanding Doctoral Thesis Research in Atomic, Molecular, or Optical Physics Award Vol. 1: 3125
Outstanding Doctoral Thesis Research in Beam Physics Award Vol. 1: 3126
Outstanding Donor Recruiter Award Vol. 1: 1011
Outstanding Earth Science Teacher Award Vol. 1: 12539
Outstanding Educator Award
AGC Education and Research Foundation Vol. 1: 236
American Ceramic Society Vol 1: 1492
Association for Women Geoscientists Vol 1: 4998
Public Relations Society of America Vol 1: 15429
Radiological Society of North America Vol 1: 15539
Outstanding Educators Award Vol. 2: 3073
Outstanding Electrical Engineering Junior Award Vol. 1: 8540
Outstanding Elementary Social Studies Teacher of the Year Award Vol. 1: 12988
Outstanding Engineer Award Vol. 1: 9822
Outstanding Environmental and Engineering Geologic Project Award Vol. 1: 5139
Outstanding Executive Director of a State, Provincial, and Territorial Association (SPTA) Award Vol. 1: 3334
Outstanding Explorer Award Vol. 1: 1221
Outstanding Extension Educator Award Vol. 1: 3723
Outstanding Faculty Adviser Award Vol. 1: 15058
Outstanding Faculty Development Award Vol. 1: 5720
Outstanding Federal Healthcare Executive Award Vol. 1: 5250
Outstanding Field Chapter Vol. 1: 15057
Outstanding Financial Manager Vol. 1: 4636
Outstanding Fluid Power Educator Vol. 1: 10433
Outstanding Fluid Power Student Vol. 1: 10434
Outstanding Football Official Award Vol. 1: 13217

Outstanding Forest Steward of the Year Vol. 1: 14082
Outstanding Forestry Journalism Award Vol. 1: 16510
Outstanding Foundation Award Vol. 1: 5167
Outstanding Friend of the Society Award Vol. 1: 6497
Outstanding Fruit Cultivar Award Vol. 1: 3724
Outstanding Fund Raising Executive Award Vol. 1: 5161
Outstanding Genealogist Award Vol. 1: 14021
Outstanding German Educator Award Vol. 1: 1301
Outstanding Government Service Award Vol. 1: 2910
Outstanding Graduate Educator Award Vol. 1: 3725
Outstanding Graduate Student Award Vol. 1: 17643
Outstanding Graduate Student Leadership Award Vol. 1: 4849
Outstanding Graduate Student Member of the Year Award Vol. 1: 7856
Outstanding Health Care Professional Award Vol. 1: 8267
Outstanding Health Worker Vol. 1: 17999
Outstanding Hearing Conservationist Award Vol. 1: 13328
Outstanding High School Senior in German Vol. 1: 1302
Outstanding Human Performance Intervention Award Vol. 1: 10655
Outstanding Human Service Student Vol. 1: 13495
Outstanding Humanitarian Service Award Vol. 1: 649
Outstanding IIE Publication Award Vol. 1: 9870
Outstanding Individual Achievement Vol. 1: 12457
Outstanding Individual at the Local Level Vol. 1: 14251
Outstanding Individual Volunteer Award Vol. 1: 2626
Outstanding Individual with Autism of the Year Vol. 1: 5552
Outstanding Industry Activist Vol. 1: 14392
Outstanding Industry Scientist Award Vol. 1: 3726
Outstanding Information Science Teacher Award Vol. 1: 3744
Outstanding Instructional Communication Award Vol. 1: 10656
Outstanding Instructional Product Vol. 1: 10657
Outstanding Instructional Product or Intervention Award Vol. 1: 10657
Outstanding International Horticulturist Award Vol. 1: 3727
Outstanding JADARA Article Award Vol. 1: 152
Outstanding Jazz Educator Award Vol. 1: 12743
Outstanding Jazz Student Award Vol. 1: 12744
Outstanding Journalism Award Vol. 1: 1798
Outstanding Judge Award Vol. 1: 11153
Outstanding Junior Investigator of the Year Vol. 1: 16699
Outstanding Junior Member Contest Vol. 1: 13713
Outstanding Junior Shorthorn Breeder Award Vol. 1: 2608
Outstanding Large Chapter Award Vol. 1: 9821
Outstanding Lawyer Award Vol. 1: 11154
Outstanding Leader in Oregon Blueberry Industry Vol. 1: 14669
Outstanding Leadership Vol. 1: 19051
Outstanding Leadership Award
Africa Travel Association Vol. 1: 219
American Rental Association Vol 1: 3481
Council for Exceptional Children Vol 1: 7857
Outstanding Leadership in the Industry Vol. 1: 14392
Outstanding Leadership Medal Vol. 1: 12208
Outstanding Lecture Award Vol. 1: 13329
Outstanding Librarian Award Vol. 1: 9675
Outstanding Library Award Vol. 1: 9676
Outstanding Library Board Award Vol. 1: 4607
Outstanding Library Service Award Vol. 1: 4608
Outstanding Lithuanian Woman Award Vol. 1: 11383
Outstanding Local Leadership Award Vol. 1: 5310
Outstanding Local Section Member Award Vol. 1: 17395
Outstanding Logging Operator Vol. 1: 14392
Outstanding Male and Female Athlete of the Year Vol. 1: 12913
Outstanding Management Innovator Award Vol. 1: 10310
Outstanding Management of Resources Vol. 1: 14392
Outstanding Master's Thesis Award Vol. 1: 780
Outstanding Medical Information Management Executive Award Vol. 1: 5251
Outstanding Member Vol. 1: 4486
Outstanding Member Award Vol. 1: 13957
Outstanding Member of the Year Vol. 1: 12793
Outstanding Mentor Award Vol. 1: 4961
Outstanding Merchandising Achievement Awards Competition Vol. 1: 15138
Outstanding Middle Level Social Studies Teacher of the Year Vol. 1: 12989
Outstanding Mother Award Vol. 1: 13460
Outstanding New Biology Teacher Achievement Award Vol. 1: 12410
Outstanding New Librarian Award Vol. 1: 9677
Outstanding New Systematic Application Award Vol. 1: 10659
Outstanding Newcomer Award Vol. 1: 9471
Outstanding Newsletter Award
Amateur Athletic Union Vol. 1: 495
Federation of Historical Bottle Collectors Vol 1: 8665
National Press Photographers Association Vol 1: 13569
Outstanding Offensive and Defensive Linemen of the Year Awards Vol. 1: 13232
Outstanding Organization Vol. 1: 12939
Outstanding Organization at the Local Level Vol. 1: 14252
Outstanding Organization Development Article of the Year Award Vol. 1: 14683
Outstanding Organization Development Projects of the Year Award Vol. 1: 14684
Outstanding Organization of the Year Vol. 1: 9705
Outstanding Original Script Vol. 1: 9196
Outstanding Paper Award
American Society for Engineering Education Vol. 1: 3665
International Association for Bridge and Structural Engineering Vol 2: 4776
National Association for Research in Science Teaching Vol 1: 12354
Outstanding Paper Awards
American Society for Nondestructive Testing Vol. 1: 3781
International Council on Hotel, Restaurant and Institutional Education Vol 1: 10369
Outstanding Paper Presented at Convention Vol. 1: 16408
Outstanding Paralegal Award Vol. 1: 7258
Outstanding Pennsylvania Author and/or Illustrator Vol. 1: 14940
Outstanding Performance Aid Award Vol. 1: 10658
Outstanding Performance Awards Vol. 1: 15941
Outstanding Philanthropic Organization Vol. 1: 5171
Outstanding Philanthropist Award Vol. 1: 5165
Outstanding Physician Assistant of the Year Award Vol. 1: 734
Outstanding Physician Award Vol. 1: 15456
Outstanding Planning Awards Vol. 1: 3212
Outstanding Power Engineering Educator Award Vol. 1: 9823
Outstanding Product Achievement Vol. 1: 6163
Outstanding Professional Achievement in Metropolitan Transportation Planning Vol. 1: 5233
Outstanding Professional Designee Vol. 1: 10137
Outstanding Professor Award Vol. 1: 15640
Outstanding Program Awards Vol. 1: 18220
Outstanding Program Awards for Credit and Non-Credit Programs Vol. 1: 18221
Outstanding Project Award Vol. 1: 8086
Outstanding Project Award for Biomedical Research in Aging Vol. 1: 9469
Outstanding Project Awards Vol. 1: 17272
Outstanding Project in Ground Water Protection Award Vol. 1: 13294
Outstanding Project in Ground Water Remediation Award Vol. 1: 13295
Outstanding Project in Ground Water Supply Award Vol. 1: 13296
Outstanding Promoter Award Vol. 1: 13807
Outstanding Promotional Service Award Vol. 1: 220
Outstanding Psychologist Award Vol. 1: 3335
Outstanding Public Affairs Award Vol. 1: 4646
Outstanding Public Library Services Award Vol. 1: 6702
Outstanding Public Service Announcement Vol. 1: 12181
Outstanding Public Service Award Vol. 1: 19052
Outstanding Public Service Award
Archaeological Institute of America Vol. 1: 4580
Council for Exceptional Children Vol 1: 7858
Outstanding Publication Award
American Association of Colleges for Teacher Education Vol. 1: 1051

National Press Photographers Association Vol 1: 13569
Ohio Academy of History Vol 1: 14460
Outstanding Reference Sources Vol. 1: 2692
Outstanding Region Advisor Vol. 1: 4644
Outstanding Region Executive Officer Award Vol. 1: 4644
Outstanding Regional Director Vol. 1: 8258
Outstanding Research Award Vol. 1: 10659
Outstanding Researcher Vol. 2: 3356
Outstanding Researcher Award
American Society for Horticultural Science Vol. 1: 3728
Council for Learning Disabilities Vol 1: 7870
National Rural Health Association Vol 1: 13652
Radiological Society of North America Vol 1: 15540
Outstanding ROTC Cadet Award Vol. 1: 14661
Outstanding ROTC Cadet of the Year Vol. 1: 296
Outstanding Rural Health Program Award Vol. 1: 13653
Outstanding Rural Physician Assistant Award Vol. 1: 8268
Outstanding Sawmill Operator Vol. 1: 14392
Outstanding Scholar Award Vol. 1: 8678
Outstanding Scholarly Publication in Family Therapy Research Award Vol. 1: 935
Outstanding School Award Vol. 1: 8405
Outstanding Science Teacher Educator of the Year Vol. 1: 4962
Outstanding Scientific Achievement for Clinical Investigation Award Vol. 1: 2130
Outstanding Scientific Achievements by a Young Investigator Vol. 1: 887
Outstanding Scientific Materials Managers Award Vol. 1: 12656
Outstanding Sculpture Educator Award Vol. 1: 10618
Outstanding Secondary Social Studies Teacher of the Year Vol. 1: 12990
Outstanding Section Awards
AACE International Vol. 1: 25
American Institute of Aeronautics and Astronautics Vol 1: 2395
Outstanding Section Campus Representative Award Vol. 1: 3666
Outstanding Section/Student Chapter Partnership Award Vol. 1: 16586
Outstanding Service Award
National Space Society of Australia Vol. 2: 581
Professional Convention Management Association Vol 1: 15296
States Organization for Boating Access Vol 1: 17273
Outstanding Service Award
Africa Travel Association Vol. 1: 221
American Academy of Family Physicians Vol 1: 613
American Association of Meat Processors Vol 1: 1157
ASPRS - The Imaging and Geospatial Information Society Vol 1: 4746
Association of Building Engineers Vol 2: 5116
Canadian Sociology and Anthropology Association Vol 1: 7039
Chicago Book Clinic Vol 1: 7322
Colorado River Watch Network Vol 1: 7567
Council on Governmental Ethics Laws Vol 1: 7921
International Federation for Information Processing Vol 2: 795
International Wild Waterfowl Association Vol 1: 10836
National Association of Underwater Instructors Vol 1: 12711
Private Practice Section/American Physical Therapy Association Vol 1: 15247
Soil and Water Conservation Society Vol 1: 16934
Specialty Graphic Imaging Association Vol 1: 17114
TRI-M Music Honor Society Vol 1: 17604
Outstanding Service Award for Military Pediatrics Vol. 1: 707
Outstanding Service Award - Karate Vol. 1: 496
Outstanding Service Awards
National Agricultural Aviation Association Vol. 1: 12220
National Interscholastic Swimming Coaches Association of America Vol 1: 13389
Outstanding Service Medallion Vol. 1: 838
Outstanding Service to a Chapter Award Vol. 1: 15297
Outstanding Service to Environmental Education Award Vol. 1: 14253
Outstanding Service to Environmental Education by an Individual Award Vol. 1: 14254
Outstanding Service to Environmental Education by an Organization Award Vol. 1: 14255
Outstanding Service to Librarianship Award Vol. 1: 6692
Outstanding Service to People with Disabilities Vol. 1: 7454
Outstanding Service to the Forest Industry Vol. 1: 14392
Outstanding Short Course Vol. 1: 16332
Outstanding Show Poster Award Vol. 1: 8666
Outstanding Small Chapter Award Vol. 1: 9821
Outstanding Society Awards Vol. 1: 11356
Outstanding Southeastern Author Award Vol. 1: 17007
Outstanding Southeastern Library Program Award Vol. 1: 17008
Outstanding SPS Chapter Advisor Award Vol. 1: 2544
Outstanding Squadron Advisor Vol. 1: 4643
Outstanding State ACES Division Award Vol. 1: 4850
Outstanding State Association Award Vol. 1: 12245
Outstanding State Federation Vol. 1: 19096
Outstanding State Leader Award Vol. 1: 5310
Outstanding State Representative Award Vol. 1: 8135
Outstanding Statistical Application Awards Vol. 1: 4315
Outstanding Student Achievement in Contemporary Sculpture Award Vol. 1: 10619
Outstanding Student Award
American Medical Technologists Vol. 1: 2755
Resort and Commercial Recreation Association Vol 1: 15638
Resort and Commercial Recreation Association Vol 1: 15640
Outstanding Student Award for Undergraduate Research Vol. 1: 16818
Outstanding Student Chapter Award Vol. 1: 16356
Outstanding Student Recognition Awards Vol. 1: 13079
Outstanding Student Research Award Vol. 1: 10660
Outstanding Support Staff Award Vol. 1: 9678
Outstanding Teacher Award
Council for Learning Disabilities Vol. 1: 7871
National Marine Educators Association Vol 1: 13425
Pennsylvania Association of Private School Administrators Vol 1: 14921
Outstanding Teacher Awards Vol. 1: 17460
Outstanding Teacher Educator in Reading Award Vol. 1: 10591
Outstanding Teacher of American History Contest Vol. 1: 13714
Outstanding Teacher of the Year Awards Vol. 1: 1306
Outstanding Teacher of Theatre in Higher Education Award Vol. 1: 4995
Outstanding Technical Achievement Award Vol. 1: 69
Outstanding Technical Paper Award Vol. 1: 11704
Outstanding Technologist Award Vol. 1: 16780
Outstanding Ticketing Professional Award Vol. 1: 10796
Outstanding Total Community Service Vol. 1: 7455
Outstanding Total Youth Vol. 1: 7456
Outstanding Trailblazer Award Vol. 1: 6
Outstanding Trustee Award Vol. 1: 9679
Outstanding Undergraduate Educator Award Vol. 1: 3729
Outstanding Undergraduate Student Member of the Year Award Vol. 1: 7859
Outstanding Use of Wood Vol. 1: 14392
Outstanding Volunteer Award Vol. 1: 15457
Outstanding Volunteer Awards Vol. 1: 13466
Outstanding Volunteer Fund Raiser Award Vol. 1: 5164
Outstanding Volunteer Fundraiser Vol. 1: 5172
Outstanding Woman Veterinarian of the Year Vol. 1: 5012
Outstanding Women in Music Award Vol. 1: 17406
Outstanding Women of Color Vol. 1: 10123
Outstanding Wrestling Official of the Year Vol. 1: 497
Outstanding Young Agents Committee Award Vol. 1: 9643
Outstanding Young Agrologist Award Vol. 1: 249
Outstanding Young Alumnus Vol. 1: 8943
Outstanding Young Dentist Award Vol. 2: 3769
Outstanding Young Electrical and Computer Engineer Award Vol. 1: 8541
Outstanding Young Farmer Awards Vol. 1: 17982
Outstanding Young Industrial Engineer Award Vol. 1: 9871
Outstanding Young Investigator Award Vol. 1: 11597

Award Index

Outstanding Young Manufacturing Engineer Award Vol. 1: 16724
Outstanding Young Member Award Vol. 1: 848
Outstanding Young Numismatist of the Year Vol. 1: 2911
Outstanding Young Range Professional Award Vol. 1: 16404
Outstanding Young Scientist Award Vol. 2: 1778
The Outstanding Young Scientists (TOYS) Vol. 2: 3983
Outstanding Young Volunteer of the Year Award Vol. 1: 11188
Outstanding Young Woman Volunteers Award Vol. 2: 3952
Outstanding Younger Member Award Vol. 1: 16587
Outstanding Youth Vol. 1: 2140
Outstanding Youth Project Vol. 1: 7457
Outstanding Youth Science Researchers Vol. 2: 3983
Outstanding Zone Campus Activity Coordinator Award Vol. 1: 3682
Overall Triathletes of the Year Vol. 1: 18461
Overly Scholarship; Helene Vol. 1: 18878
Oversattarpris Vol. 2: 4664
Overseas Premium Vol. 2: 6122
Overseas Prize Vol. 2: 6853
Owen Awards; Wilfred Vol. 2: 6041
Owen Book Prize; Walter Vol. 1: 6334
Owen Medal; Morgan Vol. 2: 5649
Owen Memorial Scholarship; Charles and Melva T. Vol. 1: 13191
Owen Memorial Trophy Vol. 1: 17903
Owen Poetry Prize; Guy Vol. 1: 17046
Owens Award; Jesse Vol. 1: 18451
Owens Scholarly Achievement Award; William A. Vol. 1: 16295
Owlglass Prize Vol. 2: 2316
Owsley Award; Frank L. and Harriet C. Vol. 1: 17036
OX5; Mr. Vol. 1: 14766
Oxford University Fellowship Vol. 2: 6600
PACC Scholarship Vol. 1: 15065
Pace Award Vol. 1: 498
Pace Award; Frank Vol. 1: 10393
PACE Awards Vol. 1: 1163
Pacemaker Award Vol. 1: 13662
Pacemaker Awards; Associated Collegiate Press Vol. 1: 14221
Pacemaker Awards; National Scholastic Press Association Vol. 1: 14222
Pacesetter Award
 Alberta Construction Safety Association Vol. 1: 363
 Manufacturers' Agents for the Foodservice Industry Vol 1: 11499
 National Academic Advising Association Vol 1: 12092
Pacesetter of the Year Award Vol. 1: 12977
Pacific Southwest Section Outstanding Community College Educator Award Vol. 1: 3667
Pacing Triple Crown Vol. 1: 18162
Package Printing and Converting's Diecutter/Diemaker of the Year Award Vol. 1: 10195
Packaging Achiever Awards Vol. 2: 596
Packaging Competition Awards Vol. 1: 13521
Packaging Hall of Fame Vol. 1: 14794
Packard International Parks Merit Award; Fred M. Vol. 2: 4917
Packard International Parks Merit Award/World Commission on Protected Areas; Fred M. Vol. 2: 4920
Packard Outstanding Educator Award; Robert L. Vol. 1: 17060
Packer Engineering Safety Award Vol. 1: 3859
PACS Technology Award Vol. 1: 6266
Padma Bhushan Vol. 2: 2580
Padma Shri Vol. 2: 2581
Padma Vibhushan Vol. 2: 2582
Padnendadlu Graduate Bursary Vol. 2: 192
Paediatric Anaesthesia Research Fund Vol. 2: 5145
Page Award; Handley Vol. 2: 6649
The Page Medal Vol. 2: 67
Page Outstanding Service Award; John A. Vol. 1: 9327
Page Prize; Gillian Vol. 2: 6731
Page Young Investigator Research Award; Irvine H. Vol. 1: 2186
Pagels Human Rights of Scientists Award; Heinz R. Vol. 1: 14109
Pahlsons pris; Margit Vol. 2: 4665
Paine Journalism Award; Thomas Vol. 1: 17526
Paine Memorial Award; Thomas O. Vol. 1: 15085
Painter Memorial Award; Robert J. Vol. 1: 5449
Painter Memorial Award; SES/ASTM Robert J. Vol. 1: 17248
Painton Award; Harry R. Vol. 1: 7807
Pake Prize; George E. Vol. 1: 3127
Pakistan Institute of Sciences Gold Medal Vol. 2: 3921
Pal Memorial Award; George Vol. 1: 121
Palaios Outstanding Paper Award Vol. 1: 16412
Palanca Memorial Awards for Literature; Carlos Vol. 2: 3978
Paleontological Society Medal Vol. 1: 14813
Paletou Award; J. Wallace Vol. 1: 9938
Paley Prize in Short Fiction; Grace Vol. 1: 4773
Palmai-Tenser Scholarship; Rose Vol. 1: 11896
Palme d'Or
 Cannes International Film Festival Vol. 2: 1730
 International Advertising Festival Vol 2: 6202
 Shark Awards Festival Vol 2: 2887
Palme Memorial Fund Scholarships; Olof Vol. 2: 4616
Palme Prize; Olof Vol. 2: 4617
Palmer Award; Joe Vol. 1: 13875
Palmer Award; Katherine Vol. 1: 14810
Palmer Memorial Prize; Edwin Vol. 1: 12115
Palmer Prize; Frederick Vol. 2: 6123
Palmera de Bronce Vol. 2: 4525
Palmera de Oro Vol. 2: 4525
Palmera de Plata Vol. 2: 4525
Palmes Academiques Vol. 2: 1824
Paloma O'Shea Santander International Piano Competition Vol. 2: 4540
PAMA/ATP Award Vol. 1: 15272
Pamplin Distinguished Awards Vol. 1: 8878
Panafrican Film and Television Festival of Ouagadougou Vol. 2: 1160
Panchaud Medallions; John Vol. 2: 5717
Pandora Award Vol. 2: 7343
Panetti International Prize with Gold Medal; Professor Modesto Vol. 2: 2969
Pannell Award; Lucile Micheels Vol. 1: 18867
Panofsky Prize in Experimental Particle Physics; W. K. H. Vol. 1: 3128
Panorama Brasilian Art Vol. 2: 1134
Panorama de Arte Brasileira Vol. 2: 1134
Panowski Playwriting Award; Mildred and Albert Vol. 1: 15687
Pantalla Abierta Award Vol. 2: 4493
Panting Award; Gerry Vol. 1: 6757
Papalia Award for Excellence in Teacher Education; Anthony Vol. 1: 1833
Papanicolaou Award Vol. 1: 4018
Paper Industry Gold Medal Vol. 2: 6519
Paper Prize Awards Vol. 1: 14981
Papers and Publications Committee Prizes Vol. 2: 6433
Papers Award Vol. 2: 6314
Pappas Research Award; Doug Vol. 1: 16172
Paracelsus Medaille Vol. 2: 2196
Paracelsus-Preis Vol. 2: 4892
Paracelsusring der Stadt Villach Vol. 2: 822
Parade - IACP Police Service Award Vol. 1: 10174
Paragon Awards Vol. 1: 12978
Paralegal of the Year Vol. 1: 8021
Param Vir Chakra Vol. 2: 2583
Param Vishisht Seva Medal Vol. 2: 2584
Parametrician of the Year Vol. 1: 10733
Parandowski Prize; Jan Vol. 2: 4019
Paraprofessional of the Year Award Vol. 1: 4611
Parbo Medal; Sir Arvi Vol. 2: 521
Parcel - Leif J. Sverdrup Civil Engineering Management Award; John I. Vol. 1: 3969
Pard'ners Award Vol. 1: 1963
Pardoe Space Award; Geoffrey Vol. 2: 6650
Parent of the Year Vol. 1: 14476
Parent-Patient Leadership Award Vol. 1: 7469
Parenteau Memorial Award; William A. Vol. 1: 334
Parents' Choice Awards Vol. 1: 14854
Parents' Choice Classic Award Vol. 1: 14854
Parents' Choice FunStuff Award Vol. 1: 14854
Parents of the Year Vol. 1: 5553
Parish Pastor of the Year Vol. 1: 119
Parisot Foundation Fellowship; Jacques Vol. 2: 4928
Park Communicator Award Vol. 1: 158
Park Educator Award Vol. 1: 158
Park Heritage Award Vol. 1: 158
Park Stewardship Award Vol. 1: 158
Parke-Davis Award Vol. 1: 3752
Parker Award; Virginia Vol. 1: 6117
Parker Awards for Spoken Business Japanese; Sir Peter Vol. 2: 7075
Parker Education Gold Ribbon Awards; Sally Vol. 1: 4344
Parker Medal for Distinguished Service to the Profession of Pharmacy; Paul F. Vol. 1: 1634
Parker Memorial Award; Jim Vol. 1: 12498
Parker Memorial Award; R. Hunt Vol. 1: 14371
Parker Memorial Medal; Ben H. Vol. 1: 2553
Parker Romantic Novel of the Year Vol. 2: 6605
Parker Trophy; Jackie Vol. 1: 6516
Parkhouse Award; Charles Vol. 2: 5184
Parkinson Award for Young British Musicians; Dorothy Vol. 2: 5969

Parkman Medal Vol. 2: 6124
Parks Photography Competition; Gordon Vol. 1: 8827
Parlin Award; Charles Coolidge Vol. 1: 2719
Parmele Award
Professional Convention Management Association Vol. 1: 15298
Specialty Graphic Imaging Association Vol 1: 17115
Parry Award; Evan Vol. 2: 3742
Parsons Award; Charles Lathrop Vol. 1: 1572
Parsons Award; Frank Vol. 2: 395
Parsons Memorial Prize; R. W. Vol. 2: 522
Parsons Prize for Social Science; Talcott Vol. 1: 554
Partee Trophy - Norfolk Dog Vol. 1: 14428
Partington Prize Vol. 2: 7119
Partisan of the Year Award, TAIKO Vol. 2: 1388
Partner in Health Award Vol. 1: 7498
Partner of the Year Vol. 1: 10901
Partners Against Leukemia and Lymphoma Award Vol. 1: 11309
Partners Award Vol. 1: 364
Partnership Award
Direct Selling Association Vol. 1: 8211
Indiana Library Federation Vol 1: 9680
Partnership Development Award Vol. 2: 3717
Partnership with AERC-Morab Vol. 1: 10519
Partnership with USDF All Breed-Morab Vol. 1: 10520
Parville; Prix Henri de Vol. 2: 1595
Pascal; Prix Paul Vol. 2: 1596
Pascatti Rotary Prize; Antonio Vol. 2: 3136
Paschal Award; James Frederick Vol. 1: 7581
Passano Foundation Award Vol. 1: 14867
Passenger Service Award Vol. 1: 341
Passow Classroom Teacher Scholarship; A. Harry Vol. 1: 12321
Past Presidents Vol. 1: 2015
Past President's Award
American Association for Clinical Chemistry Vol. 1: 888
International Federation of Biomedical Laboratory Science Vol 1: 10407
Past Presidents' Award Vol. 1: 1222
Past Presidents' Award for Merit in Transportation Vol. 1: 9950
Past Presidents' Canadian Legislator Award Vol. 1: 7069
Past President's Intermediate Brass Scholarship Vol. 1: 15881
Past-Presidents' Medal Vol. 1: 11788
Past Presidents' Memorial Medal Vol. 1: 6630
Past President's Scholarship Vol. 1: 9244
Pasteur Award Vol. 1: 9614
Pasteur Medal; Louis Vol. 2: 1563
Patch Awards; Dan Vol. 1: 17935
Pate Award; Tom Vol. 1: 6517
Pate Leadership for Children Award; Maurice Vol. 1: 17911
Paterno; Medaglia Emanuele Vol. 2: 3105
Paterno Scholar-Athlete Award; William Pearce/Joseph V. Vol. 1: 13215
Paterson Award; Donald G. Vol. 1: 11845
Paterson Kerr Book Award; Joan Vol. 1: 18690
Paterson Medal and Prize Vol. 2: 6065
Pates Prize Vol. 2: 5131
Pathfinder Award
Automotive Occupant Restraints Council Vol. 1: 5571
Institute for Public Relations Vol 1: 9756
National Association for Girls and Women in Sport Vol 1: 12327
Patient Advocacy Award Lecture Vol. 1: 3282
Patient/Family Education Materials Award Vol. 1: 5286
Patient Participation Award Vol. 2: 6696
Paton Prize; Evgenij Vol. 2: 1903
Paton Prize; William A. Vol. 1: 12116
Paton Society Award Vol. 1: 8573
Patria; Prix Bene Merenti de Vol. 1: 16145
Patriach Athenagoras Diocesan Service Award Vol. 1: 13251
Patrick Award; Dan Vol. 1: 10282
Patrick Henry Memorial Oratorical Contest Vol. 1: 13244
The Patrick Trevor-Roper Undergraduate Award Vol. 2: 6713
Patriot Award Vol. 1: 14843
Patriot Medal Vol. 1: 13773
Patriot of the Nation Vol. 1: 13962
Patriotism Award Vol. 1: 3225
Patriots Award Vol. 1: 7717
Patron of Architecture Award Vol. 2: 4333
Patron of the American Community Theatre Association Vol. 1: 1058
Patron of the Arts Award Vol. 1: 9196
Patrons and Fellows Vol. 2: 2635
Patron's Medal Vol. 2: 6767
Patron's Recognition Award Vol. 1: 10620
PatsyLu Prize Vol. 1: 10031
Patterson Award; A. Lindo Vol. 1: 1860
Patterson Grants; Alfred Nash Vol. 1: 7375
Patterson Memorial Grant; Bryan Vol. 1: 16892
Patwardhan Prize in Nutritional Sciences; Dr. V. N. Vol. 2: 2616
Paul Award; Alice Vol. 1: 11370
Paul Branton Meritorious Service Award Vol. 2: 5799
Paul Career Award; John Vol. 2: 5583
Paul Freeling Award Vol. 2: 6697
Paul Prize; Barbara Vol. 1: 15497
Paul VI Prize; International Vol. 2: 3092
Pauling Poster Prize Vol. 1: 1861
Pavarotti Trophy Vol. 2: 6393
Pavement Awards Vol. 1: 12298
Pawsey Medal Vol. 2: 121
Paxinos-Watson Prize Vol. 2: 302
Payen Award; Anselme Vol. 1: 1573
Payne Award; Ed Vol. 1: 16486
Payne Award for Most Promising Newcomer; Sam Vol. 1: 9196
Payne Medal; J.A. Vol. 1: 11641
PC World Award Vol. 2: 7432
Peabody Awards Collection Vol. 1: 18281
Peabody Awards; George Foster Vol. 1: 18281
Peabody Medal; George Vol. 1: 14877
Peace Award of Committee of 100 Vol. 2: 1357
Peace Education Awards Vol. 1: 15508
Peace Play Contest Vol. 1: 9137
Peace Prize of the German Book Trade Vol. 2: 2216
Peace Quilt Awards Vol. 1: 5834
P.E.A.C.E. Trophy Vol. 2: 2830
Peak Award Vol. 1: 14245
Peanut Research and Education Award Vol. 1: 3030
Pearce Award; William T. Vol. 1: 5450
Pearce/Joseph V. Paterno Scholar-Athlete Award; William Vol. 1: 13215
Pearl Award for Investigative Reporting; Daniel Vol. 1: 8073
Pearls Vol. 2: 2565
Pearson Award; Clarence ₤kev Vol. 1: 12582
Pearson Award; L. B. "Mike" Vol. 1: 6664
Pearson Award; Lester B. Vol. 1: 13349
Pearson Prize; Carl Bode { Norman Holmes Vol. 1: 4326
Pease Award; Theodore Calvin Vol. 1: 16496
Peaslee Brazing Award; Robert L. Vol. 1: 4464
Peat Marwick Award; KPMG Vol. 1: 18610
Peccei Scholarship Vol. 2: 805
Peck Award; Walter D. Vol. 1: 15582
Pecora Award; William T. Vol. 1: 14883
Pedersens Biblioteksfonds Forfatterpris; Edvard Vol. 2: 1285
Pederson Award in Solid-State Circuits; Donald O. Vol. 1: 9789
Pederson, CTC Award; Melva C. Vol. 1: 4257
Pediatric Dermatology Fellows/Residents Research Award Vol. 1: 16366
Pediatric Dermatology Research Grant Vol. 1: 16367
Pediatric Founders Award Vol. 1: 4026
Pedler Lectureship Vol. 2: 6978
Pedroli Prize; Castelli Vol. 2: 2108
Pedrotti; Concurso Internazionale per Direttori d'Orchestra Antonio Vol. 2: 2983
Pedrotti International Competition for Orchestra Conductors; Antonio Vol. 2: 2983
Peek Award; Cuthbert Vol. 2: 6773
Peele Memorial Award; Robert Vol. 1: 16357
Peet Travelling Prize; Thomas Eric Vol. 2: 7312
Peirce Essay Contest Award; C. S. Vol. 1: 7288
Pelander Award; Carl E. Vol. 1: 15893
Pelick Research Award; Supelco/ Nicholas Vol. 2: 2970
Pelletier; Prix Memain- Vol. 2: 1859
Pels Foundation Awards for Drama; Laura Vol. 1: 14902
Peltier Award; Leslie C. Vol. 1: 5477
Peltier Plaque Vol. 1: 16528
Pelton Award; Jeanette Siron Vol. 1: 5882
Pelzer Memorial Award; Louis Vol. 1: 14699
Pemberton Trophy Vol. 2: 5955
PEN/Faulkner Award for Fiction Vol. 1: 14909
PEN/Malamud Award for Short Fiction Vol. 1: 14910
PEN Prison Writing Awards Vol. 1: 14903
PEN Publisher Award Vol. 1: 14904
Pena; Premio Enrique Vol. 2: 11
Penanrun; Prix Le Dissez de Vol. 2: 1687
Penaud Aeromodelling Diploma; Alphonse Vol. 2: 4744
Pendergast Award; Margaret and James F. Vol. 1: 6185
Pendleton Award; S. Alden Vol. 1: 9899
Pendray Aerospace Literature Award Vol. 1: 2396
Pendray Award; G. Edward Vol. 1: 2396
Penguin Young Readers Group Award Vol. 1: 4929
Penick Award for Excellence in the Game of Life; Harvey Vol. 1: 7111

Penner Prize; Donald W. Vol. 1: 6273
Penney - University of Missouri Newspaper Awards; JC Vol. 1: 18325
Penning Award Excellence in Low-Temperature Plasma Physics Vol. 1: 10815
Penrose Award; Spencer Vol. 1: 2250
Penrose Award/University Division Coach of the Year; Spencer Vol. 1: 2258
Penrose Medal Vol. 1: 16653
Penrose Medal Award Vol. 1: 9025
PeopleFs Choice Award Vol. 1: 9471
People's Choice Award
American Numismatic Association Vol. 1: 2912
American Physicians Art Association Vol 1: 3159
Toronto International Film Festival Group Vol 1: 17560
People's Choice Awards Vol. 1: 14960
People's Choice Awards-Best Commercial-Digital Vol. 1: 15259
People's Choice Awards-Best Commercial-Photo Vol. 1: 15260
People's Choice-Best Artistic-Digital Vol. 1: 15261
People's Choice-Best Artistic-Photo Vol. 1: 15262
Peplau Award; Hildegard Vol. 1: 2944
Pepler International Award; George Vol. 2: 7050
PEPP Chair Award Vol. 1: 13747
PEPP Merit Award Vol. 1: 13748
PEPP Professional Development Awards Vol. 1: 13749
Peppe Award; Mike Vol. 1: 17732
Pepsi 400 Trophy Vol. 1: 8067
Pepys Medal; Samuel Vol. 2: 5786
Percy Sergeant Medal Vol. 2: 4143
Pereira Award; Professor E. O. E. Vol. 2: 4559
Perera Memorial Award; Aylet Lily Vol. 2: 4560
Perfect Ten (Equine Only) Award Vol. 1: 1964
Performance Citation Award Vol. 1: 7150
Performance Test Codes Medal Vol. 1: 4158
Periwinkle Award Vol. 1: 7485
Perkin Medal Vol. 2: 7189
Perkins Award; Dud Vol. 1: 2812
Perkins Award for Professional Excellence; R. Marlin Vol. 1: 4500
Perkins Award; Marlin Vol. 1: 1337
Perkins Government Relations Award; Carl D. Vol. 1: 1845
Perkins, Jr. Memorial Award; John F. Vol. 1: 3176
Perlemuter Piano Scholarship; Vlado Vol. 2: 5923
Perlman Award for Human Advancement; Jewish Women International Vol. 1: 11014
Perlman Award; Itzhak Vol. 1: 18579
Perlman Gallery Cash Award; Miriam Vol. 1: 16517
Perloff President's Prize Vol. 1: 1981
Perpetual Trophy for the Performance of Irish Contemporary Choral Music Vol. 2: 2829
Perpetual World Championship Trophies Vol. 2: 5910
Perren Research Award; S. M. Vol. 2: 3037
Perret; Prix Paul-Michel Vol. 2: 1688
Perret Prize; Auguste Vol. 2: 1925
Perrier Award Vol. 2: 5752
Perrier Pick of the Fringe Season Vol. 2: 5752
Perron Award; E. du Vol. 2: 3677
Perrot; Medaille Georges Vol. 2: 1524
Perry Award; Newel Vol. 1: 13192
Perry Awards (Tony Awards); Antoinette Vol. 1: 11261
Perry Distinguished Authors Award; J. Warren Vol. 1: 5331
Perry Research Scholarship; John Lord Vol. 2: 6744
Pershing Memorial Membership Award; Everett Vol. 1: 13098
Pershing Plaque Vol. 1: 13301
Persian Language Study in Tehran Vol. 1: 2519
Person of the Year
Canadian Construction Association Vol. 1: 6425
Minnesota Holstein Association Vol 1: 11842
Singapore Computer Society Vol 2: 4427
Person of the Year Award
Brazilian-American Chamber of Commerce Vol. 1: 5932
French-American Chamber of Commerce Vol 1: 8882
Irrigation Association Vol 1: 10902
Personal Achievement in Chemical Engineering Awards Vol. 1: 7298
Personal Service Award Vol. 1: 3429
Personal Trainer of the Year Vol. 1: 9559
Personality of the Year Vol. 2: 4159
Personality of the Year Award Vol. 2: 5196
Persons Awards Vol. 1: 17286
Persoon Medal; Christiaan Hendrik Vol. 2: 4369
Perspectives Award Vol. 1: 5154
Perten Award; The Harold Vol. 2: 783
Pertzoff Prize; Vladimir A. Vol. 1: 18357
Peryam Award; David R. Vol. 1: 5451
Pessimist of the Year Award Vol. 1: 5714
Peter Floud Award Vol. 2: 7338
Peter Isaac Award; Working for a Healthier Workplace - The Vol. 2: 5397
Peter Williamson Memorial Trust Fund Bursaries Vol. 1: 17128
Peters Award; John P. Vol. 1: 4197
Peters Historical Crime Award; Ellis Vol. 2: 5712
Petersen Award; Lt. General Frank Vol. 1: 13439
Peterson Agricultural Scholarship Award; John W. Vol. 1: 14706
Peterson Consumer Service Award; Esther
Consumer Federation of America Vol. 1: 7780
Food Marketing Institute Vol 1: 8788
Peterson Distinguished Service Award; Elaine Vol. 1: 13263
Peterson Fellows; Charles E. Vol. 1: 5490
Peterson Fellowship; Kate B. and Hall J. Vol. 1: 819
Peterson Research Fellowships and Internships; Charles E. Vol. 1: 5490
Petit d'Ormoy; Prix Vol. 2: 1597
Petrassi; Concorso Internazionale di Composizione Goffredo Vol. 2: 3049
Petrassi International Competition for Composers; Goffredo Vol. 2: 3049
Petrie Memorial Award; Dr. Vol. 1: 6267
Petrizzo Award for Career Achievement; D. Richard Vol. 1: 12979
Petro-Canada Award in New Media Vol. 1: 6118
Pets in Cities Award Vol. 1: 10218
Petsavers Award Vol. 2: 5470
Pettigrew Award; Kenneth J. Vol. 1: 18420
Pettijohn Medal; Francis J. Vol. 1: 16413
Pettinos Award; Charles E. Vol. 1: 1448
Peurifoy Construction Research Award Vol. 1: 3970
Peyches; Prix Ivan Vol. 2: 1598
Peyton Award for Cold Regions Engineering; Harold R. Vol. 1: 3971
Pezcoller Foundation - FECS Recognition for Contribution to Oncology Vol. 2: 886
Pezcoller International Award for Cancer Research; AACR- Vol. 2: 3116
Pezzano Scholarships; Chuck Vol. 1: 5898
Pfeffer Peace Prize Vol. 1: 8681
Pfeiffer Service Award; Peggy Leach Vol. 1: 5190
Pfeil Prize; Wilhelm Leopold Vol. 2: 2400
Pfister Award; Oskar Vol. 1: 3283
Pfizer Animal Health Distinguished Service Award Vol. 1: 1028
Pfizer Animal Health Physiology Award Vol. 1: 1887
Pfizer Award Vol. 1: 9442
Pfizer Award in Enzyme Chemistry Vol. 1: 1574
Pfizer Extension Award Vol. 1: 15182
Pfizer Minority Summer Fellowship Award Vol. 1: 1684
Pfizer Mycology Postdoctoral Fellowship Vol. 1: 13257
Pfizer Mycology Postdoctoral Fellowship/John P. Utz Award Vol. 1: 13256
Pfizer Outstanding Investigator Award Vol. 1: 3752
Pfizer Predoctoral Excellence in Renal Research Award; Renal Section Vol. 1: 3179
PGA Assistants Professional Championship Vol. 2: 6559
PGA Championship Vol. 1: 15320
PGA Club Professional Championship Vol. 2: 6560
PGA Cup Vol. 2: 6561
PGA Trainee of the Year Vol. 2: 6568
Phadke Oration; Dr. G.M. Vol. 2: 2808
Phadke Travelling Award; Late G.M. Vol. 2: 2809
Pharmacia and Upjohn Physiology Award Vol. 1: 1888
Pharmacia-ASPET Award for Experimental Therapeutics Vol. 1: 3809
Pharmingen Investigator Award Vol. 1: 1135
Phaup Award Vol. 2: 7435
PHBA National Youth Congress Horse Show High Point Youth Vol. 1: 14823
PhD Scholarships Vol. 2: 31
Phelan Art Awards; James Duval Vol. 1: 15830
Phelan Literary Award; James Duval Vol. 1: 15831
Phelan Memorial Award; Paul F. Vol. 1: 3503
Phenix UDA Vol. 2: 2008
Phi Alpha Theta Western Front Association Undergraduate Essay Prize Vol. 1: 14982
Phi Alpha Theta/Westerners International Award Vol. 1: 14983
Phi Alpha Theta World History Association Paper Prize Vol. 1: 14984
Phibro Animal Health Excellence in Poultry Research Award Vol. 1: 995
Phil Hedges Award Vol. 1: 14593

Philadelphia International Film Festival and Market (Philafilm Awards) Vol. 1: 409
Philadelphia Liberty Medal Vol. 1: 9192
Philadelphia Section Award Vol. 1: 1587
Philafilm Awards Vol. 1: 409
Philalethes Lecture Vol. 1: 15013
Philatelic Hall of Fame Vol. 1: 3077
Philatelic Traders Vol. 2: 6535
Philbin Award Vol. 1: 12509
Philbro Extension Award Vol. 1: 15182
Philip Morris Art Award Vol. 2: 5967
Philip Morris International Prize Vol. 2: 1752
Philippine Mathematical Olympiad Vol. 2: 3984
Philippine Physics Olympiad Vol. 2: 3985
Philips Award; Frederik Vol. 1: 9790
Philips; Prix Vol. 2: 1980
Philips Prize in Jurisprudence; Henry M. Vol. 1: 3102
Philips Scholarships; Ada Vol. 2: 5154
Philips Travel Fellowship Vol. 2: 5334
Phillips Award; A.T. Vol. 1: 10050
Phillips Award; Dr. Jackson R. E. Vol. 1: 5325
Phillips Award; Melba Newell Vol. 1: 1253
Phillips Leadership Award; Sarah Thorniley Vol. 1: 15010
Phillips Memorial Award; John Vol. 1: 1718
Phillips Memorial Medal; John C. Vol. 2: 4921
Phillips Performance Award Vol. 1: 18421
Phillips Petroleum Company ISC All-World Awards Vol. 1: 10755
Phillips Prize; A.A. Vol. 2: 57
Phillips Prize for Behind the Scenes Achievement; Mary Vol. 1: 9196
Phillips Trophy, P.T.S. Trophy Vol. 2: 6535
Philos Award - Philanthropist of the Year Vol. 1: 3472
Phoenix Award
Air Transport World Vol. 1: 341
Children's Literature Association Vol 1: 7350
Society of American Travel Writers Vol 1: 16540
Phoenix Award for Outstanding Contributions to Disaster Recovery Vol. 1: 18118
Phoenix Award for Small Business Disaster Recovery Vol. 1: 18119
Phoenix Diploma Vol. 2: 4745
Phoenix House Award for Public Service Vol. 1: 15019
Photo Contest Vol. 1: 19019
Photo of Agriculture Award Vol. 1: 13958
Photo Travel Division Awards Vol. 1: 15029
Photogrammetric (Fairchild) Award Vol. 1: 4747
Photographers' Awards Vol. 2: 5151
PhotographersF Fellowship Fund Vol. 1: 7234
Photographic Portrait Prize Vol. 2: 48
Photography Annual Vol. 1: 7638
Photography Award Vol. 1: 9983
Photography Awards
American Hemerocallis Society Vol. 1: 2210
Outdoor Writers Association of America Vol 1: 14752
Photography Contests Vol. 1: 8990
Photojournalism Division Awards Vol. 1: 15030
Physical Education School Recognition Award Vol. 1: 6200
Physical Science Award Vol. 2: 4569
Physician Assistant Award Vol. 1: 5252
Physician Assistant of the Year Vol. 1: 14676
Physician Assistant Service to the Underserved Award Vol. 1: 735
Physician Executive of the Year Award Vol. 1: 1677
Physician of the Year
American Association of Physician Specialists Vol. 1: 1240
United States Amateur Boxing, Inc. Vol 1: 17717
Physician of the Year Award Vol. 1: 8269
Physician-Scientist Training Award Vol. 1: 1916
Physiological Section Award Vol. 1: 5883
Phytochemical Society of Europe Medal Vol. 2: 4021
Pi Gamma Mu Scholarships Vol. 1: 15038
Pi Kapp Scholar Award Vol. 1: 15049
Pi Kappa Alpha Chapter and Alumni Awards Vol. 1: 15042
Pi Tau Sigma Gold Medal Vol. 1: 4159
Piafsky Young Investigator Award; K.M. Vol. 1: 5942
Piafsky Young Investigator Award of the Canadian Society for Clinical Pharmacology; K. M. Vol. 1: 5942
Piaz; Premio Giorgio Dal Vol. 2: 3128
Piccolo Prix Vol. 1: 12284
Pickell Award; Mark Vol. 1: 10752
Pickering Award for Playwriting Excellence; Robert J. Vol. 1: 7489
Picture Book Award Vol. 1: 16984
Picture Book of the Year Award Vol. 2: 408
"Picture It Painted Professionally" Awards Vol. 1: 14807
Pied Piper Award Vol. 1: 4002
Piekara Prize; Arkadiiusz Vol. 2: 4048
Piepenbrink Award for Excellence in Behavioral Healthcare Management and Service; Harold C. Vol. 1: 5047
Pier of the Year Award Vol. 2: 6481
Pierce Award; Janette Vol. 1: 8510
Pierce Medal; Lorne Vol. 1: 15765
Pierce Memorial Prize; W. H. Vol. 2: 7087
Pierce Prize in Astronomy; Newton Lacy Vol. 1: 1362
Piercy Award; Esther J. Vol. 1: 4916
Pieri Memorial Award; Louis A. R. Vol. 1: 2277
Pierre Fournier Prize Vol. 2: 1750
Pierre Robillard Award Vol. 1: 17281
Pijls Prize; Catharine Vol. 2: 1105
Pijlsprijs; Catharina Vol. 2: 1105
Pike Prize for Service to People with Disabilities Vol. 1: 5864
Pike Prize for the Handicapped Vol. 1: 5864
Pilkington Outstanding Educator Award; Theo C. Vol. 1: 3668
The Pillar Award Vol. 1: 2756
Pillsbury Bake-Off (R) Contest Vol. 1: 8994
Piloo Mody Surfa Coats Awards Vol. 2: 2640
Pilot and Feasibility Awards
Cystic Fibrosis Foundation Vol. 1: 8011
Washington University in St. Louis - Diabetes Research and Training Center Vol 1: 18612
Pilot of the Year Award Vol. 1: 9368
Pilot Project Research Awards Vol. 1: 18296
Pilot Research Award Vol. 1: 557
Pilot Safety Award
Helicopter Association International Vol. 1: 9369
National Business Aviation Association Vol 1: 12829
PIME Communications Award Vol. 2: 867
Pimentel Award in Chemical Education; George C. Vol. 1: 1575
Pimlott Award; Douglas H. Vol. 1: 13980
Pimsleur Award for Research in Foreign Language Education; Paul Vol. 1: 1834
Pinch Medal Vol. 1: 11789
Pinchot Medal; Gifford Vol. 1: 16511
Pinckney Award; Robert L. Vol. 1: 2204
Pinehurst Bronze Medal Vol. 1: 17312
Pinet; Prix Vol. 2: 1468
Pinette; Fondation Vol. 2: 1482
Pinkard Leader in Federal Equity Award; Mary D. Vol. 1: 17778
Pinkerton Prize Vol. 1: 18245
Pinkett Minority Student Award; Harold T. Vol. 1: 16497
Pinnacle Award
Association of the Wall and Ceiling Industries - International Vol. 1: 5366
Canadian Society of Association Executives Vol 1: 6980
Medical-Dental-Hospital Business Associates Vol 1: 11646
Specialized Carriers and Rigging Association Vol 1: 17100
Pinnacle Awards
Society for Human Resource Management Vol. 1: 16241
Society of National Association Publications Vol 1: 16757
Pinnacle Awards for Convention and Visitor Bureaus (CVBs) and Tourist Offices Vol. 1: 17318
Pinnacle Awards for Hotels Vol. 1: 17319
Pinnacle Design Achievement Award Vol. 1: 4039
Pinsker Award Vol. 1: 10222
Pinto Prize; Roquette Vol. 2: 1114
Pintrich Outstanding Dissertation Award; Paul R. Vol. 1: 3337
Pioneer and Century Certificates Vol. 1: 18798
Pioneer Award
AIIM - The Enterprise Content Management Association Vol. 1: 259
American Association of Petroleum Geologists Vol. 1: 1223
American Endurance Ride Conference Vol 1: 1965
American Institute of Ultrasound in Medicine Vol 1: 2565
Association for Communication Excellence in Agriculture, Natural Resources, and Life and Human Sciences Vol 1: 4801
International Embryo Transfer Society Vol 1: 10391
International Society for Traumatic Stress Studies Vol 1: 10694
National Dairy Shrine Vol 1: 13075
Nation's Restaurant News - Lebhar-Friedman Inc. Vol 1: 13969
Pioneer Citation Vol. 1: 15524
Pioneer Families of Franklin County Vol. 1: 14469
Pioneer Heritage Award Vol. 1: 14887
Pioneer Hi-Bred Forage Award Vol. 1: 1889
Pioneer in Cardiac Pacing and Electrophysiology Award Vol. 1: 9341
Pioneer in Clay Science Lecture Vol. 1: 7467
Pioneer Man-of-the-Year Chinese Martial Arts Award Vol. 1: 499

Pioneer of Safety Award Vol. 1: 365
Pioneer Pin Vol. 2: 471
Pioneers of Underwater Acoustics Medal Vol. 1: 130
Piore Award; Emanuel R. Vol. 1: 9791
Piot; Prix Eugene Vol. 2: 1469
Pipe Smoker of the Year Vol. 1: 10228
Piper General Aviation Award Vol. 1: 2397
Piper Prize; C. S. Vol. 2: 622
Pires Prize; Dr. Antonio Vol. 2: 2
Pisk Prize; Paul A. Vol. 1: 2847
Pistilli Silver VeteranFs Medal; Philip Vol. 1: 17612
Pitaluga International Composition Competition for Classical Guitar; Michele Vol. 2: 3118
Pitcher Insurance Agency Safety Award Vol. 1: 15205
Piteau Outstanding Young Member Award; Douglas R. Vol. 1: 5140
Pitt Rivers Award Vol. 2: 5227
Pittaluga International Classical Guitar Competition - City of Alessandria Award; Michelle Vol. 2: 3119
Pittman, Sr. Memorial Exhibit Award; John Jay Vol. 1: 2913
Pittman Wildlife Art Award; Major General and Mrs. Don D. Vol. 1: 13068
Pius XI Medal Vol. 2: 7410
Plain English Awards Vol. 2: 6539
Plain English Campaign Awards Vol. 2: 6539
Plain English Web Award Vol. 2: 6539
Plain Gold Jewelry Vol. 2: 2566
Plain Precious Metal Jewelry Vol. 2: 2567
Plains Poets Award Vol. 1: 13173
Plaisterers Trophy Vol. 2: 5891
Planck-Medaille; Max- Vol. 2: 2095
Planck Research Award; Max Vol. 2: 2436
Planner of the Year Award Vol. 1: 7883
Planning and Development Merit Award Vol. 1: 4381
Planning Consultancy of the Year Award Vol. 2: 7051
Plant Award; Richard Vol. 1: 4796
Plants Award for Special Events; Helen L. Vol. 1: 3669
Plarski Award; Lea Vol. 1: 13405
Plaskett Medal Vol. 1: 15739
Plasmadynamics and Lasers Award Vol. 1: 2398
Plass Award; William T. Vol. 1: 4177
Plastics Hall of Fame Vol. 1: 15099
Plata; Medalla de Vol. 1: 16739
Plateau Audience Award; Joseph Vol. 2: 891
Plateau Life Achievement Award; Joseph Vol. 2: 891
Plateau Music Award; Joseph Vol. 2: 891
Plateau Prize; Joseph Vol. 2: 891
Plateauprijzen; Joseph Vol. 2: 891
Platinum Award Vol. 1: 15579
Platinum Disc Award Vol. 2: 3948
Platinum Jubilee Endowment Trust Award Vol. 2: 2668
Platinum Jubilee Lectures Vol. 2: 2746
Platinum Video Award Vol. 1: 10607
Platinum Wing Award Vol. 1: 12826
Plaut Community Leadership Award; Johanna Cooke Vol. 1: 8336
Play Competition for Youth Theatre Vol. 1: 5745
Player of the Year
Asian Football Confederation Vol. 2: 3403
Camanachd Association Vol 2: 5577
Canadian Colleges Athletic Association Vol 1: 6414
Intercollegiate Tennis Association Vol 1: 10004
New Hampshire Golf Association Vol 1: 14078
Professional Golfers' Association of America Vol 1: 15321
United States Professional Tennis Association Vol 1: 18035
Player Portrait Award; John Vol. 2: 6483
Player to Watch Vol. 1: 10005
Players of the Year Vol. 1: 15303
PlayLabs Festival Vol. 1: 15107
Playoffs Most Valuable Player Vol. 1: 7800
Playwright Award Competition Vol. 1: 5744
Playwrights Association of New Zealand Award Vol. 2: 3805
Pleissner Memorial Award; Ogden Vol. 1: 4439
Pleissner Memorial Award; Ogden and Mary Vol. 1: 4439
Pless Graduate of the Year; J. Will Vol. 1: 14998
Plimpton Prize Vol. 1: 14860
Plumey; Prix Vol. 2: 1599
Plummer Memorial Educational Lecture Award Vol. 1: 4465
Plyler Prize for Molecular Spectroscopy; Earle K. Vol. 1: 3129
Poe Award; Edgar A. Vol. 1: 18728
Poe Awards (Edgars); Edgar Allan Vol. 1: 12055
Poehlman Award; William J. Vol. 1: 16180
Poel Memorial Festival; William Vol. 2: 7126
Poet Laureate Consultant in Poetry Vol. 1: 11347
Poetker Award; Frances Jones Vol. 1: 2295
Poetry Award
National Writers Association Vol. 1: 13945
River City Vol 1: 15676
Poetry Books Award Vol. 1: 18614
Poetry Center Prize Vol. 1: 7476
Poetry Chapbook Competition, Artist Residency Program Vol. 1: 7195
Poetry Chapbook Contest Vol. 1: 16090
Poetry Contest Vol. 1: 19020
Poetry, Fiction and Nonfiction Contest Vol. 1: 7571
Poetry International Festival Vol. 2: 3640
Poetry Society of Michigan Award Vol. 1: 13174
Poetry Society of Oklahoma Award Vol. 1: 13175
Poetry Society of Tennessee Award Vol. 1: 13176
Poetry Society of Texas Award Vol. 1: 13177
Poets Greatest Hits National Archive Vol. 1: 15448
Poets' Roundtable of Arkansas Award Vol. 1: 13178
Poggendorf Lecture; Walter Vol. 2: 644
Pohl-Preis; Robert-Wichard- Vol. 2: 2096
Points and Awards Program Vol. 1: 17071
Points Champions Vol. 1: 1901
Poirson; Prix Ayme Vol. 2: 1600
Pol Gold Medal; Balthasar van der Vol. 2: 933
Poland Restored Vol. 2: 4015
Polanyi Award; John C. Vol. 1: 6910
Polar Medal Vol. 2: 5603
Polaris Award Vol. 2: 6243
Policard-Lacassagne; Prix Andre Vol. 2: 1601
Police Bravery Award Vol. 2: 6544
Police Exemplary Service Medal Vol. 1: 6093
Police Medal of Honor Vol. 1: 3226
Police Officer of the Year Award Vol. 1: 10174
Police Overseas Service Medal Vol. 2: 222
Polish Chemical Society Medal Vol. 2: 4034
Polish Composers Union Prize Vol. 2: 4039
Polish-German Marian Smoluchowski-Emil Warburg Physics Prize Vol. 2: 4049
Polish PEN Centre Prizes Vol. 2: 4019
Polish Radio Award Vol. 2: 4002
Political Advocacy of Science Award Vol. 1: 6479
Political Journalism Award Vol. 1: 13547
Politis Composition Prize Vol. 1: 5866
Politzer Prize Vol. 2: 4984
Polk Awards; George Vol. 1: 11402
Polk Memorial Awards; George Vol. 1: 11402
Polka Music Awards Vol. 1: 10551
Pollak Fellowship; Hansi Vol. 2: 4310
Pollie Awards Vol. 1: 1260
Pollitzer Student Travel Prize; William Vol. 1: 1235
Pollock Award; Herbert C. Vol. 1: 8289
Pollock Award; R. C. Vol. 1: 2741
Pollock-Krasner Foundation Grants Vol. 1: 15152
Pollock Memorial Lecture Vol. 2: 645
Pollock Trophy; Sam Vol. 1: 2278
Polya Award; George Vol. 1: 11610
Polya Prize Vol. 2: 6403
Polya Prize; George Vol. 1: 16274
Polymer Physics Prize Vol. 1: 3130
Polytechnique Commemorative Award Vol. 1: 6490
Pomer Award; Vic Vol. 1: 12284
Pomerance Award for Scientific Contributions to Archaeology Vol. 1: 4581
Pomerance Fellowship; Harriet and Leon Vol. 1: 4582
Pomeroy Award for Outstanding Contributions to Teacher Education; Edward C. Vol. 1: 1052
Pon Memorial Award; Ernest M. Vol. 1: 12312
PONCHO Special Recognition Awards Vol. 1: 15955
Pool Postdoctoral Research Fellowship; Judith Graham Vol. 1: 13340
Poort-Prize Vol. 2: 4279
Pop Award Vol. 2: 3502
Pope Award; E. P. Vol. 1: 1331
Pope John Paul II Religious Freedom Award Vol. 1: 7154
Pope John XXI Prize Vol. 2: 7420
Popescu Prize for European Poetry Translation; Corneliu M. Vol. 2: 6542
Popp Excellence in Teaching Award; Richard Vol. 1: 4027
Poppele Broadcast Award; Jack Vol. 1: 15527
Pops Medal Award; Horace Vol. 1: 18768
Popular Annual Financial Reporting Award Program Vol. 1: 9150
Popular Choice Award Vol. 1: 589
Population Specific Research Project Award Vol. 1: 17344
Porraz International Coastal Engineering Award; Mauricio Vol. 1: 3955
Porter Award; Charles Vol. 1: 16300
Porter Award; J. Roger Vol. 1: 17898

Porter Award; USFCC/J. Roger Vol. 1: 3770
Porter Grant for Graduate Work in Composition; Ellen Jane Lorenz Vol. 1: 12000
Porter Lecture Award; William C. Vol. 1: 5253
Porter Memorial Award; Frank C. Vol. 1: 18592
Porter Memorial Book Prize; John Vol. 1: 7040
Porter Physiology Fellowships for Minorities Vol. 1: 3177
Porter Prize; Arthur Kingsley Vol. 1: 7509
Porter Prize for Fiction; Katherine Anne Vol. 1: 14241
Porter Tradition of Excellence Book Award; John Vol. 1: 7040
Porterfield Award; Robert Vol. 1: 17018
Portland International Film Festival Vol. 1: 14399
Portland Opera Lieber Awards Vol. 1: 15158
Positive Image Award Vol. 1: 17399
Posner Award; Fellows' Ernst Vol. 1: 16498
Posner Memorial Award; Louis Vol. 1: 10974
Posner Poetry Book Award Vol. 1: 7875
Post Doctoral Award Vol. 1: 10298
Post Doctoral Awards Vol. 1: 458
Post-Doctoral Research Award to Honor the Cadet Nurse Corps Vol. 1: 974
Postal History Award Vol. 2: 6535
Postal History Journal Awards Vol. 1: 15165
Postal History Society Medal Vol. 1: 15166
Postcard Story Competition Vol. 1: 19028
Postdoctoral Fellowship in Physiological Genomics Vol. 1: 3178
Postdoctoral Fellowship Program Vol. 1: 2831
Postdoctoral Fellowship Travel Awards for Minorities Vol. 1: 1685
Postdoctoral Fellowships
  Getty Grant Program Vol. 1: 9074
  Heiser Program for Research in Leprosy and Tuberculosis Vol 1: 9355
Postdoctoral Fellowships in Infectious Diseases Vol. 1: 13257
Poster Award
  European Society of Biomechanics Vol. 2: 3038
  Society for American Archaeology Vol 1: 16162
Poster Paper Prize Vol. 2: 6594
Poster Prize
  British Endodontic Society Vol. 2: 5303
  Challenger Society for Marine Science Vol 2: 5611
  International Federation of Societies of Cosmetic Chemists Vol 2: 6263
Poster Prizes Vol. 2: 2114
Poster Session Awards Vol. 1: 2345
Postgraduate Best Paper Award Vol. 1: 3057
Postgraduate Prize Vol. 2: 5376
Postgraduate QRA Meetings Award Vol. 2: 6573
Postgraduate Scholarship
  British Association for Applied Linguistics Vol. 2: 5234
  Canadian Meteorological and Oceanographic Society Vol 1: 6728
Postgraduate Student Prize
  Australian Optical Society Vol. 2: 314
  Royal Society of South Australia Vol 2: 649
Posthumous Medal of Honor Vol. 1: 3227
Postlethwait Award; Samuel Noel Vol. 1: 5884
Postsecondary Teacher of the Year Vol. 1: 12834
Potamkin Prize for Research in Pick's, Alzheimer's, and Related Diseases Vol. 1: 641
Pothuganti Award for Excellence Vol. 2: 2549
Pott Memorial Award; Anthony Vol. 2: 5061
Potter Award; Dennis Vol. 2: 5217
Potter Award of Special Recognition; Helen Vol. 1: 4968
Potter Award; Stuart G. Vol. 1: 5577
Potter Gold Medal; James Harry Vol. 1: 4160
Potter Lifetime Professional Service Award; Louis B. Vol. 1: 8136
Potter Memorial Award; Tim Vol. 2: 5443
Pottorff Professional Designee of the Year Award; Verne W. Vol. 1: 10137
Potts Memorial Award; John H. Vol. 1: 5522
Potts Memorial Fellowship Award; Ralph H. Vol. 1: 2969
Poultry Products Research Award Vol. 1: 15183
Poultry Science Association Fellows Vol. 1: 15184
Poultry Welfare Research Award Vol. 1: 15185
Poverello Medal Vol. 1: 8860
Powder Metallurgy Design Competition Vol. 1: 11705
Powder Metallurgy Pioneer Award Vol. 1: 11706
Powell Award; Cedric Vol. 1: 5452
Powell Award; Elizabeth Vol. 1: 18222
Powell Award; Maxwell
  Delta Nu Alpha Transportation Fraternity Vol. 1: 8150
  Delta Omicron Vol 1: 8152
Powell Award; Michael Vol. 2: 5756
Powell Award; William and Mousie Vol. 1: 11199
Powell Joint Warfighting Essay Contest; Colin L. Vol. 1: 18005
Powell Minority Postdoctoral Fellowship in Tropical Disease Research; Colin L. Vol. 1: 13257
Powell Prize; John Wesley Vol. 1: 16228
Power Award; General Thomas S. Vol. 1: 297
Power Strategic Combat Missle Crew Award; General Thomas S. Vol. 1: 297
Powers Fiction Book Award; Anne Vol. 1: 7875
Powers Memorial Award; Sidney Vol. 1: 1224
Pownall Award for Information Books; Eve Vol. 2: 409
Pozzetta Dissertation Research Award; George E. Vol. 1: 9626
Pozzoli International Piano Competition; Ettore Vol. 2: 3013
PPFA Hall of Fame Vol. 1: 15347
PPIC-FAI Award Vol. 2: 2558
PR Professional of the Year Vol. 1: 15430
Practical Project Award Vol. 2: 6192
Practice Award
  Accounting and Finance Association of Australia and New Zealand Vol. 2: 32
  American College of Clinical Pharmacology Vol 1: 1635
Practice Excellence Award Vol. 1: 3061
Practitioner of the Year Vol. 1: 12976
Practitioner of the Year Award Vol. 1: 809
Practitioner Research Award
  American Academy of Pediatrics Vol. 1: 708
  American Veterinary Medical Association Vol 1: 4410
PractitionerFs Award for Excellence Vol. 2: 836
Prados Prize; Miguel Vol. 1: 6828
Praemium Erasmianum Vol. 2: 3519
Praemium Imperiale Vol. 2: 3217
Prague Spring International Music Competition Vol. 2: 1264
Prairie Pasque Children's Book Award Vol. 1: 16989
Prakash Memorial Medal; Professor Brahm Vol. 2: 2703
Prakken Professional Cooperation Award Vol. 1: 10784
Prangey Award; Louis Vol. 2: 4797
Pras Hestrin Vol. 2: 2923
Pras l'Bikoret Sifrutit Vol. 2: 2897
Pras l'Roman Ivri Mekori Vol. 2: 2898
Pras l'Sefer Shira Ivri Mekori Vol. 2: 2899
Pras Zalman Shazar Le'heker Toldot Am Israel Vol. 2: 2928
Prasad Award; Dr. Rajendra Vol. 2: 2593
Prasad Memorial Lecture; Prof. M. R. N. Vol. 2: 2704
Prasad Memorial Oration Award; Dr. D. N. Vol. 2: 2617
Prather Award; Victor A. Vol. 1: 1352
Pratley Award; P. L. Vol. 1: 6919
Pratt & Whitney Canada Grand Prix Vol. 1: 10425
Pratt and Whitney Canada Grand Prize Vol. 1: 10424
Pratt Award; Haraden Vol. 1: 9792
Pratt International Library Travel Fund; Bogle/ Vol. 1: 2672
Pratt Memorial Award; Wallace E. Vol. 1: 1225
Pratt-Severn Best Student Research Paper Award Vol. 1: 3745
Pratte Memorial Scholarship; Thomas Vol. 1: 17339
Pre-College Award Vol. 1: 1248
Preakness Stakes
  Maryland Jockey Club Vol. 1: 11562
  Triple Crown Productions, Inc. Vol 1: 17609
Preedy Post-Graduate Bursary; Winifred E. Vol. 2: 193
Prego; Premio Ing. Agr. Antonio J. Vol. 2: 3
Prego Prize; Antonio J. Vol. 2: 3
Preis der Deutschen Physikalische Gesellschaft Vol. 2: 2092
Preis der Gesellschaft Deutcher Chemiker fur Schriftsteller Vol. 2: 2173
Preis der Gesellschaft Deutscher Chemiker fur Journalistein und Schriftsteller Vol. 2: 2173
Preller Prize; Gustav Vol. 2: 4277
Premi David di Donatello per la Cinematografia Internazionale Vol. 2: 3021
Premi de les Lletres Catalanes Ramon Llull Vol. 2: 4480
Premi Giosue Carducci Vol. 2: 3140
Premi Josep Pla Vol. 2: 4481
Premier Award Vol. 2: 2856
Premier Award of SADA Vol. 2: 4326
Premier Print Awards Vol. 1: 15238
Premier Property Award Vol. 1: 15639
Premier Recreation Operation Award
  Resort and Commercial Recreation Association Vol. 1: 15639

Resort and Commercial Recreation Association Vol 1: 15640
Premier Technology Shandon Award Vol. 2: 4256
Premier's Literary Award Vol. 2: 673
Premies voor de verspreiding van de betere film in Belgie Vol. 2: 1084
Premio a Investigadores Noveles Vol. 2: 4543
Premio Academia Nacional de Agronomia y Veterinaria Vol. 2: 4
Premio Academia Nacional de la Historia Vol. 2: 12
Premio Agricola Interamericano para Profesionales Jovenes Vol. 2: 1207
Premio al Desarrollo Agropecuario Vol. 2: 5
Premio al Egresado con Mejor Promedio en las Carreras de Historia Vol. 2: 13
Premio Apel-les Mestres Vol. 2: 4482
Premio Balzan Vol. 2: 3062
Premio Bayer en Ciencias Veterinarias Vol. 2: 6
Premio Biblioteca Breve Vol. 2: 4483
Premio Bolsa de Cereales de Buenos Aires Vol. 2: 7
Premio Cacho Pallero Vol. 2: 4495
Premio Campiello Vol. 2: 3003
Premio Carlos Bonvalot Vol. 2: 4092
Premio Ceresis Vol. 2: 3958
Premio Colegio Oficial de Farmaceuticos de Madrid Vol. 2: 4533
Premio Comillas de Biografia, Autobiografia y Memorias Vol. 2: 4547
Premio Compasso d'oro ADI Vol. 2: 2991
Premio Consagracion a la Geografia Vol. 2: 19
Premio Consejo General de Colegios de Farmaceuticos Vol. 2: 4534
Premio de Novela Fernando Lara Vol. 2: 4484
Premio del Rey Prize Vol. 1: 2242
Premio do Mar Rei D. Carlos Vol. 2: 4093
Premio Dr. Antonio Pires Vol. 2: 2
Premio Dotte Giuseppe Borgia Vol. 2: 2973
Premio Espasa Ensayo Vol. 2: 4485
Premio Espiritualidad Vol. 2: 4486
Premio F. Busoni Vol. 2: 2999
Premio Frederico de Menezes Veiga Vol. 2: 1122
Premio Fundacion Alfredo Manzullo Vol. 2: 8
Premio Gilberto Figueroa Nogueron Vol. 2: 3445
Premio Grinzane Cavour Vol. 2: 3005
Premio Iberoamericano Book Award Vol. 1: 11236
Premio Interamericano a la Participacion de la Mujer en el Desarrollo Rural Vol. 2: 1209
Premio Internazionale Accademia Musicale Chigiana Siena Vol. 2: 2952
Premio Internazionale di Meridionalistica Guido Dorso Vol. 2: 2987
Premio Internazionale Ennio Flaiano Vol. 2: 2985
Premio Internazionale Ferrari-Soave Vol. 2: 2968
Premio Internazionale Paladino D'Oro Vol. 2: 3084
Premio Internazionale Panetti-Ferrari Vol. 2: 2969
Premio Internazionali dell' Instituto Nazionale delle Assicurazioni Vol. 2: 2971
Premio Jean Mitry Vol. 2: 3121
Premio Jinete Iberico Vol. 2: 4495
Premio Jose Maria Bustillo Vol. 2: 9
Premio Joven Investigador Profesor Ignacio Chavez Vol. 2: 3449
Premio La Sonrisa Vertical Vol. 2: 4548
Premio Literario Branquinho da Fonseca Vol. 2: 4094
Premio Luis de Camoes Vol. 2: 4089
Premio Luis Zambrano a la Inventiva Tecnologica Nacional Vol. 2: 7428
Premio Magda Donato Vol. 2: 3431
Premio Maria Teresa Messori Roncaglia and Eugenio Mari Vol. 2: 2974
Premio Mesquite Audience Award Vol. 1: 9218
Premio Mikeldi Plata Vol. 2: 4517
Premio Municipais Joshua Benoliel de Fotografia Vol. 2: 4071
Premio Municipal Alfredo Marceneiro de Fado Vol. 2: 4072
Premio Municipal Augusto Vieira da Silva de Investigacao Vol. 2: 4073
Premio Municipal Carlos Botelho de Pintura Vol. 2: 4074
Premio Municipal Fernando Amado de Encenacao Teatral Vol. 2: 4075
Premio Municipal Joao Baptista Rosa de Video Vol. 2: 4076
Premio Municipal Jorge Colaco de Azulejaria Vol. 2: 4077
Premio Municipal Jose Simoes de Almeida de Escultura Vol. 2: 4078
Premio Municipal Julio Cesar Machado de Jornalismo Vol. 2: 4079
Premio Municipal Julio de Castilho de Olisipografia Vol. 2: 4080
Premio Municipal Maria Leonor Magro de Radio Vol. 2: 4081
Premio Municipal Rafael Bordalo Pinheiro de Banda Desenhada, Cartoon e Caricaturista Vol. 2: 4082
Premio Municipal Roberto de Araujo Pereira de Design Vol. 2: 4083
Premio Nacional
Asociacion Nacional de la Publicidad Vol. 2: 3433
Engineers' Association of Chile Vol 2: 1166
Premio Nacional de Ciencia Vol. 2: 7427
Premio Nacional de Ciencia y Tecnologia de Alimentos Vol. 2: 3441
Premio Nacional de Ciencias Vol. 2: 1162
Premio Nacional de Ciencias y Tecnologia Clodomiro Picado Twight Vol. 2: 1203
Premio Nacional de Literatura Vol. 2: 1163
Premio Nacional de Periodismo Vol. 2: 1164
Premio Nacional de Periodismo Pio Viquez Vol. 2: 1204
Premio Nacional de Teatro Vol. 2: 1205
Premio Nadal Vol. 2: 4487
Premio Nazionale del Presidente della Repubblica Vol. 2: 2972
"Premio Paolo Borciani" - International String Quartet Competition Vol. 2: 3134
Premio Planeta de Novela
Editorial Planeta SA Vol. 2: 4488
Editorial Planeta SA Vol 2: 4488
Premio Primavera de Novela Vol. 2: 4489
Premio Real Academia Nacional de Farmacia Vol. 2: 4535
Premio Riccione Ater Vol. 2: 3123
Premio Riccione per il Teatro Vol. 2: 3123
Premio Saint-Vincent per il Cinema Italiano Vol. 2: 3138
Premio Sent Sovi Vol. 2: 4550
Premio Tenco Vol. 2: 3011
Premio Tenore Vol. 2: 2977
Premio Valle Inclan Vol. 2: 7134
Premio Valmor e Municipal de Arquitectura Vol. 2: 4084
Premio Varese Vol. 2: 3086
Premios ADIRCAE Vol. 2: 4471
Premios Anuales a los Mejores Trabajos Cientificos Vol. 2: 7426
Premios de Beneficencia Alejandro Angel Escobar Vol. 2: 1193
Premios de Investigacion Cientifica Vol. 2: 3451
Premios Municipais Eca de Queiroz de Literatura Vol. 2: 4085
Premios Municipais Joly Braga Santos de Musica Vol. 2: 4086
Premios Municipais Palmira Bastos e Antonio Silva de Interpretacao Teatral Vol. 2: 4087
Premios Principe de Asturias Vol. 2: 4497
Premios Weizmann de la Academia Mexicana de Ciencias Vol. 2: 3452
Prentice Medal; Charles F. Vol. 1: 659
Prescott Award; Gerald W. Vol. 1: 15035
Prescott Award; Samuel Cate Vol. 1: 9853
Prescott Eddy Medal; Harrison Vol. 1: 18643
Presenter of the Year Vol. 2: 7047
Preservation Award
Birmingham Historical Society Vol. 1: 5787
Canadian Railroad Historical Association Vol 1: 6858
Historical Society of Frederick County Vol 1: 9421
Los Angeles Conservancy Vol 1: 11412
Preservation Awards Vol. 1: 9429
Preservation Merit Awards Vol. 1: 9409
Preservation Publication Award Vol. 1: 16499
President & Vice President's Choice Award Vol. 2: 7219
Presidential Academic Fitness Awards Vol. 1: 17819
Presidential Achievement Award Vol. 1: 12487
Presidential Award
American Academy of Otolaryngology - Head and Neck Surgery Vol. 1: 676
American Academy of Periodontology Vol 1: 729
American Association of Blood Banks Vol 1: 1015
American Society for Engineering Management Vol 1: 3690
American Society of Naturalists Vol 1: 4183
Canadian Institute of Forestry Vol 1: 6603
International Association of Diecutting and Diemaking Vol 1: 10196
International Association of Gerontology and Geriatrics Vol 2: 1130
National Association of Black Social Workers Vol 1: 12422
National Association of Recording Merchandisers Vol 1: 12638
Society for Prevention Research Vol 1: 16386
Presidential Award for Outstanding Contributions to the Promotion of Scholarship in the Third World Vol. 1: 5369
Presidential Award for Reading and Technology Vol. 1: 10592
Presidential Award of the RES - Annie R. Beasley Memorial Award Vol. 1: 16325
Presidential Citation
American College of Cardiology Vol. 1: 1620

American Mosquito Control Association Vol 1: 2804
International Association of Emergency Managers Vol 1: 10205
U.S. Hang Gliding Association Vol 1: 17927
Presidential Citation Award Vol. 1: 12272
Presidential Citations
American Congress on Surveying and Mapping Vol. 1: 1780
American Urological Association Vol 1: 4395
Presidential Citations and Awards Vol. 1: 13849
Presidential Citations for Meritorious Service Vol. 1: 4748
Presidential Citizens Medal Vol. 1: 8552
Presidential Commendation
American Psychiatric Association Vol. 1: 3284
Executive Office of the President Vol 1: 8555
Presidential Disaster Service Vol. 1: 1928
Presidential Distinguished Service Award Vol. 1: 16781
Presidential Honor Award Vol. 1: 10774
Presidential Leadership Award Vol. 1: 12526
Presidential Medal of Freedom Vol. 1: 8553
Presidential Proclamation Vol. 1: 16749
Presidential Public Safety Communication Award Vol. 1: 8555
Presidential Rank Awards Vol. 1: 18014
Presidential Recognition Award Vol. 1: 16163
Presidential Research Competition Vol. 1: 16325
Presidential Scholars in the Arts Vol. 1: 13254
Presidential Sports Award (Gold) Vol. 2: 4239
Presidential Sports Award (Silver) Vol. 2: 4240
Presidents Achievement Award Vol. 1: 17376
President's Achievement Award - 1 Vol. 1: 8614
PresidentFs Award Vol. 1: 11412
President's Award
Advertising Women of New York Vol. 1: 191
Alberta Amateur Boxing Association Vol 1: 361
American Academy of Family Physicians Vol 1: 614
American Association of Petroleum Geologists Vol 1: 1213
American Association of Petroleum Geologists Vol 1: 1225
American Handwriting Analysis Foundation Vol 1: 2158
American Lung Association Vol 1: 2707
American Probation and Parole Association Vol 1: 3263
American Society for Gravitational and Space Biology Vol 1: 3714
American Society of Cytopathology Vol 1: 4019
American Veterinary Medical Association Vol 1: 4411
Association of Consulting Engineers New Zealand Vol 2: 3697
Barbados Union of Teachers Vol 2: 840
Canadian Association for Enterostomal Therapy Vol 1: 6194
Canadian Association of Home and Property Inspectors Vol 1: 6261
Canadian Bar Association Vol 1: 6335
Canadian Institute of Food Science and Technology Vol 1: 6594
Canadian Nuclear Society Vol 1: 6766
Canadian Society for Industrial Security Vol 1: 6944
Canadian Society of Petroleum Geologists Vol 1: 7019
Canadian Veterinary Medical Association Vol 1: 7059
Chartered Institution of Water and Environmental Management Vol 2: 5643
The Chris Awards Vol 1: 7386
Document Management Industries Association Vol 1: 8242
Educational Theatre Association Vol 1: 8406
Institute for Operations Research and the Management Sciences Vol 1: 9749
Institute of Environmental Sciences and Technology Vol 1: 9838
Institution of Professional Engineers New Zealand Vol 2: 3743
International Association of Business Communicators Vol 1: 10150
International Association of Registered Financial Consultants Vol 1: 10236
International Corrections and Prisons Association Vol 1: 10342
International Ergonomics Association Vol 2: 3074
International Slurry Surfacing Association Vol 1: 10633
International Society of Explosives Engineers Vol 1: 10721
La Crosse Area Development Corporation Vol 1: 11173
Lamaze International Vol 1: 11213
Library Administration and Management Association Vol 1: 11335
Massachusetts Association of School Business Officials Vol 1: 11572
Medical Library Association Vol 1: 11665
National Association for the Advancement of Colored People Vol 1: 12367
National Council of La Raza Vol 1: 13003
National Defense Transportation Association Vol 1: 13086
National Federation of Press Women Vol 1: 13134
National Guild of Community Schools of the Arts Vol 1: 13304
National Guild of Hypnotists Vol 1: 13316
National Marine Educators Association Vol 1: 13426
National Organization for Human Service Education Vol 1: 13496
National Press Photographers Association Vol 1: 13570
National Water Safety Congress Vol 1: 13889
New York Society of Architects Vol 1: 14168
North American Association for Environmental Education Vol 1: 14256
North American Association of Food Equipment Manufacturers Vol 1: 14263
North American Society for the Psychology of Sport and Physical Activity Vol 1: 14338
Ottawa Little Theatre Vol 1: 14742
Professional Grounds Management Society Vol 1: 15329
Puppeteers of America Vol 1: 15464
Radio Club of America Vol 1: 15528
Royal Academy of Dance Vol 2: 6618
Royal Scottish Geographical Society Vol 2: 6895
Society of Cable Telecommunications Engineers Vol 1: 16615
Society of Naval Architects and Marine Engineers Vol 1: 16759
Southeastern Library Association Vol 1: 17009
U.S.A. Track and Field Vol 1: 18452
Women's Sports Foundation Vol 1: 18874
World Atlatl Association Vol 1: 18909
PresidentsF Award Vol. 1: 11758
Presidents' Award
American Society of Civil Engineers Vol. 1: 3972
Committee of Presidents of Statistical Societies Vol 1: 7622
Institute of Management Accountants Vol 1: 9900
President's Award for Best Conference Presentation Vol. 1: 13122
Presidents' Award for Communication Program of the Year Vol. 1: 9706
President's Award for Distinguished Federal Civilian Service Vol. 1: 18015
President's Award for Educational Excellence Vol. 1: 17819
President's Award for Educational Improvement Vol. 1: 17819
President's Award for Environmental Stewardship Vol. 1: 9117
President's Award for Exceptional and Innovative Leadership in Adult and Continuing Education Vol. 1: 839
PresidentFs Award for Journalism Vol. 1: 2856
President's Award for Merit Vol. 1: 16951
Presidents' Award for Public Service Vol. 1: 9707
Presidents' Award for the Air Force Reserve Command Vol. 1: 298
President's Award of Excellence Vol. 1: 15913
President's Award of Excellence, Honor and Merit Vol. 1: 4107
President's Award of Merit Vol. 1: 5352
President's Awards
Geological Society of London Vol. 2: 5934
Horatio Alger Society Vol 1: 9484
Metal Construction Association Vol 1: 11699
President's Book Award Vol. 1: 3581
President's Certificate Vol. 1: 615
President's Certificate of Merit Award Vol. 1: 7248
President's Challenge Physical Activity and Fitness Awards Program Vol. 1: 15215
President's Choice Award Vol. 2: 424
PresidentFs Choice Awards Vol. 1: 14750
President's Chris Award Vol. 1: 7386
President's Citation
American Association of Homes and Services for the Aging Vol. 1: 1121
Federation of Genealogical Societies Vol 1: 8659
Society for Imaging Science and Technology Vol 1: 16254
Society for Mining, Metallurgy, and Exploration Vol 1: 16358

President's Citation for Outstanding Section/ Chapter Partnership Vol. 1: 16586
President's Commendation Vol. 2: 7443
President's Community Volunteer Award Vol. 1: 15142
President's Conservation Achievement Award Vol. 1: 13984
President's Continuing Education Grant Vol. 1: 1424
President's Corporate Council Award Vol. 1: 3730
President's Cup
Canadian Dermatology Association Vol. 1: 6455
Mountainview Women's Nine Hole Golf Association Vol 1: 11993
Society of Ornamental Turners Vol 2: 7210
Society of Plastics Engineers Vol 1: 16833
Sports Car Club of America Vol 1: 17210
Presidents Cup Vol. 1: 14348
President's Distinguished Service Award Vol. 2: 75
Presidents' Distinguished Service Award Vol. 1: 5062
President's "E" Award for Exports Program Vol. 1: 17794
President's "E Star" Award Vol. 1: 17795
The President's Education Award Program Vol. 1: 17819
President's Environment and Conservation Challenge Awards Vol. 1: 8554
President's Environmental Merit Awards Program Vol. 1: 17894
President's Environmental Youth Awards (PEYA) Vol. 1: 17894
President's Excellence in Presentation Award Vol. 1: 1226
President's Exhibitors Award Vol. 1: 2315
President's Fishery Conservation Award Vol. 1: 2032
President's Gold Medal Vol. 2: 2810
President's Honorary Citation Vol. 2: 4976
President's Medal
American Society of Landscape Architects Vol. 1: 4106
Association of Military Colleges and Schools of the United States Vol 1: 5235
Bowling Proprietors' Association of America Vol 1: 5889
Ergonomics Society - England Vol 2: 5800
Municipal Art Society of New York Vol 1: 12011
Niagara University Vol 1: 14231
Operational Research Society of the United Kingdom Vol 2: 6509
Royal Academy of Engineering Vol 2: 6622
Society of American Military Engineers Vol 1: 16529
Presidents' Medal Vol. 1: 3973
President's Medallion Vol. 1: 11432
President's Medallist Vol. 2: 7094
President's National Medal of Science Vol. 1: 13672
President's New Researcher Awards Vol. 1: 6837
President's Pin Award Vol. 1: 8647
President's Plaque Vol. 1: 11473
President's Plaques Vol. 1: 7753
PresidentFs Prize Vol. 2: 5614
President's Prize
Actuarial Society of South Africa Vol. 2: 4124
Australian Acoustical Society Vol 2: 128
Canadian Cartographic Association Vol 1: 6386
Canadian Meteorological and Oceanographic Society Vol 1: 6729
Institute of Chartered Accountants in Australia Vol 2: 482
Institution of Engineers Australia/Engineers Australia Vol 2: 523
Ottawa Field-Naturalists' Club Vol 1: 14727
Presidents' Prize Vol. 1: 11375
President's Prize for Best Regional Business Vol. 2: 148
President's Prizes for Outstanding Achievement in Primary and Secondary Education Vol. 1: 8478
President's Pro Bono Service Award Vol. 1: 17257
President's Public Service Award Vol. 1: 13984
President's Service Award Vol. 1: 16903
President's Service Awards Vol. 1: 15142
President's Shield Vol. 1: 17148
President's Transportation Awards Vol. 1: 1291
President's Trophy
American Trucking Associations - Safety Management Council Vol. 1: 4375
Canadian Interuniversity Sport Vol 1: 6665
Confederate Stamp Alliance Vol 1: 7677
International 210 Association Vol 1: 10013
Presidio La Bahia Award Vol. 1: 16959
Press Awards Vol. 1: 12236
Press Prize for Broadcasters and Producers Vol. 2: 4883
Pressberg Memorial Scholarship Fund; Jack Vol. 1: 11500
Pressman-Burroughs Welcome Fund Career Development Award; Jack D. Vol. 1: 966
Pressure Vessel and Piping Award Vol. 1: 4161
Prestigious Award Vol. 1: 12439
Preston Manufacturer of the Year Award; Thomas F. Vol. 1: 13096
Preston Personal Service Award; Harold Kramer - John Vol. 1: 3444
Prestwich Medal Vol. 2: 5935
Prevention Science Award Vol. 1: 16387
PRI Service Medal Vol. 2: 4062
Price Child Health and Welfare Journalism Awards Vol. 1: 18343
Price Medal Vol. 2: 6690
Price Oration; Joseph Vol. 1: 2155
Price/Rod Webster Award; Derek Vol. 1: 9443
Priddle Medal; R.A. Vol. 2: 524
Pride and Progress Award Vol. 1: 11924
Pride in the Profession Awards Vol. 1: 2747
Priest Award; Jerry Vol. 1: 9499
Priestley Award; Joseph Vol. 1: 8184
Priestley Medal Vol. 1: 1576
Priestley Memorial Medal; H. T. Vol. 2: 460
Prijs der Nederlandse Letteren Vol. 2: 3623
Prijs van de Jonge Jury Vol. 2: 3496
Prijs van de Nederlandse Kinderjury Vol. 2: 3497
Prijs voor Meesterschap Vol. 2: 3672
Prime Contractor of the Year Vol. 1: 18120
Prime Movers Committee Award Vol. 1: 4162
Prince Meritorious Service Award; Max T. Vol. 1: 13609
Prince of Asturias Award for Communications and Humanities Vol. 2: 4497
Prince of Asturias Award for Concord Vol. 2: 4497
Prince of Asturias Award for International Cooperation Vol. 2: 4497
Prince of Asturias Award for Letters Vol. 2: 4497
Prince of Asturias Award for Social Sciences Vol. 2: 4497
Prince of Asturias Award for Sports Vol. 2: 4497
Prince of Asturias Award for Technical and Scientific Research Vol. 2: 4497
Prince of Asturias Award for the Arts Vol. 2: 4497
Prince of Asturias Awards Vol. 2: 4497
Prince of Wales Bowl; U.S. Match Racing Championship - Vol. 1: 18071
Prince of Wales Prizes Vol. 1: 15498
Prince of WalesFs Award for Portrait Drawing Vol. 2: 7027
Prince Philip Award Vol. 2: 6683
Prince Philip Medal Vol. 2: 6623
Prince Philip Prize Vol. 2: 7399
Prince Philip Prize for the Designer of the Year Vol. 2: 5736
The Princess Chichibu Memorial TB Global Award Vol. 2: 1917
Princess Royal Award Vol. 2: 6684
Principal of the Year Vol. 1: 6290
Principal's Leadership Award Vol. 1: 12659
Pringle Award; Thomas Vol. 2: 4172
Print Media Award Vol. 1: 10593
Print Media Festivals Vol. 1: 9315
Print Media Personality of the Year Vol. 1: 10270
Printer of the Year
Data Publishers Association Vol. 2: 5728
PrintImage International Vol 1: 15235
Printing Ink Pioneer Award Vol. 1: 12614
Prism Awards Vol. 2: 4230
Prison Writing Awards; PEN Vol. 1: 14903
Prisoner of War Medal Vol. 1: 8120
Pritchard-Higgins Design Award; R. D. Vol. 1: 15206
Pritchett Memorial Prize; V.S. Vol. 2: 7003
Pritsker Doctoral Dissertation Award Vol. 1: 9872
Pritzker Architecture Prize Vol. 1: 15240
Private Enterprise Exemplar Medal Vol. 1: 8878
Private Plant Breeding Award Vol. 1: 12995
Private Practice Professional Development Award Vol. 1: 13750
Private Sector Financial Excellence Award Vol. 1: 5186
Private Sector Hall of Fame Vol. 2: 3160
Private Sector Leadership Vol. 1: 6164
Prix Adelson Castiau Vol. 2: 997
Prix Adolphe Wetrems Vol. 2: 1027
Prix Agathon De Potter Vol. 2: 1028
Prix Albert Brachet Vol. 2: 1029
Prix Albert-Tessier Vol. 1: 15487
Prix Alfred Kastler Vol. 2: 1822
Prix Allier de Hauteroche Vol. 2: 1525
Prix Alvine-Belisle Vol. 1: 5394
Prix Ambatielos Vol. 2: 1526
Prix Ampere d'Electricite de France Vol. 2: 1602
Prix Andres Bello Vol. 2: 4767
Prix Antoine d'Abbadie Vol. 2: 1603
Prix Anton Bergmann Vol. 2: 998
Prix Armand Blanc Vol. 2: 2289
Prix Ars Electronica - International Competition for Cyberarts Vol. 2: 762

Prix Artur du Fay Vol. 2: 1604
Prix Athanase-David Vol. 1: 15488
Prix Auguste Sacre Vol. 2: 1030
Prix Auguste Teirlinck Vol. 2: 999
Prix Balleroy Vol. 2: 1860
Prix baron de Saint-Genois Vol. 2: 1000
Prix Baron Van Ertborn Vol. 2: 1031
Prix Bastien-Lepage Vol. 2: 1470
Prix Bene Merenti de Patria Vol. 1: 16145
Prix Blaise Pascal du GAMNI-SMAI Vol. 2: 1605
Prix Breaute Vol. 2: 1471
Prix Brizard Vol. 2: 1472
Prix Canada pour l'excellence Vol. 1: 13586
Prix Carlos Calvo Vol. 2: 4767
Prix Catenacci Vol. 2: 1473
Prix Cazes - Brasserie Lipp Vol. 2: 1938
Prix Champlain Vol. 1: 7734
Prix Charles Duvivier Vol. 2: 1001
Prix Charles Lagrange Vol. 2: 1032
Prix Charles Lemaire Vol. 2: 1033
Prix Charles-Louis de Saulses de Freycinet Vol. 2: 1606
Prix Charles Mentzer des Rencontres de Chimie Therapeutique Vol. 2: 1966
Prix Chaudesaigues Vol. 2: 1474
Prix Chavasse - GALF Vol. 2: 1979
Prix Cinema du Reel Vol. 2: 1732
Prix Ciudad de Huesca Vol. 2: 4495
Prix Claude Aubry Vol. 2: 4783
Prix COGEDIM Vol. 2: 1734
Prix Colmont Vol. 2: 1475
Prix Corail du Livre Vol. 2: 1799
Prix CORESTA Vol. 2: 1752
Prix d'Aeronautique Vol. 2: 1713
Prix Dagnan-Bouveret Vol. 2: 1476
Prix Danube Festival, Bratislava Vol. 2: 4452
Prix d'Astronautique Vol. 2: 1714
Prix de Boelpaepe Vol. 2: 1034
Prix de Chenier Vol. 2: 1527
Prix de Composition Musicale Vol. 2: 3472
Prix de Gnseil Regional Vol. 2: 1792
Prix de Journalisme Science et Societe Vol. 1: 6867
Prix de la Belgica Vol. 2: 1035
Prix de la Confederation Mondiale des Activites Subaquatiques Vol. 2: 1890
Prix de la Critique Internationale Vol. 1: 5396
Prix de la Federation Francaise d'Etudes et Sports Sous-Marins Vol. 2: 1890
Prix de la Fonction Publique du Canada pour Services Insignes Vol. 1: 17593
Prix de la Fondation George Montefiore Vol. 2: 943
Prix de La Fons-Melicocq Vol. 2: 1528
Prix de La Grange Vol. 2: 1529
Prix de la Marine Nationale Vol. 2: 1890
Prix de la Presse Vol. 2: 1890
Prix de la Sante et du Bien-Etre Psychologique Vol. 1: 14666
Prix de la Scam Vol. 2: 1732
Prix de la Societe Francaise de Gravure Vol. 2: 1477
Prix de la ville de Toulon Vol. 2: 1890
Prix de l'adjudant Hubert Lefebvre Vol. 2: 1036
Prix de l'Age d'Or Vol. 2: 1083
Prix de l'Association des Musiciens de Geneve Vol. 2: 4702
Prix de Lausanne Vol. 2: 4878
Prix de l'Ecole Centrale Vol. 2: 1607
Prix de l'Institut Francais du Petrole Vol. 2: 1608
Prix de Merite Vol. 1: 6797
Prix de Psychologie Vol. 2: 1002
Prix de Rome Fine Art Vol. 2: 3642
Prix de Rome in Architecture Vol. 1: 6119
Prix de Rome in Architecture for Emerging Practitioners Vol. 1: 6119
Prix de Sciences Humaines Esdras-Minville Vol. 1: 16143
Prix de Stassart Vol. 2: 1003
Prix de Stassart pour Histoire Nationale Vol. 2: 1004
Prix de West Invitational Exhibition Vol. 1: 13068
Prix de West Purchase Award Vol. 1: 13068
Prix Delalande-Guerineau Vol. 2: 1530
Prix d'Encouragement a la recherche en Chimie Therapeutique Vol. 2: 1967
Prix Denise-Pelletier Vol. 1: 15489
Prix des Ambassadeurs Vol. 2: 3553
Prix des Bibliotheques Vol. 2: 1732
Prix des Cathedrales Vol. 2: 1478
Prix des Dames Vol. 2: 1960
Prix des Deux-Magots Vol. 2: 1728
Prix des Jeunes Vol. 2: 1715
Prix des Maisons de la Presse Vol. 2: 1934
Prix des Sciences de la Mer Vol. 2: 1609
Prix d'Excellence Vol. 2: 1911
Prix d'Excellence Aliant Vol. 1: 5507
Prix d'Excellence d'Heritage Vol. 1: 9385
Prix Dr. Max-Luthi Vol. 2: 4891
Prix Doublemard Vol. 2: 1479
Prix du Commisariat a l'Energie Atomique Vol. 2: 1610
Prix du Court Metrage Vol. 2: 1732
Prix du Jeune Ecrivain Vol. 2: 1940
Prix du Jeune Ecrivain Francophone Vol. 2: 1941
Prix du Jury Vol. 2: 1730
Prix du Jury de l'Universite Paris Vol. 2: 1928
Prix du Livre de Photographie/Arles Book Award Vol. 2: 1945
Prix du Merite Motocycliste Vol. 2: 4816
Prix du Patrimoine Vol. 2: 1732
Prix du Public
Festival du Film Court de Villeurbanne Vol. 2: 1792
International Festival of Maritime and Exploration Films Vol 2: 1890
Prix du Public du Meilleur Court-Metrage Europeen Vol. 2: 850
Prix du Quebec
Center for the Study of Canada Vol. 1: 7236
Quebec Ministere de la Culture et des Communications Vol 1:
Quebec Ministere de la Culture et des Communications Vol 1:
Quebec Ministere de la Culture et des Communications Vol 1: 15488
Quebec Ministere de la Culture et des Communications Vol 1: 15489
Quebec Ministere de la Culture et des Communications Vol 1: 15491
Prix Dubois - Debauque Vol. 2: 1037
Prix Duc Vol. 2: 1480
Prix Dumas-Millier Vol. 2: 1481
Prix Edmond de Selys Longchamps Vol. 2: 1038
Prix Edouard Mailly Vol. 2: 1039
Prix Elizabeth Mrazik Cleaver pour le meilleur livre d'images canadien Vol. 2: 4784
Prix Emer de Vattel Vol. 2: 4767
Prix Emile de Laveleye Vol. 2: 1005
Prix Emile Laurent Vol. 2: 1040
Prix Emile-Nelligan Vol. 1: 17672
Prix Ernest Acker Vol. 2: 977
Prix Ernest Discailles Vol. 2: 1006
Prix Ernst Meyer Vol. 2: 4778
Prix et Fondations Concernant l'Academie de France a Rome Vol. 2: 1482
Prix et Medailles de la SFA Vol. 2: 1981
Prix Eugene Catalan Vol. 2: 1041
Prix Eugene Goblet d'Alviella Vol. 2: 1007
Prix Eugene Lameere Vol. 2: 1008
Prix Europa Vol. 2: 1757
Prix Europeens Emile Bernheim Vol. 2: 1102
Prix Ex Aequo - International Children's and Youth Radio Drama Festival Vol. 2: 4711
Prix FIT - de la Traduction Vol. 1: 10418
Prix FIT de la Traduction Astrid Lindgren Vol. 1: 10419
Prix Fonde par l'Etat Vol. 2: 1611
Prix Fontannes Vol. 2: 1837
Prix France Telecom Vol. 2: 1612
Prix Frances E. Russell Vol. 2: 4785
Prix Francis Lieber Vol. 2: 4767
Prix Francois Deruyts Vol. 2: 1042
Prix Francqui Vol. 2: 895
Prix Franz Cumont Vol. 2: 1009
Prix Frederic de Martens Vol. 2: 4767
Prix Frederic Swarts Vol. 2: 1043
Prix Fuji Vol. 2: 1792
Prix G. Rolin-Jaequemyns Vol. 2: 4767
Prix Galeano d'excellence Pedagogique Vol. 1: 5941
Prix Gaudry Vol. 2: 1838
Prix Gazzola Vol. 2: 1888
Prix Gemeaux Vol. 1: 68
Prix Georges Vanderlinden Vol. 2: 1044
Prix Gerard-Morisset Vol. 1: 15490
Prix Gilles-Corbeil Vol. 1: 17673
Prix Gosselet Vol. 2: 1839
Prix Grotius Vol. 2: 4767
Prix Gustave Camus Vol. 2: 978
Prix Guy et Lilianne Fregault Vol. 1: 9728
Prix Henri Buttgenbach Vol. 2: 1045
Prix Henri Lavachery Vol. 2: 1010
Prix Henri Wheaton Vol. 2: 4767
Prix Herman Schoolmeesters Vol. 2: 1011
Prix Honorius-Provost Vol. 1: 15485
Prix Injalbert Vol. 2: 1482
Prix Irene Fuerison Vol. 2: 979
Prix Jacques Deruyts Vol. 2: 1046
Prix Jacques Lavalleye-Coppens Vol. 2: 980
Prix Jacques Lefebvre Vol. 2: 5868
Prix Japon - Concours International de Programmes Educatifs Vol. 2: 3298
Prix Jean Cuvillier Vol. 2: 1613
Prix Jeune Chercheur Vol. 2: 1982
Prix Jeunesse International Munchen Vol. 2: 2373
Prix John L. Synge Vol. 1: 15767
Prix John Westlake Vol. 2: 4767
Prix Jos Albert Vol. 2: 981
Prix Joseph De Keyn Vol. 2: 1012
Prix Joseph-Edmond Marchal Vol. 2: 982
Prix Joseph Gantrelle Vol. 2: 1013
Prix Joseph Schepkens Vol. 2: 1047
Prix Jules Duculot Vol. 2: 1014
Prix Jules Raeymaekers Vol. 2: 983
Prix Lamarck Vol. 2: 1048
Prix Lazare Carnot Vol. 2: 1614
Prix Le Bel Vol. 2: 1815
Prix Le Fevre-Deumier de Ports Vol. 2: 1689
Prix Le Guay-Lebrun Vol. 2: 1483
Prix Leo Errera Vol. 2: 1049
Prix Leon et Henri Fredericq Vol. 2: 1050
Prix Leon Leclere Vol. 2: 1015

Prix Lionel-Groulx-Foundation Yves-Saint-Germain Vol. 1: 9729
Prix Lionel - Groulx - les Cooperants Vol. 1: 9729
Prix Litteraire Prince Pierre-de-Monaco Vol. 2: 3473
Prix Louis-Jeantet de medecine Vol. 2: 4862
Prix Louis Renault Vol. 2: 4767
Prix Louise Dehem Vol. 2: 984
Prix Mancini Vol. 2: 4767
Prix Maxime-Raymond Vol. 1: 9730
Prix Michel-Brunet Vol. 1: 9731
Prix Michener de Journalism Vol. 1: 11718
Prix Nine Choucroun Vol. 2: 1850
Prix Noel-Mailloux Vol. 1: 14665
Prix Nouveau Talent Vol. 2: 1986
Prix Octave Mirbeau et Valentine Allorge Vol. 2: 1615
Prix Osiris Vol. 2: 1861
Prix Paul and Marie Stroobant Vol. 2: 1051
Prix Paul Artot Vol. 2: 985
Prix Paul Bonduelle Vol. 2: 986
Prix Paul-Emile-Borduas Vol. 1: 15491
Prix Paul Fourmarier Vol. 2: 1052
Prix Paul Guggenheim Vol. 2: 4876
Prix Paul Streit Vol. 2: 4702
Prix Paul Vigne d'Octon Vol. 2: 1690
Prix Philips Vol. 2: 1980
Prix Pierre Carsoel Vol. 2: 987
Prix Pierre Desnuelle Vol. 2: 1616
Prix Pierre Sue Vol. 2: 1816
Prix Pol and Christiane Swings Vol. 2: 1053
Prix Polydore de Paepe Vol. 2: 1016
Prix pour le Meilleur Film d'Exploration Vol. 2: 1890
Prix pour les Droits de l'Homme Vol. 1: 17704
Prix Prestwich Vol. 2: 1840
Prix Professeur Louis Baes Vol. 2: 1054
Prix Professionel Vol. 1: 14667
Prix Pyral Vol. 2: 1792
Prix quadrennial de Bibliographie Vol. 1: 10491
Prix Rene Janssens Vol. 2: 988
Prix Samuel Pufendorf Vol. 2: 4767
Prix Sandmeyer Vol. 2: 4893
Prix Science et Defense Vol. 2: 1812
Prix Sir John William Dawson Vol. 1: 15757
Prix Special ASIFA Vol. 2: 1227
Prix Steacie Vol. 1: 17288
Prix Suisse Vol. 2: 4702
Prix Susse Freres Vol. 2: 1484
Prix Suzanne Tassier Vol. 2: 1017
Prix Theodore Ott Vol. 2: 4886
Prix Theophile de Donder Vol. 2: 1055
Prix Theophile Gluge Vol. 2: 1056
Prix Tobie Jonckheere Vol. 2: 1018
Prix TPS Vol. 2: 1792
Prix Triennal de la Societe Royale de Chimie Vol. 2: 1096
Prix Trillium Vol. 1: 14570
Prix Ugo Papi - Gaston Leduc Vol. 2: 1691
Prix Victor Tourneur Vol. 2: 1019
Prix Viquesnel Vol. 2: 1841
Prix Vitoria Vol. 2: 4767
Prix Volney Vol. 2: 1862
Prix Wegmann Vol. 2: 1842
Prixa UNDA Vol. 2: 4882
Priz UIP Vol. 2: 5756
Prize Award; Michael Vol. 2: 921
Prize Bridge Competition Awards Vol. 1: 2557
Prize for a Distinguished Bibliography Vol. 1: 11909
Prize for a Distinguished Scholarly Edition Vol. 1: 11910
Prize for a Faculty Member for Research in an Undergraduate Institution Vol. 1: 3131
Prize for a First Book Vol. 1: 11911
Prize for Achievement in Accelerator Physics and Technology Vol. 1: 18026
Prize for Bibliography Vol. 1: 10491
Prize for Children's Film Vol. 2: 2333
Prize for Distinguished Service to the Profession Vol. 1: 16275
Prize for Freedom Vol. 2: 6375
Prize for Independent Scholars Vol. 1: 11912
Prize for Industrial Applications of Physics Vol. 1: 2545
Prize for Innovative Applied Physics of the Division of Industrial and Applied Physics Vol. 1: 6285
Prize for Material Sciences Vol. 2: 2705
Prize for Meritorious Achievement Vol. 1: 18026
Prize for Television and Radio Vol. 2: 4276
Prize for the Best German Short Film Vol. 2: 2316
Prize for the Promotion, Dissemination and Teaching of International Humanitarian Law Vol. 2: 3082
Prize for the Teaching of OR/MS Practice Vol. 1: 9750
Prize for Translated Work Vol. 2: 4278
Prize for Vocational Dental Practitioners Vol. 2: 5304
Prize for Young Scientists Vol. 2: 2955
Prize in Agricultural Sciences Vol. 2: 2956
Prize in Applied Oceanography Vol. 1: 6730
Prize in Chemistry Vol. 2: 2957
Prize in Earth Sciences Vol. 2: 2958
Prize in Economic Sciences in Memory of Alfred Nobel Vol. 2: 4639
Prize in Engineering Sciences Vol. 2: 2959
Prize in Theoretical and Mathematical Physics Vol. 1: 6286
Prize of Excellence Vol. 2: 3900
Prize of INTERFILM Vol. 2: 2316
Prize of Janko Hrasko Vol. 2: 4452
Prize of the Berlin Children's Jury Vol. 2: 2048
Prize of the Catholic Film Association Vol. 2: 2316
Prize of the Children's Cinema Vol. 2: 2316
Prize of the Churches Vol. 2: 2048
Prize of the FIPRESCI Vol. 2: 2316
Prize of the German Art Film Theatre Association Vol. 2: 2048
Prize of the Mayor of the Bratislava City Vol. 2: 4452
Prize of the Photo Book Vol. 2: 1945
Prize of the Societe Internationale de Chirurgie Vol. 2: 4852
Prize of UNICEF Vol. 2: 2048
Prize of USTT and Literary Fund Vol. 2: 4452
Prize Paper Award Vol. 1: 9824
"Prized Pieces" International Film and Video Festival Vol. 1: 12781
Prizes for Short Films Vol. 2: 2334
Prizes for the Distribution of Quality Films in Belgium Vol. 2: 1084
Prizes for the Promotion of Community-Based Cultural Exchange Vol. 2: 3235
Prizes of the 150th Anniversary of the RSSL Vol. 2: 1098
Pro Bono Publico Award Vol. 1: 1376
Pro-Comm Awards Competition Vol. 1: 6025
Pro Ecclesia et Pontifice Medal Vol. 2: 7417
Pro Finlandia Medal Vol. 2: 1375
Pro Football Hall of Fame Vol. 1: 15250
PRO LABORE SECURO Statuette Vol. 2: 3997
Pro Lingua Award Vol. 1: 8815
Pro Modified World Champion Vol. 1: 10466
PRO Rally Region of the Year Vol. 1: 17212
Pro Rodeo Hall of Fame Vol. 1: 15353
Pro Stock Puller of the Year Vol. 1: 13857
Pro Urbe Budapest Award Vol. 2: 2494
Process Award Vol. 1: 10502
ProcirepFs Award for Best Producer Vol. 2: 1948
Procter & Gamble Award in Applied and Environmental Microbiology Vol. 1: 3771
Procter Prize for Scientific Achievement; William Vol. 1: 16058
Proctor Leadership Award; Charles Henry Vol. 1: 1949
Proctor Medal Vol. 1: 4954
Proctor Memorial Leadership Award; Charles Henry Vol. 1: 1949
Proctor Prize; George Vol. 1: 7055
Proctor Prize; Thomas R. Vol. 1: 12117
Proctor Research Medal Award; Francis I. Vol. 1: 4954
Procurement Awards Vol. 1: 18120
Product of the Year Vol. 1: 12819
Production Award
American Guernsey Association Vol. 1: 2141
Canadian Brown Swiss and Braunvieh Association Vol 1: 6365
Production Engineering Award Vol. 1: 16803
Production Operations Award Vol. 1: 16803
Production Technology Award Vol. 2: 2527
Prof. M.L. Khorana Memorial Award Vol. 2: 2733
Prof. M.L. Schroff Award Vol. 2: 2734
Professional Achievement Vol. 1: 11143
Professional Achievement Award
Association of Specialized and Cooperative Library Agencies Vol. 1: 5342
Canadian Association of Black Journalists Vol 1: 6229
Special Libraries Association - Transportation Division Vol 1: 17088
Professional Achievement Awards Vol. 1: 17644
Professional Achievement Citations Vol. 1: 18261
Professional Agent of the Year Vol. 1: 12624
Professional Alarm Technician of the Year Vol. 1: 12811
Professional Assistance Awards Vol. 1: 11131
Professional Associateship Vol. 2: 6896
Professional Award
American Horticultural Society Vol. 1: 2296
Association for Communication Excellence in Agriculture, Natural Resources, and Life and Human Sciences Vol 1: 4802
Ordre des Psychologues du Quebec Vol 1: 14667
Special Libraries Association Vol 1: 17080
Professional Awards
American Society of Landscape Architects Vol. 1: 4101
American Society of Landscape Architects Vol 1: 4107
Professional Care Award Vol. 1: 6721
Professional Chapter Excellence Awards and Chapter of the Year Award Vol. 1: 2720

Professional Commitment Award Vol. 2: 3744
Professional Contribution by an ACE Member Vol. 1: 5122
Professional Development Award
American Counseling Association Vol. 1: 1846
IES, Institute for the International Education of Students Vol 1: 9595
System Safety Society Vol 1: 17377
Professional Development Awards Vol. 1: 15914
Professional Development Program Awards Vol. 1: 16085
Professional Development Scholarships Vol. 1: 18865
Professional Education Project Award Vol. 1: 709
Professional Educator of the Year Award Vol. 1: 36
Professional Engineer of the Year
Institution of Engineers Australia/Engineers Australia Vol. 2: 525
Institution of Engineers Australia/Engineers Australia Vol 2: 540
Professional Engineers Citizenship Award Vol. 1: 15309
Professional Engineers Gold Medal Vol. 1: 15310
Professional Excellence in Building Awards Vol. 2: 236
Professional Flute Choir Competition Vol. 1: 13205
Professional Leadership Award Vol. 1: 4851
Professional Member of the Year Vol. 1: 12794
Professional of the Year
Association of Jewish Center Professionals Vol. 1: 5204
Government Management Information Sciences Vol 1: 9157
Ladies Professional Golf Association Vol 1: 11200
United States Professional Tennis Association Vol 1: 18036
Professional of the Year Award Vol. 1: 5204
Professional Prix de Rome in Architecture Vol. 1: 6119
Professional Progress Award for Outstanding Progress in Chemical Engineering Vol. 1: 2494
Professional Recognition Award Vol. 1: 5391
Professional Research Award Vol. 1: 13850
Professional Risk Management Services Inc Vol. 1: 3272
Professional Safety Paper Awards Vol. 1: 4233
Professional Service Award
Institute of Australian Geographers Vol. 2: 479
National Community Education Association Vol 1: 12940
States Organization for Boating Access Vol 1: 17274
Professional Service Award Vol. 1: 12474
Professional Service to Health Education Award Vol. 1: 911
Professional Teacher of the Year Award Vol. 1: 36
Professionalism Award Vol. 1: 12705
Professor Pham Bieu Tam Memorial Award Vol. 1: 18533
Professor Shambu Nath De Memorial Lecture Vol. 2: 2706
Professors' Prize Vol. 2: 5080
Program Award Vol. 1: 12249
Program Director of the Year Vol. 1: 9560
Program Director of the Year Award Vol. 1: 1183
Program Directors Awards Vol. 1: 7742
Program Excellence Award Vol. 1: 16398
Program Excellence Award Vol. 1: 10785
Program Excellence Awards Vol. 1: 10312
Program Standards Award Vol. 1: 12273
Program to Recognize Excellence in Student Literary Magazines Vol. 1: 13027
Programme Awards Vol. 2: 7044
Programme of the Year Vol. 2: 5097
Programming Systems and Languages Paper Award Vol. 1: 4815
Progress Award Vol. 1: 500
Progress in Equity Award Vol. 1: 1323
Progress Medal Vol. 2: 6879
Progress Medal Award Vol. 1: 16750
Project Funding Program Vol. 1: 4681
Project Manager of the Year Vol. 2: 5098
Project of the Year Vol. 2: 5099
Project of the Year Vol. 1: 5985
Project of the Year Award Vol. 1: 15373
Projects, Facilities and Construction Award Vol. 1: 16804
PROMAX Awards Vol. 1: 15381
PROMAX/BDA Home Entertainment Awards Vol. 1: 15381
PROMAX/BDA Latin America Awards Vol. 1: 15381
PROMAX North America Awards Vol. 1: 15381
PROMAX World Gold Awards Vol. 1: 15381
Promega Biotechnology Research Award Vol. 1: 3772
Prometheus Award Vol. 1: 11320
Promise to the Earth Award Vol. 1: 12253
Promising Performer Award Vol. 1: 375
Promising Personality Vol. 1: 17517
Promising Playwright Award Vol. 1: 7554
Promising Researcher Award Vol. 1: 13028
Promising Young Writers Program Vol. 1: 13029
Promoter of the Year Vol. 1: 17756
Promotion and Education (P&E) Awards Vol. 1: 5264
Promotion of Excellence Award Vol. 1: 9477
Promotion of Savings, Consumer Protection, and Export PerFormance Award Vol. 2: 2669
Promotional Prizes Vol. 2: 2345
Propellants and Combustion Award Vol. 1: 2399
Property Council Rider Hunt Awards Vol. 2: 601
ProQuest SIRS International Commendation Award; IASL/ Vol. 1: 10238
ProRally of the Year Vol. 1: 17211
Prosceniumprijs Vol. 2: 3679
Proskauer Prize; Edith H. and Richmond Vol. 1: 13690
Prost; Prix Gabriel-Auguste Vol. 2: 1531
Protege Awards Vol. 1: 17555
Prous Science Award on New Technologies in Drug Discovery Vol. 2: 773
Prouty and Elsie S. Prouty Memorial Award; Morton D. Vol. 1: 13179
Prouty Award; Bob Vol. 1: 17236
Provasoli Award; Luigi Vol. 1: 15036
Province of Nova Scotia Scholarship Vol. 1: 5507
Provincial Police Award Vol. 2: 5121
Proximity Achievement Award Vol. 1: 17936
Pruszynski Prize; Ksawery Vol. 2: 4019
Pruvost; Prix Fondation Pierre Vol. 2: 1843
Pruzansky Memorial Fund for Maternal and Child Health Nursing; Donna Vol. 1: 7470
Pryor Award; Susie Vol. 1: 4623
Pryor Memorial Award; Bill Vol. 1: 18592
Prys vir Televisie en Radio Vol. 2: 4276
PSA Contemporary Medal Vol. 1: 9186
PSA International Exhibition
Photographic Society of America Vol. 1: 15027
Photographic Society of America Vol 1: 15028
Photographic Society of America Vol 1: 15029
Photographic Society of America Vol 1: 15030
Photographic Society of America Vol. 1: 15031
Photographic Society of America Vol 1: 15032
PSA Medal Vol. 1: 9186
PSA Yankee Medal Vol. 1: 9186
PSJ Award Vol. 2: 3307
PSJ Award for Drug Research and Development Vol. 2: 3308
PSJ Award for Young Scientists Vol. 2: 3309
Psycho-social Award Vol. 2: 2544
Psychoanalytic Training Today Award Vol. 2: 6284
Psychological Dimensions of Peacework Award Vol. 1: 15413
Psychotherapy Prize Vol. 2: 6732
PTC Essay Prize Vol. 1: 14792
PTV National Awards Vol. 2: 3923
Public Access to Government Information Award Vol. 1: 1148
Public Affairs Competition Vol. 1: 1163
Public and Community Service Emmy Awards Vol. 1: 12181
Public Archaeology Award Vol. 2: 3763
Public Citizen of the Year Vol. 1: 12665
Public Communications Award
Canadian Archaeological Association Vol. 1: 6186
Society of Toxicology Vol 1: 16878
Public Education Award Vol. 1: 13901
Public Education Award Vol. 1: 18644
Public Education Awards Program Vol. 1: 6456
Public Health Award Vol. 1: 616
Public Health Prize Vol. 2: 1918
Public History Award Vol. 1: 14461
Public Information Program Award Vol. 1: 10138
Public Interest Award Vol. 2: 3792
Public Plant Breeding Award Vol. 1: 12996
Public Policy and Advocacy Award Vol. 1: 530
Public Policy Award Vol. 1: 2400
Public Programming Awards Vol. 1: 15594
Public Recreation Man and Woman of the Year Vol. 1: 501
Public Recreation Volunteer of the Year Award Vol. 1: 502
Public Relations Award Vol. 1: 503
Public Relations Coordinator of the Year Vol. 1: 12795
Public Relations Flim/Video Competition Vol. 1: 15426
Public Relations Recognition Award
American Association of Nurse Anesthetists Vol. 1: 1184

Institute of Management Accountants Vol 1: 9901
Public Risk Manager of the Year Award Vol. 1: 15436
Public Rose Garden Achievement Award Vol. 1: 394
Public Safety Recognition Vol. 1: 5695
Public Sector Leadership Vol. 1: 6165
Public Service Achievement Award Vol. 1: 7629
Public Service Award
American Woman's Society of Certified Public Accountants Vol. 1: 4491
Society for American Archaeology Vol 1: 16164
Society for Prevention Research Vol 1: 16388
Public Service Award
The Adirondack Council Vol. 1: 158
Advertising Council Vol 1: 182
American Crystallographic Association Vol 1: 1862
American Institute of Aeronautics and Astronautics Vol 1: 2401
American Institute of Certified Public Accountants Vol 1: 2464
American Institute of Professional Geologists Vol 1: 2551
American Public Power Association Vol 1: 3445
American Society for Cell Biology Vol 1: 3592
American Veterinary Medical Association Vol 1: 4412
Animal Transportation Association - European Office Vol 2: 5055
Associated Press Managing Editors - Managing Editors Association Vol 1: 4769
Association of Consulting Foresters of America Vol 1: 5113
Friends of Libraries U.S.A. Vol 1: 8903
National Rehabilitation Association Vol 1: 13610
National Science Foundation - National Science Board Vol 1: 13676
Oncology Nursing Society Vol 1: 14548
Society of Petroleum Engineers Vol 1: 16805
UCLA Alumni Association Vol 1: 17645
Public Service Awards
American Association of Petroleum Geologists Vol. 1: 1227
Fund for the City of New York Vol 1: 8929
Public Service Campaign of the Year Vol. 1: 14076
Public Service Citations Vol. 1: 18262
Public Service Excellence Award Vol. 2: 2535
Public Service Group Achievement Award Vol. 1: 12209
Public Service Medal
Australian Honours Secretariat Vol. 2: 223
National Aeronautics and Space Administration Vol 1: 12210
Public Service National Leadership Award Vol. 1: 2221
Public Welfare Medal Vol. 1: 12163
Publication Award
Association of Engineering Geologists Vol. 1: 5141
Canadian Society for Clinical Pharmacology Vol 1: 6935
Publication Awards Vol. 1: 15621
Publication Design Awards Vol. 1: 16843
Publication Grant Vol. 1: 15023
Publication in Counselor Education and Supervision Award Vol. 1: 4852
The Publication Medal Vol. 2: 650
Publications and Electronic Media Awards Vol. 1: 13666
Publications Award
AACE International Vol. 1: 25
Association for Industrial Archaeology Vol 2: 5093
Audio Engineering Society Vol 1: 5523
Flight Safety Foundation Vol 1: 8723
Publications Grant Vol. 1: 4583
Publisher of the Year
Association of Free Community Papers Vol. 1: 5158
Data Publishers Association Vol 2: 5729
Publisher of the Year Award Vol. 1: 6356
Publishing Award Vol. 2: 6332
Puckey Prize; Sir Walter Vol. 2: 6153
Pufendorf; Prix Samuel Vol. 2: 4767
PUK-Councilers Prize Vol. 2: 4279
Pulaski Scholarship Vol. 1: 1804
Pulitzer Fellowships Vol. 1: 15453
Pulitzer Prizes Vol. 1: 15454
Pull of the Year Vol. 1: 13858
Pullara Award Vol. 1: 2449
Puller of the Year Vol. 1: 13864
Pulliam Fellowship for Editorial Writing; Eugene C. Vol. 1: 16837
Pulliam National Journalism Writing Award; Eugene S. Vol. 1: 5641
Pulling Family of the Year Vol. 1: 13859
Pulling Hall of Fame Vol. 1: 13860
Pulp Biology Research Award Vol. 1: 10061
Pulp Press International Three-Day Novel Competition Vol. 1: 4548
Pundik Prize; Mendel and Eva Vol. 2: 2933
Punster of the Year Vol. 1: 10615
Pupin Medal Vol. 1: 7576
Puppeteers of America Award Vol. 1: 15465
Purchasing Manager of the Year Award Vol. 1: 13375
Purdy Award; Ken W. Vol. 1: 10522
Purdy Award; Ross Coffin Vol. 1: 1493
Purdy Distinguished Achievement Award; Richard B. Vol. 1: 10665
Purdy Medal Vol. 2: 151
Purina Mills, Inc. Teaching Award Vol. 1: 1881
Purina Mills, Inc. Teaching Award in Dairy Production Vol. 1: 1890
Purina Mills Teaching Award; Land O'Lakes/ Vol. 1: 15178
Purple Heart Vol. 1: 13704
Purse Doctoral Fellowship; Ross C. Vol. 1: 6751
Pursuit of Excellence Award Vol. 1: 13267
Purvis Memorial Award Vol. 2: 7177
Puschkin Prize; Alexander Vol. 2: 2401
Pushcart Prize: Best of the Small Presses Vol. 1: 15474
Pushkin Prize; Alexander Sergeovich Vol. 2: 4397
Pustovoit Award Vol. 2: 1915
- Putnam & Grosset Group Award Vol. 1: 4929
Putnam Publishing Group Award Vol. 1: 4929
Putnam Service Award; Allan Ray Vol. 1: 4707
PVA Donor Recognition Award Vol. 1: 14843
Pyramid Award Vol. 1: 4424
Pyramid Awards Vol. 1: 18619
Pyrotechnics Guild International Competition Vol. 1: 15476
Qaboos Prize for Environmental Preservation; Sultan Vol. 2: 1998
QBS Award Vol. 1: 13751
QRA-Bill Bishop Award Vol. 2: 6574
QSPA Achievement Award Vol. 2: 603
QSPA Award for Leadership in the Profession Vol. 2: 604
QSPA Lifetime Achievement Vol. 2: 605
QSPELL Awards Vol. 1: 15493
QST Cover Plaque Award Vol. 1: 37
Qualey Article Award; Carlton C. Vol. 1: 9627
Quality Awards Vol. 2: 2657
Quality in Construction Award Vol. 1: 12298
Quantum Electronics Award Vol. 1: 9590
Quantum Electronics Prize Vol. 2: 1788
Quarter-Century Honor Roll Vol. 1: 12532
Quarter Midgets of America Hall of Fame Vol. 1: 10526
Quaternary Conference Fund Vol. 2: 6575
Quaternary Research Fund Vol. 2: 6576
Queen Award; Ellery Vol. 1: 12055
Queen Elisabeth International Music Competition of Belgium Prizes Vol. 2: 947
Queen Elizabeth II Coronation Award Vol. 2: 6619
Queen Elizabeth II Silver Jubilee Endowment Fund for Study in a Second Official Language Award Program Vol. 1: 5375
Queen Fabiola Prize Vol. 2: 917
Queen Sonja International Music Competition Vol. 2: 3914
Queen's Award
Girls' Brigade Australia Vol. 2: 472
Girls' Brigade International Council Vol 2: 5941
Queen's Award for Enterprise: Innovation Vol. 2: 6578
Queen's Award for Environmental Achievement Vol. 2: 6579
Queen's Award for Export Achievement Vol. 2: 6581
Queen's Award for Forestry Vol. 2: 5675
Queen's Award for Technological Achievement Vol. 2: 6580
Queen's Awards for Enterprise Vol. 2: 6579
Queen's Awards for Enterprise in Innovation Vol. 2: 6580
Queen's Awards for Enterprise in International Trade Vol. 2: 6581
Queen's Awards for Enterprise: International Trade Vol. 2: 6582
Queen's Awards for Enterprise: Sustainable Development Vol. 2: 6583
Queen's Fire Service Medal Vol. 2: 5604
Queen's Gallantry Medal Vol. 2: 5605
Queen's Medal for Champion Shot Vol. 1: 6094
Queen's Medals Vol. 2: 6915
Queen's Police Medal for Distinguished Service Vol. 2: 5606
Queen's Prize Vol. 2: 6485
Queensland Division Chemical Branch Award Vol. 2: 526
Queeny Safety Professional of the Year Award; Edgar Monsanto Vol. 1: 4234
Queneau Palladium Medal; Joan Hodges Vol. 1: 1092
Quesada Award; General E. R. Vol. 1: 335
Quesada Memorial Award; General E. R. Vol. 1: 335
Quigley Award; R. M. Vol. 1: 6529

Quill Medal; Jeffrey Vol. 2: 5013
Quilt National Awards Vol. 1: 8019
Quilters Hall of Fame Vol. 1: 15501
QuiltFs Japan Prize Vol. 1: 8019
Quimby Regional Competitions for Young Organists Vol. 1: 2150
Quinn '50 Distinguished Service Award; George J. Vol. 1: 7173
Quinn Award; Jim Vol. 1: 12767
Quinn Award; Robert G. Vol. 1: 3670
Quinn Endowment; Frederic Ives Medal/Jarus W. Vol. 1: 14608
Quran Recitation Vol. 1: 10919
QWF Awards Vol. 1: 15493
R & D 100 Awards Vol. 1: 15505
R38 Memorial Prize Vol. 2: 6651
RAAG Award Vol. 2: 2471
Rabb Award; Sidney R. Vol. 1: 8789
Rabi Prize in Atomic, Molecular and Optical Physics; I. I. Vol. 1: 3132
Rabone Award Vol. 2: 3745
RAC Awards Vol. 1: 15648
Race Organizer of the Year Vol. 1: 17756
Racehorse of the Year Award Vol. 2: 6587
Rachel Carson Prize Vol. 1: 3701
Racial/Ethnic Minority Graduate Scholarship Vol. 1: 16464
Racial Justice Award Vol. 1: 19100
RACie Awards Vol. 1: 15647
Racolin Memorial Fellowship; The Natalie and Mendel Vol. 1: 19066
RAD Magazine Award Vol. 2: 6738
RAD Magazine Best Poster Prize Vol. 2: 5333
Radcliffe Travelling Fellowship in Reliability and Quality Assurance; Frank Vol. 2: 6652
Raddall Atlantic Fiction Award; Thomas Vol. 1: 19003
Radde Educator of the Year Award; Leon R. Vol. 1: 9881
Radin Distinguished Service Award; Alex Vol. 1: 3446
Radio Broadcasting Hall of Fame Vol. 1: 12428
Radio Mercury Awards Vol. 1: 15513
Radio Mercury Gold Award Vol. 1: 15513
Radio Mercury Public Service Award Vol. 1: 15513
Radio Programming and Promotion Awards Vol. 1: 14120
Radio Technical Commission for Aeronatics Vol. 1: 15771
Radish Marine Enlisted Aircrew of the Year Award; Danny Vol. 1: 11522
Radix Pin; Harry E. Vol. 1: 17903
Radix Trophy Vol. 1: 17903
Radix Trophy; Henry E. Vol. 1: 15325
Rafaelsen Fellowship Award Vol. 1: 7550
Raffles Award; Stamford Vol. 2: 7400
Rafto Memorial Prize; Professor Thorolf Vol. 2: 3916
Ragazzini Award; John R. Vol. 1: 2495
Raghavendra Memorial Award; Prof. B.G. Vol. 2: 2782
Raginski Award; Bernard B. Vol. 1: 16198
Rahman Prize for Computational Physics; Aneesur Vol. 1: 3133
Rahn Education Award; Ivan B. Vol. 1: 16359
RAI Prize Vol. 2: 3136
RAIA Gold Medal Vol. 2: 628
Raikes Medal Vol. 2: 4318
Railroad Calendar Color Slide Contest Vol. 1: 12057
Railway Engineering Award Vol. 2: 527
Rain Bird Engineering Concept of the Year Award Vol. 1: 3862
Rainmaker Award Vol. 1: 7998
Raise Your Sites Award Vol. 1: 9361
Rajchman Prize; Jan Vol. 1: 16309
Rajewsky; Medaille Boris Vol. 2: 1765
Raju Oration Award; Dr. P. N. Vol. 2: 2618
Raleigh Award for Fiction; Sir Walter Vol. 1: 14372
Rally Awards Vol. 1: 17212
Ralph W. Westcott Award Vol. 1: 18158
Ralston Purina Company Teaching Award in Dairy Science Vol. 1: 1881
The Ram Award Vol. 1: 5217
Rama Rao Memorial Award; P.B. Vol. 2: 2797
Ramachandran 60th Birthday Commemoration Medal; Prof. G. N. Vol. 2: 2707
Ramaermedaille Vol. 2: 3633
Ramage Grant for Graduate Study in Composition; Lillian Harlan Vol. 1: 12000
Ramah Leadership Award Vol. 1: 13590
Raman Birth Centenary Award; C. V. Vol. 2: 2747
Raman Medal; Chandrasekhara Venkata Vol. 2: 2708
Ramanathan Medal; K. R. Vol. 2: 2709
Ramanujan Birth Centenary Award; Srinivasa Vol. 2: 2748
Ramanujan Prize for Young Mathematicians Vol. 2: 2949
Ramdohr Prize; Paul Vol. 2: 2087
Ramo Medal; Simon Vol. 1: 9793
Ramos Awards; Elise Vol. 1: 4786
Ramp Safety Award Vol. 1: 8720
Rampal International Flute Competition; Jean-Pierre Vol. 2: 1749
Ramsay Medal; Erskine Vol. 1: 2533
Ramsay Memorial Fellowships for Postdoctoral Chemical Research Vol. 2: 6589
Ramsdell Award; Charles Vol. 1: 17034
Ramsdell Award; Fletcher M. Green and Charles W. Vol. 1: 17034
Ramsden Awards; John Vol. 2: 7127
Rand Medal; ASCEPT Michael Vol. 2: 96
Rand Memorial Gold Medal; Charles F. Vol. 1: 2534
Rand Trophy; Remington Vol. 1: 9902
Randall Award; Ollie A. Vol. 1: 13053
Randolph/Bayard Rustin Freedom Award; A. Philip Vol. 1: 15
Randolph Freedom Award; A. Philip Vol. 1: 15
Randolph-Perry Medal Vol. 1: 11641
Randolph Program for International Peace; Jennings Vol. 1: 17961
Raney Fund Award Vol. 1: 4078
Ranier III Special Prize; Prince Vol. 2: 3469
Ranki Prize; Gyorgi Vol. 1: 8382
Ranking Champion Vol. 2: 1109
Ransom Memorial Medals; James Vol. 2: 6173
Rao Award; Dr. T. Ramachandra Vol. 2: 2619
Rao Award; Tilak Venkoba Vol. 2: 2620
Rao Forestry Research Award; Dr. Y.S. Vol. 2: 3395
Rao Memorial Lecture; Prof. K. Rangadhama Vol. 2: 2710
Rao Oration Award in Microbiology; Dr. Y. S. Narayana Vol. 2: 2621
Raper Oral and Maxillofacial Radiology Award; Howard R. Vol. 1: 662
Raphel Memorial Award; Arnold L. Vol. 1: 17868
Rapoport Award for Excellence in Commentary; Louis Vol. 1: 2599
Rapp Archaeological Geology Award; Rip Vol. 1: 9026
Rare Books and Manuscripts Librarianship Award Vol. 1: 5085
Rasmussen Emerging Artist Memorial Award; Cathy Vol. 1: 8019
Raster Award Vol. 1: 9311
Ratcliff Trophy; Tom Vol. 2: 5910
Rating; Standard and Poor's BBB Vol. 2: 3883
Ratner Award; Bret Vol. 1: 710
Rattlesnake Award; Jimmy
Baseball Canada Vol. 1: 5679
Canadian Federation of Amateur Baseball Vol 1: 6475
Rauriser Literaturpreis Vol. 2: 743
Raven Award Vol. 1: 12055
Raven Award; Peter Vol. 1: 4225
Raven Awards Vol. 1: 15565
Rawley Prize; James A. Vol. 1: 14700
Rawlings Award for Energy Conservation (Manager and Technician); General Edwin W. Vol. 1: 299
Rawlings Awards for Environmental Achievement; General Edwin W. Vol. 1: 299
Rawlings Big Stick Award Vol. 1: 15567
Rawlings Gold Glove Award Vol. 1: 15568
Rawlings Silver Glove Award Vol. 1: 15569
Rawls-Palmer Progress in Medicine Lecture and Award Vol. 1: 3612
Rawls Prize; William E. Vol. 1: 12845
Ray Award in Memory of Margaret Sutermeister; Isaac Vol. 1: 3285
Rayleigh Book Award Vol. 2: 6159
Rayleigh Medal Vol. 2: 5985
Raymond Award; Rossiter W. Vol. 1: 2535
Raymond Literary Award; Wayte and Olga Vol. 1: 2914
RBMS Exhibition Catalogue Awards Vol. 1: 5083
Rea Award for the Short Story Vol. 1: 8301
Rea Non-Fiction Prize Vol. 1: 5854
REACH Awards Vol. 1: 5300
REACH (REcognize ACHievement) Awards Vol. 1: 19110
Reaching Out Award - DEMA Hall of Fame Vol. 1: 8234
Read Award; Sir Herbert Vol. 1: 10646
Read Medal; John E. Vol. 2: 1232
Read Memorial Award; The S.E. Group/ Les Vol. 1: 6208
Reader Prize; Ralph Vol. 2: 400
Readers' Choice Awards Vol. 1: 15194
Readers Digest Student Award Vol. 2: 5269
Readers Prizes of the *Berliner Morgenpost* Vol. 2: 2048
Reading/Literacy Research Fellowship Vol. 1: 10594
Reagan Award; John H. Vol. 1: 7673
Real Estate Journalism Competition Vol. 1: 12631
Realia Honors Vol. 1: 9765
Realtor of the Year Vol. 1: 12634
RealtorFs Choice Award Vol. 1: 9471
Reardon Award; Paul C. Vol. 1: 12875
Reason Memorial Award; George Vol. 1: 6268

Rebbot Award; Olivier Vol. 1: 14761
Recent Graduate Award Vol. 1: 11144
Reckord Trophy; Major Gen. Milton A. Vol. 1: 13301
Reclamation Researcher of the Year Vol. 1: 4178
Reclamationist of the Year Vol. 1: 4179
Recognition Award
American Association of School Personnel Administrators Vol. 1: 1284
American Society for Cybernetics Vol 1: 3620
Association for Science Teacher Education Vol 1: 4961
Gas Processors Association Vol 1: 8972
National Association of Diaconate Directors Vol 1: 12510
National Intercollegiate Soccer Officials Association Vol 1: 13384
Teachers Association of Baltimore County Vol 1: 17415
Recognition Award for Emerging Scholars Vol. 1: 1328
Recognition Award in Entomology Vol. 1: 17366
Recognition Awards
American Association of Poison Control Centers Vol. 1: 1258
Ohio Middle School Association Vol 1: 14476
Optimist International Vol 1: 14622
Recognition Awards for Outstanding Achievement in the Field of Information Technology Vol. 1: 12667
Recognition of Achievement Award Vol. 1: 4728
Recognition of Goodness Award Vol. 1: 10994
Recognition of Outstanding Service and Involvement Vol. 1: 8259
Recognition of Professional Service Award Vol. 1: 5308
Recognition of Retirees and Deceased Vol. 1: 4853
Record Houses of the Year Vol. 1: 4589
Record Interiors of the Year Vol. 1: 4590
Recorded Event of the Year Vol. 1: 10270
Recorder of the Year Vol. 1: 14478
Recording and Fieldwork Award Vol. 2: 5094
Recycler of the Year Vol. 1: 13604
Recycler of the Year Award Vol. 1: 13484
Red Award for Air National Guard Aerospace Maintenance; Chief Master Sergeant Dick Vol. 1: 300
Red Cloud Indian Art Show Vol. 1: 9389
Red Coat (Membership) Award Vol. 1: 60
Red Cross International Committee Prize Vol. 2: 3469
Red Earth Poetry Award Vol. 2: 590
Red Earth Poetry Award; Dymocks Vol. 2: 589
Red Ochre Award Vol. 2: 103
Redd Center Publication Grants; Charles Vol. 1: 15595
Redd Student Award in Women's History; Annaley Naegle Vol. 1: 15596
Reddick Memorial Scholarship Award; Dr. Lawrence Dunbar Vol. 1: 5370
Reden Plakette Vol. 2: 2235
Redhouse Student Prize; James W. Vol. 1: 17633
Redi Award Vol. 2: 2325
Redmond Award; Juanita Vol. 1: 301
Redon; Fondation Vol. 2: 1482
Redwood Lectureship; Theophilus Vol. 2: 6979
Reebok Human Rights Award Vol. 1: 15601
Reed Aeronautics Award Vol. 1: 2402
Reed and Mallik Medal Vol. 2: 6125
Reed Award; Sylvanus Albert Vol. 1: 2402
Reed Medal; Walter Vol. 1: 4261
Reed Technology Medal; Robert F. Vol. 1: 9175
Reel Current Award Vol. 1: 12080
Rees Memorial Fund; Dick Vol. 2: 6368
Reese Fellowship Vol. 1: 819
Reese Research Prize; Raymond C. Vol. 1: 3974
Reese Structural Research Award; Raymond C. Vol. 1: 1760
Reeve Memorial Award; John Peter Vol. 1: 18353
Reeves Premium; A. H. Vol. 2: 6160
Referee of the Year Vol. 2: 3403
Reference Service Press Award Vol. 1: 2693
Reference Services Award Vol. 1: 9609
REFORMA Scholarship Vol. 1: 15604
Regal Cinemas Dreammaker Award Vol. 1: 12080
Regennitter AAU Jujitsu Service Award; Professor Vol. 1: 504
Reger Memorial Award; Harley B. Vol. 1: 13620
Reggie Awards Vol. 1: 15385
Regifting Grants Program Vol. 1: 8000
Regina Medal Vol. 1: 7161
Region Achievement Award Vol. 1: 17213
Region Newsletter of the Year Award Vol. 1: 4749
Region of the Year Vol. 1: 12796
Region of the Year Award Vol. 1: 4750
Regional Achievement Award Vol. 2: 6180
Regional Airline of the Year Vol. 1: 341
Regional Assistant Coach of the Year Vol. 1: 13709
Regional Award Vol. 1: 6945
Regional Awards
National Association of Student Personnel Administrators Vol. 1: 12688
National Park Academy of the Arts Vol 1: 13528
National Water Safety Congress Vol 1: 13890
New England Theatre Conference Vol 1: 14057
Regional Best Condition Award Vol. 1: 1966
Regional Business Achievers Award Vol. 2: 4148
Regional Chapter Research Advancement Award Vol. 1: 16047
Regional Competition for Young Organists Vol. 1: 2152
Regional Director of the Year Vol. 1: 1671
Regional Director of the Year
American College of Oncology Administrators Vol. 1: 1701
National Horseshoe Pitchers Association of America Vol 1: 13355
Regional Distinguished Mid-Career Award Vol. 1: 8518
Regional Distinguished Service Award Vol. 1: 8519
Regional Distinguished Team Award Vol. 1: 8520
Regional Diver of the Year Award Vol. 1: 17667
Regional Division Art Educator Award Vol. 1: 12274
Regional Division Art Educator of the Year Vol. 1: 12274
Regional Graduate Scholarships Vol. 1: 7020
Regional Horse Awards Vol. 1: 14349
Regional Leadership Award
Mid-America Regional Council Vol. 1: 11743
National Council for Continuing Education and Training Vol 1: 12959
Regional Medallions Vol. 1: 14321
Regional Person of the Year Award Vol. 1: 3482
Regional Person of the Year Award Vol. 1: 12959
Regional Presentation Award Vol. 2: 6181
Regional Presidents Award Vol. 1: 12445
Regional Publication Awards Vol. 1: 17214
Regional Recognition Award Vol. 1: 6241
Regional Representative of the Year Vol. 1: 12797
Regional Safety Committee of the Year Vol. 1: 366
Regional Safety Professional of the Year Vol. 1: 4234
Regional Service Award Vol. 1: 11978
Register of Merit Vol. 1: 14429
Registrar Prize Vol. 2: 5146
Regnone Service Award; Debbie Vol. 1: 15640
Regrant Program Vol. 1: 14386
Rehabilitation International Presidential Award Vol. 1: 15608
Rehabilitation Prize Vol. 2: 2021
Rehnquist Award for Judicial Excellence; William H. Vol. 1: 12876
Reichart Award; Stuart R. Vol. 1: 302
Reid Memorial Award; Crawford Vol. 1: 10903
Reid Memorial Fellowship; J.H. Stewart Vol. 1: 6307
Reid Prize in Mathematics; W. T. and Idalia Vol. 1: 16276
Reiffenstein Student Award; Roderick Vol. 1: 14972
Reilly Outstanding Geography Teacher of the Year; John Vol. 1: 11580
Reinach; Prix Lucien de Vol. 2: 1692
Reiner Award; Miriam Vol. 1: 889
Reiner Diamond Pin Award; Abraham Vol. 1: 670
Reingold Prize; The Nathan Vol. 1: 9444
Reinhart and Henry Kuhlmann Award; Frank W. Vol. 1: 5453
Reinhart Award; Frank W. Vol. 1: 5454
Reinhart Ring; Hans Vol. 2: 4888
Reinhold Award for Innovation in Teaching; Van Nostrand Vol. 1: 10370
Related Industry Award Vol. 1: 12221
Relating Research to Practice Award Vol. 1: 1945
Reliability Test and Evaluation Award Vol. 1: 9839
Relief Pitcher Vol. 1: 17169
Religion Reporter of the Year Award Vol. 1: 11026
Religious Broadcasting Hall of Fame Award Vol. 1: 13624
Religious Educational Excellence Award Vol. 1: 12868
Religious Liberty Award Vol. 1: 9959
Remington Honor Medal Vol. 1: 3058
Remington Painting Award; Frederic Vol. 1: 13068
Remmers Award; H.H. Vol. 1: 15471

Remmey Memorial Award; Paul B. Vol. 1: 4440
Remodeler of the Month/Year Awards Vol. 1: 12559
Remote Sensing and Photogrammetry Society Award Vol. 2: 6595
Remote Sensing Society Medal Vol. 2: 6595
Remote Sensing Society President's Prize Vol. 2: 6598
Renaissance Awards Vol. 1: 12560
Renal Section Pfizer Predoctoral Excellence in Renal Research Award Vol. 1: 3179
Renaudot; Prix Theophraste Vol. 2: 1943
Renault; Prix Louis Vol. 2: 4767
Rencontres chorales internationales de Montreux Vol. 2: 4870
Renner Award for Outstanding Crime Reporting; Thomas Vol. 1: 10853
Renner Award; Tom Vol. 1: 10852
Renner Medal; Janos Vol. 2: 2492
Rennie Memorial Award for Excellence in Government Public Relations; Don Vol. 1: 6847
Rennie Memorial Medal Vol. 2: 623
Renold Fellowship; Albert Vol. 2: 2109
Renovated Building Award Vol. 1: 5998
Renovated Laboratory of the Year
R & D Magazine - Reed Business Information Vol. 1: 15504
Scientific Equipment and Furniture Association Vol 1: 15930
Rental E-Web Image Award Vol. 1: 3483
Rental Hall of Fame Vol. 1: 3484
Repligen Corporation Award in Chemistry of Biological Processes Vol. 1: 1577
Replogle Award for Management Improvement; Luther I. Vol. 1: 17869
Reporter/Scrapbook Award Vol. 1: 13959
Republic of Vietnam Campaign Medal Vol. 1: 8121
Research Achievement Award Vol. 1: 2187
Research Achievement Award in the Pharmaceutical Sciences Vol. 1: 3059
Research and Audit Awards Vol. 2: 5410
Research and Development Award
American Diabetes Association Vol. 1: 1909
Institute of Food Technologists Vol 1: 9854
Research and Development Team Award Vol. 2: 7046
Research and Education Award Vol. 1: 14024
Research and Education in Dentistry Fund for Post Graduate Studies in Dental Education Vol. 2: 4327
Research and Special Libraries Award Vol. 1: 5207
Research and Travel Grants Vol. 2: 4644
Research Appointments Vol. 1: 18330
Research Appointments/Fellowships Vol. 2: 6914
Research Article Award Vol. 1: 8667
Research Assistantships Vol. 1: 18288
Research Associateship Programs Vol. 1: 13629
Research Award
Accounting and Finance Association of Australia and New Zealand Vol. 2: 33
Canadian Society for the Study of Higher Education Vol 1: 6969
European Society for Paediatric Endocrinology Vol 2: 5866
Photographic Historical Society of Canada Vol 1: 15024
Research Award
Ambulatory Pediatric Association Vol. 1: 531
American Academy of Clinical Toxicology Vol 1: 563
American Alliance for Theatre and Education Vol 1: 797
American Counseling Association Vol 1: 1847
American Diabetes Association Vol 1: 1917
American Institute of Aeronautics and Astronautics Vol 1: 2374
Charcot-Marie-Tooth Association Vol 1: 7284
Council for Exceptional Children Vol 1: 7860
Emergency Nurses Association Vol 1: 8446
Fellows of the American Bar Foundation Vol 1: 8678
Hawk Mountain Sanctuary Association Vol 1: 9294
Lamaze International Vol 1: 11214
National Association of Animal Breeders Vol 1: 12379
Radiation Research Society Vol 1: 15510
Society for Human Resource Management Vol 1: 16242
World Organization of Building Officials Vol 1: 18962
Research Award Competition Vol. 1: 1826
Research Award for Outstanding Article in a Journal Vol. 1: 4996
Research Award in Teacher Education Vol. 1: 5361
Research Awards
American Society of Echocardiography Vol. 1: 4028
International Corrections and Prisons Association Vol 1: 10343
Research Awards
American Heart Association, Talbot County Branch Vol. 1: 2190
Arthritis Foundation Vol 1: 4659
National Institute of Nursing Research Vol 1: 13378
National Therapeutic Recreation Society Vol 1: 13850
Oral and Maxillofacial Surgery Foundation Vol 1: 14625
Post-Polio Health International Vol 1: 15162
Society for Theatre Research Vol 2: 7127
Research Council Awards Vol. 1: 14219
Research, Development and Demonstration Project Grants Vol. 1: 11666
Research Dissemination Award Vol. 1: 16052
Research Dissertation Award Vol. 1: 16053
Research/Educational Awards Vol. 2: 139
Research Excellence Award Vol. 1: 13652
Research Federation Award of Merit Vol. 1: 14219
Research Fellowship Vol. 1: 5222
Research Fellowship Award Vol. 1: 6277
Research Fellowship Grants Vol. 1: 15095
Research Fellowship in Iranian Studies Vol. 1: 2520
Research Fellowships
American Association for Cancer Research Vol. 1: 862
Pulmonary Hypertension Association Vol 1: 15458
Susan G. Komen Breast Cancer Foundation Vol 1: 17345
Research Fellowships and Grants Vol. 1: 11443
Research Fellowships in Cerebrovascular Disease Vol. 1: 13812
Research Grant
British Society of Periodontology Vol. 2: 5520
Photographic Historical Society of Canada Vol 1: 15025
South African Dental Association Vol 2: 4328
Research Grant
American Association of Feline Practitioners Vol. 1: 1102
Australian Society for Medical Research Vol 2: 368
National Speleological Society Vol 1: 13794
Royal Society of Tropical Medicine and Hygiene Vol 2: 7036
Research Grant of the Lupus Foundation of America Vol. 1: 11437
Research Grant Program to Assist Foreign Scholars in Chinese Studies Vol. 2: 4950
Research Grants
Alzheimer Society of Canada Vol. 1: 459
Canadian Anesthesiologists' Society Vol 1: 6181
Canadian Physiotherapy Cardio-respiratory Society Vol 1: 6808
Intensive Care Society Vol 2: 6199
Research Grants
American Association of Oral and Maxillofacial Surgeons Vol. 1: 1195
American Lung Association of Eastern Missouri Vol 1: 2711
European Society of Anaesthesiology Vol 2: 878
Plastic Surgery Educational Foundation Vol 1: 15096
Research Grants and Fellowships Vol. 1: 7079
Research in Counselor Education and Supervision Award Vol. 1: 4854
Research in Dental Caries Award Vol. 1: 10062
Research in Oral Biology Award Vol. 1: 10063
Research in Prosthodontics and Implants Award Vol. 1: 10064
Research in Prosthodontics Award Vol. 1: 10064
Research Medal
Royal Agricultural Society of England Vol. 2: 6668
Royal Scottish Geographical Society Vol 2: 6890
The Royal Society of Victoria Vol 2: 653
Research Presentation Award Vol. 1: 10233
Research Prize Vol. 2: 3296
Research Prize and Bronze Medal Vol. 2: 6733
Research Pump-Priming Grants Vol. 2: 5413
Research Recognition Award Vol. 1: 14626
Research Scholar Award Vol. 1: 2083
Research Scholar Award Vol. 1: 8834
Research Scholarships Vol. 1: 5727
Research Seed Grant Program Vol. 1: 11739
Research Starter Grant Vol. 1: 16620
Research Student Awards Vol. 2: 5485
Research Symposium Grant Vol. 1: 10120
Research Training Fellowship Vol. 1: 3023
Research Training Fellowships Vol. 2: 4932

Research Utilization Award Vol. 1: 16054
Researcher of the Year Vol. 1: 2775
Reserve Grand Award Vol. 1: 18202
Reserve Grand Champion Vol. 1: 12772
Reservoir Description and Dynamics Award Vol. 1: 16806
Reservoir Engineering Award Vol. 1: 16806
Resident Award
American College of Preventive Medicine Vol. 1: 1724
Congress of Neurological Surgeons Vol 1: 7708
Resident Award Paper Contest Vol. 1: 6296
Resident Case of the Year Award Vol. 1: 3490
Resident Community Outreach Award Vol. 1: 617
Resident Essay Award Vol. 1: 3462
Resident Essay Contest Vol. 1: 7004
Resident/Fellow Essay Award Vol. 1: 4663
Resident Physician's Prize Paper Award Vol. 1: 4017
Resident Research Award
American Academy of Pediatrics Vol. 1: 711
American Rhinologic Society Vol 1: 3490
California Society of Anesthesiologists Vol 1: 6063
Oral and Maxillofacial Surgery Foundation Vol 1: 14627
Resident Research Competition Vol. 1: 16620
Resident Research Contest Vol. 1: 6278
Resident Research Grants Vol. 1: 595
Resident Research Scholarship Vol. 1: 1740
Resident/Trainee Award Vol. 1: 3560
Resident's Award Vol. 1: 3822
Resistol Rookie of the Year Vol. 1: 15354
Resnik Award; Judith A. Vol. 1: 9794
Resnik Challenger Medal Vol. 1: 16915
Restaurant and Chef Awards Vol. 1: 10955
Restaurant Design and Graphics Awards Vol. 1: 10956
Restaurateur of the Year Vol. 1: 8145
Restoration Fund Grant Vol. 2: 3526
Restrepo; Distincion Felix Vol. 2: 1197
Restrepo Medal; Felix Vol. 2: 1197
Retail Design Awards Vol. 1: 12682
Retail Employee Development Award Vol. 1: 15653
Retail Store Design and Layout Award Vol. 2: 4203
Retailer of the Year Awards
Awards and Recognition Association Vol. 1: 5609
National Association of Recording Merchandisers Vol 1: 12639
Retired Art Educator Award Vol. 1: 12275
Retired Chaplain Award Vol. 1: 5311
The Rettig Prize Vol. 2: 4621
Return of the Child Award Vol. 1: 11310
Reuben Award Vol. 1: 12851
Reuchlinpreis der Stadt Pforzheim Vol. 2: 2391
Reuter Foundation Stanford Fellowship Vol. 2: 6601
Reuter Prize; Paul Vol. 2: 4793
Revelle Medal; Roger Vol. 1: 2122
Revenue Society of G.B. Award Vol. 2: 6535
Reves Award; Emery Vol. 1: 7405
Review of Research Award Vol. 1: 1946
Rey; Prix Henri Vol. 2: 1961
Reynaud; Prix Jean Vol. 2: 1485
Reynolds Award; Orr E. Vol. 1: 3180
Reynolds Distinguished Service Award; Orr E. Vol. 1: 3715
Reynolds Medal; Osborne Vol. 2: 6094
Reynolds Media Awards; Nancy Susan Vol. 1: 11639
RGCP/SAPC Elective Prize Vol. 2: 6698
Rhoads Lecture; Jonathan E. Vol. 1: 3801
Rhodes SGIM Service Award; Elnora M. Vol. 1: 16700
Rhodia Award; Marschall Vol. 1: 1874
Rhomberg Preis; Alexander Vol. 2: 2194
Rhone Poulenc Rorer Clinical Investigator Lecture Award Vol. 1: 8453
RHR International Award for Excellence in Consultation Vol. 1: 3407
Rhys Memorial Prize; John Llewellyn Vol. 2: 5191
Rhys Prize; *The Mail on Sunday* - John Llewellyn Vol. 2: 5191
RIAS/Acanthus Award for Measured Drawing Vol. 2: 6816
Ribalow Prize; Harold U. Vol. 1: 9230
Ribaud; Prix Gustave Vol. 2: 1617
Rica Award; Receta Vol. 1: 8994
Rice - Drama Desk Awards; Vernon Vol. 1: 8274
Rice Innovative Program Award; Robert Vol. 1: 400
Rice King Award; Thomas Vol. 1: 11955
Rice National Championship Trophy; Grantland Vol. 1: 8800
Rich Awards for Excellence in Communications; Wilmer Shields Vol. 1: 7916
Rich Memorial Moot Court Competition; Giles Sutherland Vol. 1: 2570
Richard-Allan Educational Scholarship Vol. 1: 13716
Richard Beckhard Practice Award Vol. 1: 8588
Richard III Scholarship for Medieval Studies Vol. 1: 15666
Richard Memorial Prize; Therese and Edwin H. Vol. 1: 13690
Richard; Prix Maurice- Vol. 1: 16146
Richard S. Kennedy Student Essay Prize Vol. 1: 17529
Richards Award for Media Criticism; Bart Vol. 1: 14950
Richards Award; Robert H. Vol. 1: 2536
Richards Award; Tudor Vol. 1: 5533
Richards Distinguished Alumni Award; Loretta Vol. 1: 7535
Richards Education Award Vol. 1: 14582
Richards Graduate Student Research Grant; Albert G. Vol. 1: 663
Richards Memorial Award; Charles Russ Vol. 1: 4163
Richards Prize; Audrey Vol. 2: 5006
Richards Scholarship; K.A. Vol. 2: 322
Richardson Award for Perinatal and Pediatric Health Care Research; Douglas K. Vol. 1: 16373
Richardson Award; Violet Vol. 1: 16964
Richardson Award; William D. Vol. 1: 9125
Richardson Gold Medal; Benjamin Ward Vol. 2: 6937
Richardson Medal Vol. 2: 6268
Richardson Medal; David Vol. 1: 14616
Richardson Memorial Literary Trust; Evelyn Vol. 1: 19004
Richardson Producer of the Year; Jack Vol. 1: 6141
Richardson Research Grant; Henry and Sylvia Vol. 1: 8479
Richardson Theatre Awards (Jessies); Jessie Vol. 1: 9196
Richardson Trophy Vol. 2: 6801
Richart Award; Frank E. Vol. 1: 5455
Richey Medal; Michael Vol. 2: 6830
Richmond Cerebral Palsy Center Award Vol. 1: 538
Richmond Lectureship; Dale Vol. 1: 712
Richtenberger; Prix Vol. 2: 1486
Richter Award; Edward Vol. 2: 1372
Richter Award; Jed Vol. 1: 15894
Richter Prize; Curt P. Vol. 2: 2323
Richtmyer Memorial Lecture Vol. 1: 1254
Ricker Resource Conservation Award; William E. Vol. 1: 2033
Ricketts Chapter Research Award; Donald E. Vol. 1: 9882
Rickey Medal Vol. 1: 3975
Ricks Award; Earl T. Vol. 1: 303
Ricky's Red Rose Challenge Trophy Vol. 1: 13806
Ride Managers Vol. 1: 12463
Rideal Lecture; Sir Eric Vol. 2: 7178
Rider Award Program Vol. 1: 17889
Rider Awards Vol. 1: 12464
Rider Mileage Champion - Vol. 1: 1967
Rider Mileage Program Award Vol. 1: 1968
Ridges Memorial Award; Robert V. Vol. 1: 17215
Ridgway Student Chapter Award; Robert Vol. 1: 3976
Ridley Charlton Award of Outstanding Achievement; Margaret Vol. 1: 6554
Ridley; In-Service Training Award in Memory of Clarence E. Vol. 1: 10313
Ridout Awards; Godfrey Vol. 1: 16119
Rietz Lecture Vol. 1: 9912
Rigg Memorial Award; Sir Theodore Vol. 2: 3800
Right Livelihood Award Vol. 2: 4619
Rights of the Child Prize Vol. 1: 7331
Rigo Award; Joseph T. Vol. 1: 4828
Riley Prize; Franklin L. Vol. 1: 11866
Rimet Cup; Jules Vol. 2: 4755
Rimka premija; Albino Vol. 2: 3385
Ring Award for Investigative Reporting; Selden Vol. 1: 4540
Ring Award; Nancy McNeir Vol. 1: 15795
Ringwood Award for Drama; Gwen Pharis Vol. 1: 19006
Rinkel Award; Herbert J. Vol. 1: 580
Rio National Prize in Chemistry; Andres Manuel del Vol. 2: 3437
Rio; Premio Nacional de Quimica Andres Manuel del Vol. 2: 3437
Riopelle Award; James and Marie Vol. 1: 3000
Ripperton Environmental Educator Award; Lyman A. Vol. 1: 270
Rising Moon Outstanding Youth Services Librarian Award Vol. 1: 4609
Rising Star Award
Canadian Country Music Association Vol. 1: 6445
National Association for College Admission Counseling Vol 1: 12305
United States Harness Writers' Association Vol 1: 17937
Rising Stars Secondary Art Achievement Award Vol. 1: 12276
Rising Start Award Vol. 1: 7499
Rispens Award; Bart Vol. 2: 2446

Rist Prize; David Vol. 1: 11770
RITA Award Vol. 1: 15711
Rittenhouse Award Vol. 1: 11667
Ritter Award; R. Max Vol. 1: 17733
Ritter Award; Tex Vol. 1: 10401
Rittle, Sr. Memorial Scholarship; Paul H. Vol. 1: 9939
Rivenes Award; David G. Vol. 1: 505
River Award; The Charles Vol. 1: 6209
River Bend Cup - Norwich and Norfolk Vol. 1: 14430
River Prize; Charles Vol. 1: 4413
Rivera Award in Transgender Studies; Sylvia Vol. 1: 7224
Rivis Prize; Mrs. F. E. Vol. 2: 6802
Rivkin Award; William R. Vol. 1: 2059
Rivot; Prix L. E. Vol. 2: 1618
RMA of the Year Vol. 1: 2757
Roadrunners of the Year Award Vol. 1: 15679
Roake Trophy Vol. 1: 9654
Roanoke-Chowan Award for Poetry Vol. 1: 14373
Roark Jr. Meritorious Service Award; Eldridge W. Vol. 1: 14523
Roback Scholarship; Herbert Vol. 1: 12138
Robb Fellowship; Preston Vol. 1: 11940
Robbins Award; Harold Vol. 1: 4289
Robe of Achievement Vol. 1: 15978
Robel Award Vol. 2: 4006
Robert A. Hains Award Vol. 1: 6638
Robert H. Armstrong Award Vol. 1: 4566
Roberts Award for Young Filmmakers; Bill Vol. 1: 5651
Roberts Award; Frances F. Vol. 1: 7808
Roberts Award; Summerfield G. Vol. 1: 16960
Roberts Lecture; Lloyds Vol. 2: 7017
Roberts Playwriting Award; Forest A. Vol. 1: 15687
Roberts Public Library Distinguished Service Award; William H. Vol. 1: 14366
Roberts Vocal Scholarship; W. Towyn Vol. 2: 6472
Robertson Continuing Professional Educator Award; Adelle F. Vol. 1: 18223
Robertson Memorial Lecture Vol. 1: 12164
Robertson Memorial Prize; James Alexander Vol. 1: 7700
Robertson Memorial Trophy; Heaton R. Vol. 1: 17903
Robertson Most Outstanding Undergraduate Award Vol. 1: 15043
Robeson Award; Paul Vol. 1: 140
Robeson Awards; Paul Vol. 1: 14204
Robichaux Award; Joseph Vol. 1: 18453
Robie Award for Achievement in Industry Vol. 1: 10945
Robie Humanitarianism Award Vol. 1: 10946
Robinson Award; Charlie Vol. 1: 15424
Robinson Award for Best Printed Map; Arthur Vol. 1: 1777
Robinson Award; J. Franklin Vol. 1: 558
Robinson Award; Renault Vol. 1: 12778
Robinson Awards; Robert L. Vol. 1: 3286
Robinson Coach of the Year; Eddie Vol. 1: 8801
Robinson-Cunningham Award Vol. 1: 558
Robinson Distinguished Service Award; Stanley C. Vol. 1: 18224
Robinson Grant; Helen M. Vol. 1: 10595
Robinson Lectureship; Robert Vol. 2: 6980
Robinson Marine Naval Flight Officer of the Year Award; Robert Guy Vol. 1: 11523
Robinson Memorial Medal for Begonia Hybrid; Alfred D. Vol. 1: 1395
Robinson Periodontal Regeneration Award; R. Earl Vol. 1: 730
Robinson Prize for Historical Analysis; Michael C. Vol. 1: 13049
Robinson Prize; James Harvey Vol. 1: 2243
Robinson Prize; Joan Cahalin Vol. 1: 16440
Robinson Scholar-Athlete Award; Coach Eddie Vol. 1: 13215
Robinson Scholarship Award; Thelma A. Vol. 1: 7665
Robison Foundation/B. Robison Sporck-Stegmaier Award Vol. 1: 18965
Rocard; Prix Yves Vol. 2: 1982
Rocha Medal; Manuel Vol. 2: 4065
Roche Award Vol. 2: 4258
Roche Diagnostics Award Vol. 2: 5081
Roche Junior Faculty Vol. 1: 2084
Roche New Investigator Award Vol. 1: 4249
Rochester International Film Festival Vol. 1: 15693
Rock and Roll Hall of Fame Vol. 1: 15695
Rock Mechanics Award Vol. 1: 16360
Rockefeller Prentice Memorial Award in Animal Breeding and Genetics Vol. 1: 3893
Rockefeller Prize Vol. 1: 3088
Rockefeller Trophy; William A. Vol. 1: 18715
Rockman Instruction Publication of the Year Award; Ilene F. Vol. 1: 5086
Rockower Awards for Excellence in Jewish Journalism; Simon Vol. 1: 2599
Rockwell Award; Martha Vol. 1: 18105
Rocky Mountain National Watermedia Exhibition Awards Vol. 1: 8804
Rodan Excellence in Mentorship Award; Gideon A. Vol. 1: 3582
Rodda Award Vol. 2: 668
Rodeo Hall of Fame Vol. 1: 15706
Roderick Award; Colin Vol. 2: 460
Roderick Haig-Brown Regional Prize Vol. 1: 18665
Roderick Lectures; Colin Vol. 2: 461
Roderick Prize; Colin Vol. 2: 460
Rodermund Service Award; Matthew Vol. 1: 7132
Rodgers Achievement Award; Samuel U. Vol. 1: 12459
Rodgers Award; Richard Vol. 1: 4003
Rodgers Scholarship; Paul W. Vol. 1: 10092
Rodriguez Diversity Award; Santiage Vol. 1: 7101
Roe Award; Joseph H. Vol. 1: 890
Roe Award; Kenneth Andrew Vol. 1: 1093
Roe Award; Ralph Coats Vol. 1: 3671
Roe Medal; Ralph Coats Vol. 1: 4164
Roebling Award Vol. 1: 3977
Roebling Medal Vol. 1: 11799
Roebuck Cup; Charles Vol. 2: 5306
Roelen Medal; Otto Vol. 2: 2263
Roelker Prize; Nancy Lyman Vol. 1: 16079
Roemer Conservation Awards; Elsie Vol. 1: 9107
Roentgen Resident/Fellow Research Award Vol. 1: 15541
Roeske Certificate of Recognition for Excellence in Medical Student Education; Nancy C. A. Vol. 1: 3287
Roesler Scholarship; Eldon Vol. 1: 18772
Roethke Memorial Foundation Poetry Prize; Theodore Vol. 1: 17519
Roger A. Morse Teaching/Extension/Regulatory Award Vol. 1: 8339
Rogers Award; David E. Vol. 1: 5038
Rogers Award; John Vol. 1: 7192
Rogers Award; William Vol. 1: 5973
Rogers Bursaries; Hal Vol. 1: 11158
Rogers Information Advancement Award; Frank Bradway Vol. 1: 11668
Rogers Memorial Award; Russell Hill Vol. 1: 15822
Rogers Memorial Exhibit Award; Lelan G. Vol. 1: 2915
Rohrer Consulting Psychology Practice Award; Perry L. Vol. 1: 3407
Rokkan Prize in Comparative Social Science Research; Stein Vol. 2: 1913
Rokkan Prize; Stein Vol. 2: 5823
Role Model Award Vol. 1: 7715
Role of Law Award Vol. 1: 7090
Rolex Awards for Enterprise Vol. 2: 4880
Rolex International Women's Keelboat Championship Vol. 1: 18069
Rolex Junior Championships; U.S. Sailing/ Vol. 1: 18074
Rolex Player of the Year Award Vol. 1: 11201
Rolex Player to Watch Vol. 1: 10005
Rolex Trophy Vol. 1: 8068
Rolin-Jaequemyns; Prix G. Vol. 2: 4767
The Roll of Distinguished Philatelist Vol. 2: 5111
Roll of Honor Vol. 2: 3528
Roll of Honor Award Vol. 1: 8876
Roll of Honour Vol. 2: 4945
Roll of Honour Award Vol. 2: 3157
Rolling Trophy Vol. 2: 2658
Rollins Graduate Student Research Grant; William H. Vol. 1: 664
Rollo Award; David and Linda Vol. 1: 18408
Rolls-Royce Enthusiasts Awards Vol. 2: 6603
Romance Contest Vol. 1: 19021
Romanell Lecture on Philosophical Naturalism; Patrick Vol. 1: 3089
Romanell - Phi Beta Kappa Professorship in Philosophy Vol. 1: 14991
Romanowski Medal; Miroslaw Vol. 1: 15766
Romantic Novel of the Year Vol. 2: 6605
Rombaux; Prix Egide Vol. 2: 989
Rome Awards Vol. 2: 5444
Rome Fellowship Vol. 2: 5445
Rome Memorial Award; Sidney R. Vol. 1: 437
Rome Prize Vol. 1: 540
Rome Scholarship Vol. 2: 5446
Rome Scholarship in Architecture Vol. 2: 5447
Rome Scholarship in Fine Arts Vol. 2: 5448
Romer - G. G. Simpson Medal; A. S. Vol. 1: 16893
Romer Prize; Alfred Sherwood Vol. 1: 16894
Romero Award; Oscar Vol. 1: 15726
Romero First Book Publication Prize; Lora Vol. 1: 4329
Rominger Plaque; William E. Vol. 1: 12236
Romney Citizen Volunteer Award; Lenore and George W. Vol. 1: 15143
Romney Prize; Hans Vol. 2: 7279
Romney Volunteer Center Excellence Award Vol. 1: 15144
Ronald Hicks Memorial Award Vol. 2: 3820
Rood Award; Roy S. Vol. 1: 8751
Rookie Chapter of the Year Vol. 1: 12798
Rookie Member of the Year Vol. 1: 12799
Rookie of the Year
Continental Basketball Association Vol. 1: 7801

Award Index

Sportscar Vintage Racing Association Vol 1: 17237
Western Women Professional Bowlers Vol 1: 18701
Rookie of the Year Award (National Sprint Care Div.) Vol. 1: 17757
Rookie of the Year Award (Silver Crown Div.) Vol. 1: 17758
Rookie Player of the Year Vol. 1: 10006
Rookies of the Meet Award Vol. 1: 18422
Rookies of the Year Vol. 1: 15304
Roosevelt Award for Excellence in Recreation and Park Research; Theodore and Franklin Vol. 1: 13601
Roosevelt Award for Outstanding Contributions to the Cause of Human Rights; Eleanor Vol. 1: 17870
Roosevelt Award; Franklin Delano Vol. 1: 16229
Roosevelt Award; Theodore Vol. 1: 12905
Roosevelt Distinguished Service Medal; Theodore Vol. 1: 17521
Roosevelt Four Freedoms Awards; Franklin D. Vol. 1: 8864
Roosevelt Fund Award; Eleanor Vol. 1: 1329
Roosevelt Memorial Grant; Theodore Vol. 1: 2832
Root Award; H. Paul Vol. 1: 2721
Root Award; Lt. Charles S. Vol. 1: 13452
Root Memorial Award; Charles D. Vol. 1: 17766
Roozeboom Medal; Bakhuis Vol. 2: 3659
Roquemore Memorial Award; A. D. Vol. 1: 2210
Ros Prize Vol. 2: 6699
Rosa Award; Edward Bennett Vol. 1: 17802
Rosa Camuna Vol. 2: 2995
Rosa Sabater Prize Vol. 2: 4521
Roscoe Fellowship; H. C. Vol. 2: 5371
Rose Award for Press Criticism; Arthur Vol. 1: 13551
Rose Award; Rod Vol. 1: 16850
Rose Award; William C. Vol. 1: 3566
Rose Bowl Player of the Game Vol. 1: 464
Rose-Bowl Trophy; Mackenzie Junner Vol. 2: 7205
Rose-Higgins Design Award; A.J. Vol. 1: 15206
Rose-Hulman Award Vol. 1: 10098
Rose International Cello Competition and Festival; Leonard Vol. 1: 16094
RoseMary Seymour Award Vol. 2: 3879
Rosen; Prix Raymond Vol. 2: 1820
Rosenau Silver Medallion; Ruth Vol. 1: 4677
Rosenbaum Memorial Award; Colonel Samuel Vol. 1: 13305
Rosenberg Award; Bill Vol. 1: 8592
Rosenberg Award for Poems on the Jewish Experience; Anna Davidson Vol. 1: 11460
Rosenblum Dissertation Award; Barbara Vol. 1: 16925
Rosens Linnemedalj Vol. 2: 4630
Rosenstiel Award for Distinguished Work in Basic Medical Research; Lewis S. Vol. 1: 15721
Rosenthal Award; Walter Vol. 1: 11902
Rosenthal Foundation Awards; Richard and Hinda Vol. 1: 1719
Rosenzweig Biennial Competition; Irene Vol. 1: 4675
Rosenzweig Distinguished Service Award Vol. 1: 4610
Rosewater Indiana High School Book Award; Eliot Vol. 1: 5191
Rosica, Jr. Memorial Award; Albert E. Vol. 1: 1613
Rosie Award Vol. 1: 5191
Rosie Awards Vol. 1: 372
Ross Aviation Safety Award; Pete Vol. 1: 11524
Ross Award
Canadian Paediatric Society Vol. 1: 6788
Royal College of Radiologists - United Kingdom Vol 2: 6738
Ross Award for Best New Magazine Writer; Alexander Vol. 1: 13420
Ross Award; Harland Vol. 1: 18544
Ross Award; Madeline Dane Vol. 1: 14761
Ross Award; Thomas Vol. 2: 6819
Ross Awards; Arthur Vol. 1: 9769
Ross Dissertation Award; Jacqueline A. Vol. 1: 8401
Ross Education Awards Vol. 1: 702
Ross Leadership Award Vol. 1: 7770
Ross Medal; Will Vol. 1: 2708
Ross Memorial Award; H. Browning Vol. 1: 18454
Ross Prize; John Munn Vol. 2: 6013
Ross Student Paper Award; Carl A. Vol. 1: 4560
Rosse Cup Vol. 2: 6803
Rossel; Prix Victor Vol. 2: 937
Rossi; Prix Vol. 2: 1693
Rossi Prize; Bruno Vol. 1: 1363
Rossini; Prix Vol. 2: 1487
Rossiter History of Women in Science Prize; Margaret W. Vol. 1: 9445
Roster of Fellows Vol. 1: 2957
Roster of Honor Vol. 1: 2958
Rostkowski Award; Nicolaus Vol. 1: 9389
Rostropovitch; Concours International de Violoncelle Vol. 2: 1750
Rostropovitch International Cello Competition Vol. 2: 1750
Roswell/Ancare Masters' Travel Fellowship Award; Dr. Harry Vol. 1: 6210
Roswell Dissertation Award; Virginia A. Vol. 1: 4787
Rotary Award for World Understanding and Peace Vol. 1: 15723
ROTC Award Vol. 1: 4518
ROTC Awards Vol. 1: 13780
ROTC Medals Vol. 1: 13774
Roth Award for a Translation of a Literary Work; Lois Vol. 1: 11913
Roth Manufacturing Engineering Scholarship; Edward S. Vol. 1: 16725
Rothert Award; Otto A. Vol. 1: 8693
Rothman Memorial Award; Stephen Vol. 1: 16317
Rothmans Foundation Ballet Scholarship Vol. 2: 689
Rothrock Award Vol. 1: 17010
Rothschild Challenge Cup Vol. 2: 6804
Rothstein Golden Pen Award for Scientific Writing; Jules M. Vol. 1: 3154
Rotorua Trophy Vol. 2: 3853
Roubaix; Prix Francois de Vol. 2: 1890
Roulston/COTF Innovation Award Vol. 1: 6778
Rourke Prize; Constance M. Vol. 1: 4330
Rous-Whipple Award Vol. 1: 3756
Rouse Gold Medallion Vol. 1: 4677
Rouse Hydraulic Engineering Lecture; Hunter Vol. 1: 3978
Rousseau; Prix de Composition Musicale Marcel Samuel- Vol. 2: 1488
Rousseau; Prix Gaston Vol. 2: 1619
Roussy; Prix Gustave Vol. 2: 1620
Routh Student Research Grant Vol. 1: 3409
Routman Teacher Recognition Award; Regie Vol. 1: 10596
Rouyer; Prix Vol. 2: 1489
Rowan-Legg Award; Edward K. Vol. 1: 6336
Rowe Award in Perinatal Cardiology; Richard D. Vol. 1: 16374
Rowe Medals; N. E. Vol. 2: 6653
Rowing Awards Vol. 2: 2850
Rowing Hall of Fame Vol. 1: 18048
Rowland Award; Dunbar Vol. 1: 11867
Rowland Prevention Award; Lela Vol. 1: 13450
Rowland Prize; Thomas Fitch Vol. 1: 3979
Rowlands Male Student-Athlete of the Year; David Vol. 1: 13406
Roxane Laboratories Linda Arenth Excellence in Cancer Nursing Management Award Vol. 1: 14531
Roy Award; Thomas Vol. 1: 6530
Roy Calne Award Vol. 2: 5544
Roy Memorial Lecture; Dr. Biren Vol. 2: 2711
Roy Space Science and Design Award; Dr. Biren Vol. 2: 2528
Roy Trust Award; Dr. Biren Vol. 2: 2529
Royal Academy Summer Exhibition Vol. 2: 6611
Royal Asiatic Society Award Vol. 2: 6680
Royal Canadian Mounted Police Long Service Medal Vol. 1: 6095
Royal Canin Award
American Animal Hospital Association Vol. 1: 810
American Veterinary Medical Association Vol 1: 4414
Royal College of Radiologists Award Vol. 2: 6738
Royal Conservatory of Music Scholarships Vol. 1: 15750
Royal Designer for Industry Award Vol. 2: 6921
Royal Dublin Society Crafts Competition Vol. 2: 2877
Royal Economic Society Prize Vol. 2: 6753
Royal Gold Medal Vol. 2: 6824
Royal Historical Society/*History Today* Prize Vol. 2: 6780
Royal Humane Society Awards Vol. 2: 6813
Royal Mail Trophy Vol. 2: 6535
Royal Medals Vol. 2: 6915
Royal Norwegian Order of Merit Vol. 2: 3902
Royal Norwegian Order of St. Olav Vol. 2: 3903
Royal Over-Seas League Music Competition Vol. 2: 6853
Royal Red Cross Vol. 2: 5607
Royal Society of Literature Ondaatji Prize Vol. 2: 7004
Royal Society of Western Australia Medal Vol. 2: 655
Royal Swedish Academy of Engineering Sciences Great Gold Medal Vol. 2: 4635
Royal Victorian Order
Canada Chancellery of Honors Vol. 1: 6080
Central Chancery of the Orders of Knighthood Vol 2: 5608
Royce Award for Achievement; IIE Sir Henry Vol. 2: 663
Royce Award; Sir Henry Vol. 2: 6161
Royce Lectures in the Philosophy of the Mind Vol. 1: 3090

Rozelle Trophy; Pete Vol. 1: 13227
Rs of Excellence Vol. 1: 15589
RSA Benno Schotz Prize Vol. 2: 6885
RSA Guthrie Award Vol. 2: 6885
RSA Medal for Architecture Vol. 2: 6885
RSPB/CIWEM Living Wetlands Award Vol. 2: 5644
RSPB Fine Art Award Vol. 2: 7216
Rube Goldberg Award Vol. 1: 12851
Rubens-Alcais Challenge Vol. 1: 10329
Rubincam Youth Award Vol. 1: 13281
Rubinstein Award Vol. 1: 1175
Rubinstein International Piano Master Competition in Conjuction with the Israel Philharmonic Orchestra; Arthur Vol. 2: 2893
Rubinstein Memorial Prize; The Artur Vol. 2: 7259
Rubner-Preis; Max Vol. 2: 2247
Ruby Award; National Distinguished Service Vol. 1: 8517
Rudd Award; Steele Vol. 2: 397
Rudolfs Medal; Willem Vol. 1: 18645
Rudolph Student Athlete Achievement Award; Wilma Vol. 1: 12373
Rudolphi-Medaille; Carl-Asmund- Vol. 2: 2078
Rudolphi Medal; Karl Asmund Vol. 2: 2078
Ruger World Team Trophy; William B. Vol. 1: 13648
Ruggles Travel Grant Awards; Richard and Nancy Vol. 1: 10110
Ruhlmann; Prix Vol. 2: 1490
Ruiz; Premio Santos Vol. 2: 4536
Rumbaugh Historical Oration Contest; Joseph S. Vol. 1: 13775
Rumford Medal Vol. 2: 6916
Rumford Prize Vol. 1: 555
Rumsey Buyers' Choice Award; Nona Jean Hulsey Vol. 1: 13068
Runcorn-Florensky Medal Vol. 2: 1779
Runcorn Travel Award; Keith Vol. 2: 1779
Runermark Award; Jan Vol. 2: 867
Runner of the Year Vol. 1: 18457
Runyon - Walter Winchell Cancer Fund Fellowships; Damon Vol. 1: 8035
Ruppe Distinguished Service Award; Carol Vol. 1: 16223
Ruptash-Mandryk Nurse of the Year Award Vol. 1: 376
Rural Australia Medical Undergraduate Scholarship Scheme Vol. 2: 166
Rural County Engineer of the Year Award Vol. 1: 12500
Rural Health Practitioner of the Year Vol. 1: 13654
Rural Wales Award Vol. 2: 5581
Rural Youth Europe Awards Vol. 2: 819
Rush Award; Benjamin
American Psychiatric Association Vol. 1: 3288
Dickinson College Vol 1: 8185
Rush Award; Gertrude E. Vol. 1: 12747
Russ Prize; Fritz J. and Dolores H. Vol. 1: 12130
Russell and Burch Award Vol. 1: 9526
Russell Award for Distinguished Research in the Teaching of English; David H. Vol. 1: 13030
Russell Award; Frances E. Vol. 2: 4785
Russell Award; T. Randolph Vol. 1: 7760
Russell, Jr., Award; Louis B. Vol. 1: 2188
Russell Lectureship; Henry Norris Vol. 1: 1364
Russell Memorial Medal; Peter Nicol Vol. 2: 528
Russell Naval Aviation Flight Safety Award; Adm. James S. Vol. 1: 14653
Russell Scholarship; Norman K. Vol. 1: 13512
Rustgi International Travel Awards; Moti L. and Kamla Vol. 1: 8835
Rustin Freedom Award; A. Philip Randolph/Bayard Vol. 1: 15
Rustin Human Rights Award; Bayard Vol. 1: 2005
Rutherford Medal and Prize Vol. 2: 6066
Rutherford Memorial Lecture Vol. 2: 6066
Rutherford Scholarship; Andrew Vol. 1: 9649
Rutter Gold Medal and Prize Vol. 2: 5650
Ruzicka-Preis Vol. 2: 4902
Ruzicka-Prize Vol. 2: 4902
RV Automotive Achievement Award Vol. 1: 15587
Ryan Award; Cornelius Vol. 1: 14761
Ryan Editorial Award; Robert G. Vol. 1: 8260
Ryan Trophies; John T. Vol. 1: 6631
Ryan Winners Circle Acting Awards; Irene Vol. 1: 11119
Ryan Winners Circle Evening of Scenes; Irene Vol. 1: 11119
Ryder Cup Vol. 2: 6562
Ryle Award for Excellence in Writing on the Problems of Geriatrics; Joseph D. Vol. 1: 13552
Ryle Memorial Medal Vol. 2: 6563
Ryser SGI Vol. 2: 5266
Ryskamp Research Fellowship; Charles A. Vol. 1: 1813
S. Lewis Elmer Award Vol. 1: 2146
SA Scientific Award Vol. 2: 4259
SAA Dissertation Award Vol. 1: 16165
SAACE Excellence Awards Vol. 2: 4306
SAAD Dental Student Prize Vol. 2: 7117
SAALED Bursary Vol. 2: 4300
SAAUW Fellowship Vol. 2: 4311
Saban Scholar-Athlete Award; Coach Lou Vol. 1: 13215
Sabbatical Exchange Program Vol. 1: 13118
Sabina Fund Vol. 1: 8593
Sabine Medal; Wallace Clement Vol. 1: 131
The SABR Salute Vol. 1: 16173
Saccamanno, M.D. New Frontiers in Cytology Award; Geno Vol. 1: 4020
Sacerdoti Award; Cesare Vol. 2: 6285
Sacher Student Award; George Vol. 1: 9063
Sachs Award; Curt Vol. 1: 2840
Sacre; Prix Emile Vol. 2: 990
Sadasivan Lecture; Prof. T. S. Vol. 2: 2712
Saddle Bronc of the Year Vol. 1: 15355
Saddlemyer Award; Ann Vol. 1: 4797
Sadek Award Vol. 2: 6831
Safe City Award Vol. 1: 6042
Safe Contractor of the Year Awards Vol. 1: 13588
Safe Drinking Water Award Vol. 1: 5223
Safe Driver Award Program Vol. 1: 13659
Safe Driving Award Vol. 1: 17871
Safe Mileage Award Vol. 1: 18840
Safety and Health Award Vol. 1: 4466
Safety and Occupational Health Awards Vol. 1: 15451
Safety Award
International Association of Diecutting and Diemaking Vol. 1: 10197
International Association of Wildland Fire Vol 1: 10260
National Propane Gas Association Vol 1: 13577
Safety Award for Superior Accomplishment Vol. 1: 17803
Safety Award More than 100,000 Man Hours Vol. 1: 14377
Safety Awards
Canadian Association of Oilwell Drilling Contractors Vol. 1: 6271
National Paint and Coatings Association Vol 1: 13519
New York Shipping Association Vol 1: 14155
North Carolina Utility Contractors Association Vol 1: 14378
Safety Awards of Commendation Vol. 1: 13519
Safety Awards of Excellence Vol. 1: 13519
Safety Awards of Honor Vol. 1: 13519
Safety Awards of Merit Vol. 1: 13519
Safety Codes and Standards Medal Vol. 1: 4165
Safety Contest Awards Vol. 1: 3447
Safety Director of the Year Award Vol. 1: 4376
Safety Engineer of the Year Vol. 1: 17373
Safety in Construction Medal Vol. 2: 6126
Safety in Seas Award Vol. 1: 13482
Safety Manager of the Year Vol. 1: 17375
Safety Professionals of the Year Vol. 1: 4236
Safety Recognition Award
Professional Convention Management Association Vol. 1: 15299
Specialty Graphic Imaging Association Vol 1: 17116
Safety Recognition Awards Vol. 1: 15338
Sagan Award for Public Understanding of Science Vol. 1: 7897
Sagar Award; Dr. Vidya Vol. 2: 2622
Sagarmatha Award Vol. 2: 3482
Sagebrush Award for a Young Adult Reading or Literature Program Vol. 1: 19085
Sagebrush Education Resources Literature Grant Vol. 1: 4930
Saget; Prix Julien Vol. 2: 1962
Sagittarius Prize Vol. 2: 7149
Sahitya Akademi Awards Vol. 2: 2791
Sahitya Akademi Fellowship Vol. 2: 2792
Sahitya Akademi Translation Prize Vol. 2: 2793
Saidi-Sirjani Memorial Book Prize Vol. 1: 10652
Sail Gold Medal Vol. 2: 2659
Saillet; Prix Joseph Vol. 2: 1694
Sainsbury Scholarship in Painting and Sculpture Vol. 2: 5449
St. Cuthberts Mill Award for Works on Paper Vol. 2: 6943
St. George National Award Vol. 1: 1444
St. Hubert's Giralda Trophy Vol. 1: 18715
St. John Ambulance Air Wing Travelling Fellowship Vol. 2: 5545
St. Kilda Film Festival Vol. 2: 661
Saint La Salle Medal Vol. 1: 11491
St. Lawrence Section Outstanding Educator Award Vol. 1: 3672
St. Lazarus Garnham Fellowship Vol. 2: 6369
St. Louis (Chapter 17) Scholarship Vol. 1: 16726
St. Louis Refractories Award Vol. 1: 1494
Saint Luke's Lecture Vol. 2: 2873
St. LukeFs Lecture Vol. 2: 2874

St. Olav Medal Vol. 2: 3904
St. Petersburg Yacht Club Trophy Vol. 1: 18070
Saint-Prix; Prix Berriat Vol. 2: 1695
St. Romanos the Melodist Medallion Vol. 1: 13252
Saintour; Prix Vol. 2: 1696
Saito Award Vol. 2: 3323
Sakakibara Prize; Yasuo Vol. 1: 4331
Sakharov Prize for Freedom of Thought; European Parliament Vol. 2: 5847
Saksena Memorial Medal; Professor Shyam Bahadur Vol. 2: 2713
Sakura Finetek Student Scholarship Vol. 1: 13723
Sakurai Prize for Theoretical Particle Physics; J. J. Vol. 1: 3134
Salazar Award for Communications; Ruben Vol. 1: 13004
Salcedo Jr. Science Education Award; Dr. Juan S. Vol. 2: 3986
Salem Conference Grant; Dr. Shawky Vol. 2: 3584
Sales Executive of the Year Award Vol. 1: 14214
Sales Representative of the Year Award Vol. 1: 6357
Sales to Foreign Tourists Vol. 2: 2568
Salesperson of the Year Vol. 2: 3710
Salin Prize; Kasper Vol. 2: 4599
Salinpriset; Kasper Vol. 2: 4599
Salit-Gitelson Tell Memorial Fellowship; Maria Vol. 1: 19067
Salivary Research Award Vol. 1: 10065
Salle Medal; Do La Vol. 1: 11491
Salmon Award; Dr. Daniel E. Vol. 1: 12534
Salon Culinaire Vol. 2: 4430
Salon Culinaire Mondial
National Restaurant Association Vol. 1: 13631
Society of German Cooks Vol 2: 2383
Saloutos Memorial Book Award in Immigration History; Theodore Vol. 1: 9628
Saloutos Memorial Book Award; Theodore Vol. 1: 242
Salter Award; Janet & Maxwell Vol. 1: 5744
Salter Special Award; Robert B. Vol. 1: 6784
Salters' Graduate Prizes Vol. 2: 7062
Saltire Society and The Royal Bank of Scotland - Scottish Science Award Vol. 2: 7072
Saltire Society Award Vol. 2: 5756
Saltire Society Scottish Literary Awards Vol. 2: 7069
Saltus Medal Award; J. Sanford Vol. 1: 2934
Saltus Medal; John Sanford Vol. 2: 5392
Salute to Excellence Awards
National Association of Black Journalists Vol. 1: 12413
National Restaurant Association Educational Foundation Vol 1: 13636
Salvan; Prix Eugene Vol. 2: 1697
Salvatori Prize; Henry Vol. 1: 9402
Salzberg Mentorship Award; Arnold M. Vol. 1: 713
Salzman Award for Excellence in International Economic Performance; Herbert Vol. 1: 17872
SAM/Organon Visiting Professor in Adolescent Research Award Vol. 1: 16152
Samaritan Award Vol. 1: 11202
Samashuri Vol. 2: 4564
Samoyed of the Year: Male, Female, Veteran, Senior, and Danish Champion in Sledge Racing Vol. 2: 1287
Sample Student Excellence Award; W. Frederick Vol. 1: 16648
Sampson Excellence in Teaching Award; Donald K. Vol. 1: 5947
Samson Award; J. Edouard Vol. 1: 6785
San Antonio International Piano Competition Vol. 1: 15822
San Sebastian International Film Festival Awards Vol. 2: 4538
Sanchez Memorial Award; George I. Vol. 1: 15604
Sand Dollar Awards Vol. 1: 7552
Sand et Marie Guido Triossi; Prix Gabrielle Vol. 2: 1621
Sandburg Literary Award; Carl Vol. 1: 8907
Sanders Award; Mark Vol. 1: 12678
Sanders Foundation International Schools Scholarship; Margaret Vol. 2: 2459
Sanderson Attack Squadron of the Year Award; Lawson H. M. Vol. 1: 11525
Sanderson Award; A. B. Vol. 1: 6920
Sanderson Award; Sandy Vol. 1: 6448
The Sandlot Kid Vol. 1: 17176
Sandmeyer Prize Vol. 2: 4893
Sandoz Award; Mari Vol. 1: 14018
Sandoz Oration Award for Research in Cancer Vol. 2: 2623
Sandrof Lifetime Achievement Award; Ivan Vol. 1: 12783
Sanford Award; Nevitt Vol. 1: 10742
Sanford-Springvale Rotary Scholarship Vol. 1: 15841
Sangeet Natak Akademi Fellowships Vol. 2: 2778
Sanger Award; Margaret Vol. 1: 15088
Sangiorgi; Premio Giorgio Maria Vol. 2: 2975
Sangster Memorial Award; Allan Vol. 1: 6324
Sanitarian's Award Vol. 1: 10084
Sansome President's Trophy; Hugh Vol. 2: 6314
Sansum Medal; W.E. Vol. 2: 529
Santarelli Award for Public Policy; Donald E. Vol. 1: 13503
Santos-Dumont Gold Airship Medal Vol. 2: 4746
Santos Prize; Reynaldo Dos Vol. 2: 3033
Sao Paulo International Film Festival Vol. 2: 1136
Saouma Award; Edouard Vol. 2: 3055
Sapporo International Ski Marathon Vol. 2: 3316
Sara Kirke Award Vol. 1: 6166
Sarabhai Medal; Vikram Vol. 2: 1741
Sarbadhikari Gold Medal Vol. 2: 2736
Sarchet Award; Bernard R. Vol. 1: 3691
Sargant Fellowship Vol. 2: 5450
Sargent Award; Franklin Haven Vol. 1: 571
Sargent, Jr. Award; Lowrie B. Vol. 1: 5456
Sargent Medal Vol. 1: 16530
Sargent Medal; M. A. Vol. 2: 530
Sargent Progress Award; Albert M. Vol. 1: 16727
Sarma Memorial Award; P.S. Vol. 2: 2798
Sarnat Award in Craniofacial Biology; Bernard G. Vol. 1: 10071
Sarnat Basic Science Award; Bernard G. Vol. 1: 15097
Sarnat Student Award in Craniofacial Biology; Bernard G. Vol. 1: 10066
Sarnoff Award; David Vol. 1: 9795
Sarnoff Citation Vol. 1: 15529
Sarnoff Medal Award; David Vol. 1: 16751
Sarton Award; May Vol. 1: 14047
Sarton Chair Vol. 2: 1086
Sarton Leersoel Vol. 2: 1086
Sarton Medaille Vol. 2: 1087
Sarton Medal
History of Science Society Vol. 1: 9446
Sarton Committee of the University of Ghent Vol 2: 1087
Sasakawa - DHA Disaster Prevention Award Vol. 2: 4872
Sasakawa Health Prize Vol. 2: 4929
SASEV Award Vol. 2: 4348
SASEV Journal Prize Vol. 2: 4349
SASEV Prize Vol. 2: 4350
SASEV Student Prize Vol. 2: 4351
SASEV Table Grape Award Vol. 2: 4352
Saskatchewan Choral Federation Choral Competition Vol. 1: 15850
Saskatchewan Choral Federation Choral Scholarship Vol. 1: 15882
Sasol Post-Graduate Medal Vol. 2: 4319
Sass Award for Distinguished Service to Journalism and Mass Communication; Gerald M. Vol. 1: 5333
Sass-Korktsak Award; Andrew Vol. 1: 6709
Sass Medal; Hans and Jacob Vol. 1: 11641
Satbir Award; Smt. Kamal Vol. 2: 2624
Satgur Prasad-Prag Parmeshwari Devi Memorial Award Vol. 2: 2785
Satomi Prize Vol. 2: 3209
Saturn Awards Vol. 1: 121
Saunders Award; Harold E. Vol. 1: 4191
Saunders Gold Medal; William Lawrence Vol. 1: 2537
Saunders Memorial Award; Robert G. Vol. 1: 6423
Saunders Natural History Award; W. E. Vol. 1: 14583
Saunders Sr. Award; Harris Vol. 1: 4370
Saur Award for Best Article in *College and Research Libraries*; K. G. Vol. 1: 5087
Sauveur Achievement Award; Albert Vol. 1: 4708
Savage Memorial Award; Warren F. Vol. 1: 4467
Savage "Miles From Nowhere" Memorial Award; Barbara Vol. 1: 11986
Savago New Voice Award; Joe Vol. 1: 15479
Save Our Earth Award Vol. 1: 13180
Save Our Streams Award Vol. 1: 10940
Saved by the Belt/Air Bag Awards Program; National Law Enforcement Vol. 1: 10172
Savory Award for Science Communication; Eve
BC Innovation Council Vol. 1: 5698
BC Innovation Council Vol 1: 5700
Savory Shield Award Vol. 1: 2312
Sawtelle Music Scholarship; B. Douglas Vol. 1: 12043
Sawyer Award; R. Tom Vol. 1: 4166
Saxby Award Vol. 2: 6880
Saxton Memorial Exhibit Award; Burton Vol. 1: 2916
Sayen Award; Clarence N. Vol. 2: 6244
SBET/Replacement Parts Industries BMET of the Year Award Vol. 1: 4978
SCA Distinguished Service Award Vol. 1: 12921
SCA Golden Anniversary Fund Awards Vol. 1: 12924
Scaglione Prize for a Translation of a Literary Work; Aldo and Jeanne Vol. 1: 11914

Scaglione Prize for a Translation of a Scholarly Study of Literature; Aldo and Jeanne Vol. 1: 11915
Scaglione Prize for Comparative Literary Studies; Aldo and Jeanne Vol. 1: 11916
Scaglione Prize for French and Francophone Studies; Aldo and Jeanne Vol. 1: 11917
Scaglione Prize for Italian Studies; Aldo and Jeanne Vol. 1: 11918
Scaglione Prize for Studies in Germanic Languages and Literatures; Aldo and Jeanne Vol. 1: 11919
Scaglione Prize for Studies in Slavic Languages and Literatures; Aldo and Jeanne Vol. 1: 11920
Scanstar Packaging Competition Vol. 2: 1334
Scantlebury Memorial Award; Donald L. Vol. 1: 8998
Scardina Award of Excellence; Virginia Vol. 1: 2962
Scattergood System Achievement Award; E. F. Vol. 1: 3448
SCC Award Medals Vol. 1: 15894
SCCA/CASCT North American Rally Cup Vol. 1: 17216
SCCA Road Rally Rookie of the Year Vol. 1: 17200
Scelpe Award Vol. 2: 4144
Scenic Technology Award Vol. 1: 17955
Schaar Playwright Award; Ruby Yoshino Vol. 1: 10964
Schachern Award Vol. 1: 15615
Schaefer Award; Hugo H. Vol. 1: 3060
Schaeffer Environmental Award; William D. Vol. 1: 9176
Schaeffler Award; Willy Vol. 1: 18106
Schafer Award; George E. Vol. 1: 16889
Schafer Prize; Alice T. Vol. 1: 5006
Schaff Prize; Philip Vol. 1: 3914
Schaffer Young Investigator Award; Rita Vol. 1: 5773
Schaffner Achievement Award; Franklin J. Vol. 1: 8223
Schallek Memorial Graduate Fellowship Award; William B. Vol. 1: 15664
Scharansky Freedom Award; Anatoly Vol. 1: 17675
Schary Awards; Dore Vol. 1: 4546
Schatz Award; Jack Vol. 1: 506
Schauer Memorial Scholarship; Lee E. Vol. 1: 15997
Schawlow Award; Arthur L. Vol. 1: 11229
Schawlow Prize in Laser Science; Arthur L. Vol. 1: 3135
Schechter Medal; Solomon Vol. 1: 11011
Scheel-Preis; Karl- Vol. 2: 2097
Scheele Award Vol. 2: 4678
Scheele Medal; Herbert Vol. 2: 5161
Scheele Trophy; Herbert Vol. 2: 3411
Scheelepriset Vol. 2: 4678
Scheepers Prize for Youth Literature Vol. 2: 4280
Scheffer; Prix Ary Vol. 2: 1491
Schell Memorial Intermediate Piano Scholarship; Minnie Vol. 1: 15883
Schellenberg Award Vol. 1: 17117
Schenck Award; Carl Alwin Vol. 1: 16512
Schenkel Player of the Year; Chris Vol. 1: 15276
Schenley Award - Most Outstanding Player Vol. 1: 6514
Schering Plough Clinical Lectureship Vol. 1: 14549
Schering-Plough Research Institute Award Vol. 1: 3567
Schering Veterinary Award Vol. 1: 7060
Schermerhorn Award Vol. 2: 4977
Scheveningen International Music Competition Vol. 2: 3662
Schiebold-Gedenkmunze Vol. 2: 2238
Schiefer "Old Timer's" Memorial Award; Paul Vol. 1: 17106
Schiller Award; L. Vol. 2: 4025
Schilling Award; David C. Vol. 1: 304
Schimmel Award for Distinguished Contribution to Archaeology; Percia Vol. 2: 2920
Schindler Award; Rudolf V. Vol. 1: 3709
Schlack Award; Carl A. Vol. 1: 5254
Schlafman Award; Sophie Vol. 1: 9184
Schlegel - Tieck Prize Vol. 2: 7135
Schlenz Medal; Harry E. Vol. 1: 18646
Schlich Memorial Award; Sir William Vol. 1: 16513
Schlich Memorial Trust Award Vol. 2: 5676
Schlossmann Medal; Karl Vol. 2: 1351
Schlueter Stroke Awards Vol. 1: 4338
Schlumberger Award; Conrad Vol. 2: 3530
Schlumberger; Prix Gustave Vol. 2: 1532
Schlumpf Award; Mildred Vol. 1: 2210
Schmeisser Award; William Vol. 1: 17969
Schmeisser Memorial Trophy; William Vol. 1: 17969
Schmid Service Award; John A. Vol. 1: 14506
Schmidheiny Prize for Free Enterprise and Political Liberty; Max Vol. 2: 4868
Schmidt Prize; Bernhard Vol. 2: 1352
Schmitt Award for Outstanding Corporate Leadership; Fred Vol. 1: 13604
Schmitt; Prix Florent Vol. 2: 1492
Schmitthoff Prize; Clive and Twinkie Vol. 2: 6029
Schmitz Award for Outstanding Contributions to the Frontiers in Education Conference; Ronald J. Vol. 1: 3673
Schmocker Memorial Award; Hanna Vol. 1: 7051
Schmorl-Preis; Georg- Vol. 2: 2379
Schneck Award; Shirley R. Vol. 1: 16199
Schneider Achievement Award; Dean Herman Vol. 1: 7815
Schneider Director Award; Alan Vol. 1: 17509
Schneider Prize in Linear Algebra; Hans Vol. 1: 10498
Schoeller-Junkmann-Preis Vol. 2: 2204
Schoemaker Award; Harold Jan Vol. 2: 4510
Schoenberg International Award in Neuroepidemiology; Bruce S. Vol. 1: 642
Schoenfield Media Award; Al Vol. 1: 10775
Schofield Award; Fon H. Vol. 1: 5664
Scholar/Artist Award Vol. 1: 13080
Scholar-Athlete Award Vol. 1: 10007
Scholar-Athlete Awards
National Christian College Athletic Association Vol. 1: 12889
National Football Foundation and College Hall of Fame, Valley of the Sun Chapter Vol 1: 13222
Scholar Award Vol. 1: 912
Scholar Awards
American Society of Hematology Vol. 1: 4070
Tulane University - Center for Bioenvironmental Research Vol 1: 17622
Scholarly Book of the Year Vol. 1: 5841
Scholarly Book Prizes Vol. 1: 6472
Scholarly Paper Competition Vol. 1: 13489
Scholarship Award
American Bible Society Vol. 1: 1398
Cooperstown Art Association Vol 1: 7818
Indiana Holstein Association Vol 1: 9666
United Commercial Travelers of America, Butler Council 465 Vol 1: 17691
Scholarship Awards
American Association of Blood Banks Vol. 1: 1016
Liederkranz Foundation Vol 1: 11352
Scholarship Contests Vol. 1: 13775
Scholarship Foundation Award Vol. 1: 2003
Scholarship/Grant Program Vol. 1: 16027
Scholarship Program
Poteet Strawberry Festival Association Vol. 1: 15174
Rocky Mountain Coal Mining Institute Vol 1: 15699
Wisconsin Farm Bureau Federation Vol 1: 18780
Scholarships
American Chiropractic Association Vol. 1: 1592
Old Dominion Kennel Club of Northern Virginia Vol 1: 14503
Harry S. Truman Good Neighbor Award Foundation Vol 1: 17613
Scholarships of the City of Munich Vol. 2: 2346
Scholarships, Writing Awards, Internships Vol. 1: 16041
Scholastic Achievement Awards Vol. 1: 15576
Scholastic Library Publishing National Library Week Grant Vol. 1: 2682
Scholastic Press Freedom Award Vol. 1: 17308
Scholdstroms pris; Birger Vol. 2: 4666
Scholl-Preis; Geschwister- Vol. 2: 2347
Schonfeld Award; William A. Vol. 1: 3552
Schonstedt Scholarship in Surveying Vol. 1: 1781
School Administrators Distinguished Library Service Award Vol. 1: 1274
School Librarian's Workshop Scholarship Vol. 1: 1282
School Library Media Specialist Award Vol. 1: 11427
School Nurse of the Year Vol. 1: 15907
School of Advanced Air Power Air Force Institute of Technology (AFIT) Award Vol. 1: 321
School of Advanced Air Power Award Vol. 1: 322
School of Medicine Award Vol. 1: 5941
Schooley World Team Trophy; John M. Vol. 1: 13648
Schottky-Preis fur Festkorperforschung; Walter- Vol. 2: 2098
Schottlander Prize Vol. 2: 5499
Schotz Prize; RSA Benno Vol. 2: 6885
Schoutedenprijs; Henri Vol. 2: 1075
Schreder 15-Meter Class Trophy Vol. 1: 16113
Schreiber Award; Frederick C. Vol. 1: 153
Schreiner Prize; Olive Vol. 2: 4173
Schreyer Award Vol. 1: 5110
Schroeder Award; Bill Vol. 1: 10244
Schroepfer Medal; George J. Vol. 1: 18647
Schubert and the Music of Modern Times International Competition; Franz Vol. 2: 828

Schubert Award for Teaching College Science; Leo Vol. 1: 18590
Schuchert Award; Charles Vol. 1: 14814
Schuck Award; Victoria Vol. 1: 3239
Schuckska priset Vol. 2: 4667
Schueren Award; Emmanuel van der Vol. 2: 876
Schultz High School Excellence Award; Dave Vol. 1: 13941
Schumacher Memorial Award; Max Vol. 1: 9361
Schumacher Prize; Fritz Vol. 2: 2402
Schuman Award; William Vol. 1: 7601
Schuman/Europe Trophy Vol. 2: 2830
Schumann and Piano and Song Competition; International Robert Vol. 2: 2313
Schumann Choir Competition; International Robert Vol. 2: 2314
Schumpeter-Preis Vol. 2: 2375
Schumpeter Prize Vol. 2: 2375
Schunk-Preis fur Medizin; Ludwig Vol. 2: 2336
Schunk Prize for Medicine; Ludwig Vol. 2: 2336
Schuster Award; Brady/ Vol. 1: 3418
Schutz Lecture Vol. 1: 3091
Schutz Perpetual Trophy; Heinrich Vol. 2: 2830
Schwab; Education Award in honor of Fred E. Vol. 1: 16834
Schwartz Award Vol. 1: 1663
Schwartz Children's Book Awards; Ruth and Sylvia Vol. 1: 14564
Schwartz Emergency Medical Service of the Year Award (BLS Service of the Year Award); Leo R. Vol. 1: 12527
Schwartz Fellowship; Frances M. Vol. 1: 2935
Schwartz Memorial Award; Paul Vol. 1: 4441
Schwartzwalder Professional Achievement in Ceramic Engineering (PACE) Award; Karl Vol. 1: 1495
Schwarzenberger Prize in International Law; Georg Vol. 2: 5996
Schweikert, Jr. Disability Awareness Award; Harry A. Vol. 1: 14844
Schweisguth Prize Vol. 2: 6299
Schweitzer Award; Albert Vol. 2: 6206
Schweitzer Medal; Albert Vol. 1: 4533
Schweitzer Medal; Friedrich Vol. 2: 784
Schweitzer Prize for Humanitarianism; Albert Vol. 1: 11029
Schweitzer Prizes; William P. and Gertrude Vol. 1: 12118
Schweizer Musikedition Vol. 2: 4907
Schwidefsky Medal Vol. 2: 4978
Schwiglhofer Trophy; Oscar Vol. 2: 5108
Science Award Vol. 2: 4992
Science Award Vol. 2: 4988
Science Fair Award Vol. 1: 6464
Science Fair Award Vol. 1: 17997
Science Fair Prizes Vol. 1: 5671
Science Fiction/Fantasy Short Story Contest Vol. 1: 15925
Science in Society Book Awards Vol. 1: 6866
Science in Society Journalism Awards
  Canadian Science Writers' Association Vol. 1: 6867
  National Association of Science Writers Vol 1: 12654
Science Journalism Awards Vol. 1: 953
Science to Practice Award Vol. 1: 16389
Science Writing Awards Vol. 1: 2546
Scientific Achievement Award
  Chinese American Medical Society Vol. 1: 7365
  International Union of Forest Research Organizations Vol 2: 815
  System Safety Society Vol 1: 17378
Scientific and Technical Academy Awards Vol. 1: 192
Scientific Award Vol. 1: 2297
Scientific Essay Contest Vol. 1: 15097
Scientific Freedom and Responsibility Award Vol. 1: 954
Scientific Medal Vol. 2: 7401
Scientific Poster Awards Vol. 1: 1706
Scientific Prize Vol. 2: 1919
Scientific Prize/Prix Ciardi Vol. 2: 926
Scientific Research and Development Award Vol. 1: 17378
Scientific Research Prizes Vol. 2: 3451
Scientist Award Vol. 1: 6225
Scientist of the Year Award Vol. 1: 15506
SCN Elizabeth Lowry Award Vol. 1: 19078
Scobee Lecturer Vol. 1: 1033
Scobie Memorial Award; James R. Vol. 1: 7701
Scopus Award Vol. 1: 2072
Scotchmer Essay Award; David Vol. 1: 9735
Scotlan Award for Distinguished Service; Priscilla A. Vol. 1: 903
Scotsman Fringe First Awards Vol. 2: 5753
Scott Award; Arnold H. Vol. 1: 5457
Scott Award; Elizabeth L. Vol. 1: 7623
Scott Award; Jessie M. Vol. 1: 2945
Scott Award; John Vol. 1: 5828
Scott Award of Merit; Margaret B. Vol. 1: 6697
Scott Commemoration Medal; Senior Captain Vol. 2: 4281
Scott Commemorative Medal; Junior Captain Vol. 2: 4282
Scott-Farnie Medal Vol. 2: 5014
Scott Fellowship; David B. Vol. 1: 10067
Scott FounderFs Award; John Paul Vol. 1: 4531
Scott Medal Award Vol. 1: 15934
Scott Medal for Conservation Merit; Peter Vol. 2: 4922
Scott Memorial Trophy (Doublehanded); Manton D. Vol. 1: 18079
Scott Prize Lectureship; James Vol. 2: 6999
Scott Prize; Primrose Vol. 2: 6014
Scott Prizes; James Brown Vol. 2: 4767
Scott Service Award; Chris Vol. 1: 9259
Scotti Prize; Alexander S. Vol. 2: 2316
Scottish Book of the Year Awards Vol. 2: 7069
Scottish First Book of the Year Vol. 2: 7069
Scottish Geographical Medal Vol. 2: 6897
Scottish Historical Book Award Vol. 2: 7070
Scottish International Piano Competition Vol. 2: 7081
Scottish Research Book Award Vol. 2: 7071
Scottish Salon of Photography Vol. 2: 7083
Scottish Science Award Vol. 2: 7072
Scottish Song Competition Vol. 2: 7073
Scourby Narrator of the Year Award; Alexander Vol. 1: 2070
Scoville Award Vol. 1: 18932
Scrapbook Contest Vol. 1: 8991
Screen Actors' Guild Awards Vol. 1: 15942
Screen Awards Vol. 1: 19014
Screener's Choice Award for Narrative Integrity Vol. 1: 4538
Screenwriter's Contest Vol. 1: 13950
Scribner Award; B. F. Vol. 1: 5458
Scribner Award; Belding H. Vol. 1: 4198
Scripps Award; Samuel H. Vol. 1: 1894
Scrivner Award for Creative Grantmaking; Robert W. Vol. 1: 7917
Scroll of Excellence Vol. 1: 18817
Scroll of Merit Vol. 2: 6245
Scwist Science Fair Awards Vol. 1: 16188
SDC Centenary Medal Vol. 2: 7190
SDE Fellowships Vol. 1: 16031
Sea Grant Association Award Vol. 1: 15950
Sea Grant Fellowship Vol. 1: 9182
Seaborg Award for Nuclear Chemistry; Glenn T. Vol. 1: 1578
Seaborg Award; Glenn T. Vol. 1: 2220
Seaborg National Public Leadership Award; Glenn T. Vol. 1: 2221
Seaborg SIYSS Award Vol. 1: 15927
Seal Memorial Trophy Award; George H. Vol. 1: 8228
Sealants Hall of Fame Award Vol. 1: 5459
Seaman Enlisted Awards for Outstanding Operational Support; Lewis L. Vol. 1: 5255
Seaman Memorial Scholarship; Anne Vol. 1: 15330
SEAMEO Service Award Vol. 2: 4110
SEARCA Graduate Scholarship Vol. 2: 3990
SEARCA PhD Research Scholarship Vol. 2: 3991
SEARCA Professorial Chairs Vol. 2: 3992
SEARCA Seed Fund for Research and Training Vol. 2: 3993
Search for New Music Competition Vol. 1: 10031
Search for Outstanding Contributions to Science Education Vol. 2: 3986
Searle Award Vol. 1: 9062
Sears Cup Vol. 1: 18074
SEASECS Article Prize Vol. 1: 17002
Seastrom Safety Award Vol. 1: 15205
Seavey Quality in Law Enforcement Award Program; Webber Vol. 1: 10175
Second Level Education Award Vol. 2: 2841
Secondary Teacher of the Year Vol. 1: 12835
Secretary of State's Distinguished Service Award Vol. 1: 17873
Secretary's Award Vol. 1: 17874
Section Achievement Award Vol. 1: 1644
Section Activities Award Vol. 1: 9951
Section/Chapter Partnerships of Distinction Awards Vol. 1: 16586
Section Grant Vol. 2: 7037
Section of the Year Award Vol. 1: 6604
Section Outstanding Teaching Award Vol. 1: 3674
Section Performance Award Vol. 1: 10914
Section Technical Award Vol. 1: 9951
Sector Awards Vol. 2: 6930
Security Officer of the Year Vol. 2: 2856
Security Officer of the Year Award Vol. 1: 17857
Security Professional of the Year
  Information Systems Security Association Vol. 1: 9708
  World Association of Detectives Vol 2: 7355
Seddon Award; Richard Vol. 1: 9485
Sedgwick Memorial Medal Vol. 1: 3433
Seed and Pilot Programs Vol. 1: 8317
Seed Research Awards Vol. 1: 17252
Seed Science Award Vol. 1: 7983
Seedsman of the Year Vol. 1: 5514
Seeger Prize; Charles Vol. 1: 16212

Seeker for Truth Vol. 1: 10431
Seemen Preis; Hans von Vol. 2: 2252
Seff Award; Richard Vol. 1: 145
Sefika Award Vol. 2: 4232
Segal Award; Martin E. Vol. 1: 11365
Segall Award of Merit; Harold N. Vol. 1: 6378
Seibold Prize; Eugen and Ilse Vol. 2: 2222
Seidel Distinguished Service Award; Jim Vol. 1: 714
Seidenbaum Award; Art Vol. 1: 11416
Seifert Prize; Jaroslav Vol. 2: 4578
Sejong Literacy Prize; King Vol. 2: 2002
Selby Fellowship Vol. 2: 122
Seldin Award; Joel R. Vol. 1: 15414
Seldin Distinguished Award; Donald W. Vol. 1: 13410
Selected Marine Corps Reserve Medal Vol. 1: 8122
Self-Adhesive Labelling Awards Vol. 2: 3694
Selfe Medal; Norman Vol. 2: 531
Seligman Award; Monroe Vol. 1: 9840
Seligman Crystal Vol. 2: 6269
Seligman Lecture; Richard Vol. 2: 7179
Seligson/Golden Award Vol. 1: 891
Sellin-Glueck Award Vol. 1: 4008
Seltzer Distinguished Service Recognition; Mildred M. Vol. 1: 4888
Selwyn Award Vol. 2: 6881
Selye Award; Hans Vol. 1: 2560
Selznek Outstanding Administrator of the Year; Harrie Vol. 1: 7877
Sembrich Voice Competition; Marcella Vol. 1: 11168
SEMI Award for North America Vol. 1: 15971
Seminary Award Vol. 1: 8985
Sen Award; B. R. Vol. 2: 3056
Sen Oration Award for Practice of Medicine; M. N. Vol. 2: 2625
Sen Prize; Dr. S. R. Vol. 2: 2755
Senart; Prix de la Fondation Emile Vol. 2: 1533
Senior Achievement Award Vol. 1: 646
Senior Bowler of the Year
Bowling Writers Association of America Vol. 1: 5899
Royal New South Wales Bowling Association Vol 2: 635
Women's All-Star Association Vol 1: 18850
Senior High Youth Voluntarism Award Vol. 1: 18190
Senior Investigator Award Vol. 1: 6936
Senior Ladies Bonspiel Vol. 1: 18169
Senior Ladies Trophy Vol. 1: 18169
Senior Medal for Botany Vol. 2: 4304
Senior Membership Vol. 1: 16255
Senior Moulton Medal Vol. 2: 6100
Senior Performance Competitions Vol. 1: 12035
Senior PGA Championship Vol. 2: 6564
Senior Player of the Year Vol. 1: 15277
Senior Recognition Award for Distinguished Contributors to the Division of Counseling Psychology Vol. 1: 3325
Senior Rookie of the Year Vol. 1: 15278
Senior Scientist Award Vol. 1: 14973
Senior Whitehead Prize Vol. 2: 6404
Seniors' Service Award Vol. 1: 18147
Senn Lectureship and Award; Milton J. E. Vol. 1: 715
Senne; Prix Emile Le Vol. 2: 1534
Sense of Smell Award; Olfactory Research Fund Vol. 1: 8856
Sensenbaugh Environmental Technology Award; J. Deane Vol. 1: 271
Sent Lisi Par Excellence Awards Vol. 2: 4399
Sentinels of Safety Awards Vol. 1: 13455
Sentner Short Story Award; Carl Vol. 1: 15222
Seoul International Music Festival Awards Vol. 2: 4115
Separation Science Lecture Vol. 2: 7180
Serena Medal for Italian Studies Vol. 2: 5211
Sergnese (Friends of CARHA) Category; Hockey Hall of Fame - John Vol. 1: 6154
Servaas Memorial Award; Sandi Vol. 1: 9415
Servant; Prix Vol. 2: 1622
Service Award
Australian Science Teachers Association Vol. 2: 349
Canadian Society for Clinical Pharmacology Vol 1: 6937
Turkish Academy of Sciences Vol 2: 4993
Service Award
American College of Clinical Pharmacology Vol. 1: 1636
American Crystallographic Association Vol 1: 1863
Association for Communication Excellence in Agriculture, Natural Resources, and Life and Human Sciences Vol 1: 4803
Association for Computing Machinery - Special Interest Group on Knowledge Discovery and Data Mining Vol 1: 4833
Association for Gay, Lesbian, and Bisexual Issues in Counseling Vol 1: 4884
Association for Library and Information Science Education Vol 1: 4908
Association of Indiana Media Educators Vol 1: 5190
Association of Specialized and Cooperative Library Agencies Vol 1: 5343
Canadian Society of Petroleum Geologists Vol 1: 7021
Foodservice Consultants Society International Vol 1: 8794
International Swimming Hall of Fame Vol 1: 10776
Middle East Studies Association of North America Vol 1: 11752
National Apostolate for Inclusion Ministry Vol 1: 12250
National Junior College Athletic Association Vol 1: 13407
Rider University Student Government Association Vol 1: 15670
Royal Astronomical Society of Canada Vol 1: 15740
Society for Imaging Science and Technology Vol 1: 16256
World Organization of Building Officials Vol 1: 18963
Service Awards Vol. 2: 5769
Service Awards
Association of Public Treasurers of the United States and Canada Vol. 1: 5326
Health Science Communications Association Vol 1: 9316
National Association of Underwater Instructors Vol 1: 12711
Scouting Ireland CSI Vol 2: 2885
Service Badge Vol. 1: 440
Service Bowl Award Vol. 1: 18148
Service Commendation Vol. 1: 2959
Service Medal
Irish United Nations Veterans Association Vol. 2: 2860
Textile Institute Vol 2: 7271
Service Sector Manager of the Year; Manufacturing Manager of the Year/ Vol. 1: 15450
Service to Children Television Awards Vol. 1: 12436
Service to Democracy Award Vol. 1: 831
Service to Keuka Vol. 1: 11145
Service to NACADA Award Vol. 1: 12093
Service to Others Vol. 1: 8944
Service to SPR Award Vol. 1: 16390
Servicios Distinguidos a la Fuerza Submarina Vol. 2: 1188
Servier Young Investigator Award Vol. 2: 439
Seshadri Prize in the Field of Practice of Community Medicine; Dr. M. K. Vol. 2: 2626
Seshadri Seventieth Birthday Commemoration Medal; Professor T. R. Vol. 2: 2714
Session Organizer of the Year Award Vol. 1: 10730
Sessions Memorial Award; John Vol. 1: 2694
SETAC Government Service Award Vol. 1: 16662
SETAC/Menzie Cura Environmental Education Award Vol. 1: 16663
SETAC President Citations Vol. 1: 16664
SETAC - Procter & Gamble Fellowship for Doctoral Research in Educational Science Vol. 1: 16665
Seton Award; Elizabeth Ann Vol. 1: 12869
Seton Award; Ernest Thompson Vol. 1: 10213
Seton Distinguished Volunteer Award; Fenmore R. Vol. 1: 15609
Seven State Exhibition Vol. 1: 11088
Seventy-Five Year Club Member Certificate Vol. 1: 2917
Severn Best Student Research Paper Award; Pratt- Vol. 1: 3745
Sevigne Award; Frank Vol. 1: 18455
Sewell Medal Vol. 2: 6805
Sexual Orientation and Gender Identity Conference (SOGIC) Awards Vol. 1: 6337
Seybold Vision Award Vol. 1: 15984
Seymour Award; Harold J. "Si" Vol. 1: 4894
Seymour Award; Whitney North Vol. 1: 8605
Seymour Medal Vol. 1: 16174
Seymour Vestermark Award Vol. 1: 3293
SGA Young Scientist Award Vol. 2: 1268
Sgambati Award; Fred Vol. 1: 6666
SGL Carbon Award Vol. 1: 1449
Shaara Award; Michael Vol. 1: 11429
Shaara Outstanding Writer Award; Michael Vol. 1: 17064
Shacklock Trophy Vol. 2: 5044
Shadakshara Swamy Endowment Lecture Award; Prof. M. Vol. 2: 2799
Shadle Fellowship; Albert R. and Alma Vol. 1: 4121
Shaffer Award for Academic Excellence as a Graduate Faculty Member; Robert H. Vol. 1: 12689
Shaffer Award; Robert H. Vol. 1: 5155
Shaffer Award; Thomas E. Vol. 1: 716
Shah Memorial Lecture; Professor R. C. Vol. 2: 2749
Shakespeare Award for Classical Theatre (Will Award); William Vol. 1: 15986
Shakespeare Prize Vol. 2: 2403

Award Index

Shaler Company's Rislone Most Improved Championship Driver Award Vol. 1: 17754
Shalom Peace Award Vol. 1: 11002
Shands Award Vol. 1: 14714
Shanghai Television Festival Vol. 2: 3950
Shankar Memorial Lecture; Dr. Jagdish Vol. 2: 2715
Shannon Award; National Film Board Kathleen Vol. 1: 19078
Shanti Swarup Bhatnagar Medal Vol. 2: 2716
Shantz Award; Stan Vol. 1: 15169
Shaper Prize; Radomir Vol. 2: 4781
Shapiro Award; Arthur Vol. 1: 16200
Shapiro Prize; Alec Vol. 2: 6734
Share the Wealth Packets Vol. 1: 11350
Shark Awards, the International Advertising Festival of Ireland Vol. 2: 2887
Sharman Award Vol. 2: 378
Sharp Award; A.J. Vol. 1: 5885
Sharp Memorial Prize; Frank Chapman Vol. 1: 3092
Sharpe Award; Norma Vol. 1: 6214
Sharpe Prize; Roy Vol. 2: 5327
Sharpest Knife in North America Award Vol. 1: 1158
Sharples Perpetual Award; Laurence P. Vol. 1: 345
Shatalov Award; Mikhail and Ekateryna Vol. 1: 12119
Shattuck Public Service Awards; Henry L. Vol. 1: 5860
Shaughnessy Prize; Mina P. Vol. 1: 11921
Shaurya Chakra Vol. 2: 2585
Shaw Award; Cliff Vol. 1: 13991
Shaw Award; Donna Mary Vol. 1: 6981
Shaw Deaf Australian of the Year Award; Dorothy Vol. 2: 143
Shaw Deaf Youth of the Year; Dorothy Vol. 2: 143
Shaw Memorial Award; Peter Vol. 1: 12646
Shaw Postdoctoral Prize in Acoustics; Edgar and Millicent Vol. 1: 6146
Shaw Prize; Bernard Vol. 2: 7136
Shaw-Worth Memorial Scholarship Vol. 1: 9528
Shawcross Prize; A. J. Vol. 2: 5993
Shazar Award for Research in Jewish History; Zalman Vol. 2: 2928
Shea Award; James H. Vol. 1: 12540
Shea Prize; John Gilmary Vol. 1: 1456
Sheahan Award; John Drury Vol. 1: 7900
Shedden Uhde Medal and Prize Vol. 2: 532
Sheehan Literary Award for U.S. Paper Money Studies; Catherine Vol. 1: 2918
Sheehan Memorial Educational Scholarship; Dezna C. Vol. 1: 13716
Sheeline Award for Excellence in Public Relations; Randall D. Vol. 1: 2496
Sheep Heritage Foundation Vol. 1: 3544
Sheerin, Sr. Service Award; Thomas F. Vol. 1: 14839
Sheffield Award Vol. 1: 6970
Shehadi New Writers Award; Philip Vol. 1: 11747
Shelburne Award; Tilton E. Vol. 1: 5460
Shell Playwriting Award Vol. 2: 3806
Shell Science Teaching Award Vol. 1: 13684
Shelley Memorial Award Vol. 1: 15134
Shelton Award for Sustained Excellence; Robert M. Vol. 1: 9323
Shenk Award Vol. 1: 12257
Shepard Award; Glenn Vol. 1: 13852
Shepard Award; Paul Vol. 1: 3243
Shepard Medal for Excellence in Marine Geology; Francis P. Vol. 1: 16414
Shepard Medal for Marine Geology; Francis P. Vol. 1: 16414
Shepard Science Award; Charles C. Vol. 1: 17829
Shepherd Distinguished Composer of the Year Award Vol. 1: 12036
The Shepherd Specialty Papers Poster Award Vol. 1: 6211
Shepherd Teaching Award; Margaret Vol. 1: 18553
Shepherd's Voice Award Vol. 1: 3545
Shepherd's Voice Award for Broadcast Media Vol. 1: 3546
Sheppard Award; C. Stewart Vol. 1: 7268
Sheppard Award; Eugenia Vol. 1: 7885
Sherif Award; Carolyn Wood Vol. 1: 3385
Sherlock Meritorious Service Award; Charles N. Vol. 1: 3782
Sherman Leadership Award; Simon Vol. 1: 16124
Sherrard Awards; J. M. Vol. 2: 3704
Sherrington Memorial Lecture Vol. 2: 7018
Sherry Memorial Trophy; Goodfellow Memorial Oratorio Scholarship/Helen Davis Vol. 1: 15867
Sherwin Award; Raymond J. Vol. 1: 16020
Sherwin-Williams Student Award in Applied Polymer Science Vol. 1: 1558
Shevchenko Freedom Award Vol. 1: 17650
Shiebler Award; George L. Vol. 1: 8349
Shield of Public Service Vol. 1: 6845
Shields Medal Vol. 1: 16531
Shields-Trauger Award Vol. 1: 5646
Shildrick Award; John P. Vol. 2: 5553
Shilling Award; Charles W. Vol. 1: 17663
Shin Award Vol. 1: 11012
Shinbum Kyokai Sho Vol. 2: 3241
SHINE (Sexual Health in Entertainment) Awards Vol. 1: 11639
Shinohara Memorial Award Vol. 2: 3331
Ship of the Year Vol. 1: 18958
Shipley Award; Robert M. Vol. 1: 2088
Shipman Gold Medal Award; J. Vol. 1: 9758
Shiras Institute/Mildred & Albert Panowski Playwriting Award Vol. 1: 15687
Shkwarek Plaque; Joe Vol. 1: 313
Shneidman Award; Edwin Vol. 1: 1295
Shock Compression Science Award Vol. 1: 3136
Shock New Investigator Award; Nathan Vol. 1: 9064
Shockley Memorial Award; Woodland G. Vol. 1: 5461
Shoemaker Award; Norma J. Vol. 1: 16638
Shoemaker Award of Merit; Ralph J. Vol. 1: 17086
Shoemaker Grant; Norma J. Vol. 1: 16639
Shofar Award (Ram's Horn) Vol. 1: 13395
Sholes Award; Christopher Latham Vol. 1: 7875
Shoop Preteen Scholarship Award; J. Homer Vol. 1: 1788
Shore Plaque; Eddie Vol. 1: 2279
Shorei-Sho/Young Investigator Awards Vol. 2: 3271
Shores - Greenwood Publishing Group Award; Louis Vol. 1: 2695
Short Film Award Vol. 1: 12077
Short Film Festival Prize Vol. 2: 3910
Short-Form Award Vol. 1: 15995
Short Play Awards Program Vol. 1: 11114
Short Prose Competition for Developing Writers Vol. 1: 19029
Short Story and Poetry Contest Vol. 1: 8992
Short Story Award Vol. 1: 13946
Short Story Contest
Affaire de Coeur Magazine Vol. 1: 217
Writers' Journal Vol 1: 19022
Short Story Dagger Vol. 2: 5713
Short-term Senior Fellowships in Iranian Studies Vol. 1: 2521
Shorten Award; Sarah Vol. 1: 6308
Shotwell Memorial Award; Ambrose M. Vol. 1: 4861
Shousha Foundation Prize and Fellowship; Dr. A. T. Vol. 2: 4930
Show Awards
Canadian Brown Swiss and Braunvieh Association Vol. 1: 6366
Heart of New England Chihuahua Club Vol 1: 9336
Show Canada Showmanship Awards Vol. 1: 11963
Show Hunter Ponies Awards Vol. 2: 5459
Show Me Readers Award Vol. 1: 11882
Show Ponies Awards Vol. 2: 5460
Show Trophy Vol. 1: 3001
ShowSouth Awards Vol. 1: 5495
Shri Dhanwantari Prize Vol. 2: 2717
SHRM Foundation Outstanding Graduate Student Award Vol. 1: 16243
Shrobehn Internship Program; AECT National Convention - Earl F. Vol. 1: 4878
Shryock Medal; Richard H. Vol. 1: 967
Shubin-Weil Award for Excellence Vol. 1: 16640
Shubitz Award; Simon M. Vol. 1: 18251
Shull Award; Charles Albert Vol. 1: 4220
Shulman Award; The Morton Vol. 1: 14864
Shulman Book Prize; Marshall Vol. 1: 960
Shulman Challenge Award; Neville Vol. 2: 6774
Shumavon Award; Leo Vol. 1: 13098
Shumway Award; F. Ritter Vol. 1: 15364
Shuster Memorial Award; Ben Vol. 1: 596
Shy Award; G. Milton Vol. 1: 639
SIA Service Award Vol. 1: 15969
SIAD Medal Vol. 2: 5653
SIAM Activity Group on Optimization Prize Vol. 1: 16277
SIAM Award in the Mathematical Contest in Modeling Vol. 1: 16278
SIAM Prize for Distinguished Service to the Profession Vol. 1: 16279
SIAM Prize in Numerical Analysis and Scientific Computing Vol. 1: 16286
SIAM Student Paper Prize Vol. 1: 16280
Sibelius Violin Competition; International Jean Vol. 2: 1425
Sibert Informational Book Medal; Robert F. Vol. 1: 4931
Sibley Fellowship; Mary Isabel Vol. 1: 14992
Sicher First Research Essay Award; Harry Vol. 1: 1201
Sickinger Award; Vera Vol. 1: 829
SICOT/SIROT Award Vol. 2: 929
SID Award (Store Interior Design Award) Vol. 1: 12682
Sidewalk Sale and Exhibition Vol. 1: 7256
Sidewise Awards for Alternate History Vol. 1: 15995
Sidey Medal and Prize; T. K. Vol. 2: 3872
Sidley Memorial Award; Dorothy Vol. 2: 5978
Sidney Griller Award Vol. 2: 6407
Siebert Scholarship; Ned Vol. 1: 2145

Siebold Award; Philipp Franz von Vol. 2: 2437
Siedenburg Award Vol. 1: 11433
Siefkes Justice Maker Award; Jim Vol. 1: 11449
Siegel Award; Robt. Vol. 1: 7673
Siegel Memorial Award; Joseph A. Vol. 1: 16728
Siegel Service Award; Joseph A. Vol. 1: 16728
Siesel Award for Community Service; E. Hank Vol. 1: 13283
Siess Award for Excellence in Structural Research; Chester Paul Vol. 1: 1760
Sievers Trophy; Art Vol. 1: 13647
Sievert Award Vol. 2: 1909
Sievert Award; Fred H. Vol. 1: 8137
SIG Excellence in Advanced Practice Award Vol. 1: 12600
SIG Member of the Year Award Vol. 1: 3746
SIG of the Year Award Vol. 1: 3747
SIG Publication of the Year Award Vol. 1: 3748
SIGACT Distinguished Service Prize Vol. 1: 4820
Sigal Peace and Justice Scholarship; Dr. Phillip Vol. 1: 8408
SIGCOMM Award Vol. 1: 4825
SIGCSE Award Vol. 1: 4823
Sigma Delta Chi Awards Vol. 1: 16838
Sigma Diagnostics Student Scholarship Vol. 1: 13723
Sigma Iota Epsilon Scholarships Vol. 1: 16035
Sigma Pi Sigma Undergraduate Research Award Vol. 1: 16819
Sigma Pi Sigma Undergraduate Research Award Vol. 1: 2547
SIGMOD Contributions Award Vol. 1: 4836
SIGMOD Innovations Award Vol. 1: 4835
Sign Design Competition Vol. 1: 10628
Signal Service Award Vol. 1: 2742
Signature Membership Vol. 1: 14872
Significant Achievement Award
National Wildlife Rehabilitators Association Vol. 1: 13914
Rotary International Vol 1: 15724
Significant Contribution to the Field of Marriage and Family Therapy Award Vol. 1: 936
Signis Prize Vol. 2: 3469
Signum Fidei Medal Vol. 1: 11181
Signy Foreign Fellowship; Gordon Vol. 2: 3352
Sikes Slide Sequence Award; Sarah Vol. 1: 2210
Sikkens Prize Vol. 2: 3665
Sikorsky Award for Humanitarian Service; Igor Vol. 1: 9370
Sikorsky International Trophy; Igor I. Vol. 1: 2205
Silva Service Award Vol. 1: 18022
Silver Anchor Vol. 2: 1890
Silver Anchor Award Vol. 1: 8918
Silver Anniversary Award Vol. 1: 12906
Silver Antelope Award Vol. 1: 5914
Silver Anvil Awards Vol. 1: 15431
Silver Apple Award Vol. 1: 8204
Silver Ball Award Vol. 1: 16122
Silver Beaver Award Vol. 1: 5915
Silver Berlin Bear Vol. 2: 2048
Silver Bowl Vol. 1: 10548
Silver Bowl Award Vol. 1: 14684
Silver Buffalo Award Vol. 1: 5916
Silver Combustion Medal Vol. 1: 7611
Silver Core Award Vol. 2: 796
Silver Cross for Valor Vol. 1: 11290
Silver Crown Awards Vol. 1: 7578
The Silver Dirac Medal Vol. 2: 715
Silver Edelweiss Vol. 2: 4545
Silver Elephant Award Vol. 2: 2551
Silver Gavel Awards for Media and the Arts Vol. 1: 1377
Silver-gilt Medal for Bibliography Vol. 2: 5165
Silver Good Citizenship Medal Vol. 1: 13776
Silver Hardhat Award Vol. 1: 7761
Silver Harp Vol. 2: 3503
Silver Hawk Award Vol. 1: 11526
Silver Helmet Awards Vol. 1: 4519
Silver Jewelry Vol. 2: 2569
Silver Jubilee Vol. 1: 6245
Silver Jubilee Commemoration Medal Vol. 2: 2718
Silver Kisses Vol. 2: 3495
Silver Leaf Awards
International Association of Business Communicators - BC Chapter Vol. 1: 10156
International Association of Business Communicators Manitoba Vol 1: 10159
Silver Lifesaving Medal Vol. 1: 8123
Silver Mailcoach Vol. 2: 6535
Silver Medal
Acoustical Society of America Vol. 1: 132
American Advertising Federation Vol 1: 769
American Rhododendron Society Vol 1: 3493
Brazilian Metallurgy and Materials Association Vol 2: 1125
Edinburgh Architectural Association Vol 2: 5749
French National Center for Scientific Research Vol 2: 1828
The Gardeners of America/Men's Garden Clubs of America Vol 1: 8967
Institute of Actuaries - United Kingdom Vol 2: 5990
National Association of Licensed Paralegals Vol 2: 6457
National Vegetable Society Vol 2: 6490
Royal Academy of Engineering Vol 2: 6624
Royal Academy of Medicine in Ireland Vol 2: 2874
Royal Aeronautical Society - United Kingdom Vol 2: 6654
Scarab Club Vol 1: 15899
Society of Economic Geologists Vol 1: 16654
Tau Sigma Delta Vol 1: 17411
Zoological Society of London Vol 2: 7402
Silver Medal and Associate Fellowship of the Society Vol. 2: 311
Silver Medal Award
Advertising Women of New York Vol. 1: 193
Audio Engineering Society Vol 1: 5524
Fertilizer Society of South Africa Vol 2: 4178
National Student Campaign Against Hunger and Homelessness Vol 1: 13816
Silver Medal of Honor Vol. 1: 4442
Silver Medallion Vol. 1: 5924
Silver Member Vol. 1: 10020
Silver Memorial Award; Henry K. Vol. 1: 12605
Silver Otter Award Vol. 2: 5315
Silver Page Award Vol. 1: 4036
Silver Palette Award Vol. 1: 16645
Silver Plaque Award Vol. 1: 13643
Silver Plate Award Vol. 1: 10436
Silver Playwriting Competition Prize; Dorothy Vol. 1: 10985
Silver Quill Editorial Achievement Award Vol. 1: 4468
Silver Ring Vol. 1: 6605
Silver Rope Award for Leadership Vol. 1: 442
Silver Rose Bowl Vol. 2: 3688
Silver Satellite Award Vol. 1: 8851
Silver Screen Award Vol. 1: 17980
The Silver Service Award Vol. 1: 2758
Silver Shell Awards Vol. 2: 4538
Silver Shovel Award Vol. 1: 10533
Silver Slugger Awards Vol. 1: 17192
Silver Slugger Team Vol. 1: 17193
Silver Spike Vol. 2: 4552
Silver SPUR Awards Vol. 1: 15833
Silver Star Vol. 2: 723
Silver Star: Navy Vol. 1: 8124
Silver T-Square Vol. 1: 12852
Silver Torch Award Vol. 1: 12448
Silver Trowel Award Vol. 2: 5228
Silver Turnbuckle Award Vol. 2: 6655
Silver Wings Individual Awards Vol. 1: 4644
Silver Wings Unit Award Vol. 1: 4645
Silver World Award Vol. 1: 5917
Silverfish Review Poetry Chapbook Award Vol. 1: 16062
Silverstein-Simeone Award Lecture Vol. 1: 10705
Silvert Award; Kalman Vol. 1: 11237
Sim Awards Vol. 2: 7387
Simkins Award; Francis B. Vol. 1: 17037
Simmonds Award; The David Vol. 1: 14865
Simmons First National Bank Grand Purchase Award Vol. 1: 4675
Simmons Scholarship; Morgan and Mary Vol. 1: 2145
Simmons Short Fiction Award; John Vol. 1: 10880
Simms Prize Vol. 2: 6656
Simms Scholar-Athlete Award; Robert A. Vol. 1: 13215
Simms Scholarship; Julia Viola Vol. 1: 5792
Simon/Anderson Publishing Outstanding Paper Award; William L. Vol. 1: 90
Simon/Anderson Publishing Outstanding Student Paper Award; William L. Vol. 1: 91
Simon Award Vol. 2: 5471
Simon Award; George Vol. 1: 8715
Simon Award; Norma P. Vol. 1: 5346
Simon Children's Book Award; Charlie May Vol. 1: 4615
Simon Medal; Andre Vol. 2: 6334
Simon Memorial Prize Vol. 2: 6067
Simon Sherman Industry Service Award Vol. 1: 16124
Simonaviciaus premija; Kazimiero Vol. 2: 3386
Simons Memorial Award; Bernard Vol. 2: 6231
Simons Prize; Harden Vol. 1: 3675
Simonsen Lectureship Vol. 2: 6981
Simpson Medal; A. S. Romer - G. G. Vol. 1: 16893
Simpson Technical Editors Award; Maurice Vol. 1: 9841
Sims Award; Arthur Vol. 2: 5135
Sims Encouragement Fund Award for Work in the Comedic Arts; Tim Vol. 1: 14565

Simulation and Ground Testing Award Vol. 1: 2380
Sinclair Award; David Vol. 1: 843
Sinclair Award for Broadcast Journalism; Gordon Vol. 1: 69
Sinclaire Award; Matilda W. Vol. 1: 2060
Singapore Literature Prize Vol. 2: 4424
Singapore Promising Brand Award Vol. 2: 4420
Singarimbun Research Awards; Masri Vol. 2: 2816
Singer Award; Colonel Merton Vol. 1: 15630
Singer of the Year Vol. 1: 15993
Singer Prize Vol. 2: 5493
Singh Dandass Memorial Award; IETE-Flt. Lt. Tanmaya Vol. 2: 2769
Singh Memorial Award; Harvans Vol. 2: 2786
Singh of Kalsia Memorial Cancer Research Award; Raja Ravi Sher Vol. 2: 2627
Sinha Memorial Award; Professor Umakant Vol. 2: 2750
Sinking Creek Film Celebration Vol. 1: 12080
Sintra; Prix Thomson Vol. 2: 1983
SIOP Awards Vol. 2: 6300
Sir Antony Fisher International Memorial Award Vol. 1: 5516
Sir Henry Royce Memorial Medal Vol. 2: 6182
Sir Joseph Burn Prize Vol. 2: 5993
Sir Monty Finniston Award Vol. 2: 5100
Sir Wilfred Fish Research Prize Vol. 2: 5521
Sisco Excellence in Teaching Award; John I. Vol. 1: 17054
Sise Outstanding Alpine Masters Award; Al Vol. 1: 18107
Sister Cities Expressions of Peace Youth Art Contest Vol. 1: 16071
Sister Irene Award Vol. 1: 14710
Sister Mary Arthur "Sharing the Light" Award Vol. 1: 6269
Sisyphus Award Vol. 1: 12963
Sitharman Memorial Essay Competition; Dr. R. Vol. 2: 2811
SITPRO Prize Vol. 2: 6029
Sivickis premija; Pranciskaus Vol. 2: 3387
Sixteenth Century Journal Literature Prize Vol. 1: 16080
Sixteenth Century Society and Conference Medal Vol. 1: 16081
Sixth Man Award Vol. 1: 12763
Sixty Year Membership Medal Vol. 1: 2919
Sjoberg Award; Leif and Inger Vol. 1: 3516
Skalny Scholarship Vol. 1: 1805
Skater of the Year Vol. 1: 17129
Skeffington Award; A. M. Vol. 1: 7538
Skellerup Award Vol. 2: 3746
Skerman Award for Microbial Taxonomy Vol. 2: 7370
SKF Award Vol. 2: 7444
Ski Magazine Cup Award Vol. 1: 18108
Skier of the Year
International Ski Federation Vol. 2: 4836
Ski Racing Vol 1: 16083
Skiing Magazine Development Cup Vol. 1: 18109
Skills for Chefs Competition Vol. 2: 5287
SkillsUSA Championships Vol. 1: 16086
Skinner Award; Bradley Vol. 1: 14803
Skinner Award; Clarence R. Vol. 1: 17681
Skinner Award; Constance Lindsay Vol. 1: 18868
Skinner Award; Morris F. Vol. 1: 16895
Skinner Memorial Fund Award; John E. Vol. 1: 2034
Skinner New Researcher Award; B. F. Vol. 1: 3310
Skinner Sermon Award Vol. 1: 17681
Sklodowska-Curie Award; Marie Vol. 1: 980
Skolnik Award; Herman Vol. 1: 1579
Skrzypek Award; Alexander J. Vol. 1: 9610
SLA Meckler Award for Innovations in Technology Vol. 1: 17078
Slade Prize; Ivan Vol. 2: 5494
Slagle Lectureship; Eleanor Clarke Vol. 1: 2960
Slate - MacDaniels Award Vol. 1: 14304
Slater Scholarship; Robert C. Vol. 1: 11836
Sled of the Year Vol. 1: 13861
Sleeks Prize; Ary Vol. 2: 961
Slessor Prize; Kenneth Vol. 2: 585
Slichter Award; William P. Vol. 1: 17804
Sliffe Awards for Distinguished Junior High and High School Mathematics Teaching; Edyth May Vol. 1: 11611
Slipper Gold Medal; Stanley Vol. 1: 7022
Sloan Industry Studies Fellowship; Alfred P. Vol. 1: 2498
Sloan Memorial Award; Norman J. Vol. 2: 7356
Sloan Public Service Awards Vol. 1: 8929
Slocum Award Vol. 1: 11042
Slonimsky Award for Outstanding Musical Biography; Nicolas Vol. 1: 4004
Slote Award; Bernice Vol. 1: 15195
Slovak Physical Society Award Vol. 2: 4448
Slovak Physical Society Medal Vol. 2: 4449
Smail Memorial Piano Award; Mary Winston Vol. 1: 18586
Small and Commercial Print Division Awards Vol. 1: 15031
Small and Disadvantaged Business Award Vol. 1: 336
Small Animal Practitioner Award Vol. 1: 7061
Small Animal Practitioner of the Year Vol. 2: 365
Small Business Advocates of the Year Vol. 1: 18121
Small Business Exporter of the Year Vol. 1: 18122
Small Craft Group Medal Vol. 2: 6841
Small Ecological Project Grants Vol. 2: 5299
Small Firms Merit Awards for Research and Technology Vol. 2: 7292
Small Memorial Award; Ben John Vol. 1: 7754
Small Press Publisher of the Year Award Vol. 1: 6358
Small Project and Travel Awards Vol. 2: 7305
Small Projects Award Vol. 2: 5750
Small Research Grants Program Vol. 1: 9516
SMART Vol. 2: 7293
Smart 21 Vol. 1: 9969
SMART Awards Vol. 2: 7292
Smart Competition; Harold Vol. 2: 6883
The Smart21 Communities Vol. 1: 9970
Smarties Prize for Children's Books Vol. 2: 5190
SME Education Foundation Family Scholarship Vol. 1: 16729
SME Progress Award Vol. 1: 16727
SME Research Medal Vol. 1: 16730
Smedley Memorial Award; Glenn Vol. 1: 2920
Smelik/IBBY Prize; Jenny Vol. 2: 3571
Smelik-Kiggenprijs; Jenny Vol. 2: 3571
SMFA Brass Award Vol. 1: 15881
The SMFA Senior Speech Arts Scholarship Vol. 1: 15857
The SMFA Senior Woodwind Scholarship Vol. 1: 15852
Smissman Award; Bristol-Myers Squibb Vol. 1: 1534
Smith Award; A. Lewis Vol. 1: 8143
Smith Award; Adam Vol. 1: 5306
Smith Award; Arthur Vol. 2: 1904
Smith Award; Daniel B. Vol. 1: 3061
Smith Award for Distinguished Pathology Educator; H. P. Vol. 1: 3605
Smith Award for Excellence in Nonprofit Leadership; Edward A. Vol. 1: 11760
Smith Award for Submarine Support Achievement; Levering Vol. 1: 14001
Smith Award; Georgina Vol. 1: 1321
Smith Award; Homer H. Vol. 1: 4199
Smith Award; Horton Vol. 1: 15322
Smith Award; Howard DeWitt Vol. 1: 5462
Smith Award; I. W. Vol. 1: 6954
Smith Award; Job Lewis Vol. 1: 717
Smith Award; Mary Jacobs Vol. 1: 15993
Smith Award; Merriam Vol. 1: 18729
Smith Award; Nila Banton Vol. 1: 10597
Smith Award; NZSA Lilian Ida Vol. 2: 3794
Smith Award; Reginald Heber Vol. 1: 13417
Smith Award; Robert M. Vol. 1: 718
Smith Award; Roger C. Vol. 1: 5347
Smith Award; Sir Grafton Elliot Vol. 2: 303
Smith Award; Wilbur S. Vol. 1: 3980
Smith Awards for Science Promotion; Michael Vol. 1: 13976
Smith Book Awards; Lillian Vol. 1: 17050
Smith Breeden Prizes Vol. 1: 2022
Smith Distinguished Transportation Educator Award; Wilbur S. Vol. 1: 9952
Smith Fellowship; Alice E. Vol. 1: 18784
Smith Fellowships; Al Vol. 1: 11131
Smith Hydraulic Fellowship; J. Waldo Vol. 1: 3981
Smith International Trumpet Solo Competition; Ellsworth Vol. 1: 10805
Smith Jr. Student Paper Award; W. David Vol. 1: 2498
Smith Medal; Blakely Vol. 1: 16766
Smith Medal; Gilbert Morgan Vol. 1: 12165
Smith Medal; H. G. Vol. 2: 624
Smith Medal; J. Lawrence Vol. 1: 12166
Smith Medal; Julian C. Vol. 1: 8467
Smith Medal; Waldo E. Vol. 1: 2123
Smith Medal; William Vol. 2: 5936
Smith Memorial Award; Dale A. Vol. 1: 1017
Smith Memorial Award; H. G. Vol. 2: 624
Smith Memorial Award; Svend Vol. 1: 10737
Smith Memorial Exhibit Award; Sidney W. Vol. 1: 2921
Smith Memorial Medal; S. G. Vol. 2: 7272
Smith National Award; Sidney O. Vol. 1: 9644
Smith Playwriting Award; Jean Kennedy Vol. 1: 11120
Smith Practice Excellence Award; Daniel B. Vol. 1: 3061
Smith Prize; Dwight L. Vol. 1: 18691
Smith Prize; Rufus Z. Vol. 1: 4791
Smith Research Award; Bob Vol. 2: 6555
Smith Research Fellowship; Sir Frederick Vol. 2: 6745
Smith-Scwist Endowed Scholarship; Dr. Michael Vol. 1: 16189
Smith Sr. Award; Bruce Vol. 1: 92

Smith - U.S. Water Polo Award; James R. "Jimmy" Vol. 1: 18166
Smith-Wintemberg Award Vol. 1: 6187
Smithers Award; R. Brinkley Vol. 1: 13035
Smiths Detection Award Vol. 1: 6877
Smithsonian Craft Show Vol. 1: 16100
Smithsonian Institution Fellowship Program Vol. 1: 16098
Smolar Award for Excellence in Comprehensive Coverage or Investigative Reporting; Boris Vol. 1: 2599
Smolar Award for Excellence in North American Jewish Journalism; Boris Vol. 1: 2600
Smoluchowski Award Vol. 2: 2025
Smoluchowski Medal; Marian Vol. 2: 4050
Smoot Organizational Meritorious Award; Willie Vol. 1: 12779
Smyth Salver Vol. 2: 6355
Smyth Statesman Award; Henry DeWolf Vol. 1: 14440
Smythe Award; Robert Adger Vol. 1: 15042
Smythe International Service Citation Award; Hugh H. and Mabel M. Vol. 1: 10011
Smythe Trophy; D. Verner Vol. 1: 18074
Smythies Award; Jill Vol. 2: 6389
SNC-Lavalin Plant Design Competition Vol. 1: 6894
Snedecor Award; George W. Vol. 1: 7624
Snell Premium Vol. 2: 6146
Sniadecki Medal; Jedrzej Vol. 2: 4035
Snively Memorial Award; Dr. George G. Vol. 1: 17217
Snodgrass Award; Bill Vol. 1: 14804
Snodgrass Memorial Research Award Vol. 1: 8480
Snow Award; Roland B. Vol. 1: 1496
Snow Early Career Award in Educational Psychology; Richard E. Vol. 1: 3338
Snow Foundation Prize; John Ben Vol. 1: 14287
Snowcem Award Vol. 2: 2641
Snyder Award; Walter F. Vol. 1: 14433
Soaring Hall of Fame Vol. 1: 16114
Sober Lectureship; Herbert A. Vol. 1: 3568
Soccer Coach of the Year Vol. 1: 6667
Soccer Outstanding Service Award Vol. 1: 507
Social Achievement Award Vol. 2: 922
Social Action Award Vol. 1: 16465
Social Action Leadership Award Vol. 1: 17686
Social Indicators Research Best Paper Award Vol. 1: 10677
Social Issues Dissertation Award Vol. 1: 16450
Social Research, Policy & Practice Student Research Award Vol. 1: 9065
Social Science Prize of the American Academy Vol. 1: 554
Social Service Award Vol. 2: 2805
Social Studies Programs of Excellence Vol. 1: 12991
Social Worker of the Year Vol. 1: 12665
Society Award Vol. 2: 3324
Society Awards Vol. 2: 2910
Society Citation Vol. 1: 9699
Society Diplomas Vol. 2: 5917
Society for Analytical Chemistry Silver Medal Vol. 2: 6982
Society for In Vitro Biology Student Travel Awards Vol. 1: 16259
Society for Research into Higher Education Awards Vol. 2: 7112
Society Medal Vol. 2: 140
Society of Analytical Chemistry Gold Medal Vol. 2: 6983
Society of Australasian Specialists/Oceania Medals Vol. 1: 16563
Society of Children's Book Writers and Illustrators Grants Vol. 1: 16626
Society of Cosmetic Chemists Awards Vol. 1: 16632
Society of Midland Authors Awards Vol. 1: 16741
Society of Petroleum Engineers of AIME Distinguished Service Award Vol. 1: 16796
Society of Shipping Executives Education Trust Prize Vol. 2: 6029
Society of South African Geographers Fellow Vol. 2: 4263
Society of West End Theatre Vol. 2: 7203
Society of Women Musicians Prize Vol. 2: 6853
Society's Medal Vol. 2: 646
Soderberg Memorial Scholarship; Myrtle Vol. 1: 14774
Soderbergs Pris Vol. 2: 4640
Soest Preis; Konrad von Vol. 2: 2350
Soffer Research Award; Alfred Vol. 1: 1626
Software Process Achievement Award
Carnegie Mellon University - Software Engineering Institute Vol. 1: 7117
Institute of Electrical and Electronics Engineers - Computer Society Vol 1: 9815
Software System Award Vol. 1: 4815
Soil Science Applied Research Award Vol. 1: 16939
Soil Science Distinguished Service Award Vol. 1: 16940
Soil Science Education Award Vol. 1: 16941
Soil Science Professional Service Award Vol. 1: 16942
Soil Science Research Award Vol. 1: 16943
Sokhey Award; Maj. Gen. Saheb Singh Vol. 2: 2628
Solberg Award Vol. 1: 4192
Solid-State Circuits Award Vol. 1: 9789
Solidarity Award for Lifetime Contribution to the Labor Movement Vol. 1: 18787
Solidarity Prize Vol. 1: 18904
Sollenberger Trophy; John B. Vol. 1: 2280
Sollich Award Vol. 2: 416
Sollmann Award in Pharmacology; Torald Vol. 1: 3810
Solo Competition Vol. 1: 14633
Solo Driver of Eminence Award Vol. 1: 17218
Solo II Cup Vol. 1: 17219
Solo II Divisional of the Year Award Vol. 1: 17220
Solo II Driver of Eminence Award Vol. 1: 17221
Solo II Driver of the Year Vol. 1: 17221
Solo II Rookie of the Year Vol. 1: 17222
Solomon Award; King Vol. 1: 534
Solomon Schechter Award Vol. 1: 18182
Soloviev Medal; Sergey Vol. 2: 1780
Solray Award for Clinical Research in IBS/Motility Vol. 1: 2085
Somaini; Premio Triennale per la Fisica Francesco Vol. 2: 3007
Sommer Award; Ralph F. Vol. 1: 1088
Sommerfeld Preis; Arnold Vol. 2: 2045
Sommers Award; Ben Vol. 1: 8047
Sommerville Prize; Helen Vol. 2: 6015
Somogyi-Sendroy Award Vol. 1: 892
Son Diabetes Educator Award; Allene Von Vol. 1: 1083
Song Award; John S. Vol. 1: 16263
Song Foundation Award for Plant Tissue Culture; John S. Vol. 1: 16263
Song of the Year Vol. 1: 10270
Songwriter of the Year
Dallas Songwriters Association Vol. 1: 8029
Nashville Songwriters Association International Vol 1: 12082
Songwriters Hall of Fame Vol. 1: 12134
Songwriting Award Vol. 2: 6451
Sonnenwirth Memorial Award Vol. 1: 3765
Sonning Music Prize; Leonie Vol. 2: 1336
Sonning Prize Vol. 2: 1338
Sonnings Musikpris; Leonie Vol. 2: 1336
Sonntag Award; Al Vol. 1: 16886
Sonographer Scholarships Vol. 1: 4029
Sons of Martha Medal Vol. 1: 15308
Sons of Norway Jumping Award Vol. 1: 18110
Sontheime Award Vol. 1: 4372
Sony Radio Academy Awards Vol. 2: 7226
Soo Award; Kun-Po Vol. 1: 3289
Soper Award for Excellence in Health Literature; Fred L. Vol. 1: 14832
Soper Award; Lord Vol. 2: 6362
Sorantin Award for Young Artists; Hemphill-Wells Vol. 1: 15816
Sorantin Young Artist Award Vol. 1: 15816
Sorby Medal Vol. 2: 904
Sorokin Lecture Vol. 1: 4280
Sorum Awards; Assembly William Vol. 1: 3290
Sosman Memorial Lecture Award; Robert B. Vol. 1: 1497
Souder Award; Wilmer Vol. 1: 10068
Soul Train Music Awards Vol. 1: 16967
South African Academy of Science and Arts Literary Prize Vol. 2: 4279
South African Association for the Advancement of Science Certificate of Merit Vol. 2: 4364
South African Chemical Institute Gold Medal Vol. 2: 4320
South African Institute of Architects Award for Excellence Vol. 2: 4334
South African Institute of Architects Award of Merit Vol. 2: 4335
South African Institute of Architects Best Student Award Vol. 2: 4336
South African Institute of Architects Medal of Distinction Vol. 2: 4337
South African Institute of Electrical Engineers Awards Vol. 2: 4339
South African Medal Vol. 2: 4365
South African Sports Merit Award Vol. 2: 4240
South African Veterinary Association Gold Medal Vol. 2: 4360
South Asia Foreign Language and Area Studies Fellowships Vol. 1: 18359
South Atlantic Review Essay Prize Vol. 1: 16979
Southcomb Award; Kenneth W. Vol. 1: 11527
Southeast Review Poetry Contest Vol. 1: 16999
Southern Books Competition Vol. 1: 17011
Southern Cross Award Vol. 2: 71
Southern Cross Package Design Awards Vol. 2: 597

Southgate Memorial Trophy; Hugh M. Vol. 1: 18136
Southwest Asia Service Medal Vol. 1: 8125
Southwest Fine Arts Competition Vol. 1: 12025
Southwest Juried Exhibition Vol. 1: 12025
Southwick Memorial Award; Justin A. Vol. 1: 10837
Souza Award; Felipa da Vol. 1: 10450
Sovereign Awards Vol. 1: 11018
Sower Award Vol. 1: 14014
SP USA Award Vol. 1: 15803
Spaatz Trophy Vol. 1: 13301
Space Achievement Award Vol. 1: 18128
Space Achievement Medal Vol. 2: 5338
Space Flight Award Vol. 1: 1353
Space Flight Medal Vol. 1: 12211
Space Grant Fellowship Program Vol. 1: 8757
Space Operations and Support Award Vol. 1: 2403
Space Pioneer Award Vol. 2: 582
Space Processing Award Vol. 1: 2404
Space Science Award Vol. 1: 2405
Space Systems Award Vol. 1: 2406
Space Technology Hall of Fame Vol. 1: 18129
Spacecraft Design Award Vol. 1: 2406
Spalding Player of the Year Vol. 1: 12398
Spanos Best Graduate Student Paper Award; Nicholas P. Vol. 1: 3416
Sparks Medal; Ben C. Vol. 1: 4167
Sparks-Thomas Award Vol. 1: 1580
Sparks Tutoring Award; G'anne Vol. 1: 5817
Speaker Hall of Fame; Council of Peers Award for Excellence/ Vol. 1: 13785
Spearman Medal Vol. 2: 5430
Speas Airport Award; Jay Hollingsworth Vol. 1: 2407
Special Achievement and Recognition Vol. 1: 8846
Special Achievement Award
- Academy of Motion Picture Arts and Sciences Vol. 1: 110
- Health Science Communications Association Vol 1: 9317
- National Council of Social Security Management Associations Vol 1: 13012
Special Achievement - Man/Woman of the Year Vol. 1: 10931
Special Achievements for the ACHMM Vol. 1: 80
Special Award
- AIIM - The Enterprise Content Management Association Vol. 1: 260
- American Society for Information Science and Technology Vol 1: 3749
- National Association for Interpretation Vol 1: 12348
- National Legal Aid and Defender Association Vol 1: 13416
- Polish Physical Society Vol 2: 4051
Special Award for Dedicated Service Vol. 1: 12093
Special Award of Honor Vol. 1: 10530
Special Award of Stelvio National Park Vol. 2: 3130
Special Award or Citation to Institutions and Individuals Vol. 1: 18225
Special Awards
- American Association of Petroleum Geologists Vol. 1: 1228
- Association of Engineering Geologists Vol 1: 5142
- Institute of Nuclear Materials Management Vol 1: 9924
- Journalism Education Association Vol 1: 11054
- New England Theatre Conference Vol 1: 14058
Special Awards Established by the President Vol. 1: 8555
Special Breed Master Judge Vol. 1: 13541
Special Certificate of Appreciation Vol. 1: 4396
Special Christopher Award Vol. 1: 7393
Special Citation Award Vol. 1: 2558
Special Citation in Journalism Vol. 1: 5642
Special Citations
- American Academy of Periodontology Vol. 1: 731
- National Press Photographers Association Vol 1: 13571
Special Commendation Vol. 1: 11547
Special Distinguished & Outstanding Service Awards Vol. 1: 3716
Special Education Research Vol. 1: 19053
Special Educational Merit Award for Women Vol. 1: 10793
Special Focus Awards Vol. 1: 5985
Special Grand Prix of the Jury Vol. 1: 11944
Special Honorary Member Award Vol. 2: 4160
Special Innovation Award Vol. 1: 9903
Special Interest Group (SIG) Leadership Award Vol. 1: 12600
Special Jubilee Awards Vol. 2: 7437
Special Jury Award Vol. 2: 4538
Special Merit Citation Vol. 1: 2606
Special Olympics Award Vol. 1: 4518
Special President's Award of Merit Vol. 1: 1292
Special Prize Vol. 2: 3136
Special Prize in Memoriam of Rainer Werner Fassbinder Vol. 2: 2304
Special Recognition and Presidential Awards Vol. 1: 13356
Special Recognition Award
- Alberta Construction Safety Association Vol. 1: 367
- American Camping Association Vol 1: 1438
- American College of Preventive Medicine Vol 1: 1725
- American Institute of Certified Public Accountants Vol 1: 2465
- American Meat Science Association Vol 1: 2743
- Asian American Journalists Association Vol 1: 4687
- Association for Research in Vision and Ophthalmology Vol 1: 4955
- Canadian Athletic Therapists Association Vol 1: 6318
- International Technology Education Association Vol 1: 10786
- Manufacturers' Agents for the Foodservice Industry Vol 1: 11501
- States Organization for Boating Access Vol 1: 17275
Special Recognition Awards
- Asphalt Recycling and Reclaiming Association Vol. 1: 4731
- Society for Information Display Vol 1: 16310
- United States Auto Club Vol 1: 17759
Special Recognition for Excellence in Public Relations Vol. 1: 17077
Special Recognition, Mule Vol. 1: 2823
Special Recognition, Person Vol. 1: 2824
Special Research Awards Vol. 1: 8012
Special Service/Achievement Awards Vol. 1: 16021
Special Service Award
- American Rental Association Vol. 1: 3485
- Canadian Mental Health Association - Alberta Division Vol 1: 6722
Special Service Award
- American Association of Avian Pathologists Vol. 1: 996
- Association for Educational Communications and Technology and the ECT Foundation Vol 1: 4879
- CFA Institute Vol 1: 7269
- College Gymnastics Association Vol 1: 7519
- International Reading Association Vol 1: 10598
- National Association of Conservation Districts Vol 1: 12475
Special Service Citation Vol. 1: 2408
Special Services Award Vol. 1: 15530
Special Student Awards Vol. 1: 1342
Specialised Manufacturing Exporter of the Year Vol. 2: 3811
Specialists in Blood Banking Scholarship Awards
- American Association of Blood Banks Vol. 1: 1003
- American Association of Blood Banks Vol 1: 1003
Specialty Bookseller of the Year Award Vol. 1: 6359
Spectrum Award Vol. 1: 18960
Spectrum Awards Design Competition Vol. 1: 2092
Spedding Award; Frank H. Vol. 1: 14445
Speed and Figure Skating Championships Vol. 2: 4834
Speed and Figure Skating National Championships Vol. 1: 17719
Speed Index 61 and under Vol. 1: 2825
Speed Index 62-74 Vol. 1: 2826
Speed Index 74-85 Vol. 1: 2827
Speedo/USMS Coach of the Year Award Vol. 1: 17994
Speedy Award Vol. 1: 14845
Speirs Award; Doris Huestis Vol. 1: 16618
Speiss Award; Ray H. Vol. 1: 3676
Speller Award; Frank Newman Vol. 1: 12066
Speller Award; Thomas H. Vol. 1: 16588
Spellman Award; Cardinal Vol. 1: 7167
Spellman Jazz Masters Award; A. B. Vol. 1: 13103
Spelvin Award; George Vol. 1: 11570
Spence Trophy; G. M. Vol. 2: 3854
Spencer Artistic Achievement Award; Sara Vol. 1: 798
Spencer Award; Beulah K. Vol. 1: 412
Spencer Award; William I. Vol. 1: 19115
Spencer Best After Dinner Speaker of the Year; Ivor Vol. 2: 5951
Spencer-Jones Gold Medal; Harold Vol. 2: 6832
Spencer Memorial Award; Adrian Vol. 2: 6079
Spencer Memorial Award; Norman Vol. 2: 3758
Spencer Postdoctoral Fellowship Program; NAE/ Vol. 1: 12124
Spendiarov International Geological Prize; L. A. Vol. 2: 4395
Sperry Award; Elmer A. Vol. 1: 16589

Sperry Award; Lawrence Vol. 1: 2409
Sperry Founder Award; Albert F. Vol. 1: 10915
Sperry Young Achievement Award; Lawrence Vol. 1: 2409
Speyer Memorial Prize; Ellin P. Vol. 1: 12120
SPHE International Packaging and Handling Design Competition Vol. 1: 9926
SPHE Packaging Competition Vol. 1: 9926
SPI Structural Foam Division Annual Recognition Award Vol. 1: 16859
Spielvogel Award; Carl Vol. 1: 14761
Spiers Memorial Lecture and Prize Vol. 2: 6984
Spies Superstar Awards; Henry Vol. 1: 12706
Spingarn Medal Vol. 1: 12368
Spink Award; J. G. Taylor Vol. 1: 12752
Spink Award; Topps - J. G. Taylor Vol. 1: 17549
Spinoza Award Vol. 1: 18196
Spira Lifetime Achievement Award; Patricia G. Vol. 1: 10797
Spiral of Life Award Vol. 1: 11311
Spirit Award
  Amateur Athletic Union Vol. 1: 508
  International Ticketing Association Vol 1: 10798
  Professional Convention Management Association Vol 1: 15300
Spirit of America Award Vol. 1: 18184
The Spirit of America Award Vol. 1: 4506
Spirit of Broadcasting Award Vol. 1: 12437
Spirit of Caring Award Vol. 1: 7246
Spirit of Flight Award Vol. 1: 12731
Spirit of Hospice Award Vol. 1: 10875
Spirit of Hospice Awards Vol. 1: 14088
Spirit of Saint Louis Award Vol. 1: 15796
Spirit of St. Louis Medal Vol. 1: 4168
Spiritus Awards Vol. 1: 10291
Spitler Award; Gary Vol. 1: 12583
Splenda Pure Magic Award Vol. 1: 8994
Split Summer Festival Vol. 2: 1223
Splitsko ljeto Vol. 2: 1223
Spokesperson for Agriculture Vol. 1: 13960
Sponsor Appreciation Award Vol. 1: 81
Sponsors and Endowment Award Vol. 1: 16904
Sporck-Stegmaier Award; Robison Foundation/B. Robison Vol. 1: 18965
Sport Australia Hall of Fame Vol. 2: 677
Sport in Society Hall of Fame Vol. 1: 7242
Sporting Art Award Vol. 1: 590
Sporting Goods Agents Hall of Fame Vol. 1: 17160
Sporting News Baseball Research Award Vol. 1: 16168
The Sporting News Man of the Year Vol. 1: 17194
Sportive et Sportif Europeen de l'Annee Vol. 2: 4583
Sports and Recreation Award Vol. 1: 14846
Sports Emmy Awards Vol. 1: 12182
Sports Feature of the Year Vol. 2: 7242
Sports Illustrated Sportsman/Sportswoman of the Year Vol. 1: 17227
Sports Journalism of the Year Vol. 2: 7243
Sports Lifetime Achievement Award Vol. 1: 12182
Sports Ministries Award Vol. 1: 12890
Sports Personalities of the Year (Men, Women, Team) Vol. 2: 7244
Sports Personality of the Year Award Vol. 1: 4307
Sports Philatelists International Awards Vol. 1: 17229
Sports Photographer of the Year Vol. 2: 7245
SportsMan and SportsWoman of the Year Vol. 1: 18019
Sportsman of the Year Vol. 1: 17194
Sportswoman of the Year Award Vol. 1: 18851
Sportswomen of the Year Awards Vol. 1: 18875
Spot News Photo Award Vol. 1: 14143
Spot News Video Award Vol. 1: 14144
Spotlight Awards Vol. 1: 12030
Spotton Award for Best Canadian Short Film; NFB - John Vol. 1: 17561
Sprague Memorial Award; Joseph A. Vol. 1: 13572
Sprakvardspris Vol. 2: 4668
Spraragen Memorial Membership Award; William Vol. 1: 4469
Spratt Outstanding Secondary Social Studies Teacher of the Year; William Vol. 1: 11581
Sprengel Agronomic Research Award; Carl Vol. 1: 3876
Sprent Prize; John Frederick Adrian Vol. 2: 371
Spriestersbach Award for Excellence in Teaching; Barbara Vol. 1: 14498
Sprigg Medal; Reg Vol. 2: 323
Spring Art Founder Award; John Vol. 1: 13690
Spring Conference Scholarships Vol. 1: 7560
Spring Show Award Vol. 1: 8524
Springer Award; Bonnie J. Vol. 1: 4645
Springer Award; Fred Vol. 1: 3028
Springer Award; LT GEN. Robert D. Vol. 1: 4644
Springer Award; Russell S. Vol. 1: 16590
Sprinter of the Year Vol. 1: 18457
SPRITE Undergraduate Summer Research Program Vol. 1: 17623
Sproule Aviation Maintenance Marine of the Year Award; Willie D. Vol. 1: 11528
Sproule Memorial Award; J. C. "Cam" Vol. 1: 1229
Sproule Memorial Plaque; J.C. Vol. 1: 6632
Sprout Award; Harold and Margaret Vol. 1: 10764
Spruance Safety Award; William W. Vol. 1: 13301
Spruce Award; Richard Vol. 1: 10148
Spruiell Medical Field Training Exercise Planner Award; Colonel Thomas L. Vol. 1: 5256
SPS Allied Award Vol. 1: 16820
SPS Leadership Scholarships Vol. 1: 16821
Spur Awards Vol. 1: 18703
SPUR: Support for Products Under Research Vol. 2: 7293
Spurgeon III Award; William H. Vol. 1: 8567
Squibb Award Vol. 1: 9697
Squire Award; James R. Vol. 1: 13031
Squire Distinguished Resident Award in Diagnostic Radiology; Lucy Frank Vol. 1: 981
Squires Memorial Senior Brass Award; Blanche Vol. 1: 15884
Squires Memorial Senior Chopin Scholarship; Blanche Vol. 1: 15885
Squires Memorial Woodwind Award; Blanche Vol. 1: 15886
Sreenivasan Memorial Award; IETE-Prof. K. Vol. 2: 2770
Sreenivasaya Memorial Award Vol. 2: 2800
Srinivasa Ramanujan Medal Vol. 2: 2719
Srivastav Award in the Field of Virology; Dr. J. B. Vol. 2: 2629
Srivastava Foundation Award; Prof. B. C. Vol. 2: 2630
SSC Distinguished Service Award Vol. 1: 17282
SSC Gold Medal Vol. 1: 17283
SSC Honorary Membership Award Vol. 1: 17284
St-Laurent Award of Excellence; Louis Vol. 1: 6338
Staats Award; Elmer Vol. 1: 5187
Staats Award; Elmer B. Vol. 2: 810
Staats International Journal Award; Elmer B. Vol. 2: 810
Staats Public Service Career Award; Elmer B. Vol. 1: 12650
Staatspreis fur Consulting Vol. 2: 757
Staatspreis fur das Schonste Buch Vol. 2: 758
Staatspreise fur Werbung Vol. 2: 756
Stachiewicz Medal; Jules
  Canadian Society for Chemical Engineering Vol. 1: 6895
  Canadian Society for Mechanical Engineering Vol 1: 6955
Stack Award for Interpreting Chemistry for the Public; James T. Grady - James H. Vol. 1: 1552
Staf Nees Prize Vol. 2: 1081
Staffell Visual Effects Award; Charles Vol. 2: 5505
Staffing Industry Communications Awards Vol. 1: 4311
Stafford Memorial Award; William Vol. 1: 13181
Stage Awards for Acting Excellence Vol. 2: 5754
Stage Management Award Vol. 1: 17956
Stagg Award; Amos Alonzo Vol. 1: 2046
Stagg Trophy; Amos Alonzo Vol. 1: 13218
Stahl Award; Egon Vol. 2: 2377
Stahl Preis; Egon Vol. 2: 2377
Stahr Award; Jack Vol. 1: 18149
Stainer Preis; Jakob Vol. 2: 749
Staley Prize; J. I. Vol. 1: 15919
Stals Prize for the Humanities Vol. 2: 4283
Stamp Memorial Fund; Dudley Vol. 2: 6914
Stampar Medal; Andrija Vol. 2: 1721
Stampex Exhibition Awards Vol. 2: 6535
Stand Poetry Competition Vol. 2: 7247
Standard and Poor's BBB Rating Vol. 2: 3883
Standard Bank Young Artist Awards Vol. 2: 4191
Standard Bearer Award Vol. 1: 13297
Standard Class Trophy Vol. 1: 16115
Standard Life Audience Award Vol. 2: 5756
Standards Achievement Award Vol. 1: 4062
Standards and Practices Award Vol. 1: 10916
Standards Medal Vol. 1: 2852
Standing Group Grant Vol. 2: 5824
Standish Award; Myles Vol. 1: 14746
Standish-Barry Prize Vol. 2: 6735
Stanfield Distinguished Service Award; Howard E. Vol. 1: 17139
Stanfield Trophy; Robert L. Vol. 1: 6668
Stanford Poetry Prize; Ann Vol. 1: 11591
Stanhope Gold Medal Vol. 2: 6813

Stanley Award; Edward Vol. 1: 15196
Stanley Award; Robert Vol. 1: 18545
Stanleys Vol. 1: 12554
Stannard Baker Award; J. Vol. 1: 13705
Stapp Award; John Paul Vol. 1: 210
Star Boy Award Vol. 2: 1423
Star of Courage Vol. 1: 6096
Star of Gallantry Vol. 2: 216
Star of Military Valour Vol. 1: 6097
STAR (Science to Achieve Results) Research Grants Vol. 1: 17896
Stara Planina Order Vol. 2: 1156
Stark Memorial Award; Kevin Vol. 2: 533
Starkey Award; J. W. Vol. 2: 6938
Starkey-Robinson Award Vol. 1: 6252
Starr Award; Bart Vol. 1: 5493
Starr Award; Paul Vol. 1: 4359
Starr Award; Walter A. Vol. 1: 16022
Starrett Poetry Prize Competition; Agnes Lynch Vol. 1: 18339
Stars of the Industry Awards Vol. 1: 2320
Stars of the Year Vol. 1: 12708
Starz Denver International Film Festival
  Denver Film Society Vol. 1: 8159
  Denver Film Society Vol 1: 8160
  Denver Film Society Vol 1: 8161
  Denver Film Society Vol 1: 8162
  Denver Film Society Vol 1: 8163
Starz People's Choice Award Vol. 1: 8163
Stassart; Prix Vol. 2: 1698
State Allocated Scholarship Award Vol. 1: 14925
State and Regional Intellectual Freedom Achievement Award Vol. 1: 2670
State Association Leadership Award Vol. 1: 12941
State Awards Vol. 1: 14073
State Awards and National Awards Vol. 1: 12465
State Boating Access Program Excellence Award Vol. 1: 17276
State/Canadian Province Award Vol. 1: 12358
State Chairperson of the Year Vol. 1: 18472
State Coordinator Vol. 1: 12800
State CVA Program Excellence Award Vol. 1: 17277
State Development and Construction Corporation Award Vol. 2: 4561
State Director of the Year
  American College of Managed Care Administrators Vol. 1: 1672
  American College of Oncology Administrators Vol 1: 1702
State Director of the Year Award
  American Academy of Medical Administrators Vol. 1: 630
  National Propane Gas Association Vol 1: 13578
State of Hawaii Order of Distinction for Cultural Leadership Vol. 1: 9287
State of the Art Award Vol. 1: 15203
State-of-the-Art of Civil Engineering Award Vol. 1: 3982
State President's Sport Award Vol. 2: 4239
State/Province Art Educator Award Vol. 1: 12277
State/Province Art Educator of the Year Vol. 1: 12277
State/Province Association Newsletter Award Vol. 1: 12278
State/Province Programs or Associations Award Vol. 1: 10713
State Society Publications Awards Vol. 1: 2759
State Statesman Vol. 1: 8847
Stateman in Healtcare Administration Vol. 1: 1703
States Student Award; John D. Vol. 1: 4970
Statesman in Healthcare Administration Vol. 1: 1673
Station of the Year Vol. 1: 14076
Statistics in Chemistry Award Vol. 1: 4316
Statistics New Zealand/Jacoby Prize Vol. 2: 3827
Statistics New Zealand - Jacoby Student Essay Competition Vol. 2: 3828
Statton Lecture; Henry M Vol. 1: 4071
Statuette with Pedestal Vol. 1: 10015
Staubs Precollege Outreach Award; Harry Vol. 1: 2410
Stauder Award; Alfred Vol. 2: 417
Staudinger-Preis; Hermann- Vol. 2: 2174
Stauffer Prizes; Joseph S. Vol. 1: 6120
Steacie Memorial Fellowships Vol. 1: 13977
Steacie Prize Vol. 1: 17288
Stead Prize; Christina Vol. 2: 585
Steadman Award; Richard Vol. 1: 7546
Steavenson Memorial Award Vol. 2: 5250
Stebbins Trophy; James F. Vol. 1: 18715
Steck - Vaughn Award Vol. 1: 17475
Steel Distributor of the Year Award Vol. 1: 5353
Steel Eighties Award Vol. 2: 2660
Steel Guitar Hall of Fame Vol. 1: 10759
Steel Oleander Award Vol. 1: 8948
Steele-Bodger Memorial Scholarship; Harry Vol. 2: 5564
Steele Memorial Senior Romantic Music Scholarship; Maude Vol. 1: 15887
Steen Award; Ralph W. Vol. 1: 8332
Stefanko Best Paper Award Vol. 1: 16361
Steffens Prize; Henrik Vol. 2: 2404
Stegner Award; Wallace Vol. 1: 18269
Stegner Fellowships in Creative Writing; Wallace E. Vol. 1: 7956
Steiger Memorial Award; William Vol. 1: 2346
Stein Award; Rose and Sam Vol. 1: 14474
Stein Memorial Arts Person of the Year Award; Ann G. Vol. 1: 18572
Stein Prize; Fordham- Vol. 1: 8809
Steinberg Award; S. S. Vol. 1: 3504
Steinbock Award; Max Vol. 1: 10481
Steindler Award; Arthur Vol. 1: 14715
Steiner Award for Leadership in Foreign Language Education, K-12; Florence Vol. 1: 1835
Steiner Award for Leadership in Foreign Language Education, Postsecondary; Florence Vol. 1: 1836
Steiner Medal Vol. 2: 152
Steiner Prize; Herbert Vol. 2: 792
Steinmetz Award; Charles Proteus Vol. 1: 9796
Stenback Plaquette Vol. 2: 1396
Stengel Memorial Award; Alfred Vol. 1: 1720
Stennis Student Congress Awards; John C. Vol. 1: 13245
Steno Medal Vol. 2: 1303
Steno Medaljen Vol. 2: 1303
Stephansson Award for Poetry; Stephan G. Vol. 1: 19006
Stephens Family History Award; Edyth Vol. 1: 8386
Stephens Lecture Vol. 2: 5986
Stephenson Award for Outstanding Service; William J. Vol. 1: 13795
Stephenson Medal; George Vol. 2: 6127
Stephenson Memorial Lecture; Marjory Vol. 2: 7099
Stephenson Prize; George Vol. 2: 6185
Stephenson Prize Lecture; Marjory Vol. 2: 7099
Stepinsnki Fund Award Vol. 2: 4469
Stereo Division Awards Vol. 1: 15032
Sterling Staff Competition Vol. 1: 11998
Stern Award Vol. 2: 6505
Stern Award; Philip M. Vol. 1: 18598
Stern Award; Rabbi Malcolm H. Vol. 1: 10996
Stern Humanitarian Award; Rabbi Malcolm H. Vol. 1: 8660
Sternig Award for Short Fiction; Larry and Eleanor Vol. 1: 7875
Stevens Award; Don C. Vol. 1: 2212
Stevens Award; J. C. Vol. 1: 3983
Stevens Award; K. G. Vol. 2: 7445
Stevens Competition Vol. 2: 7385
Stevens Memorial Award; Barbara Vol. 1: 13182
Stevenson - Hamilton Award Vol. 2: 4382
Stevenson Trophy Vol. 1: 9904
Stevie Award; Uncle Vol. 2: 4226
Steward Avian Research Fund; Paul Vol. 1: 9717
Stewardson, Keefe LeBrun Travel Grants Vol. 1: 2444
Stewart Award; Claude A. Vol. 2: 484
Stewart Award; James E. Vol. 1: 1001
Stewart Awards; Ada Mayo Vol. 1: 1407
Stewart Awards; Paul A. Vol. 1: 18755
Stewart Cup; Ross Vol. 1: 18179
Stewart Engineering-Humanities Award; Robert E. Vol. 1: 3863
Stewart Prize; Douglas Vol. 2: 585
Steyn Prize for Natural Science and Technical Achievement; M. T. Vol. 2: 4284
Stichting Internationaal Orgelconcours Vol. 2: 3675
Stichting Sikkensprijs Vol. 2: 3665
Stier Award; Elizabeth Fleming Vol. 1: 9855
Stiftelsen Kortfilmfestivalen Vol. 2: 3910
Stiftelsen Natur och Kulturs oversattarpris Vol. 2: 4669
Stiles Memorial Award; William C. Vol. 1: 17970
Still Medal; Percy Vol. 2: 6137
Still Medallion of Honor; Andrew Taylor Vol. 1: 672
Stillwell Award Vol. 2: 465
Stimulation of Research Award Vol. 1: 3064
Stinchcomb Memorial Lecture and Award; Wayne W. Vol. 1: 5463
Stine Award in Materials Engineering and Science; Charles M. A. Vol. 1: 2497
Stipendium ur Lena Vendelfelts minnesfond Vol. 2: 4670
Stirling Medal; John B. Vol. 1: 8468
Stirling Memorial Award; Nadin Vol. 1: 6723
Stitt Award Vol. 1: 5257
Stitt Lecture Award; Edward Rhodes Vol. 1: 5257
STLE National Award Vol. 1: 16884
Stock-Gedachtnispreis; Alfred- Vol. 2: 2175
Stock of the Year Vol. 1: 15355
Stockberger Achievement Award; Warner W. Vol. 1: 10562
Stockholm Junior Water Prize Vol. 2: 389
Stockman Award Vol. 2: 3912

Stoddart Award for Outstanding Performance; Richard R. Vol. 1: 9576
Stodghill Award; Don and Pat Vol. 1: 13183
Stoeger Composer's Chair; Elise L. Vol. 1: 7278
Stoeger Prize; Elise L. Vol. 1: 7278
Stohr Medal; A.E. Vol. 2: 534
Stoker Awards; Bram Vol. 1: 9490
Stokes Memorial Award Vol. 1: 13357
Stokes Royal Engineers Vol. 1: 15654
Stokinger Award; Herbert E. Vol. 1: 2347
Stokinger Award Lecture Vol. 1: 2347
Stokstad Award; E.L.R. Vol. 1: 3796
Stolaruk International Entertainment Competition; Vivian Vivio Vol. 1: 759
Stollery Award; Robert Vol. 1: 6425
Stompin Tom Award Vol. 1: 8326
Stone Award; Donald C. Vol. 1: 3818
Stone Award for Excellence in Education; Donald C. Vol. 1: 3454
Stone Award; I. F. Vol. 1: 12088
Stone Award; Peter Vol. 2: 5117
Stone Graduate Fellowship; Ralph W. Vol. 1: 13796
Stone Memorial Award; Walter Vol. 2: 451
Stoneman Fellowship; Bertha Vol. 2: 4312
Stora priset Vol. 2: 4671
Storch Award in Fuel Chemistry; Henry H. Vol. 1: 1581
Store of the Year Vol. 1: 12682
Storer Award Vol. 1: 4079
Storey International Award; Robert G. Vol. 1: 7193
Stork Fellow; Charles Wharton Vol. 1: 5491
Storrs Memorial Piano Scholarships; Evelyn Bonar Vol. 1: 12041
Story of the Year Vol. 1: 17369
Storywriting and Art Competition Vol. 2: 107
Stouffer Award Vol. 1: 4281
Stoughton Award for Young Teachers; Bradley Vol. 1: 4709
Stoughton Award for Young Teachers of Metallurgy; Bradley Vol. 1: 4709
Stover Memorial Award; Elizabeth Matchett Vol. 1: 17057
Stowe Award; Allen B. Vol. 1: 18150
Stowe Sportsmanship Award; Dr. Allen B. Vol. 1: 18150
Stowell-Orbison Awards Vol. 1: 17725
Stoye Awards Vol. 1: 4080
STP Most Improved Championship Driver Award Vol. 1: 17754
Strachauer Medal; Ehrma Vol. 1: 18588
Strader Memorial Award; Noel Ross Vol. 1: 7530
Stradford Award; C. Francis Vol. 1: 12748
Straelen; Prix van Vol. 2: 1844
Stranahan Award; Jason G. (Stranny) Vol. 1: 17971
Strategic HR Leadership Award Vol. 1: 16238
Strategic Leadership and Governance Awards Vol. 1: 10312
Strathglass Trophy Vol. 1: 18715
Strating Prize for Preventive Medicine; Albert Vol. 2: 4285
Stratton Award; Samuel Wesley Vol. 1: 17805
Stratton Medal; Henry M. Vol. 1: 4071
Straus Award; Flora Stieglitz Vol. 1: 7341
Straus Award; Ralph I. Vol. 1: 13467
Strausbaugh Club Relations Award; Bill Vol. 1: 15323
Strauss Award; Sidney L. Vol. 1: 14169
Street Luge Championship Vol. 2: 7249
Street Stock Endurance Championship Vol. 1: 10524
Strega Prize Vol. 2: 3132
Stresemann-Foerderung; Erwin- Vol. 2: 2209
Strickler Innovation in Instruction Award; Les B. Vol. 1: 3497
Striker Junior Paper Award; Gyorgy Vol. 2: 2508
Strimple Award; Harrell L. Vol. 1: 14815
String Teacher of the Year Award Vol. 1: 4321
Stritch Medal Vol. 1: 11434
Strive and Succeed Award Vol. 1: 9486
Strock Award; Lester W. Vol. 1: 16181
Strong Award; Dorothy and Bruce Vol. 1: 13734
Stroud Memorial Award; Clara Vol. 1: 4443
Stroud Memorial Award; Ida Wells Vol. 1: 4444
Stroud Memorial Rookie of the Year Award (National Midget Car Div.); Bob Vol. 1: 17760
Stroukoff Memorial Trophy; Larissa Vol. 1: 16116
Strousse Award Vol. 1: 15197
Structural Foam Division Awards Vol. 1: 16860
Structural Materials Distinguished Materials Scientist/Engineer Award Vol. 1: 11818
Structural Materials Distinguished Service Award Vol. 1: 11819
Structure Moved the Longest Distance on Land Vol. 1: 10255
Structure Moved with the Most Square Footage on One Floor Vol. 1: 10256
Structures, Structural Dynamics, and Materials Award Vol. 1: 2411
Strzelecki Prize; Jan Vol. 2: 4019
Stuart Certificate; Akroyd Vol. 2: 6138
Stuart Memorial Lectureship; Charles A. Vol. 1: 5975
Stuart Prize; Akroyd Vol. 2: 6657
Stubbs Medal; Oliver Vol. 2: 6000
Stubbs Research Grant; E. L. Vol. 1: 11745
Stuckenbruck Person of the Year Award; Linn Vol. 1: 15374
Stuckey Award; Bill Vol. 1: 1969
Studded Gold Jewelry Vol. 2: 2570
Studded Precious Metal Jewelry Vol. 2: 2571
Student Achievement Award Vol. 1: 6195
Student Achievement Grants Vol. 1: 14008
Student Achievement Scholarship Vol. 1: 14946
Student Advocacy Award Vol. 1: 10022
Student Aid Award Vol. 1: 18492
Student and New Investigator Travel Awards Vol. 1: 8505
Student Article Contest Vol. 1: 6693
Student Assistance Scheme Vol. 2: 5380
Student-Athlete of the Week Vol. 1: 12891
Student Award
American Society of Heating, Refrigerating and Air-Conditioning Engineers Vol. 1: 4063
Association of Consulting Engineers New Zealand Vol 2: 3698
Canadian Association for Health, Physical Education, Recreation and Dance Vol 1: 6201
Canadian Dam Association Vol 1: 6451
Canadian Society of Microbiologists Vol 1: 7011
Federation of Analytical Chemistry and Spectroscopy Societies Vol 1: 8619
National Council on Family Relations Vol 1: 13044
National Federation of State Poetry Societies Vol 1: 13184
Student Award for Excellence Vol. 1: 9873
Student Award for International Understanding Vol. 2: 5829
Student Award for Scholarly Writing Vol. 1: 16192
Student Award in Systematic Paleontology Vol. 1: 14811
Student Award - Postgraduate Division Vol. 2: 5788
Student Award - Undergraduate Division Vol. 2: 5798
Student Awards
American Institute of Chemical Engineers Vol. 1: 2498
Association of Photographers Vol 2: 5152
Czechoslovak Society of Arts and Sciences Vol 1: 8014
Dechema - Society for Chemical Engineering and Biotechnology Vol 2: 2074
Remote Sensing and Photogrammetry Society Vol 2: 6596
Sea Grant Association Vol 1: 15951
The Wildlife Society Vol 1: 18749
Student Awards for Outstanding Research Vol. 1: 16185
Student Awards for Precious Metals Research Vol. 1: 10554
Student Book Prize Vol. 1: 7970
Student Bursary Vol. 2: 7298
Student Business Initiative Award Vol. 1: 5621
Student Chapter Award Vol. 1: 9953
Student Chapter Awards Vol. 1: 1658
Student Chapter of the Year Award
American Society for Information Science and Technology Vol. 1: 3750
International Facility Management Association Vol 1: 10399
Student Chapter Sponsor Award of Excellence Vol. 1: 12279
Student Community Outreach Award Vol. 1: 618
Student Competition for Overseas Music Study Award Vol. 2: 4116
Student Competitions Vol. 1: 10806
Student Composer Awards Vol. 1: 5957
Student Composition Competition Vol. 1: 12037
Student Design Competition
Institute of Store Planners Vol. 1: 9942
Institution of Professional Engineers New Zealand Vol 2: 3747
Southeastern Theatre Conference Vol 1: 17019
Student Design Project Competition Vol. 1: 4063
Student Electives Scheme Vol. 2: 6370
Student Essay Competition in Healthcare Management Vol. 1: 1659
Student Excellence Award Vol. 1: 6809
Student Gold Quill Awards Vol. 1: 10160
Student Journalist Impact Award Vol. 1: 11054
Student Leader of the Year Award Vol. 1: 174
Student Leadership Awards Vol. 1: 3062
Student Liaison Award Vol. 1: 7755

Student Lighting Design Awards Vol. 2: 6383
Student Literary Award Vol. 1: 13081
Student Medal Vol. 1: 15732
Student Membership Challenge Vol. 1: 6810
Student of the Year Award Vol. 1: 15050
Student Paper Award
American Society for Bioethics and Humanities Vol. 1: 3572
Environmental Design Research Association Vol 1: 8501
Student Paper Awards
American Society of Agricultural and Biological Engineers Vol. 1: 3864
Society of Naval Architects and Marine Engineers Vol 1: 16767
Student Paper of the Year Award Vol. 1: 15375
Student Paper Prize Vol. 1: 16281
Student Photo Contest Vol. 1: 1375
Student Planner Award Vol. 1: 3213
Student Poster Award Vol. 1: 6246
Student Poster Prize Vol. 2: 304
Student Presentation Award
Canadian Acoustical Association Vol. 1: 6147
Canadian Cardiovascular Society Vol 1: 6379
Student Prize Vol. 2: 3780
Student Prize Essay/Project Vol. 1: 11961
Student Prize of Excellence Vol. 1: 5507
Student Prizes Vol. 2: 5857
Student Professional Paper Award Vol. 1: 5143
Student Recognition Vol. 1: 5392
Student Recognition Certificate Vol. 1: 1977
Student Research Award Vol. 2: 2320
Student Research Award
American Geriatrics Society Vol. 1: 2131
American Psychological Association - Division of Family Psychology (Division 43) Vol 1: 3332
Gerontological Society of America Vol 1: 9065
National Academic Advising Association Vol 1: 12094
Student Research Award Competition Vol. 1: 3410
Student Research Award for Clinical Child Psychology Vol. 1: 3404
Student Research Awards
American Association for Clinical Chemistry Vol. 1: 893
American Psychological Association - Adult Development and Aging Division (Division 20) Vol 1: 3298
Student Research Fellowship Award Vol. 1: 2086
Student Research Fellowships
Alpha Omega Alpha Honor Medical Society Vol. 1: 425
Foundation for Digestive Health and Nutrition Vol 1: 8836
Student Research Grant Vol. 1: 3527
Student Research Paper Vol. 1: 16399
Student Research Prize Vol. 2: 1353
Student Research Training Award Vol. 1: 14628
Student Researcher Award Vol. 2: 5103
Student/Resident Award Vol. 1: 1171
Student Scholars Award Vol. 1: 6537
Student Scholarships
Delta Omicron Vol. 1: 8153
National Society for Histotechnology Vol 1: 13723
Society of Wetland Scientists Vol 1: 16905
Student Section Advisor Award Vol. 1: 4169
Student Service Vol. 1: 11780
Student Television Awards Vol. 2: 7045
Student Translation Award Vol. 1: 4366
Student Travel Award Vol. 2: 3781
Student Travel Awards
American Psychological Association - Society for the Study of Lesbian, Gay and Bisexual Concerns (Division 44) Vol. 1: 3398
European Society for Biomaterials Vol 2: 5858
International Society of Chemical Ecology Vol 1: 10706
Society for Industrial and Applied Mathematics Vol 1: 16282
Teratology Society Vol 1: 17447
Student Writing and Development Award Vol. 1: 11336
Student Writing Contest Vol. 1: 2035
Student/Young Scientist Travel Award Vol. 2: 2122
Studentship Awards Vol. 1: 5224
Studer Preis; Willi Vol. 2: 4903
Studies Book Award Vol. 1: 16980
Study Abroad Program Vol. 1: 15472
Study Circles Challenge Trophies Vol. 2: 4571
Study Grant Awards Vol. 2: 277
Study Grants Vol. 2: 4298
Study/Internship Abroad Vol. 1: 9478
Study Scholarship Vol. 2: 4610
Study Tour Fellowships Vol. 1: 16558
Stukus Trophy - Coach of the Year; Annis Vol. 1: 6518
Stulberg International String Competition Vol. 1: 17312
Stumph Award for Excellence in Publication Vol. 1: 12335
Sturdy Oaks Award Vol. 1: 4621
Sture Centerwalls Pris Vol. 2: 4641
Sturgeon Memorial Award; Theodore Vol. 1: 7239
Sturgis Medal Vol. 1: 16532
Stuttgart Literary Prize Vol. 2: 2415
STUVA Prize Vol. 2: 2427
Styka Award; Adam Vol. 1: 1806
SubbaRow Memorial Lecture; Dr. Yellapragada Vol. 2: 2720
Subcontractor of the Year Vol. 1: 18120
Sublette Award of Excellence; Louise Vol. 1: 15915
Submarine/ASW Writing Award Vol. 1: 14002
Subscription Sales Team of the Year Vol. 2: 5730
Suburban Journalist of the Year Vol. 1: 17315
Suden/Frances Hellebrandt Professional Opportunity Awards; Caroline tum Vol. 1: 3181
Sudler Cup Vol. 1: 16972
Sudler Flag of Honor Vol. 1: 16973
Sudler International High School Marching Band Championship Video Competition Vol. 1: 16975
Sudler International Wind Band Composition Competition; Louis Vol. 1: 16974
Sudler Shield Vol. 1: 16975
Sudler Silver Scroll Vol. 1: 16976
Sudler Trophy Vol. 1: 16977
Sudman Student Paper Competition; Seymour Vol. 1: 939
Sudreys Fund Vol. 2: 7106
Suffness Young Investigators Symposium Award; Matt Vol. 1: 4213
Sugg Heritage Award Vol. 2: 6174
Suggs Rolex Rookie of the Year Award; Louise Vol. 1: 11203
Suhr Husband and Wife Team Award; Bob and Julie Vol. 1: 1970
Sukeslained Award; V.J. Vol. 2: 1367
Sullins, Jr., Award for Outstanding Service in Optometry; W. David Vol. 1: 5258
Sullivan Fishery Conservation Award; Carl R. Vol. 1: 2036
Sullivan International Membership Award; Carl R. Vol. 1: 2037
Sullivan Memorial Award; James E. Vol. 1: 509
Sullivan Trophy; Senator Joseph A. Vol. 1: 6669
Sulman Prize Vol. 2: 49
Sulzberger Memorial Award and Lectureship; Marion B. Vol. 1: 569
Summer Grants for Upper Division and Graduate Students Vol. 1: 15597
Summer Music Centers Awards Vol. 1: 13131
Summer Paid Internships Vol. 1: 17908
Summer Stipends Vol. 1: 11631
Summer Studentships Vol. 1: 6710
Summers Distinguished Merit Award; Alex J. Vol. 1: 2316
Summers Poetry Prize; Hollis Vol. 1: 14484
Summit Award Vol. 1: 16741
The Summit Award Vol. 1: 10096
Summit Awards Vol. 1: 18185
Summit Quinphos Award Vol. 2: 3801
Sumpter Excellence in Teaching Award; Robert Vol. 1: 13385
SunAmco Medal Vol. 1: 10816
Sundance Film Festival Awards Vol. 1: 17328
Sunday Times Watercolour competition; Singer Friedlander/ Vol. 2: 6523
Sunder Lal Hora Medal Vol. 2: 2721
Sunderland Award; George B. Vol. 1: 10714
Sungurlu Memorial Award for Best International Student Poster; Ozan Vol. 1: 1230
Sunkist Young Designer Award
American Society of Agricultural and Biological Engineers Vol. 1: 3848
American Society of Agricultural and Biological Engineers Vol 1: 3865
Sunshine Award
Society of Professional Journalists Vol. 1: 16839
Young Audiences of Greater Cleveland Vol 1: 19087
Suntory Prize for Community Cultural Activities Vol. 2: 3333
Suntory Prize for Social Sciences and Humanities Vol. 2: 3334
Supelco/Nicholas Pelick Research Award Vol. 1: 2970
Super Bowl Vol. 1: 13228
Super Bowl Most Valuable Player Vol. 1: 13227
Super Senior Service Award Vol. 1: 18151
Super Stock Puller of the Year Vol. 1: 13862
Superchannel Award Vol. 1: 19078
Superintendent of the Year Vol. 1: 6538
Superior Achievement Award Vol. 1: 9918
Superior Honor Award Vol. 1: 17875

Supple Religion Writer of the Year Award Vol. 1: 15616
Supplier Awards Vol. 2: 5585
Supplier Excellence Award Vol. 1: 2206
Supplier of the Year
Data Publishers Association Vol. 2: 5731
National Ground Water Association Vol 1: 13298
Supplier of the Year Award
American Meat Institute Vol. 1: 2732
Awards and Recognition Association Vol 1: 5610
National Minority Supplier Development Council Vol 1: 13458
Supplier Web Award Vol. 1: 15390
Suppliers Golden Achievement Award Vol. 1: 15391
Supply Chain Executive of the Year Vol. 1: 6575
Support of Science Award Vol. 1: 7898
Supreme Champion
International Sheep Dog Society Vol. 2: 6290
Palomino Horse Breeders of America Vol 1: 14822
Supreme Kight and Supreme Lady Vol. 1: 5967
Supreme Order of Christ (Militia of Our Lord Jesus Christ) Vol. 2: 7418
Supreme Undergraduate Award Vol. 1: 438
Surgan Victim Activist Award; Edith Vol. 1: 13504
Surrency Prize; Erwin C. Vol. 1: 3759
Survey and General Instrument Company Award Vol. 2: 5266
Surveying and Mapping Award Vol. 1: 3984
Surveying Excellence Award Vol. 1: 13756
Surveyor Award For Local Government Vol. 2: 5086
Survivability Award Vol. 1: 2412
Survivors' Club Vol. 1: 10176
Susman Prize; Gene Wise - Warren Vol. 1: 4333
Sustainability in Design and Use Award Vol. 2: 6087
Sustained Achievement Award Vol. 1: 15627
Sustained Lifetime Achievement Award Vol. 1: 16405
Sustained Superior Performance Award Vol. 1: 510
Sustaining Membership Lecture Award Vol. 1: 5259
Sutermeister; Isaac Ray Award in Memory of Margaret Vol. 1: 3285
Sutherland Award; Edwin H. Vol. 1: 4009
Sutherland Prize; Donald M. Vol. 1: 3760
Sutherland Prize; Kenneth J. G. Vol. 2: 611
Sutherland Trophy Vol. 2: 5309
Suttle Award; H. K. Vol. 2: 5901
Svenska Akademiens pris for introduktion av svensk kultur utomlands Vol. 2: 4672
Svenska Akademiens Svensklararpris Vol. 2: 4673
Svenska Akademiens Teaterpris Vol. 2: 4674
Sverdrup Civil Engineering Management Award; John I. Parcel - Leif J. Vol. 1: 3969
Sverdrup Medal Vol. 1: 16533
Svjetski Festival Animiranih Filmova Vol. 2: 1241
SW Carey Medal Vol. 2: 466
Swackhamer Peace Essay Contest Vol. 1: 14437
Swaminathan 60th Birthday Commemoration Lecture; Professor S. Vol. 2: 2722
Swan Premium Vol. 2: 6146
Swanberg Distinguished Service Award; Harold Vol. 1: 2771
Swarup Memorial Lecture; Professor Har Vol. 2: 2723
Swastek Award; Rev. Joseph V. Vol. 1: 15148
Swearingen Award for Outstanding Chapter Achievement and Excellence in Chapter Service; Harry S. Vol. 1: 3455
Swearingen Award; Noble J. Vol. 1: 5350
Sweeney; Academic Award in Memory of Stephen B. Vol. 1: 10314
Sweeney Award; Catherine H. Vol. 1: 2298
Sweeney Award; Craig Vol. 1: 18060
Sweeney Award; Michael A.J. Vol. 2: 4353
Sweeney Medal; Edward C. Vol. 1: 8562
Sweepstakes Winner Vol. 1: 13135
Sweet Fellowship; Georgina Vol. 2: 194
Swimmer of the Year Award Vol. 1: 18423
Swimming Athlete of the Year Award Vol. 1: 17734
Swimming Coach of the Year Vol. 1: 6670
Swinbank Award Vol. 2: 5632
Swiney Prize for a Work on Jurisprudence Vol. 2: 6922
Swings; Prix Pol Vol. 2: 1098
Swiss Music - Edition Vol. 2: 4907
Swiss Poster Award Vol. 2: 4905
The Swiss Re Award Vol. 2: 4125
Swissair/Crossair Special Prize Vol. 2: 4864
Swit Journalism Prize; David Vol. 1: 17104
Sword of Ignatius Loyola Award Vol. 1: 15796
Sword of Loyola Vol. 1: 11435
Swormstedt Award
Professional Convention Management Association Vol. 1: 15301
Specialty Graphic Imaging Association Vol 1: 17118
Sybesma Award; Thea Vol. 2: 3625
Sydney International Piano Competition of Australia Vol. 2: 413
Sydney Risk Prize foraOutstandingaOriginalaScript by an Emerging Playwright Vol. 1: 9196
Sydney *Sun* Aria Contest Vol. 2: 690
Sydnor Award; Charles S. Vol. 1: 17038
Sykes Memorial Award; George Vol. 2: 6521
Sylvester-Bradley Award Vol. 2: 6517
Sylvester Medal Vol. 2: 6917
Sylvia Cup Design Competition Vol. 1: 16504
Sylvie Gravel Prize Vol. 2: 1233
Syme Research Prize; David Vol. 2: 713
Symington Award; W. Stuart Vol. 1: 305
Symmes Municipal Award; Lee Vol. 1: 14584
Symons Memorial Medal Vol. 2: 6847
Symposium Paper Award Vol. 1: 4064
Syncrude Canada Innovation Award Vol. 1: 6896
Synder Excellence Award; Mayrose Vol. 1: 1408
Synge Award; John L. Vol. 1: 15767
Syngenta Award Vol. 1: 3194
Syngenta Corp Protection American Phytopathological Society Award Vol. 1: 17367
Syngenta Crop Protection Award in Agronomy Vol. 1: 17368
Syngenta Crop Protection Recognition Award Vol. 1: 3877
Syngenta Nematology Award Vol. 1: 16775
Syntex Award in Physical Organic Chemistry Vol. 1: 6903
Synthes Award Vol. 1: 14625
Szczesny Prize; Commander Kazimierz Vol. 2: 4019
Szekely Prize Vol. 1: 5649
Szigeti Violin Competition; Jozsef Vol. 2: 2504
Szilard Lectureship Award; Leo Vol. 1: 3137
Szold Award; Henrietta Vol. 1: 9232
T & R (Insurance Services) Limited Prize Vol. 2: 6029
T-Mobile All-Rookie Team Vol. 1: 12764
T-Mobile Rookie of the Year Vol. 1: 12765
Tableman Award; Betty Vol. 1: 11722
Tabler Memorial Scholarship Award; Pat Vol. 1: 7399
TAC Heptathlon Award Vol. 1: 18443
Tachau Teacher of the Year Award; Mary K. Bonsteel Vol. 1: 14701
Tacussel; Prix Jacques Vol. 2: 4846
Taggart Award; Arthur F. Vol. 1: 16362
Taggart Award for Texas Newspaper Leader of the Year; Pat Vol. 1: 17467
Taishoff Award for Excellence in Broadcast Journalism; Sol Vol. 1: 13558
Tait Award of Excellence; John Vol. 1: 6339
Tait Trophy Vol. 1: 9260
Taiwanese Film of the Year Vol. 2: 4952
Taiwanese Filmmaker of the Year Vol. 2: 4952
Tajima Prize Vol. 2: 4847
Take Pride in America Contest Vol. 1: 14750
Talbert Junior Sportsmanship Award; Bill Vol. 1: 10791
Talbert Junior Sportsmanship Awards; Bill Vol. 1: 18152
Talbot-Ponsonby Prize for Agricultural Valuation Vol. 2: 6669
Talbot Prize for African Anthropology; Amaury Vol. 2: 6676
Talley EMS Instructor/Coordinator of the Year Award; Mary Ann Vol. 1: 12528
Tallix Foundry Prize Vol. 1: 13690
Tallmadge Award for Contributions to Coating Technology; John A. Vol. 1: 2499
Tamisiea Award; John A. Vol. 1: 211
Tampere International Short Film Festival Vol. 2: 1427
Tampereen Kansainvaliset lyhytelokuvajuhlat Grand Prix Vol. 2: 1427
Tanabe Young Investigator Award Vol. 1: 1637
Tanagho Award Vol. 2: 3607
Tanaka Distinguished Achievement Award; Junichiro Vol. 1: 10555
Tanaka Memorial Dissertation Award in Psychology; Jeffrey S. Vol. 1: 3314
Tanesse; Prix Vol. 2: 1699
Tanner Award; Martin W. Vol. 1: 17223
Tanner-Vandeput-Boswick Burn Prize
International Burn Foundation Vol. 1: 10286
International Society for Burn Injuries Vol 1: 10641
Tanner-Vandeput Prize for Burn Research
International Burn Foundation Vol. 1: 10286
International Society for Burn Injuries Vol 1: 10641
Tanneyhill Award; Ann Vol. 1: 13883
Tantramar Trophy Vol. 1: 6671
Taormina Memorial Award; Silvio C. Vol. 1: 12592

Tapling Medal Vol. 2: 6856
TAPPI Fellow Award Vol. 1: 17396
TAPPI Gold Medal Vol. 1: 17394
Taran Family Memorial Award Vol. 1: 9034
Targa D'Oro Citta Di Sondrio Vol. 2: 3130
Target Award Vol. 1: 8202
Tarjan Award; George Vol. 1: 3291
Tarnopolsky Human Rights Award; The Honourable Walter S. Vol. 1: 6340
Tarnopolsky Medal; Hon. Walter S. Vol. 1: 10325
Tarrega; Certamen Internacional de Guitarra Francisco Vol. 2: 4473
Tarrega International Guitar Competition; Francisco Vol. 2: 4473
Tasker Documentary Award; Rex Vol. 1: 5505
Tata Gold Medal Vol. 2: 2661
Tate Award; Barbara Vol. 2: 7220
Tate Award for Undergraduate Academic Advising; John Vol. 1: 18322
Tate International Award; John T. Vol. 1: 2548
Tate Medal for International Leadership in Physics Vol. 1: 2548
Tau Beta Pi Laureate Vol. 1: 17404
Taubeneck Award; Marie Vol. 1: 17448
Tauber Prize; Richard Vol. 2: 5050
The Tauchi Memorial Award Vol. 2: 3279
Taurman Voice Scholarship; Mikanna Clark Vol. 1: 12000
Taussig Article Award; Frank W. Vol. 1: 14516
Tavares Award; R.C. Vol. 2: 3158
Tawara Gold Medal Vol. 2: 3210
Taxpayers Award Vol. 2: 2423
Taxpayers*F* Friend Award Vol. 1: 13838
Taylor/Alton Blakeslee Graduate Student Fellowships; Rennie Vol. 1: 7873
Taylor and Francis Award Vol. 2: 3611
Taylor and Francis Best Letter Award Vol. 2: 6597
Taylor Award; Florence Vol. 2: 735
Taylor Award for Private Gardens; Kathryn S. Vol. 1: 14074
Taylor Award for Voluntary Service; Dwain Vol. 1: 14847
Taylor Award; Franklin V. Vol. 1: 3305
Taylor Award in Modern American Poetry; Aiken Vol. 1: 15982
Taylor Award of Merit; E. P. Vol. 1: 11018
Taylor Award; Vice Admiral Rufus L. Vol. 1: 13452
Taylor Awards; Deems Vol. 1: 4004
Taylor Body-of-Work Award; Sydney Vol. 1: 5209
Taylor Book Awards; Sydney Vol. 1: 5210
Taylor Distinguished Service Award; Fan Vol. 1: 5289
Taylor Key Award Vol. 1: 16156
Taylor Manuscript Award; Sydney Vol. 1: 5211
Taylor Medal; David W. Vol. 1: 16768
Taylor Medal; Florence Vol. 2: 237
Taylor Medal; J. Hall Vol. 1: 4170
Taylor Medal; R. M. Vol. 1: 12845
Taylor Memorial Bowl; Joanna Sliski Vol. 1: 15895
Taylor Memorial Lecture; Norman Vol. 2: 3802
Taylor Memorial Medal; Braid Vol. 2: 6565
Taylor (of Australia) Prize; George Vol. 2: 6658
Taylor Prize; Lilian Coleman Vol. 1: 15499
Taylor Research Medal; Frederick W. Vol. 1: 16730
TBS, Inc. Technical Services Award Vol. 1: 9611
TCAC Grants Vol. 1: 17383
TCG/MetLife Foundation Extended Collaboration Grants for Artists Vol. 1: 17510
TCG/NEA Designer Fellows Vol. 1: 17507
Tchaikovsky Competition; International Vol. 2: 4392
TD Canadian Children's Literature Award Vol. 1: 6395
TDMA Hall of Fame Vol. 1: 5606
Te Kura Pounamu Award Vol. 2: 3753
Teacher as Researcher Grant Vol. 1: 10599
Teacher Awards Vol. 1: 7563
Teacher Educational Mini-Grants Vol. 1: 7186
Teacher Fellow Award Vol. 1: 14280
Teacher of the Year
  Correctional Education Association - Region III Vol. 1: 7831
  Ladies Professional Golf Association Vol 1: 11204
Teacher of the Year Award
  Estonian Education Personnel Union Vol. 2: 1355
  Professional Golfers' Association of America Vol 1: 15324
Teacher of the Year Awards Vol. 1: 12362
Teacher-Researcher Grants Vol. 1: 13032
Teacher Travel Fellowship Award Vol. 2: 2812
Teacher's Award Vol. 2: 6464
Teachers Who Inspire Vol. 1: 15843
Teaching Award
  Ambulatory Pediatric Association Vol. 1: 532
  American Horticultural Society Vol 1: 2299
Teaching Award of Excellence Vol. 1: 14281
Teaching Awards Vol. 1: 1588
Teaching Awards Program Vol. 1: 3400
Teaching Career Enhancement Awards Vol. 1: 3182
Teaching Excellence Awards Vol. 1: 2422
Teague Space Award; Olin E. Vol. 1: 1349
Team Awards Vol. 1: 10624
Team of the Year
  Asian Football Confederation Vol. 2: 3403
  Kansas City Barbeque Society Vol 1: 11077
  Ohio Middle School Association Vol 1: 14476
Teambuild Vol. 2: 6128
Tech-Savvy Hotels Award Vol. 1: 7719
Technical Achievement Award Vol. 1: 9577
Technical Achievement Award
  Institute of Electrical and Electronics Engineers - Computer Society Vol. 1: 9816
  NACE International: The Corrosion Society Vol 1: 12067
  National Association of Corrosion Engineers Vol 1: 12488
Technical and Feature Writing Awards Vol. 1: 2760
Technical and Scientific Communication Award Vol. 1: 13033
Technical Association of the Australian and New Zealand Pulp and Paper Industry Awards Vol. 2: 45
Technical Award Vol. 1: 16613
Technical Committee Prize Paper Awards Vol. 1: 9825
Technical Council Distinguished Individual Service Award Vol. 1: 9826
Technical Optics Award Vol. 2: 315
Technical Paper Award Vol. 1: 4065
Technical Paper Awards
  Institute of Quarrying - England Vol. 2: 6076
  Wire Association International Vol 1: 18768
Technical Standards Board Certificate of Appreciation Vol. 1: 16591
Technical Standards Board Outstanding Contribution Award Vol. 1: 16591
Technical Writing Awards Vol. 1: 337
Technician Diploma Vol. 2: 6025
Technician of the Month Award Vol. 1: 3908
Technician of the Year
  Association of Public-Safety Communications Officials - International Vol. 1: 5322
  ETA International - Electronics Technicians Association, International Vol 1: 8536
Technician of the Year Award
  American Association for Laboratory Animal Science Vol. 1: 918
  International Society of Certified Electronics Technicians Vol 1: 10702
  Professional Aviation Maintenance Association Vol 1: 15264
Technician Publication Award Vol. 1: 919
Technician Recognition Award Vol. 1: 918
Technician Safety Practitioner Scholarship Vol. 2: 6193
Technicolor/Herbert T. Kalmus Gold Medal Award Vol. 1: 16752
Technipro Best Oral Presentation Vol. 2: 141
Technologist of the Year
  American Medical Technologists Vol. 1: 2761
  American Society for Clinical Pathology Vol 1: 3604
  Society of Medical Laboratory Technologists of South Africa Vol 2: 4259
  Society of Medical Laboratory Technologists of South Africa Vol 2: 4260
Technology Achievement Award Vol. 1: 17137
Technology and Engineering Awards Vol. 1: 12183
Technology Award Vol. 1: 13299
Technology Award
  American Society of Heating, Refrigerating and Air-Conditioning Engineers Vol. 1: 4066
  Royal Agricultural Society of England Vol 2: 6670
Technology Awards Vol. 2: 7046
Technology Honor Society Vol. 1: 17426
Technology Marketing ICON Awards Vol. 1: 5930
Technology of the Year Vol. 1: 5197
Technology Teacher Educator of the Year Vol. 1: 7927
Technology Transfer Award Vol. 1: 16514
Ted Giles Clinical Vignettes Vol. 1: 7005
Teddy Award Vol. 1: 12905
Teen Buckeye Book Award Vol. 1: 5979
Teenage Festival of Life Award Vol. 2: 3881
Teer, Jr. Award; Nello L. Vol. 1: 3505
Tees Leadership Award; Richard C. Vol. 1: 6890
Teetor Educational Award; Ralph R. Vol. 1: 16592

Teichmueller Stipendium Vol. 2: 2189
Telecommunicator of the Year Vol. 1: 5323
Teleport Awards for Excellence Vol. 1: 18981
Television Journalism Awards Vol. 2: 7047
Television Journalist of the Year Vol. 2: 7047
Television Programming and Promotions Awards Vol. 1: 14121
Television-Radio Awards Vol. 1: 19015
Television Sports Awards Vol. 2: 7048
Telford Medal Vol. 2: 6129
Telford Prize; Sir Robert Vol. 2: 6153
Telly Awards Vol. 1: 17429
Temple Award for Creative Altruism Vol. 1: 10859
Templer Medal Vol. 2: 7129
Templeton Award for European Religion Writer of the Year; John Vol. 2: 4704
Templeton European Film Prize; John Vol. 2: 4705
Templeton Prize for Progress toward Research or Discoveries about Spiritual Realities Vol. 1: 11027
Templeton Religion Reporter of the Year Award Vol. 1: 15617
Templin Award; Richard L. Vol. 1: 5464
Ten Outstanding Young Americans Vol. 1: 17983
Tenant Service Award Vol. 1: 6043
TenBroek Award; Jacobus Vol. 1: 13193
Tendler Fellowship; Dora and Meyer Vol. 1: 19068
Tenhoff Award; Ray E. Vol. 1: 16672
Tennessee Children's Choice Book Award Vol. 1: 17439
Tennessee History Book Award Vol. 1: 17435
Tennessee Independent Spirit Award Vol. 1: 12080
Tennessee Resource Sharing Award Vol. 1: 17436
Tennis Educational Merit Award Vol. 1: 10792
Tennis Educational Merit Award for Men Vol. 1: 10792
Tennis Educational Merit Award for Women Vol. 1: 10793
Tennis Facility Awards Vol. 1: 18153
Tennis World Champions Vol. 2: 6308
Terman Award; Frederick Emmons Vol. 1: 3677
Terpsychsna Prize Vol. 2: 4026
Terry Historic Preservation Award; Lucille Vol. 1: 8332
Tertiary Institute Award Vol. 2: 263
Tertis Award; The Lillian Vol. 2: 7259
Tertis International Viola Competition and Workshop; Lionel Vol. 2: 7259
Terui Award Vol. 2: 3325
Terzaghi Lecture; Karl Vol. 1: 3985
Tesla Award; Nikola Vol. 1: 9797
TESOL Fellowship for Graduate Study Vol. 1: 17418
TESOL/Newbury House Award for Excellence in Teaching Vol. 1: 17422
TESOL/Regents Publishing Company Fellowship Vol. 1: 17418
TESOL Research Interest Section/Newbury House Distinguished Research Award Vol. 1: 17421
TESOL Research Interest Section/Thomson Heinle Distinguished Research Award Vol. 1: 17421
TESOL Thomson Heinle Award for Excellence in Teaching Vol. 1: 17422
TESOL Travel Grant Vol. 1: 17423
Tess Award in Coatings; Roy W. Vol. 1: 1582
Tessenow Gold Medal; Heinrich Vol. 2: 2405
Test of Time Award Vol. 2: 7232
Tesvik Odulu Vol. 2: 4989
Texas Bluebonnet Award Vol. 1: 17488
Texas Collector's Institute Award Vol. 1: 17486
Texas Service Award for Outstanding Contributions to Clinical Chemistry Vol. 1: 894
Texas Tech Law School Foundation Grants Vol. 1: 17454
Texier II; Prix Henri Vol. 2: 1700
Texier; Prix Henri Vol. 2: 1701
Text Prize Vol. 1: 226
Textile Designer of the Year, TEXO Vol. 2: 1389
Thackray Medal; John Vol. 2: 7123
Thalberg Memorial Award; Irving G. Vol. 1: 111
Thales Human Factors Integration Award Vol. 2: 5801
Thames Television Award Vol. 2: 5230
Thames Valley Award Vol. 2: 5534
Thanks Badge Vol. 2: 2884
Thant Peace Award; U Vol. 1: 17706
Thayer Award; Sylvanus Vol. 1: 18003
The Dominion Sunday Times Bruce Mason Playwrights Award Vol. 2: 3825
Theater P.E.I. Playwriting Awards Vol. 1: 15223
Theatre Grants Vol. 1: 15227
Theatre Historial Society of America Awards Vol. 1: 17512
Theatre Library Association Award Vol. 1: 17515
Theatre World Awards Vol. 1: 17517
Thebault; Prix Victor Vol. 2: 1623
Theiler Memorial Trust Award Vol. 2: 4216
Thelin Researcher of the Year Award; Dr. Murray Vol. 1: 13341
Therapeutic Frontiers Lecture Award Vol. 1: 1638
Therapy Horse of the Year Award Vol. 1: 2795
Thermo Electron Clinical Chemistry and Automation Systems Award Vol. 2: 5082
Thermoforming Institute National Awards Vol. 1: 16863
Thermophysics Award Vol. 1: 2413
Theses Award Vol. 1: 6404
Thesis and Dissertation Awards Vol. 1: 1826
Thessaloniki Film Festival Vol. 2: 2473
Thevenot Medal; Jean Vol. 2: 4799
Thew Fund Awards; H.A. Vol. 2: 6451
Thibaud; Concours International Marguerite Long et Jacques Vol. 2: 1932
Thibaud International Competition; Marguerite Long and Jacques Vol. 2: 1932
Thiele Denkmunze; Dr. Edmund Vol. 2: 2034
Thistle Student Award Vol. 2: 4261
Thom Award; Charles Vol. 1: 16301
Thom Award for Early Design Achievement; Ronald J. Vol. 1: 6121
Thomas Award; Clayton J. Vol. 1: 11771
Thomas Award; Isaiah Vol. 1: 15691
Thomas Award; Lowell Vol. 1: 14761
Thomas Award; Major General Jack E. Vol. 1: 13452
Thomas Award; Moyer D. Vol. 1: 5465
Thomas Award; Theodore Vol. 1: 7666
Thomas Bedford Memorial Prize Vol. 2: 5398
Thomas CEA Distinguished Service Award; Joe D. Vol. 1: 7514
Thomas J. McTague Memorial Award Vol. 1: 6639
Thomas L. Phillips Collegiate Journalism Vol. 1: 8924
Thomas Lecture and Prize; E. Donnall Vol. 1: 4072
Thomas Medal Vol. 2: 1905
Thomas Memorial Award; Jesse Burgess Vol. 1: 18203
Thomas Memorial Award; R. D. Vol. 1: 4470
Thomas National Memorial Trophy; Norma Vol. 2: 5045
Thomas Travel Journalism Awards; Lowell Vol. 1: 16541
Thomason, Jr. Award; Colonel John W. Vol. 1: 11537
Thompson Award Vol. 1: 12258
Thompson Award; E. H. Vol. 2: 6598
Thompson Award for Distinguished Service; George N. Vol. 1: 16605
Thompson Award; Helen M. Vol. 1: 4345
Thompson Award; Mary Anee Vol. 1: 4644
Thompson Award; S. Earl Vol. 1: 5093
Thompson Award; Sanford E. Vol. 1: 5466
Thompson Award; W. F. Vol. 1: 2513
Thompson Foundation Gold Medal; J. P. Vol. 2: 630
Thompson Medal; Mary Clark Vol. 1: 12167
Thompson Memorial Award; Arthur R. Vol. 1: 10941
Thompson Memorial Award; Robert D. Vol. 1: 5467
Thompson Premium; J. Langham Vol. 2: 6162
Thompson Trophy; Jim Vol. 1: 6645
Thomson Gale Award for Excellence in Business Librarianship Vol. 1: 2696
Thomson Gale Award for Excellence in Reference and Adult Library Services Vol. 1: 2697
Thomson Gold Medal; Sir George Vol. 2: 6052
Thomson Medal Vol. 2: 3873
Thomson Medal; J. P. Vol. 2: 630
Thomson Premium; J. J.
Institution of Electrical Engineers - England Vol. 2: 6146
Institution of Electrical Engineers - England Vol 2: 6163
Thomson Prize in Applied Meteorology; Dr. Andrew Vol. 1: 6731
Thomson Resistance Welding Award; Elihu Vol. 1: 4471
Thorarinsson Medal Vol. 2: 542
Thoreau Medal; Emerson - Vol. 1: 552
Thorel; Prix Ernest Vol. 2: 1702
Thorlet; Prix
Academie des Beaux-Arts Vol. 2: 1493
Academie des Sciences Vol 2: 1624
Academie des Sciences Morales et Politiques Vol 2: 1703
Thornburgh Family Award; Bill Vol. 1: 1971
Thorndike Award for Career Achievement in Educational Psychology; Edward L. Vol. 1: 3339
Thornton Memorial Award and Lecture; John A. Vol. 1: 5596
Thorpe Award; Jim Vol. 1: 18456
Thorvaldsen Medal Vol. 2: 1328

Thouron Fellowship Vol. 2: 6348
Threadgill Award; Michael Beall Vol. 1: 13330
Threadneedle/Spectator Parliamentarian of the Year Awards Vol. 2: 7236
Three-A-Day of Dairy Award Vol. 1: 8994
Three-Day Novel Contest Vol. 1: 4548
Thring Award Vol. 2: 5764
Thrower of the Year Vol. 1: 18457
Thulinmedaljen Vol. 2: 4689
Thunbergmedaljen Vol. 2: 4631
Thurber Prize for American Humor Vol. 1: 17535
Thurlow Award Vol. 1: 9919
Thurston Award; John B. Vol. 1: 9883
Thurston Grand President's Award; Emory W. Vol. 1: 14994
Thygesen Trophy; Jake Vol. 1: 6424
TIAA-CREF Student-Athlete of the Year Vol. 1: 17029
Tibbitts Award; Clark Vol. 1: 4889
Tibbitts Grand Champion Horse Award; Bev Vol. 1: 14350
Tibor Greenwalt Memorial Award and Lectureship Vol. 1: 1018
Tice Friend of the AphA-ASP Award; Linwood F. Vol. 1: 3063
Tickey Award; Bertha Vol. 1: 524
Tiemann Award; Walter Vol. 2: 2352
Tierney/Ernst & Young Research Award; Cornelius E. Vol. 1: 5188
Tiffany Awards for Employee Excellence Vol. 1: 3473
Tilak Lecture; Prof. B. D. Vol. 2: 2724
Tilden Award; Freeman Vol. 1: 13534
Tilden Lectureship Vol. 2: 6985
Tilleard Medal Vol. 2: 6857
Tillmanns-Skolnick Award Vol. 1: 1583
Tillyer Award; Edgar D. Vol. 1: 14617
Tilton Memorial Award; Randy Vol. 1: 3250
Time Magazine Quality Dealer Award Vol. 1: 17542
Time Out/01 - for London Awards Vol. 2: 7276
Time Out Eating and Drinking Awards Vol. 2: 7277
Time Person of the Year Vol. 1: 17543
Timmie Awards Vol. 1: 17566
Timoshenko Medal Vol. 1: 4171
Timothy Trophy Vol. 1: 5604
Tinbergen Awards for Young Statisticians from Developing Countries; Jan Vol. 2: 3617
Tindall Trophy; Frank Vol. 1: 6672
Tinkle Award; Lon Vol. 1: 17484
Tinkle Research Excellence Award; Donald W. Vol. 1: 17061
Tinsley Prize; Beatrice M. Vol. 1: 1365
Tipton Award; Royce J. Vol. 1: 3986
Tir na n-Og Awards Vol. 2: 7325
Tiroler Landespreis fur Kunst Vol. 2: 750
Tiroler Landespreis fur Wissenschaft Vol. 2: 751
Tirumurti Memorial Lecture; Dr. T.S. Vol. 2: 2725
Tison Award Vol. 2: 1875
Tissandier Diploma; Paul Vol. 2: 4747
Titan All America Hockey Squad (East and West) for Colleges Vol. 1: 2253
Titan All-America Hockey Squad (East and West) for Universities Vol. 1: 2254
Titus Award; Shirley Vol. 1: 2946
Titus Memorial Trophy; Jerry Vol. 1: 1369
TLA/SIRS Freedom of Information Award Vol. 1: 17437
Tlws y Cerddor (Composers Medal) Vol. 2: 7330
TMS/ASM Joint Distinguished Lectureship in Materials and Society Award
ASM International Vol. 1: 4710
Minerals, Metals, and Materials Society Vol 1: 11820
Tobin Award; Mrs. Edgar Vol. 1: 11710
Tobler Award for Review of the Prevention Science Literature; Nan Vol. 1: 16391
TOBY Award for Office Buildings Between 100,000 and 249,999 Square Feet Vol. 1: 5999
TOBY Award for Office Buildings Between 250,000 and 499,999 Square Feet Vol. 1: 6000
TOBY Award for Office Buildings Between 500,000 and One Million Square Feet Vol. 1: 6001
TOBY Award for Office Buildings Over One Million Square Feet Vol. 1: 6002
TOBY Award for Office Buildings Under 100,000 Square Feet Vol. 1: 6003
Today's Workplace of Tomorrow Vol. 1: 9712
TOEFL Award Vol. 1: 8401
Tofte/Betty Ren Wright Children's Literature Award; Arthur Vol. 1: 7875
Toison d'Or Vol. 2: 1846
Toit-Malherbe Prize for Genealogical Research; D. F. du Vol. 2: 4286
Toit Medal for Business Leadership; Frans du Vol. 2: 4287
Toit Memorial Lecture; DeBeers Alex L. du Vol. 2: 4189
Tokle Award; Torger Vol. 1: 18111
Tokyo International Competition for Chamber Music Composition Vol. 2: 3239
Tokyo International Competition for Guitar Compositions Vol. 2: 3239
Tokyo International Film Festival Vol. 2: 3336
Tokyo International Music Competition Vol. 2: 3338
Tokyo Video Festival Vol. 2: 3343
Tolkningspris Vol. 2: 4675
Toll Excellence Awards Vol. 1: 10278
Tollefsen Award; Lois Vol. 1: 10462
Tom Butcher Trophy Vol. 2: 5352
Tom-Gallon Award Vol. 2: 7150
Tomkinson Award; Helen Vol. 2: 5372
Tomorrow's Leader Award Vol. 1: 619
Tomorrow's Leaders of MPI Award Vol. 1: 11683
Tompkins Fellowship; Sally Kress Vol. 1: 16559
Tondelli; Premio Piervittorio Vol. 2: 3124
Toner, Jr. Memorial Award; Arthur C. Vol. 1: 511
Tonge Scholarship Award; Gwendolyn Vol. 2: 843
Tono; Medalla al Merito Logistico y Administrativo Contralmirante Rafael Vol. 2: 1189
Tony Awards Vol. 1: 11261
Tony Noon Scholarship Vol. 2: 324
Tooley Award Vol. 2: 6272
Toonder Award; Marten Vol. 2: 2823
Tooting Bec Cup Vol. 2: 6566
Top 10 Orienteers Vol. 2: 1149
Top 25 Censored Stories of the Year Vol. 1: 15369
Top 100 Companies Award Vol. 2: 4371
Top ARCite Award Vol. 1: 3514
Top Case of the Year Vol. 1: 18031
Top Exporter Vol. 2: 3479
Top Female Pilot Vol. 1: 14243
Top Packaging Awards Vol. 1: 8718
Top Seven Intelligent Communities Vol. 1: 9969
Top Seven Intelligent Communities of the Year Vol. 1: 9971
Top Tea Place of the Year Vol. 2: 7253
Top Ten Business Women of ABWA Vol. 1: 1430
Top Ten Public Works Leaders of the Year Vol. 1: 3456
Topham and Susan Redd Butler Independent Research and Creative Work Awards; John Vol. 1: 15598
Topps All-Star Rookie Team Vol. 1: 17550
Topps Minor League Player-of-the-Month Vol. 1: 17551
Topps Organization of the Year Vol. 1: 17552
Torch Award
American Society for Training and Development Vol. 1: 3836
Federation of Jewish Men's Clubs Vol 1: 8669
Torello International Festival of Mountain and Adventure Films Vol. 2: 4545
Tork Prize; Istvan Vol. 2: 305
Tornov-Loeffler; Prix Ch. M. Vol. 2: 1494
Toronto Arts Awards Vol. 1: 17556
Toronto-City Award for Best Canadian Feature Film Vol. 1: 17562
Toronto City Award for Excellence in Canadian Production Vol. 1: 17562
Toronto International Salon of Photography Vol. 1: 17564
Toronto Press Club National Newspaper Awards Vol. 1: 6759
Torrens Award; Richard R. Vol. 1: 3987
Tory; Medaille Henry Marshall Vol. 1: 15768
Tory Medal; Henry Marshall Vol. 1: 15768
Toscanini; Concorso Internazionale di Direzione d'Orchestra Arturo Vol. 2: 3050
Toscanini International Competition for Conductors; Arturo Vol. 2: 3050
Toscano Medal; Salvador Vol. 2: 3439
Toscano; Medalla Ing. Salvador Vol. 2: 3439
Toshiba/NSTA ExploraVision Awards Vol. 1: 13685
Tosney Award; Eileen M. Vol. 1: 1316
Totius Prize for Theology and Study of the Original Languages of the Bible Vol. 2: 4288
Touchstone Award Vol. 1: 6341
Touchstone Award; F. Morris Vol. 1: 17972
Toulmin Medal Vol. 1: 16534
Tour Award; Sam Vol. 1: 5468
Tour de France Vol. 2: 1708
Touring Car World Cup Vol. 2: 1882
Tourism Promotion Grant Vol. 1: 9542
Toutain-Blanchet; Prix Vol. 2: 1535
Tovey Memorial Prize; Donald Vol. 2: 7314
Tower and Carillon Prize Vol. 2: 1081
Tower Trophy Vol. 1: 17903
Towers Flight Safety Award; Adm. John H. Vol. 1: 14654
Towley Award; Carl Vol. 1: 11055
Townes Award; Charles Hard Vol. 1: 14618
Towngate Theatre National Playwriting Contest Vol. 1: 14455
Townshend Award; B. W. O. Vol. 2: 6659
Township Leader of the Year Vol. 1: 11830

Townsville Foundation for Australian Literary Studies Award Vol. 2: 460
Towson University Prize for Literature Vol. 1: 17568
Toynbee Memorial Lectureship; Joseph Vol. 2: 7019
Toyota Tapestry Grant Vol. 1: 13686
Trabajador del Ano en Salud Vol. 1: 17999
Tracey Memorial Award; Anna Vol. 1: 15059
Tracks Award Vol. 1: 7023
Tracy Fellowship; Joyce Vol. 1: 819
Trade Book of the Year Vol. 1: 5842
Trade Contractor Award of Excellence Vol. 1: 6426
Traditional Irish Music, Singing and Dancing Awards Vol. 2: 2891
Trail Achievement Award Vol. 1: 2222
Trail Grants Vol. 1: 14035
Trail Ride Award Vol. 1: 2796
Trailblazer Award
Alberta Construction Safety Association Vol. 1: 368
International Furnishings and Design Association Vol 1: 10446
National Marrow Donor Program Vol 1: 13440
Trailblazer in Philanthropy Award Vol. 1: 15015
Trainee Awards For Excellence in Research Vol. 1: 7006
Trainee Excellence in Education Award Vol. 1: 6380
Trainee of the Year; PGA Vol. 2: 6568
Trainee Travel Awards Vol. 1: 3757
Trainer of the Year Award Vol. 1: 13123
Training and Research at Italian Libraries Vol. 2: 2950
Training company of the year Vol. 2: 5898
Training Trophy Vol. 2: 6931
Trakl Preis fur Lyrik; Georg Vol. 2: 744
Trakl Prize for Poetry; Georg Vol. 2: 744
Trampoline and Tumbling National Leadership Award Vol. 1: 512
Trans-American Sedan Championship Vol. 1: 17208
Trans-Canada Trophy Vol. 1: 6172
Transactions Prize Paper Award Vol. 1: 9578
Transco Press Award Vol. 2: 5229
Transfusion Medicine Fellowship Awards Vol. 1: 1004
Translation Prize
American-Scandinavian Foundation Vol. 1: 3516
Quebec Writers' Federation Vol 1: 15493
Translators Association Unger Award Vol. 1: 4367
Transplant Recipients International Organization Scholarships Vol. 1: 17575
Transporation Person of the Year Vol. 1: 8154
Transport and Energy Processes Division Award Vol. 1: 2500
Transportation Achievement Award Vol. 1: 9954
Transportation Administrator of the Year Vol. 1: 12350
Transportation Research Board Distinguished Service Award Vol. 1: 17578
Transportation Safety Awards Vol. 1: 17101
Trask Prize and Awards; Betty Vol. 2: 7151
Trautman Award; Topps - George M. Vol. 1: 17553
Travel Agent of the Year Award Vol. 1: 4255
Travel Award
European Wound Management Association Vol. 2: 5872
Minerals Engineering Society Vol 2: 6434
National Council on Public History Vol 1: 13050
Travel Awards Vol. 1: 18237
Travel Bursaries Vol. 2: 5334
Travel Fellowship Award Vol. 1: 16606
Travel Fellowships
Association for the Study of Obesity Vol. 2: 5104
European Association for Cancer Research Vol 2: 5807
Travel Grant
American Association for Clinical Chemistry Vol. 1: 895
South African Dental Association Vol 2: 4329
Travel Grants
American Association for Cancer Research Vol. 1: 863
Association of Paediatric Anaesthetists of Great Britain and Ireland Vol 2: 5147
Endocrine Society of Australia Vol 2: 440
Travel Grants for Educators Vol. 1: 10600
Travel Hall of Fame Vol. 1: 4256
Travel Industry Awards for Excellence Vol. 1: 17589
Travel Industry Hall of Leaders Vol. 1: 17588
Travel Industry Odyssey Awards Vol. 1: 17589
Travel Journalist of the Year Vol. 1: 16541
Travel Journalist of the Year Award Vol. 1: 4257
Travel/Research Grant Vol. 1: 11790
Travel Scholarship Vol. 2: 4611
Travel Scholarships Vol. 2: 1763
Travel Writing Award Vol. 1: 19023
Traveling Fellowship Vol. 1: 1425
Travelling Fellowships
British Orthopaedic Foot and Ankle Society Vol. 2: 5414
Royal College of Physicians and Surgeons of Glasgow Vol 2: 6716
Travelling Scholarships
British Society of Rehabilitation Medicine Vol. 2: 5525
Society of Authors - England Vol 2: 7152
Travers; Prix Maurice Vol. 2: 1704
Tree of Learning Award Vol. 2: 4923
Tree of Life Award
Canadian Institute of Forestry Vol. 1: 6606
Jewish National Fund Vol 1: 11003
Leukemia and Lymphoma Society Vol 1: 11312
Tregre Award; Louis S. Vol. 1: 12974
Trejo Librarian of the Year Award Vol. 1: 15605
Tremaine Fellowship; Marie Vol. 1: 5748
Trendsetter Award Vol. 1: 8795
Trent - Crede Medal Vol. 1: 133
Trento Filmfestival Internazionale Montagna Esplorazione Vol. 2: 3136
Trento International Film Festival of Mountain and Exploration Vol. 2: 3136
Trevethan Award; P. J. Vol. 1: 9135
Trevithick Premium Vol. 2: 6130
Tri-M Leadership Award Vol. 1: 17605
Trial Lawyer of the Year Award Vol. 1: 17607
Triangle Award Vol. 1: 11965
Trianti Grand Prix; Alexandra Vol. 2: 2451
Triathletes of the Year Vol. 1: 18461
Tribute of the Film Society of Lincoln Center Vol. 1: 8691
Tribute to Women and Industry (TWIN) Vol. 1: 19104
Tribute to Women Award Vol. 1: 19100
Tribute to Women in Industry (TWIN) Award Vol. 1: 19106
Tribute to Women in International INdustry Vol. 1: 19106
TRIC Awards Vol. 2: 7255
Tricerri; Premio Vol. 2: 3109
Tricolor Medal Vol. 1: 2211
Triennial Prize Vol. 1: 16481
Trieschman Award; Albert E. Vol. 1: 1035
Trieste Science Prize Vol. 2: 2960
Trillium Book Award Vol. 1: 14570
Trillium Book Award for Poetry Vol. 1: 14570
Trimble Memorial Award; Robert E. Vol. 1: 9371
Trimmer Merit Shop Teaching Award of Excellence; John Vol. 1: 4755
Triple Crown Champion
Churchill Downs Inc. Vol. 1: 7407
New York Racing Association Vol 1: 14150
Triple Crown Trophy Vol. 1: 17609
Triple Tiara Vol. 1: 7408
Troland Research Awards Vol. 1: 12168
Troll-Preis; Thaddaeus- Vol. 2: 2140
Trollope Medal; D. H. Vol. 2: 535
Trombetta, MD Teaching Award; George C. Vol. 1: 3615
Tropham and Susan Redd Butler Faculty Fellowships; John Vol. 1: 15599
Trophee du Fairplay FIM Vol. 2: 4814
Trost Award; Jan Vol. 1: 10622
Trotter Prize; Mildred Vol. 1: 1236
Trotting Triple Crown Vol. 1: 18163
Troublemaker Awards Vol. 1: 11183
Troughton Memorial Award; Ellis Vol. 2: 281
Trouw Publieksprijs voor het Nederlandse Boek Vol. 2: 3498
Truck Awards Vol. 2: 425
Truck of the Year Vol. 1: 11969
Truck Puller of the Year Vol. 1: 13854
Truck Safety Contest Vol. 1: 4377
Trudeau Medal; Edward Livingston Vol. 1: 2709
True Value Man of the Year Vol. 1: 13229
Trueblood Award; Kenneth N. Vol. 1: 1864
Truman Award; Harry S
National Guard Association of the United States Vol. 1: 13301
National Guard Association of the United States Vol 1: 13302
Truman Book Award; Harry S Vol. 1: 9268
Truman Good Neighbor Award; Harry S. Vol. 1: 17614
Truman Prize; S. J. Wallace Vol. 1: 12121
Truman Public Service Award; Harry S. Vol. 1: 7432
Trumpeter Award Vol. 1: 12947
Trumpler Award; Robert J. Vol. 1: 5486
Truog Soil Science Award; Emil Vol. 1: 16944
Truran, Jr., Medical Materiel and Logistics Management Award; Paul F. Vol. 1: 5260
Trustee Award Vol. 1: 17438
Trustee Citation
Association for Library Trustees and Advocates Vol. 1: 4937
Illinois Library Association Vol 1: 9612
Trustee Citation Award Vol. 1: 14019
Trustee of the Year Award Vol. 1: 1129
Trustee Recognition Award Vol. 1: 14095

Trustee's Award Vol. 1: 15466
Trustees Award Vol. 1: 10300
Trustees' Honor Roll Vol. 1: 3550
Trustees Trophy Vol. 1: 7678
TSA Star Recognition Program Vol. 1: 17427
Tsao Leonardo Award; Makepeace Vol. 1: 10682
Tschumi Prize; Jean Vol. 2: 1926
TSI-FAI Award on Plant Nutrient Sulphur Vol. 2: 2559
TSL Trophy Vol. 2: 5535
Tsongas Economic Patriot Award; Paul E. Vol. 1: 7656
Tucker Architectural Awards Competition Vol. 1: 6005
Tucker Award; Gabriel F. Vol. 1: 2622
Tucker Award; IBC International John Vol. 2: 6233
Tucker Award; IBC John Vol. 2: 6233
Tucker Award; Richard Vol. 1: 17617
Tucker Medal; Bernard Vol. 2: 5549
Tucker Study Grants; Sarah Vol. 1: 17618
Tudor Medal Vol. 1: 16535
Tully Medal in Oceanography; J.P. Vol. 1: 6732
Tully Memorial Grant; Stephen R. Vol. 1: 15563
Tulsa Library Trust Award for Young Readers' Literature Vol. 1: 17627
Tunbridge Wells International Young Concert Artists Competition Vol. 2: 7279
Tunnels and Deep Science Merit Award Vol. 1: 4382
Tunner Aircrew Award; Lt. General William H. Vol. 1: 306
Tuntland Memorial Award; Paul E. Vol. 1: 16117
Tupolev Aeromodelling Diploma; Andrei Vol. 2: 4748
Tupolev Aeromodelling Medal; Andrei Vol. 2: 4749
Turbayne International Berkeley Essay Prize Competition; Colin and Ailsa Vol. 1: 18341
Turcotte Memorial Award; Robert Vol. 1: 9261
Turin International Film Festival Vol. 2: 3009
Turing Award; A. M. Vol. 1: 4816
Turnbull Award; John Vol. 1: 6884
Turnbull Award; Lt. Col. J.L. (Jack) Vol. 1: 17973
Turnbull Award; W. Rupert Vol. 1: 6173
Turnbull Lectureship; David Vol. 1: 11598
Turnbull Trophy Vol. 1: 10483
Turnbull Trophy; Jack Vol. 1: 17973
Turner Award; Alfred H. Vol. 2: 5046
Turner Award; Bob Vol. 1: 13090
Turner Award for Outstanding Service to NASPA; Fred Vol. 1: 12690
Turner Award; Frederick Jackson Vol. 1: 14702
Turner Award; Wava Banes Vol. 1: 17407
Turner Entrepreneur Award; Arthur E. Vol. 1: 14418
Turner Lecture Vol. 2: 3748
Turner Lecture; Francis C. Vol. 1: 3988
Turner Medal; Henry C. Vol. 1: 1761
Turner Prize; Dr. Lynn W. Vol. 1: 14981
Turner Prize; Ethel Vol. 2: 585
Turner - Scholefield Award Vol. 2: 7191
Turnquist Trophy Vol. 1: 7462
Turpie Award; Mary C. Vol. 1: 4332
Tutor Appreciation Awards Vol. 1: 10948
Tutor Work Study Grant Vol. 2: 3834
Tutorial Citation Award Vol. 1: 3783
Tutt Award; Wm. Thayer Vol. 1: 18402
Tuttle Award; Arnold D. Vol. 1: 212
Tuttle Award; Frederick H. Vol. 1: 18502
Tuttle Distinguished Achievement Award; Judge Elbert P.
Pi Kappa Alpha Vol. 1: 15042
Pi Kappa Alpha Vol 1: 15044
TV Week Logie Awards Vol. 2: 705
Twain Award; Mark
Missouri Association of School Librarians Vol. 1: 11883
Society for the Study of Midwestern Literature Vol 1: 16460
TWAS Award in Basic Medical Sciences Vol. 2: 2961
TWAS Award in Biology Vol. 2: 2962
TWAS Award in Chemistry Vol. 2: 2963
TWAS Award in Mathematics Vol. 2: 2964
TWAS Award in Physics Vol. 2: 2965
Tweddle Medal Vol. 2: 7211
Tweed Award; Harrison Vol. 1: 1378
Twenhofel Medal Vol. 1: 16415
Twenty-Five Year Award
American Institute of Architects Vol. 1: 2437
National Athletic Trainers' Association Vol 1: 12720
Twenty-Five Year Awards Vol. 1: 1388
Twenty-Five Year Club Member Certificate Vol. 1: 2922
Twenty-Five Year Membership Medals Vol. 1: 2923
Twin Cities Musicians Union AFM Award Vol. 1: 18587
The Two Air Forces Award Vol. 1: 323
Two Ladies from Texas Award Vol. 1: 13185
Two Wheel Drive Puller of the Year Vol. 1: 13863
Two-Year College Biology Teaching Award Vol. 1: 12411
Tyler Award; Leona Vol. 1: 3326
Tyler Ecology Award Vol. 1: 18345
Tyler Prize for Environmental Achievement Vol. 1: 18345
Tyler Prize for Stimulation of Research Vol. 1: 3064
Tyler Research Award; Dr. Ralph W. Vol. 1: 7816
Tylman Research Program; Stanley D. Vol. 1: 622
Tylman Student Essay Award; Stanley D. Vol. 1: 622
Tyndall Award; John Vol. 1: 14619
Tyndall Medal Vol. 2: 5987
Tyrrell Historical Medal; J. B. Vol. 1: 15769
Tzvi & Mara Propes Prize; Aharon Vol. 2: 2904
U S Open Three Cushion Billiard Championships Vol. 1: 17764
UCB Award for Excellence in Medicinal Chemistry Vol. 2: 774
Ucross Foundation Artists-in-Residence Program Vol. 1: 17648
Ueberroth - U.S. Water Polo Award; Peter V. Vol. 1: 18166
Uhlig Young Educator Award; H.H. Vol. 1: 12489
U.I.A.A. Prize Vol. 2: 3136
Ujima Award Vol. 1: 12423
UK Company of the Year Vol. 2: 5423
UK Fashion Export Awards Vol. 2: 7285
UKeiG Research Award Vol. 2: 7299
Ukrainian of the Year Award Vol. 1: 17652
ULI Awards for Excellence Vol. 1: 18372
Ullman Award; Edwin F. Vol. 1: 896
Ullmann Peace Prize; Liv Vol. 1: 7331
Ulmer, Jr. Applied Research Award; Walter F. Vol. 1: 7204
Ulrich's Serials Librarianship Award; CSA/ Vol. 1: 4912
Uluslararasi Istanbul Film Festivali Vol. 2: 4982
Umezawa Memorial Award; Hamao Vol. 2: 6297
Umgeni Award Vol. 2: 4377
Umweltpreis der Landeshauptstadt Stuttgart Vol. 2: 2419
Unda Dove Vol. 2: 1100
Underfashion Club Scholarship Program Vol. 1: 17658
Undergraduate Award Vol. 1: 16033
Undergraduate Award for Excellence Vol. 1: 10867
Undergraduate Certificate of Merit Vol. 1: 15077
Undergraduate Essay Award in Mesoamerican Studies Vol. 1: 9735
Undergraduate Information Systems Award Vol. 1: 5624
Undergraduate Project Prize Vol. 2: 7038
Undergraduate Report Awards Vol. 1: 6531
Undergraduate Research Assistantships Vol. 1: 11872
Undergraduate Scholarship Vol. 1: 2169
Undergraduate Scholarships
Acacia Fraternity Vol. 1: 63
Canadian Meteorological and Oceanographic Society Vol 1: 6733
Undergraduate Student Award Vol. 1: 8189
Undergraduate Student Awards for an Outstanding Horticulture Student Vol. 1: 3731
Undergraduate Student Bursaries Vol. 2: 5387
Undergraduate Student Paper Competition
Alpha Kappa Delta Vol. 1: 421
Institute of Industrial Engineers Vol 1: 9874
Undergraduate Student Scholarship Vol. 1: 14985
Undergraduate Students Award Vol. 1: 11791
Undergraduate Water Prize Vol. 2: 390
Underwater Athletes of the Year Vol. 1: 17665
Underwood Distinguished Service Award; Robert J. Vol. 1: 12607
UNEP Sasakawa Environment Prize Vol. 2: 3366
UNESCO Award for Distinguished Services to Physical Education and Sport Vol. 2: 1999
UNESCO Crafts Prize Vol. 2: 2000
UNESCO - International Music Council Music Prize Vol. 2: 2001
UNESCO Literacy Prizes Vol. 2: 2002
UNESCO Prize for Human Rights Education Vol. 2: 2003
UNESCO Prize for Landscape Architecture Vol. 2: 2004
UNESCO Prize for Peace Education Vol. 2: 2005
UNESCO Science Prize Vol. 2: 2006
Ungar German Translation Award Vol. 1: 4367
Unger Award; Heinz Vol. 1: 14566
UNICA Medal Vol. 2: 4680
UNICA-medaljen Vol. 2: 4680
UNICEF Award for Distinguished Service Vol. 1: 17912

UNICEF Award for Films Vol. 1: 17913
UNICEF Prize Vol. 2: 3298
UNICEF; Prize of Vol. 2: 2048
UNICON, the International Unicycling Convention and Championships Vol. 1: 10808
UNIMA Citation for Excellence in the Art of Puppetry Vol. 1: 17669
UNIMA-USA Scholarships Vol. 1: 17670
Union Carbide Lectureship Award Vol. 1: 3678
Union League Civic and Arts Foundation Poetry Prize Vol. 1: 15120
The Union Medal Vol. 2: 1920
Union Medal Vol. 2: 5403
Union of International Fairs Awards Vol. 2: 2010
Unique Contribution to the Theatre Award Vol. 1: 8278
Unit Awards Vol. 1: 4646
Unit Citation Vol. 1: 1929
Unit Citation for Gallantry Vol. 2: 224
Unit Citations Vol. 2: 224
Unit Leader of the Year Vol. 1: 61
Unit of the Year Award Vol. 1: 10715
Unit Performance Vol. 1: 1930
Unitas Medal Vol. 2: 4345
United Nations Environment Program Awards Vol. 2: 3367
United Nations Medal Vol. 1: 8126
United Nations Medals Vol. 1: 6080
United Nations Population Award Vol. 1: 17710
United Nations Prize in the Field of Human Rights Vol. 1: 17704
United Nations Service Medal (Korea) Vol. 1: 8127
United States Air Force Twelve Outstanding Airmen of the Year Vol. 1: 307
U.S. Bicycling Hall of Fame Vol. 1: 17762
U.S. Business Hall of Fame Vol. 1: 11061
U.S. Catholic Award Vol. 1: 17768
U.S. Chess Championship Vol. 1: 17772
United States Dressage Federation All Breed Award Vol. 1: 11379
U.S. Energy Award Vol. 1: 17892
United States Figure Skating Champions Vol. 1: 17903
U.S. Genomics Award Vol. 1: 5781
United States Hang Gliding Association Commendation Vol. 1: 17928
United States Hockey Hall of Fame Vol. 1: 17942
U.S. Independence Cup Vol. 1: 18065
U.S. Industrial Film and Video Festival Vol. 1: 17980
U.S. International Film and Video Festival Vol. 1: 17980
U.S. Junior Sailing Championships Vol. 1: 18074
U.S. Match Racing Championship - Prince of Wales Bowl Vol. 1: 18071
U.S. Medal of Remembrance Vol. 1: 17944
U.S. Men's Sailing Championship - Clifford D. Mallory Cup Vol. 1: 18072
U.S. National Hot Air Balloon Champion Vol. 1: 5647
United States of America Counties Award Vol. 1: 7944
U.S. Olympic Hall of Fame Vol. 1: 18020
United States Open Tennis Championships Vol. 1: 18154
United States Presidential Scholars Program Vol. 1: 17821
U.S. Sailing One-Design Awards Vol. 1: 18073
U.S. Sailing/Rolex Junior Championships Vol. 1: 18074
U.S. Scrabble Open Vol. 1: 13688
U.S. Senate Productivity Award for Maryland Vol. 1: 11566
U.S. Singlehanded Sailing Championship - George D. O'Day Trophy Vol. 1: 18075
United States Skill Olympics Vol. 1: 16086
United States Steel Foundation Award in Molecular Biology Vol. 1: 12153
United States Swimming Award Vol. 1: 18424
United States Swimming Life Members Vol. 1: 18425
U.S. Team Race Championship - George R. Hinman Trophy Vol. 1: 18076
United States Water Polo Award Vol. 1: 18167
U.S. Women's Sailing Championship - Mrs. Charles Francis Adams Trophy Vol. 1: 18077
U.S. Women's Sailing Championships Vol. 1: 18078
U.S. Youth Sailing Championship Vol. 1: 18079
United States Youth Soccer Association Youth Referee of the Year Vol. 1: 18180
Unity Awards in Media Vol. 1: 11373
University Cup Vol. 1: 6673
University Medal for Excellence Vol. 1: 7589
University of Cincinnati Award Vol. 1: 3264
University of Louisville Grawemeyer Award for Ideas Improving World Order Vol. 1: 18298
University of Louisville Grawemeyer Award for Music Composition Vol. 1: 18305
University of Louisville Grawemeyer Award in Education Vol. 1: 18299
University of Maryland International Music Competitions Vol. 1: 16094
University of Michigan Press Book Award Vol. 1: 18317
University of Southern Mississippi Medallion Vol. 1: 11874
University Service Award Vol. 1: 17646
Unlimited Puller of the Year Vol. 1: 13864
Uno Lamm High Voltage Direct Current Award Vol. 1: 9827
Unsinkable Heroine Award Vol. 1: 9334
Unsung Hero Award
Academy of Certified Hazardous Materials Managers Vol. 1: 82
Organization of Professional Employees of the United States Department of Agriculture Vol 1: 14707
Unsung Unitarian Universalist Award Vol. 1: 17682
UOP Technology Award Vol. 1: 10917
UPA National Championships Vol. 1: 17654
UPA Spirit of the Game Awards Vol. 1: 17655
UPE Scholarship Awards Vol. 1: 18367
Upjohn Young Investigators Award Vol. 1: 4250
Upper Secondary School Teachers Prizes Vol. 2: 1401
Uppsala Short Film Festival Vol. 2: 4693
UPS Minority Advancement Award Vol. 1: 9875
Upson-Loren B. Miller Fellowship; Lent D. Vol. 1: 7422
The Upstarts Awards Vol. 2: 6497
Upward Mobility Award Vol. 1: 16916
Urbahn Medal Vol. 1: 16536
Urban and Community Forestry Award Vol. 1: 11876
Urban Beautification Award Vol. 1: 2300
Urban Council Short Film Awards Vol. 2: 3936
Urban County Engineer of the Year Award Vol. 1: 12500
Urban Design Awards for Excellence Vol. 1: 2433
Urbanek Memorial Award; Karel Vol. 1: 15972
Ure Award for Sportsmanship; Captain James S. Vol. 1: 13905
Uren Award; Lester C. Vol. 1: 16807
Urey Medal Vol. 2: 1761
Urey Prize; Harold C. Vol. 1: 1366
Urology Medal Vol. 1: 719
URTI Prize Vol. 2: 3469
US Bowler Writing Competition Vol. 1: 1416
US/ICOMOS Fellows Vol. 1: 17780
USA/British Isles Visiting Fellowship Vol. 2: 6701
USA-CA Award Vol. 1: 7944
USA Grand National Champion Vol. 1: 4479
USA International Ballet Competition Vol. 1: 18406
USA International Harp Competition Vol. 1: 18408
USA Swimming Combined Team Traveling Trophy; William A. Lippman Jr. Vol. 1: 18418
USA Table Tennis National Championships Vol. 1: 18428
The USA Today Baseball Weekly Award Vol. 1: 16175
USA Today Sports Weekly Award Vol. 1: 16172
USAF Personnel Manager of the Year Vol. 1: 308
USAT Girls' Sportsmanship Trophy Award Vol. 1: 18049
User Feedback Award Vol. 1: 15845
USF Grant Awards Vol. 1: 15932
USGA Championships Vol. 1: 17919
USHA National Championships Vol. 1: 17922
Usher Prize; Abbott Payson Vol. 1: 16441
Usher Research Award in Dermatology; Barney Vol. 1: 6457
Ushkow Community Service Award; Martin C. Vol. 1: 720
USHWAn-of-the-Year Vol. 1: 17938
USHWAn of the Year; Bob Zellner Vol. 1: 17940
USILA Awards Vol. 1: 17974
USILA Trophy Vol. 1: 17975
USO Woman of the Year Vol. 1: 18475
USPLTA - Annual Golf Tournament Vol. 1: 18392
USPLTA - Honorary Life Membership Award Vol. 1: 18393
USPLTA - Special Recognition Award Vol. 1: 18394
USRA Presidential Award Vol. 1: 18042
USRA Scholarship Program Vol. 1: 18043
USRowing Medal Vol. 1: 18050
USSA Outstanding Alpine Masters Award Vol. 1: 18107
USSS Athlete of the Year Vol. 1: 17362
USSS Coach of the Year Vol. 1: 17363
USTA Girls' Sportsmanship Award Vol. 1: 18155

USTA Junior and Boys' Sportsmanship Award Vol. 1: 18150
USTA Tennis NJTL Chapter of the Year Award Vol. 1: 18156
USX Foundation Award in Molecular Biology Vol. 1: 12153
Utah State Poetry Society Award Vol. 1: 13186
Uteck Bowl
Canadian Interuniversity Sport Vol. 1: 6674
Canadian Interuniversity Sport Vol 1: 6675
Utility Design Awards Vol. 1: 3441
Utilization Award Vol. 1: 12344
Utmarkt Svensk Form Vol. 2: 4691
Utz Award; John P.
National Foundation for Infectious Diseases Vol. 1: 13256
National Foundation for Infectious Diseases Vol 1: 13257
Uveeler Award Vol. 2: 2944
Vachon Award; Romeo Vol. 1: 6174
Vahue Award; L. Ray Vol. 1: 14747
Vaisala Award; Prof. Dr. Vilho Vol. 2: 4936
Valdes; Premio Miguel Aleman Vol. 2: 3443
Valencia Film Festival Vol. 2: 4525
Valent Biosciences- Best Paper Awards Vol. 1: 15093
Valladolid International Film Festival Vol. 2: 4552
Valley Forge Certificate Vol. 1: 13301
Valley Forge Cross for Heroism Vol. 1: 13301
Valley, Jr., Prize; George E. Vol. 1: 3138
Vallis Agri Prize Vol. 2: 3136
Valor Award
National Association for Search and Rescue Vol. 1: 12359
World Conservation Union Vol 2: 4920
Value of Wilderness to the Outdoors Experience Contest Vol. 1: 14750
Valued Customer Award Vol. 1: 12820
van Ameringen Award in Psychiatric Rehabilitation; Arnold L. Vol. 1: 3292
Van Anda Award; Carr Vol. 1: 15948
Van Antwerpen Award for Service to the Institute; F. J. & Dorothy Vol. 1: 2501
Van Beneden; Prix Edouard Vol. 2: 1098
Van Beneden Prize; Pierre-Joseph and Edouard Vol. 2: 1057
van Buren Structural Engineering Award; Maurice P. Vol. 1: 1755
Van Cleef Memorial Medal Vol. 1: 2101
Van Couvering Memorial Award; Martin C. Vol. 1: 2554
Van de Vate Prize for Orchestral Music; Nancy Vol. 1: 10032
van de Woestijne Prize; Karel Vol. 2: 962
Van Den Heever Prize for Jurisprudence; Toon Vol. 2: 4289
Van der Hoogt-prijs; Lucy B. and C. W. Vol. 2: 3673
van der Mueren Prize; Floris Vol. 2: 1076
van der Walt Award; Johnny Vol. 2: 4222
van Drimmelen Medal; Dominee Pieter Vol. 2: 4290
Van Dyck; Prijs Albert Vol. 2: 968
Van Eck Medal; Hendrik Vol. 2: 4321
Van Ginderachter Prize; Jozef Vol. 2: 963
Van Goidsenhoven; Prijs Franz Vol. 2: 969
Van Grover Youth Exhibit Award; Melissa Vol. 1: 2924
Van Harrevold Memorial Award; Central Nervous System Section Vol. 1: 3183
Van Helmont; Prijs J. B. Vol. 2: 970
Van Leeuwenhoek Distinctive Travel Award Vol. 2: 2130
Van Leeuwenhoek Medal Vol. 2: 3660
van Looyprijs; Jacobus Vol. 2: 3550
Van Niel International Prize for Studies in Bacterial Systematics Vol. 2: 552
Van Nostrand Memorial Award; John Vol. 1: 10008
Van Nostrand Reinhold Research Award Vol. 1: 10372
Van Orman Trophy Vol. 1: 11360
van Oyeprijs; Paul Vol. 2: 1077
Van Remortel Service Award; Harold Vol. 1: 897
Van Sant Memorial Award; Gene and Mary Vol. 1: 13355
Van Slyke Foundation Award Vol. 1: 898
Van Vliet Trophy; M. L. Vol. 1: 6675
van Vught Award; Jean Vol. 2: 7433
van Wesemael Literary Prize; Guust Vol. 2: 3585
Van Winkle Award; Rip Vol. 1: 5900
van Wyk Louw Medal; N. P. Vol. 2: 4291
Van Zandt Citizenship Award; VFW James E. Vol. 1: 18519
VanArsdel Prize Vol. 1: 15632
Vance Award; James A. Vol. 1: 6921
Vance Award; John C. Vol. 1: 17583
Vance Award; Robert W. Vol. 1: 7991
Vancouver International Film Festival Vol. 1: 18485
Vandenberg Award; Hoyt S. Vol. 1: 309
Vanderlinden Prize; Henri L. Vol. 2: 1078
Vanderlinden Public Official Award; Spence Vol. 1: 3449
Vandiver Award; Willard T. Vol. 1: 513
Vanguard Award for Associates and Affiliates Vol. 1: 12838
Vanguard Award for Government and Community Relations Vol. 1: 12839
Vanguard Award for Marketing Vol. 1: 12840
Vanguard Award for Programmers Vol. 1: 12841
Vanguard Award for Public Relations Vol. 1: 12839
Vanguard Award for Public Relations/ Vanguard Award for State/Regional Association Leadership Vol. 1: 12839
Vanguard Award for Science and Technology Vol. 1: 12842
Vanguard Award for State/Regional Association Leadership Vol. 1: 12839
Vanguard Award for Young Leadership Vol. 1: 12843
Vanguard Degree Vol. 1: 13932
Vanier Cup Vol. 1: 6662
Vanier Cup Trophy Vol. 1: 6676
Vanier Medal Vol. 1: 9932
VanMeter Humanitarian Award for International Relations; Harriet Vol. 1: 10272
Vannprisen Vol. 2: 3892
Vardon Trophy Vol. 1: 15325
Vardon Trophy; Harry Vol. 2: 6567
Vare Trophy Vol. 1: 11205
Varian Award; Russell and Sigurd Vol. 1: 5597
Varietal Awards Vol. 1: 2212
Varna International Ballet Competition Vol. 2: 1158
Varnell Memorial Award for Small Business; Charles E. Vol. 1: 338
Varoujan Award; Daniel Vol. 1: 14048
Varrazzano Award Vol. 1: 10929
Vars Award; Harry M. Vol. 1: 3802
Vasconcelos World Award of Education; Jose Vol. 2: 3461
Vaucouloux; Prix Roy Vol. 2: 1625
Vaughan and Bushnell Awards (Golden Hammer Awards) Vol. 1: 12554
Vaughn Concerto Competition; Elizabeth Harper Vol. 1: 17356
VDE/ETG Award Vol. 2: 2103
Veale Prize; Sir Alan Vol. 2: 6153
Veblen - Commons Award Vol. 1: 4881
Vegetable Breeding Working Group Award of Excellence Vol. 1: 3732
Vegetarian Essay Contest Vol. 1: 18487
Vehicle Theft Award of Merit Vol. 1: 10177
Velluz; Prix Leon Vol. 2: 1626
Ventris Memorial Award; Michael Vol. 2: 5062
Venzie Award; E. F. Vol. 1: 5366
Verbatim Award Vol. 2: 5816
Verco Medal Vol. 2: 651
Verco Medal; Sir Joseph Vol. 2: 651
Vercoullie Prize; Jozef Vol. 2: 964
Verdaguer; Prix Alfred
Academie des Sciences Vol. 2: 1627
Institut de France Vol 2: 1863
Verdeyen Prize for Soil Mechanics Vol. 2: 1090
Vergers; Prix Adolphe Noel des Vol. 2: 1536
Veritas Award Vol. 1: 772
Verlanger; Prix Julia Vol. 2: 1988
Vermaak Award; Coenraad Vol. 2: 4227
Verman Award; IETE-Lal. C. Vol. 2: 2771
Vermont Playwrights Award Vol. 1: 18481
Vermont Superintendent of the Year Vol. 1: 18502
Vern Haverstick Groundwater Hero Award Vol. 1: 9212
Verner Awards; Elizabeth O'Neill Vol. 1: 16982
Vernon; Prix Frederic et Jean de Vol. 2: 1495
Verona Award; Nagrada Eva Vol. 2: 1220
Versatility Award Vol. 1: 14431
Versatility Hall of Fame Vol. 1: 1933
Versele; Prix Bernard Vol. 2: 939
Vertical Smile { La Sonrisa Vertical Vol. 2: 4548
Vertin Award; James R. Vol. 1: 7270
Very Special Arts Playwright Discovery Program Vol. 1: 18578
Very Special Arts Young Playwrights Program Vol. 1: 18578
Vesper Cup Vol. 1: 18051
Vess Avionics Marine of the Year Award; Paul G. Vol. 1: 11529
Vesta Award Vol. 1: 18804
Vestermark Award for Psychiatric Education; Seymour D. Vol. 1: 3293
Veteran's Administration Employee of the Year Award Vol. 1: 288
Veterans Award
Amateur Athletic Union Vol. 1: 514
National Association of State Workforce Agencies Vol 1: 12679
Vetlesen Prize Vol. 1: 7597
Vetter Prize for Electrochemical Kinetics; Klaus-Jurgen Vol. 2: 4848
VEWAA Service Award Vol. 1: 13614
VFP Medal Vol. 1: 18515
VFW Americanism Award Vol. 1: 18520
VFW Armed Forces Award Vol. 1: 18521
VFW Aviation and Space Award Vol. 1: 18522

VFW Congressional Award Vol. 1: 18523
VFW Dwight David Eisenhower Distinguished Service Award Vol. 1: 18524
VFW Emergency Medical Technician Award Vol. 1: 18517
VFW Firefighter Award Vol. 1: 18525
VFW Hall of Fame Award Vol. 1: 18526
VFW News Media Award Vol. 1: 18527
VGP Award Vol. 1: 2109
Vice Presidents' Award Vol. 1: 9905
Vice Presidents Emiriti Award Vol. 2: 6939
Vice Principal of the Year Vol. 1: 6291
Vick Outstanding Province President Award; A. Frank Vol. 1: 14999
Vickery Award Vol. 1: 5020
Victor Memorial Prize; Mildred Vol. 1: 13690
Victoria Cross Vol. 2: 5609
Victoria Cross for Australia Vol. 2: 216
Victoria Medal Vol. 2: 6775
Victoria Medal of Honour Vol. 2: 6806
Victorian Premier's Literary Awards Vol. 2: 683
Victory Awards Vol. 1: 13622
Video Festivals Vol. 1: 9318
Video Grand Prix Vol. 2: 3343
Viener Book Prize; Saul Vol. 1: 2596
Viennet-Damien; Prix Vol. 2: 1963
Vietnam Logistic and Support Medal Vol. 2: 225
Vietnam Medal Vol. 2: 225
Vietnam Service Medal Vol. 1: 8128
Vietnamese Youth Excellence Award Vol. 1: 18531
Vigness Memorial Award; Dr. Irwin Vol. 1: 9842
Viking Range Awards for Broadcast Media Vol. 1: 10957
Viking Society for Northern Research Awards Vol. 2: 7318
Vilardi Humanitarian Award; Emma May Vol. 1: 761
Vilella Award; Joseph R. Vol. 1: 5469
Vilenica International Literary Festival Vol. 2: 4463
Vilenica International Literary Prize Vol. 2: 4463
Vilis Vitols Award Vol. 1: 4972
Viljoen Medal for Journalism; Markus Vol. 2: 4292
Villa I Tatti Fellowships Vol. 2: 3142
Villaescusa Community Service Award; Henrietta Vol. 1: 12551
Village Award Vol. 1: 9202
The Village Voice OBIE Awards Vol. 1: 18535
Villard Award; Serge Vol. 1: 6197
Vinas; Concours International de Chant Francisco Vol. 2: 4554
Vinas; Concurs Internacional de Cant Francesc Vol. 2: 4554
Vinas International Singing Contest; Francisco Vol. 2: 4554
Vincent Lemieux Prize Vol. 1: 6822
Vincent Memorial Scholarship; Susan Vol. 1: 8270
Vincent Prize in Human Sciences; Marcel Vol. 1: 5018
Vinci World Award of Arts; Leonardo da Vol. 2: 3462
Vinifera Perpetual Monteith Trophy Award Vol. 1: 18539
Vinifera Perpetual Wine-Grape Productivity Trophy Vol. 1: 18541
Vinsant Flight Nurse of the Year Award; Dolly Vol. 1: 7614
Vintage Cup Awards Vol. 1: 17890
Vintage Fashion Award Vol. 1: 14805
Viotti; Concorso Internazionale di Musica e Danza G. B. Vol. 2: 3126
Viotti International Music and Dance Competition; Gian Battista Vol. 2: 3126
Vir Chakra Vol. 2: 2586
Virgilio Memorial Haiku Competition; Nicholas A. Vol. 1: 9239
Virgin Group Award Vol. 2: 5226
Virginia Film Festival Vol. 1: 18555
Virginia Law Enforcement Challenge Awards Vol. 1: 18551
Virginia Literacy Foundation Grants Vol. 1: 5813
Virginia Waring International Piano Competition; Joanna Hodges International Piano Competition/ Vol. 1: 18569
Virginia Wine Competition Vol. 1: 18540
Virtuoso Scholarship Award Vol. 1: 757
VISA Triple Crown Challenge Vol. 1: 17610
Vishisht Seva Medal Vol. 2: 2587
Vishwakarma Medal Vol. 2: 2726
Visible Minorities Scholarship Vol. 1: 13880
Vision Award Vol. 1: 4651
Vision for Life Award Vol. 1: 11313
Vision for Tomorrow Award Vol. 1: 8212
Vision of Justice Sermon Award Vol. 1: 17687
Visionary Award Vol. 1: 6051
Visions du Reel International Documentary Film Festival Vol. 2: 4913
Visiting Fellowship in Irish Studies Vol. 1: 10888
Visiting Professor in Adolescent Health Research Award Vol. 1: 16152
Visiting Professor in Adolescent Medicine Award Vol. 1: 16148
Visiting Research Fellowships Vol. 1: 819
Visiting Scholar Grants Vol. 1: 9075
Visiting Scholarship Vol. 2: 6200
Visitor Professorship Vol. 1: 6279
Visser-Nederlandia Prijzen Vol. 2: 3484
Vistelius Prize Vol. 1: 10106
Visual Arts Emeritus Award Vol. 2: 104
Visual Arts Emeritus Medal Vol. 2: 105
Vitarius Memorial Scholarship; Alec Vol. 1: 8872
Vitoria; Prix Vol. 2: 4767
Vlaicu Prize; Aurel Vol. 2: 4386
VMI (Virginia Military Institute) Future Captain of Industry Award Vol. 1: 18574
Vocal Competition Vol. 1: 13490
Vocal Group of the Year Vol. 1: 10270
Vocational Initiative and Club Achievement Program Awards Vol. 1: 16085
Voelcker Award for Poetry Vol. 1: 14905
Vogel Award; F. Stephen Vol. 1: 17726
Vogels, Jr. Award; David S. Vol. 1: 8661
Vohra Award; Pran Vol. 2: 2751
Voice of Democracy Scholarship Vol. 1: 18529
Voice of Democracy Scholarship Program Vol. 1: 11189
Volleyball Coach of the Year Vol. 1: 6677
Vollmer Award; August Vol. 1: 4010
Volume Sales Achievement Award Vol. 2: 5782
Volunteer Achievement Award Vol. 1: 17156
Volunteer Award
Canadian Camping Association Vol. 1: 6373
Canadian Society of Petroleum Geologists Vol 1: 7024
Nature Canada Vol 1: 13981
Volunteer Council Fundraising Gold Ribbon Awards Vol. 1: 4346
Volunteer Council Gold Ribbon Membership Awards Vol. 1: 4347
Volunteer Council Gold Ribbon Service Awards Vol. 1: 4348
Volunteer Hall of Fame Vol. 1: 515
Volunteer Leadership Award Vol. 1: 1445
Volunteer of the Year
American Health Care Association Vol. 1: 2165
Autism Society of America Vol 1: 5554
Federation of Canadian Archers Vol 1: 8627
Leavenworth Area Development Vol 1: 11279
Lupus Foundation of America, Arkansas Chapter Vol 1: 11441
Volunteer of the Year Award
Audubon Society of New Hampshire Vol. 1: 5534
Institute of Internal Auditors - UK and Ireland Vol 2: 6039
International Society of Crime Prevention Practitioners Vol 1: 10716
National Hemophilia Foundation Vol 1: 13336
National Multiple Sclerosis Society Vol 1: 13466
National Organization for Victim Assistance Vol 1: 13505
Nature Saskatchewan Vol 1: 13992
Ouachita Council on Aging Vol 1: 14744
Planned Parenthood Federation of Canada Vol 1: 15090
Volunteer of the Year - College Division Vol. 1: 12388
Volunteer of the Year - University Division Vol. 1: 12389
Volunteer Recognition Award
Canadian Association of Career Educators and Employers Vol. 1: 6242
Canadian Mental Health Association - Alberta Division Vol 1: 6724
Volunteer Service Award Vol. 1: 18157
Volunteer State Book Award Vol. 1: 17439
Volunteers in Fund Raising Awards Vol. 1: 13261
Volunteers of the Year Vol. 1: 15305
Volvo Tennis/All-America Vol. 1: 9997
Volvo Tennis/Rookie Player of the Year Vol. 1: 10006
Volvo Tennis Scholar Athletes Vol. 1: 10007
Volvo Tennis/Senior Player of the Year Vol. 1: 10001
Volvo Tennis/Tennis College Player of the Year Vol. 1: 10004
Von-Arnim Prize; Bettina Vol. 2: 2058
von-Baeyer-Denkmunze; Adolf- Vol. 2: 2176
von Bekesy Medal Vol. 1: 134
von-Bergmann-Plakette; Ernst- Vol. 2: 2197
von Braun Award for Excellence in Space Program Management Vol. 1: 2414
von Briesen Award; Arthur Vol. 1: 13418
von-Chamisso-Preis der Robert Bosch Stiftung; Adelbert- Vol. 2: 2040
von Gruber Award; Otto Vol. 2: 4979
Von Hippel Award Vol. 1: 11599
von-Hofmann-Denkmunze; August-Wilhelm- Vol. 2: 2177

von Humboldt Award for Scientific Cooperation; Alexander Vol. 2: 2438
Von Karman Award Vol. 2: 1868
von Karman Award; Theodore Vol. 1: 310
Von karman Lecture Vol. 1: 2415
von Karman Lectureship in Astronautics Vol. 1: 2415
von Karman Medal; Theodore Vol. 1: 3989
von Karman Prize; Theodore Vol. 1: 16283
Von Liebig Prize; Justus Vol. 2: 2406
von Neumann Lecture; John Vol. 1: 16284
von Neumann Theory Prize; John Vol. 1: 9751
Von-Recklinghausen-Preis Vol. 2: 2205
von Sckell-Ehrenring; Friedrich Ludwig Vol. 2: 2041
von Siemens Music Prize; Ernst Vol. 2: 4915
von Siemens-Musikpreis; Ernst Vol. 2: 4915
Von Stein Prize; Freiherr Vol. 2: 2407
Vondel Translation Prize Vol. 2: 7137
Voorhies Award; Amos E. Vol. 1: 14673
Vosges; Prix Blaise des Vol. 2: 1705
Voss Award Vol. 1: 11043
Voss Award; Walter C. Vol. 1: 5470
Voss-Preis fur Uebersetzung; Johann-Heinrich- Vol. 2: 2148
Vossen Award; John L. Vol. 1: 5598
Vouras Medal; Paul P. Vol. 1: 2102
Vrenios Memorial Award; Nick Vol. 1: 13490
VSDA Home Entertainment Awards Vol. 1: 8474
VSLS Education Foundation Scholarships Vol. 1: 18500
Vucinich Prize; Wayne S. Vol. 1: 961
W & J National Painting Show Vol. 1: 14511
W. R. Brown Medal Vol. 2: 467
WA Special Librarian of the Year Award Vol. 2: 278
Wabash Valley Juried Exhibition Vol. 1: 17354
Wachsmann Prize for Advanced and Critical Essays in Organology; Klaus P. Vol. 1: 16213
Wacker (Chapter 4) Memorial Award; Lawrence A. Vol. 1: 16731
Waddell Award; Tom Vol. 1: 8652
Waddingham/Doctor Award Vol. 1: 7687
"Waddy" Young Award; Walter R. Vol. 1: 4645
Wade Award; Jake Vol. 1: 7541
Wade Trophy Vol. 1: 18857
Wadia Medal; Darashaw Nosherwanji Vol. 2: 2727
Wadlin Distinguished Service Award; George K. Vol. 1: 3679
Wadsworth Award; Milton E. Vol. 1: 16363
Wadsworth Prize for Business History Vol. 2: 5570
Waeckerle Founder's Award; Joseph F. Vol. 1: 8438
WAFFA Salver Vol. 2: 5910
Wager Medal Vol. 2: 543
Wager Prize Vol. 2: 543
Wagggs Medal Vol. 2: 7360
Wagner Award
American Philatelic Congress Vol. 1: 3073
Canadian Society of Biblical Studies Vol 1: 6986
Wagner Memorial Award; SES/CSA Lorne K. Vol. 1: 17249
Wagner Narrative Screenwriting Award; Robert W. Vol. 1: 7387
Wagner Sanitarian Award; Davis Calvin Vol. 1: 747
Wahi Award for Cytology and Preventive Oncology; Dr. Prem Nath Vol. 2: 2631
Wahlbergska Minnesmedaljen I guld Vol. 2: 4642
Wailes Award; B. L. C. Vol. 1: 11868
Waitemata Aero Club Cup Vol. 2: 3855
Wakefield Gold Medal Vol. 2: 6660
Wakenham Prize Vol. 2: 6842
Waksman Award in Microbiology; Selman A. Vol. 1: 12169
Waksman Outstanding Teaching Award Vol. 1: 16302
Walcott Medal; Charles Doolittle Vol. 1: 12170
Wald Award; Nina Starr Braun Vol. 1: 5389
Wald Baaken Award; Joan Vol. 1: 19054
Wald Memorial Lecture Vol. 1: 9913
Waldo Award; Dwight Vol. 1: 3819
Wales Book of the Year Awards Vol. 2: 4995
Waley Medal; A. J. Vol. 2: 6807
Walford Career Achievement Awards in the Performing Arts and in Visual Arts; Paul de Hueck and Norman Vol. 1: 14560
Walker Alexander Award; CLA Margaret Vol. 1: 7523
Walker Award for Excellence in Contributions to Chemical Engineering Literature; William H. Vol. 1: 2502
Walker Award; Jack Vol. 1: 3155
Walker Award; John Vol. 2: 6139
Walker Award; R.V.L. Vol. 1: 7062
Walker Award; Stanley Vol. 1: 17485
Walker Cup Vol. 1: 17920
Walker Humanitarian Award; Bishop John T. Vol. 1: 230
Walker, Jr. Award; John K. Vol. 1: 11772
Walker Memorial Award; Morris R. Vol. 1: 5065
Walker Memorial Grant; Ronald W. Vol. 1: 7561
Walker Prize Vol. 1: 12027
Walker Prizes; T.W. Vol. 2: 3803
Walker Scholarship; Myrtle and Earl Vol. 1: 16732
Walkley Awards for Journalism; W.G. Vol. 2: 561
Wall Young Investigator Award; Patrick D. Vol. 1: 10121
Wallace Award; David H. Vol. 1: 13697
Wallace Dissertation Award; S. Rains Vol. 1: 16296
Wallace Essay and Publication Prize; Hugh Vol. 2: 7020
Wallace Memorial Award; Karl R. Vol. 1: 12930
Wallace-Reader's Digest Writers' Awards; Lila Vol. 1: 18583
Wallace's Registrars' Prize; Hugh Vol. 2: 7021
Wallach-Plakette; Otto- Vol. 2: 2178
Wallenberg Awards; Raoul Vol. 1: 15552
Wallenberg Civic Courage Award; Raoul Vol. 1: 15553
Wallenberg Hero for Our Time Award; Raoul Vol. 1: 15554
Wallenberg World of Heroes Award; Raoul Vol. 1: 15554
Wallin Education of Handicapped Children Award; J. E. Wallace Vol. 1: 7861
Wallin Special Education Lifetime Achievement Award; J. E. Wallace Vol. 1: 7861
Wallis Award; Helen Vol. 2: 6272
Wallis Memorial Intermediate Beethoven Scholarship; Gordon C. Vol. 1: 15888
Wallis Memorial Senior Beethoven Scholarship; Gordon C. Vol. 1: 15889
Wallis Memorial Silver Award Vol. 1: 15890
Walls Award; James F. Vol. 1: 12680
Walpole Gold Medal; Horace Vol. 1: 7930
Walsh Award; Edith Vol. 2: 5373
Walsh Award for Lifetime Contributions to Family Medicine; John G. Vol. 1: 620
Walsh Medal for Service to Industry; Alan Vol. 2: 256
Walsh - Weston Bronze Award Vol. 2: 5640
Walter Cronkite Award for Excellence in Journalism and Telecommunication Vol. 1: 7972
Walter Payton Man of the Year Vol. 1: 13229
Walters Award; Lt. General Vernon A. Vol. 1: 13452
Walters Jr. Sense of Smell Award; Henry G. Vol. 1: 8856
Waltham International Award for Scientific Achievement Vol. 2: 1340
Waltham Service to the Profession Award Vol. 2: 1341
Walther Cup; Fred and Barbara Vol. 1: 11641
Walton Award; A. Ronald Vol. 1: 13006
Walton/Russell L. Miller Award in Safety/Loss Prevention; Norton H. Vol. 1: 2503
WAMSO Young Artist Competition Vol. 1: 18588
Wander Lecture; Albert Vol. 2: 7022
Wang Young Investigator Award; Shih-Chun Vol. 1: 3184
Wanganui Trophy Vol. 2: 3856
Wanner Award; Vance R. Vol. 1: 11773
Wanzer, FPSA, Award; Douglas H. Vol. 1: 15027
Wapensky Award; V. A. Vol. 1: 5890
War Order Virtuti Militari Vol. 2: 4017
War Service Medal Vol. 1: 13777
Warburg-Medaille; Otto- Vol. 2: 2227
Ward Award; Arch Vol. 1: 7542
Ward Award for Outstanding New Children's Theatre Company; Zeta Phi Eta/ Winifred Vol. 1: 799
Ward Exceptional Service Award; Herb Vol. 1: 16666
Ward Library Instruction Award; James E. Vol. 1: 17440
Ward Memorial Award; Earl F. Vol. 1: 339
Ward Memorial Award; Julian E. Vol. 1: 213
Ward Memorial Film Award; Jack Vol. 1: 4530
Ward Memorial Posthumous Award; R.D. 'Bob' Vol. 1: 12246
Ward Memorial Prize; Lynd Vol. 1: 9540
Ward Outstanding New Children's Theatre Company Award; Winifred Vol. 1: 800
Ward Prize for African-American Plays; Theodore Vol. 1: 7573
Ward Prize; Zeta Phi Eta - Winifred Vol. 1: 799
Warden of the Year Vol. 1: 14267
Warder Award for Outstanding Achievement; Frederick B. Vol. 1: 14003
Wardle Award; Robert Arnold Vol. 1: 7036
Ware Award for Distinguished (Undergraduate) Teaching; L. M. Vol. 1: 3729
Wark Medal and Lecture; Ian Vol. 2: 123

Warkany Lecturer Award; Josef Vol. 1: 17449
Warm Water Fisheries Management Award Vol. 1: 8648
Warman International Students Design Award Competition Vol. 2: 536
Warmington Trophy; Ivon Vol. 2: 3857
Warnecki Prize for a Part in Radio Drama; Janusz Vol. 2: 4027
Warner Award; Edward
International Academy of Aviation and Space Medicine Vol. 1: 10017
International Civil Aviation Organization Vol 1: 10318
Warner Award; Jo Vol. 1: 6020
Warner Awards Program; William E. Vol. 1: 8513
Warner Medal; Worcester Reed Vol. 1: 4172
Warner Memorial Medal Vol. 2: 7273
Warner Memorial Medal Award; Samuel L. Vol. 1: 16753
Warner Prize for Astronomy; Helen B. Vol. 1: 1367
Warner Trophy Vol. 1: 9906
Warren Award; Gretchen Vol. 1: 14049
Warren Diffraction Physics Award; Bertram E. Vol. 1: 1865
Warren Medal; W. H. Vol. 2: 537
Warren Prize; G. K. Vol. 1: 12171
Warsash/AOS Student Prize Vol. 2: 316
Warsaw Chopin Competition Vol. 2: 2065
Warth Air Force Historical Foundation Award; Joe and Josephine Vol. 1: 324
Warwick Memorial Award; Irvin Vol. 1: 10027
Warwick Prize; O. Harold Vol. 1: 12845
Washburn Award; Bradford Vol. 1: 12028
Washburn Prize; Sherwood L. Vol. 1: 1237
Washington Award Vol. 1: 3990
Washington Correspondence Award Vol. 1: 13553
Washington Craft Show Vol. 1: 16100
Washington Crossing Foundation Scholarships Vol. 1: 18596
Washington Honor Medal; George Vol. 1: 8880
Washington International Competition Vol. 1: 8889
Washington Medal; Martha Vol. 1: 13778
The Washington Monthly Journalism Award Vol. 1: 18604
The Washington Post Award for Distinguished Community Service Vol. 1: 18610
The Washington Post Award for Excellence in Nonprofit Management Vol. 1: 7230
The Washington Post/Children's Book Guild Award for Nonfiction Vol. 1: 7343
Washington Prize Vol. 1: 18891
Washington State Reserve Police Association Trophy Vol. 1: 13648
Washington Theatre Festival Awards Vol. 1: 16969
Washingtonians of the Year Vol. 1: 18616
Wason Medal for Materials Research Vol. 1: 1762
Wason Medal for Most Meritorious Paper Vol. 1: 1763
Wasserman Foundation Prizes; Leo Vol. 1: 2597
Wasserman Memorial Award; Prof. Dr. Rene D. Vol. 1: 4472
Wasserman Student Essay Prize; Leo Vol. 1: 2597
Waste Management Award Vol. 1: 272
Watanabe Medal; G. Vol. 2: 3211
Wateler Peace Prize Vol. 2: 3488
Wateler-Vredesprijs Vol. 2: 3488
Water Environment Merit Award Vol. 2: 391
Water Works State Leadership Award Vol. 1: 14067
Waterbury Award for Outdoor Lighting; Paul Vol. 1: 9618
Watercolor U.S.A. Vol. 1: 17239
Waterfall Award; Wallace Vol. 1: 5471
Waterford Crystal Award Vol. 2: 6027
Waterford Crystal European Athlete of the Year Award Vol. 2: 2111
Waterman Award; Alan T. Vol. 1: 13673
Waters Distinguished Service Award; Gordon M. Vol. 1: 7121
Watkins Award; J. B. C. Vol. 1: 6122
Watrous Award; Harry Vol. 1: 12122
Watson Award; Clarence W. Vol. 1: 2038
Watson Award for Consular Excellence; Barbara M. Vol. 1: 17876
Watson Award; Robert C. Vol. 1: 2571
Watson, Jr.; Assistant Excellence in Leadership Award in Memory of Buford M. Vol. 1: 10315
Watson, Jr. Medal of Excellence; William C. Vol. 1: 17830
Watson Medal; Garth Vol. 2: 6131
Watson Medal; James Craig Vol. 1: 12172
Watson Prize; Albert J. Vol. 2: 6016
Watson Prize; Frank Vol. 1: 15938
Watt Award; Gladys Cameron Vol. 1: 14742
Watt International Medal; James Vol. 2: 6185
Watt International Medal; James Vol. 2: 6186
Watt Medal; James Vol. 2: 6132
Watters Memorial Scholarship; George E. Vol. 1: 14066
Wayburn Award; Edgar Vol. 1: 16023
Wayne Award; Peter Vol. 2: 6219
W.B. Lewis Medal Vol. 1: 6767
The WCA Award for Excellence in Non-Profit Management Vol. 1: 7230
WCA Honors Vol. 1: 18861
WCO Emeritus Vol. 1: 18923
WCPS Awards Vol. 1: 18918
WCS Research Fellowship Vol. 2: 5179
Weary Dunlop Award Vol. 2: 287
Weatherford Award; W. D. Vol. 1: 4554
Weatherford Awards Vol. 1: 4561
Weatherly Award; Earl Vol. 1: 7673
Weaver's Company Medal and Prize Vol. 2: 7274
Webb Award; Aileen Osborn Vol. 1: 1852
Webb Award; James E. Vol. 1: 3820
Webb Medal; William H. Vol. 1: 16769
Webb Memorial Trophy; Francis Vol. 2: 6535
Webb Prize Vol. 2: 6133
Webb Service Award; Aileen Osborn Vol. 1: 1852
Webb Studentship; Bernard Vol. 2: 5063
Weber Engineering Leadership Recognition; Ernst Vol. 1: 9798
Weber Preis; Max Vol. 2: 2046
Website Award
Construction Writers Association Vol. 1: 7762
Overseas Press Club of America Vol 1: 14761
Webster Award; Betty Vol. 1: 14637
Webster Award; Derek Price/Rod Vol. 1: 9443
WEC Gold Medal for International Corporate Achievement in Sustainable Development Vol. 1: 18925
WEC Gold Medal for International Corporate Environmental Achievement Vol. 1: 18925
Wedel Award; Cynthia Vol. 1: 3474
Wedemeyer Award; Charles A. Vol. 1: 18226
Wedgwood Sponsorship Award Vol. 2: 5230
Weed Book Prize Vol. 2: 730
Weeks Medal; Lewis G. Vol. 2: 325
Weelden Award; Arie van Vol. 2: 3531
Weems Award Vol. 1: 9920
Weetabix Trophy Vol. 2: 6355
Weetabix Women's British Open Championship Vol. 2: 6355
Weetaluktuk Award; Daniel Vol. 1: 6188
Wegener-Medaille; Alfred Vol. 2: 2083
Wegener Medal and Honorary Membership; Alfred Vol. 2: 1781
Weigley Graduate Student Travel Awards; Russell F. Vol. 1: 16339
Weil Award Vol. 1: 1176
Weil Awards; Frank L. Vol. 1: 10988
Weil Prize; Martin Eli Vol. 1: 16456
Weiler and Mildred B. Frame Piano Scholarship Fund; Eleanor B. Vol. 1: 12000
Weill; Prix de Dessin Pierre David Vol. 2: 1496
Weiller; Prix de Portrait Paul-Louis Vol. 2: 1497
Weiller; Prix Paul-Louis Vol. 2: 1498
Weinberg Memorial Award for Geriatric Psychiatry; Jack Vol. 1: 3294
Weinberg Plaque; Al Vol. 1: 12236
Weindling Prize; Rosalind G. Vol. 2: 2904
Weinsier Award for Excellence in Medical/Dental Nutrition Education; Roland L. Vol. 1: 3797
Weinstock Award; Morris F. Vol. 1: 12808
Weintal Prize for Diplomatic Reporting; Edward Vol. 1: 9030
Weintraub Award; Sandra Brand and Arik Vol. 1: 10972
Weintraub Scholarship; Mark Vol. 1: 14038
Weinzirl Award; Elizabeth Vol. 1: 13833
Weir Award for Best Original Screenplay; Michael Vol. 1: 5505
Weir Prize; C. J. Vol. 2: 6017
Weis Trophy; Bernard J. Vol. 1: 15069
Weisbrod One-Act Competition Vol. 1: 11388
Weisel Scholarship; William E. Vol. 1: 16733
Weisenfeld Award for Excellence in Ophthalmology; Mildred Vol. 1: 4956
Weisinger Award; Mort Vol. 1: 4092
Weiss Award; Rosalee G. Vol. 1: 3424
Weiss/Brown Publication Subvention Award Vol. 1: 14206
Weiss Student Scholarship; Fannie Vol. 1: 1898
Weissen Raben; Die Vol. 2: 2330
Weitzman Award; Richard E. Vol. 1: 8457
Weizmann Prizes Vol. 2: 3452
Weizmann Prizes of the Academy of Scientific Research (Premios Weizmann de la Academia de la Investigacion Cientifica) Vol. 2: 3452
Welby Memorial Recognition of Service Award; Bob Vol. 1: 10757
Welch Award in Chemistry Vol. 1: 18655
Welch Award; Medard W. Vol. 1: 5599
Welch Foundation Scholarship Vol. 2: 6316
Welch Livingstone Award; Evelyn Vol. 1: 7839
Welch Medal; William H. Vol. 1: 968

Wellcome Diagnostics Student Award Vol. 2: 4261
Wellcome Medal and Prize; Sir Henry Vol. 1: 5261
Wellcome Medal for Anthropology as Applied to Medical Problems Vol. 2: 6677
Wellcome Prize Vol. 2: 6909
Wellek Prize; Rene Vol. 1: 1743
Wellington Prize; Arthur M. Vol. 1: 3991
Wells Appreciation Award; Cliff Vol. 1: 12402
Wells Award; Ida B.
National Association of Black Journalists Vol. 1: 12413
National Association of Black Journalists Vol 1: 12414
Wells Memorial Award; Elizabeth B. Vol. 1: 12566
Wells Memorial Key Vol. 1: 16840
Wells Service Award; Kergan Vol. 1: 1950
Welsh Arts Council Prizes Vol. 2: 4995
Welsh Community Service Award; Paul Vol. 1: 4518
Welsh Society Medallion Vol. 1: 18657
Weltmeister im Pflugen Vol. 2: 3688
Welty Prize in Fiction; Eudora Vol. 1: 17052
Wenner Outstanding Award; Adrien M. Vol. 1: 16313
Wereld Muziek Concours Kerkrade Vol. 2: 3684
Werner Award; Wallace "Buddy" Vol. 1: 18112
Werner Host Club Award; Louis S. Vol. 1: 2925
Werner Medaille; Abraham-Gottlob- Vol. 2: 2088
Werner-Medaille; Golden Vol. 2: 4894
Werner-Preis Vol. 2: 4894
Wertheimer Award Vol. 2: 6216
Wesley-Logan Prize Vol. 1: 2244
Wesson Memorial Physician of the Year Award; Dr. Ray Vol. 1: 17717
West Agro Inc. Award Vol. 1: 1891
West Australia Film Awards Vol. 2: 458
West Scholarship for Feline Research Vol. 2: 6746
West Virginia Children's Book Award Vol. 1: 18670
West Virginia Poetry Society Award Vol. 1: 13187
Westbrook Local History Award; Lucille Vol. 1: 4619
Westcott USTA Family of the Year Award; Ralph W. Vol. 1: 18158
Westerfield Award; Samuel Z. Vol. 1: 13094
Western Australia Film and Video Festival Vol. 2: 458
Western Australia Week Literary Awards Vol. 2: 685
Western Australian Premier's Book Awards Vol. 2: 685
Western Auto NASCAR Mechanics Hall of Fame Vol. 1: 10526
Western Conference Trophy Vol. 1: 6507
Western Electric Fund Award Vol. 1: 3674
Western Garden Design Wards Vol. 1: 17330
Western Heritage Awards (Wrangler Award) Vol. 1: 13069
Western Home Awards Vol. 1: 17332
Western Political Science Association Awards Vol. 1: 18696
Western Regional Book Design & Production Awards Vol. 1: 15443
Western States Book Awards Vol. 1: 18698
Westfaelischer Kurstpreis Vol. 2: 2350
Westfaelischer Literaturpreis Vol. 2: 2349
Westinghouse Award; George Vol. 1: 3680
Westinghouse Medals; George Vol. 1: 4173
Westinghouse Science Talent Search Vol. 1: 15928
Westlake; Prix John Vol. 2: 4767
Weston Award for Teaching Excellence; William H. Vol. 1: 12049
Weston Award; SETAC/Roy F. Vol. 1: 16667
Weston Grant; Martha Vol. 1: 16626
Westonbirt Orchid Medal Vol. 2: 6808
Westrups beloning; Wilhelm Vol. 2: 4632
WetlandFs Appreciation Writing Award; Ducks Unlimited Canada Vol. 1: 14755
Wexner Graduate Fellow Vol. 1: 18720
Wexner Prize Vol. 1: 18718
Weyant Lifetime Achievement Award; J. Thomas Vol. 1: 13644
Weyerhaeuser Award; Charles A. Vol. 1: 8821
Weyhe Gallery Purchase Award; E. Vol. 1: 16517
Weyuker Scholarship; Matthew L. Vol. 1: 14718
WFEO Award for Engineering Excellence Vol. 2: 2016
WFEO Medal of Excellence in Engineering Education Vol. 2: 2017
Wham Leadership Medal; George S. Vol. 1: 2857
Wharton Citation of Merit for State Author; Edith Vol. 1: 14187
What the Papers Say Award Vol. 2: 6338
Wheadon Education Award; The Lynn Vol. 1: 6545
Wheatley Award; John Vol. 1: 3139
Wheatley Award; William A. Vol. 1: 18207
Wheatley Medal Vol. 2: 7198
Wheaton; Prix Henri Vol. 2: 4767
Wheeler Bursary; Alwyne Vol. 2: 7124
Wheeler Cross Country Award Vol. 1: 12892
Wheeler Legacy Award; A. O. Vol. 1: 443
Wheeler Prize; Charles B. Vol. 1: 14482
Wheeler Track and Field Awards Vol. 1: 12893
Whelan Lieder Piano Scholarship; Goodfellow Memorial Lieder Voice Scholarship/ Vol. 1: 15865
Wheldon Award; Huw Vol. 2: 5217
Wherry Award; Edgar T. Vol. 1: 5886
Wherry Award; Elizabeth Vol. 2: 5374
Wherry Award; Robert J. Vol. 1: 16297
Whetnall Lectureship; Edith Vol. 2: 7023
Whetten Award; Nellie Yeoh Vol. 1: 5600
Whipper Gold Award; Leigh Vol. 1: 409
Whipple Professional Development Grant; Gertrude Vol. 1: 10601
Whirly-Girls Helicopter Flight Training Scholarship Vol. 1: 18725
Whitaker Distinguished Lectureship Vol. 1: 5771
Whitaker Graduate Student Awards Vol. 1: 5772
Whitaker Young Investigator Award Vol. 1: 5773
Whitbread Book of the Year Vol. 2: 5194
Whitbread Literary Awards Vol. 2: 5194
Whitby Award for Distinguished Teaching and Research; George Stafford Vol. 1: 1584
Whitby Award; Kenneth T. Vol. 1: 844
Whitcombe Cox Trophy Vol. 2: 6568
White Award; Dorothy Vol. 1: 14742
White Award for Outstanding Musical Biography; Timothy Vol. 1: 4004
White Award; Marsh W.
American Institute of Physics Vol. 1: 2549
Society of Physics Students Vol 1: 16822
White Award Master List Vol. 1: 18733
White Award; Paul Vol. 1: 15536
White Award; Timothy Vol. 2: 4417
White Awards Vol. 1: 7426
White Children's Book Award; William Allen Vol. 1: 18733
White Distinguished Teacher Award; Albert Easton Vol. 1: 4711
White Fellow; Wilford L. Vol. 1: 10357
White Fellowship; Harold Vol. 2: 577
White Golden Quill Award; The Carson Vol. 1: 14328
White House Fellows Vol. 1: 15213
White House News Photographers' Association Awards Vol. 1: 18731
White Humanitarian Award; Byron "Whizzer" Vol. 1: 13233
White Medal; C. G. Vol. 1: 11641
White Medal; Clarence G. Vol. 1: 4593
White Membership Award; Sandi Vol. 1: 9262
White Memorial Award for Electronic Journalism; Paul Vol. 1: 15536
White Memorial Award; Philip R. Vol. 1: 16264
White National Defense Award; Thomas D. Vol. 1: 17715
White National Memorial Trophy; Belle Vol. 2: 5047
White Prize; Frederick Vol. 2: 124
White Prize Lecture; T. C. Vol. 2: 6717
White Ravens Vol. 2: 2330
White Scholarship; Portia Vol. 1: 5792
White Scholarship; Sir William Vol. 2: 6843
White Stag Award
United States Ski and Snowboard Association Vol. 1: 18083
United States Ski and Snowboard Association Vol 1: 18083
White Travelling Fellowship; T. C. Vol. 2: 6718
White Trophy Vol. 1: 6739
White Visiting Scholarship; T. C. Vol. 2: 6718
White Youth Award; Ryan Vol. 1: 13338
Whitehead Award for Best Design of a Trade Book; Fred Vol. 1: 17486
Whitehead Awards for Excellence in Reporting on Drug and Alcohol Problems; Nancy Dickerson Vol. 1: 8282
Whitehead Prize Vol. 2: 6405
Whitehill Prize; Walter Muir Vol. 1: 7556
Whitfield Award; Willis J. Vol. 1: 9843
Whitfield Prize Vol. 2: 6781
Whiting Award; John Vol. 2: 5071
Whiting Memorial Award Vol. 1: 10667
Whiting Writers' Award Vol. 1: 18735
Whitley Awards Vol. 2: 659
Whitley Travel Scholarship; Don Vol. 2: 7088
Whitlock Award; Marvin Vol. 1: 16593
Whitman Award; Walt Vol. 1: 65
Whitman Citation of Merit Award for State Poet; Walt Vol. 1: 14188
Whitney Award Vol. 1: 14355
Whitney Award; W. R. Vol. 1: 12068
Whitney Award; W.R. Vol. 1: 12490
Whitney Medal; Charles S. Vol. 1: 1764
Whitney Memorial Award; Edgar A. Vol. 1: 4445

Whitney Memorial Award; Eli Vol. 1: 16734
Whitney Productivity Award; Eli Vol. 1: 16734
Whitten Medal; Charles A. Vol. 1: 2124
Whitten Silver Medallion Award; E. B. Vol. 1: 13611
Whittingham Jazz Award; Peter Vol. 2: 6451
Whittington Excellence in Teaching Award; Leslie A. Vol. 1: 12651
Whittle Medal; Sir Frank Vol. 2: 6625
Whittle Safety Award Vol. 2: 6249
Whitworth Award for Educational Research Vol. 1: 6468
Whitworth Scholarship Awards for Engineering Apprentices Vol. 2: 6185
Wholesaler of the Year Awards Vol. 1: 12640
Who's Who of Food and Beverage in America Award Vol. 1: 10958
Whylie Scholarship; Dwight Vol. 1: 5792
Whyte Award; Andrew Vol. 1: 10951
Wichelns Freedom of Speech Award; Herbert A. Vol. 1: 12925
Wichelns Memorial Award for Distinguished Scholarship in Rhetoric and Public Address; James A. Winans/Herbert A. Vol. 1: 12931
Wick Scholarship; Martin M. Vol. 1: 2145
Wickham Award; The Mary Ann Vol. 1: 12021
Wiegenstein Award for Meritorious Service Vol. 1: 1649
Wiegenstein Leadership Award; John G. Vol. 1: 1649
Wiehe-Stiftung; Preis der Horst Vol. 2: 2210
Wien Awards; Mae L. Vol. 1: 15917
Wien Prize for Social Responsibility; Lawrence A. Vol. 1: 7599
Wiener Award for Social and Professional Responsibility; Norbert Vol. 1: 7651
Wiener Medal; Norbert Vol. 1: 3621
Wiener Prize; Norbert Vol. 1: 16285
Wiesel Award for Jewish Arts and Culture; Elie Vol. 1: 9398
Wiesel Prize in Ethics; Elie Vol. 1: 18740
Wiesenthal Center Humanitarian Award; Simon Vol. 1: 16069
Wiesenthal Center National Leadership Award; Simon Vol. 1: 16068
Wigan Cup Vol. 2: 6809
Wigglesworth Lecture and Medal Award Vol. 2: 6755
Wight Memorial Award; J.A. Vol. 2: 5472
Wightman Award Vol. 1: 8937
Wigilia Medal Vol. 1: 15150
Wigram Cup Vol. 2: 3858
Wigram Cup (Sub-Competition) - Instrument Flying Vol. 2: 3859
Wigram Cup (Sub-Competition) - Junior Landing Vol. 2: 3860
Wigram Cup (Sub-Competition) - Non-instrument Circuits Vol. 2: 3861
Wigram Cup (Sub-Competition) - Senior Landing Vol. 2: 3862
Wijnstroom Fund; Margaret Vol. 2: 3586
Wilborn Foreign Language Teacher of the Year Award; Graciela Vol. 1: 8816
Wilbur Award for Historic Preservation; Hervey B. Vol. 1: 1341
Wilbur Awards Vol. 1: 15611
Wilby Memorial Scholarship; Ernest Vol. 1: 15733
Wilcher Award; Denny and Ida Vol. 1: 16024
Wilcox Award; Bill Vol. 1: 2223
Wild Animal Welfare Award Vol. 2: 7306
Wild Award Vol. 1: 18830
Wild Leitz Photogrammetric Fellowship Award Vol. 1: 4744
Wildenmann Prize Vol. 2: 5825
Wildenstein; Prix Georges Vol. 2: 1499
Wilder Award; Laura Ingalls Vol. 1: 4932
Wilder Award; Russell Vol. 1: 18113
Wilder Medal Vol. 1: 3244
Wildfang Aerial Refueler/Transport Squadron of the Year Award; Henry Vol. 1: 11530
Wildlife Action Awards Vol. 2: 7334
Wildlife and Environment Zimbabwe Competitions Vol. 2: 7439
Wildlife Category Award of Merit Vol. 1: 13529
Wildlife Leadership Awards Vol. 1: 15701
Wildlife Utilisation Award Vol. 2: 4228
Wildman Medal Vol. 1: 8148
Wildy Prize for Microbiology Education; Peter Vol. 2: 7100
Wiley & Sons Award for Innovation in Teaching; John Vol. 1: 10370
Wiley & Sons Lifetime Research Achievement Award; John Vol. 1: 10371
Wiley Award for Excellence in Engineering Technology Education Vol. 1: 3630
Wiley Award; Harvey W. Vol. 1: 4550
Wiley-Berger Award for Volunteer Service Vol. 1: 1100
Wiley Distinguished Author Award; Meriam/ Vol. 1: 3681
Wiley Memorial Best Paper of the Year Research Award; Bradford Vol. 1: 10372
Wiley Memorial Novella Contest; Ruthanne Vol. 1: 7477
Wiley Professional Development Grant; First Step Award - Vol. 1: 4913
Wilhelm Award in Chemical Reaction Engineering; R. H. Vol. 1: 2504
Wilhelm Leibniz Prize; Gottfried Vol. 2: 2223
Wilhelmi-Haskell Stewardship Award Vol. 1: 12894
Wilke Memorial Award; Louis G. Vol. 1: 516
Wilkes Award Vol. 2: 5285
Wilkins Award for Outstanding Deputy Chief of Mission; Baker- Vol. 1: 17853
Wilkinson Award Vol. 1: 11695
Wilkinson Meritorious Service Award Vol. 1: 10787
Wilkinson Outstanding Young Electrical Engineer Award; Roger I. Vol. 1: 8541
Wilkinson Prize in Numerical Analysis and Scientific Computing; James H. Vol. 1: 16286
Wilks Award Vol. 1: 17062
Wilks Memorial Award Vol. 1: 4317
Will Award Vol. 1: 15986
Willan Grand Prize; Healey Vol. 1: 6361
Willan Prize; Healey Vol. 1: 6123
Willems-Orde; Militaire Vol. 2: 3490
Willems Prize; Gustave Vol. 2: 924
Willems Prize; Leonard Vol. 2: 965
Willendorf Award Vol. 2: 6217
Willensky Fund; Elliot Vol. 1: 12012
Willey Distinguished Service Award; Calvert L. Vol. 1: 9856
William Harris Award Vol. 1: 14716
William J. Eva Award Vol. 1: 6595
William Johnston Memorial Shield Vol. 2: 5993
William Kapell International Piano Competition and Festival Vol. 1: 16094
William Riley Parker Prize Vol. 1: 11922
Williams Award; Amstutz- Vol. 1: 1024
Williams Award; Boyce R. Vol. 1: 154
Williams Award; Burt Vol. 1: 13573
Williams Award for Research in Physical Therapy; Marian Vol. 1: 3156
Williams Award; George E. Vol. 1: 8662
Williams Award; Rohan Vol. 2: 6738
Williams Award; William Carlos Vol. 1: 15135
Williams Award; W.S. Gwynn Vol. 1: 10242
Williams Award; WSO James K. Vol. 1: 18967
Williams Community Publishing Prize; Raymond Vol. 2: 5072
Williams Distinguished Leadership Award; Robert H. Vol. 1: 8458
Williams History Prize; A. E. Vol. 2: 657
Williams/James S. Brown Service Award; Cratis D. Vol. 1: 4562
Williams, Jr., Design Award; Alexander C. Vol. 1: 9514
Williams Jr. International Adaptive Aquatics Award; John K. Vol. 1: 10777
Williams Medal; J E D Vol. 2: 6833
Williams Memorial Award; Edwin Vol. 2: 5879
Williams Memorial Medal
Royal Horticultural Society Vol. 2: 6802
Royal Horticultural Society Vol 2: 6810
Williams Premium; F. C. Vol. 2: 6146
Williams Prize in Louisiana History; Kemper and Leila Vol. 1: 9419
Williams Prize; Roger T. Vol. 1: 13693
Williams Prizes in Louisiana History; General L. Kemper Vol. 1: 9419
Williams Space Logistics Medal; Jack L. Vol. 1: 16952
Williams SpeakerFs Award; Warren Vol. 1: 3295
Williams Trophy; George Vol. 2: 5775
Williams Up-and-Coming Leadership Award; Nofflet Vol. 1: 18227
Williamson Best Student Paper Award; Merrit Vol. 1: 3692
Williamson Prize; The Ronald Vol. 2: 6018
Willis Award; George E. Vol. 1: 4473
Willis Award of Merit Vol. 1: 13351
Williston Medal; Arthur L. Vol. 1: 4174
Williston Medal Contest; Arthur L. Vol. 1: 4150
Wills Alliance Award; Barbara Salisbury Vol. 1: 801
Willson Award; Cedric Vol. 1: 1765
Wilmoth Medal; G.R. Vol. 2: 538
Wilson Award Vol. 2: 4378
Wilson Award; Alice E. Vol. 1: 6491
Wilson Award; E. H. Vol. 1: 14305
Wilson Award for Young Musicians; Clive Vol. 2: 5970
Wilson Award; Gayle C. Vol. 1: 12306
Wilson Award; Gill Robb Vol. 1: 311
Wilson Award in Nuclear Chemical Engineering; Robert E. Vol. 1: 2505
Wilson Award in Spectroscopy; E. Bright Vol. 1: 1585
Wilson Award; James Lee Vol. 1: 16416
Wilson Award; Ralph C. Vol. 1: 13602
Wilson Award; Thomas J. Vol. 1: 9279
Wilson Award; Tommy Vol. 1: 925
Wilson Award; Woodrow
Alumni Association of Princeton University Vol. 1: 450
American Red Cross National Headquarters Vol 1: 3475
Wilson Awards; Kenneth R. Vol. 1: 6368

Wilson Coach of the Year Award Vol. 1: 10009
Wilson Company Award; H. W. Vol. 1: 17081
Wilson Company Indexing Award; H. W. Vol. 1: 4082
Wilson Cypripedioideae Award; W. W. Vol. 1: 3002
Wilson Fiction Prize; Ethel Vol. 1: 18666
Wilson Foundation Award; Woodrow Vol. 1: 3240
Wilson Leadership Award; Janie Menchaca Vol. 1: 12552
Wilson Library Staff Development Grant; H. W. Vol. 1: 2665
Wilson Medal; E. B. Vol. 1: 3593
Wilson Memorial Lecture Award; John Arthur Vol. 1: 2632
Wilson Memorial Scholarship; Cristine Swanson Vol. 1: 11253
Wilson Memorial Vase; Guy Vol. 2: 6811
Wilson National High School Coaches - AD of the Year Vol. 1: 13343
Wilson Presentation Award Vol. 1: 17450
Wilson Prize; Alexander Vol. 1: 18756
Wilson Prize for Achievement in the Physics of Particle Accelerators; Robert R. Vol. 1: 3140
Wilson Publication Award; James G. Vol. 1: 17451
Wilson State/Regional Leadership Award; Norton Vol. 1: 12459
Wilson - Toekenning Vol. 2: 4378
Wimalasurendra Memorial Award; D. J. Vol. 2: 4562
Winans/Herbert A. Wichelns Memorial Award for Distinguished Scholarship in Rhetoric and Public Address; James A. Vol. 1: 12931
Windmill Trust Scholarship Vol. 2: 569
Wine Research Award Vol. 1: 16737
Winegrape Productivity Trophy Vol. 1: 18541
Wing Bulletin Awards Vol. 1: 313
Wing of the Year Award Vol. 1: 313
Wingate Memorial Trophy; Wilson Vol. 1: 17976
Wingate Rome Scholarship in the Fine Arts Vol. 2: 5451
Wingquist Award Vol. 2: 7444
Winkle Award; Rip Van Vol. 1: 15905
Winner Award; Lewis and Beatrice Vol. 1: 16311
Winner Memorial Award; Robert H. Vol. 1: 15136
Winners' Circle Award Vol. 1: 13188
The Winnifred C. Cory Award of Merit Vol. 1: 6546
Winokur Clinical Research Paper Abstract Award; George Vol. 1: 560
Winship Award; Laurence L. Vol. 1: 14913
Winship Secondary School Theatre Award; F. Loren Vol. 1: 802
Winsor and Newton Award Vol. 1: 4446
Winsor & Newton Choice Award Vol. 2: 7221
Winsor & Newton Young Artists Award Vol. 2: 6835
Winsor Essay Prize; Justin Vol. 1: 2678
Winston Cup (Winston Cup Series) Vol. 1: 8069
Winter Award; George
American Society of Civil Engineers Vol. 1: 3992
European Society for Biomaterials Vol 2: 5859
Winter-Klein; Prix Aniuta Vol. 2: 1628
WinterFest Spotlight Award Vol. 1: 12030
Winzen Lifetime Achievement Award; Otto C. Vol. 1: 2416
Wischmeyer Memorial Scholarship; Albert E. Vol. 1: 16735
Wisconsin Arts Board Fellowships Vol. 1: 18774
Wisconsin Historical Society Vol. 1: 18797
Wisconsin Travel Award Vol. 2: 6072
Wisdom Grant in Aid of Research; William B. Vol. 1: 17530
Wise Award; Stephen S. Vol. 1: 2591
Wise - Warren Susman Prize; Gene Vol. 1: 4333
Wisely American Civil Engineer Award; William H. Vol. 1: 3993
Wiseman Book Award; James R. Vol. 1: 4584
Wiskirchen Jazz Award; Reverend George C. Vol. 1: 12855
Wister Award; Owen Vol. 1: 18704
Wister Medal; John C. Vol. 1: 11641
Withrow Distinguished Speaker Award; Lloyd L. Vol. 1: 16573
WITI Hall of Fame Vol. 1: 18838
Witmer Award; Lightner Vol. 1: 3362
Witt Award; Robert C. Vol. 1: 3498
Witt Supplier of the Year Award; F. W. Vol. 1: 1159
Wittkamper Peace Award; Will Vol. 1: 8230
Witty Short Story Award; Paul A. Vol. 1: 10602
WMO Research Award for Young Scientists Vol. 2: 4937
WNBA Award Vol. 1: 11826
Wohelo Order Vol. 1: 6076
The Wohler Award Vol. 2: 3043
Wohler-Preis "Ressourcenschonende Prozesse" Vol. 2: 2179
Wojciech Rubinowicz Scientific Prize Vol. 2: 4052
Wolf Award; C. R. Vol. 1: 9456
Wolf Chamber Music Award; Andrew Vol. 1: 5689
Wolf-Fenton Award Vol. 1: 9456
Wolf Memorial Award for Best Portrait or Figure Study; Paul J. Vol. 1: 15032
Wolf Memorial Award; Kate Vol. 1: 18937
Wolf Officiating Award; Julian Vol. 1: 18049
The Wolf Prizes Vol. 2: 2938
Wolfe Literary Award; Thomas Vol. 1: 18694
Wolfe Medal of Honor; Catharine Lorillard Vol. 1: 4653
Wolfe Memorial Trophy; Colonel Franklin C. Vol. 1: 14643
Wolfe Sr. Youth Best of Show Exhibit Award; Charles H. Vol. 1: 2926
Wolfe Sr. Youth Exhibit Award; Charles H. Vol. 1: 2927
Wolfe Society Literary Prize; Thomas Vol. 1: 17529
Wolfensohn Award; James D. Vol. 2: 6447
Wolff Lecture Award; Harold G. Vol. 1: 2163
Wolfson History Awards Vol. 2: 7340
Wolfson Laboratory Refurbishment Grants Vol. 2: 6914
The Wolgin Foundation/Israel Museum Fellowships Vol. 2: 2921
Wolgom Award of Excellence; Jay Vol. 1: 9298
Wollaston Award; Charles Vol. 2: 6612
Wollaston Medal Vol. 2: 5937
Wolman Award; Abel Vol. 1: 3457
Wolowski; Prix Vol. 2: 1706
Wolper Best Documentary Award; David L. Vol. 1: 12078
Wolper Student Documentary Achievement Award; David L.
International Documentary Association Vol. 1: 10380
International Documentary Association Vol 1: 10381
Wolskel Industrial Chemistry Essay Award Vol. 2: 625
Wolters*F* Prize; Richard Vol. 2: 3565
Womack Outstanding Library Technician Award; Sharon G. Vol. 1: 4611
Woman CPA of the Year Award Vol. 1: 4492
Woman Entrepreneur of the Year Award Vol. 2: 4421
Woman FIDE Master Vol. 2: 2481
Woman Grandmaster Vol. 2: 2482
Woman International Master Vol. 2: 2483
Woman Lawyer of the Year Vol. 1: 18855
Woman of the Year
Federation of Fly Fishers Vol. 1: 8649
Tall Clubs International Vol 1: 17387
Women in Food Industry Management Vol 1: 18822
Woman of the Year Award
Pearl S. Buck International Vol. 1: 14881
Society for Women in Philosophy Vol 1: 16476
Women in Insurance and Financial Services Vol 1: 18826
Woman of the Year in Travel Vol. 1: 17588
Women and Politics Prize Vol. 2: 91
Women in Cell Biology Senior and Junior Career Awards Vol. 1: 3594
Women in Geography Education Scholarship Vol. 1: 12972
Women in Production Scholarship Vol. 1: 18835
Women in Spotlight Vol. 1: 18989
Women Making History Essay Contest Vol. 1: 14467
Women of Enterprise Awards Vol. 1: 5585
Women of Excellence Vol. 1: 19102
Women of Outstanding Achievement Vol. 2: 7361
Women's Action for Nuclear Disarmament Education Fund Vol. 1: 18844
Women's Advocate Award Vol. 1: 8673
Women's Artist Award Vol. 1: 11371
Women's Development Athletes-of-the-Year Vol. 1: 18457
Women's Leadership Development and Gender Equity Award Vol. 1: 1041
Women's National Book Association Award Vol. 1: 18868
Women's National Championship Cup Finals Vol. 2: 5775
Women's Opportunity Awards Vol. 1: 16965
Women's Player of the Year Vol. 1: 18403
Women's Sports Journalism Awards Vol. 1: 18876
Women's Team of the Year Vol. 2: 3403
Women's Wrestler of the Year Vol. 1: 18473
WONCA Foundation Award Vol. 2: 4436
Wood Award; Coke Vol. 1: 18709
Wood Book Award; Bryce Vol. 1: 11238
Wood Book Grant; Beryl Vol. 2: 844
Wood Building and Interiors Exporter of the Year Vol. 2: 3812
Wood Cup; A. D. Vol. 2: 5536
Wood Design Awards
Canadian Wood Council Vol. 1: 7071

Wood Design and Building Magazine - Dovetail Communications Vol 1: 18884
Wood Foundation Graduate Scholarship; Mike Vol. 1: 17030
Wood Medal and Prize; A. B. Vol. 2: 5988
Wood Memorial Award for Best of Show Exhibit; Howland Vol. 1: 2928
Wood Memorial Award for Children's Literature; Alice Louise Vol. 1: 14494
Wood Prize; J. Howard and Barbara M.J. Vol. 1: 15121
Wood Prize; R. W. Vol. 1: 14620
Wood Science Writing Award; Elizabeth A. Vol. 1: 1866
Woodard Award Vol. 1: 9389
Woodbridge Award of Excellence; Donald B. Vol. 1: 12900
Woodbury Award for Special Achievement; Franklin B.W. Vol. 1: 3693
Wooden Award; John R. Vol. 1: 11410
Wooden Horse Award Vol. 2: 452
Woodford-Williams Prize Vol. 2: 6736
Woodland Memorial Award; Woody Vol. 1: 10753
Woodrow Award Vol. 2: 5473
Woodruff Fellowship; Helen M. Vol. 1: 4585
Woods Award; K. B. Vol. 1: 17584
Woods Memorial Award; David F. Vol. 1: 11563
Woodson Book Award; Carter G. Vol. 1: 12992
Woodson Memorial Award; Grace Vol. 1: 9499
Woodward Award for Best Electronic Map; David Vol. 1: 1777
Woodward Award; Julian Vol. 1: 938
Woodward-Fondiller Prize Vol. 1: 7133
Woodwind Award; Blanche Squires Memorial Vol. 1: 15886
Woodworth Memorial Award Vol. 1: 9645
Woolbert Research Award; Charles H. Vol. 1: 12932
Woollard Award; George P. Vol. 1: 9027
Woolley Award; Davis C. Vol. 1: 5668
Woomer Award; J. W. Vol. 1: 16364
Worcester, Nelson and Turner Prizes Vol. 1: 18898
Words+ Outstanding Consumer Lecture Award Vol. 1: 10639
Work-in-Progress Grants Vol. 1: 16626
Worked 100 Nations Award Vol. 1: 18997
Worked All Zones Award Vol. 1: 7945
Working Group Recognition Award Vol. 1: 9828
Working Hunter Ponies Awards Vol. 2: 5461
Workmen's Circle/Dr. Emanuel Patt Visiting Professorship in Eastern European Jewish Studies Vol. 1: 19069
Workplace Diversity Professional Development Award Vol. 1: 10316
World and National Calendar Awards Vol. 1: 6036
World Association of Christian Radio Amateurs and Listeners Awards Vol. 2: 7351
World Athletics Series Vol. 2: 3466
World Book - ALA Goal Grant Vol. 1: 2666
World Book Award Vol. 1: 7162
World Book Prize of Underwater Pictures Vol. 2: 1799
World Boxing Council Awards Vol. 2: 3458
World Challenge Vol. 1: 17224
World Champion Vol. 2: 4771
World Champion Award Vol. 1: 10766
World Champion Cheesemaker Vol. 1: 18776
World Champions Vol. 1: 15356
World Championship Vol. 2: 1892
World Championships
International Association of Athletics Federations Vol. 2: 3467
International Canoe Federation Vol 2: 4512
World Championships in Ballroom and Latin Dancing Vol. 2: 7368
World Citizen Vol. 1: 10473
World Citizenship Award Vol. 1: 14438
World Class Awards Vol. 1: 14875
World Clean Air Congress Award Vol. 2: 6319
World Cup Vol. 2: 3391
World Cup Jumping Leaders Vol. 2: 4836
World Curling Freytag Award Vol. 2: 7366
World Development Awards for Business Vol. 2: 5612
World Festival of Animated Films Vol. 2: 1241
World Figure Skating Championships Vol. 2: 4834
World Figure Skating Hall of Fame Vol. 1: 17904
World Food Policy Award Vol. 1: 238
The World Food Prize Vol. 1: 18939
World Footbag Championships Vol. 1: 18941
World Games Competitions Vol. 2: 3619
World Golf Hall of Fame Vol. 1: 18943
World Horseshoe Tournament Vol. 1: 13358
World Hunger Media Awards Vol. 1: 18945
World Junior Figure Skating Championships Vol. 2: 4834
World Junior Short Track Speed Skating Championships for Ladies and Men Vol. 2: 4834
World Junior Speed Skating Championships for Ladies and Men Vol. 2: 4834
World Karting Hall of Fame Vol. 1: 10526
World Leisure International Scholarship Vol. 1: 18952
World Marathon Cup Vol. 2: 3467
World Methodist Peace Award Vol. 1: 18956
World Motorcycle Championships Vol. 2: 4817
World Mystical Poetry Prize Vol. 2: 4530
World of Difference Award Vol. 2: 5645
World Peace Academy Diploma Vol. 1: 10201
World Phosphate Institute Awards Vol. 2: 3475
World Piano Competition Vol. 1: 18965
World Player of the Year Vol. 1: 9120
World Ploughing Championship Awards Vol. 2: 3688
World Police Prize Vol. 2: 6280
World Press Photo Children's Award Vol. 2: 3690
World Press Photo Contest Vol. 2: 3690
World Press Photo of the Year Vol. 2: 3690
World Rainforest Awards Vol. 1: 15545
World Rally Champion Vol. 2: 1884
World Record for Game Fish Award Vol. 1: 10448
World Short Track Speed Skating Team Championships Vol. 2: 4834
World Single Distance Championships for Ladies and Men Vol. 2: 4834
World Skeet Shooting Championships Vol. 1: 13798
World Speed Skating Championship for Ladies and Men Vol. 2: 4834
World Sprint Speed Skating Championships for Ladies and Men Vol. 2: 4834
World Standards Day Paper Awards Vol. 1: 17250
World Taekwondo Federation Competitions Vol. 2: 4120
World Wide Video Festival Vol. 2: 3692
World Youth Championship for the FIFA/Coca-Cola Cup Vol. 2: 4757
World Youth Sailing Championship Vol. 1: 18079
Worlddidac Award Vol. 2: 4941
WorldFest - Houston International Film and Video Festival Vol. 1: 18993
World's Best Short Short Story Contest Vol. 1: 17000
World's Paper Trade Review Medal Vol. 2: 6519
Worldwide Awards Competition Vol. 1: 8200
Worldwide Competition for Junior Sociologists Vol. 2: 4519
Worner Essay Award; Junior NATO Manfred Vol. 2: 945
Worner Essay Award; Senior NATO Manfred Vol. 2: 945
Worner Essay Awards; Manfred Vol. 2: 945
Worner Fellowship; Manfred Vol. 2: 945
Worshipful Company of Dyers Awards for Woodwind/Brass Vol. 2: 6853
Worshipful Company of Dyers Research Medal Vol. 2: 7192
Worst-Dressed Women Vol. 1: 11996
Wortelmann-Preis der Stadt Bochum fur das Amateur-Figurentheater; Fritz Vol. 2: 2100
Wortelmann Preis of the City of Bochum for Amateur Puppetry; Fritz Vol. 2: 2100
Worth Prize; R. H. Vol. 2: 5938
Worth Silver Medal; John Edward Vol. 2: 6940
Worthingham Fellow; Catherine Vol. 1: 3157
Worthington Medal; Henry R. Vol. 1: 4175
Worths Estes Prize; J. Vol. 1: 969
Worts Staff Service Award; Grace Vol. 1: 6752
Woszczerowicz Prize; Jacek Vol. 2: 4028
WPLGA - Lentil Family of the Year Vol. 1: 18395
WPLGA - Special Recognition Award Vol. 1: 18396
WPRA Foundation Vol. 1: 18793
WPX Award Vol. 1: 7946
WPX Award of Excellence Vol. 1: 7947
WPX Honor Roll Vol. 1: 7948
Wrangler Award Vol. 1: 13069
Wrangler Jeans World Champion Bullfighter Vol. 1: 15351
Wratten Journal Award; Denis Vol. 2: 5185
Wren Prize; Dr. Peter Vol. 2: 6033
Wrench Scholarship; Jesse Vol. 1: 11878
Wrenn Award for a Humanitarian and Caring Person; Gilbert and Kathleen Vol. 1: 1848
Wrestling Coach of the Year Vol. 1: 6678
Wrestling Person of the Year Vol. 1: 517
Wright Achievement Award; Orville Vol. 1: 14655
Wright Award; Bob Vol. 1: 12360
Wright Award; E. Whitman Vol. 1: 6922
Wright Award in Olfactory Research; Frank Allison Linville's R. H. Vol. 1: 16066
Wright Award in Olfactory Research; R. H. Vol. 1: 16066
Wright Award; MacKellar Michael Vol. 2: 6747
Wright Award; Mary Tolle Vol. 1: 16049

Wright Award; Mickey Vol. 1: 9121
Wright Award of Distinction; Irving S. Vol. 1: 1997
Wright Award; Sewall Vol. 1: 4184
Wright Brothers Lecture Vol. 1: 2417
Wright Brothers Lectureship in Aeronautics Vol. 1: 2417
Wright Brothers Medal Vol. 1: 16594
Wright Brothers Memorial Trophy Vol. 1: 12191
Wright Children's Literature Award; Arthur Tofte/Betty Ren Vol. 1: 7875
Wright Cup; John Howie Vol. 1: 11474
Wright Distinguished Service Award; Logan Vol. 1: 3411
Wright League Service Award; G. R. tBobv Vol. 1: 5478
Wright Mariological Award; Cardinal John J. Vol. 1: 11549
Wright Memorial Award; Katharine Vol. 1: 12192
Wright Memorial Exhibit Award; B. P. Vol. 1: 2929
Wright Memorial Trophy; Lee O. Vol. 1: 13647
Wright Prize for Poetry; Wesley Michel Vol. 2: 711
Wright Special Recognition Award; Lin Vol. 1: 803
Wrigley-Fairchild Prize Vol. 1: 2103
Writer of the Year Vol. 1: 17369
Writers' Award Contest Vol. 1: 10966
WritersF Corner Hall of Fame Vol. 1: 17939
Writer's Digest Annual Writing Competition Vol. 1: 18999
Writers Digest Short Story Competition Vol. 1: 19000
Writer's Digest Writing Competition Vol. 1: 19001
Writers' Emeritus Award Vol. 2: 100
Writers in Performance Literary Competition Vol. 1: 15961
The Writer's Trust of Canada/McClelland and Stewart Journey Prize Vol. 1: 11625
Writing Awards
River City Vol. 1: 15676
Syngenta Corp. Vol 1: 17369
Writing for Children Competition Vol. 1: 19030
WSAVA Hills Excellence in Veterinary Healthcare Award Vol. 2: 1342
WSAVA Paatsama Award Vol. 2: 1343
WSO Award for Achievement in Scientific Research and Development Vol. 1: 18968
WSO Chapter/National Office of the Year Award Vol. 1: 18969
WSO Concerned Citizen Award Vol. 1: 18970
WSO Concerned Company/Corporation Award Vol. 1: 18971
WSO Concerned Company/Corporation Honorable Mention Certificate Vol. 1: 18972
WSO Concerned Organization Award Vol. 1: 18973
WSO Concerned Professional Award Vol. 1: 18974
WSO Educational Award Vol. 1: 18975
WSO Environmental/Occupational Safety Person of the Year Vol. 1: 18976
WSO International Award Vol. 1: 18977
WSS Achievement in Women's Studies Librarianship Awards Vol. 1: 5088
WTS National Member of the Year Vol. 1: 18879
WTS National Woman of the Year Vol. 1: 18880
Wulf Memorial Award; Hans Vol. 1: 7052
Wulff Award; Lee Vol. 1: 8650
Wurdigungspreis des Landes Tirol fur Literatur, Musik etc. Vol. 2: 750
Wurdigungspreis fur Erwadisenenbieolung des Landes Tirol Vol. 2: 752
WWF Award for Conservation Merit Vol. 2: 4946
Wyeth Award in Clinical Microbiology Vol. 1: 3764
Wyeth-Ayerst Outstanding Chapter Awards Vol. 1: 706
Wyeth Fellowship Vol. 2: 5546
Wyeth Young Investigator Award in Vaccine Development
Infectious Diseases Society of America Vol. 1: 9700
National Foundation for Infectious Diseases Vol 1: 13258
Wyeth Young Psychopharmacologist Award Vol. 1: 3420
Wyld Propulsion Award Vol. 1: 2418
Wyld Propulsion Award; James H. Vol. 1: 2418
Wyman Award; Kelley - Vol. 1: 12391
Wyman Memorial Award Vol. 1: 12391
Wyman Memorial Award; L. L. Vol. 1: 5472
Wyndham Award Vol. 2: 4223
The Wynne Prize Vol. 2: 50
WYOpoets Award Vol. 1: 13189
Xavier Medal; St. Francis Vol. 1: 19032
Xirka Gieh ir-Repubblika Vol. 2: 3429
XL Anniversary Prize Vol. 2: 4521
Xplorer of the Year Award Vol. 1: 19035
XYZ Digital Award Vol. 2: 6898
Yachtsman of the Year Award Vol. 2: 7391
Yaciuk Award; Walter Vol. 1: 18404
Yale Center for International and Area Studies Awards Vol. 1: 19041
Yale Series of Younger Poets Vol. 1: 19037
Yamagiwa-Yoshida Memorial International Cancer Study Grants Vol. 2: 4860
Yant Award; William B. Vol. 1: 2348
Yarwood Memorial Medal; John Vol. 2: 5560
YASD/*School Library Journal* Author Achievement Award Vol. 1: 19083
YASD/*School Library Journal* Young Adult Author Award Vol. 1: 19083
Yasme Award Vol. 1: 19043
Yeadon Memorial Trophy; T. M. Vol. 2: 5048
Year End Awards Vol. 1: 4570
Year-End High Score Awards Vol. 1: 9506
Year End Series Festival of New Plays Vol. 1: 14394
Yearly Award for Young ICU Investigators Vol. 2: 882
Yearly Research Award Vol. 2: 7424
Years of Dedicated Service Award Vol. 1: 377
Yennenga Stallion Trophy Vol. 2: 1160
Yerkes Award; Robert M. Vol. 1: 3377
Yitzah Rabin Award Vol. 1: 3010
Ylvisaker Award for Public Policy Engagement; Paul Vol. 1: 7918
Yoder-Heneman Human Resource Management Creative Application Award Vol. 1: 16239
Yoder-Heneman Personnel Creative Application Awards Vol. 1: 16239
Yoder-Heneman Personnel Research Award Vol. 1: 16242
Yokelson Medal Award; Marshall V. Vol. 1: 18768
Yomiuri International Cartoon Contest Vol. 2: 3354
Yomiuri International Cooperation Prize Vol. 2: 3344
Yomiuri Kokusai Kyoryoku Sho Vol. 2: 3344
Yomiuri Kokusai Manga Taisho Vol. 2: 3354
Yonge Award; Sir Charles Maurice Vol. 2: 6414
York Prize in Photography; Duke and Duchess of Vol. 1: 6105
Yorkdale Memorial Award; Alan H. Vol. 1: 5473
Yorkshire & Humberside Arts Young Composers Awards Vol. 2: 5976
Yorkshire Arts Young Composers Competition Vol. 2: 5976
Yorzyk Memorial Award; David Vol. 1: 17995
Yoshikawa Eiji Bungaku Sho Vol. 2: 3290
Yoshikawa Eiji Prize for Literature Vol. 2: 3290
Yost Distinguished Services Award; Max Vol. 1: 4771
Youden Award in Interlaboratory Testing; W. J. Vol. 1: 4318
Young Achiever Award Vol. 2: 5105
Young Adult Author Award Vol. 1: 4601
Young Adult Book Award Vol. 1: 16984
Young Adult Canadian Book Award Vol. 1: 6694
Young Adult Sequoyah Book Award Vol. 1: 14501
Young Adult Volunteer of the Year Award Vol. 1: 2167
Young Alumni Merit Award Vol. 1: 7174
Young Alumni Service Citations Vol. 1: 18263
Young American Awards Vol. 1: 5918
Young American Creative Patriotic Art Competition Vol. 1: 11190
Young American Medal for Bravery Vol. 1: 17834
Young American Medal for Service Vol. 1: 17835
Young Archeologist of the Year Award Vol. 2: 5231
Young Architects Award Vol. 1: 2438
Young Architects Forum Vol. 1: 4587
Young Artist Competition
Fort Collins Symphony Association Vol. 1: 8825
National Flute Association Vol 1: 13206
New York Flute Club Vol 1: 14125
Young Artists Auditions Competition Vol. 1: 14097
Young Artists Competition
Connecticut Alliance for Music Vol. 1: 7721
International Clarinet Association Vol 1: 10321
Sister Cities International Vol 1: 16071
Young Artists Showcase Vol. 1: 16071
Young Asian Biotechnologist Prize Vol. 2: 3326
Young Australians Best Book Award Vol. 2: 739
Young Author Best Paper Award Vol. 1: 10817
Young Award; Cy Vol. 1: 5683
Young Award; Hugh Hampton Vol. 1: 4397
Young Beekeeper of the Year Vol. 1: 6067
Young Cancer Researcher Award Vol. 2: 5808

Young Cancer Researcher Award Lecture Vol. 2: 5809
Young Chemist Award Vol. 2: 4099
Young CHMM of the Year Vol. 1: 83
Young Cinema Festival Vol. 2: 3336
Young Citizen of the Year Award Vol. 2: 725
Young Clinical Chemist Award Vol. 1: 899
Young Competitor Award Vol. 1: 7053
Young Composer Awards Vol. 1: 4005
Young Composers Awards Vol. 1: 16119
Young Composers' Competition Vol. 1: 12467
Young Concert Artists International Auditions Vol. 1: 19089
Young Concert Artists Trust Award Vol. 2: 7394
Young Consultants Award Vol. 1: 9955
Young Consulting Engineers Award Vol. 2: 5770
Young Continuing Education Travel Fellowship Award; The Robert Vol. 1: 6212
Young Contributor's Award Vol. 1: 1295
Young Crop Scientist Award Vol. 1: 7984
Young Dermatologists' Volunteer Award Vol. 1: 6458
Young Designer of the Year Prize Vol. 2: 1362
Young Dietitian of the Year Vol. 1: 11082
Young Direct Marketer of the Year Vol. 2: 181
Young Director Prize Vol. 2: 1846
Young Educator Award Vol. 1: 6297
Young Emerging Scholars Award; Alma H. Vol. 1: 18370
Young Engineer Achievement Award Vol. 1: 6439
Young Engineer Award Vol. 1: 16364
Young Engineer of the Year Vol. 2: 6164
Young Engineer of the Year Award
Canadian Society for Bioengineering Vol. 1: 6885
National Society of Professional Engineers Vol 1: 13752
Young Engineers of the Year Vol. 1: 11589
Young Engineers Speaking Competition Vol. 2: 539
Young Entrepreneur Award Vol. 2: 7233
Young FAI Artists Contest Vol. 2: 4750
Young Federal Healthcare Administrator Award Vol. 1: 5262
Young Fellows Award Vol. 2: 3259
Young Filmmaker of the Year Vol. 2: 458
Young Filmmakers Festival Vol. 1: 14400
Young Forest Landowner of the Year Vol. 1: 8823
Young Forester Leadership Award Vol. 1: 16515
Young Freight Forwarder of the Year Vol. 2: 5336
Young Government Civil Engineer of the Year Award Vol. 1: 3994
Young Handler Award Vol. 2: 6291
Young Hoosier Book Awards Vol. 1: 5192
Young Hoosier Picture Book Award Vol. 1: 5193
Young Industrialist Awards of Hong Kong Vol. 2: 3933
Young Innovator Award
BC Innovation Council Vol. 1: 5698
BC Innovation Council Vol 1: 5701
Young Investigaor Awards Vol. 1: 2862
Young Investigator Award
American College of Clinical Pharmacology Vol. 1: 1637
American Society for Bone and Mineral Research Vol 1: 3583
American Society of Echocardiography Vol 1: 4030
American Society of Nephrology Vol 1: 4200
Bristol-Myers Squibb Canada Co. Vol 1: 5942
Canadian Association of Radiologists Vol 1: 6298
Canadian Cardiovascular Society Vol 1: 6381
International College of Angiology Vol 1: 10323
International Society for Aerosols in Medicine Vol 2: 2321
National Alliance for Research on Schizophrenia and Depression Vol 1: 12233
Society for Medical Decision Making Vol 1: 16333
Society for Pediatric Research Vol 1: 16375
United States and Canadian Academy of Pathology Vol 1: 17727
Young Investigator Award Competition Vol. 1: 3798
Young Investigator Awards
Cancer Research Foundation Vol. 1: 7082
National Foundation for Infectious Diseases Vol 1: 13258
Young Investigator Awards; Shorei-Sho/ Vol. 2: 3271
Young Investigator Memorial Travel Awards Vol. 1: 1686
Young Investigator Travel Award
International Society for the Study of Hypertension in Pregnancy Vol. 2: 3612
Radiation Research Society Vol 1: 15511
Young Investigator Travel Awards Vol. 1: 17452
Young Investigator's Award
Association of Medical Microbiology and Infectious Disease Canada Vol. 1: 5225
Society of Critical Care Medicine Vol 1: 16641
Young Investigators Award
European Federation of Societies for Ultrasound in Medicine and Biology Vol. 2: 5833
International Association for Dental Research Vol 1: 10069
Young Investigators Awards Vol. 1: 9342
Young Investigators' Prizes Vol. 1: 4185
Young Jazz Composer Awards Vol. 1: 4005
Young Journalist of the Year Vol. 2: 7047
Young Jumper Award Vol. 1: 2160
Young, Jr., Award; Whitney M. Vol. 1: 2439
Young, Jr. Memorial Scholarship; Whitney M. Vol. 1: 14200
Young Lawyers' Pro Bono Award Vol. 1: 6342
Young Logistician Award Vol. 1: 16953
Young Manager of the Year Award Vol. 2: 5629
Young Medal and Prize; Thomas Vol. 2: 6068
Young Member Outstanding Service Award Vol. 1: 16808
Young Members' Award Vol. 2: 5646
Young Metallurgist of the Year Award Vol. 2: 2662
Young Musician Scholarship Vol. 1: 9081
Young NDT Professional Award Vol. 1: 3784
Young Neurosurgeons Award Vol. 1: 18933
Young Nursery Professional of the Year Vol. 1: 8750
Young OCTAN Award Vol. 1: 14671
Young Oncologist Essay Awards Vol. 1: 3462
Young Oncologist Travel Grants Vol. 1: 3463
Young Optometrist of the Year Vol. 1: 2977
Young Oration; Thomas Vol. 2: 6068
Young People's Film and Video Festival Vol. 1: 14400
Young Performers Awards Vol. 2: 696
Young Performers Competition Vol. 1: 6124
Young Persons Book of the Year Vol. 2: 3711
Young Physics Students Competition Vol. 2: 4450
Young Planner of the Year Award Vol. 2: 7052
Young Player of the Year Vol. 2: 3403
Young Playwrights Festival Vol. 1: 19093
Young Professional Activity Award Vol. 1: 2419
Young Professional Engineer of the Year Vol. 2: 540
Young Professional of the Year Vol. 2: 4428
Young Readers' Choice Award Vol. 1: 14780
Young Republican Man of the Year Vol. 1: 19097
Young Republican Woman of the Year Vol. 1: 19098
Young Researchers' Award Vol. 2: 3195
Young Sailor of the Year Award Vol. 2: 7392
Young Scholars Award Vol. 1: 1461
Young Scholars Competition Vol. 1: 5804
Young Scientific Career Award Vol. 2: 2412
Young Scientific Career Award - Light Vol. 2: 2413
Young Scientist Award
European Behavioral Pharmacology Society Vol. 2: 2115
European Federation of Food Science and Technology Vol 2: 3533
European Meteorological Society Vol 2: 2123
Geological Society of America Vol 1: 9028
Indian Society of Soil Science Vol 2: 2761
International Confederation for Thermal Analysis and Calorimetry Vol 2: 4206
International Society for Neurochemistry Vol 2: 1309
Mineralogical Association of Canada Vol 1: 11792
Phytopathological Society of Japan Vol 2: 3312
Young Scientist Award in Noninvasive Cardiovascular Dynamics Vol. 2: 4455
Young Scientist Award; Intel Foundation Vol. 1: 15927
Young Scientist Awards Vol. 2: 3025
Young Scientist's Award Vol. 1: 6977
Young Scientists' Awards Vol. 2: 2752
Young Scientists for Rainforests Vol. 2: 5695
Young Scientist's Poster Award Vol. 2: 1273
Young Scientists Publication Awards Vol. 2: 1782
Young Scientists Travel Awards Vol. 2: 1783
Young Sculptor Awards Vol. 1: 13693
Young Soloists Award Vol. 1: 18579
Young Soloists' Competition Vol. 1: 13818
Young Technologist Award Vol. 2: 7046
Young UK Cell Biologist Award Vol. 1: 3595
Young Vilenica Vol. 2: 4463

Young Wildlife Photographer of the Year Competition Vol. 2: 6493
Young Woman Engineer of the Year Award Vol. 2: 6183
Young Woman of the Region Vol. 2: 7362
Youngblood Scholarship; John Vol. 1: 18557
Younger Federal Lawyer Award Vol. 1: 8601
Younger Member Group Award Vol. 1: 3995
Younger Members*F* Award for Achievement Vol. 2: 6165
Youskevitch Award; Igor Vol. 1: 14131
Youth Ambassador Vol. 2: 426
Youth Art Month Award Vol. 1: 12280
Youth Art Month State Report Awards Vol. 1: 7843
Youth Arts Awards Vol. 1: 17620
Youth as Resources Grants Vol. 1: 11259
Youth Athletics Outstanding Association Award Vol. 1: 18442
Youth Athletics Outstanding Individual Award Vol. 1: 18455
Youth Award
American Bashkir Curly Registry Vol. 1: 1391
National Apostolate for Inclusion Ministry Vol 1: 12251
Youth Incentive Award Vol. 1: 7493
Youth Leadership
Walter Cronkite School of Journalism and Mass Communication Vol. 1: 7972
National Community Education Association Vol 1: 12942
Youth Leadership Awards Vol. 1: 6078
Youth of the Year Award Vol. 1: 2797
Youth Person of the Year Award Vol. 1: 2798
Youth Scholarship Vol. 1: 2142
Youth Service Medal Vol. 1: 13706
Youth Softball Volunteer of the Year Vol. 1: 518
Youth Theatre Director of the Year Award Vol. 1: 804
Youth World Championship Horse Show Golden Horse Awards Vol. 1: 14823
Ysgoloriaeth W. Towyn Roberts Vol. 2: 6472
Yunus Nadi Gift Vol. 2: 4964
Zaheer Medal; S. H. Vol. 2: 2728
Zaimont Prize; Judith Lang Vol. 1: 10031
Zak Award Vol. 1: 900
Zakon Lectureship; Samuel J. Vol. 1: 9431
Zakon Prize; Samuel J. Vol. 1: 9432
Zambrano National Prize for Inventive Technology; Luis Vol. 2: 7428
Zammit Award; George Vol. 1: 11489
Zangerle Award Vol. 1: 10139
Zanotti Award for Excellence in Non-Serial Publications; Christine Vol. 1: 4630
Zarem Award for Distinguished Achievement; Abe M. Vol. 1: 2420
Zarrow Award for Young Readers' Literature; Anne V. Vol. 1: 17627
ZASP President's Award Vol. 2: 4029
Zawidzki Medal; Jan Vol. 2: 4036
Zbinden Memorial Lecture Award; Gerhard Vol. 2: 1274
Zeigler Lecture Award; Earle F. Vol. 1: 14334
Zeiler Award; Geraldine Colby Vol. 1: 4021
Zeitlin-Ver Brugge Prize Vol. 1: 9443
Zeldovich Gold Medal; Ya B. Vol. 1: 7612
Zeldovich Medals Vol. 2: 1742
Zellen Golden Quill Award; Gosta Vol. 1: 18916
Zellner USHWAn of the Year; Bob Vol. 1: 17940
Zelma H. Weisfeld Costume Design & Technology Award Vol. 1: 17957
Zemanek Award; Heinz Vol. 2: 764
Zeneca Pharmaceuticals/Komen Foundation Excellence in Breast Cancer Education Award Vol. 1: 14538
ZENECA Research Scholarship Vol. 2: 878
Zenger for Freedom of the Press and the Peoples Right to Know; John Peter and Anna Catherine Vol. 1: 18239
Zerbe Memorial Award; Farran Vol. 1: 2930
Zerby and Carl T. Koerner Outstanding Electrical and Computer Engineering Student Award; Alton B. Vol. 1: 8542
Zero Accidents Award
Specialized Carriers and Rigging Association Vol. 1: 17101
Specialized Carriers and Rigging Association Vol 1: 17102
Zhizhuo Award; Wang Vol. 2: 4980
Zibetska Priset Vol. 2: 4676
Ziegler-Preis; Karl- Vol. 2: 2180
Ziering Award for Outstanding Contribution for a Publication in the *Journal of Clinical Chemistry*; Sigi Vol. 1: 901
Zimmer Award Vol. 1: 14625
Zimmerman Founder's Award; O. T. Vol. 1: 26
Zimmerman-Rand Valor Award Vol. 1: 12359
Zinam Award; Oleg Vol. 1: 10307
Zinn Memorial Award; Captain Ron Vol. 1: 18458
Ziskind-Somerfeld Research Award Vol. 1: 16607
Zittel Medaille; Karl Alfred von Vol. 2: 2367
Zlatnata Antena Vol. 2: 1146
Zlatnata Rakla Vol. 2: 1147
Zola Award Vol. 1: 14782
Zollman Award; Charles C. Vol. 1: 15203
Zonal Awards Vol. 2: 2762
Zone Outstanding Campus Representative Award Vol. 1: 3682
Zoo Animal Welfare Award Vol. 2: 7306
Zorgniotti Award Vol. 2: 3608
Zorn Disabled Swimmer of the Year Award; Trish L. Vol. 1: 18426
Zubin Award; Joseph Vol. 1: 3426
Zuck Public Courage Award; Alfred M. Vol. 1: 12652
Zue Award; Dick Vol. 1: 18114
Zumwalt Corporate Award; Admiral Vol. 1: 13441
Zuspan Award Vol. 2: 3613
Zvorikine; Prix Nicolas Vol. 2: 1629
Zwilich Prize; Ellen Taaffe Vol. 1: 10031
Zworykin Award; The IFMBE Vladimir K. Vol. 2: 1234
Zworykin Premium; Dr. V. K. Vol. 2: 6166